18.95

Notes
on the
Old Testament

Albert Barnes

ISAIAH
Volume 1

BAKER BOOK HOUSE
Grand Rapids, Michigan 49506

Barnes' Notes

Heritage Edition — Fourteen Volumes 0834-4

When ordering by ISBN (International Standard Book Number), numbers listed above should be preceded by 0-8010-.

Reprinted from the 1851 edition published by Blackie & Son, London

Reprinted 1983 by Baker Book House Company

ISBN : 0-8010-0840-9

Printed and bound in the United States of America

EDITOR'S PREFACE

So long as the church endures, shall the genius and eloquence of the son of Amoz be held in admiration. On the ruins of once flourishing empires and cities, his credentials are written ; and the more these ruins are explored, and compared with his prophetic pages, the deeper will the conviction grow, that the inspiration of God is there. In a sceptical age like the present, it cannot but be of great advantage to direct the minds of our youth to *demonstrations* like these. But Isaiah has still nobler themes than the downfall of empires. The grand subjects of this "fifth evangelist" are the person and character, and reign and glory of Christ ; the triumphs of the church ; the restoration of the Jews ; and conversion of the world ; and these are presented in a style that is by turns simple, beautiful, tender, sublime, impetuous. The majesty of Isaiah has never been surpassed.

This exposition of the prophet originally appeared in three large octavos ; it was subsequently condensed by the author, and re-issued in two volumes of smaller size. From this second and latest edition, the present reprint has been made. The reader will recognize in it the same easy and perspicuous style, the same racy illustrations, the same prevailing good sense, and general full-ness of exposition, that have made the author the most popular of modern commentators. He makes no pretence, indeed, to very profound or original criticism. But while there is necessarily less of this than in works written professedly for the scholar, there is much more of it than is usually found in popular commentaries. The sense of the original is always carefully ascer-tained, and made the basis of exposition ; but while the merely philological inquiry is, for the most part, carried so far as to satisfy, it is never pushed to the length of tedium or fatigue. Thus a happy medium has been secured, and a commentary produced, acceptable alike to the scholar and the Christian. It is, perhaps, not too much to say that it is the most readable and generally useful commentary on Isaiah in the English language. The scholarship of Alexander is doubtless more exact and profound, and his exegesis more independent ; but his book is for scholars, and for scholars alone. It deals principally in philological criticism ; its avowed aim is briefly to present the true sense, along with a condensed historical synopsis of opinion. Very nearly the same may be said of Henderson, Lowth, Stock, and Noyes. The illustration in all of them is too scant to satisfy, and the public instructor in search of available materials for lectures on Isaiah, will consult them in vain ; but in these volumes will be found, in union with judicious criticism, a satisfying copiousness of illustration. In the archæological department particularly, the author excels, having added to the stores of Gesenius and other diligent cultivators of this field, much additional matter from the works of modern travellers. This feature of the book greatly enhances its value, and lends to it a peculiar charm; it is especially fitted to captivate the young, and allure them to studies which they are but too apt to imagine repulsive and dry. The author, indeed, has been blamed for disproportionate attention to this part of his subject; but readers generally will thank him for that attention, and think with himself that it is perhaps the capital excellence of the work. Yet the author has by no means prosecuted this part of his subject to the injury of other parts. The Messianic prophecies, which form so marked a portion of Isaiah, have due care bestowed on them, and the evangelical interpretation is throughout skilfully and successfully maintained. The author, indeed, does not exalt anything into a type or prediction of Christ merely because it occurs in the writings of a prophet; but, on the other hand, he has no rationalistic bias inclining him to explain away such prophecies as the Church has all along applied to the Messiah. His good sense never forsakes him. The sobriety of his judgment is seen in the manner in which he deals with the questions of the literal restoration of the Jews, and the personal reign of Christ. If the advocates of these doctrines are not satisfied with his conclusions, they will seldom or never find reason to complain of his candour.

The peculiarities of this edition are the careful revision to which the text has been subjected; additional Notes where these were required; references to supplementary Notes in former volumes, under those places where the author's views were supposed to be at variance with the received theology of our church and country; to which must be added very many additional pictorial illustrations. Numerous errors, in the Hebrew text particularly, had crept into the American edition; these have been corrected; and care has been taken to present the pointed Hebrew throughout with due accuracy. The supplementary Notes would have been perhaps more numerous, but for the fact that the author's peculiarities had been reviewed at length in the New Testament volumes, and therefore a simple reference seemed all that was needed. The aim, from the first, has been to supply no more Notes than were absolutely required, that the author might appear in his own dress, with as little foreign admixture as possible.

May this work be abundantly blessed. May it revive in our land, and especially in our youth, a taste for the literature of the Bible, deepen in their minds the conviction of its inspiration, and dispose them to its study.

PREFACE TO THE FIRST EDITION

It is with unaffected diffidence that this work is offered to the patronage of the Christian public. It has been prepared amidst the toils and responsibilities of a most laborious pastoral charge, and at such intervals as could be secured without seeming to infringe on the direct and immediate duties demanded in my station. Those hours have been, with scarcely an exception, the early morning hours; and whatever may be the manner in which this book may be received by the public, whether it shall or shall not contribute in any degree to advance the knowledge of the truth, and the love of the sacred Scriptures, its preparation, by requiring me to commence each day with the direct contemplation of an interesting portion of inspired truth, has for four years constituted one of the most delightful parts of my work. It is the production of many a laborious, but many a pleasant, hour; and while I desire to render thanks to the Giver of life and health, that he has granted me strength to engage in these studies, I shall ever look back with gratitude to the deeply interesting moments in which I have been endeavouring to illustrate the ' Visions of Isaiah.'

When I commenced the work, I designed nothing farther than an *enlargement* of Lowth on Isaiah. It occurred to me that it might be useful to retain his Notes as a *basis*, with some additional illustrations. But this plan was soon abandoned; and no other use has been made of Lowth than that which is common with other writers. Valuable as are his Notes, and beautiful as is his version, yet it was soon perceived, or thought to be perceived, that greater usefulness might be secured by enlarging the plan, and making a work entirely new. Very valuable helps have been furnished, since the time of Lowth, for the illustration of the Hebrew prophets; and it was deemed desirable to avail myself of them all, so far as it was in my power. Most of those helps will be found enumerated in the list of works on Isaiah, at the close of the Introduction, § 8.

Some of the reasons which led to the wish to illustrate Isaiah, are the following: (1.) He is one of the most beautiful and sublime of the sacred writers. (2.) In some respects his writings are among the most difficult portions of the Old Testament. (3.) His prophecies are so closely connected with interesting historical events, and furnish so much opportunity of illustration from archæology, oriental customs, and the investigations of modern travellers, that it is highly desirable that all the light should be thrown upon them which is possible from these sources. (4.) The fulfilment of prophecy is perhaps more clear.

minute, and striking in Isaiah than in any other of the prophets; and a commentary, therefore, on his writings, compared with the present state of the countries to which his prophecies refer, as reported by modern travellers, and especially with the record of the life, and doctrines, and death of Christ, will constitute itself a demonstration of the divine origin of the sacred Scriptures, and may be made one of the best antidotes against infidelity. It is impossible, it is believed, with an honest mind, to compare the predictions of Isaiah respecting Babylon, Moab, Tyre, and Idumea, with the travels of Volney, Burckhardt, Seetzen, Sir R. K. Porter, Maundrell, Laborde, and Stephens, without the fullest conviction that he who uttered these predictions, two thousand and five hundred years since, was divinely inspired. It is impossible to believe that this could have been the result of political sagacity; it is equally impossible to believe that it could have been produced by chance or conjecture. And, in like manner, it is impossible to compare his full, minute, and glowing descriptions of the Messiah, with the life of the Lord Jesus Christ; to collate minutely and critically, for example, the prophecies in the ixth, the xith, the xxxvth, the liid, the liiid chapters, with what actually occurred in the life, the sufferings, and the death of the Redeemer, without the fullest conviction that he was permitted to see, in distinct vision, events which were to take place in future times. No man can be a close student of Isaiah, and remain an infidel; no man can study his writings with prayer, who will not find his faith confirmed, his heart warmed, his mind elevated and purified, and his affections more firmly fixed on the beauty of the everlasting truth of God.

But the main reason which led to the selection of Isaiah as a subject of exposition was, his strongly evangelical character, and the fact, that he, more than any other prophet, has unfolded the future glories, and predicted the triumphs of the church on earth. He has been usually styled 'the fifth Evangelist;' and it is certain that there was vouchsafed to him a clearer view of the universal spread of the gospel, and of the blessedness of the reign of the Messiah, than was granted to any other of the ancient prophets. It was this characteristic mainly which has prompted to this attempt to make his sentiments more widely known, and more clearly understood. In an age distinguished, more than any other since that of the apostles, for efforts for the conversion of the whole world to God, nothing will so entirely fall in with the leading characteristics and efforts of the times as an attempt to establish some just views of the right interpretation of the prophecies on this subject. Men will put forth great and noble exertions when the object is clearly defined, and when they have some distinct view of what it is possible to attain. A right apprehension of what *is to be* on earth, will do much to form the plans and shape the efforts of those who seek the world's conversion. It will do much to suppress unauthorized hopes, to repress wild and visionary schemes, and to secure well-founded and judicious efforts to accomplish the object. A correct understanding of the prophecies, therefore, is necessary to direct those who are forming plans for the conversion of the world, and to uphold the hands and to encourage the hearts of those who are engaged in practically executing the work.

There is one advantage on this subject, in contemplating the *entire* prophecies in a book, above what would arise from *selecting* the portions which relate to the final triumph of the gospel, and forming a commentary on them exclusively. As the predictions now stand in the prophets, they are intermingled with predictions respecting *other* events which have been strikingly and clearly fulfilled. The mind is carried forward therefore *amidst demonstrations ;* the certain conviction of the mind that the predictions respecting Babylon, Tyre, Moab, and Idumea *have been fulfilled,* is carried to the contemplation of the predictions respecting things yet to come. The mind ranges amidst proofs of the divine origin of the book which is examined ; and these proofs strengthen the faith in regard to the events which are yet to come. He performs some service for his generation, who contributes in any degree to unfold the meaning of the ancient predictions, and to show to the Christian church what the world yet will be ; and he who contributes in any manner so to blend the arguments for the past fulfilment of prophecy with the predictions of what is yet to be on earth, does not live entirely in vain. It is doubtless with this view that the predictions respecting the Messiah, and the final universal triumph of the gospel, are *scattered along* and *intermingled with* predictions that relate to events that would be of more immediate fulfilment. The student of the prophecies thus walks amidst the monuments of their truth which time has set up along his way;—not much unlike the traveller who is seeking a distant land amidst much that is obscure and uncertain ; who encounters rapid streams and lofty crags and hills ; whose paths lead through dense and entangled forests ; but who yet finds every now and then monuments erected which show him that the road *has* been travelled, and which prove that the same path which others have trod will lead him to the place which he desires to reach. He who has attentively examined Isaiah, and compared the predictions respecting events which are now passed, with their fulfilment, is not likely to be a man whose faith will be shaken in regard to the reality of the inspiration of the Book of God, or to the final prevalence of religion all over the world. As an illustration of the influence of Isaiah in forming the opinions of Christians in regard to the character of the better days which are to bless the world, we may advert to the fact that the views of most Christians respecting the Millennium are probably derived from this prophet; and that even after the revelations of the New Testament, if we wish to obtain full and clear conceptions of what the world is yet to be under the reign of the Prince of Peace, we instinctively turn to the glowing visions of the son of Amoz. It has been one of the constant and earnest prayers of the author of these Notes, that his labours may contribute to the confirmation of the faith of Christians in respect to the final triumph of Christianity; and to the augmentation of their zeal in spreading the gospel around the world.

In the fulfilment of this design, as well as to exhibit the true meaning of the prophet, I have availed myself of all the helps within my reach, to show that the prophecies pertaining to events already passed, have been minutely and strikingly fulfilled. In these portions of the book, my first aim has been to settle, as well as I could, the exact sense of the prophet by philological investigation, and then to adduce the testimony of modern travellers in regard to the *present* condition of the countries so described. Modern travellers have contributed much to the confirmation of the truth of the prophetic statements; and if these Notes have *any* value above what is found in the common exposi-tions of Isaiah, it is probably in this respect.   In illustration of this, reference may be made to the prophecies respecting Babylon, Moab, Damascus, Tyre and Idumea, in the xiiith, xivth, xvth, xvith, xviith, xxxiiid, and xxxivth chapters.

In the preparation of these Notes I have availed myself of all the aids within my reach.   The books from which I have derived most assistance are WAL-TON's POLYGLOTT ; the Critici Sacri ; Poole's Synopsis ; Calmet's Dictionary; Vitringa ; .Rosenmüller ; Calvin ; Gesenius ; Jerome ; Bochart's Hierozoicon ; Taylor's Heb. Con. ; Lowth's and Noyes' Versions ; Keith on the Prophecies ; Newton on the Prophecies ; Hengstenberg's Christology; and the writings of oriental travellers.to which I have had access.   I have also derived considerable aid from the Biblical Repository, and from Prof. Bush's Scripture Illustra-tions.

This work is committed now to the Christian public with the fervent prayer that it may do good.   The public—for whose favourable regards thus far in life I have had abundant reason to be grateful—will receive kindly what is kindly meant.   It is not *right* to deprecate criticism, for every man who makes a book subjects himself, of his own choice, to the free remarks of all who may choose to notice his productions.   His works, henceforward, whatever they may be, belong not to himself alone, but to the public at large ; and no author has a right to complain if his style, his opinions, his arguments, his illustrations, are freely examined.   For such examination he should be grateful, come from what quarter it may—if it help him to amend his style, to correct his errors, to suggest better illustrations, to remove obscurity, to advance sounder arguments, and in any way to make his works more worthy of the patronage of the public.   *He* has a right to demand only that criticisms should be in the spirit of Christian love—that they should not be made *for the sake* of criticism, and that they should not be carping or petulant.   He has a right to ask that those who examine his positions should *presume* that he has bestowed labour and thought on them, and that labour and thought should be reciprocated in judging of them before they are condemned.   He has a right to expect that assertion in regard to his opinions should not be deemed sufficient to supply the place of argument ; and that the uttering of an opinion *ex cathedra* should not be allowed to take the place of a candid and prayerful investigation of the meaning of words, and phrases, and figures of speech ; of a careful inquiry into whatever in archæology, philology, geography, or travels, may throw light on the meaning of God's word.   Argument should meet argument ; thought conflict with thought ; and truth should be elicited by manly, liberal, and candid discussion.   The only object should be truth ; and every author should be thankful to any man who will suggest to him what he had forgotten ; com-municate what to him was unknown ; correct or refute what was erroneous ; and thus make him more useful to his fellow-men.

It is not improper, however, as a matter of mere justice to myself, to sug-gest one other thing to those who may be disposed to examine this work.   A man burdened with the cares and toils of a pastoral office, has not the advantages of preparing a work for the public which they have who are favoured with the entire command of their time, or whose professional duties *require* them to pursue a course of study that shall be in accordance with what they may choose to submit to the press. The pastors of the churches, for whose use more especially this work is intended, will know how to appreciate this remark ; and they who know the toils of that office will not judge unkindly or severely of what is designed as a means of enlarging the sphere of usefulness in which a man is placed ; or of contributing in any, the humblest degree, to illustrate the truth of the Bible, to confirm the churches in its inspiration, to unfold its beauties, and to aid in the exposition of truth. Lord Bacon has said, 'I HOLD EVERY MAN TO BE A DEBTOR TO HIS PROFESSION ;' and they who appreciate the force of this remark will look with kindness on every effort to enlarge the sphere of the usefulness of those who are by their office expositors of the word of God.

With these remarks, this work is committed to the world. The desires of my heart will be gratified if it is the means, in any degree, of confirming the faith of man in the inspiration of the Divine oracles, and of hastening the triumphs of that day when ' the wilderness and the solitary place shall be glad, and the desert shall rejoice and blossom as the rose,' and when ' the ransomed of JEHOVAH shall return and come to Zion with songs, and everlasting joy upon their heads.' Isa. xxxv. 1, 10.

ALBERT BARNES.

Philadelphia, Nov. 14, 1833.

PREFACE TO THE SECOND EDITION

Since the publication of the first edition of this work, I have twice carefully revised it. In doing this, while the main features of the exposition have been retained, I have endeavoured to render it more worthy of the patronage of the Christian public. I have availed myself of all the criticisms made on it which I have seen, and have adopted all the suggestions which appeared to me to be well founded. My principal aim has been to *condense* the work as much as possible, by removing redundant words, and by excluding whatever did not contribute to the elucidation of the Prophet. The work was originally published in three large octavo volumes. By using a different type ; by the omission of the 'New Translation' inserted in the former edition, and by the abridgments which have been made, I am now able to present it in a much narrower compass, and at a price which will make it much more easy to procure it. It may perhaps be of interest to some to know that in revising it, I have stricken out matter, besides the 'New Translation,' to the amount of about one hundred and twenty octavo pages, and have introduced new matter to the amount of about fifty pages. In a few places additions of considerable extent have been made. For the *new* matter I am under special obligations to the Biblical Researches of Dr. Robinson, and Mr. Smith, and to the work of Wilkinson on the Manners and Customs of the Ancient Egyptians. By the aid of the 'Researches' I have been enabled to correct several places relating to the geography of Palestine, and to throw important light on several passages of the Prophet. I have, in fact, incorporated in the Notes all that I have found in that invaluable work which seemed to me to illustrate in any way the writings of Isaiah, and as nothing better can be hoped for on the Holy Land, this part of the work may be considered to be complete. The favourable manner in which the first edition was received made it obligatory on me to do all that I could to make it more worthy of patronage, and again I commit it to the world, with the hope that it may contribute in some degree to the illustration of this sublime and beautiful portion of the inspired volume.

ALBERT BARNES.

Washington Square, Philadelphia, June 23, 1845.

INTRODUCTION

§ 1. *Division of the Books of the Old Testament.*

THE Jews early divided the books of the Old Testament into three parts—the *Law*, the *Prophets*, and the *Hagiographa*, or holy writings. The *Law* comprised the five books of Moses; and the priority was given to this division because it was the first composed, as well as on account of its containing their civil and ecclesiastical constitution, and their oldest historical records. The *Prophets* comprised the second and the largest division of the sacred writings of the Jews. This portion comprehended the books of Joshua, Judges, 1 and 2 Samuel, 1 and 2 Kings, which were called the *former prophets;* and Isaiah, Jeremiah, Ezekiel, and the books from Hosea to Malachi, which were called the *latter prophets.* Daniel has been excluded from this portion by the later Jews, and assigned to the third division, because they regard him not as a prophet, but as an historical writer. Formerly his work was doubtless included in the second division. The third portion, *the Hagiographa*, comprises the Psalms, Proverbs, Job, Song of Solomon, Ruth, Lamentations, Ecclesiastes, Esther, Daniel, Ezra and Nehemiah, and the two books of Chronicles. This division of the Old Testament is as old as the time of our Saviour, for he refers to it in Luke xxiv. 44. The Jews attribute the arrangement and division of the canonical books to Ezra. They say that he was assisted in this by one hundred and twenty men who constituted 'a great Synagogue;' that Daniel, and his three friends, Shadrach, Meshach, and Abednego, were of this number; and that Haggai and Zechariah, together with Simon the Just, also were connected with it. But this statement is known to be erroneous. From the time of Daniel to the time of Simon the Just, not less than two hundred and fifty years intervened (Alexander on the Canon, pp. 26, 27); and of course all these persons could not have been present. It is not, however, improbable that Ezra may have been assisted by learned and pious men who aided him in the work. What Ezra *did* is indeed unknown. It is the general opinion that he collected and arranged the books which now compose the Old Testament; that perhaps he wrote some of the historical books, or compiled them from fragments of history and documents that might have been in the public archives (comp. the ANALYSIS of Isa. ch. xxxvi.); and that he gave a finish and arrangement to the whole. As Ezra was an inspired man, the arrangement of the sacred books, and the portions which he may have added, have thus the sanction of Divine authority. There is no evidence, however, that Ezra *completed* the canon of

the Old Testament. Malachi lived after him, and in the first book of Chronicles (ch. iii.) the genealogy of the sons of Zerubbabel is carried down to the
time of Alexander the Great—about one hundred and thirty years subsequent
to the time of Ezra. The probability is, therefore, that Ezra *commenced* the
arrangement of the books, and that the canon of the Old Testament was completed by some other hand.

The 'prophets' were divided into *the former* and *the latter*. Among the
latter, Isaiah has uniformly held the first place and rank. This has been
assigned him not because he prophesied before all the others. He indeed preceded Ezekiel and Jeremiah, but Jonah, Amos, and Hosea were his contemporaries. The precedence has been given to his prophecies over theirs, probably for two reasons; first, on account of their length, dignity, and comparative
value ; and secondly, because formerly the minor prophets were bound in one
volume, or written on one roll of parchment, and it was convenient to place
them *together*, and they all had a place, therefore, after Isaiah. At all times
his prophecies have been regarded as the most important of any in the Old
Testament; and by common consent they have been deemed worthy of the
principal place among the Jewish writings.

§ 2.   *Life of Isaiah, and the Characteristics of his Writings.*

Of the time in which Isaiah lived, little more is known than he has himself
told us. In the superscription to his book (ch. i. 1), we are told that he was
the son of Amoz, and that he discharged the prophetic office under the reign
of the kings Uzziah, Jotham, Ahaz, and Hezekiah. In regard to those times,
and the character of the period in which they reigned, see Introduction, § 3.
It is evident also from the prophecies themselves, that he delivered them during
the reign of these kings. In ch. vi. 1, it is expressly said that he had a vision
of JEHOVAH in the year in which Uzziah died. Of course he must have commenced his prophetic labours at least as early as during the last year of that
king. If that chapter or vision was not designed as an inauguration of the
prophet, or an induction into the prophetic office (see Notes on the chapter),
and if his prophecies were collected and arranged as they were delivered, then
it will follow that the previous chapters (i.–v.) may have been delivered in the
reign of Uzziah, and perhaps some time before his death. There is no express
mention made of his uttering any prophecies in the time of Jotham. Hengstenberg and others suppose that the prophecies in ch. ii.–v. were delivered
during his reign. But of this there is no conclusive evidence. He might not
have *recorded* anything during his reign ; though he may, as a public preacher,
have been engaged in the prophetic office in another mode. His writings
themselves contain evidence that he was engaged in the prophetic office in the
reign of Ahaz. See ch. vii., seq. That he was engaged in the prophetic office
during the reign of Hezekiah we learn from chs. xxxvi.–xxxix. We have an
explicit statement that he was occupied in his prophetic work until the fifteenth
year of Hezekiah, at the commencement of which the ambassadors from Babylon came up to Jerusalem to congratulate him on his recovery from his illness ;
ch. xxxix. Uzziah died, according to Calmet, 754 years before Christ. Isaiah

must therefore have occupied the prophetic office at least from **754 years before** Christ to 707 years before Christ, or forty-seven years ; that is, under Uzziah one year, under Jotham sixteen years, under Ahaz sixteen years, and under Hezekiah fourteen years. It is not known at what age he entered on the prophetic office. It is probable that he lived much longer than to the fifteenth year of Hezekiah. In 2 Chron. xxxii. 32, it is said that ' the rest of the acts of Hezekiah ' were ' written in the vision of Isaiah ;' and this statement obviously implies that he survived him, and wrote the acts of his reign up to his death. As Hezekiah lived fourteen or fifteen years after this (Isa. xxxviii. 5. comp. 2 Kings xviii. 2), this would make the period of his public ministry to extend to at least sixty-one or sixty-two years. If he survived Hezekiah, he probably lived some time during the reign of Manasseh. This supposition is confirmed, not indeed by any direct historical record in the Old Testament, but by all the traditional accounts which have been handed down to us. The testimony of the Jews, and of the early fathers, is uniform that he was put to death by Manasseh by being sawn asunder. The main alleged offence was, that he had said that he had seen JEHOVAH, and that for this he ought to die, in accordance with the law of Moses (Ex. xxxiii. 20), ' No man shall see me and live.' If he lived to the time of Manasseh, and especially if he prophesied under him, it is probable the true reason why he was put to death was, that he was offensive to the monarch and his court.

The circumstances which render the supposition probable that he lived under Manasseh, and that he was put to death by him by being sawn asunder, are the following. (1.) The fact which has been stated above that he lived to complete the record of the reign of Hezekiah, and of course survived him. (2.) The testimony of the Jewish writers. There is, indeed, much that is fabulous in their writings, and even in connection with the truths which they record, there is much that is puerile and false ; but there is no reason to doubt the main *facts* which they relate. Josephus, indeed, does not expressly state that he was slain by Manasseh, but he gives an account of the reign of Manasseh which renders it probable that *if* Isaiah were then alive he would have been put to death. Thus he says (Ant. B. x. ch. iii. § 1) that ' he barbarously slew all the righteous men that were among the Hebrews ; nor would he spare the prophets, for he every day slew some of them, till Jerusalem was overflown with blood.' In the Talmud the following record occurs :—' Manasseh put Isaiah to death. The Rabbi said, he condemned him, and put him to death ; for he said to him, Moses, thy Lord said, No man shall see me and live (Ex. xxxiii. 20), but thou hast said, I saw the Lord upon a throne high and lifted up (Isa. vi. 1). Moses, thy Lord said, Who will make the Lord so near that we can call to him ; but thou hast said, Seek the Lord while he may be found, call upon him while he is near (lv. 6). Moses, thy Lord said, The number of thy days will I fulfil (Ex. xxii. 26); but thou hast said, I will add to thy days fifteen years (xxxviii. 5),' etc. See Gesenius Einlei. p. 12. The testimony of the Jews on this subject is uniform. Michaelis (Preface to Isaiah) has referred to the following places in proof on this point. Tract. Talmud. *Jabhamoth*, fol. 49; *Sanhedrin*, fol. 103; *Jalkut*, part ii. fol. 38; *Schalscheleth Hakkab*. fol. 19. Raschi and Abarbanel in their commentaries give the same statement. (3.)

The testimony of the early Christian writers is the same. Justin Martyr, in his dialogue with Trypho the Jew (p. 349), speaking of Isaiah, says, ὃν πρίονι ξύλῳ ἐπρίσατε, ' whom ye sawed asunder with a wooden saw.' —Tertullian (de patientia, c. 14) says, His patientiae viribus secatur Esaias.—Lactantius (lib. iv. c. 2) says, Esais, quem ipsi Judaei serrâ consectum crudelissime necaverunt. —Augustine (de Civit. Dei, lib. 18, c. 24) says, ' the prophet Isaiah is reputed to have been slain by the impious King Manasseh.' Jerome (on Isa. lvii. 1) says, that the prophet prophesied in that passage of his own death, for ' it is an undisputed tradition among us, that he was sawn asunder by Manasseh, with a wooden saw.' These passages and others from the Jewish writers, and from the fathers, are to be found in Michaelis' Preface to Isaiah ; in Gesenius' Introduction ; and in Carpzov. Crit. Sacr. In a matter of simple fact, there seems to be no reason to call this testimony in question. It is to be remembered that Jerome was well acquainted with Hebrew, that he dwelt in Palestine, and no doubt has given the prevalent opinion about the death of Isaiah. (4.) The character of Manasseh was such as to make it probable that if Isaiah lived at all during his reign, he would seek his death. In 2 Kings xxi. 16, it is said of him that he ' shed innocent blood very much, till he had filled Jerusalem from one end to another.' This account is in entire accordance with that of Josephus, quoted above. In the early part of his reign, it is recorded that he did evil, and especially that he reared the high places and the altars of idolatry which Hezekiah had destroyed, and endeavoured to restore again the abominations which had existed in the time of Ahab. 2 Kings xxi. 2, 3. It is scarcely credible that such a man as Isaiah would see all this done without some effort to prevent it; and it is certain that such an effort would excite the indignation of Manasseh. If, however, he cut off the righteous men of Jerusalem, as Josephus testifies, and as the author of the books of Kings would lead us to believe, there is every probability that Isaiah would also fall a sacrifice to his indignation. It is not necessary in order to this to suppose that Isaiah appeared much in public; or that, being then an old man, he should take a prominent part in the transactions of that period. That we have no *recorded* prophecy of that time, as we have of the times of Uzziah, Ahaz, and Hezekiah, leaves it probable that Isaiah had withdrawn from the more public functions of the prophetic office, and probably (see § iv. of this Introduction) had given himself to the calm and holy contemplation of future and better times under the Messiah. But still his sentiments would be known to the monarch; and his influence while he lived among the people may have been materially in the way of the designs of Manasseh. Manasseh, therefore, may have regarded it as necessary to remove him, and in the slaughter of the good men and prophets of his time, there is every probability that Isaiah would be made a victim. (5.) It affords some confirmation of this statement that Paul (Heb. xi. 37) affirms of some of the ancient saints, that they were ' sawn asunder.' There is not in the Old Testament any express mention of any one's being put to death in this manner; but it has been common with all expositors, from the earliest periods, to suppose that Paul had reference to Isaiah. The universal tradition on this subject among the Hebrews makes this morally certain. It is certain that Paul could not have made such an enumeration unless there was a well-established tradition of some one or more who had suffered in this manner; and all tradition concurs in assigning it to Isaiah. (6.) The character of the second part of the prophecies of Isaiah (chs. xl.–lxvi.) accords with this supposition. They are *mainly* employed in depicting the glories of a future age; the blessedness of the times of the Messiah. They bespeak the feelings of a holy man who was heart-broken with the existing state of things; and who had retired from active life, and sought consolation in the contemplation of future blessings. No small part of those prophecies is employed in lamenting an existing state of *idolatry* (see particularly chs. xl. xli. lvi. lvii. lxv.), and the prevalence of general irreligion. Such a description does not accord with the reign of Hezekiah; and it is evidently the language of a man who was disheartened with prevailing abominations, and who, seeing little hope of immediate reform, cast his mind forward into future times, and sought repose in the contemplation of happier days. How *long* he lived under Manasseh is unknown; and hence it is not possible to ascertain his age when he was put to death. We may reasonably suppose that he entered on his prophetic office as early as the age of twenty. From Jer. i. 6, we learn that an earlier call than this to the prophetic office sometimes occurred. On this supposition he would have been eighty-two years of age at the death of Hezekiah. There is no improbability, therefore, in the supposition that he might have lived ten or even fifteen years or more, under the long reign of Manasseh. The priest Jehoiada attained the great age of one hundred and thirty years, 2 Chron. xxiv. 15. Isaiah lived evidently a retired and a temperate life. It is the uniform tradition of the oriental Christians that he lived to the age of one hundred and twenty years ; see Hengstenberg's Christol. vol. i. p. 278.

Where he lived is not certainly known ; nor are many of the circumstances of his life known. His permanent residence, in the earlier part of his prophetic life, seems to have been at Jerusalem. During the reign of the ungodly Ahaz, he came forth boldly as the reprover of sin, and evidently spent a considerable part of his time near the court, ch. vii. seq. His counsels and warnings were then derided and disregarded. Hezekiah was a pious prince, and admitted him as a counsellor, and was inclined to follow his advice. In his reign he was treated with respect, and he had an important part in directing the public counsels during the agitating occurrences of that reign. If he lived in the time of Manasseh, he probably retired from public life; his counsel was unsought, and if offered, was disregarded. It is evident that he did not *entirely* withdraw from his office as a reprover (chs. lvi.–lviii), but his main employment seems to have been to contemplate the pure and splendid visions which relate to the happier times of the world, and which constitute the close of his prophecies, chs. xl.–lxvi.

Of the family of Isaiah little is known. The Jewish writers constantly affirm that he was of noble extraction, and was closely connected with the royal family. The name of his father was Amoz, or *Amotz*—אָמוֹץ ; not the prophet Amos, as some have supposed, for *his* name in Hebrew is אָמוֹס, Amos. Amoz, or Amotz, the father of Isaiah, the Jews affirm to have been the brother of Amaziah the son of Joash, king of Judah, 2 Kings xiv. 1. Thus D. Kimchi on Isa. i. 1, writes, 'We are ignorant of his family, from what tribe he was, except that our doctors have handed it down by tradition that Amotz and Amaziah were brothers.' And thus R. Solomon says, 'It is handed down to us from our ancestors that Amotz and Amaziah were brothers.' The same is said also by R. Levi (in Megilla, c. i. fol. 10); and by Abarbanel, Pref. fol. 1 (quoted by Michaelis, Pref. to Isa.) In this supposition there is nothing improbable: and the fact that he was admitted so freely to the counsels of Hezekiah, and that he went so boldly to Ahaz (ch. vii. 1, seq.), may seem to give some countenance to the idea that he was connected with the royal family. His father was evidently well known; see ch. i. 1, and elsewhere, where his name is introduced. Indeed, it is not improbable that most of the prophets were descended from families that were highly respectable, as they generally mention the name of their father as a name that is well known; comp. Ezek. i. 3; Jer. i. 1; Hos. i. 1; Joel i. 1; Jonah i. 1; Zeph. i. 1; Zec. i. 1. In the other prophets the name of the *father* is omitted, probably because he was obscure and unknown. It is morally certain that Isaiah was not connected with the Levitical order, since if he had been, this would have been designated as in Jer. i. 1; Ezek. i. 3. The wife of Isaiah is called a prophetess (ch. viii. 3), and it is supposed by some that she had the spirit of prophecy; but the more probable opinion is, that the wives of the prophets were called prophetesses, as the wives of the priests were called priestesses. On the question whether he had more than one wife, see Notes on chs. vii. viii. Two sons of Isaiah are mentioned, both of whom had names fitted to awaken religious attention, and who were in some sense the pledges of the fulfilment of divine predictions. The name of the one was 'SHEAR-JASHUB' (ch. vii. 3), the meaning of which is, *the remainder shall return*—designed, undoubtedly, to be a sign or pledge that the remnant of the Jews who should be carried away *at any time* would return; or that the whole nation would not be destroyed and become extinct. This was one of the *axioms*, or fundamental points in all the writings of this prophet; and whatever calamity or judgment he foretold, it was always terminated with the assurance that the nation should be still ultimately preserved, and greatly enlarged, and glorified. This idea he seems to have resolved to keep as much as possible before the minds of his countrymen, and to this end he gave his son a name that should be to them a pledge of his deep conviction of this truth. The name of the other is MAHER-SHALAL-HASH-BAZ (ch. viii. 1), *haste to the spoil; haste to the prey*—a name significant of the fact that the Assyrian (ch. vii.) would soon ravage and subdue the land, or would extensively plunder the kingdom of Judea. Tradition says that the death of Isaiah occurred in Jerusalem, near the fountain of Siloam. Just below this fountain and opposite to the point where Mount Ophel terminates, is a large mulberry-tree, with a terrace of stones surrounding its trunk, where it is said Isaiah was sawn asunder; Robinson's Bib. Research, i. 342. The tradition further is, that his body was buried here, whence it was removed to Paneas near the sources of the Jordan, and from thence to Constantinople in the year of our Lord 442.

Great respect was paid to Isaiah and his writings after his death. It is evident that Jeremiah imitated him (comp. Notes on chs. xv. xvi.); and there is abundant evidence that he was studied by the other prophets. The estimate in which he was held by the Lord Jesus, and by the writers of the New Testament, will be shown in another part of this Introduction; see § viii. Josephus (Ant. B. xi. ch. i. § 2) says that Cyrus was moved by the reading of Isaiah to the acknowledgment of the God of Israel, and to the restoration of the Jews, and to the rebuilding of the temple. After stating (§ 1) the decree which Cyrus made in favour of the Jews, he adds, ' This was known to Cyrus by his reading the book which Isaiah left behind him of his prophecies; for this prophet had said that God had spoken thus to him in a secret vision, " My will is that Cyrus, whom I have appointed to be king over many and great nations, send back my people to their own land, and build my temple." This was foretold by Isaiah one hundred and forty years before the temple was demolished. Accordingly, when Cyrus read this, and admired the divine power, an earnest desire and ambition came upon him to fulfil what was so written; so he called for the most eminent Jews that were in Babylon, and said to them, that he gave them leave to go back to their own country, and to rebuild their city Jerusalem and the temple of their God.' In this passage of Josephus there is an undoubted reference to Isa. xliv. 28; ' That saith of Cyrus, He is my Shepherd, and shall perform all my pleasure, even saying to Jerusalem, Thou shalt be built; and to the temple, Thy foundation shall be laid ;' comp. ch. xlv. 1, seq. On the genuineness of this passage of Josephus see Whiston's Note. It is justly remarked (see Jahn's observation, quoted by Hengstenberg, Christol. i. 279) that this statement of Josephus furnishes the only explanation of the conduct of Cyrus towards the Jews. It is only a commentary on Ezra i. 2, where Cyrus says, ' JEHOVAH the God of heaven and earth hath given me all the kingdoms of the earth; and he hath charged me to build him an house at Jerusalem which is in Judah.' It is incredible that Cyrus should not have seen the prophecy (Isa. xliv. 28) respecting himself before he made this proclamation.

The writings of the fathers are full of the praise of Isaiah. Jerome says of him that he is not so much to be esteemed a prophet as an Evangelist. And he adds, ' he has so clearly explained the whole mystery of Christ and the church, that you will regard him not as predicting future events, but as composing a history of the past.' In his Epistle ad Paulinum he says, ' Isaiah seems to me not to have composed a prophecy, but the gospel.' And in his Preface he says, ' that in his discourse he is so eloquent, and is a man of so noble and refined elocution, without any mixture of rusticity, that it is impossible to preserve or transfuse the beauty of his style in a translation ;' comp. the Confess. of Augus. ix. 5; De Civita. Dei. lib. viii. c. 29.   Moses Amyraldus said of Isaiah that he ' seems to thunder and lighten; he seems to confound and mingle not Greece, as was formerly said of Pericles; not Judea, and the neighbouring regions, but heaven and earth and all the elements ;' see Michælis Pref. to Isa. p. 8, 9, 10; comp. Joseph. Ant. B. x. c. 3; Sirach ch. xlviii. 22.

' The style of Isaiah,' says Hengstenberg, Christol. vol. i. p. 281, ' is in general characterized by simplicity and sublimity; in the use of imagery, he holds an intermediate place between the poverty of Jeremiah and the exuber-

ance of Ezekiel. In other respects his style is suited to the subject, and
changes with it. In his denunciations and threatenings he is earnest and
vehement ; in his consolations and instructions, on the contrary, he is mild
and insinuating ; in the strictly poetic passages, full of impetuosity and fire.
He so lives in the events he describes, that the future becomes to him as the
past and the present.'

It is now generally conceded that a considerable portion of Isaiah, like the
other prophets, is poetry. For the establishment of this opinion, we are
indebted mainly to Bishop Lowth. ' It has,' says he, (Prelim. Diss. to Isaiah)
' I think, been universally understood that the prophecies of Isaiah were
written in prose. The style, the thoughts, the images, the expressions, have
been allowed to be poetical, and that in the highest degree ; but that they were
written in verse, in measure, in rhythm, or whatever it is that distinguishes as
poetry the composition of those books of the Old Testament which are allowed
to be poetical, such as Job, the Psalms, and the Proverbs, from the historical
books, as mere prose, this has never been supposed, at least has not been at
any time the prevailing feeling.'

The main object of Lowth, in his Preliminary Dissertation, was to demonstrate that the prophecies of Isaiah have all the characteristics of Hebrew
poetry ; a position which he has abundantly established, and which is admitted
now by all to be correct. For a more extended view of the nature of Hebrew
poetry, the reader may consult my Introduction to the Book of Job, pp.
xxxix–liv.

In all ages Isaiah has been regarded as the most sublime of all writers. He
is simple, bold, rapid, elevated ; he abounds in metaphor, and in rapid transitions ; his writings are full of the sublimest figures of rhetoric, and the most
beautiful ornaments of poetry. Grotius compares him to Demosthenes. ' In
his writings we meet with the purity of the Hebrew tongue, as in the orator
with the delicacy of the Attic taste. Both are sublime and magnificent in
their style ; vehement in their emotions ; copious in their figures ; and very
impetuous when they describe things of an enormous nature, or that are grievous and odious. Isaiah was superior to Demosthenes in the honour of illustrious birth.' Comm. on 2 Kings xix. 2. It may be added here, that although
his writings are not so ancient as those of Moses, or as those of Homer and
Hesiod, yet they are more ancient than most of the admired classic productions of Greece, and are far more ancient than any of the Latin classics. As
an *ancient writer* he demands respect. And laying out of view altogether the
idea of his inspiration, and his *religious* character, he has a claim as a poet,
an orator, a writer of eminent beauty and unrivalled sublimity, to the attention of those who are seeking eminence in literature. No reason can be given
why in a course of mental training, Isaiah, and the language in which he wrote,
should be neglected, while Hesiod and Homer, with the language in which they
wrote, should be the objects of admiration and of diligent culture. In no book,
perhaps, can the mere man of taste be more gratified than in the study of
Isaiah ; by no writings would the mind be more elevated in view of the beautiful and the sublime, or the heart be more refined by the contemplation of the
pure. Few, very few of the Greek and Latin classic writers can be put into

the hands of the young without endangering the purity of their morals; but Isaiah may be studied in all the periods of youth, and manhood, and age, only to increase the virtue of the heart and the purity of the imagination, at the same time that he enriches and expands the understanding. And while no one who has just views of the inestimable value of the Greek and Latin classics in most of the respects contemplated in education, would wish to see them banished from the schools, or displaced from seminaries of learning, yet the lover of ancient writings ; of purity of thought and diction ; of sweet and captivating poetry; of the beautiful and sublime in writing; of perhaps the oldest language of the world, and of the pure sentiments of revelation, may hope that the time will come when the Hebrew language shall be deemed worthy of culture in American schools and colleges as well as the Latin and Greek; and that as a part of the training of American youth, Isaiah may be allowed to take a place *at least* as honourable as Virgil or Homer—as Cicero or Demosthenes. It is indeed a melancholy reflection which we are compelled to make on the seminaries of learning in our land—a Christian land—that the writings of the Hebrew prophets and poets have been compelled to give place to the poetry and the mythology of the Greeks; and that the books containing the only system of pure religion are required to defer to those which were written under the auspices of idolatry, and which often express sentiments, and inculcate feelings, which cannot be made to contribute to the purity of the heart, or be reconciled with the truth as revealed from heaven. As specimens of taste; as models of richness of thought and beauty of diction ; as well as for their being the vehicles in which the knowledge of the only true religion is conveyed to man, these writings have a claim on the attention of the young. Were the writings of Isaiah mere human compositions ; had they come down to us as the writings of Demosthenes and Homer have done; and had they not been connected with *religion*, we may be permitted to express the belief, that the Jewish *classics, with* the classics of Greece and Rome, would have been allowed an honourable place in all the seminaries of learning, and in all the public and private libraries of the land.

§ 3. *The Times of Isaiah.*

Isaiah, as we have seen, lived for the greater part of a century, and possibly even more than a century. It is probable also that for a period of more than seventy years he exercised the prophetic office. During that long period, important changes must have occurred ; and a knowledge of some of the leading events of his time is necessary to understand his prophecies. Indeed a simple knowledge of historical facts will often make portions of his prophecies clear which would be otherwise entirely unintelligible.

The kingdom of Israel, which during the reigns of David and Solomon had been so mighty and so magnificent, was divided into two separate kingdoms 990 years before Christ, or two hundred and forty years before Isaiah entered on his prophetic office. The glory of these kingdoms had departed ; and they had been greatly weakened by contentions with each other, and by conflicts with surrounding nations. In a particular manner, the kingdom of Israel, or

Samaria, or Ephraim, or the ten tribes, as it was indiscriminately called, had been governed by a succession of wicked princes; had become deeply imbued with idolatry, and had so far provoked God as to make it necessary to remove them to a foreign land. It was during the time in which Isaiah discharged the duties of the prophetic office that that kingdom was utterly overturned, and the inhabitants transplanted to a distant country. In the year 736 before Christ, or not far from twenty years after Isaiah entered on his work, Tiglath-Pileser king of Assyria slew Rezin king of Damascus, the ally of Pekah the king of Samaria; and he entered the land of Israel, and took many cities and captives, chiefly in Gilead and Galilee, and carried many of the inhabitants to Assyria; 2 Kings xvi. 5–9; Amos i. 5; 2 Kings xv. 29; 1 Chron. v. 26. This was the first captivity of the kingdom of Israel. Shalmaneser succeeded Tiglath-Pileser as king of Assyria B.C. 724. In the year 721 B.C. he besieged Samaria, and after a siege of three years he took it. He carried beyond the Euphrates the inhabitants which Tiglath-Pileser had not removed, and placed them in cities there; 2 Kings xvii. 3–18; Hos. xiii. 16; 1 Chron. v. 26. This was the end of the kingdom of Israel, after it had subsisted two hundred and fifty-four years. Isaiah exercised the prophetic office during about thirty of the last years of the kingdom of Israel. But his residence was principally at Jerusalem; and not many of his predictions have reference to the kingdom of Israel. Most of his prophecies which have reference to the Jews relate to the kingdom of Judah, and to Jerusalem.

The kingdom of Judah, whose capital was Jerusalem, had greatly declined from the splendour and magnificence which had existed under David and Solomon. It had been greatly weakened by the revolt of the ten tribes, and by the wars in which it had been engaged with the kingdom of Samaria, as well as with surrounding nations. Though its kings were superior in virtue and piety to the kings of Israel, yet many of them had been unworthy to be the descendants of David, and their conduct had exposed them greatly to the divine displeasure.

When Isaiah entered on his prophetic office the throne was occupied by Uzziah; or as he is elsewhere called, Azariah. He succeeded his father Amaziah, and was sixteen years old when he came to the throne, and reigned fifty-two years. He began his reign in the year 809 B.C., and of course his reign extended to the year 757 B.C. His general character was that of integrity and piety. He was a worshipper of the true God, yet he did not remove the groves and high places which had been established in the land for idolatrous worship. He greatly strengthened Jerusalem; was successful in his wars with the Philistines, with the Arabians, and the Ammonites, and extended his kingdom somewhat into surrounding regions. Near the close of his life he was guilty of an act of rashness and folly in claiming as a monarch the right of going into the temple of the Lord, and of burning incense on the altar. For this sin he became a leper and remained so till his death; 2 Kings xv; 2 Chron. xxvi. He was of course regarded as unclean, and was obliged to dwell by himself in a separate house; 2 Chron. xxvi. 21. During this period, the affairs of the government were administered by his son Jotham; 2 Chron. xxvi. 21. It is probable that Isaiah exercised the prophetic office but for a short time, perhaps for a single year, during the reign of Uzziah. None of his prophecies can be certainly proved to relate to his reign except that contained in the sixth chapter. It is more natural, however, to suppose that those in the previous five chapters were delivered in his reign.

Uzziah, or Azariah, was succeeded by his son Jotham. He ascended the throne at the age of twenty-five, and reigned sixteen years in Jerusalem. The general character of Jotham was like that of his father. He was upright; and he was not guilty of idolatry. Yet the high places were not removed ; the groves still remained : and the state of the people was corrupt ; 2 Kings xv. 32–36 ; 2 Chron. xxvii. 1–9. He carried forward the plan which his father had commenced of fortifying the city (2 Chron. xxvi. 3), and of enlarging and beautifying his kingdom. In a particular manner, he is said to have built a high gate to the house of the Lord, and to have fortified Ophel ; 2 Chron. xxvi. 3. Ophel was a mountain or *bluff*, which was situated between Mount Zion and Mount Moriah. From the base of this mountain or bluff flowed the waters of Siloam. This bluff was capable of being strongly fortified, and of contributing much to the defence of the city, and accordingly it became one of the strongest places in Jerusalem. Jotham also built cities, and castles, and towns in the mountains and forests of Judea (2 Chron. xxvi. 4), and it is evident that his great aim was to beautify and strengthen his kingdom. The principal wars in which he was engaged were with the Ammonites, whom he subdued, and laid under tribute ; 2 Chron. xxvi. 5.

It was during the reign of Jotham that very important events occurred in the vast empire of the East. The ancient empire of the Assyrians which had governed Asia for more than thirteen hundred years was dissolved on the death of Sardanapalus in the year 747 before Christ. Sardanapalus was distinguished for sloth and luxury. He sunk into the lowest depths of depravity ; clothed himself as a woman ; spun amidst the companies of his concubines ; painted his face and decked himself as a harlot. So debased was he, that his reign became intolerable. He became odious to his subjects and particularly to Arbaces the Mede, and to Belesis the Babylonian. Belesis was a captain, a priest, and an astrologer ; and by the rules of his art, he took upon him to assure Arbaces that he should dethrone Sardanapalus, and become lord of all his dominions. Arbaces hearkened to him, and promised him the chief place over Babylon if his prediction proved true. Arbaces and Belesis promoted a revolt, and the defection spread among the Medes, Babylonians, Persians, and Arabians, who had been subject to the Assyrian empire. They mustered an army of not less than four hundred thousand men, but were at first defeated by Sardanapalus, and driven to the mountains ; but they again rallied and were again defeated with great slaughter, and put to flight towards the hills. Belesis, however, persisted in the opinion that the gods would give them the victory, and a third battle was fought, in which they were again defeated. Belesis again encouraged his followers ; and it was determined to endeavour to secure the aid of the Bactrians. Sardanapalus supposing victory was secure, and that there could be no more danger, had returned to his pleasures, and given himself and his army up to riot and dissipation. Belesis and Arbaces, with the aid of the Bactrians, fell upon the army, sunk in inglorious ease, and

entirely vanquished it, and drew Sardanapalus without the walls of his capital.
Here, closely besieged, he sent away his three sons and two daughters into
Paphlagonia.   In Nineveh he determined to defend himself, trusting to an
ancient prophecy, " that Nineveh could never be taken till the river became
her enemy ;" and as he deemed this impossible, he regarded himself as secure.
He maintained his position, and resisted the attacks of his enemies for two
years, until the river, swelled by great rains, rose and overflowed a considerable part of it.   Regarding his affairs as now desperate, he caused a vast pile
of wood to be raised in a court of his palace, in which he placed his gold and
silver and royal apparel, and within which he enclosed his eunuchs and concubines, and retired within his palace, and caused the pile to be set on fire,
and was consumed himself with the rest ; Universal History, Anc. Part, vol.
iii. pp. 354–358.   Edit. Lond. 1779.

From this kingdom, thus destroyed, arose the two kingdoms of Assyria, as
mentioned in the Scriptures, and of Babylonia.   Arbaces, who, according to
Prideaux, is the same as Tiglath-Pileser (comp. however Universal History,
vol. v. 359), obtained a large part of the empire.   Belesis had Babylon,
Chaldea, and Arabia.   Belesis, according to Prideaux (Connex. book i. p.
114), was the same as Nabonassar, or Baladan (see Note on ch. xxxix. 1); and
was the king from whom was reckoned the famous era of Nabonassar commencing in the 747th year before the Christian era.   It is not improbable
that there was some degree of dependence of the Babylonian portion of the
empire on the Assyrian ; or that the king of Babylon was regarded as a
viceroy to the king of Assyria, as we know that among the colonists sent by
Shalmaneser to people Samaria after the ten tribes were carried away, were
some from Babylon, which is there mentioned in such a manner as to leave
the impression that it was a province of Assyria ; 2 Kings xvii. 24.   The
kingdom of Babylon, however, ultimately acquired the ascendency, and the
Assyrian was merged into the Chaldean monarchy.   This occurred about one
hundred years after the reign of Nabonassar, or Baladan, and was effected by
an alliance formed between Nabopolassar and Cyaxares the Median ; see Rob.
Cal. Art. Babylonia ; comp. Note on ch. xxxix. 1.   It should be observed,
however, that the history of the Assyrian empire is one of the obscurest portions of the ancient history ; see the article Assyria in Rob. Calmet.

There is not any decided evidence that Isaiah delivered any prophecies
during the reign of Jotham.   Most commentators have supposed that the
prophecies in ch. ii.—v. were delivered during his reign ; but there is no internal proof to demonstrate it ; see the Analysis of these chapters.

Jotham was succeeded by Ahaz.   He was the twelfth king of Judah.   He
came to the throne at the age of twenty years, and reigned in Jerusalem
sixteen years, and of course died at the age of thirty-six.   He ascended the
throne, according to Calmet, 738 years before the Christian era ; see 2 Kings
xvi. 2 ; 2 Chron. xxviii. 5.   The character of Ahaz was the reverse of that of
his father ; and, excepting Manasseh his grandson, there was not probably a
more impious prince that sat on the throne of Judah.   Nor was there a reign
that was on the whole more disastrous than his.   A statement of his deeds of
evil, and a brief record of the calamitous events of his reign, is given in 2 Chron.

xxviii. and in 2 Kings xvi. He imitated the kings of Israel and Samaria in all manner of abominations and disorders. He early made images of Baalim. He burnt incense in the valley of Hinnom to idol gods, and burnt his children in the fire. He established idolatrous places of worship in every part of the land ; and caused the worship of idols to be celebrated in the groves, and on all the hills in Judea. As a consequence of this idolatry, and as a punishment for his sins and the sins of the nation, his kingdom was invaded by the joint forces of the kings of Syria and of Samaria. A large number of captive Jews were carried to Damascus ; and in one day Pekah the king of Samaria killed one hundred and twenty thousand, and took captive two hundred thousand more whom he purposed to carry captive to Samaria. This he would have done but for the remonstrance of the prophet Obed, who pled with him, and represented the impropriety of his carrying his brethren into bondage ; and at his solicitation, and from the apprehension of the wrath of God, the captives were returned to Jericho, and set at liberty ; 2 Chron. xxviii. 15. It was at this juncture, and when Ahaz trembled with alarm at the prospect of the invasion of the kings of Syria and Samaria, that he resolved to call in the aid of the Assyrian, and thus to repel the apprehended invasion. Though he had been able to defeat the united armies of Syria and Samaria once (2 Kings xvi. 5), yet those armies again returned, and Ahaz in alarm determined to seek the aid of Assyria. For this purpose he sent messengers, with terms of most humble submission and entreaty, and with the most costly presents that his kingdom could furnish, to secure the alliance and aid of Tiglath-Pileser the king of Assyria ; 2 Kings xvi. 7, 8. It was at this time, when Ahaz was so much alarmed, that Isaiah met him at the conduit of the upper pool in the highway of the fuller's field (Isa. vii. 3, 4,) and assured him that he had no occasion to fear the united armies of Syria and Samaria ; that Jerusalem was safe, and that God would be its protector. He assured him that the king-doms of Syria and Samaria should not be enlarged by the accession and con-quest of the kingdom of Judah (Isa. vii. 7-9) ; and advised Ahaz to ask a sign, or demonstration, from JEHOVAH that this should be fulfilled ; Isa. vii. 10, 11. Ahaz indignantly, though with the appearance of religious scruple, said that he would *not* ask a sign, vii. 12. The *secret* reason, however, why he was not solicitous to procure a sign from JEHOVAH was, that he had formed an alliance with the king of Assyria, and scorned the idea of recognizing his dependence on JEHOVAH.—Isaiah, therefore, proceeded (vii. 13, seq.) to assure him that JEHOVAH would himself give a sign, and would furnish a demonstration to him that the land would be soon forsaken of both the kings which Ahaz dreaded ; see Notes on ch. vii. Isaiah then proceeded to state the consequences of this alliance with the king of Assyria, and to assure him that the result would be, that, under the pretence of aiding him, he would bring up his forces on the land of Judah, and spread devastation and ruin, and that Jerusalem only would be spared ; Isa. vii. 17, seq. and ch. viii. The prophecy respecting the speedy removal of the two kings of Syria and Samaria was accomplished ; see Notes on ch. vii. 16. At about the same time the kingdom of Judah was threatened with an invasion from the Edomites and Philistines ; 2 Chron. xxviii. 17, 18 In this emergency Ahaz had recourse to his old ally the king of Assyria :

2 Chron. xxviii. 20, 21.   To secure his friendship, he made him a present
obtained from the temple, from his own house, and from the princes ; 2 Chron.
xxviii. 21.   The king of Assyria professedly accepted the offer ; marched
against Rezin the king of Syria, took Damascus, and slew Rezin, agreeably to
the prediction of Isaiah, ch. vii. 16.   While Tiglath-Pileser was at Damascus,
Ahaz visited him, and being much charmed with an altar which he saw there,
he sent a model of it to Urijah the priest to have one constructed like it in
Jerusalem ; 2 Kings xvi. 10, seq.   This was done.   Ahaz returned from
Damascus ; offered sacrifice on the new altar which he had had constructed,
and gave himself up to every species of idolatry and abomination ; 2 Kings
xvi. 12, seq.   He offered sacrifice to the gods of Damascus, on the pretence
that they had defended Syria, and might be rendered propitious to defend his
own kingdom (2 Chron. xxviii. 23); he broke up the vessels of the temple,
shut up the doors, and erected altars to the heathen deities in every part of
Jerusalem ; 2 Chron. xxviii. 24, 25.   He thus finished his inglorious reign in
the thirty-sixth year of his age, and was buried in the city of Jerusalem, but
not in the sepulchres of the kings, on account of his gross abominations ;
2 Chron. xxviii. 27.

The prediction of Isaiah (ch. vii. viii.) that his calling in the aid of the
king of Assyria would result in disaster to his own land, and to *all* the land
except Jerusalem (Note, ch. viii. 8), was not accomplished in the time of Ahaz,
but was literally fulfilled in the calamities which occurred by the invasion of
Sennacherib in the times of Hezekiah ; see Notes on ch. viii. and ch. xxxvi.
–xxxix.

It is not *certainly* known what prophecies were delivered by Isaiah in the
time of Ahaz.   It is certain that those contained in ch. vii. viii. and ix.
were uttered during his reign, and there is every probability that those contained in ch. x. xi. xii. were also.   Perhaps some of the subsequent predictions
also were uttered during his reign.

Ahaz was succeeded by his son Hezekiah, one of the most pious kings that
ever sat on the throne of David.   He was twenty-five years old when he began
to reign, and he reigned twenty-nine years ; 2 Chron. xxxix. 1.   His character
was the reverse of that of his father ; and one of the first acts of his reign was
to remove the evils introduced in the reign of Ahaz, and to restore again the
pure worship of God.   He began the work of reform by destroying the high
places, cutting down the groves, and overturning the altars of idolatry.   He
destroyed the brazen serpent which Moses had made, and which had become
an object of idolatrous worship.   He ordered the doors of the temple to be
rebuilt, and the temple itself was thoroughly cleansed and repaired ; 2 Kings
xviii. 1–6. 2 Chron. xxix. 1–17.   He restored the observance of the Passover,
and it was celebrated with great pomp and joy (2 Chron. xxx. seq.), and he
restored the regular worship in the temple as it was in the time of Solomon ;
2 Chron. xxviii. 18.   Successful in his efforts to reform the religion of his
country, and in his wars with the Philistines (2 Kings xviii. 8), he resolved
to cast off the inglorious yoke of servitude to the king of Assyria ; 2 Kings
xviii. 7.   He refused, therefore, to pay the tribute which had been promised
to him, and which had been paid by his father Ahaz.   As might have been

expected, this resolution excited the indignation of the king of Assyria, and led to the resolution to compel submission. Sennacherib, therefore, invaded the land with a great army; spread desolation through no small part of it; and was rapidly advancing towards Jerusalem. Hezekiah saw his error, and, alarmed, he sought to avoid the threatened blow. He, therefore, put the city in the best possible posture of defence. He fortified it; enclosed it with a second wall; erected towers; repaired the fortification Millo in the city of David; stopped all the fountains; and made darts and shields that the city might be defended; 2 Chron. xxxii. 1–8. He endeavoured to prepare himself, as well as possible to meet the mighty foe; and he did all that he could to inspire confidence in God among the people; Notes on Isa. xxii. 9–11. Yet as if not quite confident that he could be able to hold out during a siege, and to resist an army so mighty as that of Sennacherib, he sent ambassadors to him, acknowledged his error, and sued for peace. Sennacherib proposed that he should send him three hundred talents of silver, and thirty talents of gold, and gave the *implied* assurance that if this were done his army should be withdrawn; 2 Kings xviii. 13, 14. Hezekiah readily agreed to send what was demanded; and to accomplish this he emptied the treasury, and stripped the temple of its ornaments; 2 Kings xviii. 15, 16. Sennacherib *then* went down to Egypt (see Notes on ch. xxxvi. xxxvii.), and was repelled before Pelusium by the approach of Tirhakah king of Ethiopia, who had come to the aid of the Egyptian monarch. On his return, Sennacherib sent messengers from Lachish, and a portion of his army to Jerusalem to demand its surrender; Isa. xxxvi. 2. To this embassy no answer was returned by the messengers of Hezekiah (Isa. xxxvi. 21, 22); and the messengers of Sennacherib returned again to him to Libnah; Note on Isa. xxxvii. 8. At this period, Sennacherib was alarmed by the rumour that Tirhakah, whom he had so much reason to dread, was advancing against him (Isa. xxxvii. 9), and he again sent messengers to Hezekiah to induce him to surrender, intending evidently to anticipate the news that Tirhakah was coming, and to secure the conquest of Jerusalem without being compelled to sit down before it in a regular siege. This message, like the former, was unsuccessful. Hezekiah spread the case before Jehovah (ch. xxxvii. 15–20), and received the answer that Jerusalem was safe. Sennacherib advanced to attack the city; but in a single night 185,000 of his men were destroyed by an angel of the Lord, and he himself fled to his capital, where he was slain by his two sons; ch. xxxvii. 36–38.

These events were among the most important in Jewish history. Isaiah lived during their occurrence; and a large portion of his prophecies from ch. xiv. to ch. xxxix. are occupied with allusions to and statements of these events. He gave himself to the work of preparing the nation for them; assuring them that they would come, but that Jerusalem should be safe. He seems to have laboured to inspire the mind of Hezekiah and the minds of the people with confidence in God, that when the danger should arrive, they might look to him entirely for defence. In this he was eminently successful; and Hezekiah and the nation put unwavering confidence in God. An accurate acquaintance with the causes, and the various events connected with the overthrow of Sennacherib, is indispensable to a clear understanding of Isaiah; and these causes and events I have endeavoured to present in Notes on the several chapters which refer to that remarkable invasion. Soon after this, Hezekiah became dangerously ill; and Isaiah announced to him that he must die; Isa. xxxviii. 1. Hezekiah prayed to God for the preservation of his life, and an assurance was given to him that he should live fifteen years longer; Isa. xxxviii. 5. In attestation of this, and as a demonstration of it, the shadow on the sun-dial of Ahaz was made to recede ten degrees; see Notes on ch. xxxviii. 8.

Hezekiah, after his signal success over his foe, and the entire deliverance of his kingdom from the long dreaded invasion, and his recovery from the dangerous illness, became eminently prosperous and successful. He was caressed and flattered by foreign princes; presents of great value were given him, and he encompassed himself with the usual splendour and magnificence of an oriental monarch; 2 Chron. xxxii. 23, 27, 28. As a consequence of this, his heart was lifted up with pride; he gloried in his wealth, and magnificence, and even became proud of the divine interposition in his favour. To show what was in his heart, and to humble him, he was left to display his treasures in an ostentatious manner to the ambassadors of Merodach-Baladan king of Babylon (2 Chron. xxxii. 25, 31), and *for this* received the assurance that all his treasures and his family should be carried in inglorious bondage to the land from whence the ambassadors came; 2 Kings xx. 12–18; Notes on Isa. xxxix. The remnant of the life of Hezekiah was peace; Isa. xxxix. 8. He died at the age of fifty-four years; and was buried in the most honoured of the tombs of the kings of Judah (2 Chron. xxxii. 33); and was deeply lamented by a weeping people at his death.

The reign of Hezekiah stretched through a considerable portion of the prophetic ministry of Isaiah. A large part of his prophecies are, therefore, presumed to have been uttered during this reign. It is probable that to this period we are to attribute the entire series from ch. xiii. to ch. xxxix. inclusive. The *most* important of his prophecies, from ch. xl. to ch. lxvi., I am disposed to assign to a subsequent period—to the reign of Manasseh. The reasons for this may be seen, in part, in § 2 of this Introduction.

Hezekiah was succeeded by his son Manasseh. The reasons for thinking that any part of the life of Isaiah was passed under the reign of this wicked prince have been stated above. He was the fifteenth king of Judah, and was twelve years old when he began to reign, and reigned fifty-five years. It was during his reign, and by him, as it is commonly supposed, that Isaiah was put to death. He forsook the path of Hezekiah and David, restored idolatry, worshipped the idols of Canaan, rebuilt the high places which Hezekiah had destroyed, set up altars to Baal, and planted groves to false gods. He raised altars to the whole host of heaven even in Jerusalem and in the courts of the temple, made his son pass through the fire to Moloch, was addicted to magic and divination, set up the idol of Astarte in the house of God, and caused the people to sin in a more aggravated form than had been done by the heathen who had formerly inhabited the land of Canaan. To all this he added cruelty in the highest degree, and 'shed innocent blood very much, till he had filled Jerusalem from one end to another.' Probably most of the distinguished men of piety were cut off by him, and among them, it is supposed, was Isaiah ; see 2 Kings xxi.; 2 Chron. xxxiii.

So great were his crimes that God brought upon the land the king of Assyria, who took Manasseh from the hiding place where he sought a refuge amidst briers and thorns, and bound him, and carried him to *Babylon* (2 Chron. xxxii. 11),—another proof that Babylon was at this time a dependent province of the Assyrian monarchy. In Babylon, Manasseh repented of his sins and humbled himself, and he was again returned to his land and his throne. After his restoration he removed the worship of idols, and re-established the worship of JEHOVAH. He built a wall on the west side of Gihon, and extended it around to Mount Ophel, and put Jerusalem in a posture of defence. He broke down and removed the altars which he had erected in Jerusalem, and in the temple ; and he removed all traces of idolatrous worship except the high places, which he suffered still to remain. There is evidence of his reformation ; and the latter part of his reign appears to have passed in comparative happiness and virtue.

It was only during the early part of his reign that Isaiah lived, and there is in his prophecies no express mention made of Manasseh. If he lived during any part of it, it is evident that he withdrew entirely, or nearly so, from the public exercise of his prophetic functions, and retired to a comparatively private life. There is evidently between the close of the xxxixth chapter of his prophecy, and the period when the latter part of his prophecies commences (ch. xl.) an interval of considerable duration. It is not a violation of probability that Isaiah after the death of Hezekiah, being an old man, withdrew much from public life ; that he saw and felt that there was little hope of producing reform during the impious career of Manasseh; and that, in the distress and anguish of his soul, he gave himself up to the contemplation of the happier times which should yet occur under the reign of the Messiah. It was during this period, I suppose, that he composed the latter part of his prophecies, from the xlth to the lxvith chapter. The nation was full of wickedness. An impious prince was on the throne. Piety was banished, and the friends of JEHOVAH were bleeding in Jerusalem. The nation was given up to idolatry. The kingdom was approaching the period of its predicted fall and ruin. Isaiah saw the tendency of events ; he saw how hopeless would be the attempt at reform. He saw that the captivity of Babylon was hastening on, and that the nation was preparing for that gloomy event. In this dark and disastrous period, he seems to have withdrawn himself from the contemplation of the joyless present, and to have given his mind to the contemplation of happier future scenes. An interval perhaps of some ten or fifteen years may be supposed to have elapsed between his last public labours in the time of Hezekiah, and the prophecies which compose the remainder of the book. During this interval he may have withdrawn from public view, and fixed his mind on the great events of future times. In his visions he sees the nation about to go into captivity. Yet he sees also that there would be a return from bondage, and he comforts the hearts of the pious with the assurance of such a return. He announces the name of the monarch by whom that deliverance would be accomplished, and gives assurance that the captive Jews should again return to their own land. But he is not satisfied with the announcement of this comparatively unimportant deliverance. With that he connects a far greater and more important deliverance, that from sin, under the Messiah. He fixes his eye, therefore, on the future glories of the kingdom of God ; sees the long promised Messiah; describes his person, his work, his doctrine, and states in glowing language the effects of his coming on the happiness and destiny of mankind. As he advances in his prophetic descriptions, the deliverance from Babylon seems to die away and is forgotten ; or it is lost in the contemplation of the event to which it had a resemblance—the coming of the Messiah—as the morning star is lost in the superior glory of the rising sun. He throws himself forward in his descriptions ; places himself *amidst* these future scenes, and describes them as taking place around him, and as events which he saw. He thinks and feels and acts as if *in* that period ; his mind is full of the contemplation ; and he pours out, in describing it, the most elevated language and the sublimest thoughts. It was in contemplations such as these, I suppose, that he passed the close of his life ; and in such visions of the glorious future, that he sought a refuge from the gloom and despondency which must have filled a pious mind during the early part of the reign of the impious and blood-thirsty Manasseh.

Isaiah was cotemporary with the prophets Jonah, Hosea, and Micah. They, however, performed a less important public part, and were not favoured with visions of the future glory of the church, like his. In a single chapter, however, the same language is used by Isaiah and by Micah ; see Isa. ii. 2-4 ; comp. Micah iv. 1-4. In which prophet the language is original, it is impossible now to determine.

The period of the world in which Isaiah lived was in some respects a *forming* period. We have seen that it was during his life that the kingdom of Assyria, which had so long swayed a sceptre of entire dominion over the East, began to wane, and that its power was broken. The kingdom of Babylon, which ultimately became so vast and mighty, and which destroyed Assyria itself, was established during his life on a basis that secured its future independence and grandeur. The kingdom of Macedon, whose rise was followed by so great events under the emperor Alexander, was founded about the time when Isaiah began his prophetic life (B.C. 814), by Caranus. Carthage had been founded about half a century before (B.C. 869); and Rome was founded during his life, B.C. 753. Syracuse was built by Archias of Corinth, during his life, B.C. 769. It is of some importance in recollecting the events of ancient history to *group* them together, and some advantage may be derived to the student from connecting these events with the name and life of Isaiah.

The following tables, copied mainly from Jahn's Biblical Archaeology, will give a correct view of the principal chronological events in the time of Isaiah, and may be of use in the correct understanding of his prophecies.

TABLE I.

B.C.	JUDAH.	ISRAEL.	ASSYRIA.	MEDIA.	BABYLON.	OTHERS.
825	Amaziah.	Jeroboam II. 41 yrs.		Arbaces, 29 years.		
814		*Jonah,* the prophet.				Mace- donia.
811	Uzziah, 52 years.	*Amos,* the prophet.				
797				Interreg- num,79 yrs.		
784		*Hosea,* the prophet. Interreg- num, 12 ys.				
773		Zechariah, 6 months. Shallum, 1 month.	Phul, 21 yrs.			
772		Menahem, 10 years.				
761	*Isaiah.*	Pekahiah, 2 years.				
759	Jotham, 16 years. *Micah.*	Pekah, 20 years.				
753			Tiglath- Pileser, 19 years.			Rome.
747					Nabonassar 14, or Mero- dach-Bala- dan.	
743	Ahaz, 16 ys.					
740			Conquers Da- mascus, Gali- lee & Gilead.			
739		Interreg- num, 9 yrs.				
734			Shalmaneser, 14 years.		Nadius, 2 years.	
730		Hosea,9 ys.			Porus,5 ys.	
728	Hezekiah, 29 years.				Jugaeus, 5 years.	
722		OVERTHROW OF ISRAEL.				

TABLE II.

B.C.	JUDAH.	ASSYRIA.	MEDIA.	BABYLON.
721	Hezekiah.			
720		Sennacherib, 7 ys.		
718			Dejoces, 53 yrs.	
714		Senn. in Judea.		
713		Essar-haddon, 35 years.		
709				Arkianus, 5 yrs.
704				Interreg. 2 yrs.
702				Belibus, 3 years.
699	Manasseh, 55 ys.			Apronadius,6 yrs.
693				Rigebelus, 1 yr.
692				Messomordacus, 4 years.

§ 4. *Divisions of Isaiah.*

Various modes of classifying the prophecies of Isaiah have been proposed, in order to present them in the most lucid and clear manner. Gesenius divides the whole into four parts, exclusive of the historical portion (ch. xxxvi.–xxxix.); the first, comprising ch. i.–xii.; the second, ch. xiii.–xxiii.; the third, ch. xxiv.–xxxv.; and the fourth, ch. xl.–lxvi. Horne proposes the following division : Part I. ch. i.–v.; II. ch. vii.–xii.; III. ch. xiii.–xxiv.; IV. ch. xxiv.–xxxiii.; V. ch. xxxvi.–xxxix.; VI. ch. xl.–lxvi.; see his Introduction, vol. ii. 157, seq. Vitringa divides the book into the following portions :—

I. PROPHETIC.

(1.) Five prophetic addresses directly to the Jews, including the Ephraimites, reprehending, denouncing, and accusing them, ch. i.–xii.

(2.) Eight addresses or prophetic discourses, in which the destiny of foreign nations is foretold, particularly the destiny of Babylon, Philistia, Moab, Syria, Assyria, Ethiopia, Egypt, Arabia and Tyre, ch. xiii.–xxiii.

(3.) Penal judgments against the Jews and their foes, with ample promises of the final preservation and future prosperity of the Jews, ch. xxiv.–xxxvi.

(4.) Four consolatory addresses, respecting the coming of the Messiah, and particularly describing the events which would be introductory to it; especially the liberation from the captivity at Babylon, ch. xl.–xlix.

(5.) A description of the coming and work of the Messiah—his person, his doctrines, his death, and the success of the gospel and its final triumph, ch. xlix.–lxvi.

II. HISTORIC. The events recorded in ch. xxxvi.–xxxix.

The natural and obvious division of Isaiah is into two parts, the first of which closes with the xxxixth chapter, and the latter of which comprises the remainder of the book (xl.–lxvi). In this division the latter portion is regarded as substantially a *continuous* prophecy, or an *unbroken* oracle or vision, relating to far distant events, and having little reference to existing things at the time when Isaiah lived, except the implied censures which are passed on the idolatry of the Jews in the time of Manasseh. The main drift and scope, however, is to portray events to come—the certain deliverance of the Jews from the bondage in Babylon, and the higher deliverance of the world under the Messiah, of which the former was the *suggester* and the *emblem.*

The former part (ch. i.–xxxix.) comprises a collection of independent prophecies and writings composed at various periods during the public ministry of the prophet, and designed to produce an *immediate* effect on the morals, the piety, the faith, and the welfare of the nation. The general drift is, that Jerusalem was secure ; that the kingdom of God on earth could not be destroyed ; that however much his people might be subjected to punishment for their sins, and however long and grievous might be their calamities, and however mighty their foes, yet that the kingdom of God could not be overturned, and his promises set at nought. Hence in all the predictions of judgment and calamity ; in all the reproofs for crime, idolatry, and sin ; there is usually found a *saving clause*,—an assurance that the people of God would finally triumph, and be secure. And hence so large a portion of this division of the book is occupied with a prophetic statement of the entire and utter overthrow of the formidable states, nations, and cities with which they had been so often engaged in war, and which were so decidedly hostile to the Jews. The prophet, therefore, goes over in detail these cities and nations, and depicts successively the destruction of the Assyrians, of Babylon, Tyre, Moab, Damascus, Edom, &c., until he comes to the triumphant conclusion in ch. xxxv. that ALL the enemies of the people of God would be destroyed, and his kingdom be established on an imperishable basis under the Messiah ; see Notes on ch. xxxv. This is the scope of this part of the prophecy; and this is the reason why there is such fearful denunciation of surrounding nations. In the course of the predictions, however, there are frequent reproofs of the Jews for their sins, and solemn warnings and assurances of judgments against *them ;* but there is the uniform assurance that they should be delivered, as a people, from all bondage and calamity, and be restored to ultimate freedom and prosperity.

This part of the book comprises the prophecies which were uttered during the reigns of Uzziah, Jotham, Ahaz, and Hezekiah ; see § 3. For convenience it may be divided in the following manner :—

FIRST. Independent prophecies, relating to Judah and Israel, ch. i.–xii. These are seven in number.

I. Reproof of national crimes, ch. i.

II. JUDAH, its sins, ch. ii. iii. iv.

III. JUDAH, a vineyard, ch. v.

IV. VISION OF JEHOVAH, ch. vi.

V. AHAZ ; impending calamity ; prediction of the birth and character of the Messiah, ch. vii. viii. ix. 1–7.

VI. SAMARIA, ch. ix. 8–21 ; x. 1–4.

VII. SENNACHERIB ; deliverance from him ; advent and work of the Messiah, ch. x. 5–34; xi. xii.

SECOND. Independent prophecies, mainly relating to surrounding nations which had been regarded as hostile to the Jews, or which were their natural enemies, or which for their sins were to be cut off to make way for the introduction and permanent establishment of the kingdom of God, ch. xiii.–xxiii. These prophecies are fourteen in number, and relate to the following kingdoms and people.

VIII. BABYLON, ch. xiii. xiv. 1–27.

IX. PHILISTIA, ch. xiv. 28–32.

X. MOAB, ch. xv. xvi.

XI. DAMASCUS, ch. xvii. 1–11.

XII. SENNACHERIB, ch. xvii. 12–24.

XIII. NUBIA, or ETHIOPIA, ch. xviii.

XIV. EGYPT, ch. xix.

XV. EGYPT and ASSYRIA, ch. xx.

XVI. The destruction of BABYLON, ch. xxi. 1–10.

XVII. DUMAH OR IDUMEA, ch. xxi. 11, 12.

XVIII. ARABIA, ch. xxi. 13–17.

XIX. JERUSALEM, when about to be besieged by Sennacherib, ch. xxii. 1–14.

XX. The fall of SHEBNA, and the promotion of ELIAKIM, ch. xxii. 15–25.

XXI. TYRE, ch. xxiii.

THIRD. Independent prophecies, relating mainly to the times of Hezekiah, and to the prospect of the Assyrian invasion under Sennacherib; with a statement of the ultimate safety of the people of God, and the overthrow of all their enemies, ch. xxiv.–xxxv. These prophecies are eight in number, and relate to the following events.

XXII. Desolation of the land of JUDEA, its delivery and triumph, ch. xxiv.–xxvii.

XXIII. EPHRAIM to be destroyed, and JUDAH preserved, ch. xxviii.

XXIV. The siege and deliverance of Jerusalem, ch. xxix.

XXV. An alliance with Egypt condemned, ch. xxx.

XXVI. Denunciation on account of the contemplated alliance with Egypt, ch. xxxi.

XXVII. The virtuous and yet unsuccessful reign of Hezekiah, ch. xxxii.

XXVIII. The destruction of the ASSYRIAN ARMY, ch. xxxiii.

XXIX. The destruction of EDOM, and of *all* the enemies of God, and the final triumph and security of the people, ch. xxxiv. xxxv.

FOURTH. The historical portion (ch. xxxvi.–xxxix.), relating to the destruction of Sennacherib, and the sickness and recovery of Hezekiah.

One great cause of the difficulty of understanding Isaiah arises from the manner in which the division into CHAPTERS has been made. This division is known to be of recent origin, and is of no authority whatever. It was first adopted by Cardinal Hugo in the 13th century, who wrote a celebrated commentary on the Scriptures. He divided the Latin Vulgate into chapters nearly the same as those which now exist in the English version. These chapters he divided into smaller sections by placing the letters A, B, C, &c., at equal distances from each other in the margin. The division into verses is of still later origin. It was made by Stephens on a journey from Lyons to Paris in 1551, and was first used in his edition of the New Testament. The Jews formerly divided the books of the Old Testament into greater and smaller sections.

It is obvious that these divisions are of no authority; and it is *as* obvious that they were most injudiciously made. A simple glance at Isaiah will show that prophecies have been divided in many instances which should have been retained in the same chapter; and that prophecies, and parts of prophecies, have been thrown into the same chapter which should have been kept distinct. It is not usually difficult to mark the commencement and the close of the prophecies in Isaiah; and an indication of such a natural division throws material light on the prophecy itself. The proper divisions have been indicated above.

§ 5. *The Historical Writings of Isaiah.*

It is evident that Isaiah wrote more than we have in the book which bears his name. In 2 Chron. xxvi. 22, it is said, ' Now the rest of the acts of Uzziah, first and last, did Isaiah the prophet, the son of Amoz, write.' But the only portion of the book of Isaiah which can with any *certainty* be referred to the time of Uzziah is chapter vi. And even if, as we may suppose, the five previous chapters are to be referred to his time, yet they contain no historical statement; no record of public events sufficient to constitute a history of 'the acts of Uzziah, first and last.' It is therefore morally certain that there were other writings of Isaiah which we have not in this collection of his prophecies.

Again, in 2 Chron. xxxii. 32, it is said, 'Now the rest of the acts of Hezekiah, and his goodness, behold, they are written in the vision of Isaiah the prophet, the son of Amoz.' In the book of Isaiah we have a record of some very important events connected with the life of Hezekiah; see ch. xxxvi.–xxxix. But there is no formal *record* of the events of the early part of his reign, or of his death. What is said relates to the invasion of Sennacherib (ch. xxxvi. xxxvii.); to the sickness and recovery of Hezekiah (ch. xxxviii.); and to the visit of the ambassadors from Babylon, ch. xxxix. But this would scarcely deserve to be called a record, or history of his 'acts,' and his 'goodness,' (marg. *kindnesses*); that is, his doings or plans of beneficence to promote the happiness and piety of his people. It is not, however, on this passage so much that reliance is to be placed to prove that he wrote other documents, as on the passage quoted from 2 Kings.

In regard to these historical records which are not now found in the book of Isaiah, there can be but two opinions.

(1.) One is, that they are lost; that they formed a part of the record of his times which was then of value, and which was lost when more full and complete records were made in the books of Kings and Chronicles. Many such writings are mentioned which are now lost, or which are not found under the names of their authors. Thus we have accounts of the writings of Gad, and Iddo the Seer, and Nathan, and the prophecy of Ahijah the Shilomite, and the book of Jehu (1 Chron xxix. 29; 2 Chron. ix. 29; xx. 34; 1 Kings xvi. 1); all of which are now lost, unless they have come down to us under some other name. Nor is there any improbability that some portions of the once inspired writings are lost. They may have been inspired to accomplish a certain object; and, when that object was gained, they may have been lost or destroyed as not farther necessary, or as superseded by superior clearness of revelation. No man can tell why it should be regarded as more improbable that divine communications which are *written* should be lost when they have accomplished their purpose, than it is that divine communications *spoken* should be lost. In the mere act of writing there is no peculiar sacredness that should make it necessary to preserve it. And yet no one can doubt (comp. John xxi. 25) that a very large portion of what our blessed Lord spoke, who always spoke inspired truth, is now irrecoverably lost. It never was recorded; and there can be no impropriety in supposing that portions of truth that have been recorded have likewise perished. The whole Bible will be consumed in the conflagration of the last day—but truth will live. God has preserved, with remarkable care, as much truth as he saw was necessary to illuminate and edify his church to the end of time. There is, however, no indispensable necessity of supposing that *in fact* any part of the sacred record has been destroyed. For,

(2.) The records which were made by Isaiah, Iddo, Nathan, Ahijah, &c., may have been public documents that were laid up in the archives of the state, and that were subsequently *incorporated* into the historical books which we now have. It is probable that the history of each reign was recorded by a prophet, a scribe, or a *historiographer;* see Note, Isa. xxxvi. 3. From the following extract from the travels of Mr. Bruce, it is evident that such an officer is known in modern times as attached to a court. The extract will also be descriptive of the duties of such an officer, and perhaps may be regarded as descriptive of some of the functions discharged by the prophets. 'The king has near his person an officer who is meant to be his HISTORIOGRAPHER. He is also keeper of his seal; and is *obliged to make a journal of the king's actions, good or bad, without comment of his own upon them.* This, when the king dies, or at least soon after, is delivered to the council, who read it over, and erase every thing false in it, whilst they supply every material fact that may have been omitted, whether purposely or not.' Travels, vol. ii. p. 596. Such a record is also kept of all the sayings and purposes of the Emperor of China by an officer appointed for this purpose. It is carefully made, and sealed up during his life, and is not opened until he dies. This is regarded in that empire as an important public security that the Emperor will say or do nothing that he will be unwilling should be known by posterity; see Edin. Ency., Art. China. It would seem probable, therefore, that this is an oriental custom extensively prevalent. There is every reason to believe that a part of these royal biographies, or records of important events in each reign, were written by prophets; see the Analysis of Isa. xxxvi. These records would be deposited in the archives of state, and would be regarded as authentic documents, and placed under the custody of proper officers. When the connected history of the nation came to be written; when the books of the 'Kings' and the 'Chronicles' were composed, nothing would be more natural than to take these documents or historical records, and arrange and embody them *as a part* of the sacred history. They may have been incorporated entire into the narratives which we now have; and the name of the writer simply referred to as the *authority* for the document, or to preserve the recollection of the original author of each fragment or part of the history. This I regard as by far the most probable supposition; and if this be correct, then we have still substantially the portions of history which were composed by Isaiah, Gad, &c., and they have been, with perhaps some slight changes necessary to constitute a continuous narrative, or to supply some omissions, incorporated into the historical records which we now possess. These requisite changes may have been made by Ezra when the canon of the Old Testament was completed. The reasons for this opinion may be seen more at length in the Analysis of chapter xxxvi.

§ 6. *Quotations of Isaiah in the New Testament.*

Isaiah refers more fully to the times of the Messiah than any other of the prophets. It is natural, therefore, to expect to find his writings often quoted or appealed to in the New Testament. The frequency of the reference, and the manner in which it is done, will show the estimate in which he was held by the Saviour, and by the apostles. It may also contribute in some degree to the explanation of some of the passages quoted to have them convenient for reference, or for examination. The meaning of Isaiah may be often determined by the inspired statement of the event referred to in the New Testament ; and the meaning of a New Testament writer likewise by a reference to the passage which he quotes. In regard to these quotations, also, it may be of use to bear in remembrance that a portion is made directly and literally from the Hebrew, and agrees also with the Septuagint version, or is in the words of the Septuagint ; a portion agrees with the Hebrew in sense but not in words ; a portion is made from the Septuagint translation even when the Septuagint differs from the Hebrew ; and in some cases there is a bare allusion to a passage. It may be useful to furnish a classification of the entire passages which are quoted in the New Testament, under several heads, that they may be seen at one view, and may be compared at leisure. For this selection and arrangement, I am mainly indebted to Horne. Intro. vol. ii. p. 343, seq.

I. *Quotations agreeing exactly with the Hebrew.*

Isa. liii. 4.	quoted in	Matt. viii. 17.
Isa. liii. 12.		Mark xv. 28; Luke xxii. 37.
Isa. liii. 1.		John xii. 38; comp. Rom. x. 16.
Isa. lii. 15.		Rom. xv. 21.
Isa. xxii. 13.		1 Cor. xv. 32.
Isa. xxv. 8.		1 Cor. xv. 54.
Isa. xlix. 8.		2 Cor. vi. 2.
Isa. liv. 1.		Gal. iv. 27.
Isa. viii. 17, 18.		Heb. ii. 13.

II. *Quotations nearly agreeing with the Hebrew.*

Isa. vii. 14.	quoted in	Matt. i. 23.
Isa. vi. 9, 10.		Matt. xiii. 14, 15; comp. Acts xxviii. 26; Mark iv. 12; Luke viii. 10.
Isa. liv. 13.		John vi. 45.
Isa. lxvii. 1, 2.		Acts vii. 49, 50.
Isa. xlix. 6.		Acts xiii. 47.
Isa. lii. 5.		Rom. ii. 24.
Isa. i. 9.		Rom. ix. 29.
Isa. viii. 14.		Rom. ix. 33.
Isa. lii. 7.		Rom. x. 15.
Isa. lxv. 1, 2.		Rom. x. 20, 21.
Isa. xxix. 14.		1 Cor. i. 19.
Isa. xl. 13.		1 Cor. 2. 16.
Isa. xxxviii. 11, 12.	Comp. Rom. xi. 34.	1 Cor. xiv. 21.
Isa. xl. 6, 7, 8.		1 Pet. i. 24, 25.
Isa. liii. 9.		1 Pet. ii. 22.
Isa. liii. 5.		1 Pet. ii. 24.
Isa. viii. 12, 13.		1 Pet. iii. 14, 15.

III.   *Quotations agreeing with the Hebrew in sense, but not in words.*

Isa. xl. 3, 4, 5.   Matt. iii. 3.   Comp. Mark i. 3.   Luke iii. 4–6.

Isa. xlii. 1–4.   .   .   .   .   Matt. xii. 18–21.

Isa. lix. 7, 8.   .   .   .   .   Rom. iii. 15–17.

Isa. x. 22, 23.   .   .   .   .   Rom. ix. 27, 28.

Isa. xlv. 23.   .   .   .   .   Rom. xiv. 11.

Isa. xi. 10.   .   .   .   .   Rom. xv. 12.

Isa. lii. 11, 12.   .   .   .   .   2 Cor. vi. 17.

IV.   *Quotations which give the general sense, but which abridge, or add to it.*

Isa. vi. 9, 10.   .   .   John xii. 40; Matt. xiii. 14, 15; Mark iv. 12.

Luke viii. 10; Acts xxviii. 26.

Isa. xxix. 10.   .   .   .   .   Rom. xi. 8.

V.   *Quotations which are taken from several different places.*

Isa. xxvi. 16; viii. 14.   .   quoted in   .   Rom. ix. 33.

Isa. xxix. 10; vi. 9; Ezek. xii. 2.   .   .   .   Rom. xi. 8.

Isa. lxii. 11; Zech. ix. 9.   .   .   .   .   .   Matt. xxi. 5.

VI.   *Quotations differing from the Hebrew, but agreeing with the Septuagint.*

Isa. xxix. 13.   .   .   .   .   Matt. xv. 8, 9.

Isa. lv. 3.   .   .   .   .   Acts xiii. 34.

VII.   *Quotations in which there is reason to suspect a different reading in the Hebrew, or that the words were understood in a sense different from that expressed in our Lexicons.*

Isa. lx. 1, 2.   .   .   .   .   .   .   Luke iv. 18, 19.

Isa. liii. 7, 8.   .   .   .   .   .   .   Acts viii. 32, 33.

Isa. lix. 20, 21.   .   .   .   .   .   Rom. xi. 26, 27.

Isa. lxiv. 4.   .   .   .   .   .   .   1 Cor. ii. 9.

Isa. xlii. 2, 4.   .   .   .   .   .   .   Matt. xii. 18, 21.

VIII.   *Allusion to a passage in Isaiah.*

Isa. xii. 3.   .   .   .   .   .   .   John viii. 37, 38.

IX.   *Quotations made from the Septuagint.*

Many of the passages above referred to are made also from the Septuagint, when that version agrees with the Hebrew. I refer here to a few passages which have not been noted before. The apostles wrote in the Greek language, and for the use of those among whom the Septuagint was extensively used. Occasionally, however, they quoted directly from the Hebrew, that is, made a *translation* themselves, or quoted according to the general sense. *All* the quotations that are in accordance with the Septuagint, or that vary from it, may be seen in Horne's Introd. vol. ii. p. 387, 428.

Isa. xlix. 6,	.	.	.	Acts xiii. **47.**
Isa. lxv. 1, 2.	.	.	.	Rom. x. 20, **21.**
Isa. lii. 15.	.	.	.	Rom. v. 21.
Isa. xlix. 8.	.	.	.	2 Cor. vi. 2.
Isa. xxix. 13.	.	.	.	Matt. xv. 8, **9.**
Isa. lv. 3.	.	.	.	Acts xiii. 34.
Isa. liii. 12.	.	.	.	Mark xv. 28; Luke xxii. **37.**

X. *Quotations which differ from the Hebrew, and the Septuagint, and which were perhaps taken from some version or paraphrase, or which were so rendered by the sacred writers themselves.*

Isa. ix. 1, 2.	.	.	.	.	.	Matt. iv. 15, 16.
Isa. xlii. 1, 4.	.	.	.	.	.	Matt. xii. 18, 21.

So numerous are these quotations, and so entirely do the writings of Isaiah harmonize with those of the New Testament, that it may be regarded almost as an indispensable part of the work of explaining the New Testament to explain Isaiah. They seem to be parts of the same work; and an exposition of the apostles and evangelists can hardly be deemed complete without the accompaniment of the evangelical prophet.

§ 7. *The Character and Nature of Prophecy.*

1. The words prophet and prophecy are used in the Bible in a larger sense than they are commonly with us. We have attached, in common usage, to the word prophet, the idea simply of one who foretels future events, προφήτης from πρόφημι *to speak before, to foretel.* To a correct understanding of the prophetic functions, and of the writings of the prophets, however, it is necessary to bear in remembrance that the office of foretelling future events comprised but a small portion of their public duties. They were the messengers of God to his people and to the world; they were appointed to make known his will; to denounce his judgments; to rebuke the crimes of rulers and people; to instruct in the doctrines of religion; and generally to do whatever was needful in order effectually to promulgate the will of God. The prophet was, therefore, a man who was commissioned to teach and rebuke kings and nations, as well as to predict future events. With the idea of a prophet there is *necessarily* connected the idea that he spoke not his own thoughts, but that what he uttered was received directly from God in one of the modes in which that will was made known. He was God's ambassador to men; and of course was a man who was raised up or designated by God himself. He was not *trained* for this office, since a man could not be trained for inspiration; though it was a matter of fact that several of the prophets were taken from the ' school of the prophets,' or from among the 'sons of the prophets;' 1 Kings xx. 35; 2 Kings ii. 3, 5, 7, 15; iv. 1, 38; v. 22; vi. 1. Yet the choice from among them of any one to perform the functions of the prophet under divine inspiration, seems to have been incidental, and not in a uniform mode. A large part of the prophets had no connection with those schools. Those schools were doubtless usually under the direction of some inspired man, and were probably

designed to train those educated there for the functions of public teachers, of for the stations of learning under the theocracy; but they could not have been regarded as intended to train for that office which depended wholly on the direct inspiration of God.

The word rendered prophet, נָבִיא *Nâbî*, is derived from נָבָא *Nâbâ*, not used in Kal, which is probably, according to Gesenius, the same as נָבַע *Nâbăng* —the ע *Ayin* being softened into *Aleph* א —and which means to boil up, to boil forth, as a fountain ; hence to pour forth words as they do who speak with fervour of mind, or under divine inspiration. The word, therefore, properly means, to speak under a peculiar fervour, animation, inspiration of mind produced by a divine influence ; to speak, either in foretelling future events, or denouncing the judgments of God when the mind was full, and when the excited and agitated spirit of the prophet poured forth words as water is driven from the fountain.

But the word also denotes all the forms or modes in which the prophet communicated the will of God, or discharged the functions of the prophetic office. Hence it is used to denote, (1) the predicting of future events (see Taylor's Heb. Con. or Cruden); (2) to speak in the name of God, or as his messenger, and by his authority, Ex. vii. 1; iv. 16; (3) to chant or sing sacred praises to God while under a divine influence—1 Sam. x. 11; xix. 20; 1 Chron. xxv. 2, 3—because this was often done by the inspired prophets ; (4) to rave, as e. g. to utter the frantic ravings of the prophets of Baal, 1 Kings xviii. 29; 1 Sam. xviii. 10. This latter meaning is in accordance with the customs among the heathen, where the prophet or the prophetess professed to be full of the divine influence, and where that influence was manifested by writhings and contortions of the body, or by a pretended suspension of the powers of conscious agency, and the manifestation of conduct not a little resembling the ravings of delirium. Hence the Greeks applied the word μαντις, *mantis* (from μαίνομαι to be mad, to rave, to be delirious) to the frenzied manner of the soothsayers, prophetic oracles, &c. It is possible that the true prophets, occasionally under the power of inspiration, exhibited similar agitations and spasmodic affections of the body (comp. Num. xxiv. 4; Ezek. i. 28; Dan. x. 8–10; 1 Sam. xix. 24; Jer. xx. 7), and that this was imitated by the false prophets. The two main ideas in the word *prophecy* relate, (*a*) to the prediction of future events, and (*b*) to declaring the will of God, denouncing vengeance, threatening punishment, reproving the wicked, &c., under the influence of inspiration, or by a divine impulse.

II. In order to obtain a clear idea of the nature of prophecy, it is important to have a correct apprehension of the *modes* in which God communicated his will to the prophets, or of the manner in which they were influenced, and affected by the prophetic *afflatus* or inspiration. Of course all the light which can be obtained on this subject is to be derived from the Scriptures ; but the subject is involved still in much obscurity. Perhaps the following will include all the modes in which the will of God was made known to the prophets, or in which they received a knowledge of what they were to communicate to others.

(1.) A direct commission by an audible voice from heaven, spoken in a solemn manner, and in circumstances in which there could be no doubt of the call.

Thus Moses was called by God at the Bush, Ex. iii. 2–6; Isaiah in the temple, Isa. vi. 8, seq.; Samuel by God, 1 Sam. iii. 4, 6, 8, 10; Jeremiah, Jer. i. 4, Ezek. i. 3; and perhaps Joel, i. 1, Amos, i. 1, Jonah, Jon. i. 1, Micah, Mic. i. 1, &c. In these cases there was no doubt on the mind of the prophet of his call, as it was usually in such circumstances, and probably in such a manner, as to leave the fullest demonstration that it was from God. There is no evidence, however, that the whole message was usually communicated to the mind of the prophet in this manner. Perhaps the first call to the prophetic office was made in this mode, and the nature of the message imparted in the manner that will be specified soon. All that is essential to the correct understanding of this is, that there was a clear designation to the prophetic office.

(2.) The will of God was made known by dreams. Instances of this kind are common in the sacred Scriptures, as one of the earliest modes of communication between God and the soul. The idea seems to be that the senses were locked up, and that the soul was left free to hold communication with the invisible world, and to receive the expressions of the will of God. The belief that God made known his will in this manner was by no means confined to the Jewish nation. God informed Abimelech in a dream that Sarah was the wife of Abraham, Gen. xx. 3, 6. Joseph was early favoured with prophetic dreams, which were so clear in their signification as to be easily interpreted by his father and brethren, Gen. xxxvii. 4, 5, 6. The butler and baker in Egypt both had dreams predicting their future destiny, Gen. xl. 5; and Pharaoh had a dream of the future condition of Egypt, which was interpreted by Joseph, Gen. xli. 7, 25. God spake to Jacob in a dream, Gen. xxxi. 11; and it was in a dream that he made his promise to impart wisdom to Solomon, 1 Kings iii. 5. Nebuchadnezzar had dreams respecting his future destiny, and the kingdoms that should arise after him, Dan. ii. 1, 5; and the will of God was made known to Daniel in a dream, Dan. i. 17; vii. 1. God expressly declared that he would make known his will by dreams. Num. xii. 6: 'If there be a prophet among you, I the Lord will make myself known to him in a vision, and will speak unto him in a dream.' Thus also in Joel ii. 28: ' Your sons and your daughters shall prophesy, your old men shall dream dreams, your young men shall see visions.' The false prophets pretended also to have dreams which conveyed to them the will of God. The ancient belief on this subject is expressed in a most sublime manner in the language of Elihu as addressed to Job:—

> For God speaketh once,
> Yea, twice, when man regardeth it not;
> In a dream, in a vision of the night,
> When deep sleep falleth upon men,
> In slumberings upon the bed—
> Then he openeth the ears of men,
> And sealeth up for them admonition,
> That he may turn man from his purpose,
> And remove pride from man.

Ch. xxxiii. 14—17.

It is now impossible to determine in what way God thus communicated his will; or how it was known that the thoughts in sleep were communicated by God; or what criterion the prophet or other person had, by which to distinguish these from common dreams.   The *certainty* that they were from God is demonstrated by the fact that the event was accurately fulfilled, as in the case of Joseph, of Pharaoh, of Nebuchadnezzar, of Daniel.   There is no instance in which the will of God seems to have been communicated to Isaiah in this manner ; and it is not needful to my purpose to pursue this part of the inquiry any further.   The mode in which the will of God was made known to Isaiah was mainly, if not entirely, by *visions*, ch. i. 1 ; and that mode will demand a more full and distinct examination.   It may just be remarked here, that no man can demonstrate that God *could* not convey his will to man in the visions of the night, or in dreams ; or that he could not then have access to the soul, and give to the mind itself some certain indications by which it might be known that the communication was from him.   It is possible that the mode of communicating the will of God by the *dream* חֲלוֹם *hhalom*—did not differ *essentially* from the mode of *the vision*— חִזָּיוֹן —*hh'zon*—by causing a *vision* of the subject as in a landscape to pass before the mind.

(3.) The prophets were brought under such an influence by the divine Spirit as to overpower them, and while in this state the will of God was made known to them.   In what way his will was *then* communicated we may not be able to determine.   I speak only of an overpowering influence which gave them such views of God and truth as to weaken their animal frame, and as, in some instances, to produce a state of *ecstacy*, or a *trance*, in which the truth was made to pass before them by some direct communication which God had with their minds.   In these cases, in some instances at least, the communication with the external world was closed, and God communicated his will immediately and directly.   Reference to this is not unfrequently made in the Scriptures, where there was such a powerful divine influence as to prostrate the frame, and take away the strength of the body.   Thus in Ezek. i. 3, ' The hand of JEHOVAH was then upon me.'   Cornelius à Lapide remarks on this passage, that ' the prophets took their station by the side of a river, that in the stillness and delightful scenery around them they might, through the soft pleasing murmur of the waters, be refreshed, enlivened, and prepared for the divine ecstacies.'   Bib. Repository, vol. ii. p. 141.   It is more natural, however, to suppose that they did not court or solicit these influences, but that they came upon them by surprise.   Jer. xx. 7, ' Lord, thou hast persuaded me, and I have suffered myself to be persuaded ; thou hast been too strong for me, and hast prevailed.'   This influence is referred to in 1 Sam. xix. 20, ' The Spirit of God was upon the messengers [of Saul] and they also prophesied.'   In 1 Sam. xix. 24, the *power* of the prophetic impulse is indicated by the fact that it led Saul to strip off his clothes, probably his robes, and to prophesy in the same manner as Samuel ; and in the statement that ' he lay down naked all that day, and all that night,' under the prophetic impulse.

The *effect* of this strong prophetic impulse on the body and the mind is indicated in the following passages.   It is said of Abraham in Gen. xv. 12, when he had a vision, ' Behold terror and great darkness came upon him.'   It was evinced in a remarkable manner in the case of Balaam, Num. xxiv. 4, 16.   It is said of him, that he ' saw the vision of the Almighty, falling *into a trance* (LXX. " who saw the vision of God ἐν ὕπνῳ, *in sleep*,") but having his eyes open.' He was probably overcome, and fell to the ground, and yet his eyes were open, and *in* that state he uttered the predictions respecting Israel. The same effect is indicated in regard to John, Rev. i. 17, 'And when I saw him, I fell at his feet as dead.' So of Ezekiel (ch. i. 28, 'And when I saw it, I fell upon my face, and I heard a voice of one that spoke.' And in a more remarkable manner in the case of Daniel (ch. x. 8), 'Therefore I was left alone, and saw this great vision, and there remained no strength in me; for my comeliness was turned in me into corruption, and I retained no strength.' And again (ch. viii. 27), 'And I Daniel fainted, and was sick certain days.' That there was a remarkable agitation of the body, or suspension of its regular functions so as to resemble in some degree the ravings of delirium, is apparent from 2 Kings ix. 11; Jer. xxix. 26. The nature of the strong prophetic impulse is perhaps indicated also in the expression in 2 Pet. i. 21, 'Holy men of God spake as they were moved—(φερόμενοι—*borne along, urged, impelled*) by the Holy Ghost.'

That it was supposed that the prophetic impulse produced such an effect on the body as is here represented, is well known to have been the opinion of the heathens. The opinion which was held by them on the subject is stated in a beautiful manner by Plato : ' While the mind sheds its light around us, pouring into our souls a meridian splendour, we being in possession of ourselves, are not under a supernatural influence. But after the sun has gone down, as might be expected, an ecstasy, a divine influence, and a frenzy falls upon us. For when the divine light shines, the human goes down ; but when the former goes down, the latter rises and comes forth. This is what ordinarily happens in prophecy. Our own mind retires on the advent of the divine Spirit ; but after the latter has departed, the former again returns.' Quoted in Bib. Repos. vol. ii. p. 163. In the common idea of the Pythia, however, there was the conception of derangement, or raving madness. Thus Lucan :—

> ——Bacchatur demens aliena per antrum
> Colla ferens, vittasque Dei, Phœbaeaque serta
> Erectis discussa comis, per inania templi
> Ancipiti cervice rotat, spargitque vaganti
> Obstantes tripodas, magnoque exaestuat igne
> Iratum te, Phœbe, ferens.   *Pharsalia*, V.

' She madly raves through the cavern, impelled by another's mind with the fillet of the god, and the garland of Phœbus, shaken from her erected hair: she whirls around through the void space of the temple, turning her face in every direction ; she scatters the tripods which come in her way, and is agitated with violent commotion, because she is under thy angry influence, O Apollo.' Virgil has given a similar description of a demoniacal possession of this kind:—

> ——Ait : Deus, ecce, Deus ! cui talia fanti
> Ante fores, subitò non vultus, non color unus,
> Nec comptae mansere comae ; sed pectus anhelum,
> Et rabie fera corda tument : majorque videri
> Nec mortale sonans ; afflata est numine quando
> Iam propriore Dei.   *Æneid.* vi. 46, seq.

> I feel the god, the rushing god ! she cries—
> While thus she spoke enlarged her features grew
> Her colour changed, her locks dishevelled flew.

> The heavenly tumult reigns in every part,
> Pants in her breast and swells her rising heart;
> Still spreading to the sight the priestess glowed,
> And heaved impatient of the incumbent god.
> Then to her inmost soul, by Phœbus fired,
> In more than human sounds she spoke inspired.   *Pitt.*
> See also *Æneid.* vi. 77, seq.

From all such mad and unintelligible ravings the true prophets were distinguished. The effect of inspiration on the physical condition of their bodies and minds may be expressed in the following particulars. (*a.*) It prostrated their strength; it threw them on the ground, as we have seen in the case of Saul, and of John, and was attended occasionally with sickness, as in the case of Daniel. There seems to have been such a view of God, and of the events which were to come to pass, as to take away for a time their physical strength. Nor is there any thing improbable or absurd in this. In the language of Prof. Stuart (Bib. Repos. ii. p. 221), we may ask, ' Why should not this be so ? How could it be otherwise than that the amazing disclosures sometimes made to them should affect the whole corporeal system ? Often does this happen when one and another scene opens upon us in a natural way, and which has respect merely to things of the present world. But when the future glories of the Messiah's kingdom were disclosed to the mental eye of a prophet or a seer, when the desolation of kingdoms, and the slaughter of many thousands, the subjugation and massacre of God's chosen people, famine, pestilence, and other tremendous evils were disclosed to his view, what could be more natural than that agitation, yea, swooning, should follow in some cases ? ' It may be added, that in the experience of Christians in modern times the elevated views which have been taken of God, of heaven, of the hopes of glory, and of the plan of salvation, have produced similar effects on the bodily frame. *Any* deep, absorbing, elevated emotion may produce this state. ' The flesh is weak,' and that there *may* be such a view of glory or of calamity ; such hope or fear ; such joy or sorrow as to prostrate the frame and produce sickness, or faintness, is nothing more than what occurs every day. (*b.*) There is no evidence that the true prophets were divested of intelligent consciousness so that they were ignorant of what they uttered ; or that the Spirit made use of them *merely* as organs, or as unconscious agents to utter his truth. They everywhere speak and act as men who understood what they said, and do not rave as madmen. Indeed, the very fact to which I have adverted, that the view of future events had such an effect as to take away their strength, shows that they were conscious, and had an intelligent understanding of what they saw, or spoke. That the prophet had *control* of his own mind ; that he could speak or not as he pleased ; that he acted as a conscious, voluntary, intelligent agent, is more than once intimated, or expressly affirmed. Thus in one of the strongest cases of the overpowering nature of the inspiration which can be adduced—the case of Jeremiah—it is intimated that the prophet *even then* was a voluntary agent, and could speak or not, as he pleased. The *strength* of this overpowering agency is intimated in Jer. xx. 7.

> Thou didst allure me, O JEHOVAH, and I was allured ;
> Thou didst encourage me, and didst prevail ;

I am become a laughing stock every day,
Ridicule hath spent its whole force upon me.

Blayney's Trans.

And yet, in immediate connection with this, the prophet *resolved* that he
would cease to prophesy, and that he would no more speak in the name of
JEHOVAH.

Then I said, I will not make mention of him,
Nor speak any more in his name;
But his word was in my heart as a burning fire shut up in my bones,
And I was weary with forbearing,
And I could not stay. ver. 9.

This proves, that Jeremiah was, even under the full power of the prophetic
impulse, a free and conscious agent. If he was a mere passive instrument in
the hands of the Spirit, how could he determine no more to prophesy? And
how could he carry this purpose into execution, as he actually did for a while?
But this inquiry has been settled by the express authority of the apostle Paul.
He affirms, in a manner which leaves no room to doubt, that the prophets were
conscious agents, and that they had control over their own minds, when he
says (1 Cor. xiv. 32), 'the spirits of the prophets are subject to the prophets;'
and on the ground of this he requires those who were under the prophetic
inspiration to utter their sentiments in such a manner as not to produce confusion and irregularity in the churches, 1 Cor. xiv. 29–31, 33, 40. How
could he reprove their disorder and confusion, if they had no control over the
operations of their own minds; and if they were not conscious of what they
were uttering? The truth seems to have been that they had the same control
over their minds that any man has; that they were urged, or impelled by the
Spirit to utter the truth, but that they had power to refuse; and that the
exercise of this power was subjected to substantially the same laws as the
ordinary operations of their minds. The true idea has been expressed, probably, by Bishop Lowth. 'Inspiration may be regarded not as suppressing or
extinguishing for a time the faculties of the human mind, but of purifying,
and strengthening, and elevating them above what they would otherwise
reach.' Nothing can be more rational than this view; and according to this,
there was an essential difference between the effect of true inspiration on the
mind, and the wild and frantic ravings of the pagan priests, and the oracles of
divination. Every thing in the Scriptures is consistent, rational, sober, and
in accordance with the laws of the animal economy; every thing in the heathen
idea of inspiration was wild, frantic, fevered, and absurd. (*c.*) It may be
added, that this is the common view of prophecy which prevailed among the
fathers of the church. Thus Epiphanius says, 'In whatever the prophets have
said, they have been accompanied with an intelligent state of mind;' Ad.
Haeres. Mont. c. 4. Jerome in his Preface to Isaiah says, 'Nor indeed, as
Montanus and insane women dream, did the prophets speak in an ecstasy, so
that they did not know what they uttered, and, while they instructed others,
did not themselves understand what they said.' Chrysostom says, 'For this
is characteristic of the diviners, to be in a state of frenzy, to be impelled by
necessity, to be driven by force, to be drawn like a madman. A prophet, on
the contrary, is not so; but utters his communication with sober intelligence,

and in a sound state of mind, knowing what he says,' Homil. xxix. in Ep. ad Cor., Bib. Repos. ii. 141.

(4.) The representation of future scenes was made known to the prophets by VISIONS. This idea may not differ from the two former, except that it intimates that *in* a dream, and *in* the state of prophetic ecstasy, events were made known to them not by *words*, but by causing the scene to pass before their mind or their mental visions, *as if* they saw it. Thus the entire series of the prophecies of Isaiah is described as a VISION in ch. i. 1, and in 2 Chron. xxxii. 32. It is of importance to have a clear understanding of what is implied by this. The name *vision* is often elsewhere given to the prophecies, Num. xxiv. 4, 16; 1 Sam. iii. 1; 2 Sam. vii. 17; Prov. xxix. 18; Obad. i. 1; Isa. xxi. 2; xxii. 1, 5; Jer. xiv. 14; Lam. ii. 9; Ezek. vii. 13; Dan. ii. 19; vii. 2; viii. 1, 13, 16, 17, 26; ix. 21, 23, 24; x. 1, 7, 8, 14, 16; 2 Chron. ix. 29; Ezek. i. 1. The prophets are called *Seers* רֹאִים *rōyîm;* and חֹזִים *Hhōzim,* and their prophecies are designated by words which denote that which *is seen,* as מַחֲזֵה הַזָּיוֹן חָזוֹן מַרְאֶה, &c.—all of which are words derived from the verbs rendered *to see,* חָזָה and רָאָה. It would be unnecessary to quote the numerous passages where the idea of *seeing* is expressed. A few will show their general charac·ters. They may be *classified* according to the following arrangement.

(*a.*) Those which relate to an *open* vision, a distinct and clear *seeing,* 1 Sam. iii. 1: ' And the word of the LORD was precious in those days ; there was no open vision '—חָזוֹן נִפְרָץ—no vision spread abroad, common, open, public, usual. It was a rare occurrence, and hence the divine communications were regarded as peculiarly precious and valuable.

(*b.*) Those which pertain to the prophetic ecstasy, or trance—probably the more usual, and proper meaning of the word. Num. xxiv. 3, 4, ' The man whose eyes are open hath said ; he hath said which heard the words of God, which saw the vision of the Almighty, falling, but having his eyes open.' Num. xxiv. 17, ' I see him, but not now; I behold him, but not near ; there shall come a Star out of Jacob, and a Sceptre shall rise out of Israel.' That is, I see, or have a vision of that Star, and of that Sceptre *in the distance,* as if looking on a landscape, and contemplating an indistinct object in the remote part of the picture. Thus Ezek. i. 1, ' The heavens were opened, and I saw the visions of God ; ' viii. 3.; xl. 2, ' In visions he brought me to the land of Israel,' comp. Luke i. 22.

(*c.*) Instances where it is applied to DREAMS: Dan. ii. 19, 28; iv. 5; vii. 2; viii. 1, 13, 16, 17, 26, 27; ix. 21, 23, 24; Gen. xlvi. 2, ' God spake to Israel in visions of the night,' Job. iv. 13.

(*d.*) Instances where the prophets represent themselves as standing on a *watch-tower,* and looking off on a distant landscape to descry future and distant events.

> ' I will stand upon my watch,
> And will set me upon the tower,
> And will watch to see what he will say unto me,
> And what I shall answer when I am reproved.'   Habak. ii. 1.

' For thus hath the Lord said unto me, Go, set a watchman, let him declare what he seeth ;' Notes, Isa. xxi. 6; comp. ver. 8, 11; Micah vii. 4; comp.

Jer. vi. 17; Ezek. iii. 17; xxxiii. 7. In these passages, the idea is that of one who is stationed on an elevated post of observation, who can look over a large region of country, and give timely warning of the approach of an enemy

The general idea of prophecy which is presented in these passages, is that of a scene which is made to pass before the mind like a picture, or a landscape, where the mind contemplates a panoramic view of objects around it, or in the distance ; where, as in a landscape, objects may appear to be grouped together, or lying near together, which may be in fact separated a considerable distance. The prophets described those objects which were presented to their minds as they *appeared* to them, or as they seem to be drawn on the picture which was before them. They had, undoubtedly, an intelligent consciousness of what they were describing ; they were not mad, like the priestesses of Apollo ; they had a clear view of the *vision*, and described it as it appeared to them. Let this idea be kept in mind, that the prophets saw IN VISION ; that probably the mode in which they contemplated objects was somewhat in the manner of a *landscape* as it passes before the mind, and much light and beauty will be cast on many of the prophecies which now seem to be obscure.

III. From the view which has now been taken of the nature of prophecy, some important remarks may be made, throwing additional light on the subject.

(1.) It is not to be expected that the prophets would describe what they saw in all their connections and relations ; see Hengstenberg, in Bib. Repos. ii. p. 148. They would present what they saw as we describe what we witness in a landscape. Objects which *appear* to be near, may be in fact separated by a considerable interval. Objects on the mountain side may seem to lie close to each other, between which there may be a deep ravine, or a flowery vale. In describing or painting it, we describe or paint the points that appear ; but the ravine and the vale cannot be painted. They are not seen. So in a prophecy, distant events may appear to lie near to each other, and may be so described, while *between* them there may be events happy or adverse, of long continuance and of great importance.

(2.) Some SINGLE VIEW of a future event may attract the attention and engross the mind of the prophet. A multitude of comparatively unimportant objects may pass unnoticed, while there may be one single absorbing view that shall seize upon, and occupy all the attention. Thus in the prophecies which relate to the Messiah. Scarcely any one of the prophets gives any connected or complete view of his entire life and character. It is some single view of him, or some single event in his life, that occupies the mind. Thus at one time his birth is described ; at another his kingdom ; at another his divine nature ; at another his sufferings ; at another his resurrection ; at another his glory. *The prophetic view is made up, not of one of these predictions, but of all combined;* as the life of Jesus is not that which is contained in *one* of the Evangelists, but in all combined. Illustrations of this remark might be drawn in abundance from the prophecies of Isaiah. Thus in ch. ii. 4, he sees the Messiah as the Prince of Peace, as diffusing universal concord among all the nations, and putting an end to war. In ch. vi. 1–5, comp. John xii. 41, he sees him as the Lord of glory, sitting on a throne, and filling the temple. In ch. vii. 14, he

sees him as a child, the son of a virgin. In ch. ix. 1, 2, he sees him as having
reached manhood, and having entered on his ministry, in the land of Galilee
where he began to preach. In ch. ix. 6, 7, he sees him as the exalted Prince,
the Ruler, the mighty God, the Father of eternity. In ch. xi. he sees him as
the descendant of Jesse—a tender sprout springing up from the stump of an
ancient decayed tree. In ch. xxv. 8, he sees him as destroying death, and
introducing immortality; comp. 1 Cor. xv. 54. In ch. xxxv. the happy effects
of his reign are seen; in ch. liii. he views him as a suffering Messiah, and contemplates the deep sorrows which he would endure when he should die to make
atonement for the sins of the world. Thus in all the prophets we have one
view presented at one time, and another at another; and the entire prediction
is made up of *all* these when they are combined into one. It may be observed
also of Isaiah, that in the first part of his prophecy the idea of an exalted or
triumphant Messiah is chiefly dwelt upon; in the latter part, he presents more
prominently the idea of the suffering Messiah. The reason may have been,
that the object in the first part was to console the hearts of the nation under
their deep and accumulated calamities, with the assurance that their great
Deliverer would come. In the latter part, which may not have been published
in his life, the idea of a suffering Messiah is more prominently introduced. This
might have been rather designed for posterity than for the generation when
Isaiah lived; or it may have been designed for the more pious individuals in
the nation rather than for the nation at large, and hence, in order to give a *full*
view of the Messiah, he dwelt then on his sufferings and death; see Hengstenberg's Christol. vol. i. pp. 153, 154.

(3.) Another peculiarity, which may arise from the nature of prophecy as
here presented, may have been that the mind of the prophet glanced rapidly
from one thing to another. By very slight associations or connections, as they
may now appear to us, the mind is carried from one object or event to another;
and almost before we are aware of it, the prophet seems to be describing some
point that has, as appears to us, scarcely *any* connection with the one which
he had but just before been describing. We are astonished at the transition,
and perhaps can by no means ascertain the *connection* which has subsisted in
view of the mind of the prophet, and which has led him to pass from the one
to the other. The mental association to us is lost or unseen, and we deem him
abrupt, and speak of his rapid transitions, and of the difficulties involved in the
doctrine of a double sense. The views which I am here describing may be
presented under the idea of what may be called THE LAWS OF PROPHETIC SUGGES-
TION; and perhaps a study of those laws might lead to a removal of most of the
difficulties which have been supposed to be connected with the subject of a
spiritual meaning, and of the double sense of the prophecies. In looking over
a landscape; in attempting to describe the objects as they lie in view of the
eye—if that landscape were not seen by others for whom the description is
made—the transitions would seem to be rapid, and the objects might seem to
be described in great disorder. It would be difficult to tell why this object was
mentioned in connection with that; or by what laws of association the one was
suggested by the other. A house or tree; a brook, a man, an animal, a valley,
a mountain, might all be described, and between them there might be no appa-

rent laws of close connection, and all the real union may be that they lie in the same range, in view of him who contemplates them. The *laws of prophetic suggestion* may appear to be equally slight ; and we may not be able to trace them, because we have not the entire view or grouping which was presented to the mind of the prophet. We do not see the associations which in his view connected the one with the other. To him, there may have been no double sense. He may have described objects singly as they appeared to him. But they may have lain near each other. They may have been so closely grouped that he could not separate them even in the description. The words appropriate to the one may have naturally and easily fallen into the form of appropriate description of the other. And the objects may have been so contiguous, and the transition in the mind of the prophet so rapid, that he may himself have been scarcely conscious of the change, and his narrative may seem to flow on as one continued description. Thus the object with which he commenced, may have sunk out of view, and the mind be occupied entirely in the contemplation of that which was at first secondary. Such seems to have been, in a remarkable manner, the peculiarity of the mind of Isaiah. Whatever is the object or event with which he *commences*, the description usually *closes* with the Messiah. His mind glances rapidly from the object immediately before him, and fixes on that which is more remote, and the first object gradually sinks away; the language rises in dignity and beauty; the mind is full, and the description proceeds with a statement respecting the Prince of Peace. This is not double sense : it is RAPID TRANSITION under the laws of PROPHETIC SUGGESTION; and though at first some object immediately before the prophet was the subject of his contemplation, yet before he closes, his mind is totally absorbed in some distant event that has been presented, and his language is designedly such as is adapted to that. It would be easy to adduce numerous instances of the operation of this law in Isaiah. For illustration we may refer to the remarkable prophecy in ch. vii. 14; comp. ch. viii. 8; ix. 1–7. See Notes on those passages. Indeed, it may be presented, I think, as one of the prominent characteristics of the mind of Isaiah, that in the prophetic visions which he contemplated, the Messiah always occupied some place ; that whatever prophetic landscape, so to speak, passed before him, the Messiah was always in some part of it ; and that consequently wherever he *began* his prophetic annunciations, he usually *closed* with a description of some portion of the doctrines, or the work of the Messiah. It is this law of the mental associations of Isaiah which gives such value to his writings in the minds of all who love the Saviour.

(4.) It follows from this view of prophecy, that the prophets would speak of occurrences and events as they appeared to them. They would speak of them as actually present, or as passing before their eyes. They would describe them as being what they *had* seen, and would thus throw them into the past tense, as we describe what we have seen in a landscape, and speak of what we *saw*. It would be comparatively infrequent, therefore, that the event would be described as *future*. Accordingly we find that this is the mode actually adopted in the prophets. Thus in Isa. ix. 6, ' Unto us a child *is* born, unto us a son *is* given.' Isa. xlii. 1, ' Behold my servant whom I *uphold*, mine elect in whom

my soul *delighteth.*' So in the description of the sufferings of the Messiah :
' He *is* despised.' ' He *hath* no form or comeliness,' ch. liii. 2, 3. Thus in ch.
xiv. 1–8, Cyrus is addressed as if he were personally present. Frequently
events are thus described as *past*, or as events which the prophet *had seen* in
vision. ' The people that walked in darkness *have seen* a great light ; they
that dwell in the land of the shadow of death, upon them hath the light shined,'
ch. ix. 2. So especially in the description of the sufferings of the Messiah :
' As many *were* astonished at thee.' ' His visage *was* so marred.' ' He *hath*
borne our griefs.' ' He *was* oppressed, and he *was* afflicted.' ' He *was* taken
from prison.' ' He *was* cut off out of the land of the living.' ' He *made* his
grave,' &c. &c.; Isa. lii. 14, 15; liii. 4–9. In some cases, also, the prophet
seems to have placed himself in vision *in the midst* of the scenes which he
describes, or to have taken, so to speak, a station where he might contemplate
a part as past, and a part as *yet to come.* Thus in Isa. liii. the prophet seems
to have his station *between* the humiliation of the Saviour and his glorification,
in which he speaks of his sufferings as *past*, and his glorification, and the success of the gospel, as *yet to come;* comp. particularly ver. 9–12. This view of
the nature of prophecy would have saved from many erroneous interpretations ;
and especially would have prevented many of the cavils of sceptics. It is a
view which a man would be allowed to take in describing a landscape ; and
why should it be deemed irrational or absurd in prophecy?

(5.) From this view it also follows, that the prophecies are usually to be
regarded as seen *in space* and not *in time;* or in other words, the time would
not be actually and definitely marked. They would describe the *order*, or the
succession of events ; but between them there might be a considerable, and an
unmeasured interval of time. In illustration of this we may refer to the idea
which has been so often presented already—the idea of a landscape. When
one is placed in an advantageous position to view a landscape, he can mark
distinctly the *order* of the objects, the succession, the *grouping.* He can tell
what objects appear to him to lie *near* each other ; or what are apparently in
juxtaposition. But all who look at such a landscape know very well that there
are objects which the eye cannot take in, and which will not be exhibited by
any description. For example, hills in the distant view may seem to lie *near*
to each other ; one may seem to rise just back of the other, and they may
appear to constitute parts of the same mountain range, and yet *between* them
there may be wide and fertile vales, the *extent* of which the eye cannot measure,
and which the mind may be wholly unable to conjecture. It has no means of
measuring the distance, and a description of the whole scene as it *appeared* to
the observer would convey no idea of the distance of the intervals. So in the
prophecies. Between the events seen in vision there may be long intervals,
and the length of those intervals the prophet may have left us no means of
determining. He describes the scene as it appeared to him in vision. In a
landscape the distance, the length, the nature of these intervals might be
determined in one of three ways : (1) by the report of one who had gone over
the ground and actually *measured* the distances ; (2) by going ourselves and
measuring the distances ; or (3) by a revelation from heaven. So the *distance
of time* occurring between the events seen in vision by the prophets, may be

determined either by the actual *admeasurement* as the events occur, or by direct revelation either made to the prophet himself, or to some other prophet. Accordingly we find in the prophecies these facts. (*a*) In many of them there are no marks of *time*, but only of *succession*. It is predicted only that one event should succeed another in a certain order. (*b*) Occasionally the time of some *one* event is marked in the succession, as e. g. the time of the death of the Messiah, in Dan. ix. 26, 27. (*c*) Events are apparently connected together, which in fact were to be separated by long intervals. Thus Isaiah ch. xi. makes the deliverance which was to be effected by the Messiah, to follow immediately the deliverance from the yoke of the Assyrians, without noticing the long train of intermediate occurrences. And in the same manner Isaiah, Hosea, Amos, and Micah very often connect the deliverance under the Messiah with that which was to be effected from the captivity at Babylon, without noticing the long train of intermediate events. There was such a resemblance between the two events that, by the laws of *prophetic suggestion*, the mind of the prophet glanced rapidly from one to the other, and the description which *commenced* with the account of the deliverance from the Babylonish captivity, *closed* with the description of the triumphs of the Messiah. And yet not one of the prophets ever intimate that the Messiah would be the leader from the exile at Babylon. (*d*) The *time* is sometimes revealed to the prophets themselves, and they mark it distinctly. Thus to Jeremiah it was revealed that the exile at Babylon would continue seventy years (ch. xxv. 11, 12), and although this event had been the subject of revelation to other prophets, yet to no one of them was there before an intimation of the *time* during which it was to continue. So also of the *place*. That the Jews would be carried away to a distant land if they were disobedient, had been predicted by Moses, and threatened by many of the prophets; and yet there was no intimation of the *place* of their bondage until the embassy of the king of Babylon to Hezekiah, and the sin of Hezekiah in showing them his treasure, led Isaiah to declare that *Babylon was the place* to which the nation was to be carried; see Notes on Isa. xxxix. 6. Marks of time are thus scattered, though not very profusely, through the prophecies. They were, on the whole, so definite as to lead to the general expectation that the Messiah would appear about the time when Jesus was born; see Notes on Matt. ii.

(6.) It is a consequence of this view also, that many of the prophecies are obscure. It is not to be expected that the *same* degree of light should be found in the prophecies which we have now. And yet so far as the prophecy *was* made known, it might be clear enough; nor was there any danger or need of mistake. The facts themselves were perfectly plain and intelligible; but there was only a partial and imperfect development of the facts. The *fact*, e.g. that the Messiah was to come; that he was to be born at Bethlehem; that he was to be a king; that he was to die; that his religion was to prevail among the nations; and that the Gentiles were to be brought to the knowledge of him, were all made known, and were as clear and plain as they are now. Much is known now, indeed, of the *mode* in which this was to be done which was not then; and the want of this knowledge served to make the prophecies appear obscure. We take the information which we *now* have, and go back to the times when the prophecies were uttered, and finding them obscure, we seem to infer that because *all* was not known, *nothing* was known. But wo are to remember that *all* science at the beginning is elementary; and that knowledge on all subjects makes its advances by slow degrees. Many things in the prophecies were obscure, in the sense that there had been only a partial revelation; or that only a few facts were made known; or that the time was not marked with certainty; and yet the facts themselves may have been as clear as they are now, and the *order of succession* may have been also as certainly and clearly determined. The *facts* were revealed; the manner in which they were to occur may have been concealed.

It may be added here, in the words of Prof. Stuart, ' that many prophecies have respect to kingdoms, nations, and events, that for thousands of years have been buried in total darkness. In what manner they were fulfilled we know not; when, we know not. We do not even know enough of the geography of many places and regions that are named in them, to be able to trace the scene of such fulfilment. Customs, manners, and many other things alluded to by such prophecies, we have no present means of illustrating in an adequate manner. Of course, and of necessity, then, there must be more or less in all such prophecies, that is obscure to us.' Bib. Repository, vol. ii. p. 237.

§ 8. *Works illustrative of Isaiah.*

Probably no book of the Bible has occupied so much the attention of critics, of commentators, and of private Christians, as Isaiah. The beauty, grandeur, and power of his prophecies; their highly evangelical character; the fact that they are so frequently quoted in the New Testament; the number and minuteness of his predictions in regard to cities and kingdoms; as well as the intrinsic difficulty of many portions of his writings, all have contributed to this. Of the numerous works which may be consulted in reading, or in explaining Isaiah, the following are among the principal:

I. THE ANCIENT VERSIONS.

(1.) The Septuagint, so called from the seventy interpreters who are supposed to have been engaged in it. This is the most ancient, and in some respects the most valuable of all the versions of the Bible, and was formerly esteemed so valuable as to be read in synagogues and in churches. Much uncertainty exists in regard to the *real* history of this version. According to the common Jewish legend respecting it, Ptolemy Philadelphus, who reigned king of Egypt from 284 to 246 B. C., formed the wish, through the advice of his librarian, Demetrius Phalerius, to possess a Greek copy of the Jewish Scriptures, for the Alexandrian Library, and sent to Jerusalem for this object. The Jews sent him a Hebrew manuscript, and seventy-two men of learning to translate it. They all laboured together, being shut up in the island of Pharos, where having agreed on the translation by mutual conference, they dictated it to Demetrius, who wrote it down, and thus in the space of seventy-two days the whole was finished. This legend is given in an epistle said to have been written by Aristeas, to his brother in Alexandria. Josephus also relates the story, Ant. xii. II. 2-14, But it has every mark of fiction ; and an examination of the Septuagint itself will convince any one that it was not all made by the same persons, or at the same time. The most probable supposition is, that after the Jews had settled in great numbers in Egypt, and had in some measure forgotten the Hebrew Language, a Greek version became necessary for the public use in their temple there (Notes, Isa. xix. 18), and in their synagogues. There is no improbability that this was done under the sanction of the Sanhedrim, or Council of LXXII. in Egypt, and that it thus received its name and authority. The translation was probably commenced about 250 years before Christ. The Pentateuch would be first translated, and the other books were probably translated at intervals between that time and the time of Christ. ' The Pentateuch is best translated, and exhibits a clear and flowing Greek style ; the next in rank is the translation of Job and the Proverbs ; the Psalms and the Prophets are translated worst of all, and indeed often without any sense. Indeed, the real value of the Septuagint, as a version, stands in no sort of relation to its reputation.'—*Calmet*. ' Isaiah has had the hard fate to meet a translation unworthy of him, there being hardly any book of the Old Testament that is so ill rendered in that version as Isaiah.'—*Lowth*. The authority of this version, however, soon became so great as to supersede the use of the Hebrew among all the Jews who spoke Greek. It was read in the synagogues in Egypt, and was gradually introduced into Palestine. It had the highest reverence among the Jews, and was used by them everywhere ; and is the version that is most commonly quoted in the New Testament. From the Jews the reputation and authority of this version passed over to Christians, who employed it with the same degree of credence as the original. The *text* of this version has suffered greatly, and great efforts have been made to restore it ; and yet probably after all these efforts, and after all the reputation which the version has enjoyed in former times, there has not been any where, or scarcely in any language, any version of the Scriptures that is more incorrect and defective than the Septuagint. Probably there is *no* version from which, as a whole, a more correct idea would not be derived of the real meaning of the sacred Scriptures, and this is true in a special manner of Isaiah. It is valuable as the oldest version ; as having been regarded with so much respect in former times : and as, notwithstanding its faults, and the imperfection of the text, throwing much light on various parts of the Old Testament. But as an *authority* for correcting the Hebrew text, it is of little or no value. The history of the Septuagint may be seen in Hody, de Biblior. Textibus orig. Ox. 1705; Horne's Intro. vol. ii. 163, seq.; Prideaux's Connexions ; Walton's Proleg. c. ix. § 3-10; Isaac Vossius de LXX. Inter. Hag. Com. 1661; and Brett, Diss. on the Septuagint, in Watson's Theo. Tracts, vol. iii. p. 18, seq.

(2.) The Latin Vulgate—the authorized version of the Papal communion. When Christianity had extended itself to the West, where the Latin language was spoken, a version of the Scriptures into that language became necessary. In the time of Augustine there were several of these, but only one of them was adopted by the church. This was called *common vulgata*, because it was made from the common Greek version, η κοινή. In modern times this version is often called *Itala,* or the Italic version. This version, in the Old Testament, was made literally from the Septuagint, and copied all its mistakes. To remedy the evils of this, and to give a correct translation of the Scriptures, Jerome undertook a translation directly from the Hebrew. He went to Palestine and enjoyed the oral instructions of a learned Jew. He availed himself of all the labours of his predecessors, and furnished a translation which surpassed all that preceded his in usefulness. In the seventh century this version had supplanted all the old ones. It was the first book ever printed. By the Council of Trent, it was declared to be ' authentic '—and is the authorized or standard version of the Papists ; and is regarded by them as of equal authority with the original Scriptures. This version is allowed generally to be a very faithful translation ; and it undoubtedly gives a much more correct view of the original than the Septuagint.

(3.) The Syriac versions. Of these there are two, both of which are of Christian origin ; having been made by Christians of the Syrian church who dwelt in Mesopotamia. The earliest, and most celebrated of these is the Peshito ; i. e. *the clear,* or *the literal.* It is the authorized version of the Syrian church, and is supposed by them to have been made in the time of Solomon. It was probably made in the first century. It follows, in general, the Hebrew literally; and is VERY VALUABLE as an aid in ascertaining the meaning of the Hebrew Scriptures. The other Syriac version was made from the Septuagint about the year 616, for the use of the Monophysites. It is of value, therefore, only for the interpretation of the Septuagint. It is the former of these which is printed in the Polyglotts. Of the latter no portion has been printed except Jeremiah and Ezekiel, 1787, and Daniel, 1788. —*Calmet.*

(4.) The Arabic versions. The Scriptures have been at various times translated into Arabic. After the time of Mohammed, the Arabic became the common language of many of the Jews, and of numerous bodies of Christians in the East. Sometimes the translations were made from the Hebrew, sometimes from the Septuagint, from the Peshito, or the Vulgate. The version of R. Saadias Gaon, director of the Jewish Academy at Babylon, was made in the tenth century. It comprised originally the Old Testament ; but there have been printed only the Pentateuch, and Isaiah. The Pentateuch is found in the Polyglotts. Isaiah was published by Paulus in 1791. The Mauritanian version was made in the thirteenth century, by an Arabian Jew, and was published by Erpenius in 1629. The Arabic version in the Polyglotts was made by a Christian of Alexandria, and was made from the Septuagint.—*Robinson.* Of course these are of little value in illustrating the Hebrew text. The chief and great value of the Arabic consists in the light which is thrown upon the meaning of Hebrew words, phrases, and customs, from the Arabic language, manners, and literature.

(5.) The Targums or Chaldee versions. All these are the works of Jews living in Palestine and Babylon, from a century before Christ, to the eighth, or ninth century after. They bear the name *Targum,* i. e. *translation.* They comprise the Targum of Onkelos on the Pentateuch ; of Jonathan Ben Uzziel on the historical books, and the prophets ; of Jerusalem on the Pentateuch ; and of smaller and separate Targums on the books of Daniel, Ezra, and Nehemiah. That of Jonathan Ben Uzziel, which was made about the time of the Saviour, and which includes Isaiah, is far inferior to that of Onkelos. It often wanders from the text in a wordy, allegorical explanation ; admits many explanations which are arbitrary, and especially such as honour the Pharisees ; and often gives a *commentary* instead of a translation ; see Gesenius, Comm. uber den Isa. Einl. § 11. It is valuable, as it often gives a literal translation of the Hebrew, and adheres to it closely, and as it gives a statement of what was the prevailing interpretation of the sacred writings in the time when it was made. It may, therefore, be used in an argument with the modern Jews, to show that many of the passages which they refuse to refer to the Messiah were regarded by their fathers as having a relation to him.

The more modern versions of the Scriptures are evidently of little or no use in interpreting the Bible, and of no authority in attempting to furnish a correct text. On the general character of the versions above referred to, the reader may consult Horne's Intro. vol. ii. 156, seq. ; Gesenius, Einl. § 10–20.

II. COMMENTARIES. The following are among the principal, which may be referred to in illustration of Isaiah :

(1.) Commentarius in Librum Prophetiarum Isaiæ, Cura et Studio Campegii Vitringa, 2 vol. fol. 1714, 1720, 1724. This great work on Isaiah first appeared at Leuwarden in 1714. It has been several times reprinted. Vitringa was professor of theology at Franecker, and died in 1722. In this great work, Vitringa surpassed all who went before him in the illustration of Isaiah ; and none of the subsequent efforts which have been made to explain this prophet have superseded this, or rendered it valueless. It is now indeed indispensable to a correct understanding of this prophet. He is the fountain from which most subsequent writers on Isaiah have copiously drawn. His excellencies are, great learning ; copious investigation ; vast research ; judicious exposition ; an excellent spirit, and great acuteness. His faults—for faults abound in his work—are (1.) Great diffuseness of style. (2.) A leaning to the allegorical mode of interpretation. (3.) A minute, and anxious, and often fanciful effort to find something in history that accords with his view of each prediction. Often these parts of his work are forced and fanciful ; and though they evince great research and historical knowledge, yet his application of many of the prophecies must be regarded as wholly arbitrary and unsatisfactory. (4.) He did not seem to be fully acquainted with the poetic and figurative character of the prophetic style. Hence he is often forced to seek for fulfilment of particular expressions when a more complete acquaintance with the character of that style would have led him to seek for no such minute fulfilment. Yet no one can regard himself as furnished for a correct and full examination of Isaiah, who is not in possession of this elaborate work.

(2.) The collection of commentaries in the Critici Sacri, 9 vols. fol. This great work contains a collection of the best commentaries which were known at the time in which it was made. Valuable critical notes will be found in the commentary of Drusius, and occasional remarks of great value in the brief commentary of Grotius. Grotius is the father of commentators ; and especially on the New Testament, he has furnished more *materials* which have been worked up into the recent commentaries, than all other expositors united. He is especially valuable for the vast amount of classical learning which he has brought to illustrate the Scriptures. His main faults are, a want of spirituality, and a laxness of opinions; but no man who wishes to gain a large and liberal view of the sacred writings, will deem his library complete who has not the commentary of this great man. His notes, however, on Isaiah and the Old Testament generally, are very brief.

(3.) The same work abridged and arranged by Poole, in 5 vols. fol. This work has often been reprinted, and is well known as Poole's Synopsis. It is a work of great labour. It consists in arranging in one continuous form the different expositions contained in the work last mentioned. With all the learning and labour expended on it, it is, like most other abridgements, a work which will make him who consults it regret that an abridgement had been attempted, and sigh for the original work. It is an arrangement of *opinions*, without any *reasons* for those opinions as they existed in the minds of the original authors. To a man disposed to collect *opinions* merely, this work is invaluable; to a man who wishes to know on what opinions are based, and what is their true value, it will be regarded generally as of comparatively little use. The original work—the Critici Sacri—is of infinitely more value than this Synopsis by Poole.

(4.) The commentary of Calvin. This may be found in his works printed at Amsterdam in 1667. This commentary on Isaiah was originated in discourses which were delivered by him in his public ministry, and which were committed to writing by another hand, and afterwards revised by himself. The critical knowledge of Calvin was not great; nor does he enter minutely into criticisms, or philology. He aims at giving the sense of Isaiah, often somewhat in the form of a paraphrase. There is little criticism of words and phrases; little attempt to describe customs, or to illustrate the geography of the places referred to; and there is often in the writings of this great man a want of vivacity and of point. But he is judicious and sound. His practical remarks are useful; and his knowledge of the human heart, and his good sense, enabled him to furnish a commentary that is highly valuable.

(5.) Rosenmüller on Isaiah. This distinguished and very valuable work was first published in 1793, in three parts, and afterwards in a completely revised edition in 1810, in three volumes. The merit of Rosenmüller consists in his great learning; in his cautious and careful collection of all the materials which existed to throw light on the prophet; and in his clear and simple arrangement and statement. The *basis* of this work is indeed Vitringa; but Rosenmüller is by no means confined to him. He has gathered from all sources what he regarded as necessary to an explanation of the prophet. He is judicious in his criticisms; and not rash and reckless in attempting to modify and amend the text. He does not resemble Grotius, who is said to have 'found Christ nowhere;' but he is almost always, particularly in the first part, an advocate for the Messianic interpretation. There can be found nowhere a more valuable collection of *materials* for an understanding of Isaiah than in Rosenmüller.

(6.) Philologisch-Kritischer und Historischer Commentar über den Isaiah, von W. Gesenius, 3 Th. Leipzig, 1821. ' The commentary of Gesenius has not rendered superfluous the work of Rosenmüller. Gesenius has certainly been more independent in ascertaining the meaning of words, and in this respect has rendered a great service to the prophet. His diligence has considerably increased the materials of exegesis by collecting a number of striking parallel passages, especially from Arabian and Syrian writers, which though not numerous, have been very accurately read. His historical illustrations, especially of the prophecies relating to foreign nations, are for the most part very valuable ; and his acuteness has made new discoveries.'—*Hengstenberg.* The great value of Gesenius consists in his explanation of words and phrases ; in his bringing to bear his vast learning in the Hebrew, and the cognate languages, to an explanation of the prophet ; in his acuteness and skill in philological investigations ; and in his use of illustrations of customs, geography, &c., from modern travellers. A favourable specimen of his manner of exposition may be seen in his commentary on the prophecy respecting Moab, ch. xv. xvi. This is translated in the Biblical Repository for January 1836. See also a translation of ch. xvii. 12–14. xviii. 1–7, in the Biblical Repository for July, 1836. Of this exposition Prof. Stuart says, ' I consider it the only successful effort which has been made, to unravel the very difficult passage of which it treats. I consider it a kind of *chef d' œuvre* among the philological efforts of this distinguished writer ; ' Bib. Rep. July, 1836, p. 220. For the general merits of Gesenius, see the article ' Hebrew Lexicography,' by Prof. Stuart, in Bib. Repository, 1836, p. 468, seq.

(7.) Isaiah ; a New Translation with a Preliminary Dissertation, and Notes, Critical, Philological, and Explanatory. By Robert Lowth, D. D., Lord Bishop of London. This very beautiful translation of Isaiah was first published in London, in quarto, in 1778, and has been several times reprinted. A German translation was published by M. Koppe, with notes and additions, at Göttingen, 1779, 1780, in 4 vols. 8vo. It is the *only* work in English, with which I am acquainted, of any very great value on Isaiah ; and it will doubtless continue to hold its rank as a standard work in sacred literature. Of all the interpreters of Isaiah, Lowth has probably most clearly discerned the true nature of the prophetic visions ; has been enabled most clearly to apprehend and express the sense of the prophet ; and has presented a translation which has been universally admired for its beauty. The faults of the work are, that his translation is often too paraphrastic ; that he indulges in great caprice of criticism ; that he often changes the Hebrew text on very slight authority ; and that there is a want of copiousness in the notes for the purpose of those who would obtain a full and accurate view of Isaiah. Lowth made good use of the aids which in his time might be derived from the researches of Oriental travellers. But since his time, this department of literature has been greatly enlarged, and important light has been thrown upon many passages which in his time were obscure.

(8.) A new translation of the Hebrew Prophets, arranged in chronological order. By George Noyes, Boston, 1833. This work professes to be simply a literal translation of the prophets, without an extended commentary. A very

few notes are appended. The translation is executed with great skill and
fidelity, and gives in general very correctly the meaning of the original. The
translator has availed himself of the labours of Gesenius, and of the other
modern critics. For a further view of this work, see North American Review
for January, 1838.

(9.) Esaias ex recensione Textus Hebraei, ad fidem Codd. et verss. Latine,
vertit, et Notas subjecit, J. C. Doederlin. Altdorf, 8vo. 1780. Norimbergæ,
1789.

(10.) The Book of the Prophet Isaiah, in Hebrew and English. The
Hebrew text metrically arranged, the translation altered from that of Bishop
Lowth. By the Right Rev. Joseph Stock, D. D., Bishop of Killala, 1804, 4to.
'There is a variety of notes, critical and explanatory, supplied partly by the
translator, and partly by others. Many of these are uncommonly valuable
for their depth and acuteness, and tend to elucidate in a high degree the
subject matter of these prophecies ;' British Critic, vol. xxviii. p. 466.

(11.) Lectures on the Prophecies of Isaiah, by Robert Macculoch. London,
1791, 4 vols. 8vo.

(12.) Hierozoicon, Sive de animalibus Sacræ Scripturæ. Auctore Samuele
Bocharto. Folio, Lond. 1663. This great work has been several times
reprinted. It is a work of immense research and learning ; and is invaluable
to all who desire to obtain a knowledge of the subjects on which it treats.
Great use may be made of it in the interpretation of the Scriptures ; and its
authority has often been used in the following translation and notes. There
is repeated mention of *animals* in Isaiah ; and in no other work known to me
can so accurate and valuable a description of those animals be found as in
Bochart.

(13.) Christology of the Old Testament and a commentary on the Predictions of the Messiah, by the prophets. By E. W. Hengstenberg, Doctor of
Phil. and Theol., Professor of the latter in the University of Berlin. Translated from the German by Reuel Keith, D. D. Alexandria, 1836. For a
notice of Prof. Hengstenberg, and the character of his writings, see Biblical
Repository, vol. i. p. 21. The first vol. of this work was published in 1829
It is a very valuable accession to sacred literature, and should form a part of
every theological library. It evinces great learning ; accurate research ; and
is deeply imbued with the spirit of piety. Its fault on Isaiah is, that there
are many parts of this prophet which should be regarded as predictions of the
Messiah, which are not noticed, or so regarded in his work. His expositions
of those parts which he *has* examined (Isa. ii. iv. vii. viii. 23. ix. 1-6. xi. xii.
xl. seq.) are very valuable.

(14.) Oriental Travellers. In regard to these, the main design is not
usually to demonstrate the truth of the predictions of the prophets, or to
furnish formal expositions of the meaning of the passages of Scripture. The
illustration of the sacred writings which is to be derived from them, is mainly
incidental, and often is as far as possible from the intention of the traveller
himself. The illustrations which are derived from these travels, relate particularly to manners, rites, customs, usages, modes of travelling, conversation,
and laws ; to the animals which are mentioned in the Bible ; to houses, articles

of dress and furniture ; and more especially to the fulfilment of the prophecies. In this respect almost a new department pertaining to the truth of the Bible has been opened by the researches of modern travellers. Many of the older commentaries were exceedingly defective and unsatisfactory for the want of the information which can now be derived from such researches ; and the principal advance which can be anticipated in the interpretation of the prophecies, is probably to be derived from this source. In this respect such researches are invaluable, and particularly in the exposition of Isaiah. Some of the most complete and irrefragable demonstrations of the inspiration of the sacred writings are furnished by a simple comparison of the predictions with the descriptions of places mentioned by modern travellers. In this work, I have endeavoured to embody the results of these inquiries in the notes. As an illustration of the kind of aid to be expected from this quarter, I may refer to the notes on ch. xiii. xiv. respecting Babylon ; ch. xv. xvi. respecting Moab ; ch. xxiii. of Tyre ; and ch. xxxiv. xxxv. of Edom. Perhaps no part of the world has excited more the attention of travellers than those where the scenes of Scripture history and of prophecy are laid. Either for commercial purposes, or by a natural desire to visit those parts of the earth which have been the scenes of sacred events, or by the mere love of adventure, most of the places distinguished either in history or in prophecy have been recently explored. The sites of Babylon, Nineveh, Tyre, Damascus, and Jerusalem have been examined ; Lebanon, Egypt, Arabia, and Palestine in general have been visited ; and even Moab and Arabia have been traversed. The ancient land of Idumea, long deemed inaccessible, now Arabia Petræa, has been explored by Burckhardt, by Captains Irby and Mangles, by Laborde, and still more recently by our own countrymen, Mr. Stephens, and by Messrs. Smith and Robinson. The capital of that once celebrated kingdom has been discovered and examined after it had been unknown for ages, and a most striking fulfilment of the sacred predictions has thus been furnished ; see Notes on ch. xvi. and xxxiv. Perhaps there is no department of sacred learning that promises so much to illustrate the Scriptures, as that of modern travels. It is to be remembered (to use the words of Prof. Bush), that as ' the Bible, in its structure, spirit, and costume, is essentially an Eastern book, it is obvious that the natural phenomena and the moral condition of the East should be made largely tributary to its elucidation. In order to appreciate fully the truth of its descriptions, and the accuracy, force and beauty of its various allusions, it is indispensable that the reader, as far as possible, separate himself from his ordinary associations, and put himself by a kind of mental transmutation into the very circumstances of the writers. He must set him. self down in the midst of Oriental scenery—gaze upon the sun, sky, mountains and rivers of Asia—go forth with the nomade tribes of the desert— follow their flocks—travel with their caravans—rest in their tents—lodge in their khans—load and unload their camels—drink at their watering places— pause during the heat of the day under their palms—cultivate the fields with their own rude implements—gather in or glean after their harvests—beat out and ventilate the grain in their open threshing floors—dress in their costume— note their proverbial or idiomatic forms of speech, and listen to the strain of song or story with which they beguile their vacant hours ; ' Pref. to Illustrations of the Scriptures. To use the words of a late writer in the London Quarterly Review, ' we confess that we have felt more surprise, delight, and conviction in examining the account which the travels of Burckhardt, Mangles, Irby, Leigh, and Laborde have so recently given of Judea, Edom, &c., than we have ever derived from any similar inquiry. It seems like a miracle in our own times. Twenty years ago, we read certain portions of the prophetic Scriptures with a belief that they were true, because other similar passages had, in the course of ages, been proved to be so, and we had an indistinct notion that all these (to us) obscure and indefinite denunciations had been— we know not very well when or how—accomplished ; but to have graphic descriptions, ground plans and elevations, showing the actual existence of all the heretofore vague and shadowy denunciations of God against Edom, does, we confess, excite our feelings, and exalt our confidence in prophecy to a height that no *external* evidence has hitherto done. Here we have, bursting upon our age of incredulity, by the labours of accidental, impartial, and sometimes incredulous witnesses, the certainty of existing facts, which fulfil what were hitherto considered the most vague and least intelligible of all the prophecies. The value of one such contemporaneous proof is immense.' ' It is,' to use the language of the Biblical Repository (vol. ix. pp. 456, 457), ' *sensible* evidence, graven on the eternal rocks, and to endure till those rocks shall melt in the final catastrophe of earth. The exactness between the prediction and the fulfilment is wonderful. The evidence for the truth of the prophecies is sometimes said to be cumulative ; but here we have a new volume at once opened to our view; a sudden influx of overpowering light. It is a monumental miracle, an attestation to the truth of God wrought into the very framework of the globe ; ' Review of Laborde's Journey to Petra. It may be added, that the sources of information on these interesting subjects are becoming very numerous, and already leave little to be desired. To see this, it is sufficient to mention the following :—Roberts' Oriental Illustrations ; Maundrell's Journey from Aleppo to Jerusalem ; Volney's Travels through Egypt and Syria ; Mariti's Travels through Cyprus, Syria and Palestine ; Russell's Natural History of Aleppo ; Clarke's Travels in the Holy Land ; Burckhardt's Travels in Syria ; ——— Travels in Nubia and Egypt ; Keppel's Narrative of a Journey from India to England ; Morier's Journey through Persia ; Jowett's Christian Researches ; Burnes' Travels in Bokhara ; Laborde's Journey to Petra, and the travels of Chandler, Pococke, Shaw, Pitts, Niebuhr—the ' prince of travellers'—Porter, Seetzen ; from all of whom valuable illustrations may be derived, and confirmations of the truths of the Scripture prophecies. Of all the works of this description, the most valuable for an accurate exposition of the Scriptures, in relation to the geography of the Holy Land, is the recent work of our own countrymen—' Biblical Researches in Palestine, Mount Sinai, and Arabia Petræa,' a journal of Travels in the year 1838, by E. Robinson and E. Smith, 3 vols. 8vo, 1841.

THE BOOK

OF

THE PROPHET ISAIAH

CHAPTER I.

ANALYSIS OF THE CHAPTER.

THIS chapter contains, I. the Inscription or title to the whole book of Isaiah (ver. 1); and, II. an entire prophecy respecting the land of Judah. In regard to the title see the Notes on ver. 1.

The remainder of the chapter (ver. 2-31) comprises a single prophecy, complete in itself, and evidently delivered on a single occasion. It has no immediate connection with that which follows, though it may have been delivered about the same period. When it was delivered is not known. We are informed (ch. vi. 1) that the vision of Jehovah, which Isaiah had in the temple, occurred during the last year of the reign of Uzziah. The only indication which we can have of the time when this prophecy was uttered, is to be derived from its *location*, and from the accordance of its contents with the state of things in Judea. It is evident that the author of the arrangement, whoever he was, regarded it as properly placed in the order of time before the account of the vision of Jehovah, i.e. as having been uttered before the death of Uzziah. Nor are the contents of such a nature as to render it improbable that the collector has followed the natural order in which the prophecies were delivered. On some accounts, indeed, it might better be regarded as spoken during the reign of Ahaz; but at any time of the Jewish history in which Isaiah lived, it is not an inappropriate description of the character of the Jewish people. There is one internal indication indeed that it was not delivered in the time of Ahaz. Ahaz had filled the land with the groves and altars of idolatry. See the Introduction, § 3. But this prophecy does not allude to idolatry, as the leading and characteristic sin. It is a description of a people who still kept up the *form* of the worship of Jehovah; of a people deeply depraved indeed, and suffering under the tokens of the Divine displeasure, but who were professedly the

worshippers of the true God. It is descriptive of a time when the nation was distinguished for *hypocrisy* rather than *idolatry*. It naturally falls, therefore, into the time of Uzziah, or Jotham—as it cannot be supposed that if delivered during the reign of Hezekiah, it would be so far misplaced as to constitute the introductory chapter to the whole series of prophecies. In regard to the *time* when it was uttered, and the *time* to which it refers, there have been very different opinions. Abarbanel, Grotius, and Rosenmüller, suppose that it refers to the times of Uzziah; De Wette supposes that it relates to the reign of Jotham; Piscator, Hensler, Arnold, regard it as relating to the reign of Ahaz; and Jarchi, Vitringa, and Eichhorn, refer it to the times of Hezekiah. In such a variety of opinion it is impossible to fix the time with any certainty. Nor is it very material. It was not an inappropriate description of the general character of the Jewish people; and there can be no doubt that there were times during the long prophetic life of Isaiah, when it would be found to accord fully with the condition of the nation. Unhappily, also, there are times in the church now, when it is fully descriptive of the character of the professed people of God, and it contains truths, and fearful denunciations, not less appropriate to them, than they were to the people who lived in the time of Isaiah.

The prophecy is highly objurgatory and severe in its character. It is made up of reproof, and of assurances that the evils which they were suffering were for their hypocrisy, and other sins. It commences with a solemn and very sublime address to heaven and earth to witness the deep depravity, and the pervading corruption of the land of Judah. It was such as was adapted to attract the attention, and to amaze all beings in heaven and on earth, v. 2-4. The prophet then proceeds to state that the existing calamities of the nation had been inflicted on account of their sins, and that for those sins the land was laid waste, v. 5-9. Yet they kept up the appearance of religion. They were constant and regular, externally, in offering sacrifices. But their character was deeply hypocritical. The services of God were so false and hollow, that he spurned and despised them. They were a weariness to him, and a burden, v. 10–15. The prophet then calls on the sinful nation to turn from their sins, and to seek God, with the assurance that he was willing to re-admit them to his favour ; to pardon all their crimes, and to receive them as his own children, v. 16–20. If they did not do it, he assures them that heavier judgments would come upon them than they had yet experienced,

v. 21–25 ; and that God would so deal with them as to effect a change in the nation, and to restore the happier and purer state of things existing in former days. The wicked would be punished, and Zion would be redeemed, v. 26-31.

THE vision *a* of Isaiah, the son of Amoz, which he saw concerning Judah and Jerusalem, in the days *b* of Uzziah, Jotham, Ahaz, *and* Hezekiah, kings of Judah.

a Num.12.6.   *b* 2Ch.26.32.

---

1. *The vision.* The first verse evidently is a *title,* but whether to the whole book or only to a part of it has been questioned. As it stands here, however, it seems clearly intended to include the entire book, because it embraces all that was seen during the reigns of Uzziah, Jotham, Ahaz, and Hezekiah ; that is, during the whole prophetic life of the prophet. The same title is also given to his prophecies in 2 Chron. xxxii. 32: ' Now the rest of the acts of Hezekiah, and his goodness, behold they are written in the vision of Isaiah.' Vitringa supposes that the former part of this title, ' the vision of Isaiah,' was at first affixed to the single prophecy contained in the first chapter, and that the latter part was inserted afterwards as an introduction to the whole book. This might have been done by Isaiah himself if he collected his prophecies into a volume, or by some other inspired man who collected and arranged them ; see the Introduction to ch. xxxvi. —The word *vision,* חָזוֹן *hhăzōn,* denotes properly that which is *seen,* from the verb, חָזָה *hhăzâ, to see, to behold.* It is a term which is often used in reference to the prophecies of the Old Testament ; Num. xii. 6; xxiv. 4; 1 Sam. iii. 1; Ps. lxxxix. 19; Dan. ii. 19; vii. 2; viii. 1; Nah. i. 1; Gen. xv. 1; Isa. xxi. 2; xxii. 1. Hence the prophets were anciently called *Seers,* as those who *saw* or witnessed events which were yet to come ; comp. 1 Sam. ix. 9 : ' He that is now called a Prophet was beforetime called *a Seer ;'* 1 Sam. ix. 11, 18, 19; 1 Chron. ix. 22; xxix. 29; 2 Kings xviii. 13. In these *visions* the objects probably were made to pass before the mind of the prophet

as *a picture,* in which the various events were delineated with more or less distinctness, and the prophecies were spoken, or recorded, as the visions appeared to the observer. As many events could be represented only by *symbols,* those symbols became a matter of record, and are often left without explanation. On the nature of the prophetic visions, see Introduction, § 7. (4.) ¶ OF ISAIAH. The name Isaiah יְשַׁעְיָהוּ from יֶשַׁע *Yĕsha'*— salvation, help, deliverance—and יְהֹוָה *Yehovâ* or JEHOVAH, means ' salvation of JEHOVAH,' or ' JEHOVAH will save.' The Vulgate renders it ISAIAS ; the LXX. Ησαΐας *Esaias.* This is also retained in the New Testament ; Mat. iii. 3; iv. 14; xii. 17; xv. 7; Mar. vii. 6; Luke iv. 17; John xii. 39; Acts viii. 28; Rom. ix. 27, &c., &c. In the book of Isaiah itself we find the form יְשַׁעְיָהוּ *Yesha'yâhu,* but in the inscription the Rabbins give the form יְשַׁעְיָה *Yesha'yâ.* It was common among the Hebrews to incorporate the name JEHOVAH, or a part of it, into their proper names; see Note on ch. vii. 14. Probably the object of this was to express veneration or regard for him—as we now give the name of a parent or friend to a child ; or in many cases the name may have been given to record some signal act of mercy on the part of God, or some special interposition of his goodness. The practice of incorporating the name of the God that was worshipped into proper names was common in the East. Thus the name *Bel,* the principal idol worshipped in Babylon, appears in the proper names of the kings, as Belshazzar, &c.; comp. Note ch. xlvi. 1. It is not known that the name was given to Isaiah

2 Hear, *a* O heavens; and give ear, O earth; for the Lord hath spoken: I have nourished and brought up children,*b* and they have rebelled against me:

a De.32.1.Je.2 12.Mi.1.2. *b* ch.63.16.

with any reference to the nature of the prophecies which he would deliver; but it is a remarkable circumstance that it coincides so entirely with the design of so large a portion of his predictions. The substance of the latter portion of the book, at least, is the *salvation* which Jehovah would effect for his people from their oppressors in Babylon, and the far mightier deliverance which the world would experience under the Messiah. ¶ *The son of Amoz.* See the Introduction, § 2. ¶ *Concerning Judah.* The Jews after the death of Solomon were divided into two kingdoms; the kingdom of Judah, and of Israel, or Ephraim. The kingdom of *Judah* included the tribes of Judah and Benjamin. Benjamin was a small tribe, and it was not commonly mentioned, or the name was lost in that of Judah. The kingdom of Israel, or Ephraim, included the remaining ten tribes. Few of the prophets appeared among them; and the personal ministry of Isaiah does not appear to have been at all extended to them. ¶ *Jerusalem.* The capital of the kingdom of Judah. It was on the dividing line between the tribes of Judah and Benjamin. It is supposed to have been founded by Melchizedek, who is called king of Salem (Gen. xiv. 18), and who is supposed to have given this name *Salem* to it. This was about 2000 years before Christ. About a century after its foundation as a city, it was captured by the *Jebusites*, who extended its walls and built a citadel on Mount Zion. By them it was called Jebus. In the conquest of Canaan, Joshua put to death its king (Josh. x. 23), and obtained possession of the town, which was jointly occupied by the Hebrews and Jebusites until the latter were expelled by David, who made it the capital of his kingdom under the name of *Jebus-Salem*, or, for the sake of easier pronunciation by changing the ב B into ר R, *Jerusalem*. After the revolt of the ten tribes, it of course became the capital of the kingdom of Judah. It was built on hills, or rocks, and was capable of being strongly fortified, and was well adapted to be the

capital of the nation. For a more full description of Jerusalem, see Notes on Mat. ii. 1. The vision which is here spoken of as having been seen respecting Judah and Jerusalem, pertains only to this chapter; see ch. ii. 1. ¶ *In the days of Uzziah.* In the *time*, or during the *reign* of Uzziah; 2 Chron. xxvi.; comp. Intro. § 3. He was sixteen years old when he began to reign, and reigned fifty-two years. It is not affirmed or supposed that Isaiah began to prophesy at the *commencement* of his reign. The first part of the long reign of Uzziah was prosperous. He gained important victories over his enemies, and fortified his kingdom; 2 Chron. xxvi. 5–15. He had under him an army of more than three hundred thousand men. But he became proud—attempted an act of sacrilege—was smitten of God, and died a leper. But though the kingdom under Uzziah was flourishing, yet it had in it the elements of decay. During the previous reign of Joash, it had been invaded and weakened by the Assyrians, and a large amount of wealth had been taken to Damascus, the capital of Syria; 2 Chron. xxiv. 23, 24. It is not improbable that those ravages were repeated during the latter part of the reign of Uzziah; comp. Isa. i. 7. ¶ *Jotham.* He began to reign at the age of twenty-five years, and reigned sixteen years; 2 Chron. xxvii. 1, 2. ¶ *Ahaz.* He began to reign at the age of twenty, and reigned sixteen years. He was a wicked man, and during his reign the kingdom was involved in crimes and calamities; 2 Chron. xxviii. ¶ *Hezekiah.* He was a virtuous and upright prince. He began his reign at the age of twenty-five years, and reigned twenty-nine; 2 Chron. xxix; see the Introduction § 3.

2. *Hear, O heavens.* This is properly the beginning of the prophecy. It is a sublime commencement; and is of a highly poetic character. The heavens and the earth are summoned to bear witness to the apostacy, ingratitude, and deep depravity of the chosen people of God. The address is expressive of deep feeling,—the bursting forth

of a heart filled with amazement at a wonderful and unusual event. The same sublime beginning is found in the song of Moses, Deut. xxxii. 1:

Give ear, O ye heavens, and I will speak;
And hear, O earth, the words of my mouth.

comp. Ps. iv. 3, 4. Thus also the prophets often invoke the hills and mountains to hear them; Ezek. vi. 3: ' Ye mountains of Israel, hear the words of the Lord God: Thus saith the Lord God to the mountains, and to the hills, and to the rivers, and to the valleys;' comp. Ezek. xxxvi. 1. ' Be astonished, O ye heavens, at this, and be horribly afraid, be ye very desolate, saith the Lord,' Jer. ii. 12. By the *heavens* therefore, in this place, we are not to understand the *inhabitants* of heaven, i. e. the angels, any more than by *the hills* we are to understand the *inhabitants* of the mountains. It is high poetic language, denoting the *importance* of the subject, and the remarkable and amazing truth to which the attention was to be called. ¶ *Give ear. O earth.* It was common thus to address the earth on any remarkable occasion, especially any one implying warm expostulation, Jer. v. 19; xxii. 29; Micah i. 2; vi. 2; Isa. xxxiv. 1; xlix. 13. ¶ *For.* Since it is Jehovah that speaks, all the universe is summoned to attend; comp. Ps. xxxiii. 8, 9: ' Let all the earth fear the Lord; let all the inhabitants of the world stand in awe of him. For he spake and it was done; he commanded and it stood fast.' ¶ *The* LORD.—יְהֹוָה *Yehŏvâ,* or JEHOVAH. The small *capitals* used here and elsewhere throughout the Bible, in printing the word LORD, denote that the original word is JEHOVAH. It is derived from the verb הָיָה *hâyâ, to be;* and is used to denote *being,* or the fountain of being, and can be applied only to the true God; comp. Ex. iii. 14: ' And God said unto Moses, I AM THAT I AM,' אֶהְיֶה אֲשֶׁר אֶהְיֶה; Ex. vi. 3; Num. xi. 21; Isa. xlvii. 8. It is a name which is never given to idols, or conferred on a creature; and though it occurs often in the Hebrew Scriptures, as is indicated by the small capitals, yet our translators have retained it but four times; Ex. vi. 3; Ps. lxxxiii. 18; Isa. xii. 2; xxvi. 4. In *combination,* however, with

other names, it occurs often. Thus in *Isaiah,* meaning the salvation of Jehovah; *Jeremiah,* the exaltation or grandeur of Jehovah, &c.; comp. Gen. xxii. 14: ' Abraham called the name of the place *Jehovah-jireh,*' Ex. xvii. 15; Judg. vi. 24; Ezek. xlviii. 35. The Jews never pronounced this name, not even in reading their own Scriptures. So sacred did they deem it, that when it occurred in their books, instead of the word JEHOVAH, they substituted the word ADONAI, אֲדֹנָי *Lord.* Our translators have shown respect to this feeling of the Jews in regard to the sacredness of the name; and hence, have rendered it by the name of LORD—a word which by no means conveys the sense of the word JEHOVAH. It would have been an advantage to our version if the word JEHOVAH had been retained wherever it occurs in the original. ¶ *I have nourished.* Heb. *I have made great;* גִּדַּלְתִּי. In Piel, the word means *to make great, to cause to grow;* as e. g. the hair; Num. vi. 5, plants, Isa. xliv. 14; then to educate or bring up children; Isa. xlix. 21, 41, 13; 2 Kings x. 6. ¶ *And brought up.* רוֹמַמְתִּי *rōmămtī,* from רוּם *rūm,* to lift up or exalt. In Piel it means to bring up, nourish, educate; Isaiah xxiii. 4. These words, though applied often to the training up of children, yet are here used also to denote the *elevation* to which they had been raised. He had not merely trained them up, but he had trained them up to *an elevated station;* to peculiar honour and privileges. ¶ *Children.* Heb. בָּנִים *bânim—sons.* They were the adopted children of God; and they are represented as being weak, and ignorant, and helpless as children, when he took them under his fatherly protection and care; Hos. xi. 1: ' When Israel was a child, then I loved him, and called my son out of Egypt;' comp. Note, Mat. ii. 15; Isa. lxiii. 8–16. ¶ *They have rebelled.* This complaint was often brought against the Jews; comp. Isa. lxiii. 10; Jer. ii. 6, 7, 8.—This is the sum of the charge against them. God had shown them peculiar favours. He recounted his mercy in bringing them out of Egypt; and on the ground of this, he demanded obedience and love; comp. Ex. xx. 1, 2, 3. And yet they

3 The ox[a] knoweth his owner, and the ass his master's crib : *but* Israel doth not know, my people doth not consider.

4 Ah, sinful nation, a people laden [1] with [b] iniquity, a seed of evil-doers, children that are corrupters ! they have forsaken the LORD, they have provoked the Holy One of Israel unto anger, they are [2]gone away backward.

a Jer.8.7.   1 *of heaviness.*   b Mat.11.21.
2 *alienated,* or *separated,* Ps.58.3.

had forgotten him, and rebelled against him. The Targum of Jonathan, an ancient Chaldee version, has well expressed the idea here. ' Hear, O heavens, which were moved when I gave my law to my people : give ear, O earth, which didst tremble before my word, for the Lord has spoken. My people, the house of Israel, whom I called sons,—I loved them,—I honoured them, and they rebelled against me.' The same is true substantially of all sinners; and alas, how often may a similar expostulation be made with the professed people of God ! 3. *The ox, &c.* The design of this comparison is to show the great stupidity and ingratitude of the Jews. Even the least sagacious and most stupid of the animals, destitute as they are of reason and conscience, evince knowledge and submission far more than the professed people of God. The ox is a well known domestic animal, remarkable for patient willingness to toil, and for submission to his owner. ¶ *Knoweth his owner.* Recognizes, or is submissive to him. ¶ *The ass.* A well known animal, proverbial for dulness and stupidity. ¶ *His master's crib.* אבוס from אבם *âbăs,* to heap up, and then to fatten. Hence it is applied to the stall, barn, or crib, where cattle are fed, or made fat ; Job xxxix. 9 ; Prov. xiv. 4. The ass has sufficient knowledge to understand that his *support* is derived from that. The idea is, that the ox was more submissive to laws than the Jews ; and that even the most stupid animal better knew whence support was to be derived, than they did the source of their comfort and protection. The ass would not wander away, and the ox would not rebel as they had done. This comparison was very striking, and very humiliating, and nothing could be more fitted to bring down their pride. A similar comparison is elsewhere used. Thus, in Jer. viii. 7, the Jews are contrasted with the stork : ' Yea, the stork in the heaven knoweth her appointed times ; and the turtle [dove], and the crane, and the swallow, observe the time of their coming ; but my people know not the judgment of the Lord.' This idea has been beautifully expressed by Watts :

> The brutes obey their God,
> And bow their necks to men ;
> But we more base, more brutish things,
> Reject his easy reign.

Comp. Hos. xi. 4. ¶ *But Israel.* The name *Israel,* though after the division of the tribes into two kingdoms specifically employed to denote that of the ten tribes, is often used in the more general sense to denote the whole people of the Jews, including the kingdom of Judah. It refers here to the kingdom of Judah, though a name is used which is not inappropriately characteristic of the whole people. ¶ *Doth not know.* The Latin Vulgate, the Septuagint, and the Arabic, add the word ' me.' The word *know* is used in the sense of *recognizing* him as their Lord ; of acknowledging him, or submitting to him. ¶ *Doth not consider.* Heb. Do not *understand.* They have a stupidity greater than the brute.

4. *Ah ! sinful nation.* The word rendered ' ah !'— הוֹי *hoy*—is not a mere exclamation, expressing astonishment. It is rather an interjection denouncing threatening, or punishment. ' Wo to the sinful nation.' Vulg. ' Vae genti peccatrici.' The corruption pertained to the *nation,* and not merely to a part. It had become general. ¶ *Laden with iniquity.* The word translated *laden*— כֶּבֶד —denotes properly any thing *heavy,* or burdensome ; from כָּבַד *kâbhădh, to be heavy.* It means that they were oppressed, and borne down with the *weight* of their sins. Thus we say, Sin sits *heavy* on the conscience. Thus Cain said, ' My punishment is greater than I can bear ;' Gen. iv. 13. The word

5 Why *a* should ye be stricken
any more? ye will ¹revolt more and

a Je.2,30.   1 *increase revolt.*

is applied to an *employment* as being
burdensome; Exod. xviii. 18: 'This
thing is too *heavy* for thee.' Num. xi.
14: 'I am not able to bear all this people alone; it is too *heavy* for me.' It is
applied also to a *famine*, as being heavy,
severe, distressing. Gen. xii. 10: 'For
the famine was *grievous* (כָּבֵד *heavy*) in
the land;' Gen. xli. 31. It is also applied
to *speech*, as being heavy, dull, unintelligible. Ex. iv. 10: 'I am slow (heavy
כְּבַד) of speech, and of a slow (heavy כְּבַד)
tongue.' It is not applied to *sin* in the
Scriptures, except in this place, or except in the sense of making atonement
for it. The idea however is very striking—that of a *nation*—an entire people,
bowed and crushed under the enormous
weight of accumulated crimes. To pardon iniquity, or to *atone* for it, is represented by *bearing it*, as if it were a heavy
burden. Ex. xxviii. 38, 43, 'That
Aaron may *bear* the iniquity of the holy
things.' Lev. x. 17: 'God hath given
it you to *bear* the iniquity of the congregation.' Lev. xxii. 9; xvi. 22; Num.
xviii. 1; Isa. liii. 6: 'JEHOVAH hath laid
on him the iniquity of us all.' 11: 'He
shall *bear* their iniquities.' 1 Pet. ii.
24: 'Who his own self bare our sins
in his own body on the tree.' ¶ *A seed.*
זֶרַע *zērā'*, from זָרַע *zārā'*, to sow, to
scatter, to disperse. It is applied to
seed sown in a field; Judg. vi. 3; Gen.
i. 11, 12; xlvii. 23; to plants set out, or
engrafted; or to planting, or transplanting a nation. Isa. xvii. 10: 'And thou
shalt *set it* [תִּזְרָעֶנּוּ shalt sow, or plant it]
with strange slips.' Hence it is applied
to children, posterity, descendants, from
the resemblance of seed sown, and to a
harvest springing up, and spreading.
The word is applied by way of eminence
to the Jews, as being THE *seed* or posterity of Abraham, according to the
promise that his seed should be as the
stars of heaven; Gen. xii. 7; xiii. 15,
16; xv. 5, 18; xvii. 7, &c. ¶ *Children.*
Heb. *sons*—the same word that is used
in ver. 2. They were the adopted people or sons of God, but they had now become corrupt. ¶ *That are corrupters.*

more. The whole head is sick, and
the whole heart faint.

מַשְׁחִיתִים *mǎshhītlīm*, from שָׁחַת *shāh-
hǎth*, to destroy, to lay waste, as an invading army does a city or country;
Josh. xxii. 33; Gen. xix. 13. To destroy a vineyard; Jer. xii. 10. To break
down walls; Ezek. xxvi. 4. Applied to
conduct, it means to *destroy*, or lay
waste virtuous principles; to break
down the barriers to vice; to corrupt
the morals. Gen. vi. 12: 'And God
looked upon the earth, and it was *corrupt*—נִשְׁחָתָה;—for all flesh had corrupted his way—הִשְׁחִית—upon the
earth;' Deut. iv. 16; xxxi. 29; Judg.
ii. 19. They were not merely corrupt
themselves, but they corrupted others
by their example. This is always the
case. When men become infidels and
profligates themselves, they seek to
make as many more so as possible.
The Jews did this by their wicked lives.
The same charge is often brought against
them; see Judg. ii. 12; Zeph. iii. 7.
¶ *They have provoked.* Heb. נִאֲצוּ.
'They have *despised* the Holy One;'
comp. Prov. i. 30; v. 12; xv. 5. Vulg.
'They have *blasphemed*.' Septuagint,
παρωργίσατε. 'You have *provoked* him
to anger.' The meaning is, that they
had so *despised* him, as to excite his
indignation. ¶ *The Holy One of Israel.*
God; called the Holy One of Israel because he was revealed to them as *their*
God, or they were taught to regard him
as the sacred object of their worship.
¶ *They are gone away backward.*
Lowth: 'They have turned their backs
upon him.' The word rendered *they are
gone away*, נָזֹרוּ *nāzōrū*, from זוּר *zūr*,
means properly, *to become estranged* ;
to be alienated. Job. xix. 13: 'Mine
acquaintance are verily *estranged* from
me.' It means especially that declin-
ing from God, or that alienation, which
takes place when men commit sin; Ps.
lxxviii. 30.

5. *Why*, &c. The prophet now, by
an abrupt change in the discourse, calls
their attention to the *effects* of their
sins. Instead of saying that they *had*
been smitten, or of saying that they
had been punished *for their sins*, he

assumes both, and asks why it should be repeated. The Vulgate reads this: 'Super quo—on what part—shall I smite you any more?' This expresses well the sense of the Hebrew—עַל־מֶה —*upon what;* and the meaning is, 'what part of the body can be found on which blows have not been inflicted? On every part there are traces of the stripes which have been inflicted for your sins.' The idea is taken from a body that is all covered over with *weals* or marks of blows, and the idea is, that the whole frame is one continued bruise, and there remains no sound part to be stricken. The particular chastisement to which the prophet refers is specified in ver. 7–9. In ver. 5, 6, he refers to the calamities of the nation, under the image of a person wounded and chastised for crimes. Such a figure of speech is not uncommon in the classic writers. Thus Cicero (de fin. iv. 14) says, 'quae hic reipublicae vulnera imponebat hic sanabat.' See also Tusc. Quaes. iii. 22; Ad Quintum fratrem, ii. 25; Sallust; Cat. 10. ¶ *Should ye be stricken.* Smitten, or punished. The manner in which they *had* been punished, he specifies in ver. 7, 8. Jerome says, that the sense is, ' there is no medicine which I can administer to your wounds. All your members are full of wounds; and there is no part of your body which has not been smitten before. The more you are afflicted, the more will your impiety and iniquity increase.' The word here, תֻּכּוּ *thŭkkū,* from נָכָה, means to smite, to beat, to strike down, to slay, or kill. It is applied to the infliction of punishment on an individual ; or to the judgments of God by the plague, pestilence, or sickness. Gen. xix. 2: 'And they *smote* the men that were at the door with blindness.' Num. xiv. 12: 'And I will *smite* them with the pestilence.' Ex. vii. 25: 'After that the Lord *had* smitten the river,' i.e. had changed it into blood ; comp. verse 20 ; Zech. x. 2. Here it refers to the judgments inflicted on the nation as the punishment of their crimes. ¶ *Ye will revolt.* Heb. You will *add* defection, or revolt. The effect of calamity, and punishment, will be only to increase rebellion. Where the heart is right with God, the tendency

of affliction is to humble it, and lead it more and more to God. Where it is evil, the tendency is to make the sinner more obstinate and rebellious. This effect of *punishment* is seen every where. Sinners revolt more and more. They become sullen, and malignant, and fretful ; they plunge into vice to seek temporary relief, and thus they become more and more alienated from God. ¶ *The whole head.* The prophet proceeds to specify more definitely what he had just said respecting their being stricken. He designates each of the members of the body—thus comparing the Jewish people to the human body when under severe punishment. The word *head* in the Scriptures is often used to denote the *princes, leaders,* or *chiefs* of the nation. But the expression here is used as a figure taken from the human body, and refers solely to the *punishment* of the people, not to their *sins.* It means that *all* had been smitten—all was filled with the effects of punishment—as the human body is when the head and all the members are diseased. ¶ *Is sick.* Is so smitten— so punished, that it has become sick and painful. Heb. לָחֳלִי—*for sickness,* or *pain.* The preposition לְ denotes a *state,* or condition of any thing. Ps. lxix. 21. ' And in [לְ] my thirst, they gave me vinegar to drink.' The expression is *intensive,* and denotes that the head was entirely sick. ¶ *The whole heart faint.* The *heart* is here put for the whole region of the chest or stomach. As when the head is violently pained, there is also sickness at the heart, or in the stomach, and as these are indications of *entire* or *total* prostration of the frame so the expression here denotes the perfect desolation which had come over the nation. ¶ *Faint.* Sick, feeble, without vigour, attended with nausea. Jer. viii. 18: ' When I would comfort myself in my sorrow, my heart is faint within me;' Lam. i. 22. When the body is suffering ; when severe punishment is inflicted, the effect is to produce languor and faintness at the seat of life. This is the idea here. Their punishment had been so severe for their sins, that the heart was languid and feeble—still keeping up the figure drawn from the human body.

6 From the sole of the foot even unto the head *there is* no soundness in it ; *but* wounds, and bruises, and putrifying sores : they have not been closed, neither bound up, neither mollified with ointment.[1]

1 or, *oil.*

6. *From the sole of the foot,* &c. Or as we say, ‘ from head to foot,’ that is, in every part of the body. There may be included also the idea that this extended from the lowest to the highest among the people. The Chaldee paraphrase is, ‘ from the lowest of the people even to the princes—all are contumacious and rebellious.’ ¶ *No soundness.* מְתֹם *methōm,* from תָּמַם *thâmăm,* to be perfect, sound, uninjured. There is no part unaffected ; no part that is sound. It is all smitten and sore. ¶ *But wounds.* The precise shade of difference between this and the two following words may not be apparent. *Together,* they mean such wounds and contusions as are inflicted upon man by scourging, or beating him. This mode of punishment was common among the Jews ; as it is at the East at this time. Abarbanel and Kimchi say that the word here rendered *wounds* (פֶּצַע, a verbal from פָּצַע to wound, to mutilate), means an open wound, or a cut from which blood flows. ¶ *Bruises.* חַבּוּרָה *hhăbbūrâ.* This word means a contusion, or the effect of a blow where the skin is not broken ; such a contusion as to produce a swelling, and livid appearance ; or to make it, as we say, black and blue. ¶ *Putrifying sores.* The Hebrew rather means *recent,* or *fresh* wounds ; or rather, perhaps, a running wound, which continues fresh and open ; which cannot be cicatrized, or dried up. The LXX. render it elegantly πληγὴ φλεγμαίνουσα, a swelling, or tumefying wound. The expression is applied usually to inflammations, as of boils, or to the swelling of the tonsils, &c. ¶ *They have not been closed* That is, the lips had not been pressed together, to remove the blood from the wound. The meaning is, that nothing had been done towards healing the wound. It was an unhealed, undressed, all-pervading sore. The art of medicine, in the East, consists chiefly in external applications ; accordingly the prophet’s images in this place are all taken from surgery. Sir John Chardin, in his note on Prov. iii. 8,

‘ It shall be health to thy navel, and marrow to thy bones,’ observes, that the comparison is taken from the plasters, ointments, oils, and frictions, which are made use of in the East in most maladies. ‘ In Judea,’ says Tavernier, ‘ they have a certain preparation of oil, and melted grease, which they commonly use for the healing of wounds.’ *Lowth.* Comp. Note on ch. xxxviii. 21. ¶ *Neither mollified with ointment.* Neither made *soft,* or *tender,* with ointment. Great use was made, in Eastern nations, of *oil,* and various kinds of unguents, in medicine. Hence the good Samaritan is represented as pouring in *oil* and wine into the wounds of the man that fell among thieves (Luke x. 34) ; and the apostles were directed to anoint with oil those who were sick ; James v. 14 ; comp. Rev. iii. 18. ¶ *Ointment.* Heb. *oil.* שֶׁמֶן. The oil of olives was used commonly for this purpose. The whole figure in these two verses relates to their *being punished* for their sins. It is taken from the appearance of a man who is severely beaten, or scourged for crime ; whose wounds had not been dressed ; and who was thus a continued bruise, or sore, from his head to his feet. The *cause* of this the prophet states afterwards, ver. 10, seq. With great skill he first reminds them of what they saw and knew, that they were severely punished ; and then states to them the *cause* of it. Of the calamities to which the prophet refers, they could have no doubt. They were every where visible in all their cities and towns. On these far-spreading desolations, he fixes the eye distinctly first. Had he *begun* with the statement of their *depravity,* they would probably have revolted at it. But being presented with a statement of their sufferings, which they all saw and felt, they were prepared for the statement of the cause.—To find access to the consciences of sinners, and to convince them of their guilt, it is often necessary to remind them first of the calamities in which they are actually

7 Your country *is* desolate,[a] your cities *are* burned with fire : your land, strangers devour it in your presence, and *it is* desolate, as overthrown[1] by strangers.

8 And the daughter of Zion is

a Deut.28.51.

1 *the overthrow of.*

involved; and then to search for the cause. This passage, therefore, has no reference to their moral character. It relates solely to their punishment. It is often indeed adduced to prove the doctrine of depravity; but it has no direct reference to it, and it should *not* be adduced to prove that men are depraved, or applied as referring to the moral condition of man. The account of their *moral* character, as the cause of their calamities, is given in ver. 10–14. That statement will fully account for the many woes which had come on the nation.

7. *Your country is desolate.* This is the *literal* statement of what he had just affirmed by a figure. In this there was much art. The figure (ver. 6) was striking. The resemblance between a man severely beaten, and entirely livid and sore, and a land perfectly desolate, was so impressive as to arrest the attention. This had been threatened as one of the curses which should attend disobedience; Lev. xxvi. 33 :

And I will scatter you among the heathen,
And will draw out a sword after you:
And your land shall be desolate,
And your cities waste.

Comp. ver. 31, 32; Deut. xxviii. 49–52. It is not certain, or agreed among expositors, to what time the prophet refers in this passage. Some have supposed that he refers to the time of *Ahaz*, and to the calamities which came upon the nation during his reign; 2 Chron. xxviii. 5–8. But the probability is, that this refers to the time of Uzziah; see the Analysis of the chapter. The reign of Uzziah was indeed prosperous; 2 Chron. xxvi. But it is to be remembered that the land had been ravaged just before, under the reigns of Joash and Amaziah, by the kings of Syria and Israel; 2 Kings xiv. 8–14; 2 Chron. xxiv.; xxv.; and it is by no means probable that it had recovered in the time of Uzziah. It was lying under the effect of the former desolation, and not improbably the enemies of the Jews were even then hovering around it, and possibly still in the

very midst of it. The kingdom was going to decay, and the reign of Uzziah gave it only a temporary prosperity. ¶ *Is desolate.* Heb. Is desolation. שְׁמָמָה *shemâmâ.* This is a Hebrew mode of emphatic expression, denoting that the desolation was so universal that the land might be said to be entirely in ruins. ¶ *Your land.* That is, the *fruit*, or *productions* of the land. Foreigners consume all that it produces. ¶ *Strangers* זָרִים *zârim,* from זוּר *zur,* to be alienated, or estranged, ver. 4. It is applied to *foreigners,* i. e. those who were not Israelites, Ex. xxx. 33; and is often used to denote an enemy, a foe, a barbarian; Ps. cix. 11 :

Let the extortioner catch all that he hath,
And let the *strangers* plunder his labour.

Ezek. xi. 9; xxviii. 10; xxx. 12; Hos. vii. 9; viii. 7. The word refers here particularly to the Syrians. ¶ *Devour it.* Consume its provisions. ¶ *In your presence.* This is a circumstance that greatly heightens the calamity, that they were compelled to look on and witness the desolation, without being able to prevent it. ¶ *As overthrown by strangers.* כְּמַהְפֵּכַת זָרִים—from הָפַךְ *hâphâkh,* to turn, to overturn, to destroy as a city; Gen. xix. 21–25; Deut. xxix. 22. It refers to the changes which an invading foe produces in a nation, where every thing is subverted; where cities are destroyed, walls are thrown down, and fields and vineyards laid waste. The land was as if an invading army had passed through it, and completely overturned everything. Lowth proposes to read this, ' as if destroyed by an inundation ;' but without authority. The desolation caused by the ravages of foreigners, at a time when the nations were barbarous, was the highest possible image of distress, and the prophet dwells on it, though with some appearance of repetition.

8. *And the daughter of Zion.* Zion, or *Sion,* was the name of one of the hills on which the city of Jerusalem was built. On this hill formerly stood the

left as *a* a cottage in a vineyard, | as a lodge in a garden of cucumbers, as a besieged city.

a Lam.2.6.

city of the *Jebusites*, and when David took it from them he transferred to it his court, and it was called the city of David, or the holy hill. It was in the southern part of the city. As Zion became the residence of the court, and was the most important part of the city, the name was often used to denote the city itself, and is often applied to the whole of Jerusalem. The phrase ' daughter of Zion' here means Zion itself, or *Jerusalem*. The name *daughter* is given to it by a personification in accordance with a common custom in Eastern writers, by which beautiful towns and cities are likened to young females. The name *mother* is also applied in the same way. Perhaps the custom arose from the fact that when a city was built, towns and villages would spring up round it—and the first would be called the *mother-city* (hence the word metropolis). The expression was also employed as an image of *beauty*, from a fancied resemblance between a beautiful town and a beautiful and well-dressed woman. Thus Ps. xlv. 13, the phrase *daughter of Tyre*, means Tyre itself; Ps. cxxxvii. 8, *daughter of Babylon*, i. e. Babylon; Isa. xxxvii. 22, ' The virgin, the daughter of Zion;' Jer. xlvi. 2; Isa. xxiii. 12; Jer. xiv. 17; Num. xxi. 23, 32, (Heb.); Jud. xi. 26. *Is left*. נוֹתְרָה. The word here used denotes left as *a part* or *remnant* is left—not left *entire*, or *complete*, but in a weakened or divided state. ¶ *As a cottage*. Literally, *a shade*, or *shelter*—כְּסֻכָּה *kesŭkkâ*, a temporary habitation erected in vineyards to give shelter to the grapegatherers, and to those who were appointed to *watch* the vineyard to guard it from depredation; comp. Note Matt. xxi. 33. The following passage from Mr. Jowett's ' Christian Researches,' describing what he himself saw, will throw light on this verse. ' Extensive fields of ripe melons and cucumbers adorned the sides of the river (the Nile). They grew in such abundance that the sailors freely helped themselves. Some guard, however, is placed upon them. Occasionally, but at long and desolate intervals, we may observe a little hut,

made of reeds, just capable of containing one man ; being in fact little more than a fence against a north wind. In these I have observed, sometimes, a poor old man, perhaps lame, protecting the property. It exactly illustrates Isa. i. 8.' ' Gardens were often probably unfenced, and formerly, as now, esculent vegetables were planted in some fertile spot in the open field. A custom prevails in Hindostan, as travellers inform us, of planting in the commencement of the rainy season, in the extensive plains, an abundance of melons, cucumbers, gourds, &c. In the centre of the field is an artificial mound with a hut on the top, just large enough to shelter a person from the storm and the heat ;' Bib. Dic. A.S.U. The following cut will convey a clear idea of such a cottage.

LODGE IN A GARDEN OF CUCUMBERS.

Such a cottage would be designed only for a *temporary* habitation. So Jerusalem seemed to be left amidst the surrounding desolation as a temporary abode, soon to be destroyed. ¶ *As a lodge*. The word *lodge* here properly denotes a place for *passing the night*, but it means also a *temporary abode*. It was erected to afford a shelter to those who guarded the enclosure from thieves, or from jackals, and small foxes. ' The jackal,' says Hasselquist, ' is a species of mustela, which is very common in Palestine, especially during the vintage,

9 Except *a* the LORD of hosts had left unto us a very small remnant, we should have been as Sodom,*b* *and*

we should have been like unto Gomorrah.

a Lam.3.22. Rom.9.29.
b Gen.19.24.

and often destroys whole vineyards, and gardens of cucumbers. ¶ *A garden of cucumbers.* The word *cucumbers* here probably includes every thing of the *melon* kind, as well as the cucumber. They are in great request in that region on account of their cooling qualities, and are produced in great abundance and perfection. These things are particularly mentioned among the luxuries which the Israelites enjoyed in Egypt, and for which they sighed when they were in the wilderness. Num. xi. 5: 'We remember—the cucumbers and the melons,' &c. The cucumber which is produced in Egypt and Palestine is large—usually a foot in length, soft, tender, sweet, and easy of digestion (*Gesenius*), and being of a cooling nature, was peculiarly delicious in their hot climate. The meaning here is, that Jerusalem seemed to be left as a temporary, lonely habitation, soon to be forsaken and destroyed. ¶ *As a besieged city.* כְּעִיר נְצוּרָה. *Lowth.* 'As a city taken by siege.' *Noyes.* " ' So is the delivered city.' This translation was first proposed by Arnoldi of Marburg. It avoids the incongruity of comparing a city with a city, and requires no alteration of the text except a change of the vowel points. According to this translation, the meaning will be, that all things round about the city lay desolate,' like the withered vines of a cucumber garden around the watchman's hut; in other words, that the city alone stood safe amidst the ruins caused by the enemy, like the hut in a gathered garden of cucumbers." *Noyes.* According to this interpretation, the word נְצוּרָה *netzŭrâ* is derived not from עוּר *tzŭr*, to besiege, to press, to straiten; but from נָעַר *nâtzăr*, to preserve, keep, defend; comp. Ezek. vi. 12. The Hebrew will bear this translation; and the concinnity of the comparison will thus be preserved. I rather prefer, however, the common interpretation, as being more obviously the sense of the Hebrew, and as being sufficiently in ac-

cordance with the design of the prophet. The idea then is, that of a city straitened by a siege, yet standing as a temporary habitation, while all the country around was lying in ruins. Jerusalem, alone preserved amidst the desolation spreading throughout the land, will resemble a temporary lodge in the garden—itself soon to be removed or destroyed. The essential idea, whatever translation is adopted, is that of the solitude, loneliness, and temporary continuance of even Jerusalem, while all around was involved in desolation and ruin.

9. *Except, &c.* It is owing entirely to the mercy of God, that we are not like Sodom. The prophet traces this not to the goodness of the nation, not to any power or merit of theirs, but solely to the mercy of God. This passage the apostle Paul has used in an argument to establish the doctrine of divine sovereignty in the salvation of men; see Note Rom. ix 29. ¶ *The Lord.* Heb. JEHOVAH. Note ver. 2. ¶ *Of hosts.* צְבָאוֹת *Tzebhâôth*—the word sometimes translated *Sabaoth*; Rom. ix. 29; James v. 4. The word means literally *armies* or *military hosts*. It is applied however to the *angels* which surround the throne of God; 1 Kings xxii. 19; 2 Chron. xviii. 18; Ps. ciii. 21; and to *the stars* or constellations that appear to be marshalled in the sky; Jer. xxxiii. 22; Isa. xl. 26. This *host*, or the " host of heaven," was frequently an object of idolatrous worship; Deut. iv. 19; xvii. 3; 2 Kings xvii. 16. God is called JEHOVAH *of hosts* because he is at the head of all these armies, as their leader and commander; he marshals and directs them —as a general does the army under his command. 'This,' says Gesenius, ' is the most common name of God in Isaiah, and in Jeremiah, Zechariah, and Malachi. It represents him as the ruler of the hosts of heaven, i.e., the angels and the stars. Sometimes, but less frequently, we meet with the appellation Jehovah, *God* of hosts. Hence, some suppose the expression *Jehovah of hosts* to be elliptical. But it is not a correct

10 Hear the word of the LORD, ye rulers of Sodom; give ear unto the law of our God, ye people of Gomorrah:

11 To what purpose ^a is the multitude of your sacrifices unto me? saith the LORD: I am full of the

a Ps.50.8,&c. Amos 5 21,22.

assertion that Jehovah, as a proper name, admits of no genitive. But such relations and adjuncts as depend upon the genitive, often depend upon proper names. So in Arabic, one is called *Rebiah of the poor* in reference to his liability.' The name is given *here*, because to save any portion of a nation so wicked implied the exercise of the same power as that by which he controlled the hosts of heaven. ¶ *Remnant.* A small part—that which is left. It means here, that God had spared a portion of the nation, so that they were not entirely overthrown. ¶ *We should have been as Sodom*, &c. This does not refer to the *character* of the people, but to their *destiny*. If God had not interposed to save them they would have been overwhelmed *entirely* as Sodom was; comp. Gen. xix. 24, 25.

10. *Hear the word of the Lord.* The *message* of God. Having stated the *calamities* under which the nation was groaning, the prophet proceeds to address the rulers, and to state the *cause* of all these woes. ¶ *Ye rulers of Sodom.* The incidental mention of Sodom in the previous verse gives occasion for this beautiful transition, and abrupt and spirited address. Their character and destiny were almost like those of Sodom, and the prophet therefore openly addresses the rulers as being called to preside over a people like those in Sodom. There could have been no more severe or cutting reproof of their wickedness than to address them as resembling the people whom God overthrew for their enormous crimes.

11. *To what purpose.* לָמָּה לִי. 'What is it to me; or what profit or pleasure can I have in them?' God here replies to an *objection* which might be urged by the Jews to the representation which had been made of their guilt. The objection would be, that they were strict in the duties of their religion, and that they even abounded in offering victims of sacrifice. God replies in this and the following verses,

that all this would be of no use, and would meet with no acceptance, unless it were the offering of *the heart*. He demanded righteousness; and without that, all external offerings would be vain. The same sentiment often occurs in the Old Testament.

Hath Jehovah as great delight in burnt-offerings and sacrifices
As in obeying the voice of the Lord?
Behold, to obey is better than sacrifice,
And to hearken than the fat of rams.
                               1 Sam. xv. 22.

To what purpose shall frankincense be brought unto me from Sabah?
Or the rich aromatic reed from a far country?
Your burnt-offerings are not acceptable,
Nor your sacrifices pleasant unto me.
                     Jer. vi. 20. *Blaney.*

For I desired mercy and not sacrifice;
And the knowledge of God more than burnt-offerings.   Hosea vi. 6.
I hate, I despise your solemn feast days,
And I will not smell in your solemn assemblies;
Though ye offer me your burnt-offerings,
And your meat-offerings,
I will not accept them;
Neither will I regard the thank-offerings of your fat beasts.
Take thou away from me the noise of thy songs;
For I will not hear the melody of thy viols.
But let judgment run down as waters,
And righteousness as a mighty stream.
                     Amos v. 21—24.

¶ *Is the multitude.* There was no deficiency in the amount of offerings. It was admitted that they complied in this respect with the requirements of the law; and that they offered an *abundance* of sacrifices, so numerous as to be called a *multitude*—רֹב *rōbh*, a vast number. Hypocrites abound in outward religious observances just in proportion to their neglect of the spiritual requirements of God's word; comp. Matt. xxiii. 23. ¶ *Your sacrifices.* זִבְחֵיכֶם *zibhhhēkhĕm*, from זָבַח, to slay; especially to slay for sacrifice. The word used here denotes any sacrifice which was made by blood; but is distinguished from the burnt-offering from the fat, that this was not entirely consumed. It is applied to the sin-offering, trespass-offering, thank-offering. The word also stands opposed to the offerings which

burnt-offerings of rams, and the fat of fed beasts; and I delight not in the blood of bullocks, or of lambs, or of ¹ he-goats.

12 When ye come to ²appear before me, who hath required this at your hand to tread my courts?

1 *great he-goats.* 2 *be seen.*

were made *without* blood (מִנְחָה *mĭn-hhâ*). Any offering that consisted in an animal that was slain came under this general denomination of *sacrifice*, Ex. x. 25; Lev. xvii. 8; Num. xv. 5. ¶ *Burnt-offerings.* עֹלוֹת *ŏlŏth*, from עָלָה, *âlâh*, to go up, ascend. It is applied to a sacrifice that was wholly consumed, or made to ascend on an altar. It answers to the Greek ὁλόκαυστον— *holocaust*, that which is entirely consumed. Such offerings abounded among the Hebrews. The burnt-offering was wholly consumed on the altar, excepting the skin and the blood. The blood was sprinkled round the altar, and the other parts of the animal which was slain, were laid upon the altar and entirely burned; see Lev. i. This was commonly a *voluntary* offering; and this shows their zeal to comply with the external forms of religion. ¶ *I am full.* שָׂבַעְתִּי, I am *satiated.* The word is usually applied to food and drink, denoting satisfaction, or satiety. It is used here with great force, denoting that their offerings had been so numerous and so incessant, that God was *satiated* with them. It means that he was weary, tired, disgusted with them. Thus, in Job vii. 4: 'I am full—שָׂבַעְתִּי—of tossings to and fro unto the dawning of the day.' Prov. xxv. 17:

Withdraw thy foot from thy neighbour's house, Lest he be weary (Heb. *full*) of thee, and hate thee.

¶ *Fat, &c.* They were required to offer, not the lame, or the diseased (Deut. xv. 21; xvii. 1; Lev. xvii. 20; Mal. i. 7, 8); and God admits here that they had *externally* complied with this requirement. The fat was burned on the altar. ¶ *I delight not.* That is, I delight not in them when offered without the heart; or I delight not in them in comparison with works of righteousness; see Amos v. 21–24; Ps. iv. 9–13; li. 16–19.

12. *When you come to appear before me.* The temple was in Jerusalem, and

was regarded as the *habitation*, or *dwelling-place*, of the God of Israel. Particularly, the most holy place of the temple was deemed the place of his sacred abode. The Shekinah—from שָׁכַן *shâkhăn, to dwell*—the visible symbol of his presence, rested on the cover of the ark, and from this place he was accustomed to commune with his people, and to give responses to their requests. Hence, 'to appear before God,' Heb. 'to be seen before my face,' לִרְאוֹת פָּנַי for אֶת פָּנַי, means to appear in his temple as a worshipper. The phrase occurs in this sense in the following places: Exod. xxxiv. 23, 24; Deut. xxxi. 11; 1 Sam. i. 22; Ps. xlii. 3. ¶ *Who hath required this.* The Jews were required to appear there to worship God (Exod. xxiii. 17; Deut. xvi. 16); but it was not required that they should appear with that spirit and temper. A similar sentiment is expressed in Ps. l. 16. ¶ *At your hand.* From you. The emphasis in this expression is to be laid on *your*. 'Who has asked it of *you?*' It was indeed the duty of the humble, and the sincere, to tread those courts, but who had required such hypocrites as *they* were to do it? God sought the offerings of pure worshippers, not those of the hypocritical and the profane. ¶ *To tread my courts.* The *courts* of the temple were the different *areas* or open spaces which surrounded it. None entered the temple itself but the priests. The people worshipped God in the *courts* assigned them around the temple. In one of those courts was the altar of burnt-offerings; and the sacrifices were all made there; see Notes on Matt. xxi. 12. *To tread his courts* was an expression therefore, equivalent to, to worship. To *tread the courts* of the Lord here, has the idea of profanation. Who has required you to tread those courts with this hollow, heartless service? It is often used in the sense of *treading down*, or *trampling on*, 2 Kings vii. 17–20; Dan. viii. 7–10; Isa. lxiii. 3–16.

13 Bring no more vain oblations: ^aincense is an abomination unto me; the new moons and sabbaths,

a Lu.11.42.

the calling of assemblies, I cannot away with; *it is* ¹ iniquity, even the solemn meeting.

1 or, *grief.*

---

13. *Bring no more.* God does not intend absolutely to forbid this kind of worship, but he expresses his strong abhorrence of the *manner* in which it was done. He desired a better state of mind; he preferred purity of heart to all this external homage. ¶ *Vain.* Heb. '*offering of vanity*'—שָׁוְא *shâv*—offerings which were hollow, false, deceitful, and hypocritical. ¶ *Oblations.* מִנְחַת *minhhâth.* This word properly denotes a gift, or present, of any kind (Gen. xxxii. 13), and then especially a *present* or *offering* to the Deity, Gen. iv. 3–5. It does not denote a *bloody* offering, but what is improperly rendered in the Old Testament, a *meat-offering* (Lev. ii. 1; vi. 14; ix. 17)—an offering made of flour or fruits, with oil and frankincense. A small part of it was burned upon the altar, and the remainder was eaten by Aaron and his sons with salt, Lev. ii. 1, 9, 13. The proper translation would have been *meal* or *flour-offering* rather than *meat-offering*, since the word *meat* with us now denotes animal food only. ¶ *Incense.* More properly *frankincense.* This is an aromatic or odoriferous gum, which is obtained from a tree called *Thurifera.* Its leaves were like those of a pear-tree. It grew around Mount Lebanon, and in Arabia. The gum was obtained by making incisions in the bark in dog days. It was much used in worship, not only by the Jews, but by the heathen. When burned, it produced an agreeable odour; and hence it is called a *sacrifice of sweet smell*, an odour acceptable to God; comp. Phil. iv. 18. That which was burned among the Jews was prepared in a peculiar manner, with a mixture of sweet spices. It was offered by the priest alone, and it was not lawful to prepare it in any other way than that prescribed by the law; see Ex. xxx. 34, &c. ¶ *Is an abomination.* Is hateful, or an object of abhorrence; that is, as it was offered by them, with hollow service, and with hypocritical hearts. ¶ *The new moons.*

On the appearance of the new moon, in addition to the daily sacrifices, two bullocks, a ram, and seven sheep, with a meal-offering, were required to be offered to God, Num. x. 10; xxviii. 11–14. The new moon in the beginning of the month Tisri (October), was the beginning of their civil year, and was commanded to be observed as a festival, Lev. xxiii. 24, 25. The appearance of the new moon was announced by the blowing of silver trumpets, Num. x. 10. Hence the annual festival was called sometimes, ' the memorial of the blowing of trumpets.' The time of the appearance of the new moon was not ascertained, as with us, by astronomical calculation; but persons were stationed, about the time it was to appear, on elevated places in the vicinity of Jerusalem, and when it was discovered, the trumpet was sounded. Moses did not command that this should be observed as a festival except at the beginning of the year, but it is not improbable that the Jews observed each return of the new moon as such. ¶ *And sabbaths.* שַׁבָּת *shăbbâth*, from שָׁבַת *shâbăth*, to cease to do anything; to rest from labour. The words here used are all in the singular number, and should have been rendered ' the new moon, and the sabbath, and the calling of the assembly; ' though used in a collective sense. The sabbaths here refer not only to the weekly sabbaths, but to *all* their days of rest. The word *sabbath* means properly a day of rest (Gen. ii. 2, 3); and it was applied not only to the seventh day, but particularly to the beginning and the close of their great festivals, which were days of unusual solemnity and sacredness, Lev. xvi. 31; xxiii. 24–39. ¶ *The calling of assemblies.* The solemn convocations or meetings at their festivals and fasts. ¶ *I cannot away with.* Heb. לֹא אוּכַל —I cannot bear, or endure. ¶ *It is iniquity.* That is, in the way in which it is conducted. This is a strong emphatic expression. It is not merely evil, and tending to evil; but it is *ini-*

14 Your new moons and your
appointed feasts my soul hateth:
they are a trouble unto me; I am
weary to bear *them*.

15 And when ye *a* spread forth
your hands I will hide mine eyes
from you; yea, when ye [1] make

quity itself. There was no mixture of
good. ¶ *Even the solemn meeting.*
The word which is here used—עֲצָרָה—
comes from the verb עָצַר *âtzar*, which
signifies *to shut up,* or *to close;* and is
applied to the solemnities which *concluded* their great feasts, as being periods
of unusual interest and sacredness. It
was applied to such solemnities, because
they *shut up,* or *closed* the sacred festivals. Hence that day was called *the
great day of the feast,* as being a day
of peculiar solemnity and impressiveness; see Note, John vii. 37; comp. Lev.
xxiii. 3–36. In the translation of this
word, however, there is a great variety
in the ancient versions. Vulg., ' Your
assemblies are iniquitous.' LXX.,
' Your new moons, and sabbaths, and
great day, I cannot endure; fasting and
idleness.' Chald. Paraph., ' Sacrifice
is abominable before me; and your new
moons, and sabbaths, *since you will not
forsake your sins, so that your prayer
may be heard in the time of your assembling.*' Syriac, ' In the beginning
of your months, and on the sabbath,
you convene an assembly, but I do not
eat that [*i.e.,* sacrifices] which has been
obtained by fraud and violence.' The
English translation has, however, probably expressed the correct sense of the
Hebrew.

14. *Your appointed feasts.* That is,
your assemblies convened on *regular set
times*—מוֹעֵד *moêdh,* from יָעַד *yââdh, to
fix, to appoint.* Hengstenberg (Chris.
iii. p. 87) has shown that this word
(מֹלְעֲדִים) is applied in the Scriptures
only to the sabbath, passover, pentecost,
day of atonement, and feast of tabernacles. Prof. Alexander, *in loc.* It is
applied to those festivals, because they
were fixed by law to certain periods of
the year. This verse is a very impressive repetition of the former, as if the
soul was full of the subject, and disposed to dwell upon it. ¶ *My soul
hateth.* I hate. Ps. xi. 5. The nouns
נֶפֶשׁ *nephesh, soul,* and רוּחַ *ruâhh, spirit,*
are often used to denote the *person*

himself, and are to be construed as *I.*
Thus, Isa. xxvi. 9: ' With my soul have
I desired thee in the night; yea, with
my spirit within me will I seek thee
early; ' that is, ' I myself seek thee;
I myself do desire thee.' So the phrase,
' deliver my soul,'—נַפְשִׁי—that is, *deliver me,* Ps. xxii. 20; lxxxiv. 3; lxxxvi.
13, 14; *that thy soul may bless me,*
Gen. xxvii. 19; *his soul shall dwell at
ease,* Ps. xxv. 13; comp. Num. xi. 6;
Lev. xvi. 29; Isa. lv. 2, 3; Job. xvi. 4.
So the word *spirit:* ' Thy watchfulness hath preserved my spirit '—רוּחִי
—Job x. 12; comp. Ps. xxxi. 6; 1 Kings
xxi. 5. The expression here is emphatic, denoting *cordial* hatred: *odi ex
animo.* ¶ *They are a trouble.* טֹרַח
tôrăhh. In Deut. i. 12, this word
denotes a *burden,* an oppressive load
that produces weariness in bearing it.
It is a strong expression, denoting that
their acts of hypocrisy and sin had
become so numerous, that they became
a heavy, oppressive load. ¶ *I am weary
to bear them.* This is language which
is taken from the act of carrying a
burden till a man becomes weary and
faint. So, in accordance with human
conceptions, God represents himself as
burdened with their vain oblations, and
evil conduct. There could be no more
impressive statement of the evil effects
of sin, than that even Omnipotence was
exhausted as with a heavy, oppressive
burden.

15. *Ye spread forth your hands.*
This is an expression denoting the act
of *supplication.* When we ask for help,
we naturally stretch out our hands, *as
if* to receive it. The expression therefore is equivalent to ' when ye pray, or
implore mercy.' Comp. Ex. ix. 29;
xvii. 11, 12; 1 Kings viii. 22. ¶ *I will
hide mine eyes,* &c. That is, I will not
attend to, or regard your supplications.
The Chaldee Paraphrase has, ' When
your priests expand their hands to pray
for you.' ¶ *Your hands,* &c. This
is given as a reason why he would not
hear. The expression *full of blood,*

many prayers, I will not hear: your hands are full of [1]blood.

16 Wash[a] you, make you clean, put away the evil of your doings

from before mine eyes; cease[b] to do evil;

17 Learn to do well: seek judgment, [2]relieve the oppressed; judge

denotes crime and guilt of a high order —as, in murder, the hands would be dripping in blood, and as the stain on the hands would be proof of guilt. It is probably a figurative expression, not meaning literally that they were murderers, but that they were given to rapine and injustice; to the oppression of the poor, the widow, &c. The sentiment is, that *because* they indulged in sin, and came, even in their prayers, with a determination still to indulge it, God would not hear them. The same sentiment is elsewhere expressed; Ps. lxvi. 18 : 'If I regard iniquity in my heart, the Lord will not hear me;' Prov. xxviii. 9: 'He that turneth away his ear from hearing the law, even his prayer shall be abomination;' Jer. xvi. 10–12; Zech. vii. 11, 12; Prov. i. 28, 29. This is the reason why the prayers of sinners are not heard.—But the truth is abundantly taught in the Scriptures, that if sinners will forsake their sins, the *greatness* of their iniquity is no obstacle to forgiveness; Isa. i. 18; Matt. xi. 28; Luke xvi. 11–24.

16. *Wash you.* This is, of course, to be understood in a moral sense; meaning that they should put away their sins. Sin is represented in the Scriptures as *defiling* or *polluting* the soul (Ezek. xx. 31; xxiii. 30; Hos. v. 8; ix. 4); and the removal of it is represented by the act of washing; Ps. li. 2: 'Wash me thoroughly from mine iniquity, and cleanse me from my sin;' Jer. iv. 14: 'O Jerusalem, wash thine heart from wickedness, that thou mayest be saved;' Job ix. 30; 1 Cor. vi. 11; Heb. x. 22; 2 Peter ii. 22; Rev. i. 5; vii. 14. It is used here in close connection with the previous verse, where the prophet says that their *hands were filled with blood.* He now admonishes them to *wash away* that blood, with the implied understanding, that *then* their prayers would be heard. It is worthy of remark, also, that the prophet directs them to do this *themselves.* He addresses them as moral agents, and as

having ability to do it. This is the uniform manner in which God addresses sinners in the Bible, requiring them to put away their sins, and to make themselves a new heart.* Comp. Ezek. xviii. 31, 32. ¶ *The evil of your doings.* This is a Hebraism, to denote *your evil doings.* ¶ *From before mine eyes.* As God is omniscient, to put them away from before *his* eyes, is to put them away altogether. To pardon or forgive sin, is often expressed by *hiding it;* Ps. li. 9 :

Hide thy face from my sins.

¶ *Cease to do evil.* Comp. 1 Peter iii. 10, 11. The prophet is specifying what was necessary in order that their prayers might be heard, and that they might find acceptance with God. What he states here is a universal truth. If sinners wish to find acceptance with God, they must come renouncing *all* sin; resolving to put away *every* thing that God hates, however dear it may be to the heart. Comp. Mark ix. 43–47.

17. *Learn to do well.* To *learn* here is *to become accustomed to,* to practise it. *To do well* stands opposed to all kinds of evil. ¶ *Seek judgment.* The word *judgment*—מִשְׁפָּט—here means *justice.* The direction refers particularly to *magistrates,* and it is evident that the prophet had them particularly in his view in all this discourse. Execute justice between man and man with impartiality. The word *seek*—דִּרְשׁוּ—means to pursue, to search for, as an object to be gained; to regard, or care for it, as the main thing. Instead of seeking gain, and bribes, and public favour, they were to make it an object of intense interest to do justice. ¶ *Relieve*—אַשְּׁרוּ—literally, *make straight,* or *right* (margin, *righten*). The root—אָשַׁר *âshǎr*—means *to proceed,* to *walk*

* See the subject of moral inability discussed in the Notes and Supplementary Notes, under 1 Cor. ii. 14; Gal. v. 17. The author's language here is certainly unguarded.

the fatherless; plead for the widow.

18 Come now, and let us reason [a]

together, saith the LORD : though your sins be as scarlet, they shall be

[a] ch. 43. 26.

forward in a direct line; and bears a relation to יָשַׁר *yâshăr,* to be straight. Hence it often means to be successful or prosperous—to go straight forward to success. In Piel, which is the form used here, it means to *cause* to go straight ; and hence, applied to leaders, judges, and guides, to conduct those under their care in a straight path, and not in the devices and crooked ways of sin ; Prov. xxiii. 19 :

Hear thou, my son, and be wise,
And guide (אַשֵּׁר *make straight*) thine heart in the way.

¶ *The oppressed.* Him to whom injustice has been done in regard to his character, person, or property ; comp. Notes on ch. lviii. 6. ¶ *Judge the fatherless.* Do justice to him—vindicate his cause. Take not advantage of his weak and helpless condition—his ignorance and want of experience. This charge was particularly necessary on account of the *facilities* which the guardians of orphans have to defraud or oppress, without danger of detection or punishment. Orphans have no experience. Parents are their natural protectors ; and therefore God especially charged on their guardians to befriend and do justice to them ; Deut. xxiv. 17 : ' Thou shalt not pervert the judgment of the stranger, nor the fatherless, nor take the widow's raiment to pledge.' ¶ *Plead for.* Contend for her rights. Aid her by vindicating her cause. She is unable to defend herself ; she is liable to oppression ; and her rights may be taken away by the crafty and designing. It is remarkable that God so often insists on this in the Scriptures, and makes it no small part of religion ; Deut. xiv. 29 ; xxiv. 17 ; Ex. xxii. 22 : ' Ye shall not afflict any widow, or fatherless child.' The ancient views of piety on this subject are expressed in the language, and in the conduct of Job. Thus, *impiety* was said to consist in oppressing the fatherless and widow :

They drive away the ass of the fatherless,
They take the widow's ox for a pledge.
Job xxiv. 3.

He evil-entreateth the barren that beareth not,
And doeth not good to the widow. Ver. 21.

Job's own conduct was an illustration of the elevated and pure views of ancient piety :

When the ear heard me, then it blessed me ;
And when the eye saw me, it gave witness to me ;
Because I delivered the poor that cried,
And the fatherless,
And him that had none to help him.
The blessing of him that was ready to perish came upon me ;
And I caused the widow's heart to leap for joy.
Job xxix. 11-13.

See also Jer. vii. 6; Mal. iii. 5; Jas. i. 27. Hence God is himself represented as the vindicator of the rights of the widow and orphan :

A father of the fatherless,
And a judge of the widows,
Is God in his holy habitation. Ps. lxviii. 5.
Leave thy fatherless children, I will preserve them alive ;
And let thy widows trust in me.
Jer. xlix. 11.

18. *Come now.* This is addressed to the nation of Israel; and the same exhortation is made to all sinners. It is a solemn act on the part of God, submitting the claims and principles of his government to *reason,* on the supposition that men *may* see the propriety of his service, and of his plan. ¶ *Let us reason together.* וְנִוָּכְחָה from יָכַח, not used in Kal, but in Hiphil ; meaning to *show,* to *prove.* Job xiii. 15: ' Surely I will *prove* my ways (righteous) before him ;' *i.e.,* I will justify my ways before him. Also *to correct, reprove, convince,* Job xxxii. 12 ; *to rebuke, reproach, censure,* Job vi. 25; *to punish,* Job v. 17; Prov. iii. 12; *to judge, decide,* Isa. xi. 3; *to do justice,* Isa. xi. 4; or *to contend,* Job xiii. 3; xvi. 21; xxii. 4. Here it denotes the kind of contention, or argumentation, which occurs in a court of justice, where the parties reciprocally state the grounds of their cause. God had been addressing magistrates particularly, and commanding them to seek judgment, to relieve the oppressed, to do justice to the orphan and widow ; all of which terms are taken from courts

as white as ^a snow; though they be | red like crimson, they shall be as

wool.

of law. He here continues the language, and addresses them as accustomed to the proceedings of courts, and proposes to submit the case as if on trial. He then proceeds (vers. 18–20), to adduce the *principles* on which he is willing to bestow pardon on them ; and submits the case to them, assured that those principles will commend themselves to their reason and sober judg-ment. ¶ *Though your sins be as scarlet.* The word used here—שָׁנִים *shânim*—denotes properly a bright red colour, much prized by the ancients. The Arabic verb means to *shine*, and the name was given to this colour, it is supposed by some, on account of its splendour, or bright appearance. It is mentioned as a merit of Saul, that he clothed the daughters of Israel in *scar-let*, 2 Sam. i. 24. Our word *scarlet*, denoting a bright red, expresses the colour intended here. This colour was obtained from the eggs of the *coccus ilicis*, a small insect found on the leaves of the oak in Spain, and in the coun-tries east of the Mediterranean. The cotton cloth was dipped in this colour *twice;* and the word used to express it means also *double-dyed*, from the verb שָׁנָה *shânâ, to repeat.* From this *double-dying* many critics have supposed that the name given to the colour was de-rived. The interpretation which derives it from the sense of the Arabic word *to shine*, however, is the most probable, as there is no evidence that the *double-dying* was peculiar to this colour. It was a more *permanent* colour than that which is mentioned under the word *crimson.* White is an emblem of inno-cence. Of course *sins* would be repre-sented by the opposite. Hence we speak of crimes as *black*, or *deep-dyed*, and of the soul as *stained* by sin. There is another idea here. This was a *fast*, or *fixed* colour. Neither dew, nor rain, nor washing, nor long usage, would remove it. Hence it is used to repre-sent the *fixedness* and *permanency* of sins in the heart. No human means will wash them out. No effort of man, no external rites, no tears, no sacrifices,

no prayers, are of themselves sufficient to take them away. They are *deep fixed* in the heart, as the scarlet colour was in the web of cloth, and an almighty power is needful to remove them. ¶ *Shall be as white as snow.* That is, the deep, fixed stain, which no human power could remove, shall be taken away. In other words, sin shall be pardoned, and the soul be made pure. White, in all ages, has been the emblem of innocence, or purity ; comp. Ps. lxviii. 14; Eccl. ix. 8; Dan. vii. 9; Matt. xvii. 2; xxviii. 3; Rev. i. 14; iii. 4, 5; iv. 4; vii. 9, 13. ¶ *Though they be red.* The idea here is not materially different from that expressed in the former part of the verse. It is the Hebrew poetic form of expressing substantially the same thought in both parts of the sen-tence. Perhaps, also, it denotes *inten-sity*, by being repeated ; see Intro. § 8. ¶ *Like crimson,* כַּתּוֹלָע. The differ-ence between *scarlet* and *crimson* is, that the former denotes a *deep red; the* latter a deep red slightly tinged with *blue.* Perhaps this difference, however, is not marked in the original. The *purple* or *crimson* colour was obtained commonly from a shell-fish, called *mu-rex*, or *purpura*, which abounded chiefly in the sea, near Tyre; and hence the *Tyrian dye* became so celebrated. That, however, which is designated in this place, was obtained, not from a shell-fish, but a worm (Heb. תּוֹלָע *tôlâ*), snail, or conchylium—the *Helix Janthina* of Linnæus.* This colour was less per-

---

* *Helix Janthina.* is a mollusc or shell-fish, called the violet snail. It inhabits the deep sea in warm latitudes, and, when the water is calm,

Helix Janthina.

may be seen in large numbers floating on its surface. By the Heb. תּוֹלָע *tôlâ*, is probably meant the *Coccus ilicis* of Linnæus, which attains the size and form of a pea, is of a violet black colour, covered with a whitish powder, adhering to plants, chiefly various species of oak, and so

19 If ye be willing and obedient, ye shall eat the good of the land:

20 But if ye refuse and rebel, ye shall be devoured with the sword:

for the mouth of the Lord *a* hath spoken *it*.

21 How is the faithful city be-

a Lev. 26, 33.

---

manent than the *scarlet;* was of a *bluish* cast; and is commonly in the English Bible rendered *blue*. It was employed usually to dye *wool*, and was used in the construction of the tabernacle, and in the garments of the high-priest. It was also in great demand by princes and great men, Judg. viii. 26; Luke xiv. 19. The prophet has adverted to the fact that it was employed mainly in dying *wool*, by what he has added, *'shall be as wool.' ¶ As wool.* That is, as wool *undyed*, or from which the colour is removed. Though your sins appear as deep-stained, and as permanent as the fast colour of crimson in wool, yet they shall be removed—as if that stain should be taken away from the wool, and it should be restored to its original whiteness.

19. *If ye be willing.* If you submit your wills, and become voluntary in your obedience to my law. ¶ *And obedient.* Heb. If you will *hear; i.e.,* my commands. ¶ *Ye shall eat,* &c. That is, the land shall yield its increase; and you shall be saved from pestilence, war, famine, &c. The productions of the soil shall no more be devoured by strangers, ver. 7; comp. Notes on ch. lxv. 21–23. This was in accordance with the promises which God made to their fathers, and the motives to obedience placed before them, which were drawn from the fact, that they should possess a land of distinguished fertility, and that obedience should be attended with eminent national prosperity. Such an appeal was adapted to the infancy of society, and to the circumstances of the people. It should be added, however, that with this they connected the idea, that God would be *their* God and Protector; and, of course, the idea that all the blessings resulting from that fact would be theirs; Ex. iii. 8: ' And I am come down to deliver them out of the hand of the Egyptians, and to bring

closely resembling grain, that its insect nature was not known for many centuries, &c.—*Kitto's Cyclop.*, Art. *Purple.*

them up out of that land unto a good land and a large, unto a land flowing with milk and honey; ' comp. Ex. iii. 17; xiii. 5; Deut. xxviii. 1–9. In accordance with this, the *language* of promise in the New Testament is, that of inheriting the earth, *i.e.*, the land, Note, Matt. v. 5. The expression here means, that if they obeyed God they should be under his patronage, and be prospered. It refers, also, to ver. 7, where it is said, that strangers devoured the land. The promise here is, that if they were obedient, this calamity should be removed.

20. *But if ye refuse, ye shall be devoured with the sword.* Your enemies shall come in, and lay waste the land. This prediction was fulfilled, in consequence of their continuing to rebel, when the land was desolated by Nebuchadnezzar, and the nation was carried captive to Babylon. It illustrates a *general* principle of the Divine government, that if men persevere in rebelling against God, they shall be destroyed. The word *devour* is applied to the *sword*, as if it were insatiable for destruction. Whatever *destroys* may be figuratively said to *devour;* see Notes on ch. xxxiv. 5, 6; comp. Isa. v. 24; Lam. ii. 3; Ezek. xv. 4; Joel ii. 3; Rev. xi. 5—where *fire* is said to devour. ¶ *The mouth of the Lord.* Jehovah himself This had been spoken by the mouth of the Lord, and recorded, Lev. xxvi. 33:

And I will scatter you among the heathen,
And will draw out a sword after you;
And your land shall be desolate,
And your cities waste.

On these points God proposed to *reason;* or rather, perhaps, these principles are regarded as *reasonable*, or as commending themselves to men. They are the great principles of the Divine administration, that if men obey God they shall prosper; if not, they shall be punished. They commend themselves to men as just and true; and they are seen and illustrated every where.

21. *How is.* This is an expression

come an harlot! ^a*it* was full of judgment: righteousness lodged in it; but now murderers.

a Jer.2.20,21.

of *deploring*, or *lamenting*. It indicates that that had occurred which was matter of grief. The prophet had stated the principles of the Divine government; had urged the people to reason with God; and had affirmed his willingness to pardon. But it was seen that they *would not* repent. They were *so* wicked and perverse, that there was no hope of their reformation. His mind is full of this subject; he repeats the charge of their wickedness (21-23), and states what *must be* the consequences. ¶ *The faithful city.* Jerusalem. It is represented here under the image of *a wife*—once faithful to her husband; once a devoted and attached partner. Jerusalem *was* thus once. In former days, it was the seat of the pure worship of God; the place where his praise was celebrated, and where his people came to offer sincere devotion. In the Scriptures, the *church* is often represented under the image of a wife, to denote the tenderness and sacredness of the union; Hos. ii. 19, 20; Isa. lxii. 5; liv. 6; Rev. xxi. 9. ¶ *An harlot.* She has proved to be false, treacherous, unfaithful. The unfaithfulness of the people of God, particularly their idolatry, is often represented under the idea of unfaithfulness to the marriage contract; Jer. iii. 8, 9; v. 7; xiii. 27; xxiii. 14; Ezek. xvi. 32; xxiii. 37; Hos. ii. 2; iv. 2. ¶ *It was full of judgment.* It was distinguished for *justice* and righteousness. ¶ *Lodged in it.* This is a figurative expression, meaning that it was characterized as a righteous city. The word ‏לִין‏ is from ‏לוּן‏ *lun*, to pass the night, to remain through the night (Gen. xix. 2); and then to lodge, to dwell; Ps. xxv. 13; Job xvii. 2; xxix. 19. In this place it has the sense of *abiding, remaining, continuing permanently.* Jerusalem was *the home* of justice, where it found protection and safety. ¶ *Now murderers.* By *murderers* here are meant probably unjust judges; men who did not regard the interests of the poor,

22 Thy silver is become dross, thy wine mixed with water:

23 Thy princes *are* rebellious, and companions of thieves: every

the widow, and the orphan; and who therefore, by a strong expression, are characterized as murderers. They had displaced justice from its home; and had become the permanent inhabitants of the city; comp. Note, ver. 15.

22. *Thy silver.* The sentiment in this verse, as it is explained by the following, is, thy princes and people have become corrupt, and polluted. Silver is used here to denote what should have been more valuable—virtuous princes. ¶ *Dross.* This word—‏סִיג‏—means the *scoriae*, or baser metal, which is separated from the purer in smelting. It is of little or no value; and the expression means, that the rulers had become debased and corrupt, as if pure silver had been converted wholly to dross. ¶ *Thy wine.* Wine was regarded as the most pure and valuable drink among the ancients. It is used, therefore, to express that which *should have been* most valued and esteemed among them —to wit, their rulers. ¶ *Mixed with water.* Diluted, made weak. According to Gesenius, the word rendered *mixed*—‏מָהוּל‏ *mâhûl*—is from ‏מָהַל‏ *mâhûl*, the same as ‏מוּל‏ *mûl*, to circumcise; and hence, by a figure common with the Arabians, to *adulterate*, or dilute wine. The word does not occur in this sense elsewhere in the Scriptures, but the connection evidently requires it to be so understood. Wine mixed with water is that which is weakened, diluted, rendered comparatively useless. So with the rulers and judges. They had lost the strength and purity of their integrity, by intermingling those things which tended to weaken and destroy their virtue, pride, the love of gifts, and bribes, &c. Divested of the figure, the passage means, that the rulers had become wholly corrupt.

23. *Thy princes*, &c. This is an explanation of the previous verse. Princes mean here those attached to the royal family; those who by rank, or office, had an influence over the

one loveth gifts, and followeth after rewards: they judge not the fatherless, neither doth the cause of the widow come unto them.

24 Therefore saith the Lord, the LORD of hosts, the mighty One of Israel, Ah, I will ease *a* me of mine

a Deut.28.63; Eze.5.13.

people. ¶ *Rebellious.* Against God. The corruption of a nation commonly begins with the rulers. ¶ *Companions of thieves.* That is, they connive at the doings of robbers; they do not bring them to justice; they are their accomplices, and are easily bribed to acquit them. ¶ *Every one loveth gifts.* Every magistrate can be *bribed.* ¶ *Followeth after rewards.* רֹדֵף. This word denotes the act of *pursuing after* in order to obtain something; and means here that they made it an object to obtain rewards by selling or betraying justice. They sell justice to the highest bidder. No more distressing condition of a people can be conceived than this, where justice could not be secured between man and man, and where the wicked could oppress the poor, the widow, and the orphan, as much as they pleased, because they knew they could bribe the judge. ¶ *They judge not.* They do not render justice to; ver. 17. The Chaldee has well expressed the sense of a part of this verse: 'They say, each one to his neighbour, Favour me in my judgment, or do me good in it, and I will recompense you in your cause.' ¶ *The cause of the widow come unto them.* Or, rather, come *before* them. They would not take up her cause, but rather the cause of those who were esteemed able to offer a bribe, and from whom a gift might be expected, if a decision was made in their favour.

24. *Therefore saith the Lord, &c.* The prophet having stated the guilt of the nation, proceeds to show the consequences of their crimes; or to foretell what would happen. The name of God is repeated, to attract attention; to fill the mind with awe; and to give emphasis to the solemn sentence which was about to be uttered. ¶ *The Lord.* אָדוֹן. This word properly denotes *master, lord, owner.* Gen. xxiv. 9: Lord *over his whole house.* 1 Kings xvi. 24: *Owner of the hill Samaria.* It is applied here to JEHOVAH, not as a peculiar title, or as one of the names which he

assumes to himself, but as owner, proprietor, master, ruler of the nation. The word, when applied to God as one of his peculiar titles, has the form of an ancient plural termination, אֲדֹנָי *ădōnâi.* The root is probably דּוּן *dhŭn,* to judge, which in ancient times was also closely connected with the idea of *ruling.* ¶ *The Lord of hosts.* JEHOVAH—ruling in the hosts of heaven, and therefore able to accomplish his threatenings; Note, ver. 9. ¶ *The mighty One of Israel.* He who had been their defender in the days of their peril; who had manifested his mighty power in overthrowing their enemies; and who had shown, therefore, that he was able to inflict vengeance *on them.* ¶ *Ah.* הוֹי. This is an expression of *threatening.* It is that which is used when an *affront* is offered, and there is a purpose of revenge; see ver. 4. ¶ *I will ease me.* This refers to what is said in ver. 14, where God is represented as *burdened* with their crimes. The Hebrew word is, I will be consoled, or comforted— *i.e.,* by being delivered from my foes— אֶנָּחֵם from נָחַם, in Niphil, to suffer pain, to be grieved; and hence, to have pity, to show compassion. In Piel, to console or comfort one's-self; to take revenge. The idea included in the word is that of *grief* or *distress,* either in beholding the sufferings of others, or from some injury received from others. Hence, in Piel, it denotes to obtain relief from that distress, either by aiding the distressed object, or by taking revenge. In both instances, the mind, by a law of its nature, finds relief. The passion expends itself on its proper object, and the mind is at ease. It is used here in the *latter* sense. It is an instance where God uses the language which men employ to denote *passion,* and where they obtain relief by *revenge.* When applied to God, it is to be understood in accordance with *his* nature, as implying simply, that he would punish them; comp. Note on ver. 13. It means that he had been *pained* and *grieved* by their crimes;

adversaries, and avenge me of mine enemies:

25 And ^a I will turn my hand upon thee, and purely ¹ purge away

thy dross, and take away all thy tin:

26 And I will restore thy judges as at the first, and thy counsellors

his patience had been put to its utmost trial; and now he would seek relief from this by inflicting due punishment on them. An expression explaining this may be seen in Ezek. v. 13: 'Then shall mine anger be accomplished, and I will cause my fury to rest upon them, and *I will be comforted.*' Also, Deut. xxviii. 63: 'As the Lord rejoiced over you, to do you good; so the Lord will rejoice over you, to destroy you.' ¶ *Mine adversaries.* The enemies to his law and government among the rebellious Jews. The expression in this verse is a remarkable instance of God's adapting himself to our apprehension, by using our language. Instances occur often in the Scriptures where language expressive of human passions is applied to God; and as human language must be employed in revelation, it was indispensable. But those expressions are not to be understood as they are when applied to the passions of men. In God, they are consistent with all that is pure, and glorious, and holy, and should be so understood. The Chaldee renders this verse, 'I will console the city of Jerusalem; but woe to the impious, when I shall be revealed to take vengeance on the enemies of my people.' But this is manifestly a false interpretation; and shows how reluctant the Jews were to admit the threatenings against *themselves.*

25. *And I will turn my hand upon thee.* This expression is capable of two significations. The hand may be stretched out for two purposes, either to inflict punishment, or to afford help and protection. The phrase here refers evidently to the latter, to the act of rdeeming and restoring his people, ver. 26, 27. The idea may be thus expressed: 'I will stretch out my hand to punish my enemies (ver. 24), and will *turn my hand* upon thee for protection, and recovery.' ¶ *Purge away.* This refers to the process of smelting, or purifying metals in the fire. It means, I will

remove all the dross which has accumulated (ver. 22), and will make the silver pure. This was commonly done by fire; and the idea is, that he would render his own people pure by those judgments which would destroy his enemies who were intermingled with them. ¶ *Purely.* The original word here— בַּבֹּר *kābbōr*—has been commonly understood to mean, *according to purity; i.e.,* effectually or entirely pure. Thus it is translated by the Septuagint, and by the Latin Vulgate. But by the Chaldee it is translated, 'I will purify thee as with *the herb borith.*' The word *may* mean *lye, alkali,* or *potash,* (Job ix. 30); and it may mean also *borax*— a substance formed of alkali and boracic acid, much used in purifying metals. The essential idea is, I will make you effectually, or entirely pure. ¶ *Thy tin.* Tin is with us a well-known white metal. But the word used here does not mean *tin.* It denotes the *stannum* of the ancients; a metal formed of lead mixed with silver ore. Here it means, I will take away all the impure metal mixed with thee; varying the idea but little from the former part of the verse.

26. *And I will restore,* &c. That is, I will give you such judges as the nation had in former days—in the times of Moses, Joshua, &c. Most of the charges in this chapter are against the *magistrates.* The calamities of the nation are traced to *their* unfaithfulness and corruption, ver. 17-23. God now says that he will remove this cause of their calamity, and give them pure magistrates. ¶ *Thy counsellors.* Thy advisers; that is, those occupying places of trust and responsibility. *When* this should be, the prophet does not say. The Jewish commentators suppose that he refers to the time after the return from captivity, and to such men as Zerubbabel, Ezra, and Nehemiah; and to the times of Hyrcanus and Herod. Jerome supposes that the times of the Messiah are referred to. It is impos-

as at the beginning : afterward thou shalt be called, The city of righteousness, The faithful city.

1 or, *they that return of her.*

27 Zion shall be redeemed with judgment, and her converts [1] with [a] righteousness.

[a] 1Cor.1.30.

---

sible to determine which is the correct opinion; though, as the Babylonish captivity was the *punishment* of those national sins which the prophet was denouncing, it is more probable that he refers to the time immediately *succeeding* that punishment, when the nation would be restored. I am inclined, therefore, to the opinion, that the prophet had reference solely to the prosperity of the Jewish nation, under a succession of comparatively virtuous princes, after the Babylonish captivity. ¶ *Thou shalt be called,* &c. The principal *cause* of your wickedness and calamity, *i.e.* your unfaithful rulers being removed and punished, you shall afterwards be distinguished as a city of righteousness. ¶ *The faithful city.* That is, faithful to Jehovah—faithful in keeping his laws, and maintaining the rites of his religion as formerly; comp. ver. 21. 27. *Zion.* See Note, ver. 8. The word *Zion* here is used to designate the whole Jewish people to whom the prophet had reference ; that is, the inhabitants of Judah and Jerusalem, ver. 1. ¶ *Shall be redeemed.* The word used here—פָּדָה—is employed in two senses in the Scriptures. It implies *always* the idea of *deliverance,* as from captivity, danger, punishment, slavery, sin. But this idea occurs (1) sometimes without any reference to a *price* paid, but simply denoting to deliver, or to set at liberty; and (2) in other instances the price is specified, and then the word occurs under the strict and proper sense of redeem ; *i.e.,* to rescue, or deliver, by a ransom price. Instances of the former general sense occur often ; as *e.g.,* to deliver from slavery without mention of a price ; Deut. vii. 8: 'The Lord loved you, and *redeemed* you out of the house of bondmen.' See also Jer. xv. 21; xxxi. 11. The idea of delivering in any way from danger occurs often ; Job v. 20: 'In famine he shall *redeem* thee from death, and in war from the power of the sword ;' 1 Kings i. 29: 'As Jehovah liveth, that hath *redeemed*

my soul out of all distress.' 1 Sam. iv. 9. But the word often occurs in connection with the mention of the *price,* and in this sense the words rendered *redeem* are commonly used in the New Testament ; see Ex. xiii. 13 ; Num. xviii. 15, 16, 17 ; comp. Gal. iii. 13. 1 Pet. i. 18 ; Rev. v. 9 ; Eph. i. 17. Matt. xx. 28 ; 1 Tim. ii. 6. In these last places, the blood of Christ, or his atoning sacrifice, is mentioned as the *price,* or the *valuable consideration,* by which deliverance from sin is effected ; comp. Note, ch. xliii. 3. In the case now before us, however, the word is used in the *general* sense, to denote that God would *rescue* and save his people from the calamities and judgments to which they were to be subjected on account of their sins. Though they were to be taken captive for their sins, yet they should again be delivered and restored to their land. The Septuagint evidently so understands it : ' Her captivity shall be saved with judgment and with mercy.' The Chaldee Paraphrase renders it in a manner somewhat similar: ' But Zion, when judgment shall have been accomplished in her, shall be redeemed ; and they who keep the law shall be returned to it in righteousness.' ¶ *With judgment.* In a righteous, just manner. That is, God shall evince his justice in doing it; his justice to a people to whom so many promises had been made, and his justice in delivering them from long and grievous oppression. All this would be attended with the displays of *judgment,* in effecting their deliverance. This might be evinced (1) in keeping his promises made to their fathers ; (2) in delivering an oppressed people from bondage ; and (3) in the displays of *judgment* on the nations necessary in accomplishing the deliverance of the Jews. This is the common interpretation. It *may be,* however, that the expression does not refer to the *character of God,* which is not at all the subject of discourse, but to the *character of the people* that should be

28 And the ¹destruction of the
transgressors and of the sinners
shall be together, ᵃ and they that

1 *breaking.*   a Ps.125.5; Lu.12.45,46.

forsake ᵇ the LORD shall be consumed.
29 For they shall be ashamed of

b Zeph.1.6.

redeemed. Before, the nation was corrupt ; after the captivity, they would be
just. Zion should be redeemed ; and
the effect of that redemption would be,
that the people would be reformed, and
holy, and just. This does not refer,
properly, to redemption by the Lord
Jesus, though it is equally true that
that will be accomplished with justice,
i.e., in entire consistency with the
character of a just and holy God. ¶ *Her
converts.* This is an unhappy translation. The Hebrew here means simply,
' they that return of her ' (marg.) ;
that is, those who return from captivity.
It is implied that *all* would not return
—which was true—but those who *did*
return, would come back in righteousness. ¶ *With righteousness.* This refers
to the *character* of those who shall return.
The prediction is, that the character of
the nation would be reformed (ver. 26) ;
that it would be done by means of this
very captivity ; and that they who returned would come back with a different
character from the nation at the time
that Isaiah wrote. They would be a
reformed, righteous people. The character of the nation was greatly improved
after the captivity. Their propensity
to idolatry, in a particular manner, was
effectually restrained ; and probably the
character of the people *after* the captivity, for morals and religion, was not
inferior to the best periods of their
history before.

28. *And the destruction.* Heb. שֶׁבֶר
—the *breaking,* or *crushing, i.e.,* the
punishment which was about to come
upon them ; comp. Lam. ii. 11 ; iii. 47 ;
Prov. xvi. 18. ¶ *Of the transgressors.*
Revolters, or those that rebel against
God. ¶ *And of the sinners.* Of all
the sinners in the nation, of all kinds
and degrees. ¶ *Together.* At the same
time with the redemption of Zion.
¶ *Shall be consumed.* יִכְלוּ, from כָּלָה
kâlâ, to be completed, or finished ; to be
consumed, wasted away ; to vanish, or
disappear. It denotes complete and

entire extinction ; or the *completing* of
any thing. It is applied to a cloud
of smoke, that entirely dissolves and
disappears :

As the cloud is *consumed* and vanisheth away:
So he that goeth down to the grave shall come
up no more.   Job vii. 9.
But the wicked shall perish,
And the enemies of the Lord shall be as the fat
of lambs ;
They shall *consume,*
Into smoke shall they *consume* away.
Ps. xxxvii. 20.

It is applied to *time,* as vanishing and
disappearing (Job vii. 6) ; and to the
destruction or perishing of men ; Jer.
xvi. 4; Ezek. v. 13. The idea is that
of *complete* and *entire* consumption and
destruction, so that *none shall be left.*
Applied to future punishment, it means
that the destruction of sinners shall be
total and complete. There shall be no
sinner who shall not be destroyed ; and
there shall be none destroyed whose
destruction shall not be entire and total.
The expression here refers to the heavy
calamities which were about to come
upon the guilty nation, but it is *as*
descriptive of the future punishment
that shall come upon the wicked.

29. *For they shall be ashamed.* That
is, when they see the punishment that
their idolatry has brought upon them,
they shall be ashamed of the folly and
degradation of their worship. Moreover, the gods in which they trusted
shall yield them no protection, and shall
leave them to the disgrace and confusion
of being forsaken and abandoned. ¶ *Of
the oaks. Groves,* in ancient times, were
the favourite places of idolatrous worship.
In the city of Rome, there were thirty-
two groves consecrated to the gods.
Those were commonly selected which
were on hills, or high places ; and they
were usually furnished with temples,
altars, and all the implements of idolatrous worship. Different kinds of groves
were selected for this purpose, by
different people. The *Druids* of the
ancient Celtic nations in Gaul, Britain,
and Germany, offered their worship in

the oaks which ye have desired, and | ye shall be confounded for the gardens that ye have chosen.

groves of *oak*—hence the name *Druid*, derived from δρῦς, *drus*, an oak. Frequent mention is made in the Scriptures of groves and high places ; and the Jews were forbidden to erect them ; Deut. xvi. 21 ; 1 Kings xvi. 23 ; 2 Kings xvi. 4 ; Ezek. vi. 13 ; xvi. 16, 39 ; Ex. xxxiv. 13 ; Judg. iii. 7 ; 1 Kings xviii. 19 ; Isa. xvii. 8 ; Mic. v. 14. When, therefore, it is said here, that they should be ashamed of the *oaks*, it means that they should be ashamed of their *idolatrous worship*, to which they were much addicted, and into which, under their wicked kings, they easily fell. Their calamities were coming upon them mainly for this idolatry.—It is not certainly known what species of tree is intended by the word translated *oaks*. The LXX. have rendered it by the word *idols*—ἀπὸ τῶν εἰδώλων αὐτῶν. The Chaldee, ' ye shall be confounded *by the groves of idols.*' The Syriac version also has *idols*. Most critics concur in supposing that it means, not the *oak*, but the *terebinth* or *turpentine* tree—a species of fir. This tree is the *Pistacia Terebinthus* of Linnæus, or the common turpentine tree, whose resin or juice is the Chian or Cyprus turpentine, used in medicine. The tree grows to a great age, and is common in Palestine. The *terebinth*—now called in Palestine the but'm-tree—' is not an evergreen, as is often represented ; but its small, feathered, lancet-shaped leaves fall in the autumn, and are renewed in the spring. The flowers are small, and are followed by small oval berries, hanging in clusters from two to five inches long, resembling much the clusters of the vine when the grapes are just set. From incisions in the trunk there is said to flow a sort of transparent balsam, constituting a very pure and fine species of turpentine, with an agreeable odour like citron or jessamine, and a mild taste, and hardening gradually into a transparent gum. The tree is found also in Asia Minor, Greece, Italy, the south of France, and in the north of Africa, and is described as not usually rising to the height of more than twenty feet.'—

Robinson's *Bib. Researches*, iii. 15, 16. It produces the nuts called the pistachio nuts. They have a pleasant, unctuous taste, resembling that of almonds, and they yield in abundance a sweet and pleasant oil. The best Venice turpentine, which, when it can be obtained pure, is superior to all the rest of its kind, is the produce of this tree. The following cut will give an idea of the appearance of the *terebinth*.

Turpentine Tree. *(Pistacia Terebinthus.)*

The Hebrew word אֵילִים *ēlīm*, from אֵיל *ēl*, or more commonly אֵלָה *ēlâ*, seems to be used sometimes as the Greek δρῦς is, to denote *any* large tree, whether evergreen or not ; and especially any large tree, or cluster of trees, where the worship of idols was celebrated. ¶ *Which ye have desired*. The Jews, until the captivity at Babylon, as all their history shows, easily relapsed into idolatry. The meaning of the prophet is, that the punishment at Babylon would be so long and so severe as to make them *ashamed* of this, and turn them from it. ¶ *Shall be confounded*. Another word meaning to be ashamed. ¶ *For the gardens*. The places planted with trees, &c., in which idolatrous worship was practised. ' In the language of the Hebrews, every place where plants and trees were cultivated with greater care than in the open field, was called a garden. The idea of such an enclosure was certainly borrowed from the garden of Eden, which the

30 For ye shall be as an oak whose leaf fadeth, and as a garden that hath no water.

31 And the strong shall be as tow, and the maker of it as a spark, and they shall both burn together, and none shall quench them.

bountiful Creator planted for the reception of his favourite creature. The garden of Hesperides, in Eastern fables, was protected by an enormous serpent; and the gardens of Adonis, among the Greeks, may be traced to the same origin; for the terms *horti Adonides*, the gardens of Adonis, were used by the ancients to signify gardens of pleasure, which corresponds with the name of Paradise, or the garden of Eden, as *horti Adonis* answers to the garden of the Lord. Besides, the gardens of primitive nations were commonly, if not in every instance, devoted to religious purposes. In these shady retreats were celebrated, for a long succession of ages, the rites of pagan superstition.'—*Paxton*. These groves or gardens were furnished with the temple of the god that was worshipped, and with altars, and with every thing necessary for this species of worship. They were usually, also, made as shady and dark as possible, to inspire the worshippers with religious awe and reverence on their entrance; comp. Note, lxvi. 17.

30. *For ye*, &c. The mention of the *tree* in the previous verse, gives the prophet occasion for the beautiful image in this. They had desired the oak, and they should be like it. *That*, when the frost came, was divested of its beauty, and its leaves faded, and fell; so should their beauty and privileges and happiness, as a people, fade away at the anger of God. ¶ *A garden that hath no water.* That is therefore withered and parched up; where nothing would flourish, but where all would be desolation—a most striking image of the approaching desolation of the Jewish nation. In Eastern countries this image would be more striking than with us. In these hot regions, a constant supply of water is necessary for the cultivation, and even for the very existence and preservation of a garden. Should it want water for a few days, every thing in it would be burnt up with neat. and totally destroyed. In all gardens, therefore, in those regions,

there must be a constant supply of water, either from some neighbouring river, or from some fountain or reservoir within it. To secure such a fountain became an object of indispensable importance, not only for the coolness and pleasantness of the garden, but for the very existence of the vegetation. Dr. Russell, in his *Natural History of Aleppo*, says, that 'all the gardens of Aleppo are on the banks of the river that runs by that city, or on the sides of the rill that supplies their aqueduct;' and all the rest of the country he represents as perfectly burnt up in the summer months, the gardens only retaining their verdure, on account of the moistness of their situation.

31. *And the strong.* Those who have been *thought* to be strong, on whom the people relied for protection and defence —their rulers, princes, and the commanders of their armies. ¶ *As tow.* The coarse or broken part of flax, or hemp. It means here that which shall be easily and quickly kindled and rapidly consumed. As tow burns and is destroyed at the touch of fire, so shall the rulers of the people be consumed by the approaching calamities. ¶ *And the maker of it.* This is an unhappy translation. The word פֹּעֲלוֹ *may be* indeed a participle, and be rendered 'its maker,' but it is more commonly *a noun*, and means his *work*, or his *action*. This is its plain meaning here. So the Latin Vulgate, the Septuagint, and the Chaldee. It means, that as a spark enkindles tow, so *the works* or *deeds* of a wicked nation shall be *the occasion* or *cause* of their destruction. The ambition of one man is the cause of his ruin; the sensuality of a second is the cause of his; the avarice of a third is the cause of his. These passions, insatiable and ungratified, shall be the occasion of the deep and eternal sorrows of hell. So it means here, that the crimes and hypocrisy of the nation would be the real cause of all the calamities that would come upon them as a people. ¶ *Shall both burn together.*

CHAPTER II.

THE prophecy in this and the two following chapters, constitutes one continued discourse. At what time it was delivered is not known, and cannot be ascertained by the prophecy itself. Bishop Lowth supposes it was in the time of Jotham, or Uzziah, and this opinion is probably correct; for it is to be presumed that in collecting the prophecies, those would be placed first which were first delivered. Besides, the prophecy relates to a time of prosperity, when the fruits of commerce abounded, and did much to corrupt the people (see ch. ii. 7, 16, 20; iii. 18–23), and this accords best with the time of Uzziah, or the time of Jotham. Some have referred it to the return from Babylon, others to the times of the Messiah. The description in ch. ii. 2–4, and iv. 5, 6, cannot easily be referred to any other times than those of the Messiah.

The main scope of the prophecy is, to denounce the crimes which prevailed in the time when it was delivered; to threaten certain punishment for these crimes; and to assure the nation that there would be happier times when those crimes should have received their appropriate punishment, and when the nation should be reformed. The prophecy has relation solely to the kingdom of Judah, ch. ii. 1. The prophet opens the prophecy (ch. ii. 2) by a brief but striking statement of the happy period when the Messiah should come, and the happy influence of his advent, ch. ii. 2–4. It would seem, in looking at the entire prophecy, as if he had been contemplating the sins of the nation which then abounded, until his heart was sickened, and he involuntarily cast his mind forward to brighter and happier days when these things should cease, and the Messiah should reign in his glory. See Introduction, § 7. The future times of the Messiah he exhibits, by showing (ch. ii. 2) that the benefits of the true religion would be extended to all people, and would be so conspicuous as to attract their attention, as if the temple, the place of the worship of the true God, should be made conspicuous in the sight of all nations. It would excite a deep interest, and a spirit of earnest inquiry every where (ver. 3), and the effect of his reign would be to put an end to wars, and to introduce ultimately universal peace (ver. 4). In view of that, the prophet (ver. 5) exhorts all the people to turn from their sins, and to walk in the light of Jehovah. This leads him to a statement of the crimes which he would seem to have been contemplating, and the punishment which must follow from their prevalence. The statement of the crimes and their punishment is somewhat intermingled, but they may be exhibited so as to be contemplated separately and distinctly.

Crimes.

Forsaking Jehovah;
Patronage of soothsayers;
Alliance with strangers (ver. 6);
Accumulation of treasures;
Preparation of war-chariots (ver. 7);
Universal and debasing idolatry (ver. 8, 9).

Punishments.

God would so judge them as to produce universal consternation (ver. 10).

He would humble their pride, and bring them low (ver. 11, 12).

He would smite and destroy all their wealth, and the sources of national corruption and depravity (ver. 13–17).

He would entirely destroy the idols (ver. 13).

He would produce universal terror and alarm (ver. 19–21).

In view of these heavy judgments, the prophet calls on the people (ver. 22) to cease to trust in men, since all were mortal, and unworthy of their confidence.

In chapter iii., the description of the punishment of the nation is continued (ver. 1–15), intermingled with the account of their sins.

The spark and the flame from the kindled flax mingle, and make one fire. So the people and their works would be enkindled and destroyed together. They would burn so rapidly, that nothing could extinguish them. The meaning is, that the nation would be punished; and that all their works of idolatry and monuments of sin would be the occasion of their punishment, and would perish at the same time. The *principle* involved in this passage teaches us the following things:—(1.) That the wicked, however mighty, shall be destroyed. (2.) That their works will be the *cause* of their ruin—a cause necessarily leading to it. (3.) That the works of the wicked—all that they do and all on which they depend—shall be destroyed. (4.) That this destruction shall be final. Nothing shall stay the flame. No tears of penitence, no power of men or devils, shall *put out* the fires which the works of the wicked shall enkindle.

There would be calamity, the removal of the means of support, and the removal of the men in whom the nation had reposed confidence (ver. 1–4).

There would be oppression, and a violation of, and disregard of all the proper laws of social life (ver. 5).

There would be a state of anarchy and calamity, so that no one would be willing to be a leader, or undertake to remove the difficulties of the nation, or hold an office of trust (ver. 6, 7).

Jerusalem would be ruined (ver. 8).

The cause of this was pride and hypocrisy (ver. 8, 9).

The prophet states the principles of the Divine administration—that it should be well with the righteous, but ill with the wicked (ver. 12–15).

The rulers of the nation were corrupt and oppressive (ver. 12–15).

The chapter closes (ver. 16–26) with a graphic description of the gaiety, pride, and folly of the female part of the Jewish community, and with the assurance that they would be involved in the calamities which were coming upon the nation.

Chapter iv. is a continuation of the same prophecy. It contains the following parts:—

1. A statement of the general calamity of the nation, indicated by the fact that the *men* would be destroyed, and that the women would apply to the few that remained that they might be called by their name, and their reproach be taken away (ver. 1).

2. At that future time there would be a looking to the Messiah; a feeling that God only could interpose and save them; and a high estimate placed on the 'Branch of Jehovah'—the Messiah, to whom alone they could look for deliverance (ver. 2).

3. The people would turn to God, and there would be a reformation from their national sins (ver. 3, 4). The judgments of Jehovah would be effectual to the removal of the peculiar crimes which the prophet had denounced, and the nation would become holy.

God would, in that future time, become the protector of his people, and the symbols of his presence and protection would be manifest every where in the midst of them (ver. 5, 6).

It is evident, therefore, that this prophecy was uttered when the nation was proud, haughty, and hypocritical; when they had been successfully engaged in commerce, and when the means of luxury abounded; when the national pride and vanity were manifested in dress, and luxury, and in the oppressive acts of the rulers; when general disorder and anarchy prevailed, and when a part of the nation at least was idolatrous. The entire prophecy may be regarded as a condemnation of these sins, and a solemn declaration that *for* these sins, wherever they prevail, the judgments of God will be poured out on a people. The prophecy, also, contemplates happier and purer times, and contains the assurance that the *series* of judgments which God would bring on a guilty people would *ultimately* have the effect to purify them, and that all these crimes and calamities would be succeeded by the pure and peaceful reign of the Messiah. It is in accordance with the manner of Isaiah, when he surveys existing crimes; when he sees the degradation of his countrymen, and is deeply distressed; when he portrays the judgments that must *certainly* come upon them; and when, as if sickened with the contemplation of their crimes and calamities, his mind seeks repose in the contemplation of the purer and happier period when the Messiah should reign, and peace, prosperity, and purity should prevail.

T HE word that Isaiah the son of Amoz saw concerning Judah and Jerusalem.

2 And *a* it shall come to pass in the last days, *that* the mountain of the Lord's house shall be

a Mic.4.1,&c.

CHAPTER II.

1. *The word.* This indicates that this is the commencement of a new prophecy. It has no immediate connection with the preceding. It was delivered doubtless at a different time, and with reference to a different class of events. In the previous chapter the term *vision* is used (ver. 1), but the meaning is substantially the same. The term *word* דָּבָר *dâbâr*, denotes a command, a promise, a doctrine, an oracle, a revelation, a message, a thing, &c. It means here, that Isaiah foresaw certain *future events* or *things* that would happen in regard to Judah and Jerusalem. ¶ *Judah*, &c. ; see Notes, ch. i. 1.

2. *In the last days.* בְּאַחֲרִית הַיָּמִים *bĕăhhărith hăyyâmîm.* In the *after* days ; in the *futurity* of days ; *i.e.*, in the time to come. This is an expres-

established [1] in the top of the mountains, and shall be exalted above

the hills; and all [a] nations shall flow unto it.

sion that often occurs in the Old Testament. It does not of itself refer to any *particular* period, and especially not, as our translation would seem to indicate, to the end of the world. The expression properly denotes *only future time* in general. But the prophets were accustomed to concentrate all their hopes on the coming of the Messiah. They saw his advent as giving character, and sublimity, and happiness to all coming times. Hence the expression came to denote, by way of eminence, the times of the Messiah, and is frequently used in the New Testament, as well as the Old, to designate those times; see Acts ii. 17; comp. Joel ii. 28; Heb. i. 2; 1 Pet. i. 5, 20; 1 John ii. 18; Gen. xlix. 1; Mic. iv. 1; Deut. iv. 30; Jer. xlviii. 47; Dan. xi. 28. The expressions which follow are figurative, and cannot well be interpreted as relating to any other events than the times of the Messiah. They refer to that future period, then remote, which would constitute the *last* dispensation of things in this world—the *last* time—the period, however long it might be, in which the affairs of the world would be closed. The patriarchal times had passed away; the dispensation under the Mosaic economy would pass away; the times of the Messiah would be the *last* times, or the last dispensation, under which the affairs of the world would be consummated. Thus the phrase is evidently used in the New Testament, as denoting the *last* time, though without implying that that time would be short. It might be longer than *all* the previous periods put together, but it would be the *last* economy, and under that economy, or *in* that time, the world would be destroyed, Christ would come to judgment, the dead would be raised, and the affairs of the world would be wound up. The apostles, by the use of this phrase, never intimate that the time would be short, or that the day of judgment was near, but only that *in* that time the great events of the world's history would be consummated and

closed; comp. 2 Thess. ii. 1–5.—This prophecy occurs in Micah (ch. iv. 1–5) with scarcely any variation. It is not known whether Isaiah made use of Micah, or Micah of Isaiah, or both of an older and well-known prophecy. Hengstenberg (*Chris.* i., pp. 289, 290) supposes that Isaiah copied from Micah, and suggests the following reasons:—1. The prediction of Isaiah is disconnected with what goes before, and yet begins with the copulative *Vav* ‫ו‬, *and.* In Micah, on the contrary, it is connected with what precedes and follows. 2. In the discourses of the prophets, the promise usually follows the threatening. This order is observed by Micah; in Isaiah, on the contrary, the promise contained in the passage precedes the threatening, and another promise follows. Many of the older theologians supposed that the passages were communicated alike by the Holy Spirit to both writers. But there is no improbability in supposing that Isaiah may have availed himself of language used by Micah in describing the same event. ¶ *The mountain of the Lord's house.* The temple was built on mount Moriah, which was hence called the mountain of the Lord's house. The temple, or the mountain on which it was reared, would be the object which would express the public worship of the true God. And hence, to say that that should be elevated higher than all other hills, or mountains, means, that the worship of the true God would become an object so conspicuous as to be seen by all nations; and so conspicuous that all nations would forsake other objects and places of worship, being attracted by the glory of the worship of the true God. ¶ *Shall be established.* Shall be fixed, rendered permanent. ¶ *In the top of the mountains.* To be in the top of the mountains, would be to be *conspicuous,* or seen from afar. In other words, the true religion would be made known to all people. ¶ *Shall flow unto it.* This is a figurative expression, denoting that they would be converted to the true re-

3 And many people shall go and say, Come *a* ye, and let us go up to the mountain of the LORD, to the house of the God of Jacob: and he will teach us of his ways, and we will walk in his paths; for out of Zion *b* shall go forth the law, and the word of the LORD from Jerusalem.

a Jer.31.6; 50.5; Zec.8.21,23.　　*b* Lu.24.47.

ligion. It indicates that they would come in multitudes, like the flowing of a mighty river. The idea of the *flowing* of the nations, or of the movement of many people towards an object like a broad stream, is one that is very grand and sublime; comp. Psal. lxv. 7. This cannot be understood of any period previous to the establishment of the gospel. At no time of the Jewish history did any events occur that would be a complete fulfilment of this prophecy. The expressions evidently refer to that period elsewhere often predicted by this prophet (Isa. xi. 10· xlii. 1, 6; xlix. 22; liv. 3; lx. 3, 5, 10; lxii. 2; lxvi. 12, 19), when *the Gentiles* would be brought to the knowledge of the true religion. In Isa. lxvi. 12, there occurs a passage remarkably similar, and which may serve to explain this:

'Behold I will extend peace to her [to Zion] as a river;
And the glory of the Gentiles like a flowing stream.'

Under the Messiah, through the preaching of the apostles and by the spread of the gospel, this prophecy was to receive its full accomplishment.

3. *And many people shall go.* This denotes a prevalent *desire* to turn to the true God, and embrace the true religion. It is remarkable that it speaks of an inclination among them *to seek* God, as if they were satisfied of the folly and danger of their ways, and felt the necessity of obtaining a better religion. In many cases this has occurred. Thus, in modern times, the people of the Sandwich Islands threw away their gods and remained without any religion, as if waiting for the message of life. Thus, too, the heathen not unfrequently come from a considerable distance at missionary stations to be instructed, and to receive the Bible and tracts. Perhaps this is to be extensively the mode in which Christianity is to be spread. God, who has all power over

human hearts, may excite the heathen to anxious inquiry; may show them the folly of their religion; and may lead them to this *preparation* to embrace the gospel, and this disposition to *go* and seek it. He has access to all men. By a secret influence on the understanding, the heart, and the conscience of the heathen, he can convince them of the folly of idolatry and its vices. He can soften down their prejudices in favour of their long-established systems; can break down the barriers between them and Christians; and can dispose them to receive with joy the messengers of salvation. He can raise up, among the heathen themselves, reformers, who shall show them the folly of their systems. It cannot be doubted that the universal triumph of the gospel will be preceded by some such remarkable preparation among the nations; by a secret, silent, but most mighty influence from God on the heathen generally, that shall loosen their hold on idolatry, and dispose them to welcome the gospel. And the probability that this state of things exists already, and will more and more, should be an inducement to Christians to make more vigorous efforts to send every where the light of life. ¶ *He will teach us of his ways.* He will make us acquainted with his will, and with the doctrines of the true religion. ¶ *For out of Zion.* These are the words of the *prophet*, not of the people. The prophet declares that the law would go from Zion; that is, Zion would be the centre from which it would be spread abroad; see Note, ch. i. 8. Zion is put here for Jerusalem, and means that the message of mercy to mankind would be spread *from* Jerusalem. Hence the Messiah commanded his disciples to tarry 'in Jerusalem until they should be endued with power from on high.' Luke xxiv. 49. Hence, also, he said that repentance and remission of sins should 'be preached among all nations, *beginning at Jerusalem* '—

4 And he shall judge among the | nations, and shall rebuke many

perhaps referring to this very passage in Isaiah; Luke xxiv. 47. ¶ *The law.* This is put here for the doctrines of the true religion in general. The law or will of God, under the reign of the Messiah, would proceed from Zion. ¶ *The word of the Lord.* The message of his mercy to mankind; that which he has *spoken* respecting the salvation of men.—The truth which is here taught is, *that Zion or the church is the source of religious truth, and the centre of religious influence in the world.* This is true in the following respects:— (1.) Zion was the source of religious truth to the ancient world. Knowledge was gained by travel; and it is capable of about as clear demonstration as any fact of ancient history, that no inconsiderable part of the knowledge pertaining to God in ancient Greece was obtained by intercourse with the sages of distant lands, and that the truths held in Zion or Jerusalem thus radiated from land to land, and mind to mind. (2.) The church is now the centre of religious truth to the world around it. (*a.*) The world by its philosophy never originates a system of religion which it is desirable to retain, and which conveys any just view of God or the way of salvation. (*b.*) The most crude, unsettled, contradictory, and vague opinions on religion prevail in this community called ' *the world.*' (*c.*) If *in* this community there are any opinions that are true and valuable, they can in most instances be traced to *the church.* They are owing to the influence of the pulpit; or to an early training in the Bible; or to early teaching in the Sabbath-school, or to the instructions of a pious parent, or to the *general* influence which Christianity exerts on the community. (3.) The church holds the power of *reformation* in her hands, every cause of morals advancing or retarding as she enters into the work, or as she withdraws from it. (4.) The heathen world is dependent on the church for the knowledge of the true religion. There are *no* systems of truth that start up on a pagan soil. There is no elastic energy in a heathen mind.

There is no recuperative power to bring it back to God. There is no *advance* made toward the truth in any heathen community. There is no well-spring of life to purify the soul. The effect of time is only to deepen the darkness, and to drive them farther from God. They only worship mere shapeless blocks; they bow down before worse looking idols; they enter less elegant and more polluted temples. The idols of the heathen are not constructed with half the skill and taste evinced two thousand years ago; nor are their temples built with such exquisite art. No idol of the heathen world now can compare with the statue of Minerva at Athens; no temple can be likened to the Parthenon; no sentiment of heathenism in China, India, or Africa, can be compared with the views of the sages of Greece. The heathen world is becoming worse and worse, and if ever brought to better views, it must be by a *foreign* influence; and that influence will not go forth from philosophy or science, but *from the church.* If light is ever to spread, it is to go forth from Zion; and the world is dependent on *the church* for any just knowledge of God and of the way to life. The ' law is to go forth from Zion;' and the question whether the millions of the human family are to be taught the way to heaven, is just a question whether the church can be roused to diffuse abroad the light which has arisen on her.

4. *And he shall judge.* Or he shall exercise the office of a judge, or umpire. This *literally* refers to the God of Jacob (ver. 3), though it is clear that the meaning is, that he will do it by the Messiah, or under his reign. One office of a judge is to decide controversies; to put an end to litigations, and thus to promote peace. The connection shows that this is the meaning here. Nations that are contending shall be brought to peace by the influence of the reign of the Messiah, and shall beat their swords into ploughshares. In other words, the influence of the reign of the Messiah shall put a period to wars, and reduce contending nations to peace. ¶ *And*

people; and they [a] shall beat their swords into ploughshares; and their spears into [1] pruning-hooks: nation shall not lift up sword against

a Ps.46.9; Hos.2.18.   1 or, *scythes.*

shall rebuke. Shall *reprove* them for their contentions and strifes.

Lowth: 'Shall work conviction in many peoples.'
Noyes: 'He shall be a judge of the nations,
        And an umpire of many kingdoms.'

He shall show them the evil of war; and by reproving them for those wicked passions which cause wars, shall promote universal peace. This the gospel every where does; and the tendency of it, if obeyed, would be to produce universal peace. In accordance with predictions like these, the Messiah is called the Prince of Peace (Isa. ix. 6); and it is said that of his peace there shall be no end; Isa. ix. 7. ¶ *And they shall beat,* &c. They shall change the arts of war to those of peace; or they shall abandon the pursuits of war for the mild and useful arts of husbandry; comp. Ps. xlvi. 9; Hos. ii. 20. A similar prophecy is found in Zech. ix. 10. The following extracts may serve to illustrate this passage :—'The Syrian plough, which was probably used in all the regions around, is a very simple frame, and commonly so light, that a man of moderate strength might carry it in one hand. Volney states that in Syria it is often nothing else than the branch of a tree, cut below a bifurcation, and used without wheels. The ploughshare is a piece of iron, broad but not large, which tips the end of the shaft. So

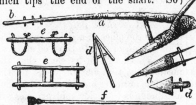

MODERN ORIENTAL PLOUGH.—From Fellow's Asia Minor.

a, the plough; *b,* the pole; *c,* the handle or plough-tail, *d d d,* shares; *e e,* yokes; *f,* the goad, or instrument for driving.

much does it resemble the short sword used by the ancient warriors, that it may, with very little trouble, be converted into that deadly weapon; and when the work of destruction is over, reduced again to its former shape, and

applied to the purposes of agriculture.' ¶ *Their spears.* Spears were much used in war. They were made of wood, with a sharpened piece of iron or other metal attached to the end. The pruning-hook, made for cutting the limbs of vines or trees, is, in like manner, a long piece of wood with a crooked knife attached to it. Hence it was easy to convert the one into the other. ¶ *Pruning-hooks.* Hooks or long knives for trimming vines. The word here, however, means any thing employed in *reaping* or *mowing,* a sickle, or a scythe, or any instrument to *cut with,* as well as a pruning-hook. These figures, as images of peace, are often used by the prophets. Micah (iv. 4) has added to this description of peace in Isaiah, the following :

But they shall sit
Every man under his vine,
And under his fig-tree;
And none shall make them afraid:
For the mouth of Jehovah hath spoken it.

Joel (iii. 10) has reversed the figure, and applied it to war prevailing over peace :

Beat your ploughshares into swords;
And your pruning-hooks into spears.

The same emblems to represent peace, which are here used by Isaiah, also occur in heathen poets. Thus Martial; Epigr. xiv. 34:

Falx ex ense.
Pax me certa ducis placidos conflavit in usus,
Agricolae nunc sum, militis ante fui.

So Virgil; Georg. 1, 507:

Squalent abductis arva colonis,
Et curvae rigidum falces conflantur in ensem.

So also Ovid; Fast. 1, 699:

Sarcula cessabunt, versique in pila ligones.

¶ *Nation shall not lift up,* &c. This is a remarkable prediction of universal peace under the gospel. The prediction is positive, that the time will come when it shall prevail. But it has not yet been fully accomplished. We may remark, however, in relation to this:

nation, neither shall they learn war any more.

5 O house of Jacob, come ye, and let us walk ^a in the light of the LORD.

a Eph.5.8.   1 or, *more than.*

6 Therefore thou hast forsaken thy people, the house of Jacob, because they be replenished ¹from the east, and *are* soothsayers ^b like the Philistines, and they ²please

b Deut.18.14.   2 or, *abound with.*

(1.) That the tendency of the gospel is to promote the arts, and to produce the spirit of peace. (2.) It will dispose the nations to do right, and thus to avoid the occasions of war. (3.) It will fill the mind with horror at the scenes of cruelty and blood that war produces. (4.) It will diffuse honour around the arts of peace, and teach the nations to prize the endearments of home and country, and the sweet scenes of domestic life. (5.) Just so far as it has influence over princes and rulers, it will teach them to lay aside the passions of ambition and revenge, and the love of conquest and 'glory,' and indispose them to war. (6.) The tendency of things now is towards peace. The laws of nations have been established under the gospel. Difficulties can even now be adjusted by negotiation, and without a resort to arms. (7.) Wars are far less barbarous than they were formerly. The gospel has produced humanity, mildness, and some degree of justice even in war. It has put an end to the unmerciful treatment of prisoners ; has prevented their being sold as slaves ; has taught even belligerents not to murder women and children. (8.) Nothing remains to be done to make peace universal but to send the gospel abroad through every land. When that is done, the nations will be disposed to peace ; and the prophet, therefore, has predicted the universal prevalence of peace *only* when all nations shall be brought under the influence of the gospel.

5. *O house of Jacob.* This is a direct address, or exhortation, of the prophet to the Jews. It is made in view of the fact that God had gracious purposes towards them. He intended to distinguish them by making them the source of blessings to all nations. As this was to be their high destiny, he exhorts them to devote themselves to him, and to live to his honour. The word *house* here means the *family*, or *nation.* The

phrase is applied to the Jews because their tribes were descended from the twelve sons of Jacob. ¶ *Let us walk.* Let us *live.* The word *walk* is often used to denote human life or conduct ; comp. ver. 3 ; Rom. vi. 4 ; viii. 1 ; 1 Cor. v. 7 ; Gal. vi. 16, &c. ¶ *In the light of the* LORD. The sense of this is : Let us obey the commandments of JEHOVAH ; or, as the Chaldee expresses it, 'Let us walk in the doctrine of the law of the Lord.' The idea may be thus expressed : 'Let us not walk in the darkness and error of sin and idolatry, but in the light or instruction which God sheds upon us by his law. He teaches us what we should do, and let us obey him.' *Light* is often, in the Scriptures, thus put for instruction, or teaching ; comp. Note, Matt. iv. 16 ; John i. 4 ; also, Eph. v. 8.

6. *Therefore.* The prophet proceeds in this and the following verses, to state the reasons of their calamities, and of the judgments that had come upon them. Those judgments he traces to the crimes which he enumerates—crimes growing chiefly out of great commercial prosperity, producing pride, luxury, and idolatry. ¶ *Thou hast forsaken.* The address is changed from the exhortation to the house of Jacob (ver. 5) to God, as is frequently the case in the writings of Isaiah. It indicates a state where the mind is full of the subject, and where it expresses itself in a rapid and hurried manner. ¶ *Hast forsaken.* Hast withdrawn thy protection, and given them over to the calamities and judgments which had come upon them. ¶ *They be replenished.* Heb. They are *full.* That is, these things abound. ¶ *From the East.* Marg. *More than the East.* The meaning of the expression it is not easy to determine. The word translated *East*, קֶדֶם, denotes also *antiquity*, or that which is *of old*, as well as the East. Hence the LXX. render it, 'their land is, *as of old*, filled.' The Chaldee, 'their land is filled with idols *as at the*

themselves in the children of
strangers. [b]

7 Their [b] land also is full of silver
and gold, neither *is there any* end

beginning.' Either idea will suit the
passage ; though our translation more
nearly accords with the Hebrew than
the others. The *East, i.e.,* Arabia,
Persia, Chaldea, &c., was the country
where astrology, soothsaying, and divination particularly abounded ; see Dan.
ii. 2 ; Deut. xviii. 9–11. ¶ *And* are
soothsayers. Our word *soothsayers*
means *foretellers, prognosticators,* persons who pretend to predict future events
without inspiration, differing in this
from true prophets. What the Hebrew
word means, it is not so easy to determine. The word עֹנְנִים *ōnénim* may be
derived from עָנַן *ânân, a cloud*—and
then would denote those who augur from
the appearance of the clouds, a species
of divination from certain changes
observed in the sky ; comp. Lev. xix.
26 : ' Neither shall ye—*observe times.*'
2 Kings xxi. 6. This species of divination was expressly forbidden ; see Deut.
xviii. 10, 11, 12 : ' There shall not be
found among you any one that useth
divination, or *an observer of times,* or
an enchanter,' &c. Or the word may
be derived from עַיִן *ain, an eye,* and
then it will denote those who fascinate,
enchant, or bewitch by the eye. It is
probable that the word includes *augury,
necromancy,* and *witchcraft,* in general
—all which were expressly forbidden by
the law of Moses ; Deut. xviii. 10–12.
¶ *Like the Philistines.* The Philistines occupied the land in the south-
west part of Palestine. The LXX. use
the word *foreigners* here, as they do
generally, instead of the Philistines.
¶ *And they please themselves.* The
word here used—שָׂפַק—means literally
to clap the hands in token of joy. It
may also mean, *to join the hands, to
shake hands,* and then it will signify
that they *joined hands* with foreigners ;
that is, they made compacts or entered
into alliances with them contrary to the
law of Moses. The LXX. seem to understand it of unlawful marriages with the
women of surrounding nations—τέκνα
πολλὰ ἀλλόφυλλα ἐγενήθη αὐτοῖς ; comp.
Neh. xiii. 23. It means probably, in

general, that they entered into improper
alliances, whether they were military,
matrimonial, or commercial, with the
surrounding nations. The words *children of strangers* may mean, with the
descendants of the foreigners with whom
Moses forbade any alliances. The Jews
were to be a separate and peculiar
people, and, in order to this, it was
necessary to forbid all such foreign
alliances ; Ex. xxiii. 31, 32 ; xxxiv.
12–15 ; Ps. cvi. 3, 5 ; Ezra ix.

7. *Their land also is full of silver
and gold.* This *gold* was brought
chiefly from Ophir. Solomon imported
vast quantities of silver and gold from
foreign places ; 2 Chron. viii. 18 ; ix.
10 ; 1 Chron. xxix. 4 ; comp. Job xxviii.
16 ; 1 Kings x. 21, 27 ; 2 Chron. ix. 20.
' And the king made silver to be in
Jerusalem as stones.'—' It was nothing
accounted of in the days of Solomon.'
From these expressions we see the force
of the language of Isaiah—' their land
is *full,*' &c. This accumulation of
silver and gold was expressly forbidden
by the law of Moses ; Deut. xvii. 17 :
' Neither shall he [the king of Israel]
greatly multiply to himself silver and
gold.' The reason of this prohibition
was, that it tended to produce luxury,
effeminacy, profligacy, the neglect of
religion, and vice. It is on this account
that it is brought by the prophet as an
accusation against them that their land
was thus filled. ¶ *Treasures.* Wealth
of all kinds ; but chiefly silver, gold,
precious stones, garments, &c. ; comp.
Note, Matt. vi. 19. ¶ *Their land also
is full of horses.* This was also forbidden in the law of Moses ; Deut. xvii. 16 :
' But he shall not multiply horses to
himself, nor cause the people to return
to Egypt, to the end that he should
multiply horses.' This law, however,
was grossly violated by Solomon ; 1
Kings x. 26 : ' And Solomon gathered
together chariots and horsemen ; he had
a thousand and four hundred chariots,
and twelve thousand horsemen.' It is
not quite clear *why* the use of horses
was forbidden to the Jews. Perhaps
several reasons might have concurred :

of their treasures; their land is also full of horses, neither *is there any* end of their chariots:

8 Their land also is full of *a* idols; they worship the work of their

a Jer.2.28.

(1.) Egypt was distinguished for producing fine horses, and the Egyptians used them much in war (Deut. xvii. 16); and one design of God was to make the Jews distinguished in all respects from the Egyptians, and to keep them from commerce with them. (2.) Horses were chiefly used *in war*, and the tendency of keeping them would be to produce the love of war and conquest. (3.) The tendency of keeping them would be to lead them to put *trust* in them rather than in God for protection. This is hinted at in Ps. xx. 7: 'Some trust in chariots, and some in horses; but we will remember the name of JEHOVAH our God.' (4.) *Horses* were regarded as consecrated *to the sun;* see *Univ. Hist. Anc. P.*, vol. x., 177. Ed. 1780. They were sacrificed in various nations to the sun, their swiftness being supposed to render them an appropriate offering to that luminary. There is no evidence, however, that they were used for sacrifice among the Hebrews. They were probably employed to draw the chariots in the solemn processions in the worship of the sun. The ancient Persians, who were sun-worshippers, dedicated white horses and chariots to the sun, and it is supposed that other nations derived the practice from them. The sun was supposed to be drawn daily in a chariot by four wondrous coursers, and the fate of Phaeton, who undertook to guide that chariot and to control those coursers, is known to all. The use of horses, therefore, among the Hebrews in the time of Ahaz, when Isaiah lived (see 2 Kings xxxiii. 11), was connected with idolatry, and it was mainly on this account that the prophet rebuked their use with so much severity; 2 Kings xxiii. 11. It may be added, that in a country like Judea, abounding in hills and mountains, cavalry could not be well employed even

in war. On the plains of Egypt it could be employed to advantage; or in predatory excursions, as among the Arabs, horses could be used with great success and effect, and Egypt and Arabia therefore abounded with them. Indeed, these may be regarded as the native countries of the horse. As it was the design of God to separate, as much as possible, the Jews from the surrounding nations, the use of horses was forbidden. ¶ *Chariots.* *Chariots* were chiefly used in war, though they were sometimes used for pleasure. Of those intended for war there were two kinds; one for the generals and princes to ride in, the other to break the enemy's ranks. These last were commonly armed with hooks or scythes. They were much used by the ancients; Josh. xi. 4; Judg. i. 19. The Philistines, in their war against Saul, had 30,000 chariots, and 6000

EGYPTIAN CHARIOT.

horsemen; 1 Sam. xiii. 5. There is no evidence, however, that the Jews used chariots for war. Solomon had many of them (1 Kings x. 26), but they do not appear to have been used in any military expedition, but to have been kept for display and pleasure. Judea was a mountainous country, and chariots would have been of little or no use in war.

8. *Their land also is full of idols;*

own hands, the work which their
own fingers have made;

9 And the mean man boweth
down, and the great man humbleth
himself ; therefore forgive them not.

10 Enter [a] into the rock, and hide
thee in the dust, for fear of the
LORD, and for the glory of his
majesty.

a ver.19.21; Rev.6.15,16.

comp. Hos. viii. 4; x. 1. Vitringa supposes that Isaiah here refers to idols
that were kept in private houses, as
Uzziah and Jotham were worshippers
of the true God, and in their reign
idolatry was not publicly practised. It
is certain, however, that though Uzziah
himself did right, and was disposed to
worship the true God, yet he did not
effectually remove idolatry from the
land. The high places were not removed, and the people still sacrificed
and burnt incense on them ; 2 Kings
xv. 4. It was customary with the
heathen to keep in their houses *Penates*
or *household gods*—small images, which
they regarded as *protectors*, and to
which they paid homage : comp. Gen.
xxx. 19; Judg. xvii. 5; 1 Sam. xix. 13;
Hos. iii. 4. ' This is a true and literal
description of India. The traveller
cannot proceed a *mile* through an inhabited country without seeing idols,
and vestiges of idolatry in every direction. See their vessels, their implements of husbandry, their houses, their
furniture, their ornaments, their sacred
trees, their *domestic* and public temples ; and they all declare that the land
is full of idols.'—*Roberts.* ¶ *The work
of their own hands,* &c. Idols. It is
often brought as proof of their great
folly and degradation that they paid
homage to what *they* had themselves
made. See this severely satirized in
Isa. xl. 18–20; xli. 67; xliv. 9–17.

9. *And the mean man.* That is, the
man in humble life, the poor, the low
in rank—for this is all that the Hebrew
word here—אָדָם—implies. The distinction between the two words here
used—אָדָם as denoting a man of humble
rank, and אִישׁ as denoting one of elevated rank—is one that constantly occurs in the Scriptures. Our word *mean*
conveys an idea of moral baseness and
degradation, which is not implied in the
Hebrew. ¶ *Boweth down.* That is,
before idols. Some commentators, however, have understood this of bowing

down in *affliction,* but the other is probably the true interpretation. ¶ *And
the great man.* The men in elevated
rank in life. The expressions together
mean the same as *all ranks of people.*
It was a common or universal thing.
No rank was exempt from the prevailing idolatry. ¶ *Therefore forgive
them not.* The Hebrew is *future*—לָהֶם
וְאַל־תִּשָּׂא. Thou wilt not *bear* for them ;
that is, thou wilt not bear away their
sins [by an atonement], or ' thou wilt
not forgive them ;'—but agreeable to a
common Hebrew construction, it has the
force of the imperative. It involves a
threatening of the prophet, in the form
of an address to God. ' So great is
their sin, that thou, Lord, wilt not pardon them.' The prophet then proceeds,
in the following verses, to denounce the
certainty and severity of the judgment
that was coming upon them.

10. *Enter into the rock.* That is,
into the *holes* or *caverns* in the rocks,
as a place of refuge and safety; comp.
ver. 19, and Rev. vi. 15, 16. In times
of invasion by an enemy, it was natural
to flee to the fastnesses or to the caverns
of rocks for refuge. This expression is
highly figurative and poetic. The prophet warns them to flee from danger.
The sense is, that such were their
crimes that they would certainly be
punished ; and he advises them to flee
to a place of safety. ¶ *And hide thee
in the dust.* In ver. 19, this is ' caves
of the dust.' It is parallel to the former, and probably has a similar meaning. But *may* there not be reference
here to the mode prevailing in the East
of avoiding the monsoon or poisonous
heated wind that passes over the desert?
Travellers there, in order to be safe, are
obliged to throw themselves down, and
to place their mouths close to the earth
until it has passed. ¶ *For fear of the
Lord.* Heb. ' From the face of the
terror of the Lord.' That is, the punishment which God will inflict will sweep
over the land, producing fear and terror.

11 The lofty looks ^a of man shall be humbled, and the haughtiness of men shall be bowed down; and the LORD alone shall be exalted in that ^b day.

12 For the day of the LORD of

hosts *shall be* upon every *one that is* proud and lofty, and upon every *one that* is lifted up, and he shall be brought low;

13 And upon all the ^c cedars of Lebanon, *that are* high and lifted

a ver.17; ch.5.16; Ps.13.27.   b Zep.3.11,16; Zec 9.16.   c Eze.31.3; Zec.11.1,2.

¶ *And for the glory,* &c. That is, the honour or splendour which will attend him when he comes forth to inflict judgment on the people; ver. 19, 20.

11. *The lofty looks.* Heb. ' The *eyes of pride,*' *i.e.,* the proud eyes or looks. Pride commonly evinces itself in a lofty carriage and supercilious aspect; Ps. xviii. 27. ¶ *Shall be humbled.* By the calamities that shall sweep over the land. This does not mean that he shall be brought *to be* humble, or to have a humble heart, but that that on which he so much prided himself would be taken away. ¶ *The Lord alone,* &c. God will so deal with them as to vindicate his honour; to turn the attention entirely on himself, and to secure the reverence of all the people. So terrible shall be his judgments, and so *manifestly* shall they come from *him,* that they shall look away from every thing else to *him* alone. ¶ *In that day.* In the day of which the prophet speaks, when God would punish them for their sins, Reference is probably made to the captivity at Babylon.—It may be remarked, that one design of punishment is to lead men to regard and honour God. He will humble the pride of men, and so pass before them in his judgments, that they shall be compelled to *acknowledge* him as their just Sovereign and Judge.

12. *The day,* &c. This expression evidently denotes that the Lord would inflict severe punishment upon every one that was lofty. Such a severe infliction is called *the day of the Lord of hosts,* because it would be a time when *he* would particularly manifest himself, and when *he* would be recognised as the inflicter of that punishment. *His* coming forth in this manner would give *character* to that time, and would be the prominent *event.* The punishment of the wicked is thus frequently called *the day of the Lord;* Isa. xiii. 6, 9: ' Behold the day of the

Lord cometh, cruel both with wrath and fierce anger,' &c.; Jer. xlvi. 10: ' The day of the Lord God of hosts, a day of vengeance.' Ezek. xxx. 3; Zeph. i. 7, 14; Joel ii. 31; see also in the New Testament, 1 Thess. v. 2; 2 Pet. iii. 10. ¶ *Every* one that is *proud and lofty.* Or, rather, every *thing* that is high and lofty. The phrase is not restricted to *persons,* though it embraces them. But though the language here is general, the reference is doubtless, mainly, to the princes, magistrates, and nobility of the nation; and is designed not only to designate them as men of rank and power, but as men who were haughty in their demeanour and feelings. At the same time, there is included in the language, as the subsequent verses show, all on which the nation prided itself.

13. *And upon all the cedars of Lebanon.* This is a beautiful specimen of the poetic manner of writing, so common among the Hebrews, where spiritual and moral subjects are represented by grand or beautiful imagery taken from objects of nature. Mount Lebanon bounded Palestine on the north. It was formerly much celebrated for its large and lofty cedars. These cedars were from thirty-five to forty feet in girth, and very high. They were magnificent trees, and were valuable for ceiling, statues, or roofs, that required durable and beautiful timber. The roof of the temple of Diana of Ephesus, according to Pliny, was of cedar, and no small part of the temple of Solomon was of this wood. A few lofty trees of this description are still remaining on Mount Lebanon. ' After three hours of laborious travelling,' says D'Arvieux, ' we arrived at the famous cedars about eleven o'clock. We counted twenty-three of them. The circumference of these trees is thirty-six feet. The bark of the cedar resembles that of the pine;

the leaves and cone also bear consider-able resemblance. The stem is upright, the wood is hard, and has the reputa-tion of being incorruptible. The leaves are long, narrow, rough, very green, ranged in tufts along the branches; they shoot in spring, and fall in the beginning of winter. Its flowers and fruit resemble those of the pine. From the full grown trees, a fluid trickles naturally, and without incision; this is clear, transparent, whitish, and after a time dries and hardens; it is supposed to possess great virtues. The place where these great trees are stationed, is in a plain of nearly a league in circum-ference, on the summit of a mount which is environed on almost all sides by other mounts, so high that their summits are always covered with snow. This plain is level, the air is pure, the heavens always serene.'

LEBANON, AND ITS CEDARS.   (*Cedrus Libani Conifera.*)

Maundrell found only sixteen cedars of large growth, and a natural planta-tion of smaller ones, which were very numerous. One of the largest was twelve yards six inches in girth, and thirty-seven yards in the spread of its boughs. At six yards from the ground, it was divided into five limbs, each equal to a great tree. Dr. Richardson visited them in 1818, and found a small clump of large, tall, and beautiful trees, which he pronounces the most pic-turesque productions of the vegetable world that he had ever seen. In this clump are two generations of trees; the oldest are large and massy, rearing their heads to an enormous height, and spreading their branches to a great extent. He measured one, not the largest in the clump, and found it thirty-two feet in circumference. Seven of these trees appeared to be very old, the rest younger, though, for want of space, their branches are not so spread-ing.—Bush's *Illustrations of Scripture.* 'The celebrated cedar-grove of Leba-non,' says Dr. Robinson, 'is at least two days' journey from Beïrût, near the northern, and perhaps the highest sum-mit of the mountain. It has been often and sufficiently described by travellers for the last three centuries; but they

up, and upon all the oaks of Bashan,

14 And upon all the high mountains, and upon all the hills *that
are* lifted up,

15 And upon every high tower,
and upon every fenced wall,

16 And upon all the ships of
Tarshish, and upon all [1] pleasant
pictures.

1 pictures of desire.

all differ as to the number of the oldest
trees, inasmuch as in counting, some
have included more and some less of the
younger ones. At present, the number
of trees appears to be on the increase,
and amounts in all to several hundred.
This grove was long held to be the
only remnant of the ancient cedars of
Lebanon. But Seetzen, in 1805, discovered two other groves of greater
extent; and the American Missionaries,
in travelling through the mountains,
have also found many cedars in other
places. The trees are of all sizes, old
and young; but none so ancient and
venerable as those usually visited.'—
Bib. Researches, iii., 440, 441. The
cedar, so large, lofty, and grand, is
used in the Scriptures to represent
kings, princes, and nobles; comp. Ezek.
xxxi. 3; Dan. iv. 20–22; Zech. xi. 1, 2;
Isa. xiv. 8. Here it means the princes
and nobles of the land of Israel. The
Chaldee renders it, 'upon all the strong
and mighty kings of the people.' ¶ *And
upon all the oaks of Bashan.* Bashan
was east of the river Jordan, in the
limits of the half tribe of Manasseh. It
was bounded on the north and east by
Gilead, south by the river Jabbok, and
west by the Jordan. It was celebrated
for pasturage, and for producing fine
cattle; Num. xxi. 33; xxxii. 33; Ps.
xxii. 12; Ezek. xxxix. 18; Amos iv. 1;
Mic. vii. 14. Its lofty oaks are also
particularly celebrated; Ezek. xxvii. 6;
Amos ii. 9; Zech. xi. 2. The sense here
is not different from the former member
of the sentence—denoting the princes
and nobles of the land.

14. *And upon all the high mountains.*
Judea abounded in lofty mountains,
which added much to the grandeur of
its natural scenery. Lowth supposes
that by mountains and hills are meant
here, ' kingdoms, republics, states,
cities;' but there are probably no
parallel places where they have this
meaning. The meaning is probably
this:—high mountains and hills would

not only be objects of beauty or grandeur, but also places of defence, and
protection. In the caverns and fastnesses of such hills, it would be easy for
the people to find refuge when the land
was invaded. The meaning of the
prophet then is, that the day of God's
vengeance should be upon the places of
refuge and strength; the strongly fortified places, or places of sure retreat in
cases of invasion; comp. Notes on ver.
19. ¶ *Hills that are lifted up.* That
is, high, elevated hills.

15. *Every high tower.* Towers, or
fortresses, were erected for defence and
protection. They were made on the
walls of cities, for places of observation
(comp. Note, ch. xxi. 5), or in places
of strength, to be a refuge for an army,
and to be a point from which they
might sally out to attack their enemies.
They were *high* to afford a defence
against being scaled by an enemy, and
also that from the top they might look
abroad for observation; and also to
annoy an enemy from the top, when the
foe approached the walls of a city.
¶ *Every fenced wall.* בְּצוּרָה חוֹמָה.
The word *fenced*, בְּצוּרָה *betzūrā*, is
from בָּצַר *bâtzăr*, to make inaccessible,
and hence to fortify. It denotes a wall
that is inaccessible, or strongly fortified.
Cities were commonly surrounded by
high and strong walls to defend them
from enemies. The sense is, God would
overturn all their strong places of refuge
and defence.

16. *And upon all the ships of Tarshish.* Ships of Tarshish are often
mentioned in the Old Testament, but
the meaning of the expression is not
quite obvious; see 1 Kings x. 22; 2
Chron. ix. 21; xx. 36, 37; Ps. xlviii. 7,
&c. It is evident that *Tarshish* was
some distant land from which was imported silver, iron, lead, tin, &c. It is
now generally agreed that *Tartessus* in
Spain is referred to by the Tarshish of
Scripture. Bruce, however, supposes

17 And ^a the loftiness of man shall be bowed down, and the haughtiness of men shall be laid low: and the LORD alone shall be exalted in that day.

18 And the idols ¹ he shall utterly abolish.

19 And they shall go into the holes of the rocks, and into the

a ver. 11.   1 or, *shall utterly pass away.*

that it was in Africa, south of Abyssinia; see Note on ch. lx. 9. That it was in the *west* is evident from Gen. x. 4; comp. Ps. lxxxii. 10. In Ezek. xxviii. 13, it is mentioned as an important place of trade; in Jer. x. 9, it is said that silver was procured there; and in Ezek. xxviii. 12, it is said that iron, lead, silver, and tin, were imported from it. In 2 Chron. ix. 21, it is said that the ships of Tarshish returned every three years, bringing gold and silver, ivory, apes and peacocks. These are productions chiefly of India, but they might have been obtained in trade during the voyage. In Isa. xxiii. 1; lx. 9, the phrase, 'ships of Tarshish,' seems to denote ships that were bound on long voyages, and it is probable that they came to denote a particular kind of ships adapted to long voyages, in the same way as the word *Indiaman* does with us. The precise situation of *Tarshish* is not necessary to be known in order to understand the passage here. The phrase, 'ships of Tarshish,' denotes clearly ships employed in foreign trade, and in introducing articles of commerce, and particularly of luxury. The meaning is, that God would embarrass, and destroy this commerce; that his judgments would be on their articles of luxury. The LXX. render it, 'and upon every ship of the sea, and upon every beautiful appearance of ships.' The Targum, 'and upon those who dwell in the isles of the sea, and upon those who dwell in beautiful palaces.' ¶ *And upon all pleasant pictures.* Margin, 'pictures of desire;' that is, such as it should be esteemed desirable to possess, and gaze upon; pictures of value or beauty. Targum, 'costly palaces.' The word rendered 'pictures,' שְׂכִיּוֹת, denotes properly *sights*, or objects to be looked at; and does not designate *paintings* particularly, but every thing that was designed for ornament or luxury. Whether the art of painting was much known among the

Hebrews, it is not now possible to determine. To a certain extent, it may be presumed to have been practised; but the meaning of this place is, that the Divine judgment should rest on all that was designed for mere ornament and luxury; and, from the description in the previous verses, there can be no doubt that such ornaments would abound.

17. *And the loftiness*, &c.; see Note, ver. 11. The repetition of this makes it strongly emphatic.

18. *And the idols*; Note, ver. 8. ¶ *Abolish.* Heb. 'Cause to pass away or disappear.' He shall entirely cause their worship to cease. This prediction was most remarkably fulfilled. Before the captivity at Babylon, the Jews were exceedingly prone to idolatry. It is a remarkable fact that no such propensity was ever evinced *after* that. In their own land they were entirely free from it; and scattered as they have been into all lands, they have in every age since kept clear from idolatry. Not an instance, probably, has been known of their relapsing into this sin; and no temptation, or torture, has been sufficient to induce them to bow down and worship an idol. This is one of the few instances that have occurred where affliction and punishment have *completely* answered their design.

19. *And they shall go.* That is, the worshippers of idols. ¶ *Into the holes of the rocks.* Judea was a mountainous country, and the mountains abounded with caves that offered a safe retreat for those who were in danger. Many of those caverns were very spacious. At En-gedi, in particular, a cave is mentioned where David with six hundred men hid himself from Saul in the *sides* of it; 1 Sam. xxiv. Sometimes caves or dens were artificially constructed for refuge or defence in danger; Judg. vi. 2; 1 Sam. xiii. 6. Thus, 'because of the Midianites, the children of Israel made them the dens which are

caves of the [1] earth, for fear of the Lord, and for the glory of his majesty, when he ariseth to shake terribly [a] the earth.

20 In that day a man shall cast

[1] or, *dust.*   [a] Hag.2,6,21; He.12.26,27.

his idols of silver,[2] and his idols of gold, which they made [3] *each one* for himself to worship, to the moles and to the bats ;

[2] *the idols of his silver.*

[3] or, *for him.*

---

in the mountains, and caves, and strong holds.' Judg. vi. 2. To these they fled in times of hostile invasion. ' When the men of Israel saw that they were in a strait (for the people were distressed), then the people did hide themselves in caves, and in thickets, and in rocks, and in high places, and in pits;' 1 Sam. xiii. 6; comp. Jer. xli. 9. Mahomet speaks of a tribe of Arabians, the tribe of Thamud, who ' hewed houses out of the mountains to secure themselves;' Koran, ch. xv. and xxvi. Grots or rooms hewed out of rocks for various purposes are often mentioned by travellers in Oriental regions ; see Maundrell, p. 118, and Burckhardt's *Travels in Syria,* and particularly Laborde's *Journey to Arabia Petrea.* Such caves are often mentioned by Josephus as affording places of refuge for banditti and robbers ; *Ant.,* B. xiv. ch. 15, and *Jewish Wars,* B. i. ch. 16. To enter into the caves and dens, therefore, as places of refuge, was a very natural image to denote consternation. The meaning here is, that the worshippers of idols should be so alarmed as to seek for a place of security and refuge ; comp. ver. 10. ¶ *When he ariseth.* This is an expression often used in the Scriptures to denote the commencement of doing any thing. It is here derived, perhaps, from the image of one who has been in repose—as of a lion or warrior, rousing up suddenly, and putting forth mighty efforts. ¶ *To shake terribly the earth.* An image denoting the presence of God, for judgment or punishment. One of the magnificent images which the sacred writers often use to denote the presence of the Lord is, that the earth shakes and trembles; the mountains bow and are convulsed ; 2 Sam. xxii. 8 : ' Then the earth shook and trembled ; the foundations of heaven moved, because he was wroth ;' see also ver. 9–16; Judg. v. 4; Hab. iii. 6-10: ' The mountains saw thee and trembled;'

Heb. xii. 26: ' Whose voice then shook the earth.' The image here denotes that he would come forth in such wrath that the very earth should tremble, as if alarmed his presence. The mind cannot conceive more sublime images than are thus used by the sacred writers.

20. *In that day.* That is, in the time when God would come forth to inflict punishment. Probably the day to which the prophet refers here was the time of the captivity at Babylon. ¶ *A man shall cast,* &c. That is, *all* who have idols, or who have been trusting in them. Valuable as they may be—made of gold and silver ; and much as he may *now* rely on them or worship them, yet he shall then see their vanity, and shall cast them into dark, obscure places, or holes, where are moles and bats. ¶ *To the moles.* לַחְפֹּר פֵּרוֹת. Probably this should be read as a single word,' and it is usually interpreted *moles.* Jerome interprets it mice, or moles, from חָפַר *hhâphăr, to dig.* The word is formed by doubling the radical letters to give *intensity.* Similar instances of words being divided in the Hebrew, which are nevertheless to be read as one, occur in 2 Chron. xxiv. 6; Jer. xlvi. 20; Lam. iv. 3; Ezek. xxvii. 6. The mole is a well-known animal, with exceedingly small eyes, that burrows under ground, lives in the dark, and subsists on roots. The bat lives in old ruins, and behind the bark of trees, and flies only in the night. They *resemble* each other, and are used here in connection, because *both* dwell amidst ruins and in obscure places ; both are regarded as animals of the lowest order ; both are of the same genus, and both are almost blind. The sense is, therefore, that the idols which had before been so highly venerated, would now be despised, and cast into obscure places, and amidst ruins, as worthless ; see Bochart's *Hieroz.,* P. i., Lib. iii., p. 1032.

21 To go into the clefts of the rocks, and into the tops of the ragged rocks, for fear of the LORD, and for the glory of his majesty,

a Ps.146.3,4; Jer.17.5.

when he ariseth to shake terribly the earth.

22 Cease [a] ye from man, whose breath is in his nostrils; for wherein is he to be accounted of?

Ed. 1663. ¶ *And to the bats.* 'The East may be termed the country of bats; they hang by hundreds and thousands in caves, ruins, and under the roofs of large buildings. To enter such places, especially after rain, is *most* offensive. I have lived in rooms where it was sickening to remain, on account of the smell produced by those creatures, and whence it was almost impossible to expel them. What from the appearance of the creature, its sunken diminutive eye, its short legs (with which it cannot walk), its leather-like wings, its half-hairy, oily skin, its offensive ordure ever and anon dropping on the ground, its time for food and sport, darkness, makes it one of the most disgusting creatures to the people of the East.

GREAT TERNATE BAT (*Pteropus Edwardsii*).
From a Specimen in the British Museum.

No wonder, then, that its name is used by the Hindoos (as by the prophet) for an epithet of contempt. When a house ceases to please the inhabitants, on account of being haunted, they say, Give it to the *bats.* "Alas! alas! my wife and children are dead; my houses, my buildings, are all given to the bats." People ask, when passing a tenantless house, "Why is this habitation given to the bats?"'—*Roberts.* The meaning is, that the man would throw his idols into such places as the bats occupy —he would so see their vanity, and so

despise them, as to throw them into old ruins and dark places.

21. *To go.* That is, that he may go. ¶ *Clefts of the rocks;* see Note on ver. 19. ¶ *Into the tops,* &c. The tops of such rocks were not easily accessible, and were therefore deemed places of safety. We may remark here, how vain were the refuges to which they would resort—as if they were safe from *God,* when they had fled to the places in which they sought safety from *man.* The image here is, however, one that is very sublime. The earth shaking; the consternation and alarm of the people; their renouncing confidence in all to which they had trusted; their rapid flight; and their appearing on the high projecting cliffs, are all sublime and terrible images. They denote the severity of God's justice, and the image is a faint representation of the consternation of men when Christ shall come to judge the earth; Rev. vi. 15–17.

22. *Cease ye from man.* That is, cease to confide in or trust in him. The prophet had just said (ver. 11, 17) that the proud and lofty men would be brought low; that is, the kings, princes, and nobles would be humbled. They in whom the people had been accustomed to confide should show their insufficiency to afford protection. And he calls on the people to cease to put their reliance on any of the devices and refuges of men, implying that trust should be placed in the Lord only; see Ps. cxlvi. 3, 4; Jer. xvii. 5. ¶ *Whose breath is in his nostrils.* That is, who is weak and short-lived, and who has no control over his life. All his power exists only while he breathes, and his breath is in his nostrils. It may soon cease, and we should not confide in so frail and fragile a thing as the breath of man; see Ps. cxlvi. 3–5:

Put not your trust in princes,
Nor in the son of man, in whom there is no help.
His breath goeth forth, he returneth to his earth;
In that very day his thoughts perish.

CHAPTER III.

FOR, behold, the Lord, the LORD of hosts, doth take away *a* from Jerusalem, and from Judah, the stay and the *b* staff, the whole stay

a ch.36.12; Jer.38.9. *b* Lev.26.26.

of bread, and the whole stay of water.

2 The mighty *c* man, and the man of war, the judge, and the prophet, and the prudent, and the ancient.

c 2Ki.24.14.

Happy is he that hath the God of Jacob for his help,
Whose hope is in the Lord his God.

The Chaldee has translated this verse, 'Be not subject to man when he is terrible, whose breath is in his nostrils; because to-day he lives, and to-morrow he is not, and shall be reputed as nothing.' It is remarkable that this verse is omitted by the LXX., as Vitringa supposes, because it might seem to exhort people not to put confidence in their rulers. ¶ *For wherein,* &c. That is, he is unable to afford the assistance which is needed. When God shall come to judge men, what can *man* do, who is weak, and frail, and mortal? Refuge should be sought in God. The exhortation of the prophet here had respect to a particular time, but it may be applied in general to teach us not to confide in weak, frail, and dying man. For life and health, for food and raiment, for home and friends, and especially for salvation, we are dependent on God. He alone can save the sinner; and though we should treat men with all due respect, yet we should remember that God alone can save us from the great day of wrath.

CHAPTER III.

1. *For.* This is a continuation of the previous chapter. The same prophecy is continued, and the force of the argument of the prophet will not be seen unless the chapters are read together; see the Analysis prefixed to ch. ii. In the close of the second chapter (ver. 22), the prophet had cautioned his countrymen against confiding in man. In this chapter, a reason is given here why they should cease to do it—to wit, that God would soon take away their kings and princes. ¶ *The Lord.* הָאָדוֹן ; see Note on ch. i. 24. ¶ *The Lord of hosts;* see Note ch. i. 9. The prophet calls the attention of the Jews particularly to the fact that this was about to be done by JEHOVAH *of hosts*—a title which he gives

to God when he designs to indicate that that which is to be done implies peculiar strength, power, and majesty. As the work which was now to be done was the removal of the mighty men on which the nation was depending, it is implied that it was a work of power which belonged peculiarly to the God of armies— the Almighty. ¶ *Doth take away.* Is about to remove. In the Hebrew, the word here is a *participle,* and does not mark the precise time. It has reference here, however, to the future. ¶ *From Jerusalem,* &c., Note ch. i. 1. ¶ *The stay.* In the Hebrew, the words translated *stay* and *staff* are the same, with the exception that the former is in the masculine, and the latter in the feminine gender. The meaning is, that God would remove *all kinds of support,* or *every thing* on which they relied. The reference is undoubtedly to the princes and mighty men on whose counsels and aid the nation was resting for defence; see ver. 2, 3. ¶ *The whole stay of bread.* We use a similar expression when we say that *bread is the staff of life.* The Hebrews often expressed the same idea, representing the *heart* in man as being *supported* or *upheld* by bread, Gen. xviii. 5 (*margin*); Judg. xix. 5 (*margin*); Lev. xxvi. 26; Ps. cv. 16. ¶ *Stay of water.* He would reduce them from their luxuries introduced by commerce (ch. ii.) to absolute want. This often occurred in the sieges and wars of the nation; and in the famines which were the consequence of the wars. The reference here is probably to the invasion of the land by Nebuchadnezzar. The famine consequent on that invasion is described in Jer. xxxviii. 21; xxxviii. 9; Lam. iv. 4: 'The tongue of the sucking child cleaveth to the roof of his mouth for thirst; the young children ask bread, and no man breaketh it unto them."

2. *The mighty man.* The hero. The idea expressed is not simply that of

3 The captain of fifty, and the honourable [1] man, and the counsellor, and the cunning artificer, and the [2] eloquent orator.

4 And I will give children *a to be their princes,* and babes shall rule over them.

1 *a man eminent in countenance.*
2 *or, skilful of speech.*   *a* Eccl.10.16.

personal strength and prowess, but the higher one of military eminence or heroism.—*Prof. Alexander.* This was fully accomplished in the time of Nebuchadnezzar ; 2 Kings xxiv. 14. ¶ *And the prudent.* This word in the original —םסק—means properly *a diviner,* or a *soothsayer.* But it is sometimes used in a good sense ; see Prov. xvi. 10, *margin.* The Chaldee understands it of a man *who is consulted,* or whose opinion is asked, in times of perplexity or danger. The word was originally applied to false prophets, diviners, and soothsayers, who claimed the power of looking into futurity. It came, however, to denote also the man of sagacity, the statesman, the experienced counsellor, who from the records of the past could judge of the future, and to whom, therefore, the nation could look in times of perplexity and danger. Vitringa supposes that it may refer here to the false prophets on whose advice the nation might be relying. ¶ *The ancient.* The old man. Such men, especially among the Hebrews, were deemed particularly qualified to give advice. They had experience ; they kept the traditions of their fathers ; they had conversed with the wise of the preceding generation ; and in a land where there were few books, and knowledge was to be gained mainly by conversation and experience, great respect was shown them ; see Lev. xix. 32; 2 Chron. xxxi. 17; 1 Kings xii. 6, 8.

3. *The captain of fifty.* By this was probably denoted an officer in the army. The idea is, that the commanders of the various divisions of the army should be taken away. ¶ *The honourable man.* Heb. פנים נשׂוא *nĕsū pânim.* The *man of elevated countenance.* That is, the man high in office. He was so called from the aspect of dignity which a man in office would assume. In the previous chapter, the phrase is used to denote rather the *pride* which attended such officers, than the dignity of the office itself. ¶ *And the counsellor;* Note,

ch. i. 26. ¶ *The cunning artificer.* Heb. The man wise in mechanic arts ; skilled in architecture, &c. ¶ *And the eloquent orator.* לחשׁ נבון *nĕbhōn lāhhăsh.* Literally, skilled or learned in whispering, in conjuration, in persuasion. The word לחשׁ *lāhhăsh* denotes properly a whispering, sighing, or calling for help ; (Isa. xxvi. 16, 'they have poured out a prayer,' לחשׁ—a secret speech, a feeble sigh for aid.) It is applied to the charm of the serpent—the secret breathing or gentle noise by which the charm is supposed to be effected ; Ps. lviii. 6; Jer. viii. 17; Eccl. x. 11. In ver. 20 of this chapter it denotes a charm or amulet worn by females ; see Note on that verse. It is also applied to magic, or conjuration—because this was usually done by gentle whispering, or incantation ; see Note, ch. viii. 19. From this use of the word, it comes to denote one that influences another ; one who persuades him in any way, as an orator does by argument and entreaty. Ancient orators also probably sometimes used a species of recitative, or measured cadence, not unlike that employed by those who practised incantations. Jerome says that it means here, ' a man who is learned, and acquainted with the law, and the prophets.' Chaldee, ' The prudent in council.' It *may be* used in a good sense here ; but if so, it is probably the only place where the word is so used in the Old Testament. A prophecy similar to this occurs in Hos. iii. 4: ' For the children of Israel shall abide many days without a king, and without a prince, and without a sacrifice, and without an image, and without an ephod, and without teraphim.'

4. *And I will give children.* Not children in respect to age so much as in regard to talent for governing. I will commit the land to the government of weak and imbecile princes. This would naturally occur when the wise and great were removed ; comp. Eccl. x. 16: ' Wo to thee, O land, when thy king is a

5 And the people shall be oppressed, every one by another, and every one by his neighbour : the child shall behave himself proudly against the ancient, and the base against the honourable.

6 When a man shall take hold of his brother, of the house of his father, *saying*, Thou hast clothing, be thou our ruler, and *let* this ruin *be* under thy hand :

---

child ;' comp. Isa. iii. 12. ¶ *And babes shall rule,* &c. That is, babes in experience and knowledge. This was fully accomplished in the succession of weak and wicked princes that succeeded Isaiah, until the time of Zedekiah, the last of them, when the temple was taken by Nebuchadnezzar.—*Lowth.*

5. *And the people shall be oppressed.* This describes the state of anarchy and confusion which would exist under the reign of children and babes (ver. 4), when all law would be powerless, and all rights violated, and when the feeble would be oppressed and borne down by the strong. The word used here, properly denotes that *unjust exactions or demands* would be made, or that the people would be *urged* to fulfil them. ¶ *Every one by another.* In turn they shall oppress and vex one another. Heb. ' man by man ; and man by his neighbour'—a strong mode of expression, denoting that there would be a state of mutual strife, and violation of rights ; comp. 1 Kings xx. 20. ¶ *The child,* &c. All ranks of society shall be broken up. All respect due from one rank in life to another shall be violated. ¶ *Shall behave himself proudly.* The word here used means rather to *urge,* or *press on.* The child shall *crowd on* the old man. This was particularly descriptive of a state of anarchy and disorder, from the fact that the Jews inculcated so much respect and deference for age ; see Note on ver. 2. ¶ *The ancient.* The old man. ¶ *And the base.* The man of low rank in life. The word properly means the man that is despised, the vile, the ignoble ; 1 Sam. xviii. 23 ; Prov. xii. 9. ¶ *The honourable.* All the forms of respect in life would be broken up ; all the proper rules of deference between man and man would be violated. Neither dignity, age, nor honour would be respected.

6. *When a man shall take hold,* &c. In this verse, and the following verses, the prophet continues to describe the calamitous and ruined state that would come upon the Jews ; when there would be such a want of wealth and men, that they would seize upon any one that they thought able to defend them. The act of *taking hold* here denotes *supplication* and *entreaty,* as when one in danger or distress clings to that which is near, or which may be likely to aid him ; comp. ch. iv. 1 ; 1 Sam. xv. 27. ¶ *His brother.* His kinsman, or one of the same tribe and family—claiming protection because they belonged to the same family. ¶ *Of the house of his father.* Descended from the same paternal ancestors as himself. Probably this refers to one of an ancient and opulent family—a man who had kept himself from the civil broils and tumults of the nation, and who had retained his property safe in the midst of the surrounding desolation. In the previous verse, the prophet had said that one characteristic of the times would be a want of respect for *the aged* and *the honourable.* He here says that such would be. the distress, that a man would be *compelled* to show respect to rank ; he would look to the ancient and wealthy families for protection. ¶ *Thou hast clothing.* In ancient times wealth consisted very much in changes of garments ; and the expression ' thou hast clothing,' is the same as ' you are *rich,* you are able to assist us ;' see Ex. xii. 34 ; xx. 26 ; Gen. xlv. 22 ; 2 Kings v. 5. ¶ *And let this ruin,* &c. This is an expression of entreaty. ' Give us assistance, or defence. We commit our ruined and dilapidated affairs to thee, and implore thy help.' The LXX. read this, ' and let my food,' *i.e.,* my support, ' be under thee '—do thou furnish me food. There are some other unimportant variations in the ancient versions, but the sense is substantially given in our translation. It is expressive of great distress and anarchy—when there would be no ruler, and every man would seek one for himself. The whole deportment evinced

7 In that day shall he ¹swear, saying, I will not be an ²healer; for in my house *is* neither bread nor clothing: make me not a ruler of the people.

8 For Jerusalem is ruined, *a* And

1 *lift up the* hand, Ge.14.22.　2 *binder up.*　a Mic.3.12.

Judah is fallen; because *b* their tongue and their doings *are* against the LORD, to provoke the *c* eyes of his glory.

9 The show of their *d* countenance doth witness against them, and they

b Lam.5.16,17.　c 1Cor.10.22.　d Jer.3.3.

here by the suppliant is one of submission, distress, and humility.

7. *In that day shall he swear.* Hebrew, יִשָּׂא 'Shall he lift up'—*i.e.*, the voice, or the hand. To lift up the hand was one of the modes of taking an oath. Perhaps it means only that he should lift up *the voice*—*i.e.*, should *answer;* comp. Num. xiv. 1. The Vulgate, the LXX., and the Chaldee, read it simply 'he shall *answer.*' ¶ *I will not be an healer.* Heb. '*a binder up*,' ch. i. 6. The Vulgate renders it, 'I am not a physician.' The LXX. and the Chaldee, 'I am not sufficient to be a leader.' The meaning is, that the state of affairs was so ruinous and calamitous that he would not attempt to restore them; as if, in the body, disease should have so far progressed that he would not undertake to restore the person, and have him *die* under his hands, so as to expose himself to the reproach of being an unsuccessful and unskilful physician. ¶ *Is neither bread nor clothing.* I am not rich. I have not the means of providing for the wants of the people, or to maintain the rank of a ruler. 'It is customary,' says Sir John Chardin, 'to gather together an immense quantity of clothes, for their fashions never alter.' 'The kings of Persia have great wardrobes, where they have always many hundreds of habits ready, designed for presents, and sorted.'—*Lowth.* The description here is one of very great calamity and anarchy. So great would be the ruin and danger, that men would be unwilling to be chosen to the office of princes and rulers, and none could be found who would desire to possess the highest honours of the nation. Generally men *aspire* to office; here they were unwilling, on account of the disordered and ruined state of affairs, even to accept of it.

8. *For Jerusalem, &c.* The prophet proceeds to show the cause of this state

of things. 'These are the words of the *prophet,* and not of him who was chosen leader.'—*Jerome.* ¶ *Is ruined.* It would be so ruined, and the prospect of preserving it would be so completely taken away, that no one could be induced to undertake to defend and protect it. ¶ *Judah.* The kingdom of Judah, of which Jerusalem was the capital ; Note ch. i. 1. ¶ *Is fallen.* Heb. *falls; i.e.*, is about to fall—as a tower or a tree falls to ruin. If the *capital* fell and was ruined, the kingdom would also fall as a matter of course. ¶ *Because their tongue,* &c. This is the *reason* why Judah was ruined. By word and deed —that is, in every way they opposed God. The *tongue* here represents their *language,* their manner of speaking. It was proud, haughty, rebellious, perhaps blasphemous. ¶ *To provoke.* To irritate ; to offend. ¶ *The eyes of his glory.* This is a Hebrew expression to denote *his glorious eyes.* The eye quickly expresses anger or indignation. We perceive these passions in the flashing of the eye sooner than in any other part of the countenance. Hence, to *provoke the eyes,* is an expression signifying simply to excite to anger, or to excite him to punish them. Lowth proposes to render this 'to provoke the *cloud* of his glory'—referring to the Shekinah or cloud that rested over the ark in the temple. By a slight variation of the Hebrew text, reading עֲנַן instead of עֵנֵי, it may be so read, and the Syriac so translates it ; but the change in the Hebrew text does not seem to be authorized.

9. *The show of their countenance.* The word rendered *the show* is probably derived from a word signifying *to know,* or *to recognise,* and here denotes *impudence* or *pride.* LXX., 'The *shame* of their face.' ¶ *Doth witness against them.* *Answers* to them ; or *responds* to them (עָנְתָה). There is a correspondence between the feelings of

declare their sin as Sodom, they hide *it* not. Wo unto their soul! for they have rewarded evil unto themselves.

10 Say ye to the righteous, that *it shall be* well *with him:*[a] for they shall eat the fruit of their doings.

11 Wo unto the wicked! *it shall*

be ill *with him:* for the reward of his hands shall be [1] given him.

12 *As for* my people, children *are* their oppressors, and women rule over them. O my people, they which [2] lead thee cause *thee* to err, and [3] destroy the way of thy paths.

a Eccl. 8. 12, 13.   1 *done to.*   2 or, *call thee blessed.*   3 *swallow up.*

---

the heart and the looks, an *answering* of the countenance to the purposes of the soul that shows their true character, and betrays their plans. The prophet refers here to the great law in physiology that the emotions of the heart will be usually *expressed* in the countenance ; and that by the marks of pride, vanity, and malice there depicted, we may judge of the heart ; or as it is expressed in our translation, that the expression of the face will *witness* against a wicked man. ¶ *They declare,* &c. By their deeds. Their crimes are open and bold. There is no attempt at concealment. ¶ *As Sodom*; see Gen. xix. 5; comp. Note, Isa. i. 10. ¶ *Wo unto their soul.* They shall bring woe upon themselves ; they deserve punishment. This is an expression denoting the highest abhorrence of their crimes. ¶ *They have rewarded evil*, &c. They have brought the punishment upon themselves by their own sins.

10. *Say ye to the righteous.* The meaning of this verse and the following is sufficiently plain, though expositors have given some variety of interpretation. They declare a great principle of the Divine administration similar to what is stated in ch. i. 19, 20. Lowth reads it, 'Pronounce ye a blessing on the just ; verily good (shall be to him).' ¶ *That* it shall be *well*, &c. The word rendered 'well,' means 'good.' The sense evidently is, that in the Divine administration it shall be well to be righteous. The LXX. have rendered this in a remarkable manner, connecting it with the previous verse : ' Wo unto their soul, for they take evil counsel among themselves, saying, *Let us bind the righteous, for he is troublesome unto us;* therefore they shall eat the fruit of their doings.' ¶ *They shall eat,* &c. That is, they shall receive the appro-

priate *reward* of their works, and that reward shall be happiness. As a husbandman who sows his field and cultivates his farm, eats the fruit of his labour, so shall it be with the righteous. A similar expression is found in Prov. i. 31 :

Therefore shall they eat of the fruit of their own way,
And be filled with their own devices.

Also Jer. vi. 19: ' I will bring evil upon this people, *even* the fruit of their thoughts;' comp. Gal. vi. 8.

11. *Wo unto the wicked.* To all the wicked—but here having particular reference to the Jews whom Isaiah was addressing. ¶ It shall be *ill* with him. The word *ill* is the only word here in the original. It is an emphatic mode of speaking—expressing deep abhorrence and suddenness of denunciation. ' Woe to the impious ! Ill !' ¶ *For the reward of his hands.* Of his conduct. The hands are the instruments by which we accomplish any thing, and hence they are put for the whole man. ¶ *Shall be given him.* That is, shall be repaid to him ; or he shall be justly recompensed for his crimes. This is the principle on which God rules the world. It shall be well here and hereafter, with those who obey God ; it shall be ill here and for ever, with those who disobey him.

12. As for *my people, children* are *their oppressors.* This refers, doubtless, to their civil rulers. They who *ought* to have been their *protectors,* oppressed them by grievous taxes and burdens. But whether this means that the rulers of the people were *literally* minors, or that they were so in *disposition* and *character,* has been a question. The original word is in the singular number (מְעוֹלֵל), and means a *child,* or an infant. It may, however, be taken collectively

13 The LORD standeth up to plead,[a] and standeth to judge the people.

14 The LORD will enter into judgment with the ancients of his people, and the princes thereof: for ye have eaten[1] up the [b] vineyard;

the spoil of the poor *is* in your houses.

15 What mean ye *that* ye beat my people to pieces,[c] and grind the faces of the poor? saith the LORD GOD of hosts.

16 Moreover, the LORD saith,

a Mic.6.2.   1 or, *burnt.*   *b* Mat.21,33.   *c* ch.58,4.

---

as a noun of multitude, or as denoting more than one. To whom reference is made here cannot easily be determined, but possibly to *Ahaz*, who began to reign when he was twenty years old; 2 Kings xvi. 2. Or it may mean that the *character* of the princes and rulers was that of inexperienced children, unqualified for government. ¶ *Are their oppressors.* Literally, 'are their *exactors*,' or their *taxers*—the collectors of the revenue. ¶ *And women rule over them.* This is not to be taken literally, but it means either that the rulers were under the influence of the *harem*, or the females of the court; or that they were effeminate and destitute of vigour and manliness in counsel. The LXX. and the Chaldee render this verse substantially alike: ' Thy exactors strip my people as they who gather the grapes strip the vineyard. ¶ *They which lead thee.* Heb. *They who bless thee, or call thee blessed.* (See margin.) This refers, doubtless, to the public teachers, and the false prophets, who *blessed* or flattered the people, and who promised them safety in their sins. ¶ *Cause* thee *to err.* Lead you astray; or lead you into sin and danger. ¶ *And destroy.* Heb. *Swallow up.*

13. *The Lord standeth up.* To *stand up* may mean the same as to *arise.* God would not sit in silence and see their wicked conduct; but he would come forth to inflict on them exemplary and deserved chastisement. ¶ *To plead.* To *litigate,* to contend with, *i.e.,* to condemn, to inflict punishment.

14. *With the ancients,* &c. With the old men, the counsellors. ¶ *Ye have eaten up the vineyard.* Heb. ' Ye have *burnt up* '—that is, you have consumed or destroyed it. By the vineyard is represented the Jewish republic or people; Ps. lxxx. 9–13; comp.

Notes, Isa. v. 1–7. The princes and rulers had, by their exactions and oppressions, ruined the people, and destroyed the country. ¶ *The spoil of the poor.* The *plunder* of the poor; or that which you have taken from the poor by exactions and oppressions. The word *spoil* commonly means the plunder or booty which is obtained in war.

15. *What mean ye.* What is your object? Or, What advantage is it to you? Or, By what right or pretence do you do this? ¶ *Beat my people to pieces.* That is, that you trample on them; or cruelly oppress them; Ps. xciv. 5. ¶ *And grind the faces of the poor.* This is an expression also denoting great oppression. It is taken from the act of grinding a substance on a stone until it is worn away and nothing is left. So, by their cruel exactions, by their injustice to the poor, they exhausted their little property until nothing was left. The word *faces* here is synonymous with *persons*—or with the poor themselves. The word *face* is often used in the sense of *person;* Ex. xxxiii. 14; 2 Sam. xviii. 11. A similar description, though in still stronger language, is found in Micah iii. 2, 3:

Who pluck off their skin from off them,
And their flesh from off their bones;
Who also eat the flesh of my people,
And flay their skin from off them;
And they break their bones, and chop them in pieces,
As for the pot, and as flesh within the caldron.

16. *Moreover, the Lord saith.* In the previous parts of this prophecy, the prophet had rebuked the princes, magistrates, and the people generally. In the remainder of this chapter, he reproves with great severity the pride, luxury, and effeminacy of the female part of the Jewish community. Some interpreters have understood this as designed to reprove the the pride and luxury of the *cities* and

Because the daughters of Zion are naughty, and walk with stretched-forth necks, and [1] wanton eyes, walking and [2] mincing *as they go*, and making a tinkling with their feet.

[1] *deceiving with their eyes.*

[2] *tripping nicely.*

He teacheth with his fingers;
Frowardness is in his heart,
He deviseth mischief continually.

towns of Judah, regarded as *daughters of Zion;* see Note, ch. i. 8. But this interpretation is far-fetched and absurd. On this principle every thing in the Bible might be turned into allegory. ¶ *The daughters of Zion.* Jewish females; they who dwelt in Zion. Perhaps he means particularly those who dwelt in *Zion*, the capital—or the females connected with the court. It is probable that the prophet here refers to the prosperous reign of Uzziah (2 Chron. xxvi. 5, &c.), when by successful commerce luxury would naturally abound. ¶ *Are haughty.* Are proud. ¶ *And walk with stretched-forth necks.* Displaying the neck ostentatiously ; elevating or extending it as far as possible. Septuagint, ὑψηλῷ τραχήλῳ, with elevated or exalted neck ; *i.e.*, with that indication of pride and haughtiness which is evinced by a lofty demeanour. ' When the females dance [in India], they stretch forth their necks, and hold them away, as if their heads were about to fall from their shoulders.'—*Roberts.* ¶ *And wanton eyes.* וּמְשַׁקְּרוֹת עֵינָיִם. The word שָׁקַר *shâqăr* usually means *to lie, to deceive*, and may here refer to the art of alluring by a wanton or fascinating glance of the eye. There has been great diversity of opinion about the meaning of this expression. Lowth proposes to read it, ' and falsely setting off their eyes with paint,' in allusion to a custom known to prevail in the East, of colouring the eye-lids with stibium, or the powder of lead ore. This was done the better to exhibit the white of the eye, and was supposed by many to contribute to the healthful action of the eye itself. This practice is known to prevail extensively now ; but it is not clear that the prophet here has reference to it. The expression is usually interpreted to mean ' *deceiving with the eyes*,' that is, *alluring* or *enticing* by the *motion* of the eyes. The *motion* of the eyes is mentioned (Prov. vi. 13, 14) as one mode of *deceiving* a person :

He winketh with his eyes,
He speaketh with his feet,

Comp. Notes on Job xlii. 14. The meaning here, doubtless, is, that they attempted to entice by the *motion* or *glance* of the eye. The Chaldee seems to have understood this of staining the eyes with stibium. ¶ *Mincing* as *they go.* Margin, 'Tripping nicely ;' that is, walking with an affected gait—a mode which, unhappily, is too well known in all ages to need a more particular description. Roberts, speaking of the dance in India, says, ' Some parts of the dance consist of a tripping or mincing step, which they call *tatte-tattee.* The left foot is put first, and the inside of the right keeps following the heel of the former.' ¶ *And making a tinkling with their feet.* That is, they adorn themselves with *ankle rings*, and make a tinkling or noise with them to attract attention. The custom of wearing rings on the fingers and wrists has been common every where. In addition to this, Oriental females often wore them on the *ankles*—a custom in

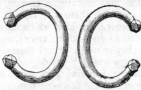

ANKLETS, one-sixth the real size.
From Lane's Egyptians.

itself not more unreasonable or absurd. The custom is mentioned by travellers in Eastern countries in more modern times. Thus, Michaelis says, ' In Syria and the neighbouring provinces, the more opulent females bind ligaments around their feet, like chains, or bracelets, united by small chains of silver and gold, and exhibit them by their sound as they walk.' And Pliny (*Nat. Hist.*, lib. xxiii., ch. 12) says, ' Silver has succeeded to gold in the luxury of the females who form bracelets for their feet of that, since an ancient custom forbids

17 Therefore the LORD will smite with a scab the crown of the head of the daughters of Zion, and the LORD will discover [1] their secret parts.

1 *make naked.*

18 In that day the LORD will take away the bravery of *their* tinkling ornaments *about their feet*, and *their* [2] cauls, and *their* round tires like the moon,

2 or, *net-works.*

them to wear gold.' Frequent mention is made of these ornaments, says Rosenmüller, in the Arabic and Persian poems. Roberts, speaking of the ornaments on the feet of females in India, says, ' The first is a large silver curb like that which is attached to a bridle ; the second is of the same kind, but surrounded by a great number of small BELLS ; the third resembles a bracelet ; and the fourth is a convex hoop, about two inches deep.'

17. *Therefore the Lord will smite with a scab.* There is some diversity of rendering to this expression. The LXX. read it, ' The Lord will humble the principal daughters of Zion '—those who belong to the court, or to the families of the princes. The Chaldee, ' The Lord will prostrate the glory of the daughters of Zion.' The Syriac is the same. The Hebrew word שִׂפַּח *sippăhh,* translated ' will smite with a scab,' means to *make bald,* particularly to make the hair fall off by sickness. Our translation conveys the idea essentially, that is, that God would visit them with disease that would remove the hair which they regarded as so great an ornament, and on which they so much prided themselves. Few things would be so degrading and humiliating as being thus made bald. The description in this verse means, that God would humble and punish them ; that they who so adorned themselves, and who were so proud of their ornaments, would be divested of their gay attire, and be borne naked into captivity in a foreign land.

18. *In that day.* That is, in the time when he would inflict this exemplary punishment on them—probably the calamitous times of the Babylonish captivity. ¶ *The Lord will take away.* By the agents that he shall choose to employ in this work.—The prophet proceeds to specify the various ornaments that composed the female apparel in his time. It is not easy to describe

them particularly, nor is it necessary. The *general* meaning of the passage is plain : and it is clear from this, that they greatly abounded in ornaments. ¶ *The bravery.* This word *we* apply to valour or courage. The word here used, however, means *ornament, adorning,* or *glory.* ¶ *Of* their *tinkling ornaments.* This is the same word which is used in ver. 16, and refers to the chains or clasps with which they ornamented their feet and ankles, and which made a tinkling noise as they walked. ¶ *And* their *cauls.* Margin, ' *net-works.*' The LXX. is the same. It is commonly supposed to mean *caps of net-work* worn on the head. According to others, the word refers to small *suns* or *spangles* worn on the hair, answering to the following word *moons.* ' The caul is a strap, or girdle, about four inches long, which is placed on the top of the head, and which extends to the brow, in a line with the nose. The one I have examined is made of gold, and has many joints ; it contains forty-five rubies, and nine pearls, which give it a net-work appearance.'—*Roberts.* ¶ Their *round tires like the moon.* Heb. *moons.* This refers to small ornaments in the shape of crescents, or half-moons, commonly worn on the neck. They were also sometimes worn by men, and even by camels ; Judg. viii. 21 (margin), 26. It is probable that these ornaments might originally have had some reference to the moon as an object of worship, but it does not appear that they were so worn by the females of Judea.—They are still worn by the females of Arabia. —*Rosenmüller.* Roberts says of such ornaments in India, ' The crescent is worn by Parvati and Siva, from whom proceed the LINGAM, and the principal impurities of the system. No dancing girl is in full dress without her round tires like the moon.' This ornament is still found in the form which the annexed engraving exhibits—under the

19 The ¹ chains, and the brace- | lets, and the ² mufflers,

1 or, *sweet balls.*   2 or, *spangled ornaments.*

---

name of *chumarah.* 'The *chumarah,* | ment worn by the women of western
which signifies moon, is a splendid orna- | Asia in front of their head-dresses. It

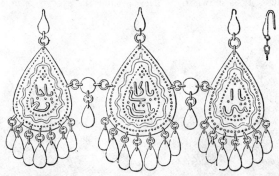

THE CHUMARAH, one-half the real size.—From Lane's Egyptians.

is usually made of gold, set with precious stones and pearls. They are sometimes made of the crescent form, but the most common are such as the engraving represents. They often have Arabic characters inscribed upon them, and sometimes a sentence from the Koran is used by the Mahometan women of Arabia Felix.'

19. *The chains.* Margin, *sweet balls.* The word used here is derived from the verb נָטַף *nâtăph, to drop, to fall in drops,* or *to distil,* as juice from a plant. Hence it means that which *resembles drops*—as pearls, or precious stones, used as ornaments for the neck or ears. We retain a similar word as applicable to the ornaments of the ears, by calling them *drops.* The Chaldee renders this *chains,* and so also the Vulgate. The LXX. understand it of a *hanging* or *pendant* ornament—and this is its undoubted meaning—an ornament pendant like gum distilling from a plant. 'These consist, first, of one most beautifully worked, with a pendant ornament for the neck; there is also a profusion of others which go round the same part, and rest on the bosom. In making curious chains, the goldsmiths of England do not surpass those of the East.'— *Roberts.* ¶ *And the bracelets.* For the wrists. The Chaldee translates it, ' bracelets for the hands.' These ornaments were very ancient ; see Gen. xxiv.

22; Num. xxi. 50.—Mahomet promises to those who shall follow him, gold and silver bracelets. 'The bracelets are large ornaments for the wrists, in which are sometimes inclosed small BELLS.'—

ANCIENT BRACELETS, half the real size.

Roberts. ¶ *Mufflers.* Margin, *spangled ornaments.* The word used here is derived from a verb, *to tremble, to shake*— רָעַל *ra'ăl*—and the name is given to the ornament, whatever it was, probably from its *tremulous* motion. Perhaps it means *a light, thin veil;* or possibly, as in the margin, spangled ornaments, producing a tremulous, changing aspect. In Zech. xii. 2, the word is used to denote ' trembling '— giddiness, or intoxication. It was early customary, and is still common in Oriental countries, for the females to wear veils. No female ventures abroad without her veil. That which is supposed to be intended here, is described

20 The bonnets, and the ornaments of the legs, and the head-
bands, and the ¹ tablets, and the
ear-rings,

1 *houses of the soul.*

by the Arabian scholiast Safieri, quoted
by Gesenius. It is drawn tight over
the upper part of the head, but the part
around the eyes is open, and a space

FACE-VEILS AND WALKING-WRAPPERS OF MODERN EGYPTIAN WOMEN.
From Description de l'Egypte.

left to see through, and the lower part
is left loose and flowing, and thus produces the *tremulous* appearance indicated in this place; see the Notes and
illustrations on ver. 24.

20. *The bonnets.* The *tiara, head-
dress,* or *turban.* The word comes
from the verb *to adorn.* The *turban*
is almost universally worn in the East.
It was worn by the priests, Ex. xxxix.
28; by the bridegroom, Isa. lxi. 10;
Ezek. xxiv. 17; and by women. Its
form is well known. ¶ *And the ornaments for the legs.* The word used
here is derived from a verb signifying
to walk, to go, particularly to walk in a
stately and formal manner—with a
measured step, הַצְּעָדוֹת, from צָעַד;
and thus refers to a proud and lofty
gait. The *ornament* which is here
referred to is supposed to have been a
short chain extending from one foot to
the other, worn by the Eastern women
to give them a measured and stately
gait.—*Gesenius.* This *chain* is supposed to have been attached by hooks
or clasps to the 'tinkling ornaments'
mentioned in ver. 16. Safieri mentions
these ornaments, and thus describes
them : ' The word denotes a small chain,
with which females, when they walk,
connect their feet, in order to make
their steps equal.' Happily these ornaments are unknown in modern times, at
least in Western countries. They are
still retained in the East. ¶ *And the
head-bands.* This word means *girdles*
of any kind, still commonly worn on the
head. The following cut will illustrate
one of the usual forms of the head-
band. ¶ *And the tablets.* The Hebrew
is, as in the margin, '*the houses of the
soul.*' The word translated *soul* means
also the *breath;* and hence, as one of its
meanings, that which is *breathed,* or
which is smelled ; *scent, fragrancy,*

odour. The word *houses* here may denote also *boxes*—as boxes of perfumes. The phrase here means, undoubtedly, *smelling boxes* or *bottles,* containing perfumes or fragrant odours. The word *tablets* has no meaning here. ¶ *And the ear-rings.* It is by no means certain that the original means *ear-rings*

THE KUSSAH OR HEAD-BAND.—From Lane's Modern Egyptians.

The word לְחָשִׁים is derived from the verb לָחַשׁ signifying *to whisper,* and then *to conjure, to charm* (see Note on ver. 3); and here probably denotes precious stones worn by the females as *amulets* or *charms.* The word is often used to denote charming *serpents*—from their *hissing*—and it has been supposed probable that these amulets were small images of serpents. There is no doubt that such ornaments were worn by Oriental females. 'These ornaments seem to have been *amulets,* often gems and precious stones, or plates of gold and silver, on which certain magic formulas were inscribed, which were worn suspended from the neck or ears by Oriental females.'—*Gesenius.*

ORNAMENTED HEAD-DRESS.
From an Egyptian Sculpture.

The following extract will furnish an explanation of these ornaments:—' Besides ornamental rings in the nose and the ears, they [Oriental females] wore others round the legs, which made a tinkling as they went. This custom has also descended to the present times; for Rauwolf met with a number of Arabian women on the Euphrates, whose ankles and wrists were adorned with rings, sometimes a good many together, which, moving up and down as they walked, made a great noise. Chardin attests the existence of the same custom in Persia, in Arabia, and in very hot countries, where they commonly go without stockings, but ascribes the tinkling sound to little bells fastened to those rings. In the East Indies, golden bells adorned the feet and ankles of the ladies from the earliest times; they placed them in the flowing tresses of their hair; they suspended them round their necks, and to the golden rings which they wore on their fingers, to announce their superior rank, and extort the homage which they had a right to expect from the lower orders; and from the banks of the Indus, it is probable the custom was introduced into the other countries of Asia. The Arabian females in Palestine and Syria delight in the same ornaments, and, according to the statements of Dr. Clarke, seem to claim the honour of leading the fashion.'—' Their bodies are covered with a long blue tunic; upon their heads they wear two handkerchiefs, one as a hood, and the other bound over it, as a fillet across the temples. Just above the right nostril, they place a small button, sometimes studded with pearl, a piece of glass, or any other glittering substance; this is fastened by a plug, thrust through the cartilage of the nose. Sometimes they have the cartilaginous separation between the nostrils bored for a ring, as large as those ordinarily used in Europe for hanging curtains; and this pendant in the upper lip covers the mouth; so that, in order to eat, it

21 The rings, and nose-jewels,
22 The changeable suits of apparel, and the mantles, and the wimples, and the crisping-pins,

is necessary to raise it. Their faces, hands, and arms are tatooed, and covered with hideous scars; their eyelashes and eyes being always painted, or rather dirtied, with some dingy black or blue powder. Their lips are dyed of a deep and dusky blue, as if they had been eating blackberries. Their teeth are jet black; their nails and fingers brick red; their wrists, as well as their ankles, are laden with large metal cinctures, studded with sharp pyramidical knobs and bits of glass. Very ponderous rings are also placed in their ears.'—*Paxton.*

21. *The rings.* Usually worn on the fingers. ¶ *And nose-jewels.* The custom of wearing jewels in the *nose* has generally prevailed in savage tribes, and was common, and is still, in Eastern nations—among the Arabians, Persians, &c. Sir John Chardin says, ‘It is the custom in almost all the East for the women to wear rings in their noses, in the left nostril, which is bored low down in the middle. These rings are of gold, and have commonly two pearls and one ruby between, placed in the ring. I never saw a girl or young woman in Arabia, or in all Persia, who did not wear a ring in this manner in her nostrils.'—Harmer's *Obs.*, iv., p. 318. The annexed cut will illustrate the usual form of this ornament in the East.

22. The articles which are mentioned

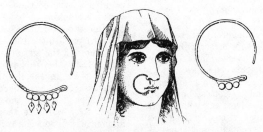

THE KHIZAM OR NOSE-JEWEL OF MODERN EGYPT, one-third the real size.
From Lane's Egyptians.

in the remaining part of this description, are entire articles of apparel; those which had preceded were chiefly single ornaments. ¶ *The changeable suits of apparel.* The word which is used here in the original comes from a verb signifying *to pull of* as a shoe; to unclothe one's-self; and it here denotes the more *costly* or *valuable* garments, which are not worn on common occasions, and which are *laid aside* in ordinary employments. This does not refer to any *particular* article of dress, but to splendid and costly articles in general. ‘The Eastern ladies take great pride in having many changes of apparel, because their fashions NEVER alter. Thus the net brocades worn by their grandmothers are equally fashionable for themselves.' —*Roberts.* ¶ *And the mantles.* From the verb *to cover,* or *to clothe.* The word *mantle* does not quite express the force of the original. It means the fuller *tunic* which was worn over the common one, with sleeves, and which reached down to the feet. ‘A loose robe,' says Roberts, ‘which is gracefully crossed on the bosom.' ¶ *And the wimples.* Our word *wimple* means a *hood,* or *veil,* but this is not the meaning of the Hebrew word in this place. It means a wide, broad garment, which could be thrown over the whole, and in which the individual usually slept. ‘Probably the fine muslin which is sometimes thrown over the head and body.'—*Roberts.* ¶ *And the crisping-pins.* This phrase with us would denote *curling-irons.* But the Hebrew here denotes a very different article. It means *money-bags,* or *purses.* These were often made very large, and were highly ornamented; comp. 2 Kings v. 23. Frequently they were attached to the girdle.

23 The glasses, and the fine linen, | and the hoods, and the veils.

23. *The glasses.* These is a great variety of opinion about the expression used here. That the ancient Jews had *looking-glasses*, or *mirrors*, is manifest from the account in Ex. xxxviii. 8. These *mirrors* were made of polished plates of brass. The Vulgate and Chaldee understand this of *mirrors*. The LXX. understand by it a *thin, transparent covering like gauze*, perhaps like silk. The word is derived from the verb *to reveal, to make apparent*, &c., and applies either to mirrors or to a splendid shining garment. It is probable that their excessive vanity was evinced by carrying small mirrors in their hands— that they might examine and adjust their dress as might be necessary. This is now done by females of Eastern nations. Shaw informs us that, ' In the Levant, looking-glasses are a part of female dress. The Moorish women in Barbary are so fond of their ornaments, and particularly of their looking-glasses, which they hang upon their breasts, that they will not lay them aside, even when, after the drudgery of the day, they are obliged to go two or three miles with a pitcher or a goat-skin to fetch water.' —*Burder.* In Egypt, the mirror was made of mixed metal, chiefly of copper, and this metal was so highly polished, that in some of the mirrors discovered at Thebes, the lustre has been partially restored, though they have been buried in the earth for many centuries. The mirror was nearly round, inserted in a handle of wood, stone, or metal, whose form varied according to the taste of the owner. The following cut will give an idea of the ancient form of the mirror, and will show that they might be easily

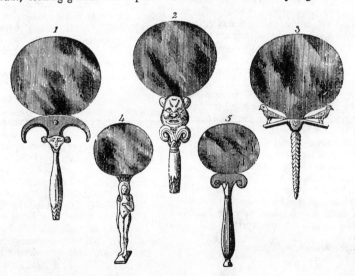

ANCIENT METAL MIRRORS.—From Wilkinson's Egyptians.

1, 3. In Mr. Salt's collection.   4. In the museum of Alnwick Castle.
2. In the possession of Dr. Hogg.   5. From a painting at Thebes.

carried abroad as an ornament in public; comp. Wilkinson's *Manners and Customs of the Ancient Egyptians*, vol. iii., pp. 384-386. ¶ *And the fine linen.* Anciently, the most delicate and fine garments were made from linen which was obtained chiefly from Egypt; see Note, Luke xvi. 19. ¶ *And the hoods.* Or, *turbans.* ¶ *And the veils.* This does not differ probably from the veils worn now, except that those worn by Eastern females are *large*, and made so as to cover

24 And it shall come to pass, *that* instead of sweet smell, there shall be stink; and instead of a girdle, a rent; and instead of well-set hair, baldness;[a] and instead of a stomacher, a girding of sackcloth: *and* burning instead of beauty.

the head and the shoulders, so that they may be drawn closely round the body, and effectually conceal the person; comp. Gen. xxiv. 65.

24. *And it shall come to pass.* The prophet proceeds to denounce the *judgment* or *punishment* that would come upon them for their pride and vanity. In the calamities that would befall the nation, all their ornaments of pride and vainglory would be stripped off; and instead of them, they would exhibit the marks, and wear the badges of calamity and grief. ¶ *Instead of sweet smell.* Hebrew בֹּשֶׂם *bôsĕm*, aromatics, perfumes, spicy fragrance; such as they used on their garments and persons. 'No one ever enters a company without being well perfumed; and in addition to various scents and oils, they are adorned with numerous garlands, made of the most odoriferous flowers.'—*Roberts.* 'The persons of the Assyrian ladies are elegantly clothed and scented with the richest oils and perfumes. When a queen was to be chosen to the king of Persia, instead of Vashti, the virgins collected at Susana, the capital, underwent a purification of twelve months' duration, to wit: "six months with oil of myrrh, and six months with sweet odours." The general use of such precious oil and fragrant perfumes among the ancient Romans, particularly among the ladies of rank and fashion, may be inferred from these words of Virgil:

Ambrosiaeque comae divinum vertice odorem
Spiravere:—   *Æn.* i. 403.

"From her head the ambrosial locks breathed divine fragrance." '—*Paxton.* ¶ *A stink.* This word properly means the fetor or offensive smell which attends the decomposition of a deceased body. It means that the bodies which they so carefully adorned, and which they so assiduously endeavoured to preserve in beauty by unguents and perfumes, would die and turn to corruption. ¶ *And instead of a girdle.* Girdles were an indispensable part of an Oriental dress. Their garments were loose and flowing, and it became necessary to gird them up when they ran, or danced, or laboured. ¶ *A rent.* There has been a great variety of opinion about the meaning of this word. The most probable signification is that which is derived from a verb meaning *to go around, encompass;* and hence that it denotes *a cord.* Instead of the beautiful girdle with which they girded themselves, there shall be *a cord*—an emblem of poverty, as the poor had nothing else with which to gird up their clothes;—a humiliating description of the calamities which were to come upon proud and vain females of the court. ¶ *And instead of well-set hair.* Hair that was curiously braided and adorned. 'No ladies pay more attention to the dressing of the hair than these [the dancing girls of India]; for as they never wear caps, they take great delight in this their natural ornament.' —*Roberts.* Miss Pardoe, in '*The City of the Sultan,*' says, that after taking a bath, the slaves who attended her spent an hour and a half in dressing and adorning her hair; comp. 1 Pet. iii. 3. ¶ *Instead of a stomacher.* It is not certainly known what is meant by this, but it probably means some sort of *girdle,* or a plaited or stiffened ornament worn on the breast. ' I once saw a dress beautifully plaited and stiffened for the front, but I do not think it common.'—*Roberts.* ¶ *A girding of sackcloth.* This is a coarse cloth that was commonly worn in times of affliction, as emblematic of grief; 2 Sam. iii. 31; 1 Kings xx. 31; xxi. 27; Job xvi. 15; Isa. xxxii. 11. ¶ *And burning.* The word here used does not occur elsewhere. It seems to denote *a brand, a mark burnt in, a stigma;* pehaps a sun-burnt countenance, indicating exposure in the long and wearisome journey of a captivity over burning sands and beneath a scorching sun. ¶ *Instead of beauty.* Instead of a fair and delicate complexion, cherished and nourished with care. Some of the

25 Thy men shall fall by the sword, and thy [1] mighty in the war.

26 And [a] her gates shall lament and mourn; and she, *being* [2] desolate, shall sit upon [b] the ground.

1 *might.*
a Lam.1.4.   2 *cleansed*, or *emptied.*   *b* Lam 2.10.

---

articles of dress here referred to may be illustrated by the following cut [and those p. 106], which exhibit several varieties of the costume of an Oriental female.

A LADY ADORNED WITH THE SAFA AND TURBAN.—From Lane's Modern Egyptians.

To what *particular* time the prophet refers in this chapter is not known, perhaps, however, to the captivity at Babylon. To whatever he refers, it is one of the most striking reproofs of vanity and pride, especially the pride of female ornament, any where to be found. And although he had *particular* reference to the Jewish females, yet there is no impropriety in regarding it as applicable to all such ornaments wherever they may be found. They indicate the same state of the heart, and they must meet substantially the same rebuke from God. The body, however delicately pampered and adorned, must become the prey of corruption. 'The worm shall feed sweetly on it, and the earth-worm shall be its covering;' comp. Isa. xiv. 2; Job xxiv. 20. The single thought that the body must die—that it must lie and moulder in the grave—should check the love of gay adorning, and turn the mind to a far more important matter—the salvation of the soul, which cannot die; to 'the ornament of a weak and quiet spirit, which is in the sight of God of great price;' 1 Pet. iii. 4.*

25. *Thy men.* This is an address to Jerusalem itself, by a change not uncommon in the writings of Isaiah. In the calamities coming on them, their strong men should be overcome, and fall in battle.

26. *And her gates.* Cities were sur-

---

* On this portion of Isaiah (iii. 16–24), the following works may be consulted:—N. G. Schroederi comm. Philo. Crit. de vestitu mulierum Hebraeorum, 1745, 4to.; Disserta Philolo. Polycarpi Lyceri, ad Esa. iii. 16–18 illustrandum, in Thesau. Antiq. Ugolini, tom. xxix., pp. 438–452; also Bynaeus, de Calceis Hebrae. ch. viii.; Thesau. Antiq. Sacr., tom. xxix., p. 756, *seq.*

CHAPTER IV.

FOR AN ANALYSIS OF THIS CHAPTER, SEE CH. II.

AND in that day seven women shall take hold of one man, say-

ing, We will eat our own bread, and wear our own apparel; only let ¹us be called by thy name, to take away ² our reproach.

1 thy name be called upon us.   2 or, take thou away.

rounded with walls, and were entered through gates opening into the principal streets. Those gates became, of course, the places of chief confluence and of business; and the expression here means, that in all the places of confluence, or amidst the assembled people, there should be lamentation on account of the slain in battle, and the loss of their mighty men in war. ¶ *And she.* Jerusalem is often represented as a female distinguished for beauty. It is here represented as a female sitting in a posture of grief. ¶ Being *desolate, shall*

sit upon the ground. To sit on the ground, or in the dust, was the usual posture of grief and mourning, denoting great depression and humiliation; Lam. ii. 10; iii. 28; Jer. xv. 17; Job iii. 13; Ezra ix. 3–5. It is a remarkable coincidence, that in the medals which were made by the Romans to commemorate the captivity of Judea and Jerusalem, Judea is represented under the figure of a female sitting in a posture of grief, under a palm tree, with this inscription —JUDEA CAPTA—in the form which is exhibited in the annexed engraving.

JUDEA MEDALS OF CAPTIVITY.—From Calmet.

The passage here, however, refers not to the captivity by the Romans, but to the first destruction by Nebuchadnezzar. It is a tender and most affecting image of desolation. During the captivity at Babylon, it was completely fulfilled; and for ages since, Judea might be appropriately represented by a captive female sitting pensively on the ground.

CHAPTER IV.

1. *In that day.* The time of calamity referred to in the close of the previous chapter. This is a continuation of that prophecy, and there was no reason why these six verses should have been made a separate chapter. That the passage refers to the Messiah, is apparent from what has been stated in the Notes on the commencement of the

prophecy (ch. ii. 1–4), and from the expressions which occur in the chapter itself; see Notes on ver. 2, 5, 6. ¶ *Seven women.* The number *seven* is used often to denote a *large* though *indefinite* number; Lev. xxvi. 28; Prov. xxiv. 16; Zech. iii. 9. It means that so great should be the calamity, so many *men* would fall in battle, that many women would, contrary to their natural modesty, become suitors to a single man, to obtain him as a husband and protector. ¶ *Shall take hold.* Shall apply to. The expression, 'shall take hold,' denotes the *earnestness* of their application. ¶ *We will eat our own bread,* &c. We do not ask this in order to be maintained. We will forego that which the law (Ex. xxi. 10) enjoins as the duty of the husband in case he has more than one wife.

2 In that day shall the *a* branch of the LORD be [1] beautiful and glorious, and the fruit of the earth *shall be* excellent and comely for them [2] that are escaped of Israel.

a Jer.23.5,6; Zec.6.12,13.

1 *beauty and glory.*   2 *the escaping of Israel.*

¶ *Only let us be called by thy name.* Let us be regarded as *thy wives.* The wife then, as now, assumed the name of the husband. A remarkably similar expression occurs in Lucan (B. ii. 342). Marcia there presents a similar request to Cato :

Da tantum nomen inane
Connubii; liceat tumulo scripsisse, Catonis Marcia.

'Indulge me only with the empty title of wife. Let there only be inscribed on my tomb, "Marcia, wife of Cato." '
¶ *To take away my reproach.* The reproach of being unmarried; comp. Gen. xxx. 23; 1 Sam. i. 6.

2. *The branch of the* LORD. צֶמַח יְהֹוָה. *The sprout of* JEHOVAH. This expression, and this verse, have had a great variety of interpretations. The LXX. read it, ' In that day God shall shine in counsel with glory upon the earth, to exalt, and to glorify the remnant of Israel.' The Chaldee renders it, ' In that day, the *Messiah* of the Lord shall be for joy and glory, and the doers of the law for praise and honour to those of Israel who are delivered.' It is clear that the passage is designed to denote some signal blessing that was to succeed the calamity predicted in the previous verses. The only question is, to what has the prophet reference? The word ' branch ' (צֶמַח) is derived from the verb (צָמַח *tzâmăhh*) signifying *to sprout, to spring up,* spoken of plants. Hence the word *branch* means properly that which *shoots up,* or *sprouts* from the root of a tree, or from a decayed tree; comp. Job xiv. 7–9. The Messiah is thus said to be ' a root of Jesse,' Rom. xi. 12; comp. Note, Isa. xi. 1, 10, and ' the root and offspring of David,' Rev. xxii. 16, as being a *descendant* of Jesse; *i.e.,* as if Jesse should fall like an aged tree, yet the *root* would sprout up and live. The word ' branch ' occurs several times in the Old Testament, and in most, if not all, with express reference to the Messiah ; Jer. xxiii. 5: ' Behold, the days come, saith the Lord,

that I will raise unto David a righteous *Branch,* and a king shall reign;' Jer. xxxiii. 15: ' In those days, and at that time, will I cause the Branch of righteousness to grow up unto David ;' Zech. iii. 8; vi. 12. In all these places, there can be no doubt that there is reference to him who was *to spring up* from David, as a sprout does from a decayed and fallen tree, and who is therefore called a *root,* a *branch* of the royal stock. There is, besides, a peculiar beauty in the figure. The family of David, when the Messiah was to come, would be fallen into decay and almost extinct. Joseph, the husband of Mary, though of the royal family of David (Matt. i. 20; Luke ii. 4), was poor, and the family had lost all claims to the throne. In this state, as from the decayed root of a fallen tree, a *sprout* or *branch* was to come forth with more than the magnificence of David, and succeed him on the throne. The name ' branch,' therefore, came to be significant of the Messiah, and to be synonymous with ' the son of David.' It is so used, doubtless, in this place, as denoting that the coming of the Messiah would be a joy and honour in the days of calamity to the Jews. Interpreters have not been agreed, however, in the meaning of this passage. Grotius supposed that it referred to Ezra or Nehemiah, but ' mystically to Christ and Christians.' Vogellius understood it of the *remnant* that should return from the Babylonish captivity. Michaelis supposed that it refers to the Jews, who should be a *reformed* people after their captivity, and who should spring up with a new spirit. Others have regarded it as a poetic description of the extraordinary fertility of the earth in future times. The reasons for referring it to the Messiah are plain—(1.) The word has this reference in other places, and the representation of the Messiah under the image of a branch or shoot, is, as we have seen, common in the Scriptures. Thus, also, in ch. liii. 2, he is called also שֹׁרֶשׁ *shōrĕsh, root,* and

יוֹנֵק *yōnĕq*, a tender plant, a sucker, sprout, shoot, as of a decayed tree; comp. Job viii. 16; xiv. 7; xv. 30; Ezek. xvii. 22. And in reference to the same idea, perhaps, it is said, Isa. liii. 8, that he was נִגְזָר *nighzăr, cut off*, as a branch, sucker, or shoot is cut off by the vine-dresser or farmer from the root of a decayed tree. And thus, in Rev. v. 5, he is called ῥίζα Δαβὶδ—the root of David. (2.) This interpretation accords best with the *magnificence* of the description, ver. 5, 6 ; and, (3.) It was so understood by the Chaldee interpreter, and, doubtless, by the ancient Jews. ¶ *Shall be beautiful and glorious.* Heb. ' Shall be beauty and glory ;' that is, shall be the chief ornament or honour of the land ; shall be that which gives to the nation its chief distinction and glory. In such times of calamity, his coming shall be an object of desire, and his approach shall shed a rich splendour on that period of the world. ¶ *And the fruit of the earth,* פְּרִי הָאָרֶץ correctly rendered *fruit of the earth,* or *of the land.* The word ' earth ' is often in the Scriptures used to denote the land of Judea, and perhaps the article here is intended to denote that that land is particularly intended. This is the parallel expression to the former part of the verse, in accordance with the laws of Hebrew poetry, by which one member of a sentence expresses substantially the same meaning as the former ; see Introduction, § 8. If the former expression referred to the *Messiah,* this does also. The ' fruit of the earth ' is that which the earth produces, and is here not different in signification from the *branch* which springs out of the ground. Vitringa supposes that by this phrase the Messiah, according to his human nature, is meant. So Hengstenberg (*Christol., in loc.*) understands it ; and supposes that as the phrase ' branch of Jehovah ' refers to his Divine origin, as proceeding from Jehovah ; so this refers to his human origin, as proceeding from the earth. But the objections to this are obvious—(1.) The second phrase, according to the laws of Hebrew parallelism, is most naturally an echo or repetition of the sentiment

in the first member, and means substantially the same thing. (2.) The phrase ' branch of Jehovah ' does not refer of necessity to his Divine nature. The idea is that of a decayed tree that has fallen down, and has left a living root which sends up a shoot, or sucker ; and can be applied with great elegance to the decayed family of David. But how, or in what sense, can this be applied to Jehovah ? Is Jehovah thus fallen and decayed ? The idea properly is, that this shoot of a decayed family should be nurtured up by JEHOVAH ; should be appointed by him, and should thus be *his* branch. The parallel member denotes substantially the same thing ; ' the fruit of the earth '—the shoot which the earth produces—or which springs up from a decayed family, as the sprout does from a fallen tree. (3.) It is as true that his human nature proceeded from God as his Divine. It was produced by the Holy Ghost, and can no more be regarded as ' the fruit of the earth ' than his Divine nature ; Luke i. 35; Heb. x. 5. (4.) This mode of interpretation is fitted to bring the whole subject into contempt. There are plain and positive passages enough to prove that the Messiah had a Divine nature, and there are enough also to prove that he was a man ; but nothing is more adapted to produce disgust in relation to the whole subject, in the minds of sceptical or of *thinking* men, than a resort to arguments such as this in defence of a great and glorious doctrine of revelation. ¶ Shall be *excellent.* Shall be *for exaltation,* or *honour.* ¶ *Comely.* Heb. ' For an ornament ;' meaning that *he* would be an honour to those times. ¶ *For them that are escaped of Israel.* Marg. ' The escaping of Israel.' For the remnant, the small number that shall escape the calamities—a description of the pious portion of Israel which now escaped from all calamities—would rejoice in the anticipated blessings of the Messiah's reign, or would participate in the blessings of that reign. The idea is not, however, that the number who would be saved would be *small,* but that they would be characterized as those who had *escaped,* or who had been rescued.

3 And it shall come to pass, *that he that is* left in Zion, and *he that* remaineth in Jerusalem, shall be called *a* holy, *even* every one that

a ch.60.21.

is written [1] among the living in Jerusalem :

4 When the LORD shall have washed *b* away the filth of the

1 or, *to life*, Rev.21.27.　　　*b* Zec.13.1.

---

3. He that is *left in Zion.* This *properly* refers to the remnant that should remain after the mass of the people should be cut off by wars, or be borne into captivity. If it refer to the few that would come back from Babylon, it means that they would be reformed, and would be a generation different from their fathers—which was undoubtedly true. If it refer, as the connection seems to indicate, to the times of the Messiah, then it speaks of those who are 'left,' while the great mass of the nation would be unbelievers, and would be destroyed. The mass of the nation would be cut off, and the remnant that was left would be holy; that is, all true friends of the Messiah would be holy. ¶ *Shall be called holy.* That is, shall *be* holy. The expression ' to be called,' is often used in the Scriptures as synonymous with ' to be.' ¶ *Every one that is written among the living.* The Jews were accustomed to register the names of all the people. Those names were written in a catalogue, or register, of each tribe or family. To be written in that book, or register, meant to be alive, for when a death occurred, the name was stricken out; Ex. xxxii. 32; Dan. xii. 1; Ezek. xiii. 9. The expression came also to denote all who were truly the friends of God ; they whose names are written in *his* book—the book of life. In this sense it is used in the New Testament ; Phil. iv. 3; Rev. iii. 5; xvii. 5. In this sense it is understood in this place by the Chaldee Par.: 'Every one shall be called holy who is written to *eternal* life ; he shall see the consolation of Jerusalem.' If the reference here is to the Messiah, then the passage denotes that under the reign of the Messiah, all who should be found enrolled as his followers, would be holy. An effectual separation would subsist between them and the mass of the people. They would be *enrolled* as his friends, and they would be a separate, holy community ; comp. 1 Pet. ii. 9.

4. *When the Lord.* That is, *after* God has done this, then all that are written among the living shall be called holy. The prophet in this verse states the benefits of *affliction* in purifying the people of God. He had said, in the previous verse, that all who should be left in Zion should be called holy. He here states that *previous* to that, the defilement of the people would be removed by judgment. ¶ *Shall have washed away.* The expression, *to wash,* is often used to denote to *purify* in any way. In allusion to this fact is the beautiful promise in Zech. xiii. 1; see Note, ch. i. 16. ¶ *The filth.* This word here refers to their *moral* defilement— their pride, vanity, haughtiness ; and perhaps to the idolatry and general sins of the people. As the prophet, however, in ch. iii. 16–23, had particularly specified the sins of the female part of the Jewish people, the expression here probably refers especially to them, and to the judgments which were to come upon them ; ch. iii. 24. It is not departing from the spirit of this passage to remark, that the church is purified, and true religion is often promoted, by God's humbling the pride and vanity of females. A love of excessive ornament ; a fondness for dress and display ; and an exhibition of great gaiety, often stand grievously in the way of pure religion. ¶ *The daughters of Zion;* see ch. iii. 16. ¶ *And shall have purged.* This is synonymous with the expression *to wash.* It means to purify, to remove, as one removes blood from the hands by washing. ¶ *Blood of Jerusalem.* Crime, blood-guiltiness— particularly the crime of *oppression, cruelty,* and *robbery,* which the prophet (ch. i. 15) had charged on them. ¶ *By the spirit of judgment.* This refers, doubtless, to the *calamities,* or *punishment,* that would come upon the nation ; principally, to the Babylonish captivity. After God should have humbled and reformed the nation by a series of

daughters of Zion, and shall have purged tho blood of Jerusalem from the midst thereof by the spirit of judgment, and by the spirit of burning.

5 And the LORD will create upon every dwelling-place of mount Zion, and upon her assemblies, a cloud

a Zec.3.5.   1 or, *above*.   2 *covering*.   b ch.25.4.

and smoke by day, and the shining of a flaming fire *a* by night; for upon 1 all the glory *shall be* a 2 defence.

6 And there shall be a tabernacle for a shadow in the day-time from the heat, and for a place of *b* refuge, and for a covert from storm and from rain.

judgments, then they who were purified by them should be called holy. The word *spirit* here cannot be shown to be the Holy Spirit; and especially as the Holy Spirit is not represented in the Scriptures as the agent in executing judgment. It perhaps would be best denoted by the word *influence*, or *power*. The word properly denotes *wind, air, motion* (Gen. viii. 1; Job i. 19); then *breathing, exhalation*, or *breath* (Job vii. 7; Ps. xxxiii. 6); hence it means the *soul;* and it means also God's *influence*, or his putting forth his power and life-giving energy in animating and sustaining the universe; and also, as here, his putting forth *any* influence in accomplishing his works and designs. ¶ *And by the spirit of burning. Fire* is often, in the Scriptures, the emblem of punishment, and also of purifying; comp. Note, Matt. iii. 11, 12; see Mal. iii. 2, 3. The Chaldee translates this, 'by the *word* of judgment, and by the *word* of consuming.' The reference is to the *punishments* which would be sent to purify the people *before* the coming of the Messiah.

5. *And the* LORD *will create*. The meaning of this verse and the next is, that God would take his people into his holy care and protection. The idea is expressed by images drawn, in this verse, from the protection which he afforded to the Israelites in their journeying from Egypt. The word *create* means here, he will afford, or furnish, such a defence. ¶ *Upon every dwelling-place*, &c. Upon all the habitations of his people; that is, they shall be secure, and regarded as under his protection. The word *upon* refers to the fact that the pillar of cloud stood *over* the tabernacle in the wilderness, **as a** symbol of the Divine favour and presence. So his protection should be

on or *over* the houses of all his people; comp. Ps. xcii. 4–6. ¶ *Of mount Zion;* comp. Note, ch. i. 8. ¶ *And upon her assemblies.* Their convocations; their sacred assemblies, such as were called together on the Sabbath; Lev. xxiii. 2; Num. xxviii. 18. It refers here to their *future* assemblies, and therefore includes the Christian church assembled to worship God. ¶ *A cloud and smoke by day.* This refers to the pillar of cloud that went before the Israelites in their journey in the wilderness; Ex. xiii. 21; xiv. 20. ¶ *By day.* By day, this appeared to them as a cloud; by night, as a pillar of fire; Ex. xiii. 21, 22. That is, it was always conspicuous, and could be seen by all the people. A pillar of cloud could not have been seen by night; and God changes the symbols of his presence and protection, so that at all times his people may see them. The meaning here is, that as God gave to the Israelites a symbol of his presence and protection, so he would be the protector and defender of his people hereafter. ¶ *For upon all the glory.* Above all the *glorious object;* that is, his church, his people. It is here called 'the glory,' as being a glorious, or an honourable object. ¶ *A defence.* This word properly means *a covering, a protection*, from the verb *to cover*, and means that God will protect, or defend his people.

6. *And there shall be a tabernacle.* The reference here is to the *tabernacle*, or sacred *tent* that God directed Moses to make in the wilderness. The image of the cloudy pillar mentioned in the previous verses, seems to have suggested to the mind of the prophet the idea of the tabernacle over which that pillar rested. The principal idea here is, however, not a tabernacle as a symbol of the Divine protection, or of Divine

CHAPTER V.

ANALYSIS.

This chapter commences a new subject, and is in itself an entire prophecy, having no connection with the preceding or the following chapter. *When* it was delivered is unknown; but from the strong resemblance between the circumstances referred to here, and those referred to in ch. ii., it is probable it was at about the same period. The fact, also, that it is closely connected with that in the place which has been assigned it in the collection of the prophecies of Isaiah, is a circumstance which strongly corroborates that view. The general design of the chapter is to denounce the prevalent vices of the nation, and to proclaim that they will be followed with heavy judgments. The chapter may be conveniently regarded as divided into three parts.

I. A beautiful parable illustrative of the care which God had shown for his people, ver. 1–7. He states what he had done for them; calls on them to judge themselves whether he had not done for them all that he could have done; and, since his vineyard had brought forth no good fruit, he threatens to break down its hedges, and to destroy it.

II. The various vices and crimes which prevailed in the nation are denounced, and punishment threatened, ver. 8–23.

1. The sin of covetousness, ver. 8–10.
2. The sins of intemperance, revelry, and dissipation, ver. 11–17.
3. The sin of despising and contemning God, and of practising iniquity as if he did not see it, or could not punish it, ver. 18, 19.
4. The sin of those who pervert things, and call evil good and good evil, ver. 20.
5. The sin of vain self-confidence, pride, and inordinate self-esteem, ver. 21.
6. The sin of intemperance is again reproved, and the sin of receiving bribes; probably because these were in fact connected, ver. 22, 23.

III. Punishment is denounced on the nation for indulgence in these sins, ver. 24–30. The punishment would be, that he would call distant nations to invade their land, and it should be laid waste.

"The subject of this prophecy," says Lowth, "does not differ materially from ch. i., but it is greatly superior to it in force, in severity, in variety, in elegance."

N OW will I sing to my well-beloved a song of my beloved

worship, but of a place of refuge from a tempest; that is, that they should be *safe* under his protection. In Eastern countries they dwelt chiefly in tents. The idea is, therefore, that God would furnish them a place of shelter, a hiding-place from the storm. ¶ *In the day-time from the heat.* The heat in those regions was often very intense, particularly in the vast plains of sand. The *idea* here is, therefore, one that is very striking. It means, that God would furnish to them a refuge that would be like the comfort derived from a tent in a burning desert. ¶ *For a place of refuge.* A place to which to flee in the midst of a storm, as a tent would be. ¶ *A covert.* A place of retreat, a safe place to retire to. The figure here used is not unfrequently employed in the prophets; ch. xxv. 4; xxxii. 2. In eastern countries this idea would be very striking. While traversing the burning sands of a desert, exposed to the rays of a tropical sun, nothing could be more grateful than the cool shadow of a rock. Such figures are therefore common in oriental writings, to denote protection and agreeable shelter from

calamities; see Note on ch. xxxii. 2. The idea in these verses is—(1.) That God will be a defender of his people. (2.) That he will protect their families, and that his blessing will be upon their dwelling-places; comp. Note on ch. lix. 21. (3.) They may expect his blessing on their religious assemblies. (4.) God, through the promised Messiah, would be a refuge and defence. The sinner is exposed to the burning wrath of God, and to the storms of Divine vengeance that shall beat for ever on the naked soul in hell. From all this burning wrath, and from this raging tempest, the Messiah is the only refuge. Through him God forgives sin; and united to him by faith, the soul is safe. There are few images more beautiful than this. Soon the storms of Divine vengeance will beat on the sinner. God will summon him to judgment. But then, he who has fled to the Messiah—the Lord Jesus—as the refuge of his soul, shall be safe. He shall have nothing to fear, and in his arms shall find defence and salvation.

CHAPTER V.

1. *Now will I sing.* This is an indi-

touching his vineyard. My well-
beloved hath a *a* vineyard in ¹ a very
fruitful hill :

a Lu.20.9,&c.   *1 the horn of the son of oil.*

2 And he ² fenced it, and gathered out the stones thereof, and
planted it with the choicest *b* vine,

2 or, *made a wall about it.*   b Jer.2.21.

cation that what follows is poetic, or is
adapted to be sung or chanted. ¶ *To
my well-beloved.* The word used here
—יָדִיד—is a term of endearment. It
properly denotes a friend ; a favourite ;
one greatly beloved. It is applied to
saints as being the beloved, or the
favourites of God, in Ps. cxxvii. 2 ;
Deut. xxxiii. 12. In this place, it is
evidently applied to Jehovah, the God
of the Jewish people. As there is some
reason to believe that the God of the
Jews—the manifested Deity who undertook their deliverance from Egypt, and
who was revealed as *their* God under
the name of ' the Angel of the Covenant '—was the Messiah, so it may be
that the prophet here meant to refer to
him. It is not, however, to the Messiah *to come.* It does not refer to the God
incarnate—to Jesus of Nazareth ; but
to the God of the Jews, in his capacity
as their lawgiver and protector in the
time of Isaiah ; not to him in the capacity of an incarnate Saviour. ¶ *A song
of my beloved.* Lowth, ' A song of
loves,' by a slight change in the Hebrew.
The word דֹּוד usually denotes ' an uncle,'
a father's brother. But it also means
one beloved, a friend, a lover ; Cant. i.
13, 14, 16 ; ii. 3, 8, 9 ; iv. 16, 17. Here
it refers to Jehovah, and expresses the
tender and affectionate attachment
which the prophet had for his character and laws. ¶ *Touching his vineyard.* The Jewish people are often
represented under the image of a vineyard, planted and cultivated by God ;
see Ps. lxxx ; Jer. ii. 21 ; xii. 10. Our
Saviour also used this beautiful figure
to denote the care and attention which
God had bestowed on his people ; Matt.
xxi. 33, *sq.* ; Mark xii. 1, *sq.* ¶ *My
beloved.* God. ¶ *Hath a vineyard in
a very fruitful hill.* Heb. ' On a horn
of the son of oil.' The word *horn* used
here in the Hebrew, denotes the *brow*,
apex, or sharp point of a hill. The
word is thus used in other languages to
denote a hill, as in the Swiss words
shreckhorn, buchorn. Thus *Cornwall*,

in England, is called in the old British
tongue *Kernaw*, as lessening by degrees, like a horn, running out into
promontories, like so many horns ; for
the Britons called a horn *corn*, and in
the plural *kern*. The term ' horn ' is
not unfrequently applied to hills. Thus,
Pococke tells us (vol. ii. p. 67), that
there is a low mountain in Galilee which
has both its ends raised in such a manner
as to look like two mounts, which are
called the ' Horns of Hutin.' Harmer,
however, supposes that the term is used
here to denote the land of Syria, from
its resemblance to the shape of a horn ;
Obs. iii. 242. But the idea is, evidently, that the land on which God
respresents himself as having planted
his vineyard, was like an elevated hill
that was adapted eminently to such a
culture. It may mean either the *top*
of a mountain, or a little mountain, or
a *peak* divided from others. The most
favourable places for vineyards were on
the sides of hills, where they would be
exposed to the sun.—Shaw's *Travels*,
p. 338. Thus Virgil says :

—— denique apertos
Bacchus amat colles.

' Bacchus loves open hills ;.' *Georg.* ii.
113. The phrase, *son of oil*, is used in
accordance with the Jewish custom,
where *son* means descendant, relative,
&c. ; see Note, Matt. i. 1. Here it
means that it was so fertile that it
might be called the very *son of oil*, or
fatness, *i.e.*, fertility. The image is
poetic, and very beautiful ; denoting that
God had planted his people in circumstances where he had a right to expect
great growth in attachment to him.
It was not owing to any want of care
on his part, that they were not distinguished for piety. The Chaldee renders
this verse, ' The prophet said, I will sing
now to Israel, who is compared to a vineyard, the seed of Abraham my beloved :
a song of my beloved to his vineyard.'

2. *And he fenced it.* Marg. ' Made
a wall about it.' The word used here
is supposed rather to mean *to dig about*,

and built a tower in the midst of it, and also [1] made a wine-press therein: and he looked that it should bring forth grapes, and it brought forth wild grapes.

1 *hewed.*

to grub, as with a pick-axe or spade.—*Gesenius.* It has this signification in Arabic, and in one place in the Jewish Talmud.—*Kimchi.* The Vulgate and the LXX. understand it of making a hedge or fence, probably the first work in preparing a vineyard. And as 'a hedge' is expressly mentioned in ver. 5, it seems most probable that that is its meaning here. ¶ *And gathered out the stones,* &c. That it might be easily cultivated. This was, of course, a necessary and proper work. ¶ *And planted it with the choicest vine.* Heb. 'With the sorek.' This was a choice species of vine, the grapes of which, the Jewish commentators say, had very small and scarcely perceptible stones, and which, at this day, is called *serki* in Morocco; in Persia, *kishmis.*—*Gesenius.* ¶ *And built a tower.* For the sake of watching and defending it. These towers were probably placed so as to overlook the whole vineyard, and

WATCH-TOWER IN A VINEYARD.

were thus posts of observation; comp. Note, ch. i. 8; see also Note, Matt. xxi. 33. ¶ *And also made a wine-press.* A place in which to put the grapes for the purpose of expressing the juice; see Note, Matt. xxi. 33. ¶ *And he looked.* He waited in expectation; as a husbandman waits patiently for the vines to grow, and to bear grapes. ¶ *Wild grapes.* The word here used is derived from the verb באש *baäsh, to be offensive, to corrupt, to putrify;* and is supposed by Gesenius to mean *monk's-hood,* a poisonous herb, offensive in smell, which produces berries like grapes. Such a meaning suits the connection better than the supposition of grapes that were wild or uncultivated. The Vulgate understands it of the weed called *wild vine—labruscas.* The LXX. translate it by *thorns, ἄκανθας.* That there were vines in Judea which produced such poisonous berries, though resembling grapes, is evident; see 2 Kings iv. 39–41: 'And one went out into the fields to gather pot herbs, and he found a field vine, and he gathered from it wild fruit.' Moses also refers to a similar vine; Deut. xxxii. 32, 33: 'For their vine is as the vine of Sodom; their grapes are grapes of gall; their clusters are bitter.' Hasselquist thinks that the prophet here means the *nightshade.* The Arabs, says he, call it *wolf-grapes.* It grows much in vineyards, and is very pernicious to them. Some poisonous, offensive berries, growing on wild vines, are doubtless intended here.

3 And now, O inhabitants of Jerusalem, and men of Judah, judge, I pray you, betwixt me and my vineyard.

4 What could have been done more to my vineyard that I have not done in it? Wherefore, when I looked that it should bring forth

The general meaning of this parable it is not difficult to understand ; comp. Notes on Matt. xxi. 33. Jerome has attempted to follow out the allegory, and explain the particular parts. He says, ' By the metaphor of the vineyard is to be understood the people of the Jews, which he surrounded or inclosed by *angels;* by gathering out the stones, the removal of *idols;* by the tower, the *temple* erected in the midst of Judea ; by the wine-press, the *altar.*' There is no propriety, however, in attempting thus minutely to explain the particular parts of the figure. The general meaning is, that God had chosen the Jewish people ; had bestowed great care on them in giving them his law, in defending them, and in providing for them ; that he had omitted nothing that was adapted to produce piety, obedience, and happiness, and that they had abused it all, and instead of being obedient, had become exceedingly corrupt.

3. *And now,* &c. This is an appeal which God makes to the Jews themselves, in regard to the justice and propriety of what he was about to do. A similar appeal he makes in Mic. vi. 3 : ' O my people, what have I done unto thee? and wherein have I wearied thee? Testify against me.' He intended to *punish* them (ver. 5, 6), and he appeals to them for the justice of it. He would do to them as they would do to a vineyard that had been carefully prepared and guarded, and which yet was value-less. A similar appeal he makes in ch. i. 18; and our Saviour made an application remarkably similar in his parable of the vineyard, Matt. xxi. 40–43. It is not improbable that he had his eye on this very place in Isaiah ; and it is, therefore, the more remarkable that the Jews did not understand the bearing of his discourse.

4. *What could I,* &c. As a man who had done what is described in ver. 2, would have done all that *could* be done for a vineyard, so God says that he has done all that he could, in the

circumstances of the Jews, to make them holy and happy. He had chosen them ; had given them his law; had sent them prophets and teachers; had defended them ; had come forth in judgment and mercy, and he now appeals *to them* to say what *could* have been done more. This important verse implies that God had done all that he could have done; that is, all that he could consistently do, or all that justice and goodness required him to do, to secure the welfare of his people. It cannot, of course, be meant that he had no physical ability to do any thing else, but the expression must be interpreted by a reference to the point in hand ; and that is, an appeal to others to determine that he had done all that could be done in the circumstances of the case. In this respect, we may, without impropriety, say, that there *is* a limit to the power of God. It is impossible to conceive that he *could* have given a law more holy; or that he could append to it more solemn sanctions than the threatening of eternal death ; or that he could have offered higher hopes than the prospect of eternal life; or that he could have given a more exalted Redeemer. It has been maintained (see the *Princeton Bib. Repert.,* April 1841) that the reference here is to the future, and that the question means, ' what remains now to be done to my vineyard as an expression of displeasure?' or that it is asked with a view to introduce the expression of his purpose to punish his people, stated in ver. 5. But that the above is the meaning of the passage, or that it refers to what God had actually done, is evident from the following considerations:—(1.) He had specified at length (ver. 2) what he had done. He had performed *all* that was usually done to a vineyard ; in fencing it, and clearing it of stones, and planting in it the choicest vines, and building a wine-press in it. Without impropriety, it might be said of a man that, whatever wealth he had, or what-

grapes, brought it forth wild grapes?

5 And now, go to; I will tell you what I will do to my vineyard: I will take away the *a* hedge thereof,

a Ps.80.12,13.

and it shall be eaten up; *and* break down the wall thereof, and it shall be ¹ trodden down.

6 And I will lay it waste: it shall not be pruned nor digged; but there

¹ *for a treading.*

ever power he had to do *other* things, he *could do nothing more to perfect a vine-yard.* (2.) It is the meaning which is most naturally suggested by the original. Literally, the Hebrew is, ' *What to do more?*' — מַה־לַעֲשׂוֹת עוֹד. Coverdale renders this, as it is in our translation, ' What more could have been done for it?' Luther, ' What should one do more to my vineyard, that I have done for it?'—Was sollte man doch mehr thun an meinem Weinberge, das ich nicht gethan habe an ihm? Vulg., Quid est quod debui ultra facere— ' What is there which I *ought* to do more?' Sept., Τί ποιήσω ἔτι—' What shall I do yet?' implying that he had done all that he could for it. The Chaldee renders it, ' What good thing —מה טבא—shall I say that I will do to my people that I have not done for them?' implying that he had done for them all the good which could be spoken of. The Syriac, ' What remains to be done to my vineyard, and I have not done it?' In all these versions, the sense given is substantially the same— that God had done all that could be done to make the expectation that his vineyard would produce fruit, proper. There is no reference in one of these versions to what he *would* do after-wards, but the uniform reference is to what he *had* done to make the expecta-tion *reasonable,* that his vineyard would produce fruit. (3.) That this is the fair interpretation is apparent farther, because, when, in ver. 5, he says what he *would do,* it is entirely different from what he said he *had done.* He *had* done all that could be done to make it proper to expect fruit; he now *would* do what would be a proper expression of his displeasure that no fruit had been produced. He would take away its hedge; break down its walls, and lay it waste. But in the interpretation of the passage proposed by the *Princeton Repert.,* there is an entire omission of

this part of the verse—' that I have not done in it.' It is not improper, there-fore, to use this passage to show that God had done all that could be con-sistently done for the salvation of man, and the same appeal may now be made to sinners everywhere; and it may be asked, what God *could* have done for their salvation more than has been done? *Could* he have given them a purer law? *Could* he present higher con-siderations than have been drawn from the hope of an *eternal* heaven, and the fear of an *eternal* hell? Could he have furnished a more full atonement than has been made by the blood of his own Son? The conclusion to which we should come would be in accordance with what is said in the prophet, that God has done *all* for the salvation of sinners that in the circumstances of the case could be done, and that if they are lost, they only will bear the blame.

5. *Go to.* The Hebrew word here is one that is commonly rendered, ' I pray you,' and is used *to call the attention* to what is said. It is the word from which we have derived the adverb *now,* נָא. ¶ *I will take away the hedge.* A *hedge* is a fence of thorns, made by suffering thorn-bushes to grow so thick that nothing can pass through them. Here it means that God would withdraw his protection from the Jews, and leave them exposed to be overrun and trodden down by their enemies, as a vineyard would be by wild beasts if it were not protected. ¶ *The wall,* &c. Vineyards, it seems, had a *double* enclosure.— *Gesenius.* Such a double protection might be necessary, as some animals might scale a wall that would yet find it impossible to pass through a thorn-hedge. The sense here is, that though the Jews had been protected in every way possible, yet that protection would be withdrawn, and they would be left defenceless.

6. *I will lay it waste,* &c. The de-

shall come up briers and thorns ; I will also command the clouds that they rain no rain upon it.

7 For the vineyard of the LORD of hosts *is* the house of Israel, and

1 *plant of his pleasures.*

the men of Judah [1] his pleasant plant ; and he looked for judgment, but behold [2] oppression ; for righteousness, but behold a cry.

8 Wo unto them that join *a* house

2 *a scab.* a Mic.2.2.

---

scription here is continued from ver. 5. The image is carried out, and means that the Jews should be left utterly without protection. *¶ I will also command the clouds,* &c. It is evident here, that the parable or figure is partially dropped. A husbandman could not command the clouds. It is God alone who could do that; and the figure of the vineyard is dropped, and God is introduced speaking as a sovereign. The meaning is, that he would withhold his Divine influences, and would abandon them to desolation. The sense of the whole verse is plain. God would leave the Jews without protection; he would remove the guards, the helps, the influences, with which he had favoured them, and leave them to their own course, as a vineyard that was unpruned, uncultivated, unwatered. The Chaldee has well expressed the sense of the passage: 'I will take away the house of my sanctuary [the temple], and they shall be trodden down. I will regard them as guilty, and there shall be no support or defence for them ; they shall be abandoned, and shall become wanderers. I will command the prophets, that they shall not prophesy over them.' The lesson taught here is, that when a people become ungrateful, and rebellious, God will withdraw from them, and leave them to desolation ; comp. Rev. ii. 3.

7. *For the vineyard,* &c. This is the application of the parable. God had treated the Jews as a husbandman does a vineyard. This was *his* vineyard— the object of his faithful, unceasing care. This was his *only* vineyard ; on this people alone, of all the nations of the earth, had he bestowed his peculiar attention. *¶ His pleasant plant.* The plant in which he delighted. As the husbandman had been at the pains to plant the *sorek* (ver. 2), so had God selected the ancient stock of the Jews as his own, and made the race the object of his chief attention. *¶ And he looked*

for judgment. For justice, or righteousness. *¶ But behold oppression.* The word rendered *oppression* means properly- *shedding of blood.* In the original here, there is a remarkable *paranomasia,* or play upon words, which is not uncommon in the Hebrew Scriptures, and which was deemed a great beauty in composition :

He looked for *judgment,*	מִשְׁפָּט	*mishpat,*
and lo! *shedding of blood,*	מִשְׂפָּח	*mispáhh;*
For *righteousness,*	צְדָקָה	*tzdahakd,*
but lo! *a clamour,*	צְעָקָה	*tze'aká.*

It is impossible, of course, to retain this in a translation. *¶ A cry. A clamour;* tumult, disorder ; the clamour which attends anarchy, and covetousness, and dissipation (ver. 8, 11, 12), rather than the soberness and steadiness of justice.

8. *Wo unto them,* &c. The prophet now proceeds to *specify* some of the crimes to which he had referred in the parable of the vineyard, of which the Jews had been guilty. The first is *avarice.* *¶ That join house to house.* That seek to possess many houses ; or perhaps that seek to live in large and magnificent palaces. A similar denunciation of this sin is recorded in Mic. ii. 2: Neh. v. 1–8. This, together with what follows, was contrary to the law of Moses. He provided that when the children of Israel should enter the land of Canaan, the land should be equitably divided ; and in order to prevent avarice, he ordained the *jubilee,* occurring once in fifty years, by which every man and every family should be restored to their former possession ; Lev. xxv. Perhaps there could have been no law so well framed to prevent the existence, and avoid the evils of covetousness. Yet, in defiance of the obvious requirements and spirit of that law, the people in the time of Isaiah had become generally covetous. *¶ That lay field to field.* That purchase one farm after another.

to house, *that* lay field to field, till *there be* no place, that [1]they may be placed alone in the midst of the earth !

9 In mine ears, *said* the LORD of hosts, Of [2]a truth many houses shall be desolate, *even* great and fair, without inhabitant.

1 *ye*.   2 *if not*.

10 Yea, [a]ten acres of vineyard shall yield one bath, and the seed of an homer shall yield an ephah.

11 Wo unto them that rise up early in the morning, *that* they may follow strong drink ; that continue until night, *till* wine [3]inflame them !

a Hag.1.9,11.   3 or, *pursue them*.

The words 'that lay,' mean *to cause to approach;* that is, they *join on* one farm after another.   ¶ *Till* there be *no place.* Till they reach the *outer limit* of the land; till they possess all.   ¶ *That they may be placed alone.* That they may displace all others ; that they may drive off from their lands all others, and take possession of them themselves. ¶ *In the midst of the earth.* Or rather, in the midst of the *land.* They seek to obtain the whole of it, and to expel all the present owners.   Never was there a more correct description of avarice. It is satisfied with no present possessions, and would be satisfied only if *all* the earth were in its possession. Nor would the covetous man be satisfied then.   He would sit down and weep that there was nothing more which he could desire. How different this from that *contentment* which is produced by religion, and the love of the happiness of others !

9. *In mine ears.* This probably refers to the prophet. As if he had said, 'God has revealed it to me,' or 'God has said in my ears,' *i.e*, to me. The LXX. read it, 'These things are heard in the ears of the Lord of hosts,' *i.e.*, the *wishes* of the man of avarice. The Chaldee, 'The prophet said, In my ears I have heard ; a decree has gone from the Lord of hosts,' &c. ¶ *Many houses shall be desolate.* Referring to the calamities that should come upon the nation for its crimes.

10. *Yea, ten acres.* In this verse a reason is rendered why the houses mentioned in the previous verse should become desolate. The reason is, that the land would become sterile and barren, as a Divine judgment for their oppression. To what particular time the prophet refers, here, is not apparent. It is certain, however, that the land of

Canaan was frequently given up to sterility.   The withholding of the early and latter rains, or the neglect of cultivation from any cause, would produce this.   At present, this formerly fertile country is among the most unproductive on the face of the earth.   ¶ *Ten acres.* An *acre*, among the Hebrews, was what could be ploughed by one yoke of oxen in a day.   It did not differ materially from our acre.   ¶ *Shall yield one bath.* One bath of wine.   The *bath* was a Jewish measure for liquids, containing about seven gallons and a half.   To say that *ten acres* should produce no more wine than this, was the same as to say that it would produce almost nothing.   ¶ *And the seed of an homer.* An *homer* was a Hebrew measure for grain, containing about eight bushels. ¶ *An ephah.* The *ephah* contained about three pecks.   Of course, to say that an homer of seed should produce about three pecks, would be the same as saying that it would produce almost nothing.

11. *Wo unto them.* The prophet, having denounced *avarice*, proceeds now to another vice—that of *intemperance*, or *dissipation.*   ¶ *That rise up early,* &c.   That rise *for this purpose*, when nothing else would rouse them.   It may illustrate this somewhat, to remark, that it was not common among the ancients to become intoxicated at an early hour of the day; see Note on Acts ii. 15; comp. 1 Thess. v. 7. It indicated then, as it does now, a confirmed and habitual state of intemperance when a man would do this early in the morning.   'The Persians, when they commit a debauch, arise betimes, and esteem the morning as the best time for beginning to drink wine, by which means they carry on their excess till night.'— *Morier.*   ¶ That *they may follow strong*

12 And *a* the harp, and the viol, the tabret, and the pipe, and wine, are in their feasts: but they *b* regard

not the work of the LORD, neither consider the operation of his hands.

drink—שֵׁכָר *shēkhâr*, or sichar. This word is derived from a verb signifying to drink, to become intoxicated. All nations have found out some intoxicating drink. That which was used by the Hebrews was made from grain, fruit, honey, dates, &c., prepared by fermentation. The word sometimes means the same as wine (Num. xxviii. 7), but more commonly it refers to a stronger drink, and is distinguished from it, as in the common phrase, 'wine and strong drink;' Lev. x. 9; Num. vi. 3; Judg. xiii. 4,7. Sometimes it may be used for *spiced wine*—a mixture of wine with spices, that would also speedily produce intoxication. The Chaldee renders the word חֲמַר עַתִּיק 'old fermented liquor;' denoting the *mode* in which strong drink was usually prepared. It may be remarked here, that whatever may be the *form* in which intoxicating drink is prepared, it is substantially the same in all nations. Intoxication is caused by *alcohol*, and that is produced by fermentation. It is never created or increased by distillation. The only effect of distillation is, to collect and preserve the alcohol which existed in the beer, the wine, or the cider. Consequently, the same substance produces intoxication when wine is drank, which does when brandy is drank; the same in cider or other fermented liquor, as in ardent spirits. ¶ *That continue until night*. That drink all day. This shows that the *strong drink* intended here, did not produce *sudden* intoxication. This is an exact description of what occurs constantly in oriental nations. The custom of sitting long at the wine, when they have the means of indulgence, prevails everywhere. D Arvieux says, that while he was staying among the Arabs on mount Carmel, a wreck took place on the coast, from which one of the emirs obtained two large casks of wine. He forthwith sent to the neighbouring emirs, inviting them to come and drink it. They gladly came, and continued drinking for two days and two nights, till not a

drop of the wine was left. In like manner, Tavernier relates that the king of Persia sent for him early one morning to the palace, when, with other persons, he was obliged to sit all the day, and late at night, drinking wine with the shah; but at last, 'the king growing sleepy, gave us leave to depart, which we did very willingly, having had hard labour *for seventeen hours together*.' ¶ *Inflame them*. Excite them; or stimulate them. We have the same phrase—denoting the *burning* tendency of strong drink. The American Indians appropriately call it *fire-water*.

12. The prophet proceeds to state still further the extent of their crimes. This verse contains an account of their dissipated habits, and their consequent forgetfulness of God. That they commonly had musical instruments in their feasts, is evident from many passages of the Old Testament ; see Amos vi. 5, 6. Their feasts, also, were attended with songs ; Isa. xxiv. 8, 9. ¶ *The harp*—כִּנּוֹר, *kĭnnōr*. This is a well-known stringed instrument, employed commonly in sacred music. It is often mentioned as having been used to express the pious feelings of David ; Ps. xxxii. 2 ; xliii. 4 ; xlix. 5. It is early mentioned as having been invented by Jubal ; Gen. iv. 21. It is supposed usually to have had ten strings (Josephus, *Ant.* B. x. ch. xii. § 3). It was played by the hand ; 1 Sam. xvi. 23 ; xviii. 9. The *root* of the word כִּנּוֹר, *kĭnnōr*, is unknown. The word *kinnor* is used in all the languages cognate to the Hebrew, and is recognised even in the Persian. It is probable that the instrument here referred to was common in all the oriental nations, as it seems to have been known before the Flood, and of course the knowledge of it would be extended far. It is an oriental name and instrument, and from this word the Greeks derived their word κινύρα. The LXX. render it κιθάρα and κινύρα. Once they substitute for it ὄργανον, Ps. cxxxvi. 2 ; and five times ψαλτήριον, Gen. iv. 20; Ps. xlviii. 4;

lxxx. 2; cxlix. 3; Ezek. xxvi. 13. The harp—*kinnor*—is not only mentioned as having been invented by Jubal, but it is also mentioned by Laban in the description which he gives of various solemnities, in regard to which he assures the fleeing Jacob that it had been his wish to accompany him with all the testimonials of joy—'with music—*toph* and *kinnor*;' Gen. xxxi. 27. In the first age it was consecrated to joy and exultation. Hence it is referred to as the instrument employed by David to drive away the melancholy of Saul (1 Sam. xvi. 16–22), and is the instrument usually employed to celebrate the praises of God ; Ps. xxxiii. 1, 2; xliii. 4; xlix. 5; lxxi. 22, 23. But the harp was not only used on sacred occasions. Isaiah also mentions it as carried about by courtezans (ch. xxiii. 16), and also refers to it as used on occasions of gathering in the vintage, and of increasing the joy of the festival occasion. So also it was used in military triumphs. Under the reign of Jehoshaphat, after a victory which had been gained over the Moabites, they returned in triumph to Jerusalem, accompanied with playing on the *kinnor;* 2 Chron. xx. 27, 28. The harp was generally used on occasions of joy. Only in one place, in Isaiah (xvi. 11), is it referred to as having been employed in times of mourning. There is no ancient figure of the *kinnor* that can be relied on as genuine. We can only say that it was an instrument made of sounding wood, and furnished with strings. Josephus says that it was furnished with ten strings, and was played with the plectrum (*Ant.* B. viii. ch. x.) Suidas, in his explanation of it, makes express mention of strings or sinews (p. 318); and Pollux speaks of goats' claws as being used for the plectrum. David made it out of the *berosh*, or fir, and Solomon out of the almug. Pfeiffer supposes, that the strings were drawn over the belly of a hollow piece of wood, and that it had some resemblance to our violin. But it is more probable that the common representation of the harp as nearly in the form of a triangle, with one side or the front part wanting, is the correct one. For a full discussion of the subject, see Pfeiffer on the Music of the ancient Hebrews, *Bib. Repos.* vol. vi. pp. 366–373. Montfaucon has furnished a drawing of what was supposed to be the ancient *kinnor*, which is represented in the annexed cut. But, after all, the usual form is not quite certain.

THE HARP OR KINNOR.
From Description de l'Egypte.

Bruce found a sculpture of a harp resembling that usually put into the hands of David, or nearly in the form of a triangle, and under circumstances which led him to suppose that it was as old as the times of Sesostris. ¶ *And the viol.* נֶבֶל *nĕbhĕl.* From this word is derived the Greek word ναβλίον, and the Latin *nablium* and *nabla.* But it is not very easy to form a correct idea of this instrument. The derivation would lead us to suppose that it was something in the shape of a *bottle,* and it is probable that it had a form in the shape of a leathern bottle, such as is used in the East, or at least a vessel in which wine was preserved ; 1 Sam. x. 3; xxv. 18; 2 Sam. xvi. 1. It was at first made of the בְּרוֹשׁ *bĕrōsh* or fir; afterwards it was made of the almug tree, and occasionally it seems to have been made of metal ; 2 Sam. vi. 5; 1 Chron. xiii. 8. The external parts of the instrument were of wood, over which strings were drawn in various ways. Josephus says it had twelve strings (*Ant.* B. viii. ch. x.) He says also that it was played with the fingers.— *Ibid.* Hesychius and Pollux reckon it among stringed instruments. The resonance had its origin in the vessel or the bottom part of the instrument, upon which the strings were drawn. According to Ovid, this instrument was played on with both hands :

Quaravis mutus erat, voci favisse putatur
Piscis, Aroniae fabula nota lyrae.
Disce etiam duplicè genialia palmâ
Verrere.   *De Arte Amandi*, lib. iii. 327.

According to Jerome, Isodorus, and Cassiodorus, it had the form of an inverted Greek Delta ▽. Pfeiffer supposes that this instrument was probably the same as is found represented on ancient monuments. The belly of the instrument is a wooden bowl, having a small hole in the under part, and is covered over with a stretched skin, which is higher in the middle than at the sides. Two posts, which are fastened together at the top by a cross piece, pass obliquely through this skin. Five strings pass over this skin, having a bridge for their support on the cross piece. The instrument has no pins or screws, but every string is fastened by means of some linen wound with it around this cross piece. The description of this instrument is furnished by Niebuhr (*Th.* i. p. 179). It is played on in two ways, either by being struck with the finger, or by a piece of leather, or perhaps a quill hung at its side and drawn across the strings. It cannot with certainty be determined when this instrument was invented, or when it

LYRE.—From some of the Ancient Sculptures.

came into use among the Hebrews. It is first mentioned in the time of Saul (1 Sam. x. 5), and from this time onward it is frequently mentioned in the Old Testament. It was used particularly in the public worship of God; 2 Sam. vi. 5; 1 Kings x. 12: 2 Chron.

xx. 28; xxix. 25; 1 Chron. xv. 16; xvi. 5. It was usually accompanied with other instruments, and was also used in festivals and entertainments; see *Bib.Repos.* vol. vi. pp. 357–365. The usual form of representing it is shown in the preceding cut, and is the form in which the lyre appears on ancient monuments, in connection with the statues of Apollo.

The annexed cut is a representation of a lyre from a Jewish shekel of the time of Simon Maccabeus, and may have been, not improbably, a form in frequent use among the Jews.

LYRE.
From the Medals of Simon Maccabeus.

Niebuhr has furnished us with an instrument from the East, which is supposed to have a very near resemblance to that which is referred to by Isaiah. This instrument is represented in the following cut.

EASTERN LYRE.
From Description de l'Egypte.

¶ *The tabret.* תֹף *tŏph.* This was one of the instruments which were struck with the hands. It was the kettle-drum of the ancients, and it is more easy to determine its form and use than it is of most of the instruments used by the Hebrews. The LXX. and other Greek translators render it by τύμπανον. This word, as well as the Latin tympanum, is manifestly derived from the Hebrew. The Arabic word *duf* applied to the same instrument is also derived from the same Hebrew word. It was an instrument of wood, hollowed out, and covered over with leather and struck with the hands—a species of drum. This form of the drum is used by the Spaniards, and they have preserved it ever since the time of the Moors. It was early used. Laban wished to accompany Jacob with its sound; Gen. xxxi. 27. Miriam, the sister of Moses, and the females with her, accompanied the song of victory with this instrument; Ex. xv. 20. Job was acquainted with it (Job xvii. 6; xxi. 12), and David employed it in the festivities of religion; 2 Sam. vi. 5. The occasions on which it is mentioned as being used are joyful occasions, and for the most part those who play on it are females, and on this account they are called 'drum-beating women' (Ps. lxviii. 26)—in our transla-tion, 'damsels playing with timbrels.' In our translation it is rendered *tabret,* Isa. v. 12; 1 Sam. x. 5; Gen. xxxi. 26; Isa. xxiv. 8; xxxi. 22; 1 Sam. xviii. 6; Ezek. xxxviii. 13; Jer. xxxi. 4; Job xvii. 6; *tabering,* Nah. ii. 7; and *timbrel,* Ps. lxxxi. 2; Ex. xv. 20; Job xxi. 12; Ps. cxlix. 3; cl. 4; Judg. xi. 34; Ps. lxviii. 25. It is no where mentioned as employed in war or warlike transactions. It was sometimes made by merely stretching leather over a wooden hoop, and thus answered to the instrument known among us as the tambourine. It was in the form of a sieve, and is often found on ancient monuments, and particularly in the hands of Cybele. In the East, there is now no instrument more common than this. Niebuhr (*Th.* i. p. 181) has given the following description of it :—' It is a broad hoop covered on one side with a stretched skin. In the rim there are usually thin round pullies or wheels of metal which make some noise, when this drum, held on high with one hand, is struck with the fingers of the other hand. No musical instrument perhaps is so much employed in Turkey as this. When the females in their harems dance or sing, the time is always beat on this instrument. It is called *doff.*' The fol-lowing figures are representations of it.

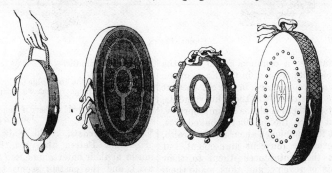

TAMBOURINES OF EASTERN ORIGIN.—From Description de l'Egypte.

See *Bib. Repos.* vol. vi. pp. 398–402. It is commonly supposed that from the word *toph, Tophet* is derived—a name given to the valley of Jehoshaphat near Jerusalem, because this instrument was used there to drown the cries of chil-dren when sacrificed to Moloch. ¶ *And*

pipe. חָלִיל *hhâlîl.* This word is de-rived either from חָלַל *hhâlâl, to bore through,* and thence conveys the idea of a flute bored through, and furnished with holes (*Gesenius*); or from חָלַל *hhâlăl, to leap* or *dance;* and thence it conveys the idea of an instrument that was played on at the dance.—*Pfeiffer*. The Greek translators have always rendered it by αὐλός. There are, in all, but four places where it occurs in the Old Testament; 1 Kings i. 40; Isa. v. 12; xxx. 29; Jer. xlviii. 36 ; and it is uniformly rendered *pipe* or *pipes*, by our translators. The origin of the pipe is unknown. It was possessed by most ancient nations, though it differed much in form. It was made sometimes of wood, at others of reed, at others of the bones of animals, horns, &c. The *box-wood* has been the common material out of which it was made. It was

sometimes used for plaintive music (comp. Matt. ix. 23); but it was also employed in connection with other instruments, while journeying up to Jerusalem to attend the great feasts there ; see Note on Isa. xxx. 29. Though employed on plaintive occasions, yet it was also employed in times of joy and pleasure. Hence, in the times of Judas Maccabeus, the Jews complained 'that all joy had vanished from Jacob, and that the flute and cithera were silent ;' 1 Mac. iii. 45 ; see *Bib. Repos.* vol. vi. pp. 387–392. The following graceful figures will show the manner of playing the flute or pipe among the Greeks.

GREEK FLUTE PLAYERS.

It was also a common art to play the double flute or pipe, in the East, in the manner represented in the cut on next page. In the use of these instruments, in itself, there could be no impropriety. That which the prophet rebuked was, that they employed them not for praise, or even for innocent amusement, but that they introduced them to their feasts of revelry, and thus made them the occasion of forgetting God. Forgetfulness of God, in connection with music and dancing, is beautifully described by Job :

They send forth their little ones like a flock,
And their children dance;
They take the timbrel and harp,
And rejoice at the sound of the organ;
They spend their days in mirth,
And in a moment go down to the grave.

And they say unto God—
'Depart from us;
For we know not the knowledge of thy ways.
What is the Almighty, that we should serve him?
And what profit should we have if we pray unto him?'   Job xxi. 11–15.

¶ *In their feasts.* 'The Nabathæans of Arabia Petrea always introduced music at their entertainments (*Strabo*, xvi.), and the custom seems to have been very general among the ancients. They are mentioned as having been essential among the Greeks, from the earliest times ; and are pronounced by Homer to be requisite at a feast:

Μολπή τ' ὀρχηστύς τε τά γάρ τ' ἀναθήματα
    δαιτός.   *Od.* i. 152.

Aristoxenus, quoted by Plutarch, *De*

13 Therefore my people are gone into captivity, because *a they have no knowledge*; and their 1 honourable men *are* famished, and their multitude dried up with thirst.

a Ho.4.6; Lu.19.44.   1 *glory are men of famine.*

14 Therefore hell hath enlarged herself, and opened her mouth without measure : and their glory, and their multitude, and their pomp, and he that rejoiceth, shall descend into it.

Musicâ, says, that 'the music was designed to counteract the effects of ine-

DOUBLE FLUTE PLAYER.

briety; for as wine discomposes the body and the mind, so music has the power of soothing them, and of restoring their previous calmness and tranquillity.' *See* Wilkinson's *Manners and Customs of the Ancient Egyptians*, vol. ii. pp. 248. 249. ¶ *But they regard not*, &c. The reproof is especially, that they forget him in their entertainments. They employ music to inflame their passions; and amid their songs and wine, their hearts are drawn away from God. That this is the tendency of such feasts, all must know. God is commonly forgotten in such places; and even the sweetest music is made the occasion for stealing the affections from him, and of inflaming the passions, instead of being employed to soften the feelings of the soul, and raise the heart to God. ¶ *The operation of his hands.* The work of his hands—particularly his dealings

among the people. God is round about them with mercy and judgment, but they do not perceive him.

13. *Therefore my people are gone.* This is evidently used with reference to the *future.* The prophet described events as *passing before his eyes* as a vision (Note, ch. i. 1); and he here seems to *see* the people going into captivity, and describes it as an event actually occurring. ¶ *Into captivity.* Referring, doubtless, to the captivity at Babylon. ¶ *Because* they have *no knowledge.* Because they do not choose to retain the knowledge of God. ¶ *And their honourable men.* The Hebrew is, ' The glory of the people became men of famine;' that is, they shall be destroyed with famine. This was to be a *punishment* for their dissipation at their feasts. ¶ *And their multitude.* The mass, or body of the nation; the common people. ¶ *Dried up with thirst.* Are punished in this manner for their indulgence in drinking. The punishment here specified, refers particularly to a journey through an arid, desolate region, where drink could be obtained only with difficulty. Such was the route which the nation was compelled afterwards to take in going to Babylon.

14. *Therefore hell.* The word translated *hell*, שׁאול *shĕôl*, has not the same meaning that we now attach to that word; its usual signification, among the Hebrews, was *the lower world, the region of departed spirits.* It corresponded to the Greek ᾅδης, *hades*, or place of the dead. This word occurs eleven times in the New Testament (Matt. xi. 23; xvi. 18; Luke x. 15; xvi. 23; Acts ii. 27, 31; 1 Cor. xv. 55; Rev. i. 18; vi. 8; xx. 13, 14), in all of which places, except 1 Cor. xv. 55, it is rendered *hell*, though denoting, in most of those places, as it does in the Old Testament, the abodes of the dead. The LXX., in this place, and usually, translate the word *sheol* by ᾅδης, *hades.* In

15 And the mean man shall be brought down, and the mighty man shall be humbled, and the eyes of the lofty shall be humbled :

16 But the LORD of hosts shall be exalted in judgment, and [1] God,

that is holy, shall be sanctified in righteousness.

17 Then shall the lambs feed after their manner, and the waste places of the fat ones shall strangers eat.

1 *the God the holy*, or, *the holy God.*

was represented by the Hebrews as *low down*, or *deep* in the earth—contrasted with the height of heaven; Deut. xxxii. 22; Job xi. 8; Ps. cxxxix. 7, 8. It was a place where thick darkness reigns; Job x. 21, 22 : 'The land of darkness and the shadow of death ; a land of darkness, as darkness itself.' It is described as having *valleys*, or *depths*, Prov. ix. 18. It is represented also as having *gates*, Isa. xxxviii. 10; and as being inhabited by a great multitude, some of whom sit on thrones, occupied in some respects as they were on earth; see Note, Isa. xiv. 9. And it is also said that the wicked descend into it by openings in the earth, as Korah, Dathan, and Abiram did ; Num. xv. 30, &c. In this place, it means evidently the *regions of the dead*, without the idea of punishment ; and the poetic representation is, that so many of the Jews would be cut off by famine, thirst, and the sword, that those vast regions would be obliged *to enlarge themselves* in order to receive them. It means, therefore, that while many of them would go into captivity (ver. 13), vast multitudes of them would be cut off by famine, thirst, and the sword. ¶ *Opened her mouth.* As if to absorb or consume them ; as a *cavern*, or opening of the earth does ; comp. Num. xvi. 30. ¶ *Without measure.* Without any limit. ¶ *And their glory.* All that they esteemed their pride and honour shall descend together into the yawning gulf. ¶ *Their multitude.* The multitude of people ; their vast hosts. ¶ *Their pomp.* Noise, tumult ; the bustle, and shouting, and display made in battle, or war, or victory ; Isa. xiii. 4; Amos ii. 2; Hos. x. 14. ¶ *And he that rejoiceth.* All that the nation prided itself on, and all that was a source of joy, should be destroyed.

15, 16. *And the mean man—the mighty man.* The expressions here mean that *all* ranks would be subdued

and punished; see Note, ch. ii. 9. ¶ *The eyes of the lofty*, &c.; see Note, ch. ii. 11, 17. ¶ *Shall be exalted in judgment.* In his justice ; he shall so manifest his justice as to be exalted in the view of the people. ¶ *Shall be sanctified.* Shall be *regarded* as holy. He shall so manifest his righteousness in his dealings, that it shall be seen and felt that he is a holy God.

17. *Then shall the lambs feed.* This verse is very variously interpreted. Most of the Hebrew commentators have followed the Chaldee interpretation, and have regarded it as designed to console the pious part of the people with the assurance of protection in the general calamity. The Chaldee is, 'Then the just shall feed, as it is said, to them ; and they shall be multiplied, and shall possess the property of the impious.' By this interpretation, *lambs* are supposed, as is frequently the case in the Scriptures, to represent the people of God. But according to others, the probable design of the prophet is, to denote the state of utter desolation that was coming upon the nation. Its cities, towns, and palaces would be destroyed, so as to become a vast pasturage where the flocks would roam at pleasure. ¶ *After their manner.* Heb. 'According to their *word*,' *i.e.*, under their own *command*, or at pleasure. They would go where they pleased without being obstructed by fences. ¶ *And the waste places of the fat ones.* Most of the ancient interpreters suppose, that the waste places of the fat ones here refer to the desolate habitations of the rich people ; in the judgments that should come upon the nation, they would become vacant, and strangers would come in and possess them. This is the sense given by the Chaldee. The Syriac translates it, 'And foreigners shall devour the ruins which are yet to be restored.' If this is the sense, then it accords with the *first* interpretation

18 Wo unto them that draw iniquity with cords of vanity, and sin as it were with a cart-rope!

19 That say, *a* Let him make speed, *and* hasten his work, that

a 2 Pe. 3, 3, 4.

we may see *it:* and let the counsel of the Holy One of Israel draw nigh and come, that we may know *it.*

20 Wo unto them that [1] call evil good, and good evil; that put dark-

[1] *say concerning evil, it is good.*

---

suggested of the previous verse—that the pious should be fed, and that the proud should be desolate, and their property pass into the hands of strangers. By others (Gesenius, &c.), it is supposed to mean that strangers, or foreigners, would come in, and fatten their cattle in the desert places of the nation. The land would be so utterly waste, that they would come there to fatten their cattle in the rank and wild luxuriancy that would spontaneously spring up. This sense will suit the connection of the passage; but there is some difficulty in making it out from the Hebrew. The Hebrew which is rendered 'the waste places of the fat ones,' may, however, be translated 'the deserts that are rich—rank—luxuriant.' The word *stranger* denotes *foreigners;* or those who are not *permanent* dwellers in the land.

18. *Wo unto them,* &c. This is a new denunciation. It introduces another form of sin, and threatens its appropriate punishment. ¶ *That draw iniquity with cords of vanity.* The general idea in this verse and the next, is, doubtless, that of plunging deeper and deeper into sin. The word *sin* here, has been sometimes supposed to mean *the punishment* for sin. The word has that meaning sometimes, but it seems here to be taken in its usual sense. The word *cords* means strings of any kind, larger or smaller; and the expression *cords of vanity,* is supposed to mean *small, slender, feeble* strings, like the web of a spider. The word vanity שָׁוְא, *may,* perhaps, have the sense here of falsehood or deceit; and the cords of deceit may denote the schemes of evil, the plans for deceiving men, or of bringing them into a snare, as the fowler springs his deceitful snare upon the unsuspecting bird. The Chaldee translates it, 'Woe to those who begin to sin by little and little, drawing sin by cords of vanity; these sins grow

and increase until they are strong, and are like a cart-rope.' The LXX. render it, ' Woe to those who draw sin with a long cable;' *i.e.,* one sin is added to another, until it comes to an enormous length, and the whole is drawn along together. Probably the true idea is that of the ancient interpretation of the Rabbins, 'An evil inclination is at first like a fine hair string, but the finishing like a cart-rope.' At first, they draw sin with a slender cord, then they go on to greater deeds of iniquity that urge them on, and draw them with their main strength, as with a cart-rope. They make a strong *effort* to commit iniquity.

19. *That say,* &c. They add one sin to another for *the purpose* of *defying* God, and provoking him to anger. They pretend that he will not punish sin; and hence they plunge deeply into it, and defy him to punish them. ¶ *Let him make speed.* Let him come quick to punish. ¶ And *hasten his work.* His punishment. ¶ *That we may see* it. An expression of defiance. We would like to see him undertake it. ¶ *The counsel of the Holy One,* &c. His threatened purpose to punish. This is the language of all sinners. They plunge deep into sin; they mock at the threatenings of God; they defy him to do his utmost; they do not believe his declarations. It is difficult to conceive more dreadful and high-handed iniquity than this.

20. *Wo unto them that call evil good,* &c. This is the fourth class of sins denounced. The sin which is reprobated here is that of *perverting* and *confounding* things, especially the distinctions of morality and religion. They prefer erroneous and false doctrines to the true; they prefer an evil to an upright course of conduct. The Chaldee renders this, ' Wo to those who say to the impious, who are prospered in this age, You are good; and who say to the meek,

ness for light, and light for darkness ; that put bitter for sweet, and sweet for bitter !

21 Wo unto *them that are* wise in their own *a* eyes, and prudent [1] in their own sight !

a Pro.26.12.   [1] *before their face.*

22 Wo unto *them that are* mighty to drink wine, and men of strength to mingle strong drink :

23 Which justify the wicked for reward, and take away the righteousness of the righteous from him !

Ye are impious.' Jarchi thinks that the prophet here refers to those who worship idols, but he evidently has a more general reference to those who confound all the distinctions of right and wrong, and who prefer the wrong. ¶ *That put darkness for light. Darkness*, in the Scriptures, is the emblem of ignorance, error, false doctrine, crime. Light denotes truth, knowledge, piety. This clause, therefore, expresses in a figurative, but more emphatic manner, what was said in the previous member of the verse. ¶ *That put bitter. Bitter* and *bitterness* are often used to denote *sin;* see Note on Acts viii. 23; also Rom. iii. 14; Eph. iv. 31; Heb. xii. 15; Jer. ii. 19; iv. 18. The meaning here does not differ from that expressed in the other parts of the verse, except that there is *implied* the additional idea that sin *is* bitter; and that virtue, or holiness, is sweet : that is, that the one is attended with painful consequences, and the other with pleasure.

21. *Wo unto* them that are *wise*, &c. This is the fifth crime specified. It refers to those who are inflated with a false opinion of their own knowledge, and who are therefore self-confident and vain. This is expressly forbidden ; Prov. iii. 7 : ' Be not wise in thine own eyes ;' comp. Prov. xxvi. 12. ¶ *In their own eyes.* In their own opinion, or estimation. ¶ *And prudent.* Knowing; self-conceited. This was, doubtless, one characteristic of the times of Isaiah. It is known to have been strikingly the characteristic of the Jews—particularly the Pharisees—in the time of our Saviour. The evil of this was, (1.) That it evinced and fostered *pride.* (2.) That it rendered them unwilling to be instructed, and especially by the prophets. As they supposed that they were already wise enough, they refused to listen to others. This is always the effect of such self-confidence : and hence the Saviour

required his disciples to be meek, and humble, and teachable as children.

22. *Wo unto* them that are *mighty*, &c. This is the sixth specification of crime. He had already denounced the intemperate in ver. 11. But probably this was a prevailing sin. Perhaps there was no evidence of reform ; and it was needful to *repeat* the admonition, in order that men might be brought to regard it. The prophet repeats a similar denunciation in ch. lvi. 12. ¶ *Mighty.* Perhaps those who prided themselves on their ability to drink *much* without becoming intoxicated ; who had been so accustomed to it, that they defied its effects, and boasted of their power to resist its usual influence. A similar idea is expressed in ch. lvi. 12. ¶ *Men of strength.* The Chaldee understands this of *rich* men ; but, probably, the reference is to those who boasted that they were able to bear *much* strong drink. ¶ *To mingle.* To mix wine with spices, dates, drugs, &c., to make it more intoxicating ; Prov. ix. 2, 5. They boasted that they were able to drink, without injury, liquor of extraordinary intoxicating qualities. ¶*Strong drink ;* Note, ver. 11. On the subject of the strong drink used in the East, *see* Harmer's *Observations,* vol. ii. pp. 140–148. Ed. Lond. 1808.

23. *Which justify.* This refers, doubtless, to magistrates. They gave unjust decisions. ¶ *For reward.* For bribes. ¶ *And take away the righteousness.* That is, they do not decide the cause in favour of those who have just claims, but are determined by a bribe ; see Note, ch. i. 23. It is remarkable, that this is introduced in immediate connection with their being mighty to mingle strong drink. One effect of intemperance is to make a man ready to be *bribed.* Its effect is seen as clearly in courts of justice, and in the decisions of such courts, as any where. A man

24 Therefore as the [1] fire devour- eth the stubble, and the flame consumeth [a] the chaff, so their root shall be as rottenness, and their blossom shall go up as dust. Because they have cast away the law of the LORD of hosts, and despised the word of the Holy One of Israel;

1 *tongue of fire.*   *a* Mat.3.12.

25 Therefore is the anger of the LORD kindled against his people, and he hath stretched forth his hand against them, and hath smitten them : and the hills did [b] tremble, and their carcasses *were* torn [2] in the midst of the streets. For all this [c] his anger is not turned away, but his hand *is* stretched out still.

b Hab.3.6.   2 or, *as dung.*   *c* Le.26.14,&c.

that is intemperate, or that indulges in strong drink, is not qualified to be a judge.

24. *Therefore as the fire,* &c. The remainder of this chapter is occupied with predicting *judgments,* or punishments, upon the people for their sins which had been specified. The Hebrew here is, ' The *tongue* of fire.' The figure is beautiful and obvious. It is derived from the pyramidal, or tongue-like appearance of *flame.* The concinnity of the metaphor in the Hebrew is kept up. The word *devoureth* is in the Hebrew *eateth:* ' As the tongue of fire eats up,' &c. The use of the word *tongue* to denote *flame* is common in the Scriptures ; see Note on Acts ii. 3. ¶ *And the flame consumeth the chaff.* The word rendered *chaff* here, means rather *hay,* or *dried grass.* The word rendered ' consumeth,' denotes properly *to make to fall,* and refers to the appearance when a fire passes through a field of grain or grass, consuming the stalks near the ground, so that the upper portion *falls down,* or sinks gently into the flames. ¶ So *their root shall be as rottenness.* Be rotten ; or decayed—of course furnishing no moisture, or suitable juices for the support of the plant. The idea is, that all the sources of national prosperity among the Jews would be destroyed. The word *root* is often used to denote the source of *strength* or *prosperity;* Is. xiv. 30; Hos. ix. 16; Job xviii. 16. ¶ *And their blossom.* This word rather means germ, or tender branch. It also means the flower. The figure is kept up here. As the *root* would be destroyed, so would all that was supported by it, and all that was deemed beautiful, or ornamental. ¶ *As dust.* The Hebrew denotes *fine dust,* such as is easily blown

about. The root would be rotten ; and the flower, wanting nourishment, would become dry, and turn to dust, and blow away. Their strength, and the sources of their prosperity would be destroyed ; and all their splendour and beauty, all that was ornamental, and the source of national wealth, would be destroyed with it. ¶ *They have cast away.* They have refused to *obey* it. This was the cause of all the calamities that would come upon them.

25. *Therefore is the anger of the Lord kindled.* The Lord is *enraged,* or is angry. Similar expressions often occur ; Num. xi. 33; 2 Kings xxiii. 26: Deut. xi. 17; Ps. lvi. 40; Job xix. 11, Ps. ii. 12. The *cause* of his anger was the crimes which are specified in this chapter. ¶ *And he hath stretched forth his hand.* To stretch forth the hand may be an action expressive of protection, invitation, or punishment. Here it is the latter ; comp. Isa. xiv. 27. ¶ *And hath smitten them.* Punished them. To what this refers particularly is not clear. Gesenius supposes that the expressions which follow are descriptive of pestilence. Lowth and Rosenmüller suppose that they refer to the earthquakes which occurred in the days of Uzziah, and in the time of the prophets; Amos i. 1; Zech. xiv. 5. The words, perhaps, will bear either construction. ¶ *And the hills did tremble.* This expression is one that is often used in the Scriptures to denote the presence and anger of God. It is well adapted to describe an earthquake ; but it is also often used poetically, to describe the presence and the majesty of the Most High ; comp. Ps. cxliv. 5; Job ix. 6; xxvi. 11; Ps. cxiv. 7; Jer. iv. 24; Hab. iii. 10; Ps. xviii. 7; xcvii. 5; civ. 32. The image is one that is very sublime. The earth,

26 And he will lift up an ensign to the nations from far, and will hiss unto them from the end of the earth; and, behold, they shall come with speed swiftly.

a Joel 2.3-11.

27 None [a] shall be weary nor stumble among them; none shall slumber nor sleep; neither shall the girdle of their loins be loosed, nor the latchet of their shoes be broken:

---

as if conscious of the presence of God, is represented as alarmed, and trembling. Whether it refers here to the earthquake, or to some other mode of punishment, cannot be determined. The fact, however, that such an earthquake had occurred in the time of Isaiah, would seem to fix the expression to that. Isaiah, from that, took occasion also to denounce future judgments. This was but the beginning of woes. ¶ *And their carcasses* were *torn*. The margin here is the more correct translation. The passage means that their dead bodies were strewed, unburied, like filth, through the streets. This expression would more naturally denote a pestilence. But it may be descriptive of an earthquake, or of any calamity. ¶ *For all this*. Notwithstanding all this calamity, his judgments are not at an end. He will punish the nation more severely still. In what way he would do it, the prophet proceeds in the remainder of the chapter to specify; comp. ch. ix. 12; x. 4.

26. *And he will lift up an ensign,* &c. The idea here is, that the nations of the earth are under his control, and that he can call whom he pleases to execute his purposes. This power over the nations he often claims; comp. Isa. xliv. 28; xlv. 1–7; x. 5–7; ix. 11; viii. 18. An *ensign* is the *standard*, or *flag* used in an army. The elevation of the standard was a signal for assembling for war. God represents himself here as simply raising the standard, expecting that the nations would come at once. ¶ *And will hiss unto them.* This means that he would *collect* them together to accomplish his purposes. The expression is probably taken from the manner in which bees were hived. Theodoret and Cyril, on this place, say, that in Syria and Palestine, they who kept bees were able to draw them out of their hives, and conduct them into fields, and bring them back again, with

the sound of a flute or the noise of hissing. It is certain also that the ancients had this idea respecting bees. Pliny (lib. xi. ch. 20) says: Gaudent plausu, atque tinnitu aeris, cóque convocantur. 'They rejoice in a sound, and in the tinkling of brass, and are thus called together.' Ælian (lib. v. ch. 13) says, that when they are disposed to fly away, their keepers make a musical and harmonious sound, and that they are thus brought back as by a siren, and restored to their hives. So Virgil says, when speaking of bees:

Tinnitusque cie, et Matris quate cymbala circum.
Georg. iv. 64.

'On brazen vessels beat a tinkling sound,
And shake the cymbals of the goddess round;
Then all will hastily retreat, and fill
The warm resounding hollow of their cell.'
Addison.

So Ovid:

Jamque erat ad Rhodopen Pangaeaque flumina ventum,
Aeriferae comitum cum crepuere manus.
Ecce! novae coeunt volucres tinnitibus actae
Quosque movent sonitus aera sequuntur apes.
Fastor, lib. iii., 739.

See also Columella, lib. x. ch. 7; Lucan, lib. ix. ver. 288; and Claudian, *Panegyric. in sextum consul. Honorii,* ver. 259; comp. Bochart, *Hieroz.* P. ii. lib. iv. ch. x. pp. 506, 507. The prophets refer to that fact in several places, Isa. viii. 18; Zech. x. 8. The simple meaning is, that God, at his pleasure, would collect the nations around Judea like bees, *i.e.*, in great numbers. ¶ *The end of the earth.* That is, the remotest parts of the world. The most eastern nations known to them were probably the Babylonians, Medes, Persians, and perhaps the inhabitants of India. The general idea is, that he would call in the distant nations to destroy them. In Isa. vii. 18, Egypt and Assyria are particularly specified. This was in accordance with the prediction in Deut. xxviii. 49.

27. *None shall be weary.* In this verse and the following, the prophet

28 Whose arrows *are* sharp, and all their bows bent, their horses' hoofs shall be counted like flint, and their wheels like a whirlwind :

29 Their roaring *shall be* like a lion, they shall roar like young lions ; yea, they shall roar, and lay hold of the prey, and shall carry *it* away safe, and none shall deliver *it*.

---

describes the condition of the army that would be summoned to the destruction of Judea. It would be composed of bold, vigorous, courageous men ; they would be unwearied by long and painful journies ; they would be fierce and violent ; they would come fully prepared for conquest. None would be *weary*, *i.e.*, fatigued with long marches, or with hard service ; Deut. xxv. 18 ; 2 Sam. xvi. 14. ¶ *Nor stumble.* They shall be chosen, select men ; not those who are defective, or who shall easily fall by any impediments in the way of their march. ¶ *None shall slumber.* They shall be unwearied, and indefatigable, pursuing their purpose with ever watchful vigilance—so much as not to be off their guard. They cannot be taken by surprise. ¶ *Neither shall the girdle of their loins be loosed.* The ancients wore a loose, large, flowing robe, or upper garment. When they laboured, or ran, it was necessary to *gird* this up round the body, or to lay it aside altogether. The form of expression here may mean, that they will not relax their efforts ; they will not unloose their girdle ; they will not unfit themselves for vigorous action, and for battle. *In* that girdle, with which they bound up their robes, the orientals usually carried their dirks and swords ; see Neh. iv. 18 ; Ezek. xxii. 15. It means that they should be fully, and at all times, prepared for action. ¶ *Nor the latchet of their shoes be broken.* They will be constantly prepared for marches. The shoes, sandals, or *soles* were attached to the feet, not by upper leather, but were girded on by thongs or strings ; see Notes on Matt. iii. 2.

28. *Whose arrows* are *sharp.* Bows and arrows were the common instruments of fighting at a distance. Arrows were, of course, made sharp, and usually pointed with iron, for the purpose of penetrating the shields or coats of mail which were used to guard against them. ¶ *And all their bows bent.* All

ready for battle. ¶ *Their horses' hoofs shall be counted like flint.* It is supposed that the ancients did not usually shoe their horses. Hence a hard, solid hoof would add greatly to the value of a horse. The prophet here means, that their horses would be prepared for any fatigue, or any expedition ; see a full description of horses and chariots in Bochart's *Hieroz.* P. i. lib. ii. ch. viii. ix. ¶ *And their wheels like a whirlwind.* That is, the wheels of their chariots shall be swift as the wind, and they shall raise a cloud of dust like a whirlwind. This comparison was very common, as it is now ; see *Bochart.* See, also, a magnificent description of a war-horse in Job xxxix. 19–25.

29. *Their roaring*, &c. Their battle cry, or their shout as they enter into an engagement. Such a *shout,* or cry, was common at the commencement of a battle. War was very much a personal conflict ; and they expected to accomplish much by making it as frightful and terrible as possible. A shout served not only to excite their own spirits, but to produce an impression of their numbers and courage, and to send dismay into the opposite ranks. Such *shouts* are almost always mentioned by Homer, and by other writers, in their accounts of battles. They are often mentioned, also, in the Old Testament ; Ex. xxxii. 18 ; Jos. vi. 10, 16, 20 ; Jer. l. 15 ; 1 Sam. xvii. 20, 52 ; 2 Chron. xiii. 15 ; Job xxxix. 25. ¶ *Like a lion.* This comparison is common in the Bible ; Jer. li. 38 ; Hos. xi. 10 ; Amos iii. 4 ; comp. Num. xxiii. 24. ¶ *Like young lions.* This variation of the expression, from the lion to the young lion, is very common. It is the Hebrew form of poetry, where the second member expresses little more than the first. Here the description is that of a lion, or more probably a *lioness* and her whelps, all ravenous, and all uniting in roaring for prey. The idea is, that the army that would come up would be

30 And in that day shall they
roar against them like the roaring
of the sea ; and if *one* look unto the
land, behold darkness *and* 1 sorrow,
and 2 the light is darkened in the
heavens thereof.

1 or, *distress.*　　　　2 or, *when it is light, it shall
be dark in the destructions thereof.*

greedy of plunder ; they would rush on
to rapine in a frightful manner.

30. *They shall roar against them.*
The army that shall come up shall roar
against the Jews. The image of *the
roaring of the sea* indicates the great
number that would come; that of the
roaring of the *lion* denotes their fierceness and terror. ¶ *And if* one *look
unto the land.* This expression has
given some perplexity, because it is supposed not to be full or complete. The
whole image, it has been supposed (see
Lowth), would be that of looking *upward* to the heaven for help, and then
to the land, or *earth;* comp. ch. viii. 22,
where the same expression is used.
But there is no need of supposing the
expression defective. The prophet
speaks of the vast multitude that was
coming up and roaring like the tumultuous *ocean.* On *that* side there was
no safety. The waves were rolling, and
every thing was fitted to produce alarm.
It was natural to speak of the *other*
direction, as the *land*, or the shore; and
to say that the people would look there
for safety. But, says he, there would
be no safety there. All would be darkness. ¶ *Darkness* and *sorrow.* This
is an image of distress and calamity.
There should be no light ; no consolation ; no safety ; comp. ch. lix. 9; Amos
v. 18, 20; Lam. iii. 2. ¶ *And the light
is darkened,* &c. That which gave
light is turned to darkness. ¶ *In the
heavens thereof.* In the *clouds,* perhaps, or by the gloomy thick clouds.
Lowth renders it, 'the light is obscured
by the gloomy vapour.' The main
idea is plain, that there would be
distress and calamity; and that there
would be no light to guide them on their
way. On the one hand a roaring,
raging multitude, like the sea; on the
other distress, perplexity, and gloom.
Thus shut up, they must perish, and
their land be utterly desolate.

CHAPTER VI.

ANALYSIS OF THE CHAPTER.

This chapter contains a very sublime description of the manifestation of Jehovah to Isaiah,
and of a solemn commission to him to declare
his purposes to the Jews. It has been supposed
by many to be a solemn *inauguration* to the prophetic office, and to have been the *first* of his
prophecies. But this supposition is not to be
considered as just. It is evident (Isa. i. 1) that
he prophesied *before* the death of Uzziah, and
there is reason to suppose that the order of *time*
is observed in the previous chapters; see Introduction, § 2. The most probable supposition of
the occasion of this prophecy, is this, that the
people were extremely guilty; that they were
strongly indisposed to listen to the message of
the prophet, and that he was therefore favoured
with this extraordinary commission in order to
give his message more success and higher authority in the minds of the people. It is a new
commission to make his message as impressive
as possible—as if it came direct from the lips of
the Almighty. The Jews say, that for this pre-
tension that he had seen Jehovah, he was sawn
asunder by *Manasseh.* And to this fact Paul has
been supposed to refer in Heb. xi. 37, where he
says of those who had been eminent in faith,
'they were sawn asunder;' see Introduction, § 2.

This vision is expressed in the language appropriate to Eastern monarchs. God is represented
as sitting on a *throne,* and attended by ministers,
here called seraphim. His throne is elevated,
and the posture of sitting denotes dignity and
majesty. The language of the description is
taken from the temple. The image is that of
God sitting in the most holy place. Surrounding him are seen the seraphim, and the cloud
filling the temple. Isaiah is represented as
without the temple, near the altar. The great
altar of sacrifice stood directly in front of the
temple, so that if the doors of the temple had
been open, and the veil separating the holy from
the most holy place had been withdrawn, he
would have had a distinct view of the mercy-
seat. That veil between is supposed to be withdrawn, and he is permitted directly to contemplate the sacred and solemn manifestation made
in the immediate dwelling-place of God. The
chapter comprises, properly, three parts.

I. The vision, ver. 1–4. Jehovah is seen upon
a throne, clad in the manner of an ancient monarch, with a robe and a train which filled the
whole temple. He sits as a king, and is adorned
in the robes of royalty, ver. 1. He is encompassed with ministering spirits—with the seraphim, in the manner of a magnificent king, ver. 2.

They are seen, by the prophet, to be solemnly engaged in his worship, and to stand in the attitude of the most profound veneration, ver. 3. So awful and sublime was the worship, that even the posts of the temple were moved; the whole sacred edifice trembled at the presence of God, and at the voice of those who were engaged in his praise; and the whole temple was filled with the symbol of the Divine presence and majesty, ver. 4.

II. The *effect on the prophet*, ver. 5–7. He was overcome with a sense of his unworthiness, and felt that he could not live. He had seen Jehovah, and he felt that he was a ruined man, ver. 5. Yet one of the seraphim flew to the altar, and bore thence a live coal, and touched his lips, and assured him that his sin was taken away, and that he was pardoned, ver. 6, 7.

III. The *commission of the prophet*, ver. 8–13.

God inquires who will go for him to the people, and bear his message, and the prophet expresses his readiness to do it, ver. 8. The nature of the message is stated, ver. 9, 10. The *duration*—the state of things which he predicted would follow from this—is asked, and the answer is returned, ver. 11–13. It was to be until utter desolation should spread over the land, and the mass of the nation was cut off, and all were destroyed, except the small portion which it was necessary to preserve, in order to prevent the nation from becoming wholly extinct.

IN the year *a* that king Uzziah died, I saw *b* the Lord sitting upon a throne, high and lifted up, and 1 his train filled the temple.

a 2Ki.15.7. *b* 1Ki.22.19. 1 or, *the skirts thereof.*

CHAPTER VI.

1. *In the year.* This naturally denotes a period *after* the death of Uzziah, though in the same year. The mention of the time was evidently made when the prophecy was composed, and it is to be presumed that the death of Uzziah *had* occurred at the time when the prophet saw this vision. If so, it is clear that this was not the *first* of his prophecies, for he saw his visions '*in the days* of Uzziah;' ch. i. 1. The Chaldee, however, reads this: 'in the year when Uzziah was smitten with the leprosy;' and most of the Jewish commentators so understand it; 2 Chron. xxvi. 19, 20. The Rabbins say that the meaning is, that he then became *civilly* dead, by ceasing to exercise his functions as a king, and that he was cut off as a leprous man from all connection with the people, and from all authority; see Introduction, § 3. This is, doubtless, true; but still, the more natural signification is, that this occurred in the year in which he actually died. ¶ *I saw.* That is, he saw in a *vision;* see Introduction, § 7, (4.) A similar vision is described by Micaiah; 1 Kings xxii. 19; see also Amos vii. 1; viii. 1; ix. 1; Dan. vii. 13, &c. ¶ *The Lord.* In the original here the word is not *Jehovah,* but אֲדֹנָי *ădōnai ;* see Notes on ch. i. 24. Here it is applied to Jehovah ; see also Ps. cxiv. 7, where it is also so applied ; and see Isa. viii. 7, and Job xxviii. 28, where Jehovah calls

himself *Adonai.* The word does not itself denote essential divinity ; but it is often applied to God. In some MSS., however, of Kennicott and De Rossi, the word Jehovah is found. We may make two remarks here. (1.) That Isaiah evidently meant to say that it was Jehovah who appeared to him. He is expressly so called in ver. 5, 8, 11. (2.) It is equally clear, from the New Testament, that Isaiah saw The Messiah. John quotes the words in this chapter, ver. 10, as applicable to Jesus Christ, and then adds (John xii. 41), 'these things said Esaias when he saw his glory, and spake of him.' An inspired man has thus settled this as referring to the Messiah, and thus had established the propriety of applying to him the name Jehovah, *i.e.*, has affirmed that the Lord Jesus is Divine. Jerome says, that this vision was designed to represent the doctrine of the Trinity.— In John i. 18, it is said, 'No man hath seen God at any time; the only begotten Son, who is in the bosom of the Father, he hath declared him.' In Ex. xxxiii. 20, God says, 'Thou canst not see my face, for there shall no man see me and live ;' see also 1 Tim. vi. 16. These passages may be reconciled with what is here said by Isaiah, in the following manner :—(1.) Isaiah does not say that he saw the Divine essence ; and all that his words fairly imply, is, that he saw a manifestation, or vision of Jehovah— some striking symbolical representation

2 Above it stood the seraphims : each one had six wings ; with twain he covered his face, and with twain

he *a* covered his feet, and with twain he did fly.

a Eze.1.11.

of him. (2.) It was the manifestation of JEHOVAH in the person of the Messiah, of the 'only begotten Son who hath revealed or declared him,' that he saw. Such manifestations of God have been made often, and all that the declaration of Isaiah implies, of necessity, is, that he had a vision of God incarnate seated in glory, from whom he now received a new commission to go out and proclaim the truth to that wicked and rebellious generation. ¶ *Sitting upon a throne.* God is thus often represented as a king, sitting on a throne ; 1 Kings xxii. 19; Ezek. xliii. 7; Jer. xvii. 12. ¶ *High and lifted up.* That is, the *throne ;* an indication of state and majesty. ¶ *And his train.* The word *train* שׁוּלָיו, properly signifies the skirt of a garment, or a robe ; Ex. xxviii. 33, 34. Here it is evidently designed as a representation of a large, flowing robe, that filled all the most holy part of the temple. The Orientals regarded such large robes as indicative of grandeur and state. The Messiah was seen seated on a throne as a king ; clothed in a large, loose, flowing robe, in the manner of oriental monarchs, and surrounded by his ministers. The design of this magnificent vision was not only to impress the prophet with a sense of the holiness of God, but also to give additional weight to his commission, as having been derived immediately from the Divine majesty; comp. ver. 9, 10. It is remarkable that Isaiah attempts no representation of JEHOVAH himself. He mentions his robes; the throne; the seraphim; but mentions no form or appearance of God himself. In this there is great sublimity. There is enough mentioned to fill the mind with awe; there is enough concealed to impress as deeply with a sense of the Divine majesty. It is remarkable, also, that it is not the *usual* appearance of God in the temple to which he refers. That was the *Shekinah,* or visible symbol of God. That was on the mercy-seat, this was on a throne; that was a cloud, of this no form is mentioned; over that

the cherubim stretched forth their wings, over this stood the seraphim ; that had no clothing, this was clad in a full flowing robe. ¶ *Filled the temple.* Probably, the most holy place only is intended. The large, full, magnificent robe seemed to fill up the entire holy of holies. Some have supposed that this vision was represented as appearing in the *heavens.* But the expression here evidently implies, that it was seen in the *temple* at Jerusalem.

2. *Above it.* Either above the throne, or above him. The LXX. render it, 'Round about him '—κύκλῳ αὐτοῦ. The Chaldee, 'The holy ministers stood on high in his presence.' ¶ *The seraphims.* The verb שָׂרַף *sârăph,* from which this word is derived, is uniformly translated *to burn,* and is used frequently ; see *Taylor.* The noun שָׂרָף denotes, according to Bochart, the *chersydros,* a serpent that lives in lakes and moist places ; but when those places are dried up, it becomes a land serpent, and then its bite is very fierce, and is attended with a most dreadful inflammation all over the body. Rabbi Solomon says, that 'serpents are called *seraphim* because they burn men with the poison of their teeth,' perhaps because the idea of *heat* and *poison* were connected. The word is applied to the fiery flying serpents which bit the children of Israel, and in imitation of which a brazen serpent was erected on a pole by Moses. It is translated 'a fiery serpent' in Num. xxi. 8; Isa. xiv. 29; xxx. 6. In Deut. viii. 15; Num. xxi. 6, it is rendered 'fiery,' and in the passage before us, *seraphims.* The word שְׂרֵפָה often occurs in the sense of *burning ;* Deut. xxix. 23 ; 2 Chron. xvi. 14; xxi. 19, &c. The LXX. render it *seraphim,* σεραφίμ ; so the Vulgate and the Syriac. The Chaldee, 'his holy ministers.' Probably it is now impossible to tell why this name was given to the representations that appeared to Isaiah. Perhaps it may have been from their *burning* ardour and zeal in the service of God; perhaps from the *rapidity* of their

3 And [1] one cried unto another, and said, Holy, holy, holy *is* the

1 *this cried to this.*

LORD of hosts ; the [2] whole earth *is* full of his glory.

2 *his glory is the fulness of the whole earth.*

motion in his service—derived from the rapid motion of the serpent. Gesenius supposes that the name was derived from a signification of the word denoting *noble* or *excellent*, and that it was on this account applied to princes, and to celestial beings. Kimchi says, that the name was given with reference to their bright, shining appearance ; comp. Ezek. i. 13 ; 2 Kings ii. 2 ; vi. 17. The word is applied to celestial beings no where else, except in this chapter. There is no reason to think that the seraphim described here partook of the *form* of the serpent, as the representation seems to be rather that of a man. Thus each one (ver. 2) is represented as covering his *face* and his *feet* with his wings—a description that does not pertain to the serpentine form. God is usually represented as surrounded or encompassed by heavenly beings, as his ministers ; Ps. civ. 4 ; Dan. vii. 10 ; 1 Kings xxii. 19 ; Ps. lxviii. 17 ; Heb. xii. 22. The idea is one of peculiar magnificence and grandeur. It is derived especially from the customs of monarchs, particularly Eastern monarchs, who had numerous princes and nobles to attend them, and to give magnificence to their court. ¶ *Each one had six wings.* Wings are emblematic of the *rapidity* of their movement ; the number here, perhaps, denoting their celerity and readiness to do the will of God. ¶ *With twain he covered his face.* This is designed, doubtless, to denote the *reverence* and *awe* inspired by the immediate presence of God ; comp. Amos vi. 9, 10. The Chaldee adds, ' He covered his face *so that he could not see.*' To cover the face in this manner is the natural expression of reverence ; comp. Note on ch. lii. 15. And if the pure and holy seraphim evinced such reverence in the presence of Jehovah, with what profound awe and veneration should we, polluted and sinful creatures, presume to draw near to him ! Assuredly *their* position should reprove our presumption when we rush thoughtlessly and irreverently into his presence, and should teach us to bow with lowly veneration

and deep humility ; comp. Rev. iv. 9–11. ¶ *He covered his feet.* In a similar description of the cherubim in Ezek. i. 11, it is said that they covered *their bodies.* In Isaiah, the expression clearly denotes not the feet only, but the lower extremities. This was also an expression of reverence drawn from our conceptions of propriety. The seraphim stood covered, or as if *concealing themselves* as much as possible, in token of their nothingness and unworthiness in the presence of the Holy One. ¶ *He did fly.* He was quick to execute the commands of God. It may be observed, also, that among the ancients, *Mercury*, the messenger of Jupiter, was always represented with wings. Milton has copied this description of the seraphim :

'A seraph winged:—six wings he wore to shade
His lineaments divine; the pair that clad
Each shoulder broad, came mantling o'er his breast
With regal ornament; the middle pair
Girt like a starry zone his waist, and round
Skirted his loins and thighs with downy gold,
And colours dipt in heaven; the third his feet
Shadowed from either heel with feathered mail,
Sky-tinctured grain.'
                            Par. Lost, Book v.

3. *And one cried to another.* Heb. 'This cried to this.' That is, they cried to each other in alternate responses. One cried ' holy ;' the second repeated it ; then the third ; and then they probably united in the grand chorus, ' Full is all the earth of his glory.' This was an ancient mode of singing or recitative among the Hebrews ; see Ex. xv. 20, 21, where Miriam is represented as going before in the dance with a timbrel, and the other females as following her, and *answering*, or responding to her, Ps. cxxxvi. 1 ; comp. Lowth, *on the Sacred Poetry of the Hebrews,* Lect. xix. ¶ *Holy, holy, holy.* The *repetition* of a name, or of an expression, three times, was quite common among the Jews. Thus, in Jer. vii. 4, the Jews are represented by the prophet as saying, ' the temple of the Lord, the temple of the Lord, the temple of the Lord, are these.' Thus, Jer. xxii. 29: ' O earth, earth, earth, hear the word of the Lord ;' Ezek.

4 And the posts of the [1]door moved at the voice of him that cried, and the house was filled with smoke.

5 Then said I, Wo *is* me ! for I am [2]undone ; because *a* I *am* a man

[1] *thresholds.*   [2] *cut off.*   *a* Zec.3.1-7.

xxi. 27 : 'I will overturn, overturn, overturn;' see also 1 Sam. xviii. 23: 'O my son Absalom! my son, my son ;' see also the repetition of the form of benediction among the Jews, Num. vi. 24–26:

JEHOVAH bless thee and keep thee;
JEHOVAH make his face to shine upon thee, and be gracious unto thee;
JEHOVAH lift up his countenance upon thee, and give thee peace.

In like manner, the number *seven* is used by the Hebrews to denote a great, indefinite number ; then a full or complete number ; and then perfectness, completion. Thus, in Rev. i. 4; iii. 1; iv. 5, the phrase, 'the seven spirits of God,' occurs as applicable to the Holy Spirit, denoting his fulness, completeness, perfection. The Hebrews usually expressed the superlative degree by the repetition of a word. Thus, Gen. xiv. 10: 'The vale of Siddim, *pits, pits* of of clay,' *i.e.*, was full of pits ; see Nordheimer's *Heb. Gram.* § 822–824. The form was used, therefore, among the Jews, to denote *emphasis ;* and the expression means in itself no more than 'thrice holy;' that is, supremely holy. Most commentators, however, have supposed that there is here a reference to the doctrine of the Trinity. It is not probable that the Jews so understood it ; but applying to the expressions the fuller revelations of the New Testament, it cannot be doubted that the words will express that. Assuming that that doctrine is true, it cannot be doubted, I think, that the seraphs laid the foundation of their praise in that doctrine. That there was a distinct reference to the second person of the Trinity, is clear from what John says, ch. xii. 41. No *argument* can be drawn directly from this in favour of the doctrine of the Trinity ; for the repetition of such phrases thrice in other places, is merely *emphatic*, denoting the superlative degree. But when the doctrine is *proved* from other places, it may be presumed that the heavenly beings were apprized of it, and that the foundation of their ascriptions of praise was laid in that.

The Chaldee has rendered this, 'Holy in the highest heavens, the house of his majesty ; holy upon the earth, the work of his power; holy for ever, and ever, and ever, is the Lord of hosts.' The whole expression is a most sublime ascription of praise to the living God, and should teach us in what manner to approach him. ¶ *The* LORD *of hosts;* see Note, ch. i. 9. ¶ *The whole earth.* Marg. 'The earth is the fulness of his glory.' All things which he has made on the earth express his glory. His wisdom and goodness, his power and holiness, are seen every where. The whole earth, with all its mountains, seas, streams, trees, animals, and men, lay the foundation of his praise. In accordance with this, the Psalmist, in a a most beautiful composition, calls upon all things to praise him ; see Ps. cxlviii.

Praise the Lord from the earth,
Ye dragons, and all deeps:
Fire and hail; snow and vapours;
Stormy wind fulfilling his word:
Mountains, and all hills;
Fruitful trees, and all cedars;
Beasts, and all cattle;
Creeping things, and flying fowl.

4. *And the posts of the door.* Marg. 'Thresholds.' There is some difficulty in the Hebrew here, but the meaning of the expression is sufficiently apparent. It means that there was a tremour, or concussion, as if by awe, or by the sound attending the cry. It is evidently a poetic expression. ¶ *The house.* The temple. ¶ *Was filled with smoke.* There is here, doubtless, a reference to *the cloud* that is so often mentioned in the Old Testament as the visible symbol of the Divinity; see Note, Isa. iv. 5. A similar appearance is recorded when Solomon dedicated the temple; 1 Kings viii. 10; 2 Chron. v. 13; Ezek. x. 4.

5. *Wo is me !* That is, I am filled with overwhelming convictions of my own unworthiness, with alarm that I have seen JEHOVAH. ¶ *For I am undone.* Marg. 'Cut off.' Chaldee, 'I have sinned.' LXX., 'I am miserable, I am *pierced through.*' Syriac, 'I am

of unclean lips, and I dwell in the midst of a people of unclean lips ; for mine eyes have seen the King, the LORD of hosts.

6 Then flew one of the seraphims

1 and in his hand a live coal.

unto me, [1] having a live coal in his hand, *which* he had taken with the tongs from off the *a* altar ;

7 And he [2] laid *it* upon my mouth, and said, Lo, this hath touched thy

a Rev.8.3.   2 caused it to touch.

---

struck dumb.' The Hebrew word may sometimes have this meaning, but it also means *to be destroyed, to be ruined, to perish;* see Hos. x. 15; Zeph. i. 2; Hos. iv. 6; Isa. xv. 1. This is probably the meaning here, 'I shall be ruined, or destroyed.' The reason of this, he immediately states. ¶ *A man of unclean lips.* This expression evidently denotes that he was a *sinner,* and especially that he was unworthy either to join in the praise of a God so holy, or to deliver a message in his name. The vision; the profound worship of the seraphim; and the attendant majesty and glory, had deeply impressed him with a sense of the holiness of God, and of his own unfitness either to join in worship so holy, or to deliver the message of so pure a God. A similar effect is recorded in reference to Abraham; Gen. xviii. 27; see also Ex. iv. 10, 12; Jer. i. 6. A deep consciousness of guilt, in view of the holiness and majesty of God, is also described by Job:

I have heard of thee by the hearing of the ear,
But now mine eye seeth thee.
Wherefore I abhor myself,
And repent in dust and ashes.—Job xlii. 5, 6.

An effect also remarkably similar is described in reference to the apostle Peter, Luke v. 8: " When Simon Peter saw it [the miracle which Jesus had wrought], he fell down at Jesus' knees, saying, Depart from me, for I am a sinful man, O Lord.' ¶ *A people of unclean lips.* A people who are unworthy to celebrate the praises of a God so pure and exalted. ¶ *Mine eyes have seen.* In Ex. xxxiii. 20, it is said : ' Thou canst not see my face ; for there shall no man see me and live;' comp. John i. 18; 1 Tim. vi. 16. Perhaps it was in recollection of this, that Isaiah said he was undone. It is not, however, to be understood that the prophet saw JEHOVAH himself, but only the *symbol* of his presence. It was for this expression, according to the tradition of the Jews, that Manasseh took occasion

to put the prophet to death ; see Introduction, § 2. ¶ *The Lord of hosts.* JEHOVAH of hosts. John applies this to the Lord Jesus, and this proves that he is Divine ; see John xii. 41.

6. *Then flew.* Isaiah is represented as standing *out* of the temple ; the seraphim as *in* it. ¶ *Having a live coal.* The Vulgate renders this, 'A stone.' This is, probably, the original meaning of the word ; see 1 Kings xix. 6. It at first denoted a hot stone which was used to roast meat upon. It may also mean a coal, from its resemblance to such a stone. ¶ *From off the altar.* The altar of burnt-offering. This stood in the court of the priests, in front of the temple; see Notes on Matt. xxi. 12. The fire on this altar was at first kindled by the Lord, Lev. ix. 24, and was kept continually burning ; Lev. vi. 12, 13.

7. *And he laid it upon my mouth.* Marg. ' And he caused it to touch my mouth.' This is the more correct rendering. It was a slight, momentary touch, sufficient merely to be a *sign* or *token* that he was cleansed. ¶ *Thine iniquity is taken away.* That is, whatever obstacle there existed to your communicating the message of God to this people, arising from your own consciousness of unworthiness, is taken away. You are commissioned to bear that message, and your own consciousness of guilt should not be a hinderance. To understand this, it should be remembered that *fire,* among the orientals, has been always regarded as an emblem of *purifying.* Thus the Sabeans, the followers of Zoroaster in Persia, worshipped *fire,* as the emblem of a pure divinity ; see Mal. iii. 2, 3 ; comp. Matt. iii. 2. Every minister of the gospel, though conscious of personal unworthiness and unfitness, should yet go freely and cheerfully to his work, if he has evidence that he is called and commissioned by God. ¶ *Is purged.* Is purified, is removed —תְּכֻפַּר from כָּפַר *kâphăr, to cover, to*

lips, and thine iniquity is taken away, and thy sin purged.

8 Also I heard the voice of the Lord, saying, Whom shall I send, and who will go for us? Then said I, [1] Here *am* I; send me.

[1] Behold me.

overlay; then to make an atonement for, to expiate, to cover sin, to pardon it, to affect or to procure forgiveness; and then to purify in general, to make whole; comp. Note on ch. xliii. 3. This does not mean, that the fire from the altar had any physical effect to purify him from sin, but that it was *emblematic* of such a purifying; and probably, also, the fact that it was taken from the altar of sacrifice, was to him an indication that he was pardoned through the *atonement*, or expiation there made. The Jews expected pardon in no other mode than by sacrifice; and the offering on their altar pointed to the great sacrifice which was to be made on the cross for the sins of men. There is here a beautiful *union* of the truths respecting sacrifice. The great doctrine is presented that it is only by sacrifice that sin can be pardoned; and the Messiah, the sacrifice himself, is exhibited as issuing the commission to Isaiah to go and declare his message to men.

8. *The voice of the* Lord. Heb. ' The voice of Jehovah.' He had before been addressed by one of the seraphim. ¶ *Whom shall I send, and who will go for us?* The change of number here, from the singular to the plural, is very remarkable. Jerome, on this place, says that it indicates the 'sacrament' of the Trinity. The LXX. render it, ' Whom shall I send, and who will go to this people?' The Chaldee, ' Whom shall I send to prophesy, and who will go to teach?' The Syriac, ' Whom shall I send, and who will go?' The Arabic has followed the LXX. The use of the plural pronouns *we* and *us*, as applicable to God, occurs several times in the Old Testament. Thus, Gen. i. 26 : ' And God said, Let us make man in our image;' Gen. xi. 6, 7 : ' And Jehovah said, Go to, let us go down, and there confound their language.' Such a use of the name of God in the plural is very common, but it is not clear that there is a reference to the doctrine of the Trinity. In some cases, it is evi-

dent that it cannot have such a reference, and that no *argument* can be drawn from the use of that plural form in favour of such a doctrine. Thus, in Isa. xix. 4, the expression ' a cruel lord,' is in the Hebrew in the plural, yet evidently denoting but one. The expression translated ' the most Holy One,' or ' the Holy,' is in the plural in Prov. ix. 10; xxx. 3. In 1 Sam. xix. 13, 16, the plural form is applied to a *household god*, or an image; and the plural form is applied to God in Job xxxv. 20, ' my Makers' (Heb.); Eccl. xii. 1, ' thy Creators' (Heb.); Ps. cxxi. 5, ' Jehovah is thy keepers' (Heb.); see also Isa. liv. 5; xxii. 2; xliii. 5; lxii. 5. This is called by grammarians *pluralis excellentiæ*, or the plural form indicating majesty or honour. It is, in all countries, used in reference to kings and princes; and as God often represents himself as a *king* in the Scriptures, and speaks in the language that was usually applied to kings in oriental countries, no argument can be drawn from expressions like these in defence of the doctrine of the Trinity. There are unanswerable arguments enough in support of that doctrine, without resorting to those which are of doubtful authority.

[That there are clearer intimations of the doctrines of the Trinity, than that contained in this and similar texts, is indubitable; but we must not set aside the early and somewhat obscure intimations of a doctrine, simply because it comes afterwards to be exhibited with more fulness. Such is the plan of revelation; and, instead of despising early announcements, or deeming them useless, because better *proofs* of the doctrine in question can be found, we ought to admire the wisdom and goodness of God in this gradual development of truth. The same interest belongs to the work of thus tracing the rise and progress of truth in the Bible, as belongs to that of him who traces rivers to their fountain head, and proves that, far up amid mountains all but inaccessible, rises the tiny stream, on whose broad waters, as it nears the sea, navies float in proud array. No more visible, in its earlier outflowings, is this doctrine of the Trinity; yet by and by it is the element on which Christianity floats, and in which it lives and moves. Thus we see the unity and harmony of revelation in all ages; the doctrine is the same; the degree of manifestation only is different. The necessity of preserving and exhibiting this unity, gives to these early intimations an unspeakable importance; though some, through an excess of candour, would abandon them to the enemy. This text, and its parallels, Gen. i. 26; iii. 22; xi. 7, exhibit the Trinity in Revelation's dawn indistinctly—partially disclosed—revealing only a *plurality* of persons. As the light increases, the *three* persons are seen moving under the lifting shadows, till, in the New Testament, baptism is commanded in the name of the Father, Son, and Holy Ghost; and the existence and functions of each person are clearly unfolded.

The problem is, to account for the use of the plural number in these passages, consistently with the unity of God. The doctrine of the Trinity seems to furnish an easy and beautiful solution; but this solution has been rejected, not by Unitarians only, but by Trinitarians not a few. Various hypotheses have been offered: as, that in the creation of man (Gen. i. 26), God associated with himself the heavens and the earth; or, that he consulted with angels; or, meant simply to indicate the importance of the work; or, perhaps, to supply a lesson of deliberation! These crudities are by most, however, long ago abandoned as untenable; and the solution most generally approved by such as reject that of the Trinity, is that furnished by an appeal to the *style of majesty.* Oriental princes, it is alleged, from the most ancient times, used the plural number in publishing their decrees; and such is the style of royalty to this day. But, unfortunately for this theory, there is no evidence whatever that ancient potentates employed this style. *The use of the plural number by kings and princes, is quite a modern invention.* The Bible does not furnish any example of it. Nor is there any evidence that God himself, on peculiarly solemn occasions, keeping out of sight, of course, the text in question, used such style; there is abundant evidence to the contrary, the singular number being used by Jehovah in the most sublime and awful declarations.

Besides this strange use of the plural number on the part of God himself, plural names (Elohim, Adonim) are frequently given to him by the writers of the Bible; the instances in which these names occur in the singular form, are the exceptions. The name usually rendered *God* in the English Bible, is almost invariably plural—Elohim, Gods. That these plural forms are used of idols, as well as of the true God, is admitted;

but as the peculiar names of the true God came, in process of time, to be applied to idols, so would the peculiar *form* of these names, and to tell us that these forms *are* so applied, is quite beside the question. We wish to know why, originally, such forms were applied to the *true* God; and it is no answer to tell us they are also applied to idols. 'There is nothing more wonderful in the name being so used *in the plural form*, than in its being so used *at all.* The same principle which accounts for the name GOD being given to heathen deities *at all*, will equally well account for its being given to them in the *particular form* in which it is applied to the true God.'—*Wardlaw.* This is pointed and decisive; and renders it needless to speculate here on the *mode* in which the name, or the plural form of it, came to be transferred to false gods, or great men. On this point, see Dr. J. Pye Smith's *Scripture Testimony to the Messiah.* It is further remarkable, that these plural appellatives are, for the most part, combined with verbs and adjectives in *the singular number;* as, ' Gods (he) created,' Gen. i. 1; and with plural adjuncts 'but rarely. Now, the ordinary rule of grammar might have been followed invariably, as well as in these few instances, or the departures from it might have been but few in number. That this is not the case, implies the existence of some very cogent reason, and cannot be regarded as the result, merely, of accident. To account for the use of these plural names, our author has recourse to what is called the *pluralis majestaticus*, or *excellentiæ*, according to which, nouns of dignity and majesty, in Hebrew, are said to be used in the plural form. But the existence of this *pluralis majestaticus* has never been proved. Its defence is now abandoned by the most skilful grammarians. Ewald repudiates it. And it is not a little remarkable, that some of the examples most relied on for proof of this *dignified plural*, are found, on examination, to possess nothing of the dignity, while more exact scholarship has reduced their plurality also. The examples alluded to, are, Exod. xxi. 29, 34; xxii. 10, 13; Isa. i. 3; where the supposed plural form denotes the owner of oxen, of sheep, and of asses!—fit parties, doubtless, to be honoured with the *pluralis majestaticus.* In truth, leaving out of view the plural appellatives applied to the Deity, *i.e.*, the appellatives in question, and which, therefore, cannot be adduced, there is no evidence whatever of this pretended rule. Had any rule of the kind existed, we should, without doubt, have found it exemplified, when kings, princes, nobles, generals, priests, and prophets figure on the sacred pages. That the *pluralis excellentiæ* is not applied to them, is sufficient proof of its non-

9 And he said, Go and tell this people, Hear ye [1]indeed, but understand not ; and see ye [2]indeed, but perceive not.

10 Make the heart of this people fat, and make their ears heavy,

[1] *in hearing,* or *without ceasing.*

and shut their eyes: lest they see with their eyes, and hear with their ears, and understand with their heart, and convert, and be healed.

11 Then said I, LORD, how long? And he answered, Until the cities

[2] *in seeing.*

---

existence; and should dispose rational and candid inquirers to acquiesce in the solution of the grammatical anomalies we have been considering, that is furnished by the doctrine of Trinity in Unity—the solution which, to say the least of it, is beset with fewest difficulties.]

The language here indicates the *design* for which this vision was shown to Isaiah. It was to commission him to exhibit truth that would be extremely unpleasant to the nation, and that would have the certain effect of hardening their hearts. In view of the nature and effect of this message, God is represented as inquiring who would be willing to undertake it? Who had courage enough to do it? Who would risk his life? And it indicates, perhaps, that there were *few* in the nation who would be willing to do it, and that it was attended with self-denial and danger. ¶ *Here am I.* This shows at once his confidence in God, and his zeal. He had been qualified for it by the extraordinary commission, and he was now ready to bear the message to his countrymen. In this attitude *we* should stand, prompt to deliver *any* message that God shall intrust to our hands, and to engage in *any* service that he calls on us to perform.

9. *And he said,* &c. The expressions which follow are those which denote hardness of heart and blindness of mind. They would hear the *words* of the prophet, but they would not understand him. They were so obstinately bent on iniquity that they would neither believe nor regard him. This shows the spirit with which ministers must deliver the message of God. It is their business to deliver the message, though they should know that it will neither be understood nor believed. ¶ *Hear ye indeed.* Heb. ' In hearing, hear.' This is a mode of expressing emphasis. This passage is quoted in Matt. xiii. 14 ; see Note on that place.

10. *Make the heart.* The word *heart*

here is used in the sense of the *mind*— to denote all their mental powers. It is commonly used in this sense in the Scriptures. ¶ *Fat.* Gross, heavy, dull, stupid. That is, go and proclaim such *truth* to them as shall have this effect— as shall irritate, provoke, enrage them ; truth, whose delivery shall be attended, in their gross and corrupt hearts, with this blinding and infatuating influence. The effect would be produced by the corrupt state of their hearts, not by any native tendency of the truth, and still less by any direct Divine influence. ' Go, and *proclaim truth* to a corrupt and sensual people, and the *result* will be that they will not hear ; they are so wicked that they will not attend to it ; they will become even *more* hardened ; yet go, and though certain of producing this effect, still proclaim it ;' see this passage explained in the Notes on John xii. 40. ¶ *Their ears heavy.* Dull, stupid, insensible. ¶ *And shut their eyes.* The word here used means *to spread over,* and then to close. It denotes here the state of mind which is more and more indisposed to attend to the truth. ¶ *And be healed.* Be restored from the malady of sin ; be recovered and pardoned. Sin is often represented as a painful, loathsome malady, and forgiveness as restoration from such a malady ; Isa. xxx. 26 ; Ps. ciii.; xli. 3, 4 ; 2 Chron. vii. 14 ; Jer. iii. 22 ; xvii. 14. We may learn here, (1.) That the effect of truth is often to irritate men and make them more wicked. (2.) The truth must, nevertheless, be proclaimed. This effect is not the fault of the truth ; and it is often well that the heart should be known, and the true effect should be seen.

11. *How long.* The prophet did not dare to pray that this effect should not follow. He asked merely therefore *how long* this state of things must continue ; how long this message was to be

be wasted without inhabitant, and the houses without man, and the land be ¹ utterly desolate ;

12 And the Lord have removed men *a* far away, and *there be* a great forsaking in the midst of the land.

1 *desolate with desolation.*　　a 2 Ki.25.21.

13 But yet in it *shall be* a tenth, and ² *it* shall return, and shall be eaten : as a teil-tree, and as an oak, whose ³ substance *is* in them when they cast *their leaves, so* the holy seed *shall be* the substance thereof.

2 or, *when it is returned and hath been broused.*
3 or, *stock* or *stem.*

delivered, and how long it should be attended with these painful effects. ¶ *Until the cities,* &c. They will remain perverse and obstinate until the land is completely destroyed by Divine judgments. Still the truth is to be proclaimed, though it is known it will have no effect in reforming the nation. This refers, doubtless, to the destruction that was accomplished by the Babylonians. ¶ *The houses without man.* This is strong language, denoting the certain and wide-spread desolation that should come upon the nation.

12. *And the Lord have removed,* &c. The land shall be given up to desolation. The men—the strength of the nation—shall be taken to a distant land. ¶ *And* there be *a great forsaking.* A great desolation ; the cities and dwellings shall be abandoned by the inhabitants ; comp. Isa. xvii. 2 ; Jer. iv. 29 ; Zeph. ii. 4.

13. *But yet,* &c. The main idea in this verse is plain, though there is much difficulty in the explanation of the particular phrases. The leading thought is, that the land should not be *utterly* and finally abandoned. There would be the remains of life—as in an oak or terebinth tree when the tree has fallen ; comp. Notes on ch. xi. 1. ¶ *A tenth.* That is, a tenth of the inhabitants, or a very small part. Amidst the general desolation, a small part should be preserved. This was accomplished in the time of the captivity of the Jews by Nebuchadnezzar. We are not to suppose that *literally* a tenth part of the nation would remain ; but a part that should bear somewhat the same proportion to the entire nation, in strength and resources, that a tenth does to the whole. Accordingly, in the captivity by the Babylonians we are told (2 Kings xxv. 12), that ' the captain of the guard left the poor of the land to be vinedressers and husbandmen ;' comp. 2 Kings xxiv.

14, where it is said, that ' Nebuchadnezzar carried away all Jerusalem, and all the princes, and all the mighty men of valour, even ten thousand captives, and all the craftsmen and smiths, none remained *save the poorer sort of the people of the land.*' Over this remnant, Nebuchadnezzar made Gedaliah king ; 2 Kings xxv. 22. ¶ *And it shall return.* This expression can be explained by the history. The prophet mentions the *return,* but he has omitted the fact that this remnant should go away ; and hence all the difficulty which has been experienced in explaining this. The history informs us, 2 Kings xxv. 26, that this remnant, this tenth part, ' *arose and came to Egypt, for they were afraid of the Chaldees.*' A part also of the nation was scattered in Moab and Edom, and among the Ammonites ; Jer. xl. 2. By connecting this idea with the prophecy, there is no difficulty in explaining it. It was of the return from Egypt that the prophet here speaks ; comp. Jer. xlii. 4–7. After this flight to Egypt they returned again to Judea, together with those who were scattered in Moab, and the neighbouring regions ; Jer. xl. 11, 12. This remnant thus collected was what the prophet referred to as *returning* after it had been scattered in Egypt, and Moab, and Edom, and among the Ammonites. ¶ *And shall be eaten.* This is an unhappy translation. It has arisen from the difficulty of making sense of the passage, by not taking into consideration the circumstances just adverted to. The word translated ' eaten ' means to feed, to graze, to consume by grazing, to consume by fire, to consume or destroy in any way, to remove.—*Gesenius* on the word בָּעַר. Here it means that this remnant shall be for *destruction ;* that judgments and punishments shall follow them after their return from Egypt and Moab. Even this remnant shall be the object of Divine displeasure, and shall feel the weight of his indignation; see Jer. xliii.; xliv. ¶ *As a teil-tree.* The word *teil* means the *linden,* though there is no evidence that the linden is denoted here. The word here used—אֵלָה—is translated *elm* in Hos. iv. 13, but generally *oak;* Gen. xxxv. 4; Judg. vi. 11, 19; 2 Sam. xviii. 9, 14. It is here distinguished from the אַלּוֹן *oak.* It probably denotes the *terebinth,* or turpentine tree; for a description of which, see Notes on ch. i. 29. ¶ *Whose substance.* Marg. 'Stock' or 'Stem.' The margin is the more correct translation. The word usually denotes the upright shaft, stem, or stock of a tree. It means here, whose *vitality* shall remain; *i.e.,* they do not entirely die. ¶ *When they cast* their leaves. The words 'their leaves' are not in the original, and should not be in the translation. The Hebrew means, 'in their falling'—or when they fall. As the evergreen did *not* cast its leaves, the reference is to the falling of the *body* of the tree. The idea is, that when the tree should fall and decay, still the life of the tree would remain. In the root there would be life. It would send up new *shoots,* and thus a new tree would be produced; see Notes on ch. iv. 2; xi. 1. This was particularly the case with the terebinth, as it is with the fir, the chestnut, the oak, the willow, &c.; see Job xiv. 7. The idea is, that it would be so with the Jews. Though desolate, and though one judgment would follow another, and though even the remnant would be punished, yet the race would not be extinguished. It would spring up again, and survive. This was the case in the captivity of Babylon; and again the case in the destruction of Jerusalem; and in all their persecutions and trials since, the same has always occurred. They survive; and though scattered in all nations, they still live as demonstrative of the truth of the Divine predictions; Deut xviii. ¶ *The holy seed.* The few remaining Jews. They shall not be utterly destroyed, but shall be like the life remaining in the root of the tree. No prophecy, perhaps, has been more remarkably fulfilled than that in this verse. 'Though the

cities be waste and the land be desolate, it is not from the poverty of the soil that the fields are abandoned by the plough, nor from any diminution of its ancient and natural fertility, that the land has rested for so many generations. Judea was not forced only by artificial means, or from local and temporary causes, into a luxuriant cultivation, such as a barren country might have been, concerning which it would not have needed a prophet to tell that, if once devastated and abandoned, it would ultimately revert to its original sterility. Phenicia at all times held a far different rank among the richest countries of the world; and it was not a bleak and sterile portion of the earth, nor a land which even many ages of desolation and neglect could impoverish, that God gave in possession and by covenant to the seed of Abraham. No longer cultivated as a garden, but left like a wilderness, Judea is indeed greatly changed from what it was; all that human ingenuity and labour did devise, erect, or cultivate, men have laid waste and desolate; all the "plenteous goods" with which it was enriched, adorned, and blessed, have fallen like seared and withered leaves when their greenness is gone; and stripped of its "ancient splendour," it is left *as an oak whose leaf fadeth:*—but its inherent sources of fertility are not dried up; the natural richness of the soil is unblighted; *the substance is in it,* strong as that of the teil tree or the solid oak, which retain their substance when they cast their leaves. And as the leafless oak waits throughout winter for the genial warmth of returning spring, to be clothed with renewed foilage, so the once glorious land of Judea is yet full of latent vigour, or of vegetative power, strong as ever, ready to shoot forth, even "better than at the beginning," whenever the sun of heaven shall shine on it again, and "the holy seed" be prepared for being finally "the substance thereof." *The substance that is in it*—which alone has here to be proved—is, in few words, thus described by an enemy: "The land in the plains is *fat* and *loamy,* and exhibits every sign of the *greatest fecundity.* Were nature assisted by art, the fruits of the most distant countries might be produced within the distance of

CHAPTER VII.

ANALYSIS.

PROBABLY no portion of the Bible has been regarded as so difficult of interpretation, and has given rise to so great a variety of expositions, as the prophecy which is commenced in this chapter, and which is closed in ch. ix. 7. The importance of the prophecy respecting the Messiah (vii. 14, *sq.*; viii. 7; ix. 1–7), is one reason why interpreters have been so anxious to ascertain the genuine sense; and the difficulties attending the supposition that there is reference to the Messiah, have been among the causes why so much anxiety has been felt to ascertain its true sense.

The prophecy which commences at the beginning of this chapter, is continued to ch. ix. 7. All this was evidently delivered at the same time, and constitutes a single vision, or oracle. This should have been indicated in the division of the chapters. Great obscurity arises from the arbitrary, and, in many instances, absurd mode of division into chapters which has been adopted in the Bible.

This chapter, for convenience of illustration, may be regarded as divided into four parts:—

I. The historical statement with which the whole account is introduced in ver. 1, 2. The principal occurrences referred to in the chapter took place in the time of Ahaz. For an account of his character and reign, see Introduction, § 3. He was an idolater, and erected the images, and altars, and groves of idolatry everywhere. He sacrificed to Baalim, and burned his children in the valley of Hinnom in honour of Moloch, and filled Jerusalem everywhere with abominations, 2 Kings xvi. 2–4; 2 Chron. xxviii. 1–4. For these abominations, he was delivered into the hand of the king of Syria, and was subjected to calamities from the threatened invasion of the united armies of Syria and Samaria. At this time Rezin was king of Syria, of which Damascus was the capital; and Pekah was king of Israel, or Samaria. These kings, during the concluding part of the reign of Jotham, the predecessor of Ahaz, had formed an alliance and had gone up towards Jerusalem to make war upon it, but had not been able to take it. The formation of this confederacy in the time of Jotham is distinctly declared in 2 Kings xv. 37. To this confederacy Isaiah refers in ver. 1, where he says that it occurred in the days of Jotham. The statement is made by Isaiah here, doubtless, in order to trace the important matter to which

he alludes to its commencement, though what he subsequently says had particular relation to Ahaz. Though the confederacy was formed in the time of Jotham, yet the consequences were of long continuance, and were not terminated until the defeat of Sennacherib in the time of Hezekiah; see ch. xxxvii. Isaiah here, in general, says (ver. 1) that they went up against Jerusalem, and could not take it. He may refer here to an expedition which they made in the time of Jotham, or he may design this as a *general* statement, indicating the result of *all* their efforts, that they could not take Jerusalem. If the latter is the proper interpretation, then the statement in ver. 1, was made by Isaiah at a subsequent period, and is designed to state *all* that occurred. It is more natural, however, to suppose that they made an attempt in the time of Jotham to take Jerusalem, but that they were unsuccessful. When Ahaz came to the throne, the alliance was continued, and the effort was renewed to take Jerusalem. Formidable preparations were made for the war, and an invading army came up upon the land. Many of the subjects of Ahaz were taken captive and carried to Damascus. Pekah slew in one day an hundred and twenty thousand men, and took two hundred thousand captives, and carried them towards Samaria. They were released from bondage by the solicitation of Oded, a prophet, who represented to them the impropriety of taking their brethren captive, and they were re-conveyed to Jericho; 2 Chron. xxviii. 5–15. At about the same time, the Assyrians took Elath, and retained it as a city belonging to them; 2 Kings xvi. 6. From the report of this strong alliance, and from the ravages which were committed by their united forces, Ahaz was alarmed, and trembled for the safety of Jerusalem itself, ver. 3. But instead of looking to God for aid, he formed the purpose of securing the alliance of the king of *Assyria*, and for this purpose sent messengers to Tiglath-pileser with professions of deep regard, and with the most costly presents which could be procured by exhausting the treasury (2 Kings xvi. 7, 8), to secure his friendship and co-operation. To this the king of Assyria agreed, and entered into the war by making an assault on Damascus; 2 Kings xvi. 9. It was this alliance, and the confidence which Ahaz had in it, that produced his answer to Isaiah (vii. 12), and his refusal to ask a sign of the Lord; and it was this alliance which subsequently involved Jerusalem in so much difficulty from the invasion of the Assyrians. The Assyrians, as might have been fore-

twenty leagues." "Galilee," says Malte Brun, " would be a paradise, were it in-

habited by an industrious people, under an enlightened government." '

seen, consulted their own advantage, and not
the benefit of Ahaz. They meant to avail themselves of the opportunity of subduing, if possible,
Judea itself; and, consequently, the land was
subsequently invaded by them, and Jerusalem
itself put in jeopardy. This consequence was
distinctly foretold by Isaiah, ch. vii. 17–25; viii.
7, 8. Yet before the alliance was secured, Ahaz
was in deep consternation and alarm, and it was
at this point of time that Isaiah was sent to him,
ver. 2, 3.

II. At this time of consternation and alarm,
Isaiah was sent to Ahaz to assure him that
Jerusalem would be safe, and that there was no
real cause of alarm, ver. 3–9. His main object
was to induce the monarch to repose confidence
in Jehovah, and to believe that his kingdom,
protected by God, could not be overthrown.
Isaiah was directed to take with him his son,
whose name (Shear-jashub—*the remnant shall
return*) was itself a sign or pledge that the
nation should not be *utterly* destroyed, and
that, consequently, it could not become permanently subject to Syria or Samaria, ver. 3. He
went to meet Ahaz at the upper pool, whither,
probably, Ahaz had gone, attended by many of
the court, to see whether it was practicable to
stop the water, so as to prevent an enemy from
procuring it; comp. 2 Chron. xxxii. 4. He
directed him not to be afraid of the enemies
that were coming, for they were like smoking,
half-extinguished brands that could do little
injury, ver. 4. He assured him that the purpose of the confederated kings should not be
accomplished; that Jehovah had said that their
design could not be established; and that the
limits of their respective kingdoms should be
the same that they were then, and should not
be enlarged by the conquest and accession of
Jerusalem—for that Damascus should still remain the capital of Syria, and Samaria of Ephraim, and that within sixty-five years the kingdom of Ephraim should be totally destroyed,
and of course Jerusalem and Judah could not
be permanently added to it. So far from having
Jerusalem as a tributary and dependent province, as Remaliah had anticipated, his own
kingdom was to be completely and finally destroyed, ver. 4–9. The design of all this was to
allay the fears of Ahaz, and to induce him to
put confidence in God.

III. A sign is promised—a proof or demonstration of the truth of what the prophet had
spoken, ver. 10–17. To the assurance which
Isaiah (ver. 4–9) had given of the safety of Jerusalem, Ahaz makes no reply. His whole conduct, however, shows that he is wholly unim-
pressed and unaffected by what he had said,

and that he put no confidence in the assurances
of the prophet. He was not looking to God for
aid, but to the king of Assyria; and he, doubtless,
felt that if his aid was not obtained, his kingdom
would be destroyed. He evidently had no belief
in God, and no confidence in the prophet. His
mind was in a restless, uneasy condition from
the impending danger, and from uncertainty
whether the aid of the king of Assyria could be
procured. In order to induce him to turn his
attention to God, the only Protector, and to
calm his fears, Ahaz is commanded to ask of
Jehovah any sign or miracle which he might
desire, in order to confirm what the prophet had
spoken, ver. 10, 11. This Ahaz refuses, ver. 12.
He does it under the semblance of piety, and an
unwillingness to appear to tempt Jehovah. But
the *real* cause was, doubtless, that he had no
confidence in Jehovah; he had no belief in what
he had spoken; and he was secretly depending
on the aid of the king of Assyria. His reply
was couched in respectful terms, and had the
appearance of piety, and was even expressed in
language borrowed from the law, Deut. v. 16.
Yet important purposes were to be answered, by
there being a sign or proof that what the prophet
had said should take place. It was important
that Ahaz, as the king of Judah, and as the head
of the people, should have evidence that what
was said was true. It was important that a
suitable impression should be made on those
who were present, and on the mass of the people,
inducing them to put confidence in Jehovah.
It was important that they should look to future
times; to the certain security of the nation, and
to the evidence that the nation *must* be preserved until the great Deliverer should come.
A sign is, therefore, forced upon the attention
of Ahaz. The prophet tells him that however
reluctant he may be to seek a sign, or however
incredulous he might be, yet that Jehovah would
give a token, proof, or demonstration, which
would be a full confirmation of all that he had
said. *That would be done which could be done
only by Jehovah, and which could be known only
by him;* and *that* would be the demonstration
that Jerusalem would be safe from this impending invasion. A virgin should bear a son, and
before he should arrive at years of discretion, or
be able to discern the difference between good
and evil—*i.e.*, in a short space of time, the land
would be forsaken of both its kings, ver. 14–16.
Who this virgin was, and what is the precise
meaning of this prediction, has given, perhaps,
more perplexity to commentators than almost
any other portion of the Bible. The *obvious*
meaning seems to be this. Some young female,
who was then a virgin, and who was unmarried

at the time when the prophet spoke, would conceive, and bear a son. To that son a name would be given, or his birth, in the circumstances in which it occurred, would make such a name proper, as would indicate that God was with them, and would be their Protector. Maternal affection would give the child the name Immanuel. The child would be nurtured up in the usual way among the Jews (ver. 15) until he would be able to discern between good and evil —i e., until he should arrive at years of discretion. Between the time which should elapse from the conception of the child, and the time when he should arrive at an age to distinguish good from evil, that is in about three years, the land should be forsaken of the hostile kings, ver. 16. This seems to be the obvious meaning of this passage; and in this way only could this be a clear and satisfactory evidence to Ahaz of the certainty that the land would be entirely and permanently free from the invasion. God only could know this; and, therefore, this was a proof of the certainty of what Isaiah had said. But though this is the obvious meaning, and though such an event only could be a sign to Ahaz that the land would be forsaken of both the invading kings, yet there is no reason to doubt that the prophet so couched what he said—so expressed this by the direction of the Holy Ghost, as to be applicable also to another much more important event, which was to be also, and in a much more important sense, a sign of the protection of God —the birth of the Messiah. He, therefore, selected words which, while they were applicable to the event immediately to occur, would also cover much larger ground, and be descriptive of more important events—and events which were in the same line and direction with that immediately to come to pass—the certainty of the Divine protection, and of ultimate freedom from all danger. The language, therefore, has, at the commencement of the prophecy, a fulness of meaning which is not entirely met by the immediate event which was to occur, and which can be entirely fulfilled only by the great event which Isaiah ever had in his eye—the birth of the Messiah. The mind of Isaiah would very naturally be carried forward to that future event. In accordance with the laws of what may be called prophetic suggestion or association, see Introduction, §7, iii. (3), and which are constantly exemplified in Isaiah, his mind would fix on better times, and more happy events. He saw the birth of a child in a future age, of which this was but the emblem. That was to be born literally of a virgin. His appropriate name, from his nature, and from his being the evidence of the Divine favour and presence, would be Imma-

nuel—as the appropriate name of this child would be Immanuel, because he would be the pledge of the Divine protection and presence. The idea is, that there is a fulness of meaning in the words used, which will apply to future events more appropriately than to the one immediately before the writer. That there is rapid transition—a sudden carrying the mind forward to rest on a future more important event, which has been suggested by the language used, and which is in the mind of the speaker or writer so much more important than that which was first mentioned, as completely to absorb the attention. The reasons for the view here given are detailed at length in the Notes on ch. vii. ver. 14-16.

IV. The prophet had thus far directed all his efforts to convince Ahaz that from the quarter from which they had apprehended danger, nothing was to be feared. He now, however (ver. 17-25), proceeds to assure them that danger would come from the quarter where they least expected it—from the very quarter where Ahaz was seeking aid and deliverance—the king of Assyria. He assures him that the king of Assyria would take advantage of the alliance, and, under pretence of aiding him, would turn every thing to his own account, and would ultimately bring desolation on the land of Judah. The calamities which would follow from this unhappy alliance, the prophet proceeds to state and unfold, and with that concludes the chapter. It is evident from 2 Kings xvi. 7, that the discourse of Isaiah made no impression on the mind of Ahaz. He sent messengers with valuable presents to Tiglath-pileser, king of Assyria. Tiglath-pileser professedly entered into the views of Ahaz, and promised his aid. He went up against Damascus and took it (2 Kings xvi. 9), after Ahaz had suffered a terrible overthrow from the united armies of Rezin and Pekah. The land of Samaria was laid waste by him, and a large part of the inhabitants carried captive to Assyria, 2 Kings xv. 29. Thus the prediction of Isaiah, that the land should be forsaken by two kings (ch. vii. 16), was fulfilled. But this deliverance from their invasion was purchased by Ahaz at a vast price. The real purpose of Tiglath-pileser was not to aid Ahaz, but to make him and his kingdom dependent and tributary (2 Chron. xxviii. 21); and this alliance was the first in the succession of calamities which came upon Judah and Jerusalem, and which ended only under Hezekiah by the entire destruction of the army of Sennacherib ; see ch. xxxvii. During the remainder of the reign of Ahaz, he was tributary to Assyria; and when Hezekiah (2 Kings xvii. 7) endeavoured to throw off the yoke of Assyria, the attempt involved him in war; subjected his kingdom to invasion; and was attended with a loss of no small part of the cities and towns of his kingdom; see 2 Kings xviii.; xix.; xx.; Isa. xxxvi.; xxxvii.; comp. Notes on ch. viii.; x. 28–32. Thus the second part of this prophecy was fulfilled. The fuller statement of these important transactions will be found in the Notes on the various passages which relate to these events.

AND *a* it came to pass in the days of Ahaz the son of Jotham, the

son of Uzziah king of Judah, *that* Rezin the king of Syria, and Pekah the son of Remaliah, king of Israel, went up toward Jerusalem, to war against it, but could not prevail against it.

2 And it was told the house of David, saying, Syria ¹ is confederate with Ephraim: and his heart was moved and the heart of his

a 2 Kings 16.5.   1 *resteth on.*

CHAPTER VII.

1. *In the days of Ahaz.* Ahaz began to reign about 738 years before Christ. By a comparison of 2 Kings xvi. 5, &c., with 2 Chron. xxviii. 5, &c., it will be seen that Judea was twice invaded by Rezin and Pekah in the reign of Ahaz; see the Analysis of the chapter. ¶ That *Rezin*, &c. This confederacy was formed in the time of Jotham; 2 Kings xv. 37. But it was not carried into execution during his reign. It is evident from this place, that it was executed in the early part of the reign of Ahaz; probably in the first or second year of his reign. ¶ *Syria*—אֲרָם *Arâm*, so called from Aram (Gen. x. 22, 23), a son of Shem, and who peopled its chief provinces. It comprehended the country lying between the Euphrates east, the Mediterranean west, Cilicia north, and Phenicia, Judea, and Arabia south; see Notes on ch. xvii. Syria of the two rivers is Mesopotamia. Syria of Damascus, so called because Damascus was its capital, extended eastward along Mount Libanus, but its limits varied according to the power of the princes of Damascus. After the reign of the Seleucidae, Syria came to denote the kingdom or region of which Antioch was the capital. Here it denotes the Syria lying around Damascus, and of which Damascus was the capital.—*Calmet.* ¶ *King of Israel.* Of the ten tribes, called the kingdom of Israel, or Samaria; Note, ch. i. 1. ¶ *Went up.* Jerusalem was situated on hills, and on the highest part of the land. But it is possible that this language is derived from the fact that it was the capital. The language is used even when the region from which the traveller comes

does not lie lower than the city. Thus it is not uncommon to speak of *going up* to London, Paris, &c. ¶ *Could not prevail.* Heb. ' Could not fight against it,' *i.e.*, with happy result, or with success. He was not able to take it. That the allied kings really besieged Ahaz, is evident from 2 Kings xvi. 5: They ' came up to Jerusalem to war, and they besieged Ahaz, but they could not overcome him.' The reason why they could not take Jerusalem was, probably, not only because it was a strong place and well defended, but because there was intelligence that their own dominions were threatened with an invasion by the Assyrians, and they could not protract their siege of Jerusalem long enough to take it.

2. *And it was told the house of David.* That is, the royal family; or the king and princes; the government. Ahaz was the descendant and successor of David. ¶ *Syria is confederate with Ephraim.* Ephraim was one of the tribes of Israel, and the kingdom of Israel was often called *Ephraim*, or the kingdom of Ephraim; in the same way as the tribes of Judah and Benjamin were called the kingdom of Judah. The phrase, ' is confederate with,' is in Hebrew ' resteth on;' see margin. The meaning is, that Syria was *supported by* Ephraim, or was allied with Ephraim. The kingdom of Israel, or Ephraim, was situated *between* Syria and Jerusalem. Of course, the latter could not be attacked without marching through the former, and without their aid. In this sense it was that Syria, or the Arameans, relied or *rested* on Ephraim. Though Syria was by far the stronger power, yet it was not strong enough to attack Jerusalem

people, as the trees of the wood are moved with the wind.

3 Then said the LORD unto Isaiah, Go forth now to meet Ahaz, thou

and [1] Shear-jashub thy son, at the end of the conduit of the upper pool, in the [2] highway of the fuller's field ;

---

1 *i.e., the remnant shall return.*

2 or, *causeway.*

---

had the kingdom of Israel been opposed to it. ¶ *And his heart.* The heart of the king—of Ahaz. ¶ *Was moved as the trees of the wood.* This is a very beautiful and striking image. It expresses universal trembling, consternation, and alarm, as the trees are moved *together* when the wind passes violently over them. A similar expression is found in Ovid—in *Canaces,* Epist. xi. ver. 76, 77:

Ut quatitur tepido fraxina virga noto
Sic mea vibrari pallentia membra videres.

3. *Then said the Lord.* In regard to the purposes for which Isaiah was sent to meet Ahaz, and the reason why this place was selected, see the Analysis of the chapter. ¶ *Thou and Shear-jashub.* The meaning of the name *Shear-jashub* is, 'the remnant shall return.' The names which Isaiah gave to his sons were significant or emblematic of some important events which were to occur to the Jews. They were for *signs* to the people, and had been given in order to keep before the nation the great truth that God was their protector, and that however much they might suffer or be punished, yet the nation would not be totally destroyed until the great Deliverer should come ; see Note on ver. 14, and ch. viii. 3. Why this name was given to this son, or on what occasion, is not certainly known. It is probable, however, that was with reference to the future calamities and captivity of the Jews, denoting that a part of the people would return to the land of their fathers ; comp. ch. x. 21, 22. The name was a remembrancer given by him as a prophet, perhaps, some time before this, that the nation was not to be wholly annihilated—a truth which Isaiah everywhere keeps before them in his prophecies ; comp. Note ch. vi. 13. *Why* Shear-jashub accompanied Isaiah now is not recorded. It might be as a pledge to Ahaz of the purpose of the Lord, that the people should not be

destroyed. Ahaz may have been apprized of the reason why the name was given, and his presence might serve to mitigate his fears. ¶ *At the end of the conduit.* A *conduit* is a pipe, or other conductor of water. The water flowed from a fountain, but was conducted to different receptacles for the supply of the city. ¶ *Of the upper pool.* Or the upper receptacle, or pond. Robinson (*Bib. Researches,* i. p. 483) and Pococke (*Descr. of the East,* ii. p. 25, 26) suppose that the upper and lower pools referred to by Isaiah, were on the west side of the city, the ruins of which now remain. The upper pool is now commonly called by the monks *Gihon,* and by the natives *Birket el Mamilla.* It lies in the basin forming the head of the valley of Hinnom or Gihon, about seven hundred yards west-northwest from the Yâfa gate, on the west of Jerusalem. The sides of this pool are built of hewn stones laid in cement, with steps at the corners by which to descend into it. The bottom is level. The dimensions are as follows :

Length from east to west.....316 Eng. feet.
Breadth at the west end......200
Breadth at the east end.......218
Depth at each end............... 18

There is no water-course, or other visible means, by which water is now brought into this reservoir, but it is probable that it was filled in the rainy seasons by the waters which flowed from the higher ground round about. From this upper pool a part of the water was conveyed into the city to the pool of Hezekiah, lying within the walls, and situated some distance to the north-eastward of the Yâfa gate. 'Hezekiah stopped the upper watercourse of Gihon, and brought it straight down to the west side of the city of David;' 2 Chron. xxxii. 30; comp. Notes on ch. xxii. 9. This upper pool had a trench or 'conduit,' and a considerable part of the waters were allowed to flow through this to the lower pool. The 'lower pool' is

4 And say unto him, Take heed, and be quiet; fear not, [1] neither be faint-hearted for the two tails of these smoking firebrands, for the

fierce anger of Rezin with Syria, and of the son of Remaliah.

5 Because Syria, Ephraim, and

1 *let not thy heart be tender.*

mentioned in the Old Testament only once, and that by Isaiah (ch. xxii. 9), and there without any hint of its locality. There is now a large lower pool on the western side of Jerusalem, which is not improbably the one intended, and which stands in contrast with the one here mentioned. This pool is called by the Arabs *Birket es-Sultân.* There is, at present, no other pool in the vicinity of Jerusalem to which the description in Isaiah can be well applied. This reservoir is situated in the valley of Hinnom or Gihon, southward from the Yâfa gate. Its northern end is nearly upon a line with the southern wall of the city. The pool was formed by throwing strong walls across the bottom of the valley, between which the earth was wholly removed. A road crosses on the causeway at the southern end. The following are the measurements of this pool:

Length along the middle......592 Eng. feet.
Breadth at the north end.....245
Breadth at the south end.....275
Depth at north end............ 35
Depth at south end............ 42

This reservoir was probably filled from the rains, and from the superfluous waters of the upper pool. It is now in ruins. The water from this pool would flow off into the valley of Hinnom, and thence into the valley of Jehoshaphat or Kedron, or subsequently into the pool of Hezekiah, situated *within* the city; see Notes on ch. xxii. 9, 11. Why Ahaz was at that place, the prophet does not say. It is possible he was examining it, to see whether the fountain could be stopped up, or the water diverted, so that it could not be used by the enemy, and so that they could be prevented from maintaining a protracted siege; comp. 2 Chron. xxxii. 4. It is probable that the king had gone to this place attended by many of his counsellors, and as this was the main source of the supply of water to the city, a multitude would be there, and Isaiah could have an opportunity not only to deliver his message to Ahaz

and his court, but in the presence of a considerable concourse of people, and might thus inspire confidence among the alarmed and dejected inhabitants of the city. ¶ *In the highway of the fuller's field.* In the place occupied as a situation on which to spread, or suspend cloth that was bleached, or dyed. This situation would be chosen because much water was needed in bleaching or dyeing cloth. The name 'highway' denotes the public path, or road that led to this field. Probably, on one side of this highway was the aqueduct, and on the other the fuller's field. Of the fuller's field, Eusebius and Jerome merely say that it was shown in their day in the suburbs of the city.—*Onom.* art. *Ager Fullonis.*

4. *Take heed.* Heb. 'Keep thyself;' that is, from fear. ¶ *Neither be faint-hearted.* Heb. 'Let not thy heart be tender;' that is, let it not be easily moved; be strong, fearless. ¶ *For the tails,* &c. There is much beauty and force in this comparison. The *design* of Isaiah is to diminish the fear of Ahaz. Instead, therefore, of calling them *firebrands*—burning and setting on fire every thing in their way—he calls them the *tails, i.e.,* the *ends,* or remains of firebrands—almost consumed themselves, and harmless. And instead of saying that they were *burning* and *blazing,* he says that they were merely *smoking*—the half-burnt, decaying remains of what might have been once formidable. The prophet also is just about to announce their approaching destruction by the Assyrians; see ver. 8. He therefore speaks of them as already almost extinguished, and incapable of doing extensive injury. ¶*Son of Remaliah.* Pekah, ver. 1. 'It is by way of contempt that the king of Israel is not called by his own name. The Hebrews and Arabians, when they wish to speak reproachfully of any one, omit his proper name and call him merely the son of this or that, especially when his father is but little known or respected. So Saul names David, in con-

the son of Remaliah have taken evil counsel against thee, saying,

6 Let us go up against Judah, and [1]vex it, and let us make a breach therein for us, and set a king in the midst of it, *even* the son of Tabeal:

7 Thus saith the Lord GOD, It shall not stand, neither shall it come to pass.

8 For the head of Syria *is* Damascus, and the head of Damascus *is* Rezin; and within threescore and five years shall Ephraim be broken, that [2] it be not a people.

1 or, *weaken.*   2 *from a.*

tempt, the son of Jesse; 1 Sam. xx. 27, 31.'—*Hengstenberg.*

6. *And vex it.* Marg. ' Weaken it.' Probably the word means to throw into consternation or fear, by besieging it.—*Gesenius.* ¶ *And let us make a breach therein.* Let us break down the walls, &c. ¶ *And set a king.* Subdue it, and make it tributary to the allied kingdoms of Syria and Ephraim. ¶ *The son of Tabeal.* Nothing more is known of this person. He might have been some disaffected member of the royal family of David, who had sought the aid of Rezin and Pekah, and who would be allied to them, or tributary to them. It is possible that he had already a party in Jerusalem in his favour; comp. ch. viii. 12. Probably, the two kings wished to cut off such portions of the territory of Judah as should be convenient to them, and to set a king over the remainder, who should be under their control; or to divide the whole between themselves, by setting up a king who would be tributary to both.

8. *For the head of Syria.* The *capital.* The *head* is often used in this sense. ¶ Is *Damascus.* For an account of this city, see Notes on ch. xvii. 1; comp. Notes, Acts ix. 2. The sense of this passage is, ' Do not be alarmed as if Rezin was about to *enlarge* his kingdom, by taking Judea and making Jerusalem his capital. The revolution which these kings contemplate cannot be accomplished. The kingdoms of Syria and Israel shall not be enlarged by the conquest of Judah. The centre of their power shall remain where it is now, and their dominion shall not be extended by conquest. The capital of Syria is, and shall continue to be, Damascus. The king of Syria shall be confined within his present limits, and Jerusalem therefore shall be safe.' ¶ *The head of Damascus.* The *ruler,* or *king* of

Damascus is Rezin. ¶ *And within threescore and five years.* There has been some inquiry why *Ephraim* is mentioned here, as the prophet in the former part of the verse was speaking of *Syria.* But it should be remembered that he was speaking of Syria and Ephraim as *confederate.* It was natural, therefore, to intimate, in close connection, that no fear was to be apprehended from either of them. There has been much difficulty experienced in establishing the fact of the exact fulfilment of this, and in fixing the precise event to which it refers. *One* catastrophe happened to the kingdom of Ephraim or Israel within one or two years of this time, when Tiglath-pileser, king of Assyria, invaded the land and carried no small part of the people to Assyria; 2 Kings xv. 29. *Another* occurred in the next reign, the reign of Hoshea, king of Israel, when Shalmaneser king of Assyria took Samaria, and carried Israel away captive into Assyria; 2 Kings xvii. 1–6. This occurred in the twelfth year of Ahaz. But that the Israelites remained in Samaria, and kept up the forms of a civil community, and were not finally carried away until the time of Esarhaddon, is evident; comp. 2 Chron. xxxiv. 6, 7, 33; xxxv. 18; 2 Kings xxiii. 19, 20. Manasseh, king of Judah, was taken captive by the king of Assyria's captains (2 Chron. xxxiii. 2) in the twenty-second year of his reign; that is, sixty-five years from the second year of Ahaz, when this prophecy is supposed to have been delivered. And it is also supposed that at this time Esarhaddon took away the remains of the people in Samaria, and put an end to the kingdom, and put in their place the people who are mentioned in Ezra iv. 3.—*Dr. Jubb, as quoted by Lowth.* The entire extinction of the people of Israel and the kingdom did

9 And the head of Ephraim *is* Samaria, and the head of Samaria *is* Remaliah's son. ¹ If ye will not

believe, surely ye shall not be established.

not take place till Esarhaddon put new colonists from Babylon, and from Cuthah, and from Ava, and from Hamath, and from Sepharvaim in the cities of Samaria, instead of the children of Israel; 2 Kings xvii. 24; comp. Ezra iv. 2, 10. Long before this, indeed, the power of the kingdom had been on the wane; a large portion of the people had been removed (2 Kings xvii. 5, 6, 18); but its *entire* extinction was not accomplished, and ̦the kingdom utterly destroyed, until this was done. Till this occurred, the land might be still regarded as in the possession somewhat of its former people, and all hopes of their rising again to the dignity of a kingdom was not extinguished. But when foreigners were introduced, and took possession of the land; when all the social organization of the ancient people was dissolved; then it might be said that 'Ephraim was *for ever* broken,' and that it was demonstrated that it 'should be no more a people.' Its inhabitants were transferred to a distant land, no longer to be organized into a peculiar community, but to mingle with other people, and finally all traces of their origin as Jews were to be lost. This event, of placing the foreigners in the cities of Samaria, occurred just sixty-five years after it had been predicted by Isaiah.—*Archbishop Usher.*

It may be asked here, how the statement of what was to occur at so remote a period as sixty-five years could be any consolation to Ahaz, or any security that the designs of the kings of Syria and Samaria should *then* fail of being accomplished? To this we may reply, —(1.) It was the assurance that Jerusalem could not be finally and permanently reduced to submission before these dreaded enemies. *Their* power was to cease, and of course Jerusalem had nothing *ultimately* and *finally* to dread. (2.) The design was to inspire confidence in JEHOVAH, and to lead Ahaz to look directly to him. If these formidable powers could not ultimately prevail, and if there was a certain prediction that they should be destroyed,

then it was possible for God, if Ahaz would look to him, *now* to interpose, and save the city. To inspire that confidence in JEHOVAH was the leading purpose of Isaiah. (3.) This prediction is in accordance with many which occur in Isaiah, that all the enemies of the people of God would be *ultimately* defeated, and that God, as the head of the theocracy, would defend and deliver his people; see Notes on ch. xxxiv. A kingdom that was so soon to be destroyed as Ephraim was, could not be an object of great dread and alarm. Rosenmüller conjectures, that Isaiah refers to some unrecorded prophecy made before his time, that in sixty-five years Israel would be destroyed; and that he refers here to that prophecy to encourage the heart of Ahaz, and to remind him that a kingdom could not be very formidable that was so soon to come to an end. At all events, there is no contradiction between the prophecy and the fulfilment, for *within* the time here mentioned, Ephraim ceased to be a kingdom. The ancient Jewish writers, with one consent, say, that Isaiah referred here to the prophecy of Amos, who prophesied in the days of Uzziah, and whose predictions relate mainly to the kingdom of Israel. But as Amos, does not specify any particular *time* when the kingdom should be destroyed, it is apparent that Isaiah here could not have referred to any *recorded* prophecy of his. ¶ *Be broken.* Its power shall be destroyed; the kingdom, as a kingdom, shall come to an end.

9. *And the head of Ephraim.* The capital city of Ephraim, or of Israel. ¶ *Is Samaria.* This was long the capital of the kingdom of Israel. For a description of this city, see Notes on ch. xxviii. 1. The meaning of the prophet is, that Samaria should *continue* to be the head of Ephraim; that is, Jerusalem should not be made its capital. ¶ *If ye will not believe, surely ye shall not be established.* There is considerable variety in the interpretation of these words, though the general sense is evident. The Chaldee renders them,

10 Moreover, [1] the LORD spake again unto Ahaz, saying,

11 Ask thee a sign *a* of the LORD thy God: ask [2] it either in the depth, or in the height above.

1 And the LORD added to speak.
a ch.38.7,22.   *2 or, make thy petition deep.*

'If ye will not believe *the words of the prophet*, ye shall not remain.' It is probable that Ahaz, who was greatly alarmed, and who trembled at the formidable power of Syria and Israel united, received the annunciation of the prophet with much distrust. He was anxious about the means of defence, but did not trust in the promise of God by the prophet. Isaiah, therefore, assures him, that if he did not believe him; if he did not put confidence in God, and his promises, he *should* not be protected from Syria and Ephraim. They would come and destroy his kingdom. 'You have no occasion,' is the language of the prophet, 'to fear. God has resolved to protect you, and no portion of your land shall be taken by your enemies. Nevertheless, in order that you may obtain deliverance, you must believe his promise, and put your confidence in him, and not in the aid of the Assyrians. If you do this, your mind shall be calm, peaceful, and happy. But if you do *not* do this; if you rely on the aid of Assyria, you shall be troubled, alarmed, unsuccessful, and bring ruin upon yourself and nation.' This, therefore, is an exhortation to confide solely in the promises of God, and is one of the instances constantly occurring in the Old Testament and the New, showing, that by faith or confidence in God only, can the mind be preserved calm when in the midst of dangers.

11. *Ask thee.* Ask for *thyself;* ask a sign that shall be convincing to *thyself,* since thou dost not fully credit the words of the prophet. It is evident that the words of the prophet had made no impression on the mind of Ahaz. God, therefore, proposes to him to ask any *proof* or *demonstration* which he might select; any thing that would be an indication of Divine power that should put what the prophet had said beyond doubt. Had Ahaz put confidence in God, he would have believed what the prophet said without miraculous proof. But he had no such confi-dence. The prophet, therefore, proposes that he should ask *any* miraculous demonstration that what he said would come to pass. This proposition was made, probably, not so much from respect to Ahaz as to leave him without excuse, and in order that *the people* might have the assurance that the city and kingdom were safe. ¶ *A sign.* A demonstration that shall confirm the promise now made, and that shall be an evidence that Jerusalem shall be safe. The word used here, and translated *sign*—אות *oth*—means *a flag*, or *standard*, Num. ii. 2; *a memorial* or *pledge* of a covenant, Gen. xvii. 11; any *pledge, token,* or *proof* of a Divine mission, Judg. vi. 17; or a miracle wrought in attestation of a Divine promise or message. This is its sense here. That which Isaiah had spoken seemed highly improbable to Ahaz, and he asked him to seek a proof of it, if he doubted, by any prodigy or miracle. It was customary for miracles or prodigies to be exhibited on similar occasions; see ch. xxxviii. 7, where the shadow on the dial of this same Ahaz was carried backward ten degrees, in proof of what the prophet Isaiah had spoken; comp. 1 Sam. ii. 27–34; 1 Kings xiii. 1–3; Ex. iii. 12; Judg. vi. 36–40. That the word here refers to some event which could be brought about only by Divine power, is evident from the whole connection. No mere *natural* occurrence could have satisfied Ahaz, or convey to the people a demonstration of the truth of what the prophet was saying. And if the prophet had been unable or unwilling to give a miraculous sign, where is the fitness of the answer of Ahaz? How could he be regarded as in any way tempting God by asking it, unless it was something which God only could do? And how could the prophet bring the charge (ver. 13), that he had not merely offended men, but God also? It is clear, therefore, that Isaiah was conscious that he was invested by God with the power of working a miracle, and that he pro-

12 But Ahaz said, I will not ask, | neither will I tempt the LORD.

posed to perform any miracle which Ahaz should suggest that would serve to remove his doubts, and lead him to put confidence in God. ¶ *Ask it either in the depth*, &c. He gave him his *choice* of a miracle—any sign or wonder in heaven, or on earth—above or below; a miracle in the sky, or from beneath the earth. Many of the versions understand the expression 'the depth,' as referring to *the grave*, or to the region of departed souls—*hades*. So the Vulgate, Aquila, Symmachus. The Chaldee reads it, ' Seek that there may be a miracle to thee upon the earth, or a sign in the heavens.' The literal meaning of the Hebrew is, 'make low, ask for;' that is, ask for a sign below; obtain, by asking for thyself, a miracle that shall take place below. It may refer to the earth, or to the region under the earth, since it stands in contrast with that which is above. If it refers to the region under the earth, it means that Isaiah would raise the dead to life if Ahaz desired it; if to the earth, that any wonder or miracle that should take place in the elements—as a tempest, or earthquake—should be performed. ¶ *The height above*. The heaven, or the sky. So the Pharisees desired to see a sign from heaven, Matt. xvi. 1.

12. *I will not ask*. In this case Ahaz assumed the appearance of piety, or respect for the command of God. In Deut. vi. 16, it is written, ' Thou shalt not tempt the Lord thy God ;' and Ahaz perhaps had this command in his eye. It was a *professed* reverence for God. But the *true* reason why he did not seek this sign was, that he had already entered into a negotiation with the king of Assyria to come and defend him ; and that he was even stripping the temple of God of its silver and gold, to secure this assistance ; 2 Kings xvi. 7, 8. When men are depending on their own devices and resources, they are unwilling to seek aid from God ; and it is not uncommon if they excuse their want of trust in him by some appearance of respect for religion. ¶ *Tempt*. Try, or do a thing that shall provoke his displeasure, or seek his interposition in a case where he has not promised it. To tempt God

is the same as to put him to the proof ; to see whether he is able to perform what he proposed. It is evident, however, that here there would have been no *temptation* of God, since a sign had been offered him by the prophet in the name of God. ' The answer of Ahaz can be regarded either as one of bitter scorn, as if he had said, " I will not put thy God to the proof, in which he will be found wanting. I will not embarrass thee by taking thee at thy word ; " or as the language of a hypocrite who assumes the mask of reverence for God and his command.' — *Hengstenberg*. Chrysostom and Calvin regard the latter as the correct interpretation. If it be asked here *why* Ahaz did not put Isaiah to the test, and *secure*, if possible, the Divine confirmation to the assurance that Jerusalem would be safe, the following may be regarded as the probable reasons :—(1.) He was secretly relying on the aid of Assyria. He believed that he could fortify the city, and distress the enemy by turning away the supply of water, so that they could not carry on a siege, and that all the further aid which he needed could be derived from the Assyrians. (2.) If the miracle had been *really wrought*, it would have been a proof that JEHOVAH was the true God—a proof which Ahaz had no desire of witnessing. He was a gross idolater ; and he was not anxious to witness a demonstration which would have convinced him of the folly and sin of his own course of life. (3.) If the miracle could not be wrought, as Ahaz seems to have supposed would be the case, then it would have done much to unsettle the confidence of the people, and to have produced agitation and alarm. It is probable that a considerable portion of the people were worshippers of JEHOVAH, and were looking to him for aid. The pious, and the great mass of those who conformed to the religion of their fathers, would have been totally disheartened ; and this was a result which Ahaz had no desire to produce. (4.) Michaelis has suggested another reason, drawn from the character of idolatry. According to the prevailing notions at that period, every nation had its own gods. Those

13 And he said, Hear ye now, O house of David; *Is it* a small thing for you to weary men, but will ye weary my God also?

a Lu.1.31-35.   b Mat.1.23.
1 or, *thou,* O Virgin, *shalt.*

14 Therefore the LORD himself shall give you a sign: Behold, *c* a virgin shall conceive, and bear a son, and *b* shall call his ¹ name Immanuel.

---

of one people were more, and those of another less powerful; see Isa. x. 10, 11; xxxvi. 18–20; xxxvii. 10–13. If a miracle had been performed, Ahaz *might* have believed that it was performed by the god of the country, who might have had the disposition, but not the power, to defend him. It would have been to the mind of the idolater no proof that the god of Syria or Samaria was not more powerful, and might not have easily overcome him. Ahaz seems to have regarded JEHOVAH as such *a* God—as one of the numerous gods which were to be worshipped, and perhaps as not the most powerful of the tutelary divinities of the nations. This was certainly the view of the surrounding idolaters (ch. x. 10, 11; xxxvi. 18–20); and it is highly probable that this view prevailed among the idolatrous Israelites.

13. *O house of David* (ver. 2). By this is to be understood not only the king himself, but the princes and rulers. Perhaps in addressing him thus, there was implied no small irony and reproach. David confided in God. But *Ahaz,* his descendant, feared to *tempt* God! As if God could not aid him! Worthy descendant he of the pious and devoted David!! ¶ Is it *a small thing.* You are not satisfied with wearying men, but you would also fatigue and wear out the patience of God. ¶ *Weary.* Exhaust their patience; oppose them; prevent their sayings and messages; try their spirits, &c. ¶ *Men.* Prophets; the men who are sent to instruct, and admonish. ¶ *Will ye weary my God also?* Will you refuse to keep his commands; try his patience; and exhaust his long-suffering? comp. ch. i. 14. The sense of this passage seems to be this: When Ahaz refused to believe the bare prediction of the prophet, his transgression was the more excusable. He had wearied and provoked him, but Isaiah had as yet given to Ahaz no direct demonstration that he was from God; no outward proof of his Divine mission; and the offence of

Ahaz might be regarded as in a sense committed against man. It was true, also, that Ahaz had, by his unbelief and idolatry, greatly tried the feelings of the pious, and wearied those who were endeavouring to promote true religion. But now the case was changed. God had offered a sign, and it had been publicly rejected. It was a direct insult to God; and an offence that demanded reproof. Accordingly, the manner of Isaiah is at once changed. Soft, and gentle, and mild before, he now became bold, open, vehement. The honour of God was concerned; a direct affront had been offered to him by the sovereign of the people of God; and it was proper for the prophet to show that *that* was an offence which affected the Divine Majesty, and demanded the severest reproof.

14. *Therefore.* Since you will not *ask* a pledge that the land shall be safe, JEHOVAH will furnish one unasked. A sign or proof is desirable in the case, and JEHOVAH will not withhold it because a proud and contemptuous monarch refuses to seek it. Perhaps there is no prophecy in the Old Testament on which more has been written, and which has produced more perplexity among commentators than this. And after all, it still remains, in many respects, very obscure. Its general original meaning is not difficult. It is, that in a short time—within the time when a young woman, then a virgin, should conceive and bring forth a child, and that child should grow old enough to distinguish between good and evil—the calamity which Ahaz feared would be entirely removed. The confederacy would be broken up, and the land forsaken by both those kings. The conception and birth of a child—which could be known only by him who knows *all* future events—would be the evidence of such a result. His appropriate *name* would be such as would be a *sign,* or an indication that God was the protector of the nation, or was

still with them. In the examination of
this difficult prophecy, my first object
will be to give an explanation of the
meaning of the *words* and *phrases* as
they occur in the passage, and then to
show, as far as I may be able, what
was the design of the passage. ¶ *The*
LORD *himself.* Heb. ' Adonai ;' see this
word explained in the Note on ch. i.
24. He will do it without being asked
to do it ; he will do it though it is rejected and despised ; he will do it because it is important for the welfare
of the nation, and for the confirmation
of his religion, to furnish a demonstration to the people that he is the only
true God. It is clearly implied here,
that the sign should be such as JEHOVAH
alone could give. It would be such as
would be a demonstration that he presided over the interests of the people.
If this refers to the birth of a child,
then it means that this was an event
which could be known only to God, and
which could be accomplished only by his
agency. If it refers to the miraculous
conception and birth of the Messiah,
then it means that *that* was an event
which none but God could accomplish.
The true meaning I shall endeavour to
state in the Notes, at the close of ver. 16.
¶ *Shall give you.* Primarily to the
house of David ; the king and royal
family of Judah. It was especially
designed to assure the government that
the kingdom would be safe. Doubtless,
however, the word ' you ' is designed to
include the nation, or the people of the
kingdom of Judah. It would be so
public a sign, and so clear a demonstration, as to convince *them* that their city
and land must be ultimately safe. ¶ *A*
sign. A pledge; a token; an evidence
of the fulfilment of what is predicted.
The word does not, of *necessity*, denote
a miracle, though it is often so applied ;
see Notes on ver. 11. Here it means a
proof, a demonstration, a certain indication that what he had said should be
fulfilled. As that was to be such a
demonstration as to show that he was
able to deliver the land, the word *here*
denotes that which was miraculous, or
which could be effected *only* by JEHOVAH.
¶ *Behold.* הִנֵּה. This interjection is
a very common one in the Old Testa-

ment. It is used to arrest attention ;
to indicate the importance of what was
about to be said. It serves to designate
persons and things ; places and actions.
It is used in lively descriptions, and
animated discourse ; when any thing
unusual was said, or occurred ; or any
thing which peculiarly demanded attention ; Gen. xii. 19; xvi. 16; xviii. 9;
i. 29; xl. 9; Ps. cxxxiv. 1. It means
here, that an event was to occur which
demanded the attention of the unbelieving monarch, and the regard of the
people—an event which would be a full
demonstration of what the prophet had
said, that God would protect and save
the nation. ¶ *A virgin.* This word
properly means a girl, maiden, virgin,
a young woman who is unmarried, and
who is of marriageable age. The word
עַלְמָה, *ălmâ*, is derived from the verb
עָלַם, *ălăm, to conceal, to hide, to cover.*
The word עֶלֶם, *ĕlĕm*, from the same
verb, is applied to a *young man*, in
1 Sam. xvi. 56; xx. 22. The word here
translated a virgin, is applied to Re-
bekah (Gen. xxiv. 43), and to Miriam,
the sister of Moses, Ex. ii. 8. It occurs
in only seven places in the Old Testament. Besides those already mentioned,
it is found in Ps. lxviii. 25; Cant. i. 3;
vi. 8; and Prov. xxx. 19. In all these
places, except, perhaps, in Proverbs, it
is used in its obvious natural sense, to
denote a young, unmarried female. In
the Syriac, the word ܥܠܡ, *alĕm*,
means to grow up, *juvenis factŭs est;*
juvenescere fecit. Hence the derivatives are applied to youth; to young
men ; to young women—to those who
are growing up, and becoming youths.
The etymology of the word requires us
to suppose that it means one who is
growing up to a marriageable state, or
to the age of puberty. The word
maiden, or virgin, expresses the correct
idea. Hengstenberg contends, that it
means one *in the unmarried state;*
Gesenius, that it means simply the
being of marriageable age, the age of
puberty. The Hebrews usually employed the word בְּתוּלָה, *bĕthûlâ*, to
denote a pure virgin (a word which the
Syriac translation uses here); but the
word here evidently denotes one who

was *then* unmarried; and though its primary idea is that of one who is growing up, or in a marriageable state, yet the whole connection requires us to understand it of one who was *not then married*, and who was, therefore, regarded and designated as a virgin. The Vulgate renders it ' virgo.' The LXX. ἡ παρθίνος, *a virgin*—a word which they use as a translation of the Hebrew בְּתוּלָה in Ex. xxii. 16, 17; Lev. xxi. 3, 14; Deut. xxii. 19, 23, 28; xxxii. 25; Judg. xix. 24; xxi. 12; and in thirty-three other places (see Trommius' *Concord.*); of נַעֲרָה, *naǎrâ*, a girl, in Gen. xxiv. 14, 16, 55; xxxiv. 3 (twice); 1 Kings i. 2; and of עַלְמָה, *ălmâ*, only in Gen. xxiv. 43; and in Isa. vii. 14. The word, in the view of the LXX. translators, therefore, conveyed the proper idea of a virgin. The Chaldee uses substantially the same word as the Hebrew. The idea of a *virgin* is, therefore, the most obvious and natural idea in the use of this word. It does not, however, imply that the person spoken of should be a virgin *when* the *child* should be born; or that she should ever after be a virgin. It means simply that one who was *then* a virgin, but who was of marriageable age, should conceive, and bear a son. Whether she was *to be* a virgin *at the time* when the child was born, or was to remain such afterwards, are inquiries which cannot be determined by a philological examination of the word. It is evident, also, that the word is not opposed to *either* of these ideas. *Why* the name which is thus given to an unmarried woman was derived from the verb to *hide*, to *conceal*, is not agreed among lexicographers. The more probable opinion is, that it was because to the time of marriage, the daughter was supposed to be hidden or concealed in the family of the parents; she was kept shut up, as it were, in the paternal dwelling. This idea is given by Jerome, who says, ' the name is given to a virgin because she is said to be hidden or secret; because she does not expose herself to the gaze of men, but is kept with great care under the custody of parents.' The sum of the inquiry here, into the meaning of the word translated *virgin*, is, that it does

not differ from that word as used by us. The expression means no more than that one who was then a virgin should have a son, and that this should be a sign to Ahaz. ¶ *And shall call his name.* It was usual for *mothers* to give names to their children; Gen. iv. 1; xix. 37; xxix. 32; xxx. 18. There is, therefore, no reason to suppose, as many of the older interpreters did, that the fact that it is said the mother should give the name, was a proof that the child should have no human father. Such arguments are unworthy of notice; and only show to what means men have resorted in defending the doctrines, and in interpreting the pages of the Bible. The phrase, 'she will name,' is, moreover, the same as ' they shall name,' or he shall be named. ' We are not, then, to suppose that the child should actually receive the name Immanuel as a proper name, since, according to the usage of the prophet, and especially of Isaiah, that is often ascribed to a person or thing as a name which belongs to him in an eminent degree as an attribute; see ch. ix. 5; lxi. 6; lxii. 4.'—*Hengstenberg.* The idea is, that that would be a name that might be *appropriately* given to the child. Another name was also given to this child, expressing substantially the same thing, with a circumstantial difference; see Note on ch. viii. 3. ¶ *Immanuel.* Heb. ' God with us '—עִמָּנוּאֵל—from אֵל, *God*, and עִמָּנוּ, *with us.* The name is designed to denote that God would be with the nation as its protector, and the birth of this child would be a sign or pledge of it. The mere circumstance that this name is given, however, does not imply any thing in regard to the nature or rank of the child; for nothing was more common among the Jews than to incorporate the name, or a part of the name, of the Deity with the names which they gave to their children. Thus, *Isaiah* denotes the salvation of JEHOVAH; *Jeremiah*, the exaltation or grandeur of JEHOVAH, each compounded of two words, in which the name JEHOVAH constitutes a part. Thus, also, in *Elijah*, the two names of God are combined, and it means literally, *God the* JEHOVAH. Thus, also, *Eliab*, God my father; *Eliada*,

15 Butter and honey shall he eat, that he may know to refuse the evil, and choose the good.

knowledge of God; *Eliakim*, the resurrection of God; *Elihu*, he is my God; *Elisha*, salvation of God. In none of these instances is the fact, that the name of God is incorporated with the proper name of the individual, any argument in respect to his rank or character. It is true, that Matthew (ch. i. 23) uses this name as properly expressing the rank of the Messiah; but all that can be demonstrated from the use of the name by Matthew is, that it *properly* designated the nature and rank of the Lord Jesus. It was a pledge, then, that God was with his people, and the name designated by the prophet had a complete fulfilment in its use as applied to the Messiah. Whether the Messiah be regarded as himself a pledge and demonstration of the presence and protection of God, or whether the name be regarded as descriptive of his nature and dignity, yet there was an *appropriateness* in applying it to him. It was fully expressive of the event of the incarnation. Jerome supposes that the name, Immanuel, denotes nothing more than Divine aid and protection. Others have supposed, however, that the name must denote the assumption of our nature by God in the person of the Messiah, *i.e.*, that God became man. So Theodoret, Irenæus, Tertullian, Lactantius, Chrysostom, Calvin, Rosenmüller, and others. The true interpretation is, that no *argument* to prove that can be derived from the use of the name; but when the fact of the incarnation has been demonstrated from other sources, the *name is appropriately expressive of that event.* So it seems to be used by Matthew.

[It may be quite true, that no argument can be founded on the bare name, Immanuel; yet that name, *in its connection here*, may certainly be regarded as a designed prediction of the incarnation of Christ. Such a design our author allows in the prophecy generally. 'The prophet,' says he, '*designedly* made use of language which would be appropriate to a future and most glorious event.' Why, then, does he speak of the most pregnant word in the prophecy as if Matthew had accidentally stumbled on it, and, finding it would appropriately express the nature of Christ, accommodated it for that purpose? Having originally rejected the Messianic reference, and been convinced only by a more careful examination of the passage, that he was in error, something of his old view seems still to cling to this otherwise admirable exposition. 'The name Immanuel,' says Professor Alexander, 'although it might be used to signify God's providential presence merely (Ps. xlvi. 8, 12; lxxxix. 25; Josh. i. 5; Jer. i. 8; Isa. xliii. 2), has a latitude and pregnancy of meaning which can scarcely be fortuitous; and which, combined with all the rest, makes the conclusion almost unavoidable, that it was here intended to express a personal, as well as a providential presence. . . . When we read in the Gospel of Matthew, that Jesus Christ was actually born of a virgin, and that all the circumstances of his birth came to pass that this very prophecy might be fulfilled, it has less the appearance of an unexpected application, than of a conclusion rendered necessary by a series of antecedent facts and reasonings, the last link in a long chain of intimations more or less explicit (referring to such prophecies as Gen. iii. 15; Micah v. 2). The same considerations seem to show that the prophecy is not merely accommodated, which is, moreover, clear from the emphatic form of the citation ($\tau o\tilde{v}\tau o$ $\ddot{o}\lambda o\nu$ $\gamma\acute{\epsilon}\gamma o\nu\epsilon\nu$ $\ddot{\iota}\nu\alpha$ $\pi\lambda\eta\rho\omega\theta\tilde{\eta}$), making it impossible to prove the existence of any quotation in the proper sense, if this be not one.' But, indeed, the author himself admits all this, though his language is less decided and consistent than could be wished on so important a subject.]

15. *Butter and honey.* The word rendered *butter* (הֶמְאָה *hĕmâh*), denotes not butter, but thick and curdled milk. This was the common mode of using milk as an article of food in the East, and is still. In no passage in the Old Testament does butter seem to be meant by the word. Jarchi says, that this circumstance denotes a state of plenty, meaning that the land should yield its usual increase notwithstanding the threatened invasion. Eustatius on this place says, that it denotes delicate food. The more probable interpretation is, that it was the usual food of children, and that it means that the child should be nourished in the customary manner. That this was the common nourishment

16 For before the child shall know to refuse the evil, and choose the good, the land that thou abhor-rest shall be forsaken of both her kings.

---

of children, is abundantly proved by Bochart; *Hieroz.* P. i. lib. xi. ch. li. p. 630. Barnabas, in his epistle, says, 'The infant is first nourished with honey, and then with milk.' This was done usually by the prescription of physicians. Paulus says, 'It is fit that the first food given to a child be honey, and then milk.' So Aëtius, 'Give to a child, as its first food, honey;' see *Bochart.* Some have, indeed, supposed that this refers to the fact that the Messiah should be *man* as well as God, and that his eating honey and butter was expressive of the fact that he had a *human nature!* But against this mode of interpretation, it is hoped, it is scarcely needful now to protest. It is fitted to bring the Bible into contempt, and the whole science of exegesis into scorn. The Bible is a book of sense, and it should be interpreted on principles that commend themselves to the sober judgment of mankind. The word rendered *honey*—שַׁבַּד—is the same word—*dibs*—which is now used by the Arabs to denote the syrup or jelly which is made by boiling down wine. This is about the consistence of molasses, and is used as an article of food. Whether it was so employed in the time of Isaiah, cannot now be determined, but the word here may be used to denote honey; comp. Note, ver. 22. ¶ *That he may know.* As this translation now stands, it is unintelligible. It would *seem* from this, that his eating butter and honey would *contribute* to his knowing good and evil. But this cannot be the meaning. It evidently denotes '*until* he shall know,' or, 'at his knowing;' Nord. *Heb. Gram.*, § 1026. 3. He shall be nourished in the usual way, *until* he shall arrive at such a period of life as to know good from evil. The LXX. render it, Πριν ἢ γνωναι αὐτὸν—'*Before* he knows.' The Chaldee, '*Until* he shall know.' ¶ *To refuse the evil,* &c. Ignorance of good and evil denotes infancy. Thus, in Nineveh, it is said there were 'more than sixscore thousand persons that cannot discern be-

tween their right hand and left hand;' commonly supposed to denote infants; Jonah iv. 11; comp. Deut. i. 39. The meaning is, that he should be nourished in the usual mode in infancy, and before he should be able to discern right from wrong, the land should be forsaken of its kings. At what particular period of life this occurs, it may not be easy to determine. A capability to determine, in some degree, between good and evil, or between right and wrong, is usually manifest when the child is two or three years of age. It is evinced when there is a capability of understanding *law*, and feeling that it is wrong to disobey it. This is certainly shown at a very early period of life; and it is not improper, therefore, to suppose that here a time was designated which was not more than two or three years.

16. *The land that thou abhorrest.* The land concerning which thou art so much *alarmed* or *distressed;* that is, the united land of Syria and Ephraim. It is mentioned here as 'the land,' or as one land, because they were united then in a firm alliance, so as to constitute, in fact, or for the purposes of invasion and conquest, one people or nation. The phrase, 'which thou abhorrest,' means properly, which thou loathest, the primary idea of the word—קוץ, *qûtz*—being to feel a nausea, or to vomit. It then means to fear, or to feel alarm; and this, probably, is the meaning here. Ahaz, however, evidently looked upon the nations of Syria and Samaria with disgust, as well as with alarm. This is the construction which is given of this passage by the Vulgate, Calvin, Grotius, Junius, Gataker, and Piscator, as well as by our common version. Another construction, however, has been given of the passage by Vitringa, J. D. Michaelis, Lowth, Gesenius, Rosenmüller, Hengstenberg, and Hendewerk. According to this, the meaning is not that the *land* should be the object of abhorrence, but that the kings themselves were the objects of dislike or

dread ; and not merely that the two kings should be removed, but that the land itself was threatened with desolation. This construction is free from the objections of an exegetical kind to which the other is open, and agrees better with the idiom of the Hebrew. According to this, the correct translation would be :

For before the child shall learn to refuse the evil and to choose the good,
Desolate shall be the land, before whose two kings thou art in terror.'

¶ *Of both her kings.* Ahaz took the silver and gold that was found in the temple, and sent it as a present to the king of Assyria. Induced by this, the king of Assyria marched against Damascus and slew Rezin, 2 Kings xvi. 9. This occurred but a short time after the threatened invasion of the land by Rezin and Remaliah, in the *third* year of the reign of Ahaz, and, consequently, about one year after this prophecy was delivered. Pekah, the son of Remaliah, was slain by Hoshea, the son of Elah, who conspired against him, slew him, and reigned in his stead. This occurred in the fourth year of the reign of Ahaz, for Pekah reigned twenty years. Ahaz began to reign in the seventeenth year of the reign of Pekah, and as Pekah was slain after he had reigned twenty years, it follows that he was slain in the fourth year of the reign of Ahaz—perhaps not more than two years after this prophecy was delivered ; see 2 Kings xv. 27, 30 ; xvi. 1. We have thus arrived at a knowledge of the time intended by Isaiah in ver. 16. The whole space of time was not, probably, more than two years.

A great variety of opinions have oeen entertained by interpreters in regard to this passage (ver. 14–16). It may be useful, therefore, to state briefly what those opinions have been, and then what seems to be the true meaning.

(i.) The first opinion is that which supposes that by the ' virgin ' the wife of Ahaz is referred to, and that by the child which should be born, the prophet refers to Hezekiah. This is the opinion of the modern Jewish commentators

generally. This interpretation prevailed among the Jews in the time of Justin. But this was easily shown by Jerome to be false. Ahaz reigned in Jerusalem but sixteen years (2 Kings xvii. 2), and Hezekiah was twenty-five years old when he began to reign (2 Kings xviii. 2), and of course was not less than nine years old when this prophecy was delivered. Kimchi and Abarbanel then resorted to the supposition that Ahaz had a second wife, and that this refers to a child that was to be born of her. This supposition cannot be *proved* to be false, though it is evidently a *mere* supposition. It has been adopted by the Jews, because they were pressed by the passage by the early Christians, as constituting an argument for the divinity of Christ. The ancient Jews, it is believed, referred it mainly to the Messiah.

(ii.) Others have supposed, that the prophet designated some virgin who was then present when the king and Isaiah held their conference, and that the meaning is, ' as surely as this virgin shall conceive, and bear a son, so surely shall the land be forsaken of its kings.' Thus Isenbiehl, Bauer, Cube, and Steudel held, as quoted by Hengstenberg, *Christol.* i. p. 341.

(iii.) Others suppose that the ' virgin ' was not an actual, but only an ideal virgin. Thus Michaelis expresses it : ' By the time when one who is yet a virgin can bring forth (*i.e.,* in nine months), all will be happily changed, and the present impending danger so completely passed away, that if you were yourself to name the child, you would call him Immanuel.' Thus Eichhorn, Paulus, Hensler, and Ammon understand it ; see *Hengstenberg.*

(iv.) Others suppose that the ' virgin ' was the prophet's wife. Thus Aben Ezra, Jarchi, Faber, and Gesenius. Against this supposition there is only one objection which has been urged that is of real force, and that is, that the prophet already had a son, and of course his wife could not be spoken of as a virgin. But this objection is entirely removed by the supposition, which is by no means improbable, that the former wife of the prophet was dead, and that he was about to be united in marriage to another who was a virgin.

In regard to the prophecy itself, there have been three opinions :—

(i.) That it refers *exclusively* to some event in the time of the prophet ; to the birth of a child then, either of the wife of Ahaz, or of the prophet, or of some other unmarried female. This would, of course, exclude all reference to the Messiah. This was formerly my opinion ; and this opinion I expressed and endeavoured to maintain, in the first composition of these Notes. But a more careful examination of the passage has convinced me of its error, and satisfied me that the passage has reference to the Messiah. The reasons for this opinion I shall soon state.

(ii.) The second opinion is, that it has *exclusive* and *immediate* reference to the Messiah ; that it does not refer at all to any event which was *then* to occur, and that to Ahaz the future birth of a Messiah from a virgin, was to be regarded as a pledge of the Divine protection, and an assurance of the safety of Jerusalem. Some of the objections to this view I shall soon state.

(iii.) The third opinion, therefore, is that which *blends* these two, and which regards the prophet as speaking of the birth of a child which would soon take place of some one who was then a virgin —an event which could be known only to God, and which would therefore constitute a sign, or demonstration to Ahaz of the truth of what Isaiah said ; but that the prophet intentionally so used language which would *also* mark a more important event, and direct the minds of the king and people onward to the future birth of one who should more fully answer to all that is here said of the child that would be born, and to whom the name Immanuel would be more appropriately given. This, I shall endeavour to show, must be the correct interpretation. In exhibiting the reasons for this opinion, we may, FIRST, state the evidence that the prediction refers to some child that would be born *soon* as a pledge that the land would be forsaken of its kings ; and SECONDLY, the evidence that it refers also to the Messiah in a higher and fuller sense.

I. EVIDENCE THAT THE PROPHECY REFERS TO SOME EVENT WHICH WAS SOON TO OCCUR—TO THE BIRTH OF A CHILD OF SOME ONE WHO WAS THEN A VIRGIN, OR UNMARRIED.

(i.) It is the *obvious* interpretation. It is that which would strike the great mass of men accustomed to interpret language on the principles of common sense. If the passage stood by itself ; if the seventh and eighth chapters were *all* that we had ; if there were no allusion to the passage in the New Testament ; and if we were to sit down and merely look at the circumstances, and contemplate the narrative, the unhesitating opinion of the great mass of men would be, that it *must* have such a reference. This is a good rule of interpretation. That which strikes the mass of men ; which appears to men of sound sense as the meaning of a passage on a simple perusal of it, is likely to be the true meaning of a writing.

(ii.) Such an interpretation is demanded by the circumstances of the case. The immediate point of the inquiry was not about the *ultimate* and *final* safety of the kingdom—which would be demonstrated indeed by the announcement that the Messiah would appear—but it was about a present matter ; about impending danger. An alliance was formed between Syria and Samaria. An invasion was threatened. The march of the allied armies had commenced. Jerusalem was in consternation, and Ahaz had gone forth to see if there were any means of defence. In this state of alarm, and at this juncture, Isaiah went to assure him that there was no cause for fear. It was not to assure him that the nation should be ultimately and finally safe— which might be proved by the fact that the Messiah would come, and that, therefore, God would preserve the nation ; but the pledge was, that he had no reason to fear *this* invasion, and that within a short space of time the land would 'be forsaken of both its kings.' How could the fact that the Messiah would come more than seven hundred years afterwards, prove this ? Might not Jerusalem be taken and subdued, as it was afterwards by the

Chaldeans, and yet it be true that the Messiah would come, and that God would manifest himself as the protector of his people ? Though, therefore, the assurance that the Messiah would come would be a *general* proof and pledge that the nation would be preserved and ultimately safe, yet it would not be a pledge of the *specific* and *immediate* thing which occupied the attention of the prophet, and of Ahaz. It would not, therefore, be a ' sign' such as the prophet offered to give, or a proof of the fulfilment of the specific prediction under consideration. This argument I regard as unanswerable. It is so obvious, and so strong, that all the attempts to answer it, by those who suppose there was an immediate and exclusive reference to the Messiah, have been entire failures.

(iii.) It is a circumstance of *some* importance that Isaiah regarded himself and his children as ' signs' to the people of his time ; see ch. viii. 18. In accordance with this view, it seems he had named one child Shear-jashub, vii. 3 ; and in accordance with the same view, he afterwards named another Maher-shalal-hash-baz—both of which names are significant. This would *seem* to imply that he meant here to refer to a similar fact, and to the birth of a son that should be a sign also to the people of his time.

(iv.) An unanswerable reason for thinking that it refers to some event which was soon to occur, and to the birth of a child *before* the land should be forsaken of the two kings, is the record contained in ch. viii. 1-4. That record is evidently connected with this account, and is intended to be a public assurance of the fulfilment of what is here predicted respecting the deliverance of the land from the threatened invasion. In that passage, the prophet is directed to take a great roll (ver. 1), and make a record concerning the son that was to be born ; he calls public witnesses, men of character and well-known reputation, in attestation of the transaction (ver. 2); he approaches the prophetess (ver. 3); and it is expressly declared (ver. 4) that before the child should have ' knowledge to say, My father, and my mother,' *i.e.,* be able to discern between good and evil

(ch. vii. 16), ' the riches of Damascus and the spoil of Samaria' should be ' taken away before the king of Assyria.' This is so evidently a completion of the prophecy in ch. vii., and a solemn fulfilling of it in a manner that should be satisfactory to Ahaz and the people, that it is impossible, it seems to me, to regard it any otherwise than as a *real* transaction. Hengstenberg, and those who suppose the prophecy to refer *immediately* and *exclusively* to the Messiah, are obliged to maintain that that was a ' symbolical transaction ' — an opinion which might, with the same propriety, be held of any historical statement in the Bible ; since there is nowhere to be found a more simple and unvarnished account of mere matter of historical fact than that. The statement, therefore, in ch. viii., is conclusive demonstration, I think, that there was a reference in ch. vii. 14–16, to a child of the prophet that would be soon born, and that would be a *pledge* of the Divine protection, and a *proof* or *sign* to Ahaz that his land would be safe.

It is no objection to this that Isaiah then had a son (ch. vii. 3), and that therefore the mother of that son could not be a virgin. There is no improbability in the supposition that the mother of that son was deceased, and that Isaiah was about again to be married. Such an event is not so uncommon as to make it a matter of ridicule (see *Hengstenberg,* p. 342) ; or to render the supposition wholly incredible.

Nor is it any objection that another name was given to the child that was born to Isaiah ; ch. viii. 1, 3. Nothing was more common than to give two names to children. It might have been true that the name usually given to him was Maher-shalal-hash-baz ; and still true that the circumstances of his birth were such an evidence of the Divine protection, and such an emblem of the Divine guardianship, as to make proper the name Immanuel ; see Note on ver. 14. It may be observed, also, that on the supposition of the strict and exclusive Messianic interpretation, the same objection might be made, and the same difficulty would lie. It was no more true of Jesus of Nazareth than of the child of Isaiah, that he was commonly called Immanuel. He had another name also, and was called by that other name. Indeed, there is not the slightest evidence that the Lord Jesus was *ever* designated by the name Immanuel as a proper name. All that the passage means is, that such should be the circumstances of the birth of the child as to render the name Immanuel *proper;* not that it would be applied to him in fact as the usual appellation.

Nor is it any objection to this view, that the mind of the prophet is evidently directed onward *to* the Messiah; and that the prophecy terminates (ch. viii. 8; ix. 1–7) with a reference to him. That this is so, I admit; but nothing is more common in Isaiah than for him to *commence* a prophecy with reference to some remarkable deliverance which was soon to occur, and to *terminate* it by a statement of events connected with a higher deliverance under the Messiah. By the laws of *prophetic suggestion,* the mind of the prophet seized upon resemblances and analogies; was carried on to future times, which were *suggested* by something that he was saying or contemplating as about to occur, until the mind was absorbed, and the primary object forgotten in the contemplation of the more remote and glorious event; see Introduction to Isaiah, § 7. III. (3.)

II. EVIDENCE THAT THE PROPHECY REFERS TO THE MESSIAH.

(i.) The passage in Matt. i. 22, 23, is an evidence that *he* regarded this as having a reference to the Messiah, and that it had a complete fulfilment in him. This quotation of it also shows that that was the common interpretation of the passage in his time, or he would not thus have introduced it. It cannot be *proved,* indeed, that Matthew means to affirm that this was the primary and original meaning of the prophecy, or that the prophet had a direct and exclusive reference to the Messiah; but it proves that in his apprehension the words had a *fulness* of meaning, and an adaptedness to the actual circumstances of the birth of the Messiah, which would accurately and appropriately express that event; see Notes on the passage in Matthew. The prophecy was not completely *fulfilled, filled up, fully and*

adequately met, until applied to the Messiah. That event was so remarkable; the birth of Jesus was so strictly of a virgin, and his nature so exalted, that it might be said to be a *complete* and *entire* fulfilment of it. The language of Isaiah, indeed, was applicable to the event referred to immediately in the time of Ahaz, and expressed that with clearness; but it more appropriately and fully expressed the event referred to by Matthew, and thus shows that the prophet designedly made use of language which would be appropriate to a future and most glorious event.

(ii.) An argument of no slight importance on this subject may be drawn from the fact, that this has been the common interpretation in the Christian church. I know that this argument is not conclusive; nor should it be pressed beyond its due and proper weight. It is of force only because the united and almost uniform impression of mankind, for many generations, in regard to the meaning of a written document, is not to be rejected without great and unanswerable arguments. I know that erroneous interpretations of many passages have prevailed in the church; and that the interpretation of many passages of Scripture which have prevailed from age to age, have been such as have been adapted to bring the whole subject of scriptural exegesis into contempt. But we should be slow to reject that which has had in its favour the suffrages of the unlearned, as well as the learned, in the interpretation of the Bible. The interpretation which refers this passage to the Messiah has been the prevailing one in all ages. It was followed by all the fathers and other Christian expositors until the middle of the eighteenth century (*Hengstenberg*); and is the prevailing interpretation at the present time. Among those who have defended it, it is sufficient to mention the names of Lowth, Koppe, Rosenmüller, and Hengstenberg, in addition to those names which are found in the well-known English commentaries. It has been opposed by the modern Jews, and by German neologists; but has *not* been regarded as false by the great mass of pious and humble Christians. The argument here is simply that which would be applied in the interpretation of a passage in Homer or Virgil; that where the great mass of readers of all classes have concurred in any interpretation, there is *presumptive evidence* that it is correct—evidence, it is true, which may be set aside by argument, but which is to be admitted to be of *some* account in making up the mind as to the meaning of the passage in question.

(iii.) The reference to the Messiah in the prophecy accords with the *general strain and manner* of Isaiah. It is in accordance with his custom, at the mention of some occurrence or deliverance which is soon to take place, to suffer the mind to fix ultimately on the more remote event of the *same general character*, or lying, so to speak, *in the same range of vision* and of thought; see the Introduction, § 7. It is also the custom of Isaiah to hold up to prominent view the idea that the nation would not be ultimately destroyed till the great Deliverer should come; that it was safe amidst all revolutions; that vitality would remain like that of a tree in the depth of winter, when all the leaves are stripped off (ch. vi. 13); and that all their enemies would be destroyed, and the true people of God be ultimately secure and safe under their great Deliverer; see Notes on ch. xxxiv.; xxxv. It is true, that this argument will not be *very* striking except to one who has attentively studied this prophecy; but it is believed, that no one can profoundly and carefully examine the manner of Isaiah, without being struck with it as a very important feature of his mode of communicating truth. In accordance with this, the prophecy before us means, that the nation was safe from this invasion. Ahaz feared the extinction of his kingdom, and the *permanent* annexation of Jerusalem to Syria and Samaria. Isaiah told him that that could not occur; and proffered a demonstration, that in *a very few years* the land would be forsaken of both its kings. —*On another ground also it could not be.* The people of God were safe. His kingdom could not be permanently destroyed. It must continue until the Messiah should come, and the eye of the prophet, in accordance with his usual custom, glanced to that future event,

and he became *totally* absorbed in its contemplation, and the prophecy is finished (ch. ix. 1–7) by a description of the characteristics of the light that he saw in future times rising in dark Galilee (ch. ix. 1, 2), and of the child that should be born of a virgin then.

In accordance with the same view, we may remark, as Lowth has done, that to a people accustomed to look for a great Deliverer; that had fixed their hopes on one who was to sit on the throne of David, the *language* which Isaiah here used would naturally suggest the idea of a Messiah. It was so animated, so ill adapted to describe his own son, and so fitted to convey the idea of a most remarkable and unusual occurrence, that it could scarcely have been otherwise than that they should have *thought* of the Messiah. This is true in a special manner of the language in ch. ix. 1–7.

(iv.) An argument for the Messianic interpretation may be derived from the public expectation which was excited by some such prophecy as this. There is a striking similarity between it and one which is uttered by Micah, who was contemporary with Isaiah. Which was penned *first* it would not be easy to show; but they have internal evidence that they both had their origin in an expectation that the Messiah would be born of a virgin; comp. Note, ch. ii. 2. In Micah v. 2, 3, the following prediction occurs: 'But thou, Bethlehem Ephratah, though thou be little among the thousands of Judah, yet out of thee shall he come forth unto me that is to be ruler over Israel; whose goings forth have been from of old, from the days of eternity. Therefore will he give them up, until the time when she which travaileth hath brought forth.' That this passage refers to the birth of the Messiah, is demonstrable from Matt. ii. 6. Nothing can be clearer than that this is a prediction respecting the place of his birth. The Sanhedrim, when questioned by Herod respecting the place of his birth, answered without the slightest hesitation, and referred to this place in Micah for proof. The expression, 'she which travaileth,' or, 'she that bears shall bear'—יָֽלָדָה׃, *she bearing shall bear*—refers evi dently to some prediction of such a birth; and the word 'she that bears' (יֹלֶדֶת) seems to have been used somewhat in the sense of a proper name, to designate one who was well known, and of whom there had been a definite prediction. Rosenmüller remarks, 'She is not indeed expressly called a virgin, but that she is so is self-evident, since she shall bear the hero of Divine origin (from everlasting), and consequently not begotten by a mortal. The predictions throw light on each other; Micah discloses the Divine origin of the person predicted, Isaiah the wonderful manner of his birth.'—*Ros.*, as quoted by Hengstenberg. In his first edition, Rosenmüller remarks on Micah v. 2: 'The phrase, "she who shall bear shall bear," denotes the *virgin* from whom, in a miraculous manner, the people of that time hoped that the Messiah would be born.' If Micah refers to a well-known existing prophecy, it must evidently be this in Isaiah, since no other similar prophecy occurs in the Old Testament; and if he wrote subsequently to Isaiah, the prediction in Micah must be regarded as a proof that this was the prevailing interpretation of his time.

That this was the prevailing interpretation of those times, is confirmed by the traces of the belief which are to be found extensively in ancient nations, that some remarkable person would appear, who should be born in this manner. The idea of a Deliverer, to be born of a *virgin*, is one that somehow had obtained an extensive prevalence in Oriental nations, and traces of it may be found almost everywhere among them. In the Hindoo Mythology it is said, respecting *Budhu*, that he was born of *Maya*, a goddess of the imagination—a virgin. Among the Chinese, there is an image of a beautiful woman with a child in her arms, which child, they say, was born of a virgin. The passage in Virgil is well known:

Jam redit et Virgo, redeunt Saturnia regna:
Jam nova progenies coelo demittitur alto.
Tu modo nascenti puero, quo ferrea primum
Desinet, ac toto surget gens aurea mundo.
Casta fave Lucina: tuus jam regnat Apollo.
                         Eclog. iv. 4, *sq.*

Comes the last age, by Cumæ's maid foretold;
Afresh the mighty line of years unrolled.

The Virgin now, now Saturn's sway returns;
Now the blest globe a heaven-sprung child adorns,
Whose genial power shall whelm earth's iron race,
And plant once more the golden in its place.—
Thou chaste Lucina, but that child sustain,
And lo! disclosed thine own Apollo's reign.
                         Wrangham.

This passage, though applied by Virgil to a different subject, has been usually regarded as having been suggested by that in Isaiah. The coincidence of thought is remarkable on any supposition; and there is no improbability in the supposition that the expectation of a great Deliverer to be born of a virgin had prevailed extensively, and that Virgil wrought it up in this beautiful manner, and applied it to a prince in his own time. On the prevalent expectation of such a Deliverer, see Note on Matt. ii. 2.

(v.) But the great and the unanswerable argument for the Messianic interpretation is derived from the conclusion of the prophecy in ch. viii. 8, and especially in ch. ix. 1–7. The prophecy in ch. ix. 1–7 is evidently connected with this; and yet *cannot* be applied to a son of Isaiah, or to any other child that should be then born. If there is any passage in the Old Testament that *must* be applied to the Messiah, that is one; see Notes on the passage. And if so, it proves, that though the prophet at first had his eye on an event which was soon to occur, and which would be to Ahaz full demonstration that the land would be safe from the impending invasion, yet that he employed language which would describe also a future glorious event, and which would be a fuller demonstration that God would protect the people. He became *fully* absorbed in that event, and his language at last referred to that alone. The child then about to be born would, in most of the circumstances of his birth, be an apt emblem of him who should be born in future times, since both would be a demonstration of the Divine power and protection. To both, the name Immanuel, though not the common name by which either would be designated, might be appropriately given. Both would be born of a virgin —the former, of one who was then a virgin, and the birth of whose child could be known only to God,—the

17 The LORD shall bring upon thee, and upon thy people, and upon thy father's house, days that have not come, from the day that

Ephraim departed from Judah; *even* the king of Assyria.

18 And it shall come to pass in that day, *that* the LORD shall hiss

latter, of one who should be appropriately called *the* virgin, and who should remain so at the time of his birth. This seems to me to be the meaning of this difficult prophecy. The considerations in favour of referring it to the birth of a child in the time of Isaiah, and which should be a pledge to him of the safety of his kingdom *then*, seem to me to be unanswerable. And the considerations in favour of an ultimate reference to the Messiah—a reference which becomes in the issue total and absorbing — are equally unanswerable ; and if so, then the twofold reference is clear.

17. *The Lord shall bring*, &c. The prophet having assured Ahaz that his kingdom should be free from the invasion that then threatened it, proceeds, however, to state to him that it would be endangered from another source. ¶ *Thy father's house.* The royal family —the princes and nobles. ¶ *Days that have not come.* Times of calamity that have not been equalled. ¶ *From the day that Ephraim departed from Judah.* From the time of the separation of the ten tribes from the tribes of Judah and Benjamin. ¶ Even *the king of Assyria.* This was done in the following manner. Though the siege which Rezin and Pekah had undertaken was not at this time successful, yet they returned the year after with stronger forces, and with counsels better concerted, and again besieged the city. This was in consequence of the continued and increasing wickedness of Ahaz ; 2 Chron. xxviii. 1–5. In this expedition, a great multitude were taken captives, and carried to Damascus; 2 Chron. xxviii. 5. Pekah at this time also slew 120,000 of the Jews in one day (2 Chron. xxviii. 6); and Zichri, a valiant man of Ephraim, slew Maaseiah the son of Ahaz. At this time, also, Pekah took no less than 200,000 of the kingdom of Judah, proposing to take them to Samaria, but was prevented by the influence of the prophet Oded ; 2 Chron. xxviii. 8–15. In this calamity, Ahaz stripped the temple of its treasures and ornaments,

and sent them to Tiglath-pileser, king of Assyria, to induce him to come and defend him from the united arms of Syria and Ephraim. The consequence was, as might have been foreseen, that the king of Assyria took occasion, from this, to bring increasing calamities upon the kingdom of Ahaz. He first, indeed, slew Rezin, and took Damascus; 2 Kings xvi. 7. Having subdued the kingdoms of Damascus and Ephraim, Tiglath-pileser became a more formidable enemy to Ahaz than both of them. His object was not to aid Ahaz, but to distress him (2 Chron. xxviii. 20); and his coming professedly and at the request of Ahaz, to his help, was a more formidable calamity than the threatened invasion of both Rezin and Pekah. God has power to punish a wicked nation in his own way. When they seek human aid, he can make this a scourge. He has kings and nations under his control ; and though a wicked prince may seek earthly alliance, yet it is easy for God to allow such allies to indulge their ambition and love of rapine, and make them the very instruments of punishing the nation which they were called to defend. It should be observed that this phrase, 'even the king of Assyria,' is by many critics thought to be spurious, or a marginal reading, or gloss, that has by some means crept into the text. The ground of this opinion is, that it does not harmonize entirely with the following verse, where *Egypt* is mentioned as well as Assyria, and that it does not agree with the poetical form of the passage.

18. *In that day the Lord shall hiss ;* see Note, ch. v. 26. ¶ *For the fly.* That is, for the army, or the multitude of people. The comparison of a numerous army with *flies* is not uncommon ; *see* Homer's *Iliad*, B. ii. 469, &c.

———— Thick as insects play,
The wandering nation of a summer's day,
That, drawn by milky streams at evening hours
In gathered swarms surround the rural bowers;
From pail to pail with busy murmur run
The gilded legions, glittering in the sun.
                                        Pope.

The comparison is drawn probably from

for the fly that *is* in the uttermost part of the rivers of Egypt, and | for the bee that *is* in the land of Assyria:

the *number*, but also is intended to indicate the *troublesome* character, of the invaders. Perhaps, also, there is an allusion here to the well-known fact that one of the ten plagues of Egypt was caused by numerous swarms of flies ; Ex. viii. 21–24. An army would be brought up from that country as numerous, as troublesome, and as destructive as was that swarm of flies. The following description, by Bruce, of a species of flies in Abyssinia and the adjacent regions, will give an idea of the character of this calamity, and the force of the language used here :—

'This insect is called Zimb ; it has not been described by any naturalist. It is, in size, very little larger than a bee, of a thicker proportion, and has wings, which are broader than those of a bee, placed separate, like those of a fly : they are of pure gauze, without colour or spot upon them ; the head is large, the upper jaw or lip is sharp, and has at the end of it a strong pointed hair, of about a quarter of an inch long ; the lower jaw has two of these pointed hairs ; and this pencil of hairs, when joined together, makes a resistance to the finger, nearly equal to that of a strong hog's bristle ; its legs are serrated in the inside, and the whole covered with brown hair or down.

Zimb or Dog-Fly of Abyssinia.
From Bruce's Travels.

As soon as this plague appears, and their buzzing is heard, all the cattle forsake their food, and run wildly about the plain, till they die, worn out with fatigue, fright, and hunger. No remedy remains, but to leave the black earth, and hasten down to the sands of Atbara ; and there they remain, while the rains last, this cruel enemy never daring to pursue them further. Though his size be immense, as is his strength, and his body covered with a thick skin, defended with strong hair, yet even the camel is

not capable to sustain the violent punctures the fly makes with his pointed proboscis. He must lose no time in removing to the sands of Atbara ; for when once attacked by this fly, his body, head, and legs, break out into large bosses, which swell, break, and putrefy, to the certain destruction of the creature. Even the elephant and rhinoceros, who, by reason of their enormous bulk, and the vast quantity of food and water they daily need, cannot shift to desert and dry places as the season may require, are obliged to roll themselves in mud and mire, which, when dry, coats them over like armour, and enables them to stand their ground against this winged assassin ; yet I have found some of these tubercles upon almost every elephant and rhinoceros that I have seen, and attribute them to this cause. All the inhabitants of the sea-coast of Melinda, down to Cape Gardefan, to Saba, and the south coast of the Red Sea, are obliged to put themselves in motion, and remove to the next sand, in the beginning of the rainy season, to prevent all their stock of cattle from being destroyed. This is not a partial emigration ; the inhabitants of all the countries, from the mountains of Abyssinia northward, to the confluence of the Nile, and Astaboras, are once a year obliged to change their abode, and seek protection in the sand of Beja ; nor is there any alternative, or means of avoiding this, though a hostile band were in their way, capable of spoiling them or half their substance. This fly has no sting, though he seemed to me to be rather of the bee kind ; but his motion is more rapid and sudden than that of the bee, and resembles that of the gad-fly in England. There is something particular in the sound or buzzing of this insect ; it is a jarring noise, together with a humming, which induces me to believe it proceeds, at least in part, from a vibration made with the three hairs at his snout.' ¶ *The uttermost part of the rivers of Egypt.* The remotest part of the land—that is, from the whole country. Egypt was watered by a single river ; the Nile. But this river emptied into the Medi-

19 And *a*they shall come, and shall rest all of them in the desolate valleys, and in the holes of the rocks, and upon all thorns, and upon all ¹ bushes.

a Je.16.16.   1 or, *commendable trees.*

20 In the same day shall the LORD shave with a razor that is hired, *namely*, by them beyond the river, by the king of Assyria, the head, and the hair of the feet: and it shall also consume the beard.

---

terranean by several mouths; and from this river also were cut numerous canals to water the land. These are intended by the *rivers* of Egypt; see Notes, ch. xix. 6, 7. Those canals would be stagnant for no small part of the year; and around them would be produced, as is usual near stagnant waters, great quantities of flies. This prophecy was fulfilled by the invasion of the land in subsequent times by the Egyptians; 2 Kings xxiii. 33, 34; 2 Chron. xxxv. 20, 24; xxxvi. 1, 2. ¶ *And for the bee.* That is, for the *army.* An army is compared to *bees* on account of their number; perhaps also on account of the pungency and severity of the sting. The comparison is common; see Deut. i. 44; vii. 20; Ps. cxviii. 12. The Chaldee has rendered this verse, 'The Lord shall call to a people girded with the armies of the brave, who are numerous as flies, and shall bring them from the ends of the land of Egypt; and strong armies, strong as bees, and shall bring them from the land of Assyria.' No prophecy was ever more completely fulfilled than this by the successive invasions of Pharaoh-Necho, Esarhaddon and Nebuchadnezzar; see Isa. xxxvi.; xxxvii.; 2 Chron. xxxvi. 7–21.

19. *And they shall come.* The idea in this verse is, that they would spread over the land, and lay it waste. The poetic image of flies and bees is kept up; meaning, that the armies would be so numerous as to occupy and infest all the land. ¶ *And shall rest.* As bees do. Thus the *locusts* are said to have *rested* in all the land of Egypt; Ex. x. 14. ¶ *In the desolate valleys.* The word translated *valleys* usually means *a valley with a brook,* or a brook itself. The Chaldee translates it, 'In the streets of cities.' But the idea is derived from the habits of flies and bees. The meaning is, that they should fill all the land, as innumerable swarms of flies and bees—would settle down everywhere,

and would infest or consume everything. Bees, probably, chose situations near to running streams. Virgil, in his directions about selecting a place for an apiary, gives the following among others:—

At liquidi fontes, et stagna virentia musco
Adsint, et tenuis fugiens per gramina rivus.
Georg. iv. 18, 19.

But there let pools invite with moss arrayed,
Clear fount and rill that purls along the glade.
Sotheby.

¶ *In the holes of the rocks.* Probably the same image is referred to here. It is well known that in Judea, as well as elsewhere, bees were accustomed to live in the holes or caverns of the rocks. They were very numerous; and the figure here is, that the Assyrians would be numerous as the swarms of bees were in that land, even in the high and inaccessible rocks; comp. Isa. ii. 19–21. ¶ *Upon all thorns.* The image here is kept up of flies and bees resting on everything. *Thorns* here refer to those trees and shrubs that were of little value; but even on these they would rest. ¶ *All bushes.* Heb. 'All trees that are commendable, or that are to be praised;' see margin. The word denotes those shrubs and trees that were objects of *praise;* that is, that were cultivated with great attention and care, in opposition to *thorns* that grew wild, and without cultivation, and that were of little value. The meaning of the passage is, that the land would be invaded in every part, and that everything, valuable or not, would be laid waste.

20. *In the same day,* &c. The idea in this verse is the same as in the preceding, though presented in a different form. The meaning is, that *God* would bring upon them this punishment, but that he would make use of the Assyrian as an *instrument* by which to do it. ¶ *Shave.* The act of shaving off the hair denotes punishment or disgrace;

21 And it shall come to pass in that day, *that* a man shall nourish a young cow and two sheep:

22 And it shall come to pass, for the abundance of milk *that* they shall give, that he shall eat butter: for butter and honey shall every one eat *that* is left [1] in the land.

1 *in the midst of.*

comp. 2 Sam. x. 4. : 'Hanun took David's servants, and shaved off one half of their beards ;' 1 Chron. xix. 4. ¶ *With a razor.* Using them as an instrument. God here claims the power of directing them, and regards them as employed by him ; see ch. x. 5-7. ¶ *That is hired.* This is an allusion to the custom of *hiring* soldiers, or employing *mercenary armies.* Thus Great Britain employed *mercenary* troops, or hired of the Germans bodies of *Hessians* to carry on the war in America. The meaning here is, that God would employ the Assyrians as *his* instruments, to effect *his* purposes, as though they were *hired* and paid by the plunder and spoil of the nation. ¶ *By them beyond the river.* The river *Euphrates.* The Euphrates is usually meant in the Scriptures where 'the river' is mentioned without specifying the name ; Ps. lxxii. 8; lxxx. 2. This was the river which Abraham had passed ; and this, perhaps, was, for a long time, the eastern boundary of their geographical knowledge ; see Note, ch. xi. 15. ¶ *The head.* The hair of the head. ¶ *The hair of the feet.* Or the other parts of the body ; of the lower parts of the body. ¶ *Shall consume the beard.* Shall cut off the beard. This was esteemed particularly disgraceful among the Jews. It is, at this day, among all Eastern nations. The *beard* is regarded as a distinguished ornament ; among the Mahometans, it is *sworn* by, and no higher insult can be offered than to treat the beard with indignity ; comp. Note, Isa. l. 6. The meaning is here, that God would employ the Assyrian as his instrument to lay waste the land.

21. *In that day.* In the time specified in the previous verses—in the judgments that should be brought upon the land by the Egyptians and Assyrians. ¶ *A man shall nourish.* Heb. 'Make to live ;' that is, he shall own, or feed. ¶ *A young cow.* The Hebrew denotes a heifer that gives milk. The state

which is denoted by this is that of great *poverty.* Instead of being engaged in agriculture, of possessing great resources in that time, a man should depend, for the subsistence of himself and his family, on what a single cow and two sheep would yield. Probably this is intended also as a description of the general state of the nation, that it would be reduced to great poverty. ¶ *And two sheep.* Two here seems to be used to denote a very small number. A man, *i.e.*, the generality of men, would be so reduced as to be able to purchase and keep no more.

22. *For the abundance of milk,* &c. On account, or by means of the great quantity of milk. This image also denotes that the land should be desolate, and abandoned by its inhabitants. Such a range would the cow and sheep have in the lands lying waste and uncultivated, that they would yield abundance of milk. ¶ *For butter and honey.* This shall be the condition of all who are left in the land. Agriculture shall be abandoned. The land shall be desolate. The few remaining inhabitants shall be dependent on what a very few cows and sheep shall produce, and on the subsistence which may be derived from honey obtained from the rocks where bees would lodge. Perhaps, also, the swarms of *bees* would be increased, by the fact that the land would be forsaken, and that it would produce abundance of wild flowers for their subsistence. The general idea is plain, that the land would be desolate. Butter and honey, that is, butter mingled with honey, is a common article of food in the East ; see Note on ver. 15. D'Arvieux being in the camp of an Arab prince who lived in much splendour, and who treated him with great regard, was entertained, he tells us, the first morning of his being there, with little loaves, *honey, new-churned butter,* and cream more delicate than any he ever saw, together with coffee.—*Voy. dans la Pal.*, p. 24. And in another

23 And it shall come to pass in that day, *that* every place shall be, where there were a thousand vines at a thousand silverlings, it shall *even* be for briers and thorns.

24 With arrows and with bows shall *men* come thither; because all the land shall become briers and thorns.

25 And *on* all hills that shall be digged with the mattock, there shall not come thither the fear of briers and thorns; but it shall be for the sending forth of oxen, and for the treading of lesser cattle.

---

place, he assures us that one of the principal things with which the Arabs regale themselves at breakfast is cream, or new butter mingled with honey.—P. 197. The statement of the prophet here, that the poor of the land should eat butter and honey, is not inconsistent with this account of D'Arvieux, that it is regarded as an article of food with which even princes treat their guests; for the idea of the prophet is, that when the land should be desolate and comparatively uninhabited, the natural luxuriant growth of the soil would produce an abundance to furnish milk, and that honey would abound where the bees would be allowed to multiply, almost without limit; see Harmer's *Obs.*, vol. ii. p. 55. Ed. Lond. 1808.

23. The remainder of this chapter is a description of great desolation produced by the invasion of the Assyrians. ¶ *Where there were a thousand vines.* Where there was a valuable vineyard. In every place, that is, that was well cultivated and valuable. ¶ *At a thousand silverlings.* The word rendered 'silverlings' here — כֶּסֶף, *kĕsĕph* — denotes, properly, *silver*, of any amount. But it is also used to denote the silver coin which was in use among the Jews, *the shekel.* Perhaps this was the only silver coin which, in early times, they possessed, and hence the word *shekel* is omitted, and so many pieces of *silver* are mentioned. Thus, in Gen. xx. 16, Abimelech says, that he had given Abraham 'a thousand of silver'—that is, a thousand shekels. The shekel was worth about two shillings of our money. It is probable that a vineyard would be valued, in proportion to the number of vines that could be raised on the smallest space; and the meaning is here, that the land that was most fertile, and that produced the most, would be desolate, and would produce only briers and

thorns. The land in Judea admits of a high state of cultivation, and requires it, in order to make it productive. When neglected, it becomes as remarkably sterile. At present, it generally bears the marks of great barrenness and sterility. It is under the oppression of Turkish power and exactions; and the consequence is, that, to a traveller, it has the appearance of great barrenness. But, in the high state to which the Jews brought it, it was eminently fertile, and is capable still of becoming so, if it should be placed under a government that would encourage agriculture and bestow freedom. This is the account which all travellers give of it now.

24. *With arrows and with bows, &c.* This is a continuation of the description of its desolation. So entirely would it be abandoned, so utterly desolate would it be, that it would become *a vast hunting-ground.* It would be covered with shrubs and trees that would afford a convenient covert for wild beasts; and would yield to its few inhabitants a subsistence, not by cultivation, but by the bow and the arrow. There can scarcely be a more striking description of utter desolation. But, perhaps, the long captivity of seventy years in Babylon literally fulfilled it. Judea was a land that, at all times, was subject to depredations from wild beasts. On the banks of the Jordan—in the marshes, and amid the reeds that sprung up in the lower bank or border of the river—the lion found a home, and the tiger a resting-place; comp. Jer. xlix. 19. When the land was for a little time vacated and forsaken, it would be, therefore, soon filled with wild beasts; and during the desolations of the seventy years' captivity, there can be no doubt that this was literally fulfilled.

25. *And* on *all hills, &c.* All the fertile places in the mountains that

CHAPTER VIII.

ANALYSIS OF THE CHAPTER.

IN ch. vii. the prophet had told Ahaz that God would give him a sign that the land of Judah should be safe from the threatened invasion of the united armies of Syria and Israel. In this chapter, there is a record of the primary fulfilment of that promise, ver. 1–4. From ver. 5 to ver. 8, the prophet resumes and repeats what he had said before in ch. vii. 17–25, that although the land should be safe from *this* invasion, yet one more formidable would occur by the armies of Assyria. The cause of this is stated to be, that Judah had despised the Lord, and had sought alliances with Syria and Israel. The prophet then proceeds to exhort the people to put confidence in Jehovah—assuring them that if they refused to confide in him, they must expect to be destroyed, ver. 9–18; and the chapter concludes with denouncing punishment on those that looked to necromancers and diviners, rather than to the true God. The prophecy is intimately connected with that in the previous chapter; and was delivered, evidently, not far from the same time.

MOREOVER the LORD said unto me, Take thee a great roll, and write in it with a man's pen concerning [1] Maher-shalal-hash-baz.

[1] *in making speed to the spoil, he hasteneth the prey,* or, *make speed, &c.*

used to be cultivated with the spade. Vineyards were often planted on the sides of hills; and those places were among the most productive and fertile in the land; see ch. v. 1. ¶ *The mattock.* The spade; the garden hoe; or the weeding-hook. An instrument chiefly used, probably, in vineyards. ¶ *There shall not come thither.* There shall not be. ¶ *The fear of briers and thorns.* This does not make sense; or if it does, it is not a sense consistent with the connection. The idea of the whole passage is, that the land, even the most fertile parts of it, should be given up to briers and thorns; that is, to desolation. The Hebrew here, is ambiguous. It may mean, '*thou* shalt not come there, for fear of the briers and thorns.' That is, the place that was formerly so fertile, that was cultivated with the spade, shall now be so completely covered with thorns, and shall furnish so convenient a resting-place for wild beasts and reptiles, as to deter a man from going there. The LXX., and the Syriac, however, understand it differently—as denoting that those places should be still cultivated. But this is evidently a departure from the sense of the connection. Lowth understands it in the *past* tense; 'where the fear of briers and thorns never came.' The general idea of the passage is plain, that those places, once so highly cultivated, would now be desolate. ¶ *Shall be for the sending forth,* &c. Shall be wild, uncultivated, and desolate—vast *commons* on which oxen and sheep shall feed at large. ¶ *Lesser*

cattle. Heb. 'Sheep, or the flock.' Sheep were accustomed to range in deserts and uncultivated places, and to obtain there, under the guidance of the shepherd, their subsistence. The description, therefore, in these verses, is one of extensive and wide desolation; and one that was accomplished in the calamities that came upon the land in the invasions by the Egyptians and Assyrians.

CHAPTER VIII.

1. *Take thee a great roll.* The word which is here translated 'roll' more properly signifies *tablet.* So the Chaldee renders it. Those *tablets* were made of wood, metal, or stone, for the purpose of writing on; see ch. xxx. 8; Hab. ii. 2. On these tablets, or smooth plates, writing was performed by cutting the letters with an iron *stylus,* or small chisel. The process was slow, but the writing was permanent. They sometimes used the skins of animals, or the bark of trees, and subsequently the *papyrus* of Egypt (comp. Note, ch. xix. 7); and it is possible that Isaiah may have used such a roll or volume on this occasion; comp. ver. 16. ¶ *With a man's pen.* The word *pen* here (חֶרֶט) denotes the iron *stylus,* which was used to *engrave* or *cut* the letters in the metal or wood. The phrase 'a man's pen,' has been variously interpreted. The Chaldee renders it, 'Write in it an open, or clear writing, or an expanded writing;' meaning that he should make it clear and distinct, so as to be easily read. The Syriac, 'Write on it in the [usual] custom of men.' The word which is translated 'man's' (אֱנוֹשׁ)

2 And 1 took unto me faithful witnesses to record, Uriah *a* the priest, and Zechariah the son of Jeberechiah.

3 And I 1 went unto the pro-

phetess; and she conceived and bare a son. Then said the LORD to me, Call his name Maher-shalal-hash-baz:

4 For *b* before the child shall have

usually denotes *common men*, the lower ranks, in opposition to the higher ranks of society. And probably the direction means simply, 'write on it in letters such as men commonly use ; in a plain, open, distinct manner—without using any mysterious emblems or characters, but so that men may read it distinctly and easily.' A parallel place occurs in Hab. ii. 2 : 'Write the vision and make it plain upon tables, that he may run that readeth it.' ¶ *Concerning.* Heb. ‫ל‬. This preposition may denote *concerning, of,* or *to.* I understand it here as referring to the *heading* or *title* of the prophecy. This was to be set *over* the prophecy, as a running title, to denote the main subject of it. The subject is indicated in the name which is immediately added. ¶ *Maher.* Hasten ; or, he shall hasten. ¶ *Shalal.* Spoil, or prey. ¶ *Hash.* Hasten, or make speed. ¶ *Baz.* Spoil, or prey. The name used here is a repetition of the same idea—denoting haste in seizing prey, or spoil ; and is repeated to give emphasis, and to excite attention. The idea is, that the Assyrian would hasten to his plunder—that it would be accomplished with speed. This name was to be given to a child of Isaiah ; and this child was to be a *sign* of the event which was signified by the name ; see ver. 18 ; comp. Hab. ii. 2, 3.

2. *And I took unto me faithful witnesses.* What was the precise object in calling in these witnesses is not known. Some have supposed that it was to bear testimony to the marriage of the prophet at that time. But it may have been for the purpose of a public record of the prophecy ; a record so made, that *the precise time* when it was delivered could be attested without dispute. The prophecy was an important one ; and it was important to know, in the most authentic and undisputed manner, that such a prophecy had been delivered. It is probable that the prophecy, attested

by the names of those two men, was suspended in some public place in the temple, so that it might be seen by the people, and allay their fears ; and in order to remove from the multitude every suspicion that it was *a prophecy after the event.* That this was a real, and not a symbolical transaction, is perfectly manifest, not only from the narrative itself, but from ver. 18. They are called 'faithful,' not on account of their private character, but because their public testimony would be credited by the people. ¶ *To record.* To bear witness. ¶ *Uriah the priest.* This is, doubtless, the same man that is mentioned in 2 Kings xvi. 10. He was a man of infamous character ; the accomplice of Ahaz in corrupting the true religion ; but still his testimony might be the more valuable to Ahaz, as he was associated with him in his plans. ¶ *And Zechariah,* &c. It is not certainly known who this was. Perhaps he was one of the Levites whose name is mentioned in 2 Chron. xxix. 13.

3. *Then said the* LORD, &c. The name thus given was to be emblematic of a particular event—that Assyria would soon take away the spoil of Damascus and Samaria. It is not remarkable that the name Immanuel should also be given to the same child, as signifying the presence and protection of God in defending the nation from the invaders ; see Notes on ch. vii. 14, 15. Calvin thinks that all this passed in *a vision* before the prophet ; but it has every mark of being a literal narrative of the birth of a son to Isaiah ; and without this supposition, it is impossible to understand the account contained here.

4. *For before,* &c. This must have occurred in a short time—probably before the expiration of three years. A child would usually learn to address his parents in that time. *In fact,* the event here predicted occurred in less than three years from the time when the prophecy

knowledge to cry, My father, and my mother, the [1] riches of Damascus and the spoil of Samaria shall be taken away *a* before the king of Assyria.

1 or, *he that is before the king of Assyria shall take away the riches.*

5 The LORD spake also unto me again, saying,

6 Forasmuch as this people refuseth the waters of Shiloah *b* that go softly, and rejoice in Rezin and Remaliah's son;

a 2 Ki.15.29; 16.9; 17.3.   *b* Neh.3.15; Jn.9.7.

---

was spoken; see Notes on ch. vii. 16. ¶ *Before the king of Assyria.* By the king, or by his conquests. By the spoil of Samaria here, is to be understood, not the plunder which should be carried away from the city, but from the kingdom of Samaria. In other places, the land is called by the name of the capital; comp. 2 Kings xvii. 26; xxiii. 19; Jer. xxxi. 5. The *city* of Samaria was not plundered until eighteen years after the time here mentioned by the prophet; 5, 6. These verses introduce again what was predicted in ch. vii. 17, *sq.*, respecting the invasion of the land by the king of Assyria. The *cause* of the invasion is specified, and the consequences are foretold.

6. *Forasmuch as this people.* There has been a considerable difference of opinion among interpreters respecting the 'people' to whom the prophet here refers. Some have supposed that it refers to the kingdom of Judah alone; others to a *party* in that kingdom; and others to the kingdom of Judah in connection with the ten tribes, or the kingdom of Israel also. The latter is probably the correct interpretation. The prophet reproves the *whole* nation of the Jews for despising the mild and gentle reign of the family of David, and for seeking the aid of foreign nations; the ten tribes as seeking an alliance with Rezin and Pekah; and the kingdom of Judah as seeking an alliance with the king of Assyria. It was characteristic of the nation—both of the ten tribes, and of the tribe of Judah—that they forsook the defence which they had in themselves, and sought foreign alliances. Hence God says, that he will bring upon them the judgments which they deserve. That there is a joint reference to both the kingdoms of Israel and Judah, is apparent from ver. 14. It cannot refer to the kingdom of Judah alone, for it could not be brought as an accusation

against them, that they took pleasure in Rezin. In the opinion that it refers to the kingdoms of Israel and of Judah —to the whole Jewish people, Vitringa, Lowth, and Hengstenberg concur. ¶ *The waters of Shiloah that go softly.* That flow gently. The name Siloah, or Siloam, is found only three times in the Scriptures as applied to waters; once in this place, where it is spoken of a running water; once as a pool in Nehemiah —בְּרֵכַת הַשֶּׁלַח—ch. iii. 15, and again as a pool, in the account of the miracle of healing the man who was born blind; John ix. 7, 11. Siloam is on the east side of the city of Jerusalem, to the south-east of the site of the temple, and its waters flow into the valley of Jehoshaphat. The name means *sent*, or *sending*, from שָׁלַח *to send*, and was probably given to it because the waters were *sent* or made to pass through a subterranean passage or aqueduct.

At present, it properly consists of two receptacles or reservoirs, the waters from one of which flow into the other. The first, or upper one, is now called the 'Fountain of the Virgin,' from a tradition that it was here that the Virgin Mary resorted before her purification, in order to wash her child's linen. This fountain is on the west side of the valley of Jehoshaphat, and is about 1550 feet from the south-east corner of the city wall. The cavity of this fountain is wholly excavated in the solid rock. To enter it there is at first a descent of sixteen steps, to a level place or platform of twelve feet in diameter, and then another descent of ten steps to the water, making the whole depth twenty-five feet. The basin here is about fifteen feet long by five or six wide, and the height six or eight feet. There is some reason to suppose that this is supplied by a fountain lying under the mosque of Omar, on the site of the temple of Solomon. From this fountain the water is conducted by a subterranean passage, in a direction a little to the west of south to what is properly called the fountain of Siloam. This passage runs under the extremity of mount Ophel; is cut entirely from the solid rock, and is found by measurement to be 1750 feet in length. At the lower part it is from ten to fifteen feet in height by two in breadth; but in the middle so low, that it can be passed only by creeping on the hands and knees. The passage is partly filled up with sand. From this aqueduct the water is conveyed into the pool of Siloam, situated near where the Ty-

7 Now therefore, behold, the Lord bringeth up upon them the waters of the river, strong and many, *even* ᵃthe king of Assyria, and all his glory: and he shall come up over all his channels, and go over all his banks:

a ch.7.1-6.

ropeon, or 'valley of cheesemongers,' opens into the valley of Jehoshaphat. This reservoir is

POOL OF SILOAM.—From Forbin.

fifty-three feet long, eighteen feet broad, and nineteen feet deep, though now there is usually no water remaining within it. From this reservoir the water flows off into the vale below, furnishing water for the gardens, which are constructed in terraces on the side of the valley. The water in both these fountains is the same. It is sweet, and slightly brackish, but not disagreeable. It is the common water now used by the inhabitants of the neighbouring village of Kefr Selwâne—or the straggling village of Siloam. For a full description of this fountain, *see* Robinson's *Bib. Researches*, vol. i. pp. 493-514. This fountain was probably formerly included within the walls, and furnished a part of the supply of water to the city.

The meaning of this passage is this. The waters of Siloam denote the reign of Jehovah, as manifesting itself in the administration of the family of David—a mild, gentle, and munificent reign, beautifully represented by the unfailing and gently-flowing waters on which the happiness of Jerusalem so much depended. That reign a large part of the nation—the ten tribes—had rejected, and had set up a separate kingdom, and had sought the aid of the king of Damascus. The remainder—the kingdom of Judah—were in like manner now disposed to reject the aid of Jehovah, and sought an alliance

with the king of Assyria—beautifully represented here by the river Euphrates. The waters of Siloam—a gentle, small, sweetly-flowing stream, represented the government of Jehovah. The waters of the Euphrates—violent, rapid, impetuous, and overflowing, represented the government of Assyria. The one they despised; the other they sought and admired. The power of the kingdom of David was then feeble and decayed. That of the Assyrian monarch was vigorous, mighty, vast. They despised the one, and sought the alliance of the other. ¶ *And rejoice.* That is, they confide in, and feel that in their protection they are safe. ¶ *In Rezin.* King of Syria. ¶ *And Remaliah's son.* Pekah, king of Samaria; ch. vii. 1. The crime here mentioned was peculiar to the kingdom of Israel; showing that the prophet, in part at least, had reference to them.

7. *The waters of the river.* By *the river*, in the Scripture, is commonly meant the river Euphrates, as being, by way of eminence, the largest river with which they were acquainted; and also as being that distinguished by the fact that Abraham had lived beyond it, and crossed it; see Note, ch. vii. 20. In this verse the image is kept up which was commenced in ver. 6. The Jews rejected the gentle waters of Siloah, and sought the alliance of a foreign king, whose kingdom stretched along, and extended beyond the Euphrates. It was natural, therefore, to compare the invasion of the land to the overflowing of mighty waters that would sweep everything away. A similar comparison is found in Juvenal, who, in describing the introduction of Eastern customs into Rome, represents the *Orontes* as flowing into the Tiber:—

Jampridem Syrus in Tiberim defluxit Orontes.

The comparison of an invading army with an overflowing stream, or an inundation, is not uncommon; see Lucan's *Phars.* vi. 272. Hor. *Car.* iv. 14, 15, *sq.* ¶ *Strong and many.* Violent

8 And he shall pass through Judah; he shall overflow and go over; he shall reach *even* to the

1 *fulness of the breadth of thy land shall be the stretchings out of his wings.*

neck: and the [1] stretching out of his wings shall fill *a* the breadth of thy land, O Immanuel.

a ch.36.1, &c.

waves, and numerous. It means that a mighty host would come up upon the land. ¶ *Even the king of Assyria.* It has been supposed by many that this is a *gloss*, or explanation, which has crept into the text. There is no doubt that it expresses the true sense of the passage, but it is remarkable that Isaiah himself should furnish a *literal* explanation in the midst of a figurative description. ¶ *And all his glory.* Eastern kings marched in the midst of vast splendour. They moved with all the magnificence of. the court, and were attended usually with their princes and nobles; with a splendid retinue; and with all the insignia of royalty. Such was the case with Xerxes when he invaded Greece; and such, too, with Darius, and with most of the Oriental conquerors. ¶ *And he shall come up,* &c. The figure of overflowing waters is here retained. To understand this, it is necessary to remark, that the Euphrates annually overflows its banks to a very considerable extent. It rises in the mountains of Armenia, and, flowing for a considerable distance in a region where the mountains are covered with snow, it falls into the level region of Mesopotamia or Syria, and flows through that region, almost parallel with the Tigris, towards the Persian Gulf. From its banks, vast numbers of canals were made, as in Egypt, to receive the water, and to render the country fertile. By the melting of the snows in Armenia, in the summer, the stream becomes greatly enlarged, and overflows vast portions of the adjacent country in a manner similar to the Nile. Usually the river is *not* very large. Otho says, that on the 12th of March, when he crossed the Euphrates, it was not more than 200 paces in width, but in its height, it extends 500 or 600 paces into the plains on the right. Thevenot observes, that near to Bir, the Euphrates seemed no larger than the Seine at Paris, but was very large when it was swollen. At Baby-

lon, it is said to be about four hundred feet in breadth. That it overflows its banks, is abundantly attested by ancient as well as modern travellers; see Rosenmüller and Gesenius on this verse. ¶ *Its channels.* This word means either *brooks*, or *valleys*, or *canals*, or *channels* of a river. The Euphrates flowed through a level region, and it is not improbable that it had at various times made for itself many channels. Besides this, there were many *canals* cut in various directions to convey its waters to the gardens, farms, &c. All these the prophet says would be full—and the water would extend even far beyond them.

8. *He shall,* &c. That is, the Assyrian—though still retaining the idea of an overflowing stream, or a deluge of waters. ¶ *Reach* even *to the neck.* Chaldee, 'They shall come even to Jerusalem.' 'The prophet compares Jerusalem here,' says Kimchi, 'to the head of the human body. As when the waters reach to the *neck* of a man, he is very near drowning, so here, the prophet intimates that the whole land would be deluged, and that it would be nearly *utterly* destroyed.' The figure thus understood is a very sublime one Jerusalem was situated on hills—elevated above the surrounding country, and, in reference to the whole land, might be aptly compared to the human head. Thus Josephus (*De Bello,* lib. iii. ch. ii.), describing Jerusalem, says,— Ἱεροσόλυμα προανίσχουσα τῆς περιοίκου πάσης, ὥσπερ ἡ κεφαλὴ σώματος—*Jerusalem, eminent above all the surrounding region, as the head of the body.* The country is represented as being laid under water—a vast sea of rolling and tumultuous waves — with Jerusalem alone rising above them, standing in solitary grandeur amidst the heaving ocean, and itself in danger each moment of being ingulphed; see a similar figure, Isa. xxx. 28:

His spirit is like a torrent overflowing
It shall reach to the middle of the neck.

9 Associate yourselves, O ye people, and [1]ye shall be broken[a] in
pieces; and give ear, all ye of far

1 or, *yet*.　　　　*a* ch.37.36.

And so also, Hab. iii. 13:

Thou didst go forth for the salvation of thy peo-
ple,
For the salvation of thine anointed:
Thou didst smite the head from the house of the
wicked,
Destroying the foundation even to the neck.

¶ *And the stretching out of his wings.*
This is a continuation of the same idea
under a new figure. The term *wings*
is often applied to an army, as well in
modern as in ancient writings. It
denotes that the invading army would
be so vast as, when expanded or drawn
out, to fill the land. ¶ *Shall fill the
breadth.* Shall occupy the entire land,
so that there shall be no city or town
which he shall not invade. ¶ *Thy
land, O Immanuel;* see Note, ch. vii. 14.
If this be understood as referring to the
son of Isaiah that was to be born, then
it means that the child was given as a
pledge that the land would be safe from
the threatened invasion. It was natural,
therefore, to address the child in that
manner; as reminding the prophet that
this land, which was about to be invaded,
belonged to God, and was yet under his
protection. Its meaning may be thus
paraphrased: 'O thou who art a pledge
of the protection of God—whose birth
is an assurance that the land is under
his care, and who art given as such a
sign to the nation. Notwithstanding
this pledge, the land shall be full of
foes. They shall spread through every
part, and endanger all.' Yet the name,
the circumstances of the birth, the promise at that time, would all remind the
prophet and the king, that, notwithstanding this, the land would be still
under the protection of God. If the
language be understood as referring to
the future Messiah, and as an address
made to him then, by calling the land
his land, it is intimated that it could
not be brought to utter desolation, nor
could the country where he was to be
born remain wasted and ruined. It
would be indeed invaded; the armies of
the Assyrian would spread over it, but
still it was the land of Immanuel; and

countries: gird yourselves, and ye
shall be broken in pieces; gird yourselves, and ye shall be broken in
pieces.

was to be the place of his birth, and it
was to be secure until the time should
arrive for him to come. The probability is, I think, that the address is
here solely to the Messiah; and that the
purpose of God is to fix the mind of the
prophet on the fact that the Messiah
must come, as an assurance that the
land could not be wholly and perpetually desolate; see Notes on ch. vii. 14.
9. *Associate yourselves.* In the previous verses the prophet had seen the
Assyrian coming up on the land like
an overwhelming flood. He looked
upon the danger, and his mind was
turned to the pledge of safety which
God had given. The name Immanuel,
and the promise connected with the
giving of that name (ch. vii. 16), reminded him of the perfect safety of the
nation; for it was a pledge that God
was with them; see ver. 10. In view
of this pledge of the protection of God,
this verse is a spirited apostrophe to the
mighty host that was about to invade
the land. Though confederated and
vast, yet they could not prevail. They
should be scattered, much as they might
be prepared for victory, for God had
given a pledge that he would defend his
people. ¶ *Associate.* There has been
much variety among interpreters about
the meaning of the original word used
here. It may mean *to be terrified, to
be alarmed,* as well as to associate or
become confederate. The Vulgate and
Chaldee render it, 'Be assembled, or
congregated.' The LXX., 'Know, ye
nations,' &c. The Syriac, 'Tremble,
ye people,' &c. Still the notion of
associating, confederating, or entering
into an alliance, suits the connection
better; answers to the parallelism in the
latter part of the verse, and is equally
consonant with the original. ¶ *O ye
people.* Ye people of Assyria. This
is an apostrophe to the mighty multitudes that were to come up upon the
land from that country. ¶ *And ye
shall be broken in pieces.* That is,
though the confederacy be mighty, yet
it shall not prevail. It shall not ac-

10 Take counsel together, and it shall come to nought; speak the word, and it shall not stand: for God *a is* with us.

11 For the LORD spake thus to

a Ps.46.1,7.   *1 in strength of.*

me with [1] a strong hand, and instructed me, that I should not walk *b* in the way of this people, saying,

12 Say ye not, A confederacy, to

b Prov.1.15.

complish that which you purpose—the entire destruction of the land of Judah. ¶ *Give ear, all ye of far countries.* That should be particularly engaged in the confederacy—Assyria, and the kingdoms allied with it. ¶ *Gird yourselves.* As if for war; that is, prepare yourselves thoroughly for conquest; see Note, ch. v. 27. The *repetition* of this shows the excited and agitated state of the prophet's mind. It is a strong, emphatic mode of expression—denoting that they should be *certainly* broken in pieces, notwithstanding the strength of their confederacy.

10. *Take counsel together.* This is an address to the same foreign nations. It refers to the designs which they would form to destroy the Jewish state. ¶ *Speak the word.* That is, give the command—to overturn the nation of the Jews. ¶ *It shall not stand.* It shall not be accomplished. ¶ *For God is with us.* Heb. 'For Immanuel.' It indicates the confidence of the prophet in view of the promise and the pledge. His reliance was there. Though the enemies were strong and mighty; though the confederacy was formidable; yet his simple reliance was in the name *Immanuel!* In this he had confidence, in spite of all the violent efforts and designs of the foes of Judah; see Num. xiv. 9:

Only, rebel not ye against the Lord:
Neither fear ye the people of the land;
For they are bread for us;
Their defence is departed from them,
And JEHOVAH *is with us,*
Fear them not.

See also Ps. xlvi. 6, 7:

The heathen raged,
The kingdoms were moved.
He uttered his voice, the earth dissolved.
JEHOVAH *of hosts is with us;*
The God of Jacob is our refuge.

11. *For the* LORD *spake thus.* Spake that which immediately follows in the next verse. Warned him not to unite in the alliance with foreign kingdoms which the nation was about forming. ¶ *With a strong hand.* Marg. 'With

strength of hand.' That is, when the hand of God *urged* me. A strong prophetic impulse is often represented as being produced by God's laying his *hand* on the prophet; or by his being thus, as it were, *urged* or *impelled* to it; Ezek. iii. 14: 'The hand of JEHOVAH was strong upon me;' 2 Kings iii. 15: 'And it came to pass, that when the minstrel played, the hand of the LORD came upon him;' Jer. xx. 7: 'O LORD, thou art stronger than I, and hast prevailed;' see also Eccl. ii. 24; 1 Kings xviii. 46; 2 Kings iii. 15; Ezek. xxxiii. 22; xl. 1; comp. Introduction, § 7.11. (3.) The meaning is, that the prophet was strongly, and almost irresistibly, urged by the Divine influence, to say what he was about to say. ¶ *That I should not walk,* &c. That I should not approve, and fall in with, the design of Ahaz, and of the nation, in calling in the aid of the Assyrian armies.

12. *Say ye not.* Do not join in their purposes of forming a confederacy. Do not unite with the king and the people of Judah in their alarms about the threatened invasion by the kings of Syria and Samaria, and in their purpose to form an alliance with the king of Assyria. The reason why they should not do this, he states in ver. 13, where he exhorts the nation to put confidence in the Lord rather than in man. There has been, however, great diversity in the interpretation of this passage. The LXX. render the word קֶשֶׁר *qĕshĕr,* 'confederacy,' by the word σκληρόν— 'Everything which this people say, is *hard.*' The Syriac, 'Do not say, *rebellion,*' &c. The Chaldee understands the word in the same sense. Lowth proposes to change the word קֶשֶׁר *qĕshĕr,* into קָדֹשׁ *qádhŏsh,* because Archbishop Secker possessed one MS. in which this reading was found; and he translates the passage:

' Say ye not it is holy,
Of every thing of which this people shall say
it is holy.'

all *them to* whom this people shall say, A confederacy; neither *a* fear ye their fear, nor be afraid.

13 Sanctify the LORD of hosts himself; and *let* him *b be* your fear, and *let* him *be* your dread.

a 1 Pet.3.14,15.   *b* Lu.12.5.

That is, 'call not their idols holy; nor fear ye the object of their fear; that is, the gods of the idolaters.' But it is plain that this does not suit the connection of the passage, since the prophet is not reproving them for their idolatry, but is discoursing of the alliance between the kings of Syria and Samaria. Besides, the authority of *one* MS., without the concurrence of any ancient version, is not a sufficient authority for changing the Hebrew text. Most commentators have understood this word 'confederacy' as referring to the alliance between the kings of Syria and Samaria; as if the prophet had said, ' Do not join in the cry so common and almost universal in the nation, *There is a confederacy between those two kingdoms; there is an alliance formed which endangers our liberty*—a cry that produces alarm and trepidation in the nation.' Thus Rosenmüller and Gesenius explain it. Aben Ezra, and Kimchi, however, understand it of a *conspiracy*, which they suppose was formed in the kingdom of Ahaz, against him and the house of David; and that the prophet warns the people against joining in such a conspiracy. But of the existence of such a conspiracy there is no evidence. Had there *been* such a conspiracy, it is not probable that it would have been so well known as to make it a proper subject of public denunciation. Conspiracies are usually secret and concealed. I regard this, however, as a caution to the prophet not to join in the prevailing demand for an alliance with the king of Assyria. Ahaz trembled before the united armies of Syria and Samaria. He sought, therefore, foreign assistance—the assistance of the king of Assyria. It is probable that in this he was encouraged by the leaders of the people, and that this would be a popular measure with the mass of the nation. Yet it implied distrust of God (Note, ver. 6); and,

14 And he shall be for a *c* sanctuary; but for a stone of *d* stumbling, and for a rock of offence,*e* to both the houses of Israel; for a gin and for a snare to the inhabitants of Jerusalem.

c Eze.11.16.   *d* 1 Pet.2.8.   *e* Mat.13.57.

therefore, the prophet was directed not to unite with them in seeking this ' confederacy,' or alliance, but to oppose it. The word translated 'confederacy,' קֶשֶׁר, *qĕshĕr*, is derived from the verb קָשַׁר, *qâshăr, to bind, to fetter;* to enter into a conspiracy. It usually refers to a *conspiracy*, but it may mean a combination or alliance of any kind. Or, if it here means a *conspiracy*, a union between Ahaz and the Assyrians may be regarded as a species of *conspiracy*, as it was an unnatural alliance; a species of combination against the natural and proper government of Judah—the theocracy. ¶ *Neither fear ye their fear.* Do not partake of their alarm at the invasion of the land by the united armies of Syria and Samaria. Rather put confidence in God, and believe that he is able to save you; comp. 1 Pet. iii. 13–15.

13. *Sanctify, &c.* Regard JEHOVAH as holy; *i.e.*, worship and honour him with pious fear and reverence. Regard *him* as the source of safety, and the true defence. Ahaz and his people sought for aid from Assyria against the armies of Syria and Samaria. The direction here is rather to seek aid from God. ¶ Let *him* be *your fear.* Do not be alarmed at what man can do (ver. 12), but fear and honour God. Be afraid to provoke his wrath by looking to other sources of help when his aid only should be sought.

14. *And he shall be for a sanctuary.* The word translated *sanctuary* means, literally, *a holy place, a consecrated place*, and is usually applied to the tabernacle, or to the temple; Ex. xxv. 8; Lev. xii. 4; xxi. 12; Jer. li. 51. It also means *an asylum*, or *a refuge*, to which one might flee in case of danger, and be safe; see Ezek. xi. 16. Among all ancient nations, *temples* were regarded as safe places to which men might flee when pursued, and when in danger. It

15 And many among them shall stumble, and fall, and be broken, and be snared, and be taken.

16 Bind up the testimony, *a* seal the law among *b* my disciples.

a Rev.5.1,5.   b Prov.8.8,9.

was deemed sacrilege to tear a man away from a temple or an altar. That the temple was so regarded among the Jews is manifest; see 1 Kings i..50; ii. 28. In allusion to this, the prophet says, that JEHOVAH would be a sanctuary; that is, an asylum, or refuge, to whom they should flee in times of danger, and be safe; see Psal. xlvi. 1: ' God is our refuge and strength;' Prov. xviii. 10: 'The name of the LORD is a strong tower; the righteous runneth into it, and is safe.' It is also well known that temples and altars were regarded as *asyla* among the Greeks and Romans. The reference here is rather to *an altar*, as the asylum, than to a city or temple; as, in the other member of the sentence, the same object is said to be a stone of stumbling— a figure which would not be applicable to a temple or a city. ¶ *A stone of stumbling.* A stone against which one should impinge, or over which he should fall. The idea is, that none could run against a hard, rough, fixed stone, or rock, without injuring himself. So the Jews would oppose the counsels of God; instead of making him their refuge and strength, they would resist his claims and appeals, and the consequence would be their destruction. It is also to be remembered, that God is often represented in the Scriptures as a *rock*, a firm defence, or place of safety, to those who trust in him. But instead of their thus taking refuge in him, they would oppose themselves to this firm rock, and ruin themselves; see Deut. xxxii. 4, 15,18,30, 31, 37; Ps. xix. 14; xxviii. 1; xxxi. 2, 3; xli. 2; xlii. 9. Many of the ancient Jewish commentators applied this to the Messiah.—*Gesenius in loco.* It is also applied to Christ in the New Testament, 1 Pet. ii. 8. ¶ *A rock of offence.* A rock over which they should fall. The English word *offence*, had that meaning formerly, and retains it in our translation of the Bible. ¶ *To both the houses of Israel.* To the two kingdoms of Judah and Israel; that is, to the wicked portion of them, not to those who were truly pious. ¶ *For a*

gin. A *net*, or *snare*, to take birds. The idea is the same as in the former part of the verse. By rejecting the counsel of God; by despising his protection, and by resisting his laws, they would be unexpectedly involved in difficulties, as birds which are caught in a snare.

15. *And many among them.* Many by the invasion under the Assyrian. Many were taken captive; many killed, and many were carried to Babylon. The repetition here of so many expressions so nearly synonymous is emphatic, and shows that it would be certainly done.

16. *Bind up.* This expression is one that is applicable to a *volume,* or *roll* of writing. Thus far the prophet seems to have had the *roll* opened, which is mentioned in ver. 1. Now the prophecy is complete, and he directs to bind it up, or close it. Perhaps, also, it is implied that it would be useless any further to address a rebellious and headstrong people. He had delivered his message, but they disregarded it. ¶ *The testimony.* The message; especially that of which Uriah and Zechariah had been called *to bear witness,* ver. 2. Any message from God is, however, sometimes called a *testimony,* as being that to which a prophet bears witness; Ps. xix. 7; 2 Kings xi. 12; Deut. iv. 45; vi. 17, 20; 1 Kings ii. 3; Neh. ix. 34. ¶ *Seal.* Books were made in the form of rolls, and were often sealed when completed—as we seal a letter. The mode of sealing them was not by wax only, but by uniting them by any adhesive matter, as paste, or glue. Wax in warm climates would be generally rendered useless by the heat. The meaning here is, to secure, to close up—perhaps by passing a cord or string around the volume, and making it secure, denoting that it was finished; see Dan. viii. 26; xii. 4. ¶ *.The law.* The communication or command which he had delivered, and which, being given by inspiration, had now the force of a *law.* ¶ *Among my disciples.* Most of the Jewish commentators suppose that the volume, when

17 And *a* I will wait upon the
LORD, that hideth *b* his face from
the house of Jacob, and I will look
for him.

18 Behold,*c* I and the children

a ch.50.11; 45.8.　　*b* Hab.2.3.　　*c* Heb.2.13.

completed by a prophet, was given for
safe keeping to his disciples, or to some
employed to preserve it securely. The
word *disciples* means those who are
taught, and here means those who were
taught by the prophet; perhaps the
pious and holy part of the people who
would listen to his instructions. The
Chaldee translates this verse, 'O prophet, preserve the testimony, lest ye
testify to those who will not obey; seal
and hide the law, because they will not
learn it.'

17. *And I will wait upon the* LORD.
This is the commencement of a new
subject. The prophet had closed his
former message; but had seen that in
regard to the great mass of the nation,
his exhortation had been in vain. He
now says, that having delivered his message, he would patiently look to God
alone. His hope was in him, though the
nation looked elsewhere; and though
calamities were coming, yet he would
still trust in God only. ¶ *That hideth
his face.* This is a figurative expression,
denoting the withdrawing of his favour
and protection. He would leave them,
and give them to deserved punishment;
comp. Job xxiii. 9; xiii. 24; Ps. xliv.
24; x. 1; civ. 29. ¶ *And I will look
for him.* I will expect aid from him,
and will believe that his promises of
final protection will yet be fulfilled;
comp. Hab. ii. 3:

For the vision is yet for an appointed time,
But at the end it shall speak, and not lie:
Though it tarry, wait for it;
Because it will surely come, it will not tarry.

18. *Behold, I,* &c. By 'signs and
wonders,' here, it is meant that they,
by the names given them, were intended
to teach important lessons to the Jewish
people. Their names were significant,
and were designed to illustrate some important truth; and especially the prophet here intimates that they were to
inculcate the truth in regard to the presence and protection of God, to induce
the people to look to him. Thus the

whom the LORD hath given me, *are*
for signs and for wonders in Israel
from the LORD of hosts, which
dwelleth in mount Zion.

19 And when they shall say unto
you, Seek unto them that have

name *Immanuel*, 'God with us,' ch.
vii. 14; and *Shear-jashub*, 'the remnant shall return,' ch. vii. 3, were both
significant of the fact that none but God
could be the protector of the nation.
And in like manner, it is possible that
his own name, signifying the *salvation
of Jehovah*, had been given him with
such a reference. But at all events, it
was a name which would remind them
of the truth that he was *now* inculcating, that salvation was to be found in
JEHOVAH, and that they should look to
him. Names of children were often thus
emblematic (see Hos. i.); and the
prophets themselves were regarded as
signs of important events; Ezek. xxiv.
24; comp. Note, Isa. xx. 3. This passage is quoted with reference to the
Messiah in Heb. ii. 13. ¶ *Which
dwelleth in mount Zion.* Mount Zion
was the residence of the house of David,
or of the court, and it was often used to
signify Jerusalem itself. The sense here
is, that God was the protector of Jerusalem, or regarded that as his home; see
Note, ch. i. 8.

19. *And when they shall say.* When
the people, instead of putting confidence
in God, shall propose to apply to necromancers. In the time of Ahaz the people
were, as they were often, much inclined
to idolatry; 2 Kings xvi. 10. In their
troubles and embarrassments, instead
of looking to JEHOVAH, they imitated
the example of surrounding nations, and
applied for relief to those who professed
to be able to hold converse with spirits.
That it was common for idolatrous people
to seek direction from those who professed that they had the power of divin-
ing, is well known; see Isa. xix. 3;
xxix. 4. It was expressly forbidden to
the Jews to have recourse to those who
made such professions; Lev. xx. 6; Deut.
xviii. 10, 11. Yet, notwithstanding this
express command, it is evident that it
was no uncommon thing for the Jews
to make application for such instructions; see the case of Saul, who made

familiar spirits, and unto wizards that peep and that mutter; should

application to the woman of Endor, who professed to have a familiar spirit, in 1 Sam. xxviii. 7-25. Among heathen nations, nothing was more common than for persons to profess to have intercourse with spirits, and to be under the influence of their inspiration. The oracle at Delphi, of this nature, was celebrated throughout Greece, and throughout the world. Kings and princes, warriors and nations, sought of the priestess who presided there, responses in undertaking any important enterprise, and were guided by her instructions; *see* the *Travels of Anacharsis*, vol. ii. 376, *sq.* ¶ *Seek unto.* Apply to for direction. ¶ *That hath familiar spirits.* Heb. אֹבוֹת *ôbhôth*. The word 'familiar,' applied to spirit, is supposed to have been used by our translators to imply that they were attended by an invisible spirit that was subject to their call, or that would inspire them when they sought his direction. The Hebrew word is used to denote a necromancer, a conjuror; particularly one who was supposed to have power to call up the dead, to learn of them respecting future events; see 1 Sam. xxviii. 7-19; Deut. xviii. 11. The word is most commonly applied to *women;* as it was almost entirely confined to women to profess this power; Lev. xix. 31; xx. 6; 1 Sam. xxviii. The idea was, that they could call up the spirits of the dead who were supposed to have seen objects invisible to the living, and who could, therefore, inform them in regard to things which mortals on earth could not see. The Vulgate renders this by ' Pythons and diviners.' A *Python*, among the Greeks and Romans, denoted one that had the spirit of prophesying, and was particularly applied to the priestess of Apollo at Delphi. The LXX. render the place thus: ' And if they say to you, Seek the *ventriloquists*, ἐγγαστριμύθους, and those speaking from the earth, and speaking vain things, who speak from the belly,' οἳ ἐκ τῆς κοιλίας φωνοῦσιν. From this it is evident, that the art of the *ventriloquist*, so well known now, was known then; and it is highly probable that the secret of the art of soothsayers consisted

not a people seek unto their God? for the living to the dead?

very much in being able to throw the voice, with various modifications, into different places, so that it would seem to come from a grave, or from an image of a dead person, that was made to appear at the proper time. ¶ *And unto wizards.* The word used here—יִדְּעֹנִים —is derived from the verb יָדַע *to know;* and means *a wise man, a soothsayer, a magician*, or one possessed with a spirit of divination. The arts of the magician, or soothsayer, were often the arts of one skilled in natural magic; acquainted somewhat with the laws of chemistry; and able, therefore, to produce appearances among an ignorant people that would surprise them; *see* Brewster's *Natural Magic*, where this art is fully explained. ¶ *That peep.* This word is properly used of young birds, and means *to chirp, to pip;* and also to make a small noise by the gentle opening of the mouth. It is then applied to the *gentle whispering* which the ancients ascribed to departed spirits; the small, low, shrill voice which they were supposed to use, and which, probably, those attempted to imitate who claimed the power of raising them to the earth. It was believed among all the ancient nations, that departed spirits did not speak out openly and clearly, but with an indistinct, low, gentle, suppressed voice. Thus, in Virgil :—

　　　　—— pars tollere vocem
Exiguam.　　　　*Æneid*, vi. 492.

　　　　—— gemitus lachrymabilis imo
Auditur tumulo, et vox reddita fertur ad aures.
　　　　　　　　Æneid, iii. 39.

Thus Horace :—

Umbræ cum Sagana resonarint triste et acutum.
　　　　　　　　Sat. lib i. 8, 40.

Thus Homer, speaking of the shade or spirit of Patroclus, says that it went with a whizzing sound: Ὤχετο τετριγυῖα. —*Iliad*, Ψ-101.

He said, and with his longing arms essay'd
In vain to grasp the visionary shade;
Like a thin smoke he sees the spirit fly,
And hears a feeble, lamentable cry.

This might my friend, so late in battle lost,
Stood at my side a pensive, plaintive ghost.
　　　　　　　　Pope.

So, also, Lucian says of the infernal

20 To _a_ the law and to the testimony: if they speak not according

_a_ Lu.16.29; Jn.5.39.

to this word, _it is_ because _there is_
no ¹ light in them.

1 _morning._

regions, ' The whizzing shades of the
dead fly around us ;' see _Gesenius in
loc._ and _Rosenmüller ;_ also Bochart's
Hieroz., Part i. B. iii. ch. ii. p. 731.
¶ _And that mutter._ The word used
here—הָגָה _hâghâ_—usually means _to meditate, to consider;_ and then _to speak,
to utter._ It also means _to sigh, to
mourn,_ Jer. xlviii. 31; Isa. xvi. 7 ; _to
coo,_ as a dove, Isa. xxxvii. 14 ; lix. 11;
and then _to roar_ like a lion ; not the
loud roar, but the _grumbling,_ the _sup-
pressed_ roar _(Bochart);_ Isa. xxxi. 4.
The idea here is, probably, that of _gently
sighing,_ or _mourning_—uttering feeble,
plaintive lamentations or sighs, as departed shades were supposed to do ; and
this was, probably, imitated by necromancers. By thus feigning that they
conversed with the dead, they imposed
on the ignorant populace, and led them
to suppose that they had supernatural
powers. ¶ _Should not a people seek,_
&c. Is it not proper that a people
should inquire of the God that is worshipped, in order to be directed in per-
plexing and embarrassing events ? Some
have understood this to be a question of
the _idolaters,_ asking whether it was not
right and proper for a people to seek
counsel of those whom they worshipped
as God. I understand it, however, as
a question asked by the prophet, and as
the language of strong and severe rebuke. ' You are seeking to idols, to the
necromancers, and to the dead. But
JEHOVAH is your God. And should not
a people so signally favoured, a people
under his peculiar care, apply to him,
and seek his direction ?' ¶ _For the liv-
ing._ On account of the affairs of the
living. To ascertain what will be their
lot, what is their duty, or what will occur
to them. ¶ _To the dead._ The necromancers pretended to have intercourse
with the spirits of the dead. The prophet strongly exposes the absurdity of
this. What could the _dead_ know of
this ? How could they declare the
future events respecting the living ?
Where was this authorized? Men should
seek God—the living God—and not

pretend to hold consultation with the
dead.
　20. _To the law,_ &c. To the revelation which God has given. This is a
solemn call of the prophet to try everything by the revealed will of God ; see
ver. 16. ¶ _If they speak not._ If the
necromancers—those that pretended to
have intercourse with the dead. ¶ _Ac-
cording to this word._ According to
what God has revealed. By this standard all their pretended revelations were
to be tried. By this standard all doctrines are still to be tried. ¶ _It is be-
cause._ There has been a great variety
of criticism upon this verse, but our
translation expresses, probably, the true
idea. The word rendered here ' _be-
cause,_' אֲשֶׁר _ãshẽr,_ commonly denotes
' which;' but it seems here to be used in
the sense of the Syriac ? _Dolath,_ or the
Greek ὅτι. ¶ _No light._ Marg. ' Morning.' Heb. שָׁחַר _shâhhăr._ The word
usually means the morning light ; the
mingled light and darkness of the
aurora; daybreak. It is an emblem of
advancing knowledge, and perhaps, also,
of prosperity or happiness after calamity, as the break of day succeeds the
dark night. The meaning here may
be, ' If their teachings do not accord
with the law and the testimony, it is
proof that they are _totally_ ignorant,
without even the _twilight_ of true knowledge ; that it is _total darkness_ with
them.' Or it may mean, ' If they do
not speak according to this word, _then
no dawn will arise, i.e.,_ no prosperity
will smile upon _this people.'—Gesenius._
Lowth understands it of _obscurity, darkness :—_
　' If they speak not according to this word,
　　In which there is no obscurity.'
But there is no evidence that the word
is ever used in this sense. Others
suppose that the Arabic sense of the
word is to be retained here, _deception,_
or _magic._ ' If they speak not according to this oracle, in which there is no
deception.' But the word is not used
in this sense in the Hebrew. The
meaning is, probably, this : ' The law

21 And they shall pass through it hardly bestead and hungry; and it shall come to pass, that, when they shall be hungry, they shall fret *a* themselves, and curse *b* their

a Prov.19.3.   b Rev.16.11.

king and their God, and look upward.

22 And they shall look unto the earth; and behold trouble and darkness, dimness of anguish; and *they shall be* driven to darkness.

---

of God is the standard by which all professed communications from the invisible world are to be tested. If the necromancers deliver a doctrine which is not sustained by that, and not in accordance with the prophetic communications, it shows that they are in *utter* ignorance. There is not even the *glimmering* of the morning twilight; all is total night, and error, and obscurity with them, and they are not to be followed.'

21. *And they shall pass.* The people who have been consulting necromancers. This represents the condition of those who have sought for counsel and direction, and who have not found it. They shall be conscious of disappointment, and shall wander perplexed and alarmed through the land. ¶ *Through it.* Through the land. They shall wander in it from one place to another, seeking direction and relief. ¶ *Hardly bestead.* Oppressed, borne down, agitated. The meaning is, that the people would wander about, oppressed by the calamities that were coming upon the nation, and unalleviated by all that soothsayers and necromancers could do. ¶ *And hungry.* Famished; as one effect of the great calamities that would afflict the nation. ¶ *They shall fret themselves.* They shall be irritated at their own folly and weakness, and shall aggravate their sufferings by self-reproaches for having trusted to false gods. ¶ *Their king and their God.* The Hebrew interpreters understand this of the *false gods* which they had consulted, and in which they had trusted. But their *looking upward*, and the connection, seem to imply that they would rather curse the *true* God—the 'king and the God' of the Jewish people. They would be subjected to the proofs of his displeasure, and would vent their malice by reproaches and curses. ¶ *And look upward.* For relief. This denotes the condition of those in deep distress,

instinctively casting their eyes to heaven for aid. Yet it is implied that they would do it with no right feeling, and that they would see there only the tokens of their Creator's displeasure.

22. *And they shall look unto the earth.* They would look upward and find no relief, and then in despair cast their eyes to the earth to obtain help there. Yet equally in vain. The whole image is one of intense anguish brought on the nation for leaving the counsel of the true God. ¶ *And behold*, &c.; see Note, ch. v. 30. ¶ *Trouble.* Anguish, oppression, צָרָה *tzârâ*, from צוּר *tzŭr*, to oppress, to straiten, to afflict. This is a remarkable instance of the prophet Isaiah's manner—of a rapid, impetuous, and bold style of utterance. He accumulates images; piles words on each other; and deepens the anxiety by each additional word, until we almost feel that we are enveloped by the gloom, and see objects of terror and alarm on every side. ¶ *Dimness of anguish.* These words should be kept separate in the translation—מְעוּף צוּקָה *mĕŭph tzŭkâ, darkness, oppression*—accumulated epithets to heighten the gloom and terror of the scene. ¶ *And they shall be driven to darkness.* Heb. וַאֲפֵלָה מְנֻדָּה a darkness that is *driven*, or that is urged upon itself; that becomes condensed, accumulated, until it becomes terrible and frightful. The idea is that of a driving tempest, or an involving obscurity (מְנֻדָּה *menŭddâ* from נָדָה *nâdhâ*, to push, thrust, impel, urge on, as a driving storm). The prophet has thus accumulated every possible idea of gloom and obscurity, and probably there is not anywhere a more graphic description of gathering darkness and trouble, and of the consternation of those involved in it, than this. So fearful and terrific are the judgments of God when he comes forth to punish men !

CHAPTER IX.

THIS chapter is a continuation of the prophecy begun in ch. vii., and continued in ch. viii.
It is composed of mingled threats and promises.
Its characteristic may be said to be *rays of light
thrown into the midst of shades.* It promises
comfort and deliverance, while at the same time
it denounces the sins of the nation, and assures
the nation that the anger of the Lord is not
turned away. The previous chapter had closed
by describing a time of general calamity and
darkness. This begins (ver. 1–4) by showing
that the calamity would not be so great as in
former times. It would be mitigated. There
would be light—particularly in the dark regions
of Zebulun and Naphtali—the provinces lying
most exposed to the Syrian invasion. This light
or deliverance was connected with the birth of
the promised child (ver. 6, 7); and the mention

of this leads the prophet into a magnificent description of his names, character, and reign.
The prophet then returns to the threatened
destruction of Israel, and denounces the Divine
judgment against it. By the Syrians and the
Philistines it would be invaded and destroyed,
ver. 8–12. The *effects* of this, in cutting off their
sources of strength, and producing general dismay and ruin, are described in the remainder of
the chapter, ver. 13–21. The chapter, therefore, would impart consolation to the inhabitants
of Judah, and is designed to confirm the promise
that it should be safe from the threatened invasion; comp. ch. viii. 1–4.

NEVERTHELESS, the dimness
shall not *be* such as *was* in her
vexation, when at the first he lightly
afflicted the land of Zebulun and the
land of Naphtali, and afterward did

CHAPTER IX.

1. *Nevertheless.* Notwithstanding
what is said in the previous chapter of
the calamities that are coming upon
Israel. Hengstenberg renders this whole
verse : ' For darkness shall not be upon
the land upon which there is distress ;
as the former time has dishonoured the
land of Zebulun and the land of Naphtali ; so shall the time come to honour
it, the region on the border of the sea,
by the side of the Jordan, Galilee of
the Gentiles.' ¶ *The dimness.* The
Hebrew word here denotes obscurity, or
darkness ; and is here used, as the word
darkness often is in the Scriptures, to
denote calamity or affliction. The dimness, or calamity, here referred to, is that
which is threatened, ch. viii. 21, 22.
¶ Shall *not* be *such.* It shall not be
unbroken darkness, and unalleviated
calamity ; but it shall be interrupted by
the rising of the great light that shall
shine on the dark land of Zebulun and
Naphtali. ¶ *In her vexation.* The
word ' *her* ' refers to the whole land of
Palestine, to the afflictions that came
upon the whole region. The word
vexation, מוּצָק, means oppression, calamity, or being *straitened,* or *pressed.*
¶ *When at the first.* In the former
time ; on a former occasion. ¶ *He
lightly afflicted.* The word here used,
קָלַל, means properly, to be, or make
light, or small ; and in Hiphil, the form

which occurs here, it often means *to
esteem lightly, to despise, to hold in
contempt;* 2 Sam. xix. 44; Ezek. xxii.
7. It probably has that sense here, as
the design of the prophet is evidently
to speak, not of a *light* affliction in the
former time, but of a grievous, heavy
calamity—a calamity which would be
well denoted by the expression, ' he
made them vile ; he exposed them to
contempt and derision.' The time to
which reference is made here, was probably the invasion of the land by Tiglath-pileser ; 2 Kings xv. 29; 1 Chron.
v. 26. In that invasion, the parts of
Zebulun and Naphtali were particularly
afflicted. ' Tiglath-pileser took Ijon,
and Gilead, and Galilee, and all the
land of Naphtali, and carried them captive to Assyria ;' 2 Kings xv. 29. This
region had also been invaded by Ben-
hadad two hundred years before the
time of Isaiah ; 1 Kings xv. 20, and
there might have been a reference to
these various invasions to which this
northern part of the land of Palestine
had been subjected. ¶ *The land of
Zebulun.* The region occupied by the
tribe of Zebulun. This tribe was located
between the sea of Tiberias, or the lake
Gennesareth, and the Mediterranean. It
extended entirely across from the one
to the other, and as it was thus favoured
with a somewhat extended sea-coast, the
people were more given to commerce
than the other tribes, and hence mingled

more grievously afflict *her* by the
way of the sea, beyond Jordan, in Galilee [1] of the nations.

---

more with surrounding nations. ¶ *And the land of Naphtali.* The region which was occupied by this tribe was directly north of Zebulun, and of the sea of Galilee, having that sea and the tribe of Zebulun on the south and south-east, Asher on the west, and a part of the tribe of Manasseh, on the east. ¶ *And afterward.* That is, in subsequent times ; meaning times that were to come *after* the prophecy here delivered. The previous part of the verse refers to the calamities that had come upon that region in former times. The expression here refers to what was seen by the prophet as *yet* to occur. ¶ *Did more grievously afflict.* הִכְבִּיד. This verb has very various significations. It properly means *to be heavy, to be grievous, to lie* or *fall heavy on any one, to be dull, obstinate;* also, *to be honoured, respected; i.e.,* of *weight,* or influence in society. It means, in Hiphil, the form which is used here, *to make heavy,* or *grievous;* 1 Kings xii. 10; Isa. xlvii. 6; *to oppress,* Neh. v. 15; and it *also* means *to cause to be honoured,* or *distinguished, to favour.* — *Gesenius.* The connection requires that it should have this sense here, and the passage means, that the land which he had *made vile* in former times, or had suffered to be despised, he had purposed to *honour,* or to render illustrious by the great light that should rise on it. So Lowth, Rosenmüller, and Gesenius, translate it ; see a similar use of the word in Jer. xxx. 19; 2 Chron. xxv. 19; 1 Sam. ii. 30. ¶ *By the way of the sea.* The sea of Galilee, or Gennesareth. All this region was in the vicinity of that sea. The word *way* here, דֶּרֶךְ *dĕrĕkh,* means *towards,* or *in the vicinity of.* The extensive dark region lying in the vicinity of that sea. Both those tribes bordered on the sea of Tiberias, or had that as a part of their boundary. ¶ *Beyond Jordan.* This expression— עֵבֶר הַיַּרְדֵּן —means in the vicinity of Jordan ; the land by the side of the Jordan, or perhaps that large region through which the upper part of the Jordan passed. It does not

mean strictly on the *east* of Jordan, but rather the northern portion of the land. It is such language as a man would use who was describing the upper and imperfectly known regions of the country—the dark, uncivilized region through which the upper part of the Jordan flowed, and the word עֵבֶר, here rendered *beyond,* means *side*—by the side of the Jordan. ¶ *Galilee of the nations.* This was sometimes called *upper Galilee.* It was called ' Galilee of the nations,' or of the *Gentiles,* because it was surrounded by them, and because the heathen were extensively intermingled with the Jews. In this region, Solomon had given to Hiram, king of Tyre, twenty cities; 1 Kings ix. 2. Adjacent to this region were the countries of Phenicia, Tyre, and Sidon ; and the people would naturally mingle much with them in commerce. The country abounded with hills and caverns, and, consequently, it was never possible completely to dislodge from the fastnesses the former inhabitants of the land. Strabo enumerates among the inhabitants of Galilee, Arabians and Phenicians. The inhabitants of this country are represented as having been bold and courageous, but as seditious, and prone to insolence and rebellion. If it be asked here, in what way this land had been made contemptible, or why it was regarded as an object of contempt ? we may reply, (1.) The district in which these two tribes dwelt constituted the border-land towards the heathen nations. (2.) The Galileans not only dwelt in the vicinity of the heathen, but a large number of them had actually remained in the country, and it had been found impossible to expel them from it ; Judg. i. 30–35. (3.) The Phenicians, with whom they held commercial intercourse, and with whom they dwelt intermingled, were among the most corrupt of the heathen nations. To this may be added, (4.) They were far from Jerusalem, and, consequently, the influence of religion may be supposed to have been less felt among them than among the other Jews. The true

2 The ^apeople that walked in darkness have seen a great light: they that dwell in the land of the

a Mat. 4.15,16.   1 or, *to him.*

shadow of death, upon them hath the light shined.

3 Thou hast multiplied the nation, *and* not ¹ increased the joy: they

---

religion was, in a great measure, lost upon them, and ignorance and superstition took its place. Hence, in the New Testament, they are spoken of as almost proverbially rude and ignorant.

2. *The people that walked in darkness.* The inhabitants of the region of Galilee. They were represented as walking in darkness, because they were far from the capital, and from the temple; they had few religious privileges; they were intermingled with the heathen, and were comparatively rude and uncultivated in their manners and in their language. Allusion to this is several times made in the New Testament; John i. 46: ' Can any good thing come out of Nazareth ?' vii. 52: 'Search and look, for out of Galilee ariseth no prophet;' Matt. xxvi. 69; Mark xiv. 70. The word *walked* here is synonymous with *lived*, and denotes that thick darkness brooded over the country, so that they *lived*, or walked amidst it. ¶ *Have seen a great light. Light* is not only an emblem of knowledge in the Scriptures, but of joy, rejoicing, and deliverance. It stands opposed to moral darkness, and to times of judgment and calamity. What is the particular reference here, is not agreed by expositors. The immediate connection seems to require us to understand it of deliverance from the calamities that were impending over the nation then. They would be afflicted, but they would be delivered. The tribes of Israel would be carried captive away; and Judah would also be removed. This calamity would particularly affect the ten tribes of Israel—the northern part of the land, the regions of Galilee—*for those tribes would be carried away not to return.* Yet this region also would be favoured with a peculiarly striking manifestation of light. I see no reason to doubt that the language of the prophet here is adapted to extend into that future period when the Messiah should come to that dark region, and become both its light and its deliverer. Isaiah *may* have referred to the immediate deliverance of the nation from impend-

ing calamities, but there is a fulness and richness of the language that seems to be applicable only to the Messiah. So it is evidently understood in Matt. iv. 13–16. ¶ *They that dwell.* The same people are referred to here as in the former member of the verse. ¶ *In the land of the shadow of death.* This is a most beautiful expression, and is peculiar to the Hebrew poets. The word צַלְמָוֶת *tzălmăvĕth,* is exceedingly poetical. The *idea* is that of *death,* as a dark substance or being, casting a long and chilly *shade* over the land—standing between the land and the light—and thus becoming the image of ignorance, misery, and calamity. It is often used, in the Scriptures, to describe those regions that were lying as it were in the *penumbra* of this gloomy object, and exposed to all the chills and sorrows of this melancholy darkness. Death, by the Hebrews, was especially represented as extending his long and baleful shadow over the regions of departed spirits; Job xxxviii. 17:

Have the gates of death been opened to thee?
Hast thou seen the gates of the shadow of death?

Job x. 21:

Before I go—I shall not return—
To the land of darkness
And of the shadow of death.

It is thus an image of chills, and gloom, and night—of anything that resembles the still and mournful regions of the dead. The Chaldee renders these two verses thus : ' In a former time Zebulun and Naphtali emigrated ; and those who remained after them a strong king shall carry into captivity, because they did not remember the power which was shown in the Red Sea, and the miracles which were done in Jordan, and the wars of the people of the cities. The people of the house of Israel who walked in Egypt as in the midst of shades, came out that they might see a great light.'

3. *Thou hast multiplied the nation.* Thou hast rendered the nation strong, powerful, mighty. Several interpreters, as Calvin, Vitringa, and Le Clerc, sup-

jcy before thee according to the joy in harvest, *and* as *men* rejoice when they divide the spoil.

4 For [1] thou hast broken the yoke of his burden, and the staff of his shoulder, the rod of his oppressor, as in the day *a* of Midian.

---

1 or, *when thou breakest.*   *a* Judg.7.21, &c.

---

pose that the prophet here, and in the two following verses, speaks in the first instance of the prosperity near at hand, and of the rapid increase of the Israelites after the return from the Babylonish exile, in which the inhabitants of Galilee must have participated, as may be inferred from the accounts of Josephus respecting the great population of that province in his time ; see *Jewish Wars,* i. 20, 3. Vitringa also directs our attention to the fact, that the Jewish people, after the exile, not only filled Judea, but spread themselves into Egypt, Syria, Mesopotamia, Asia Minor, Greece, and Italy. But there seems to be no necessity for referring it to such an increase of the inhabitants. It may refer to the great increase of the Messiah's kingdom, or of the kingdom which he would set up, and whose commencement would be in Galilee ; *see* Hengstenberg, *Christol.,* vol. i. p. 354. ¶ And *not increased the joy.* The Masorites here read in the margin לֹו *to it,* instead of לֹא *not.* Eleven MSS., two of them ancient, have this reading. This reading is followed by the Chaldee Paraphrase, the Syriac, and the Arabic. The LXX. seem also to have so understood it. So also it is in the margin, and so the connection demands ; and it is unquestionably the correct reading. It would then read, 'thou hast increased for it [the nation] the joy.' Hengstenberg, however, suggests that the phrase may mean, 'whose joy thou didst not before enlarge,' that is, upon whom thou hast before inflicted heavy sufferings. But this is harsh, and I see no reason to doubt that an error may have crept into the text. ¶ *They joy before thee according to the joy of harvest.* This is a beautiful figure ; and is found frequently in ancient writings. The harvest was a time of exultation and joy, and was commonly gathered amid songs and rejoicings, and concluded with a festival. The phrase ' before thee' refers to the fact that the first-fruits of the harvest among the Hebrews were presented with thanksgiving before God

in the temple ; Deut. xii. 7 ; xiv. 22–26. ¶ And *as* men *rejoice,* &c. This is also an expression of great joy and rejoicing. Such an occasion, at the close of a battle, when great spoil or plunder had been taken, would be one of great rejoicing ; see Judg. v. 30 ; 1 Sam. xxx. 16 ; 2 Chron. xx. 25–28.

4. *For thou hast broken.* This verse, and the following, show the way in which the occasion of the joy had been furnished. The expression ' thou *hast* ' does not necessarily refer to *the past,* but is a form of expression derived from the nature of the prophetic visions, where that is described as *past* which is seen to pass before the eyes of the prophet ; see Introduction, § 7. ¶ *The yoke.* This word is often used to denote *oppression,* or *tyranny;* Lev. xxvi. 13 ; Deut. xxviii. 48—where oppression is described as 'an iron yoke;' comp. 1 Kings xii. 4; Isa. xlvii. 6; lviii. 6. ¶ *The staff of his shoulder.* The word rendered *staff* here may mean a bough, a branch, a staff, stick, or rod. Gesenius supposes that the expression here means the rod by which punishment is inflicted, and that the phrase ' rod of, or for the shoulder,' denotes oppression and servitude. Rosenmüller thinks, that it refers rather to the custom among the ancients of placing a piece of wood, not unlike a yoke, on the necks and shoulders of slaves, as a mark of servitude. Hengstenberg understands it, ' the staff which strikes the neck or back.' ¶ *The rod of his oppressor.* This, doubtless, refers to the chastisement which was inflicted on those in bondage, and is a phrase denoting oppression and servitude. The word ' his ' here refers to *Israel.* ¶ *As in the day of Midian.* This refers to the deliverance that was accomplished under Gideon against the Midianites ; see Judg. vii.; viii. That deliverance was a remarkable interposition of God. It was accomplished not by human strength ; but was a signal manifestation of the power of God in delivering the nation from the long oppression of the Midianites. So the prophet says here,

5 For [1] every battle of the warrior *is* with confused noise, and garments

1 or, *when the whole.*

rolled in blood; [2] but *this* shall be with burning *and* [3] fuel of fire.

2 or, *and it was.*   3 *meat.*

that the deliverance will be as signal a proof of the presence and power of God as is was in that day. Herder (*Heb. Poetry*, vol. ii. p. 296) says, ' At that period, in the north part of the country, a great deliverance was wrought. Then, in the obscure forests of Naphtali and Zebulun, the light of freedom went forth over all the land. So now, also, in this northern press of nations, in the way along the sea of Galilee, where now the hostile Syrians are exercising their oppressions, the light of freedom is going forth, and there shall be joy and jubilee, like that of the song of Deborah.'

5. *For every battle of the warrior.* The expression used here has caused great difficulty, from the fact that it occurs nowhere else in the Scriptures. The word סְאוֹן *seon*, rendered here *battle*, is supposed to mean rather *greaves*, or the armour of the warrior which covered the feet and the legs. It would be literally translated, ' Every greave of those armed with greaves.'—*Gesenius.* The Chaldee renders it, ' For every gift of theirs is for evil.' The Syriac, ' For every tumult [of battle] is heard with terror.' Hengstenberg renders it, ' For all war-shoes put on at the noise of battle, all garments dipped in blood, shall be burnt, shall be the food of fire.' The idea, according to him, is, that the great future redemption will be like the deliverance under Gideon ; ' because, far from being accomplished by force of arms, with it all contention and war shall cease.' Gesenius regards the figurative expression as a general designation of that peace which shall never end. All the armour used in war shall then be burnt, as being of no further use. ¶ *Is with confused noise.* The word used here—רַעַשׁ *ra'ash*—denotes, properly, a shaking, as of a spear ; a concussion, tumult, noise, as of a battle. Here it is supposed to refer to the noise which the armour of the soldiers made —particularly to the noise made by the *greaves*, or war-shoes, worn on the feet and legs. Those greaves were fitted up, it is said, by numerous large iron hooks, or clasps, and were fastened sometimes

with large nails ; comp. Josephus, *Jewish Wars*, B. vi. ch. i. § 8. ¶ *And garments.* This word here refers, doubtless, to the soldier's cloak or blanket. ¶ *Rolled in blood.* This is a description of the usual effect of war. The image of war is that of a clangour made by the armour of soldiers, and by garments that have been dipped in human blood. It is a most revolting but just image. ¶ *But this shall be.* In regard to this threatened invasion and danger, this shall be the result. The meaning is this. The prophet sees the image of war and of threatened invasion. He hears the clangour of their greaves—the sound of their march ; and he sees the usual emblem of battle — bloody garments. But he says here, that this invasion shall not be successful. There was no occasion of alarm. The very armour of the warrior should be burned up. The enemy should be defeated— and their greaves, and their bloody garments, should be consumed. ¶ *With burning.* For burning ; that is, it shall be consumed. ¶ And *fuel of fire.* Heb. ' Food of fire.' This is a strong, emphatic expression—' it shall be to be burned— the food of fire.' It denotes the certainty that they would be vanquished ; that the invading foe would not be successful ; and that his very armoury and garments would be stripped off and burned. To understand this, it is necessary to remark, that in ancient times it was customary to strip the dead which were slain in a vanquished army, and to collect their armour, their chariots, &c., and consume them. The more valued spoils of battle were reserved as the prey of the victors, or to be suspended in temples consecrated to the gods ; see Ps. xlvi. 9, 10 :

He maketh wars to cease unto the end of the earth;
He breaketh the bow;
And cutteth the spear in sunder;
He burneth the chariot in the fire.

Ezekiel has carried out this description more at length :

And the inhabitants of the cities of Israel shall go forth,
And shall set on fire and burn the weapons,

6 For unto us a child is born, unto *a* us a son is given, and the

a Lu.2.11.

government *b* shall be upon his shoulder; and his name shall be

b Mat.28.18.

Both the shields and the bucklers,
The bows and the arrows,
And the clubs and the lances.

Ezek. xxxix. 9.

Zechariah has a similar figure, as descriptive of the time of the Messiah:

Rejoice greatly, O daughter of Zion;
Shout, O daughter of Jerusalem;
Behold, thy king cometh unto thee.

. . . .

And I will cut off the chariot from Ephraim,
And the horse from Jerusalem,
And the battle bow shall be cut off, &c.

Zech. ix. 9, 10.

This custom prevailed among several nations. Thus Virgil:

— scutorumque incendi victor acervos.

Æneid, viii. 562.

There can be no doubt, I think, that the prophet here has his eye on the victories of the Messiah, and that he means to say, that in those victories all armour would be for fuel of fire; that is, that they would be achieved without hostile arms. Applied to the Messiah, it means either that his victories would be complete, or that *in* his victories all necessity of such armour would cease. According to this, the passage teaches that peace should be introduced by him without a conflict, and thus harmonizes with the numerous parallel passages in which peace is represented as a characteristic mark of the times of the Messiah, when contention, war, and destruction shall cease; see ch. xi. 6, 7.

6. *For.* This is given as a *reason* of the victories that were predicted in the previous verses. That it has reference to the Messiah has been almost universally conceded; and indeed it does not seem possible to doubt it. The eye of the prophet seems to have been fixed on this great and glorious event—as attracting all his attention. The scenes of coming times, like a *panorama*, or *picture*, passed before him. Most of the picture seems to have been that of battles, conflicts, sieges, dimness, and thick darkness. But in one portion of the passing scene there was light. It was the light that he saw rising in the distant and darkened Galilee. He saw the joy of the people; the armour of

war laid aside; the image of peace succeeding; the light expanding and becoming more intense as the darkness retired, until he saw in this region the Prince of Peace—the Sun of Righteousness itself. The eye of the prophet gazed intently on that scene, and was fixed on that portion of the picture: he sees the Messiah in his office, and describes him as already come, and as born unto the nation. ¶ *Unto us.* For our benefit. The prophet saw in vision the darkness and gloom of the nation, and saw also the son that would be born to remove that darkness, and to enlighten the world. ¶ *A child* (יֶלֶד). This word usually denotes a lad, a boy, a youth. It is commonly applied to one in early life; but no particular stress is to be laid on the word. The vision of the prophet is, that the long-expected Messiah is born, and is seen growing up amidst the surrounding darkness of the north of Palestine, ver. 1. ¶ *Is born.* Not that he was born when the prophet spake. But in prophetic vision, as the events of the future passed before his mind, he saw that promised son, and the eye was fixed intently on him; see the Introduction, § 7, and Note, ch. i. 1. ¶ *A son.* בֵּן *bēn.* This word does not differ materially from the word translated *child.* In the future scenes, as they passed before the mind of the prophet, he saw the child, the son that was to be born, and described him as he appeared to his view —as a child. Fixing the eye on him, he proceeds at once to designate his character by stating the appropriate names which he would bear. ¶ *Is given.* The Messiah is often represented as having been *given*, or *sent;* or as the rich gift of God; Note, Acts iv. 12; John iii. 16; Eph. i. 22; John xvii. 4. The Messiah was pre-eminently the *gift* of the God of love. Man had no claim on him, and God voluntarily gave his Son to be a sacrifice for the sins of the world. ¶ *And the government shall be upon his shoulder.* The sense of this passage is, that he shall *rule*, or that the government shall be vested in him. Various

called Wonderful, Counsellor, The

a Heb.1.8.   b Eph.2.14.

interpretations have, however, been given of the phrase 'upon his shoulder.' Some have supposed, that it means simply he shall sustain the government, as the shoulder is that by which we uphold any thing. Pliny and Cicero thus use the phrase ; see Rosenmüller. Others, that it means that he should wear the royal purple from a child.—*Grotius.* Lowth supposes that it refers to the ensign of government—the sceptre, the sword, the keys, or the like, that were borne upon the shoulder, or suspended from it ; see Note on ch. xxii. 22. It is evident, from this latter place, that some ensign of office was usually borne upon the shoulder. The sense is, that he should be a king, and under this character the Messiah is often predicted. ¶ *And his name shall be called.* That is, his attributes shall be such as to make all these applications appropriate descriptions of his power and work. *To be called,* and *to be,* in the Hebrew, often mean the same thing. The word וַיִּקְרָא *may* possibly mean, Jehovah shall call him ; or it may be regarded as taken impersonally. Such a use of a verb is not uncommon in Isaiah. ' *One calls him,*' is, according to the usage in Isaiah, as much as to say, he will justly bear this name ; or simply, he will be. ¶ *Wonderful.* פֶּלֶא. This word is derived from the verb פָּלָא *pâlâ,* to separate, to distinguish, or to make great. It is applied usually to anything that is great or wonderful, as a miracle ; Ex. xv. 2; Lam. i. 9; Dan. xii. 6. It is applied here to denote the unusual and remarkable assemblage of qualities that distinguished the Messiah. Those are specified more particularly in the other part of the verse ; such an assemblage of qualities as to make proper the names Mighty God, &c. ' The proper idea of the word,' says Hengstenberg, ' is *miraculous.* It imports that the personage here referred to, in his being and in his works, will be exalted above the ordinary course of nature, and that his whole manifestation will be a miracle.' Yet it seems to me, that the proper idea of the word is not that of *miraculous.* It

mighty God, *a* The everlasting Father, the Prince of Peace.*b*

is rather that which is *separated* from the ordinary course of events, and which is fitted to excite amazement, wonder, and admiration, whether it be miraculous or not. This will be apparent if the following places are examined, where the word occurs in various forms. It is rendered *marvellous,* Ps. cxviii. 23; cxxxix. 14; xcviii. 1; Job v. 9; *wonderful,* 2 Sam. i. 26; Ps. cxxxix. 14; Prov. xxx. 18; Job xlii. 3; Ps. lxxii. 18; lxxxvi. 10; *hidden,* Deut. xxx. 2; *things too high,* Ps. cxxxi. 1; *miracles,* Judg. vi. 13; Ex. xv. 2; Ps. lxxvii. 14; lxxxviii. 10; lxxxix. 5; the word is translated *wonders,* in the sense of *miracles,* in several places ; and *hard,* Deut. xvii. 8; Jer. xxxii. 17. From these passages, it is clear that it *may* denote that which is miraculous, but that this idea is not necessarily connected with it. Anything which is fitted to excite wonder and amazement, from any cause, will correspond with the sense of the Hebrew word. It is a word which expresses with surprising accuracy everything in relation to the Redeemer. For the Messiah was *wonderful* in all things. It was wonderful love by which God gave him, and by which he came ; the manner of his birth was wonderful ; his humility, his self-denial, his sorrows were wonderful ; his mighty works were wonderful ; his dying agonies were wonderful ; and his resurrection, his ascension, were all fitted to excite admiration and wonder. ¶ *Counsellor.* This word has been sometimes joined with ' wonderful,' as if designed to qualify it thus—*wonderful counsellor;* but it expresses a distinct attribute, or quality. The name *counsellor* here, יוֹעֵץ, denotes one of honourable rank ; one who is fitted to stand near princes and kings as their adviser. It is expressive of great wisdom, and of qualifications to guide and direct the human race. The LXX. translate this phrase, ' The angel of the mighty counsel.' The Chaldee, ' The God of wonderful counsel.' ¶ *The mighty God.* Syriac, ' The mighty God of ages.' This is one, and but one out of many, of the instances in which the name *God* is applied to the Messiah ; comp. John i. 1; Rom. ix. 5; 1 John v. 20; John xx. 28; 1 Tim. iii. 16; Heb. i. 8. The name ' mighty God,' is unquestionably attributed to the true God in ch. x. 21. Much controversy has arisen in relation to this expression ; and attempts have been made to show that the word translated God, אֵל, may refer to a hero, a king, a conqueror. Thus Gesenius renders, it ' Mighty hero ;' and supposes that the name ' God ' is here used in accordance with the custom of the Orientals, who ascribe Divine attributes to kings. In like manner Plüschke (see *Hengstenberg*) says, ' In my opinion this name is altogether symbolical. The Messiah shall be called strength of God, or strong God, Divine hero, in order by this name to remind the people of the strength of God.' But after all such controversy, it still remains certain that the natural and obvious meaning of the expression is to denote a Divine nature. So it was evidently understood by the ancient versions ; and the fact that the name God is so often applied to Christ in the New Testament, proves that it is to be understood in its natural and obvious signification. ¶ *The everlasting Father.* The Chaldee renders this expression, ' The man abiding for ever.' The Vulgate, ' The Father of the future age.' Lowth, ' The Father of the everlasting age.' Literally, it is the Father of eternity, אֲבִי עַד. The word rendered *everlasting,* עַד, properly denotes *eternity,* and is used to express *for ever;* see Ps. ix. 6, 19; xix. 10. It is often used in connection with עוֹלָם, thus, וַעֲדֵי עִילָם, *for ever and ever;* Ps. x. 16; xxi. 5; xlv. 7. The Hebrews used the term *father* in a great variety of senses —as a literal father, a grandfather, an ancestor, a ruler, an instructor. The phrase may either mean the same as the Eternal Father, and the sense will be, that the Messiah will not, as must be the case with an earthly king, however excellent, leave his people destitute after a short reign, but will rule over them and bless them for ever (*Hengstenberg);* or it may be used in accordance with a custom usual in Hebrew and in Arabic, where he who possesses a thing is called the father of it. Thus,

the *father of strength* means strong ; the *father of knowledge,* intelligent ; the *father of glory,* glorious ; the *father of goodness,* good ; the *father of peace,* peaceful. According to this, the meaning of the phrase, the *Father of eternity,* is properly *eternal.* The application of the word here is derived from this usage. The term *Father* is not applied to the Messiah here with any reference to the distinction in the Divine nature ; for that word is uniformly, in the Scriptures, applied to the *first,* not to the second person of the Trinity. But it is used in reference to *duration,* as a Hebraism involving high poetic beauty. He is not merely represented as everlasting, but he is introduced, by a strong figure, as even the *Father of eternity,* as if even *everlasting duration* owed itself to his paternity. There could not be a more emphatic declaration of strict and proper eternity. It may be added, that *this* attribute is often applied to the Messiah in the New Testament ; John viii. 58; Col. i. 17; Rev. i. 11, 17, 18; Heb. i. 10, 11; John i. 1, 2. ¶ *The Prince of Peace.* This is a Hebrew mode of expression denoting that he would be *a peaceful prince.* The tendency of his administration would be to restore and perpetuate peace. This expression is used to distinguish him from the mass of kings and princes who have delighted in conquest and blood. In contradistinction from all these, the Messiah would seek to promote universal concord, and the tendency of his reign would be to put an end to wars, and to restore harmony and order to the nations ; see the tendency of his reign still further described in ch. xi. 6–9; Note, ch. ii. 4; see also Mic. v. 4; Hos. ii. 18. It is not necessary to insist on the coincidence of this description with the uniform character and instructions of the Lord Jesus. In this respect, he disappointed all the hopes of the Jewish nation, who, in spite of the plain prophecies respecting his peaceful character, expected a magnificent prince, and a conqueror. The expressions used here imply that he would be more than human. It is impossible to believe that these appellations would be given under the Spirit of inspiration to a mere man. They express a higher nature ; and they

7 Of the increase of *his* government and peace *there shall be* no end,*a* upon the throne of David,

and upon his kingdom, to order it, and to establish it with judgment

a Dan.2.44; 1 Cor.15.25.

coincide with the account in the New Testament throughout, that he would be Divine. It is true, indeed, that expressions of a pompous and high-sounding character were commonly assumed by Oriental princes. The following is a single instance of their arrogance, ostentation, and pride. 'Chosröes, king of kings, lord of lords, ruler of the nations, *prince of peace*, saviour of men ; among the gods, a man good and eternal, but among men, a god most illustrious, glorious, a conqueror rising with the sun, and giving vision at night.' — Theoph. *Simocatta Chron.*, iv. 8, quoted by Gesenius. But it cannot be pretended, that the Spirit of inspiration would use titles in a manner so unmeaning and so pompous as this. Besides, it was one great object of the prophets to vindicate the name and character of the true God, and to show that all such appellations belonged to him alone. However such appellations might be used by surrounding nations, and given to kings and princes by the heathen, yet in the Scriptures they are not given to earthly monarchs. That this passage refers to the Messiah has been generally conceded, except by the Jews, and by a few later critics. Jarchi and Kimchi maintain that it refers to Hezekiah. They have been driven to this by the use which Christians have made of the passage against the Jews. But the absurdity of this interpretation has been shown in the Notes on ch. vii. 14. The *ancient* Jews incontestably referred it to the Messiah. Thus the Targum of Jonathan renders it, 'His name shall be called God of wonderful counsel, man abiding for ever, THE MESSIAH, מָשִׁיחַ, whose peace shall be multiplied upon us in his days.' Thus Rabbi Jose, of Galilee, says, 'The name of the Messiah is שָׁלוֹם *Shālōm*, as is said in Isa. ix. 6, "Father of Eternity, Prince of Peace."' Ben Sira (fol. 40, of the Amsterdam Edition, 1679) numbers among the eight names of the Messiah those also taken from this passage, Wonderful, Counsellor, Mighty God, Prince of Peace. The

later Jews, however, have rejected this interpretation, because the Messiah is here described as God.

7. *Of the increase, &c.* The word rendered *government* here, מִשְׂרָה, means properly his government *as a prince—his principality*, and is a continuation of the idea in the previous verse, 'the Prince of Peace.' It means that his reign as a prince of peace—in extending and promoting peace, shall be unlimited, ¶ *And peace.* This does not signify in the original, as our translation would seem to do, that there should be no end to the increase of his peace, but that there should be no limit to *peace*, that is, that his reign should be one of unlimited peace. The whole is a description of a prosperous, wide-extended, ever-growing and unlimited empire of peace. ¶ *No end.* The word here used—קֵץ—may refer either to space or time. The connection, however, seems to confine it to *time*, and to mean simply that over his wide-extended and peaceful principality he should reign for ever. ¶ *Upon the throne of David;* see Note, Acts ii. 30. This was in accordance with the promise made to David; 1 Kings viii. 25; 2 Sam. vii. 12, 13; Ps. cxxxii. 11. This promise was understood as referring to the Messiah. The primary idea is, that he should be descended in the line of David, and accordingly the New Testament writers are often at pains to show that the Lord Jesus was of that family; Luke ii. 4. When it is said that he would sit upon the throne of David, it is not to be taken literally. The peculiarity of the reign of David was, *that he reigned over the people of God.* He was chosen for this purpose from humble life ; was declared in his administration to be a man after God's own heart; and his long and prosperous reign was a reign over the people of God. To sit upon the throne of David, therefore, means to reign over the people of God ; and in this sense the Messiah sat on his throne. There is also a similarity in the two administrations, in the fact that the Messiah was taken from humble life.

and with justice, from henceforth even for ever. The zeal of the LORD of hosts will perform this.

8 The Lord sent a word into

Jacob, and it hath lighted upon Israel.

9 And all the people shall know, *even* Ephraim and the inhabitants

and that his reign will be far-extended and prosperous. But the main idea of resemblance is, that the reign of each extended over the people of God. ¶ *And upon his kingdom.* That is, over the kingdom of the people of God. It does not mean particularly the Jews, but all those over whom the Divine administration should be set up. ¶ *To order it.* To raise up, or confirm it. The word, also, is sometimes used to denote to *found* a kingdom. Here it means to *confirm* it, to cause it to stand. ¶ *And to establish it.* To place it on a firm foundation; to make it firm. ¶ *With judgment,* &c. That is, under an administration that shall be just and right. Most kingdoms have been those of blood, and have been established by iniquity, and by the unjust overthrow of others. But the administration of the Messiah shall be established in righteousness, and shall be destined to extend and perpetuate justice and righteousness for ever. ¶ *From henceforth.* That is, from the time which was the period of the prophet's vision, when he saw in vision the Messiah rising in the dark parts of Galilee; Notes, ver. 1, 2. ¶ *The zeal.* The word here used denotes *ardour,* intense desire in accomplishing an object; and means that the establishment of this kingdom was an object of intense and ardent desire on the part of JEHOVAH. It is also implied that nothing else than the zeal of JEHOVAH could do it. We may remark here—(1.) That if JEHOVAH feels so intense a desire for this, then the subjects of the Messiah's reign should also feel this. (2.) If JEHOVAH feels this zeal, and if he will certainly accomplish this, then Christians should be encouraged in their efforts to spread the gospel. His *purpose* to do this is their only encouragement—and a sufficient encouragement—to excite *their* zeal in this great and glorious work.

8. *The Lord sent.* Not JEHOVAH here, but *Adonai.* It is apparent that this verse is the commencement of a new prophecy, that is not connected with that which precedes it. The strain of

the preceding prophecy had respect to Judah; this is confined solely to Israel, or Ephraim. Here the division of the chapter should have been made, and should not have been again interrupted till the 4th verse of ch. x., where the prophecy closes. The prophecy is divided into *four* parts, and each part is designed to threaten a distinct judgment on some particular, prominent vice. I. *Crime*—their pride and ostentation, ver. 8, 9. *Punishment*—the land would be invaded by the Syrians and the Philistines, ver. 11, 12. II. *Crime*—they had apostatized from God, and the leaders had caused them to err, ver. 13, 16. *Punishment*—JEHOVAH would cut off the chief men of the nation, ver. 14, 15, 17. III. *Crime*—prevalent wickedness in the nation, ver. 18. *Punishment*— the anger of JEHOVAH, consternation, anarchy, discord, and want, ver. 19–21. IV. *Crime*—prevalent injustice; ch. x. 1, 2. *Punishment*—foreign invasion, and captivity; ch. x. 3, 4. The poem is remarkably regular in its structure (*Lowth*), and happy in its illustrations. At what *time* it was composed is not certain, but it has strong internal evidence that it immediately followed the preceding respecting Judah. ¶ *A word.* A message, or prediction; Note, ch. ii. 1. ¶ *Into Jacob.* Jacob was the ancestor of the nation. But the name came to be appropriated to the ten tribes, as constituting the majority of the people. It was at first used to denote *all* the Jews (Num. xxiii. 7, 10, 23; xxiv. 17, 19; Deut. xxxii. 9; 1 Chron. xvi. 13 · Ps. xiv. 7; xx. 1); but it came, after the revolt of the ten tribes under Jeroboam, to be used often to denote them alone; Amos vi. 8; Mic. i. 5; iii. 1; v. 8. The word or message which was sent, refers undoubtedly to that which immediately follows. ¶ *And it hath lighted upon.* Heb. 'It fell.' This is but a varied expression for, he sent it to Israel. ¶ *Israel.* The same as Jacob—the ten tribes—the kingdom of Ephraim.

9. *And all the people shall know.* Shall know the message; or shall know

of Samaria, that say in the pride and stoutness of heart,

10 The bricks are fallen down, but we will build with hewn stones: the sycamores are cut down, but we will change *them into* cedars.

the judgment which God denounces against their crimes. The Chaldee renders this, ' All the people have exalted themselves, Ephraim and the inhabitants of Samaria, in their magnitude, and in the pride of the heart.' ¶ *Ephraim.* This is another name for Israel, as Ephraim was the principal tribe ; Note, ch. vii. 2. ¶ *And the inhabitants of Samaria.* The capital of Ephraim or Israel ; Note, ch. vii. 9. ¶ *That say in the pride.* This is a description of general and prevalent pride ; and it is traced to the source of all pride—*the heart.* It was a desire of splendour, power, and magnificence, originating in the heart, and manifesting itself by the language of self-confidence and defiance at the judgments of God. ¶ *Stoutness.* Heb. ' Greatness.' It means a self-confident purpose; and indicates the state of feeling in a man when he trusts to his own resources, and not to God.

10. *The bricks are fallen down.* The language of this verse is figurative ; but the sentiment is plain. It contains the confession of the inhabitants of Samaria, that their affairs were in a ruinous and dilapidated state; but also their self-confident assurance that they would be able to repair the evils, and restore their nation to more than their former magnificence.

Bricks, in oriental countries, were made of clay and straw, and were rarely burned. Hence, exposed to suns and rains, they soon dissolved. Walls and houses constructed of such materials would not be very permanent, and to build with them is strongly contrasted with building in a permanent and elegant manner with hewn stone. The meaning is, that their former state was one of less splendour than they designed that their subsequent state should be. Desolation had come in upon their country, and this they could not deny. But they confidently boasted that they would more than repair the evil. ¶ *We will build.* Our ruined houses and walls. ¶ *With hewn stones.* At once more permanent and elegant than the structures of bricks had been. ¶ *The sycamores.* These trees grew abundantly on the low lands of Judea, and were very little esteemed; 1 Ki. x. 27; 2 Ch. i. 15; ix. 27. 'This curious tree seems to partake of the

nature of two different species,' says Calmet, 'the mulberry and the fig; the former in its leaf, and the latter in its fruit. Its Greek name, συκόμορος, is plainly descriptive of its character, being compounded of συκος, a fig tree, and μορος, a mulberry tree. It is thus described by Norden:

SYCAMORE (*Ficus sycomorus*).

"They have in Egypt divers sorts of figs; but if there is any difference between them, a particular kind differs still more. I mean that which the sycamore bears, that they name in Arabic *giomez.* This sycamore is of the height of a beech, and bears its fruit in a manner quite different from other trees. It has them on the trunk itself, which shoots out little sprigs in form of a grapestalk, at the end of which grows the fruit close to one another, most like bunches of grapes. The tree is always green, and bears fruit several times in the year, without observing any certain seasons, for I have seen some sycamores which had fruit two months after others. This sort of tree is pretty common in Egypt."' They were not highly valued, though it is probable they were often employed in building.

They are contrasted with cedars here— (1.) Because the cedar was a much more rare and precious wood. (2.) Because it was a much more smooth and elegant article of building. (3.) Because it was more permanent. The grain and texture of the sycamore is remarkably coarse and spongy, and could, therefore, stand in no competition with the cedar for beauty and ornament. ¶ *We will change* them. We will employ in their stead.

¶ *Cedars.* The cedar was a remarkably fine, elegant, and permanent wood for building. It was principally obtained on mount Lebanon, and was employed in temples, palaces, and in the houses of the rich; see Note on ch. ii. 18.

The sycamore is contrasted with the cedar in 1 Kings x. 27 : ' Cedars he made

11 Therefore the LORD shall set up the adversaries of Rezin against him, and ¹join his enemies together:

12 The Syrians before, and the Philistines behind ; and they shall devour Israel with ²open mouth. For all this his anger is not turned

1 *mingle.*   2 *whole.*

away, but his hand is stretched out still.

13 For the people turneth not unto him that smiteth them, neither do they seek the LORD of hosts.

14 Therefore the LORD will cut off from Israel head and tail, branch and rush, in one day.

---

to be as sycamore trees.' The whole passage denotes self-confidence and pride; an unwillingness to submit to the judgments of God, and a self-assurance that they would more than repair all the evils that would be inflicted on them.

11. *Therefore.* This verse indicates the *punishment* that would come upon them for their pride. ¶ *The* LORD *shall set up.* Heb. 'Shall exalt.' That is, they shall overcome and subdue him. ¶ *The adversaries of Rezin.* King of Syria, ch. vii. 1. It should be observed here, that twenty-one MSS., instead of *adversaries*, read *princes* of Rezin. The sense seems to require this; as in the following verse, it is said that the *Syrians* will be excited against them. ¶ *Against him.* Against Ephraim. ¶ *And join his enemies together.* Heb. 'Mingle them together.' They shall be excited into wild and agitated commotion, and shall pour down together on the land and devour it. In what way this would be done is specified in ver. 12.

12. *The Syrians;* chap. vii. 1. The Syrians had been the allies of the Israelites. But after the death of Rezin, it is probable that they joined the Assyrians, and united with them in the invasion of Samaria.— *Aben Ezra; Grotius.* ¶ *Before.* Heb. ' From the east.' Syria was situated to the east of Samaria, and the meaning is here, that they would pour in upon Samaria from that side. ¶ *And the Philistines.* The Philistines occupied the country south-west of Samaria, lying along on the shores of the Mediterranean. It is not particularly mentioned in the Scriptures that they invaded Samaria after this prediction of Isaiah, but such a thing is by no means improbable. They were long unsubdued ; were full of hostility to the Jewish people ; and were many times engaged with them in wars, and several

times subdued them ; Judg. xiii.; xiv.; 2 Chron. xxviii. 18. The name Palestine is derived from Philistine, although this people occupied but a small part of the country ; *see* Reland's *Palestine,* c. vii. ¶ *Behind.* That is, from *the west* — the region where they dwelt. The sacred writers speak as if looking toward the east, the rising sun, and they speak of the west as the region behind them ; see Notes on Job xxiii. 8, 9. ¶ *And they shall devour.* Heb. ' They shall eat.' This figure is taken from a ravenous beast ; and means that they should come up with raging desires, and fierce impetuosity, to destroy the nation. ¶ *With open mouth.* Heb. ' With the whole mouth.' The metaphor is derived from raging and furious animals. Chaldee, ' In every place.' ¶ *For all this.* Notwithstanding all this. ¶ *His anger,* &c.; see Note, ch. v. 25.

13. *For the people,* &c. This is a reason why his anger would not cease, and it is, at the same time, the suggestion of a new crime for which the Divine judgment would rest upon them. It commences the second part of the oracle. ¶ *Turneth not.* It is *implied* here that it was the design of the chastisement to turn them to God. In this case, as in many others, such a design had not been accomplished. ¶ *Unto him that smiteth them.* To God, who had punished them. ¶ *Neither do they seek.* They do not seek his protection and favour ; they do not worship and honour him. ¶ *The* LORD *of hosts ;* Note, ch. i. 9.

14. *Will cut off head and tail.* This is a proverbial expression, which is explained in the following verse ; see also Deut. xxviii. 13, 14. The head is often used to denote those in honour and authority. The tail is an expression applicable to the lower ranks, and would

15 The ancient and honourable, he *is* the head; and the prophet that teacheth lies, he *is* the tail.

16 For [1] the leaders of this people cause *them* to err; and *they that are* [2] led of them *are* [3] destroyed.

17 Therefore the LORD shall have no joy in their young men, neither shall have mercy on their father-

less and widows: for every one *is* an hypocrite and an evil-doer, and every mouth speaketh [4] folly. For all this his anger is not turned away, but his hand *is* stretched out still.

18 For wickedness [a] burneth as the fire: it shall devour the briers and thorns, and shall kindle in the

1 or, *they that call them blessed.*   2 or, *called blessed.*   3 *swallowed up.*   4 or, *villany.*   a Mal.4.1.

commonly indicate more than simply the common people. It would imply contempt; a state of great abjectness and meanness. ¶ *Branch and rush.* This is also a proverbial expression, meaning the highest and lowest; see Note, Isa. xix. 15. The word here translated *branch,* means properly the bough or top of the palm tree. The palm grew to a great height before it gave out any branches, and hence the image is a beautiful one to denote those *high* in office and authority. The word *rush* means the coarse, long-jointed reed, that grows in marshes—an apt emblem of the base and worthless classes of society.

15. *The ancient.* The elder; the old man. ¶ *And honourable.* Heb. ' The man of elevated countenance.' The man of rank and office. ¶ *The prophet that teacheth lies.* The false prophet. Of those there were many; and probably at this time many in Samaria.

16. *For the leaders of this people,* &c.; Note, ch. iii. 12. Heb. ' They that call this people blessed '—referring more particularly to the false prophets. ¶ They that are *led of them.* Heb. ' They that are called blessed by them.' ¶ *Are destroyed.* Heb. ' Are swallowed up;' see Note, ch. iii. 12. They are ruined; or swallowed up as in a vast whirlpool or vortex.

17. *Shall have no joy.* He shall not delight in them so as to preserve them. The parallel part of the verse shows that the phrase is used in the sense of having mercy. ¶ *In their young men.* The hope and strength of the nation. The word here used commonly denotes those *who are chosen,* particularly for purposes of war. The sense is, that the hope and strength of the nation, that

on which the chief reliance would be placed, would be cut off. ¶ *Neither shall have mercy,* &c. Judgment would sweep through the nation, even over those who were the usual objects of the Divine protection—widows and orphans; comp. Ps. x. 14, 18; xlviii. 5; Deut. x. 18; Jer. xlix. 11; Hos. xiv. 3. These passages show that the fatherless and the widow are the special objects of the Divine favour; and when, therefore, it is said that the Lord would not have mercy even on these, it shows the extent and severity of the Divine judgments that were coming on the nation. ¶ *For every one* is *a hypocrite.* A deceiver; a dissembler. The word used here, however, חָנֵף *hhânêph,* means rather a profane or profligate man, a man who is *defiled* or *polluted,* than a dissembler. It is applied often to idolaters and licentious persons, but not to hypocrites; see Job viii. 13; xiii. 16; xv. 34; xvii. 8; Dan. xi. 32. ¶ *Every mouth speaketh folly.* The word rendered *folly,* may denote foolishness, but it is also used to denote wickedness or crime; 1 Sam. xxv. 23. Probably this is the meaning here. That the character here given of the Ephraimites is correct, is abundantly shown also by other prophets; see particularly Hosea. ¶ *For all this.* Notwithstanding all the judgments that should come thus upon the young men, and widows, and orphans, still his anger was not turned away. This is the close of the second *strophe* or part of this pro- phecy.

18. *For wickedness.* This commences the *third* part of the prophecy, which continues to the end of the chapter. It is a description of prevailing impiety. The effects and prevalence of it are de- scribed by the image of a raging, burn-

thickets of the forest: and they shall mount up *like* the lifting up of smoke.

19 Through the wrath of the LORD of hosts is the land darkened,*a* and the people shall be as

the ¹fuel of the fire: no man shall spare his *b* brother.

20 And he shall ²snatch on the right hand, and be hungry; and he *c* shall eat on the left hand, and they shall not be satisfied: they

a Acts 2.20.　　　1 *meat.*　　　*b* Mic.7.2,6.　　　2 *cut.*　　　*c* Lev.26.26; Jer.19 9.

ing flame, that spreads everywhere; first among the humble shrubbery—the briers and thorns, then in the vast forests, until it spreads over the land, and sends a mighty column of flame and smoke up to heaven. ¶ *Burneth as the fire.* Spreads, rages, extends as fire does in thorns and in forests. In what respects it burns like the fire, the prophet immediately specifies. It spreads rapidly everywhere, and involves all in the effects. Wickedness is not unfrequently in the Scriptures compared to *a fire* that is shut up long, and then bursts forth with raging violence. Thus Hos. vii. 6:

Truly, in the inmost part of it, their heart is like an oven,
While they lie in wait;
All the night their baker sleepeth;
In the morning it burneth like a blazing star.

' As an oven conceals the lighted fire all night, while the baker takes his rest, and in the morning vomits forth its blazing flame ; so all manner of concupiscence is brooding mischief in their hearts, while the ruling faculties of reason and conscience are lulled asleep, and their wicked designs wait only for a fair occasion to break forth.'—*Horsely* on Hosea ; see also Isa. l. 2 ; lxv. 5. ¶ *It shall devour.* Heb. ' It shall eat.' The idea of devouring or eating, is one which is often given to fire in the Scriptures. ¶ *The briers and thorns.* By the briers and thorns are meant, doubtless, the lower part of the population ; the most degraded ranks of society. The idea here seems to be, first, that of impiety spreading like fire over all classes of people ; but there is also joined with it, in the mind of the prophet, the idea of punishment. Wickedness would rage like spreading fire ; but like fire, also, it would sweep over the nation accomplishing desolation and calamity, and consuming everything in the fire of God's vengeance. The wicked are often

compared to thorns and briers—fit objects to be burned up ; Isa. xxxiii. 12 :

And the people shall be as the burnings of lime;
As thorns cut up shall they be burned in the fire.

¶ *And shall kindle.* Shall burn, or extend, as sweeping fire extends to the mighty forest. ¶ *In the thickets of the forests.* The dense, close forest or grove. The idea is, that it extends to all classes of people—high as well as low. ¶ *And they shall mount up.* The Hebrew word here used—יִתְאַבְּכוּ from אָבַךְ—occurs nowhere else. The image is that of a far-spreading, raging fire, sending columns of smoke to heaven. So, says the prophet, is the rolling, raging, consuming fire of the sins of the nation spreading over all classes of people in the land, and involving all in wide-spread desolation.

19. *Through the wrath.* By the anger, or indignation. This spreading desolation is the proof of his anger. ¶ *Is the land darkened.* The word here used —עָתַם—occurs nowhere else. According to Gesenius, it is the same as תָּמַם to be or make complete ; and hence means, in this place, to be consumed, or laid waste. Kimchi and Aben Ezra render it, ' The land is darkened.' Sept. Σνγκέκαυται. Chald. צְרוֹבַת.—' Is scorched.' Jerome renders it, *Conturbata est terra*—' The land is disturbed.' The effect is doubtless such as ascending and spreading columns of fire and smoke would produce, and perhaps the general word *desolate* had better be used in translating the word. ¶ *And the people shall be as fuel of the fire.* This is an image of wide-spread ruin. The idea is, that they shall destroy one another as pieces of wood, when on fire, help to consume each other. The way in which it shall be done is stated more fully in the next verse. ¶ *No man shall spare his brother.* There shall be such a state of wickedness, that it shall lead to anar-

shall eat every man the flesh of his own arm :

21 Manasseh, Ephraim; and Ephraim, Manasseh; *and* they

together *shall be* against Judah. For all this his anger is not turned away, but his hand *is* stretched out, still.

---

chy, and strife, and mutual destruction. The common ties of life shall be dissolved, and a man shall have no compassion on his own brother.

20. *And he shall snatch.* Heb. ' He shall cut off.' Many have supposed that this refers to a state of famine ; but others regard it as descriptive of a state of faction extending throughout the whole community, dissolving the most tender ties, and producing a dissolution of all the bonds of life. The context (ver. 19, 21) shows, that the latter is meant ; though it is not improbable that it would be attended with famine. When it is said that he ' would cut off his right hand,' it denotes a condition of internal anarchy and strife. ¶ *And be hungry.* And not be satisfied. Such would be his rage, and his desire of blood, that he would be insatiable. The murder of those on one side of him would not appease his insatiable wrath. His desire of carnage would be so great that it would be like unappeased hunger. ¶ *And he shall eat.* The idea here is that of contending factions excited by fury, rage, envy, hatred, contending in mingled strife, and spreading death with insatiable desire everywhere around them. ¶ *They shall eat.* Not literally ; but shall destroy. To eat the flesh of any one, denotes to seek one's life, and is descriptive of blood-thirsty enemies ; Ps. xxvii. 2 : ' When the wicked, *even* mine enemies and foes, came upon me *to eat up my flesh,* they stumbled and fell ;' Job xix. 22 :

Why do ye persecute me as God, And are not satisfied with my flesh?

comp. Deut. vii. 16; Jer. x. 25; xxx. 15; l. 17; Hos. vii. 7; see Ovid's *Metam.* 8, 867 :

Ipse suos artus lacero divellere morsu Cœpit; et infelix minuendo corpus alebat.

¶ *The flesh of his own arm.* The Chaldee renders this, ' Each one shall devour the substance of his neighbour.' Lowth proposes to read it, ' The flesh of his

neighbour,' but without sufficient authority. The expression denotes a state of dreadful faction—where the ties of most intimate relationship would be disregarded, represented here by the appalling figure of a man's appetite being so rabid that he would seize upon and devour his own flesh. So, in this state of faction and discord, the rage would be so great that men would destroy those who were, as it were, their own flesh, *i.e.,* their nearest kindred and friends.

21. *Manasseh, Ephraim.* This verse is a continuation of the statement in regard to the extent and fearfulness of the faction. Those who were hitherto most tenderly and intimately allied to each other, would now be engaged in furious strife. Manasseh and Ephraim were the two sons of Joseph (Gen. xlvi. 20), and their names are used as expressive of tender union and friendship; comp. Gen. xlviii. 20. The tribes of Ephraim and Manasseh were near each other, and they always were allied together. The expression here denotes that they who had hitherto been joined in tender alliance, would be rent into contending factions, thirsting for each other's blood. ¶ And *they together.* They would be united in opposing Judah while they were devouring each other, as it is not an uncommon thing for those who are opposed to each other to unite in hostility to a common foe ; comp. Luke xxiii. 12. This is an image that heightens the description of the anarchy — introducing implacable animosity against another tribe, while they were contending among themselves. That such anarchies and factions existed, is apparent from all the history of the kingdom of Israel ; comp. 2 Kings xv 10, *sq.;* 2 Kings xv. 30. In this last passage, the death of Pekah is described as having occurred in a conspiracy formed by Hoshea. ¶ *For all this,* &c.; see ver. 12, Note v. 25. This closes the third *strophe* or part of the prophecy under consideration. The fourth and last strophe occurs in ch. x. 1-4.

CHAPTER X.
ANALYSIS.

This chapter is composed of two parts: the first (ver. 1–4) closes the prophecy commenced in ch. ix. 8, and should have been connected with that in the division into chapters; and the second part commences an entirely *new* prophecy, respecting the destruction of the Assyrians; see the Analysis prefixed to ver. 5. The first four verses of this chapter constitute the *fourth* strophe, or part of the prophecy, commenced in ch. ix. 8, and contains a specification of a crime, and its punishment:—*the crime*, prevalent injustice and oppression (ch. ix. 1, 2);

the punishment, foreign invasion, ch ix. 3, 4; see Note on ch. ix. 8.

WO [a] unto them that decree unrighteous decrees, and [1] that write grievousness *which* they have prescribed;

2 To turn aside the needy from judgment, and to take away the right from the poor of my people, that widows may be their prey, and *that* they may rob the fatherless!

a Ps.94.20.   1 *to the writers that.*

CHAPTER X.

1. *Wo unto them that decree unrighteous decrees.* To those who frame statutes that are oppressive and iniquitous. The prophet here refers, doubtless, to the rulers and judges of the land of Judea. A similar description he had before given; chap. i. 10, 23, &c. ¶ *And that write*, &c. Heb. 'And to the writers who write violence.' The word translated *grievousness*, עָמָל, denotes properly *wearisome labour, trouble, oppression, injustice.* Here, it evidently refers to the judges who declared oppressive and unjust sentences, and caused them to be recorded. It does not refer to the mere scribes, or recorders of the judicial opinions, but to the judges themselves, who pronounced the sentence, and caused it to be recorded. The manner of making Eastern decrees differs from ours : they are first written, and then the magistrate authenticates them, or annuls them. This, I remember, is the Arab manner, according to D'Arvieux. When an Arab wanted a favour of the emir, the way was to apply to the secretary, who drew up a decree according to the request of the party ; if the emir granted the favour, he printed his seal upon it ; if not, he returned it torn to the petitioner. Sir J. Chardin confirms this account, and applies it, with great propriety, to the illustration of a passage which I never thought of when I read over D'Arvieux. After citing Isa. x. 1, ' *Wo unto them that decree unrighteous decrees, and to the writers that write grievousness,*' for so our translators have rendered the latter part of the verse in the margin, much

more agreeably than in the body of the version, Sir John goes on, ' The manner of making the royal acts and ordinances hath a relation to this ; they are always drawn up according to the request ; the first minister, or he whose office it is, writes on the side of it, " according to the king's will," and from thence it is sent to the secretary of state, who draws up the order in form.' —*Harmer.*

2. *To turn aside.* Their sentences have the effect, and are designed to have, to pervert justice, and to oppress the poor, or to deprive them of their rights and just claims ; comp. ch. xxix. 21; Prov. xxvii. 5. ¶ *The needy.* דַּלִּים. Those of humble rank and circumstances ; who have no powerful friends and defenders. ¶ *From judgment.* From obtaining justice. ¶ *And to take away.* To take away by violence and oppression. The word גָּזַל *gâzăl*, is commonly applied to robbery, and to oppression ; to the taking away of spoils in battle, &c. ¶ *That widows may be their prey.* That they may rob widows, or obtain their property. This crime has always been one particularly offensive in the sight of God ; see Note ch. i. 23. The widow and the orphan are without protectors. Judges, by their office, are particularly bound to preserve their rights ; and it, therefore, evinces peculiar iniquity when they who should be their protectors become, in fact, their oppressors, and do injustice to them without the possibility of redress. Yet this was the character of the Jewish judges ; and for this the vengeance of Heaven was about to come upon the land.

3 And what *a* will ye do in the day of visitation, and in the desolation *which* shall come from far? to whom will ye flee for help? and where will ye leave your glory?

a Job 31.14; Hos.9.7; Rev.6.17.

4 Without me they shall bow down under the prisoners, and they shall fall under the slain. For all this his anger is not turned away, but his hand *is* stretched out still.

3. *And what will ye do.* The prophet here proceeds to denounce the judgment, or punishment, that would follow the crimes specified in the previous verses. That punishment was the invasion of the land by a foreign force. 'What will ye do? To whom will you fly? What refuge will there be?' Implying that the calamity would be so great that there would be no refuge, or escape. ¶ *In the day of visitation.* The word *visitation* (פְּקֻדָּה) is here used in the sense of God's coming to punish them for their sins; comp. Job xxxi. 14; xxxv. 15; Isa. xxvi. 14; Ezek. ix. 1. The idea is probably derived from that of a master of a family who comes to take account, or to investigate the conduct of his servants, and where the visitation, therefore, is one of reckoning and justice. So the idea is applied to God as designing to *visit* the wicked; that is, to punish them for their offences; comp. Hos. ix. 7. ¶ *And in the desolation.* The destruction, or overthrowing. The word used here--שׁוֹאָה--usually denotes a storm, a tempest (Prov. i. 27); and then sudden destruction, or calamity, that sweeps along irresistibly like a tempest; Zeph. i. 15; Job xxx. 3, 14; Ps. xxxv. 8. ¶ Which *shall come from far.* That is, from Assyria, Media, Babylonia. The sense is, 'a furious storm of war is about to rage. To what refuge can you then flee? or where can you then find safety?' ¶ *Where will ye leave your glory.* By the word *glory* here, some have understood the prophet as referring to their aged men, their princes and nobles, and as asking where they would find a safe place for them. But he probably means their *riches, wealth, magnificence.* Thus Ps. xlix. 17:

For when he dieth, he shall carry nothing away;
His *glory* shall not descend after him.

See also Hos. ix. 2; Isa. lxvi. 12. The word *leave* here, is used in the sense

of *deposit,* or commit for safe keeping; comp. Job xxxix. 14. 'In the time of the invasion that shall come up like a tempest on the land, where will you deposit your property so that it shall be safe?'

4. *Without me.* בִּלְתִּי. There has been a great variety of interpretation affixed to this expression. The sense in which our translators understood it was, evidently, that they should be forsaken of God; and that, as the effect of this, they should bow down under the condition of captives, or among the slain. The Vulgate and the LXX, however, and many interpreters understand the word here as a simple negative. 'Where will you flee for refuge? Where will you deposit your wealth *so as not* to bow down under a chain?' Vulgate, *Ne incurvemini sub vinculo.* LXX. Τοῦ μὴ ἐμπεσεῖν εἰς ἀπαγωγήν—'Not to fall into captivity.' The Hebrew will bear either mode of construction. Vitringa and Lowth understand it as our translators have done, as meaning that God would forsake them, and that without him, that is, deprived of his aid, they would be destroyed. ¶ *They shall bow down.* They shall be subdued, as armies are that are taken captive. ¶ *Under the prisoners.* That is, under the *condition* of prisoners; or *as* prisoners. Some understand it to mean, that they should bear down *in the place* of prisoners; that is, in prison. But it evidently means, simply, that they should be captives. ¶ *They shall fall under the slain.* They shall be slain. Gesenius renders it, '*Among* the prisoners, and *among* the slain.' The Chaldee reads it, 'You shall be cast into chains out of your own land, and beyond your own cities you shall be cast out slain.' Vitringa supposes that the prophet, in this verse, refers to the custom, among the ancients, of placing prisoners in war under a yoke of wood to indicate their captivity. That such

GENERAL ANALYSIS OF CHAPTERS X. 5–34; XI.; XII.

At ver. 5, in this chapter, there is evidently the commencement of a new prophecy, or vision; and the division into chapters should have indicated such a commencement. The prophecy is continued to the close of the 12th chapter. Its general scope is a threatening against Assyria, and the prediction of ultimate safety, happiness, and triumph to the people of Judah. It has no immediate connection with the previous vision any further than the subjects are similar, and one seems to have suggested the other. In the previous vision, the prophet had described the threatened invasion of *Ephraim* or *Israel*, by the *Syrians;* in this, he describes the threatened invasion of *Judah* by the *Assyrians.* The result of the invasion of Ephraim would be the desolation of Samaria, and the captivity of the people; but the result of the invasion of Judah would be that God would interpose and humble the Assyrian, and bring deliverance to his people. This chapter is occupied with an account of the threatened invasion of Judea by the Assyrian, (ver. 5–7); with a statement of his confident boasting, and defiance of God (ver. 8–14); with encouraging the people to confide in God, and not to be afraid of him; and with the assurance that he would be discomfited and overthrown, ver. 15–34. The mention of this deliverance gives occasion for the elevated and beautiful statement respecting the *future* deliverance of the nation by the Messiah, and the glorious triumph that would attend his reign, which occurs in ch. xi.; xii.

When the prophecy was uttered, and in regard to whom, has been a question. Vitringa supposes that it was uttered in immediate connection with the foregoing, and that it is in fact a part of it. But from ver. 9, 11, it is evident that at the time this prophecy was uttered, Samaria was destroyed; and from ver. 20, it is clear that it was after the ten tribes had been carried into captivity, and when the Assyrian supposed that he could accomplish the same

destruction and captivity, in regard to Jerusalem and Judah, that had taken place in regard to Samaria and Ephraim. As to the remark of Vitringa, that the prophet anticipated these future events, and spoke of them as already passed, it may be observed, that the structure and form of the expressions suppose that they were *in fact* passed at the time he wrote; see the Notes on ver. 9, 11, 20. Lightfoot (*Chronica Temporum*) supposes that the prophet here refers to the threatened invasion of the land by Tiglath-pileser, king of Assyria, after he had destroyed Damascus, and when, being about to advance upon Jerusalem, Ahaz stripped the temple of its valuable ornaments, and sent them to him; 2 Kings xvi. 17, 18. Lowth supposes that the threatened invasion here refers to that of Sennacherib. This is, probably, the correct reference. This took place in the fourteenth year of Hezekiah, 725 years before the Christian era. Hezekiah, alarmed at the approach of Sennacherib, sent messengers to him to Lachish (2 Kings xviii. 14), to obtain a cessation of hostilities. Sennacherib agreed to such a peace, on condition that Hezekiah should pay him three hundred talents of silver, and thirty of gold. In order to meet this demand, Hezekiah was obliged to advance all the silver and gold in the treasury, and even to strip the temple of its ornaments. Having done this, he hoped for safety; and on this occasion, probably, this prophecy was uttered. It was designed to show that the danger of invasion was not passed; to assure them the king of Assyria would still come against the nation (comp. 2 Kings viii. 17, &c.); but that still God would interpose, and would deliver them. A further reference to this is made in Isa. xx., and a full history given in ch. xxxvii.; xxxviii.; see Notes on those chapters.

5 1 O 2 Assyrian, the rod *a* of mine anger, 3 and the staff in their hand is mine indignation.

1 *wo to the Assyrian.*　　2 *Asshur.*
a Jer.51.20,21.　　3 or, *though.*

a custom obtained, there can be no doubt; but it is not probable that Isaiah refers to it here. The simple idea is, that many of them should be taken captive, and many of them slain. This prediction was fulfilled in the invasion of Tiglath-pileser; 2 Kings xv.; xvi. ¶ *For all this.* Notwithstanding these calamities. The cup of punishment is not filled by these, but the Divine judgment shall still be poured

out further upon the nation. The anger of God shall not be fully expressed by these *minor* inflictions of his wrath, but his hand shall continue to be stretched out until the whole nation shall be overwhelmed and ruined; see Note on ver. 12.

5. *O Assyrian.* The word הוֹי *hō,* is commonly used to denounce wrath, or to indicate approaching calamity; as an interjection of threatening; Isa. i. 4,

6 I will send him against an
hypocritical nation, and against
the people of my wrath will I give
him a charge, ^ato take the spoil,

and to take the prey, and to ¹ tread
them down ^b like the mire of the
streets.

'Wo sinful nation;' ver. 8, 11, 18, 20,
21; Jer. xlviii. 1; Ezek. xiii. 2. The
Vulgate so understands it here: ' Væ
Assur;' and the LXX. Οὐαὶ 'Ασσυρίοις
—'Wo to the Assyrians.' So the Chaldee and the Syriac. It is not then a
simple *address* to the Assyrian ; but a
form denouncing wrath on the invader.
Yet it was not so much designed to intimidate and appal the Assyrian himself, as to comfort the Jews with the
assurance that calamity should overtake him. The ' Assyrian' referred to
here was the king of Assyria—Sennacherib, who was leading an army to
invade the land of Judea. ¶ *The rod
of mine anger.* That is, the rod, or
instrument, by which I will inflict punishment on a guilty nation. The Hebrew would bear the interpretation that
the Assyrian was an object against
which God was angry ; but the former
is evidently the sense of the passage,
as denoting that the Assyrian was the
agent by which he would express his
anger against a guilty people. Wo
might be denounced against him for
his wicked intention, at the same time
that God might design to make use of
his plans to punish the sins of his own
people. The word *anger* here, refers
to the indignation of God against the
sins of the Jewish people. ¶ *And the
staff.* The word *staff* here, is synonymous with *rod*, as an instrument of
chastisement or punishment ; ch. ix. 4;
comp. ver. 24; Nah. i. 13; Ezek. vii.
10. ¶ *In their hand.* There has been
considerable variety in the interpretation of this passage. Lowth and Noyes
read it, ' The staff in whose hand is the
instrument of my indignation.' This
interpretation Lowth adopts, by omitting the word הוא on the authority
of the Alexandrine copy of the LXX.,
and five MSS., two of them ancient.
Jerome reads it, ' Wo to the Assyrian !
He is the staff and the rod of my fury;
in their hand is my indignation.' So
Forerius, Ludovicus, de Dieu, Cocceius,
and others. Vitringa reads it, ' And
in the hands of those who are my rod

is my indignation.' Schmidius and
Rosenmüller, ' And the rod which is in
their hands, is the rod of mine indignation.' There is no necessity for any
change in the text. The Hebrew,
literally, is, ' Wo to the Assyrian ! Rod
of my anger ! And he is the staff. In
their hands is my indignation.' The
sense is sufficiently clear, that the Assyrian was appointed to inflict punishment on a rebellious people, as the
instrument of God. The Chaldee renders it, ' Wo to the Assyrian ! The
dominion [power, ruler] of my fury,
and the angel sent from my face,
against them, for a malediction. LXX.
' And wrath in their hands.' ¶ *In their
hand.* In the hand of the Assyrians,
where the word ' Assyrian' is taken as
referring to the king of Assyria, as the
representative of the nation.

6. *I will send him.* Implying that
he was entirely in the hand of God, and
subject to his direction ; and showing
that God has control over kings and
conquerors ; Prov. xxi. 1. ¶ *Against
an hypocritical nation.* Whether the
prophet here refers to Ephraim, or to
Judah, or to the Jewish people in general, has been an object of inquiry among
interpreters. As the designs of Sennacherib were mainly against Judah, it is
probable that that part of the nation
was intended. This is evidently the
case, if, as has been supposed, the prophecy was uttered after the captivity
of the ten tribes ; see ver. 20. It need
scarcely be remarked, that it was eminently the characteristic of the nation
that they were hypocritical ; comp.
Isa. ix. 17; Matt. xv. 17; Mark vii. 6.
¶ *And against the people of my wrath.*
That is, those who were the objects of
my wrath ; or the people on whom I
am about to pour out my indignation.
¶ *To take the spoil.* To plunder them.
¶ *And to tread them down.* Heb. ' And
to make them a treading down.' The
expression is drawn from war, where
the vanquished and the slain are trodden down by the horses of the conquering army. It means here, that the

7 Howbeit *a* he meaneth not
so, neither doth his heart think
so ; but *it is* in his heart to

a xi.4.12.

destroy and cut off nations not
a few.

8 For he saith, *Are* not my
princes altogether kings ?

Assyrian would humble and subdue the
people ; that he would trample indignantly on the nation, regarding them
with contempt, and no more to be
esteemed than the mire of the streets.
A similar figure occurs in Zech. x. 5 :
' And they shall be as mighty men
which tread down their enemies in the
mire of the streets in battle.'

7. *Howbeit he meaneth not so.* It
is not his purpose to be the instrument,
in the hand of God, of executing his
designs. He has a different plan ; a
plan of his own which he intends to
accomplish. ¶ *Neither doth his heart
think so.* He does not intend or design
it. The *heart* here, is put to express
purpose, or *will*. ¶ It is *in his heart
to cut off nations.* Utterly to destroy
or to annihilate their political existence.
¶ *Not a few.* The ambitious purpose
of Sennacherib was not confined to
Judea. His plan was also to invade
and to conquer Egypt; and the destruction of Judea was only a part of his
scheme ; Isa. xx. This is a most remarkable instance of the supremacy
which God asserts over the purposes of
wicked men. Sennacherib formed his
own plan without compulsion. He devised large purposes of ambition, and
intended to devastate kingdoms. And
yet God says that he was under his
direction, and that his plans would be
overruled to further his own purposes.
Thus ' the wrath of man would be made
to praise him ;' Ps. lxxvi. 10. And
from this we may learn—(1.) That
wicked men form their plans and devices with perfect freedom. They lay
their schemes as if there were no superintending providence ; and feel, correctly, that they are not under the laws
of compulsion, or of fate. (2.) That
God presides over their schemes, and
suffers them to be formed and executed
with reference to his own purposes.
(3.) That the plans of wicked men often,
though they do not intend it, go to
execute the purposes of God. Their
schemes result in just what they did
not intend—the furtherance of his

plans, and the promotion of his glory.
(4.) That their plans are, nevertheless,
wicked and abominable. They are to
be judged according to what they are
in themselves, and not according to the
use which God may make of them by
counteracting or overruling them. *Their*
intention is evil; and by that they must
be judged. That God brings good out
of them, is contrary to their design,
and a thing for which *they* deserve no
credit, and should receive no reward.
(5.) The wicked are in the hands of
God. (6.) There is a superintending
providence ; and men cannot defeat the
purposes of the Almighty. This extends to princes on their thrones ; to
the rich, the great, and the mighty, as
well as to the poor and the humble—
and to the humble as well as to the
rich and the great. Over all men is
this superintending and controlling providence ; and all are subject to the di
rection of God. (7.) It has often happened, *in fact*, that the plans of wicked
men have been made to contribute to
the purposes of God. Instances like
those of Pharaoh, of Cyrus, and of
Sennacherib ; of Pontius Pilate, and of
the kings and emperors who persecuted
the early Christian church, show that
they are in the hand of God, and that
he can overrule their wrath and wickedness to his glory. The madness of
Pharaoh was the occasion of the signal
displays of the power of God in Egypt.
The wickedness, and weakness, and
flexibility of Pilate, was the occasion
of the atonement made for the sins of
the world. And the church rose, in its
primitive brightness and splendour, amid
the flames which persecution kindled,
and was augmented in numbers, and in
moral loveliness and power, just in proportion as the wrath of monarchs raged
to destroy it.

8. *For he saith.* This verse, and the
subsequent verses to ver. 11, contain
the vaunting of the king of Assyria,
and the descriptions of his own confidence of success. ¶ *Are not my princes
altogether kings?* This is a confident

9 ^a *Is* not ^b Calno as ^c Carche- | mish? *is* not Hamath as Arpad?

a 2 Ki.18.33;19.12,13.   *b* Amos 6.2. | *is* not Samaria as ^d Damascus?
c 2 Chron.35.20.   *d* 2 Ki.16.9.

boast of his *own* might and power. His own dominion was so great that even his princes were endowed with the ordinary power and *regalia* of kings. The word *princes*, may here refer either to those of his own family and court— to the *satraps* and officers of power in his army, or around his throne; or more probably, it may refer to the subordinate governors whom he had set over the provinces which he had conquered. 'Are they not clothed with royal power and majesty? Are they not of equal splendour with the other monarchs of the earth?' How great, then, must have been his *own* rank and glory to be placed *over* such illustrious sovereigns! It will be recollected, that a common title which oriental monarchs give themselves, is that of King of kings; see Ezek. xxvi. 7; Dan. ii. 37; Ezra vii. 12. The oriental princes are still distinguished for their sounding titles, and particularly for their claiming dominion over all other princes, and the supremacy over all other earthly powers.

9. Is *not Calno as Carchemish?* The meaning of this confident boasting is, that none of the cities and nations against which he had directed his arms, had been able to resist him. All had fallen before him; and all were alike prostrate at his feet. Carchemish had been unable to resist him, and Calno had shared the same fate. Arpad had fallen before him, and Hamath in like manner had been subdued. The words which are used here are the same nearly that Rabshakeh used when he was sent by Sennacherib to insult Hezekiah and the Jews; Isa. xxxvi. 19; 2 Kings xviii. 34. *Calno* was a city in the land of Shinar, and was probably the city built by Nimrod, called in Gen. x. 10, *Calneh*, and at one time the capital of his empire. It is mentioned by Ezekiel, xxvii. 23. According to the Targums, Jerome, Eusebius, and others, Calno or Calneh, was the same city as *Ctesiphon*, a large city on the bank of the Tigris, and opposite to Seleucia.— *Gesenius* and *Calmet.* ¶ *Carchemish.* This was a city on the Euphrates, be-

longing to Assyria. It was taken by Necho, king of Egypt, and re-taken by Nebuchadnezzar in the fourth year of Jehoiachin, king of Judah; 2 Kings xxiii. 29. Probably it is the same city as Cercusium, or Kirkisia, which is situated in the angle formed by the junction of the Chebar and the Euphrates; comp. Jer. xlvi. 2; 2 Chron. xxv. 20. ¶ *Hamath.* This was a celebrated city of Syria. It is referred to in Gen. x. 18, as the seat of one of the tribes of Canaan. It is often mentioned as the northern limit of Canaan, in its widest extent; Num. xiii. 21; Josh. xiii. 5; Judg. iii. 3. The Assyrians became masters of this city about 753 years before Christ; 2 Kings xvii. 24. Burckhardt mentions this city as situated on both sides of the river Orontes. The town is at present of considerable extent, and contains about 30,000 inhabitants. There are four bridges over the Orontes, in the town. The trade of the town now is with the Arabs, who buy here their tent-furniture, and their clothes. This city was visited by the Rev. Eli Smith, in 1834. It lies, says he, on the narrow valley of the 'Asy; and is so nearly concealed by the high banks, that one sees little of it until he actually comes up to the gates; *see* Robinson's *Bib. Researches*, vol. iii. App. pp. 176, 177. ¶ *Arpad.* This city was not far from Hamath, and is called by the Greeks Epiphania; 2 Kings xviii. 34. ¶ *Samaria.* The capital of Israel, or Ephraim. From the mention of this place, it is evident that this prophecy was written *after* Samaria had been destroyed; see Notes on ch. vii. 9; xxviii. 1. ¶ *As Damascus.* The capital of Syria; see Note, ch. vii. 9, and the Analysis of ch. xvii. The LXX. have varied in their translation here considerably from the Hebrew. They render these verses, 'And he saith, Have I not taken the region beyond Babylon, and Chalane, where the tower was built? and I have taken Arabia, and Damascus, and Samaria.' The *main idea*, however—the *boast* of the king of Assyria, is retained.

10 As my hand hath found the kingdoms of the idols, and whose graven images did excel them of Jerusalem and of Samaria;

11 Shall I not, as I have done

unto Samaria and her idols, so do to Jerusalem and her idols?

12 Wherefore it shall come to pass, *that*, when the Lord hath performed his whole work upon

---

10, 11. The argument in these two verses is this: 'The nations which I have subdued were professedly under the protection of idol gods. Yet those idols were not able to defend them—though stronger than the gods worshipped by Jerusalem and Samaria. And is there any probability, therefore, that the protection on which you who are Jews are leaning, will be able to deliver you?' Jerusalem he regarded as an idolatrous city, like others; and as all others had hitherto been unable to retard his movements, he inferred that it would be so with Jerusalem. This is, therefore, the confident boasting of *a man* who regarded himself as able to vanquish all *the gods* that the nations worshipped. The same confident boasting he uttered when he sent messengers to Hezekiah; 2 Kings xix. 12: 'Have the gods of the nations delivered them which my father destroyed; as Gozan, and Haran, and Rezeph, and the children of Eden, which were in Thelasar?' Isa. xxxvi. 18–20: 'Hath any of the gods of the nations delivered his land out of the hand of the king of Assyria? Where are the gods of Hamath and of Arphad? Where are the gods of Sepharvaim? And have they delivered Samaria out of my hand?' ¶ *Hath found.* That is, 'I have found them unable to defend themselves by their trust in their idols, and have subdued them.' ¶ *The kingdoms of the idols.* The kingdoms that worship idols. ¶ *And whose graven images.* That is, whose idols; or whose representations of the gods. The word properly signifies that which is hewn or cut out; and then the block of wood, or stone, that is carved into an image of the god. Here it refers to the gods themselves, probably, as having been found to be impotent, though he supposed them to be more powerful than those of Jerusalem and Samaria. ¶ *Did excel.* Heb. 'More than Jerusalem,' where the preposition מ, *mem*, is used to denote comparison. They were *more* to be dreaded; or more mighty than

those of Jerusalem. ¶ *Of Jerusalem.* Jerusalem and Samaria had often been guilty of the worship of idols; and it is probable that Sennacherib regarded them as idolaters in the same sense as other nations. They had given occasion for this suspicion by their having often fallen into idolatrous habits; and the Assyrian monarch did not regard them as in any manner distinguished from surrounding nations. It is not improbable that he was aware that Jerusalem worshipped Jehovah (comp. Isa. xxxvi. 20); but he doubtless regarded Jehovah as a mere tutelary divinity—the peculiar god of that land, as Baal, Ashtaroth, &c., were of the countries in which they were adored. For it was a common doctrine among ancient idolaters, that each nation had its peculiar god; that the claims of that god were to be respected and regarded *in* that nation; and that thus all nations should worship their own gods undisturbed. Jehovah was thus regarded as the tutelary god of the Jewish nation. The sin of Sennacherib consisted in confounding Jehovah with false gods, and in then setting him at defiance.

11. *Shall I not*, &c. 'Shall I not meet with the same success at Jerusalem that I have elsewhere? As I have overcome all others, and as Jerusalem has no peculiar advantages; as the gods of other nations were more in number, and mightier than those of Jerusalem, and yet were unable to resist me; what is there in Jerusalem that can stay my progress?'

12. *Wherefore*, &c. In this verse God, by the prophet, threatens punishment to the king of Assyria for his pride, and wicked designs. ¶ *His whole work.* His entire plan in regard to the punishment of the Jews. He sent the king of Assyria for a specific purpose to execute his justice on the people of Jerusalem. That plan he would execute *entirely* by the hand of Sennacherib, and would *then* inflict deserved punishment on Sennacherib himself, for his

mount Zion and on Jerusalem, I will [1] punish [a] the fruit of the [2] stout heart of the king of Assyria, and the glory of his high [b] looks.

1 visit upon.   a Jer.50.15.

13 For he saith, By the strength of my hand I have done *it*, and by my wisdom; for I am prudent: and I have removed the bounds of the

2 greatness of the heart.   b Ps.18.27.

wicked purposes. ¶ *Upon mount Zion.* Mount Zion was a part of Jerusalem (see Note, ch. i. 8), but it was the residence of the court, the dwelling-place of David and his successors; and perhaps here, where it is mentioned as distinct from Jerusalem, it refers to the court, the princes, nobles, or the government. ' I will execute my purposes against the government, and the people of the city.' ¶ *I will punish.* Heb. ' I will visit;' but here, evidently used to denote punishment; see Note, ver. 3. ¶ *The fruit of the stout heart.* Heb. ' The fruit of the greatness of the heart.' The 'greatness of the heart,' is a Hebraism for pride of heart, or great swelling designs and plans formed in the heart. *Fruit* is that which a tree or the earth produces; and then anything which is produced or brought forth in any way. Here it means that which a proud heart had produced or designed, that is, plans of pride and ambition; schemes of conquest and of blood. ¶ *The glory of his high looks.* Heb. ' The glory of the lifting up of his eyes '— an expression indicative of pride and haughtiness. The word *glory*, here, evidently refers to the self-complacency, and the air of majesty and haughtiness, which a proud man assumes. In this verse we see—(1.) That God will accomplish all the purposes of which he designs to make wicked men the instruments. *Their* schemes shall be successful just so far as they may contribute to *his* plans, and no further. (2.) When that is done, they are completely in *his* power, and under his control. He can stay their goings when he pleases, and subdue them to his will. (3.) The fact that they have been made to further the plans of God, and to execute his designs, will not free them from deserved punishment. They meant not so; and they will be dealt with according to *their* intentions, and not according to God's design to overrule them. *Their* plans were wicked; and if God brings good out of them, it is

contrary to *their* intention; and hence, they are not to be screened from punishment because he brings good out of their plans, contrary to their designs. (4.) Wicked men *are in fact* often thus punished. Nothing is more common on earth; and all the woes of hell will be an illustration of the principle. Out of all evil God shall educe good; and even from the punishment of the damned themselves, he will take occasion to illustrate his own perfections, and, in that display of his just character, promote the happiness of holy beings.

13. *For he saith.* The king of Assyria saith. This verse and the following are designed to show the reason why the king of Assyria should be thus punished. It was on account of his pride, and wicked plans. He sought not the glory of God, but purposed to do evil. ¶ *For I am prudent.* I am wise; attributing his success to his own understanding, rather than to God. ¶ *I have removed the bounds of the people.* That is, ' I have changed the limits of kingdoms; I have taken away the old boundaries, and made new ones at my pleasure. I have divided them into kingdoms and provinces as I pleased.' No higher assumption of power could have been made than thus to have changed the ancient limits of empires, and remodelled them at his will. It was claiming that he had so extended his own empire, as to have effectually blotted out the ancient lines which had existed, so that they were now all one, and under his control. So a man who buys farms, and annexes them to his own, takes away the ancient limits; he runs new lines as he pleases, and unites them all into one. This was the claim which Sennacherib set up over the nations. ¶ *Have robbed their treasures.* Their hoarded wealth. This was another instance of the claim which he set up, of power and dominion. The treasures of kingdoms which had been hoarded for purposes of peace or war, he had plundered, and appropriated to his

people, and have robbed their treasures, and I have put down the inhabitants like [1] a valiant *man:*

14 And my hand hath found, as a nest, the riches of the people: and as one gathereth eggs *that are* left, have I gathered all the earth; and there was none that moved

[1] or, *many peopl3.*

the wing, or opened the mouth, or peeped.

15 Shall the axe boast itself against him that heweth therewith? or shall the saw magnify itself against him that shaketh it? as if the [2] rod should shake *itself* against them that lift it up, *or* as if the

[2] or, *a rod should shake them.*

own use; comp. Note on ch. xlvi. 3. ¶ *I have put down the inhabitants.* I have subdued them; have vanquished them. ¶ *As a valiant* man. כַּאֲבִיר. Marg. 'Many people.' The Keri, or Hebrew marginal reading, is כְּבִיר, without the א, 'a mighty, or, strong man.' The sense is not materially different. It is a claim that he had evinced might and valour in bringing down nations. Lowth renders it, ' Them that were strongly seated.' Noyes, 'Them that sat upon thrones.' The Chaldee renders the verse, not literally, but according to the sense, 'I have made people to migrate from province to province, and have plundered the cities that were the subjects of praise, and have brought down by strength those who dwelt in fortified places.' Our translation has given the sense correctly.

14. *And my hand hath found, as a nest.* By a beautiful and striking figure here, the Assyrian monarch is represented as describing the *ease* with which he had subdued kingdoms, and rifled them of their treasures. No resistance had been offered. He had taken them with as little opposition as a rustic takes possession of a nest, with its eggs or young, when the parent bird is away. ¶ *Eggs* that are *left.* That is, eggs that are left of the parent bird ; when the bird from fright, or any other cause, has gone, and when no resistance is offered. ¶ *Have I gathered all the earth.* That is, I have subdued and plundered it. This shows the height of his self-confidence and his arrogant assumptions. ¶ *That moved the wing.* Keeping up the figure of the nest. There was none that offered resistance ; as an angry bird does when her nest is about to be robbed. ¶ *Or opened the mouth.* To make a noise in alarm. The dread of him produced perfect silence and sub-

mission. ¶ *Or peeped.* Or that chirped —the noise made by young birds ; Note, ch. viii. 19. The idea is, that such was the dread of his name and power that there was universal silence. None dared to resist the terror of his arms.

15. *Shall the axe, &c.* In this verse God reproves the pride and arrogance of the Assyrian monarch. He does it by reminding him that he was the mere instrument in his hand, to accomplish *his* purposes ; and that it was just as absurd for him to boast of what he had done, as it would be for the axe to boast when *it* had been wielded with effect. In the axe there is no wisdom, no skill, no power ; and though it may lay the forest low, yet it is not by any skill or power which it possesses. So with the Assyrian monarch. Though nations had trembled at his power, yet he was in the hand of God, and had been directed by an unseen arm in accomplishing the designs of the Ruler of the universe. Though himself free, yet he was under the direction of God, and had been *so* directed as to accomplish *his* designs. ¶ *The saw magnify itself.* That is, boast or exalt itself *against* or *over* him that uses it. ¶ *That shaketh it.* Or moves it backwards and forwards, for the purpose of sawing. ¶ *As if the rod.* A rod is an instrument of chastisement or punishment ; and such God regarded the king of Assyria. ¶ *Should shake* itself, &c. The Hebrew, in this place, is as in the margin : ' A rod should shake them that lift it up.' But the sense is evidently retained in our translation, as this accords with all the other members of the verse, where the leading idea is, the absurdity that a mere instrument should exalt itself against him who makes use of it. In this manner the preposition עַל *over,* or *against,* is evidently understood

staff should lift up ¹ *itself, as if it were* no wood.

16 Therefore *ᵃ* shall the Lord, the LORD of hosts, send among his fat ones *ᵇ* leanness; and under his

1 or, *that which is not wood.*   *a* Acts 12.23.

So the Vulgate and the Syriac. ¶ *The staff.* This word here is synonymous with *rod*, and denotes an instrument of chastisement. ¶ *As if it were no wood.* That is, as if it were a moral agent, itself the actor or deviser of what it is made to do. It would be impossible to express more strongly the idea intended here, that the Assyrian was a mere instrument in the hand of God to accomplish *his* purposes, and to be employed at his will. The statement of this truth is designed to humble him : and if there be *any* truth that will humble sinners, it is, that they are in the hands of God ; that he will accomplish his purposes by them ; that when they are laying plans against him, he will overrule them for his own glory ; and that they will be arrested, restrained, or directed, just as he pleases. Man, in his schemes of pride and vanity, therefore, should not boast. He is under the God of nations ; and it is one part of his administration, to control and govern ALL THE INTELLECT IN THE UNIVERSE. In all these passages, however, there is not the slightest intimation that the Assyrian was not *free*. There is no fate ; no compulsion. He regarded himself as a free moral agent ; he did what he pleased ; he never supposed that he was urged on by any power that violated his own liberty. If he did what he pleased, he was free. And so it is with all sinners. They do as they please. They form and execute such plans as they choose ; and God overrules *their* designs to accomplish his own purposes. The Targum of Jonathan has given the sense of this passage ; ' Shall the axe boast against him who uses it, saying, I have cut [wood] ; or the saw boast against him who moves it, saying, I have sawed ? When the rod is raised to smite, it is not the rod that smites, but he who smites with it.'

16. *Therefore shall the Lord.* Heb. אָדוֹן *Adŏn.* ¶ *The Lord of hosts.* In the present Hebrew text, the original

glory he shall kindle a burning like the burning of a fire.

17 And the light of Israel shall be for a fire, *ᶜ* and his Holy One for a flame ; and it shall burn and

b Ps. 106.15.   *c* Heb. 12.29.

word is also אֲדֹנָי *adŏnâi,* but fifty-two MSS. and six editions read JEHOVAH. On the meaning of the phrase, *the Lord of hosts,* see Note, ch. i. 9. This verse contains a threatening of the punishment that would come upon the Assyrian for his insolence and pride, and the remainder of the chapter is mainly occupied with the details of that punishment. The punishment here threatened is, that while he appeared to be a victor, and was boasting of success and of his plunder, God would send leanness—as a body becomes wasted with disease. ¶ *His fat ones.* That is, those who had *fattened* on the spoils of victory ; his vigorous, prosperous, and flourishing army. The prophet here evidently intends to describe his numerous army glutted with the trophies of victory, and revelling on the spoils. ¶ *Leanness.* They shall be emaciated and reduced ; their vigour and strength shall be diminished. In Ps. cvi. 15, the word *leanness,* רָזוֹן *râzōn,* is used to denote destruction, disease. In Mic. vi. 10, it denotes diminution, scantiness—' the scant ephah.' Here it denotes, evidently, that the army which was so large and vigorous, should waste away as with a pestilential disease ; comp. ver. 19. The *fact* was, that of that vast host few escaped. The angel of the Lord slew 185,000 men in a single night ; 2 Kings xviii. 35 ; see Notes on ch. xxxviii. 36. ¶ *And under his glory.* That is, beneath the boasted honour, might, and magnificence of the proud monarch. ¶ *He shall kindle.* That is, God shall suddenly and entirely destroy his magnificence and pride, as when a fire is kindled beneath a magnificent temple. A similar passage occurs in Zech. xii. 6 :

In that day I will make the governors of Judah
Like a hearth of fire among the wood,
And like a torch of fire in a sheaf ;
And they shall devour all the people round about.

17. *And the light of Israel.* That is, JEHOVAH. The word *light* here, אוֹר, is used also to denote a *fire,* or that

devour his thorns and his briers in one *a* day.

18 And shall consume the glory of his forest, and of his fruitful

field, 1 both soul and body: and they shall be as when a standard-bearer fainteth.

a ch.37.36.   1 *from the soul, and even to the flesh.*

---

which causes light and heat; see Ezek. v. 2; Isa. xliv. 16; xlvii. 14. Here it is used in the same sense, denoting that JEHOVAH would be *the fire* (אוֹר) that would cause the *flame* (שֵׁשׁ) which would consume the Assyrian. JEHOVAH is often compared to a burning flame, or fire; Deut. iv. 24; ix. 3; Heb. xii. 29. ¶ *Shall be for a fire.* By his power and his judgment he shall destroy them. ¶ *His Holy One.* Israel's Holy One; that is, JEHOVAH—often called in the Scriptures the Holy One of Israel. ¶ *And it shall burn.* That is, the flame that JEHOVAH shall kindle, or his judgments that he shall send forth. ¶ *And devour his thorns and his briers.* An expression denoting the utter impotency of all the mighty armies of the Assyrian to resist JEHOVAH. As dry thorns and briers cannot resist the action of heat, so certainly and speedily would the armies of Sennacherib be destroyed before JEHOVAH; comp. Note, ch. ix. 18. Lowth supposes, that by 'briers and thorns'·here, the common soldiers of the army are intended, and by 'the glory of his forest' (ver. 18), the princes, officers, and nobles. This is, doubtless, the correct interpretation; and the idea is, that all would be completely consumed and destroyed. ¶ *In one day.* The army of Sennacherib was suddenly destroyed by the angel; see Notes on ch. xxxvii. 36.

18. *The glory of his forest.* In these expressions, the army of Sennacherib is compared with a beautiful grove thick set with trees; and as all the beauty of a grove which the fire overruns is destroyed, so, says the prophet, it will be with the army of the Assyrian under the judgments of God. If the 'briers and thorns' (ver. 17) refer to the common soldiers of his army, then the glory of the forest—the tall, majestic trees—refer to the princes and nobles. But this mode of interpretation should not be pressed too far. ¶ *And of his fruitful field.* וְכַרְמִלּוֹ. The word used here—*carmel*—is applied commonly to

a rich mountain or promontory on the Mediterranean, on the southern boundary of the tribe of Asher. The word, however, properly means a fruitful field, a finely cultivated country, and was given to Mount Carmel on this account, In this place it has no reference to that mountain, but is given to the army of Sennacherib to *keep up the figure* which the prophet commenced in ver. 17. That army, numerous, mighty, and well disciplined, was compared to an extensive region of hill and vale; of forests and fruitful fields; but it should all be destroyed as when the fire runs over fields and forests, and consumes all their beauty. Perhaps in all this, there may be allusion to the proud boast of Sennacherib (2 Kings xix. 23), that he would 'go up the sides of Lebanon, and cut down the cedars thereof, and the choice fir-trees thereof, and enter into the forest of Carmel.' In allusion, possibly, to this, the prophet says that God would cut down the tall trees and desolate the fruitful field—the 'carmel' of his army, and would lay all waste. ¶ *Both soul and body.* Heb. 'From the soul to the flesh;' *i.e.*, entirely. As the soul and the flesh, or body, compose the entire man, so the phrase denotes the *entireness* or *totality* of anything. The army would be totally ruined. ¶ *And they shall be as when a standard-bearer fainteth.* There is here a great variety of interpretation. The LXX. read it, 'And he shall flee as one that flees from a burning flame.' This reading Lowth has followed; but for this there is not the slightest authority in the Hebrew. The Vulgate reads it, 'And he shall fly for terror,' *et erit terrore profugus.* The Chaldee, 'And he shall be broken, and shall fly.' The Syriac, 'And he shall be as if he had never been.' Probably the correct idea is, *and they shall be as when a sick man wastes away.* The words which are used (כִּמְסֹס נֹסֵס) are brought together for the sake of a *paronomasia*—a figure of speech common in the Hebrew. The word rendered in our

19 And the rest of the trees of his forest shall be [1] few, that a child may write them.

20 And it shall come to pass in that day, *that* the remnant of Israel,

1 *number.*

and such as are escaped of the house of Jacob, shall no more again stay upon him that smote them; but *a* shall stay upon the *b* LORD, the Holy One of Israel, in truth.

a 2 Chro.28.20.   *b* Hos.14.3.

---

version *fainteth* (מְסֹס *mĕsōs*) is probably the infinitive construct of the verb מָסַס *māsăs*, to melt, dissolve, faint. It is applied to the manna that was dissolved by the heat of the sun, Ex. xvi. 21; to wax melted by the fire, Ps. lxviii. 2; to a snail that consumes away, Ps. lviii. 8; or to water that evaporates, Ps. lviii. 7. Hence it is applied to the heart, exhausted of its vigour and spirit, Job vii. 5; to things decayed that have lost their strength, 1 Sam. xv. 9; to a loan or tax laid upon a people that wastes and exhausts their wealth. It has the general notion, therefore, of melting, fainting, sinking away with the loss of strength; Ps. xxii. 14; cxii. 10; xcvii. 5; Isa. xix. 1; xiii. 7; Josh. ii. 11; v. 1; vii. 5. The word rendered standard-bearer (נֹסֵס) is from the verb נָסַס *nāsăs*. This word signifies sometimes *to lift up*, to elevate, or to erect a flag or standard to public view, to call men to arms; Isa. v. 26; xi. 10, 12; xiii. 2; xviii. 3; xlix. 22; and also to lift up, or to exhibit anything as a judgment or public warning, and may thus be applied to Divine judgments. Gesenius renders the verb, *to waste away, to be sick*. In Syriac it has this signification. Taylor (*Heb. Con.*) says, that it does not appear that this word ever has the signification of a military standard under which armies fight, but refers to a standard or ensign to *call* men together, or to indicate alarm and danger. The probable signification here, is that which refers it to a man wasting away with sickness, whose strength and vigour are gone, and who becomes weak and helpless. Thus applied to the Assyrian army, it is very striking. Though mighty, confident, and vigorous—like a man in full health—yet it would be like a vigorous man when disease comes upon him, and he pines away and sinks to the grave.

19. *And the rest of the trees, &c.* Keeping up still the image of a large

and once dense forest, to which he had likened the Assyrian army. ' *The rest* ' here means that which shall be left after the threatened judgment shall come upon them. ¶ *That a child may write them.* That a child shall be able to number them, or write their names; that is, they shall be very few. A child can number or count but few; yet the number of those who would be left, would be so very small that even a child could count them with ease. It is probable that a few of the army of Sennacherib escaped (see Note, ch. xxxvii. 37); and compared with the whole army, the remnant might bear a striking resemblance to the few decaying trees of a once magnificent forest of cedars.

20. *And it shall come to pass.* The prophet proceeds to state the effect on the Jews, of the judgment that would overtake the army of the Assyrian. One of those effects, as stated in this verse, would be, that they would be led to see that it was in vain to look to the Assyrians any more for aid, or to form any further alliance with them, but that they should trust in the Lord alone. ¶ *The remnant of Israel.* Those that would be left after the Assyrian had invaded and desolated the land. ¶ *Shall no more again stay.* Shall no more depend on them. Alliances had been formed with the Assyrians for aid, and they had resulted as all alliances formed between the friends and the enemies of God do. They are observed as long as it is for the interest or the convenience of God's enemies to observe them; and then his professed friends are made the victims of persecution, invasion, and ruin. ¶ *Upon him that smote them.* Upon the Assyrian, who was about to desolate the land. The calamities which he would bring upon them would be the main thing which would open their eyes, and lead them to forsake the alliance. One design of God's permitting the Assyrians to invade the land, was, to punish them

21 The remnant *a* shall return,
even the remnant of Jacob, unto
the mighty God.

22 For though thy people Israel

a ch. 6.13; 65.8,9.　　*b* Ro.9.27,28.　　1 *in, or, among.*

be as the sand of the sea, *yet* *b* a
remnant 1 of them shall return: the
consumption *c* decreed shall overflow 2 with righteousness.

c ch.28.22; Dan.9.27.　　2 or, *in.*

for this alliance, and to induce them to
trust in God. ¶ *But shall stay,* &c.
They shall depend upon JEHOVAH, or
shall trust in him for protection and
defence. ¶ *The Holy One of Israel;*
see ver. 17. ¶ *In truth.* They shall
serve him sincerely and heartily, not
with feigned or divided service. They
shall be so fully satisfied that the Assyrian cannot aid them, and be so severely
punished for ever, having formed an
alliance with him, that they shall now
return to JEHOVAH, and become his
sincere worshippers. In this verse,
the prophet refers, doubtless, to the
times of Hezekiah, and to the extensive
reformation, and general prevalence of
piety, which would take place under his
reign; 2 Chron. xxxii. 22–33. Vitringa,
Cocceius, Schmidius, &c., however, refer
this to the time of the Messiah; Vitringa
supposing that the prophet refers *immediately* to the times of Hezekiah, but *in
a secondary sense,* for the complete fulfilment of the prophecy, to the times of
the Messiah. But it is not clear that
he had reference to any other period
than that which would immediately
follow the invasion of Sennacherib.

21. *The remnant,* &c. That is, those
who shall be left after the invasion of
Sennacherib. ¶ *Shall return.* Shall
abandon their idolatrous rites and places
of worship, and shall worship the true
God. ¶ *The mighty God.* The God
that had evinced his power in overcoming and destroying the armies of
Sennacherib.

22. *For though,* &c. In this verse,
and in ver. 23, the prophet expresses
positively the idea that *but* a remnant
of the people should be preserved amidst
the calamities. He had said (ver. 20,
21), that a remnant should return to
God. He now carries forward the idea,
and states that *only* a remnant should
be preserved out of the multitude, however great it was. Admitting that the
number was then very great, yet the
great mass of the nation would be cut
off, and only a small portion would re-

main. ¶ *Thy people Israel.* Or rather,
' thy people, O Israel,' making it a direct
address to the Jews, rather than to God.
¶ *Be as the sand of the sea.* The sands
of the sea cannot be numbered, and
hence the expression is used in the Bible
to denote a number indefinitely great;
Ps. cxix. 18; Gen. xxii. 17; xli. 49; Josh
xi. 4; Judg. vii. 12; 1 Sam. xiii. 5, &c.
¶ *Yet a remnant.* The word *yet* has
been supplied by the translators, and
evidently obscures the sense. The idea
is, that a remnant ONLY—a very small
portion of the whole, should be preserved.
Though they were exceedingly numerous
as a nation, yet the mass of the nation
would be cut off, or carried into captivity, and only a few would be left. ¶ *Shall
return.* That is, shall be saved from
destruction, and return by repentance
unto God, ver. 21. Or, if it has reference to the approaching captivity of
the nation, it means that but a few of
them would return from captivity to the
land of their fathers. ¶ *The consumption.* The general sense of this is plain.
The prophet is giving a reason why only
a few of them would return, and he says,
that the judgment which God had determined on was inevitable, and would overflow the land in justice. As God had
determined this, their *numbers* availed
nothing, but the consumption would be
certainly accomplished. The word *consumption* (כִּלָּיוֹן from כָּלָה *kâlâ* to
complete, to finish, to waste away,
vanish, disappear) denotes a languishing, or wasting away, as in disease;
and then *destruction,* or that which
completes life and prosperity. It denotes
such a series of judgments as would be
a *completion* of the national prosperity,
or as should *terminate* it entirely.
¶ *Decreed.* הָרוּץ *hhârûtz.* The word
here used is derived from הָרַץ *hhârâtz,*
to sharpen, or bring to a point; to rend,
tear, lacerate; to be quick, active,
diligent; and then to decide, determine,
decree; because that which is decreed
is brought to a point, or issue.— *Taylor.*

23 For the Lord God of hosts shall make a consumption, even determined, in the midst of all the land.

24 Therefore thus saith the Lord God of hosts, O my people that

dwellest in Zion, be not *a* afraid of the Assyrian : he shall smite thee with a rod, [1] and shall lift up his staff against thee, after the manner of Egypt.

a ch.37.6.   [1] *but he shall.*

It evidently means here, that it was fixed upon or decreed in the mind of God, and that being thus decreed, it must certainly take place. ¶ *Shall overflow.* שׁוֹטֵף *shŏtēph.* This word is usually applied to an inundation, when a stream rises above its banks and overflows the adjacent land ; Isa. xxx. 28; lxvi. 12; Ps. lxxviii. 20. Here it means evidently, that the threatened judgment would spread like an overflowing river through the land, and would accomplish the devastation which God had determined. ¶ *With righteousness.* With justice, or in the infliction of justice. Justice would abound or overflow, and the consequence would be, that the nation would be desolated.

23. *For the Lord God of hosts ;* Note, ch. i. 9. ¶ *Shall make a consumption.* The Hebrew of this verse might be rendered, 'for its [destruction] is completed, and is determined on ; the Lord Jehovah of hosts will execute it in the midst of the land.' Our translation, however, expresses the force of the original. It means that the destruction was fixed in the mind or purpose of God, and would be certainly executed. The translation by the LXX., which is followed in the main by the apostle Paul in quoting this passage, is somewhat different. ' For he will finish the work, and cut it short in righteousness ; for a short work will the Lord make in the whole habitable world '—ἐν τῇ οἰκουμένῃ ὅλῃ ; as quoted by Paul, 'upon the earth' —ἐπὶ τῆς γῆς. For the manner in which this passage is quoted by Paul, see Notes on Rom. ix. 27, 28. ¶ *In the midst of all the land.* That is, the land of Israel, for the threatened judgment extended no further.

24. *Therefore, &c.* In this verse the prophet returns to the main subject of this prophecy, which is to comfort the people of Jerusalem with the assurance that the army of the Assyrian would be destroyed. ¶ *O my people.* An expres-

sion of tenderness, showing that God regarded them as his children, and notwithstanding the judgments that he would bring upon them for their sins. In the midst of severe judgments, God speaks the language of tenderness; and, even when he punishes, has towards his people the feelings of a father ; Heb. xii. 5–11. ¶ *That dwelleth in Zion.* Literally, in mount Zion ; but here taken for the whole city of Jerusalem ; see Note, ch. i. 8. ¶ *Be not afraid,* &c. For his course shall be arrested, and he shall be repelled and punished ; ver. 25–27. ¶ *He shall smite thee.* He shall, indeed, smite thee, but shall not utterly destroy thee. ¶ *And shall lift up his staff.* Note, ver. 5. The *staff* here is regarded as an instrument of punishment ; comp. Note, ch. ix. 4 ; and the sense is, that by his invasion, and by his exactions, he would oppress and punish the nation. ¶ *After the manner of Egypt.* Heb. ' In the way of Egypt.' Some interpreters have supposed that this means that Sennacherib would oppress and afflict the Jews in his going down to Egypt, or on his way thither to attack the Egyptians. But the more correct interpretation is that which is expressed in our translation—*after the manner of Egypt.* That is, the nature of his oppressions shall be like those which the Egyptians under Pharaoh inflicted on the Jews. There are *two* ideas evidently implied here. (1.) That the oppression would be heavy and severe. Those which their fathers experienced in Egypt were exceedingly burdensome and cruel. So it would be in the calamities that the Assyrian would bring upon them. But, (2.) their fathers had been delivered from the oppressions of the Egyptians. And so it would be now. The Assyrian would oppress them ; but God would deliver and save them. The phrase, ' in the way of,' is used to denote *after the manner of,* or, as an example, in Amos iv. 10, ' I have sent among you

25 For yet a very little while, and the indignation *a* shall cease, and mine anger in their *b* destruction.

26 And the LORD of hosts shall stir up a scourge for him, according to the slaughter of Midian *c* at the

rock of Oreb: and *as* his rod *was* upon the sea, so shall he lift it up after the manner of Egypt.

27 And it shall come to pass in that day, *that* his burden shall [1] be taken away from off thy shoulder, and thy yoke from off thy neck, and

a Dan.11.36.   b 2 Ki.19.35.   c Judg.7.25.   1 remove.

the pestilence after the manner of Egypt;' Heb. ' In the way of Egypt;' comp. Ezek. xx. 30.

25. *For yet a very little while.* This is designed to console them with the hope of deliverance. The threatened invasion was brief, and was soon ended by the pestilence that swept off the greater part of the army of the Assyrian. ¶ *The indignation shall cease.* The anger of God against his offending people shall come to an end ; his purposes of chastisement shall be completed; and the land shall be delivered. ¶ *In their destruction.* עַל־תַּבְלִיתָם from בָּלָה *bâlâ,* to wear out ; to consume ; to be annihilated. It means here, that his anger would terminate in the entire annihilation of their power to injure them. Such was the complete overthrow of Sennacherib by the pestilence; 2 Kings xix. 35. The word here used, occurs in this form in no other place in the Hebrew Bible, though the verb is used, and other forms of the noun. *The verb,* Deut. vii. 4; xxix. 5 ; Josh. ix. 13 ; Neh. ix. 21, &c. *Nouns,* Ezek. xxiii. 43 ; Isa. xxxviii. 17 ; Jer. xxxviii. 11, 12 ; Isa. xvii. 14, *et al.*

26. *And the* LORD *of hosts shall stir up.* Or shall raise up that which shall prove as a scourge to him. ¶ *A scourge for him.* That is, that which shall punish him. The scourge, or rod, is used to denote severe punishment of any kind. The nature of this punishment is immediately specified. ¶ *According to the slaughter of Midian.* That is, as the Midianites were discomfited and punished. There is reference here, doubtless, to the discomfiture and slaughter of the Midianites by Gideon, as recorded in Judg. vii. 24, 25. That was signal and entire ; and the prophet means to say, that the destruction of the Assyrian would be also signal and total. The country of Midian, or Ma-

dian, was on the east side of the Elanitic branch of the Red Sea ; but it extended also north along the desert of mount Seir to the country of the Moabites ; see Note on ch. lx. 6. ¶ *At the rock of Oreb.* At this rock, Gideon slew the two princes of the Midianites, Oreb and Zeeb (Judg. vii. 25) ; and from this circumstance, probably, the name was given to the rock : Lev. xi. 15 ; Deut. xiv. 14. It was on the east side of the Jordan. ¶ *And as his rod,* &c. That is, as God punished the Egyptians in the Red Sea. ¶ *So shall he lift it up after the manner of Egypt.* As God overthrew the Egyptians in the Red Sea, so shall he overthrow and destroy the Assyrian. By these two comparisons, therefore, the prophet represents the complete destruction of the Assyrian army. In both of these cases, the enemies of the Jews had been completely overthrown, and so it would be in regard to the hosts of the Assyrian.

27. *His burden shall be taken away.* The oppressions and exactions of the Assyrian. ¶ *From off thy shoulder.* We bear a burden on the shoulder ; and hence any grievous exaction or oppression is represented as borne upon the shoulder. ¶ *And his yoke,* &c. Another image denoting deliverance from oppression and calamity. ¶ *And the yoke shall be destroyed because of the anointing.* In the interpretation of these words, expositors have greatly differed. The Hebrew is literally, ' From the face of oil,' מִפְּנֵי־שָׁמֶן. The Vulgate renders it, literally, *à facie olei.* The LXX. ' His fear shall be taken from thee, and his yoke *from thy shoulders.*' The Syriac, ' His yoke shall be broken before the oxen.' The Chaldee Paraphrase, ' The people shall be broken before the Messiah.' Lowth renders it, ' The yoke shall perish from off your shoulders ;' following the Septuagint. Grotius sug-

the yoke shall be destroyed because of the *a* anointing.

28 He is come to Aiath, he is

passed to Migron; at Michmash he hath laid up his carriages:

a Dan.9.24.

gests that it means that the yoke which the Assyrians had imposed upon the Jews would be broken by Hezekiah, the king who had been anointed with oil. Jarchi also supposes that it refers to one who was anointed—to the king; and many interpreters have referred it to the Messiah, as the anointed of God. Vitringa supposes that the Holy Spirit is here intended. Kimchi supposes, that the figure is derived from the effect of oil on wood in destroying its consistency, and loosening its fibres; and that the expression means, that the yoke would be broken or dissolved as if it were penetrated with oil. But this is ascribing a property to oil which it does not possess. Archbishop Secker supposes that, instead of *oil*, the text should read *shoulder*, by a slight change in the Hebrew. But for this conjectural reading there is no authority. Cocceius supposes, that the word *oil* here means *fatness*, and is used to denote prosperity and wealth, and that the prophet means to say, that the Assyrian would be corrupted and destroyed by the great amount of wealth which he would amass. The Rabbins say, that this deliverance was wrought on account of the great quantity of oil which Hezekiah caused to be consumed in the synagogues for the study of the law—a striking instance of the weak and puerile methods of interpretation which they have everywhere evinced. I confess that none of these explanations seem to me to be satisfactory, and that I do not know what is the meaning of the expression.

28. *He is come to Aiath.* These verses (28–32) contain a description of the march of the army of Sennacherib as he approached Jerusalem to invest it. The description is expressed with great beauty. It is rapid and hurried, and is such as one would give who was alarmed by the sudden and near approach of an enemy—as if, while the narrator was stating that the invader had arrived at one place, he had already come to another; or, as if while one messenger should say, that he had come to one

place, another should answer that he was still nearer, and a third, that he was nearer still, so as to produce universal consternation. The prophet speaks of this as if he *saw* it (comp. Note, ch. i.); as if, with the glance of the eye, he sees Sennacherib advancing rapidly to Jerusalem. The general course of this march is from the north-east to the south-west towards Jerusalem, and it is possible still to follow the route by the names of the places here mentioned, and which remain at present. All the places are in the vicinity of Jerusalem, and this shows how much his rapid approach was fitted to excite alarm. The name *Aiath* עַיָּת does not occur elsewhere; but *Ai* עַי is often mentioned, and *Aijah* עַיָּא is found in Neh. xi. 31. Doubtless, the same city is meant. It was situated near Bethel eastward; Josh. vii. 2. It was at this place that Joshua was repulsed on account of the sin of Achaz, though the city was afterwards taken by Joshua, the king seized and hanged, and the city destroyed. It was afterwards rebuilt, and is often mentioned; Ezra ii. 28; Neh. vii. 32. It is called by the LXX. Ἀγγαι; and by Josephus, *Aina.* In the time of Eusebius and Jerome, its site and scanty ruins were still pointed out, not far distant from Bethel towards the east. The name, however, has at present wholly perished, and no trace of the place now remains. It is probable that it was near the modern Deir Diwân, about three miles to the east of Bethel; see Robinson's *Bib. Researches,* ii. pp. 119, 312, 313. ¶ *He is passed to Migron.* That is, he does not remain at Aiath, but is advancing rapidly towards Jerusalem. This place is mentioned in 1 Sam. xiv. 2, from which it appears that it was near Gibeah, and was in the boundaries of the tribe of Benjamin, to the southwest of Ai and Bethel. No trace of this place now remains. ¶ *At Michmash.* This was a town within the tribe of Ephraim, on the confines of Benjamin; Ezra ii. 27; Neh. vii. 31. This place is now called Mukhmâs, and is situated on a slope or

29 They are gone over the passage: they have taken up their
lodging at Geba; Ramah *a* is afraid;
Gibeah of Saul is fled.

a Jer. 31. 15.

low ridge of land between two small
wadys, or water-courses. It is now
desolate, but bears the marks of having
been a much larger and stronger place
than the other towns in the neighbourhood. There are many foundations of
hewn stones; and some columns are
lying among them. It is about nine
miles to the north-east of Jerusalem,
and in the immediate neighbourhood
of Gibeah and Ramah. — Robinson's
Bib. Researches, ii. p. 117. In the
time of Eusebius it was a large village.
— *Onomast.* Art. *Machmas.* ¶ *He
hath laid up his carriages.* Heb.
'He hath deposited his weapons.' The
word rendered *hath laid up*—יִפְקִיד—
may possibly mean, *he reviewed*, or he
took an account of; that is, he made
that the place of *review* preparatory to
his attack on Jerusalem. Jerome says,
that the passage means, that he had
such confidence of taking Jerusalem,
that he deposited his armour at Michmash, as being unnecessary in the siege
of Jerusalem. I think, however, that
the passage means simply, that he had
made Michmash one of his *stations* to
which he had come, and that the expression 'he hath deposited his armour
there,' denotes merely that he had come
there as one of his stations, and had
pitched his camp in that place on the
way to Jerusalem. The English word
carriage, sometimes meant formerly,
that which is carried, baggage, vessels,
furniture, &c. — *Webster.* In this
sense it is used in this place, and also
in 1 Sam. xvii. 22; Acts xxi. 15.

29. *They are gone over the passage.*
The word *passage* (מַעְבָּרָה) may refer
to any passage or ford of a stream, a
shallow part of a river where crossing
was practicable; or it may refer to any
narrow pass, or place of passing in
mountains. The Chaldee Paraphrase
renders this, 'They have passed the
Jordan;' but this cannot be the meaning, as all the transactions referred to
here occurred in the vicinity of Jerusalem, and long after they had crossed the
Jordan. In 1 Sam. xiii. 23, the ' passage of Michmash' is mentioned as the
boundary of the garrison of the Philistines. Between Jeb'a and Mükhmâs
there is now a steep, precipitous valley,
which is probably the 'passage' here
referred to. This wady, or valley, runs
into another that joins it on the north,
and then issues out upon the plain not
far from Jericho. In the valley are
two hills of a conical form, having steep
rocky sides, which are probably the
rocks mentioned, in connection with
Jonathan's adventure, as a narrow defile
or way between the rock Bozez on the
one side, and Seneh on the other;
1 Sam. xiv. 4, 5. This valley appears
at a later time to have been the dividing line between the tribes of Ephraim
and Benjamin, for Geba on the south
side of this valley was the northern
limit of Judah and Benjamin (2 Kings
xxiii. 8); while Bethel on its north side
was on the southern border of Ephraim;
Judg. xvi. 1, 2.—Robinson's *Bib. Researches*, ii. p. 116. Of course it was
an important place, and could be easily
guarded—like the strait of Thermo-
pylæ. By his having passed this place
is denoted an advance towards Jerusalem, showing that nothing impeded his
progress, and that he was rapidly hastening with his army to the city. ¶ *They
have taken up their lodging at Geba.*
They have pitched their camp there,
being entirely *through* the defile of
Michmash. Heb. 'Geba is a lodging
place for us;' that is, for the Assyrians.
Perhaps, however, there is an error in
the common Hebrew text here, and
that it should be לָמוֹ *lâmō*, 'for them,'
instead of לָנוּ *lânû*, 'for us.' The LXX.
and the Chaldee so read it, so our
translators have understood it. *Geba*
here is not be confounded with ' Gibeah
of Saul,' mentioned just after. It was
in the tribe of Benjamin (1 Kings xv.
22); and was on the line, or nearly on
the line, of Judah, so as to be its northern boundary; 2 Kings xxiii. 8. It was
not far from Gibeah, or Gibeon. There
are at present no traces of the place
known. ¶ *Ramah.* This city was in

30 Lift [1] up thy voice, O daughter

1 *cry shrill with.*

the tribe of Benjamin. It was between Geba and Gibea. It was called *Ramah,* from its being on elevated ground; comp. Note, Matt. ii. 18. Ramah, now called *er-Râm,* lies on a high hill a little east of the road from Jerusalem to Bethel. It is now a miserable village, with few houses, and these in the summer mostly deserted. There are here large square stones, and also columns scattered about in the fields, indicating an ancient place of some importance. A small mosque is here with columns, which seems once to have been a church. Its situation is very conspicuous, and commands a fine prospect. It is near Gibeah, about six Roman miles from Jerusalem. So Jerome, *Comm.* in Hos. v. 8: ' Rama quæ est juxta Gabaa in septimo lapide a Jerosolymis sita.' Josephus places it at forty stadia from Jerusalem; *Ant.* viii. 12, 3. ¶ *Is afraid.* Is terrified and alarmed at the approach of Sennacherib —a beautiful variation in the description, denoting his rapid and certain advance on the city of Jerusalem, spreading consternation everywhere. ¶ *Gibeah of Saul.* This was called ' Gibeah of Saul,' because it was the birthplace of Saul (1 Sam. xi. 4; xv. 34; 2 Sam. xxi. 6); and to distinguish it from Gibea in the tribe of Judah (Josh. xv. 57); and also a Gibeah where Eleazar was buried; Josh. xxiv. 33. Jerome mentions Gibeah as in his day level with the ground.— *Epis.* 86, *ad Eustoch.* It has been almost wholly, since his time, unnoticed by travellers. It is probably the same as the modern village of Jeba, lying in a direction to the southwest of Mŭkhmâs. This village is small, and is half in ruins. Among these there are occasionally seen large hewn stones, indicating antiquity. There is here the ruin of a small tower almost solid, and a small building having the appearance of an ancient church. It is an elevated place from which several villages are visible.— Robinson's *Bib. Researches,* ii. p. 113. ¶ *Is fled.* That is, the inhabitants have fled. Such was the consternation produced by the march of the army of Sennacherib, that the city

of Gallim: cause it to be heard unto Laish, O poor Anathoth.

was thrown into commotion, and left empty.

30. *Lift up thy voice.* That is, cry aloud from alarm and terror. The prophet here changes the manner of describing the advance of Sennacherib. He had described his rapid march from place to place (ver. 28, 29), and the consternation at Ramah and Gibeah; he now changes the mode of description, and calls on Gallim to lift up her voice of alarm at the approach of the army, so that it might reverberate among the hills, and be heard by neighbouring towns. ¶ *Daughter.* A term often applied to a beautiful city or town; see Note on ch. i. 8. ¶ *Gallim.* This was a city of Benjamin, north of Jerusalem. It is mentioned only in this place and in 1 Sam. xxv. 44. No traces of this place are now to be found. ¶ *Cause it to be heard.* That is, cause thy voice to be heard. Raise the cry of distress and alarm. ¶ *Unto Laish.* There was a city of this name in the northern part of Palestine, in the bounds of the tribe of Dan; Judg. xviii. 7, 29. But it is contrary to all the circumstances of the case to suppose, that the prophet refers to a place in the north of Palestine. It was probably a small village in the neighbourhood of Gallim. There are at present no traces of the village; in 1 Mac. ix. 9, a city of this name is mentioned in the vicinity of Jerusalem, which is, doubtless, the one here referred to. ¶ *O poor Anathoth.* Anathoth was a city of Benjamin (Josh. xxi. 18), where Jeremiah was born; Jer. i. 1. 'Anàta, which is, doubtless, the same place here intended, is situated on a broad ridge of land, at the distance of one hour and a quarter, or about three miles, from Jerusalem. Josephus describes Anathoth as twenty stadia distant from Jerusalem (*Ant.* x. 7, 3); and Eusebius and Jerome mention it as about three miles to the north of the city. 'Anàta appears to have been once a walled town, and a place of strength. Portions of the wall still remain, built of large hewn stones, and apparently ancient, as are also the foundations of some of the houses. The houses are few, and the people are poor

31 Madmenah is removed; the inhabitants of Gebim gather themselves to flee.

32 As yet shall he remain at Nob that day: he shall shake his hand *against* the mount of the daughter of Zion, the hill of Jerusalem.

---

and miserable. From this point there is an extensive view over the whole eastern slope of the mountainous country of Benjamin, including all the valley of the Jordan, and the northern part of the Dead Sea. From this place, also, several of the villages here mentioned are visible. — Robinson's *Bib. Researches,* ii. pp. 109–111. The word *poor,* applied to it here (עֲנִיָּה) denotes *afflicted,* oppressed; and the language is that of pity, on account of the impending calamity, and is not designed to be descriptive of its ordinary state. The language in the Hebrew is a paranomasia, a species of writing quite common in the sacred writings; see Gen. i. 2; iv. 12; Isa. xxviii. 10, 13; Joel i. 15; Isa. xxxii. 7; Micah i. 10, 14; Zeph. ii. 4; comp. Stuart's *Heb. Gram.* Ed. 1, § 246. The figure abounded not only in the Hebrew but among the Orientals generally. Lowth reads this, 'Answer her, O Anathoth;' following in this the Syriac version, which reads the word rendered poor (עֲנִיָּה) as a verb from עָנָה *ânâ,* to answer, or respond, and supposes that the idea is retained of an *echo,* or reverberation among the hills, from which he thinks *Anathoth,* from the same verb, took its name. But the meaning of the Hebrew text is that given in our translation. The simple idea is that of neighbouring cities and towns lifting up the voice of alarm, at the approach of the enemy.

31. *Madmenah.* This city is mentioned nowhere else. The city of Madmanna, or Medemene, mentioned in Josh. xv. 31, was in the bounds of the tribe of Simeon, and was far south, towards Gaza. It cannot be the place intended here. ¶ *Is removed.* Or, the inhabitants have fled from fear; see ver. 29. ¶ *Gebim.* This place is unknown. It is nowhere else mentioned. ¶ *Gather themselves to flee.* A description of the alarm prevailing at the approach of Sennacherib.

32. *As yet shall he remain.* This is still a description of his advancing

towards Jerusalem. He would make a station at Nob and remain there a day, meaning, perhaps, *only* one day, such would be his impatience to attack and destroy Jerusalem. ¶ *At Nob.* Nob was a city of Benjamin, inhabited by priests; Neh. xi. 32. When David was driven away by Saul, he came to this city, and received supplies from Ahimelech 'the priest; 1 Sam. xxi. 1–6. Nob must have been situated somewhere upon the ridge of the mount of Olives, to the northeast of the city. So Jerome, professedly from Hebrew tradition, says, ' Stans in oppidulo Nob et procul urbem conspiciens Jerusalem.'—*Comm. in loc.* Messrs. Robinson and Smith sought all along the ridge of the mount of Olives, from the Damascus road to the summit opposite to the city, for some traces of an ancient site which might be regarded as the place of Nob; but without the slightest success.—*Bib. Researches,* ii. p. 150. ¶ *He shall shake his hand.* That is, in the attitude of menace, or threatening. This language implies, that the city of Nob was so near to Jerusalem that the latter city could be seen from it; and the description denotes, that at the sight of Jerusalem Sennacherib would be full of indignation, and utter against it the threat of speedy and complete ruin. ¶ *The mount of the daughter of Zion;* see Note, ch. i. 8. The Chaldee renders this, ' He shall come, and stand in Nob, the city of the priests, over against the wall of Jerusalem, and shall answer and say to his army, " Is not this that city of Jerusalem against which I have assembled all my armies, and on account of which I have made an exaction on all my provinces? And lo, it is less and more feeble than any of the defences of the people which I have subjected in the strength of my hand." Over against that he shall stand, and shake his head, and shall bring his hand against the mount of the sanctuary which is Zion, and against the court which is in Jerusalem.' Jarchi and Kimchi say, that Nob was so near to Jerusalem that it could be seen from

33 Behold, the Lord, the Lord of hosts, shall lop the bough with terror: and the high ones of stature *shall be* hewn down, and the haughty shall be humbled.

34 And he shall cut down the thickets of the forests with iron, and Lebanon shall fall [1] by a mighty one.

CHAPTER XI.

ANALYSIS OF THE CHAPTER.

This chapter is connected with the preceding as part of the same general prophecy. In that, the prophet had described the invasion of Sennacherib, and had given the assurance that Jerusalem should be safe, notwithstanding the threatened invasion. The general design of that

[1] or, *mightily.*

---

thence ; and hence this is mentioned as the last station of the army of the Assyrian, the end of his march, and where the prize seemed to be within his grasp.

33. *Behold, the Lord,* &c. The prophet had described, in the previous verses, the march of the Assyrians towards Jerusalem, station by station. He had accompanied him in his description, until he had arrived in full sight of the city, which was the object of all his preparation. He had described the consternation which was felt at his approach in all the smaller towns. Nothing had been able to stand before him ; and now, flushed with success, and confident that Jerusalem would fall, he stands before the devoted city. But here, the prophet announces that his career was to close ; and here his arms to be stayed. Here he was to meet with an overthrow, and Jerusalem would still be safe. This is the design of the prophecy, to comfort the inhabitants of Jerusalem with the assurance that they still would be safe. ¶ *Will lop the bough.* The word *bough* here (פֻּארָה) is from פֵּאר to adorn, to beautify ; and is given to a branch or bough of a tree on account of its beauty. It is, therefore, descriptive of that which is beautiful, honoured, proud ; and is applied to the Assyrian on account of his pride and magnificence. In ver. 18, 19, the prophet had described the army of the Assyrian as a magnificent forest. Here

prophecy was *to console the people with the assurance of their deliverance from impending calamity.* But it was a general principle with the Hebrew prophets, and particularly with Isaiah, when *any* event tending to console the people, or to excite the nation's gratitude, occurred, to cast the eye forward to that great future deliverance which they anticipated under the Messiah; see Introduction, § 7, (3.) The contemplation of *present* objects dies away; the mind fixes more intently on the glories of the Messiah's reign; the prophetic vision ranges over the beauties of his person, and the glories of his kingdom, until the prophet seems to have forgotten the subject with which he commenced. This was perfectly natural. It was by an obvious law of association in the mind, by which the mention of deliverance, in any form, however humble, would suggest that great deliverance on which the eye of every Jew would rest. It

he says that the glory of that army should be destroyed, as the vitality and beauty of the waving bough of a tree is quickly destroyed when it is lopped with an axe. There can scarcely be conceived a description, that would more beautifully represent the fading strength of the army of the Assyrian than this. ¶ *With terror.* In such a way as to inspire terror. ¶ *The high ones of stature.* The chief men and officers of the army.

34. *And he shall cut down the thickets of the forest.* The army of the Assyrians, described here as a thick, dense forest; comp. ver. 18, 19. ¶ *With iron.* As a forest is cut down with an axe, so the prophet uses this phrase here, to *keep up and carry out the figure.* The army was destroyed with the pestilence (2 Kings xix. 35); but it fell as certainly as a forest falls before the axe. ¶ *And Lebanon.* Lebanon is here evidently descriptive of the army of the Assyrian, retaining the idea of a beautiful and magnificent forest. Thus, in Ezek. xxxi. 3, it is said, 'the king of the Assyrians was a cedar of Lebanon with fair branches.' Lebanon is usually applied to the Jews as descriptive of them (Jer. xxii. 6, 23; Zech. x. 10; xi. 1), but it is evidently applied here to the Assyrian army ; and the sense is, that that army should be soon and certainly destroyed, and that, therefore, the inhabitants of Jerusalem had no cause of alarm ; see Notes on ch. xxxvii.

hence follows, that wherever the prophet *begins*, he usually *ends* with a glowing description of the reign of the Messiah. However far from this central object of revealed religion he may commence, yet there is a tendency everywhere to *it* in the prophetic writings; and the moment that, by any law of association, this object is suggested, or the eye catches a glimpse of it, the former object sinks out of view, and the person and reign of the Messiah becomes the sole theme of the prophetic description. This is the case here. Isaiah had commenced the prophecy with an account of the invasion of Sennacherib; ch. x. 5, &c. He had described the deliverance from that danger; ch. x. 33, 34. The mention of this deliverance directs his thoughts to that far greater deliverance which would take place under the Messiah; and immediately (ch. xi.) he commences a glowing description of his coming and his reign. The *language* with which he commenced the prophecy, is retained; the illustrations are drawn from the subject *before* under consideration; but the description pertains to the glories of the reign of the Mes-

siah. The proof of this will appear in the Notes on particular passages in the chapter. Its general design is, to console the people by the prospect of a great future deliverance under the Messiah, and by a prospect of the glories of his reign. He describes, (i.) The certainty that he would come, and his character; ver. 1–5. (ii.) The peace and prosperity which would follow from his advent; ver. 6–9. (iii.) The fact that the Gentiles would be called to partake of the privileges of his reign; ver. 10. (iv.) The restoration of the exiles to their native land under his reign; ver. 11, 12. (v.) The fact, that his reign would put a period to dissensions and strifes between the contending nations of the Jews; ver. 13; and (vi.) The universal prevalence of his religion, and the deliverance of his people; ver. 14–16.

A ND *a* there shall come forth a rod out of the stem *b* of Jesse, and a branch *c* shall grow out of his roots:

　　a ch.53.2.　　*b* Acts 13.23; Rev.22.16.　　*c* Zec.6.12.

CHAPTER XI.

1. *And there shall come forth a rod.* In the previous chapter, the prophet had represented the Assyrian monarch and his army under the image of a dense and flourishing forest, with all its glory and grandeur. In opposition to this, he describes the illustrious personage who is the subject of this chapter, under the image of a slender twig or shoot, sprouting up from the root of a decayed and fallen tree. Between the Assyrian, therefore, and the person who is the subject of this chapter, there is a most striking and beautiful contrast. The one was at first magnificent—like a vast spreading forest—yet should soon fall and decay; the other was the little sprout of a decayed tree, which should yet rise, expand, and flourish. ¶ *A rod* (חֹטֶר *hhōtĕr*). This word occurs in but one other place; Prov. xiv. 3: ' In the mouth of the foolish is *a rod* of pride.' Here it means, evidently, *a branch, a twig, a shoot,* such as starts up from the roots of a decayed tree, and is synonymous with the word rendered *branch* (צֶמַח *tzēmăhh*) in ch. iv. 2; see the Note on that place. ¶ *Out of the stem.* (מִגֶּזַע). This word occurs but three times in the Old Testament; see Job xiv. 8; where it is rendered *stock:*

Though the root thereof wax old in the earth,
And the *stock* thereof die in the ground;

and in Isa. xl. 24: ' Yea, their *stock* shall not take root in the earth.' It means, therefore, the stock or stump of a tree that has been cut down—a stock, however, which may not be quite dead, but where it may send up a branch or shoot from its roots. It is beautifully applied to an ancient family that is fallen into decay, yet where there may be a descendant that shall rise and flourish ; as a tree may fall and decay, but still there may be vitality in the root, and it shall send up a tender germ or sprout. ¶ *Of Jesse.* The father of David. It means, that he who is here spoken of should be of the family of Jesse, or David. Though Jesse had died, and though the ancient family of David would fall into decay, yet there would arise from that family an illustrious descendant. The beauty of this description is apparent, if we bear in recollection that, when the Messiah was born, the ancient and much honoured family of David had fallen into decay ; that the mother of Jesus, though appertaining to that family, was poor, obscure, and unknown ; and that, to all appearance, the glory of the family had departed. Yet from that, as from a long-decayed root in the ground, he

2 And the Spirit of the LORD shall rest upon *a* him, the spirit of

a Mat.3.16; Jn.3.34.

wisdom *b* and understanding, the spirit of counsel and might, the

b 1Cor.1.30.

should spring who would restore the family to more than its ancient glory, and shed additional lustre on the honoured name of Jesse. ¶ *And a branch* (נֵצֶר *nētzĕr*). A twig, branch, or shoot; a slip, scion, or young sucker of a tree, that is selected for transplanting, and that requires to be watched with peculiar care. The word occurs but four times; Isa. lx. 21: 'They shall inherit the land for ever, THE BRANCH of my planting;' Isa. xiv. 19: 'But thou art cast out of thy grave as an abominable branch;' Dan. xi. 7. The word rendered BRANCH in Jer. xxiii. 5; xxxiii. 15, is a different word in the original (צֶמַח *tzĕmăhh*), though meaning substantially the same thing. The word *branch* is also used by our translators, in rendering several other Hebrew words; *see* Taylor's *Concordance*. Here the word is synonymous with that which is rendered *rod* in the previous part of the verse—a shoot, or twig, from the root of a decayed tree. ¶ *Out of his roots.* As a shoot starts up from the roots of a decayed tree. The LXX. render this, 'And a *flower* (ἄνθος) shall arise from the root.' The Chaldee, 'And a king shall proceed from the sons of Jesse, and the Messiah from his sons' sons shall arise;' showing conclusively that the ancient Jews referred this to the Messiah.

That this verse, and the subsequent parts of the chapter, refer to the Messiah, may be argued from the following considerations:—(1.) The fact that it is expressly applied to him in the New Testament. Thus Paul, in Rom. xv. 12, quotes the tenth verse of this chapter as expressly applicable to the times of the Messiah. (2.) The Chaldee Paraphrase shows, that this was the sense which the ancient Jews put upon the passage. That paraphrase is of authority, only to show that this was the sense which appeared to be the true one by the ancient interpreters. (3.) The description in the chapter is not applicable to any other personage than the Messiah. Grotius supposes that the passage refers to Hezekiah; though, 'in

a more sublime sense,' to the Messiah. Others have referred it to Zerubbabel. But none of the things here related apply to either, except the fact that they had a descent from the family of Jesse; for neither of those families had *fallen into the decay* which the prophet here describes. (4.) The peace, prosperity, harmony and order, referred to in the subsequent portions of the chapter, are not descriptive of any portion of the reign of Hezekiah. (5.) The terms and descriptions here accord with other portions of the Scriptures, as applicable to the Messiah. Thus Jeremiah (xxiii. 5; xxxiii. 15) describes the Messiah under the similitude of a *branch*. a germ or shoot—using, indeed, a different Hebrew word, but retaining the same idea and image; comp. Zech. iii. 8. It accords also with the description by Isaiah of the same personage in ch. iv. 2; see Note on the place. (6.) I may add, that nearly all commentators have referred this to the Messiah; and, perhaps, it would not be possible to find greater unanimity in regard to the interpretation of any passage of Scripture than on this.

2. *And the Spirit of the* LORD. The Spirit of JEHOVAH. Chaldee, 'And there shall rest upon him the spirit of prophecy from before JEHOVAH.' In the previous verse, the prophet had announced his origin and his birth. In this, he proceeds to describe his extraordinary endowments, as eminently holy, pure, and wise. There can be no doubt that reference is here had to the Holy Spirit, the third person of the sacred Trinity, as descending upon him in the fulness of his influences, and producing in him perfect wisdom, knowledge, and the fear of the Lord. The Spirit of JEHOVAH shall rest upon him —a Spirit producing wisdom, understanding, counsel, might, &c. All these are in the Scriptures traced to the agency of the Holy Spirit; see 1 Cor. xii. 8–11. The meaning here is, that the Messiah should be endowed with these eminent prophetic gifts and qualifications for his ministry by the agency

spirit of knowledge, and of the fear of the LORD;

3 And shall make him of [1] quick

understanding in the fear of the LORD: and he shall not judge after the sight of his eyes, neither reprove after the hearing of his ears:

1 *scent*, or, *smell*.

---

of the Holy Spirit. It was by that Spirit that the prophets had been inspired (see 2 Pet. i. 21; 2 Tim. iii. 16); and as the Messiah was to be a prophet (Deut. xviii. 15, 18), there was a fitness that he should be endowed in the same manner. If it be asked how one, who was Divine in his own nature, could be thus endowed by the aid of the Spirit, the answer is, that he was also to be a man descended from the honoured line of David, and that *as* a man he might be furnished for his work by the agency of the Holy Ghost. His human nature was kept pure; his mind was made eminently wise; his heart always retained the fear and love of God, and there is no absurdity in supposing that these extraordinary endowments were to be traced to God. That he *was* thus under the influence of the Holy Spirit, is abundantly taught in the New Testament. Thus, in Matt. iii. 16, the Holy Spirit is represented as descending on him at his baptism. In John iii. 34, it is said, 'For he whom God hath sent speaketh the words of God; for God giveth not the Spirit by measure unto him;' comp. Col. i. 19. ¶ *Shall rest upon him.* That is, shall descend on him, and remain with him. It shall not merely *come* upon him, but shall attend him permanently; comp. Num. xi. 25, 26. ¶ *The spirit of wisdom.* The spirit producing wisdom, or making him wise. Wisdom consists in the choice of the best means to secure the best ends. This attribute is often given to the Messiah in the New Testament, and was always evinced by him; comp. 1 Cor. i. 30; Eph. i. 17; Col. ii. 3: 'In whom are hid all the treasures of wisdom and knowledge.' ¶ *And understanding.* The difference between the words here rendered *wisdom* and *understanding* is, that the former denotes wisdom properly; and the latter, that judgment resulting from wisdom, by which we distinguish things, or decide on their character. ¶ *The spirit of counsel.* That by which he shall be qualified to *give* counsel or advice; the

qualification of a public instructor and guide; see Note on ch. ix. 6. ¶ *And might.* Strength, vigour, energy; that strength of heart and purpose which will enable a man to meet difficulties, to encounter dangers, to be bold, open, and fearless in the discharge of his duties. It is not necessary to remark, that this characteristic was found in an eminent degree in the Lord Jesus Christ. ¶ *Of knowledge.* That is, the knowledge of the attributes and plans of JEHOVAH; comp. Matt. xi. 27: 'Neither knoweth any man the Father save the Son.' John i. 18: 'No man hath seen God at any time; the only begotten Son, which is in the bosom of the Father, he hath declared him;' 1 John v. 20. ¶ *And of the fear of the* LORD. The fear of JEHOVAH is often used to denote piety in general, as consisting in a reverence for the Divine commands, and a dread of offending him; *i.e.*, a desire to please him, which is piety; comp. Job xxviii. 28; Ps. xix. 9; cxi. 10; Prov. i. 7; iii. 13; xv. 33; xix. 23. That this characteristic was found eminently in the Lord Jesus, it is not necessary to attempt to prove.

3. *And shall make him of quick understanding.* (וַהֲרִיחוֹ.) The LXX. render this, ' And the spirit of the fear of God shall fill him.' The Chaldee, ' And the Lord shall draw him near to him in his fear.' The Syriac, ' And he shall be resplendent (like the sun, or the stars) in the fear of the Lord.' The Hebrew word here used is probably derived from רִיחַ *riähh*, used only in Hiphil, *to smell;* and is kindred with רוּחַ *rüäh*, *wind, breath*, for fragrant substances *breathe out* an odour.—*Gesenius.* It then denotes *to take delight in smelling* (Ex. xxx. 38; Lev. xxvi. 31); and thence, by an easy transition, to take delight in anything; Amos v. 21. The reason is, that the objects of smell are usually pleasant and agreeable; and especially such as were the aromatics used in public worship. The sense here is, probably, that he would take pleasure

4 But *a* with righteousness shall
he judge the poor, and ¹ reprove

a Ps.72.2,4; Rev.19.1.

with equity for the meek of the
earth: and he shall smite the earth

1 *argue.*

in the fear of Jehovah, that is, in piety,
and in devoting himself to his service.
The interpretation given in our translation, is that given by many expositors; though that above suggested is
probably the correct one. The word is
used to denote *pleasure* in a thing; it
is not used anywhere, it is believed, to
denote a quick understanding; comp.
Ex. v. 21; Phil. iv. 18. The idea which
is conveyed by our translators is, probably, derived from *the discernment of
the quality of objects* by an acute sense
of *smell*, and hence they interpreted the
word to denote an acute discrimination
of any objects. ¶ *And he shall not judge
after the sight of his eyes.* He shall
not judge of things by their external
appearance, or with partiality. This is
language which is applicable to a magistrate, and is spoken of the Messiah
as the descendant of David, and as
sitting on his throne as a ruler of his
people. He who judges ' after the sight
of his eyes,' does it according to external appearances, showing favour to
rank, to the rich, and the great; or judging as things *appear* without a close
and careful inquiry into their true nature and bearings; comp. John vii. 24:
' Judge not according to the appearance,
but judge righteous judgment;' Deut.
i. 16, 17. ¶ *Neither reprove.* רוֹכִיחַ.
This word means *to show, to prove; to
correct, reprove, convince; to reproach,*
or *censure; to punish; to judge, decide,*
&c. Here it is evidently used as synonymous with ' shall he judge ' in the
former part of the parallelism—retaining the idea of a just judge, who decides
not according to the hearing of the ears,
but according to justice. ¶ *After the
hearing of his ears.* Not by plausible
statements, and ingenious defences, but
by weighing evidence, and by an impartial examination of the true merits of
the case. This belonged to the Lord
Jesus, because, (1.) He was never influenced by any undue regard to rank,
honour, or office. His opinions were
always impartial; his judgments without bias or favouritism. (2.) He was

able to discern the true merits of every
case. He knew what was in man, saw
the true state of the heart, and, therefore, was not deceived or imposed upon
as human judges are; see John ii. 24,
25; comp. Rev. ii. 23; John vi. 64.
4. *Shall he judge the poor.* That is,
he shall see that impartial justice is done
them; he shall not take part with the
rich against the poor, but shall show that
he is the friend of justice. This is the
quality of a just and upright magistrate,
and this character the Lord Jesus everywhere evinced. He chose his disciples
from among the poor; he condescended
to be their companion and friend; he
provided for their wants; and he pronounced their condition blessed; Matt.
v. 3. There may be a reference here
to the poor in spirit—the humble, the
penitent; but the main idea is, that he
would not be influenced by any undue
regard for the higher ranks of life, but
would be the friend and patron of the
poor. ¶ *And reprove.* הוֹכִיחַ. And
judge, decide, or argue for; that is, he
shall be their friend and their impartial judge; ver. 3. ¶ *With equity.*
With uprightness, or uncorrupted integrity. ¶ *For the meek of the earth.*
עַנְוֵי־אָרֶץ. For the humble, the
lower class; referring to those who
were usually passed by, or oppressed
by those in power. ¶ *And he shall
smite the earth.* By the *earth* here, or
the land, is meant evidently *the wicked*,
as the following member of the parallelism shows. Perhaps it is intended to
be implied, that the earth, when he
should come, would be eminently depraved; which was the fact. The
characteristic here is that of an upright
judge or prince, who would punish the
wicked. To *smite* the earth, or the
wicked, is expressive of punishment;
and this characteristic is elsewhere attributed to the Messiah; see Ps. ii. 9–12;
Rev. ii. 27. The trait is that of a just,
upright, impartial exercise of power—
such as would be manifested in the defence of the poor and the innocent, and
in the punishment of the proud and the

with the ^arod of his mouth, and with the breath of his lips shall he slay the wicked.

a Rev.2.16; 19.15.

5 And righteousness shall be the girdle ^bof his loins, and faithfulness the girdle of his reins.

b Eph.6.14.

---

guilty. ¶ *With the rod of his mouth.* The word שֵׁבֶט here rendered ' *rod,*' denotes properly a stick, or staff; a rod for chastisement or correction (Prov. x. 13; xiii. 24; Job ix. 34; xxi. 9); the staff, or sceptre of a ruler—as an emblem of office; a measuring rod; a spear, &c.; Note, ch. x. 5. It is not elsewhere applied to the mouth, though it is often used in other connections. It means that which goes out of the mouth—a word, command, threatening, decision; and it is implied that it would go forth to pronounce sentence of condemnation, and to punish. His word would be so just, impartial, and authoritative, that the effect would be to overwhelm the wicked. In a sense similar to this, Christ is said to have been seen by John, when 'out of his mouth went a sharp two-edged sword' (Rev. i. 16); that is, his commands and decisions were so authoritative, and so certain in their execution, as to be like a sharp sword; comp. Heb. iv. 12; Isa. xlix. 2: ' And he hath made my mouth like a sharp sword.' The discriminating preaching, the pungent discourses, the authoritative commands of the Lord Jesus, when on earth, showed, and his judicial decisions in the day of judgment will show, the manner of the fulfilment of the prediction. ¶ *And with the breath of his lips.* This is synonymous with the previous member of the parallelism. ' The breath of his lips ' means that which goes forth from his lips—his doctrines, his commands, his decisions. ¶ *Shall he slay the wicked.* That is, he shall condemn the wicked; or, he shall sentence them to punishment. This is descriptive of a prince or ruler, who by his commands and decisions effectually subdues and punishes the wicked; that is, he does justice to all. Grotius interprets this, ' by his prayers,' referring it to Hezekiah, and to the influence of his prayers in destroying the Assyrians. The Chaldee Paraphrast translates it, ' And by the word of his lips he shall slay the impious Armillus.' By *Armillus,* the Jews mean the last

great enemy of their nation, who would come after Gog and Magog and wage furious wars, and who would slay the Messiah Ben Ephraim, whom the Jews expect, but who would be himself slain by the rod of the Messiah Ben David, or the son of David.—*Castell.*

5. *And righteousness shall be the girdle of his loins.* The sense of this verse is plain. He will always exhibit himself as a just and faithful king. The *girdle of the loins* refers to the cincture, or band, with which the ancients girded themselves. A part of their dress consisted of an outward, loose, flowing robe. This robe it was necessary to gird up, or to confine close to the body in active labour, or in running; and the meaning of the figure here used is, probably, that the virtues of righteousness and justice would *adhere* to him as closely and inseparably as the garment does to the body to which it was bound. The figure of representing the virtues as *clothing,* or describing them as parts of *dress* with which we are invested, is common in the Scriptures:

I put on righteousness, and it clothed me;
My judgment was as a robe and a diadem.
Job xxix. 14.

I will greatly rejoice in the Lord,
My soul shall be joyful in my God;
For he hath clothed me with the garments of salvation,
He hath covered me with the robe of righteousness,
As a bridegroom decketh himself with ornaments,
And as a bride adorneth herself with her jewels.
Isa. lxi. 10.

Comp. Rev. xix. 8, and Paul's beautiful description in Eph. vi. 13–17. In like manner, vice and wickedness are sometimes represented as so closely *adhering* to a man as to be a part of his very clothing; Ps. cix. 18, 19:

He clothed himself with cursing, like as with a garment.
Let it be unto him as the garment which covereth him,
And for a girdle, wherewith he is girded continually.

The Chaldee renders this, ' And the just shall be round about him on every side — סְהוֹר כְּהוֹר — and the servants

6 The *a* wolf also shall dwell with the lamb, and the leopard shall lie down with the kid; and the calf, and the young lion, and the fatling together; and a little child shall lead them.

a ch.65.25.

of truth shall come near to him.' The idea is, that he shall be distinguished for justice and truth, and that a zeal for these shall make him strong and active in executing the purposes of his reign. This closes the description of the *personal* qualities of the Messiah. The account of the effects of his reign follows in the subsequent verses.

6. *The wolf also.* In this, and the following verses, the prophet describes the effect of his reign in producing peace and tranquillity on the earth. The description is highly poetical, and is one that is common in ancient writings in describing a golden age. The two leading ideas are those of *peace* and *security.* The figure is taken from the condition of animals of all descriptions living in a state of harmony, where those which are by nature defenceless, and which are usually made the prey of the strong, are suffered to live in security. By nature the wolf preys upon the lamb, and the leopard upon the kid, and the adder is venomous, and the bear, and the cow, and the lion, and the ox, cannot live together. But if a state of things should arise, where all this hostility would cease; where the wild animals would lay aside their ferocity, and where the feeble and the gentle would be safe; where the adder would cease to be venomous, and where all would be so mild and harmless that a little child would be safe, and could lead even the most ferocious animals, that state would represent the reign of the Messiah. Under his dominion, such a change would be produced as that those who were by nature violent, severe, and oppressive; those whose disposition is illustrated by the ferocious and blood-thirsty propensities of the lion and the leopard, and by the poison of the adder, would be changed and subdued, and would be disposed to live in peace and harmony with others. This is the *general* idea of the passage. We are not to cut the interpretation to the quick, and to press the expressions to know what particular class of men are represented by the lion, the bear, or the adder. The *general* image that is before the prophet's mind is that of peace and safety, *such as that would be* if a change were to be produced in wild animals, making them tame, and peaceful, and harmless.

This description of a golden age is one that is common in Oriental writers, where the wild beasts are represented as growing tame; where serpents are harmless; and where all is plenty, peace, and happiness. Thus Jones, in his commentary on Asiatic poetry, quotes from an Arabic poet, *Ibn Onein*, p. 380:

Justitia, a qua mansuetus fit lupus fame astric-
tus,
Esuriens, licet hinnulum candidum videat—

'Justice, by which the ravening wolf, driven by hunger, becomes tame, although he sees a white kid.' Thus, also, Ferdusi, a Persian poet:

Rerum Dominus, Mahmud, rex potens,
Ad cujus aquam potum veniunt simul agnus et
lupus—

'Mahmud, mighty king, lord of events, to whose fountain the lamb and the wolf come to drink.' Thus Virgil, Eclogue iv. 21:

Ipsæ lactæ domum referent distenta capellæ
Ubera; nec magnos metuent armenta leones—

Home their full udders, goats, unurged shall
bear,
Nor shall the herd the lordly lion fear.

And immediately after:

Occidet et serpens, et fallax herba veneni
Occidet—

The snake, and poison's treacherous weed shall
die.　　　　　　　　　　　　*Wrangham.*

Again, Eclogue, v. 60:

Nec lupus insidias pecori, nec retia cervis
Ulla dolum mediantur: amat bonus otia Daphnis.

So also Horace, *Epod.* xvi. 53, 54:

Nec vespertinus circumgemit ursus ovile,
Nec intumescit alta viperis humus.

See also *Claudian*, Lib. ii. v. 25, *sq.;* and Theocritus, Idyl xxiv. 84, as quoted by Gesenius and Rosenmüller.

These passages are beautiful, and highly poetic; but they do not equal the beauty of the prophet. There is an exquisite sweetness in the passage of Isaiah—in the picture which he has drawn—particularly in the introduction of the security of the young child, which does not occur in the quotations from the heathen poets.

That this passage is descriptive of the times of the Messiah, there can be no doubt. It has been a question, to what particular part of his reign the prophet has reference. Some have referred it to the time when he came, and to the influence of his gospel in mitigating the ferocity of his enemies, and ultimately disposing them to suffer Christians to live with them—the infuriated enemies of the cross, under the emblem of the wolf, the bear, the leopard, and the adder, becoming willing that the Christian, under the emblem of the lamb, and the kid, should live with them without molestation. This is the interpretation of Vitringa. Others have referred it to the Millennium—as descriptive of a state of happiness, peace, and universal security then. Others have referred it to the second coming of the Messiah, as descriptive of a time when it is supposed that he will reign personally on the earth, and when there shall be universal security and peace, and when the nature of animals shall be so far changed, that the ferocity of those which are wild and ravenous shall cease, and they shall become harmless to the defenceless. Without attempting to examine these opinions at length, we may, perhaps, express the sense of the passage by the following observations :—(1.) The eye of the prophet is fixed upon the reign of the Messiah, not with reference to time, but with reference to the actual facts of that reign. He saw the scene pass before his mind in vision (see the Introduction, § 7, iii. (4.) (5.), and it is not the nature of such descriptions to mark the *time*, but the order, the passing aspect of the scene. *Under the reign of the Messiah*, he saw that this would occur. Looking down distant times, as on a beautiful landscape, he perceived, under the mild reign of the Prince of peace, a state of things which would be well represented by the wolf dwelling with the lamb, the leopard crouching down with the kid,

and a little child safe in their midst. (2.) It was, *in fact*, partially fulfilled in the earliest times of the gospel, and has been everywhere. Under that gospel, the mad passions of men have been subdued ; their wild ferocious nature has been changed ; their love of conquest, and war, and blood taken away ; and the change has been such as would be beautifully symbolized by the change of the disposition of the wolf and the leopard—suffering the innocent and the harmless to live with them in peace. (3.) The scene will not be fully realized until the reign of the Messiah shall be extended to all nations, and his gospel shall everywhere accomplish its full effects. The vision of Isaiah here has not yet received a full completion ; nor will it until the earth shall be full of the knowledge of the Lord, ver. 9. The mind is, therefore, still directed onward. In future times, UNDER THE REIGN OF THE MESSIAH, what is here described shall occur—a state of security, and peace, and happiness. Isaiah saw that splendid vision, as in a picture, pass before the mind ; the wars, and persecutions, and trials of the Messiah's kingdom were, for a time at least, thrown into the back ground, or not represented, and, in that future time, he saw what is here represented. It has been partially fulfilled—in all the changes which the Messiah's reign has made in the natural ferocity and cruelty of men ; in all the peace which at any time the church has been permitted to enjoy ; in all the revolutions promoting human safety, welfare, and happiness, which Christianity has produced. It is to receive the complete fulfilment—τὸ ἀποτελίσμα —only in that future time when the gospel shall be everywhere established on the earth. The essential thing, therefore, in the prophecy, is the representation of the peace, safety, and harmony which shall take place under the Messiah. So to speak, it was a taking out, and causing to pass before the mind of the prophet, all the circumstances of harmony, order, and love in his reign —as, in a beautiful panoramic view of a landscape, the beauties of the whole scene may be made to pass before the mind ; the circumstances that might even then, if surveyed closely, give pain, were hid from the view, or lost in the loveliness of the whole scene. (4.) That it does not refer to any literal change in the nature of animals, so that the ferocity of the untamed shall be wholly laid aside, the disposition to prey on one another wholly cease, and the poisonous nature of the adder be destroyed, seems to me to be evident— (a) Because the whole description has a highly figurative and poetical cast. (b) Because such figurative expressions are common in all poetry, and especially among the Orientals. (c) Because it does not appear how the gospel has any tendency to change the nature of the lion, the bear, or the serpent. It acts on men, not on brutes; on human hearts, not on the organization of wild animals. (d) Because such a state of things could not occur without a perpetual miracle, changing the *physical* nature of the whole animal creation. The lion, the wolf, the panther, are made to live on flesh. The whole organization of their teeth and digestive powers is adapted to this, and this alone. To fit them to live on vegetable food, would require a change in their whole structure, and confound all the doctrines of natural history. The adder is poisonous, and nothing but a miracle would prevent the poisonous secretion, and make his bite innocuous. But where is a promise of any such continued miracle as shall change the whole structure of the animal creation, and make the physical world different from what it is? It is indeed probable that wild animals and venomous serpents will wholly retire before the progress of civilization and Christianity, and that the earth may be inhabited everywhere with safety—for such is the tendency of the advance of civilization—but this is a very different thing from a change in the physical nature of the animal creation. The fair interpretation of this passage is, therefore, that revolutions will be produced in the wild and evil passions of men—the only thing with which the gospel has to do—as great *as if* a change were produced in the animal creation, and the most ferocious and the most helpless should dwell together.—*The wolf* (זְאֵב *zĕebh*) is a

well-known animal, so called from his yellow or golden colour. The Hebrew name is formed by changing ה *hē* in the word זָהָב *zâhâbh, gold,* to א *aleph.* —Bochart. The wolf, in the Scriptures, is described as ravenous, fierce, cruel; and is the emblem of that which is wild, ferocious, and savage among men; Gen. xlix. 27: 'Benjamin shall ravin as a wolf;' Ezek. xxii. 27: 'Her princes in the midst thereof are like wolves ravening the prey;' Matt. vii. 15: 'Beware of false prophets, which come to you in sheep's clothing, but inwardly they are ravening wolves;' John x. 12; Matt. x. 16; Luke x. 3; Acts xx. 29. The wolf is described as sanguinary and bloody (Ezek. xxii. 27), and as taking its prey by night, and as therefore particularly an object of dread; Jer. v. 6: 'A wolf of the evenings shall spoil them; Hab. i. 8: 'Their horses are more fierce than the evening wolves;' Zeph. iii. 3: 'Her judges are evening wolves, they gnaw not the bones till to-morrow.' In the Scriptures, the wolf is constantly represented in contrast with the lamb; the one the emblem of ferocity, the other of gentleness and innocence; Matt. x. 16; Luke x. 3. The heathen poets also regard the wolf as an emblem of ferocity and cruelty:

Inde lupi ceu
Raptores, atra in nebula, quos improba ventris
Exegit cæcos rabies, etc.—
(Virg. *Æn.* ii. 355, *sq.*)

As hungry wolves, with raging appetite,
Scour through the fields, nor fear the stormy night—
Their whelps at home expect the promised food,
And long to temper their dry chaps in blood—
So rushed we forth at once. *Dryden.*

Cervi, luporum præda rapacium.
Hor. *Car. Lib.* iv. Ode iv. 50.

See a full illustration of the nature and habits of the wolf in Bochart, *Hieroz.* Part i. B. iii. ch. x. pp. 821–830. ¶*Shall dwell.* יָגוּר. Shall sojourn, or abide. The word usually denotes a residence for a time only, away from home, not a permanent dwelling. The idea here is, that they shall remain peacefully together. The same image occurs in ch. lxv. 25, in another form: 'The wolf and the lamb shall feed together.' ¶*The lamb.* Everywhere the emblem of mildness, gentleness, and innocence;

7 And the cow and the bear shall feed; their young ones shall lie down together: and the lion shall eat straw like the ox.

and, therefore, applied often to the people of God, as mild, inoffensive, and forbearing; John xxi. 15; Luke x. 3; Isa. xl. 2. It is very often applied, by way of eminence, to the Lord Jesus Christ; John i. 29; Acts viii. 32; Isa. ii. 7; 1 Pet. i. 19; Rev. v. 6, 8, 12, 13; vi. 16; vii. 9, 10, 14, 17, *et al.* ¶ *And the leopard.* נָמֵר *nâmēr* The leopard, a well-known wild beast, was regarded in Oriental countries as second in dignity only to the lion. The Arabic writers say, 'He is second in rank to the lion, and, as there is a natural hatred between them, victory is alternate between them.' Hence, in the Scriptures, the lion and the leopard are often joined together as animals of the same character and rank; Cant. iv. 8:

From the lions' den,
From the mountains of the leopards.

See Jer. v. 6, and Hos. xiii. 7:

Therefore I will be unto them as a lion,
As a leopard by the way will I observe them.

The leopard is distinguished for his spots; Jer. xiii. 23: 'Can the Ethiopian change his skin, or the leopard his spots?' it has small white eyes, wide jaws, sharp teeth, and is represented as extremely cruel to man. It was common in Palestine, and was an object of great dread. It lurked for its prey like the lion, and seized upon it suddenly (Jer. v. 6; Hos. xiii. 7), and was particularly distinguished for its velocity (Hab. i. 8), and is often referred to in the classic writers as an emblem of fleetness. See *Bochart.* The image here used by Isaiah, that 'the leopard should lie down with the kid,' as an emblem of peace and safety, occurs almost in the same form in the Sybilline oracles, Lib. iii:

παρδάλιές τ' ἐριφοῖς ἅμα βοσκήσονται,—

'Leopards shall feed together with kids.' *See* Bochart, *Hieroz.* Part i. B. iii. ch. vii. pp. 786–791. ¶ *With the kid.* The young of the goat; Gen. xxxvii. 21; Lev. xxiii. 19; Luke xv. 29. Like the lamb, it was an emblem of gentleness, mildness, and inoffensiveness. ¶ *And the calf.* Another emblem of inoffen-

siveness and innocence. ¶ *And the young lion.* The Hebrew word here used—כְּפִיר—denotes one that is old enough to go abroad for prey. It is employed as emblematic of dangerous enemies (Ps. xxxiv. 2; xxxv. 17; lviii. 7); and also as emblematic of young heroes, or defenders of a state; Ezek. xxxviii. 15; Nah. ii. 14. ¶ *And the fatling.* The calf or other animal that was well fed, and that would be therefore particularly an object of desire to a wild beast. The beauty of the image is heightened, by the circumstance that now the ravenous beast would live with that which usually excites its keenest appetite, without attempting to injure it. ¶ *And a little child shall lead them.* This is a peculiarly beautiful image introduced into the picture of peace and prosperity. Naturally, the lion and the leopard are objects of dread to a young child. But here, the state of peace and safety is represented as not only so entire that the child might live with them in safety, but their natural ferocity is so far subdued and tamed, that they could be led by him at his will. The verisimilitude of the picture is increased by the circumstance, that these wild beasts *may be* so far tamed as to become subject to the will of a man, and even of a child.

7. *And the cow and the bear shall feed.* That is, together. Animals that by nature do not dwell together, where by nature the one would be the prey of the other, shall dwell together—an image of safety and peace. ¶ *And the lion shall eat straw like the ox.* A representation of the change that will take place under the reign of the Messiah in the natural disposition of men, and in the aspect of society; as great *as if* the lion were to lose his natural appetite for blood, and to live on the usual food of the ox. This cannot be taken literally; for such an interpretation would suppose a change in the physical organization of the lion—of his appetites, his teeth, his digestive organs—a change which it would be absurd to suppose will ever exist. It would in fact make him a different being. And it is clear, therefore, that the whole passage is to be

8 And the sucking child shall play on the hole of the asp, and the weaned child shall put his hand on the ¹cockatrice' den.

1 or, *adder's*.   *a* Job.5.23; ch.35.9; Rev.21.7.
                     b Ps.72.19; Hab.2.14.

9 They shall not hurt *a* nor destroy in all my holy mountain: for *b* the earth shall be full of the knowledge of the LORD, as the waters cover the sea.

interpreted in a *moral* sense, as denoting great and important changes in society, and in the hearts of men.

8. *And the sucking child.* An emblem here of harmlessness and innocence. The change in the world, under the Messiah, shall be as great as if a sucking infant should be able to play unharmed with a venomous serpent. ¶ *Shall play.* Shall delight himself (שׁעֲשַׁע) as children usually engage in their sports; comp. Prov. viii. 30, 31; Ps. cxix. 24. ¶ *On the hole of the asp.* Over, or around the cavern, hole, or place of retreat of the asp. He shall play over that place as safely as if the nature of the asp was changed, and it had become innocuous. The Hebrew word here rendered *asp* (פֶּתֶן *pêthên*) denotes the serpent usually called the asp, whose poison is of such rapid operation that it kills almost instantly; see Job xx. 14, 16; Ps. lviii. 4; xci. 13; Deut. xxxii. 33. The word occurs in no other places in the Old Testament. This serpent is small. It is found particularly in Egypt, though also in other places; see Note on Job xx. 14. It is here used as the emblem of the more sudden, malignant, and violent passions; and the idea is, that under the Messiah a change would be wrought in men of malignant and deadly passions as signal *as if* the asp or adder were to lose his venom, and become innocuous to a child. ¶ *And the weaned child.* But still, a young and helpless child. The image is varied, but the same idea is retained. ¶ *Shall put his hand.* That is, he shall do it safely, or uninjured. ¶ *On the cockatrice' den.* Marg. ' Adder's.' The word here rendered *cockatrice* (צִפְעוֹנִי *tziphōni*) occurs only in the following places: Isa. xiv. 29; xi. 8; lix. 5; Prov. xxiii. 32; Jer. viii. 17. In all these places, it is rendered cockatrice, except in Prov. xxiii. 32. The *cockatrice* was a fabulous kind of serpent, supposed to be hatched from the

egg of a cock. The serpent here designated is, doubtless, a species of the *adder*, more venomous, perhaps, than the *pethen*, but still belonging to the same species. Bochart (*Hieroz.* P. ii. lib. iii. ch. ix.) supposes that the *basilisk* is intended—a species of serpent that, he says, was supposed to poison even with its breath. The general idea is the same here as above. It is in vain to attempt to spiritualize these expressions, and to show that they refer to certain individuals, or that the animals here designated refer to particular classes of the enemies of the gospel. It is a mere poetic description, denoting great peace and security; and all the changes in the mad, malignant, and envenomed passions of men, that may be necessary to produce and perpetuate that peace. Pope has versified this description in the following beautiful manner:

The lambs with wolves shall graze the verdant mead,
And boys, in flowery bands, the tigers lead.
The steer and lion at one crib shall meet,
And harmless serpents lick the pilgrim's feet.
The smiling infant in his hand shall take
The crested basilisk, and speckled snake;
Pleased, the green lustre of the scales survey,
And, with their forked tongue, shall innocently
play.   *Messiah.*

9. *They shall not hurt.* That is, those who are designated above under the emblems of the lion, the leopard, the bear, and the adder. ¶ *Nor destroy in all my holy mountain.* Mount Zion; here used, as elsewhere, to denote the seat of his reign on the earth, or his church; Notes, ch. i. 8; ii. 4. The disposition of men, naturally ferocious and cruel, shall be changed so entirely, that the causes of strife and contention shall cease. They shall be disposed to do justice, and to promote each other's welfare everywhere. ¶ *For the earth.* That is, in the times of the Messiah. It does not say that it shall be *immediate* under his reign, but *under* his reign this shall occur on the earth.

10 And in that day there shall be a *a*root of Jesse, which shall stand for an ensign of the people; to it shall the *b*Gentiles seek: and his rest *c* shall be ¹glorious.

¶ *The knowledge of the Lord.* This is put for piety, as the *fear* of the Lord often is. The earth shall be full of a correct understanding of the existence, perfections, plans, and claims of God; and shall be disposed to yield to those claims—thus producing universal peace. ¶ *As the waters cover the sea.* That is, the depths or the bottom of the sea; comp. Hab. ii. 14. The vast waters of the ocean cover all its depths, find their way into all the caverns, flow into all the recesses on the shore—and thus shall the knowledge of JEHOVAH spread like deep, flowing waters, until the earth shall be pervaded and covered with it. It is evident that a time is here spoken of which has not yet fully come, and the mind is still directed onward, as was that of the prophet, to a future period when this shall be accomplished. The prophecy has been indeed in part fulfilled. Wherever the gospel has spread, its effect has been just that which is predicted here. It has calmed and subdued the angry passions of men; changed their feelings and their conduct; disposed them to peace; and tended to mitigate national ferocity, to produce kindness to captives, and to those who had been oppressed. It has mitigated laws that were cruel and bloody; and has abolished customs, games, sports, and pastimes that were ferocious and savage. It has often changed the bitter persecutor, as it did Saul of Tarsus, to the mildness and gentleness of a lamb; and it has spread an influence over nations tending to produce humanity and benevolence. It has produced mildness, gentleness, and love, in the domestic circle; changed the cruel and lordly husband to a companion and friend; and the character of the stern and inexorable father to one of paternal kindness and peace. Wherever it has spread *in truth* and not *in form merely*, it has shed a mild, calming, and subduing influence over the passions, laws, and customs of men. But its effects have been but partially felt; and we are led, therefore, to look forward to future times, when the prophecy shall be entirely fulfilled, and the power of the gospel shall be felt in all nations.

10. *And in that day.* That future time when the reign of the Messiah shall be established; Note, ch. iii. 2; iv. 1. The prophet, having described the birth, and the personal characteristics of the great personage to whom he referred, together with the peaceful effects of his reign, proceeds to state the *result* of that reign in some other respects. The first is (ver. 10), that the *Gentiles* would be brought under his reign; the second (ver. 14), that it would be attended with the restoration of the scattered people of Judea; and the third (ver. 15, 16), that it would be followed by the destruction of the enemies of the people of God. ¶ *There shall be a root of Jesse.* There shall be a sprout, shoot, or scion of the ancient and decayed family of Jesse; see Note, v. 1. Chaldee, 'There shall be a son of the sons of Jesse.' The word *root* here—שֹׁרֶשׁ—is evidently used in the sense of a root that is alive when the tree is dead; a root that sends up a shoot or sprout; and is thus applied to him who should proceed from the ancient and decayed family of Jesse; see ch. liii. 2. Thus in Rev. v. 5, the Messiah is called 'the *root* of David,' and in Rev. xxii. 16, 'the root and the offspring of David.' ¶ *Which shall stand.* There is reference here, doubtless, to the fact that military ensigns were sometimes raised on mountains or towers which were *permanent*, and which, therefore, could be rallying points to an army or a people. The idea is, that the root of Jesse, *i.e.*, the Messiah, should be conspicuous, and that the nations should flee to him, and rally around him as a people do around a military standard. Thus the Saviour says (John xii. 32): 'And I, if I be lifted up from the earth, will draw all men unto me.' ¶ *For an ensign.* For a standard, or a sign around which they shall rally. ¶ *Of the people.* That is, as the parallelism

11 And it shall come to pass in that day, that the LORD shall set his hand again the second time to recover the remnant of his people, which shall be left, from *a* Assyria,

and from Egypt, and from Pathros, and from Cush, and from Elam, and from Shinar, and from Hamath, and from the islands of the sea.

a Zec.10.10,11.

shows, of the Gentiles. ¶ *To it shall the Gentiles seek.* The heathen world shall look to it for safety and deliverance. In the Scriptures, the world is spoken of as divided into Jews and Gentiles. All who are not Jews come under this appellation. This is a distinct prophecy, that other nations than the Jews should be benefited by the work of the Messiah, and constitute a part of his kingdom. This fact is often referred to by Isaiah, and constitutes a very material feature in his prophecies; ch. xlii. 1, 6; xlix. 22; liv. 3; lx. 3, 5, 11, 16; lxi. 6, 9; lxii. 2; lxvi. 12, 19. The word *seek* here, is used in the sense of seeking as a Deliverer, or a Saviour: they shall apply to him for instruction, guidance, and salvation; or they shall apply to him as a nation looks to its deliverer to protect it; comp. ch. viii. 19; 2 Kings i. 3; Isa. lxv. 1. ¶ *And his rest.* The rest, peace, and quietness, which he shall give. This evidently includes *all* the rest or peace which he shall impart to those who seek him. The word מְנוּחָה *mĕnūhhâ* sometimes denotes *a resting-place*, or a habitation (Num. x. 33; Micah ii. 10; Ps. cxxxii. 8); but it also denotes a *state of rest, quietness;* Ruth i. 9; Jer. xlv. 3; Ps. xxiii. 2; xcv. 11; Deut. xii. 9; Isa. xxviii. 12; lxvi. 1. Here it evidently means the latter. It may refer, (1.) To the peace which he gives to the conscience of the awakened and troubled sinner (Matt. xi. 28–30); or (2.) to the prosperity and peace which his reign shall produce. ¶ *Shall be glorious.* Heb. 'Shall be glory.' That is, shall be full of glory and honour. It shall be such as shall confer signal honour on his reign. The Chaldee understands this of his *place* of residence, his palace, or court. 'And the place of his abode shall be in glory.' The Vulgate renders it, 'and his sepulchre shall be glorious.'

['By his rest, we are not to understand his grave—or his death—or his Sabbath—or the rest

he gives his people—but his place of rest, his residence. There is no need of supplying a preposition before *glory*, which is an abstract used for a concrete—glory, for glorious. *The church, Christ's home*, shall be glorious from his presence, and the accession of the Gentiles.'— (Alexander.) This is a beautiful rendering; it is, moreover, consistent with the letter and spirit of the passage. Some include both ideas.]

11. *And it shall come to pass.* The prophet having, in the previous verse, stated the effect of the reign of the Messiah on the *Gentile* world, proceeds to state the result on the scattered Jews. Whether it is to be a *literal* re-collecting of the scattered tribes to the land of their fathers, has been a subject of debate, and is still so by expositors. We may be able to determine what is the correct general interpretation after the particular phrases have been examined. ¶ *In that day.* That future time referred to in this whole prophecy. The word *day* is often used to denote a long time—or the time during which anything continues, as *the day* denotes all the hours until it is terminated by night. So *day* denotes the time of a man's life—' his day;' or time in general; or the time when one shall be prominent, or be the principal object at that time. Thus it is applied to the time of the Messiah, as being the period of the world in which *he* will be the prominent or distinguished object; John viii. 56: ' Abraham rejoiced to see my day;' Luke xvii. 24: 'So shall the Son of man be in his day.' The expression here means, that somewhere in that future time, when the Messiah should appear, or when the world should be put under him as the Mediator, the event would take place which is here predicted. As the word 'day' includes *all* the time of the Messiah, or all his reign from his first to his second advent, it is not to be supposed that the event would take place when he was personally on earth. Isaiah saw it in vision, as *one* of the

events which was to occur after the 'root of Jesse' should stand as an ensign to the nations. ¶ That *the* LORD *shall set his hand.* That JEHOVAH shall undertake this, and accomplish it. To set the hand to anything is to undertake to perform it. ¶ *The second time.* שֵׁנִית. This word properly means, as it is here translated, the second time, implying that the prophet here speaks of a deliverance which would resemble, in some respects, a *former* deliverance or recovery. By the former recovery to which he here refers, he cannot mean the deliverance from Egypt under Moses, for at that time there was no recovery from scattered and distant nations. Besides, if *that* was the reference by the former deliverance, then that here mentioned as the 'second' deliverance would be that from the Babylonish captivity. But on the return from that captivity, there was *not* a collecting of the Jews from all the nations here specified. When the Jews were led back to Judea under Nehemiah, there is no record of their having been collected from 'Egypt,' or from 'Cush,' or from 'the islands of the sea.' It is evident, therefore, I think, that by the former deliverance to which the prophet here alludes—the deliverance which was to precede that designated here as the *second*—he refers to the return from the captivity of Babylon ; and by the 'second,' to some still more future recovery that should take place under the administration of the Messiah. This is further confirmed from the fact that the whole scope of the prophecy points to that future period. ¶ *To recover.* Heb. 'To possess,' or, to obtain possession of—לִקְנוֹת *liqnoth.* This word properly means to obtain possession of by purchasing or buying anything. But it is also applied to *any* possession obtained of an object by power, labour, skill, or by delivering from bondage or captivity, and is thus synonymous with *redeem* or *deliver.* Thus it is applied to the deliverance of the people from Egypt ; Deut. xxxii. 6 ; Ex. xv. 16 ; Ps. lxxiv. 2. It means here, that JEHOVAH would redeem, rescue, recover his people ; but it does not specify the *mode* in which it would be done. Any mode—

either by collecting and rescuing them from the regions into which they were scattered into one place, or by a *spiritual* turning to him, wherever they might be, would meet the force of this word. If *in* the lands where they were scattered, and where they had wandered away from the true God, they were converted, and should become again his people, the event would correspond with all that is meant by the word here. They would *then* be purchased, possessed, or recovered to himself, by being delivered from their spiritual oppression. It is not necessary, therefore, to resort to the interpretation that they should, in the 'second' deliverance, be restored *literally* to the land of Canaan. Any argument for *that* doctrine from this passage must be drawn from the word here used—'recover'—and that *that* idea is not necessarily involved in this word is abundantly manifest from its familiar use in the Old Testament. All that that word implies, is, that they should *be possessed* by God as his people ; an idea which is fully met by the supposition that the scattered Jews everywhere will be converted to the Messiah, and thus become his true people. For this use of the word, see Gen. xxv. 10 ; xlvii. 22 ; xlix. 30 ; l. 13 ; Josh. xxiv. 32 ; 2 Sam. xii. 3 ; Ps. lxviii. 54 ; Lev. xxvii. 24 ; Neh. v. 8. In no place does it necessarily imply the idea of *collecting* or *restoring* a scattered people to their own land. ¶ *The remnant of his people.* That is, the remnant of the Jews, still called his people. In all the predictions respecting the calamities that should ever come upon them, the idea is *always* held out that the nation would not be wholly extinguished ; but that, however great the national judgments, a remnant would still survive. This was particularly true in regard to the fearful judgments which Moses denounced on the nation if they should be disobedient, and which have been so strikingly fulfilled ; Deut. xxviii. As the result of those judgments, Moses does not say that JEHOVAH would annihilate the nation, or extinguish their name, but that they would be 'left few in number,' (Deut. xxviii. 62) ; that JEHOVAH would scatter them among all people, from the one end of the earth even to the other,

(Deut. xxviii. 64); and that among those nations they should find no ease, neither should the sole of their foot have rest, ver. 65. In like manner it was predicted that they should be scattered everywhere. 'I will scatter them also among the heathen, whom neither they nor their fathers have known. I will deliver them to be removed into all the kingdoms of the earth for their hurt, to be a reproach, a proverb, a taunt, and a curse, in all places whither I will drive them ;' Jer. ix. 16; xxiv. 9, 10. 'I will execute judgments in thee, and the whole remnant of thee will I scatter into all the winds ;' Ezek. v. 10. 'I will also scatter them among the nations, among the heathen, and disperse them in the countries ;' Ezek. xii. 15. 'I will sift the house of Israel among the nations, like as corn is sifted in a sieve, yet shall not the least grain fall upon the earth. They shall be wanderers among the nations ;' Amos ix. 9. 'I will make a full end of the nations whither I have driven thee, but I will not make a full end of thee, but correct thee in measure; yet will I not leave thee wholly unpunished ;' Jer. xlvi. 28. From all these, and from numerous other passages in the Old Testament, it is evident that it was designed that the Jewish nation should never be wholly destroyed ; that though they were scattered among the nations, they should still be a distinct people ; that while other nations would wholly cease to exist, yet that a remnant of the Jewish people, with the national peculiarities and customs, would still survive. How entirely this has been fulfilled, the remarkable history of the Jewish people everywhere testifies. Their present condition on the earth, as a people scattered in all nations, yet surviving; without a king and a temple, yet preserving their national prejudices and peculiarities, is a most striking fulfilment of the prophecy ; see Keith's *Evidence of the Fulfilment of Prophecy*, p. 64–82. ¶ *From Assyria*. The name Assyria is commonly applied to that region of country which lies between Media, Mesopotamia, Armenia, and Babylon, and which is now called Kurdistan. The boundaries of the kingdom have often varied, and, as a kingdom or separate nation, it has long since ceased to exist. The name *Assyria* in Scripture is given, (1.) To ancient Assyria, lying east of the Tigris, and between Armenia, Susiana, and Media— the region comprising mostly the modern kingdoms and the pashalic of Mosul. (2.) Most generally the name Assyria means *the kingdom of Assyria*, including Babylonia and Mesopotamia, and extending to the Euphrates ; Isa. vii. 20; viii. 7. (3.) After the overthrow of the Assyrian empire, the name continued to be applied to those countries which were formerly held under its dominion—including Babylonia (2 Kings xxiii. 29; Jer. ii. 18), Persia (Ezra vi. 22), and Syria.—*Robinson ; Calmet*. It is in this place applied to that extensive region, and means that the Jews scattered there—of whom there have always been many—shall be brought under the dominion of the Messiah. If the Nestorian Christians in the mountains of Kurdistan are the descendants of the lost ten tribes (see Note on ver. 12), then the reference here is, doubtless, to them. There are, however, other Jews there, as there always has been ; see Dr. Grant's work on '*The Nestorians, or, the Lost Ten Tribes*,' New York, 1841. ¶ *And from Egypt*. The well-known country in Africa, watered by the Nile. In all ages, there have been many Jews there. Its vicinity to Palestine ; its remarkable fertility, and the advantages which it offered to them, attracted many Jews there ; and at some periods they have composed no inconsiderable part of the population. It was in this country that the translation of the Hebrew Scriptures into the Greek language, called the Septuagint, was made, for the use of the numerous Jews residing there. At present they are numerous there, though the exact number is unknown. During the reign of Bonaparte, an estimate was made, for his information, of the number of Jews in the world, and, in that estimate, 1,000,000 was assigned to the Turkish empire—probably about a third part of all on the earth. A large portion of this number is in Egypt. ¶ *And from Pathros*. This was one of the three ancient divisions of Egypt. It was the same as Upper Egypt, or the southern part of Egypt, the *Coptic* portion of that country. The inhabitants of that country are called *Pathrusim*. To that place many of the Jews retired in the calamities of the nation, notwithstanding the remonstrances of Isaiah; Jer. xliv. 1, 15. For this act God severely threatened them; see Jer. xliv. 26–29. ¶ *And from Cush.* The Chaldee reads this, 'And from Judea.' The Syriac, 'And from Ethiopia.' This country denotes, properly, the regions settled by the descendants of Cush, the eldest son of Ham; Gen. x. 8. Commentators have differed very much about the region understood in the Scriptures by the name *Cush.* Bochart supposes that by it the southern parts of Arabia are always meant. Gesenius supposes, that by Cush is always meant a region in Africa. Michaelis supposes that by Cush the southern part of Arabia and the African Ethiopia were both intended. In the Scriptures, however, it is evident that the name is given to different regions. (1.) It means what may be called the *Oriental Cush,* including the region of the ancient Susiana, and bounded on the south by the Persian Gulf, and on the west and southwest by the Tigris, which separates it from the Arabian Irak. This province has the name Chusastan, or Chusistan, and was, probably, the ancient *Cush* mentioned in Zeph. iii. 10: 'From beyond the rivers of Ethiopia, (Heb. *Cush*), my suppliants, even the daughter of my dispersed, shall bring mine offering.' The principal rivers there were the Ulai, the Kur, the Chobar, and the Choaspes. The same place is referred to in 2 Kings xvii. 24, where the king of Assyria is said to have 'brought men from Babylon, and from *Cuthah*, and from Ava,' where the word *Cuthah* evidently refers to *Cush,* the Armenian mode of pronouncing Cush by exchanging the letters *Shin* for *Tav,* as they always do in pronouncing *Ashur,* calling it *Athur,* &c.; see the Chaldee Paraphrase, and the Syriac version, *passim.* (2.) *Cush,* as employed by the Hebrews, *usually* denoted the southern parts of Arabia, and was situated chiefly along the coast of the Red Sea, since there are several passages of Scripture where the name *Cush* occurs, which can be applied to no other country,

and least of all to the African Cush or Ethiopia; see Num. xii. 1, where the woman whom Moses married is called an 'Ethiopian,' (Heb. 'Cushite'). It can be scarcely supposed that she came from the distant regions of Ethiopia in Africa, but it is evident that she came from some part of Arabia. Also Habakkuk iii. 7, says:

I saw the tents of *Cushan* in affliction;
And the curtains of the land of Midian did tremble.

From which it is evident, that *Cushan* and *Midian* were countries adjacent; that is, in the southern part of Arabia; comp. 2 Chron. xxi. 16; xiv. 9. (3.) The word *Cush* is applied to Ethiopia, or the country south of Egypt, now called Abyssinia. This country comprehended not only Ethiopia above Syene and the cataracts, but likewise Thebais, or Upper Egypt; comp. Jer. xiii. 23; Dan. xi. 3; Ezek. xxx. 4, 5; Isa. xliv. 14; see Notes on Isa. xviii. 1. To which of these regions the prophet here refers, it is not easy to determine. As the other countries here mentioned, however, are chiefly in the East, it is most natural to suppose that he refers to *the Oriental Cush* mentioned under the first division. The general idea of the prophet is plain, that the scattered Jews should be gathered back to God. ¶ *And from Elam.* This was the name of a country originally possessed by the Persians, and so called from the son of Shem of the same name; Gen. xiv. 1. It was the southern part of Persia, situated on the Persian Gulf, and included, probably, the whole of the region now called Susiana or Chusistan. The city Susa or Shushan was in it; Dan. viii. 2. ¶ *And from Shinar.* This was a part of Babylonia, and is supposed to be the plain lying between the Tigris and the Euphrates; Gen. x. 10; xi. 2; Dan. i. 2; Zech. v. 11. It was the region elsewhere called Mesopotamia. The LXX. render it, 'And from Babylon;' and it is remarkable that Luke (Acts ii. 9), where he has reference, probably, to the place, speaks of 'the dwellers in Mesopotamia' as among those who heard 'the wonderful works of God' in their own language. It was in this plain that the tower of Babel was commenced; Gen. x. ¶ *And from*

12 And he shall set up an ensign *a* for the nations, and shall
assemble the *b* outcasts of Israel,

a ch.18.3.　　　*b* Ps.147.2; ch.27.13; 56.8.

and gather together the *c* dispersed
of Judah from the four corners [1] of
the earth.

c Jn.7.35; Js.1.1.　　　1 *wings.*

Hamath ; see Note, ch. x. 9. ¶ *And
from the islands of the sea.* This expression probably denotes the islands
situated in the Mediterranean, a part
of which were known to the Hebrews.
But, as geography was imperfectly
known, the phrase came to denote the
regions lying west of the land of Canaan ; the unknown countries which
were situated in that sea, or west of it,
and thus included the countries lying
around the Mediterranean. The word
translated ' islands ' here (אִיִּים) means
properly *habitable dry land*, in opposition to water ; Isa. xlii. 13: ' I will make
the rivers *dry land ;*' where to translate
it *islands* would make nonsense. Hence,
it means also land adjacent to water,
either washed by it, or surrounded by
it, that is, a maritime country, coast, or
island. Thus it means *coast* when applied to Ashdod (Isa. xx. 6); to Tyre
(Isa. xxii. 2, 6); to Peloponnesus or
Greece (called Chittim, Ezek. xxvii. 6).
It means an *island* when applied to
Caphtor or Crete (Jer. xlvii. 4; Amos
ix. 7). The word was commonly used
by the Hebrews to denote *distant regions
beyond the sea*, whether coasts or islands,
and especially the maritime countries
of the West, to them imperfectly known
through the voyages of the Phenicians ;
see Note on ch. xli. 1 ; comp. Isa. xxiv.
15; xl. 15; xlii. 4, 10, 12; li. 5.

12. *And he shall set up an ensign ;*
see ver. 10. The Messiah shall stand
in view of the nations, as a standard is
erected by a military leader. An ensign or standard was usually lifted up
on the mountains or on some elevated
place (comp. ch. xviii. 3); and the
meaning here is, that the Messiah would
be the conspicuous object around which
the nations would rally. ¶ *And shall
assemble.* This word, אָסַף *âsăph*, properly means, to gather, collect, to assemble together, as fruits are collected
for preservation (Ex. xxiii. 10); to collect a people together (Num. xxi. 16);
to gather or collect gold ; 2 Kings xxii. 4.
It may also mean to gather or collect

any thing for destruction (Jer. viii. 13);
and hence to take out of the way, to
kill, destroy ; 1 Sam. xv. 6; Ezek. xxiv.
29. Here, it is evidently synonymous
with the word ' recover ' in ver. 11. It
cannot be proved that it means that
God will *literally* re-assemble all the
scattered Jews ; for the *collecting them*,
or regathering them to himself *as his
people*, though they may be still scattered among the nations, is all that the
words necessarily imply. Thus when
the word is used, as it is repeatedly, to
denote the death of the patriarchs, where
it is said they were ' gathered to their
fathers,' it does not mean that they
were buried in the same grave, or the
same vicinity, but that they were united
to them in death ; they partook of the
same lot ; they all alike went down to
the dead ; Gen. xxv. 8; xxxv. 29; xlix.
29; Num. xx. 24; Deut. xxxii. 50. ¶ *The
outcasts of Israel.* The name ' Israel,'
applied at first to all the descendants
of Jacob, came at length to denote the
' kingdom of Israel,' or of the ' ten
tribes,' or of ' Ephraim,' as the tribes
which revolted under Jeroboam were
called. In this sense it is used in the
Scriptures after the time of Jeroboam,
and thus it acquired a technical signification, distinguishing it from Judah.
¶ *The dispersed of Judah.* ' Judah,'
also, though often used in a general
sense to denote the Jews as such, without
reference to the distinction in tribes, is
also used technically to denote the kingdom of Judah, as distinguished from the
kingdom of Israel. The tribe of Judah
was much larger than Benjamin, and
the name of the latter was lost in the
former. A considerable part of the ten
tribes returned again to their own land,
with those of the tribes of Judah and
Benjamin ; a portion remained still in
the countries of the East, and were intermingled with the other Jews who
remained there. All distinctions of the
tribes were gradually abolished, and
there is no reason to think that the
' ten tribes,' here referred to by the name
' Israel,' have now anywhere a distinct

13 The *a* envy also of Ephraim shall depart, and the adversaries

a Jer.3.18; Eze.37.17,22; Hos.1.11.

of Judah shall be cut off; Ephraim shall not envy Judah, and Judah shall not vex Ephraim.

and separate existence ; see this point fully proved in a review of Dr. Grant's work on ' *The Nestorians, or, the Lost Ten Tribes,*' in the *Bib. Rep.* for October 1841, and January 1842, by Prof. Robinson. The literal meaning here then would be, that he would gather the remains of those scattered people, whether pertaining to ' Israel ' or ' Judah,' from the regions where they were dispersed. It does not necessarily mean that they would be regathered in their distinctive capacity *as* ' Israel ' and ' Judah, or that the distinction would be still preserved, but that the people of God would be gathered together, and that all sources of alienation and discord would cease. The meaning, probably, is, that under the Messiah all the remains of that scattered people, in all parts of the earth, whether originally appertaining to ' Israel ' or ' Judah,' should be collected into one spiritual kingdom, constituting one happy and harmonious people. To the fulfilment of this, it is not necessary to be supposed that they would be literally gathered into one place, or that they would be restored to their own land, or that they would be preserved as a distinct and separate community. The leading idea is, that the Messiah would set up a glorious kingdom in which all causes of alienation and discord would cease. ¶ *From the four corners of the earth.* Chaldee, ' From the four *winds* of the earth.' The LXX. render it, ' From the four wings (πτερύγων) of the earth.' It means, that they should be collected to God from each of the four parts of the earth—the east, the west, the north, and the south. The Hebrew word here rendered 'corners,' means properly *wings.* It is applied, however, to the *corner,* or border of a thing, as a skirt, or mantle (1 Sam. xxiv. 5, 11; Deut. xxiii. 1); and hence to the boundaries, or corners of the earth, because the earth seems to have been represented as a quadrangular plain ; Ezek. vii. 2.

13. *The envy also.* The word *envy* here, is used in the sense of *hatred,* or the hatred which arose from the *ambi-*

tion of Ephraim, and from the *prosperity* of Judah. Ephraim here, is the name for the kingdom of Israel, or the ten tribes. The *reasons* of their envy and enmity towards Judah, all arising from their ambition, were the following :—(1.) This tribe, in connection with those which were allied to it, constituted a very large and flourishing part of the Jewish nation. They were, therefore, envious of any other tribe that claimed any superiority, and particularly jealous of Judah. (2.) They occupied a central and commanding position in Judea, and naturally claimed the pre-eminence over the tribes on the north. (3.) They had been formerly highly favoured by the abode of the ark and the tabernacle among them, and, on that account, claimed to be the natural *head* of the nation ; Josh. xviii. 1, 8, 10 ; Judg. xviii. 31; xxi. 19; 1 Sam. i. 3, 24. (4.) When Saul was king, though he was of the tribe of Benjamin (1 Sam. ix. 2), they submitted peaceably to his reign, because the Benjaminites were in alliance with them, and adjacent to them. But when Saul died, and the kingdom passed into the hands of David, of the tribe of Judah, their natural rival, thus exalting that powerful tribe, they became dissatisfied and restless. David kept the nation united ; but on his death, they threw off the yoke of his successor, and became a separate kingdom. From this time, their animosities and strifes became an important and painful part of the history of the Jewish nation, until the kingdom of Ephraim was removed. The language here is evidently figurative, and means, that in the time here referred to UNDER THE MESSIAH, the causes of animosity, before existing, would cease ; that contentions between those who are, by nature, brethren, and who ought to evince the spirit of brethren, would come to an end ; and that those animosities and strifes would be succeeded by a state of amity and peace. When the scattered Jews shall be regathered to God under the Messiah, all the contentions among them

14 But they shall fly upon the shoulders of the Philistines toward the west; they shall spoil ¹ them of

1 *the children.*   2 *Edom and Moab* shall be *the laying on of their hand.*

the east together; ² they shall lay their hand upon Edom and Moab; and *a* the children of Ammon ³ shall obey them.

a ch.60.14.   3 *their obedience.*

shall cease, and they shall be *united* under one king and prince. All the causes of contention which had so long existed, and which had produced such disastrous results, would come to an end. The strifes and contentions of these two kingdoms, once belonging to the same nation, and descended from the same ancestors—the painful and protracted *family broil*—was the object that most prominently attracted the attention, then, of the prophets of God. The most happy idea of future blessedness which was presented to the mind of the prophet, was that period when all this should cease, and when, under the Messiah, all should be harmony and love. ¶ *And the adversaries of Judah shall be cut off* That is, Judah shall be safe; the people of God shall be delivered from their enemies—referring to the future period under - the Messiah, when the church should be universally prosperous. ¶ *Judah shall not vex Ephraim.* Shall not oppress, disturb, or oppose. There shall be peace between them. The church prospers only when contentions and strifes cease; when Christians lay aside their animosities, and love as brethren, and are *united* in the great work of spreading the gospel around the world. That time will yet come. *When* that time comes, the kingdom of the Son of God will be established. *Until* that time, it will be in vain that the effort is made to bring the world to the knowledge of the truth; or if not wholly in vain, the efforts of Christians who seek the conversion of the world will be retarded, embarrassed, and greatly enfeebled. How devoutly, therefore, should every friend of the Redeemer pray, that all causes of strife may cease, and that his people may be united, as the heart of one man, in the effort to bring the whole world to the knowledge of the truth.

14. *But they shall fly.* The design of this verse is, to show the rapid and certain spiritual conquests which would

result from the conversion of the scattered Jewish people. The Jews understood this literally, as referring to the conquests over their enemies. But if the exposition which has been given of this chapter thus far is correct, the passage is to be interpreted as a figurative description of the triumph of the people of God under the Messiah. The *time* to which it refers, is that which shall succeed the conversion of the scattered Jews. The *effect* of the gospel is represented under an image which, to Jews, would be most striking—that of conquest over the neighbouring nations with whom they had been continually at war. Philistia, Edom, Moab, and Ammon, had been always the enemies of Judea; and to the Jews, no figurative representation could be more striking than that, *after* the union of Judah and Ephraim, they should proceed in rapid and certain conquest to subdue their ancient and formidable enemies. The meaning of the phrase 'they shall fly,' is, they shall hasten with a rapid motion, like a bird. They shall do it quickly, without delay, as an eagle hastens to its prey. It indicates their *suddenly* engaging in this, and the celerity and certainty of their movements. As the united powers of Judah and Ephraim would naturally make a sudden descent on Philistia, so the Jews, united under the Messiah, would go to the rapid and certain conversion of those who had been the enemies of the cross. ¶ *Upon the shoulders.* בְּכָתֵף. There has been a great variety in the interpretation of this passage; and it is evident that our translation does not express a very clear idea. The LXX. render it, 'And they shall fly in the ships of foreigners, and they shall plunder the sea.' The Chaldee, 'And they shall be joined with one shoulder [that is, they shall be *united* shoulder to shoulder], that they may smite the Philistines who are in the west.' The Syriac, 'But they shall *plough* the Philistines;' that is,

15 And the LORD shall utterly
destroy the tongue of the Egyptian

they shall subdue them, and cultivate
their land. The word rendered 'shoulder,' means, properly, *the shoulder*, as
of a man or beast (ch. xlvi. 7; xlix. 22;
Num. vii. 9; Job xxxi. 22; Ezek. xxiv.
4); the *undersetters* or shoulders to
support the lavers (1 Kings vii. 30);
a corner or side of a building (Ex.
xxxviii. 14); and is applied to *the side*
of anything, as the side of a building,
the border of a country, a city, or sea
(1 Kings vi. 8; vii. 39; Num. xxxiv. 11;
Josh. xv. 8, 10, 11, &c.) Here it
seems to mean, not that the Jews
would be borne *upon* the shoulder of
the Philistines, but that they would
make a sudden and rapid descent *upon
their borders;* they would invade their
territory, and carry their conquest ' toward the west.' The construction is,
therefore, 'they shall make a rapid
descent on the borders of the Philistines,' or, in other words, the spiritual
conquest over the enemies of the church
of God shall be certain and rapid.
¶ *The Philistines.* Philistia was situated on the southwestern side of the
land of Canaan. The Philistines were
therefore adjacent to the Jews, and
were often involved in war with them.
They were among the most constant
and formidable enemies which the Jews
had. ¶ *Toward the west.* This does
not mean that they should be borne
on the shoulders of the Philistines *to*
the west; but that they should make a
sudden and rapid descent on the Philistines, who *were* west of them. It stands
opposed to the nations immediately
mentioned as lying *east* of the land of
Judea. ¶ *They shall spoil.* They
shall plunder; or, they shall take them,
and their towns and property, as the
spoil of war. That is, they shall vanquish them, and make them subject to
them. According to the interpretation
which has been pursued in this chapter,
it means, that the enemies of God shall
be subdued, and brought to the knowledge of the truth, in a rapid and decisive manner. The *language* is that
which is drawn from the idea of conquest; the *idea* is that of a rapid and
far-spreading conversion among the na-

sea; and with his mighty wind
shall he shake his hand over tho

tions, to the gospel. ¶ *Them of the
east.* Heb. ' The sons of the east;' that
is, the nations east of Judea. ¶ *They
shall lay their hand.* Heb. ' Edom and
Moab shall be the laying on of their
hand;' that is, they shall lay their
hand on those nations for conquest and
spoil; they shall subdue them. ¶ *Edom.*
Idumea; the country settled by the
descendants of Esau—a country that
was south of Judea, and extended from
the Dead Sea to the Elanitic gulf of
the Red Sea. They were an independent people until the time of David,
and were reduced to subjection by him,
but they afterwards revolted and became again independent. They were
often engaged in wars with the Jews,
and their conquest was an object that
was deemed by the Jews to be very
desirable (see Notes on ch. xxxiv.)
¶ *And Moab.* The country of the
Moabites was east of the river Jordan,
on both sides of the river Arnon, and
adjoining the Dead Sea. Their capital
was on the river Arnon. They also
were often involved in wars with tho
Jews (comp. Deut. xxiii. 3; see Notes
on ch. xv., xvi.) ¶ *And the children
of Ammon.* The Ammonites, the descendants of Ammon, a son of Lot.
Their country lay southeast of Judea
(Deut. ii. 19-21). Their territory extended from the river Arnon north to
the river Jabbok, and from the Jordan
far into Arabia. It was directly north
of Moab. They were often engaged,
in alliance with the Moabites, in waging
war against the Jews. ¶ *Shall obey
them.* Heb. ' Shall be their obedience.'
All these descriptions are similar. They
are not to be interpreted literally, but
are designed to denote the rapid triumphs
of the truth of God *after* the conversion
of the Jews; and the sense is, that tho
conquests of the gospel will be as sudden, as great, and as striking over its
enemies, as *would have been* the complete subjugation of Philistia, Moab,
Ammon, and Edom, to the victorious
army of the Jews.

15. *And the* LORD. The prophet
goes on with the description of the
effect which shall follow the return of

river, and shall smite it in the seven streams, and make *men* go
over ¹ dry-shod.

1 in shoes.

the scattered Jews to God. The language is figurative, and is here drawn from that which was the great storehouse of all the imagery of the Jews— the deliverance of their fathers from the bondage of Egypt. The general sense is, that all the embarrassments which would tend to impede them would be removed; and that God would make their return as easy and as safe, as *would* have been the journey of their fathers to the land of Canaan, if the 'Egyptian Sea' had been removed entirely, and if the 'river,' with its 'seven streams,' by nature so formidable a barrier, had been dried up, and a path had been made to occupy its former place. Figuratively, the passage means, that all the obstructions to the peace and safety of the people of God would be removed, and that their way would be easy and safe. ¶ *The tongue.* The Hebrews applied the word 'tongue' to anything that resembled a tongue—to a bar of gold (Josh. vii. 21, 24); to a flame of fire (Note, Isa. v. 24; comp. Acts ii. 3); to a bay of the sea, or a gulf, from its shape (Josh. xv. 5; xviii. 19). So we speak of a tongue of land. When it is said that the Lord would 'utterly destroy' it, it is equivalent to saying that it would be entirely dried up; that is, so as to present no obstruction. ¶ *Of the Egyptian Sea.* Some interpreters, among whom is Vitringa, have supposed that by the tongue of the Egyptian Sea here mentioned, is meant the river Nile, which flows into the Mediterranean, here called, as they suppose, the Egyptian Sea. Vitringa observes that the Nile, before it flows into the Mediterranean, is divided into two streams or rivers, which form the Delta or the triangular territory lying between these two rivers, and bounded on the north by the Mediterranean. The eastern branch of the Nile being the largest, he supposes is called the tongue or *bay* of the Egyptian Sea. But to this interpretation there are obvious objections—(1.) It is not known that the Mediterranean is elsewhere called the Egyptian Sea. (2.) This whole description pertains to the departure

of the children of Israel from Egypt The imagery is all drawn from that. But, in their departure, the Nile constituted no obstruction. Their place of residence, in Goshen, was east of the Nile. All the obstruction that they met with, from any sea or river, was from the Red Sea. (3.) The Red Sea is divided, at its northern extremity, into two bays, or forks, which may be called the *tongues* of the sea, and across one of which the Israelites passed in going from Egypt. Of these branches, the western one was called the Hero-öpolite branch, and the eastern, the Elanitic branch. It was across the western branch that they passed. When it is said that Jehovah would 'destroy' this, it means that he would dry it up so that it would be no obstruction; in other words, he would take the most formidable obstructions to the progress of his people out of the way. ¶ *And with his mighty wind.* With a strong and powerful wind. Michaelis supposes that by this is meant a tempest. But there is, more probably, a reference to a strong and steady *hot* wind, such as blows over burning deserts, and such as would have a tendency to dry up even mighty waters. The illustration is, probably, derived from the fact that a strong east wind was employed to make a way through the Red Sea (Ex. xiv. 21). If the allusion here be rather to a mighty wind or a tempest, than to one that is hot, and that tends to evaporate the waters even of the rivers, then it means that the wind would be so mighty as to part the waters, and make a path through the river, as was done in the Red Sea and at the Jordan. The *idea* is, that God would remove the obstructions to the rapid and complete deliverance and conversion of men. ¶ *Shall he shake his hand.* This is to indicate that the mighty wind will be sent from God, and that it is designed to effect this passage through the rivers. The shaking of the hand, in the Scripture, is usually an indication of anger, or of strong and settled purpose (see ch. x. 32; xiii. 2; Zech. ii. 9). ¶ *Over the*

16 And there shall be an highway for the remnant of his people, which shall be left, from Assyria; like as it was *a* to Israel in the day that he came up out of the land of Egypt.

river. Many have understood this as referring to the Nile; but two considerations show that the Euphrates is rather intended—(1.) The term 'THE river' (הַנָּהָר, *hănnâhâr*) is usually applied to the Euphrates, called THE RIVER, by way of eminence; and when the term is used without any qualification, that river is commonly intended (see Notes, ch. vii. 20; viii. 7; comp. Gen. xxxi. 21; xxxvi. 37; 1 Kings iv. 21; Ezra iv. 10, 16; v. 3). (2.) The effect of this smiting of the river is said to be (ver. 16) that there would be a highway for the people *from Assyria*, which could be caused only by removing the obstruction which is produced by the Euphrates lying between Judea and some parts of Assyria. ¶ *And shall smite it.* That is, to dry it up, or to make it passable. ¶ *In the seven streams.* The word 'streams' here (נְחָלִים) denotes streams of much less dimensions than a river. It is applied to *a valley* with a brook running through it (Gen. xxvi. 19); and then to any small brook or stream, or rivulet (Gen. xxxii. 24; Ps. lxxiv. 15). Here it denotes brooks or streams that would be fordable. When it is said that the river should be smitten '*in* the seven streams,' the Hebrew does not mean that it was *already* divided into seven streams, and that God would smite *them*, but it means, that God would smite it *into* seven streams or rivulets; that is, into *many* such rivulets (for the number seven is often used to denote a large indefinite number, Note, ch. iv. 1); and the expression denotes, that though the river presented an obstruction, in its natural size, which they could not overcome, yet God would make new channels for it, and scatter it into innumerable rivulets or small streams, so that they could pass over it dry-shod. A remarkable illustration of this occurs in Herodotus (i. 189): 'Cyrus, in his march to Babylon, arrived at the river Gyndes, which, rising in the mountains of Matiene, and passing through the country of the Dar-

neans, loses itself in the Tigris; and this, after flowing by Opis, is finally discharged into the Red Sea. While Cyrus was endeavouring to pass this river, which could not be performed without boats, one of the white consecrated horses boldly entering the stream, in his attempts to cross it, was borne away by the rapidity of the current, and totally lost. Cyrus, exasperated by the accident, made a vow that he would render this stream so very insignificant, that women should hereafter be able to cross it without so much as wetting their feet. He accordingly suspended his designs on Babylon, and divided his forces into two parts; he then marked out with a line, on each side of the river, one hundred and eighty trenches; these were dug according to his orders, and so great a number of men were employed that he accomplished his purpose; but he thus wasted the whole of that summer' (see also Seneca, *De Ira.* iii. 21). ¶ *Go over dry-shod.* Heb. 'In shoes, or sandals.' The waters in the innumerable rivulets to which the great river should be reduced, would be so shallow, that they could even pass them in their sandals without wetting their feet—a strong figurative expression, denoting that the obstruction would be completely removed. 'The prophet, under these metaphors, intends nothing else than that there would be no impediment to God when he wished to deliver his people from captivity.'—(Calvin.)

16. *And there shall be an highway.* All obstructions shall be removed, and they shall be permitted to return without hinderance (comp. Note on ch. xxxv. 8). ¶ *For the remnant of his people from Assyria* (Note, ver. 11). ¶ *Like as it was to Israel,* &c. That is, God will remove all obstructions as he did at the Red Sea; he will subdue all their enemies; he will provide for their wants; and he will interpose by the manifest marks of his presence and protection, as their God and their friend.—The

CHAPTER XII.

ANALYSIS OF THE CHAPTER.

THIS chapter is a part of the vision which was commenced in ch. x. 5. The prophet had foretold the deliverance of the nation from the threatened invasion of Sennacherib (ch. x.); he had then looked forward to the times of the Messiah, and described the certainty, the character, and the consequences of his reign (ch. xi.) The eleventh chapter closes with a reference to the deliverance of the nation from the oppression of the Egyptians. That deliverance was celebrated with a beautiful ode, which was sung by Miriam and ' all the women,' who ' went out after her with timbrels and with dances' (Ex. xv. 1–21). In imitation of that deliverance, Isaiah says, in this chapter, that the deliverance of which he speaks shall be celebrated also with a song of praise; and this chapter, therefore, is properly an

expression of the feelings of the redeemed people of God, in view of his great mercy in interposing to save them. It should be read in view of the great and glorious deliverance which God has wrought for us in the redemption of his Son; and with feelings of lofty gratitude that he has brought us from worse than Egyptian bondage—the bondage of sin. The song is far better applied to the times of the Messiah, than it could be to anything which occurred under the Jewish dispensation. The Jews themselves appear to have applied it to his time. On the last day of the feast of tabernacles, they brought water in a golden pitcher from the fountain of Siloam, and poured it, mingled with wine, on the sacrifice that was on the altar, with great rejoicing (see Notes, John vii. 14, 37). This custom was not required by Moses, and probably arose from the command in ver. 3 of this chapter. Our Saviour applied it to himself, to the benefits of

general view of the chapter is, therefore, that it refers to the triumph of the Messiah's kingdom; that it is not yet fully accomplished; and that the time is coming when the scattered Jews shall be regathered to God—not returned to their own land, but brought again under his dominion under the administration of the Messiah; and that this event shall be attended with a sudden removal of the obstructions to the gospel, and to its rapid spread everywhere among the nations. Comparing this with the present state of the Jews, we may remark, in regard to this prospect—(1.) That they are now, and will continue to be, scattered in all nations. They have been driven to all parts of the earth—wanderers without a home —yet continuing their customs, rites, and peculiar opinions; and continuing to live, notwithstanding all the efforts of the nations to crush and destroy them. (2.) They speak nearly all the languages of the world. They are acquainted with all the customs, prejudices, and opinions of the nations of the earth. They would, therefore, be under no necessity of engaging in the laborious work of learning language—which now occupies so much of the time, and consumes so much of the strength of the modern missionary. (3.) The law of God is thus in all nations. It is in every synagogue; and it has been well said, that the law there is like extin-

guished candles, and that all that is needful to illuminate the world, is to light those candles. Let the Jew everywhere be brought to see the true meaning of his law; let the light of evangelical truth shine into his synagogue, and the world would be at once illuminated. The truth would go with the rapidity of the sunbeams from place to place, until the whole earth would be enlightened with the knowledge of the Redeemer. (4.) The Jews, when converted, make the best missionaries. There is a freshness in their views of the Messiah when they are converted, which Gentile converts seldom feel. The apostles were all Jews; and the zeal of Paul shows what converted Jews will do when they become engaged in making known the true Messiah. If it has been a characteristic of their nation that they would ' compass sea and land to make one proselyte,' what will their more than three millions accomplish when they become converted to the true faith of the Redeemer ? We have every reason, therefore, to expect that God intends to make great use yet of the Jews, whom he has preserved scattered everywhere—though they be but a ' remnant' —in converting the world to his Son. And we should most fervently pray, that they may be imbued with love to their long-rejected Messiah, and that they may everywhere become the missionaries of the cross.

his gospel, and to the influences of the Spirit (John vii.); and the ancient Jews so applied it also. 'Why is it called the house of drawing? Because from thence they draw the Holy Spirit; as it is written, "and ye shall draw water with joy from the fountains of salvation."'—(*Jerusalem Talmud*, as quoted by Lowth.)

A ND in that day thou shalt say, O Lord, I *a* will praise thee:

CHAPTER XII.

1. *And in that day.* The day referred to in the previous chapter, the time of the Messiah, when the effects of his reign shall be seen everywhere. The duty of praise, however, is couched in such language as to make it applicable to the event predicted in the former part of the prophecy (ch. x.)—the delivering of the nation from the invasion of Sennacherib, as well as the more glorious event on which the prophet fixed his eye (ch. xi.)—the coming and reign of the Messiah. The language of this song of praise would be appropriate to both these events. ¶ *Thou shalt say.* The address to an individual here, in the term 'thou,' is equivalent to *every one*, meaning that *all* who were thus interested in the Divine interposition should say it. ¶ *O Lord.* O Jehovah —the great author of this interposition. ¶ *I will praise thee: though thou wast angry with me.* If this language is applied to the Jews, and supposed to be used by them in regard to the invasion of Sennacherib, it means, that God suffered their land to be invaded, and to be subjected to calamities, in consequence of their sins (ch. x. 6, *sq.*) If it is supposed to be applied to the time of the Messiah, then it is language which every redeemed sinner may use, that God was angry with him, but that his anger is turned away. As applicable to the redeemed, it is an acknowledgment which they all feel, that they have no claim to his mercy, and that it lays the foundation for unceasing praise that his anger is turned away by the plan of salvation.

2. *Behold, God is my salvation.* Or, God is the author, or source, of my salvation. It has not been brought about by any human hands, but is to be traced directly to him. The value of a gift is

though *b* thou wast angry with me, thine anger is turned away, and thou comfortedst me.

2 Behold, God *is* my salvation; I will trust, and not be afraid: for the *c* Lord JEHOVAH *is* my strength and *my* song; he also is become my salvation.

a Ps.34.1,&c.   *b* Ps.30.5; ch.54.7,8; Hos.6.1.   *c* Ps.118.14.

always enhanced by the dignity and excellency of the giver, and it confers an inestimable value on the blessings of salvation, that they are conferred by a being no less than the infinite God. It is not by human or angelic power; but it is to be traced directly and entirely to Jehovah. ¶ *I will trust, and not be afraid.* Since God is its author; since he is able to defend me, and to perfect that which he has begun, I will confide in him, and not be afraid of the power or machinations of any enemy. In his hands I am safe. God is the foundation of our confidence; and trusting in him, his people shall never be moved. ¶ *For the* Lord JEHOVAH. This is one of the four places in which our translators have retained the original word Jehovah, though the Hebrew word occurs often in the Scriptures. The other places where the word Jehovah is retained in our version are, Ex. vi. 3; Ps. lxxviii. 18; Isa. xxvi. 4. The original in this place is יָהּ יְהוָה (Jah, Jehovah). The word Jah (יָהּ) is an abbreviation of the word Jehovah. The abbreviated form is often used for the sake of conciseness, particularly in the Psalms, as in the expression *Hallelujah* (הַלְלוּ־יָהּ), *i.e.*, praise Jehovah (Ps. lxxxix. 9; xciv. 7, 12; civ. 35; cv. 15; cvi. 1, 48; cxi. 1; cxiii. 1, *et al.*) In this place, and Isa. xxvi. 4, the *repetition* of the name seems to be used to denote *emphasis;* or perhaps to indicate that Jehovah is the same always—an unchangeable God. In two codices of Kennicott, however, the name Jah (יָהּ) is omitted, and it has been conjectured by some that the repetition is an error of transcribers; but the best MSS. retain it. The LXX., the Chaldee, and the Syriac, however, omit it. ¶ *Is my strength and* my *song.* The same expression occurs in the hymn

3 Therefore with joy *a* shall ye draw water *b* out of the wells of salvation.

4 And in that day shall ye say, Praise *c* the LORD, ¹ call upon his

a Cant.2.3.   *b* Jn.4.10,14.

name, declare his doings among the people, make mention that his name is exalted.

5 Sing *d* unto the LORD; for he

c Ps.145.4-6.   1 or, *proclaim.*
d Ex.15.1,21; Ps.98.1.

that Moses composed after the passage of the Red Sea, in imitation of which this song is evidently composed; Ex. xv. 2:

JEHOVAH is my strength and my song,
And he is become my salvation.

The word 'strength' means, that he is the source of strength, and implies that all who are redeemed are willing to acknowledge that all their strength is in God. The word 'song' implies that he is the proper object of praise; it is to celebrate *his* praise that the 'song' is composed. ¶ *He also is become my salvation.* This is also found in the song of Moses (Ex. xv. 2). It means that God had become, or was the author of salvation. It is by his hand that the deliverance has been effected, and to him should be the praise.

3. *Therefore.* In view of all his mercies. The Hebrew is, however, simply, '*and* ye shall draw.' It has already been intimated that the Jews applied this passage to the Holy Spirit: and that probably on this they based their custom of drawing water from the fountain of Siloam at the feast of the dedication (Note, John vii. 37). The fountain of Siloam was in the eastern part of the city, and the water was borne from that fountain in a golden cup, and was poured, with every expression of rejoicing, on the sacrifice on the altar. It is not probable, however, that this custom was in use in the time of Isaiah. The language is evidently figurative; but the meaning is obvious. A fountain, or a well, in the sacred writings, is an emblem of that which produces joy and refreshment; which sustains and cheers. The figure is often employed to denote that which supports and refreshes the soul; which sustains man when sinking from exhaustion, as the bubbling fountain or well refreshes the weary and fainting pilgrim (comp. John iv. 14). It is thus applied to God as an overflowing fountain, fitted to supply the wants of all his creatures (Jer. ii. 13; xvii. 13;

Ps. xxxvi. 9; Prov. xiv. 27); and to his plan of salvation—the sources of comfort which he has opened in the scheme of redeeming mercy to satisfy the wants of the souls of men (Zech. xiii. 1; Isa. xli. 18; Rev. vii. 17). The word 'rivers' is used in the same sense as 'fountains' in the above places (Isa. xlii. 15; xliii. 19, 20). Generally, in the Scriptures, streams, fountains, rivers, are used as emblematic of the abundant fulness and richness of the mercies which God has provided to supply the spiritual necessities of men. The idea here is, therefore, that they should partake abundantly of the mercies of salvation; that it was free, overflowing, and refreshing —like waters to weary pilgrims in the desert; and that their partaking of it would be with joy. It would fill the soul with happiness; as the discovery of an abundant fountain, or a well in the desert, fills the thirsty pilgrim with rejoicing.

4. *And in that day* (see ver. 1). ¶ *Call upon his name.* Marg. 'Proclaim.' It denotes to call upon him in the way of celebrating his praise. The whole hymn is one of praise, and not of prayer. ¶ *Declare among the people.* Among all people, that they may be brought to see his glory, and join in the celebration of his praise. ¶ *His doings.* Particularly in regard to the great events which are the subject of the previous predictions—his interposition in saving men by the Messiah from eternal death. ¶ *Make mention.* Heb. 'Cause it to be remembered' (see Note on ch. lxii. 6). ¶ *That his name is exalted.* That it is worthy of adoration and praise. It is worthy to be exalted, or lifted up in view of the nations of the earth (2 Sam. xxii. 47; Ps. xxi. 13; xlvi. 10).

5. *Sing unto the Lord.* This is the same expression which occurs in the song of Moses (Ex. xv. 21). Isaiah evidently had that in his eye. ¶ *He hath done excellent things.* Things that are exalted (נֵאוּת); that are worthy

hath done excellent things: this *is* known in all the earth.

6 Cry *a* out and shout, thou 1 inhabitant of Zion: for *b* great *is* the Holy One of Israel in the midst of thee.

a Zep.3.14. 1 *inhabitress.* *b* Ps.89.18.

CHAPTER XIII.

ANALYSIS OF CHAPTERS XIII.; XIV. 1–27.

THE thirteenth chapter of Isaiah commences a new prophecy, and, according to the division of Vitringa, a new book or part of his prophecies. The first book, according to him, extending from ch. i. to the close of ch. xii., is occupied with a series of prophecies respecting the Jews. The second portion, from ch. xiii. to ch. xxxv. inclusive, consists of a number of separate predictions respecting other nations, with which the Jews were in various ways more or less connected. See Introduction.

The thirteenth and the fourteenth chapters, with the exception of the last five verses of ch. xiv., contain one entire prophecy foretelling the destruction of Babylon. The main design is to predict the destruction of that city: but it is also connected with a design to furnish consolation to the Jews. They were to be carried captive there; and the purpose of the prophet was to assure them that the city to which they should yet be borne as exiles would be completely destroyed.

It is not easy to ascertain with certainty the precise time when this prophecy was delivered, nor is it very material. It is certain that it was delivered either during the reigns of Uzziah, Jotham, Ahaz, or Hezekiah (ch. i. 1), the reign of the last of whom closed 710 years before the Christian era; and, since the Jews were carried captive to Babylon 586 years before that era, the prophecy must have been delivered 124 years before that event; and, as Babylon was taken by Cyrus 536 years before Christ, it must have been delivered at least 174 years before its accomplish-

to be celebrated, and had in remembrance; things that are majestic, grand, and wonderful. ¶ *This is known in all the earth.* Or, more properly, 'Let this be known in all the earth.' It is worthy of being celebrated everywhere. It should be sounded abroad through all lands. This expresses the sincere desire of all who are redeemed, and who are made sensible of the goodness and mercy of God the Saviour. The instinctive and the unceasing wish is, that the wonders of the plan of redeeming mercy should be everywhere known among the nations, and that all flesh should see the salvation of our God.

6. *Cry out* (צַהֲלִי). This word is usually applied to the neighing of a horse (Jer. v. 8; viii. 16). It is also used to express joy, pleasure, exultation, by a clear and loud sound of the voice (Isa. x. 30; xii. 6; xiv. 14; liv. 1; Jer. xxxi. 7; l. 11). It is here synonymous with the numerous passages in the Psalms, and elsewhere, where the people of God are called on to exult, to shout, to make a noise as expressive of their joy (Ps. xlvii. 1; cxlviii.; cxlix.; Isa. xlii. 11; xliv. 23; Jer. xxxi. 7; Zeph. iii. 14; Zech. ix. 9). ¶ *And shout* (רֹנִּי). This word properly means to cry aloud (Prov. i. 20; viii. 3); to cry for help (Lam. ii. 19); to raise a shout of joy,

to rejoice, or exult (Lev. ix. 24; Job xxxviii. 7); to praise, or celebrate with joy (Ps. xxxiii. 1; li. 15; lix. 17; lxxxix. 13). Here it denotes the joy in view of God's mercies, which leads to songs of exalted praise. ¶ *Thou inhabitant of Zion.* Thou that dwellest in Zion; that is, thou who art numbered with the people of God (Note, ch. i. 8). The margin here is in accordance with the Hebrew — 'Inhabitress of Zion;' and the word here used is applicable to *the people,* rather than to an individual. ¶ *For great is the Holy One of Israel.* That is, God has shown himself great and worthy of praise, by the wonderful deliverance which he has wrought for his people. Thus he closes this beautiful hymn. It is worthy of the theme —worthy to be sung by all. O, may all the redeemed join in this song of deliverance; and may the time soon come, when the beautiful vision of the poet shall be realized, in the triumphant song of redemption echoing around the world:

'One song employs all nations; and all cry,
"Worthy the Lamb, for he was slain for us!"
The dwellers in the vales and on the rocks
Shout to each other, and the mountain-tops
From distant mountains catch the flying joy;
Till, nation after nation taught the strain,
Earth rolls the rapturous hosanna round.'

The Task, Book vi.

ment. Theodoret supposed that this prophecy was published during the latter part of the reign of Hezekiah. Cocceius and Lightfoot supposed that it was delivered about the same period as the former, and this also is the opinion of Vitringa. All that is of importance, is, that if it was a true prophecy of Isaiah, as there is the fullest demonstration, it must have been delivered *at least* 170 years before the event which it foretells was accomplished. The *material* points to settle in regard to the prophecies are— (1) Whether they were delivered before the event; (2) whether the things predicted could have been foreseen by human sagacity; (3) whether the prediction is so clear, and particular, as to correspond with the event, or not to be mere vague conjecture; and (4) whether there is such an occurrence of events as to constitute in fact a fulfilment of the prophecy. If these things meet, there is the fullest evidence that the prediction was from God.

At the time when this prophecy was delivered, the Jews were in the secure possession of their own capital and country. They were harassed, indeed, by surrounding nations, but they were still free. They had no controversy with Babylon; nor had they reason to apprehend danger from that distant people. Their being borne to that land, was itself, in the time of Isaiah, a distant event, and one that then was not likely to occur. It is remarkable that Isaiah does not distinctly *foretell* that event here, but throws himself to a period of time *beyond* that, when they *would be* in captivity, and predicts their deliverance. His prophecy *supposes* that event to have occurred. It is a vision passing before his mind *after* that event had taken place; when they would be.*in* Babylon; and when they would be sighing for deliverance (ch. xiv. 1, 2). The prophet, therefore, may be conceived in this vision as taking his stand *beyond* an event which had not yet occurred—the captivity of the Jews and their removal to Babylon—and predicting *another* event still more future, which would result in their deliverance—the complete overthrow of the city, and the consequent deliverance of the Jewish people. We are to conceive him standing, as it were, amidst the captive Jews, and directing his eye onward to the complete recovery of the nation by the destruction of Babylon itself. (ch. xiv. 1, 2). See Introduction, § 7, III. (4.)

This prophecy of the destruction of Babylon was delivered, we have seen, at least 174 years before the event occurred. At the time when it was delivered, nothing was more improbable than the ruin of that city as described by Isaiah (ch. xiii. 19-22). It was one of the largest, most

flourishing, and perhaps the most strongly fortified city of the world. The prediction that it should be like 'Sodom and Gomorrah;' that it should 'never be inhabited;' that the wild beast of the desert should lie there; and that dragons should be in their pleasant palaces, was wholly improbable; and could have been foreseen *only* by God. There were no natural causes that were leading to this which man could perceive, or of which a stranger and a foreigner, like Isaiah, could have any knowledge. This will appear evident by a brief description of the condition of this celebrated city.—BABYLON (derived from BABEL, and probably built on the same spot as the tower of Babel) was the capital of Babylonia, or Chaldea, and was probably built by Nimrod; but it was a long period before it obtained its subsequent size and splendour. It was enlarged by Belus, and so greatly beautified and improved by Semiramis, that she might be called not improperly the foundress of it. It was ·subsequently greatly increased and embellished by Nebuchadnezzar. It stood in the midst of a large plain, and on a very deep and fertile soil. It was on both sides of the river Euphrates, and of course was divided by that river into two parts. The two parts were connected by a bridge near the centre of the city; and there is also said to have been a *tunnel,* or subterranean passage, made from the palace on the east of the river to the palace on the west, made under the river. The old city was on the east, and the new city, built by Nebuchadnezzar, was on the west. Both these divisions were enclosed by one wall, and the whole formed a complete square, which Herodotus, who visited it, and who is the most ancient author who has written on it, says, was 480 furlongs in compass, or 120 furlongs on each side: that is, it was fifteen miles on each side, or sixty miles in compass. Public belief has been greatly staggered by the accounts which are thus given of the size of Babylon. But the account of the extent of the walls given, by ancient authors, is nearly uniform. Thus Herodotus says it was 480 stadia, or furlongs, in circumference. Pliny and Solinus make it the same. Strabo says it was 385 stadia in circumference; Diodorus, 360; Clitarchus, who accompanied Alexander, says it was 365, and Curtius says it was 368. According to the lowest of these estimates, it could not have been less than twelve miles square, or forty-eight miles in circumference; and was at least eight times as large in extent as London and its appendages; and somewhat larger than the entire district of Columbia.—(Calmet, and *Edin. Ency.*) It is not to be inferred, however, that all this vast space was compactly built. It was enclosed with a wall; but a considerable portion of it might have been occupied with the public squares, with palaces, and with hanging gardens, or, possibly, might have been unoccupied.

The walls of Babylon are said by Herodotus to have been eighty-seven feet thick, and 350 high. They were built of brick, or clay dried in the sun, and not burned; and were cemented by a kind of glutinous earth, or bitumen, with which the adjacent region abounded. The whole city was surrounded by an immense ditch, from which this clay had been taken to make the walls of the city, and which, being always filled with water, contributed materially to its defence. There were 100 gates to the city, twenty-five on each side. These gates were of solid brass. Between every two of them there were three towers, raised ten feet above the walls. From the gates there were streets, each 151 feet in width, which ran through the city, so that there were fifty streets in all, cutting each other at right angles, and forming 676 squares in the city. A bridge sixty feet in width crossed the Euphrates in the centre of the city, and at the extremities of the bridge were two palaces, the old palace on the east, and the new palace on the west. The temple of Belus, which occupied almost a square, was near the old palace on the east. Babylon was celebrated for its hanging gardens, built on arches, near 400 feet square, and which were elevated one above another, by terraces, until they reached the height of the walls of the city. On the highest terrace was an aqueduct for watering the gardens, supplied with water by a pump, or probably by the *Persian wheel*, by which the water of the Euphrates was raised to this extraordinary height. In order to prevent the danger of being overflown by the rise in the Euphrates, two canals were cut from the river at a considerable distance above the town, by which the superabundant waters were carried into the Tigris. It is to be borne in mind, however, in order to a just view of this prophecy, that Babylon did not attain its highest splendour and magnificence until *after* the time of Isaiah. It was under Nebuchadnezzar, who ascended the throne of Babylon about 100 years after Isaiah died, that it rose to its highest degree of splendour and power. When Isaiah lived, though it was a city of great wealth and power, and distinguished for great commercial advantages, yet it was then dependent on Assyria. It did not become the capital of the vast kingdom of Chaldea until 680 years before Christ, according to the chronology of Hales, when Assaradon became master of Babylon, and reunited the empires of Assyria and Chaldea.

Babylon was the natural seat of empire in the East, and was early distinguished for its commercial advantages. A simple glance at the map of Asia will convince any one that somewhere in the vicinity of Babylon is the natural seat of power in the East, and that few places on the globe are more eligibly situated for a vast trade, as it was conducted before the discovery of the Cape of Good Hope. The commerce from the rich regions of Asia naturally passed through Babylon on its way to Europe, and to Western Asia. It was the centre of a vast fertile region, the productions of which were conveyed to Babylon, and from which they would naturally be borne down on the Euphrates to the ocean; see Note on ch. xliii. 14. The first empire of which the earliest historians furnish any trace, was in the land of Shinar, the land of the Chaldeans (Gen. x. 8–10; xi. 1–9). Syria, Arabia, Tyre with all her wealth, and distant Egypt, were subject and tributary to it. The natural advantages of that *region* for a vast capital, are shown by the fact, that amidst all changes and revolutions, empire has been disposed to fix her permanent seat somewhere on the banks of the Tigris or the Euphrates. Thus, Nineveh, the capital of Assyria, was long a mighty and magnificent commercial city, as well as the proud capital of a vast empire. Thus, when Babylon fell, Seleucia rose on the banks of the Tigris, as if prosperity and power were unwilling to leave the fertile plains watered by those rivers. Thus, near Seleucia, arose Ctesiphon, the winter residence of the Parthian monarchs. And thus, under the sway of the Arabians, long after Nineveh, and Babylon, and Seleucia had fallen, Bagdad and Ormus rivalled Babylon and Seleucia, and "became, like them, the resort of the merchant, and the home of the learned.' 'At this time Bagdad and Bussora are faded tokens of the splendour of those which have faded and fallen.' The fact that there was in that vicinity such a succession of celebrated cities, demonstrates that there were there some important commercial advantages. Among those advantages respecting Babylon, was the fact that it was the centre of a vast fertile region; that it naturally received the productions of Armenia on the north; and that its midway position rendered it the natural thoroughfare for the caravan trade between Eastern and Western Asia. Accordingly, Babylon was early distinguished for its commerce and manufactures. Babylonian garments, of uncommon value, had made their way to Palestine as early as the times of Joshua (Josh. vii. 21). Tapestries embroidered with figures of griffons, and other monsters of Eastern imagination, were articles of export. Carpets were wrought there of the finest material and workmanship, and formed an article of extensive exportation. They were in high repute in the time of Cyrus, whose tomb at Pasargada was adorned with them.—(Arrian, *Exped. Alex.*, vi. 29.) Babylonian robes were also highly esteemed for the fineness of their texture and the brilliancy of their purple, and were used by the royal family of Persia. The *commerce* of that city and of Babylonia consisted in the traffic in emeralds and other precious stones; silver and gold; carpets, tapestries, and other manufactured cloths; cotton and pearls; cinnamon and other spicery, obtained from the East; and, in general, of whatever articles were produced in the eastern parts of Asia, which were naturally brought to Babylon on the way to Western Asia and to Europe. For a learned and interesting article on the commerce of Babylon, see *Bib. Rep.* vol. vii. pp. 364–390. Thus, by the fertility of the soil; by its size and strength; by its strong and lofty walls; by its commercial advantages; and by everything that could contribute to the defence of an ancient city, Babylon seemed to be safe; and if there was any ancient city that appeared to bid defiance to the attacks of enemies, or to the ravages of time, it was Babylon. Yet Isaiah said that it should be destroyed; and in the course of our exposition we shall be greatly struck, not only with the certain fulfilment of the prediction, but with the wonderful accuracy and minuteness of the entire prophetic statement.

The vision opens (ch. xiii. 2, 3), with the command of God to assemble his forces to go forth, and accomplish his work in regard to the city. By a beautiful poetic image, the prophet represents himself as *immediately*, on the issuing of this command, listening to the tumult and noise caused by those who were assembling for war; by the gathering together of nations; by their

assembling from a far country to destroy the whole land (ver. 4, 5). He then proceeds to depict the consternation that would follow; the alarm of the people; and their distress, when the day of the Lord should come (6–10). Then, changing the mode of address from himself to God, he sets forth, in a variety of the most distressing and appalling images, the destruction that would come upon the *inhabitants* of Babylon—the humbling of their pride (11); the almost entire destruction of the men (12); the flight of the inhabitants (13, 14); the murder of those who should flee; and the destruction of their wives and children (15, 16). He then specifies (17) the instruments by which this should be done, and closes the chapter (19–22) with a minute and most particular account of the complete and final overthrow of the city; of its entire and everlasting desolation. The subsequent chapter, which is a continuation of this prophecy, is occupied with an account of the deliverance of the Jews from their captivity, and with a further description of the humbling of that proud city and of its monarch. See an analysis of it at the commencement of the chapter.

The thirteenth chapter 'is one of the most beautiful examples that can be given of elegance of composition, variety of imagery, and sublimity of sentiment and diction in the prophetic style.' —(Lowth.) It may be added, that it is one of the clearest predictions of a future event that can anywhere be found; and that the exact and minute fulfilment of it furnishes the highest possible evidence that Isaiah 'spake as he was moved by the Holy Ghost.'

T HE burden of Babylon,[a] which Isaiah the son of Amoz did see.

a ch. xxi.; xlvii.; Jer. l.; li.

CHAPTER XIII.

1. *The burden of Babylon.* Or, the burden *respecting*, or *concerning* Babylon. This prophecy is introduced in a different manner from those which have preceded. The terms which Isaiah employed in the commencement of his previous prophecies, were VISION (see Note, ch. i. 1), or WORD (ch. ii. 1). There has been considerable diversity of opinion in regard to the meaning of the word 'burden,' which is here employed. The Vulgate renders it, *Onus*—' Burden,' in the sense of *load*. The LXX. Ὅρασις—' Vision.' The Chaldee, 'The burden of the cup of malediction which draws near to Babylon.' The Hebrew word (מַשָּׂא *mássâ,* from נָשָׂא *nâsâ, to lift,*

to raise up, to bear, to bear away, to suffer, to endure), means properly that which is borne; that which is heavy; that which becomes a burden; and it is also applied to a gift or present, as that which is borne *to* a man (2 Chron. xvii. 11). It is also applied to a proverb or maxim, probably from the *weight* and *importance* of the sentiment condensed in it (Prov. xxx. 1; xxxi. 1). It is applied to an oracle from God (2 Kings iv. 25). It is often translated ' burden' (Isa. xv.; xix. 1; xxi. 11, 13; xxii. 1; xxiii. 1; xxx. 6; lxvii. 1; Jer. xxiii. 33, 34, 38; Neh. i. 1; Zech. i. 1; xii. 1; Mal. i. 1). By comparing these places, it will be found that the term is applied to those oracles or prophetic declarations

2 Lift ye up a banner upon the high mountain, exalt the voice unto them, shake the hand, that they may go into the gates of the nobles.

which contain sentiments peculiarly weighty and solemn; which are employed chiefly in denouncing wrath and calamity; and which, therefore, are represented as weighing down, or *oppressing* the mind and heart of the prophet. A similar usage prevails in all languages. We are all familiar with expressions like this. We speak of news or tidings of so melancholy a nature as to weigh down, to sink, or depress our spirits; so heavy that we can scarcely bear up under it, or endure it. And so in this case, the view which the prophet had of the awful judgments of God, and of the calamities which were coming upon guilty cities and nations, was so oppressive, that it weighed down the mind and heart as a heavy burden. Others, however, suppose that it means merely a message or prophecy which is *taken up*, or borne, respecting a place, and that the word indicates nothing in regard to the nature of the message. So Rosenmüller, Gesenius, and Cocceius, understand it. But it seems to me the former interpretation is to be preferred. Grotius renders it, 'A mournful prediction respecting Babylon.' ¶ *Did see.* Saw in a vision; or in a scenical representation. The various events were made to pass before his mind in a vision, and he was permitted to see the armies mustered; the consternation of the people; and the future condition of the proud city. This verse is properly the *title* to the prophecy.

2. *Lift ye up a banner.* A military ensign or standard. The vision opens here; and the first thing which the prophet hears, is the solemn command of God addressed to the nations as subject to him, to rear the standard of war, and to gather around it the mighty armies which were to be employed in the destruction of the city. This command, 'Lift ye up a banner,' is addressed to the leaders of those armies to assemble them, and to prepare them for war. ¶ *Upon the high mountain.* It was customary for military leaders to plant a standard on a tower, a fortress, a city, a high mountain, or any elevated spot, in order that it might be seen afar, and be the rallying point for the people to collect together (see Note, ch. xi. 10). Here, the prophet does not refer to any particular *mountain*, but means simply, that a standard should be raised, around which the hosts should be assembled to march to Babylon. The Chaldee renders it, 'Over the city dwelling in security, lift up the banner.' ¶ *Exalt the voice.* Raise up the voice, commanding the people to assemble, and to prepare for the march against Babylon. Perhaps, however, the word 'voice' here (קוֹל *qōl*) refers to the *clangour*, or sound, of a trumpet used for mustering armies. The word is often used to denote *any* noise, and is frequently applied to thunder, to the trumpet, &c. ¶ *Unto them.* That is, to the Medes and Persians, who were to be employed in the destruction of Babylon. ¶ *Shake the hand.* In the way of *beckoning;* as when one is at so great a distance that the voice cannot be heard, the hand is waved for a sign. This was a command to *beckon* to the nations to assemble for the destruction of Babylon. ¶ *That they may go into the gates of the nobles.* The word here rendered 'nobles' (נְדִיבִים) means, properly, *voluntary, free, liberal;* then those who are noble, or liberally-minded, from the connection between nobleness and liberality; then those who are noble or elevated in rank or office. In this sense it is used here; comp. Job xii. 21; xxxiv. 18; 1 Sam. ii. 8; Ps. cvii. 40; and Prov. viii. 16, where it is rendered 'princes;' Num. xxi. 18, where it is rendered 'nobles.' Lowth renders it here 'princes.' Noyes renders it 'tyrants'—a sense which the word has in Job xxi. 28 (see Note on that place). There is no doubt that it refers to Babylon; and the prophet designs probably to speak of Babylon as a magnificent city—a city of princes, or nobles. The Chaldee renders it, 'That they may enter its gates, which open to them of their own accord;' retaining the original signification of *voluntariness* in the Hebrew word, and expressing the idea that the conquest would be easy. Our common translation has expressed the correct sense.

3 I have commanded my sanctified ones, I have also called my
mighty *a* ones for mine anger, *even*
them that rejoice in my highness.

4 The noise of a multitude in the

a Joel 2,11.

mountains, 1 like as of a great people; a tumultuous noise of the kingdoms of nations gathered together:
the LORD of hosts mustereth the
host of the battle.

1 *the likeness.*

---

3. *I have commanded.* This is the
language of God in reference to those
who were about to destroy Babylon.
He claimed the control and direction of
all their movements; and though the
command was not understood by *them*
as coming from him, yet it was by his
direction, and in accordance with his
plan (comp. Notes on ch. x. 7; xlv. 5,
6). The *command* was not given by
the prophets, or by an audible voice;
but it was his secret purpose and direction that led them to this enterprise.
¶ *My sanctified ones.* The Medes and
Persians; not called 'sanctified' because they were holy, but because they
were *set apart* by the Divine intention
and purpose to accomplish this. The
word 'sanctify' (קָדַשׁ) often means *to
set apart*—either to God; to an office;
to any sacred use; or to any purpose
of religion, or of accomplishing any of
the Divine plans. Thus, it means to
dedicate one to the office of priest (Ex.
xxviii. 41); to set apart or dedicate an
altar (Ex. xxxix. 36); to dedicate a
people (Ex. xix. 10–14); to appoint, or
institute a fast (Joel i. 14; ii. 15); to
sanctify a war (Joel iii. 9), that is, to
prepare one's-self for it, or make it
ready. Here it means, that the Medes
and Persians were *set apart,* in the purpose of God, to accomplish his designs
in regard to Babylon (comp. Note. ch.
x. 5, 6). ¶ *My mighty ones.* Those
who are strong; and who are so entirely
under my direction, that they may be
called mine. ¶ *For mine anger.* To
accomplish the purposes of my anger
against Babylon. ¶ *Even them that
rejoice in my highness.* It cannot be
supposed that the Medes and Persians
really exulted, or rejoiced in God or in
his plans; for it is evident that, like
Sennacherib (ch. x.), they were seeking
to accomplish their *own* purposes, and
were not solicitous about the plans of
God (comp. Note on ch. xlvii. 6). The
word rendered 'my highness' (גַּאֲוָתִי)

means, properly, *my majesty,* or *glory.*
When applied to men, as it often is, it
means pride or arrogance. It means
here, the high and exalted plan of God
in regard to Babylon. It was a mighty
undertaking; and one in which the
power, the justice, and the dominion of
God over nations would be evinced. In
accomplishing this, the Medes and Persians would rejoice or exult, not *as* the
fulfilling of the plan of God; but they
would exult *as if* it were their *own*
plan, though it would be *really* the glorious plan of God. Wicked men often
exult in their success; they glory in
the execution of their purposes; but
they are really accomplishing the plans
of God, and executing his great designs.

4. *The noise of a multitude in the
mountains.* The prophet here represents himself as hearing the confused
tumult of the nations assembling to the
standard reared on the mountains (ver.
2). This is a highly beautiful figure—
a graphic and vivid representation of
the scene before him. Nations are seen
to hasten to the elevated banner, and to
engage in active preparations for the
mighty war. The sound is that of a *tumult,* an *excited multitude* hastening to
the encampment, and preparing for the
conquest of Babylon. ¶ *Like as of a great
people.* Heb. 'The likeness of a great
people.' That is, such a confused and
tumultuous sound as attends a great
multitude when they collect together
¶ *A tumultuous noise.* Heb. 'The
voice of the tumultuous noise of the
kingdoms of nations gathered together.'
¶ *The* LORD *of hosts.* JEHOVAH, the
God of hosts, or armies (Note, ch. i. 9).
¶ *Mustereth.* Collects; puts in military array. Over all this multitude of
nations, hastening with confused sounds
and tumult like the noise of the sea,
putting themselves in military array,
God, unseen, presides, and prepares
them for his own great designs. It is
not easy to conceive a more sublime

5 They come from a far country, from the end of heaven, *even* the LORD and the weapons of his indignation, to destroy the whole land.

6 Howl ye: for the day *a* of the

LORD *is* at hand; it shall come as a destruction from the Almighty.

7 Therefore shall all hands ¹ be faint, and every man's heart shall melt:

1 or, *fall down.*

---

image than these mighty hosts of war, unconscious of the hand that directs them, and of the God that presides over them, moving as he wills, and accomplishing his plans.

5. *They come.* That is, 'JEHOVAH and the weapons of his indignation'— the collected armies come. The prophet sees these assembled armies with JEHOVAH, as their leader, at their head. ¶ *From a far country.* The country of the Medes and Persians. These nations, indeed, bordered on Babylonia, but still they stretched far to the north and east, and, probably, occupied nearly all the regions to the east of Babylon which were then known. ¶ *From the end of heaven.* The LXX. render this, Ἀπ' ἄκρου θεμιλίου τοῦ οὐρανοῦ— 'From *the extreme foundation* of the heaven.' The expression in the Heb., 'From the end, or extreme part of heaven,' means, the distant horizon by which the earth appears to be bounded, where the sky and the land seem to meet. In Ps. xix. 6, the phrase ' from the end of the heaven' denotes the east, where the sun appears to rise; and ' unto the ends of it' denotes the west:

His going forth is from the end of the heaven;
And his circuit unto the ends of it.

It is here synonymous with the phrase, 'the end of the earth,' in Isa. v. 26. ¶ *Even the* LORD. The word 'even,' introduced here by the translators, weakens the force of this verse. The prophet means to say that JEHOVAH is coming at the head of those armies, which are the weapons of his indignation. ¶ *The weapons of his indignation.* The assembled armies of the Medes and Persians, called 'the weapons of his indignation,' because by them he will accomplish the purposes of his anger against the city of Babylon (see Note, ch. x. 5). ¶ *To destroy the whole land.* The whole territory of Babylonia, or Chaldea. Not only the city, but the nation and kingdom.

6. *Howl ye.* ' Ye inhabitants of Babylon, in view of the approaching destruction. ¶ *The day of the* LORD. The time when JEHOVAH will inflict vengeance on you draws near (see Note, ch. ii. 12; comp. ver. 9). ¶ *As a destruction from the Almighty.* Not as a desolation from man, but as destruction sent from him who has all power in heaven and on earth. Destruction meditated by man might be resisted; but destruction that should come from the Almighty must be final and irresistible. The word 'Almighty' (שַׁדַּי *Shăddai*), one of the names given to God in the Scriptures, denotes, properly, *one who is mighty,* or who has all power; and is correctly rendered Almighty, or Omnipotent; (Gen. xvii. 1; xxviii. 3; xlviii. 3; Ex. vi. 3; Ruth i. 20; Job v. 17; vi. 4, 14; viii. 3, 5; xi. 7; xiii. 4; xv. 25). In the Hebrew here, there is a paronomasia or *pun*—a figure of speech quite common in the Scriptures, which cannot be retained in the translation— 'It shall come as *a destruction* (כְּשֹׁד *keshŏdh*) from the Almighty (מִשַּׁדַּי *misshăddai*).'

7. *Therefore shall all hands be faint.* This is designed to denote the consternation and alarm of the people. They would be so terrified and alarmed that they would have no courage, no hope, and no power to make resistance. They would abandon their plans of defence, and give themselves up to despair (comp. Jer. l. 43: 'The king of Babylon hath heard the report of them, and his hands waxed feeble; anguish took hold of him, and pangs as of a woman in travail;' Ezek. vii. 17; Zeph. iii. 16). ¶ *And every man's heart shall melt.* Or, shall faint, so that he shall have no courage or strength (comp. Deut. xx. 8). The fact was, that the destruction of Babylon took place in the night. It came suddenly upon the city, while Belshazzar was at his impious feast; and the alarm was so unexpected

8 And they shall be afraid: pangs and sorrows shall take hold of them; they shall be in pain as a woman that travaileth; they shall be ¹ amazed ² one at another; their faces *shall be as* ³ flames.

1 *wonder.*   2 *every man at his neighbour.*

9 Behold, the day ᵃ of the LORD cometh, cruel both with wrath and fierce anger, to lay the land desolate; and he shall destroy the sinners thereof out of it.

10 For the stars of heaven, and

3 *faces of the flames.*   ᵃ Mal.4.1.

and produced such consternation, that no defence was attempted (see Dan. v. 30; comp. Notes on ch. xlv. 1).

8. *They shall be in pain as a woman that travaileth.* This comparison is often used in the Scriptures to denote the deepest possible pain and sorrow, as well as the *suddenness* with which any calamity comes upon a people (Ps. xlviii. 6; Isa. xxi. 3; xlii. 14; Jer. vi. 24; xiii. 21; xxii. 33; xlix. 24; l. 43; Hos. xiii. 13; Mic. iv. 9, 10; John xvi. 21; Gal. iv. 19; 1 Thess. v. 3). ¶ *They shall be amazed one at another.* They shall stare with a stupid gaze on one another, indicating a state of great distress, anxiety, and alarm. They shall look to each other for aid, and shall meet in the countenances of others the same expressions of wonder and consternation. ¶ *Their faces* shall be as *flames.* Their faces shall glow or burn like fire. When grief and anguish come upon us, the face becomes inflamed. The face *in fear* is usually pale. But the idea here is not so much that of *fear* as of *anguish;* and, perhaps, there is mingled also here the idea of *indignation* against their invaders.

9. *The day of the* LORD *cometh;* see ver. 6. ¶ *Cruel* (אַכְזָרִי). This does not mean that *God* is cruel, but that the 'day of JEHOVAH' that was coming should be unsparing and destructive to them. It would be the exhibition of *justice,* but not of *cruelty;* and the word stands opposed here to *mercy,* and means that God would not spare them. The *effect* would be that the inhabitants of Babylon would be destroyed. ¶ *Fierce anger.* Heb. (אַף חָרוֹן) 'A glow, or burning of anger.' The phrase denotes the most intense indignation (comp. Num. xxv. 4; xxxii. 14; 1 Sam. xxviii. 18). ¶ *To lay the land desolate.* Chaldea (ver. 5).

10. *For the stars of heaven.* This verse cannot be understood literally,

but is a metaphorical representation of the calamities that were coming upon Babylon. The meaning of the figure evidently is, that those calamities would be such as would be appropriately denoted by the sudden extinguishment of the stars, the sun, and the moon. As nothing would tend more to anarchy, distress, and ruin, than thus to have all the lights of heaven suddenly and for ever quenched, this was an apt and forcible representation of the awful calamities that were coming upon the people. Darkness and night, in the Scriptures, are often the emblem of calamity and distress (see Note, Matt. xxiv. 29). The revolutions and destructions of kingdoms and nations are often represented in the Scriptures under this image. So respecting the destruction of Idumea (Isa. xxxiv. 4):

And all the hosts of heaven shall be dissolved,
And the heavens shall be rolled together as a
   scroll;
And all their host shall fall down,
As the leaf falleth from off the vine,
And as a falling fig from the fig-tree.

So in Ezek. xxxii. 7, 8, in a prophecy respecting the destruction of Pharaoh, king of Egypt:

And when I shall put thee out,
I will cover the heavens, and make the stars
   thereof dark,
I will cover the sun with a cloud,
And the moon shall not give her light.
And the bright lights of heaven will I make dark
   over thee.
And set darkness upon thy land.

(comp. Joel ii. 10; iii. 15, 16.) Thus in Amos viii. 9:

I will cause the sun to go down at noon,
And I will darken the earth in a clear day.

see also Rev. vi. 12–14:

And I beheld when he had opened the sixth seal,
   and lo,
The sun became black as sackcloth of hair,
And the moon became as blood;
And the stars of heaven fell unto the earth,
Even as a fig-tree casteth her untimely figs
When she is shaken of a mighty wind:
And the heaven departed as a scroll when it is
   rolled together.

the constellations thereof, shall not
give their light: the sun shall be
darkened in his going forth, and
the moon shall not cause her light
to shine.

11 And I will punish the world
for *their* evil, and the wicked for

their iniquity; and I will cause the
arrogancy of the proud to cease,
and will lay low the haughtiness of
the terrible.

12 I will make a man more precious than fine gold; even a man
than the golden wedge of Ophir.

Many have supposed that these expressions respecting the sun, moon, and
stars, refer to kings, and princes, and
magistrates, as the *lights* of the state;
and that the sense is, that their power
and glory should cease. But it is rather
a figurative representation, denoting
calamity *in general*, and describing a
state of extreme distress, such as *would
be* if all the lights of heaven should
suddenly become extinct. ¶ *And the
constellations thereof* (וּכְסִילֵיהֶם). The
word (כְּסִיל *khesil*) means properly *a
fool;* Prov. i. 32; x. 1, 18; xiii. 19,
20, *et al.* It also denotes *hope, confidence, expectation* (Job xxxi. 24; Prov.
iii. 26; Job viii. 14); also the *reins*, the
flanks or *loins* (Lev. iii. 4, 10, 15; Ps.
xxxviii. 7). It is also, as here, applied
to a constellation in the heavens, but
the connection of this meaning of the
word with the other significations is
uncertain. In Job ix. 9, and xxxviii.
31, it is translated 'Orion.' In Amos v.
8, it is translated the 'seven stars'—the
Pleiades. In Arabic, that constellation
is called 'the giant.' According to an
Eastern tradition, it was Nimrod, the
founder of Babylon, afterwards translated to the skies; and it has been
supposed that the name *the impious* or
foolish one was thus given to the deified
Nimrod, and thus to the constellation. The Rabbins interpret it *Simis.*
The word 'constellations' denotes clusters of stars, or stars that appear to be
near to each other in the heavens, and
which, on the celestial globe, are reduced to certain figures for the convenience of classification and memory,
as the bear, the bull, the virgin, the
balance. This arrangement was early
made, and there is no reason to doubt
that it existed in the time of Isaiah
(comp. Notes on Job ix. 9).

11. *And I will punish the world.* By
the 'world' here is evidently meant the
Babylonian empire, in the same way as

'all the world' in Luke ii. 1, means
Judea; and in Acts xi. 28, means the
Roman empire. Babylonia, or Chaldea,
was the most mighty empire then on
earth, and might be said to comprehend
the whole world. ¶ *And I will cause
the arrogancy.* This was the prevailing
sin of Babylon, and it was on account
of this *pride* mainly that it was overthrown (see Notes on ch. xiv.; xlvii.
1–7; comp. Dan. iv. 22, 30).

12. *I will make a man,* &c. I will
so cut off and destroy the men of Babylon, that a single man to defend the city
will be more rare and valuable than fine
gold. The expression indicates that
there would be a great slaughter of the
men of Babylon. ¶ *Than fine gold.*
Pure, unalloyed gold. The word here
used (פָּז *pâz*) is often distinguished from
common gold (Ps. xix. 11; cxix. 127;
Prov. viii. 19). ¶ *Than the golden
wedge of Ophir.* The word (כֶּתֶם
këthëm) rendered 'wedge' means properly *gold;* yellow gold; what is hidden,
precious, or hoarded; and is used only
in poetry. It indicates nothing about
the *shape* of the gold, as the word *wedge*
would seem to suppose. 'Ophir' was a
country to which the vessels of Solomon
traded, and which was particularly distinguished for producing gold; but respecting its particular situation, there
has been much discussion. The 'ships
of Tarshish' sailed from Ezion-geber
on the Red Sea, and went to Ophir
(1 Kings ix. 26; x. 22; xxii. 48). Three
years were required for the voyage; and
they returned freighted with gold, peacocks, apes, spices, ivory, and ebony
(1 Kings ix. 28; x. 11, 12; comp. 2 Chron.
viii. 18). The gold of that country was
more celebrated than that of any other
country for its purity. Josephus supposes that it was in the East Indies;
Bruce that it was in South Africa;
Rosenmüller and others suppose that it
was in Southern Arabia. It is probable

13 Therefore *a* I will shake the heavens, and the earth *b* shall remove out of her place, in the wrath of the LORD of hosts, and in the day of his fierce anger.

a Hag. 2.6.

14 And it shall be as the chased roo, and as a sheep that no man taketh up: they shall every man turn to his own people, and flee every one into his own land.

b 2 Pet. 3.10,11.

that the situation of Ophir must ever remain a matter of conjecture. The Chaldee Paraphrase gives a different sense to this passage. ' I will love those who fear me, more than gold in which men glory ; and those who observe the law more than the tried gold of Ophir.' (On the situation of Ophir the following works may be consulted :—*The Pictorial Bible*, vol. ii. pp. 364–369; Martini Lipenii, *Dissert. de Ophir;* Joan. Christophori Wichmanshausen *Dissert. de Navig. Ophritica ;* H. Relandi, *Dissert. de Ophir ;* Ugolini, *Thes. Sac. Ant.* vol. viii.; and Forster *On Arabia.*)

13. *Therefore I will shake the heavens.* A strong, but common figure of speech in the Scriptures, to denote great commotions, judgments, and revolutions. The figure is taken from the image of a furious storm and tempest, when the sky, the clouds, the heavens, appear to be in commotion ; comp. 1 Sam. xxii. 8 :

Then the earth shook and trembled,
The foundation of heaven moved and shook,
Because he was wroth.

See also Isa. xxiv. 19, 20; Hag. ii. 6, 7.
¶ *And the earth shall remove out of her place.* A common figure in the Scriptures to denote the great effects of the wrath of God ; as if even the earth should be appalled at his presence, and should tremble and flee away from the dread of his anger. It is a very sublime representation, and, as carried out often by the sacred writers, it is unequalled in grandeur, probably, in any language. Thus the hills, the mountains, the trees, the streams, the very heavens, are represented as shaken, and thrown into consternation at the presence of God ; see Hab. iii. 6, 10 :

He stood and measured the earth ;
He beheld and drove asunder the nations ;
And the everlasting mountains were scattered.
The perpetual hills did bow;
His ways are everlasting.

The mountains saw thee and they trembled ;
The overflowing of the water passed by ;
The deep uttered his voice,
And did lift up his hands on high.

See Rev. xx. 11: ' And I saw a great white throne, and him that sat on it, from whose face the earth and the heaven fled away.' The figure in Isaiah is a strong one to denote the terror of the anger of God against Babylon.

14. *And it shall be.* Babylon shall be. ¶ *As the chased roe.* Once so proud, lofty, arrogant, and self-confident ; it shall be as the trembling gazelle, or the timid deer pursued by the hunter, and panting for safety. The word (צְבִי *tzĕbhi*) denotes a deer of the most delicate frame ; the species that is most fleet and graceful in its movements; properly the *gazelle* (see Bochart's *Hieroz.* i. 3. 25). ' To hunt the antelope is a favourite amusement in the East, but which, from its extraordinary swiftness, is attended with great difficulty. On the first alarm, it flies like an arrow from the bow, and leaves the best-mounted hunter, and the fleetest dog, far behind. The sportsman is obliged to call in the aid of the falcon, trained to the work, to seize on the animal, and impede its motions, to give the dogs time to overtake it. Dr. Russel thus describes the chase of the antelope: " They permit horsemen, without dogs, if they advance gently, to approach near, and do not seem much to regard a caravan that passes within a little distance ; but the moment they take the alarm, they bound away, casting from time to time a look behind : and if they find themselves pursued, they lay their horns backwards, almost close on the shoulders, and flee with incredible swiftness. When dogs appear, they instantly take the alarm ; for which reason the sportsmen endeavour to steal upon the antelope unawares, to get as near as possible before slipping the dogs ; and then, pushing on at full speed, they throw off the falcon, which being taught to strike or fix upon the cheek of the game, retards its course by repeated attacks, till the greyhounds have time to get up." '—(Burder's *Orient. Cus.*)

15 Every one that is found shall be thrust through; and every one that is joined *unto them* shall fall by the sword.

16 Their children also shall be dashed *a* to pieces before their eyes;

a Ps.137.8,9.

their houses shall be spoiled, and their wives ravished.

17 Behold, I will stir up the Medes *a* against them, which shall not regard silver; and *as for* gold, they shall not delight in it.

b Dan.5.28,31.

¶ *As a sheep.* Or like a scattered flock of sheep in the wilderness that has no shepherd, and no one to collect them together; an image also of that which is timid and defenceless. ¶ *That no man taketh up.* That is astray, and not under the protection of any shepherd. The meaning is, that that people, once so proud and self-confident, would become alarmed, and scattered, and be afraid of everything. ¶ *They shall every man turn unto his own people.* Babylon was the capital of the heathen world. It was a vast and magnificent city; the centre of many nations. It would be the place, therefore, where numerous foreigners would take up a temporary residence, as London and other large cities are now. Jeremiah (ch. l. 37) describes Babylon as containing a mingled population—'and upon all the mingled people that are in the midst of her'—*i.e.*, the *colluvies gentium*, as Tacitus describes Rome in his time. Jeremiah also (ch. l. 28) describes this mingled multitude as fleeing and escaping out of the land of Babylon, when these calamities should come upon them. The idea in Isaiah is, that this great and mixed multitude would endeavour to escape the impending calamities, and flee to their own nations.

15. *Every one that is found.* In Babylon, or that is overtaken in fleeing from it. This is a description of the capture of the city, and of the slaughter that would ensue, when the invaders would spare neither age nor sex. ¶ *Every one that is joined* unto them. Their allies and friends. There shall be a vast, indiscriminate slaughter of all that are found in the city, and of those that attempt to flee from it. Lowth renders this, 'And all that are collected in a body;' but the true sense is given in our translation. The Chaldee renders it, 'And every one who enters into fortified cities shall be slain with the sword.'

16. *Their children also shall be dashed to pieces.* This is a description of the horrors of the capture of Babylon; and there can be none more frightful and appalling than that which is here presented. That this is done in barbarous nations in the time of war, there can be no doubt. Nothing was more common among American savages, than to dash out the brains of infants against a rock or a tree, and it was often done before the eyes of the afflicted and heart-broken parents. That these horrors were not unknown in Oriental nations of antiquity, is evident. Thus, the Psalmist implies that it would be done in Babylon, in exact accordance with this prediction of Isaiah; Ps. cxxxvii. 8, 9:

O daughter of Babylon, who art to be destroyed:
Happy shall he be who rewardeth thee as thou hast served us;
Happy shall he be who taketh and dasheth thy little ones against the stones.

Thus, also, it is said of Hazael, that when he came to be king of Syria, he would be guilty of this barbarity in regard to the Jews (2 Kings viii. 13; comp. Nahum iii. 10). It was an evidence of the barbarous feelings of the times; and a proof that they were far, very far, from the humanity which is now deemed indispensable even in war. ¶ *Their houses shall be spoiled.* Plundered. It is implied here, says Kimchi, that this was to be done also 'before their eyes,' and thus the horrors of the capture would be greatly increased.

17. *Behold, I will stir up.* I will cause them to engage in this enterprise. This is an instance of the control which God claims over the nations, and of his power to excite and direct them as he pleases. ¶ *The Medes.* This is one of the places in which the prophet specified, *by name*, the instrument of the wrath of God. Cyrus himself is subsequently mentioned (Isa. xliv. 28; xlv. 1) as the agent by which God would accomplish his purposes. It is remarkable, also, that 'the Medes' are here mentioned many years before they became a separate and independent nation. It was elsewhere predicted that the Medes would be employed in this siege of Babylon; thus, in Isa. xxi. 2: 'Go up, O Elam (that is, Persia), besiege, O Media;' Jer. li. 11: 'Jeho-vah hath raised up the spirit of the kings of the Medes, for his device is against Babylon to destroy it.' Media was a country east of Assyria, which is supposed to have been peopled by the descendants of Madai, son of Japheth (Gen. x. 2). Ancient Media extended on the west and south of the Caspian Sea, from Armenia, on the north, to Faristan or Persia proper, on the south. It was one of the most fertile regions of Asia. It was an ancient kingdom. Ninus, the founder of the Assyrian monarchy, is said to have encountered one of its kings, whom he subdued, and whose province he made a part of the Assyrian empire. For 520 years, the Medes were subject to the Assyrians; but, in the time of Tiglath-pileser and Shalmaneser, they revolted, and, by the destruction of the army of Sennacherib before Jerusalem—an event which was itself *subsequent* to the delivery of this prophecy respecting Babylon—they were enabled to achieve their independence. At the time when this prophecy was uttered, therefore, Media was a dependent province of the kingdom of Assyria. Six years they passed in a sort of anarchy, until, about 700 years B.C., they found in Dejoces an upright statesman, who was proclaimed king by universal consent. His son and successor, Phraortes, subdued the Persians, and all upper Asia, and united them to his kingdom. He also attacked Assyria, and laid siege to Nineveh, the capital, but was defeated. Nineveh was finally taken by his successor, Cyaxares, with the aid of his ally, the king of Babylon; and Assyria became a province of Media. This widely-extended empire was delivered by him to his son Astyages, the father of Cyrus. Astyages reigned about 35 years, and then delivered the vast kingdom to Cyrus, about 556 years B.C., under whom the prediction of Isaiah respecting Babylon

was fulfilled. In this way arose the Medo-Persian kingdom, and henceforward *the laws of the Medes and Persians* are always mentioned together (Est. i. 9; x. 2; Dan. vi. 8, 12). From this time, all their customs, rites, and laws, became amalgamated.—(Herod. i. 95-130). In looking at this prophecy, therefore, we are to bear in mind—(1.) the fact that, when it was uttered, Media was a dependent province of the kingdom of Assyria; (2.) that a long time was yet to elapse before it would become an independent kingdom; (3.) that it was yet to secure its independence by the aid of that very Babylon which it would finally destroy; (4.) that no human foresight could predict these revolutions, and that every circumstance conspired to render this event *improbable.* The great strength and resources of Babylon; the fact that Media was a dependent province, and that such great revolutions must occur *before* this prophecy *could* be fulfilled, render this one of the most striking and remarkable predictions in the sacred volume. ¶ *Which shall not regard silver,* &c. It is remarkable, says Lowth, that Xenophon makes Cyrus open a speech to his army, and, in particular, to the Medes, who made the principal part of it, with praising them for their disregard of riches. 'Ye Medes and others who now hear me, I well know, that you have not accompanied me in this expedition with a view of acquiring wealth.'—(*Cyrop.* v.) That this was the character of the Medes, is further evident from several circumstances. 'He reckoned, says Xenophon, that his riches belonged not any more to himself than to his friends. So little did he regard silver, or delight in gold, that Crœsus told him that, by his liberality, he would make himself poor, instead of storing up vast treasures for himself. The Medes possessed, in this respect, the spirit of their chief, of which an instance, recorded by Xenophon, is too striking and appropriate to be passed over. When Gobryas, an Assyrian governor, whose son the king of Babylon had slain, hospitably entertained him and his army, Cyrus appealed to the chiefs of the Medes and Hyrcanians, and to the noblest and

18 *Their* bows also shall dash the young men to pieces; and they shall have no pity on the fruit of the womb; their eye shall not spare children.

19 And Babylon, the glory of kingdoms, the beauty of the Chaldees' excellency, shall be [1] as when God [a] overthrew Sodom and Gomorrah.

1 *the overthrowing of.*

a Gen.19.24.

---

most honourable of the Persians, whether, giving first what was due to the gods, and leaving to the rest of the army their portion, they would not overmatch his generosity by ceding to him their whole share of the first and plentiful booty which they had won from the land of Babylon. Loudly applauding the proposal, they immediately and unanimously consented; and one of them said, "Gobryas may have thought us poor, because we came not loaded with coins, and drink not out of golden cups; but by this he will know, that men can be generous even without gold." ' (*See* Keith *On the Prophecies*, p. 198, Ed. New York, 1833.) This is a remarkable prediction, because this is a very unusual circumstance in the character of conquerors. Their purpose has been chiefly to obtain plunder, and, especially, gold and silver have been objects to them of great value. Few, indeed, have been the invading armies which were not influenced by the hope of spoil; and the want of that characteristic among the Medes is a circumstance which no human sagacity could have foreseen.

18. *Their bows also.* Bows and arrows were the usual weapons of the ancients in war; and the Persians were particularly skilled in their use. According to Xenophon, Cyrus came to Babylon with a great number of archers and slingers (*Cyrop.* ii. 1). ¶ *Shall dash the young men*, &c. That is, they shall dash the young men to pieces, or kill them by their bows and arrows. Vulgate, ' And with their arrows shall they slay the young.' The meaning of the word here rendered ' dash to pieces,' is to smite suddenly to the ground.

19. *And Babylon, the glory of kingdoms.* That is, the capital, or chief ornament of many nations. Appellations of this kind, applied to Babylon, abound in the Scriptures. In Dan. iv. 30, it is called ' great Babylon;' in

Isa. xiv. 4, it is called ' the golden city;' in Isa. xlvii. 5, ' the lady of kingdoms;' in Jer. li. 13, it is spoken of as ' abundant in treasures;' and, in Jer. li. 41, as ' the praise of the whole earth.' All these expressions are designed to indicate its immense wealth and magnificence. It was the capital of a mighty empire, and was the chief city of the heathen world. ¶ *The beauty of the Chaldees' excellency.* Heb. ' The glory of the pride of the Chaldees;' or the ornament of the proud Chaldees. It was their boast and glory; it was that on which they chiefly prided themselves. How well it deserved these appellations we have already seen. ¶ *Shall be as when God overthrew Sodom and Gomorrah* (Gen. xix. 24). That is, shall be completely and entirely overthrown; shall cease to be inhabited, and shall be perfectly desolate. It does not mean that it shall be overthrown in the same manner as Sodom was, but that it should be as completely and entirely ruined. The successive steps in the overthrow of Babylon, by which this prophecy was so signally fulfilled, were the following: (1.) The taking of the city by Cyrus. This was accomplished by his clearing out the *Pallacopas*, a canal that was made for the purpose of emptying the superfluous waters of the Euphrates into the lakes and marshes formed by it in the south-west borders of the province towards Arabia. Into this canal he directed the waters of the Euphrates, and was thus enabled to enter the city in the channel of the river under the walls (see Notes on ch. xlv. 1, 2). He took the city by surprise, and when the inhabitants, confident of security, had given themselves up to the riot of a grand public festival; and the king and the nobles were revelling at a public entertainment. From this cause, also, it happened that the waters, which were thus diverted from their usual channel, converted the whole country

into a vast, unhealthy morass, that
contributed greatly to the decline of
Babylon. (2.) The *second* capture of
Babylon by Darius Hystaspes. Cyrus
was not the destroyer of the city, but
he rather sought to preserve its magnificence, and to perpetuate its pre-eminence among the nations. He left it to
his successor in all its strength and
magnificence. But, after his death, it
rebelled against Darius, and bade defiance to the power of the whole Persian empire. Fully resolved not to
yield, they adopted the resolution of
putting every woman in the city to
death, with the exception of their mothers and one female, the best beloved
in every family, to bake their bread.
All the rest, says Herodotus (iii. 150),
were assembled together and strangled.
The city was taken at that time by
Darius, by the aid of Zopyrus, son of
Megabyzus, who, in order to do it,
mutilated himself beyond the power of
recovery. He cut off his nose and ears,
and having scourged himself severely, He
presented himself before Darius. He
proposed to Darius to enter the city,
apparently as a deserter who had been
cruelly treated by Darius, and to deliver the city into his hands. He was
one of the chief nobles of Persia; was
admitted in this manner within the
walls; represented himself as having
been punished because he advised Darius to raise the siege; was admitted
to the confidence of the Babylonians;
and was finally intrusted with an important military command. After several
successful conflicts with the Persians,
and when it was supposed his fidelity
had been fully tried, he was raised to
the chief command of the army; and
was appointed to the responsible office
of τειχοφύλαξ, or guardian of the walls.
Having obtained this object, he opened
the gates of Babylon to the Persian
army, as he had designed, and the city
was taken without difficulty (Herod. iii.
153–160). As soon as Darius had
taken the city, he 'levelled the walls,
and took away the gates, neither of
which things had Cyrus done before.
Three thousand of the most distinguished of the nobility he ordered to
be crucified; the rest he suffered to
remain.'—(Herod. iii. 159.)   (3.) After

its conquest by Darius, it was always
regarded by the Persian monarchs with
a jealous eye. Xerxes destroyed the
temples of the city, and, among the rest,
the celebrated temple or tower of Belus
(Strabo, xvi. 1, 5.) 'Darius,' says Herodotus, 'had designs upon the golden
statue in the temple of Belus, but did
not dare to take it; but Xerxes, his
son, took it, and slew the priest who
resisted its removal.'   (4.) The city
was captured a third time, by Alexander the Great. Mazæus, the Persian
general, surrendered the city into his
hands, and he entered it with his army
—*velut in aciem irent*—'as if they
were marching to battle.'—(Q. Curtius,
v. 3.) It was afterwards taken by Anti-
gonus, by Demetrius, by Antiochus the
Great, and by the Parthians; and each
successive conquest contributed to its
reduction. (5.) Cyrus transferred the
capital from Babylon to *Susa* or Shu-
san (Neh. i. 1; Ezra ii. 8; iv. 16; ix.
11, 15), which became the capital of
the kingdom of Persia, and, of course,
contributed much to diminish the importance of Babylon itself. (6.) Seleu-
cus Nicator founded Seleucia in the
neighbourhood of Babylon, on the Tigris, chiefly with a design to draw off
the inhabitants of Babylon to a rival
city, and to prevent its importance. A
great part of its population migrated to
the new city of Seleucia (Plin. *Nat.
Hist.* vi. 30). Babylon thus gradually
declined until it lost all its importance,
and the very place where it stood was,
for a long time, unknown. About the
beginning of the first century, a small
part of it only was inhabited, and the
greater portion was cultivated (Diod.
Sic. ii. 27). In the second century,
nothing but the walls remained (Pausa-
nius, *Arcad.* c. 33). It became gradually a great desert; and, in the fourth
century, its walls, repaired for that
purpose, formed an enclosure for wild
beasts, and Babylon was converted into
a hunting place for the pastime of the
Persian monarchs. After this, there is
an interval of many ages in the history
of its mutilated remains, and of its
mouldering decay (Keith, *On the Prophecies*, p. 216; Jerome, *Comm. on Isa.*
ch. xiv.) Benjamin of Tudela vaguely
alludes to the palace of Nebuchadnez-

20 It ^a shall never be inhabited, neither shall it be dwelt in from generation to generation; neither

a Jer.50.3,39; 51.29,62; Rev.18.2,&c.

shall the Arabian pitch tent there; neither shall the shepherds make their fold there:

---

zar, which, he says, could not be entered, on account of its being the abode of dragons and wild beasts. Sir John Maundeville, who travelled over Asia, A.D. 1322, says, that 'Babylone is in the grete desertes of Arabye, upon the waye as men gon towarde the kyngdome of Caldee. But it is full longe sithe ony man durste neyhe to the toure; for it is alle deserte and full of dragons and grete serpentes, and fulle dyverse veneymouse bestes all abouten.' 20. *It shall never be inhabited.* This has been completely fulfilled. It is now, and has been for centuries, a scene of wide desolation, and is a heap of ruins, and there is every indication that it will continue so to be. From Rauwolff's testimony it appears, that in the sixteenth century 'there was not a house to be seen;' and now the 'eye wanders over a *barren desert*, in which the ruins are nearly the only indication that it had ever been inhabited. It is impossible to behold this scene and not be reminded how exactly the predictions of Isaiah and Jeremiah have been fulfilled, even in the appearance Babylon was doomed to present, *that she should never be inhabited.*'—(Keppel's *Narrative*, p. 234.) 'Babylon is spurned alike by the heel of the Ottoman, the Israelites, and the sons of Ishmael.'—(Mignan's *Travels*, p. 108.) 'It is a *tenantless* and desolate metropolis.'—(Ibid. p. 235; see Keith *On Prophecy*, p. 221.) ¶ *Neither shall it be dwelt in,* &c. This is but another form of the expression, denoting that it shall be utterly desolate. The following testimonies of travellers will show *how* this is accomplished:—'Ruins composed, like those of Babylon, of heaps of rubbish impregnated with nitre, cannot be cultivated.'—(Rich's *Memoir*, p. 16.) 'The decomposing materials of a Babylonian structure doom the earth on which they perish, to lasting sterility. On this part of the plain, both where traces of buildings are left, and where none stood, all seemed equally *naked* of vegetation; the whole ground appearing as if it had been washed over and over again by the

coming and receding waters, till every bit of genial soil was swept away; its half-clay, half sandy surface being left in ridgy streaks, like what is often seen on the flat shores of the sea after the retreating of the tide.'—(Sir R. K. Porter's *Travels*, vol. ii. p. 392.) 'The ground is low and marshy, and presents not the slightest vestige of former buildings, of any description whatever.'—(Buckingham's *Travels,* vol. ii. p. 278.) 'The ruins of Babylon are thus *inundated* so as to render many parts of them inaccessible, by converting the valleys among them into morasses.'—(Rich's *Memoir,* p. 13.) ¶ *Neither shall the Arabian pitch tent there.* The Arabians dwelt chiefly in tents; and were a wandering people, or engaged in traffic which was conducted in caravans travelling from place to place. The idea here is, that Babylon, so far from being occupied as a *permanent* residence for any people, would be unfit even for a resting place. It would be so utterly desolate, so forsaken, and so unhealthy, that the caravan would not even stop there for a night. What a change this from its former splendour! How different from the time when it was the place of magnificent palaces, when strangers flocked to it, and when people from all nations were collected there! ¶ *Neither shall the shepherds,* &c. This is an additional image of desolation. Babylon was situated in the midst of a most fertile region. It might be supposed that, though it was to be destroyed, it would still furnish pasturage for flocks. But no, says the prophet, it shall be so utterly and entirely desolate, that it shall not even afford pasturage for them. The reasons of this are—(1) that the whole region round about Babylon was laid under water by the Euphrates after the city was taken, and became a stagnant pool, and of course an unfit place for flocks; and (2) that Babylon was reduced to an extended scene of ruins; and on those ruins — those extended wastes of broken walls, of bricks and cement—no grass would grow. The

21 But [1] wild beasts of the desert shall lie there: and their houses shall be full of [2] doleful creatures: and [3] owls shall dwell there, and satyrs shall dance there.

1 ziim.   2 ochim, or, ostriches.   3 daughters of the owl.

prophecy has been remarkably fulfilled. It is said that the Arabs cannot be persuaded to remain there even for a night. They traverse these ruins by day without fear ; but at night the superstitious dread of evil spirits deters them from remaining there. 'Captain Mignan was accompanied by six *Arabs* completely armed, but he " could not induce them to remain towards night, from the apprehension of evil spirits. It is impossible to eradicate this idea from the minds of these people, who are very deeply imbued with superstition... And when the sun sunk behind the Mujelibé, and the moon would have lighted his way among the ruins, it was with infinite regret that he obeyed the summons of his guides." ' — (Mignan's *Travels*, as quoted by Keith, pp. 221, 222.) ' All the people of the country assert that it is extremely dangerous to approach the mound' [the mound in Babylon called Kasr, or Palad] 'after nightfall, on account of the multitude of evil spirits by which it is haunted.'—(Rich's *Memoir on the Ruins of Babylon*, p. 27.) The Rev. Joseph Wolff, speaking of his visit to Babylon, says, 'I inquired of them (the Yezeedes), whether the Arabs ever pitched their tents among the ruins of Babylon. No, said they, the Arabs believe that the ghost of Nimrod walks amidst them in the darkness, and no Arab would venture on so hazardous an experiment.'

21. *But wild beasts of the desert shall lie there.* Heb. צִיִּים (*tziyim*). This word denotes properly those animals that dwell in *dry* and desolate places, from צִי, *a waste, a desert.* The ancient versions have differed considerably in the interpretation. The LXX. in different places render it, Θηρία—' Wild animals ;' or δαιμόνια—' Demons.' The Syriac, 'Wild animals, spirits, sirens.' Vulg. 'Beasts, demons, dragons.' Abarbanel renders it, 'Apes.' This word is applied to *men*, in Ps. lxx. 9 ; lxxiv. 14 ; to *animals*, Isa. xxiii. 13 ; xxxiv. 14 ; Jer. l. 39. Bochart supposes that *wild cats* or *catamounts* are here intended. He has

proved that they abound in eastern countries. They feed upon dead carcasses, and live in the woods, or in desert places, and are remarkable for their howl. Their yell resembles that of infants. (*See* Bochart's *Hieroz.* i. 3. 14. pp. 860–862.) ¶ *And their houses shall be full of doleful creatures.* Marg. ' Ochim,' or ' Ostriches.' אֹחִים. The LXX. render this 'Clamours,' or 'Howlings,' without supposing that it refers to any particular animals. The Hebrew word is found nowhere else. Bochart supposes that the yell or howl of wild animals is intended, and not animals themselves (*Hieroz.* i. 3. 15). ¶ *And owls shall dwell there.* Heb. ' Daughters of the owl or ostrich.' The owl is a well-known bird that dwells only in obscure and dark retreats, giving a doleful screech, and seeking its food only at night. It is not certain, however, that the owl is intended here. The LXX. render it, Σειρῆνες—' Sirens.' The Chaldee, ' The daughter of the ostrich.' Bochart has gone into an extended argument to prove that the ostrich is intended here (*Hieroz.* xi. 2. 14). The Hebrew does not particularly denote the kind of bird intended, but means those that are distinguished for their sound—' the daughters of sound or clamour.' ' The ostrich is a sly and timorous creature, delighting in solitary barren deserts. In the night they frequently make a very doleful and hideous noise ; sometimes groaning as if they were in the greatest agonies.'— (Shaw's *Travels*, vol. ii. p. 348, 8vo ; Taylor's *Heb. Con.; see* Job xxx. 29; Isa. xxxiv. 13; xliii. 20; Jer. l. 39; Mic. i. 8; Lev. xi. 16; Deut. xiv. 15; Lam. iv. 3.) The word does not elsewhere occur. ¶ *And satyrs shall dance there* (שְׂעִירִים). A *satyr*, in mythology, was a sylvan deity or demigod, represented as a monster, half man and half goat, having horns on his head, a hairy body, with the feet and tail of a goat (Webster). The word here used properly denotes that which is *hairy*, or *rough*, and is applied to *goats* in Gen. xxv. 25; Ps. lxviii. 21; Lev. xiii. 10, 25, 26, 30,

22 And ¹ the wild beasts of the islands shall cry in their ² desolate houses, and dragons in *their*

1 *Jim.*   2 or, *palaces.*

pleasant palaces: and her time *is* near ᵃ to come, and her days shall not be prolonged.

a Deut.32,35,36.

32. It is often rendered *hair* (*see* Taylor). In Isa. xxxiv. 14, it is rendered 'satyr;' in Deut. xxxii. 2, it is rendered 'the small ram;' in Lev. xvii. 7, and 2 Chron. xi. 15, it is rendered 'the devils,' meaning objects of worship, or idols. Bochart supposes that it refers to the idols that were worshipped among the Egyptians, who placed *goats* among their gods. Döderlin supposes that it means either *fawns,* or a species of the monkey tribe, resembling in their rough and shaggy appearance the wild goat. They are here represented as 'dancing;' and in Isa. xxxiv. 14, as 'crying to each other.' It is evident that the prophet intends animals of a rough and shaggy appearance; such as are quick and nimble in their motions; such as dwell in deserts, in forests, or in old ruins; and such as answer to each other, or chatter. The description would certainly seem more applicable to some of the *simia* or monkey tribe than to any other animals. It is *possible,* indeed, that he means merely to make use of language that was well known, as describing animals that the ancients *supposed* had an existence, but which really had not, as the imaginary beings called satyrs. But it is possible, also, that he means simply wild goats (comp. Bochart's *Hieroz.* xi. 6. 7). The LXX. render it, Δαιμόνια—'Demons, or devils.' The Vulgate, *Pilosi*—'Shaggy, or hairy animals.' The Chaldee, 'Demons.' The essential idea is, that such wild animals as are supposed to dwell in wastes and ruins, would hold their revels in the forsaken and desolate palaces of Babylon. The following remarks of the Rev. Joseph Wolff may throw light on this passage : 'I then went to the mountain of Sanjaar, which was full of Yezeedes. One hundred and fifty years ago, they believed in the glorious doctrine of the Trinity, and worshipped the true God ; but being severely persecuted by the neighbouring Yezeedes, they have now joined them, and are worshippers of the devil. These men frequent the ruins of Babylon, and

dance around them. On a certain night, which they call the Night of Life, they hold their dances around the desolate ruins, in honour of the devil. The passage which declares that "satyrs shall dance there," evidently has respect to this very practice. The original word translated "satyr," literally means, according to the testimony of the most eminent Jewish Rabbins, *devil worshippers.*' 'It is a curious circumstance,' says Mr. Rich, in his *Memoir on the Ruins of Babylon,* p. 30, in describing the Mujelibé, 'that here I first heard the oriental account of satyrs. I had always imagined the belief of their existence was confined to the mythology of the west ; but a Chôadar who was with me when I examined this ruin, mentioned by accident, that in this desert an animal is found resembling a man from the head to the waist, but having the thighs and legs of a sheep or a goat ; he said also that the Arabs hunt it with dogs, and eat the lower parts, abstaining from the upper on account of their resemblance to the human species.' 'The Arabians call them Sied-as-sad, and say that they abound in some woody places near Semava on the Euphrates.'

22. *And the wild beasts of the islands* (אִיִּים) ; see Notes, ch. xi. 11 ; xli. 1, on the word rendered 'islands.' The word denotes islands, or coasts, and as those coasts and islands were unknown and unexplored, the word seems to have denoted unknown and uninhabited regions in general. Bochart supposes that by the word here used is denoted a species of wolves, the jackal, or the *thoes.* It is known as a wild animal, exceedingly fierce, and is also distinguished by alternate howlings in the night (*see* Bochart's *Hieroz.* i. 3. 12). The word wolf probably will not express an erroneous idea here. The Chaldee renders it, 'Cats.' ¶ *Shall cry.* Heb. 'Shall *answer,* or *respond* to each other.' This is known to be the custom of wolves and some other wild animals, who send forth those dismal howls in alternate responses

at night. This alternation of the howl or cry gives an additional impressiveness to the loneliness and desolation of forsaken Babylon. ¶ *And dragons* (תַּנִּים). This word, in its various forms of *tannim, taninim, tannin,* and *tannoth,* denotes sometimes *jackals* or *thoes,* as in Job xxx. 29 ; Ps. xliv. 19 ; Micah i. 8 ; Mal. i. 3. But it also denotes a great fish, a whale, a sea monster, a dragon, a serpent. It is translated ' a whale' in Gen. i. 21 ; Job vii. 12 ; Ezek. xxxii. 2 ; ' serpents,' Ex. vii. 9, 10, 12 ; ' dragons,' or ' dragon,' Deut. xxxii. 33 ; Neh. ii. 13 ; Ps. xliv. 19 ; lxxiv. 13 ; xci. 13 ; cxlviii. 7 ; Isa. xxvii. 1 ; li. 9 ; Jer. xiv. 6 ; li. 34 ; Mal. i. 3, *et al.;* and once 'sea monsters,' Lam. iv. 3. A *dragon* properly means a kind of winged serpent much celebrated in the dark ages. Here it may not improperly be rendered *jackal* (*see* Bochart's *Hieroz.* i. 1. 9, p. 69). ¶ *In* their *pleasant palaces.* Heb. ' Their palaces of luxury and pleasure.' The following testimonies from travellers will show how minutely this was accomplished :—' There are many dens of wild beasts in various parts.' ' There are quantities of porcupine quills.' ' In most of the cavities are numberless bats and owls.' ' These caverns, over which the chambers of majesty may have been spread, are now the refuge of jackals and other savage animals. The mouths of their entrances are strewed with the bones of sheep and *goats ;* and the loathsome smell that issues from most of them is sufficient warning not to proceed into the den.'—(Sir R. K. Porter's *Travels,* vol. ii. p. 342.) ' The mound was full of large holes ; we entered some of them, and found them strewed with the carcasses and skeletons of animals recently killed. The ordure of wild beasts was so strong, that prudence got the better of curiosity, for we had no doubt as to the savage nature of the inhabitants. Our guides, indeed, told us that all the ruins abounded in lions and other wild beasts ; so literally has the Divine prediction been fulfilled, that wild beasts of the deserts should lie there.'—(Keppel's *Narrative,* vol. i. pp. 179, 180.) ¶ *And her time* is *near to come.* This was spoken about 174 years before the destruction of Babylon.

But we are to bear in mind that the prophet is to be supposed to be speaking to the captive Jews *in* Babylon, and speaking to them respecting their release (see ch. xiv. 1, 2 ; comp. remarks on the Analysis of this chapter). Thus considered, supposing the prophet to be addressing the Jews in captivity, or ministering consolation to them, the time was near. Or if we suppose him speaking as in his own time, the period when Babylon was to be destroyed was at no great distance.

On this whole prophecy, we may observe—(1.) That it was uttered at least 170 years before it was fulfilled. Of this there is all the proof that can be found in regard to any ancient writings. (2.) When uttered, there was the strongest improbability that it would be fulfilled. This improbability arose from the following circumstances : (*a*) The Jews were secure in their own land, and they had no reason to dread the Babylonians ; they had no wars with them, and it was improbable that they would be plucked up as a nation and carried there as captives. Such a thing had never occurred, and there were no circumstances that made it probable that it would occur. (*b*) The great strength and security of Babylon rendered it improbable. It was the capital of the heathen world ; and if there was any city that seemed impregnable, it was this. (*c*) It was improbable that it would be overthrown by *the Medes.* Media, at the time when the prophecy was uttered, was a dependent province of Assyria (Note, ver. 17), and it was wholly improbable that the Medes would revolt ; that they would subdue their masters ; that they would be united to the Persians, and that thus a *new* kingdom would arise, that should overthrow the most mighty capital of the world. (*d*) It was improbable that Babylon would become uninhabitable. It was in the midst of a most fertile country ; and by no human sagacity could it have been seen that the capital would be removed to Susa, or that Seleucia would be founded, thus draining it of its inhabitants ; or that by the inundation of waters it would become unhealthy. How could mere human sagacity have foreseen that there would not be a house

CHAPTER XIV.

ANALYSIS.

THIS chapter is a continuation of the prophecy respecting Babylon, which was commenced in the previous chapter. The prophecy is concluded at ver. 27. A considerable portion of the chapter is a poem of unequalled beauty and sublimity. It is to be remembered that this prophecy was uttered at least 174 years before they were carried into captivity; and the design of the prophet is, to declare the *certainty* of their release after they should be subjected to this bondage. He, doubtless, intended that this prophecy should be borne with them, in memory at least, to Babylon, and that it should comfort and sustain them when there (see Introduction to ch. xiii). He, therefore, opens the vision by a summary statement of the *certainty* of their deliverance (1–3). This general declaration respecting the deliverance of the Jews, is followed by a triumphant song on that subject, that is singularly beautiful in its imagery, and sublime in its conception. 'It moves in lengthened elegiac measure, like a song of lamentation for the dead, and is full of lofty scorn and contumely from beginning to the end.'—(Herder's *Spirit of Hebrew Poetry*, by Marsh, vol. ii. p. 206.) It may be called *the triumphal song of the Jews when delivered from their long and oppressive bondage.* The parts and design of this poem may be thus expressed:

I. A chorus of Jews is introduced, expressing

their surprise at the sudden and entire downfall of Babylon, and the complete destruction of the proud and haughty city. The whole earth is full of joy and rejoicing that the city, so long distinguished for oppressions and arrogance, is laid low; and even *the cedars* of Lebanon are introduced as uttering a most severe taunt over the fallen tyrant, and expressing their security now that he is no more (4–8).

II. The scene is immediately changed from earth to hell. Hades, or the region of the dead, is represented as moved at the descent of the haughty king of Babylon to those abodes. Departed monarchs rise from their thrones, and insult him on being reduced from his pride and magnificence to the same low state as themselves (9–11). This portion of the ode is one of the boldest personifications ever attempted in poetry: and is executed with remarkable brevity and force—so much so that we almost seem to *see* the illustrious shades of the dead rise from their couches to meet the descending king of Babylon.

III. The Jews now resume the speech (12–17). They address the king of Babylon as fallen from heaven—like the bright star of the morning. They speak of him as the most magnificent and proud of the monarchs of the earth. They introduce him as expressing the most extravagant purposes of ambition; as designing to ascend to heaven, and to make his throne above the stars; and as aiming at equality with God.

---

in it in the sixteenth century; or that now, in 1839, it would be a wide and dreary waste? Can any man now tell what London, or Paris, or New York, or Philadelphia, will be two years hence? Yet a prediction that those cities shall be the residence of 'wild beasts of the desert,' of 'satyrs' and 'dragons,' would be as probable now as was the prediction respecting Babylon at the time when Isaiah uttered these remarkable prophecies. (3.) The prophecy is not vague conjecture. It is not a *general* statement. It is minute, and definite, and particular; and it has been as definitely, and minutely, and particularly fulfilled. (4.) This is one of the evidences of the Divine origin of the Bible. How will the infidel account for this prophecy and its fulfilment? It will not do to say that it is *accident*. It is too minute, and too particular. It is not *human sagacity*. No human sagacity could have foretold it. It is

not *fancied fulfilment*. It is real, in the most minute particulars. And if so, then Isaiah was commissioned by JEHOVAH as he claimed to be—for none but the omniscient JEHOVAH can foresee and describe future events as the destruction of Babylon was foreseen and described. And if *this* prophecy was inspired by God, by the same train of reasoning it can be proved that the whole Bible is a revelation from heaven. For a very interesting account of the present state of the ruins of Babylon, furnishing the most complete evidence of the fulfilment of the prophecies in regard to it, the reader may consult an article in the *Am. Bib. Rep.*, vol. viii. pp. 177–189. (See also the two *Memoirs on the Ruins of Babylon*, by C. J. Rich, Esq. London, 1816 and 1818.) The frontispiece to this volume, compiled from the sketches of recent travellers, gives accurate and interesting views of those ruins.

They then speak of him as cast down to hell, and as the object of reproach by all those who shall behold him.

IV. The scene is again changed. Certain persons are introduced who are represented as seeing the fallen king of Babylon—as looking narrowly upon him, to make themselves sure that it was he—and as taunting him with his proud designs and his purposes to make the world a wilderness (15–20). They see him cast out and naked; lying among the undistinguished dead, and trodden under feet; and contrast his condition with that of monarchs who are usually deposited in a splendid mausoleum. But the once haughty king of Babylon is represented as denied even a common burial, and as lying undistinguished in the streets.

V. The whole scene of the poem is closed by introducing God as purposing the certain ruin of Babylon; as designing to cut off the whole of the royal family, and to convert the whole city into pools of water, and a habitation for the bittern (21–23). This is declared to be the purpose of JEHOVAH; and a solemn declaration is made, that when *he* makes a purpose none can disannul it.

VI. A confirmation of this is added (24–27) in a fragment respecting the destruction of the army of the Assyrian under Sennacherib, by

which the exiles in Babylon would be comforted with the assurance, that he who had destroyed the Assyrian host with such ease could also effect his purposes respecting Babylon (see the remarks introductory to ver. 24).

'I believe it may be affirmed,' says Lowth, that there is no poem of its kind extant in any language, in which the subject is so well laid out, and so happily conducted, with such a richness of invention, with such a variety of images, persons, and distinct actions, with such rapidity and ease of transition in so small a compass, as in this ode of Isaiah. For beauty of disposition, strength of colouring, greatness of sentiment, brevity, perspicuity, and force of expression, it stands, among all the monuments of antiquity, unrivalled.'

The king of Babylon, who was the subject of this prediction, and who reigned when Babylon was taken, was Belshazzar (see Dan. v.; and Notes on ver. 22).

FOR *a* the LORD will have mercy on Jacob, and will yet *b* choose Israel, and set them in their own land: and the strangers shall be joined with them, and they shall cleave to the house of Jacob.

a Ps.102.13.   *b* Zec.1.17; 2.12.

CHAPTER XIV.

1. *For the* LORD *will have mercy on Jacob.* That is, he will pity the captive Jews in Babylon. He will not abandon them, but will remember them, and restore them to their own land. ¶ *And will yet choose Israel.* Will show that he regards them as still his chosen people ; or will again *choose* them by recovering them from their bondage, and by restoring them to their country as his people. The names 'Jacob' and 'Israel' here simply denote the Jews. They do not imply that *all* of those who were to be carried captive would return, but that as a people they would be restored. ¶ *And set them,* &c. Heb. 'Will cause them to rest in their own country ;' that is, will give them peace, quietness, and security there. ¶ *And the stranger shall be joined to them.* The 'stranger,' here, probably refers to those foreigners who would become proselytes to their religion, while they were in Babylon. Those proselytes would be firmly united with them, and would return with them to their own land. Their captivity would be attended

with this advantage, that many even of those who led them away, would be brought to embrace their religion, and to return with them to their own country. If it is asked what *evidence* there is that any considerable number of the people of Chaldea became Jewish proselytes, I answer, that it is expressly stated in Esther viii. 17 : 'And many of the people of the land became Jews ; for the fear of the Jews fell upon them.' Ezra, indeed, has not mentioned the fact, that many of the people of Babylonia became proselytes to the religion of the Jews, but it is in accordance with all that we know of their history, and their influence on the nations with which, from time to time, they were connected, that many should have been thus joined to them. We know that in subsequent times many of other nations became proselytes, and that multitudes of the Egyptians, the Macedonians, the Romans, and the inhabitants of Asia Minor, embraced the Jewish religion, or became what were called ' proselytes of the gate.' They were circumcised, and were regarded as entitled to a part

2 And the people shall take them, and bring *a* them to their place: and the house of Israel shall possess them in the land of the LORD for servants and handmaids: and they shall take them captives, whose captives¹ they were; and they shall rule over their oppressors.

a ch.18.7; 60.4,&c.; 66.20.
1 *that had taken them captives.*

3 And it shall come to pass in the day that the LORD shall give thee rest *b* from thy sorrow, and from thy fear, and from the hard bondage wherein thou wast made to serve.

4 That *c* thou shalt take up this proverb ² against the king of Ba-

b Eze.28.24.   *c* Hab.2.6.
2 or, *taunting speech.*

of the privileges of the Jewish people (see Acts ii. 9–11; comp. Acts xvii. 4, 17). Tacitus, speaking of his time, says, that ‘every abandoned man, despising the religion of his country, bears tribute and revenue to Jerusalem, whence it happens that the number of the Jews is greatly increased.’ — (*Hist.* v. 5.) That the Jews, therefore, who were in Babylon should induce many of the Chaldeans during their long captivity to become proselytes, is in accordance with all their history.

2. *And the people shall take them.* That is, the people in Babylon. ¶ *And bring them to their place.* That is, they shall attend them to the land of Judea, and aid in restoring them to their own country. There is reference here, doubtless, to the fact that Cyrus would assist them (comp. Ezra ch. i.), and that many of the inhabitants of Chaldea who would become proselytes, would be willing to accompany them to their own land. ¶ *And the house of Israel shall possess them in the land of the* LORD. Not in a foreign land, and among strangers and foes, but in their own land, and among the institutions of their own religion. They would be willing to return with them, and occupy a humble place among them, as servants, for the sake of enjoying the privileges of the true religion. It was a matter of course among the Hebrews, that proselytes would be regarded as occupying a less elevated place in society than native-born Jews. ¶ *And they shall take them captive, &c.* That is, they shall induce them to become proselytes; to be willing to accompany them to their own homes, and to become their servants there. It does not mean that they would subdue them by force; but that they would be able, by their influence

there, to disarm their opposition; and to induce them to become the friends of their religion. ¶ *And they shall rule over their oppressors.* This is one instance where the people of God would show that they could disarm their oppressors by a mild and winning demeanour, and in which they would be able to induce others to join with them. Such would be the force of their example and conduct, of their conversation and of their deportment, even in the midst of proud and haughty Babylon, that their oppressors would be won to embrace the religion of their captives. If, in proud and haughty Babylon, those who loved the Lord could thus do good; if, when they were *captives*, they could have such an influence over their haughty masters, where is there a place in which the friends of God may not be useful by their example, their conversation, and their prayers?

3. *And it shall come to pass.* That is, then thou shalt take up a taunting song against the king of Babylon (ver. 4). ¶ *That the* LORD *shall give thee rest* (comp. ch. xxxviii. 12). The nature of this predicted rest, is more fully described in Ezek. xxviii. 25, 26. ¶ *From thy sorrow.* The long pain of thy captivity in Babylon. ¶ *And from thy fear.* Heb. ‘Trembling.’ That is, the apprehension of the ills to which they were continually exposed. Trembling is usually one effect of fear. ¶ *And from thy hard bondage.* The severe and galling servitude of seventy years.

4. *That thou shalt take up.* Thou shalt utter, declare, or commence. The word ‘take up,’ is used in the sense of utter, speak, or declare, in Ex. xx. 7; xxiii. 1; Ps. xv. 2. ¶ *This proverb* (הַמָּשָׁל). Vulg. ‘Parable.’ Sept. Τὸν θρῆνον, — ‘Lamentation.’ The Hebrew

bylon, and say, How hath the oppressor ceased! the ¹ golden ᵃ city
ceased!

5 The LORD hath broken the staff

1 or, *exactress of gold.*   ᵃ Rev.18.16.

of the wicked, *and* the sceptre of
the rulers.

6 He who smote ᵇ the people in
wrath with a ² continued stroke, he

ᵇ ch.33.1.   2 *a stroke without removing.*

word *mâshâl,* usually rendered *proverb,*
is also rendered *a parable,* or *a by-word.*
It properly denotes *a metaphor, a comparison, a similitude;* and is applied
usually to a brief and pungent sentiment
or maxim, where wisdom is embodied
in few words. In these the ancients
abounded. They had few books; and
hence arose the necessity of condensing
as much as possible the sentiments of
wisdom, that they might be easily
remembered, and transmitted to future
times. These maxims were commonly
expressed in figurative language, or by
a brief comparison, or short parable, as
they are with-us. The word also means,
figurative discourse generally; and
hence, a song or poem (Num. xxiii. 7,
18; Job xxvii. 1; xxix. 1; Ps. xlix. 5).
It is also used to denote a *satire,* or a
song of triumph over enemies (Micah
ii. 4; Heb. iv. 6; Joel ii. 17). It is
evidently used in this sense here—to
denote a taunting speech, a song of
triumph over the prostrate king of
Babylon. In this beautiful song, there
are all the elements of the most pungent
satire, and all the beauties of the highest
poetry. ¶ *Against the king of Babylon.*
Over the king of Babylon, or in regard
to him. It is not certain that any
particular king of Babylon is here intended. If there was, it was probably
Belshazzar, in whose reign the city was
taken (see Notes on ver. 22). It may,
however, be designed to denote the
Babylonian empire—the kingdom that
had oppressed the Jews; and thus *the
king* may be referred to as the head of
the nation, and as the representative of
the whole people. ¶ *How hath the
oppressor ceased!* The word 'oppressor'
(נֹגֵשׂ) denotes, properly, *the exactor of
tribute,* and refers here to the fact that
Babylon had oppressed its dependent
provinces, by exacting large revenues
from them, and thus cruelly oppressing
them. ¶ *Ceased.* Ceased to exact
tribute; or (Heb.) 'is at rest.' It is
now at rest, and no more puts forth its

power in oppressing its dependent provinces. ¶ *The golden city.* Babylon.
The word used here (מַדְהֵבָה) occurs
nowhere else in the Bible. According
to the Jewish Commentators, it means
an exactress of gold, as if derived from
זָהָב (*dĕhăbh*), used for זָהָב (*zĕhăbh*), gold.
Gesenius and Michaelis prefer another
reading (מַרְהֵבָה *mărhēbhâ,* from רָהַב
râhăbh), and suppose that it means
oppression. The Vulgate renders it
tribute — 'The tribute hath ceased.'
The LXX. 'Επισπουδαστής—'Solicitor,
or exactor (of gold).' Vitringa supposes
that the word means *gold,* and that it
refers to the golden sceptre of its kings
that had now ceased to be swayed over
the prostrate nations. The most probable sense is, that it means the exactress
of gold, or of tribute. This best expresses
the force of the word, and best agrees
with the parallelism. In this sense it
does not refer to the magnificence of the
city, but to its oppressive acts in demanding tribute of gold from its dependent provinces.

5. *The LORD hath broken.* JEHOVAH,
by the hand of Cyrus. ¶ *The staff of
the wicked.* That is, the sceptre of the
king of Babylon. The word rendered
'staff' (מַטֶּה) may mean either a bough,
stick, staff, rod, or a sceptre. The sceptre
was the symbol of supreme power. It
was in the form of a staff, and was made
of wood, ivory, or gold. It here means
that JEHOVAH had taken away the power
from Babylon, and destroyed his dominion.

6. *He who smote.* This may either
refer to the king of Babylon, or to the
rod or sceptre which he had used, and
which was now broken. Herder refers
it to the sceptre, 'that which smote the
nations.' (On the meaning of the word
smote, see Notes on ch. x. 20.) ¶ *The
people.* The nations that were subject
to his authority. ¶ *With a continual
stroke.* Marg. 'A stroke without removing.' Vulg. *Plagâ insanabili—*

that ruled the nations in anger, is persecuted, *and* none hindereth.

7 The whole earth is at rest, *and* is quiet ; they break forth into singing.

8 Yea, the fir trees *a* rejoice at thee, *and* the cedars of Lebanon, *saying,* Since thou art laid down, no feller is come up against us.

a Eze.31.16.

' With an incurable plague.'—Sept. the same—Πληγῇ ἀνιάτῳ. The Hebrew is, as in the margin, 'A smiting without removing,' or without cessation. There was no relaxation in its oppressions, it was *always* engaged in acts of tyranny. ¶ *He that ruled the nations.* Babylon was the capital of a vast empire, and that empire was composed of many dependent nations. ¶ *Is persecuted.* By those that make war upon it. *Its* turn had come to be oppressed, and overthrown. ¶ And *none hindereth.* No nation opposes the invader. None of the dependent kingdoms of Babylon have any real attachment to it, but all rejoice at its downfall. The most mighty kingdom of the earth is helpless and ruined. What a change was this ! How sudden and striking the revolution ! And what a warning to proud and guilty cities !

7. *The whole earth is at rest.* The kingdom of Babylonia, or Chaldea, extended nearly over the whole heathen world. Now that Babylon was fallen, and that those oppressions would cease, the world is represented as in peace and quietness. ¶ *They break forth into singing.* That is, the inhabitants of all the nations that were subject to Babylon now rejoice that they are released from its galling and oppressive yoke.

8. *Yea, the fir trees rejoice at thee.* They join with the inhabitants of the nations in rejoicing at thy downfall— for they now, like those inhabitants, are suffered to remain undisturbed. (On the word rendered *fir trees,* see Notes on ch. i. 29.) It is evident that a species of evergreen is meant ; and probably some species that grew in Syria or Palestine. The idea is plain. The very forest is represented as rejoicing. It would be safe from the king of Babylon. He could no longer cut it down to build his palaces, or to construct his implements of war. This figure of representing the hills and groves, the trees, the mountains, and the earth, as exulting,

or as breaking forth into joy, is common in the Scriptures :

Let the heavens rejoice, and let the earth be glad;
Let the sea roar, and the fulness thereof.
Let the field be joyful, and all that is therein :
Then shall all the trees of the wood rejoice
Before the Lord.　　　　　Ps. xcvi. 11-13.

Let the floods clap their hands;
Let the hills be joyful together
Before the Lord.　　　　　Ps. xcviii. 8, 9.

Praise the Lord from the earth,
Ye dragons and all deeps;
Fire and hail; snow and vapour;
Stormy wind fulfilling his word:
Mountains and all hills;
Fruitful trees and all cedars.
　　　　　　　Ps. cxlviii. 7-12.

(Comp. 1 Chron. xvi. 31; Hab. iii. 10, 11.) ¶ *The cedars of Lebanon* (Note, ch. x. 34). The cedars of Lebanon were much celebrated for building ; and it is not impossible that the king of Babylon had obtained timber from that mountain with which to construct his palaces at Babylon. They are now represented as rejoicing that he is fallen, since they would be safe and undisturbed. A similar figure of speech occurs in Virgil, *Ecl.* v. 68 :

Peace, peace, mild Daphnis loves; with joyous cry
The untill'd mountains strike the echoing sky;
And rocks and towers the triumph spread abroad—
' A god! Menalcas! Daphnis is a god!'
　　　　　　　　　　Wrangham.

It is a beautiful figure ; and is a fine specimen of the poetry of the Hebrews, where everything is animated, and full of life. ¶ *Since thou art laid down.* Since thou art dead. ¶ *No feller.* No one to cut us down. Jowett (*Chris. Res.*) makes the following remarks on this passage on his visit to Lebanon :— ' As we passed through the extensive forest of fir trees situated between Deir-el-Kamr and Ainep, we had already heard, at some distance, the stroke of one solitary axe, resounding from hill to hill. On reaching the spot, we found a peasant, whose labour had been so far successful, that he had felled his tree and lopped his branches. He was now

9 ¹ Hell ªfrom beneath is moved for thee to meet *thee* at thy coming: it stirreth up the dead for thee,

even all the ² chief ones of the earth: it hath raised up from their thrones all the kings of the nations.

1 or, *the graves.*   ª Eze.32.21.

2 *leaders,* or, *great goats.*

hewing it in the middle, so as to balance the two halves upon his camel, which stood patiently by him waiting for his load. In the days of Hiram, king of Tyre, and subsequently under the kings of Babylon, this romantic solitude was not so peaceful; that most poetic image in Isaiah, who makes these very trees vocal, exulting in the downfall of the destroyer of nations, seems now to be almost realized anew—*Yea, the fir trees rejoice at thee, and the cedars of Lebanon, saying, Since thou art laid down, no feller is come up against us.*'

9. *Hell from beneath.* The scene is now changed. The prophet had represented the people of all the subject nations as rejoicing that the king of Babylon had fallen, and had introduced even the trees of the forest as breaking forth into joy at this event. He now transfers the scene to the mournful regions of the dead; follows the spirit of the departed king of Babylon—the man who once gloried in the magnificence of his kingdom and his court, and who was more distinguished for pride and arrogance than all other monarchs—down to the land of darkness, and describes his reception there. This portion of the ode is signally sublime, and is managed with great power and skill. It is unequalled, perhaps, by any writings for boldness, majesty, and, at the same time, for its severe sarcasm. The word 'hell' here (שְׁאוֹל *sheōl*) is rendered by the Vulgate *infernus;* and by the LXX. Ὁ ᾅης—*Hades.* It properly means the grave, and then the dark regions of the lower world—the region of ghosts and shades: a place where thick darkness reigns. The verb from which it is derived means, properly, *to ask, to demand, to require, to seek;* and this name (*sheol*) is supposed to have been given to the grave, and to the regions of departed spirits, from the insatiable *demand* which they are constantly making of the living (see Note on ch. v. 14, where the word is explained). The word denotes, says Taylor (*Heb. Con.*), 'The underground parts of the earth, other-

wise called the nether, or lower parts of the earth; the earth beneath in opposition to the earth above, where men and other animals live. In *sheol* are the foundations of the mountains (Deut. xxxii. 22). In *sheol* men penetrate by digging into the earth (Amos ix. 2). Into *sheol* the roots of trees do strike down (Ezek. xxxi. 16). Into *sheol*, Korah, Dathan, and Abiram went down alive (Num. xvi. 30, 33). In *sheol* the body is corrupted and consumed by worms (Job xvii. 13, 14; Ps. xvi. 10; xlix. 14). They that rest together in the dust are said to go down *to the bars,* or *strong gates of sheol* (Job xvii. 16). In *sheol* there is no knowledge, nor can any praise God or give thanks there (Ps. vi. 5; Eccl. ix. 10; Isa. xxxviii. 10, 11). *Sheol* and the pit, death and corruption, are synonymous (Ps. xvi. 10; lxxxix. 48; Prov. i. 12; vii. 27; Ezek. xxxi. 16; Hos. xiii. 14). A grave is one particular cavity purposely digged for the interment of a dead person; *sheol* is a collective name for all the graves. He that is in the grave is in *sheol;* but he that is in *sheol* may not be in a grave, but in any pit, or in the sea. In short, it is the region of the dead; which is figuratively considered as a city or large habitation with gates and bars in which there are many chambers (Prov. vii. 27).' *Sheol* is never full, but is always asking or craving more (Prov. xxvii. 20; Heb. ii. 5). Here it means, not a place of punishment, but the region of the dead, where the ghosts of the departed are considered as residing together. ¶ *From beneath.* From beneath the earth. *Sheol* was always represented as being *in* or *under* the ground, and the grave was the avenue or door that led to it (see Note on ch. v. 14. ¶ *Is moved for thee.* Is roused to meet thee; is surprised that a monarch once so proud and magnificent is descending to it. The image here is taken from the custom of the ancients in burying, especially of burying princes and kings. This was usually done in caves or sepulchres excavated from a rock (see the

Notes and illustrations on ch. lxvi. 4). Mr. Stephens, in his *Travels in Egypt, Arabia Petrea, and the Holy Land,* has given an account of the manner in which he passed a night in Petra, which may serve to illustrate this passage : ' We ascended the valley, and rising to the summit of the rocky rampart [of Petra], it was almost dark when we found ourselves opposite a range of tombs in the suburbs of the city. Here we dismounted ; and selecting from among them one which, from its finish and dimensions, must have been the last abode of some wealthy Edomite, we prepared to pass the night within its walls. In the front part of it was a large chamber, about twenty-five feet square, and ten feet high ; and behind this was another of smaller dimensions, furnished with receptacles of the dead, not arranged after the manner of shelves along the wall, as in the catacombs I had seen in Italy and Egypt, but cut lengthwise in the rock, like ovens, so as to admit the insertion of the body with the feet foremost. My plans for the morrow being all arranged, the Bedouins stretched themselves out in the outer chamber, while I went within ; and seeking out a tomb as far back as I could find, I crawled in feet first, and found myself very much in the condition of a man buried alive. I had just room enough to turn round ; and the worthy old Edomite for whom the tomb was made, never slept in it more quietly than I did.'—(Vol. ii. pp. 82, 83, 86.) To understand the passage before us, we are to form the idea of an immense and gloomy cavern, all around which are niches or cells made to receive the bodies of the dead. In this vast vault monarchs repose in grandeur suitable to their former rank, each on his couch, ' in glory,' with their arms beside them (see ver. 18). These mighty shades— these departed monarchs—are represented as rising from their couches to meet the descending king of Babylon, and receive him with insults on his fall. —The Hebrew word for *moved* denotes more than our translation conveys. It means that they were *agitated*—they *trembled*—they advanced towards the descending monarch with trepidation. The idea of the shades of the mighty

dead thus being troubled, and rising to meet the king of Babylon, is one that is exceedingly sublime. ¶ *It stirreth up. Sheol* stirreth up ; that is, they are stirred up or excited. So the LXX. render it ' All the giants who rule the earth rise up to thee.' ¶ *The dead.* Heb. רְפָאִים (*rĕphâim*). The LXX. render this, Οἱ γίγαντες—' Giants.' So the Vulgate and the Chaldee. The meaning of this word has been a subject of great difference of opinion among lexicographers. It is sometimes found as a gentile noun to denote the sons of Raphah, called *Rephaim* (2 Sam. xxi. 16, 18), a Canaanitish race of giants that lived beyond Jordan (Gen. xiv. 5 ; xv. 20), from whom Og the son of Bashan was descended (Deut. iii. 11). It is sometimes used to denote all the giant tribes of Canaan (Deut. ii. 11, 20) ; and is particularly applied to men of extraordinary strength among the Philistines (2 Sam. xxi. 16, 18.) Vitringa supposes that the term was given to the spirits of the dead on account of the fact that they appeared to be *larger* than life ; that they in their form and stature resembled giants. But a more probable opinion is, that it is applied to the shades of the dead as being weak, feeble, or without power or sensation, from the word רָפָא (*râphâ*), weak, feeble, powerless. This interpretation is strongly confirmed by the place before us (ver. 10), ' Art thou become weak as we ? ' The word is rendered ' giants ' in the following places : Deut. ii. 11, 20 ; iii. 13 ; Josh. xii. 4 ; xv. 8 ; xvii. 15 ; xviii. 16 ; 2 Sam. xxi. 16, 18, 20, 22 ; 1 Chron. xx. 5, 6, 8. It is rendered ' Rephaims,' Gen. xiv. 5 ; xv. 20 ; 2 Sam. v. 18, 22 ; xxiii. 13. It is rendered ' the dead ' Job xxvi. 5 ; Ps. lxxxviii. 10 ; Prov. ii. 18 ; ix. 18 ; xxi. 16 ; Isa. xxvi. 29 ; and once it is rendered ' deceased,' Isa. xxvi. 14. It here means the departed spirits of the dead—the inhabitants of that dark and dismal region, conceived by the Hebrews to be situated beneath the ground, where dwell the departed dead before their final destiny is fixed— called *sheol* or *hades*. It is not the residence of the wicked only—the place of punishment—but the place where *all* the dead are supposed to be

10 All they shall speak and say unto thee, Art thou also become weak as we ? art thou become like unto us ?

11 Thy pomp is brought down to the grave, *and* the noise of thy viols : the worm is spread under thee, and the worms cover thee.

congregated before their final doom is pronounced.

[The author entertains peculiar views of the state of knowledge among the Hebrews regarding the future world—views which will be found fully canvassed in the preface to the volumes on Job. As to the alleged notion of *all* the dead dwelling in some dismal region before their final doom is pronounced, we have there taken pains to show that the righteous in ancient times entertained no such gloomy expectations. The opinions of the ancient Hebrews on this subject, must be taken from passages in which they expressly treat of it, and intimate plainly what their belief is, and not from passages confessedly full of poetical imagery. Nor are we to construe popular and poetical phraseology so strictly and literally as to form a theological creed out of it, in contradiction to the actual belief of those who daily used that phraseology. Because Englishmen speak of the dead *indiscriminately* as having *gone to the grave, and to the land of spirits*, must we, out of this, construct a Popish purgatory as the national belief? Yet this would be just as reasonable in the case of the English, as in the case of the Jews. The reader will appreciate the following observations of Professor Alexander on the place:—'Two expressions have been faithfully transcribed by interpreters, from one another, in relation to this passage, with a very equivocal effect upon its exposition. The one is, that it is full of biting sarcasm—an unfortunate suggestion of Calvin's, which puts the reader on the scent for irony, and even wit, instead of opening his mind to impressions of sublimity and tragic grandeur. The other, for which Calvin is in no degree responsible, is, that we have before us not a mere prosopopeia, or poetical creation of the highest order, but a chapter from the popular belief of the Jews, as to the locality, contents, and transactions of the unseen world. Thus Gesenius, in his Lexicon and Commentary, gives a minute topographical description of *Sheol*, as the Hebrews believed it to exist. With equal truth, a diligent compiler might construct a map of hell, as conceived of by the English Puritans, from the descriptive portions of the Paradise Lost. The infidel interpreters of Germany regard the scriptural and classical mythology precisely in the same light. But when Christian writers copy their expressions or ideas, they should take pains to explain

whether the popular belief of which they speak was true or false, and, if false, how it could be countenanced and sanctioned by inspired writers. This kind of exposition is, moreover, chargeable with a rhetorical incongruity, in lauding the creative genius of the poet, and yet making all his grand creations commonplace articles of popular belief. The true view of the matter, as determined both by piety and taste, appears to be, that the passage now before us comprehends two elements, and only two religious verities or certain facts, and poetical embellishments. The admission of a *tertium quid*, in the shape of superstitious fables, is as false in rhetoric as in theology.']

¶ *The chief ones of the earth.* Marg. 'Leaders,' or 'great goats.' The Hebrew word means properly *great goats*, or goats that are leaders of the flock. Perhaps there is intended to be a slight degree of sarcasm in applying this word to princes and monarchs. It is nowhere else applied to princes, though the word is often used or applied to *rams*, or to the chief goats of a flock. ¶ *From their thrones.* In *hades*, or *sheol*. They are there represented as occupying an eminence similar to that which distinguished them on earth.

10. *All they shall speak*, &c. Language of astonishment that one so proud, and who apparently never expected to die, should be brought down to that humiliating condition. It is a severe taunt at the great change which had taken place in a haughty monarch.

11. *Thy pomp.* Thy magnificence (see Note on ch. v. 14). ¶ *The noise of thy viols.* Instruments of music were often used in their feasts ; and the meaning here is, that instead of being surrounded with splendour, and the instruments of music, the monarch was now brought down to the corruption and stillness of the grave. The instrument referred to by the word 'viol' (בֶל *nēbhĕl*, plur. *nebhâlim*, Gr. νάβλα, Lat. *nablium*), was a stringed instrument usually with twelve strings, and played by the pecten or by the hand (see Notes and illustrations on ch. v. 12). Addi-

12 How art thou fallen from heaven, O ¹ Lucifer, son of the morning! *how* art thou cut down to the

1 or, *day star.*

ground, which didst weaken the
nations!

13 For thou hast said in thine
heart, I will ascend into heaven,

tional force is given by all these expressions if they are read, as Lowth reads
them, as questions asked in suprise, and
in a taunting manner, over the haughty
king of Babylon—'Is thy pride then
brought down to the grave?' &c. ¶ *The
worm.* This word, in Hebrew (רִמָּה
rimmâ), denotes a worm that is found
in putrid substances (Ex. xvi. 25; Job
vii. 5; xxi. 26). ¶ *Is spread under
thee.* Is become thy couch—instead of
the gorgeous couch on which thou wert
accustomed to repose. ¶ *And the worm*
(תּוֹלֵעָה *tōleâ*)—the same word which
occurs in ch. i. 18, and there rendered
crimson (see Note on that verse). This
word is usually applied to the insect from
which the crimson dye was obtained;
but it is also applied to the worm which
preys upon the dead (Ex. xvi. 20; Isa.
lxvi. 24). ¶ *Cover thee.* Instead of the
splendid covering which was over thee
when reposing on thy couch in thy palace.
What could be more humiliating than
this language? How striking the contrast between his present situation and
that in which he reposed in Babylon!
And yet this language is as applicable
to all others as to that proud and haughty
king. It is equally true of the great
and mighty everywhere; of the rich,
the gay, the beautiful, and the proud,
who lie on beds of down, that they will
soon lie where worms shall be their couch
and their covering. How ought this
reflection to humble our pride! How
should it lead us to be prepared for that
hour when the grave shall be our bed;
and when far away from the sound of
the viol and the harp; from the sweet
voice of friendship and the noise of
revelry, we shall mingle with our native
dust!

12. *How art thou fallen from heaven.*
A new image is presented here. It is
that of the bright morning star; and a
comparison of the once magnificent monarch with that beautiful star. He is
now exhibited as having fallen from his
place in the east to the earth. His glory
is dimmed; his brightness quenched.

Nothing can be more poetic and beautiful than a comparison of a magnificent monarch with the bright morning
star! Nothing more striking in representing his death, than the idea of that
star falling to the earth! ¶ *Lucifer.*
Marg. 'Day-star' (הֵילֵל *hēlēl*, from
הָלַל *hâlăl, to shine*). The word in Hebrew occurs as a noun nowhere else.
In two other places (Ezek. xxi. 12;
Zech. xi. 2), it is used as a verb in the
imperative mood of Hiphil, and is
translated 'howl' from the verb יָלַל
(*yâlăl*), *to howl* or *cry*. Gesenius and
Rosenmüller suppose that it should be
so rendered here. So Noyes renders it,
'Howl, son of the morning!' But the
common translation seems to be prefer-
able. The LXX. render it, 'Εωσφόρος,
and the Vulgate, 'Lucifer, the morning
star.' The Chaldee, 'How art thou
fallen from high, who wert splendid
among the sons of men.' There can be
no doubt that the object in the eye of
the prophet was the bright morning
star; and his design was to compare
this magnificent oriental monarch with
that. The comparison of a monarch
with the sun, or the other heavenly
bodies, is common in the Scriptures.
¶ *Son of the morning.* This is a Hebraism (see Note, Matt. i. 1), and signifies that that bright star is, as it were,
the production, or the offspring of morning; or that it *belongs to* the morning.
The word 'son' often thus denotes *possession,* or that one thing belongs to
another. The same star in one place
represents the Son of God himself; Rev.
xxi. 16: 'I am—the bright and morning star.' ¶ *Which didst weaken the
nations.* By thy oppressions and exactions, rendering once mighty nations
feeble.

13. *For thou hast said in thine heart.*
It was thy purpose or design. ¶ *I will
ascend into heaven.* Nothing could
more strikingly show the arrogance of
the monarch of Babylon than this impious design. The meaning is, that he
intended to set himself up as supreme;

1 will exalt my throne above the stars *a* of God : I will sit also upon the mount of the congregation, in the sides *h* of the north!

he designed that all should pay homage to him ; he did not intend to acknowledge the authority of God. It is not to be understood literally ; but it means that he intended *not* to acknowledge any superior either in heaven or earth, but designed that himself and his laws should be regarded as supreme. ¶ *Above the stars of God.* The stars which God has made. This expression is equivalent to the former that he would ascend into heaven. ¶ *I will sit also upon the mount of the congregation.* The word rendered 'congregation' (מוֹעֵד from יָעַד *to fix, appoint*), properly means a fixed or definite time ; then an *appointed* place of meeting ; then a meeting itself ; an assembly, a congregation. What is referred to here it is difficult to determine. The LXX. render it, ' On a high mountain, on the lofty regions which lie to the north.' The Chaldee, ' I will sit in the mount of covenant, in the regions of the north.' Grotius supposes that when the king of Babylon said he would ascend into heaven, he meant the land of Judea, which was called heaven because it was dedicated to God ;—that when he said he would ascend above the stars, he meant to denote those ' who were learned in the law ;' that by the ' mount of the congregation,' he meant mount Moriah where was the temple ; and that by the ' side of the north,' he meant mount Zion, which, he says, was on the north of Jerusalem. It is remarkable that the usually accurate Grotius should have fallen into this error, as mount Zion was not on the north of Jerusalem, but was south of mount Moriah. Vitringa defends the same interpretation in the main, but supposes that by the ' mount of the congregation' is meant mount Zion, and by ' the sides of the north,' is meant mount Moriah lying north of Zion. He supposes that mount Zion is called ' the mount of the congregation,' not because the congregation of Israel assembled there, but because it was the *appointed place* where God met his people, or where he manifested himself to them, and appeals to the following places where the word which is here

rendered ' congregation' is applied, in various forms, to the manifestation which God thus made (Ex. xxv. 22 ; xxix. 42, 43 ; Ps. lxxiv. 8). So Lowth supposes that it refers to the place where God promised to meet with his people (Ex. xxv. 22 ; xxix. 42, 43), and to commune with them, and translates it ' the mount of the Divine presence.' But to this interpretation there are great objections —(1.) The terms here employed ' the mount of the congregation,' ' the sides of the north,' are not elsewhere applied to mount Zion, and to mount Moriah. (2.) It does not correspond with the evident design of the king of Babylon. His object was not to make himself master of Zion and Moriah, but it was to exalt himself above the stars ; to be elevated above *all* inferior beings ; and to be above the gods. (3.) It is a most forced and unnatural interpretation to call the land of Judea ' heaven,' to speak of it as being ' above the stars of God,' or as ' above the heights of the clouds ;' and it is clear that the king of Babylon had a much higher ambition, and much more arrogant pretensions, than the conquest of what to him would be the comparatively limited province of Judea. However important that land appeared to the Jews as their country and their home ; or however important it was as the place of the solemnities of the true religion, yet we are to remember that it had no such consequence in the eyes of the king of Babylon. He had no belief in the truth of the Jewish religion, and all Judea compared with his other vast domains would appear to be a very unimportant province. It is evident, therefore, I think, that the king of Babylon did not refer here to Judea, or to Zion. The leading idea of his heart, which ought to guide our interpretation, was, that he designed *to ascend in authority over all inferior beings, and to be like the Most High.* We are to remember that Babylon was a city of idolatry ; and it is most probable that by ' the mount of the congregation, in the sides of the north,' there is reference to a belief prevalent in

Babylon that the gods had their residence on some mountain of the north. This was a common opinion among the ancients. The Hindoos call that mountain *Meru;* the Persians, who are followers of Zoroaster, *Al Bordsch;* the Arabs, *Kafe;* and the Greeks, *Olympus.* The common opinion was that this mountain was in the centre of the world, but the Hindoos speak of it as to the north of themselves in the Himalaya regions; the followers of Zoroaster in the mountains of Caucasus, lying to the north of their country; and the Greeks speak of Olympus, the highest mountain north of them in Thessaly. The Hindoo belief is thus referred to by Ward :—' In the book of Karma-Vipaka, it is said that the heavenly Vishnu, Brahma, and Siva, are upon the three peaks of the mountain Su-Meru, and that at the foot of this mountain are the heavens of twenty-one other gods.'—(*View of the History, Literature, and Religion of the Hindoos,* vol. i. p. 13.) So Wilford, in a Treatise on the mountain Caucasus, in the *Asiatic Researches,* vol. vi. p. 488, says, ' The Hindoos regard the mountain Meru as the dwelling-place of the gods. In the Puranas it is said, that upon the mountain Meru there is eternal day, for a space of fourteen degrees around the mountain Su-Meru, and consequently eternal night for the same space on the opposite side ; so the Hindoos are constrained to admit that Su-Meru is directly upon the top of the shadow of the earth, and that from the earth to that peak there is a vast cone-formed hill, dense as other earthly bodies, but invisible, impalpable, and impassable by mortals. On the side of this hill are various abodes, which, the higher one ascends, become the more beautiful, and which are made the dwellings of the blessed, according to the degrees of their desert. God and the most exalted of the divine beings have their abodes on the sides of the north, and on the top of this mountain.' According to the Zendavesta, the Al Bordsch is the oldest and the highest of the mountains; upon that is the throne of Ormuzd, and the assemblage of the heavenly spirits (Feruer ; see Rosenmüller, *Alterthumskunde,* vol. i. pp. 154-157). Thus in Babylon, some of the mountains north

in Armenia may have been supposed to be the peculiar dwelling-place of the gods. Such a mountain would *appear* to be under the north pole, and the constellations would seem to revolve around it. It is not improbable that the Aurora Borealis, playing often as it does in the north with peculiar magnificence, might have contributed to the belief that this was the peculiar abode of the gods. Unable to account—as indeed all moderns are—for these peculiar and magnificent lights in the north, it accorded with the poetic and mythological fancy of the ancients to suppose that they were designed to play around, and to adorn the habitation of the gods. This disposition to make the mountains of the north the seat of the gods, may have arisen also in part from the fact that the country on the north of Babylon was a volcanic region, and that the light emitted from volcanoes was an appropriate manifestation of the glory of superior invisible beings. ' On the borders of the Caspian [Sea], in the country around the Bakir, there is a tract called The Field of Fire, which continually emits inflammable gas, while springs of naphtha and petroleum occur in the same vicinity, as also mud volcanoes. In the chain of Elburs, to the south of this sea, is a lofty mountain, which, according to Morier, sometimes emits smoke, and at the base of which there are several craters where sulphur and saltpetre are procured in sufficient abundance to be used in commerce.'— (Lyell's *Geology,* vol. i. p. 297.) We find some traces of these ideas in the Scriptures. The *north* is often mentioned as the seat of the whirlwind, the storm, and especially as the residence of the cherubim. Thus in Ezekiel's vision of the cherubim, the whole magnificent scene is represented as coming from the *north*—as if the appropriate abode of the cherubim :

' I looked, and lo! a whirlwind *from the north*
Came sweeping onward, a vast cloud that rolled
In volumes, charged with gleaming fire, along,
And cast its splendours all around.
Now from within shone forth, what seemed
    the glow
Of gold and silver molten in the flame,
And in the midst thereof the form expressed,
As of a fourfold living thing—a shape
That yet contained the semblance of a man.'
      Ezek. i. 4, 5, trans. in Marsh's *Herder.*

14 I will ascend above the heights of the clouds: I will be *a* like the Most High.

15 Yet *b* thou shalt be brought down to hell, to the sides of the pit.

a 2 Thes.2.4.

16 They that see thee shall narrowly look upon thee, and consider thee, *saying, Is* this the man that made the earth to tremble, that did shake kingdoms;

b Mat.11.23.

Thus, in Ezek. xxviii. 14, Tyre is said to be 'the anointed cherub that covereth,' and to have been 'upon the holy mountain of God,' or *the gods*—evidently meaning, not Zion, but some mountain in the vicinity of Eden (see ver. 13). Thus also, in Zech. vi. 1–8, four chariots are represented as coming out of the mountains, the first chariot with red horses, the second with black horses, the third with white horses, and the fourth with bay horses. The horses that have gone through the earth are (ver. 8) represented as going to the *north* as their place of rest. These passages, particularly the one from Ezekiel, show that the northern regions were regarded as the seat of striking and peculiar manifestations of the Divine glory (comp. Notes on Job xxiii. 9; xxxvii. 22). And it is probable that, in the view of the Babylonians, the northern mountains of Armenia, that seemed to be near the north pole, around which the constellations revolved, and that appeared to be surmounted and encompassed by the splendid light of the Aurora Borealis, were regarded as the peculiar place where the gods held their assemblies, and from whence their power went forth through the nations. Over all their power it was the intention of the king of Babylon to ascend, and even to rise above the stars that performed their revolutions around the seats of the gods in the north; to be *supreme* in that assembly of the gods, and to be regarded there as the supreme and incontrollable director of even all the gods. It is probable, says Mitford (*Life of Milton*, vol. i. p. 73), that from this scarcely intelligible hint Milton threw up his palace for his fallen angels—thus:

At length into the limits of the north
They came, and Satan to his royal seat,
High on a hill, far blazing as a mount
Raised on a mount, with pyramids and towers,
From diamond quarries hewn, and rocks of gold.
The palace of great Lucifer, so call

That structure in the dialect of men
Interpreted; which not long after he
Affecting an equality with God,
In imitation of that mount, whereon
Messiah was declared in sight of heaven,
The mountain of the congregation called, &c.

14. *I will be like the Most High.* There is a remarkable resemblance between this language and that used in 2 Thess. ii. 4, in regard to Antichrist: ' He, as God, sitteth in the temple of God, showing himself that he is God.' And this similarity is the more remarkable, because Antichrist is represented, in Rev. xvii. 4, 5, as seated in Babylon—the spiritual seat of arrogance, oppression, and pride. Probably Paul had the passage in Isaiah in his eye when he penned the description of Antichrist.

15. *Yet thou shalt be brought down to hell.* Heb. ' To sheol ' (comp. ver. 9). ¶ *To the sides of the pit.* The word ' pit,' here, is evidently synonymous with *hell* or *hades*, represented as a deep, dark region under ground. The dead were often buried in caves, and the descent was often dark and dreary, to the vaults where they reposed. Hence it is always represented as going *down;* or, as the *inferior* regions. The ' sides of the pit ' here stand opposed to the ' sides of the north.' He had sought to *ascend* to the one; he should be *brought down* to the other. The reference here is, doubtless, to the land of shades; to the dark and dismal regions where the departed dead are supposed to dwell—to *sheol.* So the parallelism proves. But the image or figure is taken from the custom of burying, where, in a deep natural cavern, or a sepulchre excavated from a rock, the dead were ranged around the *sides* of the cavern in niches or recesses excavated for that purpose (see Note on ver. 9).

16. *They that see thee.* That is, after thou art dead. The scene here changes, and the prophet introduces those who would contemplate the body

17 *That* made the world as a wilderness, and destroyed the cities thereof ; ¹ *that* opened not the house of his prisoners?

18 All the kings of the nations, *even* all of them, lie in glory, every one in his own house:

1 or, *did not let his prisoners loose homewards.*

of the king of Babylon after he should be slain—the passers-by arrested with astonishment, that one so proud and haughty was at last slain, and cast out among the common dead (ver. 19). ¶ *Shall narrowly look upon thee.* To be certain that they were not deceived. This denotes great astonishment, as if they could scarcely credit the testimony of their senses. It also expresses insult and contempt. They ask whether it is possible that one who so recently shook the kingdoms of the earth should now lie cast out as unworthy of a burial. ¶ *That made the earth to tremble.* That agitated the world by his ambition.

17. That *made the world as a wilderness.* That made cities and kingdoms desolate. ¶ That *opened not the house of his prisoners.* This is a description of his oppression and cruelty. Of course many prisoners would be taken in war. Instead of giving them liberty,

he threw them into prison and kept them there. This may be rendered, 'his prisoners he did not release that they might return home' (see the Margin). The Chaldee renders it, 'To his prisoners he did not open the door.' The sense is substantially the same. The idea is, that he was cruel and oppressive. He threw his captives into dungeons, and found pleasure in retaining them there.

18. *All the kings of the nations.* That is, this is the common way in which the kings are buried. ¶ *Lie in glory.* They lie in a magnificent mausoleum; they are surrounded with splendour even in their tombs. It is well known that vast sums of money were expended to rear magnificent mausoleums as the burial place of kings. With this design, probably, the pyramids of Egypt were reared; and the temple of Bel in Babylon, we are told, was employed for this purpose. Jose-

THE PYRAMIDS OF GHIZEH, LOWER EGYPT.

phus says that vast quantities of money were buried in the sepulchre of David. The kings of Israel were buried in a royal burying place on Mount Zion (2 Chron. xxi. 20; xxxv. 24 ; Neh. iii. 16). For a description of the sepul-

19 But thou art cast out of thy grave, like an abominable branch, *and as* the raiment of those that are slain, thrust through with a sword, that go down to the stones of the pit; as a carcase trodden under feet.

20 Thou shalt not be joined with them in burial, because thou hast destroyed thy land, *and* slain thy people: the *a* seed of evil-doers shall never be renowned.

a Job 18.16; Ps.37.28.

---

chre of David, and of sepulchres in general, *see* Calmet's *Dict.* Art. *Sepulchre* (comp. Ezek. xxxii.) ¶ *Every one in his own house.* In a sepulchre constructed for himself. It was usual for kings to have a splendid tomb constructed for themselves.

19. *But thou art cast out of thy grave.* Thou art not buried like other kings in a magnificent sepulchre, but art cast out like the common dead. This was a mark of the highest infamy (see Isa. xxxiv. 3; Ezek. xxix. 5; Jer. xxii. 19). Nothing was considered more disgraceful than to be denied the privileges of an honourable burial (see Note on ch. liii. 9). On the fulfilment of this prophecy, see Note on ver. 20. ¶ *As an abominable branch* (כְּנֵצֶר נִתְעָב). The LXX. render this, 'And thou shalt be cast upon the mountains as a dead body that is abominable, with many dead that are slain by the sword, descending to Hades.' The Chaldee, 'And thou shalt be cast out of thy sepulchre as a branch that is hid.' Lowth supposes that by 'abominable branch' there is allusion to a tree on which a malefactor was hanged, that was regarded as detestable, and cursed. But there are obvious objections to this interpretation. One is, that the word *branch* (*netzer*) is never applied to a *tree*. It means *a shoot, a slip, a scion* (Note, ch. xi. 1). Another objection is, that there seems here to be no necessary allusion to such a tree; or to anything that would lead to it. Jerome says, that the word *netzer* denotes a shoot or sucker that starts up at the root of a plant or tree, and that is useless to the husbandman, and which he therefore cuts off. So, says he, the king of Babylon shall be cast off—as the farmer throws away the useless sucker. This is probably the correct idea. The word *abominable* means, therefore, not only that which is *useless*, but indicates that the shoot or sucker is *troublesome* to

the husbandman. It is an object that he *hates*, and which he gets clear of as soon as possible. So the king of Babylon would be cast out as useless, hateful, abominable; to be thrown away, as the noxious shoot is, as unfit for use, and unworthy to be preserved. ¶ *As the raiment of those that are slain.* As a garment that is all defiled with gore, and that is cast away and left to rot. The garments of those slain in battle, covered with blood and dirt, would be cast away as polluted and worthless, and so would be the king of Babylon. Among the Hebrews such garments were regarded with peculiar abhorrence (Rosenmüller); perhaps from the dread which they had of touching a dead body, and of course of anything that was found on a dead body. ¶ *Thrust through with a sword.* That is, the slain thrust through. The effect of this was to pollute the garment with blood, and to render it useless. ¶ *That go down to the stones of the pit.* The 'pit' here means the grave or sepulchre (ver. 15). The phrase 'stones of the pit,' conveys the idea that the grave or sepulchre was usually either excavated from the solid rock, or constructed of stones. The idea is simply, that those who were slain with the sword were buried in the usual manner, though their bloody garments defiled were cast away. But the king of Babylon should not have even the honour of such a burial as was given to those who fell in battle. ¶ *As a carcase trodden under foot.* Unburied; as the body of a brute that is exposed to the air, and denied the honour of a sepulchre.

20. *Thou shalt not be joined with them in burial.* That is, even with those who are slain with the sword in battle, and to whom is granted the privilege of a decent burial. ¶ *Hast destroyed thy land.* Hast been a cruel, harsh, and oppressive prince. ¶ *The seed of evil-doers.* The posterity of

21 Prepare slaughter for his children *a* for the iniquity of their fathers; that they do not rise, nor possess the land, nor fill the face of the world with cities.

a Ex.20.5.

22 For I will rise up against them, saith the LORD of hosts, and cut off from Babylon the name, and remnant, and son, and nephew, saith the LORD.

---

the wicked. ¶ *Shall never be renowned.* Heb. 'Shall never be called,' or 'named' (לֹא־יִקָּרֵא); that is, shall never be distinguished, celebrated, or honoured. This is a general proposition; but the prophet here possibly designs to apply it to the king of which he is speaking, as having been descended from ancestors that were wicked; or more probably it is a new circumstance, more fully explained in the following verse, that *his* posterity should be cut off from the honour of succeeding him on the throne, and that they, as well as he, should be loaded with disgrace. The design is to affirm the fact that the Babylonian dynasty would end with him; and that his posterity would be reduced from the honours which they had hoped to have inherited. At the same time, the general proposition is applicable not only to the posterity of the king of Babylon, but to all. It is a great truth pertaining to the Divine administration, that the descendants of wicked men shall be dishonoured. So it is with the posterity of a traitor, a pirate, a drunkard, a man of profligacy. They are involved in disgrace, poverty, and calamity, as the result of the sin of their ancestor.

21. *Prepare slaughter for his children.* That is, cut them off not only from inheriting the honour of their father, but from life. This command seems to be directed to the Medes and Persians, and denotes that they *would* thus cut off his children. ¶ *For the iniquity of their fathers.* On account of the crimes of their ancestors—the pride, haughtiness, and oppression of the kings of Babylon. This is the statement of a general principle of the Divine administration, that the consequences of crime often pass over from the perpetrator, and impinge on his descendants (see Ex. xx. 5). ¶ *That they do not rise.* That they do not rise to occupy the places of their fathers; that they be degraded and reduced from

their elevation and honours. ¶ *Nor fill the face of the world with cities.* The LXX. render this, 'And fill the land with wars.' The Chaldee, 'And fill the face of the world with *enemies.*' The Syriac, 'And fill the face of the earth with *war.*' These versions evidently took the word עָרִים (*ârîm*) to mean *enemies* or *wars*—a sense which the word sometimes may have. But the common interpretation is to be preferred. The apprehension was, that they would fill the land, if they lived, with such cities of pride, magnificence, and wickedness, as *Babylon* was, and that thus crimes would be multiplied and prolonged; and hence the purpose of God was not only to cut off Babylon—the *model* of all cities of arrogance and pride—but also to cut off those who would be disposed to rear similar cities, and to fill the land again with crime.

22. *For I will rise up against them, saith the* LORD *of hosts.* That is, against the family of the king of Babylon. ¶ *And cut off from Babylon the name.* That is, all the *males* of the royal family, so that the name of the monarch shall become extinct (comp. Ruth iv. 5; Isa. lvi. 5). ¶ *And remnant.* All that is left of them; so that the family shall cease to exist. ¶ *The son and nephew.* Every one of the family who could claim to be an heir of the throne. The dynasty shall cease; and the proud and haughty family shall become wholly extinct. This is the solemn purpose in regard to the *family* of the monarch of Babylon. It only remains to inquire when and how it was fulfilled.

The circumstances which it was said would exist in regard to the king of Babylon here spoken of, are the following:—(1.) That he would be a proud, haughty, and oppressive prince (ver. 17, and throughout the prophecy). (2.) That when he died he would be cast out with the common dead, and denied the common honours of the sepulchre—

especially the honours which all other monarchs have in their burial (ver. 18–20). (3.) That his posterity would be cut off, and that he would have no one to succeed him on his throne; or that the dynasty and the kingdom would terminate in him (ver. 21, 22).

In regard to the application and the fulfilment of this prophecy there have been three opinions.

I. That it does not refer to an *individual* sovereign, but to the kings of Babylon in general; that the description is designed to be applicable to the succession or the dynasty, as signally haughty, proud, and oppressive; and that the prophet means to say that that haughty and wicked reign of kings should cease. To this, the objections are obvious—(1.) The whole aspect and course of the prophet seems to have reference to an *individual*. Such an individual the prophet seems to have constantly in his eye. He descends to *sheol* (ver. 9); he is proud, ambitious, oppressive, cast out; all of which circumstances refer naturally to an individual, and not to a *succession* or dynasty. (2.) The main circumstance mentioned in the prophecy is applicable only to an individual—that he should be *unburied* (ver. 18–21). It was not true of *all* the kings of Babylon that they were unburied, and how could it be said respecting a *succession* or a dynasty at all that it should be cast out of the grave as an abominable branch; and that it should not be joined with others in burial? All the circumstances, therefore, lead us to suppose that the prophet refers to an individual.

II. The Jews, in general, suppose that it refers to Nebuchadnezzar. But to this interpretation, the objections are equally obvious—(1.) It was not true that Nebuchadnezzar had no one to succeed him on the throne; or that his family was totally cut off, as it was foretold of this king of Babylon that his would be (ver. 21, 22). (2.) It was not true that he was denied the privileges of a burial which kings commonly enjoy. To meet this difficulty, the Jews have invented the following story. They say that when Nebuchadnezzar was driven from men during his derangement (Dan. iv.), and when he was with the beasts of the field seven years, the people made his son, Evil-Merodach, king; but that when Nebuchadnezzar was restored to his right mind and to his throne, he threw Evil-Merodach into prison, where he lay until he died. At the death of Nebuchadnezzar, the people released him to make him king, but he refused because he did not believe that his father was dead, and said that if his father should find him he would kill him; and that in order to convince him that his father was dead he was taken out of the grave. But this is manifestly a fiction. Besides, the prophecy was not that the king should be taken out of the grave, but that he should not be buried. Nebuchadnezzar was succeeded in the kingdom by his son Evil-Merodach, and he by Belshazzar, in whom the line of kings ended.

III. The only other interpretation of which this is susceptible, is that which refers it to Belshazzar, in whose reign the city of Babylon was taken. This king, called in Scripture Belshazzar (Dan. v.), was the son of Evil-Merodach, and the grandson of Nebuchadnezzar. His name, as it occurs in heathen writers, was *Nabonadius*. In him the circumstances of the prophecy agree—(1.) He was an impious prince (Xen. *Cyr.* vii. Dan. v). (2.) In his reign the city and the kingdom came to an end, as it was foretold. (3.) Every circumstance of the taking of Babylon would lead us to suppose that he was denied the privilege of a magnificent sepulture. (*a*.) He was slain in the night (Dan. v. 30). (*b*.) It was in the confusion of the capture of the city—amidst the tumult caused by the sudden and unexpected invasion of Cyrus. It is therefore altogether improbable that he had a regular and an honoured burial. Like the common dead, he would lie in the palace where he fell, or in the street. (*c*.) There is no evidence that Cyrus gave him an honourable sepulchre. (4.) None of his posterity occupied the throne to give honour to the memory of their father. (5.) In him the dynasty and the kingdom ended. Immediately the kingdom on his death was given to the Medes and Persians (Dan. v. 28–31). None of the names of his posterity, if he had any, are known; and God cut off from

23 I will also make it a possession for the bittern and pools of
water; and I will sweep it with the

besom of destruction, saith the
LORD of hosts.

24 The LORD of hosts hath sworn,

him 'the name and remnant, the son and
nephew,' as was predicted (see Prideaux's
Connection, i. 2. 257–271, Ed. 1815).

23. *I will also make it a possession
for the bittern.* The word 'bittern,' in
English, means a bird with long legs
and neck, that stalks among reeds and
sedge, feeding upon fish. The Hebrew

THE BITTERN.   *(Ardea Stellaries)*

word (קִפֹּד, *qippōdh*), occurs but five times
(Isa. xxxiv. 11; Zeph. ii. 14). According to Bochart and Gesenius, it means
the hedgehog. It has been variously
rendered. Some have supposed it to be
a land animal; some an aquatic animal;
and most have regarded it as a fowl.
Bochart has proved that the hedgehog
or porcupine is found on the shores of
the Euphrates. He translates this place,
'I will place Babylon for an habitation
of the porcupine, *even* the pools of
water;' that is, the pools that are round
about Babylon shall become so dry that
porcupines may dwell there (see Bochart,
Hieroz. iii. 36. pp. 1036–1042). ¶ *And
pools of water.* Bochart supposes this
means, *even* the pools of water shall become dry. But the common interpretation is to be preferred, that Babylon
itself should become filled with pools of
water. This was done by Cyrus' directing the waters of the Euphrates from

their channel when the city was taken,
and by the fact that the waters never
returned again to their natural bed, so
that the region was overflowed with
water (see Notes on ch. xiii.) ¶ *And I
will sweep it with the besom of destruction.* A *besom* is a broom; and the
sense here is, that God would entirely
destroy Babylon, and render it wholly
uninhabitable.

24. *The* LORD *of hosts* (see Note on
ch. i. 9). It is evident that this verse
and the three following, is not directly
connected with that which goes before,
respecting Babylon. This pertains to
the Assyrian; that had relation to Babylon. Vitringa says that this is attached to the prophecy respecting Babylon, and is a peculiar yet not altogether
foreign argument, and is a sort of epilogue to the prophecy respecting Babylon. The design, he says, is this. As the
events which had been foretold respecting Babylon seemed so great and wonderful as to be almost incredible, the
prophet, in order to show the Jews how
easily it could be accomplished, refers
them to the case of Sennacherib, and
the ease with which he and his army
had been destroyed. Lowth supposes
that the Assyrians and Babylonians here
are one people. Rosenmüller supposes
that this prophecy respecting Sennacherib has been *displaced* by the collector of the prophecies of Isaiah, and
that it should have been attached to the
prophecy respecting the Assyrian monarch (see ch. x.) The probable sense
of the passage is that which makes it
refer to the predicted destruction of
Sennacherib (ch. x.); and the design of
the prophet in referring to that here is,
to assure the Jews of the certain destruction of Babylon, and to comfort them
with the assurance that they would be
delivered from their captivity there.
The prophecy respecting Babylon was
uttered *before* the destruction of Sennacherib; but it is to be remembered that
its design was to comfort the Jews *in*
Babylon. The prophet therefore throws
himself *beyond* the period of their captivity—though it was to occur many

saying, Surely as I have thought, so shall it come to pass; and as I have purposed, *so* shall it stand;

25 That I will break the Assyrian in my land, and upon my mountains tread him under foot: then *a* shall his yoke depart from off them, and his burden depart from off their shoulders.

26 This *is* the purpose that is purposed, upon the whole earth; and this *is* the hand that is stretched out upon all the nations.

27 For *b* the LORD of hosts hath purposed, and who shall disannul *it?* and his hand *is* stretched out, and who shall turn it back?

a ch.10.27.   *b* 2Ch.20.6; Job 23.13; Pr.21.30; Dan.4.35.

---

years *after* the prophecy respecting Babylon was uttered; and with this view he introduces the subject of the Assyrian. At that future time, Sennacherib would have been destroyed. And as God would have fulfilled the prophecy respecting the proud and self-confident Assyrian, so they might have the assurance that he *would* fulfil his predictions respecting the *no less* proud and self-confident 'king of Babylon; and as he would have delivered his people from the invasion of the Assyrian, even when he was at the gates of Jerusalem, so he *would* deliver them in their captivity in Babylon. ¶ *Hath sworn* (see Gen. xxiv. 7; Ex. xiii. 5, 11; xxxiii. 1; Num. xxxii. 10; Heb. iii. 18; vi. 13). JEHOVAH is often represented as making use of an oath to denote the strong confirmation, the absolute certainty of what he utters. The oath here was designed to comfort the Jews, when they should be in Babylon, with the assurance that what he had thus solemnly promised would assuredly come to pass. ¶ *As I have thought.* As I have designed, or intended. God's promises never fail; his purposes shall all be accomplished (comp. ch. xlvi. 10, 11). This passage is full proof that God does not *change:* that whatever his purposes are, they are inflexible. Change supposes imperfection; and it is often affirmed that God is immutable (1 Sam. xv. 29; Mal. iii. 6; James i. 17.)

25. *That I will break.* That I will break his power; that I will discomfit and destroy his army. ¶ *The Assyrian.* Sennacherib (see ch. x.) ¶ *In my land.* That is, in the land of Canaan. This is often called his land; and this expression shows that the passage does not and cannot refer to the king of Babylon, for he was destroyed in his own city (Dan. v.) ¶ *And upon my mountains.* That is, upon the mountains of Palestine.

The army of Sennacherib was destroyed on the mountains that were near to Jerusalem (see Notes on ch. x. 33, 34). ¶ *Then shall his yoke.* The yoke of the Assyrian (see Note on ch. x. 27).

26. *This* is *the purpose.* This is the sum of the whole design—a design that embraces the destruction both of the king of Assyria, and of Babylon. ¶ *Upon the whole earth.* The successive kingdoms of Assyria and Babylonia embraced the whole earth, and to destroy them would in fact affect all the nations.

27. *For the* LORD *of hosts* (see Note on ch. i. 9). ¶ *Who shall disannul* it? Who has power to defeat his purposes? Difficult as they may be in appearance, and incredible as their fulfilment may seem, yet his purposes are formed in full view of all the circumstances; and there is no power to resist his arm, or to turn him aside from the execution of his designs. By this assurance God designed to comfort his people when they should be in Babylon in a long and dreary captivity (comp. Psal. cxxxvii.) And by the same consideration his people may be comforted at all times. His plans shall stand. None can disannul them. No arm has power to resist him. None of the schemes formed against him shall ever prosper. Whatever ills, therefore, may befall his people; however thick, and gloomy, and sad their calamities may be; and however dark his dispensations may appear, yet they may have the assurance that all his plans are wise, and that they all shall stand. No matter how many, or how mighty may be the foes of the church; no matter how strong their cities, or their ramparts; no matter how numerous their armies, or how self-confident may be their leaders, they have no power to resist God. If *their* plans are in his way they will be thrown down; if revolutions are

28 In the year that *a* king Ahaz died was this burden.

29 Rejoice not thou, whole Palestina, because *b* the rod of him that

a 2 Ki.16.20.   *b* 2 Ch.26.6.

smote thee is broken : for out of the serpent's root shall come forth a cockatrice,[1] and his fruit *c shall be* a fiery flying serpent.

1 or, *adder.*   *c* 2 Ki.18.3.

needful among men to accomplish *his* purposes, they will be brought about ; if cities and armies need to be destroyed in order that *his* plans may succeed, and his church be safe, they will be demolished, just as the army of Sennacherib was laid pale in death, and as Babylon— the haughtiest of cities—was overthrown. Who can stand against God ? and who can resist the execution of his will ?

28. *In the year that king Ahaz died.* This is the caption or title to the following prophecy, which occupies the remainder of this chapter. This prophecy has no connection with the preceding ; and should have been separated from it in the division into chapters. It relates solely to Philistia ; and the design is to comfort the Jews with the assurance that they had nothing to apprehend from them. It is not to call the Philistines to lamentation and alarm, for there is no evidence that the prophecy was promulgated among them (Vitringa) ; but it is to assure the Jews that they would be in no danger from their invasion under the reign of the successor of Ahaz, and that God would more signally overthrow and subdue them than had been done in his time. It is not improbable that at the death of Ahaz, and with the prospect of a change in the government on the accession of his successor, the Philistines, the natural enemies of Judah, had meditated the invasion of the Jews. The Philistines had been subdued in the time of Azariah (2 Kings xv. 1–7), or Uzziah, as he is called in 2 Chron. xxvi. 1, who was the son and successor of Amaziah. He broke down the wall of Gath, and the wall of Gabneh, and the wall of Ashdod, and effectually subdued and humbled them (2 Chron. xxvi. 6). In the time of Ahaz, and while he was engaged in his unhappy controversies with Syria and Ephraim, the Philistines took advantage of the enfeebled state of Judah, and made successful war on it, and took several of the towns (2 Chron. xxviii. 18) ; and at his death they had

hope of being able to resist Judah, perhaps the more so as they apprehended that the reign of Hezekiah would be mild, peaceable, and unwarlike. Isaiah, in the prophecy before us, warns them not to entertain any such fallacious expectations, and assures them that his reign would be quite as disastrous to them as had been the reign of his predecessors. ¶ *Was this burden* (see Note on ch. xiii. 1).

29. *Rejoice not thou.* Rejoice not at the death of Ahaz, king of Judah. It shall be no advantage to thee. It shall not be the means of making an invasion on Judah more practicable. ¶ *Whole Palestina.* We apply the name *Palestine* to the whole land of Canaan. Formerly, the name referred only to Philistia, from which we have derived the name *Palestine.* The word פְּלֶשֶׁת (*Pelêshĕth*) means properly the land of sojourners or strangers, from פָּלַשׁ (*pâlăsh*), *to rove about, to wander, to migrate.* The LXX. render it, 'Αλλοφυλοι—' Strangers,' or ' Foreigners,' and Γῆ ἀλλοφύλων—'Land of strangers.' Philistia was situated on the south-western side of the land of Canaan, extending along the Mediterranean Sea from Gaza on the south, to Lydda on the north. The Philistines were a powerful people, and had often been engaged in wars with Judah. They had made a successful attack on it in the time of Ahaz ; and amidst the feebleness and distractions which they supposed might succeed on the change of the government of Judah, and the administration of an inexperienced prince like Hezekiah, they hoped to be still more successful, and would naturally rejoice at the death of Ahaz. When the prophet says '*whole* Palestina,' he means to say that no part of Philistia would have occasion to rejoice at the succession of Hezekiah (see ver. 31). ¶ *Because the rod of him that smote thee is broken.* It was not true that they had been smitten during the reign of Ahaz, but it had been done by his predecessor Uzziah. Perhaps the prophet refers to

30 And the first-born of the poor
shall feed, and the needy shall lie
down in safety: and I will kill thy

root with famine, and he shall slay
thy remnant.

31 Howl, O gate; cry, O city;

---

that prince, and to his death. He had
smitten and subdued them. At his
death they would rejoice; and their joy
had been continued during the reigns
of Jotham and Ahaz. They would now
rejoice the more that a young and inexperienced prince was to ascend the
throne. Their joy had been that *Uzziah*
had died, and that joy had been augmenting since his death. But the prophet now tells them that they will have
no further occasion for such joy. ¶ *For
out of the serpent's root.* That is, there
shall spring forth from the serpent, or
shall succeed the serpent, as a shoot or
sprout springs from the root of a decayed
tree (see Note on ch. xi. 1). By the
serpent here, is undoubtedly intended
king Uzziah, who had so severely chastised the Philistines. The word 'serpent'
(נָחָשׁ) denotes a serpent of any kind,
and usually one far less venomous than
that which is meant by the word translated cockatrice. Probably the prophet
does not give this name *serpent* to Uzziah
or to Ahaz, or the name *cockatrice* to
Hezekiah, because *he* regarded the
names as properly descriptive of their
character, but because they were so regarded by the Philistines. They were
as odious and offensive to them, and as
destructive of their plans, as venomous
reptiles would be. ¶ *Shall come forth
a cockatrice* (see Note on ch. lix. 5).
A basilisk, or adder, a serpent of most
venomous nature (see Note on ch. xi.
8). That is, though Uzziah is dead,
yet there shall spring up from him one
far more destructive to you than he was;
one who shall carry the desolations of
war much further, and who shall more
effectually subdue you. Most commentators have concurred in supposing that
Hezekiah is here referred to, who 'smote
the Philistines even unto Gaza and the
borders thereof, from the tower of the
watchmen to the fenced city' (2 Kings
xviii. 8). This is, doubtless, the correct
interpretation. The Chaldee renders
it, however, 'Because there shall proceed from the descendants of Jesse the
Messiah, and his works shall be among

you as a flying serpent.' This interpretation Rosenmüller supposes is correct; but it is evidently foreign to the
scope of the passage.

30. *And the first-born of the poor
shall feed.* That is, there shall be safety
to those parts of Judah which have long
been exposed to the invasions of the
Philistines. Philistia bordered on Judea,
and was constantly making wars upon
it, so that there was no safety felt.
Isaiah now says, that Hezekiah would
so effectually and completely subdue
them that there should be no danger
from their invasion. The phrase 'the
first-born of the poor' is an Hebraism,
a strong, emphatic expression, denoting
those who are the most poor; the most
abject sons of poverty; those who have
an eminence or a double portion of want,
as the first-born among the Hebrews
were entitled to peculiar distinctions and
privileges. The idea is, that even the
most poor and defenceless would be safe.
¶ *Shall feed.* That is, they shall be
supplied with food; they shall feed safely
as a flock does that is guarded from wild
beasts. They shall be no longer alarmed,
but shall dwell in security, peace, and
plenty. ¶ *And I will kill thy root.* The
word rendered 'root' denotes properly
the root of a plant, which being dried
up or killed, the plant of course withers
and dies. So God says that he would
effectually and entirely destroy the power
of the Philistines. ¶ *Slay thy remnant.*
That is, shall slay all that appertains to
thee. Or, he shall dry up the root, and
the branches shall wither and die also.
The whole power of the nation shall be
withered and destroyed.

31. *Howl, O gate.* That is, ye who
throng the gate. The *gates* of a city
were the chief places of concourse.
¶ *Cry, O city.* The prophet here fixes
the attention upon some principal city
of Philistia, and calls upon it to be
alarmed in view of the judgments that
were about to come upon the whole land.
¶ Art *dissolved.* The word 'dissolved'
(מוּג) is applied to that which melts, or
which wastes away gradually, and then

thou, whole Palestina, *art* dissolved: for there shall come from the north a smoke, and [1]none *shall be* alone in his [2]appointed times.

32 What shall *one* then answer

1 or, he shall *not*. 2 or, *assemblies*.

to that which faints or disappears. It means here that the kingdom of Philistia would disappear, or be destroyed. It probably conveys the idea of its fainting, or becoming feeble from fear or apprehension. ¶ *From the north a smoke.* From the regions of Judah, which lay north and east of Philistia. The 'smoke' here probably refers to a cloud of dust that would be seen to rise in that direction made by an invading army. ¶ *And none shall be alone in his appointed times.* There has been a great variety of interpretation in regard to this passage. Lowth renders it, ' And there shall not be a straggler among his levies.' The Hebrew is, as in the margin, ' And not solitary in his assemblies.' The LXX. render it, Καὶ οὐκ ἔσται τοῦ εἶναι— ' And it is not to be endured.' The Chaldee, ' And there shall be none who shall retard him in his times.' The Arabic, ' Neither is there any one who can stand in his footsteps.' The Vulgate, ' Neither is there any one who can escape his army.' Aben Ezra renders it, ' No one of the Philistines shall dare to remain in their palaces, as when a smoke comes into a house all are driven out.' Probably the correct idea is given by Lowth ; and the same interpretation is given by Gesenius, Rosenmüller, Dathe, and Michaelis. No one of the invading army of Hezekiah shall come by himself ; no one shall be weary or be a straggler : the army shall advance in close military array, and in dense columns ; and this is represented as the cause of the cloud or smoke that the prophet saw rising, the cloud of dust that was made by the close ranks of the invading host (comp. Isa. v. 27).

32. *What shall one then answer.* The design of this verse is obvious. It is to show that Judea would be safe from the invasions of the Philistines, and that God was the protector of Zion. For this purpose the prophet refers to messengers or ambassadors who should be sent for any purpose to Jerusalem, either

the messengers of the nation? That [a]the LORD hath founded Zion, and the [b]poor of his people shall [3]trust in it.

a Ps.87.1-6. b Zep.3.12.
3 *betake themselves unto.*

to congratulate Hezekiah, or to form an alliance with the Jews. The prophet asks what answer or information should be given to such messengers when they came respecting their state ? The reply is, that JEHOVAH had evinced his purpose to protect his people. ¶ *Of the nation.* Of any nation whose ambassadors should be sent into Judea. ¶ *That the LORD hath founded Zion.* That he is its original founder, and that he has now shown his regard for it by protecting it from the Philistines. It would be safe from their attacks, and JEHOVAH would thus show that he had it under his own protection. The LXX. render this, ' And what shall the kings of the Gentiles then answer ? That the Lord hath founded Zion.' The scope of the passage is the assurance that Zion would be safe, being founded and preserved by JEHOVAH ; and that the Philistines had no cause of triumph at the death of Ahaz, since God would still be the protector of his people. The doctrine established by this passage is, that in all the changes which take place by the death of kings, princes, magistrates, and ministers ; and in all the revolutions which occur in kingdoms, the enemies of the people of God have no cause for rejoicing. God is the protector of his church ; and he will show that he has founded Zion, and that his people are safe. No weapon that is formed against his people shall prosper, and the gates of hell shall not prevail against his church. ¶ *Shall trust in it.* In Zion. It was a strongly fortified city, God was its protector, and in times of calamity his people could betake themselves there in safety. In this strong place the most weak and defenceless—the poorest of the people, would be safe. In the church of God, the poor are the objects of as deep regard as the rich ; the humble, the meek, the weak, the feeble, are there safe, and no power of an enemy can reach or affect them. God is their defender and their friend ; and in his arms they are secure.

CHAPTER XV.

ANALYSIS OF CHAPTERS XV., XVI.

§ I. *The time of the prophecy.*

THIS and the following chapter make one
entire prophecy, and should not have been
divided. At what time it was delivered is unknown. The only period which is designated
is, that it was to be fulfilled in three years from
the time when it was uttered (ch. xvi. 14).
Lowth supposes that it was delivered soon after
the former, in the first years of the reign of
Hezekiah, and that it was fulfilled in the fourth
year of his reign, when Shalmanezer invaded
the kingdom of Israel. He supposes that he
might have marched through Moab, and secured
its strong places on his way to Judea. Gesenius supposes that it was uttered by some contemporary of Isaiah, or by some earlier prophet, without the epilogue (ch. xvi. 14), as a
general denunciation against Moab; and that it
was adopted by Isaiah and applied to the Moabites during his own time. This he argues
because of the repetition of geographical names;
the play upon those names; the roughness and
harshness of the expressions; and many favourite phrases which, he says, are foreign to 'the
genuine Isaiah.' He supposes that it had its
origin in the national animosity which subsisted
between the Jews and the Moabites; and that
it might have been composed on account of the
tribute which had been withheld, B.C. 896; or
on account of the corruption of the Moabites,
B.C. 949; or on the taking possession of the
territory by Reuben and Gad. But this is evidently conjectural. It is fair to presume that
it is a production of Isaiah himself, unless it can
be proved that he did not write it; and the
argument from the style, to prove that it was
written by some other person than Isaiah, does
not seem to be sufficient. It *may* have been
written by Isaiah at an early period of his life,
and subsequently incorporated into his prophecies, and adapted by himself to a state of things
existing in an advanced period of his prophetic
life (see Note on ch. xvi. 14). Compare, however,
the arguments of Gesenius in his Commentary,
and in the *Bib. Rep.*, vol. vii. pp. 120, 121. It is
certain that it was composed when the tribute
was withheld from Judah which was due from
the Moabites (see ch. xvi. 1).

§ II. *History of Moab.*

THE land of Moab, so called from Moab the
son of Lot, by his eldest daughter (Gen. xix. 31-
37), was situated on the east side of the river
Jordan, and adjacent to the Dead Sea, and on
both sides of the river Arnon, although, strictly
and properly speaking, the river Arnon was re-

garded as its northern boundary. Its capital
city was on the river Arnon. The first residence of Lot, after fleeing from Sodom, was
Zoar (Gen. xix. 30), on the south-east of the Dead
Sea; from thence he removed into the mountainous region where his two sons were born
(Gen. xix. 30). The country was originally
occupied by a race of giants called *Emim* (Deut.
ii. 10), whom the Moabites conquered and expelled. A considerable part of this country was
subsequently conquered by Sihon, king of the
Amorites, who made the Arnon the boundary
of the land of Moab, and Heshbon his capital
(Num. xxi. 26; comp. Num. xxi. 13; Judg. xi.
18). The Israelites passed by their land in
journeying to Canaan, without distressing or
embarrassing them; because God had said that
he had given 'Ar to the children of Lot for a
possession' (Deut. ii. 9). But the adjacent
region in the possession of the Amorites, the
Israelites took, after a signal victory, and gave
to the tribes of Reuben and Gad (Num. xxi.
31-35). Thus the territory of the Jews, being
bounded by the river Arnon, was adjacent to
that of Moab. It is evident, however, though
the Arnon was the proper boundary of Moab,
yet that a considerable portion of country on
the north of that river was usually regarded
as lying in the land of Moab, though strictly
within the limits of the territory formerly of
the Amorites, and subsequently of the tribes
of Reuben and Gad. Thus mount Nebo is said
to be in the land of Moab (Deut. xxxii. 49;
xxxiv. 1), though it was properly within the
limits of the Amorites. And thus many of the
places in the prophecy before us were on the north
of that river, though specified as in the country
of Moab. It is probable that the boundary was
never regarded as permanently fixed, though
the river Arnon was its natural and usual limit.

There was always a great antipathy between
the Jews and the Moabites, and they were the
natural and constant enemies of the Jewish
nation. The foundation of the enmity was laid
far back in their history. Balaam seduced the
Israelites to sin by means of the daughters of
Moab (Num. xxv. 1, 2); and God ordered that
this people should not enter into the congregation of his people, or be capable of office, to the
tenth generation, because they had the inhu-
manity to refuse the children of Israel a passage through their land in their journey to
Canaan (Deut. xxiii. 3).

Eglon, king of the Moabites, was the first
who oppressed Israel after the death of Joshua.
Ehud killed him and subdued the Moabites
(Judg. iii. 21). Toward the end of this period,
however, peace and friendship were restored,
mutual honours were reciprocated, as the his-

tory of Ruth shows, and Moab appears to have been a place of refuge for outcasts and emigrant Hebrews (Ruth i. 1; 1 Sam. xxii. 3; Jer. xl. 11; Isa. xvi. 3). David subdued Moab and Ammon, and made them tributary (2 Sam. viii. 2–12; xxiii. 20). The right to levy this tribute seems to have been transferred to Israel after the division of the kingdom; for after the death of Ahab, they refused to pay the customary tribute of 100,000 lambs and as many rams (2 Kings i. 1; iii. 4; Isa. xvi. 1). Soon after the death of Ahab they began to revolt (2 Kings iii. 4, 5). They were subsequently engaged in wars with the Jews. Amos (i. 13, *sq.*) denounced great calamities on them, which they probably suffered under Uzziah and Jotham, kings of Judah (2 Chron. xxvi. 7, 8; xxvii. 5). Calmet supposes that they were carried captive by Nebuchadnezzar beyond the Euphrates, as the prophets had threatened (Jer. ix. 26; xii. 14, 15; xxv. 11, 12; xlviii. 47; xlix. 3, 6, 39; l. 16); and that they were restored by Cyrus to their land, as many other captive nations were. It is probable that, in the latter times, they were subject to the Asmonean kings, and finally to Herod the Great.—(Robinson; Calmet.) It is remarkable that Jeremiah has introduced much of this chapter into his prophecy in his 48th chapter.

§ III. *Comparison of Isaiah with Jeremiah.*

In order to see the resemblance between the two prophecies, I insert here a comparison of the corresponding parts, following the order of Isaiah.

ISAIAH XV.	JEREMIAH XLVIII.
2. On all their heads shall be baldness, And every beard cut off.	37. For every head shall be bald, And every beard clipped. Upon all the hands shall be cuttings, And upon the loins sackcloth.
3. In their streets they shall gird themselves with sackcloth; On the tops of their houses, and in their streets, every one shall howl.	38. There shall be lamentations, generally, upon the housetops of Moab, and in the streets thereof.
4. And Heshbon shall cry, and Elealeh; Their voice shall be heard unto Jahaz: Therefore the armed soldiers of Moab shall cry out: His life shall be grievous unto him.	34. From the cry of Heshbon even unto Elealeh And unto Jahaz have they uttered their voice.
5. His fugitives shall flee unto Zoar, an heifer of three years old; For by the mounting up of Luhith with weeping shall they go it up; For in the way of Horonaim they shall raise up a cry of destruction.	34. From Zoar even unto Horonaim, As an heifer of three years old; For in the going up of Luhith, Continual weeping shall go up. 3. A voice of crying shall be from Horonaim. 5. For in the going down of Horonaim, The enemies have heard a cry of destruction
6. For the waters of Nimrim shall be desolate.	34. For the waters also of Nimrim shall be desolate.
7. Therefore the abundance they have gotten, And that which they have laid up, Shall they carry away to the brook of the willows.	36. Because the riches that he hath gotten is perished.
[8, 9; xvi. 1–5, are wanting in Jeremiah.]	
xvi. 6. We have heard of the pride of Moab; He is very proud; Even his haughtiness, and his pride, and his wrath; But his lies shall not be so.	29. We have heard of the pride of Moab; he is exceeding proud; His loftiness and his arrogancy, And his pride and the haughtiness of his heart:
	30. I know his wrath, saith the Lord; But it shall not be so: His lies shall not so effect it.
7. Therefore shall Moab howl for Moab, Every one shall howl: For the foundation of Kir-hareseth shall ye mourn; Surely are they stricken.	31. Therefore will I howl for Moab, And I will cry out for all Moab; Mine heart shall mourn for the men of Kir-heres.
8. As to the vine of Sibmah, the lords of the heathen have broken down the principal plants thereof; They have come even unto Jazer, They wandered through the wilderness; Her branches are stretched out, They are gone over the sea.	32. O vine of Sibmah! Thy plants are gone over the sea; They reach even unto the sea of Jazer.

9. Therefore I will bewail with the weeping of
Jazer, the vine of Sibmah;
For the shouting of thy summer fruits,
And for thy harvest is fallen.

10. And gladness is taken away, and joy out of
the plentiful field;
The treaders shall tread out no wine in their
presses;
I have made their vintage-shouting to cease.

11. Wherefore my bowels shall sound like an
harp for Moab.
And mine inward parts for Kir-haresh.

32. O vine of Sibmah!
I will weep for thee with the weeping of Jazer:
The spoiler is fallen upon thy summer fruits
and upon thy vintage.

33. And joy and gladness is taken from the plen-
tiful field, and from the land of Moab;
And I have caused wine to fail from the
wine presses;
None shall tread with shouting;
Their shouting shall be no shouting.

36. Therefore my heart shall sound for Moab
like pipes;
And mine heart shall sound like pipes for
the men of Kir-heres.

§ IV. *Moab after the exile.*

AFTER the exile, intimate connections took
place between the Jews and the Moabites by
marriages (Ezra ix. 1, *sq.*; Neh. xiii. 1). These
marriages, however, were dissolved by Ezra as
being, in his view, contrary.to the law of Moses.
In the time of the Maccabees little mention is
made of them (comp. Dan. xi. 41); but Josephus
mentions them in the history of Alexander Jan-
næus. Heshbon and Nadaba, Lemba and
Oronas, Gelithon and Zara, cities of Moab, are
there mentioned as being at that time in the
possession of the Jews (Jos. *Ant.* xiii. 15. 4).
After that, their name is lost under that of the
Arabians, as was also the case with Edom and
Ammon. At the time of Abulfeda, Moab proper, south of the river Arnon, bore the name of
Karrak, from the city of that name (comp. Note
on ch. xv. 1); the territory north of the Arnon,
the name of Belka, which includes also the
country of the Amorites. Since that time the
accounts of the country are exceedingly meagre,
and it is only until quite recently that the state
of Moab has attracted the attention of travellers.
It has been ranged and ravaged by the predatory tribes of Arabs, and, through fear of them,
few travellers have ventured to visit it. In
February and March, 1806, however, Mr. Seetz-
en, not without danger of losing his life, undertook a tour from Damascus down to the south
of the Jordan and the Dead Sea, and thence to
Jerusalem; and, in his journey, threw much
unexpected light on the prophecy before us,
especially in regard to the places here mentioned. He found a multitude of places, or the
ruins of places, still bearing the old names, and
thus has set bounds to the perfectly arbitrary
designations of the old maps. In September
1812, that distinguished German traveller, I. L.
Burckhardt, made the same tour from Damascus
down to Karrak, whence he pursued his journey
over Wady Mousa, or Petra, and thence to Cairo
in Egypt. In 1818, a company of intelligent
English travellers (Bankes, Irby, Mangles, and
Legh), made a journey from Karrak to the land
of the Edomites, particularly to Petra, and

thence back, on the other side of the Jordan, to
Tiberius. In some respects they confirmed,
and, in others, extended the accounts of Seetzen
(see Gesenius' *Commentary*). In the Notes on
these chapters, I have endeavoured to embody
the principal information found in these writers
on the topography of Moab.

§ V. *Analysis of this prophecy.*

'THE prophecy,' says Prof. Stuart (*Bib. Rep.*,
vii. 110), 'is a piece replete with vivid description, with animated and impassioned thought,
with poetic diction, and with scenes which are
adapted to make a deep impression on the mind
of the reader.' The prophecy in the two chapters contains the following parts:—

I. The capitals of Moab are destroyed suddenly in one night (ch. xv. 1).

II. In the midst of the consternation, the
people hasten to the high places, and to the
altars and temples of the gods, to implore protection. They are seen in the streets with sackcloth, and on the tops of the houses, crying out
with loud lamentations, and every expression
of sorrow and despair (xv. 2–4).

III. Some of the fugitives flee to Zoar for protection, and others to Luhith and Horonaim,
hastening to countries beyond their own borders, because everything in their own land was
withered and dried up (xv. 5–7).

IV. Consternation and desolation are spread
throughout the land, and even the streams are
full of blood, and wild beasts are seen coming
up upon the land (xv. 8, 9).

V. The prophet pities them, weeps with them
(xv. 5; xvi. i. 11), and advises them to seek the
favour of Judah by sending to them the customary tribute which was due, and which had
been for a long time withheld (xvi. 1).

VI. Some of the fugitives are seen at the
fords of Arnon endeavouring to escape to Judea,
and making supplication for reception, and imploring blessings on the land (xvi. 2–6). But
see the Notes on ch. xvi. 2–7, for another view of
the design of this passage. The view here given
is that suggested by Gesenius and Prof. Stuart.

VII. They are repulsed, and the answer to their supplication is given in such a tone as to show the deep sense of the injury received from Moab which the Jewish people entertained (xvi. 7).

VIII. The prophet then proceeds in his description of the utter wasting of the country of Moab—desolation which excited the deepest feelings in his heart, and so great as to move his most tender compassion (xvi. 8–12).

IX. Then follows a limitation of the time when all this would take place. Within three years all this would be fulfilled (xvi. 13, 14).

THE [a] burden of Moab. Because in the night Ar of Moab is laid waste, and brought[1] to silence; because in the night Kir of Moab is laid waste, and brought to silence;

[a] Jer.48; Eze.25.8–11; Amos 21.3.   1 or, cut off.

CHAPTER XV.

1. *The burden of Moab* (see Note on ch. xiii. 1). This is the *title* of the prophecy. The Chaldee renders this, 'The burden of the cup of malediction which is to come upon Moab.' ¶ *Because in the night.* The fact that this was to be done in the night denotes the *suddenness* with which the calamity would come upon them. Thus the expression is used in Job to denote the suddenness and surprise with which calamities come :

Terrors take hold on him as waters,
A tempest stealeth him away in the night.
Job xxvii. 20.

So a thief is represented as coming in the night—in a sudden and unexpected manner (Job xxiv. 14):

The murderer in the night is as a thief.

See also Matt. xxiv. 43; 1 Thess. v. 2; 2 Pet. iii. 10; Rev. iii. 3; xvi. 15. ¶ *Ar of Moab.* This was the capital of Moab. It was situated on the south of the river Arnon. It was sometimes called *Rabbath Moab.* Isaiah (ch. xvi. 7–11) calls it the city 'with walls of burnt brick.' Under the name of Areopolis it occurs in Eusebius and Stephen of Byzantium, and in the acts of many Synods of the fifth and sixth centuries, when it was the seat of a bishop (Reland's *Palestine*, pp. 577, 578). Abulfeda says that in his time it was a small town. Jerome says that the city was destroyed by an earthquake when he was young, probably about A.D. 315. Burckhardt found a place called Rabba about twenty miles south of the river Arnon, which he supposed to be the ancient Ar. Seetzen found there ruins of considerable compass; especially the ruins of an old palace or temple, of which portions of the wall and some pillars are still standing. Legh says, 'There are no traces of fortifications to be seen; but, upon an eminence, were a dilapidated Roman temple and some tanks.' ¶ *Is laid waste.* That is, is about to be laid waste. This passed before the mind of Isaiah in a vision, and he represents it as it appeared to him, as already a scene of desolation. ¶ And *brought to silence.* Marg. 'Cut off.' The word may mean either. The sense is, that the city was to be destroyed, for so the word דָמָה (*dâmâ*) often means (Hos. iv. 5, 6; x. 7, 15; Jer. vi. 2; xlvii. 5; Zeph. i. 11). ¶ *Kir of Moab.* Probably this city was the modern *Kerek* or *Karak.* The Chaldee renders it by the name כְּרַכָּא (*Kĕrăkkâ*), or 'fortress,' hence the name *Kerek* or *Karak.* According to Burckhardt, it lies about three hours, and according to Abulfeda twelve Arabic miles, south of Ar Moab, upon a very high and steep rocky hill, from which the prospect extends even to Jerusalem, and which, formed by nature for a fortress, overlooks the whole surrounding country. In the wars of the Maccabees (2 Macc. xii. 17) it is mentioned under the name of Κάρακα (*Karaka*), and it is now known by the name of *Kerek* or *Karak.* In the time of the crusades, a heathen prince built there under king Fulco (in the year 1131) a very important castle, which was very serviceable to the Franks, and in 1183 it held out successfully against a formidable siege of a month by Saladin. Abulfeda speaks of it as so strong a fortress that one must abandon even the wish to take it. It has been visited in modern times by Seetzen, Burckhardt, and the company of English travellers referred to above. The place has still a castle, into which the whole surrounding country brings its grain for safe keeping. The small and poor town is built upon the remains of once important edifices, and is inhabited by Moslems and Christians. It is the seat of a bishop, though the

2 He is gone up to Bajith, and to Dibon, tho high places, to woop: Moab shall howl over Nebo, and over Medeba: on all their heads *shall be* baldnose, *and* every beard cut off.

bishop resides at Jerusalem (see Gesenius, *Comm. in loc.*)

2. *He is gone up.* That is, the inhabitants of Moab in consternation have fled from their ruined cities, and have gone up to other places to weep. ¶ *To Bajith, and to Dibon.* Lowth supposes that these two words should be joined together, and that one place is denoted. The Chaldee renders it, ' Ascend into the houses of Dibon.' Kimchi supposes that the word (בַּיִת) denotes a temple. It usually means *house*, and hence may mean a temple of the gods ; that is, the principal *house* in the land. This interpretation is adopted by Gesenius and Noyes. Vitringa supposes it to mean Beth-Meon (Jer. xlviii. 24), or Beth-Baal-Meon (Josh. xiii. 17), north of the Arnon, now *Macin*. I have adopted the translation proposed by Kimchi as better expressing the sense in my view than that which makes it a proper name. Dibon, perhaps the same place as Dimon in ver. 9, was a city given by Moses to Gad, and afterwards yielded to Reuben (Num. xxxii. 3, 33, 34; Josh. xiii. 9). It was again occupied by the Moabites (Jer. xlviii. 18, 22). Eusebius says it was a large town on the north of the river Arnon. Seetzen found there ruins under the name of Dibân in a magnificent plain. Hence *Dibon* is here appropriately described as *going up* from a plain to weep ; and the passage may be rendered, ' Dibon is weeping upon the high places.' ¶ *To weep.* Over the sudden desolation which has come upon the principal cities. ¶ *Moab shall howl over Nebo.* Nebo was one of the mountains on the east of the Jordan. It was so high that from it an extended view could be taken of the land of Canaan opposite. It was distinguished as being the place where Moses died (Deut. xxii. 49 ; xxxiv. 1). The meaning of this is, that *on* mount Nebo, Moab should lift up the voice of wailing. Jerome says that the idol Chamos, the principal idol of Moab, was on mount Nebo, and that this was the place of its worship. This mountain was

near the northern extremity of the Dead Sea. Mount Nebo was completely barren when Burckhardt passed over it, and the site of the ancient city had not been ascertained (*Travels in Syria*, p. 370.) On its summit, says Burckhardt, was a heap of stones overshadowed by a very large wild pistacia tree. At a short distance below, to the south-west, is the ruined place called Kereyat. ¶ *And over Medeba.* This was a city east of the Jordan in the southern part of the territory allotted to Reuben. It was taken from the Reubenites by the Moabites. Burckhardt describes the ruins of this town, which still bears the same name. He says of it, it is ' built upon a round hill ; but there is no river near it. It is at least half an hour in circumference. I observed many remains of private houses, constructed with blocks of silex ; but not a single edifice is standing. There is a large birket [tank, or cistern], which, as there is no spring at Medeba, might be still of use to the Bedouins, were the surrounding ground cleared of the rubbish to allow the water to flow into it ; but such an undertaking is far beyond the views of the wandering Arab. On the west side of the town are the foundations of a temple built with large stones, and apparently of great antiquity. A part of its eastern wall remains, constructed in the same style as the castle wall at Ammon. At the entrance to one of the courts stand two columns of the Doric order. In the centre of one of the courts is a large well.'—(*Travels in Syria*, pp. 366, 367.) ¶ *On all their heads* shall be *baldness*, &c. To cut off the hair of the head and the beard was expressive of great grief. It is well known that the Orientals regard the beard with great sacredness and veneration, and that they usually dress it with great care. Great grief was usually expressed by striking external acts. Hence they lifted up the voice in wailing ; they hired persons to howl over the dead ; they rent their garments ; and for the same reason, in times of great

3 In their streets they shall gird themselves with sackcloth: on the tops of their houses, and in their

1 *descending into weeping*, or, *coming down with weeping.*

streets, every one shall howl, 1 weeping abundantly.

4 And Heshbon shall cry, and Elealeh; their voice shall be heard *even* unto Jahaz: therefore the

---

calamity or grief, they cut off the hair, and even the beard. Herodotus (ii. 36) speaks of it as a custom among all nations, except the Egyptians, to cut off the hair as a token of mourning. So also Homer says, that on the death of Patroclus they cut off the hair as expressive of grief (*Iliad*, xxiii. 46, 47) :

Next these a melancholy band appear,
Amidst lay dead Patroclus on a bier;
O'er all the course their scattered locks they
threw.   *Pope.*

See also *Odyss.* iv. 197. This was also the custom with the Romans (Ovid. *Amor.* 3, 5, 12); the Egyptians (Diod. i. 84); the Scythians (Herod. iv. 71); and the modern Cretans. The *principle* on which this is done is, that thereby they are deprived of what is esteemed the most beautiful ornament of the body ; an idea which lies at the foundation of mourning in all countries and ages. The loss of the beard, also, was the highest calamity, and would be expressive of the deepest grief. 'It is,' says D'Arvieux, who has devoted a chapter to the exposition of the sentiments of the Arabs in regard to the *beard*, 'a greater mark of infamy in Arabia to cut a man's beard off, than it is with us to whip a fellow at the cart's tail, or to burn him in the hand. Many people in that country would far rather die than incur that punishment. I saw an Arab who had received a musket shot in the jaw, and who was determined rather to perish than to allow the surgeon to cut his beard off to dress his wound. His resolution was at length overcome ; but not until the wound was beginning to gangrene. He never allowed himself to be seen while his beard was off ; and when at last he got abroad, he went always with his face covered with a black veil, that he might not be seen without a beard ; and this he did till his beard had grown again to a considerable length.'—(*Pic. Bib.*, vol. ii. p. 109.) Burckhardt also remarks, that the Arabs who have, from any cause, had the misfortune to lose

their beards invariably conceal themselves from view until their beards are grown again (comp. Isa. iii. 24; xxii. 12; Jer. xli. 5 ; Micah i. 16). The idea is, that the Moabites would be greatly afflicted.   Jeremiah has stated the same thing of Moab (xlviii. 37) :

For every head shall be bald, and every beard
he clipt;
And upon all hands shall be cuttings,
And upon the loins sackcloth.

3. *In their streets.* Publicly. Everywhere there shall be lamentation and grief. Some shall go into the streets, and some on the tops of the houses. ¶ *They shall gird themselves with sackcloth.* The common token of mourning ; and also worn usually in times of humiliation and fasting. It was one of the outward acts by which they expressed deep sorrow (Gen. xxxvii. 34 ; 2 Sam. iii. 31 ; 1 Kings xxi. 27; 2 Kings xix. 1 ; Job xvi. 15 ; Note on ch. iii. 24). ¶ *On the tops of the houses.* The roofs of the houses in the East were, and still are, made flat, and were places of resort for prayer, for promenade, &c. The prophet here says, that all the usual places of resort would be filled with weeping and mourning. In the streets, and on the roofs of the houses, they would utter the voice of lamentation. ¶ *Shall howl.* It is known that, in times of calamity in the East, it is common to raise an unnatural and forced howl, or long-continued shriek. Persons are often hired for this purpose (Jer. ix. 17). ¶ *Weeping abundantly.* Heb. 'Descending into weeping ;' *i.e.*, going, as we would say, *deep into it*, or weeping much ; immersed as it were in tears (comp. Jer. xiii. 17; xiv. 17).

4. *And Heshbon shall cry.* This was a celebrated city of the Amorites, twenty miles east of the Jordan (Josh. xiii. 17). It was formerly conquered from the Moabites by Sihon, and became his capital, and was taken by the Israelites a little before the death of Moses (Num. xxi. 25). After the carrying away of the ten tribes it was re-

armed soldiers of Moab shall cry out; his life shall be grievous unto him.

5 My ^aheart shall cry out for

covered by the Moabites. Jeremiah (xlviii. 2) calls it 'the pride of Moab.' The town still subsists under the same name, and is described by Burckhardt. He says, it is situated on a hill, south-west from El Aal [Elealeh]. 'Here are the ruins of an ancient town, together with the remains of some edifices built with small stones; a few broken shafts of columns are still standing, a number of deep wells cut in the rock, and a large reservoir of water for the summer supply of the inhabitants.' —(*Travels in Syria*, p. 365.) ¶ *And Elealeh.* This was a town of Reuben about a mile from Heshbon (Num. xxxii. 37). Burckhardt visited this place. Its present name is El Aal. 'It stands on the summit of a hill, and takes its name from its situation—Aal, meaning "the high." It commands the whole plain, and the view from the top of the hill is very extensive, comprehending the whole of the southern Belka. El Aal was surrounded by a well built wall, of which some parts yet remain. Among the ruins are a number of large cisterns, fragments of walls, and the foundations of houses, but nothing worthy of notice. The plain around it is alternately chalk and flint.'—(*Travels in Syria*, p. 365.) ¶ Even *unto Jahaz.* This was a city east of Jordan, near to which Moses defeated Sihon. It was given to Reuben (Deut. ii. 32), and was situated a short distance north of Ar, the capital of Moab. ¶ *The armed soldiers of Moab.* The consternation shall reach the very army. They shall lose their courage, and instead of defending the nation, they shall join in the general weeping and lamentation. ¶ *His life shall be grievous.* As we say of a person who is overwhelmed with calamities, that his life is wearisome, so, says the prophet, shall it be with the whole nation of Moab.

5. *My heart shall cry out for Moab.* This is expressive of deep compassion; and is proof that, in the view of the prophet, the calamities which were coming

Moab;¹ his fugitives *shall flee* unto Zoar, an heifer of three years old: for by the mounting up of Luhith with weeping shall they go it up;

upon it were exceedingly heavy. The same sentiment is expressed more fully in ch. xvi. 11; see also Jer. xlviii. 36: 'My heart shall sound for Moab like pipes.' The phrase denotes great inward pain and anguish in view of the calamities of others; and is an expression of the fact that we feel ourselves oppressed and borne down by sympathy on account of their sufferings (see Note on ch. xxi. 3). It is worthy of remark, that the LXX. read this as if it were '*his* heart'—referring to the Moabites, 'the heart of Moab shall cry out.' So the Chaldee; and so Lowth, Michaelis, and others read it. But there is no authority for this change in the Hebrew text; nor is it needful. In the parallel place in Jer. xlviii. 36, there is no doubt that the heart of the prophet is intended; and here, the phrase is designed to denote the deep compassion which a holy man of God would have, even when predicting the ills that should come upon others. How much compassion, how much deep and tender feeling should ministers of the gospel have when they are describing the final ruin —the unutterable woes of impenitent sinners under the awful wrath of God in the world of woe! ¶ *His fugitives.* Marg. 'Or to the borders thereof, even as an heifer' (בְּרִיחֶיהָ). Jerome and the Vulgate render this 'her *bars*,' and it has been explained as meaning that the voice of the prophet, lamenting the calamity of Moab, could be heard as far as the *bars*, or gates, of Zoar; or that the word *bars* means *princes*, *i.e.*, protectors, a figure similar to *shields of the land* (Ps. xlvii. 10; Hos. iv. 18.) The LXX. render it, 'Εν αὐτῇ—' The voice of Moab in her is heard to Zoar.' But the more correct rendering is, undoubtedly, that of our translation, referring to the fugitives who should attempt to make their escape from Moab when the calamities should come upon her. ¶ *Unto Zoar.* Zoar was a small town in the southern extremity of the Dead Sea, to which Lot fled when Sodom was

for in the way of Horonaim they shall raise up a cry of [1] destruction.

6 For the waters of Nimrim shall

be desolate : [2] for the hay is withered away, the grass faileth, there is no green thing.

1 *breaking.*

2 *desolations.*

overthrown (Gen. xix. 23). Abulfeda writes the name Zoghar, and speaks of it as existing in his day. The city of Zoar was near to Sodom, so as to be exposed to the danger of being overthrown in the same manner that Sodom was, Zoar being exempted from destruction by the angel at the solicitation of Lot (Gen. xix. 21). That the town lay on the east side of the Dead Sea, is apparent from several considerations. Lot ascended from it to the mountain where his daughters bore each of them a son, who became the ancestors of the Moabites and the Ammonites. But these nations both dwelt on the east side of the Dead Sea. Further, Josephus, speaking of this place, calls it Ζοάρων τῆς 'Αραβίας—' Zoar of Arabia' (*Bell. Jud.* iv. 8, 4). But the Arabia of Josephus was on the east of the Dead Sea. So the crusaders, in the expedition of King Baldwin, A.D. 1100, after marching from Hebron, proceeded around the lake, and came, at length, to a place called *Segor*, doubtless the Zoghar of Abulfeda. The probability, therefore, is, that it was near the southern end of the sea, but on the eastern side. The exact place is now unknown. In the time of Eusebius and Jerome, it is described as having many inhabitants, and a Roman garrison. In the time of the crusaders, it is mentioned as a place pleasantly situated, with many palm trees. But the palm trees have disappeared, and the site of the city can be only a matter of conjecture (see Robinson's *Bib. Researches*, vol. ii. pp. 648–651). ¶ *An heifer of three years old.* That is, their fugitives flying unto Zoar shall lift up the voice like an heifer, for so Jeremiah in the parallel place explains it (xlviii. 34). Many interpreters have referred this, however, to Zoar as an appellation of that city, denoting its flourishing condition. Bochart refers it to Isaiah, and supposes that he designed to say that *he* lifted his voice as an heifer. But the more obvious interpretation is that given above, and is that which

occurs in Jeremiah. The expression, however, is a very obscure one. See the various senses which it may bear, examined in Rosenmüller and Gesenius *in loc.* Gesenius renders it, 'To Eglath the third ;' and supposes, in accordance with many interpreters, that it denotes a place called *Eglath*, called the third in distinction from two other places of the same name ; though he suggests that the common explanation, that it refers to a heifer of the age of three years, may be defended. In the third year, says he, the heifer was most vigorous, and hence was used for an offering (Gen. xv. 9). Until that age she was accustomed to go unbroken, and bore no yoke (Pliny, 8, 4, 5). If this refers to Moab, therefore, it may mean that hitherto it was vigorous, unsubdued, and active; but that now, like the heifer, it was to be broken and brought under the yoke by chastisement. The expression is a very difficult one, and it is impossible, perhaps, to determine what is the true sense. ¶ *By the mounting up of Luhith.* The *ascent* of Luhith. It is evident, from Jer. xlviii. 5, that it was a mountain, but where, is not clearly ascertained. Eusebius supposes it was a place between Areopolis and Zoar (see Reland's *Palestine,* pp. 577–579). The whole region there is mountainous. ¶ *In the way of Horonaim.* This was, doubtless, a town of Moab, but where it was situated is uncertain. The word means *two holes.* The region abounds to this day with caves, which are used for dwellings (Seetzen). The place lay, probably, on a declivity from which one descended from Luhith. ¶ *A cry of destruction.* Heb. ' Breaking.' A cry *appropriate to* the great calamity that should come upon Moab.

6. *For the waters of Nimrim.* It is supposed by some that the prophet here states the cause why the Moabites would flee to the cities of the south, to wit, that the *waters* of the northern cities would fail, and the country become desolate, and that they would

7 Therefore the abundance they have gotten, and that which they have laid up, shall they carry away to the ¹brook of the willows.

8 For the cry is gone round about the borders of Moab, the howling

1 or, *valley of the Arabians.*   2 *additions.*
a 2 Ki.17.25.

thereof unto Eglaim, and the howling thereof unto Beer-elim.

9 For the waters of Dimon shall be full of blood: for I will bring more ² upon Dimon, lions *a* upon him that escapeth of Moab, and upon the remnant of the land.

seek support in the south. But it is more probable that he is simply continuing the description of the desolation that would come upon Moab. Nimrah, or Beth Nimra, meaning *a house of limpid waters*, was a city of Reuben east of the Dead Sea (Num. xxxii. 3; comp. Jer. xlviii. 34). It was, doubtless, a city celebrated for its pure fountains and springs of water. Here Seetzen's chart shows a brook flowing into the Jordan called *Nahr Nimrim*, or *Wady Shoaib*. 'On the east of the Jordan over against Jericho, there is now a stream called *Nimlim*— doubtless the ancient *Nimrim*. This flows into the Jordan, and as it flows along gives fertility to that part of the country of Moab.'—(Rev. Eli Smith.) It is possible that the waters failed by a common practice in times of war, when an enemy destroyed the fountains of a country by diverting their waters, or by casting into them stones, trees, &c. This destructive measure of war occurs, with reference to Moab, in 2 Kings iii. 25, when the Israelites, during an incursion into Moab, felled the fruit trees, cast stones into the ploughed grounds, and *closed the fountains*, or *wells*. ¶ *For the hay is withered away.* The waters are dried up, and the land yields nothing to support life.

7. *Therefore the abundance they have gotten.* Their wealth they shall remove from a place that is utterly burnt up with drought, where the waters and the grass fail, to another place where they may find water. ¶ *To the brook of willows.* Marg. 'The valley of the Arabians.' The LXX. render it, 'I will lead them to the valley of the Arabians, and they shall take it.' So Saadias. It might, perhaps, be called the valley of the Arabians, because it was the boundary line between them and Arabia on the south. Lowth renders it, 'To Babylon.' The probability is,

that the prophet refers to some valley or brook that was called the brook of the willows, from the fact that many willows grew upon its bank. Perhaps it was the small stream which flows into the southern extremity of the Dead Sea, and which forms the boundary of Arabia Petrea of the province of Jebal. They withdrew towards the south, where towards Petra or Sela they had their property in herds (ch. xvi. 1); for probably the invader came from the north, and drove them in this direction. Lowth, and most commentators, suppose that 'they' in this verse refers to the enemies of Moab, and that it means that they would carry away the property of Moab to some distant place. But the more probable meaning is, that when the waters of the Nimrim should fail, they would remove to a place better watered; that is, they would leave their former abode, and wander away. It is an image of the desolation that was coming upon the land.

8. *For the cry is gone round about*, &c. The cry of distress and calamity has encompassed the whole land of Moab. There is no part of the land which is not filled with lamentation and distress. ¶ *The howling.* The voice of wailing on account of the distress. ¶ *Unto Eglaim.* This was a city of Moab east of the Dead Sea, which, Eusebius says, was eight miles south of Ar, and hence, says Rosenmüller, it was not far from the south border of Moab. It is mentioned by Josephus (*Ant.* xiv. 1), as one of the twelve cities in that region which was overthrown by Alexander the Great. ¶ *Unto Beer-elim.* Literally, *the well of the princes.* Perhaps the same as that mentioned in Num. xxi. 14–18, as being in the land of Moab, and near to Ar:

The princes digged the well,
The nobles of the people digged it.

9. *For the waters of Dimon.* Probably the same as *Dibon* (ver. 2). Euse-

CHAPTER XVI.

ANALYSIS.

This chapter is a continuance of the former, and the scope of it is, to give advice to the Moabites, and to threaten them with punishment in case, as the prophet foresaw, they should neglect or refuse to follow it. The advice was (1-5), to send the customary tribute to the king of Judah; to seek his protection, and to submit themselves to him. But the prophet foresaw that, through the pride of Moab (6), they would refuse to recognize their subjection to Judah, and that, as a consequence, they would be doomed to severe punishment (7-11), and to a certain overthrow within a specified time (12-14). See the *Analysis* prefixed to ch. xv.

SEND ye the lamb *a* to the ruler of the land from 1 Sela to the wilderness, unto the mount of the daughter of Zion.

a 2 Ki.3.4.   1 *a rock, or, Petra.*

bius says it was a large town on the northern bank of the river Arnon. Jerome says that the letters *m* and *b* are often interchanged in oriental dialects (see Note on ver. 2). ¶ *Shall be full of blood.* That is, the number of the slain of Moab shall be so great, that the blood shall colour the waters of the river—a very common occurrence in times of great slaughter. Perhaps by the *waters* of Dimon the prophet does not mean the river Arnon, but the small rivulets or streams that might flow into it near to the city of Dibon. Probably there were winter brooks there, which do not run at all seasons. The Chaldee renders it, ' The waters of Dimon shall be full of blood, because I will place upon Dimon an assembly of armies.' ¶ *For I will bring more upon Dimon.* Heb. ' I will bring *additions;*' that is, I will bring upon it additional calamities. Jerome says, that by those additional calamities, the prophet refers to the *lions* which are immediately after mentioned. ¶ *Lions upon him that escapeth of Moab.* Wild beasts upon those who escaped from the slaughter, and who took refuge in the wilderness, or on the mountains. The Chaldee renders it, ' A king shall ascend with an army, and shall destroy the remainder of their land.' Aben Ezra interprets it of the king of Assyria; and Jarchi of Nebuchadnezzar, who is called a lion in Jer. iv. 7. Vitringa also supposes that Nebuchadnezzar is meant. But it is more probable that the prophet refers to wild beasts, which are often referred to in the Scriptures as objects of dread, and as bringing calamities upon nations (see Lev. xxvi. 22; Jer. v. 6; xv. 3; 2 Kings xviii. 25). ¶ *Upon the remnant of the land.* Upon all those who escaped the desolation of the war. The LXX. and the

Arabic render this, ' Upon the remnant of *Adama,*' understanding the word rendered ' land' (אֲדָמָה *ădhâmâ*), as the name of a city. But it more probably means the land.

CHAPTER XVI.

1. *Send ye the lamb.* Lowth renders this, ' I will send forth the son from the ruler of the land;' meaning, as he supposes, that under the Assyrian invasion, even the young prince of Moab would be obliged to flee for his life through the desert, that he might escape to Judea; and *that* thus God says that *he* would send him. The only authority for this, however, is, that the LXX. read the word ' send' in the future tense (ἀποστιλῶ) instead of the imperative; and that the Syriac reads בַּר (*băr*) instead of כַּר (*kăr*), *a lamb.* But assuredly this is too slight an authority for making an alteration in the Hebrew text. This is one of the many instances in which Lowth has ventured to suggest a change in the text of Isaiah without sufficient authority. The LXX. read this, ' I will send reptiles (ἑρπετὰ) upon the land. Is not the mountain of the daughter of Zion a desolate rock?' The Chaldee renders it, ' Bear ye tribute to the Messiah, the anointed of Israel, who is powerful over you who were in the desert, to Mount Zion.' And this, understanding by the Messiah the anointed king of Israel, is probably the true rendering. The word ' lamb' (כַּר *kăr*) denotes, properly, a pasture lamb, a fat lamb, and is usually applied to the lamb which was slain in sacrifice. Here it probably means a lamb, or *lambs* collectively, as a tribute, or acknowledgment of subjection to Judah. Lambs were used in the daily sacrifice in the temple, and in the other sacrifices of the Jews. Large numbers

of them would, therefore, be needed, and it is not improbable that the *tribute* of the nations subject to them was often required to be paid in animals for burnt offering. Perhaps there might have been this additional reason for that— that the sending of such animals would be a sort of incidental acknowledgment of the truth of the Jewish religion, and an offering to the God of the Hebrews. At all events, the word here seems to be one that designates *tribute* ; and the counsel of the prophet is, that they should send their *tribute* to the Jews. ¶ *To the ruler of the land.* To the king of Judah. This is proved by the addition at the close of the verse, 'unto the mount of the daughter of Zion.' It is evident from 2 Sam. viii. 2, that David subdued the Moabites, and laid them under tribute, so that the 'Moabites became David's servants, and brought gifts.' That *lambs* were the specific kind of tribute which the Moabites were to render to the Jews as a token of their subjection, is clearly proved in 2 Kings iii. 4 : 'And Mesha, king of Moab, was a sheep-master, and rendered unto the king of Israel an hundred thousand rams, with the wool.' This was in the time of Ahab. But the Moabites after his death revolted from them, and rebelled (2 Kings iv. 5). It is probable that as this tribute was laid by *David* before the separation of the kingdoms of Judah and Israel, and as the kings of Judah claimed to be the true successors of David and Solomon, they demanded that the tribute should be rendered to *them*, and not to the kings of Israel, and this is the claim which Isaiah enforces in the passage before us. The command of the prophet is to regain the lost favour of Israel by the payment of the tribute that was due.—The territory of Moab was in early times, and is still, rich in flocks of sheep. Seetzen made his journey with some inhabitants of Hebron and Jerusalem who had purchased sheep in that region. Lambs and sheep were often demanded in tribute. The Persians received fifty thousand sheep as a tribute annually from the Cappadocians, and one hundred thousand from the Medes (Strabo, ii. 362). ¶ *From Sela in the wilderness.* The word 'Sela'

(סֶלַע) means *a rock;* and by it here there can be no doubt that there is intended the city of that name which was the capital of *Arabia Petrea*. The city was situated within the bounds of Arabia or Idumea, but was probably at this time in the possession of the Moabites. It was, therefore, the remotest part of their territory, and the sense may be, 'Send tribute even from the remotest part of your land ;' or it may be, that the region around that city was particularly favourable to pasturage, and for keeping flocks. To this place they had fled with their flocks on the invasion from the north (see Note on ch. xv. 7). Vitringa says that that desert around Petra was regarded as a vast common, on which the Moabites and Arabians promiscuously fed their flocks. The situation of the city of *Sela*, or (πέτρα) *Petra*, meaning the same as *Sela*, a rock, was for a long time unknown, but it has lately been discovered. It lies about a journey of a day and a half south-east of the southern extremity of the Dead Sea. It derived its name from the fact that it was situated in a vast hollow in a rocky mountain, and consisted almost entirely of dwellings hewn out of the rock. It was the capital of the Edomites (2 Kings xix. 7); but might have been at this time in the possession of the Moabites. Strabo describes it as the capital of the Nabatheans, and as situated in a vale well watered, but encompassed by insurmountable rocks (xvi. 4), at a distance of three or four days' journey from Jericho. Diodorus (19, 55) mentions it as a place of trade, with caves for dwellings, and strongly fortified by nature. Pliny, in the first century, says, 'The Nabatheans inhabit the city called Petra, in a valley less than two [Roman] miles in amplitude, surrounded by inaccessible mountains, with a stream flowing through it' (*Nat. Hist.* vi. 28). Adrian, the successor of Trajan, granted important privileges to that city, which led the inhabitants to give his name to it upon coins. Several of these are still extant. In the fourth century, Petra is several times mentioned by Eusebius and Jerome, and in the fifth and sixth centuries it appears as the metropolitan see of the Third

Palestine (see the article *Petra* in Reland's *Palestine*). From that time, Petra disappeared from the pages of history, and the metropolitan see was transferred to Rabbah. In what way Petra was destroyed is unknown.

Whether it was by the Mahometan conquerors, or whether by the incursions of the hordes of the desert, it is impossible now to ascertain. All Arabian writers of that period are silent as to Petra. The name became changed to

VIEW OF PETRA (SELA) FROM THE TOP OF THE THEATRE.—LABORDE.

that which it bears at present—Wady Musa, and it was not until the travels of Seetzen, in 1807, that it attracted the attention of the world. During his excursion from Hebron to the hill Madŭrah, his Arab guide described the place, exclaiming, 'Ah! how I weep when I behold the ruins of Wady Musa.' Seetzen did not visit it, but Burckhardt passed a short time there, and described it. Since his time it has been repeatedly

visited (see Robinson's *Bib. Researches,* vol. ii. pp. 573–580).

This city was formerly celebrated as a place of great commercial importance, from its central position and its being so securely defended. Dr. Vincent (in his *Commerce of the Ancients,* vol. xi. p. 263, quoted in Laborde's *Journey to Arabia Petrea,* p. 17) describes Petra as the capital of Edom or Sin, the Idumea or Arabia Petrea of the Greeks, the Nabatea considered both by geographers, historians, and poets, as the source of all the precious commodities of the East. The caravans in all ages, from Minea in the interior of Arabia, and from Gerka on the gulf of Persia, from Hadramont on the ocean, and some even from Sabea in Yemen, appear to have pointed to Petra as a common centre ; and from Petra the trade seems to have branched out into every direction—to Egypt, Palestine, and Syria, through Arsinoe, Gaza, Tyre, Jerusalem, Damascus, and a variety of intermediate roads that all terminated on the Mediterranean. Strabo relates, that the merchandise of India and Arabia was transported on camels from Leuke Kome to Petra, and thence to Rhinocolura and other places (xvi. 4, 18, 23, 24). Under the Romans the trade was still more prosperous. The country was rendered more accessible, and the passage of merchants facilitated by military ways, and by the establishment of military posts to keep in check the predatory hordes of the neighbouring deserts. One great road, of which

RUINS OF A TRIUMPHAL ARCH (PETRA).

traces still remain, went from Petra to Damascus ; another went off from this road west of the Dead Sea to Jerusalem, Askelon, and other parts of the Mediterranean (Laborde, p. 213 ; Burckhardt, 374, 419). At a period subsequent to the Christian era there always reigned at Petra, according to Strabo, a king of the royal lineage, with whom a prince was associated in the government (Strabo, p. 779). The very situation of this city, once so celebrated, as

has been remarked above, was long unknown. Burckhardt, under the assumed name of Shelkh Ibrahim, in the year 1811, made an attempt to reach Petra under the pretext that he had made a vow to sacrifice a goat in honour of Aaron on the summit of Mount Hor near to Petra. He was permitted to enter the city, and to remain there a short time, and to *look* upon the wonders of that remarkable place, but was permitted to make no notes or drawings on the spot. His object was supposed to be to obtain treasures, which the Arabs believe to have been deposited there in great abundance, as all who visit the ruins of ancient cities and towns in that region are regarded as having come there solely for that purpose. If assured that they have no such design, and if the Arabs are reminded that they have no means to remove them, it is replied ' that, although they may not remove them in their presence, yet when they return to their own land, they will have the power of *commanding* the treasures to be conveyed to them, and it will be done by magic.'—(Burckhardt's *Travels in Syria*, pp. 428, 429.)

Burckhardt's description of this city, as it is brief, may be here given *verbatim :*—' Two long days' journey northeast from Akaba [a town at the extremity of the Elanitic branch of the Red Sea, near the site of the ancient Eziongeber], is a brook called Wady Musa, and a valley of the same name. This place is very remarkable for its antiquities, and the remains of an ancient city, which I take to be Petra, the capital of Arabia Petrea, a place which, so far as I know, no European traveller has ever explored. In the red sandstone of which the vale consists, there are found more than two hundred and fifty sepulchres, which are entirely hewn out of the rock, generally with architectural ornaments in the Grecian style. There is found there a mausoleum in the form of a temple [obviously the same which Legh and Laborde call the temple of victory], on a colossal scale, which is likewise hewn out of the rock, with all its apartments, portico, peristylum, &c. It is an extremely fine monument of Grecian architecture, and in a fine state of preservation. In the same place there are yet other mausoleums with obelisks, apparently in the Egyptian style ; a whole amphitheatre hewn out of the solid rock, and the remains of a palace and many temples.'

TEMPLE IN ROCK (PETRA).

Mr. Bankes, in company of Mr. Legh, and Captains Irby and Mangles, have the merit of being the first persons who, as Europeans, succeeded to any extent in making researches in Petra. Captains Irby and Mangles spent two days amongst its temples, tombs, and ruins, and have furnished a description of what they saw. But the most full and satisfactory investigation which has been made of these ruins, was made by M. de Laborde, who visited the city in 1829, and was permitted to remain there eight days, and to examine it at leisure. An account of his journey, with splendid plates, was published in Paris in 1830, and a translation in London in 1836. To this interesting account the reader must be referred. It can only be remarked here, that Petra, or Sela, was a city entirely encompassed with lofty rocks, except in a single place, where was a deep ravine between the rocks which constituted the principal entrance. On the east and west it was enclosed with lofty rocks, of from three to five hundred feet in height ; on the north and south the ascent was gradual from the city to the adjacent hills. The ordinary entrance was through a deep ravine, which has been, until lately, supposed to have been the only way of access to the city. This ravine approaches it from the east, and is about a mile in length. In the narrowest part it is twelve feet in width, and the rocks are on each side about three hundred feet in height. On the northern side, there are tombs excavated in the rocks nearly the entire distance. The stream which watered Petra runs along in the bottom of the ravine, going through the city, and descending through a ravine to the west (see Robinson's *Bib. Researches*, vol. ii. pp. 514, 538). Of this magnificent entrance, the following cut will furnish an illustration. The city is wholly uninhabited, except when the wandering Arab makes use of an excavated tomb or palace in which to pass the night, or a caravan pauses there. The rock which encompasses it is a soft freestone. The tombs, with which almost the entire city was encompassed, are cut in the solid rock, and are adorned in the various modes of Grecian and Egyptian architecture. The surface of the solid rock was first made smooth, and then a plan of the tomb or temple was drawn on the smoothed surface, and the workmen began at the top and cut the various pillars, entablatures, and capitals. The tomb was then excavated from the rock, and was usually entered by a single door. Burck-

ENTRANCE TO A ROCK-HEWN TOMB (PETRA).

hardt counted two hundred and fifty of these tombs, and Laborde has described minutely a large number of them. For a description of these splendid monuments, the reader must be referred to the work of Laborde, pp. 152–193. Lond. Ed.

2 For it shall be, *that* as a wandering bird cast ¹ out of the nest, *so* the daughters of Moab shall be at the fords of ᵃ Arnon.

1 or, *a nest forsaken.*   a Num.21.13.   2 *bring.*

That this is the Sela referred to here there can be no doubt; and the discovery of this place is only one of the instances out of many, in which the researches of oriental travellers contribute to throw light on the geography of the Scriptures, or otherwise illustrate them. For a description of this city, see Stephen's *Incidents of Travel in Egypt, Arabia Petrea, and the Holy Land,* vol. ii. ch. iv. p. 65, *sq.;* the work of Laborde referred to above; and Robinson's *Bib. Researches,* vol. ii. pp. 573–580, 653–659. ¶ *To the mount of the daughter of Zion.* To Mount Zion; *i.e.,* to Jerusalem (Note, ch. i. 8). The meaning of this verse, therefore, is, ' Pay the accustomed tribute to the Jews. Continue to seek their protection, and acknowledge your subjection to them, and you shall be safe. They will yield you protection, and these threatened judgments will not come upon you. But refuse, or withhold this, and you will be overthrown.'

2. *For it shall be.* It shall happen in the time of the calamity that shall come upon Moab. ¶ *As a wandering bird.* (See ch. x. 14.) The same idea is presented in Prov. xxvii. 8 :

As a bird that wanders from her nest,
So is a man that wandereth from his place.

The idea here is that of a bird driven away from her nest, where the nest is destroyed, and the young fly about without any home or place of rest. So would Moab be when the inhabitants were driven from their dwellings. The reason why this is introduced seems to be, to enforce what the prophet had said in the previous verse—the duty of paying the usual tribute to the Jews, and seeking their protection. The time is coming, says the prophet, when the Moabites shall be driven from their homes, and when they will need that protection which they can obtain by paying the usual tribute to the Jews. ¶ *The daughters of Moab.* The females shall be driven from their homes, and

3 Take ² counsel, execute judgment; make thy shadow as the night in the midst of the noonday; hide the outcasts, bewray not him that wandereth.

shall wander about, and endeavour to flee from the invasion which has come upon the land. By the apprehension, therefore, that their wives and daughters would be exposed to this danger, the prophet calls upon the Moabites to secure the protection of the king of Judah. ¶ *At the fords of Arnon.* Arnon was the northern boundary of the land of Moab. They would endeavour to cross that river, and thus flee from the land, and escape the desolations that were coming upon it. The river Arnon, now called Mujeb, flows in a deep, frightfully wild, and rocky vale of the same name (Num. xxi. 15; Deut. ii. 24; iii. 9), in a narrow bed, and forms at this time the boundary between the provinces of Belka and Karrak (Seetzen). Bridges were not common in the times here referred to; and, indeed, permanent bridges among the ancients were things almost unknown. Hence they selected the places where the streams were most shallow and gentle, as the usual places of crossing.

3. *Take counsel.* Heb. ' Bring counsel ;' or cause it to come (הָבִיאוּ, or as it is in the *keri,* הביאי). The Vulgate renders this in the singular number, and so is the *keri,* and so many MSS. J. D. Michaelis, Lowth, Eichhorn, Gesenius, and Noyes, regard verses 3–5 as a supplicatory address of the fugitive Moabites to the Jews to take them under their protection, and as imploring a blessing on the Jewish people if they would do it; and ver. 6 as the negative answer of the Jews, or as a refusal to protect them on account of their pride. But most commentators regard it as addressed to the Moabites by the prophet, or by the Jews, calling upon the Moabites to afford such protection to the Jews who might be driven from their homes as to secure their favour, and confirm the alliance between them; and ver. 6 as an intimation of the prophet, that the pride of Moab is such that there is no reason to suppose the

4 Let mine outcasts dwell with thee, Moab: be thou a covert to them from the face of the spoiler: for the [1]extortioner is at an end, the spoiler ceaseth, the [2]oppressors are consumed out of the land.

1 *wringer.*   2 *treaders down.*

advice will be followed. It makes no difference in the sense here, whether the verb 'give counsel' be in the singular or the plural number. If singular, it may be understood as addressed to *Moab* itself; if plural, to the *inhabitants* of Moab. Vitringa supposes that this is an additional advice given to the Moabites by the prophet, or by a chorus of the Jews, to exercise the offices of kindness and humanity towards the Jews, that thus they might avoid the calamities which were impending. The *first* counsel was (ver. 1), to pay the proper tribute to the Jewish nation; *this* is (ver. 3–5) to show to those Jews who might be driven from their land kindness and protection, and thus preserve the friendship of the Jewish nation. This is, probably, the correct interpretation, as if he had said, 'take counsel; seek advice in your circumstances; be not hasty, rash, impetuous, unwise; do not cast off the friendship of the Jews; do not deal unkindly with those who may seek a refuge in your land, and thus provoke the nation to enmity; but let your land be an asylum, and thus conciliate and secure the friendship of the Jewish nation, and thus mercy shall be reciprocated and shown to you by him who shall occupy the throne of David' (ver. 5). The *design* is, to induce the Moabites to show kindness to the fugitive Jews who might seek a refuge there, that thus, in turn, the Jews might show them kindness. But the prophet foresaw (ver. 6) that Moab was so proud that he would neither pay the accustomed tribute to the Jews, nor afford them protection; and therefore the judgment is threatened against them which is finally to overthrow them. ¶ *Execute judgment.* That is, do that which is equitable and right; which you would desire to be done in like circumstances. ¶ *Make thy shadow.* A *shadow* or *shade*, is often in the Scriptures an emblem of protection from the burning heat of the sun, and thence of those burning, consuming judgments, which

are represented by the intense heat of the sun (Note on Isa. iv. 6; comp. Isa. xxv. 4; xxxii. 2; Lam. iv. 20). ¶ *As the night.* That is, a deep, dense shade, such as the night is, compared with the intense heat of noon. This idea was one that was very striking in the East. Nothing, to travellers crossing the burning deserts, could be more refreshing than the shade of a far-projecting rock, or of a grove, or of the night. Thus Isaiah counsels the Moabites to be to the Jews—to furnish protection to them which may be like the grateful shade furnished to the traveller by the rock in the desert. The figure here used is common in the East. Thus it is said in praise of a nobleman: 'Like the sun, he warmed in the cold; and when Sirius shone, then was he coolness and shade.' In the *Sunna* it is said: 'Seven classes of men will the Lord overshadow with his shade, when no shade will be like his; the upright Imam, the youth,' &c. ¶ *Hide the outcasts.* The outcasts of Judah—those of the Jews who may be driven away from their own homes, and who may seek protection in your land. Moab is often represented as a place of refuge to the outcast Hebrews (see the Analysis to ch. xv.) ¶ *Bewray not him that wandereth.* Reveal not (תְּגַלִּי), do not show them to their pursuer; *i.e.*, give them concealment and protection.

4. *Let mine outcasts.* This may be understood as the language of Judea, or of God. '*Mine* outcasts' may mean the exiles of Judea, or God may call them *his*. The sense is essentially the same. It denotes those who were fugitives, wanderers, exiles from the land of Judea, and who took refuge in the land of Moab; and God claims for them protection. ¶ *Dwell with thee.* Not dwell permanently, but sojourn (יָגוּרוּ), let them remain with you as exiles; or let them find a refuge in your land. ¶ *Be thou a covert to them.* A refuge; a hiding-place; a place of secresy (סֵתֶר *sēthĕr*). ¶ *From the face*

5 And in mercy shall the throne be ¹ established ; and ᵃ he shall sit upon it in truth in the tabernacle of David, ᵇ judging and seeking

1 or, *prepared.* a Dan.7.14,27; Mic.4.7; Lu.1.32,33.

of the spoiler. That is, the conqueror from whose desolating career they would seek a refuge in the land of Moab. Who this *spoiler* would be, is not known. It would seem to be some invader who was carrying desolation through the land of Judea. It may be observed, however, that Lowth, by setting the points aside, supposes that this should be read, 'Let the outcasts of Moab sojourn with thee, O Zion.' So Noyes. But this seems to me not to suit the connection and the design ; which is, to persuade the Moabites to conciliate the favour of the Jews by affording a hiding-place to their fugitives. ¶ *For the extortioner is at an end.* Literally, 'there is an end, or there will be an end of the oppressor ; or he will be wanting.' The Chaldee renders it, ' The *enemy* is at an end.' The idea here seems to be, that the oppressor in the land of Judea would not continue there always ; the exiles of the Jews might soon return ; and Judea be able *then* to return kindness to Moab. Judea did not ask that her exiles should permanently abide in Moab, but asked only a temporary refuge, with the certainty that she would be soon delivered from her oppressions, and would then be able to furnish aid to Moab in return. ¶ *The oppressors are consumed.* Or, ' the treader down,' he that has trodden down the nations *shall* soon be removed, and *then*, in turn, Judea will be able to repay the kindness which is now asked at the hand of Moab, in permitting her exiles to remain in their land.

5. *And in mercy.* In benignity ; kindness ; benevolence. ¶ *Shall the throne be established.* The throne of the king of Judah. That is, he that shall sit upon the throne of David shall be disposed to repay the kindness which is now sought at the hand of Moab, and shall be able to do it. ¶ *And he shall sit upon it.* The king of Israel. ¶ *In truth.* In faithfulness ; that is, shall be true and faithful. His character shall be such that he will do justice,

judgment, and hasting righteousness.

6 We have heard of the pride of Moab ; *he is* very proud : *even* of

b Ps.72.2.

and will furnish protection and aid to the Moabites, if they now receive the fugitives of Israel. ¶ *In the tabernacle of David.* In the dwelling place ; the palace of David ; for so the word *tabernacle*, or *tent* (אֹהֶל *ōhĕl*) seems to be used here. It means *temple* in Ezek. xli. 1. It denotes a habitation, or dwelling place, in general, in Prov. xiv. 11 ; Ps. lii. 7 ; xci. 10. The palace, court, or *citadel* of David, was on mount Zion ; and the sense here is, that the king to whom Israel refers would be a worthy successor of David—just, true, faithful, benignant, and disposed to repay the favours now sought at the hand of Moab. ¶ *Seeking judgment.* Anxious to do right ; and seeking an opportunity to recompense those who had shown any favour to the people of the Jews. Moab, therefore, if she would now afford protection to the Jews, might be certain of a recompense. ¶ *And hasting righteousness.* Not tardy and slow in doing what should be done—anxious to do justice to all. It is implied here also, that a king who would be so just, and so anxious to do *right* to all, would not only be ready to show kindness to the Moabites, if they protected the fugitives of Judea, but would also be disposed to do *right* if they refused that protection ; that is, would be disposed to inflict *punishment* on them. Alike, therefore, by the hope of the protection and favour of the king of the Jews, and by the dread of punishment, the prophet endeavours to persuade Moab now to secure their favour by granting protection to their exiles.

6. *We have heard of the pride of Moab.* We Jews ; we have *all* heard of it ; that is, we *know* that he is proud. The evident design of the prophet here is, to say that Moab was so proud, and was well known to be so haughty, that he would *reject* this counsel. He would neither send the usual tribute to the land of Judea (ver. 1), thus acknowledging his dependence on them ; nor would he give protection to the exiled

his haughtiness, and his pride, and his wrath: *but* his lies *shall* not *be* so.

7 Therefore shall Moab howl for Moab; every one shall howl: for

the foundations of [a] Kir-hareseth shall ye [1] mourn; surely *they are* stricken.

8 For the fields of Heshbon lan-

Jews as they should wander through his land, and *thus* endeavour to conciliate their favour, and secure their friendship. As a consequence of this, the prophet proceeds to state that heavy judgments would come upon Moab as a nation. ¶ He is *very proud.* The same thing is stated in the parallel place in Jer. xlviii. 29 (comp. ver. 11). Moab was at ease; he was confident in his security; he feared nothing; he sought *no* means. therefore, of securing the friendship of the Jews. ¶ *And his wrath.* As the result of pride and haughtiness. Wrath or indignation is excited in a proud man when he is opposed, and when the interests of others are not made to give way to his. ¶ But *his lies* shall *not* be *so.* The Hebrew phrase (לֹא־כֵן—'not so') here seems to be used in the sense of 'not right;' 'not firm, or established;' that is, his vain boasting, his false pretensions, his *lies* shall not be confirmed, or established; or they shall be vain and impotent. In the parallel place in Jeremiah, it is, 'But it shall not be so; his lies shall not effect it.' The word rendered 'his lies' here (בַּדָּיו), means his boasting, or vain and confident speaking. In Isa. xliv. 25, it is connected with the vain and confident responses of diviners and soothsayers. Here it means that Moab boasted of his strength and security, and did not feel his need of the friendship of the Jews; but that his security was false, and that it should not result according to his expectations. That Moab was proud, is also stated in ch. xxv. 8; and that he was disposed to give vent to his pride by reproaching the people of God, is apparent from Zech. ii. 8:

I have heard the reproach of Moab,
And the revilings of the children of Ammon,
Whereby they have reproached my people,
And boasted themselves upon their border.

7. *Therefore shall Moab howl for Moab.* One part of the nation shall mourn for another; they shall howl, or

lament, in alternate responses. Jerome renders it, 'the people (shall howl) to the city; the city to the provinces.' The general idea is, that there would be an universal lamentation throughout the land. This would be the punishment which would result from their pride in neglecting to send the tribute and seeking the favour of the Jews; or they would lament because of the expectation of finding a refuge among the Israelites was taken away. ¶ *For the foundations.* On account of the foundations of Kir-hareseth, for they shall be overthrown; that is, that city shall be destroyed. The word here rendered 'foundations' (אֲשִׁישֵׁי), occurs nowhere else but in this place, and in Hos. iii. 1. The LXX. render it, 'The inhabitants.' The Chaldee, 'Men.' Jeremiah, in the parallel place, renders it also 'men' (xlviii. 31). In Hos. iii. 1, it is rendered 'flagons of wine'—and it has been supposed by many that it has this sense here, as this would agree with what is immediately added of the fields of Heshbon, and the vine of Sibmah. Rosenmüller renders it by 'strong men, or *heroes;*' and supposes that it means that the *strong* men of Kir-hareseth would be destroyed, and that they would mourn on that account. The probable sense is, that that on which the city rested, or was based, was to be destroyed. So Kimchi, Jarchi, and the Syriac understand it. ¶ *Kir-hareseth.* Literally, *wall of potsherds,* or *of bricks.* Aquila renders it, Τοιχῷ ὀστρακίνῳ. Symmachus, Τείχει ὀστρακίνῳ. This was a city of Moab, but where it was situated is unknown. Vitringa supposes that it was the same as Kir Moab (ch. xv. 1), which, Gesenius says, is not improbable, for it is now mentioned as in ruins, and as one of the chief cities.

8. *For the fields of Heshbon.* (See Note, ch. xv. 4.) ¶ *Languish.* They are parched up with drought. The 'fields' here evidently mean *vineyards,*

guish, *and* the vine of Sibmah : the lords of the heathen have broken down the principal plants thereof, they are come *even* unto Jazer, they

wandered *through* the wilderness: her branches are [1] stretched out, they are gone over the sea :

1 or, *plucked up.*

for so the parallelism demands.   So in Deut. xxxii. 32:

> Their vine is of the vine of Sodom,
> And of the fields of Gomorrah.

¶ And *the vine of Sibmah.* Sibmah, or Shibmah, was a city of Reuben (Num. xxxii. 38 ; Josh. xiii. 19). Jeremiah, in the parallel place (xlviii. 32) speaks of the vine of Sibmah also. He also says that the enemies of Moab had taken Sibmah, and that the vine and wine had been destroyed (xlviii. 33). There was no more certain mode of producing desolation in a land where grapes were extensively cultivated than to cut down the vines. The Turks constantly practise that in regard to their enemies, and the result is, that wide desolation comes upon the countries which they invade. At this time it is probable that Sibmah belonged to the Moabites. It is mentioned here as being distinguished for the luxuriant production of the grape. Seetzen still found the vine cultivated in that region. Jerome says, that between Sibmah and Heshbon there was scarcely a distance of five hundred paces, half a Roman mile. ¶ *The lords of the heathen.* The princes of the heathen nations that had come to invade Moab. The words ' have broken down ' (הֶלְמוּ) may be taken in either of two senses, either to beat, strike, or break down, as in our version ; or *to be* beaten, or smitten with wine—*i.e.,* to become intoxicated—like the Greek οἰνοπλὴξ—*smitten with wine.* The former is doubtless the sense here. ¶ *The principal plants thereof.* The choice vines of it—*her sorek* (שֹׁרֻקֶיהָ). (See Notes on ch. v. 2.) ¶ *They are come.* That is, the vines of Sibmah had spread or extended themselves even to Jazer, indicating their great luxuriance and fertility. Jazer was a city at the foot of the mountains of Gilead which was given to Gad, and afterwards to the Levites (Josh. xxi. 39). Jerome says it was about fifteen miles from Heshbon. Seetzen found the ruins of a city called Szâr, and another place called

Szir, from which a small stream (Nahar Szir) flows into the Jordan (Gesenius). That the shoots of the vine of Sibmah reached unto Jazer and the desert, is a beautiful poetic expression for the extensive spread and luxuriance of the vine in that region. ¶ *They wandered.* The vines *wandered* in the desert. They found no twig or tree to which they could attach themselves, and they spread around in wild luxuriancy. ¶ Through *the wilderness.* The wilderness or desert of Arabia, which encompassed Moab. ¶ *Her branches are stretched out.* Are extended far, or are very luxuriant. ¶ *They are gone over the sea.* Called in the parallel place in Jer. xlviii. 32, ' the Sea of Jazer ;' probably some lake that had that name near the city of Jazer. It may *possibly* mean the Dead Sea, but that name is not elsewhere given to the Dead Sea in the Scriptures. It has been objected by some to this statement that modern travellers have not found any such place as the ' Sea of Jazer ;' or any lake in the vicinity of Jazer. But we may observe—(1.) that Seetzen found a stream flowing into the Jordan near Jazer ; and (2.) that it is possible that a pond or lake may have once there existed which may have been since, in the course of ages, filled with sand. It is known, for example, that in the vicinity of Suez the ancient narrow gulf there, and the large inland sea made by the Bitter lakes, have been choked up by the sand of the desert. Seetzen also says that he saw some pools near the source of the stream called Nahar Szir (*river Szir*).—Prof. Stuart. *Bib. Rep.* vol. vii. p. 158. The whole description of the vines of Sibmah is poetic ; designed, not to be literally understood, but to denote their remarkable luxuriance and fertility. A similar description of a *vine*—though there used to denote the Jewish people—occurs in Psal. lxxx. 8–11 :

> Thou hast brought a vine out of Egypt ;
> Thou hast cast out the heathen and planted it ;
> Thou preparedst room before it,
> And didst cause it to take deep root,
> And it filled the land.

9 Therefore [a] I will bewail with the weeping of Jazer the vine of Sibmah : I will water thee with my tears, O Heshbon, and Elealeh ; for [1] the shouting for thy summer fruits and for thy harvest is fallen.

10 And [b] gladness is taken away, and joy out of the plentiful field ;

a Jer.48.32, &c.   1, or, the alarm is fallen upon.

The hills were covered with the shadow of it,
And the boughs thereof were like the goodly
    cedars.
She sent out her boughs unto the sea,
And her branches unto the river.

9. *Therefore I will bewail.* So great is the desolation that I, the prophet, will lament it, though it belongs to another nation than mine own. The expression indicates that the calamity will be great (see Note on ch. xv. 5). ¶ *With the weeping of Jazer.* That is, I will pour out the same lamentation for the vine of Sibmah which I do for Jazer ; implying that it would be deep and bitter sorrow (see Jer. xlviii. 32). ¶ *I will water thee with my tears.* Indicating the grievous calamities that were coming upon those places, on account of the pride of the nation. They were to Isaiah foreign nations, but he had a heart that could feel for their calamities. ¶ *For the shouting for thy summer fruits.* The shouting attending the ingathering of the harvest (Note on ch. ix. 3). The word used here (הֵידָד), denotes, properly, a joyful acclamation, a shout of joy or rejoicing, such as was manifested by the vintager and presser of grapes (Jer. xxv. 30; xlviii. 33); or such as was made by the warrior (Jer. li. 14). Here it means, that in the time when they would expect the usual shout of the harvest, it should not be heard, but instead thereof there should be the triumph of the warrior. Literally, ' upon thy summer fruits, and upon thy harvests has the shouting fallen ;' that is, the shout of the warrior has fallen upon that harvest instead of the rejoicing of the husbandman. So Jeremiah evidently understands it (xlviii. 32): ' The *spoiler* is fallen upon thy summer fruits, and upon thy vintage.' Lowth proposes here a correction of the Hebrew text, but without necessity or authority.

10. *And gladness, &c.* The gladness

and in the vineyards there shall be no singing, neither shall there be shouting : the treaders shall tread out no wine in *their* presses ; I have made *their vintage* shouting to cease.

11 Wherefore my bowels [c] shall sound like an harp for Moab, and mine inward parts for Kir-haresh.

b ch.24.8.   c ch.63.15.

and joy that was commonly felt in the field producing a rich and luxuriant harvest. ¶ *Out of the plentiful field.* Heb. ' From Carmel ;' but Carmel means a fruitful field as well as the mountain of that name (see Note on ch. x. 18). ¶ *I have made* their vintage *shouting to cease.* That is, by the desolation that has come upon the land. The vineyards are destroyed ; and of course the shout of joy in the vintage is no more heard.

11. *Wherefore my bowels.* This is also an expression of the deep grief of the prophet in view of the calamities which were coming upon Moab. The *bowels* in the Scriptures are everywhere represented as the seat of compassion, pity, commiseration, and tender mercy (Gen. xiii. 30): ' His bowels did yearn upon his brother '—he deeply felt for him, he greatly pitied him (1 Kings iii. 26 ; Ps. xxv. 6 ; Prov. xii. 10 ; Cant. v. 4 ; Isa. lxiii. 15 ; Jer. iv. 19 ; xxxi. 20 ; Phil. i. 8 ; ii. 1). In classic writers, the word ' bowels ' denotes the *upper* viscera of victims—the heart, the lungs, the liver, which were eaten during or after the sacrifice (Robinson, *Lex.*, on the word σπλάγχνον). In the Scriptures, it denotes the *inward parts*—evidently also the upper viscera, regarded as the seat of the emotions and passions. The word as we use it—denoting the lower *viscera*—by no means expresses the sense of the word in the Scriptures, and it is this change in the signification which renders the use of the very language of the Bible unpleasant or inappropriate. We express the idea by the use of the word *heart*—the seat of the affections. ¶ *Shall sound like an harp.* The *bowels* are represented in the Scriptures as affected in various modes in the exercise of pity or compassion. Thus, in Lam. i. 20, Jeremiah says, ' My bowels are troubled ' (see Lam. ii. 1 ; Jer. xxxi. 20). Job (ch. xxx. 27,) says, ' My

12 And it shall come to pass, when it is seen that Moab is *a* weary on the high place, that he shall

a ch.26.16.

come to his sanctuary to pray ; but he *b* shall not prevail.

13 This *is* the word that the

b Pr.1.28.

bowels *boiled*, and rested not ; ' there was great agitation ; deep feeling. Thus, Jer. iv. 19 :

My bowels ! My bowels ! I am pained at my very heart.
My heart *maketh a noise* in me.

So Isa. lxiii. 15 : ' Where is the *sounding* of thy bowels and mercies ?' The word ' sound ' here means to make a tumultuous noise ; and the whole expression here denotes that his heart was affected with the calamities of Moab as the strings of the harp vibrate when beaten with the plectrum or the hand. His heart was deeply pained and affected by the calamities of Moab, and responded to those calamities, as the strings of the harp did to the blow of the plectrum. ¶ *Mine inward parts.* The expressions here used are somewhat analogous to ours of the *beating of the heart*, to denote deep emotion. Forster says of the savages of the South Sea that they call compassion *a barking of the bowels*. ¶ *For Kirharesh.* (See Note on ver. 7.)

12. *When it is seen.* When it occurs ; that is, when Moab actually *becomes* weary. ¶ *Is weary on the high place.* The *high place* denotes the place of idolatrous worship, and here means the same as the temple of Chemosh or his sanctuary. Temples and altars were usually constructed on such places, and especially the temples of the heathen gods. Moab is represented here as looking to her gods for protection. Weary, exhausted, worn down with calamities, she is represented as fleeing from the desolate towns and cities, and taking refuge at the altar, and seeking assistance there. This, says Jerome, is the final misery. She is now forsaken of those aids to which she had always trusted, and on which she had relied. Her men slain ; her towns destroyed ; her strong places broken down ; her once fertile fields languishing and desolate, she flees to the shrine of her god, and finds even her god unable to aid and defend her. ¶ *Shall come to his sanctuary.* To his *principal* sanctuary ; or

to the temple of the principal god which they worshipped — the god *Chemosh* (1 Kings xi. 7). This does not mean the temple at Jerusalem, though Kimchi so understands it ; but the temple of the chief divinity of Moab. Jerome says that this temple was on mount Nebo. ¶ *Shall not prevail.* That is, her prayer shall not be heard.

13. *This is the word.* This is the substance of the *former* predictions respecting Moab. This has been the *general course* or sense of the prophecies respecting Moab, during all its history. ¶ *Since that time.* Formerly ; from former times. There had been a course of predictions declaring in general that Moab should be destroyed, and the prophet says here that he had expressed their general sense ; or that *his* predictions accorded with them all —for they all predicted the complete overthrow of Moab. He now says (ver. 14) that these general prophecies respecting Moab which had been of so long standing were now to be speedily accomplished. The prophecies respecting Moab, foretelling its future ruin, may be seen in Ex. xv. 15 ; Num. xxi. 29 ; xxiv. 17 ; Ps. lx. 8 ; cviii. 9 ; Amos ii. 2 ; Zeph. ii. 9. It *may*, however, be intended here that the former portion of this prophecy had been uttered by Isaiah himself during the early part of his prophetic life. He is supposed to have prophesied some sixty or more years (*see* Introduction, § 3); and it may be that the prophecy in the fifteenth and the previous part of the sixteenth chapter had been uttered during the early part of his life without specifying the time when it would be fulfilled ; but now he says, that it would be accomplished in three years. Or it may be that some other prophet had uttered the prediction which he now repeats with additions at the close. The fact that Isaiah had done this on some occasions seems probable from the beginning of ch. ii., which appears to be a quotation from Mic. iv. 1–3 (see the Analysis to ch. xv., and Notes on ch. ii. 2).

LORD hath spoken concerning Moab since that time.

14 But now the LORD hath spoken, saying, Within three years, as the *a* years of an hireling, and the glory of Moab shall be contemned, with all that great multitude ; and the remnant *shall be* very small *and* feeble.[1]

a ch.21.16.   1 or, *not many.*

---

14. *But now the* LORD *hath spoken.* This refers to the particular and specific prophecy of Isaiah that destruction should come upon them in three years. Instead of a *general* but *indefinite* prediction of calamity to the Moabites, such as had been uttered by the former prophets, or by Isaiah himself before, it was now specific and definite in regard to the *time* when it should be fulfilled. ¶ *Within three years.* We have no means of ascertaining the exact fulfilment of this prediction, nor do we certainly know by whom it was accomplished. ¶ *As the years of an hireling.* A man that is hired has a certain time specified during which he is to labour ; the years, the months, the days for which he is engaged are agreed on, nor will he suffer any addition to be made to it. So the prophet says that the very time is fixed. It shall not be varied. It will be adhered to by God—as the time is adhered to between a man who employs another and him who is hired. And it means, that *exactly at the time* which is here specified, the predicted destruction should come upon Moab. ¶ *The glory of Moab.* That in which it glories, or boasts—its wealth, its armies, its cities, towns, &c. ¶ *Shall be contemned.* Shall be esteemed of no value ; shall be destroyed. ¶ *And the remnant.* There shall be few cities, few men, and very little wealth that shall escape the desolation (comp. ch. x. 25 ; xxiv. 6). Jerome says that 'this prophecy was delivered after the death of Ahaz, and in the reign of Hezekiah, during whose reign the ten tribes were led by Sennacherib, king of the Assyrians, into captivity. And therefore after three years, the Assyrians came and destroyed Moab, and very few were left in the land who could inhabit the deserted cities, or cultivate the desolate fields.' But it is not certainly known to what particular time the prophecy refers.—In regard to the present state of Moab, and the complete fulfilment of the prophecies respecting it, the following works may be consulted :—Newton, *On the Prophecies;* Keith, *On the Prophecies;* Burckhardt's *Travels in Syria;* and Captains Irby and Mangles' *Travels.* In regard to the fulfilment of these predictions respecting the destruction of Moab, it may be sufficient to refer to the remarks which I have made on the particular places which are mentioned in these two chapters, and to the writers mentioned above. All travellers concur in the general desolation of that country which was once so thickly studded with towns, and that abounded so richly in flocks, and produced so luxuriantly the grape. It is now strewed with ruins. All the cities of Moab have disappeared. Their place is characterized in the map of Volney's *Travels,* by *the ruins of towns.* Burckhardt, who encountered many difficulties in so desolate and dangerous a land, thus records the brief history of a few of them : 'The ruins of Eleale, Heshbon, Meon, Medaba, Dibon, Arver, all situated on the north side of the Arnon, still subsist to illustrate the history of the Beni-Israel' (*Life and Travels,* prefixed to the *Travels in Nubia,* pp. 48, 49). ' And it might be added,' says Keith, ' that they still subsist to confirm the inspiration of the Jewish Scriptures, for the desolation of each of these cities was the theme of a distinct prediction' (*Prophecies,* p. 129). Within the boundaries of Moab, Burckhardt enumerates about *fifty* ruined cities, many of them extensive. In general they are a broken down and undistinguishable mass of ruins ; but, in some instances, there are remains of temples, sepulchral monuments, traces of hanging gardens, entire columns lying on the ground, and dilapidated walls made of stones of large dimensions (see *Travels in Syria,* pp. 311–456).

In view of these two chapters, constituting one prophecy, and the facts in regard to the present state of the country of Moab, we may observe that we

CHAPTER XVII.

ANALYSIS.

THE prophecy which comprises verses 1–11 of this chapter, professes, by its title, to be against Damascus only. But it relates to the kingdom of Samaria no less than to Damascus. The reason is, that the kingdoms of Israel and Damascus were confederated against the king-

dom of Judah. The design of the prophecy may have been to warn the kingdom of Israel of the approaching destruction of the city of Damascus, and, by this means, to keep them from forming an alliance with them against Judah. When it was delivered is unknown. Lowth supposes that it was immediately after the prophecies in the seventh and eighth chapters, in the reign of Ahaz, and this supposition

---

have here clear and unanswerable evidence of the genuineness and truth of the sacred records. That evidence is found in the *particularity* with which *places* are mentioned ; and in the fact that impostors would not *specify* places, any further than was unavoidable. Mistakes, we all know, are liable to be made by those who attempt to describe the *geography* of places which they have not seen. Yet here is a description of a land and its numerous towns, made nearly three thousand years ago, and in its *particulars* it is sustained by all the travellers in modern times. The ruins of the same towns are still seen ; their places, in general, can be designated ; and there is a moral certainty, therefore, that this prophecy was made by one who *knew* the locality of those places, and that, therefore, the prophecy is ancient and genuine. An impostor would never have attempted such a description as this ; nor could he have made it so accurate and true. In the language of Prof. Stuart (*Bib. Rep.*, vol. vii. pp. 108, 109), we may say, 'How obviously everything of this kind serves to give confirmation to the authority and credibility of the sacred records ! Do sceptics undertake to scoff at the Bible, and aver that it is the work of impostors who lived in later ages? Besides asking them what *object* impostors could have in forging a book of such high and lofty principles, we may ask—and ask with an assurance that need not fear the danger of being put to the blush—whether impostors of later ages could possibly have so managed, as to preserve all the *localities* in complete order which the Scriptures present? Rare impostors they must indeed have been—men possessed of more knowledge of antiquity than we can well imagine could ever be possessed by such as would condescend to

an imposition of such a character. In fact the thing appears to be morally impossible, if one considers it in the light of *antiquity*, when so little knowledge of a geographical kind was in existence, and when mistakes respecting countries and places with which one was not personally familiar, were almost, if not altogether, unavoidable.

'How happens it, now, that the authors of the Old Testament Scriptures should have possessed such a wonderful tact in geography, as it would seem they did, unless they lived at the time and in the countries of which they have spoken? This happens not elsewhere. It is but yesterday since one of the first scientific writers on geology in Great Britain, published to the world the declaration that our Mississippi and Missouri rivers *belong to the tropics*. Respectable writers, even in Germany, the land of classical attainments, have sometimes placed Cœlo-Syria on the east of the Anti-Libanus ridge, or even seemed to transfer Damascus over the mountains, and place it between the two Lebanon ridges in the valley.' No such mistakes occur in the sacred writers. They write as men who were familiar with the geography of places named ; they mention places with the utmost familiarity ; and, after a lapse of three thousand years, every successive traveller who visits Moab, Idumea, or Palestine, does something to confirm the accuracy of Isaiah. Towns, bearing the same name, or the ruins of towns, are located in the same relative position in which he said they were ; and the ruins of once splendid cities, broken columns, dilapidated walls, trodden down vineyards, and half-demolished temples, proclaim to the world that those cities are what he said they would be, and that he was under the inspiration of God.

is not improbable, though it is not quite certain. He also supposes that it was fulfilled when Damascus was taken captive by Tiglath-pileser, and its inhabitants carried to Kir (2 Kings xvi. 9), and when he overran, also, a great part of the kingdom of Israel, and carried its inhabitants captive to Assyria.

In regard to the *time* when it was uttered, there can be little doubt that it was when the alliance existed between Damascus and the kingdom of Ephraim, or Samaria, for on no other supposition can it be accounted for, that the two kingdoms were united in the prophecy (see ver. 3). The scope or design of the prophecy is indicated in the close (ver. 14): 'This is the portion of them that spoil us, and the lot of them that rob us;' and one design, at least, was to give an assurance to the kingdom of Judah, that the alliance between Damascus and Samaria was not to be dreaded, but that the kingdom of Judah would be safe. No alliance formed against them would be successful; no purpose to destroy them should be an object of dread.

The prophecy may be regarded as consisting of three parts. I. The prediction of the Divine judgment against Damascus (1, 2). II. The prediction respecting Ephraim, the ally of Damascus, and its fulfilment (3–11). III. A prediction respecting the Assyrians, and the calamities that should come upon them as a nation (12–14).

The kingdom of Syria, or Damascus, was overthrown in the fourth year of the reign of Ahaz. It is clear, therefore, that the prophecy was delivered before that time. And if so, its proper place, in the collection of the prophecies of Isaiah, would have been immediately after the ninth chapter. The reason why it is placed here, Lightfoot supposes to be, that in the seventh and eighth chapters the special design was to denounce judgment on the two kingdoms of Damascus and Ephraim; but that the design here was to connect the prediction of those judgments with the surrounding kingdoms, and to show how they would be affected by it. The prophecy is, therefore, placed amidst those which relate to foreign nations; or to kingdoms out of the land of Canaan.

Damascus was a celebrated city of Syria, and was long the capital of the kingdom of Damascus. It was a city in the time of Abraham, for the steward in his house, Eliezer, was said to be of Damascus (Gen. xv. 2). It is situated in a very fertile plain at the foot of mount Anti-Libanus, and is surrounded by hills. It is watered by a river which the ancients called *Chrysorrhoas,* as if it flowed with gold. This

river was divided into several canals, which were conducted to various parts of the city. It rose in the mountains of Anti-Libanus, and it is probable that the branches of that river were anciently called Abana and Pharpar (2 Kings v. 12). This river is now called the Bar-raday, and the peculiar beauty and fertility of Damascus is owing wholly to it. It rises in the adjacent mountains of Anti-Libanus, and, by numerous natural and artificial channels, is made to spread over the plain on which the city stands. It waters the whole extent of the gardens—an extent of country about nine miles in diameter, in the midst of which the city is situated—and when this is done, the water that is left flows off to the south-east through the plain, where, amid the arid sands, it is soon absorbed or evaporated, and the river disappears. The gardens are planted with all kinds of trees; mostly such as produce fruit, among which the apricot holds the ascendancy. Pomegranate, orange, lemon, and fig trees abound, and rising above these are other trees of huge proportions, intermingled with the poplar and sometimes the willow. Into every garden of the city water is carried, and this river, thus divided, gives to Damascus the beauty for which it has been so celebrated. The Persian geographers say, that the plain of Damascus is one of the four paradises of the East, and it is now said that there is not in all Syria a more delightful place.

From the time of Abraham until David, the Scripture says nothing of Damascus. In his time it was subdued, and brought under his authority. Towards the end of the reign of Solomon, the authority of the Jews was cast off by Rezin, and Damascus became again independent. Jeroboam, king of Israel, again conquered Damascus, and brought Syria into subjection (2 Kings xiv. 25); but after his death the Syrians again established their independence. Rezin became king of Damascus, and entered into an alliance with Pekah, king of Israel, and, unitedly, they invaded Judah, and made great havoc in its territories (see Notes on ch. vii.; comp. 2 Kings xvi. 5). Tiglath-pileser, however, king of Assyria, came to the assistance of the king of Judah and took Damascus, and destroyed it, and killed Rezin, and carried the Syrians into captivity beyond the Euphrates. To this event, probably, Isaiah refers in the prophecy before us. He, however, did not foretell its utter and *perpetual* ruin as he did that of Babylon. Damascus again recovered from its calamities. Holofernes again took it (Judith ii. 27). It is spoken of as flourishing in the time of Ezekiel (xxvii. 2). The Romans took it in the time, and by the agency, of Pompey the Great, about sixty years before Christ. It afterwards fell into the hands of the Arabians. It was taken by the Ottomans A.D. 1517; and has since been in the possession of the Turks. At present, it has a population of about 100,000. The name by which it is now known is *El-Sham.* It is a part of the pashalic of Damascus, which extends to the southern extremity of the Dead Sea. Mehemet Ali of Egypt obtained possession of it without resistance, in June 1832, and since that time it has been under the jurisdiction of his son Ibrahim. It is regarded by Mussulmans as a place of peculiar sanctity. According to them, Mecca has the first place, Jerusalem the next, and Damascus the third.

The prophecy respecting Damascus occupies verses 1–11 of the chapter. The general sense is, that Damascus and its allies would be greatly enfeebled and almost destroyed. Its fulfilment is to be referred to the invasion of Damascus by Tiglath-pileser and the Assyrians. The remainder of the chapter (12–14) is a distinct prophecy (see Notes on ver. 12).

THE ^a burden of Damascus. Behold, ^b Damascus is taken away from *being* a city, and it shall be a ruinous heap.

2 The cities of Aroer *are* forsaken ; they shall be for flocks which shall lie down, and none ^c shall make *them* afraid.

3 The fortress also shall cease from Ephraim, and the kingdom from Damascus, and the remnant of Syria : they shall be as the glory of the children of Israel, saith the LORD of hosts.

a Jer.49.23,&c.; Amos 1.3-5; Zec.9.1, fulfilled.
b 2 Ki.16.9.   c Jer.7.33.

CHAPTER XVII.

1. *The burden of Damascus.* The oracle indicating calamity or destruction to Damascus (see Note on ch. xiii. 1). ¶ *Damascus is taken away.* That is, it shall be destroyed. It was represented to the prophet in vision as destroyed (see Note on ch. i. 1). ¶ *And it shall be a ruinous heap* (see ch. xxxv. 2.) This took place under the kings of Assyria, and particularly under Tiglath-pileser. This was in the fourth year of Ahaz (2 Kings xvi. 9).

2. *The cities of Aroer.* By *Aroer* here seems to be meant a tract or region of country pertaining to Damascus, in which were situated several cities. Grotius supposes that it was a tract of country in Syria which is called by Ptolemy *Aueira* — Αὔιρα Vitringa supposes that one part of Damascus is meant by this, as Damascus was divided by the river in the same manner that Babylon was. There were several cities of the name of *Aroer.* One was on the river Arnon in the land of Moab (Deut. ii. 36 ; iii. 12 ; Josh. xii. 3). Burckhardt found this city under the name of Araayr. There was another city of this name further north, over against Rabbath-Ammon (Josh. xiii. 25). There was a third city of this name in the tribe of Judah (1 Sam. xxx. 28). Of the city of Araayr which Burckhardt visited, nothing is now remarkable but its entire desolation. Gesenius supposes (*Comm. in loc.*) that the phrase ' the cities of Aroer ' means the cities round about Aroer, and that were connected with it, similar to the phrase ' daughters of a city.' This city he supposes was near the river Arnon, within the limits of Moab, and that the prediction here was fulfilled by Tiglath-pileser, when he carried away the inhabitants of Galilee, Gilead, and other places mentioned in 2 Kings xv. 29. There can be no doubt that it was under the jurisdiction of Damascus. ¶ Are *forsaken.* Are desolate, and the inhabitants have fled. ¶ *They shall be for flocks,* &c. (See Note on ch. v. 17.)

3. *The fortress.* The strong place of defence ; the fortified place. ¶ *Shall cease.* Shall come to an end ; shall cease to be, for so the word עָבַר (*shâbath*) is often used, (Gen. viii. 22 ; Isa. xxiv. 8 ; Lam. v. 15). ¶ *From Ephraim.* The name given to the kingdom of Israel, or to the ten tribes, because Ephraim was the largest of the ten, and was a leading tribe in their councils (see Note on ch. vii. 2). Ephraim, or the kingdom of Samaria, is here mentioned in connection with Damascus or Syria, because they were confederated together, and would be involved in the same overthrow. ¶ *And the remnant of Syria.* That which is left of the kingdom of Syria after the capital Damascus shall be destroyed. ¶ *They shall be as the glory of the children of Israel.* That

4 And in that day it shall come to pass, *that* the glory of Jacob shall be made thin, and ^a the fatness of his flesh shall wax lean.

5 And ^b it shall be as when the harvest-man gathereth the corn,

a ch.10.16.　　b Jer.51.33.

and reapeth the ears with his arm ; and it shall be as he that gathereth ears in the valley of Rephaim.

6 Yet gleaning-grapes shall be left in it, as the shaking of an olive-tree, two *or* three berries in the top of the uppermost bough, four *or*

is, as the defences, or the strongly fortified towns and fastnesses of the kingdom of Israel shall pass away or be destroyed, so shall it be with the kingdom of Damascus. As they are allied with each other, they shall fare alike. The Chaldee reads this, ' And the dominion shall cease from Ephraim, and the kingdom from Damascus.'

4. *The glory of Jacob.* Jacob is here used to denote the kingdom of Israel, or Samaria. The word ' glory ' here denotes dignity, power ; that on which they relied, and of which they boasted. ¶ *Shall be made thin.* Shall be diminished, as a body wastes away by disease, and becomes feeble. The prophet sets forth the calamities of Ephraim by two figures ; the first is that of a *body* that becomes emaciated by sickness, the other that of the harvest when all the fruits are gathered except a few in the upper branches (ver. 5, 6). ¶ *And the fatness of his flesh shall wax lean.* He shall become feeble, as a man does by wasting sickness. Chaldee, ' The riches of his glory shall be removed.'

5. *And it shall be, &c.* This is the other figure by which the prophet sets forth the calamities that were coming upon Ephraim—an image designed to denote the fact that the inhabitants and wealth of the land would be collected and removed, as the husbandman gathers his harvest, and leaves only that which is inaccessible in the upper boughs of the tree, or the gleanings in the field. ¶ *As when the harvest-man gathereth the corn.* The wheat, the barley, &c.; for so the word *corn*—now applied by us almost exclusively to maize — means in the Scriptures. The sense in this passage is plain. As the farmer cuts down and collects his grain and removes it from the harvest field, so the enemies of Ephraim would come and remove the people and their wealth to a distant land. This received a complete fulfil-

ment when the ten tribes were removed by the Assyrians to a distant land. This was done by Tiglath-pileser (2 Kings xv. 29), and by Shalmaneser (2 Kings xvii. 6). ¶ *And reapeth the ears with his arm.* As he collects the standing grain with one arm so that he can cut it with the sickle in the other hand The word rendered ' reapeth ' (קָצִיר) means here *to collect together* as a reaper does the standing grain in his arm. The word rendered 'ears' (שִׁבֳּלִים *shibbolim*), means here rather the spires or stalks of standing grain. ¶ *In the valley of Rephaim.* The valley of Rephaim is mentioned in 2 Sam. v. 18, 22 ; xxiii. 13 ; 1 Chron. xi. 15 ; xiv. 9. The name means ' the Giants ;' but why it was given to it is now unknown. In passing from Bethlehem to Jerusalem, it lies on the left, and descends gradually to the south-west, until it contracts in that direction into a deeper and narrower valley, called wady el - Werd, which unites further on with wady Ahmed, and finds its way to the Mediterranean. The plain extends nearly to Jerusalem, and is terminated by a slight rocky ridge forming the brow of the valley of Hinnom (see Josephus, *Ant.* vii. 4. 1 ; viii. 12. 4 ; also Robinson's *Bib. Researches,* vol. i. pp. 323, 324). It seem to have been distinguished for its fertility, and is here used to denote a fertile region in general.

6. *Yet gleaning-grapes, &c.* They shall not all be removed, or destroyed. A *few* shall be left, as a man who is gathering grapes or olives will leave a few that are inaccessible on the topmost boughs, or the furthest branches. Those would be usually the poorest, and so it may be implied that those left in Israel would be among the poorer inhabitants of the land. ¶ *Two* or *three.* A very few—such as would be left in gathering grapes, or in endeavouring to shake olives from a tree. ¶ *Four* or *five.* A

five in the outmost fruitful branches thereof, saith the Lord God of Israel.

7 At that day shall a man [a]look to his Maker, and his eyes shall have respect to the Holy One of Israel.

8 And he shall not look to the altars, the work of his hands, neither shall respect *that* which his fingers have made, either the groves or the [1]images.

9 In that day shall his strong cities be as a forsaken bough, and an uppermost branch, which they

a Mic.7.7.   1 or, *sun images*, Jer.17.13.

very few that would remain on the furthest branches, and that could not be shaken off or reached.

7. *At that day shall a man look to his Maker.* Instead of confiding in their strongly fortified places and armies, they shall look for aid and protection to the God that made them, and who alone can help them. National afflictions and judgments often have the effect to turn the eyes of even a wicked and rebellious people to God. They feel their danger; they are convinced of their guilt; they see that no one but God can protect them; and for a time they are willing, even by humiliation and fasting, to seek the Divine protection. ¶ *His eyes shall have respect,* &c. He shall look up to, or regard. ¶ *The Holy One of Israel.* The God of Israel; the true God. As the Syrians were allied with the kingdom of Samaria or Ephraim, they were, of course, acquainted with the true God, and in some sense acknowledged him. In these times of impending calamity, they would be led to seek him, and implore his aid and protection. There is no reason to believe, however, that they would turn permanently to him, or become his true worshippers.

8. *And he shall not look to the altars.* That is, the altars of the gods which the Syrians worshipped, and the altars of the false gods which had been erected in the land of Israel or Samaria by its wicked kings, and particularly by Ahaz. Ahaz fancied an altar which he saw at Damascus when on a visit to Tiglath-pileser, and ordered Urijah the priest to construct one like it in Samaria, on which he subsequently offered sacrifice (2 Kings xvi. 10–13). It is well known, also, that the kings of Israel and Judah often reared altars to false gods in the high places and the groves of the land (see 2 Kings xxi. 3, 4, 5). The Ephraimites were particularly guilty in this respect

(Hos. viii. 11): ' Because Ephraim hath made many altars to sin, altars shall be unto him to sin.' ¶ *Which his fingers have made.* Perhaps indicating that the idols which they worshipped had been constructed with special art and skill (see ch. ii. 8). ¶ *Either the groves.* The altars of idols were usually erected in groves, and idols were worshipped there before temples were raised (see Ex. xxxiv. 13; Deut. vii. 5; xii. 3; Judg. iii. 7; 1 Kings xiv. 23; xviii. 19; 2 Chron. xxxiii. 3; comp. Notes on ch. i. 29). ¶ *Or the images.* Marg. ' Sun images' (הַחַמָּנִים *hhămmânîm*). This word is used to denote idols in general in Lev. xxvi. 30; 2 Chron. xxiv. 4. But it is supposed to denote properly images erected to the sun, and to be derived from חַמָּה (*hhămma*), *the sun.* Thus the word is used in Job xxx. 28; Isa. xxiv. 23; xxx. 26; Cant. vi. 10. The word, according to Gesenius, is of Persian origin (*Comm. in loc.*) The sun was undoubtedly worshipped by the ancient idolaters, and altars or images would be erected to it (see Notes on Job xxxi. 26).

9. *His strong cities.* The cities of the united kingdoms of Damascus and Samaria. ¶ *Be as a forsaken bough.* There has been much difficulty in the interpretation of this passage. Lowth says, ' No one has ever been able to make any tolerable sense of these words;' and proposes himself the translation,

In that day shall his strongly fenced cities become

Like the desertion of the Hivites and the Amorites;

following in this the translation of the LXX., but doing violence to the Hebrew text. Rosenmüller translates it, ' As the remnant of a grove when the thicket is cut down, and when few trees are left.' The word rendered 'bough' (חֹרֶשׁ *hhōrĕsh*) means, properly, a thicket, or thick foliage, a wood that is entangled

left because of the children of Israel: and there shall be desolation.

10 Because ^a thou hast forgotten the God of thy salvation, and hast not been mindful of the Rock of thy strength; therefore shalt thou

<small>a Jer.17.13.</small>

plant pleasant plants, and shalt set it with ^b strange slips:

11 In the day shalt thou make thy plant to grow, and in the morning shalt thou make thy seed to flourish; *but* the harvest *shall be*

<small>b Jer.5.21.</small>

---

or intricate (1 Sam. xxiii. 15, 16, 18; 2 Chron. xxvii. 4); and probably this is the idea here. The phrase may be rendered, 'as the *leavings* or *residue* of a grove, copse, or entangled wood;' and the idea is, that as a *few* trees might be left when the axeman cuts down the grove, so a few inferior and smaller towns should be left in the desolation that would come upon Damascus. ¶*And an uppermost branch* (ver. 6). As a few berries are left in the topmost branch of the olive, or the vine, so shall a few cities or people be left in the general desolation. ¶ *Which they left.* Which *are* left, or which the invaders would leave. ¶ *Because of the children of Israel.* Literally, 'from the face,' *i.e.*, before the children of Israel. Lowth supposes that it refers to the Amorites, who left their land before the Israelites, or gave up their land for them. Vitringa renders it, ' On account of the children of Israel;' and supposes that it means that a few cities were spared by the purpose of God in the invasion by Tiglath-pileser, to be a residence of the Israelites that should remain; or that, for some reason which is not known, the Assyrians chose to spare a few towns, and not wholly to destroy the country. The *general* idea is plain, that a few towns would be left, and that it would be *before* the children of Israel, or in their presence, or in order that they might continue to dwell in them. Jerome interprets the whole as referring to the time when the land of Judea was forsaken on the invasion of the Romans. ¶ *And there shall be desolation.* The land shall be desolated, except the few cities and towns that shall be left, like the gleaning of the olive tree.

10. *Because thou,* &c. Because the kingdom of Israel or Samaria had done it. ¶ *The God of thy salvation.* The God in whom alone was salvation; or who alone could protect thee (comp. Mic. vii. 7· Hos. ii. 15). ¶ *The rock of*

thy strength. God. A rock of strength is a strongly fortified place; or a rock which an enemy could not successfully assail. High rocks were selected as a place of refuge from an invading foe (see Notes on ch. i. 10, 21). In allusion to this, God is often called *a Rock,* and a strong tower (Deut. xxxii. 4, 15, 18, 30, 31, 37; 1 Sam. ii. 2; 2 Sam. xxii. 2, 3, 32; Ps. xviii. 31, 46; xix. 14; xxviii. 1; xxx. 1, 2). ¶ *Shalt thou plant pleasant plants.* Plants that are fitted to produce pleasure or delight; that is, you shall cultivate your fields, and set them out with choice vines and plants in hope of a future harvest, but you shall be disappointed. ¶ *And shall set it with strange slips.* The word 'slips' means the *cuttings* of the vine that are set in the ground to grow; or the shoot or sucker that is taken off and *set out,* or put in the earth to take root and grow, as is often done by farmers and gardeners. The word 'strange' here means *foreign,* those which are procured from a distance, and which are therefore esteemed valuable; plants selected with care. This does not mean, as Lowth supposes, strange and idolatrous worship, and the vicious practices connected with it; but it means that, though they should be at great pains and expense in cultivating their land, yet the enemy would come in and make it desolate.

11. *In the day,* &c. Thou shalt cultivate it assiduously and constantly. Thou shalt be at special pains that it may be watered and pruned, in order that it may produce abundantly. ¶ *And in the morning.* With early care and attention—denoting the pains that would be bestowed on the young plant. ¶ *The harvest* shall be *a heap.* The margin reads this, 'the harvest shall be removed in the day of inheritance, rendering it as if the word בֵּד (*nēdh*) usually meaning a heap, were derived from נוד (*nūdh*), to shake, move, wan-

a¹ heap in the day of grief and of desperate sorrow.

12 Wo to the ² multitude of many people, *which* make a noise like the noise of the seas ; and to the rushing of nations, *that* make

1 or, *removed in the day of inheritance, and there shall be deadly sorrow.*

a rushing like the rushing of mighty ³ waters !

13 The nations shall rush like the rushing of many waters: but God *a* shall rebuke them, and they shall flee far off, and shall be chased as the chaff of the mountains be-

2 or, *noise.*   3 or, *many.*   a Ps.9.5.

der; or, as if it were to be removed. Probably the translation in the text is correct; and the sense is, 'When from the plant which was so beautiful and valuable, and which you cherished with so much care, you expected to obtain a rich harvest, you had only sorrow and inexpressible disappointment.' The figure used here is supposed by Rosenmüller to be that of hendiadys (*ἐν διὰ δυοῖν*), by which the phrases 'shall be an heap,' and 'desperate sorrow,' are to be taken together, meaning 'the heap of the harvest shall be inexpressible sorrow.' ¶ *In the day of grief.* The word rendered 'grief' here (נַחֲלָה) means, properly, *inheritance, heirship, possession,* and should have been so rendered here. It means that in the day when they *hoped* to possess the result of their planting, or in the time of the usual harvest, they would obtain only grief and disappointment. ¶ *And desperate sorrow.* The word rendered 'desperate' (אָנוּשׁ, *ánush*), denotes that which is *weak, mortal, incurable* (Job xxxiv. 6; Jer. xvii. 16; xxx. 12, 15). The sense here is, that there would be grievous disappointment, and that there would be no remedy for it; and the idea of the whole is, that calamities were coming upon the nation which would blast all their hopes, and destroy all their prospects. The prophecy was fulfilled in the invasion by Tiglath-pileser, and the army of the Assyrians.

The twelfth verse commences a new prophecy, which has no connection with that which precedes it; and which in itself gives no certain indication of the time when it was uttered, or of the people to which it relates. It is a broken and detached piece, and is evidently the description of some army rushing to conquest, and confident of success, but which was to be overtaken with sudden calamity. The entire

description is so applicable to the invasion of the land of Judah by the army of Sennacherib, and his overthrow by the angel of JEHOVAH, that by the common consent of interpreters it has been regarded as referring to it (see Notes on ch. x). But when it was spoken, or why it was placed here, is unknown. It may be added that many commentators, and, among the rest, Gesenius, have supposed that the following chapter is a part of this prophecy. The general sense of the prophecy is, that numerous hostile nations would overrun Palestine, but that JEHOVAH would destroy them all.

12. *Wo to the multitude,* &c. The word 'wo' (הוֹי *hō*) may be either an interjection simply directing the attention to them, or it may be a word indicating approaching calamity and judgment (see Note on ch. v. 6). Gesenius supposes that it is rather the language of compassion, on account of the evil which they threatened to bring upon the people of God, like 1 Kings xiii. 30, 'Ah! wo, my brother!' ¶ *The multitude of many people.* Or, the tumult of many nations—a description of the noise attending an invading army made up of many nations mingled together, such as was that of Sennacherib. ¶ *Which make a noise,* &c. This is a beautiful description of a vast army, and of the shouting, the tumult, the din, which attends its march. The same comparison occurs in Jer. vi. 23; Psal. lxv. 7 (see Ezek. xliii. 2; Rev. i. 15; xiv. 2; xix. 6). ¶ *And to the rushing of nations.* The rushing of mighty armies to conquest.

13. God *shall rebuke them.* The word 'God' is not here in the original, but is evidently to be supplied. The word 'rebuke' means that he would disarrange their plans, prevent their success, and defeat their purposes. It

fore the wind, and like ¹ a rolling thing before the whirlwind.

14 And, behold, at evening-tide trouble; *and* before the morning he *is* not. This *is* the portion of them *ª* that spoil us, and the lot of them that rob us.

CHAPTER XVIII.

ANALYSIS.

'THE eighteenth chapter of Isaiah,' says bishop Horsley, 'is one of the most obscure passages of the ancient prophets. It has been considered as such by the whole succession of interpreters from Jerome to Bishop Lowth.' 'The object of it,' says Bishop Lowth, 'the end and design of it; the people to whom it is addressed; the history to which it belongs; the person who sends the messengers; and the nation to whom they are sent, are all obscure and doubtful. Much of the obscurity lies in the highly figurative cast of the language, and in the ambiguity of some of the principal words, arising from the great variety of the senses often comprehended under the primary meaning of a single root.'

Lowth supposes that Egypt is the country referred to; that the prophecy was delivered before the return of Sennacherib's expedition to Egypt; and that it was designed to give to the Jews, and perhaps likewise to the Egyptians, an intimation of the destruction of their great

1 or, *thistle-down.*   *a* Jer.2 3.

and powerful enemy. Taylor, the editor of Calmet's *Dictionary,* supposes that it relates to a people lying in southern, or Upper Egypt, or the country above the cataracts of the Nile, *i.e.,* Nubia; and that the people to whom the message is sent are those who were situated north on the river Nile, where the various streams which go to form the Nile become a single river; and that the nation represented as 'scattered and peeled,' or as he renders it, 'a people contracted and deprived,' *i.e.,* in their persons, refers to the Pigmies, as they are described by Homer, Strabo, and others (see this view drawn out in the *Fragments* appended to Calmet's *Dict.* No. cccxxii.) Rosenmüller says of this prophecy, that 'it is involved in so many, and so great difficulties, on account of unusual expressions and figurative sentences, and the history of those times, so little known to us, that it is impossible to explain and unfold it. We seem to be reading mere *enigmas,* in explaining which, although many learned interpreters have taken great pains, yet scarcely two can be found who agree.' Gesenius connects it with the closing verse of the previous chapter; and so does also Vitringa. Gesenius supposes that it refers to a nation in alliance with Ethiopia in alliance with Israel. To this, says he, and to all the nations of the earth, the prophet addresses himself, in order to draw their attention to the sudden overthrow which God would bring upon the enemy, after he has quietly looked upon their violence for a long time. According to this view, the prophecy belongs to the period immediately pre-

shows the great power of God, that he can thus by a *rebuke*—a word—arrest mighty nations, and discomfit them when they are tumultuously hastening onward in the confidence of victory. This discomfiture refers, doubtless, to the overthrow of Sennacherib and his army by the pestilence (2 Kings xix. 35; see Notes on ch. xxxvii. 36). ¶ *And they shall flee far off.* The whole army of Sennacherib was not destroyed, but a part with himself returned to Assyria (2 Kings xix. 36). ¶ *And shall be chased as the chaff,* &c. Denoting the case with which God would do it, and the certain and entire discomfiture of the army. The figure is one that is very striking in describing an army that is routed, and that flies in disorder (comp. Job xxi. 18; Ps. i. 4; xxxv. 5; Isa. xxix. 5; Hos. xiii. 3). ¶ *And like a rolling thing.* Marg. 'Thistle-down.' It means, literally, anything that *rolls* (בַּלְגַּל *găl-*

găl, from בָּלַל *gălăl,* to roll). It is applied to chaff, stubble, or anything that is driven about by a whirlwind (Psal. lxxxiii. 14).

14. *At evening-tide trouble.* In the time of evening—that is, in the night. ¶ *Before the morning he is not.* That is, he is destroyed. This is strikingly descriptive of the destruction of the army of Sennacherib on that fatal night when the angel of the Lord slew one hundred and eighty-five thousand men (see Note on ch. xxxvii. 36). ¶ *This is the portion of them that spoil us.* Of those who would plunder us. This is a *general* declaration in regard to the enemies of the Jewish people. This is the lot, the end, the destiny of all who attempt to destroy them. That is, the people of God shall be safe whoever rises up against them; and whatever may be the number, or the power of their foes, they shall be overthrown.

ceding the 14th year of Hezekiah, when the Assyrian armies had already overrun, or were about to overrun Palestine on their way to Egypt, and the prophet confidently predicts their destruction. At this time, he remarks, Tirhakah, king of Ethiopia, with a part of Egypt, had armed himself against the Assyrians; for which purpose he had probably entered into an alliance with the Hebrews. To this friend and ally of Israel, the prophet gives the assurance that God was about to destroy completely the common enemy, the Assyrian.—By some, the land here referred to has been supposed to be Egypt; by others, Ethiopia in Africa; by others, Judea; by others, the Roman empire; and others have supposed that it refers to the destruction of Gog and Magog in the times of the Messiah. Vitringa supposes that the prophecy must be referred either to the Egyptians or the Assyrians; and as there is no account, he says, of any calamity coming upon the Egyptians like that which is described in ver. 4–6, and as that description is applicable to the destruction of the Assyrians under Sennacherib, he regards it as referring to him. Calvin says that many have supposed that the Troglodytes of Upper Egypt are meant here, but that this is improbable, as they were not known to have formed any alliances with other nations. He supposes that some nation is referred to in the vicinity of Egypt and Ethiopia, but what people he does not even conjecture. Amidst this diversity of opinion, it may seem rash to hazard a

conjecture in regard to the situation of the nation who *sent* the messengers, and the nation to whom they were sent; and it is obviously improper to hazard such a conjecture without a careful examination of the phrases and words which occur in the prophecy. When that is done—when the characteristics of the nation have been fully determined, then, perhaps, we may be able to arrive at some satisfactory conclusion in regard to this very difficult portion of the Bible. The prophecy consists of the following parts:—1. The prophet addresses him self to the nation here described as a 'land shadowing with wings,' and as sending ambassadors, in a manner designed to call their attention to the great events soon to occur (1, 2). 2. He addresses all nations, calling upon them also to attend to the same subject (3). 3. He says that God had revealed to him that destruction should come upon the enemies here referred to, and that the immense host should be left to the beasts of the earth, and to the fowls of the mountains (4–6). 4. The consequence, he says, of such events would be, that a present would be brought to Jehovah from the distant nation 'scattered and peeled,' and whose land the rivers had spoiled (7).

W O to the land shadowing with wings, which *is* beyond the rivers *a* of Ethiopia:

a ch.20.3–5; Eze.30.4–9; Zep.2.12.

CHAPTER XVIII.

1. *Woe to the land* (הוֹי). This word, as has been already remarked (Note on ch. xvii. 12), may be a mere interjection or salutation, and would be appropriately rendered by ' Ho !' Or it may be a word denouncing judgment, or wrath, as it is often used in this prophecy (Note on ch. v. 8). ¶ *Shadowing with wings* (צִלְצַל כְּנָפָיִם). This is one of the most difficult expressions in the whole chapter; and one to which as yet, probably, no satisfactory meaning has been applied. The LXX. render it, Οὐαὶ γῆς πλοίων πτέρυγες —' Ah! wings of the land of ships.' The Chaldee, ' Woe to the land in which they come in ships from a distant country, and whose sails are spread out as an eagle which flies upon its wings.' Grotius renders it, ' The land whose extreme parts are shaded by mountains.' The word rendered ' shadowed' (צִלְצַל *tzîl-tzăl*), occurs only in this place, and in

Job xli. 7, where it is translated ' fish-spears '—but as we know nothing of the *form* of those spears, that place throws no light on the meaning of the word here. The word is derived, evidently, from צָלַל (*tzâlăl*), which has three significations :—(1.) *To be shady, dark, obscure;* and hence its derivatives are applied to anything that *makes* a shade or shadow—particularly *shady trees* (Job xl. 21, 22); the shades of night (Cant. ii. 17; iv. 6); or anything that produces obscurity, or darkness, as a tree, a rock, a wing, &c. (2.) It means *to tingle,* spoken of the ears (1 Sam. iii. 11; 2 Kings xxi. 13); *to quiver*, spoken of the lips (Hab. iii. 16); and hence its derivatives are applied to anything that makes a sound by *tinkling*—an instrument of music; a cymbal made of two pieces of metal that are struck together (2 Sam. vi. 5; 1 Chron. xv. 16; xvi. 42; xxv. 6; 2 Chron. v. 12; Neh. xii. 27; Ps. cl. 5.) (3.) It means *to sink*

(Ex. xv. 10).—From the sense of making a *shade*, a derivative of the verb צָלַל (*tzĕlâtzál*)—the same as used here except the points—is applied to locusts, because they appear in such swarms as to obscure the rays of the sun, and produce an extended shade, or shadow, over a land as a cloud does; or because they make a rustling with their wings. The word here used, therefore, may mean either *shaded*, or *rustling*, or *rattling*, in the manner of a cymbal or other tinkling instrument. It may be added, that the word *may* mean a *double shade*, being a doubling of the word צֵל (*tzēl*), a *shade*, or *shadow*, and it has been supposed by some to apply to Ethiopia as lying between the tropics, having a *double shadow*; that is, so that the shadow of objects is cast one half of the year on the north side, and the other half on the south. The word 'wings' is applied in the Scriptures to the following things, viz.—(1.) The wing of a fowl. This is the literal, and common signification. (2.) The skirts, borders, or lower parts of a garment, from the resemblance to wings (Num. xv. 38; 1 Sam. xxiv. 5, 11; Zech. viii. 13). Also a bed-covering (Deut. xxxiii. 1). (3.) The extremities or borders of a country, or of the world (Job xxxvii. 3; Isa. xxiv. 16; Ezek. xvii. 3, 7). (4.) The *wing* or extremity of an army, as we use the word *wing* (Isa. viii. 8; Jer. xlviii. 40; Dan. ix. 27). (5.) The expanding rays of the morning, because the light *expands* or *spreads out* like wings (Ps. cxxxix. 9; Mal. iv. 2). (6.) The *wind*—resembling wings in rapid motion (Ps. xviii. 10, 21; civ. 3; Hos. iv. 19). (7.) The battlement or pinnacle of the temple—or perhaps the porches extended on each side of the temple like wings (Dan. ix. 27; comp. Matt. iv. 5). (8.) *Protection*—as wings are a protection to young birds in their nest (see Ps. xviii. 8; xxxvi. 7; lxi. 4; xci. 4; Matt. xxiii. 37). It has been proposed by some to apply this description to *ships*, or the sails of vessels, as if a land was designated which was covered with *sails*, or the *wings* of vessels. So the LXX., and the Chaldee. But there is no instance in which the word *wings* is so applied in the Scriptures.

The expression here used *may*, therefore, be applied to many things; and it is not easy to determine its signification. The *general* idea is, that of *something* that abounds in the land that is stretched out or expanded; that, as it were, *covers* it, and so abounds as to make a shade or shadow everywhere. And it may be applied—(1.) to a nation that abounds with birds or fowls, so that they might be said to shade the land; (2.) to a nation abounding with locusts, shading the land or making a rustling noise; or (3.) to a nation furnishing protection, or stretching out its wings, as it were, for the defence of a feeble people. So Vitringa interprets this place, and supposes that it refers to Egypt, as being the nation where the Hebrews sought protection. Or (4.) to a country that is shaded with trees, mountains, or hills. So Grotius supposes it means here, and thinks that it refers to Ethiopia, as being bounded by high hills or mountains. (5.) It *may* mean a people distinguished for navigation—abounding in *sails* of vessels—as if they were everywhere spread out like wings. So the LXX. and the Chaldee understand this; and the interpretation has some plausibility, from the fact that light vessels are immediately mentioned. (6.) The editor of Calmet's *Dictionary* supposes that it refers to the *winged Cnephim* which are sculptured over the temple gates in Upper Egypt. They are emblematic representatives of the god *Cneph*, to which the temples are dedicated, and abound in Upper Egypt. The symbol of the *wings* is supposed to denote the *protection* which the god extended over the land. (7.) Gesenius (*Com. on Isaiah*) renders it, 'Land rustling with wings,' and supposes that the word rendered 'shadowing,' denotes the *rustling* sound that is made by the clangour of weapons of war. Amidst this variety of interpretation, it is, perhaps, not possible to determine the meaning of the phrase. It has no parallel expression to illustrate it; and its meaning must be left to conjecture. Almost any one of the above significations will suit the connection; and it is not very material which is chosen. The one that, perhaps, best suits the connection, is that of the LXX.

2 That sendeth ambassadors by
the sea, even in vessels of bulrushes
upon the waters, *saying*, Go, ye
swift messengers, to a nation ¹ scattered and peeled, to a people terri-

1 or, *outspread and polished.*

ble from their beginning hitherto:
a nation ²meted out and trodden
down, whose land the rivers ³have
spoiled!

2 *of line line, and treading under foot, or, that meteth
out and treadeth down.*   3 or, *despise.*

---

and the Chaldee, which refers it to the
multitude of ships that expand their
sails, and appear to fill all the waters
of the land with wings. ¶ *Which* is
beyond (מֵעֵבֶר). This does not, of necessity, mean *beyond*, though that is its
usual signification. It properly means
*from the passing, the passages, the
crossing over*, of a river ; and may be
rendered what is on the other side; or
over against. It sometimes means on
this side, as if used by one living on the
other side (Deut. iv. 49 ; Josh. xiii. 27 ;
1 Kings iv. 24) ; in which places it has
not the sense of *beyond*, but means
either on this side, or lying alongside.
The sense here is, probably, that this
country was situated *not far* from the
rivers of Cush, *probably* beyond them,
but still it is implied that they were
not *far* beyond them, but were rather
at their passings over, or crossing-
places; that is, near them. ¶ *The
rivers of Ethiopia.* Heb. 'Rivers of
Cush.' (On the meaning of the word
'Cush,' see Note on ch. xi. 11.) It is
sometimes applicable to Ethiopia or
Nubia—that is, the portion of Egypt
above the cataracts of the Nile. Comp.
Jer. xiii. 23 : ' Can the Ethiopian [the
Cushite] change his skin?' (see also
Ezek. xxix. 10). This word does not
determine with certainty the country to
which reference is made—for the country of Cush *may* mean that east of the
Euphrates, or southern Arabia, or
southern Egypt.   Egypt and Cush are,
however, sometimes connected (2 Kings
xix. 9 ; Ps. lxviii. 31 ; Isa. xx. 3 ; xliii.
3; Nah. iii. 9; comp. Dan. xi. 43).
The *probability* from the use of this
word is, that some part of Upper Egypt
is intended.   Ethiopia in part lies
beyond the most considerable of the
streams that make up the river Nile.
2. *That sendeth ambassadors.* That
is, *accustomed* to send messengers.
What was the design of their thus sending ambassadors does not appear. The

prophet simply intimates the fact ; a
fact by which they were well known.
It may have been for purposes of commerce, or to seek protection.   Bochart
renders the word translated ' ambassadors ' by *images*, and supposes that it
denotes an image of the god Osiris made
of the papyrus ; but there does not seem
to be any reason for this opinion.   The
word צִיר (*tzir*) *may* mean an idol or
image, as in Isa. xlv. 16 ; Ps. xlix. 15.
But it usually denotes ambassadors, or
messengers (Josh. ix. 4 ; Prov. xxv.
13; xiii. 17; Isa. lvii. 9; Jer. xlix. 14 ;
Obad. 1). ¶ *By the sea.* What *sea* is
here meant cannot be accurately determined.   The word 'sea' (יָם) is applied
to various collections of water, and may
be used in reference to a sea, a lake, a
pond, and even a large river.   It is
often applied to the Mediterranean ;
and where the phrase *Great Sea* occurs,
it denotes that (Num. xxxiv. 6, 7 ; Deut.
xi. 24).   It is applied to the Lake of
Gennesareth or the Sea of Galilee (Num.
xxxiv. 11); to the Salt Sea (Gen. xiv.
3); to the Red Sea often (Ex. xiii. 10 ;
Num. xiv. 25; xxi. 4; xxxiii. 10, *et al.*)
It is also applied to *a large river*, as,
e.g., the *Nile* (Isa. xix. 5 ; Neh. iii. 8) ;
and to the Euphrates (Jer. li. 36).   So
far as this *word* is concerned, therefore,
it may denote either the Mediterranean,
the Red Sea, the Nile, or the Euphrates.
If the country spoken of is Upper Egypt
or Nubia, then we are naturally led to
suppose that the prophet refers either
to the Nile or the Red Sea. ¶ *Even
in vessels of bulrushes.* The word rendered 'bulrushes' (גֹּמֶא) is derived
from the verb גָּמָא (*gâmâ*), *to swallow,
sip, drink ;* and is given to a reed or
bulrush, from its *imbibing* water. It is
usually applied in the Scriptures to the
Egyptian *papyrus*—a plant which grew
on the banks of the Nile, and from
which we have derived our word *paper.*
' This plant,' says Taylor (*Heb. Con.*),

'grew in moist places near the Nile, and was four or five yards in height. Under the bark it consisted wholly of thin skins, which being separated and spread out, were applied to various uses. Of these they made boxes and chests, and even boats, smearing them over with pitch.' These *laminæ*, or skins, also served the purpose of paper, and were used instead of parchment, or plates of lead and copper, for writing on. This plant, the *Cyperus Papyrus* of modern botanists, mostly grew in Lower Egypt, in marshy land, or in shallow brooks and ponds, formed by the inundation of the Nile. 'The papyrus,'

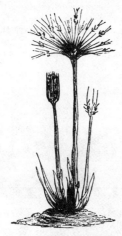

PAPYRUS (*Cyperus Papyrus*).

says Pliny, 'grows in the marsh lands of Egypt, or in the stagnant pools left inland by the Nile, after it has returned to its bed, which have not more than two cubits in depth. The root of the plant is the thickness of a man's arm; it has a triangular stalk, growing not higher than ten cubits (fifteen feet), and decreasing in breadth towards the summit, which is crowned with a thyrsus, containing no seeds, and of no use except to deck the statues of the gods. They employ the roots as firewood, and for making various utensils. They even construct small boats of the plant; and out of the rind, sails, mats, clothes, bedding, ropes; they eat it either crude or cooked, swallowing only the juice;

and when they manufacture paper from it, they divide the stem by means of a kind of needle into thin plates, or laminæ, each of which is as large as the plant will admit. All the paper is woven upon a table, and is continually moistened with Nile water, which being thick and slimy, furnishes an effectual species of glue. In the first place, they form upon a table, perfectly horizontal, a layer the whole length of the papyrus, which is crossed by another placed transversely, and afterwards enclosed within a press. The different sheets are then hung in a situation exposed to the sun, in order to dry, and the process is finally completed by joining them together, beginning with the best. There are seldom more than twenty slips or stripes produced from one stem of the plant.' —(Pliny, xiii. 11, 12.) Wilkinson remarks, that 'the mode of making papyri was this: the interior of the stalks of the plant, after the rind had been removed, was cut into thin slices in the direction of their length, and these being laid on a flat board, in succession, similar slices were placed over them at right angles, and their surfaces being cemented together by a sort of glue, and subjected to the proper degree of pressure, and well dried, the papyrus was completed.'—(*Ancient Egyptians*, vol. iii. p. 148.) The word here used is translated 'bulrushes' in Ex. ii. 3, where the little ark is described in which Moses was laid near the Nile; the 'rush' in Job viii. 11; and 'rushes,' in Isa. xxxv. 7. It does not elsewhere occur. That the ancients were in the practice of making light boats or vessels from the papyrus is well known. Thus Theophrastus (in the *History of Plants*, iv. 9) says, that 'the papyrus is useful for many things; for from this they make vessels,' or ships (πλοῖα). Thus, Pliny (xiii. 11, 22) says, *ex ipso quidem papyro navigia texunt*—'from the papyrus they weave vessels.' Again, (vi. 56, 57): 'Even now,' says he, 'in the Britannic Ocean useful vessels are made of bark; on the Nile from the papyrus, and from reeds and rushes.' Plutarch describes Isis going in search of the body of Osiris, 'through the fenny country in a bark made of the papyrus (ἐν βαρίδι παπυρίνη); where it is supposed that persons using boats of this description (ἐν παπυρίνοις ὀκαφίσι πλίοντας) are never attacked by crocodiles out of respect to the goddess,' (*De Is.* 18.) Moses, also, it will be remembered, was exposed on the banks of the Nile in a similar boat or ark. 'She took for him an ark of bulrushes, and daubed it with slime and with pitch, and put the child therein' (Ex. ii. 3). The same word occurs here (גֹּמֶא) which is used by Isaiah, and this fact shows that such boats were known as early as the time of Moses. Lucan also mentions boats made of the papyrus at Memphis :

Conseritur bibula Memphitis cymba papyro.—
Phar. iv. 136.

At Memphis boats are woven together from the marshy papyrus

The sculptures of Thebes, Memphis, and other places, abundantly show that they were employed as punts, or canoes for fishing, in all parts of Egypt, during the inundation of the Nile.'—(Wilkinson's *Ancient Egyptians,* vol. iii. p. 186.) In our own country, also, it will be remembered, the natives were accustomed to make canoes, or vessels, of the bark of the birch, with which they often adventured on even dangerous navigation. The circumstance here mentioned of the גֹּמֶא (the papyrus), seems to fix the scene of this prophecy to the region of the Nile. This reed grew nowhere else ; and it is natural, therefore, to suppose, that some nation living near the Nile is intended. Taylor, the editor of Calmet, has shown that the inhabitants of the upper regions of the Nile were accustomed to form floats of hollow earthen vessels, and to weave them together with rushes, and thus to convey them to Lower Egypt to market. He

EGYPTIAN POTTERY FLOAT ON THE NILE.

supposes that by 'vessels of bulrushes,' or rush floats, are meant such vessels. (For a description of the *floats* made in Upper Egypt with *jars,* see Pococke's *Travels,* vol. i. p. 84, Ed. London, 1743.) 'I first saw in this voyage [on the Nile] the large floats of earthenware ; they are about thirty feet wide, and sixty long, being a frame of palm boughs tied together about four feet deep, on which they put a layer of large jars with the mouths uppermost ; on these they make another floor, and then put on another layer of jars, and so a third, which last are so disposed as to trim the float, and leave room for the men to go between. The float lies across the river, one end being lower down than the other ; toward the lower end on each side they have four long poles with which they row and direct the boat, as well as forward the motion down.' Mr. Bruce, in his *Travels,* mentions vessels made of the papyrus in Abyssinia. ¶ *Upon the waters.* The waters of the Nile, or the Red Sea.

¶ *Saying.* This word is not in the Hebrew, and the introduction of it by the translators gives a peculiar, and probably an incorrect, sense to the whole passage. As it stands here, it would seem to be the language of the inhabitants of the land who sent the ambassadors, usually saying to their messengers to go to a distant nation; and this introduces an inquiry into the characteristics of the nation to *whom* the ambassadors are sent, as if it were a *different* people from those who are mentioned in ver. 1. But probably the words which follow are to be regarded as the words of the prophet, or of God (ver. 4), giving commandment to those messengers to *return* to those who sent them, and deliver the message which follows : ' You send messengers to distant nations in reed boats upon the rivers. Return, says God, to the land which sent you forth, and announce to them the will of God. Go rapidly in your light vessels, and bear this message, for it shall speedily be executed, and I will sit calmly and see it done ' (ver. 4–6). A remarkably similar passage, which throws great light on this, occurs in Ezek. xxx. 9 : ' In that day shall messengers go forth from me [God] in ships to make the careless Ethiopians afraid, and great pain shall come upon them, as in the day of Egypt ; for lo, it cometh.' ¶ *Go, ye swift messengers.* Heb. ' Light messengers.' This is evidently addressed to the boats. Achilles Tatius says that they were frequently so light and small, that they would carry but one person (Rosenmüller). ¶ *To a nation.* What nation this was is not known. The *obvious* import of the passage is, that it was some nation to whom they were *accustomed* to send ambassadors, and that it is here added merely as *descriptive* of the people. Two or three characteristics of the nation are mentioned, from which we may better learn what people are referred to. ¶ *Scattered* (מְמֻשָּׁךְ). This word is derived from מָשַׁךְ (*mâshăkh*), *to seize, take, hold fast;* to draw out, extend, or prolong ; to make double or strong ; to spread out. The LXX. render it, "Εθνος μετέωρον— ' A lofty nation.' Chaldee, ' A people suffering

violence.' Syraic, ' A nation distorted.' Vulg., ' A people convulsed, and lacerated.' It *may* denote a people *spread out* over a great extent of country ; or a people *drawn out in length*—i.e., extended over a country of considerable length, but of comparatively narrow breadth, as Egypt is ; so Vitringa understands it. Or it may mean a people *strong, valiant;* so Gesenius understands it. This best suits the connection, as being a people 'terrible hitherto.' Perhaps all these ideas may be united by the supposition, that the nation was drawn out or extended over a large region, and was *therefore* a powerful or mighty people. The idea of its being *scattered* is not in the text. Taylor renders it, ' A people of short stature ; contracted in height ; that is, dwarfs.' But the idea in the text is not one that is descriptive of *individuals*, but of the *collected* nation ; the people. ¶ *And peeled* (מוֹרָט, from מָרַט [*mârăt*] *to make smooth*, or *sharpen*, as a sword, Ezek. xxi. 14–32 ; then, to make smooth the head of any one, to pluck off his hair, Ezra ix. 3 ; Neh. xiii. 25 ; Isa. l. 6). The LXX. render it, Ξένον λαὸν καὶ χαλεπόν—'A foreign and wicked people.' Vulg., ' To a people lacerated.' The Syriac renders the whole verse, ' Go, swift messengers, to a people perverse and torn ; to a people whose strength has been long since taken away ; a people defiled and trodden down ; whose land the rivers have spoiled.' The word here used is capable of two significations :—(1.) It may denote a people who are shaved or made smooth by removing the hair from the body. It is known to have been the custom with the Egyptians to make their bodies smooth by shaving off the hair, as Herodotus testifies (xi. 37). Or, (2.) It may be translated, as Gesenius proposes, a people valiant, fierce, bold, from the sense which the verb has *to sharpen* a sword (Ezek. xxi. 15, 16). The former is the most obvious interpretation, and agrees best with the proper meaning of the Hebrew word ; the latter would, perhaps, better suit the connection. The editor of Calmet supposes that it is to be taken in the sense of *diminished*, *small, dwarfish*, and would apply it to

the *pigmies* of Upper Egypt. ¶ *To a*
people terrible. That is, warlike, fierce,
cruel. Heb. ' A people feared.' If the
Egyptians are meant, it may refer to
the fact that they had always been an
object of terror and alarm to the Israelites from their early oppressions there
before their deliverance under Moses.
¶ *From their beginning hitherto.* Heb.
' From this time, and formerly.' It has
been their general character that they
were a fierce, harsh, oppressive nation.
Gesenius, however, renders this, ' To the
formidable nation (and) further beyond ;'
and supposes that two nations are referred to, of which the most remote and
formidable one, whose land is washed by
streams, is the proper Ethiopian people.
By the other he supposes is meant the
Egyptian people. But the scope of the
whole prophecy rather requires us to
understand it of one people. ¶ *A nation
meted out.* Heb. ' Of line line ' (קָו־קָו
qăv-qăv). Vitringa renders this, ' A
nation of precept and precept ;' that is,
whose religion abounded with rites and
ceremonies, and an infinite multitude
of *precepts* or *laws* which prescribed
them. Michaelis renders it, ' A nation
measured by a line ;' that is, whose land
had been divided by victors. Döderlin
renders it, ' A nation which uses the
line ;' *i.e.*, as he supposes, which extended its dominion over other provinces. The LXX. render it, "Εθνος
ἀνέλπιστον—' A nation without hope.'
Aquila, "Εθνος ὑπόμενον—' A nation enduring or patient.' Jonathan, the Chaldee, ובוידא עמא אגירא—' A nation oppressed and afflicted.' Aben Ezra
explains it as meaning ' A nation like
a school-boy learning line after line.'
Theodore Hasæus endeavours to prove
that the reference here is to Egypt, and
that the language is taken from the
fact that the Egyptians were early
distinguished for surveying and mensu-
ration. This science, he supposes, they
were led to cultivate from the necessity
of ascertaining the height of the Nile
at its annual inundation, and from the
necessity of an accurate survey of the
land in order to preserve the knowledge
of the right of property in a country
inundated as this was. In support of
this, he appeals to Servius (*ad* Virg.

Ecl. iii. 41), where he says of the *radius*
mentioned there, ' The Radius is the
rod of the philosophers, by which they
denote the lines of geometry. This art
was invented in the time when the Nile,
rising beyond its usual height, confounded the usual marks of boundaries,
to the ascertaining of which they employed philosophers who divided the
land by *lines*, whence the science was
called geometry.' Comp. Strabo (*Geo.*
xvii. 787), who says that Egypt was
divided into thirty *nomes*, and then
adds, ' that these were again subdivided
into other portions, the smallest of which
were *farms* (αἱ ἄρουραι). But there was
a necessity for a very careful and subtle
division, on account of the continual
confusion of the limits which the Nile
produced when it overflowed, adding to
some, taking away from others, changing the forms, obliterating the signs by
which one farm was distinguished from
another. Hence it became necessary
to re-survey the country ; and hence,
they suppose, originated the science of
geometry' (see also Herodot. *Euterpe*,
c. 109). Hence it is supposed that
Egypt came to be distinguished by the
use of *the line*—or for its skill in surveying, or in geometry—or a nation *of
the line* (see the Dissertation of Theodore
Hasæus, גוי קו קו—*De Gente kav kav*,
in Ugolin's *Thes. Ant. Sac.* vii. 1588–
1580). The word קָו (*qăv*) means, properly, *a cord, a line*, particularly a
measuring line (Ezek. xlvii. 3 ; 2 Kings
xxi. 13): ' I will stretch over Jerusalem
the measuring line of Samaria,' *i.e.*, I
will destroy it like Samaria. Hence
the phrase here may denote a people
accustomed *to stretch out such lines*
over others ; that is, to lay them waste.
It is applied usually to the line connected
with a plummet, which a carpenter uses
to mark out his work (comp. Job xxxviii.
5 ; Isa. xxviii. 17; xxxiv. 11 ; Zeph. ii.
1); or to a line by which a land or
country is measured by the surveyor.
Sometimes it means *a precept*, or *rule*,
as Vitringa has rendered it here (comp.
Isa. xxviii. 10). But the phrase ' to
stretch out a line,' or ' to measure a
people by a line,' is commonly applied
to their destruction, as if a conqueror
used a line to mark out what he had to

3 All ye inhabitants of the world, and dwellers on the earth, see ye, when he lifteth up an ^aensign on the mountains; and when he bloweth a trumpet, hear ye.

a ch. 5. 26.

do (see this use of the word in 2 Kings xxi. 13; Isa. xxviii. 17; xxxiv. 11; Lam. ii. 8; Zech. i. 16). This is probably its sense here—a nation terrible in all its history, and which had been distinguished for stretching lines over others; that is, for marking them out for destruction, and dividing them as it pleased. It is therefore a simple description, not of the nation as *being itself* measured out, but as extending its dominion over others. ¶ *And trodden down* (מְבוּסָה). Marg. 'And treading under foot,' or, 'that meteth out and treadeth down.' The margin here, as is frequently the case, is the more correct rendering. Here it does not mean that *they were trodden down*, but that it was a characteristic of their nation that *they trod down others;* that is, conquered and subdued other nations. Thus the verb is used in Psal. xliv. 6; Isa. xiv. 25; liii. 6; lxiii. 18; Jer. xii. 10. Some, however, have supposed that it refers to the fact that the land was trodden down by their feet, or that the Egyptians were accustomed to lead the waters of the Nile, when it overflowed, by *treading* places for it to flow in their fields. But the former is the more correct interpretation. ¶ *Whose land the rivers have spoiled*. Marg. 'Despise.' The Hebrew word (בָּזְאוּ) occurs nowhere else. The Vulgate renders it, *Diripuerunt*—'Carry away.' The Chaldee reads it, 'Whose land the people plunder.' The word is probably of the same signification as בָּזַז (*bâzăz*), to plunder, lay waste. So it was read by the Vulgate and the Chaldee; and this reading is found in four MSS. The word is in the present tense, and should be rendered not 'have spoiled,' but 'spoil.' It is probably used to denote a country the banks of whose rivers are washed away by the floods. This description is particularly applicable to Nubia or Abyssinia—the region above the cataracts of the Nile. One has only to remember that these streams continually wash away the banks and bear the earth to deposit it *on* the lands of Lower Egypt, to see that the prophet had this region particularly in his eye. He could not have meant Egypt proper, because instead of *spoiling* the lands, or washing them away, the Nile constantly brings down a deposit from the upper regions that constitutes its great fertility. The *rivers* that are here mentioned are doubtless the various branches of the Nile (see Bruce's *Travels*, ch. iii., and Burckhardt's *Travels in Nubia*. The Nile is formed by the junction of many streams or branches rising in Abyssinia, the principal of which are the Atbara; the Astapus or Blue River; and the Astaboras or White River. The principal source of the Nile is the Astapus or Blue River, which rises in the Lake Coloe, which Bruce supposes to be the head of the Nile. This river on the west, and the various branches of the Atbara on the east, nearly encompass a large region of country called Meroë, once supposed to be a large island, and frequently called such. The whole description, therefore, leads us to the conclusion that a region is mentioned *in* that country called in general *Cush;* that it was a people living on rivers, and employing reed boats or skiffs; that they were a fierce and warlike people; and that the country was one that was continually washed by streams, and whose soil was carried down by the floods. All these circumstances apply to Nubia or Abyssinia, and there can be little doubt that this is the country intended.

3. *All ye inhabitants of the world*. These are to be regarded as the words of the prophet summoning all nations to attend to that which was about to occur. Grotius, however, and some others, suppose that they are the words of the Ethiopians. The meaning is, that the events which are here predicted would be of so public a nature as to attract the attention of all the world. ¶ *When he*. Vitringa supposes that this means the Assyrians lifting up a standard on the mountains of Judea. But the better interpretation is that which refers it to the people of Nubia,

4 For so the Lord said unto me, I will take my rest, and I will consider[1] in my dwelling-place like a clear heat [2] upon herbs, *and* like a cloud of dew in the heat of harvest:

1 or, *regard my set dwelling.*　2 or, *after rain.*

mustering their forces for war. ' All nations behold when that people collects an army ; sounds the trumpet for war ; and arrays its military forces for battle. See then the judgments that God will inflict on them—their discomfiture (ver. 4–7), and their turning to Jehovah, and sending an offering to him (ver. 7).' According to this interpretation, it will refer to the people making preparation for battle ; and perhaps it may mean that they were preparing to join the enemies of Judea—*not improbably preparing to join the forces of Sennacherib, and to invade Judea.* For this purpose it may have been that the messengers were sent to negotiate the terms of alliance with Sennacherib ; and the object of the prophecy is, to assure the Jews that this people, as well as Sennacherib, would be discomfited, and that they would yet bring an offering to God (ver. 7). ¶ *Lifteth up an ensign.* A military standard (see Note on ch. v. 26). ¶ *And when he bloweth a trumpet.* Also a signal for an army to assemble (see Note on ch. xiii. 2).

4. *For so the* Lord *said unto me.* So Jehovah has revealed his purpose, that is, to execute punishment on the people who have been described in the previous verses. Their state as there described is that of a fierce people making ready for war, and probably designing an alliance with the enemies of Judea, and marshalling their armies for that purpose. Jehovah here reveals to the prophet that they shall be discomfited, and shows the manner in which it will be done. He says he will sit calm while these preparations are going on—as the sun shines serenely on the earth while the harvest is growing, and the dew falls gently on the herb ;—but that *before* their plans are completed, he will interpose and destroy them, as if one should appear suddenly before the harvest is ripe and cut it down. The *design,* therefore, of this part of the prophecy is to comfort the Jews, and to assure them that there is no danger to them from the

preparations which were made against them—for Jehovah calmly beholds the proud rage of the enemy. ¶ *I will take my rest.* I will not interpose. I will remain calm—not appearing to oppose them, but keeping as calm, and as still, as if I seemed to favour their plans—as the sun shines on the herb, and the gentle dew falls on the grass, until the proper time for me to interpose and defeat them shall arise (ver. 5, 6). ¶ *I will consider.* I will look on ; that is, I will not now interpose and disarrange their plans before they are complete. We learn here, (1.) that God sees the plans of the wicked ; (2.) that he sees them *mature* them without attempting then to interpose to disarrange them ; (3.) that he is calm and still, because he designs that those plans shall be developed ; and (4.) that the wicked should not indulge in any dreams of security and success because God does not interpose to thwart their plans while they are forming them. He will do it in the proper time. ¶ *In my dwelling-place.* In heaven. I will sit in heaven and contemplate leisurely the plans that are going forward. ¶ *Like a clear heat.* A serene, calm, and steady sunshine, by which plants and herbs are made to grow. There seem to be two ideas blended here : the first, that of the *stillness* with which the sun shines upon the herbs ; and the other, that of the fact that the sun shines that the herbs *may grow.* ¶ *Upon herbs.* Marg. ' After rain ' (עֲלֵי־אֹיר). The word אֹיר usually signifies *light,* or *fire.* The plural form (אוֹרֹת) is used to denote herbs or vegetables in two places, in 2 Kings iv. 39, and Isa. xxvi. 19. For in the Shemitic languages the ideas of *sprouting, being grown, growing,* &c., are connected with that of the shining of the sun, or of light ; that which grows in the light ; that is, vegetables. But in the singular form the word is not thus used, unless it be in this place. That it may have this signification cannot be doubted ; and this interpretation makes good sense, and suits the connection. The

5 For afore the harvest, when the bud is perfect, and the sour grape is ripening in the flower, he shall both cut off the sprigs with pruning-hooks, and take away *and* cut down the branches.

6 They shall be left together unto the fowls of the mountains, and to

Rabbins generally interpret it as it is in the margin—'rain.' In proof of this they appeal to Job xxxvi. 30, and xxxvii. 11; but the word in these passages more properly denotes a cloud of light or of lightning, than rain. The common interpretation is probably correct, which regards the word אוֹר here as the same as אוֹרָה—'herbs' (see Vitringa). The Syriac reads it עַל יְאֹר —'upon the river.' The parallelism seems to require the sense of *herb*, or something that shall answer to 'harvest' in the corresponding member. ¶ And *like a cloud of dew.* Such a dew was still, and promoted the growth of vegetables. The idea is that of stillness and rest: where there is no storm or tempest to dissipate the gently-falling dew. This is an emblem of the perfect quietness with which God would regard the preparations for war until the proper time would come for him to interpose. The whole passage is similar to Ps. ii. 4, 5:

He that sitteth in the heavens shall laugh; Jehovah shall have them in derision. Then shall he speak unto them in his wrath, And vex them in his hot displeasure.

The idea is, that he would be as calm as the sun is upon the herb, or the dew upon the harvest field, until the time should come when it would be proper for him to interpose, and disconcert their counsels. When and how this would be done is stated in the following verses; and the whole passage is a most striking illustration of the manner with which God contemplates the machinations and evil designs of the wicked.

5. *For afore the harvest.* This verse is evidently figurative, and the image is drawn from that which is commenced in the previous verse. There, God is represented as calmly regarding the plans of the people here referred to— as the sun shines serenely on the herb, or the dew falls on the grass. *That* figure supposes that they had *formed* plans, and that they were advancing to maturity, like a growing harvest, while God surveyed them without interposition. This verse continues the figure, and affirms *that those plans shall not be mature;* that God will interpose and defeat them *while* they are maturing—as if a man should enter the harvest field and cut it down after it had been sown, or go into the vineyard, and cut down the vines while the green grape was beginning to ripen. It is, therefore, a most beautiful and expressive figure, intimating that all their plans would be foiled even when they had the prospect of a certain accomplishment. ¶ *When the bud is perfect.* The word 'bud' here (פֶּרַח) denotes either a *blossom*, or a sprout, shoot, branch. Here it denotes probably the *blossom* of the grain; or it may be the grain when it is *set.* Its meaning is, when their plans are maturing, and there is every human prospect that they will be successful. ¶ *And the sour grape is ripening.* Begins to turn; or is becoming mature. ¶ *In the flower* (נִצָּה). The blossom. This should be read rather, 'and the flower is becoming a ripening grape.' The common version does not make sense; but with this translation the idea is clear. The sense is the same as in the former phrase—when their plans are maturing. ¶ *He shall cut off the sprigs.* The shoots; the small limbs on which the grape is hanging, as if a man should enter a vineyard, and, while the grape is ripening, should not only cut off the grape, but the small branches that bore it, thus preventing it from bearing again. The idea is, not only that God would disconcert their *present* plans, but that he would prevent them from forming any in future. Before their plans were matured, and they obtained the anticipated triumph, he would effectually prevent them from forming such plans again.

6. *They shall be left together.* The figure here is dropped, and the literal

the beasts of the earth: and the fowls shall summer upon them, and all the beasts of the earth shall winter upon them.

7 In that time shall the *a* present be brought unto the Lord of hosts of a people scattered ¹ and peeled,

and from a people terrible from their beginning hitherto; a nation meted out and trodden under foot, whose land the rivers have spoiled, to the place of the name of the Lord of hosts, the mount Zion.

a Ps.68.31; 72.10; ch.16.1.

1 or, *outspread and polished.*

---

narration is resumed. The sense is, that the army shall be slain and left unburied. Perhaps the *branches* and *twigs* in the previous verse denoted military leaders, and the captains of the armies, which are now represented as becoming food for beasts of the field and for birds of prey. ¶ *To the fowls of the mountains.* Their dead bodies shall be unburied, and shall be a prey to the birds that prey upon flesh. ¶ *And to the beasts of the earth.* The wild animals; the beasts of the forest. ¶ *And the fowls shall summer upon them.* Shall pass the summer, *i.e.,* they shall continue to be unburied. ¶ *And the beasts of the earth shall winter upon them.* They shall be unburied through the winter; probably indicating that they would furnish food for the fowls and the wild beasts for a long time. On the multitude of carcases these animals will find nourishment for a whole year, *i.e.,* they will spend the summer and the winter with them. When this was fulfilled, it is, perhaps, not possible to tell, as we are so little acquainted with the circumstances of the people in relation to whom it was spoken. If it related, as I suppose, to the people of Nubia or Ethiopia forming an alliance with the Assyrians for the purpose of invading Judea, it was fulfilled probably when Sennacherib and his assembled hosts were destroyed. Whenever it was fulfilled, it is quite evident that the design of the prophecy was to give comfort to the Jews, alarmed and agitated as they were at the prospect of the preparations which were made, by the assurance that those plans would fail, and all the efforts of their enemies be foiled and disconcerted.

7. *In that time.* When their plans shall thus be disconcerted, and their armies be overthrown. ¶ *Shall the present be brought,* &c. The word

'present' (שַׁי) denotes a gift, and is found only in the phrase 'to bring gifts,' or 'presents' (Ps. lxviii. 30; lxxvi. 11). It means here evidently a tribute, or an offering to Jehovah as the only true God; and possibly may mean that the people would be converted to him, and embrace the true religion. ¶ *Of a people,* &c. From a people. The description which follows is the same precisely as in ver. 2. Numerous repetitions of this kind will be recollected by the classic reader in the *Iliad.* ¶ *To the place of the name,* &c. The place where Jehovah is worshipped, *i.e.,* Jerusalem (comp. Notes, ch. i. 8, 9). We have no means of knowing with certainty when or how this prophecy was fulfilled. That the Jewish religion spread into Upper Egypt, and that the Christian religion was afterwards established there, there can be no doubt. The Jews were scattered into nearly every nation, and probably many of this people became proselytes, and went with them to Jerusalem to worship (see Acts ii. 10; viii. 27). ' The Abyssinian annals represent the country as converted to Judaism several centuries before the Christian era; and it certainly retains many appearances bearing the stamp of that faith. In the fourth century, the nation was converted to Christianity by the efforts of Frumentius, an Egyptian, who raised himself to high favour at court. Abyssinia remained impenetrable to the arms or the creed of the followers of Mahomet, and, affording shelter to the refugees from Egypt and Arabia, it became more decidedly Christian.'— ' The Abyssinians profess the same form of Christianity with the Copts of Egypt, and even own the supremacy of the Patriarch at Cairo. They combine with their Christian profession many Judaical observances, such as circumcision, abstinence from meats,

CHAPTER XIX.

ANALYSIS.

THIS prophecy respecting Egypt extends only through this chapter. Its general scope and design is plain. It is intended to describe the calamities that would come upon Egypt, and the effect which they would have in turning the people to God. The scene is laid *in* Egypt; and the following things passed before the mind of the prophet in vision:—1. He sees JEHOVAH coming in a cloud to Egypt (1). 2. The effect of this is to produce alarm among the idols of that nation (2). 3. A state of internal commotion and discord is described as existing in Egypt; a state of calamity so great that they would seek relief from their idols and necromancers (2, 3). 4. The consequence of these dissensions and internal strifes would be, that they would be subdued by a foreign and cruel prince (4). 5. To these political calamities there would be added *physical* sufferings (5–10)—the Nile would be dried up, and all that grew on its banks would wither (5–7); those who had been accustomed to fish in the Nile would be thrown out of employment (8); and those that were engaged in the manufacture of linen would, as a consequence, be driven from employment (9, 10). 6. All counsel and wisdom would fail from the nation, and the kings and priests be regarded as fools (11–16). 7. The land of Judah would become a terror to them (17). 8. This would be followed by the conversion of many of the Egyptians to the true religion (18–20); JEHOVAH would become their protector, and would repair the breaches that had been made, and remove the evils which they had experienced (21, 22), and a strong alliance would be formed between the Egyptians, the Assyrians, and the Jews, which should secure the Divine blessing and favour (23–25).

This is the outline of the prophecy. In regard to the *time* when it was delivered, we have no certain knowledge. Lowth supposes that it refers to times succeeding the destruction of the army of Sennacherib. After that event, he says, the affairs of Egypt were thrown into confusion; intestine broils succeeded; these were followed by a tyranny of twelve princes, who

divided the country between them, until the distracted affairs settled down under the dominion of Psammetichus, who held the sceptre for fifty-four years. Not long after this, the country was invaded and conquered by Nebuchadnezzar; and then by the Persians under Cambyses, the son of Cyrus. Alexander the Great subsequently invaded and took the country, and made Alexandria the capital of his empire. Many Jews were invited thither by Alexander, and under the favour of the Ptolemies they flourished there; the true religion became prevalent in the land, and multitudes of the Egyptians, it is supposed, were converted to the Jewish faith. Bishop Newton (*Diss.* xii. *on the Prophecies*) supposes, that there was a *general* reference here to the conquest by Nebuchadnezzar, and a *particular* reference to the conquest under Cambyses the son of Cyrus. He supposes that the anarchy described in ver. 2, refers to the civil wars which arose between Apries and Amasis in the time of Nebuchadnezzar's invasion, and the civil wars between Tachos, Nectanebus, and the Mendesians, a little before the country was subdued by Ochus. The cruel king mentioned in ver. 4, into whose hands they were delivered, he supposes was Nebuchadnezzar, or more probably Cambyses and Ochus, one of whom put the yoke on the neck of the Egyptians, and the other riveted it there. The Egyptians say that Cambyses, after he killed Apis, a god worshipped in Egypt, was stricken with madness; but his actions, says Prideaux, show that he was mad long before. Ochus was the most cruel of the kings of Persia. The final deliverance of the nation, and the conversion to the true God, and the alliance between Egypt, Assyria, and Israel (18–25), he supposes, refers to the deliverance that would be introduced by Alexander the Great, and the protection that would be shown to the Jews in Egypt under the Ptolemies.

Vitringa, Gesenius, Grotius, Rosenmüller, and others, suppose that the anarchy described in ver. 2, refers to the discord which arose in the time of the δωδεκαρχία (*dodekarchy*), or the reign of the twelve kings, until Psammetichus prevailed over the rest, and that he is intended by the 'cruel lord' and 'fierce king,' described in ver. 4. In other respects, their interpretation

and the observance of Saturday as well as Sunday as a Sabbath.'—(*Encyc. of Geography*, vol. ii. pp. 585, 588.) In these facts—in the prevalence of the true religion there in former periods, the prophecy may be regarded as having been in part fulfilled. Still, as is the case with a large portion of the

prophecies of Isaiah, we must regard this as having reference to a period of greater light and truth than has yet existed there; and as destined to receive a more complete fulfilment when all lands shall be full of the knowledge of the Lord.

326 ISAIAH. [B.C. 713.

of the prophecy coincides, in the main, with that proposed by Bishop Newton.

A slight glance at some of the leading events in the history of Egypt, may enable us more clearly to determine the application of the different parts of the prophecy.

Egypt, a well-known country in Africa, is, for the most part, a great valley through which the Nile pours its waters from south to north, and is skirted on the east and west by ranges of mountains which approach or recede more or less from the river in different parts. Where the valley terminates towards the north, the Nile divides itself, about forty or fifty miles from the Mediterranean, into several parts, enclosing the territory called the Delta—so called because the various streams flowing from the one river diverge as they flow towards the sea, and thus form with the coast a triangle in the shape of the Greek letter Δ. The southern limit of Egypt proper is Syene (Ezek. xxix. 10; xxx. 6), or Essuan, the border of Ethiopia. Here the Nile issues from the granite rocks of the cataracts and enters Egypt proper. This is N. lat. 24°.

Egypt was anciently divided into forty-two *nomes* or districts, which were little provinces or counties. It was also divided into Upper and Lower Egypt. Upper Egypt was called Thebais, from Thebes the capital, and extended south to the frontier of Ethiopia. Lower Egypt contained principally the Delta and the parts on the Mediterranean. The capital was Cairo.

The most common division, however, was into three parts, Lower, Middle, and Upper Egypt. In Lower Egypt, lying on the Mediterranean, were the cities of Pithon, Raamses, Heliopolis, &c. In this division, also, was the land of Goshen. In Middle Egypt was Moph, or Memphis, Hanes, &c. In Upper Egypt was No-Ammon, or Thebes, and Syene, the southern limit of Egypt.

The ancient history of Egypt is obscure. It is agreed on all hands, however, that it was the early seat of civilization; and that this civilization was introduced from the south, and especially from Meroë. The country in the earliest times was possessed by several kings or states, which were at length united into one great kingdom. Not long after the death of Joseph, it came into the possession of the Hyksos or Shepherd kings, probably an Arabian nomadic tribe. After they were driven out, the whole country came again under one sovereign, and enjoyed great prosperity. The first king of the 19th dynasty, as it is called by Manetho, was the celebrated Sesostris, about 1500 years B.C. His successors were all called by the general

name of Pharaoh, *i.e.*, kings. The first who is mentioned by his proper name is Shishak (1 Kings xiv. 25, 26), supposed to be the Sesonchosis of Manetho, who reigned about 970 years B.C. Gesenius says, that in the time of the Jewish king Hezekiah, there reigned at the same time in Egypt three dynasties; an Ethiopic (probably over Upper Egypt), a Saïtish, and a Tanitish dynasty—of which at last sprung the dodekarchy, and whose dominion ultimately lost itself in the single reign of Psammetichus. The Ethiopic continued forty years, and consisted of three kings—Sabaco, Sevechus, and Tarakos, or Tearko—of which the two last are mentioned in the Bible, Sevechus under the name of So, סוֹא probably סְוֵא Sevechus—as the ally of Hosea, king of Israel (2 Kings xvii. 4), 722 B.C., and Tarakos, the same as Tirhakah, about the time of the 16th year of the reign of Hezekiah (714 B.C.) Instead of this whole dynasty, Herodotus (ii. 137, 139), and Diodorus (i. 65), give us only one name, that of Sabaco. Contemporary with these were the four, or according to Eusebius, five, first kings of the dynasty of Saïte, Stephinates, Nerepsus, Nichao I., who was slain by an Ethiopian king, and Psammetichus, who made an end of the dodekarchy, and reigned fifty-four years. Of the Tanitish dynasty, Psammus and Zeth are mentioned (Introduction to ch. xix.) Different accounts are given of the state of things by Herodotus and by Diodorus. The account by Diodorus, which is the most probable, is, that a state of anarchy prevailed in Egypt for two whole years; and that the troubles and commotions suggested to the chief men of the country the expediency of assuming the reins of government, and restoring order to the state. With this view, twelve of the most influential men were chosen to preside with regal power. Each had a particular province allotted to him, in which his authority was permanent; and though independent of one another, they bound themselves with mutual oaths to concord and fidelity.

During fifteen years, their relations were maintained with entire harmony: but during that time Psammetichus, whose province extended to the Mediterranean, had availed himself of his advantages, and had maintained extensive commercial intercourse with the Phenicians and Greeks, and had amassed considerable wealth. Of this his colleagues became jealous, and supposing that he meant to secure the government of the whole country, they resolved to deprive him of his province. They therefore prepared to attack him, and he was thrown upon the necessity of self defence.

Apprised of their designs, he sent to Arabia, Caria, and Ionia, for aid, and having secured a large body of troops, he put himself at their head, and gave battle to his foes at Momemphis, and completely defeated them, drove them from the kingdom, and took possession of an undivided throne (Diod. i. 66). The account of Herodotus may be seen in his history (ii. 154). Psammetichus turned his attention to the internal administration of the country, and endeavoured to ingratiate himself with the priesthood and the people by erecting splendid monuments, and beautifying the sacred edifices. There was a strong jealousy, however, excited by the fact that he was indebted for his crown to foreign troops, and from the fact that foreigners were preferred to office over the native citizens (Diod. i. 67). A large part of his troops—to the number, according to Diodorus, of 240,000—abandoned his service at one time, and moved off in a body to Ethiopia, and entered the service of the monarch of that country. His reign appears to have been a military despotism, and though liberal in its policy towards foreign governments, yet the severity of his government at home, and the injustice which the Egyptians supposed he showed to them in relying on foreigners, and preferring them, justified the appellation in ver. 4, that he was a 'cruel lord.'

Egypt was afterwards conquered by Cambyses, and became a province of the Persian empire about 525 B.C. Thus it continued until it was conquered by Alexander the Great, 350 B.C., after whose death it formed, together with Syria, Palestine, Lybia, &c., the kingdom of the Ptolemies. After the battle of Actium, 30 B.C., it became a Roman province. In A.D. 640, it was conquered by the Arabs, and since that time it has passed from the hands of the Caliphs into the hands of the Turks, and since A.D. 1517 it has been regarded as a province of the Turkish empire. This is an outline of the principal events of the Egyptian history. The events predicted in this chapter will be stated in their order in the comments on the particular verses. The two leading points which will guide our interpretation will be, that Psammetichus is intended in ver. 4, and that the effects of Alexander's conquest of Egypt are denoted from ver. 18 to the end of the chapter. Keeping these two points in view, the interpretation of the chapter will be easy. On the history of Egypt, and the commotions and revolutions there, the reader may consult Wilkinson's *Manners and Customs of the Ancient Egyptians*, vol. i., particularly pp. 143–180.

THE burden of *a* Egypt. Behold, the LORD rideth *b* upon a swift cloud, and shall come into Egypt; and the idols *c* of Egypt shall be moved at his presence, and the heart of Egypt shall melt in the midst of it.

a Jer. 46; Eze. xxix. & xxx.   *b* Ps. 18. 10; 104. 3.
c Ex. 12. 12; Jer. 43. 12.

CHAPTER XIX.

1. *The burden of Egypt.* This is the title to the prophecy. For the meaning of the word *burden*, see Note on ch. xiii. 1. The word 'Egypt' in the original is מִצְרַיִם (*Mitzraim*); and it was so called after Mizraim the second son of Ham, and grandson of Noah. Sometimes it is called Mazor (2 Kings xix. 24; Isa. xix. 6; xxxvii. 25; Mic. vii. 12); where, however, our English version has rendered the word by *besieged place* or *fortress*. The ancient name of the country among the inhabitants themselves was *Chimi* or *Chami* (Χημυ). The Egyptian word signified *black*, and the name was probably given from the black deposit made by the slime of the Nile. 'Mizraim, or Misrim, the name given to Egypt in the Scriptures, is in the plural form, and is the Hebrew mode of expressing the "two regions of Egypt" (so commonly met with in the hieroglyphics), or the "two Misr," a name still used by the Arabs, who call all Egypt, as well as Cairo, Musr or Misr.'—(Wilkinson's *Ancient Egyptians*, vol. i. p. 2). The origin of the name 'Egypt' is unknown. Egyptus is said by some to have been an ancient king of this country. ¶ *Behold, the* LORD. This is a bold introduction. JEHOVAH is seen advancing to Egypt for the purpose of confounding its idols, and inflicting punishment. The leading idea which the prophet wishes probably to present is, that national calamities—anarchy, commotion, revolution, as well as physical sufferings—are under the government and direction of JEHOVAH. ¶ *Rideth upon a swift cloud.* JEHOVAH is often thus represented as riding on a cloud, especially when he comes for purposes of vengeance or punishment:

And he rode upon a cherub and did fly,
Yea, he did fly upon the wings of the wind.
Ps. xviii. 10.

2 And I will ¹ set the Egyptians against the Egyptians ; and they shall fight every one against his brother, and every one against his

1 *mingle.*

Who maketh the clouds his chariot,
Who walketh upon the wings of the wind.
                                        Ps. civ. 3.

'I saw in the night visions, and behold, one like the Son of Man came with the clouds of heaven' (Dan. vii. 13). So the Saviour is represented as coming to judgment in the clouds of heaven (Matt. xxiv. 30). Compare the sublime description in Hab. iii. 3–10. ¶ *And the idols of Egypt.* It is well known that Egypt was celebrated for its idolatry. They worshipped chiefly the heavenly bodies ; but they worshipped also all kinds of animals, probably as living symbols of their gods. ¶ *Shall be moved.* That is, shall tremble, be agitated, alarmed ; or shall be removed from their place, and overthrown. The word will bear either construction. Vitringa inclines to the latter. ¶ *And the heart of Egypt.* The strength ; the courage ; the vigour. We use the word *heart* in the same sense now, when we speak of a stout heart ; a courageous heart, &c. ¶ *Shall melt.* The word here used denotes *to dissolve ;* and is applied to the heart when its courage fails—probably from the sensation of weakness or fainting. The fact alluded to here was probably the disheartening circumstances that attended the civil commotions in Egypt, when the people felt themselves oppressed by cruel rulers. See the Analysis of the chapter.

2. *And I will set* (סִכְסַכְתִּי). This word (from סָכַךְ) means properly *to cover*, to spread over, to hide, conceal, to protect. Another signification of the verb is, to weave, to intermingle. It may mean here, ' I will *arm* the Egyptians against each other' (Gesenius) ; or, as in our version, ' I will mingle, confound, or throw them into discord and strife.' The LXX. render it, 'Ἐπιγερθήσονται — ' They shall be excited,' or, ' raised up.' Symmachus, Συμβαλῶ. Syriac and Chaldee, ' I will excite.' The sense is, that there would

neighbour ; city against city, *and* kingdom against kingdom.
3 And the spirit of Egypt shall fail² in ᵃthe midst thereof ; and I

2 *be emptied.*   a Eze.22.14.

be discord and civil war, and this is traced to the agency or overruling providence of God—meaning that he would *permit* and *overrule* it. Compare Notes on Isa. xlv. 7 : ' I make peace, and I create evil ; I, JEHOVAH, do all these things ;' Amos iii. 6 : ' Shall there be evil in a city and JEHOVAH hath not done it ?' The civil war here referred to was probably that which arose between the twelve kings in the time of the dodekarchy (see the Analysis to the chapter), and which resulted in the single dominion of Psammetichus. Bishop Newton (*On the Prophecies*, xii.) supposes, however, that the prophet refers to the civil wars between Apries and Amasis at the time of the invasion by Nebuchadnezzar. But it agrees much better with the former discord than with this. The description which follows is that of anarchy or civil strife, where *many* parties are formed, and would naturally lead to the supposition that there were more than two engaged. ¶ And *kingdom against kingdom.* Sept. Νόμος ἐπὶ νόμων—' Nome against nomes.' Egypt was formerly divided into forty-two *nomes* or districts. The version by the LXX. was made in Egypt, and the translators would naturally employ the terms which were in common use. Still the event referred to was probably not that of one *nome* contending against another, but a civil war in which one dynasty would be excited against another (Gesenius), or when there would be anarchy and strife amongst the different members of the dodekarchy. See the Analysis of the chapter.

3. *And the spirit of Egypt* (see ver. 1). They shall be exhausted with their long internal contentions and strifes ; and seeing no prospect of deliverance, and anxious that the turmoils should end, they shall seek counsel and refuge in their gods and necromancers, but in vain. ¶ *Shall fail* (נָבְקָה). Marg. ' Be emptied.' The word means, literally, *to pour out, empty, depopu-*

will [1] destroy the counsel thereof ; and they shall seek [a] to the idols, and to the charmers, and to them that have familiar spirits, and to the wizards.

> [1] *swallow up.*   [a] ch.8.19; 47.12.

4 And the Egyptians will I [2] give over into the hands of a cruel [b] lord ; and a fierce king shall rule over them, saith the LORD, the LORD of hosts.

> [2] or, *shut up.*   [b] ch.20.4.

---

late. Here it means that they would become disheartened and discouraged. ¶ *And I will destroy.* Marg., as the Heb., 'I will swallow up.' So the word is used in Ps. cvii. 27, ' All their wisdom is destroyed' (Heb. 'swallowed up).' ¶ *And they shall seek to the idols.* According to Herodotus (ii. 152), Psammetichus had consulted the oracle of Latona at Butos, and received for answer that the sea should avenge his cause by producing brazen men. Some time after, a body of Ionians and Carians were compelled by, stress of weather to touch at Egypt, and landed there, clad in brazen armour. Some Egyptians, alarmed at their appearance, came to Psammetichus, and described them as brazen men who had risen from the sea, and were plundering the country. He instantly supposed that this was the accomplishment of the oracle, and entered into an alliance with the strangers, and by their aid was enabled to obtain the victory over his foes. Compare the different accounts of Diodorus in the Analysis of this chapter. The whole history of Egypt shows how much they were accustomed to consult their idols (see Herodot. ii. 54, *sq.*, 82, 83, 139, 152). Herodotus says (ii. 83), that the art of divination in Egypt was confined to certain of their deities. There were in that country the oracles of Hercules, of Apollo, of Mars, of Diana, and of Jupiter ; but the oracle of Latona in Butos was held in greater veneration than any of the rest. ¶ *And to the charmers* (אִטִּים). This word occurs nowhere else. The root אָטַט, in Arabic, means *to mutter, to make a gentle noise;* and this word probably denotes conjurors, diviners (see Note on ch. viii. 19). The LXX. render it, ' Their idols.' ¶ *And to them that have familiar spirits* (see Note on ch. viii. 19). The LXX. render this, ' Those who speak from the ground.' ¶ *And to*

the wizards. LXX., 'Εγγαστριμύθους —'Ventriloquists.' The Hebrew word means a wise man, a soothsayer, a magician (יִדְּעֹנִים from יָדַע *to know ;* see Lev. xix. 31; xx. 6; Deut. xviii. 11). This false science abounded in Egypt, and in most Oriental countries.

4. *And the Egyptians.* The Egyptian nation ; the entire people, though divided into factions and contending with each other. ¶ *Will I give over.* Marg. 'Shut up.' The Hebrew word (סָכַר) usually has the sense of shutting up, or closing. Here it means that these contentions would be *closed* or concluded by their being delivered to the dominion of a single master. The LXX. render it, Παραδώσω—'I will surrender.' ¶ *Into the hands of a cruel lord.* Heb. 'Lords of cruelty, or severity.' The word rendered 'lord,' meaning master, is in the Hebrew in the plural number (אֲדֹנִים). It is, however, generally supposed that it is *pluralis excellentiæ* —denoting majesty and dignity, and applicable to a *single* monarch. The connection requires this, for the state here described would be different from that where *many* rule, and it seems to suppose that *one* should succeed to the many who had been contending. In the parallel member, also, a name in the singular number is used—' a fierce king ;' and as this evidently denotes the same, it follows that the word here is used to denote a single monarch. The plural form is often thus used in the Hebrew (see Ps. vii. 10 ; Ezek. xxix. 3 ; Hos. xii. 1). God here claims jurisdiction over the nation, and says that *he* will do it—a most striking illustration of the power which he asserts over contending people to deliver them to whomsoever he will. Bishop Newton supposes that this was Nebuchadnezzar, or more properly Cambyses, by whom Egypt was made subject to the authority of Persia, and who was eminently a cruel man, a

5 And the waters shall fail from the sea, and the river shall be wasted and dried up.

6 And they shall turn the rivers far away, *and* the brooks *a* of de-

a 2 Ki. 19.24.

madman. But the more probable interpretation is that which refers it to Psammetichus. Twelve kings were in contention, of whom he was one. He called in the aid of the Arabians, and the pirates of Caria and Iona (Herodot. ii. 152; see the Analysis of the chapter; Diod. i. 66). This was in the twentieth year of the reign of Manasseh. Psammetichus reigned fifty-four years and was succeeded by Nechus his son, called in Scripture Pharaoh-Necho, and often mentioned under that name. Psammetichus, during a considerable part of his reign, was engaged in wars with Assyria and Palestine. He is here called a 'cruel lord;' that is, an oppressive monarch, probably because he secured the kingdom by bringing in to his aid foreign mercenaries—robbers and pirates, and because his wars made his government oppressive and burdensome. ¶ *A fierce king.* Heb. 'A king of strength'—a description particularly applicable to one who, like Psammetichus, had subdued eleven rivals, and who had obtained the kingdom by conquest.

5. *And the waters shall fail.* Here commences a description of the *physical* calamities that would come upon the land, which continues to ver. 10. The previous verses contained an account of the national calamities by civil wars. It may be observed that discord, anarchy, and civil wars, are often connected with physical calamities; as famine, drought, pestilence. God has the elements, as well as the hearts of men, under his control; and when he chastises a nation, he often mingles anarchy, famine, discord, and the pestilence together. Often, too, civil wars have a *tendency* to produce these calamities. They annihilate industry, arrest enterprise, break up plans of commerce, and divert the attention of men from the cultivation of the soil. This might have been in part the case in Egypt; but it would seem also that God, by direct agency, intended to afflict them by drying up

their streams in a remarkable manner. ¶ *From the sea.* The parallelism here, as well as the whole scope of the passage, requires us to understand this of the Nile. The word יָם is sometimes used to denote a large river (see Notes on ch. xi. 15; xviii. 2). The Nile is often called a sea. Thus Pliny (*Nat. Hist.* ii. 35) says, 'The water of the Nile resembles the sea.' Thus, Seneca (*Quæst. Nat.* v. 2) says, 'By continued accessions of water, it stagnates (*stagnat*) into the appearance of a broad and turbid sea.' Compare Herodot. ii. 97; Diod. i. 12, 96: 'To this day in Egypt, the Nile is named *el-Bahr*, "the sea," as its most common appellation.' 'Our Egyptian servant,' says Dr. Robinson, 'who spoke English, always called it "the sea."'—(*Bib. Researches,* vol. i. p. 542). ¶ *And the river.* The Nile. ¶ *Shall be wasted.* This does not mean *entirely,* but its waters would fail so as to injure the country. It would not *overflow* in its accustomed manner, and the consequence would be, that the land would be desolate. It is well known that Egypt derives its great fertility entirely from the overflowing of the Nile. So important is this, that a public record is made at Cairo of the daily rise of the water. When the Nile rises to a less height than twelve cubits, a famine is the inevitable consequence, for then the water does not overflow the land. When it rises to a greater height than sixteen cubits, a famine is almost as certain—for then the superabundant waters are not drained off soon enough to allow them to sow the seed. The height of the inundation, therefore, that is necessary in order to insure a harvest, is from twelve to sixteen cubits. The annual overflow is in the month of August. The prophet here means that the Nile would not rise to the height that was desirable—or the waters should *fail*— and that the consequence would be a famine.

6. *And they shall turn the rivers far away* (הֶאֶזְנִיחוּ), probably from זָנַח, to

fence shall be emptied and dried up: the reeds and flags shall wither.

7 The paper reeds by the brooks, by the mouth of the brooks, and everything sown by the brooks,

shall wither, be driven away, and be[1] no *more*.

8 The fishers also shall mourn, and all they that cast angle into

1 *shall not be.*

---

have an offensive smell; to be rancid, or *putrid.* The word in this form occurs nowhere else. It is in the Hiphil conjugation, and is probably a form made from a mixture with the Chaldee. The sense is not doubtful. It means 'the rivers shall become putrid—or have an offensive smell;' that is, shall become stagnant, and send forth unwholesome *miasmata* producing sickness, as stagnant waters often do. The Vulgate renders it, 'And the rivers shall fail.' The LXX., 'And the Egyptians shall drink the waters from the sea, but the river shall fail, and be dried up, and the rivers shall fail, and the streams ($\delta\iota\hat{\omega}\rho\upsilon\chi\epsilon\varsigma$) of the river, and all the assembling ($\sigma\upsilon\nu\alpha\gamma\omega\gamma\dot{\eta}$) of waters shall be dried up.' ¶ And *the brooks of defence.* Heb. 'The rivers of מָצוֹר (*mâtzōr*).' The word מָצוֹר often means *straitness, affliction;* then a siege, a wall, a bulwark, a fortification. But, probably, it here means *Egypt,* or the same as מִצְרַיִם (*Mĭtzrāim*) (comp. ch. xxxvii. 25; 2 Kings xxx. 24; Mark vii. 12). Perhaps the Hebrews may have thought of Egypt as a strongly fortified place, and thus have given the name to it; or possibly this may have been a modification of the name *Mitzraim.* ¶ *The reeds and flags.* Which grew on the banks of the Nile—the papyrus, &c. (see Note on ch. xviii. 2.)

7. *The paper reeds* (עָרוֹת *ârōth*). This is not the word which occurs in ch. xviii. 2, and which, it is supposed, means there the papyrus (see Note on that place). Interpreters have been divided in regard to the meaning of the word here. Gesenius derives it from עָרָה (*ârâ*), *to be naked, open, bare;* and supposes that it means an open place, a place naked of wood, and that it here denotes the pastures on the banks of the Nile. So Rosenmüller interprets it of the green pastures on the banks of the Nile; and the Hebrew commentators generally so understand it. The

Vulgate renders it, 'And the bed (*alveus*) of the river shall be dried up from the fountain.' So the Chaldee, 'And their streams shall be desolate.' It probably denotes, not paper reeds, but the green pastures that were beside the brooks, or along the banks of the Nile. ¶ *By the brooks.* Heb. 'Rivers' (יְאֹרֵי). By the 'brooks' here, in the plural number, the prophet probably means the artificial canals which were cut in every direction from the Nile for the purpose of conveying the waters to various parts of the land. ¶ *By the mouth of the brooks.* At the mouth of the canals, or where they emptied into the Nile. Such meadows, being *near* the Nile, and most sure of a supply of water, would be more valuable than those which were remote, and are, therefore, particularly specified. ¶ *Shall wither,* &c. That is, there shall be utter and entire desolation. If the Nile ceased to overflow; if the streams, reservoirs, and canals, could not be filled, this would follow as a matter of course. Everything would dry up.

8. *The fishers also.* In this verse, and the two following, the prophet describes the calamities that would come upon various classes of the inhabitants, as the consequence of the failing of the waters of the Nile. The first class which he mentions are the fishermen. Egypt is mentioned (Num. xi. 5), as producing great quantities of fish. 'We remember the fish which we did eat in Egypt freely.' 'The Nile,' says Diodorus (i.), 'abounds with incredible numbers of all sorts of fish.' The same was true of the artificial canals, and lakes, and reservoirs of water (ver. 10). Herodotus (ii. 93) says that large quantities of fish were produced in the Nile : 'At the season of spawning,' says he, 'they move in vast multitudes towards the sea.—As soon as that season is over they leave the sea, return up the river, and endeavour to regain their accustomed haunts.'—As a specimen of his

the brooks shall lament, and they that spread nets upon the waters shall languish.

a 1 Ki.10.28.

9 Moreover they that work in fine *a* flax, and they that weave net-works,[1] shall be confounded.

1 or, *white-works.*

credulity, however, and also of the attention which he bestowed on natural history, the reader may consult the passage here referred to in regard to the mode of their propagation.—He also says that it is observed of the fish that are taken in their passage to the sea, that they have 'the left. part of their heads depressed.' Of those that are taken on their return, the *right* side of the head is found to be depressed. This he accounts for by observing, that 'the cause of this is obvious : as they pass to the sea they rub themselves on the banks on the left side ; as they return they keep closely to the same bank, and, in both instances, press against it, that they may not be obliged to deviate from their course by the current of the stream.' Speaking of the Lake Moeris, Herodotus says, that 'for six months the lake empties itself into the Nile, and the remaining six, the Nile supplies the lake. During the six months in which the waters ebb, the fishing which is here carried on furnishes the royal treasury with a talent of silver (about £180) every day' (ii. 149). 'The silver which the fishery of this lake produced, was appropriated to find the queen with clothes and perfumes.'—(Diod. i. 52.) The Lake Moeris is now farmed for 30 purses (about £193) annually. Michaud says that the Lake Menzaleh now yields an annual revenue of 800 purses,' about £5364. 'The great abundance of fish produced in the Nile was an invaluable provision of nature, in a country which had neither extended pasture grounds, nor large herds of cattle, and where corn was the principal production. When the Nile inundated the country, and filled the lakes and canals with its overflowing waters, these precious gifts were extended to the most remote villages in the interior of the valley, and the plentiful supply of fish which they obtained was an additional benefit conferred upon them at this season of the year.'—(Wilkinson's *Ancient Egyptians*, vol. iii. pp. 62, 63.) Hence the great-

ness of the calamity here referred to by the prophet when the lakes and canals should be dried up. The whole country would feel it. ¶ *And all they that cast angle.* Two kinds of fishermen are mentioned—those who used a hook, and those who used the net. The former

FISHING WITH THE HOOK.
From Wilkinson's Ancient Egyptians.

FISHING WITH THE NET.
From Wilkinson's Ancient Egyptians.

would fish mainly in the *brooks* or canals that were cut from the Nile to water their lands. For the various methods of fishing, illustrated by drawings, the reader may consult Wilkinson's *Ancient Egyptians*, vol. ii. p. 21 ; vol. iii. p. 53, *sq.*

9. *Moreover.* In addition to the calamities that will come upon the fishermen, the drying up of the river will affect all who are supported by that which the overflowing of its waters produced. ¶ *They that work in fine flax.* Egypt was celebrated anciently for producing flax in large quantities, and of a superior quality (see Ex. ix. 31 ; 1 Kings x. 28). The fine linen of Egypt which was manufactured from this is celebrated in Scripture (Prov. vii. 16 ; Ezek. xxvii. 7). The Egyptians had early carried the art of manufacturing linen to a great degree of per-

fection. As early as the exode of the Hebrews, we find that the art was known by which stuffs made of linen or other materials were curiously worked and embroidered. ' And thou shalt make an hanging for the door of the tent, of blue, and purple, and scarlet, and *fine-twined linen, wrought with needle-work*' (Ex. xxvi. 36; comp. xxvii. 16; xxxvi. 37). So Ezek. xxvii. 7: ' Fine linen, with broidered work from Egypt.' So also Martial refers to embroidery with the needle in Egypt:

Hæc tibi Memphitis tellus dat munera; victa
    est
Pectine Niliaco jam Babylonis acus.
          Martial, xiv. Ep. 50.

In regard to the *fineness* of the linen which was produced and wrought in Egypt, we may introduce a statement made by Pliny when speaking of the *nets* which were made there. ' So delicate,' says he, ' were some of them, that they would pass through a man's ring, and a single person could carry a sufficient number of them to surround a whole wood. Julius Lupus, who died while governor of Egypt, had some of those nets, each string of which consisted of 150 threads; a fact perfectly surprising to those who are not aware that the Rhodians preserve to this day, in the temple of Minerva, the remains of a linen corslet, presented to them by Amasis, king of Egypt, whose threads are composed each of 365 fibres.'— (Pliny, xix. 1.) Herodotus also mentions this corslet (iii. 47), and also another presented by Amasis to the Lacedemonians, which had been carried off by the Samians: ' It was of linen, ornamented with numerous figures of animals, worked in gold and cotton. Each thread of the corslet was worthy of admiration. For though very fine, every one was composed of 360 other threads, all distinct; the quality being similar to that dedicated to Minerva at Lindus, by the same monarch.' Pliny (xix. 1) mentions four kinds of linen that were particularly celebrated in Egypt—the Tanitic, the Pelusiac, the Butine, and the Tentyritic. He also says that the quantity of flax cultivated in Egypt was accounted for, by their exporting linen to Arabia and India.—It is now known, also, that the cloth used for

enveloping the dead, and which is now found in abundance on the mummies, was *linen*. This fact was long doubted, and it was until recently supposed by many that the cloth was made of cotton. This fact that it is linen was settled beyond dispute by some accurate experiments made by Dr. Ure, Mr. Bauer, and Mr. Thompson, with the aid of powerful microscopes. It was found that linen fibres uniformly present a cylindrical form, transparent, and articulated, or jointed like a cane, while the fibres of cotton have the appearance of a flat ribbon, with a hem or border at the edge. In the mummy cloths, it

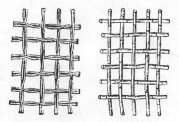

FIBRES OF COTTON AND LINEN.

was found, without exception, that the fibres were linen. Vast quantities of linen must, therefore, have been used. —The linen of the mummy cloths is generally coarse. The warp usually contains about 90 threads in the inch; the woof about 44. Occasionally, however, very fine linen cloth is found, showing the skill with which the manufacture was executed. Sir J. G. Wilkinson observes, that a piece of linen in his possession from Egypt had 540 (or 270 double) threads in one inch in the warp. Some of the cambric which is now manufactured has but 160 threads in the inch in the warp, and 140 in the woof. It is to be remembered, also, that the linen in Egypt was spun by hand, and without the aid of machinery (see, on this whole subject, Wilkinson's *Ancient Egyptians*, vol. iii. pp. 113–142. Ed. Lond. 1837). The word rendered ' fine ' here denotes, according to Gesenius, *combed* or *hatchelled*. The word ' fine,' however, expresses the idea with sufficient accuracy. Fine linen was used for clothing; but was so expensive that it was worn chiefly

10 And they shall be broken in
¹ foundations   ³ of living things.

by the rich and by princes (Luke xvi.
19). ¶ *They that weave networks.*
Marg. 'White-works.' According to
Gesenius the word דוֹרָי means *white
linen*—that which is fully bleached.
The word דוֹד means *a hole* or *cavern,*
but is not applied to cloth. The parallelism seems rather to require that the
word should mean 'white,' or that which
would correspond to 'fine,' or valuable ;
and it is not known that the Egyptians
had the art of working lace from linen.
Saadias supposes that *nets* are meant,
as being made with holes or meshes ;
but it is evident that a finer work is intended than that. ¶ *Shall be confounded.* Heb. 'Shall be ashamed.' That is,
they shall be thrown out of employment,
and not know what to do.

10. *And they shall be broken.* There
has been a great variety of opinion in
regard to the interpretation of this
verse, and much difficulty in the construction of the Hebrew words. The
Vulgate renders it, 'And its wet places
shall fail ; all who make ponds to take
fish.' The LXX., 'And all who make
beer (ζύθον) shall lament, and shall afflict
their souls.' This ζύθον was a sort of
malt liquor made of fruits by fermentation, and was used in Egypt in the
place of wine, as the grape did not
flourish there. Jerome on this place
says, that this was much used also in
Dalmatia and Pannonia, and was commonly called *Sabaium.* The Chaldee
renders this, 'And the place where they
weave cloth shall be trodden down, and
the place where they make fish ponds,
and where they collect waters, each one
for his own life.' This variety of reading arises chiefly from the different
modes of *pointing* the Hebrew words.
The word rendered 'broken' (מְדֻכָּאִים)
means *trodden down,* from דָּכָא *to tread,*
or *trample down,* and agrees in the
Hebrew with the word rendered 'purposes'—'the purposes shall be trodden
down.' The word 'purposes' (שְׁתֹתֶיהָ)
is found only in the plural, and is translated in Ps. xi. 3, 'foundations,' from
שִׁית, *foundation* or *pillar.* According
to this, it would mean that all *the pillars*

the purposes ¹ thereof, all that make
sluices *and* ponds ² for fish.

or *foundations, i.e.,* probably all the
nobles of Egypt, would be trodden down.
But this does not well suit the connection. Others derive it from שָׁתָה
(*shâthâ*), *to drink ;* and suppose that it
means that which is prepared for drink
shall be trodden down or destroyed.
Others suppose that it is derived from
שָׁתָה (*shâthâ*), *to weave,* and that it refers to the places where they wove the
cloth, *i.e.,* their looms ; or to the places
where they made their nets. And others
suppose that it is not the *places* where
they wove which are intended, but the
weavers themselves. Forerius supposes
it to be derived from שָׁתַת (*shâthăth*), *to
place, lay,* and that it refers to the
banks or *dykes* that were made to retain the waters in the canals, and that
these would be trodden down. This,
it seems to me, is the most probable
interpretation, as it suits the connection,
and agrees with the derivation of the
word. But the meaning cannot be
certainly ascertained. ¶ *All that make
sluices.* There has been quite as great
a variety in the interpetation of this
passage as in the former. The word
rendered 'sluices' (שֶׂכֶר), our translators
understand in the sense of places where
the water would be retained for fish
ponds—made by artificial banks confining the waters that overflow from the
Nile. This sense they have given to
the word, as if it were derived from סָכַר
(*sâkhăr*), *to shut up, to enclose.* The
LXX. read it as if it meant the Hebrew
שֵׁכָר (*shêkhâr*), or strong drink ; and so
also the Syriac renders it—as if from
שָׁכַר (*shâkhăr*), *to drink.* There is no
doubt that by a difference of pointing
it may have this signification. But the
most probable interpretation, perhaps, is
that which derives it from שָׂכַר (*sâkhăr*),
to hire, and means that they made those
places for reward, or for gain. They
thus toiled for hire ; and the prophet
says, that they who thus made enclosures
for fish in order to make a livelihood,
would be trodden down—that is, they
would fail of their purposes. ¶ *Ponds
for fish.* The word rendered 'fish'

11 Surely the princes of [a] Zoan *are* fools, the counsel of the wise counsellors of Pharaoh is become brutish : how say ye unto Pharaoh, I *am* the son of the wise, the son of ancient kings ?

12 Where [b] *are* they ? where *are* thy wise *men?* and let them tell

a Num.13.22.　　　b 1 Cor.1.20.　　　c ch.44.7,8.

thee now, and let them know what the [c] LORD of hosts hath purposed upon Egypt.

13 The princes of Zoan are become fools, [d] the princes of Noph are [e] deceived ; they have also seduced Egypt, *even* [1] *they that are* the stay of the tribes thereof.

d Rom.1.22.　　e Jer.2.16.　　1 *the corners,* or, *governors.*

(נֶפֶשׁ *nêphêsh*), denotes properly any living thing (*see marg.*), but if the usual interpretation is given of this verse, it is evident that fish are intended. The description, therefore, in this entire passage, from verse fifth to verse tenth, is designed to denote the calamities which would come upon Egypt from the failure of the waters of the Nile ; and the slightest knowledge of the importance of the Nile to that country will show that all these calamities would follow from such a failure.

11. *Surely the princes.* The following verses, to ver. 16, are designed to describe further the calamities that were coming upon Egypt by a want of wisdom in their rulers. They would be unable to devise means to meet the impending calamities, and would actually increase the national misery by their unwise counsels. The word 'princes' here is taken evidently for the rulers or counsellors of state. ¶ *Of Zoan.* The Vulgate, LXX., and Chaldee, render this 'Tanis.' Zoan was doubtless the Tans of the Greeks (Herod. ii. 166), and was a city of Lower Egypt, built, according to Moses (Num. xiii. 22), seven years after Hebron. It is mentioned in Ps. lxxviii. 12; Isa. xix. 11, 13; xxx. 4; Ezek. xxx. 14. It was at the entrance of the Tanitic mouth of the Nile, and gave name to it. Its ruins still exist, and there are seen there at present numerous blocks of granite, seven obelisks of granite, and a statue of Isis. It was the capital of the dynasty of the Tanitish kings until the time of Psammetichus; it was at this place principally that the miracles wrought by Moses were performed. 'Marvellous things did he in the sight of their fathers in the land of Egypt; in the field of Zoan' (Ps. lxxviii. 12). Its ruins are still called *San,* a slight change

of the word *Zoan.* The Ostium Taniticum is now the *Omm Faredje.* ¶ *Are fools.* They are unable to meet by their counsels the impending calamities. Perhaps their folly was evinced by their flattering their sovereign, and by exciting him to plans that tended to the ruin, rather than the welfare of the kingdom. ¶ *The wise counsellors of Pharaoh.* Pharaoh was the common name of the kings of Egypt in the same way as *Cæsar* became afterwards the common name of the Roman emperors—and the king who is here intended by Pharaoh is probably Psammetichus (see Note on ver. 4). ¶ *How say ye,* &c. Why do you *flatter* the monarch ? Why remind him of his ancestry ? Why attempt to inflate him with the conception of his own wisdom ? This was, and is, the common practice of courtiers ; and in this way kings are often led to measures most ruinous to their subjects.

12. *Where* are *they?* This whole verse is an appeal by the prophet to the king of Egypt respecting the counsellors and soothsayers of his kingdom. The sense is, ' a time of distress and danger is evidently coming upon Egypt. They pretend to be wise ; and there is now occasion for all their wisdom, and opportunity to evince it. Let them show it. Let them declare what is coming upon the nation, and take proper measures to meet and remove it ; and they will then demonstrate that it would be proper for Pharaoh to repose confidence in them.' But if they could not do this, then he should not suffer himself to be deluded, and his kingdom ruined, by their counsels.

13. *The princes of Zoan* (Note on ver. 11). This *repetition* is intensive and emphatic, and shows the deep conviction of the prophet of their folly. The design is to show that *all* the counsellors

14 The ^aLORD hath mingled a
perverse ¹ spirit in the midst thereof : and they have caused Egypt to
err in every work thereof, as a

a 1 Ki.22.22,23.   1 *spirit of perverseness.*

drunken *man* staggereth in his
vomit.

15 Neither shall there be *any*
work for Egypt, which the head
or tail, branch or rush, may do.

on which the Egyptians depended were
fools. ¶ *The princes of Noph.* The
Vulgate, the LXX., and the Chaldee,
render this 'Memphis,' and there is no
doubt that this is the city intended.
The name Memphis may have easily
arisen from Noph. It was written also
Moph, and hence Memphis. It is called
Menouf by the Copts and Arabians.
According to Plutarch, the name Memphis means *the port of the good.* The
situation of Memphis has been a subject
of considerable dispute, and has afforded
matter for long and laborious investigation. Sicard and Shaw fix its site at
Djezeh or Ghizeh, opposite to old Cairo.
Pococke, D'Anville, Niebuhr, and other
writers and travellers, place Memphis
more in the direction of Mitraheny,
about fifteen miles further south, on the
banks of the Nile, at the entrance of
the plain of the mummies, at the north
of which the pyramids are placed. It
was the residence of the ancient kings
of Egypt until the time of the Ptolemies,
who commonly resided at Alexandria.
Memphis retained its splendour until it
was conquered by the Arabians, about
A.D. 641. At the supposed site of Memphis south of Ghizeh, there are large
mounds of rubbish, a colossal statue sunk
in the ground, and a few fragments of
granite, which remain to test the existence of this renowned capital. In
Strabo's time, although partly in ruins,
it was yet a populous city, second only
to Alexandria. The total disappearance
of the ancient edifices of Memphis is
easily accounted for by the circumstance,
that the materials were employed for
the building of adjacent cities. Fostâl
rose out of the ruins, and when that
city was again deserted, these ruins
migrated again to the more modern
Cairo (see Robinson's *Bib. Researches,*
vol. i. p. 40). ¶ *They have also seduced
Egypt.* That is, they have by their
counsels caused it to err, and have led
it into its present embarrassment. ¶ *The
stay,* &c. Heb. פִּנָּה (*pinnâ*)—the cor-

ner ; *i.e.*, those who should have been
the support. So the word is used to
denote the head or leader of a people in
Judg. xx. 2, 14 ; 1 Sam. xiv. 38 ; Ps.
cxviii. 22 ; Isa. xxviii. 16 ; Zec. x. 4.
14. *The LORD hath mingled.* The
word מָסַךְ (*mâsăkh*), *to mingle*, is used
commonly to denote the act of mixing
spices with wine to make it more intoxicating (Prov. ix. 2, 5 ; Isa. v. 22).
Here it means, that JEHOVAH has poured
out into the midst of them a spirit of
giddiness ; that is, has produced consternation among them. National commotions and calamities are often thus
traced to the overruling providence of
God (see Note on ver. 2 ; comp. ch. x.
5, 6). ¶ *A perverse spirit.* Heb. 'A
spirit of perverseness.' The word rendered 'perverse' is derived from עָוָה,
to be crooked or *perverted.* Here it
means, that their counsels were unwise,
and such as tended to error and ruin.
¶ *To err as a drunken* man, &c. This
is a very striking figure. The whole
nation was reeling to and fro, and unsettled in their counsels, as a man is
who is so intoxicated as to reel and to
vomit. Nothing could more strikingly
express, first, the *fact* of their perverted
counsels and plans, and secondly, God's
deep abhorrence of the course which
they were pursuing.

15. *Neither shall there be* any *work.*
The sense is, that there shall be such
discord that no man, whether a prince,
a politician, or a priest, shall be able to
give any advice, or form any plan for
the national safety and security, which
shall be successful. ¶ *Which the head
or tail.* High or low ; strong or weak :
those in office and those out of office ;
all shall be dispirited and confounded.
Rosenmüller understands by the head
here, the *political* orders of the nation,
and by the tail the *sacerdotal* ranks.
But the meaning more probably is, the
highest and the lowest ranks—all the
politicians, and priests, and princes, on

16 In that day shall Egypt be like *a* unto women ; and it shall be afraid and fear, because of the shaking of the hand of the Lord of hosts, which he shaketh over it.

17 And the land of Judah shall be a terror unto Egypt: every one that maketh mention thereof shall

a Jer.51.30; Nah.3.13.   1 *lip.*

be afraid in himself, because of the counsel of the Lord of hosts, which he hath determined against it.

18 In that day shall five cities in the land of Egypt speak 1 the language *b* of Canaan, and swear to the Lord of hosts: one shall be called, The city of 2 destruction.

b Zep.3.9.   2 or, *Heres,* or, *the sun.*

the one hand, as the prophet had just stated (ver. 11–15); and all the artificers, fishermen, &c., on the other, as he had stated (ver. 8–10). This verse, therefore, is a *summing up* of all he had said about the calamities that were coming upon them. ¶ *Branch or rush.* See these words explained in the Note on ch. ix. 14.

16. *In that day shall Egypt be like unto women.* Timid ; fearful ; alarmed. The Hebrews often, by this comparison, express great fear and consternation (Jer. li. 30; Nah. iii. 13). ¶ *Because of the shaking of the hand.* The shaking of the hand is an indication of threatening or punishment (Note on ch. x. 32; xi. 15).

17. *And the land of Judah.* The fear and consternation of Egypt shall be increased when they learn what events are occurring there, and what Jehovah has purposed in regard to it. ¶ *Shall be a terror.* This cannot be understood to mean that they were in danger from an invasion by the Jews, for at that time they were not at war, and Judah had no power to overrun Egypt. Jarchi and Kimchi suppose that the passage means that the Egyptians would hear what had occurred to the army of Sennacherib on its overthrow, and that they would be alarmed as if a similar fate was about to come upon them. But the more probable interpretation is that which refers it to the *invasion* of Judah by Sennacherib. The Egyptians would know of that. Indeed, the leading design of Sennacherib was to invade Egypt, and Judah and Jerusalem were to be destroyed only *in the way* to Egypt. And when the Egyptians heard of the great preparations of Sennacherib, and of his advance upon Judah (see ch. x. 28–31), and knew that his design was to invade

them, 'the land of Judah' would be ' a terror,' because they apprehended that he would make a rapid descent upon them. Vitringa, however, supposes that the sense is, that the Egyptians in their calamities would remember the prophecies of Jeremiah and others, of which they had heard, respecting their punishment ; that they would remember that the prophecies respecting Judah had been fulfilled, and that thus Judah would be a terror to them *because* those predictions had come out of Judah. This is plausible, and it may be the correct explanation. ¶ *Which he hath determined against it.* Either against Judah, or Egypt. The Hebrew will bear either. It may mean that they were alarmed at the counsel which had been formed by Jehovah against Judah, and which was apparently about to be executed by the invasion of Sennacherib, and that thus they feared an invasion themselves, or that they learned that a purpose of destruction was formed by Jehovah against themselves, and that Judah became thus an object of terror, because the prophecies which were spoken there were certain of being fulfilled. The latter is the interpretation given by Vitringa, and perhaps is the most probable.

18. *In that day.* The word ' day ' is used in Scripture in a large signification, *as including the whole period under consideration,* or the whole time that is embraced in the scope of a prophecy. In this chapter it is used in this sense ; and evidently means that the event here foretold would take place *somewhere* in the period that is embraced in the design of the prophecy. That is, the event recorded in this verse would occur in the series of events that the prophet saw respecting

Egypt (see ch. **iv. 1**). The sense is, that somewhere in the general time here designated (ver. 4–17), the event here described would take place. There would be an extensive fear of JEHOVAH, and an extensive embracing of the true religion, in the land of Egypt. ¶ *Shall five cities.* The number 'five' here is evidently used to denote an *indefinite* number, in the same way as ' seven ' is often used in the Scriptures (see Lev. xxvi. 8). It means, that several cities in Egypt would use that language, one of which only is specified. ¶ *The language of Canaan.* Marg. 'Lip of Canaan.' So the Hebrew; but the word often means ' language.' The language of Canaan evidently means the *Hebrew* language; and it is called ' the language of Canaan ' either because it was spoken by the original inhabitants of the land of Canaan, or more probably because it was used by the Hebrews who occupied Canaan as the promised land; and then it will mean the language spoken in the land of Canaan. The phrase here used is employed probably to denote that they would be converted to the Jewish religion; or that the religion of the Jews would flourish there. A similar expression, to denote conversion to the true God, occurs in Zeph. iii. 9: 'For there I will turn to the people a pure language, that they may call upon the name of the Lord, to serve him with one consent.' ¶ *And swear to the* LORD *of hosts.* That is, they shall *devote* themselves to him; or they shall bind themselves to his service by solemn covenant; compare Deut. x. 20; Isa. xlv. 20, where conversion to God, and a purpose to serve him, is expressed in the same manner by *swearing* to him, *i.e.*, by solemnly devoting themselves to his service. ¶ *One shall be called.* The name of one of them shall be, &c. Why *one* particularly is designated is not known. ¶ *The city of destruction.* There has been a great variety of interpretation in regard to this expression. Marg. 'Heres,' or, ' The sun.' The Vulgate, 'The city of the sun;' evidently meaning Heliopolis. The LXX. Ασιδικ—'The city Asedek.' The Chaldee, ' The city of the house of the sun (בֵּית שֶׁמֶשׁ), which is to be destroyed.'

The Syriac, ' The city of *Heres.*' The common reading of the Hebrew text is, עִיר הַהֶרֶס ('*Ir Hăĕrĕs*). This reading is found in most MS. editions and versions. The word הֶרֶס (*hĕrĕs*) commonly means *destruction,* though it may also mean *deliverance*; and Gesenius supposes the name was to be given to it because it was to be a *delivered* city; *i.e.*, it would be the city to which ' the saviour' mentioned in ver. 20, would come, and which he would make his capital. Ikenius contends that the word '*Heres*' is taken from the Arabic, and that the name is the same as Leontopolis—' The city of the lion,' a city in Egypt. But besides other objections which may be made to this interpretation, the signification of *lion* is not given to the word in the Hebrew language. The common reading is that which occurs in the text—the city of *Heres.* But another reading (הַחֶרֶס) is found in sixteen MSS., and has been copied in the Complutensian Polyglot. This word (חֶרֶס *Hhĕrĕs*) properly means the *sun,* and the phrase means the city of the sun; *i.e.*, Heliopolis. Onias, who was disappointed in obtaining the high-priesthood (B.C. 149) on the death of his uncle Menelaus, fled into Egypt, and ingratiated himself into the favour of Ptolemy Philometer and Cleopatra, and was advanced to the highest rank in the army and the court, and made use of his influence to obtain permission to build a temple in Egypt like that at Jerusalem, with a grant that he and his descendants should always have a right to officiate in it as high priests. In order to obtain this, he alleged that it would be for the interest of Egypt, by inducing many Jews to come and reside there, and that their going annually to Jerusalem to attend the great feasts would expose them to alienation from the Egyptians, to join the Syrian interest (*see* Prideaux's *Connection,* under the year 149 B.C. Josephus expressly tells us (*Ant.* xiii. 3. 1–3), that in order to obtain this favour, he urged that it had been predicted by Isaiah six hundred years before, and that in consequence of this, Ptolemy granted him permission to build the temple, and that it was built at Leontopolis. It resembled that at Jerusalem, but was smaller and less splendid. It was within the Nomos or prefecture of Heliopolis, at the distance of twenty-four miles from Memphis. Onias pretended that the very place was foretold by Isaiah; and this would seem to suppose that the ancient reading was that of 'the city of the sun.' He urged this prediction in order to reconcile the Jews to the idea of another temple besides that at Jerusalem, because a temple erected in Egypt would be an object of disapprobation to the Jews in Palestine. Perhaps for the same reason the translation of Isaiah in the Septuagint renders this, 'Ασιδίκ—' The city of Asedek,' as if the original were צִדְקָה tzedâkâ—' The city of righteousness'—i.e., a city where righteousness dwells; or a city which was approved by God. But this is manifestly a corruption of the Hebrew text. It may be proper to remark that

the change in the Hebrew between the word rendered 'destruction' (הֶרֶס hĕrĕs), and the word 'sun' (חֶרֶס hhĕrĕs), is a change of a single letter where one might be easily mistaken for the other—the change of ה into ח. This might have occurred by the error of a transcriber, though the circumstances would lead us to think it not improbable that it may have been made designedly, but by whom is unknown. It may have been originally as Onias pretended, and have been subsequently altered by the Jews to counteract the authority which he urged for building a temple in Egypt; but there is no certain evidence of it. The evidence from MSS. is greatly in favour of the reading as in our translation (חֶרֶס hĕrĕs), and this may be rendered either 'destruction,' or more probably, according to Gesenius, ' deliverance,' so called from the deliverance that would be brought to it by the

PLAIN AND OBELISK OF HELIOPOLIS.

promised saviour (ver. 20). It may be added, that there is no evidence that Isaiah meant to designate the city where Onias built the temple, but

merely to predict that many cities in Egypt would be converted, one of which would be the one here designated. Onias took advantage of this, and made an

19 In that day shall there be an altar to the Lord in the midst of the land of Egypt, and a pillar *a* at the border thereof to the Lord.

artful use of it, but it was manifestly not the design of Isaiah. Which is the true reading of the passage it is impossible now to determine; nor is it important. I think the most probable interpretation is that which supposes that Isaiah meant to refer to a city *saved* from destruction, as mentioned in ver. 20, and that he did not design to designate any particular city by name.—The city of Heliopolis was situated on the Pelusian branch of the Nile, about five miles below the point of the ancient Delta. It was deserted in the time of Strabo; and this geographer mentions its mounds of ruin, but the houses were shown in which Eudoxus and Plato had studied. The place was celebrated for its learning, and its temple dedicated to the sun. There are now no ruins of ancient buildings, unless the mounds can be regarded as such; the walls, however, can still be traced, and there is an entire obelisk still standing. This obelisk is of red granite, about seventy feet high, and from its great antiquity has excited much attention among the learned. In the neighbouring villages there are many fragments which have been evidently transferred from this city. Dr. Robinson, who visited it, says, that 'the site is about two hours N.N.E. from Cairo. The way thither passes along the edge of the desert, which is continually making encroachments, so soon as there ceases to be a supply of water for the surface of the ground.—The site of Heliopolis is marked by low mounds, inclosing a space about three quarters of a mile in length, by half a mile in breadth, which was once occupied by houses, and partly by the celebrated temple of the sun. This area is now a ploughed field, a garden of herbs; and the solitary obelisk which rises in the midst is the sole remnant of the splendour of the place.—Near by it is a very old sycamore, its trunk straggling and gnarled, under which legendary tradition relates that the holy family once rested.'—(*Bib. Researches,* vol. i. pp. 36, 37.) The preceding cut, from the Pictorial Bible, will give an idea of the present appearance of Heliopolis.

19. *In that day shall there be an altar.* An *altar* is properly a place on which sacrifices are offered. According to the Mosaic law, but one great altar was to be erected for sacrifices. But the word 'altar' is often used in another sense to denote a place of *memorial;* or a place of worship in general (Josh. xxii. 22–26. It is clear that Isaiah did not intend that this should be taken *literally,* or that there should be a rival temple and altar erected in Egypt, but his description is evidently taken in part from the account of the religion of the patriarchs who erected altars and pillars and monuments to mark the places of the worship of the true God. The parallelism here, where 'pillars' are mentioned, shows in what sense the word 'altar' is used. It means that the worship of the true God would be established in Egypt, and that certain *places* should be set apart to his service. *Altars* were among the first places reared as connected with the worship of God (see Gen. viii. 20; xii. 7; xxxv. 1; Ex. xvii. 15). ¶ *To the* Lord. To Jehovah—the true God. ¶ *And a pillar.* That is, a memorial to God. Thus Jacob set up the stone on which he had lain 'for a pillar,' and poured oil on it (Gen. xxviii. 18). Again (Gen. xxxv. 14), he set up a pillar to mark the place where God met him and talked with him (comp. Gen. xxxi. 13; Lev. xxvi. 1; Deut. xvi. 22). The word 'pillar,' when thus used, denotes a stone, or column of wood, erected as a monument or memorial; and especially a memorial of some manifestation of God or of his favour. Before temples were known, such pillars would naturally be erected; and the description here means simply that Jehovah would be worshipped in Egypt. ¶ *At the border thereof.* Not in one place merely, but in all parts of Egypt. It is not improbable that the *name* of Jehovah, or some rude designation of the nature of his worship, would be inscribed on such pillars. It

20 And it shall be for a *a* sign and for a witness unto the LORD of hosts in the land of Egypt: for

a Jos.4.20.

they shall cry unto the LORD because of the oppressors, and he shall send them a saviour, and a great one, and he shall deliver them.

is known that the Egyptians were accustomed to rear pillars, monuments, obelisks, &c., to commemorate great events, and that the names and deeds of illustrious persons were engraven on them; and the prophet here says, that such monuments should be reared to JEHOVAH. In regard to the fulfilment of this prophecy, there can be no question. After the time of Alexander the Great, large numbers of Jews were settled in Egypt. They were favoured by the Ptolemies, and they became so numerous that it was deemed necessary that their Scriptures should be translated into Greek for their use, and accordingly the translation called the Septuagint was made. See Introduction, § 8, 1, (1).

20. *And it shall be for a sign.* The altar, and the pillar. This shows that the altar was not to be for sacrifice, but was a *memorial*, or designed to designate a place of worship. ¶ *They shall cry to the* LORD *because of the oppressors.* That is, oppressed and borne down under the exactions of their rulers, they shall seek deliverance from the true God—one instance among many of the effect of affliction and oppression in leading men to embrace the true religion. ¶ *And he shall send them a saviour.* Who this *saviour* would be, has been a subject on which there has been a great difference of opinion. Grotius supposes that it would be *the angel* by which the army of Sennacherib would be destroyed. Gesenius thinks it was Psammetichus, who would deliver them from the tyranny of the eleven kings who were contending with each other, or that, since in ver. 4, he is called a 'severe lord,' it is probable that the promise here is to be understood of a delivering or protecting angel. But it is evident that some person is here denoted who would be sent *subsequently* to the national judgments which are here designated. Dr. Gill supposes that by the saviour here is meant the Messiah; but this interpretation does not suit the connection,

for it is evident that the event here predicted, was to take place before the coming of Christ. Vitringa and Bishop Newton suppose with more probability that Alexander the Great is here referred to, who took possession of Egypt after his conquest in the East, and who might be called *a saviour*, inasmuch as he delivered them from the reign of the oppressive kings who had tyrannized there, and inasmuch as his reign and the reigns of those who succeeded him in Egypt, would be much more mild than that of the former kings of that country. That Alexander the Great was regarded by the Egyptians as a saviour or deliverer, is apparent from history. Upon his coming to Egypt, the people submitted to him cheerfully, out of hatred to the Persians, so that he became master of the country without any opposition (Diod. Sic. xvii. 49; Arrian, iii. 3, 1; Q. Curtius, iv. 7, 8, as quoted by Newton). He treated them with much kindness; built the city of Alexandria, calling it after his own name, designing to make it the capital of his empire; and under him and the Ptolemies who succeeded him, trade revived, commerce flourished, learning was patronized, and peace and plenty blessed the land. Among other things, Alexander transplanted many Jews into Alexandria, and granted them many privileges, equal to the Macedonians themselves (Jos. *Bell. Jud.* ii. 18. 7; *Contra Ap.* ii. 4). 'The arrival of Alexander,' says Wilkinson (*Ancient Egyptians,* vol. i. pp. 213, 214), 'was greeted with universal satisfaction. Their hatred of the Persians, and their frequent alliances with the Greeks, who had fought under the same banners against a common enemy, naturally taught the Egyptians to welcome the Macedonian army with the strongest demonstrations of friendship, and to consider their coming as a direct interposition of the gods; and so wise and considerate was the conduct of the early Ptolemies, that they almost ceased to regret the period when they were

21 And the LORD shall be known to Egypt, and the Egyptians shall know the LORD in that day, and shall do ^a sacrifice and oblation ; yea, they shall vow a vow unto the LORD, and perform *it*.

22 And the LORD shall smite Egypt; he shall smite and heal *it :* and they shall return *even* to the LORD, and he shall be entreated of them, and shall heal them.

23 In that day shall there be a highway ^b out of Egypt to Assyria ; and the Assyrian shall come into Egypt, and the Egyptian into Assyria ; and the Egyptians shall serve with the Assyrians.

^a Mal.1.11.   ^b ch.11.16.

governed by their native princes.' Under the Ptolemies, large numbers of the Jews settled in Egypt. For their use, as has been remarked, the Old Testament was translated into Greek, and a temple was built by Onias, under the sixth Ptolemy. Philo represents the number of the Jews in Egypt in his time at not less than one million. They were settled in nearly all parts of Egypt; but particularly in Heliopolis or the city of the sun, in Migdol, in Tahpanes, in Noph or Memphis, in Pathros or Thebais (Jer. xliv. 1)—perhaps the five cities referred to in ver. 18. ¶ *And a great one* (וָרָב). A mighty one ; a powerful saviour. The name 'great' has been commonly assigned to Alexander. The LXX. render this, 'Judging (κρίνων), he shall save them ;' evidently regarding רָב as derived from רִיב, *to manage a cause,* or *to judge*. Lowth renders it, 'A vindicator.' The word means *great, mighty ;* and is repeatedly applied to a prince, chief, or captain (2 Kings xxv. 8; Esth. i. 8; Dan. i. 3; ii. 48; v. 11).

21. *And the* LORD *shall be known to Egypt*. Shall be worshipped and honoured by the Jews who shall dwell there, and by those who shall be proselyted to their religion. ¶ *And the Egyptians shall know the* LORD. That many of the Egyptians would be converted to the Jewish religion there can be no doubt. This was the result in all countries where the Jews had a residence (comp. Notes on Acts ii. 9–11). ¶ *And shall do sacrifice*. Shall offer sacrifices to JEHOVAH. They would naturally go to Jerusalem as often as practicable, and unite with the Jews there, in the customary rites of their religion. ¶ *And oblation*. The word מִנְחָה (*mĭnhhâ*) 'oblation,' denotes any

offering that is not a *bloody* sacrifice—a thank-offering ; an offering of incense, flour, grain, &c. (see Notes on ch. i. 13.) The sense is, that they should be true worshippers of God. ¶ *They shall vow a vow*, &c. They shall be sincere and true worshippers of God. The large numbers of the Jews that dwelt there ; the fact that many of them doubtless were sincere ; the circumstances recorded (Acts ii. 9–11), that Jews were in Jerusalem on the day of Pentecost ; and the fact that the true religion was carried to Egypt, and the Christian religion established there, all show how fully this prediction was fulfilled.

22. *And the* LORD *shall smite Egypt*. That is, in the manner described in the previous part of this prophecy (ver. 2–10). ¶ *And heal* it. Or restore it to more than its former splendour and prosperity, as described in the previous verses (18–20). He shall send it a saviour ; he shall open new sources of prosperity ; and he shall cause the true religion to flourish there. These advantages would be more than a compensation for all the calamities that he would bring upon it. ¶ *And they shall return,* &c. These calamities shall be the means of their conversion to JEHOVAH.

23. *There shall be a highway*. A communication ; that is, there shall be an alliance between Egypt and Assyria, as constituting parts of one empire, and as united in the service of the true God. The same figure of a *highway* is found in ch. xi. 16 (see Note on that place). The truth was, that Alexander, by his conquests, subjected Assyria and Egypt, and they constituted parts of his empire, and were united under him. It was true, also, that there were large numbers of Jews in both these countries, and

24 In that day shall Israel be the third with Egypt and with Assyria, *even* a blessing in the midst of the land.

25 Whom the LORD of hosts shall bless, saying, Blessed *be* Egypt my people, *a* and Assyria the work *b* of my hands, and Israel mine inheritance.

CHAPTER XX.

ANALYSIS.

This prophecy occupies this single chapter. Its design and scope it is not difficult to understand. The time when it was delivered is designated in ver. 1, and was manifestly in the reign

a 1 Pet.2.10.   *b* Eph.2.10.

that they were united in the service of the true God. They worshipped him *in* those countries; and they met at Jerusalem at the great feasts, and thus Judah, Assyria, and Egypt, were united in his worship. ¶ *And the Assyrian shall come into Egypt.* There shall be free and uninterrupted intercourse between the two nations, as parts of the same empire. ¶ *And the Egyptians shall serve with the Assyrians.* In the same armies; under the same leader. This was the case under Alexander the Great. Or the word 'serve' may mean that they would serve God unitedly. So Lowth and Noyes render it.

24. *In that day shall Israel be the third.* That is, the three shall be united as one people. Instead of being rival, hostile, and contending kingdoms, they shall be united and friendly; and instead of having different and jarring religions, they shall all worship the same God. The prophecy rather refers to the spread of the true religion, and the worship of the true God, than to a political or civil alliance. ¶ *Even a blessing.* It shall be a source of blessing, because from Judea the true religion would extend into the other lands. ¶ *In the midst of the land.* That is, *the united land*—composed of the three nations now joined in alliance. Judea was situated in the *midst* of this united land, or occupied a central position between the two. It was also true that it occupied a central position in regard to the whole earth, and that from

of Hezekiah. The Assyrian empire had extended its conquests over Syria, Damascus, and Ephraim or Samaria (2 Kings xviii. 9–12). The king of Assyria had sent Tartan to take possession of Ashdod, or Azotus, the maritime key of Palestine, and there was evident danger that the Assyrians would overthrow the government of Judah, and secure also the conquest of Egypt. In these circumstances of danger, the main reliance of Judah was on the aid which they hoped to derive from Egypt and Ethiopia (ver. 5), as being alone able to repel the Assyrians. They relied rather on that aid than on God. To *recall* them from this, and to show them the vanity of such a dependence, and to lead them to rely on God, Isaiah was sent to them to be a sign; or to indicate by a symbolical action what would be the fate of the Egyptians on whom they were placing their reliance (ver. 4). By it, as a radiating point, the true religion was disseminated throughout all nations.

25. *Whom the* LORD *of hosts shall bless.* That is, which united country he shall acknowledge as truly worshipping him, and on which he shall bestow his favours as his favoured people. ¶ *Assyria the work of my hands.* This is synonymous with the expression 'my people.' It means that the arrangements by which the true religion would be established among them, were the work of God. Conversion to God is everywhere in the Scriptures spoken of as his work, or creation; see Eph. ii. 10: 'For we are his workmanship; created in Christ Jesus unto good works' (comp. 2 Cor. v. 17; Ps. c. 3). ¶ *Israel mine inheritance.* The land and people which is peculiarly my own —a name not unfrequently given to Israel. For a learned examination of the various hypotheses in regard to the fulfilment of this prophecy, see Vitringa. He himself applies it to the times succeeding Alexander the Great. Alexander he regards as the 'saviour' mentioned in ver. 20; and the establishment of the true religion referred to by the prophet as that which would take place under the Ptolemies. Vitringa has proved—what indeed is known to all who have the slightest knowledge of history—that there were large numbers of Jews under the Ptolemies in Egypt, and that multitudes became proselytes to the Jewish faith.

showing the Jews what would be the destiny of Egypt, he designed to withdraw them from resting on their assistance, and to turn them to God for protection and aid.

IN the year *a* that Tartan came unto Ashdod, (when Sargon the king of Assyria sent him,) and

a 2 Ki.18.17.		1 *by the hand of.*

CHAPTER XX.

1. *In the year that Tartan came unto Ashdod.* Tartan was one of the generals of Sennacherib. Ashdod, called by the Greeks Azotus, was a seaport on the Mediterranean, between Askelon and Ekron, and not far from Gaza (Reland's *Palestine,* iii.) It was one of the five cities of the Philistines, assigned to the tribe of Judah, but never conquered by them (Josh. xiii. 8; xv. 46, 47). The temple of Dagon stood here ; and hither the ark of God was brought after the fatal battle of Eben-ezer (1 Sam. v. 1, *sq.*) It sustained many sieges, and was regarded as an important place in respect to Palestine, and also to Egypt. It was taken by Tartan, and remained in the possession of the Assyrians until it was besieged by Psammetichus, the Egyptian king, who took it after a siege of twenty-nine years (Herod. ii. 157). It was about thirty miles from Gaza. It is now a small village, and is called *Esdud.* It was besieged and taken by Tartan as preparatory to the conquest of Egypt ; and if the king who is here called *Sargon* was Sennacherib, it is probable that it was taken before he threatened Jerusalem. ¶ *Sargon the king of Assyria.* Who this *Sargon* was is not certainly known. Some have supposed that it was Sennacherib ; others that it was Shalmaneser the father of Sennacherib, and others that it was Esar-haddon the successor of Sennacherib—(Michaelis). Rosenmüller and Gesenius suppose that it was a king who reigned *between* Shalmaneser and Sennacherib. Tartan is known to have been a general of Sennacherib (2 Kings xviii. 17), and it is natural to suppose that he is here intended. Jerome says that Sennacherib had seven names, and Kimchi says that he had eight ; and it is not improbable that *Sargon* was one of those names. Oriental princes often

fought against Ashdod and took it;

2 At the same time spake the LORD [1] by Isaiah the son of Amoz, saying, Go, and loose the sackcloth from off thy loins, and put off thy shoe from thy foot. And he did so, walking naked and barefoot.

had several names ; and hence the difficulty of identifying them. See Vitringa on this place.

2. *By Isaiah.* Marg. ' By the hand of Isaiah.' So the Hebrew. That is, by the instrumentality of Isaiah. He sent him to make known the fate of the Egyptians, and the folly of trusting in them on this occasion. ¶ *Go, and loose the sackcloth.* For the meaning of the word *sackcloth,* see Note on ch. iii. 24. It was commonly worn as an emblem of mourning. But there is reason to believe that it was worn also by the prophets, and was regarded, in some degree, as their appropriate dress. It was made usually of the coarse hair of the goat, and was worn as a zone or girdle around the loins. That this was the dress of Elijah is apparent from 2 Kings i. 8: ' He was an hairy man, and girt with a girdle of leather ;' that is, he was clothed in a garment made of hair. The same was true of John the Baptist (Matt. iii. 4). That the prophets wore ' a rough garment ' is apparent also from Zech. xiii. 4 : ' Neither shall they (the false prophets) wear a rough garment (Heb. A garment of hair) to deceive ;' *i.e.,* the false prophets shall not assume the dress of the true prophets for the purpose of deluding the people, or to make them think that they are true prophets. It is evident, therefore, that this hairy garment was regarded as a dress that appertained particularly to the prophets. It is well known, also, that the ancient Greek philosophers had a peculiar dress to distinguish them from the common people. Probably the custom of wearing *hair cloth* among the monks of later ages took its rise from this example of the prophets. His removing this garment was designed to be a sign or an emblem to show that the Egyptians should be stripped of all their possessions, and

3 And the LORD said, Like as my servant Isaiah hath walked

carried captive to Assyria. ¶ *Walking naked.* That is, walking *without this peculiar prophetic garment.* It does not mean that he was in a state of entire nudity; for all that he was directed to do was to lay this garment—this emblem of his office—aside. The word *naked,* moreover, is used in the Scriptures, not to denote an absolute destitution of clothing, but that the *outer* garment was laid aside (see Note on John xxi. 7). Thus it is said of Saul (1 Sam. xix. 24) that he 'stripped off his clothes also, and prophesied before Samuel, and lay down naked all that day;' *i.e.,* he stripped off his royal robes, and was *naked* or *unclothed* in that respect. He removed his *peculiar* dress as a king, or military chieftain, and appeared in the ordinary dress. It cannot be supposed that the king of Israel would be seen literally without raiment. So David is said to have danced *naked* before the ark, *i.e.,* with his royal robes laid aside. How *long* Isaiah walked in this manner has been a matter of doubt (see Note on ver. 3). The prophets were accustomed to use symbolical actions to denote the events which they foretold (see Note on ch. viii. 18). Thus the children of Isaiah, and the names given to them, were significant of important events (ch. viii. 1, 2, 3; comp. Jer. xviii. 1–6; xliii. 8, 9); in both of which places he used emblematic actions to exhibit the events concerning which he prophesied in a striking manner. Thus also the prophets are expressly called '*signs and wonders*' (Zech. iii. 8; Ezek. xii. 6).

3. *Like as.* That is, 'as Isaiah has gone stripped of his peculiar garment as a prophet, so shall the Egyptians and Ethiopians be stripped of all that they value, and be carried captive into Assyria.' ¶ *Hath walked—three years.* A great deal of difficulty has been felt in the interpretation of this place, from the strong improbability that Isaiah should have gone in this manner for a space of time so long as our translation expresses. The LXX. render this, 'As my servant Isaiah hath walked naked and barefoot three years, three years shall be for signs and wonders to the Egyptians and Ethiopians.' The phrase in the Hebrew, 'three years,' *may* either be taken in connection with the preceding part of the sentence, as in our translation, meaning that he actually walked so long; or it may be taken with that which follows, and then it will denote that he was a sign and wonder with reference to the captivity of the Egyptians and Ethiopians; and that by this symbolical action he in some way indicated that they would be carried away captive for that space of time; or, as Aben Ezra and Abarbanel suppose, that he signified that their captivity would commence after three years. Lowth supposes that it means that his walking was for three days, and that the Hebrew text has been corrupted. Vitringa also seems to suppose that this is possible, and that a day was a symbolical sign for a year. Rosenmüller supposes that this prophetic action was continued during three years *at intervals,* so that the subject might be kept before the mind of the people. But the supposition that this means that the symbolic action of walking naked and barefoot continued for so long a time in any manner, is highly improbable. (1.) The Hebrew does not necessarily require it. It *may* mean simply that his actions were a sign and wonder with reference to a three years' captivity of the Egyptians. (2.) It is in itself improbable that he should so long a time walk about Jerusalem expressly as a sign and wonder, when a much shorter period would have answered the purpose as well. (3.) Such a sign would have hardly met the circumstances of the case. Ashdod was taken. The Assyrian king was advancing. The Jews were in consternation and looking to Egypt for help; and amidst this agitation and alarm, there is the highest improbability that Isaiah would be required to remain a sign and wonder for the long space of three years, when decided action was needed, and when, unless prevented, the Jews would have formed a speedy alliance with the Egyptians. I suppose, therefore, that the entire sense of the phrase will be expressed by translating it, 'my servant Isaiah hath walked naked and

naked and barefoot three years *for* a sign and wonder upon Egypt and upon Ethiopia ;

4 So shall the king of Assyria lead away the [1] Egyptians prisoners, and the Ethiopians captives, young and old, naked and barefoot, even with *their* buttocks uncovered, to the [2] shame of Egypt.

5 And they shall be afraid and ashamed of Ethiopia their expectation, and of Egypt their glory.

6 And the inhabitant of this isle [3] shall say in that day, Behold, such *a is* our expectation, whither we flee for help to be delivered from the king of Assyria: and how shall we escape ?

1 *captivity of Egypt.*   2 *nakedness.*

3 *or, country,* Jer.47.4.   *a* Job 6.20.

barefoot, *a three years' sign and wonder ;'* that is, a sign and indication that *a three years' calamity* would come upon Egypt and Ethiopia. Whether this means that the calamity would *commence* in three years from that time, or that it should *continue* three years, perhaps we cannot determine. Grotius thinks that it means that it would occur *after* three years ; that is, that the war between the Assyrians and Ethiopians would continue during that time only. In what manner Isaiah indicated this, is not certainly known. The conjecture of Lowth is not improbable, that it was by appearing three *days* naked and barefoot, and that each day denoted a year. Or it may have been that he appeared in this manner for a short period—though but once—and *declared* that this was the design or purport of the action. ¶ *Upon Egypt, &c.* With reference to ; or as a sign in regard to Egypt. It does not mean that he was *in* Egypt, but that his action *had reference to* Egypt. ¶ *And Ethiopia.* Heb. כוּשׁ—*Cush* (see Note on ch. xi. 11). Whether this denotes the African Cush or Ethiopia, or whether it refers to the *Cush* in Arabia, cannot be determined. The latter is the more probable supposition, as it is scarcely probable that the Assyrian would extend his conquests south of Egypt so as to subdue the African Ethiopia. Probably his conquest embraced the *Cush* that was situated in the southern regions of Arabia.

4. *So shall the king of Assyria.* The emphasis here is on the word *so.* As Isaiah has walked naked, *i.e.,* stripped off his usual clothing, *so* shall the Egyptians and Ethiopians be led away *stripped* of all their possessions. ¶ *The Egyptians prisoners, and the Ethiopians captives.* The Egyptians

and Ethiopians, or Cushites, were often united in an alliance, and appear to have been when this prophecy was delivered. Thus Nahum iii. 8 :

Ethiopia and Egypt were her strength, and it was infinite;
Put and Lubim were thy helpers.

¶ *To the shame of Egypt.* It shall be a disgrace to them to be subdued, and to be carried captive in so humiliating a manner. It is remarked by Belzoni (' *Operations and Recent Discoveries in Egypt and Nubia* '), that in the figures on the remains of their temples, prisoners are often represented as naked, or only in aprons, with dishevelled hair, and with their hands chained. He also remarks, that on a *bas-relief*, on the recently-discovered graves of the kings of Thebes, a multitude of *Egyptian* and *Ethiopian prisoners* are represented—showing that Egypt and Ethiopia were sometimes *allied*, alike in mutual defence and in bondage (comp. Isa. xlvii. 2, and Nah. iii. 5).

5. *And they shall be afraid.* The Jews, or the party or faction among the Jews, that were expecting aid from allied Ethiopia and Egypt. When they shall see them vanquished, they shall apprehend a similar danger to themselves ; and they shall be ashamed that they ever confided in a people so little able to aid them, instead of trusting in the arm of God. ¶ *Egypt their glory.* Their boast, as if Egypt was able to save them. The word here rendered 'glory' (תִּפְאָרֶת) means properly, *ornament, praise, honour ;* and then it may mean the *object* of glory, or that in which men boast or confide. That is its sense here (comp. Isa. x. 12 ; xiii. 19 ; Zech. xii. 7).

6. *And the inhabitant.* The dwellers generally. ¶ *Of this isle.* The word

CHAPTER XXI.

ANALYSIS OF VER. 1–10.

THE prophecy which commences this chapter occupies the first ten verses. That it relates to Babylon is apparent from ver. 2 and 9. The object is to foretell the destruction of that city by the Medes and Persians, and the design is the same as in the more extended and minute description of the same event in ch. xiii., xiv. Whether it was delivered at the same, or at another time, cannot be determined from the prophecy. The purpose, however, of the prophecy is the same as there—to give consolation to the Jews who should be carried captive to that city; to assure them that Babylon would be destroyed, and that they would be delivered from their long and severe bondage. This is indicated in a brief and graphic manner in ver. 10.

This oracle, or ode, is one of singular beauty. It is distinguished for its brevity, energy, and force; for the variety and the rapidity of the action, and for the vivid manner in which the events are made to pass before the mind. It is the language of strong excitement and of alarm; language that expresses rapid and important movements; and language appropriate to great vigour of conception and sublimity in description. In the oracle the prophet supposes himself in Babylon, and the events which are described are made to pass rapidly in vision (see Intro. § 7, 4) before him. He first sees (ver. 1) the dreadful storm coming at a distance (the hostile armies), approaching like a whirlwind and threatening destruction to everything in its way. He then (ver. 2) hears God's direction to the invading armies; represents himself as made acquainted with the design of the vision, and

hears the command of God to Elam (Persia) and Media to go up and commence the siege. Regarding himself as among the exiles in the midst of Babylon, he (ver. 3, 4) describes himself as deeply affected in view of this sudden invasion, and of the calamities that were coming upon Babylon. In ver. 5, he describes the state of the Babylonians. They are represented, first as preparing the table, making ready for feasting and revelry, setting the watch on the watchtower, and giving themselves up to dissipation; and secondly, as suddenly alarmed, and summoned to prepare for war. He then (ver. 6–9 declares the way in which the princes of Baby lon would be roused from their revelry. But i⁺ is described in a very remarkable manner. He does not *narrate* the events, but he represents himself as directed to appoint a watchman (ver. 6) to announce what he should see. That watchman (ver. 7) sees two chariots—representing two nations coming rapidly onward to execute the orders of God. So rapid is their approach, so terrible their march, that the watchman cries out (ver. 9) that Babylon is fallen, and will be inevitably destroyed. The prophecy is then closed (ver. 10) by an address to the afflicted Jews whom God had 'threshed,' or punished, by sending them captive to Babylon, and with the declaration that this was intended by the Lord of hosts to be declared unto them. The whole design of the prophecy, therefore, is to console them, and to repeat the assurance given in ch. xiii., xiv., that Babylon would be destroyed, and that they would be delivered from bondage.

T̲HE burden of the desert of the sea. As whirlwinds ᵃin the south pass through; *so* it cometh

ᵃ Zec.9.14.

אִי (*isle*) is used here in the sense of *coast*, or *maritime* country, and is evidently applied to Palestine, or the land of Canaan, which is a narrow coast lying on the Mediterranean. That the word is often used in this sense, and may be applied to a maritime country, see Notes on ch. xiii. 22 ; xli. 1. The connection here requires us to understand it of Palestine. ¶ *Shall say*, &c. Shall condemn their own folly in trusting in Egypt, and seeking deliverance there. ¶ *And how shall we escape?* They shall be alarmed for their own safety, for the very nation on which they had relied had been made captive. And when the *stronger* had been subdued, how could the feeble

and dependent escape a similar overthrow and captivity? All this was designed to show them the folly of trusting in the aid of another nation, and to lead them to put confidence in the God of their fathers.

CHAPTER XXI.

1. *The burden* (see Note on ch. xiii. 1). ¶ *Of the desert.* There have been almost as many interpretations of this expression, as there have been interpreters. That it means Babylon, or the country about Babylon, there can be no doubt ; but the question why this phrase was applied, has given rise to a great diversity of opinions. The term 'desert' (מִדְבָּר) is usually applied to a wilderness, or to a comparatively

from the desert, from a terrible land,

2 A ¹ grievous vision is declared unto me; the treacherous ᵃ dealer

barren and uncultivated country—a place for flocks and herds (Ps. lxv. 13; Jer. ix. 9, &c.); to an actual waste, a sandy desert (Isa. xxxii. 15; xxxv. 1); and particularly to the deserts of Arabia (Gen. xiv. 6; xvi. 7; Deut. xi. 24). It may here be applied to Babylon either historically, as having been *once* an unreclaimed desert ; or by *anticipation*, as descriptive of what it *would be* after it should be destroyed by Cyrus, or possibly both these ideas may have been combined. That it was *once* a desert before it was reclaimed by Semiramis is the testimony of all history ; that it is *now* a vast waste is the united testimony of all travellers. There is every reason to think that a large part of the country about Babylon was formerly overflowed with water *before* it was reclaimed by dykes ; and as it was naturally a waste, when the artificial dykes and dams should be removed, it would again be a desert. ¶ *Of the sea* (רָם). There has been also much difference of opinion in regard to this word. But there can be no doubt that it refers to the Euphrates, and to the extensive region of marsh that was covered by its waters. The name 'sea' (יָם) is not unfrequently given to a large river, to the Nile, and to the Euphrates (see Note on ch. xi. 15; comp. ch. xix. 5). Herodotus (i. 184), says, that ' Semiramis confined the Euphrates within its channel by raising great dams against it ; for before, it overflowed the whole country like a sea.' And Abydenus, in Eusebius, (*Prepara. Evang.*, ix. 457) says, respecting the building of Babylon by Nebuchadnezzar, that ' it is reported that all this was covered with water, *and was called a sea*'— λέγεται δὲ πάντα μὲν ἐξ ἀρχῆς ὕδωρ εἶναι, θαλασσῶν καλουμένην. (Comp. Strabo, *Geog.* xvi. 9, 10; and Arrianus, *De Expedit. Alexandri*, vii. 21). Cyrus removed these dykes, reopened the canals, and the waters were suffered to remain, and again converted the whole country into a vast marsh (see Notes on ch. xiii., xiv.) ¶ *As whirl-*

dealeth treacherously, and the spoiler spoileth. Go ᵇ up, O Elam: besiege, O Media: all the sighing thereof have I made to cease.

winds. That is, the army comes with the rapidity of a whirlwind. In ch. viii. 8 (comp. Hab. i. 11), an army is compared to an overflowing and rapid river. ¶ *In the south.* Whirlwinds or tempests are often in the Scriptures represented as coming from the south, Zech. ix. 14; Job xxxvii. 9 :

Out of the south cometh the whirlwind,
And cold out of the north.

So Virgil :

———creberque procellis
Africus—   *Æneid,* i. 85.

The deserts of Arabia were situated to the south of Babylon, and the south winds are described as the winds of the desert. Those winds are represented as being so violent as to tear away the tents occupied by a caravan (Pietro della Valle, *Travels,* vol. iv. pp. 183, 191). In Job i. 19, the whirlwind is represented as coming 'from the wilderness ;' that is, from the *desert* of Arabia (comp. Jer. xiii. 24; Hos. xiii. 15). ¶ *So it cometh from the desert* (see ch. xiii. 4, and the Note on that place). God is there represented as collecting the army for the destruction of Babylon ' on the mountains,' and by mountains are probably denoted the same as is here denoted by the desert. The country of the *Medes* is doubtless intended, which, in the view of civilized and refined Babylon, was an uncultivated region, or a vast waste or wilderness. ¶ *From a terrible land.* A country rough and uncultivated, abounding in forests or wastes.

2. *A grievous vision.* Marg. as in Heb. ' Hard.' On the word 'vision,' see Note on ch. i. 1. The sense here is, that the vision which the prophet saw was one that indicated great calamity (ver. 3, 4). ¶ *Is declared unto me.* That is, is caused to pass before me, and its meaning is made known to me. ¶ *The treacherous dealer* (הַבּוֹגֵד). The perfidious, unfaithful people. This is the usual signification of the word ; but the connection here does not seem to require the signification of treachery

3 Therefore *a* are my loins filled with pains ; pangs have taken hold upon me, as the pangs of a woman

a ch.15.5.

that travaileth : I was bowed down at the hearing *of it ;* I was dismayed at the seeing *of it.*

or perfidy, but of *violence.* The word has this meaning in Hab. ii. 5, and in Prov. xi. 3, 6. It refers here to the Medes ; and to the fact that oppression and violence were now to be exercised towards Babylon. Lowth renders this : 'The plunderer is plundered, and the destroyer is destroyed ;' but the authority for so rendering it is doubtful. He seems to suppose that it refers to Babylon. The Hebrew evidently means, that there is to be plundering and devastation, and that this is to be accomplished by a nation accustomed to it, and which is immediately specified ; that is, the united kingdom of Media and Persia. The Chaldee renders it, ' They who bring violence, suffer violence ; and the plunderers are plundered.' Jarchi says, that the sense of the Hebrew text according to the Chaldee is, ' Ah! thou who art violent! there comes another who will use thee with violence ; and thou plunderer, another comes who will plunder thee, even the Medes and Persians, who will destroy and lay waste Babylon.' But the Hebrew text will not bear this interpretation. The sense is, that desolation was about to be produced by a nation *accustomed* to it, and who would act towards Babylon in their true character. ¶ *Go up.* This is an address of God to Media and Persia (see Note on ch. xiii. 17). ¶ *O Elam.* This was the name of the country originally possessed by the Persians, and was so called from Elam a son of Shem (Gen. x. 22). It was east of the Euphrates, and comprehended properly the mountainous countries of Khusistan and Louristan, called by the Greek writers *Elymais.* In this country was Susa or Shushan, mentioned in Dan. viii. 2. It is here put for Persia in general, and the call on Elam and Media to go up, was a call on the united kingdom of the Medes and Persians. ¶ *Besiege.* That is, besiege Babylon. ¶ *O Media* (see Note on ch. xiii. 17). ¶ *All the sighing thereof have I made to cease.* This has been very differently interpreted by

expositors. Some understand it (as Rosenmüller, Jerome, and Lowth,) as designed to be taken in an *active* sense ; that is, all the groaning *caused* by Babylon in her oppressions of others, and particularly of God's people, would cease. Others refer it to the army of the Medes and Persians, as if *their* sighing should be over ; *i.e.,* their fatigues and labours in the conquest of Babylon. Calvin supposes that it means that the Lord would be deaf to the sighs of Babylon ; that is, he would disregard them and would bring upon them the threatened certain destruction. The probable meaning is that suggested by Jerome, that God would bring to an end all the sighs and groans which Babylon had caused in a world suffering under her oppressions (comp. ch. xiv. 7, 8).

3. *Therefore.* In this verse, and the following, the prophet represents himself as *in* Babylon, and as a witness of the calamities which would come upon the city. He describes the sympathy which he feels in her sorrows, and represents himself as deeply affected by her calamities. A similar description occurred in the pain which the prophet represents himself as enduring on account of the calamities of Moab (see Note on ch. xv. 5 ; xvi. 11). ¶ *My loins* (see Note on ch. xvi. 11). ¶ *With pain.* The word here used (חלחלה) denotes properly the pains of parturition, and the whole figure is taken from that. The sense is, that the prophet was filled with the most acute sorrow and anguish, in view of the calamities which were coming on Babylon. That is, the sufferings of Babylon would be indescribably great and dreadful (see Nah. ii. 11 ; Ezek. xxx. 4, 9). ¶ *I was bowed down.* Under the grief and sorrow produced by these calamities. ¶ *At the hearing of it.* The Hebrew may have this sense, and mean that these things were made to pass before the eye of the prophet, and that the sight oppressed him, and bowed him down. But more probably

4 My [1]heart panted, fearfulness affrighted me: the *a* night of my pleasure hath he [2] turned into fear unto me.

5 Prepare the table, watch in the watch-tower, eat, drink; arise, ye princes, *and* anoint the shield.

1 or, *my mind wandered.* *a* Dan.5.5,&c. 2 *put.*

the מ in the word מִשְׁמֹעַ is to be taken *privatively*, and means, 'I was so bowed down or oppressed that I *could not* see; I was so dismayed that *I could not hear ;*' that is, all his senses were taken away by the greatness of the calamity, and by his sympathetic sufferings. A similar construction occurs in Ps. lxix. 23: 'Let their eyes be darkened that they see not' (מֵרְאוֹת) *i.e., from* seeing.

4. *My heart panted.* Marg. 'My mind wandered.' The Hebrew word rendered 'panted' (תָּעָה) means to wander about ; to stagger ; to be giddy ; and is applied often to one that staggers by being intoxicated. Applied to the heart, it means that it is disquieted or troubled. The Hebrew word *heart* here is to be taken in the sense of *mind*. ¶ *The night of my pleasure.* There can be no doubt that the prophet here refers to the night of revelry and riot in which Babylon was taken. The prophet calls it the night of *his* pleasure, because he represents himself as being *in* Babylon when it should be taken, and therefore uses such language as an inhabitant of Babylon would use. *They* would call it the night of their pleasure, because it was set apart to feasting and revelry. ¶ *Hath he turned into fear.* God has made it a night of consternation and alarm. The prophet here refers to the fact that Babylon would be taken by Cyrus during that night, and that consternation and alarm would suddenly pervade the affrighted and guilty city (see Dan. v).

5. *Prepare the table.* This verse is one of the most striking and remarkable that occurs in this prophecy, or indeed in any part of Isaiah. It is language supposed to be spoken in Babylon. The first direction—perhaps supposed to be that of the king—is to prepare the table for the feast. Then follows a direction to set a watch—to make the city safe, so that they might revel without fear. Then a command to eat and drink : and then immediately a sudden order, as if alarmed at an unexpected attack, to arise and anoint the shield, and to

prepare for a defence. The *table* here refers to a feast—that impious feast mentioned in Dan. v. in the night in which Babylon was taken, and Belshazzar slain. Herodotus (i. 195), Xenophon (*Cyr.* 7, 5), and Daniel (v.) all agree in the account that Babylon was taken in the night in which the king and his nobles were engaged in feasting and revelry. The words of Xenophon are, ' But Cyrus, when he heard that there was to be such a feast in Babylon, in which all the Babylonians would drink and revel through the whole night, on that night, as soon as it began to grow dark, taking many men, opened the dams into the river ;' that is, he opened the dykes which had been made by Semiramis and her successors to confine the waters of the Euphrates to one channel, and suffered the waters of the Euphrates again to flow over the country so that he could enter Babylon beneath its wall in the channel of the river. Xenophon has also given the address of Cyrus to the soldiers. ' Now,' says he, ' let us go against them. Many of them are asleep ; many of them are intoxicated ; and all of them are unfit for battle (ἀσύντακτοι).' Herodotus says (i. 191), ' It was a day of festivity among them, and while the citizens were engaged in dance and merriment, Babylon was, for the first time, thus taken.' Compare the account in Daniel v. ¶ *Watch in the watch-tower.* Place a guard so that the city shall be secure. Babylon had on its walls many *towers*, placed at convenient distances (see Notes on ch. xiii.), in which guards were stationed to defend the city, and to give the alarm on any approach of an enemy. Xenophon has given a similar account of the taking of the city : ' They having arranged their guards, drank until light.' The annexed group of oriental watch-towers is introduced here for the purpose of illustrating a general subject often referred to in the Scriptures. ¶ *Eat, drink.* Give yourselves to revelry during the night (see Dan. v.) ¶ *Arise, ye princes.* This language indicates sudden alarm. It is the language either of the prophet, or more probably of the king of Babylon, alarmed at the sudden approach of the enemy, and calling upon his nobles to arm themselves and make, a defence. The army of Cyrus entered Babylon by two divisions—one on the north where the waters of the Euphrates

GROUP OF ORIENTAL WATCH TOWERS, SELECTED FROM EXAMPLES IN THE TOWNS OF
LOWER EGYPT.

entered the city, and the other by the channel of the Euphrates on the south. Knowing that the city was given up to revelry on that night, they had agreed to imitate the sound of the revellers until they should assemble around the royal palace in the centre of the city. They did so. When the king heard the noise, supposing that it was the sound of a drunken mob, he ordered the gates of the palace to be opened to ascertain the cause of the disturbance. When they were thus opened, the army of Cyrus rushed in, and made an immediate attack on all who were within. It is to this moment that we may suppose the prophet here refers, when the king, aroused and alarmed, would call on his

6 For thus hath the Lord said unto me, Go, set a watchman, let him declare what he seeth.

7 And he saw a chariot *with* a

nobles to arm themselves for battle (see Jahn's *Hebrew Commonwealth*, p. 153, Ed. Andover, 1828). ¶ *Anoint the shield.* That is, prepare for battle. Gesenius supposes that this means to rub over the shield with oil to make the leather more supple and impenetrable (comp. 2 Sam. i. 21). The Chaldee renders it, ' Fit, and polish your arms.' The LXX. ' Prepare shields.' Shields were instruments of defence prepared to ward off the spears and arrows of an enemy in battle. They were usually made of a rim of brass or wood, and over this was drawn a covering of the skin of an ox or other animal in the manner of a drum-head with us. Oc-

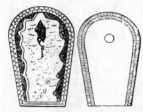

ANCIENT LEATHER SHIELDS.

casionally the hide of a rhinoceros or an elephant was used. Burckhardt (*Travels in Nubia*) says that the Nubians use the hide of the hippopotamus for the making of shields. But whatever skin might be used, it was necessary occasionally to rub it over with oil lest it should become hard, and crack, or lest it should become so rigid that an arrow or a sword would easily break through it. Jarchi says, that ' shields were made of skin, and that they anointed them with the oil of olive.' The sense is, ' Prepare your arms ! Make ready for battle !'

6. *Go, set a watchman.* This was said to Isaiah in the vision. He represents himself as in Babylon, and as hearing God command him to set a watchman on the watch-tower who would announce what was to come to pass. All this is designed merely to bring the manner of the destruction of the city more vividly before the eye.

couple of horsemen, a chariot of asses, *and* a chariot of camels; and he hearkened diligently with heed.

7. *And he saw a chariot* with *a couple of horsemen.* This passage is very obscure from the ambiguity of the word רֶכֶב (*rĕkhĕbh*)—' chariot.' Gesenius contends that it should be rendered ' cavalry,' and that it refers to cavalry two abreast hastening to the destruction of the city. The word רֶכֶב denotes properly a chariot or waggon (Judg. v. 28); a collection of waggons (2 Chron. i. 14; viii. 6; ix. 25); and sometimes refers to the *horses* or *men* attached to a chariot. ' David houghed all the chariots ' (2 Sam. viii. 4); that is, all the *horses* belonging to them. ' David killed of the Syrians seven hundred chariots ' (2 Sam. x. 18); that is, all *the men* belonging to seven hundred chariots. According to the present Masoretic pointing, the word רֶכֶב does not mean, perhaps, anything else than a chariot strictly, but other forms of the word with the same letters denote *riders* or *cavalry*. Thus, the word רָכָב denotes a horseman (2 Kings ix. 17); a charioteer or driver of a chariot (1 Kings xxii. 34; Jer. li. 21). The verb רָכַב means *to ride*, and is usually applied to riding on the backs of horses or camels; and the sense here is, that the watchman saw *a riding*, or persons riding two abreast; that is, *cavalry*, or men borne on horses, and camels, and asses, and hastening to attack the city. ¶ With *a couple of horsemen.* The word ' couple ' (צֶמֶד *tzemĕdh*) means properly a *yoke* or *pair;* and it means here that the cavalry was seen *in pairs*, *i.e.*, two abreast. ¶ *A chariot of asses.* Or rather, as above, *a riding* on asses —an approach of men in this manner to battle. Asses were formerly used in war where horses could not be procured. Thus Strabo (xv. 2, 14) says of the inhabitants of Caramania, ' Many use asses for war in the want of horses.' And Herodotus (iv. 129) says expressly that Darius Hystaspes employed asses in a battle with the Scythians. ¶ And *a chariot of camels.* A *riding* on camels. Camels also were used in war, perhaps

8 And he cried, ¹ A lion : My lord, I stand continually upon the watch-tower in ᵃ the day-time, and I am set in my ward ² whole nights ; 9 And, behold, here cometh a

chariot of men, *with* a couple of horsemen. And he answered and said, Babylon ᵇ is fallen, is fallen ; and ᶜ all the graven images of her gods he hath broken unto the ground.

1 or, *as a lion.*
a Hab.2.1.   2 or, *every night.*

b Jer.51.8,&c.; Rev.14.8.   *c* Jer.50.2.

usually to carry the baggage (see Diod. ii. 54 ; iii. 44 ; Livy, xxxvii. 40 ; Strabo, xvi. 3). They are used for all purposes of burden in the East, and particularly in Arabia.

8. *And he cried, A lion.* Marg. ' As a lion.' This is the correct rendering. The particle כ — ' as,' is not unfrequently omitted (see Isa. lxii. 5 ; Ps. xi. 1). That is, ' I see them approach with the fierceness, rapidity, and terror of a lion ' (comp. Rev. x. 3). ¶ *My lord, I stand continually upon the watch-tower.* This is the speech of the watchman, and is addressed, not to JEHOVAH, but to him that appointed him. It is designed to show the *diligence* with which he had attended to the object for which he was appointed. He had been unceasing in his observation ; and the result was, that now at length he saw the enemy approach like a lion, and it was certain that Babylon now must fall. The language here used has a striking resemblance to the opening of the *Agamemnon* of Æschylus ; being the speech of the watchman, who had been very long upon his tower looking for the signal which should make known that Troy had fallen. It thus commences :

' For ever thus ! O keep me not, ye gods,
For ever thus, fixed in the lonely tower
Of Atreus' palace, from whose height I gaze
O'erwatched and weary, like a night-dog, still
Fixed to my post ; meanwhile the rolling year
Moves on, and I my wakeful vigils keep
By the cold star-lignt sheen of spangled skies.'
Symmons, quoted in the *Pictorial Bible.*

¶ *I am set in my ward.* My place where one keeps watch. It does not mean that he was confined or imprisoned, but that he had kept his watch station (מִשְׁמֶרֶת from שָׁמַר, *to watch, to keep, to attend to*). ¶ *Whole nights.* Marg. ' Every night.' It means that he had not left his post day or night.

9. *And, behold—a chariot of men.* This place shows that the word ' chariot' (רֶכֶב) may denote something else than

a waggon or carriage, as a chariot drawn by men cannot be intended. The sense can be expressed, perhaps, by the word *riding,* ' I see a *riding* of men approach ;' that is, I see *cavalry* drawing near, or men riding and hastening to the battle. ¶ *With a couple of horsemen.* The word ' with ' is not in the Hebrew. The meaning is, ' I see a riding of men, or cavalry ; and they come in pairs, or two abreast.' A part of the sentence is to be supplied from ver. 7. He saw not only horsemen, but riders on asses and camels. ¶ *And he answered.* That is, the watchman answered. The word ' answer,' in the Scriptures, means often merely to commence a discourse after an interval ; to begin to speak (Job iii. 2 ; Dan. ii. 26 ; Acts v. 8). ¶ *Babylon is fallen.* That is, her ruin is certain. Such a mighty army is drawing near, and they approach so well prepared for battle, that the ruin of Babylon is inevitable. The *repetition* of this declaration that ' Babylon is fallen,' denotes emphasis and certainty. Comp. Ps. xcii. 9 :

For lo, thine enemies, O Lord,
For lo, thine enemies shall perish.

Ps. xciii. 3 :

The floods have lifted up, O Lord ;
The floods have lifted up their waves.

A similar description is given of the fall of Babylon in Jer. l. 32 ; li. 8 ; and John has copied this description in the account of the overthrow of the mystical Babylon (Rev. xviii. 1, 2). Babylon was distinguished for its pride, arrogance, and haughtiness. It became, therefore, the emblem of all that is haughty, and as such is used by John in the Apocalypse ; and as such it was a most striking emblem of the pride, arrogance, haughtiness, and oppression which have always been evinced by Papal Rome. ¶ *And all the graven images.* Babylon was celebrated for its idolatry, and perhaps was the place where the worship of idols commenced.

10 O my threshing, and the [1] corn of my floor: that which I have heard of the LORD of hosts, the God of Israel, have I [a] declared unto you.

ANALYSIS OF VER. 11, 12.—VISION XVII.

Dumah, or Idumea.

THIS prophecy is very obscure. It comprises but two verses. When it was delivered, or on what occasion, or what was its design, it is not easy to determine. Its brevity has contributed much to its obscurity; nor, amidst the variety of interpretations which have been proposed, is it possible to ascertain with entire certainty the true explanation. Perhaps no portion of the Scriptures, of equal length, has been subjected to a greater variety of exposition. It is not the design of these Notes to go at length into a detail of opinions which have been proposed, but to state as accurately as possible the sense of the prophet. Those who wish to see at

1 *son.*   a Eze.3.17-19; Acts 20.26,27.

length the opinions which have been entertained on this prophecy, will find them detailed in Vitringa and others.

The prophecy relates evidently to Idumea. It stands in connection with that immediately preceding respecting Babylon, and it is probable that it was delivered at that time. It has the appearance of being a reply by the prophet to language of *insult* or *taunting* from the Idumeans, who had been spoken when calamities were coming rapidly on the Jews. But it is not certain that that was the time or the occasion. It is certain only that it is a prediction of calamity succeeding to prosperity—perhaps prosperity coming to the afflicted Hebrews in Babylon, and of calamity to the taunting Idumeans, who had exulted over their downfall and captivity, and who are represented as sneeringly inquiring of the prophet what was the prospect in regard to the Jews. This is substantially the view given by Vitringa, Rosenmuller, and Gesenius.

According to this interpretation, the scene is laid in the time of the Babylonish captivity. The prophet is represented as having been

---

The principal god worshipped there was Belus, or Bel (see Note on ch. xlvi. 1). ¶ *Are broken*, &c. That is, shall be destroyed; or, in spite of its idols, the whole city would be ruined.

10. *O my threshing.* The words 'to thresh,' 'to tread down,' &c., are often used in the Scriptures to denote punishments inflicted on the enemies of God. An expression likes this occurs in Jer. li. 33, in describing the destruction of Babylon: 'The daughter of Babylon is like a threshing floor; it is time to thresh her.' In regard to the mode of threshing among the Hebrews, and the pertinency of this image to the destruction of the enemies of God, see Note on Isa. xxviii. 27. Lowth, together with many others, refers this to Babylon, and regards it as an address of God to Babylon in the midst of her punishment: 'O thou, the object on which I shall exercise the severity of my discipline; that shall lie under my afflicting hand like corn spread out upon the floor to be threshed out and winnowed, to separate the chaff from the wheat.' But the expression can be applied with more propriety to the Jews; and may be regarded as the language of *tenderness* addressed by God through the prophet to his people when they should be oppressed and

broken down in Babylon: 'O thou, my people, who hast been afflicted and crushed; who hast been under my chastening hand, and reduced to these calamities on account of your sins; hear what God has spoken respecting the destruction of Babylon, and your consequent certain deliverance.' Thus it is the language of consolation; and is designed, like the prophecies in ch. xiii., xiv., to comfort the Jews, when they should be in Babylon, with the certainty that they would be delivered. The language of *tenderness* in which the address is couched, as well as the connection, seems to demand this interpretation. ¶ *And the corn of my floor.* Heb. 'The son of my threshing floor'—a Hebraism for grain that was on the floor to be threshed. The word 'son' is often used in this peculiar manner among the Hebrews (see Note on Matt. i. 1). ¶ *That which I have heard*, &c. This shows the scope or design of the whole prophecy—to declare to the Jews the destruction that would come upon Babylon, and their own consequent deliverance. It was important that they should be *assured* of that deliverance, and hence Isaiah *repeats* his predictions, and minutely states the manner in which their rescue would be accomplished.

placed on a watch-tower long and anxiously
looking for the issue. It is night; *i e.*, it is a
time of calamity, darkness, and distress. In
this state of darkness and obscurity, some one
is represented as calling to the prophet from
Idumea, and tauntingly inquiring, what of the
night, or what the prospect was. He asks,
whether there was any prospect of deliverance;
or whether these calamities were to continue,
and perhaps whether Idumea was also to be
involved in them with the suffering Jews. To
this the prophet answers, that the morning
began to dawn—that there *was* a prospect of
deliverance. But he adds that calamity was
also coming;—calamity probably to the nation
that made the inquiry—to the land of Idumea
—*perhaps* calamity that should follow the deliverance of the Hebrew captives, who would
thus be enabled to inflict vengeance on Edom,
and to overwhelm it in punishment. The
morning dawns, says the watchman; but there
is darkness still beyond. Light is coming—
but there is night also: light for us—darkness
for you. This interpretation is strengthened
by a remarkable coincidence in an independent
source, and which I have not seen noticed, in
the 137th Psalm. The irritated and excited
feelings of the captive Jews against Edom; their
indignation at the course which Edom pursued
when Jerusalem was destroyed; and their desire
of vengeance, are all there strongly depicted,
and accord with this interpretation, which supposes the prophet to say that the glad morning
of the deliverance of the *Jews* would be succeeded by a dark night to the taunting Idumean. The feelings of the captured and exiled
Jews were expressed in the following language
in Babylon (Ps. cxxxvii. 7):—

Remember, O JEHOVAH, the children of Edom
    in the day of Jerusalem;
Who said, Rase it, rase it, even to the founda-
    tion.

That is, we desire vengeance on Idumea, who
joined with our enemies when Jerusalem was
destroyed; and when Jerusalem shall be again
rebuilt, we pray that they may be remembered,
and that punishment may be inflicted on them
for exulting over our calamities. The watchman
adds, that if the Idumean was disposed to inquire
further, he could. The result could be easily
ascertained. It was clear, and the watchman
would be disposed to give the information. But
he adds, 'return, come;' perhaps meaning,

'repent; then come and receive an answer;'—
denoting that if the Idumeans *wished* a favourable answer, they should repent of their treatment of the Jews in their calamities, and that
then a condition of safety and prosperity would
be promised them.

As there is considerable variety in the ancient
versions of this prophecy, and as it is brief, they
may be presented to advantage at a single view.
The Vulgate does not differ materially from the
Hebrew. The following are some of the other
versions:

Septuagint.

The vision of Idumea.
—Unto me he called out
of Seir, Guard the for-
tresses — (Φυλάσσετε
ἐπάλξεις). I guard
morning and night. If
you inquire, inquire,
and dwell with me. In
the grove (δρυμῷ) thou
shalt lie down, and in
the way of Dedan
(Δαιδάν).

Chaldee.

The burden of the
cup of malediction
which is coming upon
Duma.—He cries to me
from heaven, O pro-
phet, prophesy; O pro-
phet, prophesy to them
of what is to come.
The prophet said,
There is a reward to

the just, and revenge to
the unjust. If you will
be converted, be con-
verted while you can
be converted.

Syriac.

The burden of Duma.
—The nightly watch-
man calls to me out of
Seir. And the watch-
man said, The morning
cometh and also the
night. If ye will in-
quire, inquire, and then
at length come.

Arabic.

A prophecy respect-
ing Edom and Seir, the
sons of Esau.—Call me
from Seir. Keep the
towers. Guard thyself
morning and evening.
If you inquire, inquire.

It is evident, from this variety of translation,
that the ancient interpreters felt that the prophecy was enigmatical and difficult. It is not
easy, in a prophecy so brief, and where there is
scarcely any clue to lead us to the historical
facts, to give an interpretation that shall be
entirely satisfactory and unobjectionable. Perhaps the view given above may be as little liable
to objection as any one of the numerous interpretations which have been proposed.

11 The burden of *a* **Dumah. He
calleth to me out of Seir, Watchman, what of the night? Watchman, what of the night?**

a 1 Ch.1.30; Jer.49.7,&c.; Eze.35.2,&c.; Ob.1,&c.

---

11. *The burden* (see Note on ch. xiii.
1). This word ' burden' naturally leads
to the supposition that *calamity* in some
form was contemplated in the prophecy.
This is also indicated in the prophecy
by the word ' night.' ¶ *Of Dumah.*

Dumah (דוּמָה) is mentioned in Gen.
xxv. 14, and 1 Chron. i. 30, as one of
the twelve sons of Ishmael. It is
known that those sons settled in Arabia, and that the Arabians derive their
origin from Ishmael. The name

'Dumah,' therefore, properly denotes one of the wandering tribes of the Ishmaelites. The LXX. evidently read this as if it had been אֱדֹם—Edom or Idumea — 'Ιδουμαία. Jakut mentions two places in Arabia to which the name 'Dumah' is given, Dumah Irak, and Dumah Felsen. The former of these, which Gesenius supposes is the place here intended, lies upon the borders of the Syrian desert, and is situated in a valley seven days' journey from Damascus, according to Abulfeda, in lon. 45° E.; and in lat. 29° 30' N; and about three and a half days' journey from Medina. Niebuhr mentions Dumah as a station of the Wehabites (see Gesenius, *Comm. in loc.*) There can be little doubt that the place referred to is situated on the confines of the Arabian and Syrian deserts, and that it is the place called by the Arabians *Duma the stony*, or *Syrian Duma* (Robinson's Calmet). It has a fortress, and is a place of strength. Jerome says, 'Duma is not the whole province of Idumea, but is a certain region which lies toward the south, and is twenty miles distant from a city of Palestine called Eleutheropolis, near which are the mountains of Seir.' It is evident from the prophecy itself that Idumea is particularly referred to, for the prophet immediately adds, that the voice came to him from mount 'Seir,' which was the principal mountain of Idumea. Why the name 'Dumah' is used to designate that region has been a matter on which critics have been divided. Vitringa supposes that it is by a play upon the word 'Dumah,' because the word *may* be derived from דָּמַם (*dâmăm*) to be silent, to be still; and that it is used to denote the *silence*, or the *night*, which was about to come upon Idumea; that is, the calamity of which this was a prediction. Kocher supposes that the prophet used the word denoting '*silence*' (דוּמָה) by a paranomasia, and by derision for אֱדֹם, as if Idumea was soon to be reduced to silence, or to destruction. Idumea, or the country of Edom, is frequently referred to by the prophets (see Jer. xlix. 7-10, 12-18; Ezek. xxxv. 1-4, 7, 9, 14, 15; Joel iii. 19; Amos i. 11; Obad. 2-18; Mal. i.

3, 4).—For a description of Idumea, and of the prophecies respecting it, see Notes on Isa. xxxiv. ¶ *He calleth.* One calleth; there is a voice heard by me from Seir. Lowth renders it, 'A voice crieth unto me.' But the sense is, that the prophet hears one crying, or calling (קֹרֵא) to him from the distant mountain. ¶ *Unto me.* The prophet Isaiah. ¶ *Out of Seir.* The name 'Seir' was given to a mountainous tract or region of country that stretched along from the southern part of the Dead Sea, to the eastern branch of the Red Sea, terminating near Ezion-geber. Mount Hor formed a part of this range of mountains. Esau and his descendants possessed the mountains of Seir, and hence the whole region obtained the name of Edom or Idumea. Mount Seir was anciently the residence of the *Horites* (Gen. xiv. 6), but Esau made war upon them and destroyed them (comp. Gen. xxxvi. 8, 9; Deut. ii. 5, 12). Here it is put for the country of Idumea, and the sense is, that the whole land, or the inhabitants of the land, are heard by the prophet in a taunting manner asking him what of the night. ¶ *Watchman* (see Note on ver. 6). The prophet Isaiah is here referred to (comp. ch. lii. 8; lvi. 10). He is represented as being in the midst of the calamities that had come upon Judea, and as having his station in desolate Jerusalem, and looking for the signs of returning day. The eye is turned towards the east—the source whence light comes, and whence the exiles would return to their own land. Thus anxiously waiting for the indications of mercy to his desolate country, he hears this taunting voice from Idumea, asking him what was the prospect? what evidence there was of returning prosperity? ¶ *What of the night?* (comp. Hab. ii. 1). 'How stands the night? What is the prospect? What have you to announce respecting the night? How much of it is passed? And what is the prospect of the dawn?' 'Night' here is the emblem of calamity, affliction, oppression, as it often is in the Scriptures (comp. Job xxxv. 10; Mic. iii. 6); and it refers here probably to the calamities which had come upon Judea. The

12 The watchman said, The morning cometh, and also the night:

if ye will inquire, inquire ye: return, come.

---

inquiry is, How much of that calamity had passed? What was the prospect? How long was it to continue? How far was it to spread? The inquiry is *repeated* here to denote *intensity* or *emphasis*, manifesting the deep interest which the inquirer had in the result, or designed to give emphasis and point to the cutting taunt.

12. *The watchman said.* Or rather *saith;* indicating that this is the answer which the prophet returned to the inquiry from Idumea. ¶ *The morning cometh.* There are signs of approaching day. The 'morning' here is an emblem of prosperity; as the light of the morning succeeds to the darkness of the night. This refers to the deliverance from the captivity of Babylon, and is to be supposed as having been spoken near the time when that captivity was at an end;—or nearly at break of day after the long night of their bondage. This declaration is to be understood as referring to a different people from those referred to in the expression which immediately follows— 'and also the night.' 'The morning cometh'—to the captive Jews; '*and also the night*'—to some other people— to wit, the Idumeans. It *might* mean that the morning was to be succeeded by a time of darkness to the same people; but the connection seems to demand that we understand it of others. ¶ *And also the night.* A time of calamity and affliction. This is emphatic. It refers to the Idumeans. 'The morning cometh to the captive Jews; it shall be *closely* succeeded by a night—a time of calamity—to the taunting Idumeans.'—During the captivity of the Jews in Babylon, the Idumeans invaded and took possession of the southern part of Judea. The prophet here refers to the fact, perhaps, that on the return of the Jews to their native land, they would revenge this by expelling them, and by inflicting punishment on the land of Edom. For a full proof that calamities came upon the land of Idumea, see Keith *On the Prophecies,* Art. *Idumea,* and Notes on Isa. xxxiv.) ¶ *If ye will inquire, in-*

quire ye. If you choose to ask anything further in regard to this, you can. The sense is probably this: ' You Idumeans have asked respecting *the night* in derision and reproach. An answer has been given somewhat agreeably *to* that inquiry. But if you seriously wish to know anything further respecting the destiny of your land, you can ask me (Isaiah) or any other prophet, and it will be known. But ask it in seriousness and earnestness, and with a suitable regard for the prophetic character and for God. And especially if you wish a more favourable answer to your inquiries, it is to be obtained only by forsaking sin and turning to God, and *then* you may come with the hope of a brighter prospect for the future.' The design of this is, therefore—(1) to *reprove* them for the manner in which they had asked the question; (2) to assure them that God was willing to direct humble and serious inquirers; and (3) to show in what way a favourable answer could be obtained—to wit, by repentance. And this is as true of sinners now as it was then. *They* often evince the reproachful and taunting spirit which the Idumeans did. *They* hear only a similar response—that prosperity and happiness await the Christian, though now in darkness and affliction; and that calamity and destruction are before the guilty. They *might* have the same answer — an answer that God would bless them and save them, if they would inquire in a humble, serious, and docile manner. ¶ *Return.* Turn from your sins; come back to God, and show respect for him and his declarations. ¶ *Come.* Then come and you shall be accepted, and the watchman will also announce *morning* as about to dawn on you.—This seems to be the sense of this very dark and difficult prophecy. It is brief, enigmatical, and obscure. Yet it is beautiful; and if the sense above given be correct, it contains most weighty and important truth—alike for the afflicted and persecuted friends, and the persecuting and taunting foes of God. With reference to the interpretation here pro-

ANALYSIS OF VER. 13–17.—VISION XVIII.
Arabia.

THE remainder of this chapter is occupied with a single prophecy respecting Arabia. It was *probably* delivered about the time that the former was uttered—during the reign of Hezekiah, and before the invasion of Sennacherib. It had reference, I suppose, to Sennacherib; and was designed to foretell the fact that, either in his march to attack Judea, or on his return from Egypt, he would pass through Arabia, and perhaps oppress and overthrow some of their clans. At all events, it was to be fulfilled within a year after it was uttered (ver. 16), and refers to *some* foreign invasion that was to come upon their land. Rosenmüller supposes that it relates to the same period as the prophecy in Jer. xlix. 28, *sq.*, and refers to the time when Nebuchadnezzar sent Nebuzaradan to overrun the lands of the Ammonites, the Moabites, the Philistines, the Arabians, the Idumeans, and others who had revolted from him, and who had formed an alliance with Zedekiah.

The sentiment of the prophecy is simple—that within a year the country of Arabia would be overrun by a foreign enemy. The form and posed, which supposes, as will have been seen—(1) a state of excited feeling on the part of the Jews towards the Idumeans, for the part which they took in the destruction of their city; (2) the prospect of speedy deliverance to the Jews in Babylon; and (3) a consequent desolation and vengeance on the Idumeans for the feelings which they had manifested in the destruction of Jerusalem, see the prophecy of Obadiah, ver. 8–21:—

Shall I not in that day, saith the LORD,
Even destroy the wise men out of Edom,
And understanding out of the mount of Esau?
And thy mighty men, O Teman, shall be dismayed,
To the end that every one of the mount of Esau may be cut off by slaughter.
For thy violence against thy brother Jacob shame shall cover thee,
And thou shalt be cut off for ever.
In the day that thou stoodest on the other side;
In the day that the stranger carried away captive his forces;
And foreigners entered into his gates, and cast lots upon Jerusalem;
Even thou wast as one of them.
But thou shouldest not have looked on the day of thy brother in the day that he became a stranger;
Neither shouldest thou have rejoiced over the children of Judah in the day of their destruction;
Neither shouldest thou have spoken proudly in the day of distress.

* * * * *

manner of the prophecy is highly poetic and beautiful. The images are drawn from customs and habits which pertain to the Arabians, and which characterize them to this day. In ver. 13, the prophecy opens with a declaration that the caravans that were accustomed to pass peacefully through Arabia would be arrested by the apprehension of war. They would seek a place of refuge in the forests and fastnesses of the land. Thither also the prophet sees the Arabians flocking, as if to exercise the rites of hospitality, and to minister to the wants of the oppressed and weary travellers. But the reasons why *they* are there, the prophet sees to be that *they* are oppressed and driven out of their land by a foreign invader, and *they* also seek the same places of security and of refuge (ver. 14, 15). All this would be accomplished within a year (ver. 16); and the result would be, that the inhabitants of Arabia would be greatly diminished (ver. 17).

13 The burden upon Arabia. In the forest in Arabia shall ye lodge, O ye travelling companies of Dedanim.

For the day of the LORD is near upon all the heathen;
As thou hast done, it shall be done unto thee;
Thy reward shall return upon thine own head, &c.

In this prophecy these circumstances are all to be found: (1) The hostility of the Edomites against Jerusalem, and the part which they took in the destruction of the city, in ver. 10–14; (2) the fact of the deliverance of the Jews from captivity, in ver. 17; (3) the consequent vengeance upon the Idumeans (ver. 18–21). This remarkable coincidence in an independent prophecy is a strong circumstance to prove that the interpretation above proposed is correct. In regard to the general reasons for the interpretation here proposed, and the lessons which the prophecy is fitted to convey, I may be permitted to refer to my *Practical Sermons*, pp. 325–341.

13. *The burden* (see Note on ch. xiii. 1). ¶ *Upon Arabia* (בַּעְרָב). This is an unusual form. The title of the prophecies is usually without the ב, rendered 'upon.' Lowth supposes this whole title to be of doubtful authority, chiefly because it is wanting in most MSS. of the LXX. The LXX. connect it with the preceding prophecy respect-

ing Dumah, and make this a continuance of that. The preposition (בְּ)—'upon,' means here *respecting, concerning,* and is used instead of עַל, as in Zech. ix. 1. Arabia is a well-known country of western Asia, lying south and south-east of Judea. It was divided into three parts, Arabia Deserta, on the east ; Arabia Petrea, lying south of Judea ; and Arabia Felix, lying still further south. What part of Arabia is here denoted it may not be easy to determine. It is probable that it was Arabia Petrea, because this lay between Judea and Egypt, and would be exposed to invasion by the Assyrians should they invade Egypt; and because this part of Arabia furnished, more than the others, such retreats and fastnesses as are mentioned in ver. 13–15. ¶ *In the forest* (בַּיַּעַר). The word (יַעַר) ' forest ' usually denotes a grove, a collection of trees. But it may mean here, any place of refuge from a pursuing foe ; a region of thick underwood ; an uncultivated, inaccessible place, where they would be concealed from an invading enemy. The word rendered ' forest ' is commonly supposed to mean a forest in the sense in which that word is now used by us, meaning an extensive wood —a large tract of land covered with trees. It is doubtful, however, whether the word is so used in the Bible. The Rev. Eli Smith stated to me that he had visited several of the places in Palestine to which the word (יַעַר) ' forest ' or ' grove ' is given, and that he was satisfied that there never was a forest there in our use of the word. The same word *vaar*—the י not being used to begin a word in Arabic, but the ו being used instead of it—occurs often in Arabic. It means, as used by the Arabs, a rough, stony, impassable place ; a place where there are no roads ; which is inaccessible ; and which is a safe retreat for robbers—and it is not improbable that the word is so used here. ¶ *In Arabia* (בֶּעְרָב). The LXX., the Vulgate, and the Chaldee, understand this of the *evening*—' In the evening.' The word עֶרֶב, with different points from those which the Masorites have used here, means *evening,* but there is no

necessity of departing from the translation in our English version. The sense would not be materially affected whichever rendering should be preferred. ¶ *Shall ye lodge.* Shall you pass the night. This is the usual signification of the word. But here it may be taken in a larger sense, as denoting that they would pitch their tents there, or that they would seek a refuge there. The sense I suppose to be this : ' O ye travelling caravans of Dedan ! Ye were accustomed to pass through Arabia, and to find a safe and hospitable entertainment there. But now, the Arabians shall be overrun by a foreign enemy ; they shall be unable to show you hospitality, and to insure your safety in their tents, and for fear of the enemy still in the land you will be obliged to seek a lodging in the inaccessible thickets of the forests.' The passage is intended to denote the *change* that had taken place, and to show the *insecurity* for caravans. ¶ *O ye travelling companies.* Ye *caravans* (אֹרְחֹת). This word usually signifies *ways, paths, cross roads.* But it is here used evidently to denote those who *travelled* in such ways or paths ; that is, caravans of merchants. So it is used in Job vi. 19 : ' The *caravans* of Tema.' It is well known that in the East it is usual for large companies to travel together, called *caravans.* Arabia Petrea was a great thoroughfare for such companies. ¶ *Of Dedanim.* Descendants of *Dedan.* There are two men of this name mentioned in the Old Testament—the son of Raamah, the son of Cush, mentioned in Gen. x. 7; and the son of Jokshan, the son of Abraham by Keturah (Gen. xxv. 3). The descendants of the latter settled in Arabia Petrea, and the descendants of the former near the Persian Gulf. It is not easy to determine which is here intended, though most probably those who dwelt near the Persian Gulf, because they are often mentioned as merchants. They dealt in ivory, ebony, &c., and traded much with Tyre (Ezek. xxvii. 21), and doubtless also with Egypt. They are here represented as passing through Arabia Petrea on their way to Egypt, and as compelled by the calamities in the

14 The inhabitants of the land
of Tema brought ¹water to him

1 or, *bring ye.*

---

country to find a refuge in its fastnesses and inaccessible places.

14. *Of the land of Tema.* Tema was
one of the sons of Ishmael (Gen. xxv.
15), and is supposed to have peopled
the city of Thema in Arabia Deserta.
The word denotes here one of the
tribes of Ishmael, or of the Arabians.
Job speaks (vi. 19) of 'the troops of
Tema,' and Jeremiah (xxv. 23) connects Tema and Dedan together. Jerome and Eusebius say that the village
of Theman (Θαιμάν) existed in their
time. It was, according to Jerome,
five, and according to Eusebius, fifteen
miles from Petra, and was then occupied as a Roman garrison (*Onomas
Urb. et Locor*). Ptolemy speaks of a
city called Themme (Θέμμη) in Arabia
Deserta. This city lies, according to
D'Anville, in lon. 57° E., and lat. 27°
N. According to Seetzen, it is on the
road usually pursued by caravans from
Mecca to Damascus. Lowth renders
it 'The southern country,' but without
authority. The LXX. render it, Θαιμάν
—'Thaiman.' ¶ *Brought water.* Marg.
'Bring ye.' This might be rendered
in the imperative, but the connection
seems rather to require that it be read
as a declaration that they did so. To
bring water to the thirsty was an act
of hospitality, and especially in eastern
countries, where water was so scarce,
and where it was of so much consequence to the traveller in the burning
sands and deserts. The idea is, that
the inhabitants of the land would be
oppressed and pursued by an enemy;
and that the Arabians, referred to by
the prophet (ver. 13), would be driven
from their homes; and be dependent on
others; that they would wander through
the vast deserts, deprived of the neces-
saries of life; and that they would be
dependent on the charity of the people
of Tema for the supply of their wants.
The following illustration of this passage has been kindly furnished me by
the Rev. Eli Smith, missionary to
Syria, showing that Isaiah, in mentioning *hospitality* as one of the virtues
of the inhabitants of Tema, drew from

that was thirsty, they prevented
with their bread him that fled.

---

the life. 'Even in Hebrew prophecy
hospitality is distinctly recognized as a
trait in the Arab character. Isaiah
says, "the inhabitants of Tema," &c.
Tema is known as an oasis in the heart
of Arabia, between Syria and Mecca.
And among the scraps of ante-Mahom-
etan poetry that have reached us, is
one by Samaciel, a prince of this same
Tema. In extolling the virtues of his
tribe he says—

وما أُحمِدت نارُلنا دونَ طارِق
ولا ذَمّنا في النازِلينَ نزيلُ

"No fire of ours was ever extinguished
at night without a guest, and of our
guests never did one disparage us."
'In the passage quoted from Isaiah,
it is to the thirsty and hungry in flight,
that the inhabitants of Tema are represented as bringing water and bread, as
if hastening to afford them protection.
The extent to which this protection is
sometimes carried, is finely illustrated
by a traditionary anecdote in the life
of Samaciel, the prince and poet of
Tema just mentioned. In some feud
among the tribes in his neighbourhood,
a prince [Amru el-Keis] fled to Samaciel, left with him his treasures, and
was conducted by him beyond the reach
of his enemies. They assembled their
forces, and marched upon Tema. On
their way Samaciel's son fell into their
hands. Presenting the young man before his castle, they proposed to the
father the dreadful alternative, of delivering up to them what his guest had
left, or seeing his son massacred. Samaciel's sense of honour dictated the
reply—

اجلنى فاجله .... الغدر
طوق لا يبلى

"He honoured me, and I'll honour him
... Treachery is a chain to the neck
that never wears out." So he defended
the rights of his guest, and his son was

15 For *a*they fled [1]from the swords, from the drawn sword, and from the bent bow, and from the grievousness of war.

16 For thus hath the LORD said unto me, Within a year, according to the years of an hireling, *b* and all the glory of Kedar *c* shall fail.

17 And the residue of the number of [2] archers, the mighty men of the children of Kedar, shall be diminished: for the LORD God of Israel hath spoken *it*.

CHAPTER XXII.
ANALYSIS OF VER. 1–14.

THIS chapter is made up of *two* prophecies, one comprising the first fourteen verses, and addressed to the city of Jerusalem; and the other (ver. 15–25) relating to the fall of Shebna, the prefect of the palace, and to the promotion of Eliakim in his place. They may have been delivered nearly at the same time, but the subjects are distinct.

a Job 6.19,20.　　　1 *from the face of*, or, *for fear.*
b Job 7.1.　　　c ch.60.7.　　　2 *bows.*

---

slain.' ¶ *They prevented.* Our word 'prevent' usually means at present, to hinder, to obstruct. But in the Scriptures, and in the old English sense of the word, it means to anticipate, to go before. That is the sense of the word קִדְּמוּ here. They *anticipated* their wants by bread; that is, they supplied them. This was an ancient and an honourable rite of hospitality. Thus Melchizedek (Gen. xiv. 17, 18) is said to have come out and met Abraham, when returning victorious from the slaughter of Chedorlaomer, with bread and wine. ¶ *Him that fled.* The inhabitant of the land of Arabia that fled before the invader, perhaps the inhabitants of Kedar (ver. 16), or of some other part of Arabia. It is not meant that the *whole* land of Arabia would be desolate, but that the invasion would come upon certain parts of it; and the inhabitants of other portions—as of Tema—would supply the wants of the fugitives.

15. *For they fled.* The inhabitants of one part of the land. ¶ *The grievousness of war.* Heb. כֹּבֶד—the *weight*, the *heaviness*, the *oppression* of war; probably from the calamities that would result from the march of the Assyrian through their land, either on his way to Judea or to Egypt.

16. *Within a year.* What has been said before was figurative. Here the prophet speaks without a metaphor, and fixes the time when this should be accomplished. It is not usual for the prophets to designate the exact *time* of the fulfilment of their prophecies in this manner. ¶ *According to the years of an hireling.* Exactly; observing

the precise time specified (Job vii. 1). See the phrase explained on ch. xvi. 14. ¶ *All the glory.* The beauty, pride, strength, wealth, &c. ¶ *Of Kedar.* Kedar was a son of Ishmael (Gen. xxv. 15). He was the father of the Kedareneans or *Cedrai*, mentioned by Pliny (*Nat. Hist.* v. 11). They dwelt in the neighbourhood of the Nabatheans, in Arabia Deserta. These people lived in tents, and were a wandering tribe, and it is not possible to fix the precise place of their habitation. They resided, it is supposed, in the south part of Arabia Deserta, and the north part of Arabia Petrea. The name 'Kedar' seems to be used sometimes to denote Arabia in general, or Arabia Deserta particularly (see Ps. cxx. 5; Cant. i. 5; Isa. xlii. 11; lx. 7; Jer. ii. 10; xlix. 28; Ezek. xxvi. 21). ¶ *Shall fail.* Shall be consumed, destroyed (כָּלָה).

17. *And the residue of the number.* That is, those who shall be left in the invasion. Or perhaps it may be read, 'There shall be a remnant of the number of bowmen; the mighty men of Kedar shall be diminished.' ¶ *Of archers.* Heb. 'Of the bow;' that is, of those who use bows in war. The bow was the common instrument in hunting and in war among the ancients. ¶ *Shall be diminished.* Heb. 'Shall be made small;' they shall be reduced to a very small number. We cannot indeed determine the precise historical event to which this refers, but the whole connection and circumstances seem to make it probable that it referred to the invasion by the Assyrian when he went up against Judah, or when he was on his way to Egypt.

The first (ver. 1-14) relates to Jerusalem. It has reference to some period when the city was besieged, and when universal consternation spread among the people. The prophet represents himself as in the city, and as a witness of the alarm. 1. He describes (1-3) the consternation that prevailed in the city at the approach of the enemy. The inhabitants flee to the tops of the houses, either to observe the enemy or to make a defence, and the city is filled with distress, mingled with the tumultuous mirth of a portion who regard defence as hopeless, and who give themselves up to revelry and gluttony, because they apprehended that they must at all events soon die. 2. The prophet then describes (4-8) his own grief at the impending calamity, and especially at the state of things within the city. He portrays the distress; describes those who cause it, and the people engaged in it; and says that the valleys around the city are filled with chariots, and that the horsemen of the enemy have come to the very gate. 3. He then describes the preparations which are made *in* the city for defence (9-11). The inhabitants of the city had endeavoured to repair the breaches of the walls; had even torn down their houses to furnish materials, and had endeavoured to secure the *water* with which the city was supplied from the enemy; but they had not looked to God as they should have done for protection. The scope of the prophecy therefore is, to reprove them for not looking to God, and also for their revelry in the very midst of their calamities. 4. The prophet then describes the state of *morals* within the city (12-14). It was a time when they should have humbled themselves, and looked to God. He called them to fasting and to grief; but they supposed that the city *must* be taken, and that they must die, and a large portion of the inhabitants, despairing of being able to make a successful defence, gave themselves up to riot and drunkenness. To reprove this, was one design of the prophet; and perhaps, also, to

teach the general lesson that men, in view of the certainty of death, should *not* madly and foolishly give themselves to sensual indulgence.

There has been a difference of opinion in regard to the event to which this prophecy refers. Most have supposed that it relates to the invasion by Sennacherib; others have supposed that it relates to the destruction of the city by Nebuchadnezzar. Vitringa and Lowth suppose that the prophet had *both* events in view; the former in ver. 1-5, and the latter in the remainder of the prophecy. But it is not probable that it has a twofold reference. It has the appearance of referring to a *single* calamity; and this mode of interpretation should not be departed from without manifest necessity. The general aspect of the prophecy has reference, I think, to the invasion by Sennacherib. He came near the city; the city was filled with alarm; and Hezekiah prepared himself to make as firm a stand against him as possible, and put the city in the best possible state of defence. The description in ver. 9-11 agrees exactly with the account given of the defence which Hezekiah made against Sennacherib in 2 Chron. xxxii. 2, *sq.*; and particularly in regard to the effort made to secure the fountains in the neighbourhood for the use of the city, and to prevent the Assyrians from obtaining it. In 2 Chron. xxxii. 2, *sq*, we are told that Hezekiah took measures to stop all the fountains of water without the city, and the brook 'that ran through the midst of the land,' in order that the Assyrians under Sennacherib should not find water; and that he repaired the walls, and built new towers of defence in the city, and placed guards upon them. These circumstances of *coincidence* between the history and the prophecy, show conclusively that the reference is entirely to the invasion under Sennacherib. This occurred B.C. 710.

THE burden of the valley of vision. What aileth thee now,

CHAPTER XXII.

1. *The burden* (see Note on ch. xiii. 1). ¶ *The valley* (אִיְא). Sept. Φά-ραγγος—'Valley.' Chaldee, 'The burden of the prophecy respecting the city which dwells (*i.e.*, is built) in the valley, which the prophets have prophesied concerning it.' There can be no doubt that Jerusalem is intended (see ver. 9, 10). It is not usual to call it *a valley*, but it may be so called, either (1.) because there were several valleys *within* the city and adjacent to it, as the vale between mount Zion and Moriah; the

vale between mount Moriah and mount Ophel; between these and mount Bezetha; and the valley of Jehoshaphat, without the walls of the city; or (2.) more probably it was called *a valley* in reference to its being *encompassed with hills*, rising to a considerable elevation above the city. Thus mount Olivet was on the east, and overlooked the city. Jerusalem is also called a *valley*, and a *plain*, in Jer. xxi 13: 'Behold, I am against thee, O inhabitant of the valley, and rock of the plain, saith the Lord.' Thus it is described in Reland's *Pales-*

that thou art wholly gone up to the house-tops? [a]

2 Thou that art full of stirs, a

tumultuous city, a [b]joyous city: thy slain *men are* not slain with the sword, nor dead in battle.

a Deut. 22. 8.   b ch. 32. 13.

tine:—' The city was in the mountain region of Judea, in an elevated place, yet so that in respect to the mountains by which it was surrounded, it seemed to be situated in a humble place, because mount Olivet, and other mountains surrounding it, were more elevated.' So Phocas says, ' The holy city is placed in the midst of various valleys and hills, and this is wonderful (θαυμαστόν) in it, that at the same time the city seems to be elevated and depressed; for it is elevated in respect to the region of Judea, and depressed in respect to the hills around it.' — (Reland's *Palestine*, iii. 802, in Ugolini's *Thesaurus*, vi.) It was common with Isaiah and the other prophets to designate Jerusalem and other places, not by their proper names, but by some appellation that would be descriptive (see ch. xxi. 1; xxix. 1). ¶ *Of vision* (see Note on ch. i. 1). The word here means that Jerusalem was eminently the place where God made known his will to the prophets, and manifested himself to his people by *visions*. ¶ *What aileth thee now?* What is the cause of the commotion and tumult that exists in the city? The prophets throws himself at once into the midst of the excitement; sees the agitation and tumult, and the preparations for defence which were made, and asks the *cause* of all this confusion. ¶ *That thou art wholly gone up to the house-tops*. That all classes of the people had fled to the house-tops, so much that it might be said that all the city had gone up. Houses in the East were built in a uniform manner in ancient times, and are so to this day. (See a description of the mode of building in Notes on

Matt. ix. 1, *sq.*) The roofs were always flat, and were made either of earth that was trodden hard, or with large flat stones. This roof was surrounded with a balustrade (Deut. xxii. 8), and furnished a convenient place for walking, or even for eating and sleeping. Whenever, therefore, anything was to be seen in the street, or at a distance; or when there was any cause of alarm, they

HOUSE TOPS IN THE EAST.

would naturally resort to the roof of the house. When there was a tower in the city, the inhabitants fled to that, and took refuge on its top (see Judg. x. 50 –53). The image here is, therefore, one of consternation and alarm, as if on the sudden approach of an enemy.

2. *Thou that art full of stirs*. Of tumult, of commotion, of alarm. Or, perhaps, this whole description may mean that it was formerly a city distinguished for the hum of business, or for pleasure; a busy, active, enterprising city. The Hebrew will bear this, but I prefer the former interpretation, as indicating mingled alarm and consternation, and at the same time a disposition to engage in riot and revelry. ¶ *A joyous city*. A city exulting; rejoicing; given to pleasure, and to riot. (See

3 All thy rulers are fled ^a together, they are bound ¹ by the
archers : all that are found in thee

are bound together, *which* have fled
from far.

a 2 Ki.25.5,11.   1 *of the bow.*

the description of Nineveh in Zeph. ii.
15.) It is remarkable that the prophet
has blended these things together, and
has spoken of the tumult, the alarm, and
the rejoicing, in the same breath. This
may be either because it was the *general*
character of the city thus to be full of
revelry, dissipation, and riot, and he
designates it by that which *usually* and
appropriately described it ; or because
it was, even then, notwithstanding the
general consternation and alarm, given
up to revelry, and the rather on account
of the approaching danger. So he describes the city in ver. 12, 13. ¶ *Thy
slain* men are *not slain with the sword.*
The words 'thy slain' here (חֲלָלַיִךְ),
seem to be intended to be applied to the
soldiers on whom the defence of the city
rested ; and to mean those who had not
died an honourable death *in* the city in
its defence, but who had *fled* in consternation, and who were either taken in
their flight and made captive, or who
were pursued and put to death. To be
slain with the sword here is equivalent
to being slain in an honourable engagement with the enemy. But here the
prophet speaks of their consternation,
their cowardice, and of their being partly
trampled down in their hasty and ignominious flight by each other ; and partly
of the fugitives being overtaken by the
enemy, and thus put to death.

3. *All thy rulers are fled together.*
The general idea in this verse is plain.
It is designed to describe the consternation which would take place on the
approach of the invader, and especially
the timidity and flight of those on whom
the city relied for protection and defence.
Hence, instead of entering calmly and
firmly on the work of defence, no inconsiderable part of the rulers of the city
are represented as fleeing from the city,
and refusing to remain to protect the
capital. The word rendered 'thy rulers'
(קְצִינַיִךְ) denotes either the civil rulers
of the city, or military leaders. It is
most usually applied to the latter (Josh.
x. 24 ; Judg. xi. 6, 11 ; Dan. xi. 18),
and probably refers here to military

commanders. ¶ *They are bound by the
archers.* Heb. as in the margin, ' Of
the bow.' There has been a great
variety in the interpretation of this
passage. The LXX. read it, Σκληρῶς
δεδεμένοι εἰσί—' And the captives are
bound with severity.' The Chaldee,
' And the captives migrate from before
the extending of the bow.' Jarchi renders it, ' Who from the fear of arrows
were bound so that they shut themselves
up in the city.' Houbigant and Lowth
render it, ' They are fled from the bow,'
reading it הָסִרוּ instead of the present
Hebrew text אֻסָּרוּ, but without the
slightest authority. Vitringa renders
it, ' They were bound from treading, *i.e.*,
extending, or using the bow ;' or ' They
were bound *by* those who tread, *i.e.*,
use the bow ;' indicating that they were
so bound that they could not use the
bow in defence of the city. I think that
the *connection* here requires that the
word אֻסָּרוּ should be used in the sense
of being *bound* or influenced by fear—
they were so intimidated, so much under
the influence of terror, so entirely un-
manned and disabled by alarm, that they
could not use the bow ; or this was caused
by the bow, *i.e.*, by the bowmen or
archers who came to attack the city.
It is true that no other instance occurs
in which the word is used in precisely
this sense, but instances in abundance
occur where strong passion is represented as having a controlling or dis-
abling influence over the mind and body ;
where it takes away the energy of the
soul, and makes one timid, feeble,
helpless, *as if* bound with cords, or
made captive. The word אָסַר commonly
means to bind with cords, or to fetter ;
to imprison (Gen. xlii. 24 ; Judg. xvi.
5 ; 2 Kings xvii. 4) : to yoke (1 Sam.
vi. 7, 10) ; and then to bind with a vow
(Num. xxx. 3). Hence it may mean to
bind with fear or consternation. ¶ Which
have fled from far. That is, either they
have fled far away ; or they had fled
from far in order to reach Jerusalem
as a place of safety. Probably the latter
is the sense.

4 Therefore said I, Look away from me; I will [1] weep bitterly, labour [a] not to comfort me; because of the spoiling of the daughter of my people.

5 For *it is* a day of trouble, and of treading down, and of perplexity

by the LORD God of hosts in the valley of vision, breaking down the walls, and of crying to the mountains.

6 And Elam [b] bare the quiver with chariots of men *and* horsemen, and Kir [2] uncovered the shield.

1 *be in bitter weeping.*　　a Jer.4.19; 9.1; Lam.1.2.

b Jer.49.35.　　　　2 *made naked.*

---

4. *Look away from me.* Do not look upon me—an indication of deep grief, for sorrow seeks to be alone, and grief avoids publicity and exposure. ¶ *I will weep bitterly.* Heb. ' I will be bitter in weeping.' Thus we speak of *bitter* sorrow, indicating excessive grief (see Note on ch. xv. 5; comp. Jer. xiii. 17; xiv. 17; Lam. i. 16; ii. 11; Mic. i. 8, 9). ¶ *Labour not.* The sense is, ' My grief is so great that I cannot be comforted. There are no topics of consolation that can be presented. I must be alone, and allowed to indulge in deep and overwhelming sorrow at the calamities that are coming upon my nation and people.' ¶ *Because of the spoiling.* The desolation ; the ruin that is coming upon them. ¶ *The daughter of my people.* Jerusalem (see Note on ch. i. 8; comp. Jer. iv. 11; vi. 14; viii. 19, 21, 22; Lam. ii. 11; iv. 3, 6, 10).

5. *For it is a day of trouble and of treading down.* When our enemies trample on everything sacred and dear to us, and endanger all our best interests (see Ps. xliv. 6; Luke xxi. 24). ¶ *And of perplexity.* In which we know not what to do. We are embarrassed, and know not where to look for relief. ¶ *By the* LORD *God of hosts.* That is, he is the efficient cause of all this. It has come upon us under his providence, and by his direction (see Note on ch. x. 5). ¶ *In the valley of vision.* In Jerusalem (see Note on ver. 1). ¶ *Breaking down the walls.* There has been much variety in the interpretation of this place. The LXX. render it, ' In the valley of Zion they wander, from the least to the greatest ; they wander upon the mountains.' See a discussion of the various senses which the Hebrew phrase may admit, in Rosenmüller and Gesenius. Probably our common version has given the true sense, and the reference is to the fact that the walls of the city be-

came thrown down, either in the siege or from some other cause. If this refers to the invasion of Sennacherib, though his army was destroyed, and he was unable to take the city, yet there is no improbability in the supposition that he made some breaches in the walls. Indeed this is implied in the account in 2 Chron. xxxii. 5. ¶ *And of crying to the mountains.* Either for help, or more probably of such a loud lamentation that it reached the surrounding hills, and was re-echoed back to the city. Or perhaps it may mean that the shout or clamour of those engaged in building or defending the walls, reached to the mountains. Comp. Virg. *Æneid,* iv. 668 :

— resonat magnis plangoribus æther.

Rosenmüller renders it, ' A cry—to the mountains ! ' That is, a cry among the people to escape to the hills, and to seek refuge in the caves and fastnesses there (comp. Judg. vi. 2; Matt. xxiv. 16; Mark xiii. 14).

6. *And Elam.* The southern part of Persia, perhaps here used to denote Persia in general (see Note on ch. xxi. 2). Elam, or Persia, was at this time subject to Assyria, and their forces were united doubtless in the invasion of Judea. ¶ *Bare the quiver.* A ' quiver ' is a case in which arrows are carried. This was usually hung upon the shoulders, and thus *borne* by the soldier when he entered into battle. By the expression here, is meant that Elam was engaged in the siege, and was distinguished particularly for skill in shooting arrows. That the Elamites were thus distinguished for the use of the bow, is apparent from Ezek. xxxii. 24, and Jer. xlix. 35. ¶ *With chariots of men* and *horsemen.* Lowth proposes, instead of ' men,' to read אָרָם, *Syria,* instead of אָדָם, *man,* by the change of the single letter ד into ר　This mis-

7 And it shall come to pass, *that* thy [1] choicest valleys shall be full of chariots, and the horsemen shall set themselves in array [2] at the gate

1 the choice of thy.　　　2 or, toward.

8 And he discovered the covering of Judah, and thou didst look in that day to the armour of the house *a* of the forest.

a 1 Ki.7.2; 10.17.

take might have been easily made where the letters are so much alike, and it would suit the parallelism of the passage, but there is no authority of MSS. or versions for the change. The words 'chariots of men—horsemen,' I understand here, as in ch. xxi. 7, to mean *a troop* or *riding* of men who were horsemen. Archers often rode in this manner. The Scythians usually fought on horseback with bows and arrows. ¶ *Kir.* Kir was a city of Media, where the river Kyrus or Cyrus flows (2 Kings xvi. 9; Amos i. 5; ix. 7). This was evidently then connected with the Assyrian monarchy, and was engaged with it in the invasion of Judea. Perhaps the name 'Kir' was given to a region or province lying on the river Cyrus or Kyrus. This river unites with the Araxes, and falls into the Caspian Sea. ¶ *Uncovered the shield* (see Note on xxi. 5). Shields were protected during a march, or when not in use, by a covering of cloth. Among the Greeks, the name of this covering was Σάγμα. Shields were made either of metal or of skin, and the object in covering them was to preserve the metal untarnished, or to keep the shield from injury. To *uncover the shield*, therefore, was to prepare for battle. The Medes were subject to the Assyrians in the time of Hezekiah (2 Kings xvi. 9; xvii. 6), and of course in the time of the invasion of Judea by Sennacherib.

7. *Thy choicest valleys.* Heb. 'The choice of thy valleys;' meaning the most fertile and most valued lands in the vicinity of the city. The rich and fertile vales around Jerusalem would be occupied by the armies of the Assyrian monarch. What occurs in this verse and the following verses to ver. 14, is a prophetic description of what is presented historically in Isa. xxxvi., and 2 Chron. xxxii. The coincidence is so exact, that it leaves no room to doubt that the invasion here described was that which took place under Sen-

nacherib. ¶ *Set themselves in array.* Heb. 'Placing shall place themselves;' *i.e.*, they shall be drawn up for battle; they shall besiege the city, and guard it from all ingress or egress. Rabshakeh, sent by Sennacherib to besiege the city, took his station at the upper pool, and was so near the city that he could converse with the people on the walls (Isa. xxxvi. 11-13).

8. *And he discovered.* Heb. וַיְגַל —'He made naked, or bare.' The expression, 'He discovered,' means simply that it *was* uncovered, without designating the agent. ¶ *The covering of Judah.* The word here used (מָסָךְ) denotes properly *a covering*, and is applied to the *curtain* or vail that was before the tabernacle (Ex. xxvi. 36: xxxix. 38); and to the curtain that was before the gate of the court (Ex. xxxv. 17; xxxix. 40). The LXX. understand it of the *gates* of Judah, 'They revealed the gates (τὰς πύλας) of Judah.' Many have understood it of the defences, ramparts, or fortifications of Judah, meaning that they were laid open to public view, *i.e.*, were demolished. But the more probable meaning, perhaps, is, that the invading army exposed Judah to every kind of reproach; stripped off everything that was designed to be ornamental in the land; and thus, by the figure of exposing one to reproach and shame by stripping off all his clothes, exposed Judah in every part to reproach. Sennacherib actually came up against all the fortified cities of Judah, and took them and dismantled them (2 Kings xviii. 13; Isa. xxxvi. 1). The land was thus laid bare, and unprotected. ¶ *And thou didst look.* Thou Judah; or the king of Judah. Thou didst cast thine eyes to that armoury as the last resort, and as the only hope of defence. ¶ *To the armour.* Or rather, perhaps, the *armoury*, the *arsenal* (נֶשֶׁק). The LXX. render it, 'To the choice houses of the city' (comp. Neh. iii. 19). ¶ *Of the house*

9 Ye *a* have seen also the breaches of the city of David, that they are many ; and ye gathered together the waters of the lower pool :

10 And ye have numbered the

---

houses of Jerusalem, and the houses have ye broken down to fortify the wall.

11 Ye made also a ditch between the two walls for the water of the old pool : but ye have not looked

---

of the forest. This was built within the city, and was called the house of the forest of Lebanon, probably from the great quantity of cedar from Lebanon which was employed in building it (1 Kings vii. 2–8). In this house, Solomon laid up large quantities of munitions of war (1 Kings x. 16, 17); and this vast storehouse was now the principal reliance of Hezekiah against the invading forces of Sennacherib.

9. *Ye have seen also the breaches.* You who are inhabitants of the city. That such breaches were actually made, see 2 Chron. xxxii. 5. ¶ *Of the city of David.* Of Jerusalem, so called because it was the royal residence of David. Zion was usually called the city of David, but the name was given also to the entire city. ¶ *And ye gathered together,* &c. That is, Hezekiah and the people of the city collected those waters. ¶ *Of the lower pool.* (For a description of the upper and lower pool, see Notes on ch. vii. 3). The superfluous waters of the lower pool usually flowed into the valley of Hinnom, and thence into the valley of Jehoshaphat, mingling with the waters of the brook Kedron. It would seem from the passage here that those waters were not usually retained for the use of the city, though it was possible to retain them in case of a drought or a siege. At present, the lower pool is without the walls, but Hezekiah appears to have extended a temporary wall around it so as to enclose it (see Note on ver. 11). This he did, probably for two purposes ; (1.) to cut off the Assyrians from the supply of water; and (2.) to retain *all* the water in the city to supply the inhabitants during the siege ; see 2 Chron. xxxii. 4, where it is expressly declared that Hezekiah took this measure to distress the Assyrians.

10. *And ye have numbered the houses of Jerusalem.* That is, you have taken

an estimate of their number so as to ascertain how many can be spared to be pulled down to repair the walls ; or you have made an estimate of the amount of materials for repairing the walls, which would be furnished by pulling down the houses in Jerusalem. ¶ *To fortify the wall.* The houses in Jerusalem were built of stone, and therefore they would furnish appropriate materials for repairing the walls of the city. In 2 Chron. xxxii. 5, it is said that Hezekiah not only repaired the broken walls of the city on the approach of Sennacherib, but ' raised up the towers, and another wall without, and repaired Millo in the city of David, and made darts and shields in abundance.'

11. *Ye made also a ditch.* That is, they made a *reservoir* to retain the water. The word ' ditch,' however, will well describe the character of the pool of Gihon on the west side of the city (see Notes on ch. vii. 3). ¶ *Between the two walls for the water of the old pool.* Hezekiah built one of these walls himself (2 Chron xxxii. 5, 30; comp. 2 Kings xxv. 5, and Jer. xxxix. 4). Between these two walls the water would be collected so as to be accessible to the inhabitants of the city in case of a siege. Before this, the water had flowed without the walls of the city, and in a time of siege the inhabitants would be cut off from it, and an enemy would be able easily to subdue them. To prevent this, Hezekiah appears to have performed two works, one of which was particularly adapted to the times of the siege, and the other was of permanent utility. (1.) He made a wall on the west side of Gihon, so as to make the pool accessible to the inhabitants of the city, as described here by Isaiah ; and (2.) he ' stopped the upper water-course of Gihon, and brought it straight down to the west side of the city of David ' (2 Chron.

unto the maker thereof, neither had respect unto him that fashioned it long ago.

12 And in that day did the LORD God of hosts call [a] to weeping, and to mourning, and to

baldness,[b] and to girding with sackcloth :

13 And behold, joy and gladness, slaying oxen and killing sheep, eating flesh and drinking wine : let us [c] eat and drink, for to-morrow we shall die.

a Joel 1.13.　b Job 1.20; Mic.1.16.　c ch.56.12.

xxxii. 30). By this is not improbably meant that he constructed the pool which is now known as the ' pool of Hezekiah.' This reservoir lies within the walls of the city, some distance north-eastward of the Yâfa Gate, and just west of the street that leads to the church of the Holy Sepulchre. Its sides run towards the cardinal points. Its breadth at the north end is 144 feet, its length on the east side about 240 feet. The depth is not great. The bottom is rock, and is levelled and covered with cement. The reservoir is now supplied with water during the rainy season by the small aqueduct or drain brought down from the upper pool, along the surface of the ground and under the wall at or near the Yâfa Gate (comp. Robinson's *Bib. Researches*, vol. i. p. 487). This was deemed a work of great utility, and was one of the acts which particularly distinguished the reign of Hezekiah. It is not only mentioned in the Books of Kings and Chronicles, but the son of Sirach has also mentioned it in his encomium on Hezekiah : ' Hezekiah fortified his city, and brought in water into the midst thereof ; he digged the hard rock with iron, and made wells for water' (Ecclus. xlviii. 17). ¶ *But ye have not looked.* You have not relied on God. You have depended on your own resources ; and on the defences which you have been making against the enemy. This probably described the *general* character of the people. Hezekiah, however, was a pious man, and doubtless really depended on the aid of God. ¶ *The maker thereof.* God ; by whose command and aid all these defences are made, and who has given you ability and skill to make them. ¶ *Long ago.* God had made this fountain, and it had *long* been a supply to the city. He had a claim, therefore, to their gratitude and respect.

12. *And in that day.* In the invasion of Sennacherib. It might be rendered, ' And the Lord, JEHOVAH of hosts, *on such a day calls* to weeping ;' intimating that in such a time it was a general truth that God required those who were thus afflicted to weep, and fast, and pray. ¶ *Call to weeping.* That is, by his providence ; or, it was *proper* that at such a time they should weep. Affliction, oppression, and calamity are indications from God *always* that we ought to be humbled, and to prostrate ourselves before Him. ¶ *And to baldness.* To plucking off the hair, or shaving the head—one of the emblems of grief among the ancients (Job i. 20; Micah i. 16). ¶ *And to girding with sackcloth* (see Note on ch. iii. 24).

13. *And behold, &c.* When they ought to give themselves to fasting and prayer, they gave themselves up to revelry and riot. ¶ *Let us eat and drink.* Saying, Let us eat and drink. That is, it is inevitable that we must soon die. The army of the Assyrian is approaching, and the city cannot stand against him. It is in vain to make a defence, and in vain to call upon God. Since we *must* soon die, we may as well enjoy life while it lasts. This is always the language of the epicure ; and it seems to be the language of no small part of the world. Probably if the *real* feelings of the great mass of worldly men were expressed, they could not be better expressed than in this passage of Isaiah : ' We must soon die at all events. We cannot avoid that, for it is the common lot of all. And since we have been sent into a dying world ; since we had no agency in being placed here ; since it is impossible to prevent this doom, we may as well *enjoy* life while it lasts, and give ourselves to pleasure, dissipation, and revelry. While we can, we will take our com-

fort, and when death comes we will submit to it, simply because we cannot avoid it.' Thus, while God calls men to repentance and seriousness; and while he would urge them, by the consideration that this life is short, to prepare for a better; and while he designs that the nearness of death should lead them to think solemnly of it, they abuse all his mercies, endeavour to thwart all his arrangements, and live and die like the brutes.—This passage is quoted by Paul in his argument on the subject of the resurrection in 1 Cor. xv. 32. Sentiments remarkably similar to this occur in the writings of the Greek and Roman poets. Among the Egyptians, the fact that life is short was urged as one argument for promoting soberness and temperance, and in order to produce this effect, it was customary at their feasts to have introduced, at some part of the entertainment, a wooden image of Osiris in the form of a human mummy standing erect, or lying on a bier, and to show it to each of the guests, warning him of his mortality, and of the transitory nature of human pleasures. He was reminded that one day he would be like that; and was told that men ' ought to love one another, and to avoid those evils which tend to make them consider life too long, when in reality it is too short, and while enjoying the blessings of this life, to bear in mind that life was precarious, and that death would soon close all their comforts.' (See Wilkinson's *Ancient Egyptians*, vol. ii. pp. 409–411.) With the Greeks and Romans, however, as well as the Jews in the time of Isaiah, the fact of the shortness of life was used to produce just the contrary effect—to prompt them to dissipation and licentiousness. The fact of the temporary pilgrimage of man served as an inducement to enjoy the pleasures of life while they lasted, since death was supposed to close the scene, and no prospect was held out of happiness in a future state. This sentiment was expressed in their songs at their entertainments to urge themselves on to greater indulgence in wine and in pleasure. Thus, in Anacreon, Ode 4:

Εις εαυτον.

Ο δ' Ερως χιτωνα δησας
Υπερ αυχενος παπυρω
Μεθυ μοι διηκονειτο·

Τροχος αρματος γαρ οια
Βιοτος τρεχει κυλισθεις
Ολιγη δε κεισομεσθα
Κονις, οστεων λυθεντων·

Τι σε δει λιθον μυριζειν;
Τι δε γη χεειν ματαια;
Εμε μαλλον, ως ετι ζω,
Μυρισον, καλει δ' εταιρην.

Πριν, Ερως, εκει με απελθειν
Υπο νερτερων χορειας,
Σκεδασαι θελω μεριμνας.

'In decent robe behind him bound,
Cupid shall serve the goblet round;
For fast away our moments steal,
Like the swift chariot's rolling wheel;
The rapid course is quickly done,
And soon the race of life is run.
Then, then, alas! we droop, we die;
And sunk in dissolution lie:
Our frame no symmetry retains,
Nought but a little dust remains.
Why o'er the tomb are odours shed?
Why poured libations to the dead?
To me, far better, while I live,
Rich wines and balmy fragrance give.
Now, now, the rosy wreath prepare,
And hither call the lovely fair.
Now, while I draw my vital breath,
Ere yet I lead the dance of death,
For joy my sorrows I'll resign,
And drown my cares in rosy wine.'

A similar sentiment occurs in Horace. *Od.* iii. 13:

Huc vina, et unguente, et nimium brevis
Flores amœnos ferre jube rosæ.
Dum res, et ætas, et sororum
Fila trium patiuntur atra.

And still more strikingly in Petronius, *Satyric.* c. 34, *ad finem:*

Heu, heu, nos miseros, quam totus homuncio nil est!
Sic erimus cuncti, postquam nos auferat Orcus:
Ergo vivamus, dum licet esse, bene.

The same sentiments prevailed among the Jews in the time of the author of the Book of Wisdom (xi. 1–9):—' Our life is short and tedious, and in the death of a man there is no remedy: neither was there any man known to have returned from the grave. For we are born at all adventure; and we shall be hereafter as though we had never been, for the breath in our nostrils is as smoke, and a little spark in the moving of our heart. Come on, therefore, let us enjoy the good things that are present; let us

14 And it was revealed in mine ears by the LORD of hosts, Surely this iniquity shall not be purged from you till ye die, saith the Lord GOD of hosts.

ANALYSIS OF VER. 15–25.—VISION XX.

THE remainder of this chapter (ver. 15–25) is occupied with a prediction respecting Shebna, and the promotion of Eliakim in his place. From the prophecy itself it appears that Shebna was prefect of the palace (15), or that he was in the highest authority in the time of Hezekiah. That he was an unprincipled ruler is evident from the prophecy, and hence Isaiah was directed to predict his fall, and the elevation of another in his place. Whether this Shebna is the same that is mentioned in ch. xxxvi. 3, is not known. The Shebna there mentioned is called a *scribe* (22), and that was *after* the fall of Shebna here mentioned, for it occurred after Eliakim had been placed over the palace. Eliakim was then in office, and was sent on that

embassy to Sennacherib (xxxvi. 2, 22; xxxvii. 2). The probability is, therefore, that this was some other man of the same name, unless it may have been that *Shebna*, after being degraded from the rank of prefect of the palace or prime minister, became *a scribe*, or had an inferior office under Eliakim. The prophecy contains the following things:—1. A *command* to Isaiah to go to Shebna, and to reprove him for his self-confidence in his sin (15, 16). 2. A declaration that he should be carried captive to a foreign land (17, 18). 3. A declaration that he should be deposed and succeeded by Eliakim (20). 4. A description of the character and honours of Eliakim, and his qualifications for the office (21–24), and 5. A confirmation of the whole prophecy, or a summing up the whole in a single declaration (25).

15 Thus saith the Lord GOD of hosts, Go, get thee unto this treasurer, *even* unto Shebna, *a*which *is* over the house, *and say*,

a 2 Ki.18.37.

fill ourselves with costly wine and ointments, and let no flower of the spring pass by us ; let us crown ourselves with rose buds before they be withered ; let none of us go without his part of our voluptuousness ; let us leave tokens of our joyfulness in every place.' It was with reference to such sentiments as these, that Dr. Doddridge composed that beautiful epigram which Dr. Johnson pronounced the finest in the English language :

' Live while you live,' the sacred preacher cries,
' And give to God each moment as it flies ;'
' Live while you live,' the Epicure would say,
' And seize the pleasures of the present day.'
Lord, in my view, let both united be,
I live to pleasure when I live to thee.

14. *It was revealed in mine ears, Surely this iniquity shall not be purged from you till ye die.* That is, the sin is so aggravated that it shall never be expiated or pardoned. Few sins can be more aggravated than revelry and riot, thoughtlessness and mirth over the grave. Nothing can show a more decided disregard of God, and nothing a more grovelling and sensual disposition. And yet, it is the common sin of the world ; and there can be nothing more melancholy than that a race hastening to the grave should give itself to riot and dissipation. One would think that the

prospect of a speedy and certain death would deter men from sin. But the very reverse is true. The nearer they approach death, the more reckless and abandoned do they often become. The *strength* and *power* of depravity is thus shown in the fact that men CAN sin thus when near the grave, and with the most fearful warnings and assurances that they are soon to go down to eternal wo.

15. *Thus saith the Lord* GOD *of hosts* (see Note on ch. i. 9). ¶ *Go, get thee.* Heb. ' Go, come to.' This was one of the instances in which the prophets were directed to go personally, and even at the hazard of their life, to those who were high in office, and to denounce on them the Divine judgment for their sins. ¶ *Unto this treasurer* (הַסֹּכֵן). The Vulgate renders this, ' To him who dwells in the tabernacle.' The LXX. render it, Εἰς τὸ παστοφόριον, denoting properly what is borne into a recess, cell, or chapel, and referring properly to a place where an idol was placed in a temple ; and then any recess, or chamber, as a treasury, and referring here to the room which the treasurer of the temple occupied. The Hebrew word סָכַן means *to dwell with any one ;* then to be an associate or friend, and hence the participle is applied to one intrusted

16 What hast thou here, and whom hast thou here, that thou hast hewed thee out a sepulchre here, ¹ *as* he that heweth him out a sepulchre on high, *and* that graveth an habitation for himself in a rock?

1 or, *O he.*

with the care of anything, a steward, a treasurer. Jerome explains this in his Commentary as meaning, ' go to him who dwells in the tabernacle, which in Hebrew is called *Sochen.*' He understands by this some room, or recess in the temple, where the treasurer or the prefect of the temple dwelt. Our translators have expressed probably the true sense by the word 'treasurer.' ¶ *Which is over the house.* That is, either who is over the temple, or over the palace. I understand it of the latter. Shebna was not high priest, and the expression, ' over the house,' more properly denotes one who had the rule of the palace, or who was the principal minister of the king. See 1 Kings xviii. 3: ' And Ahab called Obadiah, which was the governor of his house.' What was the offence or crime of Shebna, it is impossible to say. The Jewish commentators say that he was intending to betray the city to Sennacherib, but although this is possible it has no direct proof.

16. *What hast thou here?* This verse contains a severe repoof of the pride and ostentation of Shebna, and of his expectation that he would be buried where he had built his own tomb. It also contains an *implied* declaration that he would not be permitted to lie there, but would be removed to a distant land to be buried in some less honourable manner. It is probable that Isaiah met him when he was *at* the sepulchre which he had made, and addressed this language to him there: ' What hast thou here? What right to expect that thou wilt be buried here, or why do you erect this splendid sepulchre, as if you were a holy man, and God would allow you to lie here?' Probably his sepulchre had been erected among the sepulchres of holy men, and perhaps in some part of the royal burying place in Jerusalem. ¶ *And whom hast thou here?* Who among the dead that are entombed here are connected with you, that you should deem yourself entitled to lie with them? If this was the royal cemetery, these

words might be designed to intimate that he had no connection with the royal family; and thus his building a tomb there was an evidence of vainglory, and of an attempt to occupy a place, even in death, to which he had no title. ¶ *That thou hast hewed thee out a sepulchre here.* Sepulchres were hewn or cut out of rocks (see Note on ch. xiv. 9). It was usual also for princes and rich men to have their sepulchres or tombs constructed while they were themselves alive (see Matt. xxvii. 60). Shebna was doubtless a man of humble birth, none of whose ancestors or family had been honoured with a burial in the royal cemetery, and hence the prophet reproves his pride in expecting to repose with the royal dead. ¶ *He that heweth him out a sepulchre on high.* On some elevated place, that it might be more conspicuous. Thus Hezekiah (2 Chron. xxxii. 33) was buried ' in the chiefest of the sepulchres of the sons of David.' Heb. בַּמָּרוֹם.—'In the highest.' LXX.'Εν ἀναβάσει. Such sepulchres are still found in Persia. They consist of several tombs, each hewn in a high rock near the top, the front of the rock being adorned with figures in *relievo.* ' Sepulchres of this kind are remarkably exemplified in the very ancient tombs excavated in the cliffs of the mountain of sepulchres at Naksh-i-Roustan, a full description of which may be found in Sir Robert Ker Porter's *Travels.* They are excavated in an almost perpendicular cliff of about 300 feet high. There are two rows, of which the uppermost are the most ancient and interesting, presenting highly sculptured fronts about fifty-three feet broad, crowned by a representation of an act of Sabean worship. To the lowest of them, which, however, he describes as not less than sixty feet from the ground, Sir Robert could gain access only by being drawn up by means of a rope fastened around his waist, by some active natives who had contrived to clamber up to the ledge in front of the tomb. These appear to be royal sepul-

17 Behold, the Lord [1] will carry thee away with a [2] mighty captivity, and will surely cover thee.

18 He will surely violently turn,

1 or, *who covered thee with an excellent covering, and clothed thee gorgeously, shall surely*, ver.18.

and toss thee *like* a ball into a large [3] country : there shalt thou die, and there the chariots of thy glory *shall be* the shame of thy lord's house.

2 *the captivity of a man.*   3 *large of spaces.*

chres, and probably not later than the time of the kings of Persia mentioned in Scripture.' — (*Pict. Bible.*)   Two

objects were probably contemplated by such sepulchres.   One was security from desecration.   The other was ostentation

Tombs in the Rocks at Naski Roustan.—From Flandin, Voyage en Perse.

—sepulchres thus excavated furnishing an opportunity for the display of architectural taste in front, and being conspicuous objects.   Such sepulchres are found at Petra (see Notes on ch. xvi. 1), and it is probable that Shebna sought this kind of immortality.—Many a man who has done nothing to deserve celebrity by his noble deeds while living, seeks it by the magnificence of his tomb.

17. *Behold, the* Lord *will carry thee away.*   Of the historical fact here referred to we have no other information.   To what place he was to be carried, we know not.   It is probable, however, that it was to Assyria.   ¶ *With a mighty captivity.*   Heb. נֶבֶר—'Of a man,' or perhaps, ' O man.'   If it means 'the captivity of a man,' the sense is, a strong, irresistible, mighty captivity, where the word *man* is emphatic, and means such as a mighty man would make.   Comp. Job xxxviii. 3: ' Gird up now thy loins like a man.'   The margin reads this, he ' who covered thee with an excellent covering, and clothed thee gorgeously, shall surely turn and toss thee.'   But the text conveys more nearly the idea of the Hebrew word,

which denotes the action of *casting away*, or *throwing* from one as a man throws a stone.   See the same use of the word טול in 1 Sam. xviii. 2; xx. 33; Jer. xvii. 13; xxii. 26, 28; Jonah i. 5, 12, 16.   *And will surely cover thee.*   ' Thy face,' says Lowth ; for this was the condition of mourners.   The Chaldee is, ' Shall cover thee with confusion.'   So Vitringa, who supposes that it means that although Shebna was endeavouring to rear a monument that should perpetuate his name and that of his family, God would cover them with ignominy, and reduce them to their primitive, obscure, and humble condition.

18. *He will surely violently turn.*   Lowth has well expressed the sense of this:

He will whirl thee round and round, and cast thee away.

Thus it refers to the action of throwing a stone with a *sling*, when the sling is whirled round and round several times before the string is let go, in order to increase the velocity of the stone.   The idea is here, that God designed to cast him into a distant land, and that he would give such an *impulse* to him that

19 And I will drive thee from thy station, and from thy state shall he pull thee down.

20 And it shall come to pass in that day, that I will call my servant *a* Eliakim, the son of Hilkiah :

a 2 Ki.18.18.

he would be sent afar, so far that he would not be able to return again. ¶ Like *a ball.* A stone, ball, or other projectile that is cast from a sling. ¶ *Into a large country.* Probably Assyria. When this was done we have no means of determining. ¶ *And there the chariots of thy glory* shall be *the shame of thy lord's house.* Lowth renders this,

―――― and there shall thy glorious chariots
Become the shame of the house of thy lord.

Noyes renders it,

There shall thy splendid chariots perish,
Thou disgrace of the house of thy lord.

The Chaldee renders it, ' And there the chariots of thy glory shall be converted into ignominy, because thou didst not preserve the glory of the house of thy lord.' Probably the correct interpretation is that which regards the latter part of the verse, ' the shame of thy lord's house,' as an address to him as the shame or disgrace of Ahaz, who had appointed him to that office, and of Hezekiah, who had continued him in it. The phrase ' the chariots of thy glory,' means splendid or magnificent chariots ; and refers doubtless to the fact that in Jerusalem he had affected great pride and display, and had, like many weak minds, sought distinction by the splendour of his equipage. The idea here is, that the ' chariot of his glory,' *i.e.*, the vehicle in which he would ride, would be in a distant land, not meaning that *in* that land he would ride in chariots as magnificent as those which he had in Jerusalem, but that he would be conveyed there, and probably be borne in an ignominious manner, instead of the splendid mode in which he was carried in Jerusalem. The Jews say that when he left Jerusalem to deliver it into the hands of the enemy, they asked him where his army was ; and when he said that they had turned back, they said,

21 And I will clothe him with thy robe, and strengthen him with thy girdle, and I will commit thy government into his hand ; and he shall be a father to the inhabitants of Jerusalem, and to the house of Judah.

' thou hast mocked us ;' and that thereupon they bored his heels, and tied him to the tails of horses, and that thus he died.

19. *And from thy state.* From thy office ; thy place of trust and responsibility. ¶ *Shall he pull thee down.* That is, *God* shall do it. The prophet here uses the third person instead of the first. Such a change of person is very common in the writings of the prophets (see Stuart's *Heb. Gram.* § 563–565, sixth Ed.)

20. *My servant Eliakim.* A man who will be faithful to me ; who will be trustworthy, and to whom the interests of the city may be safely confided ; a man who will not seek to betray it into the hands of the enemy. Of Eliakim we know nothing more than what is stated here, and in ch. xxxvi. From that account it appears that he was prefect of the palace ; that he was employed in a negotiation with the leader of the army of the Assyrians ; and that he was in all things faithful to the trust reposed in him. ¶ *The son of Hilkiah.* Kimchi supposes that this was the same as Azariah the son of Hilkiah, who might have had two names, and who was a ruler over the house of God in the time of Hezekiah (1 Chron. vi. 13).

21. *And I will clothe him with thy robe.* He shall succeed thee in the office, and wear the garments which are appropriate to it. ¶ *And strengthen him with thy girdle.* That is, he shall wear the same girdle that thou didst (see Note on ch. iii. 24). In that girdle was usually the purse, and to it was attached the sword. Often, among the Orientals, the girdle was adorned with gold and precious stones, and was regarded as the principal embellishment of the dress. ¶ *And he shall be a father,* &c. A counsellor ; a guide ; one who can be trusted in time of danger and difficulty. We use the word

22 And the key of the house of David will I lay upon his shoulder : so *a* he shall open, *b* and none shall shut ; and he shall shut, and none shall open.

23 And I will fasten him *as* a nail *c* in a sure place ; and he shall be for a glorious throne to his father's house.

a ch.9.6.　　*b* Job 12.14; Rev.3.7　　*c* Ezra 9 8.

father in the same sense, when we speak of the ' father of his country.'

22. *And the key.* A key is that by which a house is locked or opened. To possess that is, therefore, to have free access to it, or control over it. Thus we give possession of a house by giving the *key* into the hands of a purchaser, implying that it is his ; that he has free access to it ; that he can close it when he pleases, and that no other one, without his permission, has the right of access to it. ¶ *Of the house of David.* Of the house which David built for his royal residence ; that is, of the palace. This house was on Mount Zion ; and to have the key of that house was to have the chief authority at court, or to be prime minister (see Note on ver. 15). To be put in possession of that key, therefore, was the mark of office, or was a sign that he was intrusted with the chief authority in the government. ¶ *Will I lay upon his shoulder* (see ch. ix. 6). This seems to have been designed as an emblem of office. But in what way it was done is unknown. Lowth supposes that the key was of considerable magnitude, and was made crooked, and that thus it would lie readily on the shoulder. He has observed also, that this was a well-known badge or emblem of office. Thus the priestess of Ceres is described as having a key on the shoulder (Callim. *Ceres,* ver. 45); and thus in Æschyl. *Supp.* 299, a female high in office is described as having a key. But it is not known in what way the key was borne. It may have been borne on the shoulder, being so made as to be easily carried there ; or it may have been attached to the shoulder by a belt or strap, as a sword is ; or it may have been a mere emblem or figure inwrought into the robe, and worn as a sign of office ; or the figure of a key may have been worn on the shoulder as an epaulet is now, as a sign of office and authority. If the locks were made of wood, as

we have reason to suppose, then the key was probably large, and would answer well for a sign of office. ' How much was I delighted when I first saw the people, especially the Moors, going along the streets with each his key on his shoulder. The handle is generally made of brass (though sometimes of silver), and is often nicely worked in a device of filigrane. The way it is carried is to have the corner of a kerchief tied to the ring ; the key is then placed on the shoulder, and the kerchief hangs down in front. At other times they have a bunch of large keys, and then they have half on one side of the shoulder, and half on the other. For a man thus to march along with a large key on his shoulder, shows at once that he is a person of consequence. " Raman is in great favour with the Modeliar, for he now carries the key." " Whose key have you got on your shoulder?" " I shall carry my key on my own shoulder." ' —(Roberts.) ¶ *So he shall open,* &c. This phrase means, that he should have the highest authority in the government, and is a promise of unlimited power. Our Saviour has made use of the same expression to denote the unlimited power conferred on his apostles in his church (Matt. xvi. 19); and has applied it also to himself in Rev. iii. 7.

23. *And I will fasten him* as *a nail in a sure place.* The word ' nail ' here (יָתֵד) means properly a peg, pin, or spike ; and is applied often to the pins or large spikes which were used to drive into the ground to fasten the cords of tents. It is also applied to the nails or spikes which are driven into walls, and on which are suspended the garments or the utensils of a family. In ancient times, every house was furnished with a large number of these pegs, or nails. They were not *driven* into the walls after the house was made, but they were *worked in* while the walls were going up. The houses were usually made of stone ; and strong iron hooks,

24 And they shall hang upon him all the glory of his father's house, the offspring and the issue, all ves- | sels of small quantity, from the vessels of cups, even to all the vessels ¹ of flagons.

1 or, *instruments of viols.*

or spikes, were worked into the mortar while soft, and they answered the double purpose of nails to hang things on, and of cramp-irons, as they were so bent as to hold the walls together. These spikes are described by Sir John Chardin (Harmer's *Observations,* vol. i. p. 191) as 'large nails with square heads like dice, well made, the ends being so bent as to make them cramp-irons. They commonly,' says he, ' place them at the windows and doors, in order to hang upon them, when they like, veils and curtains.' It was also the custom to suspend in houses, and especially temples, suits of armour, shields, helmets, swords, &c., that had been taken in war as spoils of victory, or which had been used by illustrious ancestors, and these spikes were used for that purpose also. The word is here applied to a leader, or officer ; and it means that he would be fixed and permanent in his plans and office ; and that as a pin in the wall sustained the ornaments of the house *safely,* so all the glory of the house of David, all that was dear and valuable to the nation, might be reposed on him (ver. 24). ¶ *And he shall be for a glorious throne to his father's house.* A glorious seat ; that is, all his family and kindred would be sustained, and honoured by him ; or their honour and reputation might rest securely on him, and his deeds would diffuse a lustre and a glory over them all. Every virtuous, patriotic, benevolent, and pious son diffuses a lustre on all his kindred ; and this is one of the incitements to virtuous and elevated deeds which God has presented in the government of the world.

24. *And they shall hang upon him.* This figure is a continuation of that commenced in the previous verse ; and is derived from the custom of *hanging* clothes or ornaments on the spikes that were fixed in the walls ; and, perhaps, more particularly from the custom of suspending shields, swords, suits of armour, &c., taken in battle, around the walls of a temple. A great portion of the wealth of the ancients consisted

in gold and silver vessels, and in changes of raiment. These would be hung around a house in no inconsiderable degree for ostentation and parade. ' Solomon's drinking vessels were of gold ; and all the vessels of the forest of Lebanon were of pure gold ; none were of silver ' (1 Kings x. 21). ' The vessels in the house of the forest of Lebanon were two hundred targets and three hundred shields of beaten gold' (1 Kings x. 16, 17). That these were hung on spikes or pins around the house is apparent from Cant. iv. 4 : ' Thy neck is like the tower of David, builded for an armoury, whereon there hang a thousand bucklers, all shields of mighty men.' Eliakim is considered as a principal support like this, whereon would be suspended all the glory of his father's family, and all the honour of his house ; that is, he would be the principal support of the whole civil and ecclesiastical polity. ¶ *The offspring and the issue.* All that proceeded from the family ; all that were connected with it. Kimchi and Aben Ezra render it, ' Sons and daughters.' The LXX. ' From the least to the greatest.' The Chaldee, ' Sons and grandsons, youth and children.' The idea is, that all the prosperity, near and remote, would depend on him ; and that his character would sustain and give dignity to them all. The word which is rendered ' issue ' (הַצְּפִעוֹת), according to Vitringa and Rosenmüller, denotes those that were of humble condition ; and the passage means that honour would be conferred even on these by the virtues of Eliakim. ¶ *From the vessels of cups.* Literally, goblets, or bowls (אֲגָנוֹת). The idea probably is, simply that of vessels of *small capacity,* whatever was the material of which they were composed ; and hence the reference here is to those of the family of Eliakim who were of humble rank, or who were poor. ¶ *To all the vessels of flagons.* Marg. ' Instruments of viols.' Heb. נְבָלִים. This word is often applied to instruments of music, the *nebel,*

25 In that day, saith the LORD
of hosts, shall the nail that is fastened in the sure place be removed,
and be cut down, and fall ; and the
burden that *was* upon it shall be
cut off : for the LORD hath spoken
it.

CHAPTER XXIII.

ANALYSIS.

THIS prophecy respects Tyre, and extends only
to the end of this chapter. It is made up of a
succession of *apostrophes* directed either to Tyre
itself, or to the nations with which it was accustomed to trade. The first part of the prophecy (1–13) is occupied with the account of the
judicial sentence which God had passed upon
Tyre. This is not done in a direct and formal
manner, but by addresses to the various people
with whom the Tyrians had commercial intercourse, and who would be particularly affected
by its destruction. Thus (1) the prophet calls
on the ships of Tarshish to 'howl' because their
advantageous commerce with Tyre must cease.
This intelligence respecting the calamities that
had come upon Tyre, he says would be brought
to them 'from the land of Chittim' (1), that is,
from the islands and coasts of the Mediterra-

nean. In ver. 2, the calamity is described as
coming directly on the island on which Tyre was
built. In the subsequent verses, the prophet
describes the sources of the wealth of Tyre (3),
and declares that her great luxury and splendour would be destroyed (5–12). In ver. 13, the
prophet says that this would be done by the
'Chaldeans;' and this verse serves to fix the
time of the fulfilment to the siege of Tyre by
Nebuchadnezzar. In this all commentators probably (except Grotius, who supposes that it refers to Alexander the Great) are agreed. Indeed,
it seems to be past all doubt, that the events
here referred to pertain to the siege of Tyre by
Nebuchadnezzar. In the remainder of the prophecy (ver. 14 to the end of the chapter), the
prophet declares the *time* during which this
calamity would continue. He declares that it
would be only for seventy years (14), and that
after that, Tyre would be restored to her former
splendour, magnificence, and successful commerce (16, 17); and that then her wealth would
be consecrated to the service of Jehovah (18).

The *design* of the prophecy is, therefore, to
foretell the calamities that would come upon a
rich, proud, and luxurious city; and thus to
show that God was Governor and Ruler over
the nations of the earth. Tyre became distinguished for pride, luxury, and consequent

---

viol (see it described in Notes on ch. v.
12 ; xiv. 11); but it properly denotes a
bottle made of skin for holding wine,
and which, being made of the whole skin
of a goat or sheep, indicated the vessels
of large dimensions. Here it refers to
the members of the family of Eliakim
who were more wealthy and influential
than those denoted by the small vessels.
The glory of the whole family would
depend on him. His virtues, wisdom, integrity, and valour in defending and saving the Hebrew commonwealth, would
diffuse honour over the whole family connection, and render the name illustrious.

25. *In that day shall the nail.* Not
Eliakim, but Shebna. Eliakim was to
be fastened, *i.e.*, confirmed in office.
But Shebna was to be removed. ¶ *That
is fastened in the sure place.* Or, that
was once fastened, or was supposed to
be fastened—a phrase appropriate to an
office which the incumbent supposed to
be firm or secure. It here refers to
Shebna. He was regarded as having a
permanent hold on the office, and was
making provisions for ending his days
in it. ¶ *Be removed.* To a distant

land (ver. 17, 18), or simply taken
down. ¶ *And be cut down, and fall.*
As a spike, pin, or peg would be taken
away from the wall of a house. ¶ *And
the burden that* was *upon it.* All that
it sustained—as the spikes in the wall
of a house sustained the cups of gold,
the raiment, or the armour that belonged
to the family. Here it means, all that
was dependent on Shebna—the honour
of his family, his emoluments, his hope
of future fame, or of an honoured burial.
All these would fail, as a matter of
course, when he was removed from his
office. This is one instance of the usual
mode of the Divine administration. The
errors of a man intrusted with office
entail poverty, disgrace, and misery on
all who are connected with him. Not
only is his own name disgraced, but his
sin *diffuses itself*, as it were, on all connected with him. It involves them in
want, and shame, and tears ; and the
design is to deter those in office from sin,
by the fact that their crimes and errors
will thus involve the innocent in calamity, and shed disgrace and woe on
those whom they love.

dissipation; and the destruction that was to come upon it was to be a demonstration that wicked nations and cities would incur the displeasure of God, and would be destroyed.

Tyre, the subject of the prophecies, particularly of Isaiah and Ezekiel, who both predicted its overthrow (Isa. xxiii.; Ezek. xxvi.–xxix.), was a celebrated city of Phenicia, and is usually mentioned in connection with Sidon (Matt. xi. 21, 22; xv. 21; Mark iii. 8; vii. 24, 31; Luke x. 13, 14). It was on the coast of the Mediterranean, about lat. 33° 20′ N., and was about twenty miles south of Sidon. It was one of the cities allotted to the tribe of Asher (Josh. xix. 29), but it is probable that the ancient inhabitants were never driven out by the Israelites. It seems to have been occupied by the Canaanites, and is always mentioned as inhabited by a distinct people from the Jews (2 Sam. xxiv. 7; 1 Kings vii. 13, 14; ix. 12; Ezra iii. 7; Neh. xiii. 16; Ps. lxxxiii. 7; lxxxvii. 4). It was probably built by a colony from Sidon, since Isaiah (xxiii. 12) calls it the 'daughter of Zidon,' and it is said (ver. 2) to have been replenished by Sidon. That Sidon was the most ancient city there can be no doubt. *Sidon* was the eldest son of Cannan (Gen. x. 15), and the city of Sidon is mentioned by the patriarch Jacob (Gen. xlix. 13), and in the time of Joshua it is called 'Great Sidon' (Josh. xi. 8). Strabo affirms that *after Sidon*, Tyre was the most celebrated city of the Phenicians. Justin (xviii. 1, 5), expressly declares that the Sidonians, being besieged by the king of Ascalon, went in ships and built Tyre. But though Tyre was the 'daughter' of Sidon, yet it soon rivalled it in importance, and in commercial enterprise.

Among the ancient writers, Tyre is mentioned as Palæo-Tyrus (Παλαίτυρος), or ancient Tyre, and as Insular Tyre. The former was built on the *coast*, and was doubtless built first, though there is evidence that the latter was early used as a place for anchorage, or a harbour. In Old Tyre, or Tyre on the coast, undoubtedly also the most magnificent edifices would be built, and the principal business would there be at first transacted. Probably Insular Tyre was built either because it furnished a better harbour, or because, being inaccessible to an invading army, it was more secure. Insular Tyre, as the name imports, was built on an island, or a *rock*, about three quarters of a mile from the coast, or from Old Tyre. Probably the passage from one to the other was formerly by a ferry, or in boats only, until Alexander the Great, in his siege of the city, built a mole from the ruins of the old city to the new. This mole, or embankment, was not less than 200 feet in breadth, and con-

stituted a permanent connection between Tyre and the mainland. Insular Tyre was remarkably safe from the danger of invasion. It commanded the sea, and of course had nothing to dread from that quarter; and the only mode in which it could become accessible to Alexander, was to build this gigantic causeway from the mainland.

Tyre was distinguished for its enterprise, its commercial importance, its luxury, and its magnificence. Few, perhaps none, of the cities of antiquity, were more favourably situated for commerce. It was the natural seaport of Palestine and Syria, and it was favourably situated for commerce with all the cities and states bordering on the Mediterranean, and, indeed, with all the known world. The luxuries of the East passed through Tyre (see Ezek. xxvii., where there is an extended description of the various nations that trafficked with and enriched it), and the productions of distant climes from the West were introduced to the East through this seaport. It rose, therefore, to great opulence, and to consequent luxury and sin.

It was also a place of great strength. Old Tyre was defended by a wall, which was regarded as impregnable, and which is said to have resisted the attacks of Nebuchadnezzar for thirteen years. New, or Insular Tyre, was inaccessible, until Alexander constructed the immense mole by which he connected it with the mainland, and as they had the command of the sea, the city was regarded unapproachable. Alexander could not have taken it had he not possessed resources, and patience, and power, which perhaps no other ancient conqueror possessed; and had he not engaged in an enterprise which perhaps all others would have regarded as impracticable and hopeless. Josephus, indeed, states, that Shalmaneser, king of Assyria, made war against the Tyrians, with a fleet of sixty ships, manned by 800 rowers. The Tyrians had but twelve ships, yet they obtained the victory, and dispersed the Assyrian fleet, taking 500 prisoners. Shalmaneser then besieged the city for five years, but was unable to take it. This was in the time of Hezekiah, A.M. 3287, or about 717 B.C.

Nebuchadnezzar took the city after a siege of thirteen years, during the time of the Jewish captivity, about 573 years before Christ. This was in accordance with the prophecy in this chapter (see Note, ver. 13), and according to the predictions also of Ezekiel. The desolation was entire. The city was destroyed, and the inhabitants driven into foreign lands (see Notes, ver. 7, 12). The city lay desolate for seventy years (see Note on ver. 15, 17), and Old Tyre was in ruins in the time of the invasion of Alexander the Great. A new city had risen, however, on the island, called New Tyre, and this city was taken by Alexander, after a siege of eight months. Near the shore the water is said to have been shallow, but near the new city it was three fathoms, or nineteen feet in depth. The city of Tyre was taken by Alexander 332 B.C., and 241 years after its destruction by Nebuchadnezzar, and consequently about 170 years after it had been rebuilt. It was not, however, entirely destroyed by Alexander, and became an object of contention to his successors. It was successively invested by Antigonas and Ptolemy, and fell into the hands of the latter. In the apostolic age it seems to have regained somewhat of its ancient splendour. There were some Christians here (Acts xxi. 3, 4). At present it belongs to Syria. It was often an object of contention during the crusades, and was distinguished as the first archbishopric under the patriarchate of Jerusalem. It gradually sunk into decay, lost its importance, and became a place of utter ruin. Volney noticed there, in 1784, the choir of the ancient church, the remains of the walls of the city which can still be traced, and some columns of red granite, a species unknown in Syria. In the time when it was visited by Volney and Maundrell, it was a miserable village, where the inhabitants subsisted chiefly by fishing. Its exports consist only of a few sacks of corn and cotton; and the only merchant of which it could boast in the time when Volney was there, was a solitary Greek, who could hardly gain a livelihood. At present, Tyre, or, as it is called, Sur, is nothing more than a mar-

ket town, a small seaport, hardly deserving the name of a city. Its chief export is the tobacco raised on the neighbouring hills; with some cotton, and also charcoal and wood from the more distant mountains. The houses are for the most part mere hovels, very few being more than one story high, with flat roofs. The streets are narrow lanes, crooked, and filthy. Yet the many scattered palm trees throw over the place an oriental charm; and the numerous Pride of India trees interspersed among the houses and gardens, with their beautiful foliage, give it a pleasing aspect. It has a population of less than three thousand souls. In 1837, an earthquake was felt here to a very considerable extent. A large part of the eastern wall was thrown down, and the southern wall was greatly shattered, and several houses were destroyed (see Robinson's *Bib. Researches*, vol. iii. p. 400; Robinson's Calmet; *Edin. Ency.*; Newton, *On the Prophecies*, vol. xi.; Keith, *On the Prophecies*; and the *Travels* of Volney and Maundrell. On the ancient commercial importance of Tyre, also, and its present situation, and the *cause* of its decline, the reader may consult an article in the *Am. Bib. Rep.* for October 1840).

THE burden of Tyre. *a* Howl, ye ships of Tarshish; for it is laid waste so that there is no house, no entering in : from the land of Chittim *b* it is revealed to them.

a Jer.25.22;47.4; Eze.26.28; Amos 9.10; Zec.9.2-4.
b ver.12; Jer.2.10.

CHAPTER XXIII.

1. *The burden of Tyre* (see Note on ch. xiii. 1). ¶ *Howl.* This is a highly poetic description of the destruction that was coming on Tyre. The ships of Tarshish traded there ; and the prophet now addresses the ships, and calls upon them to lament because the commerce by which they had been enriched was to be destroyed, and they were to be thrown out of employ. ¶ *Ye ships of Tarshish* (see Note on ch. ii. 16). The 'Tarshish' here referred to, was doubtless a city or country in Spain (Ταρτησσὸς, *Tartessus*), and was the most celebrated emporium to which the Phenicians traded. It is mentioned by Diod. Sic., v. 35-38; Strabo, iii. 148; Pliny, *Nat. Hist.* iii. 3. According to Jer. x. 9, it exported silver; according to Ezek. xxvii. 12, 25, it exported silver, iron,

tin, and lead, to the Tyrian market. In this chapter (ver. 1, 6, 10), it is represented as an important Phenician or Tyrian colony. All the circumstances agree with the supposition that *Tartessus* in Spain is the place *here* referred to. The name 'Tartessus' (Ταρτησσὸς) is derived from the Hebrew תַּרְשִׁישׁ by a change simply in the pronunciation (see Bochart, *Geo. Sacra*, iii. 7, and J. D. Michaelis, *Spicileg. Geo. Heb.* i. 82-103). ¶ *For it is laid waste.* Tyre is laid waste ; that is, in vision it was made to pass before the mind of the prophet *as* laid waste, or as it *would* be (see Notes on ch. i. 1). ¶ *So that there is no house.* It would be completely destroyed. This was the case with old Tyre after the conquest by Nebuchadnezzar, and it remained so. See the analysis of the chapter. ¶ *No entering in.* No harbour; no port; where the ships could remain, and with which they could continue to trade. Tyre was once better situated for commerce, and had greater natural advantages, than any port in the Mediterranean. Those advantages have, however, to a great extent passed away, and natural causes combine to confirm the truth of the Divine predictions that it should cease to be a place of commerce. The merchandise of India, which was once conveyed overland through Babylon and Palmyra, and which found its natural outlet at Tyre, is now carried around the Cape of Good Hope, and will never again be restored to its old channel. Besides, Tyre itself, which once had so fine a harbour, has ceased to be a safe haven for large vessels. Robinson (George) says of its harbour, in 1830, ' It is a small circular basin, now quite filled up with sand and broken columns, leaving scarcely space enough for small boats to enter. The few fishing boats that belong to the place are sheltered by some rocks to the westward of the island '—(*Travels in Syria and Palestine*, vol. i. p. 269). Shaw, who visited Tyre in 1738, says of the harbour, ' I visited several creeks and inlets, in order to discover what provision there might have been formerly made for the security of their vessels. Yet, notwithstanding that Tyre was the chief maritime power of this country, I could not discover the least token of either *cothon* or harbour that could have been of extraordinary capacity. The coasting ships, indeed, still find a tolerably good shelter from the northern winds, under the southern shore, but are obliged immediately to return when the winds change to the west or south; so that there must have been some better station than this for their security and reception. In the N.N.E. part, likewise, of the city, we see the traces of a safe and commodious basin, lying within the walls; but which, at the same time, is very small, scarce forty yards in diameter. Yet even this port, small as it is at present, is, notwithstanding, so choked up with sand and rubbish, that the boats of those poor fishermen who now and then visit this renowned emporium, can, with great difficulty, only be admitted' (*Travels*, pp. 330, 331. Ed. fol. Oxon. 1738). Dr. Robinson says of the port of Tyre, ' The inner port or basin on the north was formerly enclosed by a wall, running from the north end of the island in a curve towards the main land. Various pieces and fragments of this wall yet remain, sufficient to mark its course; but the port itself is continually filling up more and more with sand, and now-a-days boats only can enter it. Indeed, our host informed us, that even within his own recollection, the water covered the open place before his own house, which at present is ten or twelve rods from the sea, and is surrounded with buildings; while older men remember, that vessels formerly anchored where the shore now is' (*Bib. Researches*, vol. iii. p. 397). ¶ *From the land of Chittim.* This means, probably, from the islands and coasts of the Mediterranean. In regard to the meaning of the word *Chittim*, the following is the note of Gesenius on this verse : ' Among the three different opinions of ancient and modern interpreters, according to which they sought for the land of Chittim in Italy, Macedonia, and Cyprus, I decidely prefer the latter, which is also the opinion of Josephus (*Ant.* i. 6. 1). According to this, Chittim is the island Cyprus, so called from the Phenician colony Κίτιον (Citium), in the southern part of the island, but still in such a sense, that this name Chittim was, at a later period, employed also in a wider sense, to designate other islands and countries adjacent to the coasts of the Mediterranean, as, *e.g.*, Macedonia (Dan. xi. 30; 1 Mac. i. 1; viii. 5). This is also mentioned by Josephus. That Κίτιον (Citium) was sometimes used for the whole island of Cyprus, and also in a wider sense for other islands, is expressly asserted by Epiphanius, who himself lived in Cyprus, as a well-known fact (*Adv. Hæres.* xxx. 25); where he says, " it is manifest to all that the island of Cyprus is called Κίτιον (Citium), for the Cyprians and *Rhodians* ('Ρόδιοι) are called *Kitians* (Κίτιοι)." It could also be used of the Macedonians, because they were descended from the Cyprians and Rho-

2 Be [1] still, ye inhabitants of the isle ; thou whom tho merchants of

1 *silent.*

Zidon, that pass over the sea, have replenished

3 And by great waters the seed

dians. That most of the cities of Cyprus were Phenician colonies, is expressly affirmed by Diodorus (ii. 114; comp. Herod. vii. 90), and the proximity of the island to Phenicia, together with its abundant supply of productions, especially such as were essential in shipbuilding, would lead us to expect nothing else. One of the few passages of the Bible which give a more definite hint in regard to Chittim is Ezek. xxvii. 6, which agrees very well with Cyprus: " Of the oaks of Bashan do they make them oars ; thy ships' benches do they make of ivory, encased with cedar from the isles of Chittim." The sense of this passage is, that the fleets coming from Tarshish (Tartessus) to Tyre, would, on their way, learn from the inhabitants of Cyprus the news of the downfall of Tyre.' ¶ *It is revealed to them.* If we understand *Chittim* to denote the islands and coasts of the Mediterranean, it means that the navigators in the ships of Tarshish would learn the intelligence of the destruction of Tyre from those coasts or islands where they might stop on their way. Tyre was of so much commercial importance that the news of its fall would spread into all the islands of the Mediterranean.

2. *Be still.* This is the description of a city which is destroyed, where the din of commerce, and the sound of revelry is no longer heard. It is an address of the prophet to Tyre, indicating that it would be soon still, and destroyed. ¶ *Ye inhabitants of the isle* (of Tyre). The word ' isle ' (אִי) is sometimes used to denote a *coast* or *maritime region* (see Note on ch. xx. 6), but there seems no reason to doubt that here it means the island on which New Tyre was erected. This may have been occupied even before Old Tyre was destroyed by Nebuchadnezzar, though the main city was on the coast. ¶ *Thou whom the merchants of Zidon.* Tyre was a colony from Sidon ; and the merchants of Sidon would trade to Tyre as well as to Sidon. ¶ *Have replen-*

ished. Heb. ' Have filled,' *i.e.*, with merchandise, and with wealth. Thus, in Ezek. xxvii. 8, Tyre is represented as having derived its seamen from Sidon : ' The inhabitants of Sidon and of Arvad were thy mariners.' And in Ezek. xxvii. 9–23, Tyre is represented as having been filled with shipbuilders, merchants, mariners, soldiers, &c., from Gebal, Persia, Lud, Phut, Tarshish, Javan, Tubal, Mesheck, Dedan, Syria, Damascus, Arabia, &c.

3. *And by great waters.* That is, by the abundant waters, or the overflowing of the Nile. Tyre was the mart to which the superabundant productions of Egypt were borne (see Ezek. xxvii.) ¶ *The seed of Sihor.* There can be no doubt that by 'Sihor' here is meant the river Nile in Egypt (see Josh. xiii. 3 ; 1 Chron. xiii. 5 ; Jer. ii. 18). The word שִׁחֹר (*Shǐhhōr*) is derived from שָׁחַר (*Shâhhǎr*), *to be black* (Job xxx. 30), and is given to the Nile from its colour when it brings down the slime or mud by which Egypt is rendered so fertile. The Greeks gave to the river the name Μίλας (*black*), and the Latins call it *Melo*—(Serv. ad Virg. *Geor.* iv. 291). It was called *Siris* by the Ethiopians ; perhaps the same as Sihor. The upper branches of the Nile in Abyssinia all receive their names from the *colour* of the water, and are called the White River, the Blue River, &c. ¶ *The harvest of the river.* The productions caused by the overflowing of the river. Egypt was celebrated for producing grain, and Rome and Greece derived no small part of their supplies from that fertile country. It is also evident that the inhabitants of Palestine were early accustomed to go to Egypt in time of scarcity for supplies of grain (see Gen. xxxvii. 25, 28, and the history of Joseph, Gen. xli.–xliii.) That the *Tyrians* traded with Egypt is also well known. Herodotus (ii. 112) mentions one entire quarter of the city of Memphis that was inhabited by the Tyrians. ¶ Is *her revenue.* Her re-

of Sihor, the harvest of the river, *is* her revenue ; and she is a mart of nations.

4 Be thou ashamed, O Zidon ; for the sea hath spoken, *even* the strength of the sea, saying, I travail not, nor bring forth chil-

dren, neither do I nourish up young men, *nor* bring up virgins.

5 As at the report ^aconcerning Egypt, *so* shall they be sorely pained at the report of Tyre.

6 Pass ye over to Tarshish ; howl, ye inhabitants of the isle.

a ch.19.16.

---

sources are brought from thence. ¶ *She is a mart of nations.* How true this was, see Ezek. xxvii. No place was more favourably situated for commerce ; and she had engrossed the trade nearly of all the world.

4. *Be thou ashamed, O Zidon.* Tyre was a colony of Sidon. Sidon is here addressed as the *mother* of Tyre, and is called on to lament over her daughter that was destroyed. In ver. 12, Tyre is called the ' daughter of Sidon ;' and such appellations were commonly given to cities (see Note on ch. i. 8). Sidon is here represented as *ashamed*, or grieved—as a mother is who is bereft of all her children. ¶ *The sea hath spoken.* New Tyre was on a rock at some distance from the land, and seemed to *rise out* of the sea, somewhat as Venice does. It is described here as a production of the sea, and the sea is represented as speaking by her. ¶ *Even the strength of the sea.* The fortress, or strong place (מָעֹז) of the sea. Tyre, on a rock, might be regarded as the strong place, or the defence of the Mediterranean. Thus Zechariah (ix. 3) says of it, ' And Tyrus did build herself a stronghold ' (מָצוֹר). ¶ *Saying, I travail not.* The expressions which follow are to be regarded as the language of Tyre—the founder of colonies and cities. The sense is, ' My wealth and resources are gone. My commerce is annihilated. I cease to plant cities and colonies, and to nourish and foster them, as I once did, by my trade.' The idea of the whole verse is, that the city which had been the mistress of the commercial world, and distinguished for founding other cities and colonies, was about to lose her importance, and to cease to extend her colonies and her influence over other countries. Over this fact, Sidon, the mother and founder of Tyre herself,

would be humbled and grieved that her daughter, so proud, so rich, and so magnificent, was brought so low.

5. *As at the report concerning Egypt.* According to our translation, this verse would seem to mean that the Sidonians and other nations had been pained or grieved at the report of the calamities that had come upon Egypt, and that they would be similarly affected at the report concerning Tyre. In accordance with this, some (as Jarchi) have understood it of the plagues of Egypt, and suppose that the prophet means to say, that as the nations were astonished at that, *so* they would be at the report of the calamities that would come upon Tyre. Others refer it to the calamities that would come upon Egypt referred to in ch. xix., and suppose that the prophet means to say, that as the nations would be amazed at the report of these calamities, so they would be at the report of the overthrow of Tyre. So Vitringa. But the sense of the Hebrew may be expressed thus : ' As the report, or tidings of the destruction of Tyre shall reach Egypt, they shall be pained at the tidings respecting Tyre.' So Lowth, Noyes, Rosenmüller, Grotius, Calvin. They would be grieved, either (1) because the destruction of Tyre would injure the commerce of Egypt ; or (2) because the Egyptians might fear that the army of Nebuchadnezzar would come upon them, and that they would share the fate of Tyre. ¶ *Sorely pained.* The word here used (יָחִילוּ) is commonly applied to the severe pain of parturition.

6. *Pass ye over.* That is, ye inhabitants of Tyre. This is an address to Tyre, in view of her approaching destruction ; and is designed to signify that when the city was destroyed, its inhabitants *would* flee to its colonies, and seek refuge and safety there. As

7 *Is* this your joyous *city*, whose antiquity *is* of ancient days? her own feet shall carry her [1] afar off to sojourn.

1 *from afar off.*

8 Who hath taken this counsel against Tyre, the crowning *city*, whose merchants *are* princes, whose traffickers *are* the honourable of the earth?

Tarshish was one of its principal colonies, and as the ships employed by Tyre would naturally sail to Tarshish, the inhabitants are represented as fleeing there on the attack of Nebuchadnezzar. That the inhabitants of Tyre did flee in this manner, is expressly asserted by Jerome upon the authority of Assyrian histories which are now lost. 'We have read,' says he, 'in the histories of the Assyrians, that when the Tyrians were besieged, after they saw no hope of escaping, they went on board their ships, and fled to Carthage, or to some islands of the Ionian and Ægean Sea' (Jerome *in loco.*) And again (on Ezek. xxix.) he says, 'When the Tyrians saw that the works for carrying on the siege were perfected, and the foundations of the walls were shaken by the battering rams, whatever precious things in gold, silver, clothes, and various kinds of furniture the nobility had, they put them on board their ships, and carried to the islands. So that the city being taken, Nebuchadnezzar found nothing worthy of his labour.' Diodorus (xvii. 41) relates the same thing of the Tyrians during the siege of Alexander the Great, where he says that they took their wives and children to Carthage. ¶ *Howl*. Deep grief among the Orientals was usually expressed by a loud, long, and most dismal howl or shriek (see Note on ch. xv. 2). ¶ *Ye inhabitants of the isle.* Of Tyre. The word 'isle,' however, *may* be taken as in ch. xx. 6 (see Note on that place), in the sense of *coast*, or *maritime country* in general, and possibly may be intended to denote Old Tyre, or the coast of Phenicia in general, though most naturally it applies to the city built on the island.

7. Is *this your joyous* city. Is this the city that was just now so full of happiness, of revelry, of business, of gaiety, of rejoicing? (see Note on ch. xxii. 2.) ¶ *Whose antiquity* is *of ancient days*. Strabo (xvi. 756) says, 'After Sidon, Tyre, a splendid and

most ancient city, is to be compared in greatness, beauty, and antiquity, with Sidon.' Curtius (*Hist. Alex.* iv. 4) says, 'The city was taken, distinguished both by its antiquity, and its great variety of fortune.' Arrian (ii. 16) says, that 'the Temple of Hercules at Tyre was the most ancient of those which the memory of men have preserved.' And Herodotus (ii. 44) says, that in a conversation which he had with the priest of that Temple, he informed him that it had then existed for 2300 years. Josephus, indeed, says (*Ant.* viii. 3. 1) that Tyre was built but 240 years before the temple was built by Solomon—but this was probably a mistake. Justin (xviii. 3) says that Tyre was founded in the year of the destruction of Troy. Its very high antiquity cannot be doubted. ¶ *Her own feet shall carry her afar off.* Grotius supposes that by *feet* here, the 'feet of ships' are intended, that is, their sails and oars. But the expression is designed evidently to stand in contrast with ver. 6, and to denote that a part of the inhabitants would go by land into captivity. Probably many of them were taken prisoners by Nebuchadnezzar; and perhaps many of them, when the city was besieged, found opportunity to escape and flee by land to a distant place of safety.

8. *Who hath taken this counsel?* To whom is this to be traced? Is this the work of man, or is it the plan of God?—questions which would naturally arise at the contemplation of the ruin of a city so ancient and so magnificent. The object of this question is to trace it all to God; and this perhaps indicates the scope of the prophecy—to show that God reigns, and does all his pleasure over cities and kingdoms. ¶ *The crowning* city. The distributer of crowns; or the city from which dependent towns, provinces, and kingdoms had arisen. Many colonies and cities had been founded by Tyre. Tartessus in Spain, Citium in Cyprus,

9 The LORD of hosts hath purposed it, to [1] stain the pride of all glory, and to bring [a] into contempt all the honourable of the earth.

10 Pass through thy land as a river, O daughter of Tarshish : there is no more [2] strength.

1 pollute.　　*a* 1 Cor. 1.28,29.　　*2 girdle.*

Carthage in Africa, and probably many other places were Phenician colonies, and derived their origin from Tyre, and were still its tributaries and dependants (comp. Ezek. xxvii. 33). ¶ *Whose merchants* are *princes.* Princes trade with thee ; and thus acknowledge their dependence on thee. Or, thy merchants are splendid, gorgeous, and magnificent like princes. The former, however, is probably the meaning. ¶ *Whose traffickers* (כְּנָעֶנֶיהָ, *Canaanites*). As the ancient inhabitants of Canaan were *traffickers* or *merchants*, the word came to denote merchants in general (see Job xli. 6; Ezek. xvii. 4; Hos. xii. 7; Zeph. i. 11). So the word *Chaldean* came to mean *astrologers*, because they were celebrated for astrology.

9. *The* LORD *of hosts hath purposed it* (see Note on ch. i. 9). It is not by human counsel that it has been done. Whoever is the instrument, yet the overthrow of wicked, proud, and vicious cities and nations is to be traced to the God who rules in the empires and kingdoms of the earth (see Notes on ch. x. 5-7). ¶ *To stain the pride of all glory.* Marg. 'Pollute.' The Hebrew word (חָלַל) means properly *to bore,* or *pierce through;* to open, make common (Lev. xix. 29); then to profane, defile, pollute, as, *e.g.,* the sanctuary (Lev. xix. 8; xxi. 9), the Sabbath (Exod. xxxi. 14), the name of God (Lev. xviii. 21; xix. 12). Here it means that the destruction of Tyre would show that God could easily level it all with the dust. The destruction of *Tyre* would show this in reference to *all* human glory, because (1) it was one of the most *ancient* cities ; (2) it was one of the most magnificent ; (3) it was one of the most strong, secure, and inaccessible ; (4) it was the one of most commercial importance, most distinguished in the view of nations ; and (5) its *example* would be the most striking and impressive. God often selects the most distinguished and important cities and men to make them examples to others, and to show

the ease with which he can bring all down to the earth. ¶ *To bring into contempt, &c.* To bring their plans and purposes into contempt, and to show how unimportant and how foolish are their schemes in the sight of a holy God.

10. *Pass through thy land as a river.* This verse has been very variously understood. Vitringa supposes that it means that all that held the city together —its fortifications, walls, &c., would be laid waste, and that as a river flows on without obstruction, so the inhabitants would be scattered far and near. Everything, says he, would be levelled, and the field would not be distinguishable from the city. Grotius thus renders it : ' Pass to some one of thy colonies ; as a river flows from the fountain to the sea, so do you go to the ocean.' Lowth understands it also as relating to the time of the destruction of Tyre, and to the escape which the inhabitants would then make.

'Overflow thy land like a river,
O daughter of Tarshish ; the mound [that kept
in thy waters] is no more.'

The LXX. render it, ' Cultivate (Ἐργάζον) thy land, for the ships shall no more come from Carthage' (Καρχηδόνος). Probably the true meaning is that which refers it to the time of the siege, and to the fact that the inhabitants would seek other places when their defence was destroyed. That is, ' Pass through thy *territories,* thy dependent cities, states, colonies, and seek a refuge there ; or wander there like a flowing stream.' ¶ *As a river.* Perhaps the allusion is to the Nile, as the word יְאֹר is usually given to the Nile ; or it may be to *any* river that flows on with a mighty current when all obstructions are removed. The idea is, that as waters *flow on* when the barriers are removed, so the inhabitants of Tyre would *pour forth* from their city. The idea is not so much that of *rapidity,* as it is they should go like a stream that has no dikes, barriers, or obstacles now to confine its flowing waters. ¶ *O daughter of Tarshish.* Tyre ; so called either be-

11 He stretched out his hand over the sea ; he shook the kingdom : the Lord hath given a command- ment ¹ against ² the merchant *city*, to destroy the ³ strong holds thereof.

1 or, *concerning a merchantman.*   2 *Canaan.*

12 And he said, Thou shalt *ᵃ* no more rejoice, O thou oppressed virgin, daughter of Zidon ; arise, pass over to *ᵇ* Chittim ; there also shalt thou have no rest.

3 *strengths.*   a Rev.18.22   b ver.1.

cause it was in some degree *sustained* and supplied by the commerce of Tar- shish ; or because its inhabitants would become the inhabitants of Tarshish, and it is so called by anticipation. The Vul- gate renders this, *Filia maris*—'Daugh- ter of the sea.' Junius supposes that the prophet addresses those who were then in the city who were natives of Tarshish, and exhorts them to flee for safety to their own city. ¶ There is *no more strength.* Marg. 'Girdle.' The word מֵזַח means properly a *girdle* (Job xii. 31). It is applied to that which *binds* or secures the body ; and *may* be applied here perhaps to that which *secured* or *bound* the city of Tyre ; that is, its forti- fications, its walls, its defences. They would all be levelled ; and nothing would *secure* the inhabitants, as they would flow forth as waters that are pent up do, when every barrier is removed.

11. *He stretched out his hand.* That is, Jehovah (see ver. 9). To stretch out the hand is indicative of punishment (see Notes on ch. v. 25, and ix. 12), and means that God has resolved to inflict exemplary punishment on Tyre and its dependent colonies. ¶ *Over the sea.* That is, over the *sea coast* of Phenicia ; or over the cities that were built on the coast. This alludes to the fact that Nebuchadnezzar would lay siege to these cities, and would ravage the maritime coast of Phenicia. It is not improbable also that, having taken Tyre, he would extend his conquests to *Citium*, on the island of Cyprus, and destroy as many of the dependent cities of Tyre as pos- sible. ¶ *The* Lord *hath given a com- mandment.* The control here asserted over Nebuchadnezzar is similar to that which he asserted over the Assyrian Sennacherib (see Note on ch. x. 5). ¶ *Against the merchant* city. Heb. 'Against Canaan' (אֶל־כְּנַעַן). The word ' Canaan ' *may* here be used as in ver. 8, to denote a place given to merchandise or traffic, since this was the principal

employment of the inhabitants of this region ; but it is rather to be taken in its obvious and usual sense in the Scrip- tures, as denoting the land of Canaan, and as denoting that Nebuchadnezzar would be sent against that, and espe- cially the maritime parts of it, to lay it waste. ¶ *To destroy the strongholds thereof.* That is, the strongholds of Canaan ; as Tyre, Sidon, Accho, &c. Tyre, especially, was strongly fortified, and was able long to resist the arms of the Chaldeans.

12. *And he said.* God said (ver. 9). ¶ *Thou shalt no more rejoice.* The sense is, that Tyre was soon to be de- stroyed. It does not mean that it should *never* afterwards exult or rejoice, for the prophet says (ver. 17), that *after* its destruction it would be restored, and again be filled with exultation and joy. ¶ *O thou oppressed virgin.* Lowth renders this, 'O thou deflowered virgin,' expressing the sense of the word הַמְעֻשָּׁקָה. ¶ *O daughter of Zidon* (ver. 4). ¶ *Pass over to Chittim* (see Note on ver. 1). The idea is, that under the siege the inhabitants of Tyre would seek refuge in her colonies, and the cities that were dependent on her. ¶ *There also shalt thou have no rest.* It is not improbable that Nebuchadnezzar would carry his arms to Cyprus—on which the city of Citium was—where the Tyrians would take refuge first. Megasthenes, who lived about 300 years before Christ, says of Nebuchadnezzar that he subdued a great part of Africa and Spain, and that he carried his arms so far as the Pillars of Hercules (see Newton, *On the Prophecies*, xi. 11). But whether this refers to the oppressions which Nebu- chadnezzar would bring on them or not, it is certain that the colonies that sprung from Phenicia were exposed to constant wars after this. Carthage was a colony of Tyre, and it is well known that this city was engaged in hostility with the Romans until it was utterly destroyed.

13 Behold, the land of the Chaldeans : this people was not *till* the

Assyrian founded it for them *a* that

a Ps.72.9.

Indeed all the dependent colonies of ancient Tyre became interested and involved in the agitations and commotions which were connected with the conquests of the Roman empire.

13. *Behold the land of the Chaldeans.* This is a very important verse, as it expresses the source whence these calamities were coming upon Tyre ; and as it states some historical facts of great interest respecting the rise of Babylon. In the previous verses the prophet had foretold the certain destruction of Tyre, and had said that whoever was the agent, it was to be traced to the overruling providence of God. He here states distinctly that the agent in accomplishing all this would be the Chaldeans—a statement which fixes the time to the siege of Nebuchadnezzar, and proves that it does not refer to the conquest by Alexander the Great. A part of this verse should be read as a parenthesis, and its general sense has been well expressed by Lowth, who has followed Vitringa :—

'Behold the land of the Chaldeans;
This people was of no account ;—
(The Assyrian founded it for the inhabitants of the desert ;
They raised the watch towers, they set up the palaces thereof ;)
This people hath reduced her to a ruin.'

¶ *Behold.* Indicating that what he was about to say was something unusual, remarkable, and not to be expected in the ordinary course of events. That which was so remarkable was the fact that a people formerly so little known, would rise to such power as to be able to overturn the ancient and mighty city of Tyre. ¶ *The land of the Chaldeans.* Nebuchadnezzar was the king of Chaldea or Babylonia. The names Babylon and Chaldea are often interchanged as denoting the same kingdom and people (see ch. xlviii. 14, 20; Jer. l. 1; li. 24; Ezek. xii. 13). The sense is, ' Lo! the power of Chaldea shall be employed in your overthrow.' ¶ *This people.* The people of Babylonia or Chaldea. ¶ *Was not.* Was not known ; had no government or power ; was a rude, nomadic, barbarous, feeble, and illiterate people. The same phrase occurs in Deut. xxxii.

21, where it also means a people unknown, rude, barbarous, wandering. That this was formerly the character of the Chaldeans is apparent from Job i. 17, where they are described as a nomadic race, having no established place of abode, and living by plunder. ¶ Till *the Assyrian.* Babylon was probably founded by Nimrod (see Notes on ch. xiii.), but it was long before it rose to splendour. Belus or Bel, the Assyrian, is said to have reigned at Babylon A.M. 2682, or 1322 B.C., in the time of Shamgar, judge of Israel. He was succeeded by Ninus and Semiramis, who gave the principal celebrity and splendour to the city and kingdom, and who may be said to have been its founders. They are probably referred to here. ¶ *Founded it.* Semiramis reclaimed it from the waste of waters ; built dikes to confine the Euphrates in the proper channel ; and made it the capital of the kingdom. This is the account given by Herodotus (*Hist.* i.) :—' She (Semiramis) built mounds worthy of admiration, where before the river was accustomed to spread like a sea through the whole plain.' ¶ *For them that dwell in the wilderness.* Heb. לְצִיִּים—' For the tziim.' This word (from צִי or צִיָּה, *a waste* or *desert*) denotes properly the inhabitants of the desert or waste places, and is applied to men in Ps. lxxii. 9; lxxiv. 14; and to animals in Isa. xiii. 21 (Notes); xxxiv. 14. Here it denotes, I suppose, those who had been formerly inhabitants of the deserts around Babylon—the wandering, rude, uncultivated, and predatory people, such as the Chaldeans were (Job i. 17) ; and means that the Assyrian who founded Babylon collected this rude and predatory people, and made use of them in building the city. The same account Arrian gives respecting Philip of Macedon, the father of Alexander the Great, who says, that ' Philip found them wandering and unsettled (πλανήτας καὶ ἀπόρους), feeding small flocks of sheep upon the mountains, that he gave them coats of mail instead of their shepherd's dress, and led them from the mountain to the plain, and gave them cities to dwell in, and established them with good

dwell in the wilderness : they set
up the towers thereof ; *and* he
brought it to ruin.

14 Howl, ye ships of Tarshish :
for your strength is laid waste.

15 And it shall come to pass in
that day that Tyre shall be for-

gotten seventy years, according to
the days of one king : after the end
of seventy years ¹ shall Tyre sing
as an harlot.

16 Take an harp, go about the
city, thou harlot that hast been

<hr>

1 *it shall be unto Tyre as the song of.*

<hr>

and wholesome laws.'—(*Hist. Alex.* vii.)
¶ *They set up the towers thereof.* That
is, the towers in Babylon, not in Tyre
(see Notes on ch. xiii.) Herodotus expressly says that the Assyrians built the
towers and temples of Babylon (i. 84).
¶ And *he brought it to ruin.* That is,
the Babylonian or Chaldean brought
Tyre to ruin : to wit, Nebuchadnezzar,
the king of a people formerly unknown
and rude, would be employed to destroy
the ancient and magnificent city of Tyre.

14. *Howl,* &c. (ver. 1). ¶ *For your
strength.* That which has been your
support and strength ; to wit, Tyre
(comp. Ezek. xxvi. 15–18).

15. *Tyre shall be forgotten.* Shall
cease to be a place of importance in commerce ; shall be unheard of in those
distant places to which ships formerly
sailed. ¶ *Seventy years, according to
the days of one king.* ' That is, of one
kingdom (see Dan. vii. 17 ; viii. 20).'
—(Lowth.) The word ' king ' may denote dynasty, or kingdom. The duration of the Babylonian monarchy was
properly but seventy years. Nebuchadnezzar began his conquest in the first
year of his reign, and from thence to the
taking of Babylon by Cyrus was seventy
years. And at that time the nations
that had been conquered and subdued
by the Babylonians would be restored to
liberty. Tyre was, indeed, taken towards the middle of that period, and its
subjugation referred to here was only
for the remaining part of it. ' All these
nations,' says Jeremiah (xxv. 11), ' shall
serve the king of Babylon seventy years.'
Some of them were conquered sooner,
and some later ; but the end of this
period was the common time of deliverance to them all. So Lowth, Newton,
Vitringa, Aben Ezra, Rosenmüller, and
others, understand this. That ' the
days of one king ' may denote here kingdom or dynasty, and be applied to the
duration of the kingdom of Babylon, is

apparent from two considerations, viz.
(1.) The word ' king ' must be so understood in several places in the Scriptures ;
Dan. vii. 17 : ' These great beasts which
are four, are four great *kings* which
shall arise out of the earth,' that is,
dynasties, or *succession* of kings (Dan.
viii. 20 ; so Rev. xvii. 12). (2.) The
expression is peculiarly applicable to
the Babylonian monarchy, because, during the entire seventy years which that
kingdom lasted, it was under the dominion of one family or dynasty. Nebuchadnezzar founded the Babylonian empire, or raised it to so great splendour,
that he was regarded as its founder, and
was succeeded in the kingdom by his
son Evil-Merodach, and his grandson
Belshazzar, in whose reign the kingdom
terminated ; comp. Jer. xxvii. 7 : ' And
all nations shall serve him, and his son,
and his son's son.' The period of seventy
years is several times mentioned, as a
period during which the nations that
were subject to Babylon would be oppressed, and *after* that they should be
set at liberty (see Jer. xxv. 11, 12 ;
xxix. 10 ; comp. Jer. xlvi. 26). ¶ *Shall
Tyre sing as an harlot.* Marg. as the
Hebrew, ' It shall be unto Tyre as the
song of an harlot.' That is, Tyre shall
be restored to its former state of prosperity and opulence ; it shall be adorned
with the rich productions of other climes,
and shall be gay and joyful again. There
are two ideas here ; one that Tyre would
be again prosperous, and the other that
she would sustain substantially the
same character as before. It was common to compare cities with females,
whether virtuous or otherwise (see Note
on ch. i. 8). The same figure which is
here used occurs in Rev. xvii. 3–19
(comp. Isa. xlvii. 1 ; Nah. iii. 4 ; Rev.
xviii. 3, 9).

16. *Take an harp.* This is a continuation of the figure commenced in
the previous verse, a direct command to

forgotten : make sweet melody, sing many songs, that thou mayest be remembered.

17 And it shall come to pass, after the end of seventy years, that the LORD will visit Tyre, and she shall turn to her hire, and *a* shall commit fornication with all the king-

a Rev.17.2.   *b* Zec.14.20,31.   1 *old.*

doms of the world upon the face of the earth.

18 And her merchandise and her hire shall be holiness *b* to the LORD : it shall not be treasured nor laid up ; for her merchandise shall be for them that dwell before the LORD, to eat sufficiently, and for 1 durable clothing.

Tyre as an harlot, to go about the city with the usual expressions of rejoicing. Thus Donatus, in *Terent. Eunuch.,* iii. 2, 4, says :—

'Fidicinam esse meretricum est;'

And thus Horace :—

'Nec meretrix tibicina, cujus
    Ad strepitum salias.'   1 *Epis.* xiv. 25.

¶ *Thou harlot that hast been forgotten.* For seventy years thou hast lain unknown, desolate, ruined. ¶ *Make sweet melody,* &c. Still the prophet keeps up the idea of the harlot that had been forgotten, and that would now call her lovers again to her dwelling. The sense is, that Tyre would rise to her former splendour, and that the nations would be attracted by the proofs of returning prosperity to renew their commercial intercourse with her.

17. *The* LORD *will visit Tyre.* He will restore her to her former wealth and magnificence. ¶ *And she shall turn to her hire.* The word 'hire' here denotes the wages or reward that is given to an harlot ; and the idea which was commenced in the previous verses is here continued—of Tyre as an harlot—gay, splendid, licentious, and holding intercourse with strangers and foreigners. The *gains* of that commerce with other nations are here represented as her *hire.* ¶ *And shall commit fornication,* &c. Shall again be the mart of commerce (ver. 3); shall have intercourse with all the nations, and derive her support, splendour, luxury, from all. The idea is, that she would be restored to her former commercial importance, and perhaps, also, the prophet intends to intimate that she would procure those gains by dishonest acts, and by fraudulent pretexts. After the destruction of Tyre by Nebuchadnezzar, it remained desolate until the close of the Babylonian monarchy. Then a new city was

built on the island, that soon rivalled the former in magnificence. That new city was besieged and taken by Alexander the Great, on his way to the conquests of the East.

18. *And her merchandise.* The prophecy here does not mean that this would take place *immediately* after her rebuilding, but that *subsequent* to the seventy years of desolation this would occur. ¶ *Shall be holiness to the* LORD. This undoubtedly means, that at some future period, after the rebuilding of Tyre, the true religion would prevail there, and her wealth would be devoted to his service. That the true religion prevailed at Tyre subsequently to its restoration and rebuilding there can be no doubt. The Christian religion was early established at Tyre. It was visited by the Saviour (Matt. xv. 21), and by Paul. Paul found several disciples of Christ there when on his way to Jerusalem (Acts xxi. 3–6). It suffered much, says Lowth, under the Diocletian persecution. Eusebius (*Hist.* x. 4.) says that 'when the church of God was founded in Tyre, and in other places, much of its wealth was consecrated to God, and was brought as an offering to the church, and was presented for the support of the ministry agreeable to the commandments of the Lord.' Jerome says, 'We have seen churches built to the Lord in Tyre ; we have beheld the wealth of all, which was not treasured up nor hid, but which was given to those who dwelt before the Lord.' It early became a Christian bishopric ; and in the fourth century of the Christian era, Jerome (*Comm.* in Ezek. xxvi. 7 ; xxvii. 2) speaks of Tyre as the most noble and beautiful city of Phenicia, and as still trading with all the world. Reland enumerates the following list of bishops as having been present from Tyre at

CHAPTER XXIV.

THE previous chapters, from the thirteenth to the twenty-third inclusive, have been occupied mainly in describing the destruction of nations that were hostile to the Jews, or great and distressing calamities that would come upon them. The prophet had thus successively depicted the calamities that would come upon Babylon, Damascus, Moab, Nubia, Egypt, Dumah, and Tyre. In ch. xxii., he had, however, described the calamities which would come upon Judea and Jerusalem by the invasion of Sennacherib.

In this chapter, the prophet returns to the calamities which would come upon the people of God themselves. This chapter, and the three following, to the end of the twenty-seventh, seem to have been uttered about the same time, and perhaps may be regarded as constituting one vision, or prophecy. So Noyes, Lowth, and Rosenmuller, regard it. If these chapters be included in the prophecy, then it consists (1) of a description of *calamities* in ch. xxiv. , (2) of a song of praise expressive of deliverance from those calamities, and of the consequent spread of the true religion, in ch. xxv.; (3) of a song of praise suitable to celebrate the triumphs of the true religion in ch. xxvi.; and (4) of the effect of this deliverance in purifying the Jews in ch. xxvii.

When the prophecy was uttered is wholly unknown. In regard to the events to which it relates, there has been a great diversity of opinion, and scarcely are any two interpreters agreed. Grotius regards it as relating to the carrying away of the ten tribes by Shalmaneser. Hensler supposes that it refers to the invasion of Sennacherib. Vitringa supposes that it relates to the times of the Maccabees, and to the trials and calamities which came upon the Jews under the persecutions of Antiochus Epiphanes. Noyes regards it as descriptive of the destruction of

the land by Nebuchadnezzar, and of the return of the Jews from exile. Calvin considers the account in these four chapters as a *summing up,* or *recapitulation* of what the prophet had said in the previous prophecies respecting Babylon, Moab, Egypt, &c.; and then of the prosperity, and of the spread of the true religion which would succeed these general and far-spread devastations. Subsequently to *each* of these predictions respecting calamity, the prophet had foretold prosperity and the advance of truth; and he supposes that this is a mere condensing or summing up of what he had said more at length in the preceding chapters. Lowth supposes that it may have a reference to *all* the great desolations of the country by Shalmaneser, by Nebuchadnezzar, and by the Romans, especially to that of the Romans, to which some parts of it, he says, seem to be peculiarly applicable. It is certain that the prophet employs *general* terms; and as he gives no *certain* indications of the time, or the circumstances under which it was delivered, it is exceedingly difficult to determine either. The *general* drift of the prophecy is, however, plain. It is a prediction of prosperity, and of the prevalence of true religion *after* a series of oppressive judgments should have come upon the land. It is designed, therefore, to be *consolatory* to the Jews under impending calamities, and to convey the assurance that though they would be oppressed, yet their sufferings would be succeeded by occasions of gratitude and joy. In this respect, it accords with the general strain of the prophecies of Isaiah, that the people of God would be protected; that their name and nation should not be wholly obliterated; and that the darkest seasons of trial would be succeeded by deliverance and joy.

On the whole, it seems to me, that the prophecy relates to the calamities that would come upon the nation by the invasion of Nebuchadnezzar, and the carrying away to Babylon, and the sub-

various councils; viz., Cassius, Paulinus, Zeno, Vitalis, Uranius, Zeno, Photius, and Eusebius (see Reland's *Palestine,* pp. 1002–1011, in Ugolin vi.) Tyre continued Christian until it was taken by the Saracens in A.D. 639; but was recovered again by Christians in 1124. In 1280, it was conquered by the Mamelukes, and was taken by the Turks in 1516. It is now under the dominion of the Sultan as a part of Syria. ¶ *It shall not be treasured,* &c. It shall be regarded as consecrated to the Lord, and freely expended in his

service. ¶ *For them that dwell before the* LORD. For the ministers of religion. The *language* is taken from the custom of the Jews, when the priests *dwelt* at Jerusalem. The meaning is, that the wealth of Tyre would be consecrated to the service and support of religion. ¶ *For durable clothing.* Wealth formerly consisted much in changes of raiment; and the idea here is, that the wealth of Tyre would be devoted to God, and that it would be furnished for the support of those who ministered at the altar.

sequent deliverance from the oppressive bond-age, and the joy consequent on that. Accord-ing to this interpretation, the twenty-fourth chapter is occupied mainly with the description of the *calamities* that would come upon the land by the invasion of Nebuchadnezzar; the twenty-fifth describes the *deliverance* from that oppressive bondage, and the re-establishment of the true religion on Mount Zion, with a rapid glance at the ultimate prevalence of religion under the Messiah, suggested by the deliver-ance from the Babylonish bondage; the twenty-sixth chapter is a *song* expressive of joy at this signal deliverance—in language, in the main, so general that it is as applicable to the redemption under the Messiah as to the deliver-ance from Babylon; and the twenty-seventh chapter is descriptive of the *effect* of this capti-vity and subsequent deliverance in purifying Jacob (ch. xxvii. 6–9), and recovering the nation to righteousness.

The twenty-fourth chapter is composed of three parts. The first (1–12) contains a descrip-tion of the calamities that would come upon the whole land, amounting to far-spread and wide desolation—with a graphic description of the effects of it on the inhabitants (2), on the land (3–6), on the wine, the amusements, the song, &c. (7–12), causing all gaiety and prosperity to come to an end. The second (13–17) contains a statement by the prophet that a *few* would be left in the land amidst the general desolation, and that they would be filled with joy that they had escaped. From their retreats and refuges, their fastnesses and places of security, they would lift up the song of praise that they had been preserved. The third (18–23) contains a further description of augmented judgment that would come upon the land—a more severe and lengthened calamity stretching over the coun-try, agitating it like an earthquake. Yet there is even here (22, 23), an indication that there would be deliverance, and that the Lord of hosts would reign on Mount Zion—a description which is extended through the next chapter, and which constitutes the scope and substance of that chapter. In the division of the prophecy into chapters, that chapter should have been connected with this as a part of the same pro-phecy, and a continuance of the same subject. Indeed, but for the *length* of the prophecy, these four chapters should have been thrown into one, or if the prophecy had been broken up into chap-ters, important aids would have been rendered to a correct understanding of it had there been some indication in the margin that they consti-tuted one prophecy or vision.

B EHOLD, the Lord maketh the earth empty; and maketh it waste, and turneth [1] it upside down, and scattereth abroad the inhabit-ants thereof.

2 And it shall be, as with the people, so with *a* the [2] priest; as with *b* the servant, so with his master; as with the maid, so with her mistress; as with the buyer, so with the seller; as with the lender, so with the borrower; as with the taker of usury, so with the giver of usury to him.

1 *perverteth the face thereof.*　*a* Hos.4.9.
2 or, *prince*; Gen.41.45.　*b* Ep.6.8,9.

CHAPTER XXIV.

1. *Maketh the earth empty.* That is, will depopulate it, or take away its inhabitants, and its wealth. The word ' earth ' here (אֶרֶץ) is used evidently not to denote the whole world, but the land to which the prophet particularly refers —the land of Judea. It should have been translated *the land* (see Joel i. 2). It is possible, however, that the word here may be intended to include so much of the nations that surrounded Palestine as were allied with it, or as were con-nected with it in the desolations under Nebuchadnezzar. ¶ *And turneth it up-side down.* Marg. ' Perverteth the face thereof.' That is, everything is thrown into confusion; the civil and religious institutions are disorganized, and de-rangement everywhere prevails. ¶ *And scattereth abroad,* &c. This was done in the invasion by the Chaldeans by the carrying away of the inhabitants into their long and painful captivity.

2. *As with the people, so with the priest.* This does not mean in moral character, but in destiny. It does not mean that the character of the priest would have any influence on that of the people, or that because the one was cor-rupt the other would be; but it means that all would be involved in the same calamity, and there would be no favoured class that would escape. The prophet, therefore, enumerates the various ranks of the people, and shows that all classes would be involved in the impending calamity. ¶ *As with the taker of usury.*

3 The land shall be utterly emptied, and utterly spoiled : for the LORD hath spoken this word.

4 The earth mourneth, *and* fadeth away : the world languisheth and fadeth away ; the haughty people [1] of the earth do languish.

5 The earth also is defiled under the inhabitants thereof, because they [a] have transgressed the laws, changed the ordinance, broken the everlasting covenant.

6 Therefore [b] hath the curse devoured the earth, and they that dwell therein are desolate : therefore the inhabitants of the earth are burned, [c] and few men left.

1 *height of the.*   [a] Gen.3.17; Num.35.33.
[b] Mal.4.6.   [c] 2 Pet.3.10.

He who lends his money at interest. It was contrary to the Mosaic law for one Israelite to take interest of another (Lev. xxv. 36 ; Deut. xxiii. 19 ; Neh. v. 7, 10) ; but it is not probable that this law was very carefully observed, and especially in the corrupt times that preceded the Babylonian captivity.

3. *The land.* Heb. ' The earth,' as in ver. 1. It is here rendered correctly ' the land,' as it should have been there —meaning the land of Canaan. ¶ *And spoiled.* Its valuable possessions shall become the prey of the invading foe. This is an emphatic repetition of the declaration in ver. 1, to show the absolute certainty of that which was threatened.

4. *The earth mourneth.* The word ' earth ' here, as in ver. 1, means the land of Judea, or that and so much of the adjacent countries as would be subject to the desolation described. The figure here is taken from flowers when they lose their beauty and languish ; or when the plant that lacks moisture, or is cut down, loses its vigour and its vitality, and soon withers (comp. Note, ch. i. 30 ; ch. xxxiv. 4 ; Ps. i. 3). ¶ *The world* (תֵּבֵל) Literally, the inhabitable world, but used here as synonymous with the ' land,' and denoting the kingdoms of Judah and Israel (comp. Note, ch. xiii. 11). ¶ *The haughty people.* Marg. as in the Hebrew, 'Height of the people.' It denotes the great, the nobles, the princes of the land. The phrase is expressive of *rank*, not of their moral character.

5. *The earth also is defiled under the inhabitants thereof.* The statements in this verse are given as a reason why the curse had been pronounced against them, and why these calamities had come upon them, ver. 6. The first reason is, that the very earth had become polluted by their crimes. This phrase may denote that injustice and cruelty prevailed to such an extent that the very earth was stained with gore, and covered with blood *under* the guilty population. So the phrase is used in Num. xxxiii. 33 ; Ps. cvi. 38. Or it may mean in general, that the wickedness of the people was great, and was accumulating, and the very earth under them was polluted by sustaining such a population. But the former is probably the correct interpretation. ¶ *Changed the ordinance.* Or, the *statute* (חֹק). This word, from חָקַק, *to engrave*, and then to make or institute a law or an ordinance, is usually applied to the *positive* statutes appointed by Moses. The word *statute* accurately expresses the idea. These they had changed by introducing new statutes, and had in fact, if not in form, repealed the laws of Moses, and introduced others. ¶ *Broken the everlasting covenant.* The word ' covenant ' here is evidently used, as it is often, in the sense of *law*. By the term ' everlasting covenant,' Vitringa correctly supposes is denoted the laws of nature, the immutable laws of justice and right, which are engraven on the conscience, and which are inflexible and perpetual.

6. *Therefore hath the curse devoured.* Eaten it up ; a figurative expression that is common in the Scriptures, denoting that the desolation is wide-spread and ruinous. ¶ *Are burned* (חָרוּ). Instead of this reading, Lowth proposes to read חָרְבוּ, ' Are destroyed.' The LXX. read it, ' Therefore the inhabitants of the land shall be poor.' The Syriac, ' The inhabitants of the land shall be slain.' But there is no authority from the MSS. to change the text as proposed by Lowth. Nor is it necessary. The prophet does not mean that the inhabitants of the land were *consumed by fire.*

7 The ^a new wine mourneth, the vine languisheth, all the merry-hearted do sigh.

8 The mirth of ^b tabrets ceaseth, the noise of them that rejoice endeth, the joy of the harp ceaseth.

^a ch.16.8,9; Joel 1.10,12.

9 They shall not drink wine with a song ; strong drink shall be bitter to them that drink it.

10 The city of confusion is broken down : every house is shut up, that no man may come in.

^b Jer.7.34; Hos.2.11; Rev.18.22.

The expression is evidently figurative. He is speaking of the effect of *wrath* or the *curse*, and that effect is often described in the Scriptures as burning, or consuming, as a fire does. The sense is, that the inhabitants of the land are brought under the withering, burning, consuming effect of that wrath ; and the same effects are produced by it as are seen when a fire runs over a field or a forest. Hence the word here used (חָרָה, *to burn, to be kindled*) is often used in connection with wrath, to denote burning or raging anger. Ex. xxii. 23 : ' His anger burns.' Gen. xxx. 2 : ' And the anger of Jacob was kindled against Rachel ; Gen. xliv. 18 ; Job xxvii. 2, 3 ; xlii. 7 ; Gen. xxxi. 6 : ' His anger was kindled.' (Ps. xxxvii. 1, 7, 8 ; Prov. xxiv. 19.) Comp. Job xxx. 30 :

> My skin is black upon me,
> And my bones are burnt with heat.

The sense is, that the inhabitants of the land were wasted away under the wrath of God, so that few were left ; as the trees of the forest are destroyed before a raging fire. ¶ *And few men are left.* This was literally true after the invasion of the land by the Chaldeans (2 Kings xxiv. 14–16).

7. *The new wine languisheth.* The new wine (תִּירוֹשׁ, *tirōsh*), denotes properly *must*, or wine that was newly expressed from the grape, and that was not fermented, usually translated ' new wine,' or ' sweet wine.' The expression here is poetic. The wine languishes or mourns because there are none to drink it ; it is represented as grieved because it does not perform its usual office of exhilarating the heart, and the figure is thus an image of the desolation of the land. ¶ *The vine languisheth.* It is sickly and unfruitful, because there are none to cultivate it as formerly. The idea is, that all nature sympathizes in the general calamity. ¶ *All the merry-hearted.* Probably the reference is

mainly to those who were once made happy at the plenteous feast, and at the splendid entertainments where wine abounded. They look now upon the wide-spread desolation of the land, and mourn.

8. *The mirth of tabrets.* The joy and exultation which is produced by tabrets. On the words ' tabret' (תֹּף) and ' harp ' (כִּנּוֹר), see Notes on ch. v. 12.

9. *Drink wine with a song.* That is, accompanied with a song, as the usual mode was in their feasts. ¶ *Strong drink.* On the word שֵׁכָר, see Note on ch. v. 11. ¶ *Shall be bitter,* &c. They shall cease to find pleasure in it in consequence of the general calamities that have come upon the nation.

10. *The city of confusion.* That Jerusalem is here intended there can be no doubt. The name ' city of confusion.' is probably given to it by *anticipation* of what it would be ; that is, as it appeared in prophetic vision to Isaiah (see Note on ch. i. 1). He gave to it a name that would describe its state when these calamities should have come upon it. The word rendered ' confusion ' (תֹּהוּ, *tōhū*) does not denote *disorder* or *anarchy,* but is a word expressive of emptiness, vanity, destitution of form, waste. It occurs Gen. i. 2 : ' And the earth was *without form.*' In Job xxvi. 7, it is rendered ' the empty place ;' in 1 Sam. xii. 21 ; Isa. xlv. 18, 19, ' in vain ;' and usually ' emptiness,' ' vanity,' ' confusion ' (see Isa. xxiv. 10 ; xl. 17 ; xli. 29). In Job xii. 24 ; Ps. cvii. 40, it denotes a wilderness. Here it means that the city would be desolate, empty, and depopulated. ¶ *Is broken down.* Its walls and dwellings are in ruins. ¶ *Every house is shut up.* That is, either because every man, fearful of danger, would fasten his doors so that enemies could not enter ; or more probably, the entrance to every house would be so obstructed by ruins as to render it impossible to enter it.

11 *There is* a crying for wine in
the streets ; all joy is darkened, the
mirth of the land is gone.

12 In *a* the city *is* left desolation,
and the gate *b* is smitten with destruction.

13 When thus it shall be in the
midst of the land among the people,
there shall be c as the shaking of an

a Lam.1.1.   *b* Lam.2.9.
c ch.6; 13; 17.5,6; Mic.2.12.   *d* Zep.2.14,15.

11. There is *a crying for wine in the
streets*. The inhabitants of the city,
turned from their dwellings, would cry
for wine to alleviate their distress, and
to sustain them in their calamity (comp.
ch. xvi. 8–10). ¶ *All joy is darkened*.
Is gone, or has departed, like the joyful
light at the setting of the sun.

12. *And the gate is smitten with destruction*. The word rendered ‘destruction’ may denote ‘a crash’ (Gesenius).
The idea is, that the gates of the city,
once so secure, are now battered down
and demolished, so that the enemy can
enter freely. Thus far is a description
of the calamities that would come upon
the nation. The following verses show
that, though the desolation would be
general, a few of the inhabitants would
be left—a circumstance thrown in to
mitigate the prospect of the impending
ruin.

13. *In the midst of the land*. That
is, in the midst of the land of Canaan.
¶ There shall be *as the shaking of an
olive-tree*. A few shall be left, as in
gathering olives a few will remain on
the highest and outermost boughs (see
Notes on ch. xvii. 5, 6).

14. *They shall lift up their voice*.
They who are left in the land ; or who
are not carried away to Babylon. ‘ To
lift up the voice ’ in the Scriptures may
denote either grief or joy ; compare
Gen. xxi. 6 ; 1 Sam. xxiv. 16 ; Judg. ii.
4 ; Ruth i. 9, &c., where to lift up the
voice is conected with weeping ; and
Ezek. xxi. 22 ; Ps. xciii. 3 ; Isa. xl. 29 ;
xlii. 11, &c., where it is connected with
exultation and joy. The latter is evidently the idea here, that the few who
would escape from captivity by fleeing
to neighbouring countries, would lift up
their voice with exultation that they

olive-tree, and as the gleaning-
grapes when the vintage is done.

14 They *d* shall lift up their voice,
they shall sing for the majesty of
the LORD, they shall cry aloud from
the sea.

15 Wherefore *e* glorify ye the
LORD in the ¹ fires, *even* the name
of the LORD God of Israel in the
isle *f* of the sea.

e 1 Pe.3.15.   1 or, *valleys*.   *f* Zep.2.11.

had escaped. ¶ *They shall sing for the
majesty of the* LORD. They shall sing
on account of the glory, or goodness of
JEHOVAH, who had so mercifully kept
and preserved them. ¶ *They shall cry
aloud from the sea*. From the isles and
coasts of the Mediterranean whither
they would have escaped, and where
they would find a refuge. No doubt
many of the inhabitants adjacent to the
sea, when they found the land invaded,
would betake themselves to the neighbouring islands, and find safety there
until the danger should be overpast.
Lowth renders this,

‘ The waters shall resound with the exaltation of
Jehovah,’

where he supposes מים should be rendered as if pointed מַיִם, ‘ waters,’ not
as it is in the present Hebrew text, מִיָּם
‘ from the sea.’ The sense is not materially different ; but there seems to be
no good reason for departing from the
usual interpretation.

15. *Wherefore glorify ye the* LORD.
The prophet, in this verse, calls upon
the people to join in the praise of JEHO-
VAH wherever they are scattered. In the
previous verse he describes the scattered
few who were left in the land, or who had
escaped to the adjacent islands in the sea,
as celebrating the praises of God where
they were. In this verse he calls on *all*
to join in this wherever they were scattered. ¶ *In the fires*. Marg. ‘ Valleys.’
The LXX. read, Ἐν τοῖς νήσοις—‘ In the
islands.’ The Chaldee, ‘ Therefore, when
light shall come to the just, they shall
glorify the Lord.’ Lowth supposes that
the word בָּאֻרִים should have been בָּאִיִּים,
‘ in the islands,’ or ‘ coasts.’ But the
MSS. do not give authority for this
reading ; the only authority which Lowth

16 From the ¹uttermost part of the earth have we heard songs, *even* glory to the righteous. But I said, My ²leanness, my leanness, woe unto me! the treacherous dealers have dealt treacherously; *a* yea, the treacherous dealers have dealt very treacherously.

1 wing. *2 leanness to me, or, my secret to me.*

a ch.48.8; Jer.5.11.

refers to being that of the LXX. Other conjectures have been made by others, but all without any authority from MSS. The Hebrew word in the plural form does not occur elsewhere in the Scriptures. The proper signification of the word אוֹר (*ōr*) is *light*, and it is applied (*a*) to *daylight*, or daybreak, 1 Sam. xiv. 36; Neh. viii. 3; (*b*) to light from daybreak to mid-day, Job xxiv. 14; (*c*) the sun, Job xxxi. 26; xxxvii. 21; (*d*) light as the emblem of happiness; (*e*) light as the emblem of knowledge. It is also used to denote *fire*, Ezek. v. 2; Isa. xliv. 16; xlvii. 14. In the plural form it is applied, in connection with the word *Thummim*, to the gems or images which were on the breastplate of the high priest, and from which responses were obtained. Ex. xxviii. 30: 'And thou shalt put in the breastplate of judgment the Urim (הָאוּרִים) and the Thummim' (comp. Lev. viii. 8; Ezra ii. 63). Probably it was thus used to denote the *splendour* or beauty of the gems there set, or perhaps the *light* or instruction which was the result of consulting the oracle. The proper meaning of the word is, however, *light*, and it usually and naturally suggests the idea of the *morning light*, the aurora; perhaps, also, the *northern* light, or the aurora borealis. It in no instance means *caves*, or *valleys*. Vitringa supposed it referred to *caves*, and that the address was to the *Troglodytes*, or those who had been driven from their homes, and compelled to take up their residence in caves. The word probably refers either to the regions of the morning light, the rising of the sun; or of the northern light, the aurora borealis; and in either case, the reference is doubtless to those who would be carried away to Babylon, and who were called on there by the prophet to glorify God. 'In those regions of *light*, where the morning dawns; or where the northern skies are illuminated at night, there glorify God' (see Note on ch. xiv. 13). The reasons for this opinion are, (1.) That such is the natural and proper sense of the word. It properly refers to light, and *not* to caves, to valleys, or to islands. (2.) The parallelism, the construction, demands such an interpretation. It would then be equivalent to calling on the scattered people to glorify God in the East, and in the West; in the regions of the rising sun and in the coasts of the sea; or wherever they were scattered. And the sense is, (1) that they should be *encouraged* to do this by the prospect of a return; (2) that it was their *duty* still to do this wherever they were; and (3) that the worship of the true God would be in fact continued and celebrated, though his people were scattered, and driven to distant lands. ¶ *In the isle of the sea.* The coasts and islands of the Mediterranean (ver. 14).

16. *From the uttermost part of the earth.* The word 'earth' here seems to be taken in its usual sense, and to denote countries without the bounds of Palestine, and the phrase is equivalent to *remote regions*, or *distant countries* (see Note on ch. xi. 12). The prophet here represents himself as *hearing* those songs from distant lands as a grand chorus, the sound of which came in upon and pervaded Palestine. The worship of God would be still continued, though the temple should be destroyed, the inhabitants of the land dispersed, and the land of Judea be a wide-spread desolation. Amidst the general wreck and woe, it was *some* consolation that the worship of JEHOVAH was celebrated anywhere. ¶ *Have we heard songs.* Or, we *do* hear songs. The distant celebrations of the goodness of God break on the ear, and amidst the general calamity these songs of the scattered people of God comfort the heart. ¶ *Glory to the righteous.* This is the burden and substance of those songs. Their general import and design is, to show that there shall be honour to the people of God. They are now afflicted

17 Fear, *and the pit, and the snare, *are* upon thee, O inhabitant of the earth.

a Jer. 10. 10, 11.

and scattered. Their temple is destroyed, their land waste, and ruin spreads over the graves of their fathers. Yet amidst these desolations, their confidence in God is unshaken; their reliance on him is firm. They still believe that there shall be honour and glory to the just, and that God will be their protector and avenger. These assurances served to sustain them in their afflictions, and to shed a mild and cheering influence on their saddened hearts. ¶ *But I said.* But I, the prophet, am constrained to say. This the prophet says respecting *himself*, viewing himself as left in the land of Canaan; or more probably he personifies, in this declaration, Jerusalem, and the inhabitants of the land that still remained there. The songs that came in from distant lands; the echoing praises from the exiles in the east and the west seeming to meet and mingle over Judea, only served to render the abounding desolation more manifest and distressing. Those distant praises recalled the solemn services of the temple, and the happiness of other times, and led each one of those remaining, who witnessed the desolations, to exclaim, 'my leanness.' ¶ *My leanness, my leanness.* The language of Jerusalem, and the land of Judea. This language expresses calamity. The loss of flesh is emblematic of a condition of poverty, want, and wretchedness—as sickness and affliction waste away the flesh, and take away the strength; Ps. cix. 24:

> My knees are weak through fasting,
> And my flesh faileth of fatness.

Ps. cii. 5:

> By reason of the voice of my groaning
> My bones cleave to my flesh.

See also Job vi. 12; xix. 20; Lam. iii. 4. Leanness is also put to denote the displeasure of God, in Ps. cvi. 15:

> And he gave them their request;
> But sent leanness into their soul.

Comp. Isa. x. 16. ¶ *The treacherous dealers.* The foreign nations that disregard covenants and laws; that pursue their object by deceit, and stratagem, and fraud. Most conquests are made by what are called the *stratagems* of war; that is, by a course of perfidy and deception. There can be no doubt that the usual mode of conquest was pursued in regard to Jerusalem. This whole clause is exceedingly emphatic. The word implying *treachery* (בָּגַד) is repeated no less than *five* times in various forms in this single clause, and shows how strongly the idea had taken possession of the mind of the prophet. The passage furnishes one of the most remarkable examples of the *paronomasia* occurring in the Bible. בֹּגְדוּ בָּגְדוּ וּבֶגֶד בּוֹגְדִים —*Baghadu boghedim baghadu wegehd boghedhim.* In fact, this figure abounds so much in this chapter that Gesenius contends that it is not the production of Isaiah, but a composition belonging to a later and less elegant period of Hebrew literature.

17. *Fear, and the pit.* This verse is an explanation of the cause of the wretchedness referred to in the previous verse. The same expression is found in Jer. xlviii. 43, in his account of the destruction that would come upon Moab, a description which Jeremiah probably copied from Isaiah.— There is also here in the original a *paronomasia* that cannot be retained in a translation—פַּחַד וָפַחַת וָפָח *pahhădh vâpahhŭth vâpâhh*— where the form *pahh* occurs in each word. The sense is, that they were nowhere safe; that if they escaped one danger, they immediately fell into another. The expression is equivalent to that which occurs in the writings of the Latin classics:

> Incidit in Scyllam cupiens vitare Charybdin.

The same idea, that if a man should escape from one calamity he would fall into another, is expressed in another form in Amos v. 19:

> As if a man did flee from a lion, and a bear met him;
> Or went into a house, and leaned his hand on the wall,
> And a serpent bit him.

18 And it shall come to pass, *that* he who fleeth from the noise of 'the fear shall fall into the pit; and he that cometh up out of the midst of the pit shall be taken in the snare : for the *a* windows from

20 The earth shall reel *d* to and

a Gen.7.11.   *b* Ps.18.7.   *c* Jer.4.23.   *d* ch.19.14.

on high are open, and the foundations *b* of the earth do shake.

19 The earth *c* is utterly broken down, the earth is clean dissolved, the earth is moved exceedingly.

In the passage before us, there is an *advance* from one danger to another, or the subsequent one is more to be dreaded than the preceding. The figure is taken from the mode of taking wild beasts, where various nets, toils, or pitfalls were employed to secure them. The word 'fear' (פַּחַד), denotes anything that was used to frighten or arouse the wild beasts in hunting, or to drive them into the pitfall that was prepared for them. Among the Romans the name 'fears' (*formidines*) was given to lines or cords strung with feathers of all colours, which, when they fluttered in the air or were shaken, frightened the beasts into the pits, or the birds into the snares which were prepared to take them (Seneca, *De Ira,* ii. 12 ; Virg. *Æn.* xii. 749 ; *Geor.* iii. 372). It is possible that this may be referred to here under the name of 'fear.' The word 'pit' (פַּחַת) denotes the pitfall ; a hole dug in the ground, and covered over with bushes, leaves, &c., into which they might fall unawares. The word 'snare' (פַּח) denotes a net, or gin, and perhaps refers to a series of nets enclosing at first a large space of ground, in which the wild beasts were, and then drawn by degrees into a narrow compass, so that they could not escape.

18. *From the noise of the fear.* A cry or shout was made in hunting, designed to arouse the game, and drive it to the pitfall. The image means here that calamities would be multiplied in all the land, and that if the inhabitants endeavoured to avoid one danger they would fall into another. ¶ *And he that cometh up out of the midst of the pit.* A figure taken still from hunting. It was *possible* that some of the more strong and active of the wild beasts driven into the pitfall would spring out, and attempt to escape, yet they might be secured by snares or gins purposely con-

trived for such an occurrence. So the prophet says, that though a few might escape the calamities that would at first threaten to overthrow them, yet they would have no security. They would immediately fall into others, and be destroyed. ¶ *For the windows on high are open.* This is evidently taken from the account of the deluge in Gen. vii. 11: ' In the six hundredth year of Noah's life, in the second month, the seventeenth day of the month, the same day were all the fountains of the great deep broken up, and the windows (or *flood-gates,* Margin) of heaven were opened.' The word 'windows' here (אֲרֻבּוֹת) is the same which occurs in Genesis, and properly denotes *a grate, a lattice, a window,* and then any opening, as a sluice or floodgate, and is applied to a tempest or a deluge, because when the rain descends, it seems like opening sluices or floodgates in the sky. The sense here is, that calamities had come upon the nation *resembling* the universal deluge. ¶ *And the foundations of the earth do shake.* An image derived from an earthquake —a figure also denoting far-spreading calamities.

19. *The earth is utterly broken down.* The effect as it were of an earthquake where everything is thrown into commotion and ruin. ¶ *The earth is moved exceedingly.* Everything in this verse is intense and emphatic. The verbs are in the strongest form of emphasis : ' By breaking, the land is broken ;' ' by scattering, the land is scattered ;' ' by commotion, the land is moved.' The repetition also of the expression in the same sense three times, is a strong form of emphasis ; and the whole passage is designed to denote the utter desolation and ruin that had come upon the land.

20. *The earth shall reel to and fro like a drunkard.* This is descriptive of the agitation that occurs in an earthquake when everything is shaken from

fro like a drunkard, and shall-be removed *a* like a cottage ; and the transgression thereof shall be heavy upon *b* it : and it shall fall, and not rise again.

a Rev.21.1.　　　　b Zec.5.5-8.

21 And it shall come to pass in that day, *that* the LORD shall punish[1] the host of the high ones *that are* on high, and the kings of *c* the earth upon the earth.

1 *visit upon.*　　　　c Ps.76.12.

its foundation, and when trees and towers are shaken by the mighty concussion. The same figure is used in ch. xxix. 9. See also the description of a tempest at sea, in Ps. cvii. 27 :

> They reel to and fro,
> And stagger like a drunken man,
> And are at their wit's end.

¶ *And shall be removed like a cottage.* Or rather, shall *move* or *vacillate* (הִתְנוֹדְדָה) like a cottage. The word cottage (מְלוּנָה from לוּן, *to pass the night, to lodge for a night*) means properly a temporary shed or lodge for the watchman of a garden or vineyard (see Note on ch. i. 8). Sometimes these cottages were erected in the form of a hut ; and sometimes they were a species of *hanging bed* or *couch*, that was suspended from the limbs of trees. They were made either by interweaving the limbs of a tree, or by suspending them by cords from the branches of trees, or by extending a cord or cords from one tree to another, and laying a couch or bed on the cords. They were thus made to afford a convenient place for observation, and also to afford security from the access of wild beasts. Travellers in the East even now resort to such a temporary lodge for security (see Niebuhr's *Description of Arabia*). These lodges were easily moved to and fro, and swung about by the wind—and this is the idea in the verse before us. The whole land was agitated as with an earthquake ; it reeled like a drunkard ; it moved, and was unsettled, as the hanging couch on the trees was driven to and fro by the wind. ¶ *And the transgression thereof shall be heavy upon it.* Like a vast incumbent weight on a dwelling which it cannot sustain, and beneath which it is crushed. ¶ *And it shall fall, and not rise again.* This does not mean, as I apprehend, that the nation should never be restored to its former dignity and rank as a people ; for the prophet immediately (ver. 23) speaks of such a

restoration, and of the re-establishment of the theocracy ; but it must mean that IN *those convulsions* it would not rise. It would not be able to recover itself ; it *would certainly* be prostrated. As we say of a drunkard, he may stumble often, and partially recover himself, yet he will certainly fall so as not then to be able to recover himself, so it would be with that agitated and convulsed land. They would make many efforts to recover themselves, and they would partially succeed, yet they would ultimately be completely prostrate in the dust.

21. *In that day.* In the time of the captivity at Babylon. ¶ *Shall punish.* Heb. as the Marg., 'Shall visit upon' (see Note on ch. x. 12). ¶ *The host of the high ones.* There have been various interpretations of this expression. Jerome understands it of the host of heaven, and thinks it refers to the fact that in the day of judgment God will judge not only earthly things but celestial, and especially the sun and moon and stars, as having been the objects of idolatrous worship (see Deut. iv. 19 ; Dan. viii. 10 ; xi. 13). Comp. Ps. xviii. 17 ; Jer. xxv. 30, where the words 'on high' are used to denote heaven. Aben Ezra supposes that by the phrase is meant *angels*, who preside over the governors and kings of the earth, in accordance with the ancient opinion that each kingdom was under the tutelage of guardian angels. To this Rosenmüller seems to assent, and to suppose that the beings thus referred to were *evil* spirits or demons to whom the kingdoms of the world were subject. Others, among whom is Grotius, have supposed that the reference is to the images of the sun, moon, and stars, which were erected in high places, and worshipped by the Assyrians. But probably the reference is to those who occupied places of power and trust in the *ecclesiastical* arrangement of Judea, the high priest and priests, who exercised a vast dominion over the nation, and who, in many respects, were re-

22 And they shall be gathered together [1] *as* prisoners are gathered in [2] the pit, and shall be shut up in the prison, and after many days shall they be [3] visited.

[1] *with the gathering of prisoners.*   [2] or, *dungeon.*

23 Then [a] the moon shall be confounded, and the sun ashamed, when the LORD of hosts shall reign in mount Zion, and in Jerusalem, and [4] before his ancients, gloriously.

[3] or, *found wanting.*   [a] Eze. 32. 7.
[4] or, *there shall be glory before his ancients*

garded as elevated even over the kings and princes of the land. The comparison of rulers with the sun, moon, and stars, is common in the Scriptures; and this comparison was supposed peculiarly to befit *ecclesiastical* rulers, who were regarded as in a particular manner the lights of the nation. ¶ *Upon the earth.* Beneath, or inferior to those who had places of the highest trust and honour. The ecclesiastical rulers are represented as occupying the superior rank; the princes and rulers in a civil sense as in a condition of less honour and responsibility. This was probably the usual mode in which the ecclesiastical and civil offices were estimated in Judea.

22. *And they shall be gathered together.* That is, those who occupy posts of honour and influence in the ecclesiastical and civil polity of the land. ¶ *As prisoners.* Margin, as in the Heb. 'With the gathering of prisoners.' The reference is to the custom of collecting captives taken in war, and chaining them together by the hands and feet, and thrusting them in large companies into a prison. ¶ *In the pit.* Marg. 'Dungeon.' The sense is, that the rulers of the land should be made captive, and treated as prisoners of war. This was undoubtedly true in the captivity under Nebuchadnezzar. The people were assembled; were regarded as captives; and were conveyed together to a distant land. ¶ *And shall be shut up in the prison.* Probably this is not intended to be taken *literally*, but to denote that they would be as secure *as if* they were shut up in prison. Their prison-house would be Babylon, where they were enclosed *as in a prison* seventy years. ¶ *And after many days.* If this refers, as I have supposed, to the captivity at Babylon, then these 'many days' refer to the period of seventy years. ¶ *Shall they be visited.* Marg. 'Found wanting.' The word here used (פָּקַד) may be used either in a good or bad

sense, either to visit for the purpose of reviewing, numbering, or aiding; or to visit for the purpose of punishing. It is probably, in the Scriptures, most frequently used in the latter sense (see 1 Sam. xv. 2; Job xxxi. 14; xxxv. 15; Ps. lxxxix. 33; Isa. xxvi. 14; Jer. ix. 24). But it is often used in the sense of taking account of, reviewing, or mustering as a military host (see Num. i. 44; iii. 39; 1 Kings xx. 15; Isa. xiii. 4). In this place it may be taken in either of these senses, as may be best supposed to suit the connection. To me it seems that the connection seems to require the idea of a visitation for the purpose of relief or of deliverance; and to refer to the fact that at the end of that time there would be a reviewing, a mustering, an enrolment of those who should have been carried away to their distant prison-house, to ascertain how many remained, and to *marshal* them for their return to the land of their fathers (see the books of Ezra and Nehemiah). The word here used has *sometimes* the sense expressed in the margin, 'found wanting' (comp. 1 Sam. xx. 6; xxv. 15; Isa. xxxviii. 10); but such a sense does not suit the connection here. I regard the verse as an indication of future mercy and deliverance. They would be thrown into prison, and treated as captives of war; but after a long time they would be visited by the Great Deliverer of their nation, their covenant-keeping God, and reconducted to the land of their fathers.

23. *Then the moon shall be confounded.* The heavenly bodies are often employed in the sacred writings to denote the princes and kings of the earth. These expressions are not to be pressed *ad unguem* as if the sun denoted one thing and the moon another; but they are *general* poetic expressions designed to represent rulers, princes, and magistrates of all kinds (comp. Ezek. xxxii. 7; Joel ii. 30, 31). ¶ *Shall be confounded.* Shall be covered with shame.

CHAPTER XXV.

ANALYSIS.

For the general design and scope of this chapter, see the Analysis to ch. xxiv. It is a song of praise to God for the anticipated deliverance of his people from the bondage in Babylon. The desolation of Jerusalem and Judah had been described in ch. xxiv.; that chapter had closed with an intimation that JEHOVAH would again reign in glory on Mount Zion (ver. 23); and in view of this future deliverance the prophet breaks out into this beautiful song of praise. It was not unusual for the prophets to express, by anticipation, such songs of praise as would be celebrated by the people in times of signal deliverance (see Notes on ch. xii.) This song of praise is one of the most beautiful that is to be found in the writings of Isaiah. The essential idea is that which was hinted at in ch. xxiv. 23, that JEHOVAH would reign with a glory that would obscure the brightness of the sun and the moon on Mount Zion. Filled with the idea, the prophet fixes the eye on those future glories, and declares

what shall occur *under* that reign. He sees JEHOVAH reigning there for a long series of years; and *during* that reign he sees (6) that he would provide a way by which the darkness might be removed from all nations (7); that he would originate that plan by which death would be swallowed up in victory (8); and that there he would execute a plan by which all his enemies would be laid low (9–12). The hymn is designed, therefore, to celebrate the faithfulness of God in fulfilling his ancient promises, and delivering his people from their long captivity by the destruction of Babylon (1–5); and the future glories that would shine forth under the reign of JEHOVAH on Mount Zion, including the arrangements of redeeming mercy for the world.

O LORD, thou *art* my God; I will *a* exalt thee, I will praise thy name: for thou hast done wonderful *things ;* thy counsels of old *are* faithfulness *b and* truth.

a Ps.46.10.   b Num.23.19.

That is, shall appear to shine with diminished beauty, as if it were *ashamed* in the superior glory that would shine around it. The sense is, that when the people should be returned to their land, the theocracy would be restored, and the magnificence of the kings and other civil rulers would be dimmed in the superior splendour of the reign of God. Probably there is reference here to the time when JEHOVAH would reign in Jerusalem through, or by means of, THE MESSIAH. ¶ *In Mount Zion* (see Note on ch. i. 8). This would take place subsequently to the captivity, and pre-eminently under the reign of THE MESSIAH. ¶ *And before his ancients.* That is, before the elders of the people ; in the presence of those intrusted with authority and rule. ¶ *Gloriously.* He would reign gloriously when his laws should be respected and obeyed; when his character as King and Ruler should be developed ; and when, under his sceptre, his kingdom should be augmented and extended. On this glad prospect the eye of the prophet was fixed ; and this was the bright and splendid object in the 'vision' that served to relieve the darkness that was coming upon the nation. Present calamities may be borne, with the hope that JEHOVAH will reign more gloriously hereafter ; and when the effect of all

shall be such as to exalt JEHOVAH in the view of the nations. It may be added that when JEHOVAH, by the Messiah, shall reign over all the earth, all the glory of princes and monarchs shall be dimmed ; the celebrity of their wisdom and power and plans shall be obscured in the superior splendour of the wisdom of God, in reigning through his Son over the human race. Come that blessed day; and speedily let the glory of the moon be confounded, and the sun be ashamed, and all inferior magnificence fade away before the splendour of the Sun of righteousness !

CHAPTER XXV.

1. *O Lord, thou* art *my God.* The prophet speaks, not in his own name, but in the name of the people that would be delivered from bondage. The sense is, that JEHOVAH had manifested himself as their covenant-keeping God ; and that in view of his faithfulness in keeping his promises, they now had demonstration that he was *their* God. ¶ *I will exalt thee.* A form of expression often used to denote *praise* (Ps. cxviii. 28; cxlv. 1), meaning that the worshipper would exalt God in the view of his own mind, or would regard him as above all other beings and objects. ¶ *For thou hast done wonderful* things. On the meaning of the Heb. פֶּלֶא—'wonderful,'

2 For thou hast made of a city an heap ; *of* a defenced city a ruin : a *a* palace of strangers to be no city ; it shall never be built.

a Jer.51.37.   *b* Rev.11.13.

3 Therefore shall the strong people glorify *b* thee, the city of the terrible nations shall fear thee.

4 For thou hast been a strength to the poor, a strength to the needy

---

see Note on ch. ix. 6. ¶ Thy *counsels of old.* Which were formed and revealed long since. The counsels referred to are those respecting the delivery of his people from bondage, which had been expressed even long before their captivity commenced, and which would be now completely and triumphantly fulfilled. ¶ Are *faithfulness.* Have been brought to pass ; do not fail. ¶ And *truth.* Heb. אֶמֶן—whence our word *Amen.* LXX. Γένοιτο — ' Let it be.' The word denotes that the purposes of God were *firm,* and would certainly be fulfilled.

2. *For thou hast made.* This is supposed to be uttered by the Jews who should return from Babylon, and therefore refers to what *would have been* seen by them. In their time it would have occurred that God had made of the city an heap. ¶ *Of a city.* I suppose the whole scope of the passage requires us to understand this of Babylon. There has been, however, a great variety of interpretation of this passage. Grotius supposed that Samaria was intended. Calvin that the word is used *collectively,* and that various cities are intended. Piscator that Rome, the seat of Antichrist, was intended. Jerome says that the Jews generally understand it of Rome. Aben Ezra and Kimchi, however, understand it to refer to many cities which they say will be destroyed in the times of Gog and Magog. Nearly all these opinions may be seen subjected to an examination, and shown to be unfounded, in Vitringa. ¶ *An heap.* It is reduced to ruins (see Notes on ch. xiii., xiv.) The ruin of Babylon *commenced* when it was taken by Cyrus, and the Jews were set at liberty ; it was not *completed* until many centuries after. The form of the Hebrew here is, ' Thou hast placed *from* a city *to* a ruin :' that is, thou hast changed it *from* being a city *to* a pile of ruins. ¶ Of *a defenced city.* A city fortified, and made strong against the approach of an enemy. How

true this was of Babylon may be seen in the description prefixed to chapter xiii. ¶ *A palace.* This word properly signifies the residence of a prince or monarch (Jer. xxx. 18 ; Amos i. 4, 7, 10, 12). Here it is applied to Babylon on account of its splendour, as if it were a vast palace, the residence of princes. ¶ *Of strangers.* Foreigners ; a term often given to the inhabitants of foreign lands, and especially to the Babylonians (see Note on ch. i. 7 ; comp. Ezek. xxviii. 7 ; Joel iii. 17). It means that this was, by way of eminence, THE city of the foreigners ; the capital of the whole Pagan world ; the city where foreigners congregated and dwelt. ¶ *It shall never be built.* (See Notes on ch. xiii. 19–22.)

3. *The strong people.* The reference here is not probably to the Babylonians, but to the surrounding nations. The deliverance of the Jews, and the destruction of Babylon, would be such striking events that they would lead the surrounding nations to acknowledge that it was the hand of God. ¶ *The city of the terrible nations.* The word ' city ' here is taken probably in a collective sense, to denote the *cities* or the strong places of the surrounding nations which would be brought thus to tremble before God. The destruction of a city so proud and wicked as Babylon would alarm *them,* and would lead them to *fear* that they might share the same fate, especially as many of them had been associated in oppressing the now delivered people of the land of Judea.

4. *For thou hast been a strength to the poor.* Thou hast sustained and upheld them in their trials, and hast delivered them. God is often spoken of as the *strength* of his people. Isa. xxvi. 4 : ' In the Lord JEHOVAH is everlasting strength.' Ps. xxvii. 1 : ' The Lord is the strength of my life, of whom shall I be afraid ?' Ps. xxviii. 8 ; xxix. 11 ; xxxi. 2 ; xlvi. 1 ; Isa. xlv. 24.—By the ' poor ' and the ' needy ' here undoubtedly are meant the captive Jews

in his distress, a refuge from the storm, a shadow from the heat, when the blast of the terrible ones *is* as a storm *against* the wall.

5 Thou shalt bring down the noise of strangers, as the heat in a dry place ; *even* the heat with the shadow of a cloud : the branch

a ch.2.2,3.   *b* Mat.22.2,&c.

who had been stripped of their wealth, and carried from their homes, and confined in Babylon. ¶ *A refuge.* A place of safety; a retreat ; a protection. God is often spoken of as such a *refuge;* Deut. xxxiii. 27 : 'The eternal God is thy refuge.' (2 Sam. xxii. 3 ; Ps. ix. 9 ; xiv. 6; xlvi. 1, 7, 11 ; lvii. 1; lix. 16.) ¶ *From the storm.* This word (זֶרֶם) usually denotes a tempest of wind and rain. Here it is put for calamity and affliction. The figure is common in all languages. ¶ *A shadow from the heat.* (See Note on ch. iv. 6; xvi. 3; comp. ch. xxxii. 2.) ¶ *When the blast of the terrible ones.* Of the fierce, mighty, invading enemies. When they sweep down all before them as a furious tempest does. ¶ Is *as a storm* against *the wall.* For 'wall' here (קִיר), Lowth proposes to read קוּר, from קָרַר, *to be cold* or *cool,* and supposes that this means a winter's storm. In this interpretation also Vitringa and Cappellus coincide. But there is no need of supposing an error in the text. The idea is, probably, that of a fierce driving storm that would prostrate walls and houses ; meaning a violent tempest, and intending to describe in a striking manner the severity of the calamities that had come upon the nation.

5. *Thou shalt bring down the noise.* The tumult ; the sound which they make in entering into battle ; or the note of triumph, and the sound of revelry. The phrase may refer either to their shout of exultation over their vanquished foes; or to the usual sound of revelry ; or to the hum of business in a vast city. ¶ *Of strangers.* Of foreigners (see Note on ver. 2). ¶ *As the heat in a dry place.* The parallelism here requires that we should suppose the phrase ' with the shadow of a cloud ' to be supplied in this hemistich, as it is obscurely ex-

of the terrible ones shall be brought low.

6 And in this mountain *a* shall the LORD of hosts make unto all people a feast *b* of fat things, a feast of wines on the lees, of fat things full of marrow, of *c* wines on the lees well refined.

c Cant.5.1.

pressed in our translation by the word ' even,' and it would then read thus :

As the heat in a dry place [by the shadow of a cloud],
The noise of the strangers shalt thou humble;
As the heat by the shadow of a cloud,
The exultation of the formidable ones shalt thou bring low.

The idea thus is plain. Heat pours down intensely on the earth, and if unabated would wither up every green thing, and dry up every stream and fountain. But a cloud intervenes, and checks the burning rays of the sun. So the wrath of the 'terrible ones,' the anger of the Babylonians, raged against the Jews. But the mercy of God interposed. It was like the intervening of a cloud to shut out the burning rays of the sun. It stayed the fury of their wrath, *and rendered them impotent to do injury, just as the intense burning rays of the sun are completely checked by an interposing cloud.* ¶ *The branch of the terrible ones.* This is a very unhappy translation. The word זָמִיר (*zâmir*) is indeed used to denote a branch, or bough, as derived from זָמַר, *to prune a vine;* but it also has the sense of *a song;* a song of praise, or a song of exultation, from a second signification of זָמַר, *to sing; perhaps* from the song with which the work of the vineyard was usually accompanied. See the verb used in this sense in Judg. v. 3 ; Ps. ix. 12 ; xxx. 5; xlvii. 7; and the word which occurs here (*zâmir*) used in the sense of *a song* in Ps. cxix. 54; 2 Sam. xxiii. 1; Job xxxv. 10. Here it is undoubtedly used in the sense of *a song,* meaning either a shout of victory or of revelry; and the idea of the prophet is, that this would be brought low by the destruction of Babylon, and by the return of the captive Jews to their own land.

6. *And in this mountain.* In mount

7 And he will ¹destroy in this mountain the face of the covering cast² over all people, and the vail that ᵃ is spread over all nations.

1 _swallow up._　　　2 _covered._　　　ᵃ 2 Cor.3.16,18.

Zion, _i.e.,_ in Jerusalem. The following verses undoubtedly refer to the times of the Messiah. Several of the expressions used here are quoted in the New Testament, showing that the reference is to the Messiah, and to the fact that his kingdom would commence in Jerusalem, and then extend to all people. ¶ _Shall the_ LORD _of hosts._ (See Note on ch. i. 9.) ¶ _Make unto all people._ Provide for all people. He shall adapt the provisions of salvation not only to the Jews, but to men everywhere. This is one of the truths on which Isaiah loved to dwell, and which in fact constitutes one of the peculiarities of his prophecy. It is one of the chief glories of the gospel, that it is _unto all people._ See Isa. lvii. 7; Dan. v. 19; vii. 14; comp. Luke ii. 10: ' I bring you good tidings of great joy, which shall be _unto all people._' ¶ _A feast._ A feast, or entertainment, was usually observed, as it is now, on occasion of a great victory, or any other signal success. It is, therefore, emblematic of an occasion of joy. Here it is used in the twofold sense of an occasion of joy, and of an abundance of provisions for the necessities of those who should be entertained. This feast was to be prepared on mount Zion—in the provision which would be made in Jerusalem by the Messiah for the spiritual wants of the whole world. The arrangements for salvation are often represented under the image of an ample and rich entertainment (see Luke xiv. 16; Rev. xix. 19; Mat. xiii. 11). ¶ _Of fat things._ Of rich delicacies. Fat things and marrow are often used as synonymous with a sumptuous entertainment, and are made emblematic of the abundant provisions of Divine mercy (see Isa. lv. 2; Ps. lxiii. 5; xxxvi. 8: ' I shall be satisfied with the fatness of thy house.') ¶ _A feast of wines on the lees._ The word which is here used (שְׁמָרִים) is derived from שָׁמַר, _to keep, preserve, retain,_ and is applied usually to the _lees_ or _dregs_ of wine, because they _retain_ the strength and colour of the wine which is left to stand on them. It is also in this place applied to _wine_ which has been kept on the lees, and is therefore synonymous with _old wine;_ or wine of a rich colour and flavour. This fact, that the colour and strength of wine are retained by its being suffered to remain without being poured from one vessel into another, is more fully expressed in Jer. xlviii. 11 :

Moab hath been at ease from his youth,
And he hath settled on his lees,
And hath not been emptied from vessel to vessel,
Neither hath he gone into captivity;
Therefore his taste remaineth in him,
And his scent is not changed.

Comp. Zeph. i. 12. It is well known that wines, unless retained for a considerable time on the lees, lose their flavour and strength, and are much less valuable (comp. Notes on John ii. 10, 11). ¶ _Of fat things full of marrow._ Marrow is also an emblem of richness, or the delicacy of the entertainment (Ps. lxiii. 5). ¶ _Of wines on the lees well refined._ The word rendered ' well refined ' (מְזֻקָּקִים) is usually applied to the purifying of metals in a furnace (1 Chron. xxviii. 18; xxix. 4; Job xxviii. 1). When applied to wine, it denotes that which has been suffered to remain on the lees until it was entirely refined and purified by fermentation, and had become perfectly clear.

7. _And he will destroy._ Heb. ' He will swallow up,' that is, he will abolish, remove, or take away. ¶ _In this mountain the face of the covering._ In mount Zion, or in Jerusalem. This would be done in Jerusalem, or on the mountains of which Jerusalem was a part, where the great transactions of the plan of redemption would be accomplished. The word ' face ' here is used as it is frequently among the Hebrews, where the face of a thing denotes its aspect, or appearance, and then the thing itself. Thus ' the face of God ' is put for God himself; the ' face of the earth ' for the earth itself; and the ' face of the vail ' means the vail itself, or the appearance of the vail. To cover the head or the face was a common mode of expressing _grief_ (see 2 Sam. xv. 30; xix. 5; Es.

8 He will ^aswallow up death in victory ; and the Lord God will wipe ^baway tears from off all faces ;

^a Hos.13.14; 1Cor.15.54.

and the rebuke of his people shall be taken away ^cfrom off all the earth : for the Lord hath spoken *it*.

^b Rev.21.4.　　　^c Mal.3.17,18.

vi. 12). It is probable that the expression here is taken from this custom, and the vail over the nations here is to be understood as expressive of the ignorance, superstition, crime, and wretchedness that covered the earth.

8. *He will swallow up.* This image is probably taken from a whirlpool or mælstrom in the ocean that absorbs all that comes near it. It is, therefore, equivalent to saying he will destroy or remove (ver. 7). In this place it means that he will abolish death ; that is, he will cause it to cease from its ravages and triumphs. This passage is quoted by Paul in his argument respecting the resurrection of the dead (1 Cor. xv. 54). He does not, however, quote directly from the Hebrew, or from the LXX., but gives the substance of the passage. His quoting it is sufficient proof that it refers to the resurrection, and that its primary design is to set forth the achievements of the gospel—achievements that will be fully realized only when death shall cease its dominion, and when its reign shall be for ever at an end. ¶ *Death.* Vitringa supposes that by ' death ' here is meant the wars and calamities with which the nation had been visited, and which would cease under the Messiah. In this interpretation Rosenmüller concurs. It is possible that the word may have this meaning in some instances ; and it is possible that the calamities of the Jews may have *suggested* this to the prophet, but the primary sense of the word here, I think, is death in its proper signification, and the reference is to the triumphs of God through the Messiah in completely abolishing its reign, and introducing eternal life. This was designed, doubtless, to comfort the hearts of the Jews, by presenting in a single graphic description the gospel as adapted to overcome *all* evils, and even to remove the greatest calamity under which the race groans — death. ¶ *In victory.* Heb. חֵצַנָל. Paul, in 1 Cor. xv. 54, has translated this, Εἰς νῖκος—' Unto victory.' The word νῖκος (victory) is often

the translation of the word (see 2 Kings ii. 26 ; Job xxxvi. 7 ; Lam. iii. 18 ; Amos i. 2 ; viii. 7) ; though here the LXX. have rendered it ' strong (or prevailing) death shall be swallowed up.' The word may be derived from the Chaldee verb חֵצַנָ, *to conquer, surpass;* and then may denote *victory.* It often, however, has the sense of permanency, duration, completness, eternity ; and may mean *for ever*, and then *entirely* or *completely.* This sense is not materially different from that of Paul, ' unto victory.' Death shall be completely, permanently, destroyed ; that is, a complete *victory'* shall be gained over it. The Syriac unites the two ideas of victory and perpetuity. ' Death shall be swallowed up *in victory for ever.'* This will take place under the reign of the Messiah, and shall be completed only in the morning of the resurrection, when the power of death over the people of God shall be completely and for ever subdued. ¶ *Will wipe away tears from off all faces.* This is quoted in Rev. xxi. 4, as applicable to the gospel. The sense is, that Jehovah would devise a plan that would be fitted to furnish perfect consolation to the afflicted ; to comfort the broken-hearted ; and that would in its final triumphs remove calamity and sorrow from men for ever. The *fulness* of this plan will be seen only in heaven. In anticipation of heaven, however, the gospel now does much to alleviate human woes, and to wipe away tears from the mourner's eyes. This passage is exquisitely beautiful. The poet Burns once said that he could never read it without being affected to tears. It may be added that nothing but the gospel will do this. No other religion can furnish such consolation ; and no other religion is, therefore, adapted to man. ¶ *And the rebuke of his people.* The reproach ; the contempt ; the opposition to them. This refers to some future period when the church shall be at peace, and when pure religion shall everywhere prevail. Hitherto the people of God have been

9 And it shall be said in that day, Lo, this *is* our God ; we have waited *a* for him, and he will save us : this *is* the LORD ; we have waited for him, we will be glad and rejoice in his salvation.

10 For in this mountain shall the hand of the LORD rest, and Moab shall be trodden [1] down under

him, even as straw [2] is trodden down for the dunghill.

11 And he shall spread forth his hands in the midst of them, as he that swimmeth spreadeth forth *his hands* to swim : and he shall bring down their pride together with the spoils of their hands.

a Tit.2.13.   1 *threshed.*   2 or, *threshed in Madmenah.*

scorned and persecuted, but the time will come when persecution shall cease, the true religion shall everywhere prevail, the church shall have rest, and its triumphs shall spread everywhere on the earth.

9. *And it shall be said in that day.* By the people of God. This shall be the language of exultation and joy which they shall use. ¶ *Lo, this is our God.* This is the language of those who now see and hail their Deliverer. It implies that *such* deliverance, and *such* mercy could be bestowed only by God, and that the fact that such mercies had been bestowed was proof that he was *their* God. ¶ *We have waited for him.* Amidst many trials, persecutions, and calamities, we have looked for the coming of our God to deliver us, and we will rejoice in the salvation that he brings. ¶ *This* is the LORD. This is JEHOVAH. It is JEHOVAH that has brought this deliverance. None but he could do it. The plan of redeeming mercy comes from him, and to him is to be traced all the benefits which it confers on man.

10. *For in this mountain.* In mount Zion. ¶ *Shall the hand of the LORD rest.* The *hand* in the Scriptures is often used as the symbol of protection and defence. By the expression that the hand of JEHOVAH should REST on mount Zion, is meant probably that he would be its defender; his protection would not be withdrawn, but would be *permanent* there. For an illustration of the phrase, see a similar use of the word *hand* as denoting protection, in Ezra vii. 6, 28; viii. 18, 22, 31; Neh. ii. 8. ¶ *And Moab.* (For an account of Moab, see Notes on ch. xv., xvi.) Moab here seems to be used in a general sense to denote the enemies of God, and the declaration that it would be

trodden down seems designed to indicate that the foes of God and his people would all be destroyed (comp. Notes on ch. xxxiv.) ¶ *Under him.* The Chaldee renders this, ' In his own place.' The phrase has the sense of ' in his place,' in Ex. xvi. 29; 2 Sam. ii. 23. Here it may mean that Moab, or the enemies of God, would be trodden down and destroyed in their own land. ¶ *As straw is trodden down for the dunghill.* As straw is suffered to lie in the yard where cattle lie, to be trodden down by them for the purpose of making manure. Lowth renders this, ' As the straw is threshed under the wheels of the car.'

The LXX. render it in the same way. Lowth supposes that there has been an error in transcribing the Hebrew text, and that the former reading was מרכבה instead of מדמנה. But there is not the slightest evidence from the MSS. that any such mistake has occurred. Nor is it necessary to suppose it. The image is one that is not of unfrequent occurrence in the Scriptures, to denote the complete and disgraceful prostration of an enemy (see Ps. lxxxiii. 10; 2 Kings ix. 37; Jer. viii. 2; ix. 22; xvi. 4; xxv. 33).

11. *And he shall spread forth his hands.* The sense is, that JEHOVAH would stretch out his hands everywhere, prostrating his enemies, and the enemies of his people. Lowth, however, applies this to Moab, and supposes that it is designed to represent the action of one who is in danger of sinking, and who, in swimming, stretches out his hands to sustain himself. In order to this, he supposes that there should be a slight alteration of a single letter in the Hebrew. His main reason for suggesting this change is, that he cannot conceive how the act of the stretch-

12 And the fortress of the high fort of thy walls shall he bring down, lay low, *and* bring to the ground, *even* to the dust.

CHAPTER XXVI.

ANALYSIS.

FOR the general scope and design of this chapter, see the remarks at the commencement of ch. xxiv. and xxv. It is a song of praise supposed to be sung by the Jews on their return to their own land, and in the re-establishment of the government of God with the ordinances of worship on Mount Zion. It was usual, as has been already remarked, to celebrate any great event with a song of praise, and the prophet supposes that the recovered Jews would thus be disposed to celebrate the goodness of JEHOVAH in again restoring them to their own land, and to the privileges of their own temple service. There are some indications that this was designed to be sung with a chorus, and with alternate responses, as many of the Psalms were. The ode opens with a view of Jerusalem as a strong city, in which they might find protection under the guardianship of God (1). Then there is a response, or a call, that the gates of the strong city should be open to receive the return-

ing nation (2). This is followed by a declaration of the safety of trusting in JEHOVAH, and a call on all to confide in him (3, 4). The reason of this is stated (5–7), that JEHOVAH humbled the proud, and guarded the ways of the just. The confidence of the Jews in JEHOVAH is next described (8, 9); and this is followed by a declaration (10, 11) that the wicked would not recognize the hand of God; and by an assertion that all their deliverance had been wrought by God (12). This is succeeded by an acknowledgment that they had submitted to other lords than JEHOVAH; but that now they would submit to him alone (13, 14). The declaration succeeds that God had enlarged their nation (15); and this is followed by a description of their calamities, and their abortive efforts to save themselves (16–18). Many had died in their captivity, yet there is now the assurance that they should live again (19); and a general call on the people of God to enter into their chambers, and hide themselves there until the indignation should be overpast (20), with the assurance that JEHOVAH would come forth to punish the oppressors for their iniquity (21). With this assurance the poem closes.

I N that day shall this song be sung in the land of Judah ; We

out of the hands of a swimmer can be any illustration of the action of God in extending his hands over Moab to destroy it. It must be admitted that the figure is one that is very unusual. Indeed it does not anywhere else occur. But it is the obvious meaning of the Hebrew text ; it is so understood in the Vulgate, the Chaldee, the Syriac, and the figure is one that is not unintelligible. It is that of a swimmer who extends his hands and arms as far as possible, and who by force removes all that is in his way in passing through the water. So JEHOVAH would extend his hands over all Moab. He would not confine the desolation to any one place, but it would be complete and entire. He would subject all to himself, as easily as a swimmer makes his way through the waters. ¶ *With the spoils of their hands.* The word here rendered 'spoils' (אַרְבֹּת), Lowth renders, ' The sudden gripe.' The Chaldee renders it substantially in the same manner, 'With the laying on of his hands,' *i.e.,* with all his might. Kim-

chi also understands it of the gripe of the hands or the arms. The LXX. render it, ' Upon whatsoever he lays his hands,' *i.e.,* God shall humble the pride of Moab in respect to everything on which he shall lay his hands. The word properly and usually signifies *snares, ambushes, craft;* and then, by a natural metonymy, the plunder or spoils which he had obtained by snares and ambushes—which seems to be the sense here. It would all perish with Moab, and the land would thus be completely subdued.

12. *And the fortress,* &c. Thy strong defences shall be destroyed. This is spoken of Moab (comp. Notes on ch. xv., xvi.), and is designed to be emblematic of the enemies of the people of God (comp. Notes on ch. xxxiv.) The *repetition* of the expressions ' bring down,' ' lay low,' and ' bring to the ground,' is designed to make the sentence emphatic, and to indicate that it would certainly be accomplished.

CHAPTER XXVI.

1. *In that day shall this song be*

have a strong *a* city ; salvation will God appoint *for* walls *b* and bulwarks.

2 Open *c* ye the gates, that the

a Ps. 31.21.   *b* ch 60.18.   c Ps.118.19.
1 *truths.*   2 *peace, ᵠpeace.*   d Ph.4.7.

sung. By the people of God, on their restoration to their own land. ¶ *We have a strong city.* Jerusalem. This does not mean that it was then strongly fortified, but that God would guard it, and that thus it would be strong. Jerusalem was easily capable of being strongly fortified (Ps. xxv. 2) ; but the idea here is, that Jehovah would be a protector, and that this would constitute its strength. ¶ *Salvation will* God *appoint* for *walls.* That is, he will himself be the defender of his people in the place of walls and bulwarks. A similar expression occurs in ch. lx. 18 (see also Jer. iii. 23, and Zech. ii. 5). ¶ *Bulwarks.* This word means properly bastions, or ramparts. The original means properly a *pomœrium,* or antemural defence ; a space without the wall of a city raised up like a small wall. The Syriac renders it, *Bar shuro,* —' Son of a wall,' meaning a small wall. It was usually a breastwork, or heap of earth thrown up around the city, that constituted an additional defence, so that if they were driven from that they could retreat within the walls.

2. *Open ye the gates.* This is probably the language of a chorus responding to the sentiment in ver. 1. The captive people are returning ; and this cry is made that the gates of the city may be thrown open, and that they may be permitted to enter without obstruction (comp. Ps. xxiv. 7, 9; cxviii. 19). ¶ *That the righteous nation which keepeth the truth.* Who, during their long captivity and intercourse with heathen nations, have not apostatized from the true religion, but have adhered firmly to the worship of the true God. This was doubtless true of the great body of the captive Jews in Babylon.

3. *Thou wilt keep* him. The following verses to ver. 11, contain moral and religious reflections, and seem designed to indicate the resignation

righteous nation which keepeth the truth[1] may enter in.

3 Thou wilt keep *him* [2] in perfect peace, *d whose* [3] mind *is* stayed *on thee :* because he trusteth in thee.

3 or, *thought,* or, *imagination.*

evinced by the ' righteous nation ' during their long afflictions. Their own feelings they are here represented as uttering in the form of *general truths* to be sources of consolation to others. ¶ *In perfect peace.* Heb. as in the Marg., ' Peace, peace ;' the repetition of the word denoting, as is usual in Hebrew, emphasis, and here evidently meaning undisturbed, perfect peace. That is, the mind that has confidence in God shall not be agitated by the trials to which it shall be subject ; by persecution, poverty, sickness, want, or bereavement. The inhabitants of Judea had been borne to a far distant land. They had been subjected to reproaches and to scorn (Ps. cxxxvii.) ; had been stripped of their property and honour ; and had been reduced to the condition of prisoners and captives. Yet their confidence in God had not been shaken. They still trusted in him ; still believed that he could and would deliver them. Their mind was, therefore, kept in entire peace. So it was with the Redeemer when he was persecuted and maligned (1 Pet. ii. 23; comp. Luke xxiii. 46). And so it has been with tens of thousands of the confessors and martyrs, and of the persecuted and afflicted people of God, who have been enabled to commit their cause to him, and amidst the storms of persecution, and even in the prison and at the stake, have been kept in perfect peace. ¶ Whose *mind* is *stayed* on thee. Various interpretations have been given of this passage, but our translation has probably hit upon the exact sense. The word which is rendered ' mind ' (יֵצֶר) is derived from יָצַר (*yâtzăr*) *to form, create, devise ;* and it properly denotes that which *is* formed or made (Ps. ciii. 14; Isa. xxix. 16, Heb. ii. 18). Then it denotes anything that is formed by the mind — its thoughts, imaginations, devices (Gen. viii. 21; Deut. xxxi. 21). Here it may

4 Trust *a* ye in the Lord for ever: *b* for in the Lord JEHOVAH *is* ¹ everlasting strength.

5 For he bringeth down them that dwell on high; the lofty city, he layeth it low; he layeth it low,

a Ps.62.8.　　*b* Ps.125.1.　　1 *the rock of ag s.*

even to the ground; he bringeth it *even* to the dust.

6 The foot *c* shall tread it down, *even* the feet of the poor, *and* the steps of the needy.

7 The way *d* of the just *is* upright-

c Mal.4.3.　　　*d* Ep.2.10.

---

mean the *thoughts* themselves, or the mind that forms the thoughts. Either interpretation suits the connection, and will make sense. The expression, 'is stayed on thee,' in the Hebrew does not express the idea that the mind is stayed *on God*, though that is evidently implied. The Hebrew is simply, whose mind is *stayed, supported* (סָמוּךְ); that is, evidently, supported by God. There *is* no other support but that; and the connection requires us to understand this of him.

4. *Trust ye in the Lord for ever.* The sense is, 'Let your confidence in God on no occasion fail. Let no calamity, no adversity, no persecution, no poverty, no trial of any kind, prevent your reposing entire confidence in him.' This is spoken evidently in view of the fact stated in the previous verse, that the mind that is stayed on him *shall* have perfect peace. ¶ *For in the* Lord JEHOVAH. This is one of the four places where our translators have retained the original word JEHOVAH (comp. Ex. vi. 3; Ps. lxxxiii. 18; Notes on Isa. xii. 2). The original is יְהֹוָה בְּיָהּ (BeJah Jehovah); the first word, יָהּ (Jah), (comp. Ps. lxviii. 4), being merely an abridged form of Jehovah. The same form occurs in ch. xii. 2. The *union* of these two forms seems designed to express, in the highest sense possible, the majesty, glory, and holiness of God; to excite the highest possible reverence where language fails of completely conveying the idea. ¶ *Is everlasting strength.* Heb. as in the Marg., 'The rock of ages;' a more poetic and beautiful expression than in our translation. The idea is, that God is firm and unchangeable like an eternal rock; and that in him we may find protection and defence for everlasting ages (see Deut. xxxii. 4, *et al.*; 1 Sam. ii. 2; 2 Sam. xxii. 32, 47; xxiii. 3;

Ps. xviii. 31; xix. 14; xxviii. 1; xlii. 9; lxii. 2, 6, 7, &c., where God is called 'a rock').

5. *The lofty city, he layeth it low.* The city of Babylon (see Note on ch. xxv. 12; comp. Notes on ch. xiii., xiv.)

6. *The foot shall tread it down,* even *the feet of the poor.* That is, evidently, those who had been despised by them, and who had been overcome and oppressed by them. The obvious reference here is to the Jews who had been captives there. The idea is not necessarily that the 'poor' referred to here would be among the conquerors, but that *when* the Babylonians should be overcome, and their city destroyed, those who were then oppressed should be in circumstances of comparative prosperity. No doubt the Jews, who in subsequent times travelled to the site of Babylon for purposes of traffic, would trample indignantly on the remains of the city where their fathers were captives for seventy years, and would exult in the idea that their own once down-trodden city Jerusalem was in a condition of comparative prosperity. That there were many Jews in Babylon after that city began to decline from its haughtiness and grandeur, we learn expressly from both Philo and Josephus. Thus Philo (*De Legatione ad Caium*, p. 792) says, that 'it is known that Babylon and many other satraps were possessed by the Jews, not only by rumour, but by experience.' So Josephus (*Ant.* xv. 2.) says, that there were in the time of Hyrcanus many Jews at Babylon.

7. *The way of the just is uprightness.* The Hebrew is literally, 'The way *to* the just is uprightness;' the word 'way' probably refers to God's way, or his dealings with the righteous. The sentiment is, that his dealings with them are just; that though they are afflicted and oppressed, yet that

ness: *a* thou, most upright, dost weigh the path of the just.

8 Yea, in the way of thy *b* judgments, O LORD, have we waited for thee; the desire *c* of our soul *is* to thy name, and to the remembrance of thee.

a Ps.37.23.   *b* Ps.65.6.   *c* Is.63.1,6.

9 With my soul have I desired thee in the night; *d* yea, with my spirit within me will I seek thee early; for when *e* thy judgments are in the earth, the inhabitants of the world will learn righteousness.

d Ca.3.1.   *e* Ps.58.11.

---

his ways are right, and they will yet perceive it. This is language supposed to be used by the captive Jews after they had seen the proud city of Babylon taken, and after God had come forth to restore them to their own land. The word 'uprightness' in the original is in the plural number, but is often used in the sense of *straightness* (Prov. xxiii. 31; Cant. vii. 10); of sincerity, or uprightness (Cant. i. 4); or of righteousness as a judge (Ps. ix. 9; lviii. 2; xcix. 4). ¶ *Thou most upright.* Evidently an address to God, as being most just, and as having now evinced his uprightness in the deliverance of his people. The same epithet is applied to him in Deut. xxxii. 4; Ps. xxv. 8; xcii. 16. ¶ *Dost weigh the path of the just.* The word here used (פָּלַס) may mean to weigh as in a balance (Ps. lviii. 3); but it may also mean, and does usually, to make straight or smooth; to beat a path; to make level (Ps. lxxviii. 50; Prov. iv. 26; v. 21). Here it probably means, that God had made the way smooth, or exactly level. He had removed all obstacles, and had conducted his people in a plain and levelled way (see Notes on ch. xl. 3, 4).

8. *Yea, in the way of thy judgments.* The word 'judgments' often refers to the statutes or laws of God. But it may also refer to the afflictions and trials with which he visits or judges men; the punishments which they endure for their sins. In which sense the word is used here it is not easy to determine. Lowth understands it of the 'laws' of JEHOVAH. So Kimchi, who says that the sense is, that during their captivity and trials, they had not remitted anything of their love and piety towards God. I am inclined to the belief that this is the true interpretation, because in the corresponding member of the parallelism they are

represented as saying that the desire of their soul was to God, and to the remembrance of him, implying that they sought by an observance of his laws to please him, and to secure his favour. ¶ *The desire of our soul is to thy name.* The word 'name' is here used, as it is often, to denote God himself. They desired that he would come and deliver them; they earnestly wished that he would manifest himself to them as their friend. ¶ *And to the remembrance of thee.* The word 'remembrance' (זֵכֶר) is often equivalent to *name, appellation,* or that by which any one is remembered, or known. Thus Ex. iii. 15:

This is my name for ever;
And this is my memorial זִכְרִי unto all generations.

So Ps. xxx. 4:

Sing unto JEHOVAH, O ye saints of his;
And give thanks at the remembrance of his holiness;

that is, at his holy memorial (Marg.) or name. In the place before us it seems to be used in the sense of *name* or *appellation;* that is, that by which God would be remembered or known.

9. *With my soul—in the night.* By desiring God in the night, and by seeking him early, is meant that the desire to seek him was unremitted and constant. The prophet speaks of the pious Jews who were in captivity in Babylon; and says that it was the object of their unremitted anxiety to please God, and to do his will. ¶ *For when thy judgments are in the earth.* This is given as a reason for what had just been said, that in their calamity they had sought God without ceasing. The reason is, that the punishments which he inflicted were intended to lead men to learn righteousness. The sentiment is expressed in a general form, though there is no doubt that the immediate

10 Let ^a favour be shewed to the
wicked, *yet* will he not learn righteousness : in ^b the land of uprightness will he deal unjustly, and will
not behold the majesty ^c of the
Lord.

_a Ec.8.11; Re.2.21. _b Ec.3.16. _c ch.2.10. _d Je.5.3.

reference is to the calamities which the
Jews had suffered in their removal to
Babylon as a punishment for their sins.
¶ *Learn righteousness.* The design is
to warn, to restrain, and to reform
them. The immediate reference here
was undoubtedly to the Jews, in whom
this effect was seen in a remarkable
manner in their captivity in Babylon.
But it is also true of other nations ;
and though the effect of calamity is
not always to turn a people to God, or
to make them permanently righteous,
yet it restrains them, and leads them
at least to an external reformation. It
is also true in regard to nations as well
as individuals, that they make a more
decided advance in virtue and piety in
days of affliction than in the time of
great external prosperity (comp. Deut.
vi. 11, 12).

10. *Let favour be showed to the wicked.* This is designed as an illustration
of the sentiment in the previous verse
—that judgments were needful in order
that wicked men might be brought to
the ways of righteousness. The truth
is general, that though wicked men
are favoured with success in their enterprises, yet the effect will not be to
lead them to the ways of virtue and
religion. How often is this illustrated
in the conduct of wicked men ! How
often do they show, when rolling in
wealth, or when surrounded with the
comforts of the domestic circle, that
they feel no need of the friendship of
God, and that their heart has no response of gratitude to make for all his
mercies ! Hence the necessity, according to the language of the song before
us, that God should take away their
property, remove their friends, or destroy their health, in order that they
may be brought to honour him. To do
this, is benevolence in God ; for whatever is needful to bring the sinner to
the love of God and to the ways of
virtue, is kindness to his soul. ¶ *In*

11 Lord, *when* thy hand is lifted
up, they ^d will not see · but they
shall ^e see, and be ashamed for
their envy ¹ at the people ; yea, the
fire ^f of thine enemies shall devour
them.

_e Re.1.7.   ¹ or, *toward thy.*   _f Da.3.22,25.

the land of uprightness. Even when
others are just and pious around him ;
when this is so much the general characteristic that it may be called ' the
land of integrity,' yet he will pursue
his way of iniquity, though in it he may
be solitary. Such is his love of sin,
that neither the favour of God nor the
general piety around him—neither the
mercy of his Maker nor the influence
of holy examples, will lead him in the
way of piety and truth. ¶ *Will not
behold the majesty of the* Lord. Will
not see that which makes the Lord
glorious in his dealings with men, so
as to love and adore him. He is blind,
and sees no evidence of loveliness in
the character of God.

11. Lord, when *thy hand is lifted
up.* This is an explanation of the sentiment expressed in the former verse.
The lifting up of the hand here refers,
doubtless, to the manifestations of the
majesty and goodness of the Lord.
¶ *They will not see.* They are blind
to all the exhibitions of power, mercy,
and goodness. ¶ But *they shall see.*
They shall yet be brought to recognize
thy hand. They shall see thy favour
towards thy children, and thy judgment on thy foes. The Divine dealings
will be such that they shall be constrained to recognize him, and to
acknowledge his existence and perfections. ¶ *And be ashamed.* Be confounded because they did not sooner
recognize the Divine goodness. ¶ *For*
their *envy at thy people.* The word
' their ' is not in the Hebrew, and the
sense is, that they shall see the zeal of
Jehovah in behalf of his people, and
shall be ashamed that they did not
sooner recognize his hand. The word
rendered 'envy' (קִנְאָה) may mean envy
(Eccl. iv. 4 ; ix. 6), but it more properly
and frequently means *zeal, ardour*
(2 Kings x. 16 ; Isa. ix. 6). ¶ *Yea, the
fire of thine enemies shall devour them.*
Or rather, ' Yea, the fire in regard to

12 LORD, thou wilt ordain peace for *a* us : for thou also hast wrought all our works ¹ in us.

13 O LORD our God, *other* *b* lords beside thee have had dominion over us : *but* *c* by thee only will we make mention of thy name.

a ver.3.   1 or, *for*.

14 *They are* dead, they shall not live ; *they are* deceased, they shall not rise : therefore hast thou visited and destroyed them, and made all their memory to perish.

15 Thou hast increased the nation, O LORD, thou hast increased

b 2 Ch.28.5,6; Ro.6.16 18.   *c* Ps.71.15,16.

thy enemies shall devour them.' The sense is, that when his people were delivered, his foes would be destroyed ; his zeal for his people would also be connected with indignation against his foes. The deliverance of his people from Babylon, and the commencement of the downfall of that city, were simultaneous, and the cause was the same.

12. *Thou wilt ordain peace.* The word 'peace' here seems to stand opposed to the evils of various kinds which they had experienced in the captivity at Babylon ; and to refer not only to peace, but also to prosperity, and to the continued Divine favour. ¶ *For thou hast wrought all our works in us.* Or rather, '*for* us' (לָנוּ). It is owing to thy hand that we are saved.

13. Other *lords beside thee have had dominion.* The allusion here is to the kings of Babylon who had subdued and oppressed them, and who in their long captivity had held them in subjection to their laws. ¶ But *by thee only will we make mention of thy name.* This may be better rendered, '*but* only thee, thy name will we henceforward commemorate.' The words 'by thee,' and 'thy name,' are put in apposition, and denote the same thing. The word 'make mention' (נַזְכִּיר) means literally to cause to be remembered ; to commemorate ; to celebrate. The idea is, that during their long captivity they had been subject to the dominion of other lords than JEHOVAH ; but now that they were restored to their own land, they would acknowledge only JEHOVAH as their Lord, and would henceforward celebrate only his name.

14. They are *dead.* That is, the kings and tyrants to whom reference is made in ver. 13. The principal enemies of the Jews, who had oppressed them, were slain when Babylon was

taken by Cyrus (see Notes on ch. xiii., xiv.) ¶ *They shall not live.* They shall not again live, and be permitted to harass and enslave us. ¶ They are *deceased.* Heb. רְפָאִים—a name given to the *shades* or *manes* of the dead, from an idea that they were weak and powerless (see Notes on ch. xiv. 9, 10 ; comp. Ps. lxxxviii. 11 ; Prov. ii. 18 ; ix. 18 ; xxi. 16). The sense here is, that they had died and gone to the land of shades, and were now unable any more to reach or injure the people of God. ¶ *Therefore.* Or rather, *for ;* the word לָכֵן being used evidently in the sense of *because that*, as in Gen. xxxviii. 26 ; Num. xi. 31 ; xiv. 13 ; Ps. xlii. 7 ; xlv. 3. The declaration that follows is given as the reason why they were dead, and incapable of again injuring or annoying them. ¶ *Hast thou visited*, &c. (see Note on ch. xxiv. 22.) The word 'visit' here is used in the sense of *to punish*. ¶ *And made all their memory to perish.* Hast blotted out their name ; hast caused their celebrity to cease.

15. *Thou hast increased the nation.* That is, the Jewish nation (see Note on ch. ix. 3). The nation was not only enlarged by its regular increase of population, but many converts attended them on their return from Babylon, and probably many came in from surrounding nations on the rebuilding of their capital. ¶ *Thou hadst removed* it *far,* &c. Or rather, thou hast extended far all the borders of the land. The word rendered 'removed' (רָחַק) means usually to put far away, and here it may mean to put far away the borders or boundaries of the nation ; that is, to extend them far. The word 'unto' is not in the original ; and the phrase rendered 'ends of the earth,' may mean the borders, or boundaries of the land. The parallelism requires

the nation: thou art glorified: thou hadst removed *it* far *unto* all the ends of the earth.

16 LORD, in trouble *a* have they visited thee, they poured out a prayer[1] *when* thy chastening *was* upon them.

17 Like as a woman with child, *that* draweth near the time of her delivery, is in pain, *and* crieth out

a Hos.5.15.   1 *secret speech.*

in her pangs; so have we been in thy sight, O LORD.

18 We have been with child, we have been in pain, we have as it were brought forth wind; we have not wrought any deliverance in the earth, neither have the inhabitants of the world fallen.

19 Thy dead *men* shall live, *together with* my dead body shall they arise. Awake and sing, ye

---

this construction, and it is indeed the obvious one, and has been adopted by Lowth and Noyes.

16. *Poured out a prayer.* Marg. 'Secret speech.' The Hebrew word לַחַשׁ means properly a whispering, muttering; and then a sighing, a calling for help. This is the sense here. In their calamity they sighed, and called on God for help.

17. *Like as a woman with child,* &c. This verse is designed to state their griefs and sorrows during the time of their oppression in Babylon. The comparison here used is one that is very frequent in the sacred writings to represent any great suffering (see Ps. xlviii. 6; Jer. vi. 24; xiii. 21; xxii. 23; xlix. 24; l. 43; Mic. iv. 9, 10).

18. *We have been,* &c. This refers to sorrows and calamities which they had experienced in former times, when they had made great efforts for deliverance, and when those efforts had proved abortive. Perhaps it refers to the efforts of this kind which they had made during their painful captivity of seventy years. There is no direct proof, indeed, that during that time they attempted to revolt, or that they organized themselves for resistance to the Babylonish power; but there can be no doubt that they earnestly desired deliverance, and that their condition was one of extreme pain and anguish —a condition that is strikingly represented here by the pains of childbirth. Nay, it is not improbable that during that long period there may have been abortive efforts made at deliverance, and that here they refer to those efforts as having accomplished nothing. ¶ *We have as it were brought forth wind.* Our efforts have availed nothing. Mi-

chaelis, as quoted by Lowth, explains this figure in the following manner: 'Rariorem morbum describi, empneumatosin, aut ventosam molam dictum; quo quæ laborant diu et sibi, et peritis medicis gravidæ videntur, tandemque post omnes veræ gravitatis molestias et labores ventum ex utero emittant; quem morbum passim describunt medici.'—(*Syntagma Comment.* vol. ii. p. 165.) Grotius thinks that the reference is to birds, ' Quæ edunt ova subventanea,' and refers to Pliny x. 58. But the correct reference is, doubtless, that which is mentioned by Michaelis. ¶ *Neither have the inhabitants of the world fallen.* We had no power to subdue them; and notwithstanding all our exertions their dominion was unbroken. This refers to the Babylonians who had dominion over the captive Jews.

19. *Thy dead* men *shall live.* Very various interpretations have been given of this verse, which may be seen at length by comparing Vitringa, Rosenmüller, Gesenius, and Poole's *Synopsis.* In ver. 14, the chorus is represented as saying of the dead men and tyrants of Babylon that had oppressed the captive Jews, that they should not rise, and should no more oppress the people of God. In contradistinction from this fate of their enemies, the choir is here introduced as addressing JEHOVAH (comp. ver. 16), and saying ' THY dead shall live;' that is, thy people shall live again; shall be restored to vigour, and strength, and enjoyment. They had been dead; that is, *civilly* dead in Babylon; they were cut off from their privileges, torn away from their homes, made captives in a foreign land. Their king had been dethroned; their temple

that *a* dwell in dust; for thy dew *is as* the dew of herbs, and the earth shall cast out the dead.

a Dan.12.2.

demolished; their princes, priests, and people made captive; their name blotted from the list of nations; and to all intents and purposes, as a people, they were *deceased.* This figure is one that is common, by which the loss of privileges and enjoyments, and especially of civil rights, is represented as *death.* So we speak now of a man's being dead in law; dead to his country; spiritually dead; dead in sins. I do not understand this, therefore, as referring primarily to the doctrine of the resurrection of the dead; but to the captives in Babylon, who were civilly dead, and cut off by their oppressors from their rights and enjoyments as a nation. ¶ *Shall live.* Shall be restored to their country, and be reinstated in all their rights and immunities as a people among the nations of the earth. This restoration shall be as striking as would be the resurrection of the dead from their graves. Though, therefore, this does not refer primarily to the resurrection of the dead, yet the illustration is drawn from that doctrine, and implies that that doctrine was one with which they were familiar. An image which is employed for the sake of illustration must be one that is familiar to the mind, and the reference here to this doctrine is a demonstration that the doctrine of the resurrection was well known. ¶ *Together with my dead body shall they arise.* The words 'together with' are not in the original. The words rendered 'my dead body' (נְבֵלָתִי) literally means, 'my dead body,' and may be applied to a man, or to a beast (Lev. v. 2; vii. 24). It is also applied to the dead in general: to the deceased; to carcasses, or dead bodies (see Lev. xi. 11; Ps. lxxix. 2; Jer. vii. 33; ix. 22; xvi. 18; xxvi. 23; xxxiv. 20). It may, therefore, be rendered, 'My deceased, my dead;' and will thus be parallel with the phrase 'thy dead men,' and is used with reference to the same species of resurrection. It is not the language of the prophet Isaiah, as if he referred to *his* own body when it should be

dead, but it is the language of the *choir* that sings and speaks in the name of the Jewish people. *That people* is thus introduced as saying *my* dead, that is, *our* dead, shall rise. Not only in the address to JEHOVAH is this sentiment uttered when it is said '*thy* dead shall rise,' but when the attention is turned to themselves as a people, they say '*our* dead shall rise;' those that appertain to our nation shall rise from the dust, and be restored to their own privileges and land. ¶ *Awake and sing.* In view of the cheering and consolatory fact just stated that the dead shall rise, the chorus calls on the people to awake and rejoice. This is an address made directly to the dejected and oppressed people, as if the choir were with them. ¶ *Ye that dwell in dust.* To sit in dust, or to dwell in the dust, is emblematic of a state of dejection, want, oppression, or poverty (Ps. xliv. 25; cxix. 25; Isa. xxv. 12; xxvi. 5; xlvii. 1). Here it is supposed to be addressed to the captives in Babylon, as oppressed, enslaved, dejected. The *language* is derived from the doctrine of the resurrection of the body, and proves that that doctrine was understood and believed; the *sense* is, that those who were thus dejected and humbled should be restored to their former elevated privileges. ¶ *For thy dew.* This is evidently an address to JEHOVAH. *His* dew is that which he sends down from heaven, and which is under his direction and control. Dew is the emblem of that which refreshes and vivifies. In countries where it rains but seldom, as it does in the East, the copious dews at night supply in some sense the want of rain. Thence *dew* is used in Scripture as an emblem of the graces and influences of the Spirit of God by which his people are cheered and comforted, as the parched earth and the withered herbs are refreshed by the copious dews at night. Thus in Hos. xiv. 5:

I will be as the dew unto Israel;
He shall grow as the lily,
And cast forth his roots as Lebanon.

The prophet here speaks of the captivity in Babylon. Their state is repre-

20 Come, my people, enter thou into thy chambers, and shut thy doors about thee : hide thyself as it were for a little moment, until the indignation be overpast.

21 For, behold, the LORD cometh

out *a* of his place to punish the inhabitants of the earth for their iniquity : the earth also shall disclose her 1 blood, and shall no more cover her slain.

a Jude 14,15.   1 *bloods.*

---

sented as a state of death—illustrated by the parched earth, and the decayed and withered herbs. But his grace and favour would visit them, and they would be revived. ¶ As *the dew of herbs.* As the dew that falls on herbs. This phrase has, however, been rendered very variously. The Vulgate renders it, ' Thy dew is as the dew of light.' The LXX. ' Thy dew shall be healing (*ἴαμα*) unto them.' The Chaldee, ' Thy dew shall be the dew of light.' But the most correct and consistent translation is undoubtedly that which renders the word אורת, *herbs* or *vegetables* (comp. 2 Kings ix. 19). ¶ *And the earth shall cast out the dead.* This is language which is derived from the doctrine of the resurrection of the body ; and shows also that that doctrine was understood by the Hebrews in the time of Isaiah. The sense is, that as the earth shall cast forth its dead in the resurrection, so the people of God in Babylon should be restored to life, and to their former privileges in their own land.

20. *Come, my people.* This is an *epilogue* (Rosenmüller), in which the choir addresses the people, and entreats them to be tranquil during that convulsion by which their oppressors would be punished, and the way made for their deliverance. The image is taken from seeking a shelter when a storm rages, until its fury is spent. The address is to the captive Jews in Babylon. The tempest that would rage would be the wars and commotions by which Babylon was to be overthrown. While that storm raged, *they* were exhorted to be calm and serene. ¶ *Enter thou into thy chambers.* Into places of retirement, where the storm of indignation on your enemies shall not reach or affect you. ¶ *Hide thyself as it were,* &c. Do not mingle in the scenes of battle, lest you should partake of the general calamity. ¶ *For a little mo-*

ment. Implying that the war would not rage long. Babylon was taken in a single night (see Notes on ch. xiii., xiv.), and the call here is for the people of God to be calm while this battle should rage in which the city should be taken. ¶ *Until the indignation,* &c. Not, as Lowth supposes, the indignation of God against his people, but the storm of his indignation against their enemies the Babylonians. That would be soon 'overpast,' the city would be taken, the storms of war would cease to rage, and *then* they would be delivered, and might safely return to their own land.

21. *For, behold, the* LORD *cometh out of his place.* That is, from heaven, which is the dwelling-place or residence of God (Ps. cxv. 3 ; Ezek. iii. 12 ; Mic. i. 3). When God executes vengeance, he is represented as coming from his abode, his dwelling-place, his capitol, as a monarch goes forth to war to destroy his foes. ¶ *To punish the inhabitants of the earth.* The land of Chaldea, or of Babylon. ¶ *The earth also shall disclose her blood.* Blood, in the Scriptures, often denotes *guilt.* The sense here is, that the land of Chaldea would reveal its guilt ; that is, the punishment which God would inflict would be a revelation of the crimes of the nation. There is a resemblance here to the language which was used respecting the blood of Abel, Gen. iv. 10 : ' The voice of thy brother's blood (Heb. as here, *bloods*) crieth unto me from the ground.' ¶ *And shall no more cover her slain.* Shall no more be able to conceal its guilt in slaying the people of God. By these hopes, the Jews were to be comforted in their calamity ; and no doubt this song was penned by Isaiah long before that captivity, in order that, in the midst of their protracted and severe trials, they might be consoled with the hope of deliverance, and might know what to

CHAPTER XXVII.

ANALYSIS.

FOR the general design of this chapter, see the analysis of ch. xxiv. Many different expositions have been given of its design, and indeed almost every commentator has had his own theory, and has differed from almost every other. Some of the different views which have been taken may be seen in the Notes on ver. 1, and may be examined at length in Vitringa. I regard the most simple and obvious interpretation as the correct one; and that is, that it is a continuation of the vision commenced in ch. xxiv., and referring to the same great event—the captivity at Babylon and the deliverance from that captivity. This subject has been pursued through the 24th, the 25th, and the 26th chapters. In the 25th and the 26th chapters, the main design was to show the joy which would be evinced on their rescue from that land. The main purpose of this is to show the effect of that captivity and deliverance in purifying the Jews themselves, and in overcoming their propensity to idolatry, on account of which the captivity had been suffered to take place. The *design* of the chapter is, like that of many others in Isaiah, to comfort

them when they should be oppressed during their long and painful exile. The general plan of the chapter is—1. A statement that their great enemy, the leviathan, should be destroyed (1); and, 2. A song, in alternate responses, respecting the people of God, under the image of a vineyard yielding rich wines (2-13). In this song JEHOVAH'S protection over the vineyard is shown (3); he declares that he is not actuated by fury (4); his people are exhorted to trust in him (5); a full promise that the Jews shall yet flourish is given (6); JEHOVAH says that his judgments are mild on them (7, 8), and that the design is to purify his people (9); for their sins they should be punished (10, 11); yet that they should be restored to their own land, and worship him in the holy mount at Jerusalem (12, 13).

IN that day the LORD, with his sore, and great, and strong sword, shall punish leviathan *a* the piercing[1] serpent, even leviathan that crooked serpent; and he shall slay the dragon that *is* in the sea.

a Ps.74.14.   1 or, *crossing like a bar.*

do when the storms of war should rage around the place of their captivity, and when the proud city was to fall. They were not to mingle in the strife; were to take no part with either their foes or their deliverers; but were to be calm, gentle, peaceful, and to remember that all this was to effect their deliverance. Compare Ex. xiv. 13, 14: 'Fear ye not, stand still, and see the salvation of JEHOVAH; JEHOVAH shall fight for you, and ye shall hold your peace.'—There are times when the children of God should look calmly on the conflicts of the men of this world. They should mingle with neither party; for they should remember that JEHOVAH presides over these agitations, and that their ultimate end is to bring deliverance to his church, and to advance the interests of his kingdom on the earth. Then they should be mild, gentle, prayerful; and should look up to God to make all these agitations and strifes the means of advancing the interests of his kingdom.

CHAPTER XXVII.

1. *In that day.* In that future time when the Jews would be captive in Babylon, and when they would sigh for

deliverance (see Note on ch. xxvi. 1). This verse might have been connected with the previous chapter, as it refers to the same event, and then this chapter would have more appropriately commenced with the poem or song which begins in ver. 2. ¶ *With his sore.* Heb. הַקָּשָׁה—' Hard.' Sept. Tὴν ἁγίαν—' Holy.' The Hebrew means a sword that is hard, or well-tempered and trusty. ¶ *And great, and strong sword.* The sword is an emblem of war, and is often used among the Hebrews to denote war (see Gen. xxvii. 40; Lev. xxvi. 25). It is also an emblem of justice or punishment, as punishment then, as it is now in the Turkish dominions, was often inflicted by the sword (Deut. iii. 41, 42; Ps. vii. 12; Heb. xi. 37). Here, if it refers to the overthrow of Babylon and its tyrannical king, it means that God would punish them by the armies of the Medes, employed as his sword or instrument. Thus in Ps. xvii. 13, David prays, ' Deliver my soul from the wicked, which is thy sword' (comp. Notes on ch. x. 5, 6). ¶ *Leviathan* (לִוְיָתָן). The LXX. render this, Tὴν δράκοντα—' The dragon.' The word 'leviathan' is probably derived from לָוָה in Arabic, *to weave, to twist* (Gesenius); and literally means, *the twisted animal.* The word occurs in six places in the Old Testament, and is translated in Job iii. 8, 'mourning,' Marg. 'leviathan;' in Job xli. 1, 'leviathan'—in which chapter is an extended description of the animal; in Ps. lxxiv. 14, it is rendered 'leviathan,' and seems to be applied to Pharaoh; and in Ps. civ. 26, and in the passage before us, where it is twice also rendered 'leviathan.' Bochart (*Hieroz.* ii. 5. 16–18) has gone into an extended argument to show that by the leviathan the *crocodile* is intended; and his argument is in my view conclusive. On this subject, Bochart, Dr. Good (on Job xli.), and Robinson's Calmet, may be consulted. The crocodile is a natural inhabitant of the Nile and of other Asiatic and African rivers; is of enormous voracity and strength, as well as of fleetness in swimming; attacks mankind and all animals with prodigious impetuosity; and is furnished with a coat of mail so scaly and callous that it will resist the force of a musket ball in every part except under the belly. It is, there-

CROCODILE.

fore, an appropriate image by which to represent a fierce and cruel tyrant. The sacred writers were accustomed to describe kings and tyrants by an allusion to strong and fierce animals. Thus, in Ezek. xxix. 3–5, the dragon, or the crocodile of the Nile, represents Pharaoh; in Ezek. xxii. 2, Pharaoh is compared to a young lion, and to a whale in the seas; in Ps. lxxiv. 13, 14, Pharaoh is compared to the dragon, and to the leviathan. In Dan. vii., the four monarchs that should arise

are likened to four great beasts. In Rev. xii., Rome, the new Babylon, is compared to a great red dragon. In the place before us, I suppose that the reference is to Babylon; or to the king and tyrant that ruled there, and that had oppressed the people of God. But among commentators there has been the greatest variety of explanation. As a *specimen* of the various senses which commentators often assign to passages of Scripture, we may notice the following views which have been taken of this passage. The Chaldee Paraphrast regards the leviathans, which are twice mentioned, as referring, the first one to some king like Pharaoh, and the second to a king like Sennacherib. Rabbi Moses Haccohen supposes that the word denotes the most select or valiant of the rulers, princes, and commanders that were in the army of the enemy of the people of God. Jarchi supposes that by the first-mentioned leviathan is meant Egypt, by the second Assyria, and by the dragon which is in the sea, he thinks *Tyre* is intended. Aben Ezra supposes that by the dragon in the sea, Egypt is denoted. Kimchi supposes that this will be fulfilled only in the times of the Messiah, and that the sea monsters here mentioned are Gog and Magog—and that these denote the armies of the Greeks, the Saracens, and the inhabitants of India. Abarbanel supposes that the Saracens, the Roman empire, and the other kingdoms of Gentiles, are intended by these sea monsters. Jerome, Sanctius, and some others suppose that *Satan* is denoted by the leviathan. Brentius supposes that this was fulfilled in the day of Pentecost when Satan was overcome by the preaching of the gospel. Other Christian interpreters have supposed, that by the leviathan first mentioned *Mahomet* is intended; by the second, *heretics;* and by the dragon in the sea, *Pagan India.* Luther understood it of Assyria and Egypt; Calvin supposes that the description properly applies to the king of Egypt, but that under this image other enemies of the church are embraced, and does not doubt that *allegorically* Satan and his kingdom are intended. The more simple interpretation, however, is that which refers

2 In that day sing ye unto her,

A vineyard *a* of red wine.

a Lu.20.9,&c.

it to Babylon. This suits the connection ; accords with the previous chapters ; agrees with all that occurs in this chapter, and with the image which is here used. The crocodile, the dragon, the sea monster—extended, vast, unwieldy, voracious, and odious to the view — would be a most expressive image to denote the abhorrence with which the Jews would regard Babylon and its king. ¶ *The piercing serpent.* The term ' serpent' (נָחָשׁ) may be given to a dragon, or an extended sea monster. Comp. Job xxvi. 13. The term ' piercing,' is, in the Marg., ' Crossing like a bar.' The LXX. render it, Ὄφιν φεύγοντα—' Flying serpent. The Heb. בָּרִיחַ, rendered ' piercing,' is derived from בָּרַח, *to flee ;* and then to stretch across, or pass through, as a bar through boards (Ex. xxxvi. 33). Hence this word may mean fleeing ; extended ; a cross bar for fastening gates ; or the cross piece for binding together the boards for the tabernacle of the congregation (Ex. xxvi. 26 ; xxxvi. 31). Lowth renders it, ' The rigid serpent ;' probably with reference to the hard scales of the crocodile. The word *extended, huge, vast,* will probably best suit the connection. In Job xxvi. 13, it is rendered, ' the crooked serpent ;' referring to the constellation in the heavens by the name of the Serpent (see Notes on that place). The idea of *piercing* is not in the Hebrew word, nor is it ever used in that sense. ¶ *That crooked serpent.* This is correctly rendered ; and refers to the fact that the monster here referred to throws itself into immense volumes or folds, a description that applies to all serpents of vast size. Virgil has given a similar description of sea monsters throwing themselves into vast convolutions :

' Ecce autem gemini a Tenedo tranquilla per alta —— immensis orbibus angues.'—*Æn.* ii. 203.

And again :

' Sinuantque immensa volumine terga.'
Idem. 208.

The reference in Isaiah, I suppose, is not to *different* kings or enemies of the people of God, but to the same. It is customary in Hebrew poetry to refer to the same subject in different members of the same sentence, or in different parts of the same parallelism. ¶ *The dragon.* Referring to the same thing under a different image—to the king of Babylon. On the meaning of the word ' dragon,' see Note on ch. xiii. 22. ¶ *In the sea.* In the Euphrates; or in the marshes and pools that encompass Babylon (see Notes on ch. xi. 15; xviii. 2). The sense of the whole verse is, that God would destroy the Babylonish power that was to the Jews such an object of loathsomeness and of terror.

2. *Sing ye unto her.* That is, sing unto, or respecting the vineyard. The word rendered ' sing ' (עַנּוּ) signifies properly, *answer, respond to ;* and then, sing a responsive song, where one portion of the choir responds to another (see Ex. xv. 21). This has been well expressed here by Lowth in his translation :

' To the beloved Vineyard, sing ye a responsive song.'

It is the commencement of a song, or hymn respecting Judea, represented under the image of a vineyard, and which is probably continued to the close of the chapter. ¶ *A vineyard* (see Notes on ch. v. 1, &c.) The Hebrew phrase rendered ' a vineyard of red wine ' is the title to the song ; or the responsive song respects the ' vineyard of red wine.' ¶ *Of red wine* (חֶמֶר, *hhēmer*). Lowth proposes to read instead of this, חֶמֶד (*hhēmedh*), *pleasantness, beauty,* or *beloved.* He observes that many MSS. have this meaning, and that it is followed by the LXX. and the Chaldee. The LXX. read it, Ἀμπελὼν καλλὸς— ' Beautiful vineyard.' This would well suit the connection, and this slight error in transcribing might have easily occurred. But the authority in the MSS. for the change is not conclusive. The word which now occurs in the text denotes properly *wine,* from חָמַר, *to ferment.* The word חָמַר also has the signification *to be red* (Ps. lxxv. 9 ; Job

3 I ^a the LORD do keep it ; I will water it every moment ; lest *any* hurt it, I will keep it night and day.

4 Fury *is* not in me : who would set the briers *and* thorns against

a Ps.121 4,5.   1 or, *march against.*

me in battle ? I would ¹ go through them, I would burn them together.

5 Or let him take hold of my strength, ^b *that* he may make peace ^c with me ; *and* he shall make peace with me.

b ch.45.24.   *c* Job 22.21.

---

xvi. 16); and according to this, our translators have rendered it ' of red wine.' Bochart (*Geog. Sac.* ii. 1, 29) renders it, ' A vineyard fertile in producing wine.' The correct translation would be one that would not seem very congruous in our language, ' a vineyard of wine,' or ' a wine-vineyard.'

3. *I the* LORD *do keep it.* There is understood here or implied an introduction ; as ' JEHOVAH said ' (comp. Ps. cxxi. 35). ¶ *I will water it every moment.* That is, constantly, as a vine-dresser does his vineyard.

4. *Fury* is *not in me.* That is, I am angry with it no more. He had punished his people by removing them to a distant land. But although he had corrected them for their faults, yet he had not laid aside the affection of a Father. ¶ *Who would set.* Heb. ' Who would give me.' The LXX. render this, ' Who would place me to keep the stubble in the field ? ' Great perplexity has been felt in regard to the interpretation of this passage. Lowth translates it :

' O that I had a fence of the thorn and the brier;'

evidently showing that he was embarrassed with it, and could not make of it consistent sense. The whole sentence must refer either to the people of God, or to his enemies. If to his people, it would be an indication that they were like briers and thorns, and that if his fury should rage they would be consumed, and hence he calls upon them (ver. 5) to seize upon his strength, and to be at peace with him. If it refers to his enemies, then it expresses a *wish* that his enemies were in his possession ; or a purpose to go against them, as fire among thorns, and to consume them if they should presume to array themselves against his vineyard. This latter I take to be the true sense of the passage. The phrase ' who would set me,' or in Heb. ' who will give me,' may be ex-

pressed by *utinam*, indicating strong desire ; and may be thus paraphrased : ' I retain no anger against my people. I have indeed punished them ; but my anger has ceased. I shall now defend them. If they are attacked by foes, I will guard them. When their foes approach, *I desire, I earnestly wish*, that they may be in my possession, that I may destroy them—as the fire rages through briers and thorns.' It expresses a firm determination to defend his people and to destroy their enemies, unless (ver. 5), which he would prefer, they should repent, and be at peace with him. ¶ *The briers* and *thorns.* His enemies, and the enemies of his people (comp. Notes on ch. ix. 17; x. 17). Perhaps the phrase is here used to denote enemies, because briers and thorns are so great enemies to a vineyard by impeding growth and fertility. ¶ *I would go through them.* Or, rather, I would go against them in battle to destroy them. ¶ *I would burn them up together.* As fire devours the thorns and briers ; that is, I would completely destroy them.

5. *Or let him.* The Hebrew word rendered here ' or ' (אִם) means *unless;* and the sense is, the enemies of the Jewish people shall be completely destroyed as briers are by fire, *unless* they flee to God for a refuge. ¶ *Take hold of my strength.* That is, let the enemy take hold of me to become reconciled to me. The figure here is taken probably from the act of fleeing to take hold of the horns of the altar for refuge when one was pursued (comp. 1 Kings i. 50 ; ii. 28) ¶ That *he may make peace with me.* With me as the guardian of the vineyard. If this were done they would be safe. ¶ And *he shall make peace with me.* That is, even the enemy of me and of my vineyard *may* be permitted to make peace with me. Learn, (1.) That God is willing to be reconciled to his enemies. (2.) That that peace

6 He shall cause them that come of Jacob to take root : *a* Israel shall blossom and bud, and *b* fill the face of the world with fruit.

7 Hath he smitten him, 1 as he smote those that smote him ? *or is*

a Ps.92.13-15; Hos.14.5,6.   *b* Rom.11.12.
1 *according to the stroke of.*

he slain according to the slaughter of them that are slain by him ?

8 In measure, when 2 it shooteth forth, thou wilt debate with it : he 3 stayeth his *c* rough wind in the day of the east wind.

2 or, *thou sendest it forth.*
3 or, *when he removeth it.*   *c* ch.57.16.

---

must be obtained by seeking his protection; by submitting to him, and laying hold of his strength. (3.) That if this is not done, his enemies must be inevitably destroyed. (4.) He will defend his people, and no weapon that is formed against them shall prosper.

6. *He shall cause them that come of Jacob to take root.* This language is derived from the vine, as the shoots or cuttings of the vine take root and flourish. To take root, therefore, is an emblem denoting that the descendants of Jacob, or the people of God, would increase and prosper. ¶ *Shall blossom and bud.* An image also taken from the vine, or from fruit trees in general, and meaning that they should greatly flourish in the time succeeding their return from the captivity. ¶ *And fill the face of the world with fruit.* On the meaning of the word 'face,' see Note on ch. xxv. 7. The sense is, that the people of God would so increase and flourish that the true religion would ultimately fill the entire world. The same idea of the universal prevalence of the true religion is often advanced by this prophet, and occurs in various parts of the hymns or songs which we are now considering (see ch. xxv. 6–8). The figure which is here used, drawn from the vine, denoting prosperity by its increase and its fruit, is beautifully employed in Ps. xcii. 13, 14 :

Those that be planted in the house of Jehovah,
Shall flourish in the courts of our God.
They shall still bring forth fruit in old age ;
They shall be rich and green.

7. *Hath he smitten him, as he smote those that smote them ?* Has God punished his people in the same manner and to the same extent as he has their enemies? It is implied by this question that he had not. He had indeed punished them for their sins, but he had not destroyed them. Their enemies

he had utterly destroyed. ¶ *According to the slaughter of those that are slain by him.* Heb. 'According to the slaying of his slain.' That is, not as our translation would seem to imply, that their enemies had been slain BY them; but that they were '*their* slain,' inasmuch as they had been slain on their account, or to promote their release and return to their own land. It was not true that their enemies had been slain *by* them; but it was true that they had been *slain on their account,* or in order to secure their return to their own country.

8. *In measure,* &c. This verse in our translation is exceedingly obscure, and indeed almost unintelligible. Nor is it much more intelligible in Lowth, or in Noyes; in the Vulgate, or the Septuagint. The various senses which have been given to the verse may be seen at length in Vitringa and Rosenmüller. The idea, which I suppose to be the true one, without going into an examination of others which have been proposed, is the following, which is as near as possible a literal translation :

In moderation in sending her [the vineyard] away didst thou judge her,
Though carrying her away with a rough tempest in the time of the east wind.

The word rendered 'measure' (סַאסְּאָה) occurs nowhere else in the Scriptures. It is probably derived from סְאָה, *a measure;* usually denoting a measure of grain, containing, according to the Rabbins, a third part of an ephah, *i.e.,* about *a peck.* The word here used is probably a contraction of סְאָה סְאָה, literally, *measure by measure,* i.e., *moderately,* or in moderation. So the Rabbins generally understand it. The idea is 'small measure by small measure,' not a large measure at a time ; or, in other words, *moderately,* or in moderation. It refers, I suppose, to

9 By this therefore shall the iniquity of Jacob be purged ; *a* and this *is* all the fruit to take away his sin ; when he maketh all the stones of the altar as chalk stones that are beaten in sunder, the groves and ¹ images shall not stand up.

10 Yet the defenced city *shall*

a Heb.12.6.　　　1 or, *sun images.*

the fact that in inflicting judgment on his people, it had not been done with intolerable severity. The calamity had not been so overwhelming as entirely to cut them off, but had been tempered with mercy. ¶ *When it shooteth forth.* This expression does not convey an intelligible idea. The Hebrew בְּשַׁלְחָהּ —literally, *in sending her forth,* from שָׁלַח *to send,* or *to put forth*—refers, I suppose, to the fact that God had sent her, *i.e.,* his vineyard, his people, forth to Babylon ; he had cast them out of their own land into a distant country, but when it was done it was tempered with mercy and kindness. In this expression there is indeed a mingling of a metaphor with a literal statement, since it appears rather incongruous to speak of sending forth a *vineyard;* but such changes in expressions are not uncommon in the Hebrew poets. ¶ *Thou wilt debate with it.* Or, rather, thou hast *judged* it ; or hast punished it. The word רִיב means sometimes to debate, contend, or strive ; but it means also to take vengeance (1 Sam. xxv. 39), or to punish ; to contend with any one so as to overcome or punish him. Here it refers to the fact that God *had* had a contention with his people, and had punished them by removing them to Babylon. ¶ *He stayeth* (הָגָה). This word means in one form *to meditate,* to think, to speak ; in another, *to separate,* as dross from silver, to remove, to take away (Prov. xxv. 4, 5). Here it means that he *had* removed, or separated his people from their land as with the sweepings of a tempest. The word 'stayeth' does not express the true sense of the passage. It is better expressed in the margin, 'when he removeth it.' ¶ *His rough wind.* A tempestuous, boisterous wind, which God sends. Winds are emblematic of judgment, as they sweep away everything before them. Here the word is emblematic of the calamities which came upon Judea by which the nation was removed to

Babylon ; and the sense is, that they were removed *as in* a tempest ; they were carried away as if a violent storm had swept over the land. ¶ *In the day of the east wind.* The east wind in the climate of Judea was usually tempestuous and violent ; Job xxvii. 21 :

The east wind carrieth him away and he departeth ;
And, as a storm, hurleth them out of his place.

Jer. xviii. 17 :

I will scatter them as with an east wind before the enemy.

(Comp. Gen. xli. 6 ; Ex. x. 13 ; xiv. 21 ; Job xxxviii. 24 ; Ps. lxxviii. 26 ; Hab. i. 6). This wind was usually hot, noxious, blasting, and scorching (Taylor).

9. *By this.* This verse states the whole design of the punishment of the Jews. They were taken away from their temple, their city, and their land ; they were removed from the groves and altars of idolatry by which they had been so often led into sin ; and the design was to preserve them henceforward from relapsing into their accustomed idolatry. ¶ *The iniquity of Jacob.* The sin of the Jewish people, and particularly their tendency to idolatry, which was their easily besetting sin. ¶ *Be purged* (see Note on ch. i. 25). ¶ *And this is all the fruit.* And this is all the *object* or *design* of their captivity and removal to Babylon. ¶ *When he maketh all the stones of the altar as chalk stones.* That is, JEHOVAH shall make the stones of the altars reared in honour of idols like chalk stones ; or shall throw them down, and scatter them abroad like stones that are easily beaten to pieces. The sense is, that JEHOVAH, during their captivity in Babylon, would overthrow the places where they had worshipped idols. ¶ *The groves and images shall not stand up.* The groves consecrated to idols, and the images erected therein (see Note on ch. xvii. 8).

10. *Yet the defenced city.* Gesenius supposes that this means Jerusalem. So Calvin and Piscator understand it.

be desolate, *and* the habitation forsaken, and left like a wilderness: there shall the calf feed, and there shall he lie down and consume the branches thereof.

11 When the boughs thereof are withered, they shall be broken off: the women come *and* set them on fire ; for *a* it *is* a people of no understanding : therefore he that made

them will not have mercy on them, and he that formed them will shew them no favour.

12 And it shall come to pass in that day, *that* the Lord shall beat off from the channel of the river unto the stream of Egypt, and *b* ye shall be gathered one by one, O ye children of Israel.

a De.32.28; Ho.4.6.　　　　*b* Jn.6.37.

Others understand it of Samaria, others of Babylon (as Vitringa, Rosenmüller, and Grotius), and others of cities in general, denoting those in Judea, or in other places. To me it seems plain that Babylon is referred to. The whole description seems to require this; and especially the fact that this song is supposed to be sung *after* the return from the captivity to celebrate their deliverance. It is natural, therefore, that they should record the fact that the strong and mighty city where they had been so long in captivity, was now completely destroyed. For the meaning of the phrase 'defenced city,' see Note on ch. xxv. 2. ¶ Shall be *desolate* (see ch. xxv. 2; comp. Notes on ch. xiii.) ¶ *The habitation forsaken.* The *habitation* here referred to is Babylon. It means the habitation or dwelling-place where *we* have so long dwelt as captives (comp. Prov. iii. 33; xxi. 20; xxiv. 15). ¶ *And left like a wilderness.* See the description of Babylon in the Notes on ch. xiii. 20–22. ¶ *There shall the calf feed.* It shall become a vast desert, and be a place for beasts of the forest to range in (comp. ch. vii. 23; see Note on ch. v. 17). ¶ *And consume the branches thereof.* The branches of the trees and shrubs that shall spring up spontaneously in the vast waste where Babylon was.

11. *When the boughs thereof are withered.* This is a further description of the desolation which would come upon Babylon. The idea is, that Babylon would be forsaken until the trees should grow and decay, and the branches should fall to be collected for burning. That is, the desolation should be entire, undisturbed, and long continued. The idea of the desolation is, therefore, in this verse carried forward, and a new

circumstance is introduced to make it more graphic and striking. Lowth, however, supposes that this refers to the vineyard, and to the fact that the vine-twigs are collected in the East from the scarcity of fuel for burning. But it seems to me that the obvious reference is to Babylon, and that it is an image of the great and prolonged desolation that was coming upon that city. ¶ *They shall be broken off.* That is, by their own weight as they decay, or by the hands of those who come to collect them for fuel. ¶ *The women come.* Probably it was the office mainly of the women to collect the fuel which might be necessary for culinary purposes. In eastern climates but little is needed; and that is collected of the twigs of vineyards, of withered stubble, straw, hay, dried roots, &c., wherever they can be found. ¶ And *set them on fire.* That is, to burn them for fuel. ¶ *Of no understanding.* Of no right views of God and his government—wicked, sinful (Prov. vi. 32; xviii. 2; Jer. v. 21).

12. *And it shall come to pass in that day,* that *the Lord shall beat off.* The word which is here used (חָבַט) means properly to beat off with a stick, as fruit from a tree (Deut. xx. 20). It also means to beat out grain with a stick (Judg. vi. 11; Ruth xi. 17). The word which is rendered in the other member of the sentence, 'shall be gathered' (לָקַט), is applied to the act of *collecting* fruit after it has been beaten from a tree, or grain after it has been threshed. The use of these words here shows that the image is taken from the act of collecting fruit or grain after harvest; and the expression means, that as the husbandman gathers in his fruit, so God would gather in his people. In the

13 And it shall come to pass in that day, *that* the great trumpet shall*a* be blown, and they shall come which were ready to perish in the land of Assyria, and the outcasts in the land of Egypt, and shall worship the LORD in the holy mount at Jerusalem.

CHAPTER XXVIII.

ANALYSIS.

THIS chapter comprises a new prophecy and

a Mat.24.31; 1 Thes.4.16; Rev.11.15.

relates to a new subject. Gesenius supposes that it is to be connected with the following to to the close of ch. xxxiii., and that they relate to the same subject, and were delivered at the same time. Munster supposes that the prophecy here commenced continues to the close of ch. xxxv., and that it relates to the Assyrian war in which the ten tribes were carried away captive. Dœderlin supposes that this chapter and the two following were uttered at the same time, and relate to the same subject; Hensler, that the prophecy closes at the 33d chapter.

It is not improbable that this chapter and the following were delivered at the same time, and

figure, it is supposed that the garden or vineyard of JEHOVAH extends from the Euphrates to the Nile; that his people are scattered in all that country; that there shall be agitation or a shaking in all that region as when a farmer beats off his fruit from the tree, or beats out his grain; and that the result would be that all those scattered people would be gathered into their own land. The time referred to is, doubtless, after Babylon should be taken; and in explanation of the declaration it is to be remembered that the Jews were not only carried to Babylon, but were scattered in large numbers in all the adjacent regions. The promise here is, that from all those regions whither they had been scattered they should be re-collected and restored to their own land. ¶ *From the channel of the river.* The river here undoubtedly refers to the river Euphrates (see Note on ch. xi. 15). ¶ *Unto the stream of Egypt.* The Nile. ¶ *And ye shall be gathered one by one.* As the husbandman collects his fruits one by one—collecting them carefully, and not leaving any. This means that God will not merely collect them as a nation, but as *individuals.* He will see that none is overlooked, and that all shall be brought in safety to their land.

13. *The great trumpet shall be blown.* This verse is designed to describe in another mode the same fact as that stated in verse 12, that JEHOVAH would re-collect his scattered people. The figure is derived from the trumpet which was blown to assemble a people for war (Grotius); or from the blowing of the trumpet on occasion of the great feasts and festivals of the Jews (Vitringa). The idea is, that God would summon

the scattered people to return to their own land. The *way* in which this was done, or in which the will of God would be made known to them, is not specified. It is probable, however, that the reference here is to the decree of Cyrus (Ezra i. 1), by which they were permitted to return to their own country. ¶ *Which were ready to perish.* Who were reduced in numbers, and in power, and who were ready to be annihilated under their accumulated and long-continued trials. ¶ *In the land of Assyria.* The ten tribes were carried away into Assyria (2 Kings xvii. 6); and it is probable that many of the other two tribes were also in that land. A portion of the ten tribes would also be re-collected, and would return with the others to the land of their fathers. Assyria also constituted a considerable part of the kingdom of the Chaldeans, and the name Assyria may be given here to that country in general. ¶ *And the outcasts.* Those who had fled in consternation to Egypt and to other places when these calamities were coming upon the nation (see Jer. xli. 17, 18; xlii. 15–22). ¶ *And shall worship the* LORD. Their temple shall be rebuilt; their city shall be restored; and in the place where their fathers worshipped shall they also again adore the living God.—This closes the prophecy which was commenced in ch. xxiv.; and the design of the whole is to comfort the Jews with the assurance, that though they were to be made captive in a distant land, yet they would be again restored to the land of their fathers, and again worship God there. It is almost needless to say that this prediction was completely fulfilled by the return of the Jews to their own country under the decree of Cyrus.

that they relate to the same general subject—the approaching calamities and wars with the Assyrians, which would terminate only in the removal of the people to a distant land, and in the destruction of the entire city and nation. But the prophecy in this chapter has not any necessary connection with those which follow, and it may be regarded as separate.

When it was uttered is not certainly known. It is clear, however, that it was before the carrying away of the ten tribes, or while the kingdom of Ephraim or Samaria was still standing. Yet it would seem that it was when that kingdom was exceedingly corrupt, and was hastening to a fall (ver. 1–4). Perhaps it was in the time of Ahaz, or in the beginning of the reign of Hezekiah, when Samaria or Ephraim had entered into a league with Rezin, king of Damascus, and may therefore synchronize with ch. vii., viii. Whenever it was uttered, it is certain that its purpose was to predict the overthrow of Ephraim or Samaria, and the fact, that when that kingdom should be overthrown, the kingdom of Judah would still survive.

The prophecy consists of two parts:—1. The overthrow of Samaria or Ephraim (1–4). 2. The fact that JEHOVAH would preserve and defend a portion of his people—those who comprise the kingdom of Judah (5–29). The following brief view will present an analysis of the prophecy:—

I. Ephraim or Samaria, for its sins, particularly for intemperance, would be overthrown (1–4).

II. God would preserve the residue of his people, yet they also deserved rebuke, and would be also subjected to punishment (5–29). 1. He would preserve them (5, 6) and be their glory and strength. 2. Yet they deserved, on many accounts, to be reproved, particularly because many even of the priests and prophets were intemperate (7–8). 3. They also disregarded the

messengers of God, and treated their messages with contempt and scorn, as being vain repetitions and a mere stammering (9–13). 4. They regarded themselves as safe, since they were firm and united, and had as it were made a league with death (14, 15). 5. God, in view of their sins, threatens them with deserved punishment (16–21). This would occur in the following manner:—(a.) He would lay in Zion a corner stone, tried and precious, and all that regarded that should be safe (16). (b.) Yet heavy judgments would come upon the guilty and the unbelieving. Judgment would be laid to the line, and the storms of Divine vengeance would sweep away their false refuges, and their covenant with death should not avail them (17–21). (c.) The people are therefore admonished to attend to this, for the destruction was determined upon the whole land (22). (d.) The whole account of their punishment is concluded by a reference to the conduct of a husbandman, and an illustration is drawn from the fact that he takes various methods to secure his harvest. He ploughs, he sows, and in various ways he thrashes his grain. So in various ways God would deal with his people. He would instruct, admonish, correct, and punish them, in order that he might secure the *greatest amount of piety and good fruits from them.* Chastisement was just as necessary for them as it was for the husbandman in various modes to beat out his grain (23–29).

WO to the crown of pride, to the drunkards of Ephraim, whose glorious beauty *is* a fading flower, which *are* on the head of the fat valleys of them that are overcome [1] with wine !

1 broken.

CHAPTER XXVIII.

1. *Wo* (see Note on ch. xviii. 1). The word here is used to denounce impending judgment. ¶ *To the crown of pride.* This is a Hebrew mode of expression, denoting the *proud* or *haughty crown.* There can be no doubt that it refers to the capital of the kingdom of Ephraim; that is, to Samaria. This city was built by Omri, who purchased ' the hill Samaria ' of Shemer, for two talents of silver, equal in value to £792, 11s. 8d., and built the city on the hill, and called it, after the name of Shemer, Samaria (1 Kings xvi. 24). Omri was king of Israel (B.C. 925), and he made this city the capital of his kingdom. The city was built on a pleasant and fertile hill,

and surrounded with a rich valley, with a circle of hills beyond ; and the beauty of the hill on which the city was built suggested the idea of a wreath or chaplet of flowers, or a *crown.* After having been destroyed and reduced to an inconsiderable place, it was restored by Herod the Great, B.C. 21, who called it *Sebaste* (Latin, *Augusta*), in honour of the Emperor Augustus. It is usually mentioned by travellers under the name of Sebaste. Maundrell (*Travels,* p. 58) says, ' Sebaste, the ancient Samaria, is situated on a long mount of an oval figure ; having first a fruitful valley, and then a ring of hills running round it.' The following is the account which is given by Richardson :—' Its situation

2 Behold, the Lord hath a | mighty and strong one, *which as*

is extremely beautiful, and strong by nature; more so, I think, than Jerusalem. It stands on a fine large insulated hill, compassed all round by a broad, deep valley. The valley is surrounded by four hills, one on each side, which are cultivated in terraces to the top, sown with grain, and planted with fig and olive trees, as is also the valley. The hill of Samaria, likewise, rises in terraces to a height equal to any of the adjoining mountains.' Dr. Robinson, who visited this place in 1838, says, ' The find round swelling hill, or almost mountain of Samaria, stands alone in the midst of the great basin of some two hours [seven or eight miles] in diameter, surrounded by higher mountains on every side. It is near the eastern side of the basin ; and is connected with the eastern mountains, somewhat after the manner of a promontory, by a much lower ridge, having a wady both on the south and on the north. The mountains and the valleys around are to a great extent arable, and enlivened by many villages and the hand of cultivation. From all these circumstances, the situation of the ancient Samaria is one of great beauty. The hill itself is cultivated to the top ; and, at about midway of the ascent, is surrounded by a narrow terrace of level land like a belt, below which the roots of the hill spread off more gradually into the valleys. The whole hill of Sebästich [the Arabic form for the name Sebaste] consists of fertile soil ; it is cultivated to the top, and has upon it many olive and fig trees. It would be difficult to find, in all Palestine, a situation of equal strength, fertility, and beauty combined. In all these particulars, it has very greatly the advantage over Jerusalem.'—(*Bib. Researches*, vol. iii. pp. 136—149). Standing thus by itself, and cultivated to the top, and exceedingly fertile, it was compared by the prophet to a crown, or garland of flowers—such as used to be worn on the head, especially on festival occasions. ¶ *To the drunkards of Ephraim.* Ephraim here denotes the kingdom of Israel, whose capital was Samaria (see Note on ch. vii. 2). That intemperance was the prevailing sin in

the kingdom of Israel is not improbable. It prevailed to a great extent also in the kingdom of Judah (see ver. 7, 8; comp. Notes on ch. v. 11, 22). ¶ *Whose glorious beauty* is *a fading flower.* That is, it shall soon be destroyed, as a flower soon withers and fades away. This was fulfilled in the destruction that came upon Samaria under the Assyrians when the ten tribes were carried into captivity (2 Kings xvii. 3–6). The allusion in this verse to the ' crown' and ' the fading flower' encircling Samaria, Grotius thinks is derived from the fact that among the ancients, drunkards and revellers were accustomed to wear a crown or garland on their heads, or that a wreath or chaplet of flowers was usually worn on their festival occasions. That this custom prevailed among the Jews as well as among the Greeks and Romans, is apparent from a statement by the author of the Book of Wisdom :

' Let us fill ourselves with costly wine and ornaments,
And let no flower of the spring pass by us;
Let us crown ourselves with rose-buds before
   they are withered.'—*Wisdom*, ii. 7, 8.

¶ *Which* are *on the head.* Which flowers or chaplets are on the eminence that rises over the fat valleys ; that is, on Samaria, which seemed to stand as the head rising from the valley. ¶ *Of the fat valleys of them that are overcome with wine.* That are occupied by, or in the possession of, those who are overcome with wine. Marg. ' Broken' with wine. Heb. (חֲלוּמֵי יָיִן) 'Smitten with wine ;' corresponding to the Greek οἰνοπλήξ; that is, they were overcome or subdued by it. A man's reason, conscience, moral feelings, and physical strength are all overcome by indulgence in wine, and the entire man is prostrate by it. This passage is a proof of what has been often denied, but which further examination has abundantly confirmed, that the inhabitants of wine countries are as certainly intemperate as those which make use of ardent spirits.

2. *Behold, the Lord hath a mighty and strong one.* The Hebrew of this passage is, ' Lo ! there is to the Lord (לַאדֹנָי) mighty and strong.' Lowth renders it,

a tempest *a* of hail, *and* a destroying storm, as a flood of mighty waters overflowing, shall cast down to the earth with the hand.

3 The crown of pride, the drunkards of Ephraim, shall be trodden under [1] feet.

a Ezek. 13. 11.   1 *with.*

---

4 And the glorious beauty which *is* on the head of the fat valley shall be *b* a fading flower, *and* as the hasty fruit before the summer; which *when* he that looketh upon it seeth, while it is yet in his hand he eateth [2] it up.

b Ps. 73. 19, 20.   2 *swalloweth.*

'Behold the mighty one, the exceedingly strong one,'

and supposes that it means the Lord himself. It is evident, however, that something must be understood as being that which the Lord ' hath,' for the Hebrew properly implies that there is something strong and mighty which is under his control, and with which, as with a tempest, he will sweep away and destroy Ephraim. Jarchi supposes that רוּחַ (*wind*) is understood; Kimchi that the word is יוֹם (*day*); others that חַיִל (*an army*) is understood. But I think the obvious interpretation is to refer it to the Assyrian king, as the agent by which JEHOVAH would destroy Samaria (2 Kings xvii. 3–6). This power was entirely under the direction of JEHOVAH, and would be employed by him in accomplishing his purpose on that guilty people (comp. Notes on ch. x. 5, 6). ¶ *As a tempest of hail.* A storm of hail is a most striking representation of the desolation that is produced by the ravages of an invading army (comp. Job xxvii. 21; Note on ch. xxx. 30; also Hos. xiii. 15). ¶ *A flood of mighty waters.* This is also a striking description of the devastating effects of an invading army (comp. Ps. xc. 5; Jer. xlvi. 7, 8. ¶ *Shall cast down to the earth.* To cast it to the earth means that it should be entirely humbled and destroyed (see Note on ch. xxv. 12). ¶ *With the hand.* LXX. Βίᾳ—' Force,' ' violence.' This is its meaning here; as if it were taken in the hand, like a cup, and dashed indignantly to the ground.

4. *As the hasty fruit before the summer.* The word rendered ' hasty fruit' (בִּכּוּרָה *bikkurah;* in Arabic, *bokkore;* in Spanish, *albacore*), denotes the *early fig.* This ripens in June; the common fig does not ripen until August. Shaw,

in his *Travels*, p. 370, says : ' No sooner does the *boccore* (the early fig) draw near to perfection in the middle or latter end of June, than the *kermez* or summer fig begins to be formed, though it rarely ripens before August, about which time the same tree frequently throws out a third crop, or the winter fig, as we may call it. This is usually of a much longer shape and darker complexion than the kermez, hanging and ripening on the tree after the leaves are shed; and provided the winter be mild and temperate it is gathered as a delicious morsel in the spring.' Robinson [George], (*Travels in Palestine and Syria*, vol. i. p. 354), says, ' The fig tree, which delights in a rocky and parched soil, and is therefore often found in barren spots where nothing else will grow, is very common in Palestine and the East. The fruit is of two kinds,

FIG (*Ficus carica*).

the *boccore* and the *kermouse*. The black and white boccore, or early fig, is produced in May; but the kermouse, or the fig properly so called, which is preserved and exported to Europe, is rarely ripe before September.' Compare Hos. ix. 10. The phrase ' before the summer' means before the heat of the summer, when the common fig was usually ripe.

5 In that day shall the LORD of hosts be for a crown of glory, and for a diadem of beauty, unto the residue of his people.

6 And for a spirit of judgment to him that sitteth in judgment, and for strength to them that turn the battle to the gate.

7 But they also have erred through wine, *a* and through strong drink are out of the way : the priest *b* and the prophet have erred through strong drink, they are swallowed up of wine, they are out of the way through strong drink ; they err in vision, they stumble *in* judgment.

a Ho.4.11.   *b* ch.56.10-12.

The idea here is this, the early fig would be plucked and eaten with great greediness. So the city of Samaria would be seized upon and destroyed by its enemies. ¶ *Which* when *he that looketh upon it seeth,* &c. That is, as soon as he sees it he plucks it, and eats it at once. He does not lay it up for future use, but as soon as he has it in his hand he devours it. So soon as the Assyrian should see Samaria he would rush upon it, and destroy it. It was usual for conquerors to *preserve* the cities which they took in war for future use, and to make them a part of the strength or ornament of their kingdom. But Samaria was to be at once destroyed. Its inhabitants were to be carried away, and it would be demolished as greedily as a hungry man plucks and eats the first fig that ripens on the tree.

5. *In that day.* This verse commences a new subject, and affirms that while the kingdom of Israel should be destroyed, the kingdom of Judah would be preserved, and restored (comp. ch. vii.–ix.) ¶ *Be for a crown of glory.* He shall reign there as its king, and he shall guard and defend the remnant of his people there. This reign of JEHOVAH shall be to them better than palaces, towers, walls, and fruitful fields, and shall be a more glorious ornament than the proud city of Samaria was to the kingdom of Israel. ¶ *And for a diadem of beauty.* A beautiful garland. The phrase stands opposed to the wreath of flowers or the diadem which was represented (ver. 1, 3) as adorning the kingdom and capital of Israel. JEHOVAH and his government would be to them their chief glory and ornament. ¶ *Unto the residue of his people.* To the kingdom of Judah, comprising the two tribes of Judah and Benjamin. This doubtless refers to the comparatively prosperous and happy times of the reign of Hezekiah.

6. *And for a spirit of judgment* (comp. Note on ch. i. 26; ch. xi. 2). The sense of this passage is, that JEHOVAH would enlighten the judges of the land, so that they should understand what was right, and be disposed to do it. ¶ *To him that sitteth in judgment.* This is to be understood *collectively,* and means those who sat upon the bench of justice ; that is, the magistracy in general. ¶ *And for strength to them that turn the battle to the gate.* That is, to the very gate of their enemies ; who not only repel their foes from their own city, but who drive them even to the gates of their own cities, and besiege them there. Thus 2 Sam. xi. 23 : 'And we were upon them even unto the entering of the gate ;' that is, we drove them back unto their own gates.

7. *But they also have erred through wine.* In the previous verses the prophet had said that the kingdom of Judah should be saved, while that of Ephraim should be destroyed. Yet he does not deny that they also were guilty of crimes for which punishment would come upon them. To portray these crimes, and to declare the certain judgment which awaited them, is the design of the remainder of the chapter. The word rendered 'have erred' (שָׁגוּ) refers usually to the fact that men *stagger* or *reel* through wine, and is applied commonly to those who are intoxicated (Prov. xx. 1). The subsequent part of this verse shows, however, that it does not refer merely to the fact that they stagger and reel as intemperate men do, but that it had an effect on their 'vision' and 'judgment ;' that is, it disqualified them for the discharge of their duties as priests and as prophets. In this part of the verse, however, the simple idea

8 For all tables are full of vomit *and* filthiness, *so that there is* no place *clean.*

9 Whom *a* shall he teach know-

a Jer.6.10.

ledge? and whom shall he make to understand doctrine? [2] *them that are* weaned from the milk, *and* drawn from the breasts.

[2] *the hearing.*

ls, that they reel or stagger through wine, *i.e.,* they are addicted to intoxication. In the subsequent part of the verse the prophet states the effect in producing indistinctness of vision and error of judgment. ¶ *And through strong drink* (see Note on ch. v. 11). ¶ *They are out of the way* (תָּעוּ). They wander; stagger; reel (comp. Notes on ch. xix. 14). ¶ *The priest and the prophet.* Probably these persons are specified to denote the higher classes of society. It is probable that the prophet also designs to indicate the enormity of the sins of the nation, from the fact that those who were specially devoted to religion, and who were supposed to have immediate communication with God, were addicted to intemperance. ¶ *They are swallowed up of wine.* They are completely absorbed by it (see Note on ch. xxv. 7); they not only themselves indulge in its use, but they are themselves, as it were, swallowed up by it, so that their reason, and strength, and virtue are all gone—as a vessel is absorbed in a mælstrom or whirlpool. ¶ *They err in vision.* For the sense of the word 'vision,' see Note on ch. i. 1. The prophet here states the effect of the use of wine and strong drink on their mental and moral powers. It was the office of the prophets to declare the will of God; probably also to explain the sense of the sacred Scriptures, and to address the people on their duty. Here the prophet says that the effect of their intemperance was that they had themselves no correct and clear views of the truth, and that they led the people into error. ¶ *They stumble* in *judgment.* There were many important subjects on which the priests sat in judgment among the Hebrews, particularly in all matters pertaining to religion. By the influence of intoxicating liquors they were disqualified for the high and holy functions of their office; and the consequence was, that the nation was corrupt, and was exposed to the heavy judgments of God.

8. *For all tables,* &c. The tables at

which they sit long in the use of wine (see Note on ch. v. 11). There was no place in their houses which was free from the disgusting and loathsome pollution produced by the use of wine.

9. *Whom shall he teach knowledge?* This verse commences a statement respecting another form of sin that prevailed among the people of Judah. That sin was contempt for the manner in which God instructed them by the prophets, and a disregard for his communications as if they were suited to children and not to adults. That *scoffing* was the principal sin aimed at in these verses, is apparent from ver. 14. Vitringa supposes that these words (ver. 9, 10) are designed to describe the manner of teaching by the priests and the prophets as being puerile and silly, and adapted to children. Michaelis supposes that the prophet means to signify that it would be a vain and fruitless labour to attempt to instruct these persons who were given to wine, because they were unaccustomed to sound and true doctrine. Others have supposed that he means that these persons who were thus given to wine and strong drink were disqualified to instruct others, since their teachings were senseless and incoherent, and resembled the talk of children. But the true sense of the passage has undoubtedly been suggested by Lowth. According to this interpretation, the prophet speaks of them as deriders of the manner in which God had spoken to them by his messengers. 'What!' say they, 'does God treat us as children? Does he deal with us as we deal with infants just weaned, perpetually repeating and inculcating the same elementary lessons, and teaching the mere rudiments of knowledge?' The expression, therefore, 'Whom shall he teach knowledge?' or, 'Whom does he teach?' is an expression of contempt supposed to be spoken by the intemperate priests and prophets—the leaders of the people. 'Whom does God take us to be?

10 For precept ¹ *must be* upon precept, precept upon precept; line upon line, line upon line; here a little, *and* there a little :

1 *or,* hath been.

11 For with ² stammering lips, and another tongue, ³ will he speak to his people.

12 To whom he said, This *is* the

2 *stammerings of.*		3 *or, he hath spoken.*

Does he regard us as mere children? Why are we treated as children with an endless repetition of the same elementary inſtruction?' ¶ *To understand doctrine.* Heb. as Marg. 'Hearing,' or 'report' (Isa. liii. 1). The sense is, For whom is that instruction intended? Whom does he wish to be taught by it? ¶ Them that are *weaned from the milk,* &c. Does he regard and treat us as mere babes?

10. *For precept* must be *upon precept.* This is probably designed to ridicule the concise and sententious manner of the prophets, and especially the fact that they dwelt much upon the same elementary truths of religion. In teaching children we are obliged to do it by often repeating the same simple lesson. So the profane and scoffing teachers of the people said it had been with the prophets of God. It had been precept upon precept, and line upon line, in the same way as children had been instructed. The meaning is, 'there is a constant repetition of the command, without ornament, imagery, or illustration; without an appeal to our understanding, or respect for our reason; it is simply *one mandate after another,* just as lessons are inculcated upon children.' ¶ *Line upon line.* This word (קַו *qăv*), properly means a *cord,* a *line;* particularly a measuring cord or line (2 Kings xxi. 13; Ezek. xlvii. 13; see Note on ch. xviii. 2). Here it seems to be used in the sense of a *rule, law,* or *precept.* Grotius thinks that the idea is taken from schoolmasters who instruct their pupils by making lines or marks for them which they are to trace or imitate. There is a repetition of similar sounds in the Hebrew in this verse which cannot be conveyed in a translation, and which shows their contempt in a much more striking manner than any version could do—

כִּי צַו לָצָו צַו לָצָו קַו לָקָו קַו לָקָו.

—*kī tzăv lâtzâv tzăv lâtzâv qăv lâqâv qăv lâqâv.* ¶ *Here a little* and *there*

a little. In the manner of instructing children, inculcating elementary lessons constantly. It may be observed here that God's method of imparting religious truth has often appeared to a scoffing world to be undignified and foolish. Sinners suppose that he does not sufficiently respect their understanding, and pay a tribute to the dignity of their nature. The truths of God, and his modes of inculcating them, are said to be adapted to the understandings of childhood and of age; to imbecility of years, or to times when the mind is enfeebled by disease.

11. *For.* This verse is to be understood as a response to what the complaining and dissatisfied people had said, as expressed in the previous verse. God says that he will teach them, but it should be by another tongue—a foreign language in a distant land. Since they refused to hearken to the messages which he sent to them, and which they regarded as adapted only to children, he would teach them in a manner that should be *much more* humiliating; he would make use of the barbarous language of foreigners to bring them to the true knowledge of God. ¶ *With stammering lips.* The word which is used here is derived from a verb (לָעֵג), which means to speak unintelligibly; especially to speak in a foreign language, or to stammer; and then to mock, deride, laugh at, scorn (comp. Isa. xxxiii. 19; Prov. i. 26; xvii. 5; Ps. ii. 4; lix. 9; Job xxii. 19). Here it means in a foreign or barbarous tongue; and the sense is, that the lessons which God wished to teach would be conveyed to them through the language of foreigners—the Chaldeans. They should be removed to a distant land, and there, in hearing a strange speech, in living long among foreigners, they should learn the lesson which they refused to do when addressed by the prophets in their own land.

12. *To whom he said.* To whom

rest *wherewith* ye may cause the weary to rest; and this *is* the refreshing; yet they would not hear.

13 But *a* the word of the LORD was unto them precept upon precept, precept upon precept; line upon line, line upon line; here a little, *and* there a little; that *b* they might go, and fall backward, and be broken, and snared, and taken.

14 Wherefore hear the word of

a Ho.6.5; 8.12.   b Mat.13.14.

the LORD, ye scornful men, that rule this people which *is* in Jerusalem.

15 Because ye have said, We have made a covenant with death, and with hell are we at agreement; when the overflowing scourge shall pass through, it shall not come *c* unto us: for we have made lies our refuge, and under falsehood have we hid ourselves.

c Eccl.8.8.

God had said; *i.e.*, to the Jews. He *had* taught them the way of rest through the prophets, but they had refused to learn. ¶ *This* is *the rest*. That is, this is the true way of happiness, to wit, by keeping the commands of God which had been so often repeated as to become to them objects of satiety and disgust. ¶ *This* is *the refreshing*. This is the way in which the mind may be comforted.

13. *But the word of the* LORD *was unto them*. Or, rather, but the word of JEHOVAH *shall be* unto them. This refers to the mode in which God said he would instruct them in a foreign land. They had complained (ver. 9, 10) that his instructions had been like a short lesson constantly repeated, as we instruct children. God here says that it should be as they said it was—they would be carried away to a distant land, and long abide among strangers; they would have ample time there to acquire instruction, and all that they would receive would be lesson after lesson of the same kind—line upon line, one judgment following another, until the lesson of their disobedience had been fully inculcated, and they had been brought to true repentance. ¶ *Here a little*, and *there a little*. So they had said (ver. 10) the lessons of God were to them by the prophets. So God says his lessons *shall be* to them by judgment. It shall not come in one sudden and overpowering burst of indignation, but it shall be, as it were, dealt out to them in small portions that it may not be soon exhausted. ¶ *That they might go*, &c. That they may go into captivity, and stumble, and be broken by the judgments of God. God will so

deal out the lessons of his judgment and wrath, that as a people they shall be broken up, and made prisoners, and be borne to a distant land.

14. *Wherefore*, &c. This verse commences a direct address to the scoffing and scornful nation, which is continued to the close of ver. 22. It is addressed particularly to the rulers in Jerusalem, as being the leaders in crime, and as being eminently deserving of the wrath of God. ¶ *Ye scornful men*. Ye who despise and reproach God and his message; who fancy yourselves to be secure, and mock at the threatened judgments of the Almighty.

15. *We have made a covenant with death*. We are not to suppose that they had formally said this, but that their conduct was *as if* they had said it; they lived as securely as if they had entered into a compact with death not to destroy them, and with hell not to devour them. The figure is a very bold one, and is designed to express the extraordinary stupidity of the nation. It is most strikingly descriptive of the great mass of men. They are as little anxious about death and hell as if they had made a compact with the king of terrors and the prince of darkness not to destroy them. They are as little moved by the appeals of the gospel, by the alarms of God's providence, by the preaching of his word, and by all the demonstrations that they are exposed to eternal death, as though they had proved that there was no hell, or had entered into a solemn covenant that they should be unmolested. A figure similar to this occurs in Job v. 23:

For thou shalt be in league with the stones of the field;

16 Therefore thus saith the Lord God, Behold I lay in Zion for a foundation a stone, *a* a tried stone,

a Ps.118.22; Mat.21.42; Acts 4.11; Rom.9.33; Eph.2.20.

a precious corner-*stone*, a sure foundation: he *b* that believeth shall not make haste.

b Rom.10.11.

And the beasts of the field shall be at peace with thee.
Comp. Hos. ii. 18. ¶ *And with hell.* Heb. 'Sheol'—the land of shades, or of departed spirits (see Note on ch. v. 14). It is nearly synonymous here with death. ¶ *When the overflowing scourge shall pass through.* There is here, in our translation, a little confusion of metaphor, since we speak usually of an overflowing *stream,* and not of an overflowing *scourge.* The word 'scourge' (שׁוֹט) means usually *a whip, a scourge,* the same as שׁוֹט, and then means any punishment or calamity (see Note on ch. x. 26; comp. Job ix. 23; v. 21. Here its means severe judgments or calamities, as *overflowing* like water, or inundating a people. ¶ *We have made lies,* &c. That is, they acted *as if* they had a safe refuge in falsehood. They sought security in false doctrines, and regarded themselves as safe from all that the prophets had denounced.

16. *Therefore thus saith the Lord God.* This verse is introductory to the solemn threatening which follows. Its design seems to be this. The prophet was about to utter an awful threatening of the judgment of God upon the nation. It might be supposed, perhaps, that the intention was completely to sweep them, and destroy them—that the threatened calamity would remove every vestige of the Jewish people and of the true religion together. To meet this supposition, God says that this should not occur. Zion was founded on a rock. It should be like an edifice that was reared on a firm, well-tried corner-stone—one that could endure all the storms that should beat around it, and be unmoved. The general sentiment of the verse is, therefore, that though a tempest of calamity was about to beat upon the people for their sins; though the temple was to be destroyed, the city laid in ashes, and many of the people slain; yet it was the purpose of God that his empire on earth should not be destroyed. A foundation, a corner-stone was to be laid that would

be unshaken and unmoved by all the assaults of the foes of God, and all who were truly resting on that should be safe. The perpetuity of his kingdom, and the safety of his true people, is, therefore, the essential idea in this passage. That it refers to the Messiah, and is designed to show that his kingdom will be perpetual *because* it is reared on him, we shall see by an examination of the words which occur in the verse. ¶ *In Zion* (see Note on ch. i. 8). Zion here is put for his empire, kingdom, or church in general on earth. To lay a corner-stone in Zion, means that his kingdom would be founded on a rock, and would be secure amidst all the storms that might beat upon it. ¶ *For a foundation a stone.* That is, I lay a firm foundation which nothing can move; I build it on a rock so that the storms and tempests of calamity cannot sweep it away (comp. Matt. vii. 24, 25). The Targum renders this, 'Lo! I appoint in Zion a king, a strong, mighty, and terrible king.' That the passage before us has reference to the Messiah there can be no doubt. The writers of the New Testament so understood and applied it. Thus it is applied by Peter (1 Pet. ii. 6), 'Wherefore, also, it is contained in the Scripture, Behold I lay in Zion a chief corner-stone, elect, precious; and he that believeth on him shall not be confounded' (see Notes on Rom. ix. 33; comp. Rom. x. 11; Matt. xxi. 42; Luke xx. 17, 18; ii. 34; Eph. ii. 20). Such a reference also exactly suits the conection. The stability of the kingdom of God on earth rests on the Messiah. God had determined to send him; and, consequently, amidst all the agitations and revolutions that could take place among his ancient people, this promise was sure, and it was certain that he would come, and that his church would be preserved. ¶ *A tried stone.* The word which is used here is applied commonly to *metals* which are tried in the fire to test their quality (see Job xxiii. 10; Ps. lxvi. 10; Jer ix. 6; Zech. xiii.

17 Judgment also will I lay to the line, and righteousness to the plummet ; and the hail shall sweep away the refuge of lies, and the waters shall overflow the hiding-place.

1 a treading down to it.

18 And your covenant with death shall be disannulled, and your agreement with hell shall not stand ; when the overflowing scourge shall pass through, then ye shall be ¹ trodden down ᵃ by it.

a Mal.4.3.

9). The idea is, that God would lay for a foundation not a stone whose qualities are unknown, and whose stability might be doubtful, but one whose firmness and solidity were so fully known, that the foundation and the superstructure would be secure. ¶ *A precious corner-stone.* The word 'precious' (LXX., and 1 Pet. ii. 6, ἔντιμον) refers to the fact that the most solid stone would be used to sustain the corner of the edifice. The principal weight of the superstructure rests on the corners, and hence, in building, the largest and firmest blocks are selected and placed there. ¶ *He that believeth.* He that confides in that ; he that believes that that foundation is firm, and that he is secure in trusting in that, shall not make haste. The great doctrine of faith in the Messiah as a ground of security and salvation, on which so much stress is laid in the New Testament, is here distinctly adverted to. The sense is, that confidence in him should keep the mind firm, and preserve him that believes in safety. ¶ *Shall not make haste.* The LXX. render it, Οὐ μὴ καταισχυνθῇ —'Shall not be ashamed.' So Peter, 1 Pet. ii. 6 ; and Paul, Rom. ix. 33. The Hebrew word יָחִישׁ, from חוּשׁ, means properly *to make haste;* and then to urge on ; and then to be afraid, to flee. The idea is derived from one who is alarmed, and flees to a place of safety. The specific thought here is that of a man on whose house the tempest beats, and who apprehends that the foundation is insecure, and leaves it to seek a more safe position. The prophet says here, that the foundation on which Zion was reared would be so firm that if a man trusted to that he would have no cause of alarm, however much the storms should beat around it. The same idea essentially is conveyed in the version of the LXX., and by Paul and Peter, where it is ren-

dered 'shall not be ashamed,' or 'confounded.' That is, he shall have no reason to be ashamed of his confidence in the firm foundation ; he shall not flee from it as a man does who puts his trust in that which fails him in the day of trial.

17. *Judgment also will I lay to the line.* The sense of this is, I will judge them *according to the exact rule of law,* as an architect frames everything according to the rule which he uses. In other words, there shall be no mercy intermingled. The *line* is used by a carpenter for measuring ; the plummet consists of a piece of lead attached to a string, and is also used by carpenters to obtain a perpendicular line. A carpenter works exactly according to the lines which are thus indicated, or his frame would not be properly adjusted. So God says that he would judge the people of Jerusalem according to the exact rule, without any intermingling of mercy. ¶ *And the hail,* &c. (see Note on ver. 2). Hail, hailstones, and floods of waters are frequent images of the Divine vengeance and wrath (Ps. cv. 32 ; Isa. xxii. 19 ; xxx. 30 ; Ezek. xiii. 13 : xxxviii. 22 ; Rev. viii. 7 ; xi. 19 ; xvi. 21).

18. *And your covenant with death* (see Note on ver. 15). ¶ *Shall be disannulled.* The word rendered 'shall be disannulled,' (וְכֻפַּר from כָּפַר), properly means *to cover, overlay;* then to pardon, forgive ; then to make atonement, to expiate. It has the idea of blotting out, forgiving, and obliterating—because a writing in wax was obliterated or *covered* by passing the *stylus* over it. Hence, also, the idea of abolishing, or rendering nought, which is the idea here. ¶ *When the overflowing scourge* (see Note on ver. 15). ¶ *Then ye shall be trodden down by it.* There is in this verse a great intermingling of metaphor, not less than three figures

19 From the time that it goeth forth it shall take you: for morning by morning shall it pass over, by day and by night; and it shall be a vexation only [1] *to* understand the report.

20 For the bed is shorter than that a *man* can stretch himself *on it;* and the covering narrower than that he can wrap himself *in it.*

21 For the LORD shall rise up as [a]*in* mount Perazim, he shall be wroth as [b]*in* the valley of Gibeon, that he may do his work, his strange [c]work; and bring to pass his act, his strange act.

[1] or, when *he shall make* you *to understand doctrine.*
a 2 Sa.5.20.   b Jos.10.10,&c.; 1 Ch.14.16.   c La.3.33.

---

being employed to denote the calamity. There is first the scourge, an instrument of punishment; there is then the idea of inundating waters or floods; then there is also the idea of a warrior or an invading army that treads down an enemy. All the images are designed to denote essentially the same thing, that the judgments of God would come upon the land, and that nothing in which they had trusted would constitute a refuge.

19. *From the time that it goeth forth it shall take you.* It shall not delay, or be hindered, or put back. As soon as the judgment is sent forth from God it shall come upon you. ¶ *For morning by morning.* Continually; without intermission. It shall be like floods and tempests that have no intermission; that are repeated every day, and continued every night, until everything is swept before them. ¶ *And it shall be a vexation.* It shall be an object of alarm, of agitation, of distress—זְוָעָה from זוּעַ, *to move one's self;* to tremble with alarm; to be troubled (Eccl. xii. 3; Dan. v. 19; vi. 27; Heb. ii. 7). Here it means that the calamity would be so great that it would fill the mind with horror only to hear of it. For similar expressions denoting the effect of hearing a report of the judgments of God, see 1 Sam. iii. 11; 2 Kings xxi. 12; Jer. xix. 3. ¶ *The report.* Marg. 'Doctrine' (see Note on ver. 9).

20. *For the bed is shorter,* &c. This is evidently a proverbial saying, and means that they would find all their places of defence insufficient to secure them. They seek repose and security —as a man lies down to rest at night. But they find neither. His bed furnishes no rest; his scanty covering furnishes no security from the chills of the night. So it would be with those who sought protection in idols, in the promises of false prophets, and in the aid which might be obtained from Egypt. —So it is with sinners. Their vain refuges shall not shield them. The bed on which they seek rest shall give them no repose; the covering with which they seek to clothe themselves shall not defend them from the wrath of God.

21. *For the* LORD *shall rise up.* To rise up is indicative of going forth to judgment, as when one rises from his seat to accomplish anything. ¶ *As in mount Perazim.* There is reference here, doubtless, to the event recorded in 2 Sam. v. 20, 21, and 1 Chron. xiv. 11, where David is said to have defeated the Philistines at Baal-Perazim. This place was near to the valley of Rephaim (2 Sam. v. 19), and not far from Jerusalem. The word 'Perazim' is from פָּרַץ (*pârâtz*), *to tear,* or *break forth,* as waters do that have been confined; and is indicative of sudden judgment, and of a complete overthrow. It was on that account given to the place where David obtained a signal and complete victory (2 Sam. v. 20); and it is here referred to, to denote that God would come forth in a sudden manner to destroy Jerusalem and Judea. He would come upon them like bursting waters, and sweep them away to a distant land. ¶ *As in the valley of Gibeon.* In 1 Chron. xiv. 16, it is said that after the victory of Baal-Perazim, 'David smote the host of the Philistines from Gibeon even to Gaza.' This victory is doubtless referred to here, and not the victory of Joshua over the Gibeonites (Josh. x. 10), as Vitringa and others suppose. ¶ *That he may do his work, his strange work.* This is called his

22 Now therefore be ye not mockers, lest your bands be made strong : for I have heard from the Lord God of hosts a consumption,

a Dan.9.27.

even *d* determined upon the whole earth.

23 Give ye ear, and hear my voice ; hearken, and hear my speech.

strange work because it would be inflicted on his people. He had destroyed their enemies often, but now he was about to engage in the unusual work of coming forth against his own people, and sweeping them away to a distant land. The work of judgment and punishment may be called the *strange* work of God always, inasmuch as it is not that in which he delights to engage, and is foreign to the benevolence of his heart. It is peculiarly so when his own people are the objects of his displeasure, and when their sins are such as to demand that he should visit them with the tokens of his wrath.

22. *Now therefore.* In view of the certain judgment which God will bring upon you. ¶ *Be ye not mockers.* This was the prevailing sin (ver. 9–14), and on account of this sin in part the judgment of God was about to come upon the guilty nation. ¶ *Lest your bands be made strong.* Lest your confinement should be more severe and protracted. God would punish them according to their sins, and if they now ceased to mock and deride him it would greatly mitigate the severity of their punishment (comp. ch. xxiv. 22). ¶ *For I have heard,* &c. I, the prophet, have heard Jehovah of hosts threaten a consumption. ¶ *A consumption,* &c. (see this phrase explained in the Note on ch. x. 23.) ¶ *Upon the whole earth.* The whole land of Judea (see Note on ch. xxiv. 1).

23. *Give ye ear.* In this verse the prophet introduces an important and striking illustration drawn from the science of agriculture. It is connected with the preceding part of the chapter, and is designed to show the propriety of what the prophet had said by an appeal to what they all observed in the cultivation of their lands. The previous discourse consists mainly of reproofs, and of threatenings of punishment on God's people for their profane contempt of the messengers of God. He had threatened to destroy their nation, and

to remove them for a time to a distant land. This the prophet had himself said (ver. 21) was his 'strange work.' To vindicate this, and to show the propriety *of God's adopting every measure, and of not always pursuing the same course in regard to his people,* he draws an illustration from the farmer. He is not always doing the same thing. He adopts different methods to secure a harvest. He adapts his plans to the soil and to the kind of grain ; avails himself of the best methods of preparing the ground, sowing the seed, collecting the harvest, and of separating the grain from the chaff. He does not *always* plough ; nor *always* sow ; nor *always* thresh. He does not deal with all kinds of land and grain in the same way. Some land he ploughs in one mode, and some in another ; and in like manner, some grain he threshes in one mode, and some in another — adapting his measures to the nature of the soil, and of the grain. Some grain he beats out with a flail ; some he bruises ; but yet he will be careful not to break the kernel, or destroy it in threshing it. However severe may appear to be his blows, yet his object is not to crush and destroy it (ver. 28), but it is to remove it from the chaff, and to save it. In all this he acts the part of wisdom, for God has taught him what to do (ver. 26, 29). So, says the prophet, God will not deal with all of his people in the same manner, nor with them always in the same mode. He will *vary* his measures as a husbandman does. When mild and gentle measures will do, he will adopt them. When severe measures are necessary, he will resort to them. His object is not to destroy his people, any more than the object of the farmer in threshing is to destroy his grain. The general design of this allegory is, therefore, to vindicate the propriety of God's engaging in what the prophet calls his 'strange act,' and 'strange work,' in punishing his people. The allegory is one of great

24 Doth the ploughman plough all day to sow? doth he open and break the clods of his ground?

25 When he hath made plain the face thereof, doth he not cast

1 or, *the wheat in the principal* place, *and barley in the appointed* place.

abroad the fitches, and scatter the cummin, and cast in [1] the principal wheat, and the [2] rye, in their place [3]?

2 or, *spelt.*   3 *border.*

beauty, and its pertinency and *keeping* are maintained throughout; and it furnishes a most important practical lesson in regard to the mode in which God deals with his people.

24. *Doth the ploughman,* &c. The question here asked implies that he does *not* plough all the day. The interrogative form is often the most emphatic mode of affirmation. ¶ *All day.* The sense is, does he do nothing else but plough? Is this the only thing which is necessary to be done in order to obtain a harvest? The idea which the prophet intends to convey here is this. A farmer does not suppose that he can obtain a harvest by doing nothing else but plough. There is much else to be done. So it would be just as absurd to suppose that God would deal with his people always in the same manner, as it would be for the farmer to be engaged in nothing else but ploughing. ¶ *Doth he open,* &c. That is, is he always engaged in opening, and breaking the clods of his field? There is much else to be done besides this. The word 'open' here refers to the *furrows* that are made by the plough. The earth is laid open as it were to the sunbeams, and to the showers of rain, and to the reception of seed. The word rendered 'break' (יְשַׂדֵּד) properly means *to harrow*, that is, to break up the clods by harrowing (Job xxxix. 10; Hos. x. 11).

25. *When he hath made plain,* &c. That is, when he has *levelled,* or made smooth the surface of the ground by harrowing, or rolling it. ¶ *Doth he not scatter abroad.* He does not sow one kind of grain merely, but different species according to the nature of the soil, or according to his wishes in regard to a crop. ¶ *The fitches* (קֶצַח). Vulg. *Gith;* a kind of cockle (*Nigella Romana*), an herb of sweet savour. LXX. Μικρὸν μελάνθιον. The word 'fitch' denotes a small species of pea. The Hebrew word, however, which occurs

nowhere else but here, probably denotes fennel, or dill, an herb whose seed the ancients mixed with their bread in order to give it a more agreeable relish. ¶ *And scatter the cummin* (כַּמֹּן). Vulg. *Cyminum*—'Cummin.' LXX. Κύμινον —also 'Cummin.' The word properly denotes an annual plant whose seeds have a bitterish warm taste with an aromatic flavour (Webster). The seeds of this plant were used as a condiment in sauces. ¶ *And cast in the principal wheat.* Marg. 'The wheat in the principal place.' Vulg. *Per ordinem*—'In its proper order, place, proportion.' So Lowth, 'In due measure.' So Aben Ezra and Kimchi render it, 'By measure;' and they suppose it means that if too much wheat be sown on the land, it will grow too thick, and that the spires will crowd and suffocate each other. Our translators have rendered the word שׂרָה, 'principal,' as if it were derived from שָׂרָה, *to rule,* and seem to have supposed that it denoted wheat that was peculiarly excellent, or distinguished for its good qualities. Ge-

EGYPTIAN WHEAT (*Triticum compositum*).

senius supposes that it means 'fat wheat,' from an Arabic signification of

26 For ¹his GOD doth instruct | him to discretion, *and* doth teach him.

1 or, and he bindeth it in such sort as his God doth teach him.

27 For the fitches are not

the word. Probably the word is designed to denote *quality*, and to convey the idea that wheat is the principal, or chief grain that is sown ; it is that which is most valued and esteemed. ¶ *And the appointed barley.* The barley is a well-known grain. The word rendered ‘appointed’ (נִסְמָן), occurs nowhere else in the Scriptures. Castellio, Taylor, Grotius, Calvin, our translators, and others, suppose that it is derived from a Hebrew word which does not now occur —סָמַן, *to designate, to mark, to seal;* and that it means barley that had been put aside and *marked* as peculiarly excellent, or seed-barley. In Chaldee, the word סְמַן occurs in the sense of *to seal, to mark, to designate* (Chaldee Par. Num. xvii. 3 : 2 Kings ix. 13 ; Esth. v. 1). The LXX., who translated it κέγχρον, and the Vulgate, Aquila, and Theodotion, understand the word as denoting a species of grain, *the millet.*

MILLET (*Holcus sorghum*).

The idea is probably that expressed by Grotius, and in our version—of barley that had been selected as seed-barley on account of its excellent quality. ¶ *And the rye.* Marg. ‘Spelt.’ The word usually denotes *spelt*—a kind of wheat now found in Flanders and Italy, called German wheat. It may, however, denote rye. ¶ *In their place.* Literally, ‘In the border.’ LXX. 'Εν τοῖς ὁρίοις σου—‘ In thy borders.’ The

idea seems to be that the spelt or rye was sown in the borders of the field while the wheat was sown in the middle ; or that the rye was sown in its *proper bounds*, or in the places which were adapted to it, and best fitted to promote its growth.

26. *For his* GOD *doth instruct him*, &c. Marg. ‘ He bindeth it in such sort as his God doth teach him.’ The more correct idea is conveyed in the text. The word יִסְּרֹו, properly means, he instructs, admonishes, or teaches him. The idea that skill in agriculture is communicated by God is not one that is discordant to reason, or to the general teachings of the Bible. Thus the architectural and mechanical skill of Bezaleel and Aholiab, by which they were enabled to make the tabernacle, is said expressly to have been imparted to them by God (Ex. xxxi. 2–6). Thus also Noah was taught how to build the ark (Gen. vi. 14–16). We are not, indeed, to suppose that the farmer is inspired ; or that God communicates to him by special revelation where, and when, and how he shall sow his grain, but the sense is, that God is the author of all his skill. He has endowed him with understanding, and taught him by his providence. It is by the study of what God teaches in the seasons, in the soil, in the results of experience and observation, that he has this art. He teaches him also by the example, the counsel, and even by the failures of others ; and all the knowledge of agriculture that he has is to be traced up to God.

27. *For the fitches are not threshed with a threshing instrument.* The word here used (חָרִיץ) denotes properly that which is pointed or sharp, and is joined with מוֹרַג in Isa. xli. 15—meaning there the threshing dray or sledge ; a plank with iron or sharp stones that was drawn by oxen over the grain (comp. 2 Sam. xxiv. 22 ; 1 Chron. xxi. 23). In the passage before us, several methods of threshing are mentioned as adapted to different

threshed with a threshing instrument, neither is a cart wheel turned about upon the cummin ; | but the fitches are beaten out with a staff, and the cummin with a rod.

kinds of grain, all of which are at the present time common in the East. Those which are mentioned under the name of the 'threshing instrument,' and 'a cart wheel,' refer to instruments which are still in use in the East. Niebuhr, in his *Travels in Arabia,* says, (p. 299,) ' In threshing their corn, the Arabians lay the sheaves down in a certain order, and then lead over them two oxen dragging a large stone.' ' They use oxen, as the ancients did, to beat out their corn, by trampling on the sheaves, and dragging after them a clumsy machine. This machine is not a stone cylinder ; nor a plank with sharp stones, as in Syria ; but a sort of sledge consisting of three rollers, fitted with irons, which turn upon axles. A farmer chooses out a level spot in his fields, and has his corn carried thither in sheaves, upon asses or dromedaries. Two oxen are then yoked in a sledge ; a driver then gets upon it, and drives them backwards and forwards upon the sheaves ; and fresh oxen succeed in the yoke from time to time. By this operation the chaff is very much cut down ; it is then winnowed, and the grain thus separated.' ' This machine,' Niebuhr adds, ' is called Nauridj. It has three rollers which turn on three axles ; and each of them is furnished with some irons which are round and flat. Two oxen were made to draw over the grain again and again the sledge above mentioned, and this was done with the greatest convenience to the driver ; for he was seated in a chair fixed on a sledge.' The annexed cut

THRESHING WITH THE SLEDGE.—From Description de l'Egypte.

will give an idea of this mode of threshing, and of the instruments that were employed. ¶ *Neither is a cart wheel.* This instrument of threshing is described by Bochart (*Hieroz.* i. 2. 32. | 311), as consisting of a cart or waggon fitted with wheels adapted to crush or thresh the grain. This, he says, was used by the Carthagenians who came from the vicinity of Canaan. It

28 Bread *corn* is bruised; because he will not ever be threshing it, nor break it *with* the wheel of his cart, nor bruise it *with* his horsemen.

appears to have been made with serrated wheels, perhaps almost in the form of circular saws, by which the straw was cut fine at the same time that the grain was separated from the chaff. ¶ *But the fitches are beaten out with a staff.* With a stick, or flail. That is, pulse in general, beans, pease, dill, cummin, &c., are easily beaten out with a stick or flail. This mode of threshing is common everywhere. It was also practised, as with us, in regard to barley and other grain, where there was a small quantity, or where there was need of special haste (see Ruth ii. 17; Judg. vi. 11).

28. *Bread* corn. Heb. לֶחֶם—'Bread.' But the word evidently denotes the material from which bread is made. The word is used in the same sense in ch. xxx. 23. ¶ *Is bruised.* That is, is more severely bruised than the dill and the cummin; it is pressed and crushed by passing over it the sledge, or the wain with serrated wheels. The word דָּקַק means often to break in pieces; to make small or fine. It is, however, applied to threshing, as consisting in beating, or crushing (Isa. xli. 15: 'Thou threshest the mountains,

and beatest them small'—וְדִקְ. ¶ *Because he will not ever be threshing it.* The word rendered 'because' (כִּי) evidently here means *although* or *but;* and the sense is, that he will not *always* continue to thresh it; this is not his only business. It is only a *part* of his method by which he obtains grain for his bread. It would be needless and injurious to be *always* engaged in rolling the stone or the sledge over the grain. So God takes various methods with his people. He does not always pursue the same course. He sometimes smites and punishes them, as the farmer beats his grain. But he does not *always* do it. He is not engaged in this method alone; nor does he pursue this constantly. It would crush and destroy them. *He, therefore, smites them just enough to secure, in the best manner, and to the fullest extent, their obedience; just as the farmer bruises his sheaves enough to separate all the grain from the chaff.* When this is done, he pursues other methods. Hence the various severe and heavy trials with which the people of God are afflicted. ¶ *Nor bruise it* with *his horsemen.* Lowth renders this, 'With

TREADING OUT CORN IN THE EAST BY HORSES.—From Description de l'Egypte.

the hoofs of his cattle;' proposing to read פרסיו instead of פָּרָשָׁיו by a change of a single letter ס *Samekh,* instead of שׁ *Shin.* So the Syriac and

29 This also cometh forth from the Lord of hosts, *which* is won- derful *a* in counsel, *and* excellent in working.

a Ps.92.5; Jer.32.19; Rom.11.33.

the Vulgate; and so Symmachus and Theodotion. But the word פָּרָשׁ may denote not only a *horseman*, but the *horse* itself on which one rides (see Bochart, *Hieroz.* i. 2, 6. p. 98. Comp. Note on Hab. i. 8; 2 Sam. i. 6; Isa. xxi. 7, 9). That horses were used in treading out grain there can be no doubt. They are extensively used in this country; and though in Palestine it is probable that oxen were chiefly employed (Deut. xxv. 4) in the early times, yet there is no improbability in supposing that in the times subsequent to Solomon, when horses abounded, they were preferred. Their more rapid motion, and perhaps the hardness of their hoofs, makes them more valuable for this service (see Michaelis' *Commentary on the Laws of Moses*, vol. ii. App. pp. 430–514, Lond. Ed. 1814). There are here, therefore, four modes of threshing mentioned, all of which are common still in the East. 1. The sledge with rollers, on which were pieces of iron, or stone, and which was dragged over the grain. 2. The cart or wain, with serrated wheels, and which was also drawn over the grain. 3. The flail, or the stick. 4. The use of cattle and horses.

29. *This also cometh*, &c. That is, these various devices for threshing his grain comes from the Lord no less than the skill with which he tills his land. (see ver. 26). ¶ And *excellent in working*. Or rather, who magnifies (וְהִגְדִּיל) his wisdom (תּוּשִׁיָּה). This word properly means wisdom, or understanding (Job xi. 6; xii. 16; xxvi. 3; Prov. iii. 21; viii. 14; xviii. 1). The idea of the prophet is, that God, who had so wisely taught the husbandman, and who had instructed him to use such various methods in his husbandry, would also be himself wise, and would pursue similar methods with his people. He would not always pursue the same unvarying course, but would vary his dispensations as they should need, and as would best secure their holiness and happiness. We see—1. The reason of afflictions. It is for the same cause which induces the farmer to employ various methods on his farm. 2. We are not to expect the same unvarying course in God's dealings with us. It would be as unreasonable to expect that the farmer would be always ploughing, or always threshing. 3. We are not to expect always the same *kind* of afflictions. The farmer uses different machines and modes of threshing, and adapts them to the nature of the grain. So God uses different modes, and adapts them to the nature, character, and disposition of his people. One man requires one mode of discipline, and another another. At one time we need one mode of correction to call us from sin and temptation; at another another. We may lay it down as a general rule, that *the Divine judgments are usually in the line of our offences ;* and by the nature of the judgment we may usually ascertain the nature of the sin. If a man's besetting sin is *pride*, the judgment will usually be something that is fitted to humble his pride; if it be covetousness, his property may be removed, or it may be made a curse; if it be undue attachment to children or friends, they may be removed. 4. God will not crush or destroy his people. The farmer does not crush or destroy his grain. In all the various methods which he uses, he takes care not to pursue it too far, and not to injure the grain. So with God's dealings with his people. His object is not to destroy them, but it is to separate the chaff from the wheat; and he will afflict them only so much as may be necessary to accomplish this. He will not be *always* bruising his people, but will in due time remit his strokes—just as the thresher does. 5. We should, therefore, bear afflictions and chastisements with patience. God deals with us in mercy—and the design of all his dispensations toward us in prosperity and adversity; in sickness and in health; in success and in disappointment, is to produce the richest and most abundant fruits of righteousness, and to prepare us to enter into his kingdom above.

CHAPTER XXIX.

ANALYSIS.

THIS chapter relates solely to Jerusalem—here called Ariel (see Note on ver. 1). It is not immediately connected with the preceding or the following chapters, though it is not improbable they were delivered about the same time. At what time this .was delivered is not known, though it is evident that it was before the invasion by Sennacherib, and probably before the time of Hezekiah. The prophecy in the chapter consists of two parts:—I. The invasion of Judea by Sennacherib, and its sudden deliverance (1-8). II. A reproof of the Jews for their infidelity and impiety.

I. The invasion of Judea, and the distress that would be brought upon Jerusalem, and its sudden deliverance (1-8). 1. Ariel would be filled with grief and distress (1, 2). 2. JEHOVAH would encamp against it and besiege it, and it would be greatly straitened and humbled (3, 4). 3. Yet the besieging army would be visited with sudden calamity and destruction—represented here by thunder, and tempest, and flame (5, 6). 4. The enemy would vanish as a dream, and all his hopes would be disappointed, as the hopes of a hungry and thirsty man are disappointed who dreams of having satisfied his hunger and thirst (7, 8).

There can be no doubt, I think, that this portion of the prophecy refers to the sudden and dreadful overthrow of Sennacherib; and the design of this portion of the prophecy is to give the assurance, that though Jerusalem would be in imminent danger, yet it would be suddenly delivered.

II. The second part consists of reproofs of the inhabitants of Jerusalem for their infidelity and impiety. 1. They were full of error, and all classes of people were wandering from God—reeling under error like a drunken man (9). 2. A spirit of blindness and stupidity everywhere prevailed among the people (10-12). 3. Formality and external regard for the institutions of religion prevailed, but without its life and power (13). 4. They attempted to lay deep and skilful plans to hide their wickedness from JEHOVAH (15). 5. They were unjust in their judgments, making a man an offender for a word, and perverting just judgment (21). 6. For all this they should be punished. (*a.*) The wisdom of their wise men should fail (14). (*b.*) The scorner would be consumed (20). 7. There would be an overturning, and the people would be made acquainted with the law of God, and the truly pious would be comforted (16-19). Those who had erred would be reformed, and would come to the true knowledge of God (22-24).

W O [1] to Ariel, to Ariel, [2] the city *where* [a] David dwelt! add ye year to year; let them [3] kill sacrifices.

    1 or, *O Ariel,* i.e., *the lion of God.*
    2 or, *of the city.*   a 2 Sam.5.9.   3 *cut off the heads.*

CHAPTER XXIX.

1. *Wo* (comp. Note on ch. xviii. 1). ¶ *To Ariel.* There can be no doubt that Jerusalem is here intended. The declaration that it was the city where David dwelt, as well as the entire scope of the prophecy, proves this. But still, it is not quiet clear why the city is here called *Ariel.* The margin reads, ' O Ariel, *i.e.*, the lion of God.' The word *Ariel* (אֲרִיאֵל) is compounded of two words, and is usually supposed to be made up of אֲרִי, *a lion,* and אֵל, *God;* and if this interpretation is correct, it is equivalent to a strong, mighty, fierce lion—where the word ' God ' is used to denote greatness in the same way as the lofty cedars of Lebanon are called cedars of God ; *i.e.*, lofty cedars. The *lion* is an emblem of strength, and a strong lion is an emblem of a mighty warrior or hero. 2 Sam. xxiii. 20 : ' He slew two *lion-like* (אֲרִיאֵל) men of Moab' (1 Chron. xi. 22). This use of the word to denote a hero is common in Arabic (see Bochart, *Hieroz.*, i. 3. 1). If this be the sense in which it is used here, then it is applied to Jerusalem under the image of a hero, and particularly as the place which was distinguished under David as the capital of a kingdom that was so celebrated for its triumphs in war. The word ' Ariel ' is, however, used in another sense in the Scriptures, to denote an *altar* (Ezek. xliii. 15, 16), where in the Heb. the word is *Ariel.* This name is given to the altar, Bochart supposes (*Hieroz.*, i. 3. 1), because the altar of burnt - offering *devours* as it were the sacrifices as a lion devours its prey. Gesenius, however, has suggested another reason why the word is given to the altar, since he says that the word אֲרִי is the same as one used in Arabic to denote *a fire-hearth,* and that the altar was so called because it was the place of perpetual burnt-offering. The name *Ariel,* is, doubtless, given in

2 Yet I will distress Ariel, and there shall be heaviness and sorrow : and it shall be unto me as Ariel.

Ezekiel to an altar ; and it may be given here to Jerusalem because it was the place of the altar, or of the public worship of God. The Chaldee renders it, ' Wo to the altar, the altar which was constructed in the city where David dwelt.' It seems to me that this view better suits the connection, and particularly ver. 2 (see Note), than to suppose that the name is given to Jerusalem because it was like a lion. If this be the true interpretation, then it is so called because Jerusalem was the place of the burnt-offering, or of the public worship of God ; the place where the fire, as on a hearth, continually burned on the altar. ¶ *The city* where *David dwelt.* David took the hill of Zion from the Jebusites, and made it the capital of his kingdom (2 Sam. v. 6–9). Lowth renders this, ' The city which David besieged.' So the LXX. 'Επολέμησε ; and so the Vulgate, *Expugnavit.* The word הָנָה properly means *to encamp*, to pitch one's tent (Gen. xxvi. 17), to station one's self. It is also used in the sense of encamping *against* any one, that is, to make war upon or to attack (see ver. 3, and Ps. xxvii. 3 ; 2 Sam. xii. 28) ; and Jerome and others have supposed that it has this meaning here in accordance with the interpretation of the LXX. and the Vulgate. But the more correct idea is probably that in our translation, that David pitched his tent there ; that is, that he made it his dwelling-place. ¶ *Add ye year to year.* That is, ' go on year after year, suffer one year to glide on after another in the course which you are pursuing.' This seems to be used ironically, and to denote that they were going on one year after another in the observance of the feasts ; walking the round of external ceremonies as if the fact that David had dwelt there, and that that was the place of the great altar of worship, constituted perfect security. One of the sins charged on them in this chapter was *formality* and *heartlessness* in their devotions (ver. 13), and this seems to be referred to here. ¶ *Let them kill sacrifices.* Marg. ' Cut off the heads.' The word here rendered 'kill' (נָקַף) may mean to

smite ; to hew ; to cut down (Isa. x. 34 ; Job xix. 26). But it has also another signification which better accords with this place. It denotes to make a circle, to revolve ; to go round a place (Josh. vi. 3, 11) ; to surround (1 Kings vii. 24 ; 2 Kings vi. 14 ; Ps. xvii. 9 ; xxii. 17 ; lxxxviii. 18). The word rendered ' sacrifices ' (חַגִּים) may mean a sacrifice (Ex. xxiii. 18 ; Ps. cxviii. 27 ; Mal. ii. 3), but it more commonly and properly denotes feasts or festivals (Ex. x. 9 ; xii. 14 ; Lev. xxiii. 39 ; Deut. xvi. 10, 16 ; 1 Kings viii. 2, 65 ; 2 Chron. vii. 8, 9 ; Neh. viii. 14 ; Hos. ii. 11, 13). Here the sense is, ' let the festivals go round ;' that is, let them revolve as it were in a perpetual, unmeaning circle, until the judgments due to such heartless service shall come upon you. The whole address is evidently ironical, and designed to denote that all their service was an unvarying repetition of heartless forms.

2. *Yet I will distress Ariel.* The reference here is doubtless to the siege which God says (ver. 3) he would bring upon the guilty and formal city. ¶ *And there shall be heaviness and sorrow.* This was true of the city in the siege of Sennacherib, to which this probably refers. Though the city was delivered in a sudden and remarkable manner (see Note on ver. 7, 8), yet it was also true that it was reduced to great distress (see ch. xxxvi., xxxvii.) ¶ *And it shall be unto me as Ariel.* This phrase shows that in ver. 1 Jerusalem is called ' Ariel,' because it contained the great altar, and was the place of sacrifice. The word *Ariel* here is to be understood in the sense of *the hearth of the great altar;* and the meaning is, ' I will indeed make Jerusalem like the great altar ; I will make it the burning place of wrath where my enemies shall be consumed as if they were on the altar of burnt sacrifice.' Thus in ch. xxx. 9, it is said of Jehovah that his ' fire is in Zion, and his furnace in Jerusalem.' This is a strong expression, denoting the calamity that was approaching ; and though the main reference in this whole passage is to the distress that would

3 And I will camp against thee round about, and will lay siege against *a* thee with a mount, and I will raise forts against thee.

4 And thou shalt be brought down, *b and* shalt speak out of the ground, and thy speech shall be low out of the dust, and thy voice shall be as of one that hath a fa-

a 2 Ki.25.1,&c. *b* La. 1.9. 1 *peep*, or, *chirp.*

miliar spirit, out of the ground, and thy speech shall [1] whisper out of the dust.

5 Moreover the multitude of thy strangers shall be like small dust, and the multitude of the terrible ones *shall be* as chaff *c* that passeth away : yea, it shall be at an instant suddenly.*d*

c Job 21.18. *d* 1 Th.5.3.

come upon them in the invasion of Sennacherib, yet there is no impropriety in supposing that there was presented to the mind of the prophet in vision the image of the total ruin that would come yet upon the city by the Chaldeans—when the temple, the palaces, and the dwellings of the magnificent city of David would be in flames, and like a vast blazing altar consuming that which was laid upon it.

3. *And I will camp against thee.* That is, I will cause an army to pitch their tents there for a siege. God regards the armies which he would employ as under his control, and speaks of them as if he would do it himself (see Note on ch. x. 5). ¶ *Round about* (כַּדּוּר). As in a circle ; that is, he would encompass or encircle the city. The word here used (דּוּר) in ch. xxii. 18, means *a ball*, but here it evidently means a circle ; and the sense is, that the army of the besiegers would encompass the city. A similar form of expression occurs in regard to Jerusalem in Luke xix. 43 : ' For the days shall come upon thee, that thine enemies shall cast a trench (χάρακα—a rampart, a mound) about thee (σοι against thee), and compass thee round (περικυκλώσουσί σι, encircle thee).' So also Luke xxi. 20. The LXX. render this, ' I will encompass thee as David did ;' evidently reading it as if it were כַּדּוּר; and Lowth observes that two MSS. thus read it, and he himself adopts it. But the authority for correcting the Hebrew text in this way is not sufficient, nor is it necessary. The idea in the present reading is a clear one, and evidently means that the armies of Sennacherib would encompass the city. ¶ *With a mount.* A rampart ; a fortification. Or, rather, perhaps, the word מַצָּב means a post, a military sta-

tion, from יָצַב, *to place, to station.* The word in this form occurs nowhere else in the Scriptures, but the word מַצָּב occurs in 1 Sam. xiii. 23; xiv. 1, 4 ; 2 Sam. xxiii. 14, in the sense of a military post, or garrison. ¶ *I will rise forts.* That is, ramparts, such as were usually thrown up against a besieged city, meaning that it should be subjected to the regular process of a siege. The LXX. read, Πύργους—' Towers ;' and so also two MSS. by changing the letter ר into ד. But there is no necessity for altering the Hebrew text. Lowth prefers the reading of the LXX.

4. And *shalt speak out of the ground* (see Note on ch. viii. 19). The sense here is, that Jerusalem, that had been accustomed to pride itself on its strength would be greatly humbled and subdued. Its loud and lofty tone would be changed. It would use the suppressed language of fear and alarm as if it spoke from the dust, or in a shrill small voice, like the pretended conversers with the dead. ¶ *And thy speech shall whisper out of the dust.* Marg. ' Peep,' or ' Chirp,' (see Note on ch. viii. 19).

5. *Moreover.* These verses (5, 7, 8) contain a beautiful description of the destruction of the army of Sennacherib. Though they had laid the plan of a regular siege ; though the city, in itself, would not be able to hold out against them, and all was alarm and conscious imbecility within ; yet in an instant the siege would be raised, and the advancing hosts of the Assyrians would all be gone. ¶ *The multitude of thy strangers.* The multitude of the strangers that shall besiege thee ; called '*thy* strangers,' because they besieged, or oppressed thee. The word ' strangers ' here, as elsewhere, means *foreigners* (see Note on ch. i. 7; comp. ch. ii. 6 ; v. 17; xiv. 1 ; xxv. 2, 5;

6 Thou ^ashalt be visited of the Lord of hosts with thunder, and with earthquake, and great noise, with storm and tempest, and the flame of devouring fire.

7 And the multitude of all the nations that fight against Ariel, even all ^b that fight against her and her munition, and that distress her, shall be as a dream ^cof a night vision.

8 It shall even be as when an hungry man dreameth, and, behold, he eateth ; but he awaketh, and his soul is empty : or when a thirsty man dreameth, and, behold, he drinketh ; but he awaketh, and behold, *he is* faint, and his soul hath appetite : so shall the multitude of all the nations be that fight against mount Zion.

a ch.30.30.   b ch.41.11,12.   c ch.37.36.

xxix. 5 ; lx. 10). ¶ *Shall be like small dust.* Light, fine dust that is easily dissipated by the wind. ¶ *Of the terrible ones.* Of the invading, besieging army, that is so much the object of dread. ¶ *As chaff that passeth away* (see Note on ch. xvii. 13). This image of chaff driven before the wind, to denote the sudden and entire discomfiture of enemies, is common in the Scriptures (see Job xxi. 18; Ps. i. 4; xxxv. 5; Hos. xiii. 13). ¶ *Yea, it shall be at an instant suddenly.* The forces of Sennacherib were destroyed in a single night by the angel of the Lord (Isa. xxxvii. 36; Notes on ch. x. 12, 28–34), and the siege of Jerusalem was of course immediately raised.

6. *Thou shalt be visited.* This is an address to the mighty army of the Assyrian. Such transitions are not uncommon in the writings of Isaiah. His eye seems to have been directed in vision to the hosts of Sennacherib, and to their sudden dispersion and destruction (ver. 5), and by a sudden, but not unnatural transition, he turns and addresses the army itself, with the assurance that it should be punished (comp. ch. xxx. 30). ¶ *With thunder,* &c. The army of the Assyrian was cut off by an angel sent forth from God (ch. xxxvii. 36). It is *possible* that all the agents here referred to may have been employed in the destruction of the Assyrian host, though they are not particularly specified in the history. But it is not absolutely necessary to understand this verse in this manner. The image of thunder, earthquakes, and lightning, is an impressive representation of sudden and awful judgment in any manner. The sense is, that they should be suddenly destroyed by the direct visitation of

God (see ch. ix. 5; xxvi. 11). ¶ *And the flame of devouring fire.* Lightning, that seems to *devour*, or that suddenly consumes.

7. *And the multitude of all the nations.* The Assyrians, and their allied hosts. ¶ *And her munition.* Her fortresses, castles, places of strength (2 Sam. v. 7; Eccl. ix. 14; Ezek. xix. 9). ¶ *Shall be as a dream of a night vision.* In a dream we seem to see the objects of which we think as really as when awake, and hence they are called *visions,* and *visions of the night* (Gen. xlvi. 2; Job iv. 13; vii. 14; Dan. ii. 28; iv. 5; vii. 1, 7, 13, 15). The specific idea here is not that of the *suddenness* with which objects seen in a dream appear and then vanish, but it is that which occurs in ver. 8, of one who dreams of eating and drinking, but who awakes, and is hungry and thirsty still. So it was with the Assyrian. He had set his heart on the wealth of Jerusalem. He had earnestly desired to possess that city—as a hungry man desires to satisfy the cravings of his appetite. But it would be like the vision of the night ; and on that fatal morning on which he should awake from his fond dream (ch. xxxvii. 36), he would find all his hopes dissipated, and the long-cherished desire of his soul unsatisfied still.

8. *It shall even be,* &c. This is a most striking figure representing the earnest desire of the Assyrian to possess the city of Jerusalem, and his utter disappointment. The comparison is elegant and beautiful in the highest degree. It is wrought up to great perfection ; and is perfectly suited to illustrate the object in view. The same image substantially is found in the

9 Stay yourselves, and wonder; cry [1] ye out, and cry: they are drunken, [a] but not with wine; they stagger, but not with strong drink.

1 or, *take your pleasure and riot.*

a ch.51.21.

---

classic writers; and this, says Lowth, may, for beauty and ingenuity, fairly come in competition with one of the most elegant of Virgil (greatly improved from Homer, *Iliad* xxii. 119), where he has applied to a different purpose, but not so happily, the same image of the ineffectual workings of the imagination in a dream:

Ac veluti in somnis oculos ubi languida pressit
Nocte quies, nequicquam avidos extendere cursus
Velle videmur, et in mediis conatibus ægri
Succidimus; non lingua valet, non corpore notæ
Sufficiunt vires; nec, vox, nec verba sequuntur.
Æniad xii. 908.

And as when slumber seals the closing sight,
The sick wild fancy labours in the night,
Some dreadful visionary foe we shun,
With airy strides, but strive in vain to run;
In vain our baffled limbs their powers essay,
We faint, we struggle, sink, and fall away;
Drained of our strength we neither fight nor fly,
And on the tongue the struggling accents die.
Pitt.

See also Lucretius (iv. 10–19), who also expresses the same image as Isaiah. As the simile of the prophet is drawn from nature, an extract which describes the actual occurrence of such a circumstance will be agreeable. 'The scarcity of water,' says Park, 'was greater here at Bubaker than at Benown. Day and night the wells were crowded with cattle lowing, and fighting with each other to come at the trough. Excessive thirst made many of them furious; others being too weak to contend for the water, endeavoured to quench their thirst by devouring the black mud from the gutters near the wells; which they did with great avidity, though it was commonly fatal to them. This great scarcity of water was felt by all the people of the camp; and by none more than myself. I begged water from the negro slaves that attended the camp, but with very indifferent success; for though I let no opportunity slip, and was very urgent in my solicitations both to the Moors and to the negroes, I was but ill supplied, and frequently passed the night in the situation of Tantalus. No sooner had I shut my eyes, than fancy would convey me to the streams and rivers of my native land; there, as I wandered along the verdant bank, I surveyed the clear stream with transport, and hastened to swallow the delightful draught; but alas! disappointment awakened me, and I found myself a lonely captive, perishing of thirst amid the wilds of Africa.'—(*Travels in Africa*).

9. *Stay yourselves.* Thus far the prophet had given a description of the siege of Jerusalem by Sennacherib, and of his sudden overthrow. He now turns to the Jews, and reproves their stupidity, formality, and hypocrisy; and the remainder of the chapter is occupied with a statement of the prevalence of these sins, of the judgments that must follow, and of the fact that there should yet be an extensive reformation, and turning to the Lord. The word rendered 'stay yourselves' (הִתְמַהְמְהוּ) means properly *to linger,* tarry, delay (Gen. xix. 16; xliii. 10; 2 Sam. xv. 28). Here it seems to denote that state of mind in which any one is *fixed in astonishment;* in which one stops, and stares at some strange and unexpected occurrence. The object of amazement which the prophet supposes would excite astonishment, was the stupidity, dulness, and hypocrisy of a people who had been so signally favoured (comp. Hab. i. 5). ¶ *Cry ye out, and cry.* There is in the original here a paronomasia which cannot be conveyed in a translation. The word which is used (הִשְׁתַּעַשְׁעוּ) is one form of the verb שָׁעַע, which means, usually, to make smooth, rub, spread over; hence, in the Hithpael form which is here used, to be spread over; and hence is applied to the eyes (Isa. vi. 10), to denote blindness, *as if* they were overspread with something by reason of which they could not see. Here it probably means, 'be ye dazzled and blinded,' that is, ye be astonished, as in the former part of the verse. The idea seems to be that of some object of sudden astonishment that dims the sight, and takes away all the powers of vision. The word is used in the same sense in

10 For *a* the LORD hath poured out upon you the spirit of deep sleep, and hath closed your eyes; the prophets and your [1] rulers the seers *b* hath he covered.

11 And the vision of all is become unto you as the words of a [2] book that is sealed, *c* which *men* deliver

to one that is learned, saying, Read this, I pray thee: and he saith, I cannot; for it *is* sealed.

12 And the book is delivered to him that is not learned, saying, Read this, I pray thee: and he saith, I am not learned.

13 Wherefore the Lord said,

a Ro.11.8.   1 *heads.*   *b* 1 Sa.9.9.   2 or, *letter.*   *c* Da.12.4,9; Re 5.1-9.

ch. xxxii. 3; comp. ch. xxxv. 5; xlii. 19. Probably the idea here would be well expressed by our word *stare*, 'stare and look with a stupid surprise;' denoting the attitude and condition of a man who is amazed at some remarkable and unlooked for spectacle. ¶ *They are drunken, but not with wine.* The people of Jerusalem. They reel and stagger, but the cause is not that they are drunken with wine. It is a moral and spiritual intoxication and reeling. They err in their doctrines and practice; and it is with them as it is with a drunken man that sees nothing clearly or correctly, and cannot walk steadily. They have perverted all doctrines; they err in their views of God and his truth, and they are irregular and corrupt in their conduct.

10. *For the* LORD *hath poured out upon you.* The word rendered 'hath poured out' (יָסַךְ) is usually referred to the act of pouring out a libation, or drink-offering in worship (Ex. xxx. 9; Hos. ix. 4; Isa. xxx. 1). Here it means that JEHOVAH had, as it were, *drenched them* (LXX. πεπότικε) with a spirit of stupefaction. This is traced to God in accordance with the usual custom in the Bible, by which his providential agency is recognized in all events (see Notes on ch. vi. 9, 10). Compare Notes on Rom. xi. 8), where this passage is quoted from the LXX., and is applied to the Jews in the time of the apostle Paul. ¶ *The spirit of deep sleep.* The word rendered ' deep sleep,' is the same as is used in Gen. ii. 21, to denote the sleep that God brought on Adam; and in Gen. xv. 12, to denote the deep sleep that fell on Abraham, and when a horror of great darkness fell upon him; and in 1 Sam. xxvi. 12, to denote the deep sleep that came upon Saul when David approached and took away

the spear and the cruise of water from his bolster. Here it means spiritual sluggishness, inactivity, stupidity, that prevailed everywhere among the people in regard to the things of religion. ¶ *The seers.* Those that see visions, another name for the prophets (see Note on ch. i. 1). ¶ *Hath he covered.* That is, he has covered their eyes; or they are all blind.

11. *And the vision of all.* The vision of all the prophets; that is, all the revelations which God has made to you (see Note on ch. i. 1). The prophet refers not only to his own communications, but to those of his contemporaries, and of all who had gone before him. The sense is, that although they had the communications which God had made to them, yet they did not understand them. They were as ignorant of their true nature as a man who can read is of the contents of a letter that is sealed up, or as a man who cannot read is of the contents of a book that is handed to him. ¶ *As the words of a book.* Marg. ' Letter.' The word סֵפֶר may mean either. It properly means anything which is *written* (Deut. xxiv. i. 3; Jer. xxxii. 11; Dan. i. 4), but is commonly applied to a book (Ex. xvii. 14; Josh. i. 8; viii. 34; Ps. xl. 8). ¶ *That is sealed* (see Note on ch. viii. 16).

12. *And the book is delivered, &c.* That is, they are just as ignorant of the true nature and meaning of the revelations of God as a man is of the contents of a book who is utterly unable to read.

13. *Wherefore the Lord said.* This verse, with the following, is designed to denounce the Divine judgment on their formality of worship. They kept up the forms of religion, but they withheld the affections of their hearts from God; and he, therefore, says that he will pro-

Forasmuch as this people draw near *me* with their mouth, *a* and with their lips do honour me, but have removed their heart far from me, and their fear toward me is taught by the precept of *b* men :

14 Therefore, behold, I will proceed ¹ to do a marvellous *c* work among this people, *even* a marvellous work and a wonder : for *d* the wisdom of their wise *men* shall

a Eze.33.31; Mat.15.6-9.		*b* Col.2.22.		1 *add.*
c Hab.1.5.		*d* Jer.49.7; Ob.8; 1 Co.1.19.

ceed to inflict on them exemplary and deserved punishment. ¶ *This people draw near* me. That is, in the temple, and in the forms of external devotion. ¶ *And with their lips do honour me.* They professedly celebrate my praise, and acknowledge me in the forms of devotion. ¶ *But have removed their heart.* Have withheld the affections of their hearts. ¶ *And their fear toward me.* The worship of God is often represented as *fear* (Job xxviii. 28; Ps. xix. 9; xxxiv. 11; Prov. i. 7). ¶ *Is taught by the precept of men.* That is, their views, instead of having been derived from the Scriptures, were drawn from the doctrines of men. Our Saviour referred to this passage, and applied it to the hypocrites of his own time (Matt. xv. 8, 9). The latter part of it is, however, not quoted literally from the Hebrew, nor from the LXX., but retains the sense : ' But in vain do they worship me, teaching for doctrines the commandments of men.' He quoted it as strikingly descriptive of the people when he lived, not as saying that Isaiah referred directly to his times.

14. *I will proceed to do.* Heb. ' I will add to do ;' that is, I will do it. ¶ *For the wisdom of their wise men shall perish.* I will bring calamity upon them which shall baffle all the skill and wisdom of their wise men. ¶ *Shall be hid.* That is, shall not appear ; shall vanish. It shall not be sufficient to prevent the calamities that shall come upon the nation.

15. *Wo unto them that seek deep,* &c. That is, who attempt to conceal their *real* intentions under a plausible exterior, and correct outward deportment.

perish, and the understanding of their prudent *men* shall be hid.

15 Wo unto them that seek deep to hide *e* their counsel from the LORD, and their works are in the dark, and they say, Who *f* seeth us ? and who knoweth us ?

16 Surely your turning of things upside down shall be esteemed as the potter's clay : for *g* shall the work say of him that made it, He

e Ps.139.7,&c.; ch.30.1.		*f* Ps.94.7.
g ch.45.9; Ro.9.20.

This is most strikingly descriptive of the character of a hypocrite who seeks to conceal his plans and his purposes from the eyes of men and of God. His external conduct is fair ; his observance of the duties of religion exemplary ; his attendance on the means of grace and the worship of God regular ; his professions loud and constant, but the whole design is to *conceal* his real sentiments, and to accomplish some sinister and wicked purpose by it. ¶ *From the* LORD. This proves that the design of the hypocrite is not always to attempt to deceive his fellowmen, but that he also aims to deceive God.

16. *Surely your turning of things upside down.* Your *perversion* of all things. They had no just views of truth. They deemed mere formality to be all that was required. They attempted to conceal their plans even from JEHOVAH ; and everything in the opinions and practice of the nation had become perverted and erroneous. There has been much diversity in rendering this phrase. Luther renders it, ' O how perverse ye are.' Lowth renders it,

' Perverse as ye are! shall the potter be esteemed as the clay ?'

Rosenmüller also accords with this interpretation, and renders it, ' O your perversity,' &c. The sense of the passage seems to be this : ' Your *changing of things* is just as absurd as it would be for the thing formed to say to him that formed it, why hast thou made me thus? It is as absurd for you to find fault with the government of God as it would be for the clay to complain of

made me not? or shall the thing framed say of him that framed it, He had no understanding?

17 *Is* it not yet a very little while,

and Lebanon shall be turned *ª* into a fruitful field, and the fruitful field shall be esteemed as a forest?

want of skill in the potter. You complain of God's laws, and worship him according to the commandments of men. You complain of his requirements, and offer to him the service of the mouth and the lip, and withhold the heart. You suppose that God does not see you, and do your deeds in darkness. All this supposes that God is destitute of wisdom, and cannot see what is done, and it is just as absurd as it would be in the clay to complain that the potter who fashions it has no understanding.' ¶ *Shall be esteemed*, &c. The *literal* translation of this passage would be, ' Your perverseness is as if the potter should be esteemed as the clay;' that is, as if he was no more qualified to form anything than the clay itself. ¶ *For shall the work*, &c. This passage is quoted by the apostle Paul (Rom. ix. 20, 21) to show the right which God has to do with his creatures as shall seem good in his sight, and the impropriety of complaining of his distinguishing mercy in choosing to life those whom he pleases. The sense of the passage is, that it would be absurd for that which is made to complain of the maker as having no intelligence, and no right to make it as he does. It would be absurd in the piece of pottery to complain of the potter as if he had no skill; and it is equally absurd in a man to complain of God, or to regard him as destitute of wisdom.

17. Is *it not yet a very little while.* The idea here is, ' you have greatly perverted things in Jerusalem. The time is at hand when there shall be *other* overturnings—when the wicked shall be cut off, and when there shall be poured out upon the nation such judgments that the deaf shall hear, and the blind see, and when those who have erred in spirit shall come to understanding' (ver. 18-24). ¶ *And Lebanon shall be turned into a fruitful field.* This is evidently a proverbial expression, denoting any great revolution of things. It is probable that in the times

of Isaiah the whole chain of Lebanon was uncultivated, as the word is evidently here used in opposition to a fruitful field (see Note on ch. ii. 13). The word which is rendered ' fruitful field ' (כַּרְמֶל, *carmel*) properly denotes *a fruitful field*, or a finely cultivated country (see Isa. x. 18). It is also applied to a celebrated mountain or promontory on the Mediterranean Sea, on the southern boundary of the tribe of Asher. It runs north-west of the plain of Esdraelon, and ends in a promontory or cape, and forms the bay of Acco. The mountain or promontory is about 1500 feet high; and abounds in caves or grottoes, and was celebrated as being the residence of the prophets Elijah and Elisha (see 1 Kings xviii. 19, 42; 2 Kings ii. 25; iv. 25; xix. 23; comp. Note on Isa. xxxv. 2). More than a thousand caves are said to exist on the west side of the mountain, which it is said were formerly inhabited by monks. But the word here is to be taken, doubtless, as it is in our translation, as denoting a well-cultivated country. Lebanon, that is now barren and uncultivated, shall soon become a fertile and productive field. That is, there shall be changes among the Jews that shall be as great *as if* Lebanon should become an extensively cultivated region, abounding in fruits, and vines, and harvests. The idea is this : ' The nation is now perverse, sinful, formal, and hypocritical. But the time of change shall come. The wicked shall be reformed; the number of the pious shall be increased; and the pure worship of God shall succeed this general formality and hypocrisy.' The prophet does not say *when* this would be. He simply affirms that it would be before *a great while*—and it may, perhaps, be referred to the times succeeding the captivity (comp. ch. xxxii. 15; xxxv. i. 6). ¶ *And the fruitful field be esteemed as a forest.* That is, there shall be great changes in the nation, *as if* a well-cultivated field should be

18 And ^a in that day shall the deaf hear the words of the book, and the eyes of the blind shall see out of obscurity, and out of darkness.

19 The meek ^b also shall ¹ increase *their* joy in the LORD, and the poor ^c among men shall rejoice in the Holy One of Israel.

^a ch.35.5; Lu.7.22.   ^b ch.61.1.   ¹ add.
^c Ja.2.5.

20 For the terrible one is brought to nought, ^d and the scorner is consumed, and all that watch ^e for iniquity are cut off ;

21 That make a man an offender for a word, and ^f lay a snare for him that reproveth in the gate, and turn aside the just for a thing of nought.

^d ch.51.13; Re.12.10.   ^e Ps.64.6; Jer.20.10.
^f Amos 5.10,12.

---

allowed to lie waste, and grow up into a forest. Perhaps it means that that which was then apparently flourishing would be overthrown, and the land lie waste. Those who were apparently in prosperity, would be humbled and punished. The effect of this revolution is stated in the following verses.

18. *Shall the deaf hear the words of the book.* They who now have the law and do not understand it, the people who seem to be deaf to all that God says, shall hear and understand it. ¶ *Shall see out of obscurity,* &c. That is, the darkness being removed, they shall see clearly the truth of God, and discern and love its beauty. Their eyes are now blinded, but then they shall see clearly.

19. *The meek.* The word 'meek' usually refers to those who are patient in the reception of injuries, but the Hebrew word used here (עֲנָיִם) means properly the oppressed, the afflicted, the unhappy (Ps. ix. 13 ; x. 12, 17; Prov. iii. 34; Isa. xi. 4). It involves usually the idea of humility or *virtuous suffering* (comp. Ps. xxv. 9; xxxvii. 11; lxix. 33). Here it may denote the pious of the land who were oppressed, and subjected to trials. ¶ *Shall increase.* Marg., as in Heb. 'Add.' It means, that they should greatly rejoice in the Lord. They should see the evidence of the fulfilment of his predictions ; they should see the oppressors punished (ver. 20, 21), and JEHOVAH coming forth to be their protector and defender (ver. 22–24). ¶ *And the poor among men.* The poor men ; or the needy. Doubtless the idea is that of the pious poor ; those who feared God, and who had been subjected to the trials of oppression and poverty.

20. *For the terrible one.* The violent one (עָרִיץ), the oppressor, who had exercised cruelty over them. This, I suppose, refers to the haughty among the Jews themselves ; to those who held offices of power, and who abused them to oppress the poor and needy. ¶ *And the scorner* (see ch. xxviii. 14, 22). ¶ *Is consumed.* Shall be entirely destroyed. ¶ *And all that watch for iniquity.* That is, who anxiously seek for opportunities to commit iniquity.

21. *That make a man an offender.* Literally, 'who cause a man to sin' (מַחֲטִיאֵי) ; that is, who hold a man to be guilty, or a criminal. Lowth renders this singularly enough :

'Who bewildered the poor man in speaking.'

Grotius supposes it means, 'Who on account of the word of God, that is, the true prophecy, treat men as guilty of crime.' Calvin supposes it means, 'Who bear with impatience the reproofs and denunciation of the prophets, and who endeavour to pervert and distort their meaning.' Hence, he supposes, they proposed artful and captious questions by which they might ensnare them. Others suppose that it refers to the fact that they led men into sin by their new doctrines and false views. The connection, however, seems to require that it should be understood of judicial proceedings, and the sense is probably correctly expressed by Noyes:

'Who condemned the poor man in his cause.'

This interpretation is also that which is proposed by Rosenmüller and Gesenius. According to the interpretation above suggested, the word rendered 'who make an offender,' means the same as who holds one guilty, that is, condemns. ¶ *A man* (אָדָם). It is

22 Therefore thus saith the LORD,[a] who redeemed Abraham, concerning the house of Jacob,

a Jos. 24. 3.

Jacob shall not [b] now be ashamed, neither shall his face now wax pale.

b ch. 54. 4.

well known that this word stands in contradistinction to שׁישׁ, and denotes usually a poor man, a man in humble life, in opposition to one who is rich or of more elevated rank. This is probably the sense here, and the meaning is, that they condemned the poor man; that is, that they were partial in their judgments. ¶ For a word (בְּדָבָר). In a word; denoting the same as a cause that is tried before a court of justice. So Ex. xviii. 16: 'When they have a matter (דָּבָר a word), they come unto me.' So Ex. xviii. 22: 'And it shall be that every great matter (Heb. every great word) that they shall bring unto me.' So Ex. xxii. 8 (in the English version 9): 'For all manner of trespass,' Heb. for every word of trespass; i.e., for every suit concerning a breach of trust. So also Ex. xxiv. 14: 'If any man have any matters to do,' (Heb. 'any words,') that is, if any one has a law suit. ¶ And lay a snare. To lay a snare is to devise a plan to deceive, or get into their possession; as birds are caught in snares that are concealed from their view. ¶ That reproveth. Or rather, that contended or pleaded; that is, that had a cause. The word יָכַח means often to contend with any one; to strive; to seek to confute; to attempt to defend or justify, as in a court of law (Job xiii. 15; xix. 5; xvi. 21; xxii. 4). It is also applied to deciding a case in law, or pronouncing a decision (Isa. xi. 3, 4; Gen. xxxi. 37; Job ix. 33). Here it means one who has brought a suit, or who is engaged in a legal cause. ¶ In the gate. Gates of cities being places of concourse, were usually resorted to for transacting business, and courts were usually held in them (Gen. xxiii. 10, 18; Deut. xvii. 5, 8; xxi. 19; xxii. 15; xxv. 6, 7; Ruth iv. 1). The sense is, they endeavoured to pervert justice, and to bring the man who had a cause before them, completely within their power, so that they might use him for their own purposes, at the same time that they seemed to

be deciding the cause justly. ¶ And turn aside the just. The man who has a just or righteous cause. ¶ For a thing of nought. Or a decision which is empty, vain (בַּתֹּהוּ), and which should be regarded as null and void.

22. Therefore. In consequence of the happy change which shall take place in the nation when the oppressor shall be removed (ver. 20, 21), and when the poor and the meek shall rejoice (ver. 19), and the ignorant shall be instructed (ver. 18), Jacob shall not be ashamed of his descendants as he was before, nor have cause to blush in regard to his posterity. ¶ Who redeemed Abraham. That is, who brought him out of a land of idolaters, and rescued him from the abominations of idolatry. The word 'redeem,' here (פָּדָה), properly denotes to ransom, i.e., to redeem a captive, or a prisoner with a price paid (Ex. xiii. 13; xxxiv. 20). But it is also used as meaning to deliver in general, without reference to a price, to free in any manner (2 Sam. iv. 9; 1 Kings i. 29; Job v. 20; Ps. lxxi. 23). It is used in this general sense here; and means that JEHOVAH had rescued Abraham from the evils of idolatry, and made him his friend. The connection, also, would seem to imply that there was a reference to the promise which was made to Abraham that he should have a numerous posterity (see ver. 23). ¶ Jacob shall not now be ashamed. This is a poetical introduction of Jacob as the ancestor of the Jewish people, as if the venerable patriarch were looking upon his children. Their deportment had been such as would suffuse a father's cheeks with shame; henceforward in the reformation that would occur he would not be ashamed of them, but would look on them with approbation. ¶ Neither shall his face wax pale. The face usually becomes pale with fear; but this may also occur from any strong emotion. Disappointment may produce paleness as well as fear; and perhaps the idea may be that the face of Jacob

23 But when he seeth his children, the work *a* of mine hands, in the midst of him, they shall sanctify my name, and sanctify the Holy One of Jacob, and shall fear the God of Israel.

24 They *b* also that erred in spirit shall [1] come to understanding, and they that murmured shall learn doctrine.

CHAPTER XXX.

ANALYSIS.

It is probable that the prophecy in this chapter was delivered about the same time as that in the previous chapter, and on the same general occasion. It is evident that it refers to the time of Hezekiah, when the Jews were alarmed by an apprehended invasion of the king of Assyria. Hezekiah had revolted from the king of Assyria (2 Kings xviii. 7); and it is probable that many of the leaders of the Jews began to be alarmed at the prospect that their land would be invaded by him, especially as it was known that it was the intention of Sennacherib to make war on Egypt, and that he could easily take Judea in his way. In such circumstances it was natural that they should propose an alliance with the Egyptians, and seek to unite their forces with theirs to repel the common danger. Instead of looking to God, and relying on his aid, they had probably entered into such an alliance, offensive and defensive (ch. xxxi. 1). To see the impropriety of such a league, it is to be remembered that God had promised to be the protector of his people, and that he had prohibited alliances with the surrounding nations; that it was a leading part of the Jewish policy,

a ch 60.21; Eph.2.10.   *b* 1 Co.6.11.
[1] *know understanding.*

as instituted by Moses, to keep them a distinct and independent people; and that special care had been exercised to keep them from returning to the customs, or depending on the aid of the Egyptians. This alliance had been formed unquestionably contrary to the solemn counsel and warning of Isaiah (ch. xx.), and he now reproves them for it, and endeavours to recall them again to confidence in God.

The following is a summary of the contents of the chapter:—I. The prophet denounces 'wo' on them for seeking the aid of Egypt (1, 2). II. He assures them that Egypt would be unable to help them, and that the effect would be that they would yet be ashamed themselves of the alliance (3–7). III. The prophet is directed to make a solem record that the prevailing character of the Jews was that of a rebellious people (8–11). IV. The judgment of God is denounced against them for forming this alliance, under the image of a wall that is ready to fall on them, and destroy them (12–14). V. The prophet tells them of the true way in which they may have peace and confidence, and that is, by putting their trust in God, and assures them that God waits to become their defender (15–18). VI. God *would* yet bless them. The people would see the vanity of their reliance on Egypt, and would turn unto God, and their turning to him would be attended with most rich and valuable blessings. These blessings are described in highly figurative and beautiful language (19–26) VII. Jehovah would show himself the protector of his people; and would, in a signal and sudden manner, overthrow and destroy the Assyrian, and deliver his people (27–33). The *scope*, therefore, of the chapter is to lead them to look away from Egypt, and to put confidence in God, at whose hand they were about to experience so signal a deliverance from the much dreaded invasion of Sennacherib.

---

should no more become pallid *as if* he had been disappointed in regard to the hopes which he had cherished of his sons.

23. *But when he seeth his children.* The sense is, ' he shall not be ashamed of his sons, for he shall see them henceforward walking in the ways of piety and virtue.' ¶ *The work of my hands.* That is, this change (ver. 17–19) by which the nation will be reformed, will be produced by the agency of God himself. The sentiment is in accordance with the doctrines of the Scriptures everywhere, that men are recovered from sin by the agency of God alone (comp. Isa. lx. 21; Eph. ii. 10). ¶ *In*

the midst of him. In the midst of his people. The name Jacob is often employed to denote all his posterity, or the whole nation of the Jews.

24. *They also that erred in spirit* (see ver. 9, 10). ¶ *Shall learn doctrine.* *When* this would occur the prophet does not state. It *may* be intended to denote the times of Hezekiah; or the times subsequent to the captivity; or possibly it may refer to the times under the Messiah. All that the prophet teaches is, that at some future period in the history of the Jews, there would be such a reform that they should be regarded as the worthy descendants of the pious patriarch Jacob.

WO *a* to the rebellious children, saith the Lord, that take counsel, but not of me ; and that cover *b* with a covering, but not of my Spirit, that they may add *c* sin to sin :

2 That *d* walk to go down into Egypt, and have not asked at my

a De.29.19.   *b* ch.29.15.   *c* Ro.2.5.   *d* ch.31.1.

CHAPTER XXX.

1. *Wo* (see Note on ch. xviii. 1). ¶ *To the rebellious children.* To those whom he had nourished as children, and who had rebelled against him (see Note on ch. i. 23). ¶ *That take counsel, but not of me.* They look to Egypt, and depend on a human arm. ¶ *And that cover with a covering.* The idea here, according to our translation, is, that they seek protection or a covering from the impending calamity. Lowth renders this, ' Who ratify covenants ;' supposing that the reference is to the fact that in ancient times compacts were formed by offering sacrifices, and by pouring out libations. The Hebrew, according to Lowth, means, ' who pour out a libation.' So the LXX. render it, Συνθήκας—' And thou hast made covenants.' The Syriac renders it, ' Who pour out libations.' The Hebrew word נָסַךְ (*nâsăkh*) properly conveys the idea of *pouring out,* and is applied—(1) to the act of pouring out wine as a drink offering, or as a libation to God (Gen. xxxv. 14 ; Ex. xxx. 9 ; 1 Chron. xi. 18; Hos. ix. 4); (2) to the act of pouring out oil, that is, to anointing kings and rulers (Ps. ii. 6 ; Dan. xi. 8) ; (3) to the act of pouring out melted metals, that is, to cast them (Isa. xl. 19 ; xliv. 10). The word also may have a meaning kindred to סָכַךְ (*sâkhăkh*), and denote *to cover,* as in Isa. xxv. 7. Various derivatives from the word are rendered ' to cover withal' (Num. iv. 7); 'the covering ' (Isa. xxviii. 20); ' the web,' that is, that which is woven for a covering (Judg. xvi. 13, 14). The idea, however, which best suits the connection here is probably that suggested by Lowth, in accordance with the LXX., and the Syriac, and adopted by Rosenmüller, Gesenius, and others, *to make a libation;* that is, to ratify a covenant,

mouth ; to strengthen themselves in the strength of Pharaoh, and to trust in the shadow of Egypt !

3 Therefore shall the strength of Pharaoh be your shame, and the trust in the shadow of Egypt *your* confusion.

4 For his princes were at Zoan, and his ambassadors came to Hanes.

---

or compact. ¶ *But not of my Spirit.* It was not such as was suggested by his Spirit, and not such as he would approve. ¶ *That they may add sin to sin.* They add to the sin of rebellion against God that of forming an alliance. Sins do not usually stand alone. When one is committed, it is often necessary to commit others in order to carry out and complete the plan which that contemplated.

2. *That walk to go down to Egypt.* Heb. ' Going in the descent to Egypt.' That is, they do it by their ambassadors (ver. 4). The journey to Egypt from Palestine is always represented as going down (Gen. xii. 10; xlii. 3; xliii. 15; Num. xx. 15; Deut. x. 22). ¶ *To strengthen themselves in the strength of Pharaoh.* To form an alliance with Pharaoh, that thus they might be able to repel the threatened invasion. Pharaoh was the general name of the kings of Egypt, in the same manner as *Cæsar* was the common name of the emperors of Rome. ¶ *To trust in the shadow of Egypt.* A ' shadow' (צֵל) is an emblem of protection and defence, as a shade is a protection from the burning rays of the sun (see Note on ch. iv. 6).

3. *Therefore shall the strength of Pharaoh be your shame* (see Note on ch. xx. 5). ¶ *Your confusion.* Heb. ' For reproach.' It would either occur that the Egyptians *would* not enter into an alliance ; or that if they did, they *could* not defend them, and in either case it would be the source of deep regret and shame.

4. *For his princes.* The sense of this verse seems to be this. The prophet is stating the fact that the Jews would be ashamed of their attempted alliance with Egypt. In this verse, and the following, he states the manner in which they would be made sensible of their

5 They were all ashamed [a] of a people *that* could not profit them, nor be an help nor profit, but a shame, and also a reproach.

6 The burden of the beasts of the south : into the land of trouble

a Jer. 2. 36.

and anguish, from whence *come* the young and old lion, the viper and fiery flying serpent, they will carry their riches upon the shoulders of young asses, and their treasures upon the bunches of camels, to a people *that* shall not profit *them*.

folly in seeking this alliance. He therefore enumerates several circumstances in regard to the manner in which the alliance had been sought, and the disappointment that would follow after all their vain confidence. He therefore states (ver. 4), that the Jews had employed persons of the highest respectability and honour, even princes, to secure the alliance ; that they had gone to Egypt with much difficulty—through a land where lions, and vipers, and fiery serpents abounded ; that they had at much hazard taken their treasures down to Egypt in order to secure the alliance (ver. 5, 6), and that after all, the Egyptians could not aid them. The phrase ' his princes,' refers to the princes of Judah, the ambassadors that the Jews sent forth, and the idea is, that they regarded the alliance as of so much importance that they had employed their most honourable men—even their princes—to secure it. ¶ *Were at Zoan.* Had come to Zoan, or were there on the business of their embassy. On the situation of Zoan, see Notes on ch. xix. 11, 13. It was the residence of the kings in Lower Egypt, and would be the place to which the ambassadors would naturally resort to negotiate an alliance. ¶ *Came to Hanes.* Respecting the situation of this place there has been much diversity of opinion among interpreters. The Chaldee renders it by the more full word *Tahpanhes ;* and Grotius supposes that the word is contracted from Tahpanhes (Jer. xliii. 7, 8), and that the name was sometimes abbreviated and written חָנֵם (*Hanes*). Vitringa supposes that it was Anusis, situated in the Delta of the Nile, and the residence of the king of the same name. Herodotus (ii. 137) mentions a city of that name, "Ἄνυσις. Anusis was a king of Egypt before the irruption of the Ethiopians, and it was not uncommon for a king to give his own name to a

city. Probably Anusis is the city intended here ; and the sense is, that they had come to the royal residence for the purpose of negotiating an alliance. It is known that in the time of Jeremiah (588 years before Christ) *Tahpanhes* was the capital of the nation (see Jer. xliii. 9).

5. *They were all ashamed.* That is, all the legates or ambassadors. When they came into Egypt, they found them either unwilling to enter into an alliance, or unable to render them any aid, and they were ashamed that they had sought their assistance rather than depend on God (comp. Jer. ii. 36).

6. *The burden of the beasts of the south.* The word ' south ' here refers doubtless to the country to the south of Judea, and particularly to Egypt. Thus it is used in Dan. xi. 5, 6. The phrase ' beasts of the south,' here refers to the animals that were travelling to Egypt. Isaiah, in vision, sees the caravan heavily laden with treasures pursuing a southern direction on its way to Egypt. The word ' burden ' is used in two senses, to denote that which is borne, a heavy burden ; or an oracle, a solemn prophetic message (see Notes on ch. xv. 1 ; xvii. 1 ; xix. 1). Many understand the word here in the latter sense, and regard this as the title of a prophetic message similar to those in ch. xv. 1 ; xvii. 1 ; xix. 1. But the word is doubtless used here in its ordinary signification, to denote the load which is borne on animals, and here especially the treasures which were borne down to Egypt, for the purpose of securing their friendly alliance. The prophet sees the caravan, or the beasts of the ambassadors heavily laden with rich treasures, travelling southward towards Egypt, and cries out, ' O the heavy burden, the load of treasures going to the south !' ¶ *Into the land of trouble and anguish.* Egypt ; so called either because it was the land where the He-

7 For *a* the Egyptians shall help in vain, and to no purpose: there-

fore have I cried [1] concerning this, Their *b* strength *is* to sit still.

brews had formerly suffered so severe oppressions; or because it was a land where the subjects were now grievously oppressed, and borne down with cruel laws; or because it was yet to be a land of trouble, from which the Jews could expect no aid. The general idea is, that Egypt was not a land of liberty and happiness, but a country where cruelty, oppression, and woe abounded. One source of trouble, as emblematic of all, the prophet immediately mentions when he designates that it abounded with venomous reptiles. ¶ *The viper* (אֶפְעֶה, *epheh*). LXX. 'Ασπίδος—'Asps' (see Isa. lix. 5). This is a well-known species of serpent. It is probably the same as the *El-Effah* of the Arabs, which is thus described by Mr. Jackson: ‘It is remarkable for its quick and penetrating poison; it is about two feet long and as thick as a man's arm, beautifully spotted with yellow and brown, and sprinkled over with blackish specks, similar to the horn-nosed snake. They have a wide mouth, by which they inhale a great quantity of air, and when inflated therewith they eject it with such force as to be heard at a considerable distance.’ It is well known that

VIPER (*El-Effah*).

Egypt produced venomous reptiles in abundance. Cleopatra destroyed herself with the bite of an asp which she had concealed for that purpose. ¶ *And fiery flying serpent* (שָׂרָף מְעוֹפֵף). LXX. Ἔκγονα ἀσπίδων πετομένων. This is the flying serpent so often referred to in the Scriptures. See a description of it in Notes on ch. xiv. 29. It is known to have abounded in the Arabian deserts, and was doubtless found also in Egypt as being in the same latitude, and in-

fested with similar reptiles. Niebuhr thus describes a species of serpent which answers to this account. ‘There is at Bakra a sort of serpents which they call *Heie Sursurie*, or *Heie Thiâre*. They commonly keep upon the date trees; and as it would be laborious for them to come down from a very high tree in order to ascend another, they twist themselves by the tail to a branch of the former, which, making a spring, by the motion they give it, throw themselves to the second. Hence it is that the modern Arabs call them the flying serpents—*Heie Thiâre.*’ Lord Anson, as quoted by Niebuhr, also speaks of them as follows:—‘The Spaniards informed us that there was often found in the woods a most mischievous serpent, called the flying snake, which, they said, darted itself from the boughs of trees on either man or beast that came within its reach, and whose sting they took to be inevitable death.’ There was a species of serpent which the Greeks called *Acontias*, and the Roman *Jaculus*, from their *swift darting motion*, and perhaps the same species is here referred to which Lucan calls *Jaculique volucres.* That these venomous reptiles abounded in Egypt is expressly testified by profane writers. Thus Ammianus says (xxii. 15), that ‘Egypt nourishes innumerable serpents, basilisks, and two-headed serpents [amphisbænas], and the scytalus [a serpent of a glistening colour], and the acontias [Latin, *Jaculus*], and adders, and vipers, and many others.’ ¶ *They will carry their riches.* Presents, designed to induce the Egyptians to enter into the alliance. That it was a common custom to make presents when one king sent an embassy to another, whether the design was to show friendship or civility, or to form an alliance, is well known in regard to all the nations of the East. The custom prevails at the present day, and is often referred to in Scripture (see 1 Kings xv. 19; 2 Kings xvi. 8; xviii. 14, 15).

7. *For the Egyptians shall help in vain.* That is, if they enter into the alliance, they shall not be able to defend

8 Now go, write it before them in a table, and note it in a book, that it may be for the ¹time to come for ever and ever.

1 *latter day.*

you from the invader. The other member of the sentence would seem to imply that they would make promises of aid, and would even boast of being able to deliver them, but that they would fail in their promises. ¶ *Therefore have I cried.* Therefore have I the prophet cried, *i.e.*, I do call her so. ¶ *Concerning this.* Concerning this country; that is, Egypt. Some have understood this as referring to Jerusalem, but the connection requires us to understand it of Egypt. ¶ *Their strength is to sit still.* This is evidently designed to be an expressive appellation of Egypt. The word here rendered, without much propriety, 'strength' (רַהַב, *râhâbh*) is a proper name of Egypt, and is several times applied to it; Isa. li. 9 :

Art thou not it that hath cut *Rahab*
And wounded the dragon ?

In this passage there can be no doubt that it refers to Egypt. So in Ps. lxxxvii. 4; lxxxix. 10 (see margin). Why it was given to Egypt is unknown, and can only be conjectured. Bochart (*Geog. Sacra*, i. 4. 24) supposes that it is derived from the word ῥιβι, which signifies *a pear*, and that it was given to the Delta or Lower Egypt on account of its form, as somewhat resembling a pear. But there is not clear evidence that such was the meaning of the word, and there is no reason why we should forsake the usual sense of the Hebrew word. The verb רָהַב (*râhâbh*) means to urge, press on, attack (Prov. vi. 3); to be high-spirited, fierce, full of courage ; to behave proudly (Isa. iii. 5); and has, in most instances, a relation to pride, to arrogance, to boasting (Job ix. 13; Ps. xl. 4). The noun *Rahab* indicates ferocity, haughtinesss, boasting, insolence ; and the name was doubtless given to Egypt on account of its insolence and pride. It is used here because Egypt would be full of self-confidence, and would boast that she could aid the suppliant Jews, and deliver them from the threatened invasion. The

phrase rendered 'to sit still,' is a part of the name which the prophet gave to her. Though she boasted, yet would she sit still ; she would be inefficient, and would do nothing ; and the whole name, therefore, may be rendered, ' I call her the blusterer that sitteth still ;' that is, ' they are courageous in talking; cowards in acting.'—(Taylor.)

8. *Now go.* This is a direction to the prophet to make a permanent record of the character of the Jewish people. The fact to be recorded was, that they were rebellious (ver. 9); the design for which the record was to be made was to show to future times that this had been the uniform character of the nation. The record was to be preserved that it might be a proof of the care of God towards the nation even in the midst of their long-continued and obstinate perverseness. ¶ *Write it before them.* Before the Jews themselves, that they may see the record, and may have it constantly before them. ¶ *In a table.* Or *on a* table. The word לוּחַ denotes a tablet either of stone to engrave upon (Deut. ix. 9; Ex. xxxi. 18); or of wood (1 Kings vii. 36). It is not improbable that this was to be exposed to public view in

ANCIENT ROLL AND SEAL.

ANCIENT STYLES.

some conspicuous place near the temple. ¶ *And note it.* Engrave it ; that is, record it. ¶ *In a book.* On parchment, or in the usual way of writing (see Note

9 That this *is* a rebellious *a* people, lying children, children *that* will not hear the law of the Lord:

10 Which say *b* to the seers, See not; and to the prophets, Prophesy not unto us right things; speak unto us *c* smooth things, prophesy deceits:

11 Get ye out of the way, turn

a De.32.20; Mic.2 6,11.　b Jer.11.21; Amos2.12; 7.13.

on ch. viii. 1). ¶ *For the time to come.* Heb. as Marg. ' The latter day.' It was to be made in order that future ages might know what had been the character of that people, and what had been the patience and forbearance of God in regard to them.

9. *That this* is *a rebellious people* (see Note on ch. i. 2). ¶ *Lying children.* They had promised in solemn covenant to take Jehovah as their God, but they had been unfaithful to their vows.

10. *Which say to the seers.* The prophets (see Note on ch. i. 1). ¶ *See not.* They desire not that they should communicate to them the will of Jehovah. ¶ *Prophesy not unto us right things.* It is not probable that they *openly* demanded of the prophets that they should declare falsehood and deceit, but their conduct was *as if* they had required that. The sense is, they bore with impatience the theatenings and commands of the true prophets; they were offended at their plainness and their reproofs of their vices; and they preferred the false prophets, who fell in with their prejudices, and who did not denounce the judgment of God for their crimes. ¶ *Speak unto us smooth things.* That is, those things which are in accordance with our feelings, prejudices, and desires; which assure us of prosperity and success, and which will not disturb us with the apprehension of punishment. This was spoken *particularly* of their desire to make a league with Egypt, an enterprise for which the true prophets threatened them with the Divine displeasure, but which probably the false prophets encouraged. ¶ *Prophesy deceits.* Not that they would openly and avowedly demand to be deceived, but they demanded that which the prophet says *would be* deceits. No man *professedly*

aside out of the path, cause the Holy One of Israel to cease from before us.

12 Wherefore thus saith the Holy One of Israel, Because ye despise this word, and trust *d* in ¹ oppression and perverseness, and stay thereon:

c 1 Ki.22.13.　d Ps.62.10.　1 or, *fraud.*

desires to be deceived; but many a man is willing to put himself under that kind of teaching which *is* deceit, and which he might know to be falsehood if he would examine it.

11. *Get ye out of the way.* Or, rather, ' Recede from the way;' or ' Turn aside from the way.' The words *way* and *path* are used to denote the true religion, or the true doctrines of God (Matt. vii. 14; xxii. 16; John xiv. 4; Acts xviii. 26; xix. 9, 23; 2 Pet. ii. 15). The request here was that the true prophets would recede from the stern and true precepts of religion, and turn to the ways of falsehood and deceit. ¶ *Cause the Holy One of Israel to cease from before us.* The sense of this is, ' Let us hear no more of this name. We are weary of constantly hearing it, as if there was nothing else but the ceaseless repetition of the name *The Holy One of Israel.*' It is to be remembered that the prophets spoke in this name, and often commenced their prophecies with the announcement, ' thus saith the Holy One of Israel.' No one more frequently used this than Isaiah (see ver. 12, 15; comp. ch. i. 4; v. 19, 24; x. 20; xii. 6; xvii. 7; xxix. 19; xxxi. 1; xli. 14). It is probable that a reference constantly to the fact that he was HOLY, was that which most troubled them. How descriptive of the feelings of sinners! How striking an illustration of the fact that they do not wish to hear of the name or laws of the Holy Lord God! And what a melancholy proof of depravity is it when men pursue such a course that they do not wish to hear of him, and desire no more to be troubled with his name and laws!

12. *Wherefore thus saith the Holy One.* Jehovah. There may be some reference here to the fact adverted to in ver. 11, that they were weary of the

13 Therefore this iniquity shall be to you as a breach *a* ready to fall, swelling out in a high wall, whose breaking cometh suddenly at an instant.

14 And he shall break *b* it as the

a Ps.62.3.　　　*b* Ps.2.9; Jer.19.11.

breaking of the [1] potter's vessel that is broken in pieces ; he shall not spare: so that there shall not be found in the bursting of it a sherd to take fire from the hearth, or to take water *withal* out of the pit.

[1] *bottle of potters.*

name of the Holy One of Israel, and of the perpetual reiteration of his commands. Isaiah, as if to show them how little he was disposed to comply with their prejudices, again makes an appeal to that name, and urges the authority of JEHOVAH. It is often proper to *repeat* the very doctrine to which sinners object, and which has given them offence. That they are offended, shows that their minds are *awake* to the truth, and gives some indication that their consciences trouble them. Ministers of God should never shrink from their duty because men oppose them ; they should never cease to speak in the name and by the authority of the Holy One of Israel, because that name may excite opposition and disgust. ¶ *Ye despise this word.* That is, the word or message of JEHOVAH (ch. xxviii. 13, 14); or perhaps it means the word 'Holy One of Israel.' The sense is, that they did not trust in the promise and protection of JEHOVAH, but relied on human aid. ¶ *And trust in oppression.* Marg. 'Fraud.' The word עשׁק properly denotes oppression, or extortion (Eccl. v. 7; Ezek. xxii. 7, 12); then, that which is obtained by extortion, and also by fraud (Lev. vi. 4 ; Ps. lxii. 11; Eccl. vii. 7). It may refer here to the fact that they had, by unjust and oppressive exactions, obtained the treasures referred to in ver. 6, by which they hoped to conciliate the favour of Egypt ; or it may mean that they trusted in their fraudulent purposes towards God, that is, to a false and perfidious course, by which they were unfaithful to him. ¶ *Perverseness.* A crooked, perverse, rebellious course. They refused submission to JEHOVAH, and relied on the aid of strangers.

13. *Therefore this iniquity.* That is, this refusing to trust in JEHOVAH, and this intention to seek the alliance

of Egypt. The general sense of the figure here is, that their depending on Egypt would involve them ultimately in complete and awful ruin—ruin that should come upon them as suddenly as when a wall that had been long swelling out gives way. ¶ *As a breach ready to fall.* Like a breaking forth, or a bursting in a wall. ¶ *Swelling out in a high wall.* That is, where the foundation is not firm, and where one part of the wall sinks, and it inclines to one side until it suddenly bursts forth. A similar figure is used by the Psalmist (lxii. 3):

Ye shall be slain all of you
As a bowing wall shall ye be, and as a tottering fence.

¶ *Whose breaking cometh suddenly.* Though it has been long leaning and swelling, yet the actual bursting forth would be in an instant. So would it be with the destruction that would come upon the Jews. Though by their sins they had been long preparing for it, yet it would come upon them by a sudden and tremendous crash. So it will be with all sinners. Destruction may seem to be long delayed—as a wall may be long inclining, and may seem to prepare imperceptibly to fall ; but in due time it will come suddenly upon them, when too late to obtain relief.

14. *And he shall break it as the breaking.* That is, its breaking shall be like the breaking of a potter's vessel. The LXX. read it, ' And its fall (τὸ πτῶμα) shall be like the breaking of an earthen vessel,' ¶ *As the breaking of the potter's vessel.* That is, as an earthen, fragile vessel, which is easily dashed to pieces. The image here is all drawn from the bursting forth, or the complete ruin of the swelling wall ; but the sense is, that the Jewish republic would be entirely broken, scattered, demolished. ¶ *He shall not spare in the bursting of it.* Figuratively in

15 For thus saith the Lord God, the Holy One of Israel, In returning and rest *a* shall ye be saved; in

a ver.7.

quietness and in confidence shall be your strength; and ye would not.

16 But ye said, No; for we will flee upon horses; therefore shall ye

---

the bursting of the wall; literally in the destruction of the Jewish state and polity. ¶ *A sherd.* A piece of pottery; a fragment. ¶ *To take fire from the hearth.* Large enough to carry coals on. ¶ *Or to take water* withal *out of the pit.* Out of the fountain, or pool; that is, it shall be broken into small fragments, and the ruin shall be complete — as when a wall tumbles down and is completely broken up. The sense is, that the republic of Israel would be completely ruined, so that there should not be found a man of any description who could aid them. The prophet does not specify when this would be. It is not necessary to suppose that it would occur on the invasion of Sennacherib, or that it would be the *immediate* consequence of seeking the aid of Egypt, but that it would be *a* consequence, though a remote one. Perhaps the figure used would lead us to look to some remote period. A high wall will begin to give way many years before its fall. The swell will be gradual, and perhaps almost imperceptible. For some time it may appear to be stationary; then perhaps some new cause will produce an increase of the projecting part, until it can no longer sustain itself, and then the ruin will be sudden and tremendous. So it would be with the Jews. The seeking of the alliance with Egypt was *one* cause—though a remote one—of their final ruin. Their forsaking God and seeking human aid, was gradually but certainly *undermining* the foundations of the state—as a wall may be gradually undermined. Frequent repetitions of that would more and more impair the real strength of the republic, until, for their accumulated acts of want of confidence, the patience of God would be exhausted, and the state would fall like a mighty, bursting wall. The prophecy was fulfilled in the invasion of Jerusalem by the Chaldeans; it had a more signal and awful fulfilment in its destruction by the Romans.

15. *For thus saith the Lord God.* The design of this verse is to give a *reason* for the destruction that should come upon them. That reason was, that God had indicated to them the path of truth and safety, but they chose not to follow it, and refused to put confidence in him. ¶ *In returning.* In returning to God; that is, if you are converted to him. ¶ *And rest.* That is, by calmly reposing on God for assistance, and not seeking the alliance of Egypt (see Ex. xiv. 13). ¶ *In quietness.* In a collected, quiet state of mind. ¶ *In confidence.* By putting simple trust in God. ¶ *Shall be your strength.* You shall be safe; your enemies shall not be able to overcome and subdue you. ¶ *But ye would not.* When Jerusalem was threatened by Sennacherib, Hezekiah *did* put this confidence in God, and reposed calmly and securely on his promises (Isa. xxxvi. 15, 18, 21); but it is not improbable that when the city was first threatened, and Hezekiah heard of the preparations made by the Assyrians, he had joined with the party in Jerusalem who proposed an alliance with Egypt, and that this was known to Sennacherib (Isa. xxxvi. 6). Probably, however, before the invasion had actually commenced he had seen the impropriety of this, either because the aid of Egypt could not be secured, or because Isaiah had warned him of this, and had been brought to put his trust entirely in Jehovah. Yet the offence *had been* committed of refusing to put implicit confidence in Jehovah, and of seeking the aid of Egypt, and for that the punishment is threatened in this chapter (ver. 16, 17).

16. *But ye said, No.* Ye who proposed an alliance with Egypt. ¶ *For we will flee upon horses.* The word 'flee' (נוס), usually signifies to flee before or from any person or thing. But here it seems to have the notion of making a rapid motion in general, and not to refer to the fact that they ex-

flee: and, We will ride upon the
swift; therefore shall they that pursue *a* you be swift.

17 One thousand *b shall flee* at
the rebuke of one; at the rebuke of

a 2 Ki.25.5.   *b* De.32.30.

pected to flee *from* their enemy, for it
does not seem to have been a part of
their expectation. The idea seems to
be that by their alliance with Egypt
they would secure the means of *rapid
motion*, whatever might be the neces-
ity or occasion for it, whether against
or from an enemy. The sense is, 'we
will by this alliance secure the assistance
of cavalry;' and, doubtless, the design
was to employ it in the attack and discomfiture of their foes. It will be recollected that Moses (Deut. xvii. 16)
strictly forbade that the future monarch
of the Jews should 'multiply horses to
himself, to cause the people to return
to Egypt,' and that consequently the
employment of cavalry was against the
laws of the nation. For the reasons of
this prohibition, see Note on ch. ii. 7.
The attempt, therefore, in the time of
Hezekiah to call in the aid of the
cavalry of Egypt, was a violation of
both the letter and the spirit of the
Jewish institutions (comp. ch. xxxi. 1;
Hos. xiv. 4). ¶ *Therefore shall ye flee.*
You shall fly before your enemies; you
shall be defeated and scattered. ¶ *We
will ride upon the swift.* That is, upon
fleet horses or coursers. Arabia was celebrated, and is still, for producing fleet
coursers, and the same was formerly true
of Egypt (see Note on ch. ii. 7).

17. *One thousand*, &c. The sense
of this is, that you shall be easily
alarmed and overcome by those who
are inferior in numbers and strength.
The number 'one thousand,' is put
for a large indefinite number; probably
meaning all. ¶ *At the rebuke of one.*
The number *one* here is put to denote
a very small number; a number in the
ordinary course of warfare entirely disproportionate to those who would be
vanquished. There is probably a reference here to the prediction in Deut.
xxxii. 30:

> How should one chase a thousand,
> And two put ten thousand to flight,

five shall ye flee; till ye be left as a
beacon [1] upon the top of a mountain,
and as an ensign on an hill.

18 And therefore will the LORD
wait, *c* that he may be gracious

1 or, *a tree bereft of branches*, or, *boughs*: or, *a mast.*
c Ho.5.15.

> Except their Rock had sold them,
> And JEHOVAH had shut them up?

¶ *At the rebuke of five.* Of a very
small number. ¶ *Till ye be left as a
beacon upon the top of a mountain.*
The word rendered 'beacon' (הֹרֶן), [Gr.
ἱστός, *a mast*], denotes properly the
mast of a ship (Isa. xxxiii. 23; Ezek.
xxvii. 5); then anything resembling a
mast, a flagstaff, or a beacon of any
kind. It may refer to a staff or mast
erected on a promontory to warn sailors,
or to be a landmark—as it is not improbable that the *masts* of ships would
be employed for that purpose; or it may
refer to a flagstaff, erected on a conspicuous place, to which the nation
could rally in time of war. On the
sea coasts of America such beacons are
often erected. Those which I have seen
consist of a pole erected on an eminence
or rising ground, with a cask or barrel
painted white on the top. The idea
seems to be, that of a long pole erected
for any purpose, and which was standing alone, stripped of its leaves and
branches, and without ornament. So
would be the few, solitary, and scattered
Jews when driven before their enemies.
¶ *And as an ensign on a hill* (see Note
on ch. v. 26; xi. 12). The idea is, that
those who should escape would be few in
number, and would stand alone, as a
beacon in view of all the nations, to admonish them of the justice of God, and
the truth of his threatenings—like an
ensign floating on a hill that can be
seen from afar. What a striking description is this of the condition of
the Jews in our times, and indeed in
all ages since their dispersion! Their
strength, and influence, and power as a
people are gone. They stand as beacons
to warn the nations of the evils of a
want of confidence in God, and of his
justice.

18. *And therefore.* The sense of the
words rendered 'and therefore,' may
be better expressed by the phrase, 'yet

unto you, and therefore will he be exalted, that he may have mercy upon you; for the LORD *is* a God of judgment: *a* blessed *are* all they that wait for him.

19 For the people shall dwell *b* in Zion at Jerusalem; thou shalt weep no more: he will be very gracious unto thee at the voice of thy cry;

when *c* he shall hear it, he will answer thee.

20 And *though* *d* the LORD give you the bread of adversity, and the water of affliction,[1] yet shall not thy teachers be *e* removed into a corner any more, but thine eyes shall see thy teachers:

a Ps.34.8.   *b* ch.65.9,24.   *c* Jer.29.12-14.
d Ps.30.5.   1 or, *oppression.*   *e* Ps.74.8; Am.8.11,12.

moreover,' meaning, that notwithstanding their sins, and the necessity of punishing them, JEHOVAH would be long-suffering, and would yet bring the nation to repentance. ¶ *And therefore will he be exalted.* Lowth renders this in accordance with a conjecture of Houbigant, 'Shall he expect in silence,' by reading יְחַכֶּה instead of יָרוּם. But there is no authority for this except a single MS. Rosenmüller supposes it means, in accordance with the interpretation of Jarchi, that he would delay, *i.e.*, that his mercy would be *long* or his judgment remote. But the sense seems to be, that God would be so forbearing that his character would be *exalted, i.e.*, that men would have more elevated conceptions of his truth, mercy, and faithfulness. ¶ *For the* LORD *is a God of judgment.* He will do what is right. He will spare the nation still; and yet establish among them the true religion, and they shall flourish. ¶ *Blessed* are *all they that wait for him.* This seems to have been recorded to encourage them, when the threatened calamities should come upon them, to put their confidence in God, and to trust that he would yet appear and restore the nation to himself. This verse is the commencement of the annunciation of the blessings which should yet be conferred on them. The description of these blessings is continued to ver. 26.

19. *For the people shall dwell in Zion* (see Note on ch. i. 8). The *language* here is evidently adapted to a return from the captivity. The whole design of the passage (ver. 19-26) is to describe a future state of prosperity by images mainly drawn from the idea of temporal enjoyment. The sense is, that in some period subsequent to the calami-

ties that would befall them for their improper reliance on the aid of Egypt (ver. 16, 17), there would be prosperity, peace, and joy in Jerusalem. The order of events, as seen by the prophet in vision, seems to be this. He sees the people threatened with an invasion by Sennacherib. He sees them forget their reliance on God and seek the aid of Egypt. He sees, as a consequence of this, a long series of calamities resulting in the downfall of the republic, the destruction of the city, and the captivity at Babylon. Yet he sees, in the distant prospect, prosperity, happiness, security, piety, the blessing of God, and rich and abundant future mercies resting on his people. That the blessings under the Messiah constitute a part of this *series* of mercies no one can doubt who attentively considers the language in ver. 25, 26. ¶ *Thou shalt weep no more* (see Note on ch. xxv. 8). ¶ *He will be very gracious unto thee at the voice of thy cry.* When in your calamities you shall cry unto him for deliverance, he shall hear you, and restore you to your own land. This is in accordance with the statements in ch. xxvi. 8, 9 (see Notes on these verses), that in their captivity in Babylon they would seek God. ¶ *He will answer thee* (see Jer. xxix. 12-14).

20. *And though the* LORD *give you the bread of adversity.* The bread that is eaten in a time of calamity; that is, he would bring upon them sore distress and want. ¶ *The water of affliction.* Marg. 'Oppression.' That is, water drank in times of affliction and oppression, or in the long and weary days of captivity. ¶ *Yet shall not thy teachers.* Your public instructors and guides (Ps. lxxiv. 9; Isa. xliii. 27; Dan. xii. 3; Amos viii. 11, 12). This refers to *all*

21 And thine ears shall hear a word behind thee, saying, This *a is* the way, walk ye in it, when ye turn to the right hand, and when ye turn to the left.

22 Ye shall defile also the cover-

a Ps. 32.8.　　1 *the graven images of thy silver.*

ing of thy [1] graven images of silver, and the ornament of thy molten images of gold: thou shalt [2] cast them away as a menstruous cloth; thou shalt say unto it, Get thee hence.*b*

2 *scatter.*　　*b* Ho. 14.8.

---

those who would be the true guides and teachers of the people of God in subsequent times; and relates, therefore, not only to prophets and pious men whom God would raise up under their own dispensation, but also to all whom he would appoint to communicate his will. It is a promise that the church of God should never want a pious and devoted ministry qualified to make known his will and defend his truth. ¶ *Be removed into a corner.* The word here used (יִכָּנֵף from כָּנַף) occurs nowhere else in the Scriptures. It is probably derived from כָּנָף, *a wing;* and in the Syriac and Chaldee, it means to collect together. The LXX. render this, 'And they who deceived thee shall no more come near unto thee.' The Syriac, 'And he (*i.e.*, the Lord) shall no more collect thy seducers.' The Chaldee, 'And he shall no more take away his own glory from the house of his sanctuary.' Rosenmüller, in accordance with Schultens, renders it, 'And thy teachers shall no more hide themselves,' referring to the fact that the wing of a fowl furnishes a hiding-place or shelter. This would accord with the general idea that they should not be removed from public view. Lowth, singularly, and without authority from the versions or MSS., renders it,

'Yet the timely rain shall no more be restrained.'

The general idea is, evidently, that they should be no more taken away ; and probably the specific idea is that proposed by Taylor (*Heb. Con.*), that thy teachers shall no more, as it were, *be winged,* or fly away; that is, be removed by flight, or as a flock of birds moving together rapidly on the wing.

21. *And thine ears shall hear a word.* A command or admonition. You shall not be left without spiritual guides and directors. ¶ *Behind thee* That is,

says Vitringa, the voice of conscience, as an *invisible* guide, shall admonish you. The idea, however, seems to be that if they were ignorant of the way, or if they were inclined to err, they should be admonished of the true path which they ought to pursue. The idea is taken either from the practice of teachers who are represented as *following* their pupils and admonishing them if they were in danger of going astray (Grotius); or from shepherds, who are represented as following their flocks, and directing them when they wandered. The Jews understand this voice ' from behind ' to be the *Bath Kol*—' the daughter of the voice ; ' a Divine admonition which they suppose attends the pious. The essential thought is, that they would not be left without a guide and instructor; that, if they were inclined to go astray, they would be recalled to the path of truth and duty. *Perhaps* there is the idea, also, that the admonition would come from some *invisible* influence, or from some unexpected quarter, as it is often the case that those who are inquiring on the subject of religion receive light from quarters where they least expected, and from sources to which they were not looking. It is also true that the admonitions of Providence, of conscience, and of the Holy Spirit, seem often to come from *behind us;* that is, they *recall* us from the path in which we were going, and restrain us from a course that would be fraught with danger. ¶ *When ye turn to the right hand,* &c. When you shall be in danger of wandering from the direct and straight path. The voice shall recall you, and direct you in the way in which you ought to go.

22. *Ye shall defile also.* That is, you shall regard them as polluted and abominable. This is language which is often used respecting their treatment of the images and altars of idolatry when they became objects of abomina-

23 Then shall he give the rain of thy seed, that thou shalt sow the ground withal; and bread of the increase of the earth, and it shall be fat and plenteous: in that day shall thy cattle feed in large pastures.

24 The oxen likewise, and the young asses that ear the ground, shall eat clean[1] provender which hath been winnowed with the shovel and with the fan.

1 *leavened*, or, *savoury*.

tion, and when they were induced to abandon them (see 2 Kings xxiii. 8, 10, 16). It is not improbable that before destroying them they would express their abhorrence of them by some act of polluting or defiling them, as significant of their contempt for the objects of degraded idolatry (see Note on ch. ii. 20). The sense of the whole passage is, that the effect of the judgments which God was about to bring upon the nation would be, to turn them from idolatry, to which as a nation they had been signally prone. ¶ *The covering.* The images of idols were usually made of wood or clay, and overlaid with gold. That gold and silver were used *to plate* them is apparent from Deut. vii. 25; and the whole process of making them from wood, and then of overlaying them with plates of gold and silver is described with graphic power and severity of irony in Isa. xl. 19, 20; xli. 6, 7. ¶ *Thy graven images of silver.* Marg. 'The graven images of thy silver.' Probably the construction in the text is correct, as meaning that the images were not made of entire silver, but of wood or clay, plated with silver. ¶ *And the ornament.* The golden plates or the covering of the images. ¶ *Thy molten images.* The word 'molten' refers to those which were made by *casting* (see Notes on ch. xl. 19, 20). ¶ *Thou shalt cast them away* (see Note on ch. ii. 20). This would be in accordance with the express direction of Moses; Deut. vii. 25: 'The graven images of their gods shall ye burn with fire; thou shalt not desire the silver or gold that is on them, nor take it unto thee, lest thou be snared therein; for it is an abomination unto the LORD thy God.'

23. *Then shall he give the rain of thy seed.* That is, he shall send rain on the seed which is sown. You will be allowed to cultivate the soil without molestation, and God will give you

fruitful seasons and abundant harvests. This is a poetic description of a happy or golden age, when there would be peace and prosperity (comp. Notes on ch. xi. 6, 7). ¶ *And bread of the increase of the earth.* And bread which the ground shall produce. ¶ *And it shall be fat and plenteous.* It shall be rich and abundant; that is, there shall be prosperity and an ample supply for your wants. ¶ *Feed in large pastures.* This is a description of security when their cattle should be permitted to roam at large, and have abundant pasturage —an image of prosperity that would be very gratifying to a people whose main conception of wealth consisted in abundance of flocks and herds.

24. *The young asses that ear the ground.* Heb. 'Labouring,' or 'cultivating the ground,' that is, ploughing it. The old English word *ear* (from the Latin *aro*) meant to till, to cultivate. The word is now obselete, but this is the sense which it has in the Bible (Gen. xlv. 6; Ex. xxxiv. 21; Deut. xxi. 4; 1 Sam. viii. 12). ¶ *Shall eat clean provender.* Marg. 'Leavened,' or 'savoury.' The word rendered 'provender' (בְּלִיל) is a verbal from בָּלַל, *to mix, mingle, confuse;* and denotes provender that is made by *mixing* various substances, *maslin* or *farago,* a mixture of barley, oats, vetches, and beans, which seem to have been sown together, and reaped at the same time (Job vi. 5; xxiv. 6). The word rendered 'clean,' (חָמִיץ) is not quite so plain in its signification. Kimchi explains it by נָקִי, *pure, clean.* Gesenius renders it 'salted,' and supposes that it refers to fodder that was mixed with salted hay. The LXX. render it, 'Provender mixed with winnowed barley.' But the real notion of the word is that which is *fermented,* from חָמֵץ, *to be sour;* to be leavened. Lowth renders it, 'well fermented.' Noyes, 'well seasoned.' The

25 And there shall be upon every high mountain, and upon every [1] high hill, rivers *and* streams of waters in the day of the great slaughter, when the towers fall.

26 Moreover, the light *a* of the

[1] *lifted up.*　　　*a* ch 60.19,20.

moon shall be as the light of the sun, and the light of the sun shall be seven-fold, as the light of seven days, in the day that the LORD bindeth up the breach of his people, and healeth the stroke of their wound.

---

idea seems to be that of a provender made of a mixture of various substances—as of grain, beans, vetches, herbs, hay, and probably salt, which, when mixed, *would* ferment, and which was regarded as nutritious and wholesome for cattle. A similar compound is used by the Arabs still (see Bochart, i. 2, 7; and Faber, and Harmer's *Observations,* i. 409). ¶ *Which hath been winnowed.* That is, which is the pure grain, which is not fed to them as it is sometimes, before it is separated from the chaff. Grain shall be so abundant in that time of prosperity that even the cattle may be fed with grain prepared as it is usually for man. ¶ *With the shovel.* The large shovel by which the grain in the chaff was thrown up in the wind that the grain might be separated from the chaff. ¶ *The fan.* This word properly means that by which any thing is *scattered*—a shovel by which the grain is thrown or tossed into the wind. 'Those who form their opinion of the latter article by an English *fan,* will entertain a very erroneous notion. That of the East is made of the fibrous part of the palmirah or cocoa-tree leaves, and measures about a yard each way.' —(Roberts).

25. *In the day of the great slaughter.* When the enemies of the people of God shall have been destroyed—probably in a time subsequent to the slaughter of the army of the Assyrians. ¶ *When the towers fall.* The towers of the enemy; perhaps referring here to the towers of Babylon. After they should fall, the Jews would be favoured with the time of prosperity to which the prophet here refers.

26. *Moreover.* In addition to all the blessings which are enumerated above. ¶ *The light of the moon.* Light is in the Scriptures an emblem of purity, intelligence, happiness, prosperity; as darkness is an emblem of ignorance,

calamity, and sin. This figure is often used by the poets. Thus Horace:

Soles melius nitent.　　　*Carm.* liv.: *Od.* v 8.

The figure of augmenting light to denote the blessings of religion, and especially of the gospel, is often employed by Isaiah (comp. Notes on ch. ii. 5; ix. 2; x. 17; xiii. 10; lviii. 8, 10; lx. 1, 3, 19, 20). The sense of this passage is, that in those future days the light would shine intensely, and without obscurity; that though they had been walking in the light of the true religion, yet that their light would be greatly augmented, and that they would have much clearer views of the Divine character and government. That this refers to the times of the Messiah there can be little or no room to doubt. It is language such as Isaiah commonly employs to describe those times; and there is a fulness and splendour about it which can suit no other period. There is nothing in the connection, moreover, which forbids such an interpretation of the passage. ¶ *Shall be as the light of the sun.* Shall be clear, bright, intense. The sense is, there shall be a great increase of light, as if the light of the moon were suddenly increased to the brightness of the meridian sun. ¶ *Shall be seven-fold.* Seven times as intense and clear as usual, as if the light of seven days were concentrated into one. The word 'seven' in the Scriptures often denotes a complete or perfect number; and indicates *completeness* or *perfection.* The phrase 'as the light of seven days,' Lowth supposes is a gloss which has been introduced into the text from the margin. The reasons which he adduces for this supposition are, that it is wanting in the LXX., and that it interrupts the rhythmical construction. But this is not sufficient authority for rejecting the words from the text. No authority of MSS. is adduced for thus rejecting them, and they are found in the Vulgate,

27 Behold, the name of the LORD
cometh from far, burning *with* his
anger, and [1]the burden *thereof is*
heavy;[2] his lips are full of indignation, and his tongue as a devouring
fire: *a*

1 or, *grievousness of flame.*   2 *heaviness.*

28 And his breath, as an overflowing stream, shall reach to the
midst of the neck, to sift *b* the nations with the sieve of vanity: and
there shall be a bridle *c* in the jaws of
the people, causing *them* to err.

a Zep.3.8.   *b* Lu.22.31.   *c* ch.37.29.

---

the Chaldee, and the Syriac. They are
wanting, however, in the Arabic. ¶ *In
the day.* Vitringa supposes that this refers to the time of the Maccabees; but
although there may be a reference to
that time, yet the idea is evidently designed to include the future times of the
Messiah. The sense of the prophet is,
that *subsequent* to the great calamities
which were to befall them, there would
be a time of glorious prosperity, and the
design of this was to comfort them with
the assurance that their nation would
not be wholly destroyed. ¶ *Bindeth
up the breach of his people.* Or the
wound. The calamity that should come
upon them is thus represented as a
wound inflicted on them by the stripes
of punishment (see Notes on ch. i. 5).
JEHOVAH would heal it by restoring them
to their own land, and to their former
privileges.

27. *Behold, the name of the* LORD
cometh (comp. Notes on ch. xix. 1). The
verses following, to the end of the chapter,
are designed evidently to describe the
destruction of the army of Sennacherib.
This is expressly declared in ver. 31,
and all the circumstances in the prediction accord with that event. There is
no necessity of supposing that this is the
commencement of a new prophecy, for it
is connected with the main subject in
the previous part of the chapter. The
whole prophecy was composed evidently
in view of that threatened invasion. In
the apprehension of that, they sought
the aid of Egypt (ver. 1–6); for that,
the prophet denounces judgment on them
(ver. 8, *et sq.*); in view of these judgments, however, he promises a more
happy state (ver. 18–26); and now, in
the close of the chapter, in order to deter
them from the alliance, he assures them
that, without any foreign aid, the Assyrian would be destroyed by JEHOVAH
himself. The phrase 'name of JEHOVAH,'
is probably another mode of designating

JEHOVAH himself; as the *name* of God
is often put for God himself (see Acts
iii. 6, 7, 12, 30; iv. 10; 1 Cor. i. 10).
The idea is, that the destruction of the
Assyrian hosts would be accomplished
by the immediate power of JEHOVAH
himself without any need of the aid of
the Egyptian or of any foreign alliances.
¶ *From afar.* That is, from heaven
(comp. Note on ch. xix. 1). ¶ *Burning*
with *his anger.* Or, rather, his anger
is enkindled. ¶ *And the burden* thereof.
Marg. 'Grievousness of flame.' Lowth
renders it, 'The flame rageth violently.'
Noyes, 'Violent is the flame.' The
LXX. render it, 'A burning wrath.' The
word מַשָּׂאָה, from נָשָׂא *to bear, lift up,
carry,* means properly a lifting up (Ps.
cxli. 2); a burden (Zeph. iii. 18); then
a mounting up, particularly of a flame
or smoke in a conflagration (Judg. xx.
38). This seems to be the idea here,
that the anger of God would be like a
heavy, dark column of mingled smoke
and flame bursting out, and rising up
over a city. ¶ *His lips are full of indignation.* All this language is of course
figurative, and means that he would
issue a command to destroy the Assyrians, or that they would be destroyed
in such a manner as most effectively to
exhibit his displeasure. ¶ *And his
tongue as a devouring fire.* That is,
he shall issue a command that shall
destroy like a raging and devouring
fire.

28. *And his breath.* The word רוּחַ
properly means *wind,* air in motion;
then a breathing, an exhalation, a breath;
then the soul, spirit, &c. The idea here
seems to be that of excited, and rapid,
and agitated breathing, as when one is
in anger (comp. Judg. viii. 3; Zech. vi.
8). ¶ *As an overflowing stream.* This
figure is common to express desolating
judgments (see Notes on ch. viii. 8; x.
22; xxviii. 17; comp. Ps. lxix. 2, 15).
¶ *Shall reach to the midst of the neck.*

29 Ye shall have a song, as *a* in the night, *when* a holy solemnity is kept; and gladness of heart, as when one goeth with a pipe to come into the mountain of the LORD, to the ¹Mighty One of Israel.

a Ps.42.4.　　1 *Rock.*　　2 *the glory of his voice.*

Isaiah (ch. viii. 8), in describing the invasion of Sennacherib, and comparing it to an overflowing torrent, says it would 'reach even to the neck;' that is, it would overflow the land, and even approach the head, the capital, but that that would be spared. By the use of a similar figure, and perhaps referring to that, he here says, that the judgment of God would overflow the army of the Assyrians, but that it would approach *only* to the neck, the head would still be spared; the commander and sovereign would not be destroyed. In accordance with this prediction, the angel in one night, as with an overflowing flood, cut off the army, and yet spared the sovereign, Sennacherib, who escaped with his life (Isa. xxxvii. 36, 37). The word rendered 'shall reach' (רֵהָצָה) properly means *shall divide*, or cut into two parts (Gen. xxxiii. 8; Num. xxxi. 37, 42; Judg. ix. 43); and the idea here seems to be that a man who is in the water seems to be *divided* into two parts, one part above, and one in the water. ¶ *To sift the nations.* Doubtless many nations were laid under requisition to furnish an army so large as that of Sennacherib, as the kingdom of Assyria was made up of a number of tributary people and provinces. The word rendered 'to sift' refers to the act of winnowing or fanning grain, in which the grain is *tossed* or thrown from the shovel into the air. As the chaff is driven away by the wind, so the nations in the army of Sennacherib would be scattered. ¶ *With the sieve of vanity.* That is, of emptiness or perdition; he would so scatter them that nothing would be left. ¶ *A bridle in the jaws of the people.* The idea is, that he had all these nations as much under his control as a man has a horse with a bridle in his mouth. The same idea the prophet has used in reference to the same subject in ch. xxxvii. 29:

30 And the LORD shall cause ²his glorious voice to be heard, and shall show the lighting down of his arm, with the indignation of *his* anger, and *with* the flame of a devouring fire, *with* scattering, and tempest, and hailstones.

I will put my bridle in thy jaws, And I will turn thee back by the way by which thou camest.

¶ *Causing* them *to err.* That shall cause them to wander; that is, he would turn them from the path in which they had designed to go. They had purposed to go to Jerusalem, but he would lead them *back* to their own land, discomfited and disheartened (see ch. xxxvii. 29).

29. *Ye shall have a song.* That is, ye inhabitants of Jerusalem shall rejoice when the army of the Assyrian is destroyed. ¶ *As in the night,* when *a solemnity is kept.* The word 'solemnity' here (חַג) denotes a festival, or feast; and refers, by way of eminence, to the Passover, which is usually designated as THE *feast;* that is, the principal festival of the Jews (see Matt. xxvii. 15; John v. 1, 11, 13, 23). This festival was kept at first at night, and was required to be so celebrated ever afterwards (Ex. xii. 42; Deut. xvi. 1–6). ¶ *As when one goeth with a pipe.* Music was used in the daily service of the temple, and their processions and celebrations were all with instrumental music. The simple idea is, that the sudden and complete destruction of the army of Sennacherib would be the occasion of the highest joy.

30. *And the LORD shall cause his glorious voice to be heard.* That is, he would give command to destroy them. They could not fail to recognize his voice, and to feel that it was accomplished by him. ¶ *The lighting down of his arm.* The descent of his arm— alluding to the act of striking, as with a sword, by which an army is cut down. ¶ With *the flame* (see Note on ch. xxix. 6). ¶ *And tempest, and hailstones.* With us it is rare that a storm of hail would be severe enough to destroy an army. But in oriental countries and in tropical climates, storms of hail are not unfrequently of sufficient violence to do it if the army were encamped in the open

31 For through the voice of the
Lord shall the Assyrian be beaten
down, *which* smote with a rod.

32 And [1] *in* every place where the

1 *every passing of the rod founded.*

grounded staff shall pass, which the
Lord shall [2] lay upon him, *it* shall be
with tabrets and harps: and in battles
of shaking will he fight [3] with it.

2 *cause to rest.*   3 *or, against them.*

field. The following extract of a letter
from one of our own countrymen, will
show that this would be by no means an
improbable occurrence :—' We had got
perhaps a mile and a half on our way,
when a cloud rising in the west gave
indications of approaching rain. In a
few minutes we discovered something
falling from the heavens with a heavy
splash, and with a whitish appearance.
I could not conceive what it was, but
observing some gulls near, I supposed
it to be them darting for fish ; but soon
after discovered that they were large
balls of ice falling. Immediately we
heard a sound like rumbling thunder, or
ten thousand carriages rolling furiously
over the pavement. The whole Bos-
phorus was in a foam, as though heaven's
artillery had been charged upon us and
our frail machine. Our fate seemed
inevitable ; our umbrellas were raised
to protect us, the lumps of ice stripped
them into ribbons. We fortunately had
a bullock's hide in the boat, under which
we crawled and saved ourselves from
further injury. One man of the three
oarsmen had his hand literally smashed,
another much injured in the shoulder,
Mr. H. received a blow on the leg, my
right hand was somewhat disabled, and
all more or less injured. It was the
most awful and terrific scene I ever
witnessed, and God forbid that I should
be ever exposed to another. Balls of
ice as large as my two fists fell into the
boat, and some of them came with such
violence as certainly to have broken an
arm or leg, had they struck us in those
parts. One of them struck the blade
of an oar and split it. The scene lasted
perhaps five minutes ; but it was five
minutes of the most awful feeling I ever
experienced. When it passed over, we
found the surrounding hills covered with
masses of ice, I cannot call it hail, the
trees stripped of their leaves and limbs,
and everything looking desolate. The
scene was awful beyond all description.
I have witnessed repeated earthquakes ;
the lightning has played, as it were,

about my head ; the wind roared, and
the waves at one moment have thrown
me to the sky, and the next have sunk
me into a deep abyss. I have been in
action, and have seen death and destruction around me in every shape of horror ;
but I never before had the feeling of
awe which seized upon me on this occasion, and still haunts, and I fear for ever
will haunt me. My porter, the boldest
of my family, who had ventured an instant from the door, had been knocked
down by a hailstone, and had they not
dragged him in by the heels, would have
been battered to death. Two boatmen
were killed in the upper part of the village, and I have heard of broken bones
in abundance. Imagine to yourself the
heavens suddenly frozen over, and as
suddenly broken to pieces in irregular
masses of from half a pound to a pound
weight, and precipitated to the earth.'
—(Commodore Porter's *Letters from
Constantinople and its Environs*, vol. i.
p. 44.)

31. *For through the voice of the* Lord
By the command of the Lord ; that is,
his voice going forth in the manner
specified in ver. 30. ¶ Which *smote
with a rod.* Who was accustomed to
smite as with a rod ; that is, his government was tyrannical and severe. As
he had been accustomed to smite in
that manner, so he would now meet the
proper reward of his oppression of the
nations.

32. *And* in *every place.* Marg. ' Every
passing of the rod founded.' Lowth renders it, ' Whenever shall pass the rod of
correction.' The whole design of the
passage is evidently to foretell the sudden
destruction of the army of the Assyrians,
and to show that this would be accomplished by the agency of God. The
idea seems to be, that in all those places
where the rod of the Assyrian would
pass, that is, where he would cause devastation and desolation, there would
be the sound of rejoicing with instruments of music when he should be overthrown. ¶ *The grounded staff.* The

33 For Tophet *a is* ordained[1] of old ; yea, for the king it is prepared ; he hath made *it* deep *and* large : the

a Jer.7.31.   1 *from yesterday.*

pile thereof *is* fire and much wood ; the breath of the LORD, like a stream of brimstone, *b* doth kindle it.

b Rev.14.9,10.

word 'staff' here, or *rod*, seems to refer to that by which the Assyrian smote the nations (ver. 31) ; or rather perhaps the Assyrian king himself as a rod of correction in the hand of JEHOVAH (see ch. x. 5). The word rendered 'grounded' (מוּסָדָה, *musâdhâh*) has given great perplexity to commentators. Lowth supposes it should be מוּסָרֹה (*correction*), according to a conjecture of Le Clerc. Two MSS. also read it in the same way. But the authority from the MSS. is not sufficient to justify a change in the present Hebrew text. This word, which is not very intelligibly rendered 'grounded,' is derived from יָסַד (*yâsâdh*), *to found, to lay the foundation of a building* (Ezra iii. 12; Isa. liv. 11) ; then to establish, to appoint, to ordain (Ps. civ. 8; Hab. i. 12). The idea here is, therefore, that the rod referred to had been *appointed, constituted, ordained* by God ; that is, that the Assyrian had been designated by him to accomplish important purposes *as a rod*, or as a means of punishing the nations. ¶ *Shall pass.* In his march of desolation and conquest. ¶ *Which the* LORD *shall lay upon him.* Or rather, as it should be translated, 'upon which JEHOVAH should lay,' *i.e.,* the rod, meaning that in all those places where JEHOVAH should lay this appointed scourge there would be yet rejoicing. ¶ It *shall be with tabrets and harps.* Those places where he had passed, and which he had scourged, would be filled with joy and rejoicing at his complete overthrow, and at their entire deliverance from the scourge. For a description of the tabret and harp, see Notes on ch. v. 12. ¶ *And in battles of shaking.* In the Hebrew there is an allusion here to what is said in ver. 28, that he would 'sift,' that is, agitate or toss the nations as in a winnowing shovel. ¶ *Will he fight with it.* Marg. 'Against them.' JEHOVAH would fight against the 'rod,' to wit, the Assyrian, and destroy him (see ch. xxxvii. 36).

33. *For Tophet.* The same idea is conveyed in this verse as in the pre-

ceding, but under another form, and with a new illustration. The sense is, that the army of the Assyrians would be completely destroyed, as if it were a large pile of wood in the valley of Hinnom that should be fired by the breath of God. The word 'Tophet' (תָּפְתֶּה with ה paragogic), denotes properly what causes loathing or abhorrence ; that which produces disgust and vomiting (from the Chaldee תִּיף (*Tûph*) to spit out) ; Job xvii. 6, 'I was an *abhorrence*' (תֹּפֶת), improperly rendered in our version, 'I was among them as a tabret.' The word occurs only in 2 Kings xxiii. 10; Jer. vii. 31, 32 ; xix. 6, 11, 13, 14, and in this place. It is applied to a deep valley on the south-east of Jerusalem, celebrated as the seat of idolatry, particularly of the worship of Moloch. The name also of 'the valley of Hinnom' was given to it ; and hence the name *Gehenna* (γἰεννα, Matt. v. 22, 29, 30; x. 28; xviii. 9; xxiii. 15, 33; Mark ix. 43, 45, 47; Luke xii. 5; James iii. 6), as denoting the place of future torments, of which the valley of Hinnom, or Tophet, was a striking emblem. This valley was early selected as the seat of the worship of Moloch, where his rites were celebrated by erecting a huge brazen image with a hollow trunk and arms, which was heated, and within which, or on the arms of which, children were placed as a sacrifice to the horrid idol. To drown their cries, drums were beaten, which were called תֹּף (*Toph*), or תֹּפִים (*Tophim*), and many suppose the name Tophet was given to the place on this account (see 2 Kings xvi. 3; xxi. 6; xxiii. 10). The name 'valley of Hinnom,' or Gehenna, was probably from the former possessor or occupier of that name. In subsequent times, however, this place was regarded with deep abhorrence. It became the receptacle of all the filth of the city ; and hence, in order to purify the atmosphere, and prevent contagion, it was needful to keep fires there continually burning. It was thus

CHAPTER XXXI.

ANALYSIS.

It is evident that this chapter was composed at about the same time as the preceding, and relates to the same subject. The general object, like the former, is to dissuade the Jews from their contemplated alliance with Egypt, and to lead them to rely on God. In doing this, the prophet first denounces a woe on those who went down to Egypt to seek aid (1); he then states that God will punish them for it (2); he then urges the utter inability of the Egyptians to furnish the aid which was needed, since JEHO-VAH was about to stretch out his arm over them also, and they, as well as those who sought their

a most striking emblem of hell-fire, and as such is used in the New Testament. Hezekiah was firmly opposed to idolatry; and it is not improbable that he had removed the images of Moloch, and made that valley the receptacle of filth, and a place of abomination, and that the prophet refers to this fact in the passage before us. ¶ Is *ordained.* Was fitted up, appointed, constituted. The prophet by a figure represents Hezekiah as having *fitted up* this place as if for the appropriate punishment of the Assyrians. ¶ *Of old.* Marg. as in Heb. 'From yesterday.' This expression may mean simply 'formerly, some time since,' as in Ex. iv. 10; 2 Sam. iii. 17. The idea here seems to be, that Tophet had been formerly, or was already prepared *as if* for the destruction of Sennacherib and his army. His ruin would be as certain, and as sudden, *as if,* in the valley of Tophet, the breath of JE-HOVAH should set on fire the vast materials that had been collected, and were ready to be kindled. It does not mean that Tophet had actually been prepared *for* the army of Sennacherib; it does not mean that his army would actually be destroyed there—for it was on the other side of the city that they were cut off (see Notes on ch. x. 32); it does not mean that they would be consigned to hell-fire;—but it means that that place had been fitted up *as if* to be an emblematic representation of his ruin; that the consuming fires in that valley were a striking representation of the sudden and awful manner in which the abhorred enemies of God

aid, should suffer under his displeasure (3). The prophet, then, in order to recall them from this contemplated alliance, and to induce them to put confidence in JEHOVAH, assures them by two most beautiful figures (4, 5) that God would protect their city in the threatened invasion, and save it from destruction. He calls on them, therefore (6), to turn unto God; assures them (7) that at that time every man would see the folly of trusting in idols; and finally (8, 9), assures them of the complete overthrow of the army of the Assyrian. The scope of the prophecy is, therefore, simple and direct; the argument condensed, impressive, and beautiful. It is not improbable, by any means, that these exhortations of Isaiah had a sensible effect on the conduct of

would be destroyed. ¶ *For the king it is prepared.* For Hezekiah; as if the place had been fitted up for his use in order to consume and destroy his enemies. It is not meant that Hezekiah actually had this in view, but the whole language is figurative. It was *as if* that place had been fitted up by Hezekiah as a suitable place in which entirely to destroy his foes. ¶ *He hath made* it *deep* and *large.* Vast; as if able to contain the entire army that was to be destroyed. ¶ *The pile thereof.* The wood that was collected there to be consumed. ¶ *The breath of the* LORD. As if JEHOVAH should breathe upon it, and enkindle the whole mass, so that it should burn without the possibility of being extinguished. The meaning is, that the destruction of the Assyrian would as really come from JEHOVAH as if he should, by his own agency, ignite the vast piles that were collected in the valley of Hinnom. ¶ *Like a stream of brimstone.* Brimstone, or sulphur, is used in the Scriptures to denote a fire of great intensity, and one that cannot be extinguished (Gen. xix. 24; Ps. xi. 6; Ezek. xxxviii. 22; Rev. ix. 17, 18). Hence it is used to denote the eternal torments of the wicked in hell (Rev. xiv. 10; xix. 20; xxi. 8). ¶ *Doth kindle it.* The army of the Assyrians would be destroyed in a manner which would be well represented by JEHOVAH's sending down upon a vast pile collected in the valley of Hinnom, a burning stream of sulphurous flame that should ignite and consume all before it (see Notes on ch. xxxvii. 36).

Hezekiah. The whole narrative respecting the invasion of Sennacherib would lead to the conclusion, that at first Hezekiah himself joined in the purpose of seeking the alliance with Egypt, but that he was afterwards led to abandon it, and to use all his influence to induce his people also to rely on the aid of God; compare ch. xxxvi. 6, with ver. 18.

WO to them that go down to Egypt for help, and stay on horses, and trust in chariots, because *they are* many; and in horsemen, because they are very strong: but *a* they look not unto the Holy One of Israel, neither seek the LORD.

2 Yet he also *is* wise, and will bring evil, and will not ¹call back his words: but will arise against the house of the evil-doers, and

against the help of them that work iniquity.

3 Now the Egyptians *are* men, and not God; and their horses flesh, and not spirit. When the LORD shall stretch out his hand, both he that helpeth shall fall, and he that is holpen shall fall down, and they all shall fail together.

4 For thus hath the LORD spoken unto me, Like as the lion *b* and the young lion roaring on his prey, when a multitude of shepherds is called forth against him, *he* will not be afraid of their voice, nor abase himself for the ²noise of them: so shall the LORD of hosts come down to fight for mount Zion, and for the hill thereof.

a Ho.7.7.　　1 *remove*.　　*b* Ho.11.10.　　2 or, *multitude*.

CHAPTER XXXI.

1. *Wo* (see Note on ch. xxx. 1). ¶ *To them that go down to Egypt* (see Note on ch. xxx. 2). ¶ *And stay on horses* (see Note on ch. xxx. 16). ¶ *And trust in chariots* (see Note on ch. xxi. 7). That they were often used in war, is apparent from the following places (Josh. xi. 4; Judg. i. 19; 1 Sam. xiii. 5; 2 Sam. viii. 4). ¶ *Because* they are *many*. Because they hope to secure the aid of many. See the references above. It is evident that their confidence in them would be in proportion to the number which they could bring into the field. ¶ *But they look not*, &c. (see Note on ch. xxx. 1.)

2. *Yet he also* is *wise*. God is wise. It is in vain to attempt to deceive him, or to accomplish such purposes without his knowledge. ¶ *And will bring evil*. The punishment which is due to such want of confidence in him. ¶ *But will arise against the house of the evil-doers*. This is a general proposition, and it is evidently just as true now as it was in the time of Isaiah.

3. *Now the Egyptians* are *men*. They are nothing but men; they have no power but such as other men possess. The idea here is, that the case in reference to which they sought aid was one in which *Divine* help was indispensable, and that, therefore, they relied on the

aid of the Egyptians in vain. ¶ *And their horses flesh, and not spirit*. There is need, not merely of *physical* strength, but of wisdom, and intelligence, and it is in vain to look for that in mere brutes. ¶ *Both he that helpeth*. Egypt, whose aid is sought. ¶ *And he that is holpen*. Judah, that had sought the aid of Egypt. Neither of them would be able to stand against the wrath of God.

4. *For thus hath the* LORD *spoken*. The design of this verse and the following is to assure the Jews of the certain protection of JEHOVAH, and thus to induce them to put their trust in him rather than to seek the alliance with Egypt. To do this the prophet makes use of two striking illustrations, the first of which is, that JEHOVAH would be no more alarmed at the number and power of their enemies than a fierce lion would be that was intent on his prey, and could not be frightened from it by any number of men that should come against him. The *point* of this comparison is, that as the lion that *was intent on his purpose* could not be frightened from it by numbers, so it would be with JEHOVAH, who *was equally intent on his purpose*—the defence of the city of Jerusalem. It does not mean, of course, that the purpose of God and of the lion resembled each other, but merely that there was simi-

5 As birds flying, so will the LORD of hosts defend *a* Jerusalem : defending also he will deliver *it, and* passing over he will preserve *it.*

6 Turn *b* ye unto *him from* whom

the children of Israel have deeply revolted, *c*

7 For in that day every man shall cast away his idols of silver,

a Ps.46.5.   *b* Jer.3.12.   *c* He.9.9.

lar *intensity of purpose,* and similar adherence to it notwithstanding all opposition. The figure is one that denotes the highest vigilance, firmness, steadiness, and a determination on the part of JEHOVAH that Jerusalem should not fall into the hands of the Assyrians. ¶ *Like as the lion.* The Divine nature and purposes are often represented in the Scriptures by metaphors, allegories, and comparisons taken from animals, and especially from the lion (see Deut. xxxiii. 20; Job x. 16; Ps. vii. 2; Hos. xi. 10). ¶ *And the young lion.* The vigorous, strong, fierce lion. The use of the two here, gives intensity and strength to the comparison. It is observable that the lion is seldom mentioned alone in the Scriptures. ¶ *Roaring on his prey.* Roaring as he seizes on his prey. This is the moment of the greatest *intensity of purpose* in the lion, and it is therefore used by Isaiah to denote the intense purpose of JEHOVAH to defend Jerusalem, and not to be deterred by any number of enemies. ¶ *When a multitude of shepherds is called forth.* When the neighbourhood is alarmed, and all the inhabitants turn out to destroy him. This comparison is almost exactly in the spirit and language of Homer, *Il.* xii. 209, *sq.* :

So pressed with hunger from the mountain's brow,
Descends a lion on the flocks below;
So stalks the lordly savage o'er the plain,
In sullen majesty and stern disdain:
In vain loud mastiffs bay him from afar,
And shepherds gall him with an iron war;
Regardless, furious, he pursues his way;
He foams, he roars, he rends the panting prey.
                                        Pope.

So also *Il.* xviii. 161, 162 :

—But checked he turns; repulsed attacks again.
With fiercer shouts his lingering troops he fires,
Nor yields a step, nor from his post retires;
So watchful shepherds strive to force in vain,
The hungry lion from the carcass slain. *Pope.*

¶ He *will not be afraid.* He will be so intent on his prey that he will not heed their shouting. ¶ *Nor abase himself.* That is, he will not be frightened, or disheartened. ¶ *So shall the*

LORD *of hosts.* That is, with the same intensity of purpose; with the same fixedness of design. He will be as little dismayed and diverted from his purpose by the number, the designs, and the war shout of the Assyrian armies.

5. *As birds flying.* This is another comparison indicating substantially the same thing as the former, that JEHOVAH would protect Jerusalem. The idea here is, that He would do it in the same manner as birds defend their young by hovering over them, securing them under their wings, and leaping forward, if they are suddenly attacked, to defend them. Our Saviour has used a similar figure to indicate his readiness to have defended and saved the same city (Matt. xxiii. 27), and it is possible that he may have had this passage in his eye. The phrase 'birds flying,' may denote the *rapidity* with which birds fly to defend their young, and hence the rapidity with which God would come to defend Jerusalem ; or it may refer to the fact that birds, when their young are attacked, fly, or flutter around them to defend them ; they will not leave them. ¶ *And passing over* (פָּסוֹחַ, *pâsõähh*). Lowth renders this, 'Leaping forward.' This word, which is usually applied in some of its forms to the Passover (Ex. xii. 13, 23, 27; Num. ix. 4; Josh. v. 11: 2 Chron. xxx. 18), properly means, as a verb, *to pass over,* and hence to preserve or spare. The idea in the passage is, that JEHOVAH would protect Jerusalem, as a bird defends its young.

6. *Turn ye unto* him. In view of the fact that he will assuredly defend Jerusalem, commit yourselves unto him rather than seek the aid of Egypt. ¶ *Have deeply revolted.* For the meaning of this phrase, see Note on ch. xxix. 15.

7. *For in that day.* That is, in the invasion of Sennacherib, and the events that shall be consequent thereon. ¶ *Every man shall cast away his idols*

and [1] his idols of gold, which your own hands have made unto you *for* a sin.

8 Then shall the Assyrian *a* fall with the sword, not of a mighty man ; and the sword, not of a mean man, shall devour him : but he shall

1 *the idols of his gold.*　　　*a* ch.87.63.
2 or, *for fear of.*
3 *for melting,* or, *tribute,* or, *tributary.*

(see Note on ch. xxx. 22 ; comp. Note on ch. ii. 20). ¶ For *a sin.* Or rather, the sin which your own hands have made. The sense is, that the making of those idols had been a sin, or sin itself. It had been *the* sin, by way of eminence, which was chargeable upon them.

8. *Then shall the Assyrian fall with the sword.* The *sword* is often used as an instrument of punishment. It is not meant here literally that the sword would be used, but it is employed to denote that complete destruction would come upon them. ¶ *Not of a mighty man.* The idea here is, that the army should not fall by the valour of a distinguished warrior, but that it should be done by the direct interposition of God (see ch. xxxvii. 36). ¶ *Of a mean man.* Of a man of humble rank. His army shall not be slain by the hand of mortals. ¶ *But he shall flee.* The Assyrian monarch escaped when his army was destroyed, and fled towards his own land ; ch. xxxvii. 37. ¶ *From the sword.* Marg. 'For fear of.' The Heb. is ' From the face of the sword ;' and the sense is, that he would flee in consequence of the destruction of his host, here represented as destroyed by the sword of JEHOVAH. ¶ *And his young men.* The flower and strength of his army. ¶ *Shall be discomfited.* Marg. ' For melting ;' or ' tribute,' or 'tributary.' LXX. Εἰς ἥττημα—' For destruction.' The Hebrew word (מַס *măs,* derived probably from מָסַס *măsăs, to melt away, to dissolve*) is most usually employed to denote a levy, fine, or tax— so called, says Taylor, because it *wastes* or *exhausts* the substance and strength of a people. The word is often used to denote that men become tributary, or vassals, as in Gen. xlix. 15 ; Deut. xx. 11 ; comp. Josh. xvi. 10 ; 2 Sam. xx. 24 ; 1 Kings iv. 6 ; v. 13 ; Esth. x. 1. Pro-

flee [2] from the sword, and his young men shall be [3] discomfited.

9 And [4] he shall pass over to his [5] stronghold for fear, and his princes shall be afraid of the ensign, saith the LORD, whose fire *is* in Zion, and his furnace in Jerusalem.

4 *his rock shall pass away for fear.*　　5 or, *strength.*

bably it does not here mean that the strength of the Assyrian army would become literally tributary to the Jews, but that they would be *as if* they had been placed under a levy to them ; their vigour and strength would melt away ; as property and numbers do under taxation and tribute.

9. *And he shall pass over.* Marg. ' His rock shall pass away for fear.' The Hebrew would bear this, but it does not convey a clear idea. The sense seems to be this. The word rendered ' stronghold' (Heb. ' His rock ') denotes his fortifications, or the places of strength in which he trusted. Probably the Assyrian monarch had many such places which he regarded as perfectly secure, both in the limits of his own kingdom, and on the line of his march towards Judea. Those places would naturally be made strong, in order to afford a refuge in case of a defeat. The idea here is, that so great would be his alarm at the sudden destruction of his army and the failure of his plans, that in his flight he would *pass over* or *beyond* these strong places ; he would not even stop to take refuge there and reorganize his scattered forces, but would flee with alarm *beyond* them, and make his way to his own capital. This appears to have been most strikingly fulfilled (see ch. xxxvii. 37). ¶ *And his princes.* Those, perhaps, that ruled over his dependent provinces. ¶ *Shall be afraid of the ensign.* That is, of *any* standard or banner that they saw. They would suppose that it was the standard of an enemy. This denotes a state of great consternation, when all the princes and nobles under the command of the Assyrian would be completely dismayed. ¶ *Whose fire is in Zion,* &c. That is, whose altar is there, and always burns there. That was the place where he

CHAPTER XXXII.

ANALYSIS

This chapter has been regarded by many as a continuation and conclusion of the prediction commenced in the preceding chapter. Though it was, however, probably uttered at about the same time, and with reference to the same general subject, yet there is no impropriety in its being separated. The previous chapter closes with a prediction that the Assyrian army, which had been so much the object of dread, would be totally destroyed. This would be of course followed with important consequences, some of which are depicted in this chapter. The prophet, therefore, states (1–8) that the defeat of Sennacherib would be followed by the peaceful and prosperous state of the kingdom under a righteous prince;—under whose reign there would be ample protection (2); at which time the advantages of instruction would prevail, and the ignorant would be enlightened (3, 4); when there would be a proper estimate put on moral worth, and when illiberality, hypocrisy, and falsehood would be no longer held in repute (5–7); and when the character of the nation would be that of a people which devised and executed large and liberal purposes (8). That this has a reference to the reign of Hezekiah, has been abundantly shown by Vitringa; and, indeed, must be obvious on the slightest inspection. For, 1. It is immediately connected with the account of the destruction of Sennacherib, and evidently means that the state of things here described would immediately succeed that. 2. There is nothing in the account that does not fully accord with the prosperous and happy times of the reign of Hezekiah. 3. There are statements in it which cannot be applied directly, or with propriety literally to the times of the Messiah. For example, the statement in the first verse that 'princes shal' rule in judgment' cannot be applied with any propriety to the apostles, since they are not anywhere designated by that name.

That, after the usual manner of Isaiah, he might not also, in the progress of this description, have glanced at the times of the Messiah, perhaps there can be no reason to doubt. But the main and leading purpose was, doubtless, to give a description of the happy times that would succeed the destruction of the army of the Assyrian. Calvin supposes, not improbably, I think, that this prophecy may have been uttered in the time of Ahaz, in whose reign wickedness so much abounded, and ignorance and idolatry so much prevailed. But whether the prophecy was actually *uttered* in the time of Ahaz or not—which cannot now be determined—yet it may have been uttered in view of the ignorance, and superstition, and hypocrisy, which prevailed in his reign, and which extended their influence into the time of his successor, and on account of which the nation was to be subjected to the calamities arising from the invasion of Sennacherib. After that, the king Hezekiah would rule in righteousness, and his kingdom would enjoy the blessings of his mild and virtuous reign.

The prophet then (10–14) proceeds to show, that *previous* to the prosperous times predicted, there would be a state of desolation and alarm. This is indicated by his calling on the daughters of luxury and fashion, who were reposing in security and confidence, to rise up in consternation at the calamities which were impending (10, 11), and by the assurance that there would be a time when they would sigh for the luxuries which they had before enjoyed (12–14). This is descriptive of the calamities which would attend the invasion of the Assyrian. Yet the prophet says, as is usual with him, that these calamities would be succeeded by more happy times (15–20). They would continue until the Spirit should be poured out from on high (15), and the result of this would be the prevalence of righteousness in the nation (16), and peace and safety (17,18); there would be safety, and the privilege of pursuing the peaceful pursuits of agriculture, and of cultivating the entire land without molestation (19, 20).

was worshipped, and it was a place, therefore, which he would defend. The meaning is, that they would be as certainly destroyed as the God whose altar was in Jerusalem was a God of truth, and would defend the place where he was worshipped. ¶ *And his furnace,* &c. (see Note on ch. xxix. 1). Where his altar continually burns. The word rendered 'furnace' (תַנּוּר) means properly *a baking oven* (Ex. vii. 28; Lev. ii. 4; vii. 9; xi. 35). This was either a large conical pot which was heated, in

which the cakes were baked at the sides; or an excavation made in the earth which was heated by putting wood *in* it, and when that was removed, the dough was put in it. Perhaps the whole idea here is, that Jehovah had a home in Jerusalem, with the usual appendages of a house; that his fire and his oven were there, an expression descriptive of a dwelling-place. If so, then the meaning is, that he would defend his own home, and that the Assyrian could not expect to prevail against it.

BEHOLD, a king shall reign in righteousness, *a* and princes shall rule in judgment.

2 And a man shall be as an hiding-place from the wind, and a covert *b* from the tempest; as rivers *c* of water in a dry place; as the shadow of a [1] great rock in a weary land.

a Ps.45.6,7; Jer.23.5,6.
b ch.4.6.　　　*c* ch.44.3.　　　1 *heavy.*

CHAPTER XXXII.

1. *Behold, a king.* That is, Hezekiah. That it refers to him is apparent from the connection. The reign of Ahaz had been one of oppression and idolatry. This was to be succeeded by the reign of one under whom the rights of the people would be secured, and under whom there would be a state of general prosperity. This *may* have been uttered while Ahaz was on the throne, or it may have been when Hezekiah began to reign. Perhaps the latter is the more probable, as Ahaz might not have tolerated anything that would have looked like a reflection on his own reign ; nor, perhaps, while he was on the throne would Isaiah have given a description that would have been a contrast between his reign and that of his successor. ¶ *Shall reign in righteousness.* That is, a righteous king shall reign ; or his administration shall be one of justice, and strongly in contrast with that of his predecessor. This was certainly the general characteristic of the reign of Hezekiah. ¶ *And princes shall rule.* Heb. ' For princes,' or, ' as to princes ' (לְשָׂרִים). Lowth proposes to read this without the ל, as the ancient versions do. But it is not necessary to change the text. It may be rendered, ' As to princes, they shall rule ' (comp. Ps. xvi. 3). The ' princes ' here denote the various officers of government, or those to whom the administration was confided. ¶ *In judgment.* That this is a just description of the reign of Hezekiah is apparent from the history, see 2 Kings xviii. 3–6 : ' He removed the high places, and broke the images, and cut down the grove. He trusted in the Lord God of Israel, so that after him was none like him among all the kings of Judah, nor any that were before him, for he clave unto the Lord, and departed not from following him.'

2. *And a man.* That is, evidently, the man referred to in the previous verse, to wit, Hezekiah. ¶ *Shall be as an hiding-place from the wind.* A place where one may take refuge from a violent wind and tempest (see Note on ch. xxv. 4). ¶ *A covert.* A place of shelter and security. Wind and tempest are emblematic of calamity and oppression ; and the sense is, that Hezekiah would be the protector of his people, and would save them from the calamities to which they had been subjected in former reigns. ¶ *As rivers of water.* This figure is often used in Isaiah (see ch. xxxv. 6, 7 ; and Notes on xli. 18). It means that the blessings of such a reign would be as grateful and refreshing as gushing fountains and running streams were to a thirsty traveller. Here it refers to the benefits that would be conferred by the reign of Hezekiah—a reign which, compared with that of his father, would be like a refreshing fountain to a weary pilgrim in a pathless desert. ¶ *As the shadow of a great rock.* In a burning desert of sand nothing is more grateful than the cooling shade of a far-projecting rock. It not only excludes the rays of the sun, but it has itself a refreshing coolness that is most grateful to a weary traveller. The same figure is often used by the classic writers (see Virgil, *Georg.* iii. 145 ; Hesiod, ii. 106). ¶ *In a weary land.* A land where there is fatigue and weariness. Probably here it is used to denote a land destitute of trees, and groves, and pleasant abodes ; a land where one expects weariness and fatigue without any refreshment and shelter. The following description from Campbell's *Travels in Africa* will explain this : ' Well does the traveller remember a day in the wilds of Africa, where the country was chiefly covered with burning sand ; when, scorched with the powerful rays of an almost vertical sun, the thermometer in the shade standing at 100°. He remembers long looking hither and thither for something that would afford protection from the

3 And the eyes of them that see shall not be dim : and the ears of them that hear shall hearken.

4 The heart also of the ¹ rash

shall understand knowledge, and the tongue of the stammerers shall be ready to speak ² plainly.

1 *hasty.*   2 or, *elegantly.*

almost insupportable heat, and where the least motion of air felt like a flame coming against the face. At length he espied a huge loose rock leaning against the front of a small cliff which faced the sun. At once he fled for refuge underneath its inviting shade. The coolness emitted from this rocky canopy he found exquisitely exhilarating. The wild beasts of the deserts were all fled to their dens, and the feathered songsters were all roosting among the thickest foliage they could find of the evergreen trees. The whole creation around seemed to groan, as if their vigour had been entirely exhausted. A small river was providentially at hand, to the side of which, after a while, he ventured, and sipped a little of its cooling water, which tasted better than the best Burgundy, or the finest old hock in the world. During all this enjoyment, the above apropos text was the interesting subject of the traveller's meditation ; though the allusion as a figure, must fall infinitely short of that which is meant to be prefigured by it. '

[The whole of this passage is capable of beautiful application to the Messiah and his times ; while the language of the second verse cannot be supposed descriptive of any *creature*; it is so associated in our minds with the character and functions of the Divine Redeemer, that we cannot easily acquiesce in any meaner application. 'To interpret the sublime imagery of this verse (2) in application to a mere human being, would be quite repugnant to the spirit of the sacred writers, by whom Jehovah alone is represented as the source of protection and refreshment to his people, and all trust in creatures solemnly interdicted ' (Henderson). Doubtless, if Hezekiah be at all intended, it is in a typical or inferior sense only. A greater than Hezekiah is here ; the language and figures used are precisely such as are elsewhere by the prophet applied to Jehovah (ch. iv. 6 ; xxv. 4) ; while the particulars characteristic of the times predicted, are just such as elsewhere he connects with gospel times (comp. ch. xxix. 18 ; xxxv. 5). The things predicted, according to this view, are a righteous administration under Messiah the prince (1) ; protection and refreshment to his subjects ; protection from ' the

wrath of God and the temptations of Satan, and the rage of the world ; refreshment by the consolations and graces of his Spirit, which are as rivers of water in this dry land ' (2) ; a desire for knowledge and such facility in the acquisition of it, that even persons ordinarily supposed disqualified should both clearly understand, and easily and accurately express the truth (3, 4) ; a just appreciation of character and estimation of men in accordance therewith (5) ; and, finally, the prevalence of a loving, liberal spirit, setting itself to devise and execute plans of benevolence on a scale hitherto unprecedented (8) ; Ps. cx. 3 ; Acts ii. 44, 45 ; 2 Cor. viii. 1, 4 ; ix. 2.]

3. *And the eyes of them that see,* &c. The sense of this verse is, that there shall be, under the reign of this wise and pious prince, on the part of the prophets and teachers, a clear view of Divine truth, and on the part of the people who hear, a disposition to hearken and to attend to it. The phrase ' of them that see,' refers probably to the *prophets,* as those who were called *seers* (see Notes on ch. xxix. 10 ; xxx. 10 ; comp. 1 Sam. ix. 9), or those who had *visions* (see Note on ch. i. 1) of the things that God would communicate to men. The word rendered ' be dim ' (תִּשְׁעֶינָה), is derived from שָׁעָה, which usually signifies *to see, to look,* but it also has a meaning similar to שָׁעַע, *to spread over, to close, to make blind.* Of this fact Lowth seems not to have been aware when he proposed, without the authority of any MS., to change the text. The sense is, that those who were prophets and religious teachers should no more see obscurely, but should have clear and just views of Divine truth. ¶ *And the ears of them that hear.* Of the people who were instructed by their religious teachers. ¶ *Shall hearken.* It shall be a characteristic of those times that they shall be disposed to attend to the truth of God.

4. *The heart also of the rash.* Marg. 'Hasty.' The Hebrew word denotes *those who hasten;* that is, those who are precipitate in forming a judgment, or deciding on a course of action. They

5 The vile person shall be no more called liberal, nor the churl said *to be* bountiful.

6 For the vile person will *a* speak villany, and his heart will work iniquity, to practise hypocrisy, and to utter error against the LORD, to make empty the soul of the hungry;

and he will cause the drink of the thirsty to fail.

7 The instruments also of the churl *are* evil : he deviseth wicked devices to destroy the poor with lying words, even when [1] the needy speaketh right.

a Jer.13.23.

1 or, *he speaketh* against *the poor in judgment.*

---

do not take time to deliberate, and consequently they are led headlong into error, and into improper courses of life. ¶ *Shall understand knowledge.* They shall take time to deliberate ; and they shall consequently form a more enlightened judgment. ¶ *And the tongue of the stammerers.* The 'stammerers' (comp. Note, ch. xxviii. 11) seem here to denote those who had indistinct and confused views of subjects, or who were incapable of expressing clear and intelligible views of Divine truth. ¶ *Shall be ready to speak plainly.* Marg. 'Elegantly.' The Hebrew is צָחוֹת 'clear,' 'white,' usually applied to a bright, clear, white light. The sense is, that there should be no indistinctness or obscurity in their views and modes of utterance.

5. *The vile person.* Heb. 'Fool.' But the connection requires us to understand this as the opposite of *liberal;* and it means a person who is close, miserly, narrow-minded, covetous. This person is designated, very appropriately, as a fool. ¶ *Shall be no more called liberal.* It is probable that under the reign of former princes, when all views of right and wrong had been perverted, men of unprincipled character had been the subjects of flattery, and names of virtue had been attributed to them by their friends and admirers. But it would not be so under the virtuous reign of the prince here celebrated. Things would be called by their right names, and flattery would not be allowed to attribute to men qualities which they did not possess. ¶ *Nor the churl.* The word 'churl' means properly a rude, surly, ill-bred man ; then a miser, a niggard. The Hebrew word means properly a deceiver, a fraudulent man (Gesenius). The word *avaricious,* however, seems to suit the connection. Lowth renders it, ' Niggard.' Noyes, ' Crafty.'

¶ *Bountiful.* Flattery shall no more ascribe to a miserly man a character which does not belong to him.

6. *For the vile person.* Heb. ' The fool.' This word more properly expresses the idea than ' vile person.' The Hebrews used the name *fool* to denote not only one destitute of understanding, but a knave, a dishonest man—regarding sin as the highest folly (see 1 Sam. xxv. 25 ; 2 Sam. iii. 33 ; Job ii. 10). ¶ *Will speak villany.* Heb. ' Will speak folly.' That is, he will act in accordance with his nature ; it is his nature to speak folly, and he will do it. Under a wicked and unjust administration such persons might be the subjects of flattery (ver. 5), and might be raised to office and power. But under the administration of a virtuous king they would not be admitted to favour ; and the reason was, that they would act out their nature, and would corrupt all around them. A monarch, therefore, who regarded the honour of his own throne, and the welfare of his subjects, would exclude them from his counsels. ¶ *To make empty the soul of the hungry.* Probably this refers to spiritual hunger and thirst ; and means that such a person would take away the means of knowledge from the people, and leave them to error, ignorance, and want. The sense is, that if such persons were raised to office, they would corrupt the nation and destroy their confidence in God ; and *this* was a reason why a virtuous prince would exclude them from any participation in his government.

7. *The instruments also.* In the Hebrew here there is a *paronomasia* which cannot be imitated in a translation. The word ' instruments ' here denotes evidently *the means* by which the churl accomplishes his object ; whether it be by words, by judicial decisions, or by crafty devices. This is also a kind of proverbial expression, and is given as a

8 But the liberal deviseth liberal things; and by liberal things shall he [1] stand.

9 Rise up, ye women that are at

1 or, *be established.*   a Amos 6.1.

ease; [a] hear my voice, ye careless daughters; give ear unto my speech

10 Many [2] days and years shall ye be troubled, ye careless women:

2 *days above a year.*

---

further reason why such a person would not be employed by a wise and virtuous prince. ¶ *Are evil.* He will make use of any unprincipled means, any wicked plan or device, to accomplish his purpose. ¶ *With lying words.* With false representations; or with deceitful promises and assurances. His aim would be particularly directed to the poor and humble, as more easily deprived of their rights than the rich and powerful. It was also of greater importance to defend the rights of the poor, and therefore the prophet says that such a person should not be in the employ of a just and virtuous ruler. ¶ *Even when the needy speaketh right.* That is, although the cause of the needy is one of truth and equity. When this would be manifest, the unprincipled man in power would deprive him of his rights, and, therefore, under a wise and virtuous administration, such a person should not be employed.

8. *But the liberal.* This seems also to have the force of a proverbial expression. The word ‘liberal’ means generous, noble, large-hearted, benevolent; a man of large views and of public spirit; a man above covetousness, avarice, and self-seeking; a man who is willing to devote himself to the welfare of his country, and to the interests of his fellow-men. It is *implied* here that such persons would be selected to administer the affairs of the government under the wise and virtuous prince of whom the prophet speaks. ¶ *Deviseth liberal things.* He purposes those things which will tend to promote the public welfare, and not those merely which will conduce to his private ends and gratification. ¶ *And by liberal things shall he stand.* Marg. ‘Be established.’ That is, according to the connection, he shall be confirmed, or approved in the government of the virtuous king referred to. It is, however, a proposition in a general form, and means also that a man by a liberal course shall be established; that is, his character, reputation, hopes, shall be established by it. This is true

now. If a man wishes to obtain permanent peace and honour, the esteem of his fellow-men, or the evidence of Divine approbation, it can be best done by large and liberal schemes to advance the happiness of a dying world. He who is avaricious and narrow-minded has no happiness, and no durable reputation; he who is large-hearted and benevolent, has the approbation of the wise and good, the favour of God, and a firm and unshaken support in the trials of life, and in the agonies of death.

9. *Rise up,* &c. Rosenmüller supposes that this commences a new vision or prophecy; and that the former part (ver. 9–14) refers to the desolation of Judea by the invasion of Sennacherib, and the latter (ver. 15–20) to the prosperity which would succeed that invasion. It cannot be doubted that this is the general reference of the passage, but there does not seem to be a necessity of making a division here. The entire prophecy, including the whole chapter, relates in general to the reign of Hezekiah; and as these events were to occur during his reign, the prophet groups them together, and presents them as constituting important events in his reign. The general design of *this* portion of the prophecy (ver. 9–14) is to show the desolation that would come upon the land of Judea in consequence of that invasion. This he represents in a poetical manner, by calling on the daughters of fashion and ease to arouse, since all their comforts were to be taken away. ¶ *Ye women that are at ease.* They who are surrounded by the comforts which affluence gives, and that have no fear of being reduced to want (comp. ch. iii. 16–26). ¶ *Ye careless daughters.* Heb. ‘Daughters confiding;’ that is, those who felt no alarm, and who did not regard God and his threatenings.

10. *Many days and years.* Marg. ‘Days above a year.’ This is a literal translation of the Hebrew. LXX. ‘Make mention of a day of a year in sorrow, with hope.’ Targum, ‘Days

for the vintage shall fail, the gathering shall not come.

11 Tremble, ye women that are at ease ; be troubled, ye careless ones ; strip ye, and make ye bare, and gird *sackcloth* upon *your* loins.

12 They shall lament for the

teats, for the [1] pleasant fields, for the fruitful vine.

13 Upon the land of my people shall come up thorns *a and* briers, yea, [2] upon all the houses of joy in the joyous city.

14 Because the palaces shall be forsaken ; the multitude of the city

---

1 *fields of desire.*   *a* Ho.10.8.   2 *or, burning upon.*

---

with years.' Kimchi supposes it means 'two years.' Grotius supposes it means 'within three years.' Various other interpretations may be seen in Poole's *Synopsis.* Gesenius renders it, ' For a year's time,' according to the vulgar expression ' a year and a day,' denoting a complete year, and supposes that it means a considerable time, a long period. The phrase literally means ' the days upon [or beyond] a year,' and may denote a long time ; as the entire days in a year would denote a long period of suffering. Lowth renders it, not in accordance with the Hebrew, ' Years upon years.' Noyes, ' One year more, and ye shall tremble.' *Perhaps* this expresses the sense ; and *then* it would denote not the length of time which they would suffer, but would indicate that the calamities would soon come upon them. ¶ *For the vintage shall fail.* A large part of the wealth and the luxury of the nation consisted in the vintage. When the vine failed, there would be, of course, great distress. The sense is, that in consequence of the invasion of the Assyrians, either the people would neglect to cultivate the lands, or they would fail to collect the harvest. This might occur either from the dread of the invasion, or because the Assyrian would destroy everything in his march.

11. *Strip ye, and make ye bare.* That is, take off your gay and splendid apparel, and put on the habiliments of mourning, indicative of a great calamity. ¶ *And gird* sackcloth (see Note on ch. iii. 24).

12. *They shall lament for the teats.* Interpreters have been not a little perplexed by this expression. Lowth supposes it is to be taken in connection with the previous verse, and that it denotes that sackcloth was to be girded upon the breast as well as upon the loins.

Others have supposed that it denotes to ' smite upon the breasts,' as a token of grief ; others, that the word ' breast ' here denotes children by a *synecdoche*, as having been nourished by the breast, and that the women here were called to mourn over their children. But it is evident, I think, that the word *breasts* here is used to denote that which nourishes or sustains life, and is synonymous with fruitful fields. It is so used in Homer (*Iliad*, ix. 141), where οἴθαρ ἀρούρης denotes fertility of land. And here the sense doubtless is, that they would mourn over the fields which once contributed to sustain life, but which were now desolate. In regard to the *grammatical* difficulties of the place, Rosenmüller and Gesenius may be consulted. ¶ *The pleasant fields.* Marg. as in Heb., ' Fields of desire.'

13. *Upon the land of my people.* A description similar to this, in regard to the consequences of the invasion of Sennacherib, is given in ch. vii. 20–25 (see Notes on that passage). ¶ *Yea, upon all the houses of joy.* Marg. ' Burning upon.' The marginal reading has originated from the supposition that the word כִּי is derived from כָּוָה, *to be burned.* This conjecture has been adopted by Junius and Tremellius, and by some others. But it is evidently mere conjecture, and is not demanded. The word ' yea ' will express the sense, meaning that desolation, indicated by the growth of thorns and briers, would come upon the cities that were then filled with joy. This does not refer to Jerusalem, which was not taken by Sennacherib, but to the other cities that were destroyed by him in his march, and this account accords with the statement in ch. vii. 20–25.

14. *Because the palaces shall be forsaken.* That is, the palaces in the cities and towns which Sennacherib would

shall be left : the [1] forts and towers
shall be for dens for ever, a joy of
wild asses, a pasture of flocks ;

15 Until the Spirit [a] be poured

1 or, *cliffs and watch-towers.*

---

lay waste. Or, if it refers, as Lowth
supposes, to the invasion of the land
in the time of the Chaldeans, then it
relates to the palaces in Jerusalem.
Vitringa supposes that the temple at
Jerusalem is particularly designated by
the word rendered *palaces.* But that
is not the usual word to denote the
temple, and it is not necessary to suppose that that is particularly referred
to. The word אַרְמוֹן usually denotes *a
palace,* or royal residence in some part
of the royal citadel (see 1 Kings xvi. 18;
Isa. xxv. 2 ; Jer. xxx. 18; Amos i. 4, 7,
10, 12). ¶ *The forts.* Marg. ' Cliffs
and watch-towers.' Heb. עֹפֶל (*ophel*).
This word properly denotes a hill or a
cliff, such as is an advantageous situation for fortresses. It is translated in
Mic. iv. 8, ' the stronghold ;' in 2 Kings
v. 24, ' the tower;' in 2 Chron. xxvii. 3;
xxx. 14; Neh. iii. 27; xi. 21, 'Ophel.'
With the article (THE *hill*) it was given,
by way of eminence, to a bluff or hill
lying north-east of mount Zion, and
south of mount Moriah, which was surrounded and fortified with a wall (Jos.
Jewish Wars, vi. 6). It extends south
from mount Moriah, running down to
the fountain of Siloam, lying between
the valley of Jehoshaphat on the east,
and the Tyropeon or valley of Cheesemongers on the west. It terminates
over the pool of Siloam in a steep point
of rock forty or fifty feet high. The
top of the ridge is flat, and the ground
is now tilled, and planted with olive and
other fruit trees (see Robinson's *Bib.
Researches,* vol. i. pp. 341, 394). It
may be used here, however, to denote a
hill or cliff, a strongly-fortified place in
general, without supposing of necessity
that it refers to the mountain in Jerusalem. ¶ *Towers.* Towers were erected
on the walls of cities at convenient
distances for purposes of observation.
¶ *Shall be for dens.* Shall become
places where banditti and robbers may
abide, and secure themselves. ¶ *For
ever.* This is evidently one instance in

upon us from on high, and the
wilderness be a fruitful field, and
the [b] fruitful field be counted for a
forest.

a Joel 2.28.   b Ps.107.33,&c.

which the word ' for ever ' (עַד־עוֹלָם),
denotes *a long time,* because in the verse
following there is a *period* specified
when the desolation would terminate.
When the word is used without any such
limitation, it denotes proper eternity.
¶ *A joy of wild asses.* A place where
wild animals will have unlimited range.

15. *Until the Spirit.* The Spirit of
God, as the source of all blessings, and
especially as able to meet and remove
the ills of the long calamity and desolation. This evidently refers to some
future period, when the evils which the
prophet was contemplating would be
succeeded by the spread of the true religion. If the prophet meant to confine
his description of calamities to those
which would attend the invasion of Sennacherib, then this refers to the piety
and prosperity which would prevail after
that during the reign of Hezekiah. If
he designed, as Lowth supposes, to describe the calamities which would attend
the invasion of the Chaldeans and the
desolation of the city of Jerusalem during the captivity, then this refers to the
prosperous times that would occur after
their return to their own land. And if
he looked forward beyond even that,
then this refers to the times of the Messiah also, and he designed to describe
the happy period when the Messiah
should have come, and when the Spirit
should be poured out. Vitringa supposes that all three of these events are
referred to. But although the *expressions* are such as are used in reference
to the times of the Messiah, yet the
word ' until ' seems to limit the prediction to some event previous to that.
The plain sense of the passage is, that
the city would lie waste, and would be
a pasture for flocks, *until* the Spirit
should be poured out ; that is, would lie
waste a long time, and then be succeeded by the merciful interposition of
God restoring them to their land and
privileges. This idea would seem to
limit it, at the utmost, to the return

16 Then judgment shall dwell in the wilderness, and righteousness remain in the fruitful field.

17 And the work of righteousness shall be peace ; *a* and the effect of righteousness, quietness and assurance for ever.

a Ps.85.10; Ja.3.18.   *b* Heb.4.9.

18 And my people shall dwell in a peaceable *b* habitation, and in sure dwellings, and in quiet resting-places,

19 When it shall hail, *c* coming down on the forest ; and the city shall be [1] low in a low place.

c ch.30.30.   1 or, *utterly abased.*

from Babylon. ¶ *Be poured out.* This is a common and usual mode of indicating that the influences of the Spirit of God would be imparted (Isa. xliv. 3; Ezek. xxxix. 29; Joel ii. 28, 29; Acts ii. 17, 18). ¶ *From on high.* From heaven (comp. Luke xxiv. 49). ¶ *And the wilderness be a fruitful field.* Until that change shall come when the places that are desolate shall become fertile, and the places which are now fertile and prosperous shall become desolate and barren. This may refer to the time when Jerusalem, that would have lain so long waste, would be again inhabited and cultivated, and when Babylon, then so prosperous, would become desolate and ruined. The expression has a proverbial cast, and denotes change and revolution (see Note on ch. xxix. 17).

16. *Then judgment shall dwell.* Or, justice shall make its appropriate dwelling-place there. ¶ *In the wilderness.* In the place that *was* a wilderness, but that shall now be turned to a fruitful field. ¶ *In the fruitful field.* In the nation that is like a fruitful field; in Judea restored.

17. *And the work of righteousness.* That which righteousness produces; or the effect of the prevalence of righteousness on the nation. ¶ *Shall be peace.* There shall be no internal agitation, and no conflicts with foreign nations. ¶ *Quietness and assurance.* This is a beautiful description of the happy effect of the prevalence of piety; and it is as true now as it was in the time of Isaiah. True religion would put an end to strifes and litigations; to riots and mobs; to oppressions and tumults; to alarms and robbery; to battle, and murder, and conflict.

18. *And my people shall dwell in a peaceable habitation.* In cities and towns that would not be alarmed by internal or external foes. ¶ *And in*

sure dwellings. In dwellings . that would be secure from invasion.—All this is descriptive of the peaceful times, and the general security which followed the return from Babylon. To this period of happiness and prosperity, Isaiah, as well as the other prophets, often refers.

19. *When it shall hail.* Heb. בָּרַד בָּרֶד—'And it shall hail in coming down.' There is a *paranomasia* in the original here, which cannot be expressed in a translation—a figure of speech, which, as we have seen, is common in Isaiah. 'Hail' is an image of Divine vengeance or punishment ; and the reference here is, doubtless, to the storms of indignation that would come on the enemies of the Jews, particularly on the Assyrians (see Notes on ch. xxx. 30). ¶ *Coming down on the forest.* Coming down on the army of the Assyrian, which is here called 'a forest.' The same term 'forest' is given to the army of the Assyrians in ch. x. 18, 19, 33, 34. The sense is, that the Divine judgment would come down on that army with as much severity as a storm of hail descends on a forest—stripping the leaves from the trees, destroying its beauty, and laying it waste. ¶ *And the city.* According to Gesenius, this is Nineveh, the capital of the Assyrian empire. According to Rosenmüller, Grotius, and others, it is Babylon. Hensler supposes that it is Jerusalem, and that the sense is, that as a city that is situated in a valley is safe when the storm and tempest sweep over the hills, so would it be to Jerusalem when the storm of wrath should sweep away the army of the Assyrian. But the connection evidently requires us to understand it of the capital of the enemy ; though whether it be Nineveh or Babylon perhaps cannot be determined. ¶ *Shall be low in a low place.*

20 Blessed *are* ye that sow beside all waters, *a* that send forth *thither* the feet of the ox and the ass.

CHAPTER XXXIII.

ANALYSIS.

THIS chapter comprises a new and distinct prophecy, though manifestly relating to the same general subject as the preceding. In ver. 19 of the previous chapter, the prophet had foretold the destruction of the army of Sennacherib; and this chapter is designed still further to set forth the circumstances and the effects of that destruction. That it refers to Sennacherib is apparent from the whole structure of the prophecy. So it is understood by Lowth, Rosenmüller, Grotius, and Calvin, though Vitringa supposes that it refers to the destruction of the Syrians, instead of the *Assyrians*, and particularly after the time, and for the crimes of Anti-

a Ec.11.1,2.

ochus Epiphanes. All the circumstances, as well as the connection, however, agree with the invasion by Sennacherib, and agree far better with that than either with the destruction of Babylon, or the judgments that came upon the *Syrians*. The *design* of the prophecy is to assure the Jews that their nation and city would be safe notwithstanding the invasion of the Assyrian, and that JEHOVAH would be to them a source of constant protection and consolation (21). The object of the prophecy, therefore, is to comfort them in this threatened invasion, and to lead them to look up to God.

The prophecy, or poem, is one of uncommon beauty in its structure, and is peculiarly elegant in its expressions. It abounds, indeed, in transitions; but they are easily seen, and can be distinctly marked. The structure and design of the poem may be seen in the following analysis:—

I. Woe is denounced against the Assyrian who had invaded Judea without provocation, and who

---

Marg. 'Utterly abased.' Heb. 'In humility shall be humbled.' The sense is, shall be completely prostrate. Those who refer this to Jerusalem suppose it refers to the time when God should humble it by bringing the enemy so near, and exciting so much consternation and alarm. Those who refer it to Babylon suppose it relates to its destruction. If referred to Nineveh, it must mean when the pride of the capital of the Assyrian empire should be humbled by the complete overthrow of their army, and the annihilation of their hopes. The connection seems to require us to adopt this latter interpretation. The whole verse is very obscure; but perhaps the above will express its general sense.

20. *Blessed are ye.* The sense of this verse is, that while the enemies of the Jews would be overthrown, they themselves would be permitted to cultivate their lands in security. Instead of *predicting* this directly, the prophet *implies* that this would occur, by declaring that those who were permitted to do this were happy. ¶ *That sow beside all waters.* Heb. 'Upon (לְבַ) all waters.' This *may* mean that they selected places near running streams as being most fertile; or it may refer, as Lowth supposes, to the manner of sowing grain, and particularly rice, in east-

ern countries. This is done by casting the seed upon the water. This custom is referred to in Eccl. xi. 1: 'Cast thy bread,' *i.e.*, thy seed, 'upon the waters, for thou shalt find it after many days;' —that is, cast thy seed upon the waters when the river overflows the banks, and the seed will sink into the slime and mud, and will spring up when the waters subside, and you will find it again after many days in a rich and luxuriant harvest. Sir John Chardin thus describes this mode of sowing: 'They sow it (the rice) upon the water; and before sowing, while the earth is covered with water, they cause the ground to be trodden by oxen, horses, and asses, who go mid-leg deep; and this is the way they prepare the ground for sowing' (Harmer's *Obs.* vol. i. p. 280). ¶ *That send forth thither the feet of the ox and the ass.* That is, for the purpose of treading the earth while the water is on it, and preparing it for the seed. In this way the ground would need no ploughing, but the seed would fall into the slime, and be sufficiently covered when the waters should subside. The idea in this verse is, that there would be a state of security succeeding the destruction of their enemies; and that they would be permitted to pursue the cultivation of the soil, unannoyed and undisturbed.

was spreading desolation over a nation that had not injured him (1). This contains the *general* scope and *purport* of the chapter.

II. The Jews are introduced (2) as offering up supplications to Jehovah in view of the threatened invasion, and beseeching him to be merciful to them, and expressing their confidence in him.

III. God himself is introduced declaring the overthrow of Sennacherib (3, 4). This he represents (3) under the image of the people—that is, the people in his army—fleeing at the noise of the tumult caused by the desolating tempest that should sweep them away, and at the act of God's lifting up himself to scatter the nations.

IV. A chorus of Jews is introduced (5, 6) extolling the greatness and mercy of God (5); and also celebrating the wisdom and piety of Hezekiah, who had put his confidence in God (6).

V. In ver. 7–9, the despair and alarm of the Jews are described on the approach of Sennacherib. This is exhibited in the following manner: —1. The messengers whom Hezekiah had sent to Sennacherib with three hundred talents of silver and thirty talents of gold, to propitiate his favour (2 Kings xviii. 14–16), return without success and weeping bitterly (7). 2. The desolation is described that attended the march of Sennacherib—a desolation that extended to the highways, the cities, and to the most beautiful and fertile places, represented by hewing down Lebanon, and turning Carmel into a wilderness (8, 9).

VI. God is now introduced (10–13) as saying that he would take the work of the destruction of the Assyrian into his own hand, and showing that he would be himself exalted (10); that he would disappoint their expectations (11); that they should be totally destroyed as if by fire (12), and calling on the nations near and remote to hear what he had done (13).

VII. The various effects of the invasion on the inhabitants of Jerusalem are [described (14–19). 1. The effect on the hypocrites, producing consternation and alarm of the highest degree (14). 2. This is finely contrasted with the confidence and security of the righteous in that time. They would confide in God (15, 16); they would see the king in his beauty (17); and they would see their foe completely destroyed (18, 19).

VIII. The whole account is closed with a statement of the fact that Jerusalem was safe, and that the enemy would be completely destroyed (20–24).

WO to thee that spoilest, *a* and thou *wast* not spoiled; and dealest treacherously, and they dealt not treacherously with thee! when thou shalt cease to spoil, thou shalt *b* be spoiled; *and* when thou shalt make an end to deal treacherously, they shall deal treacherously with thee.

a ch.21.2; Hab.2.8.   *b* Rev.13.10.

CHAPTER XXXIII.

1. *Wo to thee that spoilest.* This description accords entirely with Sennacherib and his army, who had plundered the cities and countries which they had invaded, and who were about to advance to Jerusalem for the same purpose (comp. ch. xxix. 7, 8; xxxvii. 11). ¶ *And thou* wast *not spoiled.* That is, thou hadst not been plundered by the Jews against whom thou art coming. It was because the war was so unprovoked and unjust, that God would bring so signal vengeance on them. ¶ *And dealest treacherously* (see Note on ch. xxi. 2). The treachery of the Assyrians consisted in the fact that when their assistance was asked by the Jews, in order to aid them against the combined forces of Syria and Samaria (see ch. vii. 1, 2), they had taken occasion from that invitation to bring desolation on Judah (see ch. vii. 17, 20; Notes on ch. viii. 6–8; x. 6). Hezekiah

also gave to Sennacherib thirty talents of gold and three hundred talents of silver, evidently with an *understanding* that this was all that he demanded, and that if this was paid, he would leave the nation in peace. But this implied promise he perfidiously disregarded (see 2 Kings xviii. 14, 15). ¶ *When thou shalt cease to spoil.* This does not refer to his having *voluntarily* ceased to plunder, but to the fact that God would put an end to it. ¶ *Thou shalt be spoiled.* This was literally fulfilled. The Assyrian monarchy lost its splendour and power, and was finally merged in the more mighty empire of Babylon. The nation was, of course, subject to the depredation of the conquerors, and compelled to submit to them. ¶ *When thou shalt make an end.* The idea is, that there would be a *completion*, or a finishing of his acts of treachery towards the Jews, and that would be when God should overthrow him and his army.

2 O LORD, be gracious unto us; we have waited for thee: be thou their arm every morning, our salvation also in the time of trouble.

3 At the noise of the tumult the people fled; at the lifting up of thyself the nations were scattered.

¶ *They shall deal treacherously with thee.* The words 'they shall,' are here equivalent to, 'thou shalt be dealt with in a treacherous manner.' The result was, that Sennacherib was treacherously slain by his own sons as he was 'worshipping in the house of Nisroch his god' (Isa. xxxvii. 38), and thus the prophecy was literally fulfilled. The sense of the whole is, that God would reward their desire of plundering a nation that had not injured them by the desolation of their own land; and would recompense the perfidiousness of the kings of Assyria that had sought to subject Jerusalem to their power, by perfidiousness in the royal family itself.

2. *O LORD.* This is a solemn prayer to JEHOVAH, made by the Jews in the apprehension of the invasion of the Assyrian. It is not meant that this prayer was actually offered, but it is a prophetic representation indicating the alarm of the Jews at his approach, and their disposition to throw themselves upon the mercy of God. ¶ *We have waited for thee.* That is, we have looked for deliverance from this threatened invasion from thy hand (comp. Note on ch. xxvi. 8). ¶ *Be thou their arm.* The *arm* is a symbol of *strength.* It is used in the Scriptures as emblematic of the Divine protection, or of the interposition of God in time of calamity and danger (Ex. xv. 16; Job xl. 9; Ps. xliv. 3; lxxvii. 15; lxxxix. 21; xcviii. 1). Lowth proposes to read 'our arm' instead of 'their arm;' and the connection would seem to demand such a reading. The Vulgate and the Chaldee read it in this manner, but there is no authority from MSS. for a change in the text. The truth seems to be, that Isaiah, impelled by prophetic inspiration, here interposes *his own* feelings as a Jew, and offers *his own* prayer that God would be the strength of the nation. The form, however, is *immediately* changed, and he presents the prayer of the people. ¶ *Every morning.* Constantly; at all times. ¶ *In the time*

of trouble. Referring particularly to the trouble consequent on the invasion of the Assyrians.

3. *At the noise of the tumult.* Lowth supposes that this is addressed by the prophet in the name of God, or rather by God himself to the Assyrian, and that it means that notwithstanding the terror which he had caused the invaded countries, he would himself fall and become an easy prey to those whom he intended to subdue. But probably it should be regarded as a part of the address which the Jews made to JEHOVAH (ver. 2), and the word ' tumult '—הָמוֹן, *sound, noise,* as of rain (1 Kings xviii. 41), or of music (Ezek. xxvi. 13; Amos v. 23), or the bustle or tumult of a people (1 Sam. iv. 11; xiv. 19; Job xxxix. 7)—refers here to the voice of God by which the army was overthrown. JEHOVAH is often represented as speaking to men in a voice fitted to produce consternation and alarm. Thus it is said of the vision which Daniel saw of a man by the side of the river Hiddekel, 'his words' were 'like the voice of a multitude' (הָמוֹן), (Dan. x. 6). And thus, in Rev. i. 10, the voice of Christ is said to have been 'like the voice of a trumpet;' and in ver. 15, 'like the sound of many waters.' It will be recollected also that it was said that God would send upon the Assyrian army 'thunder, and an earthquake, and a great noise, with storm and tempest, and a flame of devouring fire' (Isa. xxix. 6; comp. ch. xxx. 30); and it is doubtless to this prediction that the prophet refers here. God would come forth with the voice of indignation, and would scatter the combined armies of the Assyrian. ¶ *The people fled.* The people in the army of the Assyrian. A large part of them were slain by the angel of the Lord in a single night, but a portion of them with Sennacherib escaped and fled to their own land (Isa. xxxvii. 36, 37. ¶ *At the lifting up of thyself.* Of JEHOVAH; as when one rouses himself to strike. ¶ *The nations.* The army of Sennacherib was doubtless

4 And your spoil shall be gathered
like the gathering of the caterpillar;
as the running to and fro of locusts
shall he run upon them.

5 The LORD is exalted; *a* for he

a Ps.97.9.   b Ro.3.26.   1 *salvation.*
c Pr.14.27.   2 or, *messengers.*

made up of levies from the nations that
had been subdued, and that composed
the Assyrian empire.

4. *And your spoil.* The booty that
the Assyrian army had gathered in their
march towards Jerusalem, and which
would now be left by them to be collected by the Jews. ¶ *Shall be gathered
like the gathering of the caterpillar.*
The grammatical construction here is
such that this may admit of two interpretations. It may either mean, as the
caterpillar or the locust *is* gathered; or
it may mean, as the caterpillar gathers
its spoil. It often occurred that in
countries where the locust was an article
of food, they were scraped together in
large quantities, and thrown into ditches,
or into reservoirs, and retained to be
eaten. This is the custom in some
parts of Africa. But the meaning here

LOCUST (*Gryllus migratorius*).

is, undoubtedly, that the plunder of the
Assyrian army would be collected by
the Jews, as the locust gathered its food.
The sense is, that as locusts spread
themselves out over a land, as they go
to and fro without rule and without
molestation, gathering whatever is in
their way, and consuming everything,
so the Jews in great numbers, and without regular military array, would run
to and fro collecting the spoils of the
Assyrian army. In a country where
such devastation was made by the caterpillar and locust as in Palestine, this
was a very striking figure. The word
rendered 'caterpillar' here (חָסִיל from
חָסַל *to cut off, consume*), properly de-

notes *the devourer*, and is applied usually
to a species of locust. So it is understood here by most of the versions. The
LXX. render it, 'As if one were gathering locusts, so will they insult you.'

5. *The* LORD *is exalted* (comp. Ps.
xcvii. 9). The prophet here introduces
a chorus of the Jews, celebrating the
praises of God for delivering them from
the Assyrian. ¶ *He hath filled Zion
with judgment.* That is, the effect of
his destroying his enemies will be to fill
Jerusalem with reverence for his name.
The deliverance would be so signal, and
the manifestation of the Divine mercy so
great, that the effect would be that the
nation would turn to God, and acknowledge his gracious interposition (see ch.
xxx. 22–26, 29; xxxi. 6; xxxii. 15–18).

6. *And wisdom and knowledge shall
be.* This verse contains evidently an
address to Hezekiah, and asserts that
his reign would be characterized by the
prevalence of piety and knowledge. This
chapter abounds in sudden transitions;
and it accords with its general character
that when JEHOVAH had been addressed
(ver. 5), there should then be a direct
address to Hezekiah. ¶ *The stability.*
This word denotes firmness, steadiness,
constancy; and means that in his times
knowledge and the fear of the Lord
would be settled on a firm foundation.
The whole history of the virtuous reign
of Hezekiah shows that this was fulfilled
(see 2 Kings xviii.) ¶ And *strength of
salvation.* Or saving strength; that is,
mighty or distinguished salvation. Thy
times shall be distinguished for great
reforms, and for the prevalence of the
doctrines of salvation. ¶ *The fear of
the* LORD *is his treasure.* The principal
riches of Hezekiah. His reign shall not
be distinguished for wars and conquests,
for commercial enterprise, or for external splendour, but for the prevalence
of piety, and the fear of the LORD.

7. *Behold.* This verse introduces a

shall cry without ; the ambassadors
of peace shall weep bitterly.

8 The highways lie waste, the way-

faring man ceaseth : he hath broken
the covenant, he hath despised the
cities, he regardeth no man.

new subject by a very sudden transition.
It is designed, with the two following,
to exhibit the desolation of the land on
the invasion of Sennacherib, and the
consternation that would prevail. For
this purpose, the prophet introduces
(ver. 7) the ambassadors who had been
sent to sue for peace, as having sought
it in vain, and as weeping now bitterly ;
he represents (ver. 8) the desolation that
abounded, and the fact that Sennacherib
refused to come to any terms ; and (ver. 9)
the extended desolations that had come
upon the fairest portions of the land.
¶ *Their valiant ones*. The ' valiant
ones ' of the Jews who had been sent
to Sennacherib to obtain conditions of
peace, or to enter into a negotiation
with him to spare the city and the
nation. The word which is here rendered ' valiant ones ' (אֶרְאֶלָּם) has given
great perplexity to expositors. It occurs
nowhere else in the Scriptures. The
LXX. render the verse, ' With the dread
of you shall they be terrified ; they, of
whom you have been afraid, will, for fear
of you, raise a grievous cry.' Jerome
renders it, ' Behold, they seeing, cry
without,' as if the word was derived
from רָאָה, *to see*. The Chaldee renders
it, ' And when it shall be revealed to
them, the messengers of the people who
went to announce peace, shall cry bitterly.' The Syriac, ' If he shall permit
himself to be seen by them, they shall
weep bitterly.' Symmachus and Theodotion render it, Ἰδοὺ ὀφθήσομαι αὐτοῖς—
' Lo, I will appear to them.' So Aquila,
Ὀραθήσομαι αὐτοῖς. Most or all the versions seem to have read it as if it were
compounded of אֶרְאֶה לָם—' I will appear
to them.' But probably the word is
formed from אֲרִאֵל, the same as אֲרִיאֵל
(*Ariel*), ' a hero ' (see Note ch. xxix. 1),
and means *their hero* in a collective
sense, or *their heroes ;* that is, their
men who were distinguished as military
leaders, and who were sent to propose
terms of peace with Sennacherib. The
most honourable and valiant men would
be selected, of course, for this purpose
(comp. Note on ch. xxx. 4), but they had

made the effort to obtain peace in vain,
and were returning with consternation
and alarm. ¶ *Shall cry without*. They
would lift up their voice with weeping
as they returned, and publicly proclaim
with bitter lamentation that their efforts
to obtain peace had failed. ¶ *The ambassadors of peace*. When Sennacherib
invaded the land, and had advanced as
far as to Lachish, Hezekiah sent messengers to him with a rich present,
having stripped the temple of its gold,
and sent him all the silver which was
in his treasury, for the purpose of propitiating his favour, and of inducing
him to return to his own land (2 Kings
xviii. 14–16). But it was all in vain.
Sennacherib sent his generals with a
great host against Jerusalem, and was
unmoved by all the treasures which
Hezekiah had sent to him, and by his
solicitations for peace (2 Kings xviii.
17). It was to the *failure* of this embassy that Isaiah refers in the passage
before us.

8. *The highways lie waste*. This
verse contains a description of the desolations that had been caused by the
invasion of Sennacherib. Some have
understood it as containing the account
which the ambassadors sent by Hezekiah gave of the effects of the invasion.
Thus Grotius interprets it. But it is
probably a description made by the
prophet himself, and is designed to state
one cause why the messengers that had
been sent out wept bitterly. They had
not only failed of inducing Sennacherib
to abandon his purpose of attacking
Jerusalem, but they had witnessed the
effects of his invasion already. The
public ways were desolate. In the
consternation and alarm that was produced by his approach, the roads that
had been usually thronged were now
solitary and still. A mournful desolation already prevailed, and they apprehended still greater calamities, and
hence they wept. ¶ *The wayfaring
man ceaseth*. Heb. ' He that passes
along the road ceases.' That is, there
is a cessation of travel. No one is seen
passing along the streets that used to

9 The earth mourneth *and* languisheth ; Lebanon is ashamed *and* hewn¹ down ; Sharon is like a wil-

1 or, *withered away.*

derness ; and Bashan and Carmel shake off *their fruits.*

10 Now will I rise, saith the

---

be thronged. ¶ *He hath broken the covenant.* This may either mean that the Assyrian king had violated the compact which had been made with him by Ahaz, by which he was to come and *aid* Jerusalem against the allied armies of Syria and Samaria (see Notes on ch. vii.), or it may mean that he had violated an implied compact with Hezekiah. When Judea was threatened with an invasion by Sennacherib, Hezekiah had sent to him when he was at Lachish, and had sought for peace (2 Kings xviii. 14). In that embassy Hezekiah said, ' I have offended, return from me ; that which thou puttest on me I will bear. And the king of Assyria appointed unto Hezekiah king of Judah three hundred talents of silver and thirty talents of gold.' To pay this, Hezekiah exhausted his treasury, and even stripped the temple of its golden ornaments (2 Kings xviii. 15, 16). A compact was thus made by which it was understood that Sennacherib was to withdraw his army, and depart from the land. But notwithstanding this, he still persisted in his purpose, and immediately despatched a part of his army to lay siege to Jerusalem. *All* the treaties, therefore, had been violated. He had disregarded that which was made with Ahaz, and that which he had now himself made with Hezekiah, and was advancing in violation of all to lay siege to the city. ¶ *He hath despised the cities.* That is, he disregards their defences, and their strength ; he invades and takes all that comes in his way. He *speaks* of them with contempt and scorn as being unable to stand before him, or to resist his march. See his vain and confident boasting in ch. x. 9, and xxxvi. 19. ¶ *He regardeth no man.* He spares no one, and he observes no compact with any man.

9. *The earth mourneth.* The land through which he has passed. For the sense of this phrase, see Note on ch. xxiv. 4. ¶ *Lebanon is ashamed* and *hewn down.* For the situation of Lebanon, see Note on ch. x. 34. Lebanon

was distinguished for its ornaments of beautiful cedars. Here it is represented as being stript of these ornaments, and as covered with shame on that account. There is not any direct historical evidence that Sennacherib *had* advanced to Lebanon, though there are some intimations that this had occurred (see Note on ch. xiv. 8), and it was certainly a part of his boast that he had done it (see ch. xxxvii. 24). There is no improbability in supposing that he had sent a part of his army to plunder the country in the vicinity of Lebanon (see ch. xx. 1). ¶ *Sharon is like a wilderness.* Sharon was the name of a district south of mount Carmel along the coast of the Mediterranean, extending to Cesarea and Joppa. The name was almost proverbial to express any place of extraordinary beauty and fertility (see 1 Chron. v. 16 ; xxvii. 29 ; Cant. ii. 1 ; Isa. xxxv. 2 ; lxv. 10). There was also another Sharon on the east side of the Jordan, and in the vicinity of Bashan, which was also a fertile region (1 Chron. v. 16). To this, it is more probable that the prophet here refers, though it is not certain. The *object* seems to be to mention the most fertile places in the land as being now desolate. ¶ *Bashan.* For an account of the situation of Bashan, subsequently called Batanea, see Note on ch. ii. 13. ¶ *And Carmel* (see Note on ch. xxix. 17). ¶ *Shake off* their fruits. The words ' their fruits,' are not in the Hebrew. The LXX. read this, ' Galilee and Carmel are made bare ' (φανερὰ ἔσται, x τ.λ.) The Hebrew word נָעַר probably means *to shake; to shake out* or *off;* and refers here to the fact probably that Bashan and Carmel are represented as having shaken off *their leaves,* and were now lying desolate as in winter.

10. *Now.* This verse commences another transition. In the previous verses, the desolation of the land had been described, and the hopelessness of obtaining any terms of favour from Sennacherib, or of binding him to any

LORD ; now will I be exalted ; now *a* will I lift up myself.

11 Ye shall conceive chaff ; ye shall bring forth stubble : your breath *as* fire shall devour you.

12 And the people shall be *as* the burnings of lime ; *as* thorns cut up shall they be burned in the fire.

13 Hear, ye *that are* far off, what I have done ; and ye *that are* near, acknowledge my might.

14 The sinners in Zion are afraid; fearfulness hath surprised *b* the hypocrites : who among us shall dwell with the devouring fire? who among us shall dwell with everlasting burnings ?

compact, had been stated. In this state of things, when inevitable ruin seemed to be coming upon the nation, God said that he would interpose. ¶ *Will I rise.* To vengeance ; or to punish the invading host. The emphasis in this passage should be placed on ' I,' indicating that JEHOVAH would himself do what could not be effected by men. ¶ *Now will I be exalted.* That is, God would so interpose that it should be manifest that it was *his* hand that brought deliverance.

11. *Ye shall conceive chaff.* An address of God to the Assyrians. The figure is one that denotes that their counsels would be in vain. Chaff and stubble are used in the Scriptures, in contrast with grain, to denote anything which is not solid, nutritious, or substantial ; then anything which is frivolous, useless, vain. A similar image occurs in ch. xxvi. 18 (see Note on that place ; comp. ch. lix. 4). ¶ *Your breath as fire shall devour you.* The word ' breath ' here (רוּחַ, *spirit*) is evidently used in the sense of the Θυμός, and denotes *anger*, as in ch. xxx. 28. It refers to the haughty and arrogant spirit of Sennacherib ; the enraged and excited mind intent on victory and plunder. The sense is, that his mind, so intent on conquest—so proud, excited, and angry, would be the means of his own destruction. Lowth proposes to read ' my spirit,' but for this change there is no authority from MSS. (see Notes on ch. i. 31).

12. *And the people.* In the army of Sennacherib. ¶ As *the burnings of lime.* As if placed in a burning lime-kiln, where they must certainly be destroyed (see ch. xxx. 33; comp. Amos ii. 1). ¶ As *thorns cut up.* As thorns, or small brushwood, that has been long cut up and perfectly dried are speedily con-

sumed, so shall it be with the Assyrian army. This is an image like many that are employed, denoting that the destruction of the army of the Assyrians would be sudden and entire.

13. *Hear, ye* that are *far off.* This is an address of JEHOVAH, indicating that the destruction of the Assyrian army would be so signal that it would be known to distant nations, and would constitute an admonition to them. ¶ *Ye* that are *near.* Ye Jews ; or the nations immediately adjacent to Judea. The phrase ' far and near,' is equivalent to *all.*

14. *The sinners in Zion are afraid.* This verse is evidently designed to describe the alarm that was produced in Jerusalem on impenitent sinners and hypocrites by a view of the judgment of God on the army of Sennacherib. They would see his wrath on his enemies then, and in view of the terrors of his indignation in relation to that army they would be alarmed, and would ask how it would be possible for them to endure such wrath for ever. If the effect of the wrath of God even *for a night*, when it should blaze against that great army, was so terrible, how could it be borne for ever ? This seems to be the general idea of the passage. A great variety of interpretations have been proposed, which may be seen in Vitringa and Poole. The phrase, ' sinners in Zion ' here refers to the wicked and rebellious in Jerusalem. ¶ *Fearfulness hath surprised the hypocrites.* Those who professed to serve God, and yet who were secretly depending on the aid of Egypt (see ch. xxxi.; comp. Note on ch. ix. 17). The sentiment here is, that those who professedly are the friends of God, but who are secretly and really his enemies, are often alarmed at his judgments. When the judgments of

15 He ^a that walketh ¹ righteously
and speaketh ² uprightly ; he that
despiseth the gain of ³ oppressions,
that shaketh his hands from holding
of bribes, that stoppeth his ears from
hearing of ⁴ blood, and shutteth his
eyes ^b from seeing evil ;

a Ps.15,2.　　1 *in righteousness.*　2 *uprightness.*
3 or, *deceits.*　4 *bloods.*　*b* Ps.119.37.

God overtake sinners, they are conscious
that they deserve also his wrath, and
their minds are filled with consternation.
So in a time of prevailing sickness, or
of pestilence, they who have really no
confidence in God, and no evidence that
they are prepared to die, are filled with
alarm. A true friend of God will be
calm in such scenes; a hypocrite will
show by his consternation that he has
no religion. ¶ *Who among us shall
dwell with the devouring fire?* Some
have understood this as referring to the
fires which they supposed the Assyrian
would kindle in Jerusalem, apprehend-
ing that he would take and burn the
city. But the more probable interpretation is that which refers it to the
judgment that would be brought upon
the Assyrians—the burning wrath of
God like fire that would consume them.
The destruction of the Assyrians is repeatedly represented under the image
of a storm and tempest, where there
would be the 'flame of devouring fire'
(see Note on ch. xxix. 6). The sense is
this : 'God has suddenly consumed
that immense army of his foes. Such
must be the awful punishment of the
wicked. How can *we* abide it? We
also, though among his people, are his
foes, and are exposed to his wrath.
How *can* we endure the terrors of that
day when his burning indignation shall
also overtake us?' ¶ *Shall dwell with
everlasting burnings.* Who among us
could endure to suffer amid such burning wrath for ever? If that wrath is so
fierce as to consume such an immense
host in a single night, who could abide
it should it be continued for ever and
for ever? This is the obvious sense of
this passage; and it implies—1. That
hypocrites will be greatly alarmed when
they see punishment come upon the
open and avowed enemies of God. 2.
That in such times they will have none
of the peace and quiet confidence which
his true friends have. 3. That such an
alarm is evidence of conscious guilt and
hypocrisy. 4. That the persons here

spoken of had a belief of the doctrine of
eternal punishment — a belief which
hypocrites and sinners always have, else
why should they be alarmed? 5. That
the punishment of hypocrites in the
church will be dreadful and terrific.
This seems to have been the conviction
here. They saw that if *such* judgments
came upon those who had no knowledge
of the true God, it must be infinitely
more terrible on those who had been
trained amidst the institutions of religion, and who had professed attachment
to JEHOVAH. And so it will be in a pre-
eminent degree among those who have
been trained in the Christian church,
and who have been the professed but
insincere followers of the Lord Jesus
Christ.

15. *He that walketh righteously.* In
this and the following verses the prophet
presents, in contrast, the confidence and
the security of the righteous. He first,
in this verse, describes the characteristics of the righteous, and in the following verses their confidence in God,
and their security and safety. The first
characteristic of the righteous man is
that he walks righteously ; that is, he
lives righteously ; he does right. ¶ *And
speaketh uprightly.* The second characteristic—his *words* are well-ordered.
He is not false, perfidious, slanderous,
or obscene in his words. If a private individual, his words are simple, honest,
and true ; if a magistrate, his decisions
are according to justice. ¶ *He that despiseth the gain of oppressions.* Marg.
'Deceits.' The third characteristic—
he abhors the gain that is the result
of imposition, false dealing, and false
weights. Or if it mean *oppressions*, as
the word usually does, then the sense
is, that he does not oppress the poor, or
take advantage of their needy condition,
or affix exorbitant prices, or extort payment in a manner that is harsh and
cruel. ¶ *That shaketh his hands from
holding of bribes.* The fourth characteristic — this relates particularly to
magistrates. They adjudge causes ac-

16 He shall dwell on [1] high; his place of defence *shall be* the munitions of rocks; bread shall be given him, his waters *shall be* sure.

[1] *heights, or, high places.*

17 Thine eyes shall see [a] the king in his beauty: they shall behold the land that [2] is very far off.

18 Thine heart shall meditate ter-

[a] Jn.17.24.   [2] *of far distances.*

cording to justice, and do not allow their judgment to be swayed by the prospect of reward. ¶ *That stoppeth his ears from hearing of blood.* This is the fifth characteristic. It means, evidently, he who does not listen to a proposal to shed blood, or to any scheme of violence, and robbery, and murder (see Note on ch. i. 15). ¶ *And shutteth his eyes from seeing evil.* He does not *desire* to see it; he is not found in the places where it is committed. A righteous man should not only have no part in evil, but he will keep himself if possible from being a witness of it. A man who sees all the evil that is going forward; that is present in every brawl and contention, is usually a man who has a fondness for such scenes, and who may be expected to take part in them. It is a remarkable fact that very few of the Society of Friends are ever seen in courts of justice as *witnesses.* The reason is, that they have no fondness for seeing the strifes and contentions of men, and are not found in those places where evil is usually committed. This is the sixth characteristic of the righteous man; and the sum of the whole is, that he keeps himself from all forms of iniquity.

16. *He shall dwell on high.* See the margin. Heights, or high places, were usually places of safety, being, inaccessible to an enemy. The sense here is, that such a man as is described in ver. 15, should be preserved from alarm and danger, *as if* his habitation were on a lofty cliff or rock. The particular and special meaning is, that he should be safe from the anger, wrath, and consuming fire, which the sinner and the hypocrite dreaded (ver. 14). ¶ *The munitions of rocks.* The literal translation of this place would be, ' The strongholds of the rocks shall be his lofty fortress ' (comp. Note on ch. ii. 21). ¶ *Bread shall be given him.* He shall be sustained, and his life shall be preserved.

17. *Thine eyes.* The eyes of the righteous, described in ver. 15. ¶ *Shall*

see the king in his beauty. Some understand this of the Assyrian king. Thus Kimchi understands it, and supposes it means that they shall see him at the walls of Jerusalem; that is, shall see him destroyed. Vitringa supposes it means JEHOVAH himself, as the king of his people, and that they should see him in his glory. Others suppose it refers to the Messiah. But the immediate connection requires us to understand it of Hezekiah (comp. Note on ch. xxxii. 1, 2). The sense is, ' You shall be defended from the hostile army of the Assyrian. You shall be permitted to live under the peaceful and prosperous reign of your pious monarch, and shall see him, not with diminished territory and resources, but with the *appropriate* magnificence which becomes a monarch of Israel.' ¶ *The land that is very far off.* You shall be permitted to look to the remotest part of the land of Judea as delivered from enemies, and as still under the happy sceptre of your king. You shall not be confined by a siege, and straitened within the narrow walls of Jerusalem. The empire of Hezekiah shall be extended over the wide dominions that appropriately belong to him, and you shall be permitted to range freely over the whole land, even over the parts that are now occupied by the forces of the Assyrian. Virgil has a beautiful passage remarkably similar to this:

— juvat ire, et Dorica castra,
Desertosque videre locos, litusque relictum.
Æn. ii. 28.

18. *Thine heart.* The heart of the people of Jerusalem. ¶ *Shall meditate terror.* This is similar to the expression in Virgil:

— forsan et hæc olim meminisse juvabit.
Æn. ii. 203.

The sense here is, ' You shall hereafter *think over* all this alarm and distress. When the enemy is destroyed, the city saved, and the king shall reign in magnificence over all the nation then enjoying peace and prosperity, you shall

ror. Where *is* the scribe? where *is* the [1] receiver? where *is* he that counted the towers?

19 Thou shalt not see a fierce people; a people of a deeper speech than thou canst perceive; of a stammering [2] tongue, *that thou canst* not understand.

20 Look upon Zion, the city of our solemnities: thine eyes shall see Jerusalem a quiet habitation, a tabernacle *that* shall not be taken down; not one of the stakes thereof shall ever *a* be removed, neither shall any of the cords thereof be broken.

[1] *weigher.*   [2] *or, ridiculous.*   *a* Rev.3.12.

recall these days of terror and alarm, and shall then ask with gratitude and astonishment, Where are they who caused this alarm? Where are now they who so confidently calculated on taking the city? They are all gone—and gone in a manner fitted to excite astonishment and adoring gratitude.' 'Sweet is the recollection,' says Rosenmüller, 'of dangers that are passed.' ¶ *Where* is *the scribe?* How soon, how suddenly has he vanished! The word 'scribe' here (כָּפֵר) evidently refers to some prominent class of officers in the Assyrian army. It is from סָפַר, *to count, to number, to write;* and probably refers to a secretary, perhaps a secretary of state or of war, or an inspector-general, who had the charge of reviewing an army (2 Kings xxv. 19; Jer. xxxvii. 15; lii. 25). ¶ *Where* is *the receiver?* Marg. as in Heb. 'Weigher.' Vulg. 'Where is he that ponders the words of the law?' The LXX. 'Where are the counsellors (συμβουλεύοντες)?' Probably the word refers to him who *weighed* the tribute, or the pay of the soldiers; and means, doubtless, some officer in the army of the Assyrian; probably one whose office it was to have charge of the *military chest,* and to pay the army. ¶ *Where* is *he that counted the towers?* That is, who made an estimate of the strength of Jerusalem—either Sennacherib, or some one appointed by him to reconnoitre and report on the means which the city had of defence (comp. ch. xxxvi. 4).

19. *Thou shalt not see a fierce people.* Or, rather, 'this fierce and boasting people you shall not see.' They shall not enter the city; but though they are advancing with so much confidence, they shall be suddenly cut off and destroyed. The word rendered 'fierce,' (נוֹעָז from נָעַז), probably means *strong,* or *wicked.*

Lowth renders it, 'barbarous people,' as if it were לוֹעֵז. Michaelis also adopts this reading by supposing an error in transcribing, a change of נ into ל. Such a change *might* have easily occurred, but there is no authority from the MSS. for making an alteration in the text. The word *strong,* or *mighty,* agrees well with the connection. ¶ *A people of a deeper speech.* A people whose language is so *deep, i.e.,* so dark, or obscure, that it cannot be understood by you. This refers to the army of the Assyrians, who spoke the Syrian language, which was understood by some of the Jews, but which was unintelligible to the mass (see ch. xxxvi. 11). ¶ *Than thou canst perceive.* Than you can understand. ¶ *Of a stammering tongue* (see Note on ch. xxviii. 11). Marg. 'Ridiculous;' a sense which the Hebrew will bear, but the more appropriate meaning is that of a barbarous, or unintelligible foreign language.

20. *Look upon Zion.* Lowth renders this, 'Thou shalt see Zion,' by changing the Hebrew text in conformity with the Chaldee. There is no doubt that this accords with the sense of the passage, but there is no authority for the change. It stands in contrast with what had been said in ver. 19. There, the prophet had said that they should no more see those foreign armies that were coming to invade them. Here he directs them to look upon Zion, implying that they should be permitted to behold Zion in a situation such as he proceeds to describe it. 'You shall not see that foreign army carrying desolation as they design through the city and the land. They shall be destroyed. But behold Zion! Her you shall see quiet, prosperous, happy, peaceful.' ¶ *The city of our solemnities.* Where the religious solemnities of the nation were celebrated.

21 But there the glorious LORD *will be* unto us a place [1]of broad

rivers and streams ; wherein shall go no galley with oars, neither shall gallant ship pass thereby.

1 *broad of spaces,* or, *hands.*

¶ *A quiet habitation.* Free from invasion, and from the terrors of war. ¶ *A tabernacle.* A tent ; a dwelling, such as was common in the nomadic mode of life in the East. The whole city is described under the image of a *tent* that is fixed and undisturbed, where the family may reside in safety and comfort. ¶ *Not one of the stakes thereof.*

The 'stakes' here refer to the poles or fixtures which were driven into the ground in order to fasten the tent, to enable them to spread it, or to the small stakes or pins that were driven in the ground in order to secure the cords by which the tent was extended. The following cut will give an idea of the mode in which tents were commonly

ARABS PITCHING THEIR TENT.—From Laborde.

pitched, and will serve to explain this passage, as well as the similar passage in ch. liv. 2. ¶ *Shall ever be removed.* It shall be a fixed and permanent habitation. The word 'ever' must mean an indefinite period of duration. Sennacherib had designed to blot out the name of the people of God, and destroy their separate and independent existence. The prophet says that that should never be done. Jerusalem, the residence of his people and the emblem of his church, would be safe, and would not be destroyed. There would *always* be a safe and quiet abode for the friends of the Most High. In this sense it accords with the declaration of the Saviour, that the gates of hell should not prevail

against his church. ¶ *Neither shall any of the cords thereof be broken.* Cords were used in tents to fasten the cloth to the poles, or to fasten it to the pins which had been driven into the ground, in order to extend the cloth, and to make it firm.

21. *But there.* In Jerusalem ; or in his church, of which Jerusalem was the emblem. ¶ *The glorious* LORD. Lowth renders it, 'The glorious name of JE-HOVAH,' taking שֵׁם to be a noun, as if it were pointed שֵׁם. So the Syriac and the LXX. read it. The word 'glorious' (אַדִּיר) means magnificent ; denoting that JEHOVAH would manifest himself there as magnificent or great in the destruction

22 For the Lord *is* our judge, the
1 *statute-maker.*

Lord *is* our [1] law-giver, the Lord
is our king ; he will save us.

of his enemies, and in the protection of
his people. ¶ Will be *unto us a place.*
It seems to be harsh to say that Jehovah
would be *a place ;* but the meaning is,
that he would be to them *as* such a
place ; that is, his presence and blessing
would be such as would be represented
by broad rivers and streams flowing
through a land, or encompassing a city.
Rivers and streams are sources of fertility, the channels of commerce, and
objects of great beauty. Such seems
to be the idea here. The presence of
Jehovah would be to them a source of
great prosperity and happiness ; and a
beauty would be thrown around the city
and nation like majestic and useful
rivers. It is *possible* that there may
have been some allusion here to cities
that were encompassed or penetrated
by rivers and canals, like Babylon, or
Thebes in Egypt. Such cities derived
important advantages from rivers. But
Jerusalem had nothing of this nature to
contribute to its prosperity or beauty.
The prophet says, that the presence of
Jehovah would be to them what these
rivers were to other cities. ¶ *Of broad
rivers and streams.* Heb. ' Rivers,
streams broad of hands.' The sense
seems to be, broad rivers that are made
up of confluent streams ; or rivers to
which many streams are tributary—
like the Nile—and which are therefore
made *broad,* and capable of navigation.
The phrase here used—in the Heb.
' broad of hands '—properly denotes
broad on both hands, or as we would
say, *on both sides ;* that is, the shores
would be separated far from each other.
The word *hand* is often used in Hebrew
to denote the *side,* the shore, or the
bank of a river. The following extract
will show the importance of such rivers :
' In such a highly cultivated country as
England, and where great drought is
almost unknown, we have not an opportunity to observe the fertilizing influence
of a broad river ; but in South Africa,
where almost no human means are employed for improving the land, the be-
nign influence of rivers is most evident.
The Great, or Orange River, is a remarkable instance of this. I travelled

on its banks, at one time, for five or six
weeks, when, for several hundred miles,
I found both sides of it delightfully
covered with trees of various kinds, all
in health and vigour, and abundance of
the richest verdure ; but all the country
beyond the reach of its influence was
complete desert. Everything appeared
to be struggling for mere existence ; so
that we might be said to have had the
wilderness on one side, and a kind of
paradise on the other.'—(Campbell.)
¶ *Wherein shall go.* The mention of
broad rivers here seems to have suggested to the prophet the idea that
navigable rivers, while they were the
channels of commerce, also gave to an
enemy the opportunity of approaching
easily with vessels of war, and attacking
a city. He therefore says that no such
consequence would follow, from the fact
that Jehovah would be to them in the
place of broad rivers. No advantage
could be taken from what was to them
a source of prosperity and happiness.
While other cities were exposed to an
enemy from the very sources from which
they derived their wealth and prosperity,
it would not be so with them. From
what constituted their glory—the protection of Jehovah—no danger ever
could be apprehended. It had all the
advantages of broad rivers and streams,
but with none of their attendant exposures and perils. ¶ *No galley with oars.*
That is, no *small* vessel—for larger vessels were propelled by sails. Still the
reference is doubtless to a vessel of war ;
since vessels of commerce would be an
advantage, and it would not be an object
of congratulation that none of them
should be there. ¶ *Neither shall gallant ship.* No *great* (אַדִּיר) or magnificent ship ; no ship fitted out for purposes of war. The sense is, therefore,
that though Jerusalem should be thus
favoured, yet it would be unapproachable
by an enemy.

22. *For the* Lord *is our judge.* Jehovah will be to us nothing but a source
of happiness, truth, and prosperity. His
presence will be to us only a blessing,
and a means of success and joy. The

23 Thy [1] tacklings are loosed; they could not well strengthen their mast, they could not spread the sail; then is the prey of a great spoil divided; the lame [a] take the prey.

24 And the inhabitant shall not say, I am sick; [b] the people that dwell therein *shall be* forgiven [c] *their* iniquity.

1 or, *they have forsaken thy tacklings.*
a 1 Cor.1.27.   b Rev.21.4.   c Jer.50.20.

repetition of the name JEHOVAH *three times* is common in the Scriptures.

23. *Thy tacklings.* This is evidently an address to Sennacherib. The mention of the war-galley and the ship seems to have suggested the application of the figure to the enemies of the Jews, and particularly to Sennacherib. The prophet, therefore, compares the Assyrian to a ship that was rendered unserviceable; whose sails were unfastened, and whose mast could not be made firm, and which was therefore at the mercy of winds and waves. The Hebrew which is here rendered 'thy tacklings are loosed,' means 'thy cords are let go;' that is, the cords or ropes that fastened the sails, the masts, and the rudder, were loosened. In such a condition the ship would, of course, go to ruin. ¶ *They could not well strengthen their mast.* They could not fix it firm or secure. It is evident that if the *mast* cannot be made firm, it is impossible to navigate a ship. It is to be observed here, however, that the word which our translators have rendered 'well' (כֵּן), not only signifies 'well' as an adverb, but is also used as a noun, and means a stand or station (Gen. xl. 13; xli. 13; Dan. xi. 20, 21); and also a base or pedestal (Ex. xxx. 18, 28; xxxi. 9; xxxv. 16; xxxviii. 8; Lev. viii. 11; 1 Kings vii. 31. It may be used here to denote the *socket* or *base* of the ship's mast; or the cross beam which the mast passed through, and which held it firm. This was called by the Greeks ἱστοπέδη (*Odys.* xii. 51), or μισόδμη, ἱστοδόκη (*Iliad* i. 434). The translation, therefore, 'They could not make fast the base of their mast,' would better express the sense of the Hebrew. The LXX. render it, 'Thy mast gave way.' ¶ *They could not spread the sail.* Of course, as the ropes were all loosened, and the mast could not be made firm, it would be in vain to attempt to spread a sail. The sense is, that the plan of the Assyrian would be disconcerted, his scheme

discomfited, and his enterprise would come to naught. He and his army would be like a vessel at sea without sails. ¶ *Then is the prey of a great spoil divided.* The word 'divided' here means shall be distributed or apportioned, as plunder was usually among victors. The sense is, that much booty would be taken from the army of the Assyrian and distributed among the Jews (see Note on ver. 4). It is certain that Hezekiah had given to Sennacherib three hundred talents of silver, and thirty talents of gold, and had stripped the temple, and given the gold that was on the temple to him (2 Kings xviii. 14–16), and this treasure was doubtless in the camp of the Assyrians. And it is certain that *after* this invasion of Sennacherib, the treasures of Hezekiah were replenished, and his wealth so much abounded, that he made an improper and ostentatious display of it to the ambassadors that came from Babylon (2 Kings xx. 13–15); and there is every presumption, therefore, that a great amount of spoil was collected from the camp of the Assyrian. ¶ *The lame take the prey.* It shall be so abundant, and shall be so entirely abandoned by the Assyrians, that even the feeble and the defenceless shall go forth to the camp and take the spoil that is left.

24. *And the inhabitant.* The inhabitant of Jerusalem. ¶ *Shall not say, I am sick.* That is, probably, the spoil shall be so abundant, and the facility for taking it so great, that even the sick, the aged, and the infirm shall go forth nerved with new vigour to gather the spoil. ¶ *The people that dwell therein.* In Jerusalem. ¶ *Shall be forgiven* their *iniquity.* This is equivalent to saying that the calamities of the invasion would be entirely removed. This invasion is represented as coming upon them as a judgment for their sins. When the Assyrian should be overthrown, it would be a proof that the sin which had been the cause of the inva-

CHAPTER XXXIV.

ANALYSIS.

THE thirty-fourth and thirty-fifth chapters make one distinct and beautiful prophecy, consisting of two parts; the first containing a denunciation of judgment on the enemies of the Jews, particularly Edom (ch. xxxiv.); and the second a most beautiful description of the flourishing state of the people of God which would follow these judgments (ch. xxxv.)

At what time the prophecy was delivered it is uncertain, and, indeed, can be determined by nothing in the prophecy itself. It is observable, however, that it is the close of the first part of the *prophecies* of Isaiah, the remaining chapters to the fortieth, which commences the second part of the prophecies, being occupied with an historical description of the invasion of Sennacherib and his army. It has been supposed (see Introd. § 2, 3,) that between the delivery of the prophecies in the first and second portion of Isaiah, an interval of some years elapsed, and that the second part was delivered for his own consolation, and the consolation of the people, near the close of his life.

A somewhat similar purpose, as I apprehend, led to the composition and publication of the prophecy before us. The *general strain* of his prophecies thus far has been, that however numerous and mighty were the enemies of the Jews, the people of God would be delivered from them all. Such was the case in regard to the allied armies of Syria and Samaria (ch. vii., viii.); of the Assyrian (ch. x.); of Babylon (ch. xiii., xiv.); of Moab (ch. xv., xvi.); of Damascus and Ethiopia (ch. xvii., xviii.); of Egypt (xix., xx.); and more particularly of the Assyrians under Sennacherib (ch. xxv., xxix.-xxxiii.) The prophecy before us I regard as a kind of *summing up*, or recapitulation of all that he had delivered; and the general idea is, *that the people of God would be delivered from all their foes, and that happier times under the Messiah would succeed all their calamities.* This he had expressed often in the *particular* prophecies; he here expresses it in a summary and condensed manner.

Keeping this general design of the prophecy in view, we may observe that it consists of the following parts:—

I. A *general statement* that all the enemies of the people of God would be destroyed (ch. xxxiv. 1-4). 1. The nations of the earth are summoned to see this, and to become acquainted with the purpose of God thus to destroy all his enemies (1). 2. The destruction of the enemies of God described under the image of a great slaughter (2,3). 3. The same destruction described under the image of the heavens rolled together as a scroll (4).

II. This *general truth* paricularly applied to Edom or Idumea as among the most virulent of their enemies (5-17). 1. JEHOVAH's vengeance would come upon the land of Idumea, and the land would be covered with the slain, and soaked in blood (5-8). 2. The entire and utter desolanion of the land of Idumea is foretold. The kingdom should be destroyed, the land laid waste, and the whole country become a dwelling-place of wild beasts (9-17).

III. The happy times that would succeed— the times of the Messiah—are exhibited (ch. xxxv.) in language of great beauty and sublimity. This is the substance of all that the prophet had predicted, and all his visions terminate there. The wilderness shall blossom; and the sick and afflicted shall be healed; the desolate lands shall be fertile; there shall be no enemy to annoy, and the ransomed of the Lord shall return and come to Zion with songs and everlasting joy upon their heads.

As so large a part of this prophecy relates to Edom, or Idumea, it may be proper to preface the exposition of the chapter with a brief notice of the history of that country, and of the causes for which God denounced vengeance upon it.

Idumea was the name given by the Greeks to the land of Edom, the country which was settled by Esau. The territory which they occupied extended originally from the Dead Sea to the Elanitic gulf of the Red Sea. Their territory, however, they extended considerably by conquest, and carried their arms to the east and north-east of Moab, and obtained possession of the country of which Bozrah was the chief city. To this they had access through the intervening desert without crossing the country of the Moabites or Ammonites. The capital of East Idumea was Bozrah; the capital of South Edom was Petra or Selah, called, in 2 Kings xiv. 7, Joktheel (see Notes on ch. xvi. 1).

---

sion had been forgiven, and that God was now disposed to show them favour and mercy. It.is common in the Scriptures to represent any calamity as the consequence of sin, to identify the removal of the calamity and the forgiveness of the sin. Thus the Saviour said (Mark ii. 5) to the man afflicted with the palsy, ' Son, thy sins be forgiven thee.' And when the scribes murmured, he urged that the power of forgiving sins and of healing disease was the same, or that the forgiveness of sin was equivalent to the removal of disease (Mark ii. 9).

This country received its name from Esau, the son of Isaac, and the twin brother of Jacob. He was called Edom, which signifies *red*, from the colour of the red pottage which he obtained from Jacob by the sale of his birthright (Gen. xxv. 30). After his marriage, he removed to mount Seir, and made that his permanent abode, and the country adjacent to it received the name of Edom. Mount Seir had been occupied by a people called Horites, who were displaced by Esau, when he took possession of their country and made it his own (Deut. ii. 12). The Edomites were at first governed by princes, improperly translated 'dukes' in Gen. xxxvi. 9–31. They were an independent people until the time of David. They seem to have continued under the government of separate princes, until the apprehension of foreign invasion compelled them to unite under one leader, and to submit themselves to a king, When the children of Israel were passing through the wilderness, as the land of Edom lay between them and Canaan, Moses sent ambassadors to the king of Edom soliciting the privilege of a peaceful passage through their country, on the ground that they were descended from the same ancestor, and promising that the property of the Edomites should not be injured, and offering to pay for all that they should consume (Num. xx. 14–19). To this reasonable request the king of Edom sent a positive refusal, and came out with a strong army to resist them (Num. xx. 20). This refusal was long remembered by the Jews, and was one cause of the hostile feeling which was cherished against them. The kingdom of Edom seems to have risen to a considerable degree of prosperity. There is, indeed, no direct mention made of it after this until the time of David; but it seems to have then risen into so much importance as to have attracted his attention. David carried his arms there after having obtained a victory over the Syrians, Moabites, and Ammonites. It is not known, indeed, what was the cause of this war, but it is known that he slew eighteen thousand Edomites in the valley of Salt (2 Sam. viii. 13; 1 Chron. xviii. 12), and the rest of them were either brought into subjection under Joab, or forced to fly into foreign countries. Hadad, their young king, fled to Egypt, and was favourably received by Pharaoh, and was highly honoured at his court. He was married to the sister of Tahpanes, who was the queen of Egypt (1 Kings xi. 15–20). Yet though he lived at the court of Pharaoh, he waited only for an opportunity to recover his kingdom, and when David and Joab were dead, he proposed to the king of Egypt to make an effort to accomplish it. He returned to Idumea, but was unsuccessful in

his attempts to overcome the garrisons which David had stationed to guard and secure the country (Jos. *Ant.* viii. 2). The kingdom of Edom continued under the house of David until the time of Jehoshaphat, and was probably governed by deputies or viceroys appointed by the kings of Judah. In the reign of Jehoshaphat they joined the Moabites and Ammonites in an attempt to recover their freedom, but they were unsuccessful. In the reign of Jehoram, the son of Jehoshaphat, however, they rose in a body, and though they suffered great slaughter, yet they regained their liberty (2 Chron. xxi. 8–10). After this, no attempts were made to subdue them for more than sixty years. In the reign of Amaziah, king of Judah, however, they were attacked, and ten thousand of them fell in battle in the valley of Salt, and many were made prisoners; their capital, Selah, was taken by storm, and the two thousand captives were by Amaziah's orders thrown down the ragged precipices near the city, and dashed in pieces (2 Kings xiv. 7; 2 Chron. xxv. 12; *Universal History*, vol. i. p. 380; Ed. Lond. 1779, 8vo). When the Jews were subdued by the Babylonians, and carried captive, they seem to have regarded it as a favourable opportunity to avenge all the injustice which they had suffered from the hands of the Jews. They joined the Babylonians in their attempts to subdue Jerusalem, and exulted in the fall and ruin of the city.

Remember, O LORD, the children of Edom
In the day of Jerusalem; who said
Rase it, rase it, even to the foundation thereof.
Ps. cxxxvii. 7.

They seem to have resolved to take full vengeance for the fact that their nation had been so long subjected by David and his successors; to have cut off such of the Jews as attempted to escape; to have endeavoured to level the whole city with the ground; to have rejoiced in the success of the Babylonians, and to have imbrued their hands in the blood of those whom the Chaldeans had left—and were thus held to be guilty of the crime of fratricide by God (see particularly Obad. 10–12, 18; Ezek. xxv. 12–14; xxxv. 3–15). It was *for this especially* that they were denounced and threatened by the prophets with heavy judgment, and with the utter destruction of the nation (Isa. xxxiv. 5, 10–17; Jer. xlix. 7–10, 12–18; Ezek. xxv. 12–15; xxxv. 1–15; Joel iii. 19; Amos i. 11; Obad. 2, 3, 8, 17, 18; Mal. i. 3, 4). This refusing to aid their brethren the Jews, and joining with the enemies of the people of God, and exulting in their success, was the great crime in their history which was to call down the Divine vengeance, and terminate in their complete and utter ruin.

But their exultation does not long continue, and their cruelty to the Jews did not long remain unpunished. Five years after the taking of Jerusalem, Nebuchadnezzar humbled all the states around Judea, and particularly Idumea (Jer. xxv. 15-26; Mal. i. 3, 4).

During the Jewish exile, it would appear the Edomites pressed forward into the south of Palestine, of which they took possession as far as to Hebron. Here they were subsequently attacked and subdued by John Hyrcanus, and compelled to adopt the laws and customs of the Jews. The name Idumea was transferred to this part of the land of Judea which they occupied, and this is the Idumea which is mentioned by Pliny, Ptolemy, Strabo, and other ancient writers. Indeed the name Idumea was sometimes given by the Roman writers to the whole of Palestine (Reland's *Palestine*). Idumea, including the southern part of Judea, was henceforth governed by a succession of Jewish prefects. One of these, Antipater, an Idumean by birth, by the favour of Cæsar, was made procurator of all Judea. He was the father of Herod the Great, who become king of Judea, including Idumea. While the Edomites had been extending themselves to the north-west, they had in in turn been driven out from the southern portion of their own territory, and from their chief city itself, by the Nabatheans, an Arabian tribe, the descendants of Nebaioth, the eldest son of Ishmael. This nomadic people had spread themselves over the whole of desert Arabia, from the Euphrates to the borders of Palestine, and finally to the Elanitic gulf of the Red Sea. They thus grew up into the kingdom of Arabia Petrea, occupying very nearly the same territory which was comprised within the limits of ancient Edom. A king of this country, Aretas, is mentioned as cotemporary with Antiochus Epiphanes, about B.C. 166. From this time to the destruction of Jerusalem, the sovereigns of Arabia Petrea came into frequent contact with the Jews and Romans, both in war and peace. —The nominal independence of this kingdom continued for some thirty years after the destruction of Jerusalem. Under the reign of Trajan, about A.D. 105, it was overrun and conquered by Cornelius Palma, then governor of Syria, and formally annexed to the Roman empire (Dio. Cass. lxviii. 14; Amm. Marcell. xiv. 8).—The kingdom of Edom was thus blotted out, and their name was lost. In their own land they ceased to be a separate people, and mingled with the other descendants of Ishmael; in Judea they became, under John Hyrcanus, converts to the Jewish faith; received the rite of circumcision; and were incorporated with the Jews. Very interesting remains of cities and towns of Idumea, and particularly of Petrea, have been recently discovered by the travellers Burckhardt, and Seetzen (see *Universal History*, vol. i. pp. 370-383; *Amer. Bib. Repository*, vol. iii. pp. 247-270; Gesenius's Introduction to his *Com.* on this chapter; the *Travels* of Burckhardt, Legh, Laborde, and Stephens; Keith, *On Prophecy*, pp. 135-168; and Robinson's *Bib. Researches*, vol. ii. p. 551, *sq.*)

C OME *a* near, ye nations, to hear; and hearken, ye people: let the earth *b* hear, and [1] all that is therein; the world, and all things that come forth of it.

2 For *c* the indignation of the LORD *is* upon all nations, and *his* fury upon all their armies: he hath utterly destroyed them, he hath delivered them to the slaughter.

a Ps.49.1.   *b* De.32.1.   1 *the fulness thereof.*
c Zep.3.8.

CHAPTER XXXIV.

1. *Come near, ye nations, to hear.* That is, to hear of the judgments which God was about to execute, and the great purposes which he was about to accomplish. If the supposition be correct, that this and the following chapter contain a *summing up* of all that the prophet had thus far uttered; a declaration that ALL the enemies of the people of God would be destroyed—the most violent and bitter of whom was Idumea; and that this was to be succeeded by the happy times of the Messiah, then we see a plain reason why all the nations are summoned to hear and attend. The events pertain to them all; the truths communicated are of universal interest. ¶ *And all that is therein.* Heb. as in Marg., 'fulness thereof;' that is, all the inhabitants of the earth. ¶ *All things that come forth of it.* All that proceed from it; that is, all the inhabitants that the world has produced. The LXX. render it, 'The world and the people (ὁ λαὸς) who are therein.'

2. *For the indignation of the* LORD. JEHOVAH is about to express his wrath against all the nations which are opposed to his people. ¶ *He hath utterly destroyed them.* In his purpose, or intention. The prophet represents this

3 Their slain also shall be cast out, and their stink shall come up out of their carcases, and the mountains shall be melted with their blood.

4 And ^a all the host of heaven shall be dissolved, and the heavens

<small>a Ps.102.26; Exo.32.7,8; Joel2.31; 3.15,16; Mat.24.29; 2 Pet.3.10; Rev.6.13,14.</small>

shall be rolled together as a scroll: and all their host shall fall down, as the leaf falleth off from the vine, and as a falling *fig* from the fig-tree.

5 For my sword shall be bathed in heaven: behold, it shall come down upon Idumea, ^b and upon the people of my curse, to judgment.

<small>b Jer.49.7.</small>

as so certain that it may be exhibited as already done.

3. *Their slain also shall be cast out.* They would lie unburied. The slaughter would be so extensive, and the desolation would be so entire, that there would not remain enough to bury the dead (comp. Notes on ch. xiv. 19). ¶ *And the mountains shall be melted with their blood.* The expression here is evidently hyperbolical, and means that as mountains and hills are wasted away by descending showers and impetuous torrents, so the hills would be washed away by the vast quantity of blood that would be shed by the anger of JEHOVAH.

4. *And all the host of heaven.* On the word ' host ' (צָבָא), see Note on ch. i. 9. The heavenly bodies often represent kings and princes (comp. Note on ch. xxiv. 21). ¶ *Shall be dissolved* (וְנָמַקּוּ). This figure Vitringa supposes to be taken from the vulgar prejudice by which the stars appear to be crystals, or gems, set in the azure vault of heaven, which may *melt* and flow down by the application of heat. The sense is, that the princes and nobles who had opposed God and his people would be destroyed, *as if* the sparkling stars, like gems, should *melt* in the heavens, and flow down to the earth. ¶ *And the heavens shall be rolled together as a scroll.* The word ' scroll ' here (סֵפֶר *sĕphĕr*) means *a roll*, or a book. Books were made of parchment, leaves, &c., and were *rolled together* instead of being *bound*, as they are with us. The figure here is taken from what strikes the eye, that the heaven above us is *an expanse* (רָקִיעַ) Gen. i. 8; Ps. civ. 2,) which is *spread out ;* and which might be *rolled together*, and thus pass away. It is possible that there may be a reference also to the fact, that in a

storm, when the sky is filled with dark rolling clouds, the heavens seem to be *rolled together*, and to be passing away. The sense is, that there would be great destruction among those high in office and in power—a destruction that would be well represented by the rolling up of the firmament, and the destruction of the visible heavens and their host, and by leaving the world to ruin and to night. ¶ *And all their host shall fall down.* That is, their stars ; either by being as it were *melted*, or by the fact that the *expanse* in which they are apparently located would be rolled up and removed, and there being no *fixtures* for them they would fall. The same image occurs in Rev. vi. 13. One somewhat similar occurs in Virgil, *Georg.* i. 365, *sq.* ¶ *As the leaf falleth off from the vine,* &c. That is, in a storm, or when violently shaken.

5. *For my sword shall be bathed in heaven.* A sword is an instrument of vengeance, and is often so used in the Scriptures, because it was often employed in capital punishments (see Note on ch. xxvii. 1). This passage has given much perplexity to commentators, on account of the apparent want of meaning of the expression that the sword would be *bathed in heaven.* Lowth reads it :

For my sword is made bare in the heavens;

following in this the Chaldee which reads תִּתְגְּלֵי 'shall be revealed.' But there is no authority from MSS. for this change in the Hebrew text. The Vulgate renders it, *Quoniam inebriatus est in cœlo gladius meus*—' My sword is intoxicated in heaven.' The LXX. render it in the same way, 'Ἐμεθύσθη ἡ μάχαιρά μου ἐν τῷ οὐρανῷ; and the Syriac and Arabic in the same manner. The Hebrew word רִוְּתָה, from רָוָה, means properly *to drink to the full ;* to be

6 The sword of the LORD is filled with blood ; it is made fat with fatness, *and* with the blood of lambs and goats, with the fat of the kid-

neys of rams: for the LORD hath a sacrifice in Bozrah, *a* and a great slaughter in the land of Idumea.

satisfied, or sated with drink ; and then to be full or satiated with intoxicating liquor, to be drunk. It is applied to the sword, as satiated or made drunk with blood, in Jer. xlvi. 10 :

And the sword shall devour,
And it shall be satiate, and made drunk with
   their blood.

And thus in Deut. xxxii. 42, a similar figure is used respecting arrows, the instruments also of war and vengeance :

I will make mine arrows drunk with blood ;
And my sword shall devour flesh.

A similar figure is often used in Oriental writers, where the sword is represented as glutted, satiated, or made drunk with blood (see Rosenmüller on Deut. xxxii. 42). Thus Bohaddinus, in the life of Saladin, in describing a battle in which there was a great slaughter, says, ' The swords drank of their blood until they were intoxicated.' The idea here is, however, not that the sword of the Lord was made drunk *with blood* in heaven, but that it was intoxicated, or made furious with wrath ; it was excited as an intoxicated man is who is under ungovernable passions ; it was in heaven that the wrath commenced, and the sword of Divine justice rushed forth as if intoxicated, to destroy all before it. There are few figures, even in Isaiah, that are more bold than this. ¶ *It shall come down upon Idumea* (see the Analysis of the chapter for the situation of Idumea, and for the causes why it was to be devoted to destruction). ¶ *Upon the people of my curse.* The people devoted to destruction.

6. *The sword of the* LORD *is filled with blood.* The idea here is taken from the notion of sacrifice, and is, that God would devote to sacrifice, or to destruction, the inhabitants of Idumea. With reference to that, he says, that his sword, the instrument of slaughter, would be satiated with blood. ¶ *It is made fat with fatness.* The allusion here is to the sacrifices which were made for sin, in which the blood

and the fat were devoted to God as an offering (see Lev. vii.) ¶ *With the blood of lambs and goats.* These were the animals which were usually offered in sacrifice to God among the Jews. and to speak of a *sacrifice* was the same as to speak of the offering of rams, lambs, bullocks, &c. Yet it is evident that they denote here *the people* of Idumea, and that these terms are used to keep up the image of *a sacrifice.* The idea of sacrifice was always connected with that of *slaughter,* as the animals were slaughtered before they were offered. So here, the idea is, that there would be a great *slaughter* in Idumea ; that it would be so far of the nature of a sacrifice that they would be *devoted* to God and to his cause. It is not probable that any particular classes of people are denoted by the different animals here mentioned, as the animals here mentioned include all, or nearly all those usually offered in sacrifice, the expressions denote simply that all classes of people in Idumea would be devoted to the slaughter. Grotius, however, supposes that the following classes are intended by the animals specified, to wit, by *the lambs,* the people in general ; by *the goats,* the priests ; by *the rams,* the opulent inhabitants. ¶ *For the* LORD *hath a sacrifice in Bozrah.* Bozrah is here mentioned as one of the chief cities of Idumea. It was a city of great antiquity, and was known among the Greeks and Romans by the name of BOSTRA. It is generally mentioned in the Scriptures as a city of the Edomites (Isa. lxiii. 1; Jer. xlix. 13, 22; Amos i. 12); but once it is mentioned as a city of Moab (Jer. xlviii. 24). It probably belonged at different periods to both nations, as in their wars the possession of cities often passed into different hands. Bozrah lay south-east of Edrei, one of the capitals of Bashan, and was thus not properly within the limits of the Edomites, but was north of the Ammonites, or in the region of Auranitis, or in what is now called tho

7 And the [1] unicorns shall come down with them, and the bullocks with the bulls; and their land shall be [2] soaked with blood, and their dust made fat with fatness.

1 or, *rhinoceros.*   2 or, *drunken.*

Houran.* It is evident, therefore, that in the time of Isaiah, the Edomites had extended their conquests to that region. According to Burckhardt, who visited the Houran, and who went to Bozrah, it is at this day one of the most important cities there. 'It is situated,' says he, 'in the open plain, and is at present the last inhabited place in the south-east extremity of the Houran; it was formerly the capital of the *Arabia Provincia,* and is now, including its ruins, the largest town in the Houran. It is of an oval shape, its greatest length being from east to west; its circumference is three quarters of an hour. It was anciently encompassed with a thick wall, which gave it the reputation of great strength. Many parts of this wall, especially on the west side, remain; it was constructed of stones of moderate size, strongly cemented together. The south, and south-east quarters are covered with ruins of private dwellings, the walls of many of which are still standing, but the roofs are fallen in. The style of building seems to have been similar to that observed in all the other ancient towns of the Houran. On the west side are springs of fresh water, of which I counted five beyond the precincts of the town, and six within the walls; their waters unite with a rivulet whose source is on the north-west side, within the town, and which loses itself in the southern plain at several hours' distance; it is called by the Arabs, El Djeheir. The principal ruins of Bozrah are the following:—A square building which within is circular, and has many arches and niches in the wall. The diameter of the rotunda is four paces; its roof has fallen in, but the walls are entire. It appears to have been a Greek church.—An oblong square building, called by the natives Deir Boheiry, or the Monastery of the priest Boheiry. —The gate of an ancient house com- municating with the ruins of an edifice, the only remains of which is a large semicircular vault.—The great mosque of Bozrah, which is certainly coeval with the first era of Mahometanism, and is commonly ascribed to Omar el Khattab. The walls of the mosque are covered with a fine coat of plaster, upon which are many Cufic inscriptions in bas-relief, running all round the wall. The remains of a temple, situated on the side of a long street which runs across the whole town, and terminates at the western gate,' &c. Of these, and other magnificent ruins of temples, theatres, and palaces, all attesting its former importance, Burckhardt has given a copious description in his *Travels in Syria,* pp. 226–235, Quarto Ed. Lond. 1822.

7. *And the unicorns.* Marg. ' Rhinoceros' (רְאֵמִים) from (רָאַם). This was evidently an animal well known in Palestine, since it is frequently mentioned in the Old Testament (Num. xxiii. 22; Deut. xxxiii. 17; Job xxxix. 9, 10; Ps. xxii. 21; xxix. 6; xcii. 10, in all which places it is translated *unicorn,* or *unicorns*). The derivation of the word is uncertain, and it has been regarded as doubtful what animal is intended. The corresponding Arabic word denotes the *oryx,* a large and fierce species of the antelope. Gesenius, Schultens, De Wette, and Rosenmüller suppose that the *buffalo* is intended by the word. Bochart regards it as denoting the *gazelle,* or a species of the antelope. It can hardly, however, be regarded as so small an animal as the *gazelle.* The gazelle is common in the neighbourhood of mount Sinai; and when Laborde passed through that region his companions killed four, 'the father and mother, and two little animals a fortnight old.' He says of them: 'These creatures, which are very lively in their movements, endeavoured to bite when they were caught; their hair is a brown yellow, which becomes pale and long as the animals grows old. In appearance they resemble the Guinea pig. Their legs are of the same height,

* Burckhardt and many others spell this word *Haouran.* The Rev. E. Smith, however, says that it should be spelled without the *a*—*Houran.*

8 For *it is* the day *a* of the Lord's vengeance, *and* the year of recompenses for the controversy *b* of Zion.

9 And *c* the streams thereof shall

a Jer. 46.10.   b Mic.6.1.

but the form of their feet is peculiar; instead of nails and claws, they have three toes in front and four behind, and they walk, like rabbits, on the whole length of the foot.

GAZELLES.

The Arabs call it El Oueber, and know no other name for it. It lives upon the scanty herbage with which the rain in the neighbourhood of springs supplies it. It does not burrow in the earth, its feet not being calculated for that purpose; but it conceals itself in the natural holes or clefts which it finds in the rocks.' —(*Journey through Arabia Petrea*, pp. 106, 107. Lond. 8vo. 1836.) Taylor (*Heb. Con.*) supposes it means the rhinoceros; a fierce animal that has a single horn on the nose, which is very strong, and which sometimes grows to the height of thirty-seven inches. The ancient versions certainly regarded the word as denoting an animal with a single horn. It denotes here, evidently, some strong, fierce, and wild animal that was horned (Ps. xxii. 21), but perhaps it is not possible to determine precisely what animal is meant. For a more full investigation in reference to the kind of animal denoted by the word *reem*, see Notes on Job xxxix. 9. Here it represents that portion of the people which was strong, warlike, and hitherto unvanquished, and who regarded themselves as invincible. ¶ *Shall come down*. Shall be subdued, humbled, destroyed. ¶ *With them*. With the lambs and goats mentioned in ver. 6. All classes of the people shall be subdued and

be turned into pitch, and the dust thereof into brimstone, and the land thereof shall become burning pitch.

10 It shall not be quenched night

c De.29.33.

subjected to the slaughter. ¶ *And the bullocks with the bulls*. The young bulls with the old. All shall come down together—the fierce and strong animals representing the fierce and strong people. ¶ *And their land shall be soaked with blood*. Marg. 'Drunken;' the same word which is rendered 'bathed' in ver. 5. ¶ *Their dust made fat*. Their land manured and made rich with the slain. A battle-field is usually distinguished afterwards for its fertility. The field of Waterloo has thus been celebrated, since the great battle there, for producing rank and luxuriant harvests.

8. *For* it is *the day of the* Lord's *vengeance*. A time when Jehovah will take vengeance. ¶ *The year of recompenses for the controversy of Zion*. The time when he will recompense, *i.e.*, punish those who have had a controversy with Zion.

9. *And the streams thereof*. The idea here is, that there would be as great and awful a destruction as if the streams everywhere should become pitch or resin, which would be set on fire, and which would fill the land with flame. This image is very striking, as we may see by supposing the rivers and streams in any land to flow not with water, but with heated pitch, turpentine, or tar, and that this was all suddenly kindled into a flame. It cannot be supposed that this is to be taken literally. The image is evidently taken from the destruction of Sodom and Gomorrah (Gen. xix. 25–28), an image which is more fully used in reference to the same subject in Jer. xlix. 17, 18 : ' And Edom shall be a desolation ;...as in the overthrow of Sodom and Gomorrah, and the neighbour cities thereof, saith the Lord, no man shall abide there, neither shall a son of man dwell in it.' ¶ *And the dust thereof into brimstone*. The ruin shall be as entire as if all the soil were turned into brimstone, which should be ignited and left burning.

10. *It shall not be quenched night nor day*. That is, the burning brimstone

nor day; the ^asmoke thereof shall go up for ever: from generation to generation it shall lie waste; none-

shall pass through it for ever and ever:

a Rev.19.2,3.

and pitch (ver. 9), the emblem of perpetual and entire desolation, shall not be extinguished. ¶ *The smoke thereof shall go up for ever.* Every river and rivulet is supposed to be heated pitch, and every particle of dust sulphur, and all on fire, sending up from an extended region dense columns of smoke to heaven. No idea of ruin could be more sublime; no idea of the vengeance of God more terrible. This image has been copied by John to describe the future woes of the wicked (Rev. xiv. 11), and of mystical Babylon (Rev. xviii. 9, 18; xix. 2. 3). ¶ *From generation to generation it shall lie waste.* Full confirmation of this may be seen in the travels of Seetzen, of Burckhardt, of Volney, of Irby, and Mangles, extracts of which have been collected and arranged by Keith (*Evidences of Prophecy*, pp. 135–168). Thus Volney says, 'From the reports of the Arabs of Bakir, and the inhabitants of Gaza, who frequently go to Maan and Karak, on the road of the pilgrims, there are to the south-east of the lake Asphaltites (Dead Sea), *within three days' journey*, upwards of thirty ruined towns, *absolutely deserted.* Several of them have large edifices, with columns that may have belonged to the ancient temples, or at least to Greek churches. The Arabs sometimes make use of them to fold cattle in; but, in general, avoid them on account of the enormous scorpions with which they swarm.'—(Volney's *Travels*, vol. ii. pp. 344–346.) It is remarkable that an *infidel*, as Volney was, should in this, as in numerous other instances, have given a minute confirmation of the ancient prophecies. Seetzen says (*Travels*, p. 46), that he was told, that, 'at the distance of two days and a half from Hebron he would find considerable ruins of the ancient city of Abde, and that for all the rest of the journey he would see *no place of habitation;* he would meet only with a few tribes of wandering Arabs.' Burckhardt has given the following description of the eastern boundary of Edom, and of the adjoining part of Arabia Petrea: —' It might with truth be called Petrea,

not only on account of its rocky mountains, but also of the elevated plain already described' [*i.e.*, Shera (*Seir*), the territory of the Edomites, *Travels*, pp. 410, 435], 'which is so much covered with stones, especially flints, that it may with great propriety be called a stony desert, although susceptible of culture; in many places it is grown over with wild herbs, and must once have been thickly inhabited, for the traces of many towns and villages are met with on both sides of the Hadj road between Maan and Akaba, as well as between Maan and the plains of Houran, in which direction also are many springs. At present all this country is a desert, and Maan is the only inhabited place in it.'—(Burckhardt's *Travels*, p. 436.) Of the remains of ancient cities still exposed to view in different places throughout Idumea, Burckhardt describes the ruins of a large town, of which nothing remains but broken walls and heaps of stones; the ruins of several villages in its vicinity (p. 418); the ruins of an ancient city, consisting of large heaps of hewn blocks of siliceous stone; and the extensive ruins of Arindela, an ancient town of Palestina Tertia (p. 441). 'The following ruined places are situated in Djebal Shera (Mount Seir), to the south and south-west of Wady Musa,—Kalaat Beni Madha, Djerba, Basta, Eyl, Ferdakh, Anyk, Bir el Beytar, Shemakh, and Syk' (p. 444). Burckhardt also gives a most interesting description of the ruins of the ancient Petra which he discovered, the ancient capital of Edom, but which is too long to be transcribed here (see his *Travels*, pp. 422–432; comp. Note on ch. xvi. 1). ¶ *None shall pass through it for ever and ever.* That is, it shall not be a country through which caravans shall pass; there shall be no roads, and it shall not be deemed safe to travel through it. It will be recollected that the original source of all their calamities, and the cause of all the judgments that came upon them, was the fact that they would not let the children of Israel pass peaceably through

11 But the [1]cormorant [a]and the bittern shall possess it; the owl also and the raven shall dwell in it: and

1 or, *pelican.*   a Zep.2.14; Rev.18.2.

their land on their way to Canaan (see the Introduction to the chapter). As a punishment for this, God now says that their land shall *not be passed through;* it shall not be a thoroughfare; there shall be no travellers in it. —God usually directs his punishment of individuals and of nations *in the line of their offences,* and thus his judgments become commonly *a recompence in kind.* Thus in 2 Sam. xxii. 26, 27, it is said :—

With the merciful, thou wilt show thyself merciful;
And with the upright man thou wilt show thyself upright.
With the pure thou wilt show thyself pure;
And with the froward thou wilt show thyself unsavoury.

In accordance with this prediction that no one should pass through Edom, Volney (*Travels,* vol. ii. p. 344) says, 'The country has *not been visited by any traveller,* but it well merits such an attention.' Thus Burckhardt (*Travels,* p. 421) says, after he had entered, on the *north-east,* the territories of the Edomites, that he ' was without protection in the midst of a desert *where no traveller had ever before been seen.* It was then,' he adds, ' that for the first time he had ever felt fear during his travels in the desert, and his route thither was the most dangerous he had ever travelled ' (p. 400). ' Seetzen, on a piece of paper pasted against the wall, notified his having penetrated the country in a direct line between the Dead Sea and Mount Sinai (through Idumea), *a route never before accomplished.*'—(Burckhardt's *Syria,* p. 553.) Burckhardt had determined to attempt to pass the same way as being the shortest way to Jerusalem; but he was repeatedly told it was *impossible;* and the difficulty of the journey is illustrated in the *Travels* of Captains Irby and Mangles. They offered five hundred piastres to an Arab tribe if they would conduct them to Wady Musa, but nothing would induce them to consent. ' They said they would not go if we would give them five thousand piastres, observing that money was

he shall stretch out upon it the [b] line of confusion and the stones of emptiness.

b 2 Ki.21.13.

of no use to a man if he lost his life ' (p. 349). So strikingly has this prediction been fulfilled.

11. *But the cormorant.* This and the following verses contain a description of the desolations of Edom in language remarkably similar to that employed in the account of the destruction of Babylon (ch. xiii. 20–22; xiv. 23). The word here translated 'cormorant' (קָאַת), occurs in this place and in Zeph. ii. 14, where it is rendered ' cormorant,' and in Lev. xi. 18; Deut. xiv. 17; Ps. cii. 6, where it is rendered ' pelican.' Bochart supposes it is the *ardea stellaris,* or *bitourn,* which frequents watery places in deserts, and makes a horrible noise. The pelican is a sea-fowl, and cannot be intended here. The cormorant or water raven is a large fowl of the pelican kind, which occupies the cliffs by the sea, feeds on fish, and which is extremely voracious, and which is the emblem of a glutton. It is not

CORMORANT.

certain *what* fowl is intended here, but the word properly denotes a water-fowl, and evidently refers to some bird that inhabits desolate places. ¶ *And the bittern shall possess it.* For a description of the *bittern,* see Note on ch. xiv. 23. ¶ *The owl also and the raven.* Well known birds that occupy deserts,

12 They shall call the nobles thereof to the kingdom, but none *shall be* there, and all her princes shall be nothing.

13 And thorns shall come up in her palaces, nettles and brambles in the fortresses thereof; and it shall be an habitation of dragons, *and* a court for [1] owls.

1 *daughters of the owl,* or, *ostriches;* ch.13.21,22.

---

and old ruins of houses or towns. The image here is that of desolation and ruin; and the sense is, that the land would be reduced to a waste that would not be inhabited by man, but would be given up to wild animals. How well this agrees with Edom, may be seen in the *Travels* of Burckhardt, Seetzen, and others. In regard to the fact that the cormorant (קָאַת, *kââth*) should be found there, it may be proper to introduce a remark of Burckhardt, who seems to have had no reference to this prophecy. 'The bird *katta*,' says he, 'is met with in immense numbers. They fly in such large flocks that the boys often kill two or three of them at a time, merely by throwing a stick among them.' So also in regard to the fact that the owl and the raven shall dwell there, the following statements are made by travellers:—Captain Mangles relates that while he and his fellow-travellers were examining the ruins and contemplating the sublime scenery of Petra, 'the screaming of the eagles, hawks, and owls, which were soaring above their heads in considerable numbers, seemingly annoyed at any one approaching their lonely habitation, added much to the singularity of the scene.' So says Burckhardt : ' The fields of Tafyle (situated in the immediate vicinity of Edom) are frequented by an immense number of crows.' ¶ *And he shall stretch out upon it.* This is an illusion to the fact that an architect uses a *line*, which is employed to lay out his work (see Note on ch. xxviii. 17). ¶ *The line of confusion.* A similar expression occurs in 2 Kings xxi. 13: 'I will stretch over Jerusalem the line of Samaria, and the plummet of the house of Ahab;' *i.e.,* I will apply the same measure and rule of destruction to Jerusalem that has been applied to Samaria. So Edom would be marked out for desolation. It was the work which God had *laid out*, and which he intended to perform. ¶ *And the stones of emptiness.* Prob-

ably the *plummet* which the architect commonly employed with his line (see Note on ch. xxviii. 17). It is a fact, however, that Edom is at present an extended waste of stones and barren rocks. ' We had before us an immense expanse of dreary country, entirely covered with black flints, with here and there some hilly chain rising from the plain.'— (Burckhardt's *Travels in Syria*, p. 445.) 12. *They shall call the nobles thereof to the kingdom.* A more correct rendering of this would be, ' As to the nobles, they shall call them, but there shall be there no kingdom.' The idea is, that the kingdom would be desolate; there would be no people to rule. Or, there will be no nobles there who shall survive the destruction, and who can undertake the government of the state. The idea is taken from a government or constitution where the monarch is chosen from the ranks of the nobility. Idumea was formerly governed, as we have seen (see the Introduction to the chapter), by *dukes* or princes ; and it is probable that when it became a monarchy it was a part of the constitution that the sovereign should be chosen from their ranks. The idea here is, that none would be left who could be called to the throne ; or if any were left, they would be unwilling to undertake the government of a country where all was disorder and confusion. ¶ *And all her princes shall be nothing.* Long since Idumea has ceased to be a kingdom, and there are neither nobles nor princes there, nor are there any remains of an organized and independent government.

13. *And thorns, &c.* (see Note on ch. v. 6.) ¶ *It shall be an habitation of dragons.* On the meaning of the word ' dragons,' see Note on ch. xiii. 22. ¶ *Court for owls.* A place of resort, a residence of owls. The word rendered ' court ' (חָצִיר) means a dwelling-place, a habitation, as well as an enclosure or court. The margin is, ' Daughters of

14 The [1] wild beasts of the desert shall also meet with [2] the wild beasts of the island, and the satyr shall cry to his fellow ; the [3] screech-owl also shall rest there, and find for herself a place of rest.

15 There shall the great owl make her nest, and lay, and hatch, and gather under her shadow ; there shall the vultures also be gathered, every one with her mate.

1 Ziim.   2 Ijim.   3 or, night-monster.

the owl,' or 'ostriches' (see Note on ch. xiii. 21).—' I would,' says Stephens, when standing amidst the ruins of Petra, the capital of Idumea (see Note on ch. xvi. 1), and with this passage of Isaiah in his eye, ' I would that the sceptic could stand as I did, among the ruins of this city among the rocks, and there open the sacred book, and read the words of the inspired penman, written when this desolate place was one of the greatest cities in the world. I see the scoff arrested, his cheek pale, his lip quivering, and his heart quaking with fear, as the ancient city cries out to him in a voice loud and powerful as one risen from the dead ; though he would not believe Moses and the prophets, he believes the hand-writing of God himself, in the desolation and eternal ruin around him.' —(Incidents of Travel in Egypt, &c., vol. ii. p. 76.)

14. The wild beasts of the desert. There is in the original here a paronomasia, which cannot be conveyed in a translation.—The word rendered ' wild beasts of the desert' (צִיִּים), is rendered by the LXX., δαιμόνια, 'demons.' On the meaning of the word, see Note on ch. xiii. 21. ¶ The wild beasts of the island. Marg. 'Ijim.' Heb. אִיִּים (see Note on ch. xiii. 22). Probably the term denotes the jackal. Gesenius supposes it is so called from its howl, or nocturnal cry—from an Arabic word signifying to howl. ¶ And the satyr (see Note on ch. xiii. 21). ¶ Shall cry to his fellow. A most striking description of the desolation, when all that is heard among the ruins shall be the doleful cry of wild beasts. ¶ The screech-owl. Marg. ' Night-monster.' The word לִילִית (from לַיִל, night) properly denotes a night-spectre—a creature of Jewish superstition. The Rabbins describe it in the form of a female elegantly dressed that lay in wait for children at night—either to carry them off, or to murder them. The Greeks

had a similar idea respecting the female ἔμπουσα, and this idea corresponds to the Roman fables respecting the Lamiæ, and Striges, and to the Arabic notions of the Ghûles, whom they described as female monsters that dwell in deserts, and tear men to pieces (see Gesenius, Com. in loco; and Bochart, Hieroz. ii. 831). The margin in our version expresses the correct idea. All this is descriptive of utter and perpetual desolation—of a land that should be full of old ruins, and inhabited by the animals that usually make such ruins their abode.

15. There shall the great owl (קִפּוֹז). Gesenius supposes that this is the arrow-snake, so called from its darting or springing, in the manner of the rattle-snake—from an obsolete root to draw one's self together, to contract. Bochart (Hieroz. ii. 3. 11. 408–419) has examined the meaning of the word at length, and comes to the conclusion that it means the serpent which the Greeks called acontias, and the Latins, jaculus—the arrow-snake. The serpent is oviparous, and nourishes its young. The ancient versions, however,

EGYPTIAN VULTURE (Nephron perenopterous).

understand it in the same sense as the kippod in ver. 11—the hedgehog or por-

16 Seek ^a ye out of the book of the LORD, and read ; no one ^b of these shall fail, none shall want

a Is.8.20; Jn.5.39; 2 Pe.1.19.

her mate : for my mouth it hath commanded, and his spirit it hath gathered them.

b Mat.5.18; Lu 21.33.

cupine. ¶ *Under her shadow.* This might be done by the serpent that should coil up and cherish her young. ¶ *The vultures, &c.* The black vulture, ac-

ASH VULTURE (*Vultur cinereus*).

cording to Bochart ; according to Gesenius, the kite, or falcon—so called from its swift flight. Either of them will suit the connection. ¶ *Also be gathered, every one with her mate.* They shall make their nests there ; that is, this shall be their secure, undisturbed retreat.

16. *Seek ye out.* Look carefully at the prediction, and its fulfilment. This seems to be addressed to the inhabitants of that land, or to any who might doubt, or be disposed to examine. They were invited to compare the prediction with the fulfilment, and see how literally all would be fulfilled—an examination which may be made now, and the prediction will be seen to have been accomplished with most surprising particularity and accuracy. ¶ *The book of the* LORD. The book of JEHO-VAH, which he has caused to be written, referring, perhaps, especially to what Isaiah has here recorded ; including also what had been uttered by the other prophets in regard to Edom. The main reference is, however, doubtless, to what Isaiah has written ; and the invitation is to compare his predictions with the certain and remarkable evidence of the fulfilment. 'The pro-

phet evidently contemplated the insertion of his prophecy among the sacred books of the Jews, from which those that followed him might judge of the correctness of the prophecy' (Noyes). That a collection of the various prophetic books was made, constituting one book or volume, and regarded as the work of inspiration, is well known, and is referred to during the captivity in Babylon by Daniel (ch. ix. 2). The direction to search that book accords with the command of the Saviour (John v. 39), and the direction of Nicodemus (John vii. 32), to search the Scriptures. ¶ *No one of these shall fail.* Not one of these predictions, or these things which have been spoken. ¶ *None shall want her mate.* That is, none of the things which I have spoken shall want a fulfilment as its companion. The *language* is here evidently taken from the *pairing* of animals, and denotes that all that is spoken shall be entirely fulfilled. Some have understood this as referring to the wild animals of which he had spoken, and as meaning that in desolate Idumea they should be appropriately paired, and should breed and increase in abundance. But the more natural interpretation is to refer it to the predictions of the prophet, as meaning that no one thing which he had uttered should want a complete fulfilment. ¶ *For my mouth.* The word ' my ' is not in the Hebrew. The Hebrew phrase is כִּי־פִי הוּא, ' For the mouth, he hath commanded.' The word הוּא stands for *He,* that is, JEHO-VAH, and the phrase means the same as *his* mouth, that is, the mouth of God. The LXX. render it, 'For the Lord hath commanded them.' Lowth renders it, ' For the mouth of JEHOVAH,' changing הוּא into יְהוָֹה in accordance with five MSS. and the translation of the LXX. ¶ *And his spirit.* The Spirit of God ; that is, JEHOVAH himself. ¶ *Hath gathered them.* Will collect, or assemble ; *i.e.,* the wild beasts spoken of in the previous verses that shall occupy

17 And he hath cast the lot for them, and his hand hath divided it unto them by line : they shall possess it for ever, from generation to generation shall they dwell therein.

CHAPTER XXXV.

ANALYSIS.

THIS chapter is a continuation of the prophecy commenced in the previous chapter. See the Analysis of ch. xxxiv. for a general view of the design of the prophecy. The object of the whole is, to show that all the enemies of the people of God, and particularly Edom, which had so peculiarly and grievously offended them, would be destroyed; and that the destruction of their foes would be followed by times of security, prosperity, and joy.

That this chapter refers to the Messiah is apparent from the slightest inspection of it. It so clearly describes the times of the gospel; so distinctly speaks of the very works which the Redeemer in fact performed; and is so full, and rich, and beautiful, that it cannot be regarded as referring to any other period. It has, in many respects, a strong resemblance to the predictions in ch. xi. and xii., and is incontestably among the most beautiful of the prophecies of Isaiah.

The chapter may be divided into the following portions :—

I. The consolations which would follow the destruction of all their enemies—as great a change as if the wilderness were to blossom like the rose, and the glory and beauty of Lebanon and Carmel were given to the desert (1, 2).

II. The exhortation addressed to those in office and authority to comfort the feeble, and strengthen the weak, with the assurance that those blissful times would come (3, 4).

III. The description of the actual condition of the future period of happiness which is foretold. 1. The eyes of the blind would be opened, the deaf made to hear, and the lame man be cured (5–7). 2. It would be a time of holiness. The way of access to these blessings would be open and free to all—even to all nations, but it would be a way for the pure only (8). 3. It would be a time of safety. There would be no enemy that could overcome and subdue them (9). 4. It would be a time of elevated joy—represented by the return to Zion from a long and painful captivity (10). In the fulness of the blessings of the reign of the Messiah all their sorrow and sighing would flee away (10).

THE wilderness and the solitary place shall be glad for them ; and ^athe desert shall rejoice, and blossom as the rose.

a ch. 55.12,13.

desolate Idumea. It shall be the agency of God that shall bring them up upon the land to occupy it for ever.

17. *And he hath cast the lot for them.* He hath assigned to them the land of Edom to be occupied by them as their portion. This *language* is taken from the fact that countries were commonly apportioned, particularly among conquerors, by the lot. In this way Judea was divided among the tribes of Israel (Num. xxvi. 55, 56). ¶ *His hand hath divided it unto them by line.* He has marked out, as a surveyor does, the land of Edom as the dwelling-place of the beasts of the forest. A land was usually surveyed and divided into proper parts or portions before the lot was cast (Josh. xviii. 4–6). ¶ *They shall possess it.* The wild beasts mentioned in the previous verses. The testimony of all travellers demonstrates that thus far this prediction has been strikingly fulfilled.

CHAPTER XXXV.

1. *The wilderness and the solitary* *place.* This is evidently figurative language, such as is often employed by the prophets. The word rendered ' solitary place ' (צִיָּה), denotes properly *a dry place,* a place without springs and streams of water ; and as such places produce no verdure, and nothing to sustain life, the word comes to mean a desert. Such expressions are often used in the Scriptures to express *moral* or *spiritual desolation;* and in this sense evidently the phrase is used here. It does not refer to the desolations of Judea, but to all places that might be properly called a moral wilderness, or a spiritual desert ; and thus aptly expresses the condition of the world that was to be benefited by the blessings foretold in this chapter. The parallel expressions in ch. xli. 17–19 ; xliv. 3, 4, show that this is the sense in which the phrase is here used ; and that the meaning is, that *every* situation which might be appropriately called a moral wilderness— that is, the whole heathen world—would ultimately be made glad. The sense is,

2 It shall blossom abundantly, and rejoice even with joy and singing: the glory of Lebanon *a* shall

a Ho.14.5,6.

be given unto it, the excellency of Carmel and Sharon ; they shall see the glory of the LORD, *and* the excellency of our God.

that as great and happy changes would take place in regard to those desolations *as if* the wilderness should become a vast field producing the lily and the rose; or as if (ver. 2) there should be imparted to such places the glory of Lebanon, and the beauty of Sharon and Carmel. ¶ *Shall be glad for them.* This is evidently a personification, a beautiful poetic figure, by which the wilderness is represented as expressing joy. The sense is, the desolate moral world would be filled with joy on account of the blessings which are here predicted. The phrase 'for them,' expressed in Heb. by the affix ם, means, doubtless, *on account* of the blessings which are foretold in this prophecy. Lowth supposes, however, that the letter has been added to the word ' shall be glad' (יְשִׂשׂוּ), by mistake, because the following word begins with a מ. The reading of the present Hebrew text is followed by none of the ancient versions; but it is nevertheless probably the correct reading, and there is no authority for changing it. The sense is expressed above by the phrase 'shall rejoice on account of the things contained in this prophecy;' to wit, the destruction of all the foes of God, and the universal establishment of his kingdom. Those who wish to see a more critical examination of the words here used, may find it in Rosenmüller and Gesenius. ¶ *And blossom as the rose.* The word rendered 'rose' (הֲבַצֶּלֶת) occurs only here and in Cant. ii. 1, where it is also rendered a ' rose.' The LXX. render it, Κρίνον—' Lily.' The Vulgate also renders it, *Lilium*—the lily. The Syriac renders it also by a word which signifies the lily or narcissus; or, according to the Syriac lexicographers, ' the meadow-saffron,' an autumnal flower springing from poisonous bulbous roots, and of a white and violet colour. The sense is not, however, affected materially whatever be the meaning of the word. Either the rose, the lily, or the saffron, would convey the idea of beauty compared with

the solitude and desolation of the desert· The word ' rose ' with us, as being a flower better known, conveys a more striking image of beauty, and there is no impropriety in retaining it.

2. *It shall blossom abundantly.* Heb. ' Blossoming it shall blossom '—a common mode of expression in Hebrew, denoting *certainty, abundance, fulness*—similar to the expression (Gen. ii. 17), ' Dying thou shalt die,' *i.e.*, thou shalt surely die. The sense here is, it shall blossom in abundance. ¶ *And rejoice even with joy.* Strong figurative language, denoting the greatness of the blessings; *as* great as if in the waste wilderness there should be heard the voice of joy and rejoicing. The LXX. render this, ' The deserts *of Jordan* also bloom and rejoice;' and Jerome applies this to the preaching of John in the wilderness adjacent to Jordan. The LXX. evidently read הַיַּרְדֵּן instead of the Hebrew רְנֵן. Lowth has followed this, and rendered it, ' The well-watered plain of Jordan shall rejoice,' but without any authority from Heb. MSS. for the change. ¶ *The glory of Lebanon.* The glory or ornament of Lebanon was its cedars (see Note on ch. x. 34). The sense here·is, that the change would be as great under the blessings of the Messiah's reign *as if* there should be suddenly transferred to the waste wilderness the majesty and glory of mount Lebanon. ¶ *The excellency of Carmel.* Carmel was emblematic of beauty, as Lebanon was of majesty, and as Sharon was of fertility. For a description of Carmel, see Note on ch. xxix. 17; of Sharon, see Note on ch. xxxiii. 9. The sense is clear. The blessings of the times of the Messiah would be as great, compared with what had existed before, as if the desert were made as lovely as Carmel, and as fertile as Sharon. The world that, in regard to comfort, intelligence, and piety, might be compared to a pathless desert, would be like the beauty of Carmel and the fertility of Sharon. ¶ *They shall see the glory of*

3 Strengthen ^aye the weak hands, and confirm the feeble knees.

4 Say to them *that are* of a fearful¹ heart, Be strong, fear ^bnot; behold, your God will come *with*

<small>a He.12.12. 1 hasty. b ch.44.2.</small>

vengeance, *even* God *with* a recompence ; he will come and save ^cyou.

5 Then ^dthe eyes of the blind shall be opened, and the ears of the deaf shall be unstopped.

<small>c ch.25.9; Lu.21.28. d Mat.11.5.</small>

the LORD. As manifested under the Messiah.

3. *Strengthen ye.* That is, you who are the religious teachers and guides of the people. This is an address made by the prophet *in view* of what he had said and was about to say of the promised blessings. The sense is, strengthen and sustain the feeble and the desponding by the promised blessings; by the assurances (ch. xxxiv.) that all the enemies of God and his people will be destroyed; and that he will manifest himself as their Protector, and send upon them the promised blessings. Or it may be regarded as addressed to the officers and ministers of religion *when* these blessings should have come ; and as being an exhortation to them to make use of the influences, the promises, and the consolations which would attend the coming of the Messiah, to strengthen the feeble, and confirm those who were faint-hearted. ¶ *The weak hands, and confirm the feeble knees.* Strength resides mainly in the arms, and in the lower limbs, or the knees. If these are feeble, the whole frame is feeble. *Fear* relaxes the strength of the arms, and the firmness of the knees; and the expressions 'weak hands,' and 'feeble knees,' become synonymous with saying, of a *timid, fearful,* and *desponding* frame of mind. Such were to be strengthened by the assurance of the favour of God, and by the consolations which would flow from the reign of the Messiah. The Jews, who looked abroad upon the desolations of their country, were to be comforted by the hope of future blessings; those who lived in those future times were to be consoled by the assurances of the favour of God through the Messiah (comp. Notes on ch. xl. 1).

4. *Say to them.* This is still an address to the ministers of religion, to make use of all the consolations which these truths and predictions furnish to confirm and strengthen the people of God. ¶ *Of a fearful heart.* Of a

timid, pusillanimous heart; those who tremble before their enemies. The Hebrew is, as in the Marg., 'Of a *hasty* heart;' that is, of those who are disposed to *flee* before their enemies (see Note on ch. xxx. 16). ¶ *Behold, your God will come* with *vengeance.* That is, in the manner described in the previous chapter ; and, *generally,* he will take vengeance on *all* the enemies of his people, and they shall be punished. The language in this chapter is, in part, derived from the captivity at Babylon (ver. 10), and the general idea is, that God would take vengeance on *all* their enemies, and would bring them complete and final deliverance. This does not mean that when the Messiah should come *he* would be disposed to take vengeance; nor do the words 'your God' here refer to the Messiah ; but it is meant that their God, JEHOVAH, would certainly come and destroy all their enemies, and prepare the way thus for the coming of the Prince of peace. The general promise is, that however many enemies might attack them, or however much they might fear them, yet that JEHOVAH would be their protector, and would completely humble and prostrate all their foes.—The Hebrew will admit of 'a somewhat different translation, which I give in accordance with that proposed by Lowth. The sense is not materially varied.

<small>Say ye to the faint-hearted, Be ye strong; fear
ye not; behold your God !
Vengeance will come ; the retribution of God :
He himself will come, and will deliver you.</small>

5. *Then the eyes of the blind shall be opened.* The images in this verse and the following are those of joy and exultation. They describe the times of happiness when God would come to save them from their foes. This passage is so accurate a description of what the Messiah, the Lord Jesus, did, that it doubtless refers to the miracles which he would perform. In not a few instances did he in fact restore the

6 Then shall the lame *man* leap as an hart, and the tongue of the dumb sing : for in the wilderness shall waters *a*break out, and streams in the desert.

a ch. 43.19.

7 And the parched ground shall become a pool, and the thirsty land springs *b* of water : in the habitation of dragons where each lay, *shall be* grass,[1] with reeds and rushes.

b Jn.4.14; 7.38.   1 or, *a court for.*

blind to sight, giving thus the most unequivocal proof that he was the Messiah sent from God (Matt. ix. 27; xx. 30; Mark viii. 23; x. 46; Luke vii. 21). It is a full confirmation of the opinion that this passage refers to Christ, that the Saviour himself appeals to the fact that he restored the blind to sight, as demonstration that he was the Messiah, implying that it was predicted that this would be a part of his appropriate work (Matt. xi. 5; comp. Luke iv. 18). ¶ *And the ears of the deaf be unstopped.* Another demonstration of Divine power, and another proof that would be furnished that the Messiah was from God. The Lord Jesus often gave this demonstration that he was invested with Divine power (Matt. xi. 5 ; Mark vii. 32, 37; ix. 25).

6. *Then shall the lame* man *leap.* This was literally fulfilled after the coming of the Messiah (Acts xiv. 10; iii. 8). It is an *emblem* of the general joy which the coming of the Messiah would impart, and is an *instance* of the blessings which it would convey. ¶ *As an hart.* The word here used denotes the stag, or male deer. In Arabic it denotes the wild, or mountain-goat. The word sometimes refers to any species of deer or antelope, and this is referred to here from its quick and sprightly nature. ¶ *And the tongue of the dumb sing.* Shall be able to sing, and to praise God. On the restoration of the dumb to the benefits of language, see Matt. ix. 32, 33; xii. 22; xv. 30, 31; Mark ix. 17; Luke xi. 14. ¶ *For in the wilderness shall waters break out.* The joy shall be as great, and the blessings as numerous and refreshing, *as if* running fountains should suddenly break out in the desert, and the thirsty and weary traveller should be thus unexpectedly and fully supplied. The world, in regard to its real comforts without the gospel, may be not unaptly compared to a vast waste of pathless sands and arid plains. Nothing will more strongly

express the blessings of the gospel than the idea of cool, refreshing, abundant fountains and streams bursting forth in such pathless wastes. This is an image which would be very expressive to those who were accustomed to cross such deserts, and it is one which is frequently employed by the sacred writers, and especially by Isaiah (see ch. xliii. 19, 20; xlviii. 21; xlix. 10, 11; lv. 1; lviii. 11). 'Lameness and dumbness are the uniform effects of long walking in a desert; the sand and gravel produce the former, fatigue the latter. In such cases some of us have walked hours together without uttering a sentence ; and all walked as if crippled, from the sand and gravel getting into the shoes ; but the sight of water, especially if unexpected, unloosed every tongue, and gave agility to every limb; men, oxen, goats, sheep, and dogs, ran with speed and expressions of joy to the refreshing element.' —(Campbell's *Travels in Africa.*) The Chaldee Paraphrast understands this as referring entirely to the return from the captivity at Babylon. ' Then shall they see the exiles of Israel assembled, ascend to their own land as the swift stags, so that they shall not be hindered.'

7. *And the parched ground shall become a pool.* The idea is the same here as in the previous verse, that under the Messiah there would be blessings as great *as if* ' the parched ground ' should become a lake of pure and refreshing water. The words ' parched ground,' however, probably do not convey the sense which Isaiah intended. The image which he had in his eye is much more beautiful than that which is denoted by the ' parched ground.' Lowth translates it, ' The glowing sand.' The LXX. Ἄνυδρος — ' The dry place. The Hebrew word (שָׁרָב *shârâb*), properly denotes the heat of the sun (Isa. xlix. 10); and then the phenomenon which is produced by the refraction of the rays of the sun on the glowing sands of a desert, and which gives the appearance of a sea

or lake of water. This phenomenon is witnessed in the deserts of Arabia and Egypt, and has been also seen occasionally in the south of France and in Russia. We have no word in English to express it. The French word by which it is commonly designated is *mirage*. It is caused by the refraction of the rays of the sun, an explanation of which may be found in the *Edin. Encyclopædia,* vol. xiv. pp. 753–755. It is often described by travellers, and is referred to in the Koran, ch. xxiv. 39:

The works of unbelievers are like *the serab* in a plain,
Which the thirsty man takes to be water, until he comes to it, and finds that it is not.

Mr. Sale's Note on this place in the Koran is, ' The Arabic word *serab* signifies that false appearance which in the eastern countries is often seen in sandy plains about noon, resembling a large lake of water in motion, and is occasioned by the reverberation of the sunbeams, "by the quivering undulating motion of that quick succession of vapours and exhalations which are extracted by the powerful influence of the sun " (Shaw's *Travels*, p. 378). It sometimes tempts thirsty travellers out of their way, but deceives them when they come near, either going forward (for it always appears at the same distance), or quite vanishes.' Q. Curtius (vii. 5) also has mentioned it, in the description of the march of Alexander the Great across the Oxus to Sogdiana : ' The vapour of the summer sun inflamed the sands, which when they began to be inflamed all things seemed to burn. A dense cloud, produced by the unusual heat of the earth, covered the light, and the *appearance of the plains was like a vast and deep sea.*' The Arabians often refer to this in their writings, and draw images from it. ' Like the serab of the plain, which the thirsty take to be water.' ' He runs for the spoil of the serab ; ' a proverb. ' Deceitful as the appearance of water ; ' also a proverb. ' Be not deceived by the glimmer of the serab ; ' another proverb. This appearance has been often described by modern travellers (see Shaw's *Travels*, p. 375 ; Clarke's *Travels*, vol. ii. p. 295 ; Belzoni's *Travels and Operations in Egypt*

and Nubia, p. 196). The same appearance has been observed in India, and in various parts of Africa. ' During the French expedition to Egypt, the phenomena of unusual refractions were often seen. The uniformity of the extensive sandy plains of Lower Egypt is interrupted only by small eminences, on which the villages are situated, in order to escape the inundations of the Nile. In the morning and the evening, as many have remarked, objects appear in their natural position ; but when the surface of the sandy ground is heated by the sun, the land seems at a certain distance terminated by a general inundation. The villages which are beyond it appear like so many islands situated in the middle of a great lake ; and under each village is an inverted image of it. As the observer approaches the limits of the apparent inundation, the imaginary lake which seemed to encircle the village withdraws itself, and the same illusion is reproduced by another village more remote.'—(*Edin. Encyclopædia*, vol. xiv. p. 754.) ' In the desert,' says Prof. Robinson, ' we had frequent instances of the *mirage* presenting the appearance of lakes of water and islands ; and as we began to descend towards Suez, it was difficult to distinguish between these appearances and the distant real waters of the Red Sea.'—(*Travels in Palestine and the adjacent regions*, in 1838, *Bib. Repos.* April, 1839, p. 402.) Major Skinner, in his recently published *Journey Overland to India*, describes the appearance of the serab in that very desert, between Palestine and the Euphrates, which probably supplied the images which the prophet employs : ' About noon the most perfect deception that can be conceived exhilarated our spirits, and promised an early resting-place. We had observed a slight *mirage* two or three times before, but this day it surpassed all I have ever fancied. Although aware that these appearances have often led people astray, I could not bring myself to believe that this was unreal. The Arabs were doubtful, and said that, as we had found water yesterday, it was not improbable that we should find some to-day. The seeming lake was broken in several parts by little islands of sand that gave strength

8 And an high way shall be there, and a way, and it shall be

to the delusion. The dromedaries of the Sheikhs at length reached its borders, and appeared to us to have commenced to ford as they advanced, and became more surrounded by the vapour. I thought they had got into deep water, and moved with greater caution. In passing over the sand banks their figures were reflected in the water. So convinced was Mr. Calmun of its reality, that he dismounted and walked towards the deepest part of it, which was on the right hand. He followed the deceitful lake for a long time, and to our sight was strolling on the bank, his shadow stretching to a great length beyond. There was not a breath of wind; it was a sultry day, and such an one as would have added dreadfully to our disappointment if we had been at any time without water.'

Southey has beautifully described this appearance and its effects on the traveller :—

Still the same burning sun! no cloud in heaven!
The hot air quivers, and the sultry mist
Floats o'er the desert, with a show
Of distant waters mocking their distress.

The idea of the prophet, if he refers to this phenomenon, is exceedingly beautiful. It is that the *mirage*, which has the appearance only of a sheet of water, and which often deceives the traveller, shall become a *real* lake; that there shall be hereafter no deception, no illusion; that man, like a traveller on pathless sands, weary and thirsty, shall no more be deceived by false appearances and unreal hopes. The hopes and promises which this world can furnish are as delusive as is the *mirage* to the exhausted and thirsty traveller. Man approaches them, and, like that delusive appearance, they recede or vanish. If they are still seen, they are always at a distance, and he follows the false and deceptive vision till he comes to the end of life. But the promises of God through the Messiah, are like *real* lakes of water and running streams to the thirsty traveller. They never deceive, never recede, never vanish, never are unsatisfactory. Man may approach them, knowing that there is no illusion; he may satisfy his wants, and still the sup-

ply is unexhausted and inexhaustible. Others also may approach the same fountain of pure joy, with as much freedom as travellers may approach the running stream in the desert. ¶ *In the habitation of dragons* (see Note on ch. xiii. 22). The sense of this is, that the blessings which are promised shall be as great as if in such dry and desolate places there should be verdure and beauty. ¶ *Where each lay.* In every place which the wild beast had occupied. ¶ Shall be *grass.* Marg. ' A court for.' The Hebrew word (חָצִיר) may mean either *grass*, or *a court*, or habitation. The latter is undoubtedly the meaning of the word here, and thus it responds in the parallelism to the ' *habitation* of dragons.'

In *the habitation* where each lay,
Shall be *a court* for reeds and rushes.

¶ *Reeds and rushes.* These usually grew by ponds and marshes. The image which the prophet had been employing was that of a desert of sands and arid plains. He here says, that there would be *verdure.* In those pathless wastes there would spring up that which was nourished by water. The sense is, that those portions of the earth which are covered with moral desolation, like the pathless wastes of the desert, shall put on the appearance of moral cultivation and verdure.

8. *And an highway shall be there* (see Note on ch. xi. 16). This is *language* which is derived from the return of the Jews from captivity. The idea is, that there would be easy and uninterrupted access to their own land. The more remote, though main idea in the mind of the prophet seems to have been, that the way of access to the blessings of the Messiah's reign would be open and free to all (comp. ch. xl. 3, 4). ¶ *And a way.* It is not easy to mark the difference between the word *way* (דֶּרֶךְ) and a highway (מַסְלוּל). Probably the latter refers more particularly to a *raised* way (from סָלַל, *to cast up*), and would be expressed by our word *causeway* or *turnpike.* It was such a way as was usually made for the march of armies by removing obstructions, filling valleys, &c. The

called, The way of holiness ; the
unclean *a* shall not pass over it ;
but 1 it *shall be* for those : the wayfaring men, though fools, shall not
err *therein.*

a ch.52.1; Joel 3.17; Rev.21.27.

9 No *b* lion shall be there, nor
any ravenous beast shall go up
thereon, it shall not be found
there : but the redeemed shall
walk *there :*

1 or, *for he shall be with them.*   *b* Eze.34.25.

word *way* (דֶּרֶךְ) is a more general term,
and denotes a path, or road of any kind.
¶ *And it shall be called the way of holiness.* The reason why it should be so
called is stated ; — no impure person
should travel it. The idea is, that all
who should have access to the favour of
God, or who should come into his kingdom, should be holy. ¶ *The unclean
shall not pass over it.* There shall be
no idolater there ; no one shall be admitted who is not a pure worshipper of
JEHOVAH. Such is the design of the
kingdom which is set up by the Messiah, and such the church of Christ
should be (see ch. xl. 3, 4 ; xlix. 11 ;
lxii. 10). ¶ *But it* shall be *for those.*
For those who are specified immediately ;
for the ransomed of the Lord. The
Margin is, ' For he shall be with them.'
Lowth reads it,

But he himself shall be with them, walking in
the way.'

And this, it seems to me, is the more
probable sense of the passage, indicating
that they should not go alone or unprotected. It would be a holy way, because
their God would be with them ; it would
be safe, because he would attend and
defend them. ¶ *The wayfaring men.*
Heb. ' He walking in the way.' According to the translation proposed
above, this refers to God, the Redeemer,
who will be with his people, walking in
the way with them. ¶ *Though fools.*
Heb. ' And fools.' That is, the simple,
the unlearned, or those who are regarded as fools. It shall be a highway
thrown up, so direct, and so unlike other
paths, that there shall be no danger of
mistaking it.—The friends of God are
often regarded as fools by the world.
Many of them *are* of the humbler class
of life, and are destitute of human learning, and of worldly wisdom. The sense
here is, that the way of salvation shall
be so plain, that no one, however ignorant and unlearned, need err in regard
to it. In accordance with this, the

Saviour said that the gospel was preached to the poor; and he himself always represented the way to life as such that the
most simple and unlettered might find it.

9. *No lion shall be there.* Lions
abounded in all the countries adjacent
to Palestine. They are, therefore, often
referred to by the sacred writers, as
objects of dread and alarm. The leading idea in the *language* of Isaiah in
this whole passage, is that of a way
constructed from Babylon to Judea, so
straight and plain that the most simple
of the people might find it and walk in
it. But *such* a path would lie through
desert sands. It would be in the region
infested with lions and other wild beasts.
The prophet, therefore, suggests that
there should be no cause for such dread
and alarm. The sense is, that in that
kingdom to which he had made reference all would be *safe.* They who
entered it should find security and defence as they travelled that road. And
it *is* true. They who enter the path
that leads to life, find there no cause
of alarm. Their fears subside ; their
apprehensions of punishment on account of their sins die away ; and they
walk that path with security and confidence. There is nothing *in* that way
to alarm them ; and though there may
be many foes—fitly represented by lions
and wild beasts—lying *about* the way,
yet no one is permitted to ' go up
thereon.' This is a most beautiful
image of the safety of the people of
God, and of their freedom from all
enemies that could annoy them. ¶ *But
the redeemed shall walk* there. The
language here referred at first doubtless
to those who would be rescued from the
captivity at Babylon ; but the main
reference is to those who would be redeemed by the blood of the atonement,
or who are properly called ' the redeemed of the LORD.' That Isaiah
was acquainted with the doctrine of
redemption is apparent from his fifty-
third chapter. There is not here, in-

10 And the ransomed ^a of the Lord shall return, and come to Zion with songs, ^b and everlasting

^a ch.51.11.　　　　　^b Rev.5.9.

joy ^c upon their heads : they shall obtain joy and gladness, and sorrow ^d and sighing shall flee away.

^c Jude 24.　　　　　^d Rev.7.17; 21.4.

deed, any express mention made of the *means* by which they would be redeemed, but the language is so general that it may refer either to the deliverance from the captivity at Babylon, or the future more important deliverance of his people from the bondage of sin by the atoning sacrifice of the Messiah. On the word rendered ' redeem,' see Note on ch. xliii. 1. The idea is, that the path here referred to is appropriately designed only for the redeemed of Lord. It is not for the profane, the polluted, the hypocrite. It is not for those who live for this world, or for those who love pleasure more than they love God. The church should not be entered except by those who have evidence that they are redeemed. None should make a profession of religion who have no evidence that they belong to ' the redeemed,' and who are not disposed to walk in the way of holiness. But, *for* all such it is a highway on which they are to travel. It is made by levelling hills and elevating valleys ; it is made across the sandy desert and through the wilderness of this world ; it is made through a world infested with the enemies of God and his people. It is made straight and plain, so that none need err ; it is defended from enemies, so that all may be safe ; it is rendered secure, because ' He,' their Leader and Redeemer, shall go with and guard that way.

10. *And the ransomed of the* Lord. The word here rendered ' ransomed,' is different from the word rendered ' redeemed ' in ver. 9. This word is פְּדוּיֵי from פָּדָה ; though it is not easy, perhaps not possible, to designate the difference in the sense. Doubtless there was a shade of difference among the Hebrews, but what it was is not now known. See this word explained in the Note on ch. i. 27. The *language* here is all derived from the deliverance from Babylon, and the images employed by the prophet relate to that event. Still, there can be no doubt that he meant to describe the deliverance under

the Messiah. ¶ *Shall return, and come to Zion.* This language also is that which expresses the return from Babylon. In a more general sense, and in the sense intended particularly by the prophet, it means, doubtless, that *all* who are the redeemed of God shall be gathered under his protection, and shall be saved. ¶ *With songs.* With rejoicing—as the ransomed captives would return from Babylon, and as all who are redeemed enter the church on earth, and will enter into heaven above. ¶ *And everlasting joy upon their heads.* This *may be* an expression denoting the fact that joy is manifest in the face and aspect (Gesenius). Thus we say that joy lights up the countenance, and it is possible that the Hebrews expressed this idea by applying it to the head. Thus the Hebrews say (Ps. cxxvi. 2):

Then was our mouth filled with laughter,
And our tongue with singing.

Or it may refer to the practice of *anointing* the head with oil and perfume in times of festivity and joy—in contrast with the custom of throwing ashes on the head in times of grief and calamity (Rosenmüller). Or it may refer to a custom of wearing a wreath or chaplet of flowers in times of festivity, as is often done now, and as was commonly done among the ancients in triumphal processions (Vitringa). Whichever exposition be adopted, the idea is the same, that there would be great joy, and that that joy would be perpetual and unfading. This is true of all who return to Zion under the Messiah. *Joy* is one of the first emotions ; joy at redemption, and at the pardon of sin ; joy in view of the hopes of eternal life, and of the everlasting favour of God. But this joy is not short-lived and fading, like the garland of flowers on the head ; it is constant, increasing, everlasting. ¶ *And sorrow and sighing shall flee away* (see Note on ch. xxv. 8).

This is a most beautiful close of the *series* or succession of prophecies which we have been thus far contemplating. The result of all is, that the redeemed of the Lord shall have joy and rejoicing; that all their enemies shall be subdued, and that they shall be rescued from all their foes. In the analysis of the prophecy contained in the thirty-fourth and thirty-fifth chapters, it was stated that this prophecy seemed to be a *summary* of all that Isaiah had before uttered, and was designed to show that all the enemies of the people of God would be destroyed, and that they would be triumphantly delivered and saved. All these minor deliverances were preparatory to and emblematic of the greater deliverance under the Messiah; and accordingly all his predictions look forward to, and terminate in that. In the portions of prophecy which we have been over, we have seen the people of God represented as in danger from the Syrians, the Assyrians, the Egyptians, the Moabites, the Edomites, the Babylonians; and in reference to them *all*, the same result has been predicted, that they would be delivered from them, and that their enemies would be destroyed. This has been, in the chapters which we have passed over, successively foretold of Damascus, of Egypt, of Moab, of Ethiopia, of Babylon, of Edom, and of Sennacherib; and the prophet has reached the conclusion that ALL the enemies of God's people would ultimately be destroyed, and that they would be safe under the reign of the Messiah, to which all their deliverances were preparatory, and in which they all would terminate. Having pursued this course of the prophecy; having looked at all these foes; having seen them in vision all destroyed; having seen the Prince of Peace come; having seen the wonders that he would perform; having seen all danger subside, and the preparation made for the eternal security and joy of all his people, the prophet closes this series of predictions with the beautiful statement now before us, 'the redeemed of JEHOVAH shall return, and come to Zion with songs, and everlasting joy; and sorrow and sighing shall flee away.'

Notes
on the
Old Testament

Albert Barnes

ISAIAH
Volume 2

BAKER BOOK HOUSE

Grand Rapids, Michigan 49506

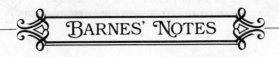

Heritage Edition Fourteen Volumes 0834-4

1. Genesis (Murphy)	0835-2	8. Minor Prophets (Pusey)	0842-5
2. Exodus to Esther (Cook)	0836-0	9. The Gospels	0843-3
3. Job	0837-9	10. Acts and Romans	0844-1
4. Psalms	0838-7	11. I Corinthians to Galatians	0846-8
5. Proverbs to Ezekiel (Cook)	0839-5	12. Ephesians to Philemon	0847-6
6. Isaiah	0840-9	13. Hebrews to Jude	0848-4
7. Daniel	0841-7	14. Revelation	0849-2

When ordering by ISBN (International Standard Book Number), numbers listed above should be preceded by 0-8010-.

Reprinted from the 1851 edition published by Blackie & Son, London

Reprinted 1983 by Baker Book House Company

ISBN : 0-8010-0840-9

Printed and bound in the United States of America

NOTE BY THE EDITOR

In this Edition of Barnes on Isaiah, the "New Translation," given with the first Edition of the Work, is withheld, because the Author himself has suppressed it in his second and last Edition, and the Editor did not feel himself at liberty to disturb that arrangement. "My principal aim," says Mr. Barnes in his preface, "has been to *condense* the work as much as possible, by removing redundant words, and by excluding whatever did not contribute to the elucidation of the prophet. In revising it I have stricken out matter, besides the 'New Translation,' to the amount of about one hundred and twenty octavo pages." For the omission of the Translation in the recent Edition, the want of room was one reason, and probably the character of the Translation itself was another. The Author never claimed much for it, and his profound countryman, Alexander, observes regarding it, that "it seems to be wholly independent of the Commentary, and can hardly be considered an improvement, either on the Common Version or on that of Lowth." It is on the Commentary that the Author has rested his fame, and there assuredly it has a solid and lasting foundation.

For peculiarities of this Edition, see the Editor's Preface in the first volume.

THE BOOK

OF

THE PROPHET ISAIAH

CHAPTER XXXVI.

ANALYSIS.

THIS chapter commences the historical portion of Isaiah, which continues to the close of the thirty-ninth chapter. The main subject is the destruction of Sennacherib and his army. It contains also an account of the sickness and recovery of Hezekiah; the song with which he celebrated his recovery; and an account of his ostentation in showing his treasures to the ambassadors of the king of Babylon. In 2 Chron. xxxii. 32, the following record occurs:—' Now the rest of the acts of Hezekiah, and his goodness, behold they are written in the vision of Isaiah, the son of Amoz;' and it is to this portion of Isaiah to which the author of the Book of Chronicles doubtless refers.

There was an obvious propriety in Isaiah's making a record of the invasion and destruction of Sennacherib. That event has occupied a considerable portion of his prophetic announcements; and as he lived to see them fulfilled, it was proper that he should record the event. The prophecy and its fulfilment can thus be compared together; and while there is the strongest internal testimony that the prophecy was uttered before the event, there is also the most striking and clear fulfilment of all the predictions on the subject.

A parallel history of these transactions occurs in 2 Kings xvii.–xx., and in 2 Chron. xxxii. The history in Chronicles, though it contains an account of the same transaction, is evidently by another hand, as it bears no further resemblance to this, than that it contains an account of the same transactions. But between the account here and in 2 Kings there is a most striking resemblance, so much so as to show that they were mainly by the same hand. It has been made a matter of inquiry whether Isaiah was the original author, or whether he copied a history which he found in the Book of Kings, or whether both he and the author of the Book of Kings copied from some original document which is now lost, or whether the collectors of the prophetic writings after the return from the captivity at Babylon, judging that such a history would appropriately explain the prophecies of Isaiah, copied the account from some historical record, and inserted it among his prophecies. This last is the opinion of Rosenmüller—an opinion which evidently lacks all historical evidence, and indeed all probability. The most obvious and fair supposition undoubtedly is, that this history was inserted here by Isaiah, or, that he made this record according to the statement in 2 Chron. xxxii. 32. Gesenius also accords substantially with Rosenmüller in supposing that this history is an *elaboration* of that in the Book of Kings, and that it was reduced to its present form by some one who collected and edited the Books of Isaiah after the Babylonish captivity. Vitringa supposes that both the accounts in Kings and in Isaiah have been derived from a common historical document, and have been adopted and somewhat abridged and modified by the author of the Book of Kings and by Isaiah.

It is impossible now to determine the truth in regard to this subject; nor is it of much importance. Those who are desirous of seeing the subject discussed more at length may consult Vitringa, Rosenmüller, and Gesenius. The view of Gesenius is chiefly valuable because he has gone into a comparison of the account in Isaiah with that in Kings. The following remarks are all that occur to me as desirable to make, and express the conclusion which I have been able to form on the subject:—

I. The two accounts have a common origin, or are substantially the production of the same hand. This is apparent on the face of them. The same course of the narrative is pursued, the same expressions occur, and the same style of composition is found. It is *possible*, indeed, that the Holy Spirit *might* have inspired two different authors to adopt the same style and expressions in recording the same events, but this is not the mode elsewhere observed in the Scriptures. Every sacred writer is allowed to pursue his own method of narration, and to express himself in a style and manner of his own.

2. There is no *evidence* that the two accounts were abridged from a more full narrative. Such a thing is *possible;* nor is there any impropriety in the supposition. But it lacks historical support. That there *were* histories among the Jews which are now lost; that there were public records which were the'fountains whence the authors of the histories which we now have drew their information, no one can doubt who reads the Old Testament. Thus we have accounts of the writings of Gad, and Iddo the seer, and Nathan, and the prophecy of Ahijah the Shilonite, and of the Book of Jehu the prophet (2 Chron. ix. 29; xx. 34; 1 Kings xvi. 1), all of which are now lost, except so far as they are incorporated in the historical and prophetical books of the Old Testament. It is *possible,* therefore, that these accounts may have been abridged from some such common record, but there is no historical testimony to the fact.

3. There is no *evidence* that these chapters in Isaiah were inserted by Ezra, or the other inspired men who collected the Sacred Writings, and published a *recension,* or an edition of them after the return from Babylon. That there was such a work performed by Ezra and his contemporaries is the testimony of all the Jewish historians (see Dr. Alexander *On the Canon of Scripture*). But there is no historical evidence that they thus introduced into the writings of Isaiah an entire historical narrative from the previous histories, or that they composed this history to be inserted here. It is done nowhere else. And had it been done on this occasion, we should have had reason to expect that they would have inserted historical records of the fulfilment of *all* the other prophecies which had been fulfilled. We should have looked, therefore, for historical statements of the downfall of Damascus and Syria; of the destruction of Samaria, of Moab, of Babylon, and of Tyre, as proofs of the fulfilment of the predictions of Isaiah. There can be no reason why the account of the destruction of Sennacherib should have been singled out and inserted in preference to others. And this is especially true in regard to *Babylon.* The prophecy of Isaiah (ch. xiii., xiv.) had been most striking and clear; the fulfilment had also been most remarkable; Ezra and his contemporaries must have felt a much deeper interest in that than in the destruction of Sennacherib; and it is unaccountable, therefore, if they inserted this narrative respecting Sennacherib, that they did not give us a full account also of the overthrow of Babylon, and of their

deliverance, as showing the fulfilment of the prophecies on that subject.

4. The author of the Books of Kings is unknown. There is reason to believe that these books, as well as the Books of Chronicles, and some other of the historical books of the Old Testament, were written *by* the prophets; or at least compiled and arranged by some inspired man, from historical sketches that were made by the prophets. To such sketches or narratives we find frequent reference in the books themselves. Thus Nathan the prophet, and Ahijah the Shilonite, and Iddo the seer, recorded the acts of Solomon (2 Chron. ix. 29); thus the same Iddo the seer, and Shemaiah the prophet, recorded the acts of Rehoboam (2 Chron. xii. 15); thus the acts of Jehoshaphat were written in the Book of Jehu (2 Chron. xx. 34); and thus Isaiah wrote the acts of king Uzziah (2 Chron. xxvi. 22), and also of Hezekiah (2 Chron. xxxii. 32). Many of these historical sketches or fragments have not come down to us; but all that was essential to us has been doubtless incorporated into the sacred narrative, and transmitted to our own times. It is not improbable that many of these histories were mere fragments or public documents; narratives or sketches of a single reign, or some important fact in a reign, which were subsequently revised and inserted in the more extended history, so that, after all, it may be that we have all, or nearly all, of these fragments incorporated in the histories which we now possess.

5. As Isaiah is thus known to have written some portions of the history of the kings, it is probable that his history would be incorporated into the record of the kings by whomsoever that record might be composed. Indeed, the composition of the entire Books of Kings has been ascribed by many writers to Isaiah, though Grotius and some others ascribe it to Jeremiah. The general, and the probable opinion is, however, that the Books of the Kings were digested into their present form by Ezra. It is probable, therefore, I think, that Isaiah wrote the chapters in Kings respecting the invasion of Sennacherib; that the compiler of the Books of Kings, whoever he might be, adopted the fragment as a part of his history, and that the portion which we have here in Isaiah is the same fragment revised, abridged in some places, and enlarged in others, to adapt it to his purpose in introducing it into his book of prophecy. But it is admitted that this is conjecture. Every consideration, however, must lead us to suppose that this is the work of Isaiah (comp. Introd. § 5).

The portion of history contained in these chapters differs from the record in the Kings in several respects. There is no difference in regard to the historical facts, but the difference has respect to the fulness of the narratives, and to the change of a few words. The most material difference is that a few sentences, and members of sentences, are omitted in Isaiah which are found in Kings. These variations will be noticed in the exposition, and it is not necessary more particularly to refer to them here.

The thirty-sixth chapter contains the following parts, or subjects:—1. Sennacherib, having taken most of the strongholds of Judea, sent Rabshakeh with a great force to besiege Jerusalem, and to summon it to surrender (1, 2). 2. Hezekiah sent an embassy to meet with Rabshakeh, evidently to induce him to depart from the city (3). 3. This embassy Rabshakeh addressed in a proud, insolent, and taunting speech, reproaching them with putting their trust in Egypt, and with their feebleness, and assuring them that Sennacherib had come up against the city at the command of JEHOVAH (4–10). 4. The Jewish embassy requested Rabshakeh to speak in the Aramean or Syrian language, that the common people on the wall might not hear (11). 5. To this he replied, that he came that *they might hear ;* to endeavour to draw them off from trusting to Hezekiah, and to induce them to submit to Sennacherib, promising them abundance in the land to which he would take them (12–20). 6. To all this, the embassy of Hezekiah said nothing, but returned, as they had been instructed, into the city, with deep expressions of sorrow and grief (21, 22).

N OW *a* it came to pass in the fourteenth year of king Hezekiah, *that* Sennacherib king of Assyria came up against all the defenced cities of Judah, and took them.

a 2 Ki.18.13,&c.; 2 Ch.32.1,&c.

CHAPTER XXXVI.

1. *In the fourteenth year of Hezekiah.* Of his reign, B.C. 709. ¶ *That Sennacherib.* Sennacherib was son and successor of Shalmaneser, king of Assyria, and began to reign A.M. 3290, or B.C. 714, and reigned, according to Calmet, but four years, according to Prideaux eight years, and according to Gesenius eighteen years. The immediate occasion of this war against Judah was the fact that Hezekiah had shaken off the yoke of Assyria, by which his father Ahaz and the nation had suffered so much under Tiglath-pileser, or Shalmaneser (2 Kings xviii. 7). To reduce Judea again to subjection, as well as to carry his conquests into Egypt, appears to have been the design of this celebrated expedition. He ravaged the country, took the strong towns and fortresses, and prepared then to lay siege to Jerusalem itself. Hezekiah, however, as soon as the army of Sennacherib had entered Judea, prepared to put Jerusalem into a state of complete defence. At the advice of his counsellors he stopped the waters that flowed in the neighbourhood of the city, and that might furnish refreshment to a besieging army, built up the broken walls, enclosed one of the fountains within a wall, and prepared shields and darts in abundance to repel the invader (2 Chron. xxxii. 2–5). Sennacherib, seeing that all hope of easily taking Jerusalem was taken away, apparently became inclined to hearken to terms of accommodation. Hezekiah sent to him to propose peace, and to ask the conditions on which he would withdraw his forces. He confessed his error in not paying the tribute stipulated by his father, and his willingness to pay now what should be demanded by Sennacherib. Sennacherib demanded three hundred talents of silver, and thirty talents of gold. This was paid by Hezekiah, by exhausting the treasury, and by stripping even the temple of its gold (2 Kings xviii. 13–16). It was evidently understood in this treaty that Sennacherib was to withdraw his forces, and return to his own land. But this treaty he ultimately disregarded (see Note on ch. xxxiii. 8). He seems, however, to have granted Hezekiah some respite, and to have delayed his attack on Jerusalem until his return from Egypt. This war with Egypt he prosecuted at first with great success, and with a fair prospect of the conquest of that country. But having laid siege to Pelusium, and having spent much time before it without success, he was compelled at length to raise the siege, and to retreat. Tirhakah king of Ethiopia having come to the aid of Sevechus, the reigning monarch of Egypt, and advancing to the relief of Pelusium, Sennacherib was compelled to raise the siege, and retreated to Judea. Here, having taken Lachish, and disregarding his compact with He-

2 And the king of Assyria sent Rabshakeh from Lachish to Jerusalem unto king Hezekiah with a great army. And he stood by the conduit of the upper pool in the highway of the fuller's field.

3 Then came forth unto him Eliakim, Hilkiah's son, which was over the house, and Shebna the scribe, [1] and Joah, Asaph's son, the recorder.

4 And Rabshakeh said unto them, Say ye now to Hezekiah, Thus saith the great king, the king of Assyria, What confidence is this wherein thou trustest?

5 I say, sayest thou (but they are

1 or, secretary.

---

zekiah, he sent an army to Jerusalem under Rabshakeh to lay siege to the city. This is the point in the history of Sennacherib to which the passage before us refers (see Prideaux's *Connection*, vol. i. pp. 138–141 ; Jos. *Ant.* x. 1 ; Gesenius *in loco;* and Robinson's Calmet). ¶ *All the defenced cities.* All the towns on the way to Egypt, and in the vicinity of Jerusalem (see Notes on ch. x. 28–32).

2. *And the king of Assyria sent Rabshakeh.* In 2 Kings xviii. 17, it is said that he sent Tartan, and Rabsaris, and Rabshakeh. In regard to Tartan, see Note on ch. xx. 1. It is probable that Rabshakeh only is mentioned in Isaiah because the expedition may have been mainly under his direction, or more probably because he was the principal speaker on the occasion to which he refers. ¶ *From Lachish.* This was a city in the south of the tribe of Judah, and was south-west of Jerusalem (Josh. x. 23; xv. 39). It was situated in a plain, and was the seat of an ancient Canaanitish king. It was rebuilt and fortified by Rehoboam (2 Chron. xi. 9). It was in some respects a border town, and was a defence against the incursions of the Philistines. It was therefore situated between Jerusalem and Egypt, and was in the direct way of Sennacherib in his going to Egypt, and on his return. It lay, according to Eusebius and Jerome, seven Roman miles from Eleutheropolis towards the south. No trace of the town, however, is now to be found (see Robinson's *Bib. Researches*, vol. ii. pp. 388, 389). ¶ *With a great army.* Sennacherib remained himself for a time at Lachish, though he followed not long after. It is probable that he sent forward a considerable portion of his immense army, retaining only so many forces as he judged would be necessary

to carry on the siege of Lachish. In 2 Chron. xxxii. 9, it is said that Sennacherib, while he sent his servants to Jerusalem, ' laid siege to Lachish and all his power with him ;' but this must mean that he retained with him a considerable part of his army, and doubtless all that contributed to his magnificence and splendour. The word ' power ' in 2 Chron. xxxii. 9, means also ' dominion ' (see the margin), and denotes all the insignia of royalty ; and this might have been retained while a considerable part of his forces had been sent forward to Jerusalem. ¶ *And he stood.* He halted ; he encamped there ; he intended to make that the point of attack. ¶ *By the conduit, &c.* (see Notes on ch. vii. 3.)

3. *Then came forth unto him.* Isaiah has here omitted what is recorded in 2 Kings xviii. 18, viz., that Rabshakeh and his companions ' called to the king,' and as the result of that probably Hezekiah sent out Eliakim. ¶ *Eliakim, Hilkiah's son, which was over the house.* Respecting Eliakim, and his character, see Notes on ch. xxii. 20–25. ¶ *And Shebna the scribe.* This may have been some other man than the one mentioned in ch. xxii. 15. He is there said to have been ' over the house,' and it is stated that he should be degraded from that office, and succeeded by Eliakim. It is possible, however, that Hezekiah retained him as *scribe*, or as *secretary* (see the analysis of ch. xxii. 15–25). ¶ *And Joah, Asaph's son, the recorder.* The *chronicler ;* the officer to whom was intrusted the keeping of the records of state. The Hebrew word means ' the remembrancer ;' him by whose means former events might be recalled and remembered, perhaps an officer such as would be called *historiographer.*

4. *What confidence.* What is the ground of your confidence ? on what do

but vain [1] words) [2] *I have* counsel and strength for war : now on whom dost thou trust, that thou rebellest against me ?

6 Lo, thou trustest in the staff of this broken reed, on Egypt ; whereon if a man lean, it will go into his hand, and pierce it : so *is*

1 *a word of lips.*
2 or, but *counsel and strength* are *for the war.*

Pharaoh king of Egypt to all that trust in him.

7 But if thou say to me, We trust in the LORD our God : *is it* not he whose high places and whose altars Hezekiah hath taken away, and *a* said to Judah and to Jerusalem, Ye shall worship before this altar ?

a 2 Ki.18.4.

you trust? The appellation 'great king' was the customary title of the kings of the Persians and Assyrians.

5. *I say*, sayest thou. In 2 Kings xviii. 20, this is 'thou sayest ;' and thus many MSS. read it here, and Lowth and Noyes have adopted that reading. So the Syriac reads it. But the sense is not affected whichever reading is adopted. It is designed to show to Hezekiah that his reliance, either on his own resources or on Egypt, was vain. ¶ *But* they are but *vain words.* Marg. as Heb. 'A word of lips ;' that is, mere words ; vain and empty boasting. ¶ *On whom dost thou trust, that thou rebellest against me ?* Hezekiah had revolted from the Assyrian power, and had refused to pay the tribute which had been imposed on the Jews in the time of Ahaz (2 Kings xviii. 7).

6. *Lo, thou trustest.* It is possible that Sennacherib might have been apprised of the attempt which had been made by the Jews to secure the co-operation of Egypt (see Notes on ch. xxx. 1–7 ; xxxi. 1, *sq.*), though he might not have been aware that the negotiation was unsuccessful. ¶ *In the staff of this broken reed.* The same comparison of Egypt with a broken reed, or a reed which *broke* while they were trusting to it, occurs in Ezek. xxix. 6, 7. *Reeds* were doubtless used often for staves, as they are now. They are light and hollow, with long joints. The idea here is, that as a slender reed would break when a man leaned on it, and would pierce his hand, so it would be with Egypt. Their reliance would give way, and their trusting to Egypt would be attended with injury to themselves (comp. ch. xxx. 5, 7 ; xxxi. 3).

7. *But if thou say to me.* If you shall make this plea, that you believe

JEHOVAH will protect you in your revolt. The word 'thou' here refers to Hezekiah, or to the ambassadors speaking in his name. In 2 Kings xviii. 22, it is, 'but if *ye* say unto me ;' that is, you ambassadors. The sense is substantially the same. ¶ Is it *not he*, &c. This is given as a reason why they should not put their confidence in JEHOVAH. The reason is, that he supposed that Hezekiah had removed all the altars of JEHOVAH from all parts of the land, and that they could not calculate on the protection of a God whose worship had been abolished. It is probable that Sennacherib and Rabshakeh had heard of the reformation which had been effected by Hezekiah ; of his destroying the groves and altars which had been consecrated in the reign of his father to idolatry, and perhaps of the fact that he had even destroyed the brazen serpent which Moses had made, and which had become an object of idolatrous worship (2 Kings xviii. 4), and he may have supposed that all these altars and groves had been devoted to JEHOVAH, and were connected with his worship. He did not seem to understand that all that Hezekiah had done was only to establish the worship of JEHOVAH in the land. ¶ *High places.* The worship of idols was usually performed in groves on high places ; or on the tops of hills and mountains. It seems to have been supposed that worship in such places was more acceptable to the Deity. Perhaps it may have been because they thus seemed *nearer* the residence of the gods ; or, perhaps, because there is sublimity and solemnity in such places—a stillness and elevation above the world which seem favourable to devotion (see 1 Sam. ix. 12 ; 1 Kings iii. 4 ; 2 Kings xii. 2 ; 1 Chron. xiii. 29). Chapels, temples, and

8 Now therefore give ¹pledges, I pray thee, to my master the king of Assyria, and I will give thee two thousand *a* horses, if thou be able on thy part to set riders upon them.

9 How then wilt thou turn away the face of one captain of the least

of my master's servants, and put thy trust on Egypt *b* for chariots and for horsemen?

10 And am I now come up without the LORD against this land to destroy it? The LORD *c* said unto me, Go up against this land, and destroy it.

1 or, *hostages.*　*a* Ps.20.*l*,8; Hos.14.3.　*b* Jer.2 36.　　*c* ch.45.7; Am.3.6.

altars, were erected on such places (1 Kings xiii. 22; 2 Kings xvii., xxix), and ministers and priests attended there to officiate (1 Kings xii. 32; 2 Kings xvii. 32). Even the kings of Judah, notwithstanding the express prohibition of Moses (Deut. xii.), were engaged in such acts of worship (2 Kings xii. 4; xiv. 4; xv. 4, 35; 2 Chron. xv. 17; xx. 33); and Solomon himself sacrificed in chapels of this kind (1 Kings iii. 2). These places Hezekiah had destroyed; that is, he had cut down the consecrated groves, and had destroyed the chapels and temples which had been erected there. The fact that Ahaz, the father of Hezekiah, had been distinguished for worshipping in such places had probably led the king of Assyria to suppose that this was the proper worship of the God of the Jews; and now that Hezekiah had destroyed them all, he seems to have inferred that he was guilty of gross irreligion, and could no longer depend on the protection of JEHOVAH. ¶ *And said to Judah and Jerusalem.* He had commanded them to worship only in Jerusalem, at the temple. This was in strict accordance with the law of Moses; but this seems to have been understood by Sennacherib as in fact almost or quite banishing the worship of JEHOVAH from the land. Probably this was said to alienate the minds of the people from Hezekiah, by showing them that he had taken away their rights and privileges of worshipping God where they chose.

8. *Now, therefore, give pledges.* Marg. 'Hostages.' The Hebrew verb (עָרַב) means properly *to mix* or *mingle;* then, to exchange commodities by barter or traffic; then, to become surety for any one, to exchange with him, to stand in his place; then, to pledge, to pledge one's life, or to give security of any kind. Here it is used in a spirit of *taunting* or *derision,* and is equiva-

lent to what would be said among us, ' I will bet you, or I will lay a wager, that if we should give you only two thousand horses, you could not find men enough to ride them, or men that had knowledge of horsemanship enough to guide them.' There was much severity in this taunt. The Jews hoped to defend themselves. Yet here was an immense army coming up to lay siege against them. What hope had they of defence? So weak and feeble were they, that Rabshakeh said they could not furnish even two thousand horsemen to resist all the host of the Assyrians. There was also, doubtless, much *truth* in this taunt. It was not permitted by the law of Moses for the Jews to keep cavalry, nor for their kings to multiply horses. The reason of this may be seen in the Notes on ch. ii. 7. Though some of the kings, and especially Solomon, had disregarded this law of Moses, yet Hezekiah had endeavoured to restore the observance of the law, and it is probable that he *had* no cavalry, and that the art of horsemanship *was* little known in Jerusalem. As the Assyrians prided themselves on their cavalry, they consequently looked with contempt on a people who were destitute of this means of defence.

9. *How then wilt thou turn away the face.* The most unimportant captain in the army of Assyria commands more horsemen than this, and how can you expect to oppose even him, much more how can you be able to resist all the mighty army of the Assyrians? ¶ *One captain of the least.* The word 'captain' here (פֶּחַת, construct state from פֶּחָה) denotes a *prefect* or *governor* of a province less than a satrap, an officer who was under the satrap, and subject to him. It is applied to an officer in the Assyrian empire (2 Kings xviii. 24); in the Chaldean empire (Jer.

11 Then said Eliak.m, and Sheb-na, and Joab, unto Rabshakeh, Speak, I pray thee, unto thy servants in the Syrian language ; for we understand *it:* and speak not to us in the Jews' language, in the ears of the people that *are* on the wall.

---

li. 23); the Persian (Esth. viii. 9; ix. 3); and to the prefects of Judea in the time of Solomon (1 Kings x. 15). The word is of foreign origin.

10. *And am I now come 'up without the* LORD. Am I come up without his permission or command? Rabshakeh here speaks in the name of his master ; and he means to say that he had the express command of JEHOVAH to inflict punishment on the Jews. It is *possible* that there had been conveyed to Sennacherib a rumour of what Isaiah had said (see ch. x. 5, 6) that God would bring the Assyrians upon the Jewish people to punish them for their sins, and that Rabshakeh now pleads that as his authority, in order to show them that resistance would be vain. Or it may be that he uses the name JEHOVAH here as synonymous with the name of GOD, and means to say that he had been *divinely directed* to come up in that expedition. All the ancient warriors usually consulted the gods, and endeavoured by auguries to obtain the Divine approbation of their plans of conquest, and Rabshakeh may mean simply to say that his master came now under the divine sanction and direction. Or, which is more probable, he made use of this as a mere pretence for the purpose of influencing the people who heard him, and to whom he said he was sent (ver. 12), in order to alienate their minds from Hezekiah, and to induce them to surrender. He knew that it was one of the *principles* of the Jews, however little they regarded it in practice, to yield to his authority. Wicked men will be glad to plead Divine authority for their purposes and plans when they can have the slightest pretence for it.

11. *Speak, I pray thee, unto thy servants in the Syrian language.* Heb. אֲרָמִית —' Aramean.' Aram, or Aramea, properly meaning *a high region*, or the *highlands*, was of wider extent than Syria Proper, and comprehended not only Syria, but Mesopotamia. It usually denotes however Syria Proper, of which the capital was Damascus. The language of all this country was probably the same—the Syrian or Aramean, a language of the same family as the Hebrew, and having a strong resemblance to that and to the Chaldee. This was not properly the language of *Assyria,* where probably a dialect composed of the language of the Medes and Persians was employed. But the Syriac language was spoken in different parts of Assyria. It was spoken in Mesopotamia, and doubtless in some of the provinces of the Assyrian empire, and might be presumed to be understood by Rabshakeh, and those with him. The Jews had intercourse with the Syrians, and those who had been sent out by Hezekiah had learned to speak that. It is not probable that they understood the Medo-Persian tongue that was spoken by the Assyrians usually. The Syriac or Aramean was probably the most common language which was spoken in that region. Its knowledge prevailed in the time of the Saviour, and was that which he usually spoke. ¶ *In the Jews' language* (יְהוּדִית). The language of *Judah.* It is remarkable that they did not call it the *Hebrew* language. But there might have been some national pride in regard to this. The Hebrew language had been the common language of all the Jews, and had been spoken by those of the kingdom of Israel or Samaria, as well as by those of the kingdom of Judah. But after the revolt of the ten tribes it is possible that they might have claimed the *language* as their own, and regarded the Hebrew — the venerable language of their fathers—as belonging to them peculiarly, as they claimed everything that was sacred or venerable in the nation, and hence they spoke of it as the language of *Judah.* The name of *Judah,* or *Jews,* which is derived from Judah, was, after the removal of the ten tribes, given to the entire nation—a name which is retained to the present time. In Isa. xix. 18, it is called the language of Canaan (see Note on that

12 But Rabshakeh said, Hath my *a* master sent me to thy master and to thee to speak these words?

Ps. 31. 18.

hath he not *sent me* to the men that sit upon the wall, that they may eat their own dung and drink their own piss with you?

place). ¶ *In the ears of the people that are on the wall.* This conference took place evidently near the city, and within hearing distance. Doubtless the people of the city, feeling a curiosity to hear the message of the Assyrian, crowded the walls. The Jewish ambassadors were apprehensive that what was said by Rabshakeh would alienate their minds from Hezekiah, and requested that the conference might be conducted in a language which they could not understand.

12. *Hath my master sent me to thy master and to thee?* To Hezekiah, and to you *alone.* A part of my purpose is to address the *people,* to induce them to leave Hezekiah, and to offer no resistance to the Assyrian. ¶ *To the men that sit on the wall,* &c. The meaning of this is, that the inhabitants of the city, if they do not surrender, will be subjected to the severest evils of famine. If they did not surrender, it was the purpose of the Assyrian to lay siege to the city, and to reduce it. But it was often the work of years to reduce and take a city. Nebuchadnezzar spent thirteen years before Tyre, and the Greeks employed ten in reducing ancient Troy. The sense here is, therefore, that unless the people could be induced to surrender to Sennacherib, they would be subjected to all the horrors of a siege, when they would be reduced to the most deplorable state of necessity and want. The idea in the whole verse is clearly expressed in the parallel place in 2 Chron. xxxii. 11: ' Doth not Hezekiah persuade you to give over yourselves to die by famine and by thirst, saying, The LORD our God shall deliver us out of the hand of the king of Assyria?'—In regard to the indelicacy of this passage, we may observe—1. That the Masorites in the Hebrew text have so *pointed* the words used, that in reading it the offensiveness would be considerably avoided. It is common in the Hebrew Scriptures, when a word is used in the text that is indelicate, to place another word in the

margin, and the vowel-points that belong to the word in the margin are applied to the word in the text, and the word in the margin is thus commonly read. In accordance with this custom among the Jews, it is evident that more delicacy might have been observed by our translators in this, and in some other places of the Scriptures. 2. The customs, habits, and modes of expression of people in different nations and times, differ. What appears indelicate at one time or in one country, may not only be tolerated, but common in another. Many things are esteemed indelicate among us which are not so in polite and refined France; many expressions are so regarded now which were not in the time when the Bible was translated into English. Many things may be to us offensive which were not so to the Syrians, the Babylonians, and the Jews; and many modes of expression which are common now, and consistent with all our notions of refinement, *may* appear improper in some other period of the world. There are many things in Shakspere, and in most of the old English writers, which cannot now be read without a blush. Yet need I say that those expressions will be heard with unconcern in *the theatre* by those whose delicacy is most offended by some expression in the Bible? There are things infinitely more offensive to delicacy in Byron, and Moore, and even Burns, than there are in the Scriptures; and yet are these not read without a murmur by those who make the loudest complaints of the slightest departure from delicacy in the Bible? 3. There is another remark to be made in regard to this. Isaiah is not at all responsible for the indelicacy of the language here. He is simply a historian. He did not *say* it; nor is he responsible for it. If there is indelicacy in it, it is not in *recording* it, but in *saying* it; and the responsibility is on Rabshakeh. If Isaiah undertook to make a record of an important transaction, what right

13 Then Rabshakeh stood, and cried with *a* a loud voice in the Jews' language, and said, Hear ye the words of the *b* great king, the king of Assyria.

14 Thus saith the king. Let not Hezekiah deceive you : for he shall not be able to deliver you.

15 Neither *c* let Hezekiah make you trust in the LORD, saying, The LORD will surely deliver us :

a Ps.17.10-13.   *b* Ps.82.6,7; Dan.4.37.   *c* Ps.71.10,11.

this city shall not be delivered into the hand of the king of Assyria.

16 Hearken not to Hezekiah : for thus saith the king of Assyria, Make ¹ *an agreement* with me *by* a present, and come out to me : and eat ye every one of his vine, *d* and every one of his fig-tree, and drink ye every one the waters of his own cistern ;

1 *with me a blessing,* or, *seek my favour by a present.*
d Zech.3.10.

had he to abridge it, or contract it, or to make it different from what it was ? 4. And again : it was of importance to give the *true character* of the attack which was made on Jerusalem. The coming of Sennacherib was attended with pride, and insolence, and blasphemy ; and it was important to state the true character of the transaction, and to record *just what was said and done.* Hence Isaiah, as a faithful historian, recorded the coming of the Assyrians ; the expressions of their haughtiness, insolence, and pride ; their vain boasting, and their reproaches of JEHOVAH ; and for the same reason he has recorded the gross and indelicate *language* which they used to add to the trials of the Jews. Let him who *used* the language, and not him who *recorded* it, bear the blame.

13. *Then Rabshakeh stood.* Indicating the posture of a man who intends to speak to them at a distance. ¶ *And cried with a loud voice.* So that those on the wall could hear. ¶ *The words of the king,* &c. (see Note on ver. 4.)

14. *Let not Hezekiah deceive you.* By inducing you to put your trust in JEHOVAH or in himself, or with promises that you will be delivered. ¶ *Not be able to deliver you.* In 2 Kings xviii. 29, it is added, ' out of his hand ;' but the sense is substantially the same.

15. *Make you trust in the* LORD. Rabshakeh knew that Hezekiah was professedly devoted to JEHOVAH, and that he would endeavour to induce the people to trust in him. The Jews had now no other refuge but God, and as long as they put their confidence there, even Rabshakeh knew that it was hazardous to attempt to take and de-

stroy their city. It was his policy, therefore, first to endeavour to undermine their reliance on God, before he could have any hope of success. The enemies of God's people cannot succeed in their designs against them until they can unsettle their confidence in Him.

16. *Hearken not to Hezekiah.* Do not listen to his entreaties to confide in him, and in JEHOVAH ; do not unite with him in endeavouring to make any resistance or opposition to us. ¶ *Make* an agreement *with me* by *a present.* The LXX. read this, Εἰ βούλεσθε εὐλογηθῆναι—' If you wish to be blessed, or happy, come out to me.' The Hebrew is literally, ' Make with me a blessing ' (בְּרָכָה). The idea of its being done ' by a present,' is not in the Hebrew text. The word ' blessing ' here probably means the same as *peace.* ' Make peace with me,' perhaps because peace was regarded as a blessing ; and perhaps the word is used with a reference to one of the significations of בָּרַךְ, which is *to kneel down,* and this word may refer to their *kneeling down ;* that is, to their offering allegiance to the king of Assyria. The former is, however, the more probable sense, that the word means *peace,* because this was an evident blessing, or would be the source of rich blessings to them. It is not, however, used in this sense elsewhere in the Bible. The Chaldee renders it, ' Make peace (שְׁלָמָא) with me.' ¶ *And come out to me.* Surrender yourselves to me. It is evident, however, that he did not mean that he would *then* remove them from their city and country, but he demanded a surrender, intending to come and re-

17 Until *a* I come and take you
away to a land like your own land,
a land of corn and wine, a land of
bread and vineyards.

18 *Beware* lest Hezekiah persuade you, saying, The LORD will
deliver us : *b* Hath any of the gods

of the nations delivered his land
out of the hand of the king of Assyria ?

19 Where *are* the gods of Hamath and Arphad ? where *are* the
gods of Sepharvaim ? and have

a Prov.12.10.   b Dan.3.15.

move them at some other period (ver.
17). ¶ *And eat ye every one of his
own vine.* An emblem of safety, when
every man might be permitted to partake of the fruit of his own labour. All
that he now professed to desire was,
that they should surrender the city,
and give up their means of defence,
and *then* he would leave them in
security and quietness, *until* it should
please his master to come and remove
them to a land as fertile as their own.
¶ *And drink ye every one.* Another
emblem of security and happiness. This
promise was made to induce them to
surrender. On the one hand, he threatened them with the dreadful evils of
famine if they refused and allowed their
city to be besieged (ver. 12) ; and on
the other, he promised them, for a time
at least, a quiet and secure residence in
their own city, and then a removal to a
land not inferior to their own.

17. *Until I come.* These are the
words of the king of Assyria delivered
by Rabshakeh. It was proposed that
they should remain safely in Jerusalem
until Sennacherib should himself come
and remove them to his own land. He
was now engaged in the siege of Lachish
(ver. 2), and it is probable that he purposed to take some other of the unsubdued towns in that part of Palestine.
¶ *And take you away.* It was common
for conquerors in ancient times to remove a vanquished people from their
own country. They did this either by
sending them forth in colonies to people
some unsettled region, or by removing
the body of them to the land of the
conqueror. This was done for various
purposes. It was sometimes to make
slaves of them ; sometimes for the purposes of triumph ; but more commonly
to secure them from revolt.   In this
manner the ten tribes were removed
from the kingdom of Samaria ; and
thus also the Jews were carried to

Babylon. Suetonius says (ch. xxi.) of
Augustus, that he removed the Suevi
and the Sicambri into Gaul, and stationed them on the Rhine. The same
thing was also practised in Egypt, for
the purpose of securing the people from
revolt (Gen. xlvii. 21). ¶ *A land like
your own land.* A fertile land, abounding in the same productions as your
own. ¶ *And wine.* Palestine was
celebrated for the vine. The idea is,
that in the land to which he would
remove them, they should not want.

18. *Hath any of the gods of the nations,* &c. This is said to show them
the impossibility, as he supposed, of
being delivered from the arm of the
king of Assyria. He had conquered
all before him, and not even the gods
of the nations had been able to rescue
the lands where they were worshipped
from the hands of the victorious invader.
He *inferred,* therefore, that JEHOVAH,
the God of Palestine, could not save
their land.

19. *Where* are *the gods of Hamath,*
&c. In regard to these places, see
Notes on ch. x. 9–11. ¶ *Where* are
the gods of Sepharvaim? Sepharvaim
was probably in Mesopotamia. Ptolemy
mentions a city there of the name of
Sipphara, as the most southern city of
Mesopotamia, which is probably the
same. It is evident that it was in the
vicinity of Hamath and Arphad, and
these are known to have been in Mesopotamia. When Shalmaneser carried
Israel away captive from Samaria, he
sent colonies of people into Palestine in
their stead, among whom were the
Sepharvaim (2 Kings xvii. 24, 31).
¶ *And have they delivered Samaria*
(see Note on ch. x. 11). The author
of the Books of Chronicles expresses
this in a more summary manner, and
says, that Rabshakeh joined JEHOVAH
with the gods of the nations in the
same language of reproach : ' And he

they delivered Samaria out *a* of my hand?

20 Who *are they* among all the gods *b* of these lands that have delivered their land out of my hand, that the LORD should deliver Jerusalem out of my hand?

21 But they held their peace, and answered him not a word: for

a 2 Ki.18.10.

the king's commandment was, saying, Answer him *c* not.

22 Then came Eliakim the son of Hilkiah, that *was* over the household, and Shebna the scribe, and Joah the son of Asaph, the recorder, to Hezekiah with *their* clothes rent, and told him the words of Rabshakeh.

b ch.37.18,19; 45.16,17.   *c* Prov.26.4.

spake against the God of Jerusalem, as against the gods of the people of the

earth, which were the work of the hands of man ' (2 Chron. xxxii. 19).

HAMATH, VIEW OF THE CITY AND AQUEDUCT.—From Laborde's Syria.

21. *But they held their peace.* Hezekiah had commanded them not to answer. They were simply *to hear* what Rabshakeh had to propose, and to report to him, that he might decide on what course to pursue. It was a case also in which it was every way proper that they should be silent. There was so much insolence, self-confidence, blasphemy, the proposals were so degrading, and the claims were so arrogant, that it was not proper that they should enter into conference, or listen a moment to the terms proposed. Their minds also were so horror-stricken with the language of insolence and blasphemy, and their hearts so pained by the circumstances of the city, that they would not feel like replying to him.—There *are* circumstances when it is proper to maintain a profound silence in the presence

of revilers and blasphemers, and when we should withdraw from them, and go and spread the case before the LORD. This was done here (ch. xxxvii. 1), and the result showed that this was the course of wisdom.

22. *With* their *clothes rent.* This was a common mark of grief among the Jews (see 2 Sam iii. 21; 1 Kings xxi. 27; Ezra ix. 3; Job i. 20; ii. 12; Jer. xxxvi. 24; and Notes on Matt. xxvi. 65; Acts xiv. 14). The *causes* of their griefs were the insolence and arrogance of Rabshakeh ; the proposal to surrender the city ; the threatening of the siege on the one hand, and of the removal on the other, and the blasphemy of the name of their God, and the reproach of the king. All these things filled their hearts with grief, and they hastened to make report to Hezekiah.

CHAPTER XXXVII.

ANALYSIS.

This chapter contains a continuation of the historical narrative commenced in the previous chapter. Hezekiah went with expressions of grief to the temple, to spread the cause of his distress before the Lord (1). He sent an embassage to Isaiah to ask his counsel in the time of the general distress (2–5). Isaiah replied that he should not be afraid of the Assyrian, for that he should soon be destroyed (6, 7). The return of Rabshakeh to Sennacherib (8). Sennacherib heard that Tirhakah, king of Ethiopia, was preparing to make war upon him, and sent another embassay, with substantially the same message as the former, to induce him to surrender (9–13). Hezekiah having read the letter which he sent, went again to the temple, and spread it before the Lord (14). His prayer is recorded (15–20). Isaiah, in answer to his prayer, reproves the pride and arrogance of Sennacherib, and gives the assurance that Jerusalem shall be safe, and that the Assyrian shall be destroyed (21–35). The chapter closes

CHAPTER XXXVII.

1. *When king Hezekiah heard* it. Heard the account of the words of Rabshakeh (ch. xxxvi. 22). ¶ *That he rent his clothes* (see Note on ch. xxxvi. 22). ¶ *He covered himself with sackcloth* (see Note on ch. iii. 24). ¶ *And went into the house of the* Lord. Went up to the temple to spread out the case before Jehovah (ver. 14). This was in accordance with the usual habit of Hezekiah ; and it teaches us that when we are environed with difficulties or danger, and when the name of our God is blasphemed, we should go and spread out our feelings before God, and seek his aid.

2. *And he sent Eliakim* (see Note on ch. xxxvi. 3). ¶ *And the elders of the priests.* It was a case of deep importance, and one that pertained in a special manner to the interests of religion ; and he, therefore, selected the most respectable embassage that he could to present the case to the prophet. ¶ *Covered with sackcloth.* Religion had been insulted. The God whom the priests served had been blasphemed, and the very temple was threatened, and it was proper that the *priests* should go with the habiliments of mourning. ¶ *Unto Isaiah.* It was customary on occasions

with an account of the destruction of the army of the Assyrians, and the death of Sennacherib (36–38).

AND *a* it came to pass when king Hezekiah heard *it*, that he rent *b* his clothes, and covered himself with sackcloth, and went *c* into the house of the Lord.

2 And he sent Eliakim, who *was* over the household, and Shebna the scribe, and the elders of the priests, covered with *d* sackcloth, unto Isaiah the prophet the son of Amoz.

3 And they said unto him, Thus saith Hezekiah, This day *is* a day of *e* trouble, and of rebuke, *f* and of blasphemy : [1] for the children are come to the birth, and *there g is* not strength to bring forth.

a 2 Ki 19.1,&c.   b Job 1.20.   c ver. 14.
d Joel 1.13.   e Ps 50.15.   f ch.25.8; Rev.3.19.
1 or, *provocation.*   g ch.66.9.

of danger to consult prophets, as those who had direct communication with God, and seek counsel from them. Thus Balak sent messengers to Balaam to consult him in a time of perplexity (Num. xxii. 5, *sq.*) ; thus Jehoshaphat and the king of Israel consulted Micaiah in time of danger from Syria (1 Kings xxii. 1–13) ; thus Ahaziah, when sick, sent to consult Elijah (2 Kings i. 1–9) ; and thus Josiah sent an embassage to Huldah the prophetess to inquire in regard to the book which was found in the temple of the Lord (2 Kings xxii. 14.)

3. *This is a day of rebuke.* This may refer either to the reproaches of Rabshakeh, or more probably to the fact that Hezekiah regarded the Lord as *rebuking* his people for their sins. The word which is here used (תּוֹכֵחָה), means more properly *chastisement* or *punishment* (Ps. cxlix. 7 ; Hos. v. 9). ¶ *And of blasphemy.* Marg. ' Provocation.' The word here used (נְאָצָה), means properly *reproach* or *contumely ;* and the sense is, that God and his cause had been vilified by Rabshakeh, and it was proper to appeal to him to vindicate the honour of his own name (ver. 4). ¶ *For the children are come,* &c. The meaning of this figure is plain. There was

4 It may be the LORD thy God will hear the words of Rabshakeh, whom the king of Assyria his master hath sent to reproach *a* the living God, and will reprove the words which the LORD thy God hath heard : wherefore lift up *thy* prayer for the *b* remnant that is left. 1

5 So the servants of king Hezekiah came to Isaiah.

a ver.23,24; ch.51,7,8.　　*b* Ro.9.27.　　1 *found.*

6 And Isaiah said unto them, Thus shall ye say unto your master. Thus saith the LORD, Be not afraid of *c* the words that thou hast heard, wherewith the servants of the king of Assyria have blasphemed me.

7 Behold, I will ² send a blast upon him, and he shall hear a rumour, and return to his own land ; and I will cause him to fall by the sword in his own land.

c ch.43.1,2; 51.12,13.
2 or, *put a spirit into him;* 1 Ki.22.23.

the highest danger, and need of aid. It was as in childbirth in which the pains had been protracted, the strength exhausted, and where there was most imminent danger in regard to the mother and the child. So Hezekiah said there was the most imminent danger in the city of Jerusalem. They had made all possible preparations for defence. And now, in the most critical time, they felt their energies exhausted, their strength insufficient for their defence, and they needed the interposition of God.

4. *It may be the* LORD *thy God.* The God whom thou dost serve, and in whose name and by whose authority thou dost exercise the prophetic office. ¶ *Will hear the words.* Will come forth and vindicate himself in regard to the language of reproach and blasphemy which has been used. See a similar use of the word 'hear' in Ex. ii. 24 ; iii. 7. ¶ *To reproach the living God.* The revilings of Rabshakeh were really directed against the true God. The reproach of the 'living God' consisted in comparing him to idols, and saying that he was no more able to defend Jerusalem than the idol-gods had been able to defend their lands (see Note on ch. xxxvi. 18). The phrase 'the *living* God' is often applied to JEHOVAH in contradistinction from idols, which were mere blocks of wood or stone. ¶ *For the remnant that is left.* For those who survive ; or probably for those parts of the land, including Jerusalem, that have not fallen into the hands of the Assyrian. Sennacherib had taken many towns, but there were many also that had not yet been subdued by him.

6. *Wherewith the servants,* &c. Heb.

נְעָרֵי —The 'youth,' or the young men. The word properly denotes boys, youths, young men ; and is used here probably by way of disparagement, in contradistinction from an embassy that would be truly respectable, made up of aged men. ¶ *Have blasphemed me.* God regarded these words as spoken against himself, and he would vindicate his own honour and name.

7. *Behold, I will send a blast upon him.* Marg. 'Put a spirit into him.' The word rendered 'blast' (רוּחַ) is commonly rendered 'spirit.' It *may* denote breath, air, soul, or spirit. There is no reason to think that the word is here used in the sense of *blast* of wind, as our translators seem to have supposed. The sense is probably, ' I will infuse into him a spirit of *fear,* by which he shall be alarmed by the rumour which he shall hear, and return to his own land.' The word is often used in this sense (comp. 1 Sam. xvi. 14; see also Isa. xxxi. 8, 9). Gesenius understands it here in the sense of *will* or *disposition.* ' I will change his will or disposition, so that he will return to his own land.' ¶ *And he shall hear a rumour.* The rumour or report here referred to, was doubtless that respecting Tirhakah king of Ethiopia (ver. 9). It was this which would alarm him, and drive him in haste from the cities which he was now besieging, and be the means of expelling him from the land. ¶ *And I will cause him,* &c. This is said in accordance with the usual statements in the Scriptures, that *all* events are under God's providential control (comp. Note on ch. x. 5, 6). ¶ *By the sword in his own land* (see Note on ver. 38).

8 So Rabshakeh returned, and found the king of Assyria warring against Libnah : *a* for he had heard that he was departed from *b* Lachish.

9 And he heard say concerning

a Num.33.20,21; Jos.21.13; 2 Ch.21.10.

Tirhakah king of Ethiopia, He is come forth to make war with thee. And when he heard *it*, he sent messengers to Hezekiah, saying,

10 Thus shall ye speak to Heze-

b Jos.10.31-34.

---

8. *So Rabshakeh returned.* Returned from Jerusalem to the camp of his master. He had received no answer to his insulting message (ch. xxxvi. 21); he saw there was no prospect that the city would surrender ; and he therefore returned again to the camp. ¶ *And found the king of Assyria warring against Libnah.* He had departed from Lachish. Why he had done this is unknown. It is possible that he had taken it, though this is not recorded anywhere in history. Or it is possible that he had found it impracticable to subdue it as speedily as he had desired; and had withdrawn from it for the purpose of subduing other places that would offer a more feeble resistance. Libnah was a city in the south of Judah (Josh. xv. 42), given to the priests, and declared a city of refuge (1 Chron. vi. 54, 57). Eusebius and Jerome say it was in the district of Eleutheropolis (Calmet). It was about ten miles to the north-west of Lachish. This city was taken by Joshua, and all its inhabitants put to the sword. After taking this, Joshua next assaulted and took Lachish (Josh. x. 29-32).

9. *And he heard say.* The report or rumour referred to in ver. 7. In what way he heard this is not intimated. It is probable that the preparations which Tirhakah had made, were well known to the surrounding regions, and that he was already on his march against Sennacherib. ¶ *Tirhakah.* This king, who, by Eusebius and by most ancient writers, is called Ταρακὸς (*Tarakos*), was a celebrated conqueror, and had subdued Egypt to himself. He reigned over Egypt eighteen years. When Sennacherib marched into Egypt, Sevechus or Sethon was on the throne. Sennacherib having laid siege to Pelusium, Tirhakah came to the aid of the city, and, in consequence of his aid, Sennacherib was compelled to raise the siege and returned to Palestine, and laid

siege to Lachish. Tirhakah succeeded Sevechus in Egypt, and was the third and last of the Ethiopian kings that reigned over that country. He probably took advantage of the distracted state that succeeded the death of Sevechus, and secured the crown for himself. This was, however, after the death of Sennacherib. The capital which he occupied was Thebes (see Prideaux's *Connection*, vol. i. pp. 141, 145, 149. Ed. 1815). As he was celebrated as a conqueror, and as he had driven Sennacherib from Pelusium and from Egypt, we may see the cause of the alarm of Sennacherib when it was rumoured that he was about to follow him into Palestine, and to make war on him there. ¶ *He is come forth.* He has made preparations, and is on his way. ¶ *He sent messengers*, &c. With letters or despatches (ver. 14). Hezekiah was probably ignorant of the approach of Tirhakah, or at all events Sennacherib would suppose that he was ignorant of it ; and as Sennacherib knew that there would be no hope that Hezekiah would yield if he knew that Tirhakah was approaching to make war on him, he seems to have resolved to anticipate the intelligence, and to see if it were possible to induce him to surrender. He, therefore, sent substantially the same message as before, and summoned him to capitulate.

10. *Let not thy God deceive thee.* The similar message which had been sent by Rabshakeh (ch. xxxvi. 14, 15) had been sent mainly *to the people* to induce them not to put confidence in Hezekiah, as if he would deceive them by leading them to rely on the aid of JEHOVAH. As that had failed, he, as a last resort, sent a similar message to Hezekiah himself, designed to alienate *his mind* from God, and assuring him that resistance would be vain. To convince him, he referred him (ver. 11-13) to the conquests of the Assyrians,

kiah king of Judah, saying, Let not thy God, in whom thou trustest, deceive thee, saying, Jerusalem shall not be given into the hand of the king of Assyria.

11 Behold, thou hast heard what the kings of Assyria have done to *a* all lands by destroying

a ch.14.17.   b 2 Ki.17.6; 18.11.

them utterly ; and shalt thou be delivered ?

12 Have the gods of the nations delivered them which my fathers have destroyed, *as* *b* Gozan, and Haran,*c* and Rezeph, and the children of *d* Eden which *were* in Telassar ?

c Gen.12.4; 28.10.   d Amos 1.5

and assured him that it would be impossible to resist a nation that had subdued so many others. He had it not in his power to add *Egypt* to the list of subdued kingdoms, or it would have been done.

11. *And shalt thou be delivered ?* How will it be possible for you to stand out against the conquerors of the world ?

12. *My fathers.* My predecessors on the throne. ¶ *Gozan.* This was a region or country in the northern part of Mesopotamia, and on the river Chaboras. There was a river of the name of *Gozan* in Media, which ran through the province, and gave it its name. The river fell probably into the Chaboras. This region is known to have been under the dominion of Assyria, for Shalmaneser, when he had subdued the ten tribes, carried them away beyond the Euphrates to a country bordering on the river Gozan (2 Kings xvii. 6). According to Gesenius, the river which is referred to, is the Chaboras itself. He translates the passage in 2 Kings xvii. 6, thus: 'And placed them in Chaleitis (Halah), and on the Chabor (Habor), a river of Gozan, and in the cities of the Medes.' According to this, the river was the Chaboras, the Chabor of Ezekiel, and the region was situated on the Chaboras. This river falls into the Euphrates from the east. Ptolemy calls the region lying between the Chaboras and Laocoras by the name of *Gauzanitis,* which is doubtless the same as the Hebrew *Gozan.* Gozan is usually mentioned in connection with cities of Mesopotamia (2 Kings xix. 42; 1 Chron. v. 26). ¶ *And Haran.* This was a city of Mesopotamia, to which Abraham went after he left Ur of the Chaldees. His father died here; and from this place he was called to go

into the land of promise (Gen. xi. 31, 32; comp. Notes on Acts vii. 4). It is now called *Harran,* and is situated in lat. 36° 52′ N. ; lon. 39° 5′ E., in a flat and sandy plain, and is only peopled by a few wandering Arabs, who select it as the place of residence on account of the delicious waters it contains. It belonged by conquest to the Assyrian empire. ¶ *And Rezeph.* According to Abulfeda, there were many towns of this name. One, however, was more celebrated than the others, and is probably the one here referred to. It was situated about a day's journey west of the Euphrates, and is mentioned by Ptolemy by the name of 'Ρησαφα (*Resapha*). ¶ *And the children of Eden.* Eden was evidently a country well known in the time of Isaiah, and was, doubtless, the tract *within* which man was placed when he was created. The garden or Paradise was *in* Eden, and was not properly itself called Eden (Gen. ii. 8). It is probable that Eden was a region or tract of country of considerable extent. Its situation has been a subject of anxious inquiry. It is not proper here to go into an examination of this subject. It is evident from the passage before us that it was either in Mesopotamia, or in the neighbourhood of that country, since it is mentioned in connection with cities and towns of that region. It is mentioned by Amos (B.C. 787), as a country then well known, and as a part of Syria, not far from Damascus :

I will break also the bar of Damascus,
And cut off the inhabitant from the plain of Aven,
And him that holdeth the sceptre *from the house of* Eden,
And the people of Syria shall go into captivity to Kir,
Saith the Lord.   Amos i. 5.

In Isa. li. 3, Eden is referred to as a

13 Where *is* the king of *a* Hamath, and the king of Arphad, and the king of the city of Sepharvaim, Ilena, and Ivah?

14 And Hezekiah received the letter from the hand of the messengers, and read it: and Hezekiah went up *b* unto the house of

a ch.x.9; Jer.49.23.   *b* ver.1; Joel 2.17-20.
c Ex.25.22; Ps 80.1; 99.1.   *d* ch.43.10,11.   *e* Ps.86.10.

the LORD, and spread it before the LORD.

15 And Hezekiah prayed unto the LORD, saying,

16 O LORD of hosts, God of Israel, that dwellest *c between* the cherubims, thou *d art* the God, *even* thou *e* alone, of all the kingdoms of the earth: thou hast made heaven and earth.

country well known, and as distinguished for its fertility:

For JEHOVAH shall comfort Zion;
He will comfort all her waste places,
And he will make her wilderness *like Eden*,
And her desert like the garden of JEHOVAH.

Thus also in Ezek. xxvii. 23, we find Eden mentioned in connection with Haran and Canneh. Canneh was probably the same as Calneh (Gen. x. 10), the Calno of Isaiah (ch. x. 9), and was, doubtless, situated in Mesopotamia, since it is joined with cities that are known to have been there (comp. also Ezek. xxxi. 9, 16, 18). All these passages demonstrate that there was such a country, and prove also that it was either in Mesopotamia, or in a country adjacent to Mesopotamia. It is not, however, possible now to designate its exact boundaries. ¶ *In Telassar.* This place is nowhere else mentioned in the Scriptures. Nothing, therefore, is known of its situation. The connection demands that it should be in Mesopotamia. The names of ancient places were so often lost or changed that it is often impossible to fix their exact locality.

13. *The king of Hamath* (see Note on ch. xxxvi. 19). ¶ *Hena and Ivah.* Hena is mentioned in 2 Kings xviii. 34; xix. 13. It was evidently in Mesopotamia, and was probably the same which was afterwards called *Ana*, situated near a ford of the Euphrates. The situation of Ivah is not certainly known. It was under the Assyrian dominion, and was one of the places from which colonists were brought to Samaria (2 Kings xvii. 24, 31). Michaelis supposes that it was between Berytus and Tripoli, but was under the dominion of the Assyrians.

14. *And Hezekiah received the letter.* Heb. 'Letters' (*plural*). It is

not mentioned in the account of the embassy (ver. 9), that a letter was sent, but it is not probable that an embassage would be sent to a monarch without a written document. ¶ *Went up into the house of the* LORD. The temple (ver. 1). ¶ *And spread it before the* LORD. Perhaps unrolled the document there, and spread it out; or perhaps it means simply that he spread out the contents of the letter, that is, made mention of it in his prayer. Hezekiah had no other resource. He was a man of God; and in his trouble he looked to God for aid. He, therefore, before he formed any plan, went up to the temple, and laid his case before God. What an example for all monarchs and rulers! And what an example for all the people of God, in times of perplexity!

16. *O* LORD *of hosts* (see Note on ch. i. 9). ¶ *That dwellest* between *the cherubims.* On the cherubim, see Note on ch, xiv. 13. The reference here is doubtless to the fact that the symbol of the Divine presence in the temple—the Shechinah (from שָׁכַן *shákhán, to dwell, to inhabit;* so called because it was the symbol of God's *dwelling* with his people or *inhabiting* the temple)—rested on the cover of the ark in the temple. Hence God is frequently represented as dwelling between the cherubim (Ex. xxv. 22; Ps. lxxx. 1; xcix. 1). On the whole subject of the cherubim, the reader may consult an article in the *Quarterly Christian Spectator* for September 1836. ¶ *Thou* art *the God.* The only God (ch. xliii. 10, 11). ¶ Even *thou alone.* There is none besides thee —a truth which is often affirmed in the Scriptures (Deut. xxxii. 39; Ps. lxxxvi. 10; 1 Cor. viii. 4). ¶ *Thou hast made heaven and earth.* It was on the ground of this power and universal

17 Incline *a* thine ear, O LORD, and hear ; open thine eyes, *b* O LORD, and see: and hear all the words of Sennacherib, which hath sent to reproach the living God.

18 Of a truth, LORD, the kings of Assyria have laid waste all the nations, [1] and their countries,

19 And have [2] cast their gods

into the fire: for they *were* no gods, but *c* the work of men's hands, wood and stone: therefore they have destroyed them.

20 Now, therefore, O LORD our God, save us from his hand, that all the kingdoms of the earth may know *d* that thou *art* the LORD, *even* thou only.

a Dan.9.18.   *b* Job 36.7.   1 *lands.*   2 *given.*

c Ps.115.4,&c.; ch.40.19,20; 41.7; 44.9,&c.
d ch.42.8; Ps.46.10.

dominion that Hezekiah pleaded that God would interpose.

17. *Incline thine ear.* This is evidently language taken from what occurs among men. When they are desirous of hearing distinctly, they incline the ear or apply it close to the speaker. Similar language is not unfrequently used in the Scriptures as applicable to God (2 Kings xix. 16; Ps. lxxxvi. 1; xxxi. 2; lxxxviii. 2; Dan. ix. 18). ¶ *Open thine eyes.* This is similar language applied to God, derived from the fact that when we wish to see an object, the eyes are fixed upon it (comp. Job xiv. 3; xxvii. 19). ¶ *And hear all the words.* That is, attend to their words, and inflict suitable punishment. This was the burden of the prayer of Hezekiah, that God would vindicate his own honour, and save his name from reproach. ¶ *Which he hath sent.* In the letters which he had sent to Hezekiah, as well as the words which he had sent to the people by Rabshakeh (ch. xxxvi. 18–20). ¶ *To reproach the living God* (see Note on ver. 4).

18. *Of a truth.* It is as he has said, that all the nations had been subjected to the arms of the Assyrian. He now intends to add Jerusalem to the number of vanquished cities and kingdoms, and to boast that he has subdued the nation under the protection of JEHOVAH, as he had done the nations under the protection of idol-gods. ¶ *Have laid waste all the nations.* Heb. as Marg. ' All the lands.' But this is evidently an elliptical form of expression, meaning all the inhabitants or people of the lands. In 2 Kings xix. 17, it is thus expressed : ' The kings of Assyria have destroyed the nations and their lands.'

19. *And have cast their gods into*

the fire. This appears to have been the usual policy of the Assyrians and Babylonians. It was contrary to the policy which the Romans afterwards pursued, for they admitted the gods of other nations among their own, and even allowed them to have a place in the Pantheon. Their design seems not to have been to alienate the feelings of the vanquished, but to make them feel that they were a part of the same people. They supposed that a vanquished people would be conciliated with the idea that their gods were admitted to participate in the honours of those which were worshipped by the conquerors of the world. But the policy of the Eastern conquerors was different. They began usually by removing the people themselves whom they had subdued, to another land (see Note on ch. xxxvi. 17). They thus intended to alienate their minds as much as possible from their own country. They laid everything waste by fire and sword, and thus destroyed their homes, and all the objects of their attachment. They destroyed their temples, their groves, and their household gods. They well knew that the civil policy of the nation was founded *in religion*, and that, to subdue them effectually, it was necessary to abolish their religion. Which was the wisest policy, may indeed admit of question. Perhaps in each case the policy was well adapted to the particular end which was had in view. ¶ *For they* were *no gods.* They were not truly gods, and therefore they had no power of resistance, and it was easy to destroy them.

20. *That all the kingdoms of the earth may know.* Since he has been able to subdue all others ; and since Judea alone, the land under the pro-

21 Then Isaiah the son of Amoz sent unto Hezekiah, saying, Thus saith the LORD God of Israel, Whereas thou hast prayed *a* to me against Sennacherib king of Assyria:

22 This *is* the word which the LORD hath spoken concerning him; The virgin, the daughter of Zion,

hath despised *b* thee, *and* laughed thee to scorn ; the daughter of Jerusalem hath shaken her head at thee.

23 Whom hast thou reproached and blasphemed ? and against whom hast thou exalted *thy* voice, and lifted up thine eye on high? *even* against the Holy One of Israel.

a Prov.15.29; Lu.18.1.   *b* Ps.31.18; 46.1,2.

---

tection of JEHOVAH, would be saved, all the nations would know that it could not be by the power of an idol. The desire of Hezekiah, therefore, was not primarily that of his own personal safety or the safety of his kingdom. It was that JEHOVAH might vindicate his great and holy name from reproach, and that the world might know that he was the only true God. A supreme regard to the glory of God influenced this pious monarch in his prayers, and we have here a beautiful model of the object which we should have in view when we come before God. It is not primarily that we may be saved ; it is not, as the leading motive, that our friends or that the world may be saved ; it is *that the name of God may be honoured.* This motive of prayer is one that is with great frequency presented in the Bible (comp. ch. xlii. 8; xliii. 10, 13, 25; Deut. xxxii. 39 ; Ps. xlvi. 10; lxxxiii. 18; Neh. ix. 6; Dan. ix. 18, 19).—Perhaps there could have been furnished no more striking proof that JEHOVAH was the true God, than would be by the defeat of Sennacherib. No other nation had been able to resist the Assyrian arms. The great power of that empire was now concentrated in the single army of Sennacherib. He was coming with great confidence of success. He was approaching the city devoted to JEHOVAH—the city where the temple was, and the city and people that were everywhere understood to be under his protection. The affairs of the world had arrived at a crisis ; and the time had come when the great JEHOVAH could strike a blow which would be felt on all nations, and carry the terror of his name, and the report of his power throughout the earth. Perhaps this was one of the main motives of the

destruction of that mighty army. God intended that his power should be felt, and that monarchs and people that arrayed themselves against him, and blasphemed him, should have a striking demonstration that he was God, and that none of the devices of his enemies could succeed.

21. *Whereas thou hast prayed.* Because thou hast come to me instead of relying on thy own resources and strength. In 2 Kings xix. 20, it is, 'That which thou hast prayed to me against Sennacherib, king of Assyria, I have heard.'

22. *The virgin, the daughter of Zion.* Jerusalem (see Note on ch. i. 8; comp. Note on ch. xxiii. 12). The parallelism in this and the following verses shows that the poetic form of speech is here introduced. ¶ *Hast despised thee.* That is, it is secure from thy contemplated attack. The idea is, that Jerusalem would exult over the ineffectual attempts of Sennacherib to take it, and over his complete overthrow. ¶ *Hath laughed thee to scorn.* Will make thee an object of derision. ¶ *Hath shaken her head at thee.* This is an indication of contempt and scorn (comp. Ps. xxii. 7; cix. 25; Jer. xviii. 16; Zeph. ii. 15; Matt. xxvii. 39).

23. *Whom hast thou reproached ?* Not an idol. Not one who has no power to take vengeance, or to defend the city under his protection, but the living God. ¶ *Exalted thy voice.* That is, by thy messenger. Thou hast spoken in a loud, confident tone ; in the language of reproach and threatening. ¶ *And lifted up thine eyes on high.* To lift up the eyes is an indication of haughtiness and pride. He had evinced arrogance in his manner, and he was yet to learn that it was against the living and true God.

24 By [1] thy servants hast thou reproached the LORD, and hast said, By the multitude of my chariots am I come up to the height of the mountains, to the sides of Leba-non; and I will cut down the [2] tall cedars thereof, *and* the choice fir-trees thereof: and I will enter into the height of his border, [3] *and* the forest of his Carmel.

1 *the hand of thy.*

2 *tallness of the cedars thereof, and the choice of the fir-trees thereof.* 3 or, and *his fruitful field.*

24. *By thy servants.* Heb. 'By the hand of thy servants.' That is, by Rabshakeh (ch. xxxvi.), and by those whom he had now sent to Hezekiah with letters (ver. 9, 14). ¶ *And hast said.* Isaiah does not here quote the precise *words* which Rabshakeh or the other messengers had used, but quotes the substance of what had been uttered, and expresses the real feelings and intentions of Sennacherib. ¶ *By the multitude of my chariots.* The word ' chariots' here denotes *war-chariots* (see Notes on ch. ii. 7; lxvi. 20). ¶ *To the height of the mountains.* Lebanon is here particularly referred to. Chariots were commonly used, as cavalry was, in plains. But it is probable that Lebanon was accessible by chariots drawn by horses. ¶ *To the sides of Lebanon.* On the situation of Lebanon, see Notes on ch. x. 34; xxix. 17. Sennacherib is represented as having carried desolation to Lebanon, and as having cut down its stately trees (see Note on

CYPRESS TREE (*Cupressus Sempervirens*).

ch. xxxiii. 9). ¶ *I will cut down the tall cedars thereof.* Marg. 'The tall-ness of the cedars thereof.' The boast of Sennacherib was that he would strip it of its beauty and ornament; that is, that he would lay the land waste. ¶ And *the choice fir-trees thereof* (see Note on ch. xiv. 8). The LXX. render it, Υπαρξισσου—'The beauty of the cypress.' The word here denotes the *cypress*, a tree resembling the white cedar. It grew on Lebanon, and, together with the cedar, constituted its glory. Its wood, like that of the cedar, was employed for the floors and ceilings of the temple (1 Kings v. 22, 24; vi. 15, 34). It was used for the decks and sheathing of ships (Ezek. xxvii. 5); for spears (Neh. ii. 4); and for musical instruments (2 Sam. vi. 5). ¶ *The height of his border.* The extreme retreats; the furthest part of Lebanon. In 2 Kings xix. 23, it is, ' I will enter the lodgings of his borders;' perhaps referring to the fact that on the ascent to the top of the mountain there was a place for the repose of travellers; a species of inn or caravansera which *bounded* the usual attempts of persons to ascend the mountain. Such a lodging-place on the sides or tops of mountains which are frequently ascended, is not uncommon. ¶ And *the forest of his Carmel.* On the meaning of the word Carmel, see Note on ch. xxix. 17. Here it means, as in that passage, a rich, fertile, and beautiful country. It is known that Lebanon was covered on the top, and far down the sides, with perpetual snow. But there was a region lying on its sides, between the snow and the base of the mountain, that was distinguished for fertility, and that was highly cultivated. This region produced grapes in abundance; and this cultivated part of the mountain, thick set with vines and trees, might be called a beautiful grove. This was doubtless the portion of Lebanon which is here intended. At a distance, this tract on the sides of Lebanon ap-

25 I have digged, and drunk water; and with the sole of my feet have I dried up all the rivers of the ¹ besieged places.

¹ or, *fenced and closed.*

peared doubtless as a *thicket* of shrubs and trees. The phrase 'garden-forest,' will probably express the sense of the passage. 'After leaving Baalbec, and approaching Lebanon, towering walnut-trees, either singly or in groups, and a rich carpet of verdure, the offspring of numerous streams, give to this charming district the air of an English park, majestically bordered with snow-tipped mountains. At Deir-el-Akmaar, the ascent begins—winding among dwarf oaks, hawthorns, and a great variety of shrubs and flowers. A deep bed of snow had now to be crossed, and the horses sunk or slipped at every moment. To ride was impracticable, and to walk dangerous, for the melting snow penetrated our boots, and our feet were nearly frozen. An hour and a half brought us to the cedars.'—(Hogg.)

25. *I have digged.* That is, I have digged wells. This was regarded among eastern nations as an important achievement. It was difficult to find water, even by digging, in sandy deserts; and in a country abounding with rocks, it was an enterprise of great difficulty to sink a well. Hence the possession of a well became a valuable property, and was sometimes the occasion of contention between neighbouring tribes (Gen. xxvi. 20). Hence also to stop up the wells of water, by throwing in rocks or sand, became one of the most obvious ways of distressing an enemy, and was often resorted to (Gen. xxvi. 15, 18; 2 Kings iii. 19, 25). To dig wells, or to furnish water in abundance to a people, became also an achievement which was deemed worthy to be recorded in the history of kings and princes (2 Chron. xxvi. 10). Many of the most stupendous and costly of the works of the Romans in the capital of their empire, and in the principal towns of their provinces, consisted in building aqueducts to bring water from a distance into a city. An achievement like this I understand Sennacherib as boasting he had performed; that he had furnished water for the cities and towns of his mighty empire; that he had accomplished what was deemed so difficult, and what required so much expense, as digging wells for his people; and that he had secured them from being stopped up by his enemies, so that he and his people drank of the water in peace. Gesenius, however, understands this as a boast that he had extended the bounds of his empire beyond its original limits, and unto regions that were naturally destitute of water, and where it was necessary to dig wells to supply his armies. Rosenmüller understands it as saying: 'I have passed over, and taken possession of foreign lands.' Drusius regards it as a proverbial saying, meaning 'I have happily and successfully accomplished all that I have undertaken, as he who digs a well accomplishes that which he particularly desires.' Vitringa regards it as saying, 'that to dig wells, and to drink the water of them, is to enjoy the fruit of our labours, to be successful and happy.' But it seems to me that the interpretation above suggested, and which I have not found in any of the commentators before me, is the correct exposition. ¶ *And drunk water.* In 2 Kings xix. 24, it is, 'I have drunk *strange* waters;' that is, the waters of foreign lands. I have conquered them, and have dug wells in them. But the sense is not materially changed. ¶ *And with the sole of my feet.* Expressions like this, denoting the desolations of a conqueror, are found in the classic writers. Perhaps the idea there is, that their armies were so numerous that they drank up all the waters in their march—a strong hyperbole to denote the number of their armies, and the extent of their desolations when even the waters failed before them. Thus Claudian (*De Bello Getico*, 526) introduces Alaric as boasting of his conquests in the same extravagant manner, and in language remarkably similar to this:

Cum cesserit omnis
Obsequiis natura meis. Subsidere nostris
Sub pedibus montes; arescere vidimus amnes—
Fregi Alpes, galeisque Padum victricibus hausi.

26 Hast thou not heard [1] long ago, *how* I have done it ; *and* of ancient times, that I have formed it ? now have I *a* brought it to pass, that thou shouldest be to lay waste defenced cities *into* ruinous heaps.

1 or, how *I have made it long ago, and formed it of ancient times ? should I now bring it to be laid waste,* and *defenced cities* to be *ruinous heaps.*

27 Therefore their inhabitants were [2] of small power, they were dismayed and confounded : they were *as* the grass of the field, and *as* the green herb, *as* the grass on the house-tops, and *as corn* blasted before it be grown up.

a ch.10.5,6.　　　　2 *short of hand.*

So Juvenal (*Sat.* x. 176), speaking of the dominion of Xerxes, says:

——credimus altos
Defecisse amnes, epotaque flumina Medo
Prandente.

The boast of drying up streams with the sole of the foot, is intended to convey the idea that he had not only supplied water for his own empire by digging wells, but that he had cut off the supplies of water from the others against whom he had made war. The idea perhaps is, that if such an army as his was, should pass through the streams of a country that they should invade, and should only take away the water that would adhere to the sole or the hollow of the foot on their march, it would dry up all the streams. It is strong hyperbolical language, and is designed to indicate the number of the forces which were under his command. ¶ *Of the besieged places.* Marg. 'Fenced' or 'closed.' The word rendered 'rivers' (אוֹרֵי), may denote canals, or artificial streams, such as were common in Egypt. In ch. xix. 6, it is rendered 'brooks,' and is applied to the artificial canals of Egypt (see Note on that place). The word here rendered 'besieged places' (מָצוֹר *mátzor*), may mean distress, straitness (Deut. xxviii. 53) ; siege (Ezek. iv. 2, 7) ; mound, bulwark, intrenchment (Deut. xx. 20) ; or it may be a proper name for Egypt, being one of the forms of the name מִצְרַיִם (*Mitz-raim*) or Egypt. The same phrase occurs in ch. xix. 6, where it means Egypt (see Note on that place), and such should be regarded as its meaning here. It alludes to the conquests which Sennacherib is represented as boasting that he had made in Egypt, that he had easily removed obstructions, and destroyed their means of defence. Though he had been repulsed before Pelusium by Tirhakah king of Ethiopia (see

Note on ch. xxxvi. 1), yet it is not improbable that he had taken many towns there, and had subdued no small part of the country to himself. In his vain boasting, he would strive to forget his repulse, and would dwell on the case of conquest, and the facility with which he had removed all obstructions from his way. The whole language of the verse, therefore, is that of a proud and haughty Oriental prince, desirous of proclaiming his conquests, and forgetting his mortifying defeats.

26. *Hast thou not heard.* This is evidently the language of God addressed to Sennacherib. It is designed to state to him that he was under his control ; that this was the reason (ver. 27) why the inhabitants of the nations had been unable to resist him ; that he was entirely in his hands (ver. 28) ; and that he would control him as he pleased (ver. 29). ¶ *Long ago* how *I have done it.* You boast that all this is by your own counsel and power. Yet I have done it ; *i.e.*, I have purposed, planned, arranged it long ago (comp. ch. xxii. 11). ¶ *That thou shouldest be to lay waste.* I have raised you up for this purpose, and you have been entirely under my control (see Note on ch. x. 5).

27. *Therefore.* Not because you have so great power ; but because I have rendered them incapable of resisting you. ¶ Were *of small power.* Heb. ' Short of hand ;' they were feeble, imbecile, unable to resist you. ¶ *They were dismayed.* Heb. ' They were broken and ashamed.' Their spirits sank ; they were ashamed of their feeble powers of resistance ; and they submitted to the ignominy of a surrender. ¶ *They were as the grass of the field.* The same idea is expressed by Sennacherib himself in ch. x. 15, though under a different image (see Note on that verse). The idea here is, as the grass of the

28 But I know thy [1] abode, and thy going out, and thy coming in, and thy rage against me.

29 Because thy rage against me, and thy tumult, is come up into mine ears, therefore will I put my hook *a* in thy nose, and my bridle in thy lips, and I will turn thee

1 or, *sitting*.   *a* ch.30.28; Eze.38 4.

back by the way by which thou camest.

30 And this *shall be* a sign unto thee, Ye shall eat this year such as groweth of itself; and the second year that which springeth of the same: and in the third year sow ye, and reap, and plant vineyards, and eat the fruit thereof.

---

field offers no resistance to the march of an army, so it was with the strongly fortified towns in the way of Sennacherib. ¶ As *the grass on the house-tops*. In eastern countries the roofs of houses are always flat. They are made of a mixture of sand, gravel, or earth; and on the houses of the rich there is a firmly constructed flooring made of coals, chalk, gypsum, and ashes, made hard by being beaten or rolled. On these roofs spears of wheat, barley, or grass sometimes spring up, but they are soon withered by the heat of the sun (Ps. cxxix. 6–8). The idea here, therefore, is that of the greatest feebleness. His enemies were not simply like the grass in the field, but they were like the thin, slender, and delicate blade that sprung up in the little earth on the roof of a house, where there was no room for the roots to strike down, and where it soon withered beneath the burning sun. ¶ As corn *blasted before it is grown up*. Before it acquires any strength. The idea in all these phrases is substantially the same—that they were incapable of offering even the feeblest resistance.

28. *But I know*. The language of God. 'I am well acquainted with all that pertains to you. You neither go out to war, nor return, nor abide in your capital without my providential direction' (see Notes on ch. x. 5–7). ¶ *Thy abode*. Marg. 'Sitting.' Among the Hebrews, sitting down, rising up, and going out, were phrases to describe the whole of a man's life and actions (comp. Deut. vi. 7; xxviii. 6; 1 Kings iii. 7; Ps. cxxi. 8). God here says that he knew the place where he dwelt, and he was able to return him again to it, ver. 29. ¶ *And thy rage against me* (see ver. 4).

29. *Because thy rage and thy tumult*. Or rather, thy pride, thy insolence, thy

vain boasting. ¶ *Therefore will I put my hook in thy nose*. This is a most striking expression, denoting the complete control which God had over the haughty monarch, and his ability to direct him as he pleased. The *language* is taken from the custom of putting a ring or hook in the nose of a wild animal for the purpose of governing and guiding it. The most violent animals may be thus completely governed, and this is often done with those animals that are fierce and untameable. The Arabs often pursue this course in regard to the camel, and thus have it under entire control. A similar image is used in respect to the king of Egypt (Ezek. xxix. 4). The idea is, that God would control and govern the wild and ambitious spirit of the Assyrian, and that with infinite ease he could conduct him again to his own land. ¶ *And my bridle* (see Note on ch. xxx. 28). ¶ *And I will turn thee back* (see ver. 37).

30. *And this* shall be *a sign unto thee*. It is evident that the discourse here is turned from Sennacherib to Hezekiah. Such transitions, without distinctly indicating them, are common in Isaiah. God had in the previous verses, in the form of a direct personal address, foretold the defeat of Sennacherib, and the confusion of his plans. He here turns and gives to Hezekiah the assurance that Jerusalem would be delivered. On the meaning of the word 'sign,' see Note on ch. vii. 14. Commentators have been much perplexed in the exposition of the passage before us, to know how that which was to occur one, two, or three years after the event, could be a *sign* of the fulfilment of the prophecy. Many have supposed that the year in which this was spoken was a Sabbatic year, in which the lands were not cultivated, but were suffered

to lie still (Lev. xxxv. 2–7); and that the year following was the year of Jubilee, in which also the lands were to remain uncultivated. They suppose that the idea is, that the Jews might be *assured* that they would not experience the evils of famine which they had anticipated from the Assyrians, because the Divine promise gave them assurance of supply in the Sabbatic year, and in the year of Jubilee, and that although their fields had been laid waste by the Assyrian, yet their wants would be supplied, until on the third year they would be permitted in quietness to cultivate their land, and that this would be to them *a sign*, or a token of the Divine interposition. But to this there are two obvious objections—1. There is not the slightest evidence that the year in which Sennacherib besieged Jerusalem was a Sabbatic year, or that the following year was the Jubilee. No mention is made of this in the history, nor is it possible to prove it from any part of the sacred narrative. 2. It is still difficult to see, even if it were so, how that which was to occur two or three years after the event, could be a sign to Hezekiah then of the truth of what Isaiah had predicted. Rosenmüller suggests that the two years in which they are mentioned as sustained by the spontaneous productions of the earth were the two years in which Judea had been already ravaged by Sennacherib, and that the third year was the one in which the prophet was now speaking, and that the prediction means that in that very year they would be permitted to sow and reap. In the explanation of the passage, it is to be observed that the word 'sign' is used in a variety of significations. It may be used as an *indication* of anything unseen (Gen. i. 14); or as a military ensign (Num. ii. 2); or as a sign of something future, an omen (Isa. viii. 18); or as a token, argument, proof (Gen. xvii. 2; Exod. xxxi. 13). It may be used as a sign or token of the truth of a prophecy; that is, when some minor event furnishes a proof that the whole prophecy would be fulfilled (Ex. iii. 12; 1 Sam. ii. 34; x. 7, 9). Or it may be used as a wonder, a prodigy, a miracle (Deut. iv. 34; vi. 22). In the case before us,

it seems to mean that, in the events predicted here, Hezekiah would have a token or argument that the land was *completely freed* from the invasion of Sennacherib. Though a considerable part of his army would be destroyed; though the monarch himself would be compelled to flee, yet Hezekiah would not from that fact alone have the assurance that he would not rally his forces, and return to invade the land. There would be every inducement arising from disappointment and the rage of defeat for him to do it. To compose the mind of Hezekiah in regard to this, this assurance was given, that the land would be quiet, and that the fact *that it would remain quiet during the remainder of that year, and to the third year, would be a* SIGN, *or demonstration that the Assyrian army was* ENTIRELY *withdrawn, and that all danger of an invasion was at an end.* The sign, therefore, does not refer so much to *the past,* as to the security and future prosperity which would be consequent thereon. It would be an evidence to them that the nation would be safe, and would be favoured with a high degree of prosperity (see ver. 31, 32). It is possible that this invasion took place when it was too late to sow for that year, and that the land was so ravaged that it could not that year be cultivated. The harvests and the vineyards had been destroyed; and they would be dependent on that which the earth had spontaneously produced in those parts which had been untilled. As it was now too late to sow the land, they would be dependent in the following year on the same scanty supply. In the third year, however, they might cultivate their fields securely, and the former fertility would be restored. ¶ *Such as groweth of itself.* The Hebrew word here (סָפִיחַ), denotes grain produced from the kernels of the former year, without new seed, and without cultivation. This, it is evident, would be a scanty supply; but we are to remember that the land had been ravaged by the army of the Assyrian. ¶ *That which springeth of the same.* The word here used (שָׁחִיס), in the parallel passage in 2 Kings xix. 29 (סָחִישׁ), denotes that

31 And [1] the remnant that is escaped of the house of Judah shall again take root downward, and bear fruit upward.

32 For out of Jerusalem shall go forth a remnant, and [2] they that escape out of mount Zion: the zeal of the Lord of hosts shall do this.

33 Therefore thus saith the Lord concerning the king of Assyria, He shall not come into this city, nor shoot an arrow there, nor come before it with [3] shields, nor cast a bank against it.

1 *the escaping of the house of Judah that remaineth.*
2 *the escaping.*   3 *shield.*

which grows of itself the third year after sowing. This production of the third year would be of course more scanty and less valuable than in the preceding year, and there can be no doubt that the Jews would be subjected to a considerable extent to the evils of want. Still, as the land would be quiet; as the people would be permitted to live in peace; it would be a *sign* to them that the Assyrian was finally and entirely withdrawn, and that they might return in the third year to the cultivation of their land with the assurance that this much-dreaded invasion was not again to be feared. ¶ *And in the third year.* Then you may resume your agricultural operations with the assurance that you shall be undisturbed. Your two years of quiet shall have been a full demonstration to you that the Assyrian shall not return, and you may resume your employments with the assurance that all the evils of the invasion, and all apprehension of danger, are at an end.

31. *And the remnant that is escaped* (see Marg.) Those that are left of the Jews. The ten tribes had been carried away; and it is not improbable that the inhabitants of the kingdom of Judah had been reduced by want, and by the siege of Lachish, Libnah, &c. It is not to be supposed that Sennacherib could have invaded the land, and spread desolation for so long a time, without diminishing the number of the people. The promise in the passage is, that those who were left should flourish and increase. The land should be at rest; and under the administration of their wise and pious king their number would be augmented, and their happiness promoted. ¶ *Shall again take root downward.* Like a tree that had been prevented by any cause from growing or bearing fruit. A tree, to bear well,

must be in a soil where it can strike its roots deep. The sense is, that all obstructions to their growth and prosperity would be removed.

32. *Shall go forth a remnant.* The word 'remnant' means that which is left; and does not of necessity imply that it should be a small portion. No doubt a part of the Jews were destroyed in the invasion of Sennacherib, but the assurance is here given that a portion of them would remain in safety, and that they would constitute that from which the future prosperity of the state would arise. ¶ *And they that escape.* Marg. 'The escaping,' *i.e.*, the remnant. ¶ *The zeal* (see Note on ch. ix. 7).

33. *He shall not come into this city.* Sennacherib encamped probably on the north-east side of the city, and his army was destroyed there (see Notes on ch. x. 28, *sq.*) ¶ *Nor shoot an arrow there.* That is, nor shoot an arrow within the walls of the city. ¶ *Nor come before it with shields* (see Note on

Ancient Egyptian Battlements.
From Rosellini.

ch. xxi. 5). The meaning here is, that the army should not be permitted to

34 By the way that he came, by the same shall he return, and shall not come into this city, saith the LORD.

35 For I *a* will defend this city to save it for mine own sake, and for my servant David's sake.

a ch.38.6; Jer.17.25,26.

36 Then *b* the angel of the LORD went forth, and smote in the camp of the Assyrians an hundred and fourscore and five thousand : and when the arose early in the morning, behold, they *were* all dead corpses.

b ch.10.12,&c.

---

come before the city defended with shields, and prepared with the means of attack and defence. ¶ *Nor cast a bank against it.* A mound ; a pile of earth thrown up in the manner of a fort to defend the assailants, or to give them an advantage in attacking the walls.

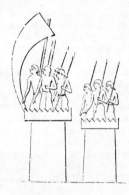

SIEGE TOWERS, FILLED WITH ARMED MEN.

Sieges were conducted by throwing up banks or fortifications, behind which the army of attack could be secure to carry on their operations. Towers filled with armed men were also constructed, covered with hides and other impenetrable materials, which could be made to approach the walls, and from which those who were within could safely conduct the attack.

34. *By the way that he came* (ver. 29; comp. ver. 37). ¶ *And shall not come into this city* (ver. 33; comp. ch. xxix. 6–8).

35. *For I will defend this city.* Notwithstanding all that Hezekiah had done to put it in a posture of defence (2 Chron. xxxii. 1, *sq.*) still it was JEHOVAH alone who could preserve it. ¶ *For mine own sake.* God had been reproached and blasphemed by Sen-

nacherib. As his name and power had been thus blasphemed, he says that he would vindicate himself, and for the honour of his own insulted majesty would save the city. ¶ *And for my servant David's sake.* On account of the promise which he had made to him that there should not fail a man to sit on his throne, and that the city and nation should not be destroyed until the Messiah should appear (see Ps. cxxxii. 10–18).

36. *Then the angel of the* LORD *went forth.* This verse contains the record of one of the most remarkable events which have occurred in history. Many attempts have been made to explain the occurrence which is here recorded, and to trace the agencies or means which God employed. It may be observed that the use of the word 'angel' here does not determine the manner in which it was done. So far as the *word* is concerned, it might have been accomplished either by the power of an invisible messenger of God—a spiritual being commissioned for this purpose ; or it might have been by some second causes under the direction of an angel—as the pestilence, or a storm and tempest ; or it might have been by some agents *sent* by God whatever they were —the storm, the pestilence, or the simoom, to which the name *angel* might have been applied. The word ' angel' (מַלְאָךְ from לָאַךְ *to send*) means properly *one sent, a messenger,* from a private person (Job i. 14); from a king (1 Sam. xvi. 19; xix. 11, 14, 20). Then it means *a messenger of God,* and is applied (1) to an angel (Ex. xxiii. 20; 2 Sam. xiv. 16; *et al.*); (2) to a prophet (Hag. i. 13; Mal. iii. 1); (3) to a priest (Eccl. v. 5; Mal. ii. 7). The word may be applied to *any* messenger sent from God, whoever or whatever that may be. Thus, in Ps. civ. 4, the

winds are said to be his angels, or messengers :

Who maketh the winds (רוּחוֹת) his angels (מַלְאָכָיו);

The flaming fire his ministers.

The general sense of the word is that of ambassador, messenger, one sent to bear a message, to execute a commission, or to perform any work or service. It is known that the Jews were in the habit of tracing all events to the agency of invisible beings sent forth by God to accomplish his purposes in this world. There is nothing in this opinion that is contrary to reason ; for there is no more improbability in the existence of a good angel than there is in the existence of a good man, or in the existence of an evil spirit than there is in the existence of a bad man. And there is no more improbability in the supposition that God employs invisible and heavenly messengers to accomplish his purposes, than there is that he employs man. Whatever, therefore, were the means used in the destruction of the Assyrian army, there is no improbability in the opinion that they were under the direction of a celestial agent sent forth to accomplish the purpose. The chief suppositions which have been made of the means of that destruction are the following :—
1. It has been supposed that it was by the direct agency of an angel, without any second causes. But this supposition has not been generally adopted. It is contrary to the usual modes in which God directs the affairs of the world. His purposes are usually accomplished by some second causes, and in accordance with the usual course of events. Calvin supposes that it was accomplished by the direct agency of one or more angels sent forth for the purpose. 2. Some have supposed that it was accomplished by Tirhakah, king of Ethiopia, who is supposed to have pursued Sennacherib, and to have overthrown his army in a single night near Jerusalem. But it is sufficient to say in reply to this, that there is not the slightest historical evidence to support it ; and had this been the mode, it would have been so recorded, and the fact would have been stated. 3. It has been attributed by some, among whom is Prideaux (*Connection*, vol. i. p. 143) and J. E. Faber (*Notes*

on *Harmer's Obs.*, i. 65), to the hot pestilential wind which often prevails in the East, and which is often represented as suddenly destroying travellers, and indeed whole caravans. This wind, called *sam, simûm, samiel,* or *simoom*, has been usually supposed to be poisonous, and almost instantly destructive to life. It has been described by Mr. Bruce, by Sir R. K. Porter, by Niebuhr, and by others. Prof. Robinson has examined at length the supposition that the Assyrian army was destroyed by this wind, and has stated the results of the investigations of recent travellers. The conclusion to which he comes is, that the former accounts of the effects of this wind have been greatly exaggerated, and that the destruction of the army of the Assyrians cannot be attributed to any such cause. See the article WINDS, in his edition of Calmet's *Dictionary*. Burckhardt says of this wind, whose effects have been regarded as so poisonous and destructive, ' I am PERFECTLY CONVINCED that all the stories which travellers, or the inhabitants of the towns of Egypt and Syria, relate of the simoom of the desert are greatly exaggerated, and I *never could hear of a* SINGLE WELL-AUTHENTICATED INSTANCE *of its having proved mortal to either man or beast.*' Similar testimony has been given by other modern travellers ; though it is to be remarked that the testimony is rather of a *negative* character, and does not entirely destroy the possibility of the supposition that this so often described pestilential wind may in some instances prove fatal. It is not, however, referred to in the Scripture account of the destruction of Sennacherib ; and whatever may be true of it in the deserts of Arabia or Nubia, there is no evidence whatever that such poisonous effects are ever experienced in Palestine. 4. It has been attributed to a storm of hail, accompanied with thunder and lightning. This is the opinion of Vitringa, and seems to accord with the descriptions which are given in the prophecy of the destruction of the army in ch. xxix. 6; xxx. 30. To this opinion, as the most probable, I have been disposed to incline ; for although these passages *may* be regarded as figurative, yet the more natural inter-

37 So Sennacherib king of Assyria departed, and went and returned, and dwelt at Nineveh.

---

pretation is to regard them as descriptive of the event. We know that such a tempest might be easily produced by God, and that violent tornadoes are not unfrequent in the East. One of the plagues of Egypt consisted in such a tremendous storm of hail accompanied with thunder, when ' the fire ran along the ground,' so that ' there was hail, and fire mingled with the hail,' and so that ' the hail smote throughout all the land of Egypt all that was in the field, both man and beast ' (Ex. ix. 22-25). This description, in its terror, its suddenness, and its ruinous effects, accords more nearly with the account of the destruction of Sennacherib than any other which has been made. See Notes on ch. xxx. 30, for a remarkable description of the effect of a storm of hail. 5. It has been supposed by many that it was accomplished by the pestilence. This is the account which Josephus gives (*Ant.* x. 1. 5), and is the supposition which has been adopted by Rosenmüller, Döderlin, Michaelis, Hensler, and many others. But there are two objections to this supposition. One is, that it does not well accord with the description of the prophet (ch. xxix. 6; xxx. 30); and the other, and more material one is, that the plague does not accomplish its work so suddenly. This was done in a single night; whereas, though the plague appears suddenly, and has been known to destroy whole armies, yet there is no recorded instance in which it has been so destructive in a few hours as in this case. It may be added, also, that the plague does not often leave an army in the manner described here. One hundred and eighty-five thousand were suddenly slain. The survivors, if there were any, as we have reason to suppose (ver. 37), fled, and returned to Nineveh. There is no mention made of any who lingered, and who remained sick among the slain. Nor is there any apprehension mentioned, as having existed among the Jews, of going into the camp, and stripping the dead, and bearing the spoils of the army into the city. Had the army been destroyed by the plague, such is the fear of the contagion in countries where it prevails, that nothing would have induced them to endanger the city by the possibility of introducing the dreaded disease. The account leads us to suppose that the inhabitants of Jerusalem immediately sallied forth and stripped the dead, and bore the spoils of the army into the city (see Notes on ch. xxxiii. 4, 24). On the whole, therefore, the most probable supposition seems to be, that, if any secondary causes were employed, it was the agency of a violent tempest—a tempest of mingled hail and fire, which suddenly descended upon the mighty army. Whatever was the agent, however, it was the hand of God that directed it. It was a most fearful exhibition of his power and justice ; and it furnishes a most awful threatening to proud and haughty blasphemers and revilers, and a strong ground of assurance to the righteous that God will defend them in times of peril.

It may be added, that Herodotus has given an account which was undoubtedly derived from some rumour of the entire destruction of the Assyrian army. He says (ii. 141) that when Sennacherib was in Egypt and engaged in the siege of Pelusium, an Egyptian priest prayed to God, and God heard his prayer, and sent a judgment upon him. ' For,' says he, ' a multitude of mice gnawed to pieces in one night both the bows and the rest of the armour of the Assyrians, and that it was on that account that the king, when he had no bows left, drew off his army from Pelusium.' This is probably a corruption of the history which we have here. At all events, the account in Herodotus does not conflict with the main statement of Isaiah, but is rather a confirmation of that statement, that the army of Sennacherib met with sudden discomfiture. ¶ *And when they arose.* At the time of rising in the morning ; when the surviving part of the army arose, or when the Jews arose, and looked toward the camp of the Assyrians.

37. *So Sennacherib departed.* Probably with some portion of his army and retinue with him, for it is by no

38 And it came to pass, as he was worshipping in the house of Nisroch his god, that Adrammelech and Sharezer his sons smote *a*him

a ch.14,9-12.

with the sword ; and they escaped into the land of [1] Armenia: and Esarhaddon his son reigned in his stead.

1 *Ararat.*

means probable that the whole army had been destroyed. In 2 Chron. xxxii. 21, it is said that the angel 'cut off all the mighty men of valour, and the leaders and captains in the camp of the king of Assyria.' His army was thus entirely disabled, and the loss of so large a part of it, and the consternation produced by their sudden destruction, would of course lead him to abandon the siege. ¶ *Went and returned.* Went from before Jerusalem and returned to his own land. ¶ *And dwelt at Nineveh.* How long he dwelt there is not certainly known. Berosus, the Chaldean, says it was 'a little while' (see Jos. *Ant.* x. 1. 5). Nineveh was on the Tigris, and was the capital of Assyria. For an account of its site, and its present situation, see the *American Biblical Repository* for Jan. 1837, pp. 139–159.

38. *As he was worshipping.* Perhaps this time was selected because he might be then attended with fewer guards, or because they were able to surprise him without the possibility of his summoning his attendants to his rescue. ¶ *In the house.* In the temple. ¶ *Of Nisroch his god.* The god whom he particularly adored. Gesenius supposes that the word *Nisroch* denotes *an eagle,* or *a great eagle.* The eagle was regarded as a sacred bird in the Persian religion, and was the symbol of Ormuzd. This god or idol had been probably introduced into Nineveh from Persia. Among the ancient Arabs the eagle occurs as an idol. Josephus calls the idol Araskes ; the author of the book of Tobit calls it Dagon. Vitringa supposes that it was the Assyrian Bel, and was worshipped under the figure of Mars, the god of war. More probably it was the figure of the eagle, though it might have been regarded as the god of war. ¶ *That Adrammelech and Sharezer his sons smote him with the sword.* What was the cause of this rebellion and parricide is unknown. These two sons subse-

quently became, in Armenia, the heads of two celebrated families there, the Arzerunii, and the Genunii (see Jos. *Ant.* x. 1, 5, *note*). ¶ *And they escaped.* This would lead us to suppose that it was some *private* matter which led them to commit the parricide, and that they did not do it with the expectation of succeeding to the crown. ¶ *Into the land of Armenia.* Heb. as Marg. 'Ararat.' The Chaldee renders this, 'The land of קַרְדּוּ (*Kardoo*,' that is, *Kardianum,* or, the mountains of the Kurds. The modern Kurdistan includes a considerable part of the ancient Assyria and Media, together with a large portion of Armenia. This expression is generally substituted for Ararat by the Syriac, Chaldee, and Arabic translators, when they do not retain the original word *Ararat.* It is a region among the mountains of Ararat or Armenia. The Syriac renders it in the same way ܕܩܘܪܕܘ —'Of Kurdoya' (*the Kurds*). The LXX. render it, 'Into Armenia.' Jerome says that ' Ararat was a champaign region in Armenia, through which the Araxes flowed, and was of considerable fertility.' Ararat was a region or province in Armenia, near the middle of the country between the Araxes and the lakes Van and Oroomiah. It is still called by the Armenians *Ararat.* On one of the mountains in this region the ark of Noah rested (Gen. viii. 4). The name *Ararat* belongs properly to the region or country, and not to any particular mountain. For an account of this region, see Sir R. K. Porter's *Travels,* vol. i. p. 178, *sq.;* Smith and Dwight's *Researches in Armenia,* vol. ii. p. 73, *sq.;* and Morier's *Second Journey,* p. 312. For a very interesting account of the situation of Ararat, including a description of an ascent to the summit of the mountain which bears that name, see the *Bib. Rep.* for April, 1836, pp. 390–416. 'The origin of the name Armenia is unknown. The Armenians call themselves after their fabulous progenitor

CHAPTER XXXVIII.

ANALYSIS.

THIS chapter contains the record of an important transaction which occurred in the time of Isaiah, and in which he was deeply interested —the dangerous sickness, and the remarkable recovery of Hezekiah. It is introduced here, doubtless, because the account was drawn up by Isaiah (see Analysis of ch. xxxvi.); and because it records his agency at an important crisis of the history. A record of the same transaction, evidently from the same hand, occurs in 2 Kings xx. 1–11. But the account differs more than the records in the two previous chapters. It is *abridged* in Isaiah by omitting what is recorded in Kings in ver. 4, and in the close of ver. 6, it is *transposed* in the statement which occurs in regard to the application of the 'lump of figs;' and it is *enlarged* by the introduction of the record which Hezekiah made of his sickness and recovery (9–20).

The contents of the chapter are—1. The state- ment of the dangerous sickness of Hezekiah, and the message of God to him by the prophet (1). 2. The prayer which Hezekiah offered for his recovery (3). 3. The assurance which God gave to him by the prophet that his days should be lengthened out fifteen years, and the sign given to confirm it by the retrocession of the shadow on the sun-dial of Ahaz (5–8). 4. The record which Hezekiah made in gratitude to God for his recovery (9–20); and 5. The statement of the manner in which his recovery was effected (21, 22).

IN *a* those days was Hezekiah sick unto death. And Isaiah the prophet, the son of Amoz, came unto him, and said unto him, Thus saith the LORD, [1] Set thine house in order: for thou shalt die, and not live.

a 2 Ki.20.1,&c.; 2 Chron.32.24.
[1] *give charge concerning thy house.*

Haig, and derive the name *Armen* from the son of Haig, Armenag. They are probably a tribe of the ancient Assyrians; their language and history speak alike in favour of it. Their traditions say also that Haig came from Babylon.'

CHAPTER XXXVIII.

1. *In those days.* That is, his sickness commenced about the period in which the army of Sennacherib was destroyed. It has been made a question whether the sickness of Hezekiah was before or after the invasion of Sennacherib. The most natural interpretation certainly is, that it occurred *after* that invasion, and probably at no distant period. The only objection to this view is the statement in ver. 6, that God would deliver him out of the hand of the king of Assyria, which has been understood by many as implying that he was then threatened with the invasion. But this may mean simply that he would be *perpetually* and *finally* delivered from his hand; that he would be secure in that independence from a foreign yoke which he had long sought (2 Kings xviii. 7); and that the Assyrian should not be able again to bring the Jews into subjection (see Notes on ch. xxxvii. 30, 31; comp. Note on ver. 6). Jerome supposes that it was brought upon him lest his heart should be elated with the signal triumph, and in order that, in his circumstances, he might be kept humble. Josephus (*Ant.* x. 2. 1) says that the sickness occurred soon after the destruction of the army of Sennacherib. Prideaux (*Connection*, vol. i. p. 137) places his sickness *before* the invasion of the Assyrians. ¶ *Was sick.* What was the exact nature of this sickness is not certainly known. In ver. 21 it is said that it was 'a boil,' and probably it was a pestilential boil. The pestilence or plague is attended with an eruption or boil. 'No one,' says Jahn, 'ever recovered from the pestilence unless the boil of the pestilence came out upon him, and even then he could not always be cured' (*Biblical Antiquities*, § 190). The pestilence was, and is still, rapid in its progress. It terminates the life of those who are affected with it almost immediately, and at the furthest within three or four days. Hence we see one ground of the alarm of Hezekiah. Another cause of his anxiety was, that he had at this time no children, and consequently he had reason to apprehend that his kingdom would be thrown into contention by conflicting strifes for the crown. ¶ *Unto death.* Ready to die; with a sickness which in the ordinary course would terminate his life. ¶ *Set thine house in order.* Heb. 'Give command (צַו) to thy house,' *i.e.*, to thy family. If you have any directions to

give in regard to the succession to the crown, or in regard to domestic and private arrangements, let it be done soon. Hezekiah was yet in middle life. He came to the throne when he was twenty-five years old (2 Kings xviii. 2), and he had now reigned about fourteen years. It is possible that he had as yet made no arrangements in regard to the succession, and as this was very important to the peace of the nation, Isaiah was sent to him to apprize him of the necessity of leaving the affairs of his kingdom so that there should not be anarchy when he should die. The direction, also, may be understood in a more general sense as denoting that he was to make whatever arrangements might be necessary as preparatory to his death. We see here—1. The boldness and fidelity of a man of God. Isaiah was not afraid to go in and freely tell even a monarch that he must die. The subsequent part of the narrative would lead us to suppose that until this announcement Hezekiah did not regard himself as in immediate danger. It is evident here, that the *physician* of Hezekiah had not informed him of it—*perhaps* from the apprehension that his disease would be aggravated by the agitation of his mind on the subject. The duty was, therefore, left, as it is often, to a minister of religion—a duty which even many ministers are slow to perform, and which many physicians are reluctant to *have* performed. 2. No danger is to be apprehended commonly from announcing to those who are sick their true condition. Friends and relatives are often reluctant to do it, for fear of agitating and alarming them. Physicians often prohibit them from knowing their true condition, under the apprehension that their disease may be aggravated. Yet here was a case in which pre-eminently there might be danger from announcing the danger of death. The disease was deeply seated. It was making rapid progress. It was usually incurable. Nay, there was here a moral certainty that the monarch would die. And this was a case, therefore, which particularly demanded, it would seem, that the patient should be kept quiet, and free from alarms. But God regarded it as of great importance that he should know his true condition,

and the prophet was directed to go to him and faithfully to state it. Physicians and friends often err in this. There is no species of cruelty greater than to suffer a friend to lie on a dying bed under a delusion. There is no sin more aggravated than that of designedly deceiving a dying man, and flattering him with the hope of recovery when there is a moral certainty that he will not, and cannot recover. And there is evidently no danger to be apprehended from communicating to the sick their true condition. It should be done tenderly, and with affection ; but it should be done faithfully. I have had many opportunities of witnessing the effect of apprizing the sick of their situation, and of the moral certainty that they must die. And I cannot now recall an instance in which the announcement has had any unhappy effect on the disease. Often, on the contrary, the effect is to calm the mind, and to lead the dying to look up to God, and peacefully to repose on him. And the effect of THAT is *always* salutary. Nothing is more favourable for a recovery than a peaceful, calm, heavenly submission to God ; and the repose and quiet which physicians so much desire their patients to possess, is often best obtained by securing confidence in God, and a calm resignation to his will. 3. Every man with the prospect of death before him should set his house in order. Death is an event which demands preparation—a preparation which should not be deferred to the dying moment. In view of it, whether it comes sooner or later, our peace should be made with God and our worldly affairs so arranged that we can leave them without distraction, and without regret. ¶ *For thou shalt die, and not live.* Thy disease is incurable. It is a mortal, fatal disease. The Hebrew is, 'for thou art *dead*' (מֵת) ; that is, you are a dead man. A similar expression occurs in Gen. xx. 3, in the address which God made to Abimelech : ' Behold thou art a dead man, on account of the woman which thou hast taken.' We have a similar phrase in our language, when a man is wounded, and when he says, ' I am a dead man.' This is all that we are required to understand here, that,

2 Then Hezekiah turned his face toward the wall, and prayed unto the LORD,

3 And said, Remember *a* now, O LORD, I beseech thee, how I have

walked before thee in truth, and with a perfect heart, and have done *that which is* good in thy sight: and Hezekiah wept [1] sore.

according to the usual course of the disease, he must die. It is evident that Isaiah was not acquainted himself with the secret intention of God ; nor did he know that Hezekiah would humble himself, and plead with God ; nor that God would by a miracle lengthen out his life.

2. *Then Hezekiah turned his face toward the wall.* The wall of the room in which he was lying. He was probably lying on a couch next the wall of his room. Eastern houses usually have such couches or ottomans running along on the sides of the room on which they recline, and on which they lie when they are sick. Hezekiah probably turned his face to the wall in order that his emotion and his tears might not be seen by the bystanders, or in order that he might compose himself the better for devotion. His prayer he wished, doubtless, to be as secret as possible. The Chaldee renders this, ' Turned his face to the wall of the house of the sanctuary ;' that is, of the temple, so that it might appear that he prayed toward the temple. Thus Daniel, when in Babylon, is said to have prayed with his windows opened towards Jerusalem (Dan. vi. 10). The Mahometans pray everywhere with their faces turned toward Mecca. But there is no evidence in the Hebrew text that Hezekiah prayed in that manner. The simple idea is, that he turned over on his couch toward the wall of his room, doubtless, for the greater privacy, and to hide his deep emotion.

3. *And said, Remember now, O* LORD, *I beseech thee.* The object which Hezekiah desired was evidently that his life might be spared, and that he might not be suddenly cut off. He therefore makes mention of the former course of his life, not with ostentation, or as a ground of his acceptance or justification, but *as a reason* why his life should not be cut off. He had not lived as many of the kings of Israel had done. He had not been a patron of idolatry. He had promoted an extensive and thorough

reformation among the people. He had exerted his influence as a king in the service of JEHOVAH, and it was his purpose still to do it ; and he, therefore, prayed that his life might be spared in order that he might carry forward and perfect his plans for the reformation of the people, and for the establishment of the worship of JEHOVAH. ¶ *How I have walked.* How I have lived. Life, in the Scriptures, is often represented as a journey, and a life of piety is represented as walking with God (see Gen. v. 24; vi. 9; 1 Kings ix. 4; xi. 33). ¶ *In truth.* In the defence and maintenance of the truth, or in sincerity. ¶ *And with a perfect heart.* With a heart sound, sincere, *entire* in thy service. This had been his leading aim ; his main, grand purpose. He had not pursued his own ends, but his whole official royal influence had been on the side of religion. This refers to his *public* character rather than to his private feelings. For though, as a man, he might be deeply conscious of imperfection ; yet as a king, his influence had been wholly on the side of religion, and he had not declined from the ways of God. ¶ *And have done* that which is *good.* This accords entirely with the account which is given of him in 2 Kings xviii. 3–5. ¶ *And Hezekiah wept sore.* Marg. as Heb. ' With great weeping.' Josephus (*Ant.* x. 2. 1) says, that the reason why Hezekiah was so much affected was that he was then childless, and saw that he was about to leave the government without a successor. Others suppose that it was because his death would be construed by his enemies as a judgment of God for his stripping the temple of its ornaments (2 Kings xviii. 16). It is possible that several things may have been combined in producing the depth of his grief. In his song, or in the record which he made to express his praise to God for his recovery, the main reason of his grief which he suggested was, the fact that he was in

4 Then came the word of the Lord to Isaiah, saying,

5 Go and say to Hezekiah, Thus saith the Lord, the God of David thy father, I have heard thy prayer, I have seen thy tears: be-

hold, I will add unto thy days fifteen years.

6 And I will deliver thee and this city out of the hand of the king of Assyria: and I will defend this city.

danger of being cut off in the midst of his days ; that the blessings of a long life were likely to be denied him (see ver. 10–12). We have here an instance in which even a good man may be surprised, alarmed, distressed, at the sudden announcement that he must die. The fear of death is natural ; and even those who are truly pious are *sometimes* alarmed when it comes.

4. *Then came the word of the* Lord. In the parallel place in 2 Kings xx. 4, it is said, ' And it came to pass, afore Isaiah was gone out into the middle court, that the word of the Lord came unto him.' That is, the message of God came to Isaiah before he had left Hezekiah ; or as soon as he had offered his prayer. This circumstance is omitted by Isaiah on the revision of his narrative which we have before us. But there is no contradiction. In this place it is implied that the message came to him soon, or immediately.

5. *The God of David thy father*. David is mentioned here, probably, because Hezekiah had a strong resemblance to him (2 Kings xviii. 3), and because a long and happy reign had been granted to David ; and also because the promise had been made to David that there should not fail a man to sit on his throne (see Note on ch. xxxvii. 35). As Hezekiah resembled David, God promised that his reign should be lengthened out ; and as he perhaps was then without a son and successor, God promised him a longer life, with the prospect that he might have an heir who should succeed him on the throne. ¶ *Behold, I will add unto thy days fifteen years.* This is perhaps the only instance in which any man has been told exactly how long he would live. Why God *specified* the time cannot now be known. It was, however, a full answer to the prayer of Hezekiah, and the promise is a full demonstration that God is the hearer of prayer, and that he can answer it at

once.—We learn here, that it is right for a friend of God to pray for life. In times of sickness, and even when there are indications of a fatal disease, it is not improper to pray that the disease may be removed, and the life prolonged. If the desire be to do good ; to advance the kingdom of God ; to benefit others ; or to perfect some plan of benevolence which is begun, it is not improper to pray that God would prolong the life. Who can tell but that he *often* thus spares useful lives when worn down with toil, and when the frame is apparently sinking to the grave, in answer to prayer ? He does not indeed work miracles as he did in the case of Hezekiah, but he may direct to remedies which had not before occurred ; or he may himself give a sudden and unlooked-for turn to the disease, and restore the sufferer again to health.

6. *And I will deliver thee and this city.* The purport of this promise is, that he and the city should be *finally* and *entirely* delivered from all danger of invasion from the Assyrians. It *might* be apprehended that Sennacherib would collect a large army, and return ; or that his successor would prosecute the war which he had commenced. But the assurance here is given to Hezekiah that he had nothing more to fear from the Assyrians (see Notes on ch. xxxi. 4, 5 ; xxxvii. 35). In the parallel place in 2 Kings xx. 6, it is added, ' I will defend this city for mine own sake, and for my servant David's sake.' In the parallel passage also, in 2 Kings xx. 7, 8, there is inserted the statement which occurs in Isaiah at the end of the chapter (ver. 21, 22). It is evident that those two verses more appropriately come in here. Lowth conjectures that the abridger of the history omitted those verses, and when he had transcribed the song of Hezekiah, he saw that they were necessary to complete the narrative, and placed them at the end of the chapter,

7 And this *shall be* a sign *a* unto thee from the LORD, that the LORD will do this thing that he hath spoken;

8 Behold, I will bring again the

a ch.7.11,14.

shadow of the degrees, which is gone down in the sun-dial 1 of Ahaz, ten degrees backward. So the sun returned ten degrees, by which degrees it was gone down.

1 *degrees by,* or, *with the sun.*

with proper marks to have them inserted in the right place, which marks were overlooked by transcribers. It is, however, immaterial *where* the statement is made; and it is now impossible to tell in what manner the transposition occurred.

7. *And this* shall be *a sign unto thee.* That is, a sign, or proof that God would do what he had promised, and that Hezekiah would recover and be permitted to go again to the temple of the Lord (ver. 22; 2 Kings xx. 8). On the meaning of the word 'sign,' see Notes on ch. vii. 11, 14; comp. Note on ch. xxxvii. 30. The promise was, that he should be permitted to go to the temple in three days (2 Kings xx. 5).

8. *Behold, I will bring again the shadow.* The shadow, or shade which is made by the interception of the rays of the sun by the gnomon on the dial. The phrase 'bring again' (Heb. מֵשִׁיב) means *to cause to return* (Hiphil, from שׁוּב, *to return*); that is, I will cause it retrograde, or bring back. LXX. Στρέψω—'I will turn back.' Few subjects have perplexed commentators more than this account of the sun-dial of Ahaz. The only other place where a sun-dial is mentioned in the Scriptures is in the parallel place in 2 Kings xx. 9, 10, where the account is somewhat more full, and the nature of the miracle more fully represented : ' This sign shalt thou have of the LORD, that the LORD will do the thing which he hath spoken : —Shall the shadow go forward ten degrees, or go back ten degrees? And Hezekiah answered, It is a light thing for the shadow to go down ten degrees; nay, but let the shadow return backward ten degrees.' That is, it would be in the usual direction which the shadow takes, for it to go *down*, and there would be less that would be decisive in the miracle. He therefore asked that it might be moved backward from its common direction, and then there could be

no doubt that it was from God ; 2 Kings xx. 11: ' And Isaiah the prophet cried unto JEHOVAH, and he brought the shadow ten degrees backward, by which it had gone down in the dial of Ahaz.' ¶ *The shadow of the degrees.* That is, the shadow made *on* the degrees ; or indicated by the degrees on the dial. But there has been much difficulty in regard to the meaning of the word *degrees.* The Hebrew word (מַעֲלָה from עָלָה, *to ascend, to go up*) means properly *an ascent;* a going up from a lower to a higher region ; then a *step* by which one ascends, applied to the steps on a staircase, &c. (1 Kings x. 19; Ezek. xl. 26, 31, 34.) Hence it may be applied to the ascending or descending figures or marks on a dial designating the ascent or descent of the sun ; or the ascent or descent of the shadow going up or down by *steps* or hours marked on its face. The word is applied to a *dial* nowhere else but here. Josephus understands this as referring to the steps in the house or palace of Ahaz. ' He desired that he would make the shadow of the sun which he had already made to go down ten steps in his house, to return again to the same place, and to make it as it was before ;' by which he evidently regarded Hezekiah as requesting that the shadow which had gone down on the steps of the palace should return to its place ten steps backward. It is possible that the time of day *may* have been indicated by the shadow of the sun on the steps of the palace, and that this may have constituted what was called the sun-dial of Ahaz; but the more probable interpretation is that which regards the dial as a distinct and separate contrivance. The LXX. render it by the word *steps,* yet understanding it as Josephus does, Ἀναβαθμοὺς τοῦ οἴκου τοῦ πατρός σου—' The steps of the house of thy father.' ¶ *Which is gone down on the sun-dial of Ahaz.* Marg. ' Degrees by,' or ' with the sun.' Heb. literally, 'which has descended on the steps, or degrees of Ahaz by, or with the sun' (בְמַעֲלוֹת), that is, by means of the sun, or caused by the progress of the sun. The shadow had gone down on the dial by the regular course of the sun. Ahaz was the father of Hezekiah ; and it is evident from this, that the dial had been introduced by him, and had been used by him to measure time. There is no mention of any instrument for keeping time in the Bible before this, nor is it possible, perhaps, to determine the origin or character of this invention, or to know where Ahaz obtained it. Perhaps all that can be known on the subject has been collected by Calmet, to whose article [Dial] in his Dictionary, and to the Fragments of Taylor appended to his Dictionary (Fragments, ii., cii.) the reader may be referred for a more full statement on this subject than is consistent with the design of these Notes. The mention of the dial does not occur before the time of Ahaz, who lived b.c. 726; nor is it certainly known that even after his time the Jews generally divided their time by hours. The word 'hour' (καιρικός) occurs first in Tobit ; and it has been supposed that the invention of *dials* came from beyond the Euphrates (Herod. ii. 109). But others suppose that it came from the Phenicians, and that the first traces of it are discoverable in what Homer says (*Odyss.* xv. 402) of 'an island called Syria lying above Ortygia, where the revolutions of the sun are observed.' The Phenicians are supposed to have inhabited this island of Syria, and it is therefore presumed that they left there this monument of their skill in astronomy. About three hundred years after Homer, Pherecydes set up a sun-dial in the same island to distinguish the hours. The Greeks confess that Anaximander, who lived b.c. 547, under the reign of Cyrus, first divided time by hours, and introduced sun-dials among them. This was during the time of the captivity at Babylon. Anaximander travelled into Chaldea, and it is not improbable that he brought the dial from Babylon. The Chaldeans were early distinguished for their attention to astronomy, and it is probable that it was in Babylon that the sun-dial, and the division of the day

into hours, was first used, and that the knowledge of that was conveyed in some way from Chaldea to Ahaz. Interpreters have differed greatly in regard to the *form* of the sun-dial used by Ahaz, and by the ancients generally. Cyril of Alexandria and Jerome believed it was a staircase so disposed, that the sun showed the hours on it by the shadow. This, as we have seen, was the opinion of Josephus ; and this opinion has been followed by many others. Others suppose it was an obelisk or pillar in the middle of a smooth pavement on which the hours were engraved, or on which lines were drawn which would indicate the hours. Grotius, in accordance with the opinion of Rabbi Elias Chomer, describes it thus : ' It was a concave hemisphere, in the midst of which was a globe, the shadow of which fell upon several lines engraved on the concavity of the hemisphere ; these lines, they say, were eight-and-twenty in number.' This description accords nearly with the kind of dial which the Greeks called *scapha*, a boat, or *hemisphere*, the invention of which the Greeks ascribed to a Chaldean named Berosus (Vitruv. ix. 9). See the plate in Taylor's Calmet, ' Sun-dial of Ahaz' (Figs. 1 and 2). Berosus was a priest of Belus in Babylon, and lived indeed perhaps 300 years after Ahaz ; but there is no necessity of supposing that he was the *inventor* of the dial. It is sufficient to suppose that he was reputed to be the first who introduced it into Greece. He went from Babylon to Greece, where he taught astronomy first at Cos, and then at Athens, where one of his dials is still shown. Herodotus expressly says (i. 109), ' the pole, the gnomon, and the division of the day into twelve parts, the Greeks received from the Babylonians.' This sun-dial was portable ; it did not require to be constructed for a particular spot to which it should be subsequently confined ; and therefore one ready-made might have been brought from Babylon to Ahaz. That he had commerce with these countries appears by his alliance with Tiglath-pileser (2 Kings xvi. 7, 8). And that Ahaz was a man who was desirous of availing himself of foreign inventions, and introducing them into his capital, appears evident from his desire to have an altar constructed in Jerusalem, similar to the one which he had seen in Damascus (2 Kings xvi. 10). The dial is now a well-known instrument, the *principle* of which is, that the hours are marked on its face by a *shadow* cast from the sun by a gnomon. In order to the understanding of this miracle, it is not necessary to be acquainted with the form of the ancient dial. It will be understood by a reference to *any* dial, and would have been substantially the same, whatever was the form of the instrument. The essential idea is, that the shadow of the gnomon which thus indicated a certain degree or hour of the day, was made to go back ten degrees or places. It may conduce,

however, to the illustration of this subject to have before the eye a representation of the usual form of the ancient dial, and I therefore annex three forms of dials which have been discovered. 'The engraving represents—1. A concave dial of white marble, found at Civita, in the year 1762. 2. Another concave dial, found at mount Tusculum, near Rome, in 1726. 3. A compound dial, preserved in the Elgin collection in the British Museum. It was found at Athens, supposed to have been used in marking the hours on one of the crossways of the city. The first two are considered to resemble, if indeed they be not identical with the famous dial of Ahaz.'

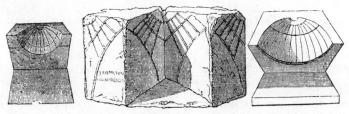

ANCIENT SUN DIALS.—From Specimens in British Museum.

In regard to this miracle, it seems only necessary to observe that all that is indispensable to be believed is, that the shadow on the dial was made suddenly to recede from *any* cause. It is evident that this may have been accomplished in several ways. It may have been by arresting the motion of the earth in its revolutions, and causing it to retrograde on its axis to the extent indicated by the return of the shadow, or it may have been by a miraculous *bending*, or inclining of the rays of the sun. As there is no evidence that the event was observed elsewhere; and as it is not *necessary* to suppose that the earth was arrested in its motion, and that the whole frame of the universe was adjusted to this change in the movement of the earth, it is most probable that it was an inclination of the rays of the sun ; or a miraculous causing of the *shadow* itself to recede. This is the whole statement of the sacred writer, and this is all that is necessary to be supposed. What Hezekiah desired was a miracle; a sign that he should recover.

That was granted. The retrocession of the shadow in this sudden manner was not a natural event. It could be caused only by God ; and *this* was all that was needed. A simple exertion of Divine power on the rays of the sun which rested on the dial, deflecting those rays, would accomplish the whole result. It may be added that it is not recorded, nor is it necessary to an understanding of the subject to suppose, that the bending of the rays was *permanent*, or that so much time was *lost*. The miracle was instantaneous, and was satisfactory to Hezekiah, though the rays of the sun casting the shadow may have again been soon returned to their regular position, and the shadow restored to the place in which it would have been had it not been interrupted. No infidel, therefore, can object to this statement, unless he can prove that this *could* not be done by him who made the sun, and who is himself the fountain of power. ¶ *By which degrees it was gone down.* By the same *steps*, or degrees on which the shadow had descended. So the

9 The writing of Hezekiah king of Judah, when he had been sick, and was recovered of his sickness:

10 I said *a*in the cutting off of

my days, I shall go to the gates of the grave: I am deprived of the residue of my years.

11 I said, I shall not see the

a Job 7.7,&c.; Ps.77,3,&c.

LXX. express it; 'so the sun re-ascended the ten steps by which the shadow had gone down.' It was the *shadow* on the dial which had gone down. The *sun* was *ascending,* and the consequence was, of course, that the shadow on a vertical dial would *descend.* The ' sun ' here means, evidently, the sun *as it appeared;* the rays, or the shining of the sun. A return of the shadow was effected such as would be produced by the recession of the sun itself.

9. *The writing of Hezekiah.* This is the title to the following hymn—a record which Hezekiah made to celebrate the goodness of God in restoring him to health. The writing itself is *poetry,* as is indicated by the parallelism, and by the general structure. It is in many respects quite obscure—an obscurity perhaps arising from the brevity and conciseness which are apparent in the whole piece. It is remarkable that this song or hymn is not found in the parallel passage in the Book of Kings. The reason why it was omitted there, and inserted here, is unknown. It is *possible* that it was drawn up for Hezekiah by Isaiah, and that it is inserted here as a part of his composition, though adopted by Hezekiah, and declared to be *his,* that is, as expressing the gratitude of his heart on his recovery from his disease. It was common to compose an ode or hymn of praise on occasion of deliverance from calamity, or any remarkable interposition of God (see Notes on ch. xii. 1; xxv. 1; xxvi. 1). Many of the Psalms of David were composed on such occasions, and were expressive of gratitude to God for deliverance from impending calamity. The hymn or song is composed of two parts. In the first part (ver. 10–14), Hezekiah describes his feelings and his fears when he was suffering, and especially the apprehension of his mind at the prospect of death; and the second part (ver. 15–20) expresses praise to God for his goodness.

10. *I said.* Probably the words ' I

said ' do not imply that he said or spoke this openly or audibly; but this was the language of his heart, or the substance of his reflections. ¶ *In the cutting off of my days.* There has been considerable diversity of interpretation in regard to this phrase. Vitringa renders it as our translators have done. Rosenmüller renders it, ' In the meridian of my days.' The LXX. 'Εν τῷ ὕψει τῶν ἡμερῶν μου—' In the height of my days,' where they evidently read ברמי instead of בדמי, by the change of a single letter. Aquila, and the Greek interpreters generally, rendered it, ' In the silence of my days.' The word here used in Hebrew (דְּמִי) denotes properly *stillness,* quiet, rest; and Gesenius renders it, ' in the quiet of my days.' According to him the idea is, ' now when I might have rest; when I am delivered from my foes; when I am in the midst of my life, of my reign, and of my plans of usefulness, I must die.' The sense is, doubtless, that he was about to be cut off in middle life, and when he had every prospect of usefulness, and of happiness in his reign. ¶ *I shall go to the gates of the grave.* Heb. ' Gates of sheol.' On the meaning of the word *sheol,* and the Hebrew idea of the descent to it through gates, see Notes on ch. v. 14; xiv. 9. The idea is, that he must go down to the regions of the dead, and dwell with departed shades (see Note on ver. 11). ¶ *The residue of my years.* Those which I had hoped to enjoy; of which I had a reasonable prospect in the ordinary course of events. It is evident that Hezekiah had looked forward to a long life, and to a prosperous and peaceful reign. *This* was the means which God adopted to show him the impropriety of his desire, and to turn him more entirely to his service, and to a preparation for death.—Sickness often has this effect on the minds of good men.

11. *I shall not see the* Lord. In the

LORD, *even* the LORD, in *a* the land of the living : I shall behold man no more with the inhabitants of the world.

12 Mine age is departed, and is

a Ps. 27. 13.

original, the Hebrew which is rendered ' LORD,' is not JEHOVAH, but יָהּ יָהּ (JAH, JAH.) On the meaning of it, see Note on ch. xii. 2 (comp. Note on ch. vii. 14). The *repetition* of the name here denotes *emphasis* or *intensity of feeling*—the deep desire which he had to see JEHO-VAH in the land of the living, and the intense sorrow of his heart at the idea of being cut off from that privilege. The idea here is, that Hezekiah felt that he would not be spared to enjoy the tokens of Divine favour on earth ; to reap the fruits of the surprising and remarkable deliverance from the army of Senna-cherib ; and to observe its happy results in the augmenting prosperity of the people, and in the complete success of his plans of reformation.   ¶ *I shall behold man no more.* I shall see the living no more ; I shall die, and go among the dead.   He regarded it as a privilege to live, and to enjoy the society of his friends and fellow-worshippers in the temple—a privilege from which he felt that he was about to be cut off. ¶ *With the inhabitants of the world.* Or rather, ' amongst the inhabitants of the land of stillness ;' that is, of the land of shades—*sheol.* He would not there see man as he saw him on earth, living and active, but would be a shade in the land of shades ; himself still, in a world of stillness.   ' I shall be associated with them there, and of course be cut off from the privileges of the society of living men.'   [See Supplementary Note on ch. xiv. 9.]   The Hebrew word rendered ' world ' (חֶדֶל), is from חָדַל, *to cease,* to leave off, to desist ; to become languid, flaccid, pendulous.   It then conveys the idea of leaving off, of rest-ing, of being still (Judg. v. 6; Job iii. 17; xiv. 6; Isa. ii. 22).   Hence the idea of *frailty* (Ps. xxxix. 5); and hence the word here denotes probably the place of rest, the region of the dead, and is synonymous with the land of *silence,* such as the grave and the region

removed from me as a shepherd's tent : I have cut off like a weaver my life : he will cut me off [1] with pining sickness : from day *even* to night wilt thou make an end of me.

1 or, *from the* thrum.

of the dead are in contradistinction from the hurry and bustle of this world.   Our translation seems to have been made as if the word was חֶלֶד, *life, lifetime* ; hence the world (Ps. xvii. 14 ; xlix. 2). The Vulgate renders it, ' *Habitatorem quietis.*'   The LXX. simply, ' I shall behold man no more.'

12. *Mine age.*   The word which is here used (דּוֹר) means properly the revolving period or circle of human life. The parallelism seems to demand, how-ever, that it should be used in the sense of *dwelling* or habitation, so as to corre-spond with the ' shepherd's tent.'   Ac-cordingly, Lowth and Noyes render it, ' Habitation.'   So also do Gesenius and Rosenmüller.   The Arabic word has this signification ; and the Hebrew verb דּוּר also means *to dwell, to remain,* as in the Chaldee.   Here the word means a dwelling, or habitation ; that is, a tent, as the habitations of the Orientals were mostly tents.   ¶ *Is departed* (נִסַּע).   The idea here is, that his dwell-ing was to be transferred from one place to another, as when a tent or encamp-ment was broken up ; that is, he was about to cease to dwell on the earth, and to dwell in the land of silence, or among the dead.   ¶ *From me as a shep-herd's tent.*   As suddenly as the tent of a shepherd is taken down, folded up, and transferred to another place. There is doubtless the idea here that he would continue to *exist,* but in another place, as the shepherd would pitch his tent or dwell in another place.   He was to be cut off from the earth, but he expected to dwell among the dead.   The whole passage conveys the idea that he expected to dwell in another state—as the shepherd dwells in another place when he strikes his tent, and it is re-moved.   ¶ *I have cut off like a weaver my life.* This is another image designed to express substantially the same idea. The sense is, as a weaver takes his web from the loom by cutting the warp, or

13 I reckoned till morning, *that*, as a lion, so will he break all my bones: from day *even* to night wilt thou make an end of me.

14 Like a crane *or* a swallow, so did I chatter; I did mourn *a* as a dove: mine eyes fail *with looking* upward: O LORD, I am oppressed; undertake for 1 me.

a ch.59.11.   1 or, *ease me.*

the threads which bind it to the beam, and thus *loosens* it and takes it away, so his life was to be cut off. When it is said, ' I cut off ' (קִפַּדְתִּי), the idea is, doubtless, I *am* cut off; or my life is cut off. Hezekiah here speaks of himself as the agent, because he might have felt that his sins and unworthiness were the cause. Life is often spoken of as a web that is woven, because an advance is constantly made in filling up the web, and because it is soon finished, and is then cut off. ¶ *He will cut me off.* God was about to cut me off. ¶ *With pining sickness.* Marg. ' From the thrum.' Lowth, 'From the loom.' The word דַּלָּה means properly something hanging down or pendulous ; anything pliant or slender. Hence it denotes *hair* or locks (Cant. vii. 6). Here it seems to denote the *threads* or *thrums* which tied the web to the weaver's beam. The image here denotes the cutting off of life as the weaver cuts his web out of the loom, or as he cuts off thrums. The word never means sickness. ¶ *From day* even *to night.* That is, in the space of a single day, or between morning and night—as a weaver with a short web accomplishes it in a single day. The disease of Hezekiah was doubtless the pestilence ; and the idea is, that God would cut him off speedily, as it were in a single day. ¶ *Wilt thou make an end of me.* Heb. ' Wilt thou perfect ' or ' finish ' me ; that is, wilt thou take my life.

13. *I reckoned.* There has been considerable variety in interpreting this expression. The LXX. render it, ' I was given up in the morning as to a lion.' The Vulgate renders it, ' I hoped until morning ;' and in his commentary, Jerome says it means, that as Job in his trouble and anguish (ch. vii. 4) sustained himself at night expecting the day, and in the daytime waiting for the night, expecting a change for the better, so Hezekiah waited during the night expecting relief in the morning. He

knew, says he, that the violence of a burning fever would very soon subside, and he thus composed himself, and calmly waited. So Vitringa renders it, ' I composed my mind until the morning.' Others suppose that the word here used (שִׁוִּיתִי), means, ' I made myself *like* a lion,' that is, in roaring. But the more probable and generally adopted interpretation is, ' I looked to God, hoping that the disease would soon subside, *but* as a lion he crushed my bones. The disease increased in violence, and became past endurance. *Then* I chattered like a swallow, and mourned like a dove, over the certainty that I must die.'—Our translators, by inserting the word ' that,' have greatly marred the sense, as if he had *reckoned* or calculated through the night that God *would* break his bones, or increase the violence of the disease, whereas the reverse was true. He hoped and expected that it would be otherwise, and with that view he composed his mind. ¶ *As a lion so will he break all my bones.* This should be in the past tense. ' He [God] *did* crush all my bones. The connection requires this construction. The idea is, that as a lion crushes the bones of his prey, producing great pain and sudden death, so it was with God in producing great pain and the prospect of sudden death. ¶ *From day* even *to night,* &c. (see Note on ver. 12.) Between morning and night. That is, his pain so resembled the crushing of all the bones of an animal by the lion, that he could not hope to survive the day.

14. *Like a crane.* The word used here (סוּס) denotes usually a *horse.* The Rabbins render it here ' a crane.' Gesenius translates it ' a swallow ;' and in his Lexicon interprets the word which is translated ' a swallow ' (עָגוּר) to mean *circling,* making gyrations ; and the whole phrase, ' as the circling swallow.' The Syriac renders this, ' As the chattering swallow.' The Vulgate, ' As the young of the swallow.' The LXX.

15 What shall I say? he hath both spoken unto me, and himself hath done *it:* I shall go softly all my years in the bitterness of my soul.

simply 'As the swallow.' That two birds are intended here, or that some fowl is denoted by the word עָגוּר, is manifest from Jer. viii. 7, where it is mentioned as distinct from the סוּס (the crane) וְסוּס עָגוּר. On the meaning of the words Bochart may be consulted (*Hieroz.* i. 2. p. 602). It is probable that the swallow and the crane are intended. The swallow is well known, and is remarkable for its twittering. The crane is also a well-known bird with long limbs made to go in the water. Its noise may be expressive of grief. ¶ *So did I chatter.* Peep, or twitter (see Note on ch. viii. 19). The idea here is doubtless that of pain that was expressed in sounds resembling that made by birds—a broken, unmeaning, unintelligible sighing ; or quick breathing, and moaning. ¶ *I did mourn as a dove.* The dove, from its plaintive sound, is an emblem of grief. It is so used in ch. lix. 11. The idea is that of the *lonely* or *solitary* dove that is lamenting or mourning for its companion :

'Just as the lonely dove laments its mate.'

¶ *Mine eyes fail.* The word here used (דַּלּוּ) means properly *to hang down,* to swing like the branches of the willow ; then to be languid, feeble, weak. Applied to the eye, it means that it languishes and becomes weak. ¶ With looking *upward.* To God, for relief and comfort. He had looked so long and so intensely toward heaven for aid, that his eyes became weak and feeble. ¶ *O* Lord, *I am oppressed.* This was his language in his affliction. He was so oppressed and borne down, that he cried to God for relief. ¶ *Undertake for me.* Marg. 'Ease me.' The word (עָרַב) more properly means, to become surety for him. See it explained in the Note on ch. xxxvi. 8. Here it means, be surety for my life ; give assurance that I shall be restored ; take me under thy protection (see Ps. cxix. 122): 'Be surety for thy servant for good.'

15. *What shall I say?* This language seems to denote surprise and gratitude at unexpected deliverance.

It is the language of a heart that is overflowing, and that wants words to express its deep emotions. In the previous verse he had described his pain, anguish, and despair. In this he records the sudden and surprising deliverance which God had granted ; which was so great that no words could express his sense of it. Nothing could be more natural than this language ; nothing would more appropriately express the feelings of a man who had been suddenly restored to health from dangerous sickness, and brought from the borders of the grave. ¶ *He hath both spoken unto me.* That is, he has *promised.* So the word is often used (Deut. xxvi. 17; Jer. iii. 19). He had made the promise by the instrumentality of Isaiah (ver. 5, 6). The promise related to his recovery, to the length of his days, and to his entire deliverance from the hands of the Assyrians. ¶ *And himself hath done* it. He himself has restored me according to his promise, when no one else could have done it. ¶ *I shall go softly.* Lowth renders this, in accordance with the Vulgate, 'Will I reflect.' But the Hebrew will not bear this construction. The word here used (אֶדַּדֶּה) occurs in but one other place in the Bible (Ps. xlii. 4): 'I *went* with them to the house of God ;' *i.e.,* I went with them in a sacred procession to the house of God ; I went with a solemn, calm, slow pace. The idea here is, 'I will go humbly, submissively, all my life ; I will walk in a serious manner, remembering that I am travelling to the grave ; I will avoid pride, pomp, and display ; I will suffer the remembrance of my sickness, and of God's mercy to produce a calm, serious, thoughtful demeanour all my life.' This is the *proper* effect of sickness on a pious mind, and it is its *usual* effect. And probably, one design of God was to keep Hezekiah from the ostentatious parade usually attendant on his lofty station ; from being elated with his deliverance from the Assyrian ; from improper celebrations of that deliverance by revelry and pomp ; and to keep him in remembrance, that though he

16 O Lord, by these *things men* live, *a* and in all these *things is* the life of my spirit: so wilt thou recover me, and make me to live.

17 Behold, [1] for peace I had great bitterness ; but thou hast [2] in love to my soul *delivered it* from the pit

of *b* corruption : for thou hast cast all my sins behind thy back.

18 For the grave *c* cannot praise thee, death cannot celebrate thee: they that go down into the pit cannot hope for thy truth.

a Mat.4.4.   1 or, *on my peace* came.
2 *loved my soul from the pit.*   *b* Ps.10.2.   *c* Ps.6.5.

---

was a monarch, yet he was a mortal man, and that he held his life at the disposal of God. ¶ *In the bitterness of my soul.* I will remember the deep distress, the bitter sorrows of my sickness, and my surprising recovery ; and will allow the remembrance of that to diffuse seriousness and gratitude over all my life.

16. *O* Lord, *by these* things men *live.* The design of this and the following verses is evidently to set forth the goodness of God, and to celebrate his praise for what he had done. The phrase 'these things,' refers evidently to the *promises* of God and their *fulfilment ;* and the idea is, that men are sustained in the land of the living only by such gracious interpositions as he had experienced. It was not because men had any power of preserving their own lives, but because God interposed in time of trouble, and restored to health when there was no human prospect that they could recover. ¶ *And in all these* things. In these promises, and in the Divine interposition. ¶ Is *the life of my spirit.* I am alive in virtue only of these things. ¶ *So wilt thou recover me.* Or so *hast* thou recovered me ; that is, thou hast restored me to health.

17. *Behold, for peace.* That is, instead of the health, happiness, and prosperity which I had enjoyed, and which I hope still to enjoy. ¶ *I had great bitterness.* Heb. ' Bitterness to me, bitterness;' an emphatic expression, denoting intense sorrow. ¶ *But thou hast in love to my soul.* Marg. ' Loved my soul from the pit.' The word which occurs here (חָשַׁק) denotes properly *to join* or *fasten together ;* then to be attached to any one ; to be united tenderly ; to embrace. Here it means that God had loved him, and had thus delivered his soul from death. ¶ Delivered *it from the pit of corruption.* The

word rendered corruption (בְּלִי), denotes consumption, destruction, perdition. It may be applied to the grave, or to the deep and dark abode of departed spirits ; and the phrase here is evidently synonymous with *sheol* or *hades.* The grave, or the place for the dead, is often represented as *a pit*—deep and dark—to which the living descend (Job xvii. 16 ; xxxiii. 18, 24, 28, 30 ; Ps. xxviii. 1 ; xxx. 3 ; lv. 23 ; lxix. 15 ; lxxxviii. 4 ; comp. Note on Isa. xiv. 15, 19). ¶ *For thou hast cast all my sins behind thy back.* Thou hast forgiven them ; hast ceased to punish me on account of them. This shows that Hezekiah, in accordance with the sentiment everywhere felt and expressed in the Bible, regarded his suffering as the fruit of sin.

18. *For the grave cannot praise thee.* The Hebrew word here is *sheol.* It is put by metonymy here for those who are *in* the grave, *i.e.,* for the dead. The word ' praise ' here refers evidently to the public and solemn celebration of the goodness of God. It is clear, I think, that Hezekiah had a belief in a future state, or that he expected to dwell with ' the inhabitants of the land of silence ' (ver. 11) when he died. But he did not regard that state as one adapted to the celebration of the public praises of God. It was a land of darkness ; an abode of silence and stillness ; a place where there was no temple, and no public praise such as he had been accustomed to. A similar sentiment is expressed by David in Ps. vi. 5 :

For in death there is no remembrance of thee ;
In the grave who shall give thee thanks ?

In regard to the Jewish conceptions of the state of the dead, see Notes on ch. xiv. 15, 19.

[See the Supplementary Note on ch. xiv. 9 ; also the Prefatory Remarks by the Editor on the Author's exposition of Job. The ideas entertained by the Author on the state of knowledge

19 The living, the living, he shall praise thee, as I *do* this day: the father *a* to the children shall make known thy truth.

20 The LORD *was ready* to save me: therefore we will sing my songs to the stringed instruments all the

a Ps.78.3,4.

days of our life in the house of the LORD.

21 For Isaiah had said, Let them take a lump of figs, and lay *it* for a plaster upon the boil, and he shall recover.

22 Hezekiah also had said, What

---

among the ancient saints regarding a future world, cannot but be regarded as peculiarly unfortunate. After the fashion of some German critics, the Old Testament worthies are reduced to the same level with the heroes of Homer and Virgil, as far as this matter is concerned at least.]

¶ *Cannot hope for thy truth.* They are shut out from all the means by which thy truth is brought to the mind, and the offers of salvation are presented. Their probation is at an end; their privileges are closed; their destiny is sealed up. The idea is, it is a privilege to live, because this is a world where the offers of salvation are made, and where those who are conscious of guilt may hope in the mercy of God.

19. *The living, the living.* An emphatic or intensive form of expression, as in ver. 11, 17. Nothing would express his idea but a repetition of the word, as if the heart was full of it. ¶ *The father to the children.* One generation of the living to another. The father shall have so deep a sense of the goodness of God that he shall desire to make it known to his children, and to perpetuate the memory of it in the earth.

20. *The* LORD was ready *to save me.* He was prompt, quick to save me. He did not hesitate or delay. ¶ *Therefore we will sing my songs.* That is, my family and nation. The song of Hezekiah was designed evidently not as a mere *record*, but to be used in celebrating the praises of God, and probably in a public manner in the temple. The restoration of the monarch was a fit occasion for public rejoicing; and it is probable that this ode was composed to be used by the company of singers that were employed constantly in the temple. ¶ *To the stringed instruments.* We will set it to music, and will use it publicly (see Notes on ch. v. 12).

21. *For Isaiah had said.* In the

parallel place in Kings the statement in these two verses is introduced *before* the account of the miracle on the sun-dial, and before the account of his recovery (2 Kings xx. 7, 8). The order in which it is introduced, however, is not material. ¶ *Let them take a lump of figs.* The word here used (דְּבֵלָה) denotes *a round cake* of dried figs pressed together in a mass (1 Sam. xxv. 18). Figs were thus pressed together for preservation, and for convenience of conveyance. ¶ *And lay it for a plaster.* The word here used (מָרַח) denotes properly *to rub*, bruise, crush by rubbing; then to rub, in, to anoint, to soften. Here it means they were to take dried figs and lay them softened on the ulcer. ¶ *Upon the boil* (הַשְּׁחִין). This word means a burning sore or an inflamed ulcer (Ex. ix. 9, 11; Lev. xiii. 18–20). The verb in Arabic means to be hot, inflamed; to ulcerate. The noun is used to denote a species of black leprosy in Egypt, called Elephantiasis, distinguished by the black scales with which the skin is covered, and by the swelling of the legs. Here it probably denotes a pestilential boil; an eruption, or inflamed ulceration produced by the plague, that threatened immediate death. Jerome says that the plaster of figs was medicinal, and adapted to reduce the inflammation and restore health. There is no improbability in the supposition; nor does any thing in the narrative prohibit us from supposing that natural means might have been used to restore him. The miracle consisted in the arrest of the shade on the sun-dial, and in the announcement of Isaiah that he would recover. That *figs*, when dried, were used in the Materia Medica of the ancients, is asserted by both Pliny and Celsus (see Pliny, *Nat. Hist.* xxiii. 7; Celsus, v. 2, quoted by Lowth.)

22. *Hezekiah also had said.* What

is the sign that I shall also go up
to the house *a* of the LORD ?

CHAPTER XXXIX.

ANALYSIS.

THIS short chapter completes the historical
part of Isaiah. The same record occurs with
some slight changes in 2 Kings xx. 12–21.
Comp. the Introduction to ch. xxxvi. The chapter is composed of the following parts :—1. The
statement that the king of Babylon sent an embassage to Hezekiah to congratulate him on his
recovery (1). This embassage contemplated also
an inquiry into the truth of the report in regard
to the miracle on the sun-dial (2 Chron. xxxii.
31). 2. Hezekiah showed them all his treasures
in an ostentatious and improper manner (2).
This was permitted, in order that he might be
tried, and might know all that was in his own

evidence or proof have I that I shall be
restored, and permitted to go to the
temple? The miracle on the sun-dial
was wrought in answer to this request,
and as a demonstration that he should
yet be permitted to visit the temple of
God (see Note on ver. 7).

CHAPTER XXXIX.

1. *At that time.* That is, soon after
his recovery; or after he had amassed
great wealth, and was surrounded with
the evidences of prosperity (2 Chron.
xxxii. 27–31). ¶ *Merodach-baladan,
the son of Baladan, king of Babylon*
In the parallel place in 2 Kings xx. 12,
this name is written Berodach-baladan,
by a change of a single letter. Probably the name was written and pronounced both ways. Merodach was an
idol of the Babylonians (Jer. l. 2) :
'Babylon is taken, Bel is confounded,
Merodach is confounded.' This idol,
according to Gesenius, was probably the
planet *Mars,* or Mars the god of war.
To this god, as well as to Saturn, the
ancient Semitic nations offered human
sacrifices (see Gesenius's *Lex.* and
Comm. in loc.) The word 'Baladan' is
also a compound word, and means 'Bel
is his lord.' The name of this idol,
Merodach, was often incorporated into
the proper names of kings, and of
others. Thus we have the names Evil-
Merodach, Messi-Mordachus, Sisimor-
dachus, Mardocentes, &c. In regard
to the statement of Isaiah in this verse,
no small degree of difficulty has been

heart, and not be lifted up with pride, and with
the conviction of his own righteousness (2 Chron.
xxxiii. 31). 0. Isaiah is sent with a message to
Hezekiah to inquire what he had done, and who
those ambassadors were (3–5). 4. He is directed
to deliver the solemn message of God that Jerusalem should be taken, and that all its inhabitants and all its treasures should be carried to
Babylon—the place whence those ambassadors
came (5–7). 5. Hezekiah expresses submission
to the just sentence and purpose of God, and
gratitude that it should not occur in his days (8).

A T *b* that time Merodach-baladan,
the son of Baladan, king of Babylon, sent letters and a present to
Hezekiah: for he had heard that he
had been sick, and was recovered.

a Ps.84.2.   *b* 2 Ki.20.12,&c.

felt by commentators, and it is not until
quite recently that the difficulty has
been removed, and it has been done in
a manner to furnish an additional and
most striking demonstration of the entire and minute accuracy of the sacred
narrative. The difficulty arose from
several circumstances—1. This king
of Babylon is nowhere else mentioned
in sacred history. 2. The kingdom
of Assyria was yet flourishing, and
Babylon was one of its dependencies.
For, only nine years before, Salmanas-
sar the Assyrian monarch is said to
have transported the inhabitants of Babylon to other parts (2 Kings xvii. 24),
and Manasseh, not many years after,
was carried captive to Babylon by the
king of Assyria (2 Chron. xxxiii. 11).
These instances incontestably prove that
at the time of Hezekiah, Babylon was
dependent on the Assyrian kings. Who,
then, it is asked, was this Merodach-
baladan, king of Babylon? If he was
governor of that city, how could he send
an embassy of congratulation to the
Jewish sovereign, then at war with his
liege lord? The canon of Ptolemy
gives us no king of this name, nor does
his chronology appear reconcilable with
sacred history.

'In this darkness and doubt,' says
Dr. Wiseman, 'we must have continued,
and the apparent contradiction of this
text to other passages would have remained inexplicable, had not the progress of modern Oriental study brought

2 And Hezekiah was glad of them and shewed them the house of his [1] precious things, the silver, and the gold, and the spices, and the precious ointment, and all the

1 or, *spicery.*

house of his [2] armour, and all that was found in his treasures: there was nothing in his house, nor in all his dominion, that Hezekiah shewed them not.

2 *vessels,* or, *instruments,* or, *jewels.*

to light a document of the most venerable antiquity. This is nothing less than a fragment of Berosus, preserved in the chronicle of Eusebius. This interesting fragment informs us, that after Sennacherib's brother had governed Babylon, as Assyrian viceroy, Acises unjustly possessed himself of the supreme command. After thirty days he was murdered by Merodach-baladan, who usurped the sovereignty for six months, when he was in turn killed, and was succeeded by Elibus. But after three years, Sennacherib collected an army, gave the usurper battle, conquered, and took him prisoner. Having once more reduced Babylon to his obedience, he left his son Assordan, the Esarhaddon of Scripture, as governor of the city.'

The only objection to this statement, or to the entire consistency of this fragment with the Scripture narrative is, that Isaiah relates the murder of Sennacherib, and the succession of Esarhaddon before Merodach-baladan's embassy to Jerusalem. But to this Gesenius has well replied, that this arrangement is followed by the prophet in order to conclude the history of the Assyrian monarch, which has no further connection with the subject, so as not to return to it again.

By this order, also, the prophecy of his murder is more closely connected with the history of its fulfilment (ch. xxxvii. 7; comp. ver. 38). And this solution, which supposes some interval to have elapsed between Sennacherib's return to Nineveh, and his death, is rendered probable by the words of the text itself. 'He went and returned, *and dwelt in Nineveh;* and it came to pass,' &c. (ch. xxxvii. 37, 38.)

Thus we have it certainly explained how there was a king, or rather a usurper in Babylon at the time when it was really a provincial city of the Assyrian empire. Nothing was more probable than that Merodach-baladan, having seized the throne, should endeavour to

unite himself in league and amity with the enemies of his master, against whom he had revolted. Hezekiah, who, no less than himself, had thrown off the Assyrian yoke, and was in powerful alliance with the king of Egypt, would be his first resource. No embassy, on the other hand, could be more welcome to the Jewish monarch who had the common enemy in his neighbourhood, and who would be glad to see a division made in his favour by a rebellion in the very heart of that enemy's kingdom. Hence arose that excessive attention which he paid to the envoys of the usurper, and which so offended Isaiah, or rather God, who, as a consequence, threatened the Babylonian captivity (see Dr. Wiseman's *Lectures on Science and Revealed Religion,* pp. 369–371. Ed. And. 1837). ¶ *Sent letters.* The LXX. add, καὶ πρέσβεις—'and ambassadors.' ¶ *And a present.* It was customary among the Orientals, as it is now, to send a valuable present when one prince sent an embassage for any purpose to another. It is stated in 2 Chron. xxxii. 31, that one object of their coming was to make inquiry ' of the wonder that was done in the land;' that is, of the miracle in regard to the retrocession of the shadow on the sun-dial of Ahaz. It is well known that, from the earliest periods, the Babylonians and Chaldeans were distinguished for their attention to astronomy. Indeed, as a science, astronomy was first cultivated on the plains of Chaldea; and there the knowledge of that science was scarcely surpassed by any of the ancient nations. The report which they had heard of this miracle would, therefore, be to them a matter of deep interest as an astronomical fact, and they came to make inquiry into the exact truth of the report.

2. *And Hezekiah was glad of them.* Possibly he regarded himself as flattered by an embassage from so great a distance, and so celebrated a place as Babylon. It is certain that he erred

3 Then came Isaiah the prophet unto king Hezekiah, and said unto him, What said these men? and from whence came they unto thee?

And Hezekiah said, They are come from a far country unto me, *even* from Babylon.

---

in some way in regard to the manner in which he received them, and especially in the ostentatious display which he made of his treasures (2 Chron. xxxii. 31). ¶ *And showed them the house of his precious things.* The LXX. render this, Νεχωθᾶ—'The house of Nechotha,' retaining the Hebrew word. The Marg. 'Spicery.' The Hebrew word (נְכֹת) properly means, according to Gesenius, *a contusion*, a breaking to pieces; hence *aromatic powder*, or spices reduced to powder, and then any kind of aromatics. Hence the word here may mean 'the house of his spices,' as Aquila, Symmachus, and the Vulgate translate it; or 'a treasury,' 'a storehouse,' as the Chaldee and the Syriac here render it. It was undoubtedly a treasure or storehouse; but it may have taken its name from the fact, that it was mainly employed as a place in which to keep spices, unguents, and the various kinds of aromatics which were used either in public worship, or for the purposes of luxury. ¶ *The silver and the gold.* Possibly Hezekiah may have obtained no small quantity of silver and gold from what was left in the camp of the Assyrians. It is certain that after he was delivered from danger he was signally prospered, and became one of the most wealthy and magnificent monarchs of the east; 2 Chron. xxxii. 27, 28: 'And Hezekiah had exceeding much riches and honour; and he made himself treasuries for silver and for gold, and for precious stones, and for spices, and for shields, and for all manner of pleasant jewels; storehouses also for the increase of corn, and wine, and oil; and stalls for all manner of beasts, and cotes for flocks.' A considerable part of this wealth arose from presents which were made to him, and from gifts which were made for the service of the temple (2 Chron. xxxii. 23). ¶ *And the precious ointment.* Used for anointing kings and priests. Or more probably the ointment here referred to was that which was in more common use, to anoint the

body after bathing, or when they were to appear in public. ¶ *And all the house of his armour.* Marg. 'Vessels,' or 'instruments,' or 'jewels.' The word כְּלִי denotes *any* article of furniture, utensil, or vessel; any trapping, instrument, or tool; and any implement of war, weapon, or arms. Probably it here refers to the latter, and denotes shields, swords, spears, such as were used in war, and such as Hezekiah had prepared for defence. The phrase is equivalent to our word *arsenal* (comp. 2 Chron. xxxii. 27). Solomon had an extensive arsenal of this description (1 Kings x. 16, 17), and it is probable that these were regarded as a part of the necessary defence of the kingdom. ¶ *Nor in all his dominion.* Everything that contributed to the defence, the wealth, or the magnificence of his kingdom he showed to them. The purpose for which Hezekiah thus showed them all that he had, was evidently display. In 2 Chron. xxxii. 25, it is stated that 'Hezekiah rendered not again according to the benefit done unto him, for his heart was lifted up;' and in ver. 31, it is said, that in regard to this transaction, 'God left him, to try him, that he might know all that was in his heart.' The result showed how much God hates pride, and how certainly he will punish all forms of ostentation.

3. *Then came Isaiah.* Isaiah was accustomed to declare the will of God most freely to monarchs (see ch. vii.) ¶ *What said these men?* What proposition have they made? What is the design of their coming? It is *implied* in the question that there had been some improper communication from them. To this question Hezekiah returned no answer. ¶ *And from whence came they?* It was doubtless known in Jerusalem that ambassadors had come, but it would not be likely to be known from what country they had come. ¶ *From a far country.* Probably this was said in order to palliate and excuse his conduct, by

4 Then said he, What have they seen in thine house? And Hezekiah answered, All that *is* in mine house have they seen : there is nothing among my *a* treasures that I have not shewed them.

5 Then said Isaiah to Hezekiah, Hear the word of the LORD of hosts :

6 Behold, the days *b* come, that all that *is* in thine house, and *that* which thy fathers have laid up in store until this day, shall be carried to *c* Babylon : nothing shall be left, saith the LORD.

a Prov.23.5.   *b* Jer.20.5.   *c* 2 Ki.25.6,&c.

intimating to the prophet that it was proper to show respectful attention to foreigners, and that he had done nothing more than was demanded by the laws of hospitality and kindness.

4. *What have they seen?* It is probable that the fact that Hezekiah had showed them the treasures of his kingdom was known in Jerusalem. Such a fact would be likely to attract attention, and to produce inquiry among the people into the cause. ¶ *All that is in mine house.* Here was the confessions of a frank, an honest, and a pious man. There was no concealment ; no disguise. Hezekiah knew that he was dealing with a man of God—a man too to whom he had been under great obligations. He knew that Isaiah had come commissioned by God, and that it would be in vain to attempt to conceal anything. Nor does he seem to have wished to make any concealment. If he was conscious that what he had done had been improper, he was willing to confess it ; and at any rate he was willing that the exact truth should be known. Had Hezekiah been like Ahaz, he might have spurned Isaiah from his presence as presenting improper inquiries. But Hezekiah was accustomed to regard with respect the messengers of God, and he was therefore willing to submit his whole conduct to the Divine adjudication and reproof. Piety makes a man willing that all that he has done should be known. It saves him from double-dealing and subterfuges, and a disposition to make vain excuses ; and it inclines him to fear God, to respect his ambassadors, and to listen to the voice of eternal truth.

5. *Hear the word of the LORD of hosts.* Hear what the mighty God that rules in heaven says of this. This is an instance of great fidelity on the part of the prophet. He felt himself sent from God

in a solemn manner to rebuke sin in a monarch, and a pious monarch. It is an instance that strikingly resembles the boldness and faithfulness of Nathan when he went to David, and said, ' Thou art the man' (2 Sam. xii. 7).

6. *Behold, the days come.* The captivity of the Jews in Babylon commenced about one hundred and twenty years after this prediction (comp. Jer. xx. 5). ¶ *That all that* is *in thine house.* That is, all the treasures that are in the treasure-house (ver. 2). ¶ *And* that *which thy fathers have laid up in store.* In 2 Kings xviii. 15, 16, we are told that Hezekiah, in order to meet the demands of the king of Assyria, had cut off even the ornaments of the temple, and taken all the treasures which were in ' the king's house.' It is *possible*, however, that there might have been other treasures which had been accumulated by the kings before him which he had not touched. ¶ *Nothing shall be left.* This was literally fulfilled (see 2 Chron. xxxvi. 18). It is remarkable, says Vitringa, that this is the first intimation that the Jews would be carried to Babylon—the first designation of the *place* where they would be so long punished and oppressed. Micah (iv. 10), a contemporary of Isaiah, declares the same thing, but probably this was not before the declaration here made by Isaiah. Moses had declared repeatedly, that, if they were a rebellious people, they should be removed from their own to a foreign land ; but he had not designated the country (Lev. xxvi. 33, 34 ; Deut. xxviii. 64–67 ; xxx. 3). Ahijah, in the time of Jeroboam (1 Kings xiv. 15), had predicted that they should be carried ' beyond the river,' *i.e.*, the Euphrates ; and Amos (v. 27) had said that God would carry them ' into captivity beyond Damascus.' But all these predictions were now concentrated on Babylon ;

7 And of thy sons that shall issue from thee, which thou shalt beget, shall they take away; and *a* they shall be eunuchs in the palace of the king of Babylon.

a Fulfilled, Dan.1.2-7.

and it was for the first time distinctly announced by Isaiah that that was to be the land where they were to suffer so long and so painful a captivity.

7. *And of thy sons.* Thy posterity (see Note on Matt. i. 1). ¶ *That shall issue from thee.* Of the royal family. The captivity at Babylon occurred more than a hundred years after this, and of course those who were carried there were somewhat remote descendants of Hezekiah. ¶ *And they shall be eunuchs.* The word here used (כָּרִיסִים *sārīsīm*) denotes properly and strictly eunuchs, or such persons as were accustomed to attend on the harems of Oriental monarchs (Est. ii. 3, 14, 15). These persons were also employed often in various offices of the court (Est. i. 10, 12, 15), and hence the word often means a minister of court, a court-officer, though not literally an eunuch (Gen. xxxvii. 6; xxxix. 1). It is not easy, however, to tell when the word is to be understood literally, and when not. The Targum understands it of those who should be *nurtured*, or become great in the kingdom of Babylon. That the Jews were advanced to some offices of trust and power in Babylon, is evident from the case of Daniel (i. 2–7). It is by no means improbable, also, that the king of Babylon would have a pride in having among the attendants at his court, or even over the harem, the descendants of the once magnificent monarchs of the Jews.

8. *Good* is *the word of the* Lord. The sense of this is, 'I acquiesce in this; I perceive that it is right; I see in it evidence of benevolence and goodness.' The grounds of his acquiescence seem to have been—1. The fact that he saw that it was just. He felt that he had sinned, and that he had made an improper display of his treasures, and deserved to be punished. 2. He felt that the sentence was mild and merciful. It was less than he deserved, and less than

8 Then said Hezekiah to Isaiah, Good *b* is the word of the Lord which thou hast spoken. He said moreover, For there shall be peace and truth in my days.

b 1 Sam.3.18.

he had reason to expect. 3. It was merciful to *him*, and to his kingdom *at that time.* God was not coming forth to cut him off, or to involve him in any more calamity. 4. His own reign and life were to be full of mercy still. He had abundant cause of gratitude, therefore, that God was dealing with *him* in so much kindness. It cannot be shown that Hezekiah was regardless of his posterity, or unconcerned at the calamity which would come upon them. All that the passage fairly implies is, that he saw that it was right; and that it was proof of great mercy in God that the punishment was deferred, and was not, as in the case of David (2 Sam. 13, 14, *sq.*), to be inflicted in his own time. The nature of the crime of Hezekiah is more fully stated in the parallel passage in 2 Chron. xxxii. 25, 26, 30, 31. ¶ *For there shall be peace.* My kingdom shall not be disturbed during my reign with a foreign invasion. ¶ *And truth.* The truth of God shall be maintained; his worship shall be kept up; his name shall be honoured. ¶ *In my days.* During my reign. He inferred this because Isaiah had said (ver. 7) that *his posterity* would be carried to Babylon. He was assured, therefore, that these calamities would not come in his own time. We may learn from this—1. That we should submit to God when he punishes us. If we have right feelings we shall always see that we deserve all that we are called to suffer. 2. In the midst of severest judgments we may find *some* evidence of mercy. There are *some* considerations on which the mind may fix that will console it with the evidence of the compassion of God, and that will not only make it submissive, but fill it with gratitude. 3. We should accustom ourselves to such views of the Divine dealings, and should *desire* to find in them the evidence of goodness and mercy, and not the evidence of wrath and severity. It is of infinite importance that we should cherish right views of God; and should believe that he is holy, good, and merciful. To do this, we should feel that we deserve *all* that we suffer; we should look at what we *might* have endured; we should look at the mercies *spared* to us, as well as at those which are *taken away;* and we should hold to the belief, as an unwaver-ing principle from which we are never to depart, that God is *good*, SUPREMELY AND WHOLLY GOOD. Then our minds will have peace. Then with Hezekiah we may say, 'Good is the word of JE-HOVAH.' Then with the suffering Redeemer of the world we may always say, 'Not my will, but THINE BE DONE' (Luke xxii. 42).

GENERAL INTRODUCTION TO CHAPTERS XL.-LXVI.

IT is admitted, on all hands, that the second part of Isaiah, comprising the prophecies which commence at the fortieth chapter, and which continue to the end of the book, is to be regarded as the most sublime, and to us the most important part of the Old Testament. In the previous portions of his prophecies there was much that was local and temporary. Indeed all, or nearly all, that occurs from ch. i. to ch. xxxix. had direct and immediate reference to the times in which the prophet lived, or was suggested by the events which occurred in those times. Not unfrequently, indeed, there were prophecies respecting the Messiah's coming (ch. ii., iv., vii., ix., xi., xxxv.), but the primary reference was to events that were then occurring, or which were soon to occur, and which were local in their character. And though the mind of the prophet is carried forward by the laws of prophetic suggestion (see Introd. § 7, III. (3), and he describes the times of the Messiah, yet the immediate and primary reference of those prophecies is to Judea, or to the kingdoms and countries in the vicinity of Judea, with which the Jews were in various ways connected.

In this portion of the prophecy, however, there is little that is local and temporary. It is occupied with a prophetic statement of events which were to occur long after the time of the prophet; and which would be of interest not only to the Jewish nation, but to the whole human family. It is a beautiful and glowing description of occurrences, in which men of the present and of all subsequent times will have as deep an interest as they who have lived at any former period. Indeed it is not improbable that as the world advances in age, the interest in this portion of Isaiah will increase; and that as the gospel is carried around the globe, the beauty and accuracy of these descriptions will be more clearly seen and highly appreciated; and that nations will yet derive their highest consolations, and see the clearest proof of the inspiration of the Sacred Volume, from the entire correspondence between this portion of Isaiah and the events which are yet to gladden the world. There is no portion of the Old Testament where there is so graphic and clear a description of the times of the Messiah. None of the other prophets linger so long, and with such apparent delight, on the promised coming of the Prince of Peace; or his character and work; on the nature of his instructions, and the manner of his reception; on the **trials** of his life, and the painful circumstances of his death ; on the dignity of his nature, and on his lowly and humble character ; on the prevalence of his religion, and on its transforming and happy effects ; on the consolations which he would furnish, and on the fact that his religion would bear light and joy around the world.

Lowth supposes that this prophecy was uttered in the latter part of the reign of Hezekiah. A more probable supposition is that of Hengstenberg, that it was uttered in the time of Manasseh. I have endeavoured to show (Introd. § 2) that Isaiah lived some time during the reign of Manasseh. According to this supposition, there was probably an interval of some twelve or fourteen years between the close of the predictions in the first part, and those which occupy this portion of the book. Manasseh was a cruel prince ; and his reign was cruel (see Introd. § 3). It was a time of the prevalence of idolatry and sin. In this state of things, it is probable that Isaiah, who was then of great age, withdrew almost entirely from the public functions of the prophetic work, and sought personal consolation, and endeavoured to furnish comfort for the pious portion of the nation, in the contemplation of the future. In this period, I suppose, this portion of the prophecy was conceived and penned. Isaiah, in the close of the previous part of the prophecies (ch. xxxix. 7), had distinctly announced that the nation would be carried to Babylon. He saw that the crimes of the monarch and of the nation were such as would certainly hasten this result. He had retired from the public functions of the prophetic office, and given himself up to the contemplation of happier and purer times. He, therefore, devoted himself to the task of furnishing consolation for the pious portion of the nation, and especially of recording prophetic descriptions which would comfort the Jews when they should be held in long captivity in Babylon. We have seen (Notes on ch. xiii. and xiv.) that Isaiah had before this laid the foundations for these consolations by the assurance that Babylon and its mighty power would be entirely destroyed, and, of course, that the Jewish people could not be held *always* in bondage there. In this part of the prophecy (ch. xl.-lxvi.) his object is to give more full and specific consolations. He therefore places himself, in vision (see Introd. § 7, I. (4), in the midst of the future scenes which he describes, and states distinctly and fully the grounds of consolation. These topics of consolation would arise from two sources—both of which he presents at great length and with great beauty. The first is, that the nation would be delivered from its long and painful captivity. This was the *primary* thing to be done, and this was needful in order to furnish to them consolation. He places himself in that future time. He sees his own nation borne to a distant land, according to his own predictions ; sees them sighing in their hard bondage ; and sees the city and the temple where they once worshipped the God of their fathers laid in ruins, and all their pleasant things laid waste (ch. lxiv. 11), and the people dispirited and sad in their long and painful captivity. He predicts the close of that captivity, and speaks of it as present to his view. He consoles the people by the assurance that it was coming to an end ; names the monarch—Cyrus—by whom their oppressors were to be punished, and by whom they were to be restored to their own land ; and describes, in the most beautiful and glowing imagery, their certain return. The second source of consolation is that which relates to the coming of a far more important deliverer than Cyrus, and to a far more important redemption than that from the captivity at Babylon. By the laws of prophetic suggestion, and in accordance with the usual manner of Isaiah, his mind is carried forward to much more momentous events. The descriptions of the prophet insensibly change from the immediate subject under contemplation to the far more important events connected with the coming and work of the Messiah. This was the common rule by which the mind of Isaiah acted ; and it is no wonder, therefore, that an event so strikingly resembling the deliverance of man from the bondage of sin by the Messiah as was the deliverance from the captivity of Babylon, should have been suggested by that, and that his thoughts should pass rapidly from one to the other, and the one be forgotten in the other. The eye of the prophet, therefore, glances rapidly from the object more immediately in view in the future, to the object more remote ; and he regards the return from the Babylonish captivity as introductory to a far more important deliverance. In the contemplation of that more distant event, therefore, he becomes wholly absorbed ; and from this he derives his main topics of consolation. He sees the author of redemption in various scenes—now as a sufferer, humble, poor, and persecuted ; and now the more distant glories of the Messiah's kingdom rise to view. He sees him raised up from the dead ; his empire extend and spread among the Gentiles ; kings and princes from all lands coming to lay their offerings at his feet ; the distant tribes of men come bending before him, and his religion of peace and joy diffusing its blessings around the world. In the contemplation of these future glories, he desires to furnish consolation for his afflicted countrymen in Babylon, and at the same time a demonstration of the truth of the oracles of God, and of the certain prevalence of the true religion, which should impart happiness and peace in all future times.

The character of the period when this portion of the prophecy was delivered, and the circumstances under which it was uttered, as well as the object which the prophet had in view, may account for some remarkable features in it which cannot fail to strike the attentive reader—1. The *name* of the prophet does not occur. It may have been designed that the consolation should be furnished rather by the *nature* of the truth, than by the name or authority of the man. When addressing monarchs, and when denouncing the vices and crimes of the age, his name is mentioned (comp. ch. vii. and xxxviii.) ; the authority under which he acted is stated ; and he utters his warnings in the name of JEHOVAH. Here he presents simple truth, in a case where it is to be presumed that his prophetic authority and character were already sufficiently established. 2. There is less of fire and impetuosity, less of severity and abruptness of manner, in this than in the former prophecies. Isaiah was now an old man, and his style, and manner of thinking and of utterance would be naturally mellowed by age. His object, also, was not reproof so much as consolation ; it was not, as formerly, to denounce judgment, but to speak of comfort. It was not to rebuke kings and nobles for their crimes, and to rouse the nation to a sense of its danger ; it was to mitigate the woes of those in bondage, and to furnish topics of support to those who were groaning in captivity far from the temple of their

God, and from the sepulchres of their fathers. The language of the second part is more gentle and flowing; more tender and mild. There is exquisite beauty and finish, and occasionally there are bursts of the highest sublimity; but there is not the compression of thought, and the struggling as it were for utterance, which there often is in the former part. There, the prophetic impulse is like waters pent up between projecting rocks and hills, it struggles and bursts forth impetuously and irresistibly; in this portion of the prophecy, it is like the placid stream—the full-flowing, majestic river—calm, pure, deep, and sublime. There are, indeed, characteristics of the same style, and of the same author, but it is in different circumstances, and with a different object in view. Homer in the Odyssey has been compared to the sun when setting with full orb, but with diminished brightness; in the Iliad to the sun in his meridian. Isaiah, in this part of his prophecies, resembles the sun shining with steady and pure effulgence without a cloud; in the former part, he resembles the sun when it bursts through clouds in the darkened heavens—the light struggling through the openings in the sky, and amidst the thunders that roll and echo along the hills and vales. 3. The portion which follows (ch. xl.–lxvi.) is a *single* prophecy, apparently uttered at one time, and having one great design. The former part consists of a number of independent and separate predictions, some of them very brief, and having no immediate connection with each other. Here, all is connected, and the same design is kept steadily and constantly in view. His beautiful descriptions roll on, to use one of his own images, 'like a river,' or the 'waves of the sea.' 4. Almost everything which occurs in the prophecy relates to that which was to be fulfilled long after the time of Isaiah. Occasionally there is a slight allusion to the prevalence of idolatry in his own time, but there is no express mention of the events which were then occurring. He does not mention his own circumstances; he does not allude to the name of the monarch who lived when he wrote. He seems to have forgotten the present, and to live and act in the scenes of the distant future. He, therefore, speaks *as if* he were among the exiled Jews in Babylon when their long captivity was about to come to an end; he exhorts, rebukes, administers, comforts, as if they were present, and as if he were directly addressing them. He speaks of the life, sufferings, and death of the Messiah also, as events which he *saw*, and seeks personal consolation and support amidst the prevailing crimes and calamities of his own times, in the contemplation of future scenes.

It will be seen, from what has been said, and from the examination of the prophecy itself, that it possesses a decidedly evangelical character. Indeed, this is so clear and apparent, that many have maintained that the primary reference is to the Messiah, and that it had no relation to the return from the captivity at Babylon. Such was the opinion of the learned Vitringa. Even Grotius, of whom it has been said, that while Cocceius found 'Christ everywhere, he found him nowhere,' admits that the prophecy has an obvious reference to the Messiah. His words are, ' Cum autem omnia Dei beneficia umbram in se contineant eorum quæ Christus præstitit, tum præcipue ista omnia quæ deinceps ab Esaia prænunciabuntur, verbis sæpissime a Deo sic directis, *ut simplicius limpidiusque in res Christi, quam in illas, quas primo significare*

Esaias voluit, convenirent.' Indeed, it is impossible to read this portion of the prophecy without believing that it had reference to the Messiah, and that it was designed to furnish consolation from the contemplation of his glorious reign. That there was a primary reference to the return from the captivity at Babylon, I shall endeavour to show as we advance in the interpretation of the prophecy. But it will also be seen that though the prophet *begins* with that, he *ends* usually with a contemplation of the Redeemer; that these events seem to have lain so near each other in the beautiful field of prophetic vision, that the one naturally suggested the other; and that the description passes from the former object to the latter, so that the contemplation of the person and work of the Messiah, and of the triumphs of his gospel, become the absorbing theme of his glowing language (see Introd. § 7).

CHAPTER XL.

ANALYSIS.

I. THE subject of the whole prophecy (ch. xl.-lxvi.) is introduced in ver. 1, 2. The general design is, to comfort the afflicted and oppressed people of God. They are contemplated as in Babylon, and as *near* the close of the exile. Jerusalem is regarded as in ruins (comp. ch. xliv. 26-28; li. 3; lii. 9; lviii. 12); the land is waste and desolate (lxiii. 18); the city and the temple are destroyed (lxiv. 10, 11). Their captivity is about to end, and the people about to be restored to their own land (ch. xliv. 28; lviii. 12; lx. 10; lxv. 9). In this situation, the prophet is directed to address words of consolation to the oppressed and long-captive Jews, and to assure them that their calamities are about to close. Jerusalem —now in ruins—was to be assured that the end of her desolation was near, for that an ample punishment had been taken for all her sins.

II. The prophet next represents the deliverance under an image taken from the march of earthly kings (3-8). The voice of a herald is heard in the wilderness making proclamation, that every obstacle should be removed, that JEHOVAH might return to Zion conducting his people. As he had conducted them from the land of Egypt, so he was about to conduct them from Babylon, and to appear again in Jerusalem and in the temple. Between Babylon and Jerusalem there was an immense tract of country which was a pathless desert. Through this land the people would naturally be conducted; and the voice of the herald is heard demanding that a highway should be made—in the manner of a herald who preceded an army, and who required valleys to be filled, and roads to be constructed, over which the monarch and his army might pass with ease and safety. It is to be observed that the *main* thing here is not that *the people* should return, and a way be made for *them*, but that JEHOVAH was about to return to Jerusalem, and that the pathway should be made for *him*. *He* was to be their leader and guide, and this was the principal source of comfort in their return. In this, the Holy Spirit, who directed and inspired the prophet, *purposely* suggests language that would be applicable to a far more important event, when the herald of the Messiah should announce *his* coming. The main thing which the voice was to cry is represented in ver. 6-8. That was, that JEHOVAH was faithful to his promises, and that his predictions would be certainly fulfilled. Everything else would fade away—the grass would wither, the flower would fail, and the people would die —but the word of JEHOVAH would be unfailing, and this would be manifest alike in the release of the people from Babylon, and in the coming of the Messiah.

III. The messenger that brought these glad tidings to Jerusalem, is exhorted to announce the happy news to the remaining cities of Judah —to go to an eminence—to lift up the voice—and to proclaim that their God had come (9).

IV. In ver. 10, 11, the assurance is given that he would come 'with a strong hand'—almighty and able to save; he would come as a tender and gentle shepherd, regarding especially the weak and feeble of his people—language alike applicable to God, who should conduct the people from exile to their own land, and to the Messiah; though more strikingly and completely fulfilled in the latter.

V. The mention of the *omnipotence* of JEHOVAH, who was about to conduct his people to their own land, leads the prophet into a most sublime description of his power, majesty, and glory, the object of which seems to be to induce them to put entire confidence in him (12–17). God measures the waters in the hollow of his hand; he metes out the heavens with a span; he measures the dust of the earth, and weighs the mountains (12). None has counselled, or can counsel him;—his understanding is superior to that of all creatures (13, 14). The nations before him are as a drop of a bucket, and as the small dust of the balance, and as nothing (15, 17). All the vast forests of Lebanon, and all the beasts that roam there, would not be sufficient to constitute a burnt-offering that should be a proper expression of his majesty and glory (16).

VI. From this statement of the majesty and glory of God, the prophet shows the absurdity of attempting to form an image or likeness of God, and the certainty that all who trusted in idols should be destroyed, as the stubble is swept away by the whirlwind (18–25).

VII. It follows also, if God is so great and glorious, that the people should put confidence in him. They should believe that he was able to save them; they should wait on him who alone could renew their strength (26–31). The entire scope and design of the chapter, therefore, is, to induce them to put their reliance in God, who was about to come to vindicate his people, and who would assuredly accomplish all his predictions and promises. The argument is a most beautiful one; and the language is unsurpassed in sublimity.

COMFORT *a* ye, comfort ye my people, saith your God.

a Heb 6.17,18.

CHAPTER XL.

1. *Comfort ye, comfort ye my people.* This is the exordium, or the general subject of this and the following chapters. The commencement is abrupt, as often happens in Isaiah and the other prophets. The *scene* where this vision is laid is in Babylon; the *time* near the close of the captivity. The *topic*, or main subject of the consolation, is stated in the following verse—that that captivity was about to end, and that brighter and happier days were to succeed their calamities and their exile. The exhortation to ' comfort ' the people is to be understood as a command of God to those in Babylon whose office or duty it would be to address them—that is, to the ministers of religion, or to the prophets. The Targum of Jonathan thus renders it: ' Ye prophets, prophesy consolations concerning my people.' The LXX. render it, ' Comfort ye, comfort ye my people, saith God. O priests, speak to the heart of Jerusalem; comfort her.' The design of Isaiah is doubtless to furnish that which should be to them a source of consolation when amidst the deep distress of their long captivity; to furnish an assurance that the captivity was about to end, and that brighter and happier times were to ensue. The exhortation or command is *repeated*, to give intensity or emphasis to it, in the

usual manner in Hebrew, where emphasis is denoted by the *repetition* of a word. The word rendered ' comfort ' (from נָחַם *năhhăm*) means properly *to draw the breath forcibly*, to sigh, pant, groan; then to lament, or grieve (Ps. xc. 13; Jer. xv. 6); then to comfort or console *one's-self* (Gen. xxxviii. 12); then to take vengeance (comp. Note on ch. i. 24). All the forms of the word, and all the significations, indicate *deep emotion*, and the *obtaining of relief* either by repenting, or by taking vengeance, or by administering the proper topics of consolation. Here the topic of consolation is, that their calamities were about to come to an end, *in accordance with the unchanging promises of a faithful God* (ver. 8), and is thus in accordance with what is said in Heb. vi. 17, 18. ¶ *My people.* The people of God. He regarded those in Babylon as his people; and he designed also to adduce such topics of consolation as would be adapted to comfort *all* his people in all ages. ¶ *Saith your God.* The God of those whom he addressed—the God of the prophets or ministers of religion whose office was to comfort the people. We may remark here, that it is an important part of the ministerial office to administer consolation to the people of God in affliction; to exhibit to them his promises; to urge

2 Speak ye [1] comfortably to Jerusalem, and cry unto her that her warfare [2] is accomplished, that her iniquity is pardoned ; for she hath received of the LORD's hand double for [a] all her sins.

1 *to the heart.*   2 or, *appointed time.*   *a* ch.61.7.

the topics of religion which are adapted to sustain them ; and especially to uphold and cheer them with the assurance that their trials will soon come to an end, and will all terminate in complete deliverance from sorrow and calamity in heaven.

2. *Speak ye comfortably.* Heb. עַל־לֵב as in the margin, ' To the heart.' The *heart* is the seat of the affections. It is there that sorrow and joy are felt. We are oppressed there with grief, and we speak familiarly of being pained at the heart, and of being of a glad or merry heart. To speak ' to the heart,' is to speak in such a way as to remove the troubles of the heart ; to furnish consolation and joy. It means that they were not merely to urge such topics as should convince the understanding, but such also as should be adopted to minister consolation to the heart. So the word is used in Gen. xxxiv. 3 : ' And his soul clave unto Dinah—and he loved the damsel, and spake kindly (Heb. to the heart) of the damsel ;' Gen. l. 21 : ' And he comforted them, and spake kindly unto them' (Heb. to their hearts) ; see also 2 Chron. xxxii. 6. ¶ *To Jerusalem.* The direction is not merely to speak to the people in Babylon, but also to comfort Jerusalem itself lying in ruins. The general direction is, therefore, that the entire series of topics of consolation should be adduced —the people were to return from their bondage, and Jerusalem was to be rebuilt, and the worship of God to be restored. ¶ *And cry unto her.* In the manner of a crier ; or one making public and loud proclamation (comp. ver. 3, 9). Jerusalem is here personified. She is addressed as in ruins, and as about to be rebuilt, and as capable of consolation from this promise. ¶ *That her warfare is accomplished.* LXX. ' That her humiliation (ταπείνωσις) is accomplished.' The Hebrew word (צָבָא, ' warfare ') properly means *an army* or *host* (comp. Note on ch. i. 9), and is usually applied to an army going forth to war, or marshalled for battle (2 Sam. viii.

16; x. 7). It is then used to denote an appointed time of service ; the discharge of a duty similar to an enlistment, and is applied to the services of the Levites in the tabernacle (Num. iv. 23) : ' All that enter in to perform the service (Heb. to war the warfare), to do the work in the tabernacle of the congregation.' Compare Num. viii. 24, 25. Hence it is applied to human life contemplated as a warfare, or enlistment, involving hard service and calamity ; an enlistment from which there is to be a discharge by death.

Is there not a set time [Heb. a warfare] to man
    upon earth ?
Are not his days as the days of an hireling ?
            Job vii. 1.

But if a man die—shall he indeed live again ?
All the days of my appointed time [Heb. my
    warfare] will I wait,
Till my change come.   Job xiv. 14.

Compare Dan. x. 1. The word then means hard service, such as soldiers endure ; an appointed time which they are to serve ; an enlistment involving hardships, toil, privation, danger, calamity. In this sense it is applied here to Jerusalem—to the trials, calamities, desolations to which she was subjected for her sins, and which were to endure *a definite and fixed time*—like the enlistment of an army. That time was now coming to an end, and to be succeeded by a release, or discharge. Vitringa, who supposes that this refers primarily and solely to the times of the Messiah, regards this as meaning that the definite time of the legal economy, a time of toil, and of vexatious and troublesome ceremonies, was about to end by the coming of the Messiah. But the more correct interpretation is, probably, that which supposes that there was a primary reference to the long and painful captivity of the Jews in Babylon. ¶ *That her iniquity.* The iniquity or sin here referred to, is that long series of acts of rebellion, corruption, and idolatry, with which the Jewish people had been chargeable, and which had rendered their captivity necessary. As a nation, that sin was now expiated, or removed by their protracted punishment in Babylon. It was a sufficient expression of the Divine displeasure at the national offences, and God was *satisfied* (נִרְצָה) with it, and could consistently restore them to their land, and to their former privileges. The whole language here has respect to *national*, and not to individual offences. ¶ *Is pardoned.* Vulg. *Dimissa est iniquitas illius.* LXX. Λέλυται αὐτῆς ἡ ἁμαρτία—' Her sin is loosed,' dissolved, remitted. The word ' pardon' does not quite express the meaning of the word in the original (נִרְצָה). The word רָצָה (*râtzâ*) properly means *to delight in any person or thing;* to take pleasure in; then to receive graciously or favourably ; to delight in sacrifices and offerings (Job xxxiii. 26; Ps. li. 18; Ezek. xx. 40); and, in the Hiphil conjugation, to satisfy, or pay off, *i.e.*, to cause to be satisfied, or pleased ; and then in Hophal, to be satisfied, to be paid off, to be pleased or satisfied with an expiation, or with an atonement for sins, so as to *delight* in the person who makes it. Here it means not strictly *to pardon*, but it means that they had endured the national punishment which God saw to be necessary ; they had *served out* the long and painful enlistment which he had appointed, and now he was *satisfied*, and took delight in restoring them to their own land. It does not refer to the pardon of men in consequence of the atonement made by the Lord Jesus; but it may be used as an *illustration* of that, when God is satisfied with that atonement ; and when he has *pleasure* or *delight* in setting the soul free from the bondage of sin, and admitting the sinner to his favour—as he had delight here in restoring his people to their own land. ¶ *For she hath received.* Jerusalem had now been desolate for almost seventy years, on the supposition that this relates to the period near the close of the exile, and that was regarded as an ample or full expression of what she *ought* to suffer for her national offences. ¶ *Of the Lord's hand.* From the hand, or by the agency of JEHOVAH. Whoever were the instruments, her sufferings were to be regarded as his appointment. ¶ *Double for all her sins.*

The word rendered ' double' (כִּפְלַיִם) is the dual form from כֵּפֶל, 'a doubling,' and occurs in Job xli. 13 :

Who will rip up the covering of his armour ?
Against *the doubling* of his nostrils who will
    advance ?   *Good.*

And in xi. 6 :

And that he would unfold to them the **secrets** of
    wisdom.
That they are *double* to that which is;

that is, there are *double-folds* to God's wisdom, or the wisdom of of God is complicated, inexplicable (Gesenius). The word in Job means ' conduplications, folds, complications, mazes, intricacies' (Good). Here the word has doubtless its usual and proper meaning, and denotes *double, twice as much* ; and the expression may denote that God had inflicted on them *double* that which had been usually inflicted on rebellious nations, or on the nation before for its sins. Or the word may be used to denote *abundance*, and the prophet may design to teach that they had been *amply*, or *abundantly* punished for their crimes. ' That is,' says Grotius, ' as much as God judged to be sufficient.' ' *Double*, here,' says Calvin, ' is to be received for large and abundant.' Some have supposed (see Rosenmüller, who approves of this interpretation) that the word ' sins' here means the punishment of sins, and that the word ' double' refers to the mercies or favours which they were about to receive, or which God had purposed to confer on them. So Lowth understands it ; and renders the word לָקְחָה ' shall receive' (in the future):

That she shall receive at the hand of JEHOVAH
[Blessings] double to the punishment of all her
    sins.

But though it was true that their favours on their return, in the hope of the Messiah, and in their renovated privileges, would be far more numerous than their sufferings had been, yet this does not so well suit the connection, where the prophet is giving *a reason* why they should be released from their bondage, and restored to the privileges of their own land. That reason manifestly is, that they had suffered what was regarded by JEHOVAH as an *ample* expression of his displeasure for their national offences. It does not refer to

3 The ^avoice of him that crieth in the wilderness, Prepare ^bye the way of the LORD, make straight in the desert a highway for our God.

^a Mat.3.3.　　　　^b Mal.3.1.

individual sinners; nor to any power which they have to make atonement for their sins; nor does it refer to the atonement made by the Messiah. But it may be remarked, by the way, that in the sufferings of the Redeemer there has been *ample* satisfaction for the sins of his people. The Chaldee interpreter understands this as Rosenmüller does, that the word 'double' refers to the mercies which they had received : ' Because she has received a cup of consolation from the presence of the Lord, *as if* (כְּאִלּוּ) she had been smitten twofold for all her sins.'

3. *The voice of him that crieth.* Lowth and Noyes render this, ' A voice crieth,' and annex the phrase ' in the wilderness' to the latter part of the sentence :

A voice crieth, 'In the wilderness prepare ye the way of JEHOVAH.'

The Hebrew (קוֹל קוֹרֵא) will bear this construction, though the Vulgate and the LXX, render it as in our common version. The sense is not essentially different, though the parallelism seems to require the translation proposed by Lowth. The design is to state the source of consolation referred to in the previous verses. The time of the exile at Babylon was about to be completed. JEHOVAH was about to conduct his people again to their own country through the pathless wilderness, as he had formerly conducted them from Egypt to the land of promise. The prophet, therefore, represents himself as hearing the voice of a herald, or a forerunner in the pathless waste, giving direction that a way should be made for the return of the people. The whole scene is represented as a march, or return of JEHOVAH at the head of his people to the land of Judea. The idea is taken from the practice of Eastern monarchs, who, whenever they entered on a journey or an expedition, especially through a barren and unfrequented or inhospitable country, sent harbingers or heralds before them to prepare the way. To do this, it was necessary for them to provide supplies, and make bridges, or find fording places over the streams; to level hills, and construct causeways over valleys, or fill them up; and to make a way through the forest which might lie in their intended line of march. This was necessary, because these contemplated expeditions often involved the necessity of marching through countries where there were no public highways that would afford facilities for the passage of an army. Thus Arrian (*Hist.* liv. 30) says of Alexander, ' He now proceeded to the river Indus, the army' *i.e.*, ἡ στρατιά, a *part* of the army, or an army sufficient for the purpose, ' going before, which made a way for him, for otherwise there would have been no mode of passing through that region.' ' When a great prince in the East,' says Paxton, ' sets out on a journey, it is usual to send a party of men before him to clear the way. The state of those countries in every age, where roads are almost unknown, and, from want of cultivation, in many places overgrown with brambles and other thorny plants, which renders travelling, especially with a large retinue, incommodious, requires this precaution. The Emperor of Hindoostan, in his progress through his dominions, as described in the narrative of Sir Thomas Roe's embassy to the court of Delhi, was preceded by a very great company, sent before him to cut up the trees and bushes, to level and smooth the road, and prepare their place of encampment. We shall be able, perhaps, to form a more clear and precise idea from the account which Diodorus gives of the marches of Semiramis, the celebrated Queen of Babylon, into Media and Persia. " In her march to Ecbatana," says the historian, " she came to the Zarcean mountain, which, extending many furlongs, and being full of craggy precipices and deep hollows, could not be passed without taking a great compass. Being therefore desirous of leaving an everlasting memorial of herself, as well as of shortening the way, she ordered the precipices to be digged down, and the hollows to be filled up; and at a great expense she made a shorter and more expeditious road; which to this day is called from her the road of Semiramis. Afterward she went into Persia, and all the other countries of Asia subjected to her dominion, and wherever she went, she ordered the mountains and precipices to be levelled, raised causeways in the plain country, and, at a great expense, made the ways passable.'' The writer of the apocryphal Book of Baruch, refers to the same subject by the same images : ' For God hath appointed that every high hill, and banks of long continuance, should be cast down, and valleys filled up, to make even the ground, that Israel may go safely in the glory of God' (ch. v. 7). It is evident that the primary reference of this passage was to the exiles in Babylon, and to their return from their long captivity, to the land of their fathers. The imagery, the circumstances, the design of the prophecy, all seem to demand such an interpretation. At the same time it is as clear, I apprehend, that the prophet was inspired to use language, of design, which should appropriately express a more important event, the coming of the forerunner of the Messiah, and the work which he should perform as preparatory to his advent. There was such a striking *similarity* in the two events, that they could be grouped together in the same part of the prophetic vision or picture ; the mind would naturally, by the laws of prophetic suggestion (Introd. § 7, III. (3), glance from one to the other, and the same language would appropriately and accurately express both. Both could be described as the coming of JEHOVAH to bless and save his people ; both occurred after a long state of desolation and bondage—the one a bondage in Babylon, the other in sin and national declension. The pathless desert was literally to be passed through in the one instance ; in the other, the condition of the Jews was that which was not unaptly likened to a desert—a condition in regard to real piety not unlike the state of a vast desert in comparison with fruitful fields. ' It was,' says Lowth, ' in this desert country, destitute at that time of all religious cultiva-

tion, in true piety and works unfruitful, that John was sent to prepare the way of the Lord by preaching repentance. That this passage *has* a reference to John as the forerunner of the Messiah, is evident from Matt. iii. 3, where it is applied to him, and introduced by this remark : ' For this is he that was spoken of by the prophet Esaias, saying, The voice,' &c. (see also John i. 23.) The events were so similar, in their main features, that the same language would describe both. John was nurtured in the desert, and passed his early life there, until he entered on his public work (Luke ii. 80). He began to preach in a mountainous country, lying east of Jerusalem, and sparsely inhabited, and which was usually spoken of as a desert or wilderness (Matt. iii. 1) ; and it was here that his voice was heard announcing the coming of the Messiah, and that he pointed him to his own followers (John i. 28, 29). ¶ *In the wilderness.* Babylon was separated from Judea by an immense tract of country, which was one continued desert. A large part of Arabia, called Arabia Deserta, was situated in this region. To pass in a direct line, therefore, from Babylon to Jerusalem, it was necessary to go through this desolate country. It was here that the prophet speaks of hearing a voice commanding the hills to be levelled, and the valleys filled up, that there might be a convenient highway for the people to return (comp. Notes on ch. xxxv. 8–10). ¶ *Prepare ye the way.* This was in the form of the usual proclamation of a monarch commanding the people to make a way for him to pass. Applied to the return of the exile Jews, it means that the command of God had gone forth that all obstacles should be removed. Applied to John, it means that the people were to prepare for the reception of the Messiah ; that they were to remove all in their opinions and conduct which would tend to hinder his cordial reception, or which would prevent his success among them. ¶ *Of the* LORD. Of JEHOVAH. JEHOVAH was the leader of his people, and was about to conduct them to their own land. The march, therefore, was regarded as that of JEHOVAH, as a monarch or king, at the head of his people,

4 Every valley shall be exalted,
and every mountain and hill shall
be made low: and the crooked ^a shall

be made ¹ straight, and the rough
places ² plain.

a ch.45,2.   1 or, *a straight place.*
2 or, *a plain place.*

conducting them to their own country;
and to prepare the way of Jehovah was,
therefore, to prepare for his march at
the head of his people. Applied to the
Messiah, it means that God was about
to come to his people to redeem them.
This language naturally and obviously
implies, that he whose way was thus to
be prepared was Jehovah, the true God.
So it was undoubtedly in regard to him
who was to be the leader of the exile
Jews to their own land, since none but
Jehovah could thus conduct them. And
if it be admitted that the language has
also a reference to the Messiah, then it
demonstrates that he was appropriately
called Jehovah. That John the Baptist
had such a view of him, is apparent
from what is said of him. Thus, John
i. 15, he says of him that, 'he was before' him—which was not true unless
he had an existence previous to his
birth; he calls him, ver. 18, 'the only-
begotten Son, which *is* in the bosom of
the Father;' and in ver. 34, he calls
him 'the Son of God' (comp. John x.
30, 33, 36). In ch. iii. 31, he says of
him, 'he that cometh from above is
ABOVE ALL; he that cometh from heaven
is ABOVE ALL.' Though this is not one
of the most direct and certain proof-
texts of the divinity of the Messiah, yet
it is one which may be applied to him
when that divinity is demonstrated from
other places. It is not one that can be
used with absolute certainty in an *argument* on the subject, to convince those
who deny that divinity—since, even on
the supposition that it refers to the Messiah, it may be said plausibly, and with
some force, that it may mean that Jehovah was about to manifest himself by
means of the Messiah; yet it is a passage which those who are convinced of
the divinity of Christ from other sources,
will apply without hesitation to him as
descriptive of his rank, and confirmatory
of his divinity. ¶ *Make straight.*
Make a straight or *direct* road; one
that should conduct at once to their
land. The Chaldee renders this verse,
'Prepare a way before the people of

Jehovah; make in the plain ways before the congregation of our God.' ¶ *A
highway* (see Note on ch. xxxv. 8).
4. *Every valley shall be exalted.*
That is, every valley, or low piece of
ground, shall be filled up so as to make
a level highway, as was done in order
to facilitate the march of armies. This
verse is evidently designed to explain
what is intended in ver. 3, by preparing
the way for Jehovah. Applied to the
return of the Jews from Babylon, it
means simply that the impassable valleys were to be filled up so as to make
a level road for their journey. If applied
to the work of John, the forerunner of
the Messiah, it means that the nation
was to be called on to put itself in a state
of preparation for his coming, and for
the success of his labours among them.
Vitringa, and others, have endeavoured
to specify what particular moral qualities in the nation are meant by the 'valley,' by the 'mountain and hill,' and by
the 'crooked' and 'rough places.' But
the illustrations are such as cannot be
demonstrated to be referred to by the
prophet. The *general* sense is plain.
The *language*, as we have seen, is taken
from the march of a monarch at the
head of his army. The general idea
is, that all obstructions were to be removed, so that the march would be without embarrassment. As applicable to
the work of John also, the language
means in general, that whatever there
was in the opinions, habits, conduct, in
the pride, self-confidence, and irreligion
of the nation that would prevent his
cordial reception, was to be removed.
¶ *Every mountain and hill.* They shall
be dug down so as to make the journey
easy. All obstructions were to be removed. ¶ *And the crooked.* The word
here used (עָקֹב) is usually rendered
'crooked;' but perhaps not by any good
authority. The verb עָקַב usually denotes
to be behind; to come from behind;
or, as Gesenius supposes, to be elevated
like a mound, arched like a hill or
tumulus, and is hence applied to the
heel from the figure (see Gen. xxv. 26;

5 And the glory of the LORD shall be revealed, and all flesh shall see *it* together: for the mouth of the LORD hath spoken *it*.

6 The voice said, Cry. And he said, What shall I cry? All *a* flesh *is* grass, and all the goodliness thereof *is* as the flower of the field.

a Ps.10.15; Ja.1.10,11.

Hos. xii. 4). According to this, the word would denote properly a hill, mound, or acclivity, which would *put back* those who attempted to ascend. ¶ *Shall be made straight.* Marg. ' A straight place.' The Hebrew word (מִישׁוֹר) denotes properly *evenness*, a level region, a plain. The hilly places would be reduced to a level. ¶ *And the rough places.* Those which are hard, *bound up*, stony, difficult to pass. Such as abounded with rocks and precipices, and which presented obstructions to a journey. Such places abounded in the region lying between Palestine and Babylon. ¶ *Plain.* Marg. 'A plain place.' A smooth, level plain.

5. *And the glory of the* LORD. The phrase here means evidently the majesty, power, or honour of JEHOVAH. He would display his power, and show himself to be a covenant-keeping God, by delivering his people from their bondage, and reconducting them to their own land. This glory and faithfulness would be shown in his delivering them from their captivity in Babylon; and it would be still more illustriously shown in his sending the Messiah to accomplish the deliverance of his people in later days. ¶ *And all flesh.* All men. The word 'flesh' is often used to denote human nature, or mankind in general (Gen. vi. 12; Ps. lxv. 3; cxlv. 21). The idea is, that the deliverance of his people would be such a display of the Divine interposition, so that all nations would discern the evidences of his power and glory. But there is a fulness and a richness in the language which shows that it is not to be confined to that event. It is more strikingly applicable to the advent of the Messiah—and to the fact that through him the glory of JEHOVAH would be manifest to all nations. Rosenmüller supposes that this should be translated,

And all flesh shall see together
That the mouth of JEHOVAH hath spoken it.

The Hebrew will bear this construction,

but there is no necessity for departing from the translation in the common version. The LXX. *add* here the words 'salvation of God,' so as to read it, 'and all flesh shall see the salvation of God,' and this reading has been adopted in Luke iii. 6; or it may be more probable that Luke (iii. 4–6) has quoted from *different parts* of Isaiah, and that he intended to quote that part, not from the version of the LXX., but from Isa. lii. 10. Lowth, on the authority of the LXX., proposes to restore these words to the Hebrew text. But the authority is insufficient. The Vulgate, the Chaldee, the Syriac, and the Hebrew MSS. concur in the reading of the present Hebrew text, and the authority of the Septuagint is altogether insufficient to justify a change. ¶ *For the mouth of the* LORD. The strongest possible confirmation that it would be fulfilled (see Note on ch. xxxiv. 16). The idea is, that God had certainly promised their deliverance from bondage; and that his interposition, in a manner which should attract the attention of all nations, was certainly purposed by him. Few events have ever more impressively manifested the glory of God than the redemption of his people from Babylon; none has occurred, or will ever occur, that will more impressively demonstrate his glory, wisdom, and faithfulness, than the redemption of the world by the Messiah.

6. *The voice said.* Or rather ' *a* voice.' Isaiah represents himself here again as hearing a voice. The word ' the ' introduced in our translation, mars the sense, inasmuch as it leads to the supposition that it was the voice of the same person or crier referred to in ver. 3. But it is different. *That* was the voice of a *crier* or herald, proclaiming that a way was to be open in the desert. *This* is introduced for a different purpose. It is to proclaim distinctly that while everything else was fading and transitory, the promise of God was firm and secure. Isaiah therefore,

represents himself as hearing *a* voice requiring the prophets (so the Chaldee) *to make a proclamation.* An inquiry was at once made, What should be the nature of the proclamation? The answer was, that all flesh was grass, &c. He had (ver. 3–5) introduced a herald announcing that the way was to be prepared for their return. He now introduces *another* voice with a distinct message to the people, that God was faithful, and that his promises would not fail. A voice, a command is heard, requiring those whose duty it was, to make proclamation. The voice of God; the Spirit speaking to the prophets, commanded them to cry. ¶ *And he said.* Lowth and Noyes read this, ' And I said.' The LXX. and the Vulgate read it also in this manner, in the first person. Two manuscripts examined by Kennicott also read it in the first person. Houbigant, Hensler, and Döderlin adopt this reading. But the authority is not sufficient to justify a change in the Hebrew text. The Syriac and Chaldee read it as it is in the present Hebrew text, in the third person. The sense is, that the person, or prophet to whom the command came to make proclamation, made answer, ' What shall be the nature of my proclamation?' It is equivalent to saying, ' It was answered;' or if Isaiah is the person to whom the voice is represented as coming, it means that *he* answered; and is, therefore, equivalent to the reading in the LXX. and Vulgate, and adopted by Lowth. This is the probable supposition, that Isaiah represents himself as hearing the voice, and as expressing a willingness to make proclamation, but as waiting to know *what* he was to proclaim. ¶ *All flesh.* This is the answer; or this is what he was to proclaim. The general design or scope of the answer was, that he was to proclaim that the promise of JEHOVAH was secure and firm (ver. 8), and that therefore God would certainly come to deliver them. To make this more impressive by way of contrast, he states that all men are weak and feeble like the grass that is soon withered.—The expression does not refer particularly to the Jews in Babylon, or to any single nation or class of people, but to all men,

in all places, and at all times. All princes, nobles, and monarchs; all armies and magistrates are like grass, and will soon pass away. On the one hand, *they* would be unable to accomplish what was needful to be done in the deliverance of the people; and on the other, their oppressors had no power to continue their bondage, since *they* were like grass, and must soon pass away. But JEHOVAH was ever-enduring, and was able to fulfil all his purposes. ¶ *Is grass.* It is *as* feeble, weak, and as easily consumed as the grass of the field. A similar sentiment is found in Ps. ciii. 15, 16:

As for man, his days are as grass;
As a flower of the field so he flourisheth;
For the wind passeth over it, and it is gone,
And the place thereof shall know it no more.

See also James i. 10, 11. The passage in Isaiah is evidently quoted by Peter, 1 Ep. i. 24, 25: ' All flesh is as grass, and all the glory of man as the flower of grass. The grass withereth, and the flower thereof falleth away: but the word of the Lord endureth for ever; *and this is the word which by the gospel is preached unto you* '—a passage which proves that Isaiah had reference to the times of the Messiah in the place before us. ¶ *And all the goodliness thereof.* The word rendered ' goodliness ' (חֶסֶד) denotes properly, *kindness,* love, goodwill, mercy, favour. Here it is evidently used in the sense of elegance, comeliness, beauty. The LXX. render it δόξα, and so does Peter (1 Ep. i. 24). Applied to *grass,* or to herbs, it denotes the flower, the beauty, the comeliness. Applied to man, it means that which makes him comely and vigorous— health, energy, beauty, talent, wisdom. His vigour is soon gone; his beauty fades; his wisdom ceases; and he falls, like the flower, to the dust. The idea is, that the plans of man must be temporary; that all that appears great in him must be like the flower of the field; but that JEHOVAH endures, and his plans reach from age to age, and will certainly be accomplished. This important truth was to be proclaimed, that the people might be induced not to trust in man, but put their confidence in the arm of God.

7 The grass withereth, the flower fadeth, because the spirit of the Lord bloweth upon it : surely the people *is* grass.

8 The *a* grass withereth, the flower fadeth : but the word *b* of our God shall stand for ever.

a 1 Pe.1.24,25.　　　　*b* Mark 13.31.

---

7. *The grass withereth.* Soon withers. Its beauty is soon gone. ¶ *The flower fadeth.* Soon fades ; or fades when the wind of Jehovah passes over it. So it is also with man. He loses his vigour, and dies at once when Jehovah takes away his strength and beauty. ¶ *Because the spirit of the* Lord *bloweth upon it.* This should be rendered, undoubtedly, ' When the *wind* of Jehovah bloweth upon it.' The word ' spirit ' here does not suit the connection, and does not express the idea of the prophet. The word רוּחַ (*ru̇ăhh*) means, properly, *breath*—a breathing, or blowing ; and is often used indeed to denote spirit, soul, life. But it *often* means a breath of wind ; a breeze ; air in motion (Job xli. 8 ; Jer. ii. 24 ; xiv. 6). It is applied to the cool breeze which springs up in the evening (Gen. iii. 8 ; comp. Cant. ii. 17 ; iv. 6). It sometimes means a strong and violent wind (Gen. viii. 1 ; Isa. vii. 2 ; xli. 16) ; and also a tempest, or hurricane (Job i. 19 ; xxx. 15 ; Isa. xxvii. 8). The ' wind of Jehovah ' means that which Jehovah sends, or causes ; and the expression here refers, doubtless, to the hot or poisonous east winds which blow in Oriental countries, and which wither and dry up everything before them (comp. Jonah iv. 8). ¶ *Surely the people* is *grass.* Lowth reads this, ' this people ;' referring to the Jewish nation. So the Syriac. Perhaps it refers to the people of Babylon (so Rosenmüller), and means *that* mighty people would fade away like grass. But the more probable interpretation is that which regards it as referring to ALL people, and of course including the Jews and the Babylonians. The sense, according to this view, is, 'all nations shall fade away. All human power shall cease. But the promise of Jehovah shall survive. It shall be unchanging amidst all revolutions ; it shall survive all the fluctuations which shall take place among men. It may, therefore, be trusted with unwavering reliance.' To *produce* that reliance was the object of the proclama-

tion. On this passage, descriptive of the state of man, the reader will at once be reminded of the beautiful language of Shakspeare :

This is the state of man ! To-day he puts forth
The tender leaves of hope : to-morrow blossoms,
And bears his blushing honours thick upon him ;
The third day comes a frost, a killing frost,
And when he thinks, good easy man, full surely
His greatness is a-ripening, nips his root,
And then he falls——
——never to hope again.
　　　　Hen. VIII., Act. ii. Sc. 2.

In the following passage from Tasso, the same image is adopted :

The gentle budding rose (quoth he) behold,
　That first scant peeping forth with virgin
　　　beams,
Half ope, half shut, her beauties doth up-fold
　In their dear leaves, and less seen fairer seems,
And after spreads them forth more broad and
　　bold,
　Then languishes and dies in last extremes.
So in the passing of a day doth pass
　The bud and blossom of the life of man,
Nor e'er doth flourish more, but, like the grass
　Cut down, becometh withered, pale, and wan.
　　　Fairfax, Edit. Windsor, 1817.

8. *The grass withereth,* &c. This is repeated from the former verse for the sake of emphasis, or strong confirmation. ¶ *But the word of our God.* The phrase ' word of our God,' refers either to his promise to be the protector and deliverer of his people in their captivity, or, in general, means that *all* his promises shall be firm and unchanging. ¶ *Shall stand for ever.* Amidst all revolutions among men, his promise shall be firm. It shall not only live amidst the changes of dynasties, and the revolutions of empires, but it shall *continue* for ever and ever. This is designed for support to an afflicted and oppressed people ; and it must have been to them, in their bondage, the source of high consolation. But it is equally so now. Amidst all the changes on earth ; the revolutions of empires ; the vanishing of kingdoms, God is the same, and his promises are unfailing. We see the grass wither at the return of autumn, or in the drought : we see the flower of the field lose its beauty, and decay ; we see

9 O ¹ Zion, that bringest good
tidings, get thee up into the high
mountain ; O ² Jerusalem, that
bringest good tidings, lift up thy

voice with strength ; lift *it* up, be
not afraid ; say unto the cities of
Judah, Behold your God !

1 or, *thou that tellest good tidings to Zion.*
2 or, *thou that t. llest good tidings to Jerusalem.*

man rejoicing in his vigour and his
health, cut down in an instant; we see
cities fall, and kingdoms lose their power
and vanish from among nations, but God
changes not. He presides in all these
revolutions, and sits calm and unmoved
amidst all these changes. Not one of
his promises shall fail ; and at the end
of all the changes which human things
shall undergo, JEHOVAH, the God of his
people, will be the same.

9. *O Zion, that bringest good tidings.*
This is evidently the continuance of
what the 'voice' said, or of the annunciation which was to give joy to an
afflicted and oppressed people. There
has been, however, much diversity of
opinion in regard to the meaning of the
passage. The margin renders it, ' Thou
that tellest good tidings to Zion,' making Zion the receiver, and not the pub-
lisher of the message that was to convey
joy. The Vulgate, in a similar way,
renders it, ' Ascend a high mountain,
thou who bringest good tidings to Zion '
(*qui evangelizas Zion*). So the Chaldee,
understanding this as an address to the
prophet, as in ver. 1, 'Ascend a high
mountain, ye prophets, who bring glad
tidings to Zion.' So Lowth, Noyes, Gesenius, Grotius, and others. The word
מְבַשֶּׂרֶת, from בָּשַׂר (*bāsăr*), means *cheering with good tidings;* announcing good
news ; bearing joyful intelligence. It
is a participle in the feminine gender ;
and is appropriately applicable to some
one that bears good tidings *to* Zion, and
not to Zion as appointed to bear glad
tidings. Lowth supposes that it is applicable to some female whose office it
was to announce glad tidings, and says
that it was the common practice for females to engage in the office of proclaiming good news. On an occasion of a
public victory or rejoicing, it was customary, says he, for females to assemble
together, and to celebrate it with songs,
and dances, and rejoicings ; and he appeals to the instance of Miriam and the
chorus of women (Ex. xv. 20, 21), and
to the instance where, after the victory

of David over Goliath, ' all the women
came out of the cities of Israel singing
and dancing to meet Saul' (1 Sam. xviii.
7). But there are objections to this interpretation ; first, if this was the sense,
the word would have been in the *plural*
number, since there is no instance in
which a female is employed alone in
this service ; and, secondly, it was not,
according to this, the office of the female
to *announce* good tidings, or to communicate a joyful message, but to *celebrate*
some occasion of triumph or victory.
Grotius supposes that the word is ' feminine in its sound, but common in its
signification ;' and thus denotes *any*
whose office it was to communicate glad
tidings. Gesenius (*Comm. in loc.*) says,
that the feminine form here is used in a
collective sense for מְבַשְּׂרִים in the plural;
and supposes that it thus refers to the
prophets, or others who were to announce
the glad tidings to Zion. Vitringa coincides with our translation, and supposes
that the sense is, that Zion was to make
proclamation to the other cities of Judah of the deliverance ; that the news
was first to be communicated to Jerusalem, and that Jerusalem was intrusted
with the office of announcing this to the
other cities of the land; and that the
meaning is, that the gospel was to be
preached first *at* Jerusalem, and then
from Jerusalem as a centre to the other
cities of the land, agreeably to Luke
xxiv. 49. In this view, also, Hengstenberg coincides (*Christol.* vol. i. p. 424).
But that the former interpretation,
which regards Zion as the *receiver*, and
not the *promulgator*, of the intelligence,
is the true one, is apparent, I think,
from the following considerations—1. It
is that which is the obvious and most
correct construction of the Hebrew.
2. It is that which is found in the ancient versions. 3. It accords with the
design of the passage. The main scope
of the passage is not to call upon Jerusalem to make known the glad tidings,
but it is to convey the good news *to*
Jerusalem; to announce to her, lying

10 Behold, the Lord God will come [1] with strong *hand*, and his arm shall rule for him ; behold, his

reward *a is* with him, and [2] his work before him.

1 or, *against the strong.*   *a* Rev. 22. 12.
2 or, *recompence for his works.*

desolate and waste, that her hard service was at an end, and that she was to be blessed with the return of happier and better times (see ver. 2). It would be a departure from this, to suppose that the subject was diverted in order to give Jerusalem a command to make the proclamation to the other cities of the land—to say nothing of the impropriety of calling on *a city* to go up into a high mountain, and to lift up its voice. On the meaning of the word ' Zion,' see Note on ch. i. 8. ¶ *Get thee up into a high mountain.* You who make this proclamation to Zion. It was not uncommon in ancient times, when a multitude were to be addressed, or a proclamation to be made, for the crier to go into a mountain, where he could be seen and heard. Thus Jotham, addressing the men of Shechem, is said to have gone and ' stood on the top of mount Gerizim, and lifted up his voice' (Judg. ix. 7; comp. Matt. v. 1). The sense is, that the messengers of the joyful news to Zion were to make themselves distinctly heard by all the inhabitants of the city, and of the land. ¶ *Lift up thy voice.* As with a glad and important message. Do not deliver the message as if you were afraid that it should be heard. It is one of joy; and it should be delivered in a clear, decided, animated manner, as if it were important that it should be heard. ¶ *With strength.* Aloud; with effort; with power (comp. ch. xxxv. 3,4). ¶ *Lift it up.* Lift up the voice. The command is repeated, to denote emphasis. The mind is full of the subject, and the prophet repeats the command, as a man often does when his mind is full of an idea. The command to deliver the message of God with animation, earnestness, and zeal is one that is not unusual in Isaiah. It should be delivered as if it were true, and as if it were believed to be true. This will not justify, however, boisterous preaching, or a loud and unnatural tone of voice—alike offensive to good taste, injurious to the health, and destructive of the life of the preacher. It

is to be remarked, also, that *this* command to lift up the voice, appertains to the glad tidings of the gospel, and not to the terrors of wrath; to the proclamation of mercy, and not to the denunciation of woe. The glad tidings of salvation should be delivered in an animated and ardent manner; the future punishment of the wicked in a tone serious, solemn, subdued. ¶ *Say unto the cities of Judah.* Not to Jerusalem only, but to all the cities of the land. They were alike to be blessed on the return from the captivity—alike in the preaching of the gospel. ¶ *Behold your God!* Lo! your God returns to the city, the temple, and the land! Lo! he comes (Note, ver. 3), conducting his people as a king to their land! Lo! he will come —under the Messiah in future times— to redeem and save! What a glad announcement was this to the desolate and forsaken cities of Judah! What a glad announcement to the wide world, ' Lo ! God has come to redeem and save; and the desolate world shall be visited with his salvation and smile, in his mercy through the Messiah!'

10. *Behold, the Lord God will come* (see Note on ver. 3). Applied to the condition of the Jews in exile, this means that God would come to deliver them. Applied to the times of the Messiah, it means that God would manifest himself in a powerful manner as mighty to save. ¶ *With strong* hand (בְּחָזָק). Marg. ' Against the strong.' So Vitringa and others understand it ; and regard it as referring to the mighty enemies of the people of God, or, as Vitringa particularly supposes, to the great foe of God and his people—the prince of darkness—the devil. Lowth also translates it in this manner, ' Against the strong one.' The LXX. render it, Μετὰ ἰσχύος —' With strength.' This is the more probable meaning—that the Lord would come with the manifestation of strength and power, able to subdue and vanquish all the enemies of his people, and to effect their complete and final salvation. ¶ *And his arm.* The *arm* is a symbol

11 He shall feed his flock like a shepherd ; *a*he shall gather the lambs with his arm, and carry *them* in his bosom, *and* shall gently lead those that [1]are with young.

a Ps.23.1; Jn.10.11.   [1] or, *give suck.*

of strength, because it is by that that we accomplish our purposes; by that a conqueror slays his enemies in battle, &c. Thus, ' Break thou the arm of the wicked;' *i.e.,* diminish or destroy his power (Ps. x. 15). ' I have broken the arm of Pharaoh king of Egypt' (Ezek. xxx. 21; comp. Jer. xlviii. 25). Thus it is said of God, ' Thou hast a mighty arm ' (Ps. lxxxix. 13), and, ' His holy arm hath gotten him the victory' (Ps. xcviii. 1 ; comp. Ex. vi. 6). The metaphor is taken from the act of stretching out the arm to fight in battle, where the *arm* is the effective instrument in subduing an enemy. ¶ *Shall rule for him.* Lowth renders the phrase, לֹו (*lo*), ' for him,' ' over him :'—' And his arm shall prevail over him ;' *i.e.,* over the strong and mighty foe. The LXX. render it, Μετά κυρίας—' With dominion.' But the meaning seems to be, ' God is mighty by himself; his power resides in his own arm ; he is not dependent on others ; he will accomplish the deliverance in such a manner that it shall be seen that he did it alone; and he shall rule for himself, without any aid, and so that it shall be manifest that he is the sovereign.' In the deliverance of his people from their captivity, he so directed it, that it was manifest that he was their deliverer and sovereign; and in the redemption of man, the same thing is apparent, that the arm of God effects the deliverance, and that it is his own power that establishes the dominion. ¶ *Behold, his reward* is *with him.* He will be ready to confer the appropriate reward on his own people. The idea seems to be taken from the custom of a conqueror, who distributes rewards among his followers and soldiers after a signal victory. This was always done in ancient wars, apparently because it seemed to be an act of justice that those who had gained the victory should share also in the result, and this participation of the booty was a stimulus to future effort, as well as a compensation for their valour. The rewards distributed consisted generally of that which was taken from the conquered ;

gold, and silver, and raiment, as well as captives or slaves (see Gen. xlix. 7 ; Ex. xv. 9; 1 Sam. xxx. 26; and particularly Judges v. 30) :

Have they not sped?
Have they not divided the prey ;
To every man a damsel or two;
To Sisera a prey of divers colours,
A prey of divers colours of needle-work,
Of divers colours of needle-work on both sides,
Meet for the necks of them that take the spoil.

The idea here is—1. That JEHOVAH would bestow appropriate rewards on his people. 2. That they would be conferred on his coming, and not be delayed. 3. That it should be done by the hand of God himself. This language was applicable to the interposition of God to save his people from their long exile, and the ' reward' would be ample in the restoration to their own land, and the re-establishment of his worship. It is applicable in a higher sense to the coming of the Messiah to bless the world. His reward was with him. He blessed his faithful followers on earth ; he will bless them more abundantly in heaven. It will be assuredly applicable to him when he shall come to gather his people to himself in the great and last day, and the language before us is used with reference to that : ' And behold, I come quickly; and my reward is with me, to give every man according as his work shall be' (Rev. xxii. 12). ¶ *And his work.* Marg. ' Recompense for his work.' The margin here is the correct rendering. The Hebrew word strictly indeed denotes work, labour, business ; but it also denotes the *wages* for work (Lev. xix. 13; Ps. cix. 20).

11. *He shall feed his flock.* In the previous verse, the fact had been asserted that God would come to subdue his foes, and to reward his people. In this verse, the mild and gentle character of his government over his people is predicted. It would not be that of a conqueror over vanquished subjects ; but it would be mild and tender, like that of a shepherd who carries the lambs, which are unable to walk, in his own arms, and gently leads along the feeble and the delicate. The word translated ' shall

feed ' (יִרְעֶה), denotes more than our word *feed* at present. It refers to all the care of a shepherd over his flock; and means to tend, to guard, to govern, to provide pasture, to defend from danger, as a shepherd does his flock. It is often applied in the Scriptures to God, represented as the tender shepherd, and especially to the Redeemer (Ps. xxiii. 1; Ezek. xxxiv. 23; John x. 14; Heb. xiii. 20; 1 Pet. ii. 25; v. 4). It is often applied to a leader or a ruler of a people (2 Sam. v. 2; vii. 7; Jer. xxxii. 2). Thus Homer often uses the phrase, ποιμήν λαῶν—'shepherds of the people,' to denote a ruler, or monarch. Here it denotes that God would evince towards his people the same tender care, guardianship and protection, which a shepherd shows for his flock. ¶ *He shall gather the lambs with his arm.* This is a most beautiful expression, denoting the care of God the Saviour for the feeblest and weakest of his people, and for the young and feeble in years and piety. A similar thing is often done by a shepherd. The tender lamb, unable to keep up with the flock, becomes weary and exhausted; and the shepherd naturally takes it in his arms and carries it. Such a shepherd as this Virgil beautifully describes:

En, ipse capellas
Protenus æger ago; hanc etiam vix, Tityre, duco;
Hic inter densas corylos modo namque gemellos,
Spem gregis, Ah! silice in nuda connixa reliquet.
Eclog. i. 12.

Lo! I my goats urge fainting o'er the mead;
This, feebler than the rest, with pains I lead.
Yean'd mid yon herds upon the flinty plain,
Her dying twins, my flock's late hope, remain.
Wrangham.

¶ And *shall gently lead*, &c. Marg. 'Give suck.' This is the more correct translation. It denotes the dams of the flock that would be easily exhausted by being overdriven, and of which there was, therefore, especial care necessary. Thus Jacob says to his brother Esau, Gen. xxxiii. 13: 'The flocks and the herds giving suck to their young are with me, and if they should be overdriven all the flock will die.' Of the necessity of such care and attention there is abundant evidence, and indeed it is manifest at a glance. Dr. Shaw, speaking of the exposure of the flocks in Syria, says: 'The greatest skill and vigilance,

and even tender care, are required in the management of such immense flocks as wander on the Syrian plains. Their prodigious numbers compel the keepers to remove them too frequently in search of fresh pastures, which proves very destructive to the young that have not strength to follow.' The following extract from Anderson's *Tour through Greece* will also serve to illustrate this passage: 'One of the great delights in travelling through a pastoral country, is to see and feel the force of the beautiful imagery in the Scriptures, borrowed from pastoral life. All day long the shepherd attends his flock, leading them into "green pastures," near fountains of water, and chooses a convenient place for them to "rest at noon." At night he drives them near his tent; and, if there is danger, encloses them in the fold. They know his voice, and follow him. When travelling, he tenderly watches over them, *and carries such as are exhausted in his arms.* Such a shepherd is the Lord Jesus Christ.' No description could more beautifully describe the character of the Redeemer. In the New Testament, he is often described as a kind and tender shepherd, and regarding the welfare of all his flock, and as ready to give his life for them (John x. 7, 9–11, 14, 15; Heb. xiii. 20; 1 Pet. ii. 25; v. 4). We are here also strikingly reminded of the solemn command which he gave to Peter, evincing his tender regard for his flock, 'Feed my lambs:' 'Feed my sheep' (John xvi. 15–17). It proves in regard to the Redeemer—1. That his nature is mild, and gentle, and tender. 2. That he has a kind regard for all his flock, and will consult the real interest of all, as a shepherd does of his flock. 3. That he has a special solicitude for the feeble and infirm, and that they will be the objects of his tender care. 4. That he feels a particular solicitude for the young. He knows their feebleness; he is acquainted with their temptations; he sees the importance of their being trained up with care; and he looks with deep interest, therefore, on all the efforts made to guard them from the ways of sin, and to train them up for his service (comp. Note on ch. xlii. 3).

12. *Who hath measured.* The ob-

12 Who hath measured the waters in the hollow of his hand, and meted out heaven with a span, and comprehended the dust of the earth in a ¹measure, and weighed the mountains in scales, and the hills in a balance?

1 *tierce.*

ject in this and the following verses to ver. 26, is to show the greatness, power, and majesty of God, by strong contrast with his creatures, and more especially with idols. Perhaps the prophet designed to meet and answer an implied objection : that the work of deliverance was so great that it could not be accomplished. The answer was, that God had made all things; that he was infinitely great; that he had entire control over all the nations; and that he could, therefore, remove all obstacles out of the way, and accomplish his great and gracious purposes. By man it could not be done; nor had idol-gods any power to do it; but the Creator and upholder of all could effect this purpose with infinite ease. At the same time that the *argument* here is one that is entirely conclusive, the passage, regarded as a description of the power and majesty of God, is one of vast sublimity and grandeur; nor is there any portion of the Sacred Volume that is more fitted to impress the mind with a sense of the majesty and glory of JEHOVAH. The question, 'who hath measured,' is designed to imply that the thing referred to here was that which had never been done, and could never be done by man; and the *argument* is, that although that which the prophet predicted was a work which surpassed human power, yet it could be done by that God who had measured the waters in the hollow of his hand. The word 'waters' here refers evidently to the vast collection of waters in the deep—the mighty ocean, together with *all* the waters in the running streams, and in the clouds. See Gen. i. 6, where the firmament is said to have been made to divide the waters from the waters. A reference to the waters *above* the heavens occurs in Ps. cxlviii. 4:

Praise him, ye heavens of heavens,
And ye waters that be above the heavens.

And in Prov. xxx. 4, a similar description of the power and majesty of God occurs:

Who hath gathered the wind in his fists?
Who hath bound the waters in a garment?
Who hath established all the ends of the earth?

And in Job xxvi. 8:

He bindeth up the waters in his thick clouds;
And the cloud is not rent under them.

The word ' waters ' here, therefore, may include *all* the water on the earth, and in the sky. The words, 'the hollow of his hand,' mean properly the hand as it is closed, forming a hollow or a cavity by which water can be taken up. The idea is, that God can take up the vast oceans, and all the waters in the lakes, streams, and clouds, in the palm of his hand, as we take up the smallest quantity in ours. ¶ *And meted out heaven.* The word rendered ' meted,' *i.e.*, measured (כּוּן), means properly *to stand erect*, to set up, or make erect; to found, fit, adjust, dispose, form, create. It usually has the idea of *fitting* or disposing. The word ' span ' (זֶרֶת) denotes the space from the end of the thumb to the end of the middle finger, when extended—usually about nine inches. The idea is, that JEHOVAH was able to compass or grasp the heavens, though so vast, as one can compass or measure a small object with the span. What an illustration of the vastness and illimitable nature of God! ¶ *And comprehended.* And measured (כָּל from כּוּל, *to hold* or *contain);* ' Lo, the heavens, and the heaven of heavens cannot *contain* thee ' (1 Kings viii. 27). ¶ *The dust of the earth.* All the earth; all the dust that composes the globe. ¶ *In a measure* (בַּשָּׁלִשׁ). Properly *three;* and then the third part of anything. Jerome supposes that it means *the three fingers,* and that the sense is, that God takes up all the dust of the earth in the first three fingers of the hand. But the more probable signification is, that the word denotes that which was *the third part* of some other measure, as of an ephah, or bath. In Ps. lxxx. 5, the word is used to denote a large measure:

Thou feedest them with the bread of tears,
And givest them tears to drink in great measure
(שָׁלִישׁ).

13 Who *a* hath directed the Spirit of the LORD, or *being* [1] his counsellor hath taught him ?

14 With whom took he counsel, and *who* [2] instructed him, and

taught him in the path of judgment, and taught him knowledge, and showed to him the way of understanding ? [3]

15 Behold, the nations *are* as a

---

a Ro.11.34.   [1] *man of his counsel.*

[2] *made him understand.*   [3] *understandings.*

The idea is, that God is so great that he can measure all the dust of the earth as easily as we can measure a small quantity of grain with a measure. ¶ *And weighed the mountains in scales.* The idea here is substantially the same. It is, that God is so mighty that he can weigh the lofty mountains, as we weigh a light object in scales, or in a balance; and perhaps, also, that he has disposed them on the earth *as if* he had weighed them out, and adapted them to their proper places and situations. Throughout this entire passage, there is not only the idea of majesty and power in God, but there is also the idea that he has *fitted* or adjusted everything by his wisdom and power, and adapted it to the condition and wants of his creatures.

13. *Who hath directed.* This passage is quoted by Paul in Rom. xi. 34, and referred to by him in 1 Cor. ii. 16. The word rendered 'directed' here (תִּכֵּן) is the same which is used in the previous verse, 'and *meted out* heaven.' The idea here is, 'Who has fitted, or disposed the mind or spirit of JEHOVAH? What superior being has ordered, instructed, or disposed his understanding? Who has *qualified* him for the exercise of his wisdom, or for the formation and execution of his plans?' The sense is, God is supreme. No one has instructed or guided him, but his plans are his own, and have all been formed by himself alone. And as those plans are infinitely wise, and as he is not dependent on any one for their formation or execution, his people may have confidence in him, and believe that he will be able to execute his purposes. ¶ *The Spirit.* The word 'spirit' is used in the Bible in a greater variety of senses than almost any other word (see Note on ver. 7). It seems here to be used in the sense of mind, and to refer to God himself. There is no evidence that it refers to the Holy Spirit particularly. ' The word *spirit*, he uses,' says Calvin, 'for reason,

judgment. He borrows the similitude from the nature of men, in order that he may more accommodate himself to them; nor, as it seems to me, does he here speak of the essential Spirit of God' (*Comm. in loco*). The design of the prophet is not to refer to the distinction in the Divine nature, or to illustrate the peculiar characteristics of the different persons of the Godhead; but it is to set forth the wisdom of JEHOVAH HIMSELF, the one infinite God, as contradistinguished from idols, and as qualified to guide, govern, and deliver his people. The passage should not be used, therefore, as a proof-text in regard to the existence and wisdom of the Holy Spirit, but is fitted to demonstrate only that God is *untaught;* and that he is independent and infinite in his wisdom. ¶ *Or being his counsellor.* Marg., as in Heb. ' Man of his counsel.' He is not dependent for counsel on men or angels. He is supreme, independent, and infinite. None is qualified to instruct him; and all, therefore, should confide in his wisdom and knowledge.

14. *With whom took he counsel.* The sentiment of the former verse is repeated here, in order, probably, to make it more emphatic. ¶ *In the path of judgment.* The way of judging correctly and wisely; or the way of administering justice. It denotes here his boundless wisdom as it is seen in the various arrangements of his creation and providence, by which all things keep their places, and accomplish his vast designs.

15. *Behold, the nations.* All the nations of the earth. This is designed to show the greatness of God, in comparison with that which strikes man as great—a mighty nation; and the main object seems to be, to show that God could accomplish his purposes without their aid, and that they could not resist him in the execution of his plans. If they were as nothing in comparison with him, how easily could he execute his

drop of a bucket, and are counted as the small dust of the balance: behold, he taketh up the isles as a very little thing.

16 And Lebanon *is* not sufficient

to burn, nor the beasts thereof sufficient for a burnt-offering.

17 All nations before him are nothing; *a* and they are counted

a Da.4.35.

purposes! If they were as nothing, how little could they resist the execution of his plans! ¶ Are *as a drop of a bucket.* In comparison with him; or are so esteemed by him. The drop that falls from the bucket in drawing water is a trifle. It has no power, and compared with the waters of the ocean it is as nothing. So small is the power of the nations in comparison with God. ¶ *And are counted.* Are thought of, regarded, esteemed by him, or in comparison with him. ¶ *As the small dust of the balance.* The small, fine dust which collects on the best finished and most accurate balance or scales, and which has no effect in making the scales uneven, or making either side preponderate. Nothing can be a more striking representation of the fact that the nations are regarded as nothing in comparison with God. ¶ *Behold, he taketh up the isles.* Or he is able to do it; he could remove the isles as the fine dust is driven before the whirlwind. A more literal translation of this passage would be, 'Lo, the isles are as the dust which is taken up,' or which one takes up; *i.e.*, which is taken up, and carried away by the wind. There is something unusual in the expression that God takes up the isles, and the idea is rather that the isles in his sight are regarded as the fine dust which the wind sweeps away. So the Chaldee renders it, 'Lo, the isles are like ashes which the wind drives away.' The word 'isles,' Vitringa and Jerome regard as denoting not the small portions of land in the sea that are surrounded by water, but lands which are encompassed and enclosed by rivers, like Mesopotamia. But there is no reason why it should not be taken here in its usual signification, as denoting the islands of the sea. They would serve well to be used in connection with mountains and hills in setting forth the vast power of God. ¶ *As a very little thing* (כְּדַּק). The word דַּק (*dăq*) means *that which is beaten small, or fine;* and then

fine dust, chaff, or any light thing which the wind easily sweeps away.

16. *And Lebanon.* The expression here refers to the trees or the cedars of Lebanon. Thus it is rendered by the Chaldee: 'And the trees of Lebanon.' For a description of Lebanon, see Note on ch. x. 34. It is probable that the word *Lebanon* here is not used in the limited sense in which it is sometimes employed, to denote a single mountain, or a single range of mountains, but includes the entire ranges lying north of Palestine, and which were comprehended under the general name of Libanus. The idea here is, that all these ranges of mountains, abounding in magnificent trees and forests, would not furnish fuel sufficient to burn the sacrifices which would be an appropriate offering to the majesty and glory of God. ¶ *To burn.* To burn for the purpose of consuming the sacrifice. ¶ *Nor the beasts thereof for a burnt-offering.* As the mountains of Lebanon were extensive forests, they would abound with wild animals. The idea is, that all those animals, if offered in sacrifice, would not be an appropriate expression of what was due to God. It may be remarked here, if all the vast forests of Lebanon on fire, and all its animals consumed as an offering to God, were not sufficient to show forth his glory, how little can our praises express the proper sense of his majesty and honour! How profound should be our reverence for God! With what awful veneration should we come before him! The image employed here by Isaiah is one of great poetic beauty; and nothing, perhaps, could give a deeper impression of the majesty and honour of the great JEHOVAH.

17. *Are as nothing.* This expresses literally what had been expressed by the beautiful and striking imagery above. ¶ *Less than nothing.* A strong hyperbolic expression denoting the utter insignificance of the nations as compared with God. Such expressions are com-

to him less than *a*nothing and vanity.

18 To whom then will ye liken God? or what likeness *b* will ye compare unto him?

19 The workman *c*melteth a graven image, and the goldsmith

spreadeth it over with gold, and casteth silver chains.

20 He that ¹is so impoverished, that he hath no oblation, chooseth a tree *that* will not rot; he seeketh unto him a cunning workman to prepare a graven image, *that* shall not be moved.

mon in the Scriptures. ¶ *And vanity.* Heb. תֹּהוּ (*thōhū*)—'Emptiness;' the word which in Gen. i. 2 is rendered 'without form.'

18. *To whom then will ye liken God?* Since he is so great, what can resemble him? What form can be made like him? The main idea here intended to be conveyed by the prophet evidently is, that God is great and glorious, and worthy of the confidence of his people. This idea he illustrates by a reference to the attempts which had been made to make a representation of him, and by showing how vain those efforts were. He therefore states the mode in which the images of idols were usually formed, and shows how absurd it was to suppose that they could be any real representation of the true God. It is possible that this was composed in the time of Manasseh, when idolatry prevailed to a great extent in Judah, and that the prophet intended in this manner incidentally to show the folly and absurdity of it.

19. *The workman.* The Hebrew word denotes an artificer of any kind, and is applied to one who engraved on wood or stone (Ex. xxviii. 2); to a workman in iron, brass, stone, wood (Ex. xxxv. 35; Deut. xxvii. 15); or an artizan, or artificer in general. It here refers manifestly to a man who worked in the metals of which idols were commonly made. Those idols were sometimes made of wood, sometimes of clay, but more frequently, as they are at present in India, of metal. It became, undoubtedly, a regular trade or business thus to make idol-gods. ¶ *Melteth.* Casts or founds. ¶ *A graven image* (פֶּסֶל). This word commonly denotes an image carved or graven from wood (Ex. xx. 4; Judg. xvii. 3; Isa. xliv. 15, 17); but it is also frequently applied to a *molten* image, or one that is cast from

metals (Jer. x. 14; li. 17). It is used in this sense here; as there is an incongruity in the idea of *casting*, or melting a *graven* image. ¶ *And the goldsmith spreadeth it over with gold.* Idols were frequently overlaid with gold or silver. Those which were in the temples of the gods were probably commonly made in this way, and probably those also which were made for private use, as far as it could be afforded. The word here rendered 'goldsmith,' however, does not of necessity mean a worker in gold, but a smith in general, or a worker in any kind of metals. ¶ *And casteth silver chains.* For the idol. These were not to fasten it, but for the purpose of ornament. The general principle seems to have been to decorate their idols with that which was regarded as the highest ornament among the people; and as chains were used in abundance as a part of their personal ornaments among the Orientals (see Notes on ch. iii. 23), so they made use of the same kind of ornaments for their idols. The idols of the Hindoos now are lavishly decorated in this manner.

20. *He that is so impoverished.* So poor. So it is generally supposed that the word here used is to be understood, though interpreters have not been entirely agreed in regard to its signification. The LXX. render the phrase, 'The carpenter chooseth a sound piece of wood.' The Chaldee, 'He cuts down an ash, a tree which will not rot.' Vulg. 'Perhaps he chooses a tree which is incorruptible.' Jarchi renders it, 'He who is accustomed to examine, and to judge between the wood which is durable, and other wood.' But the signification of the word (from כָּבַן *sākhăn, to dwell,* to be familiar with any one) given to it by our translators, is probably the correct one, that of being too poor to make a costly oblation. This notion of poverty,

21 Have *a* ye not known ? have ye not heard ? hath it not been told you *b* from the beginning ? have ye not understood from the foundations of the earth ?

a Ps.19.1; Ac.14.17; Ro.1.19,20.　　b Ro.3.1,2.

Gesenius supposes, is derived from the notion of *being seated;* and thence of sinking down from languor or debility ; and hence from poverty or want. ¶ *That he hath no oblation.* No offering ; no sacrifice ; no rich gift. He is too poor to make such an offering to his god as would be implied in an idol of brass or other metal, richly overlaid with plates of gold, and decorated with silver chains. In ver. 19, the design seems to have been to describe the more rich and costly idols that were made ; in this, to describe those that were made by the poor who were unable to offer such as were made of brass and gold. The word ' oblation,' therefore, *i.e., offering,* in this place, does not denote an offering made to the true God, but an offering made to an idol, such as an image was regarded to be. He could not afford a rich offering, and was constrained to make one of wood. ¶ *Chooseth a tree* that *will not rot.* Wood that will be durable and permanent. Perhaps the idea is, that as he could not afford one of metal, he would choose that which would be the most valuable which he could make—a piece of wood that was durable, and that would thus show his regard for the god that he worshipped. Or possibly the sense may be, that he designed it should not be moved ; that he expressed a fixed and settled determination to adhere to the worship of the idol ; and that as he had no idea of changing his religion, the permanency and durability of the wood would be regarded as a somewhat more acceptable expression of his worship. ¶ *A cunning workman.* Heb. ' A wise artificer ;' a man skilled in the art of carving, and of making images. ¶ *A graven image.* An image engraved or cut from wood, in contradistinction from one that is molten or made from metals. ¶ That *shall not be moved.* That shall stand long, as the expression of his devotion to the service of the idol. The wood that was commonly employed for this purpose as being most durable, as we learn from ch. xliv. 14, was the cedar, the cypress, or the oak (see the Note in that place). The phrase, ' shall not be moved,' does not refer so much to its being fixed in one place, as to its durability and permanency.

21. *Have ye not known?* This is evidently an address to the worshippers of idols, and either designed to be addressed to the Jews themselves in the times of Manasseh, when idolatry abounded, or to *all* idolaters. The prophet had in the previous verses shown the manner in which the idols were made, and the folly of regarding them as objects of worship. He now turns and addresses the worshippers of these idols, as being without excuse. They might have known that these were not the true God. They had had abundant opportunity of learning his existence and of becoming acquainted with his majesty and glory. Tradition had informed them of this, and the creation of the earth demonstrated his greatness and power. The prophet, therefore, asks them whether they had not known this ? Whether their conduct was the result of ignorance ? And the question implies emphatically that they *had* known, or had abundant opportunity to know of the existence and majesty of God. This was emphatically true of the Jews, and yet they were constantly falling into idolatrous worship. ¶ *From the beginning.* Heb. ' From the head,' *i.e.,* from the very commencement of the world. Has it not been communicated by tradition, from age to age, that there is one God, and that he is the Creator and upholder of all things ? This was particularly the case with the Jews, who had had this knowledge from the very commencement of their history, and they were, therefore, entirely without excuse in their tendencies to idolatry. ¶ *From the foundations of the earth.* Have you not learned the existence and greatness of God from the fact that the world has been made, and that it demonstrates the existence and perfection of God ? The sacred writers often speak of the earth as resting on a foundation, as upheld, &c. :

For he hath founded it upon the seas,
And established it upon the floods.

22 *It is* [1]he that sitteth upon the circle of the earth, and the inhabitants thereof *are* as grass-

1 or, *Him that sitteth.*

hoppers; [a]that stretcheth out the heavens as a curtain, and spreadeth them out as a tent to dwell in;

a Job 9. 8.

(Ps. xxiv. 2; see also Prov. viii. 29.) Perhaps here, however, the word 'foundation' refers rather to the *time* than to the *manner* in which the earth is made, and corresponds to the phrase 'from the beginning;' and the sense may be, 'Has it not been understood ever since the earth was founded? Has not the tradition of the existence and perfections of God been unbroken and constant?' The argument is, that the existence and greatness of God were fully known by tradition and by his works; and that it was absurd to attempt to form an image of that God who had laid the foundations of the world.

22. It is *he that sitteth.* Marg. 'Him that sitteth,' *i.e.*, have you not known him? The Hebrew literally means 'the sitter, or he sitting on the circle of the earth;' and it may be connected either with ver. 21, 'Have ye not known him sitting on the circle of the earth?' or with ver. 18, 'What likeness will ye compare to him that sitteth on the circle of the earth?' In either case the phrase is designed to show the majesty and glory of God. The word 'sitteth' refers to God as a sovereign or monarch, making the circle of the earth his throne. ¶ *The circle of the earth.* Or rather, *above* (עַל *ăl*) the circle of the earth. The word rendered 'circle' (חוּג) denotes *a circle, sphere,* or *arch;* and is applied to the arch or vault of the heavens, in Prov. viii. 27; Job xxii. 14. The phrase 'circle,' or 'circuit of the earth,' here seems to be used in the same sense as the phrase *orbis terrarum* by the Latins; not as denoting a *sphere,* or not as implying that the earth was a globe, but that it was an extended plain surrounded by oceans and mighty waters. The globular form of the earth was then unknown; and the idea is, that God sat *above* this extended circuit, or circle; and that the vast earth was beneath his feet. ¶ *And the inhabitants thereof* are *like grasshoppers.* Or rather, like locusts, for so the Hebrew word properly means. This is de-

signed to show that the inhabitants of the earth, numerous and mighty as they are, are as nothing compared with God. The *idea* is that God is so exalted, that, as he looks down from that elevated station, all the inhabitants of the world appear to him as locusts—a busy, agitated, moving, impatient multitude, spread over the vast circle of the earth beneath him—as locusts spread in almost interminable bands over the plains in the East. What a striking illustration of the insignificance of man as he is viewed from the heavens! What an impressive description of the nothingness of his mighty plans, and of the vanity of his mightiest works! ¶ *That stretcheth out the heavens.* Referring to the firmament above, as that which seems to be stretched out, or expanded over our heads. The heavens above are often thus compared to an expanse —either solid (Gen. i. 7), or to a curtain, or tent (comp. Note on ch. xxxiv. 4). ¶ *As a curtain.* The word here used (דֹּק) denotes properly *fineness, thinness;* and then a fine or thin cloth, or curtain. Here it means a thin canopy that is stretched over us. The same expression occurs in Ps. civ. 2 (comp. Job ix. 8; Isa. xliv. 24). Probably the reference here is to the veil, curtain, or awning which the Orientals are accustomed to draw over the *court* in their houses. Their houses are constructed with an open court in the centre, with the rooms ranged round it. In that court or open square there are usually fountains, if the situation is so that they can be constructed; and they are cool and refreshing places for the family to sit in the heat of the summer. In hot or rainy weather, a curtain or awning is drawn over this area. According to the image of the prophet here, the heavens are spread out over our heads as such an awning. ¶ *And spreadeth them out as a tent.* As a tent that is made for a habitation. Perhaps the idea is, that the heavens are extended like a tent in order to furnish a dwelling-place for God. Thus

23 That bringeth the princes to nothing : *a* he maketh the judges of the earth as vanity.

24 Yea, they shall not be planted ; yea, they shall not be sown ; yea, their stock shall not take root in the earth ; and he shall also blow upon them, and they shall wither, and the whirlwind shall take them away as stubble.

a Job 12.21; Ps.107.40.

the Chaldee renders it. If so, it proves that the universe, so vast, was fitted up to be the dwelling-place of the High and Holy One, and is a most impressive representation of his immensity.

23. *That bringeth the princes to nothing.* That is, all princes and kings. No matter how great their power, their wealth, and their dignity, they are, by his hand, reduced to nothing before him. The design of this passage is to contrast the majesty of God with that of princes and nobles, and to show how far he excels them all. The general truth is therefore stated, that *all* monarchs are by him removed from their thrones, and consigned to nothing. The same idea is expressed in Job xii. 21 :

He poureth contempt upon princes,
And weakeneth the strength of the mighty.

And in Ps. cvii. 40 :

He poureth contempt upon princes,
And causeth them to wander in the wilderness
    where there is no way.

The *particular* idea here, as appears from the next verse, is, that the princes and rulers who are opposed to God constitute no real resistance to the execution of his purposes. He can strip off their honours and glory, and obliterate even their names. ¶ *He maketh the judges of the earth.* Kings and princes often executed judgment *personally*, and hence the words judges and kings seem to be synonymous as they are used here, and in Ps. ii. 10 :

Be wise now, therefore, O ye kings;
Be instructed, ye judges of the earth.

24. *Yea, they shall not be planted.* The kings and rulers—especially they who oppose God in the execution of his purposes. The idea in this verse is, that their name and family should become extinct in the same way as a tree does from which no shoot starts up. Although they were great and mighty, like the tree that sends out far-spreading branches, and strikes its roots deep, yet God would so utterly destroy them that they should have no posterity, and their family become extinct. Princes and kings are often compared to lofty and majestic trees of the forest (comp. Ps. xxxvii. 35; Dan. iv. 7, *sq.*) Vitringa supposes that wicked rulers are particularly intended here, and that the idea is, that the wicked princes that persecuted his people should be entirely extinct on the earth. He refers particularly to Pharaoh, Antiochus Epiphanes, Nero, Domitian, Decius, Gallus, Galerius, Maxenus, Maximus, and some others, as instances of this kind, whose families soon became extinct. It may be remarked, in general, that the families of monarchs and princes become extinct usually much sooner than others. The fact may be owing in part to the usual luxury and vice in the families of the great, and in part to the direct arrangements of God, by which he designs that power shall not be for ever perpetuated in one family, or line. The *general* idea in the passage is, that earthly princes and rulers are as nothing when compared with God, and that he can easily destroy their families and their name. But there is no improbability in the supposition of Vitringa, that the prophet refers particularly to the *enemies* of God and his cause, and that he intends specifically to affirm that none of these enemies could prevent or embarrass the execution of his purposes— since with infinite ease he could entirely destroy their name. ¶ *They shall not be sown.* The same idea under another figure. The former referred to princes under the image of a tree ; this refers to them under the image of grain that is sown. The idea is, that their family and name should be annihilated, and should not spring up in a future generation. The same image occurs in Nahum (i. 14), in respect to the king of Assyria : ' The LORD hath given commandment concerning thee, that no more of

thy name be sown;' that is, that thy name and family should become entirely extinct. ¶ *Yea, their stock.* Their stem—referring to the stump or stock of a tree. When a tree is cut down, the roots often still live, and send up shoots, or suckers, that grow into trees. Posterity is often, in the Scriptures, compared to such suckers or shoots from old and decayed trees (see Notes on ch. xi. 1). The meaning here is, that as when a tree falls and dies without sending up any shoots, so princes should die. They should have no descendants; no one of their family should sit on their thrones. ¶ *Shall blow upon them.* As God sends a tempest upon the forest, and uproots the loftiest trees, so he will sweep away the families of princes. Or rather, perhaps, the idea here is, that God sends a strong and burning east wind, and withers up everything before it (see this wind described in the Notes on ch. xxxvii. 26). ¶ *And they shall wither.* Trees, and shrubs, and plants are dried up before that poisonous and fiery wind—the simoom—and so it would be with the princes before the blast of JEHOVAH. ¶ *And the whirlwind shall take them away as stubble.* This, in its literal signification, means that the whirlwind bears away the trees of the forest, and with the same ease God would sweep away the families of the kings and princes that opposed him and oppressed his people. It may illustrate this to observe, that the effects of whirlwinds in the East are often much more violent than they are with us, and that they often bear away to a great distance the branches of trees, and even the trees themselves. The following description of a whirlwind observed by Mr. Bruce, may serve to illustrate this passage, as well as the passage in Ps. lxxxiii. 13:

O my God, make them like a wheel;
As the stubble before the wind,

referring to the rotary action of the whirlwind, which often impels straw like a wheel set in rapid motion. 'Mr. Bruce, in his journey through the desert of Senaar, had the singular felicity to contemplate this wonderful phenomenon in all its terrific majesty, without injury, although with considerable danger and alarm. In that vast expanse of desert,

from west and to north-west of him, he saw a number of prodigious pillars of sand at different distances, moving, at times, with great celerity, at others, stalking on with majestic slowness; at intervals he thought they were coming, in a very few minutes, to overwhelm him and his companion. Again, they would retreat so as to be almost out of sight, their tops reaching to the very clouds. There, the tops often separated from the bodies; and these, once disjoined, dispersed in the air, and appeared no more. Sometimes they were broken near the middle, as if struck with a large cannon-shot. About noon, they began to advance with considerable swiftness upon them, the wind being very strong at north. Eleven of these awful visitors ranged alongside of them, about the distance of three miles. The greatest diameter of the largest appeared to him, at that distance, as if it would measure ten feet. They retired from them with a wind at south-east, leaving an impression upon the mind of our intrepid traveller, to which he could give no name, though he candidly admits that one ingredient in it was fear, with a considerable deal of wonder and astonishment. He declares it was in vain to think of flying; the swiftest horse, or fastest sailing ship, could be of no use to carry them out of this danger; and the full persuasion of this riveted him to the spot where he stood. Next day, they were gratified with a similar display of moving pillars, in form and disposition like those already described, only they seemed to be more in number and less in size. They came, several times, in a direction close upon them; that is, according to Mr. Bruce's computation, within less than two miles. They became, immediately after sunrise, like a thick wood, and almost darkened the sun; his rays shining through them for near an hour, gave them an appearance of pillars of fire. At another time, they were terrified by an army (as it seemed) of these sand pillars, whose march was constantly south, a number of which seemed once to be coming directly upon them; and though they were little nearer than two miles, a considerable quantity of sand fell around them. On the 21st of November, about

25 To whom *a* then will ye liken me, or shall I be equal? saith the Holy One.

26 Lift up your eyes on high, and behold who hath created these

a De.4.23,&c.

things, that bringeth out their hosts by number : he calleth *b* them all by names, by the greatness of his might, for that *he is* strong in power ; not one faileth.

b Ps.147.4.

eight in the morning, he had a view of the desert to the westward, as before, and the sands had already begun to rise in immense twisted pillars, which darkened the heavens, and moved over the desert with more magnificence than ever. The sun, shining through the pillars, which were thicker, and contained more sand, apparently, than on any of the preceding days, seemed to give those nearest them an appearance as if spotted with stars of gold.'—(Paxton.)

25. *To whom then will ye liken me?* (see ver. 18.) The prophet having thus set forth the majesty and glory of God, asks now with great emphasis, what *could be* an adequate and proper representation of such a God. And if God was such a Being, how great was the folly of idolatry, and how vain all their confidence in the gods which their own hands had made.

26. *Lift up your eyes on high.* Direct your eyes towards heaven, and in the contemplation of the wonders of the starry world, and of God's power there, learn the evidence of his ability to destroy his foes and to save his friends. Lowth connects this verse with the former, and renders it :

' Saith the Holy One,
Lift up your eyes on high.'

The words ' on high' here are evidently synonymous with heaven, and refer to the starry worlds. The design of the passage is to convince them of the folly of idolatry, and of the power and majesty of the true God. It is proof of man's elevated nature that he *can* thus look upward, and trace the evidences of the power and wisdom of God in the heavens; that he can raise his eyes and thoughts above the earth, and fix his attention on the works of God in distant worlds ; and in the number, the order, the greatness, and the harmony of the heavenly bodies, trace the proofs of the infinite greatness and

wisdom of God. This thought was most beautifully expressed by one of the ancient poets.

Pronaque cum spectent animalia cætera terram;
Os homini sublime dedit : cœlumque tueri,
Jussit et erectos ad sidera tollere vultus.
Ovid, *Met.* i. 84–86.

In the Scriptures, God not unfrequently appeals to the starry heavens in proof of his existence and perfections, and as the most sublime exhibition of his greatness and power (see Ps. xix. 1–6). And it may be remarked, that this argument is one that increases in strength, in the view of men, from age to age, just in proportion to the advances which are made in the science of astronomy. It is now far more striking than it was in the times of Isaiah; and, indeed, the discoveries in astronomical science in modern times have given a beauty and power to this argument which could have been but imperfectly understood in the times of the prophets. The argument is one that accumulates with every new discovery in astronomy ; but is one —such is the vastness and beauty of the system of the universe—which can be contemplated in its full power only amidst the more sublime contemplations of eternity. Those who are disposed to contemplate this argument more fully, may find it presented with great eloquence and beauty in Dr. Chalmers's *Astronomical Discourses,* and in Dick's *Christian Philosopher.* ¶ *Who hath created these* things. These heavens. This is the first evidence of the power of God in the contemplation of the heavens, that God is their *Creator.* The other demonstrations referred to are the fact, that he brings out their armies as if they were a marshalled host, and understands and calls all their names. ¶ *That bringeth out their hosts.* Their *armies,* for so the word ' hosts' means (see Note on ch. i. 9). The word here alludes to the fact that the heavenly bodies seem to be mar-

27 Why sayest thou, O Jacob, and speakest, O Israel, My *a* way
a Ps.77.7,&c. is hid from the LORD, and my

shalled, or regularly arrayed as an army; that they keep their place, preserve their order, and are *apparently led on* from the east to the west, like a vast army under a mighty leader:

Canst thou *bring forth* Mazzaroth in his season? Or canst thou *guide* Arcturus with his sons?
Job xxxviii. 32.

¶ *By number.* As if he had numbered, or named them; as a military commander would call forth his armies in their proper order, and have them so *numbered* and *enrolled* in the various divisions, that he can command them with ease. ¶ *He calleth them all by names.* This idea is also taken from a military leader, who would know the names of the individuals that composed his army. In smaller divisions of an army, this could of course be done; but the idea is, that God is intimately acquainted with *all* the hosts of stars; that though their numbers appear to us so great, yet he is acquainted with each one individually, and has that knowledge of it which we have of a person or object which we recognize by a *name*. It is said of Cyrus, that he was acquainted by name with every individual that composed his vast army. The practice of giving names to the stars of heaven was early, and is known to have been originated by the Chaldeans. Intimations of this custom we have not unfrequently in the Scriptures, as far back as the time of Job:

Which maketh Arcturus, and Orion, and Pleiades, And the chambers of the south.
Job ix. 9.

Canst thou bind the sweet influences of Pleiades? Or loose the bands of Orion? Canst thou bring forth Mazzaroth in his season? Or canst thou guide Arcturus with his sons?
Job xxxviii. 31, 32.

This power of giving names to all the stars, is beautifully ascribed to God in Ps. cxlvii. 4:

He telleth the number of the stars, He calleth them all by their names.

This view of the greatness of God is more striking now than it was in the times of David or Isaiah. Little then, comparatively, was known of the number of the stars. But since the inven-

tion of the telescope the view of the heavenly world has been enlarged almost to immensity; and though the expression 'he calleth them all by their names,' had great sublimity as used in the time of Isaiah, yet it raises in us far higher conceptions of the power and greatness of God when applied to what *we* know now of the heavens. Yet doubtless our view of the heavens is much further beneath the sublime reality than were the prevalent views in the time of the prophet beneath those which we now have. As an illustration of this we may remark, that the milky way which stretches across the heavens, is now ascertained to receive its white appearance from the mingling together of the light of an innumerable number of stars, too remote to be seen by the naked eye. Dr. Herschell examined a portion of the milky way about fifteen degrees long, and two broad, and found that it contained no fewer than fifty thousand stars, large enough to be distinctly counted, and he suspected that that portion contained twice as many more, which, for the want of sufficient light in his telescope, he saw only now and then. It is to be remembered, also, that the galaxy, or milky way, which we see with the naked eye, is only one of a *large number* of nebulæ of similar construction which are arranged apparently in *strata*, and which extend to great length in the heavens. According to this, and on every correct supposition in regard to the heavens, the number of the stars surpasses all our powers of computation. Yet God is said to lead them all forth as *marshalled armies*— how beautiful a description when applied to the *nebulæ!*—and to call all their names. ¶ *By the greatness of his might.* It is his single and unassisted arm that conducts them; his own hand alone that sustains them. ¶ *Not one faileth.* Not one is wanting; not one of the immense host is out of its place, or unnoticed. All are arranged in infinite wisdom; all observe the proper order, and the proper times. How strikingly true is this, on the slightest inspection of the heavens. How im-

judgment is passed over from my God?

28 Hast thou not known, hast thou not heard, *that* the everlasting

a ch.59.1.

God, the LORD, the Creator of the ends of the earth, fainteth not, neither *a*is weary? *there* *b*is no searching of his understanding.

b Ps.147.5.

pressive and grand is it in the higher developments of the discoveries of astronomy!

27. *Why sayest thou?* This verse is designed to reprove the people for their want of confidence in God. The idea is, ' If God is so great; if he arranges the hosts of heaven with such unerring skill, causing all the stars to observe their proper place and their exact times, the interests of his people are safe in his hands.' Piety may always find security in the assurance that He who preserves the unbroken order of the heavens will not fail to keep and save his people.—The language in this verse is to be understood as addressed to the Jews sighing for deliverance in their long and painful captivity in Babylon. Their city and temple had laid waste for many years; their captivity had been long and wearisome, and doubtless many would be ready to say, that it would never end. To furnish an argument to meet this state of despondency, the prophet sets before them this sublime description of the faithfulness and the power of God. ¶ *O Jacob.* A name often given to the Jews as the descendants of Jacob. ¶ *O Israel.* Denoting the same. The name Israel was given to Jacob because he had power to prevail as a prince with God (Gen. xxxii. 28); and it became the common name by which his descendants were known. ¶ *My way is hid from the* LORD. That is, is not seen, or noticed. The word ' way ' here denotes evidently the state or condition; the manner of life, or the calamities which they experienced. The term is often thus employed to denote the lot, condition, or manner in which one lives or acts (Ps. xxxvii. 5; Isa. x. 24; Jer. xii. 1). The phrase, ' is hid,' means that God is ignorant of it, or that he does not attend to it; and the complaint here is, that God had not regarded them in their calamities, and would not interpose to save them. ¶ *And my judgment.* My cause. The word here refers to their condition among

the people where they were captive, and by whom they were oppressed. They are represented as being deprived of their liberty; and they here complain that God disregarded their cause, and that he did not come forth to deliver them from their oppressions and their trials.

28. *Hast thou not known?* This is the language of the prophet reproving them for complaining of being forsaken, and assuring them that God was faithful to his promises. This argument of the prophet, which continues to the close of the chapter, comprises the main scope of the chapter, which is to induce them to put confidence in God, and to believe that he was able and willing to deliver them. The phrase, ' Hast thou not known?' refers to the fact that the Jewish people had had an abundant opportunity of learning, in their history, and from their fathers, the true character of God, and his entire ability to save them. No people had had so much light on this subject, and now that they were in trial, they ought to recall their former knowledge of his character, and remember his dealings of faithfulness with them and their fathers. It is well for the people of God in times of calamity and trial to recall to their recollection his former dealings with his church. That history will furnish abundant sources of consolation, and abundant assurances that their interests are safe in his hands. ¶ *Hast thou not heard?* From the traditions of the fathers; the instruction which you have received from ancient times. A large part of the knowledge of the Jews was traditionary; and these attributes of God, as a faithful God, had, no doubt, constituted an important part of the knowledge which had thus been communicated to them. ¶ *The everlasting God.* The God who has existed from eternity, unlike the idols of the heathen. If he was from eternity, he would be unchangeable, and his purposes could not fail. ¶ *The Creator of the ends of the earth.* The phrase, ' the

29 He ^agiveth power to the faint; and to *them that have* no might he increaseth strength.

30 Even the youths shall faint and be weary, and the young men shall utterly fall.

31 But they ^b that wait upon the

a 2 Co.12.9.   b Ps.84.7; 92.1,13.

ends of the earth,' means the same as the earth itself. The earth is sometimes spoken of as a vast plain having limits or boundaries (see ver. 22). It is probable that this was the prevailing idea among the ancients (comp. Deut. xxxiii. 17; 1 Sam. ii. 10; Ps. xix. 6; xxii. 27; xlviii. 10; lxv. 5; lxvii. 7; xcviii. 3; Isa. xliii. 6; xlv. 22; lii. 10). The argument here is, that he who has formed the earth could not be exhausted or weary in so small a work as that of protecting his people. ¶ *Fainteth not.* Is not fatigued or exhausted. That God, who has formed and sustained all things, is not exhausted in his powers, but is able still to defend and guard his people. ¶ There is *no searching of his understanding.* The God who made all things must be infinitely wise. There is proof of boundless skill in the works of his hands, and it is impossible for finite mind fully and adequately to search out *all* the proofs of his wisdom and skill. Man can see only a part— a small part, while the vast ocean, the boundless deep of his wisdom, lies still unexplored. This thought is beautifully expressed by Zophar in Job xi. 7–9 :—

Canst thou by searching find out God?
Canst thou find out the Almighty unto perfection?
It is as high as heaven;
  What canst thou do?
Deeper than hell;
  What canst thou know:
The measure thereof is longer than the earth,
And broader than the sea.

The *argument* here is, that that God who has made all things, *must* be intimately acquainted with the wants of his people. They had, therefore, no reason to complain that their way was hidden from the Lord, and their cause passed over by him.—*Perhaps*, also, it is implied, that as his understanding was vast, they ought not to expect to be able to comprehend the reason of all his doings; but should expect that there would be much that was mysterious and unsearchable. The *reasons* of his doings are often hid from his people; and their consolation is to be found in the assur-

ance that he *is* infinitely wise, and that he who rules over the universe *must* know what is best, and CANNOT ERR.

29. *He giveth power to the faint.* To his weak and feeble people. This is one of his attributes ; and his people, therefore, should put their trust in him, and look to him for aid (comp. 2 Cor. xii. 9). The design of this verse is to give consolation to the afflicted and down-trodden people in Babylon, by recalling to their minds the truth that it was one of the characteristics of God that he ministered strength to those who were conscious of their own feebleness, and who looked to him for support. It is a truth, however, as applicable to us as to them—a truth inestimably precious to those who feel that they are weak and feeble, and who look to God for aid.

30. *Even the youths shall faint.* The most vigorous young men, those in whom we expect manly strength, and who are best fitted to endure hardy toil. They become weary by labour. Their powers are soon exhausted. The *design* here is, to contrast the most vigorous of the human race with God, and to show that while all *their* powers fail, the power of God is unexhausted and inexhaustible. ¶ *And the young men.* The word here used denotes properly *those who are chosen* or selected (בחורים, Gr. ἐκλεκτοί), and may be applied to those who were *selected* or chosen for any hazardous enterprise, or dangerous achievement in war ; those who would be selected for vigour or activity. The meaning is, that the most *chosen* or select of the human family—the most vigorous and manly, must be worn down by fatigue, or paralyzed by sickness or death; but that the powers of God never grow weary, and that those who trust in him should never become faint.

31. *But they that wait upon the* LORD. The word rendered 'wait upon' here (from קָוָה), denotes properly *to wait*, in the sense of *expecting*. The phrase, 'to wait on JEHOVAH,' means to wait for his help ; that is, to trust in him, to put

LORD shall ¹renew ᵃ their strength: they shall mount up with wings as eagles ; they shall run ᵇand not be weary, *and* they shall walk ᶜand not faint.

¹ *change*. ᵃ Ps.103.5. ᵇ He.12.1. ᶜ Mi.4.5.

---

our hope or confidence in him. It is applicable to those who are in circumstances of danger or want, and who look to him for his merciful interposition. *Here* it properly refers to those who were suffering a long and grievous captivity in Babylon, and who had no prospect of deliverance but in him. The phrase is applicable also to *all* who feel that they are weak, feeble, guilty, and helpless, and who, in view of this, put their trust in JEHOVAH. The promise or assurance here is general in its nature, and is as applicable to his people now as it was in the times of the captivity in Babylon. Religion is often expressed in the Scriptures by 'waiting on JEHOVAH,' *i.e.*, by looking to him for help, expecting deliverance through his aid, putting trust in him (see Ps. xxv. 3, 5, 21; xxvii. 14; xxxvii. 7, 9, 34; lxix. 3; comp. Note on Isa. viii. 17; xxx. 18). It does not *imply* inactivity, or want of personal exertion; it implies merely that our hope of aid and salvation is in him—a feeling that is *as* consistent with the most strenuous endeavours to secure the object, as it is with a state of inactivity and indolence. Indeed, no man can *wait* on God in a proper manner who does not use the means which he has appointed for conveying to us his blessing. To *wait* on him without using any means to obtain his aid, is to tempt him; to expect miraculous interposition is unauthorized, and must meet with disappointment. And they only wait on him in a proper manner who expect his blessing in the common modes in which he imparts it to men —in the use of those means and efforts which he has appointed, and which he is accustomed to bless. The farmer who should *wait* for God to plough and sow his fields, would not only be disappointed, but would be guilty of provoking Him. And so the man who waits for God to do what *he* ought to do; to save him without using any of the means of grace, will not only be disappointed, but will provoke his displeasure. ¶ *Shall renew their strength.* Marg. 'Change.' The Hebrew word commonly means *to*

change, to alter; and then to revive, to renew, to cause to flourish again, as, *e.g.*, a tree that has decayed and fallen down (see Note on ch. ix. 10; comp. Job xiv. 7). Here it is evidently used in the sense of renewing, or causing to revive; to increase, and to restore that which is decayed. It means that the people of God who trust in him shall become strong in faith; able to contend with their spiritual foes, to gain the victory over their sins, and to discharge aright the duties, and to meet aright the trials of life. God gives them strength, if they seek him in the way of his appointment —a promise which has been verified in the experience of his people in every age. ¶ *They shall mount up with wings as eagles.* Lowth translates this, 'They shall put forth fresh feathers like the moulting eagle ;' and in his note on the passage remarks, that 'it has been a common and popular opinion that the eagle lives and retains his vigour to a great age ; and that, beyond the common lot of other birds, he moults in his old age, and renews his feathers, and with them his youth.' He supposes that the passage in Ps. ciii. 5, 'So that thy youth is renewed like the eagles,' refers to this fact. That this was a common and popular opinion among the ancients, is clearly proved by Bochart (*Hieroz.* ii. 2. 1. pp. 165–169). The opinion was, that at stated times the eagle plunged itself in the sea and cast off its old feathers, and that new feathers started forth, and that thus it lived often to the hundredth year, and then threw itself in the sea and died. In accordance with this opinion, the LXX. render this passage, 'They shall put forth fresh feathers (πτεροφυήσουσιν) like eagles.' Vulg. *Assument pennas sicut aquilæ.* The Chaldee renders it, 'They who trust in the Lord shall be gathered from the captivity, and shall increase their strength, and renew their youth as a germ which grows up ; upon wings of eagles shall they run and not be fatigued.' —But whatever may be the truth in regard to the eagle, there is no reason

CHAPTER XLI.

ANALYSIS.

THE design of this chapter is the same as that of the preceding, and it is to be regarded as the continuation of the argument commenced there. Its object is to lead those who were addressed, to put confidence in God. In the introduction to ch. xl. it was remarked, that this is to be considered as addressed to the exile Jews in Babylon, near the close of their captivity. Their country, city, and temple had been laid waste. The prophet represents himself as bringing consolation to them in this situation; particularly by the assurance that their long captivity was about to end; that they were about to be restored to their own land, and that their trials were to be succeeded by brighter and happier times. In the previous chapter there were general reasons given why they should put their confidence in God—arising from the firmness of his promises, the fact that he had created all things; that he had all power, &c. In this chapter there is a more definite view given, and a clearer light thrown on the mode in which deliverance would be brought to them. The prophet specifies that God would raise up a deliverer, and that that deliverer would be able to subdue all their enemies. The chapter may be conveniently divided into the following parts:—

I. God calls the distant nations to a public investigation of his ability to aid his people; to an *argument* whether he was able to deliver them; and to the statement of the reasons why they should confide in him (1).

II. He specifies that he will raise up a man from the east—who should be able to overcome the enemies of the Jews, and to effect their deliverance (2-4).

III. The consternation of the nations at the approach of Cyrus, and their excited and agitated fleeing to their idols is described (5-7).

IV. God gives to his people the assurance of his protection, and friendship (8-14). This is shown—1. Because they were the children of Abraham, his friend, and he was bound in covenant faithfulness to protect them (8, 9). 2. By direct assurance that he would aid and protect them; that though they were feeble, yet he was strong enough to deliver them (10-14).

V. He says that he will enable them to overcome and scatter their foes, as the chaff is driven away on the mountains by the whirlwind (15, 16).

VI. He gives to his people the special promise of assistance and comfort. He will meet them in their desolate condition, and will give them consolation *as if* fountains were opened in deserts, and trees producing grateful shade and fruit were planted in the wilderness (17-20).

VII. He appeals directly to the enemies of the Jews, to the worshippers of idols. He challenges them to give any evidence of the power or the divinity of their idols; and appeals to the fact that he had foretold future events; that he had raised up a deliverer for his people in proof of *his* divinity, and *his* power to save (21-29).

The *argument* of the whole is, that the idol-gods were unable to defend the nations which trusted in them; that God would raise up a mighty prince who should be able to deliver the Jews from their long and painful calamity, and

---

to believe that Isaiah here had any reference to the fact that it *moults* in its old age. The translation of Lowth was derived from the Septuagint, and not from the Hebrew text. The meaning of the Hebrew is simply, 'they shall ascend on wings as eagles,' or 'they shall lift up the wings as eagles;' and the image is derived from the fact that the eagle rises on the most vigorous wing of any bird, and ascends apparently further towards the sun. The figure, therefore, denotes strength and vigour of purpose; strong and manly piety; an elevation above the world; communion with God, and a nearness to his throne —as the eagle ascends towards the sun. ¶ *They shall run and not be weary.* This passage, also, is but another mode of expressing the same idea—that they

who trust in God would be vigorous, elevated, unwearied; that he would sustain and uphold them; and that in his service they would never faint.—This was at first designed to be applied to the Jews in captivity in Babylon to induce them to put their trust in God. But it is as true now as it was at that time. It has been found in the experience of thousands and tens of thousands, that by waiting on the Lord the heart has been invigorated; the faith has been confirmed; and the affections have been raised above the world. Strength has been given to bear trial without murmuring, to engage in arduous duty without fainting, to pursue the perilous and toilsome journey of life without exhaustion, and to rise above the world in hope and peace on the bed of death.

that they, therefore, should put their trust in JEHOVAH.

KEEP silence *a* before me, O islands; and let the people renew *their* strength: let them come near; then let them speak: let us come near together to judgment.

2 Who raised up [1] the righteous *man* from the east, called *b* him to his foot, gave *c* the nations before him, and made *him* rule over kings? he gave *them* as the dust to his sword, *and* as driven stubble to his bow.

a Zec.2.13.   1 *righteousness.*   *b* ch.46.11.   *c* Ezr.1.2.

CHAPTER XLI.

1. *Keep silence before me* (comp. Zech. ii. 13). The idea is, that the heathen nations were to be silent while God should speak, or with a view of entering into an argument with him respecting the comparative power of himself and of idols to defend their respective worshippers. The argument is stated in the following verses, and preparatory to the statement of that argument, the people are exhorted to be silent. This is probably to evince a proper awe and reverence for JEHOVAH, before whom the argument was to be conducted, and a proper sense of the magnitude and sacredness of the inquiry (comp. ver. 21). And it may be remarked here, that the same reasons will apply to *all* approaches which are made to God. When we are about to come before him in prayer or praise; to confess our sins and to plead for pardon; when we engage an argument respecting his being, plans, or perfections; or when we draw near to him in the closet, the family, or the sanctuary, the mind should be filled with awe and reverence. It is well, it is proper, to pause and think of what our emotions should be, and of what we should say, before God (comp. Gen. xxviii. 16, 17). ¶ *O islands* (אִיִּים). This word properly means *islands,* and is so translated here by the Vulgate, the LXX., the Chaldee, the Syriac, and the Arabic. But the word also is used to denote maritime countries; countries that were situated on sea-coasts, or the regions beyond sea (see Note on ch. xx. 6). The word is applied, therefore, to the islands of the Mediterranean; to the maritime coasts; and then, also, it comes to be used in the sense of *any* lands or coasts far remote, or beyond sea (see Ps. lxx. 10; Isa. xxiv. 15; Notes on ch. xl. 15; xli. 5; xlii. 4, 10, 12;

xlix. 1; Jer. xxv. 22; Dan. xi. 18). Here it is evidently used in the sense of distant nations or lands; the people who were remote from Palestine, and who were the worshippers of idols. The argument is represented as being *with* them, and they are invited to prepare their minds by suitable reverence for God for the argument which was to be presented. ¶ *And let the people renew* their *strength.* On the word 'renew,' see Note on ch. xl. 31. Here it means, 'Let them make themselves strong; let them prepare the argument; let them be ready to urge as strong reasons as possible; let them fit themselves to enter into the controversy about the power and glory of JEHOVAH' (see ver. 21). ¶ *Let us come near together to judgment.* The word 'judgment' here means evidently controversy, argumentation, debate. Thus it is used in Job ix. 32. The language is that which is used of two parties who come together to try a cause, or to engage in debate; and the sense is, that God proposes to enter into an argumentation with the entire heathen world, in regard to his ability to save his people; that is, he proposes to show the *reasons* why they should trust in him, rather than dread those under whose power they then were, and by whom they had been oppressed. Lowth renders it, correctly expressing the sense, 'Let us enter into solemn debate together.'

2. *Who raised up.* This word (הֵעִיר) is usually applied to the act of arousing one from sleep (Cant. ii. 7; iii. 5; viii. 4; Zec. iv. 1); then to awake, arouse, or stir up to any enterprise. Here it means, that God had caused the man here referred to, to arouse for the overthrow of their enemies; it was by his agency that he had been led to form the plans which should result in their de-

liverance. This is the *first* argument which God urges to induce his people to put confidence in him, and to hope for deliverance; and the fact that he had raised up and qualified such a man for the work, he urges as a proof that he would certainly protect and guard his people. ¶ *The righteous* man *from the east.* Heb. פְּדֶק *tzêdhěq*—'Righteousness.' The LXX. render it literally, Δικαιοσύνην—'Righteousness.' The Vulgate renders it, 'The just;' the Syriac as the LXX. The word here evidently means, as in our translation, the just or righteous man. It is common in the Hebrew, as in other languages, to put the abstract for the concrete. In regard to the *person* here referred to, there have been three principal opinions, which it may be proper briefly to notice. 1. The first is, that which refers it to Abraham. This is the interpretation of the Chaldee Paraphrast, who renders it, 'Who has publicly led from the east Abraham, the chosen of the just;' and this interpretation has been adopted by Jarchi, Kimchi, Abarbanel, and by the Jewish writers generally. They say that it means that God had called Abraham from the east; that he conducted him to the land of Canaan, and enabled him to vanquish the people who resided there, and particularly that he vanquished the kings of Sodom and Gomorrah, and delivered Lot from their hands (Gen. xiv.); and that this is designed by God to show them that he who had thus raised up Abraham would raise up *them* also *in* the east. There are, however, objections to this interpretation which seem to be insuperable, a few of which may be referred to. (*a.*) The country from which Abraham came, the land of Chaldea or Mesopotamia, is not commonly in the Scriptures called 'the east,' but the *north* (see Jer. i. 13–15; iv. 6; vi. 1; xxiii. 8; xxv. 9, 26; xxxi. 8; xlvi. 10; l. 3; Dan. xi. 6, 8, 11. This country was situated to the north-east of Palestine, and it is believed is nowhere in the Scriptures called the country of the east. (*b.*) The description which is here given of what was accomplished by him who was raised up from the east, is not one that applies to Abraham. It supposes more important achievements than any that signalized

the father of the faithful. There were no acts in the life of Abraham that can be regarded as subduing the 'nations' before him; as ruling over 'kings;' or as scattering them like the dust or the stubble. Indeed, he appears to have been engaged but in one military adventure—the rescue of Lot—and that was of so slight and unimportant a character as not to form the peculiarity of his public life. Had Abraham been referred to here, it would have been for some other trait than that of a conqueror or military chieftain. (*c.*) We shall see that the description and the connection require us to understand it of another—of Cyrus. 2. A second opinion is, that it refers directly and entirely to the Messiah. Many of the fathers, as Jerome, Cyril, Eusebius, Theodoret, Procopius, held this opinion. But the objections to this are insuperable. (*a.*) It is not true that the Messiah was raised up from the east. He was born in the land of Judea, and always lived in that land. (*b.*) The description here is by no means one that applies to him. It is the description of a warrior and a conqueror; of one who subdued nations, and scattered them before him. (*c.*) The connection and design of the passage does not admit of the interpretation. That design is, to lead the Jews in exile to put confidence in God, and to hope for a speedy rescue. In order to this, the prophet directs them to the fact that a king appeared in the east, and that he scattered the nations; and *from these facts* they were to infer that they would themselves be delivered, and that God would be their protector. But how would this design be accomplished by a reference to so remote an event as the coming of the Messiah? 3. The third opinion, therefore, remains, that this refers to Cyrus, the Persian monarch, by whom Babylon was taken, and by whom the Jews were restored to their own land. In support of this interpretation, a few considerations may be adverted to. (*a.*) It agrees with the fact in regard to the country from which Cyrus came for purposes of conquest. He came from the land which is everywhere in the Scriptures called the East. (*b.*) It agrees with the specifications which Isaiah elsewhere makes, where Cyrus is mentioned by name, and where there can be no danger of error in regard to the interpretation (see ch. xliv. 28; xlv. 1–4, 13). Thus in ch. xlvi. 11, it is said of Cyrus, ' Calling a ravenous bird *from the east*, the man that executeth my commandments from a far country. (*c.*) The entire description here is one that applies in a remarkable manner to Cyrus, as will be shown more fully in the Notes on the particular expressions which occur. (*d.*) This supposition accords with the design of the prophet. It was to be an assurance to them not only that God *would* raise up such a man, but that they should be delivered; and as this was intended to comfort them in Babylon, it was intended that *when* they were apprised of the conquests of Cyrus, they were to be *assured* of the fact that God was their protector; and those conquests, therefore, were to be regarded by them as a proof that God would deliver them. This opinion is held by Vitringa, Rosenmüller, and probably by a large majority of the most intelligent commentators. The only objection of weight to it is that suggested by Lowth, that the character of ' a righteous man ' does not apply to Cyrus. But to this it may be replied, that the word may be used not to denote one that is *pious*, or a true worshipper of God, but one who was disposed to do justly, or who was not a tyrant; and especially it may be applied to him on account of his delivering the Jews from their hard and oppressive bondage in Babylon, and restoring them to their own land. That was an act of eminent public justice; and the favours which he showed them in enabling them to rebuild their city and temple, were such as to render it not improper that this appellation should be given to him. It may be added also that Cyrus was a prince eminently distinguished for justice and equity, and for a mild and kind administration over his own subjects. Xenophon, who has described his character at length, has proposed him as an example of a just monarch, and his government as an example of an equitable administration. All the ancient writers celebrate his humanity and benevolence (comp. Diod.

xiii. 342, and the *Cyropedia* of Xenophon everywhere). As there will be frequent occasion to refer to Cyrus in the Notes on the chapters which follow, it may be proper here to give a very brief outline of his public actions, that his agency in the deliverance of the Jews may be more fully appreciated. Cyrus was the son of Cambyses, the Persian, and of Mandane, the daughter of Astyages, king of the Medes. Astyages is in Scripture called Ahasuerus. Cambyses was, according to Xenophon (*Cyr.* i.), king of Persia, or, according to Herodotus (i. 107), he was a nobleman. If he was the king of Persia, of course Cyrus was the heir of the throne. Cyrus was born in his father's court, A.M. 3405, or B.C. 595, and was educated with great care. At the age of twelve years, his grandfather, Astyages, sent for him and his mother Mandane to court, and he was treated, of course, with great attention. Astyages, or Ahasuerus, had a son by the name of Cyaxares, who was born about a year before Cyrus, and who was heir to the throne of Media. Some time after this, the son of the king of Assyria having invaded Media, Astyages, with his son Cyaxares, and his grandson Cyrus, marched against him. Cyrus defeated the Assyrians, but was soon after recalled by his father Cambyses to Persia, that he might be near him. At the age of sixteen, indeed, and when at the court of his grandfather, Cyrus signalized himself for his valour in a war with the king of Babylon. Evil-Merodach, the son of Nebuchadnezzar, king of Babylon, had invaded the territories of Media, but was repelled with great loss, and Cyrus pursued him with great slaughter to his own borders. This invasion of Evil-Merodach laid the foundation of the hostility between Babylon and Media, which was not terminated until Babylon was taken and destroyed by the united armies of Media and Persia. When Astyages died, after a reign of thirty-five years, he was succeeded by his son Cyaxares, the uncle of Cyrus. He was still involved in a war with the Babylonians. Cyrus was made general of the Persian troops, and at the head of an army of 30,000 men was sent to assist Cyaxares, whom the Babylonians were preparing to attack. The Babylonian monarch at this time was Neriglissar, who had murdered Evil-Merodach, and who had usurped the crown of Babylon. Cyaxares and Cyrus carried on the war against Babylon during the reigns of Neriglissar and his son Laborosoarchod, and of Nabonadius. The Babylonians were defeated, and Cyrus carried his arms into the countries to the west beyond the river Halys—a river running north into the Euxine Sea—and subdued Cappadocia, and conquered Crœsus, the rich king of Lydia, and subdued almost all Asia Minor. Having conquered this country, he returned again, re-crossed the Euphrates, turned his arms against the Assyrians, and then laid siege to Babylon, and took it (see Notes on ch. xiii., xiv.), and subdued that mighty kingdom. During the life of Cyaxares his uncle, he acted in conjunction with him. On the death of this king of Media, Cyrus married his daughter, and thus united the crowns of Media and Persia. After this marriage, he subdued all the nations between Syria and the Red Sea, and died at the age of seventy, after a reign of thirty years. Cyaxares, the uncle of Cyrus, is in the Scripture called Darius the Mede (Dan. v. 31), and it is said there, that it was by him that Babylon was taken. But Babylon was taken by the valour of Cyrus, though acting in connection with, and under Cyaxares; and it is said to have been taken by Cyaxares, or Darius, though it was done by the personal valour of Cyrus. Josephus (*Ant.* xii. 13) says, that Darius with his ally, Cyrus, destroyed the kingdom of Babylon. Jerome assigns three reasons why Babylon is said in the Scriptures to have been taken by Darius or Cyaxares; first, because he was the elder of the two; secondly, because the Medes were at that time more famous than the Persians; and thirdly, because the uncle ought to be preferred to the nephew. The Greek writers say that Babylon was taken by Cyrus, without mentioning Cyaxares or Darius, doubtless because it was done solely by his valour. For a full account of the reign of Cyrus, see Xen. *Cyr.*, Herodotus, and the ancient part of the *Universal*

History, vol. iv. Ed. Lond. 1779, 8vo. ¶ *Called him to his foot.* Lowth renders this, 'Hath called him to attend his steps.' Noyes renders it, 'Him whom victory meeteth in his march.' Grotius, 'Called him that he should follow him,' and he refers to Gen. xii. 1; Josh. xxiv. 3; Heb. xi. 8. Rosenmüller renders it, 'Who hath called from the East that man to whom righteousness occurs at his feet,' *i.e.*, attends him. But the idea seems to be, that God had influenced him to follow him as one follows a guide at his feet, or close to him. ¶ *Gave the nations before him.* That is, subdued nations before him. This is justly descriptive of the victorious career of Cyrus. Among the nations whom he subdued, were the Armenians, the Cappadocians, the Lydians, the Phrygians, the Assyrians, the Babylonians, comprising a very large portion of the world, known at that time. Cyrus subdued, according to Xenophon, all the nations lying between the Euxine and Caspian seas on the north, to the Red Sea on the south, and even Egypt, so that his own proclamation was true: 'JEHOVAH, God of heaven, hath given me all the kingdoms of the earth' (Ezra i. 2). ¶ *And made him rule over kings.* As the kings of Babylon, of Lydia, of Cappadocia, who were brought into subjection under him, and acknowledged their dependence on him. ¶ *He hath given them as the dust to his sword.* He has scattered, or destroyed them by his sword, as the dust is driven before the wind. A similar remark is made by David (Ps. xcviii. 42)—

Then did I beat them small as the dust before the wind,
I did cast them out as the dirt in the streets.

¶ *And as driven stubble.* The allusion here is to the process of fanning grain. The grain was thrown by a shovel or fan in the air, and the stubble or chaff was driven away. So it is said of the nations before Cyrus, implying that they were utterly scattered. ¶ *To his bow.* The bow was one of the common weapons of war, and the inhabitants of the East were distinguished for its use. The idea in this verse is very beautiful, and is one that is often employed in the Sacred Scriptures, and by Isaiah himself (see Job xxi. 18; Ps. i. 4; xxxv. 5;

3 He pursued them, *and* passed safely:[1] *even* by the way *that* he had not gone with his feet.

4 Who hath wrought and done *it*, calling the generations from the

[1] *in peace.*

beginning? I the LORD, the [a]first, and with the last; I *am* he.

5 The isles saw *it*, and feared; the ends of the earth were afraid, drew near, and came.

a Re.1.17; 22.13.

Notes on ch. xvii. 13; xxix. 5; comp. Hos. xiii. 3).

3. *He pursued them.* When they were driven away. He followed on, and devoted them to discomfiture and ruin. ¶ And *passed safely.* Marg. as Heb. 'In peace.' That is, he followed them uninjured; they had no power to rally, he was not led into ambush, and he was safe as far as he chose to pursue them. ¶ Even *by the way* that *he had not gone with his feet.* By a way that he had not been accustomed to march; in an unusual journey; in a land of strangers. Cyrus had passed his early years on the east of the Euphrates. In his conquests he crossed that river, and extended his march beyond even the river Halys to the western extremity of Asia, and even to Egypt and the Red Sea. The idea here is, that he had not travelled in these regions until he did it for purposes of conquest—an idea which is strictly in accordance with the truth of history.

4. *Who hath wrought and done* it? By whom has all this been accomplished? Has it been by the arm of Cyrus? Has it been by human skill and power? The design of this question is obvious. It is to direct attention to the fact that all this had been done by God, and that he who had raised up such a man, and had accomplished all this by means of him, had power to deliver his people. ¶ *Calling the generations from the beginning.* The idea here seems to be, that all the nations that dwell on the earth in every place owed their origin to God (comp. Acts xvii. 26). The word 'calling' here, seems to be used in the sense of commanding, directing, or ordering them; and the truth taught is, that all the nations were under his control, and had been from the beginning. It was not only true of Cyrus, and of those who were subdued before him, but it was true of all nations and generations. The object seems to be, to lift up the

thoughts from the conquests of Cyrus to God's universal dominion over all kingdoms from the beginning of the world. ¶ *I the* LORD, *the first.* Before any creature was made; existing before any other being. The description that God here gives of himself as 'the first and the last,' is one that is often applied to him in the Scriptures, and is one that properly expresses eternity (see ch. xliv. 6; xlviii. 12). It is remarkable also that this expression, which so obviously implies proper eternity, is applied to the Lord Jesus in Rev. i. 17, and xxii. 13. ¶ *And with the last.* The usual form in which this is expressed is simply 'the last' (ch. xliv. 6; xlviii. 12). The idea here seems to be, 'and with the last, I am the same;' *i.e.*, I am unchanging and eternal. None will subsist *after* me; since *with* the last of all created objects I shall be the same that I was in the beginning. Nothing would survive God; or in other words, he would exist for ever and ever. The argument here is, that to this unchanging and eternal God, who had thus raised up and directed Cyrus, and who had control over *all* nations, they might commit themselves with unwavering confidence, and be assured that he was able to protect and deliver them.

5. *The isles saw* it. The distant nations (see Note on ver. 1). They saw what was done in the conquests of the man whom God in this remarkable manner had raised up; and they had had demonstration, therefore, of the mighty power of JEHOVAH above the power of idols. ¶ *And feared.* Were alarmed, and trembled. All were apprehensive that *they* would be subdued, and driven away as with the tempest. ¶ *The ends of the earth.* Distant nations occupying the extremities of the globe (see Note on ch. xl. 28). ¶ *Drew near, and came.* Came together for the purpose of mutual alliance, and self-defence. The prophet evidently

6 They helped every one his neighbour; and *every one* said to his brother, Be [1] of good courage.

7 So *a* the carpenter encouraged the [2] goldsmith, *and* he that smooth-

1 *strong.*   *a* ch.40.19.   2 or, *the founder.*

eth *with* the hammer [3] him that smote the anvil, [4] saying, It *is* ready for the sodering : and he fastened it with nails, *that* it should not be moved.

3 or, *the smiting.*   4 or, *saying of the soder, It* is *good.*

refers to what he says in the following verses, that they formed treaties ; endeavoured to prepare for self-defence ; looked to their idol-gods, and encouraged each other in their attempts to offer a successful resistance to the victorious arms of Cyrus.

6. *They helped every one his neighbour.* The idolatrous nations. The idea is, that they formed confederations to strengthen each other, and to oppose him whom God had raised up to subdue them. The prophet describes a state of general consternation existing among them, when they supposed that all was in danger, and that their security consisted only in confederation ; in increased attention to their religion ; in repairing their idols and making new ones, and in conciliating the favour and securing the aid of their gods. It was natural for them to suppose that the calamities which were coming upon them by the invasion of Cyrus were the judgments of their gods, for some neglect, or some prevailing crimes, and that their favour could be secured only by a more diligent attention to their service, and by forming new images and establishing them *in* the proper places of worship. The prophet, therefore, describes in a graphic manner, the consternation, the alarm, and the haste, everywhere apparent among them, in attempting to conciliate the favour of their idols, and to encourage each other. Nothing is more common, than for men, when they are in danger, to give great attention to religion, though they may greatly neglect or despise it when they are in safety. Men fly *to* temples and churches and altars in the times of plague and the pestilence ; and as regularly flee *frcm* them when the calamity is overpast. ¶ *Be of good courage.* Marg. as Heb. 'Be strong.' The sense is, Do not be alarmed at the invasion of Cyrus. Make new images, set them up in the temples, show unusual zeal in religion, and the favour of the gods

may be secured, and the dangers be averted. This is to be understood as the language of the idolatrous nations, among whom Cyrus, under the direction of JEHOVAH, was carrying his conquests and spreading desolation.

7. *So the carpenter* (see Note on ch. xl. 19). ¶ *Encouraged the goldsmith.* Marg. ' The founder' (see Note on ch. xl. 19). The word properly means *one who melts or smelts metals of any kind ;* and may be applied either to one who works in gold, silver, or brass. The image here is that of haste, anxiety, solicitude. One workman in the manufacture of idols encouraged another, in order that the idols might be finished as soon as possible, and that thus the favour of the gods might be propitiated, and the impending danger averted. ¶ *He that smootheth* with *the hammer.* That is, he encourages or strengthens him that smites on the anvil. The idol was commonly *cast* or founded, and of course was in a rough state. This required to be *smoothed,* or polished, and this was in part done doubtless by a small hammer. ¶ *Him that smote the anvil.* The workman whose office it was to work on the anvil—forming parts of the idol, or perhaps chain. ¶ *It* is *ready for the sodering.* The parts are ready to be welded, or soldered together. All this is descriptive of haste and anxiety to have the work done ; and the object of the prophet is evidently to ridicule their vain solicitude to defend themselves against the plans and purposes of God by efforts of this kind. ¶ *And he fastened it with nails.* He fixed it to its place in the temple, or in the dwelling ; and thus showed a purpose that the worship of the idol should be permanent, and fixed. Hooks, or nails, were necessary to keep it in its place, and secure it from falling down. When the idol was thus fixed, they supposed that their kingdoms were safe. They judged that the gods would interpose to protect and defend them from

8 But thou, Israel, *art* my servant, Jacob whom I have ^a chosen, the seed of Abraham my ^b friend.

9 *Thou* whom I have taken from the ends of the earth, and called thee from the chief men thereof, and said unto thee, Thou *art* my servant, I have chosen thee, and not cast thee away.

a Ps.135.4.   b 2 Ch.20.7; Ja.2.23.

their foes.—This is a beautiful description of the anxiety, and pains, and consternation of sinners when calamity is coming upon them, and of the nature of their reliances. What could these dumb idols—these masses of brass, or silver, or stone, do to protect them? And in like manner what can all the refuges of sinners do when God comes to judge them, and when the calamities connected with death and the judgment shall overtake them? They are just as full of consternation as were the heathen who are here described; and all their refuges will be just as little to be relied on as were the senseless images which the heathen had made for their defence.

8. *But thou, Israel, art my servant.* This is an address directly to the Jews, and is designed to shew them, in view of the truths which had just been urged, that God was their protector and friend. Those who relied on idols were trusting to that which could not aid them. But those who trusted in him were safe. For their protection he had raised up Cyrus, for this purpose he had subdued the nations before him. God now expresses to them the assurance that though the nations should be destroyed, yet that he had chosen *them*, and would remember them, and his promise made to Abraham, their illustrious ancestor. The word 'servant' here is used in a mild and gentle sense, not to denote bondage or slavery, but to denote that they had been engaged in his *service*, and that he regarded them as subject to his laws, and as under his protection. ¶ *Jacob whom I have chosen.* The descendants of Jacob, whom I have selected to be my people. *Abraham my friend.* Heb. 'Loving me,' my lover. Abraham was regarded as the friend of God (see 2 Chron. xx. 7). 'And he was called the Friend of God' (James ii. 23). This most honourable appellation he deserved by a life of devoted piety, and by habitually submitting himself to the will of God. The idea in this verse is, that as they were the descendants of *his friend*, God deemed himself bound to protect and deliver them according to his gracious promises; and this is one of the many instances where the Divine favour is manifested to descendants in consequence of the piety and prayers of their ancestors.

9. Thou *whom I have taken from the ends of the earth.* From Chaldea —regarded by the Jews as the remote part of the earth. Thus in ch. xiii. 5, it is said of the Medes that they came 'from a far country, from the end of heaven' (see Note on that place). Abraham was called from Ur of the Chaldees —a city still remaining on the east of the river Euphrates. It is probably the same place as the Persian fortress *Ur*, between Nesibis and the Tigris. It was visited by Mr. Wolfe, Mr. Buckingham, and by others. ¶ *And called thee from the chief men thereof.* Or rather, from the *extremities* of the earth. The word אֲצִיל means properly *a side;* and when applied to the earth, means the sides ends, or extremities of it. In Ex. xxiv. 11, it is rendered 'nobles,' from an Arabic word signifying to be deep-rooted, and hence those who are sprung from an ancient stock (Gesenius). In this place it is evidently used in the same sense as the word (אֵצֶל) meaning *side*, in the sense of *extremity*, or *end*. The parallelism requires us to give this interpretation to the word. So Jerome renders it, *à longinquis ejus* (sc. *terræ*). The LXX. render it, 'Εκ τῶν σκωπιῶν —'From the speculations of the earth' (Thompson), or rather perhaps meaning from the extremity of *vision;* from the countries lying in the distant horizon; or from the elevated places which offered an extensive range of vision. The Chaldee renders it, 'From the kingdoms I have selected thee.' Symmachus renders it, 'Απὸ τῶν ἀγκώνων αὐτῆς—from its angles, its corners, its extremities. Some have supposed that this refers to the deliverance from Egypt,

10 Fear *a* thou not; for I *am* with thee;*b* be not dismayed, for I *am* thy God: I will *c* strengthen thee; yea, I will help thee: yea, I will uphold thee with the right hand of my righteousness.

11 Behold, all they that were incensed against thee shall be ashamed*d* and confounded: they shall be as nothing; and they 1 that strive with thee shall perish.

12 Thou shalt seek them, and

a ver. 13,14; ch.43 5.   b De.31.6,8.   c ch.40.29.

shalt not find them, *even* 2 them that contended with thee; 3 they that war against thee shall be as nothing, and as a thing of nought.

13 For I the LORD thy God will hold thy *e* right hand, saying unto thee, Fear not; I will help thee.

14 Fear not, thou worm Jacob, *and* ye 4 men of Israel; I will help thee, saith the LORD, and thy Redeemer, the Holy One of Israel.

d ch.45.24; Ze.12.3.   1 the men of thy strife.
2 the men of thy contention.   3 the men of thy war.
e De.33.26,29.   4 or, few men.

but the more probable interpretation is that which refers it to the call of Abraham from Chaldea; and the idea is, that as God had called him from that distant land, and had made him his friend, he would preserve and guard his posterity. *Perhaps* it may be implied that he would be favourable to them in that same country from whence he had called their illustrious progenitor, and would in like manner conduct them to the land of promise, *i.e.*, to their own land.

10. *Fear thou not.* This verse is plain in its meaning, and is full of consolation. It is to be regarded as addressed primarily to the exiled Jews during their long and painful captivity in Babylon; and the idea is, that they who had been selected by God to be his peculiar people had nothing to fear. But the promise is one that may be regarded as addressed to all his people in similar circumstances, and it is as true now as it was then, that those whom God has chosen have nothing to fear. ¶ *For I* am *with thee.* This is a reason why they should not be afraid. God was their protector, and of whom should they be afraid. 'If God be for us, who can be against us?' What higher consolation can man desire than the assurance that he is with him to protect him? ¶ *Be not dismayed.* The word here rendered 'dismayed' (תֵּחַת) is derived from עָשָׁה, *to see, to look;* and then to look about as one does in a state of alarm, or danger. The sense here is, that they should be calm, and under no apprehension from their foes. ¶ *For I* am *thy God.* I am able to preserve and strengthen thee. The God of heaven was their God; and as he had all

power, and that power was pledged for their protection, they had nothing to fear. ¶ *I will uphold thee.* I will enable you to bear all your trials. ¶ *With the right hand of my righteousness.* With my faithful right hand. The phrase is a Hebrew mode of expression, meaning that God's hand was faithful, that it might be relied on, and would secure them.

11. *All they that were incensed against thee.* They who were enraged against thee, *i.e.*, the Chaldeans who made war upon you, and reduced you to bondage. ¶ *Shall be ashamed and confounded.* To be ashamed and confounded is often used as synonymous with being overcome and destroyed. ¶ *They that strive with thee.* Marg. as Heb. 'The men of thy strife.' The expression refers to their enemies, the Babylonians.

12. *Thou shalt seek them.* This denotes that it would be impossible to find them, for they should cease to exist. The whole verse, with the verse following, is emphatic, repeating in varied terms what was said before, and meaning that their foes should be entirely destroyed.

14. *Fear not* (see Note on ver. 10). ¶ *Thou worm.* This word is properly applied as it is with us, to denote a worm, such as is generated in putrid substances (Ex. xvi. 20; Isa. xiv. 11; lxvi. 24); or such as destroy plants (Jonah iv. 7; Deut. xxviii. 39). It is used also to describe a person that is poor, afflicted, and an object of insignificance (Job xxv. 5, 6)—

Behold even to the moon, and it shineth not;
Yea, the stars are not pure in his sight.

15 Behold, I will make thee a new sharp threshing instrument having ¹teeth : thou shalt thresh the *ᵃ* mountains, and beat *them* small, and shalt make the hills as chaff.

¹ *mouths.*

a Mi.4.13.

How much less man, that is a worm;
And the son of man which is a worm?

And in Ps. xxii. 6—

But I am a worm, and no man ;
A reproach of men, and despised of the people.

In the passage before us, it is applied to the Jews in Babylon as poor and afflicted, and as objects of contempt in view of their enemies. It implies that in themselves they were unable to defend or deliver themselves, and in this state of helplessness, God offers to aid them, and assures them that they have nothing to fear. ¶ And *ye men of Israel* (מְתֵי יִשְׂרָאֵל *methē Israēl*.) Marg. 'Few men.' There has been a great variety in the explanation of this phrase. Aquila renders it, Τεθνεῶτες, and Theodotion, Νεκροὶ, 'dead.' So the Vulgate, *Qui mortui estis ex Israel*. The LXX. render it, 'Fear not, Jacob, O diminutive Israel' (ὀλιγοστὸς 'Ἰσραήλ). Chaldee, 'Fear not, O tribe of the house of Jacob, ye seed of Israel.' Lowth renders it, 'Ye mortals of Israel.' The Hebrew denotes properly, as in our translation, 'men of Israel;' but there is evidently included the idea of fewness or feebleness. The parallelism requires us so to understand it; and the word men, or *mortal* men, may well express the idea of feebleness. ¶ *And thy Redeemer*. On the meaning of this word, see Notes on ch. xxxv. 9 ; xliii. 1, 3. It is applied here to the rescue from the captivity of Babylon, and is used in the general sense of deliverer. God would deliver, or rescue them as he had done in times past. He had done it so often, that this might be regarded as his *appropriate appellation*, that he was THE REDEEMER of his people. ¶ *The Holy One of Israel*. The Holy Being whom the Israelites adored, and who was *their* protector, and their friend (see Note on ch. ii. 4). This appellation is often given to God (see ch. v. 19, 24 ; x. 20 ; xii. 6 ; xvii. 7 ; xxix. 19 ; xxx. 11, 12). We may remark in view of these verses—1. That the people of God are in themselves feeble and defenceless. They have no strength on which they can rely. They are often so encompassed with difficulties which they feel they have no strength to overcome, that they are disposed to apply to themselves the appellation of ' worm,' and by others they are looked on as objects of contempt, and are despised. 2. They have nothing to fear. Though they are feeble, their God and Redeemer is strong. He is *their* Redeemer, and *their* friend, and they may put their trust in him. Their enemies cannot ultimately triumph over them, but they will be scattered and become as nothing. 3. In times of trial, want, and persecution, the friends of God should put their trust alone in him. It is often the plan of God so to afflict and humble his people, that they shall feel their utter helplessness and dependence, and be led to him as the only source of strength.

15. *Behold, I will make thee*, &c. The object of the illustration in this verse and the following is, to show that God would clothe them with power, and that all difficulties in their way would vanish. To express this idea, the prophet uses an image derived from the mode of threshing in the East, where the heavy wain or sledge was made to pass over a large pile of sheaves, and to bruise out the grain, and separate the chaff, so that the wind would drive it away. The phrase, ' I will make thee,' means, ' I will constitute, or appoint thee,' *i.e.*, thou shalt be such a threshing instrument. It is not that God would make such a sledge or wain *for* them, but that they should *be* such themselves ; they should beat down and remove the obstacles in the way as the threshing wain crushed the pile of grain. ¶ *A new sharp threshing instrument*. A threshing wain, or a corn-drag. For a description of this, comp. Notes on ch. xxviii. 27, 28. ¶ *Having teeth*. Or, with double edges. The Hebrew word is applied to a sword, and means a two-edged sword (Ps. cxlix. 6). The instrument here referred to was serrated, or so made as to cut up the straw and separate the grain from the chaff. The

following descriptions from Lowth and Niebuhr, may serve still further to illustrate the nature of the instrument here referred to. 'The drag consisted of a sort of frame of strong planks made rough at the bottom with hard stones or iron; it was drawn by horses or oxen over the corn-sheaves spread on the floor, the driver sitting upon it. The wain was much like the drag, but had wheels of iron teeth, or edges like a saw. The axle was armed with iron teeth or serrated wheels throughout: it moved upon three rollers armed with iron teeth or wheels, to cut the straw. In Syria, they make use of the drag, constructed in the very same manner as above described. This not only forced out the

THRESHING WITH THE DRAG.—From Description de l' Egypte.

grain, but cut the straw in pieces, for fodder for the cattle, for in the eastern countries they have no hay. The last method is well known from the law of Moses, which forbids the ox to be muzzled, when he treadeth out the corn (Deut. xxv. 4).'—(Lowth.) 'In threshing their corn, the Arabians lay the sheaves down in a certain order, and then lead over them two oxen, dragging a large stone. This mode of separating the ears from the straw is not unlike that of Egypt. They use oxen, as the ancients did, to beat out their corn, by trampling upon the sheaves, and dragging after them a clumsy machine. This machine is not, as in Arabia, a stone cylinder, nor a plank with sharp stones, as in Syria, but a sort of sledge, consisting of three rollers, fitted with irons, which turn upon axles. A farmer chooses out a level spot in his fields, and has his corn carried thither in sheaves, upon asses or dromedaries. Two oxen are then yoked in a sledge, a driver gets upon it, and drives them backwards and forwards upon the sheaves, and fresh oxen succeed in the yoke from time to time. By this operation, the chaff is very much cut down; the whole is then winnowed, and the pure grain thus separated. This mode of threshing out the corn is tedious and inconvenient; it destroys the chaff, and injures the quality of grain.'—(Niebuhr.) In another place Niebuhr tells us that two parcels or layers of corn are threshed out in a day; and they move each of them as many as eight times, with a wooden fork of five prongs, which they call meddre. Afterwards, they throw the straw into the middle of the ring, where it forms a heap, which grows bigger and bigger; when the first layer is threshed, they replace the straw in the ring, and thresh it as before. Thus, the straw becomes every time smaller, till at last it resembles chopped straw. After this, with the fork just described, they cast the whole some yards from thence, and against the wind, which, driving back the straw, the corn and the ears not threshed out fall apart from it and make another heap. A man collects the clods of dirt, and

16 Thou shalt fan *a* them, and the wind shall carry them away, and the whirlwind shall scatter them: and thou shalt rejoice in *b* the LORD, *and* shalt glory *c* in the Holy One of Israel.

a Mat.3.12.   *b* Ro.5.11.

---

other impurities, to which any corn adheres, and throws them into a sieve. They afterwards place in a ring the heaps, in which a good many entire ears are still found, and drive over them, for four or five hours together, a dozen couples of oxen, joined two and two, till, by absolute trampling, they have separated the grains, which they throw into the air with a shovel to cleanse them. ¶ *Thou shalt thresh the mountains.* The words 'mountains' and 'hills' in this verse seem designed to denote the kingdoms greater and smaller that should be opposed to the Jews, and that should become subject to them (Rosenmüller). Grotius supposes that the prophet refers particularly to the Medes and Babylonians. But perhaps the words are used to denote simply difficulties or obstacles in their way, and the expression may mean that they would be able to overcome all those obstacles, and to subdue all that opposed them, *as if* in a march they should crush all the mountains, and dissipate all the hills by an exertion of power.

16. *Thou shalt fan them.* Keeping up the figure commenced in the previous verse. To fan here means to winnow, an operation which was performed by throwing the threshed grain up with a shovel into the air, so that the wind drove the chaff away. So all their enemies, and all the obstacles which were in their way should be scattered. ¶ *And the whirlwind shall scatter them.* The ancients believed that men might be swept away by a storm or whirlwind. See Job xxvii.—

The east wind carrieth him away and he departeth;
And as a storm hurleth him out of his place.

Comp. Homer, *Odys.* xx. 63, *sq.*, thus rendered by Pope:

Snatch me, ye whirlwinds! far from human race,
Tost through the void illimitable space;
Or if dismounted from the rapid cloud,
Me with his whelming wave let ocean shroud!

17 *When* the poor and needy seek water, and *there is* none, *and* their tongue faileth for thirst, I the LORD will hear them, *I* the God of Israel will not forsake them.

18 I will open rivers *d* in high

c ch.45.23.   *d* Ps.105.41.

See Notes on Job xxx. 22. ¶ *And thou shalt rejoice in the* LORD. In view of the aid which he has vouchsafed, and the deliverance which he has wrought for you. ¶ *Shalt glory.* Shalt boast, or shalt exult. You will regard God as the author of your deliverance, and joy in the proofs of his interposition, and of his gracious protection and care.

17. When *the poor and needy seek water.* Water is often used in the Scriptures as an emblem of the provisions of Divine mercy. Bursting fountains in a desert, and flowing streams unexpectedly met with in a dry and thirsty land, are often also employed to denote the comfort and refreshment which the gospel furnishes to sinful and suffering man in his journey through this world. The 'poor and needy' here, doubtless refer primarily to the afflicted captives in Babylon. But the expression of the prophet is general, and the description is as applicable to his people at all times in similar circumstances as it was to them. The image here is derived from their anticipated return from Babylon to Judea. The journey lay through a vast pathless desert (see Notes on ch. xl. 3). In that journey when they were weary, faint and thirsty, God would meet and refresh them as if he should open fountains in their way, and plant trees with far-reaching boughs and thick foliage along the road to produce a grateful shade, and make the whole journey through a pleasant grove. As he met their fathers in their journey from Egypt to the land of Canaan, and had brought water from the flinty rock in the desert (Ex. xv. 22, *sq.*), so in their journey through the sands of Arabia Deserta, he would again meet them, and provide for all their want.

18. *I will open rivers.* That is, I will cause rivers to flow (see Note on ch. xxxv. 7). The allusion here is doubtless to the miraculous supply of water in the

places, and fountains in the midst of the valleys; I will make the wilderness *a* a pool of water, and the dry land springs of water.

19 I *b* will plant in the wilderness

the cedar, the shittah-tree, and the myrtle, and the oil-tree; I will set in the desert the fir-tree, *and* the pine, and the box-tree together;

a Ps.107.35.   *b* ch.55.13.

desert when the Israelites had come out of Egypt. God then supplied their wants; and in a similar manner he would always meet his people, and would supply their wants *as if* rivers of pure water were made to flow from dry and barren hills. ¶ *In high places.* The word here used denotes properly barrenness or nakedness (Job xxxiii. 21); and then a hill that is bare, or destitute of trees. It is applied usually to hills in a desert (Jer. iii. 2, 21; iv. 71; vii. 29; xiv. 6). Such hills, without trees, and in a dry and lonely desert, were of course usually without water. The idea is, that God would refresh them *as if* rivers were made to flow from such hills; and it may not improperly be regarded as a promise that God would meet and bless his people in situations, and from sources where they least expected refreshment and comfort. ¶ *And fountains in the midst of the valleys* (see Note on ch. xxx. 25; xxxv. 6). ¶ *I will make the wilderness* (see Note on ch. xxxv. 7).

19. *I will plant in the wilderness.* The image in this verse is one that is frequent in Isaiah. It is designed to show that God would furnish for his people abundant consolations, and that he would furnish unanticipated sources of comfort, and would remove from them their anticipated trials and calamities. The image refers to the return of the exiles to their own land. That journey lay through Arabia Deserta—a vast desert —where they would naturally expect to meet with nothing but barren hills, naked rocks, parched plains, and burning sands. God says that he would bless them in the same manner *as if* in that desolate wilderness he should plant the cedar, the acacia, the myrtle, and the fir-tree, and should make the whole distance a grove, where fountains would bubble along their way, and streams burst forth from the hills (comp. Notes on ch. xxxii. 15). ¶ *The cedar.* The large and beautiful cedar, with lofty height, and extended branches, such as

grew on Lebanon (comp. Note on ch. ix. 10; xxxvii. 24). ¶ *The shittah-tree.* This is the Hebrew name without change, שִׁטָּה (*shittâh*). The Vulgate is *spinam*. The LXX. render it, Πύξον — 'The box.' Lowth renders it, 'The acacia.' Probably the *acacia*, or the *spina Ægyptiaca*—the Egyptian thorn of the ancients—is intended by it. It is a large tree, growing abundantly in Egypt and Arabia, and is the tree from which the gum-arabic is obtained. It is covered

ACACIA TREE (*Acacia vera*).

with large black thorns, and the wood is hard, and, when old, resembles ebony.

MYRTLE (*Myrtus communis*).

¶ *And the myrtle.* The myrtle is a tree which rises with a shrubby upright stem,

20 That they may see and know, and consider, and understand together, that the hand of the Lord

hath done this, and the Holy One of Israel hath created it.

21 Produce ¹your cause, saith

1 *cause to come near.*

eight or ten feet high. Its branches form a dense, full head, closely garnished with oval lanceolate leaves. It has numerous small pale flowers from the axillas, singly on each footstalk (*Encyc.*) There are several species of the myrtle, and they are especially distinguished for their forming a dense and close top, and thus constituting a valuable tree for shade. It is a tree that grows with great rapidity. ¶ *And the oil-tree.* Heb. 'Tree of oil;' *i.e.,* producing oil. Doubtless the *olive* is intended here, from whose fruit *oil* was obtained in abundance. This was a common tree in Palestine, and was one

OLIVE (*Olea Europea*).

of the most valued that grew. ¶ *The fir-tree.* The word here used (בְּרוֹשׁ *berōsh*) is commonly rendered, in our version, 'fir-tree' (Isa. lx. 13; lv. 13; Zech. xi. 2; Hos. xiv. 8, 9; 2 Sam. vi. 5; 1 Kings v. 8, 10; vi. 15, 34; Nah. ii. 3, and in other places). Our translators understood it evidently as referring to the cedar. It is often joined, however, with the cedar (see Note on Isa. xiv. 8; comp. ch. xxxvii. 54; Zech. xi. 1, 2), and evidently denotes another tree, probably of the same class. It is probable that the word usually denotes the *cypress.* There are various kinds of cypress. Some are evergreen, and some are deciduous, as the American

white cedar. The wood of these trees is remarkable for its durability. Among the ancients, coffins were made of it, and the tree itself was an emblem of mourning. It is here mentioned because its extended branches and dense foliage would produce a grateful shade. ¶ *And the pine.* The LXX. render this, Λεύκην —'The white poplar.' The Vulgate renders it, 'The elm.' Gesenius supposes that a species of hard oak, *holm* or *ilex,* is intended. It is not easy, however, to determine what species of tree is meant. ¶ *The box-tree.* Gesenius supposes that by this word is denoted some tall tree—a species of cedar growing on mount Lebanon that was distinguished by the smallness of its cones, and the upward direction of its branches. With us the word *box* denotes a shrub used for bordering flower-beds. But the word here denotes *a tree*—such as was sufficient to constitute a shade.

20. *That they.* The Jews, the people who shall be rescued from their long captivity, and restored again to their own land. So rich and unexpected would be the blessings—as if in a pathless desert the most beautiful and refreshing trees and fountains should suddenly spring up—that they would have the fullest demonstration that they came from God. ¶ *Hath created it.* That is, all this is to be traced to him. In the apocryphal book of Baruch there is an expression respecting the return from Babylon remarkably similar to that which is used here by Isaiah: 'Even the woods and every sweet-smelling tree shall overshadow Israel by the commandment of God' (ch. v. 8).

21. *Produce your cause.* This address is made to the same persons who are referred to in ver. 1—the worshippers of idols; and the prophet here returns to the subject with reference to a further argument on the comparative power of Jehovah and idols. In the former part of the chapter, God had urged his claims to confidence from the fact that he had raised up Cyrus; that the idols were weak and feeble

the LORD: bring forth your strong *reasons*, saith the King of Jacob.

22 Let them *a* bring *them* forth, and show us what shall happen: let them show the former things what they *be*, that we may [1] consider

them, and know the latter end of them; or declare us things for to come.

23 Show the things that are to come hereafter, that we may know

a Jn.13.19.   1 *set our heart* upon.

---

compared with him; and from the fact that it was his fixed purpose to defend his people, and to meet and refresh them when faint and weary. In the verses which follow the 21st, he urges his claims to confidence from the fact that he alone was able *to predict future events*, and calls on the worshippers of idols to show their claims in the same manner. This is the ' cause ' which is now to be tried. ¶ *Bring forth your strong* reasons. Adduce the arguments which you deem to be of the greatest strength and power (comp. Notes on ver. 1). The object is, to call on them to bring forward the most convincing demonstration on which they relied, of their power and their ability to save. The argument to which God appeals is, that he had foretold future events. He calls on them to show that they had given, or could give, equal demonstration of their divinity. Lowth regards this as a call on the idol-gods to come forth in person and show their strength. But the interpretation which supposes that it refers to their reasons, or arguments, accords better with the parallelism, and with the connection.

22. *Let them bring* them *forth*. Let the idols, or the worshippers of idols, bring forth the evidences of their divine nature and power. Or more probably it means, 'let them draw near or approach.' ¶ *And show us what shall happen*. None but the true God can discern the future, and predict what is to occur. To be able to do this, is therefore a proof of divinity to which God often appeals as a demonstration of his own Divine character (see ch. xliv. 7, 8; xlv. 3–7; xlvi. 9, 10). This idea, that none but the true God can know all things, and can with certainty foretell future events, is one that was admitted even by the heathen (see Xen. *Cyr.* i. —' The immortal gods know all things, both the past, the present, and those things which shall proceed from each

thing. It was on this belief also that the worshippers of idols endeavoured to sustain the credit of their idol-gods; and accordingly, nearly all the reputation which the oracle at Delphi, and other shrines, obtained, arose from the remarkable sagacity which was evinced in predicting future events, or the skilful ambiguity in which they so couched their responses as to be able to preserve their influence whatever might be the result. ¶ *Let them show the former things what they* be. The idea in this passage seems to be, ' Let them foretell the *entire series* of events; let them predict in their order, the things which shall *first* occur, as well as those which shall finally happen. Let them not select merely an isolated and unconnected event in futurity, but let them declare those which shall have a mutual relation and dependency, and whose causes are now hid.' The argument in the passage is, that it required a far more profound knowledge to predict the *series* of events as they should actually occur; to foretell their *order* of occurrence, than it did to foretell one single isolated occurrence. The latter, the false prophets of the heathen often undertook to do; and undoubtedly they often evinced great sagacity in it. But they never undertook to detail minutely a *series* of occurrences, and to state the *order* in which they would happen. In the Scriptures, it is the common way to foretell the *order* of events, or a *series* of transactions pertaining often to many individuals or nations, and stretching far into futurity. And it is perfectly manifest that none could do this but God (comp. ch. xlvi. 10). ¶ *Or declare us things for to come*. Declare *any* event that is to occur; anything in the future. If they cannot predict the *order* of things, or a *series* of events, let them clearly foretell *any* single event in futurity.

23. *That we may know that ye* are

that ye *are* gods: yea, do good, or do evil, that we may be dismayed, and behold *it* together.

24 Behold, ye *are* [1] of nothing, and your work [2] of nought: an abomination *is he that* chooseth you.

1 or, worse *than nothing.*

25 I [a] have raised up *one* from the north, and he shall come: from the rising of the sun shall he call upon my name; and he shall come upon princes as *upon* mortar, and as the potter treadeth clay.

2 or, worse *than of a viper.*   a ver.2.

gods. The prediction of future events is the highest evidence of omniscience, and of course of divinity. In this passage it is *admitted* that if they could do it, it would prove that they were worthy of adoration; and it is *demanded,* that *if* they were gods they should be able to make such a prediction as would demonstrate that they were invested with a Divine nature. ¶ *Yea, do good, or do evil.* *Do something;* show that you have some power; either defend your friends, or prostrate your foes; accomplish *something*—anything, good or bad, that shall prove that you have power. This is said in opposition to the character which is usually given to idols in the Scriptures—that they were dumb, deaf, dead, inactive, powerless (see Ps. cxv.) The command here to 'do evil,' means to punish their enemies, or to inflict vengeance on their foes; and the idea is, that they had no power to do anything; either to do good to their worshippers, or harm to their enemies; and that thus they showed that they were no gods. The same idea is expressed in Jer. x. 3–5 : ' They [idols] are upright as the palm-tree, but speak not; they must needs be borne, because they cannot go. Be not afraid of them, for they cannot do evil, neither also is it in them to do good.' ¶ *That we may be dismayed* (see Note on ver. 10). The word 'we' here refers to those who were the friends and worshippers of JEHOVAH. 'That I, JEHOVAH, and my friends and worshippers, may be alarmed, and afraid of what idols may be able to do.' God and his people were regarded as the foes of idols, and God here calls on them to prove that there is any reason why he and his people should be afraid of your power. ¶ *And behold it together.* That we may *all* see it; that I and my people may have full demonstration of your power.

24. *Behold, ye* are *of nothing.* Marg. ' Worse than nothing.' This refers to

idols; and the idea is, that they were utterly vain and powerless; they were as unable to render aid to their worshippers as *absolute nothingness* would be, and all their confidence in them was vain and foolish. ¶ *And your work.* All that you do, or all that it is pretended that you do. ¶ *Of nought.* Marg. ' Worse than a viper.' The word used here in the common Hebrew text (אֶפַע) occurs in no other place. Gesenius supposes that this is a corrupt reading for אֶפֶס (*nothing*), and so our translators have regarded it, and in this opinion most expositors agree. Hahn has adopted this reading in his Hebrew Bible. The Jewish Rabbins suppose generally that the word אֶפַע is the same word as אֶפְעֶה, *a viper,* according to the reading in the margin. But this interpretation is contrary to the connection, as well as the ancient versions. The Vulgate and Chaldee render it, ' Of nought.' The Syriac renders it, 'Your works are of the sword.' This is probably one of the few instances in which there has been a corruption of the Hebrew text (comp. ch. xl. 17; xli. 12, 19). ¶ *An abomination* is he that *chooseth you.* They who select idols as the object of worship, and offer to them homage, are regarded as abominable by God.

25. *I have raised up* one. In the previous verses God had shown that the idols had no power of predicting future events. He stakes, so to speak, the question of his divinity on that point, and the whole controversy between him and them is to be decided by the inquiry whether they had the power of foretelling what would come to pass. He here urges *his* claims to divinity on this ground, that he had power to foretell future events. In illustration of this, he appeals to the fact that he had raised up, *i.e., in purpose,* or *would* afterwards raise up Cyrus, in accordance with his

26 Who hath declared from the beginning, that we may know? and beforetime, that we may say, *He is* righteous? yea, *there is* none that showeth; yea, *there is* none that declareth; yea, *there is* none that heareth your words.

predictions, and in such a way that it would be distinctly seen that he had this power of foretelling future events. To see the force of this argument, it must be remembered that the Jews are contemplated as in Babylon, and near the close of their captivity; that God by the prophets, and especially by Isaiah, distinctly foretold the fact that he would raise up Cyrus to be their deliverer; that these predictions were uttered at least a hundred and fifty years before the time of their fulfilment; and that they would *then* have abundant evidence that they were accomplished. To these recorded predictions and to their fulfilment, God here appeals, and designs that in that future time when they should be in exile, his people should have evidence that He was worthy of their entire confidence, and that even the heathen should see that JEHOVAH was the true God, and that the idols were nothing. The personage referred to here is undoubtedly Cyrus (see Notes on ver. 2; comp. ch. xlv. 1). ¶ *From the north.* In ver. 2, he is said to have been raised up 'from the east.' Both were true. Cyrus was born in Persia, in the country called in the Scriptures 'the east,' but he early went to Media, and came from Media under the direction of his uncle, Cyaxares, when he attacked and subdued Babylon. Media was situated on the north and north-east of Babylon. ¶ *From the rising of the sun.* The east—the land of the birth of Cyrus. ¶ *Shall he call upon my name.* This expression means, probably, that he should acknowledge JEHOVAH to be the true God, and recognize him as the source of all his success. This he did in his proclamation respecting the restoration of the Jews to their own land : 'Thus saith Cyrus, king of Persia, JEHOVAH, God of heaven, hath given me all the kingdoms of the earth' (Ezra i. 2). There is no decided evidence that Cyrus regarded himself as a worshipper of JEHOVAH, or that he was a pious man, but he was brought to make a public recognition of him as the true God, and to feel that he owed the success of his arms to him. ¶ *And he shall come upon princes.* Upon the kings of the nations against whom he shall make war (see ver. 2, 3). The word here rendered 'princes' (from סָגַן or סֶגֶן), denotes properly *a deputy, a prefect, a governor,* or one under another, and is usually applied to the governors of provinces, or the Babylonian princes, or magistrates (Jer. li. 23, 28, 57; Ezek. xxiii. 6, 12, 33; Dan. iii. 2, 27; vi. 8). It is sometimes applied, however, to the chiefs and rulers in Jerusalem in the times of Ezra and Nehemiah (Ezra ix. 2; Neh. ii. 16; iv. 8, 13; v. 7). Here it is used as a general term; and the sense is, that he would tread down and subdue the kings and princes of the nations that he invaded. ¶ *As* upon *mortar* (see Note on ch. x. 6).

26. *Who hath declared from the beginning.* The meaning of this passage is, 'there is no one among the soothsayers, and the worshippers of idols, who has predicted the birth, the character, and the conquests of Cyrus. There is among the heathen no recorded prediction on the subject, as there is among the Jews, that when he shall have come, it may be said that a prediction is accomplished.' ¶ *And beforetime.* Formerly; before the event occurred. ¶ *That we may say.* That it may be said; that there may be evidence, or reason for the affirmation. ¶ He is *righteous.* The words 'he is' are not in the Hebrew. The original is simply 'righteous' (צַדִּיק *tzăddīq*), *just, i.e.,* it is just, or true; the prediction is fulfilled. It does not refer to the character of God, but to the certainty of the fulfilment of the prediction. ¶ There is *none that showeth.* There is no one among the worshippers of false gods, the soothsayers and necromancers, that has predicted these events. ¶ *None that heareth your words.* There is no one that has heard such a prediction among you.

27 The first *shall say* to Zion, Behold, behold them : and I will give to Jerusalem one *a* that bringeth good *b* tidings.

28 For I beheld, and *there was* no man; even among them, and *there was* no counsellor, that, when I asked of them, could ¹answer a word.

29 Behold, they *are* all vanity; their works *are* nothing; their molten images *are* wind and confusion.

a ch.40.9.   b Lu 2.10,11.   1 return.

27. *The first* shall say *to Zion.* This translation is unhappy. It does not convey any clear meaning, nor is it possible from the translation to conjecture what the word 'first' refers to. The correct rendering undoubtedly is, '*I* first said to Zion;' and the sense is, 'I, JEHOVAH, first gave to Zion the announcement of these things. I predicted the restoration of the Jews to their own land, and the raising up of the man who should deliver them ; and I only have uttered the prophecies respecting the time and circumstances in which these events would occur.' The LXX. render it, 'I will first give notice to Zion, and I will comfort Jerusalem in the way.' The Chaldee renders it, 'The words of consolation which the prophets have uttered respecting Zion in the beginning, lo, they are about to come to pass.' The sense of the passage is, that no one of the idol-gods, or their prophets, had predicted these events. The first intimation of them had been by JEHOVAH, and this had been made to Zion, and designed for its consolation. ¶ *Behold, behold them.* Lo, these events are about to come to pass. Zion, or Jerusalem, was to behold them, for they were intended to effect its deliverance, and secure its welfare. The words 'Zion' and 'Jerusalem' here seem intended to denote the Jewish people in general, or to refer to Jerusalem as the capital of the Jewish nation. The intimation had been given in the capital of the nation, and thence to the entire people. ¶ *And I will give.* Or rather, I give, or I have given. The passage means, that the bearer of the good tidings of the raising up of a deliverer should be sent to the Jewish people. To them the joyful news was announced long before the event ; the news of the raising up of such a man—an event of so much interest to them—was made to them long before the heathen had any intimation of it; and it would occur as the fulfilment of an ancient prophecy recorded among the Jews. The prophet refers here, doubtless, in the main, to his own prophecies uttered so long before the event would occur, and which would be distinctly known when they would be in exile in Babylon.

28. *For I beheld.* I looked upon the heathen world, among all the pretended prophets, and the priests of pagan idolatry. ¶ *And* there was *no man.* No man among them who could predict these future events. ¶ *No counsellor.* No one qualified to give counsel, or that could anticipate by his sagacity what would take place. ¶ *That, when I asked of them.* In the manner referred to in this chapter. There is no one of whom it could be inquired what would take place in future times. ¶ *Could answer a word.* They were unable to discern what would come to pass, or to predict the events which are referred to here.

29. *Behold, they* are *all vanity.* They are unable to predict future events ; they are unable to defend their friends, or to injure their enemies. This is the conclusion of the trial or debate (Notes, ver. 1), and that conclusion is, that they were utterly destitute of strength, and that they were entirely unworthy of confidence and regard. ¶ *Their molten images* (see Note on ch. xl. 19). ¶ *Are wind.* Have no solidity or power. The doctrine of the whole chapter is, that confidence should be reposed in God, and in him alone. He is the friend of his people, and he is able to protect them. He will deliver them from the hand of all their enemies; and he will be always their God, protector, and guide. The idols of the heathen have no power ; and it is folly, as well as sin, to trust in them, or to suppose that they can aid their friends.

CHAPTER XLII.

ANALYSIS.

Tⁿis chapter is a continuation of the same general subject which was presented in the two previous chapters. It is to be regarded (see the analysis of ch. xl.) as addressed to the exile Jews in Babylon, and near the close of their captivity, and the general object is to induce them to repose confidence in God, and to assure them of deliverance. The primary purpose of these chapters, therefore, is, to direct the attention to him who was to be raised up from the east, to rescue them from their bondage, that is, Cyrus. But in doing this, the mind of the prophet, by the laws of prophetic suggestion (see Introd. to Isaiah, § 7, III. 3), is also led to a far greater deliverer, and so entirely, and intently at times, as to lose sight altogether of Cyrus; and the restoration of the Jews to their own land is forgotten in the sublimer contemplation of the redemption of the world. In the previous chapters, the attention of the prophet had been particularly directed to Cyrus, with an occasional reference to the Messiah. In the commencement of this chapter, he seems to have lost sight of Cyrus altogether, and to have fixed the attention wholly on the future Messiah (see Notes on ver. 1). The chapter is, as I apprehend, occupied mainly, or entirely, with a description of the character and work of the Messiah. The evidence of this will be adduced in the Notes on the chapter itself. The *design* for which the Messiah is introduced is to convince the Jews that God was their protector, and that it was his purpose that the long-promised Prince and Saviour should yet arise from their restored and recovered nation. Of course, if this *was* to occur, their national existence would be preserved. There is, therefore, in the chapter, a reference to their return to their own land, though the main scope relates to the Messiah.

The chapter may be regarded as divided into two portions. In the *first* (ver. 1–9), the prophet describes the Messiah. Jehovah is introduced as speaking, and in ver. 1–4 he describes his character. He is the servant of Jehovah, endowed with the fulness of the Divine Spirit; meek, and lowly, and gentle, and kind; unobtrusive and noiseless in his movements, and

yet securing the conquest of truth. Jehovah then (5–7), addresses the Messiah himself directly, and states the object for which he had appointed him, to be a light to the Gentiles, to open the eyes of the blind, and to be the pledge of the covenant between him and his people. In ver. 8, 9, Jehovah turns to the people for whom the prophecy was given, and awakens their attention to the subject, reminds them of the predictions which had been made, and says that the fulfilment of this prophecy, like all former predictions, would demonstrate his superiority over idols, and show that he was the true God.

The *second* part of the chapter (10–25), consists mainly of a call on the world, and especially on the exile Jews, to rejoice in view of the truth here announced. This general call contains the following portions or parts:—

(1.) In the exordium (10–12) Jehovah calls on the inhabitants of all the earth to praise and glorify his name, and makes his appeal to those who are upon the sea, to the inhabitants of the isles, to the wilderness and solitary places, to the villages and the inhabitants of the rock, as all having occasion to rejoice on account of this glorious event.

(2.) In ver. 13–17, Jehovah speaks particularly of the deliverance of his people, and of the certainty of its being accomplished. He had long delayed to interpose; but now he would come forth in his strength, and annihilate his foes and redeem his people, and make darkness light before them, while all the worshippers of idols should be left without defence or aid.

(3.) The people of Israel are next addressed directly, and their character and duty presented (18–25). They are addressed as a people blind and deaf, and are admonished to rouse themselves, and to strive to attain to true knowledge. Notwithstanding all that God had done for them, and all his gracious interposition, they had hardened their hearts, and shut their eyes, and had steeled themselves against every good impression. For this God had punished them. He had given them as a spoil to their enemies, and overwhelmed them in grievous and long-continued calamities. They were now called on to attend to his instructions and promises, and henceforward be an obedient people.

It may be added, also, that it is equally vain to trust in *any* being for salvation but God. He only is able to protect and defend us; and it is a source of unspeakable consolation now, as it was in times past, that he is the friend of his people; and that, in times of deepest darkness and distress, he can raise up deliverers, as he did Cyrus, and will in his own way and time rescue his people from all their calamities.

BEHOLD my servant, whom I uphold, mine *a* elect, *in whom* my soul *b* delighteth ; I have put my Spirit upon him : he shall bring forth judgment to the Gentiles.

a Eph.1.4.   *b* Mat.17.5.

CHAPTER XLII.

1. *Behold.* This word is designed to call attention to the person that is immediately referred to. It is an intimation that the subject is of importance, and should command their regard. ¶ *My servant.* This phrase denotes properly any one who acknowledges or worships God ; any one who is regarded as serving or obeying him. It is a term which may be applied to any one who is esteemed to be a pious man, or who is obedient to the commands of God, and is often applied to the people of God (Gen. l. 17; 1 Chron. vi. 49; 2 Chron. xxiv. 9; Dan. vi. 20; ix. 2; Titus i. 1; James i. 1; 1 Pet. ii. 16; Rev. vii. 3; xv. 3). The word 'servant' may be applied either to Isaiah, Cyrus, or the Messiah ; and the question to whom it refers here is to be decided, not by the mere use of the term, but by the connection, and by the characteristics which are ascribed to him who is here designated as the 'servant' of JEHOVAH. There have been no less than five different views in regard to the personage here referred to ; and as in the interpretation of the whole prophecy in this chapter, everything depends on this question, it is of importance briefly to examine the opinions which have been entertained. I. One has been that it refers to the Jewish people. The translators of the Septuagint evidently so regarded it. They render it, 'Ιακὼβ ὁ παῖς μου, κ.τ.λ.— ' Jacob is my servant, I will uphold him ; Israel is my chosen one, my soul hath embraced him.' Jarchi also so interprets the passage, but so modifies it as to understand by it ' the righteous in Israel ; ' and among the moderns, Rosenmüller, Paulus, and some others adopt this interpretation. The principal reason alleged for this interpretation is, that the phrase ' servant of JEHOVAH,' is elsewhere used in a collective sense, and applied to the Jewish people. Rosenmüller appeals particularly to ch. xli. 8, 9; to ver. 19 of this chapter, and to ch. xliv. 21; xlv. 4; xlviii. 20; and argues that it is to be presumed that the prophet used the phrase in a uniform manner, and must therefore be supposed here also to refer to the Jewish people. But the objections are insuperable. 1. In ver. 6, the servant of JEHOVAH here referred to, is plainly distinguished *from* the people, where God says, ' I will give *thee* for a covenant of [with] the people.' 2. The description which the prophet gives here of the character of the ' servant ' of JEHOVAH, as meek, mild, gentle, quiet, and humble (ver. 2, 3), is remarkably *unlike* the character which the prophet elsewhere gives of the people, and is as remarkably *like* the character which is everywhere given of the Messiah. 3. It was not true of the Jewish people that they were appointed, as is here said of the ' servant ' of God (ver. 7), to ' open the blind eyes, and to bring the prisoners out of prison.' This is evidently applicable only to a teacher, a deliverer, or a guide ; and in no sense *can* it be applied to the collected Jewish people. II. A second opinion has been, that by the ' servant of JEHOVAH ' Cyrus was intended. Many of the Jewish interpreters have adopted this view, and not a few of the German critics. The principal argument for this opinion is, that what precedes, and what follows, relates particularly to Cyrus ; and an appeal is made particularly to ch. xlv. 1, where he is called the Anointed, and to ch. xliv. 28, where he is called the Shepherd. But to this view also, the objections are obvious. 1. The name ' servant of JEHOVAH,' is, it is believed, nowhere given to Cyrus. 2. The description here by no means agrees with Cyrus. That he was distinguished for justice and equity is admitted (see Note on ch. xli. 2), but the expressions here used, that God would ' put his Spirit upon him, that he should not cry, nor lift up his voice, so that it should be heard in the streets,' is one that is by no means applicable to a man whose life was spent mainly in the tumults of war, and in the pomp and carnage of battle and conquest. How *can* this description be applied to a man who trod down nations, and subdued kings, and who shed rivers of blood? III. Others suppose that the prophet refers to himself. Among the Jews, Aben Ezra, and among others, *Grotius* and *Döderlin* held this opinion. The only reason for this is, that in ch. xx. 3, the name 'servant' of JEHOVAH is given to Isaiah. But the objections to this are plain, and insuperable. 1. Nothing can be urged, as we have seen, from the mere use of the word 'servant.' 2. It is inconceivable that a humble prophet like Isaiah should have applied to himself a description expressive of so much importance as is here attributed to the servant of God. How could the establishment of a new covenant with the people of God, and the conversion of the heathen nations (ver. 6, 7), be ascribed to Isaiah? And in what sense is it true that *he* was appointed to open the eyes of the blind, and to lead the prisoners from the prison? IV. A fourth opinion, which it may be proper just to notice, is that which is advocated by Gesenius, that the phrase here refers to the prophets taken *collectively*. But this opinion is one that scarce deserves a serious refutation. For, 1. The name 'SERVANT of JEHOVAH,' is never given to any *collection* of the prophets. 2. Any such *collection* of the prophets is a mere creature of the fancy. When did they exist? Who composed the collection? And how could the name 'SERVANT' designate them? 3. Of what *collection* of men could it be imagined that the description here given could be applied, that such a collection should not strive, nor cry; that it should be a covenant of the people, and that it should be the means of the conversion of the Gentile world? V. The fifth opinion, therefore, is, that it refers to the Messiah; and the direct arguments in favour of this, independent of the fact that it is applicable to no other one, are so strong as to put it beyond debate. A few of them may be referred to. 1. This is the interpretation of the Chaldee Paraphrase, which has retained the exposition of the ancient and early Jews. 'Behold my servant, the MESSIAH (עַבְדִּי מְשִׁיחָא) I will cause him to come near; my chosen.' 2. There are such applications of the passage in the

New Testament to the Lord Jesus, as to leave no room to doubt that, in view of the sacred writers, the passage had this reference. Thus, in Luke ii. 32, he is spoken of as 'a light to lighten the Gentiles' (comp. ver. 6 of the chapter before us). In Acts xxvi. 18, Paul speaks of him as given to the Gentiles, 'to open their eyes, and to turn them from darkness to light' (comp. ch. xlii. 7). In Matt. iii. 17, God says of the Redeemer, 'This is my beloved Son, in whom I am well pleased,'—language remarkably similar to the passage before us (ver. 1), where he says, 'mine elect, in whom my soul delighteth.' And the whole inquiry is put to rest by the fact that Matthew (xii. 17–21) expressly and directly applies the passage to the Lord Jesus, and says that it was fulfilled in him. 3. It may be added, that the entire description is one that is exactly and entirely applicable to the Lord Jesus. It is *as* applicable as if it had been made *after* he had appeared among men, and as if it were the language of biography, and not of prophecy. It is an exceedingly beautiful and tender description of the Son of God; nor *can* there be any objection to its application to him, except what arises from a general purpose not to apply *any* part of the Old Testament to him, if it can be avoided. I shall regard the passage, therefore, as applicable to him, and him alone; and suppose that the design of the Spirit here in introducing this reference to the Messiah is, to comfort the hearts of the exile Jews with the assurance that they *must* be restored to their own land, *because* it was from them that the Messiah was to proceed, and from them that the true religion was to be spread around the world. ¶ *Whom I uphold.* Whom I sustain, or protect; *i.e.*, who is the object of my affection and care. In Matt. iii. 17, the expression is, 'in whom I am well pleased.' And so in Matt. xii. 18, it is rendered, 'my servant, whom I have chosen.' ¶ *Mine elect.* My chosen one; or the one whom I have *selected* to accomplish my great purposes. It implies that God had designated or appointed him for the purpose. In Matt. xii. 18, it is ren-

2 He shall not cry, nor lift up, nor cause his voice to be heard in the street.

3 A bruised reed shall he not break, and the [1] smoking flax shall he not [2] quench : he shall bring forth judgment unto truth.

1 or, *dimly burning.*　　　2 *quench it.*

dered 'my beloved.' It implies that he was the object of the Divine favour, and that God had chosen or appointed him to perform the work of a Messiah. ¶ In whom *my soul delighteth.* This language is applied to the Lord Jesus in Matt. iii. 17; xii. 18. God regarded him as qualified for his work; he approved of what he did; he was well pleased with all his words, and thoughts, and plans. The word 'soul' here, is equivalent to *I* myself—in whom *I* delight. ¶ *I have put my Spirit upon him* (comp. John iii. 34): 'For God giveth not the Spirit by measure unto him.' The Lord Jesus was Divine, yet as Mediator he is everywhere represented as 'the anointed' of God, or as endowed with the influences of the Holy Spirit (comp. Note on ch. xi. 2). See also ch. lxi. 1, where the Messiah says of himself, 'The Spirit of the LORD God is upon me, because he hath anointed me' (comp. Luke iv. 18). Before he entered upon his public ministry, the Spirit of God descended on him at his baptism (Matt. iii. 17), and in all his work he showed that he was endowed abundantly with that Spirit. ¶ *He shall bring forth judgment.* The word 'judgment' (מִשְׁפָּט) is used in a great variety of significations. It properly means *judgment, i.e.,* the act of judging (Lev. xix. 15); the place of judgment (Eccl. iii. 16); a cause, or suit before a judge (Num. xxviii. 5); a sentence of a judge (1 Kings iii. 28); and thence guilt or crime, for which one is judged (Jer. li. 9). It also means right, rectitude, justice; a law, or statute; a claim, privilege, or due; also manner, custom, or fashion; or an ordinance, or institution. Here it is used, probably, in the sense of the order or institution that would be introduced under the Messiah; and it means that he would set up or establish the true religion among the Gentiles. ¶ *To the Gentiles.* This is one of the many declarations which occur in Isaiah, that the Messiah would extend

the true religion to pagan nations, and that they should be brought to participate in its privileges.

2. *He shall not cry.* He will not make a clamour or noise; he will not be boisterous, in the manner of a man of strife and contention. ¶ *Nor lift up.* That is, his voice. ¶ *Nor cause his voice to be heard in the street.* He shall not use loud and angry words, as they do who are engaged in conflict, but all his teaching shall be gentle, humble, and mild. How well this agrees with the character of the Lord Jesus it is not necessary to pause to show. He was uniformly unostentatious, modest, and retiring. He did not even desire that his deeds should be blazoned abroad, but sought to be withdrawn from the world, and to pursue his humble path in perfect peace.

3. *A bruised reed.* The word 'reed' means the cane or calamus which grows up in marshy or wet places (ch. xxxvi.

REEDS (*Calamus aromaticus*).

6; see Note on ch. xliii. 24). The word, therefore, literally denotes *that which is fragile,* weak, easily waved by the wind, or broken down; and stands in contrast with a lofty and firm tree (comp. Matt. xi. 7): 'What went ye out into the wilderness to see? A reed shaken with

4 He shall not fail nor be [1]dis-
couraged, till he have set judgment

1 *broken*

in the earth : and the isles shall
wait for his *a* law.

a Ge.49.10.

the wind ?' The word here, therefore,
may be applied to men that are conscious
of feebleness and sin ; that are moved and
broken by calamity ; that feel that they
have no strength to bear up against the
ills of life. The word 'bruised' (רָצוּץ
râtzûtz) means that which is broken or
crushed, but not entirely broken off. As
used here, it may denote those who are
in themselves naturally feeble, and who
have been crushed or broken down by a
sense of sin, by calamity, or by affliction.
We speak familiarly of *crushing* or
breaking down by trials ; and the phrase
here is intensive and emphatic, denoting those who are *at best* like a reed—
feeble and fragile ; and who, in addition
to that, have been broken and oppressed
by a sense of their sins, or by calamity.
¶ *Shall he not break.* Shall he not
break off. He will not carry on the
work of destruction, and entirely crush
or break it. And the idea is, that he
will not make those already broken
down with a sense of sin and with
calamity, more wretched. He will not
deepen their afflictions, or augment their
trials, or multiply their sorrows. The
sense is, that he will have an affectionate regard for the broken-hearted, the
humble, the penitent, and the afflicted.
Luther has well expressed this : ' He
does not cast away, nor crush, nor condemn the wounded in conscience, those
who are terrified in view of their sins ;
the weak in faith and practice, but
watches over and cherishes them, makes
them whole, and affectionately embraces
them.' The expression is parallel to
that which occurs in ch. lxi. 1, where it
is said of the Messiah, ' He hath sent
me to bind up the broken-hearted ;' and
to the declaration in ch. l. 4, where it is
said, ' that I should know how to speak
a word in season to him that is weary.'
¶ *The smoking flax.* The word here
used denotes *flax*, and then a *wick* that
is made of it. The word rendered
'smoking' (כֵּהָה) means *that which is
weak*, small, thin, feeble ; then that
which is just ready to go out, or to be
extinguished ; and the phrase refers
literally to the expiring wick of a lamp,

when the oil is almost consumed, and
when it shines with a feeble and dying
lustre. It may denote here the condition
of one who is feeble and disheartened,
and whose love to God seems almost
ready to expire. And the promise that
he will not extinguish or quench that,
means that he would cherish, feed, and
cultivate it ; he would supply it with
grace, as with oil to cherish the dying
flame, and cause it to be enkindled, and
to rise with a high and steady brilliancy.
The whole passage is descriptive of the
Redeemer, who nourishes the most feeble
piety in the hearts of his people, and
who will not suffer true religion in the
soul ever to become wholly extinct. It
may seem as if the slightest breath
of misfortune or opposition would extinguish it for ever ; it may be like the
dying flame that hangs on the point of
the wick, but if there be true religion it
will not be extinguished, but will be enkindled to a pure and glowing flame, and
it will yet rise high, and burn brightly.
¶ *He shall bring forth judgment* (see
ver. 1). The word 'judgment' here
evidently denotes the true religion ; the
laws, institutions, and appointments of
God. ¶ *Unto truth.* Matthew (xii. 29)
renders this, 'unto victory.' The meaning in Isaiah is, that he shall establish
his religion according to truth ; he shall
faithfully announce the true precepts of
religion, and secure their ascendency
among men. It shall overcome all
falsehood, and all idolatry, and shall
obtain a final triumph in all nations.
Thus explained, it is clear that Matthew
has retained the general idea of the
passage, though he has not quoted it
literally.

4. *He shall not fail.* He shall not
be weak, feeble, or disheartened. However much there may be that shall tend
to discourage, yet his purpose is fixed,
and he will pursue it with steadiness and
ardour until the great work shall be fully
accomplished. There *may* be an allusion
in the Hebrew word here (יִכְהֶה *y'khhê*)
to that which is applied to the flax (כֵּהָה
khêhâ) ; and the idea *may be* that he
shall not become in *his* purposes like

5 Thus saith God the LORD, he that created the heavens, and stretched them out ; he that spread forth the earth, and that which

cometh out of it ; he that giveth breath unto the people upon it, and spirit to them that walk therein :

---

the smoking, flickering, dying flame of a lamp. There shall never be *any* indication, even amidst all embarrassments, that it is his intention to abandon his plan of extending the true religion through all the world. Such also *should* be the fixed and determined purposes of his people. Their zeal should never fail ; their ardour should never grow languid. ¶ *Nor be discouraged.* Marg. ' Broken.' The Hebrew word יָרוּץ (*yârûtz*) may be derived either from רָצַץ (*râtzătz*), *to break*, to break in pieces ; or from רוּץ (*rûtz*) *to run*, to move hastily, to rush upon any one. Our translators have adopted the former. Gesenius also supposes that this is the true interpretation of the word, and that it means, that he would not be broken, *i.e.*, checked in his zeal, or discouraged by any opposition. The latter interpretation is preferred by Vitringa, Rosenmüller, Hengstenberg, and others. The Chaldee renders it, ' Shall not labour,' *i.e.*, shall not be fatigued, or discouraged. The LXX. render it, ' He shall shine out, and not be broken.' The connection seems to require the sense which our translators have given to it, and according to this, the meaning is, ' he shall not become broken in spirit, or discouraged ; he shall persevere amidst all opposition and embarrassment, until he shall accomplish his purposes.' We have a similar phraseology when we speak of a man's being *heart-broken.* ¶ *Till he have set judgment.* Till he has secured the prevalence of the true religion in all the world. ¶ *And the isles.* Distant nations (see Note on ch. xli. 1) ; the heathen nations. The expression is equivalent to saying that the Gentiles would be desirous of receiving the religion of the Messiah, and would wait for it (see Notes on ch. ii. 3). ¶ *Shall wait.* They shall be dissatisfied with their own religions, and see that their idol-gods are unable to aid them ; and they shall be in a posture of *waiting* for some new religion that shall meet their wants. It cannot mean that they shall wait for it, in the sense of

their already having a knowledge of it, but that their being sensible that their own religions cannot save them may be represented as a condition of waiting for some better system. It has been true, as in the Sandwich Islands, that the heathen have been so dissatisfied with their own religion as to cast away their idols, and to be without *any* religion, and thus to be in a waiting posture for some new and better system. And it may be true yet that the heathen shall become extensively dissatisfied with their idolatry ; that they shall be convinced that some better system is necessary, and that they may thus be prepared to welcome the gospel when it shall be proposed to them. It may be that in this manner God intends to remove the now apparently insuperable obstacles to the spread of the gospel in the heathen world. The LXX. render this, ' And in his name shall the Gentiles trust,' which form has been retained by Matthew (xii. 21). ¶ *His law.* His commands, the institutions of his religion. The word ' law ' is often used in the Scriptures to denote the whole of religion.

5. *Thus saith God the* LORD. This verse commences a new form of discourse. It is still JEHOVAH who speaks ; but in the previous verses he had spoken *of* the Messiah in the third person ; here he is introduced as speaking *to* him directly. He introduces the discourse by showing that he is the Creator and Lord of all things. The *object* of his dwelling on this seems to have been, to show that he had *power* to sustain the Messiah in the work to which he had called him ; and to secure for him respect as having been commissioned by him who had formed the heavens and the earth, and who ruled over all. He shows that he had power to accomplish all that he had promised : and he seeks thus to elevate and confirm the hopes of the people with the assurance of their deliverance and salvation. ¶ *And stretched them out.* The heavens are often represented as stretched out as a veil (Gen. i. 6, Heb.)

6 I the LORD have called thee in righteousness, and will hold thine hand, and will keep thee, and give

thee for a covenant of the people, for a light *a* of the Gentiles.

a Lu.2.32; Ac.13.47.

or as an expanse that can be rolled up (see Note on ch. xxxiv. 4), or as a tent for the appropriate dwelling-place of God (see Note on ch. xl. 22). His great power and glory are indicated by the fact that he has stretched out what to us appears a vast expanse over our heads. On the grammatical construction of the word which occurs here in the Hebrew, *see* Rosenmüller *in loc.* ¶ *He that spread forth the earth.* He stretched it out as a plain—retaining the idea which was so common among the ancients that the earth was a vast plain, reaching from one end of the heavens to the other. The *words,* however, which are here used are not inconsistent with the idea that the earth is a sphere, since it may still be represented as stretched out, or expanded to a vast extent. The *main* idea in the passage is not to teach the *form* in which the earth is made, but to show that it has been made by God. ¶ *And that which cometh out of it.* The productions of the earth—the trees, shrubs, grain, &c. As the verb *to stretch out* cannot be applied to these, some verb must be understood; as he *produced,* or *caused to grow.* ¶ *He that giveth breath and spirit to them.* This refers, doubtless, to beasts as well as to men; and the idea is, that God is the source of life to all the creatures that live and move on the earth. The argument in the passage is, that as God is the creator and upholder of all; as he has given life to all, and has the universe entirely under his control, he has a right to appoint whom he will to be the medium of his favours to men, and to demand that suitable respect shall be shown to the Messiah whom he has designated for this work.

6. *I the* LORD *have called thee in righteousness.* The phrase 'in righteousness' has been very differently understood by different expositors (see Note on ch. xli. 10). The most probable meaning may be, ' I have done it as a righteous and just God, or in the accomplishment of my righteous purposes. I am the just moral governor of the universe, and to accomplish my

purposes of justice and fidelity, I have designated thee to this work.' Lowth has well rendered it, ' For a righteous purpose.' In this work *all* was righteousness. God was righteous, who appointed him; it was *because* he was righteous, and could not save without a mediator and an atonement, that he sent him into the world; he selected one who was eminently righteous to accomplish his purpose; and he came that he might establish righteousness on the earth, and confirm the just government of God (see ver. 21). ¶ *And will hold thine hand.* I will take thee by the hand, as one does who guides and leads another. The phrase denotes the same as to guard, or keep—as we protect a child by taking him by the hand. ¶ *And give thee for a covenant.* This is evidently an abbreviated form of expression, and the meaning is, ' I will give or appoint thee as the medium, or means by which a covenant shall be made with the people; or a mediator of the new covenant which God is about to establish with men' (see ch. xlix. 8). A similar expression occurs in Micah v. 5, where it is said of the Messiah, ' and this *man* shall be the peace;' that is, he shall be the source of peace, or peace shall be established and maintained by him. So in Eph. ii. 14, it is said of him, 'he is our peace.' ¶ *Of the people.* It has been doubted whether this means the Jewish people, or the Gentiles. Grotius, Hengstenberg, Vitringa, and others understand it of the Jews; Rosenmüller and others, of the Gentiles. It is not easy to determine which is the correct interpretation. But the meaning, as I apprehend, is, not that he would confirm the ancient covenant with the descendants of Abraham, as Hengstenberg and Vitringa suppose, but that his covenant would be established with ALL, with both Jews and Gentiles. According to this, it will refer to the Jews, not *as* Jews, or as already interested in the covenant, but as constituting one portion of the world; and the whole expression will mean, that his religion will be extended to Jews and Gentiles: *i.e.,* to the whole

7 To open the blind eyes, to bring out *a* the prisoners from the prison, and them that sit in darkness *b* out of the prison-house.

8 I *am* the LORD; that *is* my name: and *d* my glory will I not

give to another, neither my praise to graven images.

9 Behold, the former things are come to pass, and new things do I declare; before *e* they spring forth I tell you of them.

a 2 Ti.2.26. *b* 1 Pe.2.9. *c* Ps.83.18. *d* ch.40.11. *e* Ac.15.18.

world. ¶ *For a light of the Gentiles* (see Luke ii. 32). 'Light' is the emblem of knowledge, instruction, and of the true religion. The Messiah is often called 'light,' and the 'light of the world' (see Matt. iv. 16; comp. Note on Isa. ix. 2; John i. 4, 7, 9; iii. 19; viii. 12; ix. 5; xii. 35, 46; Rev. xxi. 23). This is one of the numerous declarations which occur in Isaiah, that the religion of the Messiah would be extended to the heathen world; and that they, as well as the Jews, would be brought to partake of its privileges.

7. *To open the blind eyes.* This is equivalent to saying that he would impart instruction to those who were ignorant. It relates to the Jews as well as to the Gentiles. He would acquaint them with God, and with the way of salvation. The condition of the world is often represented as one of darkness and blindness. Men see not their true character; they see not their real condition; they are ignorant of God, and of the truths pertaining to their future existence; and they need, therefore, some one who shall enlighten, and sanctify, and save them. ¶ *To bring out the prisoners from the prison* (comp. ch. lxi. 1, 2). This evidently refers to a spiritual deliverance, though the language is derived from deliverance from a prison. It denotes that he would rescue those who were confined in mental darkness by sin; and that their deliverance from the thraldom and darkness of sin would be as wonderful *as if* a prisoner should be delivered suddenly from a dark cell, and be permitted to go forth and breathe the pure air of freedom. Such is the freedom which the gospel imparts; nor can there be a more striking description of its happy effects on the minds and hearts of darkened and wretched men (comp. 1 Pet. ii. 9).

8. *I* am *the* LORD. I am JEHOVAH. Here is also a change in the address. In the previous verses, God had addressed

the Messiah. Here he turns to the people, and assures them that he is the only true God, and that he will not suffer the praise that is due to him to be given to any other, or to any graven image. The name JEHOVAH signifies *being*, or *essential existence* (see Note on ch. i. 9). It is a name which is given to none but the true God, and which is everywhere in the Scriptures used to distinguish him from all others. ¶ *That* is *my name.* That is the name which I have chosen by which to distinguish myself from all idols, and which I regard as appropriately expressive of my existence and perfections. Thus it is used in Ps. lxxxiii. 18 (comp. Ps. xcvi. 5). ¶ *And my glory.* The glory, honour, or praise that is due to me. ¶ *Will I not give.* I will not allow it to be ascribed to another; I will not allow another to assume or receive the honour which is due to me. ¶ *To another.* To *any* other; whether it be man, or whether it be an idol. God claims that all appropriate honours should be rendered to him, and that men should cherish no opinions, maintain no doctrines, indulge in no feelings, that would be derogatory to the honour of his name. This declaration is designed to counteract the propensity everywhere manifest to attribute to man that which belongs to God, or to ascribe to our own wisdom, skill, or power, that which he alone can accomplish. ¶ *Neither my praise.* The praise which is due to me. He would not permit graven images to receive the praise of having done that which he himself had accomplished.

9. *Behold, the former things are come to pass.* That is, the former things which he had foretold. This is the evidence to which he appeals in proof that he alone was God, and this is the basis on which he calls upon them to believe that what he had predicted in regard to future things would also come to pass. He had by his prophets foretold events

10 Sing unto the LORD a new song, *and* his praise from the end of the earth, ye that go down to the sea, and 1 all that is therein ; the isles, and the inhabitants thereof.

11 Let the wilderness and the cities thereof lift up *their voice,* the villages *that* Kedar doth inhabit : let the inhabitants of the rock sing, let them shout from the top of the mountains.

a Re.5.9.　　　　1 *the fulness thereof.*

---

which had now been fulfilled, and this should lead them to confide in him alone as the true God. ¶ *And new things do I declare.* Things pertaining to future events, relating to the coming of the Messiah, and to the universal prevalence of his religion in the world. ¶ *Before they spring forth.* There is here a beautiful image. The metaphor is taken from plants and flowers, the word צֶמַח (*tzâmăhh*) properly referring to the springing up of plants, or to their sending out shoots, buds, or flowers. The phrase literally means, ' before they begin to germinate,' *i.e.,* before there are any indications of life, or growth in the plant. The sense is, that God predicted the future events before there was anything by which it might be inferred that such occurrences would take place. It was not done by mere sagacity—as men like Burke and Canning may sometimes predict future events with great probability by marking certain political indications or developments. God did this when there were no such indications, and when it must have been done by mere omniscience. In this respect, all his predictions differ from the *conjectures* of man, and from all the reasonings which are founded on mere sagacity.

10. *Sing unto the* LORD *a new song.* It is common, as we have seen, to celebrate the goodness of God in a hymn of praise on the manifestation of any peculiar act of mercy (see Notes on ch. xii., xxv., xxvi.) Here the prophet calls upon all people to celebrate the Divine mercy in a song of praise in view of his goodness in providing a Redeemer. The sentiment is, that God's goodness in providing a Saviour demands the thanksgiving of all the world. ¶ *A new song.* A song hitherto unsung ; one that shall be expressive of the goodness of God in this *new* manifestation of his mercy. None of the hymns of praise that had been employed to express his former acts of goodness would appropriately express

this. The mercy was so great that it demanded a song expressly made for the occasion. ¶ And *his praise from the end of the earth.* From all parts of the earth. Let the most distant nations who are to be interested in this great and glorious plan, join in the glad celebration. On the meaning of the phrase, ' end of the earth,' see Note on ch. xl. 28. ¶ *Ye that go down to the sea.* That is, traders, navigators, merchants, seamen ; such as do business in the great waters. The sense is, that they would be interested in the plan of mercy through a Redeemer ; and hence they are called on to celebrate the goodness of God (comp. Notes on ch. lx. 5). This is referred to by the prophet, first, because of the great multitude who thus go down to the sea ; and, secondly, because their conversion will have so important an influence in diffusing the true religion to distant nations. ¶ *And all that is therein.* Marg. as Heb. ' The fulness thereof.' All that fill it ; that is, either in ships, or by dwelling on the islands and coasts. The meaning is, that *all* who were upon the sea—the *completeness,* the *wholeness* of the maritime population, being equally interested with all others in the great salvation, should join in celebrating the goodness of God. ¶ *The isles.* A large portion of the inhabitants of the world are dwellers upon islands. In modern times, some of the most signal displays of the Divine mercy, and some of the most remarkable conversions to Christianity, have been there. In the Sandwich Islands, and in Ceylon, God has poured out his Spirit, and their inhabitants have been among the first in the heathen world to embrace the gospel.

11. *Let the wilderness* (see Note on ch. xxxv. 1). The word here denotes the most uncultivated countries, intimating that even the most rude and barbarous people would have occasion to rejoice, and would be interested in the mercy

12 Let *a*them give glory unto the LORD, and declare his praise in the islands.

13 The LORD shall go forth as a mighty man, he shall stir up jealousy like a *b*man of war: he shall cry, yea, roar; he ¹shall prevail against his enemies.

a Ps.117.1.   *b* Ex.15.3.   1 or, *behave himself mightily.*

of God. ¶ *And the cities thereof.* To us there seems to be something incongruous in speaking of the ' *cities* ' in a ' wilderness.' But we are to remember that the Hebrews gave the name wilderness or desert to those regions that were mostly uncultivated, or sparsely inhabited. They were places that were chiefly devoted to pasturage, and not cultivated by the plough, or regions of vast plains of sand and far-extended barrenness, with here and there an *oasis* on which a city might be built. Josephus, speaking of the desert or wilderness lying between Jerusalem and Jericho, enumerates several villages or towns in it, showing that though it was mainly a waste, yet that it was not wholly without towns or inhabitants. We are to remember also that large towns or cities for commercial purposes, or thoroughfares, were often built in the few fertile or advantageous places which were found in the midst of desert wastes. Thus we are told of Solomon (2 Chron. viii. 4), that ' he built Tadmor *in the wilderness;*' and we know that Palmyra, and Bozrah, and Sela, were large cities that were built in the midst of regions that were generally to be regarded as deserts, or wastes. ¶ *The villages* that *Kedar doth inhabit.* Where the inhabitants of Kedar dwell. Kedar was a son of Ishmael (Gen. xxv. 13), the father of the Kedarenians or Cedrei, mentioned by Pliny (*Nat. Hist.* v. 2), who dwell in the vicinity of the Nabathæans in Arabia Deserta. They often changed their place, though it would seem that they usually dwelt in the neighbourhood of Petra, or Sela. The name Kedar is often given to Arabia Deserta, and the word may in some instances denote Arabia in general. The inhabitants of those countries usually dwell in tents, and lead a nomadic and wandering life. ¶ *Let the inhabitants of the rock sing.* It is uncertain whether the word 'rock' here (Heb. סֶלַע *Sĕlă*, Gr. Πέτραν, 'Petra' or ' rock ') is to be regarded as a proper

name, or to denote in a general sense those who dwell in the rocky part of Arabia. Sela, or Petra, was the name of the celebrated city that was the capital of Idumea (see Notes on ch. xvi. 1); and the connection here would rather lead us to suppose that this city was intended here, and that the inhabitants of the capital were called upon to join with the dwellers in the surrounding cities and villages in celebrating the goodness of God. But it may denote in general those who inhabited the desolate and stony region of Arabia Petrea, or whose home was among the cliffs of the rocks. If so, it is a call upon Arabia in general to rejoice in the mercy of God, and to give glory to him for providing a plan of redemption—an intimation that to the descendants of Ishmael the blessings of the gospel would be extended. ¶ *Let them shout from the top of the mountains.* They who had taken refuge there, or who had made their permanent abode there. Vitringa supposes that the mountains of Paran are meant, which are situated on the north of Mount Sinai. The idea in the verse is, that all the dwellers in Arabia would celebrate the goodness of God, and join in praising him for his mercy in giving a deliverer. They were yet to partake of the benefits of his coming, and to have occasion of joy at his advent. It is possible that Cowper may have had this passage in his eye in the following description of the final and universal prevalence of the gospel :—

The dwellers in the vales and on the rocks,
Shout to each other, aad the mountain-tops,
From distant mountains catch the flying joy;
Till nation after nation taught the strain,
Earth rolls the rapturous hosannas round.
                                        Task.

12. *Let them give glory — in the islands* (see Note on ch. xli. 1). Let the distant regions praise God.

13. *The Lord shall go forth.* This and the following verses give the reasons why they should praise JEHOVAH. He would go forth in his might to over-

14 I have long time holden my peace ; I have been still, *and* refrained myself : *now* *a* will I cry

a Job 32.18-20.

like a travailing woman ; I will destroy and [1] devour at once.

15 I will make waste mountains

1 *swallow*, or, *sup up*.

come and subdue his foes, and to deliver his people. In his conquests, and in the establishment of his kingdom, all people would have occasion to rejoice and be glad. ¶ *As a mighty man.* As a hero, as a warrior. JEHOVAH is often in the Scriptures represented as a hero, or a man of war :

JEHOVAH is a man of war :
JEHOVAH is his name.—Ex. xv. 3.

Who is this King of glory?
JEHOVAH, strong and mighty ;
JEHOVAH mighty in battle.—Ps. xxiv. 8.

Comp. Ps. xlv. 3 ; Isa. xxvii. 1 ; xxx. 30. ¶ *He shall stir up jealousy.* He shall rouse his vengeance, or his indignation. The word קִנְאָה means *vengeance*, or indignation, as well as jealousy. The image here is that of a warrior who rushes on impetuously to take vengeance on his foes. ¶ *He shall cry.* He shall give a shout, or a loud clamour. Warriors usually entered a battle with a loud shout, designed to stimulate their own courage, and to intimidate their foes. All this language is taken from such an entrance on an engagement, and denotes the fixed determination of God to overthrow all his enemies.

14. *I have long time holden my peace.* This is the language of JEHOVAH, and it means that he had for a long time been patient and forbearing ; but that now he would go forth as a warrior to overpower and destroy his foes. ¶ *I will destroy.* The word here used (from נָשַׁם *nâshăm*) denotes properly *to breathe hard*, to pant, as a woman in travail ; and then to breathe hard in any manner. It here denotes the hard breathing which is indicative of anger, or a purpose to execute vengeance. ¶ *And devour at once.* Marg. ' Swallow,' or ' Sup up.' The word שָׁאַף means rather *to breathe hard*, to pant, to blow, as in anger, or in the haste of pursuit. The idea in the verse is, that JEHOVAH had for a long time restrained his anger against his foes, and had refrained from executing vengeance on them. But now he would rouse his

righteous indignation, and go forth to accomplish his purposes in their destruction. All this language is descriptive of a hero or warrior ; and is, of course, not to be regarded as applicable literally to God. He often uses the language of men, and speaks of his purposes under the image of human passions. But we are not to infer that the language is literally applicable to him, nor is it to be interpreted too strictly. It means, in general, that God would go forth with a fixed and settled purpose to destroy his foes.

15. *I will make waste mountains.* This verse denotes the utter desolation which God would bring upon his foes in his anger. The meaning of this part of the verse is, that he would spread desolation over the hills and mountains that were well watered and laid out in gardens and orchards. It was common to plant vineyards on the sides of hills and mountains ; and indeed most of the mountains of Palestine and adjacent regions were cultivated nearly to the top. They were favourable to the culture of the vine and the olive ; and by making terraces, the greater portion of the hills were thus rescued for purposes of agriculture. Yet an enemy or warrior marching through a land would seek to spread desolation through all its cultivated parts, and lay waste all its fields. God, therefore, represents himself as a conqueror, laying waste the cultivated portions of the country of his foes. ¶ *And dry up all their herbs.* He would destroy all the grain and fruits on which they were depending for support. ¶ *And I will make the rivers islands.* Or rather, dry land, or deserts. I will, in the heat of my anger, dry up the streams, so that the bottoms of those streams shall be dry land. The word here rendered ' islands,' from אִי, properly denotes *dry land*, habitable ground, as opposed to water, the sea, rivers, &c., and the signification ' islands ' is a secondary signification. ¶ *And I will dry up the pools.* The pools on which they have been dependent for water for

and *a* hills, and dry up all their herbs ; and I will make the rivers islands, and I will dry up the pools.

16 And *b* I will bring the blind by *c* a way *that* they knew not ; I will lead them in paths *d that* they

a ch.49.11. *b* Ho.2.14. *c* Ep.5.8. *d* Ho.2.6.

have not known : I will make darkness light before them, and crooked things 1 straight. These things will I do *e* unto them, and not *f* forsake them.

17 They *g* shall be turned back,

1 *into straightness.* *e* Eze.14.23. *f* He.13.5. *g* Ps.97.7.

their flocks and herds. The sense of the whole passage is, I will bring to desolation those who worship idols, and the idols themselves. I will produce an entire change among them, *as great* as if I were to spread desolation over their cultivated hills, and to dry up all their streams. The reference is probably to the great changes which God would make in the heathen world. All that flourished on Pagan ground ; all that was nurtured by idolatry ; all their temples, fanes, altars, shrines, should be overturned and demolished ; and in all these things great and permanent changes would be produced. The time would have come when God could no longer bear with the growing abominations of the pagan nations, and when he would go forth as a conqueror to subdue all to himself.

16. *And I will lead the blind.* Having said in the previous verses what he would do to his enemies, God now speaks of his people. He would conduct them to their own land, as a blind people that needed a guide, and would remove whatever obstacle there was in their way. By the 'blind' here, he refers doubtless to his own people. The term is applied originally to his people in captivity, as being ignorant, after their seventy years' exile, of the way of return to their own land. It is *possible* that it may have a reference to the fact, so often charged on them, that they were characteristically a stupid and spiritually blind people. But it is more probable that it is the language of *tenderness* rather than that of objurgation ; and denotes their ignorance of the way of return, and their need of a guide, rather than their guilt, and hardness of heart. If applied to the people of God under the New Testament—as the entire strain of the prophecy seems to lead us to conclude—then it denotes that Christians will feel their need of a leader, counsellor, and guide ; and that

JEHOVAH, as a military leader, will conduct them all in a way which they did not know, and remove all obstacles from their path. ¶ *By a way* that *they knew not.* When they were ignorant what course to take ; or in a path which they did not contemplate or design. It is true of all the friends of God that they *have been led* in a way which they knew not. They did not mark out this course for themselves ; they did not at first form the plans of life which they came ultimately to pursue ; they have been led, by the providence of God, in a different path, and by the Spirit of God they have been inclined to a course which they themselves would never have chosen (comp. Note on ch. xxx. 21). ¶ *I will make darkness light before them.* Darkness, in the Scriptures, is the emblem of ignorance, sin, adversity, and calamity. Here it seems to be the emblem of adverse and opposing events ; of calamities, persecutions, and trials. The meaning is, that God would make those events which seemed to be adverse and calamitous, the means of furthering his cause, and promoting the spirit of the true religion, and the happiness of his people. This has been eminently the case with the persecutions which the church has endured. The events which have been apparently most adverse, have been ultimately overruled to the best interests of the true religion. Such was the case with the persecutions under the Roman emperors, and in general such has been the case in all the persecutions which the church has been called to suffer. ¶ *And crooked things straight.* Things which seem to be adverse and opposing—the persecutions and trials which the people of God would be called to endure. ¶ *And not forsake them* (see Notes on ch. xli. 10, 13, 14).

17. *They shall be turned back.* The phrases, to be turned back, and to be suffused with shame, are frequently used

they shall be greatly ashamed, that trust in graven images, that say to the molten images, Ye *are* our gods.

18 Hear, *a* ye deaf; and look, ye blind, *b* that ye may see.

19 Who *is* blind, but my servant? or deaf, as my messenger *that* I sent? who *is* blind as *he that is* perfect, and blind as the LORD's servant?

a ch.6.10.   *b* Jn.9.39.

in the Scriptures to denote a state of disappointment in regard to an object of trust or confidence, and especially of those who had trusted in idols (see Ps. xxxv. 4; lxx. 3; xcvii. 7; comp. Notes on ch. i. 29; xix. 9; xxxvii. 27; see also Ezek. xvi. 52; liv. 63). The sense here is, that they should find no such protection in their idol-gods as they had hoped, and that they should be covered with conscious guilt for ever, having trusted in them and given to them the homage which was due to the true God.

18. *Hear, ye deaf.* This is evidently an address to the Jews, and probably to the Jews of the time of the prophet. He had been predicting the coming of the Messiah, and the influence of his religion on the Gentile world. He had said that God would go forth to destroy the idolatry of the heathen nations, and to convince them of the folly of the worship of images, and to confound them for putting their trust in them. He seems here to have recollected that this was the easily-besetting sin of his own countrymen, and perhaps especially of the times when he penned this portion of the prophecy—under the reign of Manasseh; that that generation was stupid, blind, deaf to the calls of God, and sunk in the deepest debasement of idolatry. In view of this, and of the great truths which he had uttered, he calls on them to hear, to be alarmed, to return to God, and assures them that for these sins they exposed themselves to, and must experience, his sore displeasure. The statement of these truths, and the denouncing of these judgments, occupy the remainder of this chapter. A similar instance occurs in ch. ii., where the prophet, having foretold the coming of the Messiah, and the fact that his religion would be extended among the Gentiles, turns and reproves the Jews for *their* idolatry and crimes (see Notes on that chapter). The Jew-

ish people are often described as 'deaf' to the voice of God, and 'blind' to their duty and their interests (see ch. xxix. 18; xlii. 8). ¶ *And look—that ye may see.* This phrase denotes an attentive, careful, and anxious search, in order that there may be a clear view of the object. The prophet calls them to an attentive contemplation of the object, that they might have a clear and distinct view of it. They had hitherto looked at the subject of religion in a careless, inattentive, and thoughtless manner.

19. *Who is blind, but my servant?* Some of the Jewish expositors suppose that by 'servant' here, the prophet himself is intended, who, they suppose is here called blind and deaf by the impious Jews who rejected his message. But it is evident, that by 'servant' here, the Jewish people themselves are intended, the singular being used for the plural, in a sense similar to that where they are so often called 'Jacob' and 'Israel.' The phrase 'servants of God' is often given to his people, and is used to denote true worshippers. The word is here used to denote those who *professed* to be the true worshippers of JEHOVAH. The prophet had, in the previous verses, spoken of the blindness and stupidity of the Gentile world. He here turns to his own countrymen, and addresses them as more blind, and deaf, and stupid than they. 'Who,' he asks, 'is as blind as they are?' Where are any of the heathen nations so insensible to the appeals of God, and so hard-hearted? The idea of the prophet is, that the Jews had had far greater advantages, and yet they were so sunk in sin that it might be said that comparatively none were blind but they. Even the degradation of the heathen nations, under the circumstances of the case, could not be compared with theirs. ¶ *As my messenger* that *I sent.* Lowth renders this, 'And deaf, as he to whom I have sent

20 Seeing many things, but thou observest not ; opening the ears, but he heareth not.

21 The LORD is well pleased for

his *a*righteousness' sake ; he will magnify *b* the law, and make ¹*it* honourable.

a Ps.71.16,19; Ro.10.3,4; Phi.3.9.   *b* Mat.5.17.
1 or, *him.*

my messengers.' The LXX. render it, 'And deaf but those that rule over them ;' by a slight change in the Hebrew text. The Vulgate reads it as Lowth has rendered it. The Chaldee renders it, 'If the wicked are converted, shall they not be called my servants? And the sinners to whom I sent my prophets?' But the sense seems to be this :—The Jewish people were regarded as a people selected and preserved by God for the purpose of preserving and extending the true religion. They might be spoken of as sent for the great purpose of enlightening the world, as God's messengers in the midst of the deep darkness of benighted nations, and as appointed to be the agents by which the true religion was to be perpetuated and propagated on earth. Or perhaps, the word 'messenger' here may denote collectively the Jewish leaders, teachers, and priests, who had been sent as the messengers of God to that people, and who were, with the people, sunk in deep debasement and sin. ¶ *As* he that is *perfect* (כִּמְשֻׁלָּם). A great variety of interpretations has been offered on this word —arising from the difficulty of giving the appellation 'perfect' to a people so corrupt as were the Jews in the time of Isaiah. Jerome renders it, *Qui venundatus est*—'He that is sold.' The Syriac renders it, 'Who is blind as the prince?' Symmachus renders it, 'Ως ὁ τέλειος ; and Kimchi in a similar manner by תָּמִים (*tâmîm*)—'perfect.' The verb שָׁלַם means properly *to be whole, sound, safe;* to be completed, finished, ended : and then, to be at peace or friendship with any one. And it may be applied to the Jews, to whom it undoubtedly refers here, in one of the following senses; either (1.) *ironically*, as claiming to be perfect ; or (2.) as those who *professed* to be perfect ; or (3.) as being favoured with rites and laws, and a civil and sacred constitution that were complete (Vitringa); or (4.) as being in *friendship* with God, as Grotius and Gesenius suppose. It most prob-

ably refers to the fact that they were richly endowed by JEHOVAH with complete and happy institutions adapted to their entire welfare, and such as, in comparison with other nations, were fitted to make them perfect. ¶ *As the* LORD's *servant.* The Jewish people, professing to serve and obey God.

20. *Seeing many things.* That is, the people, the Jews, spoken of here as the servants of God. They had had an opportunity of observing many things pertaining to the law, the government, and the dealing of JEHOVAH. They had often witnessed his interposition in the days of calamity, and he often rescued them from peril. These things they could not but have observed, much as they had chosen to disregard the lessons which they were calculated to convey. ¶ *But thou observest not.* Thou dost not *keep* them (תִּשְׁמֹר); thou dost not regard them. ¶ *Opening the ears.* Thou hast thine ears open. They heard the words of the law, and the instructions conveyed by tradition from their fathers, but they did not lay them to heart, or give heed to them (see Note on ch. vi. 10).

21. *The* LORD *is well pleased for his righteousness' sake.* There is great variety in the translation and interpretation of this verse. Lowth renders it :

Yet JEHOVAH was gracious unto him for his
    truth's sake ;
He hath exalted his own praise, and made it
    glorious.

Noyes renders it :

It pleased JEHOVAH for his goodness' sake
To give him a law great and glorious ;
And yet it is a robbed and plundered people.

The LXX. render it, 'The Lord God determined that he should be justified, and magnify his praise.' The Chaldee renders it, 'JEHOVAH willed that Israel should be justified ; he magnified the doers of his law, and comforted them.' The Syriac, 'The Lord willed on account of his righteousness to magnify his law, and to commend it.' Vitringa explains it, 'God has embraced the Jewish people in his love and favour,

22 But this *is* a people robbed
and *a* spoiled ; *they* 1 *are* all of them

a ch.18.2.

snared in holes, and they are hid
in prison houses : they are for a

1 or, *insnaring all the young men of them.*

and regards them as acceptable to himself, not indeed on account of any merit of theirs, or on account of any external advantages, but on account of his own truth, fidelity, and equity, that he might fulfil the promises which he made to their fathers.' This seems to express the sense of the passage. According to this, it refers solely to the Jewish people, and not, as is often supposed, to the Messiah. The phrase, 'is well pleased,' means that JEHOVAH takes delight in his people, or looks upon them with an eye of tenderness and affection. He finds pleasure in contemplating them as *his* people, and in regarding and treating them as such. ¶ *For his righteousness'* *sake.* Not for the righteousness of his people, but on account of his *own* righteousness ; *i.e.*, his own goodness, clemency, mercy, and forbearance. It is not because he sees in them anything that should win his love, or excite his favour ; for he says (ver. 22) that they are robbed, and plundered, and hid, and bound in prison. But JEHOVAH had selected their fathers as his own people. He had made them precious promises. He had designs of mercy towards them. He had given them a holy law. He had promised to be their protector and their God. *On this account* he was pleased with them still ; and it was on account of his own fidelity and plighted protection, that he was delighted in them as his people. The word 'righteousness,' therefore (צֶדֶק), is used to denote God's purpose *to do right ; i.e.*, to adhere to his promises, and to maintain a character of fidelity and integrity. He would not fail, or violate his own pledges to his people. ¶ *He will magnify the law.* The word 'law' here is used to denote the entire series of statutes, or legislative acts of God, in regard to the Jewish people—including all his promises and pledges to them. And the meaning is, that he would so deal with them as to make that law important in their view ; so as to show that *he* regarded it as of infinite moment. He would adhere strictly himself to all his own

covenant pledges in that law, so as to show that *he* regarded it as sacred and of binding obligation ; and all his dealings with them *under* that law would be such as to magnify its importance and purity in their view. The Hebrew is, 'he will make the law great ;' that is, he will make it of great importance. ¶ *And make* it *honourable.* Or, make it glorious, by himself showing a constant regard for it, and by so dealing with them that they should be brought to see and feel its importance. According to this, which is the obvious interpretation, the passage has no reference particularly to the Messiah. It *is* true, however, that the *language* here used is such as would appropriately describe the work of the Redeemer ; and that a large part of what he did in his public ministry, and by his atonement, was 'to magnify the law and make it honourable ;'—to vindicate its equity— to urge its binding obligation—to sustain its claims—to show that it could not be violated with impunity—and to demonstrate that its penalty was just. The whole effect of the Redeemer's work is to do honour to the law of God, nor has anything occurred in the history of our world that has done so much to maintain its authority and binding obligation, as his death on the cross, in the place of sinners.

22. *But this* is *a people robbed and* *spoiled.* The Jewish people, though highly favoured, have been so unmindful of the goodness of God to them, that he has given them into the hand of their enemies to plunder them. This is to be conceived as spoken *after* the captivity, and while the Jews were in exile. Their being robbed and spoiled, therefore, refers to the invasion of the Chaldeans, and is to be regarded as spoken prophetically of the exiled and oppressed Jews while in Babylon. ¶ They are *all of them snared in holes.* This passage has been variously rendered. Lowth renders it, ' All their chosen youth are taken in the toils;' following in this the translation of Je-

prey, and none delivereth; for a spoil, [1] and none saith, Restore.

23 Who among you will give ear to this? *who* will hearken and hear for [2] the time to come?

24 Who gave Jacob for a spoil, and Israel to the robbers? did not the LORD, he *a* against whom we have sinned? for they would not

[1] *treading.*   [2] *after time.*

walk in his ways, neither were they obedient unto his law.

25 Therefore he hath poured upon him the fury of his anger, and the strength of battle: and it hath set him on fire *b* round about, yet *c* he knew not; and it burned him, yet he laid *it* not to heart.

a Ju.2.14; Ne.9.26,27.   *b* De.32.23.   *c* Ho.7.9.

rome, and rendering it as Le Clerc and Houbigant do. The LXX. read it, ' And I saw, and the people were plundered and scattered, and the snare was in all their private chambers, and in their houses where they hid themselves;' —meaning, evidently, that they had been taken by their invaders from the places where they had secreted themselves in their own city and country. The Chaldee renders it, ' All their youth were covered with confusion, and shut up in prison.' The Syriac, ' All their youth are snared, and they have hid them bound in their houses.' This variety of interpretation has arisen in part, because the Hebrew which is rendered in our version, 'in holes' (בַּחוּרִים), may be either the plural form of the word בָּחוּר (*chosen, selected*); and thence *youths*—selected for their beauty or strength; or it may be the plural form of the word חוּר, *a hole* or *cavern*, with the preposition בַ prefixed. Our translation prefers the latter; and this is probably the correct interpretation, as the *parallel* expression, ' they are hid in prison-houses,' seems to demand this. The literal interpretation of the passage is, therefore, that they were snared, or secured in the caverns, holes, or places of refuge where they sought security. ¶ *And they are hid in prison-houses.* They were concealed in their houses as in prisons, so that they could not go out with safety, or without exposing themselves to the danger of being taken captive. The land was filled with their enemies, and they were obliged to conceal themselves, if possible, from their foes. ¶ *And none saith, Restore.* There is no deliverer— no one who can interpose, and compel the foe to give up his captives. The sense is, the Jewish captives were so

strictly confined in Babylon, and under a government so powerful, that there was no one who could rescue them, or that they were so much the object of contempt, that there were none who would feel so much interest in them as to demand them from their foes.

23. *Who among you will give ear to this?* Who is there in the nation that will be so warned by the judgments of God, that he will attend to the lessons which he designs to teach, and reform his life, and return to him? It is implied by these questions that such *ought* to be the effect; it is implied also that they were so sunken and abandoned that they *would* not do it. These judgments were a loud call on the nation to turn to God, and, in time to come, to avoid the sins which had made it necessary for him to interpose in this manner, and give them to spoil.

24. *Who gave Jacob for a spoil?* Who gave up the Jewish people to be plundered? The object of this verse is, to bring distinctly before them the fact that it was JEHOVAH, the God of their fathers, and of their nation, who had brought this calamity upon them. It was not the work of chance, but it was the immediate and direct act of God on account of their sins. Probably, as a people, they were not disposed to believe this; and the prophet, therefore, takes occasion to call their attention particularly to this fact.

25. *Therefore he hath poured upon him the fury of his anger.* His righteous indignation in the overturning of their nation, the destruction of their temple and city, and in carrying them captive into a distant land. ¶ *And it hath set him on fire.* That is, the fury of JEHOVAH kindled the flame of war all around the Jewish nation, and spread

CHAPTER XLIII.

ANALYSIS.

THIS chapter is evidently a continuation of the subject discussed in the previous chapters, and refers mainly to the promised deliverance from Babylon. The people of God are still contemplated by the prophet as suffering the evils of their long and painful captivity, and his object is to comfort them with the assurances of deliverance. The chapter may be regard as composed of *a succession of arguments*, all tending to show them that God would be their protector, and that their deliverance would be certain. These arguments are not distinguished by any very clear marks of transition, and all divisions of the chapter must be in a measure arbitrary. But perhaps the following arrangement will comprise the considerations which the prophet designed to suggest.

I. In the previous chapter he had severely rebuked the Jews, as being deaf, and blind, and had showed them that it was on account of their sins that these calamities had come upon them. Yet he now turns and says, that they are the people whom he had redeemed, and whom it was his purpose to deliver, and repeats the solemn assurance that they would be rescued (1–7). This assurance consists of many *items* or considerations, showing that they would be recovered, however far they were driven from their own land. 1. God had formed and redeemed them (1). It followed from this that a God of covenant faithfulness would be with them in their trials (2). 2. They had been so precious to him and valuable, that he had given entire nations for their ransom (3). It followed from this, that he would continue to give more, if necessary, for their ransom (4). 3. It was the fixed purpose of God to gather them again, wherever they might be scattered, and they had, therefore, nothing to fear (5–7).

II. God asserts his superiority to all idol-gods. He makes a solemn appeal, as he had done in ch. xli., to show that the idols had no power; and refers to all that he had predicted and to its fulfilment in proof that he was the only true God, and had been faithful to his people (8–13). In doing this, he says—1. That none of the idols had been able to predict future events (8, 9).

2. That the Jewish people were his witnesses that he was the true God, and the only Saviour (10–12). 3. That he had existed for ever, and that none could thwart his designs (13).

III. God asserts his purpose to destroy the power of Babylon (14, 17). He says—1. That he had sent to Babylon [by Cyrus] to bring down their power, and prostrate their nobles (14, 15); and, 2. Appeals to what he had formerly done: refers to the deliverance from Egypt, and asserts it to be his characteristic that he made a way in the sea, and led forth the chariot, the horse, the army, and the power (16, 17).

IV. Yet he tells them (18–21), that all his former wonderful interpositions would be surpassed; that he would do a new thing—so strange, so wonderful, and marvellous, that all that he had formerly done should be forgotten. 1. They are commanded not to remember the former things (18). 2. He would do a new thing —a thing which in all his former interpositions had not been done (19). 3. The characteristics of the future wonder would be, that he would make a way in the wilderness, and rivers in the desert (19); and that even the wild beasts of the desert should be made to honour him (20). 4. He had formed that people for himself, and they should show forth his praise (21).

V. From these promises of protection and assistance, and these assurances of favour, God turns to remind them of their sins, and assures them that it was by no merit of theirs that he would thus interpose to deliver them. 1. He reminds them of their having neglected, as a people, to honour him, and having withheld what was his due (22–24); yet, 2. He would blot out their sins, but it was by no merit of theirs, but by his mere mercy (25, 26). 3. They had been a sinful people, and he had, therefore, humbled their power, and given the nation to reproach, and a curse (27, 28). The same subject is resumed and prosecuted in the next chapter, and they should be read together without any interruption.

B UT *a* now thus saith the LORD that created thee, O Jacob, and he that formed thee, O Israel, Fear not: for I have redeemed

a Je.33,24.26.

---

desolation everywhere. ¶ *Yet he knew not.* They refused to attend to it, and lay it to heart. They pursued their ways of wickedness, regardless of the threatening judgments, and the impending wrath of God. They did not consider that these evils were inflicted for

their crimes, nor did they turn from their sins when they were thus threatened with the wrath of God.

CHAPTER XLIII.

1. *But now.* This expression shows that this chapter is connected with the preceding. The sense is, ' Though God

thee, I have called *thee* by thy name ; thou *art* mine.

2 When *a* thou passest through the waters, *b* I *will be* with thee ; and through the rivers, they shall not overflow thee : when thou walkest through the *c* fire, thou shalt not be burned ; neither shall the flame kindle upon thee.

a Ps.66.12.   *b* Ac.27.20,25.   *c* Da.3.25,27.

has punished the nation, and showed them his displeasure (ch. xlii. 24, 25), yet *now* he will have mercy, and will deliver them.' ¶ *That created thee.* The word ' thee ' is here used evidently in a collective sense as denoting the Jewish people. It is used because the names ' Jacob ' and ' Israel ' in the singular number are applied to the people. The word ' created ' is here used to denote the idea that, as the peculiar people of God, they owed their origin to him, as the universe owed its origin to his creative power. It means that, as a people, their institutions, laws, customs, and privileges, and whatever they had that was valuable, were all to be traced to him. The same word occurs in verse 7, and again in verse 15, ' I am JEHOVAH—the Creator of Israel, your king ' (see also ch. xliv. 1 ; comp. Ps. c. 3). ¶ *Fear not.* This is to be understood as addressed to them when suffering the evils of the captivity of Babylon. Though they were captives, and had suffered long, yet they had nothing to fear in regard to their final extinction as a people. They should be redeemed from captivity, and restored again to the land of their fathers. The *argument* here is, that they were the chosen people of God ; that he had organized them as his people for great and important purposes, and that those purposes must be accomplished. It would follow from that, that they *must* be redeemed from their captivity, and be restored again to their land. ¶ *For I have redeemed thee.* The word אַל (*gâăl*) means properly *to redeem*, to ransom by means of a price, or a valuable consideration, as of captives taken in war ; or to redeem a farm that was sold, by paying back the ן rice. It is sometimes used, however, to denote deliverance from danger or bondage without specifying any price that was paid as a ransom. Thus the deliverance of the Jews from Egyptian bondage is sometimes spoken of as a redemption (Ex. vi. 6 ; xv. 13 ; comp. Gen. xviii.

16 ; Isa. xxix. 22 ; xliv. 23 ; Jer. xxxi. 11 ; see Note on ch. i. 27). It is not improbable, however, that wherever *redemption* is spoken of in the Scriptures, even in the most general manner, and as denoting deliverance from danger, oppression, or captivity, there is still retained the idea of *a ransom* in some form ; a price paid ; a valuable consideration ; or *something that was given in the place of that which was redeemed*, and which answered the purpose of a valuable consideration, or a public reason of the deliverance. Thus, in regard to the deliverance from Egypt,—Egypt, Ethiopia, and Seba are mentioned as the ransom (see Note on ver. 3) ; and so in the deliverance from the captivity, Babylon was given in the place of the ransomed captives, or was destroyed in order that they might be redeemed. So in all notions of redemption ; as, *e.g.*, God destroyed the life of the great Redeemer, or caused him to be put to death, in order that his chosen people might be saved. ¶ *I have called* thee *by thy name.* ' To call by name ' denotes intimacy of friendship. Here it means that God had *particularly* designated them to be his people. His call had not been general, addressed to the nations at large, but had been addressed to them in particular. Compare Ex. xxxi. 2, where God says that he had designated ' by name ' Bezaleel to the work of constructing the tabernacle. ¶ *Thou* art *mine.* They were his, because he had formed them as a people, and had originated their institutions ; because he had redeemed them, and because he had particularly designated them as his. The same thing may be said of his church now ; and in a still more important sense, that church is his. He has organized it ; he has appointed its peculiar institutions ; he has redeemed it with precious blood ; and he. has called his people by name, and designated them as his own.

2. *When thou passest through the*

3 For I *am* the LORD thy God, the Holy One of Israel, thy Saviour:

I gave *a* Egypt *for* thy ransom, Ethiopia and Seba for thee.

a Prov. 21. 18.

waters. This is a *general* promise, and means that whenever and wherever they should pass through water or fire, he would protect them. It had been true in their past history as a people ; and the assurance is here given in order that they might be comforted in view of the calamities which they were then suffering in Babylon. Fire and water are often used in the Scriptures to denote calamity—the latter because it overwhelms ; the former because it consumes ; see Ps. lxix. 1—' The waters are come into my soul ;' also Ps. lxxiii. 10 ; cxxiv. 4, 5 ; lxvi. 12—' We went through fire and through water.' ¶ *I* will be *with thee* (comp. Note on ch. xli. 10). ¶ *And through the rivers.* Also expressive of calamity and danger —like attempting to ford deep and rapid streams. ¶ *They shall not overflow thee.* As was the case with the Jordan when they crossed it under the guidance of Joshua, and a pathway was made for the armies of Israel. ¶ *When thou walkest through the fire.* This is expressive of calamity and danger in general *like* passing through fire. Yet it had a literal fulfilment in the case of the three pious Jews who were cast by Nebuchadnezzar into the burning furnace (Dan. iii. 25, 27). ¶ *Neither shall the flame kindle upon thee.* It shall not only not consume thee, but it shall not even burn, or injure thee (see Dan. iii. 27). The Chaldee Paraphrase refers this verse to the passage through the Red Sea, and to the protection which God gave his people there. It is rendered, ' In the beginning, when you passed through the Red Sea, my word was your aid. Pharaoh and Egypt, who were mighty like the waters of a river, were not able to prevail against you. And when thou didst go among a people who were formidable like fire, they could not prevail against you, and the kingdoms which were strong like flame could not consume you.' It is, however, to be understood rather as a promise pertaining to the future ; though the *language* is mainly derived, un-

doubtedly, from God's protecting them in their perils in former times.

3. *For I* am *the* LORD *thy God.* This verse continues the statement of the reasons why he would protect them. He was JEHOVAH *their* God. He was not only the true God, but he was the God who had entered into solemn covenant with *them*, and who would therefore protect and defend them. ¶ *The Holy One of Israel.* It was one of his characteristics that he was the God of Israel. Other nations worshipped other gods. He was THE God of Israel ; and as it was presumed that a god would protect his own people, so he bound himself to deliver them. ¶ *Thy Saviour.* This was another characteristic. He *had* saved them in days of peril ; and he had assumed towards them the relation of a Saviour ; and he would maintain that character. ¶ *I gave Egypt* for *thy ransom.* This is a very important passage in regard to the meaning of the word ' ransom.' The word נָתַתִּי (*năthăttĭ*)— ' I gave ' is rendered by Gesenius (*Comm. in loc.*), and by Noyes, in the future, ' I will give.' Gesenius supposes that it refers to the fact that the countries specified *would* be made desolate, in order to effect the deliverance of the Jews. He observes that although Cyrus did not conquer them, yet that it was done by his successors. In particular, he refers to the fact that Cambyses invaded and subdued Egypt (Herod. iii. 15) ; and that he then entered into, and subdued Ethiopia and Meroë (Strabo xvii. ; Jos. *Ant.* ii. 10. 2). But the word properly refers to the past time, and the scope of the passage requires us to understand it of past events. For God is giving a *reason* why his people might expect protection, and the reason here is, that he *had* been their deliverer, and that his purpose to protect them was so fixed and determined, that he had even brought ruin on nations more mighty and numerous than themselves, in order to effect their deliverance. The *argument* is, that *if* he had suffered Egypt, Ethiopia, and Seba to be desolated and

ruined *instead of them*, or in order to effect their deliverance, they had nothing to fear from Babylon or any other hostile nation, but that he would effect their deliverance even at the expense of the overthrow of the most mighty kingdoms. The word rendered ' ransom ' here is כֹּפֶר (*kōphěr*). It is derived from כָּפַר (*kāphǎr*)—whence the Latin *cooperio;* the Italian *coprire*, the French *couvrir;* the Norman *coverer*, and *converer;* and the English *cover*, and means literally to cover ; to cover over ; to overlay with anything, as pitch, as in Gen. vi. 14. Hence to cover over sins ; to overlook ; to forgive ; and hence to make an expiation for sins, or to atone for transgression so that it may be forgiven (Gen. xxxii. 21; Ex. xxx. 15; Lev. iv. 20; v. 26; xi. 24; xvi. 6; Ps. lxv. 4; lxxviii. 38; Prov. xvi. 14; Jer. xviii. 25; Ezek. xlv. 20; Dan. ix. 24). The noun (כֹּפֶר) means—1. A *village* or *hamlet*, as being a *cover* or shelter to the inhabitants (1 Sam. vi. 18; comp. the word כָּפָר in 1 Chron. xxvii. 25; Neh. vi. 2; Cant. vi. 12). 2. *Pitch*, as a material for overlaying (Gen. vi. 14). 3. The *cypress-flower*, the *alhenna* of the Arabs, so called because the powder of the leaves was used to *cover over* or besmear the nails in order to produce the reddish colour which Oriental females regarded as an ornament (Simonis ; Cant. i. 14; iv. 13, marg.) 4. A *ransom;* a price of redemption, or an expiation ; so called because by it sins were covered over, concealed, or removed (Ex. xxix. 36; xxx. 10, 16). In such an expiation, that which was offered as the ransom was supposed to take the place of that for which the expiation was made, and this idea is distinctly retained in the versions of this passage. Thus the LXX., Ἐποίησα ἄλλαγμά σου Αἴγυπτον, κ.τ.λ.— ' I made Egypt, &c., thy ἄλλαγμα—a commutation for thee ; a change for thee ; I put it in thy place, and it was destroyed instead of thee.' So the Chaldee, ' I gave the Egyptians as a commutation for thee' (חֲלִיפָךְ). So the Syriac, ' I gave Egypt *in thy place* ' (ܚܠܦܝܟ.). The true interpretation, therefore, is, that Egypt was regarded as having been given up to desolation and destruction

instead of the Israelites. One of them must perish ; and God chose that Egypt, though so much more mighty and powerful, should be reduced to desolation *in order* to deliver his people. They took their place, and were destroyed *instead* of the Hebrews, in order that they might be delivered from the bondage under which they groaned. This may be used as a striking *illustration* of the atonement made for sin, when the Lord Jesus, the expiatory offering, was made to suffer in the stead—ἄλλαγμα—of his people, and in order that sinners might live. And if God's giving up the Egyptians to destruction—themselves so guilty and deserving of death—in order to save his people, was a proof of his love for them, how much greater is the demonstration of his love when he gives his own holy Son to the bitter pains of death on a cross, in order that his church may be redeemed ! There has been much variety, as has already been intimated, in the interpretation of this, and in regard to the time and events referred to. It has, by many, been supposed to refer to the invasion by Sennacherib, who, when he was about to fall upon Jerusalem, turned his arms against the Egyptians and their allies, by which means Jerusalem was saved by devoting those nations to desolation. Vitringa explains it of Shalmaneser's design upon the kingdom of Judah, after he had destroyed that of Samaria, from which he was diverted by carrying the war against the Egyptians, Cusheans, and Sabeans. But of this, Lowth says, there is no clear proof in history. Secker supposes that it refers to the fact that Cyrus overcame those nations, and that they were given him for releasing the Jews. Lowth says, ' perhaps it may mean, generally, that God had often saved his people at the expense of other nations, whom he had as it were in their stead given up to destruction.' The exact historical facts in the case cannot be clearly made out ; nor is this to be wondered at, that many things of this nature should remain obscure for want of the light of history, which in regard to those times is extremely deficient. In regard to Egypt, however, I think the case is clear. Nothing is more manifest than that the prophet refers to that

4 Since thou wast precious in my sight, thou hast been honourable, and I have loved thee: therefore will I give men for thee, and people for thy [1] life.

5 Fear not; for I *am* with thee:

1 or, *person.*

---

great and wonderful fact—the commonplace illustration of the sacred writers—that the Egyptians were destroyed in order to effect the deliverance of the Jews, and were thus given as a ransom for them. ¶ *Ethiopia.* Heb. ' Cush.' In regard to this country, see Note on ch. xviii. 1. It is not improbable that the prophet here refers to the facts referred to in that chapter, and the destruction which it is there said would come upon that land. ¶ *And Seba.* This was the name of a people descended from Cush (Gen. x. 7); and hence the name of the country which they occupied. According to Josephus (*Ant.* ii. 10. 2), it seems to have been *Meroë,* a province of Ethiopia, distinguished for its wealth and commerce, surrounded by the two arms or branches of the Nile. There still remain the ruins of a metropolis of the same name, not far from the town of Shandy (Keppel's *Travels in Nubia and Arabia,* 1829). Meroë is a great island or peninsula in the north of Ethiopia, and is formed by the Nile, and the Astaboras, which unites with the Nile. It was probably anciently called *Seba,* and was conquered by Cambyses, the successor of Cyrus, and by him called *Meroë,* after his sister. That it was near to Ethiopia is apparent from the fact that it is mentioned in connection with it (comp. Ps. lxx. 10; Isa. xlv. 14;—Herod. iii. 20). They would naturally ally themselves to the Ethiopians, and share the same fate.

4. *Since thou wast precious in my sight.* This verse contains another reason why God would defend and deliver them. That reason was, that he had loved them as his people; and he was willing, therefore, that other people should be overcome in order that they might be saved. ¶ *Thou hast been honourable.* This does not refer so much to their personal character, as to the fact that they had been honoured by him with being the depository of the precious truths of his religion. It means that *he* had made them honourable by the favours bestowed on them; not that they were honourable

in reference to their own personal character and worth. ¶ *Therefore will I give men for thee.* As in the case of Egypt, Ethiopia, and Seba (ver. 3). He would cause other nations to be destroyed, if it were necessary, in order to effect their deliverance, and to restore them to their own land. We learn here —1. That nations and armies are in the hand of God, and at his disposal. 2. That his people are dear to his heart, and that it is his purpose to defend them. 3. That the revolutions among nations, the rise of one empire, and the fall of another, are often in order to promote the welfare of his church, to defend it in danger, and deliver it in time of calamity. 4. That his people should put the utmost confidence in God as being able to defend them, and as having formed a purpose to preserve and save them. Expressions similar to those used in this verse occur frequently among the Arabians (see Rosenmüller *in loco*). ¶ *For thy life.* Marg. 'Person.' Heb. ' For thy soul;' that is, on account of thee; or in thy place (see Notes on ver. 3).

5. *Fear not* (see Note on ch. xli. 10, 14; comp. ch. xliii. 1). ¶ *I will bring thy seed.* Thy children; thy descendants. The sense is, I will re-collect my scattered people from all parts of the world. The passage appears to have been taken from Deut. xxx. 3, where God promises to gather his people together again if they should be scattered among the nations, and should then repent. Vitringa understands this of the *spiritual* descendants of the Jews, or of those who should believe on the Messiah among the Gentiles, and who should *become* the people of God. But the more natural interpretation is, to refer it to the Jews who were scattered abroad during the exile at Babylon, and as a promise to re-collect them again in their own land. ¶ *From the east,* &c. From all parts of the earth; from all lands where they were scattered. That they were driven to other places than Babylon on the invasion of their land by the Chaldeans, is abundantly manifest in

I will bring thy seed from the east, and gather thee from the west;

6 I will say to the north, Give up ; and to the south, Keep not back : bring *a* my sons from far, and my daughters from the ends of the earth :

7 *Even* every one that is called by *b* my name : for I have created him for my glory, I have formed him ; yea, I have made *c* him.

8 Bring forth the blind *d* people that have eyes, and the deaf that have ears.

9 Let all the nations be gathered together, and let the people be assembled : who among them can declare this, and show us former things ? let them bring forth their witnesses that they may be justified : or let them hear, and say, *It is* truth.

a ch.18.7.   *b* Ja.2.7.   *c* Ep.2.10.   *d* Eze.12.2.

the historical records (Jer. ix. 16; Eze. v. 12; xvii. 21; Amos ix. 9; Zech. ii. 6).

6. *I will say to the north, Give up.* Give up my people, or restore them to their own land. ¶ *Bring my sons,* &c. Bring all my people from the distant lands where they have been driven in their dispersion. This is a beautiful passage. As if all lands were under the control of God, and he could at once command and they would obey, he calls on them to yield up his people to their own country. He issues a commandment which is heard in all quarters of the globe, and the scattered people of God come flocking again to their own land.

7. *Every one that is called by my name.* To be called by the name of any one, is synonymous with being regarded as his son, since a son bears the name of his father (see ch. xliv. 5; xlviii. 1). The expression, therefore, means here, all who were regarded as the children of God; and the promise is, that all such should be re-gathered to their own land. ¶ *For I have created him* (see Note on ver. 1). ¶ *For my glory.* In order to show forth, and illustrate my glory. They shall be, therefore, defended and protected ; and my glory shall be shown in their recovery and salvation.

8. *Bring forth the blind people.* Many have understood this of the Jews. So Vitringa, Rosenmüller, Grotius, and others understand it. But Lowth, more correctly, regards it as referring to the Gentiles. It is designed as an argument to show the superiority of God over all idols, and to demonstrate that he was able to deliver his people from

captivity and exile. He appeals, therefore (ver. 9), to his own people in proof of his divinity and power. None of the heathen (ver. 8) had been able to predict future events, none of the heathen gods, therefore, could save ; but JEHOVAH, who had so often foretold events that were fulfilled, *was* able to deliver, and of that fact his own people had had abundant evidence. ¶ *That have eyes.* They had natural faculties to see and know God (comp. Rom. i. 20), but they had not improved them, and they had, therefore, run into the sin and folly of idolatry. The phrase 'bring forth,' implies a solemn appeal made by God to them to enter into an argument on the subject (comp. Note on ch. xli. 1).

9. *Let all the nations be gathered together.* Let them be assembled to give evidence, or to adduce proofs that their idols are worthy of confidence (ch. xli. 1). ¶ *Who among them can declare this ?* Who among them *hath* predicted this state of things? Who has foretold the events which are now occurring? It is implied here, that JEHOVAH *had* done this, but none of the heathen gods had done it (see Note on ch. xli. 21). ¶ *And show us former things* (see Note on ch. xli. 22). The *order* of events, the manner in which one event shall succeed another. Not merely, who can declare *one single event,* but who can declare the *succession,* the *order* in which many events shall follow each other—a far more difficult thing than to declare one single future event. Neither had been done by the heathen ; both had been done by God. ¶ *That they may be justified.* That it may be demonstrated that they are what they pretend to be, and that they are worthy of the confi-

10 Ye *are* my witnesses, saith the LORD, and my servant *b* whom I have chosen: that ye may know and believe me, and understand that I *am* he: before me *c* there was no [1] God formed, neither shall there be after me.

11 I, *even* I, *am* the LORD ; and beside me *there* is no *d* Saviour.

12 I have declared and have saved, and I have showed, when *there was* no strange *god* among you: therefore ye *are* my witnesses, saith the LORD, that I *am* God.

a ch.44.8.   *b* Ph.2.7.   *c* Col.1.17.

1 or, *nothing formed of God.*   *d* Ho.13.4; Ac.4.12.

dence of men. The word 'justified' here, is used in the sense of being *right,* or *true ;*—let them in this manner show that their claims are just, and well founded. ¶ *Or let them hear, and say,* It is *truth* (see Note on ch. xli. 26).

10. *Ye* are *my witnesses.* They were his witnesses, because, first, he had given to them predictions of future events which had been literally fulfilled ; secondly, by his power of delivering them so often manifested, he had shown that he was a God able to save. Neither of these had been done by the idol-gods (comp. ch. xliv. 8). ¶ *And believe me.* Or rather, confide in me. ¶ *Before me there was no God formed.* I am the only true, the eternal God. In this expression, JEHOVAH says that he was the *first* being. He derived his existence from no one. Perhaps the Hebrew will bear a little more emphasis than is conveyed by our translation. 'Before me, God was not formed,' implying that *he* was God, and that he existed anterior to all other beings. It was an opinion among the Greeks, that the same gods had not always reigned, but that the more ancient divinities had been expelled by the more modern. It is possible that some such opinion may have prevailed in the oriental idolatry, and that God here means to say, in opposition to that, that he had not *succeeded* any other God in his kingdom. His dominion was original, underived, and independent. ¶ *Neither shall there be after me.* He would never cease to live; he would never vacate his throne for another. This expression is equivalent to that which occurs in the Book of Revelation, 'I am Alpha and Omega, the first and the last' (Rev. i. 11); and it is remarkable that this language, which obviously implies eternity, and which in Isaiah is used expressly to prove the

divinity of JEHOVAH, is, in the passage referred to in the Book of Revelation, applied no less unequivocally to the Lord Jesus Christ.

11. *I,* even *I,* am *the* LORD. The repetition of the pronoun ' I ' makes it emphatic. The design is, to affirm that there was no other being to whom the name ' JEHOVAH' appertained. There was no other one who had the attributes which the name involved ; there was, therefore, no other God. On the meaning of the word JEHOVAH, see Note on ch. i. 2. ¶ *And beside me* there *is no Saviour.* There is no one who can deliver from oppression, and captivity, and exile, such as the Jews suffered in Babylon ; there is no one but he who can save from sin, and from hell. All salvation, therefore, must come from God ; and if we obtain deliverance from temporal ills, or from eternal death, we must seek it from him.

12. *I have declared.* I have announced or predicted future events ; I have warned of danger ; I have marked out the path of safety. He had thus shown that he was the true God (see Note on ch. xli. 22, 23). ¶ *And have saved.* I have delivered the nation in former times of danger, and have thus shown that I would protect them. ¶ *And have showed.* Heb. ' Caused to hear.' I have made known future events, and have thus showed that I was God. ¶ *When* there was *no strange* god *among you.* Before the time when there was any idol in the nation, and when, therefore, it could not be pretended that deliverance was to be traced to any one but to JEHOVAH. The word 'god' here is not in the original, but is properly supplied. The word זָר is evidently used instead of אֵל זָר, as in Ps. xliv. 20 ; lxxxi. 9. It denotes a god that is worshipped by foreigners. The sense is, that their former deliverance

13 Yea, before the day *was*, I *am* he ; and *there is* none that can deliver out of my hand : I will work, and who *a* shall [1] let it ?

14 Thus saith the Lord, your

a ch.46.10.   [1] *turn it back.*

could in no sense be traced to any such foreign god. ¶ *Therefore, ye* are *my witnesses.* You who have so often been defended ; you who have the predictions respecting future events, can be appealed to as evidence that I am the only true God, able to deliver. The doctrine taught in this passage is, that God may appeal to his dealings with his people as a demonstration that he is the true God, and that he is faithful and able to deliver—an appeal which may be made to his church at large in view of its trials, persecutions, and deliverances ; and to every one who is his true friend and worshipper.

13. *Yea, before the day* was. Before the first day, or before the beginning of time ; from eternity. The LXX. render it correctly, 'Aπ' αρχης, and the Vulgate (*Ab initio*), 'From the beginning.' ¶ *I* am *he.* I am the same (ver. 10). ¶ *I will work.* I will accomplish my designs. ¶ *And who shall let it ?* Marg. as Heb. ' Turn it back.' The meaning is, ' Who can hinder it ?' And the doctrine taught here is—1. That God is from everlasting ; for if he was before *time*, he must have been eternal. 2. That he is unchangeably the same—a doctrine which is, as it is here designed to be used, the only sure foundation for the security of his people—for who can trust a being who is fickle, changing, vacillating ? 3. That he can deliver his people always, no matter what are their circumstances. 4. That he will accomplish all his plans ; no matter whether to save his people, or to destroy his foes. 5. That no one—man or devil—can hinder him. How can the feeble arm of a creature resist God ? 6. That opposition to him is as fruitless as it is wicked. If men wish for happiness, they must *fall in* with his plans, and aid in the furtherance of his designs.

14. *Thus saith the* Lord *your Redeemer.* This verse commences another argument for the safety of his people. It

Redeemer, the Holy One of Israel ; For your sake I have sent to Babylon, and have brought down all their nobles,[2] and the Chaldeans, whose cry *is* in the ships.

[2] *bars.*

is the assurance to the Jews in Babylon that he had sent to them a deliverer, and would bring down the pride of the Chaldeans, and demolish their city. ¶ *Your Redeemer* (see Note on ver. 1). ¶ *I have sent to Babylon.* That is, the Persians and Medes, under the command of Cyrus (comp. Note on ch. xiii. 3). This implies that God had command over all their armies and had the power of sending them where he pleased (comp. Notes on ch. x. 5, 6). This is to be understood as seen by the prophet in vision. He sees the armies of Cyrus encompass Babylon and the haughty city fall, and then says that God had sent or directed them there. ¶ *And have brought down all their nobles.* Marg. 'Bars.' But the word in this place probably means neither, but rather *fugitives* (comp. Notes on ch. xxvii. 1). The word used (בְּרִיחִם, *bărĭăhh*) means sometimes *bar, cross-bar*, that which passed from one side of the tabernacle to the other through rings, in order to carry it ; then a bar, or bolt of any kind (Judg. xvi. 3 ; Neh. iii. 3). But the word may also denote one who flies ; a fugitive ; and is properly used in that sense here. The verb בָּרַח, from which the word is derived, means often *to break away, to flee* (Gen. xvi. 8 ; xxxv. 1, 7 ; 1 Sam. xix. 12 ; Job xxvii. 22 ; Jonah i. 3). Here it means those who endeavoured to escape from the impending calamity and destruction ; or it *may* refer to those who had taken refuge in Babylon from other lands, as Babylon was doubtless composed in part of those who had sought a refuge there from other nations—a conflux of strangers. But the former is the more probable interpretation ; and the idea seems to be, that Jehovah had brought them down to their ships, or had led them to take refuge in their ships from the impending judgments. Jerome, however, understands it of removing the strong bars with which the prisoners of the exile Jews were protected, so that they

15 I *am* the LORD, your Holy One, the Creator of Israel, your King.

would be permitted to go forth in peace and safety. Lowth renders it, ' I will bring down all her strong bars.' The LXX. render it, Φεύγοντες πάντας—' All that fly.' So the Syriac. ¶ *And the Chaldeans*. The inhabitants of Babylon. ¶ *Whose cry is in the ships*. Lowth renders this, ' Exulting in their ships.' Noyes, ' Ships of their delight.' The Vulgate, ' Glorying in their ships.' The LXX. ' The Chaldeans shall be bound (δεθήσονται) in ships.' The Syriac, ' Who glory in their ships.' The sense is, probably, that the Chaldeans, when their city was taken, would seek to take refuge in their ships in which they would raise a shout (Rosenmüller). Or it may be, as Lowth supposes, that it was one of the characteristics of the Chaldeans, that they boasted of their ships, and of their commerce. Babylon was, as he remarks, favourably situated to be a commercial and naval power. It was on the large river Euphrates, and hence had access to the Persian Gulf and the ocean; and there can be no doubt that it was engaged, in the height of its power, in commercial enterprises. On the north of the city, the Euphrates was united to the Tigris by the canal called Nahar Malca or the Royal River, and thus a large part of the produce of the northern countries, as far as the Euxine and Caspian seas, naturally descended to Babylon (Herod. i. 194). Semiramis, the founder of Babylon, is said to have had a fleet of three thousand galleys. After the taking of the city by Cyrus, we hear indeed little of the commerce of Babylon. The Euphrates was diverted from its course, and spread over the adjacent country; and the Persian monarchs, in order to prevent the danger of invasion from that quarter, purposely obstructed the navigation, by making dams across both the Tigris and the Euphrates (Strabo xvi.) It is not to be deemed remarkable, therefore, that, in the times of its prosperity, the city of Babylon should be noted for its commerce; or as a city exulting in its shipping, or raising the sailor's cry—a cry

16 Thus saith the LORD, which maketh *a* a way in the sea, and a path in the mighty waters:

a Ex.14.16,22; Ps.77.19.

such as is heard in any port now where shipping abounds. The word rendered ' cry ' (רִנָּה) denotes properly *a shout of rejoicing* or joy (1 Kings xxii. 36; Ps. xxxi. 6; xlii. 5); and then also a mournful cry, an outcry, wailing (Ps. xvii. 1; lxi. 2). Here it may mean the joyful cry of commerce; the shout of the mariner as he leaves the port, or as he returns to his home—the shout, the clamour, which is heard at the wharfs of a commercial city. Such a cry is alluded to by Virgil in the naval games which Æneas celebrated:—

—— ferit athera clamor
Nauticus. *Æneid*, v. 140, 1.

The sense here is, that God had sent to bring down that exulting city, and to destroy all the indications of its commercial importance and prosperity.

15. *I* am *the* LORD. I am JEHOVAH—proved to be such, as the connection demands that we should interpret this, by sending to Babylon and bringing down your oppressors. This interposition in destroying Babylon would be a demonstration that he was JEHOVAH, the only true God, and their God. ¶ *The Creator of Israel* (see Note on ver. 1). ¶ *Your King*. Ruling over you, and showing the right to do it by delivering you from your foes.

16. *Thus saith the* LORD. This verse contains a reference to the deliverance from Egyptian servitude — the great storehouse of argument and illustration with the sacred writers; the standing demonstration of God's merciful interposition in behalf of their nation, and proof that he was their God. ¶ *Which maketh*. Whose characteristic it is to open a path of safety for his people even when deep and rapid floods are before them. The standing proof of this, which undoubtedly the prophet had in his eye, was the deliverance from Egypt. Still, I think, he did not mean to refer to that alone, but to that as an illustration of what God was, and had ever been to his people. ¶ *A way in the sea*. Referring to the path made through the waters

17 Which bringeth forth the chariot and horse, the army, and the power; they shall lie down together, they shall not rise: they are extinct, they are quenched as tow.

18 Remember ye not the former things, neither consider the things of old.

19 Behold, I will do a new thing:

now it shall spring forth; shall ye not know it? I will even make a way in the wilderness, *and* rivers in the desert.

20 The beast of the field shall honour me, the dragons and the owls:[1] because I gave waters in the wilderness, *and* rivers in the desert, to give drink to my people, my chosen.

1 *daughters of the owl,* or, *ostriches.*

---

of the Red Sea when the children of Israel were permitted to go on dry ground.

17. *Which bringeth forth the chariot and horse.* The reference here is, undoubtedly, to the occurrences which are recorded in Ex. xiv. 4, *sq.*, when Pharaoh and his host are said to have followed the Israelites, but were all submerged in the sea. God is said to have brought them forth in accordance with the general statement so often made, that he controls and directs princes and nations (see Notes on ch. x. 5, 6). ¶ *They shall lie down together.* They shall sink together to death, as Pharaoh and his army sunk together in a watery grave.

Thou didst blow with thy wind, the sea covered them;
They sank as lead in the mighty waters.
　　　　　　　　　　　Ex. xv. 10.

The depths have covered them:
They sank into the bottom as a stone.
　　　　　　　　　　　Ex. xv. 5.

¶ *They are extinct.* They are destroyed, as the wick of a lamp is quenched suddenly when immersed in water. This is a striking figure, to denote the suddenness with which it was done, and the completeness of their destruction. As a flame is entirely put out when plunged beneath the water, so the whole host of the Egyptians were suddenly and completely destroyed in the Red Sea. The sentiment in this verse is, that God has power over the nations to control them; that it is one of his characteristics to lead on the enemies of his people to destruction; and that they are suddenly destroyed, and their hopes, and joys, and triumphs put out for ever. If it was so in regard to the Egyptians, it will be also in regard to all his foes. And if this took place in regard to a nation, it

shall also in regard to individual sinners who oppose themselves to God.

How oft is the candle of the wicked put out?
And how oft cometh their destruction upon them?
God distributeth sorrows in his anger.
They are as stubble before the wind,
And as chaff that the storm carrieth away.
　　　　　　　　　　　Job xxi. 17, 18.

18. *Remember ye not,* &c. So great and wonderful shall be God's future interpositions in your behalf, that what he has done, great as that was, shall be comparatively forgotten. ¶ *The former things.* The deliverance from Egypt, and the overthrow of his enemies there. ¶ *The things of old.* The things that were formerly done.

19. *I will do a new thing.* Something that has not hitherto occurred, some unheard of and wonderful event, that shall far surpass all that he had formerly done (see Note on ch. xlii. 9). ¶ *Now it shall spring forth* (see Note on ch. xlii. 9). It shall spring up as the grass does from the earth; or it shall *bud forth* like the opening leaves and flowers—a beautiful figure, denoting the manner in which the events of Divine Providence come to pass. ¶ *I will even make a way in the wilderness.* In this part of the verse, the prophet describes the anxious care which God would show in protecting his people, and providing for them in conducting them to their native land. See the expressions fully explained in the Notes on ch. xli. 17–19.

20. *The beast of the field shall honour me.* The sense of this passage is plain, and the image is highly poetical and beautiful. God would pour such copious floods of waters through the waste sandy deserts to supply his people, that even the wild beasts would be sensible of his

21 This people have I formed for myself; they shall *a* show forth my praise.

22 But thou hast not called upon me, O Jacob; but thou hast been weary *b* of me, O Israel.

a Ep.1.6,12.   *b* Mal.1.13.

23 Thou hast not brought me the small[1] cattle of thy burnt-offerings; neither hast thou honoured me with thy sacrifices: I have not caused thee to *c* serve with an offering, nor wearied thee with incense.

[1] *lambs,* or, *kids.*   *c* Mat. 11.30.

---

abundant goodness, and would break forth into thanksgiving and praise for the unusual supply. ¶ *The dragons* (see Note on ch. xiii. 22). The LXX. render the word here used (תַּנִּים *tănnīm*), by σειρῆνες—'sirens'—among the ancients a marine monster that was fabled to use sweet and alluring tones of music. It is probable, however, that the LXX. understood here some species of wild-fowl which responded to one another. The Syriac translator here interprets it as denoting some wild animal of the canine species—a wood-dog. ¶ *And the owls.* Marg. as Heb. 'Daughters of the owl, or ostrich' (see Note on ch. xiii. 21).

21. *This people have I formed for myself.* To preserve the remembrance of my name; to transmit the knowledge of the true God to future times, and to celebrate my praise (see Notes on ver. 1). ¶ *They shall show forth my praise.* They shall celebrate my goodness; or, by their restoration to their own land, they shall show manifestly that they are my people.

22. *But thou hast not called upon me.* The design of this and the following verses, is to show them that they were indebted to the Divine mercy alone for their deliverance from bondage. It was not because they had been either meritorious or faithful; it was not because they had deserved these favours at his hand; for they had been a people that had been distinguished for neglecting their God. On that account, these calamities had come upon them, and their deliverance, therefore, was to be an act of mere unmerited favour. ¶ *Thou hast been weary.* As a people, you have been weary of my service. They had accounted his laws grievous and oppressive; and they had groaned under what they regarded as burdensome rites and ceremonies (see Amos viii. 5, 6; Mal. i. 13). God here refers, doubtless, to the times before the captivity, and is

stating what was the general characteristic of the people.

23. *Thou hast not brought me.* As a people you have withheld from me the sacrifices which were commanded. They had not maintained and observed his worship as he had required. ¶ *The small cattle.* Marg. 'Lambs,' or 'kids.' The Hebrew word (שֶׂה) denotes properly one of a flock—a sheep or a goat. It should have been so rendered here. These animals were used for burnt-offerings, and the Jews were required to offer them daily to God. ¶ *Of thy burnt-offerings* (comp. Ex. xxix. 38; Num. xxviii. 3). The burnt-offering was wholly consumed on the altar. ¶ *With thy sacrifices.* Bloody offerings. There is little difference between this word and that rendered 'burnt-offerings.' If there is any, it is that the word rendered 'sacrifice' (זֶבַח) is of wider signification, and expresses sacrifice in general; the word rendered 'burnt-offering' (עֹלָה), denotes that which is consumed, or which *ascends* as an offering. The holocaust refers to its being burned; the sacrifice to the offering, however made. ¶ *I have not caused thee to serve with an offering.* 'I have not made *a slave* of thee; I have not exacted such a service as would be oppressive and intolerable—such as is imposed on a slave.' The word here used (עָבַד), is often used in such a sense, and with such a reference (Lev. xxv. 39); 'Thou shalt not compel him to serve the service of a bondman' (Ex. i. 14; Jer. xxii. 13; xxv. 14; xxx. 8). The sense is, that the laws of God on the subject, were not grievous and oppressive. ¶ *With an offering.* The word here used (מִנְחָה *mĭnhhâ*) denotes properly a *bloodless* oblation, and is thus distinguished from those mentioned before. It consisted of flour mingled with salt, oil, and incense; or of the fruits of

24 Thou hast bought me no sweet cane with money, neither hast thou ¹filled me with the fat of thy sacrifices: but thou hast made me to serve with thy sins, thou hast wearied *a* me with thine iniquities.

1 *made me drunk*, or, *abundantly moistened.*
a Mal.1.17.

the earth, &c. (see Notes on ch. i. 11; comp. Lev. ii. 2; Num. xxviii. 5.) ¶ *Nor wearied thee.* By exacting incense. I have not so exacted it as to make it burdensome and wearisome to you. ¶ *With incense* (see Note on ch. i. 13). The word לְבֹנָה (Gr. λίβανος) denotes properly *frankincense*, a substance so called from its white colour, from לָבַן, *to be white.* It is found in Arabia (Isa. lx. 6; Jer. vi. 20), and in Palestine (Cant. iv. 6; 14), and was obtained by making incisions in the bark of trees. It was much used in worship among the Jews as well as by other nations. It was *burned* in order to produce an agreeable fragrance (Ex. xxx. 8; xxxvii. 29; Lev. xvi. 13).

24. *Thou hast bought me.* You have not purchased this—implying that it was not produced in Palestine, but was an article of commerce. It was to be obtained only from abroad. This is expressly affirmed in Jer. vi. 20: 'To what purpose cometh there to me incense from Sheba, *and the sweet cane from a far country?*' That it was an article of commerce is also apparent from Ezek. xxvii. 19: 'Dan also and Javan going to and fro occupied in thy fairs (*i.e.* Tyre): bright iron, cassia, and calamus (קָנֶה), were in thy market.' ¶ *Sweet cane.* The word here used (קָנֶה), denotes properly *cane, reed, calamus* (Gr. κάννα and κάννη, Latin *canna*, whence the English *cane*, Fr. *canne*, It. *canna*). It usually refers to a reed growing in wet or marshy ground. It denotes also sweet cane, *calamus aromaticus.* It is sometimes joined with the word בֹּשֶׂם (*bōsĕm*), aromatic, odour, fragrance, spice, as in Ex. xxx. 23; see also Jer. vi. 20. According to Pliny (xii. 22) it grew in Arabia, Syria, and India; according to Theophrastus, in the vales of Lebanon (*Hist. Plant.* ix. 7). It was used among the Hebrews in compounding the sacred perfumes (Ex. xxx. 23). It is a knotty root, of a reddish colour, and contains a soft white pith—in resemblance probably not unlike the calamus so well known in this country. Strabo and Diodorus Siculus say that it grew in Saba. Hasselquist says that it is common in the deserts of the two Arabias. It is gathered near Jambo, a port town of Arabia Petrea, from whence it is brought into Egypt. The Venetians purchase it, and use it in the composition of their *theriaca.* It is much esteemed among the Arabs on account of its fragrance. *See* Calmet (Art. *Cane*), and Gesenius (*Lex.* and *Comm. in loco*). It was not probably used in the worship of God anywhere except among the Hebrews. The heathens made use of incense, but I do not know that they used the calamus. ¶ *Neither hast thou filled me.* Marg. 'Made me drunk,' or 'abundantly moistened.' The word here used (רָוָה *rāvâ*), means properly *to drink to the full*, to be satisfied, sated with drink. See it explained in the Notes on ch. xxxiv. 6. It is applied to water which is drank, or to *fat* which is sucked in or drank rather than eaten (Ps. xxxvi. 9); or to a sword as drinking up blood. Here it means to satiate, or to satisfy. They had not offered the fat of sacrifices so as to satiate God. Probably this passage does not mean that the Jews had wholly neglected the public worship of God; they had not worshipped him with a proper spirit, and had thus served him with their sins, and wearied him with their transgressions. It is true, also, that while they were abundant in external rites and ceremonies, they frequently made oblations to idols, rather than to the true God. Perhaps, therefore, an emphasis is to be placed on the word 'me' in this passage, meaning, that however diligent and regular they had been in the performance of the external rites and duties of religion, yet that *God* had been neglected. ¶ *Thou hast made me to serve with thy sins.* You have made it oppressive, burdensome, wearisome for me, like the hard and onerous service of a

25 I, *even* I, *am* he that blotteth out *a* thy transgressions for mine own *b* sake, and will not remember thy *c* sins.

26 Put me in remembrance : let us plead together : declare thou, that thou mayest be *d* justified.

a Je.50.20.   *b* Eze 36.22,32.   *c* Je.31.34.   *d* Ro.8.33.

slave (see Note on ver. 23; comp. Note on ch. i. 14).

25. *I, ever I, am he.* This verse contains a gracious assurance that their sins would be blotted out, and the reason why it would be done. The pronoun 'I' is repeated to make it emphatic, as in ver. 11. Perhaps also God designs to show them the evil of the sins which are mentioned in the previous verses, by the assurance that they were committed against him who alone could forgive, and who had promised them pardon. The passage also reminds them, that it was God alone who *could* pardon the sins of which, as a nation, they had been guilty. ¶ *That blotteth out thy transgressions.* This metaphor is taken from the custom of keeping accounts, where, when a debt is paid, the charge is blotted or cancelled. Thus God says he blotted out the sins of the Jews. He cancelled them. He forgave them. Of course, when forgiven, punishment could not be exacted, and he would treat them as pardoned ; *i.e.*, as his friends. ¶ *For mine own sake.* Not because you deserve it, or have any claim, or that it would not be right to punish you. Not even primarily to promote your happiness and salvation, but for *my* sake ; 1. To show the benevolence of my character ; 2. To promote my glory by your forgiveness and salvation (see Ezek. xxxvi. 22). ¶ *And will not remember thy sins.* They shall be forgiven. Hezekiah (xxxviii. 17) expresses the same idea by saying 'thou hast cast all my sins behind thy back.' We may learn from this verse—1. That it is God only who can pardon sin. How vain, then, is it for man to attempt it ! How wicked for man to claim the prerogative! And yet it is an essential part of the papal system that the Pope and his priests have the power of remitting the penalty of transgression. 2. That this is done by God *solely* for his own sake. It is not (*a.*) because we have any *claim* to it ; for then it would not be pardon, but justice. It is not (*b.*)

because we have any power to compel God to forgive ; for who can contend with him, and how could mere *power* procure pardon? It is not (*c.*) because we have any *merit* ; for *then* also it would be justice, and we *have* no merit. Nor is it (*d.*) primarily in order that we may be happy ; for our happiness is a matter not worthy to be named, compared with the honour of God. But it is solely for his own sake—to promote his glory—to show his perfections—to evince the greatness of his mercy and compassion —and to show his boundless and eternal love. 3. They who *are* pardoned should live to his glory, and not to themselves. For *that* they were forgiven, and it should be the grand purpose of their lives so to live as to show forth the goodness, compassion, and love of that merciful Being who has blotted out their sins. 4. If men are ever pardoned, they must come to God—and to God alone. They must come, not to *justify* themselves, but to confess their crimes. And they must come with a willingness that God should pardon them on just such terms as he pleases ; at just such a time as he pleases ; *and solely with a view to the promotion of his own glory.* Unless they have this feeling, they never *can* be forgiven, nor *should* they be forgiven.

26. *Put me in remembrance.* That is, urge all the arguments in your own defence which you can urge. State everything in self-vindication which can be stated. The language here is taken from the practice of courts when a cause is on trial ; and God urges them on *their* side, to urge all in self-vindication which they can urge. On *his* part, he alleged that the princes and rulers of the nation had sinned (ver. 27) ; that the whole nation had transgressed (ver. 23, 24), and that for this they were justly punished (ver. 28). He here urges them to advance all in self-defence which they could—if they could pretend that He had forgotten anything ; that they had merits which he had not considered ; or that he had charged them with crime

27 Thy first father hath sinned,

1 *interpreters.*

and thy [1]teachers have transgressed against me.

with undue severity. ¶ *Let us plead together.* Heb. ' Let us be judged together ' (see Note on ch. xli. 1). ¶ *Declare thou, that thou mayest be justified.* That you may show that you are just, or righteous; that you may demonstrate that you are unjustly accused of crime, and punished with undue severity.

27. *Thy first father hath sinned.* This is the argument on the side of God, to show that they were neither unjustly punished, nor punished with undue severity. The argument is, that their rulers and teachers had been guilty of crime, and that therefore it was right to bring all this vengeance upon the nation. Various interpretations have been given of the phrase ' thy first father.' A slight notice of them will lead to the correct exposition. 1. Many have supposed that *Adam* is here referred to. Thus Piscator, Calovius, and most of the fathers, understand it; and, among the Jews, Kimchi. But the objections to this are plain. (*a.*) Adam was not peculiarly the first father or ancestor of the Jews, but of the whole human race. (*b.*) The Jews never boasted, or gloried in him as the founder of their nation, but they always referred to Abraham under this appellation (Mat. iii. 9; John viii. 33, 39). (*c.*) It would have been irrelevant to the design of the prophet to have referred to the sin of Adam in this case. God was vindicating his own cause and conduct in destroying their capital and temple, and in sending them as captives to a distant land. How would it prove that he was right in this, to say that Adam was a transgressor? How would it demonstrate his justice *in these peculiar inflictions* of his anger to refer to the apostacy of the ancestor of the whole human race? 2. Others refer it to Abraham. This was the sentiment of Jerome, and of some others; and by those who maintain this opinion, it is supposed to refer to his doubting the truth of the promise (Gen. xv. 8); or to the denial of his wife, and his sin in inducing her to say that she was his sister (Gen. xii. 11; xx. 2); or to the fact that when young he was an idolater.

But the obvious objection to this is, that Abraham is everywhere in the Scriptures proposed as an example of one eminently devoted to God; nor could it be said that these calamities had come upon them in consequence of his unfaithfulness, and his sins. 3. Others refer it to the rulers and princes individually. Thus Grotius refers it to Manasseh; Aben Ezra to Jeroboam, &c. 4. Others, as Vitringa, refer it to the high priest, and particularly to Uriah, who lived in the time of Ahaz, and particularly to the fact, that, in obedience to the command of Ahaz, he constructed an altar in Jerusalem like the one which he had seen and admired in Damascus (2 Kings xvi. 10–16). The objection to this interpretation is, that no reason can be given for selecting *this* particular act from a number of similar abominations on the part of the priests and rulers, as the cause of the national calamities. It was only one instance out of many of the crimes which brought the national judgments upon them. 5. Others, as Gesenius, suppose that the word is to be taken *collectively*, not as referring to any particular individual, but to the high priests in general. It is not uncommon to give the name ' father ' thus to a principal man among a people, and especially to one eminent in religious authority. The word ' first ' here does not refer to *time*, but to *rank;* not the ancestor of the people, but the one having appropriately the title of father, who had the priority also in rank. The LXX. render it, Οἱ πατέρες ὑμῶν πρῶτοι. It refers therefore, probably, to the character of the presiding officers in religion, and means that the priests, supreme in rank, and whose example was so important, had sinned; that there was irreligion at the very foundation of influence and authority; and that therefore it was necessary to bring these heavy judgments on the nation. No one acquainted with the history of the Jewish people in the times immediately preceding the captivity, can doubt that this was the character of the high priesthood.

[Gesenius and some others give the words a

28 Therefore I have profaned the | given Jacob to the curse, and Israel
princes [1] of the sanctuary, and have | to reproaches.

1 or, *holy princes.*

collective sense, as signifying either the succession of priests or ancestors in general. The interpretation which understands the phrase of Abraham, is supposed by some to be at variance with the uniform mention of that patriarch in terms of commendation. But these terms are perfectly consistent with the proposition that *he was a sinner,* which may here be the exact sense of חָטָא. To the application of the phrase to Adam, it has been objected, that he was not peculiarly the father of the Jews. To this it may be answered, that if the guilt of the national progenitor would prove the point in question, much more would it be established by the fact of their belonging to a guilty race. At the same time it may be considered as implied, that all their fathers, who had since lived, shared in the original depravity; and thus the same sense is obtained that would have been expressed by the collective explanation of *first father,* while the latter is still taken in its strict and full sense, as denoting the progenitor of all mankind.—Alexander.]

¶ *And thy teachers.* Marg. ' Interpreters.' The word here used (מְלִצֶּיךָ) is derived from לוּץ. This word means *to stammer,* to speak unintelligibly; and then to speak in a foreign and barbarous language, and then to interpret, from the idea of speaking a foreign tongue. Hence it may be used in the sense of an *internuncius,* or a messenger (2 Chron. xxxii. 31; comp. Notes on Job xxxiii. 23). That it refers here to the priests, there can be no doubt, and is properly applied to them because they sustained the office of *interpreting* his will to the people, and generally of acting as *internuncii* or messengers between God and them. The LXX. render it, Ἄρχοντες —' Rulers.'

28. *Therefore I have profaned.* The princes of the sanctuary, *i.e.,* the priests, were by their office regarded as sacred, or set apart to the service of God. To depose them from that office, to subject them to punishment, and to send them into captivity, was, therefore, regarded as *profaning* them. They were stripped of their office, and robes, and honours, and reduced to the same condition, and compelled to meet with the same treatment, as the common people. The

sense is, that he *had made them common* (for so the word חָלַל is used in Ex. xxxi. 14; xix. 22; Lev. xix. 8; xxi. 9; Mal. i. 12; ii. 2); he did not regard their office; he used them all alike. ¶ *The princes of the sanctuary.* Marg. ' Holy princes.' It means, either those who presided over and directed the services of the sanctuary, called in 1 Chron. xxiv. 5, ' governors of the sanctuary ;' or those who were holy in office. The LXX. render it, Οἱ ἄρχοντες τὰ ἅγια μου —' Who preside over my holy things,' or my sanctuary. Vulg. *Principes sanctos*—' Holy princes.' The Syriac, ' Thy princes have profaned the sanctuary.' The sense is, that God had disregarded the official character of those who were set apart to the sacred office, and had punished them in common with the people at large for their sins. ¶ *And have given Jacob to the curse.* The LXX. render it, ' I have given Jacob to be destroyed ' (ἀπωλέσαι). The Hebrew word here (חֵרֶם *hherĕm*), is that which is commonly used to denote a solemn *anathema,* excommunication, or devotion to destruction (see Note on ch. xxxiv. 5). ¶ *To reproaches.* The reproach, contempt, and scorn which they met with in their captivity, and in a land of strangers (comp. Ps. cxxxvii. 3, 4).

Thus far God states the reasons why he had punished the nation. It had been on account of the national irreligion and sins, and the destruction had come upon all, but pre-eminently on the priests and the rulers. In the arbitrary division which is made in the Bible into chapters, a very improper separation has been made by making the chapter close here. The sense of the whole passage is materially injured by this division, and the scope of the whole argument is forgotten. The design of the entire argument is, to show that God would not leave his people ; that though he punished them, he would not utterly destroy them ; and that he would appear again for their rescue, and restore them to their own land. This argument is prosecuted in the

CHAPTER XLIV.

ANALYSIS.

It has already been observed (Note on ch. xliii. 28), that the commencement of this chapter is properly a continuation and completion of the argument commenced there; and that the division should have been made at what is now the close of the fifth verse of this chapter. This chapter may be divided into the following parts:—

I. The assurance that though they had sinned (ch. xliii. 23-28) God would have mercy on them, and would restore them to his favour, and to their land (1-5). They had nothing to fear (1, 2): God would bless their offspring, and they should grow and flourish like willows by the waters (3-5), and there should be among them a general turning to the LORD, and devotion to his service (5).

II. An argument to show that JEHOVAH was the true God; and a severe and most sarcastic reproof of idolatry—designed to reprove idolaters, and to lead the people to put their confidence in JEHOVAH (6-20). This argument consists of the following parts—1. A solemn assertion of JEHOVAH himself, that there was no other God (6). 2. An appeal to the fact that he only had foretold future events, and that he only could do it (7, 8). 3. A sarcastic statement of the manner in which idols were made, and of course, the folly of worshipping them (9-20).

III. The assurance that JEHOVAH would deliver his people from all their calamities and oppressions (21-28). This part contains—1. The *assurance* that he would do it, and that their sins were blotted out (21, 22). 2. A calling upon the heavens and the earth to rejoice over so great and glorious an event (23). 3. An appeal to what JEHOVAH *had* done, and *could* do, as an evidence that he could deliver his people, to wit: he had formed the heavens—he had made the earth without aid—he made diviners mad—he frustrated the plans of the wise, and he had confirmed the promises which he had made by his servants (24-26); he said to Jerusalem that it should be inhabited, and the cities of Judah that they should be rebuilt; he had dried up the rivers; and he had raised up Cyrus for the express purpose of delivering his people (26-28); and by all this, it should be known that he would visit, and vindicate, and restore them.

YET now hear, O Jacob, my servant; and Israel, whom I have chosen:

2 Thus saith the LORD that made thee, and formed thee from the womb, *which* will help *a* thee; Fear not, O Jacob, my servant; and thou, *b* Jeshurun, *c* whom I have chosen.

a Ps.46.5; He.4.16. *b* De.32.15. *c* Ro.8.30.

following chapter; and in the commencement of that chapter the thought is pursued, that though God had thus punished them, yet he would appear and save them. The beginning of that chapter is properly the continuation and completion of the argument urged here, and *this* chapter should have closed at what is now the fifth verse of chapter xliv.

CHAPTER XLIV.

1. *Yet now hear.* This should be read in immediate connection with the previous chapter. 'Notwithstanding you have sinned, *yet* now hear the gracious promise which is made in regard to your deliverance.'

2. *Thus saith the* LORD *that made thee* (see Note on ch. xliii. 1). ¶ *And formed thee from the womb.* This is equivalent to the declaration that he was their Maker, or Creator. It means, that from the very beginning of their history as a people, he had

formed and moulded all their institutions, and directed all things in regard to them—as much as he is the former of the body from the commencement of its existence. It may be observed that the words, 'from the womb,' are joined by some interpreters with the phrase, 'that formed thee,' meaning, that he had been the originator of all their customs, privileges, and laws, from the beginning of their history; and by others with the phrase, 'will help thee,' meaning, that from the commencement of their existence as a nation, he had been their helper. According to the Masoretic marks of distinction, the former is the true sense. So the LXX., Aben Ezra, Kimchi, Lowth, &c.; but Jerome, Luther, and some others, prefer the latter mode. ¶ *Fear not* (see Note on ch. xli. 10). Though you have sinned as a people (ch. xliii. 23, 24, 27), and though all these heavy judgments have

3 For *a*1 will pour water upon him that is thirsty, and floods upon the dry ground; 1 will pour my Spirit upon thy seed, *b* and my blessing upon thine offspring.

a Jn.7.38.　　　　*b* ch.59.21.

come upon you (ch. xliii. 28), yet you have no reason to fear that God will finally abandon and destroy you. ¶ *And thou Jeshurun* (יְשֻׁרוּן). This word occurs but four times in the Bible, as a poetical name for the people of Israel, apparently expressing affection and tenderness (Deut. xxxii. 15; xxxiii. 5, 26; and in this place). It is, says Gesenius (*Comm. in loc.*), 'a flattering appellation (*schmeichelwort*) for Israel,' and is probably a diminutive from יָשׁוּר = יָשָׁר *yâshūr=yâshôr*, the passive form in an intransitive verb with an active signification. The ending וֹן *ōn*, he adds, is *terminatio charitiva*—a termination indicating affection, or kindness. In his *Lexicon*, he observes, however (as translated by Robinson), that 'it seems not improbable that it was a diminutive form of the name יִשְׂרָאֵל (*Israel*), which was current in common life for the fuller form יִשְׂרָאֵלוּן (*Israelun*), a title of affection for Israel, but, like other common words of this sort, contracted, and more freely inflected, so as at the same time to imply an allusion to the signification of *right* or *uprightness*, contained in the root יָשַׁר.' Jerome renders it, *Rectissime*— 'Most upright.' The LXX. render it, Ἠγαπημένος Ἰσραὴλ—'Beloved Israel.' The Syriac renders it, 'Israel.' So also the Chaldee. It is, doubtless, a title of affection, and probably includes the notion of uprightness, or integrity.

3. *For I will pour water*. Floods, rivers, streams, and waters, are often used in the Scriptures, and especially in Isaiah, to denote plenteous Divine blessings, particularly the abundant influences of the Holy Spirit (see Note on ch. xxxv. 6, 7). That it here refers to the Holy Spirit and his influences, is proved by the parallel expressions in the subsequent part of the verse. ¶ *Upon him that is thirsty.* Or rather, ' on the thirsty land.' The word צָמָא refers here rather to land, and the *figure* is taken from a burning sandy desert, where waters would be made to burst out in copious streams (see ch. xxxv. 6, 7). The sense is, that God would bestow blessings upon them as signal and marvellous, as if floods of waters were made to descend on the dry, parched, and desolated earth. ¶ *And floods.* The word נוֹזְלִים, from נָזַל, *to flow*, to run as liquids, means properly *flowings*, and is used for streams and rivers (Ex. xv. 8; Ps. lxxviii. 16; Prov. v. 15; Jer. xviii.) It means here that the spiritual influences which would descend on the afflicted, desolate, comfortless, and exiled people, would be like torrents of rain poured on the thirsty earth. This beautiful figure is common in the Scriptures :

He shall come down like rain upon the grass,
And as showers that water the earth.
Ps. lxxii. 6.

My doctrine shall drop as the rain
My speech shall distil as the dew,
As the small rain upon the tender herb,
And as the showers upon the grass.
Deut. xxxii. 2.

¶ *I will pour my Spirit upon thy seed* (see ch. lix. 21). This is in accordance with the promises everywhere made in the Bible to the people of God (see Gen. xii. 7; xiii. 15; xv. 18; xvii. 7, 8; Ex. xx. 6; Deut. vii. 9; Ps. lxxxix. 4; Isa. xliii. 5). It may be regarded, first, as a promise of the richest blessings to them as parents—since there is to a parent's heart no prospect so consoling as that which relates to his offspring; and, secondly, as an assurance of the perpetuity of their religion; of their return from captivity, and their restoration to their own land.

4. *And they shall spring up.* The idea is, that as plants and trees planted by water-courses, and in well-watered fields, grow and flourish, so should their children grow in virtue, hope, piety, and zeal. ¶ *As among the grass.* They shall spring up and flourish as the grass does when abundantly watered from heaven. On the meaning of the unusual form of the word בְּבֵין, in the Hebrew (*in among*), see Vitringa and Rosenmüller. The בְ here is undoubtedly an

4 And they shall spring up *a as* among the grass, as willows by the water-courses.

5 One *b* shall say, I am the LORD's; and another shall call

a Ac.2 41.

himself by the name of Jacob; and another shall subscribe *with* his hand unto the LORD, and sur-name *himself* by the name of Israel.

b Je.50.5; 2 Co.8.5.

error of the transcriber for כ (*as*)—an error which, from the similarity of the letters, might be readily made. The LXX. read it, 'Ω;—' As.' The Chaldee reads it, כ (*as*). ¶ *As willows by the water-courses.* Willows are usually planted in such places, and grow rapidly and luxuriantly. It denotes here, abundant increase, vigour and beauty ; and means that their posterity would be greatly blessed of God. A similar figure to denote the prosperity and happiness of the righteous occurs in Ps. i. 3 :

And he shall be like a tree planted by the rivers
    of water,
That bringeth forth his fruit in his season;
His leaf also shall not wither.

These two verses teach us—1. That God will pour his blessings on the children of his people—a promise which in all ages, when parents are faithful, is abundantly fulfilled. 2. That one of the richest blessings which can be imparted to a people is, that God's Spirit should descend on their children. 3. That the Spirit of God alone is the source of true happiness and prosperity to our children. All else—property, learning, accomplishment, beauty, vigour, will be vain. It is by his blessing only —by the influence of piety—that they will spring forth as among the grass, and like willows by the streams of water. 4. Parents should pray earnestly for a revival of religion. No better description can be given of a revival than that given here—the Spirit of God descending like streams and floods on the young ; and their springing forth in the graces of piety as among the grass, and growing in love to God and love to men like willows by the water-courses. Who would not pray for such a work of grace ? What family, what congregation, what people can be happy without it ?

5. *One shall say.* It shall be common to say this, or a profession of religion shall be common. The various

expressions in this verse mean substantially the same thing—that there should prevail among the people a disposition to make a profession of attachment to JEHOVAH in every proper public manner. It is in immediate connection with what is said in the previous verses, that he would pour his Spirit upon them, and especially on their children. The effect would be, that many would make a public profession of religion. This refers, doubtless, in the main, to the period after their return from the captivity, and to the general prevalence of religion then. But it is also true of the people of God at all times—especially under the Messiah. God pours his Spirit like gentle dews, or rains, on the families of his people ; and the effect is, that many publicly profess attachment to him. ¶ *I am the* LORD's. I belong to JEHOVAH ; I devote myself to him. This expresses the true nature of a profession of religion—a feeling that we are not our own, but that we belong to God. It is, that we not only feel that we are bound to worship him, but that we actually *belong* to him ; that our bodies and spirits, and all that we have and are, are to be sacredly employed in his service (see 1 Cor. vi. 20 ; 2 Cor. vii. 5 ; v. 14, 15). Nothing, in few words, can more appropriately describe the true nature of a profession of religion than the expression here used (לִיהוָה אָנִי) 'For JEHOVAH am I' —' I am wholly, and entirely, and for ever for JEHOVAH, to obey him ; to do his will ; to suffer patiently all that he appoints ; to live where he directs ; to die when, where, and how he pleases ; to moulder in the grave according to his will ; to be raised up by his power ; and to serve him for ever in a better world.' ¶ *And another shall call* himself *by the name of Jacob.* The Chaldee renders this, 'He shall pray in the name of Jacob.' The idea seems to be, that he should call himself *a friend* of Jacob—an Israelite. He should regard himself as belonging to the same family and the same religion, as Jacob; as worshipping the same God; and as maintaining the same belief. To call one's self by the same name as another, is indicative of friendship and affection; and is expressive of a purpose to be united to him, and to identify our interest with his. The idea is that which one would express by saying, that he cast in his interest with the people of God, or he became identified with them; as we now say, a man calls himself by the name of Christ, i.e., a Christian. Jerome renders this, 'He shall call by the name of Jacob,' i.e., sinners to repentance (comp. Note on ch. xliii. 7; xlviii. 1; Ps. xxiv. 6). ¶ And another shall subscribe with his hand unto the LORD. The LXX. render this, 'And another shall write with his hand (χειρὶ), I am of God.' Lowth, 'On his hand,' Aquila and Symmachus, Χειρά. Lowth supposes that the allusion here is to the marks which were made indelible by puncture with ink on the hand or on other parts of the body. He supposes that the mark thus indelibly impressed was the name of the person, or the name of the master if he was a slave, or some indication by which it might be known to whom he belonged. In this way, the soldier marked himself with the name of his commander; the idolater, with the name of his god; and in this way, Procopius says, that the early Christians marked themselves. On this passage he says, 'Because many marked their wrists or their arms with the sign of the cross, or with the name of Christ' (see Rev. xx. 4; Spencer, De Leg. Heb. ii. 20). But all this is too refined, and is evidently a departure from the true sense of the passage. The mark, or writing, was not on the hand, but with it—literally, 'and this shall write his hand to JEHOVAH;' and the figure is evidently taken from the mode of making a contract or bargain, where the name is subscribed to the instrument. It was a solemn compact or covenant, by which they enrolled themselves among the worshippers of God, and pledged themselves to his service. The manner of a contract among the Hebrews is described

in Jer. xxxii. 10, 12, 44. A public, solemn, and recorded covenant, to which the names of princes, Levites, and priests, were subscribed, and which was sealed, by which they bound themselves to the service of God, is mentioned in Neh. ix. 38. Here it denotes the solemn manner in which they would profess to be worshippers of the true God; and it is expressive of the true nature of a profession of religion. The name is given in to God. It is enrolled by the voluntary desire of him who makes the profession among his friends. It is done, after the manner of solemn compacts among men, in the presence of witnesses (Heb. xii. 1). Among Christians, it is sealed in a solemn manner by baptism, and the Lord's supper It has, therefore, all the binding force and obligation of a solemn compact; and every professor of religion should regard his covenant with God as the most sacred of all compacts, and as having a more solemn obligation than any other. And yet, how many professors are there who would shrink back with horror from the idea of breaking a compact with man, who have no alarm at the idea of having proved unfaithful to their solemn pledge that they would belong wholly to God, and would live to him alone! Let every professor of religion remember that his profession has all the force of a solemn compact that he has voluntarily subscribed his name, and enrolled himself among the friends of God; and that there is no agreement of a more binding nature than that which unites him in public profession to the cause and the kingdom of the Saviour. ¶ And surname himself by the name of Israel. Shall call himself an Israelite, and shall be a worshipper of the same God. The word rendered 'shall surname' (כָּנָה kânâ, not used in Kal, in Piel כִּנָּה kinnâ), means to address in a friendly and soothing manner; to speak kindly to any one. Gesenius renders it, 'And kindly, soothingly names the name of Israel.' But the idea is probably that expressed in our translation. The word sometimes denotes a giving of flattering titles to any one, by way of compliment (Job xxxii. 21, 22):

6 Thus saith the Lord the King of Israel, and his Redeemer the Lord *a* of hosts ; I *b am* the first, and I *am* the last ; and besides *c* me *there is* no God.

a ch.43.14.   b Re.1.8,17.
    c De.4.35; 32.39.   d ch.46.9,10.

7 And *d* who, as I, shall call, and shall declare it, and set it in order for me, since I appointed the ancient people ? and the things that are coming, and shall come, let them show unto them.

Let me not, 1 pray you, accept any man's person;
Neither let me *give flattering titles* unto man.
For I know not *to give flattering titles;*
I n so doing my Maker would soon take me away.

In Isa. xlv. 4, it is rendered, ' I have s urnamed thee [Cyrus], though thou hast n ot known me.' The word does not o ccur elsewhere. It conveys the idea of *a n honourable title;* and means here, I think, that he would call himself by t he *honourable appellation* of Israel— o r an Israelite—a worshipper of the God o f Jacob. It implies that a profession o f the true religion *is* honourable, and that it is and should be esteemed so by him who makes it. It is observable, also, that this verse contains an instance o f the parallelism in the Hebrew writ- ings where the alternate members cor- respond to each other. Here the first and third members, and the second and the fourth correspond to each other (see Introd. § 8).

6. *Thus saith the* Lord. This com- mences, as I suppose (see Analysis), the argument to prove that Jehovah is the only true God, and that the idols were vanity. The object is, to show to the Jews, that he who had made to them such promises of protection and deliver- ance was able to perform what he had pledged himself to do. ¶ *The King of Israel* (see Notes on ch. xli. 21). ¶ *And his Redeemer* (see Notes on ch. xliii. 1). ¶ *The* Lord *of hosts* (see Notes on ch. i. 9). ¶ *I am the first* (see Notes on ch. xli. 4). ¶ *And I* am *the last.* In ch. xli. 4, this is expressed ' *with* the last ;' in Rev. i. 8, ' I am Alpha and Omega.' The sense is, that God existed before all things, and will exist for ever. ¶ *And besides me* there is *no God.* This is repeatedly declared (Deut. iv. 35, 39; see Note on ch. xliii. 10–12). This great truth it was God's purpose to keep steadily before the minds of the Jews; and to keep it in the world, and ulti- mately to diffuse it abroad among the nations, was one of the leading reasons why he selected them as a peculiar peo- ple, and separated them from the rest of mankind.

7. *And who, as I.* This verse contains an *argument* to prove that he is God. In proof of this, he appeals to the fact that he alone can predict future events, and certainly declare the *order,* and the *time* in which they will come to pass (see Notes on ch. xli. 21–23; xliv. 9, 10). ¶ *Shall call.* That is, call forth the event, or command that to happen which he wills—one of the highest possible ex- hibitions of power. See a similar use of the word *call* in ch. xlvi. 2; xlviii. 15. ¶ *And shall declare it.* Declare, or an- nounce with certainty the future event. ¶ *And set it in order.* Arrange it ; secure the proper succession and place (see Notes on ch. xli. 22). The word here used (עָרַךְ) denotes properly *to place in a row;* set in order ; arrange. It is of the same signification as the Greek τάσσω or τάττω, and is applied to placing the wood upon the altar in a proper manner (Gen. xxii. 9) ; or to placing the shew-bread in proper order on the table (Lev. xxiv. 8); and especially to setting an army in order, or putting it in battle array (Gen. xiv. 8; Judg. xx. 20, 22; 1 Sam. xvii. 2). Here it means, that God would arrange the events in a proper order—as an army is marshalled and arrayed for battle. There should be no improper sequences of events; no chance; no hap-hazard ; no confusion. The events which take place under his government, occur in proper order and time, and so as best to subserve his plans. ¶ *For me.* In order to execute my plans, and to promote my glory. The events on earth are for God. They are such as he chooses to ordain, and are arranged in the manner which he chooses. ¶ *Since I appointed the ancient people.* ' From my constituting the people of old ;' that is, God had given them intimations of future events from the very period when he in times long past, had selected and

8 Fear *ye not, neither be afraid : have not I told thee from that time, and have declared *it?* ye *are* even my *b* witnesses. Is there a God besides me? yea, *there is* no ¹ God ; I know not *any.*

9 They *c* that make a graven image *are* all of them vanity : and

their ² delectable things shall not profit : and they *are* their own witnesses; they see not, nor know, that they may be ashamed.

10 Who hath formed a god, or molten a graven image *that* is profitable *d* for nothing ?

a Prov.3.25,26.   *b* 1 Jn.5.10.   1 *rock.*
c ch.41.24,29.   2 *d-sirable.*   *d* Hab.2.18; 1 Co.8.4.

---

appointed them as his people. They were, therefore, qualified to be his witnesses (8). ¶ *And the things that are coming, let them show* (see Notes on ch. xli. 22, 23).

8. *Fear ye not, neither be afraid* (see Notes on ch. xli. 10). The word here rendered ' be afraid,' occurs nowhere else in the Bible. There can be no doubt, however, in regard to its meaning. The LXX. render it, Μηδὲ πλανᾶσθε — ' Neither be deceived.' All the other ancient versions express the sense to fear, to be afraid (Gesenius, *Lex.* on the word יָרֵה). ¶ *Have not I told thee from that time.* Have I not fully declared from the very commencement of your history as a people, in the main what shall occur? ¶ *Ye are even my witnesses* (see Notes on ch. xliii. 12). ¶ *Is there a God besides me?* This is a strong mode of affirming that there is no God besides JEHOVAH (see Note on ver. 6). ¶ *Yea,* there is *no God.* Marg. ' Rock' (צוּר, *tzūr*). The word *rock* is often applied to God (see Note on ch. xxx. 29 ; comp. Deut. xxxii. 4, 30, 31; Ps. xix. 14; xxxi. 2, 3; xlii. 9; *et sæpe al.* The idea is taken from the fact that a lofty rock or fastness was inaccessible by an enemy, and that those who fled there were safe.

9. *They that make a graven image.* A graven image is one that is cut, or sculptured out of wood or stone, in contradistinction from one that is molten, which is made by being cast. Here it is used to denote an image, or an idol-god in general. God had asserted in the previous verses his own divinity, and he now proceeds to show, at length, the vanity of idols, and of idol-worship. This same topic was introduced in ch. xl. 18–20 (see Notes on that passage), but it is here pursued at greater length, and in a tone and manner far more sar-

castic and severe. *Perhaps* the prophet had two immediate objects in view; first, to reprove the idolatrous spirit in his own time, which prevailed especially in the early part of the reign of Manasseh; and secondly, to show to the exile Jews in Babylon that the gods of the Babylonians could not protect their city, and that JEHOVAH could rescue his own people. He *begins,* therefore, by saying, that the *makers* of the idols were all of them vanity. Of course, the idols themselves could have no more power than their makers, and must be vanity also. ¶ Are *all of them vanity* (see Note on ch. xli. 29). ¶ *And their delectable things.* Marg. ' De-irable.' The sense is, their valued works, their idol-gods, on which they have lavished so much expense, and which they prize so highly. ¶ *Shall not profit.* Shall not be able to aid or protect them ; shall be of no advantage to them (see Hab. ii. 18). ¶ *And they* are *their own witnesses.* They can foretell nothing ; they can furnish no aid ; they cannot defend in times of danger. This may refer either to the worshippers, or to the idols themselves —and was alike true of both. ¶ *They see not.* They have no power of discerning anything. How can they then foresee future events? ¶ *That they may be ashamed.* The same sentiment is repeated in ver. 11, and in ch. xlv. 16. The sense is, that shame and confusion *must* await all who put their trust in an idol-god.

10. *Who hath formed a god.* The LXX. read this verse in connection with the close of the previous verse, ' But they shall be ashamed who make a god, and all who sculpture unprofitable things.' This interpretation also, Lowth, by a change in the Hebrew text on the authority of a MS. in the Bodleian library, has adopted. This change is

11 Behold, all his fellows shall be ^aashamed ; and the workmen, they *are* of men : let them all be gathered together, let them stand up ; *yet* they shall fear, *and* they shall be ashamed together.

12 The smith ^b with the ¹tongs

both worketh in the coals, and fashioneth it with hammers, and worketh it with the strength of his arms : yea, he is hungry, and his strength faileth : he drinketh no water, and is faint.

<hr>

a Ps.97.7.   *b* ch.40.19,&c.   1 or, *an axe.*

made by reading קִי (*ki*) instead of מִי (*mi*) in the beginning of the verse. But the authority of the change, being that of a single MS. and the Septuagint, is not sufficient. Nor is it necessary. The question is designed to be ironical and sarcastic : ' Who is there,' says the prophet, ' that has done this ? Who are they that are engaged in this stupid work ? Do they give marks of a sound mind ? What is, and must be the character of a man that has formed *a god*, and that has made an unprofitable graven image ?

11. *Behold, all his fellows.* All that are joined in making, and in worshipping it, are regarded as the fellows, or the companions (חֲבֵרָיו) of the idol-god (see Hos. iv. 17—' Ephraim *is joined* to idols '). They and the idols constitute one company or fellowship, intimately allied to each other. ¶ *Shall be ashamed.* Shall be confounded when they find that their idols cannot aid them. ¶ *And the workmen.* The allusion to the workmen is to show that what they made could not be worthy of the confidence of men as an object of worship. ¶ *They* are *of men.* They are mortal men ; they must themselves soon die. It is ridiculous, therefore, for them to attempt to make a god that can defend or save, or that should be adored. ¶ *Let them all be gathered together.* For purposes of trial, or to urge their claims to the power of making an object that should be adored (see Note on ch. xli. 1). ¶ *Let them stand up.* As in a court of justice, to defend their cause (see Note on ch. xli. 21). ¶ *They shall fear.* They shall be alarmed when danger comes. They shall find that their idol-gods cannot defend them.

12. *The smith with the tongs.* The prophet proceeds here to show the folly and absurdity of idolatry ; and in order to this he goes into an extended state-

ment (ver. 12–19) of the manner in which idols were usually made. Lowth remarks, ' The sacred writers are generally large and eloquent on the subject of idolatry ; they treat it with great severity, and set forth the absurdity of it in the strongest light. But this passage of Isaiah far exceeds anything that was ever written on the subject, in force of argument, energy of expression, and elegance of composition. One or two of the Apocryphal writers have attempted to imitate the prophet, but with very ill success (Wisd. xiii. 11–19 ; xv. 7, &c. ; Baruch vi.)' Horace, however, has given a description of the making of idols, which, for severity of satire, and pungency of sarcasm, has a strong resemblance to this description in Isaiah:—

Olim truncus eram ficulnus, inutile lignum ;
Cum faber, incertus scannum faceretne Priapum
Maluit esse Deum.

Sat. I. viii. 1–3.

Lowth renders the phrase ' the smith with the tongs,' ' The smith cutteth off a portion of iron.' Noyes, ' The smith prepareth an axe.' The LXX. ' The carpenter sharpeneth (ὄξυνε) iron ' (σίδηρον), *i.e.*, an axe. So also the Syriac. Gesenius renders it, ' The smith makes an axe.' Many other renderings of the passage have been proposed. The idea in this verse is, I think, that the prophet describes *the commencement of the process of making a graven image.* For that purpose, he goes back even to the making of the instruments by which it is manufactured, and in this verse he describes the process of making an axe, with a view to the cutting down of the tree, and forming a god. That he does not here refer to the making of the idol itself is apparent from the fact that the process here described is that of working *in iron ;* but idols were not made of iron, and that here described especially (ver. 11, *sq.*) is one made of wood. The phrase here used, therefore, refers to the pro-

13 The carpenter stretcheth out *his* rule, he marketh it out with a line, he fitteth it with planes, and he marketh it out with the compass, and maketh it after the figure of a man, according to the beauty of a man ; that it may remain in the house.

cess of axe-making with a view to cutting down a tree to make a god ; and the prophet describes the ardour and activity with which it is done, to show how much haste they were in to complete it. The literal translation of this phrase is, 'The workman (חָרַשׁ, st. const. for חָרָשׁ) of iron [maketh] an axe.' ¶ *Both worketh in the coals.* And he works the piece of iron of which he is making an axe in the coals. He blows the coals in order to produce an intense heat (see ch. liv. 16)—'Behold, I have created the smith that bloweth the coals in the fire.' ¶ *And fashioneth it with hammers.* Forms the mass of iron into an axe. Axes were not *cast*, but *wrought*. ¶ *And worketh it with the strength of his arms.* Or, he works it with his strong arms—referring to the fact that the arm of the smith, by constant usage, becomes exceedingly strong. A description remarkably similar to this occurs in Virgil when he is describing the Cyclops :

Illi inter sese magna vi brachia tollunt
In numerum ; versantque tenaci forcipe ferrum.
Georg. iv. 174, 175.

Heaved with vast strength their arms in order rise,
And blow to blow in measured chime replies ;
While with firm tongs they turn the sparkling ore,
And Etna's caves with ponderous anvils roar.
Sotheby.

¶ *Yea, he is hungry.* He exhausts himself by his hard labour. The idea is, that he is so anxious to have it done, so engaged, so diligent, that he does not even stop to take necessary refreshment. ¶ *And his strength faileth.* He works till he is completely exhausted. ¶ *He drinketh no water.* He does not intermit his work even long enough to take a draught of water, so hurried is he. While the iron is hot, he works with intense ardour, lest it should grow cool, and his work be retarded—a very graphic description of what all have seen in a blacksmith's shop. The Rev. J. Williams states that when the South Sea islanders made an idol, they strictly abstained from food ; and although they might be, and were sometimes, three days about the work, no water, and he believes no food, passed their lips all the time. This fact would convey a satisfactory elucidation of an allusion not otherwise easily explained (*Pictorial Bible*).

13. *The carpenter.* The axe is made (ver. 12), and the carpenter now proceeds to the construction of the god. ¶ *Stretcheth out* his *rule.* For the purpose of laying out his work, or measuring it. The word here rendered ' rule,'

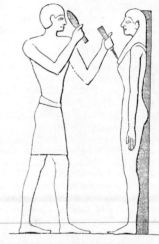

ANCIENT EGYPTIAN SCULPTORS
Blocking out stone for the formation of an Idol.
From Rosellini.

however (קַו), means properly a *line ;* and should be so rendered here. The carpenter *stretches out* a line, but not a rule. ¶ *He marketh it out with a line.* He marks out the shape ; the length, and breadth, and thickness of the body, in the rough and unhewn piece of wood He has an idea in his mind of the proper *shape* of a god, and he goes to work to make one of that form. The expression ' to mark out with a line,' is, however, not congruous. The word which is here used, and which is rendered 'line' (שֶׂרֶד) occurs nowhere else in the Bible. Lowth and Kimchi render it, 'Red ochre.' According to this the reference is to the chalk, red clay, or crayon, which a carpenter uses on a line to mark out his work. But according to Gesenius, the word means an *awl*, or a *stylus*, or *engraver*, with which the

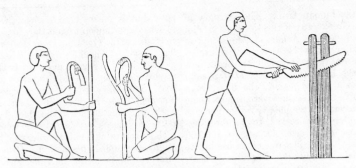

ANCIENT EGYPTIAN CARPENTERS WITH THE ADZE AND SAW.—From Rosellini.

artist sketches the outlines of the figure to be sculptured. A carpenter always uses such an instrument in laying out and marking his work. ¶ *He fitteth it with planes.* Or rather with *chisels*, or carving-tools, with which wooden images were carved. Planes are rather adapted to a smooth surface; carving is performed with chisels. The word

¶ *Marketh it out with the compass.* From הוּג (*hhūg*), *to make a circle*, to revolve, as compasses do. By a compass he accurately designates the parts, and marks out the symmetry of the form. ¶ *According to the beauty of a man.* Perhaps there may be a little sarcasm here in the thought that *a god* should be made in the shape of **a man.**

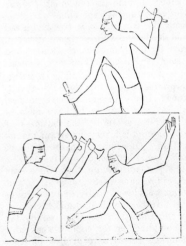

CARVING AN IDOL.—From Rosellini.

PAINTING AN IDOL.—From Rosellini.

is derived from קָצַע, *to cut off.* The Chaldee renders it, אִזְמֵל—'A knife.' The LXX. render this, 'Framed it by rule, and glued the parts together.'

It was true, however, that the statues of the gods among the ancients were made after the most perfect conceptions

14 He heweth him down cedars, and taketh the cypress and the oak, which he ¹strengtheneth for him-

1 or, *taketh courage.*

self among the trees of the forest : he planteth an ash, and the rain doth nourish *it.*

of the human form. The statuary of the Greeks was of this description, and the images of Apollo, of Venus, and of Jupiter, have been celebrated everywhere as the most perfect representations of the human form. ¶ *That it may remain in the house.* To dwell in a temple. Such statues were usually made to decorate a temple ; or rather perhaps temples were reared to be dwelling-places of the gods. It *may* be implied here, that the idol was of no use but to remain in a house. It could not hear, or save. It was like a useless piece of furniture, and had none of the attributes of God.

14. *He heweth him down cedars.* In the previous verses, the prophet had described the formation of an axe with which the work was to be done (ver. 12), and the laying out, and carving of the idol (ver. 13). In this verse he proceeds to describe the *material* of which the idol was made, and the different purposes (ver. 15–17) to which that material was applied. The *object* is to show the amazing stupidity of those who should worship a god made of the same material from which they made a fire to warm themselves, or to cook their food. For a description of cedars, see Notes on ch. ix. 10. ¶ *And taketh.* Takes to himself ; that is, makes use of. ¶ *The cypress* (תִּרְזָה *tïrzâ*). This word occurs nowhere else in the Bible. It is probably derived from a root (תָּרַז *târäz*), signifying *to be hard,* or *firm.* Hence it probably means some species of wood that derived its name from its hardness or firmness. Jerome translates it, *Ilex* (a species of oak)—'the holm-oak.' It was an evergreen. This species of evergreen, Gesenius says, was abundant in Palestine. ¶ *And the oak.* The oak was commonly used for this purpose on account of its hardness and durability. ¶ *Which he strengtheneth for himself.* Marg. 'Taketh courage.' The word אָמֵץ means properly *to strengthen,* to make strong, to repair, to replace, to harden. Rosenmüller and Gesenius sup-

pose that it means here *to choose, i.e.,* to set fast, or appoint ; and they appeal to Ps. lxxx. 15, 17, ' thou *madest strong* for thyself.' Kimchi supposes that it means, that he gave himself with the utmost diligence and care to select the best kinds of wood for the purpose. Vitringa, that he was intent on his work, and did not leave the place, but refreshed himself with food in the woods without returning home, in order that he might accomplish his design. Others interpret it to mean that he girded himself with strength, and made use of his most intense efforts in felling the trees of the forest. Lowth renders it, ' Layeth in good store of the trees of the forest.' It may mean that he gave himself with great diligence to the work ; or may it not mean that he *planted* such trees, and took great pains in watering and cultivating them for this purpose ? ¶ *He planteth an ash* (אֹרֶן). The Septuagint renders it, Πίτυν — ' Pine.' Jerome also renders it, *Pinum.* Gesenius supposes the name was given from the fact that the tree had a tall and slender top, which, when it vibrated, gave forth a tremulous, creaking sound (from רָנַן *rânän*). This derivation is, however, somewhat fanciful. Most interpreters regard it as the *ash*—a well-known tree. In idolatrous countries, where it is common to have idols in almost every family, the business of *idol-making* is a very important manufacture. Of course, large quantities of wood would be needed ; and it would be an object to procure that which was most pure, or as we say, ' clear stuff,' and which would work easily, and to advantage. It became important, therefore, to *cultivate* that wood, as we do for shipbuilding, or for cabinet-work, and doubtless groves were planted for this purpose. ¶ *And the rain doth nourish* it. These circumstances are mentioned to show the folly of worshipping a god that was formed in this manner. *Perhaps* also the prophet means to intimate that though the man planted the tree,

15 Then shall it be for a man to burn: for he will take thereof and warm himself; yea, he kindleth *it*, and baketh bread; yea, he maketh a god, and worshippeth *it :* he maketh it a graven image, and falleth down thereto.

16 He burneth part thereof in the fire: with part thereof he eateth flesh; he roasteth roast, and is satisfied, yea, he warmeth *himself,* and saith, Aha, I am warm, I have seen the fire:

17 And the residue thereof he maketh a god, *even* his graven image: he falleth down unto it, and worshippeth *it,* and prayeth unto it, and saith, Deliver me, for thou *art* my god.

18 They *a* have not known nor understood: for *b* he hath ¹ shut their eyes, that they cannot see; *and* their hearts, that they cannot understand.

a ch.45.20.   *b* ch.6.9,10.   1 *daubed.*

---

yet that he could not make it grow. He was dependent on the rains of heaven; and even in making an idol-god he was indebted to the providential care of the true God. Men, even in their schemes of wickedness, are dependent on God. Even in forming and executing plans to oppose and resist him, they can do nothing without his aid. He preserves them, feeds them, clothes them; and the instruments which they use against him are those which he has nurtured. On the rain of heaven; on the sunbeam and the dew; on the teeming earth, and on the elements which he has made, and which he controls, they are dependent; and they can do nothing in their wicked plans without abusing the bounties of his Providence, and the expressions of his tender mercy.

15. *Then shall it be for a man to burn.* It will afford materials for a fire. The design of this verse and the following is, to ridicule the idea of a man's using parts of the same tree to make a fire to cook his victuals, to warm himself, and to shape a god. Nothing could be more stupid than the conduct here referred to, and yet it is common all over the heathen world. It shows the utter debasement of the race, that they thus of the same tree make a fire, cook their food, and construct their gods.

16. *With part thereof he eateth flesh.* That is, he prepares flesh to eat, or prepares his food. ¶ *He roasteth roast.* He roasts meat.

18. *They have not known nor understood.* They are stupid, ignorant, and blind. Nothing could more strikingly show their ignorance and stupidity than

this idol worship. ¶ *He hath shut their eyes.* God hath closed their eyes. Marg. 'Daubed.' The word here used, טַח from טוּחַ denotes properly *to spread over ;* to besmear; to plaster; as, *e.g.,* a wall with mortar (Lev. xiv. 42; 1 Chron. xxix. 4; Ezek. xiii. 10, 22, 28). Here it means to cover over the eyes so as to prevent vision; and hence, metaphorically, to make them stupid, ignorant, dull. It is attributed to God in accordance with the common statement of the Scriptures, that he does what he permits to be done (see Notes on ch. vi. 9, 10). It does not mean that God had done it by any physical, or direct agency, but that it had occurred under the administration of his Providence. It is also true that the Hebrew writers sometimes employ an active verb when the signification is passive, and when the main idea is, that anything was *in fact* done. Here the main point is not the *agent* by which this was done, but *the fact* that their eyes were blinded—and perhaps all the force of the verb טַח used here would be expressed if it was rendered in an impersonal, or in a passive form, 'it is covered as to their eyes,' *i.e.*, their eyes are shut, without suggesting that it was done by God. So the LXX. render it, Ἀπημαυρώθησαν— 'They are blind,' or involved in darkness. So the Chaldee, מִטַמְטַם (also in the plural)—'Their eyes are obscured' or blind. It cannot be proved from this text that God is, by direct agency, the author by whom it was done. It was not uncommon to shut up, or seal up the eyes for various purposes in the East, and unquestionably the prophet alludes

19 And none [1] considereth [a] in his heart, neither *is there* knowledge nor understanding to say, I have burnt part of it in the fire ; yea, also I have baked bread upon the coals thereof ; I have roasted flesh, and eaten *it ;* and shall I make the residue thereof an abomination ?

shall I fall down to [2] the stock of a tree ?

20 He feedeth on ashes : a deceived heart [b] hath turned him aside, that he cannot deliver his soul, nor say, *Is there* not a lie in my right hand ?

1 *setteth to.*   [a] Ho.7.2.   2 *that which comes of.*
[b] Ho.4.12; Ro.1.21; 2 Th.2.11.

to some such custom. ' It is one of the solemnities at a Jewish wedding at Aleppo, according to Dr. Russell, who mentions it as the most remarkable thing in their ceremonies at that time. It is done by fastening the eyelids together with a gum, and the bridegroom is the person, he says, if he remembered right, that opens the bride's eyes at the appointed time. It is also used as a punishment in those countries. So Sir Thomas Roe's chaplain, in his account of his voyages to East India, tells us of a son of the Great Mogul, whom he had seen, and with whom Sir Thomas had conversed, that had before that time been cast into prison by his father, where his eyes were sealed up, by something put before them, which might not be taken off for three years ; after which time the seal was taken away, that he might with freedom enjoy the light, though not his liberty.' —(Harmer's *Obs.* vol. iii., pp. 507, 508. Ed. Lond. 8vo, 1808.)

19. *And none considereth in his heart.* Marg. ' Setteth to.' He does not place the subject near his heart or mind ; he does not think of it. A similar phrase occurs in ch. xlvi. 8 : ' Bring it again to mind.' It is a phrase drawn from the act of placing an object near us, in order to examine it closely ; and we express the same idea by the phrase ' looking at a thing,' or ' looking at it closely.' The sense is, they had not attentively and carefully thought on the folly of what they were doing—a sentiment which is as true of all sinners as it was of stupid idolaters. ¶ *An abomination.* A name that is often given to an idol (2 Kings xi. 5, 7 ; xxiii. 13). The meaning is, that an idol was abominable and detestable in the sight of a holy God. It was that which he could not endure. ¶ *Shall I fall down to the stock of a tree ?* Marg. ' That which comes of.' The

word בּוּל means properly *produce, increase,* and here evidently a stock or trunk of wood. So it is in the Chaldee.

20. *He feedeth on ashes.* There have been various interpretations of this. Jerome renders it, ' A part of it is ashes ;' the Chaldee, ' Lo ! half of the god is reduced to ashes ;' the Septuagint, ' Know thou that their heart is ashes.' The word here rendered ' feedeth' (רֹעֶה) means properly *to feed,* graze, pasture ; and then, figuratively, to delight, or take pleasure in any person or thing (Prov. xiii. 20; xv. 14 ; xxviii. 7 ; xxix. 3). In Hos. xii. 1, ' Ephraim *feedeth* on wind,' it means to strive after something vain or unprofitable ; to seek that which will prove to be vain and unsatisfactory. So here it means, that in their idol-service they would not obtain that which they sought. It would be like a man who sought for food, and found it to be dust or ashes ; and the service of an idol compared with what man needed, or compared with the true religion, would be like ashes compared with nutritious and wholesome diet. This graphic description of the effect of idolatry is just as true of the ways of sin, and of the pursuits of the world now. It is true of the gay and the fashionable ; of those who seek happiness in riches and honours; of all those who make this world their portion, that they are feeding on ashes —they seek that which is vain, unsubstantial, unsatisfactory, and which will yet fill the soul itself with disgust and loathing. ¶ *A deceived heart hath turned him aside.* This is the true source of the difficulty ; this is the fountain of all idolatry and sin. The *heart* is first wrong, and then the understanding, and the whole conduct is turned aside from the path of truth and duty (comp. Rom. i. 28). ¶ *A lie in my right hand.* The right hand is the instrument of action.

21 Remember these, O Jacob and Israel; for thou *art* my servant: I have formed thee; thou *art* my servant: O Israel, thou shalt not be *a* forgotten of me.

22 I have blotted out, *b* as a thick cloud, thy transgressions, and, as a cloud, thy sins: return

a ch. 49.14,15.   *b* ch.1.18; Ps.103.12.
c 1 Co.6.20; 1 Pe.1.18; Re.5.9.

unto me; for I have *c* redeemed thee.

23 *d* Sing, O ye heavens; for the LORD hath done *it*: shout, ye lower parts of the earth, break forth into singing, ye mountains, O *e* forest, and every tree therein: for the LORD hath redeemed Jacob, and glorified *f* himself in Israel.

d Ps.96.11,12; Re.18.20.   *e* Eze.36.1,8.   *f* ch.55.13.

A lie is a name often given to an idol as being false and delusive. The sense is, that that which they had been making, and on which they were depending, was deceitful and vain. The work of their right hand—the fruit of their skill and toil, was deceptive, and could not save them. The doctrine is, that that which sinners rely on to save their souls; that which has cost their highest efforts as a scheme to save them, is false and delusive. All schemes of religion of human origin are of this description: and all will be alike deceptive and ruinous to the soul.

21. *Remember these.* Remember these things which are now said about the folly of idolatry, and the vanity of worshipping idols. The object of the argument is, to turn their attention to God, and to lead them to put their trust in him. ¶ *Thou* art *my servant* (see Notes on ch. xlii. 19; xliii. 1).

22. *I have blotted out.* The word here used (מָחָה), means properly *to wipe away*, and is often applied to sins, as if the account was wiped off, or as we express it, blotted out (Ps. li. 3, 11; see Note on ch. xliii. 25). The phrase, ' to blot out sins like a cloud,' however, is unusual, and the idea not very obvious. The true idea would be expressed by rendering it, ' I have made them to vanish as a thick cloud;' and the sense is, as the wind drives away a thick cloud, however dark and frowning it may be, so that the sky is clear and serene, so God had caused their sins to disappear, and had removed the storm of his anger. Nothing can more strikingly represent *sin* in its nature and consequences, than a dense, dark, frowning cloud that comes over the heavens, and shuts out the sun, and fills the air with gloom; and nothing can more beautifully represent the na-

ture and effect of pardon than the idea of removing such a cloud, and leaving the sky pure, the air calm and serene, and the sun pouring down his beams of warmth and light on the earth. So the soul of the sinner is enveloped and over-shadowed with a dense cloud; but pardon dissipates that cloud, and it is calm, and joyful, and serene. ¶ *And as a cloud.* The Chaldee render this, ' As a flying cloud.' The difference between the two words here rendered ' thick cloud,' and ' cloud ' (עָב and עָנָן) is, that the former is expressive of a cloud as *dense*, thick, compact; and the latter as *covering* or veiling the heavens. Lowth renders the latter word ' Vapour;' Noyes, ' Mist.' Both words, however, usually denote a cloud. A passage similar to this is found in Demosthenes, as quoted by Lowth : ' This decree made the danger then hanging over the city pass away like a cloud.' ¶ *Return unto me.* Since your sins are pardoned, and such mercy has been shown, return now, and serve me. The *argument* here is derived from the mercy of God in forgiving them, and the *doctrine* is, that the fact that God has forgiven us imposes the strongest obligations to devote ourselves to his service. The fact that we are redeemed and pardoned is the highest argument why we should consecrate all our powers to him who has purchased and forgiven us.

23. *Sing, O ye heavens* (see ch. xlii. 10). It is common in the sacred writings to call on the heavens, the earth, and all created things, to join in the praise of God on any great and glorious event (see Ps. xcvi. 1, 11, 12; cxlviii.) The *occasion* of the joy here was the fact that God had redeemed his people—a fact, in the joy of which the heavens and earth were called to participate. An

24 Thus *saith the LORD, thy Redeemer, and he that formed thee from *the womb, I *am* the LORD that maketh all *things ;* that stretcheth *c* forth the heavens alone : that spreadeth abroad the earth by myself ;

25 That *d*frustrateth the tokens of the liars, and maketh diviners mad ; that turneth wise *men* backward, and maketh their knowledge foolish.

a ver.6.   *b* Ga.1.15.   *c* Ps.104.2.
d 2 Ch.18.11,34; Je.50.36; 1 Co.3.19.

apostrophe such as the prophet here uses is common in all writings, where inanimate objects are addressed as having life, and as capable of sharing in the emotions of the speaker. Vitringa has endeavoured to show that the various objects here enumerated are emblematic, and that by the heavens are meant the angels which are in heaven ; by the lower parts of the earth, the more humble and obscure republics of the heathen ; by the mountains, the greater and more mighty kingdoms; by the forest, and the trees, large and spacious cities, with their nobles. So Grotius also interprets the passage. But the passage is a highly-wrought expression of elevated feeling; the language of poetry, where the prophet calls on all objects to exult;—an apostrophe to the highest heavens and the lowest part of the earth—the mountains and the forests—the most sublime objects in nature—to exult in the fact that the Jewish people were delivered from their long and painful captivity, and restored again to their own land. ¶ *The* LORD *hath done* it. Has delivered his people from their captivity in Babylon. There is, however, no impropriety in supposing that the eye of the prophet also rested on the glorious deliverance of his people by the Messiah ; and that he regarded one event as emblematic of, and introductory to the other. The *language* here used will certainly appropriately express the feelings which should be manifested in view of the plan of redemption under the Messiah. ¶ *Shout, ye lower parts of the earth.* The foundations of the earth ; the parts remote from the high heavens. Let the highest and the lowest objects shout; the highest heavens, and the depths of the earth. The LXX. render it, Τὰ Θιμέλια τῆς γῆς—'The foundations of the earth.' So the Chaldee. ¶ *Ye mountains.* So in Psalm cxlviii. 9, 13: ' Mountains and all hills ; fruitful trees

and all cedars—let them praise the name of the LORD.' ¶ *O forest,* and *every tree therein.* Referring either to Lebanon, as being the most magnificent forest known to the prophet; or to any forest as a great and sublime object.

24. *Thy Redeemer* (see Note on ch. xliii. 1). ¶ *And he that formed thee from thee womb* (see Note on ver. 2). ¶ *That stretcheth forth the heavens* (see Note on ch. xl. 22). ¶ *That spreadeth abroad the earth.* Representing the earth, as is often done in the Scriptures, as a plain. God here appeals to the fact that he alone had made the heavens and the earth, as the demonstration that he is able to accomplish what is here said of the deliverance of his people. The same God that made the heavens is the Redeemer and Protector of the church, and THEREFORE the church is safe.

25. *That frustrateth.* Heb. ' Breaking : ' *i.e.,* destroying, rendering vain. The idea is, that that which necromancers and diviners relied on as certain demonstration that what they predicted would be fulfilled, God makes vain and inefficacious. The event which they predicted did not follow, and all their alleged proofs that they were endowed with Divine or miraculous power he rendered vain. ¶ *The tokens.* Heb. אֹתוֹת—' Signs.' This word is usually applied to miracles, or to signs of the Divine interposition and presence. Here it means the things on which diviners and soothsayers relied ; the tricks of cunning and sleight-of-hand which they adduced as miracles, or as demonstrations that they were under a divine influence. See the word more fully explained in the Notes on ch. vii. 2. ¶ *The liars.* Deceivers, boasters—meaning conjurers, or false prophets (comp. Jer. l. 36 ; see also Note on Isa. xvi. 6). ¶ *And maketh diviners mad.* That is, makes them foolish, or deprives

26 That confirmeth *a* the word of his servant, and performeth the counsel of his messengers ; that saith to Jerusalem, Thou shalt be inhabited ; and to the cities of Judah, Ye shall be built ; and I will raise up the ¹ decayed places thereof :

27 That saith to the deep, Be dry, and I will dry up thy rivers :

a Zec.1.6;2 Pe.1.19.

1 *wastes.*

them of wisdom. They pretend to foretell future events, but the event does not correspond with the prediction. God orders it otherwise, and thus they are shown to be foolish, or unwise. ¶ *That turneth wise* men *backward.* Lowth renders this, ' Who reverseth the devices of the sages.' The sense is, he puts them to shame. The idea seems to be derived from the fact that when one is ashamed, or disappointed, or fails of performing what he promised, he turns away his face (see 1 Kings ii. 16, *marg.*) The ' wise men,' here denote the sages ; the diviners, the soothsayers ; and the sense is, that they were not able to predict future events, and that when their prediction failed, they would be suffused with shame. ¶ *And maketh their knowledge foolish.* He makes them appear to be fools. It is well known that soothsayers and diviners abounded in the East ; and it is not improbable that the prophet here means that when Babylon was attacked by Cyrus, the diviners and soothsayers would predict his defeat, and the overthrow of his army, but that the result would show that they were utterly incapable of predicting a future event. The whole passage here has reference to the taking of Babylon by Cyrus, and should be interpreted accordingly.

26. *That confirmeth the word of his servant.* Probably the word ' servant ' here is to be taken in a *collective* sense, as referring to the prophets in general who had foretold the return of the Jews to their own land, and the rebuilding of Jerusalem. Or it may be, that the prophet refers more particularly to himself as having made a full prediction of this event. The parallel expression, ' his messengers,' however, is in the plural number, and thus it is rendered probable that the word here refers to the prophets collectively. The idea is, that it was a characteristic of God to establish the words of his servants the prophets, and that their predictions in regard to the return from the captivity in a special manner would be fulfilled. ¶ *The counsel of his messengers.* The prophets whom he had sent to announce future events, and to give counsel and consolation to the nation. ¶ *That saith to Jerusalem.* Jerusalem is here supposed to be lying in ruins, and the people to be in captivity in Babylon. In this situation, God is represented as addressing desolate Jerusalem, and saying, that it should be again inhabited, and that the cities of Judah should be rebuilt. ¶ *The decayed places.* Marg. ' Wastes.' No land, probably, was ever more completely desolated than the land of Judea when its inhabitants were carried to Babylon.

27. *That saith to the deep, Be dry.* Lowth supposes, that this refers to the fact that Cyrus took Babylon by diverting from their course the waters of the river Euphrates, and thus leaving the bed of the river dry, so that he could march his army under the walls of the city (see Notes on ch. xiii., xiv.) With this interpretation, also, Vitringa, J. H. Michaelis, Grotius, Rosenmüller, and some others, accord. Gesenius supposes that it is a description of the power of God in general ; and some others have referred it to the dividing of the waters of the Red Sea when the Hebrews came out of Egypt, as in ch. xliii. 16, 17. The most obvious interpretation is that of Lowth, Vitringa, &c., by which it is supposed that it refers to the drying up of the Euphrates and the streams about Babylon, when Cyrus took the city. The principal *reasons* for this interpretation are, first, that the entire statement in these verses has reference to the events connected with the taking of Babylon ; secondly, that it is strikingly descriptive of the manner in which the city was taken by Cyrus ; and thirdly, that Cyrus is expressly mentioned (ver.

28 That saith of Cyrus, *He is my shepherd,* and shall perform all my pleasure : even saying to Jerusalem, Thou shalt be [a]built ; and to the temple, Thy foundation shall be laid.

a Ezr.1.1,&c.

28), as being concerned in the transaction here referred to. The word rendered ' deep ' (צוּלָה) denotes properly *anything sunk;* the depth of the sea ; an abyss. But it may be applied to a deep river, and especially to the Euphrates, as a deep and mighty stream. In Jer. li. 36, the word ' sea ' is applied to the Euphrates :

' I will dry up her sea,
And make her springs dry.'

Cyrus took the city of Babylon, after having besieged it a long time in vain, by turning the waters of the river into a vast lake, forty miles square, which had been constructed in order to carry off the superfluous waters in a time of inundation. By doing this, he laid the channel of the river almost dry, and was thus enabled to enter the city above and below, under the walls, and to take it by surprise. The LXX. render the word ' deep ' here by 'Αβύσσω—'Abyss.' The Chaldee, ' Who says to Babylon, Be desolate, and I will dry up your streams.' ¶ *I will dry up thy rivers.* Referring doubtless to the numerous canals or artificial streams by which Babylon and the adjacent country were watered. These were supplied from the Euphrates, and when that was diverted from its usual bed, of course they became dry.

28. *That saith of Cyrus.* This is the first time in which Cyrus is expressly named by Isaiah, though he is often referred to. He is mentioned by him only in one other place expressly by name (ch. xlv. 1). He is several times mentioned elsewhere in the Old Testament (2 Chron. xxvi. 22, 23 ; Ezra i. 1, 2, 7; iii. 7; iv. 3; v. 13, 17; Dan. i. 21; vi. 28; x. 1). He began his reign about B.C. 550, and this prophecy was therefore delivered not far from a hundred and fifty years before he ascended the throne. None but God himself, or he whom God inspired, could have mentioned so long before, *the name* of him who should deliver the Jewish people from bondage ; and if this was delivered, therefore, by Isaiah, it proves that he was under

Divine inspiration. The name of Cyrus (כּוֹרֶשׁ, *Koresh ;* Gr. Κῦρος), the Greek writers say, means ' the sun.' It is contracted from the Persian word *khorschid,* which in that language has this signification. Cyrus was the celebrated king of the Medes and Persians, and was the son of Cambyses the Persian, and of Mandane, daughter of Astyages, king of the Medes. For an account of his character and reign, see the Notes on ch. xli. 2, where I have anticipated all that is needful to be said here. ¶ He is *my shepherd.* A shepherd is one who leads and guides a flock, and then the word denotes, by a natural and easy metaphor, a ruler, or leader of a people. Thus the name is given to Moses in Isa. xliii. 2 ; comp. Ps. lxxvii. 20, and Ezek. xxxiv. 23. The name here is given to Cyrus because God would employ him to conduct his people again to their own land. The word ' my ' implies, that he was under the direction of God, and was employed in his service. ¶ *And shall perform all my pleasure.* In destroying the city and kingdom of Babylon; in delivering the Jewish captives ; and in rebuilding Jerusalem, and the temple. ¶ *Even saying to Jerusalem.* That is, I say to Jerusalem. The Vulgate and the LXX. render this as meaning God, and not Cyrus, and doubtless this is the true construction. It was one of the things which God would do, to say to Jerusalem that it should be rebuilt. ¶ *And to the temple.* Though now desolate and in ruins, yet it shall be reconstructed, and its foundation shall be firmly laid. The phrase ' to Jerusalem,' and ' to the temple,' should be rendered ' of,' in accordance with a common signification of the preposition ל, and as it is rendered in the former part of the verse when speaking of Cyrus (comp. Gen. xx. 13 ; Judg. ix. 54). It was indeed under the direction of Cyrus that the city of Jerusalem was rebuilt, and the temple reconstructed (Ezra i. 1); but still it was to be traced to God, who raised him up

CHAPTER XLV.

ANALYSIS.

The subject which was introduced in the previous chapter (ver. 28) constitutes the main topic of this. God had there introduced the name of Cyrus as he who was to deliver his people from their captivity, and to restore them to their own land. This chapter is almost entirely occupied with a statement of the deliverance which would be effected through him—with an occasional reference to the more important deliverance which would be effected under the Messiah. The general subject of the chapter is the overthrow of Babylon, the deliverance of the Jews by Cyrus, and the events consequent on that, adapted to give consolation to the friends of God, particularly the future conversion of the Gentiles to the true religion.

I. An apostrophe to Cyrus, stating the design for which God had raised him up, and what he would do for him (1–8). This statement also comprises several items:—1. God would subdue nations before him, open brazen gates, and give him the treasures of kings (1–3). 2. The design for which God would do this would be, that he might deliver his people, and that the world might know that Jehovah was the true and only God (4–7). 3. The joyful consequences of this event—so great that the heavens are represented as dropping down righteousness, and the earth as bringing forth salvation in consequence of it (8).

II. Those who strive with their Maker are reproved and rebuked (9, 10). This is probably designed to apply to the people of Babylon, or to complainers in general in regard to the government of God.

III. God vindicates himself against the calumnies and objections of his enemies, and states the evidence that he is God, and the consequence of his interposition in raising up Cyrus. 1. He condescends to reason with men, and is willing to be inquired of respecting future events (11). 2. He had made the earth and all things, and he had raised up Cyrus for the purpose of delivering his people (12, 13). 3. He states the consequence of his raising up Cyrus, and their deliverance, for the purpose of comforting his people (14). 4. All the worshippers of idols should be ashamed and confounded (15, 16). 5. They who put their trust in God should never be confounded (17).

IV. God vindicates his own character; and calls on the nations of idolaters to come and compare the claims of idols with him, and especially appeals, in proof that he is God, to his power of predicting future events (18–21).

V. The chapter closes by a call on all nations to trust in him in view of the fact that he is the only true God; and with an assurance that all *should* yet trust in him, and that the true religion should yet spread over the world (22–25). This is designed further to comfort the people of God in their exile, and is a striking prophecy of the final universal prevalence of the gospel.

THUS saith the Lord to his anointed, to Cyrus, whose right hand I ¹have holden, to subdue nations before him; and I will loose ᵃthe loins of kings, to open before him the two-leaved gates; and the gates shall not be shut:

1 or, *strengthen'd*.   a Dan.5.6,30.

for this purpose. That this passage was seen by Cyrus is the testimony of Josephus, and is morally certain from the nature of the case, since, otherwise, it is incredible that he should have aided the Jews in returning to their own land, and in rebuilding their city and temple (see Introd. § 2). This is one of the numerous instances in the Bible, in which God claims control and jurisdiction even over heathen princes and monarchs, and in which he says that their plans are under his direction, and made subservient to his will. It is one of the proofs that God presides over all, and that he makes the voluntary purposes of men subservient to him, and a part of the means of executing his glorious designs in relation to his peo-

ple. Indeed, all the proud monarchs and conquerors of the earth have been in some sense instruments in his hand of executing his pleasure.

CHAPTER XLV.

1. *Thus saith the Lord to his anointed.* This is a direct apostrophe to Cyrus, though it was uttered not less than one hundred and fifty years before Babylon was taken by him. The word 'anointed' is that which is usually rendered *Messiah* (מָשִׁיחַ), and here is rendered by the LXX. Τῷ χριστῷ μου Κύρῳ — 'To Cyrus, my Christ,' *i.e.*, my anointed. It properly means *the anointed*, and was a title which was commonly given to the kings of Israel, because they were set apart to their office by the ceremony of anointing, who hence

were called *οἱ χριστοὶ Κυρίου*—' The anointed of the Lord' (1 Sam. ii. 10, 35; xii. 3, 5; xvi. 6; xxiv. 7, 11; xxvi. 9, 11, 23; 2 Sam. i. 14, 16; xix. 22, 23). There is no evidence that the Persian kings were inaugurated or consecrated by oil, but this is an appellation which was common among the Jews, and is applied to Cyrus in accordance with their usual mode of designating kings. It means here that God had solemnly set apart Cyrus to perform an important public service in his cause. It does not mean that Cyrus was a man of piety, or a worshipper of the true God, of which there is no certain evidence, but that his appointment as king was owing to the arrangement of God's providence, and that he was to be employed in accomplishing his purposes. The title does not designate holiness of character, but appointment to an office. ¶ *Whose right hand I have holden.* Marg. ' Strengthened.' Lowth, 'Whom I hold fast by the right hand.' The idea seems to be, that God had upheld, sustained, strengthened him—as we do one who is feeble, by taking his right hand (see Notes on ch. xli. 13; xlii. 6). ¶ *To subdue nations before him.* For a general account of the conquests of Cyrus, see Notes on ch. xli. 2. It may be added here, that ' besides his native subjects, the nations which Cyrus subdued, and over which he reigned, were the Cilicians, Syrians, Paphlagonians, Cappadocians, Phrygians, Lydians, Carians, Phenicians, Arabians, Babylonians, Assyrians, Bactrians, Sacæ, and Maryandines Xenophon describes his empire as extending from the Mediterranean and Egypt to the Indian Ocean, and from Ethiopia to the Euxine Sea, and conveys a physical idea of its extent by observing that the extremities were difficult to inhabit, from opposite causes—some from excess of heat, and others from excess of cold; some from a scarcity of water, and others from too great abundance.'—(*Pictorial Bible.*) ¶ *And I will loose the loins of kings.* The ancients dressed in a large, loose, flowing robe thrown over an under-garment or tunic, which was shaped to the body. The outer robe was girded with a sash when they toiled, or laboured, or went to war, or ran. Hence, ' to gird

up the loins' is indicative of preparation for a journey, for labour, or for war. To *unloose* the girdle, or the loins, was indicative of a state of rest, repose, or feebleness ; and the phrase here means that God would so order it in his providence that the kings would be unprepared to meet him, or so feeble that they would not be able to resist him (comp. Job xxxviii. 3; Jer. i. 17). See also Job xii. 21 :

He poureth contempt upon princes,
And weakeneth the strength of the mighty;

Marg. more correctly, ' Looseth the girdle of the strong.' There was a *literal* fulfilment of this in regard to Belshazzar, king of Babylon, when the city was taken by Cyrus. When the hand came forth on the walls of his palace, and the mysterious finger wrote his condemnation, it is said, ' Then the king's countenance was changed, and his thoughts troubled him, *so that the joints of his loins were loosed*, and his knees smote one against the other' (Dan. v. 6). The Vulgate renders this, ' I will turn the backs of kings.' ¶ *To open before him the two-leaved gates, and the gates shall not be shut.* The folding gates of a city, or a palace. It so happened in the scene of revelry which prevailed in Babylon when Cyrus took it, that the gates within the city which led from the streets to the river were left open. The city was not only *enclosed* with walls, but there were walls within the city on each side of the river Euphrates with gates, by which the inhabitants had access to the water of the river. Had not these gates been left open on that occasion, contrary to the usual custom, the Persians would have been shut up in the bed of the river, and could all have been destroyed. It also happened in the revelry of that night, that the gates of the palace were left open, so that there was access to every part of the city. Herodotus (i. 191) says, ' If the besieged had been aware of the designs of Cyrus, or had discovered the project before its actual accomplishment, they might have effected the total destruction of these troops. They had only to secure the little gates which led to the river, and to have manned the embankments on either side, and they might have in-

2 I will go before thee, and make the crooked places straight: I will break *a* in pieces the gates of

a Ps.107.17.

brass, and cut in sunder the bars of iron :

3 And I will give thee the trea-

closed the Persians in a net from which they could never have escaped ; as it happened they were taken by surprise ; and such is the extent of that city, that, as the inhabitants themselves affirm, they who lived in the extremities were made prisoners before the alarm was communicated to the centre of the palace.' None but an omniscient Being could have predicted, a hundred and fifty years before it occurred, that such an event would take place ; and this is one of the many prophecies which demonstrate in the most particular manner that Isaiah was inspired.

2. *I will go before thee.* To prepare the way for conquest, a proof that it is by the providence of God that the proud conquerors of the earth are enabled to triumph. The idea is, I will take away everything that would retard or oppose your victorious march. ¶ *And make the crooked paths straight* (see Note on ch. xl. 4). The Chaldee renders this, ' My word shall go before thee, and I will prostrate the walls.' Lowth renders it, ' Make the mountains plain.' Noyes, ' Make the high places plain.' The LXX. render it, "Ορη ὁμαλιῶ— ' Level mountains.' Vulg. *Gloriosos terræ humiliabo*—' The high places of the earth I will bring down.' The word הֲדוּרִים (*hādhūrim*) is from הָדַר (*hādhăr*), *to be large*, ample, swollen, tumid ; and probably means the swollen, tumid places, *i.e.*, the hills or elevated places ; and the idea is, that God would make them level, or would remove all obstructions out of his way. ¶ *I will break in pieces the gates of brass.* Ancient cities were surrounded by walls, and secured by strong gates, which were not unfrequently made of brass. To Babylon there were one hundred gates, twenty-five on each side of the city, which, with their posts, were made of brass. ' In the circumference of the walls,' says Herodotus (i. 179), ' at different distances, were a hundred massy gates of brass, whose hinges and frames were of the same metal.' It was to this, doubtless, that the passage before

us refers. ¶ *The bars of iron.* With which the gates of the city were fastened. 'One method of securing the gates of fortified places among the ancients, was to cover them with thick plates of iron—a custom which is still used in the East, and seems to be of great antiquity. We learn from Pitts, that Algiers has five gates, and some of these have two, some three other gates within them, and some of them plated all over with iron. Pococke, speaking of a bridge near Antioch, called the iron bridge, says, that there are two towers belonging to it, the gates of which are covered with iron plates. Some of these gates are plated over with brass ; such are the enormous gates of the principal mosque at Damascus, formerly the church of John the Baptist' (Paxton). The general idea in these passages is, that Cyrus would owe his success to Divine interposition ; and that that interposition would be so striking that it would be *manifest* that he owed his success to the favour of Heaven. This was so clear in the history of Cyrus, that it is recognized by himself, and was also recognized even by the heathen who witnessed the success of his arms. Thus Cyrus says (Ezra i. 2), ' JEHOVAH, God of heaven, hath given me all the kingdoms of the earth.' Thus Herodotus (i. 124) records the fact that Harpagus said in a letter to Cyrus, ' Son of Cambyses, Heaven evidently favours you, or you could never have thus risen superior to fortune.' So Herodotus (i. 205) says that Cyrus regarded himself as endowed with powers more than human : ' When he considered the peculiar circumstances of his birth, he believed himself more than human. He reflected also on the prosperity of his arms, and that wherever he had extended his excursions, he had been followed by success and victory.'

3. *And I will give thee the treasures of darkness.* The treasures which kings have amassed, and which they have laid up in dark and secure places. The word ' darkness,' here, means that which was

sures of darkness, and the hidden riches of secret places, that thou mayest know that I the LORD, which *a* call *thee* by thy name, am the God of Israel.

a ch 43.15.

hidden, unknown, secret (comp. Job xii. 22). The treasures of the kings of the East were usually hidden in some obscure and strong place, and were not to be touched except in cases of pressing necessity. Alexander found vast quantities of treasure thus hidden among the Persians ; and it was by taking such treasures that the rapacity of the soldiers who followed a conqueror was satisfied, and in fact by a division of the spoils thus taken that they were paid. There can be no doubt that large quantities of treasure in this manner would be found in Babylon. The following observations from Harmer (*Obs.* pp. 111, 511–513), will show that it was common to conceal treasures in this manner in the East ; ' We are told by travellers in the East, that they have met with great difficulties, very often from a notion universally disseminated among them, that all Europeans are magicians, and that their visits to those eastern countries are not to satisfy curiosity, but to find out, and get possession of those vast treasures they believe to be buried there in great quantities. These representations are very common ; but Sir J. Chardin gives us a more particular and amusing account of affairs of this kind : '' It is common in the Indies, for those sorcerers that accompany conquerors, everywhere to point out the place where treasures are hid. Thus, at Surat, when Siragi came thither, there were people who, with a stick striking on the ground or against walls, found out those that had been hollowed or dug up, and ordered such places to be opened.'' He then intimates that something of this nature had happened to him in Mingrelia. Among the various contradictions that agitate the human breast, this appears to be a remarkable one ; they firmly believe the power of magicians to discover hidden treasures, and yet they continue to hide them. Dr. Perry has given us an account of some mighty treasures hidden in the ground by some of the principal people of the Turkish empire, which, upon a revolution, were discovered by domestics privy to the se-

cret. D'Herbelot has given us accounts of treasures concealed in the same manner, some of them of great princes, discovered by accidents extremely remarkable ; but this account of Chardin's, of conquerors pretending to find out hidden treasures by means of sorcerers, is very extraordinary. As, however, people of this east have made great pretences to mighty things, in all ages, and were not unfrequently confided in by princes, there is reason to believe they pretended sometimes, by their art, to discover treasures, anciently, to princes, of which they had gained intelligence by other methods ; and, as God opposed his prophets, at various times, to pretended sorcerers, it is not unlikely that the prophet Isaiah points at some such prophetic discoveries, in those remarkable words (Isa. xlv. 3) : '' And I will give thee the treasures of darkness, and hidden riches of secret places, that thou mayest know that I the LORD, which call thee by thy name, am the God of Israel.'' I will give them, by enabling some prophet of mine to tell thee where they are concealed. Such a supposition throws a great energy into those words.' The belief that the ruins of cities abound with treasures that were deposited there long since, prevails in the East, and the inhabitants of those countries regard all travellers who come there, Burckhardt informs us, as coming to find treasures, and as having power to remove them by enchantment. ' It is very unfortunate,' says he, ' for European travellers, that the idea of treasures being hidden in ancient edifices is so strongly rooted in the minds of the Arabs and Turks ; they believe that it is sufficient for a true magician to have seen and observed the spot where treasures are hidden (of which he is supposed to be already informed by the old books of the infidels who lived on the spot), in order to be able afterwards at his ease to command the guardian of the treasure to set the whole before him. It was of no avail to tell them to follow me and see whether I searched for money. Their reply was, '' Of course you will not dare to take it out before us, but we know that if you are a skilful magician you will order it to follow you through the air to whatever place you please." If the traveller takes the dimensions of a building or a column, they are persuaded it is a magical proceeding.'—(*Travels in Syria*, pp. 428, 429. Ed. Lond. 4to, 1822.) Laborde, in his account of a visit to Petra, or Sela, has given an account of a splendid temple cut in the solid rock, which is called the Khasné, or 'treasury of Pharaoh.' It is sculptured out of an enormous block of freestone, and is one of the most splendid remains of antiquity. It is believed by the Arabs to have been the place where Pharaoh, supposed to have been the founder of the costly edifices of Petra, had deposited his wealth. 'After having searched in vain,' says Laborde, 'all the coffins and funeral monuments, to find his wealth, they supposed it must be in the urn which surmounted the Khasné. But, unhappily, being out of their reach, it has only served the more to kindle their desires. Hence whenever they pass through the ravine, they stop for a moment, charge their guns, aim at the urn, and endeavour by firing at it, to break off some fragments, with a view to demolish it altogether, and get at the treasure which it is supposed to contain.'—(Laborde's *Sinai and Petra*, p. 170. Ed. Lond. 1836.) The treasures which Cyrus obtained in his conquests are known to have been immense. Sardis, the capital of Crœsus, king of Lydia, the most wealthy monarch of his time, was, according to Herodotus (i. 84), given up to be plundered; and his hoarded wealth became the spoil of the victor (see also Xen. *Cyr.* vii.) That Babylon abounded in treasures is expressly declared by Jeremiah (ch. li. 13): 'O thou that dwellest upon many waters, abundant in treasures.' These treasures also, according to Jeremiah (ch. l. 37), became the spoil of the conqueror of the city. Pliny also has given a description of the wealth which Cyrus obtained in his conquests, which strikingly confirms what Isaiah here declares: 'Cyrus, in the conquest of Asia, obtained thirty-four thousand pounds weight of gold, besides golden vases, and gold that was wrought with leaves, and the palm-tree, and the

vine. In which victory also he obtained five hundred thousand talents of silver, and the goblet of Semiramis, which weighed fifteen talents.'—(*Nat. Hist.* 33. 3.) Brerewood has estimated that this gold and silver amounted to one hundred and twenty-six millions, and two hundred and twenty-four thousand pounds sterling.—(*De Pon. et Men.* 10.) Babylon was the centre of an immense traffic that was carried on between the eastern parts of Asia and the western parts of Asia and Europe. For a description of this commerce, see an article in the *Bib. Rep.* vol. vii. pp. 364–390. Babylonian garments, it will be remembered, of great value, had made their way to Palestine in the time of Joshua (vii. 21). Tapestries embroidered with figures of griffons and other monsters of eastern imagination were articles of export (Isaac Vossius, *Observatio*). Carpets were wrought there of the finest materials and workmanship, and formed an article of extensive exportation. They were of high repute in the times of Cyrus; whose tomb at Pasargada was adorned with them (Arrian, *Exped. Alex.* vi. 29). Great quantities of gold were used in Babylon. The vast image of gold erected by Nebuchadnezzar in the plain of Dura is proof enough of this fact. The image was sixty cubits high and six broad (Dan. iii. 1). Herodotus (i. 183) informs us that the Chaldeans used a thousand talents of frankincense annually in the temple of Jupiter. ¶ *That thou mayest know.* That from these signal successes, and these favours of heaven, you may learn that JEHOVAH is the true God. This he would learn because he would see that he owed it to Heaven (see Note on ver. 2); and because the prediction which God had made of his success would convince him that he was the true and only God. That it had this effect on Cyrus is apparent from his own proclamation (see Ezra i. 2). God took this method of making himself known to the monarch of the most mighty kingdom of the earth, in order, as he repeatedly declares, that through his dealings with kingdoms and men he may be acknowledged. ¶ *Which call thee by thy name* (see Notes on ch. xliii. 1). That thou mayest know that I, who so long before desig-

4 For Jacob my servant's sake, and Israel mine elect, I have even called thee by thy name: I have surnamed thee, though thou hast not known me.

5 I ^aam the LORD, and ^bthere is no God besides me : I girded

thee, ^cthough thou hast not known me :

6 That ^dthey may know from the rising of the sun, and from the west, that *there is* none besides me : I *am* the LORD, and *there is* none else.

---

a De.4.35,39.   b ver.14,18,22.

c Ps.18.32,39.   d ch.37.20; Mal.1.11.

---

nated thee by name, am the true God. The argument is, that none but God could have foretold *the name* of him who should be the deliverer of his people. ¶ *Am the God of Israel.* That the God of Israel was the true and only God. The point to be made known was not that he was the God of Israel, but that the God of Israel was JEHOVAH the true God.

4. *For Jacob my servant's sake* (see Note on ch. xlii. 19). The statement here is, that God had raised up Cyrus on account of his own people. The sentiment is common in the Bible, that kings and nations are in the hand of God ; and that he overrules and directs their actions for the accomplishment of his own purposes, and especially to protect, defend, and deliver his people (see Note on ch. x. 5 ; comp. ch. xlvii. 6). ¶ *I have surnamed thee.* On the meaning of the word ' surname,' see Notes on ch. xliv. 5. The reference here is to the fact that he had appointed him to accomplish important purposes, and had designated him as his ' shepherd ' (ch. xliv. 28), and his ' anointed ' (ch. xlv. 1). ¶ *Though thou hast not known me.* Before he was called to accomplish these important services, he was a stranger to JEHOVAH, and it was only when he should have been so signally favoured of Heaven, and should be made acquainted with the Divine will in regard to the deliverance of his people and the rebuilding of the temple (Ezra i. 1–3), that he would be acquainted with the true God.

5. *I* am *the* LORD, &c. (see Notes on ch. xlii. 8; xliii. 2 ; xliv. 8; and ver. 14, 18, 22, of this chapter). ¶ *I girded thee,* &c. (see Note on ver. 1). The sense is, I girded thee with the girdle—the military belt ; I prepared thee, and strengthened thee for war and conquest. Even men who are strangers to the true

God are sustained by him, and are unable to accomplish anything without his providential aid.

6. *That they may know from the rising of the sun, and from the west.* This phrase is evidently here used to designate the whole world. Kimchi says, that the reason why the north and the south are not mentioned here is, that the earth from the east to the west is perfectly inhabitable, but not so from the north to the south. That this was accomplished, see Ezra i. 1, *sq.* Cyrus made public proclamation that JEHOVAH had given him all the kingdoms of the earth, and had commanded him to rebuild the temple in Jerusalem. The purpose of all this arrangement was, to secure the acknowledgment of the truth that JEHOVAH was the only true God, as extensively as possible. Nothing could be better adapted to this than the actual course of events. For, 1. The conquest of Jerusalem by Nebuchadnezzar was an event which would be extensively known throughout all nations. 2. Babylon was then the magnificent capital of the heathen world, and the kingdom of which it was the centre was the most mighty kingdom of the earth. 3. The fact of the conquest of Babylon, and the manner in which it was done, would be known all over that empire, and would attract universal attention. Nothing had ever occurred more remarkable ; nothing more fitted to excite the wonder of mankind. 4. The hand of JEHOVAH was so manifest in this, and the prophecies which had been uttered were so distinctly fulfilled, that Cyrus himself acknowledged that it was of JEHOVAH. The existence, the name, and the truth of JEHOVAH became known as far as the name and exploits of Cyrus ; and there was a public recognition of the true God by him who had conquered the most mighty capital of the world, and whose

7 I *a*form the light, and create darkness ; I make peace, *b* and cre-

ate *c* evil. I the LORD do all these things.

a Ge.1 4.   *b* Ps.29.11.   *c* Am.5.6.

---

opinions and laws were to enter into the constitution of the Medo-Persian empire that was to succeed.

7. *I form the light, and create darkness.* Light, in the Bible, is the emblem of knowledge, innocence, pure religion, and of prosperity in general ; and darkness is the emblem of the opposite. Light here seems to be the emblem of peace and prosperity, and darkness the emblem of adversity ; and the sentiment of the verse is, that all things prosperous and adverse are under the providential control and direction of God. Of *light*, it is literally true that God made it ; and emblematically true that he is the source of knowledge, prosperity, happiness, and pure religion. Of *darkness*, it is literally true also that the night is formed by him ; that he withdraws the light of the sun, and leaves the earth enveloped in gloomy shades. It is emblematically true also that calamity, ignorance, disappointment, and want of success are ordered by him ; and not less true that all the moral darkness, or evil, that prevails on earth, is under the direction and ordering of his Providence. There is no reason to think, however, that the words 'darkness' and 'evil' are to be understood as referring to moral darkness ; that is, *sin*. A strict regard should be had to the connection in the interpretation of such passages ; and the connection here does not demand such an interpretation. The main subject is, *the prosperity which would attend the arms of Cyrus, the consequent reverses and calamities of the nations whom he would subdue, and the proof thence furnished that* JEHOVAH *was the true God;* and the passage should be limited .in the interpretation to this design. The statement is, that all this was under his direction. It was not the work of chance or hap-hazard. It was not accomplished or caused by idols. It was not originated by any inferior or subordinate cause. It was to be traced entirely to God. The successes of arms, and the blessings of peace were to be traced to him ; and the reverses of arms, and the calamities of war to him also.

This is all that the connection of the passage demands ; and this is in accordance with the interpretation of Kimchi, Jerome, Rosenmüller, Gesenius, Calvin, and Grotius. The comment of Grotius is, ' Giving safety to the people, as the Persians ; sending calamities upon the people, as upon the Medes and Babylonians.' Lowth, Jerome, Vitringa, Jahn, and some others, suppose that there is reference here to the prevalent doctrine among the Persians, and the followers of the Magian religion in general, which prevailed all over the East, and in which Cyrus was probably educated, that there are two supreme, independent, co-existent and eternal causes always acting in opposition to each other—the one the author of all good, and the other of all evil ; and that these principles or causes are constantly struggling with each other. The good being or principle, they call light ; and the evil, darkness ; the one, Oromasden, and the other Ahrimanen. It was further the doctrine of the Magians that when the good principle had the ascendency, happiness prevailed ; and when the evil principle prevailed, misery abounded. Lowth supposes, that God here means to assert his complete and absolute superiority over all other things or principles ; and that all those powers whom the Persians supposed to be the original authors of good and evil to mankind were subordinate, and must be subject to him ; and that there is no power that is not subservient to him, and under his control. That these opinions prevailed in very early times, and perhaps as early as Isaiah, there seems no good reason to doubt (Hyde, *de Relig. Veter.* Persar, xxii.) But there is no good evidence that Isaiah here referred to those opinions. Good and evil, prosperity and adversity, abound in the world at all times ; and all that is required in order to a correct understanding of this passage is the general statement that all these things are under providential direction. ¶ *1 make peace.* I hush the contending passions of men ; I dispose to peace, and prevent wars when I choose—a passage

8 Drop *a* down, ye heavens, from above, and let the skies pour down righteousness; let the earth open, and let them bring forth salvation,

and *b* let righteousness spring up together. I the LORD have created it.

a Ps.85.11.   *b* Ps.72.3.

which proves that the most violent passions are under his control. No passions are more uncontrollable than those which lead to wars; and nowhere is there a more striking display of the Omnipotence of God than in his power to repress the pride, ambition, and spirit of revenge of conquerors and kings:

Which stilleth the noise of the seas,
The noise of their waves,
And the tumult of the people.
Ps. lxv. 7.

¶ *And create evil.* The parallelism here shows that this is not to be understood in the sense of *all* evil, but of that which is the opposite of peace and prosperity. That is, God directs judgments, disappointments, trials, and calamities; he has power to suffer the mad passions of men to rage, and to afflict nations with war; he presides over adverse as well as prosperous events. The passage does not prove that God is the author of moral evil, or sin, and such a sentiment is abhorrent to the general strain of the Bible, and to all just views of the character of a holy God.

8. *Drop down, ye heavens, from above.* That is, as a result of the benefits that shall follow from the rescue of the people from their captivity and exile. The mind of the prophet is carried forward to future times, and he sees effects from that interposition, as striking as if the heavens should distil righteousness; and sees the prevalence of piety and happiness as if they should spring out of the earth. It may be designed primarily to denote the happy results of their return to their own land, and the peace and prosperity which would ensue. But there is a beauty and elevation in the language which is better applicable to the remote and distant consequences of their return—the coming and reign of the Messiah. The figure is that of the rain and dew descending from heaven, and watering the earth, and producing fertility and beauty; and the idea is, that piety and peace would prevail in a manner resembling the verdure of

the fields under such rains and dews. A figure remarkably similar to this is employed by the Psalmist (lxxxv. 11, 12):

Truth shall spring out of the earth;
And righteousness shall look down from heaven.
Yea, the LORD shall give that which is good;—
And our land shall yield her increase.

The phrase, 'drop down, ye heavens, from above,' means, pour forth, or distil, as the clouds distil, or drop down the rain or dew (Ps. xlv. 12, 13). It is appropriately applied to rain or dew, and here means that righteousness would be as abundant as if poured down like dews or showers from heaven. The LXX. however, render it, 'Let the heavens above be glad,' but evidently erroneously. ¶ *And let the skies.* The word here used (שְׁחָקִים) is derived from the verb שָׁחַק, *to rub*, pound fine, or beat in pieces; and is then applied to dust (see ch. xl. 15); to a thin cloud; a cloud of dust; and then to clouds in general (Job xxxvi. 28; xxxvii. 18; xxxviii. 37). The sense here is, that righteousness should be poured down like rain from the clouds of heaven; that is, it should be abundant, and should prevail on the earth. ¶ *Pour down righteousness.* The result of the deliverance from the captivity shall be, that righteousness shall be abundant. During the captivity they had been far away from their native land; the temple was destroyed; the fire had ceased to burn on the altars; the praises of God had ceased to be celebrated in his courts; and all the means by which piety had been nourished had been withdrawn. This state of things was strikingly similar to the earth when the rain is withheld, and all verdure droops and dies. But after the return from the exile, righteousness would abound under the re-establishment of the temple service and the means of grace. Nor can there be any doubt, I think, that the mind of the prophet was also fixed on the prevalence of religion which would yet take place under the Messiah, whose coming, though re-

9 Wo unto him that striveth
with his Maker! *Let the* ^apotsherd
strive with the potsherds of the

a Je.18.6.

earth. Shall the clay say to him
that fashioneth it, What makest
thou? or thy work, He hath no
hands?

motely, would be one of the results of
the return from the exile, and of whose
advent, that return would be so strikingly emblematic. ¶ *Let the earth open.*
As it does when the showers descend
and render it mellow, and when it brings
forth grass and plants and fruits. ¶ *And
let them bring forth salvation.* The
Chaldee renders this, 'Let the earth
open, and the dead revive, and righteousness be revealed at the same time.'
The idea is, let the earth and the heavens produce righteousness, or become
fruitful in producing salvation. Salvation shall abound *as if* it descended like
showers and dews, and as if the fertile
earth everywhere produced it. Vitringa
supposes that it means that the hearts
of men would be opened and prepared
for repentance and the reception of the
truth by the Holy Spirit, as the earth
is made mellow and adapted to the
reception of seed by the rain and dew.
¶ *And let righteousness spring up together.* Let it at the same time *germinate* as a plant does. It shall spring
forth like green grass, and like flowers
and plants in the well-watered earth.
The language in the verse is figurative,
and very beautiful. The idea is, that
peace, prosperity, and righteousness start
up like the fruits of the earth when it is
well watered with the dews and rains of
heaven; that the land and world would
be clothed in moral loveliness; and that
the fruits of salvation would be abundant
everywhere. That there was a *partial*
fulfilment of this on the return to the
land of Canaan, there can be no doubt.
The Jews were, for a time at least, much
more distinguished for piety than they
had been before. Idolatry ceased; the
temple was rebuilt; the worship of God
was re-established; and the nation enjoyed unwonted prosperity. But there
is a richness and fulness in the language
which is not met by anything that occurred in the return from the exile; and
it doubtless receives its entire fulfilment
only under that more important deliverance of which the return from Baby-

lon was but the emblem. As referred
to the Messiah, and to his reign, may
we not regard it as descriptive of the
following things? 1. The prevalence
and diffusion of the knowledge of salvation under his own preaching and that
of the apostles. Religion was revived
throughout Judea, and spread with vast
rapidity throughout almost the whole of
the known world. It seemed as if the
very heavens shed down righteousness
on all lands, and the earth, so long
barren and sterile, brought forth the
fruits of salvation. Every country partook of the benefits of the descending
showers of grace, and the moral world
put on a new aspect — like the earth
after descending dews and rains. 2. It
is beautifully descriptive of a revival of
religion like that on the day of Pentecost. In such scenes, it seems as if
the very heavens 'poured down' righteousness. A church smiles under its
influence like parched and barren fields
under rains and dews, and society puts
on an aspect of loveliness like the earth
after copious showers. Salvation seems
to start forth with the beauty of the
green grass, or of the unfolding buds,
producing leaves and flowers and abundant fruits. There cannot be found anywhere a more beautiful description of a
genuine revival of pure religion than in
this verse. 3. It is descriptive, doubtless, of what is *yet* to take place in the
better days which are to succeed the
present, when the knowledge of the Lord
shall fill the earth. All the earth shall
be blessed, as if descending showers
should produce universal fertility, and
every land, now desolate, barren, sterile,
and horrid by sin, shall become 'like
a well-watered garden' in reference to
salvation.

9. *Wo unto him that striveth with his
Maker!* This verse commences a new
subject. Its connection with the pre-
ceeding is not very obvious. It may be
designed to prevent the objections and
cavils of the unbelieving Jews who
were disposed to murmur against God,

and to arraign the wisdom of his dispensations in regard to them, in permitting them to be oppressed by their
enemies, and in promising them deliverance instead of preventing their captivity. So Lowth understands it. Rosenmüller regards it as designed to meet
a cavil, because God chose to deliver
them by Cyrus, a foreign prince, and a
stranger to the true religion, rather than
by one of their own nation. Kimchi,
and some others, suppose that it is designed to repress the pride of the Babylonians, who designed to keep the Jews
in bondage, and who would thus contend with God. But perhaps the idea
is of a more general nature. It may
be designed to refer to the fact that
any interposition of God, any mode of
manifesting himself to men, meets with
enemies, and with those who are disposed to contend with him, and *especially* any display of his mercy and grace
in a great revival of religion. In the
previous verse the prophet had spoken
of the revival of religion. Perhaps he
here adverts to the fact that *such* a
manifestation of his mercy would meet
with opposition. So it was when the
Saviour came, and when Christianity
spread around the world; so it is in
every revival now; and so it will be,
perhaps, in the spreading of the gospel
throughout the world in the time that
shall usher in the millennium. Men
thus contend with their Maker; resist the
influences of his Spirit; strive against
the appeals made to them; *oppose his
sovereignty;* are enraged at the preaching of the gospel, and often combine to
oppose him. That this is the meaning
of this passage, seems to be the sentiment of the apostle Paul, who has borrowed this image, and has applied it in
a similar manner: 'Nay but, O man,
who art thou that repliest against God?
Shall the thing formed say to him that
formed it, Why hast thou made me thus?
Hath not the potter power over the clay,
of the same lump to make one vessel
unto honour, and another unto dishonour?' (Rom. ix. 20, 21.) It is
implied that men are opposed to the
ways which God takes to govern the
world; it is *affirmed* that calamity shall
follow all the resistance which men shall
make. This we shall follow, because,

first, God has all power, and all who
contend with him must be defeated and
overthrown; and, secondly, because God
is *right*, and the sinner who opposes
him is wrong, and must and will be
punished for his resistance. ¶ Let the
potsherd strive *with the potsherds of the
earth.* Lowth renders this,

Woe unto him that contendeth with the power
    that formed him;
The potsherd with the moulder of the clay.

The word rendered 'potsherd' (חֶרֶשׂ)
means properly *a shard*, or *sherd, i.e.*,
a fragment of an earthen vessel (Deut.
vi. 21; xi. 33; Job ii. 8; xli. 22; Ps.
xxii. 16). It is then put proverbially
for anything frail and mean. Here it
is undoubtedly put for man, regarded
as weak and contemptible in his efforts
against God. Our translation would
seem to denote that it was *appropriate*
for man to contend with equals, but not
with one so much his superior as God;
or that he might have some hope of
success in contending with his fellow-
men, but none in contending with his
Maker. But this sense does not well
suit the connection. The idea in the
mind of the prophet is not that such
contentions are either proper or appropriate among men, but it is the supreme
folly and sin of contending with God;
and the thought in illustration of this
is not that men may appropriately contend with each other, but it is the superlative weakness and fragility of man.
The translation proposed, therefore, by
Jerome, ' Wo to him who contends with
his Maker—*testa de samiis terræ*—a
potsherd among the earthen pots [made
of the earth of Samos] of the earth '—
and which is found in the Syriac, and
adopted by Rosenmüller, Gesenius, and
Noyes, is doubtless the true rendering.
According to Gesenius, the particle אֵת
here means *by* or *among;* and the idea
is, that man is a potsherd among the
potsherds of the earth; a weak fragile
creature among others equally so—and
yet *presuming* impiously to contend
with the God that made him. The
LXX. render this, ' Is anything endowed
with excellence? I fashioned it like the
clay of a potter. Will the ploughman
plough the ground all the day long?
Will the clay say to the potter,' &c.

10 Wo unto him that saith unto *his* father, What begettest thou? or to the woman, What hāst thou brought forth?

11 Thus saith the LORD, the Holy One of Israel, and his Maker, Ask me of things to come concerning my sons ; *a* and concerning the work of mine hands command *b* ye me.

a Je.31.1; Ga.3.26.

b Jn.16.23.

¶ *Shall the clay,* &c. It would be absurd for the clay to complain to him that moulds it, of the form which he chooses to give it. Not *less* absurd is it for man, made of clay, and moulded by the hand of God, to complain of the fashion in which he has made him ; of the rank which he has assigned him in the scale of being ; and of the purposes which he designs to accomplish by him. ¶ *He hath no hands.* He has no skill, no wisdom, no power. It is by the *hand* chiefly that pottery is moulded ; and the hands here stand for the skill or wisdom which is evinced in making it. The Syriac renders it, 'Neither am I the work of thy hands.'

10. *Wo unto him that saith unto* his *father,* &c. It is wicked and foolish for a son to complain of his father or mother in regard to his birth, or of his rank and condition of life. Probably the idea is, that if a child is by his birth placed in circumstances less advantageous than others, he would have no right to complain of his parents, or to regard them as having acted improperly in having entered into the marriage relation. In like manner it would be *not less* improper, certainly, to complain of God who has brought us into existence by his own power, and who acts as a sovereign in the various allotments of our lives. The design is to rebuke the spirit of complaining against the allotments of Providence—a spirit which perhaps prevailed among the Jews, and which in fact is found everywhere among men ; and to show that God, as a sovereign, has a right to dispose of his creatures in the manner which he shall judge to be best. The passage proves—1. That man is formed by God, and that all his affairs are ordered by him as really as the work of the potter is moulded by the hands of the workman. 2. That God had a *design* in making man, and in ordering and arranging his circumstances in life. 3. That man is little

qualified to judge of that design, and not at all qualified to pronounce it unwise, any more than the clay could charge him that worked it into a vessel with want of wisdom ; and, 4. That God is a sovereign, and does as he pleases. He has formed man as he chose, as really as the potter moulds the clay into any shape which he pleases. He has given him his rank in creation ; given him such a body—strong, vigorous, and comely ; or feeble, deformed, and sickly, as he pleased ; he has given him such an intellect—vigorous, manly, and powerful ; or weak, feeble, and timid, as he pleased ; he has determined his circumstances in life—whether riches, poverty, an elevated rank, or a depressed condition, just as he saw fit ; and he is a sovereign also in the dispensation of his grace—having a right to pardon whom he will ; nor has man any right to complain. This passage, however, should not be adduced to prove that God, *in all respects,* moulds the character and destiny of men as the potter does the clay. Regard should be had in the interpretation to the fact that God is just, and good, and wise, as well as a sovereign ; and that man is himself a moral agent, and subject to the laws of moral agency which God has appointed. God does nothing wrong. He does not compel man to sin, and then condemn him for it. He does not *make* him a transgressor by physical power, as the potter moulds the clay, and then doom him for it to destruction. He does his pleasure according to the eternal laws of equity ; and man has no right to call in question the rectitude of his sovereign dispensations.

11. *Thus saith the* LORD. This verse is designed still further to illustrate the general subject referred to in this chapter, and especially to show them, that instead of complaining of his designs, or of finding fault with his sovereignty, it was their privilege to

12 1 ^a have made the earth, and created man upon it; I, *even* my hands, have stretched out the hea-

vens, and all their host have 1 com manded,

13 1 have raised him up in righ-

a Ps.102.25; He.11.3.

inquire respecting his dealings, and even to 'command' him. He was willing to be inquired of, and to instruct them in regard to the events which were occurring. ¶ *And his Maker* (see Note on ch. xliii. 1). ¶ *Ask me of things to come.* 'I alone can direct and order future events; and it is your duty and privilege to make inquiry respecting those events. Lowth renders this as a question, 'Do ye question me concerning my children?' But the more correct rendering is doubtless that in our translation, where it is represented as a duty to make inquiry respecting future events from God. The idea is—1. That God alone could direct future events, and give information respecting them. 2. That instead of complaining of his allotments, they should humbly inquire of him in regard to their design, and the proper manner of meeting them; and 3. That if they were made the subject of humble, fervent, believing prayer, he would order them so as to promote their welfare, and would furnish them grace to meet them in a proper manner. ¶ *Concerning my sons.* Those who are my adopted children. It is implied that God loved them as his children, and that they had the privilege of pleading for his favour and regard, with the assurance that he would be propitious to their cry, and would order events so as to promote their welfare. ¶ *And concerning the work of my hands.* In regard to what I do. This is also read as a question by Lowth; 'And do ye give me directions concerning the work of my hands?' According to this interpretation, God would reprove them for presuming to give him direction about what he should do, in accordance with the sentiment in ver. 9, 10. This interpretation also is adopted by Vitringa, Jarchi, Aben Ezra, and some others. Grotius renders it, 'Hinder, if you can, my doing what I will with them. Thus you will show what you can do, and what I can do.' Rosenmüller supposes it to mean, 'Commit my sons, and the work of my hands

to me; suffer me to do with my own what I will.' It seems to me, however, that the word 'command' is here to be taken rather as indicating the privilege of his people to present their desires in the language of fervent and respectful petition; and that God here indicates that he would, so to speak, allow them to *direct* him; that he would hear their prayers, and would conform the events of his administration to their wishes and their welfare. This is the most obvious interpretation; and this will perhaps suit the connection as well as any other. Instead of complaining, and opposing his administration (ver. 9, 10), it was their privilege to come before him and spread out their wants, and even to *give direction* in regard to future events, so far as the events of his administration would bear on them, and he would meet their desires. Thus interpreted, it accords with the numerous passages of the Bible which command us to pray; and with the promises of God that he will lend a listening ear to our cries.

12. *I have made the earth.* God here asserts that he had made all things, doubtless with a view to show that he was able to hear their cry, and to grant an answer to their requests. His agency was visible everywhere, alike in forming and sustaining all things, and in raising up for them a deliverer. They might, therefore, go before him with confidence, and spread out all their wants. ¶ *Have stretched out the heavens* (see Notes on ch. xl. 26). ¶ *And all their host.* The stars (see Notes on ch. xl. 26). ¶ *Have I commanded.* All are under my direction and control. What more can be needed by his people than the friendship and protection of him who made the heavens and the earth, and who leads on the stars!

13. *I have raised him up.* That is, Cyrus (see Notes on ch. xli. 2). ¶ *In righteousness.* In ch. xli. 2, he is called 'the righteous man.' He had raised him up to accomplish his own righteous plans. It does not necessarily mean

teousness, and I will [1] direct all his ways : he shall build [a] my city, and he shall let go my captives, not for price [b] nor reward, saith the LORD of hosts.

14 Thus saith the LORD, The labour of Egypt, and merchandise of Ethiopia and of the Sabeans, men of stature, shall come over

unto [c] thee, and they shall be thine : they shall come after thee ; in chains [d] they shall come over, and they shall fall down unto thee, they shall make supplication unto thee, *saying*, Surely [e] God *is* in thee ; and *there is* none else, *there is* no God.

1 or, *make straight*.   a 2 Ch.36.22; Ezr.1.1,&c.

b ch.52.3.   c Ps.68.31;72.10,11; ch.49.23; 60.9-16.
d Ps.149.8.   e 1 Co.14.25.

that Cyrus was a righteous man (see Notes on ch. xli. 2). ¶ *And I will direct all his ways*. Marg. 'Make straight.' This is the meaning of the Hebrew word (see Notes on ch. xl. 4). The sense here is, I will make his paths all smooth and level, *i.e.*, whatever obstacles are in his way I will remove, and give him eminent success. ¶ *He shall build my city*. Jerusalem. See Ezra i. 2, where, in his proclamation, Cyrus says, ' JEHOVAH, God of heaven, hath given me all the kingdoms of the earth ; and he hath charged me to build him an house at Jerusalem, which is in Judah.' It is very probable that Cyrus was made acquainted with these predictions of Isaiah. Nothing would be more natural than that the Jews in Babylon, when he should become master of the city, knowing that he was the monarch to whom Isaiah referred, and that he had been raised up for their deliverance, should acquaint him with these remarkable prophecies, and show him that God had long before designated him to accomplish this great work (comp. Notes on ch. xliv. 28). ¶ *And he shall let go my captives*. Heb. ' My captivity,' or ' my migration ; ' *i.e.*, those of his people who were in captivity. ¶ *Not for price*. They shall not be purchased of him as slaves, nor shall they be required to purchase their own freedom. They shall be sent away as freemen, and no price shall be exacted for their ransom (comp. ch. lii. 3). The Jews in Babylon were regarded as captives in war, and therefore as slaves. ¶ *Nor for reward*. The Hebrew word here used (שֹׁחַד) denotes properly that which is given to conciliate the favour of others, and hence often a *bribe*. Here it means, that nothing should be given to Cyrus for their purchase, or to

induce him to set them at liberty. He should do it of his own accord. It was a fact that he not only released them, but that he endowed them with rich and valuable gifts, to enable them to restore their temple and city (Ezra i. 7–11).

14. *Thus saith the* LORD. This verse is designed to denote the favours which in subsequent times would be conferred on Jerusalem, the city which (ver. 13) was to be rebuilt. It has reference, according to Lowth, to the conversion of the Gentiles, and their admission into the church of God. Grotius, however, understands it as addressed to Cyrus, and as meaning that because he had released the Jews without reward, therefore God would give him the wealth of Egypt, Ethiopia, Sabæa, and that those nations should be subject to him. But in this opinion probably he stands alone, and the objections to it are so obvious that they need not be specified. Some of the Jewish interpreters suppose that it refers to the same events as those recorded in ch. xliii. 3, and that it relates to the fact that God *had formerly* given those nations for the deliverance and protection of his people. They suppose that particular reference is had to the slaughter and destruction of the army of Sennacherib. Vitringa regards it as referring to the fact that proselytes should be made from all these nations to the true religion, and finds, as he supposes, a fulfilment of it in the times of the Saviour and the apostles. In regard to the true meaning of the passage, we may observe—1. That it refers to the times that would *succeed* their return from their exile ; and not to events that were then past. This is apparent on the face of the passage. 2. It relates to Jerusalem, or to the people

of God, and not to Cyrus. This is evident, because it was not true that these nations became subject to Cyrus after his taking Babylon, for it was not Cyrus, but his son Cambyses that invaded and subdued Egypt, and because the whole phraseology has reference to a conversion to religion, and not to the subjection involved in the conquests of war. 3. It appropriately relates to a conversion to the true God, and an embracing of the true religion. This is implied in the language in the close of the verse, 'saying, Surely God is in thee; and there is none else, there is no God.' 4. The passage, therefore, means, that subsequent to their return from Babylon, there would be the conversion of those nations; or that they—perhaps here mentioned as the representatives of great and mighty nations in general —would be converted to the true faith, and that their wealth and power would be consecrated to the cause of JEHOVAH. The *time* when this was to be, is not fixed in the prophecy itself. It is only determined that it was to be *subsequent* to the return from the exile, and to be one of the consequences of that return. The fulfilment, therefore, may be sought either under the first preaching of the gospel, or in times still more remote. A more full explanation will occur in the examination of the different parts of the verse. ¶ *The labour of Egypt.* That is, the fruit, or result of the labour of Egypt; the wealth of Egypt (see the word thus used in Job x. 3; Ps. lxxviii. 46; Isa. lv. 2; Jer. iii. 24; xx. 5; Ezek. xxiii. 9). The idea is, that Egypt would be converted to the true religion, and its wealth consecrated to the service of the true God. The conversion of Egypt is not unfrequently foretold (Ps. lxviii. 31):

Princes shall come out of Egypt.
Ethiopia shall soon stretch out her hands unto God.

See Notes on ch. xix. 18–22—where the conversion of Egypt is introduced and discussed at length. ¶ *And merchandise of Ethiopia.* On the situation of Ethiopia, see Notes on ch xviii. 1. The word 'merchandise' here means the same as wealth, since their wealth consisted in their traffic. That Cush or Ethiopia would be converted to the

true religion and be united to the people of God, is declared in the passage above quoted from Ps. lxviii. 31; and also in various other places. Thus in Ps. lxvii. 4: 'Behold Philistia, and Tyre, with Ethiopia; this man was born there;' Zeph. iii. 10: 'From beyond the ruins of Ethiopia, my suppliants, even the daughters of my dispersed, shall bring mine offering.' ¶ *And of the Sabeans, men of stature* (סְבָאִים) The inhabitants of Seba (סְבָא *Sebâ*, not שְׁבָא *Shebâ*). Sheba, and the Sabeans of that name were a country and people of Arabia Felix—comprising a considerable part of the country now known as *Yemen*, lying in the south-west part of Arabia (Joel iv. 8; Job i. 15). That country abounded in frankincense, myrrh, spices, gold, and precious stones (1 Kings x. 1; Isa. lx. 6; Jer. vi. 20). *Seba*, here referred to, was a different country. It was inhabited by a descendant of Cush (Gen. x. 7), and was probably the same as Meroë in Upper Egypt (see Notes on ch. xliii. 3). That this people was distinguished for height of stature is expressly affirmed by Herodotus (iii. 20), who says of the Ethiopians, among whom the Sabeans are to be reckoned, that they were 'the tallest of men' (λέγονται εἶναι μέγιστοι ἀνθρώπων); and Solinus affirms that the Ethiopians are 'twelve feet high.' Agatharchides, an ancient Greek poet, quoted by Bochart (*Phaleg.* ii. 26), says of the Sabeans, τὰ σώματά ἐστι τῶν κατοι- κούντων ἀξιολογώτερα—'the bodies of those who dwell there are worthy of special remark.' This shows at least a coincidence between the accounts of Scripture and of profane writers. This country is alluded to by Solomon in Psal. lxxii. 10:

The kings of Tarshish and of the isles shall bring presents;
The kings of Sheba and Seba shall offer gifts.

They are connected here with the Egyptians, and with the inhabitants of Ethiopia or Cush; and their conversion to the true religion would occur probably about the same time. Doubtless the Christian religion was early introduced into these countries, for among those converted on the day of Pentecost, were foreigners from Egypt, and the adjacent countries (Acts ii. 10, 11), who would carry the gospel with them on their return. See also the case of the eunuch of Ethiopia (Acts viii. 26–39), by whom, undoubtedly, the gospel was conveyed to that region. The first Bishop of Ethiopia was Frumentius, who was made bishop of that country about A.D. 330. There is a current tradition among the Ethiopians that the Queen of Sheba, who visited Solomon, was called *Maqueda*, and that she was not from Arabia, but was a queen of their own country. They say that she adopted the Jewish religion, and introduced it among her people; and the eunuch, who was treasurer under Queen Candace, was probably a Jew by religion if not by birth. Yet there will be in future times a more signal fulfilment of this prophecy, when the inhabitants of these countries, and the people of all other nations, shall be converted to the true religion, and shall give themselves to God (comp. Notes on ch. lx. 3–14). That prophecy has a remarkable similarity to this, and indeed is little more than a beautiful expansion of it. ¶ *Shall come over unto thee.* To thy religion; or shall be united to thee in the worship of the true God. It denotes a change not of place, but of character, and of religion. ¶ *And they shall be thine.* A part of thy people; united to thee. The whole *language* of this description, however, is taken from the custom in the conquests of war, where one nation is made subject to another, and is led along in chains. It is here figurative, denoting that the true religion would make rapid and extensive *conquests* among the heathen; that is, that the true religion would everywhere triumph over all others. The phrase 'shall come over,' denotes that their subjection would be voluntary, and that they should freely abandon their own systems; while the phrases 'shall be thine,' 'in chains,' denote the triumphant and mighty power of the truth. ¶ *They shall come after thee.* You shall precede them in the honour of having conveyed to them the true religion, and in that priority of rank which always belongs to those who are first blessed with intelligence, and with the revelation of God. ¶ *In chains shall they come over.*

Language taken from conquests, when subjugated nations are led along as captives; and here denoting the *power* of that truth which would subdue their false systems, and bring them into complete and entire *subjection* to the true religion. This does not mean that it would be against their will, or that they could not have resisted it; but merely that they would be in fact as entirely subject to the true religion as are prisoners of war, in chains, to the will of their conquerors (see Notes on ch. xiv. 1, 2). ¶ *And they shall fall down unto thee.* Recognizing thee as having the knowledge of the true God. To fall down is indicative of reverence; and it means here that Jerusalem would be honoured as being the source whence the true religion should emanate (comp. Luke xxiv. 47). An expression similar to that here used occurs in Isa. xlix. 23: ' And kings—and queens—shall bow down to thee with their face toward the earth, and lick up the dust of thy feet.' ¶ *They shall make supplication unto thee.* Lowth renders this, 'And in suppliant guise address thee.' The Hebrew properly means, they shall pray unto thee; but the idea is, that they should come as suppliants to Jerusalem, confessing that there was the knowledge of the only true God, and praying her inhabitants to impart to them an acquaintance with the true religion (see Notes on ch. ii. 3). The idea indicated by this is, that there would be a condition of anxious solicitude among heathen nations on the subject of the true religion, and that they would seek counsel and direction from those who were in possession of it. Such a state has already existed to some extent among the heathen; and the Scriptures, I think, lead us to suppose that the final spread and triumph of the gospel will be preceded by such an inquiry prevailing extensively in the heathen world. God will show them the folly of idolatry; he will raise up reformers among themselves; the extension of commercial intercourse will acquaint them with the comparative happiness and prosperity of Christian nations; and the growing consciousness of their own inferiority will lead them to desire that which has conferred so extensive benefits on other

15 Verily, thou *art* a God *a* that hidest thyself, O God of Israel, the Saviour.

16 They shall be ashamed, and also confounded, all of them : they shall go to confusion *b* together, *that are* makers of idols.

17 *But* Israel *c* shall be saved in the LORD with an everlasting salvation ; *d* ye shall not be ashamed nor *e* confounded *f* world without end.

a Ps.44.24; ch 8.17.   *b* Ps.97.7.   *c* Ro.2.28,29; 11.26.
d Je 31.3.   *e* Ps.25.2,3.   *f* 1 Pe 2.6.

lands, and lead them to come as suppliants, and ask that teachers and the ministers of religion may be sent to them.   One of the most remarkable characteristics of the present time is, that heathen nations are becoming increasingly sensible of their ignorance and comparative degradation ; that they welcome the ministers and teachers sent out from Christian lands ; and the increased commerce of the world is thus preparing the world for the final spread of the gospel.   ¶ *God* is *in thee*.   In Jerusalem ; or thou art in possession of the only true system of religion, and art the worshipper of the only true God (see ch. xlix. 7; lx. 14).

15. *Verily thou* art *a God that hidest thyself*.   That is, that hidest thy counsels and plans.   The idea is, that the ways of God seems to be dark until the distant event discloses his purpose ; that a long series of mysterious events seem to succeed each other, trying to the faith of his people, and where the reason of his doings cannot be seen.   The remark here seems to be made by the prophet, in view of the fact, that the dealings of God with his people in their long and painful exile would be to them inscrutable, but that a future glorious manifestation would disclose the nature of his designs, and make his purposes known (see ch. lv. 8, 9): 'My thoughts are not your thoughts, neither are your ways my ways' (comp. Ps. xliv. 24; Notes on Isa. viii. 17).   ¶ *The Saviour*. Still the Saviour of his people, though his ways are mysterious and the reasons of his dealings are unknown.   The LXX. render this, ' For thou art God, though we did not know it, O God of Israel the Saviour.'—This verse teaches us that we should not repine or murmur under the mysterious allotments of Providence.   They may be dark now.   But in due time they will be disclosed, and we shall be permitted to see his design,

and to witness results so glorious, as shall satisfy us that his ways are all just, and his dealings right.

16. *They shall be ashamed and confounded*.   That is, they shall find all their hopes fail, and shall be suffused with shame that they were ever so senseless as to trust in blocks of wood and stone (see Notes on ch. i. 29; xx. 5; xxx. 5; xliii. 17).   ¶ *They shall go to confusion*.   They shall all retire in shame and disgrace.   That is, when they have gone to supplicate their idols, they shall find them unable to render them any aid, and they shall retire with shame.

17. But *Israel shall be saved*.   Referring primarily to the Jews in Babylon, but affirming the universal truth that the true Israel (comp. Rom. ii. 28, 29), that is, the people of God, shall be saved from all their trials, and shall be brought to his everlasting kingdom. ¶ *In the* LORD.   By JEHOVAH—בִּיהֹוָה ; LXX. 'Aπὸ κυρίου.   It shall be done by the power of JEHOVAH, and shall be traced to him alone.   No mere human power could have saved them from their captivity in Babylon ; no human power can save the soul from hell.   ¶ *With an everlasting salvation*.   It shall not be a temporary deliverance ; but it shall be perpetual.   In heaven his people shall meet no more foes ; they shall suffer no more calamity ; they shall be driven into no exile ; they shall never die.   ¶ *Ye shall not be ashamed nor confounded*.   This means—1. That they should never find God *to fail*, *i.e.*, to be either unable or unwilling to befriend and rescue them (Ps. xlvi. 1).   2. That they should never be *ashamed*, *i.e.*, have cause to regret that they had put their trust in him.   The idea is, that they who become his friends never regret it ; never are ashamed of it.   The time never can come, when any one who has become a true friend of God

18 For thus saith the LORD that created the heavens, God himself that formed the earth and made it, he hath established it, he created it not in vain, he formed it to be inhabited; I *am* the LORD, and *there is* none else.

19 I have not spoken in secret, in a *a* dark place of the earth: I said not unto the seed of Jacob, Seek ye me in *b* vain. I the LORD speak righteousness, I declare things that are right.

a De.29.29; 30.11,&c.   *b* Ps.9.10; 69.32.

will regret it. In prosperity or adversity; in sickness or health; at home or abroad; in safety or in danger; in life or in death: there will be no situation in which they will be ashamed that they gave their hearts to God. There never have been any *true* Christians who regretted that they became the friends of the Redeemer. Their religion may have exposed them to persecution; their names may have been cast out as evil; they may have been stripped of their property; they may have been thrown into dungeons, laid on the rack, or led to the stake; but they have not regretted that they became the friends of God. Nor will they *ever* regret it. No man on a dying bed regrets that he is a friend of God. No man at the judgment bar will be ashamed to be a Christian. And in all the interminable duration of the world to come, the period never will, never *can* arrive, when any one will ever be ashamed that he gave his heart *early*, and *entirely* to the Redeemer. Why then should not all become his friends? Why will not men pursue that course which they know they never *can* regret, rather than the ways of sin and folly, which they *know* must cover them with shame and confusion hereafter?

18. *For thus saith the* LORD. This verse is designed to induce them to put unwavering confidence in the true God. For this purpose, the prophet enumerates the great things which God had done in proof that he alone was Almighty, and was worthy of trust. *¶ He hath established it.* That is, the earth. The language here is derived from the supposition that the earth is laid upon a foundation, and is made firm. The LXX. render this, 'God who displayed the earth to view, and who, having made it, divided it' (διώρισιν αὐτὴν); that is, parcelled it out to be inhabited. This accords well with the scope of the passage. *¶ He created it not in vain.* He did not form it to remain a vast desert without inhabitants. *¶ He formed it to be inhabited.* By man, and the various tribes of animals. He makes it a convenient habitation for them; adapts its climates, its soil, and its productions, to their nature; and makes it yield abundance for their support. The main idea, I think, in the statement of this general truth, is, that God designed that the earth at large should be inhabited; and that, therefore, he intended that Judea—then lying waste while the captives were in Babylon—should be re-peopled, and again become the happy abode of the returning exiles. So Grotius interprets it. The Jews, from this passage, infer, that the earth shall be inhabited after the resurrection—an idea which has every probability, since there will not be fewer reasons why the earth shall be inhabited *then* than there are now; nor can there be any reasons why the earth should *then* exist in vain any more than now. *¶ And* there is *none else* (see Note on ver. 6).

19. *I have not spoken in secret.* The word rendered 'secret' (סֵתֶר) denotes *a hiding*, or *covering;* and the phrase here means secretly, privately. He did not imitate the heathen oracles by uttering his predictions from dark and deep caverns, and encompassed with the circumstances of awful mystery, and with designed obscurity. *¶ In a dark place of the earth.* From a cave, or dark recess, in the manner of the heathen oracles. The heathen responses were usually given from some dark cavern or recess, doubtless the better to impress with awe the minds of those who consulted the oracles, and to make them more ready to credit the revelations of the fancied god. Such was the seat of the Sybil, mentioned by Virgil, *Æn.* vi. 4:—

Excisum Euboicæ latus ingens rupis in antrum

20 Assemble yourselves and come ; draw near together, ye *that are* escaped of the nations : *a* they

a Ep.2.12-16.

have no knowledge that set up the wood of their graven image, and pray unto a god *that* cannot save.

Such also was the famous oracle at Delphi. Strabo (ix.) says, 'The oracle is said to be a hollow cavern of considerable depth, with an opening not very wide.' Diodorus, giving an account of this oracle, says, ' that there was in that place a great chasm, or cleft in the earth ; in which very place is now situated what is called the Adytum of the temple.' In contradistinction from all this, God says that he had spoken openly, and without these circumstances of designed obscurity and darkness. In the *language* here, there is a remarkable resemblance to what the Saviour said of himself, and it is not improbable that he had this passage in his mind : 'I spake openly to the world ; I ever taught in the synagogue, and in the temple, whither the Jews always resort ; and in secret have I said nothing' (John xviii. 20). A similar declaration occurs in Deut. xxx. 11 : ' This commandment which I command thee this day, it is not hidden from thee, neither is it far off.' ¶ *I said not to the seed of Jacob.* The seed, or the race of Jacob, here means his people : and the idea is, that he had not commanded them to call upon him without his being ready to answer them. ¶ *Seek ye me in vain.* The phrase, 'seek ye,' may refer to worship in general ; or more properly to their calling upon him in times of calamity and trial. The sense is, that it had not been a vain or useless thing for them to serve him ; that he had been their protector, and their friend ; and that they had not gone to him, and spread out their wants for nought. It is still true, that God does not command his people to seek him in vain (comp. Deut. xxxii. 47). His service is always attended with a rich blessing to them ; and they are his witnesses that he confers on them inexpressibly great and valuable rewards. It follows from this—first, that his people have abundant encouragement to go to him in all times of trial, persecution, and affliction ; secondly, that they have

encouragement to go to him in a low state of religion, to confess their sins, to supplicate his mercy, and to pray for the influences of his Holy Spirit, and the revival of his work ; and, thirdly, that the service of God is always attended with rich reward. Idols do not benefit those who serve them. The pursuit of pleasure, gain, and ambition, is often attended with *no* reward, and is *never* attended with any benefits that satisfy the wants of the undying mind ; but the service of God meets all the wants of the soul, fills all its desires, and confers permanent and eternal rewards. ¶ *I the* LORD *speak righteousness.* This stands in opposition to the heathen oracles, which often gave false, delusive, and unjust responses. But not so with God. He had not spoken, as they did, from deep and dark places—fit emblems of the obscurity of their answers ; he had not, as they had, commanded a service that was unprofitable and vain ; and he had not, as they had, uttered oracles which were untrue and fitted to delude. ¶ *I declare things that are right.* Lowth renders this, ' Who give direct answers ;' and supposes it refers to the fact, that the heathen oracles often give ambiguous and deceitful responses. God never deceived. His responses were always true and unambiguous.

20. *Assemble yourselves, and come.* This, like the passage in ch. xli. 1, *sq.,* is a solemn appeal to the worshippers of idols, to come and produce the evidences of their being endowed with omniscience, and with almighty power, and of their having claims to the homage of their worshippers. ¶ *Ye that are escaped of the nations.* This phrase has been very variously interpreted. Kimchi supposes that it means those who were *distinguished* among the nations, their chiefs, and rulers ; Aben Ezra, that the Babylonians are meant especially ; Vitringa, that the phrase denotes *proselytes,* as those who have escaped from the idolatry of the heathen, and have embraced the true religion ; Grotius, that it denotes those who survived the

21 Tell ye, and bring *them* near; yea, let them take counsel together: who hath declared this from ancient time? *who* hath told it from that time? *have* not I the LORD? and *there is* no God else beside me; a just ^a God and a Saviour: *there is* none beside me.

_{a Ro. 3.26.}

slaughter which Cyrus inflicted on the nations. Rosenmüller coincides in opinion with Vitringa. The word here used (פָּלִיט) denotes properly one who has escaped by flight from battle, danger, or slaughter (Gen. xiv. 13; Josh. viii. 32). It is not used anywhere in the sense of a proselyte; and the idea here is, I think, that those who escaped from the slaughter which Cyrus would bring on the nations, were invited to come and declare what benefit they had derived from trusting in idol-gods. In ver. 16, God had said they should all be ashamed and confounded who thus put their trust in idols; and he here calls on them as living witnesses that it was so. Those who had put their confidence in idols, and who had seen Cyrus carry his arms over nations notwithstanding their vain confidence, could now testify that no reliance was to be placed on them, and could be adduced as witnesses to show the importance of putting their trust in JEHOVAH. ¶ *That set up the wood.* The word 'wood' is used here to show the folly of worshipping an image thus made, and to show how utterly unable it was to save.

21. *Tell ye, and bring* them *near.* That is, announce, and bring forward your strongest arguments (see Notes on ch. xli. 1). ¶ *Who hath declared this from ancient time?* Who has clearly announced the events respecting Cyrus, and the conquest of Babylon, and the deliverance from the captivity? The argument is an appeal to the fact that God had clearly foretold these events long before, and that therefore he was the true God. To this argument he often appeals in proof that he alone is God (see Note on ch. xli. 22, 23). ¶ *And* there is *no God else beside me* (see ver. 5). ¶ *A just God.* A God whose attribute it is always to do right; whose word is true; whose promises are fulfilled; whose threatenings are executed; and who always does that which, under the circumstances of the case,

ought to be done. This does not refer *particularly* to the fact that he will punish the guilty, but, in the connection here, rather seems to mean that his course would be one of equity. ¶ *And a Saviour.* Saving his people. It was a characteristic of him, that he saved or preserved his people; and his equity, or truth, or justice, was seen in his doing that. His being 'a just God' and 'a Saviour' are not set here in contrast or contradiction, as if there was any incongruity in them, or as if they needed to be reconciled; but they refer to the same thing, and mean that he was just and true *in saving* his people; it was a characteristic of him that he was *so* true to his promises, and so equitable in his government, that he *would* save them. There is here no peculiar and special reference to the work of the atonement. But the *language* is such as will accurately express the great leading fact in regard to the salvation of sinners. It is in the cross of the Redeemer that God has shown himself eminently to be just, and yet a Saviour; true, and merciful; expressing his abhorrence of sin, and yet pardoning it; maintaining the honour of his violated law, and yet remitting its penalty and forgiving the offender. It is here, in the beautiful language of the Psalmist (lxxxv. 10), that

Mercy and truth are met together,
Righteousness and peace have kissed each other.

The same idea is expressed in Rom. iii. 26: 'That he might be just, and the justifier of him that believeth in Jesus.' It is the glory of the character of God that he *can* be thus just and merciful at the same time; that he can maintain the honour of his law, secure the stability of his government, and yet extend pardon to any extent. No human administration can do this. Pardon under a human government *always* does much to weaken the authority of the government, and to set aside the majesty of the law. If *never* exercised, indeed, government

22 Look ⁿunto me, and be ye saved, all the ends of the earth ;

a Ps.22.27; Jn.3 14,15.

for 1 *am* God, and *there is* none else.

assumes the form of tyranny; if *often*, the law loses its terrors, and crime will walk fearless through the earth. But in the Divine administration, through the atonement, pardon may be extended to any extent, and yet the honour of the law be maintained, for the substituted sufferings of the innocent in the place of the guilty, will *in fact* do more to restrain from transgression than where the guilty themselves suffer. Of no human administration can it be said that it is at the same time just, and yet forgiving; evincing hatred of the violation of the law, and yet extending mercy to any extent to the violators of the laws. The blending together of these apparently inconsistent attributes belongs only to God, and is manifested only in the plan of salvation through the atonement.

22. *Look unto me, and be ye saved.* This is said in view of the declaration made in the previous verse, that he is a just God and a Saviour. It is *because* he sustains this character that all are invited to look to him; and the doctrine is, that the fact that God is at the same time just and yet a Saviour, or can save consistently *with* his justice, is an argument why they should look to him, and confide in him. If he is at the same time just—true to his promises; righteous in his dealings; maintaining the honour of his law and government, and showing his hatred of sin; and also merciful, kind, and forgiving, it is a ground of confidence in him, and we should rejoice in the privilege of looking to him for salvation. The phrase 'look unto me' means the same as, direct the attention to, as we do to one from whom we expect aid. It denotes a conviction on our part of helplessness—as when a man is drowning, he casts an imploring eye to one on the shore who can help him; or when a man is dying, he casts an imploring eye on a physician for assistance. Thus the direction to look to God for salvation implies a deep conviction of helplessness and of sin; and a deep conviction that he only can save. At the same time it shows the ease of

salvation. What is more easy than to *look* to one for help? What more easy than to cast the eyes towards God the Saviour? What more reasonable than that he should require us to do it? And what more just than that God, if men *will not* LOOK to him in order that they may be saved, should cast them off for ever?. Assuredly, if a dying, ruined, and helpless sinner will not do so simple a thing as *to look* to God for salvation, he *ought* to be excluded from heaven, and the universe will acquiesce in the decision which consigns him to despair. ¶ *All the ends of the earth.* For the meaning of this phrase, see Note on ch. xl. 28. The invitation here proves— 1. That the offers of the gospel are universal. None are excluded. The ends of the earth, the remotest parts of the world, are invited to embrace salvation, and all those portions of the world might, under this invitation, come and accept the offers of life. 2. That God is willing to save all; since he would not give an invitation at all unless he was *willing* to save them. 3. That there is ample provision for their salvation; since God could not invite them to accept of what was not provided for them, nor could he ask them to partake of salvation which had no existence. 4. That it is his serious and settled purpose that all the ends of the earth *shall be* invited to embrace the offers of life. The invitation has gone from his lips, and the command has gone forth that it should be carried to every creature (Mark xvi. 15), and now it appertains to his church to bear the glad news of salvation around the world. God intends that it shall be done, and on his church rests the responsibility of seeing it speedily executed. ¶ *For 1 am God.* This is a *reason* why they should look to him to be saved. It is clear that none but the true God can save the soul. No one else but he can pronounce sin forgiven; no one but he can rescue from a deserved hell. No idol, no man, no angel can save ; and if, therefore, the sinner is saved, he must come to the true God, and depend on

23 I have sworn *a* by myself, the word is gone out of my mouth *in* righteousness, and shall not return,

That unto me *b* every knee shall bow, every tongue shall *c* swear.

a Ge 22.16; He.6.13.   *b* Phi.2.10.   *c* De.6.13.

him. That he *may* thus come, whatever may have been his character, is abundantly proved by this passage. This verse contains truth enough, if properly understood and applied, to save the world; and on the ground of this, all men, of all ages, nations, climes, ranks, and character, might come and obtain eternal salvation.

23. *I have sworn by myself.* This verse contains a fuller statement of the truth intimated in the previous verse, that the benefits of salvation should yet be extended to all the world. It is the expression of God's solemn purpose that all nations should yet be brought to acknowledge him, and partake of the benefits of the true religion. The expression, 'I have sworn by myself,' denotes a purpose formed in the most solemn manner, and ratified in the most sacred form. God could swear by no greater (Heb. vi. 13, 16); and this, therefore, is the most solemn assurance that could be possibly given that the purpose which he had formed should be executed. To swear by himself is the same as to swear by his life, or to affirm solemnly that the event shall as certainly occur as that he exists. The same idea is often expressed by the phrase, 'as I live.' See a parallel declaration in Num. xiv. 21: ' But as truly as I live, all the earth shall be filled with the glory of the LORD' (comp. Num. xiv. 28; Isa. xlix.18; Jer. xxii. 24; Ezek. v. 11; xiv. 16, 18, 20; Zeph. ii. 9; Rom. xiv. 11). This passage is quoted by Paul in Rom. xiv. 11, where the phrase, 'I have sworn by myself' is rendered, 'as I live, saith the Lord,' showing that they are equivalent expressions. ¶ *The word is gone out of my mouth.* The LXX. render this, ' Righteousness shall proceed from my mouth, my words shall not return.' Lowth renders it, ' Truth is gone forth from my mouth; the word, and it shall not be revoked.' Jerome, 'The word of righteousness has gone forth from my mouth, and shall not return.' Rosenmüller accords with the interpretation

of Lowth. Probably the correct translation is 'righteousness (*i.e.*, the right-. eous sentence, or purpose, where the word צְדָקָה is used in the sense of *truth*, see ver. 19), has gone out of my mouth, the word (*i.e.*, the promise), and it shall not return.' In this construction the ל before לֹא (*lō*) has the force of a relative pronoun, and is to be referred to דָּבָר (*dhâbhâr*), 'the word.' The sense is, that God had spoken it, and that all which he has spoken shall certainly be fulfilled. The fact that the declaration has once passed his lips, is full proof that the purpose shall be accomplished. This is not to be understood of any promise which he had made before, but it is a solemn declaration which he now makes by the prophet. ¶ *That unto me every knee shall bow.* To bow or bend the knee, is indicative of homage or adoration; and the idea is, that all should yet acknowledge him to be God (see Note on Rom. xiv. 11). The ancient mode of offering adoration, or of paying homage, was to place the knee on the ground, and then slowly to incline the body until the head touched the earth. This is practised now in eastern countries (comp. Gen. xli. 43 ; 1 Kings xix. 18; 2 Chron. vi. 13; Matt. xxvii. 29; Rom. xi. 4; Phil. ii. 10; Eph. iii. 14). The obvious and proper signification of this is, that the time would come when God would be everywhere acknowledged as the true God. It refers therefore to the future period of glory on the earth, when all men shall have embraced the true religion, and when idolatry shall have come to an end. ¶ *Every tongue shall swear.* This expression is evidently taken from the practice of taking an oath of allegiance to a sovereign, and here means that all would solemnly acknowledge him to be the true God, and submit themselves to his government and will. See the phrase explained in the Note on ch. xix. 18. That this refers to the Messiah and his times, is apparent from the fact that it is twice referred to by the apostle Paul, and applied by him to the

24 Surely, ¹shall *one* say, In the LORD have I ²righteousness *ᵃ*and strength : *ᵇeven* to him *ᶜ* shall *men* come ; and all that are incensed against him shall be ashamed.

25 In the LORD shall all the seed of Israel be justified, *ᵈ*and shall glory.

1 or, *he shall say of me, In the LORD is all right-eousness and strength.*   2 *righteousness·s.*
a Je.23.6; 1 Co.1.30,31.   b Ze.10.6,12; Ep.6.10.
c Jn.12.32.   d Ro.5.1.

Lord Jesus and his religion (Rom. xiv. 11; Phil. ii. 10). It is a glorious promise which remains yet to be fulfilled, and there is no promise in the Bible more certain than that this earth shall yet be filled with the knowledge of the true God.

24. *Surely, shall* one *say.* Marg. ' He shall say of me, In the LORD is all righteousness and strength.' The design of the verse is, to set forth more fully the effect of the prevalence of the true religion ; and the main thought is, that there shall be an universal acknowledgment that salvation and strength were in JEHOVAH alone. Idols and men could not save ; and salvation was to be traced to JEHOVAH only. A literal translation of the passage would be, ' Truly in JEHOVAH, he said unto me,' or it is said unto me, *i.e.*, I heard it said, ' is righteousness and strength,' that is, this would be everywhere the prevailing sentiment that righteousness and strength were to be found in JEHOVAH alone. The sense is, first, that it was by him alone that they could be par-doned and justified ; and, secondly, that it was by him alone that they could ob-tain *strength* to meet their enemies, to overcome their sins, to discharge their duties, to encounter temptations, to bear afflictions, and to support them in death. These two things, righteous-ness and strength, are all that man needs. The whole of religion consists essentially in the feeling that righteous-ness and strength are to be found in God our Saviour. The LXX. render this, ' Every tongue shall swear to God, saying, Righteousness and glory shall come unto him, and all those who make distinctions among them shall be ashamed.' ¶ Even *to him shall* men *come.* For the purpose of being saved (see Notes on ch. ii. 3). ¶ *And all that are incensed against him.* All that are opposed to his government and laws. ¶ *Shall be ashamed* (see Note on ver. 16). The enemies of God shall see their own

feebleness and folly ; and they shall be ashamed that they have endeavoured to oppose one so mighty and so glorious as the living God. The multitudes that have in various ways resisted him shall see the folly of their course, and be overwhelmed with shame that they have dared to lift the hand against the God that made the heavens. Jarchi renders this, ' All who have opposed themselves to God, shall come to him, led by peni-tence on account of the things which they have done, and shall be ashamed.'

25. *In the* LORD. It shall be only in JEHOVAH that they shall find justifica-tion, and this must mean, that it is by his mercy and grace. The entire pas-sage here, I suppose, has reference to the times of the Redeemer (see Notes on ver. 21–24). If so, it means that justification can be obtained only by the mercy of God through a Redeemer. The great truth is, therefore, here brought into view, which constitutes the sum of the New Testament, that men are not justified by their own works, but by the mercy and grace of God. ¶ *All the seed of Israel.* All the spiritual seed or descendants of Jacob. It cannot mean that every individual shall be justified and saved, for the Bible abundantly teaches the contrary (see Matt. viii. 11, 12; Rom. xi.) But it must mean that all who have a character resembling that of Israel, or Jacob; all who are the true children and friends of God (see Rom. ii. 28, 29; iv. 9–13). ¶ *Be justified.* Be regarded and treated as righteous. Their sins shall be pardoned, and they shall be ac-knowledged and treated as the children of God (see Notes on Rom. iii. 24, 25). *To justify,* here, is not to pronounce them innocent, or to regard them as de-serving of his favour; but it is to receive them into favour, and to resolve to treat them *as if* they had not sinned; that is, to treat them as if they were right-eous. All this is by the mere mercy and grace of God, and is through the

CHAPTER XLVI.

ANALYSIS.

This chapter is a continuation of the argument before commenced to show the folly of idolatry, and to induce the captive and exile Jews to put their trust in JEHOVAH. The argument consists of the following particulars:—

I. The idols of Babylon should be overthrown (1, 2). The prophet sees those idols removed from their places, laid on beasts of burden, and borne away. They were unable to deliver their city from the arm of the conqueror, but were themselves carried into captivity. The exiles, therefore, had the certain prospect of deliverance.

II. God appeals to the fact, that he had always protected the Jewish people; that he had dealt with them as a parent in the infancy and youth of their nation, and he solemnly assures them that he would not leave them in their old age and their trials (3, 4).

III. He shows them the folly of idolatry, and the vanity of idols (5-7). They could not aid or defend in the day of trial; and, therefore, the people should put their trust in the true God.

IV. He appeals to them by the recollection of former events, and reminds them of his merciful interposition (8, 9).

V. He appeals to them by the fact that he had predicted future events, and especially by the fact that he had raised up a distinguished conqueror—Cyrus—who would accomplish all his pleasure (10, 11).

VI. He assures them that his righteous purpose was near to be accomplished, and that he would restore Zion to its former splendour, and that his salvation should be made known to his people (12, 13).

The *scene* of this prophecy is laid in Babylon, and at the time when the city was about to be taken by Cyrus, and the Jews about to be delivered from captivity. The idols of the Chaldeans, unable to defend their city, are borne in haste away for safety, and Cyrus is at the gates. The *design* is to give to the exiles there an assurance that when they should see these things, they should conclude that their deliverance drew near; and to furnish them thus with ample demonstration that JEHOVAH was the true God, and that he was their protector and friend. In their long and painful captivity also, they would have these promises to comfort them; and when they surveyed the splendour of the idol worship in Babylon, and their hearts were pained with the prevalent idolatry, they would have also the assurance that those idols were to be removed, and that that idolatry would come to an end.

B EL *a* boweth down, Nebo *b* stoopeth ; their idols were upon the beasts ; *c* and upon the cattle : your carriages *were* heavy loaden ; *they are* a burden to the weary *beast*.

a Je.50.51.   *b* Je.48.1,&c.   *c* Je.10.5.

---

merits of the Redeemer, who died in their place. ¶ *And shall glory.* Or rather, shall praise and celebrate his goodness. The word here used (הָלַל *hâlăl*) means, in Piel, *to sing*, to chant, to celebrate the praises of any one (1 Chron. xvi. 36; Ps. xliv. 9; cxvii. 1; cxlv. 2), and is the word of which the word *hallelujah* is in part composed. Here it means, that the effect of their being justified by JEHOVAH would be, that they would be filled with joy, and would celebrate the goodness of God. This effect of being justified, is more fully stated in Rom. v. 1-5. It is a result which always follows; and a disposition to praise and magnify the name of God in view of his boundless mercy in providing a way by which sinners may be justified, is one of the first promptings of a renewed heart, and one of the evidences that a soul is born again.

CHAPTER XLVI.

1. *Bel boweth down.* Bel or Belus (בֵּל *Bēl*, from בְּעֵל *Bĕēl*, the same as בַּעַל *Băăl*) was the chief domestic god of the Babylonians, and was worshipped in the celebrated tower of Babylon (comp. Jer. 1. 2; li. 44). It was usual to compound names of the titles of the divinities that were worshipped, and hence we often meet with this name, as in Bel-shazzar, Bel-teshazzar, Baal-Peor, Baal-zebub, Baal-Gad, Baal-Berith. The Greek and Roman writers compare Bel with Jupiter, and the common name which they give to this idol is *Jupiter Belus* (Pliny, *Nat. Hist.* xxxvii. 10 ; Cic. *De Nat. Deor.* iii. 16; Diod. ii. 8, 9). Herodotus (i. 181-183) says, that in the centre of each division of the city of Babylon (for the Euphrates divided the city into two parts) there is a circular space surrounded by a wall. In one

of these stands the royal palace, which fills a large and strongly defended space. The temple ot Jupiter Belus, says he, occupies the other, whose huge gates of brass may still be seen. It is a square building, each side of which is of the length of two furlongs. In the midst, a tower rises of the solid depth and height of one furlong; on which, resting as a base, seven other turrets are built in regular succession. The ascent on the outside, winding from the ground, is continued to the highest tower; and in the middle of the whole structure there is a convenient resting-place. In this temple there is a small chapel, which contains a figure of Jupiter in a sitting posture, with a large table before him ; these, with the base of the table, and the seat of the throne, are all of the purest gold. There was formerly in this temple a statue of solid gold, twelve cubits high. This was seized, says Herodotus, by Xerxes, who put the priest to death who endeavoured to prevent its removal. The upper room of this tower was occupied as an observatory. The idol *Baal*, or *Bel*, was peculiarly the god of the Phenicians, of the Canaanites, of the Chaldeans, of the Moabites, and of some of the surrounding nations. The most common opinion has been, that the idol was the *sun* (see Notes on ch. xvii. 8, 9), and that, under this name, this luminary received divine honours. But Gesenius supposes that by the name *Jupiter Belus* was not denoted Jupiter, ' the father of the gods,' but the planet Jupiter, *Stella Jovis*, which was regarded, together with Venus, as the giver of all good fortune; and which forms with Venus the most fortunate of all constellations under which sovereigns can be born. The planet Jupiter, therefore, he supposes to have been worshipped under the name *Bel*, and the planet Venus under the name of Astarte, or Astarcth (see Gesenius, *Comm. zu Isaiah*, ii. 333, *sq.*, and Robinson's *Calmet, Art.* Baal). The phrase ' boweth down,' means here, probably, that the idol sunk down, fell, or was removed. It was unable to defend the city, and was taken captive, and carried away. Jerome renders it, *Confractus est Bel*—' Bel is broken.' The LXX. "Επεσε Βηλ—' Bel has fallen.' Perhaps in the *language* there is allu-

sion to the fact that Dagon *fell* before the ark of God (1 Sam. v. 2, 3, 7). The sense is, that even the object of worship —that which was regarded as the most sacred among the Chaldeans—would be removed. ¶ *Nebo stoopeth*. This was an idol-god of the Chaldeans. In the astrological mythology of the Babylonians, according to Gesenius (*Comm. zu Isaiah* ii. 333, *sq.*), this idol was the planet Mercury. He is regarded as the scribe of the heavens, who records the succession of the celestial and terrestrial events; and is related to the Egyptian Hermes and Anubis. The extensive worship of this idol among the Chaldeans and Assyrians is evident from the many compound proper names occurring in the Scriptures, of which this word forms a part, as Neb-uchadnezzar, Neb-uzaradan : and also in the classics, as Nab-onad, Nab-onassar. Nebo was, therefore, regarded as an attendant on Bel, or as his scribe. The exact form of the idol is, however, unknown. The word ' stoopeth,' means that it had fallen down, as when one is struck dead he falls suddenly to the earth ; and the language denotes *conquest*, where even the idols so long worshipped would be thrown down. The scene is in Babylon, and the image in the mind of the prophet is that of the city taken, and the idols that were worshipped thrown down by the conqueror, and carried away in triumph. ¶ *Their idols were upon the beasts.* That is, they are laid upon the beasts to be borne away in triumph. It was customary for conquerors to carry away all that was splendid and valuable, to grace their triumph on their return; and nothing would be a more certain indication of victory, or a more splendid accompaniment to a triumph, than the gods whom the vanquished nations had adored. Thus in Jer. xlviii. 7, it is said, ' And Chemosh shall go forth into captivity, with his priests and his princes together' (comp. Jer. xlix. 3, marg.) ¶ *Your carriages*. That is, they were laden with the idols that were thus borne off in triumph. ¶ They are *a burden*. They are so numerous; so heavy; and to be borne so far. This is a very striking and impressive manner of foretelling that the city of Babylon would be destroyed. Instead of employing the

2 They stoop, they bow down together, they could not deliver the burden, but ¹ themselves are gone into captivity.

3 Hearken unto me, O house of Jacob, and all the remnant of the house of Israel, which are borne

1 *their soul.*

by ᵃ me from the belly, which are carried from the womb.

4 And *even to your* old age ᵇ I *am* he ; and *even* to hoar hairs will I carry *you :* I have made, and I will bear ; even I will carry, and will deliver *you.*

a Ex.19.4; Ps.71.6,18.   b Ps.92.14.

direct language of prophecy, the prophet represents himself as *seeing* the heavy laden animals and waggons moving along slowly, pressed down under the weight of the captured gods to be borne into the distant country of the conqueror. They move forth from Babylon, and the caravan laden with the idols, the spoils of victory, is seen slowly moving forward to a distant land.

2. *They stoop.* Bel, and Nebo, and all the Babylonian gods (see ver. 1). ¶ *They could not deliver the burden.* The word 'burden' here, probably means the *load* of metal, wood, and stone, of which the idols were composed. The gods whom the Babylonians worshipped had not even power to protect the images which were made to represent them, and which had now become a heavy burden to the animals and wains which were carrying them away. They could not rescue them from the hands of the conqueror; and how unable were they, therefore, to defend those who put their trust in them. The Vulgate renders this, 'They could not deliver him that bare them.' The LXX, 'You are carrying them like a burden bound on the weary, faint, and hungry; who are all without strength, and unable to escape from battle ; and as for them, they are carried away captives!' ¶ *But themselves.* Marg. as Heb. ' Their soul.' The sense is, that the gods thus worshipped, so far from being able to defend those who worshipped them, had themselves become captive, and were borne to a distant land.

3. *Hearken unto me.* From this view of the captive gods, the address is now turned to the Jews. The utter vanity of the idols had been set before them; and in view of that, God now addresses his own people, and entreats them to put their trust in him. The address he commences with words of

great tenderness and endearment, designed to lead them to confide in him as their Father and friend. ¶ *And all the remnant.* All who were left from slaughter, and all who were borne into captivity to Babylon. The language here is all full of tenderness, and is fitted to inspire them with confidence in God. The idols of the heathen, so far from being able to protect their worshippers, were themselves carried away into ignoble bondage, but JEHOVAH was himself able to carry his people, and to sustain them. ¶ *Which are borne* by me. Like an indulgent father, or a tender nurse, he had carried them from the very infancy of their nation. The same image occurs in Deut. i. 31 : 'And in the wilderness, where thou hast seen how that the LORD thy God bare thee, as a man doth bear his son, in all the way that ye went, until ye came into this place.' A similar figure occurs in Ex. xix. 4 : ' Ye have seen, how I bare you on eagles' wings, and brought you unto myself' (so Deut. xxxii. 11, 12 ; comp. Num. xi. 12 ; Isa. lxiii. 9). All this here stands opposed to the idols of the Babylonians. They were unable to protect their people. They were themselves made captive. But God had shown the part of a father and a protector to his people in all times. He had sustained and guided them; he had never forsaken them ; he had never, like the idol-gods, been *compelled* to leave them in the power of their enemies. From the fact that he had always, even from the infancy of their nation, thus protected them, they are called on to put their trust in him.

4. *And* even *to* your *old age, I* am *he.* Or rather, I am the same. I remain, unchangeably, with the same tenderness, the same affection, the same care. In this the care of God for his people surpasses that of the most tender parent, and the most kind nourisher of the

5 To whom will ye liken me, and make *me* equal, and compare me, that we may be like ?

6 They *a*lavish gold out of the bag, and weigh silver in the balance, *and* hire a goldsmith ; and he maketh it a god : they fall down ; yea, they worship.

7 They bear him upon the shoulder, they carry him, and set him in his place, and he standeth ; from his place shall he not remove : yea, *one* shall cry unto him, yet can he not answer, nor save him out of his trouble.

a ch.41.7,&c.

young. The care of the parent naturally dies away as the child reaches manhood, and he is usually removed by death before the son or daughter that excited so much solicitude in infancy and childhood, reaches old age. But not so with God. His people are always the objects of his tender solicitude. Age does not make them less dependent, and experience only teaches them more and more their need of his sustaining grace. The *argument* here is, that he who had watched over the infancy of his people with so much solicitude, would not leave them in the exposures, and infirmities, and trials of the advanced years of their history. The *doctrine* is, first, that his people *always* need his protection and care ; secondly, that he will never leave nor forsake them ; thirdly, that he who is the God of infancy and childhood will be the God of age, and that he will not leave or forsake his people, who have been the objects of his care and affection in childhood, when they become old. For though this passage refers primarily to a *people*, or a community as such, yet I see no reason why the principle should not be regarded as applicable to those who are literally aged. They *need* the care of God no less than childhood does ; and if they have walked in his ways in the vigour and strength of their life, he will not cast them off 'when they are old and gray-headed.' Hoary hairs, therefore, if 'found in the way of righteousness,' may trust in God ; and the 'second childhood' of man may find him no less certainly a protector than the first.

5. *To whom will ye liken me* (see Notes on ch. xl. 18, 25). The design of this and the following verses is to show the folly of idolatry, and the vanity of trusting in idols. This is a subject that the prophet often dwells on. The argu-

ment here is derived from the fact that the idols of Babylon were unable to defend the city, and were themselves carried away in triumph (ver. 1, 2). If so, how vain was it to rely on them ! how foolish to suppose that the living and true God could resemble such weak and defenceless blocks !

6. *They lavish gold.* The word here used means properly to shake out ; and then to pour out abundantly, or in a lavish manner. It is used in connection with the idea of *squandering* in Deut. xxi. 20 ; Prov. xxiii. 21 ; xxviii. 7. Here the idea is, that they spared no expense ; they poured out gold as if it were vile and worthless, in order to make an idol. The design of this verse is, to show the superstition of those who were idolaters ; and, particularly, how much they were willing to devote in order to maintain idol-worship. ¶ *Out of the bag.* They pour their gold out of the bag, or purse, where they have kept it ; that is, they lavish it freely. ¶ *And weigh silver in the balance.* Perhaps the idea is here, that they used silver so lavishly that they did not wait to count it, but weighed it as they would the grosser metals. The word here used and translated 'balance' (קָנֶה,), means properly *cane, reed, calamus* ; then a measuring reed or rod (Ezek. xl. 3, 5) ; then a rod, or beam of a balance, or scales (Gr. ζυγὸς). ¶ *And hire a goldsmith* (see Notes on ch. xl. 19, 20). ¶ *And he maketh it a god.* The goldsmith manufactures the gold and the silver into an image. The object of the prophet is to deride the custom of offering divine homage to a god formed in this manner (see Notes on ch. xliv. 9–19).

7. *They bear him upon the shoulder.* They carry the idol which they have made on their shoulder to the temple, or place where it is to be fixed. This cir-

8 Remember this, and show yourselves men : bring *it* again to mind,
O ye transgressors.

9 Remember the former things
of old ; for I *am* God, and *there is*

none else ; *I am* God, and *there is*
none like me ;

10 Declaring the end from the
beginning, and from ancient times
the things that are not *yet* done,

---

cumstance, with the others, is doubtless
introduced to show how ridiculous and
absurd it was to offer divine homage to
a god whom they could thus carry about
on the shoulder. ¶ *And set him in his
place.* Fix the idol on its basis or pedestal, in its proper niche, or place in
the temple. The whole design of this
verse is to contrast the idol with JEHO-
VAH. JEHOVAH is uncreated and eternal ;
the idol, on the contrary, is made by men,
is borne about, is fixed in its place, has
no power to move, remains there until it
is taken down, and has no ability either
to hear or save those who worship it.

8. *Remember this.* Bear in mind
what is now said of the manner in which
idols are made. This is addressed, doubtless, to the Jews, and is designed to keep
them from idolatry. ¶ *And show yourselves men.* Act as men ; throw away
the childish trifles of idolaters. The
word here used (הִתְאֹשָׁשׁוּ) occurs nowhere else in the Bible. It is, according
to Gesenius, derived from אִישׁ, *a man,*
and means to act *as a man.* A similar
word is used in 1 Cor. xvi. 13 (ἀνδρίζεσθε,
from ἀνήρ, *a man*), and is correctly rendered there, 'quit you like men.' This
Greek word often occurs in the Septuagint. It is used as a translation of אָמִיץ,
in Josh. i. 6, 7, 9, 18 ; 1 Chron. xxviii.
20 ; 2 Chron. xxxii. 7 ; Neh. ii. 1 ; of
גְּדל, in Ruth i.12 ; of חָזַק, in Deut. xxxi.
6, 7, 23 ; Josh. x. 25 ; 2 Kings x. 12 ; xiii.
28 ; Ps. xxvi. 20, and in several other
places. Jerome renders the Hebrew
word here, ' Be confounded ;' the LXX.
Στενάξατε—' Groan ;' the Syriac, ' Consider,' or understand. The meaning is,
that they were to act as became men—
not as children ; as became those endowed with an immortal mind, and not
as the brutes. So Kimchi renders it :
' Be men, and not brutes, which neither
consider nor understand.' ¶ *O ye transgressors.* Ye who have violated the
laws of God by the worship of idols.
In the time of Manasseh, the Israelites

were much addicted to idolatry, and
probably this is to be regarded as addressed to them, and as designed to recall them from it to the worship of the
true God.

9. *Remember the former things,* &c.
Bear in mind the repeated and constant
proofs that have been given that JEHO-
VAH is the true God—the proofs derived
from the prediction of future events, and
from the frequent interpositions of his
providence in your behalf as a nation.
¶ *For I* am God (see Notes on ch. xliv. 6).

10. *Declaring the end from the beginning.* Foretelling accurately the course
of future events. This is an argument
to which God often appeals in proof that
he is the only true God (see ch. xli. 22,
23 ; xliii. 12 ; xliv. 26). ¶ *My counsel
shall stand.* My purpose, my design,
my will. The phrase ' shall stand '
means that it shall be stable, settled,
fixed, established. This proves—1. That
God has a *purpose* or *plan* in regard to
human affairs. If he had not, he could
not predict future events, since a contingent event cannot be foreknown and
predicted ; that is, it cannot be foretold
that an event shall certainly occur in
one way, when by the very supposition
of its being *contingent* it may happen
either that way, or some other way, or
not at all. 2. That God's plan will not
be frustrated. He has *power* enough
to secure the execution of his designs,
and he will exert that power in order
that all his plans may be accomplished.
—We may observe, also, that it is a
matter of unspeakable joy that God *has*
a plan, and that it will be executed.
For (1.) If there were *no plan* in relation to human things, the mind could
find no rest. If there was no evidence
that One Mind presided over human
affairs ; that an infinitely wise plan had
been formed, and that all things had
been adjusted so as best to secure the
ultimate accomplishment of that plan,
everything would have the appearance
of chaos, and the mind must be filled

saying, My counsel shall stand, and I will do all my pleasure :

11 Calling a ravenous bird from the east, the man ¹ that executeth my counsel from a far country ; yea, I have spoken *it*, I will also

bring it to pass ; I have purposed *it*, I will also do it.

12 Hearken unto me, ye *a* stouthearted, that *are* far from righteousness :

1 *of my.*   *a* Ac.7.51.

with doubts and distractions. But our anxieties vanish in regard to the apparent irregularities and disorders of the universe, when we feel that all things are under the direction of an Infinite Mind, and will be made to accomplish his plans, and further his great designs. (2.) If his plans were *not accomplished,* there would be occasion of equal doubt and dismay. If there was any power that could defeat the purposes of God ; if there was any stubbornness of matter, or any inflexible perverseness in the nature of mind ; if there were any unexpected and unforeseen extraneous causes that could interpose to thwart his plans, then the mind must be full of agitation and distress. But the moment it can fasten on the conviction that God has formed a plan that embraces all things, and that all things which occur will be in some way made tributary to that plan, that moment the mind can be calm in resignation to his holy will. ¶ *And I will do all my pleasure.* I will accomplish all my wish, or effect all my desire. The word here rendered 'pleasure' (חֵפֶץ) means properly *delight* or *pleasure* (1 Sam. xv. 22 ; Ps. i. 2 ; xvi. 3 ; Eccl. v. 4 ; xii. 10) ; then desire, wish, will (Job xxxi. 16) ; and then business, cause, affairs (Isa. liii. 10). Here it means that God would accomplish everything which was to him an object of desire ; everything which he wished, or willed. And why should he not ? Who has power to hinder or prevent him (Rom. ix. 19) ? And why should not we rejoice that he will do all that is pleasing to him ? What better evidence have we that it is desirable that anything should be done, than that it is agreeable, or pleasing to God ? What better security can we have that it is right, than that he wills it ? What more substantial and permanent ground of rejoicing is there in regard to anything, than that it is such as God prefers, loves, and wills ?

11. *Calling a ravenous bird from the*

east. There can be no doubt that Cyrus is intended here (see Notes on ch. xli. 2, 25). The *east* here means Persia. The word rendered ' ravenous bird ' (עַיִט) is rendered *fowl* in Job xxviii. 7 ; *bird* or *birds* in Jer. xii. 9 ; *fowls* in Gen. xv. 11 ; Isa. xviii. 6 ; and *ravenous birds* in Ezek. xxxix. 4. It does not occur elsewhere in the Bible. It is here used as an emblem of a warlike king, and the emblem may either denote the rapidity of his movements—moving with the flight of an eagle ; or it may denote the devastation which he would spread —an emblem in either sense peculiarly applicable to Cyrus. It is not uncommon in the Bible to compare a warlike prince to an eagle (Jer. xlix. 22 ; Ezek. xvii. 3) ; and the idea here is, probably, that Cyrus would come with great power and velocity upon nations, like the king of birds, and would pounce suddenly and unexpectedly upon his prey. Perhaps also there may be here allusion to the standard or banner of Cyrus. Xenophon (*Cyrop*. vii.) says that it was a golden eagle affixed to a long spear ; and it is well remarked by Lowth, that Xenophon has used the very word which the prophet uses here, as near as could be, expressing it in Greek letters. The word of the prophet is עַיִט (*āyǐt*) ; the Greek word used by Xenophon is ἀετὸς (*aetos*). The Chaldee has, however, given a different rendering to this passage : 'I, who say that I will gather my captivity from the east, and will lead publicly like a swift bird from a distant land the sons of Abraham, my friend.' ¶ *The man that executeth my counsel.* Marg. as Heb. ' Of my counsel.' It may either mean the man whom he had designated by his counsel ; or it may mean the man who should execute his purpose. ¶ *Yea, I have spoken.* He spake it by the prophets ; and the idea is, that all that he had spoken should be certainly accomplished.

12. *Hearken unto me.* This is de-

13 I bring near my righteousness ; *a* it shall not be far off, and
my salvation shall not tarry : *b* and
I will place salvation in Zion for
Israel *c* my glory.

a Ro.1.17.   *b* Ps.46.1,5; Ha.2.3.   *c* Ps.14.7.

CHAPTER XLVII.

ANALYSIS.

IN the closing verse of the previous chapter,
God had given the assurance that his people
should certainly be delivered from their captivity in Babylon, and restored to their own land.
In this chapter, he describes the vengeance
which he would take on Babylon, and the entire
chapter is occupied in portraying, under various
images, the prostration and humiliation of that
proud and oppressive seat of magnificence and
of empire. Babylon is described under the
image of a lady, carefully nourished and decorated; and all the images of her destruction
are drawn from those circumstances which would
tend to humble a gay and proud female that had
been accustomed to luxury, and unused to
scenes of humiliation, poverty, and bereavement.
The *scope* of the chapter is, to state the crimes
for which she would be humbled and punished,
and the manner in which it would be done.
These are intermingled, but they may be contemplated separately. The chapter may, therefore, be regarded as consisting of the following
items :—

I. Babylon is addressed, by an apostrophe to
her, as the seat of empire, and her humiliation
is directly predicted under the image of a gay,
and delicately reared female, suddenly reduced
to circumstances of great humiliation and disgrace (1–5). She is commanded to sit down in
the dust; she should no longer be treated as
tender and delicate (1); she would be reduced
to the most abject condition—like a delicate and
tender female from elevated life compelled to
perform the most menial offices, and stripped of
all her gay attire (2, 3); she was to sit in darkness, or obscurity; her honour was to be taken
away, and she was no more to be called the lady
of kingdoms (5); and all this was to be done by
JEHOVAH, to take vengeance on the oppressors
of his people (3, 4).

II. God states the reasons why he would thus
humble and punish her (6, 7). It was because
she had shown no mercy to his people, and had
laid a heavy yoke on an ancient nation (6); and
because she had vainly calculated that her
power and magnificence would continue for
ever, notwithstanding the manner in which she
had oppressed the people whom God had given
into her hand (7).

III. The nature of the punishment which
should come upon her for this is more distinctly
and fully predicted, intermingled with further
statements of the *causes* why she should be
punished and humbled (8, 9). The *causes* were,
that luxury and effeminacy abounded; that she
was proud, and did not apprehend that it was
possible that she should be reduced from her
state of magnificence and grandeur; and that
she had cherished sorcerers and enchantments.

---

signed to call the attention of the sceptical and unbelieving Jews to the important truth which he was delivering.
Many among them might be disposed
to say that the fulfilment was delayed,
and he therefore calls upon them to attend particularly to his solemn declarations. ¶ *Ye stout-hearted.* The phrase
'stout-hearted' would naturally denote
those who were bold and courageous.
But here it evidently means those whose
hearts were *strong against God ;* who
nerved themselves to resist and oppose
his plans and government ; who were
stubborn and rebellious.

13. *I bring near my righteousness.*
The word 'righteousness' here evidently
denotes his *truth ;* the fulfilment of his
promises. His righteous and true character would be manifested to them so
plainly and clearly, that they would be
able no longer to doubt. It would not
be remote in time, or in place, but it
would be so near that they could see it,
and so plain that they could no longer
doubt or misunderstand it. ¶ *And my
salvation shall not tarry.* The people
shall be delivered from their bondage at
the exact time which has been predicted.
¶ *I will place salvation in Zion.* Zion
or Jerusalem shall be rebuilt, and salvation shall emanate from that as from a
centre to the whole world. ¶ *Israel my
glory.* The people whom he had chosen,
and who reflected his glory. God's
honour and glory on earth are seen in,
and by the church, and he designs that
the church shall be the means of making
his glory known among men. Or it
may mean, I will give my glory to Israel.
I will show to them my perfections,
and will make their nation the place
of the manifestations of my glorious
attributes.

The *punishment* was, that she should be reduced in a moment to the condition of a widow, and to the state of one who had been suddenly bereft of all her children.

IV. The crime and the punishment of the city are further stated (10, 11). The *crime* was, that she had supposed no avenging God saw her; and that she had become proud and vain of her wisdom and knowledge. The *punishment* would be, that evil would come upon her from a quarter where she little expected it, and in a manner which she could not prevent.

V. Babylon is sarcastically called on to invoke to her aid those in whom she had trusted—the astrologers, the star-gazers, and those who practised sorcery and enchantments (12, 13).

VI. The chapter concludes with a statement of the utter vanity of the sorcerers, and the absolute folly of trusting in them (14, 15). Even the flame would pass over them; and so far were they from having any power to deliver those who trusted in them, that they had no power to preserve themselves from ruin.

This chapter, therefore, contains many very particular statements about the manner in which Babylon was to be destroyed, statements which will be found to have been fulfilled with surprising accuracy. They are statements, moreover, which could not have been the result of conjecture, or mere political sagacity, for political conjecture and sagacity do not descend to minute particulars and details. It is to be borne in remembrance that this prophecy was

uttered a hundred and fifty years before its fulfilment, and that there were no circumstances existing in the time of Isaiah which could have laid the foundation for conjecture in regard to the events predicted here. The temple was then standing; the city of Jerusalem was strongly fortified; the kingdom of Judah was powerful; Babylon was just rising into magnificence; the power which ultimately overthrew it had scarcely begun to start into being: and none of the causes which ultimately led Cyrus to attack and destroy it, had as yet an existence. And if these things were so, then the conclusion is inevitable that Isaiah was under the influence of Divine inspiration. It is the *particularity* of the description in the prophets long before the events occurred, which, more than anything else, distinguishes them from mere political conjecture; and *if* the particular descriptions here and elsewhere recorded of the overthrow of Babylon, and of other future events, were actually made *before* the events occurred, then the conclusion is irresistible that they were inspired by God.

COME *a* down, and sit in the dust, O virgin daughter of Babylon; sit on the ground: *there is* no throne, O daughter of the Chaldeans; for thou shalt no more be called tender and delicate.

a Ps.18.27; Je.48.18.

CHAPTER XLVII.

1. *Come down.* Descend from the throne; or from the seat of magnificence and power. The design of this verse has already been stated in the analysis. It is to foretell that Babylon would be humbled, and that she would be reduced from her magnificence and pride to a condition of abject wretchedness. She is therefore represented as a proud female accustomed to luxury and ease, suddenly brought to the lowest condition, and compelled to perform the most menial services. ¶ *And sit in the dust.* To sit on the ground, and to cast dust on the head, is a condition often referred to in the Scriptures as expressive of humiliation and of mourning (Josh. viii. 6; Job ii. 12; x. 9; Ps. xxii. 15; Lam. iii. 29). In this manner also, on the medals which were struck by Titus and Vespasian to commemorate the capture of Jerusalem, Jerusalem is represented under the image of a female sitting on

the ground under a palm-tree, with the inscription *Judæa capta* (see Notes on ch. iii. 26). The design here is, to represent Babylon as reduced to the lowest condition, and as having great occasion of grief. ¶ *O virgin daughter of Babylon.* It is common in the Scriptures to speak of cities under the image of a virgin, a daughter, or a beautiful woman (see Notes on ch. i. 8; xxxvii. 22; comp. Lam. i. 15; Jer. xxxi. 21; xlvi. 11). Kimchi supposes that the term 'virgin' is here given to Babylon, because it had remained to that time uncaptured by any foreign power; but the main purpose is doubtless to refer to Babylon as a beautiful and splendid city, and as being distinguished for delicacy, and the prevalence of what was regarded as ornamental. Gesenius supposes that the words 'virgin daughter of Babylon,' denote not Babylon itself, but Chaldea, and that the whole land or nation is personified. But the common inter-

2 Take the millstones, and grind meal: uncover thy locks, make bare the leg, uncover the thigh, pass over the rivers.

---

pretation, and one evidently more in accordance with the Scripture usage, is to refer it to the city itself. ¶ There is *no throne.* Thou shalt be reduced from the throne ; or the throne shall be taken away. That is, Babylon shall be no longer the seat of empire, or the capital of kingdoms. How truly this was fulfilled, needs not to be told to those who are familiar with the history of Babylon. Its power was broken when Cyrus conquered it ; its walls were reduced by Darius ; Seleucia rose in its stead, and took away its trade and a large portion of its inhabitants, until it was completely destroyed, so that it became for a long time a question where it had formerly stood (see Notes on ch. xiii., xvi.) ¶ *Thou shalt no more be called tender and delicate.* A place to which luxuries flow, and where they abound. The allusion is to a female that had been delicately and tenderly brought up, and that would be reduced to the lowest condition of servitude, and even of disgrace. It is *possible* that there may be an allusion here to the effeminacy and the consequent corruption of morals which prevailed in Babylon, and which made it a place sought with greediness by those who wished to spend their time in licentious pleasures. The corruption of Babylon, consequent on its wealth and magnificence, was almost proverbial, and was unsurpassed by any city of ancient times. The following extract from Curtius (v. 1), which it would not be proper to translate, will give some idea of the prevailing state of morals :—' Nihil urbis ejus corruptius moribus, nihil ad irritandas illiciendasque immodicas voluptates instructius. Liberos conjugesque cum hospitibus stupro coire, modo pretium flagitii detur, parentes maritique patiuntur. Babylonii maxime in vinum, et quæ ebrietatem sequuntur effusi sunt. Fœminarum conviva ineuntium, in principio modestus est habitus, dein summa quæque amicula exuunt paulatimque pudorem profanant; ad ultimum (horror auribus est) ima corporum velamenta projiciunt. Nec meretricum hoc dedecus est, sed matronarum virginumque apud quas comitas habetur vulgati corporis vilitas.' See also the description of a loathsome, disgusting, and abominable custom which prevailed nowhere else, even in the corrupt nations of antiquity, except Babylon, in Herod. i. 199. I cannot transcribe this passage. The description is too loathsome, and would do little good. Its *substance* is expressed in a single sentence, πασᾶν γυναῖκα ἐπιχωρίην .... μιχθῆναι ἀνδρὶ ξείνᾳ It adds to the abomination of this custom that it was connected with the rites of religion, and was a part of the worship of the gods ! ! Strabo, speaking of this custom (iii. 348), says, ῎Εθος κατά τι λόγιον ξένῳ μίγνυσθαι. See also Baruch vi. 43. where the same custom is alluded to. For an extended description of the wealth and commerce of Babylon, see an article in the *Amer. Bib. Rep.* vol. vii. pp. 364–390.

2. *Take the millstones, and grind meal.* The design of this is plain. Babylon, that had been regarded as a delicately-trained female, was to be reduced to the lowest condition of poverty and wretchedness—represented here by being compelled to perform the most menial and laborious offices, and submitting to the deepest disgrace and ignominy. There is an allusion here to the custom of grinding in the East. The mills which were there commonly used, and which are also extensively used to this day, consisted of two stones, of which the lower one was convex on the upper side, and the upper one was concave on the lower side, so that they fitted into each other. The hole for receiving the grain was in the centre of the upper stone, and in the process of grinding the lower one was fixed, and the upper one was turned round, usually by two women (see Matt. xxiv. 41), with considerable velocity by means of a handle. Water-mills were not invented till a little before the time of Augustus Cæsar ; and windmills long after. The custom of using handmills is the primitive custom everywhere, and they are still in use in some parts of Scotland, and generally in

the East.—(See Mr. Pennant's *Tour to the Hebrides*, and the Oriental travellers

ANCIENT HANDMILL USED IN SCOTLAND.

generally. Grinding was usually performed by the women, though it was often regarded as the work of slaves. It was often inflicted on slaves as a punishment.

Molendum in pistrino; vapulandum; habendæ
    compedes.
                    Terent. *Phormio* ii. 1. 19.

In the East it was the usual work of female slaves (see Ex. xi. 5, in the

LXX.) 'Women alone are employed to grind their corn,'—(Shaw, *Algiers and Tunis*, p. 297.) 'They are the female slaves that are generally employed in the East at those handmills. It is extremely laborious, and esteemed the lowest employment in the house.'—(Sir J. Chardin, Harmer's *Obs.* i. 153.) Compare Lowth, and Gesen. *Comm. über Isaiah.* This idea of its being a low employment is expressed by Job xxxi. 10: 'Let my wife grind unto another.' The idea of its being a most humble and laborious employment was long since exhibited by Homer:

A woman next, then labouring at the mill,
Hard by, where all his numerous mills he kep⁺.
Gave him the sign propitious from within.
Twelve damsels toiled to turn them, day by day
Meal grinding, some of barley, some of wheat,
Marrow of man. The rest (their portion ground)
All slept, one only from her task as yet
Ceased not, for she was feeblest of them all;
She rested on her mill, and thus pronounced:
' Jove, Father, Governor, of heaven and earth!
                    'O grant the prayer
Of *a poor bond-woman.* Appoint their feast,
This day the last, that in Ulysses' house,
The suitors shall enjoy, for whom I drudge,
Grinding, to weariness of heart and limb,
Meal for their use.'
                            COWPER.

The sense here is, that Babylon should be reduced to the lowest state, like that

MODERN EGYPTIAN MILL FOR GRINDING CORN.

of reducing a female delicately and tenderly reared, to the hard and laborious | condition of working the handmill—the usual work of slaves. ¶ *Uncover thy locks*. Gesenius renders this, ' Raise thy veil.' The word here used (צַמָּה) is rendered 'locks,' in Cant. iv. 1, 3; vi. 7, as well as here. It occurs nowhere else in the Bible. Gesenius derives it from צָמַם (*tzâmăm*), *to braid, to plait*, and then to bind fast, as a veil ; to veil. Jerome renders it, *Denuda turpetudinem tuam*. The LXX. render it, Τὸ κατακάλυμμα σου — ' Thy veil.' The Syriac also renders it, ' Thy veil.' The Chaldee has paraphrased the whole verse thus: ' Go into servitude ; reveal the glory of thy kingdom. Broken are thy princes ; dispersed are the people of thy host ; they have gone into captivity like the waters of a river.' Jarchi says, that the word here used (צַמָּה) denotes whatever is bound up, or tied together. Kimchi says that it means the hair, which a woman disposes around her temples over her face, and which she covers with a veil, deeming it an ornament ; but that when a female goes into captivity this is removed, as a sign of an abject condition. It properly means that which is plaited, or gathered together ; and it *may* refer either to the hair so plaited as an ornament, or a covering for the head and face (comp. Note on 1 Cor. xi. 15); or it may denote a veil. To remove either would be regarded as disgraceful. It is known that oriental females pay great attention to their hair, and also that it is a universal custom to wear a close veil. To remove either, and to leave the head bare, or the face exposed, was deemed highly humiliating and dishonourable (see Notes on ch. iii. 24). ' The head,' says the Editor of the *Pictorial Bible*, ' is the seat of female modesty in the East ; and no woman allows her head to be seen bare. In our travelling experience, we saw the *faces* of very many women, but never the bare head of any except one—a female servant, whose *face* we were in the constant habit of seeing, and whom we accidentally surprised while dressing her hair. The perfect consternation, and deep sense of humiliation which she expressed on that occasion, could not easily be forgotten, and furnish a most striking illustration of the present text.' ¶ *Make bare the leg*. In the interpretation of this, also, commentators vary.

Jerome renders it, *Discoopteri humerum* —' Uncover the shoulder.' The LXX. Ἀνακάλυψαι τὰς πολιὰς—' Uncover thy gray locks.' The Syriac, ' Cut off thy hoary hairs.' Jarchi and Kimchi suppose it means, ' Remove the waters from the paths, so that they might pass over them.' The word here used (שֹׁבֶל *shōbhĕl*), is derived from שָׁבַל *shâbhăl, to go ;* to go up, to rise ; to grow ; to flow copiously. Hence the noun in its various forms means a path (Ps. lxxvii. 19 ; Jer. xviii. 15); ears of corn, *shibboleth* (Gen. xli. 5, Judg. xii. 6 ; Ruth ii. 2 ; Job xxiv. 24; Isa. xvii. 5); floods (Ps. lxix. 15); branches (Zech. iv. 12). In no place has it the certain signification of *a leg ;* but it rather refers to that which *flows :* flows copiously ; and probably here means the train of a robe (Gesenius, and Rosenmüller): and the expression means ' uncover, or make bare the train ;' that is, lift it up, as would be necessary in passing through a stream, so that the leg would be made bare. The Orientals, as is well known, wore a long, loose, flowing robe, and in passing through waters, it would be necessary to lift, or gather it up, so that the legs would be bare. The idea is, that she who had sat as a queen, and who had been clad in the rich, loose, and flowing robe which those usually wore who were in the most elevated ranks of life, would now be compelled to leave the seat of magnificence, and in such a manner as to be subject to the deepest shame and disgrace. ¶ *Uncover the thigh*. By collecting, and gathering up the train of the robe, so as to pass through the streams ¶ *Pass over the rivers*. Heb. ' Pass the rivers ;' that is, by wading, or fording them. This image is taken from the fact that Babylon was surrounded by many artificial rivers or streams, and that one in passing from it would be compelled to ford many of them. It does not mean that the *population* of Babylon would be removed into captivity by the conquerors—for there is no evidence that this was done ; but the image is that of Babylon, represented as a delicately-reared and magnificently attired female, compelled to ford the streams. The idea is, that the power and magnificence of the city would be

3 Thy nakedness shall be ^aun-covered, yea, thy shame shall be seen : I will take vengeance, and I will not meet *thee as* a man.

4 *As for* our ^b Redeemer, the LORD of hosts *is* his name, the Holy One of Israel.

a Je.13.22,26; Na.3.5.   b Je.50.34.

transferred to other places. Rosenmül-ler remarks that it is common in the countries bordering on the Tigris and the Euphrates, for females of humble rank to ford the streams, or even to swim across them.

3. *Thy nakedness.* This denotes the abject condition to which the city would be reduced. All its pride would be taken away ; and it would be brought to such a state as to fill its inhabitants with the deepest mortification and shame. Vi-tringa supposes that it means, that all the imbecility and weakness ; the vile-ness ; the real poverty ; the cruelty and injustice of Babylon, would be exposed. But it more probably means, that it would be reduced to the deepest igno-miny. No language could more forcibly express the depths of its shame and dis-grace than that which the prophet here uses. ¶ *I will take vengeance.* This expresses *literally* what had been before expressed in a figurative manner. The whole purpose of God was to inflict ven-geance on her for her pride, her luxury, and oppression, and especially for her want of kindness towards his people (see ver. 6). ¶ *And I will not meet* thee *as a man.* This phrase has been very variously interpreted. Jerome renders it, ' And man shall not resist me.' The LXX. render it, ' I will take that which is just of thee, and will no more deliver thee up to men.' The Syriac, ' I will not suffer man to meet thee.' Grotius, ' I will not suffer any man to be an in-tercessor.' So Lowth, ' Neither will I suffer man to intercede with me.' Noyes, ' I will make peace with none.' So Ge-senius (*Lex.* by Robinson) renders it, ' I will take vengeance, and will not make peace with man ; *i.e.*, will make peace with none before all are destroyed.' The word here used (עגפ) is derived from עגפ, which means, *to strike upon* or *against :* to impinge upon any one, or anything ; to fall upon in a hostile manner (1 Sam. xxii. 17); to kill, to slay (Judg. viii. 21; xv. 12); to *assail* with petitions, to urge, entreat any one

(Ruth i. 16; Jer. vii. 16); to light upon, or meet with any one (Gen. xxviii. 11), and then, according to Gesenius, to *strike* a league with any one, to make peace with him. Jarchi renders it, ' I will not solicit any man that he should take vengeance ;' *i.e.*, I will do it my-self. Aben Ezra, ' I will not admit the intercession of any man.' Vitringa ren-ders it, ' I will take vengeance, and will not have a man to concur with me ; that is, although I should not have a man to concur with me who should execute the vengeance which I meditate ; on which account I have raised up Cyrus from Persia, of whom no one thought.' In my view, the meaning which best accords with the usual sense of the word, is that proposed by Lowth, that no one should be allowed to interpose, or intercede for them. *All* the interpretations concur in the same general signification, that Babylon should be totally destroyed ; and that no man, whether, as Jerome supposes, by resistance, or as Lowth, by intercession, should be allowed to oppose the execution of the Divine purpose of vengeance.

4. As for *our Redeemer.* This verse stands absolutely, and is not connected with the preceding or the following. It seems to be an expression of admiration, or of grateful surprise, by which the prophet saw JEHOVAH as the Redeemer of his people. He saw, in vision, Ba-bylon humbled, and, full of the subject, he breaks out into an expression of grateful surprise and rejoicing. ' O ! our Redeemer! it is the work of *our Saviour*, the Holy One of Israel ! How great is his power ! How faithful is he ! How manifestly is he revealed ! Babylon is destroyed. Her idols could not save her. Her destruction has been accomplished by him who is the Redeemer of his people, and the Holy One of Israel.' Lowth regards this verse as the language of a *chorus* that breaks in upon the midst of the subject, celebrating the praises of God. The subject is resumed in the next verse.

5 Sit thou silent, and get thee into darkness, O daughter of the Chaldeans : for thou shalt no more be called The lady of kingdoms.

6 I *a* was wroth with my people;

a 2 Ch.28.9; Ze.1.15.

I have polluted mine inheritance, and given them into thine hand : thou *b* didst show them no mercy ; upon the ancient hast thou very heavily laid the yoke.

b Ob.10.16.

---

5. *Sit thou silent.* The same general sentiment is expressed here as in the preceding verses, though the figure is changed. In ver. 1–3, Babylon is represented under the image of a gay and delicately-reared female, suddenly reduced from her exalted station, and compelled to engage in the most menial and laborious employment. Here she is represented as in a posture of mourning. To sit in silence is emblematic of deep sorrow, or affliction (see Lam. ii. 10) : ' The elders of the daughter of Zion sit upon the ground and keep silence, they have cast up dust upon their heads ;'—see Note on Isa. iii. 26 : ' And she (Jerusalem) being desolate shall sit upon the ground ;' Job iii. 13 : ' So they (the three friends of Job) sat down with him upon the ground seven days and seven nights, and none spake a word unto him, for they saw that his grief was very great.' Compare Ezra ix. 4. ¶ *Get thee into darkness.* That is, into a place of mourning. Persons greatly afflicted, almost as a matter of course, shut out the light from their dwellings, as emblematic of their feelings. This is common even in this country—and particularly in the city in which I write—where the universal custom prevails of making a house dark during the time of mourning. Nature prompts to this ; for there is an obvious similarity between darkness and sorrow. That this custom also prevailed in the East is apparent (see Lam. iii. 2) : ' He hath led me, and brought me into darkness, and not into light ;' Mic. viii. 8 : ' When I sit in darkness, the LORD shall be a light unto me.' The idea is, that Babylon would be brought to desolation, and have occasion of sorrow, like a delicately-trained female suddenly deprived of children (ver. 9), and that she would seek a place of darkness and silence where she might fully indulge her grief. ¶ *O daughter of the Chaldeans* (see Notes on ver. 1). ¶ *For thou shalt no more be called The lady of kingdoms.*

The magnificence, splendour, beauty, and power, which have given occasion to this appellation, and which have led the nations by common consent to give it to thee, shall be entirely and for ever removed. The appellation, ' lady of kingdoms,' is equivalent to that so often used of Rome, as ' the mistress of the world ;' and the idea is, that Babylon sustained by its power and splendour the relation of mistress, and that all other cities were regarded as servants, or as subordinate.

6. *I was wroth with my people.* In this verse and the following, a reason is assigned why God would deal so severely with her. One of the reasons was, that in executing the punishment which *he* had designed on the Jewish people, she had done it with pride, ambition, and severity ; so that though God intended *they* should be punished, yet the feelings of Babylon in doing it, were such also as to deserve his decided rebuke and wrath. ¶ *I have polluted mine inheritance.* Jerusalem and the land of Judea (see Notes on ch. xliii. 28). He had stripped it of its glory ; caused the temple and city to be destroyed ; and spread desolation over the land. Though it had been done by the Chaldeans, yet it had been in accordance with his purpose, and under his direction (Deut. iv. 20 ; Ps. xxviii. 9). ¶ *Thou didst show them no mercy.* Though God had given up his people to be punished for their sins, yet this did not justify the spirit with which the Chaldeans had done it, or make proper the cruelty which they had evinced towards them. It is true that some of the Jewish captives, as, *e.g.*, Daniel, were honoured and favoured in Babylon. It is not improbable that the circumstances of many of them were comparatively easy while there, and that they acquired possessions and formed attachments there which made them unwilling to leave that land when Cyrus permitted them to return to their own country. But it is also true, that Ne-

7 And thou saidst, I *a* shall be a lady for ever; *so* that thou didst not lay these *things* to thy heart, neither didst remember the latter end of it.

8 Therefore hear now this, thou

that *art* given to pleasures, that dwellest *b* carelessly; that sayest in thine heart, I *am*, and none else besides me; I shall not sit *as* a widow, neither shall I know the loss of children:

b Zep.2.15.

buchadnezzar showed them no compassion when he destroyed the temple and city, that the mass of them were treated with great indignity and cruelty in Babylon. See Ps. cxxxvii. 1–3, where they pathetically and beautifully record their sufferings:

By the rivers of Babylon there we sat down,
Yea, we wept when we remembered Zion.
For there they that carried us away captive
   required of us a song;
And they that wasted us required of us mirth.
Saying, Sing us one of the songs of Zion.

Thus also Jeremiah (i. 17) describes the cruelty of their conquerors: 'Israel is a scattered sheep—the lions have driven him away; this Nebuchadnezzar hath broken his bones' (see also 2 Kings xxv. 5, 6–36; Jer. li. 34; Lam. iv. 16; v. 11–14). ¶ *Upon the ancient.* That is, upon the old man. The idea is, that they had oppressed, and reduced to hard servitude, those who were venerable by years, and by experience. To treat the aged with veneration is everywhere in the Scriptures regarded as an important and sacred duty (Lev. xix. 32; Job xxxii. 4–6); and to disregard age, and pour contempt on hoary hairs, is everywhere spoken of as a crime of an aggravated nature (comp. 2 Kings ii. 23–25; Prov. xxx. 17). That the Chaldeans had thus disregarded age and rank, is a frequent subject of complaint among the sacred writers:

They respected not the persons of the priests,
They favoured not the elders.
                            Lam. iv. 16.

Princes are hanged up by their hand.
The faces of elders were not honoured.
                            Lam. v. 12.

¶ *Laid the yoke.* The yoke in the Bible is an emblem of slavery or bondage (Lev. xxvi. 13; Deut. xxxiii. 48); of afflictions and crosses (Lam. iii. 27); of punishment for sin (Lam. i. 14); of God's commandments (Matt. xi. 29, 30). Here it refers to the bondage and affliction which they experienced in Babylon.

7. *And thou saidst, I shall be a lady for ever.* This passage describes the pride and self-confidence of Babylon. She was confident in her wealth; the strength of her gates and walls; and in her abundant resources to resist an enemy, or to sustain a siege. Babylon was ten miles square; and it was supposed to contain provisions enough to maintain a siege for many years. There were, moreover, no symptoms of internal decay; there were no apparent external reasons why her prosperity should not continue; there were no causes at work, which human sagacity could detect, which would prevent her continuing to any indefinite period of time. ¶ *Thou didst not lay these* things *to thy heart.* Thou didst not consider what, under the government of a holy and just God, must be the effect of treating a captured and oppressed people in this manner. Babylon supposed, that notwithstanding her pride, and haughtiness, and oppressions, she would be able to stand for ever. ¶ *Neither didst remember the latter end of it.* The end of pride, arrogance, and cruelty. The sense is, that Babylon might have learned from the fate of other kingdoms that had been, like her, arrogant and cruel, what must inevitably be her own destiny. But she refused to learn a lesson from their doom. So common is it for nations to disregard the lessons which history teaches; so common for individuals to neglect the warnings furnished by the destruction of the wicked.

8. *Therefore hear now this.* The prophet proceeds, in this verse and the following, to detail more particularly the sins of Babylon, and to state the certainty of the punishment which would come upon her. In the previous verses, the denunciation of punishment had been figurative. It had been represented under the image of a lady deli-

9 But these two *things* shall come to thee in a moment, in one day, the loss of children, and widowhood: they shall come upon thee in their perfection, for the multitude of thy sorceries, *and* for the great abundance of thine enchantments.

---

cately trained and nurtured, doomed to the lowest condition of life, and compelled to stoop to the most menial offices. Here the prophet uses language without figure, and states directly her crimes, and her doom. ¶ That art *given to pleasures.* Devoted to dissipation, and to the effeminate pleasures which luxury engenders (see Notes on ver. 1). Curtius, in his *History of Babylon as it was in the times of Alexander* (v. 5. 36), Herodotus (i. 198), and Strabo *Georg.* xvi.), have given a description of it, all representing it as corrupt, licentious, and dissipated in the extreme. Curtius, in the passage quoted on ver. 1, says, among other things, that no city was more corrupt in its morals; nowhere were there so many excitements to licentious and guilty pleasures. ¶ *That dwellest carelessly.* In vain security; without any consciousness of danger, and without alarm (comp. Zeph. ii. 15). ¶ *I am, and none else besides me.* The language of pride. She regarded herself as the principal city of the world, and all others as unworthy to be named in comparison with her (comp. Note on ch. xlv. 6). Language remarkably similar to this occurs in Martial's description of Rome (xii. 8):

Terrarum dea gentiumque, Roma,
Cui par est nihil, et nihil secundum—

Rome, goddess of the earth and of nations, to whom nothing is equal, nothing second.' ¶ *I shall not sit as a widow.* On the word 'sit,' see Note on ver. 1. The sense is, that she would never be lonely, sad, and afflicted, like a wife deprived of her husband, and a mother of her children. The figure is changed from ver. 1, where she is represented as a virgin; but the same idea is presented under another form (comp. Note on ch. xxiii. 4).

9. *In a moment, in one day.* This is designed, undoubtedly, to describe the suddenness with which Babylon would be destroyed. It would not decay slowly, and by natural causes, but it would be suddenly and unexpectedly destroyed. How strikingly this was fulfilled, it is not needful to pause to state (see Notes on ch. xiii., xiv.) In the single night in which Babylon was taken by Cyrus, a death-blow was given to all her greatness and power, and at that moment a train of causes was originated which did not cease to operate until it became a pile of ruins. ¶ *The loss of children, and widowhood.* Babylon would be in the situation of a wife and a mother who is instantaneously deprived of her husband, and bereft of all her children. ¶ *They shall come upon thee in their perfection.* In full measure; completely; entirely. You shall know all that is meant by this condition. The state referred to is that of a wife who is suddenly deprived of her husband, and who, at the same time, and by the same stroke, is bereft of all her children. And the sense is, that Babylon would know *all* that was meant by such a condition, and would experience the utmost extremity of grief which such a condition involved. ¶ *For the multitude of thy sorceries.* This was one of the reasons why God would thus destroy her, that sorceries and enchantments abounded there. Lowth, however, renders this, 'Notwithstanding the multitude of thy sorceries.' So Noyes, 'In spite of thy sorceries.' The Hebrew is, '*In* the multitude (בְּרֹב) of thy sorceries.' Jerome renders it, 'On account of (*propter*) the multitude of thy sorceries.' The LXX. 'In (ἐν) thy sorcery.' Perhaps the idea is, that sorcery and enchantment abounded, and that these calamities would come notwithstanding all that they could do. They would come *in the very midst* of the abounding necromancy and enchantments, while the people practised these arts, and while they depended on them. That this trust in sorcery was one cause why these judgments would come upon them, is apparent from ver. 10, 11. And that they would not be able to protect the city, or that these judgments would come in spite of all their efforts, is ap-

10 For thou hast trusted in thy wickedness; *a* thou hast said, None seeth *b* me. Thy wisdom and thy knowledge it hath ¹ perverted thee; and thou hast said in thine heart, I *am*, and none else besides me.

11 Therefore shall evil come upon

thee; thou shalt not know ² from whence it riseth: and mischief shall fall upon thee; thou shalt not be able to ³ put it off: and desolation shall come upon thee suddenly, *which* *c* thou shalt not know.

a Ec.8.8.   *b* Ps.94.7.

1 or, *caused thee to turn away.*
2 *the morning thereof.*   3 *expiate.*   *c* 1 Th.5.3.

parent from ver. 13. The idea is exactly expressed by a literal translation of the Hebrew. They would come upon her IN, *i.e.*, *in the very midst* of the multitude of sorceries and enchantments. The word here rendered 'sorceries,' means *magic*, incantation, and is applied to the work of magicians (2 Kings ix. 22; Neh. iii. 4; Micah v. 11; comp. Ex. vii. 2; Deut. xviii. 10; Dan. ii. 2; Mal. iii. 5). Magic, it is well known, abounded in the East, and indeed this may be regarded as the birthplace of the art (see Note on ch. ii. 6). ¶ And *for the great abundance of thine enchantments*. Heb. 'And in the strength;' that is, in the full vigour of thine enchantments. While they would abound, and while they would exert their utmost power to preserve the city. The word rendered 'enchantments,' means properly *society*, company, community—from being *associated*, or *bound together*; and then spells, or enchantments, from the notion that they *bound* or confined the object that was the subject of the charm. The idea was that of controlling, binding, or restraining any one whom they pleased, by the power of a spell.

10. *For thou hast trusted in thy wickedness*. The word 'wickedness' here refers doubtless to the pride, arrogance, ambition, and oppressions of Babylon. It means, that she had supposed that she was able by these to maintain the ascendancy over other nations, and perpetuate her dominion. She supposed that by her great power, her natural advantages, and her wealth, she could resist the causes which had operated to destroy other nations. Men often confide in their own wickedness—their cunning, their artifices, their frauds, their acts of oppression and cruelty, and suppose that they are secure against the judgments of God. ¶ *None seeth me*.

Compare Ps. x. 11: 'He said in his heart, God hath forgotten; he hideth his face; he will never see it.' See also Ps. xciv. 7. ¶ *Thy wisdom*. Probably the wisdom here referred to, was that for which Babylon was distinguished, the supposed science of astrology, and the arts of divination and of incantation. It may, however, refer to the purposes of the kings and princes of Babylon; and the meaning may be, that it had been perverted and ruined by relying on their counsels. But it more probably refers to the confidence in the wisdom and science which prevailed there. ¶ *Hath perverted thee*. Marg. 'Caused thee to turn away.' That is, hath turned thee away from the path of virtue, truth, and safety. It has been the cause of thy downfall. ¶ *I am*, &c. (see ver. 8.)

11. *Therefore shall evil come upon thee*. In consequence of thy pride and self-confidence; of the prevalence of corruption, licentiousness, and sin; of the prevalence of the arts of magic and of divination abounding there; and of the cruel and unfeeling oppression of the people of God;—for all these crimes ruin shall come certainly and suddenly upon thee. ¶ *Thou shalt not know from whence it cometh*. Marg. 'The morning thereof.' The margin expresses the true sense of the phrase. The word here used (שַׁחַר *shăhhăr*) means *the aurora*, the dawn, the morning (see Notes on ch. xiv. 12). Lowth has strangely rendered it, 'Evil shall come upon thee, which thou shalt not know how to deprecate.' But the word properly means the dawning of the morning, the aurora; and the sense is, that calamity should befall them whose rising or dawning they did not see, or anticipate. It would come unexpectedly and suddenly, like the first rays of the morning. It would spring up as if from no antecedent cause

12 Stand now with thy enchantments, and with the multitude of thy sorceries, wherein thou hast laboured from thy youth ; if so be thou shalt be able to profit, if so be thou mayest prevail.

13 Thou art wearied *a* in the multitude of thy counsels. Let now the astrologers,[1] *b* the star-gazers, the monthly [2] prognosticators, stand up and save thee from *these things* that shall come upon thee.

a Eze.24.12.   1 *viewers of the heavens.*   *b* Da.2.2.

2 *that give knowledge concerning the months.*

which would seem to lead to it, as the light comes suddenly out of the darkness. ¶ *And mischief.* Destruction ; ruin. ¶ *Thou shalt not be able to put it off.* Marg. 'Expiate.' This is the sense of the Hebrew (see Notes on ch. xliii. 3). The meaning is, that they could not then avert these calamities by any sacrifices, deprecations, or prayers. Ruin would suddenly and certainly come ; and they had nothing which they could offer to God as an expiation by which it could then be prevented. We need not say how strikingly descriptive this is of the destruction of Babylon. Her ruin came silently and suddenly upon her, as the first rays of morning light steal upon the world, and in such a way that she could not meet it, or turn it away.

12. *Stand now with thy enchantments* (see Notes on ver. 9). This is evidently sarcastic and ironical. It is a call on those who practised the arts of magic to stand forth, and to show whether they were able to defend the city, and to save the nation. ¶ *Wherein thou hast laboured.* Or in practising which thou hast been diligently employed. ¶ *From thy youth.* From the very commencement of thy national existence. Babylon was always distinguished for these arts. Now was a time when their value was to be put to the test, and when it was to be seen whether they were able to save the nation. ¶ *If so be.* Or, perhaps, or possibly, they may be able to profit thee—the language of irony. Perhaps by the aid of these arts you may be able to repel your foes.

13. *Thou art wearied.* Thou hast practised so many arts, and practised them so long, that thou art exhausted in them. The 'counsels' here referred to, are those which the astrologers and diviners would take in examining the prognostications, and the supposed indications of future events. ¶ *Let now the*

astrologers. Call in now the aid of the various classes of diviners on whom thou hast relied to save thee from the impending calamity and ruin. The words here rendered 'astrologers' (הֹבְרֵי שָׁמַיִם) mean properly *the dividers of the heavens;* those who divided, or cut up the heavens for the purpose of augury, or to take a horoscope (Gesenius). What this art was is not certainly known. It is probable that it referred to their designating certain stars, or constellations, or conjunctions of the planets in certain parts of the heavens, as being fortunate and propitious, and certain others as unfortunate and unpropitious. At first, astrology was synonymous with astronomy. But in process of time, it came to denote the science which professes to discover certain connections between the position and movements of the heavenly bodies, and the events which occur on the earth. It was supposed that the rising and setting, the conjunction and opposition of the planets, exerted a powerful influence over the fates of men ; over the health of their bodies, the character of their minds, and the vicissitudes of their lives. Some regarded, it would seem, the positions of the stars as mere *signs* of the events which were to follow ; and others, and probably by far the larger portion, supposed that those positions had a *positive influence* in directing and controlling the affairs of this lower world. The origin of this science is involved in great obscurity. Aristotle ascribes the invention to the Babylonians and Egyptians. Ptolemy concurs in this opinion, and Cicero traces it to the same origin. Lucian says that both these nations, as well as the Lybians, borrowed it from the Ethiopians, and that the Greeks owed their knowledge of this pretended science to the poet Orpheus. The science prevailed, it is probable, however, much more early in India ; and in China it appears to be co-

14 Behold they shall be as stubble ; ^a the fire shall burn them ; they shall not deliver ¹ themselves from the power of the flame : *there shall not be* a coal to warm at, *nor* fire to sit before it.

15 Thus shall they be unto thee with whom thou hast laboured, *even* thy merchants from thy youth : they shall wander every one to his quarter ; ^b none shall save thee.

a Na.1.10.   1 *their souls.*   *b* ch.56.11.

eval with their history. The Arabians have been distinguished for their attachment to it ; and even Tycho Brahe was a zealous defender of astrology, and Kepler believed that the conjunctions of the planets were capable of producing great effects on human affairs. It is also a remarkable fact that Lord Bacon thought that the science required to be purified from errors rather than altogether rejected. Those who wish to inquire into the various systems of astrology, and the arts by which this absurd science has maintained an influence in the world, may consult the *Edin. Encyclopedia,* Art. *Astrology,* and the authorities enumerated there. The thing referred to in the passage before us, and which was practised in Babylon, was, probably, that of *forecasting* future events, or telling what would occur by the observation of the positions of the heavenly bodies. ¶ *The star-gazers.* Those who endeavour to tell what will occur by the contemplation of the relative positions of the stars. ¶ *The monthly prognosticators.* Marg. 'That give knowledge concerning the months.' That is, at the commencement of the months they give knowledge of what events might be expected to occur during the month ;—perhaps from the dip of the moon, or its riding high or low, &c. Something of this kind is still retained by those persons who speak of a dry or wet moon ; or who expect a change of weather at the change of the moon—all of which is just as wise as were the old systems of astrology among the Chaldeans. This whole passage would have been more literally and better translated by preserving the order of the Hebrew. ' Let them stand up now and save thee, who are astrologers ; who gaze upon the stars, and who make known at the new moons what things will come upon thee.'

14. *Behold, they shall be as stubble.* They shall be no more able to resist the

judgments which are coming upon the city, than dry stubble can resist the action of the fire. A similar figure is used in ch. i. 31 (see Notes on that verse). Compare also ch. xxix. 6 ; xxx. 30, where fire is a symbol of the devouring judgments of God. ¶ *They shall not deliver themselves.* Marg. as Heb. ' Their souls.' The meaning is, that they would be unable to protect themselves from the calamities which would come upon them and the city. ¶ There shall *not* be *a coal to warm at.* The meaning is, that they would be entirely consumed—so completely, that not even a coal or spark would be left, as when stubble, or a piece of wood, is entirely burned up. According to this interpretation, the sense is, that the judgments of God would come upon them and the city, so that entire destruction would ensue. Rosenmüller, however, Cocceius, and some others, suppose this should be rendered, 'there shall not remain a coal so that bread could be baked by it.' But the more common, and more correct interpretation, is that suggested above. Compare Gesenius and Rosenmüller on the place.

15. *With whom thou hast laboured.* The multitude of diviners, astrologers, and merchants, with whom thou hast been connected and employed. The idea is, that Babylon had been the mart where all of them had been assembled. ¶ Even *thy merchants from thy youth.* Babylon was favourably situated for traffic ; and was distinguished for it. Foreigners and strangers had resorted there, and it was filled with those who had come there for purposes of trade. The sense here is, that the same destruction which would come upon the diviners, would come on all who had been engaged there in traffic and merchandise. It does not mean that the *individuals* who were thus engaged would be destroyed, but that destruction would come *upon the business;* it

would come *in spite* of all the efforts of the astrologers, and *in spite* of all the mercantile advantages of the place. The destruction would be as entire *as if* a fire should pass over stubble, and leave not a coal or a spark. What a striking description of the total ruin of the commercial advantages of Babylon! ¶ *From thy youth*. From the very foundation of the city. ¶ *They shall wander every one to his own quarter.* All shall leave Babylon, and it shall be utterly forsaken as a place of commerce, and all who have been engaged in mercantile trans-actions there shall go to other places. The phrase, 'his own quarter' (לְעֶבְרוֹ), means, *to his own way;* they shall be driven from Babylon, and wander to other places. They shall flee from the danger; and if they practise their arts, or engage in commerce, it shall be done in other places besides Babylon. ¶ *None shall save thee.* How truly this was fulfilled need not here be stated. All its arts of astrology, its wealth, its mercantile advantages, the strength of its walls and gates, were insufficient to save it, and now it lies a wide waste—

SITE OF BABYLON DURING AN INUNDATION OF THE EUPHRATES.

a scene of vast and doleful ruin (see Notes on ch. xiii., xiv.) So certainly will all the predictions of God be accomplished; so vain are the arts and devices of man, the strength of fortifications, and the advantages for commerce, when God purposes to inflict his vengeance on a guilty nation. The skill of astrology, the advantages of science, accumulated treasures, brazen gates and massive walls, and commercial advantages, the influx of foreigners, and a fertile soil, cannot save it. All these things are in the hands of God; and he can withdraw them when he pleases. Babylon once had advantages for commerce equal to most of the celebrated marts now of Europe and America. So had Palmyra, and Tyre, and Baalbec, and Petra, and Alexandria, and Antioch. Babylon was in the midst of a country as fertile by nature as most parts of the United States. She had as little prospect of losing the commerce of the world, and of ceasing to be a place of wealth and power, as Paris, or London,

CHAPTER XLVIII.

ANALYSIS.

THIS chapter contains renewed assurances of the deliverance of the exile Jews from Babylon. It is designed, in the main, to state the causes for which the captivity would occur, and to furnish the assurance also that, notwithstanding the judgment that should come upon them, God would deliver them from bondage. It contains lamentations that there was a necessity for bringing these calamities upon them; assurances that God had loved them; appeals to themselves in proof that all that they had suffered had been predicted; and a solemn command to go forth out of Babylon. It is to be regarded as addressed to the exile Jews *in* Babylon, though it is not improbable that the prophet designed it to have a bearing on the Jews of his own time, as given to idolatry, and that he intended that the former part of the chapter should be an indirect rebuke to them by showing them the consequences of their proneness to idolatry. The chapter is exceedingly tender, and full of love, and is an expression of the kindness which God has for his own people.

It is not very susceptible of division, or of easy analysis, but the following topics present probably the main points of the chapter.

I. A reproof of the Jews for their idolatrous tendencies, reminding them that this was the characteristic of the nation, and indirectly intimating that all their calamities would come upon them on account of that (1–8). This part contains—1. An address to the Jews, as those who professed to worship God, though in insincerity and hypocrisy (1, 2). 2. A solemn declaration of God that he had foretold all these events, and that they could not be traced in any manner to the power of idols, and that he, therefore, was God (3–7). 3. Their character had been that of rebellion and treachery, from the very commencement of their history (8).

II. Promises of deliverance from the evils which their sins had brought upon them, with expressions of regret that their conduct had been such as to make such judgments necessary (9–19). 1. God says that he would restrain his anger, and would not wholly cut them off (9). 2. The purpose of the calamities brought upon them was to refine and purify them, as in a furnace (10). 3. All his dealings with them had been for his own glory, and so as to promote his own honour (11). 4. An assertion of his power, and his ability to accomplish what he had purposed (12, 13). 5. He had solemnly purposed to destroy Babylon, and the Chaldeans (14). 6. He had raised up for that purpose one who should accomplish his designs (15, 16). 7. He expresses his deep regret that their conduct had been such as to make it necessary to bring these heavy judgments on them, and states what would have been the result if they had observed his commandments. Their peace would have been as a river, their righteousness as the waves of the sea, and their offspring as the sand (17–19).

III. A command to go forth from Babylon, implying the highest assurance that they should be delivered from their long and painful captivity (20–22). 1. They should go out with singing and triumph; and the ends of the earth

or Liverpool, or New York. Yet how easy was it for God, in the accomplishment of his plans, to turn away the tide of her prosperity, and reduce her to ruins. How easy, in the arrangements of his providence, to spread desolation over all the once fertile plains of Chaldea, and to make those plains pools of water. And so with equal ease, if he pleases, and by causes as little known as were those which destroyed Babylon, can he take away the commercial advantages of any city now on earth. Tyre has lost all its commercial importance; the richly-laden caravan has ceased to pause at Petra; Tadmor lies waste. Baalbec is known only by the far-strewed ruins, and Nineveh and Babylon are stripped of all that ever *made* them great, and *can* rise no more. God has taken away the importance and the power of Rome, once, like Babylon, the mistress of the world, by suffering the *malaria* to desolate all the region in her vicinity; and so with equal truth, all that contributes to the commercial importance of New York, Philadelphia, Boston, London, or Paris, are under the control of God. By some secret causes he could make these cities a wide scene of ruins; and they *may be*, if they are *like* Babylon and Tyre and Tadmor in their character, yet *like* them in their doom. They should feel that the sources of their prosperity and their preservation are not in themselves, but in the favour and protection of God. Virtue, justice, and piety, will better preserve them than wealth; and without these they *must be*, in spite of their commercial advantages, what the once celebrated cities of antiquity now are.

should see it (20). 2. God would provide for them in the deserts, and cause the waters to flow for them in their journey through the pathless wilderness (21).

The chapter concludes with a general declaration that the wicked have no peace, implying that they only have peace and security who put their trust in God (22).

HEAR ye this, O house of Jacob, which are called by the name of Israel, and are come forth out of the waters *a* of Judah ; which swear by the name of the LORD, and make mention of the God of Israel, *but* not in *b* truth, nor in righteousness.

2 For they call themselves of the holy city, *c* and stay *d* themselves upon the God of Israel ; The LORD of hosts *is* his name.

a Ps.68.26.   *b* Ie.5.28,29; Je.5.2; Jn.4.21.
c ch 52.1.   *d* Mi.3.11.

CHAPTER XLVIII.

1. *Hear ye this.* This is an address to the Jews regarded as *in* Babylon, and is designed to remind them of their origin, and of their privileges as the descendants of Jacob, and having the name of Israel (comp. Notes on ch. xlii. 1). ¶ *And are come forth out of the waters of Judah.* This metaphor is taken from a fountain which sends forth its streams of water, and the idea is, that they owed their origin to Judah, as the streams flowed from a fountain. A similar figure is used by Balaam in describing the vast increase of the Jews : (Num. xxxiv.) 'He shall pour the waters out of his buckets, and his seed shall be in many waters.' So in Deut. xxxiii. 28 : 'The fountain of Jacob shall be upon a land of corn and wine.' So Ps. lxviii. 26 :

Bless ye God in the congregations,
JEHOVAH, ye that are of the fountain of Israel.
                                        Marg.

The idea is, that *Judah* was the fountain, or origin of the people who were then exiled in Babylon. The ten tribes had revólted, and had been carried away, and the name of Benjamin had been absorbed in that of Judah, and this had become the common name of the nation. Perhaps *Judah* is here mentioned with honour as the fountain of the nation, because it was from him that the Messiah was to descend (Gen. xlix. 10); and this mention of his name would serve to bring that promise to view, and would be an assurance that the nation would not be destroyed, nor the power finally depart until He should come. ¶ *Which swear by the name.* Who worship JEHOVAH, and acknowledge him as the only true God (see Notes on ch. xix. 18; xlv. 23; comp. ch. xlviii. 1;

lxv. 16). ¶ *And make mention.* That is, in your prayers and praises. You acknowledge him, and profess to worship him. ¶ But *not in truth.* In a hypocritical manner ; not in sincerity. Compare Jer. v. 2 : ' And though they say, The Lord liveth, surely they swear falsely.'

2. *For they call themselves of the holy city.* Of Jerusalem (see ch. lii. 1; Neh. xi. 1; Matt. iv. 5 ; xxvii. 53 ; Rev. xxi. 2–27). The word rendered ' for ' here, (כִּי *kî*) means, as it often does, *although ;* and the sense is, although they call themselves of the holy city, they do not worship God in sincerity and truth. Jerusalem was called ' the holy city,' because the temple, the ark, and the symbol of the Divine presence were there, and it was the place where God was worshipped. It was deemed sacred by the Jews, and they regarded it as sufficient proof of goodness, it would seem, that they had dwelt there. Even in Babylon they would pride themselves on this, and suppose, perhaps, that it entitled them to Divine protection and favour. ¶ *And stay themselves upon the God of Israel.* In time of danger and trial they profess to seek him, and to commit their cause to him. ¶ *The LORD of hosts is his name* (see Notes on ch. i. 9). The object of the prophet in here mentioning his holy name is, probably, to show them the guilt of their conduct. He was JEHOVAH, the source of all existence. He was the God of all the hosts of heaven, and all the armies on earth. How wicked, therefore, it was to come before him in a false and hypocritical manner, and while they were professedly worshipping him, to be really offering their hearts to idols, and to be char-

3 I have declared the former things from the beginning; and they went forth out of my mouth, and I showed them; I did *them* suddenly, and they came to pass.

4 Because I knew that thou *art*

1 *hard.*

obstinate, 1 and thy neck *a is* an iron sinew, and thy brow brass;

5 I have even from the beginning declared *it* to thee; before it came to pass I showed *it* thee: lest thou shouldest say, Mine idol hath done

a De.31.27.

acteristically inclined to relapse into idolatry!

3. *I have declared the former things.* That is, in former times I have predicted future events by the prophets, which have come to pass as they were foretold. Though the fulfilment might have appeared to be long delayed, yet it came to pass at the very time, showing it to be an exact fulfilment of the prophecy. The design of thus referring to the former predictions is, to remind them of their proneness to disregard his declarations, and to recall to their attention the fact that all that he said would be certainly accomplished. As a people, they had been prone to disbelieve his word. He saw that the same thing would take place in Babylon, and that there also they would disbelieve his prophecies about raising up Cyrus, and restoring them to their own land. He therefore endeavours to anticipate this, by reminding them of their former unbelief, and of the fact that all that he *had* foretold in former times had come to pass. ¶ *From the beginning.* In regard to this, and the meaning of the phrase, 'the former things,' see Notes on ch. xli. 22; xliii. 9. The phrase, 'former things,' refers to the things which *precede* others; the series, or order of events. ¶ *I did* them *suddenly.* They came to pass at an unexpected time; when you were not looking for them, and when perhaps you were doubting whether they would occur, or were calling in question the Divine veracity. The idea is, that God in like manner would, certainly, and suddenly, accomplish his predictions about Babylon, and their release from their captivity.

4. *Because I knew that thou art obstinate.* I made these frequent predictions, and fulfilled them in this striking manner, because I knew that as a people, you were prone to unbelief, and in

order that you might have the most full and undoubted demonstration of the truth of what was declared. As they were disinclined to credit his promises, and as he saw that in their long captivity they would be prone to disbelieve what he had said respecting their deliverance under Cyrus, he had, therefore, given them these numerous evidences of the certainty of the fulfilment of all his prophecies, in order that their minds might credit what he said about their return to their own land. ¶ *That thou art obstinate.* Marg. as Heb. 'Hard,' The sense is, that they were obstinate and intractable — an expression probably taken from a bullock which refuses to receive the yoke. The word *hard,* as expressive of obstinacy, is often combined with others. Thus, in Ex. xxxii. 9; xxxiv. 9, 'hard of neck,' *i.e.,* stiff-necked, stubborn; 'hard of face' (Ezek. ii. 4); 'hard of heart' (Ezek. iii. 7). The idea is, that they were, as a people, obstinate, rebellious, and indisposed to submit to the laws of God—a charge which is often brought against them by the sacred writers, and which is abundantly verified by all their history as a people (comp. Ex. xxxii. 9; xxxiii. 3–5; xxxiv. 9; Deut. ix. 6–13; xxxi. 27; 2 Chron. xxx. 8; Ezek. ii. 4; Acts vii. 51). ¶ *Thy neck* is *an iron sinew.* The word רָיֵּד (*ghīdh*) means properly *a cord, thong,* or *band;* then a nerve, sinew, muscle, or tendon. The metaphor is taken from oxen when they make their neck stiff, and refuse to submit it to the yoke. ¶ *And thy brow brass.* Thy forehead is hard and insensible as brass. The phrase is applied to the shameless brow of a harlot (Jer. iii. 3; Ezek. iii. 7), where there is an utter want of modesty, and consummate impudence. A brow of brass is an image of insensibility, or obstinacy (so in Jer. vi. 28).

5. *I have even from the beginning*

them ; and my graven image, and
my molten image, hath commanded
them.

6 Thou hast heard, see all this ;
and will not ye declare *it?* I have
showed thee new things from this

time, even hidden things, *a* and thou,
didst not know them.

7 They are created now, and not
from the beginning ; even before the
day when thou heardest them not ;
lest thou shouldest say, Behold, I
knew them.

declared it *to thee.* He had foretold
future events, so that they had abundant demonstration that he was the true
God, and so that they could not be under
a mistake in regard to the source of their
deliverances from danger. ¶ *Mine idol
hath done them.* The idols and molten
images had not foretold these events,
and when they came to pass, it could
not, therefore, be pretended that they
had been produced by idols. By predicting them, JEHOVAH kept up the
proof that he was the true God, and
demonstrated that he alone was worthy
of their confidence and regard.

6. *Thou hast heard.* You are witnesses that the prediction was uttered
long before it was fulfilled. ¶ *See all
this.* Behold how it is all fulfilled.
Bear witness that the event is as it was
predicted. ¶ *And will ye not declare
it?* Will you not bear witness to the
entire fulfilment of the prophecy? God
appeals to them as qualified to testify
that what he had declared had come to
pass, and calls on them to make this
known as a demonstration that he alone
was God (see Notes on ch. xliv.8). ¶ *I have
showed thee new things from this time.*
From this time I make known a thing
which has not before occurred, that you
may have a similar demonstration that
JEHOVAH is God. The 'new thing'
here referred to, is, doubtless, the prediction of the deliverance from the captivity at Babylon—a new thing, in
contradistinction from those which had
been before predicted, and which were
already fulfilled (see Notes on ch. xlii.
9; xliii. 19). ¶ *Even hidden things.*
Events which are so concealed that
they could not be conjectured by any
political sagacity, or by any contemplation of mere natural causes. They are,
as it were, laid up in dark treasure-
houses (comp. ch. xlv. 3), and they can
be known only by him to whom 'the
darkness shineth as the day,' and to

whom the night and the day are both
alike (Ps. cxxxix. 12).

7. *They are created now.* The LXX.
render this, Νῦν γίνεται—' Done now ;'
and many expositors interpret it in the
sense that they are now brought into
light, as if they were created. Aben
Ezra renders it, ' They are decreed and
determined by me.' Rosenmüller supposes that it refers to the revelation, or
making known those things. Lowth
renders it, ' They are produced now,
and not of old.' Noyes, ' It is revealed
now, and not long ago.' But the sense
is probably this : God is saying that
they did not foresee them, nor were
they able to conjecture them by the
contemplation of any natural causes.
There were no natural causes in operation at the time the predictions were
made, respecting the destruction of
Babylon, by which it could be conjectured that that event would take
place ; and when the event occurred, it
was as if it had been *created* anew.
It was the result of Almighty power
and energy, and was to be traced to
him alone. The sense is, that it could
no more be predicted, at the time when
the prophecy was uttered, from the
operation of any natural causes, than
an act of creation could be predicted,
which depended on the exercise of the
Divine will alone. It was a case which
God only could understand, in the same
way as he alone could understand the
purposes and the time of his own act of
creating the world. ¶ *And not from
the beginning.* The events have not
been so formed from the beginning that
they could be predicted by the operation
of natural causes, and by political sagacity. ¶ *Even before the day when thou
heardest them not.* The sense of this is
probably, 'and before this day thou hast
not heard of them ;' that is, these predictions pertain to new events, and are
not to be found in antecedent prophecies.

8 Yea, thou heardest not; yea, thou knewest not; yea, from that time *that* thine ear was not opened: for I knew *a* that thou wouldest deal very treacherously, *b* and wast called a transgressor from the *c* womb.

9 For *d* my name's sake will I defer mine anger, and for my praise will I refrain for thee, that I cut thee not off.

a Ps.139.1-4.   *b* Je.5.11; Ho.5.7; 6.7.
   c Ps.51.5.   *d* Ps.79.9; 106.8.

The prophet did not speak now of the deliverance from Egypt, and of the blessings of the promised land, which had constituted the burden of many of the former prophecies, but he spoke of a *new* thing; of the deliverance from Babylon, and of events which they could by no natural sagacity anticipate, so that they could claim that they knew them. ¶ *Lest thou shouldest say, Behold, I knew them.* The taking of Babylon by Cyrus, and the deliverance of the exiles from their bondage, are events which can be foreseen only by God. Yet the prophet says that he had declared these events, which thus lay entirely beyond the power of human conjecture, long before they occurred, so that they could not *possibly* pretend that they knew them by any natural sagacity, or that an idol had effected this.

8. *Yea, thou heardest not.* This verse is designed to show not only that these events could not have been foreseen by them, but that when they were actually made known to them, they were stupid, dull, and incredulous. It is not only re-affirming what had been said in the previous verses, but is designed to show that they were characteristically and constantly a perverse, hardened, and insensible people. The phrase, 'thou heardest not,' therefore means that they did not attend to these things when they *were* uttered, and were prone to disregard God, and all his predictions and promises. ¶ *Yea, from that time* that *thine ear was not opened.* The word 'that' which is here supplied by our translators, greatly obscures the sense. The meaning is, 'from the first, thine ear was not open to receive them' (Lowth); that is, they were stupid, insensible, and uniformly prone to disregard the messages of God. To open the ear, denotes a prompt and ready attention to what God says (see ch. l. 5), and to close the ear denotes an un-

willingness to listen to what is spoken by him. ¶ *For I knew that thou wouldest deal very treacherously.* I knew that, as a people, you are characteristically false and perfidious. This does not refer to their conduct towards other nations, but to their conduct towards God. They were false and unfaithful to him, and the sense is, that *if* God had not foretold the destruction of Babylon and their deliverance from it so clearly that there could have been no misunderstanding of it, and no perversion, they would have also perverted this, and ascribed it to something else than to him. *Perhaps* they might, as their forefathers did, when they came out of Egypt (Ex. xxxii. 4), have ascribed it to idols (comp. ver. 5), and the result might have been a relapse into that very sin, to cure which was the design of removing them to Babylon. ¶ *And wast called.* This was thy appropriate appellation. ¶ *From the womb.* From the very commencement of your national history; from the very time when the nation was first organized (see Notes on ch. xliv. 2).

9. *For my name's sake* (see Notes on ch. xliii. 25; comp. ch. lxvi. 5). It is possible that the design of this verse may be, to answer an objection. 'If the character of the nation is such, it might be said, 'why should God *desire* to restore them again to their own land? If their sins have been so great as to make these heavy judgments proper, why not suffer them to remain under the infliction of the deserved judgment? Why should God interpose? why raise up Cyrus? why overthrow Babylon? why conduct them across a pathless wilderness, and provide for them in a sandy desert?' To this the answer is, that it was not on *their* account. It was not because they were deserving of his favour, nor was it primarily and mainly in order that they might be happy. It was *on his own*

10 Behold, I have refined *a* thee,
a Ps.60.10.   1 or, *for*, Eze.22.20-22.
        b Zec.13.9; 1 Pe.4.12.

but not [1] with silver; I have chosen thee in the furnace *b* of affliction.

account—in order to show his covenant faithfulness; his fidelity to the promises made to their fathers, his mercy, his compassion, his readiness to pardon, and his unchanging love.—And this is the reason why he 'defers his anger,' in relation to any of the children of men. His own glory, and not their happiness, is the main object in view. And this is right. The glory, the honour, and the happiness of God, are of more importance than the welfare of any of his creatures; because, first, they are *in themselves* of more importance, just in proportion as God is more elevated than any of his creatures; and, secondly, the welfare of *any* or *all* of his creatures depends on the maintaining of the honour of God, and of his government, and on the manifestation of his perfections to the universe (see the treatise of President Edwards on *The end for which God created the world*, in *Works*, vol. iii. New York Ed. 1830). ¶ *Will I defer mine anger.* That is, I will spare you, and restore you again to your own land (see Note on ver. 11). ¶ *And for my praise will I refrain for thee.* Will I refrain my anger in reference to you as a nation. The word here used (חָטַם *hhâtăm*) denotes properly *to muzzle*, and is commonly employed with reference to an animal in order to tame or subdue it. Here it means that God would restrain himself; he would not put forth his anger in order to destroy them. Learn hence—1. That God acts with reference to his own glory, in order to manifest his own perfections, and to secure his praise. 2. That the reason why the wicked are not cut off sooner in their transgressions is, that He may show his forbearance, and secure praise by long-suffering. 3. That the reason why the righteous are kept amidst their frequent failures in duty, their unfaithfulness, and their many imperfections, is, that God may get glory by showing his covenant fidelity. 4. That it is one evidence of piety—and one that is indispensable—that there should be a willingness that God should secure his

own glory in his own way, and that there should be a constant desire that *his* praise should be promoted, whatever may befall his creatures.
10. *Behold, I have refined thee.* This refers to the Jews in their afflictions and captivity in Babylon. It states *one* design which he had in view in those afflictions—to purify them. The word here used, and rendered 'refined' (צָרַף *tzârăph*), means properly *to melt;* to smelt metals; to subject them to the action of fire, in order to remove the scoria or dross from them (see Notes on ch. i. 25). Then it means to purify in any manner. Here it means that God had used these afflictions for the same purpose for which fire is used in regard to metals, in order that every impurity in their moral and religious character might be removed. ¶ *But not with silver.* Marg. 'For.' Heb. בְּכָסֶף (*bhĕkhâsĕph*). Many different interpretations of this have been proposed. Jerome renders it, *Non quasi argentum*—'Not as silver.' The LXX. Οὐχ ἕνεκεν ἀργυρίου—'Not on account of silver.' Grotius explains it, 'I have a long time tried thee by afflictions, but nothing good appears in thee;' that is, I have not found you to be silver, or to be pure, as when a worker in metals applies the usual heat to a mass of ore for the purpose of separating the dross, and obtains no silver. Gesenius explains it to mean, 'I sought to make you better by afflictions, but the end was not reached; you were not as silver which is obtained by melting, but as dross.' Rosenmüller supposes it means, that he had not tried them with that intensity of heat which was necessary to melt and refine silver; and remarks, that those skilled in metals observe that gold is easily liquified, but that silver requires a more intense heat to purify it. Jarchi renders it, 'Not by the fire of Gehenna as silver is melted by the fire.' Kimchi explains it, 'Not as one who is smelting silver, and who removes all the scoria from it, and so consumes it that nothing but pure silver remains. If that had been done, but few of you would have

11 For mine own sake, *even for* mine own sake, will I do *it :* for how *a* should *my name* be polluted?

a De.32.26,27.

and *b* I will not give my glory unto another.

12 Hearken unto me, O Jacob and

b ch.42.8.

been left.' Vitringa supposes that it means, that God had sent them to Babylon to be purified, yet it was not to be done *with* silver. It was by the agency of a people who were wicked, sinful, and unbelieving. Amidst this variety of interpretation, it is difficult to determine the sense. Probably it may be, I have melted thee, and found no silver; or the result has not been that you have been shown to be pure by all your trials; and thus it will agree with what is said above, that they were perverse, false, and rebellious as a people. ¶ *I have chosen thee.* Lowth renders this, ' I have tried thee.' The Vulgate and the LXX., however, render it, ' I have chosen thee.' The word here used (from בָּחַר *bâhhăr*) means, according to Gesenius—1. *To prove, to try, to examine;* and the primary idea, according to him, is that of *rubbing* with the *lapis* Lydius, or touchstone, or else of cutting in pieces for the purpose of examining. 2. *To approve, choose,* or *select.* This is the most common signification in the Hebrew Bible (Gen. xiii. 11; Ex. xvii. 9; Josh. xxiv. 15; Job ix. 14; xv. 5; xxix. 25). 3. *To delight in* (Gen. vi. 2; Isa. i. 29). Probably the meaning here is, ' I have proved or tried thee in the furnace of affliction.' It was true, however, that God had *chosen* or selected their nation to be his people when they were suffering in the furnace of affliction in Egypt; and it is also true that God *chooses* sinners now, or converts them, as the result of heavy affliction. Possibly this may be the idea, that their affliction had *prepared* them to embrace his offers and to seek consolation in him; and he may design to teach that one effect of affliction is to *prepare* the mind to embrace the offers of mercy. ¶ *In the furnace of affliction.* Referring particularly to their trials in Babylon. Afflictions are often likened to fire—from the fact that fire is used to purify or try metals, and afflictions have the same object in reference to the people of God.

11. *For mine own sake* (see ver. 9).

The expression here is repeated to denote emphasis. He had thrown them into the furnace of affliction on his own account, *i.e.*, in order that his own name should not be profaned by their irreligion and idolatry, and that the glory which was due to him should not be given to idols. ¶ *For how should* my name *be polluted?* The sense is, that it would be inconsistent with his perfections to see his name profaned without endeavouring to correct and prevent it; and in order to this, that he brought these afflictions upon them. They had profaned his name by their irreligion and hypocrisy. In order to correct this evil, and to prevent it in future, he had brought these national judgments on them, and removed them to Babylon. The doctrine here taught is, that when the conduct of God's professed people is such as to dishonour God, and to make his name a subject of reproach with the wicked, he will visit them with heavy judgments. He *cannot* indulge them in a course of life which will reflect dishonour on his own name. ¶ *And I will not give my glory unto another* (see Notes on ch. xlii. 8). The sense here is this. The Jews had, as a nation, been prone to ascribe to idols that which was due to God alone. To correct this, and to make an *effectual* reform, he had removed them to Babylon, and doomed them to a long and painful captivity there. It may be added that the punishment *was* effectual, and that their long trial in Babylon served entirely to correct all their idolatrous propensities as a nation.

12. *Hearken unto me.* This is a solemn call on the Jews in Babylon to attend to what he was now about to say. It is the commencement of a new part of the argument, containing the assurance that he would deliver them, and utterly destroy the Chaldeans. He begins, therefore, by asserting that he is the only true God, and that he is able to accomplish all his purposes. ¶ *My called.* The people whom I have chosen, or called. ¶ *I am he.* I am the

Israel, my called ; I *am* he : I *ᵃ am*
the first, I also *am* the last.

13 Mine *ᵇ* hand also hath laid the
foundation of the earth, and ¹my
right hand hath spanned the heavens : *when* I *ᶜ* call unto them, they
stand up together.

14 All ye, assemble yourselves,
and hear ; which among them hath

ᵃ Re.22.18.   *ᵇ* Ps.102.25;

---

declared these *things ?* The Lord
hath loved *ᵈ* him ; he will *ᵉ* do his
pleasure on Babylon, and his arm
shall be on the Chaldeans.

15 I, *even* I, have spoken ; yea,
I have called him : I *f* have brought
him, and he shall make his way
prosperous.

1 or, *the palm of my right hand hath spread out.*
ᶜ ch.40.26. *ᵈ* Mar.10.21. *ᵉ* ch.44.28. *f* Ezr.1.2.

---

same ; or I am the true and only God.
¶ *I* am *the first* (see Notes on ch.
xli. 4; xliv. 6).

13. *Mine hand also hath laid,* &c.
I am the Creator of all things, and I
have all power, and am abundantly able
to deliver you from all your foes. ¶ *And
my right hand hath spanned the heavens.*
Marg. ' The palm of my right hand
hath spread out.' The sense is, that
he by his right hand had spanned, or
measured the heavens. The phrase is
designed to show his greatness and his
power (see Notes on ch. xl. 12). ¶ *When
I call unto them* (see Note on ch. xl. 26).
The sense here is, that he who had
power thus to command the hosts of
heaven, and to secure their perfect
obedience by his word, had power also
to defend his people, and to deliver
them from their foes, and conduct them
in safety to their own land.

14. *All ye, assemble yourselves and
hear.* Ye Jews who are in Babylon,
gather together, and listen to the assurance that God is able to protect you,
and that he will certainly restore you to
your own country. ¶ *Which among
them.* Who among the heathen? ¶ *Hath
declared these* things? The things relating to the destruction of Babylon, and
the rescue of his people. This is an
appeal similar to that which God has
often made, that he alone can predict
future events. None of the astrologers,
soothsayers, or diviners of Babylon had
been able to foretell the expedition and
the conquests of Cyrus, and the capture
of the city. If they *had* been able to
foresee the danger, they might have
guarded against it, and the city might
have been saved. But God had predicted it a hundred and fifty years before it occurred, and this demonstrated,
therefore, that he alone was God. ¶ *The*

Lord *hath loved him.* Lowth renders
this, ' He whom Jehovah hath loved
will execute his will on Babylon.' The
LXX. render it, ' Loving thee, I will execute thy will against Babylon.' There
can be no doubt that it refers to Cyrus,
and that the meaning is, that he whom
Jehovah had loved would accomplish
his will on Babylon. It does not necessarily mean that Jehovah was pleased
with his moral character, or that he was
a pious man (comp. Notes on ch. xli. 2);
but that he was so well pleased with
him as an instrument to accomplish
his purposes, that he chose to employ
him for that end. ¶ *He will do his
pleasure on Babylon.* He will accomplish all his desire on that city; that is,
he will take, and subdue it. The word
' his ' here, may refer either to Cyrus
or to Jehovah. Probably it means that
Cyrus would do to Babylon what would
be pleasing to Jehovah. ¶ *And his
arm.* The arm is a symbol of strength,
and is the instrument by which we
execute our purposes.

15. *I, even I, have spoken.* The
word ' I ' is repeated to give emphasis,
and to furnish the utmost security that
it should be certainly accomplished. It
means, that Jehovah, and he alone, had
declared this, and that it was entirely
by his power that Cyrus had been raised
up, and had been made prosperous.
¶ *Yea, I have called him* (see Note on
ch. xli. 2). ¶ *I have brought him.* I
have led him on his way in his conquests. ¶ *And he shall make his way
prosperous.* There is a change of person in this verse, from the first to the
third, which is quite common in the
writings of Isaiah.

16. *Come ye near unto me* (see ver.
14). ¶ *I have not spoken in secret* (see
Notes on ch. xlv. 19). The idea here

16 Come ye near unto me, hear ye this; I have not spoken in secret from the beginning; from the time that it was, there *am* I: and now the *a* Lord God and his Spirit hath sent me.

a ch.61.11; Zec.2.8,9-11; Lu.4.18-21.

is, that he had foretold the raising up of Cyrus, and his agency in delivering his people, in terms so plain that it could not be pretended that it was *conjectured*, and so clear that there was no ambiguity. ¶ *From the time that it was, there* am *I.* From the moment when the purpose was formed, and when it began to be accomplished, I was present. The meaning is, that everything in regard to raising up Cyrus, and to the delivery of his people from Babylon, had been entirely under his direction. ¶ *And now the Lord* God *and his Spirit hath sent me.* There is evidently a change in the speaker here. In the former part of the verse, it is God who is the speaker. But here it is he who is sent to bear the message. Or, if this should be regarded, as Lowth and many others suppose, as the Messiah who is speaking to the exiled Jews, then it is an assertion that *he* had been sent by the Lord God and his Spirit. There is an ambiguity in the original, which is not retained in our common translation. The Hebrew is, 'And now the Lord Jehovah hath sent me, and his Spirit;' and the meaning may be either, as in our version, that Jehovah *and* his Spirit were united in sending the person referred to; or that Jehovah had sent him, and at the same time had also sent his Spirit to accompany what he said. Grotius renders it, 'The Lord by his Spirit has given me these commands.' Jerome understands the word 'Spirit' as in the nominative case, and as meaning that the Spirit united with Jehovah in sending the person referred to—*Dominus Deus misit me, et spiritus ejus.* The LXX., like the Hebrew, is ambiguous— Νῦν κύριος κύριος ἀπέστειλέ με, καὶ τὸ πνεῦμα αὐτοῦ. The Syriac has the same ambiguity. The Targum of Jonathan renders it, 'And now Jehovah (יְיָ) God hath sent me and his word.' It is perhaps not possible to determine, where there is such ambiguity in the form of the sentence, what is the exact meaning. As it is not common, however, in the Scriptures, to speak of the Spirit of God as sending, or commissioning his servants; and as the object of the speaker here is evidently to conciliate respect for his message as being inspired, it is probably to be regarded as meaning that he had been sent by Jehovah and was accompanied *with* the influences of his Spirit. Many of the reformers, and others since their time, have supposed that this refers to the Messiah, and have endeavoured to derive a demonstration from this verse of the doctrine of the Trinity. The argument which it has been supposed these words furnish on that subject is, that three persons are here spoken of, the person who sends, *i.e.*, God the Father; the person who is sent, *i.e.*, the Messiah; and the Spirit, who concurs in sending him, or by whom he is endowed. But the evidence that this refers to the Messiah is too slight to lay the foundation for such an argument; and nothing is gained to the cause of truth by such forced interpretations. *It would require more time, and toil, and ingenuity to demonstrate that this passage had reference to the Messiah, than it would to demonstrate the doctrine of the Trinity, and the divinity of the Redeemer, from the unequivocal declarations of the New Testament.* The remark of Calvin on this verse, and on this mode of interpretation, is full of good sense: ' This verse interpreters explain in different ways. Many refer it to Christ, but the prophet designs no such thing. *Cavendæ autem sunt nobis violentæ et coactæ interpretationes*— (such forced and violent interpretations are to be avoided).' The *scope* of the passage demands, as it seems to me, that it should be referred to the prophet himself. His object is, to state that he had not come at his own instance, or without being commissioned. He had been sent by God, and was attended by the Spirit of inspiration. He foretold events which the Spirit of God alone could make known to men. It is, therefore, a strong asseveration that his words demanded their attention, and

17 Thus saith the LORD, thy Redeemer, the Holy One of Israel; I *am* the LORD thy God which teacheth *a* thee to profit, *b* which leadeth thee *c* by the way *that* thou shouldest go.

a Mi.4.2.   *b* De.8.17,18.   *c* Ps.32.8; 73.24.

18 O *d* that thou hadst hearkened to my commandments! then had thy *e* peace been as a river, and thy righteousness as the waves of the sea :

d Ps.81.13-16.   *e* Ps.119.165.

that they had every ground of consolation, and every possible evidence that they would be rescued from their bondage. It is a full claim to Divine inspiration, and is one of the many assertions which are found in the Scriptures where the sacred writers claim to have been sent by God, and taught by his Spirit.

17. *Thy Redeemer* (see Notes on ch. xli. 14; xliii. 1). ¶ *Which teacheth thee to profit.* Teaching you what things will most conduce to your welfare. The reference here is chiefly to the afflictions which they suffered in Babylon. ¶ *Which leadeth thee.* I am thy conductor and guide. God taught them, as he does his people now, by his Providence, his revealed word, and his Spirit, the way in which they ought to go. It is one of his characteristics that he is the guide and director of his people.

18. *O that thou hadst hearkened to my commandments!* This expresses the earnest wish and desire of God. He would greatly have *preferred* that they should have kept his law. He had no wish that they should sin, and that these judgments should come upon them. The doctrine taught here is, that God greatly *prefers* that men should keep his laws. He does not desire that they should be sinners, or that they should be punished. It was so with regard to the Jews; and it is so with regard to all. In all cases, at all times, and with reference to all his creatures, he prefers holiness to sin; he sincerely desires that there should be perfect obedience to his commandments. It is to be remarked also that this is not merely prospective, or a declaration in the abstract. It relates to sin which had been actually committed, and proves that even in regard to that, God would have *preferred* that it had not been committed. A declara-

tion remarkably similar to this, occurs in Ps. lxxxi. 13–16 :

O that my people had hearkened unto me,
And Israel had walked in my ways;
I should soon have subdued their enemies,
And turned their hand against their adversaries
The haters of the Lord should have submitted themselves unto him :
But their time should have endured for ever.
He should have fed them also with the finest of the wheat;
And with honey out of the rock should I have satisfied thee.

Compare Deut. xxii. 29; Isa. v. 1–7; Ezek. xviii. 23–32; Matt. xxiii. 37; Luke xix. 21. ¶ *Then had thy peace been as a river.* The word 'peace' here (שָׁלוֹם *shâlōm*) means properly *wholeness, soundness,* and then health, welfare, prosperity, good of every kind. It then denotes peace, as opposed to war, and also concord and friendship. Here it evidently denotes prosperity in general, as opposed to the calamities which actually came upon them. ¶ *As a river.* That is, abundant—like a full, flowing river that fills the banks, and that conveys fertility and blessedness through a land. 'The heathen, in order to represent the universal power and beneficence of Jupiter, used the symbol of a river flowing from his throne; and to this the *Sycophant* in Plautus alludes (*Trium.* Act iv. Sc. 2, v. 98), in his saying that he had been at the head of that river:

Ad caput amnis, quod de cœlo exoritur, sub solio Jovis.

See also Wemyss' *Key to the Symbolical Language of Scripture,* Art. *River.* Rivers are often used by the sacred writers, and particularly by Isaiah, as symbolical of plenty and prosperity (ch. xxxii. 2; xxxiii. 31; xli. 18; xliii. 19). ¶ *And thy righteousness.* The holiness and purity of the nation. Religion, with all its inestimable benefits, would have abounded to the utmost extent. Instead of the prevailing idolatry and corruption, the hypocrisy and insin-

19 Thy seed also had been as the sand, and the offspring of thy bowels like the gravel thereof ; his name should not have been cut off nor destroyed from before me.

20 Go *a* ye forth of Babylon, flee ye from the Chaldeans, with a voice of singing declare ye, tell this, utter it *even* to the end of the earth ; say ye, The Lord hath redeemed *b* his servant Jacob.

a Je.51.6,45.   *b* 2 Sa.7.23.

cerity which had abounded, and which made it necessary for God to remove them, they would have been distinguished for sincerity, purity, love, and holy living. And this *proves* that God would have *preferred* the prevalence of holiness. ¶ *As the waves of the sea.* What can be a more beautiful or sublime image than this? What can more strikingly represent the *abundance* of the blessings which religion would have conferred on the land? The waves of the sea are an emblem of plenty. They seem to be boundless. They are constantly rolling. And so their righteousness would have been without a limit ; and would have rolled unceasingly its rich blessings over the land. Who can doubt that this would have been a better state, a condition to have been *preferred* to that which actually existed ?

19. *Thy seed also.* Instead of being reduced to a small number by the calamities incident to war, and being comparatively a small and powerless people sighing in captivity, you would have been a numerous and mighty nation. This is another of the blessings which would have followed from obedience to the commands of God ; and it proves that a people who are virtuous and pious will become numerous and mighty. Vice, and the diseases, the wars, and the Divine judgments consequent on vice, tend to depopulate a nation, and to make it feeble. ¶ *As the sand.* This is often used to denote a great and indefinite number (Gen. xxii. 17; xxxii. 12; xli. 49; Josh. xi. 4; Judg. vii. 12; 1 Sam. xiii. 5; 2 Sam. xvii. 11; 1 Kings iv. 20–29; Job xxix. 18; Ps. cxxxix. 18; Note on Isa. x. 22; Hos. i. 10; Rev. xx. 8). ¶ *And the offspring of thy bowels.* On the meaning of the word used here, see Note on ch. xxii. 24. ¶ *Like the gravel thereof.* Literally, 'and the offspring of thy bowels shall

be like its bowels,' *i.e.*, like the offspring of the sea. The phrase refers probably rather to the fish of the sea, or the innumerable multitudes of animals that swim in the sea, than to the gravel. There is no place where the word means gravel. Jerome, however, renders it, *Ut lapili ejus*—' As its pebbles.' The LXX. 'Ως ὁ χοῦς τῆς γῆς—' As the dust of the earth.' The Chaldee also renders it, ' As the stones of the sea ;' and the Syriac also. The sense is essentially the same—that the number of the people of the nation would have been vast. ¶ *His name should not have been cut off.* This does not imply of necessity that they had ceased to be a nation when they were in Babylon, but the meaning is, that if they had been, and would continue to be, obedient, their national existence would have been perpetuated to the end of time. When they ceased to be a distinct nation, and their name was blotted out among the kingdoms of the earth, it was for national crime and unbelief (Rom. xi. 20).

20. *Go ye forth of Babylon.* The prophet now directly addresses those who were in exile in Babylon, and commands them to depart from it. The design of this is, to furnish the assurance that they should be delivered, and to show them the duty of leaving the place of their long captivity when the opportunity of doing it should occur. It is also designed to show that when it should occur, it would be attended with great joy and rejoicing. ¶ *Flee ye from the Chaldeans with a voice of singing.* With the utmost exultation and joy. They should rejoice that their captivity was ended ; they should exult at the prospect of being restored again to their own land. ¶ *Utter it even to the end of the earth.* It is an event so great and wonderful that all the nations should be made acquainted with it. ¶ *The Lord hath redeemed,* &c. Jehovah has rescued from cap-

21 And they thirsted not *when* he led them through the deserts ; he caused the waters *a* to flow out of the rock for them ; he clave the

a Ex. 17.6.

rock also, and the waters gushed out.

22 *There is* no peace, *b* saith the LORD, unto the wicked.

b ch. 57.21.

---

tivity his people (see Notes on ch. xliii. 1).

21. *And they thirsted not.* This is a part of that for which they would be called to celebrate his name. It was not merely that he had redeemed them, but that he had abundantly provided for their wants in the desert, and guided them safe through the pathless wilderness to their own land (see Notes on ch. xxxv. 6, 7; xli. 17, 18). ¶ *He caused the waters to flow out of the rock for them.* The allusion here is undoubtedly to the fact that God caused the waters to flow out of the rock that Moses smote in the wilderness (Ex. xvii. 6 ; Num. xx. 11). This is not to be regarded as literally true that God would, in like manner, smite the rocks and cause waters to flow by miracle on their return from Babylon. There is no record that any such event took place, and it is not necessary so to understand this passage. It is a part of the triumphant song which they are represented as singing after their return to their own land. In that song, they celebrate his gracious interposition in language that was familiar to them, and by illustrations that were well known. They therefore speak of his mercy to them *as if* he had smitten the rock in the desert on their return, and caused the waters to flow ; and the sense is, that his mercy to them then was similar to his goodness to their fathers when he led them to the land of promise. He met all their necessities ; and his gracious interposition was experienced all the way *as really* as though he had smitten the rock, or caused cool and refreshing fountains to break out in the desert.

22. There is *no peace, saith the* LORD, *unto the wicked.* This verse contains a sentiment whose truth no one can doubt. To the transgressor of the laws of God there can be no permanent peace, enjoyment, or prosperity. The word *peace* is used in the Scriptures in all these senses (see Note on ver. 18 of this chapter). There may be the *appearance* of

joy, and there may be temporary prosperity. But there is no abiding, substantial, permanent happiness, such as is enjoyed by those who fear and love God. This sentiment occurs not unfrequently in Isaiah. It is repeated in ch. lvii. 21 ; and in ch. lvii. 20, he says that 'the wicked are like the troubled sea when it cannot rest, whose waters cast up mire and dirt.' Of the *truth* of the declaration here there can be no doubt ; but it is not perfectly apparent why it is introduced here. It is probably a part of the *song* with which they would celebrate their return ; and it may have been used for one of the following reasons :—1. As a general maxim, expressed in view of the joy which *they* had in their return to their own land. They had elevated peace and triumph and joy. This was produced by the fact that they had evidence that they were the objects of the Divine favour and protection. How natural was it in view of these blessings to say, that the wicked had no such comfort, and in general, that there was *no* peace to them of any kind, or from any quarter. Or, 2. It may have been uttered in view of the fact that many of their countrymen may have chosen to remain in Babylon when they returned to their own land. They probably formed connections there, amassed wealth, and refused to attend those who returned to Judea to rebuild the temple. And the meaning may be, that they, amidst all the wealth which they might have gained, and amidst the idolatries which prevailed in Babylon, could never enjoy the peace which *they* now had in their return to the land of their fathers. Whatever was the reason why it was here used, it contains a most important truth which demands the attention of all men. The wicked, as a matter of sober truth and verity, *have* no permanent and substantial peace and joy. They have none—1. In the *act* of wickedness. Sin may be attended with the gratifications of bad passions, but in the act of sinning, as such, there can

CHAPTER XLIX.

In the chapters which precede this, the deliverance from Babylon has been the main subject of the prophecy. There has been, indeed, decided reference in many places to the Messiah and his times: but the primary idea has been the restoration from Babylon. In this chapter, it has been commonly supposed that the Messiah is introduced directly and personally, and that there is a primary reference to him and his work. There has been, indeed, great difference of opinion among interpreters on this point; but the common sentiment has been, that the chapter has a direct reference to him. Some of the opinions which have been held may be briefly referred to as introductory to the exposition of the chapter—since the exposition of the whole chapter will be affected by the view which is taken of its primary and main design. This statement will be abridged from Hengstenberg (*Christology*, vol. i.)

1. According to some, the people of Israel are here introduced as speaking. This is the opinion of Paulus, Döderlin, and Rosenmüller. The argument on which Rosenmüller relies is, that in ver. 3, the speaker is expressly called 'Israel.' According to this idea, the whole people are represented as *a prophet* who is here introduced as speaking; who had laboured in vain; and who, though Israel was not to be gathered, was

in future times to be the instructor of the whole world (ver. 4-6). Yet this interpretation is forced and unnatural. To say nothing of the impropriety of representing the collected Jewish people as a prophet—an idea not to be found elsewhere; according to this interpretation, the people are represented as labouring in vain, when as yet they had made no effort for the conversion of the heathen, and, in ver. 5, this same people, as a prophet, is represented as 'not gathered,' and then, in ver. 6, turning to the Gentiles in order to be a light to them, and for salvation to the ends of the earth. It should be added, also, that even the ancient Jewish commentators who have applied ch. liii. to the Jewish people, have not ventured on such an interpretation here. The only argument on which Rosenmüller relies in favour of this interpretation—that drawn from the fact that the name 'Israel' is given to the speaker—will be considered in the Notes on ver. 3.

2. According to others, the prophet here refers to himself. This opinion was held by Jarchi, Aben Ezra, Kimchi, Grotius, and, among recent interpreters, by Koppe, Hensler, and Staudlin. But this interpretation has little probability. It is incredible that the prophet should speak of himself as the light of the heathen world. The speaker represents himself as not satisfied (ver. 6) that the Jewish people should be given to him, but as sent for the salvation of the ends of the earth. Before this same individual

be no substantial happiness. 2. They have no solid, substantial, elevated peace in the business or the pleasures of life. This world can furnish no such joys as are derived from the hope of a life to come. Pleasures 'pall upon the sense,' riches take wings; disappointment comes; and the highest earthly and sensual pleasure leaves a sad sense of want—a feeling that there is *something* in the capacities and wants of the undying mind which has not been filled. 3. They have no peace of conscience; no deep and abiding conviction that they are right. They are often troubled; and there is nothing which this world can furnish which will give peace to a bosom that is agitated with a sense of the guilt of sin. 4. They have no *peace* on a deathbed. There may be stupidity, callousness, insensibility, freedom from much pain or alarm. But that is not peace, any more than sterility is fruitfulness; or than death is life; or than the frost of winter is the verdure

of spring; or than a desert is a fruitful field. 5. There is often in these circumstances the reverse of peace. There is not only no positive peace, but there is the opposite. There is often disappointment, care, anxiety, distress, deep alarm, and the awful apprehension of eternal wrath. There is no situation in life or death, where the sinner can certainly *calculate* on peace, or where he will be sure to find it. There is every probability that his mind will be often filled with alarm, and that his deathbed will be one of despair. 6. There is no peace to the wicked beyond the grave. *A sinner* can *have no peace at the judgment bar of God; he* can *have no peace in hell.* In all the future world there is no place where he can find repose; and whatever this life may be, even if it be a life of prosperity and external comfort, yet to him there will be no prosperity in the future world, and no external or internal peace there.

who thus speaks, and who is rejected and despised by the Jewish people, kings and princes are represented as prostrating themselves with the deepest reverence (ver. 7). But it is certain that Isaiah never formed any such extravagant expectations for himself. Besides, there is the same objection to applying the name 'Israel' (ver. 3) to the prophet Isaiah which there is to the Messiah.

3. Gesenius supposes that this refers, not to the prophet Isaiah alone, but to the collective body of the prophets, as represented by him. But to this view also there are insuperable objections. (1.) Everything in the statement here proves that the subject is an individual, and not a mere personification. The personal pronouns are used throughout (see ver. 1, 2, 4, &c.), and the whole aspect of the account is that relating to an individual. It would be as proper to regard a statement made anywhere respecting an individual as referring to some collective body, as to interpret this in this manner. (2.) The prophets taken collectively cannot bear the name 'Israel' (ver. 3); and even Gesenius admits this, and in order to evade the force of it, denies the genuineness of the word 'Israel' in the third verse. (3.) The prophets nowhere represent themselves as called to exert an influence on the heathen world, but their representation is, that the heathen would be converted by the Messiah.

4. The only other opinion which has been extensively held, is that which refers the chapter directly to the Messiah. This was the opinion of the Christian fathers generally, and is the opinion of Lowth, Vitringa, Calvin, Hengstenberg, and of most modern interpreters. The particular reasons for this opinion will be more clearly seen in the Notes on the chapter itself, particularly ver. 1-9. In favour of this interpretation it may be observed in general:—(1.) That if the other interpretations which have been referred to are unfounded, it follows as a matter of course that it must have reference to the Messiah. (2.) The accurate agreement of the words and phrases in the prophecy with the character of the Redeemer, as developed in the New Testament, proves the same thing. (3.) It is referred to the times of the Messiah in Acts xiii. 47, and in 2 Cor. vi. 2.

The chapter may be contemplated under the following division of parts, or subjects, viz.:—

I. The Messiah is introduced as himself speaking, and stating the object of his mission, and his rejection by the Jewish nation, and the fact that he would be for a light to the Gentiles (1-6). This portion consists of the following subjects: 1. The exordium, in which he calls the distant nations to hear his voice (1). 2. His call to the office of the Messiah, and his qualifications for the work (1-3). He was called from the womb (1); he was eminently endowed for the work, as a sharp sword, or a polished shaft is for battle (2); he was the selected servant of God, by whom he designed to be glorified (3). 3. The want of success in his work (4). He had laboured in vain, yet he could commit his cause to God with the certainty of entire *future* success, and with the assurance of the Divine approbation. 4. His future success would be glorious (5, 6). He would yet gather in the tribes of Israel, and be for a light to the heathen world, and for salvation to the ends of the earth.

II. A direct promise from JEHOVAH to the Messiah of ultimate success in his work (7-12). 1. Men would indeed despise and reject him. 2. Yet kings and princes would arise and honour him (7). 3. JEHOVAH had heard him, and would yet give him for a covenant to the world; a mediator to recover the earth back to himself (8). 4. He would lead forth the prisoners, and those who sat in darkness (9): he would protect and provide for them so that the sun should not smite them, and so that their wants should be supplied (10): he would remove all obstructions from their path, and would level mountains and exalt valleys (11): and his followers would come from far, from a distant land (12).

III. A song of praise in view of the glorious results of the work of the Messiah (13).

IV. Zion is comforted with the assurance that God had not forgotten her (14-21). 1. Zion had said that JEHOVAH had forgotten her, and left her to suffer alone without pity or compassion (14). 2. God assures her that he could no more forget her than a mother could forget her child (15). 3. He had engraven her name on the palms of his hands (16). 4. All her enemies and destroyers would flee away (17). 5. She would be yet decorated and adorned as a bride, instead of being desolate (18); and would be greatly increased and enlarged by accessions from the Gentile world, so that the place where she dwelt would be too strait for her (19-21).

V. God would extend salvation, with all its blessings, to the Gentiles. Kings and queens would become the patrons of the church of God, and all the foes of himself and his cause be destroyed (22-26).

LISTEN, O isles, unto me; and hearken, ye people from far; The LORD hath called me from the *a* womb; from the bowels of my mother hath he made mention of my name.

a Je.1,5; Lu.1.15,31; Ga.1.15.

2 And he hath made my mouth like a sharp sword; *a* in *b* the shadow of his hand hath he hid me, and made me a polished shaft; *c* in his quiver hath he hid me;

a Ho 6.5; He.4.12; Re 1.16.   *b* ch.21.16.   *c* Ps.45.5.

CHAPTER XLIX.

1. *Listen.* This is the exordium, or introduction. According to the interpretation which refers it to the Messiah, it is to be regarded as the voice of the Redeemer calling the distant parts of the earth to give a respectful attention to the statement of his qualifications for his work, and to the assurances that his salvation would be extended to them (comp. ch. xli. 1). The Redeemer here is to be regarded as having already come in the flesh, and as having been rejected and despised by the Jews (see ver. 4, 5), and as now turning to the Gentile world, and proffering salvation to them. The *time* when this is supposed to occur, therefore, as seen by the prophet, is when the Messiah had preached in vain to his own countrymen, and when there was a manifest fitness and propriety in his extending the offer of salvation to the heathen world. ¶ *O isles.* Ye distant lands (see Note on ch. xli. 1). The word is used here, as it is there, in the sense of countries *beyond sea;* distant, unknown regions; the dark, heathen world. ¶ *Ye people from far.* The reason why the Messiah thus addresses them is stated in ver. 6. It is because he was appointed to be a light to them, and because, having been rejected by the Jewish nation, it was resolved to extend the offers and the blessings of salvation to other lands. ¶ *The* LORD *hath called me from the womb.* JEHOVAH hath set me apart to this office from my very birth. The stress here is laid on the *fact* that he was thus called, and not on the particular time when it was done. The idea is, that he had not presumptuously assumed this office; he had not entered on it without being appointed to it; he had been designated to it even before he was born (see ver. 5). A similar expression is used in respect to Jeremiah (i. 5): 'Before I formed thee in the belly, I knew thee; and before thou camest forth out of the womb I sanctified thee; and I ordained thee a prophet unto the nations.' Paul also uses a similar expression respecting himself (Gal. i. 15): 'But when it pleased God, who separated me from my mother's womb.' That this actually occurred in regard to the Redeemer, it is not needful to pause here to show (see Luke i. 31). ¶ *From the bowels of my mother hath he made mention of my name.* This is another form of stating the fact that he had been designated to this office from his very infancy. Many have supposed that the reference here is to the fact that Mary was commanded by the angel, before his birth, to call his name Jesus (Luke i. 31). The same command was also repeated to Joseph in a dream (Matt. i. 21). So Jerome, Vitringa, Michaelis, and some others understand it. By others it has been supposed that the phrase 'he hath made mention of my name' is the same as to call. The Hebrew is literally, 'He has caused my name to be remembered from the bowels of my mother.' The LXX. render it, 'He hath called my name.' Grotius renders it, 'He has given to me a beautiful name, by which salvation is signified as about to come from the Lord.' I see no objection to the supposition that this refers to the fact that his name was actually designated before he was born. The phrase seems obviously to imply more than merely to *call* to an office; and as his name was thus actually designated by God, and as he designed that there should be special significancy and applicability *in* the name, there can be no impropriety in supposing that this refers to that fact. If so, the idea *is,* that he was not only *appointed* to the work of the Messiah from his birth, but that he actually had a *name* given him by God before he was born, which expressed the fact that he would *save* men, and which constituted a reason why the distant heathen lands should hearken to his voice.

2. *And he hath made my mouth.* The idea here is, that he had qualified him for a convincing and powerful eloquence —for the utterance of words which would penetrate the heart like a sharp sword. The mouth here, by an obvious figure, stands for discourse. The comparison of words that are pungent, penetrating, powerful, to a sword, is common. Indeed the very terms that I have incidentally used, 'pungent,' 'penetrating,' are instances of the same kind of figure, and are drawn from a *needle*, or anything sharp and pointed, that penetrates. Instances of this occur in the following places in the Scriptures :—'The words of the wise are as goads, and as nails fastened by the masters of assemblies' (Eccl. xii. 11). 'The word of God is quick and powerful, and sharper than any two-edged sword, piercing even to the dividing asunder of soul and spirit, and of the joints and marrow' (Heb. iv. 12). In Rev. i. 16, probably in reference to this passage, the Redeemer is represented as seen by John as having a 'sharp two-edged sword' proceeding out of his mouth. So in ch. xix. 15: 'And out of his mouth goeth a sharp sword.' The bold and striking metaphor of the sword and arrow applied to powerful discourse, has been used also by heathen writers with great elegance and force. In the passages quoted by Lowth, it is said of Pericles by Aristophanes:

'His powerful speech
Pierced the hearer's soul, and left behind
Deep in his bosom its keen point infixt.'

So Pindar, *Olym.* ii. 160:

'Come on! thy brightest shafts prepare,
And bend, O Muse, thy sounding bow:
Say, through what paths of liquid air
Our arrows shall we throw?'
WEST.

A similar expression occurs in a fragment of Eupolis, in Diod. Sic. xii. 40, when speaking of Pericles:

—καὶ μόνος τῶν ῥητόρων
τὸ κέντρον ἐγκατέλειπε τοῖς ἀκροωμένοις.

A similar metaphor occurs frequently in Arabic poetry. 'As arrows his words enter into the heart.' ¶ *In the shadow of his hand hath he hid me.* This passage has been very variously interpreted. Many have understood it as meaning that the shadow of the hand of God would cover or defend him—as a shade or shadow protects from heat. The word 'shadow' is used for protection in Isa. xxv. 4; Ps. xvii. 8; xxxvi. 8. This is the interpretation which Gesenius adopts. Piscator says that it means that God protected him from the snares of the

Scribes and Pharisees. Others suppose that it means that he was hidden or protected, as the sword is in the sheath, which is under the left hand, so that it can be easily drawn by the right hand. But Vitringa remarks that the figure here is that of a drawn sword, and he supposes that the meaning is, that the shadow of the hand of God is what covers and defends it, and serves, as it were, for a scabbard. Hengstenberg coincides with this opinion, and supposes that the image is taken from a dirk which a man carries in his hand, and which he suddenly draws forth in the moment of attack. Here, the image is that of a sword under the Divine protection, and the idea is, that the shadow of the hand of God constitutes the protection, the covering of the sword. He is the defender of the Messiah, and of his words ; and his hand shall guard him as the scabbard does the sword, or as the quiver does the arrow. The Messiah, like the sword, and the polished arrow, was fitted for the execution of the plans of God, and was ready at any moment to be engaged in his cause. His words, his doctrines, would be like the sharp sword and polished arrow. They would penetrate the heart of his foes, and by his doctrines, and the truths which he would teach, he would carry his conquests around the world. ¶ *And made me a polished shaft.* The word rendered 'polished' (בָּרוּר *bârūr*), may mean either chosen, or polished. It properly means that which is separated, or severed from others ; then select, chosen. Then it may mean anything which is cleansed, or purified, and here may denote an arrow that is *cleansed* from rust; *i.e.*, polished, or made bright. The word 'shaft' (חֵץ *hhêtz*), means properly *an arrow;* and the sense here is, that the Messiah pierced the hearts of men like a pointed and polished arrow that is sped from the bow. ¶ *In his quiver.* The word 'quiver' means the covering that was made for arrows, and which was so slung over the shoulder that they could be readily reached by

3 And said unto me, Thou *art* my

a ch.43.21; Jn.13.31; 1 Pe.2.9.

the hand as they should be needed. ¶ *Hath he hid me.* 'Before his appearing,' says Hengstenberg, 'the Messiah was concealed with God like a sword kept in its sheath, or like an arrow lying in the quiver.' But perhaps this is too much refined and forced. The meaning is, probably, simply that he had protected him. 'God, by his own power,' says Calvin, 'protected Christ and his doctrine, so that nothing could hinder its course.' Yet there is, undoubtedly, the idea that he was adapted to produce rapid and mighty execution; that he was fitted, like an arrow, to overcome the foes of God; and that he was kept in the 'quiver' for that purpose.

3. *And said unto me.* That is, as I suppose, to the Messiah. God said to him that he was his servant; he by whom he would be particularly glorified and honoured. ¶ *Thou* art *my servant, O Israel.* There has been great variety, as was intimated in the analysis of the chapter, in the interpretation of this verse. The question of difficulty is, to whom does the word 'Israel' refer? And if it refer to the Messiah, why is this name given to him? There is no variety in the ancient versions, or in the MSS. The opinions which have been maintained have been referred to in the analysis, and are briefly these—1. The most obvious interpretation of the verse, if it stood alone, would be to refer it to the Jews as 'the servant of JEHOVAH,' in accordance with ch. xli. 8, by whom he would be glorified in accordance with the declaration in ch. xliv. 23. This is the opinion of Rosenmüller and of some others. But the objection to this is, that the things which are affirmed of this 'servant,' by no means apply to the Jews. It is evidently an individual that is addressed; and in no conceivable sense can that be true of the Jews at large which is affirmed of this person in ver. 4, *sq.* 2. It has been referred to Isaiah. This was the opinion of Grotius, Dathe, Saadias, Döderlin, and others. Grotius supposes it means, 'thou art my servant for the good of Israel.' So Dathe renders it: 'It is

servant, O Israel, in whom I will be glorified.*a*

for Israel's benefit that I will glorify myself in thee.' Saadias renders it, 'Thou art my ambassador to Israel.' Aben Ezra says of the passage, 'Thou art my servant, descended from Israel, in whom I will be glorified. Or, the sense is this : Thou who in my eyes art reputed as equal to all Israel.' But, as has been remarked in the analysis, this interpretation is attended with *all* the difficulty of the interpretation which refers it to the Messiah, and is inconsistent with the known character of Isaiah, and with the declarations made of the person referred to in the following verses. There is certainly no more reason why the name 'Israel' should be given to Isaiah, than there is why it should be given to the Messiah; and it is certain that Isaiah never arrogated to himself such high honour as that of being a light to the Gentiles, and a covenant of the people, and as being one before whom kings would rise up, and to whom princes would do homage. 3. Gesenius supposes that the word 'Israel' is not genuine, but has come by error into the text. But for this there is no authority except one manuscript, to which he himself attaches no weight. 4. The only other interpretation, therefore, is that which refers it to the Messiah. This, which has been the common exposition of commentators, most manifestly agrees with the verses which follow, and with the account which occurs in the New Testament. The account in ver. 4–8, is such as can be applied to no other one than he, and is as accurate and beautiful a description of him as if it had been made by one who had witnessed his labours, and heard from him the statement of his own plans. But still, a material question arises, why is this name 'Israel' applied to the Messiah? It is applied to him nowhere else, and it is certainly remarkable that a name should be applied to an individual which is usually applied to an entire people. To this question the following answers, which are, indeed, little more than conjectures, may be returned :—1. Lowth and Vitringa suppose that it is because

4 Then I said, I have laboured in vain, I have spent my strength for nought, and in vain ; *yet* surely

my judgment *is* with the LORD, and my ¹ work with my God.

1 or, *reward*, ch.40.10.

---

the name, in its full import and signification, can be given only to him ; and that there is a reference here to the fact recorded in Gen. xxxii. 28, where Jacob is said to have wrestled with God, and prevailed, and was, in consequence of that, called Israel. The full import of that name, says Lowth, pertains only to the Messiah, ' who contended powerfully with God in behalf of mankind.' 2. It is common in the Scriptures to use the *names* which occurred in the history of the Jews as descriptive of things which were to occur under the times of the Messiah, or as representing *in general* events that might occur at any time. Thus the names, *Moab, Edom, Ashur,* were used to denote the foes of God in general; the name of Elijah was given to John the Baptist (Hengstenberg). 3. In accordance with this, the name David is not unfrequently given to the Messiah, and he is spoken of under this name, as he was to be his descendant and successor. 4. For the same reason, the name *Israel* may be given to him—not as the name of the Jewish people—but the name of the illustrious ancestor of the Jewish race, because he would possess his spirit, and would, like him, wrestle with God. He was to be a prince having power with God (comp. Gen. xxxii. 28), and would prevail. In many respects there would be a resemblance between him and this pious and illustrious ancestor of the Jewish people. ¶ *In whom I will be glorified.* This means that the result of the Redeemer's work would be such as eminently to honour God. He would be glorified by the gift of such a Saviour; by his instructions, his example, the effect of his ministry while on earth, and by his death. The effect of the work of the Messiah as adapted to glorify God, is often referred to in the New Testament (see John xii. 28; xiii. 31, 32; xiv. 13; xvi. 14; xvii. 1–5). 4. *Then I said.* I the Messiah. In the previous verses he speaks of his appointment to the office of Messiah, and of his dignity. The design here is to prepare the way for the announce-

ment of the fact that he would make known his gospel to the heathen, and would be for a light to the Gentiles. For this purpose he speaks of his labours among his own countrymen ; he laments the little success which attended his work at the commencement, but consoles himself with the reflection that his cause was with God, and that his labours would not go unrewarded. ¶ *I have laboured in vain.* This is to be regarded as the language of the Messiah when his ministry would be attended with comparatively little success ; and when in view of that fact, he would commit himself to God, and resolve to extend his gospel to other nations. The expression here used is not to be taken *absolutely,* as if he had *no* success in his work, but it means that he had *comparatively* no success ; he was not received and welcomed by the united people ; he was rejected and despised by them as a whole. It is true that the Saviour *had* success in his work, and far more success than is commonly supposed (see Notes on 1 Cor. xv. 6). But it is also true that by the nation at large he was despised and and rejected. The idea here is, that there were not results in his ministry, at all commensurate with the severity of his labours, and the strength of his claims. ¶ *I have spent my strength for nought.* Comparatively for nought. This does not mean that he would not be ultimately as successful as he desired to be (comp. Notes on ch. liii. 11); but it means, that in his personal ministry he had exhausted his strength, and seen comparatively little fruit of his toils. ¶ Yet *surely my judgment* is *with the* LORD. My cause is committed to him, and he will regard it. This expresses the confidence of the speaker, that God approved of his work, and that he would ultimately give such effect to his labours as he had desired. The sense is, ' I know that JEHOVAH approves my work, and that he will grant me the reward of my toils, and my sufferings.' ¶ *And my work with my God.* Marg. ' Reward ' (see Notes on ch. xl. 10). The

5 And now, saith the Lord, that formed thee from the womb *to be* his servant, to bring Jacob again to him, [1] Though Israel be not [a] gathered, yet shall I be glorious in the eyes of the Lord, and my God shall be my strength.

[1] or, *That Israel may be gathered to him, and I may.*
[a] Mat. 23. 37.

idea is, that he knew that God would own and accept his work though it was rejected by men. It indicates perfect confidence in God, and a calm and unwavering assurance of his favour, though his work was comparatively unsuccessful—a spirit which, it is needless to say, was evinced throughout the whole life of the Redeemer. Never did he doubt that God approved his work ; never did he become disheartened and desponding, as if God would not ultimately give success to his plans and to the labours of his life. He calmly committed himself to God. He did not attempt to avenge himself for being rejected, or for any of the injuries done him. But he left his name, his character, his reputation, his plans, his labours, all with God, believing that *his* cause was the cause of God, and that *he* would yet be abundantly rewarded for all his toils. This verse teaches—1. That the most faithful labours, the most self-denying toil, and the efforts of the most holy life, may be for a time unsuccessful. If the Redeemer of the world had occasion to say that he had laboured in vain, assuredly his ministers should not be surprised that they have occasion to use the same language. It may be no fault of the ministry that they are unsuccessful. The world may be so sinful, and opposition may be got up so mighty, as to frustrate their plans, and prevent their success. 2. Yet, though at present unsuccessful, faithful labour will ultimately do good, and be blessed. In some way, and at some period, all honest effort in the cause of God may be expected to be crowned with success. 3. They who labour faithfully may commit their cause to God, with the assurance that they and their work will be accepted. The ground of their acceptance is not the success of their labours. They will be acceptable in proportion to the amount of their fidelity and self-denying zeal (see Notes on 2 Cor. ii. 15, 16). 4. The ministers of religion, when their message is rejected, and the world turns away from their ministry, should imitate the example of the Redeemer, and say, 'my judgment is with Jehovah. My cause is his cause ; and the result of my labours I commit to him.' To do this as he did, they should labour as he did ; they should honestly devote all their strength and talent and time to his service ; and then they can confidently commit all to him, and then and then only they will find peace, as he did, in the assurance that their work will be ultimately blessed, and that they will find acceptance with him.

5. *And now, saith the Lord that formed me.* This verse contains the reason why he cherished the hope that his work would not be unaccepted. The reason is, that Jehovah had said to him that he should be glorious in his eyes, and that he would be his strength. He stood so high in his favour, and he had such assurances of that favour, that he could confidently commit himself to his care. ¶ *That formed thee from the womb.* Who appointed me before I was born to the office of a servant to accomplish important purposes (see Notes on ver. 1). ¶ *To bring Jacob again to him.* To recover the Jewish people again to the pure worship of Jehovah. To them the Messiah was first to be sent, and when they rejected him, he was to proffer the same salvation to the Gentiles (see ver. 6 ; comp. Matt. xxi. 33–43). Accordingly the Saviour spent his life in preaching to the Jews, and in endeavouring to bring them back to God, and for this purpose he regarded himself as sent (Matt. xv. 24 ; see Acts iii. 26). ¶ *Though Israel be not gathered.* This metaphor is taken from a scattered flock which a shepherd endeavours to gather, or collect to himself. There is great variety in the interpretation of this expression. The margin reads it, ' That Israel may be gathered to him, and I may ' be glorious. So Lowth, ' That Israel unto him may be gathered.' So Noyes, ' To gather Israel to him.' Jerome renders

6 And he said, [1] It is a light thing that thou shouldest be my servant, to raise up the tribes of Jacob, and to restore the [2] preserved of Israel ; I will also give thee for a light *a* to the Gentiles, that thou mayest be my salvation unto the end of the earth.

[1] or, *Art thou lighter than that thou, &c.*

[2] or, *desolations.*   *a* Ac.13.47.

it, ' Israel shall not be gathered.' The LXX. render it, ' To gather Jacob unto him, and Israel.' The Syriac, ' That I may gather Jacob unto him, and assemble Israel.' This variety has arisen from the different readings in the Hebrew text. The reading in the text is לֹא (*not*) ; but instead of this the marginal reading, or the Keri of the Masorites is, לוֹ (*to him*). ' Five MSS. (two ancient),' says Lowth, ' confirm the Keri, or marginal construction of the Masorites ; and so read Aquila, and the Chaldee, LXX., and Arabic.' Gesenius and Rosenmüller adopt this, and suppose that לֹא (*lō*), is only a different form of writing לוֹ. Grotius and Hengstenberg render it as it is in our version. It is impossible to determine the true reading ; and the only guide is the context, and the views which shall be entertained of the design of the passage. To me it seems that the parallelism demands that we should adopt the reading of the Keri, the LXX., the Chaldee, and the Syriac, and which has been adopted by Lowth. According to this, it means that he had been appointed to gather in the lost sheep of the house of Israel, and gave his life to it. Other parts of this statement (ver. 4–6) show, that by them he was rejected, and that then salvation was sent to other parts of the world. Luther renders it, ' That Israel be not carried away.' ¶ *Yet shall I be.* Or, *and* (וְ) I shall be glorious. The sense is, that as the result of this appointment he would be *in some way* glorious in the sight of JEHOVAH. Though he would be rejected by the nation, yet he would be honoured by God. He would not only approve his character and work, but would secure his being honoured among men by making him the light of the Gentiles (comp. ch. xliii. 4). ¶ *And my God shall be my strength.* He might be rejected by the people, but in God he would find an unfailing source of support and consolation. It is not

needful to say, that this applies most accurately to the character of the Redeemer as exhibited in the New Testament.

6. *And he said.* That is, JEHOVAH said in his promise to the Messiah. ¶ *It is a light thing.* Marg. ' Art thou lighter than that thou,' &c. Lowth renders it, ' It is a small thing.' Hengstenberg, ' It is too little that thou shouldest be my servant to raise up the tribes of Jacob.' The sense is, that God designed to glorify him in an eminent degree, and that it would not be as much honour as he designed to confer on him, to appoint him merely to produce a reformation among the Jews, and to recover them to the spiritual worship of God. He designed him for a far more important work—for the recovery of the Gentile world, and for the spread of the true religion among all nations. The LXX. render this, ' It is a great thing for thee to be called my servant.' The Chaldee proposes it as a question, ' Is it a small thing for you that you are called my servant ?' ¶ *My servant* (see ver. 3). ¶ *To raise up the tribes of Jacob.* Heb. (לְהָקִים)—' To establish,' or confirm the tribes of Jacob ; that is, to establish them in the worship of God, and in prosperity. This is to be understood in a spiritual sense, since it is to be synonymous with the blessings which he would bestow on the heathen. His work in regard to both, was to be substantially the same. In regard to the Jews, it was to confirm them in the worship of the true God ; and in regard to the heathen, it was to bring them to the knowledge of the same God. ¶ *And to restore.* To bring back (לְהָשִׁיב) that is, to recover them from their sin and hypocrisy, and bring them back to the worship of the true and only God. The Chaldee, however, renders this, ' To bring back the captivity of Israel.' But it means, doubtless, to recover the alienated Jewish people to the pure and spiritual worship of God. ¶ *The preserved*

7 Thus saith the LORD, the Redeemer of Israel, *and* his Holy One, to him ¹ whom man despiseth, *ᵃ* to him whom the *ᵇ* nation abhorreth, to a servant of rulers, *ᶜ* Kings shall see and arise, princes also shall worship, because of the LORD that is faithful, *and* the Holy One of Israel, and he shall choose thee.

1 or, *that is despised in soul.*   *ᵃ* ch.53.3.
        ᵇ Lu.23.18-23.   *ᶜ* Ps.72.10,11.

of *Israel*. Lowth renders this, ' To restore the branches of Israel;' as if it were נְצִרֵי (*nĕtzârē*) in the text, instead of נְצוּרֵי (*nĕtzūrē*). The word נֵצֶר (*nĕtzĕr*) means *branch* (see Notes on ch. xi. 1; xiv. 9), and Lowth supposes that it means the branches of Israel; *i.e.*, the descendants of Israel or Jacob, by a similitude drawn from the branches of a tree which are all derived from the same stem, or root. The Syriac here renders it, ' The branch of Israel.' But the word properly means those who are kept, or preserved (from נָצַר, *to keep, preserve*), and may be applied either *literally* to those who were kept alive, or who survived any battle, captivity, or calamity—as a remnant ; or *spiritually*, to those who are preserved for purposes of mercy and grace out of the common mass that is corrupt and unbelieving. It refers here, I suppose, to the latter, and means those whom it was the purpose of God to *preserve* out of the common mass of the Jews that were sunk in hypocrisy and sin. These, it was the design of God to restore to himself, and to do this, was the primary object in the appointment of the Messiah. ¶ *I will also give thee for a light to the Gentiles.* I will appoint thee to the higher office of extending the knowledge of the true religion to the darkened heathen world. The same expression and the same promise occur in ch. xlii. 6 (see Notes on that verse). ¶ *That thou mayest be my salvation unto the end of the earth* (see Note on ch. xlii. 10). The true religion shall be extended to the heathen nations, and all parts of the world shall see the salvation of God. This great work was to be intrusted to the Redeemer, and it was regarded as a high honour that he should thus be made the means of diffusing light and truth among all nations. We may learn hence, first, that God will raise up the tribes of Jacob ; that is, that large numbers of the Jews shall yet be

' preserved,' or recovered to himself ; secondly, that the gospel shall certainly be extended to the ends of the earth ; thirdly, that it is an honour to be made instrumental in extending the true religion. So great is this honour, that it is mentioned as the highest which could be conferred even on the Redeemer in this world. And if *he* deemed it an honour, shall *we* not also regard it as a privilege to engage in the work of Christian missions, and to endeavour to save the world from ruin? There is no higher glory for man than to tread in the footsteps of the Son of God ; and he who, by self-denial and charity, and personal toil and prayer, does most for the conversion of this whole world to God, is most like the Redeemer, and will have the most elevated seat in the glories of the heavenly world.

7. *Thus saith the* LORD. This verse contains a promise of the future honour that should await the Redeemer, and of the success which should crown his work. The sense is, that JEHOVAH had promised to him who was despised and rejected, that kings and princes should yet rise up and honour him. ¶ *The Redeemer of Israel* (see Note on ch. xliii. 1). ¶ *To him whom man despiseth.* On the construction of the Hebrew here, see Gesenius, Vitringa, and Hengstenberg. The phrase לִבְזֹה-נֶפֶשׁ (*to the despised of soul*), means evidently one who is despised, rejected, contemned by men. The word ' soul ' here (נֶפֶשׁ) means the same as man ; *i.e.*, every man. It was a characteristic of him that he was despised and rejected by all ; and the prophet, in this verse, has given a summary of all that he has said respecting him in ch. liii. ¶ *To him whom the nation abhorreth.* The word ' nation ' here refers doubtless to the Jewish people, as in ch. i. 4 ; x. 6. The word rendered ' abhorreth ' means *for an abomination* (לִמְתָעֵב, Piel participle, from תָּעַב), and the idea is, that he was re-

garded as an abomination by the people. The same idea is more fully expressed in ch. liii. 3, 4, that the Messiah would be rejected and treated with abhorrence by the nation as such—a statement which the slightest acquaintance with the New Testament will lead any one to see has been literally fulfilled. No being ever excited more *abhorrence;* no man was ever regarded with so much abomination by any people as Jesus of Nazareth was, and still is, by the Jewish people. He was condemned by the Sanhedrim ; publicly rejected by the nation ; and at the instigation and by the desire of the assembled people at Jerusalem, he was executed as a male-factor in the most shameful and igno-minious manner then known (see Luke xxiii. 18–23). To this day, his name ex-cites the utmost contempt among Jews, and they turn from him and his claims with the deepest abhorrence. The common name by which he is desig-nated in the Jewish writings is *Tolvi*— 'the crucified ;' and nothing excites more deep abhorrence and contempt than the doctrine that they, and all others, can be saved only by the merits of 'the cru-cified.' The Chaldee renders all this in the plural, ' To those who are con-temned among the people, to those who have migrated to other kingdoms, to those who serve other lords.' ¶ *To a servant of rulers.* This probably means that the Messiah voluntarily submitted himself to human power, and yielded obedience to human rulers. The idea, if interpreted by the facts as recorded in the New Testament, is, that though he was the ruler of all worlds, yet he voluntarily became subject to human laws, and yielded submission and obe-dience to human rulers. For this pur-pose he conformed to the existing insti-tutions of his country at the time when he lived ; he paid the customary tax or tribute that was laid for the support of religion (Matt. xvii. 27); he submitted to a trial before the Sanhedrim, and before Pilate, though both were con-ducted in a manner that violated all the principles of justice ; and he sub-mitted to the unjust decree which con-demned him to die. He was, therefore, all his life, subject to rulers. He was not only exemplary and strict in obey-

ing the laws of the land ; but he be-came, in a more strict sense, their *ser-vant,* as he was deprived of his liberty, comfort, and life at their caprice. He refrained himself from exerting his Di-vine power, and voluntarily became subject to the will of others. ¶ *Kings shall see and arise.* That is, kings shall see this, and shall rise up with demonstrations of respect and reverence. They shall see the fulfilment of the Divine promises by which he is destined to be the light of the nations, and they shall render him honour as their teacher and Redeemer. To rise up, or to pros-trate themselves, are both marks of re-spect and veneration. ¶ *Princes also shall worship.* The word here used, (יִשְׁתַּחֲוּו, from שָׁחָה) means *to bow down,* to incline one's self; it then means to prostrate one's self before any one, in order to do him honour or reverence. This was the customary mode of show-ing respect or reverence in the East. It consisted generally in falling upon the knees, and then touching the forehead to the ground, and is often alluded to in the Bible (see Gen. xlii. 6; xviii. 2; xix. 1; Neh. viii. 6). This honour was paid not only to kings and princes as superior (2 Sam. ix. 8), but also to equals (Gen. xxiii. 7; xxxvii. 7, 9, 10). It was the customary form of religious homage, as it is still in the East, and denoted sometimes religious worship (Gen. xxii. 5; 1 Sam. i. 3); but not ne-cessarily, or always (see Note on Matt. ii. 11; comp. Matt. viii. 2; xiv. 33; xv. 25; xviii. 26; Mark v. 6). Here it does not mean that they would render to him religious homage, but that they would show him honour, or respect. ¶ *Because of the* Lord *that is faithful.* It is because Jehovah is faithful in the fulfilment of his promises, and will cer-tainly bring this to pass. The fact that he shall be thus honoured shall be traced entirely to the faithfulness of a covenant-keeping God. ¶ *And he shall choose thee.* Select thee to accomplish this, and to be thus a light to the heathen world. It is needless to say that this has been fulfilled. Kings and princes *have* bowed before the Redeemer; and the time will yet come when in far greater numbers they shall adore him. It is *as* needless to say, that these ex-

8 Thus saith the Lord, In an
acceptable *a* time have I heard thee,
and in a day of salvation have I
helped thee : and I will preserve

a Ps.69.13; 2 Co.6.2; Ep.1.6.

pressions can be applied to no other one
than the Messiah.   It was not true
of Isaiah that he was the light of the
heathen, or for salvation to the ends of
the earth ; nor was it true of him that
kings arose and honoured him, or that
princes prostrated themselves before
him, and did him reverence.   Of the
Messiah, the Lord Jesus alone, was all
this true ; and the assurance is thus
given, that though he was rejected by
his own nation, yet the time will come
when the kings and princes of all the
world shall do him homage.

8. *Thus saith the* Lord.   Still an
address to the Messiah, and designed
to give the assurance that he should
extend the true religion, and repair the
evils of sin on the earth.   The Messiah
is represented as having asked for the
Divine favour to attend his efforts, and
this is the answer, and the assurance
that his petition had not been offered
in vain.   ¶ *In an acceptable time.* Heb.
' In a time of *delight* or *will*,' *i.e.,* a
time when Jehovah was *willing*, or
pleased to hear him.   The word רָצוֹן
(*rátzōn*) means properly delight, satisfaction, acceptance (Prov. xiv. 35 ; Isa.
lvi. 7); will, or pleasure (Esth. viii. 1 ;
Ps. xl. 9; Dan. viii. 4-11); then also
goodwill, favour, grace (Prov. xvi. 15 ;
xix. 12).   The LXX. render this, Καιρῷ
δικτῷ—' In an acceptable time.'   So
Jerome, Gesenius, and Hengstenberg
render it, ' In a time of grace or mercy.'
The main idea is plain, that Jehovah
was well pleased to hear him when he
called upon him, and would answer his
prayers.   In a time of favour ; in a time
that shall be adjudged to be the best
fitted to the purposes of salvation, Jehovah will be pleased to exalt the Messiah to glory, and to make him the
means of salvation to all mankind.
¶ *Have I heard thee.* Have I heard
thy petitions, and the desires of thy
heart.   The giving of the world to the
Messiah is represented as in answer to
his prayer in Ps. ii. 8:

thee, and give thee for a covenant
of the people, to 1 establish the
earth, to cause to inherit the desolate heritages :

1 or, raise up.

Ask of me, and I shall give thee the heathen for
   thine inheritance,
And the uttermost parts of the earth for thy
   possession.

¶ *And in a day of salvation.* In a
time when I am disposed to grant salvation ; when the period for imparting
salvation shall have arrived.   ¶ *Have I
helped thee.* Have I imparted the assistance which is needful to accomplish
the great purpose of salvation to the
world.   This passage is quoted by Paul
in 2 Cor. vi. 2, and is by him applied
to the times of the Messiah.   It means
that the time would come, fixed by the
purpose of God, which would be a period
in which he would be disposed, *i.e.,*
well pleased, to extend salvation to the
world through the Messiah ; and that
in that time he would afford all the
requisite aid and help by his grace, for
the extension of the true religion among
the nations.   ¶ *I will preserve thee.*
That is, the cause of the Redeemer
would be dear to the heart of God, and
he would preserve that cause from being
destroyed on the earth.   ¶ *And give
thee for a covenant of the people.* The
' people ' (עַם) refers doubtless primarily
to the Jews—the better portion of the
Israelitish people—the true Israel (Rom.
ii. 28, 29).   To them he was first sent,
and his own personal work was with
them (see Notes on ver. 6).   On the
meaning of the phrase ' for a covenant,'
see Notes on ch. xlii. 6.   ¶ *To establish
the earth.* Marg. as Heb. ' To raise
up.'   The language is derived from
restoring the ruins of a land that has
been overrun by an enemy, when the
cities have been demolished, and the
country laid waste.   It is to be taken
here in a spiritual sense, as meaning
that the work of the Messiah would be
like that which would be accomplished
if a land lying waste should be restored
to its former prosperity.   In regard to
the spiritual interests of the people, he
would accomplish what would be accomplished if there should be such a restora-

9 That thou mayest say to the prisoners, *a* Go forth ; to them that *are* in darkness, *b* Show yourselves :

a Ze.9.12.

they shall feed in the ways, and their pastures *shall be* in all high places.

b 1 Pe.2.9.

tion; that is, he would recover the true Israel from the ravages of sin, and would establish the church on a firm foundation. ¶ *To cause to inherit the desolate heritages.* The image here is taken from the condition of the land of Israel during the Babylonish captivity. It was in ruins. The cities were all desolate. Such, spiritually, would be the condition of the nation when the Messiah should come; and his work would be like restoring the exiles to their own land, and causing them to re-enter on their former possessions. The one would be an appropriate emblem of the other; and the work of the Messiah would be like rebuilding dilapidated towns; restoring fertility to desolate fields ; replanting vineyards and olive gardens; and diffusing smiling peace and plenty over a land that had been subjected to the ravages of fire and sword, and that had long been a scene of mournful desolation.

9. *That thou mayest say to the prisoners, Go forth.* This language occurs also in ch. xlii. 7. For an explanation of it, see the Notes on that place. ¶ *To them that* are *in darkness.* Synonymous with being prisoners, as prisoners are usually confined in dark cells. ¶ *Show yourselves.* Heb. ' Reveal,' or manifest yourselves ; that is, as those who come out of a dark cell come into light, so do you, who have been confined in the darkness of sin, come forth into the light of the Sun of righteousness, and be manifest as the redeemed. ¶ *They shall feed in the ways.* In the remainder of this verse, and in the following verses, the Messiah is represented under the image of a shepherd, who leads forth his flock to green fields, and who takes care that they shall be guarded from the heat of the sun, and shall not hunger nor thirst. The phrase ' they shall feed in the ways,' means, probably, that in the way in which they were going they should find abundant food. They should not be compelled to turn aside for pasturage, or to go and seek for it in distant places. It is

equivalent to the language which so often occurs, that God would provide for the wants of his people, even when passing through a desert, and that he would open before them unexpected sources of supply. ¶ *And their pastures* shall be *in all high places.* This means, that on the hills and mountains, that are naturally barren and unproductive, they should find an abundance of food. To see the force of this, we are to remember that in many parts of the East the hills and mountains are utterly destitute of vegetation. This is the case with the mountainous regions of Horeb and Sinai, and even with the mountains about Jerusalem, and with the hills and mountains in Arabia Deserta. The idea here is, that in *the ways,* or paths that were commonly travelled, and where all verdure would be consumed or trodden down by the caravans, and on the hills that were usually barren and desolate, they would find abundance. God would supply them *as if* he should make the green grass spring up in the hard-trodden way, and on the barren and rocky hills vegetation should start up suddenly in abundance, and all their wants should be supplied. This is an image which we have frequently had in Isaiah, and perhaps the meaning may be, that to his people the Redeemer would open unexpected sources of comfort and joy; that in places and times in which they would scarcely look for a supply of their spiritual wants, he would suddenly meet and satisfy them *as if* green grass for flocks and herds should suddenly start up in the down-trodden way, or luxuriant vegetation burst forth on the sides and the tops of barren, rocky, and desolate hills. Harmer, however, supposes that this whole description refers rather to the custom which prevailed in the East, of making feasts or entertainments by the sides of fountains or rivers. ' To fountains or rivers,' Dr. Chandler tells us in his *Travels,* ' the Turks and the Greeks frequently repair for refreshment; especially the latter, in their fes-

10 They shall not hunger *a* nor thirst; neither shall the heat nor sun smite them; for he that hath mercy on them shall lead *b* them, even by

the springs of water shall he guide them.

11 And *c* I will make all my mountains a way, and my highways shall be exalted.

a Re.7.16.   *b* Ps.23.2.   *c* Ps.107.4,7.

tivals, when whole families are seen sitting on the grass, and enjoying their early or evening repast, beneath the trees, by the side of a rill.'—(*Travels in Asia Minor*, p. 21.)   Comp. 1 Kings i. 9.   Thus Harmer supposes that the purpose of the prophet is, to contrast the state of the Jews when they were shut up in prison in Babylon, secluded from fresh air, and even the light itself, or in unwholesome dungeons, with their state when walking at liberty, enjoying the verdure, and the enlivening air of the country; passing from the tears, the groans, and the apprehensions of such a dismal confinement, to the music, the songs, and the exquisite repasts of Eastern parties of pleasure (*see* Harmer's *Obs.*, vol. ii. pp. 18-25; Ed. Lond. 1808).   The interpretation, however, above suggested, seems to me most natural and beautiful.

10. *They shall not hunger nor thirst.* All their wants shall be abundantly provided for, as a shepherd will provide for his flock.   In the book of Revelation, this entire passage is applied (ch. vii. 16, 17) to the happiness of the redeemed in heaven, and the use which is made of it there is not foreign to the sense in Isaiah.   It means that the Messiah as a shepherd shall abundantly satisfy all the wants of his people; and it may with as much propriety be applied to the joys of heaven, as to the happiness which they will experience on earth.   Their longing desires for holiness and salvation; their hungering and thirsting after righteousness (Matt. v. 6), shall be abundantly satisfied. ¶ *Neither shall the heat nor sun smite them.*   In Rev. vii. 16, this is, 'Neither shall the sun light on them, nor any heat;' that is, the burning heat of the sun shall not oppress them—an image of refreshment, protection, and joy, as when the traveller in burning sands finds the grateful shade of a rock or of a grove (see Notes on ch. iv. 6; xiv. 3; xxv. 4; xxxii. 2).   The word here ren-

dered 'heat' (שָׁרָב *shârâbh*), denotes properly *heat, burning;* and then the heated vapour which in burning deserts produces the phenomenon of the *mirage* (see it explained in the Notes on ch. xxxv. 7).   It is equivalent here to intense heat; and means that they shall not be exposed to any suffering like that of the intense heat of the burning sun reflected from sandy wastes. ¶ *For he that hath mercy on them.*   That God and Saviour who shall have redeemed them shall be their shepherd and their guide, and they shall have nothing to fear. ¶ *Even by the springs of water.* In Rev. vii. 17, ' Shall lead them unto living fountains of waters' (see Notes on ch. xxxv. 6).   The whole figure in this verse is taken from the character of a faithful shepherd who conducts his flock to places where they may feed in plenty; who guards them from the intense heat of a burning sun on sandy plains; and who leads them beside cooling and refreshing streams.   It is a most beautiful image of the tender care of the Great Shepherd of his people in a world like this—a world in its main features, in regard to real comforts, not unaptly compared to barren hills, and pathless burning sands.

11. *And I will make all my mountains a way.*   I will make all the mountains for a highway; or an even, level way.   That is, he would remove all obstructions from their path.   The image is taken from the return from Babylon to the land of Palestine, in which God so often promises to make the hills a plain, and the crooked places straight (see Notes on ch. xl. 4). ¶ *And my highways shall be exalted.*   That is, the way shall be cast up (see ch. lvii. 14; lxii. 10), as when a road is made over valleys and gulf (see Notes on ch. xl. 4).

12. *Behold, these shall come from far.*   That is, one part shall come from a distant land, and another from the north and the west.   This is a state-

12 Behold, these shall come from far ; and lo, these from the north and from the west ; and these from the land of Sinim.

---

ment of the fulfilment of the promise made to him (ver. 6, 7), that he should be for a light to the Gentiles, and that kings and princes should rise up and honour him. The words 'from far,' denote a distant land, without specifying the particular direction from which they would come. The most distant nations should embrace his religion, and submit to him. Lowth and Secker understand it of Babylon; Grotius of the East, that is, Persia, and the other countries east of Judea. But it more properly denotes *any* distant country; and the sense is, that converts should be made from the most distant lands. ¶ *And lo, these.* Another portion. ¶ *From the north.* The regions north of Palestine. ¶ *And from the west.* Heb. 'From the sea;' that is, the Mediterranean. This word is commonly used to denote the west. The western countries known to the Hebrews were some of the islands of that sea, and a few of the maritime regions. The idea here in general is, that those regions would furnish many who would embrace the true religion. If it be understood as referring to the Messiah, and the accession to his kingdom among the Gentiles, it is needless to say that the prediction has been already strikingly fulfilled. Christianity soon spread to the west of Palestine, and the countries in Europe have been thus far the principal seat of its influence and power. It has since spread still further to the west; and, from a western world unknown to Isaiah, millions have come and acknowledged the Messiah as their Redeemer. ¶ *And these.* Another portion, carrying out the idea that they were to come from every part of the world. ¶ *From the land of Sinim.* There have been many different opinions in regard to the 'land of Sinim.' The name 'Sinim' (סינים) occurs nowhere else in the Bible, and of course it is not easy to determine what country is meant. It is evident that it is some *remote* country, and it is remarkable that it is the only land specified here by name. Some, it is said, should come from far, some from the north, others from the west, and

another portion from the country here specifically mentioned. Jerome understands it of the south in general—*Istı de terra Australi.* The LXX. understand it as denoting Persia—Ἀλλοι δὲ ἐκ γῆς Περσῶν. The Chaldee also interprets it as Jerome has done, of the south. The Syriac has not translated it, but retained the name *Sinim.* The Arabic coincides with the Septuagint, and renders it, 'From the land of Persia.' Grotius supposes that it means the region of Sinim to the south of Palestine, and Vitringa also coincides with this opinion. Bochart supposes that it means the same as Sin or Syene, *i.e.,* Pelusium, a city of Egypt; and that it is used to denote Egypt, as Pelusium was a principal city in Egypt. In Ezek. xxx. 15, *Sin* or Pelusium (marg.) is mentioned as 'the strength of Egypt.' Gesenius supposes that it refers to the *Chinese,* and that the country here referred to is Sina or China. 'This very ancient and celebrated people,' says he, 'was known to the Arabians and Syrians by the name Sin, Tcin, Tshini; and a Hebrew writer might well have heard of them, especially if sojourning in Babylon, the metropolis as it were of all Asia. This name appears to have been given to the Chinese by the other Asiatics; for the Chinese themselves do not employ it, and seem indeed to be destitute of any ancient domestic name, either adopting the names of the reigning dynasties, or ostentatiously assuming high-sounding titles, as "people of the empire in the centre of the world." ' The Rev. Peter Parker, M.D., missionary to China, remarked in an address delivered in Philadelphia, that 'the Chinese have been known from time immemorial by the name *Tschin.* Tschin means a Chinaman.' When they first received this appellation, cannot be determined, nor is the reason of its being given to them now known. As there is remarkable permanency in the *names* as well as in the *customs* of the East, it is possible that they may have had it from the commencement of their history. If so, there is no improbability in supposing that the name was known

13 Sing, O heavens; and be joyful, O earth; and break forth into singing, O mountains; for the LORD hath comforted his people, and will have mercy upon his afflicted.

14 But Zion said, *a* The LORD hath

a Ps.77.9,10.
1 *from having compassion.* *b* ch.44.21; Mat.7.11.

forsaken me, and my Lord hath forgotten me.

15 Can a woman forget her sucking child, 1 that she should not have compassion on the son of her womb? yea, they may forget, yet *b* will I not forget thee.

to the Jews in the time of Isaiah. Solomon had opened a considerable commerce with the East. For this he had built Palmyra, or Tadmor, and caravans passed constantly towards Palestine and Tyre, conveying the rich productions of India. The country of *Tschin* or *Sinim* may be easily supposed to have been often referred to by the foreign merchants as a land of great extent and riches, and it is not impossible that even at that early day a part of the merchandise conveyed to the west might have come from that land. It is not necessary to suppose that the Hebrews in the time of Isaiah had any very extensive or clear views of that country; but all that is necessary to be supposed is, that they conceived of the nation as lying far in the east, and as abounding in wealth, sufficiently so to entitle it to the pre-eminency which it now has in the enumeration of the nations that would be blessed by the gospel. If this be the correct interpretation— and I have on a re-examination come to this opinion, though a different view was given in the first edition of these Notes—then the passage furnishes an interesting prediction respecting the future conversion of the largest kingdom of the world. It may be added, that this is the only place where that country is referred to in the Bible, and there may be some plausibility in the supposition that while so many other nations, far inferior in numbers and importance, are mentioned by name, one so vast as this would not wholly be omitted by the Spirit of Inspiration.

13. *Sing, O heavens.* In view of the glorious truths stated in the previous verses, that kings should rise up, and princes worship; that the Messiah would be for a light to the Gentiles, and that the true religion would be extended to each of the four quarters of the globe. The idea in this verse is, that it was an

occasion on which the heavens and the earth would have cause to exult together. It is common in Isaiah thus to interpose a song of praise on the announcement of any great and glorious truth, and to call on the heavens and the earth to rejoice together (see Notes on ch. xii.; xlii. 10, 11; xliv. 23).

14. *But Zion said.* On the word 'Zion,' see Note on ch. i. 8. The language here is that of complaint, and expresses the deep feeling of the people of God amidst many calamities, afflictions, and trials. It may be applicable to the exile Jews in Babylon during their long captivity, as if God had forsaken them; or to those who were waiting for the coming of the Messiah, and who were sighing for the Divine interposition under him to restore the beauty of Zion, and to extend his kingdom; or in general, to the church when wickedness triumphs in a community, and when God seems to have forsaken Zion, and to have forgotten its interests. The *language* here was suggested, doubtless, by a view of the desolations of Jerusalem and Judea, and of the long and painful captivity in Babylon; but it is general, and is applicable to the people of God, in all times of similar oppression and distress. The *object* of the prophet is to furnish the assurance that, whatever might be the trials and the sufferings of his people, God had not forgotten them, and he neither could nor would forsake them. For this purpose, he makes use of two most striking and forcible arguments (ver. 15, 16), to show in the strongest possible manner that the interests of his people were safe.

15. *Can a woman forget her sucking child?* The design of this verse is apparent. It is to show that the love which God has for his people is stronger than that which is produced by the most tender ties created by any natural relation. The love of a mother for her in-

16 Behold, I have graven *a* thee upon the palms of *my* hands ; thy walls *are* continually before me.

a Ca.8.6.

17 Thy children shall make haste; thy destroyers *b* and they that made thee waste, shall go forth of thee.

b Eze.28.24; Mat.13.41,42; Re 22.15.

fant child is the strongest attachment in nature. The question here implies that it was unusual for a mother to be unmindful of that tie, and to forsake the child that she should nourish and love. ¶ *That she should not have compassion.* That she should not pity and succour it in times of sickness and distress ; that she should see it suffer without any attempt to relieve it, and turn away, and see it die unpitied and unalleviated. ¶ *Yea, they may forget.* They will sooner forget their child than God will forget his afflicted and suffering people. The phrase ' they may forget,' implies that such a thing may occur. In heathen lands, strong as is the instinct which binds a mother to her offspring, it has not been uncommon for a mother to expose her infant child, and to leave it to die. In illustration of this fact, see Notes on Rom. i. 31.

16. *Behold, I have graven thee upon the palms of* my *hands.* This is another argument in answer to the complaint of Zion in ver. 14. There have been various interpretations of this passage. Grotius supposes that it refers to a custom of placing some mark or sign on the hand, or on one of the fingers when they wished to remember anything, and appeals to Ex. xiii. 9. Lowth supposes that it is an allusion to some practice common among the Jews at that time, of making marks on their hands or arms by means of punctures in the skin with some sign or representation of the city or temple, to show their zeal and affection for it. In illustration of this, he refers to the fact that the pilgrims to the Holy Sepulchre are accustomed to get themselves marked in this manner with what are called the signs of Jerusalem. Vitringa supposes that it alludes to the custom of architects, in which they delineate the size, form, and proportions of an edifice on parchment, before they commence building it—such as we mean by the draft or model of the building ; and that the sense here is, that God, in like manner, had delineated or drawn

Jerusalem on his hands long before it was founded, and had it constantly before his eyes. According to this, the idea is, that God had *laid out* the plan of Jerusalem long before it was built, and that it was so dear to him that he had even engraven it on his hands. Others have supposed that it refers to a device on a signet, or on a ring worn on the finger or the wrist, and that the plan of Jerusalem was drawn and engraven there. To me, it seems that the view of Lowth is most accordant with probability, and is best sustained by the Oriental customs. The *essential idea* is, that Zion was dear to his heart ; and that he had sketched or delineated it as an object in which he felt a deep interest —so deep as even to delineate its outlines on the palms of his hands, where it would be constantly before him. ¶ *Thy walls.* The meaning is, that he constantly looked upon them ; that he never forgot them. He had a constant and sacred regard for his people, and amidst all their disasters and trials, still remembered them.

17. *Thy children.* The children of Zion—the true people of God. But there is considerable variety in the interpretation. The Hebrew of the present text is בָּנָיִךְ (*thy sons*). But Jerome reads it, *Structores tui*—' Thy builders;' as if it were בּוֹנַיִך. The LXX. render it, ' Thou shalt be speedily built (ταχὺ οἰκοδομηθήσῃ) by those by whom thou hast been destroyed.' The Chaldee renders it, ' Those that rebuild thy waste places shall hasten.' The Syriac reads it, ' Thy sons ;' and the Arabic, ' Thou shalt be rebuilt by those by whom thou hast been destroyed.' But there is no good authority for changing the present Hebrew text, nor is it necessary. The sense probably is, the descendants of those who dwelt in Zion, who are now in exile, shall hasten to rebuild the wastes of the desolate capital, and restore its ruins. And may it not mean, that in the great work under the Messiah, of restoring the nation to the wor-

18 Lift up thine eyes round about, and behold: all these *a* gather themselves together, *and* come to thee. *As* I live, saith the LORD, thou shalt surely clothe thee with them all as with an ornament, and bind them *on thee* as a bride *doth*.

19 For thy waste, and thy desolate places, and the land of thy destruction, shall even now be too narrow by reason of the inhabitants, and they that swallowed thee up shall be far away.

20 The children which thou shalt have, after *b* thou hast lost the other, shall say again in thy ears, The place *is* too strait for me: give place for me that I may dwell.

a ch.60.8; Zec.2.4: 10.10.

b Ro.11.11,&c.

ship of God, and of spreading the true religion, God would make use of those who dwelt in Zion; that is, of the Jews, as his ambassadors? ¶ *They that made thee waste*. Language drawn from the destruction of Jerusalem. The sense is, that they would seek no longer to retain possession, but would permit its former inhabitants to return, and engage in repairing its ruins.

18. *Lift up thine eyes round about*. That is, see the multitudes that shall be converted to thee; see thy ruined city rise again in its former beauty; see the Gentiles come and yield themselves to the worship of the true God; see kings and princes approach and do thee homage. ¶ *All these gather themselves*. That is, from a far country, from the north, the west, and the south, ver. 12. ¶ As *I live, saith the* LORD. The customary form of an oath when JEHOVAH swears. It is a solemn assurance that the event shall as certainly occur as he has an existence (see Note on ch. xlv. 23; comp. Jer. xxii. 24; Ezek. v. 11; xiv. 16, 18, 20; xvi. 48). ¶ *Thou shalt surely clothe thee with them*. Zion is here represented, as it is often elsewhere, as a female (see Note on ch. i. 8); and the accession of converts from abroad is represented under the figure of bridal ornaments. The accession of converts from the Gentiles should be to her what jewels are to a bride. ¶ *And bind them* on thee *as a bride* doth. The sentence here is manifestly incomplete. It means, as a bride binds on her ornaments. The LXX. have supplied this, and render it, 'As a bride her ornaments' (ὡς κόσμον νύμφη). The sentiment is, that the accession of the large number of converts under the Messiah to the true church of God, would be the real

ornament of Zion, and would greatly increase her beauty and loveliness.

19. *For thy waste and thy desolate places*. Thy land over which ruin has been spread, and over which the exile nation mourns. ¶ *And the land of thy destruction*. That is, thy land laid in ruins. The construction is not uncommon where a noun is used to express the sense of an adjective. Thus in Ps. ii. 6, the Hebrew phrase (*marg*.) is correctly rendered 'my holy hill.' Here the sense is, that their entire country had been so laid waste as to be a land of desolation. ¶ *Shall even now be too narrow*. Shall be too limited to contain all who shall become converted to the true God. The contracted territory of Palestine shall be incapable of sustaining all who will acknowledge the true God, and who shall be regarded as his friends. ¶ *And they that swallowed thee up*. The enemies that laid waste thy land, and that *absorbed*, as it were, thy inhabitants, and removed them to a distant land. They shall be all gone, and the land shall smile again in prosperity and in loveliness.

20. *The children which thou shalt have*. The increase of the population shall be so great. ¶ *After thou hast lost the other*. Heb. 'The sons of thy widowhood.' That is, after thou hast lost those that have been killed in the wars, and those that have died in captivity in a distant land, there shall be again a great increase *as if* they were given to a widowed mother. And perhaps the *general* truth is taught here, that the persecution of the people of God will be attended ultimately with a vast increase; and that all the attempts to obliterate the church will only tend finally to enlarge and strengthen it.

21 Then shalt thou say in thine heart, Who hath begotten me these, seeing I have lost my children, and am desolate, a captive, and moving to and fro? and who hath brought up these? Behold, I was left alone; these. where *had* they *been?*

a ch. 66. 20.

22 Thus saith *a* the Lord GOD Behold, I will lift up mine hand to the Gentiles, and set up my standard to the people: and they shall bring thy sons in *their* [1] arms, and thy daughters shall be carried upon *their* shoulders.

1 bosom.

¶ *Shall say again in thy ears.* Or, shall say to thee. ¶ *The place* is *too strait for me.* There is not room for us all. The entire language here denotes a vast accession to the church of God. It is indicative of such an increase as took place when the gospel was proclaimed by the apostles to the Gentiles, and of such an increase as shall yet more abundantly take place when the whole world shall become converted to God.

21. *Then shalt thou say in thine heart.* Thou shalt wonder at the multitude, and shalt ask with astonishment whence they all come. This verse is designed to describe the great increase of the true people of God under the image of a mother who had been deprived of her children, who should suddenly see herself surrounded with more than had been lost, and should ask in astonishment whence they all came. ¶ *Who hath begotten me these.* The idea here is, that the increase would be from other nations. They would not be the natural increase of Zion or Jerusalem, but they would come in from abroad—as if a family that had been bereaved should be increased by an accession from other families. ¶ *I have lost my children.* Jerusalem had been desolated by wars, and had become like a widow that was bereft of all her sons (comp. Notes on ch. xlvii. 8, 9). ¶ *A captive, and removing to and fro.* A captive in Babylon, and compelled to wander from my own land, and to live in a strange and distant country. ¶ *These, where* had *they* been? The image in this entire verse is one of great beauty. It represents a mother who had been suddenly deprived of all her children, who had been made a widow, and conveyed as a captive from land to land. She had seen ruin spread all around her dwelling, and regarded herself as alone. Suddenly

she finds herself restored to her home, and surrounded with a happy family. She sees it increased beyond its former numbers, and herself blessed with more than her former prosperity. She looks with surprise on this accession, and asks with wonder whence all these have come, and where they have been. The *language* in this verse is beautifully expressive of the agitation of such a state of mind, and of the effect which would be thus produced. The idea is plain. Jerusalem had been desolate. Her inhabitants had been carried captive, or had been put to death. But she should be restored, and the church of God would be increased by a vast accession from the Gentile world, so much that the narrow limits which had been formerly occupied—the territory of Palestine—would now be too small for the vast numbers that would be united to those who professed to love and worship God.

22. *Behold, I will lift up mine hand to the Gentiles.* To lift up the hand is a sign of beckoning to, or inviting; and the idea here is, that God would call the Gentiles to partake of the blessings of the true religion, and to embrace the Messiah (see Notes on ch. xi. 11). ¶ *And set up my standard to the people.* To the people of other lands; the word here being synonymous with the word Gentiles. A standard, or an ensign was erected in times of war to rally the forces of a nation around it; and the sense here is, that God would erect an ensign high in the sight of all the nations, and would call them to himself, as a military leader musters his forces for battle; that is, he would call the nations to embrace the true religion. See this phrase explained in the Note on ch. xi. 12. ¶ *They shall bring thy sons in their arms.* Marg. 'Bosom.' Jerome renders it, *In ulnis*—' In their

23 And kings shall be thy ¹ nursing fathers, and their ² queens thy nursing mothers : they shall bow down to thee with *their* face toward

1 *nourishers.*   2 *princesses.*

the earth, and lick *ª* up the dust of thy feet ; and thou shalt know that I am the LORD : for they shall not be ashamed *ᵇ* that wait for thee.

a Ps.72.9,&c.   *b* Ro 9.33.

arms.' The LXX. 'Εν κόλπω—' In the bosom.' Aquila, Symmachus, and Theodotion, 'Αγκαλας—' In their arms.' If it means bosom, as Gesenius renders it, it refers to the bosom of a garment in which things are carried. But it more probably means in the arms, as children are borne ; and the idea is, that the distant nations would come and bear with them those who were the children of Zion, that is, those who would become the true friends and worshippers of God. ¶ *And thy daughters shall be carried upon their shoulders.* Referring, doubtless, to the manner in which children were carried. In ch. lxvi. 12, the same idea is expressed by their being carried upon the sides, referring to the custom still prevalent in the East, of placing a child when it is nursed astride on the side of the mother. The following quotation will more fully explain the customs here alluded to. ' It is a custom in many parts of the East, to carry their children astride upon the hip, with the arm around the body. In the kingdom of Algiers, where the slaves take the children out, the boys ride upon their shoulders ; and in a religious procession, which Symes had an opportunity of seeing at Ava, the capital of the Burman empire, the first personages of rank that passed by were three children borne astride, on men's shoulders. It is evident, from these facts, that the Oriental children are carried sometimes the one way, sometimes the other. Nor was the custom, in reality, different in Judea, though the prophet expresses himself in these terms : " They shall bring thy sons in their arms, and thy daughters shall be carried upon their shoulders ; " for, according to Dr. Russel, the children able to support themselves are usually carried astride on the shoulders ; but in infancy they are carried in the arms, or awkwardly on one haunch. Dandini tells us that, on horseback, the Asiatics " carry their children upon their shoulders with great dexterity. These children hold by the head of him who car-

ries them, whether he be on horseback or on foot, and do not hinder him from walking or doing what he pleases." This augments the import of the passage in Isaiah, who speaks of the Gentiles bringing children thus ; so that distance is no objection to this mode of conveyance, since they may thus be brought on horseback from among the people, however remote.'—(Paxton.) ' Children of both sexes are carried on the shoulders. Thus may be seen the father carrying his son, the little fellow being astride on the shoulder, having, with his hands, hold of his father's head. Girls, however, sit on the shoulder, as if on a chair, their legs hanging in front, while they also, with their hands, lay hold of the head. In going to, or returning from heathen festivals, thousands of parents and their children may be thus seen marching along with joy.'—(Roberts.) The sense is, that converts should come from every land—that the nations should flock to the standard of the Messiah. And why may it not be regarded as a legitimate interpretation of this passage, that those who come should bring their children, their sons and their daughters, with them? That they were borne upon the arm, or upon the shoulder, is indicative of their being young children ; and that is no forced interpretation of this passage which regards it as teaching, that the parents who should be converted among the Gentiles should bring their offspring to the Redeemer, and present them publicly to God.

23. *And kings shall be thy nursing fathers.* Marg. 'Nourishers.' That is, they would patronize the church of God ; they would protect it by their laws, and foster it by their influence, and become the personal advocates of the cause of Zion. The idea is properly that of guarding, educating, and providing for children ; and the sense is, that kings and princes would evince the same tender care for the interests of the people of God which a parent or a nurse

24 Shall the prey be taken from the mighty, *a* or ¹ the lawful captive delivered ?

25 But thus saith the LORD, Even the ² captives of the mighty shall be

taken away, and the prey of the terrible shall be delivered : for I will contend with him that contendeth with thee, and I will save thy children.

---

a Mat.12.29.   1 *the captivity of the just.*   2 *captivity.*

---

does for a child. It is needless to say that this has been already to a considerable extent fulfilled, and that many princes and monarchs have been the patrons of the church, though doubtless it is destined to a more ample fulfilment still in the brighter days of this world's history, when the gospel shall spread everywhere. It is remarkable that, in the Sandwich and South Sea Islands, the Christian religion has been uniformly, almost, taken under the protection of the kings and chiefs since its first introduction there, and has been carried forward and extended under their direct authority. ¶ *They shall bow down to thee with their face toward the earth.* A posture indicating the profoundest reverence. This is the common posture of showing great respect in the East. ¶ *And lick up the dust of thy feet.* An act denoting the utmost possible respect and veneration for the church and people of God. ¶ *For they shall not be ashamed that wait for me.* They who worship me shall not be ashamed of the act requiring the deepest self-abasement, to show their reverence for me. Even those of most elevated rank shall be willing to humble themselves with the profoundest expressions of adoration.

24. *Shall the prey be taken from the mighty ?* This seems to be the language of Zion. It is not exactly the language of incredulity ; it is the language of amazement and wonder God had made great promises. He had promised a restoration of the captive Jews to their own land, and of their complete deliverance from the power of the Chaldeans. He had still further promised that the blessings of the true religion should be extended to the Gentiles, and that kings and queens should come and show the profoundest adoration for God and for his cause. With amazement and wonder at the greatness of these promises, with a full view of the difficulties to be surmounted, Zion asks here how it can

be accomplished. It would involve the work of taking the prey from a mighty conqueror, and delivering the captive from the hand of the strong and the terrible—a work which had not been usually done. ¶ *Or the lawful captive delivered ?* Marg. 'The captivity of the just.' Lowth reads this, 'Shall the prey seized by the terrible be rescued ?' So Noyes. Lowth says of the present Hebrew text, that the reading is a 'palpable mistake ;' and that instead of צַדִּיק (*the just*), the meaning should be עָרִיץ (*the terrible*). Jerome so read it, and renders it, *A robusto*—'The prey taken by the strong.' So the Syriac reads it. The LXX. render it, 'If any one is taken captive unjustly (ἀδίκως), shall he be saved ?' But there is no authority from the MSS. for changing the present reading of the Hebrew text ; and it is not necessary. The word 'just,' here may either refer to the fact that the just were taken captive, and to the difficulty of rescuing them ; or perhaps. as Rosenmüller suggests, it may be taken in the sense of *severe*, or *rigid*, standing opposed to benignity or mercy, and thus may be synonymous with severity and harshness ; and the meaning may be that it was difficult to rescue a captive from the hands of those who had no clemency or benignity, such as was Babylon. Grotius understands it of those who were taken captive in a just war, or by the rights of war. But the connection rather demands that we should interpret it of those who were made captive by those who were indisposed to clemency, and who were severe and rigid in their treatment of their prisoners. The idea is, that it was difficult or almost impossible to rescue captives from such hands, and that therefore it was a matter of wonder and amazement that that *could* be accomplished which God here promises.

25. *But thus saith the* LORD. The

26 And I will feed them that oppress thee with their own flesh; and they shall be drunken with *a* their own blood, as with ² sweet wine:

and all flesh shall know that I the LORD *am* thy Saviour and thy Redeemer, the Mighty One of Jacob.

a Re.16.6.   2 or, *new.*

meaning of this verse is, that however difficult or impracticable this might seem to be, yet it should be done. The captives taken by the terrible and the mighty should be rescued, and should be restored to their own land. ¶ *Even the captives of the mighty shall be taken away.* Marg. as Heb. ' The captivity of the mighty.' That which could not have been rescued by any ordinary means. The language here refers undoubtedly to Babylon, and to the captivity of the Jews there. ¶ *The prey of the terrible.* Of a nation formidable, cruel, and not inclined to compassion; in the previous verse described as 'just,' *i.e.*, indisposed to mercy. ¶ *For I will contend with him.* I will punish the nation that has inflicted these wrongs on thee, and will thus rescue thee from bondage.

26. *And I will feed them that oppress thee with their own flesh.* The language here used is that which appropriately describes the distresses resulting from discord and internal strifes. Similar language occurs in ch. ix. 20 (see Note on that verse). Their rage shall be excited against each other; and there shall be anarchy, internal discord, and the desire of mutual revenge. They shall destroy themselves by mutual conflicts, until they are gorged with slaughter, and drunk with blood. ¶ *And they shall be drunken with their own blood.* A similar expression occurs in Rev. xvi. 6: 'For they have shed the blood of the prophets, and thou hast given them blood to drink.' This expression describes a state of internal strife, where blood would be profusely shed, and where it would be, as it were, the drink of each other who were contending with each other. Grotius supposes that it refers to the conflicts between the Persians and the Medes, and those of the Medes and Persians with the Babylonians. Vitringa supposes it received its fulfilment in the contests which took place in the Roman empire, particularly during the

reign of Diocletian, when so many rivals contended for the sovereignty. Perhaps, however, it is in vain to attempt to refer this to any single conflict, or state of anarchy. The language is general; and it may mean in general that God would guard and protect his people; and that in doing this, he would fill the ranks of his foes with confusion, and suffer them to be torn and distracted with internal strifes; and amidst those strifes, and by means of them, would secure the deliverance and safety of his own people. It has not unfrequently happened that he has suffered or caused discord to spring up among the enemies of his people, and distracted their counsels, and thus secured the safety and welfare of those whom they were opposing and persecuting. ¶ *As with sweet wine.* Marg. 'New.' The Hebrew word (עָסִיס) means *must*, or new wine (Joel i. 5; iv. 18; Amos ix. 13). The LXX. render it, Οἶνον νέον—' New wine.' The *must*, or new wine, was the pure juice which ran first after the grapes had been laid in a heap preparatory to pressure. The ancients had the art of preserving this for a long time, so as to retain its peculiar flavour, and were in the habit of drinking it in the morning (see Hor. *Sat.* ii. 4). This had the intoxicating property very slightly, if at all; and Harmer (*Obs.* vol. ii. p. 151) supposes that the kind here meant was rather such as was used in ' royal palaces for its gratefulness,' which was capable of being kept to a great age. It is possible, I think, that there may be an allusion here to the fact that it required a *large quantity of the must* or new wine to produce intoxication, and that the idea here is that a large quantity of blood would be shed. ¶ *And all flesh.* The effect of all this shall be to diffuse the true religion throughout the world. The result of the contentions that shall be excited among the enemies of the people of God; of their civil wars and mutual slaughter; and of the consequent protection and defence of the

CHAPTER L.

ANALYSIS.

This chapter properly consists of two parts.

The first comprises the first three verses, and contains a statement of the reasons why the Jews had been rejected and punished. They are to be regarded as in exile in Babylon. It might be alleged by some of the unbelieving among them, that the calamities which came upon them were proof of caprice in God, or of want of faithfulness, or of power, and not any proof that they were suffering under his righteous displeasure. To meet these implied charges, and to show them the true cause of their suffering, is the design of this portion of the chapter. In this, God says—1. That their sufferings were not the result of mere will, or of caprice, on his part, as a husband often puts away his wife without any good reason (1). 2. There was a reason for their rejection, and that reason was, their sins. They had brought all these calamities upon themsel es, and had, in fact, sold themselves. 3. It was not for want of power on the part of God to save them. His hand was not shortened, and he had abundantly shown that he had power to defend his people (2, 3). He was able to dry up the sea, and to make the rivers a desert, and he clothed the heavens with blackness, and he was abundantly able, therefore, to save his people.

II. The second part of the chapter comprises the portion from ver. 4–11. This relates to a different subject; and, in regard to it, there has been considerable variety of interpretation. A speaker is introduced who claims to be eminently qualified for the office to which he was called (4); who has been amply endowed by God for the embassage on which he is sent (5); who meets with opposition, and who yet receives it all with meekness (6); who puts his trust in God, and confides in him alone (7–9); and who calls on all who fear the Lord to hear him (10); and who threatens to inflict punishment on all who do not listen to him (11). This portion of the chapter has been referred, by different interpreters, to different individuals. Grotius, Rosenmüller, and Gesenius, suppose that it refers to the prophet himself. Döderlein, Dathe, Koppe, August:, and some others, suppose that it refers either to the prophet himself, or to some other one living in exile at the time of the captivity. Jerome says that this, also, was the prevailing interpretation among the Jews in his time. Paulus supposes that it is not the prophet who speaks, but the better and more pious portion of the Jewish people. But the more common interpretation is that which refers it to the Messiah. In favour of this interpretation, the following considerations may be suggested :—1. The prophet himself is not known to have been in the circumstances here described (6); nor is there any evidence that this can be applied to him. Of any other prophet to whom it would apply we have no knowledge, nor would there be any propriety in so applying the language of Isaiah, if we did know of any such one. 2. The Messianic interpretation has almost universally prevailed in the Christian church—an argument of value only as showing that when so many agree in interpreting any writing, there is presumptive proof that they have not mistaken its meaning. 3. All the characteristics of the servant of God here referred to, apply to the Redeemer, and are descriptive of him and of his work. All that is said of his humiliation and meekness; of the opposition which he encountered, and of his confidence in God, applies eminently to the Lord Jesus, and to no other one. 4. The closing part (ver. 11), where the speaker threatens to the Christians in Judea ; with the successive persecutions in the Roman empire from the time of Nero to Diocletian ; with the persecution of the Waldenses in Switzerland ; of the Huguenots in France ; and of the Reformers in England, will be sufficient to convince any one that God is the protector of the church, and that no weapons formed against her shall prosper. Her enemies shall be distracted in their counsels, and left to anarchy and overthrow ; and the church shall rise resplendent from all their persecutions, and shall prosper ultimately just in proportion to their efforts to destroy it.

people whom they were endeavouring to destroy, shall be to diffuse the true religion among the nations, and to bring all men to acknowledge that he who thus protects his church is the true and only God. It would be easy to show the fulfilment of this prediction from the records of the past, and from the efforts which have been made to destroy the church of God. But that would be foreign to the design of these notes. A very slight acquaintance with the repeated efforts to destroy the ancient people of God in Egypt, in the wilderness, in Babylon, and under Antiochus Epiphanes ; with the early persecution of

inflict punishment on his foes, cannot be used with reference to Isaiah or any other prophet, but has a striking applicability to the Messiah. 5. In Luke xviii. 32, the passage (ver. 6) is applied by the Lord Jesus to himself. He says that the prophecies in regard to him must be fulfilled, and, among other things, says that the fact that he should be 'spitted on,' should be a fulfilment of a prophecy—a statement which has an obvious and manifest reference to this passage in Isaiah.

The passage, if it refers to the Messiah, relates particularly to his humiliation and sufferings, and accords with that in ch. liii. It embraces the following points:—1. He was endowed for his work, and especially fitted to comfort the afflicted and weary (4). 2. He was entirely obedient to God, and submitted to all his arrangements with cheerfulness (5). 3. He submitted with meekness to all the injuries inflicted on him by others—even to their deepest expressions of contempt (6). 4. He was sustained in these trials because he put his trust in God, and believed that he could deliver him (7-9). b. He calls upon all who feared God to put their trust in him, and stay themselves upon their God—an address to the pious portion of the nation (10). 6. He warns those who were trusting to themselves, and who were seeking their own welfare only, that he would himself inflict exemplary punishment upon them, and that they should lie down in sorrow (11).

THUS saith the LORD, Where *is* the bill of your mother's divorcement, *a* whom I have put away? or which of my creditors *is it* to whom I have sold you? Behold, for your iniquities have ye sold yourselves, *b* and for your transgressions is your mother put away.

a Je.3.8; Ho.2.?.　　　　　*b* ch.52.3.

CHAPTER L.

1. *Thus saith the* LORD. To the Jews in Babylon, who were suffering under his hand, and who might be disposed to complain that God had dealt with them with as much caprice and cruelty as a man did with his wife, when he gave her a writing of divorce, and put her away without any just cause. ¶ *Where is the bill of your mother's divorcement?* God here speaks of himself as the *husband* of his people, as having married the church to himself, denoting the tender affection which he had for his people. This figure is frequently used in the Bible. Thus in ch. lxii. 5: ' As the bridegroom rejoiceth over the bride, so shall thy God rejoice over thee ;' ' For thy Maker is thy husband' (Isa. liv. 5); ' Turn, O backsliding children, saith the Lord ; for I am married unto you' (Jer. iii. 14). Thus in Rev. xxi. 9, the church is called ' the bride, the Lamb's wife.' Compare Ezek. xvi. See Lowth on Hebrew poetry, Lec. xxxi. The phrase, ' bill of divorcement,' refers to the writing or instrument which a husband was by law obliged to give a wife when he chose to put her away. This custom of divorce Moses found probably in existence among the Jews, and also in surrounding nations, and as it was difficult if not impossible at once to remove it, he permitted it on account of the hard- ness of the hearts of the Jews (Deut. xxiv. 1; comp. Matt. xix. 8). It originated probably from the erroneous views which then prevailed of the nature of the marriage compact. It was extensively regarded as substantially like any other compact, in which the wife became a *purchase* from her father, and of course as she had been purchased, the husband claimed the right of dismissing her when he pleased. Moses nowhere defines the causes for which a man might put away his wife, but left these to be judged of by the people themselves. But he regulated the way in which it might be done. He ordained a law which was designed to operate as a material check on the hasty feelings, the caprice, and the passions of the husband. He designed that it should be with him, if exercised, not a matter of mere excited feeling, but that he should take time to deliberate upon it ; and hence he ordained that in all cases a formal instrument of writing should be executed releasing the wife from the marriage tie, and leaving her at liberty to pursue her own inclinations in regard to future marriages (Deut. xxiv. 2). It is evident that this would operate very materially in favour of the wife, and in checking and restraining the excited passions of the husband (see Jahn's *Bib. Antiq.* § 160; Michaelis's *Comm. on the Laws of Moses*, vol. i.

2 Wherefore, when I came, *was there* no man? when I called, *was there* none to answer? Is my hand shortened at all, that it cannot redeem? or have I no power to deliver? behold, at my rebuke I dry up the sea, I make the rivers a wilderness : their fish stinketh, because *there is* no water, and dieth for thirst.

---

pp. 450-478; ii. 127-40. Ed. Lond. 1814, 8vo.) In the passage before us, God says that he had not rejected his people. He had not been governed by the caprice, sudden passion, or cruelty which husbands often evinced. There was a just cause why he had treated them as he had, and he did not regard them as the children of a divorced wife. The phrase, 'your mother,' here is used to denote the ancestry from whom they were descended. They were not regarded as the children of a disgraced mother. ¶ *Or which of my creditors* is it *to whom I have sold you?* Among the Hebrews, a father had the right, by the law of Moses, if he was oppressed with debt, to sell his children (Ex. xxi. 7; Neh. v. 5). In like manner, if a man had stolen anything, and had nothing to make restitution, he might be sold for the theft (Ex. xxii. 3). If a man also was poor and unable to pay his debts, he might be sold (Lev. xxv. 39; 2 Kings iv. 1; Matt. xviii. 25). On the subject of slavery among the Hebrews, and the Mosaic laws in regard to it, see Michaelis's *Comm. on the Laws of Moses*, vol. ii. pp. 155, *sq.* In this passage, God says that he had not been governed by any such motives in his dealings with his people. He had not dealt with them as a poor parent sometimes felt himself under a necessity of doing, when he sold his children, or as a creditor did when a man was not able to pay him. He had been governed by different motives, and he had punished them only on account of their transgressions. ¶ *Ye have sold yourselves.* That is, you have gone into captivity only on account of your sins. It has been your own act, and you have thus become bondmen to a foreign power only by your own choice. ¶ *Is your mother put away.* Retaining the figure respecting divorce. The nation has been rejected, and suffered to go into exile, only on account of its transgressions.

2. *Wherefore, when I came*, was there *no man?* That is, when I came to call you to repentance, why was there no man of the nation to yield obedience? The sense is, that they had not been punished without warning. He had called them to repentance, but no one heard his voice. The Chaldee renders this, ' Wherefore did I send my prophets, and they did not turn? They prophesied, but they did not attend.' ¶ *When I called*, was there *none to answer?* None obeyed, or regarded my voice. It was not, therefore, by his fault that they had been punished, but it was because they did not listen to the messengers which he had sent unto them. ¶ *Is my hand shortened at all?* The meaning of this is, that it was not because God was unable to save, that they had been thus punished. The hand, in the Scriptures, is an emblem of strength, as it is the instrument by which we accomplish our purposes. To shorten the hand, *i.e.*, to cut it off, is an emblem of diminishing, or destroying our ability to execute any purpose (see ch. lix. 1). So in Ex. xi. 23 : ' Is the LORD's hand waxed short?' ¶ *That it cannot redeem?* That it cannot rescue or deliver you. The idea is, that it was not because he was less able to save them than he had been in former times, that they were sold into captivity, and sighed in bondage. ¶ *Behold, at my rebuke.* At my chiding— as a father rebukes a disobedient child, or as a man would rebuke an excited multitude. Similar language is used of the Saviour when he stilled the tempest on the sea of Gennesareth ; ' Then he arose and rebuked the winds and the sea, and there was a great calm' (Matt. viii. 26). The reference here is, undoubtedly, to the fact that God dried up the Red Sea, or made a way for the children of Israel to pass through it. The idea is, that he who had power to perform such a stupendous miracle as that, had power also to deliver his people at any time, and that, therefore, it was for no want of power in him that the Jews were suffering in exile. ¶ *I make*

3 I clothe the heavens with blackness, and I make sackcloth their
covering.

4 The Lord GOD hath given me
the tongue of the learned, *a* that I

a Mat. 13.54.

should know how to speak a word
in season to *him that is* weary ; *b* he
wakeneth morning by morning : he
wakeneth mine ear to hear as the
learned.

b Mat. 11.28.

the rivers a wilderness. I dry up
streams at pleasure, and have power
even to make the bed of rivers, and all
the country watered by them, a pathless,
and an unfruitful desert. ¶ *Their fish
stinketh.* The waters leave them, and
the fish die, and putrify. It is not uncommon in the East for large streams
and even rivers thus to be dried up by
the intense heat of the sun, and by being
lost in the sand. Thus the river Barrady
which flows through the fertile plain on
which Damascus is situated, and which
is divided into innumerable streams and
canals to water the city and the gardens
adjacent to it, after flowing to a short
distance from the city is wholly lost—
partly absorbed in the sands, and partly
dried up by the intense rays of the sun
(see Jones's *Excursions to Jerusalem,
Egypt, &c.*) The idea here is, that it
was God who had power to dry up those
streams, and that he who could do that,
could save and vindicate his people.

3. *I clothe the heavens with blackness.*
With the dark clouds of a tempest—
perhaps with an allusion to the remarkable clouds and tempests that encircled
the brow of Sinai when he gave the law.
Or possibly alluding to the thick darkness which he brought over the land of
Egypt (Ex. x. 21; Grotius). In the
previous verse, he had stated what he
did on the earth, and referred to the
exhibitions of his great power there.
He here refers to the exhibition of his
power in the sky; and the argument is,
that he who had thus the power to
spread darkness over the face of the sky,
had power also to deliver his people.
¶ *I make sackcloth their covering.* Alluding to the clouds. Sackcloth was a
coarse and dark cloth which was usually
worn as an emblem of mourning (see
Note on ch. iii. 24). The same image
is used in Rev. vi. 12: 'And I beheld
when he had opened the sixth seal, and
lo, there was a great earthquake; and
the sun became black as sackcloth of
hair.' To say, therefore, that the heavens

were clothed with sackcloth, is one of
the most striking and impressive figures
which can be conceived.

4. *The Lord* GOD *hath given me.*
This verse commences a new subject,
and the deliverer is directly introduced
as himself speaking. The reasons why
this is supposed to refer to the Messiah,
have been given in the analysis to the
chapter. Those reasons will be strengthened by the examination of the particular expressions in the passage, and by
showing, as we proceed in the exposition,
in what way they are applicable to him.
It will be assumed that the reference is
to the Messiah; and we shall find that
it is a most beautiful description of his
character, and of some of the principal
events of his life. This verse is designed
to state how he was fitted for the peculiar work to which he was called. The
whole endowment is traced to JEHOVAH.
It was he who had called him; he who
had given him the tongue of the learned,
and he who had carefully and attentively qualified him for his work. ¶ *The
tongue of the learned.* Heb. 'The tongue
of those who are instructed;' *i.e.*, of the
eloquent ; or the tongue of instruction
(παιδίας, LXX.); that is, he has qualified me to instruct others. It does not
mean human science or learning; nor
does it mean that any other had been
qualified as he was, or that there were
any others who were learned like him.
But it means that on the subject of religion he was eminently endowed with
intelligence, and with eloquence. In
regard to the Redeemer's power of instruction, the discourses which he delivered, as recorded in the New Testament, and especially his sermon on the
mount, may be referred to. None on
the subject of religion ever spake like
him ; none was ever so well qualified to
instruct mankind (comp. Matt. xiii. 54).
¶ *That I should know how to speak a
word in season.* The Hebrew here is,
'That I might know how to strengthen
with a word the weary ;' that is, that

5 The Lord GOD hath opened mine ^aear, and I was not ^b rebellious, neither turned away back.

6 ^c I gave my back to the smiters, and my cheeks to them that plucked off the hair : I hid not my face from shame and spitting.

_a Ps.40.6-8.   _b Mat.26.39; Jn.14.31.
_c Mat.26.67;27.26.

he might sustain, comfort, and refresh them by his promises and his counsels. How eminently he was fitted to alleviate those who were heavy laden with sin, and to comfort those who were burdened with calamities and trials, may be seen by the slightest reference to the New Testament, and the most partial acquaintance with his instructions and his life. The *weary* here are those who are burdened with a sense of guilt ; who feel that they have no strength to bear up under the mighty load, and who therefore seek relief (see Matt. xi. 28). ¶ *He wakeneth morning by morning.* That is, he wakens me every morning early. The language is taken from an instructor who awakens his pupils early, in order that they may receive instruction. The idea is, that the Redeemer would be eminently endowed, under the Divine instruction and guidance, for his work. He would be one who was, so to speak, in the school of God ; and who would be qualified to impart instruction to others. ¶ *He wakeneth mine ear.* To awaken the ear is to prepare one to receive instruction. The expressions, to open the ear, to uncover the ear, to awaken the ear, often occur in the Scriptures, in the sense of preparing to receive instruction, or of disposing to receive Divine communications. The sense here is plain. The Messiah would be taught of God, and would be inclined to receive all that he imparted. ¶ *To hear as the learned.* Many translate the phrase here ' as disciples,' that is, as those who are learning. So Lowth ; ' With the attention of a learner.' So Noyes ; ' In the manner of a disciple.' The LXX. render it, ' He has given me an ear to hear.' The idea is, probably, that he was attentive as they are who wish to learn ; that is, as docile disciples. The figure is taken from a master who in the morning summons his pupils around him, and imparts instruction to them. And the doctrine which is taught is, that the Messiah would be eminently qualified, by Divine teaching, to be the instructor of man-

kind. The Chaldee paraphrases this, ' Morning by morning, he anticipates (the dawn), that he may send his prophets, if perhaps they may open the ears of sinners, and receive instruction.'

5. *The Lord* GOD *hath opened mine ear.* This is another expression denoting that he was attentive to the import of the Divine commission (see Ps. xl. 6). ¶ *And I was not rebellious.* I willingly undertook the task of communicating the Divine will to mankind. The statement here is in accordance with all that is said of the Messiah, that he was willing to come and do the will of God, and that whatever trials the work involved he was prepared to meet them (see Ps. xl. 6–8; comp. Heb. x. 4–10).

6. *I gave my back to the smiters.* I submitted willingly to be scourged, or whipped. This is one of the parts of this chapter which can be applied to no other one but the Messiah. There is not the slightest evidence, whatever may be supposed to have been the probability, that Isaiah was subjected to any such trial as this, or that he was scourged in a public manner. Yet it was literally fulfilled in the Lord Jesus Christ (Matt. xxvii. 26 ; comp. Luke xviii. 33). ¶ *And my cheeks to them that plucked off the hair.* Literally, ' My cheeks to those who pluck, or pull.' The word here used (מָרַט) means properly *to polish,* to sharpen, to make smooth ; then to make smooth the head, to make bald ; that is, to pluck out the hair, or the beard. To do this was to offer the highest insult that could be imagined among the Orientals. The beard is suffered to grow long, and is regarded as a mark of honour. Nothing is regarded as more infamous than to cut it off (see 2 Sam. x. 4), or to pluck it out ; and there is nothing which an Oriental will sooner resent than an insult offered to his beard. ' It is a custom among the Orientals, as well among the Greeks as among other nations, to cultivate the beard with the utmost care and solicitude, so that they regard it as the highest

7 For the Lord God will help me; therefore shall I not be confounded: therefore have I set my face like a flint, and I know that I shall not be ashamed.

8 He is near that ^ajustifieth me; who will contend with me? let us stand together: who is ¹ mine adversary? ^b let him come near to me.

a Ro.8.32-34.   1 the master of my cause.
b Ze.3.1,&c.; Re.12.10.

possible insult if a single hair of the beard is taken away by violence.'— (William of Tyre, an eastern archbishop, *Gesta Dei*, p. 802, quoted in Harmer, vol. ii. p. 359.) It is customary to beg by the beard, and to swear by the beard. 'By your beard; by the life of your beard; God preserve your beard; God pour his blessings on your beard,'—are common expressions there. The Mahometans have such a respect for the beard that they think it criminal to shave (Harmer, vol. ii. p. 360). The LXX. render this, 'I gave my cheeks to buffeting' (εἰς ῥαπίσμα); that is, to being smitten with the open hand, which was literally fulfilled in the case of the Redeemer (Matt. xxvi. 67; Mark xiv. 65). The general sense of this expression is, that he would be treated with the highest insult. ¶ *I hid not my face from shame and spitting.* To spit on any one was regarded among the Orientals, as it is everywhere else, as an expression of the highest insult and indignity (Deut. xxv. 9; Num. xii. 14; Job xxx. 10). Among the Orientals also it was regarded as an insult—as it should be everywhere—to spit in the presence of any person. Thus among the Medes, Herodotus (i. 99) says that Deioces ordained that, 'to spit in the king's presence, or in the presence of each other, was an act of indecency.' So also among the Arabians, it is regarded as an offence (Niebuhr's *Travels*, i. 57). Thus Monsieur d'Arvieux tells us (*Voydans la Pal.* p. 140) 'the Arabs are sometimes disposed to think, that when a person spits, it is done out of contempt; and that they never do it before their superiors' (Harmer, iv. 439). This act of the highest indignity was performed in reference to the Redeemer (Matt. xxvi. 67; xxvii. 30); and this expression of their contempt he bore with the utmost meekness. This expression is one of the proofs that this entire passage refers to the Messiah. It is said (Luke xvii. 32) that the prophecies should be fulfilled by his being spit

upon, and yet there is no other prophecy of the Old Testament but this which contains such a prediction.

7. *For the Lord God will help me.* That is, he will sustain me amidst all these expressions of contempt and scorn. ¶ *Shall I not be confounded.* Heb. 'I shall not be ashamed;' that is, I will bear all this with the assurance of his favour and protection, and I will not blush to be thus treated in a cause so glorious, and which must finally triumph and prevail. ¶ *Therefore have I set my face like a flint.* To harden the face, the brow, the forehead, might be used either in a bad or a good sense—in the former as denoting shamelessness or haughtiness (see Note on ch. xlviii. 4); in the latter denoting courage, firmness, resolution. It is used in this sense here; and it means that the Messiah would be firm and resolute amidst all the contempt and scorn which he would meet, and would not shrink from any kind or degree of suffering which should be necessary to accomplish the great work in which he was engaged. A similar expression occurs in Ezek. iii. 8, 9: 'Behold, I have made thy face strong against their faces, and thy forehead strong against their foreheads. As an adamant, harder than a flint, have I made thy forehead; fear them not, neither be dismayed at their looks.'

8. He is *near that justifieth me.* That is, God, who will vindicate my character, and who approves what I do, does not leave nor forsake me, and I can with confidence commit myself and my cause to him (see Note on ch. xlix. 4). The word *justify* here is not used in the sense in which it is often in the Scriptures, to denote the act by which a sinner is justified before God, but in the proper, judicial sense, that he would declare him *to be* righteous; he would vindicate his character, and show him to be innocent. This was done by all the testimonies of God in his favour—by the voice which spake from heaven at his baptism—by

9 Behold, the Lord God will help me ; who *is* he *that* shall condemn me ? *a*lo, they all shall wax old as a garment ; the moth *b* shall eat them up.

10 Who *is* among you that fear-

eth the Lord, that obeyeth the voice of his servant, that walketh *in* darkness, *c* and hath no light ? let him trust *d* in the name of the Lord, and stay upon his God.

a Job 13.28.   *b* ch.51.8.   *c* Ps.23.4; Mi.7.8.
d Job 13.15; Ps.52.3; Na.1.7; He.10.35 37.

the miracles which he wrought, showing that he was commissioned and approved by God—by the fact that even Pilate was constrained to declare him innocent —by the wonders that attended his crucifixion, showing that ' he was a righteous man,' even in the view of the Roman centurion (Luke xxiii. 47), and by the fact that he was raised from the dead, and was taken to heaven, and placed at the right hand of the Father —thus showing that his whole work was approved by God, and furnishing the most ample vindication of his character from all the accusations of his foes. ¶ *Who will contend with me ?* This question indicates confidence in God, and in the integrity of his own character. The language is taken from transactions in the courts of justice ; and it is a solemn call, on any who would dare to oppose him, to enter into a trial, and allege the accusations against him before the tribunal of a holy God. ¶ *Let us stand together.* Before the seat of judgment as in a court (comp. Note on ch. xli. 1). ¶ *Who is mine adversary ?* Marg. ' Who is the master of my cause ?' The Heb. is ' Lord (בַּעַל *bául*) of judgment.' The expression means not merely one who has a lawsuit, or a cause, but one who is ' lord of the judgment,' *i.e.*, possessor of the cause, or one who has *a claim*, and can demand that the judgment should be in his favour. And the call here is on any who should have such a claim to prefer against the Messiah ; who should have any real ground of accusation against him ; that is, it is an assertion of innocence. ¶ *Let him come near to me.* Let him come and make his charges, and enter on the trial.

9. *The Lord God will help me* (see ver. 7). In the Hebrew this is, ' The Lord Jehovah,' as it is in ver. 7 also, and these are among the places where our translators have improperly rendered the word יְהֹוָה (Jehovah) by the word 'God.' ¶ *Who* is *he that shall condemn*

me ? If Jehovah is my advocate and friend, my cause *must* be right. Similar language is used by the apostle Paul : ' If God be for us, who can be against us ?' (Rom. viii. 31) ; and in Ps. cxviii. 6 :

> Jehovah is on my side ; I will not fear :
> What can man do unto me?

¶ *They all shall wax old.* All my enemies shall pass away, as a garment is worn out and cast aside. The idea is, that the Messiah would survive all their attacks ; his cause, his truth, and his reputation would live, while all the power, the influence, the reputation of his adversaries, would vanish as a garment that is worn out and then thrown away. The same image respecting his enemies is used again in ch. li. 8. ¶ *The moth shall eat them up.* The moth is a well known insect attached particularly to woollen clothes, and which soon consumes them (see Note on Job iv. 19). In eastern countries, where wealth consisted much in changes of raiment, the depredations of the moth would be particularly to be feared, and hence it is frequently referred to in the Bible. The sense here is, that the adversaries of the Messiah would be wholly destroyed.

10. *Who* is *among you that feareth the* Lord ? This whole prophecy is concluded with an address made in this verse to the friends of God, and in the next to his enemies. It is the language of the Messiah, calling on the one class to put their trust in Jehovah, and threatening the other with displeasure and wrath. The exhortation in this verse is made in view of what is said in the previous verses. It is the entreaty of the Redeemer to all who love and fear God, and who may be placed in circumstances of trial and darkness as he was, to imitate his example, and not to rely on their own power, but to put their trust in the arm of Jehovah. He had done this (ver. 7-9). He had

11 Behold, all ye that kindle a fire, that compass *yourselves* about with sparks ; walk *a* in the light of your fire, and in the sparks *that* ye have kindled. This shall ye have of mine hand, ye shall lie down *b* in sorrow.

been afflicted, persecuted, forsaken, by men (ver. 6), and he had at that time confided in God and committed his cause to him ; and he had never left or forsaken him. Encouraged by his example, he exhorts all others to cast themselves on the care of him who would defend a righteous cause. ¶ *That feareth the* LORD. Who are worshippers of JEHOVAH. ¶ *That obeyeth the voice of his servant.* The Messiah (see Note on ch. xlii. 1). This is another characteristic of piety. They who fear the Lord will also obey the voice of the Redeemer (John v. 23). ¶ *That walketh* in *darkness.* In a manner similar to the Messiah (ver. 6). God's true people experience afflictions like others, and have often trials peculiarly their own. They are sometimes in deep darkness of mind, and see no light. Comfort has forsaken them, and their days and nights are passed in gloom. ¶ *Let him trust in the name of the* LORD. The Messiah had done this (ver. 8, 9), and he exhorts all others to do it. Doing this they would obtain Divine assistance, and would find that he would never leave nor forsake them. ¶ *And stay upon his God.* Lean upon him, as one does on a staff or other support. This may be regarded still as the language of the merciful Redeemer, appealing to his own example, and entreating all who are in like circumstances, to put their trust in God.

11. *Behold, all ye that kindle a fire.* This verse refers to the wicked. In the previous verse, the Messiah had called upon all the pious to put their trust in God, and it is there implied that they would do so. But it would not be so with the wicked. In times of darkness and calamity, instead of trusting in God they would confide in their own resources, and endeavour to kindle a light for themselves in which they might walk. But the result would be, that they would find no comfort, and would ultimately under his hand lie down in sorrow. The figure is continued from the pre-

vious verse. The pious who are in darkness wait patiently for the light which JEHOVAH shall kindle for them But not so with the wicked. They attempt to kindle a light for themselves, and to walk in that. The phrase, 'that kindle a fire,' refers to all the plans which men form with reference to their own salvation ; all which they rely upon to guide them through the darkness of this world. It may include, therefore, all the schemes of human philosophy, of false religion, of heathenism, of infidelity, deism, and self-righteousness ; all dependence on our good works, our charities, and our prayers. All these are false lights which men enkindle, in order to guide themselves when they resolve to cast off God, to renounce his revelation, and to resist his Spirit. It may have had a primary reference to the Jews, who so often rejected the Divine guidance, and who relied so much on themselves ; but it also includes all the plans which men devise to conduct themselves to heaven. The confidence of the pious (ver. 10) is in the light of God ; that of the wicked is in the light of men. ¶ *That compass* yourselves *about with sparks.* There has been considerable variety in the interpretation of the word here rendered *sparks* (זִיקוֹת). It occurs nowhere else in the Bible, though the word זִקִים occurs in Prov. xxvi. 18, where it is rendered in the text 'firebrands,' and in the margin 'flames,' or 'sparks.' Gesenius supposes that these are different forms of the same word, and renders the word here, 'burning arrows, fiery darts.' The Vulgate renders it 'flames.' The LXX. φλογὶ—'flame.' In the Syriac the word has the sense of lightning. Vitringa supposes it means 'faggots,' and that the sense is, that they encompass themselves with faggots, in order to make a great conflagration. Lowth renders it, very loosely, 'Who heap the fuel round about.' But it is probable that the common version has given the true sense, and that the reference is to

CHAPTER LI.

ANALYSIS.

THIS chapter, together with ch. lii. 1–12, is one connected portion, and injury has been done by separating it. It is a part of Isaiah of exquisite beauty, and is a most suitable introduction to the important portion which follows (ch. lii. 13–18; liii.) respecting the Messiah. This is designed chiefly to comfort the Jews in their exile. They are regarded as in Babylon near the close of their captivity, and as earnestly desiring to be rescued. It is somewhat *dramatic* in its character, and is made up of alternate addresses of God and his people—the one urging the strong language of consolation, and the other fervent petitions for deliverance. The following analysis will give a correct view of the chapter:—

I. God addresses them in the language of consolation, and directs them to remember the founder of their nation, and assures them that he is able also to deliver them (1–3). 1. He speaks of them as pious, and as seeking the Lord (1). 2. They were to remember Abraham and Sarah —the *quarry*, so to speak, from which the nation had been hewed; they were to remember how feeble they were, and yet how God had made a great nation of them, and to feel assured that God was equally able to conduct them forth and to multiply them into a great nation (1, 2). 3. A direct promise that God would comfort Zion, and make it like Eden (3).

II. God calls upon his people to hearken to him, with the assurance that he would extend the true religion even to the Gentile world, and that his salvation should be more permanent than were the heavens (4–6). 1. He would make his religion a light to the Jewish people (4). Though now in darkness, yet they should be brought forth into light. 2. He would extend it to the isles—to the heathen world (5). 3. It should be everlasting. The heavens should grow old and vanish, but his salvation should not be abolished (6).

III. God assures them that they have no reason to despond on account of the number and power of their enemies. However mighty they were, yet they should be consumed as the moth eats up a garment, and as the worm consumes wool (7, 8).

IV. The people are introduced as calling upon God, and as beseeching him to interpose as he had done in former times in their behalf (9, 10). In this appeal they refer to what God had done in former periods when he cut Rahab, *i.e.*, Egypt, in pieces, and delivered his people, and they cry to him to interpose in like manner again, and to deliver them.

V. To this petition JEHOVAH replies (11–16) He assures them—1. That his redeemed shall return with joy and triumph (11). 2. He that had made the heavens was their comforter, and they had nothing to fear from man, or the fury of any oppressor (12, 13). 3. The captive exile was soon to be unloosed, and they hastened that they might be restored; that is, it would soon occur (14). 4. JEHOVAH, who had divided the

human devices, which give no steady and clear light, but which may be compared with a spark struck from a flint. The idea probably is, that all human devices for salvation bear the same resemblance to the true plan proposed by God, which a momentary spark in the dark does to the clear shining of a bright light like that of the sun. If this is the sense, it is a most graphic and striking description of the nature of all the schemes by which the sinner hopes to save himself. ¶ *Walk in the light of your fire.* That is, you will walk in that light. It is not a *command* as if he wished them to do it, but it is a declaration which is intended to direct their attention to the fact that if they did this they would lie down in sorrow. It is language such as we often use, as when we say to a young man, 'go on a little further in a career of dissipation, and you will bring your-self to poverty and shame and death.' Or as if we should say to a man near a precipice, 'go on a little further, and you will fall down and be dashed in pieces.' The essential idea is, that this course would lead to ruin. It is implied that they would walk on in this way, and be destroyed. ¶ *This shall ye have.* As the result of this, you shall lie down in sorrow. Herder renders this:

One movement of my hand upon you,
And ye shall lie down in sorrow.

How simple and yet how sublime an expression is this ! The Messiah but lifts his hand and the lights are quenched. His foes lie down sad and dejected, in darkness and sorrow. The idea is, that they would receive their doom from his hand, and that it would be as easy for him as is the uplifting or waving of the hand, to quench all their lights, and consign them to grief (comp. Matt. xxv.)

sea, was their protector. He had given them a solemn promise, and he had covered his people with the shadow of his hand, and he would defend them (15, 16).

VI. The chapter closes with a direct address to Jerusalem, and with assurances that it shall be rebuilt, and that it would be no more visited with such calamities (17-23). 1. The calamities of Jerusalem are enumerated. She had drunk the cup of the fury of JEHOVAH; she had been forsaken of those who were qualified to guide her; desolation and destruction had therefore come upon her; her sons had fainted in the streets, and had drunk of the fury of God (17-20).

2. God promises deliverance. She was drunken, but not with wine. God had taken out of her hand the cup of trembling, and she should no more drink it again; he would put that cup into the hand of those who had afflicted her, and they should drink it (21-23).

HEARKEN *a* to me, ye that *b* follow after righteousness, ye that seek the LORD : look unto the rock *whence* ye are hewn, and to the hole of the pit *whence* ye are digged.

2 Look *c* unto Abraham your fa-

a ver.7.   *b* Ro.9.30,31.   *c* He.11.8-12.

CHAPTER LI.

1. *Hearken unto me.* That is, to the God of their fathers, who now addresses them. They are regarded as in exile and bondage, and as desponding in regard to their prospects. In this situation, God, or perhaps more properly the Messiah (comp. Notes on ch. l.), is introduced as addressing them with the assurances of deliverance. ¶ *Ye that follow after righteousness.* This is addressed evidently to those who sought to be righteous, and who truly feared the Lord. There was a portion of the nation that continued faithful to JEHOVAH. They still loved and worshipped him in exile, and they were anxiously looking for deliverance and for a return to their own land. ¶ *Look unto the rock* whence *ye are hewn.* To Abraham the founder of the nation. The figure is taken from the act of quarrying stone for the purposes of building; and the essential idea here is, that God had formed the nation from the beginning, as a mason constructs a building; that he had, so to speak, taken the materials rough and unhewn from the very quarry; that he had shaped, and fitted them, and moulded them into an edifice. The idea is not that their origin was dishonourable or obscure. It is not that Abraham was not an honoured ancestor, or that they should be ashamed of the founder of their nation. But the idea is, that God had had the entire moulding of the nation; that he had taken Abraham and Sarah from a distant land, and had formed them into a great people and nation for his own purpose. The *argument* is, that he who had done this was able to raise

them up from captivity, and make them again a great people. Probably allusion is made to this passage by the Saviour in Matt. iii. 9, where he says, 'For I say unto you, that God is able of these stones to raise up children unto Abraham.' ¶ *The hole of the pit.* The word rendered 'hole' means such an excavation as men make who are taking stones from a quarry. It expresses substantially the same idea as the previous member of the verse. This language is sometimes addressed to Christians, with a view to produce humility by reminding them that they have been taken by God from a state of sin, and raised up, as it were, from a deep and dark pit of pollution. But this is not the sense of the passage, nor will it bear such an application. It *may* be used to denote that *God* has taken them, as stone is taken from the quarry; that he found them in their natural state as unhewn blocks of marble are; that he has moulded and formed them by his own agency, and fitted them into his spiritual temple; and that they owe all the beauty and grace of their Christian deportment to him; that this is an argument to prove that he who had done so much for them as to transform them, so to speak, from rough and unsightly blocks to polished stones, fitted for his spiritual temple on earth, is able to keep them still, and to fit them for his temple above. Such is the argument in the passage before us; and such a use of it is, of course, perfectly legitimate and fair.

2. *Look unto Abraham.* What was figuratively expressed in the former verse is here expressed literally. They

ther, and unto Sarah *that* bare you: for I called *a* him alone, and *b* blessed him, and increased him.

3 For the LORD shall comfort Zion : *c* he will comfort all her waste places, and he will make her wilderness like Eden, and her desert like the garden of the LORD ;

a Ge.12.1,2.   *b* Ge.22.17; 24,1,35.

joy *d* and gladness shall be found therein, thanksgiving, and the voice of melody.

4 Hearken unto me, my people, and give ear unto me, O my nation: for a law *e* shall proceed from me, and I will make my judgment to rest for a light of the people.

c ch.52.9; Ps.85.88.   *d* 1 Pe.1.8.   *e* Ro.8.2.

were directed to remember that God had taken Abraham and Sarah from a distant land, and that from so humble a beginning he had increased them to a great nation. The *argument* is, that he was able to bless and increase the exile Jews, though comparatively feeble and few. ¶ *For I called him alone.* Heb. ' For one I called him;' that is, he was alone; there was but one, and he increased to a mighty nation. So Jerome, *Quia unum vocavi eum.* So the LXX. "Οτι εἱς ἦν —' For he was one.' The point of the declaration here, is that God had called *one individual*—Abraham—and that he had caused him to increase till a mighty nation had sprung from him, and that he had the same power to increase the little remnant that remained in Babylon until they should again become a mighty people.

3. *For the* LORD *shall comfort Zion.* On the word ' Zion,' see Notes on ch. i. 8. The meaning here is, that he would again restore it from its ruins. The argument is drawn from the statement in the previous verses. If God had raised up so great a nation from so humble an origin, he had power to restore the waste places of Judea to more than their former beauty and prosperity (see Notes on ch. xl. 1). ¶ *And he will make her wilderness.* Judea is here represented as lying waste. It is to be remembered that the time to which the prophet here refers is that of the captivity, and near its close. Of course, as that would have continued seventy years, in so long a period Judea would have become almost an extended wilderness, a wide waste. Any country that was naturally as fertile as Judea, would in that time be overrun with briers, thorns, and underbrush, and even with a wild and luxuriant growth of the trees of the forest. ¶ *Like Eden*

(Gen. ii.) Like a cultivated and fertile garden—distinguished not only for its fertility, but for its beauty and order. ¶ *Her desert like the garden of the* LORD. Like the garden which the LORD planted (Gen. ii. 8). LXX. 'Ως παραδεισον κυριου —' As the paradise of the LORD.' The idea is, that it should be again distinguished for its beauty and fertility. ¶ *Joy and gladness.* The sound of rejoicing and praise shall be again heard there, where are now heard the cries of wild beasts. ¶ *The voice of melody.* Heb. ' A psalm.' The praises of God shall again be celebrated.

4. *Hearken unto me, my people.* Lowth reads this ;

Attend unto me, O ye people,
And give ear unto me, O ye nations.

The reason why he proposes this change is, that he supposes the address here is made to the Gentiles and not to the Jews, and in favour of the change he observes, that two MSS. read it in this manner. Gesenius (*Comm.*) says that three codices read עַמִּים (*peoples*), instead of עַמִּי (*my people*); and that thirteen read לְאֻמִּים (*nations*), instead of לְאֻמִּי (*my nation*). Noyes also has adopted this reading. But the authority is too slight to justify a change in the text. The Vulgate reads it in accordance with the present Hebrew text, and so substantially do the LXX. They render it, 'Hear me, hear me, my people, and ye kings, give ear unto me.' It is not necessary to suppose any change in the text. The address is to the Jews; and the design is, to comfort them in view of the fact that the heathen would be brought to partake of the privileges and blessings of the true religion. They would not only be restored to their own land, but the true religion would be extended also to the distant nations of the

5 My *a* righteousness *is* near ; my
salvation is gone forth, and mine
arms shall judge *b* the people : the
isles *c* shall wait upon me, and on
mine arm shall they trust.

6 Lift up your eyes to the heavens, and look upon the earth be-

a ch.56.1.   b Ps 98.9.   c ch.42.4; 60.9.

neath ; for *d* the heavens shall vanish
away like smoke, and the earth shall
wax old like a garment, and they
that dwell therein shall die in like
manner : but my salvation shall be
for ever, and my righteousness shall
not *e* be abolished.

d He.1.11,12; 2 Pe.3.10,12.   e Da.9.24.

earth. In view of this great and glorious truth, JEHOVAH calls on his people
to hearken to him, and receive the
glad announcement. It was a truth in
which they were deeply interested, and
to which they should therefore attend.
¶ *For a law shall proceed from me.*
The idea here is, that JEHOVAH would
give law to the distant nations by the
diffusion of the true religion. ¶ *And
I will make my judgment to rest for a
light.* The word 'judgment' here is
equivalent to *law*, or *statute*, or to the
institutions of the true religion. The
word here rendered 'to rest' (אַרְגִּיעַ from
רָגַע), Lowth renders, 'I will cause to
break forth.' Noyes renders it, 'I
will establish.' The Vulgate, *Requi-
escet*—'Shall rest.' The LXX. render
it simply, 'My judgment for a light of
the nation.' The word properly means
to make afraid, to terrify, to restrain
by threats ; rendered 'divideth' in Job
xxvi. 12 ; Isa. li. 15 ; then, to be afraid,
to shrink from fear, and hence to be
still, or quiet, *as if* cowering down from
fear. Here it means that he would
set firmly his law; he would place it
so that it would be established and
immovable.

5. *My righteousness is near.* The
word 'righteousness' is used in a great
variety of significations. Here it means,
probably, the faithful completion of his
promises to his people (Lowth). ¶ *My
salvation is gone forth.* The promise
of salvation is gone forth, and already
the execution of that purpose is commenced. He would soon deliver his
people ; he would at no distant period
extend salvation to all nations. ¶ *And
mine arm shall judge the people.* That
is, shall dispense judgment to them.
The 'arm' here is put for himself, as the
arm is the instrument by which we execute our purposes (see Notes on ver. 9).
¶ *The isles shall wait upon me.* The

distant nations ; the heathen lands (see
Note on ch. xli. 1). The idea is, that
distant lands would become interested
in the true religion, and acknowledge
and worship the true God.

6. *Lift up your eyes to the heavens.*
The design of directing their attention
to the heavens and the earth is, probably, to impress them more deeply with
a conviction of the certainty of his salvation in this manner, viz.: the heavens
and the earth appear firm and fixed ;
there is in them no apparent tendency
to dissolution and decay. Yet though
apparently thus fixed and determined,
they will all vanish away, but the promise of God will be unfailing. ¶ *For
the heavens shall vanish away.* The
word which is here rendered 'shall vanish away' (מָלַח), occurs nowhere else
in the Bible. The primary idea, according to Gesenius, is that of smoothness and softness. Then it means to
glide away, to disappear. The idea here
is, that the heavens would disappear, as
smoke is dissipated and disappears in
the air. The idea of the vanishing, or
the disappearing of the heavens and the
earth, is one that often occurs in the
Scriptures (see Notes on ch. xxxiv. 4;
comp. Ps. cii. 26 ; Heb. i. 11, 12 ; 2 Pet.
iii. 10–12). ¶ *The earth shall wax old,*
&c. Shall decay, and be destroyed
(see Ps. cii. 26). ¶ *And they that
dwell therein shall die in like manner.*
Lowth renders this, 'Like the vilest
insect.' Noyes, 'Like flies.' The Vulgate, and the LXX., however, render it
as it is in our version. Rosenmüller
renders it, 'As flies.' Gesenius renders
it, 'Like a gnat.' This variety of interpretation arises from the different explanation of the word כֵּן (*khēn*), which
usually means, *as, so, thus, in like manner*, &c. The plural form, however,
(כִּנִּים *kinnīm*), occurs in Ex. viii. 17;
Ps. cv. 31, and is rendered by the LXX.

7 Hearken *a* unto me, ye that know righteousness, the people in whose heart *b is* my law; fear ye not *c* the reproach of men, neither be ye afraid of their revilings.

8 For the moth shall eat *d* them up like a garment, and the worm shall eat them like wool: but my righteousness shall be for ever, and my salvation from generation to generation.

a ver.1.   *b* Ps.37.31.   *c* Mat.10.28.   *d* Job 4.19-21.

σκνῖφες, and by the Vulgate *sciniphes,* a species of small gnats, very troublesome from their sting, which abounds in the marshy regions of Egypt; and according to this the idea is, that the most mighty inhabitants of the earth would die like gnats, or the smallest and vilest insects. This interpretation gives a more impressive sense than our version, but it is doubtful whether it can be justified. The word occurs nowhere else in this sense, and the authority of the ancient versions is against it. The idea as given in the common translation is not feeble, as Gesenius supposes, but is a deeply impressive one, that the heavens, the earth, and all the inhabitants should vanish away together, and alike disappear. ¶ *But my salvation shall be for ever.* It is a glorious truth that the redemption which God shall give his people shall survive the revolutions of kingdoms, and the consummation of all earthly things. It is not improbable that the Saviour had this passage in his eye when he said, 'Heaven and earth shall pass away, but my word shall not pass away' (Matt. xxiv. 35).

7. *Hearken unto me, ye that know righteousness.* My people who are acquainted with my law, and who are to be saved. This is addressed to the pious part of the Jewish nation. ¶ *Fear ye not the reproach of men.* If we have the promise of God, and the assurance of his favour, we shall have no occasion to dread the reproaches and the scoffs of men (comp. Matt. x. 28).

8. *For the moth* (see ch. l. 9). The idea is, that they shall be consumed as the moth eats up a garment; or rather, that the moth itself shall consume them as it does a garment: that is, that they were so weak when compared with JEHOVAH that even the moth, one of the smallest, and most contemptible of insects, would consume them. An expression remarkably similar to this occurs in Job iv. 18-20:

Behold in his servants he putteth no confidence,
And his angels he chargeth with frailty;
How much more true is this of those who dwell
    in houses of clay,
Whose foundation is in the dust!
They are crushed before the moth-worm!
Between morning and evening they are destroyed;
Without any one regarding it, they perish for
    ever.

Perhaps the following extract from Niebuhr may throw some light on the passage, as showing that man may be crushed by so feeble a thing as a worm. 'A disease very common in Yemen is the attack of the Guiney-worm, or the *Verea-Medinensis,* as it is called by the physicians of Europe. This disease is supposed to be occasioned by the use of the putrid waters, which people are obliged to drink in various parts of Yemen; and for this reason the Arabians always pass water, with the nature of which they are unacquainted, through a linen cloth before using it. When one unfortunately swallows the eggs of this insect, no immediate consequence follows; but after a considerable time the worm begins to show itself through the skin. Our physician, Mr. Cramer, was within a few days of his death attacked by five of these worms at once, although this was more than five months after we left Arabia. In the isle of Karek I saw a French officer named Le Page, who, after a long and difficult journey, performed on foot, and in an Indian dress, between Pondicherry and Surat, through the heat of India, was busy extracting a worm out of his body He supposed he had got it by drinking bad water in the country of the Mahrattas. This disorder is not dangerous if the person who is affected can extract the worm without breaking it. With this view it is rolled on a small bit of wood as it comes out of the skin. It is slender as a thread, and two or three feet long. If unluckily it be broken, it then returns into the body, and the most disagreeable consequences ensue—palsy, a

9 Awake, awake, put on ª strength, O arm of the Lord ; awake, as in the ancient days, in the generations of old. *Art* thou not it that hath cut *b* Rahab, *and* wounded *c* the dragon ?

10 *Art* thou not it which *d* hath dried the sea, the waters of the great deep ; that hath made the depths of the sea a way for the ransomed to pass over ?

a Re.11.7.   *b* Ps.89.10.
c ch.27.1; Ps.74.13,14.   *d* Ex.14.21.

gangrene, and sometimes death.' A thought similar to that of Isaiah respecting man, has been beautifully expressed by Gray:

To contemplation's sober eye,
  Such is the race of man ;
And they that creep, and they that fly,
  Shall end where they began.

Alike the busy and the gay,
But flutter through life's little day,
  In fortune's varying colours drest ;
Brush'd by the hand of rough mischance,
Or chill'd by age, their airy dance
  They leave, in dust to rest.

¶ *And the worm shall eat them like wool.* The word rendered 'worm' (סָס), probably means the same as the moth. The Arabic renders it by *moth, weevil.* The LXX. Σής. It is of unfrequent occurrence in the Scriptures.

9. *Awake, awake.* This verse commences a new subject (see the analysis of the chapter). It is the solemn and impassioned entreaty of those who were in exile that God would interpose in their behalf, as he did in behalf of his people when they were suffering in cruel bondage in Egypt. The word 'awake' here, which is addressed to the *arm* of Jehovah, is a petition that it might be roused from its apparent stupor and inactivity, and its power exerted in their behalf. ¶ *O arm of the* Lord. The *arm* is the instrument by which we execute any purpose. It is that by which the warrior engages in battle, and by which he wields the weapon to prostrate his foes. The *arm* of Jehovah had seemed to slumber. For seventy years the prophet sees the oppressed and suffering people in bondage, and God had not come forth to rescue them. He hears them now lifting the voice of earnest and tender entreaty, that he would interpose as he had in former times, and save them from the calamities which they were enduring. ¶ *Awake, as in the ancient days.* That is, in the time when the Jews were delivered from their bondage in the land of Egypt.

¶ *Art thou not it.* Art thou not the same arm? Was it not by this arm that the children of Israel were delivered from bondage, and may we not look to it for protection still? ¶ *That hath cut Rahab.* That is, cut it in pieces, or destroyed it. It was that arm which wielded the sword of justice and of vengeance by which Rahab was cut in pieces. The word 'Rahab' here means Egypt. On the meaning of the word, see Notes on ch. xxx. 7; comp. Ps. lxxxviii. 8; lxxxix. 10. ¶ *And wounded the dragon.* The word here rendered dragon (תַּנִּין *tănnīn*) means properly any great fish or sea-monster ; a serpent, a dragon (see Notes on ch. xxvii. 1), or a crocodile. Here it means, probably, the crocodile, as emblematic of Egypt, because the Nile abounded in crocodiles, and because a monster so unwieldy and formidable and unsightly, was no unapt representation of the proud and cruel king of Egypt. The king of Egypt is not unfrequently compared with the crocodile (see Ps. xxxiv. 13, 14; Ezek. xxix. 3; xxxii. 2). Here the sense is, that he had sorely wounded, *i.e.*, had greatly weakened the power of that cruel nation, which for strength was not unfitly represented by the crocodile, one of the most mighty of monsters, but which, like a pierced and wounded monster, was greatly enfeebled when God visited it with plagues, and destroyed its hosts in the sea.

10. Art *thou not it.* Art thou not still the same? The ground of the appeal is, that the same arm that dried up the sea, and made a path for the Jewish people, was still able to interpose and rescue them. ¶ *Which hath dried the sea.* The Red Sea when the children of Israel passed over (Ex. xiv. 21). This is the common illustration to which the Hebrew prophets and poets appeal, when they wish to refer to the interposition of God in favour of their nation (comp. Ps. cv. ; see Notes on ch. xliii. 16).

11 Therefore *a* the redeemed of the LORD shall return, and come with singing unto Zion ; and everlasting joy *b shall be* upon their head: they shall obtain gladness and joy ; *and* sorrow *c* and mourning shall flee away.

12 I, *d even* I, *am* he that comforteth you: who *art* thou, that thou shouldest be afraid of a man *that*

shall die, and of the son of man *which* shall be made *as* grass ;

13 And forgettest the LORD thy Maker, that hath stretched forth the heavens, and laid the foundations of the earth ; and hast feared continually every day because of the fury of the oppressor, as if he 1 were ready to destroy ? and *e* where *is* the fury of the oppressor ?

a ch.35.10.   *b* Jude 24.   *c* Re.21.4.   *d* ver.3.

1 or, *made himself ready.*   *e* Job 20.7.

¶ *For the ransomed to pass over.* Those who had been ransomed from Egypt. The word rendered 'ransomed' is that which is commonly rendered 're-deemed.' The argument in this verse is, that he who had overcome all the obstacles in the way of their deliverance from Egypt, was able also to overcome all the obstacles in the way of their deliverance from Babylon ; and that he who had thus interposed might be expected again to manifest his mercy, and save them again from oppression. The *principle* involved in the argument is as applicable now as it was then. All God's past interpositions—and especially the great and wonderful interposition when he gave his Son for his church—constitute an argument that he will still continue to regard the interests of his people, and will interpose in their behalf, and save them.

11. *Therefore the redeemed of the LORD.* This is probably the language of JEHOVAH assuring them, in answer to their prayer, that his ransomed people should again return to Zion. ¶ *And everlasting joy* shall be *upon their head.* This entire verse occurs also in ch. xxxv. 10. See it explained in the Note on that verse. The custom of *singing* alluded to here on a journey is now very common in the East. It is practised to relieve the tediousness of a journey over extended plains, as well as to induce the camels in a caravan to move with greater rapidity. The idea here is, that the caravan that should return from Babylon to Jerusalem, across the extended plains, should make the journey amidst general exultation and joy— cheered on their way by songs, and relieving the tedium of their journey by notes of gladness and of praise.

12. *I, even I, am he that comforteth you.* The word ' I ' is repeated here to give emphasis to the passage, and to impress deeply upon them the fact that their consolation came alone from God. The argument is, that since God was their protector and friend, they had no occasion to fear anything that man could do. ¶ *Of a man* that *shall die.* God your comforter will endure for ever. But all men—even the most mighty— must soon die. And if God is our protector, what occasion can we have to fear what a mere mortal can do to us? ¶ *And of the son of man.* This phrase is common in the Hebrew Scriptures, and means the same as man. ¶ *Shall be made as grass.* They shall perish as grass does that is cut down at midday (see Notes on ch. xl. 6, 7).

13. *And forgettest the LORD thy Maker.* These verses are designed to rebuke that state of the mind—alas! too common, even among the people of God —where they are intimidated by the number and strength of their foes, and forget their dependence on God, and his promises of aid. In such circumstances God reproves them for their want of confidence in him, and calls on them to remember that he has made the heavens, and has all power to save them. ¶ *That hath stretched forth the heavens* (see Notes on ch. xl. 12, 26). ¶ *And hast feared continually every day.* They had continually feared and trembled before their oppressors. ¶ *Because of the fury of the oppressor.* Those who had oppressed them in Babylon. ¶ *As if he were ready to destroy.* Marg. ' Made himself ready.' The idea is, that he was *preparing* to destroy the people—perhaps as a marksman is making ready his bow and

14 The captive exile hasteneth that he may be loosed, and that he should not die in the pit, *a* nor that his bread should fail.

a Zec.9.11.   *b* Jn.3.34.

15 But I am the LORD thy God, that divided the sea, whose waves roared: The LORD of hosts *is* his name.

16 And I have put my words *b* in

arrows. The oppressor had been preparing to crush them in the dust, and they trembled, and did not remember that God was abundantly able to protect them. ¶ *And where is the fury of the oppressor?* What is there to dread? The idea is, that the enemies of the Jews would be cut off, and that they should therefore put their confidence in God, and rely on his promised aid.

14. *The captive exile.* Lowth renders this, evidently very improperly, 'He marcheth on with speed who cometh to set the captive free;' and supposes that it refers to Cyrus, if understood of the temporal redemption from the captivity at Babylon; in the spiritual sense, to the Messiah. But the meaning evidently is, that the exile who had been so long as it were enchained in Babylon, was about to be set free, and that the time was very near when the captivity was to end. The prisoner should not die there, but should be conducted again to his own land. The word here used, and rendered 'captive exile' (צֹעֶה from צָעָה), means properly *that which is turned on one side*, or *inclined*, as, *e.g.*, a vessel for pouring (Jer. xlviii. 12). Then it means that which is inclined, bent, or bowed down as a captive in bonds. The Chaldee renders this, 'Vengeance shall be quickly revealed, and the just shall not die in corruption, and their food shall not fail.' Aben Ezra renders it, 'Bound.' The idea is, that they who were bowed down under bondage and oppression in Babylon, should very soon be released. This is one of the numerous passages which show that the *scene* of the prophetic vision is Babylon, and the *time* near the close of the captivity, and that the design of the prophet is to comfort them there, and to afford them the assurance that they would soon be released. ¶ *And that he should not die in the pit.* That is, in Babylon, represented as a prison, or a pit. The nation would be restored

to their own land. Prisoners were often confined in a deep *pit* or cavern, and hence the word is synonymous with prison. The following extract from Paxton will illustrate this. 'The Athenians, and particularly the tribe of Hippothoontis, frequently condemned offenders to the pit. It was a dark, noisome hole, and had sharp spikes at the top, that no criminal might escape; and others at the bottom, to pierce and torment those unhappy persons who were thrown in. Similar to this place was the Lacedemonian Καιαδας, into which Aristomenes the Messenian being cast, made his escape in a very surprising manner.' Comp. also Gen. xxxvii. 20; Num. xvi. 30; Ps. ix. 15; xxviii. 1; xxx. 3, 9; xl. 2; lv. 23; cxix. 85; cxl. 10; Jer. xxxvii. 21; Zec. ix. 11. ¶ *Nor that his bread should fail.* His wants shall be supplied until he is released.

15. *But I am the* LORD *thy God.* In order to show them that he was able to save them, God again refers to the fact that he had divided the sea, and delivered their fathers from bondage and oppression. ¶ *That divided the sea.* The Red Sea. The Chaldee renders this, 'That rebuked the sea.' The LXX. Ὁ ταράσσων—'Who disturbs the sea,' or, who excites a tempest. Lowth renders it, 'Who stilleth at once the sea.' The Hebrew word is the same which occurs in ver. 4, where it is rendered, 'I will make my judgment *to rest*' (רָגַע). Probably the idea here is, that he restrains the raging of the sea *as if* by fear; *i.e.*, makes it tranquil or still by rebuking it. He had this power over all raging seas, and he had shown it in a special manner by his rebuking the Red Sea and making it rest, and causing a way to be made through it, when the children of Israel came out of Egypt. ¶ *The* LORD *of hosts is his name* (see Notes on ch. i. 9; comp. Notes on ch. xlii. 8).

16. *And I have put my words in thy mouth.* That is, he had committed his

thy mouth, and have covered thee
in the shadow *a* of mine hand, that
I may plant the heavens, *b* and lay
the foundations of the earth, and
say unto Zion, Thou *art* my people.

17 Awake, awake, stand up, O

Jerusalem, which hast drunk at the
hand of the LORD the cup of his
fury : *c* thou hast drunken the dregs
of the cup of trembling, *and* wrung
them out.

a ch.49.2.   b 2 Pe.3.13.   c ver.22; Ps.75.8.

truth to the Jewish people; to Zion.
He had intrusted them with his statutes and his laws; he had given them
the promise of the Messiah, and through
him the assurance that the true religion
would be spread to other nations. He
would, therefore, preserve them, and
restore them again to their own land.
¶ *And have covered thee in the shadow
of mine hand.* That is, I have protected thee (see Notes on ch. xlix. 2).
¶ *That I may plant the heavens.*
Lowth renders this, ' To stretch out the
heavens.' Noyes, ' To establish the
heavens.' Jerome, *Ut plantes cœlos*—
' That thou mayest plant the heavens.'
The LXX. 'Ἐν ᾗ ἔστησα τὸν οὐρανὸν—
' By which I have established heaven.'
The Chaldee renders it, ' In the shadow
of my power have I protected thee,
that I might raise up the people of
whom it was said, that they should be
multiplied as the stars of heaven.' But
the language here is evidently entirely
figurative. It refers to the restoration
of the Jews to their own land; to the
re-establishment of religion there; to
the introduction of the new economy
under the Messiah, and to all the great
changes which would be consequent on
that. This is compared with the work
of forming the heavens, and laying the
foundation of the earth. It would require almighty power; and it would
produce so great changes, that it might
be compared to the work of creating the
universe out of nothing. Probably also
the idea is included here that *stability*
would be given to the true religion by
what God was about to do—a permanency that might be compared with the
firmness and duration of the heavens
and the earth. ¶ *And say unto Zion,*
&c. That is, God would restore them
to their own land, and acknowledge
them as his own.

17. *Awake, awake* (see Notes on
ver. 9). This verse commences an address to Jerusalem under a new figure

or image. The figure employed is that
of a man who has been overcome by
the cup of the wrath of JEHOVAH, that
had produced the same effect as inebri-
ation. Jerusalem had reeled and fallen
prostrate. There had been none to sustain her, and she had sunk to the dust.
Calamities of the most appalling kind
had come upon her, and she is now
called on to arouse from this condition,
and to recover her former splendour
and power. ¶ *Which hast drunk at
the hand of the* LORD. The wrath of
JEHOVAH is not unfrequently compared
to a cup producing intoxication. The
reason is, that it produces a similar
effect. It prostrates the strength, and
makes the subject of it reel, stagger,
and fall. In like manner, all calamities
are represented under the image of a
cup that is drunk, producing a prostrating effect on the frame. Thus the
Saviour says, ' The cup which my
Father hath given me, shall I not drink
it?' (John xviii. 11; comp. Matt. xx.
22, 23; xxvi. 39, 42). The effects of
drinking the cup of God's displeasure
are often beautifully set forth. Thus,
in Ps. lxxv. 8:

In the hand of JEHOVAH there is a cup, and the
    wine is red;
It is full of a mixed liquor, and he poureth out
    of the same,
Verily the dregs thereof all the ungodly of the
    earth shall wring them out and drink them.

Plato, as referred to by Lowth, has an
idea resembling this. ' Suppose,' says
he, ' God had given to men a medicat-
ing potion inducing fear; so that the
more any one should drink of it, so
much the more miserable he should
find himself at every draught, and become fearful of everything present and
future; and at last, though the most
courageous of men, should become totally
possessed by fear; and afterwards, having slept off the effects of it, should become himself again.' A similar image
is used by Homer (*Iliad,* xvi. 527, *sq.*),
where he places two vessels at the

18 *There is* none to guide her
among all the sons *whom* she hath
brought forth ; neither *is there any*

1 *happened.*

that taketh her by the hand, of all
the sons *that* she hath brought up.

19 These two *things* [1] are come
unto thee ; who shall be sorry for

---

threshold of Jupiter, one of good, the
other of evil. He gives to some a mixed
potion of each ; to others from the evil
vessel only, and these are completely
miserable :

Two urns by Jove's high throne have ever stood,
The source of evil one, and one of good;
From thence the cup of mortal man he fills,
Blessings to these; to those distributes ills.
To most he mingles both: The wretch decreed
To taste the bad unmix'd, is curs'd indeed ;
Pursued by wrongs, by meagre famine driven,
He wanders, outcast by both earth and heaven :
The happiest taste not happiness sincere,
But find the cordial draught is dash'd with care.

But nowhere is this image handled with
greater force and sublimity than in this
passage of Isaiah. Jerusalem is here
represented as staggering under the
effects of it ; she reels and falls ; none
assist her from whence she might expect aid ; not one of them is able to
support her. All her sons had fainted
and become powerless (ver. 20); they
were lying prostrate at the head of
every street, like a bull taken in a net,
struggling in vain to rend it, and to
extricate himself. Jehovah's wrath had
produced complete and total prostration
throughout the whole city. ¶ *Thou
hast drunken the dregs.* Gesenius
renders this, ' The goblet cup.' But
the common view taken of the passage
is, that it means that the cup had been
drunk to the dregs. All the intoxicating
liquor had been poured off. They had
entirely exhausted the cup of the wrath
of God. Similar language occurs in
Rev. xiv. 10: ' The same shall drink of
the wine of the wrath of God, which is
poured out without mixture, into the
cup of his indignation.' The idea of
the *dregs* is taken from the fact that,
among the ancients, various substances,
as honey, dates, &c., were put into wine,
in order to produce the intoxicating
quality in the highest degree. The
sediment of course would remain at the
bottom of the cask or cup when the
wine was poured off. Homer, who lived
about a thousand years before Christ,
and whose descriptions are always regarded as exact accounts of the customs

in his time, frequently mentions potent
drugs as being mixed with wines. In
the *Odyssey* (iv. 220), he tells us that
Helen prepared for Telemachus and his
companions a beverage which was highly
stupefactive, and soothing to his mind.
To produce these qualities, he says that
she threw into the wine drugs which were

Νηπενθες τ' αλοχον τι κακων επιληθον
απαντων

' Grief-assuaging, rage-allaying, and
the oblivious antidote for every species
of misfortune.' Such mixtures were
common among the Hebrews. It is
possible that John (Rev. xiv. 10) refers
to such a mixture of the simple juice of
the grape with intoxicating drugs when
he uses the expression implying a seeming contradiction, κεκερασμενου ακρατου
—(*mixed, unmixed wine*)—rendered
in our version, ' poured out without
mixture.' The reference is rather to
the pure juice of the grape *mixed*, or
mingled with intoxicating drugs. ¶ *The
cup of trembling.* The cup producing
trembling, or intoxication (comp. Jer.
xxv. 15; xlix. 12; li. 7; Lam. iv. 21;
Hab. ii. 16; Ezek. xxiii. 31–33). The
same figure occurs often in the Arabic
poets (see Gesenius *Comm. zu. Isa. in
loc.*) ¶ And *wrung* them *out* (מָצִית).
This properly means, to suck out ; that
is, they had as it were sucked off all the
liquid from the dregs.

18. There is *none to guide her.* The
image here is taken from the condition
of one who is under the influence of an
intoxicating draught, and who needs
some one to sustain and guide him.
The idea is, than among all the inhabitants of Jerusalem in the time of the
calamity, there was none who could
restore to order the agitated and distracted affairs of the nation. All its
wisdom was destroyed; its counsels perplexed; its power overcome. ¶ *All the
sons* whom *she hath brought forth.* All
the inhabitants of Jerusalem.

19. *These two* things *are come unto
thee.* Marg. ' Happened.' That is, two
sources of calamity have come upon thee ;

thee? desolation, and ¹ destruction, and the famine, and the sword : by whom ᵃ shall I comfort thee?

20 Thy sons have fainted, they

¹ *breaking.*

lie at the head of all the streets, as a wild bull in a net: they are full of the fury of the LORD, the rebuke of thy God.

ᵃ La.2.11-13; Am.7.2.

to wit, famine and the sword, producing desolation and destruction; or desolation *by* famine, and destruction *by* the sword (see Lowth *on Heb. Poetry*, Lect. xix.) The idea here is, that far-spread destruction had occurred, caused by the two things, famine and the sword. ¶ *Who shall be sorry for thee?* That is, who shall be able so to pity thee as to furnish relief? ¶ *Desolation.* By famine. ¶ *And destruction.* Marg. as Heb. ' Breaking.' It refers to the calamities which would be inflicted by the sword. The land would be desolated, and famine would spread over it. This refers, doubtless, to the series of calamities that would come upon it in connection with the invasion of the Chaldeans. ¶ *By whom shall I comfort thee?* This intimates a desire on the part of JEHOVAH to give them consolation. But the idea is, that the land would be laid waste, and that they who would have been the natural comforters should be destroyed. There would be none left to whom a resort could be had for consolation.

20. *Thy sons.* Jerusalem is here represented as a mother. Her sons, that is, her inhabitants, had become weak and prostrate everywhere, and were unable to afford consolation. ¶ *They lie at the head of all the streets.* The ' head' of the streets is the same which in Lam. ii. 19; iv. 1, is denominated ' the top of the streets.' The head or top of the streets denotes, doubtless, the *beginning* of a way or street; the corner from which other streets diverge. These would be public places, where many would be naturally assembled, and where, in time of a siege, they would be driven together. This is a description of the state produced by famine. Weak, pale, and emaciated, the inhabitants of Jerusalem, in the places of public concourse, would lie prostrate and inefficient, and unable to meet and repel their foes. They would be overpowered with famine, as a wild bull is insnared in a net, and rendered incapable of any effort. This refers undoubtedly to the famine that

would be produced during the siege of the Babylonians. The state of things under the siege has been also described by Jeremiah :

Arise, cry out in the night;
In the beginning of the watches pour out thine
    heart before the Lord;
Lift up thy hands toward him for the life of thy
    young children,
That faint for hunger at the top of every street.

The young and old lie on the ground in the
    streets,
My virgins and my young men are fallen by the
    sword;
Thou hast slain them in the day of thy anger;
Thou hast killed, and not pitied.—Lam. ii. 19-21.

The tongue of the sucking child cleaveth to the
    roof of his mouth for thirst;
The young children ask bread, and no man
    breaketh it unto them;
They that did feed delicately are desolate in the
    streets;
They that were brought up in scarlet embrace
    dunghills.—Lam. iv. 4, 5.

¶ *As a wild bull in a net.* The word here rendered ' wild bull' is רּוֹא. Gesenius supposes it is the same as הַאְ, a species of *gazelle*, so called from its swiftness. Aquila, Symm. and Theod. render it here, 'Ορυξ—' Oryx ;' Jerome also renders it, *Oryx*—' A wild goat' or stag. The LXX. render it, Σιυτλίον ἡμίεφθον—' A parboiled beet !' The Chaldee, ' As broken bottles.' Bochart (*Hieroz.* i. 3. 28), supposes it means a species of mountain-goat, and demonstrates that it is common in the East to take such animals in a net. Lowth renders it, ' Oryx.' The streets of Hebrew towns, like those of ancient Babylon, and of most modern Oriental cities, had gates which were closed at night, and on some occasions of broil and danger. A person then wishing to escape would be arrested by the closed gate and if he was pursued, would be taken somewhat like a wild bull in a net. It was formerly the custom, as it is now in Oriental countries, to take wild animals in this manner. A space of ground of considerable extent—usually in the vicinity of springs and brooks, where the animals were in the habit of repair-

21 Therefore, hear now this, thou afflicted, and drunken, *a* but not with wine:

22 Thus saith thy Lord the LORD, and thy God *that* pleadeth *b* the cause of his people, Behold, I have taken out of thine hand the cup of trembling, *even* the dregs of the cup

a La.3.15.   *b* Ps.35.1; Je.50.34; Mi.7.9.

of my fury; thou shalt no more drink *c* it again.

23 But *d* I will put it into the hand of them that afflict thee; which have said to thy soul, Bow down, that we may go over: and thou hast laid thy *e* body as the ground, and as the street, to them that went over.

c ch.54.7-9.   *d* Je.25.17-29.   *e* Ps.66.11,12.

ing morning and evening—was enclosed by nets into which the animals were driven by horsemen and hounds, and when there enclosed, they were easily taken. Such scenes are still represented in Egyptian paintings (*see* Wilkinson's *Ancient Egyptians*, vol. iii. pp. 2–36), and such a custom prevailed among the Romans. Virgil represents Æneas and Dido as repairing to a wood for the purpose of hunting at break of day, and the attendants as surrounding the grove with nets or toils.

Venatum Æneas, unaque miserrima Dido,
In nemus ire parant, ubi primos crastinus ortus
Extulerit Titan, radusque retexerit orbem.
His ego nigrantem commixta grandine nimbum,
Dum trepidant alæ, *saltusque indagine cingunt,*
Desuper infundam, et tonitru cœlum omne ciebo.
                    Æn. iv. 117, *sq.*

The idea here is plain. It is, that as a wild animal is secured by the toils of the hunter, and rendered unable to escape, so it was with the inhabitants of Jerusalem suffering under the wrath of God. They were humbled, and prostrate, and powerless, and were, like the stag that was caught, entirely at the disposal of him who had thus insnared them.

21. *And drunken, but not with wine.* Overcome and prostrate, but not under the influence of intoxicating drink. They were prostrate by the wrath of God.

22. *I have taken out of thy hand the cup of trembling* (see Notes on ver. 17). This verse contains a promise that they would be delivered from the effect of the wrath of God, under which they had been suffering so long. ¶ *Thou shalt no more drink it again.* Thou shalt no more be subject to similar trials and calamities (see ch. liv. 7–9). Probably the idea here is, not that Jerusalem would never be again destroyed, which would not be true, for it was afterwards subjected to severer trials under the Ro-

mans; but that *the people* who should then return—the pious exiles—should be preserved for ever after from similar sufferings. The object of the prophet is to console *them,* and this he does by the assurance that they should be subjected to such trials no more.

23. *But I will put it into the hand of them that afflict thee.* The nations that have made war upon thee, and that have reduced thee to bondage, particularly the Babylonians. The calamities which the Jews had suffered, God would transfer to their foes. ¶ *Which have said to thy soul, Bow down, that we may go over.* This is a striking description of the pride of eastern conquerors. It was not uncommon for conquerors actually to put their feet on the necks of conquered kings, and tread them in the dust. Thus in Josh. x. 24, ' Joshua called for all the men of Israel, and said unto the captains of the men of war that went with them, Come near, put your feet upon the necks of these kings.' So David says, ' Thou has given me the necks of mine enemies ' (Ps. xviii. 40). ' The emperor Valerianus being through treachery taken prisoner by Sapor king of Persia, was treated by him as the basest and most abject slave; for the Persian monarch commanded the unhappy Roman to bow himself down and offer him his back, on which he set his foot in order to mount his chariot, or his horse, whenever he had occasion.' —(Lactantius, as quoted by Lowth.) Mr. Lane (*Modern Egyptians*, vol. i. p. 199) describes an annual ceremony which may serve to illustrate this passage:—' A considerable number of Durweeshes, says he (I am sure there were not less than sixty, but I could not count their number), laid themselves down upon the ground, side by side, as close as possible to each other, having their backs

upwards, having their legs extended, and their arms placed together beneath their foreheads. When the Sheikh approached, his horse hesitated several minutes to step upon the back of the first prostrate man ; but being pulled and urged on

CEREMONY OF THE DOSEH OR TREADING.—From Lane's Modern Egyptians.

behind, he at length stepped upon them; and then without apparent fear, ambled with a high pace over them all, led by two persons, who ran over the prostrate men, one sometimes treading on the feet, and the other on the heads. Not one of the men thus trampled on by the horse seemed to be hurt ; but each the moment that the animal had passed over him, jumped up and followed the Sheikh. Each of them received two treads from the horse, one from one of his fore-legs, and a second from a hind-leg.' It seems probable that this is a relic of an ancient usage alluded to in the Bible, in which captives were made to lie down on the ground, and the conqueror rode insultingly over them. ¶ *Thou hast laid thy body as the ground.*

That is, you were utterly humbled and prostrated (comp. Ps. lxvi. 11, 12). From all this, however, the promise is, that they should be rescued and delivered. The account of their deliverance is contained in the following chapter (ch. lii. 1–12); and the assurance of rescue is there made more cheering and glorious by directing the eye forward to the coming of the Messiah (ch. lii. 13–15; liii. 1–12), and to the glorious results which would follow from his advent (ch. liv. *sq.*) These chapters are all connected, and they should be read continuously. Material injury is done to the sense by the manner in which the division is made, if indeed any division should have been made at all.

CHAPTER LII.

ANALYSIS.

This chapter is intimately connected with the preceding, and, with that, constitutes one connected portion (see the analysis of chapter li.) This portion, however, extends only to ver. 13 of this chapter, where there commences a prophecy extending through ch. liii., relating solely to the Messiah, and constituting the most important and interesting part of the Old Testament. In this chapter, the object is to console the pious part of the Jewish community. The general topic is, the promise of a rich blessing, first at the deliverance from the captivity at Babylon, and then, in a more complete sense, at the coming of the Messiah. The chapter comprises the following topics:—

1. Jerusalem, long in bondage, is called on to arise and shake herself from the dust, and to put on her beautiful garments (1, 2). She is addressed in accordance with language that is common in Isaiah, and the other prophets, as a female sitting on the ground, covered with dust, and mourning over her desolations.

2. JEHOVAH expressly promises to deliver his people from their captivity and bondage (3–6). In stating this, he says (3), that they had sold themselves for nothing, and should be redeemed without money; he appeals to the fact that he had delivered them from Egyptian oppression in former years, and that he was as able to deliver them now (4); and he says (5, 6), that he would have compassion on them now that they were suffering under their grievous bondage, and would furnish them with the most ample demonstration that he alone was God.

3. The prophet, in vision, sees the messenger on the mountains that comes to proclaim restoration to Zion (7, 8). He speaks of the beauty of the feet of him who bears the glad message (7); and says that when that messenger is seen bearing the glad tidings, 'the watchman' should join in the exultation (8).

4. Jerusalem, and all the waste and desolate regions of Judea, are called on to break out into singing at the glad and glorious events which would occur when the people of God should be again restored (9, 10).

5. In view of all this, the people are called on to depart from Babylon, and to return to their own land (11, 12). They were to go out pure. They were not to contaminate themselves with the polluted objects of idolatry. They were about to bear back again to Jerusalem the consecrated vessels of the house of JEHOVAH, and they should be clean and holy. They should not go out with haste, as if driven out, but they would go defended by JEHOVAH, and conducted by him to their own land.

6. At ver. 13, the subject and the scene changes. The eye of the prophet becomes fixed on that greater future event to which the deliverance from Babylon was preparatory, and the whole attention becomes absorbed in the person, the manner of life, and the work of the Messiah. This part of the chapter (13–15), is an essential part of the prophecy which is continued through ch. liii., and should by no means have been separated from it. In this portion of the prophecy, all reference to the captivity at Babylon ceases; and the eye of the prophet is fixed, without vacillating, on the person of the Redeemer. In no other portion of the Old Testament is there so clear and sublime a description of the Messiah as is furnished here; and no other portion demands so profoundly and prayerfully the attention of those who would understand the great mystery of redeeming mercy and love.

A WAKE, awake ; put on thy strength, O Zion ; put on thy beautiful garments, O Jerusalem, the holy ^{a} city : for ^{b} henceforth there shall no more come unto thee the uncircumcised and the unclean.

a Ne.11.1; Re.21.2,27.   b Na.1.15.

CHAPTER LII.

1. *Awake, awake* (see Notes on ch. li. 9). This address to Jerusalem is intimately connected with the closing verses of the preceding chapter. Jerusalem is there represented as down-trodden in the dust before her enemies. Here she is described under the image of a female that had been clad in the habiliments of mourning, and she is now called on to arise from this condition, and to put on the garments that would be indicative of gladness and of joy. The idea is, that the time had come now in which she was to be delivered from her long captivity, and was to be restored to her ormer prosperity and splendour. ¶ *Put on thy strength.* Heb. ' Clothe thyself with thy strength.' The idea is, exert thyself, be strong, bold, confident ; arise from thy dejection, and become courageous as one does when he is about to engage in an enterprise that promises success, and that demands effort. ¶ *Put*

2 Shake ^c thyself from the dust ; loose thyself from the bands of thy arise, *and* sit down, O Jerusalem : neck, O captive daughter of Zion.

^a Zec.2.7.

on thy beautiful garments. Jerusalem is here addressed, as she often is, as a female (see Note on ch. i. 8). She was to lay aside the garments expressive of grief and of captivity, and deck herself with those which were appropriate to a state of prosperity. ¶ *The uncircumcised and the unclean.* The idea is, that those only should enter Jerusalem and dwell there who would be worshippers of the true God. The uncircumcised are emblems of the impure, the unconverted, and the idolatrous ; and the meaning is, that in future times the church would be pure and holy. It cannot mean that *no* uncircumcised man or idolater would ever again enter the city of Jerusalem, for this would not be true. It was a fact that Antiochus and his armies, and Titus and his army entered Jerusalem, and undoubtedly hosts of others did also who were not circumcised. But this refers to the future times, when the church of God would be pure. Its members would, in the main, be possessors of the true religion, and would adorn it. Probably, therefore, the view of the prophet extended to the purer and happier times under the Messiah, when the church should be characteristically and eminently holy, and when, as a great law of that church, none should be admitted, who did not profess that they were converted.

2. *Shake thyself from the dust.* To sit on the ground, to sit in the dust, is an expression descriptive of mourning (Job ii. 13). Jerusalem is here called on to arise and shake off the dust, as indicating that the days of her grief were ended, and that she was about to be restored to her former beauty and splendour. ¶ *Arise* and *sit down.* There is an incongruity in this expression in our translation, which does not occur in the original. The idea in the Hebrew is not that which seems to be implied in this expression to arise and sit down in *the same place,* but it means to arise from the dust, and sit in a more elevated, or honourable place. She had been represented as sitting on the earth, where her loose flowing robes would be supposed to become covered with dust. She is here called on to arise from that humble condition, and to occupy the divan, or a chair of dignity and honour. Lowth renders this, 'Ascend thy lofty seat,' and supposes it means that she was to occupy a throne, or an elevated seat of honour, and he quotes oriental customs to justify this interpretation. Noyes renders it, 'Arise and sit erect.' The Chaldee renders it, 'Rise, sit upon the throne of thy glory.' The following quotation, from Jowett's *Christian Researches,* will explain the custom which is here alluded to: 'It is no uncommon thing to see an individual, or group of persons, even when very well dressed, sitting with their feet drawn under them, upon the bare earth, passing whole hours in idle conversation. Europeans would require a chair, but the natives here prefer the ground. In the heat of summer and autumn, it is pleasant to them to while away their time in this manner, under the shade of a tree. Richly adorned females, as well as men, may often be seen thus amusing themselves. As may naturally be expected, with whatever care they may, at first sitting down, choose their place, yet the flowing dress by degrees gathers up the dust ; as this occurs, they, from time to time, arise, adjust themselves, shake off the dust, and then sit down again. The captive daughter of Zion, therefore, brought down to the dust of suffering and oppression, is commanded to arise and shake herself from that dust, and then, with grace, and dignity, and composure, and security, to *sit down;* to take, as it were, again her seat and her rank, amid the company of the nations of the earth, which had before afflicted her, and trampled her to the earth.' ¶ *Loose thyself from the bands of thy neck.* Jerusalem had been a captive, and confined as a prisoner. She is now called on to cast off these chains from her neck, and to be again at liberty. In captivity, chains or bands were attached to various parts of the body. They were usually affixed to the wrists or ankles, but it would seem also that

3 For thus saith the Lord, Ye have sold *a* yourselves for nought; and ye shall be redeemed without money.

4 For thus saith the Lord God,

a Ro.7.14-25.

sometimes collars were affixed to the neck. The idea is, that the Jews, who had been so long held captive, were about to be released, and restored to their own land.

3. *Ye have sold yourselves for nought.* You became captives and prisoners without any price being paid for you. You *cost* nothing to those who made you prisoners. The idea is, that as they who had made them prisoners had done so without paying any price for them, it was equitable that they should be released in the same manner. When their captors had paid nothing for them, God would suffer nothing to be paid for them in turn; and they should be released, as they had been sold, without a price paid for them. Perhaps God intends here to reproach them for selling themselves in this manner without *any* compensation of any kind, and to show them the folly of it; but, at the same time, he intends to assure them that no price would be paid for their ransom. ¶ *Ye shall be redeemed.* You shall be delivered from your long and painful captivity without any price being paid to the Babylonians. This was to be a remarkable proof of the power of God. Men do not usually give up captives and slaves, in whatever way they may have taken them, without demanding a price or ransom. But here God says that he designs to effect their deliverance without any such price being demanded or paid, and that as they had gone into captivity unpurchased, so they should return unpurchased. Accordingly he so overruled events as completely to effect this. The Babylonians, perhaps, in no way could have been induced to surrender them. God, therefore, designed to raise up Cyrus, a mild, just, and equitable prince; and to dispose him to suffer the exiles to depart, and to aid them in their return to their own land. In this way, they were rescued without money and without price, by the interposition of another.

4. *For thus saith the Lord God.* In

My people went down aforetime into Egypt to sojourn there; and the Assyrians oppressed them without cause.

order to show them that he could redeem them without money, God reminds them of what had been done in former times. The numerous captives in Egypt, whose services were so valuable to the Egyptians, and whom the Egyptians were so unwilling to suffer to depart, he had rescued by his own power, and had delivered for ever from that bondage. The idea here is, that with the same ease he could rescue the captives in Babylon, and restore them to their own land without a price. ¶ *My people went down.* That is, Jacob and his sons. The phrase 'went down,' is applied to a journey to Egypt, because Judea was a mountainous and elevated country compared with Egypt, and a journey there was in fact *a descent* to a more level and lower country. ¶ *To sojourn there.* Not to dwell there permanently, but to remain there only for a time. They went in fact only to remain until the severity of the famine should have passed by, and until they could return with safety to the land of Canaan. ¶ *And the Assyrians oppressed them without cause.* A considerable variety has existed in the interpretation of this passage. The LXX. render it, 'And to the Assyrians they were carried by force.' Some have supposed that this refers to the oppressions that they experienced in Egypt, and that the name 'Assyrian' is here given to Pharaoh. So Forerius and Cajetan understand it. They suppose that the name, ''the Assyrian,' became, in the apprehension of the Jews, the common name of that which was proud, oppressive, and haughty, and might therefore be used to designate Pharaoh. But there are insuperable objections to this. For the name 'the Assyrian' is not elsewhere given to Pharaoh in the Scriptures, nor can it be supposed to be given to him but with great impropriety. It is not true that Pharaoh was an Assyrian; nor is it true that the Israelites were oppressed by the Assyrians while they remained in Egypt. Others have supposed that this refers to Nebuchadnezzar

5 Now, therefore, what have I here, saith the LORD, that my people is taken away for nought? they that rule over them make them to howl, saith the LORD; that my name continually every day [a] is blasphemed.

a Ro.2.24.

and the Chaldeans in general, and that the name 'the Assyrian' is given them in a large and general sense, as ruling over that which constituted the empire of Assyria, and that the prophet here refers to the calamities which they were suffering in Babylon. But the objection to this is not the less decisive. It is true that Babylon was formerly a part or province of Assyria, and true also that in the time of the Jewish captivity it was the capital of the kingdom of which the former empire of Assyria became a subject province. But the name Babylonian, in the Scriptures, is kept distinct from that of Assyrian, and they are not used interchangeably. Nor does the connection of the passage require us to understand it in this sense. The whole passage is in a high degree elliptical, and something must be supplied to make out the sense. The general design of it is, to show that God would certainly deliver the Jews from the captivity at Babylon without money. For this purpose, the prophet appeals to the former instances of his interposition when deliverance had been effected in that way. A *paraphrase* of the passage, and a filling up of the parts which are omitted in the brief and abrupt manner of the prophet, will show the sense. 'Ye have been sold for nought, and ye shall be ransomed without price. As a proof that I can do it, and will do it, remember that my people went down formerly to Egypt, and designed to sojourn there for a little time, and that they were there reduced to slavery, and oppressed by Pharaoh, but that I ransomed them without money, and brought them forth by my own power. Remember, further, how often the Assyrian has oppressed them also, without cause. Remember the history of Sennacherib, Tiglath-pileser, and Salmaneser, and how they have laid the land waste, and remember also how I have delivered it from these oppressions. With the same certainty, and the same ease, I can deliver the people from the captivity at Babylon.' The prophet, therefore, refers to different periods and events; and the idea is, that God had delivered them when they had been oppressed *alike* by the Egyptian, and by the Assyrians, and that he who had so often interposed would also rescue them from their oppression in Babylon.

5. *Now, therefore, what have I here?* In Babylon, referring to the captivity of the Jews there. The idea is, that a state of things existed there which demanded his interposition as really as it did when his people had been oppressed by the Egyptians, or by the Assyrian. His people had been taken away for nought; they were subject to cruel oppressions; and his own name was continually blasphemed. In this state of things, it is inferred, that he would certainly come to their rescue, and that his own perfections as well as their welfare demanded that he should interpose to redeem them. The phrase, 'what have I here?' is equivalent to saying, what shall I do? what am I properly called on to do? or what reason is there now in Babylon for my interposition to rescue my people? It is implied, that such was the state of things, that God felt that there was something that demanded his interposition. ¶ *That my people is taken away for nought.* This was one thing existing in Babylon that demanded his interposition. His people had been made captive by the Chaldeans, and were now suffering under their oppressions. This had been done 'for nought;' that is, it had been done without any just claim. It was on their part a mere act of gross and severe oppression, and this demanded the interposition of a righteous God. ¶ *They that rule over them make them to howl.* Lowth renders this, 'They that are lords over them make their boast of it.' Noyes renders it, 'And their tyrants exult.' The LXX. render it, 'My people are taken away for nought: wonder ye, and raise a mournful cry' (ὀλολύζετε). Jerome renders it, 'Their lords act unjustly, and they therefore howl when they are de-

6 Therefore my people shall know my name: therefore *they shall know* in that day that I *am* he that doth speak : behold, *it is* I.

7 How beautiful *a* upon the mountains *b* are the feet of him that bring-

eth good tidings, that publisheth peace : that bringeth good tidings of *c* good, that publisheth salvation; that saith unto Zion, Thy God reigneth !

a Na.1.15; Ro.10.15. *b* ch.25.6,7; Ca.2.8. *c* Lu.2.10,11.

livered to torments.' Aben Ezra supposes that by 'their lords' here, or those who rule over them, are meant the rulers of the Jewish people, and that the idea is, that they lament and howl over the calamities and oppressions of the people. But it is probable, after all, that our translators have given the true sense of the text, and that the idea is, that they were suffering such grievous oppressions in Babylon as to make them lift up the cry of lamentation and of grief. This was a reason why God should interpose as he had done in former times, and bring deliverance. ¶ *And my name continually every day is blasphemed.* That is, in Babylon. The proud and oppressive Babylonians delight to add to the sorrows of the exiles by reproaching the name of their God, and by saying that he was unable to defend them and their city from ruin. This is the third reason why God would interpose to rescue them. The three reasons in this verse are, that they had been taken away for nought ; that they were suffering grievous and painful oppression ; and that the name of God was reproached. On all these accounts he felt that he *had* something to do in Babylon, and that his interposition was demanded.

6. *Therefore my people shall know my name.* The idea in this verse is, that his people should have such exhibitions of his power as to furnish to them demonstration that he was God.

7. *How beautiful upon the mountains.* This passage is applied by Paul to the ministers of the gospel (see Rom. x. 15). The meaning here seems to be this : Isaiah was describing the certain return of the Jews to their own land. He sees in vision the heralds announcing their return to Jerusalem running on the distant hills. A herald bearing good news is a beautiful object ; and he says that his feet are beautiful ; *i.e.,* his *running* is beautiful. He came to declare that the long and painful captivity was closed,

and that the holy city and its temple were again to rise with splendour, and that peace and plenty and joy were to be spread over the land. Such a messenger coming with haste, the prophet says, would be a beautiful object. Some have supposed (*see* Campbell *on the Gospels,* Diss. v. p. 11, § 3, 4), that the idea here is, that *the feet* of messengers when they travelled in the dust were naturally offensive and disgusting, but that the messenger of peace and prosperity to those who had been oppressed and afflicted by the ravages of war, was so charming as to transform a most disagreeable into a pleasing object. But I cannot see any such allusion here. It is true that the feet of those who had travelled far in dry and dusty roads would present a spectacle offensive to the beholder ; and it is true also, as Dr. Campbell suggests, that the consideration that they who were coming were messengers of peace and safety would convert deformity into beauty, and make us behold with delight this indication of their embassy. But it seems to me that this passage has much higher beauty. The idea in the mind of the prophet is not, that the messenger is *so near* that the sordid appearance of his feet could be seen. The beholder is supposed to be standing amidst the ruins of the desolated city, and the messenger is seen *running* on the distant hills. The long anticipated herald announcing that these ruins are to rise, at length appears. Seen on the distant hills, running rapidly, he is a beautiful object. It is his feet, his *running,* his haste, that attracts attention ; an indication that he bears a message of joy, and that the nation is about to be restored. Nahum, who is supposed to have lived after Isaiah, has evidently copied from him this beautiful image :—

Behold upon the mountains the feet of the joyful messenger,
Of him that announceth peace;

8 Thy watchmen shall lift up the voice ; with the voice together shall they sing ; for they shall see *a* eye to eye, when the LORD shall bring again Zion.

a 1 Cor.13.12.

Celebrate, O Judah, thy festivals: perform thy vows;
For no more shall pass through thee the wicked one;
He is utterly cut off.   Nah. i. 15.

¶ *That publisheth peace.* This declaration is *general*, that the coming of such a messenger would be attended with joy. The particular and special idea here is, that it would be a joyful announcement that this captivity was ended, and that Zion was about to be restored. ¶ *That bringeth good tidings of good.* He announces that which is good or which is a joyful message. ¶ *That saith unto Zion, thy God reigneth.* That is, thy God has delivered the people from their captivity, and is about to reign again in Zion. This was applied at first to the return from the captivity. Paul, as has been already observed, applies it to the ministers of the gospel. That is, it is language which will well express the nature of the message which the ministers of the gospel bear to their fellow-men. The sense is here, that the coming of a messenger bringing good tidings is universally agreeable to men. And if the coming of a messenger announcing that peace is made, is pleasant; or if the coming of such a messenger declaring that the captivity at Babylon was ended, was delightful, how much more so should be the coming of the herald announcing that man may be at peace with his Maker ?

8. *Thy watchmen.* This language is taken from the custom of placing watchmen on the walls of a city, or on elevated towers, who could see if an enemy approached, and who of course would be the first to discern a messenger at a distance who was coming to announce good news. The idea is, that there would be as great joy at the announcement of the return of the exiles, *as if* they who were stationed on the wall should see the long-expected herald on the distant hills, coming to announce that they were about to return, and that the city and temple were about to be rebuilt. It was originally applicable to the return from Babylon. But it con-

tains also the *general* truth that they who are appointed to watch over Zion and its interests, will rejoice at all the tokens of God's favour to his people, and especially when he comes to bless them after long times of darkness, depression, and calamity. It is by no means, therefore, departing from the spirit of this passage, to apply it to the joy of the ministers of religion in the visits of Divine mercy to a church and people. ¶ *Shall lift up the voice.* That is, with rejoicing. ¶ *With the voice together shall they sing.* They shall mingle their praises and thanksgivings. The idea is, that all who are appointed to guard Zion, should feel a common interest in her welfare, and rejoice when the Lord comes to visit and bless his people. The Hebrew here is more abrupt and emphatic than our common translation would make it. It is literally, ' The voice of thy watchmen ! They lift up the voice together ; they sing '—as if the prophet suddenly heard a shout. It is the exulting shout of the watchmen of Zion ; and it comes as *one* voice, with no discord, no jarring. ¶ *For they shall see eye to eye.* Lowth renders this, ' For face to face shall they see.' Noyes, ' For with their own eyes shall they behold.' Jerome renders it, *Oculo ad oculum*— ' Eye to eye.' The LXX. render it, 'Οφθαλμοὶ πρὸς ὀφθαλμοὺς, κ.τ.λ.—' Eyes shall look to eyes when the Lord shall have mercy upon Zion.' Interpreters have been divided in regard to its meaning. The sense may be, either that they shall see face to face, *i.e.*, distinctly, clearly, as when one is near another; or it may mean that they shall be *united* —they shall contemplate the same object, or look steadily at the same thing. Rosenmüller, Gesenius, Forerius, Junius, and some others, understand it in the former sense. So the Chaldee, ' For they shall see with their own eyes the great things which the Lord will do when he shall bring back his own glory to Zion.' The phrase in Hebrew occurs in no other place, except in Num. xiv. 14, which our translators have rendered,

9 Break forth into joy, sing together, ye waste places of Jerusalem : for the LORD hath comforted
his people, he hath redeemed Jerusalem.

a Ps.98.2,3.

10 The *a* LORD hath made bare
his holy arm in the eyes of all the
nations ; and all *b* the ends of the
earth shall see the salvation of our
God.

b Lu.3.6.

' For thou, LORD, art seen *face to face.*'
Heb. 'Eye to eye;' that is, near, openly,
manifestly, without any veil or interposing medium. The expression, 'face to
face,' meaning openly, plainly, manifestly, as one sees who is close to another,
occurs frequently in the Bible (see Gen.
xxxii. 30; Ex. xxxiii. 11; Deut. v. 4;
xxxiv. 10; Judg. vi. 22; Prov. xxvii. 19;
Ezek. xxx. 35; Acts xxv. 16; 1 Cor.
xiii. 12; 2 John 12; 3 John 14). So
the phrase, 'mouth to mouth,' occurs
in a similar sense (Num. xii. 8). And
there can be but little doubt, it seems
to me, that this is the sense here, and
that the prophet means to say, that the
great and marvellous doings of JEHOVAH
would be seen openly and manifestly,
and that the watchmen would thence
have occasion to rejoice. Another reason
for this opinion, besides the fact that it
accords with the common usage, is, that
the phrase, 'to see eye to eye,' in the
sense of being united and harmonious,
is not very intelligible. It is not easy
to form an image or conception of the
watchman in this attitude as denoting
harmony. To look into the eyes of
each other does not of necessity denote
harmony, for men oftentimes do this for
other purposes. The idea therefore is,
that when JEHOVAH should bring back
and bless his people, the watchmen
would have a full and glorious exhibition
of his mercy and goodness, and the result would be, that they would greatly
rejoice, and unitedly celebrate his name.
According to this interpretation, it does
not mean that the ministers of religion
would have the same precise views, or
embrace the same doctrines, however
true this may be, or however desirable
in itself, but that they would have an
open, clear, and bright manifestation of
the presence of God, and would lift up
their voices together with exultation
and praise. ¶ *When the Lord shall
bring again Zion.* Zion here denotes
the people who dwelt in Jerusalem; and
the idea is, when the Lord shall again

restore them to their own land. It is
not a departure from the sense of the
passage, however, to apply it in a more
general manner, and to use it as demonstrating that any signal interposition of
God in favour of his people should be
the occasion of joy, and shall lead the
ministers of religion to exult in God,
and to praise his name.

9. *Break forth into joy.* Jerusalem,
at the time here referred to, was lying
waste and in ruins. This call on the
waste places of Jerusalem to break out
into expressions of praise, is in accordance with a style which frequently occurs in Isaiah, and in other sacred
writers, by which inanimate objects are
called on to manifest their joy (see Notes
on ch. xiv. 7, 8; xlii. 11). ¶ *For the
LORD hath comforted his people.* That is,
he *does* comfort his people, and redeem
them. This is seen by the prophet in
vision, and to his view it is represented
as if it were passing before his eyes.
¶ *He hath redeemed Jerusalem.* On
the meaning of the word 'redeemed,'
see Notes on ch. xliii. 1–3. The idea
here is, that JEHOVAH was about to
restore his people from their long captivity, and again to cause Jerusalem to
be rebuilt.

10. *The LORD hath made bare his
holy arm.* That is, in delivering his
people from bondage. This metaphor
is taken from warriors, who made bare
the arm for battle; and the sense is,
that God had come to the rescue of his
people as a warrior, and that his interpositions would be seen and recognized
and acknowledged by all the nations. The
metaphor is derived from the manner in
which the Orientals dressed. The following extract from Jowett's *Christian
Researches* will explain the language :
—'The loose sleeve of the Arab shirt,
as well as that of the outer garment,
leaves the arm so completely free, that
in an instant the left hand passing up
the right arm makes it bare; and this
is done when a person, a soldier, for ex-

11 Depart ^aye, depart ye, go ye
out from thence, touch ^bno unclean
thing; go ye out of the midst of

her; be ^cye clean, that bear the
vessels of the LORD.

a Zec.2.6,7; 2Co.6.17; Re.18.4.
b Le.15.5,&c.; Hag.2.13.   *c* Le.22.2,&c.

ample, about to strike with the sword,
intends to give the arm full play. The
image represents JEHOVAH as suddenly
prepared to inflict some tremendous, yet
righteous judgment, so effectual "that
all the ends of the earth shall see the
salvation of God."' The phrase '*holy
arm,*' seems to mean that God would be
engaged in a holy and just cause. It
would not be an arm of conquest, or of
oppression; but it would be made bare
in a holy cause, and all its inflictions
would be righteous. ¶ *And all the ends
of the earth.* For an explanation of the
phrase 'the ends of the earth,' see Notes
on ch. xl. 28. The meaning here is,
that the deliverance of his people referred
to would be so remarkable as to be conspicuous to all the world. The most
distant nations would see it, and would
be constrained to recognize his hand.
It was fulfilled in the rescue of the nation
from the captivity at Babylon. The
conquest of Babylon was an event that
was so momentous in its consequences,
as to be known to all the kingdoms of
the earth; and the proclamation of Cyrus
(Ezra i. 1, 2), and the consequent restoration of his people to their own land,
were calculated to make the name of
JEHOVAH known to all nations.

11. *Depart ye, depart ye.* This is a
direct address to the exiles in their captivity. The same command occurs in
ch. xlviii. 20 (see Notes on that place).
It is *repeated* here for the sake of emphasis; and the urgency of the command
implies that there was some delay likely
to be apprehended on the part of the
exiles themselves. The fact seems to
have been, that though the captivity
was at first attended with every circumstance fitted to give pain, and though
they were subjected to *many* privations
and sorrows in Babylon (see Ps. cxxxvii.),
yet that many of them became strongly
attached to a residence there, and were
strongly indisposed to return. They
were there seventy years. Most of those
who were made captive would have died
before the close of the exile. Their
children, who constituted the generation

to whom the command to return would
be addressed, would have known the
land of their fathers only by report. It
was a distant land; and was to be
reached only by a long and perilous
journey across a pathless desert. They
had been born in Babylon. It was their
home; and there were the graves of their
parents and kindred. Some had been
advanced to posts of office and honour:
many, it is probable, had lands, and
friends, and property in Babylon. The
consequence would, therefore, be, that
there would be strong reluctance on
their part to leave the country of their
exile, and to encounter the perils and
trials incident to a return to their own
land. It is not improbable, also, that
many of them may have formed improper connections and attachments in that
distant land, and that they would be
unwilling to relinquish them, and return
to the land of their fathers. It was
necessary, therefore, that the most urgent
commands should be addressed to them,
and the strongest motives presented to
them, to induce them to return to the
country of their fathers. And after all,
it is evident that but comparatively a
small portion of the exile Jews ever were
prevailed on to leave Babylon, and to
adventure upon the perilous journey of
a return to Zion. ¶ *Touch no unclean*
thing. Separate yourselves wholly from
an idolatrous nation, and preserve yourselves pure. The apostle Paul (2 Cor.
vi. 17, 18) has applied this to Christians, and uses it as expressing the
obligation to come out from the world,
and to be separate from all its influences.
Babylon is regarded by the apostle as
not an unapt emblem of the world, and
the command to come out from her as
not an improper expression of the obligation to the friends of the Redeemer
to be separate from all that is evil.
John (Rev. xviii. 4) has applied this
passage also to denote the duty of true
Christians to separate themselves from
the mystical Babylon—the papal community—and not to be partaker of her
sins. The passage is applied in both

12 For ye shall not go out with haste, nor go by flight: for the LORD will go before you; and the God of Israel [1] *will be* your rereward.

1 *gather you up.*

these instances, because Babylon, in Scripture language, is regarded as emblematic of whatever is oppressive, proud, arrogant, persecuting, impure, and abominable. ¶ *That bear the vessels of the* LORD. That bear again to your own land the sacred vessels of the sanctuary. It is to be remembered that when the Jews were taken to Babylon, Nebuchadnezzar carried there all the sacred utensils of the temple, and that they were used in their festivals as common vessels in Babylon (2 Chron. xxxvii. 18; Dan. v. 2–5). These vessels Cyrus commanded to be again restored, when the exiles returned to their own land (Ezra i. 7–11). They whose office it was to carry them, were the priests and Levites (Num. i. 50; iv. 15); and the command here pertains particularly to them. They were required to be holy; to feel the importance of their office, and to be separate from all that is evil. The passage has no original reference to ministers of the gospel, but the *principle* is implied that they who are appointed to serve God as his ministers in any way should be pure and holy.

12. *For ye shall not go out with haste.* As if driven out, or compelled to flee. You shall not go from Babylon as your fathers went from Egypt, in a rapid flight, and in a confused and tumultuous manner (see Deut. xvi. 3). The idea here is, that they should have time to prepare themselves to go out, and to become fit to bear the vessels of the Lord. It was a fact that when they left Babylon they did it with the utmost deliberation, and had ample time to make any preparation that was necessary. ¶ *For the* LORD *will go before you.* JEHOVAH will conduct you, as a general advances at the head of an army. The figure here is taken from the march of an army, and the image is that of JEHOVAH as the leader or head of the host in the march through the desert between Babylon and Jerusalem (see Notes on ch. xl. 3, 4). ¶ *And the God of Israel* will be *your rereward.* Marg. 'Gather you up.' The Hebrew word used here (אָסַף)

means properly *to collect,* to gather together, as fruits, &c. It is then applied to the act of bringing up the rear of an army; and means to be a rear-ward, or guard, *agmen claudere*—as collecting, and bringing together the stragglers, and defending the army in its march, from an attack in the rear. The LXX. render it, ' The God of Israel is he who collects you ' (ὁ ἐπισυνάγων ὑμᾶς), *i.e.,* brings up the rear. The Chaldee, ' The God of Israel will collect together your captivity.'—Here the chapter should have closed, for here closes the account of the return of the exiles from Babylon. The mind of the prophet seems here to leave the captive Jews on their way to their own land, with JEHOVAH going at their head, and guarding the rear of the returning band, and to have passed to the contemplation of him of whose coming all these events were preliminary and introductory—the Messiah. *Perhaps* the *rationale* of this apparent transition is this. It is undoubtedly the doctrine of the Bible that he who was revealed as the guide of his people in ancient times, and who appeared under various names, as 'the angel of JEHOVAH,' 'the angel of the covenant,' &c., was he who afterwards became incarnate —the Saviour of the world. So the prophet seems to have regarded him; and here fixing his attention on the JEHOVAH who was thus to guide his people and be their defence, by an easy transition the mind is carried forward to the time when he would be incarnate, and would die for men. Leaving, therefore, so to speak, the contemplation of him as conducting his people across the barren wastes which separated Babylon from Judea, the mind is, by no unnatural transition, carried forward to the time when he would become a man of sorrows, and would redeem and save the world. According to this supposition, it is the same glorious Being whom Isaiah sees as the protector of his people, and almost in the same instant as the man of sorrows; and the contemplation of him as the suffering Messiah becomes so absorbing and intense, that he ab-

CHAPTERS LII. 13–15; LIII.

THE most important portion of Isaiah, and of the Old Testament, commences here, and here should have been the beginning of a new chapter. It is the description of the suffering Messiah, and is continued to the close of the next chapter. As the closing verses of this chapter are connected with the following chapter, and as it is of great importance to have just views of the design of this portion of Isaiah, it is proper in this place to give an analysis of this part of the prophecy. And as no other part of the Bible has excited so much the attention of the friends and foes of Christianity; as so various and conflicting views have prevailed in regard to its meaning: and as the proper interpretation of the passage must have an important bearing on the controversy with Jews and infidels, and on the practical views of Christians, I shall be justified in going into an examination of its meaning at considerably greater length than has been deemed necessary in other portions of the prophecy. It may be remarked in general—(1.) That if the common interpretation of the passage, as describing a suffering Saviour, be correct, then it settles the controversy with the *Jews*, and demonstrates that *their* notions of the Messiah are false. (2.) If this was written at the time when it is claimed by Christians to have been written, then it settles the controversy with infidels. The description is so particular and minute; the correspondence with the life, the character, and the death of the Lord Jesus, is so complete, that it *could* not have been the result of conjecture or accident. At the same time, it is a correspondence which could not have been brought about by an impostor who meant to avail himself of this ancient prophecy to promote his designs; for a large portion of the circumstances are such as *did not depend on himself*, but grew out of the feelings and purposes of others. *On the supposition that this had been found as an ancient prophecy, it would have been impossible for any impostor so to have shaped the course of events as to have made his character and life appear to be a fulfilment of it.* And unless the infidel could either make it out that this pro-

phecy was not in existence, or that, being in existence, it was possible for a deceiver *to create* an exact coincidence between it and his life and character and death, then, in all honesty, he should admit that it was given by inspiration, and that the Bible is true. (3.) A correct exposition of this will be of inestimable value in giving to the Christian just views of the atonement, and of the whole doctrine of redemption. Probably in no portion of the Bible of the same length, not even in the New Testament, is there to be found so clear an exhibition of the purpose for which the Saviour died. I shall endeavour, therefore, to prepare the way for an exposition of the passage, by a consideration of several points that are necessary to a correct understanding of it.

§ 1. *Evidence that it was written before the birth of Jesus of Nazareth.*

On this point there will be, and can be, no dispute among Jews and Christians. The general argument to prove this, is the same as that which demonstrates that Isaiah wrote at all before that time. For a view of this, the reader is referred to the Introduction. But this general argument may be presented in a more specific form, and includes the following particulars:— (1.) It is quoted in the New Testament as part of the prophetic writings then well known (see Matt. viii. 17; John xii. 38; Acts viii. 28–35; Rom. x. 16; 1 Pet. ii. 21–25). That the passage was in existence at the time when the New Testament was written, is manifest from these quotations. So far as the argument with the infidel is concerned, it is immaterial whether it was written 700 years before the events took place, or only fifty, or ten. It would still be prophecy, and it would still be incumbent on him to show how it came to be so accurately accomplished. (2.) It is quoted and translated by writers who undoubtedly lived before the Christian era. Thus, it is found in the Septuagint, and in the Chaldee—both of which can be demonstrated to have been made before Christ was born. (3.) There is not the slightest evidence that it has been interpolated or corrupted, or changed so as to adapt it to the Lord Jesus. It is the same in all copies, and in all versions. (4.) It has never

---

ruptly closes the description of him as the guide of the exiles to their own land. He sees him as a sufferer. He sees the manner and the design of his death. He contemplates the certain result of that humiliation and death in the spread of the true religion, and in the extension of his kingdom among men. Hencefor-

ward, therefore, to the end of Isaiah, we meet with no reference, if we except in a very few instances, to the condition of the exiles in Babylon, or to their return to their own land. The mind of the prophet is absorbed in describing the glories of the Messiah, and the certain spread of his gospel around the globe.

even been pretended that it has been introduced for the purpose of furnishing an argument for the truth of Christianity. No infidel has ever pretended that it does not stand on the same footing as any other portion of Isaiah. (5.) It is such a passage as Jews *would* not have forged. It is opposed to all their prevailing notions of the Messiah. They have anticipated a magnificent temporal prince and a conqueror: and one of the main reasons why they have rejected the Lord Jesus has been, that he was obscure in his origin, poor, despised, and put to death; in other words, because he has corresponded so entirely with the description here. No passage of the Old Testament has ever given them greater perplexity than this, and it is morally certain that if the Jews had ever forged a pretended prophecy of the Messiah, it would not have been in the language of this portion of Isaiah. They would have described him as the magnificent successor of David and Solomon; as a mighty prince and a warrior; as the head of universal empire, and would have said that by his victorious arms he would subdue the earth to himself, and would make Jerusalem the capital of the world. They never would have described him as despised and rejected of men, and as making his grave with the wicked in his death. (6.) Christians *could* not have forged and interpolated this. The Jews have always jealously guarded their own Scriptures; and nothing would have so certainly excited their attention as an attempt to interpolate a passage like this, furnishing at once an irrefragable argument against their opinions of the Messiah, and so obviously applicable to Jesus of Nazareth. It is, moreover, true, that no Jewish writer has ever pretended that the passage has either been forged, or changed in any way, so as to accommodate it to the opinions of Christians respecting the Messiah. These remarks may seem to be unnecessary, and this argument useless, to those who have examined the authenticity of the sacred writings. They are of use only in the argument with the enemies of Christianity. For, if this passage was written at the time when it is supposed to have been, and if it had reference to the Lord Jesus, then it demonstrates that Isaiah was inspired, and furnishes an argument for the truth of revelation which is irrefragable. It is incumbent on the unbeliever to destroy all the alleged proofs that it was written by Isaiah, or, as an honest man, he should admit the truth of inspiration and of prophecy, and yield his heart to the influence of the truth of the Bible. In general, it may be observed, that an attempt to destroy the credibility of this portion of Isaiah as having been written several

hundred years before the Christian era, would destroy the credibility of all the ancient writings; and that we have *as much* evidence that this is the production of Isaiah, as we have of the credibility or the authenticity of the writings of Homer or Herodotus.

§ 2. *History of the interpretation of the passage by the Jews.*

In order to a clear understanding of the passage, it is proper to give a summary view of the modes of interpretation which have prevailed in regard to it both among Jews and Christians. For this historical view, I am indebted mainly to Hengstenberg, *Chris.* i. p. 484, *sq.* The several opinions which have prevailed among the Jewish expositors are the following:—

There is the fullest evidence that the passage was applied by the early Jews, both before and after the birth of Jesus, to the Messiah, until they were pressed by its application to Jesus of Nazareth, and were compelled in self-defence to adopt some other mode of interpretation; and even after that, it is evident, also, that not a few of the better and more pious portion of the Jewish nation still continued to regard it as descriptive of the Messiah. So obvious is the application to the Messiah, so clear and full is the description, that many of them have adopted the opinion that there would be two Messiahs, one a suffering Messiah, and the other a glorious and triumphant prince and conqueror. The Old Testament plainly foretold that the Messiah would be 'God and man; exalted and debased; master and servant; priest and victim; prince and subject; involved in death, and yet a victor over death; rich and poor; a king, a conqueror, glorious; a man of griefs, exposed to infirmities, unknown, and in a state of abjection and humiliation.'—(Calmet.) All these apparently contradictory qualities had their fulfilment in the person of Jesus of Nazareth; but they were the source of great difficulty to the Jews, and have led to the great variety of opinions which have prevailed among them in regard to him. In the Lord Jesus they harmonize; but when the Jews resolved to reject him, they were at once thrown into endless embarrassment in regard to the character, coming, and work of him whom they had so long expected. The following extract from Calmet (*Dic.*) will explain some of the modern prevailing views of him, and is necessary to a clear understanding of the grounds which have been taken in the interpretation of this prophecy:—' Some of them, as the famous Hillel, who lived, according to the Jews, before Christ, maintain that the Messiah was already come in the person of Hezekiah; others, that the belief of the coming of the Messiah is no article of faith. Buxtorf says, that the greater part of the modern Rabbins believe that the Messiah has been come a good while, but keeps himself concealed in some part of the world or other, and will not manifest himself, because of the sins of the Jews. Jarchi affirms, that the Hebrews believe that the Messiah was born on the day of the last destruction of Jerusalem by the Romans. Some assign him the terrestrial paradise for his habitation; others the city of Rome, where, according to the Talmudists, he keeps himself concealed among the leprous and infirm, at the gate of the city, expecting Elias to come and manifest him. A great number believe that he is yet to come, but they are strangely divided about the time and the circumstances of his coming. Some expect him at the end of 6000 years. Kimchi, who lived in the twelfth century, believed that the coming of the Messiah was very near. Some have fixed the time of the end of their misfortunes to A.D. 1492, others to 1598, others to 1600, others yet later. Last of all, tired out with these uncertainties, they have pronounced an anathema against any who shall pretend to calculate the time of the coming of the Messiah.'

It is capable, however, of clear demonstration, that the ancient Jews, before the birth of Jesus, were not thus embarrassed in the interpretation of their own prophets. The following extracts from their writings will show that the opinion early prevailed that the passage before us had reference to the Messiah, and that they had to some extent right views of him. Even by the later Jewish interpreters who give a different exposition of the prophecy, it is admitted that it was formerly referred to the Messiah. This is admitted by Aben Ezra, Jarchi, Abarbanel, and Moses Nachmanides. Among the testimonies of the ancient Jews are the following:—The Chaldee Paraphrast, Jonathan, expressly refers it to the Messiah. Thus, in ver. 13 of this chapter, he renders the first member, 'Behold, my servant the Messiah shall prosper.' Thus, in the Medrasch Tanchuma (an old commentary on the Pentateuch), on the words 'Behold, my servant shall prosper,' it is remarked, This is the king Messiah, who is high, and lifted up, and very exalted, higher than Abraham, exalted above Moses, higher than the ministering angels.' Similar is the language of Rabbi Moses Haddarschan on Gen. i. 3: 'JEHOVAH spake: Messiah, my righteous one, those who are concealed with thee, will be such that their sins will bring a heavy yoke upon thee. The Messiah answered: Lord of the world, I cheerfully take upon myself those plagues and sorrows.

Immediately, therefore, the Messiah took upon himself, out of love, all torments and sufferings, as it is written in Isa. liii., "He was abused and oppressed."' Many other passages may be seen collected by Hengstenberg, Chris. i. 485, 486.

But this interpretation was abandoned by the Jewish interpreters when the passage was urged against them by Christians as demonstrating that Jesus of Nazareth was the Messiah, and when they could not reconcile it with their prevailing notions that the Messiah was to be a magnificent temporal prince. Gesenius asserts that 'the later Jews, no doubt, relinquished this interpretation in consequence of their controversy with Christians.' The Jews early formed the opinion that the Messiah was to be a king like David and Solomon, and was to be distinguished as a conqueror. They, therefore, looked exclusively at the passages of the Old Testament which spoke of his exaltation, and they were rendered averse to applying a passage like this to him, which spoke of his poverty, rejection, humiliation, and death. They did not, or would not, understand how passages apparently so contradictory, could be applied to the same individual; and they therefore fixed their attention on those which predicted his exaltation and majesty, and rejected the idea that the Messiah would be a sufferer. So long as they applied this portion of Isaiah to the Messiah, they could not deny that there was a remarkable correspondence between it and Jesus of Nazareth, and they were unable to meet the force of the argument thence derived in favour of his claims to the Messiahship. It became necessary, therefore, for the Jews to seek some other explanation of the passage, and to deny that it had reference to the Messiah. Accordingly, the great effort of the Jewish interpreters has been to ascertain to whom the passage can be made, with any show of probability, to apply. The great mass agree that it is not to be applied to the Messiah, and this is now the prevailing opinion among them.

Among the more modern Jewish expositors who agree that the passage is not to be applied to the Messiah, the following opinions have prevailed:—

1. The most commonly received opinion is, that it refers to the Jewish people. This is the opinion of Jarchi, Aben Ezra, Kimchi, Abarbanel, and Lipmann. According to them, the prophecy describes the condition of the Jews in their present calamity and exile; the firmness with which they endure it for the honour of God, and resist every temptation to forsake his law and worship; and the prosperity, honour, and glory which they shall obtain in the time of their redemption. In

ch. liii. 1-10, the heathen are regarded as speaking, and making an humble and penitential confession that they have hitherto mistaken the people of God, and unjustly despised them on account of their sufferings, since it now appears from their exaltation that those sufferings have not been inflicted on them on account of their sins.

2. Others take the appellation, 'salvation of JEHOVAH,' in the passage, to mean, the *pious* portion of the nation taken collectively, and regarded as making a kind of vicarious satisfaction for the ungodly. This class of interpreters among the Jews, however, has been small. They refer it to those among them who endure much affliction and suffering, but more especially to those who are publicly put to death. They mention particularly Rabbi Akiba as one who suffered martyrdom in this manner. This interpretation retains, indeed, the essential idea of *substitution* which runs through the passage, and it is not improbable that it is on this account that it has found so little favour with the modern Jews, since they reject with abhorrence the whole doctrine of vicarious sufferings as designed to make an atonement for others.

3. A few others among the Jews make the passage refer to an individual. Abarbanel, besides supposing that it refers to the Jewish people in general, suggests also that it may refer particularly to Isaiah. Rabbi Saadias Haggaon explained the whole as referring to Jeremiah. Still the passage is so plain in its general meaning, the reference to the Messiah is so obvious, that the Rabbins have not been able, with all their ingenuity, to propose an interpretation that shall be entirely satisfactory to their nation. It has probably been the means of the conversion of more Jews from the errors of their system to Christianity, than any other portion of their Scriptures. We know that, as it was explained and applied by Philip, it was the means of the conversion of the Ethiopian eunuch (Acts viii. 27-40). And so Jo. Isaac Levita, a learned Jew, says it was the means of first leading him to the Christian religion. 'I frankly confess,' says he, 'that this chapter first conducted me to the Christian faith. For more than a thousand times I read this chapter, and accurately compared it with many translations, I found that it contained a hundred more mysteries respecting Christ, than are found in any version.' Many similar instances occur, says Hengstenberg, in the reports of Missionaries among the Jews.

§ 3. *History of the interpretation of the passage by Christians.*

For seventeen centuries the view which was taken of this passage was uniform. By all the fathers of the Christian church it was regarded as having an indisputable reference to Christ. In their arguments with the Jews, it was quoted as containing a full refutation of their opinions respecting the Messiah, and as demonstrating that Jesus of Nazareth was he who had been so long announced by the prophets as 'he who was to come.' In their arguments with infidels, it was a strong proof to which they appealed of the truth of revelation; and in their homilies and expositions it was referred uniformly to the Lord Jesus. If we except Grotius, who supposed that it referred to Jeremiah, who, he says (Note on ch. lii. 13), was *figura Christi*—the type of the Messiah—it was not till the last quarter of the sixteenth century that this interpretation began to be called in question. The reason why the uniform exposition of the Christian church was abandoned then by any was, that it could *no longer be retained* consistently with the notions which prevailed, especially in Germany, of the Bible. The grand principle which began to prevail in the interpretation of the Bible was, that *all* which is there recorded is to be accounted for on natural principles. But if this passage refers to the Messiah, it harmonizes so exactly with the life and character of the Redeemer, and it is so entirely removed from the possible range of mere conjecture, that it cannot be accounted for except on the supposition of supernatural revelation. Many professed Christian interpreters, therefore, have sought other ways of explaining it, and have diligently inquired to whom it referred. As a *specimen* of the manner in which the exposition of the Bible has been conducted in Germany, we may just refer to the opinions which have prevailed in the interpretation of this, the plainest and most splendid of all the prophecies pertaining to the Messiah.

1. Comparatively the greatest number of the non-Messianic interpreters make the whole Jewish people the subject. A large number of German expositors, whose names may be seen in Hengstenberg's *Christol.* i. 494, have adopted this view. The only difference between this interpretation and that adopted by the later Jews is, that the German critics suppose it refers to the Jews in the Babylonish exile, while the Jews suppose that it refers to their nation suffering in their present exile.

2. It was held by Eckermann that it refers to the Jewish nation in the abstract, in opposition to its individual members. In other words, it seems to have been held that the nation in the abstract was guilty and was suffering, while the individual members were innocent, and escaped suffering and punishment.

3. It has been held that it refers to the pious part of the Jewish people, as contrasted with the ungodly. This opinion was defended by Paulus. His view is the following: The pious part of the Jewish people were carried into captivity with the ungodly, not on account of their own sins, but the sins of the latter. The ungodly inferred that the hope of the pious that Jehovah would help them was in vain, but as the exile came to an end, and the pious returned, they saw that they had erred, and that their hope was well-grounded. They deeply lament, therefore, that they have not long ago done penance.

4. One author has maintained that the Jewish priesthood is the subject of the prophecy, but in this he stands alone.

5. It has been maintained by others that the *prophets collectively* are referred to in the passage. This was at first the opinion of Rosenmüller, but was abandoned by him, and was then defended by De Wette, and is maintained by Gesenius.

6. Others have referred it to some individual. Thus Grotius supposes that Jeremiah is meant. Augusti supposed that Uzziah was intended. Others that Hezekiah was meant; and others that Isaiah here referred to himself; and others that it refers to some unknown prophet slain by the Jews in their exile; and others that it refers to the Maccabees!

These strange and absurd opinions are specimens of the unhappy manner of exposition which has prevailed among the German neologists; and they are specimens, too, of the reluctance of the human mind to embrace the truth as it is in Jesus, and of its proneness to the wildest aberrations, where mere human reason is suffered to take the reins in the interpretation of the Bible. Perhaps there is scarcely to be found an instance of *interpretation* that is more fitted to humble us in regard to the proneness of men to err, than in these modes of explaining this beautiful portion of Isaiah. And there is not to be found anywhere a more striking proof of the reluctance of the human mind to contemplate the sufferings and death of the Redeemer of the world, or to embrace the great and glorious truth that men can be saved only by the vicarious sacrifice of the Son of God.

§ 4. *Proof that it refers to the Messiah.*

More ample proof of this will be furnished in the exposition of the passage itself, than can now be given. But still, it may not be improper to refer to a few of the considerations which go to demonstrate that the prophet here refers to the Lord Jesus Christ.

I. He refers to an *individual*, and not to a people, or a nation. It is not either to the collective body of the Jewish people, or to the pious portion of the Jewish people, or to the collective body of the prophets. This is evident on the slightest examination of the passage. The prophet speaks of the 'servant of Jehovah;' and the whole representation is that of an individual, and not of any collective body of men. Thus his visage was marred, and his form was disfigured: he was as a tender plant; he was despised; he was rejected; he was smitten, wounded, put to death; he made his grave with the wicked and with the rich. Of what collective body of men could this be said? How absurd to apply this to a *nation*, or to any portion of a nation! It *cannot* be applied (A) *to the whole people.* In ch. liii. 3, the subject is called 'a man,' an appellation which cannot be given to a nation. Nor is there an instance in all the sacred writings where there can be found such an extended allegory as this would be, on the supposition that this refers to the Jewish people. Besides, with what possible propriety can it be said of *a nation* that it has borne the griefs and carried the sorrows of others; that it was stricken for the transgression of the people of God; that it was made an offering for sin; and that it made intercession for the sin of the transgressors? If *this* refers to a nation, then all settled views of interpretation are at an end. The circumstances which are usually supposed to mark individual existence may in all other circumstances in like manner be supposed to mean nations, and we shall have no longer any way-marks in guiding us in the interpretation of the plainest writings. Nor (B) can it refer to the pious portion of the Jewish people taken collectively. For the subject of the prophecy suffers *voluntarily;* he himself *innocent,* bears the sins of others (liii. 4–6, 9); his sufferings are the efficient cause of the righteousness of his people (ver. 11); and he suffers quietly and patiently, without allowing himself to be provoked to bitterness against the authors of his sufferings. Of all these four marks, not one belongs to the people of Israel. For (a) they went not voluntarily into the Babylonish exile, but were carried there by violence. (b) They did not suffer innocently, but suffered for their sins, (c) The sufferings of the Jews can in no sense be represented as the cause of the righteousness of others. (d) Nor did the Jews evince that patience and devotedness to the will of God which is here attributed to the subject of this prophecy. How can it be said that they were led like a lamb to the slaughter, that they did not open the mouth to complain, when even the noblest and best of them poured out their sad-

Less in complaints and lamentations? Compare Jer. xx. 7, *sq.;* xv. 10–21; Ps. cxxxvii. 8, 9. Nor (C) can it refer to the prophets taken collectively, as Gesenius supposes. On this it is sufficient to ask, Where did such a collection of the prophets ever exist? When did they suffer together? What evidence is there that they were in exile? Where and when did they take upon themselves the sins of the people, or suffer for them, or make their grave with the wicked and the rich in their death, or see of the travail of the soul, and become the means of the justification of many? All that has been said in favour of this is so entirely the work of conjecture, and is so manifestly designed to evade the obvious reference to the Messiah, that it is necessary to refer to it only as a specimen of the manner of interpretation which has prevailed, and which still prevails in the explanation of the sacred Scriptures. But if the passage does not refer either to the collective Jewish people, or to the pious portion of them, or to the prophets regarded as a collective body, then it must refer *to an individual,* and the only question is whether, it refers to the Messiah, or to some individual of the Jewish nation. As a simple and satisfactory argument that it refers to some individual, an appeal might be made to the common sense of the mass of men. Not one in a million—and he not unless he had some favourite hypothesis to defend—would ever suppose, on reading the passage, that it *could* have any reference to a collection of people of any kind. But the common sense of the mass of men is generally the best criterion of the meaning of any written document, and the best interpreter of the Bible.

II. If it refers to an individual, it must refer to the Messiah. It cannot refer to Isaiah, or Jeremiah, or Uzziah, or Akiba, for the following, among other reasons :—(*a*) The advocates of this theory have not been able to agree on any individual to whom it can be applied. Grotius suggested Jeremiah, some others Uzziah, or Isaiah, and some of the Jews Akiba. But each of these theories has been confined to the single interpreter who suggested it, and has been rejected by all the rest of the world. What better proof could there be that there is not even *plausibility* in the statement? What stronger demonstration that it is a theory *got up* on purpose to avoid the reference to the Messiah? (*b*) None of the individuals named had any claim to the statements here made respecting the individual sufferer. Did kings shut their mouths at them, and stand in awe of them? Did Jeremiah sprinkle many nations? Did Uzziah bear the griefs and the sorrows of men? Did JEHOVAH

lay on Isaiah the iniquity of all men? Did either of them make their grave with the wicked and the rich in their death? But if it cannot be shown to have reference to any other individual, then the fair inference is, that it refers to the Messiah.

III. The argument that it refers to the Messiah has all the force of tradition in its favour. We have seen that the Jews, in more ancient times, referred this prophecy to the Messiah. This fact proves that such is the *obvious* reference. When their minds were not prejudiced and blinded by their hatred of Jesus of Nazareth, and their opposition to his claims; when they were looking forward with deep anxiety to the coming of a deliverer, they applied this passage to him. And though there were embarrassments in their minds, and they were not well able to explain how this was consistent with what is elsewhere stated of his exalted nature, yet such was its obvious reference to the Messiah, that they did not dare to call it in question. Such was the fact in the Christian church for seventeen hundred years. It was the unbroken and the unvarying voice of interpretation. Now this proves, not indeed that it is *necessarily* the true interpretation, for that is to be settled on other grounds than mere tradition, but that it is the exposition which the language naturally conveys. The unvarying sense affixed to any written document for seventeen hundred years, is *likely* to be the true sense. And especially is this so, if the document in question has been in the hands of the learned and the unlearned; the high and the low; the rich and the poor; the bond and the free; and if they concur in giving to it the same interpretation, such an interpretation cannot easily or readily be set aside.

IV. The quotations in the New Testament prove that it refers to the Messiah. They go to demonstrate at the same time two points; first, that such was the prevailing mode of interpretation at that time, otherwise the passage would not have been quoted as *proof* that Jesus was the Messiah; and secondly, that such is the correct mode of interpretation. The places where it is quoted are the following:—1. In John xii. 37, 38, 'But though he had done so many miracles before them, yet they believed not on him; that the saying of Esaias the prophet might be fulfilled which he spake, Lord, who hath believed our report? And to whom hath the arm of the Lord been revealed?' In this passage, Isa. liii. 1 is quoted to explain the unbelief of the Jewish people in the time of the Saviour, with the formula *ἵνα πληρωθῇ*—'that it might be fulfilled,' the usual formula in quoting

a passage from the Old Testament which is fulfilled in the New. No one can doubt that John
meant to be understood as affirming that the
passage in Isaiah had a designed applicability to
the person and the times of the Redeemer. The
same passage is quoted by Paul in Rom. x. 16:
'But they have not all obeyed the gospel. For
Esaias saith, Lord, who hath believed our report?' 2. The passage in Luke xxii. 37 is still
more decisive. 'For I say unto you, That this
that is written must yet be accomplished in me,
And he was reckoned among the transgressors:
for the things concerning me have an end,' i.e.,
a completion, a fulfilment. Here Isa. lii. 12
is expressly and directly applied by the Saviour
himself to his own sufferings and death. No
one can doubt that he meant to say that it had
original reference to him, and would be fulfilled
in him. The same passage is applied, and in
the same sense, by Mark (ch. xv. 28), to the
sufferings and death of the Redeemer. 3. In
Acts viii. 35, Isa. liii. 7, 8 is applied by Philip
the evangelist to the Redeemer; and is explained as having a reference to him. 4. In
Matt. viii. 17, the declaration of Isaiah (liii. 4),
'Himself took our infirmities, and bore our
sicknesses,' is applied expressly to the Messiah.
These passages, directly quoting Isaiah, and applying them to the Messiah, demonstrate that
in view of the writers of the New Testament,
and of the Saviour himself, Isaiah had reference
to the Messiah. To those who admit the inspiration and the Divine authority of the New Testament, these proofs are sufficient demonstration
of the position.

V. This view is enforced by another consideration. It is, that not only is the passage expressly quoted in the New Testament, but it is
alluded to in connection with the death of the
Redeemer as an atoning sacrifice for sin, in such
a manner as to show that it was regarded by
the sacred writers as having reference to the
Messiah. It is sufficient here to refer to the
following places:—Mark ix. 12; John iii. 5;
Rom. iv. 25; 1 Cor. xv. 3; 2 Cor. v. 21; 1 Pet.
i. 19; ii. 21-25. A careful examination of these
passages would convince any one, that the
writers of the New Testament were accustomed
to regard the passage in Isaiah as having undoubted reference to the Messiah, and that this
was so universally the interpretation of the passage in their times, as to make it proper simply
to refer to it without formally quoting it. It
may be added here, that it accords with the
current and uniform statement in the New Testament about the design of the death of the
Redeemer.

VI. One other argument may be here referred

to, which I propose to state more at length when
the exposition of the fifty-third chapter shall
have been made. It arises from the exact correspondence between the passage and the events
in the life, the sufferings, and the death of the
Redeemer—a correspondence so minute that it
cannot be the result of accident; so much depending on external circumstances and on the
agency of others, that it could not have been
produced by the effort of an impostor; and so
peculiar that it can be found in no other person
but the Messiah. We shall be better able to
appreciate the force of this argument when we
have the correct exposition of the passage before
us.

To the view which has thus been taken of the
design of this portion of Isaiah, there occurs
one objection, often made by infidels, which I
deem it important here to notice. It is, that
the transactions here referred to are represented
as past, and that it must be supposed to refer
to some event which had occurred before the
time when this was written. This ground has
also been taken by Gesenius in proof that it cannot refer to the Messiah: 'The suffering, contempt, and death,' says he, 'of the servant of
God, are here represented throughout as past,
since all in ch. liii. 1-10, is in the præter.
Only the glorification is future, and is represented in the future tense.' In reply to this,
we may observe—1. That the transactions referred to are not all represented as past. The
glorification of the person referred to is described in the future tense, and of course as a
future event (ch. lii. 13-15; liii. 11, 12). It may
be added also here, that those who will examine
the Hebrew, will perceive that not everything
in regard to his sufferings is represented as past
(see ver. 7, 8, 10). But, 2. The true answer to
this objection is to be found in a correct view of
the nature of prophecy; and the objection has
been supposed to have force only because the
true character of prophecy has not been apprehended. It is a feature of the true nature of
prophecy that the prophet is placed in vision in
the midst of the scenes which he describes as
future. He describes the events as if they were
actually passing before his eyes. See this view
of prophecy explained in the Introduction, § 7.
According to this, Isaiah is to be regarded as
placed in vision amidst the scenes which he describes. He looks on the suffering Redeemer.
He describes his humiliation, his rejection, his
trial, his death, and the feelings of those who
rejected him, as if it actually occurred before his
eyes. He sees him now rejected by men and
put to death; but he also casts his eye into the
future and sees him exalted, and his religion

spreading into all the world. Though, therefore, the events which he describes were to occur
several hundred years afterwards, yet they are
portrayed, as his other prophecies are, as passing before his eyes, and as events which he was
permitted in vision to see.

ANALYSIS.

In ch. lii. 13–15, JEHOVAH speaks of his servant the Messiah, and describes the state of his
humiliation, and of his subsequent exaltation.
These verses contain, in fact, an *epitome* of what
is enlarged upon in the next chapter. The sum
of it is, that his servant should be, on the whole,
prospered and exalted (13); yet he would be
subjected to the deepest trial and humiliation
(14); but as the result of this, he would redeem
the nations of the earth, and their kings and
rulers would regard him with profound reverence (15). A display of the Divine perfections
would accompany the work of the servant of
JEHOVAH such as they had never beheld, and
they would be called on to contemplate wonders
of which they had not before heard.

Ch. liii. contains a more minute explanation
and statement of what is said in general in ch.
lii. 13–15. For convenience, it may be regarded
as divided into the following portions :—

I. An expression of amazement and lamentation at the fact that so few had embraced the
annunciation respecting the Messiah, and had
been properly affected by the important statements respecting his sufferings, his death, and
his glorification (1).

II. A description of his rejection, his sufferings, his death (2–10). Here the prophet describes the scene as actually passing before his
eyes. He speaks as if he himself were one of
the Jewish nation who had rejected him, and
who had procured his death. He describes the
misapprehension under which it was done, and
the depth of the sorrow to which the Messiah
was subjected, and the design which JEHOVAH
had in view in these sufferings. 1. His appear-

ance and rejection are described (2, 3). He is as
a shrub that grows in a parched soil without
beauty; he is a man of sorrows, instead of being,
as they expected, a magnificent prince; he has
disappointed their expectations, and there is
nothing that corresponded with their anticipa-
tions, and nothing, therefore, which should lead
them to desire him. 2. The *design* for which he
endured his sorrows is stated (4–6). He was
thought by the people to be justly put to death,
and they judged that God had judicially smitten
and afflicted him (4). But this was not the
cause. It was because he had borne the sorrows of the nation, and was wounded for their
sins (4, 5). They had all gone astray, but
JEHOVAH had caused to meet on him the iniquity of all. 3. The *manner* of his sufferings is
described (7, 8). He was patient as a lamb;
was taken from prison, and cut off. 4. The
manner of his *burial* is described (9). It was
with the rich. The *reason* why his grave was
thus distinguished from that of malefactors was,
that in fact he had done no evil. God, therefore, took care that that fact should be marked
even in his burial, and though he *died* with
malefactors, yet, as the purpose of the atonement did not require ignominy *after* death, he
should not be *buried* with them. 5. The *design*
for which all this was done is stated (10). It
was that his soul might be made an offering for
sin, and that it was thus well-pleasing or acceptable to God that he should suffer and die.

III. The result of his sufferings and humiliation is described (10–12). 1. He would see a
numerous spiritual posterity, and be abundantly
satisfied for all his pains and sorrows (10, 11).
2. By the knowledge of him, a great number
would be justified and saved (11). 3. He would
be greatly honoured, and proceed to the spiritual
conquest of all the world (12).

13 Behold, my servant shall [1] deal
prudently, he shall be exalted and
extolled, and be very high.

1 or, *prosper;* ch.53,10.

13. *Behold, my servant.* The word
' behold,' indicates here that a new object is pointed out to view, and that
it is one that claims attention on account of its importance. It is designed
to direct the mind to the Messiah. The
point of view which is here taken, is
between his humiliation and his glorification. He sees him as having been
humbled and rejected (ver. 14, 15; ch.
liii. 2–10); about to be exalted and
honoured (ver. 13–15; ch. liii. 10–12).

The word ' servant ' refers to the Messiah. Comp. Notes on ch. xlix. 5, where
the word ' servant ' is applied also to the
Messiah. It means that he would be
employed in doing the will of God, and
that he would submit to him as a servant does to the law of his master.
¶ *Shall deal prudently.* Marg. ' Prosper.' The word שָׂכַל *sâkhâl*, is used
in a twofold signification. It means
either *to act wisely,* or *to be prosperous.*
In this latter sense it is used in Josh.

14 As many were astonished at thee (his visage was so marred more than any man, and his form more than the sons of men),

i. 7, 8; 2 Kings xviii. 7; Jer. x. 21; Prov. xvii. 8. It is not easy to determine what is the meaning here. Jerome renders it, *Intelligent*—'Shall be wise or prudent.' The LXX. render it, Συνήσει ὁ παῖς μου—'My servant shall be intelligent.' The Chaldee renders it, 'Behold my servant the Messiah shall prosper' (יַצְלִיחַ). The Syriac retains the Hebrew word. Jun. and Tremell. render it, 'Shall prosper;' Castellio, 'Shall be wise.' Lowth renders it, 'Shall prosper;' and in this Gesenius and Noyes concur. Hengstenberg proposes to unite the two meanings, and to render it, 'He shall reign well,' as indicative of the prosperous and wise government of the Messiah. It seems to me that the parallelism requires us to understand this not of his personal wisdom and prudence, but of the success of his enterprise. This verse contains a summary statement of what would occur under the Messiah. The general proposition is, that he would be ultimately successful, and to this the prophet comes (ch. liii. 12). He here sees him in affliction, humble, rejected, and despised. But he says that this was not always to be. He would be ultimately exalted. It is on this that he fixes the eye, and it is this which cheers and sustains the prophet in the contemplation of the sufferings of the Messiah. ¶ *He shall be exalted.* In this part of the verse, the prophet combines the verbs which denote elevation or exaltation. The idea is, that he would be exalted to the highest pitch of honour. The word 'exalted,' with us, is often synonymous with *praise;* but here it means, he shall be elevated (נִשָּׂא), or lifted up. The reference here is, undoubtedly, to the fact that the Redeemer would be greatly honoured on earth as the Prince and Saviour of the world (ch. liii. 12), and that in view of the universe he would be elevated to the highest conceivable rank. This is described in the New Testament by his being placed 'at the right hand of God' (Mark xvi. 19); by the fact that 'angels and authorities and powers are

made subject unto him' (1 Pet. iii. 22); by the fact that God has 'set him at his own right hand in the heavenly places, far above all principality, and power, and might, and dominion, and every name that is named' (Eph. i. 20–22); and by the fact that he will return in great glory to judge the world (Matt. xxv). The idea is, that as he was the most despised among men, so he would yet be the most honoured; as he had voluntarily assumed the lowest place for the redemption of men, so he would be exalted to the highest place to which human nature could be elevated.

14. *As many were astonished at thee.* This verse is closely connected with the following, and they should be read together. The sense is, ' as many were shocked at him—his form was so disfigured, and his visage so marred—so he shall sprinkle many nations.' That is, the one fact would correspond with the other. The astonishment would be remarkable ; the humiliation would be wonderful, and fitted to attract the deepest attention; and so his success and his triumph would correspond with the depth of his humiliation and sufferings. As he had in his humiliation been subjected to the lowest condition, so that all despised him ; so hereafter the highest possible reverence would be shown him. Kings and nobles would shut their mouths in his presence, and show him the profoundest veneration. A change of person here occurs which is not uncommon in the Hebrew poets. In ver. 13, JEHOVAH speaks of the Messiah in the third person ; here he changes the form of the address, and speaks of him in the second person. In the following verse the mode of address is again changed, and he speaks of him again in the third person. Lowth, however, proposes to read this in the third person, 'As many were astonished *at him,*' on the authority of two ancient Heb. MSS., and of the Syriac and Chaldee. But the authority is not sufficient to justify a change in the text, nor is it necessary. In the word rendered 'astonished' (שָׁמְמוּ), the

primary idea is that of being struck dumb, or put to silence from sudden astonishment. Whether the astonishment is from admiration or abhorrence is to be determined by the connection. In the latter sense, it is used in ch. xviii. 16; xix. 8. Here it evidently refers to the fact that he was disfigured, and destitute of apparent beauty and attractiveness from his abject condition and his sufferings. They were struck with amazement that one so abject, and that had so little that was attractive, should presume to lay claim to the character of the Messiah. This idea is more fully expressed in the following chapter. Here it is stated *in general* that his appearance was such as to excite universal astonishment, and probably to produce universal disgust. They saw no beauty or comeliness in him (see ch. liii. 2). This expression should also be regarded as standing in contrast with what is added in verse 15. Here it is said they were amazed, astonished, silent, at his appearance of poverty and his humiliation; there it is said, ' kings should shut their mouths at him,' that is, they would be so deeply impressed with his majesty and glory that they would remain in perfect silence—the silence not of contempt, but of profound veneration. ¶ *His visage* (מִרְאֵהוּ). This word denotes properly *sight, seeing, view;* then that which is seen; then appearance, form, *looks* (Ex. xxiv. 17; Ezek. i. 16–28; Dan. x. 18). Here it means, his appearance, his looks. It does not necessarily refer to his face, but to his general appearance. It was so disfigured by distress as to retain scarcely the appearance of a man. ¶ *Was so marred* (מִשְׁחַת). This word properly means *destruction.* Here it means defaced, destroyed, disfigured. There was a disfiguration, or defacement of his aspect, more than that of man. ¶ *More than any man* (מֵאִישׁ). This may either mean, more than any other man, or that he no longer retained the appearance of a man. It probably means the latter—that his visage was so disfigured that it was no longer the aspect of a man. Castellio renders it, *Ut non jam sit homo, non sit unus de humano genere.* ¶ *And his form*

(תֹּאַר). This word denotes *a form* or *a figure* of the body (1 Sam. xxviii. 14). Here it denotes the figure, or the appearance, referring not to the countenance, but to the general aspect of the body. ¶ *More than the sons of men.* So as to seem not to belong to men, or to be one of the human family. All this evidently refers to the disfiguration which arises from excessive grief and calamity. It means that he was broken down and distressed; that his great sorrows had left their marks on his frame so as to destroy the beautiful symmetry and proportions of the human form. We speak of being crushed with grief; of being borne down with pain; of being laden with sorrow. And we all know the effect of long-continued grief in marring the beauty of the human countenance, and in bowing down the frame. Deep emotion depicts itself on the face, and produces a permanent impression there. The highest beauty fades under long-continued trials, though at first it may seem to be set off to advantage. The rose leaves the cheek, the lustre forsakes the eye, vigour departs from the frame, its erect form is bowed, and the countenance, once brilliant and beautiful, becomes marked with the deep furrows of care and anxiety. Such seems to be the idea here. It is not indeed *said* that the sufferer before this had been distinguished for any extraordinary beauty—though this may not be improperly supposed—but that excessive grief had almost obliterated the traces of intelligence from the face, and destroyed the aspect of man. How well this applies to the Lord Jesus, needs not to be said. We have, indeed, no positive information in regard to his personal appearance. We are not told that he was distinguished for manliness of form, or beauty of countenance. But it is certainly no improbable supposition that when God prepared for him a body (Heb. x. 5) in which the divinity should dwell incarnate, the human form would be rendered as fit as it could be for the indwelling of the celestial inhabitant. And it is no unwarrantable supposition that perfect truth, benevolence, and purity, should depict themselves on the

15 So shall he sprinkle *a* many nations ; the kings shall shut their mouths at him : for *that* which had

a Eze.36.25.

not been told them shall they see, and *that* which they had not heard shall they consider.

---

countenance of the Redeemer; as they will be manifested in the very aspect wherever they exist—and render him the most beautiful of men—for the expression of these principles and feelings in the countenance constitutes beauty (comp. Notes on ch. liii. 2). Nor is it an improbable supposition, that this beauty was marred by his long-continued and inexpressibly deep sorrows, and that he was so worn down and crushed by the sufferings which he endured as scarcely to have retained the aspect of a man.

15. *So* (כֵּן). This word answers to ' as ' (כַּאֲשֶׁר) in the former verse. ' In like manner as many were astonished or shocked at thee—so shall he sprinkle many nations.' The one is to be in some respects commensurate with the other. The comparison seems to consist of two points : 1. *In regard to the numbers.* Many would be shocked: many would be sprinkled by him. Large numbers would be amazed at the fact of his sorrows ; and numbers correspondently large would be sprinkled by him. 2. *In the effects.* Many would be struck dumb with amazement at his appearance ; and, in like manner, many would be struck dumb with veneration or respect. He would be regarded on the one hand as having scarce the form of a man ; on the other, even kings would be silent before him from profound reverence and awe. ¶ *Shall he sprinkle many nations.* The word here rendered ' sprinkle ' (יַזֶּה) has been very variously rendered. Jerome renders it, *Asperget* —' Shall sprinkle.' The LXX. ' So shall many nations express admiration (θαυμάσονται) at him.' The Chaldee, ' So shall he scatter,' or dissipate (יְבַדַּר) ' many people.' The Syriac renders it, ' Thus shall he purify,' cleanse, make expiation for (ﺣﺪﻛﻒ) ' many nations.' The Syriac verb used here means *to purify*, to cleanse, to make holy; and, in *aph.*, to expiate ; and the idea of the translator evidently was, that he would purify by making expiation. See the

Syriac word used in Luke iii. 17; Acts xi. 9; xxiv. 18; Heb. ix. 22 ; x. 4. Castellio renders it as Jerome does ; and Jun. and Tremell., ' He shall sprinkle many nations with stupor.' Interpreters have also varied in the sense which they have given to this word. Its usual and proper meaning is to *sprinkle*, and so it has been here commonly interpreted. But Martini, Rosenmüller, and Gesenius suppose that it is derived from an Arabic word meaning to leap, to spring, to spring up, to leap for joy, to exult ; and that the idea here is, that he should cause many nations to exult, or leap for joy. Parallel places, says Gesenius, occur in ch. xlix. 6, 7; li. 5. Against the common interpretation, ' to sprinkle,' he objects—1. That the verb could not be construed without the accusative, and that if it means that he would sprinkle with blood, the word *blood* would be specified. 2. That the connection is opposed to the idea of sprinkling, and that the antithesis requires some word that shall correspond with שָׁמֵם, ' shall be astonished,' and that the phrase ' they shall be joyful,' or ' he shall cause them to exult with joy,' denotes such antithesis. To this it may be replied, that the usual, the universal signification of the word נָזָה (*nâzâ*) in the Old Testament is *to sprinkle*. The word occurs only in the following places, and is in all instances translated ' sprinkle ' (Ex. xxix. 21; Lev. v. 9; vi. 6–17, 27; viii. 11, 30; xiv. 7, 16, 27, 51; xvi. 14, 15, 19; Num. viii. 7; xix. 4, 18, 19, 21; 2 Kings ix. 33; Isa. lxiii. 3). It is properly applicable to the act of sprinkling blood, or water; and then comes to be used in the sense of cleansing by the blood that makes expiation for sin, or of cleansing by water as an emblem of purifying. In Ezek. xxxvi. 25, the practice of sprinkling with consecrated water is referred to as synonymous with purifying—though a different word from this is used (זָרַק), ' and I will sprinkle clean water upon you, and ye shall be clean.' If the word used here means

CHAPTER LIII.

WHO hath believed *a* our ¹ report? and to whom *b* is the arm of the LORD revealed?

2 For he shall grow up before him

a Jn.1.7,12; Ep.1.18,19.   1 *hearing, or, doctrine.*

as a tender plant, and as a root out of a dry ground; he hath no form nor comeliness; and when we shall see him, *there is* no beauty that we should desire him.

b Jn.12.37; Ro.10.16.

'to sprinkle,' it is used in one of the following significations:—1. To sprinkle *with blood,* in allusion to the Levitical rite of sprinkling the blood of the sacrifice, meaning that in that way sin would be expiated and removed (Lev. xiv. 51; xvi. 14; Heb. ix. 19; x. 22); or, 2. By an allusion to the custom of sprinkling with water as emblematic of purity, or cleansing (Num. viii. 7; xix. 18; Ezek. xxxvi. 25). If used in the former sense, it means, that the Redeemer would make expiation for sin, and that his blood of purifying would be sprinkled on the nations. If in the latter, as is most probable, then it means that he would purify them, as objects were cleansed by the sprinkling of water. If in *either* sense, it means substantially the same thing—that the Redeemer would *purify,* or *cleanse* many nations, *i.e.,* from their sins, and make them holy. Still there is a difficulty in the passage which does not seem to be solved. This difficulty has been thus expressed by Taylor (*Concord.*): 'It seems here to have a peculiar meaning, which is not exactly collected from the other places where this word is used. The *antithesis* points to *regard, esteem, admiration.* "So shall he sprinkle, engage the esteem and admiration of many nations." But how to deduce this from the sense of the word I know not.' It was to meet this difficulty that Martini, Rosenmüller, and Gesenius, propose the sense of leaping, exulting, filling with joy, from the Arabic. But that signification does not accord with the uniform Hebrew usage, and probably the sense of *purifying* is to be retained. It may be remarked that whichever of the above senses is assigned, it furnishes no *argument* for the practice of sprinkling in baptism. It refers to the fact of his purifying or cleansing the nations, and not to the ordinance of Christian baptism; nor should it be used as an argument in reference to the mode in which that should be administered.   ¶ *The*

kings shall shut their mouths at him. Or rather, kings. It does not refer to any particular kings; but the idea is, that he would be honoured by kings. To shut the mouths here indicates veneration and admiration. See Job xxix. 9, 10, where reverence or respect is indicated in the same way:

The princes refrained talking,
And laid their hand upon their mouth:
The nobles held their peace,
And their tongue cleaved to the roof of their
    mouth.

See also Micah viii. 16; comp. Job v. 16; Ps. cxlvii. 42.   ¶ *For* that *which had not been told them.* In this part of the verse a reason is given for the veneration which kings would evince. It is, that they should receive intelligence of this wonderful exaltation of the messenger of God which had not before been made known to them as it had been to the Jews. Or, in other words, the great mystery of the incarnation and redemption would contain truths and wonders which they had not contemplated elsewhere. No such events would have occurred within the range of their observation; and the wonders of redemption would stand by themselves as unparalleled in all that they had heard or seen. What is here predicted has been fulfilled. The mystery of the incarnation and the atonement; the sufferings and the death of the Redeemer; his exaltation and his glory, are events which are unparalleled in the history of the world. They are events *fitted* in their nature to excite the profoundest admiration, and to induce kings and nobles to lay their hand on their mouth in token of veneration. No monarch on earth could have evinced such condescension as did the Son of God; none has been elevated to so high a rank in the universe as the Redeemer. That the Son of God should become a man; that his visage should be so disfigured by grief as to have scarcely the aspect of a human being; that he should suffer and die as he did; and that he should be exalted as he is over this whole world, and have the most elevated place in the universe at the right hand of God, are all events fitted to excite the profoundest admiration.

CHAPTER LIII.

1. *Who hath believed our report?* The main design of the prophet in all this portion of his prophecy is, undoubtedly, to state the fact that the Redeemer would be greatly exalted (see ch. lii. 13; liii. 12). But in order to furnish a fair view of his exaltation, it was necessary also to exhibit the depth of his humiliation, and the intensity of his sorrows, and also the fact that he would be rejected by those to whom he was sent. He, therefore, in this verse, to use the language of Calvin, breaks in abruptly upon the order of his discourse, and exclaims that what he had said, and what he was about to say, would be scarcely credited by any one. Preliminary to his exaltation, and to the honours which would be conferred on him, he would be rejected and despised. The word 'report' (שְׁמֻעָה) denotes properly *that which is heard*, tidings, message, news. Marg. 'Hearing,' or 'doctrine.' The LXX. render it, 'Ἀκοή —'Rumour,' 'message.' It refers to the annunciation, message, or communication which had been made respecting the Messiah. The speaker here is Isaiah, and the word 'our' refers to the fact that the message of Isaiah and of the other prophets had been alike rejected. He groups himself with the other prophets, and says that the annunciation which *they* had made of the Redeemer had been disregarded. The interrogative form is often assumed when it is designed to express a truth with emphasis; and the idea is, therefore, that the message in regard to the Messiah had been rejected, and that almost none had credited and embraced it. ¶ *And to whom is the arm of the* LORD *revealed?* The arm is that by which we execute a purpose, and is often used as the emblem of power (see Notes on ch. xxxiii. 2; xl. 10). Here it denotes the omnipotence or power of God, which would be exhibited through the Messiah. The sense is, 'Who has perceived the power evinced

in the work of the Redeemer? To whom is that power manifested which is to be put forth through him, and in connection with his work?' It refers not so much, as it seems to me, to his power in working miracles, as to the omnipotence evinced in rescuing sinners from destruction. In the New Testament, the gospel is not unfrequently called 'the power of God' (Rom. i. 16; 1 Cor. i. 18), for it is that by which God displays his power in saving men. The idea here is, that comparatively few would be brought under that power, and be benefited by it; that is, in the times, and under the preaching of the Messiah. It is to be remembered that the scene of this vision is laid in the midst of the work of the Redeemer. The prophet sees him a sufferer, despised and rejected. He sees that few come to him, and embrace him as their Saviour. He recalls the 'report' and the announcement which he and other prophets had made respecting him; he remembers the record which had been made centuries before respecting the Messiah; and he asks with deep emotion, *as if present* when the Redeemer lived and preached, who had credited what he and the other prophets had said of him. The mass had rejected it all. The passage, therefore, had its fulfilment in the events connected with the ministry of the Redeemer, and in the fact that he was rejected by so many. The Redeemer was more successful in his work as a preacher than is commonly supposed, but still it is true that by the mass of the nation he was despised, and that the announcement which had been made of his true character and work was rejected.

2. *For he shall grow up before him.* In this verse, the prophet describes the humble appearance of the Messiah, and the fact that there was nothing in his personal aspect that corresponded to the expectations that had been formed of him; nothing that should lead them to desire him as their expected deliverer, but everything that could induce them to reject him. He would be of so humble an origin, and with so little that was magnificent in his external appearance, that the nation would despise him. The word rendered 'he shall grow up'

(וַיַּעַל, from עָלָה), means properly, *to go up, to ascend*. Here it evidently applies to the Redeemer as growing up in the manner of a shoot or sucker that springs out of the earth. It means that he would start, as it were, from a decayed stock or stump, as a shoot springs up from a root that is apparently dead. It does not refer to his manner of life before his entrance on the public work of the ministry; not to the mode and style of his education; but to his starting as it were out of a dry and sterile soil where *any* growth could not be expected, or from a stump or stock that was apparently dead (see Notes on ch. xi. 1). The phrase 'before him' (לְפָנָיו), refers to Jehovah. He would be seen and observed by him, although unknown to the world. The eyes of men would not regard him as the Messiah while he was growing up, but Jehovah would, and his eye would be continually upon him. ¶ *As a tender plant*. The word used here (יוֹנֵק, from יָנַק, *to suck*, Job iii. 12; Cant. viii. 1; Joel ii. 16), may be applied either to a suckling, a sucking child (Deut. xxxii. 25; Ps. viii. 3), or to a sucker, a sprout, a shoot of a tree (Job viii. 16; xiv. 7; xv. 30; Ezek. xvii. 22; Hos. xiv. 7). Jerome here renders it, *Virgultum*. The LXX. render it, Ἀνηγγείλαμεν ὡς παιδίον ἐναντίον αὐτοῦ— 'We have made proclamation as a child before him.' But what idea they attached to it, it is impossible now to say; and equally so to determine *how* they came to make such a translation. The Chaldee also, leaving the idea that it refers to the Messiah, renders it, 'And the righteous shall be magnified before him as branches which flourish, and as the tree which sends its roots by the fountains of water; thus shall the holy nation be increased in the land.' The Syriac translates it, 'He shall grow up before him as an infant.' The idea in the passage is plain. It is, that the Messiah would spring up as from an ancient and decayed stock, like a tender shoot or sucker. He would be humble and unpretending in his origin, and would be such that they who had expected a splendid prince would be led to overlook and despise him. ¶ *And as a root* (וְכַשֹּׁרֶשׁ). The word 'root' here is evidently used by synecdoche for the sprout that starts up from a root (see Notes on ch. xi. 10, where the word is used in the same sense). ¶ *Out of a dry ground*. In a barren waste, or where there is no moisture. Such a sprout or shrub is small, puny, and withered up. Such shrubs spring up in deserts, where they are stinted for want of moisture, and they are most striking objects to represent that which is humble and unattractive in its personal appearance. The idea here is, that the Messiah would spring from an ancient family decayed, but in whose root, so to speak, there would be life, as there is remaining life in the stump of a tree that is fallen down; but that there would be nothing in his external appearance that would attract attention, or meet the expectations of the nation. Even then he would not be like a plant of vigorous growth supplied with abundant rains, and growing in a rich and fertile soil, but he would be like the stinted growth of the sands of the desert. Can anything be more strikingly expressive of the actual appearance of the Redeemer, as compared with the expectation of the Jews? Can there be found anywhere a more striking fulfilment of a prophecy than this? And how will the infidel answer the argument thus furnished for the fact that Isaiah was inspired, and that his record was true? ¶ *He hath no form*. That is, no beauty. He has not the beautiful form which was anticipated; the external glory which it was supposed he would assume. On the meaning of the word 'form,' see Notes on ch. lii. 14. It is several times used in the sense of beautiful form or figure (Gen. xxix. 17; xxxix. 6; xli. 18; Deut. xxi. 11; Esth. ii. 17; comp. 1 Sam. xvi. 18). Here it means the same as beautiful form or appearance, and refers to his *state* of abasement rather than to his own personal beauty. There is no evidence that in person he was in any way deformed, or otherwise than beautiful, except as excessive grief may have changed his natural aspect (see Note on ch. lii. 14). ¶ *Nor comeliness* (הָדָר). This word is translated honour, glory, majesty (Deut. xxxiii. 17; Ps. xxix.

4; cxlix. 9; Dan. xi. 20); excellency (Isa. xxxv. 2); beauty (Prov. xx. 29; Ps. cx. 3; 2 Chron. xx. 21). It may be applied to the countenance, to the general aspect, or to the ornaments or apparel of the person. Here it refers to the appearance of the Messiah, as having nothing that was answerable to their expectations. He had no robes of royalty; no diadem sparkling on his brow; no splendid retinue; no gorgeous array. ¶ *And when we shall see him.* This should be connected with the previous words, and should be translated, 'that we should regard him, or attentively look upon him.' The idea is, that there was in his external appearance no such beauty as to lead them to look with interest and attention upon him; nothing that should attract them, as men are attracted by the dazzling and splendid objects of this world. If they saw him, they immediately looked away from him as if he were unworthy of their regard. ¶ There is *no beauty that we should desire him.* He does not appear in the form which we had anticipated. He does not come with the regal pomp and splendour which it was supposed he would assume. He is apparently of humble rank; has few attendants, and has disappointed wholly the expectation of the nation. In regard to the personal appearance of the Redeemer, it is remarkable that the New Testament has given us no information. Not a hint is dropped in reference to his height of stature, or his form; respecting the colour of his hair, his eyes, or his complexion. In all this, on which biographers are usually so full and particular, the evangelists are wholly silent. There was evidently *design* in this; and the purpose was probably to prevent any painting, statuary, or figure of the Redeemer, that would have any claim to being regarded as correct or true. As it stands in the New Testament, there is just the veil of obscurity thrown over this whole subject which is most favourable for the contemplation of the incarnate Deity. We are told that he was a man; we are told also that he was God. The image to the mind's eye is as obscure in the one case as the other; and in both, we are directed to his moral beauty, his holiness, and benevolence, as objects of contemplation, rather than to his external appearance or form. It may be added that there is no authentic information in regard to his appearance that has come down to us by tradition. All the works of sculptors and painters in attempting to depict his form are the mere works of fancy, and are undoubtedly as unlike the glorious reality as they are contrary to the spirit and intention of the Bible. There is, indeed, a letter extant which is claimed by some to have been written by Publius Lentulus, to the Emperor Tiberius, in the time when the Saviour lived, and which gives a description of his personal appearance. As this is the *only* legend of antiquity which even claims to be a description of his person, and as it is often printed, and is regarded as a curiosity, it may not be improper here to present it in a note.* This letter is pronounced by Calmet to be spurious, and it has been abundantly *proved* to be so by Prof. Robinson (see *Bib. Rep.* vol. ii. pp. 367–393). The main arguments against its authenticity, and which entirely settle the question, are —1. The discrepancies and contradictions which exist in the various copies. 2. The fact that in the time of the

---

* 'There has a man appeared here, who is still living, named Jesus Christ, whose power is extraordinary. He has the title given to him of the great prophet; his disciples call him the Son of God. He raises the dead, and heals all sorts of diseases. He is a tall, well-proportioned man; there is an air of serenity in his countenance, which attracts at once the love and reverence of those who see him. His hair is of the colour of new wine; from the roots to his ears, and from thence to the shoulders, it is curled, and falls down to the lowest part of them. Upon the forehead it parts in two, after the manner of the Nazarenes. His forehead is flat and fair, his face without any defect, and adorned with a very graceful vermilion; his air is majestic and agreeable. His nose and his mouth are very well proportioned; and his beard is thick and forked, of the colour of his hair; his eyes are gray and extremely lively; in his reproofs he is terrible, but in his exhortations and instructions amiable and courteous; there is something wonderfully charming in his face, with a mixture of gravity. He is never seen to laugh, but he has been observed to weep. He is very straight in stature; his hands are large and spreading, and his arms very beautiful. He talks little, but with great gravity, and is the handsomest man in the world.'—(*Bib. Repos.* vol. ii. p. 368.)

3 He is despised and rejected *a* of men ; a man of sorrows, and acquainted *b* with grief : and ¹ we hid as it were *our* faces from him ; he was despised, and we esteemed him not.

a Lu.23,18,&c.   *b* He.4.15.

¹ *as an hiding of faces from him*, or, *from us; or, he hid as it were his face from us.*

Saviour, when the epistle purports to have been written, it can be demonstrated that no such man as Publius Lentulus was governor of Judea, or had any such office there, as is claimed for him in the inscriptions to the epistle. 3. That for fifteen hundred years no such epistle is quoted or referred to by any writer—a fact which *could* not have occurred if any such epistle had been in existence. 4. That the style of the epistle is not such as an enlightened Roman would have used, but is such as an ecclesiastic would have employed. 5. That the contents of the epistle are such as a Roman *would* not have used of one who was a Jew. See these arguments presented in detail in the place above referred to. It may be added, that this is the only pretended account which has come down to us respecting the personal appearance of the Saviour, except the *fable* that Christ sent his portrait to Abgar, king of Edessa, in reply to a letter which he had sent requesting him to come and heal him ; and the equally fabulous legend, that the impression of his countenance was left upon the handkerchief of the holy Veronica.

3. *He is despised.* This requires no explanation ; and it needs no comment to show that it was fulfilled. The Redeemer was eminently the object of contempt and scorn alike by the Pharisees, the Sadducees, and the Romans. In his life on earth it was so ; in his death it was still so ; and since then, his name and person have been extensively the object of contempt. Nothing is a more striking fulfilment of this than the conduct of the Jews at the present day. The very name of Jesus of Nazareth excites contempt ; and they join with their fathers who rejected him in heaping on him every term indicative of scorn. ¶ *Rejected of men.* This phrase is full of meaning, and in three words states the whole history of man in regard to his treatment of the Redeemer. The name ' THE REJECTED OF MEN,' will express all the melancholy history ;—rejected by the Jews ; by the rich ; the great and the learned ; by the mass of men of every grade, and age, and rank. No prophecy was ever more strikingly fulfilled ; none could condense more significancy into few words. In regard to the exact sense of the phrase, interpreters have varied. Jerome renders it, *Novissimum virorum* — ' The last of men ;' *i.e.*, the most abject and contemptible of mankind. The LXX. ' His appearance is dishonoured (ἄτιμον) and defective (ἐκλεῖπον) more than the sons of men.' The Chaldee, ' He is indeed despised, but he shall take away the glory of all kings ; they are infirm and sad, as if exposed to all calamities and sorrows.' Some render it, ' Most abject of men,' and they refer to Job xix. 14, where the same word is used to denote those friends who forsake the unfortunate. The word חֲדַל, used here, is derived from the verb חָדַל, which means *to cease*, to leave off, to desist ; derived, says Gesenius (*Lex.*), from the idea of becoming languid, flaccid ; and thence transferred to the act of ceasing from labour. It means usually, to cease, to desist from, to leave, to let alone (see 1 Kings xxii. 6–15 ; Job vii. 15 ; x. 20 ; Isa. ii. 22). According to Gesenius, the word here means *to be left*, to be destitute, or forsaken ; and the idea is, that he was forsaken of men. According to Hengstenberg (*Christol.*) it means ' the most abject of men,' — he who *ceases* from men, who ceases to belong to the number of men ; *i.e.*, who is the most abject of men. Castellio renders it, *Minus quam homo*—' Less than a man.' Junius and Tremellius, *Abjectissimus virorum* —' The most abject of men.' Grotius, ' Rejected of men.' Symmachus, 'Ελάχιστος ἀνδρῶν —' The least of men.' The idea is, undoubtedly, somehow that of *ceasing* from men, or from being regarded as belonging to men. There was a ceasing, or a withdrawing of that which usually appertains to man, and which belongs to him. And the thought

probably is, that he was not only ' despised,' but that there was an advance
on that—there was a *ceasing* to treat
him *as if* he had human feelings, and
was in any way entitled to human fellowship and sympathy. It does not
refer, therefore, so much to the *active*
means employed to reject him, as to the
fact that he was regarded as *cut off from
man;* and the idea is not essentially
different from this, that he was the most
abject and vile of mortals in the estimation of others ; so vile as not to be
deemed worthy of the treatment due to
the *lowest* of men. This idea has been
substantially expressed in the Syriac
translation. ¶ *A man of sorrows.* What
a beautiful expression ! A man who was
so sad and sorrowful ; whose life was so
full of sufferings, that it might be said
that that was the characteristic of the
man. A similar phraseology occurs in
Prov. xxix. 1, ' He that being often reproved,' in the margin, ' a man of reproofs ;' in the Heb. ' A man of chastisements,' that is, a man who is often
chastised. Compare Dan. x. 11: ' O
Daniel, a man greatly beloved,' Marg.
as in Heb. ' A man of desires ;' *i.e.*, a
man greatly desired. Here, the expression means that his life was characterized by sorrows. How remarkably this
was fulfilled in the life of the Redeemer,
it is not necessary to attempt to show.
¶ *And acquainted with grief.* Heb.
וִידוּעַ חֹלִי —' And knowing grief.' The
word rendered ' grief,' means usually
sickness, disease (Deut. vii. 15; xxvii.
61; Isa. i. 5); but it also means anxiety,
affliction (Eccl. v. 16); and then any
evil or calamity (Eccl. vi. 2). Many of
the old interpreters explain it as meaning, that he was known or distinguished
by disease ; that is, affected by it in a
remarkable manner. So Symm. Γνωστός
νόσῳ. Jerome (Vulg.) renders it, *Scientem
infirmitatem.* The LXX. render the
whole clause, ' A man in affliction (ἐν
πληγῇ), and knowing to bear languor,
or disease ' (εἰδὼς φέρειν μαλακίαν). But
if the word here means disease, it is
only a figurative designation of severe
sufferings both of body and of soul.
Hengstenberg, Koppe, and Ammon, suppose that the figure is taken from the
leprosy, which was not only one of the

most severe of all diseases, but was in a
special manner regarded as a Divine
judgment. They suppose that many
of the expressions which follow may be
explained with reference to this (comp.
Heb. iv. 15). The idea is, that he was
familiar with sorrow and calamity. It
does not mean, as it seems to me, that
he was to be himself sick and diseased ;
but that he was to be subject to various
kinds of calamity, and that it was to be
a characteristic of his life that he was
familiar with it. He was intimate with
it. He knew it personally ; he knew it
in others. He lived in the midst of
scenes of sorrow, and be became intimately acquainted with its various forms,
and with its evils. There is no evidence
that the Redeemer was himself sick at
any time — which is remarkable — but
there is evidence in abundance that he
was familiar with all kinds of sorrow,
and that his own life was a life of grief.
¶ *And we hid as it were* our *faces from
him.* There is here great variety of
interpretation and of translation. The
margin reads, ' As an hiding of faces
from him,' or ' from us,' or, ' He hid as
it were *his* face from us.' The Hebrew
is literally, ' And as the hiding of faces
from him, or from it ;' and Hengstenberg
explains it as meaning, ' He was as an
hiding of the face before it ;' that is,
as a thing or person before whom a
man covers his face, because he cannot
bear the disgusting sight. Jerome
(Vulg.) renders it, ' His face was as it
were hidden and despised.' The LXX.
' For his countenance was turned away '
(ἀπέστραπται. The Chaldee, ' And when
he took away his countenance of majesty
from us, we were despised and reputed
as nothing.' Interpreters have explained
it in various ways. 1. ' He was as one
who hides his face before us ;' alluding,
as they suppose, to the Mosaic law, which
required lepers to cover their faces (Lev.
iii. 45), or to the custom of covering the
face in mourning, or for shame. 2.
Others explain it as meaning, ' as one
before whom is the covering of the face,
i.e., before whom a man covers the face
from shame or disgust. So Gesenius.
3. Others, ' He was as one causing to
conceal the face,' *i.e.*, he induced others
to cover the face before him. His suf-

4 Surely he hath borne our griefs, and carried our sorrows: *yet we

a Mat.26,37.

did esteem him stricken, smitten of God, and afflicted.

ferings were so terrible as to induce them to turn away. So J. H. Michaelis. The idea seems to be, that he was as one from whom men hide their faces, or turn away. This *might* either arise from a sight of his sufferings, as being so offensive that they would turn away in pain —as in the case of a leper ; or it might be, that he was so much an object of contempt, and so unlike what they expected, that they would hide their faces and turn away in scorn. This latter I suppose to be the meaning ; and that the idea is, that he was so unlike what they had expected, that they hid their faces in affected or real contempt. ¶ *And we esteemed him not.* That is, we esteemed him as nothing ; we set no value on him. In order to give greater energy to a declaration, the Hebrews frequently express a thing positively and then negatively. The prophet had said that they held him in *positive* contempt ; he here says that they did not regard him as worthy of their notice. He here speaks in the name of his nation —as one of the Jewish people. 'We, the Jews, the nation to whom he was sent, did not esteem him as the Messiah, or as worthy of our affection or regard.'

4. *Surely.* This is an exceedingly important verse, and is one that is attended with considerable difficulty, from the manner in which it is quoted in the New Testament. The general sense, as it stands in the Hebrew, is not indeed difficult. It is immediately connected in signification with the previous verse. The meaning is, that those who had despised and rejected the Messiah, had greatly erred in contemning him on account of his sufferings and humiliation. 'We turned away from him in horror and contempt. We supposed that he was suffering on account of some great sin of his own. But in this we erred. It was not for *his* sins but for *ours.* It was not that he was smitten of God for his own sins—as if he had been among the worst of mortals—but it was because he had taken *our* sins, and was suffering for *them.* The very thing therefore that gave offence to us, and which made

us turn away from him, constituted the most important part of his work, and was really the occasion of highest gratitude.' It is an acknowledgment that they had erred, and a confession of that portion of the nation which would be made sensible of their error, that they had judged improperly of the character of the sufferer. The word rendered ' surely ' (אָכֵן, Vulg. *verē*), is sometimes a particle strongly affirming, meaning *truly, of a certain truth* (Gen. xxviii. 16 ; Ex. ii. 14 ; Jer. viii. 8). Sometimes it is an adversative particle, meaning *but yet* (Ps. xxxi. 23 ; Isa. xlix. 24). It is probably used in that sense here, meaning, that though he was despised by them, *yet* he was worthy of their esteem and confidence, for he had borne their griefs. He was not suffering for any sins of his own, but in a cause which, so far from rendering him an object of contempt, made him worthy of their highest regard. ¶ *He hath borne.* Heb. נָשָׂא *nâsâ.* Vulg. *Tulit.* LXX. Φερει— ' He bears.' Chald. ' He prayed (רְבִעִי) for, or on account of our sins.' Castellio, *Tulit ac toleravit.* In these versions, the sense is that of sustaining, bearing, upholding, carrying, as when one removes a burden from the shoulders of another, and places it on his own. The word נָשָׂא means properly *to take up,* to lift, to raise (Gen. vii. 17), ' The waters increased, and *lifted up* the ark ;' (xxix. 1), ' And Jacob *lifted up* his feet (see the margin) and came.' Hence it is applied to lifting up a standard (Jer. iv. 6 ; l. 2) ; to lifting up the hand (Deut. xxxii. 40) ; to lifting up the head (Job x. 15 ; 2 Kings xxv. 27) ; to lifting up the eyes (Gen. xiii. 10, *et sæpe*) ; to lifting up the voice, &c. It then means to bear, to carry, as an infant in the arms (Isa. xlvi. 3) ; as a tree does its fruit (Ezek. xvii. 8), or as a field its produce (Ps. lxx. 3 ; Gen. xii. 6). Hence to *endure,* suffer, permit (Job xxi. 3). ' Bear with me, suffer me and I will speak.' Hence to bear the sin of any one, to take upon one's self the suffering which is due to sin (see Notes on ver. 12 of this chapter; comp. Lev. v. 1, 17; xvii. 16; xx. 19; xxiv. 15; Num. v. 31; ix. 13; xiv. 34; xxx. 16; Ezek. xviii. 19, 20). Hence to bear chastisement, or punishment (Job xxxiv. 31): 'I have borne *chastisement*, I will not offend *any more*.' It is also used in the sense of taking away the sin of any one, expiating, or procuring pardon (Gen. l. 17; Lev. x. 17; Job vii. 21; Ps. xxxiii. 5; lxxxv. 3). In all cases there is the idea of *lifting*, sustaining, taking up, and conveying away, as by *carrying* a burden. It is not simply *removing*, but it is removing somehow by *lifting*, or carrying; that is, either by an act of power, or by so taking them on one's own self as to sustain and carry them. If applied to *sin*, it means that a man must *bear* the burden of the punishment of his own sin, or that the suffering which is due to sin is *taken up* and borne by another. If applied to *diseases*, as in Matt. viii. 17, it must mean that he, as it were, lifted them up and bore them away. It cannot mean that the Saviour literally *took* those sicknesses on himself, and *became sick* in the place of the sick, became a leper in the place of the leper, or was himself possessed with an evil spirit in the place of those who were possessed (Matt. viii. 16), but it must mean that he took them away by his power, and, as it were, lifted them up, and removed them. So when it is said (Isa. liii. 12) that he 'bare the sins of many,' it cannot mean literally that he took those sins on himself in any such sense as that he became a sinner, but only that he so took them upon himself as to *remove* from the sinner the exposure to punishment, and to *bear* himself whatever was necessary as a proper expression of the evil of sin. Peter undoubtedly makes an allusion to this passage (liii. 12) when he says (1 Pet. ii. 24), 'Who his own self bare our sins in his own body on the tree' (see Notes on ver. 12). Matthew (viii. 17) has translated it by ἔλαβε (*he took*), a word which does not differ in signification essentially from that used by Isaiah. It is almost exactly the same word which is used by Symmachus (ἀνελαβεν). ¶ *Our griefs*. The word here used (חֳלִי) means properly *sickness, disease, anxiety, af-*

fliction. It does not refer to *sins*, but to *sufferings*. It is translated 'sickness' (Deut. xxviii. 61; vii. 15; 2 Chron. xxi. 15; 1 Kings xvii. 17); 'disease' (Eccl. vi. 2; 2 Chron. xxi. 18; xvi. 12; Ex. xv. 26); 'grief' (Isa. liii. 3, 4; comp. Jer. xvi. 4). It is never in our version rendered *sin*, and never used to denote sin. 'In ninety-three instances,' says Dr. Magee (*On Atonement and Sacrifice*, p. 229, New York Ed. 1813), 'in which the word here translated (by the LXX.) ἀμαρτίας, or its kindred verb, is found in the Old Testament in any sense that is not entirely foreign from the passage before us, there occurs but this one in which the word is so rendered; it being in all other cases expressed by ἀσθενεία, μαλακία, or some word denoting bodily disease.' 'That the Jews,' he adds, 'considered this passage as referring to bodily diseases, appears from Whitby, and Lightfoot. Hor. Heb. on Matt. viii. 17.' It is rendered in the Vulgate, *Languores*—'Our infirmities.' In the Chaldee, 'He prayed for our sins.' Castellio renders it, *Morbos* — 'Diseases;' and so Junius and Tremellius. The LXX. have rendered it, in this place, 'Ἀμαρτίας—'Sins;' though, from what Dr. Kennicott has advanced in his *Diss. Gen.* § 79, Dr. Magee thinks there can be no doubt that this is a corruption which has crept into the later copies of the Greek. A few Greek MSS. of the Septuagint also read it ἀσθενείας, and one μαλακίας. Matthew (viii. 17) has rendered it, ἀσθενείας—'infirmities,' and intended no doubt to apply it to the fact that the Lord Jesus healed diseases, and there can be no doubt that Matthew has used the passage, not by way of accommodation, but in the true sense in which it is used by Isaiah; and that it means that the Messiah would take upon himself the infirmities of men, and would remove their sources of grief. It does not refer here to the fact that he would take their *sins*. That is stated in other places (ver. 6, 12). But it means that he was so afflicted, that he seemed to have taken upon himself the sicknesses and sorrows of the world; and taking them upon himself he would bear them away. I understand this, therefore, as expressing the twofold idea that he became deeply afflicted for us, and that, being thus afflicted for us, he was able to carry away our sorrows. In part this would be done by his miraculous power in healing diseases, as mentioned by Matthew ; in part by the influence of his religion, in enabling men to bear calamity, and in drying up the fountains of sorrow. Matthew, then, it is believed, has quoted this passage exactly in the sense in which it was used by Isaiah ; and if so, it should not be adduced to prove that he bore the *sins* of men—true as is that doctrine, and certainly as it has been affirmed in other parts of this chapter. ¶ *And carried.* Heb. בָל *sâbhâl.* This word means properly *to carry,* as a burden ; to be laden with, &c. (Isa. xlvi. 4, 7 ; Gen. xlix. 15.) It is applied to carrying burdens (1 Kings v. 15 ; 2 Chron. ii. 2 ; Neh. iv. 10, 17 ; Eccl. xii. 5). The verb with its derivative noun occurs in twenty-six places in the Old Testament, twenty-three of which relate to carrying burdens, two others relate to sins, and the other (Lam. v. 7) is rendered, 'We *have borne* their iniquities.' The primary idea is undoubtedly that of carrying a burden ; lifting it, and bearing it in this manner. ¶ *Our sorrows.* The word used here (מַכְאֹב, from כָּאַב, *to have pain,* sorrow, to grieve, or be sad), means properly *pain, sorrow, grief.* In the Old Testament it is rendered 'sorrow' and 'sorrows' (Eccl. i. 18; Lam. i. 12–18; Isa. lxv. 14 ; Jer. xlv. 3 ; xxx. 15); 'grief' (Job xvi. 6; Ps. lxix. 26; 2 Chron. vi. 29); 'pain' (Job xxxiii. 19; Jer. xv. 18; li. 8). Perhaps the proper difference between this word and the word translated *griefs* is, that this refers to pains of the *mind,* that of the *body ;* this to anguish, anxiety, or trouble of the soul; that to bodily infirmity and disease. Kennicott affirms that the word here used is to be regarded as applicable to griefs and distresses of the mind. 'It is evidently so interpreted,' says Dr. Magee (p. 220), 'in Ps. xxxii. 10, 'Many SORROWS shall be to the wicked ;' and again, Ps. lxix. 29, 'But I am poor and SORROWFUL ;' and again, Prov. xiv. 13, 'The heart is SORROWFUL ;' and Eccl. i. 18, 'He that increaseth knowledge increaseth sorrow ;' and so Eccl. ii. 18; Isa. lxv. 14;

Jer. xxx. 15.' Agreeably to this, the word is translated by Lowth, in our common version, and most of the early English versions, 'Sorrows.' The Vulgate renders it, *Dolores ;* the LXX. 'For us he is in sorrow' (ὀδυνᾶται), *i.e.,* is deeply grieved, or afflicted. The phrase, therefore, properly seems to mean that he took upon himself the *mental* sorrows of men. He not only took their diseases, and bore them away, but he also took or bore their mental griefs. That is, he subjected himself to the kind of mental sorrow which was needful in order to remove them. The word which is used by Matthew (viii. 17), in the translation of this, is νόσου;. This word (νόσος) means properly *sickness,* disease (Matt. iv. 23, 24; ix. 35); but it is also used in a metaphorical sense for pain, sorrow, evil (Rob. *Lex.*) In this sense it is probable that it was designed to be used by Matthew. He refers to the general subject of human ills ; to the sicknesses, sorrows, pains, and trials of life ; and he evidently means, in accordance with Isaiah, that he took them on himself. He was afflicted for them. He undertook the work of removing them. Part he removed by direct miracle— as sickness ;—part he removed by removing the *cause*—by taking away sin by the sacrifice of himself—thus removing the *source* of all ills ; and in regard to *all,* he furnished the means of removing them by his own example and instructions, and by the great truths which he revealed as topics of consolation and support. On this important passage, see Magee, *On Atonement and Sacrifice,* pp. 227–262. ¶ *Yet we did esteem him stricken.* Lowth, 'Yet we thought him judicially stricken.' Noyes, 'We esteemed him stricken from above.' Jerome (Vulg.), 'We thought him to be a leper.' The LXX. render it, 'We considered him being in trouble (or in labour, ἐν πόνῳ) and under a stroke (or in a plague or Divine judgment, ἐν πληγῇ), and in affliction.' Chaldee, 'We thought him wounded, smitten from the presence of God, and afflicted.' The general idea is, that they thought he was subjected to great and severe punishment by God for his sins, or regarded him as an object

5 But he *was* wounded [1] for our transgressions, *he was* bruised for our iniquities : the chastisement of our peace *was* upon him ; and with his [2] stripes *a* we are healed.

[1] or, *tormented.*   [2] *bruise.*   *a* 1 Pe. 2. 24, 25.

of Divine disapprobation. They *inferred* that one who was so abject and so despised ; who suffered so much and so long, must have been abandoned by God to judicial sufferings, and that he was experiencing the proper result and effect of his own sins. The word rendered 'stricken,' (נָגַע) means properly *struck*, or *smitten*. It is applied sometimes to the plague, or the leprosy, as an act by which God *smites* suddenly, and destroys men (Gen. xii. 17; Ex. xi. 1; Lev. xiii. 3, 9, 20; 1 Sam. vi. 9; Job xix. 21; Ps. lxxiii. 5), and very often elsewhere. Jerome explains it here by the word *leprous ;* and many of the ancient Jews derived from this word the idea that the Messiah would be afflicted with the leprosy. Probably the idea which the word would convey to those who were accustomed to read the Old Testament in Hebrew would be, that he was afflicted or smitten in some way corresponding to the plague or the leprosy ; and as these were regarded as special and direct Divine judgments, the idea would be that he would be smitten judicially by God, or be exposed to his displeasure and his curse. It is to be particularly observed here that the prophet does not say that he would thus be *in fact* smitten, accursed, and abandoned by God ; but only that he would be thus esteemed, or thought, viz., by the Jews who rejected him and put him to death. It is not here said that he *was* such. Indeed, it is very strongly implied that he was not, since the prophet here is introducing them as confessing their error, and saying that they were mistaken. He was, say they, bearing *our* sorrows, not suffering for his own sins. ¶ *Smitten of God.* Not that he was actually smitten of God, but we esteemed him so. We treated him as one whom we regarded as being under the Divine malediction, and we therefore rejected him. We esteemed him to be smitten *by* God, and we acted as if such an one *should* be rejected and contemned. The word here used (נָכָה) means to *smite*, to strike, and is some-

times employed to denote Divine judgment, as it is here. Thus it means to smite with blindness (Gen. xix. 11); with the pestilence (Num. xiv. 12); with emerods (1 Sam. v. 6); with destruction, spoken of a land (Mal. iii. 24); of the river (Ex. vii. 25) when he turned it into blood. In all such instances, it means that Jehovah had inflicted a curse. And this is the idea here. They regarded him as under the judicial inflictions of God, and as suffering what his sins deserved. The foundation of this opinion was laid in the belief so common among the Jews, that great sufferings always argued and supposed great guilt, and were proof of the Divine displeasure. This question constitutes the inquiry in the Book of Job, and was the point in dispute between Job and friends. ¶ *And afflicted.* We esteemed him to be punished by God. In each of these clauses the words, 'For his own sins,' are to be understood. We regarded him as subjected to these calamities on account of his own sins. It did not occur to us that he could be suffering thus for the sins of others. The fact that the Jews attempted to prove that Jesus was a blasphemer, and deserved to die, shows the fulfilment of this, and the estimate which they formed of him (see Luke xxiii. 34; John xvi. 3; Acts iii. 17; 1 Cor. ii. 8).

5. *But he* was *wounded.* Marg. 'Tormented.' Jerome and the LXX. also render this, 'He was wounded.' Junius and Tremellius, ' He was affected with grief.' The Chaldee has given a singular paraphrase of it, showing how confused was the view of the whole passage in the mind of that interpreter. ' And he shall build the house of the sanctuary which was defiled on account of our sins, and which was delivered on account of our iniquities. And in his doctrine, peace shall be multiplied to us. And when we obey his words, our sins shall be remitted to us.' The Syriac renders it in a remarkable manner, ' He is slain on account of our sins,' thus showing

that it was a common belief that the Messiah would be violently put to death. The word rendered 'wounded' (מְחֹלָל), is a participle Pual, from חָלַל (hhâlăl), to bore through, to perforate, to pierce; hence to wound (1 Sam. xxxi. 3; 1 Chron. x. 3; Ezek. xxviii. 9). There is probably the idea of painful piercing, and it refers to some infliction of positive wounds on the body, and not to mere mental sorrows, or to general humiliation. The obvious idea would be that there would be some act of *piercing*, some penetrating wound that would endanger or take life. Applied to the actual sufferings of the Messiah, it refers undoubtedly to the piercing of his hands, his feet, and his side. The word 'tormented,' in the margin, was added by our translators because the Hebrew word might be regarded as derived from חוּל (hhŭl), *to writhe*, to be tormented, to be pained—a word not unfrequently applied to the pains of parturition. But it is probable that it is rather to be regarded as derived from חָלַל, *to pierce*, or to wound. ¶ *For our transgressions.* The prophet here places himself among the people for whom the Messiah suffered these things, and says that he was not suffering for his own sins, but on account of theirs. The preposition 'for' (מִן) here answers to the Greek διά, on account of, and denotes the cause for which he suffered, and means, even according to Gesenius (*Lex.*), here, 'the ground or motive on account of, or because of which anything is done.' Compare Deut. vii. 7; Judg. v. 11; Est. v. 9; Ps. lxviii. 30; Cant. iii. 8. It is strikingly parallel to the passage in Rom. iv. 25 : 'Who was delivered for (διά) our offences.' Compare 2 Cor. v. 21; Heb. ix. 28; 1 Pet. ii. 24. Here the sense is, that the reason why he thus suffered was, that we were transgressors. All along the prophet keeps up the idea that it was not on account of any sin of which he was guilty that he thus suffered, but it was for the sins of others—an idea which is everywhere exhibited in the New Testament. ¶ He was *bruised*. The word here used (דָּכָא) means properly *to be broken to pieces*, to be bruised, to be crushed (Job vi. 9; Ps. lxxii. 4). Applied to mind, it means to break down or crush by calamities

and trials; and by the use of the word here, no doubt, the most severe inward and outward sufferings are designated. The LXX. render it, Μεμαλάκισται— 'He was rendered languid,' or feeble. The same idea occurs in the Syriac translation. The meaning is, that he was under such a weight of sorrows on account of our sins, that he was, as it were, crushed to the earth. How true this was of the Lord Jesus it is not necessary here to pause to show. ¶ *The chastisement of our peace.* That is, the chastisement by which our peace is effected or secured was laid upon him; or, he took it upon himself, and bore it, in order that we might have peace. Each word here is exceedingly important, in order to a proper estimate of the nature of the work performed by the Redeemer. The word 'chastisement' (מוּסָר), properly denotes the correction, chastisement, or punishment inflicted by parents on their children, designed to amend their faults (Prov. xxii. 15; xxiii. 13). It is applied also to the discipline and authority of kings (Job xxii. 18); and to the discipline or correction of God (Job v. 17; Hos. v. 2). Sometimes it means admonition or instruction, such as parents give to children, or God to men. It is well rendered by the LXX. by Παιδεία; by Jerome, *Disciplina*. The word does not of necessity denote *punishment*, though it is often used in that sense. It is properly that which *corrects*, whether it be by admonition, counsel, punishment, or suffering. Here it cannot properly mean *punishment*—for there is no punishment where there is no guilt, and the Redeemer had done no sin ;—but it means that he took upon himself the sufferings which would secure the peace of those for whom he died—those which, if they could have been endured by themselves, would have effected their peace with God. The word *peace* means evidently their peace with God ; reconciliation with their Creator. The work of religion in the soul is often represented as *peace ;* and the Redeemer is spoken of as the great agent by whom that is secured. 'For he is our peace' (Eph. ii. 14, 15, 17; comp. Acts x. 36; Rom. v. 1; x. 15). The phrase 'upon him,' means that the burden by which the peace of men was effected was laid upon him, and that he bore it. It is parallel with the expressions which speak of his *bearing* it, *carrying* it, &c. And the sense of the whole is, that he endured the sorrows, whatever they were, which were needful to secure our peace with God. ¶ *And with his stripes.* Marg. 'Bruise.' The word here used in Hebrew (הַחֲבוּרָה) means properly *stripe, weal, bruise, i.e.,* the mark or print of blows on the skin. Gr. Μώλωπι. Vulg. *Livore.* On the meaning of the Hebrew word, see Notes on ch. i. 6. It occurs in the following places, and is translated by stripe, and stripes (Ex. xxi. 25, *bis*); bruises (Isa. i. 6); hurt (Gen. iv. 23); blueness (Prov. xx. 30); wounds (Ps. xxxviii. 5); and spots, as of a leopard (Jer. xiii. 23). The proper idea is the weal or wound made by bruising; the mark designated by us when we speak of its being 'black and blue.' It is not a flesh wound; it does not draw blood; but the blood and other humours are collected under the skin. The obvious and natural idea conveyed by the word here is, that the individual referred to would be subjected to some treatment that would cause such a weal or stripe; that is, that he would be beaten, or scourged. How literally this was applicable to the Lord Jesus, it is unnecessary to attempt to prove (see Matt. xxvii. 26). It may be remarked here, that this could not be mere conjecture How could Isaiah, seven hundred years before it occurred, *conjecture* that the Messiah would be *scourged* and *bruised?* It is this *particularity* of prediction, compared with the literal fulfilment, which furnishes the fullest demonstration that the prophet was inspired. In the prediction nothing is *vague* and *general.* All is particular and minute, as if he saw what was done, and the description is as minutely accurate as if he was describing what was actually occurring before his eyes. ¶ *We are healed.* Literally, it is healed to us; or healing has happened to us. The *healing* here referred to, is spiritual healing, or healing from sin. Pardon of sin, and restoration to the favour of God, are not unfrequently represented as an act of *healing.* The figure is derived from

the fact that awakened and convicted sinners are often represented as crushed, broken, bruised by the weight of their transgressions, and the removal of the load of sin is represented as an act of healing. 'I said, O LORD, be merciful unto me; heal my soul; for I have sinned againt thee' (Ps. xli. 4). 'Have mercy upon me, O LORD, for I am weak; O LORD, heal me, for my bones are vexed' (Ps. vi. 2). 'Who forgiveth all thine iniquities; who healeth all thy diseases' (Ps. ciii. 3). The idea here is, that the Messiah would be scourged; and that it would be by that scourging that health would be imparted to our souls. It would be in our place, and in our stead; and it would be designed to have the same effect in recovering us, as though it had been inflicted on ourselves. And will it not do it? Is it not a fact that it has such an effect? Is not a man *as* likely to be recovered from a course of sin and folly, who sees another suffer in his place what he ought himself to suffer, as though he was punished himself? Is not a wayward and dissipated son quite as likely to be recovered to a course of virtue by seeing the sufferings which his career of vice causes to a father, a mother, or a sister, as though he himself were subjected to severe punishment? When such a son sees that he is bringing down the gray hairs of his father with sorrow to the grave; when he sees that he is breaking the heart of the mother that bore him; when he sees a sister bathed in tears, or in danger of being reduced to poverty or shame by his course, it will be far more likely to reclaim him than would be personal suffering, or the prospect of poverty, want, and an early death. And it is on this principle that the plan of salvation is founded. We shall be more certainly reclaimed by the voluntary sufferings of the innocent in our behalf, than we should be by being personally punished. Punishment would make no atonement, and would bring back no sinner to God. But the suffering of the Redeemer in behalf of men is adapted to save the world, and will in fact arrest, reclaim, and redeem all who shall ever enter into heaven.

[Sin is not only a crime for which we were

6 All we, like sheep, have gone astray; we have turned every one

1 made the iniquities of us all to meet on him.

to his own way; and the LORD hath laid ¹ on him the iniquity of us *ᵃ* all.

a Ro.4.25; 1 Pe.3.18.

condemned to die, and which Christ purchased for us the pardon of, but it is a disease which tends directly to the death of our souls, and which Christ provided for the cure of. *By his stripes, i.e.,* the sufferings he underwent, he purchased for us the Spirit and grace of God, to mortify our corruptions, which are the distempers of our souls; and to put our souls in a good state of health, that they may be fit to serve God, and prepare to enjoy him. And by the doctrine of Christ's cross, and the powerful arguments it furnisheth us with against sin, the dominion of sin is broken in us, and we are fortified against that which feeds the disease.—*Henry.*]

6. *All we, like sheep, have gone astray.* This is the penitent confession of those for whom he suffered. It is an acknowledgment that they were going astray from God; and the reason why the Redeemer suffered was, that the race had wandered away, and that JE-HOVAH had laid on him the iniquity of all. Calvin says, ' In order that he might more deeply impress on the minds of men the benefits derived from the death of Christ, he shows how necessary was that healing of which he had just made mention. There is here an elegant antithesis. For in ourselves we were scattered; in Christ we are collected together; by nature we wander, and are driven headlong towards destruction; in Christ we find the way by which we are led to the gate of life.' The condition of the race without a Redeemer is here elegantly compared to a flock without a shepherd, which wanders where it chooses, and which is exposed to all dangers. This image is not unfrequently used to denote estrangement from God (1 Pet. ii. 25): ' For ye were as sheep going astray, but are now returned to the Shepherd and Bishop of your souls.' Compare Num. xxvii. 17; 1 Kings xxii. 17; Ps. cxix. 176; Ezek. xxxiv. 5; Zech. x. 2; Matt. ix. 36. Nothing could more strikingly represent the condition of men. They had wandered from God. They were following their own paths, and pursuing their own pleasures. They were without a protector, and they were exposed on every hand to danger. ¶ *We have turned every one to his own way.*

We had all gone in the path which we chose. We were like sheep which have no shepherd, and which wander where they please, with no one to collect, defend, or guide them. One would wander in one direction, and another in another; and, of course, solitary and unprotected, they would be exposed to the more danger. So it was, and is, with man. The bond which should have united him to the Great Shepherd, the Creator, has been broken. We have become lonely wanderers, where each one pursues his own interest, forms his own plans, and seeks to gratify his own pleasures, regardless of the interest of the whole. If we had not sinned, there would have been a common bond to unite us to God, and to each other. But now we, as a race, have become dissocial, selfish, following our own pleasures, and each one living to gratify his own passions. What a true and graphic description of man! How has it been illustrated in all the selfish schemes and purposes of the race! And how is it still illustrated every day in the plans and actions of mortals! ¶ *And the* LORD *hath laid on him.* Lowth renders this, ' JEHOVAH hath made to light on him the iniquity of us all.' Jerome (Vulg.) renders it, *Posuit Dominus in eo*—' The Lord placed on him the iniquity of us all.' The LXX. render it, Κύριος παρέδωκεν αὐτὸν ταῖς ἁμαρτίαις ἡμῶν—' The Lord gave him for our sins.' The Chaldee renders it, ' From the presence of the Lord there was a willingness (רַעֲוָא) to forgive the sins of all of us on account of him.' The Syriac has the same word as the Hebrew. The word here used (פָּגַע) means, properly, *to strike upon* or *against,* to impinge on any one or anything, as the Gr. πηγνύω. It is used in a hostile sense, to denote an act of rushing upon a foe (1 Sam. xxii. 17; to kill, to slay (Judg. viii. 21; xv. 12; 2 Sam. i. 15). It also means to light upon, to meet with any one (Gen. xxviii. 11; xxxii. 2). Hence also to make peace with any one; to strike a league or compact (Isa. lxiv. 4). It is rendered, in our English version, ' reacheth to ' (Josh. xix. 11, 22, 26,

7 He was oppressed, and he was afflicted ; yet he opened not his mouth : he is brought as a lamb to the slaughter, and as a sheep before her shearers is dumb, so he opened not his mouth.

27, 34); 'came,' (Josh. xvi. 7); 'met' and 'meet' (Gen. xxxii. 1; Ex. xxiii. 4; Num. xxxv. 19; Josh. ii. 16; xviii. 10; Ruth ii. 22; 1 Sam. x. 5; Isa. lxiv. 5; Amos v. 19); 'fall' (Judg. viii. 21; 1 Sam. xxii. 17; 2 Sam. i. 15; 1 Kings ii. 29); 'entreat' (Gen. xviii. 8; Ruth i. 16; Jer. xv. 11); 'make intercession' (Isa. lix. 16; liii. 12; Jer. vii. 16; xxvii. 18; xxxvi. 25); 'he that comes betwixt' (Job xxxvi. 22); and 'occur' (1 Kings v. 4). The radical idea seems to be that of *meeting*, occurring, encountering ; and it means here, as Lowth has rendered it, that they were caused to *meet* on him, or perhaps more properly, that JEHOVAH caused them to *rush* upon him, so as to overwhelm him in calamity, as one is overcome or overwhelmed in battle. The sense is, that he was not overcome by his own sins, but that he encountered *ours*, as if they had been made to rush to meet him and to prostrate him. That is, he suffered in our stead ; and whatever he was called to endure was in consequence of the fact that he had taken the place of sinners; and having taken their place, he *met* or *encountered* the sufferings which were the proper expressions of God's displeasure, and sunk under the mighty burden of the world's atonement. ¶ *The iniquity of us all* (see Notes on ver. 5). This cannot mean that he became a sinner, or was guilty in the sight of God ; for God always regarded him as an innocent being. It can only mean that he suffered *as if* he had been a sinner ; or, that he suffered that which, *if* he had been a sinner, would have been a proper expression of the evil of sin. It may be remarked here—1. That it is impossible to find stronger language to denote the fact that his sufferings were intended to make expiation for sin. Of what *martyr* could it be said that JEHOVAH had caused to meet on him the sins of the world ? 2. This language is that which naturally expresses the idea that he suffered for *all men*. It is universal in its nature, and naturally conveys the idea that there

was no limitation in respect to the number of those for whom he died.*

7. *He was oppressed* (בגשׂ). Lowth renders this, 'It was exacted.' Hengstenberg, 'He was abased.' Jerome (Vulg.), 'He was offered because he was willing.' The LXX. 'He, on account of his affliction, opened not his mouth,' —implying that his silence arose from the extremity of his sorrows. The Chaldee renders it, 'He prayed, and he was heard, and before he opened his mouth he was accepted.' The Syriac, 'He came and humbled himself, neither did he open his mouth.' Kimchi supposes that it means, 'it was exacted;' and that it refers to the fact that taxes were demanded of the exiles, when they were in a foreign land. The word here used (בגשׂ) properly means, *to drive*, to impel, to urge ; and then to urge a debtor, to exact payment ; or to exact tribute, a ransom, &c. (see Deut. xv. 2, 3; 2 Kings xxiii. 35.) Compare Job iii. 18; Zech. ix. 8; x. 4, where one form of the word is rendered 'oppressor;' Job xxxix. 7, the 'driver;' Ex. v. 6, 'taskmasters;' Dan. xi. 20, 'a raiser of taxes.' The idea is that of *urgency*, oppression, vexation, of being hard pressed, and ill treated. It does not refer here necessarily to what was exacted by God, or to sufferings inflicted by him—though it may include those—but it refers to *all* his oppressions, and the severity of his sufferings from all quarters. He was urged, impelled, oppressed, and yet he was patient as a lamb. ¶ *And he was afflicted*. Jahn and Steudel propose to render this, 'He suffered himself to be afflicted.' Hengstenberg renders it, 'He suffered patiently, and opened not his mouth.' Lowth, 'He was made answerable; and he opened not his mouth.' According to this, the idea is, that he had voluntarily taken upon himself the sins of

* See the Supplementary Notes on imputation of sin and extent of atonement, under Rom. v. 12, 19; 2 Cor. v. 19; Gal. iii. 13; and 1 Cor. v. 14.

8 He *a* was taken ¹ from prison and from judgment: and who shall declare his generation? for he *b* was

a Ac.8.32-35.

¹ or, *away by distress and judgment; but who.*

cut off out of the land of the living; for the transgression of my people was he stricken.

b Da.9.26.

men, and that having done so, he was held answerable as a surety. But it is doubtful whether the Hebrew will bear this construction. According to Jerome, the idea is that he voluntarily submitted, and that this was the cause of his sufferings. Hensler renders it, 'God demands the debt, and he the great and righteous one suffers.' It is probable, however, that our translation has retained the correct sense. The word עָנָה, in Niphil, means *to be afflicted*, to suffer, be oppressed or depressed (Ps. cxix. 107), and the idea here is, probably, that he was greatly distressed and afflicted. He was subjected to pains and sorrows which were hard to be borne, and which are usually accompanied with expressions of impatience and lamentation. The fact that *he* did not open his mouth in complaint was therefore the more remarkable, and made the merit of his sufferings the greater. ¶ *Yet he opened not his mouth.* This means that he was perfectly quiet, meek, submissive, patient, He did not open his mouth to complain *of* God on account of the great sorrows which he had appointed to him; nor *to* God on account of his being ill-treated by man. He did not use the language of reviling when he was reviled, nor return on men the evils which they were inflicting on him (comp. Ps. xxxix. 9). How strikingly and literally was this fulfilled in the life of the Lord Jesus! It would seem almost as if it had been written after he lived, and was history rather than prophecy. In no other instance was there ever so striking an example of perfect patience; no other person ever so entirely accorded with the description of the prophet. ¶ *He is brought as a lamb to the slaughter.* This does not mean that he was led to the slaughter as a lamb is, but that as a lamb which is led to be killed is patient and silent, so was he. He made no resistance. He uttered no complaint. He suffered himself to be led quietly along to be put to death. What a striking

and beautiful description! How tender and how true! We can almost see here the meek and patient Redeemer led along without resistance; and amidst the clamour of the multitude that were assembled with various feelings to conduct him to death, himself perfectly silent and composed. With all power at his disposal, yet as quiet and gentle as though he had no power; and with a perfect consciousness that he was going to die, as calm and as gentle as though he were ignorant of the design for which they were leading him forth. This image occurs also in Jeremiah, ch. xi. 19, 'But I was like a lamb or an ox that is brought to the slaughter.' ¶ *As a sheep.* As a sheep submits quietly to the operation of shearing. Compare 1 Pet. ii. 23, 'Who when he was reviled, reviled not again.' Jesus never opened his mouth to revile or complain. It was opened only to bless those that cursed him, and to pray for his enemies and murderers.

8. *He was taken from prison.* Marg. 'Away by distress and judgment.' The general idea in this verse is, that the sufferings which he endured for his people were terminated by his being, after some form of trial, cut off out of the land of the living. Lowth renders this, 'By an oppressive judgment he was taken off.' Noyes, 'By oppression and punishment he was taken away.' The LXX. render it, 'In his humiliation (ἐν τῇ ταπεινώσει), his judgment (ἡ κρίσις αὐτοῦ), [his legal trial, *Thomson*], was taken away;' and this translation was followed by Philip when he explained the passage to the eunuch of Ethiopia (Acts viii. 33). The eunuch, a native of Ethiopia, where the Septuagint was commonly used, was reading this portion of Isaiah in that version, and the version was sufficiently accurate to express the general sense of the passage, though it is by no means a literal translation. The Chaldee renders this verse, 'From infirmities and retribution he shall collect our captivity, and the

wonders which shall be done for us in his days who can declare? Because he shall remove the dominion of the people from the land of Israel; the sins which my people have sinned shall come even unto them.' The Hebrew word which is here used (עֹצֶר, from עָצַר, *to shut up, to close,* means properly *a shutting up,* or *closure;* and then constraint, oppression, or vexation. In Ps. cvii. 39, it means violent restraint, or oppression. It does not mean *prison* in the sense in which that word is now used. It refers rather to restraint, and detention; and would be better translated by *confinement,* or by *violent oppression.* The Lord Jesus, moreover, was not confined in prison. He was bound, and placed under a guard, and was thus secured. But neither the word used here, nor the account in the New Testament, leads us to suppose that in fact he was incarcerated. There is a strict and entire conformity between the statement here, and the facts as they occurred on the trial of the Redeemer (see John xviii. 24; comp. Notes on Acts viii. 33). ¶ *And from judgment.* From a judicial decision; or by a judicial sentence. This statement is made in order to make the account of his sufferings more definite. He did not merely suffer affliction; he was not only a man of sorrows in general; he did not suffer in a tumult, or by the excitement of a mob: but he suffered under a form of law, and a sentence was passed in his case (comp. Jer. i. 16; 2 Kings xxv. 6), and in accordance with that he was led forth to death. According to Hengstenberg, the two words here 'by oppression,' and 'by judicial sentence,' are to be taken together as a hendiadys, meaning an oppressive, unrighteous proceeding. So Lowth understands it. It seems to me, however, that they are rather to be taken as denoting separate things—the *detention* or *confinement* preliminary to the trial, and the sentence consequent upon the mock trial. ¶ *And who shall declare his generation?* The word rendered 'declare' means to relate, or announce. 'Who can give a correct statement in regard to it'—implying either that there was some want of willingness or ability to do it. This

phrase has been very variously interpreted; and it is by no means easy to fix its exact meaning. Some have supposed that it refers to the fact that when a prisoner was about to be led forth to death, a crier made proclamation calling on any one to come forward and assert his innocence, and declare his manner of life. But there is not sufficient proof that this was done among the Jews, and there is no evidence that it was done in the case of the Lord Jesus. Nor would this interpretation exactly express the sense of the Hebrew. In regard to the meaning of the passage, besides the sense referred to above, we may refer to the following opinions which have been held, and which are arranged by Hengstenberg:—1. Several, as Luther, Calvin, and Vitringa, translate it, ' Who will declare the length of his life?' *i.e.,* who is able to determine the length of his future days—meaning that there would be no end to his existence, and implying that though he would be cut off, yet he would be raised again, and would live for ever. To this, the only material objection is, that the word דּוֹר *dōr (generation),* is not elsewhere used in that sense. Calvin, however, does not refer it to the personal life of the Messiah, so to speak, but to his life in the church, or to the perpetuity of his life and principles in the church which he redeemed. His words are: ' Yet we are to remember that the prophet does not speak only of the person of Christ, but embraces the whole body of the church, which ought never to be separated from Christ. We have, therefore, says he, a distinguished testimony respecting the perpetuity of the church. For as Christ lives for ever, so he will not suffer his kingdom to perish.'—(*Comm. in loco.*) 2. Others translate it, ' Who of his contemporaries will consider it,' or 'considered it?' So Storr, Döderlin, Dathe, Rosenmüller and Gesenius render it. According to Gesenius it means, ' Who of his contemporaries considered that he was taken out of the land of the living on account of the sin of my people?' 3. Lowth and some others adopt the interpretation first suggested, and render it, ' His manner of life who would declare?' In support of this, Lowth appeals to the passages from the Mishna and the Gemara of Babylon, where it is said that before any one was punished for a capital crime, proclamation was made before him by a crier in these words, 'Whosoever knows anything about his innocence, let him come and make it known.' On this passage the Gemara of Babylon adds, 'that before the death of Jesus, this proclamation was made forty days; but no defence could be found.' This is certainly false; and there is no sufficient reason to think that the custom prevailed at all in the time of Isaiah, or in the time of the Saviour. 4. Others render it, 'Who can express his posterity, the number of his descendants?' So Hengstenberg renders it. So also Kimchi. 5. Some of the fathers referred it to the humanity of Christ, and to his miraculous conception. This was the belief of Chrysostom. See Calvin *in loco.* So also Morerius and Cajetan understood it. But the word is never used in this sense. The word דּוֹר *dōr* (*generation*), means properly an age, generation of men; the revolving period or circle of human life; from דּוּר *dūr, a circle* (Deut. xxiii. 3, 4, 9; Eccl. i. 4). It then means, also, a dwelling, a habitation (Ps. xlix. 20; Isa. xxxviii. 12). It occurs often in the Old Testament, and is in all other instances translated 'generation,' or 'generations.' Amidst the variety of interpretations which have been proposed, it is perhaps not possible to determine with any considerable degree of certainty what is the true sense of the passage. The only light, it seems to me, which can be thrown on it, is to be derived from the 10th verse, where it is said, 'He shall see his seed, he shall prolong his days;' and this would lead us to suppose that the sense is, that he would have a posterity which no one would be able to enumerate, or declare. According to this, the sense would be, 'He shall be indeed cut off out of the land of the living. But his name, his *race* shall not be extinct. Notwithstanding this, his generation, race, posterity, shall be so numerous that no one shall be able to declare it.' This interpretation is not quite satisfactory, but

it has more probabilities in its favour than any other. ¶ *For* (כִּי *ki*). This particle does not here denote the *cause* of what was just stated, but points out the connection (comp. 1 Sam. ii. 21; Ezra x. 1). In these places it denotes the same as 'and.' This seems to be the sense here. Or, if it be here a *causal* particle, it refers not to what immediately goes before, but to the general strain and drift of the discourse. All this would occur to him because he was cut off on account of the transgression of his people. He was taken from confinement, and was dragged to death by a judicial sentence, and he should have a numerous spiritual posterity, *because* he was cut off on account of the sins of the people. ¶ *He was cut off.* This evidently denotes a violent, and not a peaceful death. See Dan. ix. 26: 'And after threescore and two weeks shall the Messiah be cut off, but not for himself.' The LXX. render it, 'For his life is taken away from the earth.' The word here used (נִגְזַר), means properly *to cut*, to cut in two, to divide. It is applied to the act of cutting down trees with an axe (see 2 Kings vi. 4). Here the natural and obvious idea is, that he would be violently taken away, as if he was cut down in the midst of his days. The word is never used to denote a peaceful death, or a death in the ordinary course of events; and the idea which would be conveyed by it would be, that the person here spoken of would be cut off in a violent manner in the midst of his life. ¶ *For the transgression of my people.* The meaning of this is not materially different from 'on account of our sins.' 'The speaker here—Isaiah—does not place himself in opposition to the people, but includes himself among them, and speaks of them as his people, *i.e.,* those with whom he was connected.'—(Hengstenberg.) Others, however, suppose that JEHOVAH is here introduced as speaking, and that he says that the Messiah was to be cut off for the sins of *his* people. ¶ *Was he stricken.* Marg. 'The stroke upon him;' *i.e.,* the stroke came upon him. The word rendered in the margin 'stroke' (נֶגַע), denotes properly *a blow* (Deut. xvii. 8

9 And he made his grave with the wicked, and with the rich *a* in his death ;[1] because he had done no violence, neither *was any* deceit in his mouth.

a Mat. 27. 57.   1 *deaths.*

xxi. 5); then a spot, mark, or blemish in the skin, whether produced by the leprosy or any other cause. It is the same word which is used in ver. 4 (see Note on that verse). The Hebrew, which is rendered in the margin ' upon him ' (לָמוֹ) has given rise to much discussion. It is properly and usually in the plural form, and it has been seized upon by those who maintain that this whole passage refers not to one individual but to some *collective* body, as of the people, or the prophets (see Analysis prefixed to ch. lii. 13), as decisive of the controversy. To this word Rosenmüller, in his Prolegomena to the chapter, appeals for a decisive termination of the contest, and supposes the prophet to have used this plural form for the express purpose of clearing up any difficulty in regard to his meaning. Gesenius refers to it for the same purpose, to demonstrate that the prophet must have referred to some *collective* body—as the prophets—and not to an individual. Aben Ezra and Abarbanel also maintain the same thing, and defend the position that it can never be applied to an individual. This is not the place to go into an extended examination of this word. The difficulties which have been started in regard to it, have given rise to a thorough critical examination of the use of the particle in the Old Testament, and an inquiry whether it is ever used in the singular number. Those who are disposed to see the process and the result of the investigation, may consult Ewald's *Heb. Grammar*, Leipzig, 1827, p. 365 ; Wiseman's *Lectures*, pp. 331–333, Andover Edit., 1837; and Hengstenberg's *Christology*, p. 523. In favour of regarding it as here used in the singular number, and as denoting an individual, we may just refer to the following considerations :—1. It is so rendered by Jerome, and in the Syriac version. 2. In some places the suffix מוֹ, attached to nouns, is certainly singular. Thus in Ps. xi. 7, (פָּנֵימוֹ) ' *His* face,' speaking of God; Job xxvii. 23, ' Men shall clap

their hands at him ' (עָלֵימוֹ), where it is certainly singular; Isa. xliv. 15, ' He maketh it a graven image, and falleth down thereto ' (לָמוֹ). 3. In Ethiopic the suffix is certainly singular (Wiseman). These considerations show that it is proper to render it in the singular number, and to regard it as referring to an individual. The LXX. render it, Εἰς Θάνατον—' Unto death,' and evidently read it as if it were an abbreviation of לָמוּת *lâmŭth*, and they render the whole passage, ' For the transgressions of my people he was led unto death.' This translation is adopted and defended by Lowth, and has also been defended by Dr. Kennicott. The only argument which is urged, however, is, that it was so used by Origen in his controversy with the Jews ; that they made no objection to the argument that he urged; and that as Origen and the Jews were both acquainted with the Hebrew text, it is to be presumed that this was then the reading of the original. But this authority is too slight to change the Hebrew text. The single testimony of Origen is too equivocal to determine any question in regard to the reading of the Hebrew text, and too much reliance should not be reposed even on his statements in regard to a matter of fact. This is one of the many instances in which Lowth has ventured to change the Hebrew text with no sufficient authority.

9. *And he made his grave with the wicked.* Jerome renders this, *Et dabit impios pro sepultura et divitem pro morte sua.* The LXX. render it, ' I will give the wicked instead of his burial (ἀντὶ τῆς ταφῆς), and the rich in the place, or instead of his death ' (ἀντὶ τοῦ Θανάτου). The Chaldee renders it, ' He will deliver the wicked into Gehenna, and the rich in substance who oppress, by a death that is destructive, that the workers of iniquity may no more be established, and that they may no more speak deceit in their mouth.' The Syriac renders it beautifully, ' the wicked gave ܩܒܪܐ a grave,' ܡܘܬܗ. Heng-

stenberg renders it, 'They appointed him his grave with the wicked (but he was with a rich man after his death); although he had done nothing unrighteous, and there was no guile in his mouth.' The sense, according to him, is, that not satisfied with his sufferings and death, they sought to insult him even in death, since they wished to bury his corpse among criminals. It is then incidentally remarked, that this object was not accomplished. This whole verse is exceedingly important, and every word in it deserves a serious examination, and attentive consideration. It has been subjected to the closest investigation by critics, and different interpretations have been given to it. They may be seen at length in Rosenmüller, Gesenius, and Hengstenberg. The word rendered 'he made' (וַיִּתֵּן, from נָתַן *nâthăn*) is a word of very frequent occurrence in the Scriptures. According to Gesenius, it means—1. *To give*, as (*a*) to give the hand to a victor; (*b*) to give into the hand of any one, *i.e.*, the power; (*c*) to give, *i.e.*, to turn the back; (*d*) to give, *i.e.*, to yield fruit as a tree; (*e*) to give, *i.e.*, to show compassion; (*f*) to give honour, praise, &c.; (*g*) to give into prison, or into custody. 2. *To sit*, place, put, lay; (*a*) to set before any one; (*b*) to set one over any person or thing; (*c*) to give one's heart to anything; *i.e.*, to apply the mind, &c. 3. *To make;* (*a*) to make or constitute one as anything; (*b*) to make a thing *as* something else. The notion of *giving*, or *giving over*, is the essential idea of the word, and not that of *making*, as our translation would seem to imply; and the sense is, that he was *given by design* to the grave of the wicked, or it was *intended* that he should occupy such a grave. The meaning then would be,

And his grave was appointed with the wicked;
But he was with a rich man in his death—
Although he had done no wrong,
Neither was there any guile in his mouth.

But who gave, or appointed him? I answer—1. The word may either here be used impersonally, as in Ps. lxxii. 15. ' to him shall be given,' marg. ' one shall give,' Eccl. ii. 21, meaning, that *some one* gave, or appointed his grave with the wicked; *i.e.*, his grave *was*

appointed with the wicked; or, 2. The phrase ' my people ' (עַמִּי) must be supplied; my people appointed his grave to be with the wicked; or, 3. God gave, or appointed his grave with the wicked. It seems to me that it is to be regarded as used *impersonally*, meaning that his grave was appointed with the wicked; and then the sense will be, that it was designed that he should be buried with the wicked, without designating the person or persons who intended it. So it is correctly rendered by Lowth and Noyes, ' His grave was appointed with the wicked.' ¶ *With the wicked*. It was designed that he should be buried with the wicked. The sense is, that it was not only intended to put him to death, but also to heap the highest indignity on him. Hence, it was intended to deny him an honourable burial, and to consign him to the same ignominious grave with the violators of the laws of God and man. One part of an ignominious punishment has often been to deny to him who has been eminent in guilt an honourable burial. Hence, it was said of Ahab (1 Kings xxi. 19), that the dogs should lick his blood; and of Jezebel that the dogs should eat her (1 Kings xxi. 23). Thus of the king of Babylon (Isa. xiv. 19), that he should ' be cast out of his grave as an abominable branch ' (see Note on that place). Hence those who have been peculiarly guilty are sometimes quartered, and their heads and other parts of the body suspended on posts, or they are hung in chains, and their flesh left to be devoured by the fowls of heaven. So Josephus (*Ant.* iv. 8. 6), says, ' He that blasphemeth God, let him be stoned ; and let him hang on a tree all that day, and then let him be buried in an ignominious and obscure manner.' The idea here is, that it was intended to cast the highest possible indignity on the Messiah ; not only to put him to death, but even to deny him the privilege of an honourable burial, and to commit him to the same grave with the wicked. How remarkably was this fulfilled ! As a matter of course, since he was put to death with wicked men, he would naturally have been buried with them, unless there had been some special interposition in his case. He was given up to be treated as a criminal ; he was made to take the vacated place of a murderer—Barabbas—on the cross ; he was subjected to the same indignity and cruelty to which the two malefactors were ; and it was evidently designed also that he should be buried in the same manner, and probably in the same grave. Thus in John xix. 31, it is said that the Jews, because it was the preparation, in order that their bodies should not remain on the cross on the Sabbath day, 'besought Pilate that their legs might be broken, and that they might be taken away ;' intending evidently that their death should be hurried in the same cruel manner, and that they should be buried in the same way. Who can but wonder at the striking accuracy of the prediction! ¶ *And with the rich* (עָשִׁיר). The words ' he was,' are here to be supplied. ' But he was with a rich man in his death.' The particle וֹ, rendered *and*, is properly here adversative, and means *but, yet.* The meaning is, that although he had been executed with criminals, and it had been expected that he would be interred with them, yet he was associated with a rich man in his death ; *i.e.*, in his burial. The purpose which had been cherished in regard to his burial was not accomplished. The word עָשִׁיר (from עָשַׁר, *to be straight*, to prosper, to be happy, and then to be rich), means properly *the rich*, and then the honourable and noble. It occurs very often in the Bible (*see* Taylor's *Concord.*), and is in all cases in our English version rendered ' rich.' Gesenius contends, however, that it sometimes is to be taken in a bad sense, and that it means proud, arrogant, impious, because riches are a source of pride, and pride to a Hebrew is synonymous with impiety. He appeals to Job xxvii. 19, in proof of this. But it is evident that the place in Job, ' The rich man shall lie down, but he shall not be gathered,' may be understood as speaking of a rich man as he is commonly found ; and the *word* there does not mean proud, or wicked, but it means *a rich man* who is without religion. In all places where the word occurs in the Bible, the primary idea is that of *a rich man*—though he may be righteous or wicked, pious or impious, a friend of God or an enemy. That is to be determined by the connection. And the natural and proper idea here is that of a man who is wealthy, though without any intimation with regard to his moral character. It is rather implied that the man referred to would have a character different from ' the wicked,' with whom his grave was appointed. Several interpreters, however, of the highest character, have supposed that the word here refers to *the ungodly*, and means, that in his death he was associated with the ungodly. Thus Calvin supposes that it refers to the Scribes and Pharisees, and the impious and violent Romans who rushed upon him to take his life. Luther remarks that it means, ' a rich man ; one who gives himself to the pursuit of wealth ; *i.e.*, an ungodly man.' But the objection is insuperable that the word in the Bible *never* is used in this sense, to denote simply a wicked or an ungodly man. It may denote a rich man who *is* ungodly—but that must be determined by the connection. The simple idea in the word is that of *wealth*, but whether the person referred to be a man of fair or unfair, pure or impure character, is to be determined by other circumstances than the mere use of the word. So the word ' rich ' is used in our language, and in all languages. The principal reason why it has here been supposed to mean *ungodly* is, that the parallelism is supposed to require it. But this is not necessary. It may be designed to intimate that there was a distinction between the *design* which was cherished in regard to his burial, and the *fact*. It was intended that he should have been interred with the wicked ; but in fact, he was with the rich in his death. ¶ *In his death.* Marg. ' Deaths ' (בְּמֹתָיו). Lowth renders this, ' His tomb.' He understands the letter ב as *radical* and not *servile ;* and supposes that the word is בָּמוֹת *bâmōth (hills); i.e.*, sepulchral hills. Tombs, he observes, correctly, were often hills or *tumuli* erected over the bodies of the dead ; and he supposes that the word *hill*, or *high place*, became synonymous with a *tomb*, or sepulchre. This interpretation was first suggested by Aben Ezra, and has been approved by Œcolampadius, Zuingle, Drusius, Ikin, Kuinoel, and others. But the interpretation is liable to great objections. 1. It is opposed to all the ancient versions. 2. There is no evidence that the word בָּמוֹת *bâmōth* is ever used except in one place (Ezek. xliii. 7, where it means also primarily *high places*, though there perhaps dedenoting a burial-place), in the sense of βωμός, a tomb, or place of burial. It denotes a high place or height; a stronghold, a fastness, a fortress; and then an elevated place, where the rites of idolatry were celebrated; and though it is not improbable that those places became burial-places—as we bury in the vicinity of a place of worship—yet the word simply and by itself does not denote a *tumulus*, or an elevated place of burial. The word here, therefore, is to be regarded as a noun from מָוֶת *mâvěth*, or מוֹת *môth*, plural מוֹתִים *môthim*, meaning the same as 'after his death'— 'the grave.' The plural is used instead of the singular in Ezek. xxviii. 8–10; and also Job xxi. 32: 'Yet he shall be brought to the grave;' Marg. as Heb. 'graves.' The sense, therefore, is, that after his death he would be with a man of wealth, but without determining anything in regard to his moral character. The exact fulfilment of this may be seen in the account which is given of the manner of the burial of the Saviour by Joseph of Arimathea (Matt. xxvii. 57–60. Joseph was a rich man. He took the body, and wound it in a clean linen cloth, and laid it in his own new tomb, a tomb hewn out of a rock—that is, a grave designed for himself; such as a rich man would use, and where it was designed that a rich man should be laid. He was buried with spices (John xix. 39, 40); embalmed with a large quantity of myrrh and aloes, 'about a hundred pound weight,' in the mode in which *the rich* were usually interred. How different this from the interment of malefactors! How different from the way in which he would have been buried if he had been interred with them as it had been designed! And how very

striking and minutely accurate this prophecy in circumstances which could not *possibly* have been the result of conjecture! How *could* a pretended prophet, seven hundred years before the event occurred, conjecture of one who was to be executed as a malefactor, and with malefactors, and who would in the ordinary course of events be buried *with* malefactors, conjecture that he would be rescued from such an ignominious burial by the interposition of a rich man, and buried in a grave designed for a man of affluence, and in the manner in which the wealthy are buried? ¶ *Because* (עַל *âl*). This word here has probably the signification of *although*. It is used for עַל אֲשֶׁר *âl âshēr*. Thus it is used in Job xvi. 17: 'Not for *any* injustice in my hands;' Heb. 'Although there is no injustice in my hands.' The *sense* here demands this interpretation. According to our common version, the meaning is, that he was buried with the rich man *because* he had done no violence, and was guilty of no deceit; whereas it is rather to be taken in connection with the entire strain of the passage, and to be regarded as meaning, that he was wounded, rejected, put to death, and buried by the hands of men, *although* he had done no violence. ¶ *He had done no violence.* The precise sense of the expression is, that he had not by harsh and injurious conduct provoked them to treat him in this manner, or deserved this treatment at their hands. In accordance with this, and evidently with this passage in his eye, the apostle Peter says of the Lord Jesus, 'who did no, sin, neither was guile found in his mouth' (1 Pet. ii. 20–22). ¶ *Neither* was any *deceit in his mouth.* He was no deceiver, though he was regarded and treated as one. He was perfectly candid and sincere, perfectly true and holy. No one can doubt but this was exactly fulfilled in the Lord Jesus; and however it may be accounted for, it was true to the life, and it is applicable to him alone. Of what other dweller on the earth can it be said that there was *no* guile found in his mouth? Who else has lived who has *always* been perfectly free from deceit?

10 Yet it pleased the LORD to bruise him ; he hath put *him* to grief : [1] when thou shalt make his soul an *a* offering for sin, he shall see *his* seed, he shall prolong *his* days, and the pleasure *b* of the LORD shall prosper in his hand.

[1] or, *his soul shall make.*

a 2Co.5.21; He.9,24-26.   *b* 2 Th.1.11.

10. *Yet it pleased the* LORD *to bruise him.* In this verse, the prediction respecting the final glory and triumph of the Messiah commences. The design of the whole prophecy is to state, that in consequence of his great sufferings, he would be exalted to the highest honour (see Notes on ch. lii. 13). The sense of this verse is, ‘ he was subjected to these sufferings, not on account of any sins of his, but because, under the circumstances of the case, his sufferings would be pleasing to JEHOVAH. He saw they were necessary, and he was willing that he should be subjected to them. He has laid upon him heavy sufferings. And when he has brought a sin-offering, he shall see a numerous posterity, and the pleasure of the Lord shall prosper through him.’ The LORD was ‘pleased’ with his sufferings, not because he has delight in the sufferings of innocence ; not because the sufferer was in any sense guilty or ill-deserving ; and not because he was at any time displeased or dissatisfied with what the Mediator did, or taught. But it was—1. Because the Messiah had *voluntarily* submitted himself to those sorrows which were necessary to show the evil of sin ; and in view of the great object to be gained, the eternal redemption of his people, he was *pleased* that he would subject himself to so great sorrows to save them. He was pleased with the end in view, and with all that was necessary in order that the end might be secured. 2. Because these sufferings would tend to illustrate the Divine perfections, and show the justice and mercy of God. The gift of a Saviour, such as *he* was, evinced boundless benevolence ; his sufferings in behalf of the guilty showed the holiness of his nature and law ; and all demonstrated that he was at the same time disposed to save, and yet resolved that no one should be saved by dishonouring his law, or without expiation for the evil which had been done by sin. 3. Because these sorrows would result in the pardon and recovery of an innu-merable multitude of lost sinners, and in their eternal happiness and salvation. The whole work was one of benevolence, and JEHOVAH was pleased with it *as* a work of pure and disinterested love. ¶ *To bruise him* (see Notes on ver. 5). The word here is the infinitive of Piel. ‘ To bruise him, or his being bruised, was pleasing to JEHOVAH ;’ that is, it was acceptable to him that he should be *crushed* by his many sorrows. It does not of necessity imply that there was any *positive* and *direct* agency on the part of JEHOVAH in bruising him, but only that the fact of his being thus crushed and bruised was acceptable to him. ¶ *He hath put* him *to grief.* This word, ‘ hath grieved him,’ is the same which in another form occurs in ver. 4. It means that it was by the agency, and in accordance with the design of JEHOVAH, that he was subjected to these great sorrows. ¶ *When thou shalt make his soul.* Marg. ‘ His soul shall make.’ According to the translation in the text, the speaker is the prophet, and it contains an address to JEHOVAH, and JEHOVAH is himself introduced as speaking in ver. 11. According to the margin, JEHOVAH himself speaks, and the idea is, that his soul should make an offering for sin. The Hebrew will bear either. Jerome renders it, ‘ If he shall lay down his life for sin.’ The LXX. render it in the plural, ‘ If you shall give [an offering] for sin, your soul shall see a long-lived posterity.’ Lowth renders it, ‘ If his soul shall make a propitiatory sacrifice.’ Rosenmüller renders it, ‘ If his soul, *i.e.*, he himself, shall place his soul as an expiation for sin.’ Noyes renders it, ‘ But since he gave himself a sacrifice for sin.’ It seems to me that the margin is the correct rendering, and that it is to be regarded as in the third person. Thus the whole passage will be connected, and it will be regarded as the assurance of JEHOVAH himself, that when his life should be made a sacrifice for sin, he would see a great multitude who should be saved as the result of his sufferings and death. ¶ *His soul.* The word here rendered ' soul ' (שֶׁפֶשׁ) means properly *breath*, spirit, the life, the vital principle (Gen. i. 20–30; ix. 4; Lev. xvii. 11; Deut. xii. 23). It sometimes denotes the rational soul, regarded as the seat of affections and emotions of various kinds (Gen. xxxiv. 3; Ps. lxxxvi. 4; Isa. xv. 4; xlii. 1; Cant. i. 7; iii. 1–4). It is here equivalent to *himself*—when he himself is made a sin-offering, or sacrifice for sin. ¶ *An offering for sin* (אָשָׁם). This word properly means, *blame*, guilt which one contracts by transgression (Gen. xxvi. 10; Jer. li. 5); also a sacrifice for guilt; a sin-offering; an expiatory sacrifice. It is often rendered ' trespass-offering ' Lev. v. 19; vii. 5; xiv. 21; xix. 21; 1 Sam. vi. 3, 8, 17). It is rendered ' guiltiness ' (Gen. xxvi. 10); ' sin ' (Prov. xiv. 9); ' trespass ' (Num. v. 8). The idea here is, clearly, that he would be made an offering, or a sacrifice for sin ; that by which guilt would be expiated and an atonement made. In accordance with this, Paul says (2 Cor. v. 21), that God ' made him to be sin for us ' (ἁμαρτίαν), *i.e.*, a sin-offering ; and he is called ἱλασμὸς and ἱλαστήριον, a propitiatory sacrifice for sins (Rom. iii. 25 ; 1 John ii. 2 ; iv. 10). The idea is, that he was himself innocent, and that he gave up his soul or life in order to make an expiation for sin—as the innocent animal in sacrifice was offered to God as an acknowledgment of guilt. There could be no more explicit declaration that he who is referred to here, did not die as a martyr merely, but that his death had the high purpose of making expiation for the sins of men. Assuredly this is not language which can be used of any martyr. In what sense could it be said of Ignatius or Cranmer that their souls or lives were made *an offering* (אָשָׁם or ἱλασμὸς) for sin? Such language is never applied to martyrs in the Bible; such language is never applied to them in the common discourses of men. ¶ *He shall see his seed.* His posterity ; his descendants. The language here is taken from that which was regarded as the highest blessing among the Hebrews. With them length of days and a numerous posterity were regarded as the highest favours, and usually as the clearest proofs of the Divine love. ' Children's children are the crown of old men ' (Prov. xvii. 6). See Ps. cxxvii. 5; cxxviii. 6: ' Yea, thou shalt see thy children's children, and peace upon Israel.' So one of the highest blessings which could be promised to Abraham was that he would be made the father of many nations (Gen. xii. 2; xvii. 5, 6). In accordance with this, the Messiah is promised that he shall see a numerous spiritual posterity. A similar declaration occurs in Ps. xxii. 30, which is usually applied to the Messiah. ' A seed shall serve him ; it shall be accounted to the LORD for a generation.' The natural relation between father and son is often transferred to spiritual subjects. Thus the name *father* is often given to the prophets, or to teachers, and the name *sons* to disciples or learners. In accordance with this, the idea is here, that the Messiah would sustain this relation, and that there would be multitudes who would sustain to him the relation of spiritual children. There may be emphasis on the word ' see '— he shall *see* his posterity ; for it was regarded as a blessing not only to *have* posterity, but to be permitted to live and *see* them. Hence the joy of the aged Jacob in being permitted to *see* the children of Joseph (Gen. xlviii. 11): ' And Israel said unto Joseph, I had not thought to see thy face; and lo, God hath showed me also thy seed.' ¶ *He shall prolong his days.* His life shall be long. This also is language which is taken from the view entertained among the Hebrews that long life was a blessing, and was a proof of the Divine favour. Thus, in 1 Kings iii. 14, God says to Solomon, ' if thou wilt walk in my ways, and keep my statutes and my commandments, as thy father David did walk, then I will lengthen thy days ' (see Deut. xxv. 15; Ps. xxi. 4; xci. 16; Prov. iii. 2). The meaning here is, that the Messiah, though he should be put to death, would yet see great multitudes who should be his spiritual children. Though he should die, yet he would live again, and his days should be lengthened out. It is fulfilled in

11 He shall see of the travail of
his soul, *and* shall be satisfied : by
his *a* knowledge shall my righteous

servant *b* justify *c* many ; for he shall
bear their iniquities.

a Jn.17.3; 2Pe.1.2,3.   *b* 2 Jn.1.3.   *c* Ro.5.21.

the reign of the Redeemer on earth,
and in his eternal existence and glory
in heaven. ¶ *And the pleasure of the
Lord.* That is, that which shall please
Jehovah; the work which he desires
and appoints. ¶ *Shall prosper* (see
Notes on ch. lii. 13, where the same
word occurs). ¶ *In his hand.* Under
his government and direction. Religion
will be promoted and extended through
him. The reward of all his sufferings
in making an offering for sin would be,
that multitudes would be converted and
saved ; that his reign would be permanent, and that the work which Jehovah
designed and desired would prosper
under his administration.

11. *He shall see of the travail of his
soul.* This is the language of Jehovah,
who is again introduced as speaking.
The sense is, he shall see the fruit, or
the result of his sufferings, and shall be
satisfied. He shall see *so much good*
resulting from his great sorrows ; so
much happiness, and so many saved,
that the benefit shall be an ample compensation for all that he endured. The
word here rendered ' travail ' (עָמָל), denotes properly *labour, toil ;* wearisome
labour ; labour and toil which produce
exhaustion ; and hence sometimes vexation, sorrow, grief, trouble. It is rendered ' labour ' (Ps. xc. 10; cv. 44; Jer.
xx. 18; Eccl. ii. 11–20) ; ' perverseness '
(Num. xxi. 21); ' sorrow ' (Job iii. 10);
' wickedness ' (Job iv. 8); ' trouble '
(Job v. 6, 7; Ps. lxxiii. 5); ' mischief '
(Job xv. 35 ; Ps. vii. 13; x. 7–14 ;
xciv. 20); ' travail,' meaning labour, or
toil (Eccl. iv. 4–6); ' grievousness ' (Isa.
x. 1); ' iniquity ' (Hab. i. 13); ' toil '
(Gen. xli. 51); ' pain ' (Ps. xxv. 18);
and ' misery ' (Prov. xxxi. 7). The
word ' travail ' with us has two senses,
first, labour with pain, severe toil ; and
secondly, the pains of childbirth. The
word is used here to denote excessive
toil, labour, weariness ; and refers to
the arduous and wearisome labour and
trial involved in the work of redemption, as that which exhausted the powers
of the Messiah as a man, and sunk him

down to the grave. ¶ *And shall be
satisfied.* That is, evidently, he shall
be permitted to see so much fruit of his
labours and sorrows as to be an ample
recompence for all that he has done.
It is not improbable that the image here
is taken from a husbandman who labours
in preparing his soil for the seed, and
who waits for the harvest; and who,
when he sees the rich and yellow field
of grain in autumn, or the wain heavily
laden with sheaves, is abundantly satisfied for what he has done. He has
pleasure in the contemplation of his
labour, and of the result; and he does
not regret the wearisome days and the
deep anxiety with which he made preparation for the harvest. So with the
Redeemer. There will be rich and
most ample results for all that he has
done. And when he shall look on the
multitude that shall be saved; when he
shall see the true religion spreading
over the world; when he shall behold
an immense host which no man can
number gathered into heaven ; and
when he shall witness the glory that
shall result to God from all that he has
done, he shall see enough to be an
ample compensation for all that he has
endured, and he shall look on his work
and its glorious results with pleasure.
We may remark here that this implies
that *great* and *most glorious* results
will come out of this work. The salvation of a large portion of the race, of
multitudes which no man can number,
will be necessary to be any *suitable*
remuneration for the sufferings of the
Son of God. We may be assured that
he will be ' satisfied,' only when multitudes are saved ; and it is, therefore,
morally certain that a large portion of
the race, taken as a whole, will enter
into heaven. Hitherto the number has
been small. The great mass have rejected him, and have been lost. But
there are brighter times before the
church and the world. The pure gospel
of the Redeemer is yet to spread around
the globe, and it is yet to become, and
to be for ages, the religion of the world.

Age after age is to roll on when all shall know him and obey him ; and in those future times, what immense multitudes shall enter into heaven ! So that it may yet be seen, that the number of those who will be lost from the whole human family, compared with those who will be saved, will be no greater in proportion than the criminals in a well-organized community who are imprisoned are, compared with the number of obedient, virtuous, and peaceful citizens. ¶ *By his knowledge.* That is, by the knowledge of him. The idea is, by becoming fully acquainted with him and his plan of salvation. The word *knowledge* here is evidently used in a large sense to denote *all* that constitutes acquaintance with him. Thus Paul says (Phil. iii. 10), ' That I may know him, and the power of his resurrection.' It is only by the knowledge of the Messiah ; by an acquaintance with his character, doctrines, sufferings, death, and resurrection, that any one can be justified. Thus the Saviour says (John xvii. 3), ' And this is life eternal, that they might know thee the only true God, and Jesus Christ whom thou hast sent.' Men are to become acquainted with him ; with his doctrines, and with his religion, or they can never be regarded and treated as righteous in the sight of a holy God. ¶ *Shall my righteous servant.* On the meaning of the word ' servant,' as applied to the Messiah, see Notes on ch. lii. 13. The word ' righteous ' (צַדִּיק), Lowth supposes should be omitted. His reasons are—1. That three MSS., two of them ancient, omit it. 2. That it makes a solecism in this place ; for, according to the constant usage of the Hebrew language, the adjective, in a phrase of this kind, ought to follow the substantive ; and, 3. That it makes the hemistich too long. But none of these reasons are sufficient to justify a change in the text. The phrase literally is, ' the righteous, my servant ; ' and the sense is, evidently, ' my righteous servant.' The word *righteous*, applied to the Messiah, is designed to denote not only his personal holiness, but to have reference to the fact that he would make many *righteous* (יַצְדִּיק). It is

applicable to him, because he was eminently holy and pure, and because also he was the source of righteousness to others ; and in the work of justification it is important in the highest degree to fix the attention on the fact, that he by whom the sinner was to be justified was himself perfectly holy, and able to secure the justification and salvation of all who intrusted their souls to him. No man could feel secure of salvation unless he could commit his soul to one who was perfectly holy, and able to ' bring in everlasting righteousness.' ¶ *Justify* (יַצְדִּיק). The word צָדַק is of very frequent occurrence in the Bible ; and no word is more important to a correct understanding of the plan of salvation than this, and the corresponding Greek word δικαιῶ. On the meaning of the Greek word, see Notes on Rom. i. 17. The Hebrew word means to be right, straight, as if spoken of a way (Ps. xxiii. 3). Hence, 1. To be just, righteous, spoken of God in dispensing justice (Ps. lv. 6); and of laws (Ps. xix. 10). 2. To have a just cause, to be in the right; (*a*) in a forensic sense (Gen. xxviii. 26; Job ix. 16–20 ; x. 15; xiii. 18); (*b*) of disputants, to be in the right (Job xxiii. 12); (*c*) to gain one's cause, to be justified (Isa. xliii. 9– 26). In this sense it is now often used in courts of justice, where a man who is charged with crime shows that he did not do the deed, or that having done it he had a right to do it, and the law holds him innocent. 3. To be righteous, upright, good, innocent. In this sense the word is often used in the Bible (Job xv. 14; xxiii. 9; Ps. cxliii. 2). But in this sense the Messiah will *justify* no one. He did not come to declare that men *were* upright, just, innocent. Nor will he justify them because they can show that they have not committed the offences charged on them, or that they had a right to do what they have done. The whole work of justification through the Redeemer proceeds on the supposition that men are *not* in fact innocent, and that they cannot vindicate their own conduct. 4. In Hiphil, the word means, to pronounce just, or righteous. In a forensic sense, and as applied to the act of justification before

12 Therefore will I divide him *a portion* with the great, and he shall divide the spoil with the strong; because *a* he hath poured out his soul unto death : and he was numbered with the transgressors : and he bare the sin of many, and made intercession *b* for the transgressors.

a He.12.2.

b He.7.28; 1 Jn.2.1.

God, it means to declare righteous, or to admit to favour as a righteous person ; and in connection with the pardon of sin, to resolve to treat as righteous, or as if the offence had not been committed. It is more than mere pardon; it involves the idea of a purpose to *treat as* righteous, and to acknowledge as such. It is not to declare that the person is innocent, or that he is not ill deserving, or that he had a right to do as he had done, or that he has a claim to mercy—for this is not true of any mortal; but it is to pardon, and to accept him *as if* the offence had not been committed—to regard him in his dealings with him, and treat him ever onward as if he were holy. This sense of the word here is necessary, because the whole passage speaks of his bearing sin, and suffering for others, and thus securing their justification. It does not speak of him as instructing men and thus promoting religion ; but it speaks of his dying for them, and thus laying the foundation for their justification. They are justified only in connection with his bearing their iniquities ; and this shows that the word is here used in the *forensic* sense, and denotes that they will be regarded and treated as righteous on account of what he has suffered in their behalf. ¶ *For he shall bear.* On the meaning of the word *bear*, see Notes on ver. 4. ¶ *Their iniquities.* Not that he became a sinner, or that sin can be transferred, which is impossible. Guilt and ill desert are personal qualities, and cannot be transferred from one to another. But the *consequences* of guilt may pass over to another ; the *sufferings*, which would be a proper expression of the evil of sin, may be assumed by another. And this was done by the Redeemer. *He stood between the stroke of justice and the sinner, and received the blow himself.* He *intercepted,* so to speak, the descending sword of justice that would have cut the sinner down, and thus saved him. He thus bore their iniquities ; *i.e.,* he bore in his own person what would have been a proper expression of the evil of sin if he had been himself the sinner, and had been guilty (see Notes on ver. 6). It is in connection with this that men become justified ; and it is only by the fact that he has thus borne their iniquities that they can be regarded as righteous in the sight of a holy God. *They become interested in his merits just as he became interested in their iniquities.* There is in neither case any transfer of personal properties ; but there is in both cases a participation in the *consequences* or the *results* of conduct. *He* endured the consequences or results of sin ; *we* partake of the consequences or the results of his sufferings and death in our behalf. This is the great cardinal doctrine of justification; the peculiarity of the Christian scheme ; the glorious plan by which lost men may be saved, and by which the guilty may become pardoned, and be raised up to endless life and glory; the *articulus stantis vel cadentis ecclesiæ.* LUTHER.[*]

12. *Therefore will I divide him.* I will divide *for* him (לֹו *lo*). This verse is designed to predict the triumphs of the Messiah. It is language appropriate to him as a prince, and designed to celebrate his glorious victories on earth. The words here used are taken from the custom of distributing the spoils of victory after a battle, and the idea is, that as a conqueror takes valuable spoils, so the Messiah would go forth to the spiritual conquest of the world, and subdue it to himself. Rosenmüller renders this, *Dispertsam ei multos*—'I will divide to him the many ;' *i.e.,* he shall have many as his portion. Hengsten-

[*] See Supplementary Notes, Gal. iii. 13 ; 2 Cor. v. 19, 21 ; and Rom. iv., v., in which the reader will see that the doctrine of imputation involves no such transference of moral character, no such infusion of sin or righteousness, as the author here and elsewhere alleges.

berg, 'I will give him the mighty for a portion.' So the LXX. 'Therefore he shall inherit (κληρονομήσει) many.' So Lowth, 'Therefore will I distribute to him the many for his portion.' But it seems to me that the sense is, that his portion would be *with* the mighty or the many (בְּרַבִּים) and that this interpretation is demanded by the use of the preposition בְּ in this case, and by the corresponding word אֶת prefixed to the word 'mighty.' The sense, according to this, is, that the spoils of his conquests would be *among* the mighty or the many; that is, that his victories would not be confined to a few in number, or to the feeble, but the triumphs of his conquests would extend afar, and be found among the potentates and mighty men of the earth. The word rendered here 'the great' (רַבִּים *ráb-bim*), may mean either *many* or *powerful* and *great*. The parallelism here with the word עֲצוּמִים (*the mighty*), seems to demand that it be understood as denoting the great, or the powerful, though it is differently rendered by the Vulgate, the LXX., the Chaldee, by Castellio, and by Junius and Tremellius. The sense is, I think, that his conquests would be among the great and the mighty. He would overcome his most formidable enemies, and subdue them to himself. Their most valued objects; all that constituted their wealth, their grandeur, and their power, would be among the spoils of his victories. It would not be merely his feeble foes that would be subdued, but it would be the mighty, and there would be no power, however formidable, that would be able to resist the triumphs of his truth. The history of the gospel since the coming of the Redeemer shows how accurately this has been fulfilled. Already he has overcome the mighty, and the spoils of the conquerors of the world have been among the trophies of his victories. The Roman empire was subdued; and his conquests were among these conquerors, and his were victories over the subduers of nations. It will be still more signally fulfilled in coming times, when the kingdoms of this world shall become the kingdom of our Lord and of his Christ, and he shall reign for ever and ever (Rev. **xi.** 15). ¶ *And he shall divide the spoil with the strong.* And with the mighty, or with heroes, shall he divide the plunder. The idea here is not materially different from that which was expressed in the former member of the sentence. It is language derived from the conquests of the warrior, and means that his victories would be among the great ones of the earth; his conquests over conquerors. It was from language such as this that the Jews obtained the notion, that the Messiah would be a distinguished conqueror, and hence they looked forward to one who as a warrior would carry the standard of victory around the world. But it is evident that it may be applied with much higher beauty to the spiritual victories of the Redeemer, and that it expresses the great and glorious truth that the conquests of the true religion will yet extend over the most formidable obstacles on the earth. ¶ *Because he hath poured out his soul unto death.* His triumphs would be an appropriate reward for his sufferings, his death, and his intercession. The expression 'he poured out his soul,' or *his life* (נַפְשׁוֹ; see Notes on ver. 10), is derived from the fact that the life was supposed to reside in the blood (see Notes on Rom. iii. 25); and that when the blood was poured out, the life was supposed to flow forth with it. As a reward for his having thus laid down his life, he would extend his triumphs over the whole world, and subdue the most mighty to himself. ¶ *And he was numbered with the transgressors.* That is, he shall triumph *because* he suffered himself to be numbered with the transgressors, or to be put to death with malefactors. It does not mean that he was a transgressor, or in any way guilty; but that in his death he was in fact numbered with the guilty, and put to death with them. In the public estimation, and in the sentence which doomed him to death, he was regarded and treated as if he had been a transgressor. This passage is expressly applied by Mark to the Lord Jesus (Mark **xv.** 28). ¶ *And he bare the sin of many* (נָשָׂא *n.isâ*). On the meaning of this word 'bare,' see Notes on ver. 4;

and on the doctrine involved by his bearing sin, see the Note on ver. 4–6, 10. The idea here is, that he would triumph *because* he had thus borne their sins. As a reward for this God would bless him with abundant spiritual triumphs among men, and extend the true religion afar. ¶ *And made intercession for the transgressors.* On the meaning of the word here rendered ' made intercession ' (יַפְגִּיעַ), see Notes on ver. 6, where it is rendered ' hath laid on him.' The idea is that of causing to meet, or to rush ; and then to *assail,* as it were, with prayers, to supplicate for any one, to entreat (see Isa. lix. 16; Jer. xxxvi. 25). It may not refer here to the mere act of making prayer or supplication, but rather perhaps to the whole work of the intercession, in which the Redeemer, as High Priest, presents the merit of his atoning blood before the throne of mercy and pleads for men (see Rom. viii. 34; Heb. vii. 25; 1 John ii. 1). This is the closing part of his work in behalf of his people and of the world ; and the sense here is, that he would be thus blessed with abundant and wide extended triumph, *because* he made intercession. All his work of humiliation, and all his toils and sufferings, and all the merit of his intercession, became necessary in order to his triumph, and to the spread of the true religion. In consequence of all these toils, and pains, and prayers, God would give him the victory over the world, and extend his triumphs around the globe. Here the work of the Mediator *in behalf* of men will cease. There is to be no more suffering, and beyond his intercessions he will do nothing for them. He will come again indeed, but he will come to judge the world, not to suffer, to bleed, to die, and to intercede. All his future conquests and triumphs will be in consequence of what he has already done ; and they who are not saved *because* he poured out his soul unto death, *and* bare the sin of many, *and* made intercession, will not be saved at all. There will be no more sacrifice for sin, and there will be no other advocate and intercessor.

WE have now gone through, perhaps at tedious length, this deep'y interesting and most im-

portant portion of the Bible. Assuming now (see the remarks prefixed to ch. lii. 13, *sq.*) that this was written seven hundred years before the Lord Jesus was born, there are some remarks of great importance to which we may just refer in the conclusion of this exposition.

1. The first is, the *minute* accuracy of the statements here as applicable to the Lord Jesus. While it is apparent that there has been no other being on earth, and no " collective body of men," to whom this can be applied, it is evident that the whole statement is applicable to the Redeemer. It is not the general accuracy to which I refer; it is not that there is some resemblance in the *outline* of the prediction; it is, that the statement is *minutely* accurate. It relates to his appearance, his rejection, the manner of his death, his being pierced, his burial. It describes, as minutely as could have been done after the events occurred, the manner of his trial, of his rejection, the fact of his being taken from detention and by a judicial sentence, and the manner in which it was designed that he should be buried, and yet the remarkable fact that this was prevented, and that he was interred in the manner in which the rich were buried (see Notes on vers. 2, 3, 7–10).

2. This coincidence could never have occurred if the Lord Jesus had been an impostor. To say nothing of the difficulty of attempting to fulfil a prediction by imposture and the general failure in the attempt, there are many things here which would have rendered *any* attempt of this kind utterly hopeless. A very large portion of the things referred to in this chapter were circumstances over which an impostor could have no control, and which he could bring about by no contrivance, no collusion, and no concert. They depended on the arrangements of Providence, and on the voluntary actions of men, in such a way that he could not affect them. How could he so order it as to grow up as a root out of a dry ground; to be despised and rejected of men; to be taken from detention and from a judicial sentence though innocent; to have it designed that he should be buried with malefactors, and to be numbered with transgressors, and yet to be rescued by a rich man, and placed in his tomb? This consideration becomes more striking when it is remembered that not a few men claimed to be the Messiah, and succeeded in imposing on many, and though they were at last abandoned or punished, yet between *their* lives and death, and the circumstances here detailed, there is not the shadow of a coincidence. It is to be remembered also that an impostor *would* not have aimed at what would have constituted a fulfilment of this prophecy. Notwithstanding

the evidence that it refers to the Messiah, yet it is certain also that the Jews expected no such personage as that here referred to. They looked for a magnificent temporal prince and conqueror; and an impostor *would* not have attempted to evince the character, and to go through the circumstances of poverty, humiliation, shame, and sufferings, here described. What impostor ever *would* have attempted to fulfil a prophecy by subjecting himself to a shameful death? What impostor *could* have brought it about in this manner if he had attempted it? No; it was only the true Messiah that either would or could have fulfilled this remarkable prophecy. Had an impostor made the effort, he must have failed; and it was not in human nature to attempt it under the circumstances of the case. All the claims to the Messiahship by impostors have been of an entirely different character from that referred to here.

3. We are then prepared to ask an infidel how he will dispose of this prophecy. That it existed seven hundred years before Christ is as certain as that the poems of Homer or Hesiod had an existence before the Christian era; as certain as the existence of any ancient document whatever. It will not do to say that it was forged—for this is not only without proof, but would destroy the credibility of all ancient writings. It will not do to say that it was the result of natural sagacity in the prophet—for whatever may be said of conjectures about empires and kingdoms, no natural sagacity can tell what will be the character of an individual man, or whether such a man as here referred to would exist at all. It will not do to say that the Lord Jesus was a cunning impostor and resolved to fulfil this ancient writing, and thus establish his claims; for, as we have seen, such an attempt would have belied human nature, and if attempted, could not have been accomplished. It remains then to ask what solution the infidel will give of these remarkable facts. We present him the prophecy—not a rhapsody, not conjecture, not a general statement; but minute, full, clear, unequivocal, relating to points which could not have been the result of conjecture, and over which the individual had no control. And then we present him with the record of the life of Jesus—minutely accurate in all the details of the fulfilment—a coincidence *as* clear as that between a biography and the original—and ask him to explain it. And we demand a definite and consistent answer to this. To turn away from it does not answer it. To laugh, does not answer it; for there is no argument in a sneer or a jibe. To say that it is not

worth inquiry is not true, for it pertains to the great question of human redemption. But if he *cannot* explain it, then he should admit that it is such a prediction as only God could give, and that Christianity is true.

4. This chapter proves that the Redeemer died as an atoning sacrifice for men. He was not a mere martyr, and he did not come and live merely to set us an example. Of what martyr was the language here ever used, and how could it be used? How could it be said of any martyr that he bore our griefs, that he was bruised for our iniquities, that our sins were made to rush and meet upon him, and that he bare the sin of many? And if the purpose of his coming was merely to *teach* us the will of God, or to set us an example, why is such a prominence here given to his sufferings in behalf of others? Scarcely an allusion is made to his example, while the chapter is replete with statements of his sufferings and sorrows in behalf of others. It would be impossible to state in more explicit language the truth that he died as a sacrifice for the sins of men; that he suffered to make proper expiation for the guilty. No confession of faith on earth, no creed, no symbol, no standard of doctrine, contains more explicit statements on the subject. And if the language here used does not demonstrate that the Redeemer was an atoning sacrifice, it is impossible to conceive how such a doctrine could be taught or conveyed to men.

5. This whole chapter is exceedingly important to Christians. It contains the most full, continuous statement in the Bible of the design of the Redeemer's sufferings and death. And after all the light which is shed on the subject in the New Testament; after all the full and clear statements made by the Redeemer and the apostles; still, if we wish to see a full and continuous statement on the great doctrine of the atonement, we naturally recur to this portion of Isaiah. If we wish our faith to be strengthened, and our hearts warmed by the contemplation of his sufferings, we shall find no part of the Bible better adapted to it than this. It should not only be the subject of congratulation, but of much fervent prayer. No man can study it too profoundly. No one can feel too much anxiety to understand it. Every verse, every phrase, every word should be pondered until it fixes itself deep in the memory, and makes an eternal impression on the heart. If a man understands this portion of the Bible, he will have a correct view of the plan of salvation. And it should be the subject of profound and prayerful contemplation till the heart glows with love to that merciful God who was willing

to give the Redeemer to such sorrow, and to the gracious Saviour who, for our sins, was willing to pour out his soul unto death. I bless God that I have been permitted to study it; and I pray that this exposition—cold and imperfect as it is—may be made the means yet of extending correct views of the design of the Redeemer's death among his friends, and of convincing those who have doubted the truth of the Bible, that a prophecy like this demonstrates that the Book in which it occurs must be from God.

CHAPTER LIV.

ANALYSIS.

THIS chapter, probably closely connected in sense with the preceding, and growing out of the great truths there revealed respecting the work of the Messiah, contains a promise of the enlargement, the moral renovation, and the future glory of the kingdom of God, especially under the Messiah. Like the preceding and succeeding chapters, it may have been primarily designed to give consolation to the exiles in Babylon, but it was consolation to be derived from what would occur in distant times under the Messiah, and in the spread of the true religion. Few and feeble as they were then; oppressed and captive; despised and apparently forsaken, they were permitted to look forward to future days, and had the assurance of a vast increase from the Gentile world, and of permanent glory. The design of the whole chapter is *consolatory*, and is a promise of what would certainly result from the purpose of sending the Messiah to die for the world.

The chapter may be regarded as divided into the following portions:—

I. An address to the people of God, or to Jerusalem, regarded as then feeble, and promising great enlargement (1–6). 1. Promise of a great increase, under a two-fold image; first, Of a woman who had been barren, and who subsequently had many children (1); and, secondly, Of a *tent* that was to be enlarged, in order to accommodate those who were to dwell in it (2, 3). 2. The foundation of this promise or assurance, that JEHOVAH was the husband and protector of his people (4–6).

II. The covenant which JEHOVAH had made with his people was firm and immovable (7, 10). 1. He had indeed forsaken them for a little while, but it was only to gather them again with eternal and unchanging favour (7, 8). 2. His covenant with them would be as firm as that which he had made with Noah, and which he had so steadily observed (9). 3. It would be even more firm than the hills (10). They would depart, and the mountains would be removed; but his covenant with his people would be unshaken and eternal.

III. A direct address to his people, as if agitated and tossed on a heaving sea, promising future stability and glory (11–14). 1. They were then like a ship on the stormy ocean, and without comfort. 2. Yet there would be a firm foundation laid. These agitations would cease, and she would have stability. 3. The future condition of his people would be glorious. His church would rise on the foundation—the foundation of sapphires—like a splendid palace made of precious stones (11, 12). 4. All her children would be taught of JEHOVAH, and their peace and prosperity be great (13). 5. She would be far from oppression and from fear (14).

IV. She would be safe from all her foes. No weapon that should be formed against her would prosper. All they who made any attack on her were under his control, and God would defend her from all their assaults (15–17).

S ING, *a* O barren, thou *that* didst not bear ; break forth into singing, and cry aloud, thou *that* didst not travail with child : for more *are* the children of the desolate, than the children of the married wife, saith the LORD.

a Zep.3.14; Ga.4.27.

CHAPTER LIV.

1. *Sing, O barren.* That is, shout for joy, lift up the voice of exultation and praise. The 'barren' here denotes the church of God under the Old Testament, confined within the narrow limits of the Jewish nation, and still more so in respect to the very small number of true believers, and which seemed sometimes to be deserted of God, her husband (Lowth). It is here represented under the image of a female who had been destitute of children, and who now has occasion to rejoice on the reconciliation of her husband (ver. 6; Lowth), and on the accession of the Gentiles to her family. The Chaldee renders it, 'Rejoice, O Jerusalem, who hast been as a sterile woman that did not bear.' The church is often in the Bible compared to a female, and the connection between God and his people is often compared with that between husband and wife (comp. Isa. lxii. 5;

2 Enlarge the place of thy tent, and let them stretch forth the curtains of thine habitations: spare not, lengthen thy cords, and strengthen thy stakes:

3 For thou shalt break forth on the right hand and on the left; and thy seed shall inherit the Gentiles,

and make the desolate cities to be inhabited.

4 Fear not; for thou shalt not be ashamed: neither be thou confounded; for thou shalt not be put to shame; for thou shalt forget the shame of thy youth, and shalt not remember the reproach of thy widowhood any more.

Ezek. xvi.; Rev. xxi. 2–9; xxii. 17). ¶ *Thou* that *didst not bear.* Either referring to the fact that the church was confined within the narrow limits of Judea; or that there had been in it a small number of true believers; or addressed to it in Babylon when it was oppressed, and perhaps constantly diminishing in number. I think it probable that it refers to the latter; and that the idea is, that she saw her sons destroyed in the siege and destruction of Jerusalem, and that she was not augmented by any accessions while in Babylon, but would have great occasion for rejoicing on her return, and in her future increase under the Messiah by the accession of the Gentiles. ¶ *Break forth into singing* (comp. ch. xiv. 7; xliv. 23; xlix. 13). ¶ *For more are the children of the desolate.* The 'desolate' here refers to Jerusalem, or the church. By the 'married woman,' Rosenmüller supposes the prophet means other nations which flourished and increased like a married woman. Grotius supposes that he means other cities which were inhabited, and that Jerusalem would surpass them all in her prosperity and in numbers. But the phrase seems to have somewhat of a proverbial cast, and probably the idea is that there would be a great increase, a much greater increase than she had any reason to apprehend. As if a promise was made to a barren female that she should have more children than those who were married usually had, so Jerusalem and the church would be greatly enlarged, far beyond what usually occurred among nations. The fulfilment of this is to be looked for in the accession of the Gentiles (ver. 3). 'The conversion of the Gentiles is all along considered by the prophet as a new accession of adopted children, admitted into the original church of God,

and united with it' (Lowth). See the same idea presented at greater length in ch. xlix. 20–22.

2. *Enlarge the place of thy tent.* The same idea occurs in ch. xlix. 19. 20 (see the Notes on that chapter). *The curtains of thy habitations.* The word 'curtain' does not quite express the sense here. It is commonly with us used to denote the cloth hanging round a bed or at a window, which may be spread or drawn aside at pleasure, or the hanging in theatres to conceal the stage from the spectators. The word here, however, denotes the canopy or cloth used in a tent; and the idea is, that the boundaries of the church were to be greatly enlarged, in order to accommodate the vast accession from the pagan world. ¶ *Spare not.* Do not be parsimonious in the provision of the materials for greatly enlarging the tent to dwell in. ¶ *Lengthen thy cords* (see Note on ch. xxxiii. 20).

3. *For thou shalt break forth* (see Notes on ch. xlix. 19, 20). ¶ *And make the desolate cities* (see Notes on ch. xliv. 26).

4. *Fear not,* &c. (see Notes on ch. xli. 10, 14). ¶ *Neither shalt thou be confounded.* All these words mean substantially the same thing; and the design of the prophet is to affirm, in the strongest possible manner, that the church of God should be abundantly prospered and enlarged. The image of the female that was barren is kept up, and the idea is, that there should be no occasion of the shame which she felt who had no children. ¶ *For thou shalt forget the shame of thy youth.* In the abundant increase and glory of future times, the circumstances of shame which attended their early history shall be forgotten. The 'youth' of the Jewish people refers doubtless to the bondage

5 For thy Maker *is* thine husband; the *a* LORD of hosts *is* his name; and thy Redeemer, the Holy One of Israel ; the God of the whole earth shall he be called.

6 For the LORD hath called thee as a woman forsaken and grieved in spirit, and a wife of youth, when thou wast refused, saith thy God.

a Je.3.14.

of Egypt, and the trials and calamities which came upon them there. So great should be their future prosperity and glory, that all this should be forgotten. ¶ *The reproach of thy widowhood.* The captivity at Babylon, when they were like a woman bereft of her husband and children (see Notes on ch. xlix. 21).

5. *For thy Maker* is *thine husband.* Both these words, ‘maker’ and ‘husband,’ in the Hebrew are in the plural number. But the form is evidently the *pluralis excellentiæ*—a form denoting majesty and honour (see 1 Sam. xix. 13, 16; Ps. cxlix. 2; Prov. ix. 10; xxx. 3; Eccl. xii. 1; Hos. xii. 1). Here it refers to ‘JEHOVAH of hosts,’ necessarily in the singular, as JEHOVAH is ONE (Deut. vi. 4). No argument can be drawn from this phrase to prove that there is a distinction of persons in the Godhead, as the form is so often used evidently with a singular signification.* That the words here properly have a singular signification was the evident understanding of the ancient interpreters. Thus Jerome, *Quia dominabitur tui qui fecit te*—‘Because he shall rule over thee who made thee.’ So the LXX, Ὅτι κύριος ὁ ποιῶν σε, κ.τ.λ.—‘For the Lord who made thee, the Lord of Sabaoth,’ &c. So the Chaldee and the Syriac. Lowth renders it, ‘For thy husband is thy Maker.’ The word rendered ‘husband,’ from בָּעַל, denotes properly the lord, maker, or ruler of any one; or the owner of anything. It often, however, means, to be a husband (Deut. xxi. 13; xxiv. 1; Isa. lxii. 5; Mal. ii. 11), and is evidently used in that sense here. The idea is, that JEHOVAH would sustain to his people the relation of a husband; that he who had made them, who had originated all their laws and institutions, and moulded them as a people (see Note on ch. xliii. 1), would now take his church under his protection and care (see Notes on ch. lxii. 5). ¶ *And thy Redeemer,* &c. (see Notes on

ch. xliii. 1–3.) ¶ *The God of the whole earth.* He shall no more be regarded as peculiarly the God of the Jewish people, but shall be acknowledged as the only true God, the God that rules over all the world. This refers undoubtedly to the times of the gospel, when he should be acknowledged as the God of the Gentiles as well as the Jews (see Rom. iii. 29).

6. *For the* LORD *hath called thee.* This is designed to confirm and illustrate the sentiment in the previous verse. God there says that he would be a husband to his people. Here he says, that although he had for a time apparently forsaken them, as a husband who had forsaken his wife, and although they were cast down and dejected like a woman who had thus been forsaken, yet he would now restore them to favour. ¶ *Hath called thee.* That is, will have called thee to himself—referring to the future times when prosperity should be restored to them. ¶ *As a woman forsaken.* Forsaken by her husband on account of her offence. ¶ *And grieved in spirit.* Because she was thus forsaken. ¶ *And a wife of youth.* The LXX. render this very strangely, ‘The Lord hath not called thee as a wife forsaken and disconsolate ; *nor* as a wife that hath been hated from her youth ;’ showing conclusively that the translator here did not understand the meaning of the passage, and vainly endeavoured to *supply* a signification by the insertion of the negatives, and by endeavouring to *make* a meaning. The idea is that of a wife wedded in youth ; a wife towards whom there was early and tender love, though she was afterwards rejected. God had loved the Hebrew people as his people in the early days of their history. Yet for their idolatry he had seen occasion afterwards to cast them off, and to doom them to a long and painful exile. But he would yet love them with all the former ardour of affection, and would greatly increase and prosper them. ¶ *When thou wast refused.* Or, that

* See the Supplementary Note on ch. vi. 8.

7 For a small moment *a* have I forsaken thee ; but with great mercies will I gather thee.

8 In a little wrath I hid my face

a 2 Co.4.17.

hath been rejected. Lowth, 'But afterwards rejected.' It may be rendered, 'Although (כִּי *ki* has often the sense of *although*) thou wert rejected,' or 'although she was rejected.' The idea is, that she had been married in youth, but had been afterwards put away.

7. *For a small moment.* The Chaldee and Syriac render this, 'In a little anger.' Lowth has adopted this, but without sufficient authority. The Hebrew means, 'For a little moment ;' a very short time. The reference here is probably to the captivity at Babylon, when they were apparently forsaken by JEHOVAH. Though to them this appeared long, yet compared with their subsequent prosperity, it was but an instant of time. Though this had probably a primary reference to the captivity then, yet there can be no impropriety in applying it to other similar cases. It contains an important principle ; that is, that though God appears to forsake his people, yet it will be comparatively but for a moment. He will remember his covenant, and however long their trials may seem to be, yet compared with the subsequent mercies and the favours which shall result from them, they will seem to be but as the sorrows of the briefest point of duration (comp. 2 Cor. iv. 17). ¶ *But with great mercies.* The contrast here is not that of *duration* but of *magnitude.* The forsaking was 'little,' the mercies would be 'great.' It would be mercy that they would be recalled at all after all their faults and crimes ; and the mercy which would be bestowed in the enlargement of their numbers would be inexpressibly great. ¶ *Will I gather thee.* Will I collect thee from thy dispersions, and gather thee to myself as my own people.

8. *In a little wrath.* The Syriac renders this, 'In great wrath.' The Vulgate, 'In a moment of indignation.' The LXX. 'In a little wrath.' Noyes renders it in accordance with the view of Rosenmüller, 'In overflowing wrath.'

from thee for a moment ; but with everlasting kindness will I have mercy on thee, saith the LORD thy Redeemer.

9 For this *is as* the waters of Noah

This variety of interpretation has arisen from the various meanings affixed to the unusual word רֶגַע. This word occurs nowhere else in the Bible. Gesenius supposes that it is used for the sake of paronomasia with קֶצֶף *qêtzêph,* 'wrath,' instead of שֶׁטֶף *shêtêph.* This word frequently occurs, and means a gushing out, an overflowing, an inundation, a flood (Neh. i. 8 ; Job xxxviii. 25 ; Ps. xxxii. 6 ; Prov. xxvii. 4). According to this it would mean, 'in my overflowing anger,' in accordance with the expression in Prov. xxvii. 4, 'anger is outrageous,' more correctly in the margin, 'An overflowing.' The parallelism, however, seems to demand the sense of *short* or *momentary,* as it stands opposed to 'everlasting.' But it is not possible to demonstrate that the Hebrew word has this signification. Rosenmüller agrees with Gesenius in the opinion that it should be rendered 'In overflowing wrath ;' and perhaps as the parallelism of the word 'everlasting' will be sufficiently secured by the phrase 'for a moment,' the probability is in favour of this interpretation. Then it will mean that the wrath, though it was but for a moment, was overflowing. It was like a deluge ; and all their institutions, their city, their temple, their valued possessions, were swept away. ¶ *I hid my face from thee.* This is expressive of displeasure (see Note on ch. liii. 3 ; comp. Job xiii. 24 ; xxxiv. 29 ; Ps. xxx. 7 ; xliv. 24 ; Isa. viii. 17). Here it refers to the displeasure which he had manifested in the punishment which he brought on them in Babylon. ¶ *For a moment* (see Note on ver. 7). This stands opposed to the 'everlasting kindness' which he would show to them. ¶ *But with everlasting kindness.* This is true—1. Of the church at large under the Messiah. It is the object of the unchanging affection and favour of God. 2. Of each individual Christian. He will make him blessed in an eternal heaven.

9. *For this* is as *the waters of Noah*

unto me : for *as* I have sworn that the waters of Noah should no more go over the earth ; so have I sworn that I would not be wroth with thee, nor rebuke thee.

10 For *a* the mountains shall depart, and the hills be removed ; but my kindness shall not depart from

a Ro.11.29.

thee, neither shall the covenant *b* of my peace be removed, saith the LORD that hath mercy on thee.

11 O thou afflicted, tossed with tempest, *and* not comforted, behold, I will lay thy stones *c* with fair colours, and lay thy foundation with sapphires.

b 2 Sa.23.5. *c* Re.21.18.

unto me. As it was in the time of the flood of waters, so shall it be now. ' I then solemnly promised that the waters should not again drown the earth, and I have kept that promise. I now promise with equal solemnity that I will bestow perpetual favour on my true people, and will shed upon them eternal and unchanging blessings.' ' The waters of Noah,' here mean evidently the flood that came upon the world in his time, and from which he and his family were saved. Lowth, on the authority of one MS. and of the Vulg., Syr., Sym., and Theod., reads this, ' In the days of Noah.' But the authority is not sufficient to change the Hebrew text, and the sense is as clear as if it were changed. ¶ As *I have sworn* (Gen. viii. 21, 22). God appeals to this not only because the oath and promise had been *made*, but because it had been *kept*. ¶ *That I would not be wroth.* The idea seems here to be that no calamities should spread over the *whole* church, and sweep it away, as the waters swept over the world in the time of Noah, or as desolation swept over Jerusalem and the whole land of Canaan in the time of the exile at Babylon. There would be indeed persecutions and calamities, but the church would be safe amidst all these trials. The period would never arrive when God would forsake the church, and when he would leave it to perish. One has only to recollect how God has guarded the church, even during the most dangerous periods, to see how remarkably this has been fulfilled. His covenant has been as sure as that which was made with Noah, and it will be as secure and firm to the end of time.

10. *For the mountains shall depart* (see Notes on ch.li.6). ¶ *The covenant of my peace.* That is, the covenant by which I promise peace and prosperity to thee.

11. *O thou afflicted.* In the previous verses, JEHOVAH had merely promised protection, and had in general terms assured them of his favour. Here he shows that they should not only be defended, but that his church would rise with great beauty, and be ornamented like a most splendid palace or temple. This is to be regarded as addressed primarily to the exiles in Babylon near to the close of their seventy years' captivity. But nothing forbids us to apply it to the church in all *similar* circumstances when persecuted, and when she is like a ship rolling on the heaving billows of the ocean. ¶ *Tossed with tempest.* Lowth, ' Beaten with the storm.' The idea is that of a ship that is driven by the tempest ; or any object that is tossed about with a whirlwind (סֹעֲרָה). See Jonah i. 11-13; Hos. xiii. 3; Heb. iii. 14. The figure is peculiarly striking in an Oriental country. Tempests and whirlwinds there, are much more violent than they are with us, and nothing there can stand before them (see Harmer's *Obs.* vol. i. p. 92, *sq.* Ed. Lond. 1808). ¶ And *not comforted.* They were far away from all the comforts which they had enjoyed in their own land, and they were apparently forsaken by God. ¶ *Behold, I will lay thy stones.* It is not uncommon in the Scriptures to compare the prosperity of the church to a splendid temple or palace. In the book of Tobit (ch. xiii. 16, 17) a description of Jerusalem occurs, which has all the appearance of having been copied from this, or at least shows that the writer had this passage in his eye. ' For Jerusalem shall be built up with sapphires, and emeralds, and precious stones ; thy walls, and battlements, and towers, of pure gold. And the streets of Jerusalem shall be paved with beryl, and carbuncle, and stones of Ophir.'

12 And I will make thy windows of agates, and thy gates of carbuncles, and all thy borders of pleasant stones.

And in the book of Revelation (ch. xxi. 18–21), a similar description occurs of the New Jerusalem. Possibly John had his eye upon this passage in Isaiah, though he has greatly amplified the description. The passage here undoubtedly contains a figurative description of the future prosperity and glory of the church of God. Lowth remarks on it, justly, 'These seem to be general images to express beauty, magnificence, purity, strength, and solidity, agreeably to the ideas of eastern nations ; and to have never been intended to be strictly scrutinized or minutely and particularly explained, as if they had each of them some precise moral and spiritual meaning.' The phrase ' I will lay thy stones,' refers to the work of masonry in laying down the foundation of a building, or the stones of which a building is composed, in mortar or cement. Literally, ' I cause to lie down.' The word here used (רָבַץ) is usually appropriated to an animal that crouches or lies down. ¶ With fair colours. This translation by no means conveys the idea of the original. The sense is not that the stones would have fair colours, but that the cement which would be used would be that which was commonly employed to make the most valued colours. The edifice which would be reared would be as costly and magnificent as if the very cement of the stones consisted of the most precious colouring matter; the purest vermilion. The word here rendered 'fair colours' (פּוּךְ pūkh) denotes properly, sea-weed, from which an alkaline paint was prepared ; then paint itself, dye, fucus, and also that with which the Hebrew women tinged their eyelashes (stibium). This is composed of the powder of lead ore, and was drawn with a small wooden bodkin through the eyelids, and tinged the hair and the edges of the eyelids with a dark sooty colour, and was esteemed to be a graceful ornament. This practice is of great antiquity. It was practised by Jezebel (see 2 Kings ix. 30, where the same word is used as here); it was practised among the Greeks and Romans (Xen.

Cyr. i. 11); and it is still practised in Africa (see Shaw's Travels, pp. 294, 295). The word here used is rendered 'paint,' or ' painted ' (2 Kings ix. 30; Jer. xl. 30); and 'glistening stones' (1 Chron. xxix. 2). It does not occur elsewhere. In the passage in Chronicles it may mean the carbuncle, as it is rendered here by the LXX. (ἄνθρακα); but it here denotes, doubtless, the valued paint or dye which was used as an ornament. The description here is that the very stones should be laid in cement of this description, and is of course equivalent to saying that it would be in the most costly and magnificent manner. It may be added, however, that it would not be the mere fact that the stibium would constitute the cement that the prophet seems to refer to, but probably he also means to intimate that this would contribute greatly to the beauty of the city. The cement in which bricks or stones is laid in a building is partly visible, and the beauty of the structure would be augmented by having that which was regarded as constituting the highest ornament used for cement. ¶ And thy foundations with sapphires. The sapphire is a well-known gem distinguished for its beauty and splendour. In hardness it is inferior to the diamond only. Its colours are blue, red, violet, green, white, or limpid.

12. And I will make thy windows. The word here rendered ' windows ' is rendered by Jerome propugnacula— 'fortresses,' bulwarks, ramparts ; and by the LXX. Επαλξεις—' Bulwarks,' or rather, pinnacles on the walls. The Hebrew word שִׁמְשׁוֹת is evidently derived from שֶׁמֶשׁ shêmêsh (the sun); and has some relation in signification to the sun, either as letting in light, or as having a radiated appearance like the sun. Gesenius renders it, ' notched battlements, the same as sun, or rays of the sun.' Faber (Hebrew Archæol., p. 294) supposes that the name was given to the turrets or battlements here referred to, because they had some resemblance to the rays of the sun. I think it prob-

13 And all thy children *shall be* taught of the LORD; and great *shall be* the peace of thy children.

able that the prophet refers to some radiated ornament about a building, that had a resemblance to the sun, or to some gilded turrets on the walls of a city. I see no evidence in the ancient versions that the word refers to *windows*. ¶ *Of agates.* Agates are a class of silicious, semi-pellucid gems, of many varieties, consisting of quartz-crystal, flint, horn-stone, chalcedony, amethyst, jasper, cornelian, &c., variegated with dots, zones, filaments, ramifications, and various figures. They are esteemed the least valuable of all the precious stones. They are found in rocks, and are used for seals, rings, &c. (Webster.) The Hebrew word כַּדְכֹּד *kădhkŏd*, from כָּדַד *kădhădh, to beat,* to pound, and then to strike fire, seems to denote a sparkling gem or ruby. It is not often used. It is rendered by Jerome, *Jaspidem.* The LXX. Ἴασπιν—'Jasper,' a gem of a green colour. It may be observed that it is not probable that such a stone would be used for a *window,* for the purpose of letting in light. ¶ *And thy gates.* See Rev. xxi. 21—' And the twelve gates were twelve pearls ; every several gate was of one pearl.' The gates of the city would be made of most precious stones. ¶ *Of carbuncles.* The carbuncle is a beautiful gem of a deep red colour, with a mixture of scarlet, called by the Greeks *anthrax,* found in the East Indies. It is usually about a quarter of an inch in length. When held up to the sun it loses its deep tinge, and becomes exactly the colour of a burning coal (Webster). Hence its name in Greek. The Hebrew name אֶקְדָּח is derived from קָדַח, *to burn,* and denotes a flaming or sparkling gem. The word occurs nowhere else in the Hebrew Bible. ¶ *And all thy borders.* All thy boundaries; or the whole circuit of thy walls. See Rev. xxi. 18—'And the building of the wall of it was of jasper.' The idea is, that the whole city would be built in the most splendid manner. Its foundations and all its stones would be laid in the most precious cement; its turrets, towers, battlements, gates, and the circuit of its walls, would

be made of the most precious gems. In general, there can be no doubt that this is designed to represent the future glory of the church under the Redeemer, and perhaps also to furnish an emblematic representation of heaven (comp. Rev. xxi. 2). Kimchi supposes that this may possibly be taken literally, and that Jerusalem may be yet such as is here described. Abarbanel supposes that it may refer to the time when the Oriental world, where these gems are principally found, shall be converted, and come and join in rebuilding the city and the temple. But the whole description is one of great beauty as applicable to the church of God ; to its glories on earth ; and to its glory in heaven. Its future magnificence shall be as much greater than anything which has yet occurred in the history of the church, as a city built of gems would be more magnificent than Jerusalem was in the proudest days of its glory. The language used in this verse is in accordance with the Oriental manner. The style of speaking in the East to denote unexampled splendour is well illustrated in the well-known Oriental tale of Aladdin, who thus gives his instructions : ' I leave the choice of materials to you, that is to say, porphyry, jasper, agate, lapis lazuli, and the finest marble of the most varied colours. But I expect that in the highest story of the palace, you shall build me a large hall with a dome, and four equal fronts ; and that instead of layers of bricks, the walls be made of massy gold and silver, laid alternately : and that each front shall contain six windows, the lattices of all which, except one, which must be left unfinished and imperfect, shall be so enriched with art and symmetry, with diamonds, rubies, and emeralds, that they shall exceed everything of the kind ever seen in the world.'—(*Pictorial Bible.*)

13. *And all thy children.* All that dwell in this splendid city ; all that are the true friends of the Redeemer. It shall be a part of their future glory that

14 In righteousness shalt thou be established, thou shalt be far from oppression ; for thou shalt not fear: and from terror ; for *a* it shall not come near thee.

15 Behold, they shall surely gather together, *but* not by me ; whoso ever shall gather together against thee shall fall for thy sake.

they shall be all under Divine instruction and guidance. See Jer. xxxi. 34—'And they shall teach no more every man his neighbour, and every man his brother, saying, Know the LORD ; for they shall all know me, from the least of them unto the greatest of them.' ¶ *And great* shall be *the peace of thy children.* (see Notes on ch. ii. 4 ; ix. 6).

14. *In righteousness shalt thou be established.* This is language which is appropriately addressed to a city or commonwealth. The idea is, that it would not be built up by fraud, and rapine, and conquest, as many cities had been, but by the prevalence of justice. ¶ *Thou shalt be far from oppression.* That is, thou shalt be far from being oppressed by others. So the connection demands. The Hebrew would bear an *active* signification, so that it might be read, ' be thou far from oppression,' *i.e.,* be far from oppressing others. But the design of the prophet is rather to promise than to command ; and the idea is, that they should have no occasion to fear the violence of others any more. ¶ *For it shall not come near thee.* This doubtless refers to the security, perpetuity, and prosperity of the church under the Messiah.

15. *Behold, they shall surely gather together.* The idea in this verse is, that the enemies of the people of God would indeed form alliances and compacts against them, but it would not be under the Divine direction, and they would not be able to prevail against the church. The word here rendered 'gather together' (גּוּר) means properly *to turn aside from the way ;* then to sojourn for a time ; then to assemble against any one. It seems here to refer to the gathering together of hostile forces to form an alliance, or to wage war. Great variety, however, has prevailed in the interpretation of the passage, but this seems to be the sense of it. Jerome renders it, ' Lo, a foreigner shall come who was not with me, the stranger shall

hereafter be joined to thee,' and seems to understand it of the proselytes that should be made. This sense is found expressly in the LXX., ' Lo, proselytes shall come to thee through me, and they shall sojourn with thee, and fly to thee.' The Chaldee renders it, ' Lo, the captivity of thy people shall be surely gathered unto thee, and in the end the kings of the people which were assembled to afflict thee, O Jerusalem, shall fall in the midst of thee.' But the above seems to be the correct sense. Alliances would be formed ; compacts would be entered into ; leagues would be made by the enemies of the people of God, and they would be assembled to destroy the church. This has often been done. Formidable confederations have been entered into for the purpose, and deep-laid plans have been devised to destroy the friends of the Most High. See Ps. ii. 2 : ' The kings of the earth set themselves, and the rulers take counsel together against the LORD, and against his Anointed.' No small part of history is a record of the combinations and alliances which have been entered into for the purpose of driving the true religion from the world. ¶ But *not by me.* Not under my direction, or by my command. ¶ *Shall fall for thy sake.* Heb. עָלַיִךְ—' Shall fall unto thee.' Lowth, ' Shall come over to thy side.' The phrase seems to mean that they should ' fall to them,' *i.e.,* that they should lay aside their opposition, break up their alliances *against* the church, and come over *to* it. In proof of this interpretation, Rosenmüller appeals to the following places :—1 Chron. xii. 19, 20 ; 2 Chron. xv. 9 ; Jer. xxi. 9 ; xxxix. 9. The passage, therefore, looks to the future conversion of the enemies of the church to the true faith. It has, doubtless, been partially fulfilled in the conversion of nations that have been leagued against the gospel of the Redeemer. There was a striking fulfilment in the times that succeeded the persecutions

16 Behold, I have created the smith that bloweth the coals in the fire, and that bringeth forth an instrument for his work ; and I *a* have created the waster to destroy.

17 No weapon that is formed against thee shall prosper : and every *b* tongue *that* shall rise against thee in judgment thou shalt condemn. This *is* the heritage of the servants of the LORD ; and their righteousness *c is* of me, saith the LORD.

a ch.37.26,27.   *b* Ro.8.1,33.   *c* Ps.71.16,19; Phi.3.9.

of Christians in the Roman empire. After all the power of the empire had been enlisted in ten successive persecutions to destroy the church, the very empire that had thus opposed the church was converted to the Christian faith. In a still more signal manner will this be fulfilled when all the powers of the earth now leagued against the gospel shall be converted, and when all nations shall be brought under the influences of the true religion.

16. *Behold, I have created the smith.* The sense of this verse is, ' Everything that can effect your welfare is under my control. The smith who manufactures the instruments of war or of torture is under me. His life, his strength, his skill, are all in my hands, and he can do nothing which I shall not deem it best to permit him to do. So with the enemy of the church himself—the waster who destroys. I have made him, and he is wholly under my control and at my disposal.' The smith who bloweth the coals, denotes the man who is engaged in forging instruments for war, or for any other purpose. Here it refers to him who should be engaged in forging instruments of battle to attack the church ; and why should it not refer also to him who should be engaged in making instruments *of torture*—such as are used in times of persecution ? ¶ *That bringeth forth an instrument for his work.* Lowth, ' According to his work.' Noyes, ' By his labour.' The idea is, that he produces an instrument as the result of his work. ¶ *I have created the waster to destroy.* I have formed every man who is engaged in spreading desolation by wars, and I have every such man under my control (see Notes on ch. x. 5–7; xxxvii. 26, 27; xlvi. 1–6). The sense here is, that as God had all such conquerors under his control, they could accomplish no more than he permitted them to do.

17. *No weapon that is formed.* No instrument of war, no sword, or spear ; no instrument of persecution or torture that is made by the smith, ver. 16. ¶ *Shall prosper.* On the meaning of this word, see Notes on ch. lii. 13. The sense here is, that it shall not have final and ultimate prosperity. It might be permitted for a time to appear to prosper—as persecutors and oppressors have done ; but there would not be final and complete success. ¶ *And every tongue.* No one shall be able to injure you by words and accusations. If a controversy shall arise ; if others reproach you and accuse you of imposture and deceit, you will be able ultimately to convince them of error, and, by manifestation of the truth, to condemn them. The *language* here is derived probably from courts of justice (see Notes on ch. xli. 1); and the idea is, that truth and victory, in every strife of words, would be on the side of the church. To those who have watched the progress of discussions thus far on the subject of the true religion, it is needless to say that this has been triumphantly fulfilled. Argument, sophism, ridicule, have all been tried to overthrow the truth of the Christian religion. Appeals have been made to astronomy, geology, antiquities, history, and indeed to almost every department of science, and with the same want of success. Poetry has lent the charm of its numbers ; the grave historian has interwoven with the thread of his narrative covert attacks and sly insinuations against the Bible ; the earth has been explored to prove that ' He who made the world and revealed its age to Moses was mistaken in its age ;' and the records of Oriental nations, tracing their history up cycles of ages beyond the Scripture account of the creation of the world, have been appealed to, but thus far in all these contests ultimate victory has declared in favour of the

CHAPTER LV.

ANALYSIS.

THIS chapter is closely connected in sense with the preceding chapter. It flows from the doctrines stated in ch. liii., and is designed to state what would follow from the coming of the Messiah. It would result from that work that the most free and full invitations would be extended to all men to return to God, and to obtain his favour. There would be such ample provision made for the salvation of men, that the most liberal invitations could be extended to sinners. The main idea in the chapter, I conceive to be, *that the effect of the work of the Redeemer would be to lay the foundation for a universal invitation to men to come and be saved.* So ample would be the merits of his death (ch. liii.), that *all might come* and partake of eternal life. To state this, I suppose to be the main design of this chapter. It may be regarded as comprising the following parts :—

I. A universal invitation to come and embrace the provisions of mercy. 1. All were invited to come, even they who were the most poor and needy, who had no money, as freely as to running waters and streams (1). 2. They were now regarded as spending their money and their labour for that which produced no permanent satisfaction—descriptive of the world in its vain efforts to find enjoyment (2). 3. If they would come to God they should live, and he would make with them an eternal covenant (3).

II. To encourage them to this, the assurance is presented that God had given the Messiah to be a leader of the people, and that under him distant nations should embrace the truth and be saved (4, 5).

III. In view of the fulness of the provisions of mercy, and of the fact that a great leader had been provided, all are encouraged to come and seek God. This invitation is pressed on their attention by several considerations :—1. JEHOVAH might now be found, and he was ready to pardon abundantly all sinners who were disposed to forsake the error of their way and to return to him (6, 7). 2. God shows that his plans were high above those of men, and his thoughts more elevated than theirs, and his counsels should stand. The rain descended on the earth and accomplished his great plans, and so it would be with his word. His promises would be fulfilled, and his designs would take effect, and there was, therefore, every encouragement to come, and partake of his favour and his grace (8–11). 3. There should be rich and abundant blessings attending their return to God, and universal rejoicing from their embracing the religion of the Redeemer, and becoming interested in his mercy and salvation (12, 13).

There is not to be found in the Bible a chapter more replete with rich invitations than this, nor perhaps is there anywhere to be found one of more exquisite beauty. To the end of the world it will stand as the fullest conceivable demonstration that God *intended* that the offers of salvation should be made to all men, and that he designs that his gospel shall accomplish the great plans which he had in view when he devised the scheme of redemption. While this precious chapter remains in the book of God, no sinner need despair of salvation who is disposed to return to him; no one can plead that he is too great a sinner to be saved; no one can maintain successfully that the provisions of mercy are limited in their nature or their appli-

---

Bible. And no matter from what quarter the attack has come, and no matter how much learning and talent have been evinced by the adversaries of the Bible, God has raised up some Watson, or Lardner, or Chalmers, or Buckland, or Cuvier, or Wiseman, to meet these charges, and to turn the scales in favour of the cause of truth. They who are desirous of examining the effects of the controversy of Christianity with science, and the results, can find them detailed with great learning and talent in Dr. Wiseman's *Lectures on the connection between Science and Revealed Religion*, Andover, 1837. ¶ *This* is *the heritage.* The inheritance which awaits those who serve God is truth and victory. It is not gold and

the triumph of battle. It is not the laurel won in fields of blood. But it is, the protection of God in all times of trouble ; his friendship in all periods of adversity ; complete victory in all contests with error and false systems of religion ; and preservation when foes rise up in any form and endeavour to destroy the church, and to blot out its existence and its name. ¶ *And their righteousness* is *of me.* Or rather, 'this is the righteousness, or the justification which they obtain of me ; this is that which I impart to them as their justification.' The idea is not that their righteousness is of him, but that this justification or vindication from him is a part of their inheritance and their portion.

cability to any portion of the race; and no minister of the gospel need be desponding about the success of the work in which he is engaged. The gospel shall just as certainly produce the effect which God intended, as the rain which comes down in fertilizing showers upon the dry and thirsty earth.

HO, every one that thirsteth, come *a* ye to the waters, and he that hath no money; come ye, buy *b* and eat; yea, come, buy wine *c* and milk, without money, and without price.

<hr>

a Jn.4.10,14; 7.37; Re.21.6; 22.17.

b Mat.13.44–46; Re.3.18.

c Ca.5.1.

<hr>

CHAPTER LV.

1. *Ho* (הוֹי). This word here is designed to call attention to the subject as one of importance. ¶ *Every one that thirsteth.* The word 'thirst' often indicates intense *desire*, and is thus applied to the sense of want which sinners often have, and to their anxious wishes for salvation. It is not improbable that the Saviour had this passage in his eye when he pronounced the blessing on those who hunger and thirst after righteousness (Matt. v. 6). No wants are so keen, none so imperiously demand supply, as those of hunger and thirst. They occur daily; and when long continued, as in the case of those who are shipwrecked, and doomed to wander months or years over burning sands with scarcely any drink or food, nothing is more distressing. Hence the figure is often used to denote any intense desire for anything, and especially an ardent desire for salvation (see Ps. xlii. 2; lxiii. 1; cxliii. 6; John vii. 37). The invitation here is made to all. ' Every one' (כָּל) is entreated to come. It is not offered to the elect only, or to the rich, the great, the noble; but it is made to all. It is impossible to conceive of language more universal in its nature than this; and while this stands in the Word of God, the invitation *may* be made to all, and *should* be made to all, and *must* be made to all. It *proves* that provision is made for all. Can God invite to a salvation which has not been provided? Can he ask a man to partake of a banquet which has no existence? Can he ask a man to drink of waters when there are none? Can he tantalize the hopes and mock the miseries of men by inviting them to enter a heaven where they would be unwelcome, or to dwell in mansions which have never been provided? (comp. Matt. xi. 28; Mark xvi. 15; John vii. 37; Rev. xxii. 17). ¶ *Come ye to the waters.* Water, floods, overflowing streams, or copious showers, are often used in the Scriptures to denote abundant blessings from God, and especially the blessings which would exist under the Messiah (see Isa. xxxv. 6; xliii. 20; xliv. 3). ¶ *And he that hath no money.* The poor; they who would be unable to purchase salvation if it were to be sold. The idea here is the absolute freeness of the offer of salvation. No man can excuse himself for not being a Christian because he is poor; no man who is rich can ever boast that he has *bought* salvation, or that he has obtained it on more easy terms because he had property. ¶ *Come ye, buy and eat* (comp. Matt. xiii. 44–46). That is, procure it without paying a price. The word rendered here 'buy' (שָׁבַר *shâbhăr*), properly means *to break*, then to purchase, &c. (*grain*), as that which is *broken* in a mill (Gesenius), or that which *breaks* hunger; comp. Eng. *breakfast* (Castell.) ¶ *Buy wine* (יַיִן). Wine was commonly used in their feasts, and indeed was an article of common drink (see Notes on ch. xxv. 6). Here it is emblematic of the blessings of salvation spoken of as a feast made for men. Wine is usually spoken of as that which exhilarates, or makes glad the heart (Judg. ix. 13; 2 Sam. xiii. 28; Ps. civ. 15), and it is possible that the image here may be designed specifically to denote that the blessings of salvation make men happy, or dissipate the sorrows of life, and cheer them in their troubles and woes. ¶ *And milk.* Milk, in the Scriptures, is used to denote that which nourishes, or is nutritious (Deut. xxxii. 14; Judg. iv. 1; v. 25; Isa. vii. 22; 1 Cor. ix. 7). It is mentioned as used with wine in Cant. v. 1, 'I have drunk my wine with my milk;' and with honey (iv. 11), ' Honey and milk are under my tongue.' The sense here is, that the blessings of the gospel are fitted to nourish and support the soul as well as to make it glad and

2 Wherefore do ye [1] spend money for *that which is* not bread, and your labour for *that which* satisfieth not? Hearken diligently [a] unto me, and eat ye *that which is* good, and let your soul delight itself in [b] fatness.

3 Incline your ear and come unto me ; hear, and your soul shall live ; and I will make an everlasting covenant [c] with you, *even* the sure mercies [d] of David.

1 *weigh*.   a Mat.22.4.   b Ps.63.5.
c 2 Sa.23.5; Je.32.40.   d Ac.13.34.

cheerful. ¶ *Without money*, &c. None are so poor that they cannot procure it ; none are so rich that they can purchase it with gold. If obtained at all by the poor or the rich, it must be without money and without price. If the poor are willing to accept of it as a gift, they are welcome ; and if the rich will not accept of it as a gift, they cannot obtain it. What a debt of gratitude we owe to God, who has thus placed it within the reach of all ! How cheerfully and thankfully should we accept that as a gift which no wealth, however princely, *could* purchase, and which, being purchased by the merits of the Redeemer, is put within the reach of the humblest child of Adam !

2. *Wherefore do ye spend money.* Marg. ' Weigh.' That is, in Hebrew, ' weigh silver.' Before money was coined, the precious metals were *weighed*, and hence to make a payment is represented as *weighing out silver* (Gen. xxiii. 16). ¶ *For* that which is *not bread.* The idea here is, that men are endeavouring to purchase happiness, and are disappointed. Bread is the support of life ; it is therefore emblematic of whatever contributes to support and comfort. And in regard to the pursuit of happiness in the pleasures of life, and in ambition, vanity, and vice, men are as much disappointed, as he would be who should spend his money, and procure nothing that would sustain life. ¶ *And your labour for* that which *satisfieth not.* You toil, and expend the avails of your labour for that which does not produce satisfaction. What a striking description of the condition of the world ! The immortal mind will not be *satisfied* with wealth, pleasure, or honour. It never has been. Where is the man who is *satisfied* with his wealth, and who says it is enough ? Where is there one who is satisfied with pleasure, and vanity, and gaiety ? There is a void in the heart which these things do not, cannot

fill. There is a consciousness that the soul was made for higher and nobler purposes, and that nothing but God can meet its boundless desires. Where is the man who has ever been satisfied with ambition? Alexander wept on the throne of the world ; and though Diocletian and Charles V. descended voluntarily from the throne to private life, it was because there was nothing *in* royalty to satisfy the soul, and not because they found happiness *enough* there. There never was a more simple and true description of this whole world than in this expression of Isaiah, that men are spending their money and their labour for that which satisfieth not. ¶ *Hearken diligently unto me.* The idea is, that by attending to his words and embracing his offers, they would find that without money or price which they were vainly seeking at so much expense and with so much toil. ¶ *And eat*, &c. The prophet here returns to the image in the former verse. They were invited to partake of that which would nourish the soul, and which would fill it with joy. ¶ *And let your soul delight itself in fatness.* ' Fatness' in the Scriptures is used to denote the richest food (Gen. xxvii. 28–39; Job xxxvi. 16; Ps. lxv. 11), and hence is an emblem of the rich and abundant blessings resulting from the favour of God (Ps. xxxvi. 9; lxiii. 5).

3. *Hear, and your soul shall live.* That is, if you attend to my command and embrace my promises, you shall live. Religion in the Scriptures is often represented as *life* (John v. 40; vi. 33; viii. 13; xx. 31; Rom. v. 17, 18; vi. 4; viii. 6; 1 John v. 12; Rev. ii. 7–10). It stands opposed to the death of sin—to spiritual and eternal death. ¶ *And I will make an everlasting covenant with you.* On the word ' covenant,' see Notes on ch. xxviii. 18; xlii. 6; xlix. 8. Here it means that God would bind himself to be their God, their protector, and their friend. This covenant would

4 Behold, I have given him ^a *for*
a witness ^bto the people, a leader
and commander ^c to the people.

a Eze.34.23.   *b* Jn.18.37; Re.1.5.

be made with *all* who would come to
him. It would not be with the nation
of the Jews, as such, or with any community, as such, but it would be with
all who should embrace the offers of life
and salvation. ¶ Even *the sure mercies of David.* I will confirm to you,
and fulfil in you, the solemn promises
made to David. The transaction here
referred to is that which is celebrated
in Ps. lxxxix. 2–4:—

For I have said, mercy shall be built up for ever;
Thy faithfulness hast thou established in the
    very heavens.
I have made a covenant with my chosen,
I have sworn unto David my servant,
Thy seed will I establish for ever,
And build up thy throne to all generations.

A kingdom had thus been promised to
David, and he had been assured that the
true religion should flourish among those
who were to succeed him in Israel. The
prophet here says that this solemn promise would be fulfilled in those who
should embrace the Messiah, and that
God would ratify with them this covenant. The word here rendered 'mercies' (חֶסֶד), properly means *kindness*,
goodwill, pity, compassion ; then goodness, mercy, grace. The word rendered
'sure,' denotes that which is established,
or confirmed ; that in which *confidence*
may be placed. The whole expression
denotes that the covenant made with
David was one which *promised* great
favours, and was one which was not to
be abrogated, but which was to be perpetual. With all who embraced the Messiah, God would enter into such an unchanging and unwavering covenant—a
covenant which was not to be revoked.

4. *Behold, I have given him.* This
is evidently the language of God respecting the Messiah, or of David as
representing the Messiah. Rosenmüller
supposes that the name David here is
used to designate the Messiah, and in
support of this appeals to Ezek. xxxiv.
23, 24; xxxvii. 24, 25; Jer. xxx. 9;
Hos. iii. 5. An examination of these
passages will show that they *all* refer to
the Messiah by the name of David ; and
it is morally certain that in the passage

5 Behold, thou shalt call a nation
that thou knowest not ; and nations
that ^d knew not thee shall run unto

c Ep.5.24.   *d* ch.60.5; Zec.8.23.

before us, the name David (ver. 3) suggested the Messiah. It seems to me that
this is to be regarded as a *direct address*
respecting the Messiah, and that the
object of the speaker here is to state a
reason why he should be embraced. That
reason was that God had constituted him
as a leader. The Chaldee renders this,
' Lo, I have constituted him as a prince
to the people, a king and ruler over all
kingdoms.' Kimchi says that it means
that the Messiah would be a monitor or
a mediator between men and him who
would accuse them. Grotius supposes
that *Jeremiah* is intended here ; but in
that opinion he is destined undoubtedly
to stand for ever alone. The almost unbroken interpretation, from the earliest
times, is that which refers it directly
to the Messiah. ¶ For *a witness to the
people.* Noyes renders this, ' A ruler.'
Rosenmüller, ' A monitor,'—one whose
office it was publicly to admonish, or
reprove others in the presence of witnesses. Jerome renders it, ' A witness.'
The LXX. Μαρτύριον — ' A testimony.'
The Chaldee (רַב *rábh*), ' A prince.' The
Hebrew word (עֵד) means properly a
witness (Prov. xix. 5–9) ; then testimony,
witness borne (Ex. xx. 13 ; Deut. v.
17) ; then a prince, chief, lawgiver, commander. Comp. the use of the verb in
2 Kings xvii. 13 ; Ps. l. 7 ; lxxxi. 9 ;
Lam. ii. 13. The parallelism requires
us to understand it in this sense here—
as one who stood forth to bear solemn
testimony in regard to God—to his law,
and claims, and plans ; and one who,
therefore, was designated to be the instructor, guide, and teacher of men.
¶ *A leader.* Chaldee, ' A king.' The
idea is, that he would sustain the relation of a sovereign. One of the important offices of the Messiah is that of *king.*
¶ *A commander.* Or, rather, a law-
giver. He would originate the laws and
institutions of his people.

5. *Behold, thou shalt call, &c.* This
is evidently an address to the Messiah,
and is a promise that the Gentiles should
be called by him to the fellowship of
the gospel. ¶ That *thou knowest not.*

thee, because of the LORD thy God, and for the Holy One of Israel ; for he hath glorified thee.

6 Seek ye the LORD while *a* he may be found, call ye upon him while he is near.

a Jn.7.34; He.2.3.

The phrase 'thou knowest not,' means a nation that had not been regarded as his own people. ¶ *And nations* that *knew not thee.* The heathen nations that were strangers to thee. ¶ *Shall run unto thee.* Indicating the haste and anxiety which they would have to partake of the benefits of the true religion. ¶ *Because of the* LORD *thy God.* From respect to the God who had appointed the Messiah, and who had organized the Church. ¶ *For he hath glorified thee* (John xvi. 5). God had glorified him by appointing him to be the Messiah; and he would glorify him in the future triumphs of the gospel, in the day of judgment, and in the eternal splendours of heaven.

6. *Seek ye the* LORD. The commencement of religion in the heart is often represented as seeking for God, or inquiring for his ways (Deut. iv. 29 ; Job v. 8; viii. 5; Ps. ix. 10; xiv. 2; xxvii. 8). This is to be regarded as addressed not to the Jewish exiles only or peculiarly, but to all in view of the coming and work of the Messiah. That work would be so full and ample that an invitation could be extended to all to seek after God, and to return to him. It is implied here—1. That men are by nature ignorant of God—since they are directed to 'seek' for him. 2. That if men will obtain his favour it must be sought. No man becomes his friend without desiring it; no one who does not earnestly seek for it. 3. That the invitation to seek God should be made to all. In this passage it is unlimited (comp. ver. 7). Where there are sinners, there the invitation is to be offered. 4. That the knowledge of God is of inestimable value. He would not command men to seek that which was worthless; he would not urge it with so much earnestness as is here manifested if it were not of inexpressible importance. ¶ *While he may be found.* It is implied here—1. That God may now be found. 2. That the time will come when it will be impossible to obtain his favour. The leading thought

is, that under the Messiah the offer of salvation will be made to men fully and freely. But the period will come when it will be withdrawn. If God forsakes men; if he wholly withdraws his Spirit; if they have committed the sin which hath never forgiveness ; or if they neglect or despise the provisions of mercy and die in their sins, it will be too late, and mercy cannot then be found. How unspeakably important, then, is it to seek for mercy at once—lest, slighted now, the offer should be withdrawn, or lest death should overtake us, and we be removed to a world where mercy is unknown ! How important is the present moment—for another moment may place us beyond the reach of pardon and of grace ! How amazing the stupidity of men who suffer their present moments to pass away unimproved, and who, amidst the gaieties and the business of life, permit the day of salvation to pass by, and lose their souls ! And how just is the condemnation of the sinner ! If a man will not do so simple a thing as to ASK for pardon, he OUGHT to perish. The universe will approve the condemnation of such a man ; and the voice of complaint can never be raised against that Holy Being who consigns such a sinner to hell. ¶ *Call ye upon him.* That is, implore his mercy (see Rom. x. 13; comp. Joel ii. 32). How easy are the terms of salvation ! How just will be the condemnation of a sinner if he will not call upon God ! Assuredly if men will not breathe out one broken-hearted petition to the God of heaven that they may be saved, they have only to blame themselves if they are lost. The terms of salvation *could* be made no easier ; and man *can* ask nothing more simple. ¶ *While he is near.* In an important sense God is equally near to us at all times. But this figurative language is taken from the mode of speaking among men, and it denotes that there are influences more favourable for seeking him at some periods than others. Thus God comes near to us in the preaching of his

7 Let the wicked forsake his
way, and the ¹unrighteous man
his thoughts ; ᵃand let him return
unto the LORD, and he will have

1 *man of iniquity.*   ᵃ Mar.7.21,23.
2 *multiply to pardon.*   ᵇ Ps.130.7.

mercy upon him : and to our God,
for he will ²abundantly ᵇpardon.

8 For my thoughts *are* not your
thoughts, neither *are* your ways my
ways, saith the LORD.

word, when it is borne with power to the
conscience ; in his providences, when
he strikes down a friend and comes into
the very circle where we move, or the
very dwelling where we abide ; when he
lays his hand upon us in sickness, he
is *near* us by day and by night ; in a
revival of religion, or when a pious
friend pleads with us, God is near to us
then, and is calling us to his favour.
These are favourable times for salvation ;
times which, if they are suffered to pass
by unimproved, return no more ; periods
which will all soon be gone, and when
they are gone, the sinner irrecoverably
dies.

7. *Let the wicked,* &c. In this verse
we are told what is necessary in order
to seek God and to return to him, and
the encouragement which we have to do
it. The first step is for the sinner to
forsake his way. He must come to a
solemn pause, and resolve to abandon all
his transgressions. His evil course ; his
vices ; his corrupt practices ; and his
dissipated companions, must be forsaken.
¶ *And the unrighteous man.* Marg.
' Man of iniquity.' This is a literal
translation. The address is made to all
men ; for all are such. ¶ *His thoughts.*
The Hebrew word denotes all that is
the object of *thought;* and the idea is,
that the man must abandon his plans
and purposes of life. The thoughts, in
the sight of a holy God, are not less important than the external deportment ;
and no man can obtain his favour who
is not ready to abandon his erroneous
opinions, his pride and vanity, his plans
of evil, and his purposes of life that are
opposed to God. ¶ *And let him return
unto the* LORD. Man, in the Scriptures,
is everywhere described as having wandered away from the true God. Religion consists in *returning* to him for
pardon, for consolation, for protection,
for support. The true penitent is desirous of returning to him, as the pro-
digal son returned to his father's house ;
the man who loves sin chooses to re-

main at a distance from God. ¶ *And
to our God.* The God of his people ;
the God of the speaker here. It is
the language of those who have found
mercy. The idea is, that he who has
bestowed mercy on *us,* will be ready to
bestow it on others. ' *We* have returned
to God. We have had experience of
his compassion, and we have such a
conviction of his overflowing mercy,
that we can assure all others that if
they will return to *our* God, he will
abundantly pardon them.' The doctrine is, that they who have found favour
have a deep conviction of the abounding
compassion of God, and such a sense of
the fulness of his mercy, that they are
disposed to offer the assurance to all
others, that they may also obtain full
forgiveness. Compare Rev. xxii. 17—
' And let him that heareth say, Come.'
¶ *For he will abundantly pardon.*
Marg. as Heb. ' Multiply to pardon.'
He abounds in forgiveness. This is
the conviction of those who are pardoned ; this is the promise of inestimable worth which is made to all who are
willing to return to God. On the ground
of this promise all may come to him,
and none who come shall be sent empty
away.

8. *For my thoughts* are *not your
thoughts.* Interpreters have differed in
regard to the *connection* of this verse
with the preceding. It is evident, I
think, that it is properly connected with
the subject of *pardon;* and the sense
must be, that the plans and purposes of
God in regard to forgiveness are as far
above those of men as the heavens are
higher than the earth, ver. 9. But in
what respects his plan of pardon differs
from those of men, the prophet does not
intimate, and can be understood only by
the views which are presented in other
parts of the Bible. The connection
here would seem to demand some such
view as the following—1. Men find it
difficult to pardon at all. They harbour
malice ; they seek revenge ; they are

9 For *a as* the heavens are higher than the earth, so are my ways higher than your ways, and my thoughts than your thoughts.

10 For as the rain *b* cometh down, and the snow, from heaven, and re-turneth not thither, but watereth the earth, and maketh it bring forth and bud, that it may give seed to the sower, and bread to the eater ;

a Ps.103.11.   *b* De.32.2.

slow to forgive an injury. Not so with God. He harbours no malice ; he has no desire of revenge ; he has no reluctance to forgive. 2. It may refer to *the number of offences*. Men, if they forgive once, are slow to forgive a second time, and still more reluctant to forgive a third time, and if the offence is often repeated they refuse to forgive altogether. Not so with God. No matter how often we have violated his law, yet he can multiply forgiveness in proportion to our faults. 3. *The number of the offenders*. Men *may* pardon one, or a few who injure them, but if the number is greatly increased, their compassions are closed, and they feel that the world is arrayed against them. Not so with God. No matter how numerous the offenders—though they embrace the inhabitants of the whole world—yet he can extend forgiveness to them all. 4. In regard to the *aggravation* of offences. A slight injury men forgive. But if it is aggravated, they are slow to pardon. But not so with God. No matter how aggravated the offence, he is ready to forgive. It may be added— 5. That his thoughts in regard to the *mode* of pardon are far above ours. The plan of forgiveness through a Redeemer —the scheme of pardon so fully illustrated in ch. liii., and on which the reasoning of the prophet here is based— is as far above any of the modes of pardon among men, as the heavens are above the earth. The scheme which contemplated the incarnation of the Son of God ; which proffered forgiveness only through his substituted sufferings, and in virtue of his bitter death, was one which man could not have *thought* of, and which surpasses all the schemes and plans of men. In this respect, God's ways are not our ways, and his thoughts are not our thoughts.—But at the same time that this passage refers primarily to the subject of pardon, and should be interpreted as having a main reference to that, it is also true of the

ways of God in general. His ways are not our ways, and his thoughts are not ours in regard to his plans in the creation and government of the world. He has plans for accomplishing his purposes which are different from ours, and he secures our own welfare by schemes that cross our own. He disappoints our hopes ; foils our expectations ; crosses our designs ; removes our property, or our friends ; and thwarts our purposes in life. He leads us in a path which we had not intended ; and secures our ultimate happiness in modes which are contrary to all our designs and desires. It follows from this—1. That we should form our plans with submission to the higher purposes of God. 2. We should resign ourselves to him when he chooses to thwart our plans, and to take away our comforts.

9. *For* as *the heavens*, &c. This verse is designed merely to illustrate the idea in the former. There is as great a difference between the plans of God and those of men, as between the heavens and the earth. A similar comparison occurs in Ps. ciii. 11—

For as the heaven is high above the earth,
So great is his mercy toward them that fear him.

Comp. Ps. lvii. 10—

For thy mercy is great unto the heavens,
And thy truth unto the clouds.

Also Ps. lxxxix. 2—

Mercy shall be built up for ever,
Thy faithfulness shalt thou establish in the very
    heavens.

The idea in all these passages is substantially the same—that the mercy and compassion of God are illimitable.

10. *For as the rain cometh down*. The meaning of this verse and the following is plain. This refers evidently, as the whole passage does, to the times which should succeed the coming of the Messiah. The hearts of men by nature are what the earth would be without the rains of heaven —barren and sterile. But God says that his truth shall certainly accomplish **an**

11 So shall my word be that
goeth forth out of my mouth : it
shall not return unto me void ; *a* but

it shall accomplish that which I
please, and it shall prosper *in the
thing* whereto I sent it.

a Mat.24.35.

---

effect similar to that produced by descending showers. The rain never descends in vain. It makes the earth
fertile, beautiful, and lovely. So would
it be with his truth in the moral world.
The comparison of truth with descending rain or dews is exceedingly beautiful, and occurs not unfrequently in the
Bible. See Deut. xxxii. 2—

> My doctrine shall drop as the rain,
> My speech shall distil as the dew,
> As the small rain upon the tender herb,
> And as the showers upon the grass.

Comp. 2 Sam. xxiii. 4 ; Ps. lxxii. 6 ;
Isa. v. 6 ; Note on xliv. 3. ¶ *And the
snow.* This is a part of the emblem or
symbol designed to denote the fertilizing
effect of the truth of God. The snow, as
well as the rain, accomplishes important
purposes in rendering the earth fertile.
It constitutes a covering that contributes
to the warmth and preservation of plants
and vegetation in the colder latitudes,
and on the hills and mountains is accumulated in the winter months to fill the
streams, or produce the overflowing of
the rivers in the spring and the summer.
This expression should not, however, be
pressed *ad unguem* in the interpretation, as if it contained any special spiritual signification. It is a part of the general description of that which descends
from heaven to render the earth fertile.
¶ *From heaven.* From the clouds.
¶ *And returneth not thither.* That is,
not in the form in which they descend
on the earth. They return not thither
as rain and snow. The main idea is,
they do not return without accomplishing the effect which God intends. ¶ *And
bud.* Put forth its increase ; causes it
to sprout up, or germinate. The word
'bud' is applied rather to the small
protuberance on the ends of limbs and
branches, which contains the germ of
the future leaf or flower. This word
צָמַח means rather *to germinate,* or to
cause to vegetate in general. It is applied to the putting forth of vegetation.
on the earth when the showers descend.
11. *So shall my word be.* All the

truth which God reveals is as much
adapted to produce an effect on the hard
and sterile hearts of men as the rain is
on the earth. ¶ *It shall not return unto me void.* It shall not return to me
without accomplishing that which I intend. ¶ *And it shall prosper* (see Note
on ch. lii. 13). This proves—1. That
God has a design in giving his Word to
men. He has as distinct an intention
in his Word as he has in sending down
rain upon the earth. 2. That whatever
is his design in giving the gospel, it shall
be accomplished. It is never spoken
in vain, and never fails to produce the
effect which he intends. The gospel is
no more preached in vain than the rain
falls in vain. And though that often
falls on barren rocks, or on arid sands ;
on extended plains where no vegetation
is produced, or in the wilderness 'where
no man is,' and seems to our eyes in
vain, yet it is not so. God has a design
in each drop that falls on sands or rocks,
as really as in the copious shower that
falls on fertile fields. And so the gospel often falls on the hard and barren
hearts of men. It is addressed to the
proud, the sensual, the avaricious, and
the unbelieving, and seems to be spoken
in vain, and to return void unto God.
But it is not so. He has some design
in it, and that will be accomplished.
It is proof of the fulness of his mercy.
It leaves men without excuse, and justi-
fies himself. Or when long presented
—apparently long in vain—it ultimately
becomes successful, and sinners are at
last brought to abandon their sins, and
to turn unto God. It is indeed often
rejected and despised. It falls on the
ears of men apparently as the rain falls
on the hard rock, and there are, so to
speak, large fields where the gospel is
preached as barren and unfruitful of any
spiritual good as the extended desert is
of vegetation, and the gospel seems to
be preached to almost entire communities with as little effect as is produced
when the rains fall on the deserts of
Arabia, or of Africa. But there will

12 For ye shall go out with joy, and be led forth with peace : the mountains and the hills shall break forth before you into singing, and all the trees of the field shall clap *their* hands.

a Ro.6.19.

13 Instead *a* of the thorn shall come up the fir-tree, and instead of the brier shall come up the myrtle-tree : and *b* it shall be to the LORD for a name, for an everlasting sign, *that* shall not be cut off.

b Je.13.11.

be better and happier times. Though the gospel may not now produce all the good effects which we may desire, yet it will be ultimately successful to the full wish of the widest benevolence, and the whole world shall be filled with the knowledge and the love of God.

12. *For ye shall go out with joy.* This *language* is that which is properly applicable to the exiles in Babylon, but there can be no doubt that the prophet looks also to the future happier times of the Messiah (comp. Notes on ch. lii. 7). ¶ *The mountains and the hills.* Language like this is common in Isaiah, where all nature is called on to rejoice, or where inanimate objects are represented as expressing their sympathy with the joy of the people of God (see Note on ch. xiv. 8; xxxv. 1, 2, 10; xlii. 10, 11; xliv. 23). Indeed, this imagery is common in all poetry. Thus Virgil—

Ipsi lætitia voces ad sidera jactant,
Intonsi montes : ipsæ jam carmina rupes,
Ipsa sonant arbusta.
Ec. v. 62, *sq.*

The untill'd mountains strike the echoing sky;
And rocks and towers the triumph speed abroad.
WRANGHAM.

Such language occurs especially in the poetry of the Orientals. Thus, when the god Ramar was going to the desert, says Roberts, it was said to him, ' The trees will watch for you; they will say, He is come, he is come ; and the white flowers will clap their hands. The leaves as they shake will say, Come, come, and the thorny places will be changed into gardens of flowers.' ¶ *And all the trees of the field shall clap* their *hands.* To clap the hands is expressive of joy and rejoicing (comp. 2 Kings xi. 12 ; Ps. xlvii. 1). Thus, in Ps. xcviii. 8, it is said :

Let the floods clap their hands ;
Let the hills be joyful together.

Among the Jews the language was sometimes used to express *malignant* joy

at the calamity of others (comp. Job xxvii. 3; xxxiv. 37; Lam. ii. 15; Ezek. xxv. 6). Here it is an expression of the universal rejoicing which would attend the extension of the kingdom of God on the earth.

13. *Instead of the thorn* (comp. Notes on ch. xi. 6–8; xxxv. 1, 2; xli. 19; xlii. 20). The word rendered 'thorn' (נַעֲצוּץ) occurs only here and in Isa. vii. 19. It evidently means a thorn, hedge, or thorny-bush. ¶ *Shall come up the fir-tree* (בְּרוֹשׁ *bĕrôsh;* see Notes on ch. xiv. 8; xxxvii. 24; lx. 13; Zech. xi. 2). A change would be produced in the moral condition of man as great as if in the natural world the rough and useless thorn should be succeeded by the beautiful and useful cypress (comp. ch. lx. 13). ¶ *And instead of the brier.* The brier is everywhere an emblem of desolation, and of an uncultivated country (see ch. v. 6; vii. 23, 24). ¶ *The myrtle-tree* (see Notes on ch. xli. 19). The idea here is, that under the gospel the change would be as great in the moral world as if a field all overrun with briers should at once become thick set with myrtles. ¶ *And it shall be to the* LORD. The reference here is to all that had been said in the chapter. The gift of the Messiah ; the universal offer of the gospel ; the bestowing of pardon ; the turning of the wicked unto God ; and the great and salutary changes produced by the gospel, would all be a memorial of the benevolence and glory of JEHOVAH. ¶ *For a name.* It should tend to diffuse his name ; to spread abroad a knowledge of himself. ¶ *An everlasting sign.* On the meaning of the word rendered ' sign,' see Notes on ch. vii. 14. Here it means that it would be an eternal memorial of the mercy and goodness of JEHOVAH. ¶ *That shall not be cut off.* The gospel with its rich and varied blessings shall erect enduring monuments in the earth, to the praise

CHAPTER LVI.

ANALYSIS.

THIS chapter, to ver. 9, is evidently a continuation of the same general subject which is discussed in the previous chapters, and is closely connected with the great truths communicated in ch. lii. 13-15, and ch. liii., respecting the work of the Messiah. The general design of the prophet seems to be to state the happy results which would follow his coming. In ch. liv., he states that that work would render the establishment and perpetuity of the church certain. In ch. lv., he states that it would lay the foundation for the offer of the gospel to all men, and that it should certainly be successful on the earth and finally triumph, and produce great and important changes. In this chapter (1-9) the same idea is presented in another form, that no one would be excluded from the offer of salvation, and that strangers and foreigners would become connected, with equal privileges, with the people of God. At ver. 9, a new subject is introduced—the invasion of the land of Judea by foreign armies, and the consequent punishment of the wicked and idolatrous part of the nation. This subject is continued in the following chapter. The following analysis will present a view of the design and scope of this.

I. The kingdom of God was near. The great work of man's redemption, to which the prophet referred, would not be long delayed, and those who were expecting the coming of the Messiah should be holy (1).

II. The blessedness of those who should be admitted to the privileges connected with the kingdom of God, and the coming of the Messiah. 1. Who they would be. (1.) The man who kept the Sabbath (2-4). (2.) The stranger and foreigner (3-6). (3.) The eunuch (3, 4). 2. The privileges of thus being admitted to the favour and friendship of God. (1.) They should be brought to his holy mountain. (2.) They should be made joyful in the house of prayer. (3.) Their offerings should be accepted. (4.) These favours should be extended to all people (7, 8).

III. A prophecy respecting the invasion of the land on account of the crimes of the nation. 1. The invasion is represented under the image of wild beasts coming to devour (9). 2. The cause of this. (1.) The indolence and unfaithfulness of the watchmen. (2.) Their selfishness, avarice, and covetousness. (3.) Their revelry and intemperance (10-12).

THUS saith the LORD, Keep ye ᵃjudgment, and do justice: for my salvation *is* near to come, and my righteousness to be revealed.

1 or, *equity*.

and honour of God. It will be more enduring as a memorial of him than all altars and statues, and temples erected to celebrate and perpetuate idolatry; as wide-diffused as are his works of creation, and more fruitful of blessings than anything elsewhere conferred on man.

CHAPTER LVI.

1. *Thus saith the* LORD. That is, in view of the fact that the kingdom of God was to come at no distant period, JEHOVAH states what was necessary to prepare themselves for it, and what was the character which he demanded of those who were disposed to embrace its offers, and who would be admitted to its privileges. ¶ *Keep ye judgment.* Marg. 'Equity.' Break off your sins, and be holy. A somewhat similar declaration was made by John the Baptist when he announced the coming of the Messiah: 'Repent ye, for the kingdom of heaven is at hand' (Matt. iii. 2). The general idea is, that it was not only *appropriate* that the prospect of his coming and his near approach should lead them to a holy life, but it was *necessary* in order that they might escape his indignation. ¶ *My salvation is near to come.* It is to be borne in mind that this was regarded as addressed to the Jews in exile in Babylon, and there is probably a primary reference in the words to the deliverance which they were about to experience from their long and painful captivity. But at the same time the language is appropriate to the coming of the kingdom of God under the Messiah, and the whole scope of the passage requires us to understand it of that event. Language similar to this occurs frequently in the New Testament, where the sacred writers seem to have had this passage in their eye (see Matt. iii. 2; Luke xxi. 31; Rom. xiii. 11; comp. Isa. lxii. 1-11). It is to be regarded, therefore, as having a reference to the future coming of the Messiah—perhaps as designed to describe the *series* of deliverances which were to close the painful bondage in Babylon, and to bring the people of

2 Blessed *a is* the man *that* doeth this, and the son of man *that* layeth hold on it ; that keepeth the Sabbath *b* from polluting it, and keepeth his hand from doing any evil.

3 Neither let the son of the

a Lu.12.43.   *b* ch.58.13.

God to perfect freedom, and to the full fruition of his favour. Though the actual coming of the Messiah at the time of the exile was at a period comparatively remote, yet the commencement of the great work of their deliverance was near at hand. They were soon to be rescued, and this rescue was to be but the first in the train of deliverances that would result in the entire redemption of the people of God, and was to be the public pledge that all that he had promised of the redemption of the world should be certainly effected. ¶ *To be revealed.* To be made known ; to be publicly manifested.

2. *Blessed* is *the man.* Heb. ' The blessings of the man ' (see Ps. i. 1). The sense is, ' happy is the man.' The word here rendered ' man ' (אֱנוֹשׁ) usually denotes a man in humble life or in a subordinate rank, in contradistinction from אִישׁ, a man in elevated rank. As the object of the prophet here is particularly to say, that the ' stranger ' and the ' eunuch ' would be admitted to these privileges, it is possible that he designedly used a word denoting one in humble life. The particular blessing to which he refers is specified in ver. 7, 8. ¶ *That doeth this.* That is, this which the prophet soon specifies —keeping the Sabbath, and abstaining from evil. ¶ *And the son of man.* Another form of expression denoting man. ¶ That *layeth hold on it.* Heb. ' Binds himself fast to it ;' or seizes upon it with strength. That is, he adheres firmly to the purpose, as a man seizes upon a thing with an intention not to let it go. ¶ *That keepeth the Sabbath from polluting it.* Who sacredly observes the day of holy rest which God has appointed. The Sabbath was one of the peculiar rites of the Jewish religion, and one of the most important of their institutions. Its observance entered essentially into the idea of their

stranger, *c* that hath joined himself to the Lord, speak, saying, The Lord hath utterly separated me from his people : neither let the eunuch *d* say, Behold, I *am* a dry tree.

c Nu.18.4,7; Ac.10.34,35.   *d* Ac.8.27,&c.

worship, and was designed to be the standing memorial or sign between God and the Jewish nation (Ex. xxxi. 13–17). At home, in their own nation, it kept up the constant sense of religion ; abroad, when they travelled among strangers, it would serve to remind all of the peculiar nature of their institutions, and be the public evidence that they were the worshippers of Jehovah. Hence, as this served to distinguish them from other people, it comes to be used here to signify the observance of the rites which pertained to the public worship of God ; and evidently includes whatever was to be perpetual and unchanging in the public worship of the Creator. It is remarkable that the prophet does not pronounce a blessing on him who came to bloody altars with sacrifices, or him who burned incense, or him who conformed to the peculiar rites of the Jewish religion. These rites were to pass away, and the obligation to observe them was to cease ; and in this indirect manner the sacred writer has given an intimation that there would be blessings on those who did *not* observe those rites, and that the period would arrive when the Divine favour and mercy would descend on men in a different channel. In regard to the importance of the Sabbath, see Notes on the close of chapter lviii. ¶ *And keepeth his hand,* &c. That is, is an upright, holy, honest man. He not only worships God and keeps the Sabbath, but he is upright in the discharge of all the duties which he owes to his fellow-men. These two specifications are evidently designed to include all the influences of religion—the proper service and worship of God, and an upright and holy life. Never in fact are they separated, and the religion of the Bible was designed to secure the one as much as the other.

3. *Neither let the son of the stranger.*

4 For thus saith the LORD unto the eunuchs that keep my sabbaths, and choose *the things* that please me, and take hold of my covenant;

5 Even unto them will I give in

a 1 Ti.3.15.

mine house, *a* and within my walls, a place and a name better *b* than of sons and of daughters: I will give them an everlasting name, that shall not be cut off.

b Jn.1.12.

The foreigner who shall become a proselyte to the true religion. ¶ *That hath joined himself.* That has embraced the true faith, and become a worshipper of the true God. It is evidently implied here that there would be such proselytes, and that the true religion would be extended so as to include and embrace them. The idea is, that they should be admitted to the same privileges with those who had been long recognized as the people of God. ¶ *The* LORD *hath utterly separated.* Let him not esteem himself to be an outcast, or cut off from the privileges of the people of God. This language is used with reference to the opinion which prevailed among the Jews, that the Gentiles were excluded from the privileges of the people of God, and it is designed to intimate that hereafter all such barriers would be broken down. They who entered the church as proselytes from the heathen world, were not to come in with any sense of inferiority in regard to their rights among his people; but they were to feel that all the barriers which had heretofore existed were now broken down, and that all men were on a level. There is to be no assumption of superiority of one nation or rank over another; there is to be no sense of inferiority of one class in reference to another. ¶ *Neither let the eunuch say.* This class of men was usually set over the harems of the East (Est. ii. 3, 14, 15; iv. 5); and they were employed also as high officers at court (Est. i. 10, 12, 15; Dan. i. 3; Acts viii. 27). The word is sometimes used to denote a minister of court; a court officer in general (Gen. xxxvii. 6; xxxix. 1). The Targum often renders the word by רבָּא, *a prince.* ¶ *Behold, I* am *a dry tree.* A dry tree is an emblem of that which is barren, useless, unfruitful. By the law of Moses such persons could not be enrolled or numbered in the congregation of the Lord (Deut. xxiii. 2).

The sense here is, that they should not hereafter be subjected to the religious and civil disabilities to which they had been. These external barriers to the full privileges among the people of God, would be removed. All classes and ranks would be admitted to the same privileges; all would be on the same level (see ver. 5).

4. *For thus saith the* LORD *unto the eunuchs.* Even the eunuchs, who have hitherto been excluded from the privileges of the people of God, and who have been regarded as a separated and degraded people, shall be admitted to the same privileges as others. ¶ *That keep my sabbaths.* The word is here used in the plural, though the weekly Sabbath is probably particularly intended. It may be, however, that the word is used to represent religious observances in general (see Notes on ver. 2). ¶ *And choose* the things *that please me.* Who will be willing to sacrifice their own pleasure and preferences to those things which I choose, and in which I delight. ¶ *And take hold of my covenant.* Hold fast, or steadily maintain my covenant. On the meaning of the word 'covenant,' see Notes on ch. xxviii. 18; xlii. 6; xlix. 8; liv. 10.

5. *Will I give in mine house.* That is, they shall be admitted to all the privileges of entering my house of prayer, and of being regarded as my true worshippers, and this shall be to them a more invaluable privilege than would be any earthly advantages. The word 'house' here refers undoubtedly to the temple, regarded as emblematic of the place of public worship in all ages. ¶ *And within my walls.* The walls of the city where God dwelt, referring primarily to the walls of Jerusalem. They should be permitted to dwell with God, and be admitted to all the privileges of others. All, of all classes and conditions, under the reign of the Messiah, should be regarded as on a level, and entitled

6 Also the sons of the stranger that join *a* themselves to the LORD, to serve him, and to love the name of the LORD, to be his servants, every one that keepeth the sabbath from polluting it, and taketh hold of my covenant ;

7 Even *b* them will I bring to my holy mountain ; and make them joyful in my house of prayer ; their burnt-offerings and their sacrifices *shall be c* accepted upon mine altar: for *d* mine house shall be called an house of prayer for all people.

a Je.50.5. *b* Ep.2.11-13. *c* 1 Pe.2.5. *d* Mat.21.13.

to equal advantages. There should be no religious disabilities arising from *caste*, age, country, colour, or rank of life. Those who had any physical defect should not on that account be excluded from his favour, or be regarded as not entitled to his offers of mercy. The lame, therefore, the halt, the blind ; the man of colour, the AFRICAN, the red man of the woods ; the Hindoo and the Islander ; all are to be regarded as alike invited to participate in the favour of God, and none are to be excluded from the 'house' erected to his praise, and from within the 'walls' of the holy city where he dwells. ¶ *A place.* Heb. יָד —' A hand.' The word is, however, used to denote 'a place' (Deut. xxiii. 13; Num. ii. 17; Josh. viii. 10). It is sometimes used in the sense of 'monument,' or 'trophy' (1 Sam. xv. 12; 2 Sam. xviii. 18), as if a monument were *a hand* pointing out or showing anything. The word here denotes, however, *a place*, and means that the excluded foreigner and the eunuch should be admitted to a place in the temple of God ; that is, should be admitted to the favour of God, and be permitted to dwell with him. ¶ *And a name.* As it was regarded among the Hebrews as one of the highest honours to. have a numerous posterity, the idea here is, that they should be admitted to the highest possible honour —the honour of being regarded as the children of God, and treated as his friends. ¶ *And I will give them an everlasting name.* Their memory shall not perish. They shall be admitted to eternal and unchangeable honours—the everlasting honour of being treated as the friends of God.

6. *Also the sons of the stranger* (see Note on ver. 3). The conditions on which they should be admitted to the same privileges are specified, and are the following :— 1. They were to 'join

themselves to the LORD' (see Note on ver. 3). 2. This should be with a purpose to 'serve him.' Their aim and design should be to keep his commandments and to do his will. 3. They were to 'love the name of the LORD;' that is, to love JEHOVAH himself, for the 'name' of the Lord is often used as denoting the Lord himself. 4. They were to keep his Sabbaths (see Notes on ver. 4). 5. They were to take hold of his covenant (see Notes on ver. 4). On these conditions the sons of the foreigner were to be admitted to all the privileges of the children of God, and to be united with all who love and serve him.

7. *Even them will I bring to my holy mountain* (see Notes on ch. ii. 3). That is, they should be admitted to the fellowship and privileges of his people. ¶ *And make them joyful.* In the participation of the privileges of the true religion, and in the service of God, they shall be made happy. ¶ *In my house of prayer.* In the temple—here called the house of prayer. The *language* here is all derived from the worship of the Jews, though the meaning evidently is, that under the new dispensation, all nations would be admitted to the privileges of his people, and that the appropriate services of religion which they would offer would be acceptable to God. ¶ *Their burnt-offerings.* That is, their worship shall be as acceptable as that of the ancient people of God. This evidently contemplates the future times of the Messiah, and the sense is, that in those times, the Gentiles would be admitted to the same privileges of the people of God, as the Jewish nation had been. It is true that proselytes were admitted to the privileges of religion among the Jews, and were permitted to offer burnt-offerings and sacrifices, nor can there be a doubt that they were then acceptable to God. But it is also true that there

8 The LORD God, which gathereth the outcasts *a* of Israel, saith,
Yet will I gather *others* *b* to him,

besides ¹ those that are gathered
unto him.

a Ps.147.2.   *b* Jn.10,16.   1 *to his gathered.*

was a conviction that they were admitted
as proselytes, and that there would be a
superiority felt by the native-born Jews
over the foreigners who were admitted
to their society. Under the Jewish religion this distinction was inevitable, and
it would involve, in spite of every effort
to the contrary, much of the feeling of
caste—a sense of superiority on the one
hand, and of inferiority on the other ;
a conviction on the one part that they
were the descendants of Abraham, and
the inheritors of the ancient and venerable promises, and on the other that
they had come in *as* foreigners, and
had been admitted by special favour to
these privileges. But all this was to be
abolished under the Messiah. No one
was to claim superiority on account of
any supposed advantage from birth, or
nation, or country ; no one, however
humble he might feel in respect to God
and to his own deserts, was to admit
into his bosom any sense of inferiority
in regard to his origin, his country, his
complexion, his former character. All
were to have the same near access to
God, and the offering of one was to be
as acceptable as that of another. ¶ *For
mine house.* This passage is quoted by
the Saviour (Matt. xxi. 13), to show
the impropriety of employing the temple
as a place of traffic and exchange. In
that passage he simply quotes the declaration that it should be ' a house of
prayer.' There are two ideas in the
passage as used by Isaiah ; first, that
the temple should be regarded as a house
of prayer ; and, secondly, that the privileges of that house should be extended
to all people. The main design of the
temple was that God might be there in-
voked, and the inestimable privilege of
calling on him was to be extended to
all the nations of the earth.

8. *The* LORD *God.* This verse is a
continuation of the promise made in the
previous verses, that those of other nations would be united to the ancient
people of God. The sense is, that JE-
HOVAH would not only gather back to
their country those who were scattered
abroad in other lands, but would also

call to the same privileges multitudes of
those who were now aliens and strangers.
¶ *Which gathereth the outcasts of Israel.*
Who will collect again and restore to
their own country those of the Jews who
were scattered abroad—the exiles who
were in distant lands. ¶ *Yet will I
gather* others *to him.* To Israel ; that
is, to the Jews (see John x. 16). ¶ *Besides those.* Marg. ' To his gathered.'
To those who are collected from their
exile and restored to their own country,
I will add many others of other nations.
This completes the promise referred to
in this and the previous chapters. The
next verse introduces a new subject, and
here a division should have been made
in the chapters. The great truth is here
fully expressed, that under the Messiah
the heathen world would be admitted to
the privileges of the people of God. The
formidable and long-existing barriers between the nations would be broken down.
No one nation would be permitted to
come before God claiming any peculiar
privileges ; none should regard themselves as in any sense inferior to any
other portion of the world on account of
their birth, their rank, their privileges
by nature. Under this economy we are
permitted to live—happy now in the
assurance that though we were once regarded as strangers and foreigners, yet
we are ' now fellow-citizens with the
saints and of the household of God '
(Eph. ii. 19). The whole world lies on
a level before God in regard to its origin
—for God ' has made of one blood all
the nations of men to dwell on the face
of all the earth ' (Acts xviii. 26). The
whole race is on a level in regard to
moral character—for all have sinned, and
come short of the glory of God. And
the whole race is on a level in regard to
redemption—for the same Saviour died
for all ; the same heaven is offered to
all ; and the same eternal and most
blessed God is ready to admit all to his
favour, and to confer on all everlasting
life. What thanks do we owe to the
God of grace for the blessings of the
eternal gospel ; and how anxious should
we be that the offers of salvation should

9 All ye beasts of the field, come to devour ; *yea*, all ye beasts in the forest.

10 His watchmen *are* blind ; they are all ignorant, they *are* all dumb dogs, they cannot bark ; [1] sleeping, lying down, loving to slumber.

[1] or, *dreaming;* or, *talking in their sleep.*

---

in fact be made known to all men ! The wide world may be saved, and there is not one of the human race so degraded in rank, or colour, or ignorance, that he may not be admitted to the same heaven with Abraham and the prophets, and whose prayers and praises would not be as acceptable to God as those of the most magnificent monarch who ever wore a crown.

9. *All ye beasts of the field.* This evidently commences a new subject, and refers to some invasion of the land of Judea. In the previous chapter, the prophet had comforted the people by the assurance of the coming of the Messiah, and by the fact that they should be enlarged by the accession of the Gentiles. He proceeds here to a more disagreeable part of the subject. The design is, to reprove particularly the sins of the rulers of the people, and to assure them that such conduct would incur the vengeance of Heaven. The sins reproved are indolence and inattention to duty (ver. 10-12) ; a spirit of self-indulgence and of slumber, avarice and selfishness, and luxury and intemperance. The vengeance here referred to, Lowth supposes to be the invasion of the land by the Chaldeans, and perhaps by the Romans. Grotius supposes that it refers to the Egyptians, and to bands of robbers from the Chaldeans, Syrians, Moabites, and Ammonites. Vitringa strangely enough refers it to the barbarous nations which broke in upon the Christian church to lay it waste and destroy it during the decline of the Roman empire, particularly the Huns, Saracens, Turks, Turcomans, Tartars, &c. But the connection seems to demand that it should be understood of some events, not far distant from the time of the prophet, which would be a proper punishment of the crimes then existing. According to this interpretation, the reference here, I suppose, is to the invasion of the land by the Chaldeans. They would come as wild beasts, to spread terror and devastation before them. And so great were

the national crimes, that the prophet *calls* on them to come and devour all before them. The comparison of invaders to wild beasts is not uncommon in the Scriptures. Thus Jer. xii. 9—

Mine heritage is unto me as a speckled bird,
The birds round about are against her ;
Come ye, assemble all the beasts of the field,
Come to devour.

So Jer. l. 17—

Israel is a scattered sheep ;
The lions have driven him away ;
First the king of Assyria hath devoured him,
And last this Nebuchadrezzar, king of Babylon,
    hath broken his bones.

See also Isa. ix. 11.

10. *His watchmen.* The prophet proceeds to specify the sins which had thus induced God to send the desolating armies of foreign nations. The first is specified in this verse, the apathy, indifference, and unfaithfulness, which prevailed among those who were appointed to guard their interests and defend the cause of truth. The word rendered 'his watchmen' (צֹפָו) is derived from צָפָה, *to look about;* to view from a distance ; to see afar. It is applied appropriately to those who were stationed on the walls of a city, or on a tower, in order that they might see the approach of an enemy (1 Sam. xiv. 16 ; 2 Sam. xiii. 34 ; xviii. 24). It is then applied to *prophets*, who are as it were placed on an elevated post of observation, and who are able to cast the eye far into future scenes, and to predict future events (Jer. vi. 17 ; Ezek. iii. 17 ; Note on Isa. xxi. 6–11 ; lii. 8 ; comp. lxii. 6). Here it refers undoubtedly to the public teachers of the Jews who had failed to perceive the crimes and dangers of the people ; or who, if they had seen them, had neglected to warn them of the prevalence of sin, and of the dangers to which they were exposed. ¶ *Are blind.* They have become wilfully blind to the existence of idolatry and vice, or they are so corrupt in sentiment and practice, that they fail to notice the existence of the prevailing

11 Yea, *they are* [1]greedy dogs *which* can [2]never have enough, and

they *are* shepherds *that* cannot understand ; they all look to their own

1 *strong of appetite.*   2 *know not to be satisfied.*

sins. ¶ *They are all ignorant.* Heb. 'They do not know.' This may either mean that they were not possessed of the proper qualifications for the office of prophets, or that they were so immersed in sin themselves, and so indolent, that they did not observe the existence of the national sins. In either case, they were unfit for the station. ¶ *They* are *all dumb dogs.* Dogs are appointed to guard a house or flock, and to give notice of the approach of a robber by night (Job xxx. 1). They are thus an emblem of a prophet — appointed to announce danger. Generally in the Scriptures the *dog* is mentioned as the symbol of uncleanness, of vileness, of apostasy, of that which deserved the utmost contempt (Deut. xxiii. 18; 1 Sam. xxiv. 14; 2 Sam. ix. 8; Prov. xxvi. 11; Phil. iii. 2; 2 Pet. ii. 22; Rev. xxi. 8; xxii. 15; comp. Virg. *Georg.* i. 470). But here the dog is an emblem of vigilance. The phrase ' dumb dogs,' is applicable to prophets who from any cause failed to warn the nation of their guilt and danger. ¶ *They cannot bark.* They cannot give warning of the danger which threatens. The reason why they *could* not do this the prophet immediately states. They loved to slumber—they delighted in indolence and repose. ¶ *Sleeping.* Marg. ' Dreaming,' or ' Talking in their sleep.' The word הֹזִים (*hōzim*), is from הָזָה (*hâzâ*), *to dream, to talk in one's dreams.* It is kindred to הָזָה (*hhâzâ*), to see, and the primary idea seems to be that of nocturnal *visions.* The LXX. render it, Ενυπνιαζόμενοι κοίτην—' Sleeping in bed.' Aquila, Φανταζόμενοι—' Having visions,' or phantasms. The idea is that probably of dreaming, or drowsing ; a state of indolence and unfaithfulness to their high trust. Perhaps also there is included the idea of their being deluded by vain imaginations, and by false opinions, instead of being under the influence of truth. For it is commonly the case that false and unfaithful teachers of religion are not *merely inactive ;* they act under the influence of deluding and delusive views—like men who are dream-

ing and who see nothing real. Such was probably the case with the false prophets in the time of Isaiah. ¶ *Lying down.* As dogs do who are indolent. They are inactive, unfaithful, and delighting in ease. ¶ *Loving to slumber.* Perhaps there was never a more graphic and striking description of an indolent and unfaithful ministry than this. Alas, that it should be too true of multitudes who bear the sacred office, and who are appointed to warn their fellow-men of danger ! How many come still under the description of ' dumb dogs who cannot bark, and who love to slumber !' Some are afraid of giving offence ; some have no deep sense of the importance of religious truth, and the actual danger of the ungodly ; some embrace false opinions—led on by day-dreams and fictions of the imagination, as unreal, as vain, and as inconsistent, as are the incoherent expressions which are uttered in sleep ; some engage in worldly projects, and fill up their time with the cares and plans of this life ; and some are invincibly indolent. Nothing will rouse them ; nothing induce them to forego the pleasures of sleep, and ease, and of an inactive life. The friends of God are unrebuked when they err ; and an inactive and unfaithful ministry suffers the great enemy to come and bear away the soul to death, as an unfaithful mastiff would suffer the thief to approach the dwelling without warning the inmates. But the mastiff is usually *more* faithful than an indolent ministry. To the deep shame of man be it spoken, there are more ministers of religion who are indolent, inactive, and unfaithful, than there are of the canine race. Instinct prompts *them* to act the part which God intends ; but alas, there *are* MEN —men in the ministry—whom neither instinct, nor conscience, nor reason, nor hope, nor fear, nor love, nor the command of God, nor the apprehension of eternal judgment, will rouse to put forth unwearied efforts to save souls from an eternal hell !

11. *Yea,* they are *greedy dogs.* Marg.

way, every one for his gain from his quarter.

12 Come ye, *say they,* I will fetch wine, and we will fill ourselves with

strong drink; and to-morrow shall be as this day, *and* much more abundant.

'Strong of appetite.' Literally, 'Strong of soul' (עַזֵּי־נֶפֶשׁ). Jerome renders it, *Canes impudentissimi.* So the LXX. Κύνες ἀναιδεῖς τῇ ψυχῇ—'Dogs impudent in soul.' They were greedy and insatiable in that which the soul or the appetite demands. The idea here is, that the prophets to whom reference is here made were sensual, and disposed to gorge themselves; living only for carnal indulgence, insensible to the rights of others, and never satisfied. ¶ *And they* are *shepherds* that *cannot understand.* Who are ignorant of the wants of the people, and who cannot be made to comprehend what is needed by them (see ver. 10). ¶ *They all look to their own way.* That is, they are all selfish. The ministers of religion are set apart not to promote their own interests but the welfare and salvation of others. ¶ *Every one for his gain.* For his own private ends and emoluments. ¶ *From his quarter.* Lowth, ' From the highest to the lowest.' So Rosenmüller. LXX. Κατὰ τὸ ἑαυτοῦ —'Each one according to his own purpose.' The Heb. is literally, 'From his end,' or extremity. Gen. xix. 4: ' From every quarter' (מִקָּצֶה) that is, from one end to the other; one and all, the whole. This seems to be the idea here, that one and all were given to selfishness, to covetousness, and to indulgence in luxury and sensuality.

12. *Come ye,* say they (comp. Notes on ch. xxii. 13). That is, one says to another, ' I will fetch wine;' or as *we* would say, ' I will take another glass.' The object is to describe a *drinking-bout,* or *carousal,* when the glass is shoved around, and there is drinking to excess. The language denotes the state of exhilaration and excitement when sitting at the table, and already under the influence of wine. This is not designed to be descriptive of the people at large, but of the ' watchmen,' or public teachers of the nation, and it certainly shows a state of most lamentable degeneracy and corruption. Unhappily,

however, it has not been confined to the times of Manasseh. There have been periods in the history of the Christian church, and there are still portions of that church, where the language here used with so much severity would be an appropriate description even of the Christian ministry; scenes where the professed heralds of salvation sit long at the wine, and join with the gay, the worldly, and the profane, in ' shoving round' the sparkling cup. No severer language is used in the prophets to describe and denounce any class of sinners than is appropriated to such men; at no time has the church more occasion to sit in the dust and to weep, than when her ministers ' rise up early in the morning, that they may follow strong drink; and continue until night, till wine inflame them (Isa. v. 11). ¶ *We will fill ourselves with strong drink* (see Notes on ch. v. 11). ¶ *And to-morrow,* &c. That is, indulgence of this kind was habitual. There was an *intention* to continue it. It was not that they had been once overtaken and had erred; but it was that they loved it, and meant to drink deeper and deeper. So now the guilt of ministers is greatly aggravated in the same way. It is not *merely* that they drink wine; it is not even that they on a single occasion drink too much, and say and do foolish and wicked things—liable as all are to this who indulge in drinking wine at all, and certainly as ministers will do it who indulge in the habit;— it is that they *mean* to do it; they resolve *not* to abandon it, but purpose to persevere in the habit ' to-morrow.' Hence, such men refuse to join a Society of Temperance; hence they oppose such societies as ultra and fanatical; and hence, by *not* joining them, they proclaim to the world, ' Come ye, and I will take another glass, and to-morrow shall be as this day, and much more abundant.' It is this *settled* purpose—this fixed resolution, stretching into future time, and embracing coming years, that

CHAPTER LVII.

ANALYSIS.

This chapter is evidently closely connected in sense with ch. lvi. 9-12. In the closing part of the last chapter the prophet had said that the land of Israel would be invaded by foreign armies, represented under the image of ravening beasts come to devour. One of the causes of this he had also stated, viz., the general licentiousness, avarice, and intemperance of the rulers of the nation. The same general subject is pursued in this chapter, which has been very improperly separated from the preceding. In this the prophet states specifically the sins of the nation at large, evidently as a reason why the calamities of the foreign invasion were coming upon them. It is probable that the chapter has primary reference to the times of Manasseh. Of the characteristics of his cruel reign, see the Introduction, § 3. It was a time of persecution and blood. The righteous were put to death; the public service of God was profaned and desecrated; and the evils of idolatry were seen and felt, under the royal patronage, throughout the land. Yet notwithstanding this, the nation was stupid and insensible. They were not affected as they should have been by the fact that the righteous were cut off by persecution, and that idolatry was patronized throughout the land. A few, like the prophets, felt, and deeply felt. Their hearts were desponding, and their spirits drooped. To encourage them, and to rebuke the mass of the stupid and guilty nation, was the design of this chapter.

It may be regarded as divided into three parts:—

I. The fact that the righteous were put to death, and yet that the nation was sunk in deep and deplorable stupidity. 1. The proof of the insensibility of the nation, visible in the fact that the just were taken away, and that they were unmoved (1.) 2. A statement of the comparative happy condition of the righteous, though they suffered under persecution, and were put to a violent death (ver. 1, last part, ver. 2). So far as *they* were concerned it was well, for (1.) They were taken away from more

fearful approaching evils. (2.) They entered into rest.

II. A solemn address of Jehovah, himself sitting as judge on the tribunal, and stating the crimes and demonstrating the guilt of the nation (3-14). 1. The nation summoned before him as having been apostatized—under the image so common in the prophets of their being guilty of adultery (3). 2. They were guilty of falsehood and unfaithfulness to him, and of deriding his government and laws (4). 3. The statement of the prevalence of idolatry in all parts of the nation, under every green tree, in every valley, in the clefts of the rocks, upon every mountain, and in every secret place (5-8). 4. They had gone and sought alliance with foreign powers; under the image of a woman unfaithful to her marriage vow (9). 5. They had not feared God in the prevalence of the evil and in the corruption of the nation (10, 11). 6. For all this God denounces heavy judgment (12-14). Their works should not profit them (12); nothing on which they relied could deliver them (13, first part); but the pious who confided in God should be protected (13, last part); and the stumbling-block should be taken up out of the way of his people (14).

III. Consolation and assurances of pardon, protection, and peace to those who would repent and put their trust in God. Their state contrasted with that of the wicked (15-21). 1. The righteous (15-19). (1.) Though God was high and great and holy, yet he dwelt with the lowly and the penitent. They were, therefore, encouraged to return (15). (2.) Though he had entered into controversy with his people for their sins, yet he would not continue it for ever. The feeble powers of man could not long endure the expressions of his displeasure, and he therefore would withdraw the tokens of his wrath (16). (3.) He had indeed punished his people for their covetousness, but he would restore comfort to those who mourned over their sins (17, 18). (4.) He was the author of peace, and all who were afar off, and all who were near, who would return to him, should enjoy it (19). 2. The wicked. Their condition was one strongly contrasted with that of the righteous (20, 21). (1.) They were like the troubled sea (20). (2.) They had no peace (21).

is so offensive to God. And there is not on earth a condition of more public iniquity than when the ministers of religion take this bold and open stand, and resolve that they *will not* abandon intoxicating drinks, but will continue to drink 'to-morrow,' and ever onward. Hopeless is the work of reformation when the ministers of religion take this stand; and dark is the prospect for the church on earth, when the messengers of salvation cannot be induced to stand before the church of God as examples and advocates for temperance on the most strict and uncompromising principles.

THE righteous perisheth, and no man layeth *it* to heart: and merciful [1]men *are* taken away,

none considering that the righteous *is* taken away from [2]the evil *to* come.

1 *men of kindness*, or, *godliness*.

2 *or, that which is evil.*

CHAPTER LVII.

1. *The righteous perisheth.* This refers, as I suppose, to the time of Manasseh (see Introd. § 3). Grotius supposes, that it refers to king Josiah; Vitringa, that it refers to martyrs in general. But it seems probable to me that the prophet designs to describe the state of stupidity which prevailed in his own time, and to urge as one proof of it, that the pious part of the nation was taken away by violent death, and that the nation was not affected by it. Such was the guilt of Manasseh; so violent was the persecution which he excited against the just, that it is said of him that he ' shed innocent blood very much, till he had filled Jerusalem from one end to another' (2 Kings xxii. 16). There is evidence (see Introd. § 2), that Isaiah lived to his time, and it is probable that he himself ultimately fell a victim to the rage of Manasseh. Though he had, on account of his great age, retired from the public functions of the prophetic office, yet he could not be insensible to the existence of these evils, and his spirit would not suffer him to be silent, even though bowed down by age, when the land was filled with abominations, and when the best blood of the nation was poured out like water. The word rendered 'perisheth' (אָבַד) as well as the word rendered 'taken away' (אָסַף) denotes violence, and is indicative of the fact that they were removed by a premature death. ¶ *And no man layeth it to heart.* No one is aroused by it, or is concerned about it. The sentiment of the passage is, that it is proof of great stupidity and guilt when men see the righteous die without concern. If the pious die by persecution and others are not aroused, it shows that they acquiesce in it, or have no confidence in God, and no desire that his people should be preserved; if they die in the ordinary mode and the people are unaffected, it shows their stupidity. The withdrawment of a pious man from the earth is a public calamity.

His prayers, his example, his life, were among the richest blessings of the world, and men should be deeply affected when they are withdrawn; and it shows their guilt and stupidity when they see this with indifference. It increases the evidence of this guilt when, as is sometimes the case, the removal of the righteous by death is an occasion of joy. The wicked hate the secret rebuke which is furnished by a holy life, and they often feel a secret exultation when such men die. ¶ *And merciful men.* Marg. 'Men of kindness,' or 'godliness.' Lowth and Noyes render it, 'Pious men.' The LXX. Ἄνδρες δίκαιοι—'Just men.' The Hebrew word denotes *mercy* or kindness (חֶסֶד). Here it probably means, 'Men of mercy;' that is, men who are the subjects of mercy; men who are pious, or devoted to God. ¶ Are *taken away.* Heb. ' Are gathered.' That is, they are gathered to their fathers by death. ¶ *None considering.* They were not anxious to know what was the design of Divine Providence in permitting it. ¶ *From the evil to come.* Marg. 'That which is evil.' The idea here evidently is, that severe calamities were coming upon the nation. God was about to give them up to foreign invasion (ch. lvi. 9, *sq.*); and the true reason why the just were removed was, that they may not be subject to the Divine wrath which should come upon the nation; they were not to be required to contemplate the painful state of things when an enemy should fire the cities, the palaces, and the temple, and cause the sacred services of religion to cease. It was a less evil for them to be removed by death—even by the painful death of persecution—than to be compelled to participate in these coming sorrows. At the same time this passage may be regarded as inculcating a more general truth still. It is, that the pious are often removed in order that they may not be exposed to evils which they would experience should they live. There might be the pains and sorrows of persecution; there

2 He shall ¹enter into peace: they shall rest in their beds, *each one* walking ²*in* his ᵃuprightness.

3 But draw near hither, ye sons of the sorceress, the seed of the adulterer and the whore.

1 *go in peace.*   2 or, *before him.*   a Re.14.13.

might be long and lingering disease; there might be poverty and want; there might be the prevalence of iniquity and infidelity over which their hearts would bleed; there might be long and painful conflicts with their own evil hearts, or there might be danger that *they* would fall into sin, and dishonour their high calling. For some or all these reasons the righteous may be withdrawn from the world; and could we see those reasons as God does, nothing more would be necessary to induce us to acquiesce entirely in the justice of his dealings.

2. *He shall enter into peace.* Lowth, 'He shall go in peace.' So the margin. Vulg. 'Peace shall come.' LXX. 'His sepulture (ἡ ταφὴ αὐτοῦ) shall be in peace.' The idea is, that by his death the righteous man shall enter into rest. He shall get away from conflict, strife, agitation, and distress. This may either refer to the peaceful rest of the grave, or to that which awaits the just in a better world. The direct meaning here intended is probably the former, since the grave is often spoken of as a place of rest. Thus Job (iii. 17), speaking of the grave, says:

There the wicked cease from troubling;
And there the weary be at rest.

The connection here seems also to demand the same sense, as it is immediately added, 'they shall rest in their beds.' The grave is a place of peace:

Nor pain, nor grief, nor anxious fear,
Invade thy bounds; no mortal woes
Can reach the peaceful sleeper here,
While angels watch the soft repose.—Watts.

At the same time it is true that the dying saint '*goes* in peace!' He has calmness *in his dying*, as well as peace *in his grave.* He forgives all who have injured him; prays for all who have persecuted him; and peacefully and calmly dies. He lies in a peaceful grave—often represented in the Scriptures as a place of repose, where the righteous 'sleep' in the hope of being awakened in the morning of the resurrection. He

enters into the rest of heaven—the world of perfect and eternal repose. No persecution comes there; no trial awaits him there; no calamity shall meet him there. Thus, in all respects, the righteous leave the world in peace; and thus death ceases to be a calamity, and this most dreaded of all evils is turned into the highest blessing. ¶ *They shall rest in their beds.* That is, in their graves. ¶ Each one *walking in his uprightness.* Marg. 'Before him.' The word נָכֹח means *straight, right,* and is used of one who walks straight forward. It here means an upright man, who is often represented as walking in a straight path in opposition to sinners, who are represented as walking in crooked ways (Ps. cxxv. 5; Prov. ii. 15; Isa. lix. 8; Phil. ii. 15). The sense here is, that all who are upright shall leave the world in peace, and rest quietly in their graves.

3. *But draw near hither.* That is, come near to hear the solemn sentence which God pronounces in regard to your character and doom. This is addressed to the impenitent and unbelieving part of the nation, and is designed to set before them the greatness of their sin, and the certainty that they would be punished. ¶ *Ye sons of the sorceress.* You who are addicted to sorcery and enchantments; who consult the oracles of the heathen rather than the only true God. On the meaning of the word used here, see Notes on ch. ii. 6. The Hebrews, like other inhabitants of the East, were much addicted to this, and particularly in the time of Manasseh (2 Kings xxi. 6): 'And he made his sons pass through the fire, and observed times, and used enchantments, and dealt with familiar spirits, and wizards.' So much were they devoted to this in his time, that they might be called, by way of eminence, '*the sons* of the sorceress;' as if a sorceress had been their mother, and they had grown up to walk in her steps, and to imitate her example. ¶ *The seed of the adulterer.* Implying

4 Against whom do ye sport yourselves? against whom make ye a wide mouth, *and* draw out the tongue? *are* ye not children of transgression, a seed of falsehood.

5 Inflaming yourselves [1] with idols under *a* every green tree, slaying the children *b* in the valleys under the clefts of the rocks?

1 or, *among the oaks.*   *a* 2 Ki.17.10,&c.   *b* 2 Ki.16.3.4.

that the obligations of the marriage contract were disregarded, and that licentiousness prevailed in the nation. Amidst the other abominations which existed under the wicked and corrupt reign of Manasseh (2 Kings xxi.), there is every probability that these sins also abounded. Licentiousness had been the invariable attendant on idol-worship; and dissoluteness of manners is the usual accompaniment of all other crimes. It is observable also that the Saviour often charges the same sin on the nation in his own time (Matt. xii. 39; xvi. 4; John viii. 1, *sq.*) In the language here, however, there is a reference to the fact that the nation had apostatized from God, and they were guilty of *spiritual* adultery—that is, of unfaithfulness to God. They fixed their affections on other objects than God, and loved the images of idol-worship more than they did their Creator.

4. *Against whom do ye sport yourselves?* The word here rendered 'sport' (עָנַג) means properly *to live delicately* and tenderly; then to rejoice, to take pleasure or delight. Here, however, it is evidently used in the sense of to sport one's self over any one, *i.e.*, to deride; and the idea is, probably, that they made a sport or mockery of God, and of the institutions of religion. The prophet asks, with deep indignation and emotion, against whom they did this. Were they aware of the majesty and glory of that Being whom they thus derided? ¶ *Against whom make ye a wide mouth?* That is, in derision or contempt (Ps. xxxv. 21): 'Yea, they opened their mouth wide against me.' ¶ And *draw out the tongue?* Lowth, 'Loll the tongue;' or, as we would say, 'run out the tongue.' Perhaps it was done with a rapid motion, as in mockery of the true prophets when they delivered the message of God (comp. 2 Chron. xxxvi. 16). Contempt was sometimes shown also by protruding the lips (Ps. xxii. 7): 'They shoot out the lip;' and

also by *gaping* upon a person (Ps. xxii. 13); 'They gaped upon me with their mouths.' ¶ Are *ye not children of transgression?* That is, in view of the fact that you make a sport of sacred things, and deride the laws and the prophets of God. ¶ *A seed of falsehood.* A generation that is unfaithful to God and to his cause.

5. *Inflaming yourselves.* Burning, *i.e.*, with lust. The whole language here is derived from adulterous intercourse. The sense is, that they were greatly addicted to idolatry, and that they used every means to increase and extend the practice of it. The Vulgate, however, renders this, 'Who console yourselves.' The LXX. render it, 'Invoking (παρακαλοῦντες) idols.' But the proper meaning of the Hebrew word חָמַם is, *to become warm;* to be inflamed, or to burn as with lust. ¶ *With idols.* Marg. 'Among the oaks.' Heb. בָּאֵלִים. Vulg. *In diis*—'With the gods.' LXX. Εἴδωλα—'Idols.' So the Chaldee and Syriac. The Hebrew may denote 'with gods,' *i.e.*, with idol-gods; or it may denote, as in the margin, 'among the oaks,' or the terebinth groves, from אֵיל. plural אֵילִים, or אֵלִים (*the terebinth*). See the word explained in the Note on ch. i. 29. Kimchi and Jarchi here render it by 'the terebinth tree.' Lowth renders it, 'Burning with the lust of idols;' and probably this is the correct interpretation; for, if it had meant oaks or the terebinth tree, the phrase would have been *under* (תַּחַת) instead of *in* or *with* (בְּ). ¶ *Under every green tree* (see Notes on ch. i. 29; comp. Deut. xxii. 2; 2 Kings xvii. 10; 2 Chron. xxviii. 4). ¶ *Slaying the children.* That is, sacrificing them to the idol-gods. This was commonly done by burning them, as when they were offered to Moloch, though it is not improbable that they were sometimes sacrificed in other ways. It was a common custom among the worshippers of Moloch. Thus

6 Among the smooth *stones* of
the stream *is* thy portion ; they,
they *are* thy lot ; even to them

hast thou poured a drink-offering,
thou hast offered a meat-offering.
Should I receive comfort in these ?

it is said of Ahaz (2 Chron. xxviii. 3),
that he 'burnt incense in the valley of
the son of Hinnom, and burnt his children in the fire.' The same thing is
said of Manasseh, to whose time the
prophet most probably refers. ' And
he caused his children to pass through
the fire in the valley of the son of
Hinnom ' (2 Chron. xxxiii. 6; comp.
Jer. vii. 31). The same thing was
practised in the countries of the Babylonian empire (2 Kings xvii. 31), and
from Deut. xii. 31, it is evident that it
was commonly practised by heathen
nations. The Phenicians, according to
Eusebius (Præp. Evan. iv. 16), and the
Carthagenians, according to Diodorus
Siculus (xx. 14), practised it. ¶ *In the
valleys.* The place where these abominations were practised by the Jews was
the valley of the son of Hinnom (see the
references above) ; that is, the valley of
Jehoshaphat, lying to the south and the
south-east of Jerusalem. A large hollow, brazen statue was erected, and the
fire was enkindled within it, and the
child was placed in his heated arms,
and thus put to death. The cries of
the child were drowned by the music of
the חֹף *toph,* or kettle-drums (see Notes
on ch. v. 12, where this instrument is
fully described), and hence the name of
the valley was *Tophet.* ¶ *Under the
clefts of the rocks.* Dark and shady
groves, and deep and sombre caverns
were the places where the abominable
rites of the heathen superstitions were
practised (comp. Notes on ch. xi. 21).

6. *Among the smooth stones of the
streams.* In the original here, there is
a paronomasia, which cannot be fully
retained in our English version. There
has been also considerable diversity of
opinion in regard to the sense of the
passage, from the ambiguity of the words
in the original. Jerome (Vulg.) renders
it, *In partibus torrentis pars tua*—'Thy
portion is in the parts of the torrent.'
The LXX. translate it, ' This is thy
portion ; this is thy lot.' The word
rendered in our version ' smooth stones '
(חֵלֶק *hhêlĕq*), means properly *smooth-

ness,* hence, barrenness or bare place;
and supposes that the idea is, their lot
was in the bare places of the valley, *i.e.,*
in the open (not wooded) places where
they worshipped idols—an interpretation not very consistent with the fact
that groves were commonly selected as
the place where they worshipped idols.
It seems to me, therefore, that the idea
of *smoothness* here, whether of the valley
or of the stones, is not the idea intended.
Indeed, in no place, it is believed, does
the word mean ' smooth stones ;' and
it is difficult to conceive what was the
exact idea which our translators intended to convey, or why they supposed that
such worship was celebrated among the
smooth or much-worn stones of the
running stream. The true idea can
probably be obtained by reverting to the
primitive sense of the word as derived
from the verb. The verb חָלַק *hhâhlăq*
means—1. *To smooth.* 2. *To divide,*
to distribute, to appropriate—as the
dividing of spoil, &c. Hence the noun
also means *dividing,* or portion, as that
which is *divided*—whether an inheritance, or whether the dividings of spoil
after battle. Retaining this idea, the
literal sense, as I conceive, would be
this—in which also something of the
paronomasia will be retained : 'Among
the dividings of the valley is thy dividing,' *i.e.,* thy portion. In the places
where the valley divides, is thy lot.
Thy lot is there instead of the place
which God appointed. There you
worship ; there you pour out your libations to the false gods ; and there you
must partake of the protection and
favour which the gods whom you worship
can give. You have chosen that as
your inheritance, and by the results of
that you must abide. ¶ *Of the stream.*
The word here rendered ' stream ' (נַחַל
năhhăl), means either a stream, or a
rivulet of water (Num. xxxiv. 5 ; Josh.
xv. 4–47); or it means a *valley* with a
brook or torrent; a low place with
water. Here it means evidently the
latter—as it cannot be supposed they
would worship *in* a stream, though they

7 Upon a lofty and high mountain hast thou set thy bed : even thither wentest thou up to offer sacrifice.

8 Behind the doors also and the posts hast thou set up thy remem-

a Eze.16.25,&c.; 23.2,&c.

brance ; for *a* thou hast discovered *thyself to another* than me, and art gone up : thou hast enlarged thy bed, and 1 made thee *a covenant* with them ; thou lovedst their bed where 2 thou sawest *it*.

1 or, *hewed it for thyself* larger *than theirs.*
2 or, *thou providest room.*

---

undoubtedly worshipped in a vale or low place where there was occasionally a rivulet of water. This entire description is strikingly applicable to the valley of Jehoshaphat—a low vale, broken by chasms and by projecting and overhanging rocks, and along the centre of which flowed a small brook, much swelled occasionally by the waters that fell from the adjacent hills. At some seasons of the year, however, the valley was entirely dry. The idea here is, that they had chosen their portion in the dividings of that valley instead of the adjacent hills on which the worship of God was celebrated. That valley became afterwards the emblem of punishment : and may it not be implied in this passage that they were to inherit whatever would descend on that valley; that is, that they were to participate in the punishment which would be the just expression of the Divine displeasure ? ¶ *Even to them hast thou poured out.* That is, to these idols erected in the valleys. ¶ *A drink-offering.* A libation, or drink-offering was usually poured out in the worship of heathen gods (Jer. vii. 18). It was common also in the worship of the true God (see Gen. xxxv. 14). Among the Hebrews it consisted of wine and oil (Ex. xxix. 40; Num. xv. 5–7; Lev. xxiii. 13). ¶ *Thou hast offered a meat-offering.* On the word used here (מִנְחָה *mĭnhhâ*) see Notes on ch. i. 13; xliii. 23. The word 'meat' formerly denoted in the English language *food* in general, and was not confined as it is now to animal food. Hence the word 'meat-offering' is so often used in the Scriptures when a sacrifice is intended which was not a bloody sacrifice. The *minhha* was in fact an offering of *meal*, fine flour, &c., mingled with oil (Lev. xiv. 10; Num. vii. 13), and was distinguished expressly from the bloody sacrifice. The word ' *meal*-offering' would much more

appropriately express the sense of the original than '*meat*-offering.' This was a common offering made to idols as well as to the true God, and was designed as an expression of thankfulness. ¶ *Should I receive comfort in these?* It is implied that God could not behold them but with displeasure, and that for them he would punish them. The Vulg. and the LXX. well express it, ' On account of these things shall I not be enraged?'

7. *Upon a lofty and high mountain.* The design of this verse and the following, is, to show the extent, the prevalence, the publicity, and the grossness of their idolatry. The language is that which would appropriately express adulterous intercourse, and is designed to show the abhorrence in which God held their conduct. The language is easy to be understood, and it would not be proper to go into an extended explanation of the phrases used. It is common in the Scriptures to compare idolatry among the people of God, with unfaithfulness to the marriage vow. The declaration that they had placed their bed on a high mountain, means, that in the rites of idolatrous worship, there was no concealment. It was public and shameless.

8. *Behind the doors.* In every part of their habitations—behind the doors and posts and beams of their houses, they had erected the memorials of idolatrous worship. ¶ *Hast thou set up thy remembrance.* That is, they had filled their houses with the images of tutelary gods, or with something dedicated to them. The Greeks and Romans had their *Lares* and *Penates*—their household or domestic gods—the images of which were in every family. The same was true of the apostate Hebrews. They had filled their houses with the memorials of idol-worship, and there was no part of their dwellings in which such memorials were not to be found.

9 And thou ¹wentest to the king with ointment, ᵃand didst increase

1 or, *respectedst.*   a Ho.12.1.

thy perfumes, and didst send thy messengers far off, and didst debase *thyself even* unto hell.

When a people forget God, the memorials of their apostasy will be found in every part of their habitations. The shrines of idol-gods may not be there ; the beautiful images of the Greek and Roman mythology, or the clumsy devices of less refined heathens, may not be there; but the furniture, the style of living, will reveal from 'behind every door and the posts' of the house that God is forgotten, and that they are influenced by other principles than a regard to his name. The sofa, the carpet, the chandelier, the centre-table, the instruments of music, the splendid mirror, *may be* of such workmanship as to show, as clearly as the image of a heathen god, that JEHOVAH is not honoured in the dwelling, and that his law does not control the domestic arrangements. It may be added here that this custom of the Hebrews of placing the images of idols in their dwellings, was in direct violation of the law of Moses. They were expressly directed to write the laws of God on the posts of the house and on the gates (Deut. vi. 9; xi. 20); and a curse was denounced against the man who made a graven or molten image and put it in a secret place (Deut. xxvii. 15). ¶ *For thou hast discovered* thyself. This language is taken from adulterous intercourse, and is designed to show the love which they had for idolatrous worship, and the extent of their unfaithfulness to God. ¶ *And made thee* a covenant *with them.* Marg. ' Hewed it for thyself larger than theirs.' The true sense is, that they had made an agreement with idolaters, or had entered into a covenant with them. ¶ *Thou lovedst their bed.* Marg. ' Thou providest room.' Literally, ' Thou lovest their bed ; thou hast provided a place for it.' The word ‏יד‎, here rendered ' where,' means literally *a hand ;* then a side, a place (see Notes on ch. lvi. 5). The passage means, that they had delighted in the temples, altars, groves, and sacrifices of idolatry, and had provided a place for them in their own land.

9. *And thou wentest to the king.* Marg. ' Respectedst.' Jerome renders this, ' Thou hast adorned thyself with royal ointment, and hast multiplied thy painting;' and evidently understands it as a continuation of the sentiment in the previous verses as referring to the kind of decoration which harlots used. The LXX. render it, ' Thou hast multiplied thy fornication with them, and hast done it with many who are far from thee.' The Chaldee renders it, ' When thou didst keep the law thou wert prosperous in the kingdom; and when thou didst abound in good works, then thine armies were multiplied.' Lowth supposes that the king of Egypt or Assyria is intended, and that the prophet refers to the fact, that the Hebrews had sought an alliance with them, and in order to secure it, had carried a present of valuable unguents, after the manner of the East. Rosenmüller supposes, that by the king an idol was intended, and that the sense is, that they had anointed themselves with oil, and prepared perfumes, in order to be acceptable to the idol; that is, had decorated themselves as harlots did. Grotius supposes that it means that they had imitated foreign kings, and copied the customs of other nations, and refers to the example of Ahaz (2 Kings xvi. 10). Others suppose that the word 'king' is to be taken collectively, and that it means that they had sought the alliance, and imitated the customs of foreign nations in general. It is probable that the prophet refers to some such fact. On former occasions, they had sought the alliance of the king of Assyria (see ch. vii. *sq.*); and on one occasion, at least, they had meditated an alliance with the king of Egypt (ch. xxx. 2, *sq.*) The essential idea is, that they had proved unfaithful to JEHOVAH. This idea is presented here under the image of a female unfaithful to her husband, who had decorated and perfumed herself that she might allure others. Thus the Jews had forsaken God, and had endeavoured to make themselves agreeable in the sight of other nations, and had courted

10 Thou art wearied in the greatness *a* of thy way ; *yet* saidst thou
not, There is no hope : thou hast

found the life [1] of thine hand ; therefore thou wast not grieved.

their friendship and alliance. The word
' king,' according to this, refers not to
idols, but to foreign princes, whose assistance had been sought. ¶ *And didst
increase thy perfumes.* That is, for the
purpose of rendering thyself agreeable,
after the manner of a licentious female
(see Prov. vii. 17). The custom of per-
fuming the person was common in the
East, and is still practised there. ¶ *And
didst send thy messengers.* That is, to
distant nations, for the purpose of securing their alliance. ¶ *And didst
debase* thyself even *unto hell.* On the
meaning of the word ' hell,' see Notes
on ch. v. 14. The idea is, that they
had sunk to the deepest possible debasement. In forsaking JEHOVAH; in seeking foreign alliances; in their anxiety
to secure their aid when JEHOVAH was
abundantly able and willing to protect
them, they had sunk to the lowest degradation of character and condition. The
sentiment is, that men degrade themselves when they do not put confidence
in God, and when, distrusting his ability, they put reliance on any other aid
than his. If men have God for their
protector, why should they court the
friendship of earthly princes and kings?

10. *Thou art wearied in the greatness
of thy way.* That is, in the length of
thy journeys in order to procure foreign
aid. Thou hast travelled to distant
nations for this purpose, and in doing
it, hast become weary without securing
the object in view. ¶ Yet *saidst thou
not, There is no hope.* ' Thou didst
not say it is to be despaired of (נוֹאָשׁ),
or it is vain. Though repulsed in one
place, you applied to another ; though
weary, you did not give it up. Instead
of returning to God and seeking his
aid, you still sought human alliances,
and supposed you would find assistance
from the help of men.' This is a striking
illustration of the conduct of men in seeking happiness away from God. They
wander from object to object ; they become weary in the pursuit, yet they do
not abandon it ; they still cling to hope
though often repulsed—and though the

world gives them no permanent comfort
—though wealth, ambition, gaiety, and
vice all fail in imparting the happiness
which they sought, yet they do not give
it up in despair. They still feel that it
is to be found in some other way than
by the disagreeable necessity of returning to God, and they wander from object to object, and from land to land,
and become exhausted in the pursuit,
and still are not ready to say, ' there is
no hope, we give it up in despair, and
we will now seek happiness in God.'
¶ *Thou hast found the life of thine
hand.* Marg. ' Living.' Lowth, ' Thou
hast found the support of thy life by
thy labour.' Noyes, ' Thou yet findest
life in thy hand.' Much diversity of
opinion has prevailed in regard to the
interpretation of this passage. Vitringa
interprets the whole passage of their devotion to idols, and supposes that this
means that they had borne all the expense and difficulty and toil attending
it because it gratified their hearts, and
because they found a pleasure in it
which sustained them. Calvin supposes
that it is to be understood *ironically.*
' Why didst thou not repent and turn to
me? Why didst thou not see and acknowledge thy madness? It was because thou didst find thy life in thy
hand. All things prospered and succeeded according to thy desire, and conferred happiness.' The LXX. render it,
' Because in full strength (ἐνισχύουσα)
thou hast done this ; therefore thou
shouldst not supplicate me.' Jerome
explains it to mean, ' because they have
done the things referred to in the previous verses, therefore they had not sup-
plicated the Lord, trusting more in their
own virtues than in God.' The Syriac
renders it, ' The guilt of thy hand has
contracted rust for thee, therefore thou
hast not offered supplication.' The
Chaldee renders it, ' Thou hast amassed
wealth, therefore thou didst not repent.'
Kimchi explains it to mean, ' Thou hast
found something which is as pleasant
to thee as the food is which is the life
of man.' The phrase ' life of thy hand '

11 And of whom hast thou been afraid or feared, that thou hast lied, and hast not remembered me, nor laid *it* to thy heart ? have *a* not I held my peace even of old, and thou fearest me not ?

a Ps.50.21.

occurs nowhere else. The hand is the instrument by which we execute our purposes ; and by the life of the hand here, there seems to be meant that which will give full and continued employment. They had found in these things that which effectually prevented them from repenting and returning to God. They had relied on their own plans rather than on God ; they had sought the aid of foreign powers ; they had obtained that which kept them from absolute despair, and from feeling their need of the assistance of God. Or, if it refers to their idol-worship, as Vitringa supposes, then it means that, notwithstanding all the trouble, toil, and expense which they had experienced, they had found so much to gratify them that they continued to serve them, and were unwilling to return to God. ¶ *Therefore thou wast not grieved.* Lowth, ' Thou hast not utterly fainted.' The word used here (הָלָה) means *to be polished;* then to be worn down in strength ; to be weak or exhausted (Judg. xvi. 7); then to be sick, diseased, made weak. Here it means, that either by the aid which they had obtained by foreign alliances, or by the gratification experienced in the service of idols, they had found so much to uphold them that they had not been in utter despair. And the passage may teach the general truth, that notwithstanding all the trials and disappointments of life, still sinners find *so much* comfort in the ways of sin, that they are not utterly overwhelmed in despair. They still find the ' life of their hand in them.' If a plan fails, they repeat it, or they try another. In the pursuits of ambition, of wealth, and of fashion, notwithstanding all the expense, and irksomeness, and disappointment, they find *a kind* of pleasure which sustains them, and *enough* success to keep them from returning to God. It is this imperfect pleasure and success which the world gives amidst all its disappointments, and this hope of less diminished joys and more ample success

in schemes of gain, and pleasure, and ambition, that sustains the votaries of this world in their career, and keeps them from seeking the pure and unmingled pleasures of religion. When the world becomes *all* gloom, and disappointment, and care, then there is felt the necessity of a better portion, and the mind is turned to God. Or when, as is more common, the mind becomes convinced that all the joys which the world can give—allowing the utmost limit to what is said by its friends of its powers—are poor and trifling compared with the joys which flow from the eternal friendship of God, then the blessings of salvation are sought with a full heart ; and then man comes and consecrates the fulness of his energies and his immortal vigour to the service of the God that made him.

11. *And of whom hast thou been afraid.* The sense of this verse is exceedingly obscure. The design is evidently to reprove the Jews for the course which they had been pursuing in practising idolatry, and in seeking the alliance of foreign powers. The main scope of the passage seems to be, to state that all this was proof that they did not fear God. Their conduct did not originate from any reverence for him, or any respect to his commands. And the question, ' of whom hast thou been afraid?' seems to mean that they had not been afraid of God. If they had had any reverence for any being or object that had led to the course which they had pursued, it was not for God. ¶ *That thou hast lied.* That thou hast been false and unfaithful to God. The image is here kept up of unfaithfulness to the marriage vow (ver. 6–8). ¶ *And hast not remembered me.* The proof of this was, that they had fallen into idolatry, and had sought the alliance and friendship of foreign powers. ¶ *Have not I held my peace.* The idea here seems to be, that God had been silent a long time, and they had, therefore, been emboldened to sin. He had, as it were, connived at their apostasy

12 I will declare thy righteousness, and thy works ; for they shall
not profit thee.

13 When thou criest, let thy
companies deliver thee : but the
wind shall carry them all away ;
vanity shall take *them :* but he that
putteth^a his trust in me shall pos-

a Is.37.3,9.

sess the land, and shall inherit my
holy mountain.

14 And shall say, Cast ye up,
cast ye up, prepare the way, take
up the stumbling-block *b* out of the
way of my people.

15 For thus saith the high and
lofty One that inhabiteth eternity,

b 1 Co.1.23.

and infidelity; and they had thus cast
off the fear of him, and given themselves
wholly to idolatry. Comp. Eccl. viii. 11.
12. *I will declare thy righteousness.*
This is evidently spoken ironically. The
sense is, 'you have devoted yourselves
to idols, and you have sought the aid of
foreigners. I will now announce to you
the true nature of the deliverance which
they can bring to you.' This is done
in the following verse.
13. *When thou criest.* That is, when
you are in trouble, and feel your need of
help. ¶ *Let thy companies deliver thee.*
The word here used (קִבּוּץ) means, properly, a gathering ; a throng ; a collection. Here it refers either to the *throngs*
of the idols which they had collected, and
on which they relied ; or to the collection of foreigners which they had summoned to their assistance. The idea is,
that if men trust to other objects for aid
than the arm of God, they will be left
in the day of trial to such assistance as
they can render them. ¶ *But the wind
shall carry.* They shall be like the protection which the wind sweeps away.
The Saviour expresses a similar sentiment in Matt. vii. 26, 27. ¶ *Vanity
shall take* them. Lowth and Noyes,
'A breath shall take them off.' The
word הֶבֶל *hêbhêl,* properly means *a
breath;* and probably denotes here a
gentle breeze, the slightest breath of air,
denoting the entire instability of the objects on which they trusted, when they
could be so easily swept off. ¶ *Shall
possess the land.* The assurances of
the favour and friendship of God are
usually expressed in this way (comp.
Notes on ch. xlix. 8). See Ps. xxxvii. 11;
'The meek shall inherit the earth.'
Comp. Ps. lxix. 35, 36; Matt. v. 5.
¶ *And shall inherit my holy mountain.*
In Jerusalem. That is, they shall be
admitted to elevated spiritual privileges

and joys—as great as if they had possession of a portion of the mount on
which the temple was built, and were
permitted to dwell there
14. *And shall say.* Lowth, ' Then
will I say.' Noyes, ' Men will say.'
The word אָמַר seems to be used here
impersonally, and to mean, ' One shall
say ;' *i.e.* it shall be said. The LXX.
and the Syriac render it, ' They shall
say.' The idea is, that the obstacles
would be removed from the path of those
who put their trust in God. The *language* is derived from the return from
the exile, as if persons should go before
them, and should cry, ' Cast ye up ;' or
as if the cry of the people all along their
journey should be, ' Remove the obstacles
to their return.' ¶ *Cast ye up, cast ye up.*
That is, remove the obstacles ; level the
hills ; take up any obstruction out of
the way (comp. Notes ch. xxxv. 8; xl.
3, 4). This cry is often heard before
the coming of a distinguished prince or
conqueror in the East. The Rev. Joseph
Wolff stated, in a lecture in Philadelphia (Sept. 18, 1837), that, on entering
Jerusalem from the west, in the direction of Gaza, the road, for a considerable
distance from Jerusalem, was so full of
stones, that it was impracticable to ride,
and those who were entering the city
were obliged to dismount. When the
Pasha (Ibrahim, son of Mehemet Ali)
approached Jerusalem, it was customary for a considerable number of labour-
ers to go before him, and remove the
stones from the way. This was done
amidst a constant cry, ' Cast up, cast
up the way ; remove the stones, remove
the stones.' And on a placard, or standard, it was written, ' the Pasha is coming ;' and everywhere the cry was heard,
' the Pasha is coming, the Pasha is coming; cast up the way, remove the stones.'
15. *For thus saith.* The design of

whose name *is* Holy ; I dwell in the high and *a*holy *place*, with him also *b that is* of a contrite and humble spirit, to revive *c* the spirit of the humble, and to revive the heart of the contrite ones.

16 For *d* I will not contend for ever, neither will I be always wroth: for the spirit should fail before me, and the souls *which* I have made.

a Zec.2.13.   *b* ch.66,1,2; Ps.34.18; 138.6.
c Mat.5.4.   *d* Ps.103.9; Mi.7.18.

---

this verse is, to furnish the assurance that the promise made to the people of God would certainly be accomplished. It was not to be presumed that he was so high and lofty, that he did not condescend to notice the affairs of men; but though he, in fact, dwelt in eternity, yet he also had his abode in the human heart. Many of the ancient heathens supposed that God was so lofty that he did not condescend to notice human affairs. This was the view of the Epicureans (see Notes on Acts xvii. 18); and the belief extensively prevailed in the Oriental world, that God had committed the management of the affairs of men to inferior beings which he had created. This was the basis of the Gnostic philosophy. According to this, God reposed far in the distant heavens, and was regardless of the affairs and plans of mortals, and personally unconcerned in the government of this lower world. But the Bible reveals him as a very different being. True, he is vast and illimitable in his existence and perfections; but, at the same time, he is the most condescending of all beings. He dwells with men, and he delights in making his abode with the penitent and the contrite. ¶ *The high and lofty One.* One MS. reads 'JEHOVAH,' before 'saith;' and Lowth has adopted the reading; but the authority is not sufficient. The sense is, that he who is here spoken of is, by way of eminence, THE high and holy One; the most high and the most exalted being in the universe. He is so far above all creatures of all ranks that it is not needful to specify his name in order to designate him. No one can be compared with him; no one so nearly approaches him that there can be any danger of confounding him with other beings. ¶ *That inhabiteth eternity* (comp. Notes on ch. ix. 6). The word 'eternity' here evidently stands in contrast with the 'contrite and humble spirit;' and it seems to be used to

denote the elevated *place* of an eternal dwelling or heaven. He dwells not only among men, but he dwells in eternity —where time is unknown—in a world where succession is not marked—and long before the interminable duration was broken in upon by the revolutions of years and days. ¶ *Whose name* is *Holy* (see Notes on ch. i. 4; xxx. 11; xli. 14; xliii. 3, 8, 14; xlvii. 4). ¶ *I dwell in the high and holy place.* In heaven—uniformly represented as far exalted above the earth, and as the peculiar home or dwelling-place of God. Thus, in ch. lxiii. 15, heaven is called the habitation of the holiness and glory of JEHOVAH. ¶ *With him also that is of a contrite and humble spirit.* The word 'contrite' (נִדְכָּא) means properly that which is broken, crushed, beaten small, trodden down. Here it denotes a soul that is borne down with a sense of sin and unworthiness; a heart that is, as it were, *crushed* under a superincumbent weight of guilt (see Ps. xxxiv. 18; cxxxviii. 6). ¶ *To revive the spirit.* Literally, 'to make alive.' The sense is, he imparts spiritual life and comfort. He is to them what refreshing rains and genial suns and dews are to a drooping plant.

16. *For I will not contend for ever.* I will not be angry with my people for ever, nor always refuse to pardon and comfort them (see Ps. ciii. 9). This is to be regarded as having been primarily addressed to the Jews in their long and painful exile in Babylon. It is, however, couched in general language; and the idea is, that although God would punish his people for their sins, yet his wrath would not be perpetual. If they were his children, he would visit them again in mercy, and would restore to them his favour. ¶ *For the spirit should fail before me.* Critics have taken a great deal of pains on this part of the verse, which they suppose to be very obscure. The simple meaning seems to be, that if God should con-

17 For the iniquity of his *a* covetousness was I wroth, and smote him : I hid me, and was wroth, and he went on ¹frowardly in the way of his heart.

18 I have seen his ways, and will heal *b* him : I will lead him also, and restore comforts unto him and to his mourners.

a Je.6.13.   1 *turning away.*   *b* Je.30.3; 33 6; Ho.14.4.

tinue in anger against men they would be consumed. The human soul could not endure a long-continued controversy with God. Its powers would fail; its strength decay ; it must sink to destruction. As God did not intend this in regard to his own people; as he meant that his chastisements should not be for their destruction, but for their salvation; and as he knew how much they could bear, and how much they needed, he would lighten the burden, and restore them to his favour. And the truth taught here is, that if we are his children, we are safe. We may suffer much and long. We may suffer so much that it seems scarcely possible that we should endure more. But he knows how much we can bear ; and he will remove the load, so that we shall not be utterly crushed. A similar sentiment is found in the two following elegant passages of the Psalms, which are evidently parallel to this, and express the same idea :—

But he being full of compassion,
Forgave their iniquity, and destroyed them not;
Yea many a time turned he his anger away,
And did not stir up all his wrath.
For he remembered that they were but flesh ;
A wind that passeth away and returneth not
again.   Ps. lxxviii. 38, 39.

He will not always chide ;
Neither will he keep his anger for ever.
Like as a father pitieth his children,
So the Lord pitieth them that fear him.
For he knoweth our frame;
He remembereth that we are dust.
Ps. ciii. 9, 13, 14.

The Hebrew word which is here rendered 'should fail' (עָצַף), means properly *to cover*, as with a garment; or to envelope with anything, as darkness. Then it is used in the sense of having the mind covered or muffled up with sorrow; and means to languish, to be faint or feeble, to fail. Thus it is used in Ps. lxi. 2 ; cvii. 5 ; cxlii. 3 ; Lam. ii. 11, 12, 19 ; Jonah ii. 7. Other interpretations of this verse may be seen in Rosenmüller; but the above seems to be the true sense. According to this, it furnishes ground of encouragement

and comfort to all the children of God who are afflicted. No sorrow will be sent which they will not be able to endure, no calamity which will not be finally for their own good. At the same time, it is a passage full of alarm to the sinner. How *can* he contend for ever with God ? How *can* he struggle always with the Almighty? And what *must* be the state in that dreadful world, where God *shall* contend for ever with the soul, and where all its powers shall be crushed beneath the vengeance of his eternal arm !

17. *For the iniquity of his covetousness.* The guilt of his avarice ; that is, of the Jewish people. The word here rendered 'covetousness' (בֶּצַע) means plunder, rapine, prey; then unjust gains, or lucre from bribes (1 Sam. vii. 3 ; Isa. xxxiii. 15) ; or by any other means. Here the sense is, that one of the prevailing sins of the Jewish people which drew upon them the Divine vengeance, was avarice, or the love of gain. Probably this was especially manifest in the readiness with which those who dispensed justice received bribes (comp. ch. ii. 7). See also Jer. vi. 13 : 'For from the least of them even unto the greatest of them every one is given to covetousness.' ¶ *And smote him.* That is, I brought heavy judgments on the Jewish people. ¶ *I hid me.* I withdrew the evidences of my presence and the tokens of my favour, and left them to themselves. ¶ *And he went on frowardly.* Marg. 'Turning away.' That is, abandoned by me, the Jewish people declined from my service and sunk deeper into sin. The idea here is, that if God withdraws from his people, such is their tendency to depravity, that they will wander away from him, and sink deeper in guilt—a truth which is manifest in the experience of individuals, as well as of communities and churches.

18. *I have seen his ways.* That is, either his ways of sin, or of repentance

19 I create the fruit *a* of the lips; Peace, peace to *him that is* far *b* off,

and to *him that is* near, saith the LORD ; and I will heal him.

20 But the wicked *are* like the

a Ho.14.2; He.13.15.   *b* Ep.2,13,17.

Most probably it means the former ; and the idea is, that God had seen how prone his people were to sin, and that he would now interpose and correct their proneness to sin against him, and remove from them the judgments which had been brought upon them in consequence of their crimes. ¶ *And will heal him.* That is, I will pardon and restore him. Sin, in the Scriptures, is often represented as a disease, and pardon and salvation as a healing of the disease (2 Chron. vii. 14; Ps. xli. 4; Jer. iii. 22 ; xvii. 4; xxxii. 6; Hos. xiv. 4 ; see Notes on Isa. vi. 10). ¶ *And to his mourners.* To the pious portion that mourned over their sin ; or to the nation which would sigh in their long and painful captivity in Babylon.

19. *I create the fruit of the lips.* The Chaldee and Syriac render this, ' The words of the lips.' The ' fruit ' of the lips is that which the lips produce, that is, *words;* and the reference here is doubtless to offerings of praise and thanksgiving. See Heb. xiii. 15; where the phrase, ' fruit of the lips ' (*καρπὸς χειλέων*), is explained to mean *praise.* Compare Hos. xiv. 2, where the expression, ' we will render the calves of the lips,' means that they would offer praise. The sense here is, that God bestowed such blessings as made thanksgiving proper, and thus, he ' *created* the fruit of the lips.' ¶ *Peace, peace.* The great subject of the thanksgiving would be peace. The peace here referred to probably had a primary reference to the cessation of the calamities which would soon overwhelm the Jewish nation, and their restoration again to their own land. But the whole strain of the passage also shows that the prophet had a more general truth in his view, and that he refers to that peace which would diffuse joy among all who were far off, and those who were nigh. Paul evidently alludes to this passage in Eph. ii. 14-17. Thus understood, the more general reference is to the peace which the Messiah would introduce, and which would lay the foundation for universal

rejoicing and praise (comp. Notes on ch. ii. 4 ; ix. 5). ¶ *To him that is far off.* Applied by the apostle Paul to the Gentiles, who are represented as having been far off from God, or as aliens or strangers to him (Eph. ii. 17). ¶ *And to him that is near.* That is, to the Jewish people (Eph. ii. 17), represented as having been comparatively near to God in the enjoyment of religious privileges.

20. *But the wicked.* All who are transgressors of the law and who remain unpardoned. The design of this is to contrast their condition with that of those who should enjoy peace. The proposition is, therefore, of the most general character. *All* the wicked are like the troubled sea. Whether prosperous or otherwise ; rich or poor ; bond or free; old or young; whether in Christian, in civilized, or in barbarous lands ; whether living in palaces, in caves, or in tents ; whether in the splendour of cities, or in the solitude of deserts ; ALL are like the troubled sea. ¶ *Are like the troubled sea.* The agitated (נִגְרָשׁ), ever-moving and restless sea. The sea is always in motion, and never entirely calm. Often also it lashes into foam, and heaves with wild commotion. ¶ *When it cannot rest.* Lowth renders this, ' For it never can be at rest.' The Hebrew is stronger than our translation. It means that there is no possibility of its being at rest ; it is *unable to be still* (כִּי הַשְׁקֵט לֹא יוּכָל). The LXX. render it, ' But the wicked are tossed like waves (*κλυδωνισθήσονται*), and are not able to be at rest.' The idea, as it seems to me, is not exactly that which seems to be conveyed by our translation, that the wicked are like the sea, *occasionally* agitated by a storm and driven by wild commotion, but that, like the ocean, there is *never* any peace, as there is no peace to the restless waters of the mighty deep. ¶ *Whose waters.* They who have stood on the shores of the ocean and seen the waves —especially in a storm—foam, and roll, and dash on the beach, will be able to appreciate the force of this beautiful figure,

troubled sea, when it cannot ^a rest, whose waters cast up mire and dirt.

a Pr.4.16,17.

21 *There is* no ^b peace, saith my God, to the wicked.

b 2Ki.9.22.

and cannot but have a vivid image before them of the unsettled and agitated bosoms of the guilty. The figure which is here used to denote the want of peace .n the bosom of a wicked man, is like-wise beautifully employed by Ovid :

Cumque sit hibernis agitatum fluctibus æquor,
Pectora sunt ipso turbidiora mari.

Trist. i. x. 33.

The agitation and commotion of the sinner here referred to, relates to such things as the following :—1. There is no permanent happiness or enjoyment. There is no calmness of soul in the contemplation of the Divine perfections, and of the glories of the future world. There is no substantial and permanent peace furnished by wealth, business, pleasure; by the pride, pomp, and flattery of the world. All leave the soul *un*satisfied, or *dis*satisfied ; all leave is unprotected against the rebukes of conscience, and the fear of hell. 2. Raging passions. The sinner is under their influence, and they may be compared to the wild and tumultuous waves of the ocean. Thus the bosoms of the wicked are agitated with the conflicting passions of pride, envy, malice, lust, ambition, and revenge. These leave no peace in the soul ; they make peace impossible. Men may learn in some degree to control them by the influence of philosophy ; or a pride of character and respect to their reputation may enable them in some degree to restrain them ; but they are like the smothered fires of the volcano, or like the momentary calm of the ocean that a gust of wind may soon lash into foam. To restrain them is not to subdue them ; for no man can tell how soon he may be excited by anger, or how soon the smothered fires of lust may burn. 3. Conscience. Nothing more resembles an agitated ocean casting up mire and dirt, than a soul agitated by the recollections of past guilt. A deep dark cloud in a tempest overhangs the deep ; the lightnings play and the thunder rolls along the sky, and the waves heave with wild commotion. So it is with the bosom of the sinner. Though there may be a temporary sus-

pension of the rebukes of conscience, yet there is no permanent peace. The soul *cannot* rest ; and in some way or other the recollections of guilt will be excited, and the bosom thrown into turbid and wild agitation. 4. The fear of judgment and of hell. Many a sinner has no rest, day or night, from the fear of future wrath. His troubled mind looks onward, and he sees nothing to anticipate but the wrath of God, and the horrors of an eternal hell.— How invaluable then is religion ! All these commotions are stilled by the voice of pardoning mercy, as the billows of the deep were hushed by the voice of Jesus. How much do we owe to religion ! Had it not been for this, there had been no peace in this world. Every bosom would have been agitated with tumultuous passion ; every heart would have quailed with the fear of hell. How diligently should we seek the influence of religion ! We all have raging passions to be subdued. We all have consciences that may be troubled with the recollections of past guilt. We are all travelling to the bar of God, and have reason to apprehend the storms of vengeance. We all must soon lie down on beds of death, and in all these scenes there is nothing that can give permanent and solid peace but the religion of the Redeemer. Oh ! *that* stills all the agitation of a troubled soul ; lays every billow of tumultuous passion to rest ; calms the conflicts of a guilty bosom ; reveals God reconciled through a Redeemer to our souls, and removes all the anticipated terrors of a bed of death and of the approach to the judgment bar. Peacefully the Christian can die —not as the troubled sinner, who leaves the world with a bosom agitated like the stormy ocean—but as peacefully as the gentle ripple dies away on the beach.

How blest the righteous when they die,
When holy souls retire to rest !
How mildly beams the closing eye,
How gently heaves the expiring breast !

So fades a summer cloud away ;
So sinks the gale when storms are o'er ;
So gently shuts the eye of day ;
So dies a wave along the shore.—BARBAULD.

CHAPTER LVIII.

ANALYSIS.

THE design of this chapter is to reprove the Jews for a vain dependence on the performance of the outward forms of worship. The nation is represented as diligent in the performance of the external rites of their religion, and as expecting to avert the Divine judgments by the performance of those rites. They are represented as filled with amazement, that though they were thus diligent and faithful, they had no tokens of the Divine approbation, but were left as if forsaken by God. The main scope of the chapter is to state the reasons why their religious services met with no tokens of the Divine acceptance, and the blessings which would follow the proper performance of their duties.

It is not certainly known to what period the prophet refers, whether to the Jews in his own time, or to the Jews regarded as in Babylon. Rosenmüller supposes the reference is wholly to the Jews suffering in their captivity, and practising their religious rites with a view of obtaining the Divine favour and a release. He argues this because there is no reference here to sacrifices, but merely to fasting, and the observance of the Sabbath; duties which they could perform even when far away from the temple, and from their own land. But it seems more probable that the reference here to fasting is designed as an instance or specimen of the character of the people, and that this is made so prominent because they abounded so much in it, and were so hypocritical in its observance. It is possible that it was composed at or near the time of some of the public fasts during the reign of Manasseh, and that the fact that the external rites of religion were observed amidst the abominations of that wicked reign roused the indignation of the prophet, and led him to pour forth this severe reproof of the manner in which they approached God.

The chapter comprises the following subjects:—

I. A direction to the prophet openly and boldly to reprove the sins of the nation (1).

II. The fact that the Jewish people were regular and diligent in the observance of the external duties of religion, and that they expected the Divine favour on the ground of those observances (2, 3).

III. The prophet states the reason why their excessive and punctual religious duties had not been accepted or followed with the Divine favour and blessing. 1. They still continued their heavy exactions on others, and made everything tributary to their own pleasure (3). 2. They did it for strife and debate; with hoarse contentions and angry passions (4). 3. It was with an affected and hypocritical seriousness and solemnity, not as a proper expression of a deep sense of sin (5).

IV. The prophet states the true ways in which the favour of God might be obtained, and the happy results which would follow the proper observance of his commands, and the proper discharge of the duties of religion. 1. The proper mode of fasting, and the happy results (6–9). (1.) The kind of fasting which God had chosen (6, 7). It was to loose the bands of wickedness, and undo the heavy burdens, and let the oppressed go free, and to aid the poor and needy. (2.) The consequence of this (8, 9). Their light would break forth as the morning, and the nation would prosper, and their prayers would be heard. 2. The special duty of removing the yoke of oppression, and of regarding the poor and the oppressed, and the consequences (9–12). (1.) The duty. God requires the yoke of oppression to be put away, and the oppressed and the poor to be regarded by his people (9, last clause, 10). (2.) The consequences which would follow from this (10–12). Their light would rise in obscurity, and their darkness would be as noonday; JEHOVAH would be their guide, and the waste places would be repaired, and the desolations cease. 3. The duty of keeping the Sabbath, and the consequences (13, 14). (1.) The duty (13). They were to cease to do their own pleasure, and to call it holy, and to regard it with delight. (2.) The consequences (14). They would then find delight in the service of JEHOVAH; and they would ride upon the high places of the earth, and be abundantly blessed and prospered.

CRY [1] aloud, spare not; lift up thy voice like a trumpet, and show my people their transgressions, and the house of Jacob their sins.

1 with the throat.

21. There is *no peace* (see Note on ch. xlviii. 22).

CHAPTER LVIII.

1. *Cry aloud.* Marg. ' With the throat;' that is, says Gesenius, with open throat, with full voice coming from the throat and breast ; while one who speaks low uses only the lips and tongue (1 Sam. i. 13). The Chaldee here introduces the word *prophet*, ' O

2 Yet *a* they seek me daily, and delight to know my ways, as a nation that did righteousness, and

forsook not the ordinance of their God ; they ask of me the ordinances of justice; they take delight in approaching to God.

a De.5.28,29.

prophet, cry aloud.' The LXX. render it, ' Cry with strength ' (ἐν ἰσχύϊ). ¶ *Spare not.* That is, do not spare, or restrain the voice. Let it be full, loud, and strong. ¶ *Lift up thy voice like a trumpet.* Speak loud and distinct, so that the language of reproof may be heard. The sense is, the people are insensible and stupid. They need something to rouse them to a sense of their guilt. Go and proclaim it so that all may hear. Speak not in whispers ; speak not to a part, but speak so earnestly that their attention will be arrested, and so that all shall hear (comp. Notes on ch. xl. 9). ¶ *And show my people.* This either refers to the Jewish people in the time of the prophet ; or to the same people in their exile in Babylon ; or to the people of God after the coming of the Messiah. Vitringa supposes that it refers to the nominally Christian Church when it should have sunk into the sins and formalities of the Papacy, and that the direction here is to the true ministers of God to proclaim the sins of a corrupt and degenerate church. The main reason assigned by him for this is, that there is no reference here to the temple, to the sacrifices, or to the idolatry which was the prevailing sin in the time of Manasseh. Rosenmüller, for a similar reason, supposes that it refers to the Jews in Babylon. But it has already been remarked (see the analysis to the chapter), that this reason does not appear to be satisfactory. It is true that there is no reference here to the temple or to sacrifices, and it may be true that the main sin of the nation in the time of Manasseh was idolatry ; but it is also true that formality and hypocrisy were prominent sins, and that these deserved reproof. It is true that while they adhered to the public forms of religion, the heart was not in them ; and that while they relied on those forms, and were surprised that the Divine favour was not manifested to them on

account of their observance, there was a good reason why that favour was withheld, and it was important that that reason should be stated clearly and fully. It is probable, therefore, that the reference here is to the times of the prophet himself, and that the subject of rebuke is the formality, hypocrisy, and prevalent sins of the reign of Manasseh.

2. *Yet they seek me daily.* The whole description here is appropriate to the character of formalists and hypocrites ; and the idea is, that public worship by sacrifice was celebrated daily in the temple, and was not intermitted. It is not improbable also that they kept up the regular daily service in their dwellings. ¶ *And delight to know my ways.* Probably this means, they *profess* to delight to know the ways of God ; *i.e.,* his commands, truths, and requirements. A hypocrite has no real delight in the service of God, or in his truth, but it is true at the same time that there may be a great deal of *professed* interest in religion. There may be a great deal of busy and bustling solicitude about the *order* of religious services ; the external organization of the church ; the ranks of the clergy ; and the claims of a liturgy. There may be much pleasure in theological discussion ; in the metaphysics of theology ; in the defence of what is deemed orthodoxy. There may be much pleasure in the mere *music* of devotion. There may be pleasure in the voice of a preacher, and in the power of his arguments. And there may be much pleasure in the advancement of the denomination to which we are attached ; the conversion of men not *from sin,* but from a side opposite to us ; and not *to holiness* and *to God,* but to our party and denomination.—True delight in religion is *in religion itself ;* in the service of God as such, and because it is holy. It is not mere pleasure in creeds, and liturgies, and theological discussions, and in the triumph of our cause,

3 Wherefore *a* have we fasted, *say they*, and thou seest not ? *wherefore* have we afflicted *b* our soul, and thou takest no knowledge ? Be-

hold, in the day of your fast you find pleasure, and exact all your labours.[1]

nor even in the triumph of Christianity as a mere party measure ; but it is delight in God as he is, in his holy service, and in his truth. ¶ *As a nation that did righteousness.* As a people would do who really loved the ways of righteousness. ¶ *They ask of me the ordinances of justice.* Their priests and prophets consult about the laws and institutions of religion, as if they were really afraid of violating the Divine commands. At the same time that they are full of oppression, strife, and wickedness, they are scrupulously careful about violating any of the commands pertaining to the rites of religion. The same people were subsequently so conscientious that they did not dare to enter the judgment-hall of Pilate lest they should disqualify themselves from partaking of the Passover, at the same time that they were meditating the death of their own Messiah, and were actually engaged in a plot to secure his crucifixion ! (John xix. 28.) It is often the case that hypocrites are most scrupulous and conscientious about forms just as they are meditating some plan of enormous guilt, and accomplishing some scheme of deep depravity. ¶ *They take delight in approaching to God.* There *is* a pleasure which even a hypocrite has in the services of religion, and we should not conclude that *because* we find pleasure in prayer and praise, that *therefore* we are truly pious. Our pleasure may arise from a great many other sources than any just views of God or of his truth, or an evidence that we have that we are his friends.

3. *Wherefore have we fasted.* They had fasted much, evidently with the expectation of delivering themselves from impending calamities, and securing the Divine favour. They are here introduced as saying that they had been disappointed. God had not interposed as they had expected. Chagrined and mortified, they now complain that he had not noticed their very conscientious and faithful regard for the duties of

religion. ¶ *And thou seest not ?* All had been in vain. Calamities still impended ; judgments threatened ; and there were no tokens of the Divine approbation. Hypocrites depend on their fastings and prayers as laying God under *obligation* to save them. If he does not interpose, they complain and murmur. When fasting is the result of a humble and broken heart, it is acceptable ; when it is instituted as a means of *purchasing* the Divine favour, and as laying God under *obligation*, it can be followed by no happy result to the soul. ¶ *Have we afflicted our soul.* By fasting. Twenty-one MSS. (six ancient), says Lowth, have this in the plural number —'our souls' and so the LXX., Chaldee, and Vulgate. The sense is not materially affected, however. It is evident here that they regarded their numerous fastings as laying the foundation of a claim on the favour of God, and that they were disposed to complain when that claim was not acknowledged. Fasting, like other religious duties, is proper ; but in that, as in all other services of religion, there is danger of supposing that we bring God under *obligation*, and that we are laying the foundation of a *claim* to his favour. ¶ *Thou takest no knowledge.* Thou dost not regard our numerous acts of self-denial. ¶ *Behold, in the day of your fast you find pleasure.* The prophet here proceeds to state the reasons why their fastings were not succeeded as they supposed they would be, by the Divine favour. The first reason which he states is, that even when they were fasting, they were giving full indulgence to their depraved appetites and lusts. The Syriac has well rendered this, ' In the day of your fasting you indulge your lusts, and draw near to all your idols.' This also was evidently the case with the Jews in the time of the Saviour. They were characterized repeatedly by him as ' an evil and *adulterous* generation,' and yet no generation perhaps was ever more punctual and strict in the external duties

4 Behold, ye fast for strife and debate, and to smite ^a with the fist of wickedness : ye ¹ shall not fast as *ye do this* day, to make your voice to be heard on high.

of fasting and other religious ceremonies. ¶ *And exact all your labours.* This is the second reason why their fasting was attended with no more happy results.— The margin renders this ' griefs,' or things wherewith ye grieve others.' Lowth renders it, ' All your demands of labour ye rigorously exact.' Castellio renders it, ' And all things which are due to you, you exact.' The word here rendered 'labours' denotes usually hard and painful labour ; toil, travail, &c. The LXX. render it here, ' And goad (ὑπονύσσετε) all those who are under your control' (τοὺς ὑποχειρίους ὑμῶν). The idea seems to be that they were at that time oppressive in exacting all that was due to them ; they remitted nothing, they forgave nothing. Alas, how often is this still true ! Men may be most diligent in the external duties of religion ; most abundant in fasting and in prayer, and at the same time most unyielding in demanding all that is due to them. Like Shylock—another Jew like those in the time of Isaiah— they may demand ' the pound of flesh,' at the same time that they may be most formal, punctual, precise, and bigoted in the performance of the external duties of religion. The sentiment taught here is, that if we desire to keep a fast that shall be acceptable to God, it must be such as shall cause us to unbind heavy burdens from the poor, and to lead us to relax the rigour of the claims which would be oppressive on those who are subject to us (see ver. 6).

4. *Behold, ye fast for strife and debate.* This is a third characteristic of their manner of fasting, and a third reason why God did not regard and accept it. They were divided into parties and factions, and probably made their fastings an occasion of augmented contention and strife. How often has this been seen ! Contending denominations of Christians fast, not laying aside their strifes ; contending factions in the church fast in order to strengthen their party with the solemn sanctions of religion. One of the most certain ways for bigots to excite persecution against those who are opposed to them is to ' proclaim a fast ;' and when together, their passions are easily inflamed, their flagging zeal excited by inflammatory harangues, and their purpose formed to regard and treat their dissentient brethren as incorrigible heretics and irreconcilable foes. It may be added, also, that it is possible thus to prostitute all the sacred institutions of religion for party and inflammatory purposes. Even the ordinance of the Lord's Supper may be thus abused, and violent partisans may come around the sacred memorials of a Saviour's body and blood, to bind themselves more closely together in some deed of persecution or violence, and to animate their drooping courage with the belief that what has been in fact commenced with a view to power, is carried on from a regard to the honour of God. ¶ *And to smite with the fist of wickedness.* Lowth renders this, in accordance with the LXX. ' To smite with the fist the poor ;' but this translation can be obtained only by a most violent and wholly unauthorized change in the Hebrew text. The idea is plain, that ' even when fasting' they were guilty of strife and personal combats. Their passions were unsubdued, and they gave vent to them in disgraceful personal encounters. This manifests a most extraordinary state of society, and is a most melancholy instance to show how much men may keep up the forms of religion, and even be punctual and exact in them, when the most violent and ungovernable passions are raging in their bosoms, and when they seem to be unconscious of any *discrepancy* between the religious service and the unsubdued passions of the soul. ¶ *Ye shall not fast,* &c. It is not acceptable to God. It must be offensive in his sight. ¶ *To make your voice to be heard on high.* That is, in strife and contention. So to contend and strive, says Grotius, that your voice can be heard on the mountain top. Rosenmüller, however, supposes that it means, that their fast was so conducted that they could not expect that their prayers would ascend

5 Is it such *a* a fast that I have chosen ? a [1] day for a man to afflict his soul ? *is it* to bow down his head as a bulrush, and to spread sackcloth *b* and ashes *under him?* wilt thou call this a fast, and an acceptable day to the LORD ?

a Zec.7.5.   1 or, *to afflict his soul* for a day.   *b* De.9.3.

to heaven and be heard by God. But it seems to me that the former is the correct interpretation. Their fastings were accompanied with the loud and hoarse voice of contention and strife, and on that account could not be acceptable to God.

5. *Is it such a fast that I have chosen?* Is this such a mode of fasting as I have appointed and as I approve ? ¶ *A day for a man to afflict his soul ?* Marg. 'To afflict his soul for a day.' The reading in the text is the more correct ; and the idea is, that the pain and inconvenience experienced by the abstinence from food was not the *end* in view in fasting. This seems to have been the mistake which they made, that they supposed there was something meritorious in the very *pain* incurred by such abstinence. Is there not danger of this now ? Do we not often feel that there is something meritorious in the very inconveniences which we suffer in our acts of self-denial ? The important idea in the passage before us is, that the pain and inconvenience which we may endure by the most rigid fasting are not meritorious in the sight of God. They are not that at which he aims by the appointment of fasting. He aims at justice, truth, benevolence, holiness (ver. 6, 7) ; and he esteems the act of fasting to be of value only as it will be the means of leading us to reflect on our faults, and to amend our lives. ¶ *Is it to bow down his head.* A bulrush is the large reed that grows in marshy places. It is, says Johnson, without knots or joints. In the midst of water it grows luxuriantly, yet the stalk is not solid or compact like wood, and, being unsupported by joints, it easily bends over under its own weight. It thus becomes the emblem of a man bowed down with grief. Here it refers to the sanctimoniousness of a hypocrite when fasting—a man without real feeling who puts on an air of affected solemnity, and 'appears to others to fast.' Against that the Saviour warned his disciples, and directed them, when they fasted, to do it in their ordinary dress, and to maintain an aspect of cheerfulness (Matt. vi. 17, 18). The hypocrites in the time of Isaiah seemed to have supposed that the object was gained if they assumed this affected seriousness. How much danger is there of this now ! How often do even Christians assume, on all the more solemn occasions of religious observance, a forced sanctimoniousness of manner ; a demure and dejected air ; nay, an appearance of melancholy—which is often understood by the world to be misanthropy, and which easily slides into misanthropy ! Against this we should guard. Nothing more injures the cause of religion than sanctimoniousness, gloom, reserve, coldness, and the conduct and deportment which, whether right or wrong, will be construed by those around us as misanthropy. Be it not forgotten that the seriousness which religion produces is always consistent with cheerfulness, and is always accompanied by benevolence ; and the moment we feel that our religious acts consist in merely bowing down the head like a bulrush, that moment we may be sure we shall do injury to all with whom we come in contact. ¶ *And to spread sackcloth and ashes* under him. On the meaning of the word 'sackcloth,' see Notes on ch. iii. 24. It was commonly worn around the loins in times of fasting and of any public or private calamity. It was also customary to sit on sackcloth, or to spread it under one either to lie on, or to kneel on in times of prayer, as an expression of humiliation. Thus in Est. iv. 3, it is said, 'and many lay on sackcloth and ashes ;' or, as it is in the margin, 'sackcloth and ashes were laid under many ;' (comp. 1 Kings xxi. 27). A passage in Josephus strongly confirms this, in which he describes the deep concern of the Jews for the danger of Herod Agrippa, after having been stricken suddenly with a violent disorder in the theatre of Cæsarea. 'Upon the news

6 *Is* not this the fast that I have chosen? to loose *a* the bands of wickedness, to undo the [1] heavy burdens, *b* and to let the [2] oppressed go free, *c* and that ye break every yoke?

a Jonah 3.5-10. [1] *bundles of the yoke.*   *b* Ne.5.10,12.   [2] *broken.*   *c* Je.34.8.

of his danger, immediately the multitude, with their wives and children, *sitting upon sackcloth according to their country rites*, prayed for the king ; all places were filled with wailing and lamentation ; while the king, who lay in an upper room, beholding the people below thus falling prostrate on the ground, could not himself refrain from tears.'—(*Antiq.* xix. 8. 2.) We wear crape—but for a somewhat different object. With us it is a mere *sign* of grief ; but the wearing of sackcloth or sitting on it was not a mere *sign* of grief, but was regarded as tending to *produce* humiliation and mortification. Ashes also were a symbol of grief and sorrow. The wearing of sackcloth was usually accompanied with ashes (Dan. ix. 3; Est. iv. 1, 3). Penitents, or those in affliction, either sat down on the ground in dust and ashes (Job ii. 8; xlii. 6; Jonah iii. 6) ; or they put ashes on their head (2 Sam. xiii. 19; Lam. iii. 16) ; or they mingled ashes with their food (Ps. cii. 9). The Greeks and the Romans had also the same custom of strewing themselves with ashes in mourning. Thus Homer (*Iliad*, xviii. 22), speaking of Achilles bewailing the death of Patroclus, says :

Cast on the ground, with furious hands he spread
The scorching ashes o'er his graceful head,
His purple garments, and his golden hairs;
Those he deforms, and these he tears.

Laertes (*Odys.* xxiv. 315), shows his grief in the same manner :

Deep from his soul he sighed, and sorrowing spread
A cloud of ashes on his hoary head.

So Virgil (*Æn.* x. 844), speaking of the father of Lausus, who was brought to him wounded, says :

Canitiem immundo deformat pulvere.

¶ *Wilt thou call this a fast?* Wilt thou suppose that these observances can be such as God will approve and bless? The truth here taught is, that no mere outward expressions of penitence can be acceptable to God.

6. Is *not this the fast that I have chosen?* Fasting is right and proper ; but that which God approves will prompt to, and will be followed by, deeds of justice, kindness, charity. The prophet proceeds to specify very particularly what God required, and when the observance of seasons of fasting would be acceptable to him. ¶ *To loose the bands of wickedness.* This is the first thing to be done in order that their fasting might be acceptable to the Lord. The idea is, that they were to dissolve every tie which unjustly bound their fellowmen. The Chaldee renders it, 'Separate the congregation of impiety;' but the more probable sense is, that if they were exercising any unjust and cruel authority over others ; if they had bound them in any way contrary to the laws of God and the interests of justice, they were to release them. This might refer to their compelling others to servitude more rigidly than the law of Moses allowed ; or to holding them to contracts which had been fraudulently made ; or to their exacting strict payment from persons wholly incapacitated to meet their obligations ; or it might refer to their subjecting others to more rigid service than was allowed by the laws of Moses, but it would not require a very ardent imagination for any one to see, that if he held slaves *at all*, that this came fairly under the description of the prophet. A man with a tender conscience who held slaves would have been likely to suppose that this part of the injunction applied to himself. ¶ *To undo the heavy burdens.* Marg. 'Bundles of the yoke.' The LXX. render it, 'Dissolve the obligations of onerous contracts.' The Chaldee, ' Loose the obligations of the writings of unjust judgment.' The Hebrew means, ' Loose the bands of the yoke,' a figure taken from the yoke which was borne by oxen, and which seems to have been attached to the neck by cords or bands (*see* Fragments to Taylor's *Calmet*, No. xxviii.) The yoke, in the Scripture, is usually regarded as an emblem of oppression, or compulsory toil, and is undoubtedly

so used here. The same word is used to denote 'burden' (מוּצָה), which in the subsequent member is rendered 'yoke,' and the word which is rendered 'undo' (הַתֵּר from נָתַר), is elsewhere employed to denote emancipation from servitude. The phrase here employed would properly denote the release of captives or slaves, and would doubtless be so understood by those whom the prophet addressed. Thus in Ps. cv. 17–20:

He sent a man before them, even Joseph,
Who was sold for a servant;
Whose feet they hurt with fetters;
He was laid in iron:
Until the time when his word came,
The word of the Lord tried him.
The king sent and loosed him (וַיַּתִּירֵהוּ),

Even the ruler of the people, and let him go free.

¶ *And let the oppressed go free.* Marg. 'Broken.' The Hebrew word רְצוּצִים is from the word רָצַץ, meaning *to break*, to break down (see Notes on ch. xlii. 3); to treat with violence, to oppress. It may be applied to those who are treated with violence in any way, or who are broken down by hard usage. It may refer, therefore, to slaves who are oppressed by bondage and toil; or to inferiors of any kind who are subjected to hard usage by those who are above them; or to the subjects of a tyrant groaning under his yoke. The use of the phrase here, 'go free,' however, seems to limit its application in this place to those who were held in bondage. Jerome renders it, 'Free those who are broken' (*confracti*). The LXX. Τεθραυσμένος—'Set at liberty those who are broken down.' If *slavery* existed at the time here referred to, this word would be appropriately understood as including that—at least would be so understood by the slaves themselves—for if any institution deserves to be called *oppression*, it is that of slavery. This interpretation would be confirmed by the use of the word rendered *free*. That word (חָפְשִׁים *hhǒphshǐm*) evidently refers to the act of freeing a slave. The person who had once been a slave, and who had afterwards obtained his freedom, was denominated חָפְשִׁי *hhǒphshǐ* (see Jahn, *Bib. Ant.* § 171). This word occurs, and is so used, in the following places; Ex. xxi. 12, 'And the

seventh [year] he shall go out *free;*' ver. 5, 'I will not go out *free;*' xxvi. 27, 'He shall let him go *free;*' Deut. xv. 12, 'Thou shalt let him go *free;*' ver. 13, 'When thou sendest him out *free;*' ver. 18, 'When thou sendest him away *free;*' Job iii. 19, 'The servant is *free* from his master;' that is, in the grave, where there is universal emancipation. Comp. Jer. xxxiv. 9–11, 14, 16, where the same Hebrew word is used, and is applied expressly to the emancipation of slaves. The word is used in no other places in the Bible except the following: 1 Sam. xvii. 25, 'And make his father's house *free* in Israel,' referring to the favour which was promised to the one who would slay Goliath of Gath. Job xxxix. 5: 'Who hath sent out the wild ass *free?*' Ps. lxxxviii. 5: '*Free* among the dead.' The usage, therefore, is settled that the word properly refers to deliverance from servitude. It would be naturally understood by a Hebrew as referring to that, and unless there was something in the connection which made it necessary to adopt a different interpretation, a Hebrew would so understand it of course. In the case before us, such an interpretation would be obvious, and it is difficult to see how a Jew *could* understand this direction in any other way, if he was an owner of slaves, than that he should set them at once at liberty. ¶ *And that ye break every yoke.* A yoke, in the Scriptures, is a symbol of oppression, and the idea here is, that they were to cease all oppressions, and to restore all to their just and equal rights. The prophet demanded, in order that there might be an acceptable 'fast,' that *everything* which could properly be described as a 'yoke' should be broken. How could this command be complied with by a Hebrew if he continued to retain his fellow-men in bondage? Would not its fair application be to lead him to emancipate those who were held as slaves? Could it be true, whatever else he might do, that he would fully comply with this injunction, unless this were done? If now this whole injunction were fairly complied with in *this* land, who can doubt that it would lead to the emancipation of the slaves? The language is such that it cannot well

7 *Is it* not to deal thy bread to the hungry, and that thou bring the poor that are [1] cast out to thy house? when thou seest the naked, that thou cover him; and that thou hide not thyself from thine own flesh?

8 Then *a* shall thy light break forth as the morning, and thine health shall spring forth speedily; and thy righteousness shall go before thee: the glory of the LORD shall [2] be thy rere-ward.

[1] or, *afflicted.*　　*a* Job 11. 17.　　[2] or, *gather thee up.*

be misunderstood. The prophet undoubtedly specifies those things which properly denote slavery, and demands that they should all be abandoned in order to an acceptable ' fast to the Lord,' and the fair application of this injunction would soon extinguish slavery throughout the world.

7. Is it *not to deal thy bread to the hungry?* The word renderd 'deal' (פָּרֹס), means *to divide, to distribute.* The idea is, that we are to apportion among the poor that which will be needful for their support, as a father does to his children. This is everywhere enjoined in the Bible, and was especially regarded among the Orientals as an indispensable duty of religion. Thus Job (xxxi. 16–22) beautifully speaks of his own practice:

If I have withheld the poor from his desire,
Or have caused the eyes of the widow to fail;
Or have eaten my morsel myself alone,
And the fatherless hath not eaten thereof;
If I have seen any perish for want of clothing,
Or any poor without covering;— . . . .
Then let mine arm fall from my shoulder blade,
And mine arm be broken from the bone.

¶ *And that thou bring the poor that are cast out to thy house.* Marg. 'Afflicted.' Hospitality to all, and especially to the friendless and the stranger, was one of the cardinal virtues in the Oriental code of morals. Lowth renders this, ' The wandering poor.' ¶ *When thou seest the naked,* &c. This duty is also plain, and is everywhere enjoined in the Bible (comp. Matt. xxv. 38). ¶ *And that thou hide not thyself from thine own flesh.* That is, from thine own kindred or relations who are dependent on thee. Compare Gen. xxix. 14; xxxvii. 27; where the word ' flesh ' is used to denote near relations — relations as intimate and dear as if they were a part of our flesh and blood (Gen. ii. 23). To hide one's self from them may denote either, first, to be ashamed of them on account of their poverty or humble rank in life; or, secondly, to withhold from them the

just supply of their wants. Religion requires us to treat all our kindred, whatever may be their rank, with kindness and affection, and enjoins on us the duty of providing for the wants of those poor relatives who in the providence of God are made dependent on us.

8. *Then shall thy light* (see Notes on ch. xliv. 7). The idea here is, that if they were faithful in the discharge of their duty to God, he would bless them with abundant prosperity (comp. Job xi. 17). The image is, that such prosperity would come on the people like the spreading light of the morning. ¶ *And thine health.* Lowth and Noyes render this, ' And thy wounds shall be speedily healed over.' The authority on which Lowth relies, is the version of Aquila as reported by Jerome, and the Chaldee. The Hebrew word here used, (אֲרֻכָה), means properly *a long bandage* (from אָרַךְ, *to make long*), such as is applied by surgeons to heal a wound (comp. Notes on ch. i. 6). It is then used to denote the healing which is secured by the application of the bandage; and figuratively here means their restoration from all the calamities which had been inflicted on the nation. The word rendered ' spring forth' (from צָמַח) properly relates to the manner in which plants germinate (comp. Notes on ch. xlii. 9). Here the sense is, that if they would return to God, they would be delivered from the calamities which their crimes had brought on them, and that peace and prosperity would again visit the nation. ¶ *And thy righteousness shall go before thee.* Shall be thy leader— as an army is conducted. The idea is that their conformity to the Divine laws would serve the purpose of a leader to conduct them in the ways of peace, happiness, and prosperity. ¶ *The glory of the* LORD. The allusion here is doubtless to the mode in which the children of Israel came out of Egypt (see Notes

9 Then shalt thou call, and the LORD shall answer; thou shalt cry, and he shall say, Here I *am*. If thou take away from the midst of thee the yoke, the putting forth of the finger, and speaking vanity :

10 And *if* thou draw out thy soul to the hungry, and satisfy the

afflicted soul; then shall thy light rise in obscurity, and thy darkness *be* as the noon-day.

11 And the Lord shall guide thee continually, and satisfy thy soul in ¹drought, *a* and make fat thy bones : and thou shalt be like a watered garden, and like a spring of water, whose waters ²fail not.

1 droughts.   a Ps.37.19.   2 lie, or, deceiv.

on ch. vi. 5). ¶ *Shall be thy rere-ward.* Marg. 'Shall gather thee up.' That is, shall bring up the rear (see Notes on ch. lii. 12).

9. *Then shalt thou call.* The sense is, that if we go before God renouncing all our sins, and desirous of doing our duty, then we have a right to expect that he will hear us. But if we go indulging still in sin ; if we are false and hollow and hypocritical in our worship ; or if, while we keep up the regular forms of devotion, we are nevertheless guilty of oppression, cruelty, and dishonesty, we have no right to expect that he will hear us (see Notes on ch. i. 15). ¶ *If thou take away—the yoke* (see Notes on ver. 6). ¶ *The putting forth of the finger.* That is, if you cease to contemn and despise others ; if you cease to point at them the finger of scorn. It was usual to make use of the middle finger on such occasions. Thus Martial, ii. 28, 2 :

Rideto multum ——
—— et digitum porrigito medium.

So Juvenal, *Sat.* x. 52 :

—— mediumque ostenderet unguem.

¶ *And speaking vanity.* Lowth and Noyes render it thus, ' The injurious speech.' Kimchi understands it of words of contention and strife. The word here used (אָוֶן) denotes either nothingness, vanity, a vain and empty thing (Isa. xli. 29; Zech. x. 2); or falsehood, deceit (Ps. xxxvi. 4; Prov. xvii. 4); or unworthiness, wickedness, iniquity (Job xxxvi. 21; Isa. i. 13); here it means, probably, every kind of false, harsh, and unjust speaking—all of which probably abounded among the Jews. The LXX. render it, 'Ρῆμα γογγυσμοῦ—' The word of murmuring.'

10. *And if thou draw out thy soul to the hungry.* Lowth, on the authority

of eight MSS., renders this, ' If thou bring forth *thy bread* to the hungry.' So the Syriac and Noyes. But the authority is not sufficient to justify the change in the text, nor is it necessary. The word ' soul' here is synonymous with heart, or benevolent affection ; and the idea is, if they expressed benevolent affection or kindness towards those in want. ¶ *Then shall thy light rise in obscurity.* That is, it will be as if the cheerful light of the sun should rise amidst the shades of midnight. The sense is, that their calamities and trials would be suddenly succeeded by the bright and cheerful light of prosperity.

11. *And the* LORD *shall guide thee continually.* JEHOVAH will go before you and will lead you always. ¶ *And satisfy thy soul in drought* (see Notes on ch. xli. 17, 18). The word rendered ' drought' (Marg. ' droughts ;' Heb. צַחְצָחוֹת) means *dry places*—places exposed to the intense heat of a burning sun and parched up for the want of moisture. The idea is, that God would provide for them as if in such places copious rains were to fall, or refreshing fountains to burst forth. ¶ *And make fat thy bones.* Lowth, ' Shall renew thy strength.' Noyes, ' Strengthen thy bones.' Jerome renders it, ' Shall liberate thy bones.' The LXX. ' Thy bones shall be made fat.' The idea is undoubtedly that of vigorous prosperity, and of strength. Job (xxi. 24) expresses a similar idea of a strong man dying :

'His watering places for flocks abound with milk,
And his bones are moist with marrow.'

For the propriety of this translation, which differs from the common version, see my Notes on Job, *in loco.* The word here used (חָלַץ), however, does not often, if ever, denote *to make fat.* It

12 And *they that shall be* of thee shall build the old waste places : thou shalt raise up the foundations

of many generations; and thou shalt be called, The repairer of the breach, The restorer of paths to dwell in.

---

rather means to be manful, active, brave, ready for war ; and the idea here is, probably, derived from the preparation which is made for the active services of war, rather than that of being made fat. ¶ *And thou shalt be like a watered garden.* Syriac, 'Like paradise.' This is a most beautiful image to denote continued prosperity and blessedness—an image that would be particularly striking in the East. The ideas of happiness in the Oriental world consisted much in pleasant gardens, running streams, and ever-flowing fountains, and nothing can more beautifully express the blessedness of the continued favour of the Almighty. The following extract from Campbell (*African Light*), may illustrate this passage : ' In a hot climate, where showers seldom fall, except in what is called the rainy season, the difference between a well and ill watered garden is most striking. I remember some gardens in Africa, where they could lead no water upon them, the plants were all stinted, sickly, or others completely gone, only the hole left where the faded plant had been. The sight was unpleasant, and caused gloom to appear in every countenance ; they were pictures of desolation. But in other gardens, to which the owners could bring daily supplies of water from an overflowing fountain, causing it to traverse the garden, every plant had a green, healthy appearance, loaded with fruit, in different stages towards maturity, with fragrant scent proceeding from beds of lovely flowers ; and all this produced by the virtue God hath put into the single article of water.' ¶ *Whose waters fail not.* Marg. 'Lie,' or 'Deceive.' Heb. בָּזָב—'Lie.' Waters or springs lie or deceive when they become dried up, or fail in the dry seasons of the year. They deceive the shepherd who expected to obtain water there for himself or his flock ; they deceive the caravan which had travelled to the well-known fountain where it had been often refreshed, and where, it is now found, its waters are dried up, or lost in the sand. Hence such a brook or fountain becomes

an emblem of a false and deceitful friend (Job vi. 15) :

My brethren have dealt deceitfully as a brook,
As the stream of brooks they pass away.

But in the supplies which God makes for his people there is no such deception. The fountains of pardon, peace, and joy are ever open and ever full. The streams of salvation are always flowing. The weary pilgrim may go there at any season of the year, and from any part of a desolate world, and find them always full, refreshing, and free. However far may be the pilgrimage to them from amidst the waste and burning climes of sin, however many come to slake their thirst, and however frequently they come, they find them always the same. They never fail ; and they will continue to flow on to the end of time.

12. *And* they that shall be *of thee.* They that spring from thee ; or thy people. ¶ *Shall build the old waste places.* Shall repair the old ruins, and restore the desolate cities and fields to their former beauty. This language is taken from the condition of Judea during the long captivity at Babylon. The land would have been desolated by the Chaldeans, and lain waste for a period of seventy years. Of course all the remains of their former prosperity would have gone to decay, and the whole country would be filled with ruins. But all this, says the prophet, would be restored if they were obedient to God, and would keep his law. Their descendants would be so numerous that the land would be entirely occupied and cultivated again, and cities and towns would rise with their former beauty and magnificence. ¶ *Thou shalt raise up the foundations of many generations.* That is, the foundations which had endured for generations. The word 'foundations' here (מוּסָד), means properly the foundation of a building, *i.e.*, on which a building rests. Here it means the foundation when that alone remains ; and is equivalent to ruins. The Hebrew phrase translated 'of many generations.' (דּוֹר־וָדוֹר, *generation and generation*),

13 If thou turn away thy foot from the sabbath, *from* doing thy pleasure on my holy day ; and call the sabbath a delight, the holy of the LORD, honourable ; and shalt honour him, not doing thine own ways, nor finding thine own pleasure, nor speaking *thine own* words :

---

is equivalent to one generation after another, and is the usual form of the superlative degree. The exact amount of time is not designated ; but the phrase is equivalent to a long time—while one generation passes away after another. Vitringa applies this to the gospel, and supposes that it means that the church, after long decay and desolation, would rise to its former beauty and glory. The promise is indeed *general ;* and though the *language* is taken from the recovery of Palestine from its ruins after the captivity, yet there can be no objection to applying it in a more general sense, as teaching that the people of God, if they are faithful in keeping his commandments, and in manifesting the spirit which becomes the church, will repair the ruins which sin has made in the world, and rebuild the wastes and the desolations of many ages. Sin has spread its desolations far and wide. Scarce the foundations of righteousness remain in the earth. Where they do remain, they are often covered over with ruined fragments, and are surrounded by frightful wastes. The world is full of the ruins which sin has caused ; and there could be no more striking illustration of the effects of sin on all that is good, than the ruins of Judea during the seventy years of exile, or than those of Palmyra, of Baalbec, of Tyre, of Ephesus, and of Persepolis, at present. It is for the church of God to rebuild these wastes, and to cause the beauties of cultivated fields, and the glories of cities rebuilt, to revisit the desolate earth ; in other words, to extend the blessings of that religion which will yet clothe the earth with moral loveliness, as though sin had not spread its gloomy and revolting monuments over the world. ¶ *And thou shalt be called.* The name which shall appropriately designate what you will do. ¶ *The repairer of the breach.* Lowth, 'The repairer of the broken mound.' The phrase properly means, 'the fortifier of the breach ;' *i.e.,* the one who shall build up the breach

that is made in a wall of a city, either by the lapse of time, or by a siege. ¶ *The restorer of paths to dwell in.* Lowth and Noyes render this, ' The restorer of paths to be frequented by inhabitants.' The LXX. render it, ' And thou shalt cause thy paths to rest in the midst of thee ;' and Jerome, *Avertens semitas in quietem*—' Turning the paths into rest,' which the Jewish exposition explains to mean, ' Thou shalt build walls so high that no enemy can enter them.' So Grotius renders it, ' Turning thy paths to rest ;' that is, thou shalt leave no way of access to robbers. The Chaldee renders it, ' Converting the wicked to the law.' The common English version has probably expressed correctly the sense. The idea is, that they would repair the public highways which had long lain desolate, by which access was had to their dwelling-places. It does not mean, however, that the paths or ways were to be places in which to dwell, but that the ways which led to their dwelling-places were to be restored, or repaired. These roads, of course, in the long desolations would be ruined. Thorns, and brambles, and trees would have grown upon them ; and having been long neglected, they would be impassable. But the advantages of a free intercourse from one dwelling and one city to another, and throughout the land, would be again enjoyed. Spiritually applied, it means the same as the previous expression, that the church of God would remove the ruins which sin has caused, and diffuse comfort and happiness around the world. The obstructed and overrun paths to a quiet and peaceable dwelling on earth would be cleared away, and the blessings of the true religion would be like giving free and easy access from one tranquil and prosperous dwelling-place to another.

13. *If thou turn away thy foot from the Sabbath.* The evident meaning of this is, that they were sacredly to observe the Sabbath, and not to violate or pollute it (see Notes on ch. lvi. 2). The

idea, says Grotius, is, that they were not to travel on the Sabbath-day on ordinary journeys. The 'foot' is spoken of as the instrument of motion and travel. 'Ponder the paths of thy feet' (Prov. ii. 26); *i.e.*, observe attentively thy goings. 'Remove thy foot from evil' (Prov. iv. 27); *i.e.*, abstain from evil, do not go to execute evil. So here, to restrain the foot *from* the Sabbath, is not to have the foot employed on the Sabbath; not to be engaged in travelling, or in the ordinary active employments of life, either for business or pleasure. ¶ *From doing thy pleasure on my holy day.* Two things may here be observed—1. God claims the day as *his,* and as holy on that account. While all time is his, and while he requires all time to be profitably and usefully employed, he calls the Sabbath peculiarly his own—a day which is to be observed with reference to himself, and which is to be regarded as belonging to him. To take the hours of that day, therefore, for *our* pleasure, or for work which is not necessary or merciful, is to ROB God of that which he claims as his own. 2. We are not to do our own pleasure on that day. That is, we are not to pursue our ordinary plans of amusement; we are not to devote it to feasting, to riot, or to revelry. It is true that they who love the Sabbath as they should will find 'pleasure' in observing it; for they have happiness in the service of God. But the idea is, here, that we are to do the things which God requires, and to consult *his* will in the observance. It is remarkable that the thing here adverted to, is the very way in which the Sabbath is commonly violated. It is not extensively a day of business, for the propriety of a periodical cessation from toil is so obvious, that men *will* have such days recurring at moderate intervals. But it is a day of pastime and amusement; a day not merely of relaxation from toil, but also of relaxation from the restraints of temperance and virtue. And while the Sabbath is God's great ordinance for perpetuating religion and virtue, it is also, by perversion, made Satan's great ordinance for perpetuating intemperance, dissipation, and sensuality. ¶ *And call the Sabbath a delight.* This ap-

propriately expresses the feelings of all who have any just views of the Sabbath. To them it is not wearisome, nor are its hours heavy. They love the day of sweet and holy rest. They esteem it a privilege, not a task, to be permitted once a week to disburden their minds of the cares, and toils, and anxieties of life. It is a 'delight' to them to recall the memory of the institution of the Sabbath, when God rested from his labours; to recall the resurrection of the Lord Jesus, to the memory of which the Christian Sabbath is consecrated; to be permitted to devote *a whole day* to prayer and praise, to the public and private worship of God, to services that expand the intellect and purify the heart. To the father of a family it is the source of unspeakable delight that he may conduct his children to the house of God, and that he may instruct them in the ways of religion. To the Christian man of business, the farmer, and the professional man, it is a pleasure that he may suspend his cares, and may uninterruptedly think of God and of heaven. To all who have any just feeling, the Sabbath is a 'delight;' and for them to be compelled to forego its sacred rest would be an unspeakable calamity. ¶ *The holy of the* LORD, *honourable.* This more properly means, 'and call the holy of JEHOVAH honourable.' That is, it does not mean that they who observed the Sabbath would call it 'holy to JEHOVAH *and* honourable;' but it means that the Sabbath was, in fact, 'the holy of JEHOVAH,' and that *they* would regard it as 'honourable.' A slight inspection of the Hebrew will show that this is the sense. They who keep the Sabbath aright will esteem it a day *to be honoured* (מְכֻבָּד). ¶ *And shalt honour him.* Or rather, shalt honour *it;* to wit, the Sabbath. The Hebrew will bear either construction, but the connection seems to require us to understand it of the Sabbath rather than of the LORD. ¶ *Not doing thine own ways.* This is evidently explanatory of the phrase in the beginning of the verse, 'if thou turn away thy foot.' So the LXX. understand it: Οὐκ ἀρεῖς τὸν πόδα σου ἐπ᾿ ἔργῳ—'And will not lift up thy foot to any work.' They were not

14 Then shalt thou delight thyself in the LORD ; and I will cause thee to ride upon the high places of the earth, and feed thee with

the heritage of Jacob thy father: for the mouth of the LORD hath spoken *it*.

---

to engage in secular labour, or in the execution of their own plans, but were to regard the day as belonging to God, and to be employed in his service alone. ¶ *Nor finding thine own pleasure.* The Chaldee renders this, ' And shalt not provide on that day those things which are necessary for thee.' ¶ *Nor speaking* thine own *words.* Lowth and Noyes render this, ' From speaking vain words.' The LXX. ' Nor utter a word in anger from thy mouth.' The Chaldee renders it, ' Words of violence.' It is necessary to add some epithet to make out the sense, as the Hebrew is literally, ' and to speak a word.' Probably our common translation has expressed the true sense, as in the previous members of the verse the phrase ' thine own ' thrice occurs. And according to this, the sense is, that on the Sabbath our conversation is to be such as becomes a day which belongs to God. It is not less important that our conversation should be right on the Sabbath than it is that our conduct should be.

14. *Then shalt thou delight thyself in the* LORD. That is, as a consequence of properly observing the Sabbath, thou shalt find pleasure in JEHOVAH. It will be a pleasure to draw near to him, and you shall no longer be left to barren ordinances and to unanswered prayers. The delight or pleasure which God's people have in him is a direct and necessary consequence of the proper observance of the Sabbath. It is on that day set apart by his own authority, for his own service, that he chooses to meet with his people, and to commune with them and bless them ; and no one ever properly observed the Sabbath who did not find, as a consequence, that he had augmented pleasure in the existence, the character, and the service of JEHOVAH. Compare Job xxii. 21–26, where the *principle* stated here—that the observance of the law of God will lead to happiness in the Almighty—is beautifully illustrated (see also Ps. xxxvii. 4). ¶ *And I will cause thee to ride upon*

the high places of the earth. A phrase like this occurs in Deut. xxxii. 13: ' He made him ride on the high places of the earth, that he might eat the increase of fields.' In Hab. iii. 19, the phrase also occurs : ' He will make my feet like hinds' feet, and he will make me to walk upon mine high places.' So also Ps. xviii. 33 : ' He maketh my feet like hinds' feet, and setteth me upon my high places.' In Amos iv. 13, it is applied to God: ' He maketh the morning darkness, and treadeth upon the high places of the earth.' Kimchi, Calvin, and Grotius suppose that the idea here is, that God would restore the exiled Jews to their own land—a land of mountains and elevated places, more lofty than the surrounding regions. Vitringa says that the phrase is taken from a conqueror, who on his horse or in his chariot, occupies mountains, hills, towers, and monuments, and subjects them to himself. Rosenmüller supposes it means, ' I will place you in lofty and inaccessible places, where you will be safe from all your enemies.' Gesenius also supposes that the word 'high places' here means fastnesses or strongholds, and that to walk over those strongholds, or to ride over them, is equivalent to possessing them, and that he who has possession of the fastnesses has possession of the whole country (see his *Lexicon* on the word בָּמָה, No. 2). I give these views of the most distinguished commentators on the passage, not being able to determine satisfactorily to myself what is the true signification. Neither of the above expositions seems to me to be entirely free from difficulty. The general idea of prosperity and security is undoubtedly the main thing intended ; but what is the specific sense couched under the phrase ' to *ride* on the high places of the earth,' does not seem to me to be sufficiently explained. ¶ *And feed thee with the heritage of Jacob thy father.* That is, thou shalt possess the land promised to Jacob as an inheritance. ¶ *For the mouth of the* LORD *hath spoken*

REMARKS ON THE CHAPTER.

I. From ver. 1–6, and the exposition given of these verses, particularly ver. 6, we may make the following remarks respecting slavery.

1. That the prophets felt themselves at entire liberty to animadvert on slavery as an evil. They did not feel themselves restrained from doing it by the fact that slavery was sustained by law, or by the plea that it was a civil institution, and that the ministers of religion had nothing to do with it. The holy men who were sent by God as his ambassadors, did not suppose that, in lifting up the voice against this institution, they were doing anything contrary to what fairly came within their notice as religious teachers, nor did they regard it as, in such a sense, a civil institution that they were not to advert to it.

It is often said in our country that slavery is a civil institution; that it pertains solely to political affairs; that the constitution and the laws suppose its existence, and make provision for its perpetuity; that it is not appropriate for the ministers of religion, and for ecclesiastical bodies to intermeddle with it. This plea, however, might have been urged with much more force among the Hebrews. *Their* constitution was, what ours is not, of Divine appointment, and it would have been easy for a friend of slavery to say that the prophets were interfering with what was sanctioned by the laws, and with the arrangements which were made for its perpetuity in the commonwealth. Why would not such an argument have as much weight then as it should be allowed to have now?

2. The prophet Isaiah felt himself at entire liberty to exhort the people to restore their slaves to freedom. He considered that slavery was as proper a subject for him to discuss as any other. He treated it as entirely within his province, and did not hesitate at all to express his views on it as an evil, and to demand that the evil should cease, in order to an acceptable worship of God.

3. He does not speak of it as a good and desirable institution, or as contributing to the welfare of the community. It is, in his view, a hard and oppressive system; a system which should be abandoned if men would render acceptable service to God. There is no apology made for it; no pleading for it as a desirable system; no attempt made to show that it is in

accordance with the laws of the land and with the laws of God. It would not be difficult to imagine what would be the emotions of Isaiah, if, after he had written this 58th chapter of his prophecies, it should be represented that he was the friend of slavery, or if he were to read some of the vindications of the systems published in this Christian land by ministers of the gospel, and by ecclesiastical bodies, or should hear the sentiments uttered in debate in Synods, Assemblies, Conferences, and Conventions.

4. It may be inferred from the exposition given, that Isaiah did not suppose that slavery was in accordance with the spirit of the Mosaic institutions, or that those institutions were designed to perpetuate it. His treatment of it is just such as would be natural on the supposition that the Mosaic institutions were so made that, while it was for a while *tolerated*—just as polygamy and divorce were—yet that it was the tendency and design of the Mosaic system ultimately to remove the evil entirely, and to make the Hebrews throughout a free people, and that it was therefore proper for him, as a prophet, to enjoin on them the duty of letting all the oppressed go free. It may be added, that if this was proper in the time of Isaiah, it cannot be *less* proper under the light of the gospel and in the nineteenth century.

II. From the closing portion of this chapter (ver. 13, 14), we may derive the following important inferences respecting the Sabbath:—

1. It is to be of perpetual obligation. The whole chapter occurs in the midst of statements that relate to the times of the Messiah. There is no intimation that the Sabbath was to be abolished, but it is fairly implied that its observance was to be attended with most happy results in those future times. At all events, Isaiah regarded it as of binding obligation, and felt that its proper observance was identified with the national welfare.

2. We may see the manner in which the Sabbath is to be observed. In no place in the Bible is there a more full account of the proper mode of keeping that holy day. We are to refrain from ordinary travelling and employments; we are not to engage in doing our own pleasure; we are to regard it with delight, and to esteem it a day worthy to be honoured; and we are to show respect to it by not performing our own ordinary works, or pursuing pleasures, or engaging in the common topics of conversation. In this descrip-

it. This formula often occurs when an important promise is made, and it is regarded as ample security for the fulfilment that Jehovah has promised

it. What more ample security can be required, or conceived, than the promise of the eternal God?

tion there occurs nothing of peculiar Jewish ceremony, and nothing which indicates that it is not to be observed in this manner at all times. Under the gospel, assuredly, it is as proper to celebrate the Sabbath in this way, as it was in the times of Isaiah, and God doubtless intended that it should be perpetually observed in this manner.

3. Important benefits result from the right observance of the Sabbath. In the passage before us, these are said to be, that they who thus observed it would find pleasure in JEHOVAH, and would be signally prospered and be safe. But those benefits are by no means confined to the Jewish people. It is as true now as it was then, that they who observe the Sabbath in a proper manner find happiness in the Lord—in his existence, perfections, promises, law, and in communion with him—which is to be found nowhere else. Of this fact there are abundant witnesses now in every Christian church, and they will continue to be multiplied in every coming age. And it is *as* true that the proper observance of the Sabbath contributes to the prosperity and safety of a nation now, as it ever did among the Jewish people. It is not merely from the fact that God promises to bless the people who keep his holy day; though this is of more value to a nation than all its armies and fleets; but it is, that there is in the institution itself much that tends to the welfare and prosperity of a country. It is a time when worldliness is broken in upon by a periodical season of rest, and when the thoughts are left free to contemplate higher and purer objects. It is a time when more instruction is imparted on moral and religious subjects, than on all the other days of the week put together. The public worship of God tends to enlarge the intellect, and purify the heart. No institution has ever been originated that has contributed so much to elevate the common mind; to diffuse order, peace, neatness, decency among men, and thus to perpetuate and extend all that is valuable in society, as the Sabbath. Any one may be convinced of this, who will be at the pains to compare a neighbourhood, a village, or a city where the Sabbath is *not* observed with one where it is; and the difference will convince him at once, that society owes more to the Sabbath than to any single institution besides, and that in no way possible can one-seventh portion of the time be so well employed as in the manner contemplated by the Christian day of rest.

4. Society *will* have seasons of cessation from labour, and when they are not made occasions for the promotion of virtue, they will be for the promotion of vice. Thus among the Romans an annual *Saturnalia* was granted to all, as a season of relaxation from toil, and even from the restraints of morality, besides many other days of periodical rest from labour. Extensively among heathen nations also, the seventh day of the week, or a seventh portion of the time, has been devoted to such relaxation. Thus Hesiod says, 'Ἑβδομον ἱερον ἡμαρ —' The seventh day is holy.' Homer and Callimachus give it the same title. Philo says of the seventh day. 'Ἑορτη γαρ ου μιας πολεως η χωρας εστιν αλλα του παντος —' It is a feast, not of one city or one country only, but of all.' Josephus (*Contra Apion.* ii.), says, 'There is no city, however barbarous, where the custom of observing the seventh day which prevails among the Jews is not also observed.' Theophilus of Antioch (ii.), says, 'Concerning the seventh day, which all men celebrate.' Eusebius says, 'Almost all the philosophers and poets acknowledge the seventh day as holy.' *See* Grotius, *De Veritate*, i. It is evident that this custom did not originate by chance, nor was it kept up by chance. It must have been originated by far-spreading tradition, and must have been observed either because the day was esteemed to be holy, or because it was found to be convenient or advantageous to observe such a periodical season of rest. In accordance with this feeling, even the French nation during the Revolution, while they abolished the Christian Sabbath, felt so deeply the necessity of a periodical rest from labour, that they appointed the *decade*—or one day in ten, to be observed as a day of relaxation and amusement. Whatever, therefore, may have been the origin of the Sabbath, and whatever may be the views which may be entertained of its sacredness, it is now reduced to a moral certainty that men *will* have a periodical season of cessation from labour. The only question is, In what way shall it be observed? Shall it be devoted to amusement, pleasure, and vice; or shall it be employed in the ways of intelligence, virtue, and religion? It is evident that such a periodical relaxation *may be* made the occasion of immense good to any community; and it is not less evident that it *may be* the occasion of extending far the evils of intemperance, profaneness, licentiousness, and crime. It is vain to attempt to blot out wholly the observance of the Christian Sabbath; and since it *will* and *must* be observed as a day of cessation from toil, all that remains is for society to avail itself of the advantages which may be derived from its proper observance, and to make it the handmaid of temperance, intelligence, social order, and pure religion

5. It is deeply, therefore, to be regretted that this sacred institution has been, and is so widely abused in Christian lands. As it is, it is exten-

sively a day of feasting, amusement, dissipation, and revelry. And while its observance is, more decidedly than anything else, the means of perpetuating virtue and religion on earth, it is perhaps not too much to say that it is the occasion of more intemperance, vice, and crime than all the other days of the week put together. This is particularly the case in our large cities and towns. A community cannot be disbanded from the restraints of labour one-seventh part of the time without manifest evil, unless there are salutary checks and restraints. The merchant cannot safely close his counting-room; the clerk and apprentice cannot safely be discharged; the common labourer cannot safely be dismissed from toil, unless there is something that shall be adapted on that day to enlarge the understanding, elevate the morals, and purify the heart. The welfare of the community demands that; and nowhere more than in this country. Who can doubt that a proper observance of the holy Sabbath would contribute to the prosperity of this nation? Who can doubt that the worship of God; the cultivation of the heart; the contemplation of moral and religious truth; and the active duties of benevolence, would contribute more to the welfare of the nation, than to devote the day to idleness, amusement, dissipation, and sin?

6. While the friends of religion, therefore, mourn over the desecration of the Christian Sabbath, let them remember that *their* example may contribute much to secure a proper observance of that day. On the friends of the Redeemer it devolves to rescue the day from desecration; and by the Divine blessing it may be done. The happiness of every Christian is indissolubly connected with the proper observance of the Sabbath. The perpetuity of the true religion, and its extension throughout the earth, is identified with the observance of the Sabbath. And every true friend of God the Saviour, as he values his own peace, and as he prizes the religion which he professes to love, is bound to restrain his foot on the Sabbath; to cease to find his own pleasure, and to speak his own words on that holy day; and to show that the Sabbath is to him a delight, and that he esteems it as a day to be honoured and to be loved.

CHAPTER LIX.

ANALYSIS.

This chapter is closely connected in sense with the preceding, and is designed to illustrate the same general sentiment; that the reason why the religious services of the nation were not accepted, and the nation delivered from calamity, was their hypocrisy and their other sins. The previous chapter contained a bold and energetic reproof of their expectation of the Divine favour, when they were observing only external rites without repentance, and even when they continued to practise oppression and cruelty. This beautiful chapter states more in detail their sins, and the consequences of their transgressions. The following arrangement of the parts of the chapter, will show its design and scope at a single view.

I. It was not because JEHOVAH was unable to save them that they were exposed to such judgments, and visited with such calamities (1). They were, therefore, not to blame him. This general principle is stated, in order to prevent what commonly occurs when men suffer much —a disposition to throw the blame on God.

II. It was for their sins that they were exposed to these judgments (2–8). The prophet proceeds to specify those sins in detail, with a view to bring them to conviction and to repentance. 1. The general principle is stated, that it was their sins alone which had separated between them and God (2). 2. Their hands were defiled with blood (3, part first). 3. Their lips had spoken falsehood (3, last part). 4. There was no justice among them (4, part first). 5. Their plans were mischievous (4, second part). 6. Their actions were like the egg of the cockatrice, hateful and destructive as that egg when hatched (5). 7. Their works were like the web of a spider, which could never be a covering of righteousness (6). 8. Their feet run to evil (7, part first). 9. Their thoughts were evil (7, second part). 10. They were strangers to the way of peace (8).

III. After this statement of the prevalent sins of the nation, the prophet introduces the people as making *confession*, that it was for these and similar sins that they were exposed to the Divine displeasure. Identifying himself with the people, he enumerates the calamities to which they were exposed, as a consequence of the sins which prevailed (9–14). They were in darkness; they waited in vain for light; they stumbled at noonday; they vented their sorrows like the roaring of bears, or the plaintive cry of the dove, but all in vain.

IV. JEHOVAH is represented as seeing this state of deep guilt; a state where there was deep conviction of that guilt, and a readiness to make confession; and as wondering that there was no intercessor, and as *himself* interposing to bring deliverance and salvation (15–18). The *characteristics* of him who should come to accomplish these purposes, were righteousness, salvation, vengeance, and zeal (17). He would come to take recompence on his foes, and to reward the wicked according to their deeds (18).

V. The *effect* of this would be that the name of JEHOVAH would be feared from the rising-to the setting sun. JEHOVAH would erect a barrier against the enemy when he should come in like a flood; and the Redeemer would come to Zion to effect deliverance for those who should truly repent (19–20).

VI. A covenant would be established between God and those who would turn away from transgressions (21). The *nature* of that covenant was, that its blessings would be perpetual. The spirit which God would give, and the words which he would put into their mouths, would abide with them and their posterity for ever.

'As this chapter,' says Lowth, 'is remarkable for the beauty, strength, and variety of the images with which it abounds; so it is peculiarly distinguished by the eloquence of the composition, and the exact construction of the sentences. From the first verse to the two last, it falls regularly into stanzas of four lines.' This poetical form of the chapter must be apparent to the slightest observation of the reader; and there is

---

CHAPTER LIX.

1. *Behold, the* LORD's *hand is not shortened.* On the meaning of this phrase, see Notes on ch. l. 2. ¶ *Neither his ear heavy, that it cannot hear.* On the meaning of this phrase, see Notes on ch. vi. 10.

2. *But your iniquities.* That is, the sins which the prophet had specified in the previous chapter, and which he proceeds further to specify in this. ¶ *Have separated.* The word here used (בָּדַל) conveys the idea of division, usually by a curtain or a wall (Ex. xxvi. 33; xlii. 26). Thus the 'firmament' (רָקִיעַ, *expanse*) is said to have *divided* or separated (מַבְדִּיל) the waters from the waters (Gen. i. 6). The idea here is, that their sins were like a partition between them and God, so that there was no intercourse between them and him. ¶ *And your sins have hid* his *face from you.* Marg. 'Made him hide.' The Hebrew word here is in Hiphil, meaning 'to *cause* to hide.' Kimchi and Aben Ezra understand it as *causing* him to hide his face; Vitringa as hiding his face. The metaphor, says Vitringa, is not taken from a man who turns

---

perhaps no instance of more regular construction of the various members and parts of a composition in the writings of the Hebrews.

The chapter has evidently a primary reference to the character of the nation in the times of Isaiah. The deep depravity which is described, is such as existed in the times of Manasseh; and one object of the prophet was manifestly to bring them to conviction for their sins; and to show them why they were suffering, or about to suffer, from the expressions of the Divine displeasure. But the chapter evidently also looks forward to future times, and the close of it refers so manifestly to the times of the Messiah, that it is impossible not to apply it to him.

BEHOLD, the LORD's hand is not shortened, that it cannot save; neither his ear heavy, that it cannot hear;

2 But your iniquities have separated between you and your God, and your sins have [1] hid *his* face from you, that he will not hear.

1 or, *made him hide.*

away his face from one because he does not choose to attend to what is said, but from something which comes between two persons, like a dense cloud, which hides one from the other. And, according to this, the idea is, that their sins had risen up like a thick, dark cloud between them and God, so that they had no clear view of him, and no intercourse with him—as a cloud hides the face of the sun from us. A similar idea occurs in Lam. iii. 44:

Thou hast covered thyself with a cloud,
That our prayers should not pass through.

But it seems to me more probable that the Hiphil signification of the verb is here to be retained, and that the idea is, that their sins had *caused* JEHOVAH to hide or turn away his face from their prayers from an unwillingness to hear them when they were so deeply immersed in sin. Thus the LXX. 'On account of your sins he has turned away his face (ἀπέστρεψε τὸ πρόσωπον) from you, so that he will not have mercy' (τοῦ μὴ ἐλεῆσαι). It is universally true that indulgence in sin causes God to turn away his face, and to withhold mercy and compassion. He cannot pardon those who indulge in transgression, and

3 For ^ayour hands are defiled with blood, and your fingers with iniquity ; your lips have spoken lies, your tongue hath muttered perverseness.

4 None calleth for justice, nor *any* pleadeth for truth : they trust

in vanity, and speak lies ; they conceive mischief, and bring forth iniquity.

5 They hatch ¹ cockatrices' eggs, and weave the spider's web : he that eateth of their eggs dieth,

a ch.1.15.   1 or, *adders'*.

who are unwilling to abandon the ways of sin (comp. Notes on ch. i. 15).

3. *For your hands are defiled with blood.* The prophet proceeds here more particularly to specify the sins of which they were guilty ; and in order to show the extent and depth of their depravity, he specifies the various members of the body—the hands, the fingers, the lips, the tongue, the feet, as the agents by which men commit iniquity. See a similar argument on the subject of depravity in Rom. iii. 13–15, where a part of the description which the prophet here gives is quoted by Paul, and applied to the Jews in his own time. The phrase 'your hands are defiled with blood,' means with the blood of the innocent ; that is, they were guilty of murder, oppression, and cruelty. See a similar statement in ch. i. 15, where the phrase 'your hands *are full* of blood' occurs. The word here rendered 'defiled' (גֹּאֲלוּ) means commonly *to redeem, to ransom;* then to avenge, or to demand and inflict punishment for bloodshed. In the sense of *defiling* it occurs only in the later Hebrew writers—*perhaps* used in this sense because those who were avengers became covered, *i.e.,* defiled with blood. ¶ *And your fingers with iniquity.* The *fingers* in the Scriptures are represented as the agents by which any purpose is executed (Isa. ii. 8), 'Which their own fingers have made' (comp. ch. xvii. 8). Some have supposed that the phrase here used means the same as the preceding, that they were guilty of murder and cruelty. But it seems more probable that the idea suggested by Grotius is the true sense, that it means that they were guilty of rapine and theft. The fingers are the instruments by which theft—especially the lighter and more delicate kinds of theft—is executed. Thus we use the word 'light-fingered' to denote any one who is dexterous in taking and conveying away anything,

or any one who is addicted to petty thefts. ¶ *Your lips have spoken lies.* The nation is false, and no confidence can be reposed in the declarations which are made. ¶ *Your tongue hath muttered.* On the word rendered 'muttered' (הָגָה), see Notes on ch. viii. 19. Probably there is included in the word here, the idea that they not only *spoke* evil, but that they did it with a murmuring, discontented, or malicious spirit. It may also mean that they calumniated the government of God, and complained of his laws ; or it may mean, as Grotius supposes, that they calumniated others —that is, that slander abounded among them. ¶ *Perverseness.* Heb. עַוְלָה— 'Evil'—the word from which our word *evil* is derived.

4. *None calleth for justice.* Or rather, there is no one who brings a suit with justice ; no one who goes into court for the purpose of obtaining justice. There is a love of litigation ; a desire to take all the advantage which the law can give ; a desire to appeal to the law, not for the sake of having strict justice done, but for the sake of doing injury to others, and to take some undue advantage. ¶ *Nor* any *pleadeth for truth.* Or, no one pleadeth *with* truth. He does not state the cause as it is. He makes use of cunning and falsehood to gain his cause. ¶ *They trust in vanity.* They confide in quirks and evasions rather than in the justice of their cause. ¶ *They conceive mischief.* They form plans of evil, and they execute them when they are fully ripe. Compare Job xv. 35, where the same phrase occurs. The sense is, that they form plans to injure others, and that they expect to execute them by fraud and deceit.

5. *They hatch cockatrices' eggs.* Marg. 'Adders'.' On the meaning of the word here rendered 'cockatrice,' see Notes on ch. xi. 8. Some poisonous serpent is intended, probably the adder,

and that which is crushed [1] breaketh out into a [a] viper.

1 or, *sprinkled,* as if *there brake out a viper.*

or the serpent known among the Greeks
as the basilisk, or cerastes.   This figurative expression is designed to show the
evil nature and tendency of their works.
They were as if they should carefully
nourish the eggs of a venomous serpent.
Instead of crushing them with the foot
and destroying them, they took pains
to hatch them, and produce a venomous
race of reptiles.   Nothing can more
forcibly describe the wicked character
and plans of sinners than the language
here used—plans that are as pernicious,
loathsome, and hateful as the poisonous
serpents that spread death and ruin and
alarm everywhere.   ¶ *And weave the
spider's web.*   This phrase, in itself,
may denote, as some have understood
it, that they formed plans designed to
seize upon and destroy others, as spiders
weave their web for the purpose of
catching and destroying insects.   But
the following verse shows that the language is used rather with reference to
the tenuity and gossamer character of
the web, than with any such design.
Their *works* were like the web of the
spider.   They bore the same relation
to true piety which the web of the
spider did to substantial and comfort-
able raiment.   They were vain and
useless.   The word here rendered 'web'
properly denotes the cross-threads in
weaving, the woof or filling; and is
probably derived from a word signifying a *cross-beam* (see Rosenmüller *in
loco;* also Bochart, *Hieroz.* ii. 4. 23).
¶ *He that eateth of their eggs dieth.*
That is, he who partakes of their counsels, or of the plans which they form,
shall perish.   Calvin says that the
meaning is, that ' whosoever had anything to do with them would find them
destructive and pestiferous.'   Similar
phrases, comparing the plans of the
wicked with the eggs and the brood of
the serpent, are common in the East.
'It is said,' says Roberts, speaking of
India, 'of the plans of a decidedly wicked
and talented man, "That wretch! he
hatches serpents' eggs."   ' Beware of
the fellow, his eggs are nearly hatched.''

6 Their webs shall not become
garments, neither shall they cover

a Mat.3.7; 12.34.

"Ah, my friend, touch not that affair,
meddle not with that matter; there is a
serpent in the shell." '   ¶ *And that which
is crushed breaketh out into a viper.*
On the meaning of the word here rendered ' viper,' see Notes on ch. xxx. 6.
Marg. ' Sprinkled, *is as if* there brake
out a viper.'   Jerome renders it, ' Which,
if pierced, breaks out into a basilisk.'
The LXX. render it, ' And he who was
about to eat of their eggs, having broken
one that was putrid (συντρίψας οὔριον),
found in it a basilisk (βασίλισκον).'   The
difference of translation in the text and
the margin of the common version has
arisen from the fact that the translators
supposed that the word here used (זוּרֶה)
might be derived from זָרָה *zârâh, to
sprinkle,* or *to scatter.*   But it is formed
from the word זוּר *zûr, to squeeze, to
press, to crush;* and in Job xxxix. 15,
is applied to the fact that the ostrich
might *crush* her eggs with her foot.   The
sense here is, that when their plans were
developed, they would be found to be
evil and pernicious—as when an egg
should be broken open, a venomous serpent would come forth.   The viper, it
is true, brings forth its young alive, or
is a viviparous animal.   But Bochart
has remarked, that though it produces
its young in this manner, yet that during
the period of gestation the young are included in eggs which are broken at the
birth.—This is a very impressive illustration of the character and plans of the
wicked.   The serpents here referred to
are among the most venomous and destructive that are known.   And the
comparison here includes two points—
1. That their plans resembled the *egg*
of the serpent.   The nature of the egg
cannot be easily known by an inspection.
It may have a strong resemblance to
those which would produce some inoffensive and even useful animals.   It is
only when it is hatched that its true nature is fully developed.   So it is with
the plans of the wicked.   When forming,
their true nature may not be certainly
known, and it may not be easy to determine their real character.   2. Their

themselves with their works : their works *are* works of iniquity, and the act of violence *is* in their hands.

7 Their *a* feet run to evil, and they make haste to shed innocent

blood : their thoughts *are* thoughts of iniquity ; wasting and [1] destruction *are* in their paths.

8 The way of peace they know

a Ro.3.15,&c.   1 *breaking.*

plans, when developed, are like the poisonous and destructive production of the serpent's egg. The true nature is then seen; and it is ruinous, pernicious, and evil.

6. *Their webs shall not become garments.* The spider's web is unfit for clothing; and the idea here is, that their works are as unfit to secure salvation as the attenuated web of a spider is for raiment. The sense is, says Vitringa, that their artificial sophisms avail nothing in producing true wisdom, piety, virtue, and religion, or the true righteousness and salvation of men, but are airy speculations. The works of the self-righteous and the wicked ; their vain formality, their false opinions, their subtle reasonings, and their traditions, are like the web of the spider. They hide nothing, they answer none of the purposes of a garment of salvation. The doctrine is, that men must have some better righteousness than the thin and gossamer covering which their own empty forms and ceremonies produce (comp. ch. lxiv. 6).

7. *Their feet run to evil.* In accordance with the design of the prophet to show the *entireness* of their depravity, he states that all their members were employed in doing evil. In ver. 3–6, he had remarked that depravity had extended to their hands, their fingers, their lips, and their tongue ; he here states that their *feet* also were employed in doing evil. Instead of treading the paths of righteousness, and hastening to execute purposes of mercy and justice, they were employed in journeyings to execute plans of iniquity. The words ' run,' and ' make haste,' are designed to intimate the intensity of their purpose to do wrong. They did not walk slowly ; they did not even take time to deliberate ; but such was their desire of wrong-doing, that they *hastened* to execute their plans of evil. Men usually walk slowly and with a great deal of deliberation when any *good* is to be done ; they walk rapidly, or they run

with haste and alacrity when *evil* is to be accomplished. This passage is quoted by the apostle Paul (Rom. iii. 15), and is applied to the Jews of his own time as proof of the depraved character of the entire nation. ¶ *They make haste to shed innocent blood.* No one can doubt that this was the character of the nation in the time of Manasseh (see Introd. § 3). It is not improbable that the prophet refers to the bloody and cruel reign of this prince. That it was also the character of the nation when Isaiah *began* to prophesy is apparent from ch. i. 15–21. ¶ *Their thoughts.* That is, their plans and purposes are evil. It is not merely that evil is *done*, but they *intended* that it should be done. They had no plan for doing good ; and they were constantly laying plans for evil. ¶ *Wasting.* That is, violence, oppression, destruction. It means that the government was oppressive and tyrannical ; and that it was the general character of the nation that they were regardless of the interests of truth and righteousness. ¶ *And destruction.* Marg. ' Breaking.' The word commonly means *breaking* or *breach ;* then a breaking down, or destruction, as of a kingdom (Lam. ii. 11 ; iii. 47); or of individuals (Isa. i. 28). Here it means that they broke down or trampled on the rights of others. ¶ *Are in their paths.* Instead of marking their ways by deeds of benevolence and justice, they could be tracked by cruelty and blood. The path of the wicked through the earth can be seen usually by the desolations which they make. The path of conquerors can be traced by desolated fields, and smouldering ruins, and forsaken dwelling-places, and flowing blood ; and the course of all the wicked can be traced by the desolations which they make in their way.

8. *The way of peace they know not.* The phrase ' way of peace ' may denote either peace of conscience, peace with

not; and *there is* no [1]judgment in their goings : they have made them crooked *a* paths : whosoever goeth therein shall not know peace.

9 Therefore *b* is judgment far from us, neither doth justice overtake us; we wait for light, but

behold obscurity ; for brightness, *but* we walk in darkness.

10 We *c* grope for the wall like the blind, and we grope as if *we had* no eyes : *d* we stumble at noonday as in the night; we *are* in desolate places as dead *men.*

1 or, *right.*   *a* Ps.125.5; Pr.28.18.   *b* La.5.16,17.   *c* De.28.29.   *d* Am.8.9.

God, peace among themselves, or peace with their fellow-men. Possibly it may refer to all these ; and the sense will be, that in their whole lives they were strangers to true contentment and happiness. From no quarter had they peace, but whether in relation to God, to their own consciences, to each other, or to their fellow-men, they were involved in continual strife and agitation (see Notes on ch. lvii. 20, 21). ¶ *And there is no judgment in their goings.* Marg. '*Right.*' The sense is, that there was no justice in their dealings ; there was no disposition to do right. They were full of selfishness, falsehood, oppression, and cruelty. ¶ *They have made them crooked paths.* A crooked path is an emblem of dishonesty, fraud, deceit. A straight path is an emblem of sincerity, truth, honesty, and uprightness (see Ps. cxxv. 5 ; Prov. ii. 15 ; and Notes on ch. xl. 4). The idea is, that their counsels and plans were perverse and evil. We have a similar expression now when we say of a man that he is '*straightforward,*' meaning that he is an honest man.

9. *Therefore is judgment far from us.* This is the confession of the people that they were suffering not unjustly on account of their crimes. The word 'judgment' here is evidently to be taken in the sense of vengeance or vindication. The idea is this, ' we are subjected to calamities and to oppressions by our enemies. In our distresses we cry unto God, but on account of our sins he does not hear us, nor does he come to vindicate our cause.' ¶ *Neither doth justice overtake us.* That is, God does not interpose to save us from our calamities, and to deliver us from the hand of our enemies. The word *justice* here is not to be regarded as used in the sense that they had a claim on God, or that they were now suffer-

ing unjustly, but it is used to denote the attribute of justice in God ; and the idea is, that the just God, the avenger of wrongs, did not come forth to vindicate their cause, and to save them from the power of their foes. ¶ *We wait for light.* The idea here is, that they anxiously waited for returning prosperity. ¶ *But behold obscurity.* Darkness. Our calamities continue, and relief is not afforded us. ¶ *For brightness.* That is, for brightness or splendour like the shining of the sun—an emblem of happiness and prosperity.

10. *We grope for the wall like the blind.* A blind man, not being able to see his way, feels along by a wall, a fence, or any other object that will guide him. They were like the blind. They had no distinct views of truth, and they were endeavouring to *feel* their way along as well as they could. Probably the prophet here alludes to the threatening made by Moses in Deut. xxviii. 28, 29, 'And the LORD shall smite thee with madness, and blindness, and astonishment of heart ; and thou shalt grope at noon-day as the blind gropeth in darkness, and thou shalt not prosper in thy ways.' ¶ *We stumble at noon-day as in the night.* The idea here is, that they were in a state of utter disorder and confusion. Obstacles were in their way on all hands, and they could no more walk than men could who at noon-day found their path filled with obstructions. There was no remission, no relaxation of their evils. They were continued at all times, and they had no intervals of day. Travellers, though at night they wander and fall, may look for approaching day, and be relieved by the returning light. But not so with them. It was all night. There were no returning intervals of light, repose and peace. It was as if the sun was blotted out, and all was one long,

11 We roar all like bears, and mourn [a] sore like doves; we look

a Eze.7.16.

for [b] judgment, but *there is* none; for salvation, *but* it is far from us.

b Je.7.15.

uninterrupted, and gloomy night. ¶ *We are in desolate places.* There has been great variety in the interpretation of this phrase. Noyes, after Gesenius, translates it, 'In the midst of fertile fields we are like the dead.' One principal reason which Gesenius gives for this translation (*Comm. in loc.*) is, that this best agrees with the sense of the passage, and answers better to the previous member of the sentence, thus more perfectly preserving the parallelism :

At noon-day we stumble as in the night;
In fertile fields we are like the dead.

Thus the idea would be, that even when all seemed like noon-day they were as in the night; and that though they were in places that seemed luxuriant, they were like the wandering spirits of the dead. Jerome renders it, *Caliginosis quasi mortui.* The LXX. ' They fall at mid-day as at midnight ; they groan as the dying' (ὡς ἀποθνίσκοντες στενάξουσιν). The Syriac follows this, ' We groan as those who are near to death.' The Chaldee renders it, ' It (the way) is closed before us as the sepulchre is closed upon the dead ;' that is, we are enclosed on every side by calamity and trial, as the dead are in their graves. The derivation of the Hebrew word אַשְׁמַנִּים is uncertain, and this uncertainty has given rise to the variety of interpretation. Some regard it as derived from שָׁמַם *shâmăm, to be laid waste, to be desolate;* and others from שָׁמֵן *shâmăn, to be,* or *become fat.* The word שְׁמַנִּים *shemannim,* in the sense of fatness, *i. e.,* fat and fertile fields, occurs in Gen. xxvii. 28, 39 ; and this is probably the sense here. According to this, the idea is, we are in fertile fields like the dead. Though surrounded by lands that are adapted to produce abundance, yet we are cut off from the enjoyment of them like the dead. Such is the disturbed state of public affairs; and such the weight of the Divine judgments, that we have no participation in these blessings and comforts. The idea which, I suppose, the prophet means to

present is, that the land was fitted to produce abundance, but that such was the pressure of the public calamity, that all this now availed them nothing, and they were like the dead who are separated from all enjoyments. The original reference here was to the Jew suffering for their sins, whether regarded as in Palestine under their heavy judgments, or as in Babylon, where all was night and gloom. But the *language* here is strikingly descriptive of the condition of the world at large. Sinners at noon-day grope and stumble as in the night. In a world that is full of the light of Divine truth as it beams from the works and the word of God, they are in deep darkness. They feel their way as blind men do along a wall, and not a ray of light penetrates the darkness of their minds. And in a world full of fertility, rich and abundant and overflowing in its bounties, they are still like ' the dead.' True comfort and peace they have not; and they seem to wander as in the darkness of night, far from peace, from comfort, and from God.

11. *We roar all like bears.* This is designed still further to describe the heavy judgments which had come upon them for their sins. The word here rendered ' roar' (from הָמָה *hâmâ,* like Eng. *to hum,* Germ. *hummen,* spoken of bees), is applied to any murmuring, or confused noise or sound. It sometimes means to *snarl,* as a dog (Ps. lix. 7, 15); to *coo,* as a dove (Ezek. vii. 16); it is also applied to waves that roar (Ps. xlvi. 4 ; Isa. li. 15); to a crowd or tumultuous assemblage (Ps. xlvi. 7); and to music (Isa. xvi. 11; Jer. xlviii. 36). Here it is applied to the low growl or groan of a bear. Bochart (*Hieroz.* i. 3. 9), says, that a bear produces a melancholy sound ; and Horace (*Epod.* xvi. 51), speaks of its low groan :—

Nec vespertinus circumgemit ursus ovile.

Here it is emblematic of mourning, and is designed to denote that they were suffering under heavy and long-continued calamity. Or, according to Gesenius (*Comm. in loc.*), it refers to a bear which

12 For *a* our transgressions are multiplied before thee, and our sins testify against us : for our transgressions *are* with us; and *as for* our iniquities, we know them :

13 In transgressing and lying against *b* the LORD, and departing away from our God, speaking oppression and revolt, conceiving and uttering from the *c* heart words of falsehood.

14 And judgment is turned away backward, and justice standeth afar off : for truth is fallen in the street, and equity cannot enter.

15 Yea, truth faileth ; and he *that* departeth from evil ¹ maketh himself a prey : and the LORD saw *it*, and it ² displeased him that *there was* no judgment.

a Da.9.5,&c.   *b* ch.48.8; Je.2,19-21.   *c* Mat.12.34.
1 or, *is accounted mad.*   2 or, *was evil in his eyes.*

is hungry, and which growls, impatient for food, and refers here to the *complaining*, dissatisfaction, and murmuring of the people, because God did not come to vindicate and relieve them. ¶ *And mourn sore like doves.* The cooing of the dove, a plaintive sound, is often used to denote grief (see Ezek. vii. 16 ; comp. Notes on ch. xxxviii. 14). ¶ *We look for judgment*, &c. (see Notes on ver. 9.)
12. *Our sins testify against us.* Heb. 'Answer against us.' The idea is, that their past lives had been so depraved that they became witnesses against them (comp. Notes on ch. iii. 9). ¶ *We know them.* We recognize them as *our* sins, and we cannot conceal from ourselves the fact that we are transgressors.
13. *In transgressing.* That is, we have been guilty of this as a *continuous* act. ¶ *And lying against the* LORD. We have proved false to JEHOVAH. Though we have been professedly his people, yet we have been secretly attached to idols, and have in our hearts been devoted to the service of false gods. ¶ *And departing away from our God.* By the worship of idols, and by the violation of his law. ¶ *Speaking oppression and revolt.* Forming plans to see how we might best take advantage of the poor and the defenceless, and to mature our plans of revolt against God. ¶ *Conceiving and uttering from the heart* (see Notes on ver. 4). The idea is, that they had formed in their hearts schemes of deception, and that in their conversation and their lives they had given utterance to them. All this is the language of genuine contrition, where there is a consciousness of deep guilt in the sight of God. There is an overpowering sense of the evil of sin, and a willingness to make the most full and ample acknow-

ledgment, *however mortifying it may be*, of the errors and follies of the life.
14. *And judgment is turned away backward.* The word 'judgment' is not used, as in ver. 9, to denote the Divine interposition to avenge and deliver them, but it is used in the sense of justice, or just decisions between man and man. The verse contains a further confession of the evil of their course of life ; and, among other things, they acknowledged that they had been *unjust* in their legal decisions. They had been influenced by partiality and by bribes ; they had condemned the innocent, they had acquitted the guilty. Judgment had thus been *turned back* by their sins when it seemed to be approaching and entering the city. ¶ *And justice standeth afar off.* This is a beautiful figure. Justice is represented as standing at a distance from the city. Deterred by their sins, it would not enter. They prevented its approach, and it was unknown among them. ¶ *For truth is fallen in the street.* Or rather, perhaps, *in the gate*—the place where justice was administered. The language here is all taken from courts of justice, and the idea is, that there was no justice in their decisions, but that their courts were unprincipled and corrupt. ¶ *And equity cannot enter.* It stood at a distance, and the impenetrable mass of guilt effectually prevented its approach to the capital.
15. *Yea, truth faileth.* That is, it is not to be found, it is wanting. The word here used (from עָדַר) means to be left, to remain (2 Sam. xvii. 22) ; then to be wanting or lacking (1 Sam. xxx. 19 ; Isa. xl. 26). Here it means that truth had no existence there. ¶ *And he that departeth from evil maketh*

16 And ^ahe saw that *there was* no man, and wondered that *there was* no intercessor; therefore his

a Eze.22,30.

arm ^b brought salvation unto him; and his righteousness it sustained him.

b Ps.98.1.

himself a prey. Marg. ' Is accounted mad.' Noyes renders this, ' And he that departeth from evil is plundered.' Grotius renders it, ' The innocent man lies open to injury from all.' The LXX. ' They took away the mind from understanding;' or, ' They substituted opinion in the place of knowledge.'—(Thompson's *Translation*.) The phrase, ' He that departeth from evil,' means evidently a man who did not, and would not, fall in with the prevailing iniquitous practices, but who maintained a life of honesty and piety. It was one of the evils of the times that such a man would be harassed, plundered, ill-treated. The word rendered ' maketh himself a prey' (מִשְׁתּוֹלֵל from שָׁלַל), is a word usually signifying to strip off, to plunder, to spoil. Some have supposed that the word means to make foolish, or to account mad, in Job xii. 17, 19. Thus, in the passage before us, the LXX. understood the word, and this sense of the word our translators have placed in the margin. But there is no reason for departing here from the usual signification of the word as denoting to plunder, to spoil; and the idea is, that the men of honesty and piety were subject to the rapacity of the avaricious, and the oppression of the mighty. They regarded them as lawful prey, and took every advantage in stripping them of their property, and reducing them to want. This completes the statement of the crimes of the nation, and the existence of such deeds of violence and iniquity constituted the basis on which God was led to interpose and effect deliverance. Such a state of crime and consequent suffering demanded the Divine interposition; and when JEHOVAH saw it, he was led to provide a way for deliverance and reform.

The passage before us had a primary reference to the prevalence of iniquity in the Jewish nation. But it is language also that will quite as appropriately describe the moral condition of the world as laying the foundation for the necessity of the Divine interposition

by the Messiah. Indeed, the following verses undoubtedly refer to him. No one, it is believed, can attentively read the passage, and doubt this. The mind of the prophet is fixed upon the depravity of the Jewish nation. The hands, the tongue, the eyes, the feet, the fingers, were all polluted. The whole nation was sunk in moral corruption; and this was but a partial description of what was occurring everywhere on the earth. In such a state of things in the Jewish nation, and in the whole world, the question could not but arise, whether no deliverer could be found. Was there no way of pardon; no way by which deserved and impending wrath could be diverted? From this melancholy view, therefore, the prophet turns to him who was to be the Great Deliverer, and the remainder of the chapter is occupied with a most beautiful description of the Redeemer, and of the effect of his coming. The sentiment of the whole passage is, *that the deep and extended depravity of man was the foundation of the necessity of the Divine interposition in securing salvation, and that in view of the guilt of men, God provided one who was a Glorious Deliverer, and who was to come to Zion as the Redeemer.* ¶ *And the* LORD *saw* it. He saw there was no righteousness; no light; no love; no truth. All was violence and oppression; all was darkness and gloom. ¶ *And it displeased him.* Marg. ' Was evil in his eyes.' So Jerome, ' It appeared evil in his eyes.' LXX. Καὶ οὐκ ἤρεσεν αὐτῷ— ' And it did not please him.' The Heb. וַיֵּרַע means, literally, ' It was evil in his eyes.' That is, it was painful or displeasing to him. The existence of so much sin and darkness was contrary to the benevolent feelings of his heart. ¶ *That* there was *no judgment.* No righteousness; no equity; and that iniquity and oppression abounded.

16. *And he saw that* there was *no man.* That is, no wise and prudent man qualified to govern the affairs of the people. Or, that there was no man qualified to interpose and put an end to

17 For he put on righteousness as *a* a breastplate, and an helmet of salvation upon his head ; and he

put on the garments of vengeance *for* clothing, and was clad with zeal *b* as a cloak.

a Ep.6.14,17.

b Jn.2.17.

these evils ; no one qualified to effect a reformation, and to save the nation from the calamities which their sins deserved. The reason why God provided a Redeemer was, that such was the extent and nature of human depravity, that no one on earth could arrest it, and save the world. A similar expression occurs in ch. xli. 28. ¶ *And wondered.* This is language adapted to the mode of speaking among men. It cannot be taken literally, as if God was amazed by suddenly coming to the knowledge of this fact. It is designed to express, with great emphasis, the truth, that there was no one to intercede, and that the wicked world was lying in a helpless condition. ¶ *That* there was *no intercessor.* On the meaning of the word here rendered ' intercessor,' see Notes on ch. liii. 6. The Chaldee renders it, ' There was no man who could stand and pray for them.' In ch. lxiii. 5, Isaiah expresses the idea in the following language : ' I looked, and there was none to help ; and I wondered that there was none to uphold.' ¶ *Therefore his arm.* On the meaning of this phrase, see Notes on ch. xl. 10 (comp. ch. li. 5 ; lxiii. 5). The idea is, that salvation was to be traced to God alone. It did not originate with man, and it was not accomplished by his agency or help. ¶ *And his righteousness, it sustained him.* Sustained by the consciousness that he was doing right, he went forward against all opposition, and executed his plan. This is language derived from the mode of speaking among men, and it means that as a man who is engaged in a righteous cause is sustained amidst much opposition by the consciousness of integrity, so it is with God. The cause of redemption is *the* great cause of righteousness on earth. In this cause the Redeemer was sustained by the consciousness that he was engaged in that which was designed to vindicate the interests of truth and justice, and to promote righteousness throughout the universe.

17. *For he put on righteousness.*

That is, God the Redeemer. The prophet here introduces him as going forth to vindicate his people clad like an ancient warrior. In the declaration that he ' put on righteousness,' the essential idea is, that he was pure and holy. The same image is used by the prophet in another figure in ch. xi. 5 (see Notes on that place). ¶ *As a breastplate.* The breastplate was a well-known piece of ancient armour, designed to defend the breast from the darts and the sword of an enemy. The design here is, to represent the Redeemer as a hero ; and accordingly allusion is made to the various parts of the armour of a warrior. Yet he was not to be *literally* armed for battle. Instead of being an earthly conqueror, clad in steel, and defended with brass, his weapons were moral weapons, and his conquests were spiritual. The various parts of his weapons were ' righteousness,' 'salvation,' and 'zeal.' This statement should have been, in itself, sufficient to keep the Jews from anticipating a Messiah who would be a bloody warrior, and distinguished for deeds of conquest and blood. This figure of speech is not uncommon. Paul (in Eph. vi. 14–17 ; comp. 2 Cor. vi. 7) has carried it out to greater length, and introduced more particulars in the description of the spiritual armour of the Christian. ¶ *And an helmet of salvation.* The helmet was a piece of defensive armour for the head. It was made of iron or brass, and usually surmounted by a crest of hair. It was designed to guard the head from the stroke of a sword. No particular stress should be laid on the fact, that it is said that ' salvation' would be the helmet. The design is to represent the Redeemer by the figure of a hero clad in armour, yet there seems to be no particular reason why salvation should be referred to as the helmet, or righteousness as the cuirass or breastplate. Nothing is gained by a fanciful attempt to spiritualize or explain them. ¶ *And he put on the garments of vengeance* for *clothing.* By ' garments,'

18 According to *their* [1] deeds accordingly he will repay, fury to his adversaries, recompence to his

1 *recompences.*   *a* Lu.19.27.

enemies; *a* to the islands he will repay recompence.

19 So *b* shall they fear the name

b Mal.1.11.

here, Vitringa supposes that there is reference to the *interior* garments which were worn by the Orientals corresponding to the tunic of the Romans. But it is more probable that the allusion is to the other parts of the dress or armour in general of the ancient warrior. The statement that he was clad in the garments of vengeance means, that he would go forth to vindicate his people, and to take vengeance on his foes. It would not be for mere defence that he would be thus armed for battle; but he would go forth for aggressive movements, in subduing his enemies and delivering his people (comp. ch. lxiii. 1–6). ¶ *And was clad with zeal as a cloak.* The cloak worn by men in military as well as in civil life, was a loose flowing robe or mantle that was thrown over the body, usually fastened on the right shoulder by a hook or clasp, and suffered to flow in graceful folds down to the feet. In battle, it would be laid aside, or secured by a girdle about the loins. Vitringa remarks, that, as it was usually of purple colour, it was adapted to represent the zeal which would burn for vengeance on an enemy. But the whole figure here is that drawn from a warrior or a conqueror; a hero prepared alike for defence and offence. The idea is, that he would be able to defend and vindicate his people, and to carry on aggressive warfare against his enemies. But it was not to be a warfare literally of blood and carnage. It was to be such as would be accomplished by righteousness, and zeal, and a desire to secure salvation. The triumph of righteousness was the great object still; the conquests of the Redeemer were to be those of truth.

18. *According to* their *deeds.* The general sentiment of this verse is plain, though there is not a little difficulty in the construction of the Hebrew. Lowth pronounces the former part of the verse, as it stands in the Hebrew text, to be 'absolutely unintelligible.' By a slight change in the Hebrew as it now stands (reading בַּעַל, *lord,* instead of כְּעַל *as according to*), Lowth supposes that he

has obtained the true sense, and accordingly translates it:

He is mighty to recompense;
He that is mighty to recompense shall requite.

This translation is substantially according to the Chaldee, but there is no authority from MSS. to change the text in this place. Nor is it necessary. The particle כְּעַל *kĕäl* occurs as a preposition in ch. lxiii. 7, in the sense of 'as according to,' or 'according to,' and is similar in its form to the word מֵעַל *mĕäl,* which often occurs in the sense of *from above,* or *from upon* (Gen. xxiv. 64; xl. 19; Isa. xxxiv. 16; Jer. xxxvi. 11; Amos vii. 11). The sense of the verse before us is, that God would inflict just punishment on his enemies. It is a *general* sentiment, applicable alike to the deliverance from Babylon and the redemption of his church and people at all times. In order to effect the deliverance of his people it was necessary to take vengeance on those who had oppressed and enslaved them. So in order to redeem his church, it is often necessary to inflict punishment on the nations that oppose it, or to remove by death the adversaries that stand in his way. This punishment is inflicted strictly according to their deeds. The principal thought here is, undoubtedly, that as they had opposed and oppressed the people of God, so he would take vengeance on them. He would remove his enemies, and prepare the way in this manner for the coming of his kingdom. ¶ *To the islands.* On the use of the word 'islands' in Isaiah, see Notes on ch. xli. 1. The idea here is, that he would 'repay recompence' or take vengeance on the foreign nations which had oppressed them.

19. *So shall they fear.* That is, the result of the Divine interposition to punish his enemies, shall be to secure the acknowledgment of the existence and perfections of Jehovah in every part of the world. See especially the Notes on ch. xlv. 6. ¶ *When the enemy shall come in.* There has been great variety

of the LORD from the west, and his glory from the rising of the sun. When the enemy shall come in like *a* a flood, the Spirit of the LORD shall [1] lift up a standard against him.

a Re.12.15,16.

[1] *put him to flight.*

in the interpretation of this passage, and it is remarkable that our translators have departed from all the ancient versions, and that the present translation differs from nearly all the modern expositions of the place. Lowth renders it:

When he shall come like a river straitened in
    his course,
Which a strong wind driveth along.

Jerome (Vulg.) renders it, 'When he shall come as a violent river which the Spirit of the Lord (*spiritus Domini,* or the wind of the Lord, *i.e.,* a strong wind) drives along.' The LXX. 'For the wrath of the Lord will come like an impetuous stream ; it will come with fury.' The Chaldee, 'When they shall come who oppress, like an overflowing of the river Euphrates.' The Syriac, 'Because when the oppressor shall come as a river, the Spirit of the Lord shall humble him.' The reason of this variety of interpretation is the ambiguity of the Hebrew words which occur in the verse. The word which in our common version is rendered 'the enemy' (צָר), *tzăr,* from צָרַר *tzârăr,* to press, compress, bind up together ; *intrans.* to be straitened, or compressed), may mean either—1. *An adversary, enemy, persecutor,* synonymous with אֹיֵב, as in Num. x. 9; Deut. xxxii. 27; Job xvi. 9; or, 2. *Straits, affliction* (Ps. iv. 2; xviii. 7; xliv. 11); or, 3. *Strait, narrow* (Num. xxii. 26; Job xli. 7). It may be, therefore, here either a noun meaning an enemy ; or it may be an adjective qualifying the word river, and then will denote a river that is closely confined within its banks, and that is urged forward by a mass of accumulating waters, or by a mighty wind. According to this, it will mean that JEHOVAH will come to take vengeance with the impetuosity of a river that swells and foams and is borne forward with violence in its course. The comparison of a warrior or hero with such a mighty and impetuous torrent, is exceedingly forcible and beautiful, and is not uncommon (see Notes on ch. viii. 7).

The phrase rendered 'the Spirit of the Lord' (רוּחַ יְהוָה), may denote 'the wind of JEHOVAH,' or a strong, violent, mighty wind. The appropriate signification of the word רוּחַ *ruăh,* is *wind,* or *breath ;* and it is well known that the name of God is often in the Scriptures used to denote that which is mighty or vast, as in the phrase, mountains of God, cedars of God, &c. There is no reason why it should be here regarded as denoting 'the Spirit of God,' —the great agent of enlightening and reforming the world. It may be understood, as Lowth and others have applied it, to denote a strong and violent wind —a wind urging on a mass of waters through a compressed and straitened place, and thus increasing their impetuosity and violence. The phrase 'Spirit of God' (רוּחַ אֱלֹהִים), is used to denote a strong wind, in 1 Kings xviii. 12; 2 Kings ii. 16; Isa. xl. 7; Ezek. ii. 24; iii. 14. The word rendered in our version, 'shall lift up a standard' (נֹסְסָה), rendered in the margin, 'put him to flight,' if derived from נָסַס *năsăs,* and if written with the points נָסְסָה *năsĕsăh,* would denote to lift up, to elevate, as a standard or banner, or anything to oppose and retard a foe. But the word is probably derived from נוּס *nŭs,* to *flee,* in Piel נוֹסֵס, to impel, to cause to flee. Here it means, then, that the mighty wind impels or drives on the compressed waters of the stream, and the whole passage means that JEHOVAH would come to deliver his people, and to prostrate his foes with the impetuosity of a violent river compressed between narrow banks, and driven on by a mighty wind. True, therefore, as it is, that when a violent enemy assails the church; when he comes in with error, with violence, and with allies, like a flood, JEHOVAH will rear a standard against him, and the influences of the Spirit of God may be expected to interpose to arrest the evil; yet *this* passage does not teach that doctrine, nor

20 And ᵃthe Redeemer shall come to Zion, and unto them that turn ᵇfrom transgression in Jacob, saith the LORD.

21 As for me, this *is* my ᶜcovenant with them, saith the LORD; My Spirit that *is* upon thee, and my words which I have put in thy mouth, shall not depart out of thy mouth, nor out of the mouth of thy seed, nor out of the mouth of thy seed's seed, saith the LORD, from henceforth and for ever.

a Ro.11.16.   *b* He.12.14.   *c* He.8.8,&c.

should it be so applied. It *does* teach that JEHOVAH will go forth with energy and power to defend his people and to prostrate his foes.

20. *And the Redeemer shall come.* On the meaning of the word here rendered 'Redeemer,' see Notes on ch. xliii. 1. This passage is applied by the apostle Paul to the Messiah (Rom. xi. 26); and Aben Ezra and Kimchi, among the Jews, and Christians generally, suppose that it refers to him. ¶ *To Zion.* On the word 'Zion,' see Notes on ch. i. 8. The LXX. render this, "Ενεκεν Σιὼν—'On account of Zion.' The apostle Paul (Rom. xi. 26), renders this, ' There shall come out of Zion (ἐκ Σιὼν) the Deliverer,' meaning that he would arise among that people, or would not be a foreigner. The idea in Isaiah, though substantially the same, is rather that he would come as a deliverer from abroad ; that is, he would come from heaven, or be commissioned by God. When it is said that he would come *to* Zion, it is not meant that he would come exclusively to the Jews, but that his mission would be primarily to them. ¶ *And unto them that turn from transgression in Jacob.* There is much variety in the interpretation of this passage. Paul (Rom. xi. 26) quotes it thus, ' and shall turn away ungodliness from Jacob ;' and in this he has literally followed the Septuagint. The Vulgate renders it as in our translation. The Chaldee, ' And shall turn transgressors of the house of Jacob to the law.' The Syriac, ' To those who turn iniquity from Jacob.' Lowth has adopted the rendering of the LXX., and supposes that an error has crept into the Hebrew text. But there is no good authority for this supposition. The LXX. and the apostle Paul have retained substantially, as Vitringa has remarked, the sense of the text. The main idea of the prophet is, that the effect of the coming of the Messiah would be to turn men from their sins. He would enter into covenant only with those who forsook their transgressions, and the only benefit to be derived from his coming would be that many would be thus turned from their iniquities.

21. *As for me.* In the previous part of the chapter, the prophet has spoken. Here JEHOVAH is introduced as speaking himself, and as declaring the nature of the covenant which he would establish. In the verse previous, it had been stated that the qualifications on the part of men for their partaking of the benefits of the Redeemer's work, were, that they should turn from transgression. In this verse, JEHOVAH states what he would do in regard to the covenant which was to be established with his people. ' So far as I am concerned, I will enter into a covenant with them and with their children.' ¶ *This* is *my covenant with them* (comp. Notes on ch. xlii. 6; xlix. 8; liv. 10). The covenant here referred to, is that made with men under the Messiah. In important respects it differed from that made with the Jewish people under Moses. The word ' covenant' here is evidently equivalent, as it is commonly, when applied to a transaction between God and men, to a most solemn promise on his part; and the expression is a most solemn declaration that, under the Messiah, God would impart his Spirit to those who should turn from transgression, and would abundantly bless them and their offspring with the knowledge of his truth. When it is said, ' this is my covenant,' the import evidently is, ' this is the nature or the tenure of my covenant, or of my solemn promises to my people under the Messiah. It shall certainly occur that my Spirit will be continually imparted to thy seed, and that my words will abide with thee and them for ever.' ¶ *My Spirit that is upon thee.* The

word 'thee' here does not refer, as Jerome and others suppose, to the prophet, but to the pious Hebrew people. The covenant under the Messiah, was not made peculiarly with the prophet or his posterity, but is a promise made to the church, and here evidently refers to the true people of God ; and the idea is, that the Spirit of God would be continually imparted to his people, and to their descendants for ever. It is a covenant made with true believers and with their children. ¶ *And my words.* The Chaldee understands this of prophecy. But it seems rather to refer to the truth of God in general which he had revealed for the guidance and instruction of his church. ¶ *Shall not depart out of thy mouth.* This phrase probably means, that the truth of God would be the subject of perpetual meditation and conversation. The covenant would be deemed so precious that it would constantly dwell on the tongues of those who were interested in it. ¶ *Thy seed's seed.* Thy descendants ; thy posterity. ¶ *From henceforth and for ever.* This is in accordance with the promises which everywhere occur in the Scriptures, that God would bless the posterity of his people, and that the children of the pious should partake of his favour. See Ex. xx. 6 : 'Showing mercy unto thousands (*i.e.*, thousands of generations) of them that love me and keep my commandments.' Compare Deut. iv. 37; v. 29; vii. 9; Ps. lxxxix. 24, 36; Jer. xxxii. 39, 40. There is no promise of the Bible that is more full of consolation to the pious, or that has been more strikingly fulfilled than this. And though it is true that not *all* the children of holy parents become truly pious; though there are instances where they are signally wicked and abandoned, yet it is also true that rich spiritual blessings *are* imparted to the posterity of those who serve God and who keep his commandments. The following facts are well known to all who have ever made any observation on this subject :—1. The great majority of those who become religious are the descendants of those who were themselves the friends of God. Those who now compose the Christian churches, are not those generally who have been

taken from the ways of open vice and profligacy ; from the ranks of infidelity; or from the immediate descendants of scoffers, drunkards, and blasphemers. Such men usually tread, for a few generations at least, in the footsteps of their fathers. The church is composed mainly of the descendants of those who have been true Christians, and who trained their children to walk in the ways of pure religion. 2. It is a fact that comparatively a large proportion of the descendants of the pious themselves for many generations become true Christians. I know that it is often thought to be otherwise, and especially that it is often said that the children of clergymen are less virtuous and religious than others. But it should be remembered that such cases are more prominent than others, and especially that the profane and the wicked have a malicious pleasure in making them the subject of remark. The son of a drunkard will be intemperate without attracting notice—for such a result is expected ; the son of an infidel will be an infidel ; the son of a scoffer will be a scoffer ; of a thief a thief ; of a licentious man licentious, without being the subject of special observation. But when the son of an eminent Christian treads the path of open profligacy, it at once excites remark, because *such is not the usual course, and is not usually expected ;* and because a wicked world has pleasure in marking the case, and calumniating religion through such a prominent instance of imperfection and sin. But such is not the common result of religious training. Some of the most devotedly pious people of this land are the descendants of the Huguenots who were expelled from France. A very large proportion of all the piety in this country has been derived from the ' Pilgrims,' who landed on the rock of Plymouth, and God has blessed their descendants in New England and elsewhere with numerous revivals of religion. I am acquainted with the descendants of John Rogers, the first martyr in Queen Mary's reign, of the tenth and eleventh generations. With a single exception, the oldest son in the family has been a clergymen—some of them eminently distinguished for learning and piety ;

CHAPTER LX.

ANALYSIS.

IN this chapter there is commenced a most glowing and beautiful description of the 'golden age' under the Messiah. The description is continued to the close of ch. lxii. It is adorned with the highest ornaments of poetry; the future glory of the church is displayed under the most splendid colours, and with every variety of imagery. It is designed to set forth the glory of that time when the Gentiles shall be gathered into the church, and when the whole world shall become tributary to the Messiah, and be illuminated with the light of Christian truth. The main design of the chapter is to foretell the conversion of the heathen world, and the happy and peaceful times which shall exist when that has occurred. In doing this, the highest beauties of prophetic imagery are introduced, and the powers of the inspired prophet seem to have been taxed to the utmost to convey a just view of the glory of the scene.—That it refers to the time of the Messiah no one can doubt who reads it. And that it refers to events which have not yet fully occurred is, I think, equally clear, and will be made apparent in the Notes. In accord-

ance with the usual mode in Isaiah (see Introd. § 7, 4), the prophet throws himself into the midst of the future scene (ver. 1), and the events are described as passing in vision before his eyes. He sees the light as already shining, and the glory of JEHOVAH as actually arisen upon the church;—he sees the Gentiles flocking to the Redeemer, and bringing their most valued and precious objects, and laying them at his feet.

The chapter may, for convenience, be regarded as consisting of three parts:

I. An invocation to the church to arise, and to enjoy and diffuse the light which had risen upon her (1, 2), the earth elsewhere was enveloped in deep darkness, but the light of Messiah's reign and of truth was with her.

II. The declaration that the Gentile world would be converted to the true religion, and would participate in the blessings of the reign of the Messiah. 1. The assurance that this event would occur (3). 2. The church directed to look around, and behold the multitudes that were flocking to her (4). 3. Specifications of those who would come and participate in the benefits of the reign of the Messiah. (1.) The abundance of the sea would come. (2.) The wealth of the Gentiles (5). (3.) The camels and dromedaries

and there are few families now in this land a greater proportion of whom are pious than of that. The following statistical account made of a limited section of the country, not more favoured or more distinguished for piety than many others, accords undoubtedly with similar facts which are constantly occurring in the families of those who are the friends of religion. The Secretary of the Massachusetts Sabbath School Society made a limited investigation, in the year 1838, for the purpose of ascertaining the facts about the religious character of the families of ministers and deacons with reference to the charge so often urged that the 'sons and daughters of ministers and deacons were worse than common children.' The following is the result. In 268 families which he canvassed, he found 1290 children over fifteen years of age. Of these children 884, *almost three-fourths, are hopefully pious;* 794 have united with the churches; sixty-one entered the ministry; only seventeen are dissipated, and about half only of these became so while with their parents. In eleven of these families there are 123 children, and *all* but seven pious. In fifty-six of these

families there are 249 children over fifteen, and *all* hopefully pious. When and where can any such result be found in the families of infidels, of the vicious, or of irreligious men? Indeed, it is the great law by which religion and virtue are perpetuated in the world, that God is faithful to this covenant, and that he blesses the efforts of his friends to train up generations for his service. 3. All pious parents should repose on this promise of a faithful God. They may and should believe that it is his design to perpetuate religion in the families of those who truly serve and obey him. They should be faithful in imparting religious truth; faithful in prayer, and in a meek, holy, pure, and benevolent example; they should so live *that their children may safely tread in their footsteps;* they should look to God for his blessing on their efforts, and their efforts will not be in vain. They shall see their children walk in the ways of virtue; and when they die, they may leave the world with unwavering confidence that God will not suffer his faithfulness to fail; that he will not break his covenant, nor alter the thing that is gone out of his lips (Ps. lxxxix. 33, 34).

from Midian, Ephah, and all they who resided in Sheba would come with their gold and incense (6). (4.) The flocks of Kedar, and the rams of Nebaioth would be offered (7). (5.) The multitude would be so great as to excite astonishment, and lead to the inquiry who they were. They would come like clouds; they would fly for safety as doves do to their windows in an approaching tempest (8). (6.) The distant islands —the heathen coasts, would wait for the gospel; and the commerce of the world be made tributary to the spread of truth (9). (7.) The sons of strangers would be employed in defending Zion, and kings would become the servants of the church (10). 4. So great would be the anxiety to embrace the provisions of mercy, and so numerous the converts from the Pagan world, that the gates of Zion would never be closed day or night (11). 5. The nation that refused this homage would be certainly destroyed (12). 6. Then follows a beautiful poetical description of the conversion of the Pagan world, and of the fact that the most valued and valuable objects of the Gentiles would be con-

secrated to the church, under the image of bringing the beautiful trees of Lebanon to adorn the grounds around the temple (13, 14). 7. Zion would be made an eternal excellency (15). 8. There would thus be furnished the fullest proof of the faithfulness of God, and of the fact that JEHOVAH was the Redeemer and Saviour of his people.

III. The happy state of the church in those times. 1. It would be an age when peace and justice would characterize the rulers (17). 2. Violence, contention, wasting, would be known no more (18). 3. There would be uninterrupted prosperity, and the constant reign of truth (19, 20). 4. The people would be all holy (21). 5. Their numbers would be greatly augmented, as if a small one should become a strong nation (22).

A RISE, ¹ shine; for thy light *is* ᵃ come, and the glory of the LORD is risen upon thee.

1 or, *be enlightened, for thy light cometh.*   ᵃ Ep.5.8.

CHAPTER LX.

1. *Arise.* This is evidently addressed to the church, or to Zion regarded as the seat of the church. It is represented as having been in a state of affliction and calamity (comp. Notes on ch. iii. 26; lii. 1, 2). She is now called on to arise from the dust, and to impart to others the rich privileges which were conferred on her. ¶ *Shine* (אוֹרִי). Lowth renders this, 'Be thou enlightened.' Marg. 'Be enlightened, for thy light cometh.' Noyes, 'Enjoy light.' LXX. Φωτίζου φωτίζου—' Be enlightened; be enlightened, O Jerusalem.' Herder renders it, ' Be light.' Vitringa regards the expression as equivalent to this, ' pass into a state of light. That is, enjoy light thyself, and impart it freely to others.' Gesenius renders it, ' Shine, be bright; that is, be surrounded and resplendent with light.' The idea probably is this, ' rise now from a state of obscurity and darkness. Enter into light; enter into times of prosperity.' It is not so much a command to impart light to others as it is to be encompassed with light and glory. It is the language of prophecy rather than of command; a call rather to participate in the light that was shining than to impart it to others. The LXX. and the Chaldee

here add the name ' Jerusalem,' and regard it as addressed directly to her. ¶ *Thy light* is *come.* On the word ' light,' see Notes on ch. lviii. 8, 10. The light here referred to is evidently that of the gospel; and when the prophet says that that light ' is come,' he throws himself into future times, and sees in vision the Messiah as having already come, and as pouring the light of salvation on a darkened church and world (comp. Notes on ch. ix. 2). ¶ *And the glory of the* LORD. There is reference here, doubtless, to the Shechinah or visible splendour which usually accompanied the manifestations of God to his people (see Notes on ch. iv. 5). As JEHOVAH manifested himself in visible glory to the Israelites during their journey to the promised land, so he would manifest himself in the times of the Messiah as the glorious protector and guide of his people. The Divine character and perfections would be manifested like the sun rising over a darkened world. ¶ *Is risen upon thee.* As the sun rises. The word here used (זָרַח) is commonly applied to the rising of the sun (Gen. xxxii. 31; Ex. xxii. 2; 2 Sam. xxiii. 4; Ps. civ. 22). The comparison of the gospel to the sun rising upon a dark world is exceedingly

2 For behold, the darkness shall cover the earth, and gross darkness the people ; but the LORD *a* shall arise upon thee, and his glory shall be seen upon thee.

3 And the Gentiles shall come to thy light, and kings *b* to the brightness of thy rising.

4 Lift up thine eyes round about, and see : all they gather themselves together, they come to thee : thy sons shall come from far, and thy daughters shall be nursed at *thy* side.

a Mal.4.2; 2 Co.4.6.   *b* ch.49.6,23; Re.21.24.

beautiful, and often occurs in the Bible (comp. Mal. iv. 2; Luke i. 78, marg.) ¶ *Upon thee.* Upon thee, in contradistinction from other nations and people. The gospel shed its first beams of glory on Jerusalem.

2. *For behold.* Lo, darkness covers the earth. This is designed to turn the attention to the fact that all the rest of the world would be enveloped in deep spiritual night. ¶ *Darkness* (see Notes on ch. xlv. 7). ¶ *Shall cover the earth.* Shall envelope the whole world except where it is illuminated by the gospel. It is needless to say that this was the fact when the Messiah came, and that it is still extensively true also. ¶ *And gross darkness.* Lowth renders this, 'A thick vapour.' Herder, 'Deep obscurity.' LXX. Γνόφος—Cloud, shade, tempest. The Hebrew word (עֲרָפֶל) usually denotes thick cloud, cloudy darkness, gloom ; and is often applied to the thick clouds of a tempest (Ex. xx. 18; Deut. iv. 11; Ps. xviii. 10). It is a word of intenser meaning than that which is rendered 'darkness' (חֹשֶׁךְ) and the idea here is, that the nations would be enveloped in a cloud of ignorance and sin so dense and obscure that no light could penetrate it—a description strikingly applicable to the whole heathen world. ¶ *But the LORD shall arise upon thee.* Like the sun. That is, JEHOVAH would manifest his perfections to them in a glorious manner. ¶ *Shall be seen upon thee.* There is more emphatic meaning in the original here than is conveyed in our translation. The Hebrew word (יֵרָאֶה) does not mean merely that that glory would be *visible,* but that it would be *conspicuous.* It would be so bright and luminous that it would be *seen* afar—like a cloud or column of glory standing over Jerusalem that would be conspicuous to far distant people.

3. *And the Gentiles shall come.* So splendid shall be that glory, that it will attract the distant nations, and they shall come and participate in the blessings of the gospel. This contains the main statement which it is the design of this chapter to illustrate. The prophet had frequently made this statement before in general terms (comp. ch. ii. 3; xi. 10; xlix. 22; liv. 3) ; but he here goes into a more particular account, and more fully describes the blessings which would result from this accession to the true church. ¶ *And kings* (comp. Notes on ch. xlix. 7, 23 ; lii. 15). ¶ *To the brightness of thy rising.* This does not mean that the church was to arise with the splendour of the sun; but 'thy rising' means the rising *upon her*—called *her* rising, because it would shed its beams on her. It is correctly rendered by Lowth— 'The brightness of thy sunrising;' by Noyes and Herder, 'The brightness that riseth upon thee.'

4. *Lift up thine eyes.* Jerusalem is here addressed as a female with eyes cast down from grief. She is directed to lift them up, and to see the great multitudes that were flocking to her. Wherever she could turn her eyes, she would behold them hastening to come to her. In this verse and the following verses, the prophet goes into a particular statement of what he referred to in general terms in ver. 3. The first thing which he specifies is, that the dispersed sons and daughters of the Jewish people would be gathered back. ¶ *Thy sons shall come from far.* They who have been driven into exile into distant lands shall again return. This is in accordance with the predictions so often made in Isaiah, that the scattered sons of the Jewish people would be again collected (see Notes on ch. xlix. 17, 18. ¶ *And thy daughters shall be nursed at thy*

5 Then thou shalt see, and flow together, and thine heart shall fear, and be enlarged ; because *a*the abundance[1] of the sea shall be converted unto thee, the [2]forces of the Gentiles shall come unto thee.

a Ro.11.25.

1 or, *noise of the sea shall be turned toward thee.*
2 or, *wealth,* ver. 11; ch.61.6.

side. The LXX. render this, ' And thy daughters shall be borne upon the shoulders' (ἐπ' ὥμων ἀρθήσονται). Lowth also says, that one MS. reads it ' upon the shoulders,' and another has both 'shoulders' and 'side.' The translation of the LXX., and these different readings of the MSS. have probably been caused by the supposed improbability of the fact, that children were nursed or carried on the side (comp. ch. xlix. 22). But Sir John Chardin says that it is the general custom in the East to carry the children astride upon the hip, with the arms around the body. The word, however, which is rendered ' nursed ' in our translation (תֵּאָמַנָה from אָמַן), means, properly, to stay, to sustain, support; to bear or carry a child (Num. xi. 12); hence to be faithful, firm. It is not certain that it is in any instance used in the sense of nursing; but it more probably means here, they shall be borne. It implies that the church would evince deep solicitude for the education and welfare of the young—as a mother does for her children ; and that it would be one of the blessings of those times that that solicitude should be felt and manifested.

5. *Then shalt thou see.* Lowth renders this, ' Then shalt thou fear and overflow with joy;' and supposes that it refers to the agitation and anxiety of mind attending the scene, and to the joy consequent on the numerous conversions. His authority for this change is, that forty MSS. (two of them ancient) have תִּירָא, ' thou shalt fear,' instead of תִּרְאִי, ' thou shalt see.' But though the change is of a single letter, there is not sufficient authority to make it, nor does the sense require it. The Vulgate, LXX., Chaldee, Syriac, Arabic, and Castellio, all render it in accordance with the present reading of the Hebrew text. The idea is, that Jerusalem would look with deep interest on the great multitude that would be converted to her, and that the effect would

be to cause the heart to overflow with joy. ¶ *And flow together.* This translation, it is believed, by no means conveys the true sense of the passage. Indeed, it is difficult to make sense of the translation. It is true that the Hebrew word נָהַר, *nâhăr,* means to flow, to flow together ; whence the word נָהָר, *nâhâr,* ' river.' But it may be used in the sense of flowing, or overflowing *with joy;* or it may seem to shine, to be bright, the same as נוּר, *nūr* (Gesenius) ; and thence to be cheered, to rejoice, as when the countenance is bright and cheerful (comp. Job iii. 4). Taylor (*Heb. Con.*) renders it, ' And be enlightened, or have the light flow upon thee.' The true idea is, doubtless, that of rejoicing ; denoting the happiness which will always exist in the church when many are *seen* to come and give themselves to God. ¶ *And thine heart shall fear.* The heart shall be *ruffled,* agitated, deeply excited by the view of the numbers that are converted, and by the evidence thus furnished of the Divine favour and presence. The effect of numerous simultaneous conversions in a revival of religion, is always to produce awe and reverence. There is a conviction that God is near, and that this is his work ; and a deep veneration produced by the demonstrations of his power which does not exist in other circumstances. This effect is described also by Jeremiah, ch. xxxiii. 9 : ' And they shall fear and tremble for all the goodness and for all the prosperity that I shall procure unto her' [Jerusalem]. ¶ *And be enlarged.* Shall be swelled or filled with joy. ¶ *Because the abundance of the sea.* Marg. ' Noise of the sea shall be turned unto thee.' Lowth and Noyes render it, ' The riches of the sea.' So the LXX. Πλοῦτος θαλάσσης. The Chaldee renders it, ' There shall be transferred to thee the wealth of the west' (עוֹתַר מַעַרְבָא). The Hebrew word הֲמוֹן properly denotes a noise or sound ; as of rain, of the raging of the ocean, or of

6 The multitude of camels shall cover thee, tho dromedaries of Midian *a* and Ephah ; all they from

Sheba *b* shall come: they shall bring gold *c* and incense : and they shall show forth the praises of the LORD.

a Ge.25.4,13.

b Ps.72.10.   *c* Mat.2.11.

---

a multitude of men. Then it denotes a multitude or crowd of men itself (Isa. xiii. 4; xxxiii. 3; Dan. x. 6); a host or army (Judg. iv. 7; Dan. xi. 11–13); a multitude of waters (Jer. x. 13; li. 16). It then denotes a multitude of possessions; a vast amount of wealth (Ps. xxxvii. 16; Eccl. v. 9). Here it may refer either to the multitude of the *people* that dwelt on the islands of the sea, or to their *wealth* that would be brought and devoted to Zion. As various kinds of *property* are immediately specified, it seems most natural to refer it to that; and then the idea is, that the wealth possessed by lands beyond the sea, or surrounded by the sea, would be devoted to the church of God. It will be remembered, that nearly all the wealth that was imported by Solomon and others to Judea came from beyond sea, and that it was natural to speak of such places as abounding in riches. The idea is, that the wealth of all those distant lands would be consecrated to the church—an idea denoting its great prosperity and glory when all lands should come under the influence of the truth. ¶ *Shall be converted.* Heb. 'Shall be turned.' Instead of being employed in idolatry and sin; in purposes of pleasure and mere magnificence, it *shall be turned* to a different purpose. ¶ *The forces of the Gentiles.* Marg. 'wealth.' The margin has undoubtedly the correct interpretation. The word here used (חַיִל, constr. חֵיל), usually, indeed, denotes strength, might, valour; an army, forces, host; but it also means riches, wealth (Ge. xxiv. 29; Deut. viii. 17, 18; Ruth iv. 11; Job xx. 15). The LXX. renders the passage, 'The riches of the sea, and of the nations, and of the people will come over to thee.' The sense is, that the wealth of the heathen world would be consecrated to the service of the church. To some extent, this has been the case. No small part of the great wealth of the Roman empire was devoted to the service of the Christian church; and the wealth of what was

then Pagan Europe, and of what was then Pagan and unknown America, has been, to a considerable extent, devoted to the Redeemer. The time will come when the wealth of India, of China, of Africa, and of the entire world, shall be devoted to the service of God, in a manner far more decided than has yet occurred in the most favoured Christian lands.

6. *The multitude of camels.* Lowth renders this, ' An inundation of camels.' The Hebrew word properly denotes an inundation or overflowing of waters, but it is not improperly applied to a numerous caravan or company of animals. The camel is a well-known useful animal that constitutes the principal beast of burden in Arabia, and that may, indeed, be said to constitute its wealth. It is frequently spoken of as ' the ship of the desert.' The description here is strictly applicable to Arabia; and, undoubtedly, the prophet meant to say, that that country would be blessed with the true religion, and that her merchandise and wealth would become tributary to the church of God. ¶ *Shall cover thee.* Shall come in such multitudes as to fill thee, and to be spread out all over thee. Thus we speak of a land being covered with flocks and herds. ¶ *The dromedaries.* The dromedary

DROMEDARY (*Camelus Dromedarius*).

is a species of camel that is found principally in Arabia, with one bunch or protuberance on its back, in distinction from the Bactrian camel, which has two bunches (Webster). ' It is found,' says

Dr. Shaw, 'in Barbary, though much more rarely there than in the Levant. It is chiefly remarkable for its prodigious swiftness; the Arabs affirming that it will run over as much ground in one day as one of their best horses will perform in eight or ten. The Shiekh, who conducted us to Mount Sinai rode upon a camel of this kind, and would frequently divert us with an instance of its great abilities. For he would depart from our caravan, reconnoitre another just in view, and return to us again in less than a quarter of an hour. It differeth from the common camel in being of a finer and rounder shape, and in

BACTRIAN CAMEL (Camelus Bactrianus).

having on its back a lesser bunch or protuberance.' — (Shaw's *Travels*, p. 240.) Hence, in Jer. ii. 23, the prophet speaks of the 'swift dromedary.' The idea here is, that these fleet animals, so valuable to the inhabitants of Arabia, would come bringing their merchandise for the service of the church of God; that is, the wealth of Midian and Ephah would be devoted to him. ¶ *Midian.* Midian was the fourth son of Abraham and Keturah (Gen. xxv. 2), and was the father of the Midianites. The Midianites are frequently mentioned in the Scriptures (Gen. xxxvii. 28–36; Num. xxv. 17; xxxi. 2; Judg. vi. 7–16; vii. 23, 25, *et al.*) As early as the time of Jacob they were employed in traffic, and were associated with the Ishmaelites in this business, for it was to a company of these men that Joseph was sold by his brethren (Gen. xxxvii. 28). 'The original and appropriate district of the Midianites seems to have been on the east side of the Elanitic branch of the Red Sea, where

the Arabian geographers place the city of *Madian.* But they appear to have spread themselves northward, probably along the desert coast of Mount Seir, to the vicinity of the Moabites; and on the other side, also, they covered a territory extending to the neighbourhood of Mount Sinai.'—(Robinson's *Calmet.*) Generally, the names Midianites and Ishmaelites seem to have been nearly synonymous. ¶ *Ephah.* Ephah was the eldest son of Midian (Gen. xxv. 4), and dwelt in Arabia Petræa, and gave name to the city of Ephah, called here by the LXX. Γαιφά (*Gœpha*). This city, and the small extent of country around it, constituted a part of Midian on the eastern shore of the Dead Sea, to which the territories of Midian extended. It abounded in dromedaries and camels (Judg. vi. 6). ¶ *All they from Sheba shall come.* Sheba is celebrated in the Scriptures chiefly as the place whence the Queen of that country came to visit Solomon (1 Kings x. 1; 2 Chron. ix. 1). That it abounded in wealth, may be inferred from the train which accompanied her, and from the presents with which she came to Solomon. 'And she came to Jerusalem with a very great train, with camels that bare spices, and much fine gold, and precious stones' (1 Kings x. 2). Whether it was the same country as *Seba* has been a matter of uncertainty (comp. Notes on ch. xliii. 3). It is elsewhere (Ps. lxxii. 10) mentioned as a place from whence presents should be brought to Solomon—

The kings of Tarshish and of the isles shall bring presents;
The kings of Sheba and Seba shall offer gifts.

It is usually mentioned as a place in which gold and incense abounded. 'To him shall be given the gold of Sheba (Ps. lxx. 15); 'To what purpose cometh there to me incense from Sheba' (Jer. vi. 20); 'The merchants of Sheba were thy merchants' (Ezek. xxvii. 22). According to Bruce, it was situated in Abyssinia in Ethiopa, and this has been the common opinion. It was south of Egypt, and the intercourse between Sheba and Jerusalem was not difficult; and probably a constant traffic was maintained between the two countries. In

7 All the flocks of Kedar shall be gathered together unto thee, the rams of Nebaioth shall minister unto thee: they shall come up with acceptance on mine altar, and I will *a*glorify the house of my glory.

a Hag.2.7,9.

the time of the Mamelukes, before the conquest of Egypt and Arabia by Selim, a caravan constantly set out from Abyssinia for Jerusalem (comp. Notes on ch. xlv. 14). ¶ *They shall bring gold and incense.* That this country abounded in incense, see the passages of Scripture referred to above. On the meaning of the wood ' incense,' see Notes on ch. i. 13. The idea is, that they would bring the most valuable productions of their country and devote them to God—perhaps designed to show that the wealth of Africa should yet be consecrated to the cause of the true religion. ¶ *And they shall show forth.* These distant lands shall join in the worship of JEHOVAH.

7. *All the flocks of Kedar.* On the word ' Kedar,' see Notes on ch. xxi. 16. The Kedarenians were a wandering tribe that frequently changed their residence, though it is probable they usually dwelt in the south part of Arabia Deserta, or the north of Arabia Petræa. They are mentioned as dwelling in beautiful tents (Cant. i. 5): ' I am black, but comely as the tents of Kedar,' see Ps. cxx. 5; comp. Isa. xxi. 16, 17; xlii. 11. The language here also means that that which constituted their principal wealth would come and enrich Jerusalem, or the church of God. ¶ *The rams of Nebaioth.* Nebaioth was also a son of Ishmael (Gen. xxv. 13; 1 Chron. i. 29), and was the father of the Nabatheans. They were a people of Arabia Petræa, and lived principally by plunder, trade, and the keeping of flocks. The country of Nabathea extended, it is supposed, from the Euphrates to the Red Sea, and embraced Petra, the capital of Arabia Deserta, and also Medaba. It is not possible, however, to fix the exact boundaries of the various tribes of Arabians. The general idea is, that their most valuable possessions would be devoted to God. ¶ *Shall minister unto thee.* That is, by coming up as an acceptable sacrifice on the altar. ¶ *They shall come up with acceptance on mine altar.* It is by no means necessary to understand this literally. The Jews were accustomed to express their ideas of worship by sacrifices, and the prophet naturally employed that language. The sense is, that the conversion of the wandering tribes of Arabia would be as certain and as signal as if the numerous flocks of Kedar and Nebaioth should be devoted to JEHOVAH in sacrifice. All that was valuable there would be employed in his service; the people would come with their most precious offerings and consecrate them to God. It is evident that this remains to be fulfilled. Paul, indeed, preached in Arabia (Gal. i. 17); and, doubtless, there were some conversions to Christianity there. But, as a people, they never have been converted to the true God; and in all ages they have been the victims of either idolatry or superstition. The time will come, however, when Arabia, so interesting as settled by the descendants of Abraham; so interesting in the bold, active, and energetic character of its tribes; so interesting as using a language that is one of the most refined and far-spoken of the earth; and so interesting as being, in some parts at least, among the most fertile and beautiful of the earth, shall be converted to God. Probably the most balmy, pure, and pleasant climate of the world is the southern part of Arabia Felix—the country of Yemen; and when the Arabs shall bring their energy of character to the service of the true God, and the gospel shall be preached in their language to all their tribes, no one can predict the effect which this shall have on the entire conversion of the world. ¶ *And I will glorify.* I will honour my glorious house, *i.e.,* the temple. Lowth, ' And my beauteous house I will yet beautify.' The idea is, that he would adorn the temple by bringing the distant nations, with their most valuable possessions, to worship there. That is, the true religion would yet appear glorious when the nation should acknowledge it and submit to its requirements.

8 Who *are* these *that* fly as a cloud, and as the doves to their windows?

9 Surely the isles *a* shall wait for me, and the ships of Tarshish first,

to bring thy sons from far, their silver *b* and their gold with them, unto the name of the LORD thy God, and to the Holy One of Israel, because he hath glorified thee.

---

a ch.42.4.

b Ps.68.30,31; Zec.14.14.

---

8. *Who* are *these* that *fly as a cloud?* In multitudes so numerous, that they appear as a dense cloud. The prophet, in vision, sees a vast multitude coming to Jerusalem, or hastening to embrace the true religion—so numerous as to excite surprise, and to lead to the question, Who can they be? (comp. ch. xlix. 21.) It is not uncommon to compare a multitude of persons to a cloud. Thus Livy (xxxv. 49), *Rex contra peditum equitumque nubes jactat.* Thus in Heb. xii. 1, the number of witnesses who are said to encompass Christians is compared to a cloud (νέφος μαρτύρων). So Virgil (*Geor.* iv. 60) compares a swarm of bees to a cloud—*obscuramque trahi vento mirabere nubem.* The Chaldee understands this of *swift* clouds, and takes the point of the comparison to be the *velocity* with which they would come. ' Who are these that come publicly (בְּעָב) *as swift clouds?*' But the comparison relates probably to the *number*, rather than to the *swiftness* with which they would come. Converts would be multiplied in such numbers, that they would seem to be like dense clouds making their way to Zion. This strikingly expresses the fact of the numerous conversions among the Gentiles, and is a most beautiful description of a revival of religion. ¶ *And as the doves to their windows.* Lowth renders this, ' Like doves upon the wing'—supposing with Houbigant, that there is a slight error in the Hebrew text. The LXX. render it, Σὺν νοσσοῖς—' With their young.' But the true idea is contained in the common version. Doves fly to their houses, or to their windows, in an approaching storm. In like manner converts would hasten to Zion from the heathen world. They would come in great numbers, and would feel that if there they would be safe. Morier, in his *Second Journey*, p. 140, has well illustrated this passage—' In the environs of the city' [Ispahan], says he,

' to the westward, near Zainderood, are many pigeon-houses, erected at a distance from habitations, for the purpose of collecting pigeon's dung for manure. They are large, round towers, rather broader at the bottom than at the top, crowned by conical spiracles, through which the pigeons descend. Their interior resembles a honey-comb, pierced with a thousand holes, each of which forms a snug retreat for a nest. The extraordinary flights of pigeons which I have seen upon one of these buildings affords, perhaps, a good illustration of Isa. lx. 8. Their great numbers, and the compactness of their mass, literally looked like a cloud at a distance, and obscured the sun in their passage.' The prediction here has already, in part at least, been fulfilled. The rapid conversions in the time of the apostles accorded with this prediction. In numerous revivals of religion, also, has there been a fulfilment of it; and we are yet to anticipate a far more striking and glorious completion of it in the conversion of the heathen world to the Christian faith.

9. *Surely the isles.* On the meaning of the word ' isles ' in Isaiah, see Notes on ch. xli. 1. ¶ *Shall wait for me* (see Notes on ch. xli. 4). ¶ *And the ships of Tarshish* (see Notes on ch. ii. 16). The main idea here is clear. These ships were the principal vessels known to the Hebrews as employed in foreign commerce, and the prophet employs the name to denote ships in general that sailed to distant ports. They will be employed in importing the most valuable productions of distant climes to Zion, and in collecting those who should be converted to God; that is, the commerce of the world would be made tributary to religion, and the ships that sail to distant lands would be employed in advancing the cause of salvation. ¶ *First.* Among the first, in the first rank; they shall be among the most

10 And the sons of strangers shall *a* build up thy walls, and their kings shall minister unto thee : for in *b* my wrath I smote thee, but in my favour have I had mercy on thee.

11 Therefore thy gates shall be open *c* continually . they shall not be shut day nor night ; that *men* may bring unto thee the forces of the Gentiles, and *that* their kings *may be* brought.

a Zec.6.15.   *b* ch.57.17.   *c* Re.21.25.

active and useful agents in diffusing the knowledge of the truth. Twenty-five MSS. and the Syriac read it, ' As at the first.' Jarchi and Kimchi suppose it means, as at the first ; that is, as in the time of Solomon. But the idea is, that the ships which trade to the most distant regions will be among the principal instrumentalities employed in the conversion of the heathen world to Christianity. To some extent this has already been done. The servants of God have been borne already to almost every heathen land ; and the time *may* come when it shall be deemed an essential object of those engaged in foreign commerce to diffuse a knowledge of civilization, and of the arts of life ; of science, and of pure religion. ¶ *To bring thy sons from far.* Those who shall be converted from distant lands—as if they were to come personally and worship at Jerusalem (see Notes on ch. xlix. 22). ¶ *Unto the name of the* Lord *thy God.* Lowth renders this, ' Because of the name.' So the LXX. Διὰ τὸ ὄνομα, κ.τ.λ. The idea is, that all this wealth would be devoted to Jehovah, and employed in his service. ¶ *Because he hath glorified thee.* He has honoured thee by imparting to thee the true religion, and making me the means of diffusing it around the world.

10. *And the sons of strangers.* They who have been devoted to a foreign and a false religion shall become devoted to the true religion, and engage in the service of the true God. ¶ *Shall build up thy walls.* Jerusalem is represented as a ruined city. Her walls had been thrown down, and were lying prostrate. In restoring her to her former magnificence, strangers and foreigners would lend their cheerful aid. The idea is, that they would become tributary to the church, and esteem it a privilege to be engaged in any service, however laborious, that would promote its best

interests. ¶ *And their kings* (see Notes on ch. xlix. 23). ¶ *For in my wrath I smote thee.* Referring to the calamities which he had, from time to time, brought on Jerusalem (see ch. lvii. 17). ¶ *But in my favour* (see Notes on ch. liv. 8).

11. *Therefore thy gates shall be open continually.* The main idea here is, probably, that the accession from the heathen world, and the consequent influx of converts, would be so great, that there would be a necessity that the gates should never be closed. It is *possible*, also, that the prophet meant to describe that time as a period of security and peace. The gates of cities were closed in time of war, and at night, to guard them from danger. But in those times, such would be the prevalence of peace, and such would be the purposes for which the multitude of strangers would come from all parts of the world, that the gates might be left open, and the city unguarded at all times. The sense is—1. That there will be immense multitudes that shall enter the true church from the heathen world. 2. That the gospel will be *constantly* and *unceasingly* offered to men. The doors of the church shall at no time be closed. By day and by night, at all seasons and in all places, men may come and obtain salvation. None shall be excluded because the gates shall be closed upon them; none because they are strangers and have come from distant lands ; none because there will be no room ; none because the conflux shall be so great that the provisions of mercy will be exhausted. 3. It will be a time of safety when the world shall be brought under the influence and the dominion of the Prince of Peace. There will be no need of closing the gates of cities, or of building walls around them. There will be no need to guard against hostile armies or the intrusions of hordes of

12 For the nation and kingdom that will not serve thee shall perish; yea, *those* nations shall be utterly wasted.

---

banditti. There will be no need of guarding against the fraud, oppressions, and dishonest arts of other men. If the principles of the true religion everywhere prevailed, there would be no need of walls to cities, or gates, or bars; no need of ramparts, of ships of war, and of fortifications; no need of bolts and locks and iron chests to guard our property. *No true Christian needs to guard himself or his property against another true Christian.* No lock, no bolt, no wall, no gate, no iron safe has been made in order to guard *against* a man who is the sincere friend of the Redeemer. They are made to guard against wicked men; and when universal truth and righteousness prevail, they may be suffered to rust and rot for want of use. Should the principles of Christianity be everywhere diffused, the walls of all cities might be suffered to fall down; their gates to stand open till they should decay; ships of war to lie in the dock till they should sink to the bottom; forts and fleets to be dismantled; and the whole business of making locks and shackles, and of building prisons and manufacturing instruments of war, would come to an end. ¶ *That* men *may bring unto thee.* So many shall be coming with the wealth of the Gentiles, that the gates shall be continually open. ¶ *The forces of the Gentiles.* The wealth of the heathen (see Notes on ver. 5). ¶ *And* that *their kings may be brought.* Lowth renders this, 'That their kings may come pompously attended.' Noyes, 'May come with their retinues.' The Chaldee renders it, 'And their kings be brought bound,' or in chains. But the Hebrew word used here (נְהוּגִים) denotes simply that they would be led or conducted in any way; and the idea is, that they would be induced, by the force of truth, to come and devote themselves to the service of God. They might be expected, indeed, to come, as Lowth says, pompously attended, but this idea is not in the Hebrew text.

12. *For the nation and kingdom.* Perhaps this is given as a reason for what is said in the previous verse—that kings and their subjects should come to Zion and embrace the true religion, *because* if it were not done they would perish. This is certainly one reason why sinners hasten to embrace the Saviour; and when this truth becomes deeply impressed on a community, it is one of the means of a revival of religion. An apprehension of danger; a certain anticipation of ruin if the gospel is not embraced; a conviction that 'there is salvation in no other,' is often a means of leading men to seek the Saviour. ¶ *That will not serve thee.* That will not become the servant of the church of God:—that is, that will not promote its interests, obey its laws, and maintain the true religion. ¶ *Shall perish.* This is applied particularly here to a 'nation' and a 'kingdom.' The idea is, that no nation can flourish that does not obey the law of God, or where the worship of the true God is not maintained. History is full of affecting illustrations of this. The ancient republics and kingdoms fell because they had not the true religion. The kingdoms of Babylon, Assyria, Macedonia, and Egypt; the Roman empire, and all the ancient monarchies and republics, soon fell to ruin because they had not the salutary restraints of the true religion, and lacked the protection of the true God. France cast off the government of God in the Revolution, and was drenched in blood. It is a maxim of universal truth, that the nation which does not admit the influence of the laws and the government of God must be destroyed. No empire is strong enough to wage successful war with the great JEHOVAH; and sooner or later, notwithstanding all that human policy can do, corruption, sensuality, luxury, pride, and far-spreading vice, will expose a nation to his displeasure, and bring down the heavy arm of his vengeance. There is no truth of more vital interest to *this* nation (America) than this; no declaration in any ancient writing expressive of the course of events in this world, that hangs with more portentous interest over this re-

13 The glory of Lebanon *a* shall come unto thee, the fir-tree, the pine-tree, and the box together, to beautify *b* the place of my sanctuary; and I will make the place of my feet *c* glorious.

14 The sons also of them that

a Ho.14.6,7.   *b* Ps.96.6.   *c* Ps.132.7.

afflicted thee shall come bending unto thee, and all they that despised thee shall *d* bow themselves down at the soles of thy feet; and they shall call thee, The city of the LORD, The Zion *e* of the Holy One of Israel.

d Re.3.9.   *e* He.12.22.

public, than that 'THE NATION THAT WILL NOT SERVE GOD SHALL PERISH.' As a nation, we have nothing else to depend on but our public virtue, our intelligence, our respect for the laws of Heaven. *Our defence* is not to be in standing armies —but in God, as our living and ever-watchful protector and friend. *Our hope* is not in a vast navy, in strong ramparts, in frowning battlements, but in the favour of the Most High. No martial array, no strong fortresses, no line-of-battle-ships, can save a nation that has cast off the government of God, and that is distinguished for the violation of treaties and for oppression, bribery, and corruption. The nation that violates the Sabbath; that tramples on the rights of unoffending men and women; that disregards the most solemn compacts; and that voluntarily opens upon itself the floodgates of infidelity and vice, *must* expect to meet with the displeasure of the Almighty. And it is *as* true of an individual as it is of a nation. Of any human or angelic being; of any association or combination of men or angels that does not obey God, it is true that they shall be utterly destroyed.

13. *The glory of Lebanon.* The 'glory of Lebanon,' here means the trees that grew on Lebanon (see Notes on ch. xxxv. 2). ¶ *Shall come unto thee.* That is, thy beauty and glory will be as great as if those valuable trees were brought and planted around the temple. ¶ *The fir-tree* (see Notes on ch. xli. 19; lv. 13). ¶ *The box* (see also Notes on ch. xli. 19). ¶ *To beautify the place of my sanctuary.* The site of the temple, as if they were planted around it, and as if the magnificence of Lebanon was transferred there at once. The idea is, that the most valuable and glorious objects in distant nations would be consecrated to the service of the true God. ¶ *And I will*

make the place of my feet glorious. Lowth renders this, 'I will glorify the place whereon I rest my feet;' and he supposes that the *ark* is meant as the place on which God rested his feet as a footstool. In support of this, he appeals to Ps. xcix. 5, 'Worship at his footstool;' and 1 Chron. xxviii. 2. So Rosenmüller understands it, and appeals further to Ps. cxxxii. 7. Doubtless the main idea is, that the temple was regarded as the sacred dwelling-place of God— and that he means to say, that every place in his temple, even where, to keep up the figure, he rested his feet when he sat on the throne, would be filled with magnificence and glory.

14. *The sons of them that afflicted thee.* In the previous verses the prophet had said that strangers and foreigners would become tributary to the true religion. Here, to give variety and interest to the description, he says, that even the descendants of those who had oppressed them would become tributary to them, and acknowledge them as favoured by JEHOVAH. ¶ *Shall come bending unto thee.* Shall come to thee in a posture of humiliation and respect. In regard to the fulfilment of this, we may observe—1. That there was a partial fulfilment of it in the conquest of Babylon. The *sons,* the descendants of those who had destroyed Jerusalem, and led the Jews into captivity, were constrained to acknowledge them, and, under Cyrus, to reconduct them to the land of their fathers (see Notes on ch. xiv. 1, 2). 2. It has often occurred, in times of persecution, that the immediate descendants of the persecutors, and that too by means of the persecution, became converted to the true religion, and acknowledged the God of those whom they had persecuted to be the true God. 3. It often occurs in times when there is no open and public persecution. Many of those now in the church are the chil-

15 Whereas thou hast been *a*forsaken and hated, so that no man went through *thee*, I will make thee an eternal *c* excellency, a joy of many generations.

16 Thou *d* shalt also suck the milk of the Gentiles, and shalt suck the breast of kings : and thou shalt

a Ps.78.60,61.   *b* La.1.4.   *c* Re.3.12.

know that *e* I the LORD *am* thy Saviour and thy Redeemer, the Mighty One of Jacob.

17 For brass I will bring gold, and for iron I will bring silver, and for wood brass, and for stones iron : I will also make thy officers peace, and thine exactors righteousness.

d ch.66.11,12.   *e* ch.43.3.   *f* 2 Pe.3.13.

dren or descendants of those who had been the enemies of the gospel. They themselves did all that could be done, by their lives and examples, to train up their children in opposition to it. But the sovereign mercy of God interposed, and from such he selected heralds of salvation and preachers of righteousness to a lost world, or such as should become shining lights in the more obscure walks of the Christian life. ¶ *And all they that despised thee.* There shall yet be a universal acknowledgment of the true religion even in those nations that have spurned the gospel. This does not mean that *all* who have ever despised the true religion shall be converted and saved, but that there shall be a universal acknowledgement that it is of God, and that the church is under his care. See an explanation of this sentiment in the Notes on ch. xlv. 23. ¶ *At the soles of thy feet.* In a posture of the utmost reverence and submission (see Rev. iii. 9 ; comp. Notes on ch. xlix. 23). ¶ *And they shall call thee.* They shall honour thee as the favoured of the Lord ; as the abode of the true God (see ch. ii. 3). ¶ *The Zion*, &c. The Zion, or the royal court where the holy God that is worshipped in Israel dwells.

15. *Whereas thou hast been forsaken.* Heb. ' Instead of (תַּחַת) thy being forsaken,' *i.e.*, thy subsequent prosperity shall come in the place of thy being formerly forsaken. The forsaking here refers to the various calamities, persecutions, and trials, which she had been called to endure. ¶ *So that no man went through* thee. When the country was desolate and abandoned, so that no caravan passed from one part of it to another, or made it a thoroughfare in going to other lands (comp. Lam. i. 4 ; see Notes on ch. xxxiv. 10). ¶ *I will*

make thee an eternal excellency. Lowth, 'An everlasting boast.' Noyes, 'Glory.' I will make you for ever honoured or exalted, so that you shall no more be desolate and abased. ¶ *A joy of many generations.* A subject of joy from generation to generation ; *i.e.*, one age after another.

16. *Thou shalt suck the milk of the Gentiles.* This expression means, 'Whatever is valuable and rich which they possess shall contribute to your welfare.' The idea is the same substantially which occurs in the previous parts of the chapter, that the riches of the heathen world would become tributary to the advancement of the true religion. ¶ *And thou shalt suck the breast of kings.* The Chaldee renders this, ' And thou shalt be satisfied with the riches of the people, and shalt delight thyself with the spoil of kings.' The phrase to suck the breast *of kings* is unusual ; but the sense is simple and plain, that kings and their wealth should be made to contribute to sustain the church. See the sentiment explained in the Notes on ch. xlix. 23. ¶ *And thou shalt know.* By the protection which shall be extended to thee, and by the accession which shall be made to thee, thou shalt have full proof that JEHOVAH is thy protector and friend. The conversion of the heathen world shall demonstrate that JEHOVAH is the friend of his church and people.

17. *For brass I will bring gold.* This commences the description of the happy times when the Gentiles should be led to embrace the true religion, and when the wealth of the world would be consecrated to the service of the true God. The idea is, that all things would be changed for the better. The golden age should come ; and a change from the calamities to which reference had

18 Violence shall no more be heard in thy land, wasting nor destruction within thy borders : for thou shalt call thy walls *a* Salvation, and thy gates Praise,

been made by the prophet, would take place as great as if, in all purposes of life, gold should be used where brass is commonly used ; and silver where iron is commonly used ; and brass where wood is used ; and iron where stones are used. Calvin supposes, not improbably, that allusion is here made to the temple, and that, in describing the future glory of the church, the prophet says that the change would be as glorious as if, in all places where brass and iron and wood and stone had been used, gold and silver and brass and iron should be respectively used in their places. The Chaldee renders this, ' Instead of the brass which they took away from thee, O Jerusalem, I will bring gold ; and instead of the iron I will bring silver ; and instead of the wood, brass ; and instead of the stones, iron.' Jarchi, Kimchi, and Grotius, accord with this interpretation. But it is probably designed as a poetical description of the glory of the future age, and of the great changes which would take place in human society under the influence of the gospel. No one can doubt that the gospel produces these changes ; and that the changes of society caused by the gospel are as beautiful and striking as though gold and silver should be substituted for brass and iron, and brass and iron for wood and stone. Such changes shall yet take place everywhere on the earth ; and the world shall yet be beautified, enriched, and adorned by the prevalence of the true religion. ¶ *I will also make thy officers peace.* Thy officers shall be appointed to promote peace and shall secure it. The sense is, that wars would be ended, and that universal concord and harmony would prevail in the church under the guidance of those appointed to administer to its affairs (comp. ch. ii. 4 ; ix. 6). The word ' officers,' here denotes those who should be appointed to *superintend* the affairs of the church (from פָּקַד *pâkăd*, to visit, review, superintend, oversee), and refers here to all who should be appointed to *rule* in the church. The word itself may be applicable either to civil magistrates or to the ministers of religion. The LXX. render it," Ἄρχοντας —' Rulers,' and they translate the passage, ' I will give thy rulers in peace ' (ἐν εἰρήνη). ¶ *And thine exactors.* They who should *exact*, or collect tribute or taxes. The word from which the noun here used is derived (נֹגֵשׂ), means to urge, impel, drive—hence the noun ' taskmaster '—ἐργοδιώκτης (Ex. iii. 7 ; Job iii. 18) ; then to urge a debtor, to exact a debt ; then to rule or have dominion ; to appoint and exact taxes, &c. Here it refers to magistrates, and it means that they would be mild and equal in their exactions. ¶ *Righteousness.* They shall not lay unequal or oppressive burdens ; they shall not oppress in the collection of taxes. The idea is, that righteousness would prevail in every department of the church and the state.

18. *Violence shall no more be heard in thy land.* This is a most beautiful description of the peace and prosperity which would prevail in the times of the Messiah. If the gospel, in its purity, should prevail on earth, there would be no more scenes of violence and war. The battle-shout would be heard no more ; the cry of violence, the clangour of arms, would resound no more. The pure gospel of the Redeemer has never originated one war ; never produced one scene of bloodshed ; never once prompted to violence and strife. There has been no war in any age or in any land which the principles of the gospel, if acted on by both the contending nations, would not have prevented ; there have been no scenes of bloodshed which would not have been avoided if that had been suffered to control the hearts of men. And no one who believes the Bible to be a revelation from God, can doubt that the time *will* come when the mad passions of kings and nations shall be subdued, and when wars shall cease to be known except in the melancholy and disgraceful records of past events (comp. Notes on ch. ii. 4). ¶ *Wasting.* The waste of life and property ; the burning of cities, towns, and villages ; and the de-

19 The *a* sun shall be no more thy light by day ; neither for brightness shall the moon give light unto thee: but the LORD shall be unto thee an everlasting light, and thy God *b* thy glory.

20 Thy sun shall no more go down; neither shall thy moon withdraw itself : for the LORD shall be thine everlasting light, and the days of thy *c* mourning shall be ended.

a Re.21.23; 22.5.   *b* Zec.2.5.   *c* Re.21.4.

solation which spreads over farms and plantations on the march of a victorious enemy. ¶ *Nor destruction.* Heb. שֶׁבֶר —'Breaking.' The breaking or treading down caused by the march of a triumphant army. ¶ *In thy borders.* Within thy bounds or limits. Thy whole country shall be peace and prosperity; that is, wherever the gospel shall spread there shall be security and peace. ¶ *But thou shalt call thy walls Salvation.* Thou shalt live securely within thy walls, and shalt speak of them as furnishing protection or salvation. The time will come when the church shall have no reason to apprehend danger from abroad, and when all shall be peace within. ¶ *And thy gates Praise.* Because, says Grotius, those who are appointed to watch at their gates shall announce the approach of no enemy, but shall, with the highest security, celebrate the praises of God. Praise would be celebrated in all the places of public concourse, and perfect protection would be ascribed to all her walls ; that is, in the church there would be entire security, and everywhere the praises of God would be celebrated.

19. *The sun shall be no more.* A similar expression denoting the great prosperity and happiness of the church, occurs in ch. xxx. 26 (see Notes on that place). The language here is exceedingly beautiful, and the idea is plain. It is designed to foretell the great glory which would exist in the church under the Messiah ; a glory compared with which all that is furnished by the sun, moon, and stars, would be as nothing. Expressions similar to this, and probably derived from this, are used by John in describing the glory of heaven. ' And the city had no need of the sun, neither of the moon to shine in it ; for the glory of God did lighten it, and the Lamb is the light thereof ' (Rev. xxi. 23). ' And there shall be no night there ; and they need no candle, neither light of the sun ;

for the Lord God giveth them light' (Rev. xxii. 5). The idea is, the light and beauty of truth would be so great ; the Divine perfections shine forth so illustriously under the gospel, that the eye would be attracted to *that* light as superior to all the natural splendour of the sun and moon. All the wonders and beauties of the natural world would be lost in the superior brightness that would shine in the moral world. ¶ *Neither for brightness.* In order to give light ; or, with her brightness she shall not shine on the night. ¶ *Shall the moon give light unto thee.* The beauty of the moon shall be lost in the superior effulgence of the rays of truth. ¶ *But the LORD shall be unto thee.* He will furnish a revelation that will disclose far more of his perfections and his glory, and that will be far more valuable to thee as a light and guide, than all the splendour of the heavenly bodies. ¶ *And thy God thy glory.* The honour of the church shall be that it has the true God for its protector. Its joys shall be found, not in the objects of nature—the beauty of created things—but in the glory of the Divine perfections, and in the laws and plans of the Redeemer. His name, his attributes, his laws, his protecting care, constitute her main glory. It is an honour to the church to have *such* a God and Redeemer ; an honour to share his favour, and to be under his everwatchful eye. The glory of the church is not her wealth, her numbers, her influence, nor the rank and talent of her ministers and members ; it is the character of her sovereign Lord, and in his perfections it is right that she should exult and rejoice.

20. *Thy sun shall no more go down.* There shall be no total and long night of calamity, error, and sin. This is designed to describe the flourishing and glorious state of the church. It, of course, does not mean that there should be *no* times of calamity, no period of

21 Thy people also *shall be* all righteous ; [a] they [b] shall inherit tho land for ever, [c] the branch [d] of my planting, [e] the work [f] of my hands, that I may be glorified.

a ch.4.3; Re.21.27.   b Mat.5.3.   c ch.62.4.
d Jn.15.2.   e Ps.92.13.   f Ep.2.10.

ignorance, no scenes of persecution ; but it means that there should not be total night. Truth should reign on the earth, and there never would be a time when the light of salvation would be extinct. There never would be a time like that when Jerusalem was wholly destroyed, and a long total night came over the land. There never would be a time when the Sun of righteousness would not shine, or when the world would be wholly deprived of the illumination of his beams. The church would be perpetual. It would live through all changes, and survive all revolutions, and to the end of time the light of salvation would shine upon a darkened world. Since the Messiah came, the light of revelation has never been wholly withdrawn from the world, nor has there been a period in which total and absolute night has come over all the church of God. But the prophet, probably, referred to far more glorious times than have yet occurred. The period is coming when the light of salvation will shine upon the earth with unclouded and universal splendour, as if the sun having ascended to the meridian should stand there in a blaze of glory age after age ; when there shall be no alternation of day and night ; when the light shall not be obscured by clouds ; and when there shall be no eclipse of his glory. ¶ *Neither shall thy moon.* This language is poetic, and means that there would be no such obscurity in the church as there would be in the world should the sun and moon be withdrawn. Light and beauty unobscured would fill the whole heavens, and the darkness of night would be henceforward unknown. ¶ *Withdraw itself.* Heb. יֵאָסֵף—'Be collected,' that is, shall not be withdrawn, or shall not wane. The LXX. Οὐκ ἐκλείψει —'Shall not be eclipsed,' or shall not fail. ¶ *The days of thy mourning* (see Notes on ch. xxv. 8). The description here, therefore, is one of great glory and happiness in the church. That period will yet arrive ; and no friend of God and of the happiness of man can think of that time without praying most sin-

cerely that it may soon come, when the Sun of righteousness, in the fulness of his glory, shall ascend to the meridian, and stand there without one obscuring cloud, and pour the splendour of the noontide beams all over a darkened world. Some of the ideas in this chapter, descriptive of the glorious times of the gospel, have been beautifully versified by Pope in his *Messiah :*—

Rise, crown'd with light, imperial Salem, rise!
Exalt thy tow'ry head, and lift thy eyes!
See a long race thy spacious courts adorn;
See future sons and daughters yet unborn,
In crowding ranks on every side arise,
Demanding life, impatient for the skies!
See barbarous nations at thy gates attend,
Walk in thy light, and in thy temple bend:
See thy bright altars throng'd with prostrate kings,
And heap'd with products of Sabean springs!
For thee Idumea's spicy forests blow,
And seeds of gold in Ophir's mountains glow;
See heaven its sparkling portals wide display,
And break upon them in a flood of day !
No more the rising sun shall gild the morn,
Nor evening Cynthia fill her silver horn;
But lost, dissolved in thy superior rays,
One tide of glory, one unclouded blaze,
O'erflow thy courts; the light himself shall shine
Reveal'd, and God's eternal day be thine!
The seas shall waste, the skies in smoke decay,
Rocks fall to dust, and mountains melt away;
But fix'd his word, his saving power remains ;
Thy realm for ever lasts, thine own Messiah reigns !

21. *Thy people also* shall be *all righteous* (see Notes on ch. iv. 2). ¶ *They shall inherit the land for ever* (see Notes on ch. xlix. 8; liv. 3; comp. ch. lxv. 9; Matt. v. 5). ¶ *The branch of my planting.* On the meaning of the word *branch*, see Notes on ch. xi. 1; xiv. 19. Here it means a *scion* or shoot which JEHOVAH had planted, and which had sprung up under his culture. Grotius supposes it means *posterity.* The idea seems to be, that they would inherit the land and all which would grow up under the culture of the hand of JEHOVAH. ¶ *The work of my hands.* The *language* here is taken from the cultivation of the land of Canaan ; but the sense is, that the church would inherit all that God had done for its welfare. Applied to the work of redemption, it means that the result

22 A little one shall become a thousand, and a small one a strong nation : I the LORD will hasten it in his time.

CHAPTER LXI.

ANALYSIS.

THIS chapter, in its design and structure, is intimately connected with the preceding. That it refers to the Messiah will be shown in the Notes on ver. 1–3, and the main scope and design of the chapter is to show some of the glorious results of his coming.

The chapter may be regarded as divided into the following parts, namely :—

I. The public address or proclamation of the Messiah, stating the design for which he had been appointed to his office, and the consolatory nature of his message (1–3).

II. The happy *effects* and privileges of his coming (4–9). 1. The effects of his coming in restoring the old wastes, and in building up the long-fallen ruins (4, 5). (1.) The aid of others would be called in for this. (2.) The sons of foreigners would become tributary to them, and feed their flocks and plough their fields, and dress their vines—that is, the heathen world would become subject to the church. 2. The *privileges*

---

of all the labours, self-denials, and sacrifices of the Redeemer, become the inheritance of the church. The comforts, joys, hopes, consolations of his people are the fruit of his self-denial, ' the work of his hands,' and they are permitted to enjoy it all—as if God should cultivate a fruitful field and give the avails entirely to them. ¶ *That I may be glorified* (see ch. xlix. 3 ; lxi. 3 ; Notes on ch. xlii. 8 ; xliii. 7). God would be glorified in having made so ample provision for their welfare, and in their being made happy by him. He is always glorified when others enjoy the fruits of his benevolence, and when they are made pure and happy as the result of his purposes and plans.

22. *A little one shall become a thousand.* There shall be a great increase, as if one, and that the smallest, should be multiplied to a thousand. The idea is, that the people, then small in number, would be greatly increased by the accession of the Gentile world. Lowth and Noyes render this, ' The little one.' Grotius, ' The least one.' So the LXX. 'Ο ὀλιγιστός. ¶ *I the* LORD *will hasten it in his time.* Noyes, ' Its time.' Lowth, ' Due time.' LXX. ' I will do it in the proper time' (κατα καιρόν). The sense is, that this would be done at the proper time—called, in Gal. iv. 4, ' the fulness of time.' There was a proper season when this was to be accomplished. There were important preparations to be made before it could be done. The nations, under the Divine arrangement, were to be put into a proper position to receive the Messiah. He was not to come until—1. The experiment had been fairly made to show how

weak and feeble man was without a revelation—to show that philosophy, and learning, and the policy of statesmen, could do nothing effectual for the salvation of men. 2. He was not to come until the world should be at peace, and until there would be facilities for the rapid propagation of religion in all lands. 3. Nor was he to come until all that had been said in prophecy should be fulfilled —until all the circumstances should combine, which had been foretold as favourable to the introduction of the reign of the Messiah. But *when* that period should arrive, then the LORD would ' hasten' it. There would be no unnecessary delay ; none which the circumstances of the case did not call for. So it will be in the universal spread of the gospel referred to in this chapter. When the world shall be moulded into a proper state to welcome it ; when the nations are *prepared* to receive it and profit by it ; then the universal propagation shall be *hastened*, and a nation shall be born in a day (see Notes on ch. lxvi. 8). Meantime, for the coming of that day we should pray and labour. By the diffusion of truth ; by schools ; by the spread of the Bible ; by preaching ; by the translation of the Word of God into every language ; by establishing the press in all the strong points of Pagan influence ; by placing missionaries in all the holds of power in the heathen world ; and by training up many to enter into the harvest, the Christian world should prepare for the universal conversion of the world to God. In due time it shall be hastened, and ' he that shall come, will come, and will not tarry ' (Heb. x. 37).

which would result from his coming (6–9). (1.) *absolutely*. They would be named friends of God, and enjoy the wealth of the heathen world. (2.) *Comparatively*. Their state would be far more than a recompence for all they had suffered. (3.) In the honour which would be put upon them. Their name would be known abroad, and their children be honoured as the blessed of the Lord.

III. The occasion of rejoicing which the church would have in this (10, 11). 1. In the beauty and honour with which she would be clothed. 2. In the abundant increase of righteousness and purity.

CHAPTER LXI.

1. *The Spirit of the Lord* God. Heb. The Spirit of the Lord Jehovah.' The Chaldee renders this, 'The prophet said, the spirit of prophecy from the presence of Jehovah God is upon me.' The Syriac, 'The Spirit of the Lord God.' The LXX. Πνεῦμα Κυρίου—' The Spirit of the Lord,' omitting the word *adonai* (אֲדֹנָי). So Luke quotes it in ch. iv. 18. That this refers to the Messiah is abundantly proved by the fact that the Lord Jesus expressly applied it to himself (see Luke iv. 21). Rosenmüller, Gesenius, and some others, suppose that it refers to Isaiah himself, and that the idea is, that the prophet proclaims his commission as authorized to administer consolation to the suffering exiles in Babylon. It cannot be denied that the language is such as may be applied in a subordinate sense to the office of the prophet, and that the work of the Redeemer is here described in terms derived from the consolation and deliverance afforded to the long-suffering exiles. But in a much higher sense it refers to the Messiah, and received an entire completion only as applied to him and to his work. Even Grotius, who has been said to 'find Christ nowhere in the Old Testament,' remarks, 'Isaiah here speaks of himself, as the Chaldee observes; but in him we see not an obscure image of Christ.' Applied to the Redeemer, it refers to the time when, having been baptized and set apart to the work of the Mediatorial office, he began publicly to preach (see Luke iv. 21). The phrase ' the Spirit of Jehovah is upon me,' refers to the fact that he had been publicly consecrated to his work by the Holy Spirit descending on him at his baptism (Matt. iii. 16; John i.

THE *a* Spirit of the Lord God *is* upon me ; *b* because the Lord hath *c* anointed me to preach good tidings unto the meek : he hath sent me to bind up the brokenhearted, *d* to proclaim liberty *e* to the captives, and the opening of the prison to *them that are f* bound;

a Lu.4.16-21.　　　　*b* Jn.1.32; 3.34.
c Ps.45.7.　　　　　　*d* Ps.147.3.
e Jn.3.31,6.　　　　　*f* Ro.7.23-25.

32), and that the Spirit of God had been imparted to him ' without measure ' to endow him for his great office (John iii. 34; see Notes on ch. xi. 2). ¶ *Because the* Lord *hath anointed me*. The word rendered 'hath anointed' (מָשַׁח *mâshâkh*), is that from which the word *Messiah* is derived (see Notes on ch. xlv. 1). Prophets and kings were set apart to their high office, by the ceremony of pouring oil on their heads ; and the idea here is that God had set apart the Messiah for the office which he was to bear, and had abundantly endowed him with the graces of which the anointing oil was an emblem. The same language is used in reference to the Messiah in Ps. xlv. 7 (comp. Heb. i. 9). ¶ *To preach good tidings*. On the meaning of the word (בָּשַׂר) here rendered ' to preach good tidings,' see Notes on ch. lii. 7. The LXX. render it, Εὐαγγελίσασθαι—' To evangelize,' to preach the gospel. ¶ *Unto the meek*. The word rendered ' meek ' (עֲנָוִים) properly denotes the afflicted, the distressed, the needy. The word ' meek ' means those who are *patient* in the reception of injuries, and stands opposed to revengeful and irascible. This is by no means the sense of the word here. It refers to those who were borne down by calamity in any form, and would be particularly applicable to those who had been sighing in a long captivity in Babylon. It is not improperly rendered by the LXX. by the word πτωχοῖς, ' poor,' and in like manner by Luke (iv. 18); and the idea is, that the Redeemer came to bring a joyful message to those who were oppressed and borne down by the evils of poverty and calamity (comp. Matt. xi. 5). ¶ *To bind up the brokenhearted* (see Notes on ch. i. 6). The broken-hearted are those who are deeply afflicted and distressed on any account. It may be either on account of their sins, or of captivity and oppression, or of the loss of relations and friends. The Redeemer came that he might apply the balm of consolation to all such hearts, and give them joy and peace. A similar form of expression occurs in Ps. cxlvii. 3:

He healeth the broken in heart,
And bindeth up their wounds.

¶ *To proclaim liberty to the captives.* This evidently is language which is taken from the condition of the exiles in their long captivity in Babylon. The Messiah would accomplish a deliverance for those who were held under the captivity of sin similar to that of releasing captives from long and painful servitude. The gospel does not at once, and by a mere exertion of power, open prison doors, and restore captives to liberty. But it accomplishes an effect analogous to this: it releases the *mind* captive under sin; and it will finally open all prison doors, and by preventing *crime* will prevent the necessity of prisons, and will remove all the sufferings which are now endured in confinement as the consequence of crime. It may be remarked further, that the word here rendered 'liberty' (דְּרוֹר *děrōr*) is a word which is properly applicable to the year of Jubilee, when all were permitted to go free (Lev. xxv. 10): ' And ye shall hallow the fiftieth year, and proclaim liberty (דְּרוֹר) throughout all the land unto all the inhabitants thereof.' So in Jer. xxxiv. 8, 9, it is used to denote the manumission of slaves: 'To proclaim liberty (דְּרוֹר) unto them; that every man should let his man-servant, and every man his maid-servant, being an Hebrew, or an Hebrewess, go free.' So also ver. 15, 16, of the same chapter. So also in Ezek. xlvi. 17, it is applied to the year in which the slave was by law restored to liberty. Properly, therefore, the word has reference to the freedom of those who are held in bondage, or to servitude; and it may be implied that it was to be a part of the purpose of the Messiah to proclaim, ultimately, universal freedom, and to restore all men to their just rights. If

this is the sense—and I see no reason to doubt it—while the main thing intended was that he should deliver men from the inglorious servitude of sin, it also means, that the gospel would contain principles inconsistent with the existence of slavery, and would ultimately produce universal emancipation. Accordingly it is a matter of undoubted fact that its influence was such that in less than three centuries it was the means of abolishing slavery throughout the Roman empire; and no candid reader of the New Testament can doubt that if the principles of Christianity were universally followed, the last shackle would soon fall from the slave. Be the following facts remembered—1. *No man ever made another originally a slave under the influence of Christian principle. No man ever kidnapped another, or sold another,* BECAUSE *it was done in obedience to the laws of Christ.* 2. No Christian ever manumitted a slave who did not feel that in doing it he was obeying the spirit of Christianity, and who did not have a more quiet conscience on that account. 3. No man doubts that if freedom were to prevail everywhere, and all men were to be regarded as of equal civil rights, it would be in accordance with the mind of the Redeemer. 4. Slaves are made in violation of all the precepts of the Saviour. The work of kidnapping and selling men, women, and children; of tearing them from their homes, and confining them in the pestilential holds of ships on the ocean, and of dooming them to hard and perpetual servitude, *is not the work to which the Lord Jesus calls his disciples.* 5. Slavery, in fact, cannot be maintained without an incessant violation of the principles of the New Testament. To keep men in ignorance; to withhold from them the Bible; to prevent their learning to read; to render nugatory the marriage contract, or to make it subject to the will of a master; to deprive a man of the avails of his own labour without his consent; to make him or his family subject to a removal against his will; to prevent parents from training up their children according to their own views of what is right; to fetter and bind the intellect and shut up the avenues to knowledge

2 To proclaim the acceptable year *a* of the LORD, and the day of

a Le.25.9,&c.; 2 Co.6.2.

vengeance *b* of our God ; to comfort all that *c* mourn.

b 2 Th.1.9. *c* Mar.5.4.

as a necessary means of continuing the system ; and to make men dependent wholly on others whether they shall hear the gospel or be permitted publicly to embrace it, is everywhere deemed essential to the existence of slavery, and is demanded by all the laws which rule over the regions of a country cursed with this institution. In the whole work of slavery, from the first capture of the unoffending person who is made a slave to the last act which is adopted to secure his bondage, there is an incessant and unvarying trampling on the laws of Jesus Christ. Not one thing is done to make and keep a slave in accordance with any command of Christ ; not one thing which would be done if his example were followed and his law obeyed. Who then can doubt that he came ultimately to proclaim freedom to all captives, and that the prevalence of his gospel will yet be the means of universal emancipation ? (comp. Notes on ch. lviii. 6). ¶ *And the opening of the prison.* This language also is taken from the release of those who had been confined in Babylon as in a prison ; and the idea is, that the Redeemer would accomplish a work for sinful and suffering men like throwing open the doors of a prison and bidding the man who had been long lying in a dungeon to go free. On the grammatical structure of the verb here rendered ' opening of the prison ' (פְּקַח־קוֹחַ), Gesenius (*Lex.*) and Rosenmüller may be consulted. According to Gesenius, it should be read as one word. So many MSS. read it. It occurs nowhere else. It means here *deliverance.* The LXX. render it, ' And sight to the blind,' which is followed by Luke. The *sentiment* which is found in the LXX. and in Luke, is a correct one, and one which elsewhere occurs in the prophets (see Isa. xxxiv. 5) : and as the sentiment was correct, the Saviour did not deem it necessary to state that this was not the literal translation of the Hebrew. Or more properly the Saviour in the synagogue at Nazareth (Luke iv. 19) used the Hebrew, and when Luke came to record it, he quoted

it as he found it in the version then in common use. This was the common practice with the writers of the New Testament. The Evangelist wrote probably for the Hellenists, or the Greek Jews, who commonly used the Septuagint version, and he quotes that version as being the one with which they were familiar. The sense is not materially varied whether the Hebrew be followed, or the version by the LXX. The Arabic version agrees nearly with the Evangelist. Horne (*Introduction*, ii. 403) is of opinion that the Hebrew formerly contained more than we now find in the manuscripts and the printed editions. Of that, however, I think there is no good evidence.

2. *To proclaim the acceptable year of the* LORD (see Notes on ch. xlix. 8). There is probably an allusion here to the year of Jubilee, when the trumpet was blown, and liberty was proclaimed throughout all the land (so Lev. xxv. 9, 10). In like manner the Messiah would come to proclaim universal liberty —liberty to all the world from the degrading servitude of sin. The time of his coming would be a time when JEHOVAH would be pleased to proclaim through him universal emancipation from this ignoble bondage, and to restore to all the privilege of being the freedmen of the Lord. ¶ *And the day of vengeance of our God* (see Notes on ch. xxxiv. 8). This is language adapted to the deliverance from Babylon. The rescue of his people would be attended with vengeance on their enemies. This was not quoted by the Saviour in his discourse at Nazareth, or if quoted, the fact is not recorded by Luke (see Luke iv. 19). The *text* which the Saviour took then as the foundation of his discourse (Luke iv. 21), seems to have ended with the clause before this. It is not to be inferred, however, that he did not consider the subsequent expressions as referring to himself, but it was not necessary to his purpose to quote them. Regarded as applicable to the Redeemer and his preaching, this doubtless refers to the fact that his coming

3 To appoint unto them that mourn in Zion, to give unto them beauty for ashes, the oil of joy for *ᵃ*mourning, the garment of

praise for the spirit of heaviness: that they might be called Trees of righteousness, The planting *ᵇ*of the LORD, that he might be glorified.

a Jn.16.20.

b ch.60.21.

would be attended with vengeance on his foes. It is a great truth, manifest everywhere, that God's coming forth at any time to deliver his people is attended with vengeance on his enemies. So it was in the destruction of Idumea —regarded as the general representative of all the foes of God (see Notes on ch. xxxiv., xxxv.) ; so it was in the deliverance from Egypt — involving the destruction of Pharaoh and his host ; so in the destruction of Babylon and the deliverance of the captives there. So in like manner it was in the destruction of Jerusalem ; and so it will be at the end of the world (Matt. xxv. 31–46 ; 2 Thess. i. 7–10). ¶ *To comfort all that mourn.* The expression, 'all that mourn,' may refer either to those who mourn over the loss of earthly friends and possessions, or to those who mourn over sin. In either case the gospel has afforded abundant sources of consolation (see Notes on ch. xxv. 8).

3. *To appoint unto them.* Heb. 'To place ;' *i.e.*, to place happiness before them ; to give them joy and consolation. ¶ *That mourn in Zion* (see Notes on ch. i. 8). The mourners in Zion mean those who dwelt in Jerusalem ; then all those who are connected with the church of God—his poor and afflicted people. ¶ *To give unto them beauty for ashes.* In the Hebrew there is here a beautiful paronomasia, which cannot be transferred to our language—פְּאֵר תַּחַת אֵפֶר. The word rendered 'beauty' (פְּאֵר) means properly a head-dress, turban, tiara, or diadem ; and the idea is, that the Redeemer would impart to his mourning people such an ornament instead of the ashes which in their grief they were accustomed to cast on their heads. For the use of the word, see Isa. iii. 20, and ver. 10 of this chapter ; Ex. xxxix. 29 ; Ezek. xxiv. 17–23. It was common among the Orientals to cast dust and ashes upon their heads in time of mourning, and as expressive of their grief (comp. Notes on ch. lvii. 5 ;

2 Sam. xiii. 19). ¶ *The oil of joy.* The oil of joy denotes that which was symbolical or expressive of joy. Oil or ointment was employed on occasions of festivity and joy (see Notes on ch. lvii. 9) ; but its use was abstained from in times of public calamity or grief (see 2 Sam. xiv. 2). ¶ *The garment of praise.* That is, the garment or clothing which shall be expresive of praise or gratitude instead of that which shall indicate grief. ¶ *For the spirit of heaviness.* Instead of a heavy, burdened, and oppressed spirit. The word used here (כֵּהָה), usually means faint, feeble, weak (see Notes on ch. xlii. 3). It is applied to a lamp about to go out (ch. xlii. 3) ; to eyes bedimmed, or dull (1 Sam. iii. 2) ; to a faint or pale colour (Lev. xiii. 39). Here it denotes those of a faint and desponding heart. These expressions are figurative, and are taken from the custom which prevailed more in Oriental countries than elsewhere—and which is founded in nature—of expressing the emotions of the mind by the manner of apparel. These customs are stated in the book of Judith. She 'pulled off the sackcloth which she had on, and put off the garments of her widowhood, and washed her body all over with water, and anointed herself with precious ointment, and braided the hair of her head, and put on a tire upon it (Gr. mitre), and put on her garments of gladness wherewith she was clad during the life of Manasses her husband. And she took sandals upon her feet, and put about her her bracelets, and her chains, and her rings, and her ear-rings, and all her ornaments, and decked herself bravely to allure the eyes of all men that should see her' (ch. x. 3, 4). ¶ *That they might be called.* That is, those who had mourned in Zion. ¶ *Trees of righteousness.* In the Heb. 'Oaks,' or terebinth trees. By their being oaks of righteousness is meant men distinguished for righteousness or justice. The LXX. render it,

4 And they shall build *a* the old wastes, they shall raise up the former desolations, and they shall repair the waste cities, the desolations of many generations.

5 And strangers shall stand and feed your flocks, and the sons of

the alien *shall be* your plowmen and your vine-dressers.

6 But ye shall be named the priests *b* of the LORD; *men* shall call you the *c* ministers of our God: ye shall eat the riches of the Gentiles, and in their glory shall you boast yourselves.

a ch.58.12.　　*b* Ex.19.6; 1 Pe.2.5,9; Re.1.6.
c Eze.44.11; Ep.4.11,12.

Γϵνϵαὶ—' Generations ;' Jerome, *Fortes* —' Strong ;' the Chaldee, ' Princes ;' the Syriac, ' Rams ;' but the word properly denotes the oak, or the terebinth tree—a lofty, strong, and magnificent tree. It is not uncommon to represent men by trees (see ch. i. 2.), 30; Ps. xcii. 12–14):

The righteous shall flourish like the palm-tree;
He shall grow like a cedar in Lebanon,
Those that be planted in the house of the Lord,
Shall flourish in the courts of our God.
They shall still bring forth fruit in old age;
They shall be fat and flourishing.

See also the beautiful description in Ps. i. 3, and in Jer. xvii. 8. The idea here is, that they who had been oppressed and borne down by calamity and by a sense of sin, would become vigorous and strong; and would be such as aptly to be compared to majestic trees with far-spreading branches—an image everywhere of that which is truly beautiful. ¶ *The planting of the* LORD. Those whom JEHOVAH had truly planted; that is, those who were under his care and culture (see Notes on ch. lx. 21). The same figure is used by the Saviour. ' Every plant which my heavenly Father hath not planted shall be rooted up' (Matt. xv. 13). ¶ *That he might be glorified* (see Notes on ch. lx. 21).

4. *And they shall build the old wastes* (see Notes on ch. lviii. 12).

5. *And strangers shall stand* (see Notes on ch. xiv. 1, 2 ; lx. 10). ¶ *And feed your flocks*. The keeping of flocks constituted a very considerable part of the husbandry of those who dwelt in Palestine. Of course, any considerable prosperity of a spiritual nature would be well represented by an accession of foreigners, who should come to relieve them in their toil. It is not necessary to suppose that this is to be taken literally, nor that it should be so spiritualized as to suppose that the prophet

refers to churches and their pastors, and to the fact, that those churches would be put under the care of pastors from among the heathen. The idea is, that it would be a time of signal spiritual prosperity, and when the accession would be as great and important *as if* foreigners were to come in among a people, and take the whole labour of attending their flocks and cultivating their fields. ¶ *Your ploughmen*. Heb. אִכָּר, *'ikkâr*, from which probably is derived the Greek ἀγρός; the Gothic *akr;* the German *acker;* and the English *acre*. It means properly a digger or cultivator of the soil, or husbandman (Jer. li. 26; Amos v. 16). ¶ *And vine-dressers*. The sense here accords with that which has been so repeatedly said before, that the heathen world would yet become tributary to the church (see Notes on ch. lx. 5–7, 9, 10).

6. *But ye shall be named*. The idea here literally is, ' There will be no need of your engaging in the business of agriculture. All that will be done by others; and you, as ministers of God, may engage wholly in the duties of religion. The world shall be tributary to you, and you shall enjoy the productions of all lands ; and you may, therefore, devote yourselves exclusively to the service of JEHOVAH, as a kingdom of priests.' A similar promise occurs in Ex. xix. 6 : ' And ye shall be unto me a kingdom of priests, and an holy nation.' The idea is, that there would be a degree of spiritual prosperity, as great *as if* they were permitted to enjoy all the productions of other climes ; *as if* all menial and laborious service were performed by others ; and *as if* they were to be entirely free from the necessity of toil, and were permitted to devote themselves exclusively to the services of religion. ¶ *Ye shall eat the riches of the*

7 For your shame you *shall have* double,*ᵃ* and *for* confusion they shall rejoice in their portion : therefore in their land they shall possess the double ; everlasting joy shall be unto them.

8 For I the LORD love judgment, I hate robbery for burnt-offering ; and I will direct their work in truth, and I will make an everlasting covenant *ᵇ* with them.

a ch.40.2; Zec.9.12.   b ch.55.3; Ps.50.5.

Gentiles (see Notes on ch. lx. 5–11). ¶ *And in their glory.* In what constitutes their glory, or what they regard as valuable; that is, their wealth, their talents, and their power. ¶ *Shall you boast yourselves ?* There has been considerable variety of interpretation in regard to the meaning of the word here used. Jerome renders it, *Et in gloria earum superbietis.* The LXX. 'In their wealth ye shall be admired.' (Θαυμασθήσεσθε). The Chaldee and Syriac render it, 'In their splendour ye shall glory.' The word used is יָמַר, *yâmăr.* It occurs nowhere else, it is believed, except in Jer. ii. 11, *twice,* where it is rendered 'changed.' 'Hath a nation *changed* (הַהֵימִיר) their gods, which are yet no gods? But my people have changed (הֵמִיר) their glory for that which doth not profit.' In the passage before us, it is used in Hithpael, and means properly *to exchange one's self with any one.* Here it means, ' In their splendour we shall take their places,' *i.e.,* we shall enjoy it in their stead. We shall avail ourselves of it *as if* we were to enter into their possessions, and *as if* it were our own. The sense is, it shall come to enrich and adorn the church. It shall *change places,* and shall all belong to the people of God—in accordance with that which has been so often said by Isaiah, that the wealth of the world would become tributary to the church.

7. *For your shame.* That is, instead of the reproach and humiliation which you have been called to experience. ¶ *You* shall have *double.* A double inheritance or reward (see Notes on ch. xl. 2). ¶ *And* for *confusion.* The word 'confusion' here means the same as a blush of shame, and refers to the scenes of humiliation and sorrow which the nation had passed through on account of its sins. ¶ *They shall rejoice.* There is here a change from the second to the third person—a change which is

not unfrequent in Isaiah. The same persons, however, are intended. ¶ *In their portion.* That is, you shall be permitted to rejoice in the augmented privileges which you shall enjoy. They will be more than a compensation for all the calamities which you have been called to endure. ¶ *Therefore in their land.* This is to be regarded as addressed to the exiles in Babylon, and the promise is, that the people of God would be restored again to their own land, and to more than their former privileges and blessings there. ¶ *The double.* Double of what they formerly possessed ; that is, their blessings would be greatly increased and multiplied. Applied to the times of the Messiah, to which the prophet undoubtedly refers, it means that the privileges of the friends of God would be far greater than had been enjoyed even in the most favoured times under the former dispensation. ¶ *Everlasting joy* (see Notes on ch. xxxv. 10).

8. *For I the* LORD *love judgment.* That is, ' I shall delight in rendering to my people what is right. It is right that they should enjoy my protection, and be favoured with the tokens of my kindness. Loving justice and right, therefore, I will confer on them the privileges and blessings which they *ought* to enjoy, and which will be a public expression of my favour and love.' ¶ *I hate robbery for burnt-offering.* There has been great variety in the interpretation of this phrase. Lowth renders it, ' Who hate rapine and iniquity.' Noyes, ' I hate rapine and iniquity.' Jerome, as in our translation, *Et odio habens rapinam in holocausto.* The LXX. Μισῶν ἁρπάγματα ἐξ ἀδικίας— ' Hating the spoils of injustice.' The Chaldee, ' Far from before me be deceit and violence.' The Syriac, ' I hate rapine and iniquity.' This variety of interpretation has arisen from the different views taken of the Hebrew בְּעוֹלָה.

9 And their seed shall be known among the Gentiles, and their offspring among the people : all that see them shall acknowledge them, that they *are* the seed *which* the LORD hath blessed.

10 I will greatly rejoice *a* in the LORD, my soul shall be joyful in my God : for he hath clothed me with the garments of salvation, he hath covered me with the robe of righteousness, *b* as a ¹ bridegroom decketh *himself* with ornaments, and as a bride adorneth *c herself* with her jewels.

a Ne.8.10; Hab.3.17,18; Ro.14.17.　　b Re. 19.8.
1 *as a priest.*　　　c Re.21.2.

The Syriac evidently prefixed the conjunction, ן *and,* instead of the preposition ב, *with* or *for;* and, perhaps, also the LXX. so read it. But this change, though slight, is not necessary in order to give a consistent rendering to the passage. The *connection* does not necessarily lead us to suppose that any reference would be made to 'burnt-offering,' and to the improper manner in which such offerings were made ; but the idea is rather, that God hated rapine *and* sin ; he hateth such acts as those by which his people had been removed from their land, and subjected to the evils of a long and painful captivity. And this is undoubtedly the sense of the passage. The Hebrew word עֹלָה, usually without the ן, means properly a holocaust, or that which is *made to ascend* (from עָלָה, *to ascend*) from an altar. But the word here is the construct form for עַוְלָה, *evil, wickedness;* whence our word *evil* (see Job xxiv. 20 ; Ps. cvii. 42). And the sense here is, 'I hate rapine or plunder (גֶּזֶל) *with* iniquity ;' that is, accompanied, as it always is, with iniquity and sin. And hating that as I do, I will vindicate my people who have been plundered in this way ; and who have been borne into captivity, accompanied with deeds of violence and sin. ¶ *And I will direct their work in truth.* Literally, ' I will give them work in truth or faithfulness;' that is, I will give them the reward of their work faithfully. They shall be amply recompensed for all that they have done and suffered in my cause. ¶ *And I will make* (see Notes on ch. lv. 3).

9. *And their seed.* The figure here is taken from the feelings of a parent who desires his children to be esteemed, and who regards it as an honour that they become so distinguished that their fame extends to distant lands. ¶ *Shall be known.* Shall be distinguished or honoured. For this use of the word 'known,' see Ps. lxvii. 2 ; lxxvi. 1; lxxix. 10. ¶ *And their offspring* (see Notes on ch. xlviii. 19). The Chaldee and the Syriac render this, ' Their children's children.' The sense is, that the true friends of the church shall be everywhere honoured. Distant lands shall be acquainted with them, and shall be disposed to show them distinguished respect. ¶ *Among the people.* The people of distant lands. ¶ *All that see them shall acknowledge them.* The time shall come when the true friends of the Redeemer will be universally honoured. They shall be regarded as the favoured of the Lord; and instead of being persecuted and despised, the nations of the earth will regard them as worthy of their confidence and esteem.

10. *I will greatly rejoice in the* LORD. This is the language of the prophet in the name of the church ; or, as Vitringa supposes, the language of a chorus introduced here by the prophet. The Chaldee regards it as the language of Jerusalem, and renders it, ' Jerusalem said, I will surely rejoice in the LORD.' The sentiment is, that the prosperity and enlargement of Zion is an occasion of joy, and should lead to thanksgiving and praise. The phrase, ' I will rejoice *in the Lord,*' means that the joy would arise from the view of the faithfulness and perfections of JEHOVAH manifested in the redemption of his people. See similar expressions of joy in the song of Mary (Luke i. 46, 47). ¶ *For he hath clothed me with the garments of salvation.* That is, Jerusalem or the church. ¶ *He hath covered me with the robe of righteousness.* The word rendered 'robe' here means mantle, or a large and loose garment thrown over the other parts of the dress. Such

11 For as the earth bringeth forth her bud, and as the garden causeth the things that are sown in it to spring forth ; so the Lord God will cause righteousness *a* and praise *b* to spring forth before all the nations.

a Ps.72.3; 85.11.   *b* ch.62.7.

CHAPTER LXII.

ANALYSIS.

The same general subject is pursued in this chapter which has been presented in the chapters which have gone before. The scope of the chapter is *consolatory,* and the design is to furnish such assurances of the Divine favour towards the afflicted people of God, as would uphold and comfort them in their trials. The language is such as would be addressed to the exiles in Babylon, but the main reference is undoubtedly to the times of the Messiah. The chapter may be conveniently regarded as comprising the following portions :

I. A speaker is introduced saying that he would have no rest until Zion should rise and obtain restoration from her degradation (1–5). This portion contains assurances of the Divine favour, and a promise of the future restoration and glory of Jerusalem. Who this speaker is, will be considered in ver. 1. The following are the assurances of the speaker. 1. He would give himself no peace until splendour and glory should spread over Zion (1). 2. The Gentiles would partake of the blessings conferred on Zion, and kings would come and unite with her (2). 3. Zion would be as beautiful and glorious as a royal crown in the hand of Jehovah (3). 4. She would be no more desolate and forsaken (4). 5. Jehovah would delight in Zion as a young married man delights in his bride (5).

II. The speaker says that he had set watchmen on the walls of Zion, and they are commanded to give him no rest—to be urgent and

garments are for protection and for ornament, and the image is that of the church defended and ornamented by God (see Notes on ch. xlix. 18). ¶ *As a bridegroom decketh* himself. Marg. ' As a priest.' The Hebrew is, ' As a bridegroom adorns himself as a priest' (יְכַהֵן) ; that is, as he makes splendid his head-dress in the manner of a priest. ¶ *With ornaments* (פְּאֵר). With a tiara, head-dress, diadem. See the word explained in ver. 3. The LXX. render it, Μίτραν—' Mitre.' The allusion is to the dress of the Jewish high-priest when he discharged the functions of his office, and particularly to the mitre and the plate or crown of gold which he wore in front of it (Ex. xxix. 6). It is not easy to give full force to the metaphor of the prophet in another language. The Hebrew, as near as we can express it, is, ' As a bridegroom attires himself as a priest with a crown or mitre.' The version by Aquila and Symmachus comes nearest to it—Ὡς νυμφίον ἱερατευόμενον στέφανῳ. The sense is, that the church should be adorned with the highest ornament and beauty; not for the mere purpose of decoration, but as if it were a priest engaged in offering continually the sacrifice of prayer and praise. ¶ *And as a bride.* See this explained in the Notes on ch. xlix. 18.

The word rendered ' jewels' here (כְּלִי) does not of necessity mean merely jewels. It properly means an apparatus, implement, utensil, vessel; and then dress, ornament of any kind; and would be better rendered here, in a more general sense, *bridal ornaments.*

11. *For as the earth bringeth forth.* This figure is several times used by the prophet (see Notes on ch. xlv. 8; lv. 10, 11). The idea is an exceedingly beautiful one, that, on the coming of the Messiah, truth and righteousness would spring up and abound like grass and fruits in the vegetable world when the earth is watered with rain. ¶ *Her bud.* The word ' bud' we now apply usually to the small bunch or protuberance on the branches of a plant, containing the rudiments of the future leaf or flower. The Hebrew word, however, (צֶמַח), rather means the germ, the shoot, or the young and tender plant as it comes up from the earth; that which first appears from the seed. ¶ *So the* Lord *God will cause righteousness to spring forth* (see Notes on ch. xlii. 19; xliii. 9; xliv. 4; xlv. 8). ¶ *Before all the nations.* The sense is, that righteousness would abound over all the earth, and that all the world would yet join in celebrating the praises of God.

importunate in prayer, until Jerusalem should be made glorious in the earth (6, 7),

III. The solemn assurance that JEHOVAH had sworn that there would be peace and security from the invasions of enemies (8, 9). The land would be no more subjected to plunder from abroad, but there would be that kind of safety and security which exists when a man sows and reaps without annoyance.

IV. The people are directed to prepare the way for the coming of JEHOVAH (10–12). A

crier proclaims his approach, and directs that all obstructions should be removed.

FOR Zion's sake will I not hold my peace, and for Jerusalem's sake I will not rest, *a* until the righteousness thereof go forth as brightness, *b* and the salvation thereof as a lamp *that* burneth.

a ver. 6,7.   *b* Pr.4.18.

CHAPTER LXII.

1. *For Zion's sake* (see Notes on ch. i. 8). On account of Zion; that is, on account of the people of God. ¶ *I will not hold my peace.* There have been very various opinions in regard to the person referred to here by the word 'I.' Calvin and Gesenius suppose that the speaker here is the prophet, and that the sense is, he would not intermit his labours and prayers until Zion should be restored, and its glory spread through all the earth. The Chaldee Paraphrast supposes that it is God who is the speaker, and this opinion is adopted by Grotius. Vitringa regards it as the declaration of a prophetic choir speaking in the name of the officers of the church, and expressing the duty of making continual intercession for the extension of the Redeemer's kingdom. Estius supposes it to be the petition of the Jewish people praying to God for their restoration. Amidst such a variety of interpretation it is not easy to determine the true sense. If it is the language of God, it is a solemn declaration that he was intent on the deliverance of his people, and that he would never cease his endeavours until the work should be accomplished. If it is the language of the prophet, it implies that he would persevere, notwithstanding all opposition, in rebuking the nation for its sins, and in the general work of the prophetic office, until Zion should arise in its glory. If the former, it is the solemn assurance of JEHOVAH that the church would be the object of his unceasing watchfulness and care, until its glory should fill the earth. If the latter, it expresses the feelings of earnest and devoted piety; the purpose to persevere in prayer and in active efforts to extend the cause of God until it

should triumph. I see nothing in the passage by which it can be determined with certainty which is the meaning; and when this is the case it must be a matter of mere conjecture. The only circumstance which is of weight in the case is, that the language, 'I will not be silent,' is rather that which is adapted to a prophet accustomed to pray and speak in the name of God than to God himself; and if this circumstance be allowed to have any weight, then the opinion will incline to the interpretation which supposes it to refer to the prophet. The same thing is *commanded* the watchman on the walls of Zion in ver. 6, 7; and if this be the correct interpretation, then it expresses the appropriate solemn resolution of one engaged in proclaiming the truth of God not to intermit his prayers and his public labours until the true religion should be spread around the world. ¶ *I will not rest.* While I live, I will give myself to unabated toil in the promotion of this great object (see Notes on ver. 7). ¶ *Until the righteousness thereof.* The word here is equivalent to salvation, and the idea is, that the deliverance of his people would break forth as a shining light. ¶ *Go forth as brightness.* The word here used is commonly employed 'to denote the splendour, or the bright shining of the sun, the moon, or of fire (see ch. lx. 19; comp. ch. iv. 5; 2 Sam. xxiii. 4; Prov. iv. 18). The meaning is, that the salvation of men would resemble the clear shining light of the morning, spreading over hill and vale, and illuminating all the world. ¶ *As a lamp* that *burneth.* A blazing torch—giving light all around and shining afar.

2. *And the Gentiles shall see* (see ch. xi. 10; xlii. 1–6; xlix. 22; lx. 3, 5, 16).

2 And the Gentiles shall see thy righteousness, and all kings thy glory : and thou shalt be called by a new *a*name, which the mouth of the LORD shall name.

3 Thou shalt also be a crown *b* of glory in the hand of the LORD, and a royal diadem in the hand of thy God.

4 Thou shalt no more be termed Forsaken : *c* neither shall thy land any more be termed Desolate ; but thou shalt be called ¹ Hephzi-bah, and thy land ² Beulah : for the LORD delighteth in thee, and thy land shall be *d* married.

a Re.2.17.   *b* Zec.9.16.
c Ho.1.10; He.13.5.   1 i.e., *My delight is in her.*
2 i.e., *Married.*   *d* Re.21.9,10.

¶ *And all kings thy glory* (see Notes on ch. xlix. 7, 23; lii. 15; lx. 3, 10, 11, 16). ¶ *And thou shalt be called by a new name.* A name which shall be significant and expressive of a greatly improved and favoured condition (see ver. 4). The idea is, that they would not be in a condition in which a name denoting humiliation, poverty, and oppression would be appropriate, but in circumstances where a name expressive of prosperity would be adapted to express their condition. On the custom of giving significant names, see Notes on ch. vii. 3; viii. 1. ¶ *Which the mouth of the* LORD *shall name.* Which shall be the more valuable because JE-HOVAH himself shall confer it, and which must therefore be appropriate (see Notes on ver. 4, 12.

3. *Thou shalt also be a crown of glory.* On the application of the word ' crown ' to a place, see Notes on ch. xxviii. 1, where it is applied to Samaria. Some difficulty has been felt by expositors in explaining this, from the fact that a crown or diadem was worn on the head and not held in the hand, and some have supposed that the word ' crown ' here is equivalent to any ornament which might be either borne in the hand or worn on the head ; others have supposed that the reference is to the custom of carrying a chaplet or garland in the hand on festival occasions. But probably the sense is this, ' Thou shalt be so beautiful and prosperous as to be appropriately regarded as a splendid crown or diadem. God shall keep thee as a beautiful diadem — the crown of beauty among the cities of the earth, and as that which is most comely and valuable in his sight.' This is the sense expressed by Gataker and Rosenmüller. ¶ *And a royal diadem.* Heb. ' A diadem of a kingdom.' The diadem is the

wreath or chaplet, usually set with diamonds, which is *encircled* (צָנִיף from צָנַף to roll or wind around, to encircle) around the head. It here means such as was usually worn by monarchs ; and the sense is, that Jerusalem would become exceedingly beautiful in the sight of God.

4. *Thou shalt no more be termed Forsaken.* That is, thou shalt be no more so forsaken as to make such an appellation proper. This refers to the new name which the prophet says (ver. 2) will be conferred on her. ¶ *Neither shall thy land.* Thy country shall no more be so wasted that the term desolation (שְׁמָמָה, Gr. ἔρημος) shall be properly applied to it. ¶ *But thou shalt be called Hephzi-bah.* Marg. as Heb. ' My delight is in her.' The idea is, that JE-HOVAH would show her such favour, and he would have so much pleasure in his people, that this name of endearment would be appropriately given to her. The LXX. render this, Θέλημα ἐμὸν — ' My will,' or my delight. The sense is, that Jerusalem would be eminently the object of his delight. ¶ *And thy land Beulah.* Marg. as Heb. ' Married ;' or rather, ' thou art married.' The LXX. render it, Οἰκουμένη —' Inhabited.' Lowth renders it, ' The wedded matron.' The figure is taken from a female who had been divorced, and whose appropriate name was ' Forsaken.' God says here that the appropriate name henceforward would not be the Forsaken, but *the married one*— the one favoured and blessed of God (see Notes on ch. l. 1). Language like this is common in the East. ' A sovereign is spoken of as married to his dominions; they mutually depend on each other. When a king takes possessions from another, he is said to be married to them.'—(Roberts.) ¶ *Thy*

5 For *as* a young man marrieth a virgin, so shall thy sons marry thee : and ¹ *as* the bridegroom rejoiceth over the bride, *so* shall thy God rejoice ᵃ over thee.

1 *with the joy of the bridegroom.*   a Je.32.41.

6 I have set watchmen upon thy walls, O Jerusalem, *which* shall never hold their peace day nor night ; ye that ² make mention of the LORD, keep not silence ;

2 or, *that are the Lord's remembrancers.*

---

land shall be married. See Notes on ch. liv. 4–6, where this figure is extended to greater length. By a similar figure the church is represented as the beautiful bride of the Lamb of God (Rev. xxi. 9; xix. 7).

5. *For* as *a young man marrieth a virgin.* Roberts remarks on this, ' In general no youth marries a widow. Such a thing I scarcely ever heard of [in India], nor will it ever be except under some very extraordinary circumstances, as in the case of a queen, princess, or great heiress. Even widowers also, if possible, always marry virgins.' The idea here is, that JEHOVAH would have delight in his people, which would be properly represented by the affection which a young man has for his bride. ¶ So *shall thy sons marry thee.* Lowth renders this, ' So shall thy restorer wed thee.' He supposes that the word rendered in our common version, ' thy sons ' (בָּנָיִךְ), should be pointed בֹּנָיִךְ, as a participle from בָּנָה, ' to build,' rather than from בֵּן, ' a son.' The parallelism requires some such construction as this ; and the unusual form of expression, ' *thy sons* shall be wedded to thee,' seems also to demand it. The LXX. render it, ' As a young man cohabits (συνοικῶν) with a virgin [bride] (παρθένῳ), so shall thy sons dwell with thee (κατοικήσουσιν οἱ υἱοί σου). So the Chaldee. The conjecture of Lowth has been adopted by Koppe and Döderlin. Rosenmüller supposes that there is here a mingling or confusion of figures, and that the idea is, that her sons should *possess* her—an idea which is frequently conveyed by the word בָּעַל *Bâál*, which is here used. To me it seems that there is much force in the conjecture of Lowth, and that the reference is to God as the ' builder,' or the restorer of Jerusalem, and that the sense is that he would be ' married,' or tenderly and indissolubly united to her. If it be objected that the word is in the

plural (בָּנַיִךְ) it may be observed that the word commonly applied to God (אֱלֹהִים) is also plural, and that an expression remarkably similar to the one before us occurs in Isa. liv. 5, ' For thy Maker is thy husband ' (Heb. בֹּעֲלַיִךְ, ' Thy husbands.') It is not uncommon to use a plural noun when speaking of God. It should be remembered that the points in the Hebrew are of no authority, and that all the change demanded here is in them. ¶ *And* as *the bridegroom.* Marg. as in Heb. ' With the joy of the bridegroom.' ¶ *Over the bride.* In the possession of the bride—probably the most tender joy which results from the exercise of the social affections.

6. *I have set watchmen upon thy walls* (see Notes on ch. xxi. 6–11). The speaker here is undoubtedly JEHOVAH ; and by watchmen he means those whom he had appointed to be the instructors of his people—the ministers of religion. The name ' watchmen' is often given to them (Ezek. iii. 17; xxxiii. 7 ; see Notes on Isa. lii. 8; lvi. 10). ¶ *Which shall never hold their peace.* The watches in the East are to this day performed by a loud cry as they go their rounds. This is done frequently in order to mark the time, and also to show that they are awake to their duty. ' The watchmen in the camp of the caravans go their rounds, crying one after another, "God is one, he is merciful ;" and often add, " Take heed to yourselves."'—(Tavernier.) The truth here taught is, that they who are appointed to be the ministers of religion should be ever watchful and unceasing in the discharge of their duty. ¶ *Ye that make mention of the* LORD. Marg. ' That are the LORD's remembrancers.' These are evidently the words of the prophet addressing those who are watchmen, and urging them to do their duty, as he had said (ver. 1) he was resolved to do his,

7 And give him no [1] rest, till he establish, and till he make Jerusalem a praise in the earth.

8 The LORD hath sworn by his right hand, and by the arm of his strength: Surely [2] I will no more give thy corn *to be* meat for thine enemies; and the sons of the

stranger shall not drink thy wine for the which thou hast laboured.

9 But they that have gathered it shall eat it, and praise the LORD; and they that have brought it together shall drink it in the courts of my holiness.

1 *silence.* 2 *If I give.*

Lowth renders this, ' O ye that proclaim the name of JEHOVAH.' Noyes, ' O ye that praise JEHOVAH.' But this does not express the sense of the original as well as the common version. The Hebrew word הַמַּזְכִּרִים, from זָכַר, *to remember*) means properly those bringing to remembrance, or causing to remember. It is a word frequently applied to the praise of God, or to the celebration of his worship (Ps. xx. 7; xxxviii. 1; xlv. 17; lxx. 1; cii. 12). In such instances the word does not mean that they who are engaged in his service *cause* JEHOVAH to *remember*, or bring things to his recollection which otherwise he would forget; but it means that they would keep up his remembrance among the people, or that they proclaimed his name in order that he might not be forgotten. This is the idea here. It is not merely that they were engaged in the worship of God; but it is, that they did this in order to keep up the remembrance of JEHOVAH among men. In this sense the ministers of religion are ' the remembrancers ' of the Lord. ¶ *Keep not silence.* Heb. ' Let there be no silence to you.' That is, be constantly employed in public prayer and praise.

7. *And give him no rest.* Marg. ' Silence.' In Heb. the same word (דֳמִי) as in ver. 6. The idea is, ' Keep not silence yourselves, nor let him rest in silence. Pray without ceasing; and do not intermit your efforts until the desires of your hearts shall be granted, and Zion shall be established, and the world saved.' ¶ *Till he establish.* Until he shall establish Jerusalem, and restore it to its former rank and privileges. ¶ *Till he make Jerusalem a praise in the earth.* That it may be the subject of universal commendation and rejoicing, instead of being an object of reproach and scorn. The truth taught here is, that it is the

privilege and duty of the ministers of God to pray unceasingly for the extension of his kingdom. Day and night the voice of prayer is to be urged, and urged as if they would give JEHOVAH no rest until the desires of their hearts should be granted (comp. Luke xviii. 1, *sq.*)

8. *The* LORD *hath sworn by his right hand.* An oath was taken in various forms among the ancients. It was usually done by lifting up the hand toward heaven and appealing to God. As God could swear by no greater (Heb. vi. 13), he is represented as swearing by himself (see Notes on ch. xlv. 23). Here he is represented as swearing by his right hand and by his arm—the strong instrument by which he would accomplish his purposes to defend and save his people. The sense is, that he solemnly pledged the strength of his arm to deliver them, and restore them to their own land. ¶ *Surely I will no more give.* Marg. as in Heb. ' If I give.' That is, I will not give. ¶ *Thy corn* to be *meat.* The word ' corn ' in the Scriptures means all kinds of grain—especially wheat, barley, &c. The word ' meat ' was formerly used to denote all kinds of food, and was not restricted as it is now usually to animal food. The meaning is, that they should not be subjected to the evils of foreign invasion and conquest. ¶ *And the sons of the stranger.* Foreigners, ch. lx. 10. ¶ *Shall not drink thy wine.* The productions of your toil shall be safe, and you shall enjoy them yourselves. All this denotes a state of safety and prosperity, such as there would be if they were allowed to cultivate the soil without interruption, and were permitted to enjoy the fruit of their labours.

9. *But they that have gathered it shall eat it.* There shall be a state of security, so that every man may enjoy the avails of his own labour. Nothing is a more certain indication of liberty and pros-

10 Go through, go through the gates ; prepare *a* ye the way of the people ; cast up, cast up the high-way ; gather out the stones ; lift up a standard *b* for the people.

a ch.57.14.   *b* ch.18.3; Ex.17.15.

perity than this—that every man may securely enjoy the avails of his own labour. Nothing more certainly marks the advance of civilization, and nothing so much tends to encourage industry and to promote prosperity. When a man has no security that what he sows shall be reaped by himself; when there is danger that it will be destroyed or consumed by foreign invaders ; or, when it is liable to be taken by arbitrary power to minister to the wants and luxuries of the great, there will be no industry, no incitement to labour. Such is the condition always in war. Such is the condition now in the Turkish dominions; and such is the state in savage life, and in all uncivilized communities. And as the tendency of true religion is to repress wars, to establish order, and to diffuse just views of the rights of man, it everywhere promotes prosperity by furnishing security that a man shall enjoy the avails of his own productive industry. Wherever the Christian religion prevails in its purity, there is seen the fulfilment of this prophecy ; and the extension of that religion everywhere would promote universal industry, order, and law. ¶ *And praise the* LORD. They shall not consume it on their lusts, nor shall they partake of it without gratitude. God shall be acknowledged as the bountiful giver, and they shall render him appropriate thanksgiving. ¶ *And they that have brought it together.* They who have gathered in the vintage. ¶ *Shall drink it in the courts of my holiness.* It would be drank with gratitude to God in the feasts which were celebrated at the temple (see Lev. vi. 16 ; Deut. xii. 17, 18 ; xiv. 23). The idea is, that the effect of true religion would be to produce security and liberty, and to make men feel that all their blessings came from God ; to partake of them with gratitude, and to make them the occasion of praise and thanksgiving.

10. *Go through, go through the gates.* The connection of this with what goes before is not very apparent, and there has been a great diversity of opinion in

regard to it among interpreters. Grotius supposes that it refers to the priests and Levites who are referred to also in the previous verses, and that it is a command for them to enter into the temple. Calvin supposes that it refers to the Christian church, and that the idea is, that the gates of it should be continually open for the return of penitent sinners. Rosenmüller supposes that it is an address to the cities lying between Babylon and Jerusalem, and that the idea is, that their gates would be thrown open for the return of the exiles, and that all obstacles would be taken out of the way. Others suppose that it refers to the Jews, and that the command is to them to go through the gates of Babylon, and an immediate order is added to the people to prepare the way for them. This last seems to me to be the sense of the passage. It is a direction to the exiles in Babylon to go forth and return to their own land. The gates so long closed against their return would be thrown open, and they would now have liberty to depart for their own country. Thus explained, the connection is apparent. The watchmen were commanded to pray until this was done (ver. 7) ; the prophet had said that he would not rest until it was done (ver. 1) ; JEHOVAH had promised this in a most solemn manner (ver. 8, 9) ; and now those prayers are heard, and that promise is about to be fulfilled, and they are commanded to leave the city and enter upon their journey to their own land (comp. Notes on ch. lii. 10–12). ¶ *Prepare ye the way of the people* (comp. Notes on ch. xl. 3). ¶ *Cast up, cast up the highway* (see Notes on ch. lvii. 14). ¶ *Gather out the stones.* Clear it from the stones—in other words, make a smooth path on which they can travel with ease. The word which is here used (סקל) commonly denotes to stone, or to pelt with stones, a species of capital punishment among the Hebrews (2 Sam xvi. 6–13). Hence it means to pile up stones in a heap ; and it has also the signification of removing stones from a field

11 Behold, the LORD hath proclaimed unto the end of the world, Say ye to the daughter of Zion, Behold, thy *a* salvation cometh ; behold, his reward *b is* with him, and his ¹ work before him.

12 And they shall call them, The holy people, The redeemed of the LORD : and thou shalt be called, Sought *c* out, A city not forsaken.

a Zec.9.9; Jn.12.14,15.   *b* Re.22.12.
1 or, *recompence.*   *c* Eze.34.11-16.

CHAPTER LXIII.

ANALYSIS OF CHAPTERS LXIII., LXIV.

THIS chapter and the following relate to the same general subject, and should not have been separated. The subject with which they are introduced is the destruction of the enemies of God (lxiii. 1-6), and this is followed by tender expressions of confidence in JEHOVAH, and by earnest supplications, on the part of his people, that he would interpose in their behalf. The prophet sees in vision a magnificent conqueror, stained with the blood of his enemies, returning from Edom, and from its capital Bozrah — a warrior flushed with victory, unsubdued, unweakened, and coming with the pride and stateliness of conquest. Who he is, is the object of inquiry; and the answer is, that he is a great and holy deliverer. *Why* his gorgeous robes are thus polluted with blood, becomes also a question of intense anxiety. The reply of the conqueror is, that he has been forth to subdue mighty foes; that he went alone; that there was none that could aid; and that he had trodden them down as a treader of grapes treads in the wine-press. The whole image here is that of a triumphant, blood-stained warrior, returning from the conquest of Idumea.

(Isa. v. 2), and here of removing them from the way when they are an obstruction to the traveller. Harmer supposes that the word here means to pile up stones at proper distances, as a kind of landmark in the deserts, in order to mark the way for travellers—a practice which, he says, is quite common in Arabia. But the more correct interpretation is, that they were to remove the stones from the way, in order that the journey might be made with ease. ¶ *Lift up a standard.* As when an army is about to march. They were about to be collected from their dispersions and restored to their own land, and the command is given, that the banner might be reared that they might rally around it (see Notes on ch. x. 18; lix. 19; xlix. 22).

11. *Behold the* LORD *hath proclaimed.* Proclamation is made to all nations that JEHOVAH is about to come and rescue his people. ¶ *Say ye to the daughter of Zion.* To Jerusalem (see Notes on ch. i. 8). ¶ *Thy salvation cometh.* Lowth renders this, 'Lo! thy Saviour cometh.' So the Vulgate, the LXX., the Chaldee, and the Syriac. The Hebrew word properly means *salvation,* but the reference is to God as the Deliverer or Saviour. The immediate allusion is probably to the return from Babylon, but the remote and more important reference is to the coming of the Redeemer (see Notes on ch. xl. 1-10). ¶ *Behold, his reward is with him.* See these words explained in the Notes on ch. xl. 10.

12. *And they shall call them.* It shall be the honourable and just name by which they shall be known, that they are a holy people, and that they are the redeemed of JEHOVAH. No name is so honourable as that; no one conveys so much that is elevated and ennobling as to say of one, 'he is one whom JEHOVAH has redeemed from sin and death and hell by atoning blood.' He who has a just sense of the import of this name, will desire no other record to be made of his life—no other inscription on his tomb—than that he is ONE WHO HAS BEEN REDEEMED BY JEHOVAH. ¶ *And thou shalt be called* (see Notes on ver. 2). ¶ *Sought out.* The city much sought after, or much desired—to wit, by converts who shall come from afar; by foreigners who shall come to do thee honour (see ch. ii. 3; xl. 5, 6, 10, 11 ; xlix. 18-22). Or it may mean that Jerusalem would be a city sought out and desired by JEHOVAH; *i.e.,* no more forsaken by him. So Gesenius understands it. ¶ *A city not forsaken.* No longer given up to the invasions of a foreign enemy, and abandoned to long desolation. The idea is, that the church and people of God would be the object of his kind protecting care henceforward, and would enjoy his continued smiles.

Who is referred to here has been a question in which interpreters have greatly differed in opinion. The following are some of the opinions which have been expressed.

1. Some have referred it to Judas Maccabeus. This was the opinion of Grotius, who supposed that it was designed to represent his conquest of Idumea (1 Mac. v. 1-5; Jos. *Ant.* xii. 8. 1). But against this interpretation there are insuperable objections. (1.) The attributes of the person here referred to do not agree with him. How could he announce that he was the proclaimer of righteousness and was mighty to save? (2.) The exploits of Judas Maccabeus were not such as to justify the language which the prophet here uses. He overcame the Idumeans, and slew twenty thousand men, but this event is by no means adequate to the lofty prediction of the prophet. (3.) There is another objection suggested by Lowth to this supposition. It is that the Idumea of the time of Isaiah was quite a different country from that which was laid waste by Judas. In the time of Isaiah, Idumea was known as the country south of Palestine, whose capital at one time was Petra, and at another Bozrah. But during the captivity in Babylon, the Nabatheans invaded and conquered the southern part of Judea, and took possession of a great part of what was the territory of the tribe of Judah, and made Hebron the capital. This was the Idumea known in later times, and this was the Idumea that Judas Maccabeus conquered (1 Mac. v. 65).

2. One writer, referred to by Poole (*Synopsis*), supposes that the allusion is to *Michael*, who came to assist Daniel against the Prince of the kingdom of Persia (Dan. x. 13).

3. Others have referred it to JEHOVAH subduing his enemies, and restoring safety to his people. This is the opinion of Calvin, Piscator, Junius, Noyes, and Gesenius.

4. The mass of interpreters have referred it to the Messiah. This is the opinion, among the ancients, of Origen, Jerome, Cyril, Eusebius, and Procopius; and among the moderns, of Lowth, Cocceius—*of course*, Calovius, &c. But to this opinion Calvin makes the following weighty objection; 'Christians,' says he, 'have violently distorted this passage by referring it to Christ, when the prophet simply makes an announcement respecting God. And they have feigned that Christ was red because he was covered with his own blood, which he poured out on the cross. But the simple sense is, that the Lord here goes forth in the sight of his people with red garments, that all might understand that he was their vindicator and avenger.'—(*Comm. in loc.*) The objections to an immediate and direct ap-

plication to Christ, seem to me to be insuperable. (1.) There is no reference to it in the New Testament as applicable to him. (2.) The blood with which the hero was stained, was not his own blood, but that of his foes; consequently all the applications of the words and phrases here to the Messiah as stained with his own blood are misplaced. (3.) The whole image of the prophet is that of a triumphant warrior, returning from conquest, himself unharmed and unwounded, not that of a meek and patient sufferer such as the Messiah. It is, therefore, not without the greatest perversion that it can be referred to the Messiah, nor should it be so employed.—[These objections against the application of the passage to the Messiah, seem to be fatal only to one aspect of it, viz., that which presents the Messiah as stained with his *own* blood; but though the warrior here very clearly appears stained with the blood of *others*, not his own, but the blood of vanquished foes, still that warrior *may* be the Messiah, and this one of the numerous passages in which he is represented as a victorious conqueror (Ps. xlv. 3; Rev. vi. 2; xix. 11-16). The beautiful *accommodation* of the language in the third verse to the sufferings of Christ, seems to have led to the forced application of the whole passage to the Redeemer's passion. It certainly refers, however, to a *conquering*, not a suffering, Messiah. Alexander supposes the conqueror to be JEHOVAH, or the Messiah; Henderson, the Divine Logos, the Angel or Messenger of the Divine presence, who acted as the Protector and Saviour of ancient Israel. Edom is generally taken as the type of the enemies of Israel, or of the church; and this prophecy announces their overthrow.—ED.]

5. Vitringa supposes that there is described under the emblem used here, the final and peremptory manner with which the Messiah, the vindicator and avenger of his people, will take severe vengeance, with the shedding of much blood, on the princes, people, subjects, and patrons of idolatrous and apostate Rome; that the true church on the earth would be reduced to extremities; would be destitute of protectors; and that the Messiah would interpose and by his own power destroy the foes of his people.

The whole passage (1-6) has a striking resemblance to ch. xxxiv., where the prophet predicts the overthrow of Idumea, and the long desolations that would come upon that country and people, and probably the same idea is intended to be conveyed by this which was by that —that all the enemies of the Jews would be destroyed (see the Analysis to ch. xxxix., and the Notes on that chapter). It is to be remembered that Idumea was a formidable foe to the Jews; that there had been frequent wars between them; and especially that they had greatly provoked the anger of the Hebrews, and deserved the severest Divine vengeance for uniting with the Chaldeans when they took Jerusalem, and for urging them to raze it to its foundation (Ps. cxxxvii. 7). On these accounts, Idumea was to be destroyed. Vengeance was to be taken on this foe; *and the destruction of Idumea became a kind of pledge and emblem of the destruction of all the enemies of the people of God.* Thus it is used here; and the prophet sees in vision JEHOVAH returning in triumph from the complete overthrow of the capital of that nation, and the entire destruction of the inhabitants. He sees the mighty warrior return from the conquest; his raiment stained with blood; and he inquires who he is, and receives for answer that he has been *alone* to the conquest of the foes of his people. The idea is, that all those foes would be destroyed, and that it would be done by the power of God alone. The chapter, therefore, I do not regard as immediately referring to the Messiah, but to JEHOVAH, and to his solemn purpose to destroy the enemies of his people, and to effect their complete deliverance.

It may be further remarked that the portion in ch. lxiii. 1–6, is a *responsive song;* a species of composition common in the Bible (see Ps. xxiv.; cxxxiv.; Cant. iii. 6).

The two chapters (lxiii., lxiv.) may be divided into three parts.

I. The destruction of Edom (ch. lxiii. 1–6). 1. The view of the conquering hero coming from Bozrah, and the inquiry by the people who he is (ver. 1, first part). He comes with dyed garments, yet glorious, and with the state and air of a conqueror. 2. The response of JEHOVAH the conqueror, that it was he who was mighty to save (1, last part). 3. The inquiry of the people why he was thus red in his apparel, as if he had been treading in the wine-press (2). 4. The answer of JEHOVAH (3–6). (1.) He had indeed trod the wine-press, and he had done it alone. He had trod down the people in his anger, and their blood had been sprinkled on his raiment. (2.) The day of his vengeance had arrived, and the year of his redeemed had come. (3.) No one had been able to do it, and he had gone forth alone, and had trod down their strength in his fury.

II. A hymn of thanksgiving in view of the deliverance wrought, and of the many mercies conferred on Israel (ch. lxiii. 7–14). 1. A general

acknowledgment of his mercy (7). 2. His choice of them as his people (8). 3. His sympathy for them in all their trials (9). 4. His kindness and compassion, illustrated by a reference to his leading them through the wilderness, notwithstanding their ingratitude and sin (10–14).

III. An earnest supplication in view of the condition of Israel (ch. lxiii. 15–19; lxiv.) The arguments are very beautiful and various for his interposition. 1. An appeal to JEHOVAH in view of his former mercies (15). 2. An argument from the fact that he was their Father, though they should be disowned and despised by all others (16.) 3. Earnest intercession from the fact that his enemies had trodden down the sanctuary, and that those who never acknowledged him, ruled in the land that he had given to his own people (17–19). 4. An earnest pleading with God, in view of the inestimable value of the favours which he conferred—the fact that there was nothing so much to be desired, that the world could confer nothing that was to be compared with his favour (ch. lxiv. 1–5). 5. An argument derived from the general prevalence of irreligion among the people (ch. lxiv. 6, 7). 6. Tender and affectionate pleading from the fact that they were his people (ch. lxiv. 8, 9). 7. A tender and affectionate argument from the fact that the holy city was waste; the temple in ruins; and the beautiful house where their fathers worshipped had been burned up with fire (ch. lxiv. 10–12).

This last passage (ch. lxiv. 10–12), proves that the scene of this prayer and vision is laid in Babylon. The *time* is after Jerusalem had been destroyed, the temple fired, and their sacred things transported; after Edom had joined with the Chaldeans in demanding the entire destruction of the city and temple, and had urged them on to the work of destruction (Ps. cxxxvii. 7); after the Idumeans had invaded the territories of Judea, and established a kingdom there. In their exile they are represented as calling upon God, and they are assured that the kingdom of their enemies would be wholly destroyed.

WHO *is* this that cometh from Edom, with dyed garments from Bozrah? this *that is* [1] glorious in his apparel, travelling in the greatness of his strength? I that speak in righteousness, mighty to save.

[1] *decked.*

CHAPTER LXIII.
1. *Who is this.* The language of

the people who see JEHOVAH returning as a triumphant conqueror from Idumea.

2 Wherefore *art thou* red in thine apparel, and thy garments

a Re.19.13,15.

like him that treadeth in the wine-fat?

Struck with his stately bearing as a warrior; with his gorgeous apparel; and with the blood on his raiment, they ask who he could be? This is a striking instance of the bold and abrupt manner of Isaiah. He does not describe him as going forth to war nor the preparation for battle; nor the battle itself, nor the conquests of cities and armies; but he introduces at once the *returning* conqueror having gained the victory—here represented as a solitary warrior, moving along with majestic gait from Idumea to his own capital, Jerusalem. Jehovah is not unfrequently represented as a warrior (see Notes on ch. xlii. 13).* ¶ *From Edom.* On the situation of Edom, and for the reasons of the animosity between that country and Judea, see the Aanlysis to ch. xxxiv. ¶ *With dyed garments.* That is, with garments dyed in blood. The word here rendered 'dyed' (חָמוּץ *hhâmūtz*), is derived from חָמֵץ *hhâmātz, to be sharp* and *pungent*, and is usually applied to anything that is sharp or sour. It is applied to *colour* that is bright or dazzling, in the same manner as the Greeks use the phrase χρῶμα ὀξύ—*a sharp colour*—applied to purple or scarlet. Thus the phrase πορφύραι ὀξύταται means a brilliant, bright purple (see Bochart, *Hieroz.* i. 2. 7). It is applied to the military cloak which was worn by a warrior, and may denote here either that it was originally dyed of a scarlet colour, or more probably that it was *made* red by the blood that had been sprinkled on it. Thus in Rev. xix. 13, the Son of God is represented as clothed in a similar manner: 'And he was clothed with a vesture dipped in blood.' In ver. 3, the answer of Jehovah to the inquiry why his raiment was red, shows that the colour was to be attributed to blood. ¶ *From Bozrah.* On the situation of Bozrah, see Notes on ch. xxxiv. 6. It was for a time the principal city of Idumea, though properly lying within the boundaries of Moab.

* See Supplementary Note in the *Analysis.*

In ch. xxxiv. 6, Jehovah is represented as having ' a great sacrifice in Bozrah;' here he is seen as having come from it with his garments red with blood. ¶ *This* that is *glorious in his apparel.* Marg. 'Decked.' The Hebrew word (הָדוּר) means *adorned, honourable,* or *glorious.* The idea is, that his military apparel was gorgeous and magnificent —the apparel of an ancient warrior of high rank. ¶ *Travelling in the greatness of his strength.* Noyes renders this, 'Proud in the greatness of his strength,' in accordance with the signification given by Gesenius. The word here used (צָעָה) means properly *to turn to one side,* to incline, to be bent, bowed down as a captive in bonds (Isa. li. 14); then to bend or toss back the head as an indication of pride (Gesenius). According to Taylor (*Concord.*) the word has ' relation to the actions, the superb mien or manner of a triumphant warrior returning from battle, in which he has got a complete victory over his enemies. And it may include the pomp and high spirit with which he drives before him the prisoners which he has taken.' It occurs only in this place and in ch. li. 14; Jer. ii. 20; xlviii. 12. The LXX. omit it in their translation. The sense is doubtless that Jehovah is seen returning with the tread of a triumphant conqueror, flushed with victory, and entirely successful in having destroyed his foes. There is no evidence, however, as Taylor supposes, that he is driving his prisoners before him, for he is seen alone, having destroyed all his foes. ¶ *I that speak in righteousness.* The answer of the advancing conqueror. The sense is, ' It is I, Jehovah, who have promised to deliver my people and to destroy their enemies, and who have now returned from accomplishing my purpose.' The assurance that he speaks in righteousness, refers here to the promises which he had made that he would rescue and save them. ¶ *Mighty to save.* The sentiment is, that the fact that he destroys the foes of his people is an argument that he can save those

3 I have trodden the wine-press alone; and of the people *there was* none with me: for I will tread them in mine anger, and trample them in my fury; and their blood shall be sprinkled upon my garments, and I will stain all my raiment.

who put their trust in him. The same power that destroys a sinner may save a saint; and the destruction of a sinner may be the means of the salvation of his own people.

2. *Wherefore* art thou *red?* The inquiry of the people. Whence is it that that gorgeous apparel is stained with blood? ¶ *And thy garment like him that treadeth in the wine-fat?* Or rather the 'wine-press.' The word here used (נַת) means the place where the grapes were placed to be trodden with the feet, and from which the juice would flow off into a vat or receptacle. Of course the juice of the grape would stain the raiment of him who was employed in this business, and would give him the appearance of being covered with blood. 'The manner of pressing grapes,' says Burder, 'is as follows:—having placed them in a hogshead, a man with naked feet gets in and treads the grapes; in about an hour's time the juice is forced out; he then turns the lowest grapes uppermost, and treads them for about a quarter of an hour longer; this is sufficient to squeeze the good juice out of them, for an additional pressure would even crush the unripe grapes and give the whole a disagreeable flavour.' The following statement of the Rev. I. D. Paxton, in a letter from Beyrout, March 1, 1838, will show how the modern custom accords with that in the time of Isaiah:—'They have a large row of stone vats in which the grapes are thrown, and beside these are placed stone troughs, into which the juice flows. Men get in and tread the grapes with their feet. It is hard work, and their clothes are often stained with the juice. The figures found in Scripture taken from this are true to the life.' This method was also employed in Egypt. The presses there, as represented on some of the paintings at Thebes, consisted of two parts; the lower portion or vat, and the trough where the men with naked feet trod the fruit, supporting themselves by ropes

suspended from the roof (see Wilkinson's *Ancient Egyptians*, ii. 155). Vitringa also notices the same custom.

Huc, pater O Lenæ, veni; nudataque musto
Tinge novo mecum direptis crura cothurnis.
                    Georg. ii. 7, 8.

This comparison is also beautifully used by John, Rev. xiv. 19, 20: 'And the

TREADING THE WINE-PRESS.
From a Sculpture at Thebes.

angel thrust in his sickle into the earth, and gathered the vine of the earth, and cast it into the great wine-press of the wrath of God. And the wine-press was trodden without the city, and blood came out of the wine-press even unto the horses' bridles.' And in Rev. xix. 15, 'And he treadeth the wine-press of the fierceness of the wrath of Almighty God.' The comparison of blood to wine is not uncommon. Thus in Deut. xxxii. 14, 'And thou didst drink the pure blood of the grape.' Calvin supposes that allusion is here made to the wine-press, because the country around Bozrah abounded with grapes.

3. *I have trodden the wine-press alone.* I, Jehovah, have indeed trod the wine-press of my wrath, and I have done it alone (comp. Notes on ch. xxxiv. 5, 6). The idea here is, that he had completely destroyed his foes in Idumea,

4 For the day *a* of vengeance *is* in mine heart, and the year of my redeemed is come.

5 And I looked, and *there was* none to help ; and I wondered that *there was* none to uphold : therefore mine own arm brought

salvation unto me ; and my fury, it upheld me,

6 And I will tread down the people in mine anger, and make them drunk *b* in my fury, and I will bring down their strength to the earth.

a Zep.3.8.

b Je.25.26,27.

and had done it by a great slaughter. ¶ *For I will tread.* Or rather, I trod them. It refers to what he had done ; or what was then past. ¶ *And their blood shall be sprinkled.* Or rather, their blood *was* sprinkled. The word here used (נֵצַח) does not commonly mean blood ; but splendour, glory, purity, truth, perpetuity, eternity. Gesenius derives the word, as used here, from an Arabic word meaning to sprinkle, tŏ scatter ; and hence the juice or liquor of the grape as it is sprinkled or spirted from grapes when trodden. There is no doubt here that it refers to blood—though with the idea of its being spirted out by treading down a foe. ¶ *And I will stain all my raiment.* I have stained all my raiment—referring to the fact that the slaughter was extensive and entire. On the extent of the slaughter, see Notes on ch. xxxiv. 6, 7, 9, 10.

4. *For the day of vengeance* (see Notes on ch. xxxiv. 8). ¶ *And the year of my redeemed is come.* The year when my people are to be redeemed. It is a year when their foes are all to be destroyed, and when their entire liberty is to be effected.

5. *And I looked and* there was *none to help.* The same sentiment is expressed in ch. lix. 16 (see the Notes on that verse). ¶ *None to uphold.* None to sustain or assist. The design is to express the fact that he was entirely alone in this work : that none were disposed or able to assist him. Though this has no direct reference to the plan of salvation, or to the work of the Messiah as a Redeemer, yet it is true of him also that in that work he stood alone. No one did aid him or could aid him ; but alone he ' bore the burden of the world's atonement.' ¶ *My fury, it upheld me.* My determined purpose to inflict punishment on my foes sus-

tained me. There is a reference doubtless to the fact that courage nerves the arm and sustains a man in deadly conflict ; that a purpose to take vengeance, or to inflict deserved punishment, animates one to make efforts which he could not otherwise perform. In ch. lix. 16, the sentiment is, ' his *righteousness* sustained him ; ' here it is that *his fury* did it. There the purpose was to bring salvation ; here it was to destroy his foes.

6. *And I will tread them down.* Or rather, ' I *did* tread them down.' The allusion here is to a warrior who tramples on his foes and treads them in the dust (see Notes on ch. xxv. 10). ¶ *And made them drunk.* That is, I made them reel and fall under my fury like a drunken man. In describing the destruction of Idumea in ch. xxxiv. 5, JEHOVAH says that his sword was made drunk, or that it rushed intoxicated from heaven. See Notes on that verse. But here he says that the people, under the terrors of his wrath, lost their power of self-command, and fell to the earth like an intoxicated man. Kimchi says that the idea is, that JEHOVAH extended the cup of his wrath for them to drink until they became intoxicated and fell. An image of this kind is several times used in the Scriptures (see Notes on ch. li. 17; comp. Ps. lxxv. 8). Lowth and Noyes render this, ' I crushed them.' The reason of this change is, that according to Kennicott, twenty-seven MSS. (three of them ancient) instead of the present Hebrew reading וַאֲשַׁכְּרֵם, ' And I will make them drunk,' read וַאֲשַׁבְּרֵם, ' I will break or crush them.' Such a change, it is true, might easily have been made from the similarity of the letters כ and ב. But the authority for the change does not seem to me to be sufficient, nor is it necessary. The image of making them stagger and fall

7 I will mention the *a* loving-kind-nesses of the LORD, *and* the praises of *b* the LORD, according to all that the LORD hath bestowed on us, and the great goodness towards the house of Israel, which he hath bestowed on

them according to his mercies, and according to the multitude of his loving-kindnesses.

8 For he said, Surely they *are* my people, children *that* will not lie : so he was their Saviour.

a Ho.2.19.   *b* Ps.63.4.

like a drunken man, is more poetic than the other, and is in entire accord-ance with the usual manner of writing by the sacred penman. The Chaldee renders it, ' I cast to the lowest earth the slain of their strong ones.' ¶ *And I will bring down their strength.* I subdued their strong places, and their mighty armies. Such is the sense given to the passage by our translators. But Lowth and Noyes render it, more cor-rectly, ' I spilled their life-blood upon the ground.' The word which our translators have rendered ' strength ' (נצח), is the same word which is used in ver. 3, and which is there rendered ' blood ' (see Notes on that verse). It is probably used in the same sense here, and means that JEHOVAH had brought their blood to the earth ; that is, he had spilled it upon the ground. So the LXX. render it, ' I shed their blood (κατήγαγον τὸ αἷμα) upon the earth.' This finishes the vision of the mighty conqueror returning from Edom. The following verse introduces a new subject. The sentiment in the passage is, that JEHOVAH by his own power, and by the might of his own arm, would subdue all his foes and redeem his people. Edom, in its hostility to his people, the apt emblem of all his foes, would be com-pletely humbled ; and in its subjugation there would be the emblem and the pledge that all his enemies would be destroyed, and that his own church would be safe. See the Notes on ch. xxxiv., xxxv.

7. *I will mention.* This is evidently the language of the people celebrating the praises of God in view of all his mercies in former days. See the ana-lysis to the chapter. The design of what follows, to the close of ch. lxiv., is to implore the mercy of God in view of their depressed and ruined condition. They are represented as suffering under the infliction of long and continued ills;

as cast out and driven to a distant land ; as deprived of their former privileges, and as having been long subjected to great evils. Their temple is destroyed ; their city desolate ; and their whole na-tion afflicted and oppressed. The *time* is probably near the close of the capti-vity ; though Lowth supposes that it refers to the Jews as scattered over all lands, and driven away from the country of their fathers. They begin their pe-titions in this verse with acknowledging God's great mercies to their fathers and to their nation ; then they confess their own disobedience, and supplicate, by various arguments, the Divine mercy and favour. The Chaldee commences the verse thus, ' The prophet said, I will remember the mercy of the Lord.' But it is the language of the people, not that of the prophet. The word rendered ' mention ' (אזכיר), means properly, I will *cause* to remember, or to be re-membered (see Notes on ch. lxii. 6). ¶ *And the praises of the* LORD. That is, I will recount the deeds which show that he is worthy of thanksgiving. The repetitions in this verse are designed to be emphatic ; and the meaning of the whole is, that JEHOVAH had given them abundant cause of praise, notwithstand-ing the evils which they endured.

8. *For he said.* JEHOVAH had said. That is, he said this when he chose them as his peculiar people, and en-tered into solemn covenant with them. ¶ *Surely they* are *my people.* The re-ference here is to the fact that he entered into covenant with them to be their God. ¶ *Children* that *will not lie.* That will not prove false to me—indi-cating the reasonable expectation which JEHOVAH might have, when he chose them, that they would be faithful to him. ¶ *So he was their Saviour.* Lowth renders this, ' And he became their Saviour in all their distress ; ' con-necting this with the first member of

9 In all their afflictions he ^a was afflicted, and the angel ^b of his presence saved them : in his love and in his pity he redeemed them : and he bare ^c them, and carried them all the days of old.

a Ju.10.16; Zec.2.8; Mat.25.40.45; Ac.9.4.   b Ex.14.19.   c De.32.11,12.

the following verse, and translating that, 'it was not an envoy, nor an angel of his presence that saved them.' So the LXX. render it, 'And he was to them for salvation (εἰς σωτηρίαν) from all their affliction.' The Chaldee render it, 'And his word was redemption (פְּרִיק) unto them.' But the true idea probably is, that he chose them, and *in virtue* of his thus choosing them he became their deliverer.

9. *In all their affliction he was afflicted.* This is a most beautiful sentiment, meaning that God sympathized with them in all their trials, and that he was ever ready to aid them. This sentiment accords well with the connection ; but there has been some doubt whether this is the meaning of the Hebrew. Lowth renders it, as has been already remarked, 'It was not an envoy, nor an angel of his presence that saved him.' Noyes, 'In all their straits they had no distress.' The LXX. render it, 'It was not an ambassador (οὐ πρέσβυς), nor an angel (οὐδὲ ἄγγελος), but he himself saved them.' Instead of the present Hebrew word (צָר *tzâr,* ' affliction '), they evidently read it, צִיר *tzir,* ' a messenger.' The Chaldee renders it, 'Every time when they sinned against him, so that he might have brought upon them tribulation, he did not afflict them.' The Syriac, 'In all their calamities he did not afflict them.' This variety of translation has arisen from an uncertainty or ambiguity in the Hebrew text. Instead of the present reading (לֹא, 'not') about an equal number of MSS. read לוֹ, ' to him,' by the change of a single letter. According to the former reading, the sense would be, 'in all their affliction, there was *no* distress,' —*i.e.,* they were so comforted and supported by God, that they did not feel the force of the burden. According to the other mode of reading it, the sense would be, ' in all their affliction, there was affliction to him ;' that is, he sympathized with them, and upheld them. Either reading makes good sense, and it is impossible now to ascertain which is correct. Gesenius supposes it to mean, 'In all their afflictions there would be actually no trouble to them. God sustained them, and the angel of of his presence supported and delivered them.' For a fuller view of the passage, see Rosenmüller. In the uncertainty and doubt in regard to the true reading of the Hebrew, the proper way is not to attempt to change the translation in our common version. It expresses an exceedingly interesting truth, and one that is fitted to comfort the people of God ;—that he is never unmindful of their sufferings ; that he feels deeply when they are afflicted ; and that he hastens to their relief. It is an idea which occurs everywhere in the Bible, that God is not a cold, distant, abstract being ; but that he takes the deepest interest in human affairs, and especially that he has a tender solicitude in all the trials of his people. ¶ *And the angel of his presence saved them.* This angel, called 'the angel of the presence of God,' is frequently mentioned as having conducted the children of Israel through the wilderness, and as having interposed to save them (Ex. xxiii. 20, 31; xxxii. 34 ; xxxiii. 2 ; Num. xx. 16). The phrase, 'the angel of his presence,' (Heb. מַלְאַךְ פָּנָיו, 'angel of his face,' or ' countenance '), means an angel that stands in his presence, and that enjoys his favour, as a man does who stands before a prince, or who is admitted constantly to his presence (comp. Prov. xxii. 29). Evidently there is reference here to an angel of superior order or rank, but to whom has been a matter of doubt with interpreters. Jarchi supposes that it was Michael, mentioned in Dan. x. 13–21. The Chaldee renders it, 'The angel *sent* (שְׁלִיחַ) from his presence.' Most Christian interpreters have supposed that the reference is to the Messiah, as the manifested guide and defender of the children of Israel during their long journey in the desert. This is not the place to go

10 But they rebelled, and vexed his *a* Holy Spirit : therefore he was turned to be their enemy, *b and* he fought against them.

a Ac.7.51; Ep.4.30.

b La.2.5.

into a *theological* examination of that question. The sense of the Hebrew here is, that it was a messenger sent from the immediate presence of God, and therefore of elevated rank. The opinion that it was the Son of, God is one that can be sustained by arguments that are not easily refuted. On the subject of angels, according to the Scripture doctrine, the reader may consult with advantage an article by Dr. Lewis Mayer, in the *Bib. Rep.*, Oct. 1388. ¶ *He redeemed them* (see Notes on ch. xliii. 1). ¶ *And he bare them.* As a shepherd carries the lambs of the flock, or as a nurse carries her children ; or still more probably, as an eagle bears her young on her wings (Deut. xxxii. 11, 12). The idea is, that he conducted them through all their trials in the wilderness, and led them in safety to the promised land (comp. Notes on ch. xl. 11). ¶ *All the days of old.* In all their former history. He has been with them and protected them in all their trials.

10. *But they rebelled.* Against God. This charge is often made against the Jews ; and indeed their history is little more than a record of a series of rebellions against God. ¶ *And vexed.* Or rather 'grieved.' The Heb. word עָצֵב, in Piel, means *to pain, to afflict, to grieve.* This is the idea here. Their conduct was such as *was fitted* to produce the deepest pain—for there is nothing which we more deeply feel than the ingratitude of those who have been benefited by us. Our translators have supposed that the word conveyed the idea of *provoking to wrath* by their conduct (thus the LXX. render it παρώξυναν τὸ πνεῦμα, κ.τ.λ.) ; but the more appropriate sense is, that their conduct was such as to produce pain or grief. Comp. Eph. iv. 30 : 'Grieve not (μὴ λυπεῖτε) the Holy Spirit.' Ps. lxxviii. 40 ; xcv. 10. Heb. iii. 10–17. ¶ *His Holy Spirit.* The Chaldee renders this, ' But they were unwilling to obey, and they irritated (provoked, blasphemed רְגַז) against the words of the prophets.' But the reference seems rather

to be to the Spirit of God that renewed, comforted, enlightened, and sanctified them. Grotius, Rosenmüller, and Gesenius, suppose that this means God himself—a Spirit of holiness. But, with the revelation of the New Testament before us, we cannot well doubt that the real reference here is to the third person of the Trinity—the renewer and sanctifier of the people of God. It may be admitted, perhaps, that the ancient Hebrews would refer this to God himself, and that their views of the offices of the different persons in the Divine nature were not very clearly marked, or very distinct. But this does not prove that the *real* reference may not have been to ' the Holy Ghost.' The renewer and sanctifier of the human heart at all times has been the same. And when any operations of the mind and heart pertaining to salvation are referred to in the Old Testament, nothing should forbid us to apply to the explanation of the expressions and the facts, the clear light which we have in the New Testament—in the same way as when the ancients speak of phenomena in the physical world, we deem it not improper to apply to the explanation of them the established doctrines which we now have in the physical sciences. By this we by no means design to say that the ancients had the same knowledge which we have, or that the language which they used conveyed the same idea to them which it now does to us, but that the events occurred in accordance with the laws which we now understand, and that the language may be explained by the light of modern science. Thus the word *eclipse* conveyed to them a somewhat different idea from what it does to us. They supposed it was produced by different causes. Still they described accurately *the facts in the case ;* and to the explanation of those facts we are permitted now to apply the principles of modern science. So the Old Testament describes *facts* occurring under the influence of truth. The facts were

11 Then he remembered *a* the days of old, Moses *and* his people, *saying*, Where *is* he that brought them up out of the sea with the shepherd [1] of his flock ? where *is* he that put his Holy Spirit *b* within him ?

a Le.26.42.   1 or, *shepherds*.   *b* Nu.11,17,25; Ne.9.20.

clearly understood. What shall hinder us, in explaining them, from applying the clearer light of the New Testament? Admitting this obvious principle, I suppose that the reference here was really to the third person of the Trinity ; and that the sense is, that their conduct was such as was fitted to cause grief to their Sanctifier and Comforter, in the same way as it is said in the New Testament that this is done now. ¶ *He was turned.* He abandoned them for their sins, and left them to reap the consequences. ¶ And *he fought against them.* He favoured their enemies and gave them the victory. He gave them up to a series of disasters which finally terminated in their long and painful captivity, and in the destruction of their temple, city, and nation. The sentiment is, that when we grieve the Spirit of God, he abandons us to our chosen course, and leaves us to a series of spiritual and temporal disasters.

11. *Then he remembered.* He did not forget his solemn promises to be their protector and their God. For their crimes they were subjected to punishment, but God did not forget that they were his people, nor that he had entered into covenant with them. The object of this part of the petition seems to be, to recall the fact that in former times God had never wholly forsaken them, and to plead that the same thing might occur now. Even in the darkest days of adversity, God still remembered his promises, and interposed to save them. Such they trusted it would be still. ¶ *Moses* and *his people.* Lowth renders this, ' Moses his servant,' supposing that a change had occurred in the Hebrew text. It would be natural indeed to suppose that the word 'servant' would occur here (see the Hebrew), but the authority is not sufficient for the change. The idea seems to be that which is in our translation, and which is approved by Vitringa and Gesenius. ' He recalled the ancient days when he led Moses *and* his people through the sea and the wilderness.' ¶ *Where* is *he.* The Chaldee renders this, ' Lest they should say, Where is he?' that is, lest surrounding nations should ask in contempt and scorn, Where is the protector of the people, who defended them in other times ? According to this, the sense is that God remembered the times of Moses and interposed, *lest* his not doing it should bring reproach upon his name and cause. Lowth renders it, ' How he brought them up ;' that is, he recollected his former interposition. But the true idea is that of one asking a question. ' Where now is the God that formerly appeared for their aid ?' And though it is the language of God himself, yet it indicates that state of mind which arises when the question is asked, Where is now the former protector and God of the people ? ¶ *That brought them up out of the sea.* The Red Sea, when he delivered them from Egypt. This fact is the subject of a constant reference in the Scriptures, when the sacred writers would illustrate the goodness of God in any great and signal deliverance. ¶ *With the shepherd of his flock.* Marg. ' Shepherds.' Lowth and Noyes render this in the singular, supposing it to refer to Moses. The LXX., Chaldee, and Syriac, also read it in the singular. The Hebrew is in the plural (רֹעֵי), though some MSS. read it in the singular. If it is to be read in the plural, as the great majority of MSS. read it, it probably refers to Moses *and* Aaron as the shepherds or guides of the people. Or it may also include others, meaning that Jehovah led up the people with *all* their rulers and guides. ¶ *Where* is *he that put his Holy Spirit within him ?* (see Notes on ver. 10). Heb. בְּקִרְבּוֹ—' In the midst of him,' *i.e.*, in the midst of the people or the flock. They were then under his guidance and sanctifying influence. The generation which was led to the land of Canaan was eminently pious, perhaps more so than any other of the people of Israel (comp. Josh. xxiv. 31 ; Judg. ii. 6–10).

12 That led *them* by the right hand of Moses with his glorious arm, dividing the *a* water before them, to make himself an everlasting name?

13 That led them through the

deep, as an horse in the wilderness, *that* they should not stumble?

14 As a beast goeth down into the valley, the Spirit of the LORD caused him to rest, so didst thou lead thy people, to *b* make thyself a glorious name.

a Ex.14.21,&c.   b 2 Sa.7.23.

The idea here is, that God, who then gave his Holy Spirit, had seemed to forsake them. The nation seemed to be abandoned to wickedness; and in this state, God remembered how he had formerly chosen and sanctified them; and he proposed again to impart to them the same Spirit.

12. *That led* them *by the right hand of Moses* (see Notes on ch. xli. 10–13; xlv. 1). ¶ *Dividing the water before them* (Ex. xiv. 21). ¶ *To make himself an everlasting name.* He designed to perform a work which, it would be seen, could not be performed by any false god or by any human arm, and to do it in such circumstances, and in such a manner, that it might be seen everywhere that this was the true God (comp. Notes on ch. xlv. 6). The deliverance from Egypt was attended with such amazing miracles, and with such a sudden destruction of his foes, that none but the true God could have performed it. Egypt was at that time the centre of all the science, civilization, and art known among men; and what occurred there would be known to other lands. God, therefore, in this signal manner, designed to make a public demonstration of his existence and power that shall be known in all lands, and that should never be forgotten.

13. *That led them through the deep.* They went through the deep on dry land—the waters having divided and left an unobstructed path. ¶ *As an horse in the wilderness.* As an horse, or a courser, goes through a desert without stumbling. This is a most beautiful image. The reference is to vast level plains like those in Arabia, where there are no stones, no trees, no gullies, no obstacles, and where a fleet courser bounds over the plain without any danger of stumbling. So the Israelites were led on their way without falling. All obstacles were removed, and they

were led along as if over a vast smooth plain. Our word 'wilderness,' by no means expresses the idea here. *We* apply it to uncultivated regions that are covered with trees, and where there would be numerous obstacles to such a race-horse. But the Hebrew word (מִדְבָּר) rather refers to *a desert,* a waste —a place of level sands or plains where there was nothing to obstruct the fleet courser that should prance over them. Such is probably the meaning of this passage, but Harmer (*Obs.* i. 161, *sq.*) may be consulted for another view, which may possibly be the correct one.

14. *As a beast that goeth down into the valley.* As a herd of cattle in the heat of the day descends into the shady glen in order to find rest. In the vale, streams of water usually flow. By those streams and fountains trees grow luxuriantly, and these furnish a cool and refreshing shade. The cattle, therefore, in the heat of the day, naturally descend from the hills, where there are no fountains and streams, and where they are exposed to an intense sun, to seek refreshment in the shade of the valley. The figure here is that of resting in safety after exposure; and there are few more poetic and beautiful images of comfort than that furnished by cattle lying quietly and safely in the cool shade of a well-watered vale. This image would be much more striking in the intense heat of an Oriental climate than it is with us. Harmer (*Obs.* i. 168, *sq.*) supposes that the allusion here is to the custom prevailing still among the Arabs, when attacked by enemies, of withdrawing with their herds and flocks to some sequestered vale in the deserts, where they find safety. The idea, according to him, is, that Israel lay thus safely encamped in the wilderness; that they, with their flocks and herds and riches, were suffered to remain unattacked by the king of Egypt; and that this was

15 Look down from heaven, and behold from the habitation *a* of thy holiness and of thy glory ; where *is* thy zeal and thy strength, the sounding[1] of thy bowels *b* and of thy mercies towards me ? are they restrained ?

16 Doubtless thou *art* our Father, though Abraham be ignorant of us, and Israel acknowledge us not: thou, O LORD, *art* our Father, [2] our Redeemer : thy name *is* from everlasting.

a 2 Ch.30.27.   1 or, *multitude.*   *b* Je.31.20; Ho.11.8.
2 or, *our Redeemer, from everlasting is thy name.*

---

a state of grateful repose, like that which a herd feels after having been closely pursued by an enemy, when it finds a safe retreat in some quiet vale. But it seems to me that the idea first suggested is the most correct—as it is, undoubtedly the most poetical and beautiful—of a herd of cattle leaving the hills, and seeking a cooling shade and quiet retreat in a well-watered vale. Such repose, such calm, gentle, undisturbed rest, God gave his people. Such he gives them now, amidst sultry suns and storms, as they pass through the world. ¶ *The Spirit of the* LORD (see on ver. 10). ¶ *So didst thou lead.* That is, dividing the sea, delivering them from their foes, and leading them calmly and securely on to the land of rest. So now, amidst dangers seen and unseen, God leads his people on toward heaven. He removes the obstacles in their way; he subdues their foes; he 'makes them to lie down in green pastures, and leads them beside the still waters' (Ps. xxiii. 2); and he bears them forward to a world of perfect peace.

15. *Look down from heaven.* This commences an earnest appeal that God would have mercy on them in their present calamities and trials. They entreat him to remember his former mercies, and to return and bless them, as he had done in ancient times. ¶ *And behold from the habitation* (see Notes on ch. lvii. 15). ¶ *Where* is *thy zeal.* That is, thy former zeal for thy people ; where is now the proof of the interest for their welfare which was vouchsafed in times that are past. ¶ *And thy strength.* The might which was formerly manifested for their deliverance and salvation. ¶ *The sounding of thy bowels.* Marg. ' Multitude.' The word rendered ' sounding' (הֲמוֹן), means properly a noise or sound, as of rain, 1 Kings xviii. 41; of singing, Ezek.

xxvi. 13 ; of a multitude, 1 Sam. iv. 14, xiv. 19. It also means a multitude, or a crowd of men (Isa. xiii. 4 ; xxxiii. 3). Here it relates to an emotion or affection of the mind ; and the phrase denotes compassion, or tender concern for them in their sufferings. It is derived from the customary expression in the Bible that the bowels, *i.e.,* the organs in the region of the chest—for so the word is used in the Scriptures—were the seat of the emotions, and were supposed to be affected by any strong and tender emotion of the mind (see Notes on ch. xvi. 11). The idea here is, ' Where is thy former compassion for thy people in distress ?' ¶ *Are they restrained ?* Are they withheld ? Are thy mercies to be exercised no more ?

16. *Doubtless.* Heb. כִּי — ' For; ' verily; surely. It implies the utmost confidence that he still retained the feelings of a tender father. ¶ *Thou* art *our father.* Notwithstanding appearances to the contrary, and though we should be disowned by all others, we will still believe that thou dost sustain the relation of a father. Though they saw no human aid, yet their confidence was unwavering that he had still tender compassion towards them. ¶ *Though Abraham be ignorant of us.* Abraham was the father of the nation—their pious and much venerated ancestor. His memory they cherished with the deepest affection, and him they venerated as the illustrious patriarch whose name all were accustomed to speak with reverence. The idea here is, that though *even such a man*—one so holy, and so much venerated and loved—should refuse to own them as his children, yet that God would not forget his paternal relation to them. A similar expression of his unwavering love occurs in ch. xlix. 15 : ' Can a woman forget her sucking child ?' See Notes on that place. The language here expresses the

17 O Lord, why hast thou made us to err *a* from thy ways, *and* hardened *b* our heart from thy fear ? Return *c* for thy servants' sake, tho tribes of thine inheritance.

a Ps.119.10.   *b* ch.6.10; Ro 9.17,18.   *c* Ps.90.13.

unwavering conviction of the pious, that God's love for his people would never change ; that it would live when even the most tender earthly ties are broken, and when calamities so thicken around us that we *seem* to be forsaken by God ; and *are* forsaken by our *sunshine* friends, and even by our most tender earthly connections. ¶ *And Israel acknowledge us not.* And though Jacob, another much honoured and venerated patriarch, should refuse to recognize us as his children. The Jewish expositors say, that the reason why Abraham and Jacob are mentioned here and Isaac omitted, is, that Abraham was the first of the patriarchs, and that all the posterity of Jacob was admitted to the privileges of the covenant, which was not true of Isaac. The sentiment here is, that we should have unwavering confidence in God. We should confide in him though all earthly friends refuse to own us, and cast out our names as evil. Though father and mother and kindred refuse to acknowledge us, yet we should believe that God is our unchanging friend ; and it is of more value to have such a friend than to have the most honoured earthly ancestry and the affections of the nearest earthly relatives. How often have the people of God been called to experience this ! How many times in the midst of persecution ; when forsaken by father and mother ; when given up to a cruel death on account of their attachment to the Redeemer, have they had occasion to recall this beautiful sentiment, and how unfailingly have they found it to be true ! Forsaken and despised ; cast out and rejected ; abandoned apparently by God and by men, they have yet found, in the arms of their heavenly Father, a consolation which this world could not destroy, and have experienced his tender compassions attending them even down to the grave. ¶ *Our Redeemer.* Marg. ' Our Redeemer, from everlasting is thy name.' The Heb. will bear either construction. Lowth renders it, very loosely, in accordance with the reading of *one* ancient MS., ' O deliver us, for

the sake of thy name.' Probably the idea is that which results from a deeply affecting and tender view of God as the Redeemer of his people. The heart, overflowing with emotion, meditates upon the eternal honours of his name, and is disposed to ascribe to him everlasting praise.

17. *O Lord, why hast thou made us to err from thy ways ?* Lowth and Noyes render this, ' Why dost thou suffer us to wander from thy way ?' Calvin remarks on the passage, ' The prophet uses a common form of speaking, for it is usual in the Scriptures to say that God gives the wicked over to a reprobate mind, and hardens their hearts. But when the pious thus speak, they do not intend to make God the author of error or sin, as if they were innocent —*nolunt Deum erroris aut sceleris facere auctorem, quasi sint innoxii*—or to take away their own blameworthiness. But they rather look deeper, and confess themselves, by their own fault, to be alienated from God, and destitute of his Spirit ; and hence it happens that they are precipitated into all manner of evils. God is said to harden and blind when he delivers those who are to be blinded to Satan (*Satanœ excœcandos tradit*), who is the minister and the executor of his wrath.'—(*Comm. in loc.*) This seems to be a fair account of this difficult subject. At all events, this is the doctrine which was held by the father of the system of Calvinism ; and nothing more should be charged on that system, in regard to blinding and hardening men, than is thus avowed (comp. Notes on ch. vi. 9, 10 ; Matt. xiii. 14, 15). It is not to be supposed that this result took place by direct Divine agency. It is not by positive power exerted to harden men and turn them away from God. No man who has any just views of God can suppose that he exerts a positive agency to make them sin, and then punishes them for it ; no one who has any just views of man, and of the operations of his own mind, can doubt that a sinner is voluntary in his transgression. It is true, at the same time,

18 The people of thy holiness have possessed *it* but a little while: | our adversaries have trodden down thy *a* sanctuary.

a Ps.74.6-8.

that God foresaw it, and that he did not interpose to prevent it. Nay, it is true that the wickedness of men may be favoured by his abused providence —as a pirate may take advantage of a fair breeze that God sends, to capture a merchant-man ; and true, also, that God foresaw it would be so, and yet chose, on the whole, that the events of his providence should be so ordered. His providential arrangements might be abused to the destruction of a few, but would tend to benefit and save many. The fresh gale that drove on one piratical vessel to crime and bloodshed, might, at the same time, convey many richly freighted ships towards the port. One might suffer; hundreds might rejoice. One pirate might be rendered successful in the commission of crime ; hundreds of honest men might be benefited. The providential arrangement is not to *compel* men to sin, nor is it *for the sake* of their sinning. It is to do good, and to benefit many—though this may draw along, as a consequence, the hardening and the destruction of a few. He might, by direct agency, prevent it, as he might prevent the growth of the briers and thorns in a field ; but the same arrangement, by withholding suns and dews and rains, would *also* prevent the growth of flowers and corn and fruit, and turn extended fertile lands into a desert. It is better that the thorns and briers should be suffered to grow, than to convert those fields into a barren waste. ¶ *Return.* That is, return to bless us. ¶ *The tribes of thine inheritance.* The Jewish tribes spoken of as the heritage of God on the earth.

18. *The people of thy holiness.* The people who have been received into solemn covenant with thee. ¶ *Have possessed it but a little while.* That is, the land—meaning that the time during which they had enjoyed a peaceable possession of it, compared with the perpetuity of the promise made, was short. Such is the idea given to the passage by our translators. But there is considerable variety in the interpretation of

the passage among expositors. Lowth renders it :

It is little, that they have taken possession of thy holy mountain;
That our enemies have trodden down thy sanctuary.

Jerome renders it, 'It is as nothing (*quasi nihilum*), they possess thy holy people; our enemies have trodden down thy sanctuary.' The LXX. render it, 'Return on account of thy servants, on account of the tribes of thine inheritance, that we may inherit thy holy mountains for a little time' (ἵνα μικρὸν κληρονομήσωμεν τοῦ ὄρους τοῦ ἁγίου). It has been generally felt that there was great difficulty in the place. See Vitringa. The sense seems to be that which occurs in our translation. The design is to furnish an argument for the Divine interposition, and the meaning of the two verses may be expressed in the following paraphrase :—' We implore thee to return unto us, and to put away thy wrath. As a reason for this, we urge that thy temple—thy holy sanctuary—was possessed by thy people but a little time. For a brief period there we offered praise, and met with our God, and enjoyed his favour. Now thine enemies trample it down. They have come up and taken the land, and destroyed thy holy place (ch. lxiv. 11). We plead for thine interposition, because we are thy covenant people. Of old we have been thine. But as for them, they were never thine. They never yielded to thy laws. They were never called by thy name. There is, then, no reason why the temple and the land should be in their possession, and we earnestly pray that it may be restored to the tribes of thine ancient inheritance.' ¶ *Our adversaries.* This whole prayer is *supposed* to be offered by the exiles near the close of their captivity. Of course the language is such as they would *then* use. The scene is laid in Babylon, and the object is to express the feelings which they would have then, and to furnish the model for the petitions which they would then urge. We are not, therefore, to suppose that the temple when Isaiah lived and

19 We are *thine:* thou never barest rule over them ; ¹they were not called by thy name.

1 or, *thy name was not called upon them.*

CHAPTER LXIV.

For an analysis of this chapter, see the Analysis prefixed to ch. lxiii. This chapter is closely connected with that in its design, and

wrote was in ruins, and the land in the possession of his foes. All this is seen in vision ; and though a hundred and fifty years would occur before it would be realized, yet, according to the prophetic manner, he describes the scene as actually passing before him (see Introd. § 7 ; comp. Notes on ch. lxiv. 11).

19. *We are* thine. We urge it as a reason for thy interposition to restore the land and the temple, that we are thine from ancient times. Such I take to be the meaning of the passage—in accordance with the common translation, except that the expression מֵעוֹלָם, 'from ancient times,' rendered by our translators in connection with לֹא, 'never,' is thus connected with the Jewish people, instead of being regarded as applied to their enemies. The idea is, that it is an *argument* why God should interpose in their behalf, that they had been for a long time his people, but that his foes, who then had possession of the land, had never submitted to his laws. There has been, however, great variety in interpreting the passage. Lowth renders it :

We have long been as those whom thou hast not ruled ;
We have not been called by thy name.

Noyes renders it better :

It has been with us as if thou hadst never ruled over us,
As if we had not been called by thy name.

Symmachus and the Arabic Saadias render it in the same manner. The LXX. render it, ' We have been as at the beginning when thou didst not rule over us, neither were we called by thy name ;' that is, we have gone back practically to our former heathen condition, by rejecting thy laws, and by breaking thy covenant. Each of these interpretations makes a consistent sense, but it seems to me that the one which I have

should not have been separated from it. This is one of the many instances where the division seems to have been made without any intelligent view of the scope of the sacred writer.

OH ᵃ that thou wouldest rend the heavens, that thou wouldest come down, that the mountains might ᵇ flow down at thy presence,

a Ps.144.5.   b Ju.5 5.

expressed above is more in accordance with the Hebrew. ¶ *Thou never barest rule over them.* Over our enemies— regarded in the prophetic vision as then in possession of the land. The idea is, that they have come into thy land by violence, and laid waste a nation where they had no right to claim any jurisdiction, and have now no claim to thy protection. ¶ *They were not called by thy name.* Heb. 'Thy name was not called upon them.' They were aliens and strangers who had unjustly intruded into the heritage of the Lord.

CHAPTER LXIV.

1. *Oh that thou wouldest rend the heavens.* That is, in view of the considerations urged in the previous chapter. In view of the fact that the temple is burned up (ver. 11); that the city is desolate ; that the land lies waste, and that thine own people are carried captive to a distant land. The phrase ' rend the heavens,' implies a sudden and sublime descent of Jehovah to execute vengeance on his foes, as if his heart was full of vengeance, and the firmament were violently rent asunder at his sudden appearance. It is language properly expressive of a purpose to execute wrath on his foes, rather than to confer blessings on his people. The latter is more appropriately expressed by the heavens being gently opened to make way for the descending blessings. The word here rendered 'rend' (קָרַע), means properly *to tear asunder,* as, *e.g.,* the garments in grief (Gen. xxxvii. 29 ; 2 Sam. xiii. 31); or as a wild beast does the breast of any one (Hos. xiii. 8). The LXX., however, render it by a milder word—ἀνοίξῃς—' If thou wouldst *open* the heavens,' &c. So the Syriac renders it by ' O that thou wouldst *open,*' using a word that is usually applied to

2 As *when* the ¹melting fire burneth, the fire causeth the waters to boil; to make thy name

1 *the fire of meltings.*

known to thine adversaries, *that* the nations may tremble at thy presence!

the opening of a door. God is often represented as coming down from heaven in a sublime manner amidst tempests, fire, and storms, to take vengeance on his foes. Thus Ps. xviii. 9:

He bowed the heavens also and came down;
And darkness was under his feet.

Comp. Hab. iii. 5, 6. It should be remembered that the main idea in the passage before us is that of JEHOVAH coming down to destroy his foes. His people entreat him to descend with the proofs of his indignation, so that every obstacle shall be destroyed before him, Thus he is described in Ps. cxliv. 5, 6:

Bow thy heavens, O Lord, and come down;
Touch the mountains, and they shall smoke;
Cast forth lightning, and scatter them,
Shoot out thine arrows, and destroy them.

¶ *That the mountains might flow down at thy presence.* The idea here is, that the presence of JEHOVAH would be like an intense burning heat, so that the mountains would melt and flow away. It is a most sublime description of his majesty, and is one that is several times employed in the Bible. Thus in relation to his appearance on Mount Sinai, in the song of Deborah (Judg. v. 4, 5):

The earth trembled and the heavens dropped,
The clouds also dropped water.
The mountains melted from before JEHOVAH,
Even Sinai from before JEHOVAH, the God of Israel.

So Ps. xcvii. 5:

The hills melted like wax at the presence of JEHOVAH,
At the presence of JEHOVAH [the God] of the whole earth.

So also in Micah i. 3, 4:

Lo, JEHOVAH cometh forth out of his place,
And will come down and tread upon the high places of the earth,
And the mountains shall be molten under him.
And the valleys shall be cleft,
As wax before the fire,
And as the waters pour down a precipice.

2. *As* when *the melting fire burneth.* Marg. 'The fire of meltings.' Lowth renders it, 'As when the fire kindleth the dry fuel.' So Noyes, 'As fire kindleth the dry stubble.' The LXX. render it, Ὡς κηρὸς ἀπὸ προσώπου πυρὸς τήκεται— 'As wax is melted before the fire.' So

the Syriac renders it. The Hebrew word rendered here in the margin 'meltings' (הֲמָסִים), properly means, according to Gesenius, *brushwood, twigs.* So Saadias renders it. And the true idea here is, that the presence of JEHOVAH would cause the mountains to melt, as a fire consumes light and dry brushwood or stubble. Dr. Jubb supposes that the meaning is, 'As the fire of things *smelted* burneth'—an idea which would furnish a striking comparison, but there is much doubt whether the Hebrew will bear that construction. The comparison is a very vivid and sublime one, as it is in the view given above—that the presence of JEHOVAH would set on fire the mountains, and cause them to flow down as under the operation of an intense heat. I do not know that there is reason to suppose that the prophet had any reference to a volcanic eruption, or that he was acquainted with such a phenomenon —though Syria and Palestine abounded in volcanic appearances, and the country around the Dead Sea is evidently volcanic (see Lyell's *Geology*, i. 299); but the following description may furnish *an illustration* of what would be exhibited by the flowing down of the mountains at the presence of JEHOVAH, and may serve to show the force of the language which the prophet employs in these verses. It is a description of an eruption of Vesuvius in 1779, by Sir William Hamilton. 'Jets of liquid lava,' says he, 'mixed with stones and scoriæ, were thrown up to the height of at least 10,000 feet, having the appearance of a column of fire. The falling matter being nearly as vividly inflamed as that which was continually issuing forth from the crater, formed with it one complete body of fire, which could not be less than two miles and a half in breadth, and of the extraordinary height above mentioned, casting a heat to the distance of at least six miles around it.' Speaking of the lava which flowed from the mountain, he says, 'At the point where it issued from an arched chasm in the side of the mountain, the vivid torrent rushed with

3 When thou didst *a* terrible things *which* we looked not for, thou camest down, *b* the mountains flowed down at thy presence.

4 For *c* since the beginning of the

world *men* have not heard, nor perceived by the ear, neither hath the eye [1] seen, O God, besides thee, *what* he hath prepared for him that waiteth for him.

---

a Ps.65.5.   *b* Ha.3,3,6.   *c* 1 Co.2.9. | 1 or, *seen a God beside thee* which *doeth so for him.*

---

the velocity of a flood. It was in perfect fusion, unattended with any scoriæ on its surface, or any gross material not in a state of complete solution. It flowed with the translucency of honey, in regular channels, cut finer than art can imitate, and glowing with all the splendour of the sun.'—(Lyell's *Geology,* i. 316.) Perhaps there can be conceived no more sublime representation of what was in the mind of the prophet than such an overflowing volcano. It should be observed, however, that Gesenius supposes that the word which is rendered (ver. 1–3), 'flow down' (נָזֹלּוּ), is derived, not from נָזַל *nâzăl, to flow,* to run as liquids do ; but from זָלַל *zâlăl, to shake,* to tremble, to quake as mountains do in an earthquake. But it seems to me that the connection rather demands the former signification, as the principal elements in the figure *is fire*— and the office of fire is not to cause to tremble, but to burn or melt. The effect here described as illustrative of the presence of God, was that produced by intense burning heat. ¶ *The fire causeth the waters to boil.* Such an effect was anticipated at the presence of Jehovah. The idea is still that of an intense heat, that should cause all obstacles to be consumed before the presence of the Lord. To illustrate this, the prophet speaks of that which is known to be most intense, that which causes water to boil; and the prayer is, that Jehovah would descend in the manner of such intense and glowing fire, in order that all the foes of the people might be destroyed, and all the obstacles to the restoration of his people removed. The exact point of the comparison, as I conceive, is the *intensity* of the heat, as emblematic of the majesty of Jehovah, and of the certain destruction of his foes. ¶ *To make thy name known.* By the exhibition of thy majesty and glory.

3. *When thou didst terrible things.*

In delivering the people from Egypt, and in conducting them to the promised land. ¶ *Which we looked not for.* Which we had never before witnessed, and which we had no right to expect. ¶ *Thou camest down.* As on Mount Sinai. ¶ *The mountains flowed down* (see Notes above). The reference is to the manifestations of smoke and fire when Jehovah descended on Mount Sinai (see Ex. xix. 18).

4. *For since the beginning of the world.* This verse is quoted, though not literally, by the apostle Paul, as illustrating the effects of the gospel in producing happiness and salvation (see Notes on 1 Cor. ii. 9). The meaning here is, that nowhere else among men had there been such blessings imparted, and such happiness enjoyed; or so many proofs of love and protection, as among those who were the people of God, and who feared him. ¶ Men *have not heard.* In no nation in all past time have deeds been heard of such as thou hast performed. ¶ *Nor perceived by the ear.* Paul (1 Cor. ii. 9) renders this ' neither have entered into the heart of man,' 'which,' says Lowth, 'is a phrase purely Hebrew, and which should seem to belong to the prophet.' The phrase, 'Nor perceived by the ear,' he says, is repeated without force or propriety, and he seems to suppose that this place has been either wilfully corrupted by the Jews, or that Paul made his quotation from some Apocryphal book—either the ascension of Esaiah, or the Apocalypse of Elias, in both of which the passage is found as quoted by Paul. The phrase is wholly omitted by the LXX. and the Arabic, but is found in the Vulgate and Syriac. There is no authority from the Hebrew MSS. to omit it. ¶ *Neither hath the eye seen.* The margin here undoubtedly expresses the true sense. So Lowth renders it, ' Nor hath the eye seen a God beside thee, which doeth such

5 Thou ^a meetest him that rejoiceth and worketh righteousness,
those that remember thee in thy

a Ac.10.35.

things for those that trust in him.' In
a similar manner the LXX. translate it,
' Neither have our eyes seen a God beside thee (οὐδὲ οἱ ὀφθαλμοὶ ἡμῶν εἶδον θεὸν
πλήν σου), and thy works which thou
hast done for those who wait for mercy.'
The sense is, no eye had ever seen such
a God as JEHOVAH; one who so richly
rewarded those who put their trust in
him. In the Hebrew, the word rendered
' O God,' may be either in the accusative or vocative case, and the sense is,
that JEHOVAH was a more glorious re-
warder and protector than any of the
gods which had ever been worshipped
by the nations. ¶ What *he hath pre-*
pared. Heb. יַעֲשֶׂה—' He doeth,' or will
do. So the LXX. Ἅ ποιήσεις—' What
thou wilt do.' The sense given by our
translators—' What he hath prepared,'
has been evidently adopted to *accommo-*
date the passage to the sense given by
Paul (1 Cor. ii. 9), ἃ ἡτοίμασεν, κ.τ.λ.—
' What God has prepared.' But the
idea is, in the Hebrew, not what God
has *prepared* or *laid up* in the sense of
preserving it for the future; but what
he had already done in the past. No
god had done what he had; no human
being had ever witnessed such manifestations from any other god. ¶ *For him*
that waiteth for him. Lowth and Noyes,
' For him who trusteth in him.' Paul
renders this, ' For them that love him,'
and it is evident that he did not intend
to quote this literally, but meant to
give the general sense. The idea in the
Hebrew is, ' For him who *waits* (לִמְחַכֵּה)
for JEHOVAH,' *i.e.*, who feels his helplessness, and relies on him to interpose and
save him. Piety is often represented
as an attitude of *waiting* on God (Ps.
xxv. 3, 5, 21; xxvii. 14; xxxvii. 9;
cxxx. 5). The sense of the whole verse
is, that God in his past dealings had
given manifestations of his existence,
power, and goodness, to those who were
his friends, which had been furnished
nowhere else. To those interpositions
the suppliants appeal as a reason why
he should again interpose, and why he

ways: behold, thou art wroth; for
we have sinned: in those is continuance, ^b and we shall be saved.

b Mal.3.6.

should save them in their heavy calamities.

5. *Thou meetest him*. Perhaps there
are few verses in the Bible that have
given more perplexity to interpreters
than this; and after all that has been
done, the general impression seems to
be, that it is wholly inexplicable, or
without meaning—as it certainly is in
our translation. Noyes says of his own
translation of the last member of the
verse, ' I am not satisfied with this or
any other translation of the line which
I have seen.' Lowth says, ' I am fully
persuaded that these words as they
stand at present in the Hebrew text are
utterly unintelligible. There is no doubt
of the meaning of each word separately,
but put together they make no sense
at all. I conclude, therefore, that the
copy has suffered by transcribers in this
place.' And after proposing an important change in the text, without any
authority, he says, ' perhaps these may
not be the very words of the prophet,
but, however, it is better than to impose
upon him what makes no sense at all,
as they generally do who pretend to
render such corrupted passages.' Arch.
Secker also proposed an important
change in the Hebrew text, but there is
no good authority in the MSS., it is believed, for any change. Without repeating what has been said by expositors on
the text, I shall endeavour to state what
seems to me to be its probable signification. Its *general* purpose, I think, is
clear. It is to urge, as an argument for
God's interposition, the fact that he was
accustomed to regard with pleasure
those who did well; yet to admit that
he was now justly angry on account of
their sins, and that they had continued
so long in them that they had no hope
of being saved but in his mercy. An
examination of the words and phrases
which occur, will prepare us to present
at a single view the probable meaning.
The word rendered ' thou meetest,'
(פָּגַעְתָּ) means probably to strike upon,
to impinge; then to fall upon in a hos-

tile manner, to *urge* in any way as with petitions and prayers; and then to *strike* a peace or league with any one. See the word explained in the Notes on ch. xlvii. 3. Here it means, as I suppose, to meet for purposes of peace, friendship, protection; that is, it was a characteristic of God that he met such persons as are described for purposes of kindness and favour; and it expresses the belief of the petitioners that whatever they were suffering, still they had no doubt that it was the character of God to bless the righteous. ¶ *That rejoiceth.* This translation evidently does not express the sense of the Hebrew, unless it be understood as meaning that God meets with favour those who rejoice *in* doing righteousness. So Gesenius translates it, 'Thou makest peace with him who rejoices to do justice; *i.e.*, with the just and upright man thou art in league, thou delightest in him.' So Noyes renders it, 'Thou art the friend of those who joyfully do righteousness.' Lowth, 'Thou meetest with joy those who work righteousness.' Jerome, 'Thou meetest him who rejoices and does right.' The phrase used (אֶת־שָׂשׂ) seems to me to mean, 'With joy,' and to denote the general habit of God. It was a characteristic of him to meet the just 'with joy,' *i.e.*, joyfully. ¶ *And worketh righteousness.* Heb. 'And him that doeth righteousness;' *i.e.*, 'thou art accustomed to meet the just with joy, *and* him that does right.' It was a pleasure for God to do it, and to impart to them his favours. ¶ *Those that remember thee in thy ways.* On the word 're- member,' used in this connection, see Notes on ch. lxii. 6. The idea is, that such persons remembered God in the modes which he had appointed; that is, by prayer, sacrifices, and praise. With such persons he delighted to meet, and such he was ever ready to succour. ¶ *Behold, thou art wroth.* This is language of deep feeling on the part of the suppliants. Notwithstanding the mercy of God, and his readiness to meet and bless the just, they could not be ignorant of the fact that he was now angry with them. They were suffering under the tokens of his displeasure; but they were not now disposed to blame him.

They felt the utmost assurance that he was just, whatever they might have endured. It is to be borne in mind, that this is language supposed to be used by the exiles in Babylon, near the close of the captivity; and the *evidences* that God was angry were to be seen in their heavy sorrows there, in their desolate land, and in the ruins of their prostrate city and temple (see Notes on ver. 10, 11). ¶ *In those is continuance.* Lowth has correctly remarked that this conveys no idea. To what does the word 'those' refer? No antecedent is mentioned, and expositors have been greatly perplexed with the passage. Lowth, in accordance with his too usual custom, seems to suppose that the text is corrupted, but is not satisfied with any proposed mode of amending it. He renders it, 'because of our deeds; for we have been rebellious;'—changing *entirely* the text— though following substantially the sense of the Septuagint. Noyes renders it, 'Long doth the punishment endure, until we be delivered;' but expresses, as has been already remarked, dissatisfaction even with this translation, and with all others which he has seen. Jerome renders it, *In ipsis fuimus semper* —'We have always been in them,' *i.e.*, in our sins. The LXX. Διὰ τοῦτο ἐπλανήθημεν, κ.τ.λ.—'Because of this we wandered, and became all of us as unclean, and all our righteousness as a filthy rag.' It seems to me that the phrase בָּהֶם, 'in them,' or 'in those,' refers to sins understood; and that the word rendered 'continuance' (עוֹלָם) is equivalent to a *long former period;* meaning that their sins had been of long continuance, or as we would express it, 'we have been *always* sinners.' It is the language of humble confession, denoting that this had been the characteristic of the nation, and that this was the reason why God was angry at them. ¶ *And we shall be saved.* Lowth renders this, or rather *substitutes* a phrase for it, thus, 'For we have been rebellious'—amending it wholly by conjecture. But it seems to me that Castellio has given an intelligible and obvious interpretation by regarding it as a question: 'Jamdiu peccavimus, et servabimur?' 'Long time have we sinned,

6 But we are all as an unclean *thing*, and all our *a* righteousnesses *are* as filthy rags; and we all do fade as a leaf; and our iniquities, like the wind, have carried us away.

7 And *b there is* none that calleth

upon thy name, that stirreth up himself to take hold of thee : for thou hast hid *c* thy face from us, and hast ¹ consumed us, ² because of our iniquities.

a Phi.3.9.   *b* Ho.7.7.   *c* Ho.5.15.
1 melted.   2 by the hand; Job 8.4.

and shall we be saved?' That is, we have sinned so long, our offences have been so aggravated, how can we hope to be saved ? Is salvation *possible* for such sinners ? It indicates a deep consciousness of guilt, and is language such as is used by all who feel their deep depravity before God. Nothing is more common in conviction for sin, or when suffering under great calamities as a consequence of sin, than to ask the question whether it is *possible* for such sinners to be saved.—I have thus given, perhaps at tedious length, my view of this verse, which has so much perplexed commentators. And though the view *must* be submitted with great diffidence after such a man as Lowth has declared it to be without sense as the Hebrew text now stands, and though no important *doctrine* of religion is involved by the exposition, yet some service is rendered if a plausible and probable interpretation is given to a much disputed passage of the sacred Scriptures, and if we are saved from the necessity of supposing a corruption in the Hebrew text.

6. *But we are all as an unclean* thing. We are all polluted and defiled. The word here used (טָמֵא), means properly that which is polluted and defiled in a Levitical sense ; that is, which was regarded as polluted and abominable by the law of Moses (Lev. v. 2 ; Deut. xiv. 19), and may refer to animals, men, or things ; also in a moral sense (Job xiv. 4). The sense is, that they regarded themselves as wholly polluted and depraved. ¶ *And all our righteousnesses.* The plural form is used to denote the *deeds* which they had performed—meaning that pollution extended to every *individual thing* of the numerous acts which they had done. The sense is, that all their prayers, sacrifices, alms, praises, were mingled with pollution, and were worthy only of deep detesta-

tion and abhorrence. ¶ *As filthy rags.* 'Like a garment of stated times' (עִדִּים) —from the root עָדַד (*obsol.*) to number. to reckon, to determine, *e.g.*, time. No language could convey deeper abhorrence of their deeds of righteousness than this reference—as it is undoubtedly—to the *vestis menstruis polluta.* 'Non est ambigendum,' says Vitringa, 'quin vestis עִדִּים notet *linteum* aut *pannum immundum* ex immunditie legali, eundemque fœdum aspectu ; cujusmodi fuerit imprimis *vestis, pannus,* aut *linteum* feminæ menstruo profluvio laborantis ; verisimile est, id potissimum hac phrasi designari. Sic accepit eam Alexandrinus, vertens, ὡς ῥάκος ἀποκαθημένης—*ut pannus sedentis ;* proprie : ut pannus mulieris languidæ et desidentis ex menstruo παθήματι ' (Lev. xv. 33 ; comp. xx. 18 ; Lam. i. 17). ¶ *And we all do fade as a leaf.* We are all withered away like the leaf of autumn. Our beauty is gone; our strength is fled (comp. Notes on ch. xl. 6, 7; l. 30). What a beautiful description this is of the state of man ! Strength, vigour, comeliness, and beauty thus fade away, and, like the 'sere and yellow leaf' of autumn, fall to the earth. The earth is thus strewed with that which was once comely like the leaves of spring, now falling and decaying like the faded verdure of the forest. ¶ *And our iniquities like the wind.* As a tempest sweeps away the leaves of the forest, so have we been swept away by our sins.

7. *And there is none that calleth upon thy name.* The nation is corrupt and degenerate. None worship God in sincerity. ¶ *That stirreth up himself.* The word here used (מִתְעוֹרֵר) refers to the effort which is requisite to rouse one's self when oppressed by a spirit of heavy slumber ; and the idea here is, that the nation was sunk in spiritual torpor, and that the same effort was needful to excite it which was requisite

8 But now, O Lord, thou *art* our Father ; we *ª are* the clay, and thou our potter ; and we all *are* the work of thy hand.

9 Be not wroth very sore, O Lord, neither *ᵇ* remember iniquity for ever : behold, see, we beseech thee, we *are* all thy people.

10 Thy holy cities are a wilderness, Zion is a wilderness, Jerusalem a desolation.

ª Je.18.6.   *ᵇ* Ps.79.8,&c.

to rouse one who had sunk down to deep sleep. How aptly this describes the state of a sinful world! How much disposed is that world to give itself to spiritual slumber! How indisposed to rouse itself to call upon God! No man rises to God without effort ; and unless men *make* an effort for this, they fall into the stupidity of sin, just as certainly as a drowsy man sinks back into deep sleep. ¶ *To take hold of thee.* The Hebrew word (הָזַק) means properly *to bind fast, to gird tight,* and then to make firm or strong, to strengthen ; and the idea of *strengthening one's self* is implied in the use of the word here. It means, that with the consciousness of feebleness we should seek *strength* in God. This the people referred to by the prophet were indisposed to do. This the world at large is indisposed to do. ¶ *For thou hast hid thy face.* Thou hast withdrawn thy favour from us, as a people, on account of our sins. This is an acknowledgment that one effect of his withdrawing his favour, and one evidence of it was, that no one was disposed to call upon his name. All had sunk into the deep lethargy of sin. ¶ *And hast consumed us.* Marg. 'Melted.' The Hebrew word (מוּג) means *to melt, to flow down ;* and hence, in Piel, *to cause* to melt or flow down. It is used to denote the fact that an army or host of men seem *to melt away,* or become dissolved by fear and terror (Ex. xv. 15; Josh. ii. 9–24; Job xxx. 22). 'Thou dissolvest (תְּמֹגְנֵי) my substance ;' *i.e.,* thou causest me to dissolve before thy indignation. This is described as one of the effects of the wrath of God, that his enemies vanish away, or are dissolved before him. ¶ *Because of our iniquities.* Marg. as Heb. 'By the hand ;' *i.e.,* our iniquities have been the *hand,* the agent or instrument by which this has been done.

8. *But now, O* Lord, *thou* art *our Father* (see Notes on ch. lxiii. 16). ¶ *We* are *the clay.* The idea seems to be, that their condition then had been produced by him as clay is moulded by the potter, and that they were to be returned and restored entirely by him—as they had no more power to do it than the clay had to shape itself. The sense is, that they were wholly in his hand and at his disposal (see Notes on ch. xxix. 16; xlv. 9). ¶ *And thou our potter.* Thou hast power to mould us as the potter does the clay. ¶ *And we all* are *the work of thy hand.* That is, as the vessel made by the potter is his work. We have been formed by thee, and we are dependent on thee to make us what thou wilt have us to be. This whole verse is an acknowledgment of the sovereignty of God. It expresses the feeling which all have when under conviction of sin ; and when they are sensible that they are exposed to the Divine displeasure for their transgressions. Then they feel that if they are to be saved, it must be by the mere sovereignty of God ; and then they implore his interposition to 'mould and guide them at his will.'

10. *Thy holy cities are a wilderness.* It is to be remembered that this is supposed to be spoken near the close of the exile in Babylon. In accordance with the usual custom in this book, Isaiah throws himself forward by prophetic anticipation into that future period, and describes the scene as if it were passing before his eyes (see Introd. § 7). He uses language such as the exiles would use ; he puts arguments into their mouths which it would be proper for them to use ; he describes the feelings which they would then have. The phrase, 'thy holy cities,' may either mean the cities of the Holy Land—which belonged to God, and were 'holy,' as they pertained to his people ; or it may

11 Our holy and our beautiful house, *a* where our fathers praised thee, is burnt up with fire ; and all our pleasant things are laid waste.

a La.2.7.

12 Wilt thou refrain *b* thyself for these *things*, O LORD? wilt thou hold thy peace and afflict us very sore ?

b ch.43.14.

mean, as many critics have supposed, the different parts of Jerusalem. A part of Jerusalem was built on Mount Zion, and was called the ' upper city,' in contradistinction from that built on Mount Acra, which was called the ' lower city.' But I think it more probable that the prophet refers to the cities throughout the land that were laid waste. ¶ *Are a wilderness.* They were uninhabited, and were lying in ruins. ¶ *Zion is a wilderness.* On the name ' Zion,' see Notes on ch. i. 8. The idea here is, that Jerusalem was laid waste. Its temple was burned ; its palaces destroyed ; its houses uninhabited. This is to be regarded as being uttered at the close of the exile, after Jerusalem had been lying in ruins for seventy years—a time during which any forsaken city would be in a condition which might not improperly be called *a desert.* When Nebuchadnezzar conquered Jerusalem, he burnt the temple, broke down the wall, and consumed all the palaces with fire (2 Chron. xxxvi. 19). We have only to conceive what *must* have been the state of the city seventy years after this, to see the force of the description here.

11. *Our holy and our beautiful house.* The temple. It was called ' holy,' because it was dedicated to the service of God ; and ' beautiful,' on account of its extraordinary magnificence. The original word more properly means *glorious.* ¶ *Where our fathers praised thee.* Few attachments become stronger than that which is formed for a place of worship where our ancestors have long been engaged in the service of God. It was now a great aggravation of their sufferings, that that beautiful place, consecrated by the fact that their forefathers had long there offered praise to God, was lying in ruins. ¶ *Is burned up with fire* (see 2 Chron. xxxvi. 19). ¶ *And all our pleasant things.* All that is precious to us (Heb.); all the objects of our desire. The reference is to their temples, their homes, their city—to all

that was dear to them in their native land. It would be difficult to find a passage anywhere in the Bible—or out of it—that equals this for tenderness and true pathos. They were an exiled people ; long suffering in a distant land with the reflection that their homes were in ruins ; their splendid temple long since fired and lying in desolation ; the rank grass growing in their streets, and their whole country overrun with wild beasts, and with a rank and unsubdued vegetation. To that land they longed to return, and here with the deepest emotion they plead with God in behalf of their desolate country. The sentiment here is, that we should go to God with deep emotion when his church is prostrate, and that *then* is the time when we should use the most tender pleadings, and when our hearts should be melted within us.

12. *Wilt thou refrain thyself.* Wilt thou refuse to come to our aid ? Wilt thou decline to visit us, and save us from our calamities ? ¶ *Wilt thou hold thy peace.* Wilt thou not *speak* for our rescue, and command us to be delivered ? Thus closes this chapter of great tenderness and beauty. It is a model of affectionate and earnest entreaty for the Divine interposition in the day of calamity. With such tender and affectionate earnestness may we learn to plead with God ! Thus may all his people learn to approach him as a Father ; thus feel that they have the inestimable *privilege*, in times of trial, of making known their wants to the High and Holy One. Thus, when calamity presses on us; when as individuals or as families we are afflicted ; or when our country or the church is suffering under long trials, may we go to God and humbly confess our sins, and urge his promises, and take hold of his strength, and plead with him to interpose. Thus pleading, he will hear us; thus presenting our cause, he will interpose to save.

CHAPTER LXV.

ANALYSIS.

It is generally supposed that this chapter is closely connected in sense with the preceding; and that its object is, to defend the proceedings of God in regard to the Jews, and especially with reference to the complaint in the preceding chapter. If so, it is designed to state the reasons why he had thus afflicted them, and to encourage the pious among them with the expectation of great future prosperity and safety. A general view of the chapter may be obtained by a glance at the following analysis of the subjects introduced in it.

I. God states in general that he had called another people who had not sought him, and extended the blessings of salvation to those who had been strangers to his name (1). This is evidently intended to show that many of his ancient people would be rejected, and that the blessings of salvation would be extended to others (Rom. x. 20). In the previous chapter they had pled (9), that they were 'all' his people; they had urged, because their nation had been in covenant with God, that he should interpose and save them. Here an important principle is introduced, that they were *not* to be saved of course because they were Jews; and that others would be introduced to his favour who belonged to nations which had not known him, while his ancient covenant people would be rejected. The Jews were slow to believe this; and hence Paul says (Rom. x. 20), that Isaiah was 'very bold' in advancing so unpopular a sentiment.

II. God states the true reason why he had punished them (2–7). It was on account of their sins. It was not because he was changeable, or was unjust in his dealings with them. He had punished them, and he had resolved to reject a large portion of them, though they belonged to his ancient covenant people, on account of their numerous and deeply aggravated crimes. He specifies particularly—1. That they had been a rebellious people, and that he had stretched out his hands to them in vain, inviting them to return. 2. That they were a people which had constantly provoked him by their idolatries; their abominable sacrifices; and by eating the things which he had forbidden. 3. That they were eminently proud and self-righteous, saying to others, Stand by yourselves, for we are holier than you. 4. That for these sins God could not *but* punish them. His law required it, and his justice demanded that he should not pass such offences by unnoticed.

III. Yet he said that the *whole* nation should not be destroyed. His elect would be saved; in accordance with the uniform doctrine of the Scriptures, that *all* the seed of Abraham should not be cut off, but that a remnant should be kept to accomplish important purposes in reference to the salvation of the world (8–10).

IV. Yet the wicked portion of the nation should be cut off, and God, by the prophet, describes the certain punishment which awaited them (11–16). 1. They would be doomed to slaughter. 2. They would be subjected to hunger and want, while his true servants would have abundance. 3. They would cry in deep sorrow, while his servants would rejoice. 4. Their destruction would be a blessing to his people, and the result of their punishment would be to cause his own people to see more fully the value of their religion, and to prize it more.

V. Yet there would be future glory and prosperity, such as his true people had desired, and such as they had sought in their prayers; and the chapter concludes with a glowing description of the glory which would bless his church and people (17–25). 1. God would create new heavens and a new earth—far surpassing the former in beauty and glory (17). 2. Jerusalem would be made an occasion of rejoicing (18). 3. Its prosperity is described as a state of peace, security, and happiness (19–25). (1.) Great age would be attained by its inhabitants, and Jerusalem would be full of venerable and pious old men. (2.) They would enjoy the fruit of their own labour without annoyance. (3.) Their prayers would be speedily answered—even while they were speaking. (4.) The true religion would produce a change on the passions of men *as if* the nature of wild and ferocious animals were changed, and the wolf and the lamb should feed together, and the lion should eat straw like the ox. There would be universal security and peace throughout the whole world where the true religion would be spread.

There can be no doubt, I think, that this refers to the times of the Messiah. Particular proof of this will be furnished in the exposition of the chapter. It is to be regarded, indeed, as well as the previous chapter, as primarily addressed to the exiles in Babylon, but the mind of the prophet is thrown forward. He looks at future events. He sees a large part of the nation permanently rejected. He sees the Gentiles called to partake of the privileges of the true religion. He sees still a remnant of the ancient Jewish people preserved in all their sufferings, and future glory rise upon them under the Messiah, when a new heavens and a new earth should be created. It is adapted, therefore, not only to comfort the ancient afflicted people of God, but it contains most important and cheering truth in regard to the final prevalence of the true religion, and the state of the world when the gospel shall everywhere prevail.

I ^a AM sought of *them that* asked not *for me;* I am found of *them that* sought me not : I said, Behold me, behold me, unto a nation *that* was not called by my name.

CHAPTER LXV.

1. *I am sought of* them that *asked not* for me. That is, by the Gentiles. So Paul applies it in Rom. x. 20. Lowth translates the word which is rendered, 'I am sought,' by 'I am made known.' Noyes, 'I have heard.' The LXX. render it, Ἐμφανὴς ἐγενήθην—'I became manifest.' Jerome, 'They sought me who had not before inquired for me.' The Chaldee, 'I am sought in my word by those who had not asked me before my face.' The Hebrew word דָּרַשׁ means properly *to frequent a place,* to search or seek ; and in Niphal—the form here used—to be sought unto, to grant access to any one ; hence to hear and answer prayer (Ezek. xiv. 3 ; xx. 3–31). Here there is not only the idea that he was *sought,* but that they *obtained* access to him, for he listened to their supplications. The phrase, 'That asked not for me,' means that they had not been accustomed to worship the true God. The idea is, that those had obtained mercy who had not *been accustomed* to call upon him. ¶ *I am found of* them. Paul has rendered this (Rom. x. 20), Ἐμφανὴς ἐγενόμην—'I was made manifest.' The idea is, that they obtained his favour. ¶ *I said, Behold me, behold me.* I offered them my favour, and invited them to partake' of salvation. Paul has omitted this in his quotation. ¶ *Unto a nation.* This does not refer to any particular nation, but to people who had never been admitted to favour with God. ¶ *That was not called by my name* (see Notes on ch. lxiii. 19).

2. *I have spread out my hands.* To spread out the hands is an action denoting invitation or entreaty (Prov. i. 24). The sense is, that God had invited the Jews constantly to partake of his favours,

2 I ^b have spread out my hands all the day unto a rebellious people, which walketh in a way *that was* not good, after their own thoughts.

3 A people that provoketh ^c me to anger continually to my face ; that sacrificeth ^d in gardens, and burneth incense upon ¹ altars of bricks ;

a Ro.9.24,30.　　*b* Ro.10.21.　　*c* De.32 21.
d Le.17.5　　　　　　1 *bricks.*

but they had been rebellious, and had rejected his offers. ¶ *All the day.* I have not ceased to do it. The Chaldee renders this, ' I sent my prophets all the day to a rebellious people.' ¶ *Unto a rebellious people* (see Notes on ch. i. 2). Paul renders this, Πρὸς λαον ἀπειθοῦντα καὶ ἀντιλέγοντα—' Unto a disobedient and gainsaying people ;' but the sense is. substantially preserved. ¶ *Which walketh.* In what way they did this, the prophet specifies in the following verse. This is the *general* reason why he had rejected them, and why he had resolved to make the offer of salvation to the Gentiles. This, at first, was a reason for the calamities which God had brought upon the nation in the suffering of the exile, but it also contains a *general* principle of which that was only one specimen. They had been rebellious, and God had brought this calamity upon them. It would be also true in future times, that he would reject them and offer salvation to the heathen world, and would be found by those who had never sought for him or called on his name.

3. *A people.* This verse contains a *specification* of the reasons why God had rejected them, and brought the calamities upon them. ¶ *That provoketh me to anger.* That is, by their sins. They give constant occasion for my indignation. ¶ *Continually* (תָּמִיד). It is not once merely, but their conduct as a people is *constantly* such as to excite my displeasure. ¶ *To my face.* There is no attempt at concealment. Their abominations are public. It is always regarded as an additional affront when an offence is committed *in the very presence* of another, and when there is not even the apology that it was supposed

4 Which remain among the graves, and lodge in the monuments; which eat swine's flesh,

and [1] broth of abominable *things is in* their vessels;

1 or, *pieces.*

he did not see the offender. It is a great aggravation of the guilt of the sinner, that his offence is committed in the very presence, and under the very eye, of God. ¶ *That sacrificeth in gardens* (see Notes on ch. i. 29). ¶ *And burneth incense.* On the meaning of the word 'incense,' see Notes on ch. i. 13. ¶ *Upon altars of brick.* Marg. 'Bricks.' The Hebrew is simply, 'Upon bricks.' The command of God was that the altars for sacrifice should be made of unhewn stone (Ex. xx. 24, 25). But the heathen had altars of a different description, and the Jews had sacrificed on those altars. Some have supposed that this means that they sacrificed on the roofs of their houses, which were flat, and paved with brick, or tile, or plaster. That altars were constructed sometimes on the roofs of their houses, we know from 2 Kings xxiii. 12, where Josiah is said to have beaten down the 'altars that were on the top of the upper chamber of Ahaz, which the king of Judah had made.' But it is not necessary to suppose that such sacrifices are referred to here. They had disobeyed the command of God, which required that the altars should be made only of unhewn stone. They had built other altars, and had joined with the heathen in offering sacrifices thereon. The *reason* why God forbade that the altar should be of anything but unhewn stone is not certainly known, and is not necessary to be understood in order to explain this passage. It may have been, first, in order effectually to separate his people from all others, as well in the construction of the altar as in anything and everything else; secondly, because various inscriptions and carvings were usually made on altars, and as this tended to superstition, God commanded that the chisel should not be used at all in the construction of the altars where his people should worship.

4. *Which remain among the graves.* That is, evidently for purposes of necromancy and divination. They do it to appear to hold converse with the dead,

and to receive communications from them. The idea in necromancy was, that departed spirits must be acquainted with future events, or at least with the secret things of the invisible world where they dwelt, and that certain persons, by various arts, could become *intimate* with them, or 'familiar' with them, and, by obtaining their secrets, be able to communicate important truths to the living. It seems to have been supposed that this acquaintance might be increased by lodging in the tombs and among the monuments, that they might thus be near to the dead, and have more intimate communion with them (comp. Notes on ch. viii. 19, 20). It is to be recollected, that tombs among the ancients, and especially in Oriental countries, were commonly excavations from the sides of hills, or frequently were large caves. Such places would furnish spacious lodgings for those who chose to reside there, and were, in fact, often resorted to by those who had no houses, and by robbers (see Matt. viii. 28; Mark v. 3). ¶ *And lodge in the monuments.* Evidently for some purpose of superstition and idolatry. There is, however, some considerable variety in the exposition of the word here rendered ' monuments,' as well as in regard to the whole passage. The word rendered 'lodge' (יָלִינוּ), means properly *to pass the night,* and refers not to a permanent dwelling in any place, but to remaining over night; and the probability is, that they went to the places referred to, to *sleep*—in order that they might receive communications in their dreams from idols, by being near them, or in order that they might have communication with departed spirits. The word rendered ' monuments' (נְצוּרִים) is derived from נָצַר, *nâtzăr*, to watch, to guard, to keep; then *to keep from view*, to hide—and means properly hidden recesses; and dark and obscure retreats. It may be applied either to the *adyta* or secret places of heathen temples where their oracles were consulted and many of their rites were performed;

or it may be applied to sepulchral caverns, the dark and hidden places where
the dead were buried. The LXX. render it, ' They sleep in tombs and in
caves (ἐν τοῖς σπηλαίοις) for the purpose
of dreaming' (διὰ ἐνύπνια); in allusion
to the custom of sleeping in the temples, or near the oracles of their gods,
for the purpose of obtaining from them
communications by dreams. This custom is not unfrequently alluded to by
the ancient writers. An instance of this
kind occurs in Virgil :

——— huc dona sacerdos
Cum tulit, et cæsarum ovium sub nocte silenti
Pellibus incubuit stratis, somnosque petivit :
Multa modis simulacra videt volitantia miris,
Et varias audit voces, fruiturque Deorum,
Colloquio, atque imis Acheronta affatur Avernis.
                                        Æneid, vii. 86-91.

' Here in distress the Italian nations come,
Anxious to clear their doubts and earn their
    doom ;
First on the fleeces of the slaughter'd sheep,
By night the sacred priest dissolves in sleep ;
When in a train before his slumbering eye,
Their airy forms and wondrous visions fly :
He calls the powers who guard the infernal
    floods,
And talks inspired familiar with the gods.'
                                        PITT.

In the temples of Serapis and Æscula-
pius, it was common for the sick and
infirm who came there to be cured, to
sleep there, with the belief that the proper remedy would be communicated by
dreams. The following places may also
be referred to as illustrating this custom :—Pausan. *Phoc.* 31 ; Cic. *Divin.*
i. 43; Strabo vi. 3, 9 ; S. H. Meibom.
*De incubatione in fanis Deorum olim
facta.* Helmst. 1659, 4. Lowth and
Noyes render it, ' In caverns.' The
Chaldee renders it, ' Who dwelt in
houses which are built of the dust of
sepulchres, and abide with the dead
bodies of dead men.' There can be
no doubt that the prophet here alludes
to some such custom of sleeping in the
tombs, for the alleged purpose of con-
versing with the dead, or in temples
for the purpose of communion with the
idols by dreams, or with the expectation that they would receive responses
by dreams (comp. Notes on ch. xiv. 9).
¶ *Which eat swine's flesh.* This was
expressly forbidden by the Jewish law
(Lev. xi. 7), and is held in abomination
by the Jews now. Yet the flesh of the

swine was freely eaten by the heathen ;
and when the Jews conformed to their
customs in other respects, they doubtless forgot also the law commanding a
distinction to be made in meats. Antiochus Epiphanes compelled the Jews
to eat swine's flesh as a token of their
submission, and of their renouncing
their religion. The case of Eleazer,
who chose to die as a martyr, rather
than give such a proof that he had
renounced his religion, and who preferred death rather than to dissemble,
is recorded in 2 Macc. vi. 19–31. See
also the affecting case of the mother and
her seven sons, who all died in a similar
manner, in 2 Macc. vii. Yet it seems
that, in the time of Isaiah, they had no
such devotedness to their national religion. They freely conformed to the
nations around them, and thus gave
public demonstration that they disregarded the commands of JEHOVAH. It
is also to be observed, that swine were
often sacrificed by the heathen, and were
eaten in their feasts in honour of idols.
The crime here referred to, therefore,
was not merely that of partaking of the
flesh, but it was that of joining with the
heathen in idolatrous sacrifices. Thus
Ovid says :

Prima Ceres avidæ gavisa est sanguine porcæ,
Ulta suas merita cæde nocentis opes.
                                    Fastor, i. 349.

So Horace :

——— immolet æquis
Hic porcum Laribus—
                                    Serm. ii. 164.

Thus Varro (*De Re Rustic.* ii. 4), says
' The swine is called in Greek ὗς (formerly Θῦς), and was so called from the
word which signifies *to sacrifice* (Θύειν),
for the swine seem first to have been
used in sacrifices. Of this custom we
have vestiges in the fact, that the first
sacrifices to Ceres are of the swine ; and
that in the beginning of peace, when a
treaty is made, a hog is sacrificed ; and
that in the beginning of marriage contracts in Etruria, the new wife and the
new husband first sacrifice a hog. The
primitive Latins, and also the Greeks in
Italy, seem to have done the same
thing.' Spencer (*De Leg. Heb.* i. 7) supposes that this was done often in caves
and dark recesses, and that the prophet
refers to this custom here. If this view

6 Which say, Stand by thyself, come not near to me; for I am holier than thou. These *are* a

smoke in my [1]nose, a fire that burneth all the day.

<hr>

[1] or, *anger.*

<hr>

be correct, then the offence consisted not merely in *eating* swine's flesh, but in eating it in connection with sacrifices, or joining with the heathen in their idolatrous worship. ¶ *And broth of abominable* things. Margin, 'Pieces.' Lowth says that this was for 'lustrations, magical arts, and other superstitious and abominable practices.' The word here rendered 'broth,' and in the margin 'pieces' (פָּרָק), is derived from the verb פָּרַק, *pârăk, to break* (whence the Latin *frango;* the Goth. *brikan;* the Germ. *breoken;* and the English *break*), and means that which is broken, or a fragment; and hence broth or soup, from the fragments or crumbs of bread over which the broth is poured. The LXX. render this, 'And all their vessels are polluted.' It is not improbable that the broth or soup here used was in some way employed in arts of incantation or necromancy. Compare Shakspeare's account of the witches in Macbeth:

1. *Witch.* Where hast thou been, sister?
2. *Witch.* Killing swine.   *Act* i. *Sc.* 3.

Hec. Your vessels and your spells provide,
   Your charms, and everything beside.
             Act iii. *Sc.* 5.

1. *Witch.* Round about the caldron go,
   In the poison'd entrails throw,
   Toad that under the cold stone,
   Days and nights hath thirty-one,
   Fillet of a finny snake,
   In the caldron boil and bake,
   Eye of newt, and toe of frog,
   Wool of bat, and tongue of dog,
   Adder's fork, and blind worm's sting,
   Lizard's leg, and howlet's wing,
   For a charm of powerful trouble,
   Like a hell-broth boil and bubble.
             Act iv. *Sc.* 1.

It seems probable that some such magical incantations were used in the time of Isaiah. Such things are known to have been practised in regions of idolatry (see Marco Polo, *De Region. Orient.,* iii. 24). 'When the priests of the idol,' says he, 'wish to engage in sacred things, they call the consecrated girls, and with them, in the presence of the idols, they engage in the dance, and sing aloud. These girls bear with them

vessels of food, which they place on the table before the idols, and they entreat the gods to eat of the food, and particularly they pour out broth made of flesh before them, that they may appease them.' The whole scene here described by the prophet is one connected with idolatry and magical incantations; and the prophet means to rebuke them for having forsaken God and fallen into all the abominable and stupid arts of idolaters. It was not merely that they had eaten the flesh of swine, or that they had made broth of unclean meats—which would have been minor, though real offences—it was that they had fallen into all the abominable practices connected with idolatry and necromancy.

5. *Which say, Stand by thyself.* Who at the time that they engage in these abominations are distinguished for spiritual pride. The most worthless men are commonly the most proud; and they who have wandered farthest from God have in general the most exalted idea of their own goodness. It was a characteristic of a large part of the Jewish nation, and especially of the Pharisees, to be self-righteous and proud. A striking illustration of this we have in the following description of the Hindoo Yogees, by Roberts: 'Those men are so isolated by their superstition and penances, that they hold but little intercourse with the rest of mankind. They wander about in the dark in the place of burning the dead, or "among the graves;" there they affect to hold converse with evil and other spirits; and there they pretend to receive intimations respecting the destinies of others. They will eat things which are religiously clean or unclean; they neither wash their bodies, nor comb their hair, nor cut their nails, nor wear clothes. They are counted to be *most holy* among the people, and are looked upon as beings of another world.' ¶ *These* are *a smoke in my nose.* Marg. 'Anger.' The word rendered 'nose' (אַף) means sometimes nose (Num. xi. 20; Job xl. 24), and sometimes 'anger,' because anger

6 Behold, *it is* written before me; I will not keep silence, but will re-compense, even recompense into their bosom.

7 Your iniquities, and the iniquities of your fathers together,

saith the LORD, which have burnt incense upon the mountains, and blasphemed me upon the hills: therefore will I measure their former work into their bosom.

---

is evinced by hard breathing. The LXX. render this, ' This is the smoke of my anger.' But the correct idea is, probably, that their conduct was offen-sive to God, as smoke is unpleasant or painful in the nostrils; or as smoke ex-cites irritation when breathed, so their conduct excited displeasure (Rosenmül-ler). Or it may mean, as Lowth sug-gests, that their conduct kindled a smoke and a fire in his nose as the em-blems of his wrath. There is probably an allusion to their sacrifices here. The smoke of their sacrifices constantly as-cending was unpleasant and provoking to God. ¶ *A fire that burneth all the day.* The idea here probably is, that their conduct kindled a fire of indigna-tion that was continually breathed out upon them. A similar figure occurs in Deut. xxxii. 22: ' For a fire is kindled in mine anger,' or in my nose (בְּאַפִּי), 'and shall burn unto the lowest hell.' So in Ps. xviii. 8:

There went up a smoke out of his nostrils,
And fire out of his mouth devoured.

Compare Ezek. xxxviii. 18.

6. *Behold,* it is *written before me.* That is, the crimes of which they had been guilty, or the sentence which would be consequent thereon. The allusion is to the custom of having the decrees of kings recorded in a volume or on a table, and kept in their presence, so that they might be seen and not forgotten. An allusion to this custom of opening the books containing a record of this kind on trials, occurs in Dan. vii. 10, ' The judgment was set, and the books were opened.' So also Rev. xx. 12, ' And I saw the dead, small and great, stand before God; and the books were opened; and another book was opened, which is the book of life, and the dead were judged out of those things which were written in the books, according to their works.' So here. An impartial record had been made, and God would recompense them according to their

deeds. ¶ *I will not keep silence.* Nothing shall compel me to desist from declaring a sentence which shall be just and right. ¶ *But will recompense, even recompense.* That is, I will *certainly* requite them. The word is repeated in accordance with the usual manner in Hebrew to denote emphasis. ¶ *Into their bosom* (see Ps. lxxix. 12; Jer. xxxii. 18; Luke vi. 38). The word *bosom,* here refers to a custom among the Orientals of making the bosom or front of their garments large and loose, so that articles could be carried in them, answering the purpose of our pockets (comp. Ex. iv. 6, 7; Prov. vi. 27). The sense here is, that God would *abundantly* punish them for their sins.

7. *Your iniquities.* Their idolatry and their forsaking God, and their arts of necromancy. ¶ *And the iniquities of your fathers together.* The conse-quences of your own sins, and of the long defection of the nation from virtue and pure religion, shall come rushing upon you like accumulated floods. This is in accordance with the Scripture doc-trine everywhere, that the consequences of the sins of ancestors pass over and visit their posterity (see Ex. xx. 5; xxxiv. 7; Num. xiv. 18; Job xxi. 19; Luke xi. 50, 51; Notes on Rom. v. 19). The case here was, that the nation had been characteristically prone to wander from God, and to fall into idolatry. Crime had thus been accumulating, like pent-up waters, for ages, and now it swept away every barrier. So crime *often* accumulates in a nation. Age after age rolls on, and it is unpunished, until it breaks over every obstacle, and all that is valuable and happy is swept suddenly away. ¶ *Which have burnt incense upon the mountains* (see Notes on ver. 3). ¶ *And blasphemed me upon the hills.* That is, they have dis-honoured me by worshipping idols, and by denying me in that public manner. Idols were usually worshipped on high places. ¶ *Will I measure their former*

8 Thus saith the Lord, As the new wine is found in the cluster, and *one* saith, Destroy it not ; for a blessing *is* in it : so will I do for my servants' sakes, that I may not destroy them all.

9 And I will bring forth a seed out of Jacob, and out of Judah an inheritor of my mountains : and mine elect *a* shall inherit it, and my servants shall dwell there.

10 And Sharon shall be a fold of flocks, and the valley of Achor a place for the herds to lie down in, for my people that have sought me.

a Ro 11.5,7.

work. I will recompense them ; I will pour the reward of their work or of their doings into their bosom.

8. *Thus saith the* Lord. This verse is designed to keep their minds from utter despair, and to assure them that they should not be utterly destroyed. See the analysis of the chapter. ¶ *As the new wine.* The Hebrew word here used (תִּירוֹשׁ), means properly *must* or *new wine* (see Notes on ch. xxiv. 7). The LXX. render it here, ὁ ῥάξ, a grain or berry ; meaning probably a good grape. The Chaldee renders it, ' As Noah was found pure in the generation of the deluge, and I said I would not destroy them, that I might rise up a generation from him, so will I do on account of my servants, that I may not destroy all.' Jerome renders it, *Granum*—' A kernel,' or berry. ¶ *Is found in the cluster.* Expositors have differed in the interpretation of this passage. The true image seems to be taken from collecting grapes when a large part of them were in some way damaged or spoiled—either by the quality of the vine, or by a bad season, or by having been gathered too early, or being suffered to remain too long in a heap. In such a case the vine-dresser would be ready to throw them away. But in the mass he would find a few that were ripe and good. While he was throwing away the mass, some one would say that a part was good, and would entreat him not to destroy it. So with the Jews. The mass was corrupt, and was to be cut off. But still a portion should be left. This is in accordance with the doctrine everywhere occurring in Isaiah and elsewhere in the Scriptures, that the whole Jewish nation should not be cut off, but that a remnant should be preserved (see Notes on ch. vi. 13; comp. ch. i. 9; vii. 3; x. 21;

xi. 11–16). ¶ *For a blessing.* That which is regarded as a blessing ; that is wine (comp. Judg. ix. 13). ¶ *So will I do.* The whole nation shall not be cut off, but a remnant shall be kept and saved.

9. *And I will bring forth a seed.* I will give descendants to Jacob, who shall share my favour and repossess the land. ¶ *An inheritor of my mountains.* The mountains of Palestine—Jerusalem and the vicinity—called the mountains of God because he claimed that land as his peculiar residence, and the place where his holy religion was established. ¶ *And mine elect.* They who have been chosen by me to maintain my religion in the world.

10. *And Sharon.* Sharon was properly a district south of Mount Carmel, along the coast of the Mediterranean, and extending from Cæsarea to Joppa. In the Scripture, this is almost a proverbial name to denote 'extraordinary beauty and fertility (see Notes on ch. xxx. 9; xxxii. 5). ¶ *Shall be a fold of flocks.* At the time contemplated here by the prophet—the close of the exile— that whole country would have lain waste about seventy years. Of course, during that long period it would be spread over with a wild luxuriance of trees and shrubs. Once it was celebrated pasture-ground, and was exceedingly beautiful as a place for flocks and herds. Such a place it would be again when the exiles should return, and cultivate their native land. The following description of Sharon, in the spring of 1824, by the Rev. Mr. Thompson, an American Missionary, will give an idea of the natural appearance of that part of Palestine. The view taken was from a high tower in Ramla. 'The whole valley of Sharon, from the mountains of Jerusalem to the sea, and from the

11 But ye *are* they that forsake the LORD, that forget my holy mountain, that prepare a table for that ¹troop, and that furnish the drink offering unto that ²numbei.

1 or, *Gad.*   2 or, *Meni.*

foot of Carmel to the hills of Gaza, is spread before you like a painted map, and is extremely beautiful, especially at evening, when the last rays of the setting sun gild the distant mountain tops, the weary husbandman returns from his labour, and the bleating flocks come frisking and joyful to their fold. At such a time I saw it, and lingered long in pensive meditation, until the stars looked out from the sky, and the cool breezes of evening began to shed soft dews on the feverish land. What a paradise was here when Solomon reigned in Jerusalem, and sang of the *roses of Sharon!'* ¶ *And the valley of Achor.* This was a valley near to Jericho, and was distinguished as the place where Achan was put to death by stoning (Josh. vii. 24; xv. 7; Hos. ii. 15). The word 'Achor' (עָכוֹר), means properly *causing affliction,* and the name was probably given to that valley from the trouble or affliction which was there caused to the Israelites from the sin of Achan. The phrase, 'the valley of Achor,' would probably thence become a proverbial expression to denote that which caused trouble of any kind. And the sense here probably is, that that which had been to the nation a source of calamity should become a source of blessing—*as if* a place distinguished for causing trouble should become as celebrated for producing happiness. As that valley had been a source of great trouble on their first entering into the land of Canaan, so it would become a place of great exultation, peace, and joy, on their return from their exile. They would naturally enter Canaan near to that valley, and the place which to them had been once the occasion of so much distress, would be found a quiet and peaceful place where their herds might lie down in safety (comp. Hos. ii. 15).

11. *But ye* are *they that forsake the* LORD. Or rather, 'Ye who forsake JEHOVAH, and who forget my holy mountain, I will number to the sword.' The design of this verse is to remind them of their idolatries, and to assure them that they should not escape unpunished. ¶ *That forget my holy mountain.* Mount Moriah, the sacred mountain on which the temple was built. ¶ *That prepare a table.* It was usual to set food and drink before idols—with the belief that the gods consumed what was thus placed before them (see Notes on ver. 4). The meaning here is, that the Jews had united with the heathen in thus 'preparing a table;' that is, setting it before the idols referred to, and placing food on it for them. ¶ *For that troop.* Marg. 'Gad.' Perhaps there is nowhere a more unhappy translation than this. It has been made evidently because our translators were not aware of the true meaning of the word, and did not seem to understand that it referred to idolatry. The translation *seems* to have been adopted with some reference to the *paronomasia* occurring in Gen. xlix. 19; 'Gad, a troop shall overcome him'—גָּד גְּדוּד יְגוּדֶנּוּ—where the word Gad has some resemblance to the word rendered *troop.* The word *Gad* itself, however, never means *troop,* and evidently should not be so rendered here. Much has been written on this place, and the views of the learned concerning Gad and Meni are very various and uncertain. Those who are disposed to examine the subject at length, may consult Rosenmüller, Vitringa, and Gesenius on the passage; and also the following works. On this passage the reader may consult the Dissertation of David Mills, *De Gad et Meni,* and also the Dissertation of Jo. Goth. Lakemacher, *De Gad et Meni,* both of which are to be found in Ugolin's *Thesaurus,* xxiii. pp. 671–718, where the subject is examined at length. Mills supposes that the names Gad and Meni are two names for the moon—*sidus bonum,* and μηνη (*mēnē*). He remarks that 'on account of the power which the moon is supposed to exert over sublunary things, it was often called the goddess Fortune. It is certain that the Egyptians by Τύχη (*Fortune*), which they numbered among the gods who were present at

the birth of man, understood the moon.'
Among the Arabians and Persians the
moon is said to have been denominated
Sidus felix et faustum—' The happy
and propitious star.'   See Rosenmüller
in loc. Lakemacher supposes that two
idols are meant—Hecate and Mana.
Vitringa and Rosenmüller suppose that
the sun and moon are intended.   Grotius supposes that the name *Gad* means
the same as the goddess Fortune, which
was worshipped by the Hebrews, Chaldeans, and Arabians; and that *Meni*
means a divinity of that name, which
Strabo says was worshipped in Armenia
and Phrygia.   Other opinions may be
seen in Vitringa. That two idols are
intended here, there can be no doubt.
For, 1. The circumstance mentioned of
their preparing a table for them, and
pouring out a drink-offering, is expressive of idolatry.   2. The connection
implies this, as the reproof in this
chapter is to a considerable extent for
their idolatry. 3. The universal opinion
of expositors, though they have varied
in regard to the idols intended, proves
this.   Aben Ezra, Kimchi, and the
Rabbins generally suppose that by *Gad*
the planet Jupiter was intended, which
they say was worshipped throughout
the East as the god of fortune, and this
is now the prevalent opinion.   The
word בַּד (*Gad*), says Gesenius, means *fortune,* especially the god Fortune, which
was worshipped in Babylon. He supposes that it was the same idol which
was also called Baal or Bel (comp. Notes
on ch. xlvi. 1), and that by this name
the planet Jupiter—*Stella Jovis*—was
intended, which was regarded throughout the East as the genius and giver of
good fortune, hence called by the Arabians *bona fortuna major* —' the greater
good fortune.' The word ' Meni,' on the
other hand, Gesenius supposes to denote
the planet Venus, called in the East *bona
fortuna minor*—'the lesser good fortune.'
The Vulgate renders this, *Fortunæ*—' To
Fortune.' The LXX., Τῷ δαιμονίῳ—' To
a demon ;' though, in the corresponding
member, *Meni* is rendered by τῇ τύχῃ—
' To Fortune,' and it is possible that the
order of the words has been inverted,
and that they meant to render the word
Gad by Fortune. The Chaldee renders

it simply, לְמַעְנָן—' To idols.'   It is
agreed on all hands that *some* idol is
here referred to that was extensively
worshipped in the East ; and the general
impression is, that it was an idol representing *Fortune.* But whether it was
the Sun, or the planet Jupiter, is not
easy to determine.   That it was customary to place a table before the idol
has been already remarked, and is expressly affirmed by Jerome. ' In all
cities,' says he, 'and especially in Egypt,
and in Alexandria, it was an ancient
custom of idolatry, that on the last day
of the year, and of the last month, they
placed a table filled with food of various
kinds, and a cup containing wine and
honey mixed together—*poculum mulso
mistum*—either as an expression of
thankfulness for the fertility of the past
year, or invoking fertility for the coming
year.' Thus Herodotus (iii. 18) also
describes the celebrated table of the sun
in Ethiopia. ' What they call the table
of the sun was this : A plain in the
vicinity of the city was filled, to the
height of four feet, with roasted flesh of
all kinds of animals, which was carried
there in the night under the inspection
of magistrates ; during the day, whoever
pleased was at liberty to go and satisfy
his hunger.   The natives of the place
affirm that the earth spontaneously produces all these viands ; this, however, is
what they call the table of the sun.'
¶ *And that furnish the drink-offering.*
In all ancient worship, it was customary
to pour out a libation, or a drink-offering.   This was done among idolaters,
to complete the idea of a repast. As
they placed food before the idols, so
they also poured out wine before them,
with the idea of propitiating them (see
Notes on ch. lvii. 6). ¶ *To that number.*
Marg. ' Meni.' The phrase, ' to that
number' evidently conveys no idea, and
it would have been much better to have
retained the name *Meni*, without any
attempt to translate it. The rendering,
' to that number' was adopted because
the word מְנִי *měnī* is derived from מָנָה
mânâ, to allot, to appoint, to number.
Various opinions also have been entertained in regard to this. Rosenmüller
and many others suppose that the moon
is intended, and it has been supposed

12 Therefore ^a will I number you to the sword, and ye shall all bow down to the slaughter: because when ^b I called, ye did not answer;

a Zep.1.4-6.

when I spake, ye did not hear; but did evil before mine eyes, and did choose talk wherein I delighted not.

b 2 Ch.36.15.

---

that the name *Meni* was given to that luminary because it *numbered* the months, or divided the time. Bynæus and David Mills have endeavoured to demonstrate that this was the moon, and that this was extensively worshipped in Eastern nations. Vitringa supposes that it was the same deity which was worshipped by the Syrians and Philistines by the name of *Astarte,* or *Ashtaroth,* as it is called in the Scripture; or as οὐρανίης, the queen of heaven; and if the name *Gad* be supposed to represent the sun, the name *Meni* will doubtless represent the moon. The goddess Ashtaroth or Astarte, was a goddess of the Sidonians, and was much worshipped in Syria and Phenicia. Solomon introduced her worship in Jerusalem (1 Kings xi. 33). Three hundred priests were constantly employed in her service at Hierapolis in Syria. She was called ' the queen of heaven;' and is usually mentioned in connection with Baal. Gesenius supposes that the planet Venus is intended, regarded as the source of good fortune, and worshipped extensively in connection with the planet Jupiter, especially in the regions of Babylonia. It seems to be agreed that the word refers to the worship of either the moon or the planet Venus, regarded as the goddess of good fortune. It is not very material which is intended, nor is it easy to determine. The works referred to above may be consulted for a more full examination of the subject than is consistent with the design of these Notes. The leading idea of the prophet is, that they were deeply sunken and debased in thus forsaking JEHOVAH, and endeavouring to propitiate the favour of idol-gods.

12. *Therefore will I number you to the sword.* There is undoubtedly an allusion here to the idol *Meni* mentioned in ver. 11, and a play upon the name, in accordance with a custom quite common in the sacred Scriptures. The word מָנִיתִי, *mânîthî,* ' I will number,' is derived from כָּנָה, *mânâ,* the same

word from which מְנִי, *měnî,* is derived. The idea is, since they worshipped a god whose name denoted *number*—perhaps one who was supposed to number or appoint the fates of men—God would *number* them. He would determine their destiny. It would not be done by any idol that was supposed to preside over the destinies of men; not by blind fate, or by any one of the heavenly bodies, but it would be by an intelligent and holy God. And thus *numbering* or *determining* their lot would not be in accordance with their expectations, imparting to them *a happy fortune,* but would be devoting them to the sword; that is, to destruction. The allusion is, probably, to the calamities which God afterwards brought on them by the invasion of the Chaldeans. ¶ *And ye shall all bow down to the slaughter.* This is evidently strong, and probably hyperbolic language, meaning that a large portion of the nation would be cut off by the sword. The allusion here is, I think, to the slaughter of the Jewish people in the invasion of the Chaldeans. The evil of idolatry prevailed, in the time of Isaiah, under the reign of Manasseh; and in the time of Zedekiah it had increased so much even in Jerusalem, that it was said, ' All the chief priests and the people transgressed very much after all the abominations of the heathen; and polluted the house of the Lord which he had hallowed in Jerusalem .... And they mocked the messengers of God, and despised his words, and misused his prophets, until the wrath of the Lord arose against his people, till there was no remedy. Therefore he brought upon them the king of the Chaldeans, who slew their young men with the sword, in the house of their sanctuary, and had no compassion upon young man or maiden, old man or him that stooped for age; he gave them all into their hand' (2 Chron. xxxvi. 14, 16, 17). It is possible, also, that this is intended to express a more general

13 Therefore thus saith the Lord God, Behold, my servants shall eat, but ye shall be hungry : behold, my servants shall drink, but ye shall be thirsty : behold, my servants shall rejoice, but ye shall be ashamed :

14 Behold, my servants shall

sing for joy of heart, but ye *a*shall cry for sorrow of heart, and shall howl for [1] vexation of spirit.

15 And ye shall leave your name for a curse *b* unto my chosen : for the Lord God shall slay thee, and call his servants by another name :

---

a Mat.8.12.   [1] *breaking.*   *b* Zec.8.13.

---

truth, and to intimate that when his people forsake him he will punish them; but the primary reference, it is probable, was to the slaughter caused by the Babylonians when they destroyed Jerusalem. ¶ *Because when I called.* When I called you by the prophets to repentance and to my service (see Prov. i. 24, *sq.*) ¶ *Ye did not answer.* You showed the same disregard and contempt which a child does who suffers a parent to call him, and who pays no attention to it. One of the chief aggravations of human guilt is, that the sinner pays no attention to the calls of God. He pretends not to hear; or he hears to disregard it. No more decided contempt can be shown to the Almighty; no deeper proof of the stupidity and guilt of men can be furnished. ¶ *But did evil before mine eyes* (see Notes on ver. 3).

13. *Therefore, thus saith the Lord God.* The design of this verse is to show what would be the difference between those who kept and those who forsook his commandments. The one would be objects of his favour, and have abundance; the other would be objects of his displeasure, and be subjected to the evils of poverty, grief, and want. ¶ *My servants shall eat.* Shall have abundance. They shall be objects of my favour. ¶ *But ye.* Ye who revolt from me, and who worship idols. ¶ *Shall be hungry.* Shall be subjected to the evils of want. The idea is, that the one should partake of his favour; the other should be punished.

14. *Shall sing for joy of heart.* They who serve me shall have abundant occasion of rejoicing. *But ye—shall howl.* You shall shriek under the anguish and distress that shall come upon you. ¶ *For vexation of spirit.* Marg. as in Hebrew, 'Breaking.' That is, your spirit shall be broken and crushed under

the weight of the calamities that shall come upon you.

15. *And ye shall leave your name for a curse unto my chosen.* To my people ; to those whom I have selected to be my friends. The word here rendered ' curse' (שְׁבוּעָה) means properly an oath, or *a swearing;* and then an imprecation or a curse (see Num. v. 21; Dan. ix. 11). The sense here seems to be, that their punishment would be so great that it would become the subject of imprecation when others wished to bind themselves in the most solemn manner by an oath. The pious, who wished to confirm a promise or a covenant in the most solemn manner, would say, 'If we do not perform the promise, then let us experience the same punishment at the hand of God which they have done' (comp. Jer. xxix. 22). Or it may mean, that their name would be used proverbially, like that of Sodom, as a signal example of wickedness and of the abhorrence of God. ¶ *And call his servants by another name.* So disgraceful and dishonourable shall be that name, that Jehovah will apply another name to his people. Is there not an allusion here to the designed change of the *name* by which the people of God are known ? Has it not been by the special providence of God that his true people are now known by another appellation ? Is there any name on earth now that is more the subject of reproach and execration than all the appellations by which his ancient people were known? The name *Jew*—what ideas does it convey to all the nations of the earth ? It is connected with reproach; a name regarded as belonging to a people accursed by God; a name more universally detested than any other known among men. And was it not *because* this name would be thus dishonoured, reproached, and despised, that another

16 That he who blesseth *a* himself in the earth, shall bless himself in the God of truth, and he that sweareth *b* in the earth, shall swear by the God of truth ; because the former troubles are forgotten ;

and because they are hid from mine eyes.

17 For behold, I create new heavens, *c* and a new earth : and the former shall not be remembered, nor ¹ come into mind.

a Je.4.2.　　　　*b* De.6.13; Ps.63.11.　　　*c* 2 Pe.3.13; Re.21.1.　　　1 *upon the heart.*

was given to the true people of God— the name CHRISTIAN — an honoured name—denoting true attachment to the Messiah?

16. *That he who blesseth himself in the earth.* That is, he who shall invoke blessings on himself. ¶ *Shall bless himself in the God of truth.* Or by the true God. He shall not seek a blessing from a false god; but he shall come before the true God, and seek a blessing at his hand. ¶ *And he that sweareth.* Every oath that is taken in the land shall be by the true God. There shall be no swearing by idols; but the true God shall be everywhere acknowledged. ¶ *Because the former troubles are forgotten.* The former punishments and calamities shall be passed away. The favour of God shall be restored. His pure worship shall be re-established, and his name shall be celebrated again in the land. The image here is one of returning prosperity and favour; a state when the happiness will be so great that all the former trials will be regarded as not worthy of recollection.

17. *For behold.* The idea in this verse is, that there should be a state of glory as great as if a new heaven and a new earth were to be made. ¶ *I create new heavens.* Calamity and punishment in the Bible are often represented by the heavens growing dark, and being rolled up like as a scroll, or passing away (see Notes on ch. xiii. 10; xxxiv. 4). On the contrary, prosperity, happiness, and the Divine favour, are represented by the clearing up of a cloudy sky ; by the restoration of the serene and pure light of the sun; or, as here, by the creation of new heavens (comp. Notes on ch. li. 16). The figure of great transformations in material things is one that is often employed in the Scriptures, and especially in Isaiah, to denote great spiritual changes (see ch. xi.; li. 3;

xxxv. 1, 2, 7 ; lx. 13, 17). In the New Testament, the phrase here used is employed to denote the future state of the righteous ; but whether on earth, after it shall have been purified by fire, or in heaven, has been a subject of great difference of opinion (see 2 Pet. iii. 13 ; Rev. xxi. 1). The passage before us is highly poetical, and we are not required to understand it literally. There is, so far as the language is concerned, no more reason for understanding this literally than there is for so understanding the numerous declarations which affirm that the brute creation will undergo a change in their very nature, on the introduction of the gospel (ch. xi.); and all that the language necessarily implies is, that there would be changes in the condition of the people of God as great *as if* the heavens, overcast with clouds and subject to storms, should be re-created, so as to become always mild and serene; or *as if* the earth, so barren in many places, should become universally fertile and beautiful. The immediate reference here is, doubtless, to the land of Palestine, and to the important changes which would be produced there on the return of the exiles ; but it cannot be doubted that, under this imagery, there was couched a reference to far more important changes and blessings in future times under the Messiah—changes as great *as if* a barren and sterile world should become universally beautiful and fertile. ¶ *For the former shall not be remembered.* That is, that which shall be created shall be so superior in beauty as entirely to eclipse the former. The sense is, that the future condition of the people of God would be as superior to what it was in ancient times as would be a newly created earth and heaven superior in beauty to this—where the heavens are so often obscured by clouds, and where the earth is so extensively desolate or

18 But be ye glad and rejoice for *a* ever *in that* which I create: for, behold, I create Jerusalem a rejoicing, and her people a joy.

19 And *b* I will rejoice in Jerusalem, and joy in my people: and the voice of weeping *c* shall be no more heard in her, nor the voice of crying.

20 There shall be no more thence an infant of days, nor an old man that hath not filled his days; for the child shall die an hundred years old; but the *d* sinner *being* an hundred years old shall be accursed.

a ch.51.11; 1 Th.5.16.   *b* ch.62.5.
c Re.7.17.   *d* Ec.8.12,13.

barren. ¶ *Nor come into mind.* Marg. as Heb. 'Upon the heart.' That is, it shall not be thought of; it shall be wholly forgotten. On this verse, comp. Notes on ch. li. 16.

18. *But be ye glad and rejoice* (see Notes on ch. li. 11). ¶ *For ever.* It is not to be momentary happiness—like a bright morning that is soon overcast with clouds. The joy of God's people is to endure for ever, and they shall have ceaseless cause of praise and thanksgiving. ¶ *I create Jerusalem a rejoicing.* A source of rejoicing; or a place of rejoicing. ¶ *And her people a joy.* That is, in themselves joyful, and a source of joy to all others. The idea is, that the church would be a place of the highest happiness, and that they who were redeemed would have occasion of perpetual joy. The Saviour did not come to minister gloom, nor is the true effect of religion to make his people melancholy. Religion produces seriousness; but seriousness is not inconsistent with permanent happiness. Religion produces deep thought and soberness of deportment and conversation; but this is not inconsistent with a heart at ease, or with a good conscience, or with permanent joy. Religion fills the mind with hope of ETERNAL LIFE; and the highest happiness which the soul *can* know must be in connection with the prospect of unchanging blessedness beyond the grave.

19. *And I will rejoice in Jerusalem* (see Notes on ch. lxii. 5). ¶ *And the voice of weeping shall no more be heard* (see Notes on ch. xxv. 7, 8).

20. *There shall be no more thence.* The LXX., the Syriac, and the Vulgate read this, 'There shall not be *there.*' The change requires the omission of a single letter in the present Hebrew text, and the sense seems to demand it.

The design of the prophet here is, to describe the times of happiness and prosperity which would succeed the calamities under which the nation had been suffering. This he does by a great variety of images, all denoting substantially the same thing. In ver. 17, the change is represented to be as great as if a new heaven and a new earth should be created; in this verse the image is, that the inhabitants would reach a great age, and that the comparatively happy times of the patriarchs would be restored; in ver. 21, the image is taken from the perfect security in their plans of labour, and the fact that they would enjoy the fruit of their toil; in ver. 25, the image employed is that taken from the change in the nature of the animal creation. All these are poetic images designed as illustrations of the general truth, and, like other poetic images, they are not to be taken literally. ¶ *An infant of days.* A child; a sucking child. So the Hebrew word, עוּל, denotes. The LXX. render it, 'Nor shall there be there any more an untimely birth (ἄωρος), and an old man who has not filled up his time.' The idea is not that there should be no infant in those future times—which would be an idea so absurd that a prophet would not use it even in poetic fiction—but that there will not be an infant *who shall not fill up his days,* or who will be short-lived. All shall live long, and all shall be blessed with health, and continual vigour and youth. ¶ *Nor an old man that hath not filled his days.* They shall enjoy the blessings of great longevity, and that not a longevity that shall be broken and feeble, but which shall be vigorous and happy. In further illustration of this sentiment, we may remark, 1. That there is no reason to suppose that it will be *literally* fulfilled even in the millenium. If it is to be regarded as literally to be fulfilled, then for the same reason we are to suppose that in that time the nature of the lion will be literally changed, and that he will eat straw like the ox, and that the nature of the wolf and the lamb will be so far changed that they shall lie down together (ver. 25). But there is no reason to suppose this ; nor is there any good reason to suppose that *literally* no infant or child will die in those times, or that no old man will be infirm, or that *all* will live to the same great age. 2. The promise of long life is regarded in the Bible as a blessing, and is an image, everywhere, of prosperity and happiness. Thus the patriarchs were regarded as having been highly favoured men, because God lengthened out their days ; and throughout the Scriptures it is represented as a proof of the favour of God, that a man is permitted to live long, and to see a numerous posterity (see Gen. xlv. 10 ; Ps. xxi. 4 ; xxiii. 6 ; cxxviii. 6 (Heb.); xci. 16 ; Prov. iii. 2–14 ; xvii. 6. 3. No one can doubt that the prevalence of the gospel everywhere would greatly lengthen out the life of man. Let any one reflect on the great number that are now cut off in childhood in heathen lands by their parents, all of whom would have been spared had their parents been Christians ; on the numbers of children who are destroyed in early life by the effects of the intemperance of their parents, most of whom would have survived if their parents had been virtuous ; on the numbers of young men now cut down by vice, who would have continued to live if they had been under the influence of the gospel ; on the immense hosts cut off, and most of them in middle life, by war, who would have lived to a good old age if the gospel had prevailed and put a period to wars ; on the millions who are annually cut down by intemperance and lust, and other raging passions, by murder and piracy, or who are punished by death for crime ; on the millions destroyed by pestilential disease sent by offended Heaven on guilty nations ; and let him reflect that these sources of death will be dried up by the prevalence of pure virtue and religion, and he will see that a great change *may*

yet take place literally in the life of man. 4. A similar image is used by the classic writers to denote a golden age, or an age of great prosperity and happiness. Thus the Sybil, in the *Sybilline Oracles*, B. vii., speaking of the future age, says, Στήσει δὲ τὸ γένος, ὡς πάρος ἦν σοι—'A race shall be restored as it was in the ancient times.' So Hesiod, describing the silver age, introduces a boy as having reached the age of an hundred years, and yet but a child :

'Αλλ' ἑκατὸν μὲν παῖς ἔτεα παρὰ μητίρι
        κεδνῃ,

'Ετρέφετ' ἀτάλλων μέγα νήπιος ᾧ ἐνὶ οἴκῳ.

¶ *For the child shall die an hundred years old.* That is, he that is an hundred years old when he dies, shall still be a child or a youth. This is nearly the same sentiment which is expressed by Hesiod, as quoted above. The prophet has evidently in his eye the longevity of the patriarchs, when an individual of an hundred years of age was comparatively young—the proportion between that and the usual period of life then being about the same as that between the age of ten and the usual period of life now. We are not, I apprehend, to suppose that this is to be taken literally, but it is figurative language, designed to describe the comparatively happy state referred to by the prophet, *as if* human life should be lengthened out to the age of the patriarchs, and as if he who is now regarded as an old man, should then be regarded as in the vigour of his days. At the same time it is true, that the influence of temperance, industry, and soberness of life, such as would exist if the rules of the gospel were obeyed, would carry forward the vigour of youth far into advancing years, and mitigate most of the evils now incident to the decline of life. The few imperfect experiments which have been made of the effect of entire temperance and of elevated virtue ; of subduing the passions by the influence of the gospel, and of prudent means for prolonging health and life, such as the gospel will prompt a man to use, who has any just view of the value of life, show what *may* yet be done in happier times. It is an obvious reflec-

21 And *a* they shall build houses, and inhabit *them ;* and they shall plant vineyards, and eat the fruit of them.

22 They shall not build, and another *b* inhabit; they shall not plant, and another eat ; for as the days of a tree *c are* the days of my people, and mine elect shall [1] long enjoy the work of their hands.

a Am.9.14.   *b* Le.26.16; De.28.30.   *c* Ps 92.12.   [1] *make them continue long,* or, *wear out.*

tion here, that if such effects are to be anticipated from the prevalence of true religion and of temperance, then he is the best friend of man who endeavours most sedulously to bring others under the influence of the gospel, and to extend the principles of temperance and virtue. The gospel of Christ would do more to prolong human life than all other causes combined ; and when that prevails everywhere, putting a period, as it must, to infanticide, and war, and intemperance, and murder, and piracy, and suicide, and duelling, and raging and consuming passions, then it is impossible for the most vivid imagination to conceive the effect which shall be produced on the health and long life, as well as on the happiness of mankind. ¶ *But the sinner* being *an hundred years old shall be accursed.* The sense of this appears to be, ' not all who reach to a great age shall be judged to be the friends and favourites of God. Though a sinner shall reach that advanced period of life, yet he shall be cursed of God, and shall be cut down in his sins. He shall be held to be a sinner and shall die, and shall be regarded as accursed.' Other interpretations of this expression may be seen in Poole and in Vitringa. The above seems to me to be the true exposition.

21. *And they shall build houses* (see Notes on ch. lxii. 8, 9).

22. *They shall not build, and another inhabit.* Every man shall enjoy the avails of his labour. ¶ *For as the days of a tree* are *the days of my people.* That is, in that future time, such *shall be* the length of the lives of the people (see ver. 21). The LXX. render this, ' The days of the tree of life.' The Syriac, ' As the days of trees.' The Chaldee as the LXX. The idea is, that the lives of his people would be greatly prolonged (see Notes on ver. 20). A *tree* is among the most long-lived of material objects. The oak, the tere-

binth, the cypress, the cedar, the banyan, attain to a great age. Many trees also live to a much longer period than a thousand years. The Baobab tree of Senegal (*Adansonia digitata*) is supposed to attain the age of several thousand years. Adanson inferred that one which he measured, and found to be thirty feet in diameter, had attained the age of 5150 years. Having made an incision to a certain depth, he first counted three hundred rings of annual growth, and observed what thickness the tree had gained in that period. The average rate of growth of younger trees, of the same species, was then ascertained, and the calculation made according to a supposed mean rate of increase. De Candolle considers it not improbable that the celebrated Taxodium, of Chapultepec, in Mexico, which is 117 feet in circumference, may be still more aged. In Macartney's *Embassy to China,* i. 131, an account is given of a tree of this description, which was found to be at the base no less than fifty-six feet in girth. On the longevity of trees, see *Bibliotheca Univ.,* May 1831, quoted in Lyell's *Geology,* ii. 261. The idea here is, simply, that his people would attain to an age like that of the trees of the forest ; that is, that the state of things under the Messiah would be *as if* human life were greatly prolonged (see Notes on ver. 20). ¶ *And mine elect shall long enjoy the work of their hands.* Marg. ' Make them continue long,' *or* ' wear out.' The word here used (יְבַלּוּ from בָּלָה) means properly to fall, to fall away, to fail ; to wear out, to wax old (Deut. viii. 4 ; xxix. 4 ; Isa. l. 9 ; li. 6) ; hence in Piel, *to consume.* The idea here is, that they would live to consume ; *i.e.,* to enjoy the productions of their own labour. Their property should not be wrested from them by injurious taxation, or by plunder ; but they would be permitted long to possess it, until they

23 They shall not labour in vain;
nor bring forth for trouble: for they
are [a] the seed of the blessed of the
LORD, and their offspring with them.

24 And it shall come to pass,
that before they call, I will answer;
and [b] while they are yet speaking,
I will hear.

a ch.61.9; Ro.9.7,8.

b Ps.32.5; Da.9.20,21.

should *wear it out*, or until it should be consumed. Vulg. ' The works of their hands shall be of long continuance (*inveterabunt*),' or shall be kept a long time. The LXX. ' For the works of their labours (τῶν πόνων) shall become old, or of long continuance (παλαιώσουσιν).' See Notes on ch. lxii. 8, 9.

23. *They shall not labour in vain.* That is, either because their land shall be unfruitful, or because others shall plunder them. ¶ *Nor bring forth for trouble.* Lowth renders this, ' Neither shall they generate a short-lived race.' Noyes, ' Nor bring forth children for an early death.' The LXX. render it, Οὐδὲ τεκνοποιήσουσιν εἰς κατάραν—' Nor shall they bring forth children for a curse.' The Chaldee, ' Nor shall they nourish them for death.' There can be no doubt that this refers to their posterity, and that the sense is, that they should not be the parents of children who would be subject to an early death or to a curse. The word here rendered ' bring forth' (יֵלְדוּ) is a word that uniformly means to bear, to bring forth as a mother, or to beget as a father. And the promise here is, that which would be so grateful to parental feelings, that their posterity would be long-lived and respected. The word here rendered ' trouble' (בֶהָלָה) means properly *terror*, and then the effect of terror, or that which causes terror, sudden destruction. It is derived from בָהַל *bâhâl*, to trouble, to shake, to be in trepidation, to flee, and then to punish suddenly ; and the connection here seems to require the sense that their children should not be devoted to sudden destruction. ¶ *For they* are *the seed of the blessed of the* LORD (see Notes on ch. lix. 21).

24. *Before they call, I will answer.* That is, their desires shall be anticipated, God will see their wants, and he will impart to them the blessings which they need. He will not wait to be applied to for the blessing. How many such blessings do all his people receive at the

hand of God ! How ready is he to anticipate our wants ! How watchful is he of our necessities ; and how rich his benevolence in providing for us ! Even the most faithful and prayerful of his people receive numerous favours and comforts at his hand for which they have not directly asked him. The prayer for the supply of our daily food, ' Give us this day our daily bread,' God had anticipated, and had prepared the means of answering it, long before, in the abundant harvest. Had he waited until the prayer was offered, it could not have been answered without a miracle. Ever watchful, he anticipates our necessities, and in his providence and grace lays the foundation for granting the favour long before we ask him. ¶ *And while they are yet speaking, I will hear.* So it was with Daniel (Dan. ix. 20, 21 ; comp. Ps. xxxii. 5). So it was with the early disciples when they were assembled in an upper room in Jerusalem, and when the Spirit of God descended with great power on the day of Pentecost (Acts ii. 1, 2). So when Paul and Silas, in the prison at Philippi, ' prayed and sang praises to God,' he heard them and came for their rescue (Acts xvi. 25, 26). So it has often been—and especially in revivals of religion. When his people have been deeply impressed with a sense of the languishing state of religion ; when they have gone unitedly before God and implored a blessing ; God has heard their prayers, and even while they were speaking has begun a work of grace. Hundreds of such instances have occurred, alike demonstrating the faithfulness of God to his promises, and fitted to encourage his people, and to excite them to prayer. It is one of the precious promises pertaining to the blessings of the reign of the Messiah, that the answer of prayer shall be IMMEDIATE —and for this his people should look, and this they should expect. God can as easily answer prayer at once as to

25 The *a* wolf and the lamb shall feed together, and the lion shall eat straw like the bullock: and dust *b shall be* the serpent's meat. They shall not hurt nor destroy in all my holy mountain, saith the LORD.

a ch.11.6-9.   *b* Ge.3.14.

CHAPTER LXVI.

ANALYSIS.

IT is generally supposed that this chapter is a continuation of the subject of the foregoing (Lowth). The general design is to reprove the hypocritical portion of the nation, and to comfort the pious with the assurance of the favour of God, the accession of the Gentile world, and the destruction of the foes of the church. The Jews valued themselves much upon the pomp of their temple-worship and the splendour of their ritual; they supposed that that was to be perpetual; and they assumed great merit to

delay it; and when the proper state of mind exists, he is as ready to answer it now as to defer it to a future time. What encouragement have we to pray! How faithful, how fervent should we be in our supplications! How full of guilt are we if one single blessing is withheld from our world that *might* have been imparted if we had prayed as we ought; if one single soul shall be lost who might have been saved if WE had not been unfaithful in prayer!

25. *The wolf and the lamb shall feed together* (see Notes on ch. xi.) ¶ *And the lion shall eat straw.* Shall eat hay or provender like the ox. The food of the lion now is flesh. Changes shall take place as great *as if* his nature were changed, and he should graze with the herds of the field. See a full illustration of this sentiment from the classic writers in the Notes on ch. xi. 6. ¶ *Like the bullock.* Or the ox—the cattle that *herd* together—for so the Hebrew word (בָּקָר) means. The word may be applied to a bullock, an ox, or a cow. ¶ *And dust* shall be *the serpent's meat.* There is evidently here an allusion to the sentence pronounced on the serpent in Gen. iii. 14. The meaning of the declaration here is, probably, that dust should *continue* to be the food of the serpent. The sentence on him should

themselves for the regular servives of their religion. Before the captivity in Babylon they were prone to fall into idolatry; afterwards they were kept from it, and to the present time they have not been guilty of it—so effectual was that heavy judgment in correcting this national propensity. But after their captivity their national proneness to sin assumed another form. That love of form and strict ceremony; that dependence on mere rites and the external duties of religion; that heartless and pompous system of worship commenced, which ultimately terminated in Pharisaic pride, and which was scarcely less an object of abhorrence to God than gross idolatry. To that state of things the prophet probably looked forward; and his object in this chapter was to reprove that reliance on the mere forms of external worship, and the pride in their temple and its service which he saw would succeed the return from the exile in Babylon.

It is generally agreed that the reference here is to the state of things which would follow the return from Babylon. Lowth supposes that it refers to the time when Herod would be rebuild-

be perpetual. He should be no injurious to man—either by tempting him again, or by the venom of his fangs. The state of security would be as great under the Messiah *as if* the most deadly and poisonous kinds of reptiles should become wholly innoxious, and should not attempt to prey upon men. It is to be remembered that many of the serpent kind included under the general word used here (נָחָשׁ), were dangerous to men; and indeed a large portion of them are deadly in their bite. But in future times there will be a state of security as great *as if* the whole serpent tribe were innocuous and should live on the dust alone. There can be no doubt that the prophet means here to describe the passions and evil propensities of men, which have a strong resemblance to the ferocity of the wolf, or the lion, and the deadly poison of the serpent, and to say that those passions would be subdued, and that peace and concord would prevail on the earth (see Notes on ch. xi. 8). ¶ *They shall not hurt nor destroy.* See this explained in the Notes on ch. xi. 9. All this is partially realized wherever the gospel prevails, but it will be more fully realized when that gospel shall exert its full power and shall be spread around the world.

ing the temple in the most magnificent manner, and when, notwithstanding the heavy judgment of God was hanging over their heads, the nation was formal in its worship, and proud and self-confident, as if it was the favourite of God. Vitringa supposes that it refers to the time of the introduction of the new economy, or the beginning of the times of the Messiah.

That it refers to times succeeding the captivity at Babylon, and is designed to be at once a prophetic description and a reproof of the sins which would prevail after their return, is apparent from the whole structure of the chapter, and particularly from the following considerations: 1. There is no one description, as in the former chapters, of the land as desolate, or the city of Jerusalem and the temple in ruins (see ch. lxiv. 10, 11). 2. There is no charge against them for being *idolatrous*, as there had been in the previous chapters (see especially ch. lxv. 3, 4, 11). The sin that is specified here is of a wholly different kind. 3. It is evidently addressed to them when they were either rebuilding the temple, or when they greatly prided themselves on its service (see ver. 1). 4. It is addressed to them when they were engaged in offering sacrifice with great formality, and with great reliance on the mere external services of religion; when sacrifice had degenerated into mere form, and when the spirit with which it was done was as abominable in the sight of God as the most odious of all crimes. From these considerations, it seems to me that the chapter is designed to refer to a state of things that would succeed the return from the exile at Babylon, and be a *general* description of the spirit with which they would then engage in the worship of God. They would indeed rebuild the temple according to the promise; but they would manifest a spirit in regard to the temple which required the severe reproof of JEHOVAH. They would again offer sacrifice in the place where their fathers had done it; but though they would be effectually cured of their idolatrous tendencies, yet they would evince a spirit that was as hateful to God as the worst form of idolatry, or the most heinous crimes. A large portion, therefore, of the nation would still be the object of the Divine abhorrence, and be subjected to punishment; but the truly pious would be preserved, and their number would be increased by the accession of the Gentile world.

As an additional consideration to show the correctness of this view of the time to which the chapter refers, we may remark, that a large part of the prophecies of Isaiah are employed in predicting the certain return from the exile, the re-establishment of religion in their own land,

and the resumption of the worship of God there. It was natural, therefore, that the spirit of inspiration should glance at the character of the nation *subsequent* to the return, and that the prophet should give, in the conclusion of his book, *a summary graphic description of what would occur in future times.* This I take to be the design of the closing chapter of the prophecies of Isaiah. He states in general the character of the Jewish people after the return from the exile; condemns the sins with which they would then be chargeable; comforts the portion of the nation that would be disposed in sincerity to serve God; predicts the rapid and glorious increase of the church; declares that the enemies of God would be cut off; affirms that all the world would yet come at stated seasons to worship before God; and closes the whole book by saying that the people of God would go forth and see all their enemies slain. This general view may be more distinctly seen by the following analysis of the chapter:—

I. JEHOVAH says that heaven was his throne, and the earth his footstool, and that no house which they could build for him would adequately express his glory; no external worship would suitably declare his majesty. He preferred the homage of an humble heart to the most magnificent external worship; the tribute of a sincere offering to the most costly outward devotion (1, 2).

II. He declares his sense of the evil of mere external worship, and threatens punishment to the hypocrites who should engage in this manner in his service (3, 4). In these verses it is implied that in the service of the temple after the return from the exile, there would be a spirit evinced in their public worship that would be as hateful to God as would be murder or idolatry, or as would be the cutting off a dog's neck or the sacrifice of swine; that is, that the spirit of hypocrisy, self-righteousness, and pride, would be supremely odious in his sight. They were not therefore to infer that *because* they would be restored from the exile, therefore their worship would be pure and acceptable to God. The fact would be that it would become so utterly abominable in his sight that he would cut them off and bring all their fears upon them; that is, he would severely punish them.

III. Yet even then there would be a portion of the people that would hear the word of the Lord, and to whom he would send comfort and deliverance. He therefore promises to his true church great extension, and especially the accession of the Gentiles (5–14). 1. A part of the nation would cast out and persecute the other, under pretence of promoting the glory of God and doing his will (5). Yet JEHOVAH would appear for the joy of the persecuted portion, and the persecutors would be confounded. 2. A sound is heard as of great agitation in the city; a voice indicating great and important revolutions (6). This voice is designed to produce consolation to his people; dismay to his foes. 3. A promise is given of the great and sudden enlargement of Zion—an increase when conversions would be as sudden as if a child were born without the ordinary delay and pain of parturition; as great as if a nation were born in a day (7–9). 4. All that love Zion are called on to rejoice with her, for the Gentile nations would come like a flowing stream, and the church would be comforted, as when a mother comforteth her child (10–14).

IV. God would punish his foes. He would devote idolaters to destruction (15–17).

V. He would send the message of salvation to those who were in distant parts of the world (19–21).

VI. At that time, the worship of God would everywhere be regularly and publicly celebrated. From one new moon to another, and from one Sabbath to another, all flesh would come and worship before God (23).

VII. The friends of God would be permitted to see the final and interminable ruin of all the transgressors against the Most High (24). Their destruction would be complete; their worm would not die, and their fire would not be quenched, and the whole scene of the work of redemption would be wound up in the complete and eternal salvation of all the true people of God, and in the complete and eternal ruin of all his foes. With this solemn truth—a truth relating to the final retribution of mankind, the prophecies of Isaiah appropriately close. Where more properly could be the winding up of the series of visions in this wonderful book, than in a view of the complete destruction of the enemies of God; how more sublimely than by representing the whole redeemed church as going forth together to look upon their destruction, as victors go forth to look upon a mighty army of foes slain and unburied on the battle-field?

THUS saith the LORD, The heaven *a is* my throne, and the earth *is* my footstool : where *is* the house that ye build unto me? and where *is* the place of my rest?

a 2 Ch.6.18; Mat.5.34; Ac.17.24.

CHAPTER LXVI.

1. *The heaven* is *my throne* (see Notes on ch. lvii. 15). Here he is represented as having his seat or throne there. He speaks as a king. Heaven is the place where he holds his court ; whence he dispenses his commands ; and from whence he surveys all his works (comp. 2 Chron. vi. 18; Matt. v. 34). The idea here is, that as God dwelt in the vast and distant heavens, no *house* that could be built on earth could be magnificent enough to be his abode. ¶ *The earth* is *my footstool.* A footstool is that which is placed under the feet when we sit. The idea here is, that God was so glorious that even the earth itself could be regarded only as his footstool. It is probable that the Saviour had this passage in his eye in his declaration in the sermon on the mount, 'Swear not at all ; neither by heaven, for it is God's throne; nor by the earth, for it is his footstool' (Matt. v. 34, 35). ¶ *Where* is *the house that ye build unto me?* What house can you build that will be an appropriate dwelling for him who fills heaven and earth? The same idea, substantially, was expressed by Solomon when he dedicated the temple: 'But will God indeed dwell on the earth? Behold, the heaven, and heaven of heavens cannot contain thee ; how much less this house that I have builded!' (1 Kings viii. 27.) Substantially the same thought is found in the address of Paul at Athens : 'God, that made the world, and all things therein, seeing that he is Lord of heaven and earth, dwelleth not in temples made with hands' (Acts xvii. 24). ¶ *And where* is *the place of my rest?* It has already been intimated (in the analysis) that this refers probably to the time subsequent to the captivity. Lowth supposes that it refers to the time of the rebuilding of the temple by Herod. So also Vitringa understands it, and supposes that it refers to the pride and self-confidence of those who then imagined that they were rearing a structure that was *worthy* of being a dwelling-place of JEHOVAH. Grotius supposes that it refers to the time of the Maccabees, and that it was designed to give consolation to the pious of those times when they were about to witness the profanation of the temple by Anti-

2 For all those *things* hath mine hand made, and all those *things* have been, saith the LORD : but to this *man* will I look, *even to him that is* poor *a* and of a contrite spirit, *b* and trembleth *c* at my word.

3 He that killeth an ox *is as if* he slew a man ; he that sacrificeth

a *lamb, as if* he cut off a dog's neck ; he that offereth an oblation, *as if he offered* swine's blood ; he that *2* burneth incense, *as if* he blessed an idol. Yea, they have chosen their own ways, and their soul delighteth in their abominations.

a Mat.5.3.   *b* ch.57.15.   *c* Ezr.9.4; 10.3.

1 or, *kid.*   2 *maketh a memorial of,* Le.2.2.

ochus, and the cessation of the sacrifices for three years and a half. 'God therefore shows,' says he, 'that there was no reason why they should be offended in this thing. The most acceptable temple to him was a pious mind ; and from that the value of all sacrifices was to be estimated.' Abarbanel supposes that it refers to the times of redemption. His words are these : ' I greatly wonder at the words of the learned interpreting this prophecy, when they say that the prophet in this accuses the men of his own time on account of sacrifices offered with impure hands ; for lo ! all these prophecies which the prophet utters in the end of his book have respect to future redemption.' See Vitringa. That it refers to some future time when the temple should be rebuilt seems to me to be evident. But what precise period it refers to—whether to times not far succeeding the captivity, or to the times of the Maccabees, or to the time of the rebuilding of the temple by Herod, it is difficult to find any data by which we can determine. From the whole strain of the prophecy, and particularly from ver. 3–5, it seems probable that it refers to the time when the temple which Herod had reared was finishing ; when the nation was full of pride, self-righteousness, and hypocrisy ; and when all sacrifices were about to be superseded by the one great sacrifice which the Messiah was to make for the sins of the world. At that time, God says that the spirit which would be evinced by the nation would be abominable in his sight ; and to offer sacrifice then, and with the spirit which they would manifest, would be as offensive as murder or the sacrifice of a dog (see Notes on ver. 3).

2. *For all those* things *hath mine hand made.* That is, the heaven and

the earth, and all that is in them. The sense is, ' I have founded for myself a far more magnificent and appropriate temple than you can make ; I have formed the heavens as my dwelling-place, and I need not a dwelling reared by the hand of man.' ¶ *And all those* things *have been.* That is, have been made by me, or for me. The LXX. render it, ' All those things are mine.' Jerome renders it, ' All those things *were made ;*' implying that God claimed to be the Creator of them all, and that, therefore, they all belonged to him. ¶ *But to this* man *will I look.* That is, ' I prefer a humble heart and a contrite spirit to the most magnificent earthly temple ' (see Notes on ch. lvii. 15). ¶ *That is poor.* Or rather ' humble.' The word rendered ' poor ' (עָנִי), denotes not one who has no property, but one who is down-trodden, crushed, afflicted, oppressed ; often, as here, with the accessory idea of pious feeling (Ex. xxiv. 12 ; Ps. x. 2, 9). The LXX. render it, Ταπεινὸν—' Humble ;' not πτωχόν (*poor*). The idea is, not that God looks with favour on a poor man merely *because* he is poor—which is not true, for his favours are not bestowed in view of external conditions in life—but that he regards with favour the man that is humble and subdued in spirit. ¶ *And of a contrite spirit.* A spirit that is broken, crushed, or deeply affected by sin. It stands opposed to a spirit that is proud, haughty, self-confident, and self-righteous. ¶ *And that trembleth at my word.* That fears me, or that reveres my commands.

3. *He that killeth an ox* is as if *he slew a man.* Lowth and Noyes render this, ' He that slayeth an ox, killeth a man.' This is a literal translation of the Hebrew. Jerome renders it, ' He who sacrifices an ox is *as if (quasi)* he

slew a man.' The LXX., in a very free translation—such as is common in their version of Isaiah—render it, 'The wicked man who sacrifices a calf, is as he who kills a dog; and he who offers to me fine flour, it is as the blood of swine.' Lowth supposes the sense to be, that the most flagitious crimes were united with hypocrisy, and that they who were guilty of the most extreme acts of wickedness at the same time affected great strictness in the performance of all the external duties of religion. An instance of this, he says, is referred to by Ezekiel, where he says, 'When they had slain their children to their idols, then they came the same day into my sanctuary to profane it' (ch. xxiii. 39). There can be no doubt that such offences were often committed by those who were very strict and zealous in their religious services (comp. ch. i. 11–14, with ver. 21–23. But the generality of interpreters have supposed that a different sense was to be affixed to this passage. According to their views, the particles *as if* are to be supplied; and the sense is, not that the mere killing of an ox is as sinful in the sight of God as deliberate murder, but that he who did it in the circumstances, and with the spirit referred to, evinced a spirit as odious in his sight as though he had slain a man. So the LXX., Vulgate, Chaldee, Symmachus, and Theodotion, Junius, and Tremellius, Grotius, and Rosenmüller, understand it. There is probably an allusion to the fact that human victims were offered by the heathen; and the sense is, that the sacrifices here referred to were no more acceptable in the sight of God than they were. The prophet here refers, probably, first, to the *spirit* with which this was done. Their sacrifices were offered with a temper of mind as offensive to God as if a man had been slain, and they had been guilty of murder. They were proud, vain, and hypocritical. They had forgotten the true nature and design of sacrifice, and such worship could not but be an abhorrence in the sight of God. Secondly, It may also be implied here, that the period was coming when all sacrifices would be unacceptable to God. When the Messiah should have come; when he should have

made by one offering a sufficient atonement for the sins of the whole world; then all bloody sacrifices would be needless, and would be offensive in the sight of God. The sacrifice of an ox would be no more acceptable than the sacrifice of a man; and all offerings with a view to propitiate the Divine favour, or that implied that there was a deficiency in the merit of the one great atoning sacrifice, would be odious to God. ¶ *He that sacrificeth a lamb.* Marg. 'Kid.' The Hebrew word (שֶׂה) may refer to one of a flock, either of sheep or goats (Gen. xxii. 7, 8; xxx. 32). Where the species is to be distinguished, it is usually specified, as, *e.g.*, Deut. xiv. 4, שֵׂה כְשָׂבִים וְשֵׂה עִזִּים (*one of the sheep and one of the goats*). Both were used in sacrifice. ¶ As if *he cut off a dog's neck.* That is, as if he had cut off a dog's neck for sacrifice. To offer a dog in sacrifice would have been abominable in the view of a Jew. Even the price for which he was sold was not permitted to be brought into the house of God for a vow (Deut. xxiii. 18; comp. 1 Sam. xvii. 43; xxiv. 14). The dog was held in veneration by many of the heathen, and was even offered in sacrifice; and it was, doubtless, partly in view of this fact, and especially of the fact that such veneration was shown for it in Egypt, that it was an object of such detestation among the Jews. Thus Juvenal, *Sat.* xiv. says:

Oppida tota canem venerantur, nemo Dianam.

'Every city worships the dog; none worship Diana.' Diodorus (B. i.) says, 'Certain animals the Egyptians greatly venerate (σέβονται), not only when alive, but when they are dead, as cats, ichneumons, mice, and dogs.' Herodotus says also of the Egyptians, ' In some cities, when a cat dies all the inhabitants cut off their eyebrows; when a dog dies, they shave the whole body and the head.' In Samothracia there was a cave in which dogs were sacrificed to Hecate. Plutarch says, that all the Greeks sacrificed the dog. The fact that dogs were offered in sacrifice by the heathen is abundantly proved by Bochart (*Hieroz.* i. 2. 56). No kind of sacrifice could have been regarded with higher detestation by a pious Jew. But

4 I also will choose their [1] delusious, *a* and will bring their fears upon them ; because *b* when 1 called, none did answer; when I spake, they did not hear : but they did evil before mine eyes, and chose *that* in which I delighted not.

1 or, *devices.*   *a* 2 Th.2.11.

5 Hear the word of the LORD, ye that tremble *c* at his word : Your brethren that hated you, that cast you out for my name's sake, said, Let the LORD be glorified : but he shall appear to your joy, and they shall be ashamed.

b ch.65.12; Je.7.13,14.   *c* ver.2.

God here says, that the spirit with which they sacrificed a goat or a lamb was as hateful in his sight as would be the sacrifice of a dog : or that the time would come when, the great sacrifice for sin having been made, and the necessity for all other sacrifice having ceased, the offering of a lamb or a goat for the expiation of sin would be as offensive to him as would be the sacrifice of a dog. ¶ *He that offereth an oblation.* On the word here rendered ' oblation' (מִנְחָה) see Notes on ch. i. 13. ¶ As if he offered *swine's blood.* The sacrifice of a hog was an abomination in the sight of the Hebrews (see Notes on ch. lxv. 4). Yet here it is said that the offering of the *minhhâ,* in the spirit in which they would do it, was as offensive to God as would be the pouring out of the blood of the swine on the altar, Nothing could more emphatically express the detestation of God for the spirit with which they would make their offerings, or the fact that the time would come when all such modes of worship would be offensive in his sight. ¶ *He that burneth incense.* See the word ' incense' explained in the Notes on ch. i. 13. The margin here is, ' Maketh a memorial of.' Such is the usual meaning of the word here used (זָכַר), meaning to remember, and in Hiphil to cause to remember, or to make a memorial. Such is its meaning here. Incense was burned as a *memorial* or a remembrance-offering ; that is, to keep up the remembrance of God on the earth by public worship (see Notes on ch. lxii. 6). ¶ As if *he blessed an idol.* The spirit with which incense would be offered would be as offensive as idolatry. The sentiment in all this is, that the most regular and formal acts of worship where the heart is wanting, may be as offensive to God as the worst forms of crime, or the

most gross and debasing idolatry. Such a spirit often characterized the Jewish people, and eminently prevailed at the time when the temple of Herod was nearly completed, and when the Saviour was about to appear.

4. *I also will choose their delusions.* Marg. ' Devices.' The Hebrew word here rendered ' delusions' and ' devices' (תַּעֲלוּלִים) properly denotes petulance, sauciness ; and then vexation, adverse destiny, from עָלַל, *âlăl,* to do, to accomplish, to do evil, to maltreat. It is not used in the sense of delusions, or devices ; and evidently here means the same as calamity or punishment. Comp. the Heb. in Lam. i. 22. Lowth and Noyes render it, ' Calamities ;' though Jerome and the LXX. understand it in the sense of illusions or delusions ; the former rendering it, ' *Illusiones,*' and the latter ἐμπαίγματα — ' delusions.' The parallelism requires us to understand it of calamity, or something answering to ' fear,' or that which was dreaded ; and the sense undoubtedly is, that God would choose out for them the kind of punishment which would be expressive of his sense of the evil of their conduct. ¶ *And will bring their fears upon them.* That is, the punishment which they have so much dreaded, or which they had so much reason to apprehend. ¶ *Because when I called* (see Notes on ch. lxv. 12). ¶ *But they did evil before mine eyes* (see Notes on ch. lxv. 3).

5. *Hear the word of the* LORD. This is an address to the pious and persecuted portion of the nation. It is designed for their consolation, and contains the assurance that JEHOVAH would appear in their behalf, and that they should be under his protecting care though they were cast out by their brethren. To whom this refers has been a question with expositors, and it

is perhaps not possible to determine with certainty. Rosenmüller supposes that it refers to the pious whom the ' Jews and Benjaminites repelled from the worship of the temple.' Grotius supposes that it refers to those ' who favoured Onias ;' that is, in the time of Antiochus Epiphanes. Vitringa supposes that the address is to the apostles, disciples, and followers of the Lord Jesus ; and that it refers to the persecution which would be excited against them by the Jewish people. This seems to me to be the most probable opinion : 1. Because the whole structure of the chapter (see the analysis) seems to refer to the period when the Messiah should appear. 2. Because the state of things described in this verse exactly accords with what occurred on the introduction of Christianity. They who embraced the Messiah were excommunicated and persecuted ; and they who did it believed, or professed to believe, that they were doing it for the glory of God. 3. The promise that JEHOVAH would appear for their joy, and for the confusion of their foes, is one that had a clear fulfilment in his interposition in behalf of the persecuted church. ¶ *Your brethren that hated you.* No hatred of others was ever more bitter than was that evinced by the Jews for those of their nation who embraced Jesus of Nazareth as the Messiah. If this refers to his time, then the language is plain. But to whatever time it refers, it describes a state of things where the pious part of the nation was persecuted and opposed by those who were their kinsmen according to the flesh. ¶ *That cast you out.* The word here used is one that is commonly employed to denote excommunication or exclusion from the privileges connected with the public worship of God. It is language which will accurately describe the treatment which the apostles and the early disciples of the Redeemer received at the hand of the Jewish people (see John xvi. 2, and the Acts of the Apostles generally). ¶ *For my name's sake.* This language closely resembles that which the Saviour used respecting his own disciples and the persecutions to which they would be exposed : ' But all

these things will they do unto you for my name's sake, because they know not him that sent me ' (John xv. 21; comp. Matt. x. 22; xxiv. 9). I have no doubt that this refers to that period, and to those scenes. ¶ *Said, Let the* LORD *be glorified.* That is, they profess to do it to honour God ; or because they suppose that he requires it. Or it means, that even while they were engaged in this cruel persecution, and these acts of excommunicating their brethren, they professed to be serving God, and manifested great zeal in his cause. This has commonly been the case with persecutors. The most malignant and cruel persecutions of the friends of God have been originated under the pretext of great zeal in his service, and with a professed desire to honour his name. So it was with the Jews when they crucified the Lord Jesus. So it is expressly said it would be when his disciples would be excommunicated and put to death (John xvi. 2). So it was in fact in the persecutions excited by the Jews against the apostles and early Christians (see Acts vi. 13, 14; xxi. 28–31). So it was in *all* the persecutions of the Waldenses by the Papists ; in all the horrors of the Inquisition ; in all the crimes of the Duke of Alva. So it was in the bloody reign of Mary ; and so it has ever been in all ages and in all countries where Christians have been persecuted. The people of God have suffered most from those who have been *conscientious persecutors ;* and the most malignant foes of the church have been found *in* the church, persecuting true Christians under great pretence of zeal for the purity of religion. It is no evidence of piety that a man is full of conscientious zeal against those whom he chooses to regard as heretics. And it should always be regarded as proof of a *bad* heart, and a *bad* cause, when a man endeavours to inflict pain and disgrace on others, on account of their religious opinions, under pretence of great regard for the honour of God. ¶ *But he shall appear to your joy.* The sense is, that God would manifest himself to his people as their vindicator, and would ultimately rescue them from their persecuting foes. If this is applied to

6 A voice of noise from the city, a voice from the temple, a voice of

the LORD that rendereth recompence to his enemies.

Christians, it means that the cause in which they were engaged would triumph. This has been the case in all persecutions. The effect has always been the permanent triumph and establishment of the cause that was persecuted. ¶ *And they shall be ashamed.* How true this has been of the Jews that persecuted the early Christians! How entirely were they confounded and overwhelmed! God established permanently the persecuted; he scattered the persecutors to the ends of the earth!

6. *A voice of noise from the city.* That is, from the city of Jerusalem. The prophet sees in a vision a tumult in the city. He hears a voice that issues from the temple. His manner and language are rapid and hurried—such as a man would evince who should suddenly see a vast tumultuous assemblage, and hear a confused sound of many voices. There is also a remarkable abruptness in the whole description here. The preceding verse was calm and solemn. It was full of affectionate assurance of the Divine favour to those whom the prophet saw to be persecuted. Here the scene suddenly changes. The vision passes to the agitating events which were occurring in the city and the temple, and to the great and sudden change which would be produced in the condition of the church of God. But to whom or what this refers has been a subject of considerable difference of opinion. Grotius understands it of the sound of triumph of Judas Maccabeus, and of his soldiers, rejoicing that the city was forsaken by Antiochus, and by the party of the Jews who adhered to him. Rosenmüller understands it of the voice of God, who is seen by the prophet taking vengeance on his foes. There can be no doubt that the prophet, in vision, sees JEHOVAH taking recompence on his enemies —for that is expressly specified. Still it is not easy to determine the exact time referred to, or the exact scene which passes before the mind of the prophet. To me it seems probable that it is a scene that immediately preceded

the rapid extension of the gospel, and the great and sudden increase of the church by the accession of the heathen world (see the following verses); and I would suggest, whether it is not a vision of the deeply affecting and agitating scenes when the temple and city were about to be destroyed by the Romans; when the voice of JEHOVAH would be heard in the city and at the temple, declaring the punishment which he would bring on those who had cast out and rejected the followers of the Messiah (ver. 5); and when, as a result of this, the news of salvation was to be rapidly spread throughout the heathen world. This is the opinion, also, of Vitringa. The phrase rendered here 'a voice of noise' (קוֹל שָׁאוֹן), means properly the voice of a tumultuous assemblage; the voice of a multitude. The word 'noise' (שָׁאוֹן) is applied to a noise or roaring, as of waters (Ps. lxv. 8); or of a crowd or multitude of men (Isa. v. 14; xiii. 4; xxiv. 8); and of war (Amos ii. 2; Hos. x. 14). Here it seems probable that it refers to the confused clamour of war, the battle cry raised by soldiers attacking an army or a city; and the scene described is probably that when the Roman soldiers burst into the city, scaled the walls, and poured desolation through the capital. ¶ *A voice from the temple.* That is, either the tumultuous sound of war already having reached the temple; or the voice of JEHOVAH speaking from the temple, and commanding destruction on his foes. Vitringa supposes that it may mean the voice of JEHOVAH breaking forth from the temple, and commanding his foes to be slain. But to whichever it refers, it doubtless means that the sound of the tumult was not only *around* the city, but *in* it; not merely in the distant parts, but in the very midst, and even at the temple. ¶ *A voice of the* LORD *that rendereth recompence.* Here we may observe—1. That it is recompence taken on those who had cast out their brethren (ver. 5). 2. It is vengeance taken within the city, and on the *internal,* not the *external* enemies. 3. It

7 Before she travailed, she brought forth ; before her pain came, she was delivered of a man child.

8 Who hath heard such a thing? who hath seen such things ? Shall the earth be made to bring forth in one day ? or shall a nation be born at once ? for *a* as soon as Zion travailed, she brought forth her children.

a Ac.2.44,47.

is vengeance taken in the midst of this tumult. All this is a striking description of the scene when the city and temple were taken by the Roman armies. It was the vengeance taken on those who had cast out their brethren; it was the vengeance which was to precede the glorious triumph of truth and of the cause of the true religion.

7. *Before she travailed, she brought forth.* That is, Zion. The idea here is, that there would be a great and sudden increase of her numbers. Zion is here represented, as it often is, as a female (see ch. i. 8), and as the mother of spiritual children (comp. ch. liv. 1; xlix. 20, 21). The *particular* idea here is, that the increase would be *sudden*— as if a child were born without the usual delay and pain of parturition. If the interpretation given of the 6th verse be correct, then this refers probably to the sudden increase of the church when the Messiah came, and to the great revivals of religion which attended the first preaching of the gospel. Three thousand were converted on a single day (Acts ii.), and the gospel was speedily propagated almost all over the known world. Vitringa supposes that it refers to the sudden conversion of the Gentiles, and their accession to the church. ¶ *She was delivered of a man child.* Jerome understands this of the Messiah, who was descended from the Jewish church. Grotius supposes that the whole verse refers to Judas Maccabeus, and to the liberation of Judea under him before any one could have hoped for it ! Calvin (*Comm. in loc.*) supposes that the word *male* here, or *man-child,* denotes the manly or generous nature of those who should be converted to the church ; that they would be vigorous and active, not effeminate and delicate (*generosam prolem, non mollem aut effeminatam*). Vitringa refers it to the character and rank of those who should be converted, and applies it par-

ticularly to Constantine, and to the illustrious philosophers, orators, and senators, who were early brought under the influence of the gospel. The Hebrew word probably denotes a *male,* or a man-child, and it seems to me that it is applied here to denote the character of the early converts to the Christian faith. They would not be feeble and effeminate ; but vigorous, active, energetic. It *may*, perhaps, also be suggested, that, among the Orientals, the birth of a son was deemed of much more importance, and was regarded as much more a subject of congratulation than the birth of a female. If an allusion be had to that fact, then the idea is, that the increase of the church would be such as would be altogether a subject of exultation and joy.

8. *Who hath heard such a thing ?* Of a birth so sudden. Usually in childbirth there are the pains of protracted parturition. The earth brings forth its productions gradually and slowly. Nations rise by degrees, and are long in coming to maturity. But here is such an event as if the earth should in a day be covered with a luxuriant vegetation, or as if a nation should spring at once into being. The increase in the church would be as great and wonderful as if these changes were to occur in a moment. ¶ *Shall the earth be made to bring forth in one day ?* That is, to produce its grass, and flowers, and fruit, and trees. The idea is, that it usually requires much longer time for it to mature its productions. The germ does not start forth at once; the flower, the fruit, the yellow harvest, and the lofty tree are not produced in a moment. Months and years are required before the earth would be covered with its luxuriant and beautiful productions But here would be an event as remarkable *as if* the earth should bring forth its productions in a single day. ¶ *Or shall a nation be born at once ?* Such

9 Shall I bring to the birth, and not cause [1] to bring forth? saith the LORD : shall I cause to bring forth, and shut *the womb ?* saith thy God.

10 Rejoice [a] ye with Jerusalem, and be glad with her, all ye that

love her : rejoice for joy with her, all ye that mourn for her :

11 That ye may suck, [b] and be satisfied with the breasts of her consolations ; that ye may milk out, and be delighted with the abundance [2] of her glory.

1 or, *beget.*   a Ps.26.8; 84.1-4; 122.6.   b 1 Pe.2.2.   2 or, *brightness.*

---

an event never *has* occurred. A nation is brought into existence by degrees. Its institutions are matured gradually, and usually by the long process of years. But here is an event as remarkable *as if* a whole nation should be born at once, and stand before the world, mature in its laws, its civil institutions, and in all that constitutes greatness. In looking for the fulfilment of this, we naturally turn the attention to the rapid progress of the gospel in the times of the apostles, when events occurred as sudden and as remarkable *as if* the earth, after the desolation of winter or of a drought, should be covered with rich luxuriance in a day, or as if a whole nation should start into existence, mature in all its institutions, in a moment. But there is no reason for limiting it to that time. Similar sudden changes are to be expected still on the earth ; and I see no reason why this should not be applied to the spread of the gospel in heathen lands, and why we should not yet look for the rapid propagation of Christianity in a manner as surprising and wonderful as would be such an instantaneous change in the appearance of the earth, or such a sudden birth of a kingdom.

9. *Shall I bring to the birth ?* The sense of this verse is plain. It is, that God would certainly accomplish what he had here predicted, and for which he had made ample arrangements and preparations. He would not commence the work, and then abandon it. The figure which is here used is obvious ; but one which does not render very ample illustration proper. Jarchi has well expressed it : ' Num ego adducerem uxorem meam ad sellam partus, *sc.* ad partitudinem, et non aperirem uterum ejus, ut fœtum suum in lucem produceret ? Quasi diceret ; an ego incipiam rem nec possim eam perficere ?' ¶ *Shall I cause to bring forth ?* Lowth and

Noyes render this, ' Shall I, who begat, restrain the birth ? ' This accurately expresses the idea. The meaning of the whole is, that God designed the great and sudden increase of his church ; that the plan was long laid ; and that, having done this, he would not abandon it, but would certainly effect his designs.

10. *Rejoice ye with Jerusalem.* The idea which is presented in this verse is, that it is the duty of all who love Zion to sympathize in her joys. It is one evidence of piety to rejoice in her joy ; and they who have no true joy when God pours down his Spirit, and, in a revival of religion, produces changes as sudden and transforming as if the earth were suddenly to pass from the desolation of winter to the verdure and bloom of summer ; or when the gospel makes rapid advances in the heathen world, have no true evidence that they love God or his cause. Such scenes awaken deep interest in the bosoms of angels, and in the bosom of God the Saviour ; and they who love that God and Saviour *will* rejoice in such scenes, and will mingle their joys and thanksgivings with the joys and thanksgivings of those who are thus converted and saved. ¶ *All ye that mourn for her.* That sympathize in her sorrows, and that mourn over her desolations.

11. *That ye may suck.* The same figure occurs in ch. lx. 16 ; and substantially in ch. xlix. 23. See the Notes on those places. ¶ *That ye may milk out.* The image is an obvious one. It means that they who sympathized with Zion would be nourished by the same truth, and comforted with the same sources of consolation. ¶ *And be delighted with the abundance of her glory.* Marg. ' Brightness.' Lowth renders this, ' From her abundant stores.' Noyes, ' From the fulness of her glory.'

12 For thus saith the LORD, Behold, I will extend peace to her like a river, and the glory of the Gentiles like a flowing stream : then shall ye suck, ye [a] shall be borne upon *her* sides, and be dandled upon *her* knees.

a ch.60,4,16.

Jerome (Vulg.), ' And that you may abound with delights from every kind of her glory.' The LXX. ' That sucking ye may be nourished from the commencement' (Thompson) ; ' or the entrance of her glory' (ἀπὸ εἰσόδου δόξης αὐτῆς). This variety of interpretation has arisen from the uncertain meaning of the word זִיז, *zīz*, rendered ' abundance.' Gesenius supposes that it is derived from זוּז, *zūz*, meaning, 1. *To move ;* 2. *To glance, to sparkle, to radiate,* from the idea of rapid motion ; hence, to flow out like rays, to spout like milk; and hence the noun זִיז, *zīz,* means *a breast.* This derivation may be regarded as somewhat fanciful ; but it will show why the word ' brightness' was inserted in the margin, since one of the usual significations of the verb relates to brightness, or to sparkling rays. Aquila renders it, 'Απὸ παντοδαπίας—' From every kind of abundance.' Symmachus, 'Απὸ πλήθους—' From the multitude.' The word probably refers to the abundance of the consolations which Zion possessed. Lowth proposes to change the text; but without any authority. The Chaldee renders it, ' That ye may drink of the wine of her glory;' where they probably read זִיו (*wine*), instead of the present reading, ¶ *Of her glory.* The abundant favours or blessings conferred on Zion. The glory that should be manifested to her would be the knowledge of Divine truth, and the provisions made for the salvation of men.

12. *For thus saith the* LORD. This verse contains a promise of the conversion of the Gentiles, and the fact that what constituted their glory would be brought and consecrated to the church of God. ¶ *I will extend.* The word rendered ' I will extend' (נָטָה) means properly *to stretch out,* as the hand or a measure ; then to spread out or expand, as a tent is spread out, to which it is often applied (Ge. xii. 8 ; xxvi. 5) ; or to the heavens spread out over our heads like a tent or a curtain (Isa. xl. 22).

Here it may mean either that peace would be *spread out* over the country as the waters of an overflowing river, like the Nile or Euphrates spread out over a vast region in an inundation ; or it may mean, as Gesenius supposes, ' I will *turn* peace upon her like a river ; *i.e.,* as a stream is turned in its course.' To me it seems that the former is the correct interpretation ; and that the idea is, that God would bring prosperity upon Zion like a broad majestic river overflowing all its banks, and producing abundant fertility. ¶ *Peace.* A general word denoting *prosperity* of all kinds—a favourite word with Isaiah to describe the future happiness of the church of God (see ch. ix. 6, 7 ; xxvi. 12 ; xxxii. 17 ; xlv. 7 ; xlvi. 18 ; lii. 7 ; liv. 13 ; lv. 12 ; lvii. 19). ¶ *Like a river.* That is, says Lowth. like the Euphrates. So the Chaldee interprets it. But there is no evidence that the prophet refers *particularly* to the Euphrates. The image is that suggested above—of a river that flows full, and spreads over the banks—at once an image of sublimity, and a striking emblem of great prosperity. This same image occurs in ch. xlviii. 18. See Notes on that place. ¶ *And the glory of the Gentiles* (see Notes on ch. lx. 5, 11). ¶ *Like a flowing stream.* Like the Nile, says Vitringa. But the word נַחַל is not commonly applied to a *river* like the Nile ; but to a torrent, a brook, a rivulet—either as flowing from a perennial fountain, or more commonly a stream running in a valley that is swelled often by rain, or by the melting of snows in the mountain (see Reland's *Palestine,* ch. xlv.) Such is the idea here. The peace or prosperity of Zion would be like such a swollen stream—a stream overflowing (שׁוֹטֵף) its banks. ¶ *Then shall ye suck ;* ver. 11. ¶ *Ye shall be borne upon* her *sides.* See this phrase explained in the Notes on ch. lx. 4. ¶ *And be dandled upon* her *knees.* As a child is by its nurse or mother. The idea is, that the tender-

13 As one whom his mother comforteth, so will I comfort you; and ye shall be comforted in Jerusalem.

14 And when ye see *this*, your heart shall rejoice, *a* and your bones shall *b* flourish like an herb: and the hand of the LORD shall be

known towards his servants, and *his* indignation towards his enemies.

15 For *c* behold, the LORD will come with fire, and with his chariots like a whirlwind, to render his anger with fury, and his rebuke with flames of fire.

a Jn.16.22.　*b* Pr.3.8; Eze.37.1-14.　*c* 2 Th.1.8.

est care would be exercised for the church; the same care which an affectionate mother evinces for her children. The insertion of the word ' *her* ' here by our translators weakens the sense. The meaning is, not that they should be borne upon the sides and dandled upon the knees of Zion or of the church; but that God would manifest to them the feelings of a parent, and treat them with the tenderness which a mother evinces for her children. As a mother nurses her children at her side (comp. Notes on ch. lx. 4), so would God tenderly provide for the church; as she affectionately dandles her children on her knees, so tenderly and affectionately would he regard Zion.

13. *As one whom his mother comforteth.* See the Notes on ch. xlix. 15, where the same image occurs.

14. *And when ye see* this. This great accession to the church from the Gentile world. ¶ *Your bones shall flourish like an herb.* This is an image which is often employed in the Scriptures. When the vigour of the body fails, or when it is much afflicted, the bones are said to be feeble or weakened, or to be dried (Ps. vi. 2; li. 8; xxii. 14, 17; xxxviii. 3; Lam. i. 13; Prov. xiv. 30; xvii. 22). In like manner, prosperity, health, vigour, are denoted by making the bones fat (see Notes on ch. lviii. 11; Prov. xv. 20), or by imparting health, marrow, or strength to them (Prov. iii. 8; xvi. 24). The sense here is, that their vigour would be greatly increased. ¶ *The hand of the LORD shall be known.* That is, it shall be seen that he is powerful to defend his people, and to punish their enemies.

15. *For behold, the LORD will come with fire.* The LXX. read this ' As fire' (ὡς πύρ). Fire is a common emblem to denote the coming of the Lord to judge and punish his enemies (Ps. l. 3):

Our God shall come, and shall not keep silence;
A fire shall devour before him,
And it shall be very tempestuous round about him.

So Habak. ii. 5:

Before him went the pestilence,
And burning coals went forth at his feet.

So Ps. xcvii. 3:

A fire goeth before him,
And burneth up his enemies round about.

So it is said (2 Thess. i. 8), that the Lord Jesus will be revealed ' in flaming fire, taking vengeance on them that know not God' (comp. Heb. x. 27; 2 Pet. iii. 7). So JEHOVAH is said to breathe out fire when he comes to destroy his foes:

There went up a smoke out of his nostrils,
And fire out of his mouth devoured;
Coals were kindled by it.

Ps. xviii. 8.

Comp. Notes on ch. xxix. 6; xxx. 30. This is a *general* promise that God would defend his church, and destroy his foes. To what this *particularly* applies, it may not be possible to determine, and instead of attempting that, I am disposed to regard it as a promise of a general nature, that God, in those future times, would destroy his foes, and would thus extend protection to his people. So far as the *language* is concerned, it may be applied either to the destruction of Jerusalem, to any mighty overthrow of his enemies, or to the day of judgment. The single truth is, that all his enemies would be destroyed as if JEHOVAH should come amidst flames of fire. That truth is enough for his church to know; that truth should be sufficient to fill a wicked world with alarm. ¶ *And with his chariots like a whirlwind.* The principal idea here is, that he would come with immense *rapidity*, like a chariot that was borne forward as on the whirlwind, to destroy his foes. God is often represented as coming in a chariot

16 For by fire and by his sword will the LORD plead with all flesh: and the slain of the LORD shall be many.

—a chariot of the clouds, or of a whirlwind. Ps. civ. 3:

Who maketh the clouds his chariot,
Who walketh upon the wings of the wind.

Comp. Ps. xviii. 10; see Note on ch. xix. 1. See also Jer. iv. 13:

Behold, he shall come up as clouds,
And his chariots shall be as a whirlwind.

Chariots were commonly made with two wheels, though sometimes they had four wheels, to which two horses, fiery and impetuous, were attached; and the rapid movement, the swift revolving wheels, and the dust which they raised, had no slight resemblance to a whirlwind (comp. Notes on ch. xxi. 7, 9). They usually had strong and sharp iron scythes affixed to the extremities of their axles, and were driven into the midst of the army of an enemy, cutting down all before them. Warriors sometimes fought standing on them, or leaping from them on the enemy. The chariots in the army of Cyrus are said to have been capacious enough to permit twenty men to fight from them. The following cut is a representation of the wooden war-chariot of the Parthians, and will give an idea of the general appearance and uses of the chariots of ancient times.

CHARIOT FROM SCULPTURES AT PERSEPOLIS.

¶ *To render his anger with fury.* Lowth renders this, ' To breathe forth his anger.' Jerome translates it, *Reddere,* i.e., to render. The LXX. 'Αποδοῦναι, to give, or to render. Lowth proposes, instead of the present text, as pointed by the Masorites, לְהָשִׁיב—*lĕhâshîbh,* to read it לְהַשִּׁיב—*lĕhassîbh,* as if it were derived from נָשַׁב—*nâshâbh.* But there is no necessity of a change. The idea is, that God would recompense his fury; or would cause his hand to turn upon them in fury. ¶ *With fury.* Lowth renders this, ' In a burning heat.' The word used (חֵמָה) properly means *heat,* then anger, wrath; and the Hebrew here might be properly rendered ' heat of his anger;' that is, glowing or burning wrath, wrath that consumes like fire. ¶ *With flames of fire.* His rebuke shall consume like fiery flames; or it shall be manifested amidst such flames.

16. *For by fire and by his sword.* The sword is an instrument by which punishment is executed (see Notes on ch. xxxiv. 5; comp. Rom. xiii. 4). ¶ *Will he plead with all flesh.* Or rather, he will judge (נִשְׁפָּט), that is, he will execute his purposes of vengeance on all the human race. Of course, only that part is intended who *ought* to be subject to punishment; that is, all his foes. ¶ *And the slain of the* LORD *shall be many.* The number of those who shall be consigned to woe will be immense— though in the winding up of the great drama at the close of the world, there is reason to hope that a large proportion of the race, taken as a whole, will be saved. Of past generations, indeed,

17 They *a*that sanctify themselves, and purify themselves in the gardens, *¹*behind one *tree* in the

a ch.65.3,4.

midst, eating swine's flesh, and the abomination, and the mouse, shall be consumed together, saith the LORD.

1 or, *one after another.*

there is no just ground of such hope; of the present generation there is no such prospect. But brighter and happier times are to come. The true religion is to spread over all the world, and for a long period is to prevail; and the hope is, that during that long period the multitude of true converts will be so great as to leave the whole number who are lost, compared with those who are saved, much less than is commonly supposed. Still the aggregate of those who are lost, 'the slain of the Lord,' will be vast. This description I regard as having reference to the coming of the Lord to judgment (comp. 2 Thess. i. 8); or if it refer to any other manifestation of Jehovah for judgment, like the destruction of Jerusalem by the Romans, it has a strong resemblance to the final judgment; and, like the description of that by the Saviour (Matt. xxiv.), the language is such as naturally to suggest, and to be applicable to, the final judgment of mankind.

17. *They that sanctify themselves.* That is, who attempt to purify themselves by idolatrous rites, by ablutions, and lustrations. The design here is, to describe those who will be exposed to the wrath of God when he shall come to execute vengeance. ¶ *And purify themselves in the gardens* (see Notes on ch. lxv. 3). ¶ *Behind one* tree *in the midst.* This passage has not a little exercised the ingenuity of commentators. It is quite evident that our translators were not able to satisfy themselves with regard to its meaning. In the margin they have rendered it, ' one after another,' supposing that it may mean that the idolaters engaged in their sacrifices in a solemn procession, walking one after another around their groves, their shrines, or their altars. In the translation in the text, they seem to have supposed that the religious rites referred to were celebrated behind one particular selected tree in the garden. Lowth renders it, ' After the rites of Achad.' Jerome renders it, *In hortis post januam intrinsecus*—' In the gardens they sanc-

tify themselves behind the gate within.' The LXX. ' Who consecrate and purify themselves (εἰς τοὺς κήπους, καὶ ἐν τοῖς προθύροις ἔσθοντες, κ.τ.λ.) for the gardens, and they who, in the outer courts, eat swine's flesh,' &c. The Chaldee renders the phrase סִיעָא בָּתַר סִיעָא *turba post turbam*—' Multitude after multitude.' The vexed Hebrew phrase used here, אַחַר אַחַד *ăhhăr ăhhădh*, it is very difficult to explain. The word אַחַר means properly *after ;* the after part; the extremity; behind—in the sense of following after, or going after any one. The word אַחַד, *ăhhădh*, means properly *one;* some one; any one. Gesenius (*Comm. in loc.*) says that the phrase may be used in one of the three following senses : 1. In the sense of one after another. So Sym. and Theo. render it —ὀπίσω ἀλλήλων. Luther renders it, *Einer hier, der andere da*—' one here, another there.' 2. The word אַחַד, *ăhhădh*, may be understood as the name of a god who was worshipped in Syria, by the name of Adad. This god is that described by Macrobius, *Sat.*, i. 23 : ' Understand what the Assyrians think about the power of the sun. For to the God whom they worship as Supreme they give the name Adad, and the signification of this name is *One.*' That the passage before us refers to this divinity is the opinion of Lowth, Grotius, Bochart, Vitringa, Dathe, and others. ' The image of Adad,' Macrobius adds, ' was designated by inclined rays, by which it was shown that the power of heaven was in the rays of the sun which were sent down to the earth.' The same god is referred to by Pliny (*Hist. Nat.* xxxvii. 71), where he mentions three gems which received their names from three parts of the body, and were called ' The veins of Adad, the eye of Adad, the finger of Adad ;' and he adds, ' This god was worshipped by the Syrians.' There can be no doubt that such a god was worshipped; but it is by no means certain that this idol is here referred to. It is not improbable, Vitringa

18 For I *know* their works and their thoughts: it shall come, that I will gather all nations and tongues; and they shall come, and see my glory.

---

remarks, that the name *Adad* should be written for *Ahhadh*, for the ease of pronunciation—as a slight change in letters was common for the purpose of euphony. But it is still not quite clear that this refers to any particular idol. 3. The third opinion is that of Gesenius, and accords substantially with that which our translators have expressed in the text. According to that, it should be rendered ' Those who sanctify and purify themselves in the [idol] groves after one in the midst;' *i.e.*, following and imitating the one priest who directed the sacred ceremonies. It may mean that a solemn procession was formed in the midst of the grove, which was led on by the priest, whom all followed ; or it may mean that they imitated him in the sacred rites. It seems to me probable that this refers to some sacred procession in honour of an idol, where the idol or the' altar was encompassed by the worshippers, and where they were led on by the officiating priest. Such processions we know were common in heathen worship. ¶ *In the midst.* In the midst of the sacred grove; that is, in the darkest and obscurest recess. Groves were selected for such worship on account of the sacred awe which it was supposed their dark shades would produce and cherish. For the same reason, therefore, the darkest retreat— the very middle of the grove—would be selected as the place where their religious ceremonies would be performed. I see no evidence that there is any allusion to any *tree* here, as our translators seem to have supposed ; still less, that there was, as Burder supposes, any allusion to the tree of life in the midst of the garden of Eden, and their attempts to cultivate and preserve the memory of it ; but there *is* reason to believe that their religious rites would be performed in the centre, or most shady part of the grove. ¶ *Eating swine's flesh.* That is, in connection with their public worship (see Notes on ch. lxv. 4). ¶ *And the abomination.* The thing which is held as abominable or detestable in the law of God. Thus the creeping thing and the reptile were regarded as abominations (Lev. xi. 41, 42). They were not to be eaten; still less were they to be offered in sacrifice (comp. Ex. viii. 26 ; Deut. xx. 16 ; xxix. 17 ; see Notes on ch. lxv. 3). ¶ *And the mouse.* The Hebrew word here used means the *dormouse*—a small field-mouse. Jerome understands it as meaning the *glis*, a small mouse that was regarded as a great delicacy by the Romans. They were carefully kept and fattened for food (see Varro, *De Rust.*, iii. 15). Bochart (*Hieroz.*, i. 3, 34) supposes that the name here used is of Chaldaic origin, and that it denotes a field-mouse. Mice abounded in the East, and were often exceedingly destructive in Syria (see Bochart; comp. 1 Sam. v. 4). Strabo mentions that so vast a multitude of mice sometimes invaded Spain as to produce a pestilence; and in some parts of Italy, the number of field-mice was so great that the inhabitants were forced to abandon the country. It was partly on account of its destructive character that it was held in abomination by the Hebrews. Yet it would seem that it was eaten by idolaters ; and was, perhaps, used either in their sacrifices or in their incantations (see Notes on ch. lxv. 4). Vitringa supposes that the description in this verse is applicable to the time of Herod, and that it refers to the number of heathen customs and institutions which were introduced under his auspices. But this is by no means certain. It may be possible that it is a general description of idolatry, and of idolaters as the enemies of God, and that the idea is, that God would come with vengeance to cut off all his foes.

18. *For I* know *their works.* The word ' know,' says Lowth, is here evidently left out of the Hebrew text, leaving the sense quite imperfect. It is found in the Syriac ; the Chaldee evidently had that word in the copy of the Hebrew which was used ; and the Aldine and Complutensian editions of the LXX. have the word. Its insertion is necessary in order to complete the sense ; though the proof is not clear

19 And I will set a sign *a* among them, and I will send those that escape of them unto the nations, *to* Tarshish, Pul, and Lud, that draw the bow, *to* Tubal and Javan, *to* the isles afar off that have not heard my fame, neither have seen my glory; *b* and they shall declare my glory among the Gentiles.

a ch.18,3,7; Lu.2.34.　　　　*b* Mal.1.11; Mat.28.19.

that the word was ever in the Hebrew text. The sense is, that though their abominable rites were celebrated in the deepest recesses of the groves, yet they were not concealed from God. ¶ *That I will gather all nations and tongues.* They who speak all languages (comp. Rev. vii. 9; x. 11; xi. 9). The sense is, that the period would come when Jehovah would collect all nations to witness the execution of his vengeance on his foes. ¶ *And see my glory.* That is, the manifestation of my perfections in the great events referred to here—the destruction of his enemies, and the deliverance of his people. To what particular period this refers has been a point on which expositors are by no means agreed. Grotius says it means, that such shall be the glory of the Jewish people that all nations shall desire to come and make a covenant with them. The Jewish interpreters, and among them Abarbanel (see Vitringa), suppose that it refers to a *hostile* and *warlike* assembling of all nations in the time of the Messiah, who, say they, shall attack Jerusalem with the Messiah in it, and shall be defeated. They mention particularly that the Turks and Christians shall make war on Jerusalem and on the true Messiah, but that they shall be overthrown. Vitringa supposes that it refers to the assembling of the nations when the gospel should be at first proclaimed, and when they should be called into the kingdom of God. Many of the Fathers referred it to the final judgment. It is difficult to determine, amidst this variety of opinion, what is the true meaning. Opinions are easily given, and conjectures are easily made ; and the opinions referred to above are entitled to little more than the appellation of conjecture. It seems to me, that there is involved here the idea of the judgment or punishment on the enemies of God, and at about the same time a collecting of the nations not only to witness the punishment, but also

to become participants of his favour. In some future time, Jehovah would manifest himself as the punisher of his enemies, and all the nations also would be permitted to behold his glory, as if they were assembled together.

19. *And I will set a sign among them* (see Notes on ch. xi. 12; xviii. 3). On the meaning of the word ' sign ' (אֹת), see Notes on ch. vii. 11. What is its meaning here is to be determined by the connection. That would seem to me to require some such interpretation as this: That when God should come (ver. 17, 18) to take vengeance on his foes, and to manifest his glory, he would establish some *mark* or *memorial ;* would erect some standard, or give some signal, by which his true friends would escape, and that he would send them to distant nations to proclaim his truth and gather together those who had not seen his glory. What that sign should be, he does not here say. Whether a standard, a secret communication, or some intimation beforehand, by which they should know the approaching danger and make their escape, is not declared. It is by no means easy to determine with certainty on this passage ; and it certainly becomes no one to speak dogmatically or very confidently. But it seems to me that the whole passage may have been intended, by the Holy Spirit, to refer to the propagation of the gospel by the apostles. The heavy judgments referred to may have been the impending calamities over Jerusalem. The glory of God referred to, may have been the signal manifestation of his perfections at that period in the approaching destruction of the city, and in the wonders that attended the coming of the Messiah. The gathering of the nations (ver. 18) *may* possibly refer to the collecting together of numerous people from all parts of the earth about that time ; that is, either the assembled people at the time of the Saviour's death (Acts ii. 8, 11), or the gathering of the armies

of the Romans—a commingled multitude from all nations—to inflict punishment on the Jewish nation, and to behold the manifestation of the Divine justice in the destruction of the guilty Jewish capital. The 'sign' here referred to, *may* denote the intimations which the Redeemer gave to his disciples to discern these approaching calamities, and to secure their safety by flight when they should be about to appear (Matt. xxiv. 15–18). By these warnings and previous intimations they were to be preserved. The sign was 'among them,' *i.e.*, in the very midst of the nation ; and the object of the intimation was, to secure their safety, and the speedy propagation of the true religion among all nations. Deeply sensible that there is great danger of erring here, and that the above view may be viewed as mere conjecture, I cannot, however, help regarding it as the true exposition. If there is error in it, it may be pardoned ; for it will probably be felt by most readers of these Notes that there has not been a *too frequent* reference in the interpretation proposed to the times of the Christian dispensation. ¶ *And I will send those that escape of them.* According to the interpretation suggested above, this refers to the portion of the Jewish nation that should escape from the tokens of the Divine displeasure ; that is, to the apostles and the early disciples of the Redeemer. The great mass of the nation would be abandoned and devoted to destruction. But a remnant would be saved (comp. ch. i. 9 ; xi. 11, 16). Of that remnant, God would send a portion to make his name known to those who had not heard it, and they would lead distant nations to the knowledge of his truth. The whole passage is so accurately descriptive of what occurred in the times when the gospel was first preached to the pagan world, that there can be little danger of error in referring it to those times. Compare Vitringa on the passage for a more full view of the reasons of this interpretation. The names of the places which follow are designed to specify the principal places where the message would be sent, and stand here as representatives of the whole heathen world. ¶ To *Tarshish* (see Notes on ch. ii. 16; xxiii. 1;

lx. 19). Tarshish was one of the most distant seaports known to the Hebrews ; and whether it be regarded as situated in Spain, or in the East Indies, or south of Abyssinia (see Notes above) it equally denotes a distant place, and the passage means that the message would be borne to the most remote regions. ¶ *Pul.* This is supposed to denote some region in Africa. Jerome renders it, 'Africa.' The LXX. Φούδ—'Phud.' Bochart, *Phaleg.* iv. 26, supposes that it means *Philae*, a large island in the Nile, between Egypt and Ethiopia ; called by the Egyptians *Pilak*, *i e.*, the border, or far country (see Champóllion, *l'Egypte*, i. 158). There are still on that island remains of some very noble and extensive temples built by the ancient Egyptians. ¶ *And Lud.* Jerome renders this, 'Lydia.' The LXX. 'Lud.' There was a Lydia in Asia Minor—the kingdom of the celebrated Crœsus ; but it is generally supposed that this place was in Africa. Ludim was a son of Mizraim (Gen. x. 13), and the name *Ludim*, or Lybians, referring to a people, several times occurs in the Bible (Jer. xlvi. 9 ; Ezek. xxvii. 10 ; xxx. 5). These African Lybians are commonly mentioned in connection with Pul, Ethiopia, and Phut. Bochart supposes that Abyssinia is intended, but it is by no means certain that this is the place referred to. Josephus affirms that the descendants of Ludim are long since extinct, having been destroyed in the Ethiopian wars. It is clear that some part of Egypt is intended, says Calmet, but it is not easy to show exactly where they dwelt. ¶ *That draw the bow* (קֶֽשֶׁת מֹשְׁכֵי). The LXX. here render the Hebrew phrase simply by Μοσόχ—'Mosoch,' understanding it of a place. Lowth supposes that the Hebrew phrase is a corruption of the word Moschi, the name of a nation situated between the Euxine and the Caspian seas. But there is no authority for supposing, as he does, that the word 'bow' has been interpolated. The Chaldee renders it, 'Drawing and smiting with the bow.' The idea is, that the nations here referred to were distinguished for the use of the bow. The bow was in common use in wars ; and it is by no means improbable that at that time they had acquired peculiar

20 And they shall bring all your brethren *for* an offering *a* unto the LORD, out of all nations, upon horses, and in chariots, and in litters,¹ and upon mules, and upon

swift beasts, to my holy mountain Jerusalem, saith tho LORD, as the children of Israel bring an offering in a clean vessel into the house of the LORD.

---

a Ro.15.16.   1 or, *coaches*.

---

celebrity in the use of this weapon. ¶ *To Tubal.* Tubal was the fifth son of Japhet, and is here joined with Javan because they were among the settlers of Europe. The names before mentioned together relate to Africa, and the sense there is, that the message should be sent to Africa ; here the idea is, that it should be sent to Europe. Tubal is commonly united with Meshech, and it is supposed that they peopled countries bordering on each other. Bochart labours to prove that by Meshech and Tubal are intended the Muscovites and the Tibarenians. The Tibarenians of the Greeks were the people inhabiting the country south of the Caucasus, between the Black Sea and the Araxes. Josephus says, that ' Tubal obtained *the Thobelians* (Θωβήλους) who are reckoned among the Iberians.' Jerome renders it, ' Italy.' It is not possible to determine with certainty the country that is referred to, though some part of Europe is doubtless intended. ¶ *And Javan.* Jerome renders this, ' Greece.' So the LXX. Εἰς σὴν Ἑλλάδα—' To Greece.' Javan was the fourth son of Japhet, and was the father of the Ionians and the Greeks (Gen. x. 2–4). The word ' Ionia,' Gr. Ἴων, Ἰωνία, is evidently derived from the word here rendered ' Javan' (יָוָן), and in the Scriptures the word comprehends all the countries inhabited by the descendants of Javan, as well in Greece as in Asia Minor. Ionia properly was the beautiful province on the western part of Asia Minor —a country much celebrated in the Greek classics for its fertility and the salubrity of its climate—but the word here used includes all of Greece. Thus Daniel (xi. 2), speaking of Xerxes, says, ' He shall stir up all against the realm of Javan.' Alexander the Great is described by the same prophet as ' king of Javan' (viii. 21 ; x. 20). The Hindoos call the Greeks Yavanas—the ancient Hebrew appellation. It is need-

less to say, on the supposition that this refers to the propagation of the gospel by the apostles, that it was fulfilled. They went to Greece and to Asia Minor in the very commencement of their labours, and some of the earliest and most flourishing churches were founded in the lands that were settled by the descendants of Javan. ¶ *To the isles afar off* (see Notes on ch. xli. 1). ¶ *That have not heard my fame.* Heb. ' Who have not heard my report,' *i.e.*, who were ignorant of the true God. ¶ *Neither have seen my glory.* The glory which he had manifested to the Hebrews in giving his law, and in the various exhibitions of his character and perfections among them.

20. *And they shall bring all your brethren.* That is, as great success shall attend them *as if* they should bring back all who had gone there when scattered abroad, and should present them as an offering to JEHOVAH. The image here is taken from the scene which would be presented, should the distant nations be seen bringing the scattered exiles in all lands on horses, and on palanquins, and on dromedaries, again to Jerusalem, and presenting them before JEHOVAH in the city where they formerly dwelt. It is the image of a vast caravan, conducted by the heathen world when they had become tributary to the people of God, and when they united to return them to their own land. The *spiritual* signification is, that all they who should be appropriately called ' brethren,' all who should be the true friends of God, should be brought and offered to JEHOVAH ; that is, there should be a great accession to the people of God from the heathen world. ¶ For *an offering unto the* LORD. Heb. מִנְחָה *minhhâ*—not a bloody offering or sacrifice : but an offering such as was made by flour, oil, &c. (see Notes on ch. i. 13.) ¶ *Out of all nations.* The truth shall be proclaimed in all lands, and a vast accession shall be made from all parts

of the world to the true church of God. To understand this description, we must form an idea of immense caravans proceeding from distant parts of the world to Jerusalem, bearing along the converts to the true religion to be dedicated to the service of JEHOVAH. ¶ *Upon horses.* Horses were little used by the Hebrews (see Notes on ch. ii. 7), but they are much used by the Arabs, and form an important part of the caravan that goes to distant places. ¶ *And in chariots* (comp. Notes on ver. 15). It is, however, by no means certain that the word here used refers to a wheeled vehicle. Such vehicles were not used in caravans. The editor of the *Ruins of Palmyra* tells us that the caravan they formed to go to that place, consisted of about two hundred persons, and about the same number of beasts of carriage, which were an odd mixture of horses, camels, mules, and asses; but there is no account of any vehicle drawn on wheels in that expedition, nor do we find an account of such things in other eastern journeys (Harmer). Coaches, Dr. Russel assures us, are not in use in Aleppo, nor are they commonly used in any of the countries of the East. The Hebrew word here used (רֶכֶב, *rêkhĕbh*), means properly *riding*— riders, cavalry (see it explained in the Notes on ch. xxi. 7); then *any* vehicle for riding—whether a waggon, chariot, or litter. Lowth renders it, 'In litters.' Pitts, in his account of the return from Mecca, describes a species of litter which was borne by two camels, one before and another behind, which was all covered over with searcloth, and that again with green broadcloth, and which was elegantly adorned. It is not improbable that some such vehicle is intended here, as it is certain that such things as waggons or chariots are not found in oriental caravans. ¶ *And in litters.* Marg. 'Coaches.' But the word *litters* more properly expresses the idea. Lowth renders it, 'Counes.' Thevenot tells us that *counes* are hampers, or cradles, carried upon the backs of camels, one on each side, having a back, head, and sides, like great chairs. A covering is commonly laid over them to protect the rider from wind and rain. This is a common mode of travelling in the East.

LITTERS FOR TRAVELLING IN THE EAST.—From Laborde.

The coune, or hamper, is thrown across the back of the camel, somewhat in the manner of saddle-bags with us. Some- times a person sits on each side, and they thus balance each other, and sometimes the end in which the person is placed is

21 And I will also take of them for priests, *a and* for Levites, saith the LORD.

22 For as the new *b* heavens and the new earth, which I will make, shall remain before me, saith the LORD, so shall your seed and your name remain.

23 And *c* it shall come to pass, *that* from one 1 new moon to another, and from one sabbath to another, shall all *d* flesh come to worship before me, saith the LORD.

a Re.1.6. b ch.65.17. c Zec.14.14.

1 *new moon to his new moon, and from sabbath to his sabbath.* d Ps.65.2.

balanced by provisions, or articles of furniture in the other. ' At Aleppo,' says Dr. Russel, ' women of inferior condition in long journeys are commonly stowed, one on each side of a mule, in a sort of covered cradles.' The Hebrew word here used (צָב *tzâbh*), means properly a *litter*, a *sedan coach*—what can be lightly or gently borne. The LXX. render it, Ἐν λαμπήναις ἡμιόνων μετὰ σκιαδίων—' In litters of mules, with shades or umbrellas.' Perhaps the following description of a scene in the khan at Acre, will afford an apt illustration of this passage. ' The bustle was increased this morning by the departure of the wives of the governor of Jaffa. They set off in two coaches of a curious description, common in this country. The body of the coach was raised on two parallel poles, somewhat similar to those used for sedan chairs—only that in these the poles were attached to the lower part of the coach—throwing consequently the centre of gravity much higher, and apparently exposing the vehicle, with its veiled tenant, to an easy overthrow, or at least to a very active jolt. Between the poles strong mules were harnessed, one before and one behind; who, if they should prove capricious, or have very uneven or mountainous ground to pass, would render the situation of the ladies still more critical.'—(Jowett's *Christian Researches in Syria*, pp. 115, 116, Am. Ed.) ¶ *And upon swift beasts.* Dromedaries. So Lowth and Noyes render it; and so the word here used—כִּרְכָּרוֹת —properly denotes. The word is derived from כָּרַד *kârad*, to dance; and the name is given to them for their bounding or dancing motion, their speed being also sometimes accelerated by musical instruments (Bochart, *Hieroz.* i. 2, 4). For a description of the dromedary, see Notes on ch. lx. 6. ¶ *As the children of Israel.* As the Jews bear an offer-

ing to JEHOVAH in a vessel that is pure. The utmost attention was paid to the cleanliness of their vessels in their public worship.

21. *And I will also take of them for priests.* I will give to them an honourable place in my public service; that is, I will make them ministers of religion *as if* they were priests and Levites. This cannot be taken *literally*—because the priests and Levites among the Jews were determined by law, and by regular genealogical descent, and there was no provision for substituting any in their place. But it must mean that under the condition of things described here, those who should be brought from the distant pagan world would perform the same offices in the service of God which had been performed formerly by the priests and Levites—that is, they would be ministers of religion. The services of God would no longer be performed by the descendants of Aaron, or be limited to them, but would be performed by others who should be called to this office from the heathen world.

22. *For as the new heavens and the new earth* (see Notes on ch. lxv. 17). ¶ *Shall remain before me.* They shall not pass away and be succeeded by others. The idea is, that the state of things here described would be permanent and abiding. ¶ *So shall your seed and your name remain* (see Notes on ch. lxv. 15).

23. *And it shall come to pass.* As the prophet closes the book and winds up his whole prophecy, he directs the attention to that future period which had occupied so much of his attention in vision, when the whole world should be acquainted with the true religion, and all nations should worship JEHOVAH. Of *such* a book there could be no more appropriate close; and such a contemplation peculiarly became the last pro-

24 And they shall go forth, and | look upon the carcasses of the men

phetic moments of the 'evangelical prophet' Isaiah. ¶ *From one new moon to another.* Marg. 'New moon to his new moon.' The Hebrew literally is, 'As often as the month cometh in its month;' *i.e.*, in its time, every month, every new moon (Gesenius, *Lex.*, on the word מִדֵּי). The Hebrews held a festival on the return of each month, or at every new moon (see Notes on ch. i. 14). A similar prophecy occurs in Zech. xiv. 16: 'And it shall come to pass, that every one that is left of all the nations which came up against Jerusalem, shall even go up from year to year to worship the King, the Lord of hosts, and to keep the feast of tabernacles.' In regard to the meaning of this, it is evident that it cannot be taken literally. In the nature of things it would be impossible for all nations to go literally before JEHOVAH in Jerusalem once a month, or once a year, to worship. It must then be meant that at *periodical seasons*, all the human family would worship JEHOVAH. The festivals of the new moon, the feast of tabernacles, and the Sabbaths, were the *set time* among the Hebrews for the worship of God; and the idea is, that on set times, or at regularly recurring intervals, the worship of God would yet be celebrated in all lands. I see no evidence, therefore, that this means that there should be established on the earth the habit of meeting for prayer, or for the worship of God once a month—any more than the passage above quoted from Zechariah proves that a feast like that of tabernacles would be celebrated once a year. But the idea is clear, that the time would come when JEHOVAH would be worshipped regularly and periodically everywhere; that in all nations his worship would be established in a manner similar in some respects to that which prevailed among his people in ancient times. ¶ *And from one Sabbath to another* (comp. Notes on ch. lviii. 13, 14). There can be no permanent worship of God, and no permanent religion on earth, without a Sabbath; and hence it was, that while the observance of the feasts of tabernacles, and of the Passover, and of the new moons, made a part of the *ceremonial* law, the law

respecting the Sabbaths was incorporated with the ten commandments as of moral and perpetual obligation; and it will be literally true that all the race shall yet be brought to worship God on the return of that holy day. It was instituted in paradise; and as one design of the plan of redemption is to bring man back to the state in which he was in paradise, so one effect of the true religion everywhere will be, and *is*, to make men reverence the Sabbath of the Lord. No man becomes truly pious who does not love the holy Sabbath. No nation ever has been, or ever can be converted which will not, and which *does* not, love and observe that day. Every successful effort to propagate the true religion is a successful effort to extend the practice of observing it; and just as certain as it is that Christianity will be spread around the world, so certain will it be that the Sabbath will be observed in all lands. The period is, therefore, yet to arrive when the delightful spectacle will be presented of all the nations of the earth bowing on the return of that day before the living God. The plans of this life will be suspended; toil and care will be laid aside; and the sun, as he rolls around the world, will rouse nation after nation to the worship of the true God; and the peace and order and loveliness of the Christian Sabbath will spread over all the hills and vales of the world. Who that loves the race will not desire that such a period may soon come? Who can wonder that Isaiah should have fixed his eye in the close of his prophetic labours on a scene so full of loveliness, and so replete with honour to God, and with goodwill to men? ¶ *Shall all flesh.* All the human family, all nations—a most unequivocal promise that the true religion shall yet prevail around the world. ¶ *Come to worship before me.* That is, they shall assemble for the worship of God in their respective places of devotion.

25. *And they shall go forth.* The sense of this verse evidently is, that the pious and happy worshippers of God shall see the punishment which he will execute on his and their foes, or shall

that have transgressed against me; for their worm shall *a* not die, neither shall their fire be quenched; and they shall be an abhorring *b* unto all flesh.

see, them finally destroyed. It refers to the time when the kingdom of God shall be finally and perpetually established, and when all the mighty enemies of that kingdom shall be subdued and punished. The image is probably taken from a scene where a people whose lands have been desolated by mighty armies are permitted to go forth after a decisive battle to walk over the fields of the slain, and to see the dead and the putrifying bodies of their once formidable enemies. ¶ *And look upon the carcasses of the men.* The dead bodies of the foes of God (see ver. 15, 16). ¶ *For their worm shall not die.* This image is evidently taken from the condition of unburied bodies, and especially on a battle-field. The Hebrew word (תּוֹלָע) properly refers to the worms which are generated in such corrupting bodies (see Ex. xvi. 20; Notes on Isa. xiv. 11). It is sometimes applied to the worm from which the crimson or deep scarlet colour was obtained (Notes on ch. i. 18); but it more properly denotes that which is produced in putrid substances. This entire passage is applied by the Saviour to future punishment; and is the fearful image which he employs to denote the final suffering of the wicked in hell. My views on its meaning may be seen in the Notes on Mark ix. 44, 46. ¶ *Neither shall their fire be quenched.* The fire that shall consume them shall burn perpetually. This image is taken evidently from the fires kindled, especially in the valley of Hinnom, to consume putrid and decaying substances. That was a valley on the south side of Jerusalem, into which the filth of the city was thrown. It was the place where, formerly, an image of brass was raised to Moloch, and where children were offered in sacrifice (2 Kings xvi. 3; 2 Chron. xxviii. 3). See a description of this in the Notes on Matt. v. 22. This place was subsequently regarded as a place of peculiar abomination by the Jews. The filth of the city was thrown there, and it became extremely offensive. The air was polluted and pestilential; the sight was terrific; and to preserve it in any manner pure, it was necessary to keep fires continually burning there. The extreme loathsomeness of the place, the filth and putrefaction, the corruption of the atmosphere, and the lurid fires blazing by day and by night, made it subsequently one of the most appalling and loathsome objects with which a Jew was acquainted. It was called the GEHENNA OF FIRE, and was the image which the Saviour often employed to denote the future punishment of the wicked. In that deep and loathsome vale it seems to have been the common expectation of the Jews that some great battle would be fought which would establish the supremacy of their nation over all others. Hence the Chaldee renders this, ' They shall go forth, and shall look upon the dead bodies of the sinners who have rebelled against my word; because their souls shall not die, and their fire shall not be extinguished; and the wicked shall be judged IN GEHENNA (בְּגֵיהִנָּם), until the righteous shall say, We have seen enough.' It is, however, by no means certain that Isaiah refers here especially to the valley of Hinnom. The image in his mind is evidently that of a vast army slain, and left to putrify on the field unburied, and where fires would be kindled in part to consume the heaps of the slain, and in part to save the air from pestilential influences. All the enemies of God and his church would be like such a vast host strewed on the plains, and the perpetuity of his kingdom would be finally established. ¶ *And they shall be an abhorring.* An object of loathing. So the Hebrew word דֵּרָאוֹן, means. It is derived from דָּרָא, an obsolete root, signifying, in Arabic, to thrust away, to repel. Jerome renders it, *Ad satietatem visionis*—understanding by it, that all flesh should look upon those dead bodies until they were satisfied. The LXX., Εἰς ὅρασιν—' For a vision;' or that all flesh might look upon them. It is evident that the LXX. read the word as if it were derived from the verb רָאָה, *to see.* ¶ *Unto all flesh* (see ver. 23). The sense is, that so entire would be their overthrow, and such objects of loathing would they become, that all the friends of God would turn from them in abhorrence. All the enemies of God would be destroyed; the pure religion would triumph, and the people of God would be secure.

It may be made a question, perhaps, to what period this refers. The Saviour (Mark ix. 44, 46), applied *the language* to the future punishment of the wicked, and no one, I think, can doubt that in Isaiah it *includes* that consummation of worldly affairs. The radical and essential idea in the prophet is, as it seems to me, that such would be the entire overthrow and punishment of the enemies of God; so condign their punishment; so deep their sufferings; so loathsome and hateful would they be when visited with the Divine vengeance for their sins, that they would be an object of loathing and abhorrence. They would be swept off as unworthy to live with God, and they would be consigned to punishment—loathsome like that of ever-gnawing worms on the carcasses of the slain, and interminable and dreadful like everconsuming and extinguishable fires.

This is the consummation of the series of bright visions that passed before the mind of Isaiah, and is an appropriate termination of this succession of wonderful revelations. Where could it more appropriately close than in the final triumph of the true religion, and in the complete and final destruction of all the enemies of God? The vision stretches on to the judgment, and is closed by a contemplation of those scenes which commence there, but which never end. The church is triumphant. Its conflicts cease. Its foes are slain. Its Redeemer is revealed; and its everlasting happiness is founded on a basis which can never be shaken.

Here I close my labours in endeavouring to elucidate the visions of this wonderful prophet. I thank God—the source of every right feeling and every holy desire, and the suggester of every plan that will in any way elucidate his word or promote his glory—that he ever inclined my heart to these studies. I thank him for the preservation of my life, and the continuance of my health, until I am permitted to bring this work to a close. I record, with grateful emotions, my deep conviction, that if in any way I have been enabled to explain that which was before dark; to illustrate that which was obscure; or to present any views which have not before occurred to those who may peruse this work, it is owing to the gracious influences of his Holy Spirit. And I desire to render thanks to the Great Source of light and truth, if I have been enabled to throw any light on the prophecies recorded here more than 2500 years ago; or to confirm the faith of any in the truth of the inspiration of the Bible by tracing the evidences of the fulfilment of those predictions. And I now commend the work to the blessing of God, and devote it to the glory of his name and to the advancement of the Redeemer's kingdom, with a humble prayer that it may be useful to other minds; —but with the deep conviction, that whatever may be its effect on other minds, I have been abundantly compensated for all my labour in the contemplation of the inimitable beauties, and the sublime visions of Isaiah. Thanks to God for this book;—thanks for all its beauties, its consolations, its promises, its views of the Messiah, its predictions of the certain triumph of truth, and its glowing descriptions of the future conquest of the church, when God shall extend to it 'peace like a river, and the glory of the Gentiles like a flowing stream.' Come soon that blessed day, when 'the ransomed of the Lord shall return to Zion, with songs and everlasting joy upon their heads' (ch. xxxv. 10); when 'the wilderness and the solitary place shall be glad, and the desert shall rejoice and blossom as the rose' (ch. xxxv. 1); and when it shall be announced to the church, 'thy sun shall no more go down; neither shall thy moon withdraw itself; for JEHOVAH shall be thine everlasting light, and the days of thy mourning shall be ended' (ch. lx. 20). May I be permitted to close my labours on this book in the beautiful language of Vitringa?*   'These words (ver. 23,

---

* Hæc extrema sunt (sc. ver. 23, 24) utriusque oppositi hominum generis piorum et impiorum, in quibus post varia prolusoria Dei judicia, fata

24) express the final doom of the two opposite classes of men, the righteous and the wicked, when, after various preparatory judgments of God, the fates of all ages, and our own also, shall be determined; with which also this Divine

sæculorum omnium, et nostra quoque terminabuntur; quibusque ipse quoque hic Divinus Liber Iesaiæ, magni Prophetæ, terminatur. Esto sors nostra cum sanctis, Dei reverentibus; veritatis amantibus; humilibus, mansuetis, misericordibus, et in bono opere ad finem vitæ perseverantibus, ex sententia gratiæ magni nostri Domini, Servatoris, ac Judicis Christi Jesu, sortes hasce ex voluntate Patris diribituri. Qua spe ego quoque hoc tempore affectus, prostratusque ante thronum ejus, Deo PATRI, in FILIO ejus CHRISTO JESU per SPIRITUM, submisso animo gratias ago pro gratia et lumine, quibus me indignum servum suum in commentatione hujus Libri inchoanda et absolvenda prosequutus est; supplici prece ab ejus gratia et misericordia contendens, ut aberrationibus in quas imprudens inciderim, ignoscens, hoc Opus quale est, vertere ve'it in maximam gloriam sui Nominis, usum Ecclesiæ, et solatium piorum.

''Αὐτῷ ἡ δόξα εἰς τοὺς αἰῶνας τῶν αἰώνων.'

book of Isaiah itself is terminated. Be it our lot, with those who are holy; with those who fear God and love the truth; with the humble, meek, and merciful, and with those who persevere in every good work to the end of life, from the gracious sentence of our great Lord, Saviour, and Judge, Jesus Christ, to obtain, by the will of the Father, the same portion with them. In which hope, I also, now deeply affected, and prostrate before his throne, give humble thanks to God the Father, and his Son Christ Jesus, through the Spirit, for the grace and light with which he has endowed me, his unworthy servant, in commencing and completing the commentary on this book; entreating, with earnest prayer, of his grace and mercy, that, pardoning those errors into which erroneously I may have fallen, he will employ this work, such as it is, to the glory of his name, the use of the church, and the consolation of his people; and to Him be the glory throughout all ages.'